Yearbook of National Accounts Statistics 1981

Volume I Part 1
Individual country data

United Nations
New York, 1983

NOTE

Symbols of United Nations documents are composed of capital letters combined with figures. Mention of such a symbol indicates a reference to a United Nations document.

The *Yearbook of National Accounts Statistics, 1981* consists of two volumes. The volumes are not sold separately.

The first 14 editions of the *Yearbook* were issued without series symbols.

ST/ESA/STAT/SER.O/11

UNITED NATIONS PUBLICATION

Sales No. E.83.XVII.3, Vol. I, Part 1

12500 (Vols. I and II)
(only clothbound edition for sale)

Inquiries should be directed to:

PUBLISHING DIVISION
UNITED NATIONS
NEW YORK, N.Y. 10017

Copyright © United Nations, 1983
All rights reserved
Manufactured in the United States of America

CONTENTS

	Page
Introduction	v
I. The System of National Accounts (SNA)	ix
II. The System of Material Product Balances (MPS)	xix
III. Country tables	1

	Page		Page
Afghanistan	3	Ecuador	378
Algeria	4	Egypt	413
Antigua and Barbuda	19	El Salvador	421
Argentina	20	Ethiopia	432
Australia	25	Fiji	444
Austria	60	Finland	458
Bahamas	85	France	514
Bahrain	86	French Polynesia	559
Bangladesh	87	Gabon	561
Barbados	88	German Democratic Republic	576
Belgium	91	Germany, Federal Republic of	577
Belize	113	Ghana	652
Benin	123	Greece	664
Bolivia	132	Grenada	687
Botswana	155	Guadeloupe	688
Brazil	181	Guatemala	690
British Virgin Islands	184	Guyana	696
Brunei	193	Haiti	699
Bulgaria	194	Honduras	706
Burma	199	Hong Kong	720
Burundi	204	Hungary	726
Byelorussian SSR	209	Iceland	737
Canada	210	India	750
Central African Republic	260	Indonesia	794
Chad	262	Iran (Islamic Rep. of)	797
Chile	267	Iraq	801
Colombia	275	Ireland	808
Congo	286	Israel	835
Cook Islands	289	Italy	849
Costa Rica	291	Ivory Coast	873
Cuba	314	Jamaica	887
Cyprus	315	Japan	901
Czechoslovakia	330	Jordan	989
Democratic Yemen	342	Kenya	997
Denmark	343	Kiribati	1026
Djibouti	365	Korea, Republic of	1035
Dominica	366	Kuwait	1064
Dominican Republic	370		

INTRODUCTION

This is the twenty-fifth issue of the *Yearbook of National Accounts Statistics*.1/ Like the first 24 issues, it has been prepared by the Statistical Office of the United Nations with the generous co-operation of national statistical services. It is issued in accordance with the request of the Statistical Commission 2/ that the latest available data on national accounts for as many countries and areas as possible be published regularly.

The present *Yearbook* is issued in two volumes. Volume I, (Parts I and II) "Individual country data", shows in "III. Country tables", detailed national accounts estimates for 156 countries and areas. Volume II "International tables" presents in the form of analytical tables, a summary of main national accounts aggregates, extracted from the individual country tables and supplemented by estimates made by the Statistical Office where official data are not available.

Scope of Publication

National accounts estimates for countries or areas with market economies are shown, where available, for each of the following subjects. Estimates are shown for some or all of the years 1970 through 1980.

Part 1. Summary Information

 1.1 Expenditures on the gross domestic product (current prices)
 1.2 Expenditures on the gross domestic product (constant prices)
 1.3 Cost components of the gross domestic product
 1.4 General government current receipts and expenditures, summary
 1.5 Current income and outlay of corporate and quasi-corporate enterprises, summary
 1.6 Current income and outlay of households and non-profit institutions, summary
 1.7 External transactions on current account, summary
 1.8 Capital transactions of the nation, summary
 1.9 Gross domestic product by institutional sector of origin
 1.10 Gross domestic product by kind of activity (current prices)
 1.11 Gross domestic product by kind of activity (constant prices)
 1.12 Relations among national accounting aggregates

Part 2. Final Expenditures on Gross Domestic Product: Detailed Breakdowns and Supporting Tables

 2.1 General government final consumption expenditure by function (current prices)
 2.2 General government final consumption expenditure by function (constant prices)
 2.3 Total general government outlays by function and type
 2.4 Composition of general government outlays for social security and social assistance
 2.5 Private final consumption expenditure by type (current prices)
 2.6 Private final consumption expenditure by type (constant prices)
 2.7 Gross capital formation by type of good and owner (current prices)
 2.8 Gross capital formation by type of good and owner (constant prices)
 2.9 Gross capital formation by kind of activity of owner, ISIC major divisions (current prices)
 2.10 Gross capital formation by kind of activity of owner, ISIC major divisions (constant prices)
 2.11 Gross fixed capital formation by kind of activity of owner, ISIC divisions (current prices)
 2.12 Gross fixed capital formation by kind of activity of owner, ISIC divisions (constant prices)
 2.13 Stocks of reproducible fixed assets, by type of good and owner (current prices)
 2.14 Stocks of reproducible fixed assets, by type of good and owner (constant prices)
 2.15 Stocks of reproducible fixed assets by kind of activity (current prices)
 2.16 Stocks of reproducible fixed assets by kind of activity (constant prices)
 2.17 Exports and imports of goods and services, detail

Part 3. Institutional Sector Accounts: Detailed Flow Accounts and Balance Sheets

1. General government

 3.11 Production account: Total and subsectors
 3.12 Income and outlay account: Total and subsectors
 3.13 Capital accumulation account: Total and subsectors
 3.14 Capital finance account: Total and subsectors
 3.15 Balance sheet: Total and subsectors

2. Corporate and quasi-corporate enterprises

 3.21 Production account: Total and subsectors
 3.22 Income and outlay account: Total and subsectors
 3.23 Capital accumulation account: Total and subsectors
 3.24 Capital finance account: Total and subsectors
 3.25 Balance sheet: Total and subsectors
 3.26 Financial transactions of financial institutions: detail

3. Households and private unincorporated enterprises

 3.31 Production account: Total and subsectors
 3.32 Income and outlay account: Total and subsectors
 3.33 Capital accumulation account: Total and subsectors

3.34 Capital finance account: Total and subsectors
3.35 Balance sheet: Total and subsectors

4. Private non-profit institutions serving households

   3.41 Production account
   3.42 Income and outlay account
   3.43 Capital accumulation account
   3.44 Capital finance account
   3.45 Balance sheet

5. External transactions

   3.51 Current account, detail
   3.52 Capital accumulation account
   3.53 Capital finance account

Part 4. Production by Kind of Activity: Detailed Breakdowns and Supporting Tables

   4.1 Derivation of value added by kind of activity, ISIC major divisions (current prices)
   4.2 Derivation of value added by kind of activity, ISIC major divisions (constant prices)
   4.3 Derivation of value added by kind of activity, ISIC divisions (current prices)
   4.4 Derivation of value added by kind of activity, ISIC divisions (constant prices)
   4.5 Cost components of value added, ISIC major divisions
   4.6 Cost components of value added, ISIC divisions
   4.9 Supply of goods and services (current prices)
   4.10 Supply of goods and services (constant prices)
   4.11 Disposition of goods and services (current prices)
   4.12 Disposition of goods and services (constant prices)
   4.13 Gross output of goods and services (current prices)
   4.14 Gross output of goods and services (constant prices)
   4.15 Intermediate consumption by kind of activity of user (current prices)
   4.16 Intermediate consumption by kind of activity of user (constant prices)
   4.17 Reconciliation of SNA gross domestic product with MPS net material product

For the countries with centrally planned economies, estimates are shown, where available, in terms of the System of Material Product Balances (MPS), for each of the following subjects, as a rule, for some or all of the years 1970 through 1980.

1. Net material product by use
2. Net material product by kind of activity of the material sphere
3. Primary incomes by kinds of activity of the material sphere
4. Primary incomes from net material product
5. Supply and disposition of goods and material services
6. Capital formation by kind of activity of the material and non-material spheres
7. Final consumption
8. Personal consumption according to source of supply of goods and material services
9. Total consumption of the population by object, commodity and service, and mode of acquisition

Conceptual references

The form and concepts of the statistical tables in the present volume generally conform, for the countries or areas with market economies, to the recommendations in *A System of National Accounts,* 3/ Studies in Methods, Series F, No. 2, Rev. 3. For the countries with centrally planned economies, the form and concepts generally conform to the recommendations in *Basic Principles of the System of Balances of the National Economy*, Studies in Methods, Series F, No. 17. 4/ A summary of the conceptual framework of both systems, their classifications and definitions of transactions items, is provided in chapters I and II of Volume I of the *Yearbook*.

Compilation of data

To compile the large volume of national accounts data, the Statistical Office of the United Nations each year sends to countries or areas with market economies a national accounts questionnaire; those with centrally planned economies receive a material balances questionnaire. The recipients of the questionnaires are also requested to indicate where the scope and coverage of the country estimates differ for conceptual or statistical reasons from the definitions and classifications recommended in SNA or in the System of Material Product Balances. Data obtained from these replies are supplemented by information gathered from correspondence with the national statistical services and from national and international source publications.

In this volume of the *Yearbook*, the data for each country or area are presented in separate chapters, as far as possible, under uniform table headings and classifications of the SNA or the material balances questionnaire, as the case may be. Each country chapter contains a brief introductory text (source and general note). The general note describes the extent to which the estimates conform conceptually to the recommendations of the SNA or the material balances questionnaire. Important deviations from the two systems, where known, are described in the general note, while differences in definition and coverage of specific items are indicated in foot-notes to the relevant tables.

Country data in chapter III are presented in alphabetical order.

Unless otherwise stated, the data in the *Yearbook* tables relate to the calendar year against which they are shown.

Comparability of the national estimates

Every effort has been made to present the estimates of the various countries or areas in a form designed to facilitate international comparability. To this end, important differences in concept, scope, coverage and classification have been described in the notes which precede and accompany the country tables. Such differences should be taken into account if misleading comparisons among countries or areas are to be avoided.

REVISIONS

The figures shown are the most recent estimates and revisions available at the time of compilation. In general, figures for the latest year are to be regarded as provisional. For more up to date information, reference is made to the December issue of the UN *Monthly Bulletin of Statistics* 5/.

EXPLANATION OF SYMBOLS

The following symbols have been employed:

Data not available ....
Category not applicable ....
Magnitude nil or less than half of the unit
  employed.. —
Decimal figures are always preceded by a period .. (.)

When a series is not homogeneous, this is indicated by presenting the figures in separate rows.

Details and percentages in tables do not necessarily add to totals shown because of rounding.

GENERAL DISCLAIMER

The designations employed and the presentation of material in this publication do not imply the expression of any opinion whatsoever on the part of the Secretariat of the United Nations concerning the legal status of any country, territory, city or area or of its authorities, or concerning the delimitation of its frontiers or boundaries.

Where the designation "country or area" appears in the headings of tables, it covers countries, territories, cities or areas. In prior issues of this publication, where the designation "country" appears in the headings of tables, it should be interpreted to cover countries, territories, cities or areas.

In some tables, the designation "developed" and "developing" economies is intended for statistical convenience and does not, necessarily, express a judgement about the stage reached by a particular country or area in the development process.

1/ United Nations publications. Previous editions of the *Yearbook* were issued under the following sales numbers: *1957*, 58.XVII.3; *1958*, 59.XVII.3; *1959*, 60.XVII.3; *1960*, 61.XVII.4; *1961*, 62.XVII.2; *1962*, 63.XVII.2; *1963*, 64.XVII.4; *1964*, 65.XVII.2; *1965*, 66.XVII.2; *1966*, 67.XVII.14; *1967*, 69.XVII.6; *1968*, vol. I, 70.XVII.2, vol. II. 70.XVII.3; *1969*, vol. I, 71.XVII.2, vol. II. 71.XVII.3; *1970*,72.XVII.3, vol. I, 72.XVII.3, vol. II; *1971*, (3 volumes), E.73.XVII.3; *1972*, (3 volumes), E.74.XVII.3; *1973*, (3 volumes), E.75.XVII.2; *1974*, (3 volumes), E.75.XVII.5; *1975*, (3 volumes), E.76.XVII.2; *1976* (2 volumes), E.77.XVII.2; *1977*, (2 volumes), E.78.XVII.2; *1978*, (2 volumes) E.79.XVII.8; *1979*, (2 volumes), E.80.XVII.11; l980, (2 volumes)m E.82.XVII.6.
2/ See *Official Records of the Economic and Social Council, First Year, Second Session,* annex III, chap. IV.
3/ United Nations publication, Sales No. E.69.XVII.3. The first edition of the report, published in 1953, was prepared by an expert committee appointed by the Secretary-General of the United Nations.
4/ United Nations publication, Sales. No. E.71.XVII.10.
5/ United Nations publication, ST/ESA/STAT/SER.Q.

I. THE SYSTEM OF NATIONAL ACCOUNTS (SNA)

The new System of National Accounts (SNA) was adopted by the Statistical Commission at its fifteenth session 1/ for the use of national statistical authorities and in the international reporting of comparable national accounting data. The new system is a revision and extension of the former SNA which was first formulated in 1952 2/.

A. THE STRUCTURE OF THE SNA

The SNA provides a comprehensive and detailed framework for the systematic and integrated recording of transaction flows in an economy. It brings together into an articulated and coherent system data ranging in degree of aggregation from consolidated accounts of the nation to detailed input-output and flow-of-funds tables. It includes production and goods and services and outlay and capital finance accounts for institutional sectors and subsectors.

The country tables are divided into four parts. These are listed in the Introduction. Part 1 contains summary but comprehensive information, in current and where appropriate constant prices. This part includes not only the basic gross domestic product (final expenditures and cost composition), but also summary information on government receipts and disbursements, enterprise and household income and outlay, and external transactions, a summary capital transactions account, information on gross product by institutional sector of origin and kind of activity, and finally a table showing the relations among the aggregate concepts used in the revised SNA and also commonly in national statistical systems. Tables 1.1, 1.3, 1.4, 1.5, 1.6, 1.7 and 1.8 form a simple, closed and balancing set of flow accounts, drawn from the much more complex and elaborate standard accounts of SNA; these tables can therefore be used not only to provide an overview of the operation of the economic system but also as a guide to the more detailed data that follow and as a framework to enforce conceptual and statistical consistency.

Part 2 shows detailed breakdowns of the final expenditure components of gross domestic product (consumption, capital formation, imports and exports), in current and constant prices, together with supporting tables giving additional information on government outlays and capital stock. This part also shows tables relating to stocks of reproducible tangible assets in current and constant prices.

Part 3 shows detailed institutional sector accounts. For each sector and subsector, five accounts are given: a production account, an income and outlay account, a capital formation account, a capital finance account, and a balance sheet. The last four of these are the standard SNA accounts as shown in Annex 8.3 of *A System of National Accounts* (*op.cit.*) and in Annex 8.2 of *Provisional Guidelines on National and Sector Balance Sheets and Reconciliation Accounts of the System of National Accounts* 3/. The SNA standard accounts do not include institutional sector production accounts, but provision is made for this information in the supporting tables.

The sectors and subsectors distinguished in Part 3 are: general government (central, state or provincial, local, social security funds), corporate and quasi-corporate enterprises (non-financial, financial), households and private unincorporated enterprises (farm entrepreneurial, other farm, non-farm entrepreneurial, non-farm wage earner, other) and non-profit institutions serving households.

Part 4 contains kind of activity breakdowns. Two levels of detail are employed. All of the information is asked for at the ISIC major division (1-digit) level. In some cases data are also asked for at the ISIC division (2-digit) level, with a very small amount of further breakdown to the 3-digit level. Where appropriate, both current and constant prices are specified. The tables show the derivation of value added (gross output less intermediate consumption), the cost components of value added, and employment.

B. STANDARD CLASSIFICATIONS OF THE SNA

Detailed discussions of definitions and classifications are to be found in *A System of National Accounts*, (*op.cit.*) and in the other publications on SNA cited above. The SNA distinguishes between transactor and transaction classifications. Below is given a short summary of the main characteristics of each of the classifications used by the system.

I. *Classifications of Transactors*

1. *Kind of Activity*

The kind-of-activity classification employed is the major division (1-digit) level, or in some tables the division (2-digit) level, of the *International Standard Industrial Classification of All Economic Activities*, 4/

In SNA, this classification is intended to be applied to establishment-type units, defined as the smallest units for which separate production accounts can be compiled. SNA also employs a much broader kind of activity classification, which divides producers into "industries" and three categories of "other producers". Industries are, broadly, establishments whose activities are intended to be self-sustaining, whether through production for the market or for own use, and it is to this category that the ISIC breakdown is generally applied.

All establishments falling into ISIC major divisions 1-8 should be classed as industries. Producers of government services, private non-profit services to households, and domestic services are classed as "other producers"; all of these should fall into ISIC category 9 "Community, social and personal services." ISIC category 9 also may, of course, include some establishments classed as industries. Where countries consider, however, that some establishments classed as other producers should appear in ISIC categories other than 9, the nature of the exceptions should be specified in footnotes to Tables 1.10 and 1.11.

2. Institutional Sectors

The basic SNA institutional sectoring is given in *A System of National Accounts*, (*op. cit.*) table 5.1.

Institutional sectoring, in SNA, is intended to be applied to enterprise-type units, that is, units for which complete accounts can be compiled, as opposed to the establishment-type units employed in the kind-of-activity classification. This distinction is applicable mainly to the corporate and quasi-corporate enterprise sector.

The sectoring and subsectoring employed in the institutional sector accounts in Part 3 is as follows:

General government
    Central
    State or provincial
    Local
    Social security funds
Corporate and quasi-corporate enterprises
    Non-financial
    Financial
Households and private unincorporated enterprises
    Farm entrepreneurial
    Other farm
    Non-farm entrepreneurial
    Non-farm wage earner
    Other
Non-profit institutions serving households
Rest of the world

(a) *General government*. This sector includes (1) *producers of government services*, all bodies, departments and establishments of any level of government which engage in administration, defence, regulation of the public order and health, cultural, recreational and other social services and social security arrangements which are furnished but not normally sold to the public, and (2) *industries of government*, ancillary departments and establishments mainly engaged in supplying goods and services to other units of government, such as printing plants, central transport pools and arsenals, and agencies mainly selling goods and services to the public but operating on a small scale and financially integrated with general government, such as government restaurant facilities in public buildings. Non-profit institutions which, while not an official part of any organ of government, are wholly or mainly financed and controlled by it should be included in producers of government services. Ancillary agencies may occur in any kind of activity. Producers of government services normally occur only in major division 9 (which of course may also include ancillary agencies).

Provision is made for four subsectors of general government, all of which may include the two components noted above. However, it is not intended that artificial distinctions should be introduced where they do not exist in the institutions of a particular country. It will, for instance, usually be desirable to separate state or provincial government from local government only in countries where state or provincial governments exercise a considerable degree of autonomy. Similarly, social security funds should in general be distinguished separately only where they are organized separately from the other activities of general government and exercise substantial autonomy in their operations.

(b) *Corporate and quasi-corporate enterprises*. SNA defines this sector to include enterprises which meet any one of the following criteria: (1) they are incorporated; (2) they are owned by a non-resident; (3) they are relatively large partnerships or proprietorships with complete income statements and balance sheets; (4) they are non-profit institutions mainly serving business and financed and controlled by business; or (5) they are engaged in financial activities. Because of the difficulty that may be encountered in compiling separate production account data for incorporated and unincorporated units, a combined production account for these two sectors has also been provided for.

(c) *Households and private unincorporated enterprises*. This sector includes all private unincorporated enterprises not classed as quasi-corporations. SNA also includes in this sector private non-profit institutions serving households that employ less than the equivalent of two full-time persons.

The criterion for classifying the subsectors of the household sector in these tables differs slightly from that tentatively proposed in SNA. There, the subsectoring is based upon the occupational status of the person designated "head of household". Here, the classification is based upon the most important source of household income taking all household members into account. It is considered that this criterion more accurately reflects both changing social views and changing labor force participation practices; and it responds to recent directives relating to the elimination of sex-based stereotypes.

(d) *Private non-profit institutions serving households*. This sector includes institutions not mainly financed and controlled by general governments, and employing the equivalent of two or more persons, that furnish educational, health, cultural, recreational and other social and community services to households free of charge or at prices which do not fully cover their costs of production. As in the case of general government, SNA includes two components in this sector: (1) *producers of private non-profit services to households*, which engage in the activities enumerated above, and (2) *commercial activities* of these institutions such as owning and letting dwellings, operating eating and lodging facilities, and publishing and selling books, for which it is possible to compile separate production accounts but not complete separate financial accounts. (Where separate financial accounts can be compiled, such activities would be classed as ordinary quasi-corporations.) In SNA, these commercial activities are considered to be "industries", and should be classed in the appropriate ISIC categories, whereas the non-profit services proper will all fall into ISIC category 9.

II. Classifications of Transactions

1. Classification of the Functions of Government

Table 5.3 of *A System of National Accounts* (*op. cit.*) contains a classification of the purposes of government, the 1-digit level of which was used in the previous *Yearbook* for classifying general government outlays. This classification has now been superseded by the *Classification of the Functions of Government 5/*.

2. *Household Consumption Expenditure*

Table 6.1 of SNA provides a classification of household goods and services. The classification used in this *Yearbook* is a slightly condensed version of the second level of this classification in which some second-level categories have been combined.

3. *Purposes of Private Non-Profit Bodies Serving Households*

This classification appears in Table 5.4 of SNA. It is used for classifying the final consumption expenditures of private non-profit institutions serving households.

4. *Gross Capital Formation*

Table 6.2 of SNA classifies stocks according to type, and Table 6.3 classifies gross fixed capital formation according to type. These classifications are used in this *Yearbook* in slightly modified form, calling for less detail in some areas and slightly more detail in others (specifically transport equipment).

5. *Exports and Imports of Goods and Services*

This classification is given in Table 6.4 of SNA.

6. *Transfers*

Table 7.1 of SNA contains a classification of unrequired current transfers, including direct taxes. This classification is not employed directly in the present *Yearbook* but it is the source of the definitions of a number of flows, and will be referred to in that connexion.

7. *Financial Assets and Liabilities*

Table 7.2 of SNA, gives a classification of items appearing in the capital finance account.

8. *Balance Sheet Categories*

Classifications of the various types of assets not included in the previous classification are given in *Provisional Guidelines on National and Sector Balance Sheets and Reconciliation Accounts of the System of National Accounts*, (*op.cit.*) Tables 5.1 and 5.2, dealing respectively with stocks and fixed assets, and non-reproducible tangible assets. These classifications are used in the capital stock tables in Part 2 and the balance sheet tables in Part 3.

C. DEFINITIONS OF FLOWS

The following section briefly defines the content of the flows appearing in the SNA tables of chapter III of the *Yearbook*.

I. *Total Supply of Goods and Services*

1. *Gross Output of Goods and Services*

Gross output of goods and services covers both the value of goods and services produced for sale and the value of goods and services produced for own use. It includes (a) the domestic production of goods and services which are either for sale or for transfer to others, (b) net additions to work in progress valued at cost, and to stocks of finished goods valued in producers' prices; (c) products made on own account for government or private consumption or for gross fixed capital formation; and (d) rents received on structures, machinery and equipment (but not on land) and imputed rent for owner-occupied dwellings.

Production for own consumption of households includes all own-account production of primary products (agricultural, fishing, forestry, mining and quarrying), own account production of such items as butter, flour, wine, cloth or furniture made from primary products, and other goods and services which are also commonly sold. Gross output of the distributive trades is defined as the difference between sales and purchase values of goods sold. Gross output of banks and similar financial institutions is defined as the sum of actual service charges and imputed service charges; the latter is equal to the excess of property income received over interest paid out on deposits. For casualty insurance companies gross output is defined as the excess of premiums received over claims paid, and for life insurance schemes it is the excess of premiums received over the sum of claims paid and net additions to actuarial reserves, excluding the accrued interest of the policy-holders in these reserves. Gross output of general government includes the market value of sales and goods and services produced for own use. The latter should be valued at cost, i.e., the sum of net purchases of goods and services for intermediate consumption (at purchasers' prices); consumption of fixed capital, compensation of employees, and any indirect taxes paid.

The concept of gross output appears in both Part 3 and Part 4 of the tables. In Part 3 each sector production account aggregates to its gross output. In Part 4, gross output of various kind-of-activity sectors appears in Tables 4.1 -4.4 and 4.9-4.14. In the sector production accounts (Tables 3.11, 3.21, 3.31 and 3.41) and the supply tables (4.9, 4.10, 4.13 and 4.14), gross output is divided into marketed and non-marketed components. The marketed component includes all output offered for sale (whether or not a buyer is actually found) or valued on the basis of a market transaction, even if it reaches the ultimate recipient through a transfer.

2. *Imports of Goods and Services*

Imports of goods and services include broadly the equivalent of general imports of merchandise as defined in external trade statistics, plus imports of services and direct purchases abroad made by resident households and by the government on current account. Transfer of migrants' household and personal effects and gifts between households are also included. Some additions and deductions are required, however, to move from the general trade concept to the national accounting concept. Additions required include (1) the value of purchases of bankers, stores and ballast for ships, aircraft, etc., (2) fish and salvage purchased from foreign vessels, and (3) purchases from abroad of gold ore and gold for industrial uses Deductions required include (4) goods imported solely for improvement or repair and subsequently re-exported; and (5) leased or rented machinery, equipment and other goods; the value of the repairs or leasing and rental services is included, however. The valuation of imports is c.i.f. In principle, transactions should be recorded at the moment the transfer of ownership takes place, and not when goods physically enter the domestic territory, but in practice the time of recording used in the national accounts usually must follow that used in the external trade statistics.

Total imports of goods and services appear in Tables 1.1, 1.2, 1.7 and 3.51. A detailed breakdown is given in Table 2.17.

II. *Disposition of Total Supply: Intermediate and Final uses*

1. *Intermediate Consumption*

Intermediate consumption covers non-durable goods and services used up in production, including repair and maintenance, research and development and exploration cost. It also includes indirect outlays on financing capital formation such as floatation costs for loans and transfer costs involved in the purchase and sale of intangible assets and financial claims. Intermediate consumption is, as far as possible, valued in purchasers' prices at the moment of use. For producers of government services and private non-profit services to households, intermediate consumption includes (1) purchases of goods and services on current account *less* sales of similar second-hand goods and scraps and wastes, (2) value of goods in kind received as transfers or gifts from foreign governments, except those received for distribution to households without renovation or alteration, (3) durable goods acquired primarily for military purposes, and (4) goods and services paid for by government but furnished by private suppliers to individuals (e.g medical services), provided that the individuals have no choice of supplier. However, intermediate consumption of these producers does not include (1) goods and services acquired for use in constructing capital assets, such as roads or buildings (2) goods and services paid for by government but furnished by private suppliers to individuals, when the individuals can choose the supplier, and (3) purchases of strategic materials for government stockpiles.

Intermediate consumption appears in each institutional sector production account in Part 3, and in tables 4.1-4.4 by kind of activity. In addition to the flow numbers assigned in SNA, flow numbers have been introduced for two categories of intermediate consumption not separately numbered in *A System of National Accounts.*(*op.cit*). The first is imputed bank service charges. The imputed bank service charge is defined as the excess of property income accruing to banks and similar financial institutions from the investment of deposits over the interest accruing to their depositors. This imputation is made because of the view that banks perform services for depositors for which no explicit payment is made, in return for the use of the deposits as earning assets. It is not possible to allocate the imputation to specific recipients of the services, however, so that it cannot be included, as would be desirable, as part of the intermediate consumption of each reception. It is therefore deducted as a lump sum adjustment. The adjustment appears in the tables showing kind-of-activity breakdowns of value added or intermediate consumption, including tables 1.10, 1.11 and 4.1-4.4. The second addition is intermediate consumption of industries of government, required for constructing a production account for general government (table 3.11).

2. *Government Final Consumption Expenditure*

Government final consumption expenditure is equal to the service produced by general government for its own use. Since these services are not sold, they are valued in the gross domestic product at their cost to the government. This cost is defined as the sum of (1) intermediate consumption, (2) compensation of employees, (3) consumption of fixed capital, and (4) payments of indirect taxes, less (5) the value of own-account production of fixed assets, and *less* (6) sales of goods and services. This last item, government sales, includes all payments made by individuals for services received (whether nominal or full cost), and it also includes the provision of second-hand goods from government stores as transfers in kind to foreign governments. Sales of such items as timber from forest preserves, seeds from agricultural experiment stations, and government publications would also appear here. Compensation of employees, consumption of fixed capital, and indirect taxes paid (if any) should preferably relate to all general government activity, with intra-governmental purchases and sales of goods and services eliminated in order to avoid double counting. With this treatment there will be no operating surplus for any general government unit. In cases where countries consider that ancillary agencies and/or unincorporated government enterprises selling to the general public are operated on commercial principles and that the prices charged reflect market values, treatment of these entities on a net basis is an acceptable alternative. In this treatment their sales to other government agencies will appear as intermediate consumption of the latter, and their operating surplus will appear as an item of general government income. This treatment has a number of disadvantages; the boundary between ancillary agencies and other government agencies is very difficult to specify precisely, and variations in treatment are likely to lead to incomparability among countries. Also, the net treatment makes it impossible to obtain figures for such flows as total compensation of general government employees. Finally, it has the consequence that the level of gross domestic product will vary when the government's internal transfer prices are altered, a result that is somewhat incongruous.

Total government consumption expenditures appear in Tables 1.1, 1.2, 4.11 and 4.12. A breakdown by government subsectors appears in Table 3.12. Tables 2.1-2.4 show detailed breakdowns by function.

3. *Private final consumption expenditure*

Private consumption expenditure measures the final consumption expenditure of all resident non-governmental units. Thus, it is the sum of final consumption expenditure of households and that of private non-profit institutions serving households.

(a) *Private non-profit institutions serving households*

Final consumption expenditure of these units, as in the case of government, is equal to services they produce for their own use, and it is valued at cost. Cost includes purchases and the value (in purchasers' prices) of transfers received in kind of goods and services, compensation of employees, consumption of fixed capital, and indirect taxes paid by these institutions, *less* their sales of goods and services. The definitions of purchases and sales on current account are much the same as those for general government. Private non-profit institutions serving households are defined to include units employing the equivalent of two or more full-time persons and providing educational, health, cultural, recreational, and other social and community services to households free of charge or at prices that are not intended to cover their full costs of production. Units mainly financed and controlled by general government, however, are included in general government rather than here. Units primarily serving business, such as trade associations, are included with corporate and quasi-corporate enterprises. In applying these definitions, some judgement is required, and it will often be necessary to examine intent as well as outcome. A normally profit-making unit that sustains a loss does not thereby become a non-profit institution.

Final expenditures of private non-profit institutions serving households appear in Tables 1.1, 1.2 and 3.42, and a breakdown by purpose appears in Tables 2.5 and 2.6. Definitions of the purpose categories are given in SNA classification 5.4

(b) *Resident households.* What is wanted as a component of the final uses of gross domestic product is the final consumption expenditure of resident households. What is most commonly available in the statistics, however, is not expenditure of resident units, but expenditure in the domestic market. To adjust expenditure in the domestic market to expenditure of resident units, purchases abroad and net gifts in kind received from abroad have been added, and subtracted are purchases in the domestic market of non-resident units. Corresponding adjustments are made to exports (to insure that they include purchases of non-residents in the domestic market) and to imports (to insure that they include purchases of residents abroad). These adjustments include expenditures by tourists, ships' crews, border and seasonal workers and diplomatic and military personnel on goods and services including local transportation, but they exclude expenditures reimbursible as travel expenses (which are counted as intermediate consumption). These adjustments are shown in Tables 2.5 and 2.6.

Household final consumption expenditure includes outlays on non-durable and durable goods and services, *less* sales of second hand goods and of scraps and wastes. In addition to market purchases, household final consumption expenditure includes the imputed gross rent of owner-occupied dwellings, food and other items produced on own accounts and consumed, and items provided as wages and salaries in kind by an employer, such as food, shelter or clothing, and other fringe benefits included in compensation of employees, except those considered to add to household saving. The imputed gross rent of owner-occupied dwellings should, in principle, be valued at the rent of similar facilities on the market, but has been approximated by costs, including operating, maintenance and repair charges, depreciation, mortgage interest, and interest on the owner's equity. Other non-marketed output included in final consumption is valued at producers' prices.

Total resident final consumption expenditure appears in Tables 1.1, 1.2, 1.6 and 1.12. It is broken down by institutional subsectors in Tables 3.32, and in Tables 4.11 and 4.12 it is broken down by industrial origin. A detailed breakdown by type of good is shown in Tables 2.5 and 2.6. The type-of-good categories are defined in SNA classification 6.1.

4. *Gross Capital Formation*

Gross capital formation is the sum of the increase in stocks and gross fixed capital formation, defined below. It appears in Tables 1.1, 1.2 and 1.8. Breakdowns of gross capital formation appear in Tables 2.7-2.12, 4.11 and 4.12. Gross capital formation of individual institutional sectors appears in Tables 3.13, 3.23, 3.33, and 3.43.

(a) I*ncrease in stocks.* This flow includes the value of the physical change in (a) stocks of raw materials, work in progress, and finished goods held by private producers, and (b) stocks of strategic materials held by the government. Work put in place on buildings and other structures, roads, and other construction projects is treated as gross fixed capital formation rather than increase in stocks, but it is distinguished separately there to facilitate analysis. Increases in livestock raised for slaughter should be included in the increase in stocks, but breeding and draft animals, dairy cattle, and animals raised for wool clips are treated as fixed capital. The physical change in stocks during a period of account should be valued at average purchasers' prices during the period. In some cases the available data relate to the change in the value of stocks held rather than the value of the physical change.

A classification of the increase in stocks by type is given in Tables 2.7 and 2.8, and defined in SNA classification 6.2. The increase in stocks by kind of activity of owner is shown in Tables 2.9 and 2.10.

(b) *Gross capital formation.* This flow is defined to include purchases and own account production of new producers' durable goods, reduced by net sales to the rest of the world of similar second hand or scrapped goods. Outlays of producers of government services for military purposes (except on land and certain civilian-type items such as schools, hospitals, and family-type housing, and in some cases roads when for civilian use) are, however, considered to be current expenditures. "Military purposes" are here construed in terms of final expenditures: they include the military airport, but not the bulldozer used in constructing the airport. Gross fixed capital formation includes outlays for reclaiming and improving land and for the development and extension of timber tracts, mines, plantations, orchards, vineyards, etc., and on breeding and dairy cattle, draft animals, and animals raised for wool. Outlays on alteration or extension of fixed assets which significantly extent their life or increase their productivity are included, but outlays on repair and maintenance to keep fixed assets in good working condition are not. All costs are included that are directly connected with the acquisition and installation of the fixed assets, such as customs duties and other indirect taxes, transport, delivery and installation charges, site clearing, planning and designing costs, legal fees and other transfer costs with respect to transactions in land, mineral deposits, timber tracts, etc. However, the costs of financing, such as floatation costs, underwriters' commissions, and the cost of advertising bond issues, are excluded; these items are included in intermediate consumption. The acquisition of fixed assets is to be recorded at the moment the ownership of the goods passes to the buyer. In the case of construction projects this is taken to be the time the work is put in place, but as noted above uncompleted construction projects are shown separately from completed ones.

A classification of fixed assets by type is given in Tables 2.7 and 2.8, and the categories are defined in SNA classification 6.3. A classification by kind of activity of purchaser is given in Tables 2.9, 2.10, 2.11 and 2.12, and a classification by producing industry is given in Tables 4.11 and 4.12. Breakdowns by institutional sector are given in Tables 3.13, 3.23, 3.33 and 3.43.

5. *Exports of Goods and Services*

Exports of goods and services are defined to be parallel to the definition of imports given above, and they are shown in the same tables and classifications. Exports are, however, valued f.o.b., whereas imports are valued c.i.f.

III. *Cost Components and Income Shares*

1. *Value Added and Gross Domestic Product*

The value added of industries at producers' prices is equal to the gross output of the industries at producers' prices less the value of their intermediate consumption at purchasers' prices. Value added for the total of all domestic producers (plus import duties and value added tax, which are not included in the value added of any domestic producer, and *less* imputed bank service charges which are deducted in a single line) is equal to the gross domestic product. This derivation of gross domestic product is shown in Tables 1.9-1.11, and 4.1-4.4. Gross domestic product may alternatively be defined as the sum of final expenditures in the domestic economy (Tables 1.1 and 1.2), or as the sum of incomes received in the domestic economy (Tables 1.3, 1.9 and 4.5-4.6). In principle all three methods should yield the same result but in statistical practice there are likely to be small discrepancies. Such statistical discrepancies are shown where they exist.

2. *Compensation of Employees*

Compensation of employees appears in SNA as a domestic concept and as a national concept. Table 1.3 employs the domestic concept, i.e., compensation of employees paid by resident producers. This includes payments to nonresident employees working in the country, but excludes payments to resident employees temporarily working abroad. In order to show the relation of this concept to compensation received by resident households (shown in Tables 1.6 and 3.32) and compensation paid to the rest of the world (shown in Tables 1.7 and 3.51) the two components are shown separately in Table 1.3. Each component includes (a) wages and salaries, (b) employers' contributions to social security schemes, and (c) employers' contributions to private pension, insurance and similar schemes. The national concept of compensation of employees is shown in the household sector income and outlay account (Tables 1.6 and 3.31), where compensation received by resident households from domestic producers and that received from the rest of the world are gathered together. The portion paid by resident producers appears in Table 1.3; that paid by the rest of the world appears in Table 1.7.

Wages and salaries include all payments to employees for their labor, whether in cash or in kind, before deduction of employee contributions to social security schemes, withholding taxes and the like. They include commissions, bonuses and tips, and cost of living, vacation and sick leave allowances paid directly by the employers to the employee, but they exclude reimbursement for travel and other expenses incurred by employees for business purposes, which are included in intermediate consumption. The pay and allowance of members of the armed forces, the fees, salaries and bonuses of members of boards of directors, managing directors, executives and other employees of incorporated enterprises, and the fees of ministers of religion are included. Wages and salaries in kind are valued at their cost to the employer, and include goods and services furnished to employees free of charge or at markedly reduced cost which are clearly and primarily of benefit to the employees as consumers.

Employers' contributions to social security schemes include all social security contributions that employers make on behalf of their employees, but not the employees' own share of such contributions. Social security contributions may be broader than payments to social security funds, since not all social security arrangements are funded.

Employers' contributions to pension, insurance and similar schemes includes paid and imputed contributions by employers on behalf of their employees to private funds, reserves or other schemes for providing pensions, family allowances, lay-off and severance pay, maternity leaves, workmen's compensation, health and other casualty insurance, life insurance, and the like. Where employers make payments to employees for such benefits without the establishment a formal fund for this purpose, the contributions that would be required to support such a fund are imputed both here and subsequently as an imputed transfer from households to their employers, since of course the employees do not control the use of the fund.

3. *Operating Surplus*

Operating surplus is the balancing item in the SNA production account. For an individual establishment, it is defined as the excess of value added over the sum of compensation of employees, consumption of fixed capital, and net indirect taxes. The operating surplus of all types of establishments — corporate, quasi-corporate, and unincorporated, public and private — is included in the figure shown in Table 1.3. Operating surplus for each of the institutional sectors individually is shown in Tables 3.11, 3.21 and 3.31; its breakdown by kind of activity is shown in Tables 4.5 and 4.6. It is also included in the totals for property and entrepreneurial income shown in Tables 1.4, 1.5, and 1.6.

4. *Consumption of Fixed Capital*

Consumption of fixed capital includes allowances for normal wear and tear, foreseen obsolescence and probable (normally expected) accidental damage to fixed capital not made good by repair, all valued at current replacement cost. Unforeseen obsolescence, damages due to calamities, and depletion of natural resources are not included, since these are capital losses and should appear as changes in the balance sheet. Nor is the revaluation of past allowances for consumption of fixed capital due to changes in the current replacement cost of fixed assets included; this also will appear as part of the change in accumulated allowances shown in the balance sheet. Total consumption of fixed capital appears in Tables 1.3, 1.8 and 1.12; consumption of fixed capital of individual institutional sector in Tables 3.11, 3.21, 3.31 and 3.41, and consumption of fixed capital by kind of activity in Tables 4.5 and 4.6. The accumulated consumption of fixed capital for specific types of assets and kind of activity sectors appears as the difference between the gross and net capital stock in Tables 2.13-2.16, and for individual institutional sectors it appears in Tables 3.15, 3.25, 3.35 and 3.45.

5. *Indirect Taxes*

Indirect taxes are defined as taxes chargeable to the cost of production or sale of goods and services. They include (a) import and export duties, (b) excise, sales, entertainment and turnover taxes, (c) real estate and land taxes, unless they are merely an administrative device for collecting income tax, (d) levies on value added and the employment of labor (but not social security contributions), (e) motor vehicle, driving test, licence, airport and passport fees, when paid by producers, and (f) the operating surplus of government fiscal monopolies on such items as alcoholic beverages and tobacco (in principle reduced by the normal profit margin of similar business units). In this *Yearbook* indirect taxes paid and subsidies received from supranational organizations (e..g. the European Community) are shown separately. Also, the net treatment of value added taxes recommended by the European Community has been employed.

Unlike all other indirect taxes, SNA does not allocate import duties among producers in tables by kind of activity. Indirect taxes are only allocated to a particular kind of activity where they are levied directly on the output of that activity (e.g., excise duties) or on the process of producing that output (e.g.,employment taxes). Import duties, however, are levied on the output of foreign rather than domestic producers, and are therefore shown separately in tables by kind of activity, including Tables 1.10, 1.11, 4.1, 4.2, 4.5, 4.6, 4.9 and 4.10.

Total indirect taxes appear in Table 1.3. Indirect taxes paid by individual institutional sectors appear in Tables 3.11, 3.21, 3.31, and 3.41. Indirect taxes paid to supranational organizations appear in Tables 1.7 and 1.12. Indirect taxes retained by government are shown in Table 3.12.

6. *Subsidies*

Subsidies are grants on current account by the government to (a) private enterprises and public corporations, or (b) unincorporated public enterprises when clearly intended to compensate for losses resulting from the price policies of government. Total subsidies, including those paid by supranational organizations as well as by government, appear in Table 1.3; subsidies paid by supranational organizations in Tables 1.7 and 1.12; and those paid by government in Tables 1.4 and 3.12. Subsidies received by individual institutional sectors appear in Tables 3.21, 3.31 and 3.41.

7. *Withdrawals from Quasi-Corporations*

Withdrawals from the entrepreneurial income of quasi-corporations consist of the actual payments made to the proprietors of quasi-corporations from the entrepreneurial income of these units. Entrepreneurial income of quasi-corporations is equal to their income from production (net operating surplus) *plus* their net income (receipts *less* payments) from property. In some cases, the whole of the entrepreneurial income will be treated as if paid out to the proprietors; in other cases, some of it is retained as net saving within the quasi-corporation. Withdrawals from quasi-corporations also include withdrawals from foreign branches of domestic companies or of domestic branches of foreign companies since both of these categories are treated as quasi-corporations. The withdrawals may be negative, as proprietors may provide funds to the enterprises to compensate for losses.

SNA assigns separate flow numbers to withdrawals as they appear in the paying sectors (4.4) and in the receiving sectors (4.5). As disbursements, they appear in Table 3.22 and as part of a larger total in Table 1.5. As receipts, they appear in Tables 3.12, 3.22, 3.32, and 3.42, and as parts of larger total in Tables 1.4, 1.5 and 1.6

8. *Property Income*

Property income consists of payments of interest, dividends and land rents and royalties, all of which are assigned separate SNA flow numbers both as payments and as receipts. Interest is defined as income payable and receivable on financial claims, such as bank and other deposits, bills and bonds including public debt, and the equity of households in life insurance actuarial reserves and pension funds. Dividends consist of income payable and receivable on corporate equity securities and other forms of participation in the equity of private incorporated enterprises, public corporations and co-operatives. Rent payments include, in addition to net land rent, royalty payments for concessions to exploit mineral deposits or for the use of patents, copyrights, trademarks and the like. They exclude rent payments on machinery and equipment or buildings, which are treated as the purchase of a service rather than property income and appear in gross output of the seller and intermediate consumption of the purchaser. Payments of land rent are always treated as a domestic flow since the foreign owners are for national accounting purposes dealt with as residents of the country in which the land is located. When it is not possible to separate rent of buildings and rent of the land on which the buildings stand, the whole flow is attributed to the buildings, i.e, excluded from property income and included in intermediate consumption.

Property income paid and received by individual institutional sectors is shown in Tables 3.12, 3.22, 3.32 and 3.42. As part of a larger total it appears in the summary tables 1.4, 1.5 and 1.6.

IV. *Taxes and Unrequited Transfers*

The categories of taxes and unrequited transfers are classified and defined in SNA classification 7.1. SNA does not provide the full articulation of the to-whom from-whom relationships of these flows, but assigns flow numbers to various combinations of them used in specific standard tables and accounts. In order to define the flows used in the present less ambiguously, a somewhat fuller listing of individual flow components is used.

1. *Casualty Insurance Transactions*

Casualty insurance transactions refer to health, accident fire, theft, unemployment and similar insurance schemes. The total of net premiums for the economy as a whole is equal to total premiums payable *less* an imputed service charge, which in turn is defined to be equal to the difference between premiums and claims. As a consequence, for the economy as a whole net premiums and claims are equal. However, the total service charge is distributed to sectors of receipt and disbursement in proportion to the total (not net) premiums paid, so that net premiums and claims are not necessarily equal for each sector separately. In the former SNA, these insurance transactions were considered to be in part capital items, and this practice continues in the accounts of a number of countries. In the revised SNA, however, all casualty insurance transactions, including compensation for capital losses, are considered to be current flows. They are shown in detail in Tables 3.12, 3.22, 3.331 and 3.42.

2. *Taxes and Other Government Receipts*

Taxes and other government receipts include direct taxes, compulsory fees, fines and penalties, social security contributions, and other current transfers received by general government.

Direct taxes include two components. Direct taxes on income cover levies by public authorities at regular intervals (except social security contributions) on income from employment, property, capital gains or any other source. Real estate and land taxes are included only if they are merely administrative procedures for the assessment and collection of income tax. Other direct taxes include levies by public authorities at regular intervals on the financial assets and the net of total worth of enterprises, private non-profit institutions and households, and on the possession or use of goods by households. Direct taxes received are shown in Tables 1.4 and 3.2; as payments of other sectors are shown in Tables 3.22, 3.32 and 3.42.

Compulsory fees are payments to public authorities by households for services that are obligatory and unavoidable in the only circumstances in which they are useful. Examples of such fees are payments by households for driving tests and licenses, airport and court fees, and the like. Similar payments by business units are treated as indirect taxes. Fines and penalties, however, include not only those paid by households but also those paid by corporate and quasi-corporate enterprises and private non-profit institutions serving households. They appear in the same tables as direct taxes.

Social security contributions consist of contributions for the account of employees, whether made by employees or on their behalf by employers, to the social security arrangements that are imposed, controlled or financed by the government for the purpose of providing social security benefits for the community or large sections of the community. They appear as receipts in Tables 1.4 and 3.12, and as payments in Tables 1.6 and 3.32.

Current transfers n.e.c. received by general government consist primarily of transfers received from the rest of the world and imputed employee welfare contributions. Transfers from the rest of the world include grants between governments to finance military outlays, outlays for health and educational purposes, and similar transfers in kind of military equipment, food, clothing, etc. Payments and assessments and other periodic contributions to international organizations are also included. In addition to actual transfers, this item also includes imputed transfers arising from the obligation of the government as an employer to pay directly to its employees pensions, family allowances, severance and lay-off pay and other welfare benefits, when there is no special fund, reserve or insurance for these purposes. In these circumstances, SNA provides for the establishment of an imputed fund to which imputed contributions are made, of a magnitude sufficient to support the unfunded benefit payments. The imputed contributions are included in compensation of employees, as an addition to actual payments, and are then shown as an imputed payment by the employees back to the government as an employer. These transfers appear in Table 1.4 as an aggregate, and in Table 3.12 in more detail.

xvi

3. *Household Transfer Receipts*

Household transfer receipts include social security benefits, social assistance grants, and unfunded employee welfare benefits. These flows, in varying detail, are shown in Tables 1.6, 2.4 and 3.32.

Social security benefits are payments to individuals under the social security arrangements described above. The payments are often made out of a special fund and may be related to the income of individuals from employment or to contributions to social security arrangements made on their account. Examples are unemployment insurance benefits, old-age, disability and survivors' pensions, family allowances and reimbursements for medical and hospital expenses. It may be difficult to distinguish social security benefits from social assistance grants, on the one hand, and insurance benefits, on the other. The main criterion is method of finance; the actual content will vary from country to country. Medical services, for instance, may be supplied as social assistance, as a part of social security, as a casualty insurance benefit, or as a free government service.

Social assistance grants are cash grants to individuals and households, except social security benefits and unfunded employee welfare benefits. They may be made by public authorities, private non-profit institutions, or corporate and quasi-corporate enterprises. Examples are relief payments; widows', guardians' and family allowances and payments of medical and dental expenses which are not part of social insurance schemes; war bonuses, pensions and service grants; and scholarships, fellowships and maintenance allowances for educational, training and similar purposes. They include payments by public authorities for services provided by business enterprises and private non-profit institutions directly and individually to persons, whether these payments are made to the individuals or directly to the providers of the services which the persons are considered to have purchased. They exclude, however, transfers to persons or households as indemnities for property losses during floods, wars and similar calamities; these are considered to be capital items.

Unfunded employee welfare benefits are pensions, family allowances, severance and lay-off pay, maternity leave pay, workmen's and disability compensation and reimbursements for medical expenses and other casualties which employers pay directly to their former or present employees without having special funds, reserves or insurance for these purposes.

4. *Transfers Received by Private Non-Profit Institutions*

Transfers received by private non-profit institutions serving households include grants and gifts, in cash and in kind, to non-profit institutions serving households which are intended to cover partially the cost of the provision of services by these institutions. They also include membership dues paid to political organizations, fraternal bodies and the like. They appear as a receipt in Table 3.42, and as payments sometimes as part of a larger total, in Tables 3.12, 3.22 and 3.32.

5. *Other Current Transfers n.e.c.*

Other current transfers n.e.c. include transfers to and from resident sectors that are not specifically included in any other flows. They may include migrants' remittances, transfers of immigrants' personal and household goods, and transfers between resident and non-resident households, in cash and in kind. They include allowances for bad debts.

V. *Finance of Gross Accumulation*

1. *Net Saving*

Net saving is the balancing item in the SNA income and outlay account. It is defined as the difference between current receipts and current disbursements. Net saving for the nation as a whole appears in Tables 1.8 and 1.12. Net saving for individual institutional sectors appears in Tables 3.12, 3.13, 3.22, 3.23, 3.32, 3.33, 3.42 and 3.43.

2. *Surplus of the Nation on Current Transactions*

The surplus of the nation on current transactions is the balancing item in the external transactions current accounts, Tables 1.7 and 3.51. It also appears in Table 1.8, the capital transactions account, in Table 1.12, the table showing relationships among the national accounting aggregates, and Table 3.52, the external transactions capital accumulation account.

3. *Purchases of Land, net*

Purchases of land, net, include purchases *less* sales of land, subsoil deposits, forests and inland waters, including any improvements that are an integral part of these assets except buildings and other structures. The purchases and sales are valued at the transaction (sales) price of the land, forests, etc., not including the transfer costs involved; such transfer costs are included in gross capital formation. Purchases and sales are assumed to take place when the legal title to the land passes. They are considered to take place between residents institutions only. Where the land is purchased by a non-resident, a nominal resident institution is considered to be the owner of the land. The foreign owner is assigned equity in the resident institution equivalent to the purchase price of the land. The value recorded in the flow is the same for both the buyer and the seller. For the country as a whole, therefore, purchases and sales will cancel out. If the sales value of the structures situated on the land cannot be separated from the sales value of the land itself, the entire transaction should be recorded as a purchase and sale of structures (i.e., of second-hand assets) unless the structures are intended for immediate demolition. Purchases of land appear in the capital accumulation accounts of the individual institutional sectors, in Tables 3.13, 3.23, 3.33 and 3.43.

4. *Purchases of Intangible Assets, net*

Purchases of intangible assets, net, are defined as purchases, *less* sales, of exclusive rights to mineral, fishing and other concessions and of patents, copyrights, etc. These transactions involve once-and-for-all relinquishment and acquisition of the exclusive rights, although they may be paid for over a period of years; they do not include concessions, leases, licences to use patents and permission to publish copyrighted materials which involve periodic payment of royalties or rents, with eventual reversion of the rights to the seller. The purchases and sales are valued at the transaction (sales) value of the mineral concession, lease, patent, etc., not including any transfer costs involved. (The transfer costs are included in gross capital formation.) Purchases of intangible assets appear in the individual institutional sector capital accumulation accounts (Tables 3.13, 3.23, 3.33, and 3.43) as a part of gross accumulation. Purchases from the rest of the world appear in Table 3.52.

5. *Capital Transfers*

Capital transfers are defined as unrequited transfers, in cash or in kind, which are used for purposes of capital formation or other forms of capital accumulation, are made out of wealth, or are non-recurrent. Examples of capital transfers are grants from one government to another to finance deficits in external trade, investment grants, unilateral transfers of capital goods, legacies, death duties and inheritance taxes, migrants' transfers of financial assets and indemnities in respect of calamities. Mixed transfers, considered by one party to the transaction as capital and the other as current, are treated as capital. Capital transfers appear in Tables 3.13, 3.23, 3.33, 3.43, and 3.52.

6. *Net Lending*

Net lending is defined as the excess of the sources of finance of accumulation (i.e., net saving, consumption of fixed capital, and capital transfers received) over the uses of these funds for gross capital formation, net purchases of land and intangibles, and capital transfers paid. It appears in the capital accumulation accounts of the individual institutional sectors, Tables 3.13, 3.23, 3.33 and 3.43 and 3.43, and in the external transactions capital accumulation account, Table 3.52. Net lending is also equal to the difference between a sector's net acquisition of financial assets and its net incurrence of financial liabilities. It thus also appears in the institutional sector capital finance accounts, Tables 3.14, 3.24, 3.34, 3.44 and 3.53. Not for all countries net lending derived in these two different ways are statistically identical.

VI. *Financial Assets and Liabilities*

Net acquisition of financial assets its defined as the difference between, on the one hand, acquisitions or purchases and, on the other and, relinquishment or sales by given transactors of financial claims on second parties. Net incurrence of liabilities is equal to the issue or sale less redemption or payment of financial claims of second parties. A classification and definitions of financial assets and liabilities is given in SNA classification 7.2, reproduced in Annex B. Changes in financial assets and liabilities for individual institutional sectors appear in the capital finance accounts, Tables 3.14, 3.24, 3.34, 3.44 and 3.53. Their total amount is shown in the sector balance sheets Tables 3.15, 3.25, 3.35 and 3.45.

VII. *Other Assets*

1. *Reproducible Tangible Assets*

Reproducible tangible assets are classified and defined in Table 5.1 of the *Provisional Guidelines on National and Sector Balance Sheets and Reconciliation Accounts of the System of National Accounts* (*op. cit*). They appear, classified by type of asset and broad sectors, in Tables 2.13 and 2.14, and by kind of activity in Tables 2.15 and 2.16, and for individual institutional sectors in the sector balance sheets, Tables 3.15, 3.25, 3.35, and 3.45.

2. *Non-Reproducible Tangible Assets*

Non-reproducible tangible assets are classified and defined in Table 5.2 of the publication indicated in VII.1 above. Only the total appears in the tables, in the sector balance sheets, Tables 3.15, 325, and 3.45.

3. *Non-Financial Intangible Assets*

Non-financial intangible assets include the mineral, fishing and other concessions, leases, patents, copyrights, etc., whose purchase and sale is recorded in the capital accumulation account. These intangible assets are created at the time of the purchase or sale, that is, when a once-and-for-all lump-sum payment has been made for the lease, concession, patent or copyright. They appear in the sector balance sheets, Tables 3.15, 3.25, 3.35 and 3.45.

1/ *Official records of the Economic and Social Council, Forty-fourth Session, Supplement No. 10*, paras. 8-24.
2/ The present system is published in *A System of National Accounts*, Studies in Methods, Series F, No. 2, Rev. 3 (United Nations publication, Sales No. E.69.XVII.3).
3/ Statistical Papers, Series M, No. 60 (United Nations publication, Sales No. 77.XVII.10).
4/ Statistical Papers, Series M, No. 4, Rev. 2, Add. 1 (United Nations publication, Sales No. E.71.XVII.8).
5/ Statistical Papers, Series M, No. 70 (United Nations publication, Sales No. 80.XVII.17).

II. THE SYSTEM OF MATERIAL PRODUCT BALANCES (MPS)

The System of Material Product Balances (MPS) furnishes the means for standardizing the national accounting data which the Statistical Office of the United Nations receives from countries with centrally planned economies. Data collection follows the principles found in the *Basic Methodological Rules for the Compilation of the Statistical Balance of the National Economy 1/*. This system is also described in the *Basic Principles of the System of Balances of the National Economy 2/*.

A. THE MPS STRUCTURE

The MPS is based on a system of balances. It includes material and financial balances, the balance of manpower resources and the balance of fixed capital and indicators of national wealth. The material balance is a presentation of the volume of the supply of goods and material services originating in domestically produced global product and imports and their disposition to consumption, capital formation and exports, classified by different production activity categories. The financial balance is a presentation of income flows generated in production in the material sphere, their redistribution through transactions in the non-material sphere and through other transfers flows and finally their disbursement to consumption and capital formation. The income flows of the financial balance are classified by institutional (social) sectors. The presentation is therefore comparable to that of production, income and outlay and capital finance accounts by institutional sectors in the SNA. The third type of balance, i.e., the manpower balance, presents the allocation of available manpower to production activities and institutional or social sectors. This balance is expressed in the number of persons employed. The last balance is the one of national wealth and capital assets. It is a presentation of the volume of the stocks of tangible fixed and other assets available at the beginning and the end of the year and the increase that has taken place during the year. The tangible assets are classified by type of asset and by forms of ownership and production activities of the national economy.

The tables that are presented in chapter III and are listed in the Introduction, provide further detail on the material balances. Table 1 on net material product by use is similar to the SNA table on GDP by kind of economic activity. Data regarding the production and goods and services transactions are included in tables 2, 3, 4 and 5, which present, respectively, activity breakdowns of net material product and of primary incomes of the population and of enterprises, a breakdown by socio-economic sectors of these two types of primary incomes and a breakdown of supply and disposition of goods and material services by kind of activity of the producers. Tables 6, 7, 8 and 9 present further details on the expenditure categories such as a breakdown of fixed capital formation by kind of economic activity and by socio-economic sector and of increases in material circulating assets and of stocks by kind of activity and a classification of final consumption, personal consumption and total consumption of the population by type of expenditures.

B. DIFFERENCES BETWEEN THE MPS AND THE SNA.

Apart from the differences in structure of the two systems, there are considerable differences between the coverage of the concepts used in the MPS and in the SNA. As these differences limit the use of the MPS and SNA data in cross-country types of analyses, a summary of those that are relevant to the MPS data published in chapter III of this Yearbook is reproduced below 3/.

1. *The treatment of material and non-material services*

The MPS makes a distinction contrary to the SNA, between the production of material and non-material services. Only the production of material services, together with that of goods, is covered by the gross output (global product) concept of the MPS. The production of non-material services is excluded. Material goods and services used as inputs in the production of non-material services are considered to be a part of final consumption expenditure, while income flows resulting from this type of production are treated as income transfers. The material services are those that are directly linked to the production of goods and cover the services related to repair, transportation and distribution of goods. All other services are treated as non-material services. This important difference between the MPS and the present SNA results in the following concrete differences between the two systems:

(a) Expenditures by enterprises on cultural, sports and similar facilities for their employees are excluded in the MPS from intermediate consumption. Instead a transfer between enterprises and households is included, while the material goods and services involved in the above expenditures are allocated to final consumption of the population. The SNA treats these expenditures as intermediate consumption.

(b) Depreciation of dwellings and other material goods and services involved in the provision of housing are allocated in the MPS to final consumption expenditure. As these are non-material services, no value-added contribution is included in net material product. In the SNA this contribution is included in GDP.

(c) Travel expenses in connection with business are not included in intermediate consumption in the MPS as they are in the present SNA. Instead they are treated as a part of compensation of employees and the material goods and services involved are allocated to private final consumption expenditure.

(d) The SNA and the MPS draw a different distinction between uniforms to be treated as intermediate consumption and those to be included in compensation of employees and final consumption expenditure of households. The SNA draws the distinction between civilian (intermediate consumption) and military uniforms and the MPS, between dress and working uniforms.

(e) Tips are treated in the SNA as a part of compensation of employees, while in the MPS they are treated as income transfers, when they exceed the normal service charge.

2. *Capital formation*

The MPS and SNA guidelines differ on the one hand with regard to the treatment of capital gains and losses and the coverage of depreciation and on the other in the coverage of fixed capital formation and increases in stocks. The main differences are the following:

(a) In the MPS depreciation as well as the replacement for losses due to certain foreseeable and non-forseeable damages to fixed assets and stocks - including those caused by accidents and calamities - are deducted in order to arrive at net fixed capital formation. The SNA generally uses the concept of gross fixed capital formation only. However, if net capital formation were to be estimated, only depreciation on fixed assets would have to be deducted in that system. Losses in stocks or fixed assets would never be candidates for deduction. Losses on fixed assets would be treated as capital losses and dealt with outside the national accounts flows, while losses in stocks would be treated as a part of intermediate consumption or as capital losses depending on whether they are due to normal events in production or to calamities. The dividing line between losses and depreciation of fixed assets also differs in the two systems. In the SNA, depreciation is assumed to cover among other things the average amount of accidental damage to fixed assets that is not made good by repair or replacement of parts—for example, damage arising from fire and accidents. In the MPS such damages are not reflected in depreciation but covered under losses.

(b) Depreciation in the MPS is based on the original cost of the assets. However, every eight to ten years adjustments to replacement cost are made to this asset value and these adjustments are also reflected in a corrected value of depreciation. Furthermore, differences that arise between the actual value and the written-off book value at the moment the assets are scrapped or sold are included in the value of depreciation for the year the sale or scrapping occurs. The SNA uses instead the replacement value of the assets as a basis for depreciation. Any change in this value, whether it happens at the moment the asset is sold or during the time it is used, is considered to be a capital gain or loss and is not accounted for in the national accounting flows.

(c) In addition, in depreciation the MPS includes capital consumption allowances with respect to afforestation, land improvements, roads, bridges and similar structures. The SNA does not include any imputations for depreciation of this type of asset.

(d) Expenditures on fixed assets for military purposes are treated in the MPS as a part of net fixed capital formation. In the SNA these outlays are allocated to government final consumption expenditure, except for outlays by government on the construction and alteration of family dwellings for personnel of the armed forces, which are included in gross fixed capital formation.

(e) Transfer cost with regard to purchases and sales of existing fixed assets are treated in the MPS as transfers since these are non-material services. In the SNA these costs are included in gross fixed capital formation.

(f) Work put in place on structures, roads, dams, ports and other forms of construction is allocated in the MPS to increases in material circulating assets and stocks. Only when the construction is finished is its total value transferrred to net fixed capital formation. In the SNA these outlays are immediately allocated to gross fixed capital formation.

3. *External transactions*

The third area in which the MPS and the SNA differ is in the coverage of exports and imports of goods and services, in the distinction between residents and non-residents and in the treatment of monetary *versus* non-monetary gold. The differences are the following:

(a) In the MPS embassies, consulates and international bodies are treated as residents of the country in which they are located, while in the SNA they are treated as residents of the country they represent. This difference in the residence concept has consequences for the allocation between countries of capital formation and government final consumption expenditure and also for the allocation of the income flows. Wages and salaries paid to local employees of these extraterritorial bodies are not included in the SNA concept of GDP. They are dealt with, however, as factor income from abroad and therefore accounted for in the national income concept in the SNA. In the MPS such wages and salaries, if earned in the sphere of material production, are included in primary incomes of the population as well as in net material product

(b) The MPS uses the territorial concept of final consumption expenditure, which includes purchases by non-residents in the domestic market and excludes purchases abroad by residents. As a result such flows are not accounted for in exports or imports. On the other hand, it does include in exports and imports transactions that, though they take place in the domestic market, are conducted in foreign currency. These transactions are treated as if they were transactions with non-residents. The SNA uses the national concept of final consumption expenditure and takes into account in exports and imports, respectively, the direct purchases in the domestic market by non-residents and the direct purchases abroad by non-residents. Furthermore, no distinction is made in the SNA between transactions that are conducted in local or in foreign currency.

(c) Purchases and sales by external trade organizations of goods that do not cross the border of the country in question and also imported goods that are re-exported without being processed are treated in the MPS as part respectively, of imports and of exports. In the SNA they are not accounted for in the export and import flows, except for the margins received by resident units as payments for services rendered.

(d) Gifts in kind by households to and from abroad are included in exports and imports in the SNA. In the MPS they are excluded from these flows.

(e) Transactions in intangible assets (patents, copyrights, trade-marks, exclusive rights to exploit mineral deposits etc.) with the rest of the world are included in the MPS in exports and imports. In the SNA they are treated as property income or as sales or purchases of intangible assets to our from abroad, depending on whether the payment is for the use of the right or for the outright transfer of those rights.

(f) Transactions with the rest of the world in monetary and non-monetary gold are included in the MPS in exports and imports. In the SNA exports and imports include actual transactions in non-monetary gold only. Exports in addition include newly mined gold (whether actually exported or not) in order to transform gold as a commodity into a financial asset.

C. THE STANDARD CLASSIFICATIONS OF THE MPS

Two classifications are used in the MPS standard tables presented—i.e., the kind of activity classification and the classification by socio-economic groups. Contrary to the SNA usage with respect to the activity and institutional classifications for different groups of transactions, the two MPS classifications are parallel ones that are applied to the same transaction categories: net material product and its component primary incomes and capital formation. Each of these classifications is described briefly below.

1. *Kind of Activity*

All forms of activity in production are classified according to groups or branches, depending on the nature and results of the application of labour. The two major categories constitute branches of the material sphere and branches of the non-material sphere. The first category covers the production of goods, and services that are related to the production of goods such as repair services, transportation services and goods distribution services. The second category includes the remaining services-producing activities. Each of the two categories is further broken down by branches which are similar in character to the ISIC categories used in the SNA. The unit of classification is not the organizational unit (i.e., enterprise) but a smaller unit that performs one type of activity (i.e., establishment). If an enterprise or institution or other organizational unit carries on more than one type of economic activity, it is considered to consist of two or more establishments that perform different activities.

For the subclassification of net material product by kind of activity only the activity breakdown of the material sphere is used since net material product originates in this sphere only. For capital formation, however, the activity categories of the non-material sphere are also used, since capital formation relates not only to the material sphere but also to non-material branches.

A rough correspondence based on the names of the activity categories can be established between the activity categories presented in the SNA and the MPS branches. The user should be aware, however, of the limitations that such a linkage may entail, as indicated in the following points.

(a) Mining and quarrying, manufacturing, and electricity, gas, and water are shown as three separate categories in the SNA presentation and as one category called industrial production, in the MPS presentation.

(b) Hunting and the collection of forestry products is treated as a part of agriculture in the SNA presentation and as a part of forestry and logging in the MPS.

(c) The distribution of gas, electricity and water to households is treated in the MPS as a non-material service (including in housing). This activity is therefore not reflected in net material product, while its capital formation is dealt with as capital formation of the non-material sphere. In the SNA these distribution activities are an integral part of the activity category for electricity gas and water.

(d) Printing and publishing, which is treated as a material activity in the MPS, is allocated to the MPS category called "other activities of the material sphere". In the SNA this activity is included with manufacturing.

(e) Cleaning, dyeing and repair services are included with industrial activity (manufacturing) in the MPS presentation and with community, social and personal services in the SNA.

(f) In comparing the activity breakdown of net material product and GDP, the user should be aware that the coverage of the MPS category called "other activities of the material sphere" falls far short of the combined coverage of the two SNA categories for finance, insurance, real estate and business services and for community, social and personal services. The SNA categories include all non-material activities that are excluded from the MPS coverage of net material product. In addition, the shifts between activity categories that were outlined in the previous points affect this group. Other activities in the presentation of net material product include in addition telegraph, news-gathering and editorial agencies, industrial services other than architectural design services, printing and publishing services, the production of motion pictures, phonograph records and prerecorded tapes, data-processing and tabulating services, waterway-maintenance services and the operating of flood-control systems, and services related to the conservation of natural resources and the protection of the environment.

2. *Socio-economic Sectors*

The rates of development of the national economy and the basic features of production that support this development are largely determined by the social structure of the community. In order to study the process the MPS classifies by socio-economic sectors the various activities involved in the production of material goods and services. This classification is based on the form of ownership of the fixed and circulating capital. The form of ownership of the means of production determines the forms of ownership of the product and of the incomes generated by its disposal.

The basic socio-economic sectors are the socialist sector and the private sector.

The socialist sector embraces the enterprises and institutions in public, socialist ownership. The fixed and circulating assets of these enterprises are public property. The socialist sector also includes the personal plots of employees and members of co-operatives.

Within the socialist sector the following socio-economic subsectors are distinguished: the state subsector; the co-operative subsector, which includes agricultural producer's cooperatives; associations; personal plots of employees; personal plots of members of co-operatives.

The state subsector includes the enterprises and institutions in state ownership. The state furnishes them with the fixed and circulating assets required for their operation. These economic units are administratively subordinated to central or local organs of state authority. The production of the state subsector and the income generated in it belong to the people as a country.

The co-operative subsector embraces the enterprises and institutions in collective or group onwership. The fixed and circulating assets of these economic bodies are originally built up from the entrance fees (initiation fees) of their members and the proceeds of sales of shares to them; and are later supplemented from a part of their operating surplus. The output and income of the enterprises and institutions of the co-operative sub-sector are the property of their members.

The association subsector includes the enterprises and institutions owned by voluntary or semi-voluntary associations. The fixed and circulating assets of the economic bodies of this subsector are built up from the voluntary contributions of their members and from part of the operating surplus of such bodies. The output and income of this subsector belong to the associations.

The personal plots of employees and members of co-operatives embrace agricultural output, construction and other forms of activity (gathering of wild fruits and berries, scrap collection etc.).

The private sector includes the enterprises and institutions, the fixed and circulating assets of which are privately owned. The classification of enterprises and institutions of the private sector is based on the specific economic conditions in the country concerned. Within this sector the subsector of craftsmen, artisans and peasants who are not members of co-operatives may be distinguished.

Peasants, craftsmen and artisans who do not belong to co-operatives operate small private ventures in which the productive process is carried out by their owners in person, as a rule without recourse to hired labour. This group also includes the subsidiary activities of the population occupied in the private sector of the national economy.

D. Definitions of flows

Below are given the definitions of the flows that appear in the MPS standard tables of chapter III. To make possible a comparison between the SNA and MPS data, a description of the differences between the MPS and the SNA coverage is added to each of the sections. The items needed in order to convert the MPS coverage into a coverage that conform to the SNA definition are only summarily indicated. For more information on them, the user is therefore referred to the description of the differences between the two systems in section B of this chapter. The items described below have been grouped together into similar categories to those used in chapter I section C, for the SNA flows.

I. *Total Supply and Disposition of Goods and Material Services*

1. *Gross output*

Global product covers the value of goods and material services produced. Deliveries of goods and material services within the same enterprise are generally excluded. Included are among other things the value of own-account constructed capital goods and capital repairs to fixed assets, the value of work-in-progress and the value of finished goods added to stocks. Covered is, furthermore, the value of goods and material services provided free to employees (the material services are valued at the material cost involved). In the contribution to global product by agriculture are included seeds and feed produced and consumed at the same farm and agricultural and other goods produced on personal plots for own consumption or for sale, including the cost of their processing. This concept of gross output appears in MPS table 5.

To derive gross output in producer's prices as defined in the SNA global product as described above needs to be increased with:

plus: the gross output value of non-material services including those of government, including the transfer cost on purchases and sales of existing second-hand fixed assets and land.

2. *Trade margins and transport charges*

The gross output of material goods and services is valued at both producer's and purchaser's values. The difference between the two sets of values gives the distributive trade margins (including restaurants, cafés and other catering) and the transportation margins. The gross output of the distributive-trade units is equal to the value of their gross margins on internal and external trade.

The gross margins on external trade are equivalent to the sum in domestic currency of (a) the value of imports of goods and material services in the domestic market *less* the actual value at which these imports are purchased from abroad and (b) the actual value at which exports of goods and material services are sold to abroad *less* the value of these exports in the domestic market. Trade margins and transport charges appear in MPS table 5.

3. *Intermediate material consumption including depreciation*

Intermediate material consumption consists of the value of the goods and material services used up in the production during a period of account by units of the material sphere, including the consumption of fixed assets during the period. Consistent with the scope of the gross output of goods and material services included in intermediate consumption are certain items, for example, seeds and animal feed, which are produced and used by the same unit. The intermediate outputs of raw materials etc. are valued net of the value of scraps and wastes originating in the process of production. Purchased items are valued at purchasers' values; items produced on own account are valued at cost in the case of state and co-operative enterprises and at average purchasers' prices in the case of personal plots of households. This concept of intermediate material consumption appears in MPS table 5.

Depreciation or consumption of fixed assets includes an allowance for the normal wear and tear and foreseen obsolescence of fixed assets based on standard rates of depreciation and furthermore, the difference between the book value of scrapped fixed assets and their scrap value. The allowances for depreciation are often based on the original cost of the assets which may be periodically adjusted to replacement cost.

To arrive from intermediate material consumption including depreciation as defined above, at the SNA concept of intermediate consumption, the MPS coverage needs to be increased and decreased with the following items:

plus: (i) material cost of non-material services

plus: (ii) material expenditures by enterprises on cultural, sports and similar facilities for their employees

plus: (iii) reimbursable expenditures for material goods and services purchased during business trips

minus: (iv) consumption of fixed capital in the material sphere

4. *Personal consumption*

This consists of all consumer goods, irrespective of durability, and material services (repair, transport, communication and similar services) which are purchased by households, received in kind as payment for work in state and collective enterprises and in private plots, or produced on own account on personal plots. Excluded is the purchase by households of dwellings (which is dealt with as capital formation) but included is the maintenance and depreciation of dwellings. Also included are reimbursable expenditures for material goods and services purchased during business trips. This concept of personal consumption appears in MPS tables 1 and 7. In MPS table 8 it appears according to source of supply of goods and material services. This concept of personal consumption appears in MPS tables 1 and 7. In MPS table 8 it appears according to source of supply of goods and material services. In the MPS the domestic concept of consumption is used, so that included are direct purchases by foregin tourists, diplomatic personnel and other non-residents in the domestic market, while similar purchases abroad by residents are excluded.

5. *Material consumption in the units of the non-material sphere serving*
   individuals

This flow covers expenditures on non-durable goods and material services by units of the non-material sphere serving individuals reduced by the increases in their stocks of goods. Also included is consumption of fixed assets used by these units. It appears in MPS tables 1 and 7.

6. *Material consumption in the units of the non-material sphere* serving
   the community as a whole

This flow consists of non-durable goods and material services purchased during a period of account by units of the non-material sphere serving the community as a whole, reduced by the increase of their stocks of goods during the period of account. Also included is consumption of fixed assets of these units. It appears in MPS tables 1 and 7.

To arrive from this concept at government final consumption expenditure as defined in the SNA, the following additions to and subtractions from the MPS concept have to be made:

plus: (i) the difference between the value of non-material services produced by government and their material cost and depreciation

plus: (ii) government expenditures on fixed assets that have military uses

plus: (iii) the difference between consumption expenditures (i.e., material and non-material cost, depreciation and compensation of employees) of extraterritorial bodies that represent the country abroad *minus* consumption expenditures incurred by extraterritorial bodies of other countries and international organizations located in the country in question.

plus: (iv) material expenditures by government (units in the non-material sphere serving individuals) on education, health, culture and other services provided free to individuals.

7. *Final consumption*

This flow is equal to the sum of personal consumption and material consumption and material consumption in the units of the non-material sphere that are serving individuals and of those that are serving the community as a whole. Each of these concepts has been defined above. They appear in MPS tables 5 and 7.

8. *Consumption of the population*

Consumption of the population is the sum of personal consumption and material consumption in the units of the non-material sphere serving individuals. This concept is comparable to private final consumption expenditure in the SNA can be derived from this MPS concept by adding and subtracting the following items:

plus: (i) the difference between the value of non-material services purchased by households, including housing services and the material cost and depreciation included in the value of these services.

minus: (ii) material expenditures by government (units in the non-material sphere serving individuals) on education, health, culture and other services provided free to individuals.

plus: (iii) the difference between direct purchases abroad by resident households and direct purchases in the domestic market by non-resident households as well as the difference between gifts sent abroad by household *minus* gifts received from abroad.

minus: (iv) reimbursable expenditures for material goods and services purchased during business trips.

minus: (v) material expenditures by enterprises on cultural sports and similar facilities for their employees.

9. *Total consumption of the population*

The total consumption of the population covers the consumption by the population of goods and material services and of non-material services, whether purchased by households or furnished free of charge. It therefore exceeds the consumption of the population (i.e., the sum of personal consumption and material consumption in the units of the non-material sphere serving individuals) by the value of the services of the units of the non-material sphere serving individuals, reduced by the consumption of goods and material services by these units. The value of the services of the units is equivalent to their costs of production, including operating surplus in some instances. In the case of dwellings provided by these units, their depreciation is not included when evaluating costs of production, since charges in respect of depreciation of these dwellings are included in personal consumption. Total consumption of the population appears classified by object in MPS table 9.

10. *Net fixed capital formation*

Net fixed capital formation consists of the value of new fixed assets purchased or constructed on own account and of completed capital repairs to these assets reduced by consumption of fixed assets for renewal of assets and capital repairs, and capital losses due to fire, floods and other calamities and furthermore reduced by the remaining value of scrapped fixed assets. Thus it measures the net increase in the value of fixed assets during a period of account. This flow appears in MPS table 5 and 6.

Fixed assets include completed dwellings, buildings and other structures; machinery, equipment and other durable goods acquired by units of the material and non-material sphere; cattle, excluding young cattle and cattle raised for meat; perennial plants; and expenditures on the improvement of land, forests and other natural resources. New fixed assets put into use are generally valued inclusive of acquisition and installation cost.

Capital repairs cover outlays on repairs that make up at least in part for the physical depreciation of the fixed assets and/or significantly raise the capacity and productivity of the fixed assets.

In order to convert the MPS concept of net fixed capital formation into gross fixed capital formation as defined in the SNA, the following additions and substractions from the MPS concept have to be made:

plus: (i) consumption of fixed capital in the material and non-material sphere, including that on afforestation, roads, bridges and similar structures

plus: (ii) losses due to foreseeable as well as non-foreseeable damages to fixed assets

plus: (iii) transfer cost with regard to purchases and sales of existing second-hand fixed assets, including land

plus: (iv) work in progress on construction of structures, roads, dams, ports and other forms of construction

plus: (v) the difference between outlays on fixed capital formation by extraterritorial bodies representing the country in question abroad, *less* similar outlays by extraterritorial bodies of other countries and international organizations located in the country in question

minus: (vi) government expenditures on fixed assets that have military uses.

11. *Gross fixed capital formation*

Gross fixed capital formation is equal to net fixed capital formation as defined above *plus* depreciation. Depreciation is defined in section 3 above, together with intermediate material consumption. Gross fixed capital formation classified by kind of activity appears in table 6.

12. *Increases in material circulating assets and stocks*

This item consists of increases during the period of account in the stocks of enterprises in the material sphere including wholesale and retail trade units, reduced by losses. Also covered are increases in government stockpiles including stocks of defense items and states reserves of precious metals and precious stones. The stocks in the material sphere consist of raw materials, fuels, supplies and other non-durable goods; young cattle and cattle raised for meat; work in progress including uncompleted construction projects; and finished good not yet sold. Increases in material circulating assets and stocks appear in MPS tables 1 and 6.

In order to convert the MPS concept of increases in material circulating assets and stocks into increase in stocks as defined in the SNA, the following additions to and deductions from the MPS concept are needed:

plus: (i) losses due to foreseeable and non-foreseeable damages to stocks

minus: (ii) work in progress of the construction of structures, roads, dams, ports and other forms of construction

minus: (iii) net increases in the holdings of gold ingots and other monetary gold.

13. *Losses*

This item is the sum of the value of the losses in fixed assets and losses in material circulating assets and stocks. Included are losses (a) due to fires, floods and other calamities, (b) in adult productive and working cattle, (c) due to abandoned or interrupted construction works and (d) in agricultural products in storage at state and co-operative agricultural enterprises and at farms. This flows appears in MPS tables 1 and 5.

In the SNA this final demand category is not identified separately from gross capital formation.

14. *Exports and imports of goods and material services*

Exports are defined to include: (a) outward-bound goods that cross the border of the country, including imported goods which are exported without being processed; (b) goods which are purchased outside the country by an external trade organization of the country in question and shipped directly to a third country; (c) outward-bound monetary and non-monetary gold and other precious metals; (d) unilateral transfers of goods by the government and public organizations of the country (uncompensated foreign aid); (e) material services such as transport, forwarding and communication services, rental including rental payments for time charter of ships and other transport equipment and, furthermore, export contract services rendered to other countries. The imports cover the same categories of goods and material services, which are inward bound. Exports are valued f.o.b. while imports are valued c.i.f. They appear in MPS tables 1 and 5.

To arrive at the SNA coverage of exports of goods and services, the MPS concept has to be increased and reduced as follows:

plus: (i) the difference between the exported value of non-material services and the material cost and depreciation included in these services.

plus: (ii) consumption expenditure (material and non-material cost, depreciation and compensation of employees) and outlays on fixed capital formation by extraterritorial bodies of foreign governments and international organizations located in the country in question

plus: (iii) direct purchases in the domestic market by non-resident households and gifts sent abroad by households

minus: (iv) sales abroad by an external trade organization of the country of goods that have not crossed the border of the country in question as well as of goods that have crossed the border but that are re-exported without being processed.

minus: (v) the difference between exported monetary gold and the value of sales of newly produced gold ingots and bars

MPS imports have to be adjusted in a similar manner. To be added are the imported value of non-material services minus material cost and depreciation, consumption expenditure and fixed capital formation of extraterritorial bodies that represent the country abroad and direct purchases abroad by residents. Deducted should be re-exports and purchases abroad by external trade organizations of goods that do not cross the border of the country, and also the value of imported monetary gold and gifts received households from abroad.

II. *Cost Components and Income Shares*

1. *Net material product*

Net material product is defined in the MPS and is used in countries with centrally planned economies. It can be estimated from the production income and expenditure side in the same manner as is indicated in chapter I, section C.III in which the SNA coverage of GPD is described. Following the production approach, net material product is the difference between global product (i.e., gross output) of goods and material services and intermediate material consumption including consumption of fixed assets. Net material product defined from the income side is the sum of primary incomes of the population (comparable to compensation of employees in the SNA) and primary incomes of enterprises (comparable to operating surplus in the SNA). The expenditure approach finally defines net material product as the sum of the final uses of goods and material services, i.e., personal consumption, material consumption of units in the non-material sphere serving individuals and that of similar units serving the community as a whole, net capital formation (i.e., net of depreciation), replacement for losses and the balance between exports and imports of goods and material services. These three different methods for deriving net material product are shown in MPS tables 1, 2 and 4.

To arrive at the SNA concept of GDP, net material product needs to be increased and reduced as follows:

plus: (i) the excess value of non-material services (i.e., the gross output value *minus* material cost and depreciation) consumed by households and government *plus* the difference between these excess values of exported and imported non-material services *minus*: (ii) material expenditures by enterprises on cultural, sports and similar facilities for their employees

minus: (iii) reimbursable expenditures for material goods and services purchased during business trips

plus: (iv) consumption of fixed capital in the material and non-material sphere, including that on afforestation, roads, bridges and similar structures

plus: (v) losses in fixed assets and stocks due to accidental damage such as fire, accidents, etc.

plus: (vi) transfer cost with regard to purchases and sales of existing second-hand fixed assets, including land.

2. *Primary income of the population*

The primary incomes of the population consists of (a) wages and salaries, including receipts in kind, and related incomes such as bonuses and reimbursements of expenses on business trips received from state, co-operative and private units of the material sphere; (b) the net material product (net value added) originating from the personal plots of households and (c) the net material product of self-employed craftsmen, artisans and peasants. This flow appears in MPS tables 3 and 4.

Primary income of the population is roughly comparable to the SNA concept of compensation of employees. However, several differences remain and in order to arrive from the MPS concept and compensation of employees as defined in the SNA, the following additions and deductions are needed:

plus: (i) compensation of employees including employers' contributions to social security funds, paid out in connexion with non-material activities inclusive of those that are paid out in connexion with the provision of cultural, sports and similar facilities by industries in the material sphere

plus: (ii) employers' contributions to social security funds paid out in connexion with material activities

minus: (iii) income from private enterprises

minus: (iv) reimbursable expenditures for material goods and services purchased during business trips.

3. *Primary income of enterprises*

The primary incomes of enterprises consist of the sum of the net material product of the units of the material sphere which have employees *less* the wages and salaries and related incomes which they pay out. The primary incomes of these units are the source of such items as their net income, turnover taxes, contributions to social insurance, payments of taxes, fines and other compulsory items, finance of purchases of non-material services, insurance premiums, interest on bank loans and other business costs. This flow appears in tables 3 and 4.

Although the coverage of primary incomes of enterprises is similar to that of operating surplus in the SNA, the following additions to and subtraction from the MPS are need in order to arrive at operating surplus as defined in the SNA:

plus: (i) the remaining value of non-material services (i.e., the gross output value *minus* material cost, depreciation and compensation of employees) consumed by households and government, plus the difference between the remaining values of exported and imported non-material services

minus: (ii) material expenditures by enterprises on cultural, sports and similar facilities for their employees

plus: (iii) consumption of fixed capital in the material and non-material sphere, including that on afforestation, roads, bridges and similar structures

plus: (iv) losses in fixed assets and stocks due to accidental damage such as fire, accidents etc.

plus: (v) transfer cost with regard to purchases and sales of existing fixed assets, including land

minus: (vi) employers' contributions to social security funds, paid out in connexion with material activities

plus: (vii) income from private plots and private enterprises.

---

[1] Standing Statistical Commission, Council of Mutual Economic Assistance (Moscow, 1969).
[2] Studies in Methods, Series F, No. 17 (United Nations publication, Sales No. E.71.XVII.10).
[3] For a more exhaustive list of differences between MPS and SNA, the user should refer to Comparisons of the System of National Accounts and the System of Balances of the National Economy; Part One: Conceptual Relationships (United Nations publication, Sales No. 77.XVII.6).

III. COUNTRY TABLES

Afghanistan

Source. Reply to the United Nations National Accounts Questionnaire from the Central Statistical Office, Kabul.

General note. The estimates shown in the following tables have been prepared in accordance with the System of Material Product Balances. Therefore, these estimates are not comparable in concept and coverage with those conforming to the United Nations System of National Accounts.

2b Net Material Product by Kind of Activity of the Material Sphere in Constant Market Prices

Thousand Million Afghanis — Fiscal year beginning 21 March

	1970	1971	1972	1973	1974	1975	1976	1977	1978	1979	1980
				At constant prices of:1978							
1 Agriculture and forestry	...	...	...	77.6	80.3	83.0	86.6	77.3	82.0	84.3	83.6
2 Industrial activity	...	...	...	23.7	26.1	28.6	29.3	30.4	33.2	30.7	29.3
3 Construction	...	...	...	2.7	2.7	3.8	5.7	6.9	8.6	7.6	5.8
4 Wholesale and retail trade and restaurants and other eating and drinking places	...	...	...	10.1	10.7	11.3	11.8	11.1	11.5	10.3	9.8
5 Transport and communication	...	...	...	3.3	4.0	4.8	5.3	6.0	6.1	5.2	4.8
6 Other activities of the material sphere	...	...	...	1.8	1.9	2.0	2.1	2.0	2.1	1.8	1.8
Net material product	...	...	...	119.2	125.7	133.5	140.8	133.7	143.5	139.9	135.1

Algeria

Source. Direction des Statistiques et de la Comptabilite Nationale, Secretariat d'Etat au Plan, Alger. Official estimates are published in 'Comptes Economiques'.
General note. The estimates shown in the following tables have been prepared in accordance with the United Nations System of National Accounts so far as the existing data would permit.

1.1 Expenditure on the Gross Domestic Product, in Current Prices

Million Algerian dinars

		1970	1971	1972	1973	1974	1975	1976	1977	1978	1979	1980
1	General government final consumption expenditure	3579	4097	4793	4752	6263	8421	9524	11562	15038	17257	...
2	Private final consumption expenditure	13444	14283	16772	18071	22790	26629	31818	38908	47820	55316	...
3	Gross capital formation	8752	8887	10441	13940	22846	28366	31337	41175	53424	50767	...
a	Increase in stocks	591	545	630	1523	5111	3863	568	2381	3832	1900	...
b	Gross fixed capital formation	8160	8342	9811	12417	17735	24503	30768	38794	49592	48867	...
	Residential buildings	...	...	...	...	...	...	...	...	...	...	...
	Non-residential buildings	...	...	...	...	...	...	...	...	...	...	...
	Other construction and land improvement etc.	4637	4789	6188	7125	8955	11461	14348	17479	21139	23876	...
	Other	3523	3553	3624	5293	8780	13043	16421	21315	28453	24991	...
4	Exports of goods and services	5305	4565	6163	8750	20115	19415	22821	26320	26216	37987	...
5	Less: Imports of goods and services	7007	6909	7756	10922	19580	26116	27525	36519	41875	40502	...
	Equals: Gross Domestic Product	24073	24923	30413	34592	52434	56715	67975	81446	100623	120825	...

1.2 Expenditure on the Gross Domestic Product, in Constant Prices

Million Algerian dinars

		1970	1971	1972	1973	1974	1975	1976	1977	1978	1979	1980
		\multicolumn{11}{c}{At constant prices of:1974}
1	General government final consumption expenditure	4364	4645	5129	5042	6263	6638	7346	7867	8654	...	...
2	Private final consumption expenditure	15761	16646	17878	18883	22790	24142	26449	28843	30000	...	...
3	Gross capital formation	13415	12327	13559	16087	22846	25247	24311	30787	36161	...	...
a	Increase in stocks	657	581	644	1711	5111	3512	457	1841	2342	...	...
b	Gross fixed capital formation	12758	11746	12915	14376	17735	21735	23854	28946	33819	...	...
	Residential buildings	...	...	...	...	...	...	...	...	...	...	...
	Non-residential buildings	...	...	...	...	...	...	...	...	...	...	...
	Other construction and land improvement etc.	7563	6880	8253	8288	8955	10237	11456	13482	14635	...	...
	Other	5195	4866	4662	6088	8780	11498	12398	15464	19184	...	...
4	Exports of goods and services	21880	15906	23099	23965	20115	22617	22906	24074	25452	...	...
5	Less: Imports of goods and services	11005	9648	10577	13364	19580	23369	22368	27585	29698	...	...
	Statistical discrepancy	-625	-256	-652	-84	-	213	278	482	458	...	...
	Equals: Gross Domestic Product	43790	39620	48436	50529	52433	55488	58922	64468	71027	...	...

1.3 Cost Components of the Gross Domestic Product

Million Algerian dinars

		1970	1971	1972	1973	1974	1975	1976	1977	1978	1979	1980
1	Indirect taxes, net	5470	5570	6727	7429	11020	12332	15000	19551	22702	23763	...
2	Consumption of fixed capital	1962	2149	2561	3183	3496	4729	6143	7436	7932	10191	...
3	Compensation of employees paid by resident producers to:	8407	9360	11190	11989	15033	18661	21800	26176	36253	44956	...
a	Resident households	8245	9187	10996	11794	14841	18401	21537	25828	35805	44504	...
b	Rest of the world	162	173	194	195	192	260	263	348	448	452	...
4	Net operating surplus	8233	7844	9935	11992	22883	20992	25031	28283	33736	41915	...
	Equals: Gross Domestic Product	24072	24923	30413	34592	52434	56715	67975	81446	100623	120825	...

1.4 General Government Current Receipts and Disbursements

Million Algerian dinars

		1970	1971	1972	1973	1974	1975	1976	1977	1978	1979	1980
		\multicolumn{11}{c}{Receipts}
1	Property and entrepreneurial income	971	1039	1518	1837	5276	4810	6326	5414	5158	7189	...
2	Taxes, fees and contributions	5185	5758	7527	9214	18547	19922	21246	26551	30785	38458	...
a	Indirect taxes	3106	3241	3918	4451	6150	7611	8318	9937	13978	15512	...
b	Direct taxes	1941	2360	3311	4452	12036	11906	12469	16075	16299	22399	...
c	Social security contributions	96	104	222	238	242	263	301	334	352	384	...
d	Compulsory fees, fines and penalties	42	53	76	73	119	142	158	205	156	163	...

Algeria

1.4 General Government Current Receipts and Disbursements
(Continued)

Million Algerian dinars

	1970	1971	1972	1973	1974	1975	1976	1977	1978	1979	1980
3 Other current receipts	362	1240	376	348	543	843	1149	2197	1431	1615	...
Total Current Receipts of General Government	6518	8037	9421	11399	24366	25575	28721	34162	37375	47262	...

Disbursements

	1970	1971	1972	1973	1974	1975	1976	1977	1978	1979	1980
1 General government final consumption expenditure	3579	4097	4793	4752	6263	8421	9524	11562	15038	17257	...
a Compensation of employees	2731	3163	3704	3679	4624	6447	6924	8324	10899	...	...
b Consumption of fixed capital	...	...	...	...	...	...	...	...	...	...	...
c Purchases of goods and services, net	781	870	977	1046	1581	1848	2480	3118	4019	...	...
d Less: Own account production of fixed assets	...	...	...	...	...	...	...	...	...	...	...
e Indirect taxes paid, net	67	64	112	27	58	126	120	120	120	120	...
2 Property income paid	117	131	184	180	264	510	612	796	918	1000	...
3 Subsidies	143	85	91	350	1024	4148	1507	2703	2151	1694	...
4 Other current transfers paid	1236	1956	1863	2218	4111	2566	3270	4317	4260	5166	...
a Social security benefits and social assistance grants	396	456	623	779	739	839	970	1099	1056	1396	...
b Other	840	1500	1240	1439	3372	1727	2300	3218	3204	3770	...
5 Net saving	1443	1768	2490	3899	12704	17510	13808	14784	15008	22145	...
Total Current Disbursements and Net Saving of General Government	6518	8037	9421	11399	24365	25575	28721	34162	37375	47262	...

1.7 External Transactions on Current Account, Summary

Million Algerian dinars

	1970	1971	1972	1973	1974	1975	1976	1977	1978	1979	1980

Payments to the Rest of the World

	1970	1971	1972	1973	1974	1975	1976	1977	1978	1979	1980
1 Imports of goods and services	7007	6909	7756	10922	19580	26116	27525	36519	41875	40502	...
2 Factor income paid to the rest of the world	1445	506	428	532	1111	1193	1863	2236	3266	6213	...
a Compensation of employees	162	173	194	195	192	260	263	348	448	452	...
b Property and entrepreneurial income paid	1283	333	234	337	919	933	1600	1888	2818	5761	...
3 Indirect taxes paid to supranational organizations	...	...	...	...	...	...	...	...	...	...	...
4 Current transfers to the rest of the world	83	541	47	181	1821	97	94	125	115	73	...
5 Surplus of the nation on current transactions	-1606	-767	-369	-917	147	-5586	-4023	-10293	-16653	-6154	...
Payments to the Rest of the World and Surplus of the Nation on Current Transactions	6929	7189	7861	10717	22660	21819	25459	28586	28603	40634	...

Receipts From The Rest of the World

	1970	1971	1972	1973	1974	1975	1976	1977	1978	1979	1980
1 Exports of goods and services	5305	4565	6163	8751	20115	19416	22821	26320	26216	37987	...
2 Factor income received from rest of the world	1293	1361	1456	1554	2298	2145	2369	2042	2127	2408	...
a Compensation of employees	1174	1305	1371	1468	1677	1854	2037	1680	1767	1831	...
b Property and entrepreneurial income received	119	56	85	86	621	291	332	362	360	577	...
3 Subsidies received from supranational organisations	...	...	...	...	...	...	...	...	...	...	...
4 Current transfers from rest of the world	330	1263	241	410	247	259	269	224	260	239	...
Receipts from the Rest of the World on Current Transactions	6929	7189	7861	10717	22660	21820	25459	28586	28603	40634	...

Algeria

1.8 Capital Transactions of The Nation, Summary

Million Algerian dinars

	1970	1971	1972	1973	1974	1975	1976	1977	1978	1979	1980
Finance of Gross Capital Formation											
Gross saving	7154	8130	10084	13037	23017	22799	27331	30919	36771	44613	...
1 Consumption of fixed capital	1962	2150	2561	3183	3496	4729	6143	7436	7932	10191	...
2 Net saving	5192	5980	7523	9854	19521	18070	21188	23483	28839	34422	...
Less: Surplus of the nation on current transactions	-1606	-767	-369	-917	147	-5586	-4023	-10293	-16653	-6154	...
Finance of Gross Capital Formation	8752	8887	10441	13940	22846	28366	31337	41175	53424	50767	...
Gross Capital Formation											
Increase in stocks	591	545	630	1523	5111	3863	568	2381	3832	1900	...
Gross fixed capital formation	8160	8342	9811	12417	17735	24503	30768	38794	49592	48867	...
Gross Capital Formation	8752	8887	10441	13940	22846	28366	31337	41175	53424	50767	...

1.10 Gross Domestic Product by Kind of Activity, in Current Prices

Million Algerian dinars

	1970	1971	1972	1973	1974	1975	1976	1977	1978	1979	1980
1 Agriculture, hunting, forestry and fishing	2428	2617	2828	2728	3420	4967	5315	5354	6738	7837	...
2 Mining and quarrying	3345	2451	4625	6647	18791	15904	19959	23944	24788	34103	...
3 Manufacturing	3367	3468	4052	4777	5203	5735	7428	8355	10605	14223	...
4 Electricity, gas and water	329	388	437	507	604	675	868	1031	1266	1531	...
5 Construction	2229	2642	3460	4014	5407	6634	8570	10033	13374	16154	...
6 Wholesale and retail trade, restaurants and hotels	4600	5192	5586	5683	5291	5933	7844	9776	14127	16268	...
7 Transport, storage and communication	1263	1359	1479	1767	2515	2820	3241	4123	4761	5690	...
8 Finance, insurance, real estate and business services	1951	2135	2164	2499	2946	3459	3829	4748	5750	...	...
9 Community, social and personal services	430	478	534	632	768	836	760	929	1443	...	...
Total, Industries	19942	20729	25165	29252	44945	46960	57812	68289	82850	...	...
Producers of Government Services	2732	3169	3743	3596	4579	6457	6919	8275	11213	...	...
Other Producers	...	...	...	...	...	...	...	...	...	...	...
Subtotal	22674	23897	28908	32848	49524	53417	64730	76564	94063	...	...
Less: Imputed bank service charge	243	260	...	431	630	877	1142	1359	1272	...	...
Plus: Import duties	1652	1446	1888	2047	3750	4424	4490	6551	8492	6226	...
Plus: Value added tax	...	...	...	...	...	...	...	...	...	...	...
Plus: Other adjustments	-10	-161	-383	128	-210	-249	-103	-310	-660	...	...
Equals: Gross Domestic Product	24073	24923	30413	34592	52434	56715	67975	81446	100623	120825	...

1.11 Gross Domestic Product by Kind of Activity, in Constant Prices

Million Algerian dinars

	1970	1971	1972	1973	1974	1975	1976	1977	1978	1979	1980
At constant prices of: 1974											
1 Agriculture, hunting, forestry and fishing	3376	3515	3479	3153	3420	4032	3545	3458	3826	...	...
2 Mining and quarrying	16996	12344	18691	19870	18791	17749	19568	21151	22944	...	...
3 Manufacturing	3832	3773	4339	4984	5203	5537	6173	6405	7158	...	...
4 Electricity, gas and water	336	398	454	499	604	740	945	1121	1227	...	...
5 Construction	4721	4477	5368	4950	5407	6109	6908	8068	9286	...	...
6 Wholesale and retail trade, restaurants and hotels	5207	5597	5925	5897	5291	5697	6553	7338	7996	...	...
7 Transport, storage and communication	1412	1478	1620	1967	2515	2819	2865	3014	3199	...	...
8 Finance, insurance, real estate and business services [a]	1687	1703	1718	1771	1844	2012	2130	2366	3019	...	...
9 Community, social and personal services	481	533	581	668	768	777	709	753	905	...	...
Total, Industries	38048	33818	42175	43759	43843	45472	49396	53675	59560	...	...
Producers of Government Services	...	...	...	...	...	...	...	...	...	...	...
Other Producers	...	...	...	...	...	...	...	...	...	...	...
Subtotal	...	...	...	...	...	...	...	...	...	...	...
Less: Imputed bank service charge	...	...	...	...	...	...	...	...	...	...	...
Plus: Import duties	...	...	...	...	...	...	...	...	...	...	...
Plus: Value added tax	...	...	...	...	...	...	...	...	...	...	...
Equals: Gross Domestic Product	...	...	...	...	...	...	...	...	...	...	...

a) Real estate and business services only.

Algeria

1.12 Relations Among National Accounting Aggregates

Million Algerian dinars

	1970	1971	1972	1973	1974	1975	1976	1977	1978	1979	1980
Gross Domestic Product	24073	24923	30413	34592	52434	56715	67975	81446	100623	120825	...
Plus: Net factor income received from abroad	-150	855	1029	1024	1186	952	506	-194	-1139	...	...
Factor income received	1294	1361	1457	1556	2298	2145	2369	2042	2127	...	...
Less: Factor income paid	1444	506	428	532	1112	1193	1863	2236	3266	...	...
Equals: Gross National Product	23923	25778	31442	35616	53620	57667	68481	81252	99484	...	...
Less: Consumption of fixed capital	1962	2150	2561	3183	3496	4730	6143	7436	7932	...	...
Less: Net indirect taxes paid to supranational organisations	...	...	...	...	...	...	...	...	...	...	...
Equals: National Income at Market Prices	21959	23629	28881	32434	50124	52938	62338	73817	91552	...	...
Plus: Net current transfers received from abroad	247	721	194	229	-1574	162	175	97	145	...	...
Current transfers received	330	1263	241	410	247	259	269	224	260	...	...
Less: Current transfers paid	83	541	47	181	1821	97	94	125	115	...	...
Equals: National Disposable Income at Market Prices	22207	24349	29076	32663	48550	53100	62512	73914	91698	...	...
Less: Final consumption	17023	18380	21565	22823	29053	35050	41342	50471	62859	...	...
Statistical discrepancy	8	10	12	14	24	19	17	37	-	...	...
Equals: Net Saving	5192	5980	7523	9854	19521	18070	21188	23483	28839	...	...
Less: Surplus of the nation on current transactions	-1606	-768	-370	-917	148	-5587	-4023	-10293	-16653	...	...
Statistical discrepancy	-8	-10	-12	-14	-24	-19	-17	-37	-	...	...
Equals: Net Capital Formation	6790	6737	7880	10757	19350	23637	25194	33739	45492	...	...

2.1 General Government Final Consumption Expenditure by Function, in Current Prices

Million Algerian dinars

	1970	1971	1972	1973	1974	1975	1976	1977	1978	1979	1980
1 General public services	...	...	...	723	842	1122	1471	...	...	...	...
2 Defence	...	...	...	273	546	1296	1632	...	...	...	...
3 Public order and safety	...	...	...	...	...	...	...	...	...	...	...
4 Education	...	...	...	1400	1571	2025	2197	...	...	...	...
5 Health	...	...	...	55	49	53	63	...	...	...	...
6 Social security and welfare	...	...	...	170	164	203	230	...	...	...	...
7 Housing and community amenities	...	...	...	2	-	-	-	...	...	...	...
8 Recreational, cultural and religious affairs	...	...	...	100	108	186	147	...	...	...	...
9 Economic services	...	...	...	262	226	394	332	...	...	...	...
10 Other functions	...	...	...	182	296	152	184	...	...	...	...
Total General Government Final Consumption Expenditure [a]	...	...	...	3167	3802	5438	6256	...	...	...	...

a) Excluding local authorities.

4.3 Derivation of Value Added by Kind of Activity, ISIC Divisions, in Current Prices

Million Algerian dinars

	1970 Gross Output	1970 Intermediate Consumption	1970 Value Added	1971 Gross Output	1971 Intermediate Consumption	1971 Value Added	1972 Gross Output	1972 Intermediate Consumption	1972 Value Added	1973 Gross Output	1973 Intermediate Consumption	1973 Value Added
						All Producers						
1 Agriculture, hunting, forestry and fishing	3295	867	2428	3553	936	2617	3911	1083	2828	3858	1130	2728
a Agriculture and hunting	3132	848	2283	3384	917	2468	3709	1060	2649	3604	1101	2503
b Forestry and logging	98	10	88	104	10	94	123	12	111	155	16	140
c Fishing	65	9	56	64	9	55	79	11	68	100	14	86
2 Mining and quarrying	5741	2395	3345	5132	2680	2451	7253	2628	4625	9737	3091	6647
a Coal mining	...	...	...	...	...	...	...	...	...	...	...	...
b Crude petroleum and natural gas production	5485	2270	3214	4833	2542	2290	6930	2478	4452	9400	2947	6453
c Metal ore mining	256	125	131	299	138	161	323	150	173	337	144	194
d Other mining												

Algeria

4.3 Derivation of Value Added by Kind of Activity, ISIC Divisions, in Current Prices
(Continued)

Million Algerian dinars

	1970 Gross Output	1970 Intermediate Consumption	1970 Value Added	1971 Gross Output	1971 Intermediate Consumption	1971 Value Added	1972 Gross Output	1972 Intermediate Consumption	1972 Value Added	1973 Gross Output	1973 Intermediate Consumption	1973 Value Added
3 Manufacturing	9246	5879	3367	9700	6233	3468	10942	6891	4052	12822	8045	4777
a Manufacture of food, beverages and tobacco	3267	2197	1069	3510	2330	1180	3910	2552	1358	4379	2848	1531
b Textile, wearing apparel and leather industries	2257	1573	685	2524	1776	748	2641	1839	803	3118	2079	1039
c Manufacture of wood and wood products, including furniture	740	426	314	838	500	339	937	560	377	999	589	410
d Manufacture of paper and paper products, printing and publishing	...	...	...	...	...	...	...	...	...	...	...	...
e Manufacture of chemicals and chemical petroleum, coal, rubber and plastic products	543	277	266	736	421	315	790	461	329	1232	724	508
f Manufacture of non-metallic mineral products, except products of petroleum and coal	...	...	...	...	...	...	...	...	...	...	...	...
g Basic metal industries	2006	1203	803	1628	1014	614	2102	1247	855	2589	1591	998
h Manufacture of fabricated metal products, machinery and equipment												
i Other manufacturing industries	433	203	230	464	192	272	562	232	330	505	214	291
4 Electricity, gas and water	426	96	329	520	131	388	587	150	437	669	162	507
5 Construction	5679	3450	2229	5824	3182	2642	7896	4436	3460	8132	4118	4014
6 Wholesale and retail trade, restaurants and hotels	5858	1258	4600	6547	1356	5192	7192	1606	5586	7507	1825	5683
a Wholesale and retail trade	5310	1044	4266	5970	1131	4840	6582	1368	5214	6860	1568	5292
b Restaurants and hotels	548	214	334	577	225	352	610	238	372	647	257	391
7 Transport, storage and communication	1722	459	1263	1872	512	1359	2016	536	1479	2529	762	1767
a Transport and storage	1495	431	1065	1647	486	1162	1765	500	1265	2268	715	1553
b Communication	227	29	199	225	27	198	251	36	214	261	47	214
8 Finance, insurance, real estate and business services	2240	290	1951	2414	279	2135	2445	282	2164	2809	311	2499
a Financial institutions	275	43	232	414	33	381	374	20	354	549	27	522
b Insurance	179	27	152	192	26	166	205	28	177	262	17	245
c Real estate and business services	1786	220	1567	1808	220	1588	1866	234	1633	1998	267	1732
Real estate, except dwellings	460	162	298	456	160	296	486	171	315	560	199	361
Dwellings	1326	58	1269	1352	60	1292	1380	63	1318	1438	68	1371
9 Community, social and personal services	585	155	430	650	172	478	727	192	534	857	225	632
Educational services	...	...	...	...	...	...	...	...	...	...	...	...
Medical, dental, other health and veterinary services	...	...	...	...	...	...	...	...	...	...	...	...
Total, Industries	34791	14849	19942	36212	15483	20729	42967	17802	25165	48920	19668	29252
Producers of Government Services	3402	669	2732	3918	749	3169	4590	847	3743	4510	914	3596
Other Producers	...	...	...	...	...	...	...	...	...	...	...	...
Total	38193	15519	22674	40129	16232	23897	47557	18650	28908	53430	20582	32848
Imputed bank service charge	...	243	-243	...	260	-260	...	...	...	...	431	-431
Import duties	1652	...	1652	1446	...	1446	1888	...	1888	2047	...	2047
Value added tax	...	...	...	...	...	...	...	...	...	...	...	...
Other adjustments	...	10	-10	...	161	-161	...	383	-383	...	-128	128
Total	39845	15772	24073	41575	16652	24923	49445	19033	30413	55477	20885	34592

	1974 Gross Output	1974 Intermediate Consumption	1974 Value Added	1975 Gross Output	1975 Intermediate Consumption	1975 Value Added	1976 Gross Output	1976 Intermediate Consumption	1976 Value Added	1977 Gross Output	1977 Intermediate Consumption	1977 Value Added
						All Producers						
1 Agriculture, hunting, forestry and fishing	4768	1349	3420	6661	1694	4967	7101	1786	5315	7242	1888	5354
a Agriculture and hunting	4480	1315	3166	6340	1656	4684	6736	1742	4994	6824	1836	4988
b Forestry and logging	159	16	143	169	17	152	167	17	150	162	16	146
c Fishing	129	18	111	153	22	131	199	28	171	256	36	220
2 Mining and quarrying	23406	4614	18791	22944	7041	15904	29340	9382	19959	32377	8433	23944
a Coal mining	...	...	...	...	...	...	...	...	...	...	...	...
b Crude petroleum and natural gas production	22879	4460	18418	22422	6860	15562	28811	9181	19630	31803	8218	23586

Algeria

4.3 Derivation of Value Added by Kind of Activity, ISIC Divisions, in Current Prices
(Continued)

Million Algerian dinars

		1974			1975			1976			1977		
		Gross Output	Intermediate Consumption	Value Added	Gross Output	Intermediate Consumption	Value Added	Gross Output	Intermediate Consumption	Value Added	Gross Output	Intermediate Consumption	Value Added
	c Metal ore mining	527	154	373	522	181	342	529	201	329	574	215	358
	d Other mining												
3	Manufacturing	14623	9420	5203	16816	11082	5735	19277	11849	7428	21231	12877	8355
	a Manufacture of food, beverages and tobacco	4967	3408	1559	5595	3832	1763	6309	4129	2180	6971	4467	2505
	b Textile, wearing apparel and leather industries	3701	2538	1163	3621	2423	1198	4064	2650	1414	4341	2831	1510
	c Manufacture of wood and wood products, including furniture	1177	665	512	1366	803	563	1655	916	739	1725	854	871
	d Manufacture of paper and paper products, printing and publishing	...	...	...	...	...	...	...	...	...	...	...	...
	e Manufacture of chemicals and chemical petroleum, coal, rubber and plastic products	1396	864	531	1765	1148	617	2001	1187	814	2204	1312	892
	f Manufacture of non-metallic mineral products, except products of petroleum and coal	...	...	...	...	...	...	...	...	...	...	...	...
	g Basic metal industries	2786	1721	1066	3751	2575	1176	4167	2521	1646	4644	2846	1798
	h Manufacture of fabricated metal products, machinery and equipment												
	i Other manufacturing industries	596	224	372	718	301	418	1081	446	635	1346	567	779
4	Electricity, gas and water	771	167	604	993	318	675	1221	353	868	1391	360	1031
5	Construction	10683	5277	5407	13666	7032	6634	17033	8464	8570	20693	10661	10033
6	Wholesale and retail trade, restaurants and hotels	7397	2105	5291	8746	2813	5933	10960	3117	7844	13292	3516	9776
	a Wholesale and retail trade	6653	1815	4838	7855	2472	5383	9971	2741	7231	12114	3115	8998
	b Restaurants and hotels	744	290	453	891	341	550	989	376	613	1178	401	778
7	Transport, storage and communication	3579	1063	2515	4326	1506	2820	4946	1705	3241	5983	1861	4123
	a Transport and storage	3283	1007	2277	3900	1416	2485	4451	1599	2852	5363	1764	3599
	b Communication	295	57	239	426	90	336	495	106	389	620	96	524
8	Finance, insurance, real estate and business services	3278	332	2946	3881	421	3459	4299	470	3829	5309	564	4748
	a Financial institutions	866	29	837	1086	41	1045	1243	43	1200	1711	47	1664
	b Insurance	280	15	265	375	11	364	379	11	368	437	14	424
	c Real estate and business services	2132	288	1844	2420	369	2050	2677	416	2261	3161	503	2660
	Real estate, except dwellings	616	216	400	823	293	529	985	335	650	1258	417	842
	Dwellings	1516	72	1444	1597	76	1521	1692	81	1611	1903	86	1818
9	Community, social and personal services	1044	276	768	1175	340	836	1098	338	760	1295	367	929
	Educational services	...	...	...	...	...	...	...	...	...	...	...	...
	Medical, dental, other health and veterinary services	...	...	...	...	...	...	...	...	...	...	...	...
Total, Industries		69549	24604	44945	79208	32247	46960	95274	37468	57812	108814	40524	68289
Producers of Government Services		5973	1395	4579	8035	1578	6457	9144	2225	6919	11047	2773	8275
Other Producers		...	...	...	...	...	...	...	...	...	...	...	...
Total		75522	25999	49524	87242	33825	53417	104418	39688	64730	119861	43297	76564
Imputed bank service charge		...	630	-630	...	877	-877	...	1142	-1142	...	1359	-1359
Import duties		3750	...	3750	4424	...	4424	4490	...	4490	6551	...	6551
Value added tax		...	...	...	...	...	...	...	...	...	...	...	...
Other adjustments		...	210	-210	...	249	-249	...	103	-103	...	310	-310
Total		79272	26839	52434	91666	34951	56715	108908	40933	67975	126412	44966	81446

		1978		
		Gross Output	Intermediate Consumption	Value Added

All Producers

1	Agriculture, hunting, forestry and fishing	8856	2118	6738
	a Agriculture and hunting	8426	2065	6362
	b Forestry and logging	174	17	157
	c Fishing	255	36	219
2	Mining and quarrying	34965	10177	24788

Algeria

4.3 Derivation of Value Added by Kind of Activity, ISIC Divisions, in Current Prices
(Continued)

Million Algerian dinars

		1978		
		Gross Output	Intermediate Consumption	Value Added
	a Coal mining	...	...	...
	b Crude petroleum and natural gas production	34377	9905	24472
	c Metal ore mining	588	272	316
	d Other mining			
3	Manufacturing	26575	15970	10605
	a Manufacture of food, beverages and tobacco	8636	5839	2797
	b Textile, wearing apparel and leather industries	5501	3208	2293
	c Manufacture of wood and wood products, including furniture	1774	970	804
	d Manufacture of paper and paper products, printing and publishing	...	...	...
	e Manufacture of chemicals and chemical petroleum, coal, rubber and plastic products	2087	1247	840
	f Manufacture of non-metallic mineral products, except products of petroleum and coal	...	...	...
	g Basic metal industries	6712	4092	2620
	h Manufacture of fabricated metal products, machinery and equipment			
	i Other manufacturing industries	1865	614	1251
4	Electricity, gas and water	1856	590	1266
5	Construction	24567	11193	13374
6	Wholesale and retail trade, restaurants and hotels	18341	4215	14127
	a Wholesale and retail trade	16261	3376	12885
	b Restaurants and hotels	2080	839	1242
7	Transport, storage and communication	6884	2123	4761
	a Transport and storage	6198	2035	4163
	b Communication	686	88	598
8	Finance, insurance, real estate and business services	...	...	5750
	a Financial institutions	...	...	...
	b Insurance	...	...	...
	c Real estate and business services	4566	657	3909
	Real estate, except dwellings	2140	548	1592
	Dwellings	2426	109	2317
9	Community, social and personal services	1790	347	1443
	Educational services	...	...	...
	Medical, dental, other health and veterinary services	...	...	1841
Total, Industries		...	...	82850
Producers of Government Services		15038	3826	11213
Other Producers		...	...	...
Total		...	...	94063
Imputed bank service charge		...	1272	-1272
Import duties		8492	...	8492
Value added tax		...	...	...
Other adjustments		...	660	-660
Total		...	...	100623

Algeria

4.4 Derivation of Value Added by Kind of Activity, ISIC Divisions, in Constant Prices

Million Algerian dinars

At constant prices of: 1974

All Producers

	1970 Gross Output	1970 Intermediate Consumption	1970 Value Added	1971 Gross Output	1971 Intermediate Consumption	1971 Value Added	1972 Gross Output	1972 Intermediate Consumption	1972 Value Added	1973 Gross Output	1973 Intermediate Consumption	1973 Value Added
1 Agriculture, hunting, forestry and fishing	4411	1035	3376	4608	1093	3515	4712	1233	3479	4435	1282	3153
2 Mining and quarrying	22350	5354	16996	17620	5276	12344	23379	4688	18691	24883	5014	19870
a Coal mining	...	...	...	...	...	...	...	...	...	...	...	...
b Crude petroleum and natural gas production	21938	5205	16733	17137	5118	12019	22871	4521	18350	24415	4858	19557
c Metal ore mining	412	149	263	483	158	325	508	167	341	468	156	313
d Other mining												
3 Manufacturing	10820	6988	3832	10991	7218	3773	12102	7763	4339	13867	8883	4984
a Manufacture of food, beverages and tobacco	3512	2492	1020	3726	2604	1122	4116	2807	1309	4585	3102	1483
b Textile, wearing apparel and leather industries	2711	1916	795	2935	2103	832	3042	2135	907	3435	2312	1123
c Manufacture of wood and wood products, including furniture	961	540	421	1032	605	427	1058	636	422	1074	647	427
d Manufacture of paper and paper products, printing and publishing	...	...	...	...	...	...	...	...	...	...	...	...
e Manufacture of chemicals and chemical petroleum, coal, rubber and plastic products	624	346	278	836	511	325	889	543	346	1424	860	564
f Manufacture of non-metallic mineral products, except products of petroleum and coal	...	...	...	...	...	...	...	...	...	...	...	...
g Basic metal industries	2447	1451	996	1890	1169	721	2322	1380	942	2784	1709	1075
h Manufacture of fabricated metal products, machinery and equipment												
i Other manufacturing industries	565	243	322	572	226	346	675	262	413	565	253	312
4 Electricity, gas and water	448	112	336	547	149	398	618	164	454	669	170	499
5 Construction	9598	4877	4721	8612	4135	4477	10841	5473	5368	9745	4795	4950
6 Wholesale and retail trade, restaurants and hotels	6709	1503	5207	7149	1552	5597	7720	1795	5925	7861	1964	5897
a Wholesale and retail trade	6103	1263	4841	6525	1304	5221	7078	1536	5542	7183	1689	5494
b Restaurants and hotels	606	240	366	624	248	376	642	259	383	678	275	403
7 Transport, storage and communication	1956	544	1412	2055	577	1478	2112	492	1620	2781	814	1967
8 Finance, insurance, real estate and business services	1958	271	1687	1964	261	1703	1980	262	1718	2055	284	1771
a Financial institutions	...	...	...	...	...	...	...	...	...	...	...	...
b Insurance	...	...	...	...	...	...	...	...	...	...	...	...
c Real estate and business services	1958	271	1687	1964	261	1703	1980	262	1718	2055	284	1771
9 Community, social and personal services	664	183	481	730	197	533	794	213	581	911	243	668
Total, Industries	58915	20867	38048	54276	20458	33818	64258	22083	42175	67208	23449	43759
Producers of Government Services	...	...	...	...	...	...	...	...	...	...	...	...
Other Producers	...	...	...	...	...	...	...	...	...	...	...	...
Total	...	...	...	...	...	...	...	...	...	...	...	...
Imputed bank service charge	...	...	...	...	...	...	...	...	...	...	...	...
Import duties	...	...	...	...	...	...	...	...	...	...	...	...
Value added tax	...	...	...	...	...	...	...	...	...	...	...	...
Total	...	...	...	...	...	...	...	...	...	...	...	...

At constant prices of: 1974

All Producers

	1974 Gross Output	1974 Intermediate Consumption	1974 Value Added	1975 Gross Output	1975 Intermediate Consumption	1975 Value Added	1976 Gross Output	1976 Intermediate Consumption	1976 Value Added	1977 Gross Output	1977 Intermediate Consumption	1977 Value Added
1 Agriculture, hunting, forestry and fishing	4768	1348	3420	5482	1450	4032	4914	1369	3545	4828	1370	3458
2 Mining and quarrying	23406	4615	18791	24077	6328	17749	27661	8093	19568	28149	6998	21151
a Coal mining	...	...	...	...	...	...	...	...	...	...	...	...
b Crude petroleum and natural gas production	22879	4461	18418	23602	6178	17424	27180	7944	19236	27655	6851	20804
c Metal ore mining	527	154	373	475	150	325	481	149	332	494	147	347
d Other mining												

Algeria

4.4 Derivation of Value Added by Kind of Activity, ISIC Divisions, in Constant Prices
(Continued)

Million Algerian dinars

	1974			1975			1976			1977		
	Gross Output	Intermediate Consumption	Value Added	Gross Output	Intermediate Consumption	Value Added	Gross Output	Intermediate Consumption	Value Added	Gross Output	Intermediate Consumption	Value Added
				At constant prices of: 1974								
3 Manufacturing	14623	9420	5203	15234	9697	5537	15660	9487	6173	16242	9836	6405
a Manufacture of food, beverages and tobacco	4967	3408	1559	5228	3521	1707	5214	3469	1745	5242	3539	1703
b Textile, wearing apparel and leather industries	3701	2538	1163	3106	2121	985	3281	2131	1150	3333	2187	1145
c Manufacture of wood and wood products, including furniture	1177	665	512	1221	703	518	1254	707	547	1215	620	595
d Manufacture of paper and paper products, printing and publishing	...	...	...	...	...	...	...	...	...	...	...	...
e Manufacture of chemicals and chemical petroleum, coal, rubber and plastic products	1396	864	531	1542	947	595	1681	847	834	1822	944	878
f Manufacture of non-metallic mineral products, except products of petroleum and coal	...	...	...	...	...	...	...	...	...	...	...	...
g Basic metal industries	2786	1720	1066	3442	2147	1295	3307	1990	1317	3545	2131	1414
h Manufacture of fabricated metal products, machinery and equipment												
i Other manufacturing industries	596	224	372	695	258	437	923	343	580	1085	415	670
4 Electricity, gas and water	771	167	604	1003	263	740	1221	276	945	1391	270	1121
5 Construction	10683	5276	5407	12162	6053	6109	13665	6757	6908	16078	8010	8068
6 Wholesale and retail trade, restaurants and hotels	7397	2106	5291	8083	2386	5697	8913	2360	6553	9763	2425	7338
a Wholesale and retail trade	6653	1815	4838	7273	2068	5205	8041	2026	6015	8842	2092	6750
b Restaurants and hotels	744	291	453	810	318	492	872	334	538	921	333	588
7 Transport, storage and communication	3579	1064	2515	4021	1202	2819	4098	1233	2865	4247	1233	3014
8 Finance, insurance, real estate and business services	2132	288	1844	2329	317	2012	2462	332	2130	2744	378	2366
a Financial institutions	...	...	...	...	...	...	...	...	...	...	...	...
b Insurance	...	...	...	...	...	...	...	...	...	...	...	...
c Real estate and business services	2132	288	1844	2329	317	2012	2462	332	2130	2744	378	2366
9 Community, social and personal services	1044	276	768	1069	292	777	981	272	709	1036	283	753
Total, Industries	68403	24560	43843	73460	27988	45472	79576	30180	49396	84477	30802	53675
Producers of Government Services	...	...	...	...	...	...	...	...	...	...	...	...
Other Producers	...	...	...	...	...	...	...	...	...	...	...	...
Total	...	...	...	...	...	...	...	...	...	...	...	...
Imputed bank service charge	...	...	...	...	...	...	...	...	...	...	...	...
Import duties	...	...	...	...	...	...	...	...	...	...	...	...
Value added tax	...	...	...	...	...	...	...	...	...	...	...	...
Total	...	...	...	...	...	...	...	...	...	...	...	...

	1978		
	Gross Output	Intermediate Consumption	Value Added
	At constant prices of: 1974		
	All Producers		
1 Agriculture, hunting, forestry and fishing	5210	1384	3826
2 Mining and quarrying	30960	8016	22944
a Coal mining	...	...	...
b Crude petroleum and natural gas production	30423	7827	22596
c Metal ore mining	537	189	348
d Other mining			

Algeria

4.4 Derivation of Value Added by Kind of Activity, ISIC Divisions, in Constant Prices
(Continued)

Million Algerian dinars

1978
At constant prices of: 1974

	Gross Output	Intermediate Consumption	Value Added
3 Manufacturing	18102	10944	7158
a Manufacture of food, beverages and tobacco	5572	3964	1608
b Textile, wearing apparel and leather industries	3748	2235	1513
c Manufacture of wood and wood products, including furniture	1145	642	503
d Manufacture of paper and paper products, printing and publishing	...	...	...
e Manufacture of chemicals and chemical petroleum, coal, rubber and plastic products	1643	869	774
f Manufacture of non-metallic mineral products, except products of petroleum and coal	...	...	...
g Basic metal industries	4597	2831	1766
h Manufacture of fabricated metal products, machinery and equipment			
i Other manufacturing industries	1397	403	994
4 Electricity, gas and water	1672	445	1227
5 Construction	17084	7798	9286
6 Wholesale and retail trade, restaurants and hotels	10713	2717	7996
a Wholesale and retail trade	9345	2120	7225
b Restaurants and hotels	1368	597	771
7 Transport, storage and communication	4501	1302	3199
8 Finance, insurance, real estate and business services	3818	799	3019
a Financial institutions	...	...	...
b Insurance	...	...	...
c Real estate and business services	3818	799	3019
9 Community, social and personal services	1261	356	905
Total, Industries	93320	33760	59560
Producers of Government Services	...	...	...
Other Producers	...	...	...
Total	...	...	...
Imputed bank service charge	...	...	...
Import duties	...	...	...
Value added tax	...	...	...
Total	...	...	...

4.6 Cost Components of Value Added, ISIC Divisions

Million Algerian dinars

All Producers

	1970						1971					
	Compensation of Employees	Capital Consumption	Net Operating Surplus	Indirect Taxes	Less: Subsidies Received	Value Added	Compensation of Employees	Capital Consumption	Net Operating Surplus	Indirect Taxes	Less: Subsidies Received	Value Added
1 Agriculture, hunting, forestry and fishing	796	159	1338	136	...	2428	805	185	1496	131	...	2617
a Agriculture and hunting	769	154	1228	133	...	2283	781	181	1378	129	...	2468
b Forestry and logging	12	2	74	1	...	88	10	2	82	1	...	94
c Fishing	15	3	36	2	...	56	15	3	36	1	...	55
2 Mining and quarrying	297	568	2026	454	...	3345	282	440	1251	479	...	2451
a Coal mining	...	...	...	...	...	...	...	...	...	...	...	...
b Crude petroleum and natural gas production	180	544	2046	444	...	3214	149	413	1260	469	...	2290
c Metal ore mining	117	24	-20	10	...	131	133	27	-9	10	...	161
d Other mining												

Algeria

4.6 Cost Components of Value Added, ISIC Divisions
(Continued)

Million Algerian dinars

	1970						1971					
	Compensation of Employees	Capital Consumption	Net Operating Surplus	Indirect Taxes	Less: Subsidies Received	Value Added	Compensation of Employees	Capital Consumption	Net Operating Surplus	Indirect Taxes	Less: Subsidies Received	Value Added
3 Manufacturing	1521	291	427	1127	...	3367	1580	361	284	1242	...	3468
a Manufacture of food, beverages and tobacco	332	66	122	549	...	1069	346	64	143	627	...	1180
b Textile, wearing apparel and leather industries	364	88	107	125	...	685	386	95	85	182	...	748
c Manufacture of wood and wood products, including furniture	155	22	51	87	...	314	178	24	52	84	...	339
d Manufacture of paper and paper products, printing and publishing	...	...	...	...	...	...	...	...	...	...	...	...
e Manufacture of chemicals and chemical petroleum, coal, rubber and plastic products	110	22	56	78	...	266	137	91	-13	101	...	315
f Manufacture of non-metallic mineral products, except products of petroleum and coal	...	...	...	...	...	...	...	...	...	...	...	...
g Basic metal industries	456	80	35	231	...	803	406	72	-50	186	...	614
h Manufacture of fabricated metal products, machinery and equipment					...						...	
i Other manufacturing industries	104	13	56	57	...	230	127	15	67	62	...	272
4 Electricity, gas and water	123	80	96	30	...	329	151	83	119	35	...	388
5 Construction	1097	310	472	350	...	2229	1327	435	594	286	...	2642
6 Wholesale and retail trade, restaurants and hotels	767	192	2209	1433	...	4600	900	229	2433	1630	...	5192
a Wholesale and retail trade	624	169	2153	1321	...	4266	749	205	2374	1512	...	4840
b Restaurants and hotels	143	23	56	112	...	334	151	24	59	118	...	352
7 Transport, storage and communication	714	183	328	38	...	1263	767	231	298	64	...	1359
a Transport and storage	559	125	349	31	...	1065	604	171	330	57	...	1162
b Communication	155	58	-21	7	...	199	163	60	-32	7	...	198
8 Finance, insurance, real estate and business services	297	143	1425	86	...	1951	281	145	1620	91	...	2135
a Financial institutions	138	7	226	13	...	384	120	7	403	17	...	547
b Insurance					...						...	
c Real estate and business services	159	136	1199	73	...	1567	161	138	1217	74	...	1590
Real estate, except dwellings	107	24	137	30	...	298	107	24	136	30	...	296
Dwellings	52	112	1062	43	...	1269	54	114	1081	44	...	1292
9 Community, social and personal services	202	34	139	55	...	430	224	38	154	62	...	478
Total, Industries	5814	1960	8460	3708	...	19942	6317	2147	8248	4018	...	20729
Producers of Government Services	2633	2	...	98	...	2732	3064	3	...	102	...	3169
Other Producers	...	...	...	...	...	...	...	...	...	...	...	...
Total	8447	1962	8460	3806	...	22674	9381	2150	8248	4122	...	23897
Imputed bank service charge	...	...	-243	...	...	-243	...	...	-260	...	...	-260
Import duties	...	...	...	1652	...	1652	...	...	...	1446	...	1446
Value added tax	...	...	...	...	...	...	...	...	...	...	...	...
Other adjustments	-40	...	16	12	...	-10	-21	-1	-144	2	...	-161
Total	8407	1962	8233	5470	...	24073	9360	2149	7844	5570	...	24923

	1972						1973					
	Compensation of Employees	Capital Consumption	Net Operating Surplus	Indirect Taxes	Less: Subsidies Received	Value Added	Compensation of Employees	Capital Consumption	Net Operating Surplus	Indirect Taxes	Less: Subsidies Received	Value Added

All Producers

1 Agriculture, hunting, forestry and fishing	909	169	1620	129	...	2828	989	235	1377	128	...	2728
a Agriculture and hunting	875	163	1485	127	...	2649	944	227	1208	124	...	2503
b Forestry and logging	15	2	92	2	...	111	19	5	116	2	...	140
c Fishing	20	4	43	2	...	68	26	3	53	2	...	86
2 Mining and quarrying	366	572	2847	840	...	4625	463	795	4052	1336	...	6647
a Coal mining	...	...	...	...	...	...	...	...	...	...	...	...
b Crude petroleum and natural gas production	223	543	2856	830	...	4452	307	744	4087	1315	...	6453
c Metal ore mining	143	29	-9	10	...	173	156	51	-35	21	...	194
d Other mining					...						...	

Algeria

4.6 Cost Components of Value Added, ISIC Divisions
(Continued)

Million Algerian dinars

	1972						1973					
	Compensation of Employees	Capital Consumption	Net Operating Surplus	Indirect Taxes	Less: Subsidies Received	Value Added	Compensation of Employees	Capital Consumption	Net Operating Surplus	Indirect Taxes	Less: Subsidies Received	Value Added
3 Manufacturing	1902	434	339	1377	...	4052	2071	540	762	1403	...	4777
a Manufacture of food, beverages and tobacco	396	71	182	709	...	1358	421	79	352	679	...	1531
b Textile, wearing apparel and leather industries	417	96	95	195	...	803	452	106	191	290	...	1039
c Manufacture of wood and wood products, including furniture	196	27	67	87	...	377	251	32	30	96	...	410
d Manufacture of paper and paper products, printing and publishing	...	...	...	...	...	...	...	...	...	...	...	...
e Manufacture of chemicals and chemical petroleum, coal, rubber and plastic products	147	93	-16	105	...	329	133	123	161	91	...	508
f Manufacture of non-metallic mineral products, except products of petroleum and coal	...	...	...	...	...	...	...	...	...	...	...	...
g Basic metal industries	555	125	-42	216	...	855	635	169	-5	199	...	998
h Manufacture of fabricated metal products, machinery and equipment					...						...	
i Other manufacturing industries	191	22	53	65	...	330	179	31	33	48	...	291
4 Electricity, gas and water	188	104	107	39	...	437	213	139	111	45	...	507
5 Construction	1846	574	691	349	...	3460	2160	583	858	413	...	4014
6 Wholesale and retail trade, restaurants and hotels	1043	250	2549	1746	...	5586	1173	302	2501	1708	...	5683
a Wholesale and retail trade	883	224	2487	1621	...	5214	1010	275	2431	1576	...	5292
b Restaurants and hotels	160	26	62	125	...	372	163	27	70	132	...	391
7 Transport, storage and communication	814	266	361	38	...	1479	973	318	429	47	...	1767
a Transport and storage	633	204	394	35	...	1265	773	253	484	43	...	1553
b Communication	181	62	-33	3	...	214	201	65	-55	4	...	214
8 Finance, insurance, real estate and business services	293	151	1629	94	...	2164	329	159	1880	132	...	2499
a Financial institutions	123	11	382	17	...	531	138	11	588	31	...	767
b Insurance					...						...	
c Real estate and business services	170	140	1247	77	...	1633	191	148	1292	101	...	1732
Real estate, except dwellings	114	25	145	32	...	315	131	30	147	54	...	361
Dwellings	56	115	1102	45	...	1318	60	118	1145	47	...	1371
9 Community, social and personal services	251	40	175	69	...	534	201	37	311	83	...	632
Total, Industries	7612	2560	10318	4681	...	25165	8571	3107	12281	5294	...	29252
Producers of Government Services	3585	3	...	155	...	3743	3530	3	...	63	...	3596
Other Producers	...	...	...	...	...	...	...	...	...	...	...	...
Total	11197	2563	10318	4836	...	28908	12101	3110	12281	5357	...	32848
Imputed bank service charge	...	...	...	...	...	...	...	...	-431	...	...	-431
Import duties	...	...	...	1888	...	1888	...	...	...	2047	...	2047
Value added tax	...	...	...	...	...	...	...	...	...	...	...	128
Other adjustments	...	-2	-383	3	...	-383	-112	73	142	25	...	128
Total	11190	2561	9935	6727	...	30413	11989	3183	11992	7429	...	34592

	1974						1975					
	Compensation of Employees	Capital Consumption	Net Operating Surplus	Indirect Taxes	Less: Subsidies Received	Value Added	Compensation of Employees	Capital Consumption	Net Operating Surplus	Indirect Taxes	Less: Subsidies Received	Value Added
	All Producers											
1 Agriculture, hunting, forestry and fishing	1148	234	1963	75	...	3420	1236	329	3395	8	...	4967
a Agriculture and hunting	1090	224	1781	71	...	3166	1172	317	3192	3	...	4684
b Forestry and logging	22	3	116	2	...	143	21	3	125	2	...	152
c Fishing	36	7	65	2	...	111	42	8	78	3	...	131
2 Mining and quarrying	524	793	13456	4022	...	18791	694	799	9731	4680	...	15904
a Coal mining	...	...	...	...	...	...	...	...	...	...	...	...
b Crude petroleum and natural gas production	343	737	13342	3996	...	18418	480	742	9690	4650	...	15562
c Metal ore mining	181	56	114	26	...	373	214	57	41	30	...	342
d Other mining					...						...	

Algeria

4.6 Cost Components of Value Added, ISIC Divisions
(Continued)

Million Algerian dinars

		1974					1975					
	Compensation of Employees	Capital Consumption	Net Operating Surplus	Indirect Taxes	Less: Subsidies Received	Value Added	Compensation of Employees	Capital Consumption	Net Operating Surplus	Indirect Taxes	Less: Subsidies Received	Value Added
3 Manufacturing	2546	632	286	1741	...	5203	3012	988	-66	1799	...	5735
a Manufacture of food, beverages and tobacco	590	104	177	688	...	1559	674	142	76	871	...	1763
b Textile, wearing apparel and leather industries	602	129	104	328	...	1163	623	136	85	354	...	1198
c Manufacture of wood and wood products, including furniture	311	33	57	112	...	512	388	62	-22	135	...	563
d Manufacture of paper and paper products, printing and publishing	...	...	...	...	...	...	...	...	...	...	...	...
e Manufacture of chemicals and chemical petroleum, coal, rubber and plastic products	191	139	105	97	...	531	235	148	97	136	...	617
f Manufacture of non-metallic mineral products, except products of petroleum and coal	...	...	...	...	...	...	...	...	...	...	...	...
g Basic metal industries	637	161	-149	417	...	1066	834	383	-275	233	...	1176
h Manufacture of fabricated metal products, machinery and equipment												
i Other manufacturing industries	215	66	-8	99	...	372	258	117	-27	70	...	418
4 Electricity, gas and water	257	141	155	51	...	604	291	159	168	57	...	675
5 Construction	2729	639	1502	537	...	5407	3234	1241	1436	723	...	6634
6 Wholesale and retail trade, restaurants and hotels	1371	354	3173	394	...	5291	1747	444	3725	16	...	5933
a Wholesale and retail trade	1176	323	3097	242	...	4838	1516	398	3624	-155	...	5383
b Restaurants and hotels	195	31	76	152	...	453	231	46	101	171	...	550
7 Transport, storage and communication	1220	463	761	72	...	2515	1472	518	716	114	...	2820
a Transport and storage	985	392	832	67	...	2277	1193	434	748	109	...	2485
b Communication	234	71	-71	5	...	239	279	84	-32	4	...	336
8 Finance, insurance, real estate and business services	373	168	2247	159	...	2946	468	191	2566	233	...	3459
a Financial institutions	165	12	856	69	...	1102	199	14	1091	105	...	1409
b Insurance												
c Real estate and business services	208	156	1391	90	...	1844	269	177	1475	128	...	2050
Real estate, except dwellings	144	32	184	40	...	400	202	47	204	76	...	529
Dwellings	64	124	1207	50	...	1444	67	130	1271	52	...	1521
9 Community, social and personal services	360	61	247	99	...	768	258	55	412	110	...	836
Total, Industries	10528	3485	23790	7150	...	44945	12412	4724	22083	7740	...	46960
Producers of Government Services	4450	5	...	124	...	4579	6249	4	...	204	...	6457
Other Producers	-	...	...	...	...	...	-	...	...	...	...	...
Total	14978	3490	23790	7274	...	49524	18661	4728	22083	7944	...	53417
Imputed bank service charge	...	...	-630	...	...	-630	...	...	-877	...	...	-877
Import duties	...	...	...	3750	...	3750	...	...	...	4424	...	4424
Value added tax	...	...	...	...	...	...	...	...	...	...	...	...
Other adjustments	55	6	-277	-4	...	-210	...	...	-214	-36	...	-249
Total	15033	3496	22883	11020	...	52434	18661	4729	20992	12332	...	56715

		1976					1977					
	Compensation of Employees	Capital Consumption	Net Operating Surplus	Indirect Taxes	Less: Subsidies Received	Value Added	Compensation of Employees	Capital Consumption	Net Operating Surplus	Indirect Taxes	Less: Subsidies Received	Value Added
				All Producers								
1 Agriculture, hunting, forestry and fishing	1447	350	3508	9	...	5315	1596	377	3373	8	...	5354
a Agriculture and hunting	1374	337	3279	4	...	4994	1505	360	3121	2	...	4988
b Forestry and logging	20	3	126	2	...	150	19	3	122	2	...	146
c Fishing	53	11	104	3	...	171	72	14	129	4	...	220
2 Mining and quarrying	712	953	12628	5658	...	19959	825	1045	15409	6665	...	23944
a Coal mining	...	...	...	...	...	...	...	...	...	...	...	...
b Crude petroleum and natural gas production	493	894	12614	5630	...	19630	585	968	15400	6633	...	23586
c Metal ore mining	219	59	14	38	...	329	240	77	9	32	...	358
d Other mining												

Algeria

4.6 Cost Components of Value Added, ISIC Divisions
(Continued)

Million Algerian dinars

	1976						1977					
	Compensation of Employees	Capital Consumption	Net Operating Surplus	Indirect Taxes	Less: Subsidies Received	Value Added	Compensation of Employees	Capital Consumption	Net Operating Surplus	Indirect Taxes	Less: Subsidies Received	Value Added
3 Manufacturing	3860	1204	215	2149	...	7428	4325	1325	293	2414	...	8355
a Manufacture of food, beverages and tobacco	868	208	133	971	...	2180	1063	224	83	1136	...	2505
b Textile, wearing apparel and leather industries	719	137	152	406	...	1414	772	149	122	467	...	1510
c Manufacture of wood and wood products, including furniture	447	64	59	169	...	739	504	54	110	202	...	871
d Manufacture of paper and paper products, printing and publishing	...	...	...	...	...	...	...	...	...	...	...	...
e Manufacture of chemicals and chemical petroleum, coal, rubber and plastic products	289	159	157	209	...	814	327	146	221	199	...	892
f Manufacture of non-metallic mineral products, except products of petroleum and coal	...	...	...	...	...	...	...	...	...	...	...	...
g Basic metal industries	1187	446	-267	280	...	1646	1280	588	-325	257	...	1798
h Manufacture of fabricated metal products, machinery and equipment											...	
i Other manufacturing industries	350	190	-19	114	...	635	379	164	82	153	...	779
4 Electricity, gas and water	366	174	228	100	...	868	441	208	253	130	...	1031
5 Construction	4140	1885	1675	869	...	8570	5387	2428	1035	1183	...	10033
6 Wholesale and retail trade, restaurants and hotels	2087	613	4178	965	...	7844	2579	762	4755	1679	...	9776
a Wholesale and retail trade	1827	563	4070	771	...	7231	2235	667	4642	1454	...	8998
b Restaurants and hotels	260	50	108	194	...	613	344	95	113	225	...	778
7 Transport, storage and communication	1684	696	661	200	...	3241	1992	947	882	301	...	4123
a Transport and storage	1356	609	692	195	...	2852	1606	816	890	286	...	3599
b Communication	327	87	-31	6	...	389	386	131	-8	15	...	524
8 Finance, insurance, real estate and business services	576	215	2743	292	...	3829	699	261	3498	290	...	4748
a Financial institutions	253	13	1152	149	...	1568	301	18	1641	128	...	2088
b Insurance					...						...	
c Real estate and business services	323	202	1591	143	...	2261	398	243	1857	162	...	2660
Real estate, except dwellings	251	64	246	87	...	650	322	84	336	100	...	842
Dwellings	72	138	1345	56	...	1611	76	159	1521	62	...	1818
9 Community, social and personal services	256	48	346	110	...	760	308	64	427	131	...	929
Total, Industries	15128	6138	26182	10362	...	57812	18152	7417	29925	12801	...	68289
Producers of Government Services	6693	5	...	221	...	6919	8006	21	...	248	...	8275
Other Producers	-	...	...	...	...	...	...	...	...	...	...	...
Total	21821	6143	26182	10583	...	64730	26158	7438	29925	13049	...	76564
Imputed bank service charge	...	...	-1142	...	...	-1142	...	...	-1359	...	...	-1359
Import duties	...	...	...	4490	...	4490	...	...	...	6551	...	6551
Value added tax	...	...	...	...	...	...	...	...	...	...	...	...
Other adjustments	-21	...	-9	-73	...	-103	18	-2	-283	-49	...	-310
Total	21800	6143	25031	15000	...	67975	26176	7436	28283	19551	...	81446

	1978					
	Compensation of Employees	Capital Consumption	Net Operating Surplus	Indirect Taxes	Less: Subsidies Received	Value Added

All Producers

1 Agriculture, hunting, forestry and fishing	2003	408	4551	-224	...	6738
a Agriculture and hunting	1927	393	4272	-230	...	6362
b Forestry and logging	-	-	155	2	...	157
c Fishing	76	15	124	5	...	219
2 Mining and quarrying	962	1146	15739	6942	...	24788
a Coal mining	...	...	...	...	...	...
b Crude petroleum and natural gas production	642	1074	15845	6912	...	24472
c Metal ore mining	320	72	-106	30	...	316
d Other mining					...	

17

Algeria

4.6 Cost Components of Value Added, ISIC Divisions
(Continued)

Million Algerian dinars

		1978				
		Compensation of Employees	Capital Consumption	Net Operating Surplus	Indirect Taxes	Less: Subsidies Received	Value Added
3	Manufacturing	5633	1271	1077	2627	...	10605
	a Manufacture of food, beverages and tobacco	1364	249	115	1070	...	2797
	b Textile, wearing apparel and leather industries	1070	118	481	624	...	2293
	c Manufacture of wood and wood products, including furniture	617	48	-39	178	...	804
	d Manufacture of paper and paper products, printing and publishing	...	...	...	...	...	...
	e Manufacture of chemicals and chemical petroleum, coal, rubber and plastic products	371	151	-15	334	...	840
	f Manufacture of non-metallic mineral products, except products of petroleum and coal	...	...	...	...	...	...
	g Basic metal industries	1538	424	421	237	...	2620
	h Manufacture of fabricated metal products, machinery and equipment					...	
	i Other manufacturing industries	673	281	114	184	...	1251
4	Electricity, gas and water	568	241	352	105	...	1266
5	Construction	8317	2678	1201	1178	...	13374
6	Wholesale and retail trade, restaurants and hotels	4005	975	6627	2520	...	14127
	a Wholesale and retail trade	3540	870	6024	2451	...	12885
	b Restaurants and hotels	465	105	603	69	...	1242
7	Transport, storage and communication	2577	913	983	288	...	4761
	a Transport and storage	2127	738	1025	273	...	4163
	b Communication	450	174	-42	15	...	598
8	Finance, insurance, real estate and business services	948	223	4184	394	...	5750
	a Financial institutions	397	23	1210	210	...	1841
	b Insurance					...	
	c Real estate and business services	551	200	2974	184	...	3909
	Real estate, except dwellings	414	90	964	124	...	1592
	Dwellings	137	110	2010	60	...	2317
9	Community, social and personal services	344	60	953	87	...	1443
	Total, Industries	25357	7915	35667	13917	...	82850
	Producers of Government Services	10899	18	...	296	...	11213
	Other Producers	...	...	...	...	...	...
	Total	36256	7933	35667	14213	...	94063
	Imputed bank service charge	...	...	-1272	...	...	-1272
	Import duties	...	...	...	...	...	8492
	Value added tax	...	...	...	...	...	...
	Other adjustments	...	...	-659	...	...	-660
	Total	...	...	33736	...	...	100623

Antigua and Barbuda

Source. 'Economic Survey and Projections', British Development Division in the Caribbean.

General note. The estimates shown in the following tables have been prepared in accordance with the United Nations System of National Accounts so far as the existing data would permit.

1.10 Gross Domestic Product by Kind of Activity, in Current Prices

Thousand East Caribbean dollars

	1970	1971	1972	1973	1974	1975	1976	1977	1978	1979	1980
1 Agriculture, hunting, forestry and fishing	...	...	...	6745	7750	9618	10851	11644	12820	13568	14300
2 Mining and quarrying	...	...	...	705	787	746	1068	1044	1201	1555	1800
3 Manufacturing	...	...	...	10051	9872	11056	5132	6880	9347	13307	13700
4 Electricity, gas and water	...	...	...	1109	1352	1368	1317	2086	3609	4915	7800
5 Construction	...	...	...	9035	8880	8958	10433	10934	10955	13454	15600
6 Wholesale and retail trade, restaurants and hotels	...	...	...	19584	21068	26497	28058	35592	41396	53395	60200
7 Transport, storage and communication	...	...	...	16955	18393	20068	21976	25985	29620	34932	38400
8 Finance, insurance, real estate and business services	...	...	...	20684	22849	23974	24018	28085	30391	36414	38900
9 Community, social and personal services	...	...	...	4848	6487	6669	6285	6917	8372	9979	12100
Total, Industries	...	...	...	89716	97438	108954	109138	129167	147711	181519	202800
Producers of Government Services	...	...	...	14300	18000	15300	16600	19400	23500	26000	30900
Other Producers	...	...	...	...	...	...	...	...	...	...	...
Subtotal	...	...	...	104016	115438	124254	125738	148567	171211	207519	233700
Less: Imputed bank service charge	...	...	...	4088	3809	3698	4979	6579	7061	8819	10300
Plus: Import duties	...	...	...	...	...	...	...	...	...	...	...
Plus: Value added tax	...	...	...	...	...	...	...	...	...	...	...
Equals: Gross Domestic Product	...	...	...	99928	111629	120556	120759	141988	164150	198700	223400

1.11 Gross Domestic Product by Kind of Activity, in Constant Prices

Thousand East Caribbean dollars

	1970	1971	1972	1973	1974	1975	1976	1977	1978	1979	1980
				At constant prices of: 1975							
1 Agriculture, hunting, forestry and fishing	...	...	...	10969	10302	9618	10785	10895	11879	11389	11400
2 Mining and quarrying	...	...	...	846	944	746	1028	952	1051	1238	1300
3 Manufacturing	...	...	...	11839	11629	11056	4911	6095	7841	10356	10600
4 Electricity, gas and water	...	...	...	798	1377	1368	1343	1500	1919	2206	2000
5 Construction	...	...	...	10899	9716	8958	9128	8904	8519	9415	9400
6 Wholesale and retail trade, restaurants and hotels	...	...	...	26007	27460	26497	23879	26462	29627	33535	34900
7 Transport, storage and communication	...	...	...	21895	21450	20068	16920	19325	22275	24813	25800
8 Finance, insurance, real estate and business services	...	...	...	24805	23819	23974	24024	23997	24481	24746	24700
9 Community, social and personal services	...	...	...	6576	7139	6669	5662	5474	6290	6485	6600
Total, Industries	...	...	...	114534	113836	108954	97680	103604	113882	124183	126700
Producers of Government Services	...	...	...	14300	18000	15300	16600	19400	18500	18500	22100
Other Producers	...	...	...	...	...	...	...	...	...	...	...
Subtotal	...	...	...	128834	131836	124254	114280	123004	132382	142683	148800
Less: Imputed bank service charge	...	...	...	5554	4190	3698	4482	5209	5265	5706	6100
Plus: Import duties	...	...	...	...	...	...	...	...	...	...	...
Plus: Value added tax	...	...	...	...	...	...	...	...	...	...	...
Equals: Gross Domestic Product	...	...	...	123280	127646	120556	109798	117795	127417	136977	142700

Argentina

General note. The preparation of national accounts statistics in Argentina is undertaken by Banco Central de la Republica Argentina, Buenos Aires. The official estimates are published on a quarterly basis in the 'Economic Reports'. In 1975 the publication 'Sistema de Cuentas del Producto e Ingreso de la Argentina' was presented. Volume I 'Metodologia y Fuentes' contains a detailed description of the sources and methods used for the national accounts estimation. Volume II 'Cuadros Estadisticos' presents estimates for the period 1950-1973, in accordance with the United Nations System of National Accounts (SNA). The following tables have been prepared from succesive replies to the United Nations national accounts questionnaire. When the scope and coverage of the estimates differ for conceptual or statistical reasons from the definitions and classifications recommended in SNA, a footnote is indicated to the relevant tables.

Sources and methods:

(a) Gross domestic product. The main approach used to estimate GDP is the production approach.

(b) Expenditure on the gross domestic product. The expenditure approach is used to estimate government final consumption expenditure, increase in stocks, investment in construction, and exports and imports of goods and services. The commodity-flow approach is used to estimate the current value of gross investment other than for construction. Private final consumption expenditure is taken as a residual. Government final consumption expenditure, consisting of compensation of employees and net purchases of goods and services, is obtained from government accounts. Investment in construction is estimated through the use of accounting data for the public sector, agricultural census data for the agricultural sector, and construction licenses and miscellaneous sources for the urban private construction. The estimation of domestically produced capital goods is done on the basis of the industrial censuses. For the years between censuses, the data are up-dated through a combination of indexes of physical output and price indexes. Data on exports and imports of goods and services are obtained from the balance of payments accounts. Constant values of government consumption expenditures are obtained through extrapolating wages and salaries by the number of persons employed and through deflating purchases of goods and services by the wholesale price index for non-agricultural goods. Private consumption expenditure at constant prices is obtained as a residual. The current values of construction are deflated by indexes of construction costs or extrapolated by input volumes. Domestic machinery and equipment products are deflated by index of producer prices or extrapolated by volume of production. Imported machinery and equipment are deflated by price indexes. Price deflation is used for exports and imports of goods and services.

(c) Cost-structure of the gross domestic product. The estimates of compensation of employees are based on employment data, remuneration data and collective wage agreement data. Intercensal estimates are rough, except for those activities for which accounting data are available. Operating surplus is, in general, obtained as a residual. Consumption of fixed capital is calculated on the basis of accounting data from public enterprises, capital stock data in the case of private construction, gross investment data and estimated depreciation rates in the case of durable production equipment. Information on indirect taxes is obtained by type of government authority.

(d) Gross domestic product by kind of economic activity. The table of gross domestic product by kind of economic activity is prepared in factor values. The production approach is used to estimate value added of most industries. The basic statistics on agricultural production are obtained from the Secretaria de Agricultura y Ganaderia de la Nacion. The production is valued at farmers' prices, which are obtained by subtracting transportation costs and commercial mark-ups from wholesale prices. Production estimates for beef, mutton and pork, are defined as the value of sales for slaughter, adjusted for changes in stocks and exports of live animal. Own account consumption of agricultural products and meat is included in the estimates. Since no annual information is available, indirect indicators are used to estimate the value of intermediate consumption. For mining, information on quantities and prices is obtained from the government authorities concerned. Input data are supplied by state companies and balance sheets of a representative sample of mining enterprises. The general method used in estimating industrial production is by interpolating prices and quantities between census years. After the latest industrial census of 1963, extrapolation is used, based on changes in the production volume. Information on prices is obtained from the wholesale price index and miscellaneous sources for products not included in that index. Data on the number of construction permits issued are used to estimate the value of construction in the private sector. The data are converted into value figures by using the cost of construction index. Intermediate consumption is estimated from analysis of budgets, surveys, etc. For the public sector, data are obtained from the accounts of official organizations and state enterprises. Intermediate consumption is estimated on the basis of coefficients obtained from a study of records in the field of public works. Gross output of the trade sector is estimated through applying gross percentage mark-up rates to the value of goods recorded as entering the various marketing channels. Input values are based on information from balance sheets of joint stock companies and other inquiries. Value added in the transport sector is estimated from financial statements and accounts data, direct information or from survey data. For financial intermediaries the data used is based on the financial statements of all credit institutions in the country. The data needed to calculate value added of insurance services is provided by the Super-intendencia de Seguros de la Nacion. The value of rents paid is calculated on the basis of the population censuses and the rent component of the consumer price index. In the case of owner-occupied dwellings, the average gross rent for rented dwellings is applied. The value added of the producers of government, provincial government and local government services is based on the accounts and budget data of the concerned authorities. Business services and other professional services are estimated through population census data and income data. The value of domestic services is obtained by multiplying the number of employees by their average compensation. For the estimates in constant prices, extrapolation of the base year value by indexes of production volume or output quantity and occasionally of employment data are used for all sectors except public construction, in which case the current values are deflated by an index of construction costs.

1.1 Expenditure on the Gross Domestic Product, in Current Prices

Thousand Million Argentine pesos

	1970	1971	1972	1973	1974	1975	1976	1977	1978	1979	1980
1 General government final consumption expenditure	9	13	20	42	66	188	742	1983	6152	16450	40830
2 Private final consumption expenditure a	60	86	144	237	323	891	4427	12509	30756	88820	174546
3 Gross capital formation b	19	27	45	68	95	374	2044	5695	12844	33502	72433
a Increase in stocks b	-	1	2	4	2	5	16	-	-273	21	1712
b Gross fixed capital formation	19	26	43	64	93	369	2028	5695	13117	33481	70721
4 Exports of goods and services	8	10	20	36	45	113	939	2729	6099	12579	19514
5 Less: Imports of goods and services	8	11	19	27	41	116	606	2076	4053	12245	25623
Equals: Gross Domestic Product	88	126	209	356	488	1452	7546	20840	51798	139106	281700

a) Obtained as a residual.
b) Including stocks of principal agricultural products and an important group of raw materials and manufactured goods. Other stocks are included in private final consumption expenditure.

1.2 Expenditure on the Gross Domestic Product, in Constant Prices

Million Argentine pesos

	1970	1971	1972	1973	1974	1975	1976	1977	1978	1979	1980
	\multicolumn{11}{c}{At constant prices of:1970}
1 General government final consumption expenditure	69163	71999	72787	75552	82251	82567	76469	78106	76027	85526	89512
2 Private final consumption expenditure											
3 Gross capital formation	18605	20551	20655	19742	20069	20417	21386	25610	22197	24385	26735
a Increase in stocks	-6	511	503	996	455	784	143	178	-674	49	918
b Gross fixed capital formation	18611	20040	20152	18746	19614	19634	21243	25432	22871	24336	25817
Residential buildings	6981	7290	6919	6494	7028	8140	7983	7407	7429	8258	9353
Non-residential buildings	4626	5155	5294	4401	4692	4123	5598	7560	7280	6880	7602
Other construction and land improvement etc.	...	...	...	...	...	...	...	...	...	...	...
Other	7004	7595	7939	7851	7894	7371	7662	10465	8162	9198	8862
4 Exports of goods and services	6696	7292	7410	8293	8313	7374	9705	12277	13222	12921	12419
5 Less: Imports of goods and services	7894	8621	7970	7388	8497	9071	6745	8682	7836	11852	16929
Equals: Gross Domestic Product	87970	91221	92882	96198	102136	101287	100815	107310	103610	110979	111738

Argentina

1.3 Cost Components of the Gross Domestic Product

Thousand Million Argentine pesos

	1970	1971	1972	1973	1974	1975	1976	1977	1978	1979	1980
1 Indirect taxes, net	10	12	19	31	52	85	730	1970	5594	16757	44295
2 Consumption of fixed capital	...	...	...	...	...	...	...	...	...	...	...
3 Compensation of employees paid by resident producers to:	...	...	...	...	...	...	...	...	...	...	...
4 Net operating surplus	...	...	...	...	...	...	...	...	...	...	...
Equals: Gross Domestic Product	88	126	209	356	488	1452	7546	20840	51798	139106	281700

1.10 Gross Domestic Product by Kind of Activity, in Current Prices

Thousand Million Argentine pesos

	1970	1971	1972	1973	1974	1975	1976	1977	1978	1979	1980
1 Agriculture, hunting, forestry and fishing	11	17	31	55	66	147	836	2320	5277	15138	24884
2 Mining and quarrying	2	2	4	7	10	22	130	193	755	2138	5485
3 Manufacturing	26	38	63	101	139	464	2505	6493	15098	39480	71208
4 Electricity, gas and water	2	3	4	7	10	25	191	553	1449	2865	6165
5 Construction	5	7	12	18	27	109	550	1486	3950	10605	23873
6 Wholesale and retail trade, restaurants and hotels	15	20	35	53	74	223	1240	3299	8004	22084	45427
7 Transport, storage and communication	6	12	19	30	42	122	641	1743	4336	10990	20384
8 Finance, insurance, real estate and business services	7	10	16	35	46	120	599	2534	6327	17923	40516
9 Community, social and personal services	12	16	25	49	75	219	852	2219	6601	17885	43757
Total, Industries	88	126	209	356	488	1452	7546	20840	51798	139106	281700
Producers of Government Services	...	...	...	...	...	...	...	...	...	...	...
Other Producers	...	...	...	...	...	...	...	...	...	...	...
Subtotal	88	126	209	356	488	1452	7546	20840	51798	139106	281700
Less: Imputed bank service charge	...	...	...	...	...	...	...	...	...	...	...
Plus: Import duties	...	...	...	...	...	...	...	...	...	...	...
Plus: Value added tax	...	...	...	...	...	...	...	...	...	...	...
Equals: Gross Domestic Product	88	126	209	356	488	1452	7546	20840	51798	139106	281700

1.11 Gross Domestic Product by Kind of Activity, in Constant Prices

Million Argentine pesos

At constant prices of: 1970

	1970	1971	1972	1973	1974	1975	1976	1977	1978	1979	1980
1 Agriculture, hunting, forestry and fishing	10298	10469	10644	11771	12190	11723	12262	12588	12759	13277	12424
2 Mining and quarrying	1777	1916	1972	1916	1962	1932	1979	2148	2189	2328	2417
3 Manufacturing	20986	22275	23170	24089	25504	24853	24099	25982	23248	25616	24644
4 Electricity, gas and water	1810	1979	2174	2338	2477	2627	2724	2850	2945	3261	3514
5 Construction	5025	5342	5291	4671	5041	5272	5934	6735	6697	6877	7319
6 Wholesale and retail trade, restaurants and hotels	11815	12146	12173	12327	13294	13383	12691	13621	12592	13891	14272
7 Transport, storage and communication	8962	9085	9083	9588	10178	9852	9761	10333	9959	10800	10862
8 Finance, insurance, real estate and business services	5915	5982	5850	6112	6918	6338	6074	6915	7381	7969	8928
9 Community, social and personal services	11352	11626	11934	12419	12927	13760	13798	13904	14027	14308	14620
Total, Industries	77940	80821	82292	85231	90491	89739	89321	95076	91797	98327	98999
Producers of Government Services	...	...	...	...	...	...	...	...	...	...	...
Other Producers	...	...	...	...	...	...	...	...	...	...	...
Subtotal [a]	77940	80821	82292	85231	90491	89739	89321	95076	91797	98327	98999
Less: Imputed bank service charge	...	...	...	...	...	...	...	...	...	...	...
Plus: Import duties	...	...	...	...	...	...	...	...	...	...	...
Plus: Value added tax	...	...	...	...	...	...	...	...	...	...	...
Plus: Other adjustments [b]	10030	10400	10590	10967	11645	11548	11494	12234	11813	12652	12739
Equals: Gross Domestic Product	87970	91221	92882	96198	102136	101287	100815	107310	103610	110979	111738

a) Gross domestic product in factor values.
b) Referring to indirect taxes net of subsidies.

Argentina

4.4 Derivation of Value Added by Kind of Activity, ISIC Divisions, in Constant Prices

Million Argentine pesos

At constant prices of: 1970

All Producers

	1970 Gross Output	1970 Intermediate Consumption	1970 Value Added	1971 Gross Output	1971 Intermediate Consumption	1971 Value Added	1972 Gross Output	1972 Intermediate Consumption	1972 Value Added	1973 Gross Output	1973 Intermediate Consumption	1973 Value Added
1 Agriculture, hunting, forestry and fishing	...	...	10298	...	...	10469	...	...	10644	...	...	11771
a Agriculture and hunting	...	...	10114	...	...	10233	...	...	10383	...	...	11462
b Forestry and logging	...	...	139	...	...	189	...	...	214	...	...	250
c Fishing	...	...	45	...	...	48	...	...	47	...	...	59
2 Mining and quarrying	...	...	1777	...	...	1916	...	...	1972	...	...	1916
a Coal mining	...	...	33	...	...	34	...	...	38	...	...	28
b Crude petroleum and natural gas production	...	...	1454	...	...	1565	...	...	1610	...	...	1601
c Metal ore mining	...	...	70	...	...	79	...	...	77	...	...	66
d Other mining	...	...	220	...	...	238	...	...	247	...	...	221
3 Manufacturing	...	...	20986	...	...	22275	...	...	23170	...	...	24089
a Manufacture of food, beverages and tobacco	...	...	4545	...	...	4470	...	...	4699	...	...	4779
b Textile, wearing apparel and leather industries	...	...	2769	...	...	2874	...	...	2896	...	...	2950
c Manufacture of wood and wood products, including furniture	...	...	439	...	...	457	...	...	463	...	...	466
d Manufacture of paper and paper products, printing and publishing	...	...	1186	...	...	1210	...	...	1261	...	...	1333
e Manufacture of chemicals and chemical petroleum, coal, rubber and plastic products	...	...	2846	...	...	3115	...	...	3307	...	...	3533
f Manufacture of non-metallic mineral products, except products of petroleum and coal	...	...	1176	...	...	1263	...	...	1303	...	...	1225
g Basic metal industries	...	...	1049	...	...	1174	...	...	1259	...	...	1314
h Manufacture of fabricated metal products, machinery and equipment	...	...	5527	...	...	6172	...	...	6381	...	...	6826
i Other manufacturing industries	...	...	1450	...	...	1539	...	...	1601	...	...	1664
4 Electricity, gas and water	...	...	1810	...	...	1979	...	...	2174	...	...	2338
a Electricity, gas and steam	...	...	1659	...	...	1821	...	...	2012	...	...	2166
b Water works and supply	...	...	151	...	...	158	...	...	162	...	...	172
5 Construction	...	...	5025	...	...	5342	...	...	5291	...	...	4671
6 Wholesale and retail trade, restaurants and hotels	...	...	11815	...	...	12146	...	...	12173	...	...	12327
a Wholesale and retail trade	...	...	10749	...	...	11090	...	...	11068	...	...	11161
b Restaurants and hotels	...	...	1066	...	...	1056	...	...	1105	...	...	1167
7 Transport, storage and communication	...	...	8962	...	...	9085	...	...	9083	...	...	9588
a Transport and storage	...	...	7962	...	...	8033	...	...	7981	...	...	8404
b Communication	...	...	1000	...	...	1052	...	...	1101	...	...	1184
8 Finance, insurance, real estate and business services	...	...	5915	...	...	5982	...	...	5850	...	...	6112
a Financial institutions	...	...	1921	...	...	1932	...	...	1798	...	...	2007
b Insurance	...	...	438	...	...	448	...	...	427	...	...	466
c Real estate and business services	...	...	3556	...	...	3601	...	...	3625	...	...	3640
9 Community, social and personal services	...	...	11352	...	...	11626	...	...	11934	...	...	12419
Total, Industries	...	...	77940	...	...	80821	...	...	82292	...	...	85231
Producers of Government Services	...	...	...	...	...	...	...	...	...	...	...	...
Other Producers	...	...	...	...	...	...	...	...	...	...	...	...
Total a	...	...	77940	...	...	80821	...	...	82292	...	...	85231
Imputed bank service charge	...	...	...	...	...	...	...	...	...	...	...	...
Import duties	...	...	...	...	...	...	...	...	...	...	...	...
Value added tax	...	...	...	...	...	...	...	...	...	...	...	...
Total	...	...	...	...	...	...	...	...	...	...	...	...

Argentina

4.4 Derivation of Value Added by Kind of Activity, ISIC Divisions, in Constant Prices

Million Argentine pesos

At constant prices of: 1970 — All Producers

	1974 Gross Output	1974 Intermediate Consumption	1974 Value Added	1975 Gross Output	1975 Intermediate Consumption	1975 Value Added	1976 Gross Output	1976 Intermediate Consumption	1976 Value Added	1977 Gross Output	1977 Intermediate Consumption	1977 Value Added
1 Agriculture, hunting, forestry and fishing	...	...	12190	...	...	11723	...	...	12262	...	...	12588
a Agriculture and hunting	...	...	11924	...	...	11525	...	...	12045	...	...	12339
b Forestry and logging	...	...	208	...	...	148	...	...	163	...	...	176
c Fishing	...	...	58	...	...	50	...	...	54	...	...	73
2 Mining and quarrying	...	...	1962	...	...	1932	...	...	1979	...	...	2148
a Coal mining	...	...	37	...	...	29	...	...	37	...	...	41
b Crude petroleum and natural gas production	...	...	1609	...	...	1594	...	...	1638	...	...	1757
c Metal ore mining	...	...	73	...	...	60	...	...	69	...	...	82
d Other mining	...	...	244	...	...	249	...	...	235	...	...	268
3 Manufacturing	...	...	25504	...	...	24853	...	...	24099	...	...	25982
a Manufacture of food, beverages and tobacco	...	...	5202	...	...	5238	...	...	5210	...	...	5135
b Textile, wearing apparel and leather industries	...	...	3255	...	...	3105	...	...	2936	...	...	3045
c Manufacture of wood and wood products, including furniture	...	...	534	...	...	489	...	...	400	...	...	419
d Manufacture of paper and paper products, printing and publishing	...	...	1415	...	...	1425	...	...	1248	...	...	1249
e Manufacture of chemicals and chemical petroleum, coal, rubber and plastic products	...	...	3343	...	...	3388	...	...	3445	...	...	3496
f Manufacture of non-metallic mineral products, except products of petroleum and coal	...	...	1320	...	...	1345	...	...	1298	...	...	1281
g Basic metal industries	...	...	1349	...	...	1294	...	...	1170	...	...	1344
h Manufacture of fabricated metal products, machinery and equipment	...	...	7325	...	...	6851	...	...	6726	...	...	8220
i Other manufacturing industries	...	...	1762	...	...	1717	...	...	1664	...	...	1794
4 Electricity, gas and water	...	...	2477	...	...	2627	...	...	2724	...	...	2850
a Electricity, gas and steam	...	...	2299	...	...	2447	...	...	2537	...	...	2661
b Water works and supply	...	...	178	...	...	181	...	...	188	...	...	189
5 Construction	...	...	5041	...	...	5272	...	...	5934	...	...	6735
6 Wholesale and retail trade, restaurants and hotels	...	...	13294	...	...	13383	...	...	12691	...	...	13621
a Wholesale and retail trade	...	...	12039	...	...	12094	...	...	11409	...	...	12459
b Restaurants and hotels	...	...	1255	...	...	1289	...	...	1282	...	...	1163
7 Transport, storage and communication	...	...	10178	...	...	9852	...	...	9761	...	...	10333
a Transport and storage	...	...	8970	...	...	8725	...	...	8660	...	...	9206
b Communication	...	...	1208	...	...	1127	...	...	1101	...	...	1127
8 Finance, insurance, real estate and business services	...	...	6918	...	...	6338	...	...	6074	...	...	6915
a Financial institutions	...	...	2627	...	...	1913	...	...	1499	...	...	2115
b Insurance	...	...	573	...	...	679	...	...	652	...	...	720
c Real estate and business services	...	...	3718	...	...	3746	...	...	3924	...	...	4079
9 Community, social and personal services	...	...	12927	...	...	13760	...	...	13798	...	...	13904
Total, Industries	...	...	90491	...	...	89739	...	...	89321	...	...	95076
Producers of Government Services	...	...	...	...	...	...	...	...	...	...	...	...
Other Producers	...	...	...	...	...	...	...	...	...	...	...	...
Total [a]	...	...	90491	...	...	89739	...	...	89321	...	...	95076
Imputed bank service charge	...	...	...	...	...	...	...	...	...	...	...	...
Import duties	...	...	...	...	...	...	...	...	...	...	...	...
Value added tax	...	...	...	...	...	...	...	...	...	...	...	...
Total	...	...	...	...	...	...	...	...	...	...	...	...

Argentina

4.4 Derivation of Value Added by Kind of Activity, ISIC Divisions, in Constant Prices

Million Argentine pesos

	1978 Gross Output	1978 Intermediate Consumption	1978 Value Added	1979 Gross Output	1979 Intermediate Consumption	1979 Value Added	1980 Gross Output	1980 Intermediate Consumption	1980 Value Added
				At constant prices of: 1970					
				All Producers					
1 Agriculture, hunting, forestry and fishing	...	...	12759	...	...	13277	...	...	12491
a Agriculture and hunting	...	...	12487	...	...	12979	...	...	12264
b Forestry and logging	...	...	162	...	...	178	...	...	132
c Fishing	...	...	110	...	...	120	...	...	95
2 Mining and quarrying	...	...	2189	...	...	2328	...	...	2459
a Coal mining	...	...	29	...	...	44	...	...	30
b Crude petroleum and natural gas production	...	...	1819	...	...	1934	...	...	2032
c Metal ore mining	...	...	74	...	...	67	...	...	84
d Other mining	...	...	267	...	...	282	...	...	314
3 Manufacturing	...	...	23248	...	...	25616	...	...	24644
a Manufacture of food, beverages and tobacco	...	...	5000	...	...	5262	...	...	5359
b Textile, wearing apparel and leather industries	...	...	2613	...	...	2896	...	...	2460
c Manufacture of wood and wood products, including furniture	...	...	414	...	...	460	...	...	446
d Manufacture of paper and paper products, printing and publishing	...	...	1289	...	...	1312	...	...	1224
e Manufacture of chemicals and chemical petroleum, coal, rubber and plastic products	...	...	3218	...	...	3615	...	...	3649
f Manufacture of non-metallic mineral products, except products of petroleum and coal	...	...	1286	...	...	1377	...	...	1329
g Basic metal industries	...	...	1270	...	...	1486	...	...	1368
h Manufacture of fabricated metal products, machinery and equipment	...	...	6552	...	...	7438	...	...	7107
i Other manufacturing industries	...	...	1606	...	...	1769	...	...	1702
4 Electricity, gas and water	...	...	2945	...	...	3261	...	...	3514
a Electricity, gas and steam	...	...	2763	...	...	3082	...	...	3335
b Water works and supply	...	...	182	...	...	179	...	...	179
5 Construction	...	...	6697	...	...	6877	...	...	7786
6 Wholesale and retail trade, restaurants and hotels	...	...	12592	...	...	13891	...	...	14272
a Wholesale and retail trade	...	...	11345	...	...	12557	...	...	12841
b Restaurants and hotels	...	...	1246	...	...	1334	...	...	1431
7 Transport, storage and communication	...	...	9959	...	...	10800	...	...	10862
a Transport and storage	...	...	8873	...	...	9649	...	...	9648
b Communication	...	...	1086	...	...	1151	...	...	1214
8 Finance, insurance, real estate and business services	...	...	7381	...	...	7969	...	...	8976
a Financial institutions	...	...	2504	...	...	2878	...	...	3726
b Insurance	...	...	657	...	...	721	...	...	728
c Real estate and business services	...	...	4219	...	...	4370	...	...	4522
9 Community, social and personal services	...	...	14027	...	...	14308	...	...	14744
Total, Industries	...	...	91797	...	...	98327	...	...	99747
Producers of Government Services	...	...	...	...	...	...	...	...	...
Other Producers	...	...	...	...	...	...	...	...	...
Total a	...	...	91797	...	...	98327	...	...	99747
Imputed bank service charge	...	...	...	...	...	...	...	...	...
Import duties	...	...	...	...	...	...	...	...	...
Value added tax	...	...	...	...	...	...	...	...	...
Total	...	...	...	...	...	...	...	...	...

a) Column 'Value added' is in factor values.

Australia

General note. The preparation of national accounts statistics in Australia is undertaken by the Australian Bureau of Statistics, Canberra. Preliminary estimates are published in the Budget White Paper 'National Income and Expenditure'. Estimates for each quarter are being published in 'Quarterly Estimates of National Income and Expenditure'. The most comprehensive national accounts publication is the 'Australian National Accounts, National Income and Expenditure', which contains official estimates and detailed descriptions of the conceptual framework and structure of the national accounts. Another series of publication entitled 'Estimates of Gross Product by Industry at Current and Constant Prices' contains estimates of industry gross product at current and constant prices, and of constant prices per person employed, by industry. The Australian National Accounts System corresponds closely to the United Nations System of National Accounts (SNA). Input-output tables have been published for the years 1958-59, 1962-63 and 1968-69 in 'Australian National Accounts, Input-Output Tables'. The following tables have been prepared from successive replies to the United Nations national accounts questionnaire. Estimates relate to fiscal year beginning 1 July. When the scope and coverage of the estimates differ for conceptual or statistical reasons from the definitions and classifications recommended in SNA, a footnote is indicated to the relevant tables.

Sources and methods:

(a) Gross domestic product. Gross domestic product is estimated using both the income and expenditure approaches. The difference between the two approaches is shown as a statistical discrepancy and, by convention, recorded on the expenditure side of the account.

(b) Expenditure on the gross domestic product. The expenditure approach is used to estimate government final consumption expenditure, exports and imports of goods and services, and increase in stocks. This approach, in combination with the commodity-flow approach, is also used to estimate private final consumption expenditure and gross fixed capital formation. Government final consumption expenditure is estimated from the reports and records of the government bodies. For private consumption expenditure on goods, estimates are derived from results of retail censuses, or are based on production, import and export data. For the years between censuses, results of quarterly surveys of retail sales are used to extrapolate existing census data or excise data and retail sales survey results are used. Estimates of expenditure on services are based mainly on revenue or earnings data. Rent of dwellings is estimated using a perpetual-inventory model of the stock of dwellings and the rent component of the consumer price index. Estimates of increase in stocks are based on the annual censuses of manufacturing establishments, periodic censuses of retail establishments, the 1968-69 Census of Wholesale Establishments and on the opening and closing stocks obtained from income tax tabulations. For years when censuses are not conducted, estimates are extrapolated from the latest annual bench-marks using the results of the quarterly business surveys of stocks. Estimates of public gross fixed capital formation expenditure are based on Commonwealth and State budget papers and reports of government bodies and public corporations. For the private sector, estimates are obtained from the Australian Bureau of Statistics' (ABS) quarterly collection of building statistics, the quarterly survey of new capital expenditure by private business and income tax returns. Exports and imports of goods and services are estimated from monthly customs data and quarterly survey results. For the constant price estimates, current values of government expenditure are revalued by indexes of salaries and wages and by prices of selected goods and services purchased. Private consumption expenditure is deflated by relevant components of the consumer price index or other appropriate price indexes. Prices of increase in stocks are deflated by price indexes. Gross fixed capital formation is revalued by using special purpose price indexes. Exports and imports of goods and services at constant prices are derived by direct revaluation at base-year prices and quantities of goods exported and imported.

(c) Cost-structure of the gross domestic product. The estimates of compensation of employees are based on monthly payroll tax returns, government returns and average earnings data. Estimates of operating surplus are based on income tax tabulation, survey data and annual returns of financial institutions. Information on depreciation is also based on income tax tabulations. The sources of data for net indirect taxes include Commonwealth and State budget papers and annual reports of taxation authorities.

(d) Gross domestic product by kind of economic activity. The table of GDP by kind of economic activity is prepared in factor values. The estimates are required on an establishment basis and are based on the Australian Standard Industrial Classification (ASIC). The production approach is used for agriculture, mining, manufacturing and ownership of dwellings. The income approach is used for all other sectors. For agriculture, gross value of farm production is derived from an annual census of all rural holdings with at least one hectare and from authorities concerned. The cost of production is estimated on a per unit of production basis derived from results of surveys. Estimates of output and input of mining are based on annual mining censuses. The annual census of manufacturing establishments is conducted on an integrated economic census basis, from which values of input and output are estimated. For electricity, gas and water, estimates of output are obtained from the Census of Electricity and Gas Establishments for the years 1968-69, 1969-70 and 1971-72, other years' estimates are derived by extrapolation and interpolation of census data by the revenue of electricity and gas undertakings. Input is derived by using input-output relationships based on census data. Gross output of construction is estimated as the sum of gross fixed capital formation and maintenance of buildings and construction. Estimates of intermediate input are obtained by deducting from gross output the estimates of income-based gross product. Estimates of wholesale and retail sales for 1968-69 were derived for different commodity groups from the censuses of wholesale and retail establishments. Other years' estimates are obtained through extrapolation using data on production, imports and exports and derived from sample surveys. For transport, estimates are mainly derived from revenue data supplied by the transport authorities. Gross output of the financial institutions are estimated from statistical data collected by the ABS, returns by banks and insurance offices and the Reserve Bank. For ownership of dwellings, benchmark for gross rent are based on rental data and the number of dwellings from the quinquennial censuses of population and housing. The imputed rent for owner-occupied dwellings is based on average rents for tenanted dwellings. Gross product of public administration is derived as wages, salaries and supplements paid to government employees, plus indirect taxes. Output for community services is derived from estimates of private and government expenditures on the different types of services. For the constant price estimates, double deflation is used for agriculture and mining sectors with current years' quantities revalued at base-year prices. For public administration, current price estimates of gross product are revalued by an average earnings index. For other industries, value added is extrapolated by various quantity indicators and indexes.

1.1 Expenditure on the Gross Domestic Product, in Current Prices

Million Australian dollars — Fiscal year beginning 1 July

	1970	1971	1972	1973	1974	1975	1976	1977	1978	1979	1980
1 General government final consumption expenditure [a]	4198	4788	5452	6846	9219	11462	13422	15187	16835	18804	22204
2 Private final consumption expenditure	20404	22687	25444	30054	36456	43537	49792	55182	62097	69678	78609
3 Gross capital formation [b]	9221	9636	9882	12916	15206	17140	20126	20162	24546	26058	31868
a Increase in stocks [b]	447	10	-285	1173	1018	112	1133	-481	1271	576	287
b Gross fixed capital formation [b]	8774	9626	10167	11743	14188	17028	18993	20643	23275	25482	31581
Residential buildings	1643	1860	2196	2693	2731	3567	4363	4212	4336	5143	6435
Non-residential buildings	3350	3654	3792	4330	5807	6683	6756	7597	8179	8782	10742
Other construction and land improvement etc.											
Other	3781	4112	4179	4720	5650	6778	7874	8834	10760	11557	14404
4 Exports of goods and services	5032	5578	6917	7784	9889	10979	13188	13988	16512	21617	22267
5 Less: imports of goods and services	5092	5217	5353	7782	10246	10837	13790	15028	17892	20914	24768
Statistical discrepancy	-26	205	561	1529	1224	544	406	760	-28	-779	875
Equals: Gross Domestic Product	33737	37677	42903	51347	61748	72825	83144	90251	102070	114464	131055

a) Including some transfers to private non-profit organizations servicing household.
b) Excluding livestock.

1.2 Expenditure on the Gross Domestic Product, in Constant Prices

Million Australian dollars — Fiscal year beginning 1 July

	1970	1971	1972	1973	1974	1975	1976	1977	1978	1979	1980
	At constant prices of: 1979										
1 General government final consumption expenditure	12020	12430	12994	13971	15155	16234	16937	17669	18399	18804	19793
2 Private final consumption expenditure	52061	54183	57100	60097	61883	63793	65349	66240	68383	69678	71950
3 Gross capital formation	24798	24210	23336	26569	25700	24704	26121	23730	27342	26058	28668
a Increase in stocks	1143	-10	-629	2097	1964	99	1548	-774	1686	576	267
b Gross fixed capital formation	23655	24220	23965	24472	23736	24605	24573	24504	25656	25482	28401

25

Australia

1.2 Expenditure on the Gross Domestic Product, in Constant Prices
(Continued)

Million Australian dollars — Fiscal year beginning 1 July

	1970	1971	1972	1973	1974	1975	1976	1977	1978	1979	1980
					At constant prices of: 1979						
Residential buildings	4454	4674	5015	5066	4189	4703	5149	4671	4649	5143	5725
Non-residential buildings	9672	9887	9453	9404	9809	9681	8790	9109	9135	8782	9559
Other construction and land improvement etc.											
Other	9529	9659	9497	10002	9738	10221	10634	10724	11872	11557	13117
4 Exports of goods and services	14536	15748	16335	15431	16497	17195	18521	18958	20049	21617	20583
5 Less: Imports of goods and services	15290	14722	14943	19025	19535	18531	20373	19447	21149	20914	22623
Statistical discrepancy	-46	519	1323	3180	2136	843	586	944	16	-779	826
Equals: Gross Domestic Product	88079	92368	96145	100223	101836	104238	107141	108094	113040	114464	119197

1.3 Cost Components of the Gross Domestic Product

Million Australian dollars — Fiscal year beginning 1 July

	1970	1971	1972	1973	1974	1975	1976	1977	1978	1979	1980
1 Indirect taxes, net [a]	3287	3695	4242	5302	6614	8524	9748	10340	12088	14069	16175
a Indirect taxes paid	3597	4086	4567	5686	6975	8877	10090	10840	12672	14889	17189
b Less: Subsidies received [a]	310	391	325	384	361	353	342	500	584	820	1014
2 Consumption of fixed capital [b]	2843	3117	3360	3643	4151	4892	5656	6191	6928	7725	8663
3 Compensation of employees paid by resident producers to: [c]	18447	20575	22966	28127	36115	41580	46926	51488	55415	61627	71392
a Resident households [c]	18447	20575	22966	28127	36115	41580	46926	51488	55415	61627	71392
b Rest of the world	-	-	-	-	-	-	-	-	-	-	-
4 Net operating surplus	9160	10290	12335	14275	14868	17829	20814	22232	27639	31043	34825
a Corporate and quasi-corporate enterprises	4076	4377	5058	5046	5023	6469	7682	7884	9615	11182	13685
b Private unincorporated enterprises	5084	5913	7277	9229	9845	11360	13132	14348	18024	19861	21140
c General government	-	-	-	-	-	-	-	-	-	...	...
Equals: Gross Domestic Product	33737	37677	42903	51347	61748	72825	83144	90251	102070	114464	131055

a) Subsidies on wheat and wool are recorded on an accrual basis.
b) No charges were made for consumption of fixed capital by general government services and private non-profit services to households.
c) Some government contributions to superannuation are recorded only when benefits are paid.

1.4 General Government Current Receipts and Disbursements

Million Australian dollars — Fiscal year beginning 1 July

	1970	1971	1972	1973	1974	1975	1976	1977	1978	1979	1980
					Receipts						
1 Property and entrepreneurial income [a]	985	1111	1146	1133	1121	1524	2021	2445	2733	3221	3615
2 Taxes, fees and contributions	8380	9590	10521	13484	17428	21059	24482	26652	29145	34026	40194
a Indirect taxes	3597	4086	4567	5686	6975	8877	10090	10840	12672	14889	17189
b Direct taxes	4602	5285	5702	7498	10141	11813	13946	15312	15913	18541	22343
c Social security contributions	-	-	-	-	-	-	-	-	-	...	...
d Compulsory fees, fines and penalties	181	219	252	300	312	369	446	500	560	596	662
3 Other current receipts	...	...	...	...	...	...	...	...	...	...	...
Total Current Receipts of General Government	9365	10701	11667	14617	18549	22583	26503	29097	31878	37247	43809
					Disbursements						
1 General government final consumption expenditure [b]	4198	4788	5452	6846	9219	11462	13422	15187	16835	18804	22204
a Compensation of employees	3595	4225	4821	5967	8227	9780	11358	12732	13751	15041	...
b Consumption of fixed capital [c]	-	-	-	-	-	-	-	-	-	...	...
c Purchases of goods and services, net	603	563	631	878	992	1682	2064	2455	3084	3763	...
d Less: Own account production of fixed assets	...	...	...	...	...	...	...	...	...	...	...
e Indirect taxes paid, net	...	...	...	...	...	...	...	...	...	...	...

Australia

1.4 General Government Current Receipts and Disbursements
(Continued)

Million Australian dollars — Fiscal year beginning 1 July

	1970	1971	1972	1973	1974	1975	1976	1977	1978	1979	1980
2 Property income paid	848	927	1030	1099	1326	1513	2084	2572	3084	3527	4269
3 Subsidies d	310	391	325	384	361	353	342	500	584	820	1014
4 Other current transfers paid	2010	2365	2939	3597	4945	6788	8147	9118	10027	10908	12322
a Social security benefits and social assistance grants	1823	2157	2684	3302	4585	6400	7733	8665	9512	10343	11695
b Other	187	208	255	295	360	388	414	453	515	565	627
5 Net saving	1999	2230	1921	2691	2698	2467	2508	1720	1348	3188	4000
Total Current Disbursements and Net Saving of General Government	9365	10701	11667	14617	18549	22583	26503	29097	31878	37247	43809

a) No private non-financial enterprises have been classified as quasi-corporate. All public enterprises are treated as if they were quasi-corporate. Furthermore, public non-financial enterprises are treated as if the whole of their operating surplus is withdrawn by general government.
b) Including some transfers to private non-profit organizations servicing household.
c) No charges were made for consumption of fixed capital by general government services and private non-profit services to households.
d) Subsidies on wheat and wool are recorded on an accrual basis.

1.5 Current Income and Outlay of Corporate and Quasi-Corporate Enterprises, Summary

Million Australian dollars — Fiscal year beginning 1 July

	1970	1971	1972	1973	1974	1975	1976	1977	1978	1979	1980
Receipts											
1 Net operating surplus	4076	4377	5058	5046	5023	6469	7682	7884	9615	11182	13685
2 Other property and entrepreneurial income received	1712	1972	2348	3112	3962	4526	5390	6185	6903	7987	9909
3 Current transfers received	-	-	-	-	74	-	-	-	-	-	-
Total Current Receipts	5788	6349	7406	8158	9059	10995	13072	14069	16518	19169	23594
Disbursements											
1 Property and entrepreneurial income paid	3181	3629	4098	4734	5763	6810	8065	9339	10402	12129	14414
2 Direct taxes and other current payments to general government	1379	1462	1545	1934	2344	2505	2803	3072	3002	3360	4639
3 Other current transfers paid	39	46	52	66	287	101	118	127	156	193	214
4 Net saving	1189	1212	1711	1424	665	1579	2086	1531	2958	3487	4327
Total Current Disbursements and Net Saving	5788	6349	7406	8158	9059	10995	13072	14069	16518	19169	23594

1.6 Current Income and Outlay of Households and Non-Profit Institutions

Million Australian dollars — Fiscal year beginning 1 July

	1970	1971	1972	1973	1974	1975	1976	1977	1978	1979	1980
Receipts											
1 Compensation of employees	18447	20575	22966	28127	36115	41580	46926	51488	55415	61627	71392
a From resident producers a	18447	20575	22966	28127	36115	41580	46926	51488	55415	61627	71392
b From rest of the world	-	-	-	-	-	-	-	-	-	-	-
2 Property and entrepreneurial income received	6127	7098	8599	10723	11701	13359	15542	17233	21284	23441	25490
3 Current transfers received	2099	2495	3043	3705	5101	6938	8221	9290	10206	11278	12787
a Social security benefits and social assistance grants received	1823	2157	2684	3302	4585	6400	7733	8665	9512	10343	11695
b Other	276	338	359	403	516	538	488	625	694	935	1092
Total Current Receipts	26673	30168	34608	42555	52917	61877	70689	78011	86905	96346	109669
Disbursements											
1 Private final consumption expenditure	20404	22687	25444	30054	36456	43537	49792	55182	62097	69678	78609
2 Property income paid	195	211	245	377	509	587	722	850	926	1048	1302
3 Direct taxes and other payments n.e.c. to general government	3356	3984	4336	5785	8021	9582	11493	12622	13357	15636	18205
a Social security contributions	-	-	-	-	-	-	-	-	-	-	...
b Direct taxes	...	...	...	...	...	...	...	...	...	...	...
c Fees, fines and penalties	...	...	...	...	...	...	...	...	...	...	...
4 Other current transfers paid	134	172	217	261	266	313	290	367	398	347	433
5 Net saving	2584	3114	4366	6078	7665	7858	8392	8990	10127	9637	11120
Total Current Disbursements and Net Saving	26673	30168	34608	42555	52917	61877	70689	78011	86905	96346	109669

a) Some government contributions to superannuation are recorded only when benefits are paid.

Australia

1.7 External Transactions on Current Account, Summary

Million Australian dollars — Fiscal year beginning 1 July

	1970	1971	1972	1973	1974	1975	1976	1977	1978	1979	1980
Payments to the Rest of the World											
1 Imports of goods and services	5092	5217	5353	7782	10246	10837	13790	15028	17892	20914	24768
a Imports of merchandise c.i.f.	4199	4200	4234	6378	8444	8728	11382	12229	14739	17380	20498
b Other	893	1017	1119	1404	1802	2109	2408	2799	3153	3534	4270
2 Factor income paid to the rest of the world	583	645	788	809	964	1050	1213	1426	1684	2130	2391
a Compensation of employees	.	.	.	.	.	.	.	.	.	...	...
b Property and entrepreneurial income paid	583	645	788	809	964	1050	1213	1426	1684	2130	2391
3 Indirect taxes paid to supranational organizations	...	...	...	...	...	...	...	...	...	...	...
4 Current transfers to the rest of the world [a]	321	380	472	556	626	701	704	820	913	912	1060
5 Surplus of the nation on current transactions	-580	-168	915	-609	-1052	-888	-1890	-2490	-3157	-1242	-4633
Payments to the Rest of the World and Surplus of the Nation on Current Transactions	5416	6074	7528	8538	10784	11700	13817	14784	17332	22714	23586
Receipts From The Rest of the World											
1 Exports of goods and services	5032	5578	6917	7784	9889	10979	13188	13988	16512	21617	22267
a Exports of merchandise f.o.b.	4217	4725	5986	6721	8485	9402	11518	12060	14009	18494	18845
b Other	815	853	931	1063	1404	1577	1670	1928	2503	3123	3422
2 Factor income received from rest of the world	130	183	273	390	372	266	257	276	294	368	452
a Compensation of employees	.	.	.	.	.	.	...	...	...	...	...
b Property and entrepreneurial income received [a]	130	183	273	390	372	266	257	276	294	368	452
3 Subsidies received from supranational organisations	...	...	...	...	...	...	...	...	...	...	...
4 Current transfers from rest of the world	254	313	338	364	523	455	372	520	526	729	867
Receipts from the Rest of the World on Current Transactions	5416	6074	7528	8538	10784	11700	13817	14784	17332	22714	23586

a) Including capital transfers.

1.8 Capital Transactions of The Nation, Summary

Million Australian dollars — Fiscal year beginning 1 July

	1970	1971	1972	1973	1974	1975	1976	1977	1978	1979	1980
Finance of Gross Capital Formation											
Gross saving	8615	9673	11358	13836	15378	16796	18642	18432	21361	24037	28110
1 Consumption of fixed capital	2843	3117	3360	3643	4151	4892	5656	6191	6928	7725	8663
a General government	.	.	.	.	.	.	.	.	.	...	...
b Corporate and quasi-corporate enterprises	1885	2117	2284	2524	2847	3381	3843	4230	4682	5186	5825
Public	440	484	528	579	586	761	850	963	1091	1166	1322
Private	1445	1633	1756	1945	2261	2620	2993	3267	3591	4020	4503
c Other	958	1000	1076	1119	1304	1511	1813	1961	2246	2539	2838
2 Net saving	5772	6556	7998	10193	11227	11904	12986	12241	14433	16312	19447
a General government	1999	2230	1921	2691	2698	2467	2508	1720	1348	3188	4000
b Corporate and quasi-corporate enterprises	1189	1212	1711	1424	665	1579	2086	1531	2958	3487	4327
Public	122	122	180	203	264	390	441	273	370	408	628
Private	1067	1090	1531	1221	401	1189	1645	1258	2588	3079	3699
c Other	2584	3114	4366	6078	7864	7858	8392	8990	10127	9637	11120
Less: Surplus of the nation on current transactions	-580	-168	915	-609	-1052	-888	-1890	-2490	-3157	-1242	-4633
Statistical discrepancy	26	-205	-561	-1529	-1224	-544	-406	-760	28	779	-875
Finance of Gross Capital Formation	9221	9636	9882	12916	15206	17140	20126	20162	24546	26058	31868
Gross Capital Formation											
Increase in stocks [a]	447	10	-285	1173	1018	112	1133	-481	1271	576	287

Australia

1.8 Capital Transactions of The Nation, Summary
(Continued)

Million Australian dollars — Fiscal year beginning 1 July

	1970	1971	1972	1973	1974	1975	1976	1977	1978	1979	1980
Gross fixed capital formation [a]	8774	9626	10167	11743	14188	17028	18993	20643	23275	25482	31581
1 General government	1368	1508	1668	1908	2768	3394	3434	3705	3857	4003	4329
2 Corporate and quasi-corporate enterprises	5056	5477	5246	5956	7502	8411	9171	10712	12441	13384	...
a Public	1569	1788	1815	2071	2884	3303	3699	4237	4365	4841	5610
b Private	3487	3689	3431	3885	4618	5108	5472	6475	8076	8543	...
3 Other	2350	2641	3253	3879	3918	5223	6388	6226	6977	8095	...
Gross Capital Formation	9221	9636	9882	12916	15206	17140	20126	20162	24546	26058	31868

a) Excluding livestock.

1.10 Gross Domestic Product by Kind of Activity, in Current Prices

Million Australian dollars — Fiscal year beginning 1 July

	1970	1971	1972	1973	1974	1975	1976	1977	1978	1979	1980
1 Agriculture, hunting, forestry and fishing	2042	2356	3244	4363	3910	3998	4483	4247	6839	7799	...
2 Mining and quarrying	1057	1304	1459	1775	2352	3055	3699	4211	5443	7468	...
3 Manufacturing	8942	9663	10582	12481	14484	16665	18521	19823	21435	23594	...
4 Electricity, gas and water [a]	1057	1188	1344	1525	1764	2090	2407	2689	2963	3309	...
5 Construction	2595	2897	3225	3743	4790	5587	6105	6461	6804	7315	...
6 Wholesale and retail trade, restaurants and hotels [b]	5317	5840	6658	8037	9750	11372	12856	13731	14708	15995	...
7 Transport, storage and communication	2577	2859	3102	3632	4440	5332	5942	6444	7021	7947	...
8 Finance, insurance, real estate and business services	5138	5879	6895	8004	9540	11788	14080	15918	18654	21071	...
9 Community, social and personal services [b]	3941	4538	5174	6327	8592	10461	12153	13510	14810	16574	...
Total, Industries	32666	36524	41683	49887	59622	70348	80246	87034	98677	111072	...
Producers of Government Services	1319	1505	1712	2120	2812	3275	3712	4171	4389	4634	...
Other Producers	...	...	...	...	...	...	...	...	...	...	...
Subtotal	33985	38029	43395	52007	62434	73623	83958	91205	103066	115706	...
Less: Imputed bank service charge	714	821	1005	1264	1527	1730	1966	2086	2359	2780	3433
Plus: Import duties	466	469	513	604	841	932	1152	1132	1363	1538	...
Plus: Value added tax	...	...	...	...	...	...	...	...	...	...	...
Equals: Gross Domestic Product	33737	37677	42903	51347	61748	72825	83144	90251	102070	114464	131055

a) Including sewerage.
b) Restaurants and hotels are included in item 'Community, social and personal services'.

1.11 Gross Domestic Product by Kind of Activity, in Constant Prices

Million Australian dollars — Fiscal year beginning 1 July

At constant prices of: 1974

	1970	1971	1972	1973	1974	1975	1976	1977	1978	1979	1980
1 Agriculture, hunting, forestry and fishing	3450	3747	3069	3629	3907	4150	4168	3934	5174	4747	...
2 Mining and quarrying	1718	1820	2012	2156	2367	2083	2322	2376	2476	...	...
3 Manufacturing	13349	13643	14261	15201	14544	14412	14927	14835	15457	...	...
4 Electricity, gas and water [a]	1383	1461	1561	1662	1750	1836	1987	2123	2235	...	...
5 Construction	4542	4679	4745	4968	4823	5072	4866	4827	4730	...	...
6 Wholesale and retail trade, restaurants and hotels [b]	8138	8262	8686	9556	9736	9902	10107	10082	10423	...	...
7 Transport, storage and communication	3436	3554	3771	4160	4404	4528	4879	5287	5663	...	...
8 Finance, insurance, real estate and business services	8206	8410	8810	9240	9466	9715	10057	10398	10829	...	...
9 Community, social and personal services [b]	9289	9647	10081	10509	11348	12059	12461	12943	13241	...	...
Total, Industries	53511	55223	56996	61081	62345	63757	65774	66805	70228	...	...
Producers of Government Services	...	...	...	...	...	...	...	...	...	...	...
Other Producers	...	...	...	...	...	...	...	...	...	...	...
Subtotal	53511	55223	56996	61081	62345	63757	65774	66805	70228	71620	...
Less: Imputed bank service charge	1310	1348	1405	1499	1520	1515	1518	1498	1485	1504	...
Plus: Import duties	646	607	621	842	841	786	872	812	912	891	...
Plus: Value added tax	...	...	...	...	...	...	...	...	...	...	...
Equals: Gross Domestic Product	52847	54483	56211	60424	61666	63028	65128	66119	69655	71007	...

a) Including sewerage.
b) Restaurants and hotels are included in item 'Community, social and personal services'.

Australia

1.12 Relations Among National Accounting Aggregates

Million Australian dollars — Fiscal year beginning 1 July

	1970	1971	1972	1973	1974	1975	1976	1977	1978	1979	1980
Gross Domestic Product	33737	37677	42903	51347	61748	72825	83144	90251	102070	114464	131055
Plus: Net factor income received from abroad	-453	-462	-515	-419	-592	-784	-956	-1150	-1390	-1762	-1939
Factor income received [a]	130	183	273	390	372	266	257	276	294	368	452
Less: Factor income paid	583	645	788	809	964	1050	1213	1426	1684	2130	2391
Equals: Gross National Product	33284	37215	42388	50928	61156	72041	82188	89101	100680	112702	129116
Less: Consumption of fixed capital [b]	2843	3117	3360	3643	4151	4892	5656	6191	6928	7725	8663
Less: Net indirect taxes paid to supranational organisations	...	...	...	...	...	...	...	...	...	...	...
Equals: National Income at Market Prices	30441	34098	39028	47285	57005	67149	76532	82910	93752	104977	120453
Plus: Net current transfers received from abroad [c]	-67	-67	-134	-192	-103	-246	-332	-300	-387	-183	-193
Current transfers received	254	313	338	364	523	455	372	520	526	729	867
Less: Current transfers paid [a]	321	380	472	556	626	701	704	820	913	912	1060
Equals: National Disposable Income at Market Prices	30374	34031	38894	47093	56902	66903	76200	82610	93365	104794	120260
Less: Final consumption	24602	27475	30896	36900	45675	54999	63214	70369	78932	88482	100813
Equals: Net Saving	5772	6556	7998	10193	11227	11904	12986	12241	14433	16312	19447
Less: Surplus of the nation on current transactions	-580	-168	915	-609	-1052	-888	-1890	-2490	-3157	-1242	-4633
Statistical discrepancy	26	-205	-561	-1529	-1224	-544	-406	-760	28	779	-875
Equals: Net Capital Formation [b]	6378	6519	6522	9273	11055	12248	14470	13971	17618	18333	23205

a) Including capital transfers.
b) No charges were made for consumption of fixed capital by general government services and private non-profit services to households.
c) The Australian accounts do not distinguish between current and capital transfers to the rest of the world and these items have been treated as current transfers.
d) Excluding livestock.

2.1 General Government Final Consumption Expenditure by Function, in Current Prices

Million Australian dollars — Fiscal year beginning 1 July

	1970	1971	1972	1973	1974	1975	1976	1977	1978	1979	1980
1 General public services	588	684	760	929	1242	1491	1714	1970	2125	2442	2829
2 Defence	1050	1109	1160	1373	1429	1613	1917	2102	2429	2614	3365
3 Public order and safety	259	304	356	442	618	761	888	1029	1157	1362	1611
4 Education	1028	1222	1462	1909	2766	3425	4115	4653	5061	5676	6556
5 Health	562	656	760	1029	1543	2292	2718	3036	3319	3661	4252
6 Social security and welfare	91	109	136	170	249	316	354	422	498	572	690
7 Housing and community amenities	41	45	63	92	147	187	193	200	229	278	313
8 Recreational, cultural and religious affairs	150	173	205	256	354	442	478	541	611	683	789
9 Economic services	426	485	547	641	823	926	1042	1221	1392	1506	1776
a Fuel and energy	...	...	...	...	...	...	...	...	...	...	...
b Agriculture, forestry, fishing and hunting	173	198	238	266	333	387	428	480	523	593	690
c Mining, manufacturing and construction, except fuel and energy	24	34	41	47	61	70	79	94	101	119	109
d Transportation and communication	66	79	89	110	132	143	154	159	181	191	183
e Other economic affairs	163	174	179	218	297	326	381	488	587	603	794
10 Other functions	2	2	2	3	47	9	5	12	13	9	23
Total General Government Final Consumption Expenditure [a]	4198	4788	5452	6846	9219	11462	13422	15187	16835	18804	22204

a) Including some transfers to private non-profit organizations servicing household.

2.2 General Government Final Consumption Expenditure by Function, in Constant Prices

Million Australian dollars — Fiscal year beginning 1 July

At constant prices of: 1979

	1970	1971	1972	1973	1974	1975	1976	1977	1978	1979	1980
1 General public services	...	...	...	...	...	...	...	...	...	...	...
2 Defence	...	...	...	...	...	...	...	...	...	...	...
3 Public order and safety	755	809	865	934	1038	1088	1129	1212	1281	1361	1407
4 Education	2799	3062	3317	3723	4402	4725	5119	5364	5519	5676	5817
5 Health	1907	2017	2208	2540	2939	3663	3838	3993	4138	4233	4463
6 Social security and welfare											
7 Housing and community amenities											
8 Recreational, cultural and religious affairs	...	...	...	...	...	...	...	...	...	...	...
9 Economic services	...	...	...	...	...	...	...	...	...	...	...
10 Other functions	...	...	...	...	...	...	...	...	...	...	...
Total General Government Final Consumption Expenditure	12020	12430	12994	13971	15155	16234	16937	17669	18399	18804	19793

Australia

2.3 Total General Government Outlays by Function and Type

Million Australian dollars — Fiscal year beginning 1 July

		Final Consumption Expenditures				Other Current Transfers & Property Income	Total Current Disbursements	Gross Capital Formation	Other Capital Outlays	Total Outlays
		Total	Compensation of Employees	Other	Subsidies					

1970

		Total	CoE	Other	Subsidies	Other Curr.	Total Curr. Disb.	GCF	Other Cap.	Total Outlays
1	General public services	588	...	...	-	176	764	103	5	872
2	Defence	1050	...	...	-	7	1057	-	3	1060
3	Public order and safety	259	...	...	-	1	260	26	-	286
4	Education	1028	...	...	-	109	1137	248	21	1406
5	Health	562	...	...	-	410	972	102	3	1077
6	Social security and welfare	91	...	...	-	1296	1387	11	21	1419
7	Housing and community amenities	41	...	...	2	-	43	39	13	95
8	Recreation, culture and religion	150	...	...	-	-	150	52	3	205
9	Economic services	426	...	...	303	9	738	785	33	1556
	a Fuel and energy	...	...	...	2	-	2	-	-	2
	b Agriculture, forestry, fishing and hunting	173	...	...	195	-	368	87	7	462
	c Mining (except fuels), manufacturing and construction	24	...	...	58	-	82	5	-1	86
	d Transportation and communication	66	...	...	10	1	77	682	32	791
	e Other economic affairs	163	...	...	38	8	209	12	-5	216
10	Other functions	2	...	...	5	850	857	1	-	858
	Total	4198	...	...	310	2858	7366	1368	102	8836

1971

		Total	CoE	Other	Subsidies	Other Curr.	Total Curr. Disb.	GCF	Other Cap.	Total Outlays
1	General public services	684	...	...	-	196	880	99	29	1008
2	Defence	1109	...	...	-	8	1117	-	-14	1103
3	Public order and safety	304	...	...	-	1	305	30	-	335
4	Education	1222	...	...	-	135	1357	288	20	1665
5	Health	656	...	...	1	508	1165	116	3	1284
6	Social security and welfare	109	...	...	-	1507	1616	10	25	1651
7	Housing and community amenities	45	...	...	6	-	51	44	7	102
8	Recreation, culture and religion	173	...	...	-	-	173	66	3	242
9	Economic services	484	...	...	382	10	876	855	42	1773
	a Fuel and energy	...	...	...	2	-	2	1	-	3
	b Agriculture, forestry, fishing and hunting	198	...	...	229	-	427	95	5	527
	c Mining (except fuels), manufacturing and construction	34	...	...	97	1	132	5	1	138
	d Transportation and communication	79	...	...	11	1	91	743	38	872
	e Other economic affairs	174	...	...	43	8	225	12	-2	235
10	Other functions	2	...	...	2	927	931	1	-1	931
	Total	4788	...	...	391	3292	8471	1508	113	10092

1972

		Total	CoE	Other	Subsidies	Other Curr.	Total Curr. Disb.	GCF	Other Cap.	Total Outlays
1	General public services	760	...	...	-	231	991	130	12	1133
2	Defence	1160	...	...	-	20	1180	-	2	1182
3	Public order and safety	356	...	...	-	2	358	38	-2	394
4	Education	1462	...	...	-	170	1632	328	26	1986
5	Health	760	...	...	1	581	1342	117	5	1464
6	Social security and welfare	136	...	...	-	1924	2060	9	34	2103
7	Housing and community amenities	63	...	...	7	1	71	57	5	133
8	Recreation, culture and religion	205	...	...	-	-	205	73	4	282
9	Economic services	547	...	...	316	9	872	914	29	1815
	a Fuel and energy	...	...	...	3	-	3	1	-	4
	b Agriculture, forestry, fishing and hunting	238	...	...	139	-	377	108	-18	467
	c Mining (except fuels), manufacturing and construction	41	...	...	122	1	164	10	1	175
	d Transportation and communication	89	...	...	10	-	99	784	45	928
	e Other economic affairs	179	...	...	42	8	229	12	1	242
10	Other functions	2	...	...	1	1031	1034	-	-2	1032
	Total	5452	...	...	325	3969	9746	1668	112	11526

Australia

2.3 Total General Government Outlays by Function and Type
(Continued)

Million Australian dollars — Fiscal year beginning 1 July

		Final Consumption Expenditures				Other Current Transfers & Property Income	Total Current Disbursements	Gross Capital Formation	Other Capital Outlays	Total Outlays
		Total	Compensation of Employees	Other	Subsidies					

1973

		Total	Comp.	Other	Subsidies	Other Current	Total Current Disb.	Gross Cap. Form.	Other Cap. Outlays	Total Outlays
1	General public services	929	...	...	-	278	1207	157	30	1394
2	Defence	1373	...	...	-	10	1383	-	2	1385
3	Public order and safety	442	...	...	-	2	444	43	-1	486
4	Education	1909	...	...	-	198	2107	382	34	2523
5	Health	1029	...	...	1	659	1689	147	8	1844
6	Social security and welfare	170	...	...	-	2434	2604	21	36	2661
7	Housing and community amenities	92	...	...	8	1	101	78	57	236
8	Recreation, culture and religion	256	...	...	-	-	256	75	4	335
9	Economic services	642	...	...	373	9	1024	1002	30	2056
	a Fuel and energy	...	...	...	2	-	2	-	-	2
	b Agriculture, forestry, fishing and hunting	266	...	...	189	-	455	105	-22	538
	c Mining (except fuels), manufacturing and construction	47	...	...	126	-	173	13	-	186
	d Transportation and communication	110	...	...	12	-	122	875	49	1046
	e Other economic affairs	218	...	...	44	9	271	11	3	285
10	Other functions	3	...	...	2	1105	1110	3	3	1116
	Total	6846	...	...	384	4696	11926	1908	203	14037

1974

		Total	Comp.	Other	Subsidies	Other Current	Total Current Disb.	Gross Cap. Form.	Other Cap. Outlays	Total Outlays
1	General public services	1242	...	...	-	330	1572	240	72	1884
2	Defence	1429	...	...	-	18	1447	-	35	1482
3	Public order and safety	618	...	...	-	4	622	55	1	678
4	Education	2766	...	...	-	236	3002	656	58	3716
5	Health	1543	...	...	2	817	2362	245	10	2617
6	Social security and welfare	249	...	...	-	3510	3759	21	72	3852
7	Housing and community amenities	147	...	...	8	1	156	140	134	430
8	Recreation, culture and religion	354	...	...	1	-	355	102	25	482
9	Economic services	823	...	...	350	22	1195	1301	59	2555
	a Fuel and energy	...	...	...	2	-	2	-	-	2
	b Agriculture, forestry, fishing and hunting	333	...	...	120	-	453	141	-5	589
	c Mining (except fuels), manufacturing and construction	61	...	...	172	1	234	19	6	259
	d Transportation and communication	132	...	...	12	-	144	1127	54	1325
	e Other economic affairs	297	...	...	44	21	362	14	4	380
10	Other functions	47	...	...	1	1333	1381	7	12	1400
	Total	9219	...	...	361	6271	15851	2768	477	19096

1975

		Total	Comp.	Other	Subsidies	Other Current	Total Current Disb.	Gross Cap. Form.	Other Cap. Outlays	Total Outlays
1	General public services	1491	...	...	-	336	1827	293	46	2166
2	Defence	1613	...	...	-	35	1648	-	-	1648
3	Public order and safety	761	...	...	-	5	766	75	2	843
4	Education	3425	...	...	-	287	3712	695	70	4477
5	Health	2292	...	...	1	1369	3662	387	19	4068
6	Social security and welfare	316	...	...	-	4701	5017	27	122	5166
7	Housing and community amenities	187	...	...	10	1	198	234	68	500
8	Recreation, culture and religion	442	...	...	1	1	444	139	14	597
9	Economic services	926	...	...	340	49	1315	1536	46	2897
	a Fuel and energy	...	...	...	3	-	3	-	-	3
	b Agriculture, forestry, fishing and hunting	387	...	...	98	-	485	163	-11	637
	c Mining (except fuels), manufacturing and construction	70	...	...	161	-	231	18	1	250
	d Transportation and communication	143	...	...	20	-1	162	1336	47	1545
	e Other economic affairs	326	...	...	58	50	434	20	9	463
10	Other functions	9	...	...	1	1517	1527	7	19	1553
	Total	11462	...	...	353	8301	20116	3394	406	23916

Australia

2.3 Total General Government Outlays by Function and Type
(Continued)

Million Australian dollars — Fiscal year beginning 1 July

		Final Consumption Expenditures			Subsidies	Other Current Transfers & Property Income	Total Current Disbursements	Gross Capital Formation	Other Capital Outlays	Total Outlays
		Total	Compensation of Employees	Other						

1976

		Total	Comp.	Other	Subs.	Other Curr.	Total Curr. Disb.	Gross Cap.	Other Cap.	Total Outlays
1	General public services	1714	...	...	-	360	2074	298	15	2387
2	Defence	1917	...	...	-	25	1942	-	4	1946
3	Public order and safety	888	...	...	-	5	893	85	-3	975
4	Education	4115	...	...	1	318	4434	641	57	5132
5	Health	2718	...	...	2	1141	3861	395	15	4271
6	Social security and welfare	354	...	...	-	6268	6622	27	66	6715
7	Housing and community amenities	193	...	...	11	1	205	210	31	446
8	Recreation, culture and religion	478	...	...	1	1	480	136	26	642
9	Economic services	1041	...	...	324	26	1391	1640	52	3083
	a Fuel and energy	...	...	...	3	-	3	1	-	4
	b Agriculture, forestry, fishing and hunting	428	...	...	123	-	551	188	-9	730
	c Mining (except fuels), manufacturing and construction	79	...	...	90	-	169	15	1	185
	d Transportation and communication	154	...	...	39	-1	192	1413	43	1648
	e Other economic affairs	381	...	...	69	27	477	23	17	517
10	Other functions	5	...	...	3	2086	2094	3	4	2101
	Total	13422	...	...	342	10231	23995	3434	267	27696

1977

		Total	Comp.	Other	Subs.	Other Curr.	Total Curr. Disb.	Gross Cap.	Other Cap.	Total Outlays
1	General public services	1970	...	...	-	391	2361	319	4	2684
2	Defence	2102	...	...	-	27	2129	-	6	2135
3	Public order and safety	1029	...	...	-	5	1034	108	-1	1141
4	Education	4653	...	...	1	333	4987	717	59	5763
5	Health	3036	...	...	10	1011	4057	378	12	4447
6	Social security and welfare	422	...	...	-	7320	7742	25	75	7842
7	Housing and community amenities	200	...	...	13	2	215	174	49	438
8	Recreation, culture and religion	541	...	...	2	1	544	179	42	765
9	Economic services	1221	...	...	468	27	1716	1797	-26	3487
	a Fuel and energy	...	...	...	2	-	2	-	-	2
	b Agriculture, forestry, fishing and hunting	480	...	...	271	-	751	210	-9	952
	c Mining (except fuels), manufacturing and construction	94	...	...	91	-	185	18	-79	124
	d Transportation and communication	159	...	...	48	-1	206	1546	57	1809
	e Other economic affairs	488	...	...	56	28	572	24	5	601
10	Other functions	12	...	...	6	2573	2591	9	-	2600
	Total	15187	...	...	500	11690	27377	3705	220	31302

1978

		Total	Comp.	Other	Subs.	Other Curr.	Total Curr. Disb.	Gross Cap.	Other Cap.	Total Outlays
1	General public services	2125	...	...	-	450	2575	325	2	2902
2	Defence	2429	...	...	-	25	2454	-	9	2463
3	Public order and safety	1157	...	...	-	6	1163	125	-2	1286
4	Education	5061	...	...	1	330	5392	731	62	6185
5	Health	3319	...	...	9	1199	4527	371	21	4919
6	Social security and welfare	498	...	...	-	7983	8481	28	81	8590
7	Housing and community amenities	229	...	...	14	3	246	125	28	399
8	Recreation, culture and religion	611	...	...	2	1	614	236	43	893
9	Economic services	1393	...	...	551	30	1974	1911	7	3892
	a Fuel and energy	...	...	...	2	-	2	2	-	4
	b Agriculture, forestry, fishing and hunting	523	...	...	258	-	781	187	-12	956
	c Mining (except fuels), manufacturing and construction	101	...	...	134	-	235	16	-36	215
	d Transportation and communication	181	...	...	56	-	237	1682	51	1970
	e Other economic affairs	587	...	...	101	30	718	24	4	746
10	Other functions	13	...	...	7	3084	3104	4	-1	3107
	Total	16835	...	...	584	13111	30530	3857	250	34637

Australia

2.3 Total General Government Outlays by Function and Type
(Continued)

Million Australian dollars — Fiscal year beginning 1 July

		Final Consumption Expenditures			Subsidies	Other Current Transfers & Property Income	Total Current Disbursements	Gross Capital Formation	Other Capital Outlays	Total Outlays
		Total	Compensation of Employees	Other						
					1979					
1	General public services	2442	...	...	1	493	2936	361	-28	3269
2	Defence	2614	...	...	-	30	2644	-	12	2656
3	Public order and safety	1362	...	...	-	7	1369	150	-2	1517
4	Education	5676	...	...	1	323	6000	656	51	6707
5	Health	3661	...	...	5	1342	5008	320	13	5341
6	Social security and welfare	572	...	...	1	8681	9254	28	74	9356
7	Housing and community amenities	278	...	...	16	4	298	155	52	505
8	Recreation, culture and religion	683	...	...	4	2	689	254	44	987
9	Economic services	1506	...	...	787	26	2319	2068	15	4402
	a Fuel and energy	...	...	...	2	-	2	1	-1	2
	b Agriculture, forestry, fishing and hunting	593	...	...	256	-	849	204	-15	1038
	c Mining (except fuels), manufacturing and construction	119	...	...	326	-	445	20	-36	429
	d Transportation and communication	191	...	...	66	-1	256	1800	61	2117
	e Other economic affairs	603	...	...	137	27	767	44	6	817
10	Other functions	9	...	...	5	3527	3541	11	3	3555
	Total	18804	...	...	820	14435	34059	4003	234	38296
					1980					
1	General public services	2829	...	...	1	537	3367	463	-4	3826
2	Defence	3365	...	...	-	38	3403	-	6	3409
3	Public order and safety	1611	...	...	-	5	1616	136	-3	1749
4	Education	6556	...	...	1	317	6874	608	58	7540
5	Health	4252	...	...	4	1584	5840	291	13	6144
6	Social security and welfare	690	...	...	1	9801	10492	35	68	10595
7	Housing and community amenities	313	...	...	20	4	337	183	52	572
8	Recreation, culture and religion	789	...	...	5	1	795	293	30	1118
9	Economic services	1776	...	...	970	34	2780	2286	-57	5009
	a Fuel and energy	...	...	...	24	-	24	-1	-	23
	b Agriculture, forestry, fishing and hunting	690	...	...	259	-	949	213	-16	1146
	c Mining (except fuels), manufacturing and construction	109	...	...	402	-	511	21	-92	440
	d Transportation and communication	183	...	...	69	-	252	2005	53	2310
	e Other economic affairs	794	...	...	216	34	1044	48	-2	1090
10	Other functions	23	...	...	12	4270	4305	34	-5	4334
	Total	22204	...	...	1014	16591	39809	4329	158	44296

2.4 Composition of General Government Social Security Benefits and Social Assistance Grants to Households

Million Australian dollars — Fiscal year beginning 1 July

		1970		1971		1972		1973		1974		1975	
		Social Security Benefits	Social Assistance Grants	Social Security Benefits	Social Assistance Grants	Social Security Benefits	Social Assistance Grants	Social Security Benefits	Social Assistance Grants	Social Security Benefits	Social Assistance Grants	Social Security Benefits	Social Assistance Grants
1	Education benefits	...	119	...	147	...	183	...	206	...	236	...	287
	a Pre-primary and primary	...	16	...	18	...	24	...	31	...	26	...	26
	b Secondary	...		...		...		...		...		...	
	c Tertiary	...	79	...	99	...	126	...	142	...	180	...	222
	d Other	...	24	...	30	...	33	...	33	...	30	...	39
2	Health benefits	...	399	...	496	...	569	...	651	...	817	...	1369
	a Hospital	...	124	...	163	...	200	...	227	...	304	...	362
	b Clinics and practitioners	...	115	...	160	...	191	...	205	...	250	...	723
	c Public health	...	-	...	-	...	-	...	-	...	-	...	-
	d Medicaments, etc.	...	160	...	173	...	178	...	219	...	263	...	284
3	Social security and welfare benefits	...	1293	...	1505	...	1921	...	2362	...	3411	...	4577
	a Social security	...	1288	...	1499	...	1913	...	2350	...	3393	...	4555
	Temporary sickness	...	19	...	24	...	34	...	49	...	70	...	98
	Old age and permanent disability	...	1032	...	1192	...	1527	...	1958	...	2715	...	3570

Australia

2.4 Composition of General Government Social Security Benefits and Social Assistance Grants to Households
(Continued)

Million Australian dollars — Fiscal year beginning 1 July

	1970 SSB	1970 SAG	1971 SSB	1971 SAG	1972 SSB	1972 SAG	1973 SSB	1973 SAG	1974 SSB	1974 SAG	1975 SSB	1975 SAG
Unemployment	...	11	...	26	...	47	...	58	...	303	...	515
Family assistance	...	198	...	217	...	254	...	225	...	225	...	265
Other	...	28	...	40	...	51	...	60	...	80	...	107
b Welfare	...	5	...	6	...	8	...	12	...	18	...	22
4 Housing and community amenities	...	-	...	-	...	-	...	1	...	1	...	1
5 Recreation and cultural benefits	...	-	...	-	...	-	...	-	...	-	...	1
6 Other	...	12	...	9	...	11	...	17	...	32	...	59
Total	...	1823	...	2157	...	2684	...	3237	...	4497	...	6294

	1976 SSB	1976 SAG	1977 SSB	1977 SAG	1978 SSB	1978 SAG	1979 SSB	1979 SAG	1980 SSB	1980 SAG
1 Education benefits	...	317	...	333	...	330	...	323	...	317
a Pre-primary and primary	...	26	...	31	...	31	...	31	...	...
b Secondary	...		...		...		...		...	...
c Tertiary	...	248	...	241	...	233	...	212	...	...
d Other	...	43	...	61	...	66	...	80	...	...
2 Health benefits	...	1141	...	1011	...	1199	...	1342	...	1584
a Hospital	...	355	...	387	...	389	...	435	...	568
b Clinics and practitioners	...	551	...	368	...	538	...	631	...	702
c Public health	...	-	...	-	...	·	...	1	...	5
d Medicaments, etc.	...	235	...	256	...	272	...	275	...	309
3 Social security and welfare benefits	...	6121	...	7145	...	7781	...	8459	...	9550
a Social security	...	6096	...	7116	...	7749	...	8423	...	9505
Temporary sickness	...	112	...	125	...	116	...	127	...	175
Old age and permanent disability	...	4208	...	4988	...	5532	...	6120	...	7100
Unemployment	...	618	...	794	...	910	...	925	...	996
Family assistance	...	1023	...	1038	...	998	...	1013	...	950
Other	...	135	...	171	...	193	...	238	...	284
b Welfare	...	25	...	29	...	32	...	36	...	45
4 Housing and community amenities	...	1	...	2	...	3	...	4	...	4
5 Recreation and cultural benefits	...	1	...	1	...	1	...	1	...	1
6 Other	...	31	...	34	...	36	...	33	...	32
Total	...	7612	...	8526	...	9350	...	10162	...	11488

2.5 Private Final Consumption Expenditure by Type, in Current Prices

Million Australian dollars — Fiscal year beginning 1 July

Final Consumption Expenditure of Resident Households

	1970	1971	1972	1973	1974	1975	1976	1977	1978	1979	1980
1 Food, beverages and tobacco [a]	5699	6181	6812	7974	9269	10812	12315	13760	15583	17581	19917
a Food	3819	4144	4569	5393	6213	7104	8203	9339	10585	12083	13821
b Non-alcoholic beverages											
c Alcoholic beverages	1321	1429	1575	1836	2175	2639	2942	3236	3653	4033	4515
d Tobacco	559	608	668	745	881	1069	1170	1185	1345	1465	1581
2 Clothing and footwear [b]	1830	1986	2255	2670	3156	3547	3956	4394	4749	5099	5766
3 Gross rent, fuel and power	3166	3598	4060	4700	5786	7132	8644	10073	11528	12954	14567
a Fuel and power	486	527	558	620	769	917	1075	1208	1396	1534	1687
b Other	2680	3071	3502	4080	5017	6215	7569	8865	10132	11420	12880
4 Furniture, furnishings and household equipment and operation [b]	1591	1799	2083	2717	3451	4222	4669	4770	5008	5470	6365
5 Medical care and health expenses	1219	1416	1598	1822	2302	2833	3160	3398	4019	4415	4861
6 Transport and communication	3230	3586	3932	4574	5546	6711	7667	8383	9575	11167	12593
a Personal transport equipment	1045	1150	1247	1460	1736	1894	2226	2375	2684	2897	3179
b Other	2185	2436	2685	3114	3810	4817	5441	6008	6891	8270	9414
7 Recreational, entertainment, education and cultural services	1366	1535	1738	2081	2582	3056	3491	3873	4298	4839	5451
a Education	171	196	214	208	200	218	243	255	272	293	311

35

Australia

2.5 Private Final Consumption Expenditure by Type, in Current Prices
(Continued)

Million Australian dollars — Fiscal year beginning 1 July

	1970	1971	1972	1973	1974	1975	1976	1977	1978	1979	1980
b Other	1195	1339	1524	1873	2382	2838	3248	3618	4026	4546	5140
8 Miscellaneous goods and services	2265	2487	2811	3301	4028	4760	5383	6013	6808	7734	8797
Total Final Consumption Expenditure in the Domestic Market by Households, of which c	20366	22588	25289	29839	36120	43073	49285	54664	61568	69259	78317
Plus: Direct purchases abroad by resident households	38	99	155	215	336	464	507	518	529	419	292
Less: Direct purchases in the domestic market by non-resident households											
Equals: Final Consumption Expenditure of Resident Households c	20404	22687	25444	30054	36456	43537	49792	55182	62097	69678	78609

Final Consumption Expenditure of Private Non-profit Institutions Serving Households

	1970	1971	1972	1973	1974	1975	1976	1977	1978	1979	1980
Equals: Final Consumption Expenditure of Private Non-profit Organisations Serving Households	...	...	...	...	...	...	...	...	...	...	...
Private Final Consumption Expenditure	20404	22687	25444	30054	36456	43537	49792	55182	62097	69678	78609

a) Including food, beverages and tobacco consumed in institutions except hospitals and nursing homes.
b) Drapery is included in item 'Clothing and footwear'.
c) Including private non-profit institutions serving households for which separate data are not available.

2.6 Private Final Consumption Expenditure by Type, in Constant Prices

Million Australian dollars — Fiscal year beginning 1 July

At constant prices of: 1979

Final Consumption Expenditure of Resident Households

	1970	1971	1972	1973	1974	1975	1976	1977	1978	1979	1980
1 Food, beverages and tobacco	14017	14557	15074	15428	16025	16402	16924	17366	17403	17581	18222
a Food	9349	9791	10075	10140	10653	11119	11447	11733	11969	12083	12521
b Non-alcoholic beverages											
c Alcoholic beverages	3239	3330	3557	3833	3879	3784	3955	4128	3938	4033	4193
d Tobacco	1429	1436	1442	1455	1493	1499	1522	1505	1496	1465	1508
2 Clothing and footwear	4821	4944	5291	5518	5403	5222	5037	5023	5059	5099	5369
3 Gross rent, fuel and power	8680	9117	9546	10047	10530	10970	11510	12027	12558	12954	13435
a Fuel and power	1168	1221	1255	1338	1396	1432	1517	1540	1611	1534	1498
b Other	7512	7896	8291	8709	9134	9538	9993	10487	10947	11420	11937
4 Furniture, furnishings and household equipment and operation	3272	3483	3855	4620	4959	5508	5625	5388	5384	5470	5927
5 Medical care and health expenses	...	...	...	...	...	...	...	...	...	...	...
6 Transport and communication	8048	8313	8728	9298	9435	9536	10000	10147	10728	11167	11497
a Personal transport equipment	5977	6263	6515	6816	6932	6997	7348	7369	7730	8032	8351
b Other	2071	2050	2213	2482	2503	2539	2652	2778	2998	3135	3146
7 Recreational, entertainment, education and cultural services	...	...	...	...	...	...	...	...	...	...	...
8 Miscellaneous goods and services	13223	13769	14606	15186	15531	16155	16253	16289	17251	17407	17500
Total Final Consumption Expenditure in the Domestic Market by Households, of which	52061	54183	57100	60097	61883	63793	65349	66240	68383	69678	71950
Plus: Direct purchases abroad by resident households	...	...	...	...	...	...	...	...	...	...	...
Less: Direct purchases in the domestic market by non-resident households	...	...	...	...	...	...	...	...	...	...	...
Equals: Final Consumption Expenditure of Resident Households	52061	54183	57100	60097	61883	63793	65349	66240	68383	69678	71950

Final Consumption Expenditure of Private Non-profit Institutions Serving Households

	1970	1971	1972	1973	1974	1975	1976	1977	1978	1979	1980
Equals: Final Consumption Expenditure of Private Non-profit Organisations Serving Households	...	...	...	...	...	...	...	...	...	...	...
Private Final Consumption Expenditure	52061	54183	57100	60097	61883	63793	65349	66240	68383	69678	71950

Australia

2.7 Gross Capital Formation by Type of Good and Owner, in Current Prices

Million Australian dollars — Fiscal year beginning 1 July

	\multicolumn{4}{c	}{1970}	\multicolumn{4}{c	}{1971}	\multicolumn{4}{c	}{1972}
	TOTAL	Total Private	Public Enterprises	General Government	TOTAL	Total Private	Public Enterprises	General Government	TOTAL	Total Private	Public Enterprises	General Government
Increase in stocks, total [a]	447	385	52	10	10	30	-24	4	-285	-246	-24	-15
1 Goods producing industries [a]	276	276	...	...	262	262	...	...	102	102	...	...
2 Wholesale and retail trade	405	405	...	...	229	229	...	...	368	368	...	...
3 Other, except government stocks	-11	-11	...	...	-21	-21	...	...	-60	-60	...	...
4 Government stocks	57	..	47	10	8	...	4	4	-8	...	7	-15
Statistical discrepancy	-280	-285	5	...	-468	-440	-28	...	-687	-656	-31	...
Gross Fixed Capital Formation, Total [abc]	8774	5837	1569	1368	9626	6330	1788	1508	10167	6684	1815	1668
1 Residential buildings	1643	1535	...	...	1860	1779	...	...	2196	2120	...	...
2 Non-residential buildings	3350	1392	...	...	3654	1451	...	...	3792	1364	...	...
3 Other construction	...	...	...	...	...	...	...	...	...	...	...	...
4 Land improvement and plantation and orchard development	...	...	...	...	...	...	...	...	...	...	...	...
5 Producers' durable goods	3781	2910	...	...	4112	3100	...	...	4179	3200	...	...
6 Breeding stock, dairy cattle, etc.	...	...	...	...	...	...	...	...	...	...	...	...
Total Gross Capital Formation [ad]	9221	6222	1621	1378	9636	6360	1764	1512	9882	6438	1791	1653

	\multicolumn{4}{c	}{1973}	\multicolumn{4}{c	}{1974}	\multicolumn{4}{c	}{1975}
	TOTAL	Total Private	Public Enterprises	General Government	TOTAL	Total Private	Public Enterprises	General Government	TOTAL	Total Private	Public Enterprises	General Government
Increase in stocks, total [a]	1173	1113	70	-10	1018	638	364	16	112	147	-38	3
1 Goods producing industries [a]	1126	1126	...	...	1401	1401	...	...	625	625	...	...
2 Wholesale and retail trade	716	716	...	...	1050	1050	...	...	1169	1169	...	...
3 Other, except government stocks	789	789	...	...	34	34	...	...	182	182	...	...
4 Government stocks	62	...	72	-10	402	...	386	16	3	...	-	3
Statistical discrepancy	-1520	-1518	-2	...	-1869	-1847	-22	...	-1867	-1829	-38	...
Gross Fixed Capital Formation, Total [abc]	11743	7764	2071	1908	14188	8536	2884	2768	17028	10331	3303	3394
1 Residential buildings	2693	2573	...	...	2731	2433	...	...	3567	3214	...	...
2 Non-residential buildings	4330	1591	...	...	5807	1943	...	...	6683	1967	...	...
3 Other construction	...	...	...	...	...	...	...	...	...	...	...	...
4 Land improvement and plantation and orchard development	...	...	...	...	...	...	...	...	...	...	...	...
5 Producers' durable goods	4720	3600	...	...	5650	4160	...	...	6778	5150	...	...
6 Breeding stock, dairy cattle, etc.	...	...	...	...	...	...	...	...	...	...	...	...
Total Gross Capital Formation [ad]	12916	8877	2141	1898	15206	9174	3248	2784	17140	10478	3265	3397

	\multicolumn{4}{c	}{1976}	\multicolumn{4}{c	}{1977}	\multicolumn{4}{c	}{1978}
	TOTAL	Total Private	Public Enterprises	General Government	TOTAL	Total Private	Public Enterprises	General Government	TOTAL	Total Private	Public Enterprises	General Government
Increase in stocks, total [a]	1133	1152	-16	-3	-481	-434	1	-48	1271	1433	-141	-21
1 Goods producing industries [a]	1285	1285	...	...	397	397	...	...	1116	1116	...	...
2 Wholesale and retail trade	1353	1353	...	...	754	754	...	...	1233	1233	...	...
3 Other, except government stocks	-105	-105	...	...	-186	-186	...	...	1348	1348	...	...
4 Government stocks	5	...	8	-3	-16	...	32	-48	-123	...	-102	-21
Statistical discrepancy	-1405	-1381	-24	...	-1430	-1399	-31	...	-2303	-2264	-39	...
Gross Fixed Capital Formation, Total [abc]	18993	11860	3699	3434	20643	12701	4237	3705	23275	15053	4365	3857
1 Residential buildings	4363	4032	...	...	4212	3876	...	...	4336	4056	...	...
2 Non-residential buildings	6756	1938	...	...	7597	2235	...	...	8179	2532	...	...
3 Other construction	...	...	...	...	...	...	...	...	...	...	...	...
4 Land improvement and plantation and orchard development	...	...	...	...	...	...	...	...	...	...	...	...
5 Producers' durable goods	7874	5890	...	...	8834	6590	...	...	10760	8465	...	...
6 Breeding stock, dairy cattle, etc.	...	...	...	...	...	...	...	...	...	...	...	...
Total Gross Capital Formation [ad]	20126	13012	3683	3431	20162	12267	4238	3657	24546	16486	4224	3836

Australia

2.7 Gross Capital Formation by Type of Good and Owner, in Current Prices

Million Australian dollars — Fiscal year beginning 1 July

	1979 TOTAL	1979 Total Private	1979 Public Enterprises	1979 General Government	1980 TOTAL	1980 Total Private	1980 Public Enterprises	1980 General Government
Increase in stocks, total [a]	576	567	19	-10	287	133	65	89
1 Goods producing industries [a]	2074	2074	...	...	1114	1114	...	...
2 Wholesale and retail trade	1834	1834	...	...	1464	1464	...	...
3 Other, except government stocks	-78	-78	...	...	-92	-92	...	...
4 Government stocks	31	...	41	-10	152	...	63	89
Statistical discrepancy	-3285	-3263	-22	...	-2351	-2353	2	...
Gross Fixed Capital Formation, Total [abc]	25482	16638	4841	4003	31581	21642	5610	4329
1 Residential buildings	5143	4851	...	...	6435	6132	...	...
2 Non-residential buildings	8782	2752	...	...	10742	3934	...	...
3 Other construction	...	...	...	...	...	...	...	...
4 Land improvement and plantation and orchard development	...	...	...	...	...	...	...	...
5 Producers' durable goods	11557	9035	...	...	14404	11576	...	...
6 Breeding stock, dairy cattle, etc.	...	...	...	...	...	...	...	...
Total Gross Capital Formation [ad]	26058	17205	4860	3993	31868	21775	5675	4418

a) Excluding livestock.
b) All government expenditure on defence is treated as final consumption expenditure.
c) All government expenditure on roads is treated as gross fixed capital formation.
d) Estimates are based on enterprise data and are on an ownership basis throughout.

2.8 Gross Capital Formation by Type of Good and Owner, in Constant Prices

Million Australian dollars — Fiscal year beginning 1 July

At constant prices of: 1979

	1970 TOTAL	1970 Total Private	1970 Public Enterprises	1970 General Government	1971 TOTAL	1971 Total Private	1971 Public Enterprises	1971 General Government	1972 TOTAL	1972 Total Private	1972 Public Enterprises	1972 General Government
Increase in stocks, total	1143	940	...	...	-10	7	...	...	-629	-571	...	...
1 Goods producing industries	940	...	...	...	7	...	...	...	-571	...	...	...
2 Wholesale and retail trade	...	...	...	...	...	...	...	...	...	...	...	...
3 Other, except government stocks	...	...	...	...	...	...	...	...	...	...	...	...
4 Government stocks	203	...	...	...	-17	...	...	...	-58	...	...	...
Gross Fixed Capital Formation, Total	23655	15366	...	...	24220	15559	...	...	23965	15470	...	...
1 Residential buildings	4454	4150	...	...	4674	4462	...	...	5015	4837	...	...
2 Non-residential buildings	9672	3949	...	...	9887	3835	...	...	9453	3352	...	...
3 Other construction	...	...	...	...	...	...	...	...	...	...	...	...
4 Land improvement and plantation and orchard development	...	...	...	...	...	...	...	...	...	...	...	...
5 Producers' durable goods	9529	7267	...	...	9659	7262	...	...	9497	7281	...	...
6 Breeding stock, dairy cattle, etc.	...	...	...	...	...	...	...	...	...	...	...	...
Total Gross Capital Formation	24798	16306	...	...	24210	15566	...	...	23336	14899	...	...

	1973 TOTAL	1973 Total Private	1973 Public Enterprises	1973 General Government	1974 TOTAL	1974 Total Private	1974 Public Enterprises	1974 General Government	1975 TOTAL	1975 Total Private	1975 Public Enterprises	1975 General Government
Increase in stocks, total	2097	1992	...	...	1964	1291	...	...	99	144	...	...
1 Goods producing industries	1992	...	...	...	1291	...	...	...	144	...	...	...
2 Wholesale and retail trade	...	...	...	...	...	...	...	...	...	...	...	...
3 Other, except government stocks	...	...	...	...	...	...	...	...	...	...	...	...
4 Government stocks	105	...	...	...	673	...	...	...	-45	...	...	...
Gross Fixed Capital Formation, Total	24472	16001	...	...	23736	14271	...	...	24605	14897	...	...
1 Residential buildings	5066	4833	...	...	4189	3734	...	...	4703	4227	...	...
2 Non-residential buildings	9404	3412	...	...	9809	3259	...	...	9681	2848	...	...
3 Other construction	...	...	...	...	...	...	...	...	...	...	...	...
4 Land improvement and plantation and orchard development	...	...	...	...	...	...	...	...	...	...	...	...
5 Producers' durable goods	10002	7756	...	...	9738	7278	...	...	10221	7822	...	...
6 Breeding stock, dairy cattle, etc.	...	...	...	...	...	...	...	...	...	...	...	...
Total Gross Capital Formation	26569	17993	...	...	25700	15562	...	...	24704	15041	...	...

Australia

2.8 Gross Capital Formation by Type of Good and Owner, in Constant Prices

Million Australian dollars — Fiscal year beginning 1 July

	1976 TOTAL	1976 Total Private	1976 Public Enterprises	1976 General Government	1977 TOTAL	1977 Total Private	1977 Public Enterprises	1977 General Government	1978 TOTAL	1978 Total Private	1978 Public Enterprises	1978 General Government
At constant prices of: 1979												
Increase in stocks, total	1548	1572	...	...	-774	-714	...	...	1686	1865	...	...
1 Goods producing industries	1572	...	...	...	-714	...	...	...	1865	...	...	...
2 Wholesale and retail trade	...	...	...	...	...	...	...	...	...	...	...	...
3 Other, except government stocks	...	...	...	...	...	...	...	...	...	...	...	...
4 Government stocks	-24	...	...	...	-60	...	...	...	-179	...	...	...
Gross Fixed Capital Formation, Total	24573	15296	...	...	24504	14964	...	...	25656	16458	...	...
1 Residential buildings	5149	4747	...	...	4671	4290	...	...	4649	4344	...	...
2 Non-residential buildings	8790	2503	...	...	9109	2656	...	...	9135	2799	...	...
3 Other construction	...	...	...	...	...	...	...	...	...	...	...	...
4 Land improvement and plantation and orchard development	...	...	...	...	...	...	...	...	...	...	...	...
5 Producers' durable goods	10634	8046	...	...	10724	8018	...	...	11872	9315	...	...
6 Breeding stock, dairy cattle, etc.	...	...	...	...	...	...	...	...	...	...	...	...
Total Gross Capital Formation	26121	16868	...	...	23730	14250	...	...	27342	18323	...	...

	1979 TOTAL	1979 Total Private	1979 Public Enterprises	1979 General Government	1980 TOTAL	1980 Total Private	1980 Public Enterprises	1980 General Government
At constant prices of: 1979								
Increase in stocks, total	576	567	...	...	267	131	...	...
1 Goods producing industries	567	...	...	...	131	...	...	...
2 Wholesale and retail trade	...	...	...	...	...	...	...	...
3 Other, except government stocks	...	...	...	...	...	...	...	...
4 Government stocks	9	...	...	...	136	...	...	...
Gross Fixed Capital Formation, Total	25482	16638	...	...	28401	19539	...	...
1 Residential buildings	5143	4851	...	...	5725	5458	...	...
2 Non-residential buildings	8782	2752	...	...	9559	3507	...	...
3 Other construction	...	...	...	...	...	...	...	...
4 Land improvement and plantation and orchard development	...	...	...	...	...	...	...	...
5 Producers' durable goods	11557	9035	...	...	13117	10574	...	...
6 Breeding stock, dairy cattle, etc.	...	...	...	...	...	...	...	...
Total Gross Capital Formation	26058	17205	...	...	28668	19670	...	...

2.17 Exports and Imports of Goods and Services, Detail

Million Australian dollars — Fiscal year beginning 1 July

	1970	1971	1972	1973	1974	1975	1976	1977	1978	1979	1980
Exports of Goods and Services											
1 Exports of merchandise, f.o.b. [a]	4217	4725	5986	6721	8485	9402	11518	12060	14009	18494	18845
2 Transport and communication	474	498	573	683	952	1049	1247	1326	1559	1903	2045
3 Insurance service charges	...	...	...	...	...	...	...	...	...	...	...
4 Other commodities	145	161	162	160	209	149	94	154	244	221	245
5 Adjustments of merchandise exports to change-of-ownership basis	-	-3	5	-12	-43	44	-72	-35	64	85	6
6 Direct purchases in the domestic market by non-residential households	135	131	123	164	212	258	315	390	537	801	999
7 Direct purchases in the domestic market by extraterritorial bodies	60	66	69	67	75	77	88	93	98	113	127
Total Exports of Goods and Services	5032	5578	6917	7784	9889	10979	13188	13988	16512	21617	22267
Imports of Goods and Services											
1 Imports of merchandise, c.i.f. [b]	4199	4200	4234	6378	8444	8728	11382	12229	14739	17380	20498
a Imports of merchandise, f.o.b. [c]	3790	3791	3808	5753	7660	7926	10348	11153	13494	15859	18781
b Transport of services on merchandise imports	409	409	426	625	784	802	1034	1076	1245	1521	1717
By residents	...	...	...	...	...	...	...	...	...	...	...

Australia

2.17 Exports and Imports of Goods and Services, Detail
(Continued)

Million Australian dollars — Fiscal year beginning 1 July

	1970	1971	1972	1973	1974	1975	1976	1977	1978	1979	1980
By non-residents	409	409	426	625	784	802	1034	1076	1245	1521	1717
c Insurance service charges on merchandise imports	...	...	...	...	...	...	...	...	...	...	...
2 Adjustments of merchandise imports to change-of-ownership basis	-	-	-	1	-8	-2	3	19	-1	-29	421
3 Other transport and communication [d]	382	396	440	569	713	810	961	1053	1253	1500	1619
4 Other insurance service charges	-	-	-	-	-	-	-	-	-	...	...
5 Other commodities [e]	186	232	236	271	294	253	255	399	383	321	383
6 Direct purchases abroad by government	126	124	122	112	147	175	189	223	219	264	287
7 Direct purchases abroad by resident households	199	264	321	452	656	873	999	1105	1299	1479	1561
Total Imports of Goods and Services	5092	5217	5353	7782	10246	10837	13790	15028	17892	20914	24768
Balance of Goods and Services	-61	361	1565	1	-356	142	-600	-1040	-1381	703	-2501
Total Imports and Balance of Goods and Services	5031	5578	6918	7783	9890	10979	13190	13988	16511	21617	22267

a) Representing recorded exports adjusted in respect of coverage recorded at the time the goods cross the customs frontier. Including the addition to international reserves resulting from domestic gold production. Excluding sales of ships and aircraft stores, bunkers and ballast.
b) Imports are valued on an f.o.b. basis, and freight on imports payable to non-residents is calculated separately.
c) Recorded at the time the goods cross the customs frontier. Excluding purchase of ships' and aircraft stores etc. which are included in net acquisition of foreign financial assets.
d) Including purchases of ships' stores etc. and crews' expenditure in foreign ports.
e) Including government pension payments and expenditure by foreign diplomatic and military personnel.

3.12 General Government Income and Outlay Account: Total and Subsectors

Million Australian dollars — Fiscal year beginning 1 July

	1970 Total General Government	1970 Central Government	1970 State or Provincial Government	1970 Local Government	1970 Social Security Funds	1971 Total General Government	1971 Central Government	1971 State or Provincial Government	1971 Local Government	1971 Social Security Funds
Receipts										
1 Property and entrepreneurial income [a]	985	856	...	697	...	1111	993	...	754	...
a Net operating surplus	-	-	...	-	...	-	-	...	-	...
b Withdrawals from public quasi-corporations [a]	693	232	...	461	...	797	301	...	496	...
c Interest [b]	292	624	...	236	...	314	692	...	258	...
d Dividends	-	-	...	-	...	-	-	...	-	...
e Net land rent and royalties [b]	...	...	...	...	...	...	...	...	...	...
2 Taxes, fees and contributions	8380	7105	...	1275	...	9590	7863	...	1727	...
a Indirect taxes	3597	2455	...	1142	...	4086	2519	...	1569	...
b Direct taxes	4602	4602	...	...	...	5285	5284	...	...	...
Income	4602	4602	...	...	...	5285	5284	...	...	...
Other	-	-	...	-	...	-	-	...	-	...
c Social security contributions	...	...	...	...	...	-	-	...	-	...
d Fees, fines and penalties	181	48	...	133	...	219	60	...	158	...
3 Other current transfers received	...	...	...	1672	...	...	...	...	1769	...
a Casualty insurance claims	...	...	...	-	...	...	...	...	-	...
b Transfers from other government subsectors	...	...	...	1672	...	...	...	...	1769	...
c Transfers from abroad	...	...	...	...	...	...	...	...	...	...
d Other transfers, except imputed	...	-	...	...	...	...	-	...	...	...
e Imputed unfunded employee welfare contributions	...	...	...	-	...	...	...	...	-	...
Total Current Receipts	9365	7961	...	3644	...	10701	8856	...	4250	...
Disbursements										
1 General governement final consumption expenditures [c]	4198	1958	...	2240	...	4788	2153	...	2635	...
a Compensation of employees	3595	...	...	...	...	4225	...	...	...	...
b Consumption of fixed capital [d]	...	...	...	...	...	...	...	...	...	...
c Goods and services purchased, net	603	...	...	...	...	563	...	...	...	...
d Less: Own account production of fixed assets	...	...	...	...	...	...	...	...	...	...
e Indirect taxes paid, net	...	...	...	...	...	...	...	...	...	...
2 Property income paid	848	576	...	841	...	927	616	...	947	...

Australia

3.12 General Government Income and Outlay Account: Total and Subsectors
(Continued)

Million Australian dollars — Fiscal year beginning 1 July

1970 and 1971

	Total General Government 1970	Central Government 1970	State or Provincial Government 1970	Local Government 1970	Social Security Funds 1970	Total General Government 1971	Central Government 1971	State or Provincial Government 1971	Local Government 1971	Social Security Funds 1971
a Interest	...	576	...	841	...	...	616	...	947	...
b Net land rent and royalties	...	-	...	-	...	...	-	...	-	...
3 Subsidies e	310	283	...	27	...	391	359	...	32	...
4 Other current transfers paid	2010	3594	...	88	...	2365	4016	...	119	...
a Casualty insurance premiums, net	...	...	...	-	...	...	...	...	-	...
b Transfers to other government subsectors	...	1672	...	-	...	...	1770	...	-	...
c Transfers to households	1823	1735	...	88	...	2157	2038	...	119	...
Social security benefits	-	-	...	-	...	-	-	...	-	...
Social assistance grants	1823	1735	...	88	...	2157	2038	...	119	...
Unfunded employee welfare benefits	-	-	...	-	...	-	-	...	-	...
d Transfers to private non-profit institutions serving households	...	-	...	-	...	...	-	...	-	...
e Transfers to the rest of the world f	187	187	...	-	...	208	208	...	-	...
Net saving	1999	1550	...	448	...	2230	1712	...	517	...
Total Current Disbursements and Net Saving	9365	7961	...	3644	...	10701	8856	...	4250	...

1972 and 1973

	Total General Government 1972	Central Government 1972	State or Provincial Government 1972	Local Government 1972	Social Security Funds 1972	Total General Government 1973	Central Government 1973	State or Provincial Government 1973	Local Government 1973	Social Security Funds 1973

Receipts

1 Property and entrepreneurial income a	1146	1050	...	764	...	1133	1083	...	770	...
a Net operating surplus	-	-	...	-	...	-	-	...	-	...
b Withdrawals from public quasi-corporations a	789	312	...	477	...	691	286	...	405	...
c Interest b	357	738	...	287	...	442	797	...	365	...
d Dividends	-	-	...	-	...	-	-	...	-	...
e Net land rent and royalties b	...	...	...	...	...	...	...	...	...	...
2 Taxes, fees and contributions	10521	8398	...	2124	...	13484	10880	...	2604	...
a Indirect taxes	4567	2629	...	1939	...	5686	3287	...	2399	...
b Direct taxes	5702	5702	...	...	...	7498	7498	...	...	...
Income	5702	5702	...	...	...	7498	7498	...	...	...
Other	-	-	...	...	...	-	-	...	...	...
c Social security contributions	-	-	...	-	...	-	-	...	-	...
d Fees, fines and penalties	252	67	...	185	...	300	95	...	205	...
3 Other current transfers received	...	...	...	2077	...	...	...	...	2534	...
a Casualty insurance claims	...	...	...	-	...	...	...	...	-	...
b Transfers from other government subsectors	...	...	...	2077	...	...	...	...	2534	...
c Transfers from abroad	...	...	...	...	...	...	...	...	...	...
d Other transfers, except imputed	...	-	...	...	...	...	-	...	...	...
e Imputed unfunded employee welfare contributions	...	...	...	-	...	...	...	...	-	...
Total Current Receipts	11667	9448	...	4964	...	14617	11963	...	5908	...

Disbursements

1 General government final consumption expenditures c	5452	2352	...	3101	...	6846	2887	...	3959	...
a Compensation of employees	4821	...	...	...	...	5967	...	...	...	...
b Consumption of fixed capital d	...	...	...	...	...	...	...	...	...	...
c Goods and services purchased, net	631	...	...	...	...	878	...	...	...	...
d Less: Own account production of fixed assets	...	...	...	...	...	...	...	...	...	...
e Indirect taxes paid, net	...	...	...	...	...	...	...	...	...	...
2 Property income paid	1030	676	...	1022	...	1099	717	...	1103	...
a Interest	...	676	...	1022	...	...	717	...	1103	...
b Net land rent and royalties	...	-	...	...	...	...	-	...	-	...

Australia

3.12 General Government Income and Outlay Account: Total and Subsectors
(Continued)

Million Australian dollars — Fiscal year beginning 1 July

	1972 Total General Government	1972 Central Government	1972 State or Provincial Government	1972 Local Government	1972 Social Security Funds	1973 Total General Government	1973 Central Government	1973 State or Provincial Government	1973 Local Government	1973 Social Security Funds
3 Subsidies [e]	325	295	...	30	...	384	351	...	33	...
4 Other current transfers paid	2939	4862	...	154	...	3597	5965	...	166	...
a Casualty insurance premiums, net	...	...	...	-	...	...	...	...	-	...
b Transfers to other government subsectors	...	2077	...	-	...	...	2534	...	...	...
c Transfers to households	2684	2530	...	154	...	3302	3136	...	166	...
Social security benefits	-	-	...	-	...	-	-	...	-	...
Social assistance grants	2684	2530	...	154	...	3237	3071	...	166	...
Unfunded employee welfare benefits	-	-	...	-	...	65	65	...	-	...
d Transfers to private non-profit institutions serving households	...	-	...	-	...	...	-	...	-	...
e Transfers to the rest of the world [f]	255	255	...	-	...	295	295	...	-	...
Net saving	1921	1265	...	657	...	2691	2043	...	647	...
Total Current Disbursements and Net Saving	11667	9448	...	4964	...	14617	11963	...	5908	...

	1974 Total General Government	1974 Central Government	1974 State or Provincial Government	1974 Local Government	1974 Social Security Funds	1975 Total General Government	1975 Central Government	1975 State or Provincial Government	1975 Local Government	1975 Social Security Funds
Receipts										
1 Property and entrepreneurial income [a]	1121	1120	...	805	...	1524	1413	...	991	...
a Net operating surplus	-	-	...	-	...	-	-	...	-	...
b Withdrawals from public quasi-corporations [a]	551	243	...	307	...	903	434	...	471	...
c Interest [b]	570	877	...	498	...	621	979	...	520	...
d Dividends	-	-	...	-	...	-	-	...	-	...
e Net land rent and royalties [b]	...	...	...	...	...	...	...	...	...	...
2 Taxes, fees and contributions	17428	14103	...	3326	...	21059	16901	...	4158	...
a Indirect taxes	6975	3908	...	3068	...	8877	5039	...	3838	...
b Direct taxes	10141	10141	...	...	...	11813	11813	...	...	...
Income	10141	10141	...	...	...	11813	11813	...	...	...
Other	-	-	...	...	...	-	-	...	...	...
c Social security contributions	-	-	...	-	...	-	-	...	-	...
d Fees, fines and penalties	312	54	...	258	...	369	49	...	320	...
3 Other current transfers received	...	...	...	3780	...	...	...	...	5524	...
a Casualty insurance claims	...	...	...	-	...	...	...	...	-	...
b Transfers from other government subsectors	...	...	...	3780	...	...	...	...	5524	...
c Transfers from abroad	...	...	...	-	...	...	...	...	-	...
d Other transfers, except imputed	...	-	...	-	...	...	-	...	-	...
e Imputed unfunded employee welfare contributions	...	...	...	...	...	...	...	...	...	...
Total Current Receipts	18549	15223	...	7910	...	22583	18315	...	10673	...
Disbursements										
1 General government final consumption expenditures [c]	9219	3537	...	5682	...	11462	4088	...	7375	...
a Compensation of employees	8227	...	...	...	...	9780	...	...	...	...
b Consumption of fixed capital [d]	...	...	...	...	...	...	...	...	...	...
c Goods and services purchased, net	992	...	...	...	...	1682	...	...	...	...
d Less: Own account production of fixed assets	...	...	...	...	...	...	...	...	...	...
e Indirect taxes paid, net	...	...	...	...	...	...	...	...	...	...
2 Property income paid	1326	898	...	1235	...	1513	977	...	1414	...
a Interest	...	898	...	1235	...	...	977	...	1414	...
b Net land rent and royalties	...	-	...	...	...	...	-	...	...	...

Australia

3.12 General Government Income and Outlay Account: Total and Subsectors
(Continued)

Million Australian dollars — Fiscal year beginning 1 July

	1974 Total General Government	1974 Central Government	1974 State or Provincial Government	1974 Local Government	1974 Social Security Funds	1975 Total General Government	1975 Central Government	1975 State or Provincial Government	1975 Local Government	1975 Social Security Funds
3 Subsidies [e]	361	321	...	40	...	353	307	...	46	...
4 Other current transfers paid	4945	8540	...	185	...	6788	12093	...	220	...
a Casualty insurance premiums, net	...	...	...	-	...	...	...	...	-	...
b Transfers to other government subsectors	...	3780	...	-	...	...	5525	...	-	...
c Transfers to households	4585	4400	...	185	...	6400	6180	...	220	...
Social security benefits	-	-	...	-	...	-	-	...	-	...
Social assistance grants	4497	4312	...	185	...	6294	6074	...	220	...
Unfunded employee welfare benefits	88	88	...	-	...	106	106	...	-	...
d Transfers to private non-profit institutions serving households	...	-	...	-	...	...	-	...	-	...
e Transfers to the rest of the world [f]	360	360	...	-	...	388	388	...	-	...
Net saving	2698	1927	...	768	...	2467	850	...	1618	...
Total Current Disbursements and Net Saving	18549	15223	...	7910	...	22583	18315	...	10673	...

	1976 Total General Government	1976 Central Government	1976 State or Provincial Government	1976 Local Government	1976 Social Security Funds	1977 Total General Government	1977 Central Government	1977 State or Provincial Government	1977 Local Government	1977 Social Security Funds
Receipts										
1 Property and entrepreneurial income [a]	2021	1851	...	1227	...	2445	2200	...	1432	...
a Net operating surplus	-	-	...	-	...	-	-	...	-	...
b Withdrawals from public quasi-corporations [a]	1193	657	...	536	...	1390	819	...	571	...
c Interest [b]	828	1194	...	691	...	1055	1381	...	861	...
d Dividends	-	-	...	-	...	-	-	...	-	...
e Net land rent and royalties [b]	...	...	...	...	...	...	...	...	...	...
2 Taxes, fees and contributions	24482	19688	...	4794	...	26652	21429	...	5223	...
a Indirect taxes	10090	5678	...	4412	...	10840	6041	...	4799	...
b Direct taxes	13946	13946	...	...	...	15312	15312	...	...	...
Income	13946	13946	...	...	...	15312	15312	...	...	...
Other	-	-	...	-	...	-	-	...	-	...
c Social security contributions	-	-	...	-	...	-	-	...	-	...
d Fees, fines and penalties	446	64	...	382	...	500	76	...	424	...
3 Other current transfers received	...	...	...	6115	...	...	...	...	7222	...
a Casualty insurance claims	...	...	...	-	...	...	...	...	-	...
b Transfers from other government subsectors	...	...	...	6115	...	...	...	...	7222	...
c Transfers from abroad	...	...	...	-	...	...	...	...	-	...
d Other transfers, except imputed	...	...	...	-	...	...	-	...	-	...
e Imputed unfunded employee welfare contributions	...	...	...	...	...	...	...	...	...	...
Total Current Receipts	26503	21539	...	12136	...	29097	23630	...	13877	...
Disbursements										
1 General government final consumption expenditures [c]	13422	4655	...	8767	...	15187	5210	...	9977	...
a Compensation of employees	11358	...	...	...	...	12732	...	...	...	...
b Consumption of fixed capital [d]	...	...	...	...	...	...	...	...	...	...
c Goods and services purchased, net	2064	...	...	...	...	2455	...	...	...	...
d Less: Own account production of fixed assets	...	...	...	...	...	...	...	...	...	...
e Indirect taxes paid, net	...	...	...	...	...	...	...	...	...	...
2 Property income paid	2084	1446	...	1696	...	2572	1738	...	2020	...
a Interest	...	1446	...	1696	...	...	1738	...	2020	...
b Net land rent and royalties	...	-	...	-	...	...	-	...	-	...

Australia

3.12 General Government Income and Outlay Account: Total and Subsectors
(Continued)

Million Australian dollars — Fiscal year beginning 1 July

	1976 Total General Government	1976 Central Government	1976 State or Provincial Government	1976 Local Government	1976 Social Security Funds	1977 Total General Government	1977 Central Government	1977 State or Provincial Government	1977 Local Government	1977 Social Security Funds
3 Subsidies e	342	283	...	58	...	500	410	...	89	...
4 Other current transfers paid	8147	14013	...	247	...	9118	16060	...	280	...
a Casualty insurance premiums, net	...	...	...	-	...	...	...	...	-	...
b Transfers to other government subsectors	...	6114	...	-	...	...	7222	...	-	...
c Transfers to households	7733	7485	...	247	...	8665	8385	...	280	...
Social security benefits	-	-	...	-	...	-	-	...	-	...
Social assistance grants	7612	7364	...	247	...	8526	8246	...	280	...
Unfunded employee welfare benefits	121	121	...	-	...	139	139	...	-	...
d Transfers to private non-profit institutions serving households	...	-	...	...	...	...	-	...	...	...
e Transfers to the rest of the world f	414	414	...	-	...	453	453	...	-	...
Net saving	2508	1142	...	1368	...	1720	212	...	1511	...
Total Current Disbursements and Net Saving	26503	21539	...	12136	...	29097	23630	...	13877	...

	1978 Total General Government	1978 Central Government	1978 State or Provincial Government	1978 Local Government	1978 Social Security Funds	1979 Total General Government	1979 Central Government	1979 State or Provincial Government	1979 Local Government	1979 Social Security Funds
Receipts										
1 Property and entrepreneurial income a	2733	2474	...	1552	...	3221	2608	...	2005	...
a Net operating surplus	-	-	...	-	...	-	-	...	-	...
b Withdrawals from public quasi-corporations a	1659	1011	...	648	...	1857	993	...	864	...
c Interest b	1074	1463	...	904	...	1364	1615	...	1141	...
d Dividends	-	-	...	-	...	-	-	...	-	...
e Net land rent and royalties b	...	...	...	...	...	...	...	...	...	...
2 Taxes, fees and contributions	29145	23419	...	5725	...	34026	27534	...	6492	...
a Indirect taxes	12672	7422	...	5250	...	14889	8898	...	5991	...
b Direct taxes	15913	15913	...	...	...	18541	18541	...	...	...
Income	15913	15913	...	...	...	18541	18541	...	...	...
Other	-	-	...	-	...	-	-	...	-	...
c Social security contributions	-	-	...	-	...	-	-	...	-	...
d Fees, fines and penalties	560	84	...	475	...	596	95	...	501	...
3 Other current transfers received	...	...	...	8147	...	...	...	...	9092	...
a Casualty insurance claims	...	...	...	-	...	...	...	...	-	...
b Transfers from other government subsectors	...	...	...	8147	...	...	...	...	9092	...
c Transfers from abroad	...	...	...	-	...	...	...	...	-	...
d Other transfers, except imputed	...	-	...	...	...	...	...	...	...	...
e Imputed unfunded employee welfare contributions	...	...	...	...	...	...	...	...	...	...
Total Current Receipts	31878	25893	...	15424	...	37247	30142	...	17589	...
Disbursements										
1 General government final consumption expenditures c	16835	5770	...	11065	...	18804	6168	...	12636	...
a Compensation of employees	13751	...	...	...	...	15041	...	...	...	...
b Consumption of fixed capital d	...	...	...	...	...	...	...	...	...	...
c Goods and services purchased, net	3084	...	...	...	...	3763	...	...	...	...
d Less: Own account production of fixed assets	...	...	...	...	...	...	...	...	...	...
e Indirect taxes paid, net	...	...	...	...	...	...	...	...	...	...
2 Property income paid	3084	2075	...	2301	...	3527	2361	...	2558	...
a Interest	...	2075	...	2301	...	...	2361	...	2558	...
b Net land rent and royalties	...	...	...	...	...	...	-	...	-	...

Australia

3.12 General Government Income and Outlay Account: Total and Subsectors
(Continued)

Million Australian dollars — Fiscal year beginning 1 July

	1978 Total General Government	1978 Central Government	1978 State or Provincial Government	1978 Local Government	1978 Social Security Funds	1979 Total General Government	1979 Central Government	1979 State or Provincial Government	1979 Local Government	1979 Social Security Funds
3 Subsidies [e]	584	483	...	101	...	820	708	...	113	...
4 Other current transfers paid	10027	17888	...	285	...	10908	19690	...	309	...
a Casualty insurance premiums, net	...	...	...	-	...	...	...	...	-	...
b Transfers to other government subsectors	...	8147	...	-	...	...	9092	...	-	...
c Transfers to households	9512	9226	...	285	...	10343	10033	...	309	...
Social security benefits	-	-	...	-	...	-	-	...	-	...
Social assistance grants	9350	9064	...	285	...	10162	9852	...	309	...
Unfunded employee welfare benefits	162	162	...	-	...	181	181	...	-	...
d Transfers to private non-profit institutions serving households	...	-	...	-	...	...	-	...	-	...
e Transfers to the rest of the world [f]	515	515	...	-	...	565	565	...	-	...
Net saving	1348	-323	...	1672	...	3188	1215	...	1973	...
Total Current Disbursements and Net Saving	31878	25893	...	15424	...	37247	30142	...	17589	...

	1980 Total General Government	1980 Central Government	1980 State or Provincial Government	1980 Local Government	1980 Social Security Funds
Receipts					
1 Property and entrepreneurial income [a]	3615	2858	...	2342	...
a Net operating surplus	-	-	...	-	...
b Withdrawals from public quasi-corporations [a]	2059	1014	...	1045	...
c Interest [b]	1556	1844	...	1297	...
d Dividends	...	...	...	...	...
e Net land rent and royalties [b]	...	...	...	...	...
2 Taxes, fees and contributions	40194	32727	...	7466	...
a Indirect taxes	17189	10291	...	6898	...
b Direct taxes	22343	22342	...	...	...
Income	22343	22342	...	...	...
Other	...	...	...	...	...
c Social security contributions	...	...	...	...	...
d Fees, fines and penalties	662	94	...	568	...
3 Other current transfers received	...	...	...	10307	...
a Casualty insurance claims	...	...	...	...	...
b Transfers from other government subsectors	...	...	...	10307	...
c Transfers from abroad	...	...	...	...	...
d Other transfers, except imputed	...	...	...	...	...
e Imputed unfunded employee welfare contributions	...	...	...	...	...
Total Current Receipts	43809	35586	...	20115	...
Disbursements					
1 General government final consumption expenditures [c]	22204	7552	...	14652	...
a Compensation of employees	...	...	...	...	...
b Consumption of fixed capital [d]	...	...	...	...	...
c Goods and services purchased, net	...	...	...	...	...
d Less: Own account production of fixed assets	...	...	...	...	...
e Indirect taxes paid, net	...	...	...	...	...
2 Property income paid	4269	2740	...	3114	...
a Interest	...	2740	...	3114	...
b Net land rent and royalties	...	...	...	...	...

Australia

3.12 General Government Income and Outlay Account: Total and Subsectors
(Continued)

Million Australian dollars — Fiscal year beginning 1 July

1980

	Total General Government	Central Government	State or Provincial Government	Local Government	Social Security Funds
3 Subsidies e	1014	867	...	147	...
4 Other current transfers paid	12322	22319	...	310	...
a Casualty insurance premiums, net	...	...	...	...	...
b Transfers to other government subsectors	...	10307	...	...	...
c Transfers to households	11695	11385	...	310	...
Social security benefits	...	...	...	...	...
Social assistance grants	11488	11178	...	310	...
Unfunded employee welfare benefits	207	207	...	-	...
d Transfers to private non-profit institutions serving households	...	...	...	...	...
e Transfers to the rest of the world f	627	627	...	-	...
Net saving	4000	2108	...	1892	...
Total Current Disbursements and Net Saving	43809	35586	...	20115	...

a) No private non-financial enterprises have been classified as quasi-corporate. All public enterprises are treated as if they were quasi-corporate. Furthermore, public non-financial enterprises are treated as if the whole of their operating surplus is withdrawn by general government.
b) Item 'Net land rent and royalties' is included in item 'Interest'.
c) Including some transfers to private non-profit organizations servicing household.
d) No charges were made for consumption of fixed capital by general government services and private non-profit services to households.
e) Subsidies on wheat and wool are recorded on an accrual basis.
f) The Australian accounts do not distinguish between current and capital transfers to the rest of the world and these items have been treated as current transfers.

3.13 General Government Capital Accumulation Account: Total and Subsectors

Million Australian dollars — Fiscal year beginning 1 July

1970 / 1971

	Total Gen. Gov. 1970	Central 1970	State/Prov. 1970	Local 1970	Social Sec. 1970	Total Gen. Gov. 1971	Central 1971	State/Prov. 1971	Local 1971	Social Sec. 1971
Finance of Gross Accumulation										
1 Gross saving a	1999	1550	...	448	...	2230	1712	...	517	...
a Consumption of fixed capital a	-	-	...	-	...	-	-	...	-	...
b Net saving	1999	1550	...	448	...	2230	1712	...	517	...
2 Capital transfers received	227	78	...	704	...	221	76	...	772	...
a From other government subsectors	...	...	...	...	...	...	-	...	...	...
b From other resident sectors	227	78	...	149	...	221	76	...	145	...
c From rest of the world	...	...	...	...	...	...	...	...	...	...
Finance of Gross Accumulation	2226	1628	...	1152	...	2451	1788	...	1289	...
Gross Accumulation										
1 Gross capital formation b	1378	200	...	...	...	1512	194	...	...	...
a Increase in stocks	10	8	...	2	...	4	2	...	3	...
b Gross fixed capital formation	1368	192	...	1175	...	1508	192	...	1316	...
2 Purchases of land, net c	38	-14	...	52	...	49	-14	...	63	...
3 Purchases of intangible assets, net	...	...	...	-	...	...	...	...	-	...
4 Capital transfers paid	54	593	...	17	...	60	671	...	16	...
a To other government subsectors	...	555	...	-	...	...	627	...	-	...
b To other resident sectors	54	38	...	17	...	60	44	...	16	...
c To rest of the world	...	...	...	-	...	...	...	...	-	...
Net lending	756	849	...	-94	...	830	937	...	-109	...
Gross Accumulation	2226	1628	...	1152	...	2451	1788	...	1289	...

1972 / 1973

	Total Gen. Gov. 1972	Central 1972	State/Prov. 1972	Local 1972	Social Sec. 1972	Total Gen. Gov. 1973	Central 1973	State/Prov. 1973	Local 1973	Social Sec. 1973
Finance of Gross Accumulation										
1 Gross saving a	1921	1265	...	657	...	2691	2043	...	647	...
a Consumption of fixed capital a	-	-	...	-	...	-	-	...	-	...
b Net saving	1921	1265	...	657	...	2691	2043	...	647	...
2 Capital transfers received	236	73	...	870	...	262	76	...	1087	...

Australia

3.13 General Government Capital Accumulation Account: Total and Subsectors
(Continued)

Fiscal year beginning 1 July

Million Australian dollars

	1972 Total General Government	Central Government	State or Provincial Government	Local Government	Social Security Funds	1973 Total General Government	Central Government	State or Provincial Government	Local Government	Social Security Funds
a From other government subsectors	...	-	...	...	...	...	-	...	...	...
b From other resident sectors	236	73	...	163	...	262	76	...	186	...
c From rest of the world	...	...	...	...	...	...	...	...	...	...
Finance of Gross Accumulation	2157	1338	...	1527	...	2953	2119	...	1734	...

Gross Accumulation

1 Gross capital formation [b]	1653	209	...	...	...	1898	242	...	...	...
a Increase in stocks	-15	-13	...	-	...	-10	-15	...	5	...
b Gross fixed capital formation	1668	222	...	1446	...	1908	257	...	1651	...
2 Purchases of land, net [c]	48	-30	...	77	...	112	6	...	106	...
3 Purchases of intangible assets, net	...	...	...	-	...	...	...	...	-	...
4 Capital transfers paid	79	766	...	21	...	101	970	...	31	...
a To other government subsectors	...	707	...	-	...	...	901	...	-	...
b To other resident sectors	79	59	...	21	...	101	69	...	31	...
c To rest of the world	...	...	...	-	...	...	...	...	-	...
Net lending	377	393	...	-17	...	842	901	...	-59	...
Gross Accumulation	2157	1338	...	1527	...	2953	2119	...	1734	...

	1974 Total General Government	Central Government	State or Provincial Government	Local Government	Social Security Funds	1975 Total General Government	Central Government	State or Provincial Government	Local Government	Social Security Funds

Finance of Gross Accumulation

1 Gross saving [a]	2698	1927	...	768	...	2467	850	...	1618	...
a Consumption of fixed capital [a]	-	-	...	-	...	-	-	...	-	...
b Net saving	2698	1927	...	768	...	2467	850	...	1618	...
2 Capital transfers received	278	80	...	1612	...	314	87	...	1794	...
a From other government subsectors	...	-	...	...	...	...	-	...	...	...
b From other resident sectors	278	80	...	198	...	314	87	...	227	...
c From rest of the world	...	...	...	...	...	...	...	...	...	...
Finance of Gross Accumulation	2976	2007	...	2380	...	2781	937	...	3412	...

Gross Accumulation

1 Gross capital formation [b]	2784	377	...	...	...	3397	513	...	...	...
a Increase in stocks	16	1	...	14	...	3	-	...	3	...
b Gross fixed capital formation	2768	376	...	2391	...	3394	513	...	2881	...
2 Purchases of land, net [c]	282	90	...	192	...	167	-1	...	168	...
3 Purchases of intangible assets, net	...	...	...	-	...	...	...	...	-	...
4 Capital transfers paid	179	1536	...	57	...	236	1746	...	58	...
a To other government subsectors	...	1414	...	-	...	...	1567	...	-	...
b To other resident sectors	179	122	...	57	...	236	179	...	58	...
c To rest of the world	...	...	...	-	...	...	...	...	-	...
Net lending	-269	4	...	-274	...	-1019	-1321	...	302	...
Gross Accumulation	2976	2007	...	2380	...	2781	937	...	3412	...

	1976 Total General Government	Central Government	State or Provincial Government	Local Government	Social Security Funds	1977 Total General Government	Central Government	State or Provincial Government	Local Government	Social Security Funds

Finance of Gross Accumulation

1 Gross saving [a]	2508	1142	...	1368	...	1720	212	...	1511	...
a Consumption of fixed capital [a]	-	-	...	-	...	-	-	...	-	...
b Net saving	2508	1142	...	1368	...	1720	212	...	1511	...
2 Capital transfers received	339	88	...	1797	...	343	102	...	1757	...
a From other government subsectors	...	-	...	...	...	...	-	...	...	...
b From other resident sectors	339	88	...	251	...	343	102	...	241	...
c From rest of the world	...	...	...	...	...	...	...	...	...	...
Finance of Gross Accumulation	2847	1230	...	3165	...	2063	314	...	3268	...

Australia

3.13 General Government Capital Accumulation Account: Total and Subsectors
(Continued)

Million Australian dollars — Fiscal year beginning 1 July

	1976 Total General Government	1976 Central Government	1976 State or Provincial Government	1976 Local Government	1976 Social Security Funds	1977 Total General Government	1977 Central Government	1977 State or Provincial Government	1977 Local Government	1977 Social Security Funds
Gross Accumulation										
1 Gross capital formation [b]	3431	455	...	...	...	3657	343	...	...	...
a Increase in stocks	-3	-	...	-3	...	-48	-63	...	15	...
b Gross fixed capital formation	3434	455	...	2979	...	3705	406	...	3300	...
2 Purchases of land, net [c]	110	-13	...	123	...	74	-22	...	96	...
3 Purchases of intangible assets, net	...	...	...	-	...	...	...	...	-	...
4 Capital transfers paid	160	1656	...	50	...	194	1646	...	64	...
a To other government subsectors	...	1546	...	-	...	...	1516	...	-	...
b To other resident sectors	160	110	...	50	...	194	130	...	64	...
c To rest of the world	...	...	...	-	...	...	...	...	-	...
Net lending	-854	-868	...	16	...	-1862	-1653	...	-207	...
Gross Accumulation	2847	1230	...	3165	...	2063	314	...	3268	...

	1978 Total General Government	1978 Central Government	1978 State or Provincial Government	1978 Local Government	1978 Social Security Funds	1979 Total General Government	1979 Central Government	1979 State or Provincial Government	1979 Local Government	1979 Social Security Funds
Finance of Gross Accumulation										
1 Gross saving [a]	1348	-323	...	1672	...	3188	1215	...	1973	...
a Consumption of fixed capital [a]	-	-	...	-	...	-	-	...	-	...
b Net saving	1348	-323	...	1672	...	3188	1215	...	1973	...
2 Capital transfers received	290	84	...	1698	...	220	49	...	1741	...
a From other government subsectors	...	-	...	...	...	...	-	...	...	...
b From other resident sectors	290	84	...	206	...	220	49	...	171	...
c From rest of the world	...	...	...	...	...	...	...	...	...	...
Finance of Gross Accumulation	1638	-239	...	3370	...	3408	1264	...	3714	...
Gross Accumulation										
1 Gross capital formation [b]	3836	270	...	...	...	3993	292	...	...	...
a Increase in stocks	-21	-33	...	13	...	-10	-35	...	25	...
b Gross fixed capital formation	3857	303	...	3554	...	4003	327	...	3676	...
2 Purchases of land, net [c]	66	-3	...	70	...	8	-3	...	11	...
3 Purchases of intangible assets, net	...	...	...	-	...	...	...	...	-	...
4 Capital transfers paid	205	1624	...	73	...	236	1741	...	65	...
a To other government subsectors	...	1492	...	-	...	...	1570	...	-	...
b To other resident sectors	205	132	...	73	...	236	171	...	65	...
c To rest of the world	...	...	...	-	...	...	...	...	-	...
Net lending	-2469	-2130	...	-340	...	-829	-766	...	-63	...
Gross Accumulation	1638	-239	...	3370	...	3408	1264	...	3714	...

	1980 Total General Government	1980 Central Government	1980 State or Provincial Government	1980 Local Government	1980 Social Security Funds
Finance of Gross Accumulation					
1 Gross saving [a]	4000	2108	...	1892	...
a Consumption of fixed capital [a]	-	-	...	-	...
b Net saving	4000	2108	...	1892	...
2 Capital transfers received	175	17	...	1834	...
a From other government subsectors	...	-	...	...	...
b From other resident sectors	175	17	...	158	...
c From rest of the world	...	...	...	...	...
Finance of Gross Accumulation	4175	2125	...	3726	...
Gross Accumulation					
1 Gross capital formation [b]	4418	435	...	...	...
a Increase in stocks	89	62	...	17	...
b Gross fixed capital formation	4329	373	...	3956	...

Australia

3.13 General Government Capital Accumulation Account: Total and Subsectors
(Continued)

Million Australian dollars — Fiscal year beginning 1 July

	1980 Total General Government	Central Government	State or Provincial Government	Local Government	Social Security Funds
2 Purchases of land, net c	-136	-77	...	90	...
3 Purchases of intangible assets, net	...	...	...	-	...
4 Capital transfers paid	205	1817	...	64	...
a To other government subsectors	...	1676	...	-	...
b To other resident sectors	205	141	...	64	...
c To rest of the world	...	...	...	-	...
Net lending	-312	-50	...	-401	...
Gross Accumulation	4175	2125	...	3726	...

a) No charges were made for consumption of fixed capital by general government services and private non-profit services to households.
b) Excluding livestock.
c) These are mainly purchases less sales of land and existing building, other than dwellings, from and to other sectors.

3.22 Corporate and Quasi-Corporate Enterprise Income and Outlay Account: Total and Sectors

Million Australian dollars — Fiscal year beginning 1 July

	1970 TOTAL	Non-Financial	Financial	1971 TOTAL	Non-Financial	Financial	1972 TOTAL	Non-Financial	Financial	1973 TOTAL	Non-Financial	Financial
Receipts												
1 Property and entrepreneurial income received	5788	4488	1977	6349	4840	2277	7406	5657	2648	8158	6081	3268
a Net operating surplus a	4076	4248	-172	4377	4574	-197	5058	5351	-293	5046	5632	-586
b Withdrawals from quasi-corporate enterprises	...	...	...	...	...	...	...	...	...	...	...	...
c Interest b	1669	184	2029	1925	204	2340	2290	230	2793	3004	320	3676
d Dividends	43	56	120	47	62	134	58	76	148	108	129	178
e Net land rent and royalties	...	...	...	...	...	...	...	...	...	...	...	...
2 Other current transfers received	-	-	-	-	-	-	-	-	-	-	-	-
a Casualty insurance transactions	...	...	...	...	...	...	...	...	...	...	...	...
Claims received	...	...	-	...	...	-	...	...	-	...	...	-
Net premiums received by insurance companies	...	...	...	...	...	...	...	...	...	...	...	...
b Current transfers received from the rest of the world	-	...	-	...	...	...	...	...	...	-	...	-
c Other transfers received, except imputed	...	...	...	...	...	...	...	...	...	...	...	...
d Imputed unfunded employee welfare contributions	...	...	...	...	...	...	...	...	...	...	...	...
Total Current Receipts	5788	4488	1977	6349	4840	2277	7406	5657	2648	8158	6081	3268
Disbursements												
1 Property and entrepreneurial income paid out	3181	2335	1523	3629	2627	1770	4098	2939	2058	4734	3217	2708
a Withdrawals from quasi-corporations	693	636	57	797	734	63	789	749	40	691	667	24
Public	693	636	57	797	734	63	789	749	40	691	667	24
Private	...	...	...	...	...	...	...	...	...	...	...	...
b Interest cd	1685	864	1365	1968	991	1596	2323	1170	1886	2960	1405	2547
c Dividends	803	835	101	864	902	111	986	1020	132	1083	1145	137
d Net land rent and royalties	...	...	...	...	...	...	...	...	...	...	...	...
2 Direct taxes and other current payments n.e.c. to general government	1379	1249	130	1462	1305	157	1545	1388	157	1934	1753	181
a Direct taxes ee	1379	1249	130	1462	1305	157	1545	1388	157	1934	1753	181
Income	1379	1249	130	1462	1305	157	1545	1388	157	1934	1753	181

Australia

3.22 Corporate and Quasi-Corporate Enterprise Income and Outlay Account: Total and Sectors
(Continued)

Million Australian dollars — Fiscal year beginning 1 July

	1970 TOTAL	1970 Non-Financial	1970 Financial	1971 TOTAL	1971 Non-Financial	1971 Financial	1972 TOTAL	1972 Non-Financial	1972 Financial	1973 TOTAL	1973 Non-Financial	1973 Financial
Other	-	-	-	-	-	-	-	-	-	-	-	-
b Fines, fees, penalties and other payments n.e.c.	-	-	-	-	-	-	-	-	-	-	-	-
3 Other current transfers paid	39	39	-	46	46	-	52	52	-	66	66	-
a Casualty insurance transactions	...	...	-	-	...	-	...	...	-	-	...	-
Casualty insurance premiums paid, net	...	...	...	...	...	...	...	...	...	...	...	...
Claims paid by insurance companies	-	...	-	...	...	...	...	...	-	-	...	-
b Transfers to private non-profit institutions	...	...	...	...	...	...	...	...	...	...	...	...
c Transfers to households	39	39	...	46	46	...	52	52	...	66	66	...
Unfunded employee welfare benefits	...	...	...	...	...	...	...	...	...	...	...	...
Social assistance grants and other transfers n.e.c.	39	39	...	46	46	...	52	52	...	66	66	...
d Transfers to the rest of the world	...	...	...	...	...	...	...	...	...	...	...	...
Net saving	1189	865	324	1212	862	350	1711	1278	433	1424	1045	379
Total Current Disbursements and Net Saving	5788	4488	1977	6349	4840	2277	7406	5657	2648	8158	6081	3268

	1974 TOTAL	1974 Non-Financial	1974 Financial	1975 TOTAL	1975 Non-Financial	1975 Financial	1976 TOTAL	1976 Non-Financial	1976 Financial	1977 TOTAL	1977 Non-Financial	1977 Financial
Receipts												
1 Property and entrepreneurial income received	8985	6316	4303	10995	7611	5257	13072	8908	6303	14069	9529	6962
a Net operating surplus a	5023	5788	-765	6469	7057	-588	7682	8248	-566	7884	8732	-848
b Withdrawals from quasi-corporate enterprises	...	...	...	...	...	...	...	...	...	...	...	...
c Interest b	3849	393	4865	4434	438	5607	5280	519	6603	6012	584	7490
d Dividends	113	135	203	92	116	238	110	141	266	173	213	320
e Net land rent and royalties	...	...	...	...	...	...	...	...	...	...	...	...
2 Other current transfers received	74	-	74	-	-	-	-	-	-	-	-	-
a Casualty insurance transactions	...	...	...	...	...	...	...	...	...	...	...	...
Claims received	74	...	74	...	...	-	...	...	-	...	...	-
Net premiums received by insurance companies	...	...	...	...	...	...	...	...	...	...	...	...
b Current transfers received from the rest of the world	74	...	74	-	-	-	...	...	...	-	...	-
c Other transfers received, except imputed	...	...	...	...	...	...	...	...	...	...	...	...
d Imputed unfunded employee welfare contributions	...	...	...	...	...	...	...	...	...	...	...	...
Total Current Receipts	9059	6316	4377	10995	7611	5257	13072	8908	6303	14069	9529	6962
Disbursements												
1 Property and entrepreneurial income paid out	5763	3788	3609	6810	4480	4203	8065	5101	5103	9339	5692	6069
a Withdrawals from quasi-corporations	551	536	15	903	884	19	1193	1072	121	1390	1095	295
Public	551	536	15	903	884	19	1193	1072	121	1390	1095	295
Private	...	...	...	...	...	...	...	...	...	...	...	...
b Interest cb	4039	1977	3471	4628	2195	4044	5380	2425	4797	6246	2746	5562
c Dividends	1173	1275	123	1279	1401	140	1492	1604	185	1703	1851	212
d Net land rent and royalties	...	...	...	...	...	...	...	...	...	...	...	...
2 Direct taxes and other current payments n.e.c. to general government	2344	2141	203	2505	2259	246	2803	2506	297	3072	2635	437
a Direct taxes ee	2344	2141	203	2505	2259	246	2803	2506	297	3072	2635	437
Income	2344	2141	203	2505	2259	246	2803	2506	297	3072	2635	437

Australia

3.22 Corporate and Quasi-Corporate Enterprise Income and Outlay Account: Total and Sectors
(Continued)

Million Australian dollars — Fiscal year beginning 1 July

	1974 TOTAL	1974 Non-Financial	1974 Financial	1975 TOTAL	1975 Non-Financial	1975 Financial	1976 TOTAL	1976 Non-Financial	1976 Financial	1977 TOTAL	1977 Non-Financial	1977 Financial
Other	-	-	-	-	-	-	-	-	-	-	-	-
b Fines, fees, penalties and other payments n.e.c.	-	-	-	-	-	-	-	-	-	-	-	-
3 Other current transfers paid	287	88	199	101	101	-	118	118	-	127	127	-
a Casualty insurance transactions	199	...	199	-	...	-	-	...	-	-	...	-
Casualty insurance premiums paid, net	...	...	...	...	...	...	...	...	...	...	...	...
Claims paid by insurance companies	199	...	199	-	...	-	-	...	-	-	...	-
b Transfers to private non-profit institutions	...	...	...	...	...	...	...	...	...	...	...	...
c Transfers to households	88	88	...	101	101	...	118	118	...	127	127	...
Unfunded employee welfare benefits	...	...	...	...	...	...	...	...	...	...	...	...
Social assistance grants and other transfers n.e.c.	88	88	...	101	101	...	118	118	...	127	127	...
d Transfers to the rest of the world	...	...	...	...	...	...	...	...	...	...	...	...
Net saving	665	299	366	1579	771	808	2086	1183	903	1531	1075	456
Total Current Disbursements and Net Saving	9059	6316	4377	10995	7611	5257	13072	8908	6303	14069	9529	6962

	1978 TOTAL	1978 Non-Financial	1978 Financial	1979 TOTAL	1979 Non-Financial	1979 Financial	1980 TOTAL	1980 Non-Financial	1980 Financial

Receipts

	1978 TOTAL	1978 Non-Fin	1978 Fin	1979 TOTAL	1979 Non-Fin	1979 Fin	1980 TOTAL	1980 Non-Fin	1980 Fin
1 Property and entrepreneurial income received	16518	10960	8307	19169	12922	9549	23594	15748	11967
a Net operating surplus [a]	9615	10101	-486	11182	11862	-680	13685	14441	-756
b Withdrawals from quasi-corporate enterprises	...	...	...	...	...	...	...	...	...
c Interest [b]	6738	644	8389	7762	774	9746	9682	1006	12139
d Dividends	165	215	404	225	286	483	227	301	584
e Net land rent and royalties	...	...	...	...	...	...	...	...	...
2 Other current transfers received	-	-	-	-	-	-	-	-	-
a Casualty insurance transactions	...	...	...	...	...	...	...	...	...
Claims received	...	...	-	...	...	...	...	...	...
Net premiums received by insurance companies	...	...	...	...	...	...	...	...	...
b Current transfers received from the rest of the world	-	-	-	...	...	...	-	-	-
c Other transfers received, except imputed	...	...	...	...	...	...	...	...	...
d Imputed unfunded employee welfare contributions	...	...	...	...	...	...	...	...	...
Total Current Receipts	16518	10960	8307	19169	12922	9549	23594	15748	11967

Disbursements

	1978 TOTAL	1978 Non-Fin	1978 Fin	1979 TOTAL	1979 Non-Fin	1979 Fin	1980 TOTAL	1980 Non-Fin	1980 Fin
1 Property and entrepreneurial income paid out	10402	6191	6960	12129	7380	8051	14414	-	-
a Withdrawals from quasi-corporations	1659	1278	381	1857	1487	370	2059	1708	351
Public	1659	1278	381	1857	1487	370	2059	1708	351
Private	...	...	...	...	...	...	...	...	...
b Interest [cb]	7051	3049	6297	8317	3715	7360	10204	4506	9161
c Dividends	1692	1864	282	1955	2178	321	2151	-	-
d Net land rent and royalties	...	...	...	...	...	...	...	...	...
2 Direct taxes and other current payments n.e.c. to general government	3002	2550	452	3360	2968	392	4639	-	-
a Direct taxes [ee]	3002	2550	452	3360	2968	392	4639	-	-
Income	3002	2550	452	3360	2968	392	4639	-	-

Australia

3.22 Corporate and Quasi-Corporate Enterprise Income and Outlay Account: Total and Sectors
(Continued)

Million Australian dollars
Fiscal year beginning 1 July

	1978 TOTAL	1978 Non-Financial	1978 Financial	1979 TOTAL	1979 Non-Financial	1979 Financial	1980 TOTAL	1980 Non-Financial	1980 Financial
Other	-	-	-	-	-	-	-	-	-
b Fines, fees, penalties and other payments n.e.c.	-	-	-	-	-	-	-	-	-
3 Other current transfers paid	156	156	-	193	193	-	214	214	-
a Casualty insurance transactions	-	...	-	-	...	-	-	...	-
Casualty insurance premiums paid, net	...	...	...	...	...	...	...	...	...
Claims paid by insurance companies	-	...	-	-	...	-	-	...	-
b Transfers to private non-profit institutions	...	...	...	...	...	...	...	...	...
c Transfers to households	156	156	...	193	193	...	214	214	...
Unfunded employee welfare benefits	...	...	...	...	...	...	...	...	...
Social assistance grants and other transfers n.e.c.	156	156	...	193	193	...	214	214	...
d Transfers to the rest of the world	...	...	...	...	...	...	...	...	...
Net saving	2958	2063	895	3487	2381	1106	4327	-	-
Total Current Disbursements and Net Saving	16518	10960	8307	19169	12922	9549	23594	15748	11967

a) Net operating surplus of financial enterprises includes a deduction for the imputed bank service charge.
b) Including royalties and land rent.
c) Excluding interest payments by public non-financial enterprises.
d) Excluding those paid by public non-financial enterprises.
e) Excluding those paid by public financial institutions.

3.23 Corporate and Quasi-Corporate Enterprise Capital Accumulation Account: Total and Sectors

Million Australian dollars
Fiscal year beginning 1 July

	1970 TOTAL	1970 Non-Financial	1970 Financial	1971 TOTAL	1971 Non-Financial	1971 Financial	1972 TOTAL	1972 Non-Financial	1972 Financial	1973 TOTAL	1973 Non-Financial	1973 Financial
Finance of Gross Accumulation												
1 Gross saving [a]	3074	2653	421	3329	2864	465	3995	3428	567	3948	3404	544
a Consumption of fixed capital [a]	1885	1788	97	2117	2002	115	2284	2150	134	2524	2359	165
b Net saving	1189	865	324	1212	862	350	1711	1278	433	1424	1045	379
2 Capital transfers received	19	19	-	23	23	-	31	31	-	45	45	-
a From resident sectors	19	19	-	23	23	-	31	31	-	45	45	-
b From the rest of the world	...	...	...	...	...	...	...	...	...	...	...	...
Finance of Gross Accumulation	3093	2672	421	3352	2887	465	4026	3459	567	3993	3449	544
Gross Accumulation												
1 Gross capital formation [b]	5400	4901	499	5428	4859	569	4998	4295	703	6891	6092	799
a Increase in stocks	344	343	1	-49	-53	4	-248	-249	1	935	930	5
b Gross fixed capital formation	5056	4558	498	5477	4912	565	5246	4544	702	5956	5162	794
2 Purchases of land, net [c]	-38	-37	-1	-49	-48	-1	-48	-54	6	-112	-129	17
3 Purchases of intangible assets, net	...	...	...	...	...	...	...	...	...	...	...	...
4 Capital transfers paid	...	...	...	...	...	...	...	...	...	...	...	...
5 Net lending [d]	-2269	-2192	-77	-2027	-1924	-103	-924	-782	-142	-2786	-2514	-272
Gross Accumulation	3093	2672	421	3352	2887	465	4026	3459	567	3993	3449	544

	1974 TOTAL	1974 Non-Financial	1974 Financial	1975 TOTAL	1975 Non-Financial	1975 Financial	1976 TOTAL	1976 Non-Financial	1976 Financial	1977 TOTAL	1977 Non-Financial	1977 Financial
Finance of Gross Accumulation												
1 Gross saving [a]	3512	2937	575	4960	3879	1081	5929	4678	1251	5761	4844	917
a Consumption of fixed capital [a]	2847	2638	209	3381	3108	273	3843	3495	348	4230	3769	461
b Net saving	665	299	366	1579	771	808	2086	1183	903	1531	1075	456
2 Capital transfers received	114	114	-	65	65	-	52	52	-	71	71	-
a From resident sectors	114	114	-	65	65	-	52	52	-	71	71	-
b From the rest of the world	...	...	...	...	...	...	...	...	...	...	...	...
Finance of Gross Accumulation	3626	3051	575	5025	3944	1081	5981	4730	1251	5832	4915	917
Gross Accumulation												
1 Gross capital formation [b]	8544	7631	913	8392	7075	1317	10129	8550	1579	10234	8264	1970

Australia

3.23 Corporate and Quasi-Corporate Enterprise Capital Accumulation Account: Total and Sectors
(Continued)

Million Australian dollars — Fiscal year beginning 1 July

	1974 TOTAL	1974 Non-Financial	1974 Financial	1975 TOTAL	1975 Non-Financial	1975 Financial	1976 TOTAL	1976 Non-Financial	1976 Financial	1977 TOTAL	1977 Non-Financial	1977 Financial
a Increase in stocks	1042	1044	-2	-19	-25	6	958	962	-4	-478	-486	8
b Gross fixed capital formation	7502	6587	915	8411	7100	1311	9171	7588	1583	10712	8750	1962
2 Purchases of land, net c	-282	-295	13	-167	-182	15	-110	-151	41	-74	-87	13
3 Purchases of intangible assets, net	...	...	...	...	...	...	...	...	...	...	...	...
4 Capital transfers paid	...	...	...	...	...	...	...	...	...	...	...	...
5 Net lending d	-4636	-4285	-351	-3200	-2949	-251	-4038	-3669	-369	-4328	-3262	-1066
Gross Accumulation	3626	3051	575	5025	3944	1081	5981	4730	1251	5832	4915	917

	1978 TOTAL	1978 Non-Financial	1978 Financial	1979 TOTAL	1979 Non-Financial	1979 Financial	1980 TOTAL	1980 Non-Financial	1980 Financial

Finance of Gross Accumulation

	1978 T	1978 NF	1978 F	1979 T	1979 NF	1979 F	1980 T	1980 NF	1980 F
1 Gross saving a	7640	6136	1504	8673	6780	1893	10152	...	...
a Consumption of fixed capital a	4682	4073	609	5186	4399	787	5825	4832	993
b Net saving	2958	2063	895	3487	2381	1106	4327	...	...
2 Capital transfers received	59	59	-	117	117	-	102	102	-
a From resident sectors	59	59	-	117	117	-	102	102	-
b From the rest of the world	...	...	...	...	...	...	...	...	...
Finance of Gross Accumulation	7699	6195	1504	8790	6897	1893	10254	7781	2473

Gross Accumulation

	1978 T	1978 NF	1978 F	1979 T	1979 NF	1979 F	1980 T	1980 NF	1980 F
1 Gross capital formation b	13346	11143	2203	13955	11521	2434	...	...	...
a Increase in stocks	905	897	8	571	567	4	...	...	...
b Gross fixed capital formation	12441	10246	2195	13384	10954	2430	...	...	...
2 Purchases of land, net c	-66	-76	10	-8	-27	19	...	...	...
3 Purchases of intangible assets, net	...	...	...	...	...	...	...	...	...
4 Capital transfers paid	...	...	...	...	...	...	...	...	...
5 Net lending d	-5581	-4872	-709	-5157	-4597	-560	...	...	...
Gross Accumulation	7699	6195	1504	8790	6897	1893	10254	7781	2473

a) No charges were made for consumption of fixed capital by general government services and private non-profit services to households.
b) Excluding livestock.
c) These are mainly purchases less sales of land and existing building, other than dwellings, from and to other sectors.
d) No private non-financial enterprises have been classified as quasi-corporate. All public enterprises are treated as if they were quasi-corporate. Furthermore, public non-financial enterprises are treated as if the whole of their operating surplus is withdrawn by general government.

3.32 Household and Private Unincorporated Enterprise Income and Outlay Account

Million Australian dollars — Fiscal year beginning 1 July

	1970	1971	1972	1973	1974	1975	1976	1977	1978	1979	1980
Receipts											
1 Compensation of employees a	18447	20575	22966	28127	36115	41580	46926	51488	55415	61627	71392
2 Property and entrepreneurial income received	6060	7030	8537	10088	11669	13240	15420	17169	21492	...	...
a Operating surplus of private unincorporated enterprises	4061	4756	5926	7435	7489	8594	9945	10784	14265	...	...
b Withdrawals from private quasi-corporations	...	...	...	...	...	...	4668	5455	6267	...	...
c Interest b	1463	1691	2018	2589	3485	3902					
d Dividends	536	583	593	64	695	744	807	930	960	...	...
e Net land rent and royalties	...	...	...	...	...	...	...	...	...	...	...
3 Other current transfers received	1862	2204	2736	3372	4687	6509	7859	8808	9675	...	...
a Casualty insurance claims	39	46	52	70	102	109	127	145	162	...	...
b Social security benefits	-	-	-	-	-	-	-	-	-	10343	11695
c Social assistance grants	1823	2157	2684	3302	4585	6400	7733	8526	9350		
d Unfunded employee welfare benefits	-	-	-	65	88	106	121	139	162	...	...
e Other current transfers received	...	...	...	...	...	...	...	...	...	...	...
From general government	...	...	...	...	...	...	...	...	...	...	...
From the rest fo the world	206	255	265	285	361	360	276	402	412	...	...
Other	...	...	...	...	...	...	...	...	...	...	...
Total Current Receipts	26369	29809	34239	41587	52471	61329	70205	77465	86582	...	...

53

Australia

3.32 Household and Private Unincorporated Enterprise Income and Outlay Account
(Continued)

Million Australian dollars — Fiscal year beginning 1 July

Disbursements

	1970	1971	1972	1973	1974	1975	1976	1977	1978	1979	1980
1 Final consumption expenditures c	20410	22690	25442	30039	36444	43368	49485	55016	61623	...	...
2 Property income paid	...	...	...	...	...	...	...	...	...	...	...
Consumer debt	194	213	243	368	492	572	702	824	901	...	...
Mortgage	...	...	...	...	...	...	...	...	...	...	...
Other	...	...	...	...	...	...	...	...	...	...	...
3 Direct taxes, fees, fines & other payments n.e.c. to government	...	...	...	...	...	...	...	...	...	...	...
a Social security contributions	-	-	-	-	-	-	-	-	-	-	-
b Direct taxes	...	...	...	...	...	...	...	...	...	...	...
Income taxes	3175	3765	4084	5485	7709	9213	11047	12122	12797	...	...
Other	...	...	...	...	...	...	...	...	...	...	...
c Fees, fines and penalties	...	...	...	...	...	...	...	...	...	...	...
4 Other current transfers paid	...	...	...	...	...	...	...	...	...	...	...
a Net casualty insurance premiums	...	...	...	...	...	...	...	...	...	...	...
b Transfers to private non-profit institutions serving households	...	...	...	...	...	...	...	...	...	...	...
c Transfers to the rest of the world	134	172	217	261	266	313	290	367	398	...	...
d Other current transfers, except imputed	...	...	...	...	...	...	...	...	...	...	...
e Imputed employee welfare contributions	...	...	...	...	...	...	...	...	...	...	...
Net saving	2445	2986	4264	5997	7604	7814	8519	9082	10834	...	...
Total Current Disbursements and Net Saving	26369	29809	34239	41587	52471	61329	70205	77465	86582	...	...

a) Some government contributions to superannuation are recorded only when benefits are paid.
b) Including royalties and land rent.
c) Including some expenditure of non-profit organisations.

3.51 External Transactions: Current Account: Detail

Million Australian dollars — Fiscal year beginning 1 July

Payments to the Rest of the World

	1970	1971	1972	1973	1974	1975	1976	1977	1978	1979	1980
1 Imports of goods and services	5092	5217	5353	7782	10246	10837	13790	15028	17892	20914	24768
a Imports of merchandise c.i.f.	4199	4200	4234	6378	8444	8728	11382	12229	14739	17380	20498
b Other	893	1017	1119	1404	1802	2109	2408	2799	3153	3534	4270
2 Factor income paid to the rest of the world	583	645	788	809	964	1050	1213	1426	1684	2130	2391
a Compensation of employees	-	-	-	-	-	-	-	-	-	-	-
b Property and entrepreneurial income paid	583	645	788	809	964	1050	1213	1426	1684	2130	2391
3 Indirect taxes paid to supranational organizations	...	...	...	...	...	...	...	...	...	...	...
4 Other current transfers to the rest of the world [a]	321	380	472	556	626	701	704	820	913	912	1060
a By general government	187	208	255	295	360	388	414	453	515	565	627
b By other resident sectors	134	172	217	261	266	313	290	367	398	347	433
5 Surplus of the nation on current transactions	-580	-168	915	-609	-1052	-888	-1890	-2490	-3157	-1242	-4633
Payments to the Rest of the World, and Surplus of the Nation on Current Transfers	5416	6074	7528	8538	10784	11700	13817	14784	17332	22714	23586

Receipts From The Rest of the World

	1970	1971	1972	1973	1974	1975	1976	1977	1978	1979	1980
1 Exports of goods and services	5032	5578	6917	7784	9889	10979	13188	13988	16512	21617	22267
a Exports of merchandise f.o.b.	4217	4725	5986	6721	8485	9402	11518	12060	14009	18494	18845

Australia

3.51 External Transactions: Current Account: Detail
(Continued)

Million Australian dollars — Fiscal year beginning 1 July

	1970	1971	1972	1973	1974	1975	1976	1977	1978	1979	1980
b Other	815	853	931	1063	1404	1577	1670	1928	2503	3123	3422
2 Factor income received from the rest of the world	130	183	273	390	372	266	257	276	294	368	452
a Compensation of employees	-	-	-	-	-	-	-	-	-	-	-
b Property and entrepreneurial income received [a]	130	183	273	390	372	266	257	276	294	368	452
3 Subsidies received from supranational organizations	...	...	...	...	...	...	...	...	...	...	...
4 Other current transfers from the rest of the world	254	313	338	364	523	455	372	520	526	729	867
a To general government [b]	48	58	73	79	88	95	96	118	114	141	161
b To other resident sectors	206	255	265	285	435	360	276	402	412	588	706
Receipts from the Rest of the World on Current Transfers	5416	6074	7528	8538	10784	11700	13817	14784	17332	22714	23586

a) Including capital transfers.
b) Excluding government pension payments.

3.52 External Transactions: Capital Accumulation Account

Million Australian dollars — Fiscal year beginning 1 July

	1970	1971	1972	1973	1974	1975	1976	1977	1978	1979	1980
Finance of Gross Accumulation											
1 Surplus of the nation on current transactions	-580	-168	915	-609	-1052	-888	-1890	-2490	-3157	-1242	-4633
2 Capital transfers received from the rest of the world	...	...	...	...	...	...	...	...	...	...	...
Total Finance of Gross Accumulation	-580	-168	915	-609	-1052	-888	-1890	-2490	-3157	-1242	-4633
Gross Accumulation											
1 Capital transfers paid to the rest of the world	...	...	...	...	...	...	...	...	...	...	...
2 Purchases of intangible assets, n.e.c., net, from the rest of the world	...	...	...	...	...	...	...	...	...	...	...
3 Net lending to the rest of the world	-580	-168	915	-609	-1052	-888	-1890	-2490	-3157	-1242	-4633
Total Gross Accumulation	-580	-168	915	-609	-1052	-888	-1890	-2490	-3157	-1242	-4633

3.53 External Transactions: Capital Finance Account

Million Australian dollars — Fiscal year beginning 1 July

	1970	1971	1972	1973	1974	1975	1976	1977	1978	1979	1980
Acquisitions of Foreign Financial Assets											
1 Gold and SDR's	...	...	...	...	...	...	...	...	...	...	...
2 Currency and transferable deposits	...	...	...	...	...	...	...	...	...	...	...
3 Other deposits	...	...	...	...	...	...	...	...	...	...	...
4 Bills and bonds, short term	...	...	...	...	...	...	...	...	...	...	...
5 Bonds, long term	...	...	...	...	...	...	...	...	...	...	...
6 Corporate equity securities	...	...	...	...	...	...	...	...	...	...	...
7 Short-term loans, n.e.c.	...	...	...	...	...	...	...	...	...	...	...
8 Long-term loans	...	...	...	...	...	...	...	...	...	...	...
9 Prpoprietors' net additions to accumulation of quasi-corporate, non-resident enterprises	...	...	...	...	...	...	...	...	...	...	...
10 Trade credit and advances	...	...	...	...	...	...	...	...	...	...	...
11 Other	...	...	...	...	...	...	...	...	...	...	...
Total Acquisitions of Foreign Financial Assets [a]	730	1630	1078	-336	-288	-859	-436	-54	-31	1013	1436
Incurrence of Foreign Liabilities											
1 Currency and transferable deposits	...	...	...	...	...	...	...	...	...	...	...
2 Other deposits	...	...	...	...	...	...	...	...	...	...	...
3 Bills and bonds, short term	...	...	...	...	...	...	...	...	...	...	...
4 Bonds, long term	...	...	...	...	...	...	...	...	...	...	...
5 Corporate equity securities	...	...	...	...	...	...	...	...	...	...	...
6 Short-term loans, n.e.c.	...	...	...	...	...	...	...	...	...	...	...

Australia

3.53 External Transactions: Capital Finance Account
(Continued)

Million Australian dollars   Fiscal year beginning 1 July

	1970	1971	1972	1973	1974	1975	1976	1977	1978	1979	1980
7 Long-term loans	...	...	...	...	...	...	...	...	...	...	...
8 Non-resident proprietors' net additions to accumulation of resident quasi-corporate enterprises	...	...	...	...	...	...	...	...	...	...	...
9 Trade credit and advances	...	...	...	...	...	...	...	...	...	...	...
10 Other	...	...	...	...	...	...	...	...	...	...	...
Total Incurrence of Liabilities [b]	1310	1798	163	273	764	29	1454	2436	3126	2255	6069
Net Lending	-580	-168	915	-609	-1052	-888	-1890	-2490	-3157	-1242	-4633
Total Incurrence of Liabilities and Net Lending [b]	730	1630	1078	-336	-288	-859	-436	-54	-31	1013	1436

a) Recorded at the time the goods cross the customs frontier. Excluding purchase of ships' and aircraft stores etc. which are included in net acquisition of foreign financial assets.
b) Net marine insurance payable overseas is included in item 'Net acquisition of foreign liabilities'.

4.6 Cost Components of Value Added, ISIC Divisions

Million Australian dollars   Fiscal year beginning 1 July

	1970 Compensation of Employees	1970 Capital Consumption	1970 Net Operating Surplus	1970 Indirect Taxes	1970 Less: Subsidies Received	1970 Value Added	1971 Compensation of Employees	1971 Capital Consumption	1971 Net Operating Surplus	1971 Indirect Taxes	1971 Less: Subsidies Received	1971 Value Added
All Producers												
1 Agriculture, hunting, forestry and fishing	433	433	1152	23	...	2042	436	436	1474	9	...	2356
2 Mining and quarrying	401	144	506	6	...	1057	459	184	646	15	...	1304
3 Manufacturing	5164	700	1804	1274	...	8942	5653	765	1731	1514	...	9663
4 Electricity, gas and water	446	187	407	17	...	1057	506	214	446	22	...	1188
5 Construction	1867	93	561	74	...	2595	2067	96	646	88	...	2897
6 Wholesale and retail trade, restaurants and hotels	2891	278	1525	623	...	5317	3173	295	1672	700	...	5840
7 Transport, storage and communication	1608	422	473	74	...	2577	1754	446	569	90	...	2859
8 Finance, insurance, real estate and business services	1425	501	2774	438	...	5138	1632	592	3161	494	...	5879
9 Community, social and personal services	2916	85	672	268	...	3941	3405	89	766	278	...	4538
Total, Industries	17152	2843	9874	2797	...	32666	19086	3117	11111	3210	...	36524
Producers of Government Services	1295	...	...	24	...	1319	1489	...	...	16	...	1505
Other Producers	...	...	...	...	...	...	...	...	...	...	...	...
Total	18447	2843	9874	2821	...	33985	20575	3117	11111	3226	...	38029
Imputed bank service charge	...	...	-714	...	...	-714	...	...	-821	...	...	-821
Import duties	...	...	...	466	...	466	...	...	...	469	...	469
Value added tax	...	...	...	...	...	...	...	...	...	...	...	...
Other adjustments	...	...	...	...	...	...	...	...	...	...	...	...
Total	18447	2843	9160	3287	...	33737	20575	3117	10290	3695	...	37677
of which General Government:												
1 Agriculture, hunting, forestry and fishing	30	...	...	...	...	30	37	...	...	...	...	37
2 Mining and quarrying	2	...	...	...	...	2	2	...	...	...	...	2
3 Manufacturing	88	...	...	...	...	88	92	...	...	...	...	92
4 Electricity, gas and water	-	...	...	...	...	...	-	...	...	...	...	...
5 Construction	387	...	...	...	...	387	423	...	...	...	...	423
6 Wholesale and retail trade, restaurants and hotels	1	...	...	...	...	1	1	...	...	...	...	1
7 Transport and communication	42	...	...	...	...	42	51	...	...	...	...	51
8 Finance, insurance, real estate & business services	15	...	...	...	...	15	17	...	...	...	...	17
9 Community, social and personal services	1735	...	...	...	...	1735	2113	...	...	...	...	2113
Total, Industries of General Government	2300	...	...	...	...	2300	2736	...	...	...	...	2736
Producers of Government Services	1295	...	...	24	...	1319	1489	...	...	16	...	1505
Total, General Government	3595	...	...	...	...	3619	4225	...	...	...	...	4241

Australia

4.6 Cost Components of Value Added, ISIC Divisions

Million Australian dollars — *Fiscal year beginning 1 July*

All Producers

		1972						1973				
	Compensation of Employees	Capital Consumption	Net Operating Surplus	Indirect Taxes	Less: Subsidies Received	Value Added	Compensation of Employees	Capital Consumption	Net Operating Surplus	Indirect Taxes	Less: Subsidies Received	Value Added
1 Agriculture, hunting, forestry and fishing	486	459	2158	141	...	3244	604	440	3128	191	...	4363
2 Mining and quarrying	507	217	713	22	...	1459	602	231	913	29	...	1775
3 Manufacturing	6184	785	2023	1590	...	10582	7598	863	1995	2025	...	12481
4 Electricity, gas and water	569	242	507	26	...	1344	687	254	546	38	...	1525
5 Construction	2253	101	770	101	...	3225	2629	110	880	124	...	3743
6 Wholesale and retail trade, restaurants and hotels	3561	317	1979	801	...	6658	4333	352	2320	1032	...	8037
7 Transport, storage and communication	1972	476	538	116	...	3102	2471	524	498	139	...	3632
8 Finance, insurance, real estate and business services	1862	667	3776	590	...	6895	2295	767	4239	703	...	8004
9 Community, social and personal services	3880	96	876	322	...	5174	4813	102	1020	392	...	6327
Total, Industries	21274	3360	13340	3709	...	41683	26032	3643	15539	4673	...	49887
Producers of Government Services	1692	...	...	20	...	1712	2095	...	...	25	...	2120
Other Producers	...	...	...	...	...	...	...	...	...	...	...	...
Total	22966	3360	13340	3729	...	43395	28127	3643	15539	4698	...	52007
Imputed bank service charge	...	...	-1005	...	...	-1005	...	...	-1264	...	...	-1264
Import duties	...	...	...	513	...	513	...	...	...	604	...	604
Value added tax	...	...	...	...	...	...	...	...	...	...	...	...
Other adjustments	...	...	...	...	...	...	...	...	...	...	...	...
Total	22966	3360	12335	4242	...	42903	28127	3643	14275	5302	...	51347

of which General Government:

	1972						1973					
1 Agriculture, hunting, forestry and fishing	42	...	...	...	...	42	48	...	...	...	...	48
2 Mining and quarrying	2	...	...	...	...	2	2	...	...	...	...	2
3 Manufacturing	105	...	...	...	...	105	121	...	...	...	...	121
4 Electricity, gas and water	-	...	...	...	...	...	-	...	...	...	...	...
5 Construction	492	...	...	...	...	492	576	...	...	...	...	576
6 Wholesale and retail trade, restaurants and hotels	1	...	...	...	...	1	1	...	...	...	...	1
7 Transport and communication	57	...	...	...	...	57	71	...	...	...	...	71
8 Finance, insurance, real estate & business services	19	...	...	...	...	19	24	...	...	...	...	24
9 Community, social and personal services	2411	...	...	...	...	2411	3029	...	...	...	...	3029
Total, Industries of General Government	3129	...	...	...	...	3129	3872	...	...	...	...	3872
Producers of Government Services	1692	...	...	20	...	1712	2095	...	...	25	...	2120
Total, General Government	4821	...	...	...	...	4841	5967	...	...	...	...	5992

All Producers

	1974						1975					
	Compensation of Employees	Capital Consumption	Net Operating Surplus	Indirect Taxes	Less: Subsidies Received	Value Added	Compensation of Employees	Capital Consumption	Net Operating Surplus	Indirect Taxes	Less: Subsidies Received	Value Added
1 Agriculture, hunting, forestry and fishing	735	494	2425	256	...	3910	802	541	2360	295	...	3998
2 Mining and quarrying	807	264	1230	51	...	2352	909	299	1418	429	...	3055
3 Manufacturing	9216	959	1915	2394	...	14484	10291	1069	2350	2955	...	16665
4 Electricity, gas and water	880	243	588	53	...	1764	993	288	743	66	...	2090
5 Construction	3393	129	1103	165	...	4790	3847	150	1391	199	...	5587
6 Wholesale and retail trade, restaurants and hotels	5467	420	2562	1301	...	9750	6331	503	2902	1636	...	11372
7 Transport, storage and communication	3218	622	423	177	...	4440	3666	788	651	227	...	5332
8 Finance, insurance, real estate and business services	2919	899	4912	810	...	9540	3429	1113	6177	1069	...	11788
9 Community, social and personal services	6701	121	1237	533	...	8592	8083	141	1567	670	...	10461
Total, Industries	33336	4151	16395	5740	...	59622	38351	4892	19559	7546	...	70348
Producers of Government Services	2779	...	...	33	...	2812	3229	...	...	46	...	3275
Other Producers	...	...	...	...	...	...	...	...	...	...	...	...
Total	36115	4151	16395	5773	...	62434	41580	4892	19559	7592	...	73623
Imputed bank service charge	...	...	-1527	...	...	-1527	...	...	-1730	...	...	-1730
Import duties	...	...	...	841	...	841	...	...	...	932	...	932

Australia

4.6 Cost Components of Value Added, ISIC Divisions
(Continued)

Million Australian dollars — Fiscal year beginning 1 July

	1974 Compensation of Employees	Capital Consumption	Net Operating Surplus	Indirect Taxes	Less: Subsidies Received	Value Added	1975 Compensation of Employees	Capital Consumption	Net Operating Surplus	Indirect Taxes	Less: Subsidies Received	Value Added
Value added tax	...	...	...	...	...	...	...	...	...	...	...	...
Other adjustments	...	...	...	...	...	...	...	...	...	...	...	...
Total	36115	4151	14868	6614	...	61748	41580	4892	17829	8524	...	72825

of which General Government:

1 Agriculture, hunting, forestry and fishing	67	...	...	...	...	67	75	...	...	...	...	75
2 Mining and quarrying	4	...	...	...	...	4	4	...	...	...	...	4
3 Manufacturing	164	...	...	...	...	164	188	...	...	...	...	188
4 Electricity, gas and water	-	...	...	...	...	...	-	...	...	...	...	...
5 Construction	760	...	...	...	...	760	859	...	...	...	...	859
6 Wholesale and retail trade, restaurants and hotels	1	...	...	...	...	1	1	...	...	...	...	1
7 Transport and communication	98	...	...	...	...	98	114	...	...	...	...	114
8 Finance, insurance, real estate & business services	32	...	...	...	...	32	38	...	...	...	...	38
9 Community, social and personal services	4322	...	...	...	...	4322	5272	...	...	...	...	5272
Total, Industries of General Government	5448	...	...	...	...	5448	6551	...	...	...	...	6551
Producers of Government Services	2779	...	...	33	...	2812	3229	...	...	46	...	3275
Total, General Government	8227	...	...	...	...	8260	9780	...	...	...	...	9826

	1976 Compensation of Employees	Capital Consumption	Net Operating Surplus	Indirect Taxes	Less: Subsidies Received	Value Added	1977 Compensation of Employees	Capital Consumption	Net Operating Surplus	Indirect Taxes	Less: Subsidies Received	Value Added

All Producers

1 Agriculture, hunting, forestry and fishing	807	645	2701	330	...	4483	900	656	2446	245	...	4247
2 Mining and quarrying	1054	338	1791	516	...	3699	1188	342	2033	648	...	4211
3 Manufacturing	11407	1171	2727	3216	...	18521	12275	1208	2928	3412	...	19823
4 Electricity, gas and water	1154	319	859	75	...	2407	1288	366	953	82	...	2689
5 Construction	4179	190	1522	214	...	6105	4483	204	1537	237	...	6461
6 Wholesale and retail trade, restaurants and hotels	7133	597	3260	1866	...	12856	7800	627	3304	2000	...	13731
7 Transport, storage and communication	4075	884	734	249	...	5942	4480	983	736	245	...	6444
8 Finance, insurance, real estate and business services	3969	1342	7476	1293	...	14080	4383	1629	8498	1408	...	15918
9 Community, social and personal services	9487	170	1710	786	...	12153	10577	176	1883	874	...	13510
Total, Industries	43265	5656	22780	8545	...	80246	47374	6191	24318	9151	...	87034
Producers of Government Services	3661	...	...	51	...	3712	4114	...	...	57	...	4171
Other Producers	...	...	...	...	...	...	...	...	...	...	...	...
Total	46926	5656	22780	8596	...	83958	51488	6191	24318	9208	...	91205
Imputed bank service charge	...	...	-1966	...	...	-1966	...	...	-2086	...	...	-2086
Import duties	...	...	...	1152	...	1152	...	...	...	1132	...	1132
Value added tax	...	...	...	...	...	...	...	...	...	...	...	...
Other adjustments	...	...	...	...	...	...	...	...	...	...	...	...
Total	46926	5656	20814	9748	...	83144	51488	6191	22232	10340	...	90251

of which General Government:

1 Agriculture, hunting, forestry and fishing	84	...	...	...	...	84	96	...	...	...	...	96
2 Mining and quarrying	5	...	...	...	...	5	7	...	...	...	...	7
3 Manufacturing	204	...	...	...	...	204	221	...	...	...	...	221
4 Electricity, gas and water	-	...	...	...	...	...	-	...	...	...	...	...

4.6 Cost Components of Value Added, ISIC Divisions
(Continued)

Australia

Million Australian dollars — Fiscal year beginning 1 July

	1976						1977					
	Compensation of Employees	Capital Consumption	Net Operating Surplus	Indirect Taxes	Less: Subsidies Received	Value Added	Compensation of Employees	Capital Consumption	Net Operating Surplus	Indirect Taxes	Less: Subsidies Received	Value Added
5 Construction	974	...	...	...	...	974	1073	...	...	...	...	1073
6 Wholesale and retail trade, restaurants and hotels	1	...	...	...	...	1	1	...	...	...	...	1
7 Transport and communication	126	...	...	...	...	126	143	...	...	...	...	143
8 Finance, insurance, real estate & business services	45	...	...	...	...	45	52	...	...	...	...	52
9 Community, social and personal services	6258	...	...	...	...	6258	7025	...	...	...	...	7025
Total, Industries of General Government	7697	...	...	...	...	7697	8618	...	...	...	...	8618
Producers of Government Services	3661	...	...	51	...	3712	4114	...	...	57	...	4171
Total, General Government	11358	...	...	...	...	11409	12732	...	...	...	...	12789

	1978						1979					
	Compensation of Employees	Capital Consumption	Net Operating Surplus	Indirect Taxes	Less: Subsidies Received	Value Added	Compensation of Employees	Capital Consumption	Net Operating Surplus	Indirect Taxes	Less: Subsidies Received	Value Added

All Producers

1 Agriculture, hunting, forestry and fishing	982	733	4814	310	...	6839	1092	832	5503	372	...	7799
2 Mining and quarrying	1273	369	2404	1397	...	5443	1489	425	3194	2360	...	7468
3 Manufacturing	13181	1295	3138	3821	...	21435	14649	1401	3506	4038	...	23594
4 Electricity, gas and water	1403	420	1049	91	...	2963	1568	458	1178	105	...	3309
5 Construction	4746	223	1584	251	...	6804	5141	252	1650	272	...	7315
6 Wholesale and retail trade, restaurants and hotels	8333	727	3643	2005	...	14708	9281	820	3805	2089	...	15995
7 Transport, storage and communication	4821	1087	855	258	...	7021	5431	1152	1079	285	...	7947
8 Finance, insurance, real estate and business services	4762	1864	10464	1564	...	18654	5401	2139	11731	1800	...	21071
9 Community, social and personal services	11587	210	2047	966	...	14810	13017	246	2177	1134	...	16574
Total, Industries	51088	6928	29998	10663	...	98677	57069	7725	33823	12455	...	111072
Producers of Government Services	4327	...	...	62	...	4389	4558	...	...	76	...	4634
Other Producers	...	...	...	...	...	...	...	...	...	...	...	...
Total	55415	6928	29998	10725	...	103066	61627	7725	33823	12531	...	115706
Imputed bank service charge	...	...	-2359	...	...	-2359	...	...	-2780	...	...	-2780
Import duties	...	...	...	1363	...	1363	...	...	...	1538	...	1538
Value added tax	...	...	...	...	...	...	...	...	...	...	...	...
Other adjustments	...	...	...	...	...	...	...	...	...	...	...	...
Total	55415	6928	27639	12088	...	102070	61627	7725	31043	14069	...	114464

of which General Government:

1 Agriculture, hunting, forestry and fishing	104	...	...	...	...	104	111	...	...	...	...	111
2 Mining and quarrying	7	...	...	...	...	7	8	...	...	...	...	8
3 Manufacturing	236	...	...	...	...	236	254	...	...	...	...	254
4 Electricity, gas and water	-	...	...	...	...	...	-	...	...	...	...	...
5 Construction	1148	...	...	...	...	1148	1224	...	...	...	...	1224
6 Wholesale and retail trade, restaurants and hotels	1	...	...	...	...	1	1	...	...	...	...	1
7 Transport and communication	153	...	...	...	...	153	171	...	...	...	...	171
8 Finance, insurance, real estate & business services	56	...	...	...	...	56	62	...	...	...	...	62
9 Community, social and personal services	7719	...	...	...	...	7719	8652	...	...	...	...	8652
Total, Industries of General Government	9424	...	...	...	...	9424	10483	...	...	...	...	10483
Producers of Government Services	4327	...	...	62	...	4389	4558	...	...	76	...	4634
Total, General Government	13751	...	...	...	...	13813	15041	...	...	...	...	15117

Austria

General note. The preparation of annual national accounts statistics in Austria is undertaken by the Austrian Central Statistical Office, Vienna. The official estimates are published annually in 'Oesterreichs Volkseinkommen', (Austrian Central Statistical Offce, Beitrage zur Osterreichischen Statistik). The concepts, definitions, sources of basic statistics and methods of estimation are described in the 1964-1977 issue of the above mentioned publication. The estimates are generally in accordance with the classifications and definitions recommended in the United Nations System of National Accounts (SNA). Input-output tables have been published for the years 1961, 1964 and 1976. The following tables have been prepared from successive replies to the United Nations national accounts questionnaire. When the scope and coverage of the estimates differ for conceptual or statistical reasons from the definitions and classifications recommended in SNA, a footnote is indicated to the relevant tables.

Sources and methods:

(a) Gross domestic product. Gross domestic product is estimated mainly through the production approach.

(b) Expenditure on the gross domestic product. All components of GDP by expenditure type are estimated through the expenditure approach except private final consumption expenditure of goods and gross fixed capital formation in machinery and equipment which are estimated by turnover tax statistics and the commodity-flow approach. The estimates of government final consumption expenditure are obtained directly from the accounting records of the various authorities. The value of private expenditure on goods are obtained either by multiplying the quantity data by consumer prices or by adding distributive trade margins and turnover tax and indirect taxes to the value of goods produced domestically or imported. The sources of data include statistics on agricultural produce, industrial output data by commodities and registration statistics. Decennial household surveys provide bench-mark information on average prices of items for which quantity information is available. For private expenditure on services, the estimates are mostly based on value added tax statistics. The statistics available for increase in stocks cover almost all branches, those that are not covered are included in statistical discrepancy. For gross fixed capital formation in machinery and electrical equipment, the value of domestic production plus imports minus exports is adjusted to include transport costs, trade margins, customs duties, etc. The estimates of transport equipment are based on registration statistics and are obtained by multiplying the quantity by the current prices. For construction, the gross value is derived from data on gross output of building construction. The estimates of exports and imports of goods and services are based on foreign trade statistics and the balance of payments. For the constant price estimates, various quantum indicators are used for the value added components of government services while price deflation is used for the consumption of intermediate goods. For private consumption expenditure, direct revaluation at base-year prices is used where information is available on quantities of commodities consumed. Otherwise, the current estimates are deflated by appropriate price indexes. This same method is used for increase in stocks, exports and imports of goods and services and partly for gross fixed capital formation.

(c) Cost-structure of the gross domestic product. Estimates of compensation of employees are based on contributions paid by employers on social security and wage statistics. Direct information is available on compensation of government employees. Operating surplus is basically derived as a residual item. Further breakdown is based on income tax statistics for unincorporated enterprises, independent professions and property. Corporate balance sheets and tax statistics are used for undistributed profits of corporations, and for agriculture and forestry. Operating surplus is estimated by deducting the cost-structure components from the contribution of the sector to the GDP. In the case of the public sector, data are obtained from the accounting records of public bodies. Depreciation estimates of stocks are obtained either by using the perpetual inventory concept or are extrapolated by net output at constant prices and inflated by national accounts' price index for fixed capital formation. Indirect taxes and subsidies are obtained directly from the records of the various governments.

(d) Gross domestic product by kind of economic activity. The table of GDP by kind of economic activity is prepared at market prices, i.e. producers' values. The production approach is used to estimate value added of nearly all industries. The income approach is used to estimate value added of public administration and defense. The value added of agriculture is obtained by deducting the cost of all non-factor inputs from the gross value of production, which include an imputation for produce consumed on the farms. The calculations are based on production statistics and producer prices, marketing data and food balance sheets. Mining and quarrying, electricity, gas and water as well as large-scale manufacturing are surveyed by annual over-all censuses while small-scale manufacturing is surveyed annually by samples. Bench-mark estimates have been prepared for 1964, 1971 and 1976. The bench-mark estimates were interpolated on the basis of output statistics for large-scale manufacturing and turnover statistics for small-scale manufacturing. Extrapolation is based on annual censuses, sample survey and turnover statistics. For construction, census type data on gross output and input have been available annually since 1968. The estimates of turnover in retail and wholesale trade are based on the 1964 census of non-agricultural establishments, the 1971 census of turnover and, since 1973, an annual sample survey. Estimates of restaurants and hotels are based on the 1964 industrial census and on a special survey in 1972 and 1976 Census. For the intermediate years, value added tax and turnover statistics are used. For railways and air transportation and communication, value added is derived from the accounts of concerned enterprises. For the other activities of the transport sector, bench-mark data have been provided by the 1964 and 1976 industrial census, extrapolated by various indicators. From 1973 onward, value added tax statistics provide the output indicators for most transportation other than railway and communication. For the financial institutions, value added is derived from accounting records for banking, and from statistics of the supervisory board for insurance, and for other financial institutions such as credit union, it is estimated on the basis of their share in the total volume of deposits and credits outstanding. Data on real estate are obtained from decennial housing censuses and official statistics of residential construction. In the case of owner-occupied dwellings, rents paid for comparable dwellings are applied with adjustments made to include maintenance costs and taxes. The value added of government services is estimated by adding the cost items obtained from accounting records. The estimates of other services are based on annual turnover statistics, value added tax statistics and various net to gross ratios obtained from the 1964 and 1976 census of non-agricultural establishments. The value of domestic and health services is calculated by means of social security and wage statistics. For the constant price estimates, double deflation is used for agriculture, small-scale manufacturing, electricity, gas and water, railway transportation and ownership of dwellings. The turnover of wholesale and retail trade and education and recreation is deflated by appropriate price indexes. For the producers of government services, various quantum indicators are used. For most of the remaining industries, value added is extrapolated by quantity index.

1.1 Expenditure on the Gross Domestic Product, in Current Prices

Thousand Million Austrian schillings

		1970	1971	1972	1973	1974	1975	1976	1977	1978	1979	1980
1	General government final consumption expenditure	55.22	61.98	70.10	81.91	97.43	113.05	127.79	138.74	154.18	165.89	177.51
2	Private final consumption expenditure	205.29	230.00	259.81	291.78	330.61	368.26	410.18	456.86	469.57	509.06	548.68
3	Gross capital formation	111.69	124.66	146.90	167.76	192.60	171.19	197.83	222.04	218.61	253.82	286.68
a	Increase in stocks [a]	14.51	7.76	1.99	12.79	16.88	-3.73	9.12	9.27	3.39	21.93	34.39
b	Gross fixed capital formation [b]	97.18	116.90	144.91	154.97	175.72	174.92	188.71	212.77	215.22	231.89	252.29
	Residential buildings											
	Non-residential buildings	53.48	63.85	81.09	83.32	96.01	99.50	104.92	114.43	118.05	136.89	136.17
	Other construction and land improvement etc.											
	Other	43.70	53.05	62.33	57.12	63.65	62.85	73.02	84.38	82.64	92.80	102.82
4	Exports of goods and services	121.89	133.76	150.87	176.04	218.33	220.94	251.20	274.46	295.19	343.38	388.55
5	Less: Imports of goods and services	118.21	130.78	148.14	174.03	220.41	216.72	262.25	295.92	294.86	349.16	405.49
	Equals: Gross Domestic Product	375.88	419.62	479.54	543.46	618.56	656.72	724.75	796.19	842.69	923.00	995.93

a) Including a statistical discrepancy.
b) Beginning 1973 including non-deductible value added tax and special investment tax.

1.2 Expenditure on the Gross Domestic Product, in Constant Prices

Thousand Million Austrian schillings

		1970	1971	1972	1973	1974	1975	1976	1977	1978	1979	1980
		\multicolumn{11}{c}{At constant prices of: 1976}											
1	General government final consumption expenditure	100.71	104.01	108.29	111.52	117.88	122.57	127.79	132.40	137.02	141.34	143.59
2	Private final consumption expenditure	309.31	330.09	350.16	368.97	380.01	392.35	410.18	433.57	426.92	443.05	449.58
3	Gross capital formation	160.37	165.24	181.43	198.43	200.60	176.00	197.83	210.45	198.08	219.29	232.51
a	Increase in stocks [a]	16.72	1.78	-1.87	14.49	9.36	-5.77	9.12	11.97	7.15	20.57	29.50
b	Gross fixed capital formation [b]	143.65	163.46	183.30	183.94	191.24	181.77	188.71	198.48	190.93	198.72	203.01

Austria

1.2 Expenditure on the Gross Domestic Product, in Constant Prices
(Continued)

Thousand Million Austrian schillings

	1970	1971	1972	1973	1974	1975	1976	1977	1978	1979	1980
					At constant prices of:1976						
Residential buildings											
Non-residential buildings	78.16	88.89	98.20	104.31	108.00	105.54	104.92	106.64	103.30	105.15	104.18
Other construction and land improvement etc.											
Other	57.28	65.23	72.85	70.96	72.13	66.16	73.02	81.13	77.01	83.39	88.55
4 Exports of goods and services	166.53	176.41	192.63	209.87	233.05	225.00	251.20	263.97	275.52	304.15	326.16
5 Less: Imports of goods and services	165.45	175.07	194.52	219.62	235.99	222.90	262.25	284.05	277.38	310.51	329.63
Equals: Gross Domestic Product	571.47	600.69	637.98	669.16	695.55	693.03	724.75	756.34	760.15	797.31	822.22

a) Including a statistical discrepancy.
b) Beginning 1973 including non-deductible value added tax and special investment tax.

1.3 Cost Components of the Gross Domestic Product

Thousand Million Austrian schillings

	1970	1971	1972	1973	1974	1975	1976	1977	1978	1979	1980
1 Indirect taxes, net	55.16	62.44	74.59	88.03	94.01	92.55	98.74	112.57	112.75	124.27	134.65
a Indirect taxes paid	61.68	70.00	82.49	97.23	106.92	111.53	119.55	135.87	139.30	151.20	161.76
b Less: Subsidies received	6.52	7.56	7.90	9.20	12.91	18.98	20.81	23.30	26.55	26.93	27.11
2 Consumption of fixed capital	43.85	49.52	56.20	62.37	71.47	77.42	82.51	90.61	97.80	104.14	113.25
3 Compensation of employees paid by resident producers to:	175.82	203.19	230.88	270.38	315.03	353.60	389.47	431.45	468.02	499.37	537.21
4 Net operating surplus	101.05	104.47	117.87	122.68	138.05	133.15	154.03	161.56	164.12	195.22	210.82
Equals: Gross Domestic Product	375.88	419.62	479.54	543.46	618.56	656.72	724.75	796.19	842.69	923.00	995.93

1.4 General Government Current Receipts and Disbursements

Thousand Million Austrian schillings

	1970	1971	1972	1973	1974	1975	1976	1977	1978	1979	1980
						Receipts					
1 Property and entrepreneurial income	4.45	5.50	5.22	5.51	6.72	8.65	10.20	10.25	12.21	13.23	15.52
2 Taxes, fees and contributions	136.41	155.05	181.46	210.22	242.27	256.73	279.29	320.61	355.66	384.24	417.38
a Indirect taxes	61.68	70.00	82.49	97.23	106.92	111.53	119.55	135.87	139.30	151.20	161.76
b Direct taxes	41.11	46.38	55.16	61.78	75.40	76.24	82.76	93.67	110.72	118.08	128.21
c Social security contributions	32.91	37.85	42.88	50.19	58.76	67.65	75.41	88.59	103.03	112.29	124.60
d Compulsory fees, fines and penalties	0.71	0.82	0.93	1.02	1.19	1.31	1.57	2.48	2.61	2.67	2.81
3 Other current receipts	8.33	9.49	10.65	11.98	13.76	15.87	17.92	17.38	21.45	23.07	24.55
Total Current Receipts of General Government	149.19	170.04	197.33	227.71	262.75	281.25	307.41	348.24	389.32	420.54	457.46
						Disbursements					
1 General government final consumption expenditure	55.22	61.98	70.10	81.91	97.43	113.05	127.79	138.74	154.18	165.89	177.51
a Compensation of employees	38.24	42.80	48.06	56.21	65.13	75.55	85.18	92.28	103.38	111.26	118.94
b Consumption of fixed capital	2.60	3.02	3.39	3.79	4.50	4.95	5.32	5.80	6.30	6.70	7.10
c Purchases of goods and services, net	13.61	15.26	17.62	20.75	26.50	30.93	35.47	38.65	42.48	45.83	49.20
d Less: Own account production of fixed assets	...	...	...	...	...	...	...	2.01	2.02	2.11	2.26
e Indirect taxes paid, net	0.77	0.89	1.03	1.15	1.32	1.61	1.82	14.80	18.68	21.31	24.30
2 Property income paid	4.05	4.39	4.79	5.35	6.44	8.56	12.17	14.80	18.68	21.31	24.30
3 Subsidies	6.52	7.56	7.90	9.20	12.91	18.98	20.81	23.30	26.55	26.93	27.11
4 Other current transfers paid	58.44	66.12	74.80	84.44	97.26	112.42	130.20	144.54	165.55	181.16	193.53
a Social security benefits and social assistance grants	29.83	34.07	38.35	42.80	49.26	56.37	64.74	71.61	78.78	86.71	94.80
b Other	28.61	32.05	36.45	41.64	48.00	56.05	65.46	72.93	86.77	94.45	98.73
5 Net saving	24.97	29.98	39.75	46.83	48.71	28.22	16.45	26.84	24.35	25.25	35.00
Total Current Disbursements and Net Saving of General Government	149.19	170.04	197.33	227.71	262.75	281.25	307.41	348.24	389.32	420.54	457.46

Austria

1.6 Current Income and Outlay of Households and Non-Profit Institutions

Thousand Million Austrian schillings

	1970	1971	1972	1973	1974	1975	1976	1977	1978	1979	1980
Receipts											
1 Compensation of employees	175.82	203.19	230.88	270.38	315.03	353.60	389.47	431.45	468.02	499.37	537.21
2 Property and entrepreneurial income received	73.99	77.05	80.25	79.08	86.28	92.05	103.69	109.54	110.47	131.59	140.83
3 Current transfers received	64.94	74.02	84.07	95.16	109.43	125.24	145.17	163.31	183.56	202.45	218.01
a Social security benefits and social assistance grants received	44.31	50.25	57.27	64.79	74.74	86.53	100.73	112.54	129.68	142.15	151.55
b Other	20.63	23.77	26.80	30.37	34.69	38.71	44.44	50.77	53.88	60.30	66.46
Total Current Receipts	314.75	354.28	395.20	444.61	510.73	570.89	638.33	704.31	762.05	833.40	896.05
Disbursements											
1 Private final consumption expenditure	205.29	230.00	259.81	291.78	330.61	368.26	410.18	456.86	469.57	509.06	548.68
2 Property income paid	...	...	...	...	...	...	...	...	...	...	...
3 Direct taxes and other payments n.e.c. to general government	67.32	76.90	89.94	104.32	123.95	131.83	147.39	169.12	201.71	216.63	238.13
a Social security contributions	32.91	37.85	42.88	50.20	58.75	67.65	75.42	86.59	103.03	112.29	124.60
b Direct taxes	33.70	38.23	46.13	53.10	64.01	62.87	70.40	80.05	96.07	101.67	110.72
c Fees, fines and penalties	0.71	0.82	0.93	1.02	1.19	1.31	1.57	2.48	2.61	2.67	2.81
4 Other current transfers paid	14.29	16.49	19.32	22.93	26.77	29.65	33.11	38.73	37.64	42.80	49.81
5 Net saving	27.85	30.89	26.13	25.58	29.39	41.14	47.65	39.58	53.16	64.90	59.43
Total Current Disbursements and Net Saving	314.75	354.28	395.20	444.61	510.73	570.89	638.33	704.31	762.07	833.40	896.05

1.7 External Transactions on Current Account, Summary

Thousand Million Austrian schillings

	1970	1971	1972	1973	1974	1975	1976	1977	1978	1979	1980
Payments to the Rest of the World											
1 Imports of goods and services	118.21	130.78	148.14	174.03	220.41	216.72	262.25	295.92	294.86	349.16	405.49
a Imports of merchandise c.i.f.	97.79	110.53	125.64	147.62	188.53	176.21	221.41	251.93	244.75	286.13	334.46
b Other	20.42	20.25	22.50	26.41	31.88	40.51	40.84	43.99	50.11	63.03	71.03
2 Factor income paid to the rest of the world	5.51	6.14	6.80	8.50	13.15	14.24	16.41	19.22	22.89	28.90	40.96
a Compensation of employees	...	...	...	...	...	...	...	...	...	...	...
b Property and entrepreneurial income paid	5.51	6.14	6.80	8.50	13.15	14.24	16.41	19.22	22.89	28.90	40.96
3 Indirect taxes paid to supranational organizations	...	...	...	...	...	...	...	...	...	...	...
4 Current transfers to the rest of the world	3.18	3.64	4.53	6.23	7.76	8.16	8.55	9.44	8.32	10.70	13.73
5 Surplus of the nation on current transactions	2.26	1.98	0.63	-1.61	-5.91	-0.37	-16.31	-28.93	-6.23	-12.03	-25.99
Payments to the Rest of the World and Surplus of the Nation on Current Transactions	129.16	142.54	160.10	187.15	235.41	238.75	270.90	295.65	319.84	376.73	434.19
Receipts From The Rest of the World											
1 Exports of goods and services	121.89	133.76	150.87	176.04	218.33	220.94	251.20	274.46	295.19	343.38	388.55
a Exports of merchandise f.o.b.	79.37	85.00	94.77	113.85	156.27	145.58	168.89	180.63	194.08	227.47	246.95
b Other	42.53	48.76	56.10	62.19	62.06	75.36	82.31	93.83	101.11	115.91	141.60
2 Factor income received from rest of the world	3.53	4.23	4.09	5.12	10.18	10.62	11.37	12.35	14.50	21.09	32.69
a Compensation of employees	...	...	...	...	...	...	...	...	...	...	...
b Property and entrepreneurial income received	3.53	4.23	4.09	5.12	10.18	10.62	11.37	12.35	14.50	21.09	32.69
3 Subsidies received from supranational organisations	...	...	...	...	...	...	...	...	...	...	...
4 Current transfers from rest of the world	3.73	4.54	5.13	6.00	6.91	7.19	8.33	8.84	10.15	12.26	12.95
Receipts from the Rest of the World on Current Transactions	129.16	142.54	160.10	187.15	235.41	238.75	270.90	295.65	319.84	376.73	434.19

Austria

1.8 Capital Transactions of The Nation, Summary

Thousand Million Austrian schillings

	1970	1971	1972	1973	1974	1975	1976	1977	1978	1979	1980
Finance of Gross Capital Formation											
Gross saving	113.95	126.64	147.53	166.16	186.70	170.82	181.52	193.12	212.38	241.80	260.69
1 Consumption of fixed capital	43.85	49.52	56.20	62.37	71.47	77.42	82.51	90.61	97.80	104.14	113.25
a General government	2.60	3.02	3.39	3.79	4.50	4.95	5.32	5.80	6.30	6.70	7.10
b Corporate and quasi-corporate enterprises	41.25	46.49	52.82	58.58	66.97	72.47	77.19	84.81	91.50	97.44	106.15
c Other	.	.	.	.	.	.	.	.	.	.	.
2 Net saving	70.11	77.11	91.33	103.78	115.23	93.39	99.01	102.50	114.59	137.64	147.43
a General government	24.97	29.98	39.75	46.83	48.71	28.22	16.45	26.84	24.35	25.25	35.00
b Corporate and quasi-corporate enterprises	17.29	16.24	25.45	31.37	37.13	24.03	34.91	36.08	37.08	47.49	53.00
c Other	27.85	30.89	26.13	25.58	29.39	41.14	47.65	39.58	53.16	64.90	59.43
Less: Surplus of the nation on current transactions	2.26	1.98	0.63	-1.61	-5.90	-0.37	-16.31	-28.94	-6.23	-12.03	-25.99
Finance of Gross Capital Formation	111.69	124.66	146.90	167.76	192.60	171.19	197.83	222.04	218.61	253.82	286.68
Gross Capital Formation											
Increase in stocks [a]	14.51	7.76	1.99	12.79	16.88	-3.73	9.12	9.27	3.39	21.93	34.39
Gross fixed capital formation	97.18	116.90	144.91	154.97	175.72	174.92	188.71	212.77	215.22	231.89	252.29
Gross Capital Formation	111.69	124.66	146.90	167.76	192.60	171.19	197.83	222.04	218.61	253.82	286.68

a) Including a statistical discrepancy.

1.10 Gross Domestic Product by Kind of Activity, in Current Prices

Thousand Million Austrian schillings

	1970	1971	1972	1973	1974	1975	1976	1977	1978	1979	1980
1 Agriculture, hunting, forestry and fishing	25.78	25.14	28.23	31.37	33.08	33.07	36.45	36.05	39.33	40.26	43.65
2 Mining and quarrying	2.75	2.77	2.87	2.99	3.68	4.02	3.98	4.07	4.10	4.78	4.78
3 Manufacturing	126.70	140.88	158.25	166.69	190.57	187.72	208.72	223.02	232.79	262.32	279.28
4 Electricity, gas and water	10.39	10.25	12.15	14.08	16.58	18.68	22.09	25.45	26.02	28.15	31.41
5 Construction	30.65	36.89	45.93	47.60	54.31	57.96	59.18	66.31	70.00	76.52	81.71
6 Wholesale and retail trade, restaurants and hotels	68.07	78.34	89.77	84.32	99.04	109.81	121.94	133.83	136.03	152.15	166.50
7 Transport, storage and communication	22.31	24.15	27.72	29.40	32.31	35.17	40.68	45.53	48.80	53.53	58.08
8 Finance, insurance, real estate and business services	31.58	37.15	42.49	49.24	57.78	66.68	75.06	90.34	97.29	106.46	117.98
9 Community, social and personal services	11.56	12.59	13.69	14.52	17.14	19.52	21.99	24.76	27.16	29.52	32.53
Total, Industries	329.79	368.16	421.10	440.21	504.49	532.63	590.09	649.36	681.52	753.69	815.92
Producers of Government Services	41.60	46.72	52.48	61.15	70.94	82.12	92.32	100.09	111.69	120.07	128.30
Other Producers	2.99	3.21	3.55	3.86	4.26	4.81	5.42	5.77	6.37	6.79	7.22
Subtotal	374.38	418.09	477.13	505.22	579.69	619.56	687.83	755.22	799.58	880.55	951.44
Less: Imputed bank service charge	11.74	13.70	15.24	18.89	23.32	26.49	28.02	33.68	37.25	41.01	45.33
Plus: Import duties	13.23	15.23	17.65	7.59	7.75	7.27	6.12	5.78	4.83	5.57	5.72
Plus: Value added tax	-	-	-	49.54	54.43	56.38	58.82	68.86	75.52	77.87	84.09
Equals: Gross Domestic Product	375.88	419.62	479.54	543.46	618.56	656.72	724.75	796.19	842.69	923.00	995.93

1.11 Gross Domestic Product by Kind of Activity, in Constant Prices

Thousand Million Austrian schillings

	1970	1971	1972	1973	1974	1975	1976	1977	1978	1979	1980
At constant prices of: 1976											
1 Agriculture, hunting, forestry and fishing	32.62	30.14	30.36	32.29	33.60	35.21	36.45	35.10	37.39	38.12	39.80
2 Mining and quarrying	3.99	4.11	3.85	4.12	4.36	4.03	3.98	3.56	3.51	4.06	4.08
3 Manufacturing	168.53	178.37	191.94	201.88	208.81	196.37	208.72	220.02	222.02	237.51	247.32
4 Electricity, gas and water	16.03	15.84	17.22	18.91	20.21	20.94	22.09	23.61	23.69	25.93	26.78
5 Construction	46.10	51.49	54.90	57.86	59.83	59.02	59.18	61.40	60.75	62.16	61.42
6 Wholesale and retail trade, restaurants and hotels	92.75	98.04	105.07	109.98	114.26	116.83	121.94	127.37	123.08	129.97	134.06
7 Transport, storage and communication	27.86	29.41	31.64	34.62	37.66	37.33	40.68	42.52	44.46	47.54	50.06
8 Finance, insurance, real estate and business services	53.18	57.06	60.30	64.44	67.86	70.79	75.06	81.35	83.94	88.54	92.75
9 Community, social and personal services	18.61	19.06	19.30	19.89	21.16	22.22	21.99	22.87	23.48	24.16	25.18
Total, Industries	459.67	483.52	514.58	543.99	567.75	562.74	590.09	617.80	622.32	657.99	681.45
Producers of Government Services	75.42	78.29	80.78	82.08	85.50	88.00	92.32	95.71	99.16	102.48	104.64

Austria

1.11 Gross Domestic Product by Kind of Activity, in Constant Prices
(Continued)

Thousand Million Austrian schillings

	1970	1971	1972	1973	1974	1975	1976	1977	1978	1979	1980
				At constant prices of:1976							
Other Producers	5.20	5.19	5.19	5.22	5.26	5.35	5.42	5.44	5.50	5.52	5.53
Subtotal	540.28	567.00	600.55	631.28	658.51	656.09	687.83	718.95	726.98	765.98	791.62
Less: Imputed bank service charge	17.43	19.53	20.75	22.43	24.21	25.70	28.02	30.85	33.55	37.69	39.84
Plus: Import duties	3.46	3.86	4.63	5.09	5.03	4.98	6.12	6.92	6.56	7.16	7.66
Plus: Value added tax	45.16	49.35	53.56	55.20	56.20	57.65	58.82	61.32	60.16	61.85	62.78
Plus: Other adjustments	...	...	...	...	...	...	...	...	...	...	-
Equals: Gross Domestic Product	571.47	600.69	637.98	669.16	695.55	693.03	724.75	756.34	760.15	797.31	822.22

1.12 Relations Among National Accounting Aggregates

Thousand Million Austrian schillings

	1970	1971	1972	1973	1974	1975	1976	1977	1978	1979	1980
Gross Domestic Product	375.88	419.62	479.54	543.46	618.56	656.72	724.75	796.19	842.69	923.00	995.93
Plus: Net factor income received from abroad	-1.97	-1.90	-2.70	-3.38	-2.97	-3.62	-5.04	-6.87	-8.38	-7.82	-8.27
Equals: Gross National Product	373.91	417.72	476.84	540.08	615.59	653.10	719.70	789.32	834.31	915.18	987.66
Less: Consumption of fixed capital	43.85	49.52	56.20	62.37	71.47	77.42	82.51	90.61	97.80	104.14	113.25
Less: Net indirect taxes paid to supranational organisations	...	...	...	...	...	...	...	...	...	...	...
Equals: National Income at Market Prices	330.06	368.20	420.63	477.71	544.12	575.67	637.20	698.71	736.51	811.05	874.41
Plus: Net current transfers received from abroad	0.55	0.90	0.60	-0.23	-0.85	-0.97	-0.22	-0.60	1.82	1.56	-0.78
Current transfers received	3.73	4.54	5.13	6.00	6.91	7.19	8.33	8.84	10.15	12.26	12.95
Less: Current transfers paid	3.18	3.64	4.53	6.23	7.76	8.16	8.55	9.44	8.32	10.70	13.73
Equals: National Disposable Income at Market Prices	330.61	369.10	421.24	477.47	543.27	574.70	636.98	698.11	738.33	812.61	873.63
Less: Final consumption	260.51	291.98	329.91	373.69	428.04	481.37	537.97	595.60	623.75	674.95	726.19
Equals: Net Saving	70.11	77.11	91.33	103.78	115.23	93.39	99.01	102.50	114.59	137.64	147.43
Less: Surplus of the nation on current transactions	2.26	1.98	0.63	-1.61	-5.90	-0.37	-16.31	-28.94	-6.23	-12.03	-25.99
Equals: Net Capital Formation [a]	67.85	75.13	90.70	105.39	121.13	93.76	115.32	131.44	120.82	149.67	173.42

a) Beginning 1973, including also a statistical discrepancy.

2.1 General Government Final Consumption Expenditure by Function, in Current Prices

Thousand Million Austrian schillings

		1970	1971	1972	1973	1974	1975	1976	1977	1978	1979	1980
1	General public services	1.41	1.80	1.77	2.23	3.45	2.31	2.70	4.79	5.74	5.70	...
2	Defence	4.09	4.14	4.74	5.14	6.26	7.44	8.16	8.90	9.99	11.01	11.57
3	Public order and safety	11.59	12.43	13.79	16.74	18.44	23.08	24.83	25.16	28.83	29.40	...
4	Education	10.05	11.81	13.69	16.22	19.19	22.92	26.45	29.02	32.49	35.41	...
5	Health	12.57	13.86	15.77	18.28	22.36	26.69	32.04	34.14	37.57	41.07	...
6	Social security and welfare	2.65	3.11	4.05	4.91	6.42	7.05	7.17	8.20	9.11	9.60	...
7	Housing and community amenities	1.59	1.77	2.01	2.41	2.66	2.84	2.61	2.77	3.02	3.25	...
8	Recreational, cultural and religious affairs	...	...	...	...	...	...	...	...	...	...	...
9	Economic services	1.46	1.76	1.79	1.97	2.42	2.13	3.01	2.97	2.33	3.53	...
10	Other functions [b]	9.81	11.30	12.49	14.01	16.23	18.59	20.82	22.79	25.10	26.92	28.60
	Total General Government Final Consumption Expenditure	55.22	61.98	70.10	81.91	97.43	113.05	127.79	138.74	154.18	165.89	177.51

a) Comprising consumption of fixed capital and part of pensions.
b) Comprising consumption of fixed capital, indirect taxes and part of pensions.

2.5 Private Final Consumption Expenditure by Type, in Current Prices

Thousand Million Austrian schillings

		1970	1971	1972	1973	1974	1975	1976	1977	1978	1979	1980
		Final Consumption Expenditure of Resident Households										
1	Food, beverages and tobacco	70.92	76.50	82.14	91.39	96.66	104.50	114.82	120.79	127.30	133.22	139.89
	a Food	53.62	57.59	62.01	68.85	73.78	80.34	88.18	92.05	97.53	102.60	108.52
	b Non-alcoholic beverages	1.46	1.72	1.63	1.88	1.91	2.28	2.73	3.00	3.21	3.63	3.93
	c Alcoholic beverages	9.60	10.51	11.07	12.50	12.61	12.78	13.67	14.22	14.62	14.36	14.27
	d Tobacco	6.24	6.68	7.43	8.16	8.37	9.09	10.24	11.52	11.93	12.64	13.17
2	Clothing and footwear	25.83	30.06	35.11	38.68	42.17	45.71	49.02	52.57	53.19	58.38	63.52
3	Gross rent, fuel and power	23.83	26.53	30.67	36.75	43.87	51.84	60.41	66.75	73.94	80.91	92.71
	a Fuel and power	8.87	8.99	9.86	11.80	14.10	15.69	18.30	19.19	21.47	24.12	29.19
	b Other	14.96	17.54	20.82	24.94	29.77	36.15	42.11	47.56	52.47	56.80	63.52
4	Furniture, furnishings and household equipment and operation	20.56	23.84	28.09	30.45	34.01	36.89	38.18	43.42	40.71	41.92	43.44

Austria

2.5 Private Final Consumption Expenditure by Type, in Current Prices
(Continued)

Thousand Million Austrian schillings

		1970	1971	1972	1973	1974	1975	1976	1977	1978	1979	1980
	a Household operation	3.87	4.08	4.45	5.13	5.61	5.99	6.37	7.18	6.90	7.42	7.57
	b Other	16.69	19.76	23.64	25.32	28.40	30.90	31.81	36.24	33.81	34.50	35.87
5	Medical care and health expenses	7.55	8.44	9.47	10.90	13.53	15.25	17.25	18.66	21.13	22.57	24.43
6	Transport and communication	26.83	33.23	40.61	44.17	48.60	56.13	65.34	77.24	74.71	87.79	99.68
	a Personal transport equipment	6.07	9.16	12.12	10.88	9.91	11.91	16.01	22.66	14.98	21.55	23.34
	b Other	20.76	24.07	28.49	33.29	38.69	44.22	49.33	54.58	59.73	66.24	76.34
7	Recreational, entertainment, education and cultural services	13.36	15.07	16.77	18.85	21.07	23.96	25.90	29.81	31.88	33.13	34.86
	a Education	0.80	0.86	0.84	0.83	0.84	0.99	1.16	1.43	1.56	1.84	1.95
	b Other	12.56	14.21	15.93	18.02	20.23	22.97	24.74	28.38	30.32	31.29	32.91
8	Miscellaneous goods and services	34.47	38.84	43.73	49.30	55.31	62.50	67.40	73.84	78.46	86.14	93.63
	a Personal care	7.18	7.74	8.82	10.06	11.15	12.11	13.17	14.76	14.89	15.59	16.09
	b Expenditures in restaurants, cafes and hotels	23.40	26.83	30.00	33.35	37.45	42.56	45.89	49.74	53.37	58.42	64.54
	c Other	3.89	4.27	4.92	5.89	6.71	7.84	8.35	9.34	10.22	12.13	13.02
Total Final Consumption Expenditure in the Domestic Market by Households, of which		223.35	252.51	286.60	320.49	355.22	396.77	438.34	483.10	501.31	544.06	592.16
	a Durable goods	25.65	32.13	39.97	41.10	43.68	48.86	54.33	66.88	57.07	64.81	67.73
	b Semi-durable goods	32.54	37.68	43.61	47.99	52.11	56.54	60.53	65.65	66.18	71.43	77.38
	c Non-durable goods	93.99	101.58	110.50	124.93	136.72	148.57	164.50	173.73	184.45	195.25	210.95
	d Services	71.17	81.13	92.53	106.48	122.72	142.80	158.98	176.84	193.61	212.57	236.10
Plus: Direct purchases abroad by resident households		11.72	12.94	15.99	17.33	21.51	23.77	27.48	34.44	35.90	39.53	40.93
Less: Direct purchases in the domestic market by non-resident households		29.78	35.45	42.77	46.05	46.12	52.28	55.63	60.67	67.64	74.52	84.41
Equals: Final Consumption Expenditure of Resident Households		205.29	230.00	259.81	291.78	330.61	368.26	410.18	456.86	469.57	509.06	548.68

Final Consumption Expenditure of Private Non-profit Institutions Serving Households

	1970	1971	1972	1973	1974	1975	1976	1977	1978	1979	1980
Equals: Final Consumption Expenditure of Private Non-profit Organisations Serving Households	...	...	...	...	...	...	...	...	...	...	...
Private Final Consumption Expenditure	205.29	230.00	259.81	291.78	330.61	368.26	410.18	456.86	469.57	509.06	548.68

2.6 Private Final Consumption Expenditure by Type, in Constant Prices

Thousand Million Austrian schillings

		1970	1971	1972	1973	1974	1975	1976	1977	1978	1979	1980

At constant prices of: 1976

Final Consumption Expenditure of Resident Households

		1970	1971	1972	1973	1974	1975	1976	1977	1978	1979	1980
1	Food, beverages and tobacco	99.87	104.41	105.67	110.80	109.53	110.58	114.82	115.00	118.33	121.78	122.66
	a Food	75.24	78.34	80.17	83.54	83.32	85.02	88.18	87.33	90.04	92.81	93.50
	b Non-alcoholic beverages	2.08	2.33	2.10	2.28	2.17	2.38	2.73	3.05	3.18	3.55	3.71
	c Alcoholic beverages	13.57	14.18	14.03	14.70	13.63	13.08	13.67	14.15	14.28	14.10	14.19
	d Tobacco	8.97	9.56	9.37	10.29	10.41	10.10	10.24	10.48	10.84	11.32	11.27
2	Clothing and footwear	36.35	40.77	45.55	46.98	46.55	47.70	49.02	50.32	49.52	53.14	56.00
3	Gross rent, fuel and power	44.08	45.71	48.94	53.18	54.76	57.85	60.41	62.27	66.03	68.00	70.25
	a Fuel and power	14.67	14.53	15.49	17.48	16.65	17.07	18.30	18.23	20.02	21.19	21.27
	b Other	29.41	31.18	33.45	35.71	38.11	40.78	42.11	44.05	46.01	46.82	48.98
4	Furniture, furnishings and household equipment and operation	27.55	30.80	34.80	36.18	37.51	38.59	38.18	42.34	39.07	38.90	38.30
	a Household operation	5.73	5.81	6.06	6.62	6.64	6.41	6.37	6.95	6.56	6.77	6.52
	b Other	21.82	24.99	28.74	29.56	30.87	32.18	31.81	35.39	32.51	32.13	31.78
5	Medical care and health expenses	14.78	14.67	14.67	15.54	17.01	17.09	17.25	16.94	17.31	17.57	18.24
6	Transport and communication	42.89	50.80	57.99	59.95	56.93	60.25	65.34	73.61	68.10	74.66	78.66
	a Personal transport equipment	8.78	12.39	15.23	13.24	11.52	12.74	16.01	21.94	13.02	17.91	18.84
	b Other	34.11	38.41	42.76	46.71	45.41	47.51	49.33	51.67	55.08	56.75	59.82
7	Recreational, entertainment, education and cultural services	18.47	19.93	21.25	22.92	23.94	25.19	25.90	28.47	28.62	28.59	28.89
	a Education	1.08	1.06	1.04	1.04	1.07	1.15	1.16	1.32	1.32	1.45	1.43

Austria

2.6 Private Final Consumption Expenditure by Type, in Constant Prices
(Continued)

Thousand Million Austrian schillings

	1970	1971	1972	1973	1974	1975	1976	1977	1978	1979	1980
					At constant prices of:1976						
b Other	17.39	18.87	20.21	21.88	22.87	24.04	24.74	27.15	27.30	27.14	27.46
8 Miscellaneous goods and services	57.91	60.17	62.55	62.63	63.83	66.41	67.40	67.90	67.70	70.27	70.92
a Personal care	11.17	11.46	12.25	12.59	12.70	12.84	13.17	13.92	13.10	12.66	11.43
b Expenditures in restaurants, cafes and hotels	40.24	42.06	43.26	42.55	43.49	45.49	45.89	45.35	45.95	47.93	49.97
c Other	6.50	6.65	7.03	7.50	7.64	8.08	8.35	8.63	8.65	9.69	9.53
Total Final Consumption Expenditure in the Domestic Market by Households, of which	341.89	367.27	391.41	408.20	410.07	423.66	438.34	456.85	454.68	472.92	483.92
a Durable goods	34.72	41.57	49.17	48.31	48.11	51.26	54.33	65.16	52.42	56.78	56.16
b Semi-durable goods	45.46	50.78	56.28	58.13	57.54	59.00	60.53	63.08	62.02	65.35	68.29
c Non-durable goods	138.11	145.20	150.20	160.06	156.11	158.33	164.50	166.27	172.66	177.46	177.97
d Services	123.61	129.72	135.77	141.70	148.31	155.08	158.98	162.35	167.58	173.34	181.51
Plus: Direct purchases abroad by resident households	15.39	16.25	18.85	19.67	22.97	24.37	27.48	33.10	32.33	33.19	32.99
Less: Direct purchases in the domestic market by non-resident households	47.98	53.43	60.10	58.90	53.02	55.68	55.63	56.38	60.09	63.06	67.32
Equals: Final Consumption Expenditure of Resident Households	309.31	330.09	350.16	368.97	380.01	392.35	410.18	433.57	426.92	443.05	449.59

Final Consumption Expenditure of Private Non-profit Institutions Serving Households

| Equals: Final Consumption Expenditure of Private Non-profit Organisations Serving Households | ... | ... | ... | ... | ... | ... | ... | ... | ... | ... | ... |
| Private Final Consumption Expenditure | 309.31 | 330.09 | 350.16 | 368.97 | 380.01 | 392.35 | 410.18 | 433.57 | 426.92 | 443.05 | 449.59 |

2.17 Exports and Imports of Goods and Services, Detail

Thousand Million Austrian schillings

	1970	1971	1972	1973	1974	1975	1976	1977	1978	1979	1980
	Exports of Goods and Services										
1 Exports of merchandise, f.o.b.	79.37	85.00	94.77	113.85	156.27	145.58	168.89	180.63	194.08	227.47	246.95
2 Transport and communication	...	...	...	...	...	...	...	...	...	...	...
3 Insurance service charges	...	...	...	...	...	...	...	...	...	...	...
4 Other commodities	8.70	9.75	11.37	12.76	14.26	15.27	18.72	21.10	24.35	29.61	33.84
5 Adjustments of merchandise exports to change-of-ownership basis	4.05	3.56	1.96	3.38	1.68	7.81	7.96	12.06	9.12	11.78	23.35
6 Direct purchases in the domestic market by non-residential households	29.78	35.45	42.77	46.05	46.12	52.28	55.63	60.67	67.64	74.52	84.41
7 Direct purchases in the domestic market by extraterritorial bodies	...	...	...	...	...	...	...	...	...	...	...
Total Exports of Goods and Services	121.89	133.76	150.87	176.04	218.33	220.94	251.20	274.46	295.19	343.38	388.55
	Imports of Goods and Services										
1 Imports of merchandise, c.i.f.	97.79	110.53	125.64	147.62	188.53	176.21	221.41	251.93	244.75	286.13	334.46
2 Adjustments of merchandise imports to change-of-ownership basis	1.25	-1.15	-3.14	-2.19	-1.22	2.57	-2.10	-8.21	-4.99	0.40	2.52
3 Other transport and communication	...	...	...	...	...	...	...	...	...	...	...
4 Other insurance service charges	...	...	...	...	...	...	...	...	...	...	...
5 Other commodities	7.11	8.05	9.13	10.79	10.99	13.56	14.83	17.06	18.44	22.31	26.73
6 Direct purchases abroad by government	...	...	...	...	...	...	...	...	...	...	...
7 Direct purchases abroad by resident households	12.06	13.35	16.51	17.81	22.11	24.38	28.11	35.14	36.66	40.32	41.78
Total Imports of Goods and Services	118.21	130.78	148.14	174.03	220.41	216.72	262.25	295.92	294.86	349.16	405.49
Balance of Goods and Services	3.68	2.98	2.73	2.01	-2.08	4.22	-11.05	-21.46	0.33	-5.78	-16.94
Total Imports and Balance of Goods and Services	121.89	133.76	150.87	176.04	218.33	220.94	251.20	274.46	295.19	343.38	388.55

Austria

3.11 General Government Production Account: Total and Subsectors

Thousand Million Austrian schillings

	1970 Total General Government	Central Government	State or Provincial Government	Local Government	Social Security Funds	1971 Total General Government	Central Government	State or Provincial Government	Local Government	Social Security Funds
Gross Output										
1 Sales	10.55	...	...	...	...	11.91	...	...	...	...
2 Services produced for own use	55.22	...	...	...	...	61.98	...	...	...	...
3 Own account capital formation	...	...	...	...	...	...	...	...	...	...
Gross Output	65.77	...	...	...	...	73.89	...	...	...	...
Gross Input										
Intermediate Consumption	24.16	...	...	...	...	27.17	...	...	...	...
Subtotal: Value Added	41.60	...	...	...	...	46.72	...	...	...	...
1 Indirect taxes, net	0.77	...	...	...	...	0.89	...	...	...	...
2 Consumption of fixed capital	2.60	...	...	...	...	3.02	...	...	...	...
3 Compensation of employees	38.24	...	...	...	...	42.80	...	...	...	...
4 Net Operating surplus	...	...	...	...	...	...	...	...	...	...
Gross Input	65.77	...	...	...	...	73.89	...	...	...	...

	1972 Total General Government	Central Government	State or Provincial Government	Local Government	Social Security Funds	1973 Total General Government	Central Government	State or Provincial Government	Local Government	Social Security Funds
Gross Output										
1 Sales	13.57	...	...	...	...	15.36	...	...	...	...
2 Services produced for own use	70.10	...	...	...	...	81.91	...	...	...	...
3 Own account capital formation	...	...	...	...	...	...	...	...	...	...
Gross Output	83.67	...	...	...	...	97.27	...	...	...	...
Gross Input										
Intermediate Consumption	31.19	...	...	...	...	36.11	...	...	...	...
Subtotal: Value Added	52.48	...	...	...	...	61.15	...	...	...	...
1 Indirect taxes, net	1.03	...	...	...	...	1.15	...	...	...	...
2 Consumption of fixed capital	3.39	...	...	...	...	3.79	...	...	...	...
3 Compensation of employees	48.06	...	...	...	...	56.21	...	...	...	...
4 Net Operating surplus	...	...	...	...	...	...	...	...	...	...
Gross Input	83.67	...	...	...	...	97.27	...	...	...	...

	1974 Total General Government	Central Government	State or Provincial Government	Local Government	Social Security Funds	1975 Total General Government	Central Government	State or Provincial Government	Local Government	Social Security Funds
Gross Output										
1 Sales	17.83	...	...	...	...	21.64	...	...	...	...
2 Services produced for own use	97.43	...	...	...	...	113.05	...	...	...	...
3 Own account capital formation	...	...	...	...	...	...	...	...	...	...
Gross Output	115.27	...	...	...	...	134.69	...	...	...	...
Gross Input										
Intermediate Consumption	44.33	...	...	...	...	52.57	...	...	...	...
Subtotal: Value Added	70.94	...	...	...	...	82.12	...	...	...	...
1 Indirect taxes, net	1.32	...	...	...	...	1.61	...	...	...	...
2 Consumption of fixed capital	4.50	...	...	...	...	4.95	...	...	...	...
3 Compensation of employees	65.13	...	...	...	...	75.55	...	...	...	...
4 Net Operating surplus	...	...	...	...	...	...	...	...	...	...
Gross Input	115.27	...	...	...	...	134.69	...	...	...	...

	1976 Total General Government	Central Government	State or Provincial Government	Local Government	Social Security Funds	1977 Total General Government	Central Government	State or Provincial Government	Local Government	Social Security Funds
Gross Output										
1 Sales	22.84	...	...	...	...	26.31	...	...	...	...
2 Services produced for own use	127.79	...	...	...	...	138.74	...	...	...	...
3 Own account capital formation	...	...	...	...	...	...	...	...	...	...
Gross Output	150.63	...	...	...	...	165.05	...	...	...	...

Austria

3.11 General Government Production Account: Total and Subsectors
(Continued)

Thousand Million Austrian schillings

	1976					1977				
	Total General Government	Central Government	State or Provincial Government	Local Government	Social Security Funds	Total General Government	Central Government	State or Provincial Government	Local Government	Social Security Funds
Gross Input										
Intermediate Consumption	58.31	...	...	...	...	64.96	...	...	...	...
Subtotal: Value Added	92.32	...	...	...	...	100.09	...	...	...	...
1 Indirect taxes, net	1.82	...	...	...	...	2.01	...	...	...	...
2 Consumption of fixed capital	5.32	...	...	...	...	5.80	...	...	...	...
3 Compensation of employees	85.18	...	...	...	...	92.28	...	...	...	...
4 Net Operating surplus	...	...	...	...	...	...	...	...	...	...
Gross Input	150.63	...	...	...	...	165.05	...	...	...	...

	1978					1979				
	Total General Government	Central Government	State or Provincial Government	Local Government	Social Security Funds	Total General Government	Central Government	State or Provincial Government	Local Government	Social Security Funds
Gross Output										
1 Sales	29.29	...	...	...	...	31.64	...	...	...	...
2 Services produced for own use	154.18	...	...	...	...	165.89	...	...	...	...
3 Own account capital formation	...	...	...	...	...	...	...	...	...	...
Gross Output	183.47	...	...	...	...	197.54	...	...	...	...
Gross Input										
Intermediate Consumption	71.77	...	...	...	...	77.47	...	...	...	...
Subtotal: Value Added	111.69	...	...	...	...	120.07	...	...	...	...
1 Indirect taxes, net	2.02	...	...	...	...	2.11	...	...	...	...
2 Consumption of fixed capital	6.30	...	...	...	...	6.70	...	...	...	...
3 Compensation of employees	103.38	...	...	...	...	111.26	...	...	...	...
4 Net Operating surplus	...	...	...	...	...	...	...	...	...	...
Gross Input	183.47	...	...	...	...	197.54	...	...	...	...

	1980				
	Total General Government	Central Government	State or Provincial Government	Local Government	Social Security Funds
Gross Output					
1 Sales	33.52	...	...	...	...
2 Services produced for own use	177.51	...	...	...	...
3 Own account capital formation	...	...	...	...	...
Gross Output	211.03	...	...	...	...
Gross Input					
Intermediate Consumption	82.72	...	...	...	...
Subtotal: Value Added	128.30	...	...	...	...
1 Indirect taxes, net	2.26	...	...	...	...
2 Consumption of fixed capital	7.10	...	...	...	...
3 Compensation of employees	118.94	...	...	...	...
4 Net Operating surplus	...	...	...	...	...
Gross Input	211.03	...	...	...	...

3.12 General Government Income and Outlay Account: Total and Subsectors

Thousand Million Austrian schillings

	1970					1971				
	Total General Government	Central Government	State or Provincial Government	Local Government	Social Security Funds	Total General Government	Central Government	State or Provincial Government	Local Government	Social Security Funds
Receipts										
1 Property and entrepreneurial income	4.45	3.32	...	...	...	5.50	3.81	...	...	...
2 Taxes, fees and contributions	136.42	68.49	...	...	...	155.06	77.37	...	...	...
a Indirect taxes	61.68	40.15	...	...	...	70.00	45.00	...	...	...
b Direct taxes	41.11	27.09	...	...	...	46.39	30.97	...	...	...

Austria

3.12 General Government Income and Outlay Account: Total and Subsectors
(Continued)

Thousand Million Austrian schillings

	1970					1971				
	Total General Government	Central Government	State or Provincial Government	Local Government	Social Security Funds	Total General Government	Central Government	State or Provincial Government	Local Government	Social Security Funds
c Social security contributions	32.92	0.82	...	...	...	37.85	0.90	...	...	...
d Fees, fines and penalties	0.71	0.43	...	...	...	0.82	0.50	...	...	...
3 Other current transfers received	8.33	6.95	...	...	...	9.49	7.83	...	...	...
a Casualty insurance claims	0.10	0.07	...	...	...	0.12	0.08	...	...	...
b Transfers from other government subsectors	...	1.14	...	...	...	...	1.19	...	...	...
c Transfers from abroad	0.13	0.11	...	...	...	0.16	0.11	...	...	...
d Other transfers, except imputed	...	...	...	...	...	...	...	...	...	...
e Imputed unfunded employee welfare contributions	8.10	5.63	...	...	...	9.21	6.45	...	...	...
Total Current Receipts	149.19	78.77	...	...	...	170.04	89.03	...	...	...

Disbursements

	Total General Government	Central Government	State or Provincial Government	Local Government	Social Security Funds	Total General Government	Central Government	State or Provincial Government	Local Government	Social Security Funds
1 General government final consumption expenditures	55.22	25.53	...	...	...	61.97	28.72	...	...	...
a Compensation of employees	38.24	...	...	...	...	42.80	...	...	...	...
b Consumption of fixed capital	2.60	0.52	...	...	...	3.02	0.60	...	...	...
c Goods and services purchased, net	13.61	...	...	...	...	15.26	...	...	...	...
Purchases	24.16	...	...	...	...	27.17	...	...	...	...
Less: Sales	10.55	...	...	...	...	11.91	...	...	...	...
d Less: Own account production of fixed assets	...	...	...	...	...	...	...	...	...	...
e Indirect taxes paid, net	0.77	...	...	...	...	0.89	...	...	...	...
2 Property income paid	4.05	2.87	...	...	...	4.39	3.04	...	...	...
3 Subsidies	6.52	6.03	...	...	...	7.56	6.89	...	...	...
4 Other current transfers paid	58.44	35.68	...	...	...	66.12	39.37	...	...	...
a Casualty insurance premiums, net	0.10	0.07	...	...	...	0.12	0.08	...	...	...
b Transfers to other government subsectors	...	12.85	...	...	...	...	13.76	...	...	...
c Transfers to households	43.33	10.12	...	...	...	49.19	11.34	...	...	...
Social security benefits	29.83	...	...	...	...	34.07	...	...	...	...
Social assistance grants		...	...	...	...		...	...	...	...
Unfunded employee welfare benefits	13.50	10.12	...	...	...	15.12	11.34	...	...	...
d Transfers to private non-profit institutions serving households	14.48	12.46	...	...	...	16.18	13.95	...	...	...
e Transfers to the rest of the world	0.53	0.18	...	...	...	0.63	0.24	...	...	...
Net saving	24.97	8.67	...	...	...	29.98	11.01	...	...	...
Total Current Disbursements and Net Saving	149.19	78.77	...	...	...	170.04	89.03	...	...	...

	1972					1973				
	Total General Government	Central Government	State or Provincial Government	Local Government	Social Security Funds	Total General Government	Central Government	State or Provincial Government	Local Government	Social Security Funds

Receipts

	Total General Government	Central Government	State or Provincial Government	Local Government	Social Security Funds	Total General Government	Central Government	State or Provincial Government	Local Government	Social Security Funds
1 Property and entrepreneurial income	5.22	3.53	...	...	...	5.51	3.50	...	...	...
2 Taxes, fees and contributions	181.46	90.12	...	...	...	210.22	102.62	...	...	...
a Indirect taxes	82.49	52.37	...	...	...	97.23	61.43	...	...	...
b Direct taxes	55.16	36.06	...	...	...	61.78	39.54	...	...	...
c Social security contributions	42.88	1.12	...	...	...	50.19	1.03	...	...	...
d Fees, fines and penalties	0.93	0.57	...	...	...	1.02	0.62	...	...	...
3 Other current transfers received	10.65	8.78	...	...	...	11.98	7.15	...	...	...
a Casualty insurance claims	0.13	0.08	...	...	...	0.12	0.08	...	...	...
b Transfers from other government subsectors	...	1.25	...	...	...	...	0.38	...	...	...

Austria

3.12 General Government Income and Outlay Account: Total and Subsectors
(Continued)

Thousand Million Austrian schillings

	1972					1973				
	Total General Government	Central Government	State or Provincial Government	Local Government	Social Security Funds	Total General Government	Central Government	State or Provincial Government	Local Government	Social Security Funds
c Transfers from abroad	0.18	0.12	...	...	...	0.19	0.13	...	...	...
d Other transfers, except imputed	...	...	...	...	...	...	...	...	...	...
e Imputed unfunded employee welfare contributions	10.34	7.33	...	...	...	11.67	6.55	...	...	...
Total Current Receipts	197.33	102.44	...	...	...	227.71	113.28	...	...	...
Disbursements											
1 General government final consumption expenditures	70.10	33.17	...	...	...	81.91	30.50	...	...	...
a Compensation of employees	48.06	...	...	...	...	56.21	...	...	...	...
b Consumption of fixed capital	3.39	0.68	...	...	...	3.79	0.76	...	...	...
c Goods and services purchased, net	17.62	...	...	...	...	20.75	...	...	...	...
Purchases	31.19	...	...	...	...	36.11	...	...	...	...
Less: Sales	13.57	...	...	...	...	15.36	...	...	...	...
d Less: Own account production of fixed assets	...	...	...	...	...	...	...	...	...	...
e Indirect taxes paid, net	1.03	...	...	...	...	1.15	...	...	...	...
2 Property income paid	4.79	3.09	...	...	...	5.35	3.36	...	...	...
3 Subsidies	7.90	7.19	...	...	...	9.20	8.36	...	...	...
4 Other current transfers paid	74.80	45.07	...	...	...	84.44	56.87	...	...	...
a Casualty insurance premiums, net	0.13	0.08	...	...	...	0.12	0.08	...	...	...
b Transfers to other government subsectors	...	15.75	...	...	...	...	25.38	...	...	...
c Transfers to households	55.02	12.52	...	...	...	61.38	12.04	...	...	...
Social security benefits	38.35	...	...	...	...	42.80	...	...	...	...
Social assistance grants	(	...	...	...	...	(	...	...	...	...
Unfunded employee welfare benefits	16.67	12.52	...	...	...	18.58	12.04	...	...	...
d Transfers to private non-profit institutions serving households	18.92	16.46	...	...	...	21.99	19.10	...	...	...
e Transfers to the rest of the world	0.73	0.26	...	...	...	0.95	0.27	...	...	...
Net saving	39.75	13.92	...	...	...	46.83	14.18	...	...	...
Total Current Disbursements and Net Saving	197.33	102.44	...	...	...	227.71	113.28	...	...	...

	1974					1975				
	Total General Government	Central Government	State or Provincial Government	Local Government	Social Security Funds	Total General Government	Central Government	State or Provincial Government	Local Government	Social Security Funds
Receipts											
1 Property and entrepreneurial income	6.72	3.57	...	...	...	8.65	5.49	...	...	...
2 Taxes, fees and contributions	242.26	118.21	...	...	...	256.73	123.02	...	...	...
a Indirect taxes	106.92	68.25	...	...	...	111.53	69.46	...	...	...
b Direct taxes	75.40	48.07	...	...	...	76.24	51.45	...	...	...
c Social security contributions	58.75	1.18	...	...	...	67.65	1.34	...	...	...
d Fees, fines and penalties	1.19	0.71	...	...	...	1.31	0.77	...	...	...
3 Other current transfers received	13.76	8.20	...	...	...	15.89	9.27	...	...	...
a Casualty insurance claims	0.18	0.12	...	...	...	0.15	0.10	...	...	...
b Transfers from other government subsectors	...	0.51	...	...	...	...	0.47	...	...	...
c Transfers from abroad	0.23	0.19	...	...	...	0.48	0.38	...	...	...
d Other transfers, except imputed	...	...	...	...	...	...	...	...	...	...
e Imputed unfunded employee welfare contributions	13.35	7.38	...	...	...	15.24	8.32	...	...	...
Total Current Receipts	262.75	129.97	...	...	...	281.25	137.78	...	...	...
Disbursements											
1 General government final consumption expenditures	97.43	35.58	...	...	...	113.05	42.20	...	...	...

Austria

3.12 General Government Income and Outlay Account: Total and Subsectors
(Continued)

Thousand Million Austrian schillings

		1974				1975			
	Total General Government	Central Government	State or Provincial Government	Local Government	Social Security Funds	Total General Government	Central Government	State or Provincial Government	Local Government	Social Security Funds
a Compensation of employees	65.13	...	...	...	...	75.55	...	...	...	...
b Consumption of fixed capital	4.50	0.90	...	...	...	4.95	0.99	...	...	...
c Goods and services purchased, net	26.50	...	...	...	...	30.93	...	...	...	...
Purchases	44.33	...	...	...	...	52.57	...	...	...	...
Less: Sales	17.83	...	...	...	...	21.64	...	...	...	...
d Less: Own account production of fixed assets	...	...	...	...	...	1.61	...	...	...	...
e Indirect taxes paid, net	1.32	...	...	...	...	8.56	4.94	...	...	...
2 Property income paid	6.44	3.76	...	...	...	18.98	13.84	...	...	...
3 Subsidies	12.91	11.80	...	...	...	112.42	80.19	...	...	...
4 Other current transfers paid	97.26	66.38	...	...	...	112.42	...	...	...	...
a Casualty insurance premiums, net	0.18	0.12	...	...	...	0.15	0.10	...	...	...
b Transfers to other government subsectors	...	30.40	...	...	...	...	38.00	...	...	...
c Transfers to households	70.44	13.56	...	...	...	80.70	15.55	...	...	...
Social security benefits	49.26	...	...	...	...	56.37	...	...	...	...
Social assistance grants		...	...	...	...		...	...	...	...
Unfunded employee welfare benefits	21.18	13.56	...	...	...	24.33	15.55	...	...	...
d Transfers to private non-profit institutions serving households	25.48	21.95	...	...	...	30.16	26.13	...	...	...
e Transfers to the rest of the world	1.16	0.35	...	...	...	1.41	0.41	...	...	...
Net saving	48.71	12.46	...	...	...	28.22	-3.40	...	...	...
Total Current Disbursements and Net Saving	262.75	129.97	...	...	...	281.25	137.78	...	...	...

		1976				1977			
	Total General Government	Central Government	State or Provincial Government	Local Government	Social Security Funds	Total General Government	Central Government	State or Provincial Government	Local Government	Social Security Funds

Receipts

1 Property and entrepreneurial income	10.20	7.31	...	...	...	10.25	7.23	...	...	...
2 Taxes, fees and contributions	279.29	135.27	...	...	...	320.61	152.17	...	...	...
a Indirect taxes	119.55	76.39	...	...	...	135.87	85.39	...	...	...
b Direct taxes	82.76	56.49	...	...	...	93.67	63.48	...	...	...
c Social security contributions	75.41	1.51	...	...	...	88.59	1.58	...	...	...
d Fees, fines and penalties	1.57	0.88	...	...	...	2.48	1.72	...	...	...
3 Other current transfers received	17.92	10.39	...	...	...	19.36	11.18	...	...	...
a Casualty insurance claims	0.14	0.09	...	...	...	0.15	0.10	...	...	...
b Transfers from other government subsectors	...	0.49	...	...	...	...	0.56	...	...	...
c Transfers from abroad	0.60	0.48	...	...	...	0.57	0.46	...	...	...
d Other transfers, except imputed	...	...	...	...	...	...	...	...	...	...
e Imputed unfunded employee welfare contributions	17.18	9.33	...	...	...	18.64	10.06	...	...	...
Total Current Receipts	307.41	152.97	...	...	...	348.24	170.60	...	...	...

Disbursements

1 General government final consumption expenditures	127.79	47.31	...	...	...	138.74	50.73	...	...	...
a Compensation of employees	85.18	...	...	...	...	92.28	...	...	...	...
b Consumption of fixed capital	5.32	1.06	...	...	...	5.80	1.76	...	...	...
c Goods and services purchased, net	35.47	...	...	...	...	38.65	...	...	...	...
Purchases	58.31	...	...	...	...	64.96	...	...	...	...
Less: Sales	22.84	...	...	...	...	26.31	...	...	...	...
d Less: Own account production of fixed assets	...	...	...	...	...	...	...	...	...	...
e Indirect taxes paid, net	1.82	...	...	...	...	2.01	...	...	...	...
2 Property income paid	12.17	8.04	...	...	...	14.80	10.20	...	...	...

Austria

3.12 General Government Income and Outlay Account: Total and Subsectors
(Continued)

Thousand Million Austrian schillings

	1976					1977				
	Total General Government	Central Government	State or Provincial Government	Local Government	Social Security Funds	Total General Government	Central Government	State or Provincial Government	Local Government	Social Security Funds
3 Subsidies	20.81	15.00	...	...	...	23.30	16.83	...	...	...
4 Other current transfers paid	130.20	89.17	...	...	...	144.54	98.69	...	...	...
a Casualty insurance premiums, net	0.14	0.09	...	...	...	0.15	0.10	...	...	...
b Transfers to other government subsectors	...	41.79	...	...	...	...	46.03	...	...	...
c Transfers to households	92.34	17.47	...	...	...	101.57	18.92	...	...	...
Social security benefits	64.74	...	...	...	...	71.61	...	...	...	...
Social assistance grants		...	...	...	...		...	...	...	...
Unfunded employee welfare benefits	27.60	17.47	...	...	...	29.96	18.92	...	...	...
d Transfers to private non-profit institutions serving households	35.99	29.32	...	...	...	40.94	32.95	...	...	...
e Transfers to the rest of the world	1.73	0.52	...	...	...	1.88	0.66	...	...	...
Net saving	16.45	-6.58	...	...	...	26.84	-5.82	...	...	...
Total Current Disbursements and Net Saving	307.41	152.97	...	...	...	348.24	170.60	...	...	...

	1978					1979				
	Total General Government	Central Government	State or Provincial Government	Local Government	Social Security Funds	Total General Government	Central Government	State or Provincial Government	Local Government	Social Security Funds

Receipts

1 Property and entrepreneurial income	12.21	8.91	...	...	...	13.23	9.80	...	...	...
2 Taxes, fees and contributions	355.66	168.44	...	...	...	384.24	184.66	...	...	...
a Indirect taxes	139.30	89.76	...	...	...	151.20	99.68	...	...	...
b Direct taxes	110.72	74.99	...	...	...	118.08	80.86	...	...	...
c Social security contributions	103.03	1.91	...	...	...	112.29	2.27	...	...	...
d Fees, fines and penalties	2.61	1.78	...	...	...	2.67	1.85	...	...	...
3 Other current transfers received	21.45	12.10	...	...	...	23.07	12.91	...	...	...
a Casualty insurance claims	0.16	0.11	...	...	...	0.17	0.11	...	...	...
b Transfers from other government subsectors	...	0.54	...	...	...	...	0.55	...	...	...
c Transfers from abroad	0.61	0.49	...	...	...	0.58	0.38	...	...	...
d Other transfers, except imputed	...	...	...	...	...	...	...	...	...	...
e Imputed unfunded employee welfare contributions	20.68	10.96	...	...	...	22.32	11.87	...	...	...
Total Current Receipts	389.32	189.44	...	...	...	420.54	207.36	...	...	...

Disbursements

1 General government final consumption expenditures	154.18	55.98	...	...	...	165.89	59.37	...	...	...
a Compensation of employees	103.38	...	...	...	...	111.26	...	...	...	...
b Consumption of fixed capital	6.30	1.26	...	...	...	6.70	1.34	...	...	...
c Goods and services purchased, net	42.48	...	...	...	...	45.83	...	...	...	...
Purchases	71.77	...	...	...	...	77.47	...	...	...	...
Less: Sales	29.29	...	...	...	...	31.64	...	...	...	...
d Less: Own account production of fixed assets	...	...	...	...	...	...	...	...	...	...
e Indirect taxes paid, net	2.02	...	...	...	...	2.11	...	...	...	...
2 Property income paid	18.68	13.32	...	...	...	21.31	15.42	...	...	...

Austria

3.12 General Government Income and Outlay Account: Total and Subsectors
(Continued)

Thousand Million Austrian schillings

	1978					1979				
	Total General Government	Central Government	State or Provincial Government	Local Government	Social Security Funds	Total General Government	Central Government	State or Provincial Government	Local Government	Social Security Funds
3 Subsidies	26.55	19.22	...	...	...	26.93	19.99	...	...	...
4 Other current transfers paid	165.55	108.56	...	...	...	181.16	116.30	...	...	...
a Casualty insurance premiums, net	0.16	0.11	...	...	...	0.17	0.11	...	...	...
b Transfers to other government subsectors	...	44.66	...	...	...	...	47.24	...	...	...
c Transfers to households	112.29	20.94	...	...	...	123.17	22.80	...	...	...
Social security benefits	78.78	...	...	...	...	86.71	...	...	...	...
Social assistance grants		...	...	...	...		...	...	...	...
Unfunded employee welfare benefits	33.51	20.94	...	...	...	36.46	22.80	...	...	...
d Transfers to private non-profit institutions serving households	50.90	42.24	...	...	...	55.44	45.52	...	...	...
e Transfers to the rest of the world	2.20	0.61	...	...	...	2.38	0.63	...	...	...
Net saving	24.35	-7.63	...	...	...	25.25	-3.71	...	...	...
Total Current Disbursements and Net Saving	389.32	189.44	...	...	...	420.54	207.36	...	...	...

	1980				
	Total General Government	Central Government	State or Provincial Government	Local Government	Social Security Funds

Receipts

1 Property and entrepreneurial income	15.52	11.85	...	...	...
2 Taxes, fees and contributions	417.38	194.00	...	...	...
a Indirect taxes	161.76	104.80	...	...	...
b Direct taxes	128.21	84.63	...	...	...
c Social security contributions	124.60	2.64	...	...	...
d Fees, fines and penalties	2.81	1.93	...	...	...
3 Other current transfers received	24.55	13.82	...	...	...
a Casualty insurance claims	0.18	0.12	...	...	...
b Transfers from other government subsectors	...	0.60	...	...	...
c Transfers from abroad	0.60	0.43	...	...	...
d Other transfers, except imputed	...	...	...	...	...
e Imputed unfunded employee welfare contributions	23.77	12.67	...	...	...
Total Current Receipts	457.46	219.69	...	...	...

Disbursements

1 General government final consumption expenditures	177.51	63.04	...	...	...
a Compensation of employees	118.94	...	...	...	...
b Consumption of fixed capital	7.10	...	...	...	...
c Goods and services purchased, net	49.20	...	...	...	...
Purchases	82.72	...	...	...	...
Less: Sales	33.52	...	...	...	...
d Less: Own account production of fixed assets	...	...	...	...	...
e Indirect taxes paid, net	2.26	...	...	...	...
2 Property income paid	24.30	17.60	...	...	...

Austria

3.12 General Government Income and Outlay Account: Total and Subsectors
(Continued)

Thousand Million Austrian schillings

			1980		
	Total General Government	Central Government	State or Provincial Government	Local Government	Social Security Funds
3 Subsidies	27.11	20.08	...	...	...
4 Other current transfers paid	193.53	118.69	...	...	...
a Casualty insurance premiums, net	0.18	0.12	...	...	...
b Transfers to other government subsectors	...	47.75	...	...	...
c Transfers to households	134.00	24.53	...	...	...
Social security benefits	94.80	...	...	...	...
Social assistance grants		...	...	...	...
Unfunded employee welfare benefits	39.20	24.53	...	...	...
d Transfers to private non-profit institutions serving households	56.75	45.64	...	...	...
e Transfers to the rest of the world	2.60	0.65	...	...	...
Net saving	35.00	0.27	...	...	...
Total Current Disbursements and Net Saving	457.46	219.69	...	...	...

3.13 General Government Capital Accumulation Account: Total and Subsectors

Thousand Million Austrian schillings

	1970					1971				
	Total General Government	Central Government	State or Provincial Government	Local Government	Social Security Funds	Total General Government	Central Government	State or Provincial Government	Local Government	Social Security Funds
	Finance of Gross Accumulation									
1 Gross saving	27.57	9.19	...	...	...	33.00	11.61	...	...	...
a Consumption of fixed capital	2.60	0.52	...	...	...	3.02	0.60	...	...	...
b Net saving	24.97	8.67	...	...	...	29.98	11.01	...	...	...
2 Capital transfers received	-3.72	-3.09	...	...	...	-4.01	-3.24	...	...	...
a From other government subsectors	...	-0.78	...	...	...	...	-0.82	...	...	...
b From other resident sectors	-3.72	-2.31	...	...	...	-4.01	-2.42	...	...	...
c From rest of the world	...	...	...	...	...	...	...	...	...	...
Finance of Gross Accumulation	23.84	6.10	...	...	...	28.99	8.38	...	...	...
	Gross Accumulation									
1 Gross capital formation	17.53	5.35	...	...	...	21.00	6.46	...	...	...
2 Purchases of land, net	1.82	0.60	...	...	...	1.70	0.58	...	...	...
3 Purchases of intangible assets, net	...	...	...	...	...	...	...	...	...	...
4 Capital transfers paid	...	...	...	...	...	...	...	...	...	...
Net lending	4.49	0.15	...	...	...	6.29	1.34	...	...	...
Gross Accumulation	23.84	6.10	...	...	...	28.99	8.38	...	...	...

	1972					1973				
	Total General Government	Central Government	State or Provincial Government	Local Government	Social Security Funds	Total General Government	Central Government	State or Provincial Government	Local Government	Social Security Funds
	Finance of Gross Accumulation									
1 Gross saving	43.14	14.60	...	...	...	50.62	14.94	...	...	...
a Consumption of fixed capital	3.39	0.68	...	...	...	3.79	0.76	...	...	...
b Net saving	39.75	13.92	...	...	...	46.83	14.18	...	...	...
2 Capital transfers received	-6.38	-5.69	...	...	...	-14.84	-14.25	...	...	...
a From other government subsectors	...	-1.36	...	...	...	...	-1.86	...	...	...
b From other resident sectors	-6.38	-4.33	...	...	...	-14.84	-12.38	...	...	...
c From rest of the world	...	...	...	...	...	...	-0.01	...	...	...
Finance of Gross Accumulation	36.76	8.91	...	...	...	35.77	0.68	...	...	...
	Gross Accumulation									
1 Gross capital formation	25.14	7.28	...	...	...	26.56	7.42	...	...	...
2 Purchases of land, net	1.89	0.67	...	...	...	2.30	0.89	...	...	...
3 Purchases of intangible assets, net	...	...	...	...	...	...	...	...	...	...
4 Capital transfers paid	...	...	...	...	...	...	...	...	...	...
Net lending	9.73	0.96	...	...	...	6.91	-7.63	...	...	...
Gross Accumulation	36.76	8.91	...	...	...	35.77	0.68	...	...	...

Austria

3.13 General Government Capital Accumulation Account: Total and Subsectors

Thousand Million Austrian schillings

	1974 Total General Government	1974 Central Government	1974 State or Provincial Government	1974 Local Government	1974 Social Security Funds	1975 Total General Government	1975 Central Government	1975 State or Provincial Government	1975 Local Government	1975 Social Security Funds
Finance of Gross Accumulation										
1 Gross saving	53.21	13.36	...	...	...	33.17	-2.41	...	...	...
a Consumption of fixed capital	4.50	0.90	...	...	...	4.95	0.99	...	...	...
b Net saving	48.71	12.46	...	...	...	28.22	-3.40	...	...	...
2 Capital transfers received	-11.18	-10.65	...	...	...	-12.67	-11.74	...	...	...
a From other government subsectors	...	-2.24	...	...	...	...	-2.40	...	...	...
b From other resident sectors	-11.12	-8.35	...	...	...	-12.63	-9.30	...	...	...
c From rest of the world	-0.06	-0.06	...	...	...	-0.04	-0.04	...	...	...
Finance of Gross Accumulation	42.03	2.71	...	...	...	20.50	-14.15	...	...	...
Gross Accumulation										
1 Gross capital formation	31.54	9.00	...	...	...	34.23	9.41	...	...	...
2 Purchases of land, net	2.68	0.98	...	...	...	2.51	1.15	...	...	...
3 Purchases of intangible assets, net	...	...	...	...	...	...	...	...	...	...
4 Capital transfers paid	...	...	...	...	...	...	...	...	...	...
Net lending	7.81	-7.27	...	...	...	-16.24	-24.70	...	...	...
Gross Accumulation	42.03	2.71	...	...	...	20.50	-14.15	...	...	...

	1976 Total General Government	1976 Central Government	1976 State or Provincial Government	1976 Local Government	1976 Social Security Funds	1977 Total General Government	1977 Central Government	1977 State or Provincial Government	1977 Local Government	1977 Social Security Funds
Finance of Gross Accumulation										
1 Gross saving	21.77	-5.52	...	...	...	32.64	-4.66	...	...	...
a Consumption of fixed capital	5.32	1.06	...	...	...	5.80	1.16	...	...	...
b Net saving	16.45	-6.58	...	...	...	26.84	-5.82	...	...	...
2 Capital transfers received	-12.38	-11.79	...	...	...	-11.71	-10.67	...	...	...
a From other government subsectors	...	-2.71	...	...	...	...	-2.21	...	...	...
b From other resident sectors	-12.31	-9.01	...	...	...	-11.58	-8.33	...	...	...
c From rest of the world	-0.07	-0.07	...	...	...	-0.13	-0.13	...	...	...
Finance of Gross Accumulation	9.39	-17.31	...	...	...	20.93	-15.34	...	...	...
Gross Accumulation										
1 Gross capital formation	33.72	8.97	...	...	...	36.78	9.27	...	...	...
2 Purchases of land, net	2.80	1.15	...	...	...	2.90	1.05	...	...	...
3 Purchases of intangible assets, net	...	...	...	...	...	...	...	...	...	...
4 Capital transfers paid	...	...	...	...	...	-18.75	-25.66	...	...	...
Net lending	-27.14	-27.44	...	...	...	-18.75	-25.66	...	...	...
Gross Accumulation	9.39	-17.31	...	...	...	20.93	-15.34	...	...	...

	1978 Total General Government	1978 Central Government	1978 State or Provincial Government	1978 Local Government	1978 Social Security Funds	1979 Total General Government	1979 Central Government	1979 State or Provincial Government	1979 Local Government	1979 Social Security Funds
Finance of Gross Accumulation										
1 Gross saving	30.65	-6.37	...	...	...	31.95	-2.37	...	...	...
a Consumption of fixed capital	6.30	1.26	...	...	...	6.70	1.34	...	...	...
b Net saving	24.35	-7.63	...	...	...	25.25	-3.71	...	...	...
2 Capital transfers received	-12.06	-10.90	...	...	...	-11.74	-10.13	...	...	...
a From other government subsectors	...	-2.14	...	...	...	...	-2.19	...	...	...
b From other resident sectors	-12.00	-8.70	...	...	...	-11.64	-7.85	...	...	...
c From rest of the world	-0.06	-0.06	...	...	...	-0.10	-0.09	...	...	...
Finance of Gross Accumulation	18.59	-17.27	...	...	...	20.22	-12.51	...	...	...
Gross Accumulation										
1 Gross capital formation	38.80	10.14	...	...	...	40.25	11.75	...	...	...
2 Purchases of land, net	2.93	0.87	...	...	...	3.13	1.02	...	...	...
3 Purchases of intangible assets, net	...	...	...	...	...	...	...	...	...	...
4 Capital transfers paid	...	...	...	...	...	...	...	...	...	...
Net lending	-23.14	-28.29	...	...	...	-23.16	-25.28	...	...	...
Gross Accumulation	18.59	-17.27	...	...	...	20.22	-12.51	...	...	...

Austria

3.13 General Government Capital Accumulation Account: Total and Subsectors

Thousand Million Austrian schillings

	1980				
	Total General Government	Central Government	State or Provincial Government	Local Government	Social Security Funds
Finance of Gross Accumulation					
1 Gross saving	42.10	1.69	...	...	...
a Consumption of fixed capital	7.10	1.42	...	...	...
b Net saving	35.00	0.27	...	...	...
2 Capital transfers received	-14.59	-12.24	...	...	...
a From other government subsectors	...	-1.83	...	...	...
b From other resident sectors	-14.54	-10.36	...	...	...
c From rest of the world	-0.05	-0.05	...	...	...
Finance of Gross Accumulation	27.50	-10.55	...	...	...
Gross Accumulation					
1 Gross capital formation	42.70	13.00	...	...	...
2 Purchases of land, net	3.30	1.21	...	...	...
3 Purchases of intangible assets, net	...	...	...	...	...
4 Capital transfers paid	...	...	...	...	...
Net lending	-18.49	-24.76	...	...	...
Gross Accumulation	27.50	-10.55	...	...	...

4.3 Derivation of Value Added by Kind of Activity, ISIC Divisions, in Current Prices

Thousand Million Austrian schillings

	1970			1971			1972			1973		
	Gross Output	Intermediate Consumption	Value Added	Gross Output	Intermediate Consumption	Value Added	Gross Output	Intermediate Consumption	Value Added	Gross Output	Intermediate Consumption	Value Added
All Producers												
1 Agriculture, hunting, forestry and fishing	36.48	10.70	25.78	36.73	11.59	25.14	40.90	12.67	28.23	44.81	13.45	31.37
2 Mining and quarrying	4.63	1.88	2.75	4.96	2.18	2.77	5.06	2.19	2.87	5.35	2.36	2.99
3 Manufacturing	313.30	186.61	126.70	347.53	206.65	140.88	388.61	230.36	158.25	418.41	251.73	166.69
a Manufacture of food, beverages and tobacco	61.29	39.97	21.33	66.83	42.25	24.58	72.96	46.27	26.69	79.11	52.68	26.43
b Textile, wearing apparel and leather industries	36.96	22.20	14.75	39.34	23.09	16.25	43.77	25.25	18.52	45.72	27.51	18.21
c Manufacture of wood and wood products, including furniture	23.70	14.29	9.41	26.55	15.79	10.77	30.46	17.71	12.75	34.19	21.02	13.17
d Manufacture of paper and paper products, printing and publishing	18.83	10.70	8.12	20.79	12.25	8.55	22.21	12.73	9.48	24.75	13.87	10.88
e Manufacture of chemicals and chemical petroleum, coal, rubber and plastic products	40.91	24.26	16.65	46.14	27.34	18.80	52.50	30.77	21.73	56.25	33.42	22.83
f Manufacture of non-metallic mineral products, except products of petroleum and coal	15.82	7.40	8.41	18.47	9.01	9.46	21.68	10.19	11.49	21.29	10.62	10.67
g Basic metal industries	30.99	19.35	11.64	31.34	19.41	11.92	32.58	19.47	13.11	37.34	23.33	14.01
h Manufacture of fabricated metal products, machinery and equipment	84.80	48.44	36.37	98.07	57.52	40.55	112.45	67.96	44.49	119.76	69.28	50.48
i Other manufacturing industries	...	...	...	...	...	...	...	...	...	...	...	...
4 Electricity, gas and water	14.64	4.25	10.39	15.16	4.91	10.25	17.85	5.69	12.15	20.97	6.88	14.08
a Electricity, gas and steam	13.93	3.99	9.95	14.40	4.61	9.79	17.01	5.38	11.63	19.96	6.59	13.37
b Water works and supply	0.71	0.26	0.45	0.76	0.30	0.47	0.84	0.32	0.52	1.01	0.30	0.71
5 Construction	54.27	23.62	30.65	64.44	27.54	36.89	79.21	33.28	45.93	82.99	35.39	47.60
6 Wholesale and retail trade, restaurants and hotels	99.13	31.06	68.07	112.22	33.87	78.34	127.35	37.59	89.77	123.53	39.21	84.32
a Wholesale and retail trade	73.37	16.30	57.07	82.76	18.20	64.56	94.36	21.30	73.06	90.47	22.46	68.01
b Restaurants and hotels	25.76	14.76	11.00	29.46	15.67	13.78	32.99	16.28	16.71	33.06	16.75	16.31
7 Transport, storage and communication	35.41	13.10	22.31	37.87	13.72	24.15	43.50	15.78	27.72	46.68	17.29	29.40
a Transport and storage	27.71	11.99	15.72	29.42	12.70	16.72	34.29	14.58	19.71	36.45	16.01	20.45
b Communication	7.70	1.11	6.59	8.45	1.02	7.43	9.21	1.20	8.01	10.23	1.28	8.95
8 Finance, insurance, real estate and business services	46.10	14.52	31.58	53.75	16.61	37.15	61.61	19.11	42.49	70.87	21.63	49.24
a Financial institutions	13.92	2.10	11.82	16.06	2.57	13.49	18.00	3.19	14.81	22.33	3.99	18.34

Austria

4.3 Derivation of Value Added by Kind of Activity, ISIC Divisions, in Current Prices
(Continued)

Thousand Million Austrian schillings

	1970 Gross Output	1970 Intermediate Consumption	1970 Value Added	1971 Gross Output	1971 Intermediate Consumption	1971 Value Added	1972 Gross Output	1972 Intermediate Consumption	1972 Value Added	1973 Gross Output	1973 Intermediate Consumption	1973 Value Added
b Insurance	5.37	1.66	3.71	6.75	1.97	4.78	7.91	2.06	5.85	9.30	2.37	6.93
c Real estate and business services	26.81	10.76	16.05	30.94	12.07	18.88	35.70	13.86	21.83	39.24	15.27	23.97
Real estate, except dwellings	16.79	7.83	8.95	19.66	8.81	10.86	23.12	10.23	12.89	25.86	11.29	14.57
Dwellings												
9 Community, social and personal services	17.54	5.98	11.56	18.87	6.28	12.59	20.40	6.72	13.69	21.59	7.07	14.52
Total, Industries	621.50	291.70	329.80	691.52	323.35	368.17	784.49	363.39	421.10	835.20	394.99	440.21
Producers of Government Services	65.77	24.17	41.60	73.89	27.17	46.72	83.67	31.20	52.48	97.27	36.12	61.15
Other Producers	3.31	0.32	2.99	3.59	0.39	3.21	3.98	0.42	3.55	4.34	0.48	3.86
Total a	690.58	316.19	374.39	769.00	350.91	418.09	872.14	395.01	477.13	936.81	431.59	505.22
Imputed bank service charge	...	11.74	-11.74	...	13.70	-13.70	...	15.24	-15.24	...	18.89	-18.89
Import duties	13.23	...	13.23	15.23	...	15.23	17.65	...	17.65	7.59	...	7.59
Value added tax	...	...	...	...	...	...	...	...	...	49.54	...	49.54
Total	703.81	327.93	375.88	784.23	364.61	419.62	889.79	410.25	479.54	993.94	450.48	543.46

	1974 Gross Output	1974 Intermediate Consumption	1974 Value Added	1975 Gross Output	1975 Intermediate Consumption	1975 Value Added	1976 Gross Output	1976 Intermediate Consumption	1976 Value Added	1977 Gross Output	1977 Intermediate Consumption	1977 Value Added
All Producers												
1 Agriculture, hunting, forestry and fishing	47.72	14.64	33.08	47.99	14.92	33.07	53.54	17.09	36.45	54.24	18.19	36.05
2 Mining and quarrying	7.07	3.39	3.68	7.77	3.74	4.02	7.83	3.86	3.98	7.94	3.87	4.07
3 Manufacturing	510.98	320.40	190.57	512.17	324.45	187.72	563.21	354.50	208.72	601.75	378.73	223.02
a Manufacture of food, beverages and tobacco	85.65	59.20	26.46	91.38	62.85	28.52	103.59	70.30	33.30	109.15	73.43	35.72
b Textile, wearing apparel and leather industries	48.54	30.22	18.32	46.47	28.84	17.63	49.59	29.83	19.76	52.57	32.07	20.49
c Manufacture of wood and wood products, including furniture	39.41	24.37	15.04	36.24	21.30	14.94	40.67	24.89	15.78	45.26	27.94	17.32
d Manufacture of paper and paper products, printing and publishing	32.79	19.00	13.79	31.87	18.88	12.99	34.58	20.33	14.25	35.07	20.54	14.53
e Manufacture of chemicals and chemical petroleum, coal, rubber and plastic products	87.34	57.26	30.08	84.74	56.94	27.80	90.99	61.66	29.33	95.26	64.30	30.96
f Manufacture of non-metallic mineral products, except products of petroleum and coal	25.21	13.74	11.47	25.66	13.88	11.78	27.13	14.73	12.40	29.53	16.30	13.23
g Basic metal industries	49.51	31.45	18.07	44.47	30.20	14.27	49.96	33.85	16.11	50.47	34.38	16.09
h Manufacture of fabricated metal products, machinery and equipment	142.51	85.17	57.34	151.35	91.57	59.78	166.70	98.92	67.77	184.45	109.77	74.68
i Other manufacturing industries	...	...	...	...	...	...	...	...	...	...	...	...
4 Electricity, gas and water	24.89	8.30	16.58	27.92	9.23	18.68	45.98	23.88	22.09	51.30	25.85	25.45
a Electricity, gas and steam	23.85	7.95	15.90	26.83	8.86	17.97	44.13	23.10	21.03	49.43	25.16	24.27
b Water works and supply	1.03	0.35	0.68	1.09	0.38	0.71	1.84	0.78	1.07	1.87	0.69	1.18
5 Construction	96.65	42.34	54.31	101.99	44.03	57.96	105.75	46.57	59.18	117.30	50.98	66.31
6 Wholesale and retail trade, restaurants and hotels	145.92	46.87	99.04	161.57	51.76	109.81	181.23	59.29	121.94	197.90	64.08	133.83
a Wholesale and retail trade	108.69	27.93	80.76	119.54	30.40	89.14	135.99	35.86	100.13	148.55	38.92	109.63
b Restaurants and hotels	37.23	18.95	18.28	42.03	21.36	20.67	45.25	23.43	21.82	49.36	25.16	24.20
7 Transport, storage and communication	53.78	21.46	32.31	57.84	22.67	35.17	77.35	36.67	40.68	87.41	41.88	45.53
a Transport and storage	42.70	19.74	22.95	44.55	20.64	23.91	61.26	34.41	26.85	68.76	39.37	29.39
b Communication	11.08	1.72	9.36	13.29	2.03	11.26	16.09	2.26	13.83	18.65	2.51	16.14
8 Finance, insurance, real estate and business services	82.61	24.83	57.78	94.25	27.57	66.68	106.44	31.38	75.06	125.45	35.11	90.34
a Financial institutions	27.67	4.86	22.81	31.18	5.47	25.71	32.64	6.01	26.63	38.76	6.73	32.03
b Insurance	9.97	2.62	7.35	10.81	2.84	7.97	12.80	3.28	9.52	16.37	3.69	12.68
c Real estate and business services	44.97	17.35	27.62	52.26	19.26	33.00	61.00	22.09	38.91	70.32	24.69	45.63
Real estate, except dwellings	29.94	12.85	17.09	35.23	14.19	21.04	42.28	16.52	25.76	48.51	18.14	30.37
Dwellings												
9 Community, social and personal services	25.30	8.16	17.14	28.74	9.22	19.52	32.34	10.34	21.99	36.56	11.80	24.76

Austria

4.3 Derivation of Value Added by Kind of Activity, ISIC Divisions, in Current Prices
(Continued)

Thousand Million Austrian schillings

	1974 Gross Output	1974 Intermediate Consumption	1974 Value Added	1975 Gross Output	1975 Intermediate Consumption	1975 Value Added	1976 Gross Output	1976 Intermediate Consumption	1976 Value Added	1977 Gross Output	1977 Intermediate Consumption	1977 Value Added
Total, Industries	994.91	490.40	504.51	1040.23	507.60	532.63	1173.67	583.58	590.09	1279.84	630.47	649.37
Producers of Government Services	115.27	44.33	70.94	134.69	52.57	82.12	150.63	58.31	92.32	165.05	64.96	100.09
Other Producers	4.86	0.59	4.27	5.50	0.69	4.81	6.18	0.76	5.42	6.61	0.84	5.77
Total a	1115.04	535.32	579.72	1180.42	560.86	619.56	1330.48	642.65	687.83	1451.50	696.27	755.23
Imputed bank service charge	...	23.32	-23.32	...	26.49	-26.49	...	28.02	-28.02	...	33.68	-33.68
Import duties	7.75	...	7.75	7.27	...	7.27	6.12	...	6.12	5.78	...	5.78
Value added tax	54.43	...	54.43	56.38	...	56.38	58.82	...	58.82	68.86	...	68.86
Total	1177.22	558.64	618.58	1244.07	587.35	656.72	1395.42	670.67	724.75	1526.14	729.95	796.19

	1978 Gross Output	1978 Intermediate Consumption	1978 Value Added	1979 Gross Output	1979 Intermediate Consumption	1979 Value Added	1980 Gross Output	1980 Intermediate Consumption	1980 Value Added
				All Producers					
1 Agriculture, hunting, forestry and fishing	57.76	18.43	39.33	59.72	19.46	40.26	65.50	21.85	43.65
2 Mining and quarrying	8.19	4.09	4.10	9.50	4.71	4.78	9.80	5.02	4.78
3 Manufacturing	627.88	395.09	232.79	706.36	444.04	262.32	789.51	510.23	279.28
a Manufacture of food, beverages and tobacco	116.10	79.42	36.69	125.25	86.01	39.24	135.81	95.34	40.47
b Textile, wearing apparel and leather industries	51.35	31.17	20.18	55.26	33.05	22.21	60.87	37.26	23.62
c Manufacture of wood and wood products, including furniture	45.90	28.33	17.57	51.56	32.40	19.16	58.44	37.58	20.86
d Manufacture of paper and paper products, printing and publishing	36.71	21.26	15.45	42.31	24.34	17.97	48.06	29.08	18.98
e Manufacture of chemicals and chemical petroleum, coal, rubber and plastic products	100.96	68.21	32.75	118.14	82.90	35.24	141.68	102.33	39.35
f Manufacture of non-metallic mineral products, except products of petroleum and coal	30.32	16.67	13.66	33.00	17.86	15.13	37.37	20.96	16.40
g Basic metal industries	53.32	36.54	16.78	61.90	40.82	21.08	60.64	41.96	18.67
h Manufacture of fabricated metal products, machinery and equipment	193.22	113.51	79.71	218.94	126.65	92.29	246.64	145.72	100.92
i Other manufacturing industries	...	...	...	...	...	...	...	...	...
4 Electricity, gas and water	55.24	29.21	26.02	59.14	30.99	28.15	68.16	36.74	31.41
a Electricity, gas and steam	53.25	28.51	24.74	57.04	30.25	26.79	65.85	35.93	29.93
b Water works and supply	1.99	0.71	1.29	2.10	0.74	1.36	2.30	0.82	1.49
5 Construction	122.96	52.95	70.00	133.10	56.59	76.52	142.30	60.59	81.71
6 Wholesale and retail trade, restaurants and hotels	202.91	66.87	136.03	224.93	72.78	152.15	246.93	80.43	166.50
a Wholesale and retail trade	149.93	40.34	109.58	166.93	44.35	122.59	182.96	49.65	133.31
b Restaurants and hotels	52.98	26.53	26.45	57.99	28.43	29.56	63.97	30.79	33.19
7 Transport, storage and communication	92.67	43.87	48.80	102.97	49.44	53.53	114.35	56.27	58.08
a Transport and storage	72.36	41.29	31.07	80.60	46.84	33.76	90.04	53.40	36.64
b Communication	20.31	2.58	17.73	22.37	2.60	19.77	24.31	2.87	21.44
8 Finance, insurance, real estate and business services	135.68	38.39	97.29	148.70	42.24	106.46	165.52	47.53	117.98
a Financial institutions	43.09	7.68	35.41	46.96	8.23	38.73	52.34	8.74	43.60
b Insurance	15.81	4.06	11.75	16.06	4.11	11.95	17.08	4.40	12.68
c Real estate and business services	76.78	26.65	50.13	85.68	29.90	55.78	96.10	34.39	61.70
Real estate, except dwellings	52.83	19.45	33.38	58.10	21.59	36.52	65.09	24.27	40.83
Dwellings									
9 Community, social and personal services	40.08	12.92	27.16	43.69	14.17	29.52	48.17	15.64	32.53

Austria

4.3 Derivation of Value Added by Kind of Activity, ISIC Divisions, in Current Prices
(Continued)

Thousand Million Austrian schillings

	1978 Gross Output	1978 Intermediate Consumption	1978 Value Added	1979 Gross Output	1979 Intermediate Consumption	1979 Value Added	1980 Gross Output	1980 Intermediate Consumption	1980 Value Added
Total, Industries	1343.36	661.83	681.53	1488.11	734.41	753.70	1650.23	834.31	815.92
Producers of Government Services	183.47	71.78	111.69	197.54	77.47	120.07	211.03	82.72	128.31
Other Producers	7.30	0.94	6.37	7.81	1.02	6.79	8.31	1.09	7.22
Total a	1534.13	734.54	799.59	1693.46	812.90	880.56	1869.57	918.12	951.45
Imputed bank service charge		37.25	-37.25		41.01	-41.01		45.33	-45.33
Import duties	4.83	...	4.83	5.57	...	5.57	5.72	...	5.72
Value added tax	75.52	...	75.52	77.87	...	77.87	84.09	...	84.09
Total	1614.48	771.80	842.69	1776.90	853.91	922.99	1959.38	963.45	995.93

a) Beginning 1975, estimates not yet revised, therefore not strictly comparable with those of other tables.

4.4 Derivation of Value Added by Kind of Activity, ISIC Divisions, in Constant Prices

Thousand Million Austrian schillings

At constant prices of: 1976

All Producers

	1970 Gross Output	1970 Intermediate Consumption	1970 Value Added	1971 Gross Output	1971 Intermediate Consumption	1971 Value Added	1972 Gross Output	1972 Intermediate Consumption	1972 Value Added	1973 Gross Output	1973 Intermediate Consumption	1973 Value Added
1 Agriculture, hunting, forestry and fishing	49.86	17.24	32.62	47.58	17.44	30.14	48.29	17.93	30.36	50.00	17.71	32.29
2 Mining and quarrying	7.95	3.96	3.99	8.17	4.06	4.11	7.68	3.83	3.85	8.14	4.02	4.12
3 Manufacturing	452.97	284.44	168.53	479.73	301.37	178.37	516.76	324.82	191.94	541.94	340.07	201.87
a Manufacture of food, beverages and tobacco	83.84	57.33	26.51	88.38	59.93	28.45	91.30	62.25	29.05	98.44	66.22	32.22
b Textile, wearing apparel and leather industries	47.20	28.27	18.93	48.54	29.17	19.37	52.24	31.44	20.80	53.43	32.16	21.27
c Manufacture of wood and wood products, including furniture	29.93	18.11	11.82	32.02	19.48	12.54	35.30	21.60	13.70	35.74	22.04	13.70
d Manufacture of paper and paper products, printing and publishing	28.42	16.75	11.67	29.67	17.46	12.21	31.71	18.80	12.91	33.65	19.66	13.99
e Manufacture of chemicals and chemical petroleum, coal, rubber and plastic products	67.88	45.17	22.71	74.78	50.37	24.41	81.24	54.92	26.32	87.78	59.19	28.59
f Manufacture of non-metallic mineral products, except products of petroleum and coal	22.25	12.39	9.86	24.92	13.84	11.08	26.90	14.89	12.01	26.71	14.76	11.95
g Basic metal industries	44.65	29.70	14.95	44.48	29.59	14.89	46.19	30.72	15.47	47.61	31.70	15.91
h Manufacture of fabricated metal products, machinery and equipment	128.80	76.72	52.08	136.94	81.53	55.41	151.88	90.20	61.68	158.58	94.34	64.24
i Other manufacturing industries	...	...	...	...	...	...	...	...	...	...	...	...
4 Electricity, gas and water	22.81	6.78	16.03	23.41	7.57	15.84	25.41	8.19	17.22	28.72	9.81	18.91
a Electricity, gas and steam	21.49	6.33	15.16	22.02	7.10	14.92	24.06	7.73	16.33	27.28	9.33	17.95
b Water works and supply	1.32	0.45	0.87	1.39	0.47	0.92	1.35	0.46	0.89	1.44	0.48	0.96
5 Construction	78.68	32.58	46.10	87.90	36.40	51.50	94.98	40.08	54.90	100.62	42.76	57.86
6 Wholesale and retail trade, restaurants and hotels	136.75	44.00	92.75	144.48	46.44	98.04	154.93	49.86	105.07	161.01	51.03	109.98
a Wholesale and retail trade	96.88	23.28	73.60	102.82	24.91	77.91	112.07	27.75	84.32	118.77	29.23	89.54
b Restaurants and hotels	39.87	20.72	19.15	41.66	21.53	20.13	42.86	22.11	20.75	42.24	21.80	20.44
7 Transport, storage and communication	45.51	17.65	27.86	47.73	18.32	29.41	51.33	19.69	31.64	56.59	21.97	34.62
a Transport and storage	35.41	16.34	19.07	36.78	16.90	19.88	39.32	18.14	21.18	43.21	20.28	22.93
b Communication	10.10	1.31	8.79	10.95	1.42	9.53	12.01	1.55	10.46	13.38	1.69	11.69
8 Finance, insurance, real estate and business services	75.52	22.34	53.18	80.71	23.65	57.06	85.60	25.30	60.30	90.60	26.16	64.44
a Financial institutions	20.40	3.75	16.65	22.79	4.20	18.58	24.48	4.51	19.97	26.51	4.89	21.62
b Insurance	9.49	2.44	7.05	10.23	2.62	7.61	10.84	2.78	8.06	11.34	2.91	8.43
c Real estate and business services	45.63	16.15	29.48	47.69	16.83	30.86	50.28	18.01	32.27	52.75	18.36	34.39
Real estate, except dwellings	29.29	11.33	17.96	31.01	11.90	19.11	33.24	12.96	20.28	35.20	13.17	22.03
Dwellings												
9 Community, social and personal services	27.75	9.14	18.61	28.45	9.39	19.06	28.78	9.48	19.30	29.37	9.48	19.89

Austria

4.4 Derivation of Value Added by Kind of Activity, ISIC Divisions, in Constant Prices
(Continued)

Thousand Million Austrian schillings

	1970 Gross Output	1970 Intermediate Consumption	1970 Value Added	1971 Gross Output	1971 Intermediate Consumption	1971 Value Added	1972 Gross Output	1972 Intermediate Consumption	1972 Value Added	1973 Gross Output	1973 Intermediate Consumption	1973 Value Added
				At constant prices of:1976								
Total, Industries	897.80	438.13	459.67	948.16	464.64	483.53	1013.76	499.18	514.58	1066.99	523.01	543.98
Producers of Government Services	118.70	43.28	75.42	122.62	44.33	78.29	127.59	46.81	80.78	131.50	49.42	82.08
Other Producers	5.90	0.70	5.20	5.91	0.72	5.19	5.91	0.72	5.19	5.95	0.73	5.22
Total	1022.40	482.11	540.29	1076.69	509.69	567.01	1147.26	546.71	600.55	1204.44	573.16	631.28
Imputed bank service charge	...	...	...	...	...	...	...	...	...	...	...	...
Import duties	...	...	...	...	...	...	...	...	...	...	...	...
Value added tax	...	...	...	...	...	...	...	...	...	...	...	...
Total	...	...	...	...	...	...	...	...	...	...	...	...

	1974 Gross Output	1974 Intermediate Consumption	1974 Value Added	1975 Gross Output	1975 Intermediate Consumption	1975 Value Added	1976 Gross Output	1976 Intermediate Consumption	1976 Value Added	1977 Gross Output	1977 Intermediate Consumption	1977 Value Added
				At constant prices of:1976								
				All Producers								
1 Agriculture, hunting, forestry and fishing	50.61	17.01	33.60	51.01	15.80	35.21	53.54	17.09	36.45	52.48	17.38	35.10
2 Mining and quarrying	8.71	4.35	4.36	8.01	3.98	4.03	7.84	3.86	3.98	7.09	3.53	3.56
3 Manufacturing	559.65	350.85	208.80	528.82	332.46	196.36	563.22	354.52	208.70	589.52	369.50	220.02
a Manufacture of food, beverages and tobacco	98.27	66.46	31.81	98.10	66.51	31.59	103.60	70.30	33.30	107.71	72.96	34.75
b Textile, wearing apparel and leather industries	52.19	31.43	20.76	47.80	28.70	19.10	49.59	29.83	19.76	49.87	29.98	19.89
c Manufacture of wood and wood products, including furniture	36.88	22.63	14.25	35.41	21.52	13.89	40.67	24.89	15.78	43.80	26.73	17.07
d Manufacture of paper and paper products, printing and publishing	35.43	20.80	14.63	32.26	18.94	13.32	34.58	20.33	14.25	35.39	20.78	14.61
e Manufacture of chemicals and chemical petroleum, coal, rubber and plastic products	88.62	59.85	28.77	84.80	57.22	27.58	90.99	61.66	29.33	93.61	63.48	30.13
f Manufacture of non-metallic mineral products, except products of petroleum and coal	28.37	15.48	12.89	26.77	14.62	12.15	27.13	14.73	12.40	27.94	15.10	12.84
g Basic metal industries	51.46	34.25	17.21	44.34	30.11	14.23	49.96	33.85	16.11	47.69	32.19	15.50
h Manufacture of fabricated metal products, machinery and equipment	168.43	99.95	68.48	159.34	94.84	64.50	166.70	98.93	67.77	183.51	108.28	75.23
i Other manufacturing industries	...	...	...	...	...	...	...	...	...	...	...	...
4 Electricity, gas and water	30.41	10.20	20.21	31.08	10.14	20.94	45.98	23.88	22.10	48.06	24.45	23.61
a Electricity, gas and steam	28.99	9.73	19.26	29.66	9.67	19.99	44.14	23.11	21.03	46.22	23.68	22.54
b Water works and supply	1.42	0.47	0.95	1.42	0.47	0.95	1.84	0.77	1.07	1.84	0.77	1.07
5 Construction	104.56	44.73	59.83	102.71	43.68	59.03	101.27	42.09	59.18	104.90	43.49	61.41
6 Wholesale and retail trade, restaurants and hotels	168.38	54.12	114.26	172.35	55.52	116.83	181.23	59.29	121.94	187.92	60.55	127.37
a Wholesale and retail trade	125.17	31.75	93.42	127.40	32.29	95.11	135.98	35.86	100.12	142.92	37.22	105.70
b Restaurants and hotels	43.21	22.37	20.84	44.95	23.23	21.72	45.25	23.43	21.82	45.00	23.33	21.67
7 Transport, storage and communication	61.05	23.39	37.66	61.20	23.87	37.33	77.35	36.67	40.68	81.49	38.97	42.52
a Transport and storage	46.50	21.53	24.97	46.08	21.80	24.28	61.26	34.41	26.85	64.29	36.52	27.77
b Communication	14.55	1.86	12.69	15.12	2.07	13.05	16.09	2.26	13.83	17.20	2.45	14.75
8 Finance, insurance, real estate and business services	95.50	27.64	67.86	99.85	29.06	70.79	106.44	31.38	75.06	115.27	33.92	81.35
a Financial institutions	28.56	5.26	23.30	30.07	5.55	24.52	32.64	6.01	26.63	35.35	6.51	28.84
b Insurance	11.54	2.97	8.57	11.63	2.99	8.64	12.80	3.28	9.52	16.07	4.13	11.94
c Real estate and business services	55.40	19.41	35.99	58.15	20.52	37.63	61.00	22.09	38.91	63.85	23.28	40.57
Real estate, except dwellings	37.28	14.02	23.26	39.52	14.99	24.53	61.00	22.09	38.91	63.85	23.28	40.57
Dwellings												
9 Community, social and personal services	30.99	9.83	21.16	32.49	10.27	22.22	32.34	10.35	21.99	33.67	10.80	22.87

Austria

4.4 Derivation of Value Added by Kind of Activity, ISIC Divisions, in Constant Prices
(Continued)

Thousand Million Austrian schillings

	1974 Gross Output	1974 Intermediate Consumption	1974 Value Added	1975 Gross Output	1975 Intermediate Consumption	1975 Value Added	1976 Gross Output	1976 Intermediate Consumption	1976 Value Added	1977 Gross Output	1977 Intermediate Consumption	1977 Value Added
				At constant prices of: 1976								
Total, Industries	1109.86	542.12	567.74	1087.52	524.78	562.74	1169.21	579.13	590.08	1220.40	602.59	617.81
Producers of Government Services	138.88	53.38	85.50	144.46	56.46	88.00	150.63	58.31	92.32	156.06	60.35	95.71
Other Producers	6.01	0.75	5.26	6.10	0.75	5.35	6.19	0.77	5.42	6.21	0.77	5.44
Total	1254.75	596.25	658.50	1238.08	581.99	656.09	1326.03	638.21	687.82	1382.67	663.71	718.96
Imputed bank service charge	...	...	...	...	...	...	...	...	...	...	...	...
Import duties	...	...	...	...	...	...	...	...	...	...	...	...
Value added tax	...	...	...	...	...	...	...	...	...	...	...	...
Total	...	...	...	...	...	...	...	...	...	...	...	...

	1978 Gross Output	1978 Intermediate Consumption	1978 Value Added	1979 Gross Output	1979 Intermediate Consumption	1979 Value Added	1980 Gross Output	1980 Intermediate Consumption	1980 Value Added
	At constant prices of: 1976								
	All Producers								
1 Agriculture, hunting, forestry and fishing	54.86	17.47	37.39	56.01	17.89	38.12	58.57	18.77	39.80
2 Mining and quarrying	7.02	3.51	3.51	8.05	3.99	4.06	8.19	4.11	4.08
3 Manufacturing	595.32	373.31	222.01	639.28	401.76	237.52	664.72	417.41	247.31
a Manufacture of food, beverages and tobacco	108.44	73.31	35.13	115.26	78.23	37.03	120.45	82.06	38.39
b Textile, wearing apparel and leather industries	47.40	28.50	18.90	50.47	30.37	20.10	52.17	31.34	20.83
c Manufacture of wood and wood products, including furniture	42.15	25.73	16.42	45.35	27.71	17.64	46.58	28.42	18.16
d Manufacture of paper and paper products, printing and publishing	35.61	20.94	14.67	38.81	22.77	16.04	40.37	23.67	16.70
e Manufacture of chemicals and chemical petroleum, coal, rubber and plastic products	99.46	67.49	31.97	105.31	71.63	33.68	107.48	73.34	34.14
f Manufacture of non-metallic mineral products, except products of petroleum and coal	27.66	14.92	12.74	29.74	15.86	13.88	31.34	16.57	14.77
g Basic metal industries	50.10	33.49	16.61	54.62	36.84	17.78	52.55	35.35	17.20
h Manufacture of fabricated metal products, machinery and equipment	184.50	108.93	75.57	199.72	118.35	81.37	213.78	126.66	87.12
i Other manufacturing industries	...	...	...	...	...	...	...	...	...
4 Electricity, gas and water	49.04	25.35	23.69	51.41	25.48	25.93	52.96	26.18	26.78
a Electricity, gas and steam	47.21	24.59	22.62	49.56	24.71	24.85	51.00	25.37	25.63
b Water works and supply	1.83	0.76	1.07	1.85	0.77	1.08	1.96	0.81	1.15
5 Construction	103.53	42.78	60.75	106.38	44.22	62.16	105.10	43.68	61.42
6 Wholesale and retail trade, restaurants and hotels	184.47	61.39	123.08	194.34	64.37	129.97	200.88	66.82	134.06
a Wholesale and retail trade	138.84	37.70	101.14	146.74	39.61	107.13	151.27	40.96	110.31
b Restaurants and hotels	45.63	23.69	21.94	47.60	24.76	22.84	49.61	25.86	23.75
7 Transport, storage and communication	84.41	39.95	44.46	90.33	42.79	47.54	94.69	44.63	50.06
a Transport and storage	65.71	37.41	28.30	70.52	40.21	30.31	73.15	41.82	31.33
b Communication	18.70	2.54	16.16	19.81	2.58	17.23	21.54	2.81	18.73
8 Finance, insurance, real estate and business services	118.94	35.00	83.94	125.35	36.81	88.54	131.32	38.57	92.75
a Financial institutions	38.75	7.14	31.61	43.25	7.96	35.29	46.06	8.48	37.58
b Insurance	14.61	3.75	10.86	14.15	3.63	10.52	14.68	3.77	10.91
c Real estate and business services	65.58	24.11	41.47	67.95	25.22	42.73	70.58	26.32	44.26
Real estate, except dwellings	65.58	24.11	41.47	47.32	19.03	28.29	49.31	19.92	29.39
Dwellings									
9 Community, social and personal services	34.50	11.02	23.48	35.49	11.33	24.16	37.02	11.84	25.18

Austria

4.4 Derivation of Value Added by Kind of Activity, ISIC Divisions, in Constant Prices
(Continued)

Thousand Million Austrian schillings

	1978 Gross Output	1978 Intermediate Consumption	1978 Value Added	1979 Gross Output	1979 Intermediate Consumption	1979 Value Added	1980 Gross Output	1980 Intermediate Consumption	1980 Value Added
				At constant prices of: 1976					
Total, Industries	1232.09	609.78	622.31	1306.64	648.64	658.00	1353.45	672.01	681.44
Producers of Government Services	161.48	62.32	99.16	166.60	64.12	102.48	169.31	64.67	104.64
Other Producers	6.28	0.78	5.50	6.30	0.78	5.52	6.32	0.79	5.53
Total	1399.85	672.88	726.97	1479.54	713.54	766.00	1529.08	737.47	791.61
Imputed bank service charge	...	...	...	...	...	...	...	...	...
Import duties	...	...	...	...	...	...	...	...	...
Value added tax	...	...	...	...	...	...	...	...	...
Total	...	...	...	...	...	...	...	...	...

4.6 Cost Components of Value Added, ISIC Divisions

Thousand Million Austrian schillings

	1970 Compensation of Employees	1970 Capital Consumption	1970 Net Operating Surplus	1970 Indirect Taxes	1970 Less: Subsidies Received	1970 Value Added	1971 Compensation of Employees	1971 Capital Consumption	1971 Net Operating Surplus	1971 Indirect Taxes	1971 Less: Subsidies Received	1971 Value Added
				All Producers								
1 Agriculture, hunting, forestry and fishing	...	6.38	...	0.64	0.23	25.78	...	7.14	...	0.65	0.33	25.14
2 Mining and quarrying	...	0.24	...	0.28	0.08	2.75	...	0.24	...	0.29	0.08	2.77
3 Manufacturing	...	11.16	...	22.57	3.95	126.70	...	12.50	...	25.27	4.10	140.88
4 Electricity, gas and water	...	3.20	...	0.33	0.01	10.39	...	3.45	...	0.35	0.01	10.25
5 Construction	...	1.76	...	3.15	0.18	30.65	...	2.03	...	3.67	0.19	36.89
6 Wholesale and retail trade, restaurants and hotels	...	3.95	...	13.94	0.33	68.07	...	4.38	...	16.08	0.29	78.34
7 Transport, storage and communication	...	3.97	...	2.02	1.15	22.31	...	4.40	...	2.26	2.11	24.15
8 Finance, insurance, real estate and business services	...	9.78	...	3.16	0.22	31.58	...	11.48	...	3.50	0.03	37.15
9 Community, social and personal services	...	0.49	...	1.73	0.33	11.56	...	0.53	...	1.96	0.37	12.59
Total, Industries	...	40.93	...	47.82	6.48	329.79	...	46.15	...	54.03	7.51	368.16
Producers of Government Services	...	2.60	...	0.64	-	41.60	...	3.02	...	0.74	-	46.72
Other Producers	...	0.32	...	0.01	0.04	2.99	...	0.35	...	0.02	0.05	3.21
Total	...	43.85	...	48.47	6.52	374.38	...	49.52	...	54.79	7.56	418.09
Imputed bank service charge	...	...	...	...	...	-11.74	...	...	...	...	...	-13.70
Import duties	...	...	...	13.23	...	13.23	...	...	...	15.23	...	15.23
Value added tax	...	...	...	...	...	...	...	...	...	...	...	...
Other adjustments	...	...	...	...	...	...	...	...	...	...	...	...
Total	...	43.85	...	61.70	6.52	375.87	...	49.52	...	70.02	7.56	419.62

	1972 Compensation of Employees	1972 Capital Consumption	1972 Net Operating Surplus	1972 Indirect Taxes	1972 Less: Subsidies Received	1972 Value Added	1973 Compensation of Employees	1973 Capital Consumption	1973 Net Operating Surplus	1973 Indirect Taxes	1973 Less: Subsidies Received	1973 Value Added
				All Producers								
1 Agriculture, hunting, forestry and fishing	...	7.78	...	0.73	0.37	28.23	...	8.20	...	0.62	0.48	31.37
2 Mining and quarrying	...	0.26	...	0.34	0.08	2.87	...	0.28	...	0.28	0.10	2.99
3 Manufacturing	...	14.30	...	29.91	4.06	158.25	...	15.31	...	20.76	4.57	166.69
4 Electricity, gas and water	...	3.79	...	0.49	0.01	12.15	...	4.05	...	0.41	0.01	14.08
5 Construction	...	2.31	...	4.99	0.22	45.93	...	2.43	...	2.05	0.23	47.60
6 Wholesale and retail trade, restaurants and hotels	...	5.08	...	18.29	0.35	89.77	...	5.38	...	8.71	0.38	84.32
7 Transport, storage and communication	...	5.03	...	2.63	2.32	27.72	...	5.55	...	0.53	2.78	29.40
8 Finance, insurance, real estate and business services	...	13.28	...	4.35	0.02	42.49	...	16.15	...	3.92	0.05	49.24
9 Community, social and personal services	...	0.61	...	2.25	0.42	13.69	...	0.63	...	1.83	0.52	14.52
Total, Industries	...	52.44	...	63.98	7.85	421.10	...	57.98	...	39.11	9.12	440.21
Producers of Government Services	...	3.39	...	0.85	-	52.48	...	4.01	...	0.97	-	61.15
Other Producers	...	0.39	...	0.02	0.06	3.55	...	0.40	...	0.02	0.08	3.86
Total	...	56.22	...	64.85	7.91	477.13	...	62.39	...	40.10	9.20	505.22
Imputed bank service charge	...	...	...	...	...	-15.24	...	...	...	...	...	-18.89
Import duties	...	...	...	17.65	...	17.65	...	...	...	7.59	...	7.59
Value added tax	...	...	...	...	...	...	...	...	...	49.54	...	49.54
Other adjustments	...	...	...	...	...	...	...	...	...	...	...	...
Total	...	56.22	...	82.50	7.91	479.54	...	62.39	...	97.23	9.20	543.46

Austria

4.6 Cost Components of Value Added, ISIC Divisions

Thousand Million Austrian schillings

1974 / 1975

	Compensation of Employees	Capital Consumption	Net Operating Surplus	Indirect Taxes	Less: Subsidies Received	Value Added	Compensation of Employees	Capital Consumption	Net Operating Surplus	Indirect Taxes	Less: Subsidies Received	Value Added
				All Producers								
1 Agriculture, hunting, forestry and fishing	...	9.21	...	0.96	0.63	33.08	...	9.86	...	0.99	0.70	33.07
2 Mining and quarrying	...	0.34	...	0.32	0.19	3.68	...	0.41	...	0.35	0.37	4.02
3 Manufacturing	...	17.55	...	22.41	6.59	190.57	...	18.99	...	22.89	8.21	187.72
4 Electricity, gas and water	...	4.45	...	0.49	0.49	16.58	...	4.78	...	0.57	0.29	18.68
5 Construction	...	2.78	...	2.26	0.32	54.31	...	2.97	...	2.36	0.92	57.96
6 Wholesale and retail trade, restaurants and hotels	...	6.16	...	10.05	0.50	99.04	...	6.77	...	11.01	1.49	109.81
7 Transport, storage and communication	...	6.30	...	0.56	3.56	32.31	...	6.94	...	0.63	5.56	35.17
8 Finance, insurance, real estate and business services	...	18.84	...	4.51	0.07	57.78	...	20.43	...	5.43	0.45	66.68
9 Community, social and personal services	...	0.71	...	2.03	0.56	17.14	...	0.76	...	2.26	0.98	19.52
Total, Industries	...	66.34	...	43.59	12.91	504.49	...	71.91	...	46.49	18.97	532.63
Producers of Government Services	...	4.69	...	1.13	-	70.94	...	5.04	...	1.36	-	82.12
Other Producers	...	0.45	...	0.02	-	4.26	...	0.47	...	0.02	-	4.81
Total	...	71.48	...	44.74	12.91	579.69	...	77.42	...	47.87	18.97	619.56
Imputed bank service charge				...	...	-23.32				...	...	-26.49
Import duties				...	...	7.27				7.27	...	7.27
Value added tax				7.75		7.75				56.38		56.38
Other adjustments				54.43		54.43				...		...
Total	...	71.48	...	106.92	12.91	618.55	...	77.42	...	111.52	18.97	656.72

1976 / 1977

	Compensation of Employees	Capital Consumption	Net Operating Surplus	Indirect Taxes	Less: Subsidies Received	Value Added	Compensation of Employees	Capital Consumption	Net Operating Surplus	Indirect Taxes	Less: Subsidies Received	Value Added
				All Producers								
1 Agriculture, hunting, forestry and fishing	...	10.08	...	1.45	0.90	36.45	...	10.81	...	0.80	0.96	36.05
2 Mining and quarrying	...	0.39	...	0.39	0.32	3.98	...	0.41	...	0.38	0.29	4.07
3 Manufacturing	...	20.26	...	23.57	8.67	208.72	...	22.13	...	27.02	9.61	223.02
4 Electricity, gas and water	...	5.16	...	0.69	0.54	22.09	...	5.97	...	0.84	0.56	25.45
5 Construction	...	3.19	...	2.62	1.04	59.18	...	3.37	...	3.08	1.12	66.31
6 Wholesale and retail trade, restaurants and hotels	...	7.27	...	14.57	1.38	121.94	...	8.10	...	16.39	1.55	133.83
7 Transport, storage and communication	...	7.71	...	0.75	6.42	40.68	...	8.41	...	0.98	7.50	45.53
8 Finance, insurance, real estate and business services	...	21.82	...	6.31	0.46	75.06	...	24.11	...	7.05	0.52	90.34
9 Community, social and personal services	...	0.81	...	2.69	1.08	21.99	...	0.90	...	2.94	1.19	24.76
Total, Industries	...	76.69	...	53.04	20.81	590.09	...	84.21	...	59.48	23.30	649.36
Producers of Government Services	...	5.32	...	1.57	-	92.32	...	5.87	...	1.74	-	100.09
Other Producers	...	0.50	...	0.03	-	5.42	...	0.55	...	0.03	-	5.77
Total	...	82.51	...	54.64	20.81	687.83	...	90.63	...	61.25	23.30	755.22
Imputed bank service charge				...	...	-28.02				...	...	-33.68
Import duties				...	...	...				5.78	...	5.78
Value added tax				6.12		6.12				68.86		68.86
Other adjustments				58.82		58.82				...		...
Total	...	82.51	...	119.58	20.81	724.75	...	90.63	...	135.89	23.30	796.18

1978 / 1979

	Compensation of Employees	Capital Consumption	Net Operating Surplus	Indirect Taxes	Less: Subsidies Received	Value Added	Compensation of Employees	Capital Consumption	Net Operating Surplus	Indirect Taxes	Less: Subsidies Received	Value Added
				All Producers								
1 Agriculture, hunting, forestry and fishing	...	11.29	...	0.65	1.03	39.33	...	11.56	...	0.59	1.23	40.26
2 Mining and quarrying	...	0.41	...	0.34	0.35	4.10	...	0.47	...	0.37	0.34	4.78
3 Manufacturing	...	23.82	...	25.35	11.12	232.79	...	25.39	...	28.16	11.65	262.32
4 Electricity, gas and water	...	6.58	...	0.65	0.63	26.02	...	7.04	...	0.84	0.62	28.15

83

Austria

4.6 Cost Components of Value Added, ISIC Divisions
(Continued)

Thousand Million Austrian schillings

	1978						1979					
	Compensation of Employees	Capital Consumption	Net Operating Surplus	Indirect Taxes	Less: Subsidies Received	Value Added	Compensation of Employees	Capital Consumption	Net Operating Surplus	Indirect Taxes	Less: Subsidies Received	Value Added
5 Construction	...	3.46	...	2.58	1.30	70.00	...	3.55	...	3.11	1.32	76.52
6 Wholesale and retail trade, restaurants and hotels	...	8.84	...	16.48	1.81	136.03	...	9.53	...	19.40	1.93	152.15
7 Transport, storage and communication	...	9.47	...	1.34	8.42	48.80	...	10.20	...	2.43	8.60	53.53
8 Finance, insurance, real estate and business services	...	26.00	...	7.05	0.60	97.29	...	28.05	...	7.94	-0.08	106.46
9 Community, social and personal services	...	0.97	...	2.83	1.30	27.16	...	1.04	...	3.09	1.32	29.52
Total, Industries	...	90.84	...	57.27	26.56	681.52	...	96.83	...	65.93	26.93	753.70
Producers of Government Services	...	6.37	...	1.66	-	111.69	...	6.70	...	1.80	-	120.07
Other Producers	...	0.59	...	0.03	-	6.37	...	0.62	...	0.03	0.01	6.79
Total	...	97.80	...	58.96	26.56	799.58	...	104.15	...	67.76	26.94	880.56
Imputed bank service charge	...	...	...	...	...	-37.25	...	...	...	...	...	-41.01
Import duties	...	...	...	4.83	...	4.83	...	...	...	5.57	...	5.57
Value added tax	...	...	...	75.52	...	75.52	...	...	...	77.87	...	77.87
Other adjustments	...	...	...	...	...	...	...	...	...	...	...	...
Total	...	97.80	...	139.31	26.56	842.68	...	104.15	...	151.20	26.94	923.00

	1980					
	Compensation of Employees	Capital Consumption	Net Operating Surplus	Indirect Taxes	Less: Subsidies Received	Value Added
			All Producers			
1 Agriculture, hunting, forestry and fishing	...	12.10	...	0.80	1.35	43.65
2 Mining and quarrying	...	0.44	...	0.39	0.33	4.78
3 Manufacturing	...	27.45	...	29.62	11.23	279.28
4 Electricity, gas and water	...	7.60	...	0.89	0.60	31.41
5 Construction	...	3.71	...	3.26	1.29	81.71
6 Wholesale and retail trade, restaurants and hotels	...	10.54	...	20.70	1.86	166.50
7 Transport, storage and communication	...	11.19	...	2.56	8.77	58.08
8 Finance, insurance, real estate and business services	...	31.28	...	8.47	0.22	117.98
9 Community, social and personal services	...	1.13	...	3.25	1.42	32.53
Total, Industries	...	105.44	...	69.94	27.07	815.92
Producers of Government Services	...	7.10	...	1.94	-	128.30
Other Producers	...	0.67	...	0.03	-	7.22
Total	...	113.21	...	71.91	27.07	951.44
Imputed bank service charge	...	...	...	...	...	-45.33
Import duties	...	...	...	5.72	...	5.72
Value added tax	...	...	...	84.09	...	84.09
Other adjustments	...	...	...	...	...	...
Total	...	113.21	...	161.72	27.07	996.02

Bahamas

Source. Reply to the United Nations national accounts questionnaire from the Department of Statistics, Nassau.

General note. The estimates shown in the following tables have been prepared in accordance with the United Nations System of National Accounts so far as the existing data would permit.

1.1 Expenditure on the Gross Domestic Product, in Current Prices

Million Bahamian dollars	1970	1971	1972	1973	1974	1975	1976	1977	1978	1979	1980
1 General government final consumption expenditure	...	...	...	78.6	88.6	96.9	110.8	114.0	132.0	147.2	...
2 Private final consumption expenditure	...	...	...	345.9	400.2	451.1	482.9	509.2	553.4	617.8	...
3 Gross capital formation	...	...	...	106.7	99.0	75.4	68.1	86.8	93.2	120.3	...
a Increase in stocks	...	...	...	...	...	...	...	...	...	...	...
b Gross fixed capital formation		...	...	106.7	99.0	75.4	68.1	86.8	93.2	120.3	...
Residential buildings	...	...	...	...	...	...	...	...	...	...	...
Non-residential buildings a	...	...	...	21.0	30.2	23.5	31.6	30.2	34.7	54.4	...
Other construction and land improvement etc.	...	...	...								...
Other	...	...	...	85.7	68.8	51.9	36.5	56.6	58.5	65.9	...
4 Exports of goods and services	...	...	...	465.7	598.0	605.2	667.4	702.5	820.4	947.4	...
5 Less: Imports of goods and services	...	...	...	432.1	573.2	474.8	520.5	536.5	628.5	753.2	...
Equals: Gross Domestic Product	...	...	...	564.8	612.6	753.8	808.7	876.0	970.5	1079.5	...

a) Including item 'Residential buildings'.

1.10 Gross Domestic Product by Kind of Activity, in Current Prices

Million Bahamian dollars	1970	1971	1972	1973	1974	1975	1976	1977	1978	1979	1980
1 Agriculture, hunting, forestry and fishing	...	...	...	21.3	25.1	23.6	37.1	34.8	42.0	...	...
2 Mining and quarrying	...	...	...							...	...
3 Manufacturing	...	...	...	79.4	53.9	88.1	89.8	90.9	116.9	...	...
4 Electricity, gas and water	...	...	...							...	...
5 Construction	...	...	...	13.2	19.1	14.8	20.0	19.1	22.0	...	...
6 Wholesale and retail trade, restaurants and hotels	...	...	...	147.2	157.6	166.5	182.1	213.6	248.4	...	...
7 Transport, storage and communication	...	...	...	70.6	81.2	77.4	84.8	85.8	113.4	...	...
8 Finance, insurance, real estate and business services	...	...	...	69.5	83.1	88.1	100.3	106.0	124.5	...	...
9 Community, social and personal services	...	...	...	101.7	116.7	114.7	144.2	163.3	162.8	...	...
Total, Industries	...	...	...	502.9	536.7	573.2	658.3	713.5	830.0	...	...
Producers of Government Services	...	...	...	...	...	...	...	...	...	...	...
Other Producers	...	...	...	...	...	...	...	...	...	...	...
Subtotal	...	...	...	502.9	536.7	573.2	658.3	713.5	830.0	...	...
Less: Imputed bank service charge	...	...	...	...	...	...	...	...	...	...	...
Plus: Import duties	...	...	...	64.1	71.0	64.1	71.4	81.2	96.8	...	...
Plus: Value added tax	...	...	...	...	...	...	...	...	...	...	...
Plus: Other adjustments	...	...	...	-2.2	4.9	116.5	79.0	81.3	43.7	...	...
Equals: Gross Domestic Product	...	...	...	564.8	612.6	753.8	808.7	876.0	970.5	...	...

Bahrain

Source. Reply to the United Nations National Accounts Questionnaire from the Statistics department, Directorate of Statistics, Cabinet Affairs, Manama.
General note. The estimates shown in the following tables have been prepared by the Statistics Department in accordance with the United Nations System of National Accounts so far as the existing data would permit.

1.1 Expenditure on the Gross Domestic Product, in Current Prices

Million Bahraini dinars

	1970	1971	1972	1973	1974	1975	1976	1977	1978	1979	1980
1 General government final consumption expenditure	...	...	...	...	...	67.6	88.3	111.0	132.4	150.9	...
2 Private final consumption expenditure	...	...	...	...	...	180.6	295.7	414.0	437.0	544.2	...
3 Gross capital formation	...	...	...	...	...	156.4	263.4	307.6	343.7	312.0	...
a Increase in stocks	...	...	...	...	...	...	...	...	...	...	...
b Gross fixed capital formation	...	...	...	...	...	156.4	263.4	307.6	343.7	312.0	...
4 Exports of goods and services	...	...	...	...	...	551.4	697.1	851.4	901.1	1033.8	...
5 Less: Imports of goods and services	...	...	...	...	...	542.6	770.0	960.5	967.9	1076.7	...
Equals: Gross Domestic Product	...	...	...	...	...	413.4	574.5	723.5	846.3	964.2	...

1.10 Gross Domestic Product by Kind of Activity, in Current Prices

Million Bahraini dinars

	1970	1971	1972	1973	1974	1975	1976	1977	1978	1979	1980
1 Agriculture, hunting, forestry and fishing	...	...	...	...	...	7.4	9.6	12.3	13.3	13.5	...
2 Mining and quarrying	...	...	...	...	...	133.2	167.4	193.8	211.5	244.3	...
3 Manufacturing	...	...	...	...	...	44.8	56.4	67.8	79.4	95.3	...
4 Electricity, gas and water	...	...	...	...	...	5.6	10.1	11.4	12.8	16.2	...
5 Construction	...	...	...	...	...	35.7	52.8	77.4	91.0	105.7	...
6 Wholesale and retail trade, restaurants and hotels	...	...	...	...	...	73.0	108.7	123.0	121.2	131.5	...
7 Transport, storage and communication	...	...	...	...	...	32.4	46.1	64.8	88.8	106.2	...
8 Finance, insurance, real estate and business services	...	...	...	...	...	39.5	69.7	97.7	131.6	133.1	...
9 Community, social and personal services	...	...	...	...	...	28.3	36.4	50.1	65.4	78.3	...
Total, Industries	...	...	...	...	...	399.9	557.2	698.3	815.0	924.1	...
Producers of Government Services	...	...	...	...	...	13.5	17.3	25.2	31.3	40.1	...
Other Producers	...	...	...	...	...	...	...	...	...	...	...
Subtotal	...	...	...	...	...	413.4	574.5	723.5	846.3	964.2	...
Less: Imputed bank service charge	...	...	...	...	...	...	...	...	...	...	...
Plus: Import duties	...	...	...	...	...	...	...	...	...	...	...
Plus: Value added tax	...	...	...	...	...	...	...	...	...	...	...
Equals: Gross Domestic Product	...	...	...	...	...	413.4	574.5	723.5	846.3	964.2	...

1.11 Gross Domestic Product by Kind of Activity, in Constant Prices

Million Bahraini dinars

	1970	1971	1972	1973	1974	1975	1976	1977	1978	1979	1980
				At constant prices of: 1977							
1 Agriculture, hunting, forestry and fishing	...	...	...	...	...	10.8	11.0	12.3	12.1	11.8	...
2 Mining and quarrying	...	...	...	...	...	149.0	178.6	193.8	196.2	186.4	...
3 Manufacturing	...	...	...	...	...	51.9	54.5	67.8	73.2	77.7	...
4 Electricity, gas and water	...	...	...	...	...	7.0	10.9	11.4	11.5	12.9	...
5 Construction	...	...	...	...	...	49.5	68.3	77.4	95.8	93.2	...
6 Wholesale and retail trade, restaurants and hotels	...	...	...	...	...	74.1	110.6	123.0	93.3	102.8	...
7 Transport, storage and communication	...	...	...	...	...	43.8	54.1	64.8	77.0	88.2	...
8 Finance, insurance, real estate and business services	...	...	...	...	...	58.5	82.7	97.7	123.7	121.9	...
9 Community, social and personal services	...	...	...	...	...	39.9	44.5	50.1	59.7	64.3	...
Total, Industries	...	...	...	...	...	484.5	615.2	698.3	742.5	759.2	...
Producers of Government Services	...	...	...	...	...	21.6	21.7	25.2	26.1	28.9	...
Other Producers	...	...	...	...	...	...	...	...	...	...	...
Subtotal	...	...	...	...	...	506.1	636.9	723.5	768.6	788.1	...
Less: Imputed bank service charge	...	...	...	...	...	...	...	...	...	...	...
Plus: Import duties	...	...	...	...	...	...	...	...	...	...	...
Plus: Value added tax	...	...	...	...	...	...	...	...	...	...	...
Equals: Gross Domestic Product	...	...	...	...	...	506.1	636.9	723.5	768.6	788.1	...

Bangladesh

Source. Reply to the United Nations National Accounts Questionnaire from the Bureau of Statistics, Dhake.
General note. The estimates shown in the following tables have been prepared by the Bureau of Statistics in accordance with the United Nations System of National Acounts so far as the existing data would permit.

1.1 Expenditure on the Gross Domestic Product, in Current Prices

Million Bangladesh taka — Fiscal year beginning 1 July

	1970	1971	1972	1973	1974	1975	1976	1977	1978	1979	1980
1 General government final consumption expenditure	...	...	1822	3155	4141	4642	5726	6827	9715	11509	11049
2 Private final consumption expenditure	...	...	38816	68257	122418	102623	94610	118458	124926	150162	175445
3 Gross capital formation	...	...	4027	4011	6888	9344	12348	16043	22227	27618	29526
a Increase in stocks	...	...	-	-	-	-	-	-	-	...	...
b Gross fixed capital formation	...	...	4027	4011	6888	9344	12348	16043	22227	27618	29526
4 Exports of goods and services	...	...	2711	2983	3136	5552	6670	7178	9632	10415	11208
5 Less: Imports of goods and services	...	...	2264	7320	10842	14703	13993	18216	21726	27254	31266
Equals: Gross Domestic Product	...	...	45112	71086	125741	107458	105361	130290	144774	172450	195962

1.10 Gross Domestic Product by Kind of Activity, in Current Prices

Million Bangladesh taka — Fiscal year beginning 1 July

	1970	1971	1972	1973	1974	1975	1976	1977	1978	1979	1980
1 Agriculture, hunting, forestry and fishing	...	...	26100	41501	78623	57339	53671	72248	78745	93299	104976
2 Mining and quarrying	...	...	1	2	2	2	2	2	2	2	2
3 Manufacturing	...	...	2895	4265	8376	8173	8660	9403	10315	12511	15050
4 Electricity, gas and water	...	...	130	119	131	189	231	245	260	369	470
5 Construction	...	...	1529	2899	5665	5514	5807	6155	7232	9289	11930
6 Wholesale and retail trade, restaurants and hotels [a]	...	...	3829	6508	10982	10747	10384	12832	15634	19048	21575
7 Transport, storage and communication	...	...	3366	4368	5642	6633	7334	8819	9547	11521	11902
8 Finance, insurance, real estate and business services	...	...	3013	4743	8373	9919	9026	9283	10792	13297	15145
9 Community, social and personal services [a]	...	...	3300	4878	5486	6122	6896	7846	8680	8883	9893
Total, Industries	...	...	44163	69283	123280	104638	102011	126833	141207	168219	190943
Producers of Government Services	...	...	949	1803	2461	2820	3350	3457	3567	4231	5019
Other Producers	...	...	...	...	...	...	...	...	...	...	...
Subtotal	...	...	45112	71086	125741	107458	105361	130290	144774	172450	195962
Less: Imputed bank service charge	...	...	...	...	...	...	...	...	...	...	...
Plus: Import duties	...	...	...	...	...	...	...	...	...	...	...
Plus: Value added tax	...	...	...	...	...	...	...	...	...	...	...
Equals: Gross Domestic Product	...	...	45112	71086	125741	107458	105361	130290	144774	172450	195962

a) Restaurants and hotels are included in item 'Community, social and personal services'.

1.11 Gross Domestic Product by Kind of Activity, in Constant Prices

Million Bangladesh taka — Fiscal year beginning 1 July

At constant prices of: 1972

	1970	1971	1972	1973	1974	1975	1976	1977	1978	1979	1980
1 Agriculture, hunting, forestry and fishing	...	...	26100	28827	28537	31865	30903	34019	33872	33909	36658
2 Mining and quarrying	...	...	1	2	1	1	1	1	1	1	1
3 Manufacturing	...	...	2895	3402	5481	5877	6117	6641	6938	6953	7572
4 Electricity, gas and water	...	...	130	95	86	135	163	184	184	250	266
5 Construction	...	...	1529	1713	1833	1742	2057	2188	2387	2540	2679
6 Wholesale and retail trade, restaurants and hotels [a]	...	...	3829	5142	5814	7653	7907	8008	9373	10972	11520
7 Transport, storage and communication	...	...	3366	3528	3617	3792	4095	4258	4612	4715	4790
8 Finance, insurance, real estate and business services	...	...	3013	2886	2833	2994	3060	3246	3627	3777	3965
9 Community, social and personal services [a]	...	...	3300	3678	2841	3281	3577	3756	3994	4266	4849
Total, Industries	...	...	44163	49273	51043	57340	57880	62301	64988	67383	72300
Producers of Government Services	...	...	949	1296	1239	1346	1589	1681	1778	1827	1935
Other Producers	...	...	...	...	...	...	...	...	...	...	...
Subtotal	...	...	45112	50569	52282	58686	59469	63982	66766	69210	74235
Less: Imputed bank service charge	...	...	...	...	...	...	...	...	...	...	...
Plus: Import duties	...	...	...	...	...	...	...	...	...	...	...
Plus: Value added tax	...	...	...	...	...	...	...	...	...	...	...
Equals: Gross Domestic Product	...	...	45112	50569	52282	58686	59469	63982	66766	69210	74235

a) Restaurants and hotels are included in item 'Community, social and personal services'.

Barbados

Source. Reply to the United Nations National Accounts Questionnaire from the Barbados Statistical Service, Garrison, St. Michael. Information on concepts, sources and methods of estimation utilized, are published by the same Service in 'National Income and Product, 1960-1962'.

General note. The estimates have been prepared in accordance with the United Nations System of National Accounts so far as the existing data would permit.

1.1 Expenditure on the Gross Domestic Product, in Current Prices

Million Barbados dollars

	1970	1971	1972	1973	1974	1975	1976	1977	1978	1979	1980
1 General government final consumption expenditure	...	...	...	...	130.7	134.8	151.4	172.1	189.7	210.3	257.1
2 Private final consumption expenditure	...	...	...	...	510.5	602.9	646.1	741.8	782.2	932.9	1074.1
3 Gross capital formation	...	...	...	...	169.2	156.2	235.9	194.1	254.5	302.2	381.3
a Increase in stocks	...	...	...	...	14.5	4.7	...	...	...	...	...
b Gross fixed capital formation	...	...	...	...	154.7	151.5	...	...	...	...	...
4 Exports of goods and services	...	...	...	...	362.7	402.3	406.2	492.7	645.8	871.8	1136.4
5 Less: Imports of goods and services	...	...	...	...	470.2	490.8	566.0	607.1	760.1	967.4	1190.5
Equals: Gross Domestic Product	...	...	...	...	702.9	805.4	873.5	993.6	1112.1	1349.8	1658.4

1.3 Cost Components of the Gross Domestic Product

Million Barbados dollars

	1970	1971	1972	1973	1974	1975	1976	1977	1978	1979	1980
1 Indirect taxes, net	...	...	...	...	62.4	111.8	...	...	...	...	...
2 Consumption of fixed capital	...	...	...	...	44.1	47.8	...	...	...	...	...
3 Compensation of employees paid by resident producers to:	...	...	...	...	424.0	462.6	...	...	...	...	...
4 Net operating surplus	...	...	...	...	172.4	190.2	...	...	...	...	...
Equals: Gross Domestic Product	...	...	...	...	702.9	805.4	873.5	993.6	1112.0	1349.9	1658.4

1.10 Gross Domestic Product by Kind of Activity, in Current Prices

Million Barbados dollars

	1970	1971	1972	1973	1974	1975	1976	1977	1978	1979	1980
1 Agriculture, hunting, forestry and fishing	40.3	38.0	44.0	47.0	68.5	93.5	76.8	91.7	91.7	109.1	143.7
2 Mining and quarrying	31.4	37.3	44.0	60.0	0.8	1.6	2.3	4.4	6.9	8.3	13.8
3 Manufacturing					62.7	71.9	84.8	102.6	112.4	139.6	186.6
4 Electricity, gas and water [a]	20.9	24.4	28.0	36.0	9.6	10.3	11.2	14.1	15.7	18.3	22.0
5 Construction	27.5	28.0	29.0	32.0	52.7	46.3	55.6	60.1	75.1	88.1	104.5
6 Wholesale and retail trade, restaurants and hotels [b]	71.2	78.0	84.0	96.0	182.4	192.0	230.7	269.7	314.5	403.4	493.9
7 Transport, storage and communication [a]	...	...	...	...	43.6	50.4	55.9	60.1	64.2	70.1	86.9
8 Finance, insurance, real estate and business services [c]	11.0	12.0	13.0	15.0	93.8	98.3	109.8	110.2	115.6	135.0	162.5
9 Community, social and personal services [bc]	45.0	57.0	60.0	68.0	29.2	30.8	33.1	35.0	37.8	46.1	57.6
Total, Industries	247.3	274.7	302.0	354.0	543.4	595.1	660.2	747.9	833.8	1018.0	1271.6
Producers of Government Services	42.7	47.3	55.0	72.0	97.0	105.5	127.8	142.2	150.6	179.6	218.2
Other Producers	...	...	...	...	...	...	...	...	...	...	...
Subtotal [d]	290.0	322.0	357.0	426.0	640.4	700.6	788.0	890.1	984.4	1197.6	1489.8
Less: Imputed bank service charge	...	...	...	...	...	...	...	...	...	...	...
Plus: Import duties	...	...	...	...	...	...	...	...	...	...	...
Plus: Value added tax	...	...	...	...	...	...	...	...	...	...	...
Plus: Other adjustments [e]	...	...	...	...	62.5	111.8	85.5	103.6	127.7	152.3	168.6
Equals: Gross Domestic Product	...	...	...	...	702.9	805.4	873.5	993.6	1112.0	1349.9	1658.4

a) For the first series, item 'Transport, storage and communication' is included in item 'Electricity, gas and water'.
b) For the first series, restaurants and hotels are included in item 'Community, social and personal services'.
c) For the first series, finance, insurance, real estate (except owner-occupied dwellings) and business services are included in item 'Community social and personal services'.
d) Gross domestic product in factor values.
e) Referring to indirect taxes net of subsidies.

Barbados

1.11 Gross Domestic Product by Kind of Activity, in Constant Prices

Million Barbados dollars

	1970	1971	1972	1973	1974	1975	1976	1977	1978	1979	1980
					At constant prices of: 1974						
1 Agriculture, hunting, forestry and fishing	...	...	...	...	68.5	66.2	71.0	72.4	72.3	78.3	82.6
2 Mining and quarrying	...	...	...	...	0.8	0.9	1.3	1.1	1.6	1.6	2.0
3 Manufacturing	...	...	...	...	62.6	69.3	81.0	83.6	91.2	92.8	98.4
4 Electricity, gas and water	...	...	...	...	9.6	10.1	10.8	12.3	14.2	15.8	16.8
5 Construction	...	...	...	...	52.7	44.1	49.9	43.1	46.3	52.7	56.4
6 Wholesale and retail trade, restaurants and hotels	...	...	...	...	182.4	175.8	180.1	201.7	215.7	249.0	267.7
7 Transport, storage and communication	...	...	...	...	43.6	43.4	44.3	45.5	46.6	48.3	49.7
8 Finance, insurance, real estate and business services	...	...	...	...	220.0	217.2	215.4	218.3	222.5	228.1	230.1
9 Community, social and personal services	...	...	...	...							
Total, Industries	...	...	...	...	640.4	627.0	653.9	678.0	710.5	766.7	803.8
Producers of Government Services	...	...	...	...	...	...	...	...	...	...	...
Other Producers	...	...	...	...	...	...	...	...	...	...	...
Subtotal [a]	...	...	...	...	640.4	627.0	653.9	678.0	710.5	766.7	803.8
Less: Imputed bank service charge	...	...	...	...	...	...	...	...	...	...	...
Plus: Import duties	...	...	...	...	...	...	...	...	...	...	...
Plus: Value added tax	...	...	...	...	...	...	...	...	...	...	...
Equals: Gross Domestic Product	...	...	...	...	...	...	...	...	...	...	...

a) Gross domestic product in factor values.

4.3 Derivation of Value Added by Kind of Activity, ISIC Divisions, in Current Prices

Million Barbados dollars

	1977 Gross Output	1977 Intermediate Consumption	1977 Value Added	1978 Gross Output	1978 Intermediate Consumption	1978 Value Added	1979 Gross Output	1979 Intermediate Consumption	1979 Value Added	1980 Gross Output	1980 Intermediate Consumption	1980 Value Added
						All Producers						
1 Agriculture, hunting, forestry and fishing	...	...	91.7	...	...	91.7	...	...	109.1	...	...	143.7
a Agriculture and hunting	...	...	...	...	...	84.2	...	...	99.3	...	...	133.3
b Forestry and logging	...	...	...	...	...	...	...	...	...	...	...	...
c Fishing	...	...	...	...	...	7.5	...	...	9.8	...	...	10.4
2 Mining and quarrying	...	...	4.4	...	...	6.9	...	...	8.3	...	...	13.8
3 Manufacturing	...	...	102.6	...	...	112.4	...	...	139.6	...	...	186.6
a Manufacture of food, beverages and tobacco	...	...	35.6	...	...	38.2	...	...	42.7	...	...	60.5
b Textile, wearing apparel and leather industries	...	...	23.2	...	...	23.9	...	...	32.6	...	...	42.0
c Manufacture of wood and wood products, including furniture	...	...	3.1	...	...	2.1	...	...	2.1	...	...	2.8
d Manufacture of paper and paper products, printing and publishing	...	...	7.7	...	...	9.4	...	...	14.4	...	...	17.2
e Manufacture of chemicals and chemical petroleum, coal, rubber and plastic products	...	...	11.2	...	...	13.6	...	...	18.7	...	...	24.6
f Manufacture of non-metallic mineral products, except products of petroleum and coal	...	...	...	...	...	...	...	...	...	...	...	...
g Basic metal industries	...	...	...	...	...	...	...	...	...	...	...	...
h Manufacture of fabricated metal products, machinery and equipment	...	...	15.5	...	...	15.8	...	...	19.3	...	...	26.7
i Other manufacturing industries	...	...	6.4	...	...	9.4	...	...	9.8	...	...	12.8
4 Electricity, gas and water	...	...	14.1	...	...	15.7	...	...	18.3	...	...	22.0
5 Construction	...	...	60.1	...	...	75.1	...	...	88.1	...	...	104.5
6 Wholesale and retail trade, restaurants and hotels	...	...	269.7	...	...	314.5	...	...	403.4	...	...	493.9
a Wholesale and retail trade	...	...	182.0	...	...	204.8	...	...	259.4	...	...	319.0
b Restaurants and hotels	...	...	87.7	...	...	109.7	...	...	144.0	...	...	174.9
7 Transport, storage and communication	...	...	60.1	...	...	64.2	...	...	70.1	...	...	86.9
8 Finance, insurance, real estate and business services	...	...	110.2	...	...	115.6	...	...	135.0	...	...	162.5
9 Community, social and personal services	...	...	35.0	...	...	37.8	...	...	46.1	...	...	57.6

Barbados

4.3 Derivation of Value Added by Kind of Activity, ISIC Divisions, in Current Prices
(Continued)

Million Barbados dollars

	1977 Gross Output	1977 Intermediate Consumption	1977 Value Added	1978 Gross Output	1978 Intermediate Consumption	1978 Value Added	1979 Gross Output	1979 Intermediate Consumption	1979 Value Added	1980 Gross Output	1980 Intermediate Consumption	1980 Value Added
Total, Industries	...	...	747.9	...	...	833.8	...	...	1018.0	...	...	1271.6
Producers of Government Services	...	...	142.2	...	...	150.6	...	...	179.6	...	...	218.2
Other Producers	...	...	...	...	...	...	...	...	...	...	...	...
Total a	...	...	890.1	...	...	984.4	...	...	1197.6	...	...	1489.8
Imputed bank service charge	...	...	...	...	...	...	...	...	...	...	...	...
Import duties	...	...	...	...	...	...	...	...	...	...	...	...
Value added tax	...	...	...	...	...	...	...	...	...	...	...	...
Total	...	...	...	...	...	...	...	...	...	...	...	...

a) Column 'Value added' is in factor values.

4.6 Cost Components of Value Added, ISIC Divisions

Million Barbados dollars

	1974 Compensation of Employees	1974 Capital Consumption	1974 Net Operating Surplus	1974 Indirect Taxes	1974 Less: Subsidies Received	1974 Value Added	1975 Compensation of Employees	1975 Capital Consumption	1975 Net Operating Surplus	1975 Indirect Taxes	1975 Less: Subsidies Received	1975 Value Added
					All Producers							
1 Agriculture, hunting, forestry and fishing	47.4	5.3	15.8	...	...	68.5	61.1	5.9	26.5	...	...	93.5
2 Mining and quarrying	1.8	0.2	-1.2	...	...	0.8	1.4	0.3	-0.1	...	...	1.6
3 Manufacturing	39.2	6.1	17.4	...	...	62.7	42.9	6.2	22.8	...	...	71.9
a Manufacture of food, beverages and tobacco	13.8	2.9	5.7	...	...	22.5	15.8	3.2	7.0	...	...	26.0
b Textile, wearing apparel and leather industries	9.4	0.8	1.6	...	...	11.7	10.1	0.8	3.9	...	...	14.7
c Manufacture of wood and wood products, including furniture	2.3	0.2	0.8	...	...	3.3	2.2	0.2	0.5	...	...	2.9
d Manufacture of paper and paper products, printing and publishing	3.1	0.4	1.7	...	...	5.2	3.3	0.4	2.4	...	...	6.1
e Manufacture of chemicals and chemical petroleum, coal, rubber and plastic products	4.0	0.8	1.9	...	...	6.8	4.3	0.7	4.1	...	...	9.0
f Manufacture of non-metallic mineral products, except products of petroleum and coal	...	...	...	...	...	...	...	...	...	...	...	...
g Basic metal industries	...	...	...	...	...	...	...	...	...	...	...	...
h Manufacture of fabricated metal products, machinery and equipment	4.0	0.5	2.2	...	...	6.7	4.5	0.6	2.8	...	...	7.9
i Other manufacturing industries	2.6	0.4	3.5	...	...	6.5	2.7	0.5	2.1	...	...	5.3
4 Electricity, gas and water	4.8	2.7	2.1	...	...	9.6	6.0	2.8	1.5	...	...	10.3
5 Construction	48.0	0.9	3.8	...	...	52.7	43.4	0.8	2.1	...	...	46.3
6 Wholesale and retail trade, restaurants and hotels	109.9	11.9	60.6	...	...	182.4	116.8	12.3	62.9	...	...	192.0
a Wholesale and retail trade	70.8	5.6	41.9	...	...	118.3	77.0	6.0	44.2	...	...	127.2
b Restaurants and hotels	39.1	6.3	18.7	...	...	64.1	39.8	6.3	18.7	...	...	64.8
7 Transport, storage and communication	25.6	6.5	11.5	...	...	43.6	30.3	7.2	12.9	...	...	50.4
8 Finance, insurance, real estate and business services	34.4	3.9	55.5	...	...	93.8	39.4	4.4	54.5	...	...	98.3
9 Community, social and personal services	21.9	0.5	6.8	...	...	29.2	23.2	0.5	7.1	...	...	30.8
Total, Industries	333.0	38.0	172.4	...	...	543.4	364.6	40.3	190.2	...	...	595.1
Producers of Government Services	91.0	6.1	-	...	...	97.1	98.1	7.4	-	...	...	105.5
Other Producers	...	...	...	...	...	...	...	...	...	...	...	...
Total a	424.0	44.0	172.4	...	...	640.4	462.7	47.7	190.2	...	...	700.6
Imputed bank service charge	...	...	...	...	...	...	...	...	...	...	...	...
Import duties	...	...	...	...	...	...	...	...	...	...	...	...
Value added tax	...	...	...	...	...	...	...	...	...	...	...	...
Other adjustments b	...	...	...	...	...	62.5	...	...	...	...	...	111.8
Total	...	...	...	...	...	702.9	...	...	...	...	...	805.4

a) Column 'Value added' is in factor values.
b) Referring to indirect taxes net of subsidies.

Belgium

Source. Reply to the United Nations National Accounts Questionnaire from the Institut National de Statistique, Brussels. The official estimates are published annually by the Institut National in the July-August issue of the 'Bulletin de Statistique'.

General note. The estimates shown in the following tables have been prepared in accordance with the United Nations System of National Accounts so far as the existing data would permit.

1.1 Expenditure on the Gross Domestic Product, in Current Prices

Million Belgian francs

		1970	1971	1972	1973	1974	1975	1976	1977	1978	1979	1980
1	General government final consumption expenditure	175300	201983	232444	264315	314316	388398	441000	491516	546983	590910	646683
2	Private final consumption expenditure [a]	769013	847717	947778	1083903	1255904	1421152	1623065	1772392	1898245	2058496	2228861
3	Gross capital formation	307511	324701	337987	398920	513455	499486	578023	614040	653556	681926	736358
	a Increase in stocks [b]	20437	19132	9635	24715	45590	-12442	9506	10882	8983	25236	7556
	b Gross fixed capital formation	287074	305569	328352	374205	467865	511928	568517	603158	644573	656690	728802
	Residential buildings	71778	61835	68890	94610	130524	144839	184655	202755	228675	210688	226247
	Non-residential buildings	102598	130451	138455	145767	168560	187851	202531	...	...	...	...
	Other construction and land improvement etc.								...	...	...	...
	Other	112698	113283	121007	133828	168781	179238	181331	...	...	...	...
4	Exports of goods and services	561900	608800	683000	846400	1116400	1065200	1248900	1479700	1540800	1818700	2079900
5	Less: Imports of goods and services	532800	580800	632700	811200	1109200	1061100	1264700	1514000	1582500	1888900	2208600
	Equals: Gross Domestic Product	1280924	1402401	1568509	1782338	2090875	2313136	2626288	2843648	3057084	3261132	3483202

a) Including a statistical discrepancy.
b) Including adjustment in connection with gross fixed capital.

1.2 Expenditure on the Gross Domestic Product, in Constant Prices

Million Belgian francs

		1970	1971	1972	1973	1974	1975	1976	1977	1978	1979	1980
						At constant prices of: 1975						
1	General government final consumption expenditure	302116	319982	338954	356710	370110	388398	404117	417401	443080	454391	461710
2	Private final consumption expenditure [a]	1143879	1199352	1272460	1371975	1415196	1421152	1500158	1532666	1578118	1647041	1675588
3	Gross capital formation	478405	469997	468660	522444	576956	499486	537777	537651	549165	549144	560748
	a Increase in stocks [b]	29939	28525	14887	38089	56636	-12442	10448	11062	10843	24007	6162
	b Gross fixed capital formation	448466	441472	453773	484355	520320	511928	527329	526589	538322	525137	554586
	Residential buildings	126473	99822	105243	131464	149666	144839	167611	170567	181399	158536	156515
	Non-residential buildings	173775	199262	200659	192327	188570	187851	184354	...	...	...	...
	Other construction and land improvement etc.								...	...	...	...
	Other	148218	142388	147871	160564	182084	179238	175364	...	...	...	...
4	Exports of goods and services	819200	871000	958200	1095800	1169300	1065200	1177900	1350200	1395900	1511900	1570500
5	Less: Imports of goods and services	805600	846400	916300	1092900	1175300	1061100	1180900	1372000	1419500	1556700	1601100
	Equals: Gross Domestic Product	1938000	2013931	2121974	2254029	2356262	2313136	2439052	2465918	2546763	2605776	2667446

a) Including a statistical discrepancy.
b) Including adjustment in connection with gross fixed capital.

1.3 Cost Components of the Gross Domestic Product

Million Belgian francs

		1970	1971	1972	1973	1974	1975	1976	1977	1978	1979	1980
1	Indirect taxes, net	148241	159729	165137	181151	215622	233551	271789	294924	318457	332608	362141
	a Indirect taxes paid	165224	177257	185509	206521	240636	261082	308326	335151	364957	388861	413851
	b Less: Subsidies received	16983	17528	20372	25370	25014	27531	36537	40227	46500	56253	51710
2	Consumption of fixed capital	124569	133834	148993	161636	193201	212444	231126	260546	278519	298689	305758
3	Compensation of employees paid by resident producers to:	629040	717161	821620	946269	1141213	1309930	1503065	1639313	1764722	1887933	2054816
	a Resident households	625940	713561	817420	941369	1134713	1301630	1493665	1629613	1754522	1876133	2040816
	b Rest of the world	3100	3600	4200	4900	6500	8300	9400	9700	10200	11800	14000
4	Net operating surplus	379074	391677	432759	493282	540839	557211	620308	648865	695386	741902	760487
	Equals: Gross Domestic Product	1280924	1402401	1568509	1782338	2090875	2313136	2626288	2843648	3057084	3261132	3483202

1.4 General Government Current Receipts and Disbursements

Million Belgian francs

		1970	1971	1972	1973	1974	1975	1976	1977	1978	1979	1980
						Receipts						
1	Property and entrepreneurial income	12053	8466	3771	1524	5963	6563	2815	3643	...	...	...
2	Taxes, fees and contributions	438450	491086	552631	646142	781206	926334	1052985	1178774	...	...	...
	a Indirect taxes	165224	177257	185509	206521	240636	261082	308326	335151	364957	388861	413851
	b Direct taxes	141493	163766	194421	237516	300090	374372	416222	482475	...	...	...

Belgium

1.4 General Government Current Receipts and Disbursements
(Continued)

Million Belgian francs

	1970	1971	1972	1973	1974	1975	1976	1977	1978	1979	1980
c Social security contributions	131733	150063	172701	202105	240480	290880	328437	361148	377538	405393	437207
d Compulsory fees, fines and penalties	...	...	...	...	...	...	...	...	...	...	...
3 Other current receipts	700	1200	1200	1200	1600	2300	2200	2600	2400	3300	3200
Total Current Receipts of General Government	451203	500752	557602	648866	788769	935197	1058000	1185018	1298653	1412118	1507995

Disbursements

	1970	1971	1972	1973	1974	1975	1976	1977	1978	1979	1980
1 General government final consumption expenditure	175300	201983	232444	264315	314316	388398	441000	491516	546983	590910	646683
a Compensation of employees	...	...	...	...	...	...	...	...	...	...	...
b Consumption of fixed capital	2797	3199	3567	3942	4750	5634	6463	7621	8557	9428	10481
c Purchases of goods and services, net	...	...	...	...	...	...	...	...	...	...	...
d Less: Own account production of fixed assets	...	...	...	...	...	...	...	...	...	...	...
e Indirect taxes paid, net	...	...	...	...	...	...	...	...	...	...	...
2 Property income paid	43120	46414	51778	59144	73174	82484	97756	116959	137866	166142	214409
3 Subsidies	16983	17528	20372	25370	25014	27531	36537	40227	46500	56253	51710
4 Other current transfers paid	187799	210847	242308	289303	347855	453645	520662	585165	638147	694707	764159
a Social security benefits and social assistance grants [a]	180299	199547	233308	275003	333355	433945	507262	568965	621747	680107	738959
b Other	7500	11300	9000	14300	14500	19700	13400	16200	16400	14600	25200
5 Net saving	28001	23980	10700	10734	28410	-16861	-37955	-48849	-70843	-95894	-168966
Total Current Disbursements and Net Saving of General Government	451203	500752	557602	648866	788769	935197	1058000	1185018	1298653	1412118	1507995

a) Including current transfer to private non-profit institutions serving households.

1.6 Current Income and Outlay of Households and Non-Profit Institutions

Million Belgian francs

	1970	1971	1972	1973	1974	1975	1976	1977	1978	1979	1980

Receipts

	1970	1971	1972	1973	1974	1975	1976	1977	1978	1979	1980
1 Compensation of employees	635640	724461	830520	955869	1152213	1322730	1517365	1656013	1781822	1905833	2071716
a From resident producers	625940	713561	817420	941369	1134713	1301630	1493665	1629613	1754522	1876133	2040816
b From rest of the world	9700	10900	13100	14500	17500	21100	23700	26400	27300	29700	30900
2 Property and entrepreneurial income received	352315	...	...	...	...	...	...	...	...	...	...
3 Current transfers received	190999	210747	244308	288303	347355	447545	520762	584765	640247	698307	759559
a Social security benefits and social assistance grants received	157667	176267	207193	241403	295831	384269	453684	506743	553678	604130	656569
b Other	33332	34480	37115	46900	51524	63276	67078	78022	86569	94177	102990
Total Current Receipts	1178954	...	...	...	...	...	...	...	...	...	...

Disbursements

	1970	1971	1972	1973	1974	1975	1976	1977	1978	1979	1980
1 Private final consumption expenditure	769013	847717	947778	1083903	1255904	1421152	1623065	1772392	1898245	2058496	2228861
2 Property income paid	...	...	...	...	...	...	...	...	...	...	...
3 Direct taxes and other payments n.e.c. to general government	242308	...	...	...	...	...	...	...	...	...	...
a Social security contributions	131733	150063	172701	202105	240480	290880	328437	361148	377538	405393	437207
b Direct taxes	110575	...	...	...	...	...	...	...	...	...	...
c Fees, fines and penalties		...	...	...	...	...	...	...	...	...	...
4 Other current transfers paid	8800	9100	9500	10900	13400	16600	19900	22300	24200	28000	...
5 Net saving	158833	171072	199908	213144	261451	292649	354581	348876	369380	356221	412079
Total Current Disbursements and Net Saving	1178954	...	...	...	...	...	...	...	...	...	...

1.7 External Transactions on Current Account, Summary

Million Belgian francs

	1970	1971	1972	1973	1974	1975	1976	1977	1978	1979	1980

Payments to the Rest of the World

	1970	1971	1972	1973	1974	1975	1976	1977	1978	1979	1980
1 Imports of goods and services	532800	580800	632700	811200	1109200	1061100	1264700	1514000	1582500	1888900	2208600
a Imports of merchandise c.i.f.	424900	467100	514200	665900	918800	858300	1043900	1236000	1282600	1541300	1782600
b Other	107900	113700	118500	145300	190400	202800	220800	278000	299900	347600	426000
2 Factor income paid to the rest of the world	43200	35800	34400	45000	77700	78600	75200	84900	104000	137900	230100

Belgium

1.7 External Transactions on Current Account, Summary
(Continued)

Million Belgian francs

	1970	1971	1972	1973	1974	1975	1976	1977	1978	1979	1980
a Compensation of employees	3100	3600	4200	4900	6500	8300	9400	9700	10200	11800	14000
b Property and entrepreneurial income paid	40100	32200	30200	40100	71200	70300	65800	75200	93800	126100	216100
3 Indirect taxes paid to supranational organizations	...	...	...	...	...	...	...	...	...	...	...
4 Current transfers to the rest of the world	16300	20400	18500	25200	27900	36300	33300	38500	40600	42600	57000
5 Surplus of the nation on current transactions	35100	29500	56200	33800	6700	-3600	-16100	-42300	-51300	-94800	-180200
Payments to the Rest of the World and Surplus of the Nation on Current Transactions	627400	666500	741800	915200	1221500	1172400	1357100	1595100	1675800	1974600	2315500

Receipts From The Rest of the World

	1970	1971	1972	1973	1974	1975	1976	1977	1978	1979	1980
1 Exports of goods and services	561900	608800	683000	846400	1116400	1065200	1248900	1479700	1540800	1818700	2079900
a Exports of merchandise f.o.b.	452800	487700	557300	697100	923600	856800	1012300	1161600	1214800	1453600	1647100
b Other	109100	121100	125700	149300	192800	208400	236600	318100	326000	365100	432800
2 Factor income received from rest of the world	54100	45300	46600	54300	89500	91300	92500	97000	114100	134400	211800
a Compensation of employees	9700	10900	13100	14500	17500	21100	23700	26400	27300	29700	30900
b Property and entrepreneurial income received	44400	34400	33500	39800	72000	70200	68800	70600	86800	104700	180900
3 Subsidies received from supranational organisations	...	...	...	...	...	...	...	...	...	...	...
4 Current transfers from rest of the world	11400	12400	12200	14500	15600	15900	15700	18400	20900	21500	23800
Receipts from the Rest of the World on Current Transactions	627400	666500	741800	915200	1221500	1172400	1357100	1595100	1675800	1974600	2315500

1.8 Capital Transactions of The Nation, Summary

Million Belgian francs

	1970	1971	1972	1973	1974	1975	1976	1977	1978	1979	1980
Finance of Gross Capital Formation											
Gross saving	342611	354201	394187	432720	520155	495886	561923	571740	602256	587126	556158
1 Consumption of fixed capital	124569	133834	148993	161636	193201	212444	231126	260546	278519	298689	305758
a General government	2797	3199	3567	3942	4750	5634	6463	7621	8557	9428	10481
b Corporate and quasi-corporate enterprises	121772	130635	145426	157694	188451	206810	224663	252925	269962	289261	295277
c Other	-	-	-	-	-	-	-	-	-	-	-
2 Net saving	218042	220367	245194	271084	326954	283442	330797	311194	323737	288437	250400
a General government	28001	23980	10700	10734	28410	-16861	-37955	-48849	-70843	-95894	-168966
b Corporate and quasi-corporate enterprises	31208	25315	34586	47206	37093	7654	14171	11167	25200	28110	7287
Public	3188	1205	1366	2166	1373	3164	4521	6437	6570	5810	3937
Private	28020	24110	33220	45040	35720	4490	9650	4730	18630	22300	3350
c Other	158833	171072	199908	213144	261451	292649	354581	348876	369380	356221	412079
Less: Surplus of the nation on current transactions	35100	29500	56200	33800	6700	-3600	-16100	-42300	-51300	-94800	-180200
Finance of Gross Capital Formation	307511	324701	337987	398920	513455	499486	578023	614040	653556	681926	736358
Gross Capital Formation											
Increase in stocks [a]	20437	19132	9635	24715	45590	-12442	9506	10882	8983	25236	7556
Gross fixed capital formation	287074	305569	328352	374205	467865	511928	568517	603158	644573	656690	728802
1 General government	39420	49692	54864	51429	56077	66040	77092	80310	81799	91012	106165
2 Corporate and quasi-corporate enterprises	...	...	...	...	...	...	...	...	...	...	...
3 Other	...	...	...	...	...	...	...	...	...	...	...
Gross Capital Formation	307511	324701	337987	398920	513455	499486	578023	614040	653556	681926	736358

a) Including adjustment in connection with gross fixed capital.

Belgium

1.10 Gross Domestic Product by Kind of Activity, in Current Prices

Million Belgian francs

	1970	1971	1972	1973	1974	1975	1976	1977	1978	1979	1980
1 Agriculture, hunting, forestry and fishing	45997	49290	63450	69325	62196	68208	76942	68339	76035	73242	74062
2 Mining and quarrying	12023	13721	13359	11868	15765	18866	19018	18232	16930	15708	17876
3 Manufacturing [a]	411290	424820	475741	544218	644001	634200	719595	762846	804736	858041	883165
4 Electricity, gas and water	29594	36221	40228	44888	52448	71020	77986	86483	93910	96497	109283
5 Construction	88629	95558	102775	119349	148076	167018	195663	215564	231160	235591	269054
6 Wholesale and retail trade, restaurants and hotels [bc]	163640	197440	214540	231887	250548	287303	340304	360457	396560	393365	398385
7 Transport, storage and communication	92632	105042	118990	136834	171191	182919	204876	222420	241911	267462	302587
8 Finance, insurance, real estate and business services	137379	147687	166822	191430	222325	254274	295136	329570	364476	396800	418983
9 Community, social and personal services [b]	98423	112184	126805	146631	166395	197696	227750	258762	282868	301381	324698
Total, Industries	1079607	1181963	1322710	1496430	1732945	1881504	2157270	2322673	2508586	2638087	2798093
Producers of Government Services	135035	153758	180422	207670	249512	304696	347799	387079	428669	466999	514437
Other Producers	16516	17309	18103	21706	22686	25670	27922	31920	35444	38169	40061
Subtotal	1231158	1353030	1521235	1725806	2005143	2211870	2532991	2741672	2972699	3143255	3352591
Less: Imputed bank service charge	11755	12434	15258	18684	23128	26178	35326	39625	45115	48085	47410
Plus: Import duties	59283	66823	73266	93601	134713	129662	155866	171080	168934	199622	233459
Plus: Value added tax [d]	...	...	...	...	...	...	...	...	...	...	...
Plus: Other adjustments [e]	2238	-5018	-10734	-18385	-25853	-2218	-27243	-29479	-39434	-33660	-55438
Equals: Gross Domestic Product	1280924	1402401	1568509	1782338	2090875	2313136	2626288	2843648	3057084	3261132	3483202

a) Including garages.
b) Restaurants and hotels are included in item 'Community, social and personal services'.
c) Including distribution of petroleum products.
d) Including value added tax deductible from capital formation.
e) Correction to compensate for the exclusion of certain own-account capital investments.

1.11 Gross Domestic Product by Kind of Activity, in Constant Prices

Million Belgian francs

	1970	1971	1972	1973	1974	1975	1976	1977	1978	1979	1980
					At constant prices of:1975						
1 Agriculture, hunting, forestry and fishing	70345	74367	74374	77276	80280	68208	65494	67537	74651	74882	75212
2 Mining and quarrying	23873	23887	22722	20246	20711	18866	18369	16709	15740	15143	15639
3 Manufacturing	530132	550264	594065	650835	679055	634200	687403	693784	711317	732749	730606
4 Electricity, gas and water [a]	41498	47358	55103	60261	64445	71020	75407	82610	88487	91812	93461
5 Construction	147527	150524	152746	160615	167420	167018	177864	182281	183779	177472	188510
6 Wholesale and retail trade, restaurants and hotels [bcd]	351649	370125	386321	411093	420610	416965	440583	439636	451058	468003	473951
7 Transport, storage and communication	173157	177759	180852	192602	207404	182919	189712	190235	198775	209307	222678
8 Finance, insurance, real estate and business services	206218	212309	227767	243986	252309	254274	267374	273377	285700	296825	300737
9 Community, social and personal services [b]	150734	158044	166703	180322	185382	197696	207780	213465	217372	222777	228764
Total, Industries	1695133	1764637	1860653	1997236	2077616	2011166	2129986	2159634	2226879	2288970	2329558
Producers of Government Services	239087	250620	267602	284097	298029	304696	317339	324983	341135	352746	360339
Other Producers	27286	27014	26917	26830	25744	25670	25104	25654	25756	25218	24661
Subtotal	1961506	2042271	2155172	2308163	2401389	2341532	2472429	2510271	2593770	2666934	2714558
Less: Imputed bank service charge	18248	18813	22282	25153	26726	26178	28792	30187	32986	33941	32887
Plus: Import duties [d]	...	...	...	...	...	...	...	...	...	...	...
Plus: Value added tax [e]	...	...	...	...	...	...	...	...	...	...	...
Plus: Other adjustments [f]	-5258	-9527	-10916	-28981	-18401	-2218	-4585	-14166	-14021	-27217	-14225
Equals: Gross Domestic Product	1938000	2013931	2121974	2254029	2356262	2313136	2439052	2465918	2546763	2605776	2667446

a) For 1960-1964, Steam and hot water supply are included in item 'Manufacturing'.
b) Restaurants and hotels are included in item 'Community, social and personal services'.
c) Including distribution of petroleum products.
d) Item 'Import duties' is included in item 'Wholesale and retail trade'.
e) Including value added tax deductible from capital formation.
f) Correction to compensate for the exclusion of certain own account capital investments.

1.12 Relations Among National Accounting Aggregates

Million Belgian francs

	1970	1971	1972	1973	1974	1975	1976	1977	1978	1979	1980
Gross Domestic Product	1280924	1402401	1568509	1782338	2090875	2313136	2626288	2843648	3057084	3261132	3483202
Plus: Net factor income received from abroad	10900	9500	12200	9300	11800	12700	17300	12100	10100	-3500	-18300
Factor income received	54100	45300	46600	54300	89500	91300	92500	97000	114100	134400	211800
Less: Factor income paid	43200	35800	34400	45000	77700	78600	75200	84900	104000	137900	230100
Equals: Gross National Product	1291824	1411901	1580709	1791638	2102675	2325836	2643588	2855748	3067184	3257632	3464902

Belgium

1.12 Relations Among National Accounting Aggregates
(Continued)

Million Belgian francs	1970	1971	1972	1973	1974	1975	1976	1977	1978	1979	1980
Less: Consumption of fixed capital	124569	133834	148993	161636	193201	212444	231126	260546	278519	298689	305758
Less: Net indirect taxes paid to supranational organisations	...	...	...	...	...	...	...	...	...	...	...
Equals: National Income at Market Prices	1167255	1278067	1431716	1630002	1909474	2113392	2412462	2595202	2788665	2958943	3159144
Plus: Net current transfers received from abroad	-4900	-8000	-6300	-10700	-12300	-20400	-17600	-20100	-19700	-21100	-33200
Current transfers received	11400	12400	12200	14500	15600	15900	15700	18400	20900	21500	23800
Less: Current transfers paid	16300	20400	18500	25200	27900	36300	33300	38500	40600	42600	57000
Equals: National Disposable Income at Market Prices	1162355	1270067	1425416	1619302	1897174	2092992	2394862	2575102	2768965	2937843	3125944
Less: Final consumption [a]	944313	1049700	1180222	1348218	1570220	1809550	2064065	2263908	2445228	2649406	2875544
Equals: Net Saving	218042	220367	245194	271084	326954	283442	330797	311194	323737	288437	250400
Less: Surplus of the nation on current transactions	35100	29500	56200	33800	6700	-3600	-16100	-42300	-51300	-94800	-180200
Equals: Net Capital Formation	182942	190867	188994	237284	320254	287042	346897	353494	375037	383237	430600

a) Including a statistical discrepancy.

2.1 General Government Final Consumption Expenditure by Function, in Current Prices

Million Belgian francs	1970	1971	1972	1973	1974	1975	1976	1977	1978	1979	1980
1 General public services [a,b]	65401	77180	87011	100703	119192	146298	163671	187495	211477	234144	257769
2 Defence	32120	36298	40582	44861	49763	62758	71188	76614	86088	91463	98554
3 Public order and safety	...	...	...	...	...	...	...	...	...	...	...
4 Education [b]	67055	76362	90505	101803	125594	155314	177511	194824	212727	226092	247107
5 Health [a]	...	...	...	...	...	...	...	...	...	...	...
6 Social security and welfare [b]	10724	12143	14346	16948	19767	24028	28630	32583	36691	39211	43253
7 Housing and community amenities [a]	...	...	...	...	...	...	...	...	...	...	...
8 Recreational, cultural and religious affairs	...	...	...	...	...	...	...	...	...	...	...
9 Economic services	...	...	...	...	...	...	...	...	...	...	...
10 Other functions [a]	...	...	...	...	...	...	...	...	...	...	...
Total General Government Final Consumption Expenditure	175300	201983	232444	264315	314316	388398	441000	491516	546983	590910	646683

a) Items 'Health', 'Housing and community amenities' through 'Other functions' are included in item 'General public services'.
b) Including also rent and imputed amortization of buildings.

2.2 General Government Final Consumption Expenditure by Function, in Constant Prices

Million Belgian francs	1970	1971	1972	1973	1974	1975	1976	1977	1978	1979	1980
					At constant prices of: 1975						
1 General public services [a,b]	111297	121292	126401	135602	140320	146298	150066	158864	170223	178877	182212
2 Defence	54476	55821	57703	59324	57190	62758	65978	66573	72112	72233	71915
3 Public order and safety	...	...	...	...	...	...	...	...	...	...	...
4 Education [b]	117646	123348	133781	138797	149179	155314	161964	164523	171473	173641	177319
5 Health [a]	...	...	...	...	...	...	...	...	...	...	...
6 Social security and welfare [b]	18697	19521	21069	22987	23421	24028	26109	27441	29272	29640	30264
7 Housing and community amenities [a]	...	...	...	...	...	...	...	...	...	...	...
8 Recreational, cultural and religious affairs	...	...	...	...	...	...	...	...	...	...	...
9 Economic services	...	...	...	...	...	...	...	...	...	...	...
10 Other functions [a]	...	...	...	...	...	...	...	...	...	...	...
Total General Government Final Consumption Expenditure	302116	319982	338954	356710	370110	388398	404117	417401	443080	454391	461710

a) Items 'Health', 'Housing and community amenities' through 'Other functions' are included in item 'General public services'.
b) Including also rent and imputed amortization of buildings.

2.5 Private Final Consumption Expenditure by Type, in Current Prices

Million Belgian francs	1970	1971	1972	1973	1974	1975	1976	1977	1978	1979	1980
				Final Consumption Expenditure of Resident Households							
1 Food, beverages and tobacco	241700	257472	282076	312946	351414	388813	439100	461080	481844	505648	537889
a Food	185437	195068	212701	233007	266121	293039	335143	349569	365538	381608	405431
b Non-alcoholic beverages	8543	9729	11531	13753	13647	16540	19606	18673	20204	22083	23697
c Alcoholic beverages	32339	35481	39463	45700	48558	53543	55467	60781	64173	67582	73391
d Tobacco	15381	17194	18381	20486	23088	25691	28884	32057	31931	34375	35370

Belgium

2.5 Private Final Consumption Expenditure by Type, in Current Prices
(Continued)

Million Belgian francs

		1970	1971	1972	1973	1974	1975	1976	1977	1978	1979	1980
2	Clothing and footwear	56670	64699	71755	79581	93979	99945	112920	117865	124361	136719	144526
3	Gross rent, fuel and power	117182	124992	136476	151209	180987	218152	238550	264697	290791	328338	370408
4	Furniture, furnishings and household equipment and operation	107541	126153	139619	168805	202490	212832	245833	263518	272363	286011	315618
	a Household operation	35452	38698	41698	48894	55290	62199	70000	77897	85258	92262	99652
	b Other	72089	87455	97921	119911	147200	150633	175833	185621	187105	193749	215966
5	Medical care and health expenses	48151	54120	63335	77065	92304	114228	133006	152460	169315	180506	191148
6	Transport and communication	79785	87105	103108	116684	134993	162264	190515	209185	228367	250746	275436
	a Personal transport equipment	25520	26207	34783	40377	42645	51119	64170	70291	77303	82920	83520
	b Other	54265	60898	68325	76307	92348	111145	126345	138894	151064	167826	191916
7	Recreational, entertainment, education and cultural services	30693	34169	39628	45345	55433	61242	71938	78752	86719	95136	102184
	a Education	1669	1811	1965	2121	2547	3184	3421	3724	3952	4168	4457
	b Other	29024	32358	37663	43224	52886	58058	68517	75028	82767	90968	97727
8	Miscellaneous goods and services	85591	95207	106381	124568	136204	154676	180503	213135	226085	254392	268952
	a Personal care	21363	23562	26901	30994	35000	39698	45165	50538	54387	56635	57919
	b Expenditures in restaurants, cafes and hotels	37006	42546	47164	52978	54977	61485	67879	76678	81040	86086	94589
	c Other [a]	27222	29099	32316	40596	46227	53493	67459	85919	90658	111671	116444
	Total Final Consumption Expenditure in the Domestic Market by Households, of which	767313	843917	942378	1076203	1247804	1412152	1612365	1760692	1879845	2037496	2206161
	Plus: Direct purchases abroad by resident households	20500	23800	26500	34500	37800	43000	46100	56000	61800	71600	78500
	Less: Direct purchases in the domestic market by non-resident households	18800	20000	21100	26800	29700	34000	35400	44300	43400	50600	55800
	Equals: Final Consumption Expenditure of Resident Households [b]	769013	847717	947778	1083903	1255904	1421152	1623065	1772392	1898245	2058496	2228861

Final Consumption Expenditure of Private Non-profit Institutions Serving Households

		1970	1971	1972	1973	1974	1975	1976	1977	1978	1979	1980
	Equals: Final Consumption Expenditure of Private Non-profit Organisations Serving Households	...	...	...	...	...	...	...	...	...	...	...
	Private Final Consumption Expenditure	769013	847717	947778	1083903	1255904	1421152	1623065	1772392	1898245	2058496	2228861

a) Including a statistical discrepancy.
b) Including consumption expenditure of private non-profit institutions.

2.6 Private Final Consumption Expenditure by Type, in Constant Prices

Million Belgian francs

		1970	1971	1972	1973	1974	1975	1976	1977	1978	1979	1980

At constant prices of: 1975

Final Consumption Expenditure of Resident Households

		1970	1971	1972	1973	1974	1975	1976	1977	1978	1979	1980
1	Food, beverages and tobacco	350861	361826	369001	381892	390474	388813	396226	392897	401536	416466	426898
	a Food	270909	277812	280045	286332	296713	293039	299205	296770	306838	317666	324386
	b Non-alcoholic beverages	12134	13320	14072	15198	15033	16540	18590	17393	17790	18755	19098
	c Alcoholic beverages	43887	45676	48904	53223	51782	53543	53233	54433	55039	57162	60625
	d Tobacco	23931	25018	25980	27139	26946	25691	25198	24301	21869	22883	22789
2	Clothing and footwear	78909	86306	91499	95492	102254	99945	105993	104208	104067	109931	113434
3	Gross rent, fuel and power	180602	183989	196476	207190	209164	218152	225383	231413	242168	250778	251120
4	Furniture, furnishings and household equipment and operation	157800	171216	180261	202618	220935	212832	232847	236832	237435	243660	263445
	a Household operation	56423	57856	59021	61388	62806	62199	64503	66155	67628	69526	71227
	b Other	101377	113360	121240	141230	158129	150633	168344	170677	169807	174134	192218
5	Medical care and health expenses	73253	78747	86187	98030	104038	114228	121954	131231	137717	140679	141871
6	Transport and communication	124911	126706	140483	146899	152865	162264	173781	180372	187722	194290	193812
	a Personal transport equipment	36744	34262	44014	47833	46962	51119	57213	60036	64026	64950	62749
	b Other	88167	92444	96469	99066	105903	111145	116568	120336	123696	129340	131063
7	Recreational, entertainment, education and cultural services	48776	50485	54275	58396	63075	61242	67488	69865	72743	76924	79187
	a Education	2808	2883	2961	3034	3108	3184	3259	3335	3410	3486	3561
	b Other	45968	47602	51314	55362	59967	58058	64229	66530	69333	73438	75626
8	Miscellaneous goods and services	126367	135077	147578	172658	163691	154676	166486	176248	180730	198713	189621

Belgium

2.6 Private Final Consumption Expenditure by Type, in Constant Prices
(Continued)

Million Belgian francs

	1970	1971	1972	1973	1974	1975	1976	1977	1978	1979	1980
					At constant prices of:1975						
a Personal care	34461	35697	37452	39222	39383	39698	41542	42347	42217	42029	41048
b Expenditures in restaurants, cafes and hotels	51478	53737	55819	59395	58258	61485	62739	60635	58731	60677	63226
c Other [a]	40428	45643	54307	74041	66050	53493	62205	73266	79782	96007	85347
Total Final Consumption Expenditure in the Domestic Market by Households, of which	1141479	1194352	1265760	1363175	1406496	1412152	1490158	1523066	1564118	1631441	1659388
Plus: Direct purchases abroad by resident households	29300	31300	32700	39600	40700	43000	43100	46100	47200	53200	55900
Less: Direct purchases in the domestic market by non-resident households	26900	26300	26000	30800	32000	34000	33100	36500	33200	37600	39700
Equals: Final Consumption Expenditure of Resident Households [b]	1143879	1199352	1272460	1371975	1415196	1421152	1500158	1532666	1578118	1647041	1675588

Final Consumption Expenditure of Private Non-profit Institutions Serving Households

Equals: Final Consumption Expenditure of Private Non-profit Organisations Serving Households	...	...	...	...	...	...	...	...	...	...	...
Private Final Consumption Expenditure	1143879	1199352	1272460	1371975	1415196	1421152	1500158	1532666	1578118	1647041	1675588

a) Including a statistical discrepancy.
b) Including consumption expenditure of private non-profit institutions.

2.9 Gross Capital Formation by Kind of Activity of Owner, ISIC Major Divisions, in Current Prices

Million Belgian francs

	1970			1971			1972			1973		
	Total Gross Capital Formation	Increase in Stocks	Gross Fixed Capital Formation	Total Gross Capital Formation	Increase in Stocks	Gross Fixed Capital Formation	Total Gross Capital Formation	Increase in Stocks	Gross Fixed Capital Formation	Total Gross Capital Formation	Increase in Stocks	Gross Fixed Capital Formation
						All Producers						
1 Agriculture, hunting, fishing and forestry	...	...	7492	...	...	5884	...	...	7832	...	...	10140
2 Mining and quarrying	...	...	2214	...	...	2588	...	...	2828	...	...	2319
3 Manufacturing	...	...	73453	...	...	76869	...	...	73096	...	...	80700
4 Electricity, gas and water	...	...	15724	...	...	19561	...	...	23718	...	...	19456
5 Construction	...	...	8463	...	...	6024	...	...	6352	...	...	8410
6 Wholesale and retail trade, restaurants and hotels [a]	...	...	26300	...	...	33100	...	...	35800	...	...	42200
7 Transport, storage and communication [b]	...	...	27437	...	...	32280	...	...	35877	...	...	43481
8 Finance, insurance, real estate and business services [c]	...	...	71778	...	...	61835	...	...	68890	...	...	94610
9 Community, social and personal services [d]	...	...	14793	...	...	17736	...	...	19095	...	...	21460
Total Industries	...	...	247654	...	...	255877	...	...	273488	...	...	322776
Producers of Government Services	...	...	39420	...	...	49692	...	...	54864	...	...	51429
Private Non-Profit Institutions Serving Households	...	...	...	...	...	...	...	...	...	...	...	...
Total	307511	20437	287074	324701	19132	305569	337987	9635	328352	398920	24715	374205

	1974			1975			1976			1977		
	Total Gross Capital Formation	Increase in Stocks	Gross Fixed Capital Formation	Total Gross Capital Formation	Increase in Stocks	Gross Fixed Capital Formation	Total Gross Capital Formation	Increase in Stocks	Gross Fixed Capital Formation	Total Gross Capital Formation	Increase in Stocks	Gross Fixed Capital Formation
						All Producers						
1 Agriculture, hunting, fishing and forestry	...	...	12008	...	...	10909	...	...	13471	...	...	14683
2 Mining and quarrying	...	...	2467	...	...	2088	...	...	1848	...	...	2036
3 Manufacturing	...	...	110137	...	...	106409	...	...	93468	...	...	81194
4 Electricity, gas and water	...	...	23351	...	...	35692	...	...	33736	...	...	38379
5 Construction	...	...	8308	...	...	7917	...	...	11081	...	...	12665
6 Wholesale and retail trade, restaurants and hotels [a]	...	...	48700	...	...	49500	...	...	56400	...	...	61800
7 Transport, storage and communication [b]	...	...	47205	...	...	56693	...	...	57634	...	...	61667
8 Finance, insurance, real estate and business services [c]	...	...	130524	...	...	144839	...	...	184655	...	...	202755
9 Community, social and personal services [d]	...	...	29088	...	...	31841	...	...	39132	...	...	47669
Total Industries	...	...	411788	...	...	445888	...	...	491425	...	...	522848
Producers of Government Services	...	...	56077	...	...	66040	...	...	77092	...	...	80310
Private Non-Profit Institutions Serving Households	...	...	...	...	...	...	...	...	...	...	...	...
Total	513455	45590	467865	499486	-12442	511928	578023	9506	568517	614040	10882	603158

Belgium

2.9 Gross Capital Formation by Kind of Activity of Owner, ISIC Major Divisions, in Current Prices

Million Belgian francs

	1978 Total Gross Capital Formation	1978 Increase in Stocks	1978 Gross Fixed Capital Formation	1979 Total Gross Capital Formation	1979 Increase in Stocks	1979 Gross Fixed Capital Formation	1980 Total Gross Capital Formation	1980 Increase in Stocks	1980 Gross Fixed Capital Formation
				All Producers					
1 Agriculture, hunting, fishing and forestry	...	...	17206	...	...	15963	...	...	15122
2 Mining and quarrying	...	...	2462	...	...	3053	...	...	2914
3 Manufacturing	...	...	79417	...	...	83580	...	...	101298
4 Electricity, gas and water	...	...	39820	...	...	41906	...	...	51792
5 Construction	...	...	12522	...	...	13515	...	...	11270
6 Wholesale and retail trade, restaurants and hotels [a]	...	...	62300	...	...	69400	...	...	71300
7 Transport, storage and communication [b]	...	...	73547	...	...	72409	...	...	83000
8 Finance, insurance, real estate and business services [c]	...	...	228675	...	...	210688	...	...	226247
9 Community, social and personal services [d]	...	...	46825	...	...	55164	...	...	59694
Total Industries	...	...	562774	...	...	565678	...	...	622637
Producers of Government Services	...	...	81799	...	...	91012	...	...	106165
Private Non-Profit Institutions Serving Households	...	...	...	...	...	...	...	...	...
Total	653556	8983	644573	681926	25236	656690	736358	7556	728802

a) Including banks and insurance but excluding hotels and restaurants.
b) Including state investments on rivers, canals and ports.
c) Owner-occupied dwellings only.
d) Including also hotels, restaurants, real estate except owner-occuped dwellings and business services.

2.10 Gross Capital Formation by Kind of Activity of Owner, ISIC Major Divisions, in Constant Prices

Million Belgian francs

	1970 Total Gross Capital Formation	1970 Increase in Stocks	1970 Gross Fixed Capital Formation	1971 Total Gross Capital Formation	1971 Increase in Stocks	1971 Gross Fixed Capital Formation	1972 Total Gross Capital Formation	1972 Increase in Stocks	1972 Gross Fixed Capital Formation	1973 Total Gross Capital Formation	1973 Increase in Stocks	1973 Gross Fixed Capital Formation
					At constant prices of: 1975							
					All Producers							
1 Agriculture, hunting, fishing and forestry	...	...	10888	...	...	8198	...	...	10429	...	...	12882
2 Mining and quarrying	...	...	3042	...	...	3411	...	...	3580	...	...	2860
3 Manufacturing	...	...	103370	...	...	103019	...	...	94223	...	...	100106
4 Electricity, gas and water	...	...	24402	...	...	28335	...	...	32218	...	...	25027
5 Construction	...	...	11413	...	...	7830	...	...	8069	...	...	10489
6 Wholesale and retail trade, restaurants and hotels [a]	...	...	39625	...	...	47029	...	...	48986	...	...	54692
7 Transport, storage and communication [b]	...	...	38456	...	...	43130	...	...	46702	...	...	53309
8 Finance, insurance, real estate and business services [c]	...	...	126473	...	...	99822	...	...	105243	...	...	131464
9 Community, social and personal services [d]	...	...	24236	...	...	26452	...	...	26836	...	...	27991
Total Industries	...	...	381905	...	...	367226	...	...	376286	...	...	418820
Producers of Government Services	...	...	66561	...	...	74246	...	...	77487	...	...	65535
Private Non-Profit Institutions Serving Households	...	...	...	...	...	...	...	...	...	...	...	...
Total	478405	29939	448466	469997	28525	441472	468660	14887	453773	522444	38089	484355

	1974 Total Gross Capital Formation	1974 Increase in Stocks	1974 Gross Fixed Capital Formation	1975 Total Gross Capital Formation	1975 Increase in Stocks	1975 Gross Fixed Capital Formation	1976 Total Gross Capital Formation	1976 Increase in Stocks	1976 Gross Fixed Capital Formation	1977 Total Gross Capital Formation	1977 Increase in Stocks	1977 Gross Fixed Capital Formation
					At constant prices of: 1975							
					All Producers							
1 Agriculture, hunting, fishing and forestry	...	...	13266	...	...	10909	...	...	12740	...	...	13195
2 Mining and quarrying	...	...	2686	...	...	2088	...	...	1783	...	...	1897
3 Manufacturing	...	...	120310	...	...	106409	...	...	89493	...	...	74453
4 Electricity, gas and water	...	...	26090	...	...	35692	...	...	31544	...	...	34061

Belgium

2.10 Gross Capital Formation by Kind of Activity of Owner, ISIC Major Divisions, in Constant Prices
(Continued)

Million Belgian francs

	1974 TGCF	1974 IS	1974 GFCF	1975 TGCF	1975 IS	1975 GFCF	1976 TGCF	1976 IS	1976 GFCF	1977 TGCF	1977 IS	1977 GFCF
					At constant prices of:1975							
5 Construction	...	...	9137	...	...	7917	...	...	10577	...	...	11573
6 Wholesale and retail trade, restaurants and hotels a	...	...	54542	...	...	49500	...	...	52478	...	...	54138
7 Transport, storage and communication b	...	...	50775	...	...	56693	...	...	54268	...	...	55751
8 Finance, insurance, real estate and business services c	...	...	149666	...	...	144839	...	...	167611	...	...	170567
9 Community, social and personal services d	...	...	32682	...	...	31841	...	...	36143	...	...	41170
Total Industries	...	...	459154	...	...	445888	...	...	456637	...	...	456805
Producers of Government Services	...	...	61166	...	...	66040	...	...	70692	...	...	69784
Private Non-Profit Institutions Serving Households	...	...	...	...	...	...	...	...	...	...	...	...
Total	576956	56636	520320	499486	-12442	511928	537777	10448	527329	537651	11062	526589

	1978 TGCF	1978 IS	1978 GFCF	1979 TGCF	1979 IS	1979 GFCF	1980 TGCF	1980 IS	1980 GFCF
				At constant prices of:1975					
				All Producers					
1 Agriculture, hunting, fishing and forestry	...	...	15138	...	...	13380	...	...	12406
2 Mining and quarrying	...	...	2232	...	...	2785	...	...	2630
3 Manufacturing	...	...	71277	...	...	72744	...	...	86862
4 Electricity, gas and water	...	...	33350	...	...	33042	...	...	39356
5 Construction	...	...	11057	...	...	11716	...	...	9633
6 Wholesale and retail trade, restaurants and hotels a	...	...	52702	...	...	56187	...	...	55766
7 Transport, storage and communication b	...	...	65123	...	...	61807	...	...	68622
8 Finance, insurance, real estate and business services c	...	...	181399	...	...	158536	...	...	156515
9 Community, social and personal services d	...	...	38683	...	...	43291	...	...	44242
Total Industries	...	...	470961	...	...	453488	...	...	476032
Producers of Government Services	...	...	67361	...	...	71649	...	...	78554
Private Non-Profit Institutions Serving Households	...	...	...	...	...	...	...	...	...
Total	549165	10843	538322	549144	24007	525137	560748	6162	554586

a) Including banks and insurance but excluding hotels and restaurants.
b) Including state investments on rivers, canals and ports.
c) Owner-occupied dwellings only.
d) Including also hotels, restaurants, real estate except owner-occuped dwellings and business services.

2.17 Exports and Imports of Goods and Services, Detail

Million Belgian francs

	1970	1971	1972	1973	1974	1975	1976	1977	1978	1979	1980
					Exports of Goods and Services						
1 Exports of merchandise, f.o.b.	452800	487700	557300	697100	923600	856800	1012300	1161600	1214800	1453600	1647100
2 Transport and communication											
3 Insurance service charges	90300	101100	104600	122500	163100	174400	201200	273800	282600	314500	377000
4 Other commodities											
5 Adjustments of merchandise exports to change-of-ownership basis											
6 Direct purchases in the domestic market by non-residential households	18800	20000	21100	26800	29700	34000	35400	44300	43400	50600	55800
7 Direct purchases in the domestic market by extraterritorial bodies	...	...	...	...	...	...	...	...	...	...	...
Total Exports of Goods and Services	561900	608800	683000	846400	1116400	1065200	1248900	1479700	1540800	1818700	2079900
					Imports of Goods and Services						
1 Imports of merchandise, c.i.f. a	424900	467100	514200	665900	918800	858300	1043900	1236000	1282600	1541300	1782600

Belgium

2.17 Exports and Imports of Goods and Services, Detail
(Continued)

Million Belgian francs

		1970	1971	1972	1973	1974	1975	1976	1977	1978	1979	1980
2	Adjustments of merchandise imports to change-of-ownership basis											
3	Other transport and communication											
4	Other insurance service charges	87400	89900	92000	110800	152600	159800	174700	222000	238100	276000	347500
5	Other commodities											
6	Direct purchases abroad by government											
7	Direct purchases abroad by resident households	20500	23800	26500	34500	37800	43000	46100	56000	61800	71600	78500
	Total Imports of Goods and Services	532800	580800	632700	811200	1109200	1061100	1264700	1514000	1582500	1888900	2208600
	Balance of Goods and Services	29100	28000	50300	35200	7200	4100	-15800	-34300	-41700	-70200	-128700
	Total Imports and Balance of Goods and Services	561900	608800	683000	846400	1116400	1065200	1248900	1479700	1540800	1818700	2079900

a) Imports of merchandise are estimated on f.o.b. basis.

3.12 General Government Income and Outlay Account: Total and Subsectors

Million Belgian francs

		1970					1971				
		Total General Government	Central Government	State or Provincial Government	Local Government	Social Security Funds	Total General Government	Central Government	State or Provincial Government	Local Government	Social Security Funds
		Receipts										
1	Property and entrepreneurial income	12053	-4014	...	8419	7648	8466	-8864	...	8945	8385
2	Taxes, fees and contributions	438450	285788	...	20929	131733	491086	317715	...	23308	150063
a	Indirect taxes	165224	159893	...	5331	...	177257	171483	...	5774	...
b	Direct taxes	141493	125895	...	15598	...	163766	146232	...	17534	...
c	Social security contributions	131733	...	...	...	131733	150063	...	...	...	150063
d	Fees, fines and penalties	...	...	...	...	...	...	...	...	...	...
3	Other current transfers received	700	700	...	20941	37911	1200	1200	...	22640	43208
a	Casualty insurance claims	...	...	...	...	...	...	...	...	...	...
b	Transfers from other government subsectors	...	...	...	20941	37911	...	...	...	22640	43208
c	Transfers from abroad	700	700	...	...	...	1200	1200	...	...	...
d	Other transfers, except imputed	...	...	...	...	...	...	...	...	...	...
e	Imputed unfunded employee welfare contributions	...	...	...	...	...	...	...	...	...	...
	Total Current Receipts a	451203	282474	...	50289	177292	500752	310051	...	54893	201656
		Disbursements										
1	General governement final consumption expenditures	175300	135747	...	30257	9296	201983	156469	...	35019	10495
a	Compensation of employees	...	...	...	...	...	...	...	...	...	...
b	Consumption of fixed capital	2797	1986	...	783	28	3199	2264	...	898	37
c	Goods and services purchased, net	...	...	...	...	...	...	...	...	...	...
d	Less: Own account production of fixed assets	...	...	...	...	...	...	...	...	...	...
e	Indirect taxes paid, net	...	...	...	...	...	...	...	...	...	...
2	Property income paid	43120	34599	...	8521	...	46414	36411	...	10003	...

Belgium

3.12 General Government Income and Outlay Account: Total and Subsectors
(Continued)

Million Belgian francs

	1970					1971				
	Total General Government	Central Government	State or Provincial Government	Local Government	Social Security Funds	Total General Government	Central Government	State or Provincial Government	Local Government	Social Security Funds
3 Subsidies	16983	16754	...	229	...	17528	17257	...	271	...
4 Other current transfers paid	187799	85145	...	3839	157667	210847	96416	...	4012	176267
a Casualty insurance premiums, net	...	...	...	...	...	...	...	...	...	...
b Transfers to other government subsectors	...	58852	...	...	...	...	65848	...	...	...
c Transfers to households	180299	18793	...	3839	157667	199547	19268	...	4012	176267
Social security benefits	157667	-	...	-	157667	176267	-	...	-	176267
Social assistance grants	22632	18793	...	3839	...	23280	19268	...	4012	...
Unfunded employee welfare benefits	...	...	...	...	...	...	...	...	...	...
d Transfers to private non-profit institutions serving households	...	...	...	...	...	...	...	...	...	...
e Transfers to the rest of the world	7500	7500	...	...	...	11300	11300	...	...	...
Net saving	28001	10229	...	7443	10329	23980	3498	...	5588	14894
Total Current Disbursements and Net Saving [a]	451203	282474	...	50289	177292	500752	310051	...	54893	201656

	1972					1973				
	Total General Government	Central Government	State or Provincial Government	Local Government	Social Security Funds	Total General Government	Central Government	State or Provincial Government	Local Government	Social Security Funds

Receipts

1 Property and entrepreneurial income	3771	-14022	...	9155	8638	1524	-18243	...	9259	10508
2 Taxes, fees and contributions	552631	352564	...	27366	172701	646142	414319	...	29718	202105
a Indirect taxes	185509	179341	...	6168	...	206521	199387	...	7134	...
b Direct taxes	194421	173223	...	21198	...	237516	214932	...	22584	...
c Social security contributions	172701	...	...	...	172701	202105	...	...	...	202105
d Fees, fines and penalties	...	...	...	...	...	...	...	...	...	...
3 Other current transfers received	1200	1200	...	26896	53624	1200	1200	...	30233	61228
a Casualty insurance claims	...	...	...	...	...	...	...	...	...	...
b Transfers from other government subsectors	...	...	...	26896	53624	...	...	...	30233	61228
c Transfers from abroad	1200	1200	...	...	...	1200	1200	...	...	...
d Other transfers, except imputed	...	...	...	...	...	...	...	...	...	...
e Imputed unfunded employee welfare contributions	...	...	...	...	...	...	...	...	...	...
Total Current Receipts [a]	557602	339742	...	63417	234963	648866	397276	...	69210	273841

Disbursements

1 General government final consumption expenditures	232444	180229	...	39804	12411	264315	203638	...	45963	14714
a Compensation of employees	...	...	...	...	...	...	...	...	...	...
b Consumption of fixed capital	3567	2549	...	975	43	3942	2823	...	1070	49
c Goods and services purchased, net	...	...	...	...	...	...	...	...	...	...
d Less: Own account production of fixed assets	...	...	...	...	...	...	...	...	...	...
e Indirect taxes paid, net	...	...	...	...	...	...	...	...	...	...
2 Property income paid	51778	40498	...	11280	...	59144	46488	...	12656	...

Belgium

3.12 General Government Income and Outlay Account: Total and Subsectors
(Continued)

Million Belgian francs

		1972				1973			
	Total General Government	Central Government	State or Provincial Government	Local Government	Social Security Funds	Total General Government	Central Government	State or Provincial Government	Local Government	Social Security Funds
3 Subsidies	20372	20046	...	326	...	25370	25018	...	352	...
4 Other current transfers paid	242308	111134	...	4501	207193	289303	133764	...	5597	241403
a Casualty insurance premiums, net	...	...	...	...	...	...	...	...	...	...
b Transfers to other government subsectors	...	80520	...	...	...	...	91461	...	...	...
c Transfers to households	233308	21614	...	4501	207193	275003	28003	...	5597	241403
Social security benefits	207193	-	...	-	207193	241403	-	...	-	241403
Social assistance grants	26115	21614	...	4501	...	33600	28003	...	5597	...
Unfunded employee welfare benefits	...	...	...	...	...	...	...	...	...	...
d Transfers to private non-profit institutions serving households	...	...	...	...	...	...	...	...	...	...
e Transfers to the rest of the world	9000	9000	...	...	...	14300	14300	...	...	...
Net saving	10700	-12165	...	7506	15359	10734	-11632	...	4642	17724
Total Current Disbursements and Net Saving [a]	557602	339742	...	63417	234963	648866	397276	...	69210	273841

		1974				1975			
	Total General Government	Central Government	State or Provincial Government	Local Government	Social Security Funds	Total General Government	Central Government	State or Provincial Government	Local Government	Social Security Funds

Receipts

1 Property and entrepreneurial income	5963	-17930	...	11209	12684	6563	-21259	...	14036	13786
2 Taxes, fees and contributions	781206	503864	...	36862	240480	926334	594149	...	41305	290880
a Indirect taxes	240636	232633	...	8003	...	261082	252073	...	9009	...
b Direct taxes	300090	271231	...	28859	...	374372	342076	...	32296	...
c Social security contributions	240480	...	...	...	240480	290880	...	...	...	290880
d Fees, fines and penalties	...	...	...	...	...	...	...	...	...	...
3 Other current transfers received	1600	1600	...	34744	78193	2300	2300	...	43408	119717
a Casualty insurance claims	...	...	...	...	...	...	...	...	...	...
b Transfers from other government subsectors	...	...	...	34744	78193	...	...	...	43408	119717
c Transfers from abroad	1600	1600	...	...	...	2300	2300	...	...	...
d Other transfers, except imputed	...	...	...	...	...	...	...	...	...	...
e Imputed unfunded employee welfare contributions	...	...	...	...	...	...	...	...	...	...
Total Current Receipts [a]	788769	487534	...	82815	331357	935197	575190	...	98749	424383

Disbursements

1 General government final consumption expenditures	314316	241479	...	55886	16951	388398	299223	...	68745	20430
a Compensation of employees	...	...	...	...	...	...	...	...	...	...
b Consumption of fixed capital	4750	3326	...	1363	61	5634	3862	...	1697	75
c Goods and services purchased, net	...	...	...	...	...	...	...	...	...	...
d Less: Own account production of fixed assets	...	...	...	...	...	...	...	...	...	...
e Indirect taxes paid, net	...	...	...	...	...	...	...	...	...	...
2 Property income paid	73174	56619	...	16555	...	82484	61954	...	20530	...

Belgium

3.12 General Government Income and Outlay Account: Total and Subsectors
(Continued)

Million Belgian francs

	1974					1975				
	Total General Government	Central Government	State or Provincial Government	Local Government	Social Security Funds	Total General Government	Central Government	State or Provincial Government	Local Government	Social Security Funds
3 Subsidies	25014	24656	...	358	...	27531	27157	...	374	...
4 Other current transfers paid	347855	158596	...	6365	295831	453645	224763	...	7738	384269
a Casualty insurance premiums, net	...	...	...	...	...	...	...	...	...	...
b Transfers to other government subsectors	...	112937	...	...	...	...	163125	...	...	...
c Transfers to households	333355	31159	...	6365	295831	433945	41938	...	7738	384269
Social security benefits	295831	-	...	-	295831	384269	-	...	-	384269
Social assistance grants	37524	31159	...	6365	...	49676	41938	...	7738	...
Unfunded employee welfare benefits	...	...	...	...	...	...	...	...	...	...
d Transfers to private non-profit institutions serving households	...	...	...	...	...	...	...	...	...	...
e Transfers to the rest of the world	14500	14500	...	...	...	19700	19700	...	...	...
Net saving	28410	6184	...	3651	18575	-16861	-37907	...	1362	19684
Total Current Disbursements and Net Saving [a]	788769	487534	...	82815	331357	935197	575190	...	98749	424383

	1976					1977				
	Total General Government	Central Government	State or Provincial Government	Local Government	Social Security Funds	Total General Government	Central Government	State or Provincial Government	Local Government	Social Security Funds

Receipts

1 Property and entrepreneurial income	2815	-27188	...	16392	13611	3643	-28931	...	18145	14429
2 Taxes, fees and contributions	1052985	679492	...	45056	328437	1178774	766662	...	50964	361148
a Indirect taxes	308326	298257	...	10069	...	335151	324202	...	10949	...
b Direct taxes	416222	381235	...	34987	...	482475	442460	...	40015	...
c Social security contributions	328437	...	...	...	328437	361148	...	...	...	361148
d Fees, fines and penalties	...	...	...	...	...	...	...	...	...	...
3 Other current transfers received	2200	2200	...	52052	148223	2600	2600	...	61346	175080
a Casualty insurance claims	...	...	...	...	...	...	...	...	...	...
b Transfers from other government subsectors	...	...	...	52052	148223	...	...	...	61346	175080
c Transfers from abroad	2200	2200	...	...	...	2600	2600	...	...	...
d Other transfers, except imputed	...	...	...	...	...	...	...	...	...	...
e Imputed unfunded employee welfare contributions	...	...	...	...	...	...	...	...	...	...
Total Current Receipts [a]	1058000	654504	...	113500	490271	1185018	740332	...	130455	550657

Disbursements

1 General government final consumption expenditures	441000	338414	...	78061	24525	491516	373456	...	90326	27786
a Compensation of employees	...	...	...	...	...	...	...	...	...	...
b Consumption of fixed capital	6463	4375	...	2001	87	7621	5074	...	2441	106
c Goods and services purchased, net	...	...	...	...	...	...	...	...	...	...
d Less: Own account production of fixed assets	...	...	...	...	...	...	...	...	...	...
e Indirect taxes paid, net	...	...	...	...	...	...	...	...	...	...
2 Property income paid	97756	73802	...	24396	...	116959	88825	...	28975	...

Belgium

3.12 General Government Income and Outlay Account: Total and Subsectors
(Continued)

Million Belgian francs

		1976					1977			
		Total General Government	Central Government	State or Provincial Government	Local Government	Social Security Funds	Total General Government	Central Government	State or Provincial Government	Local Government	Social Security Funds
3	Subsidies	36537	36006	...	531	...	40227	39678	...	609	...
4	Other current transfers paid	520662	258328	...	8925	453684	585165	304930	...	9918	506743
	a Casualty insurance premiums, net	...	...	...	...	...	...	...	...	...	...
	b Transfers to other government subsectors	...	200275	...	...	...	...	236426	...	...	...
	c Transfers to households	507262	44653	...	8925	453684	568965	52304	...	9918	506743
	Social security benefits	453684	-	...	-	453684	506743	-	...	-	506743
	Social assistance grants	53578	44653	...	8925	...	62222	52304	...	9918	...
	Unfunded employee welfare benefits	...	...	...	...	...	...	...	...	...	...
	d Transfers to private non-profit institutions serving households	...	...	...	...	...	...	...	...	...	...
	e Transfers to the rest of the world	13400	13400	...	...	...	16200	16200	...	...	...
	Net saving	-37955	-52046	...	1587	12062	-48849	-66497	...	627	16128
	Total Current Disbursements and Net Saving [a]	1058000	654504	...	113500	490271	1185018	740332	...	130455	550657

		1978					1979			
		Total General Government	Central Government	State or Provincial Government	Local Government	Social Security Funds	Total General Government	Central Government	State or Provincial Government	Local Government	Social Security Funds

Receipts

1	Property and entrepreneurial income	...	...	...	...	14408	...	...	...	...	13922
2	Taxes, fees and contributions	...	...	...	...	...	...	...	...	...	...
	a Indirect taxes	364957	353728	...	...	...	388861	377487	...	...	...
	b Direct taxes	...	...	...	...	...	...	...	...	...	...
	c Social security contributions	377538	...	...	...	...	405393	...	...	...	...
	d Fees, fines and penalties	...	...	...	...	...	...	...	...	...	...
3	Other current transfers received	2400	...	...	...	...	3300	...	...	...	...
	a Casualty insurance claims	...	...	...	...	...	...	...	...	...	...
	b Transfers from other government subsectors	...	...	...	...	197859	...	...	...	...	210048
	c Transfers from abroad	2400	2400	...	...	...	3300	3300	...	...	...
	d Other transfers, except imputed	...	...	...	...	...	...	...	...	...	...
	e Imputed unfunded employee welfare contributions	...	...	...	...	...	...	...	...	...	...
	Total Current Receipts [a]	1298653	827624	...	...	589805	1412118	906560	...	...	629363

Disbursements

1	General government final consumption expenditures	546983	411345	...	...	...	590910	439778	...	...	...
	a Compensation of employees	...	...	...	...	...	...	...	...	...	...
	b Consumption of fixed capital	8557	5686	...	...	122	9428	6262	...	...	138
	c Goods and services purchased, net	...	...	...	...	...	...	...	...	...	...
	d Less: Own account production of fixed assets	...	...	...	...	...	...	...	...	...	...
	e Indirect taxes paid, net	...	...	...	...	...	...	...	...	...	...
2	Property income paid	137866	106772	...	...	...	166142	131315	...	...	...

Belgium

3.12 General Government Income and Outlay Account: Total and Subsectors
(Continued)

Million Belgian francs

	1978					1979				
	Total General Government	Central Government	State or Provincial Government	Local Government	Social Security Funds	Total General Government	Central Government	State or Provincial Government	Local Government	Social Security Funds
3 Subsidies	46500	45877	...	...	...	56253	55562	...	...	...
4 Other current transfers paid	638147	...	...	...	...	694707	...	...	...	...
a Casualty insurance premiums, net	...	...	...	...	...	...	...	...	...	...
b Transfers to other government subsectors	...	268541	...	...	...	...	289295	...	...	...
c Transfers to households	621747	...	...	...	...	680107	...	...	...	...
Social security benefits	553678	...	...	...	553678	604130	...	...	...	604130
Social assistance grants	68069	...	...	...	...	75977	...	...	...	...
Unfunded employee welfare benefits	...	...	...	...	...	...	...	...	...	...
d Transfers to private non-profit institutions serving households	...	...	...	...	...	...	...	...	...	...
e Transfers to the rest of the world	16400	16400	...	...	...	14600	14600	...	...	...
Net saving	-70843	-77680	...	...	4874	-95894	-87620	...	...	-7887
Total Current Disbursements and Net Saving [a]	1298653	827624	...	...	589805	1412118	906560	...	...	629363

	1980				
	Total General Government	Central Government	State or Provincial Government	Local Government	Social Security Funds

Receipts

1 Property and entrepreneurial income	...	...	...	...	16635
2 Taxes, fees and contributions	...	...	...	...	...
a Indirect taxes	413851	401266	...	...	...
b Direct taxes	...	...	...	...	...
c Social security contributions	437207	...	...	...	...
d Fees, fines and penalties	...	...	...	...	...
3 Other current transfers received	3200	...	...	...	...
a Casualty insurance claims	...	...	...	...	...
b Transfers from other government subsectors	...	...	...	...	225234
c Transfers from abroad	3200	3200	...	...	...
d Other transfers, except imputed	...	...	...	...	...
e Imputed unfunded employee welfare contributions	...	...	...	...	...
Total Current Receipts [a]	1507995	968374	...	...	679076

Disbursements

1 General government final consumption expenditures	646683	476769	...	...	...
a Compensation of employees	...	...	...	...	...
b Consumption of fixed capital	10481	6940	...	...	153
c Goods and services purchased, net	...	...	...	...	...
d Less: Own account production of fixed assets	...	...	...	...	...
e Indirect taxes paid, net	...	...	...	...	...
2 Property income paid	214409	172556	...	...	...

Belgium

3.12 General Government Income and Outlay Account: Total and Subsectors
(Continued)

Million Belgian francs

		1980			
		Total General Government	Central Government	State or Provincial Government	Local Government	Social Security Funds
3	Subsidies	51710	50968	...	...	...
4	Other current transfers paid	764159	...	...	...	...
	a Casualty insurance premiums, net	...	...	...	...	...
	b Transfers to other government subsectors	...	307939	...	...	...
	c Transfers to households	738959	...	...	...	...
	Social security benefits	656569	...	...	...	656569
	Social assistance grants	82390	...	...	...	...
	Unfunded employee welfare benefits	...	...	...	...	...
	d Transfers to private non-profit institutions serving households	...	...	...	...	...
	e Transfers to the rest of the world	25200	25200	...	...	...
Net saving		-168966	-134398	...	...	-13498
Total Current Disbursements and Net Saving a		1507995	968374	...	...	679076

a) Column 'State or Provincial government' is included in column 'Local government'.

3.51 External Transactions: Current Account: Detail

Million Belgian francs

		1970	1971	1972	1973	1974	1975	1976	1977	1978	1979	1980
	Payments to the Rest of the World												
1	Imports of goods and services	532800	580800	632700	811200	1109200	1061100	1264700	1514000	1582500	1888900	2208600
	a Imports of merchandise c.i.f.	424900	467100	514200	665900	918800	858300	1043900	1236000	1282600	1541300	1782600
	b Other	107900	113700	118500	145300	190400	202800	220800	278000	299900	347600	426000
2	Factor income paid to the rest of the world	43200	35800	34400	45000	77700	78600	75200	84900	104000	137900	230100
	a Compensation of employees	3100	3600	4200	4900	6500	8300	9400	9700	10200	11800	14000
	b Property and entrepreneurial income paid	40100	32200	30200	40100	71200	70300	65800	75200	93800	126100	216100
3	Indirect taxes paid to supranational organizations	...	...	...	...	...	...	...	...	...	...	...
4	Other current transfers to the rest of the world	16300	20400	18500	25200	27900	36300	33300	38500	40600	42600	57000
	a By general government	7500	11300	9000	14300	14500	19700	13400	16200	16400	14600	25200
	b By other resident sectors	8800	9100	9500	10900	13400	16600	19900	22300	24200	28000	31800
5	Surplus of the nation on current transactions	35100	29500	56200	33800	6700	-3600	-16100	-42300	-51300	-94800	-180200
Payments to the Rest of the World, and Surplus of the Nation on Current Transfers		627400	666500	741800	915200	1221500	1172400	1357100	1595100	1675800	1974600	2315500
	Receipts From The Rest of the World												
1	Exports of goods and services	561900	608800	683000	846400	1116400	1065200	1248900	1479700	1540800	1818700	2079900
	a Exports of merchandise f.o.b.	452800	487700	557300	697100	923600	856800	1012300	1161600	1214800	1453600	1647100
	b Other	109100	121100	125700	149300	192800	208400	236600	318100	326000	365100	432800
2	Factor income received from the rest of the world	54100	45300	46600	54300	89500	91300	92500	97000	114100	134400	211800
	a Compensation of employees	9700	10900	13100	14500	17500	21100	23700	26400	27300	29700	30900
	b Property and entrepreneurial income received	44400	34400	33500	39800	72000	70200	68800	70600	86800	104700	180900
3	Subsidies received from supranational organizations	...	...	...	...	...	...	...	...	...	...	...
4	Other current transfers from the rest of the world	11400	12400	12200	14500	15600	15900	15700	18400	20900	21500	23800
	a To general government	700	1200	1200	1200	1600	2300	2200	2600	2400	3300	3200
	b To other resident sectors	10700	11200	11000	13300	14000	13600	13500	15800	18500	18200	20600
Receipts from the Rest of the World on Current Transfers		627400	666500	741800	915200	1221500	1172400	1357100	1595100	1675800	1974600	2315500

Belgium

3.52 External Transactions: Capital Accumulation Account

Million Belgian francs

	1970	1971	1972	1973	1974	1975	1976	1977	1978	1979	1980
Finance of Gross Accumulation											
1 Surplus of the nation on current transactions	35100	29500	56200	33800	6700	-3600	-16100	-42300	-51300	-94800	-180200
2 Capital transfers received from the rest of the world [a]	-2000	-1100	-2600	-1600	-2200	-2300	-2700	-3100	-3200	-4500	-4300
Total Finance of Gross Accumulation	33100	28400	53600	32200	4500	-5900	-18800	-45400	-54500	-99300	-184500
Gross Accumulation											
1 Capital transfers paid to the rest of the world	...	...	...	...	...	...	...	...	...	...	...
2 Purchases of intangible assets, n.e.c., net, from the rest of the world	...	...	...	...	...	...	...	...	...	...	...
3 Net lending to the rest of the world	33100	28400	53600	32200	4500	-5900	-18800	-45400	-54500	-99300	-184500
Total Gross Accumulation	33100	28400	53600	32200	4500	-5900	-18800	-45400	-54500	-99300	-184500

a) Net.

4.3 Derivation of Value Added by Kind of Activity, ISIC Divisions, in Current Prices

Million Belgian francs

	1970 Gross Output	1970 Intermediate Consumption	1970 Value Added	1971 Gross Output	1971 Intermediate Consumption	1971 Value Added	1972 Gross Output	1972 Intermediate Consumption	1972 Value Added	1973 Gross Output	1973 Intermediate Consumption	1973 Value Added
All Producers												
1 Agriculture, hunting, forestry and fishing	...	...	45997	...	...	49290	...	...	63450	...	...	69325
a Agriculture and hunting	...	...	43327	...	...	46639	...	...	60486	...	...	65562
b Forestry and logging	...	...	1932	...	...	1882	...	...	2145	...	...	2826
c Fishing	...	...	738	...	...	769	...	...	819	...	...	937
2 Mining and quarrying	...	...	12023	...	...	13721	...	...	13359	...	...	11868
a Coal mining [a]	...	...	6188	...	...	6829	...	...	6163	...	...	4825
b Crude petroleum and natural gas production	...	...	...	...	...	...	...	...	...	...	...	...
c Metal ore mining	...	...	...	...	...	...	...	...	...	...	...	...
d Other mining	...	...	...	...	...	...	...	...	...	...	...	...
3 Manufacturing	...	...	411290	...	...	424820	...	...	475741	...	...	544218
a Manufacture of food, beverages and tobacco	...	...	75750	...	...	79445	...	...	88082	...	...	95424
b Textile, wearing apparel and leather industries	...	...	44150	...	...	47093	...	...	53007	...	...	55017
c Manufacture of wood and wood products, including furniture	...	...	18097	...	...	19823	...	...	23202	...	...	26301
d Manufacture of paper and paper products, printing and publishing	...	...	20608	...	...	22298	...	...	23819	...	...	27575
e Manufacture of chemicals and chemical petroleum, coal, rubber and plastic products	...	...	38792	...	...	42570	...	...	48515	...	...	54091
f Manufacture of non-metallic mineral products, except products of petroleum and coal	...	...	21170	...	...	22026	...	...	24090	...	...	27444
g Basic metal industries	...	...	43403	...	...	35354	...	...	38805	...	...	56176
h Manufacture of fabricated metal products, machinery and equipment	...	...	134987	...	...	140045	...	...	157600	...	...	180050
i Other manufacturing industries [b]	...	...	14333	...	...	16166	...	...	18621	...	...	22140
4 Electricity, gas and water	...	...	29594	...	...	36221	...	...	40228	...	...	44888
a Electricity, gas and steam	...	...	25816	...	...	31696	...	...	35100	...	...	38410
b Water works and supply	...	...	3778	...	...	4525	...	...	5128	...	...	6478
5 Construction	...	...	88629	...	...	95558	...	...	102775	...	...	119349
6 Wholesale and retail trade, restaurants and hotels	...	...	163640	...	...	197440	...	...	214540	...	...	231887
a Wholesale and retail trade [c]	...	...	163640	...	...	197440	...	...	214540	...	...	231887
b Restaurants and hotels	...	...	...	...	...	...	...	...	...	...	...	...
7 Transport, storage and communication	...	...	92632	...	...	105042	...	...	118990	...	...	136834
8 Finance, insurance, real estate and business services	...	...	137379	...	...	147687	...	...	166822	...	...	191430
9 Community, social and personal services	...	...	98423	...	...	112184	...	...	126805	...	...	146631

Belgium

4.3 Derivation of Value Added by Kind of Activity, ISIC Divisions, in Current Prices
(Continued)

Million Belgian francs

	1970 Gross Output	1970 Intermediate Consumption	1970 Value Added	1971 Gross Output	1971 Intermediate Consumption	1971 Value Added	1972 Gross Output	1972 Intermediate Consumption	1972 Value Added	1973 Gross Output	1973 Intermediate Consumption	1973 Value Added
Total, Industries	...	...	1079607	...	...	1181963	...	...	1322710	...	...	1496430
Producers of Government Services	...	...	135035	...	...	153758	...	...	180422	...	...	207670
Other Producers	...	...	16516	...	...	17309	...	...	18103	...	...	21706
Total	...	...	1231158	...	...	1353030	...	...	1521235	...	...	1725806
Imputed bank service charge	...	...	-11755	...	...	-12434	...	...	-15258	...	...	-18684
Import duties	...	...	59283	...	...	66823	...	...	73266	...	...	93601
Value added tax	...	...	...	...	...	...	...	...	...	...	...	...
Other adjustments	...	...	2238	...	...	-5018	...	...	-10734	...	...	-18385
Total	...	...	1280924	...	...	1402401	...	...	1568509	...	...	1782338

	1974 Gross Output	1974 Intermediate Consumption	1974 Value Added	1975 Gross Output	1975 Intermediate Consumption	1975 Value Added	1976 Gross Output	1976 Intermediate Consumption	1976 Value Added	1977 Gross Output	1977 Intermediate Consumption	1977 Value Added
All Producers												
1 Agriculture, hunting, forestry and fishing	...	...	62196	...	...	68208	...	...	76942	...	...	68339
a Agriculture and hunting	...	...	58804	...	...	64705	...	...	72819	...	...	64407
b Forestry and logging	...	...	2479	...	...	2563	...	...	3137	...	...	2845
c Fishing	...	...	913	...	...	940	...	...	986	...	...	1087
2 Mining and quarrying	...	...	15765	...	...	18866	...	...	19018	...	...	18232
a Coal mining [a]	...	...	7784	...	...	10487	...	...	9458	...	...	8486
b Crude petroleum and natural gas production	...	...	...	...	...	...	...	...	...	...	...	...
c Metal ore mining	...	...	...	...	...	...	...	...	...	...	...	...
d Other mining	...	...	...	...	...	...	...	...	...	...	...	...
3 Manufacturing	...	...	644001	...	...	634200	...	...	719595	...	...	762846
a Manufacture of food, beverages and tobacco	...	...	108871	...	...	122056	...	...	131691	...	...	135533
b Textile, wearing apparel and leather industries	...	...	60448	...	...	56641	...	...	63951	...	...	61594
c Manufacture of wood and wood products, including furniture	...	...	29260	...	...	29397	...	...	34090	...	...	36630
d Manufacture of paper and paper products, printing and publishing	...	...	34865	...	...	35646	...	...	36191	...	...	39398
e Manufacture of chemicals and chemical petroleum, coal, rubber and plastic products	...	...	67641	...	...	58248	...	...	65283	...	...	74215
f Manufacture of non-metallic mineral products, except products of petroleum and coal	...	...	30180	...	...	29101	...	...	33268	...	...	37719
g Basic metal industries	...	...	77746	...	...	37882	...	...	49895	...	...	41359
h Manufacture of fabricated metal products, machinery and equipment	...	...	207702	...	...	239709	...	...	275503	...	...	300321
i Other manufacturing industries [b]	...	...	27288	...	...	25520	...	...	29723	...	...	36077
4 Electricity, gas and water	...	...	52448	...	...	71020	...	...	77986	...	...	86483
a Electricity, gas and steam	...	...	44436	...	...	61205	...	...	66150	...	...	73275
b Water works and supply	...	...	8012	...	...	9815	...	...	11836	...	...	13208
5 Construction	...	...	148076	...	...	167018	...	...	195663	...	...	215564
6 Wholesale and retail trade, restaurants and hotels	...	...	250548	...	...	287303	...	...	340304	...	...	360457
a Wholesale and retail trade [c]	...	...	250548	...	...	287303	...	...	340304	...	...	360457
b Restaurants and hotels	...	...	...	...	...	...	...	...	...	...	...	...
7 Transport, storage and communication	...	...	171191	...	...	182919	...	...	204876	...	...	222420
8 Finance, insurance, real estate and business services	...	...	222325	...	...	254274	...	...	295136	...	...	329570
9 Community, social and personal services	...	...	166395	...	...	197696	...	...	227750	...	...	258762
Total, Industries	...	...	1732945	...	...	1881504	...	...	2157270	...	...	2322673
Producers of Government Services	...	...	249512	...	...	304696	...	...	347799	...	...	387079

Belgium

4.3 Derivation of Value Added by Kind of Activity, ISIC Divisions, in Current Prices
(Continued)

Million Belgian francs

	1974 Gross Output	1974 Intermediate Consumption	1974 Value Added	1975 Gross Output	1975 Intermediate Consumption	1975 Value Added	1976 Gross Output	1976 Intermediate Consumption	1976 Value Added	1977 Gross Output	1977 Intermediate Consumption	1977 Value Added
Other Producers	...	...	22686	...	...	25670	...	...	27922	...	...	31920
Total	...	...	2005143	...	...	2211870	...	...	2532991	...	...	2741672
Imputed bank service charge	...	...	-23128	...	...	-26178	...	...	-35326	...	...	-39625
Import duties	...	...	134713	...	...	129662	...	...	155866	...	...	171080
Value added tax	...	...	...	...	...	...	...	...	...	...	...	...
Other adjustments	...	...	-25853	...	...	-2218	...	...	-27243	...	...	-29479
Total	...	...	2090875	...	...	2313136	...	...	2626288	...	...	2843648

	1978 Gross Output	1978 Intermediate Consumption	1978 Value Added	1979 Gross Output	1979 Intermediate Consumption	1979 Value Added	1980 Gross Output	1980 Intermediate Consumption	1980 Value Added

All Producers

	1978 GO	1978 IC	1978 VA	1979 GO	1979 IC	1979 VA	1980 GO	1980 IC	1980 VA
1 Agriculture, hunting, forestry and fishing	...	...	76035	...	...	73242	...	...	74062
a Agriculture and hunting	...	...	71875	...	...	68692	...	...	69350
b Forestry and logging	...	...	2876	...	...	3282	...	...	3424
c Fishing	...	...	1284	...	...	1268	...	...	1288
2 Mining and quarrying	...	...	16930	...	...	15708	...	...	17876
a Coal mining [a]	...	...	7359	...	...	5549	...	...	6578
b Crude petroleum and natural gas production	...	...	...	...	...	...	...	...	...
c Metal ore mining	...	...	...	...	...	...	...	...	...
d Other mining	...	...	...	...	...	...	...	...	...
3 Manufacturing	...	...	804736	...	...	858041	...	...	883165
a Manufacture of food, beverages and tobacco	...	...	146756	...	...	153241	...	...	160774
b Textile, wearing apparel and leather industries	...	...	61857	...	...	66988	...	...	68160
c Manufacture of wood and wood products, including furniture	...	...	36391	...	...	37936	...	...	42427
d Manufacture of paper and paper products, printing and publishing	...	...	39854	...	...	42525	...	...	44228
e Manufacture of chemicals and chemical petroleum, coal, rubber and plastic products	...	...	77911	...	...	86522	...	...	95713
f Manufacture of non-metallic mineral products, except products of petroleum and coal	...	...	36101	...	...	36279	...	...	39199
g Basic metal industries	...	...	51350	...	...	60268	...	...	46610
h Manufacture of fabricated metal products, machinery and equipment	...	...	314177	...	...	331008	...	...	339896
i Other manufacturing industries [b]	...	...	40339	...	...	43274	...	...	46158
4 Electricity, gas and water	...	...	93910	...	...	96497	...	...	109283
a Electricity, gas and steam	...	...	78867	...	...	79983	...	...	92046
b Water works and supply	...	...	15043	...	...	16514	...	...	17237
5 Construction	...	...	231160	...	...	235591	...	...	269054
6 Wholesale and retail trade, restaurants and hotels	...	...	396560	...	...	393365	...	...	398385
a Wholesale and retail trade [c]	...	...	396560	...	...	393365	...	...	398385
b Restaurants and hotels	...	...	...	...	...	...	...	...	...
7 Transport, storage and communication	...	...	241911	...	...	267462	...	...	302587
8 Finance, insurance, real estate and business services	...	...	364476	...	...	396800	...	...	418983
9 Community, social and personal services	...	...	282868	...	...	301381	...	...	324698
Total, Industries	...	...	2508586	...	...	2638087	...	...	2798093
Producers of Government Services	...	...	428669	...	...	466999	...	...	514437

Belgium

4.3 Derivation of Value Added by Kind of Activity, ISIC Divisions, in Current Prices
(Continued)

Million Belgian francs

	1978 Gross Output	1978 Intermediate Consumption	1978 Value Added	1979 Gross Output	1979 Intermediate Consumption	1979 Value Added	1980 Gross Output	1980 Intermediate Consumption	1980 Value Added
Other Producers	...	...	35444	...	...	38169	...	...	40061
Total	...	...	2972699	...	...	3143255	...	...	3352591
Imputed bank service charge	...	...	-45115	...	...	-48085	...	...	-47410
Import duties	...	...	168934	...	...	199622	...	...	233459
Value added tax	...	...	...	...	...	...	...	...	...
Other adjustments	...	...	-39434	...	...	-33660	...	...	-55438
Total	...	...	3057084	...	...	3261132	...	...	3483202

a) Including the electric plants for coal mining.
b) Including garages.
c) Including distribution of petroleum products.

4.4 Derivation of Value Added by Kind of Activity, ISIC Divisions, in Constant Prices

Million Belgian francs

		1970 Gross Output	1970 Intermediate Consumption	1970 Value Added	1971 Gross Output	1971 Intermediate Consumption	1971 Value Added	1972 Gross Output	1972 Intermediate Consumption	1972 Value Added	1973 Gross Output	1973 Intermediate Consumption	1973 Value Added
		At constant prices of: 1975 — All Producers												
1	Agriculture, hunting, forestry and fishing	...	...	70345	...	...	74367	...	...	74374	...	...	77276
	a Agriculture and hunting	...	...	66678	...	...	70598	...	...	70717	...	...	73740
	b Forestry and logging	...	...	2405	...	...	2468	...	...	2545	...	...	2599
	c Fishing	...	...	1262	...	...	1301	...	...	1112	...	...	937
2	Mining and quarrying	...	...	23873	...	...	23887	...	...	22722	...	...	20246
	a Coal mining	...	...	16770	...	...	16351	...	...	14951	...	...	12501
	b Crude petroleum and natural gas production	...	...	...	...	...	...	...	...	...	...	...	...
	c Metal ore mining	...	...	...	...	...	...	...	...	...	...	...	...
	d Other mining	...	...	...	...	...	...	...	...	...	...	...	...
3	Manufacturing	...	...	530132	...	...	550264	...	...	594065	...	...	650835
	a Manufacture of food, beverages and tobacco	...	...	102986	...	...	106942	...	...	113478	...	...	115219
	b Textile, wearing apparel and leather industries	...	...	58638	...	...	63089	...	...	64738	...	...	66864
	c Manufacture of wood and wood products, including furniture	...	...	21579	...	...	24308	...	...	27144	...	...	30363
	d Manufacture of paper and paper products, printing and publishing	...	...	33911	...	...	35637	...	...	36610	...	...	38296
	e Manufacture of chemicals and chemical petroleum, coal, rubber and plastic products	...	...	46289	...	...	50849	...	...	59468	...	...	66218
	f Manufacture of non-metallic mineral products, except products of petroleum and coal	...	...	26763	...	...	26396	...	...	28604	...	...	32144
	g Basic metal industries	...	...	40303	...	...	39004	...	...	43820	...	...	48383
	h Manufacture of fabricated metal products, machinery and equipment	...	...	181675	...	...	183278	...	...	196808	...	...	226646
	i Other manufacturing industries [a]	...	...	17988	...	...	20761	...	...	23395	...	...	26702
4	Electricity, gas and water	...	...	41498	...	...	47358	...	...	55103	...	...	60261
5	Construction	...	...	147527	...	...	150524	...	...	152746	...	...	160615
6	Wholesale and retail trade, restaurants and hotels	...	...	351649	...	...	370125	...	...	386321	...	...	411093
	a Wholesale and retail trade [bc]	...	...	351649	...	...	370125	...	...	386321	...	...	411093
	b Restaurants and hotels	...	...	...	...	...	...	...	...	...	...	...	...
7	Transport, storage and communication	...	...	173157	...	...	177759	...	...	180852	...	...	192602
8	Finance, insurance, real estate and business services	...	...	206218	...	...	212309	...	...	227767	...	...	243986
9	Community, social and personal services	...	...	150734	...	...	158044	...	...	166703	...	...	180322
Total, Industries		...	...	1695133	...	...	1764637	...	...	1860653	...	...	1997236
Producers of Government Services		...	...	239087	...	...	250620	...	...	267602	...	...	284097

Belgium

4.4 Derivation of Value Added by Kind of Activity, ISIC Divisions, in Constant Prices
(Continued)

Million Belgian francs

	1970 Gross Output	1970 Intermediate Consumption	1970 Value Added	1971 Gross Output	1971 Intermediate Consumption	1971 Value Added	1972 Gross Output	1972 Intermediate Consumption	1972 Value Added	1973 Gross Output	1973 Intermediate Consumption	1973 Value Added
					At constant prices of:1975							
Other Producers	...	...	27286	...	...	27014	...	...	26917	...	...	26830
Total	...	...	1961506	...	...	2042271	...	...	2155172	...	...	2308163
Imputed bank service charge	...	...	-18248	...	...	-18813	...	...	-22282	...	...	-25153
Import duties	...	...	...	...	...	...	...	...	...	...	...	...
Value added tax	...	...	...	...	...	...	...	...	...	...	...	...
Other adjustments	...	...	-5258	...	...	-9527	...	...	-10916	...	...	-28981
Total	...	...	1938000	...	...	2013931	...	...	2121974	...	...	2254029

	1974 Gross Output	1974 Intermediate Consumption	1974 Value Added	1975 Gross Output	1975 Intermediate Consumption	1975 Value Added	1976 Gross Output	1976 Intermediate Consumption	1976 Value Added	1977 Gross Output	1977 Intermediate Consumption	1977 Value Added
					At constant prices of:1975							
					All Producers							
1 Agriculture, hunting, forestry and fishing	...	...	80280	...	...	68208	...	...	65494	...	...	67537
a Agriculture and hunting	...	...	76947	...	...	64705	...	...	61992	...	...	64116
b Forestry and logging	...	...	2447	...	...	2563	...	...	2688	...	...	2567
c Fishing	...	...	886	...	...	940	...	...	814	...	...	854
2 Mining and quarrying	...	...	20711	...	...	18866	...	...	18369	...	...	16709
a Coal mining	...	...	12414	...	...	10487	...	...	9620	...	...	8498
b Crude petroleum and natural gas production	...	...	...	...	...	...	...	...	...	...	...	...
c Metal ore mining	...	...	...	...	...	...	...	...	...	...	...	...
d Other mining	...	...	...	...	...	...	...	...	...	...	...	...
3 Manufacturing	...	...	679055	...	...	634200	...	...	687403	...	...	693784
a Manufacture of food, beverages and tobacco	...	...	120188	...	...	122056	...	...	124658	...	...	123599
b Textile, wearing apparel and leather industries	...	...	65472	...	...	56641	...	...	61488	...	...	54668
c Manufacture of wood and wood products, including furniture	...	...	30224	...	...	29397	...	...	32305	...	...	33307
d Manufacture of paper and paper products, printing and publishing	...	...	39206	...	...	35646	...	...	34484	...	...	36435
e Manufacture of chemicals and chemical petroleum, coal, rubber and plastic products	...	...	71217	...	...	58248	...	...	71231	...	...	78673
f Manufacture of non-metallic mineral products, except products of petroleum and coal	...	...	33471	...	...	29101	...	...	32313	...	...	33557
g Basic metal industries	...	...	45149	...	...	37882	...	...	46906	...	...	42779
h Manufacture of fabricated metal products, machinery and equipment	...	...	244098	...	...	239709	...	...	255393	...	...	259069
i Other manufacturing industries [a]	...	...	30030	...	...	25520	...	...	28625	...	...	31697
4 Electricity, gas and water	...	...	64445	...	...	71020	...	...	75407	...	...	82610
5 Construction	...	...	167420	...	...	167018	...	...	177864	...	...	182281
6 Wholesale and retail trade, restaurants and hotels	...	...	420610	...	...	416965	...	...	440583	...	...	439636
a Wholesale and retail trade [bc]	...	...	420610	...	...	416965	...	...	440583	...	...	439636
b Restaurants and hotels	...	...	...	...	...	...	...	...	...	...	...	...
7 Transport, storage and communication	...	...	207404	...	...	182919	...	...	189712	...	...	190235
8 Finance, insurance, real estate and business services	...	...	252309	...	...	254274	...	...	267374	...	...	273377
9 Community, social and personal services	...	...	185382	...	...	197696	...	...	207780	...	...	213465
Total, Industries	...	...	2077616	...	...	2011166	...	...	2129986	...	...	2159634
Producers of Government Services	...	...	298029	...	...	304696	...	...	317339	...	...	324983
Other Producers	...	...	25744	...	...	25670	...	...	25104	...	...	25654
Total	...	...	2401389	...	...	2341532	...	...	2472429	...	...	2510271
Imputed bank service charge	...	...	-26726	...	...	-26178	...	...	-28792	...	...	-30187
Import duties	...	...	...	...	...	...	...	...	...	...	...	...
Value added tax	...	...	...	...	...	...	...	...	...	...	...	...
Other adjustments	...	...	-18401	...	...	-2218	...	...	-4585	...	...	-14166
Total	...	...	2356262	...	...	2313136	...	...	2439052	...	...	2465918

Belgium

4.4 Derivation of Value Added by Kind of Activity, ISIC Divisions, in Constant Prices

Million Belgian francs

	1978 Gross Output	1978 Intermediate Consumption	1978 Value Added	1979 Gross Output	1979 Intermediate Consumption	1979 Value Added	1980 Gross Output	1980 Intermediate Consumption	1980 Value Added
					At constant prices of: 1975				
					All Producers				
1 Agriculture, hunting, forestry and fishing	...	...	74651	...	...	74882	...	...	75212
a Agriculture and hunting	...	...	71202	...	...	71487	...	...	71794
b Forestry and logging	...	...	2547	...	...	2538	...	...	2600
c Fishing	...	...	902	...	...	857	...	...	818
2 Mining and quarrying	...	...	15740	...	...	15143	...	...	15639
a Coal mining	...	...	7894	...	...	7060	...	...	7253
b Crude petroleum and natural gas production	...	...	...	...	...	...	...	...	...
c Metal ore mining	...	...	...	...	...	...	...	...	...
d Other mining	...	...	...	...	...	...	...	...	...
3 Manufacturing	...	...	711317	...	...	732749	...	...	730606
a Manufacture of food, beverages and tobacco	...	...	126332	...	...	129958	...	...	131829
b Textile, wearing apparel and leather industries	...	...	53615	...	...	56801	...	...	55603
c Manufacture of wood and wood products, including furniture	...	...	33585	...	...	33228	...	...	35763
d Manufacture of paper and paper products, printing and publishing	...	...	36040	...	...	36302	...	...	35614
e Manufacture of chemicals and chemical petroleum, coal, rubber and plastic products	...	...	82422	...	...	88106	...	...	84908
f Manufacture of non-metallic mineral products, except products of petroleum and coal	...	...	32282	...	...	31759	...	...	33278
g Basic metal industries	...	...	47562	...	...	48399	...	...	45677
h Manufacture of fabricated metal products, machinery and equipment	...	...	267189	...	...	275452	...	...	275942
i Other manufacturing industries [a]	...	...	32290	...	...	32744	...	...	31992
4 Electricity, gas and water	...	...	88487	...	...	91812	...	...	93461
5 Construction	...	...	183779	...	...	177472	...	...	188510
6 Wholesale and retail trade, restaurants and hotels	...	...	451058	...	...	468003	...	...	473951
a Wholesale and retail trade [b,c]	...	...	451058	...	...	468003	...	...	473951
b Restaurants and hotels	...	...	...	...	...	...	...	...	...
7 Transport, storage and communication	...	...	198775	...	...	209307	...	...	222678
8 Finance, insurance, real estate and business services	...	...	285700	...	...	296825	...	...	300737
9 Community, social and personal services	...	...	217372	...	...	222777	...	...	228764
Total, Industries	...	...	2226879	...	...	2288970	...	...	2329558
Producers of Government Services	...	...	341135	...	...	352746	...	...	360339
Other Producers	...	...	25756	...	...	25218	...	...	24661
Total	...	...	2593770	...	...	2666934	...	...	2714558
Imputed bank service charge	...	...	-32986	...	...	-33941	...	...	-32887
Import duties	...	...	...	...	...	...	...	...	...
Value added tax	...	...	...	...	...	...	...	...	...
Other adjustments	...	...	-14021	...	...	-27217	...	...	-14225
Total	...	...	2546763	...	...	2605776	...	...	2667446

a) Including garages.
b) Item 'Import duties' is included in item 'Wholesale and retail trade'.
c) Including distribution of petroleum products.

Belize

Source. Central Planning Unit, Ministry of Finance and Economic Planning, Belize. Official estimates are published in 'National Accounts Statistics'. Information on sources and methods of estimation can be found in 'National Accounts Statistics - Sources and Methods' and in 'Economic Accounts of the Public Sector'.

General note. The estimates shown in the following tables have been prepared in accordance with the United Nations System of National Accounts so far as the existing data would permit.

1.1 Expenditure on the Gross Domestic Product, in Current Prices

Million Belize dollars

	1970	1971	1972	1973	1974	1975	1976	1977	1978	1979	1980
1 General government final consumption expenditure	...	...	...	16.5	22.0	22.8	27.1	29.5	33.9	...	...
2 Private final consumption expenditure	...	...	...	75.0	93.6	116.6	131.9	154.0	165.7	...	...
3 Gross capital formation	...	...	...	32.7	42.8	61.0	69.2	68.8	72.4	...	...
a Increase in stocks	...	...	...	5.7	4.2	8.0	11.2	5.8	3.3	...	...
b Gross fixed capital formation	...	...	...	27.0	38.6	53.0	58.0	62.9	69.1	...	...
4 Exports of goods and services	...	...	...	63.1	111.4	150.1	113.9	155.7	205.9	...	...
5 Less: Imports of goods and services	...	...	...	77.1	115.6	161.7	159.0	196.3	236.5	...	...
Equals: Gross Domestic Product	...	...	...	110.3	154.2	188.8	183.2	211.6	241.4	...	...

1.3 Cost Components of the Gross Domestic Product

Million Belize dollars

	1970	1971	1972	1973	1974	1975	1976	1977	1978	1979	1980
1 Indirect taxes, net	...	...	...	13.4	17.4	22.6	22.7	24.2	29.3	...	...
a Indirect taxes paid	...	...	...	13.4	17.4	22.6	22.7	24.5	30.5	...	...
b Less: Subsidies received	...	...	...	-	-	-	-	0.3	1.2	...	...
2 Consumption of fixed capital	...	...	...	9.5	12.8	15.3	15.7	20.1	22.6	...	...
3 Compensation of employees paid by resident producers to:	...	...	...	87.4	124.0	150.9	144.8	167.3	189.4	...	...
4 Net operating surplus	...	...	...							...	...
Equals: Gross Domestic Product	...	...	...	110.3	154.2	188.8	183.2	211.6	241.3	...	...

1.4 General Government Current Receipts and Disbursements

Million Belize dollars

	1970	1971	1972	1973	1974	1975	1976	1977	1978	1979	1980
Receipts											
1 Property and entrepreneurial income	...	...	...	2.5	2.8	3.1	2.5	1.9	2.7	...	...
2 Taxes, fees and contributions	...	...	...	18.8	25.5	34.5	37.5	38.7	50.1	...	...
a Indirect taxes	...	...	...	13.4	17.4	22.6	22.7	24.5	30.5	...	...
b Direct taxes	...	...	...	4.8	7.3	10.8	13.5	13.0	18.7	...	...
c Social security contributions	...	...	...	0.1	0.2	0.2	0.2	0.1	0.1	...	...
d Compulsory fees, fines and penalties	...	...	...	0.5	0.6	0.9	1.1	1.1	0.8	...	...
3 Other current receipts	...	...	...	0.7	1.0	0.9	1.0	0.9	1.3	...	...
Total Current Receipts of General Government	...	...	...	22.0	29.4	38.4	41.1	41.6	54.1	...	...
Disbursements											
1 General government final consumption expenditure	...	...	...	16.5	22.0	22.8	27.1	29.5	33.9	...	...
a Compensation of employees	...	...	...	...	...	12.8	16.7	18.3	20.3	...	...
b Consumption of fixed capital	...	...	...	...	...	...	...	...	...	...	...
c Purchases of goods and services, net	...	...	...	...	...	10.0	10.4	11.2	13.6	...	...
d Less: Own account production of fixed assets	...	...	...	...	...	...	...	...	...	...	...
e Indirect taxes paid, net	...	...	...	...	...	...	...	...	...	...	...
2 Property income paid	...	...	...	1.2	1.2	2.6	2.6	2.3	3.0	...	...
3 Subsidies	...	...	...	-	-	-	-	0.3	1.2	...	...
4 Other current transfers paid	...	...	...	3.4	4.3	5.1	8.5	9.2	8.4	...	...
a Social security benefits and social assistance grants	...	...	...	2.9	3.7	4.5	7.1	8.4	7.1	...	...
b Other	...	...	...	0.5	0.6	0.6	1.4	0.8	1.3	...	...
5 Net saving	...	...	...	0.9	3.7	7.9	2.9	0.3	7.6	...	...
Total Current Disbursements and Net Saving of General Government	...	...	...	22.0	29.4	38.4	41.1	41.6	54.1	...	...

Belize

1.7 External Transactions on Current Account, Summary

Million Belize dollars

	1970	1971	1972	1973	1974	1975	1976	1977	1978	1979	1980
Payments to the Rest of the World											
1 Imports of goods and services	...	...	...	77.1	115.6	161.7	159.0	...	...	...	...
a Imports of merchandise c.i.f.	...	...	...	74.9	112.4	158.0	156.0	...	...	...	...
b Other	...	...	...	2.2	3.2	3.7	3.0	...	...	...	...
2 Factor income paid to the rest of the world	...	...	...	5.2	15.3	18.9	7.1	...	...	...	...
a Compensation of employees	...	...	...	0.5	0.6	0.7	0.9	...	...	...	...
b Property and entrepreneurial income paid	...	...	...	4.7	14.7	18.2	6.2	...	...	...	...
3 Indirect taxes paid to supranational organizations	...	...	...	...	...	...	...	...	...	...	...
4 Current transfers to the rest of the world	...	...	...	0.4	0.7	0.8	1.5	...	...	...	...
5 Surplus of the nation on current transactions	...	...	...	-14.2	-12.4	-22.1	-42.7	...	...	...	...
Payments to the Rest of the World and Surplus of the Nation on Current Transactions	...	...	...	68.5	119.2	159.3	124.9	...	...	...	...
Receipts From The Rest of the World											
1 Exports of goods and services	...	...	...	63.1	111.4	150.1	113.9	...	...	...	...
a Exports of merchandise f.o.b.	...	...	...	53.2	97.5	134.5	97.0	...	...	...	...
b Other	...	...	...	9.9	13.9	15.6	16.9	...	...	...	...
2 Factor income received from rest of the world	...	...	...	1.5	1.8	2.3	2.6	...	...	...	...
a Compensation of employees	...	...	...	0.6	0.6	0.7	0.9	...	...	...	...
b Property and entrepreneurial income received	...	...	...	0.9	1.2	1.6	1.7	...	...	...	...
3 Subsidies received from supranational organisations	...	...	...	...	...	...	...	...	...	...	...
4 Current transfers from rest of the world	...	...	...	4.0	6.0	7.0	8.3	...	...	...	...
Receipts from the Rest of the World on Current Transactions	...	...	...	68.4	119.2	159.4	124.8	...	...	...	...

1.8 Capital Transactions of The Nation, Summary

Million Belize dollars

	1970	1971	1972	1973	1974	1975	1976	1977	1978	1979	1980
Finance of Gross Capital Formation											
Gross saving	...	...	...	18.5	30.4	38.9	26.4	...	...	...	...
1 Consumption of fixed capital	...	...	...	9.5	12.8	15.3	15.7	...	...	...	...
a General government	...	...	...	2.3	2.5	3.4	3.4	...	...	...	...
b Corporate and quasi-corporate enterprises	...	...	...	7.2	10.3	11.9	10.3	...	...	...	...
c Other	...	...	...					...	...	...	...
2 Net saving	...	...	...	9.0	17.6	23.6	12.7	...	...	...	...
a General government	...	...	...	0.9	3.7	6.3	2.9	...	...	...	...
b Corporate and quasi-corporate enterprises	...	...	...	8.1	13.9	17.3	9.8	...	...	...	...
c Other	...	...	...					...	...	...	...
Less: Surplus of the nation on current transactions	...	...	...	-14.2	-12.4	-22.1	-42.7	...	...	...	...
Finance of Gross Capital Formation	...	...	...	32.7	42.8	61.0	69.2	...	...	...	...
Gross Capital Formation											
Increase in stocks	...	...	...	5.7	4.2	8.0	11.2	...	...	...	...
Gross fixed capital formation	...	...	...	27.0	38.6	53.0	58.0	...	...	...	...
Gross Capital Formation	...	...	...	32.7	42.8	61.0	69.2	...	...	...	...

Belize

1.10 Gross Domestic Product by Kind of Activity, in Current Prices

Million Belize dollars

	1970	1971	1972	1973	1974	1975	1976	1977	1978	1979	1980
1 Agriculture, hunting, forestry and fishing	...	...	...	23.9	41.6	52.5	39.0	49.2	55.1	61.3	...
2 Mining and quarrying	...	...	...	0.2	0.3	0.4	0.5	0.6	0.7	0.7	...
3 Manufacturing	...	...	...	10.2	18.8	23.0	18.7	26.7	29.8	32.4	...
4 Electricity, gas and water	...	...	...	1.1	1.4	1.5	1.1	1.9	1.8	3.1	...
5 Construction	...	...	...	5.3	8.9	11.4	13.0	10.6	15.1	14.8	...
6 Wholesale and retail trade, restaurants and hotels	...	...	...	17.9	22.7	27.2	29.2	33.0	38.2	43.1	...
7 Transport, storage and communication	...	...	...	7.2	9.4	10.7	13.0	15.0	17.8	21.5	...
8 Finance, insurance, real estate and business services	...	...	...	15.3	15.7	16.1	17.2	17.8	17.3	21.8	...
9 Community, social and personal services	...	...	...	10.3	11.3	12.6	14.9	16.8	18.3	25.2	...
Total, Industries	...	...	...	91.4	130.1	155.3	146.7	171.5	194.1	223.9	...
Producers of Government Services	...	...	...	9.9	11.1	15.1	18.9	20.8	23.1	25.4	...
Other Producers	...	...	...	...	...	...	...	...	...	...	...
Subtotal [a]	...	...	...	101.3	141.2	170.4	165.6	192.3	217.2	249.3	...
Less: Imputed bank service charge	...	...	...	4.5	4.5	4.3	5.1	4.9	5.2	6.1	...
Plus: Import duties	...	...	...	...	...	...	...	...	...	...	...
Plus: Value added tax	...	...	...	...	...	...	...	...	...	...	...
Plus: Other adjustments [b]	...	...	...	13.4	17.4	22.6	22.7	24.2	29.3	...	...
Equals: Gross Domestic Product	...	...	...	110.3	154.2	188.8	183.2	211.6	241.3	...	...

a) Gross domestic product in factor values.
b) Referring to indirect taxes net of subsidies.

1.11 Gross Domestic Product by Kind of Activity, in Constant Prices

Million Belize dollars

	1970	1971	1972	1973	1974	1975	1976	1977	1978	1979	1980
				At constant prices of: 1973							
1 Agriculture, hunting, forestry and fishing	20.5	21.8	22.7	23.9	26.3	24.3	23.5	27.0	28.4	29.2	...
2 Mining and quarrying	0.2	0.2	0.2	0.2	0.2	0.3	0.4	0.3	0.4	0.4	...
3 Manufacturing	7.1	8.1	9.0	10.2	11.8	10.9	10.2	11.5	12.6	11.4	...
4 Electricity, gas and water	0.7	0.8	1.0	1.1	1.1	1.2	1.3	1.3	1.5	1.6	...
5 Construction	6.3	5.1	5.8	5.3	6.3	7.6	9.4	7.9	9.9	9.1	...
6 Wholesale and retail trade, restaurants and hotels	16.1	15.5	17.2	17.9	20.1	19.9	17.9	18.3	20.5	20.3	...
7 Transport, storage and communication	6.2	6.6	6.9	7.2	8.2	8.9	9.1	10.0	11.2	12.1	...
8 Finance, insurance, real estate and business services	14.1	14.8	15.4	15.3	15.3	15.5	16.0	15.1	14.7	16.2	...
9 Community, social and personal services	9.6	10.2	10.3	10.3	10.4	10.9	11.0	11.6	12.0	12.4	...
Total, Industries	80.8	83.1	88.5	91.4	99.7	99.5	98.8	103.0	111.2	112.7	...
Producers of Government Services	7.2	7.9	8.8	9.9	10.4	11.2	11.8	11.4	12.6	13.0	...
Other Producers	...	...	...	...	...	...	...	...	...	...	...
Subtotal [a]	88.0	91.0	97.3	101.3	110.1	110.7	110.6	114.4	123.8	125.7	...
Less: Imputed bank service charge	...	...	...	4.5	4.3	4.1	4.7	4.1	5.0	5.2	...
Plus: Import duties	...	...	...	...	...	...	...	...	...	...	...
Plus: Value added tax	...	...	...	...	...	...	...	...	...	...	...
Equals: Gross Domestic Product [a]	...	...	...	96.8	105.8	106.5	105.8	110.2	118.9	120.5	...

a) Gross domestic product in factor values.

1.12 Relations Among National Accounting Aggregates

Million Belize dollars

	1970	1971	1972	1973	1974	1975	1976	1977	1978	1979	1980
Gross Domestic Product	...	...	...	110.3	154.2	188.8	183.2	211.6	241.3	...	...
Plus: Net factor income received from abroad	...	...	...	-3.8	-13.5	-16.7	-4.5	-5.5	-7.4	...	...
Factor income received	...	...	...	1.5	1.8	2.3	2.6	...	...	...	...
Less: Factor income paid	...	...	...	5.2	15.3	18.9	7.1	...	...	...	...
Equals: Gross National Product	...	...	...	106.5	140.7	172.1	178.7	206.1	233.9	...	...

Belize

1.12 Relations Among National Accounting Aggregates
(Continued)

Million Belize dollars

	1970	1971	1972	1973	1974	1975	1976	1977	1978	1979	1980
Less: Consumption of fixed capital	...	...	...	9.5	12.8	15.3	15.7	20.1	22.6	...	...
Less: Net indirect taxes paid to supranational organisations	...	...	...	...	...	...	...	...	...	...	...
Equals: National Income at Market Prices	...	...	...	97.0	127.9	156.8	163.0	186.0	211.3	...	...
Plus: Net current transfers received from abroad	...	...	...	3.6	5.3	6.2	6.8	...	...	...	...
Current transfers received	...	...	...	4.0	6.0	7.0	8.3	...	...	...	...
Less: Current transfers paid	...	...	...	0.4	0.7	0.8	1.5	...	...	...	...
Equals: National Disposable Income at Market Prices	...	...	...	100.6	133.2	163.0	169.8	...	...	...	...
Less: Final consumption	...	...	...	91.5	115.6	139.4	159.0	...	...	...	...
Equals: Net Saving	...	...	...	9.0	17.6	23.6	12.7	...	...	...	...
Less: Surplus of the nation on current transactions	...	...	...	-14.2	-12.4	-22.1	-42.7	...	...	...	...
Equals: Net Capital Formation	...	...	...	23.2	30.0	45.7	55.5	...	...	...	...

2.7 Gross Capital Formation by Type of Good and Owner, in Current Prices

Million Belize dollars

	1973 TOTAL	Total Private	Public Enterprises	General Government	1974 TOTAL	Total Private	Public Enterprises	General Government	1975 TOTAL	Total Private	Public Enterprises	General Government
Increase in stocks, total	5.7	5.0	0.7	...	4.2	4.0	0.2	...	8.0	7.0	1.0	...
Gross Fixed Capital Formation, Total	27.0	17.5	9.5	...	38.6	25.1	13.5	...	53.0	40.0	13.0	...
1 Residential buildings	11.4	5.9	2.2		17.5	9.7	1.4		21.3	13.2	2.4	0.1
2 Non-residential buildings				...				...				
3 Other construction	2.7	...	2.7	...	4.9	...	4.9	...	4.0	...	4.0	...
4 Land improvement and plantation and orchard development	0.6	0.5	0.1	...	1.5	0.6	0.9	...	1.6	0.8	0.8	...
5 Producers' durable goods	15.6	11.1	4.5	...	21.1	14.9	6.2	...	31.7	18.0	5.6	8.1
a Transport equipment	3.7	3.3	0.4	...	4.6	4.2	0.4	...	8.2	7.4	0.7	0.1
b Machinery and equipment	11.9	7.8	4.1	...	16.5	10.7	5.8	...	23.5	10.6	4.9	8.0
6 Breeding stock, dairy cattle, etc.	...	...	...	...	...	...	...	...	...	...	...	...
Total Gross Capital Formation	32.7	22.5	10.2	...	42.8	29.2	13.6	...	61.0	39.0	13.8	8.2

	1976 TOTAL	Total Private	Public Enterprises	General Government	1977 TOTAL	Total Private	Public Enterprises	General Government	1978 TOTAL	Total Private	Public Enterprises	General Government
Increase in stocks, total	11.2	10.0	1.2	...	5.8	5.2	0.6	...	3.2	3.1	0.1	...
Gross Fixed Capital Formation, Total	58.0	44.6	13.4	...	62.9	42.3	20.5	0.1	69.1	50.7	18.4	...
1 Residential buildings	18.9	11.1	2.2		...	...	2.9		...	2.4	...	
2 Non-residential buildings				...				...			...	
3 Other construction	3.8	...	3.8	...	...	...	7.3	...	...	...	7.2	...
4 Land improvement and plantation and orchard development	1.8	0.8	1.0	...	2.0	0.9	1.1	...	5.3	1.7	3.6	...
5 Producers' durable goods	39.1	25.8	6.3	7.0	40.4	31.1	9.1	0.2	37.4	32.1	5.3	...
a Transport equipment	8.5	7.2	1.3	...	10.7	9.7	0.9	0.1	10.5	9.2	1.3	...
b Machinery and equipment	30.6	18.6	5.0	7.0	29.7	21.4	8.2	0.1	26.9	22.9	4.0	...
6 Breeding stock, dairy cattle, etc.	...	...	...	...	...	...	...	...	...	...	...	...
Total Gross Capital Formation	69.2	47.7	14.5	7.0	68.8	47.5	21.0	0.3	72.4	53.8	18.6	...

2.17 Exports and Imports of Goods and Services, Detail

Million Belize dollars

	1970	1971	1972	1973	1974	1975	1976	1977	1978	1979	1980
Exports of Goods and Services
1 Exports of merchandise, f.o.b.	...	...	...	53.2	97.5	134.5	97.0	...	...	...	...
2 Transport and communication	...	...	...	...	...	...	...	...	...	...	...
3 Insurance service charges	...	...	...	...	...	...	...	...	...	...	...
4 Other commodities	...	...	...	...	...	...	...	...	...	...	...

Belize

2.17 Exports and Imports of Goods and Services, Detail
(Continued)

Million Belize dollars

		1970	1971	1972	1973	1974	1975	1976	1977	1978	1979	1980
5	Adjustments of merchandise exports to change-of-ownership basis	...	...	...	...	...	...	...	...	...	...	...
6	Direct purchases in the domestic market by non-residential households	...	...	...	8.7	12.5	14.1	15.2	...	...	...	...
7	Direct purchases in the domestic market by extraterritorial bodies	...	...	...	...	...	...	...	...	...	...	...
	Total Exports of Goods and Services	...	...	...	63.1	111.4	150.1	113.9	...	...	...	...

Imports of Goods and Services

		1970	1971	1972	1973	1974	1975	1976	1977	1978	1979	1980
1	Imports of merchandise, c.i.f.	...	...	...	74.9	112.4	158.0	156.0	...	...	...	...
2	Adjustments of merchandise imports to change-of-ownership basis	...	...	...	...	...	...	...	...	...	...	...
3	Other transport and communication	...	...	...	...	...	...	...	...	...	...	...
4	Other insurance service charges	...	...	...	...	...	...	...	...	...	...	...
5	Other commodities	...	...	...	-0.3	-0.3	-0.4	-0.6	...	...	...	...
6	Direct purchases abroad by government	...	...	...	...	...	...	...	...	...	...	...
7	Direct purchases abroad by resident households	...	...	...	...	...	...	...	...	...	...	...
	Total Imports of Goods and Services	...	...	...	77.1	115.6	161.7	159.0	...	...	...	...
	Balance of Goods and Services	...	...	...	-14.0	-4.2	-11.6	-45.1	...	...	...	...
	Total Imports and Balance of Goods and Services	...	...	...	63.1	111.4	150.1	113.9	...	...	...	...

3.12 General Government Income and Outlay Account: Total and Subsectors

Million Belize dollars

		1973					1974				
		Total General Government	Central Government	State or Provincial Government	Local Government	Social Security Funds	Total General Government	Central Government	State or Provincial Government	Local Government	Social Security Funds

Receipts

1	Property and entrepreneurial income	2.5	0.8	...	...	...	2.8	0.6	...	...	...
	a Net operating surplus	...	...	...	...	...	...	...	...	...	...
	b Withdrawals from public quasi-corporations	...	...	...	...	...	...	...	...	...	...
	c Interest	...	...	...	...	...	...	...	...	...	...
	d Dividends	...	...	...	...	...	...	...	...	...	...
	e Net land rent and royalties	...	...	...	...	...	...	...	...	...	...
2	Taxes, fees and contributions	18.8	...	...	...	...	25.5	...	...	...	...
	a Indirect taxes	13.4	...	...	...	...	17.4	...	...	...	...
	b Direct taxes	4.8	...	...	...	...	7.3	...	...	...	...
	Income	3.6	...	...	...	...	6.3	...	...	...	...
	Other	1.2	...	...	...	...	1.0	...	...	...	...
	c Social security contributions	0.1	...	...	...	...	0.2	...	...	...	...
	d Fees, fines and penalties	0.5	...	...	...	...	0.6	...	...	...	...
3	Other current transfers received	0.7	...	...	...	...	1.0	...	...	...	...
	a Casualty insurance claims	...	...	...	...	...	...	...	...	...	...
	b Transfers from other government subsectors	...	...	...	...	...	...	...	...	...	...
	c Transfers from abroad	0.7	...	...	...	...	1.0	...	...	...	...
	d Other transfers, except imputed	...	...	...	...	...	...	...	...	...	...
	e Imputed unfunded employee welfare contributions	...	...	...	...	...	...	...	...	...	...
	Total Current Receipts	22.0	...	...	...	...	29.4	...	...	...	...

Disbursements

1	General governement final consumption expenditures	16.5	...	...	...	...	22.0	...	...	...	...

Belize

3.12 General Government Income and Outlay Account: Total and Subsectors
(Continued)

Million Belize dollars

	1973					1974				
	Total General Government	Central Government	State or Provincial Government	Local Government	Social Security Funds	Total General Government	Central Government	State or Provincial Government	Local Government	Social Security Funds
a Compensation of employees	...	...	...	...	...	...	...	...	...	...
b Consumption of fixed capital	...	...	...	...	...	...	...	...	...	...
c Goods and services purchased, net	...	...	...	...	...	...	...	...	...	...
Purchases	...	...	...	...	...	...	...	...	...	...
Less: Sales	...	...	...	...	...	...	...	...	...	...
d Less: Own account production of fixed assets	...	...	...	...	...	...	...	...	...	...
e Indirect taxes paid, net	...	...	...	...	...	...	...	...	...	...
2 Property income paid	1.2	...	...	...	...	1.2	...	...	...	...
a Interest	1.2	...	...	...	...	1.2	...	...	...	...
b Net land rent and royalties	...	...	...	...	...	...	...	...	...	...
3 Subsidies	-	...	...	...	...	-	...	...	...	...
4 Other current transfers paid	3.4	...	...	...	...	4.3	...	...	...	...
a Casualty insurance premiums, net	...	...	...	...	...	...	...	...	...	...
b Transfers to other government subsectors	...	...	...	...	...	...	...	...	...	...
c Transfers to households	3.0	...	...	...	...	3.7	...	...	...	...
Social security benefits	0.1	...	...	...	...	-	...	...	...	...
Social assistance grants	2.9	...	...	...	...	3.7	...	...	...	...
Unfunded employee welfare benefits	...	...	...	...	...	...	...	...	...	...
d Transfers to private non-profit institutions serving households	...	...	...	...	...	...	...	...	...	...
e Transfers to the rest of the world	0.4	...	...	...	...	0.6	...	...	...	...
Net saving	0.9	...	...	...	...	3.7	...	...	...	...
Total Current Disbursements and Net Saving	22.0	...	...	...	...	29.4	...	...	...	...

	1975					1976				
	Total General Government	Central Government	State or Provincial Government	Local Government	Social Security Funds	Total General Government	Central Government	State or Provincial Government	Local Government	Social Security Funds

Receipts

1 Property and entrepreneurial income	3.1	3.1	...	...	...	2.5	2.4	...	0.1	...
a Net operating surplus	0.9	0.9	...	...	...	0.2	0.3	...	...	...
b Withdrawals from public quasi-corporations	0.6	0.6	...	...	...	0.7	0.7	...	...	...
c Interest	0.5	0.5	...	...	...	0.4	0.3	...	0.1	...
d Dividends	...	...	...	...	...	...	...	...	...	...
e Net land rent and royalties	1.1	1.1	...	...	...	1.2	1.1	...	...	...
2 Taxes, fees and contributions	34.5	32.8	...	1.6	...	37.5	35.7	...	1.8	...
a Indirect taxes	22.6	21.4	...	1.1	...	22.7	21.4	...	1.3	...
b Direct taxes	10.8	10.4	...	0.4	...	13.5	13.0	...	0.5	...
Income	9.8	...	...	...	...	12.2	...	...	...	...
Other	1.0	...	...	...	...	1.3	...	...	...	...
c Social security contributions	0.2	0.2	...	...	...	0.2	0.2	...	...	...
d Fees, fines and penalties	0.9	0.8	...	0.1	...	1.1	1.1	...	...	...
3 Other current transfers received	0.9	0.9	...	0.6	...	1.0	1.0	...	0.6	...
a Casualty insurance claims	...	...	...	...	...	...	...	...	...	...
b Transfers from other government subsectors	...	...	...	0.6	...	...	...	...	0.6	...
c Transfers from abroad	0.9	0.9	...	...	...	1.0	1.0	...	...	...
d Other transfers, except imputed	...	...	...	...	...	...	...	...	...	...
e Imputed unfunded employee welfare contributions	...	...	...	...	...	...	...	...	...	...
Total Current Receipts	38.4	36.7	...	2.2	...	41.1	39.1	...	2.6	...

Disbursements

1 General government final consumption expenditures	22.8	21.2	...	1.6	...	27.1	25.3	...	1.8	...

Belize

3.12 General Government Income and Outlay Account: Total and Subsectors
(Continued)

Million Belize dollars

	1975 Total General Government	1975 Central Government	1975 State or Provincial Government	1975 Local Government	1975 Social Security Funds	1976 Total General Government	1976 Central Government	1976 State or Provincial Government	1976 Local Government	1976 Social Security Funds
a Compensation of employees	12.8	12.5	...	0.3	...	16.7	16.3	...	0.4	...
b Consumption of fixed capital	...	...	...	...	...	...	...	...	...	...
c Goods and services purchased, net	10.0	8.7	...	1.3	...	10.4	9.0	...	1.4	...
Purchases	11.1	9.8	...	1.3	...	11.5	10.1	...	1.4	...
Less: Sales	1.1	1.1	...	...	...	1.1	1.1	...	...	...
d Less: Own account production of fixed assets	...	...	...	...	...	...	...	...	...	...
e Indirect taxes paid, net	...	...	...	...	...	...	...	...	...	...
2 Property income paid	2.6	2.4	...	...	...	2.6	2.6	...	...	...
a Interest	2.5	2.4	...	...	...	2.6	2.6	...	...	...
b Net land rent and royalties	...	...	...	...	...	...	...	...	...	...
3 Subsidies	-	...	...	...	...	-	...	...	...	...
4 Other current transfers paid	5.2	5.5	...	0.2	...	8.5	8.0	...	0.3	...
a Casualty insurance premiums, net	...	...	...	...	...	...	...	...	...	...
b Transfers to other government subsectors	...	0.5	...	...	...	...	0.6	...	...	...
c Transfers to households	4.5	5.0	...	...	...	7.1	7.4	...	...	...
Social security benefits	...	...	...	...	...	...	...	...	...	...
Social assistance grants	4.5	4.5	...	...	...	7.1	7.1	...	...	...
Unfunded employee welfare benefits	...	...	...	...	...	...	...	...	...	...
d Transfers to private non-profit institutions serving households	...	...	...	...	...	...	...	...	...	...
e Transfers to the rest of the world	0.7	...	...	...	...	1.4	...	...	...	...
Net saving	7.9	7.5	...	0.4	...	2.9	3.1	...	0.5	...
Total Current Disbursements and Net Saving	38.4	36.7	...	2.2	...	41.1	39.1	...	2.6	...

	1977 Total General Government	1977 Central Government	1977 State or Provincial Government	1977 Local Government	1977 Social Security Funds	1978 Total General Government	1978 Central Government	1978 State or Provincial Government	1978 Local Government	1978 Social Security Funds
Receipts										
1 Property and entrepreneurial income	1.9	1.8	...	0.1	...	2.7	2.6	...	0.1	...
a Net operating surplus	...	...	...	...	...	...	...	...	...	...
b Withdrawals from public quasi-corporations	0.6	0.6	...	...	...	1.1	1.1	...	...	...
c Interest	0.2	0.2	...	...	...	0.3	0.2	...	0.1	...
d Dividends	...	...	...	...	...	...	...	...	...	...
e Net land rent and royalties	1.1	1.0	...	0.1	...	1.3	1.3	...	...	...
2 Taxes, fees and contributions	38.6	36.7	...	2.1	...	50.2	48.1	...	2.1	...
a Indirect taxes	24.5	23.1	...	1.5	...	30.5	29.0	...	1.5	...
b Direct taxes	13.0	12.5	...	0.5	...	18.7	18.3	...	0.5	...
Income	...	...	...	...	...	...	...	...	...	...
Other	...	...	...	...	...	...	...	...	...	...
c Social security contributions	0.1	0.1	...	...	...	0.1	0.1	...	...	...
d Fees, fines and penalties	1.1	1.0	...	0.1	...	0.8	0.7	...	0.1	...
3 Other current transfers received	0.9	0.9	...	0.9	...	1.3	1.2	...	0.9	...
a Casualty insurance claims	...	...	...	...	...	...	...	...	...	...
b Transfers from other government subsectors	...	...	...	0.9	...	...	...	...	0.9	...
c Transfers from abroad	0.9	0.9	...	...	...	1.3	1.2	...	...	...
d Other transfers, except imputed	...	...	...	...	...	...	...	...	...	...
e Imputed unfunded employee welfare contributions	...	...	...	...	...	...	...	...	...	...
Total Current Receipts	41.6	39.4	...	2.9	...	54.1	51.9	...	3.1	...
Disbursements										
1 General government final consumption expenditures	29.5	27.6	...	1.9	...	33.9	31.7	...	2.2	...

Belize

3.12 General Government Income and Outlay Account: Total and Subsectors
(Continued)

Million Belize dollars

	1977 Total General Government	1977 Central Government	1977 State or Provincial Government	1977 Local Government	1977 Social Security Funds	1978 Total General Government	1978 Central Government	1978 State or Provincial Government	1978 Local Government	1978 Social Security Funds
a Compensation of employees	18.3	17.9	...	0.4	...	20.3	19.8	...	0.4	...
b Consumption of fixed capital	...	...	...	...	...	...	...	...	...	...
c Goods and services purchased, net	11.2	9.7	...	1.5	...	13.6	11.9	...	1.8	...
Purchases	12.4	10.9	...	1.6	...	14.8	13.0	...	1.8	...
Less: Sales	1.2	1.2	...	...	...	1.2	1.1	...	...	...
d Less: Own account production of fixed assets	...	...	...	...	...	...	...	...	...	...
e Indirect taxes paid, net	...	...	...	...	...	...	...	...	...	...
2 Property income paid	2.3	2.3	...	...	...	3.0	3.0	...	...	...
a Interest	2.0	2.0	...	...	...	2.8	2.8	...	...	...
b Net land rent and royalties	0.3	0.3	...	...	...	0.2	0.2	...	...	...
3 Subsidies	0.3	0.3	...	...	...	1.2	1.2	...	...	...
4 Other current transfers paid	9.3	9.7	...	0.3	...	8.4	8.6	...	0.9	...
a Casualty insurance premiums, net	...	...	...	...	...	...	...	...	...	...
b Transfers to other government subsectors	...	0.7	...	...	...	...	0.9	...	...	...
c Transfers to households	9.3	8.9	...	...	...	8.4	7.5	...	...	...
Social security benefits	...	...	...	...	...	...	...	...	...	...
Social assistance grants	8.4	8.4	...	...	...	7.1	7.1	...	...	...
Unfunded employee welfare benefits	...	...	...	...	...	...	...	...	...	...
d Transfers to private non-profit institutions serving households	...	...	...	...	...	...	...	...	...	...
e Transfers to the rest of the world	...	0.1	...	...	...	...	0.2	...	...	...
Net saving	0.3	-0.4	...	0.7	...	7.6	7.4	...	0.1	...
Total Current Disbursements and Net Saving	41.6	39.4	...	2.9	...	54.1	51.9	...	3.1	...

3.13 General Government Capital Accumulation Account: Total and Subsectors

Million Belize dollars

	1973 Total General Government	1973 Central Government	1973 State or Provincial Government	1973 Local Government	1973 Social Security Funds	1974 Total General Government	1974 Central Government	1974 State or Provincial Government	1974 Local Government	1974 Social Security Funds
				Finance of Gross Accumulation						
1 Gross saving	3.2	...	...	...	...	6.2	...	...	...	...
a Consumption of fixed capital	2.3	...	...	...	...	2.5	...	...	...	...
b Net saving	0.9	...	...	...	...	3.7	...	...	...	...
2 Capital transfers received	5.7	...	...	...	...	8.0	...	...	...	...
a From other government subsectors	...	...	...	...	...	...	...	...	...	...
b From other resident sectors	...	...	...	...	...	...	...	...	...	...
c From rest of the world	5.7	...	...	...	...	8.0	...	...	...	...
Finance of Gross Accumulation	9.0	...	...	...	...	14.2	...	...	...	...
				Gross Accumulation						
1 Gross capital formation	10.2	...	...	...	...	13.7	...	...	...	...
2 Purchases of land, net	-0.2	...	...	...	...	-0.2	...	...	...	...
3 Purchases of intangible assets, net	-	...	...	...	...	-	...	...	...	...
4 Capital transfers paid	...	...	...	...	...	...	...	...	...	...
5 Statistical discrepancy	...	...	...	...	...	...	...	...	...	...
Net lending	-1.0	...	...	...	...	0.7	...	...	...	...
Gross Accumulation	9.0	...	...	...	...	14.2	...	...	...	...

Belize

3.13 General Government Capital Accumulation Account: Total and Subsectors

Million Belize dollars

	1975					1976				
	Total General Government	Central Government	State or Provincial Government	Local Government	Social Security Funds	Total General Government	Central Government	State or Provincial Government	Local Government	Social Security Funds
Finance of Gross Accumulation										
1 Gross saving	7.9	7.5	...	0.4	...	3.6	3.1	...	0.5	...
a Consumption of fixed capital	2.3	2.3	...	...	...	2.2	2.2	...	...	...
b Net saving	5.6	5.2	...	...	...	1.4	0.9	...	...	...
2 Capital transfers received	7.9	7.9	...	...	...	9.7	9.7	...	...	...
a From other government subsectors	...	...	...	...	...	...	...	...	...	...
b From other resident sectors	...	...	...	...	...	...	...	...	...	...
c From rest of the world	7.9	7.9	...	...	...	9.7	9.7	...	...	...
Finance of Gross Accumulation	15.8	15.4	...	0.4	...	13.3	12.8	...	0.5	...
Gross Accumulation										
1 Gross capital formation	10.2	10.0	...	0.2	...	11.4	11.3	...	0.1	...
2 Purchases of land, net	-0.2	-0.2	...	...	...	-0.2	-0.2	...	...	...
3 Purchases of intangible assets, net	.	...	...	...	...	.	...	...	...	...
4 Capital transfers paid	...	...	...	...	...	...	...	...	...	...
5 Statistical discrepancy	...	...	...	...	...	-0.4	-0.4	...	...	...
Net lending	6.0	5.8	...	0.2	...	2.5	2.1	...	0.4	...
Gross Accumulation	15.8	15.4	...	0.4	...	13.3	12.8	...	0.5	...

	1977					1978				
	Total General Government	Central Government	State or Provincial Government	Local Government	Social Security Funds	Total General Government	Central Government	State or Provincial Government	Local Government	Social Security Funds
Finance of Gross Accumulation										
1 Gross saving	0.3	-0.4	...	0.7	...	7.6	7.4	...	0.1	...
a Consumption of fixed capital	2.5	2.5	...	...	...	2.8	2.8	...	...	...
b Net saving	-2.2	-2.9	...	...	...	4.8	4.6	...	...	...
2 Capital transfers received	15.4	15.4	...	...	...	7.5	7.5	...	...	...
a From other government subsectors	...	...	...	...	...	...	...	...	...	...
b From other resident sectors	...	...	...	...	...	...	...	...	...	...
c From rest of the world	15.4	15.4	...	...	...	7.5	7.5	...	...	...
Finance of Gross Accumulation	15.7	15.0	...	0.7	...	15.1	14.9	...	0.1	...
Gross Accumulation										
1 Gross capital formation	17.5	17.3	...	0.2	...	15.3	15.1	...	0.2	...
2 Purchases of land, net	-0.2	-0.2	...	...	...	-0.5	-0.5	...	...	...
3 Purchases of intangible assets, net	...	...	...	...	...	...	...	...	...	...
4 Capital transfers paid	...	...	...	...	...	-0.3	-0.4	...	...	...
5 Statistical discrepancy	3.1	3.1	...	...	...	0.6	0.7	...	-0.1	...
Net lending	1.5	1.0	...	0.5	...	15.1	14.9	...	0.1	...
Gross Accumulation	15.7	15.0	...	0.7	...	15.1	14.9	...	0.1	...

3.51 External Transactions: Current Account: Detail

Million Belize dollars

	1970	1971	1972	1973	1974	1975	1976	1977	1978	1979	1980
Payments to the Rest of the World											
1 Imports of goods and services	...	...	...	77.1	115.6	161.7	159.0	...	...	...	...
2 Factor income paid to the rest of the world	...	...	...	5.2	15.3	18.9	7.1	...	...	...	...
a Compensation of employees	...	...	...	0.5	0.6	0.7	0.9	...	...	...	...
b Property and entrepreneurial income paid	...	...	...	4.7	14.7	18.2	6.2	...	...	...	...
3 Indirect taxes paid to supranational organizations	...	...	...	...	...	...	...	...	...	...	...
4 Other current transfers to the rest of the world	...	...	...	0.4	0.7	0.8	1.5	...	...	...	...
a By general government	...	...	...	0.4	0.6	0.7	1.4	...	...	...	...
b By other resident sectors	...	...	...	-	0.1	0.1	0.1	...	...	...	...
5 Surplus of the nation on current transactions	...	...	...	-14.2	-12.4	-22.1	-42.7	...	...	...	...
Payments to the Rest of the World, and Surplus of the Nation on Current Transfers	...	...	...	68.5	119.2	159.3	124.9	...	...	...	...

Belize

3.51 External Transactions: Current Account: Detail
(Continued)

Million Belize dollars

	1970	1971	1972	1973	1974	1975	1976	1977	1978	1979	1980
				Receipts From The Rest of the World							
1 Exports of goods and services	...	...	...	63.1	111.4	150.1	113.9	...	...	...	...
2 Factor income received from the rest of the world	...	...	...	...	...	...	...	...	...	...	...
a Compensation of employees	...	...	...	0.6	0.6	0.7	0.9	...	...	...	...
b Property and entrepreneurial income received	...	...	...	0.9	1.2	1.6	1.7	...	...	...	...
3 Subsidies received from supranational organizations	...	...	...	...	...	...	...	...	...	...	...
4 Other current transfers from the rest of the world	...	...	...	4.0	6.0	7.0	8.3	...	...	...	...
a To general government	...	...	...	0.7	0.9	0.8	0.9	...	...	...	...
b To other resident sectors	...	...	...	3.2	5.2	6.2	7.4	...	...	...	...
Receipts from the Rest of the World on Current Transfers	...	...	...	68.4	119.2	159.4	124.8	...	...	...	...

3.52 External Transactions: Capital Accumulation Account

Million Belize dollars

	1970	1971	1972	1973	1974	1975	1976	1977	1978	1979	1980
				Finance of Gross Accumulation							
1 Surplus of the nation on current transactions	...	...	...	-14.2	-12.4	-22.1	-42.7	...	...	...	...
2 Capital transfers received from the rest of the world [a]	...	...	...	6.0	8.1	8.3	15.9	...	...	...	...
Total Finance of Gross Accumulation	...	...	...	-8.2	-4.2	-13.8	-26.8	...	...	...	...
				Gross Accumulation							
1 Capital transfers paid to the rest of the world	...	...	...	...	...	...	...	...	...	...	...
2 Purchases of intangible assets, n.e.c., net, from the rest of the world	...	...	...	.	.	.	.	...	...	...	...
3 Net lending to the rest of the world	...	...	...	-8.2	-4.2	-13.8	-26.8	...	...	...	...
Total Gross Accumulation	...	...	...	-8.2	-4.2	-13.8	-26.8	...	...	...	...

a) Net.

Benin

Source. Reply to the United Nations National Accounts Questionnaire from the Institut National de la Statistique et de l'Analyse Economique, Direction Generale, Cotonou. Official estimates are published in 'Comptes de la Nation 1974-1975 et les estimations des aggregats de comptes nationaux a prix courants et a prix constants de 1970 a 1977'.

General note. The estimates shown in the following tables have been prepared in accordance with the United Nations System of National Accounts so far as the existing data would permit.

1.1 Expenditure on the Gross Domestic Product, in Current Prices

Million CFA francs	1970	1971	1972	1973	1974	1975	1976	1977	1978	1979	1980
1 General government final consumption expenditure	8976	9269	10492	11195	11802	13411	12781	14711	14414	...	...
2 Private final consumption expenditure	54081	56363	64837	70372	77940	95990	119504	147839	166553	...	...
3 Gross capital formation	11854	11990	17065	16260	22290	28793	25262	27687	28703	...	...
a Increase in stocks	1620	1700	2200	2160	2083	5958	3300	4800	5500	...	...
b Gross fixed capital formation	10234	10290	14865	14100	20207	22835	21962	22887	23203	...	...
4 Exports of goods and services	19270	23625	21620	25352	27780	30647	31613	34782	39611	...	...
5 Less: Imports of goods and services	24470	27545	30938	33180	35401	55727	54847	73817	80721	...	...
Equals: Gross Domestic Product	69711	73702	83076	89999	104411	113112	134313	151202	168560	...	...

1.2 Expenditure on the Gross Domestic Product, in Constant Prices

Million CFA francs	1970	1971	1972	1973	1974	1975	1976	1977	1978	1979	1980
					At constant prices of:1970						
1 General government final consumption expenditure	8976	9025	9824	10347	9698	9313	7536	7029	6176	...	...
2 Private final consumption expenditure	54081	53073	60709	65039	64043	66658	71417	70635	70090	...	...
3 Gross capital formation	11854	12309	16205	14479	14879	16576	12123	12321	11959	...	...
a Increase in stocks	1620	1745	2089	1923	1390	3430	1661	2136	2291	...	...
b Gross fixed capital formation	10234	10564	14116	12556	13489	13146	10462	10185	9668	...	...
4 Exports of goods and services	19270	24684	25830	23805	23805	23965	23160	19853	21342	...	...
5 Less: Imports of goods and services	24470	28280	29381	29546	23632	32082	27617	32851	33634	...	...
Equals: Gross Domestic Product	69711	70811	83187	84124	88793	84430	86619	76987	75933	...	...

1.3 Cost Components of the Gross Domestic Product

Million CFA francs	1970	1971	1972	1973	1974	1975	1976	1977	1978	1979	1980
1 Indirect taxes, net	...	...	...	...	9278	9604	13341	15890	15891	...	...
a Indirect taxes paid	...	...	...	...	9278	10144	13371	15908	15913	...	...
b Less: Subsidies received	...	...	...	...	-	540	30	18	22	...	...
2 Consumption of fixed capital	...	...	...	...	4834	5526	8529	8923	10936	...	...
3 Compensation of employees paid by resident producers to:					26598	28338	30148	35733	38932	...	...
a Resident households	...	...	...	...	26529	28255	30054	35594	38759	...	...
b Rest of the world	...	...	...	...	69	83	94	139	173	...	...
4 Net operating surplus	...	...	...	...	63701	69646	82295	90656	102802	...	...
Equals: Gross Domestic Product	69711	73702	83076	89999	104411	113114	134313	151202	168560	...	...

1.7 External Transactions on Current Account, Summary

Million CFA francs	1970	1971	1972	1973	1974	1975	1976	1977	1978	1979	1980
				Payments to the Rest of the World							
1 Imports of goods and services	24470	27545	30938	33180	35401	55727	54847	73817	80721	...	...
a Imports of merchandise c.i.f.	20350	24140	26410	28570	31500	50366	50025	68154	74210	...	...
b Other	4120	3405	4528	4610	3901	5361	4822	5663	6511	...	...
2 Factor income paid to the rest of the world	...	...	...	...	499	1103	848	1026	1083	...	...
a Compensation of employees	...	...	...	...	69	83	94	139	173	...	...
b Property and entrepreneurial income paid	...	...	...	...	430	1020	754	887	910	...	...
3 Indirect taxes paid to supranational organizations	...	...	...	...	...	...	...	...	...	...	...
4 Current transfers to the rest of the world	...	...	...	...	1762	1761	1499	1636	1780	...	...
5 Surplus of the nation on current transactions	...	...	...	...	624	-16422	-12383	-19100	-24176	...	...
Payments to the Rest of the World and Surplus of the Nation on Current Transactions	...	...	...	...	38286	42169	44811	57379	59408	...	...

Benin

1.7 External Transactions on Current Account, Summary
(Continued)

Million CFA francs

	1970	1971	1972	1973	1974	1975	1976	1977	1978	1979	1980
Receipts From The Rest of the World											
1 Exports of goods and services	19270	23625	21620	25352	27780	30647	31613	34782	39611	...	...
a Exports of merchandise f.o.b.	16090	19300	16980	20720	22700	24882	23500	27582	30000	...	...
b Other	3180	4325	4640	4632	5080	5765	8113	7200	9611	...	...
2 Factor income received from rest of the world	...	...	...	...	1216	1029	1027	1165	1197	...	...
a Compensation of employees	...	...	...	...	254	279	265	325	377	...	...
b Property and entrepreneurial income received	...	...	...	...	962	750	762	840	820	...	...
3 Subsidies received from supranational organisations	...	...	...	...	...	...	...	...	...	...	...
4 Current transfers from rest of the world	...	...	...	...	9290	10493	12171	21432	18600	...	...
Receipts from the Rest of the World on Current Transactions	...	...	...	...	38286	42169	44811	57379	59408	...	...

1.8 Capital Transactions of The Nation, Summary

Million CFA francs

	1970	1971	1972	1973	1974	1975	1976	1977	1978	1979	1980
Finance of Gross Capital Formation											
Gross saving	...	...	...	...	22914	12371	12879	8587	4527	...	...
1 Consumption of fixed capital	...	...	...	...	4834	5526	8529	8923	10936	...	...
2 Net saving	...	...	...	...	18080	6845	4350	-336	-6409	...	...
Less: Surplus of the nation on current transactions	...	...	...	...	624	-16422	-12383	-19100	-24176	...	...
Finance of Gross Capital Formation	11854	11990	17065	16260	22290	28793	25262	27687	28703	...	...
Gross Capital Formation											
Increase in stocks	...	...	...	...	2083	5958	3300	4800	5500	...	...
Gross fixed capital formation	...	...	...	...	20207	22835	21962	22887	23203	...	...
Gross Capital Formation	11854	11990	17065	16260	22290	28793	25262	27687	28703	...	...

1.10 Gross Domestic Product by Kind of Activity, in Current Prices

Million CFA francs

	1970	1971	1972	1973	1974	1975	1976	1977	1978	1979	1980
1 Agriculture, hunting, forestry and fishing	28709	30287	34245	36271	37748	39193	54005	59978	73630	...	...
2 Mining and quarrying	5932	6498	7107	7798	300	227	265	293	305	...	...
3 Manufacturing					9330	10707	9149	10259	10302	...	...
4 Electricity, gas and water	395	430	477	539	640	767	903	1168	1677	...	...
5 Construction	2310	1648	2685	3164	5480	4876	5511	5718	5995	...	...
6 Wholesale and retail trade, restaurants and hotels	12210	13654	15665	18162	25420	28050	31576	34648	35333	...	...
7 Transport, storage and communication	3832	4102	4690	5186	6780	8082	9348	11461	13471	...	...
8 Finance, insurance, real estate and business services	11593	11915	12697	13324	3695	4020	4912	4887	6816	...	...
9 Community, social and personal services					560	586	593	715	306	...	...
Total, Industries	...	...	...	...	89953	96508	116262	129127	147835	...	...
Producers of Government Services	...	...	...	...	9712	10960	11081	12880	12680	...	...
Other Producers	...	...	...	...	412	425	232	235	241	...	...
Subtotal	64981	68534	77566	84444	100077	107893	127575	142242	160756	...	...
Less: Imputed bank service charge	743	782	823	866	912	980	1482	866	3103	...	...
Plus: Import duties	5473	5950	6333	6421	5246	6201	8220	9826	10907	...	...
Plus: Value added tax	...	...	...	...	...	...	...	...	...	...	...
Equals: Gross Domestic Product	69711	73702	83076	89999	104411	113114	134313	151202	168560	...	...

Benin

1.11 Gross Domestic Product by Kind of Activity, in Constant Prices

Million CFA francs

At constant prices of: 1970

	1970	1971	1972	1973	1974	1975	1976	1977	1978	1979	1980
1 Agriculture, hunting, forestry and fishing	28577	29148	31982	31582	27362	26978	31574	33235	...	...	...
2 Mining and quarrying	5189	5490	5766	5837	7264	6646	6034	5718	...	...	...
3 Manufacturing									...	...	...
4 Electricity, gas and water	351	357	380	369	490	441	413	397	...	...	...
5 Construction	2072	2319	2203	2393	3632	2944	2663	2436	...	...	...
6 Wholesale and retail trade, restaurants and hotels	11062	12035	13452	15388	20182	18112	17429	18611	...	...	...
7 Transport, storage and communication	3546	3681	4082	4445	5786	5508	5200	5278	...	...	...
8 Finance, insurance, real estate and business services	10411	9453	10754	11562	11724	10580	8904	9672	...	...	...
9 Community, social and personal services									...	...	...
Total, Industries	...	...	...	...	...	...	...	...	...	...	...
Producers of Government Services	...	...	...	...	...	...	...	...	...	...	...
Other Producers	...	...	...	...	...	...	...	...	...	...	...
Subtotal [a]	61208	62483	68619	71576	76440	71209	72217	75347	...	...	...
Less: Imputed bank service charge	...	...	...	...	...	...	...	...	...	...	...
Plus: Import duties	...	...	...	...	...	...	...	...	...	...	...
Plus: Value added tax	...	...	...	...	...	...	...	...	...	...	...
Equals: Gross Domestic Product [a]	61208	62483	68619	71576	76440	71209	72217	75347	...	...	...

a) Gross domestic product in factor values.

1.12 Relations Among National Accounting Aggregates

Million CFA francs

	1970	1971	1972	1973	1974	1975	1976	1977	1978	1979	1980
Gross Domestic Product	69711	73702	83076	89999	104411	113114	134313	151202	168560	...	...
Plus: Net factor income received from abroad					717	-74	179	139	114	...	...
Factor income received	...	...	...	...	1216	1029	1027	1165	1197	...	...
Less: Factor income paid	...	...	...	...	499	1103	848	1026	1083	...	...
Equals: Gross National Product	...	...	...	...	105128	113040	134492	151341	168674	...	...
Less: Consumption of fixed capital	...	...	...	...	4834	5526	8529	8923	10936	...	...
Less: Net indirect taxes paid to supranational organisations	...	...	...	...	...	...	...	...	...	...	...
Equals: National Income at Market Prices	...	...	...	...	100294	107514	125963	142418	157738	...	...
Plus: Net current transfers received from abroad	...	...	...	...	7528	8732	10672	19796	16820	...	...
Current transfers received	...	...	...	...	9290	10493	12171	21432	18600	...	...
Less: Current transfers paid	...	...	...	...	1762	1761	1499	1636	1780	...	...
Equals: National Disposable Income at Market Prices	...	...	...	...	107822	116246	136635	162214	174558	...	...
Less: Final consumption	63057	65632	75329	81567	89742	109401	132285	162550	180967	...	...
Equals: Net Saving	...	...	...	...	18080	6845	4350	-336	-6409	...	...
Less: Surplus of the nation on current transactions	...	...	...	...	624	-16422	-12383	-19100	-24176	...	...
Equals: Net Capital Formation	...	...	...	...	17456	23267	16733	18764	17767	...	...

2.1 General Government Final Consumption Expenditure by Function, in Current Prices

Million CFA francs

	1970	1971	1972	1973	1974	1975	1976	1977	1978	1979	1980
1 General public services	...	...	...	...	2866	3544	2926	3019	2701	3708	...
2 Defence	...	...	...	...	1652	1684	1820	2473	1901	3267	...
3 Public order and safety	...	...	...	...							...
4 Education	...	...	...	...	2874	3450	3320	4657	5074	5004	...
5 Health	...	...	...	...	1238	1356	1212	1738	1109	1876	...
6 Social security and welfare	...	...	...	...	199	218	279	303	342	406	...
7 Housing and community amenities	...	...	...	...	22	-	10	110	127	125	...
8 Recreational, cultural and religious affairs	...	...	...	...	70	69	77	99	112	136	...
9 Economic services	...	...	...	...	1248	1171	1085	1385	1321	1622	...
10 Other functions	...	...	...	...	1633	1919	2052	927	1727	1625	...
Total General Government Final Consumption Expenditure	8976	9269	10492	11195	11802	13411	12781	14711	14414	17769	...

Benin

2.17 Exports and Imports of Goods and Services, Detail

Million CFA francs

	1970	1971	1972	1973	1974	1975	1976	1977	1978	1979	1980
Exports of Goods and Services											
1 Exports of merchandise, f.o.b.	16090	19300	16980	20720	22700	24882	23500	27582	30000	...	...
2 Transport and communication	2110	1990	2400	2790	3670	4198	5326	4894	6800	...	...
a In respect of merchandise imports	1010	950	1190	1250	1788	2286	2800	2024	3500	...	...
b Other	1100	1040	1210	1540	1882	1912	2526	2870	3300	...	...
3 Insurance service charges	20	21	22	23	22	15	10	72	95	...	...
4 Other commodities	920	919	1068	787	242	189	938	527	660	...	...
5 Adjustments of merchandise exports to change-of-ownership basis	...	...	...	...	...	...	...	...	...	...	...
6 Direct purchases in the domestic market by non-residential households	210	250	290	360	470	560	680	762	876	...	...
7 Direct purchases in the domestic market by extraterritorial bodies	1020	1145	860	672	676	788	1159	945	1180	...	...
Total Exports of Goods and Services	19270	23625	21620	25352	27780	30647	31613	34782	39611	...	...
Imports of Goods and Services											
1 Imports of merchandise, c.i.f.	20350	24140	26410	28570	31500	50366	50025	68154	74210	...	...
a Imports of merchandise, f.o.b.	...	...	...	...	...	...	...	...	...	...	...
b Transport of services on merchandise imports	-	-	-	-	-	-	25	154	210	...	...
c Insurance service charges on merchandise imports	...	...	...	...	...	...	...	...	...	...	...
2 Adjustments of merchandise imports to change-of-ownership basis	...	...	...	...	...	...	...	...	...	...	...
3 Other transport and communication	1360	1300	1560	1850	1474	2518	1842	2181	2509	...	...
4 Other insurance service charges	40	42	45	48	50	95	163	246	321	...	...
5 Other commodities	1620	798	1455	1062	701	1063	979	1411	1650	...	...
6 Direct purchases abroad by government	310	325	338	350	359	382	569	586	690	...	...
7 Direct purchases abroad by resident households	790	940	1130	1300	1318	1303	1268	1238	1341	...	...
Total Imports of Goods and Services	24470	27545	30938	33180	35402	55727	54847	73817	80721	...	...
Balance of Goods and Services	-5200	-3920	-9318	-7828	-7622	-25080	-23234	-39035	-41110	...	...
Total Imports and Balance of Goods and Services	19270	23625	21620	25352	27780	30647	31613	34782	39611	...	...

4.3 Derivation of Value Added by Kind of Activity, ISIC Divisions, in Current Prices

Million CFA francs

	1974 Gross Output	1974 Intermediate Consumption	1974 Value Added	1975 Gross Output	1975 Intermediate Consumption	1975 Value Added	1976 Gross Output	1976 Intermediate Consumption	1976 Value Added	1977 Gross Output	1977 Intermediate Consumption	1977 Value Added
All Producers												
1 Agriculture, hunting, forestry and fishing	42195	4447	37748	43614	4421	39193	60009	6004	54005	67115	7137	59978
a Agriculture and hunting	37673	3783	33890	38479	3734	34745	54277	5466	48811	60760	6438	54322
b Forestry and logging	2100	106	1994	2340	117	2223	2564	205	2359	2820	238	2582
c Fishing	2422	558	1864	2795	570	2225	3168	333	2835	3535	461	3074
2 Mining and quarrying	350	50	300	265	38	227	310	45	265	345	52	293

Benin

4.3 Derivation of Value Added by Kind of Activity, ISIC Divisions, in Current Prices
(Continued)

Million CFA francs

	1974 Gross Output	1974 Intermediate Consumption	1974 Value Added	1975 Gross Output	1975 Intermediate Consumption	1975 Value Added	1976 Gross Output	1976 Intermediate Consumption	1976 Value Added	1977 Gross Output	1977 Intermediate Consumption	1977 Value Added
3 Manufacturing	23947	14617	9330	26352	15645	10707	28718	19568	9149	32368	22109	10259
a Manufacture of food, beverages and tobacco	14908	9422	5486	15662	9821	5841	17939	12738	5201	19665	13485	6180
b Textile, wearing apparel and leather industries	3395	1797	1598	4455	2169	2286	4883	3378	1504	6025	4652	1373
c Manufacture of wood and wood products, including furniture	782	434	348	820	429	391	933	409	524	1044	479	565
d Manufacture of paper and paper products, printing and publishing	314	147	167	380	158	222	216	117	99	353	204	149
e Manufacture of chemicals and chemical petroleum, coal, rubber and plastic products	604	316	288	634	304	330	759	395	364	933	468	465
f Manufacture of non-metallic mineral products, except products of petroleum and coal	2025	1488	537	2476	1788	688	1933	1506	427	1973	1566	407
g Basic metal industries	...	...	...	...	...	...	...	...	...	...	...	...
h Manufacture of fabricated metal products, machinery and equipment	1858	982	876	1863	946	917	2055	1025	1030	2375	1255	1120
i Other manufacturing industries	61	31	30	62	30	32	-	-	-	-	-	-
4 Electricity, gas and water	1274	634	640	1323	556	767	1597	694	903	2045	877	1168
5 Construction	12624	7144	5480	10180	5304	4876	14553	9042	5511	15101	9383	5718
6 Wholesale and retail trade, restaurants and hotels	28875	3455	25420	30354	2304	28050	34749	3173	31576	38467	3819	34648
a Wholesale and retail trade	28595	3280	25315	30064	2130	27934	34413	3030	31383	38127	3680	34447
b Restaurants and hotels	280	175	105	290	174	116	336	143	193	340	139	201
7 Transport, storage and communication	12682	5902	6780	14116	6034	8082	16560	7212	9348	19545	8084	11461
a Transport and storage	11730	5729	6001	12900	5805	7095	14995	6950	8045	17898	7750	10148
b Communication	952	173	779	1216	229	987	1565	262	1303	1647	334	1313
8 Finance, insurance, real estate and business services	4750	1055	3695	4840	820	4020	5719	807	4912	5901	1014	4887
a Financial institutions	1560	460	1100	1640	380	1260	2319	331	1988	2211	479	1732
b Insurance												
c Real estate and business services	3190	595	2595	3200	440	2760	3400	476	2924	3690	535	3155
9 Community, social and personal services	860	300	560	902	316	586	928	335	593	1192	477	715
Total, Industries	127557	37604	89953	131946	35438	96508	163143	46881	116262	182079	52952	129127
Producers of Government Services	11824	2112	9712	13402	2442	10960	13149	2068	11081	15190	2310	12880
Other Producers	692	280	412	720	295	425	314	82	232	328	93	235
Total	140074	39996	100077	146068	38175	107893	176606	49031	127575	197597	55355	142242
Imputed bank service charge	...	...	...	...	...	...	...	...	...	...	...	...
Import duties	...	...	...	...	...	...	...	...	...	...	...	...
Value added tax	...	...	...	...	...	...	...	...	...	...	...	...
Total	...	...	...	...	...	...	...	...	...	...	...	...

	1978 Gross Output	1978 Intermediate Consumption	1978 Value Added

All Producers

1 Agriculture, hunting, forestry and fishing	83200	9570	73630
a Agriculture and hunting	76340	8655	67685
b Forestry and logging	3110	310	2800
c Fishing	3750	605	3145
2 Mining and quarrying	360	55	305

Benin

4.3 Derivation of Value Added by Kind of Activity, ISIC Divisions, in Current Prices
(Continued)

Million CFA francs

	1978		
	Gross Output	Intermediate Consumption	Value Added
3 Manufacturing	33374	23072	10302
a Manufacture of food, beverages and tobacco	19977	13829	6148
b Textile, wearing apparel and leather industries	5808	4575	1233
c Manufacture of wood and wood products, including furniture	1138	526	612
d Manufacture of paper and paper products, printing and publishing	448	226	222
e Manufacture of chemicals and chemical petroleum, coal, rubber and plastic products	1081	709	372
f Manufacture of non-metallic mineral products, except products of petroleum and coal	2320	1822	498
g Basic metal industries	...	...	...
h Manufacture of fabricated metal products, machinery and equipment	2602	1385	1217
i Other manufacturing industries	...	...	...
4 Electricity, gas and water	2710	1033	1677
5 Construction	15923	9928	5995
6 Wholesale and retail trade, restaurants and hotels	40132	4799	35333
a Wholesale and retail trade	39693	4605	35088
b Restaurants and hotels	439	194	245
7 Transport, storage and communication	23082	9611	13471
a Transport and storage	21158	9180	11978
b Communication	1924	431	1493
8 Finance, insurance, real estate and business services	8188	1372	6816
a Financial institutions	4113	762	3351
b Insurance			
c Real estate and business services	4075	610	3465
9 Community, social and personal services	610	304	306
Total, Industries	207579	59744	147835
Producers of Government Services	15293	2613	12680
Other Producers	341	100	241
Total	223213	62457	160756
Imputed bank service charge	...	...	...
Import duties	...	...	...
Value added tax	...	...	...
Total	...	...	...

4.6 Cost Components of Value Added, ISIC Divisions

Million CFA francs

	1974						1975					
	Compensation of Employees	Capital Consumption	Net Operating Surplus	Indirect Taxes	Less: Subsidies Received	Value Added	Compensation of Employees	Capital Consumption	Net Operating Surplus	Indirect Taxes	Less: Subsidies Received	Value Added
	All Producers
1 Agriculture, hunting, forestry and fishing	3337	1864	32356	191	...	37748	3547	1961	33475	210	...	39193
a Agriculture and hunting	2820	1624	29266	165	...	33890	2918	1658	29991	178	...	34745
b Forestry and logging	28	13	1944	17	...	1994	32	25	2146	20	...	2223
c Fishing	489	227	1146	9	...	1864	597	278	1338	12	...	2225
2 Mining and quarrying	68	6	225	1	...	300	48	5	173	1	...	227

Benin

4.6 Cost Components of Value Added, ISIC Divisions
(Continued)

Million CFA francs

	1974						1975					
	Compensation of Employees	Capital Consumption	Net Operating Surplus	Indirect Taxes	Less: Subsidies Received	Value Added	Compensation of Employees	Capital Consumption	Net Operating Surplus	Indirect Taxes	Less: Subsidies Received	Value Added
3 Manufacturing	2236	1024	5877	963	...	9330	1602	1183	6791	1131	...	10707
a Manufacture of food, beverages and tobacco	1466	617	6716	810	...	5486	733	658	3673	777	...	5841
b Textile, wearing apparel and leather industries	269	146	1326	1	...	1598	311	239	1709	27	...	2286
c Manufacture of wood and wood products, including furniture	76	44	254	5	...	348	81	25	258	6	...	391
d Manufacture of paper and paper products, printing and publishing	35	44	89	14	...	167	47	68	103	4	...	222
e Manufacture of chemicals and chemical petroleum, coal, rubber and plastic products	84	32	193	5	...	288	88	34	202	6	...	330
f Manufacture of non-metallic mineral products, except products of petroleum and coal	77	53	412	43	...	537	70	50	374	194	...	688
g Basic metal industries	...	...	...	...	...	...	...	...	...	...	...	...
h Manufacture of fabricated metal products, machinery and equipment	227	84	559	85	...	876	...	...	...	...	...	917
i Other manufacturing industries	2	4	27	-	...	30	2	4	26	-	...	32
4 Electricity, gas and water	143	258	229	10	...	640	125	80	558	4	...	767
5 Construction	2444	312	2159	565	...	5480	2090	480	2096	210	...	4876
6 Wholesale and retail trade, restaurants and hotels	4084	337	19043	1956	...	25420	4298	358	21526	1868	...	28050
a Wholesale and retail trade	4050	330	18986	1942	...	25315	4260	350	21471	1853	...	27934
b Restaurants and hotels	34	7	57	14	...	105	38	8	55	15	...	116
7 Transport, storage and communication	4328	615	1646	191	...	6780	4754	920	2258	150	...	8082
a Transport and storage	3819	510	1986	136	...	6001	4200	780	1965	150	...	7095
b Communication	509	105	112	55	...	779	554	140	293	-	...	987
8 Finance, insurance, real estate and business services	505	344	2708	138	...	3695	530	340	3005	145	...	4020
a Financial institutions	265	29	792	114	...	1100	280	30	830	120	...	1260
b Insurance					...						...	
c Real estate and business services	240	315	2203	24	...	2595	250	310	2175	25	...	2760
9 Community, social and personal services	103	50	390	17	...	560	108	50	410	18	...	586
a Sanitary and similar services	...	...	...	...	...	...	...	...	...	...	...	...
b Social and related community services	103	50	390	17	...	560	108	50	420	18	...	586
c Recreational and cultural services	...	...	...	...	...	...	...	...	...	...	...	...
d Personal and household services	...	...	...	...	...	...	...	...	...	...	...	...
Total, Industries	17248	4810	63863	4032	...	89953	17102	5377	70292	3737	...	96508
Producers of Government Services	9688	24	...	...	...	9712	10811	149	...	...	...	10960
Other Producers	412	...	...	...	...	412	425	...	...	...	...	425
Total [a]	27348	4834	63863	4032	...	100077	28338	5526	70292	3737	...	107893
Imputed bank service charge	...	...	-912	...	...	-912	...	...	-980	...	...	-980
Import duties	...	...	...	5246	...	5246	...	...	...	6201	...	6201
Value added tax	...	...	...	...	...	...	...	...	...	...	...	...
Other adjustments	...	...	...	...	...	...	...	...	...	...	...	...
Total	27348	4834	62951	9278	...	104411	28338	5526	69312	9938	...	113114

	1976						1977					
	Compensation of Employees	Capital Consumption	Net Operating Surplus	Indirect Taxes	Less: Subsidies Received	Value Added	Compensation of Employees	Capital Consumption	Net Operating Surplus	Indirect Taxes	Less: Subsidies Received	Value Added
All Producers												
1 Agriculture, hunting, forestry and fishing	4128	2132	47542	203	...	54005	5281	2424	52118	155	...	59978
a Agriculture and hunting	3328	1804	43500	173	...	48811	4362	2032	47807	121	...	54322
b Forestry and logging	148	82	2110	25	...	2359	153	87	2315	27	...	2582
c Fishing	652	246	1932	5	...	2835	766	305	1905	7	...	3074
2 Mining and quarrying	55	6	203	1	...	265	60	7	225	1	...	293

Benin

4.6 Cost Components of Value Added, ISIC Divisions
(Continued)

Million CFA francs

		1976					1977					
	Compensation of Employees	Capital Consumption	Net Operating Surplus	Indirect Taxes	Less: Subsidies Received	Value Added	Compensation of Employees	Capital Consumption	Net Operating Surplus	Indirect Taxes	Less: Subsidies Received	Value Added
3 Manufacturing	2220	2064	3708	1157	...	9149	2549	2122	4000	1588	...	10259
a Manufacture of food, beverages and tobacco	649	727	3014	811	...	5201	676	816	3732	1310	...	6180
b Textile, wearing apparel and leather industries	890	1080	-367	46	...	1504	1138	1026	-863	72	...	1373
c Manufacture of wood and wood products, including furniture	105	34	374	11	...	524	112	37	400	16	...	565
d Manufacture of paper and paper products, printing and publishing	34	17	53	-5	...	99	55	17	86	-9	...	149
e Manufacture of chemicals and chemical petroleum, coal, rubber and plastic products	65	30	261	8	...	364	71	38	345	10	...	465
f Manufacture of non-metallic mineral products, except products of petroleum and coal	85	40	136	166	...	427	79	41	128	158	...	407
g Basic metal industries	...	...	...	...	...	...	...	...	...	...	...	...
h Manufacture of fabricated metal products, machinery and equipment	392	136	382	120	...	1030	418	147	530	125	...	1120
i Other manufacturing industries	...	...	...	...	...	...	...	...	...	...	...	...
4 Electricity, gas and water	227	331	294	51	...	903	253	416	318	181	...	1168
5 Construction	2354	643	2064	450	...	5511	2454	650	2146	468	...	5718
6 Wholesale and retail trade, restaurants and hotels	5191	532	23483	2370	...	31576	5483	553	25989	2623	...	34648
a Wholesale and retail trade	5100	480	23447	2356	...	31383	5400	501	25937	2609	...	34447
b Restaurants and hotels	91	52	36	14	...	193	83	52	52	14	...	201
7 Transport, storage and communication	4108	2290	2633	317	...	9348	5566	2142	2903	850	...	11461
a Transport and storage	3500	2080	2150	315	...	8045	4880	2142	2276	850	...	10148
b Communication	608	210	483	2	...	1303	686	-	627	-	...	1313
8 Finance, insurance, real estate and business services	789	424	3159	540	...	4912	910	511	3305	161	...	4887
a Financial institutions	524	98	856	510	...	1988	574	136	885	136	...	1732
b Insurance					...						...	
c Real estate and business services	265	326	2303	30	...	2924	336	375	2419	25	...	3155
9 Community, social and personal services	115	60	397	21	...	593	125	46	518	26	...	715
a Sanitary and similar services	...	...	...	...	...	...	...	...	...	...	...	...
b Social and related community services	115	60	397	21	...	593	125	46	518	26	...	715
c Recreational and cultural services	...	...	...	...	...	...	...	...	...	...	...	...
d Personal and household services	...	...	...	...	...	...	...	...	...	...	...	...
Total, Industries	18893	8482	83777	5110	...	116262	22681	8871	91522	6053	...	129127
Producers of Government Services	11255	47	...	11	...	11081	13052	52	...	11	...	12880
Other Producers			...		...				...		...	
Total a	30148	8529	83777	5121	...	127575	35733	8923	91522	6064	...	142242
Imputed bank service charge	...	...	-1482	...	...	-1482	...	...	-866	...	...	-866
Import duties	...	...	...	8220	...	8220	...	...	...	9826	...	9826
Value added tax	...	...	...	...	...	...	...	...	...	...	...	...
Other adjustments	...	...	...	...	...	...	...	...	...	...	...	...
Total	30148	8529	82295	13341	...	134313	35733	8923	90656	15890	...	151202

	1978					
	Compensation of Employees	Capital Consumption	Net Operating Surplus	Indirect Taxes	Less: Subsidies Received	Value Added
	All Producers					
1 Agriculture, hunting, forestry and fishing	6554	3098	63642	336	...	73630
a Agriculture and hunting	5576	2681	59126	302	...	67685
b Forestry and logging	158	88	2526	28	...	2800
c Fishing	820	329	1990	6	...	3145
2 Mining and quarrying	65	8	231	1	...	305

4.6 Cost Components of Value Added, ISIC Divisions
(Continued)

Benin

Million CFA francs

		Compensation of Employees	Capital Consumption	Net Operating Surplus	Indirect Taxes	Less: Subsidies Received	Value Added
		1978					
3	Manufacturing	2704	2356	3794	1448	...	10302
	a Manufacture of food, beverages and tobacco	734	990	3436	986	...	6146
	b Textile, wearing apparel and leather industries	1134	1023	-1035	111	...	1233
	c Manufacture of wood and wood products, including furniture	123	39	432	18	...	612
	d Manufacture of paper and paper products, printing and publishing	100	29	105	-12	...	222
	e Manufacture of chemicals and chemical petroleum, coal, rubber and plastic products	80	33	240	19	...	372
	f Manufacture of non-metallic mineral products, except products of petroleum and coal	92	79	131	196	...	498
	g Basic metal industries	...	...	...	...	...	...
	h Manufacture of fabricated metal products, machinery and equipment	441	163	483	130	...	1217
	i Other manufacturing industries	...	...	...	...	...	...
4	Electricity, gas and water	448	432	602	195	...	1677
5	Construction	2776	702	1955	561	...	5995
6	Wholesale and retail trade, restaurants and hotels	5732	596	28381	624	...	35333
	a Wholesale and retail trade	5600	535	28347	605	...	35088
	b Restaurants and hotels	132	61	34	18	...	245
7	Transport, storage and communication	6586	6585	2718	1080	...	13471
	a Transport and storage	6014	2838	2046	1080	...	11978
	b Communication	572	250	922	-	...	1493
8	Finance, insurance, real estate and business services	1139	256	4414	707	...	6816
	a Financial institutions	799	145	173	675	...	3351
	b Insurance					...	
	c Real estate and business services	340	410	2683	32	...	3465
9	Community, social and personal services	80	40	166	20	...	306
	a Sanitary and similar services	...	...	...	...	...	...
	b Social and related community services	80	40	166	20	...	306
	c Recreational and cultural services	...	...	...	...	...	...
	d Personal and household services	...	...	...	...	...	...
Total, Industries		26083	10876	105904	4972	...	147835
Producers of Government Services		12849	60	...	12	...	12920
Other Producers						...	
Total [a]		38932	10936	105904	4984	...	160756
Imputed bank service charge		...	...	-3103	...	...	-3103
Import duties		...	...	...	10907	...	10907
Value added tax		...	...	...	...	...	...
Other adjustments		...	...	...	...	...	...
Total		38932	10936	102801	15891	...	168560

a) Column 4 is indirect taxes less subsidies received.

Bolivia

Source. Reply to the United Nations National Accounts Questionnaire from the Banco Central de Bolivia, La Paz. Official estimates together with information on concepts, sources and methods of estimation are published in 'Cuentas Nacionales de Bolivia'.

General note. The preparation of national accounts statistics in Bolivia is undertaken by the Banco Central de Bolivia. The official estimates together with methodological notes are published in a series of publications entitled 'Cuentas Nacionales de Bolivia'. The most detailed description of the sources and methods used for the national accounts estimation is found in 'Cuentas Nacionales, 1958-1966, Planeamiento'. The estimates are generally in accordance with the classifications and recommendations recommended in the United Nations System of National Accounts (SNA). Input-output table for 1958 has been published in 'La Matriz de Transacciones Intersectoriales de Bienes Nacionales e Importados'. The following tables have been prepared from successive replies to the United Nations national accounts questionnaire. When the scope and coverage of the estimates differ for conceptual or statistical reasons from the definitions and classifications recommended in SNA, a footnote is indicated to the relevant tables.

Sources and methods:

(a) Gross domestic product. Gross domestic product is estimated mainly through the production approach.

(b) Expenditure on the gross domestic product. All components of GDP by expenditure type are estimated through the expenditure approach except private final consumption expenditure which is obtained as a residual. The estimates of the government final consumption expenditure are based on the annual government accounts furnished by the respective government agencies. Increase in stocks estimates are based on information obtained from the enterprises. For public capital information, estimates are obtained from financial statements of the public institutions. The estimates are classified by type of goods and subdvisions of the public sector. For the estimates of private capital formation, the Instituto Nacional de Estadistica requests detailed information from the enterprises. The estimates of imported machinery and equipment are based on c.i.f. import values classified by use or economic destination. Trade margins and transport expenses are then added. The estimation of domestically produced capital goods is done on the basis of annual industrial statistics. Data on exports of goods and services are obtained from the balance of payments accounts. The value of non-monetary gold export is added to the f.o.b. figures while imports are estimated by the Banco Central. For the constant price estimates, government expenditure on wages and salaries are revalued at base-year prices while purchases of goods and services are deflated by implicit price or cost-of-living indexes. The estimates of private consumption expenditure is obtained as a residual. For the remaining items, price deflation is used.

(c) Cost-structure of the gross domestic product. The cost structure of the gross domestic product has not been estimated since 1969.

(d) Gross domestic product by kind of economic activity. The table of gross domestic product by kind of economic activity is prepared at market prices, i.e. producers' values. The production approach is used to estimate value added of most industries, but due to lack of information on intermediate consumption, value added coefficients established from the input-output table of 1958 have been utilized. The income approach is used to estimate value added of public administration and defence and some private industries. For agriculture, information relating to production volume is used, estimated on the basis of information on areas sown and production yields prepared by the Ministerio de Asuntos Campensinos y Agropecuarios and by special institutions. The gross value of production is estimated by using data on physical volumes and producer prices. Estimates of livestock production is based on existing livestock, information on meat cutting for domestic consumption and export data. The mining sector consists of the Corporacion Minera de Bolivia (COMIBOL), and of medium and small mines. The basic statistics are obtained from the accounts of COMIBOL, from Ministerio de Minera, from financial statements of medium-sized mines and from export statistics for small mines. The estimates for the manufacturing sector are based on information obtained from the annual industrial statistics published by the Instituto Nacional de Estadistica supplemented by statistics from private and public institutions and other studies. Information on electricity is obtained from the Direccion Nacional de Electricidad which controls all the public and private enterprises. The sources used for the construction estimates are the accounts of public institutions permits issued by municipalities and financial statements submitted by the construction enterprises. The value of production of private construction, which is based on permits issued and classified by surface area, is adjusted by a percentage for planned unfulfilled work. Information on trade margins and trade volumes is furnished by various concerned institutions. The gross trade margins are estimated from the price differences between the wholesale and producers prices as well as the consumer and wholesale prices for all the agricultural products and a sample of manufactured and imported goods entering the distribution channels. Restaurants and hotels estimates are based on a sample survey of the principal establishments in La Paz, blown up to cover the whole country by using the number of establishments as indicators. The estimates of railway transport are based on the accounts of the public railway enterprise. The gross value of production for urban passenger transport is estimated on the basis of the number of buses in operation, mileage, passenger volumes and average tariffs. Air transport estimates are based on the accounting statements of the national airline as well as taxes charged on foreign airlines. The accounting statements of the financial institutions are used for the financial sector. For ownership of dwellings, census information on population and housing is used supplemented by statistics on real estate. For public administration and defense, the main source is the annual financial statement requested by the Banco Central de Bolivia. Estimates for private services are obtained from concerned entities and institutions. For constant price estimates, value added for agriculture, mining and quarrying, manufacturing and transport sectors is extrapolatd by quantity index for output. Value added of construction is estimated by multiplying the annual authorized construction volume by the base-year prices. For the remaining industries, value added is deflated by appropriate price indexes.

1.1 Expenditure on the Gross Domestic Product, in Current Prices

Million Bolivian pesos

		1970	1971	1972	1973	1974	1975	1976	1977	1978	1979	1980
1	General government final consumption expenditure	1324	1520	1920	2814	4461	5699	6700	8559	10781	12276	18329
2	Private final consumption expenditure	8955	10074	12376	18081	28928	34244	39056	44940	55501	68993	100687
3	Gross capital formation	2111	2326	3420	5397	7108	12026	11949	13563	15298	16216	14888
	a Increase in stocks	319	375	797	878	558	2971	1264	1149	-98	910	-1508
	b Gross fixed capital formation	1792	1951	2623	4519	6550	9055	10685	12414	15396	15306	16396
	Residential buildings	339	346	374	636	1015	1359	1653	1864	2332	2804	...
	Non-residential buildings	184	186	198	385	594	749	1106	1346	1143	1284	...
	Other construction and land improvement etc.	379	469	750	1109	1521	1926	1986	2669	3448	3929	...
	Other	890	950	1301	2389	3420	5021	5940	6535	8473	7289	...
4	Exports of goods and services	2494	2336	2963	5878	12448	10474	12698	14512	14236	17794	25466
5	Less: Imports of goods and services	2514	2713	3430	6114	9620	13242	13956	16354	19342	23223	24383
	Equals: Gross Domestic Product	12370	13543	17249	26056	43325	49201	56447	65220	76474	92056	134987

1.2 Expenditure on the Gross Domestic Product, in Constant Prices

Million Bolivian pesos

		1970	1971	1972	1973	1974	1975	1976	1977	1978	1979	1980
		\multicolumn{11}{c}{At constant prices of:1970}
1	General government final consumption expenditure	1324	1442	1600	1789	1951	2166	2297	2368	2436	2521	2571
2	Private final consumption expenditure	8955	9275	9367	10142	10464	10894	11746	12352	13103	13690	13944
3	Gross capital formation	2111	2343	2868	2540	2520	3608	3262	3360	3392	3169	2391
	a Increase in stocks	319	371	665	390	178	794	317	247	-19	152	-174
	b Gross fixed capital formation	1792	1972	2203	2150	2342	2814	2945	3113	3411	3017	2565

Bolivia

1.2 Expenditure on the Gross Domestic Product, in Constant Prices
(Continued)

Million Bolivian pesos

	1970	1971	1972	1973	1974	1975	1976	1977	1978	1979	1980
	\multicolumn{11}{c}{At constant prices of:1970}
Residential buildings	339	328	318	313	421	492	522	546	605	619	...
Non-residential buildings	184	176	167	181	248	289	344	398	301	281	...
Other construction and land improvement etc.	379	399	557	610	593	633	598	702	787	776	...
Other	890	1069	1161	1046	1080	1400	1481	1467	1718	1341	...
4 Exports of goods and services	2494	2782	3072	3417	3383	3234	3582	3510	3405	3371	3270
5 Less: Imports of goods and services	2514	2866	3178	3242	2918	3485	3469	3439	3576	3647	2956
Equals: Gross Domestic Product	12370	12976	13729	14646	15400	16417	17418	18151	18760	19104	19220

1.3 Cost Components of the Gross Domestic Product

Million Bolivian pesos

	1970	1971	1972	1973	1974	1975	1976	1977	1978	1979	1980
1 Indirect taxes, net	942	996	1437	2723	5671	5791	6377	7724	8479	10153	...
2 Consumption of fixed capital	756	875	1149	1611	2296	2893	3413	4364	4946	5941	...
3 Compensation of employees paid by resident producers to:	4209	4872	6023	8266	13622	16364	19128	22577	26950	32982	...
a Resident households	4198	4862	6003	8234	13562	16244	18984	22389	26780	32756	...
b Rest of the world	11	10	20	32	60	120	144	188	170	226	...
4 Net operating surplus	6463	6800	8640	13456	21736	24153	27529	30555	36099	42980	...
Equals: Gross Domestic Product	12370	13543	17249	26056	43325	49201	56447	65220	76474	92056	134987

1.7 External Transactions on Current Account, Summary

Million Bolivian pesos

	1970	1971	1972	1973	1974	1975	1976	1977	1978	1979	1980
	\multicolumn{11}{c}{Payments to the Rest of the World}
1 Imports of goods and services	2514	2713	3430	6114	9620	13242	13956	16354	19342	23223	...
a Imports of merchandise c.i.f.	2302	2504	3041	5414	8586	12066	12712	14694	17556	21289	...
b Other	212	209	389	700	1034	1176	1244	1660	1786	1934	...
2 Factor income paid to the rest of the world	340	272	337	664	970	1020	1338	1914	2538	3806	...
a Compensation of employees	11	10	20	32	60	120	144	188	170	226	...
b Property and entrepreneurial income paid	329	262	317	632	910	900	1194	1726	2368	3580	...
3 Indirect taxes paid to supranational organizations	...	...	...	...	...	...	...	...	...	...	...
4 Current transfers to the rest of the world	4	1	15	46	32	76	60	60	64	72	...
5 Surplus of the nation on current transactions	-262	-476	-614	-444	2258	-3374	-1898	-3180	-6747	-8075	...
Payments to the Rest of the World and Surplus of the Nation on Current Transactions	2596	2510	3168	6380	12880	10964	13456	15148	15197	19026	...
	\multicolumn{11}{c}{Receipts From The Rest of the World}
1 Exports of goods and services	2494	2336	2963	5878	12448	10474	12698	14512	14236	17794	...
a Exports of merchandise f.o.b.	2355	2186	2718	5414	11580	9386	11480	13244	12862	15921	...
b Other	139	150	245	464	868	1088	1218	1268	1374	1873	...
2 Factor income received from rest of the world	56	93	28	176	148	228	442	230	204	234	...
a Compensation of employees	25	24	21	34	52	74	84	66	80	71	...
b Property and entrepreneurial income received	31	69	7	142	96	154	358	164	124	163	...
3 Subsidies received from supranational organisations	...	...	...	...	...	...	...	...	...	...	...
4 Current transfers from rest of the world	46	81	177	326	284	262	316	406	757	998	...
Receipts from the Rest of the World on Current Transactions	2596	2510	3168	6380	12880	10964	13456	15148	15197	19026	...

Bolivia

1.8 Capital Transactions of The Nation, Summary

Million Bolivian pesos

	1970	1971	1972	1973	1974	1975	1976	1977	1978	1979	1980
Finance of Gross Capital Formation											
Gross saving	1849	1850	2806	4953	9366	8652	10051	10383	8551	8141	...
1 Consumption of fixed capital	756	875	1149	1611	2296	2893	3413	4364	4946	5941	...
2 Net saving	1093	975	1657	3342	7070	5759	6638	6019	3605	2200	...
Less: Surplus of the nation on current transactions	-262	-476	-614	-444	2258	-3374	-1898	-3180	-6747	-8075	...
Finance of Gross Capital Formation	2111	2326	3420	5397	7108	12026	11949	13563	15298	16216	...
Gross Capital Formation											
Increase in stocks	319	375	797	878	558	2971	1264	1149	-98	910	...
Gross fixed capital formation	1792	1951	2623	4519	6550	9055	10685	12414	15396	15306	...
Gross Capital Formation	2111	2326	3420	5397	7108	12026	11949	13563	15298	16216	...

1.10 Gross Domestic Product by Kind of Activity, in Current Prices

Million Bolivian pesos

	1970	1971	1972	1973	1974	1975	1976	1977	1978	1979	1980
1 Agriculture, hunting, forestry and fishing	2240	2510	3099	4738	8265	9133	10264	11576	12937	15010	22197
2 Mining and quarrying	1273	1142	2155	3981	7567	5529	6366	7235	8491	10765	13298
3 Manufacturing	1790	1967	2403	3625	5761	6603	7822	9066	10398	12347	18885
4 Electricity, gas and water	167	181	220	306	372	469	586	732	824	929	1286
5 Construction	511	581	701	1129	1565	2017	2373	2939	3323	3848	5485
6 Wholesale and retail trade, restaurants and hotels	2182	2413	2803	4018	6862	9406	10190	11264	13403	15840	24003
7 Transport, storage and communication	931	1092	1416	1850	2783	3620	4350	5459	6570	7912	12449
8 Finance, insurance, real estate and business services	1267	1384	1647	2553	3924	4681	5521	6482	7573	8616	13488
9 Community, social and personal services	1003	1090	1384	1929	3127	3805	4325	4979	6016	7869	11701
Total, Industries	11364	12360	15828	24129	40226	45263	51797	59732	69535	83136	122792
Producers of Government Services	986	1167	1427	1990	3264	4263	5078	5986	7595	9679	13331
Other Producers	151	159	189	253	345	363	460	589	707	927	1379
Subtotal	12501	13686	17444	26372	43835	49889	57335	66307	77837	93742	137502
Less: Imputed bank service charge	131	143	195	316	510	688	888	1087	1363	1686	2515
Plus: Import duties	...	...	...	...	...	...	...	...	...	...	...
Plus: Value added tax	...	...	...	...	...	...	...	...	...	...	...
Equals: Gross Domestic Product	12370	13543	17249	26056	43325	49201	56447	65220	76474	92056	134987

1.11 Gross Domestic Product by Kind of Activity, in Constant Prices

Million Bolivian pesos

	1970	1971	1972	1973	1974	1975	1976	1977	1978	1979	1980
At constant prices of: 1970											
1 Agriculture, hunting, forestry and fishing	2240	2373	2512	2628	2725	2938	3085	3065	3130	3222	3286
2 Mining and quarrying	1273	1351	1480	1842	1705	1635	1652	1609	1464	1342	1315
3 Manufacturing	1790	1854	2004	2104	2342	2485	2692	2879	3010	3094	3063
4 Electricity, gas and water	167	179	190	211	232	237	256	285	302	318	326
5 Construction	511	524	545	563	605	679	713	791	813	804	764
6 Wholesale and retail trade, restaurants and hotels	2182	2240	2290	2362	2435	2634	2765	2834	2899	2929	2949
7 Transport, storage and communication	931	1001	1072	1141	1311	1491	1668	1891	2143	2234	2279
8 Finance, insurance, real estate and business services	1267	1313	1384	1441	1501	1614	1750	1858	1981	2019	2042
9 Community, social and personal services	1003	1038	1074	1123	1207	1321	1379	1432	1477	1516	1553
Total, Industries	11364	11873	12551	13415	14063	15034	15960	16644	17219	17478	17577
Producers of Government Services	986	1089	1186	1262	1385	1487	1585	1641	1701	1797	1820
Other Producers	151	151	147	147	133	126	147	169	174	179	183
Subtotal	12501	13113	13884	14824	15581	16647	17692	18454	19094	19454	19580
Less: Imputed bank service charge	131	137	155	178	181	230	274	303	334	350	360
Plus: Import duties	...	...	...	...	...	...	...	...	...	...	...
Plus: Value added tax	...	...	...	...	...	...	...	...	...	...	...
Equals: Gross Domestic Product	12370	12976	13729	14646	15400	16417	17418	18151	18760	19104	19220

Bolivia

1.12 Relations Among National Accounting Aggregates

Million Bolivian pesos

	1970	1971	1972	1973	1974	1975	1976	1977	1978	1979	1980
Gross Domestic Product	12370	13543	17249	26056	43325	49201	56447	65220	76474	92056	134987
Plus: Net factor income received from abroad	-284	-179	-309	-488	-822	-792	-896	-1684	-2334	-3572	...
Factor income received	56	93	28	176	148	228	442	230	204	234	...
Less: Factor income paid	340	272	337	664	970	1020	1338	1914	2538	3806	...
Equals: Gross National Product	12086	13364	16940	25568	42503	48409	55551	63536	74140	88484	...
Less: Consumption of fixed capital	756	875	1149	1611	2296	2893	3413	4364	4946	5941	...
Less: Net indirect taxes paid to supranational organisations	...	...	...	...	...	...	...	...	...	...	...
Equals: National Income at Market Prices	11330	12489	15791	23957	40207	45516	52138	59172	69194	82543	...
Plus: Net current transfers received from abroad	42	80	162	280	252	186	256	346	693	926	...
Current transfers received	46	81	177	326	284	262	316	406	757	998	...
Less: Current transfers paid	4	1	15	46	32	76	60	60	64	72	...
Equals: National Disposable Income at Market Prices	11372	12569	15953	24237	40459	45702	52394	59518	69887	83469	...
Less: Final consumption	10279	11594	14296	20895	33389	39943	45756	53499	66282	81269	119016
Equals: Net Saving	1093	975	1657	3342	7070	5759	6638	6019	3605	2200	...
Less: Surplus of the nation on current transactions	-262	-476	-614	-444	2258	-3374	-1898	-3180	-6747	-8075	...
Equals: Net Capital Formation	1355	1451	2271	3786	4812	9133	8536	9199	10352	10275	...

2.1 General Government Final Consumption Expenditure by Function, in Current Prices

Million Bolivian pesos

	1970	1971	1972	1973	1974	1975	1976	1977	1978	1979	1980
1 General public services	190	239	312	485	594	765	922	1075	1319	1466	...
2 Defence	185	171	245	383	675	902	1038	1087	1383	1629	...
3 Public order and safety	95	98	123	187	316	403	468	539	727	799	...
4 Education	427	451	505	800	1454	1606	1923	2180	2792	3687	...
5 Health	53	54	60	87	169	198	257	308	382	521	...
6 Social security and welfare	124	138	119	215	274	448	807	982	1357	1763	...
7 Housing and community amenities	59	68	67	75	90	143	126	154	156	194	...
8 Recreational, cultural and religious affairs	4	8	9	12	11	5	45	90	28	39	...
9 Economic services	187	293	480	570	878	1229	1114	2144	2637	2178	...
a Fuel and energy	1	2	2	1	3	3	4	15	10	12	...
b Agriculture, forestry, fishing and hunting	42	54	85	81	119	196	186	239	250	354	...
c Mining, manufacturing and construction, except fuel and energy	20	26	34	25	63	120	86	128	187	149	...
d Transportation and communication	89	159	293	359	362	601	532	1350	1730	1134	...
e Other economic affairs	35	52	66	104	331	309	306	412	460	529	...
10 Other functions	-	-	-	-	-	-	...	...	...	...	...
Total General Government Final Consumption Expenditure	1324	1520	1920	2814	4461	5699	6700	8559	10781	12276	18329

2.3 Total General Government Outlays by Function and Type

Million Bolivian pesos

	Final Consumption Expenditures Total	Compensation of Employees	Other	Subsidies	Other Current Transfers & Property Income	Total Current Disbursements	Gross Capital Formation	Other Capital Outlays	Total Outlays
					1970				
1 General public services	190	124	66	...	...	...	...	...	...
2 Defence	185	109	76	...	...	...	...	...	...
3 Public order and safety	95	81	14	...	...	...	...	...	...
4 Education	427	412	15	...	...	...	...	...	...
5 Health	53	41	12	...	...	...	...	...	...
6 Social security and welfare	124	62	62	...	...	...	...	...	...
7 Housing and community amenities	59	24	35	...	...	...	...	...	...
8 Recreation, culture and religion	4	3	1	...	...	...	...	...	...
9 Economic services	187	120	67	...	...	...	...	...	...

Bolivia

2.3 Total General Government Outlays by Function and Type
(Continued)

Million Bolivian pesos

	Final Consumption Expenditures Total	Compensation of Employees	Other	Subsidies	Other Current Transfers & Property Income	Total Current Disbursements	Gross Capital Formation	Other Capital Outlays	Total Outlays
a Fuel and energy	1	1	-	...	...	...	...	...	...
b Agriculture, forestry, fishing and hunting	42	31	11	...	...	...	...	...	...
c Mining (except fuels), manufacturing and construction	20	14	6	...	...	...	...	...	...
d Transportation and communication	89	52	37	...	...	...	...	...	...
e Other economic affairs	35	22	13	...	...	...	...	...	...
10 Other functions	-	-	-	...	...	...	...	...	...
Total	1324	976	348	...	...	...	...	...	...

1971

1 General public services	239	173	66	...	...	...	...	...	...
2 Defence	171	103	68	...	...	...	...	...	...
3 Public order and safety	98	80	18	...	...	...	...	...	...
4 Education	451	444	7	...	...	...	...	...	...
5 Health	54	46	8	...	...	...	...	...	...
6 Social security and welfare	138	83	55	...	...	...	...	...	...
7 Housing and community amenities	68	31	37	...	...	...	...	...	...
8 Recreation, culture and religion	8	5	3	...	...	...	...	...	...
9 Economic services	293	190	103	...	...	...	...	...	...
a Fuel and energy	2	2	-	...	...	...	...	...	...
b Agriculture, forestry, fishing and hunting	54	41	13	...	...	...	...	...	...
c Mining (except fuels), manufacturing and construction	26	21	5	...	...	...	...	...	...
d Transportation and communication	159	95	64	...	...	...	...	...	...
e Other economic affairs	52	31	21	...	...	...	...	...	...
10 Other functions	-	-	-	...	...	...	...	...	...
Total	1520	1155	365	...	...	...	...	...	...

1972

1 General public services	312	223	89	...	...	...	...	...	...
2 Defence	245	148	97	...	...	...	...	...	...
3 Public order and safety	123	100	23	...	...	...	...	...	...
4 Education	505	495	10	...	...	...	...	...	...
5 Health	60	53	7	...	...	...	...	...	...
6 Social security and welfare	119	84	35	...	...	...	...	...	...
7 Housing and community amenities	67	38	29	...	...	...	...	...	...
8 Recreation, culture and religion	9	6	3	...	...	...	...	...	...
9 Economic services	480	262	218	...	...	...	...	...	...
a Fuel and energy	2	2	-	...	...	...	...	...	...
b Agriculture, forestry, fishing and hunting	85	56	29	...	...	...	...	...	...
c Mining (except fuels), manufacturing and construction	34	22	12	...	...	...	...	...	...
d Transportation and communication	293	143	150	...	...	...	...	...	...
e Other economic affairs	66	39	27	...	...	...	...	...	...
10 Other functions	-	-	-	...	...	...	...	...	...
Total	1920	1409	511	...	...	...	...	...	...

1973

1 General public services	485	286	199	...	...	...	...	...	...
2 Defence	383	230	153	...	...	...	...	...	...
3 Public order and safety	187	160	27	...	...	...	...	...	...
4 Education	800	766	34	...	...	...	...	...	...
5 Health	87	73	14	...	...	...	...	...	...
6 Social security and welfare	215	130	85	...	...	...	...	...	...
7 Housing and community amenities	75	38	37	...	...	...	...	...	...
8 Recreation, culture and religion	12	7	5	...	...	...	...	...	...
9 Economic services	570	278	292	...	...	...	...	...	...

Bolivia

2.3 Total General Government Outlays by Function and Type
(Continued)

Million Bolivian pesos

		Final Consumption Expenditures			Subsidies	Other Current Transfers & Property Income	Total Current Disbursements	Gross Capital Formation	Other Capital Outlays	Total Outlays
		Total	Compensation of Employees	Other						
a	Fuel and energy	1	1	-	...	...	...	...	...	...
b	Agriculture, forestry, fishing and hunting	81	51	30	...	...	...	...	...	...
c	Mining (except fuels), manufacturing and construction	25	22	3	...	...	...	...	...	...
d	Transportation and communication	359	152	207	...	...	...	...	...	...
e	Other economic affairs	104	52	52	...	...	...	...	...	...
10	Other functions	-	-	-	...	...	...	...	...	...
	Total	2814	1968	846	...	...	...	...	...	...

1974

		Total	Comp.	Other						
1	General public services	594	388	206	...	...	...	...	...	...
2	Defence	675	410	265	...	...	...	...	...	...
3	Public order and safety	316	265	51	...	...	...	...	...	...
4	Education	1454	1398	56	...	...	...	...	...	...
5	Health	169	142	27	...	...	...	...	...	...
6	Social security and welfare	274	183	91	...	...	...	...	...	...
7	Housing and community amenities	90	45	45	...	...	...	...	...	...
8	Recreation, culture and religion	11	6	5	...	...	...	...	...	...
9	Economic services	878	395	483	...	...	...	...	...	...
a	Fuel and energy	3	2	1	...	...	...	...	...	...
b	Agriculture, forestry, fishing and hunting	119	72	47	...	...	...	...	...	...
c	Mining (except fuels), manufacturing and construction	63	35	28	...	...	...	...	...	...
d	Transportation and communication	362	188	174	...	...	...	...	...	...
e	Other economic affairs	331	98	233	...	...	...	...	...	...
10	Other functions	-	-	-	...	...	...	...	...	...
	Total	4461	3232	1229	...	...	...	...	...	...

1975

		Total	Comp.	Other						
1	General public services	765	522	243	...	...	...	...	...	...
2	Defence	902	532	370	...	...	...	...	...	...
3	Public order and safety	403	340	63	...	...	...	...	...	...
4	Education	1606	1549	57	...	...	...	...	...	...
5	Health	198	162	36	...	...	...	...	...	...
6	Social security and welfare	448	251	197	...	...	...	...	...	...
7	Housing and community amenities	143	88	55	...	...	...	...	...	...
8	Recreation, culture and religion	5	4	1	...	...	...	...	...	...
9	Economic services	1229	778	451	...	...	...	...	...	...
a	Fuel and energy	3	2	1	...	...	...	...	...	...
b	Agriculture, forestry, fishing and hunting	196	124	72	...	...	...	...	...	...
c	Mining (except fuels), manufacturing and construction	120	89	31	...	...	...	...	...	...
d	Transportation and communication	601	358	243	...	...	...	...	...	...
e	Other economic affairs	309	205	104	...	...	...	...	...	...
10	Other functions	-	-	-	...	...	...	...	...	...
	Total	5699	4226	1473	...	...	...	...	...	...

1976

		Total	Comp.	Other						
1	General public services	922	625	297	...	...	...	...	...	...
2	Defence	1038	668	370	...	...	...	...	...	...
3	Public order and safety	468	389	79	...	...	...	...	...	...
4	Education	1923	1875	48	...	...	...	...	...	...
5	Health	257	221	36	...	...	...	...	...	...
6	Social security and welfare	807	487	320	...	...	...	...	...	...
7	Housing and community amenities	126	84	42	...	...	...	...	...	...
8	Recreation, culture and religion	45	22	23	...	...	...	...	...	...
9	Economic services	1114	649	465	...	...	...	...	...	...

Bolivia

2.3 Total General Government Outlays by Function and Type
(Continued)

Million Bolivian pesos

	Final Consumption Expenditures Total	Compensation of Employees	Other	Subsidies	Other Current Transfers & Property Income	Total Current Disbursements	Gross Capital Formation	Other Capital Outlays	Total Outlays
a Fuel and energy	4	3	1	...	...	...	...	...	...
b Agriculture, forestry, fishing and hunting	186	138	48	...	...	...	...	...	...
c Mining (except fuels), manufacturing and construction	86	61	25	...	...	...	...	...	...
d Transportation and communication	532	274	258	...	...	...	...	...	...
e Other economic affairs	306	173	133	...	...	...	...	...	...
10 Other functions	-	-	-	...	...	...	...	...	...
Total	6700	5020	1680	...	...	...	...	...	...

1977

	Total	Compensation of Employees	Other	Subsidies	Other Current Transfers & Property Income	Total Current Disbursements	Gross Capital Formation	Other Capital Outlays	Total Outlays
1 General public services	1075	798	277	...	...	...	...	...	...
2 Defence	1087	673	414	...	...	...	...	...	...
3 Public order and safety	539	440	99	...	...	...	...	...	...
4 Education	2180	2130	50	...	...	...	...	...	...
5 Health	308	259	49	...	...	...	...	...	...
6 Social security and welfare	982	598	384	...	...	...	...	...	...
7 Housing and community amenities	154	107	47	...	...	...	...	...	...
8 Recreation, culture and religion	90	29	61	...	...	...	...	...	...
9 Economic services	2144	851	1293	...	...	...	...	...	...
a Fuel and energy	15	7	8	...	...	...	...	...	...
b Agriculture, forestry, fishing and hunting	239	165	74	...	...	...	...	...	...
c Mining (except fuels), manufacturing and construction	128	82	46	...	...	...	...	...	...
d Transportation and communication	1350	348	1002	...	...	...	...	...	...
e Other economic affairs	412	249	163	...	...	...	...	...	...
10 Other functions	-	-	-	...	...	...	...	...	...
Total	8559	5885	2674	...	...	...	...	...	...

1978

	Total	Compensation of Employees	Other	Subsidies	Other Current Transfers & Property Income	Total Current Disbursements	Gross Capital Formation	Other Capital Outlays	Total Outlays
1 General public services	1319	884	435	...	...	...	...	...	...
2 Defence	1383	846	537	...	...	...	...	...	...
3 Public order and safety	727	550	177	...	...	...	...	...	...
4 Education	2792	2720	72	...	...	...	...	...	...
5 Health	382	328	54	...	...	...	...	...	...
6 Social security and welfare	1357	842	515	...	...	...	...	...	...
7 Housing and community amenities	156	121	35	...	...	...	...	...	...
8 Recreation, culture and religion	28	21	7	...	...	...	...	...	...
9 Economic services	2637	1118	1519	...	...	...	...	...	...
a Fuel and energy	10	8	2	...	...	...	...	...	...
b Agriculture, forestry, fishing and hunting	250	196	54	...	...	...	...	...	...
c Mining (except fuels), manufacturing and construction	187	126	61	...	...	...	...	...	...
d Transportation and communication	1730	494	1236	...	...	...	...	...	...
e Other economic affairs	460	294	166	...	...	...	...	...	...
10 Other functions	...	...	...	...	...	...	...	...	...
Total	10781	7430	3351	...	...	...	...	...	...

1979

	Total	Compensation of Employees	Other	Subsidies	Other Current Transfers & Property Income	Total Current Disbursements	Gross Capital Formation	Other Capital Outlays	Total Outlays
1 General public services	1466	1066	400	...	...	...	...	...	...
2 Defence	1629	1073	556	...	...	...	...	...	...
3 Public order and safety	799	635	164	...	...	...	...	...	...
4 Education	3687	3572	115	...	...	...	...	...	...
5 Health	521	468	53	...	...	...	...	...	...
6 Social security and welfare	1763	1251	512	...	...	...	...	...	...
7 Housing and community amenities	194	155	39	...	...	...	...	...	...
8 Recreation, culture and religion	39	27	12	...	...	...	...	...	...
9 Economic services	2178	1218	960	...	...	...	...	...	...

Bolivia

2.3 Total General Government Outlays by Function and Type
(Continued)

Million Bolivian pesos

	Final Consumption Expenditures Total	Compensation of Employees	Other	Subsidies	Other Current Transfers & Property Income	Total Current Disbursements	Gross Capital Formation	Other Capital Outlays	Total Outlays
a Fuel and energy	12	10	2	...	...	...	...	...	...
b Agriculture, forestry, fishing and hunting	354	269	85	...	...	...	...	...	...
c Mining (except fuels), manufacturing and construction	149	126	23	...	...	...	...	...	...
d Transportation and communication	1134	462	672	...	...	...	...	...	...
e Other economic affairs	529	351	178	...	...	...	...	...	...
10 Other functions	...	...	...	...	...	...	...	...	...
Total	12276	9465	2811	...	...	...	...	...	...

2.7 Gross Capital Formation by Type of Good and Owner, in Current Prices

Million Bolivian pesos

	1970 TOTAL	Total Private	Public Enterprises	General Government	1971 TOTAL	Total Private	Public Enterprises	General Government	1972 TOTAL	Total Private	Public Enterprises	General Government
Increase in stocks, total [a]	319	105	...	214	375	527	...	-152	797	342	...	455
Gross Fixed Capital Formation, Total [a]	1792	790	...	1002	1951	781	...	1170	2623	1075	...	1548
1 Residential buildings	339	269	...	70	346	321	...	25	374	355	...	19
2 Non-residential buildings	184	100	...	84	186	125	...	61	198	98	...	100
3 Other construction	379	18	...	361	438	21	...	417	664	32	...	632
4 Land improvement and plantation and orchard development	-	-	...	-	31	31	...	-	86	86	...	-
5 Producers' durable goods	883	399	...	484	948	282	...	666	1297	501	...	796
a Transport equipment	417	189	...	228	364	145	...	219	537	264	...	273
b Machinery and equipment	466	210	...	256	584	137	...	447	760	237	...	523
6 Breeding stock, dairy cattle, etc.	7	4	...	3	2	1	...	1	4	3	...	1
Total Gross Capital Formation [a]	2111	895	...	1216	2326	1308	...	1018	3420	1417	...	2003

	1973 TOTAL	Total Private	Public Enterprises	General Government	1974 TOTAL	Total Private	Public Enterprises	General Government	1975 TOTAL	Total Private	Public Enterprises	General Government
Increase in stocks, total [a]	878	131	...	747	558	-910	...	1468	2971	112	...	2859
Gross Fixed Capital Formation, Total [a]	4519	2829	...	1690	6550	4351	...	2199	9055	5344	...	3711
1 Residential buildings	636	621	...	15	1015	1003	...	12	1359	1294	...	65
2 Non-residential buildings	385	268	...	117	594	429	...	165	749	515	...	234
3 Other construction	989	47	...	942	1423	68	...	1355	1658	79	...	1579
4 Land improvement and plantation and orchard development	120	107	...	13	98	96	...	2	268	260	...	8
5 Producers' durable goods	2369	1764	...	605	3393	2730	...	663	5019	3200	...	1819
a Transport equipment	1162	1000	...	162	1468	1295	...	173	2347	1700	...	647
b Machinery and equipment	1207	764	...	443	1925	1435	...	490	2672	1500	...	1172
6 Breeding stock, dairy cattle, etc.	20	22	...	-2	27	25	...	2	2	-4	...	6
Total Gross Capital Formation [a]	5397	2960	...	2437	7108	3441	...	3667	12026	5456	...	6570

	1976 TOTAL	Total Private	Public Enterprises	General Government	1977 TOTAL	Total Private	Public Enterprises	General Government	1978 TOTAL	Total Private	Public Enterprises	General Government
Increase in stocks, total [a]	1264	585	...	679	1149	125	...	1024	-98	-100	...	2
Gross Fixed Capital Formation, Total [a]	10685	4736	...	5949	12414	4484	...	7930	15396	5180	...	10216
1 Residential buildings	1653	1569	...	84	1864	1814	...	50	2332	2225	...	107
2 Non-residential buildings	1106	340	...	766	1346	300	...	1046	1143	169	...	974
3 Other construction	1879	150	...	1729	2621	113	...	2508	3383	135	...	3248
4 Land improvement and plantation and orchard development	107	104	...	3	48	48	...	-	65	50	...	15
5 Producers' durable goods	5916	2554	...	3362	6521	2201	...	4320	8449	2584	...	5865
a Transport equipment	2557	1815	...	742	2170	1743	...	427	2674	1910	...	764
b Machinery and equipment	3359	739	...	2620	4351	458	...	3893	5775	674	...	5101
6 Breeding stock, dairy cattle, etc.	24	19	...	5	14	8	...	6	24	17	...	7
Total Gross Capital Formation [a]	11949	5321	...	6628	13563	4609	...	8954	15298	5080	...	10218

Bolivia

2.7 Gross Capital Formation by Type of Good and Owner, in Current Prices

Million Bolivian pesos

	1979 TOTAL	1979 Total Private	1979 Public Enterprises	1979 General Government	1980 TOTAL	1980 Total Private	1980 Public Enterprises	1980 General Government
Increase in stocks, total a	910	143	...	767	-1508	...	...	...
Gross Fixed Capital Formation, Total a	15306	6378	...	8928	16396	...	...	...
1 Residential buildings	2804	2058	...	746	...	...	...	...
2 Non-residential buildings	1284	469	...	815	...	...	...	...
3 Other construction	3929	157	...	3772	...	...	...	...
4 Land improvement and plantation and orchard development	-	-	...	-	...	...	...	...
5 Producers' durable goods	7271	3678	...	3593	...	...	...	...
a Transport equipment	2531	1757	...	774	...	...	...	...
b Machinery and equipment	4740	1921	...	2819	...	...	...	...
6 Breeding stock, dairy cattle, etc.	18	16	...	2	...	...	...	...
Total Gross Capital Formation a	16216	6521	...	9695	14888	...	...	...

a) Column 'Public Enterprises' is included in column 'General Government'.

2.8 Gross Capital Formation by Type of Good and Owner, in Constant Prices

Million Bolivian pesos

	1970 TOTAL	1970 Total Private	1970 Public Enterprises	1970 General Government	1971 TOTAL	1971 Total Private	1971 Public Enterprises	1971 General Government	1972 TOTAL	1972 Total Private	1972 Public Enterprises	1972 General Government
				At constant prices of:1970								
Increase in stocks, total a	319	105	...	214	371	521	...	-150	665	285	...	380
Gross Fixed Capital Formation, Total a	1792	790	...	1002	1972	806	...	1166	2203	942	...	1261
1 Residential buildings	339	269	...	70	328	304	...	24	318	302	...	16
2 Non-residential buildings	184	100	...	84	176	118	...	58	167	83	...	84
3 Other construction	379	18	...	361	369	17	...	352	487	24	...	463
4 Land improvement and plantation and orchard development	-	...	...	...	30	30	...	-	70	70	...	-
5 Producers' durable goods	883	399	...	484	1067	336	...	731	1158	461	...	697
a Transport equipment	417	189	...	228	527	208	...	319	559	274	...	285
b Machinery and equipment	466	210	...	256	540	128	...	412	599	187	...	412
6 Breeding stock, dairy cattle, etc.	7	4	...	3	2	1	...	1	3	2	...	1
Total Gross Capital Formation a	2111	895	...	1216	2343	1327	...	1016	2868	1227	...	1641

	1973 TOTAL	1973 Total Private	1973 Public Enterprises	1973 General Government	1974 TOTAL	1974 Total Private	1974 Public Enterprises	1974 General Government	1975 TOTAL	1975 Total Private	1975 Public Enterprises	1975 General Government
				At constant prices of:1970								
Increase in stocks, total a	390	58	...	332	178	-292	...	470	794	30	...	764
Gross Fixed Capital Formation, Total a	2150	1298	...	852	2342	1519	...	823	2814	1662	...	1152
1 Residential buildings	313	306	...	7	421	416	...	5	492	468	...	24
2 Non-residential buildings	181	126	...	55	248	179	...	69	289	199	...	90
3 Other construction	543	26	...	517	561	26	...	535	547	26	...	521
4 Land improvement and plantation and orchard development	67	60	...	7	32	31	...	1	86	83	...	3
5 Producers' durable goods	1037	770	...	267	1072	860	...	212	1399	887	...	512
a Transport equipment	491	423	...	68	446	393	...	53	596	431	...	165
b Machinery and equipment	546	347	...	199	626	467	...	159	803	456	...	347
6 Breeding stock, dairy cattle, etc.	9	10	...	-1	8	7	...	1	1	-1	...	2
Total Gross Capital Formation a	2540	1356	...	1184	2520	1227	...	1293	3608	1692	...	1916

Bolivia

2.8 Gross Capital Formation by Type of Good and Owner, in Constant Prices

Million Bolivian pesos

	1976				1977				1978			
	TOTAL	Total Private	Public Enterprises	General Government	TOTAL	Total Private	Public Enterprises	General Government	TOTAL	Total Private	Public Enterprises	General Government
	At constant prices of: 1970												
Increase in stocks, total a	317	147	...	170	247	27	...	220	-19	-19	...	-
Gross Fixed Capital Formation, Total a	2945	1318	...	1627	3113	1166	...	1947	3411	1189	...	2222
1 Residential buildings	522	495	...	27	546	531	...	15	605	577	...	28
2 Non-residential buildings	344	106	...	238	398	89	...	309	301	45	...	256
3 Other construction	568	45	...	523	690	30	...	660	774	31	...	743
4 Land improvement and plantation and orchard development	30	29	...	1	12	12	...	-	13	10	...	3
5 Producers' durable goods	1470	634	...	836	1461	501	...	960	1709	520	...	1189
a Transport equipment	614	436	...	178	481	386	...	95	537	383	...	154
b Machinery and equipment	856	198	...	658	980	115	...	865	1172	137	...	1035
6 Breeding stock, dairy cattle, etc.	11	9	...	2	6	3	...	3	9	6	...	3
Total Gross Capital Formation a	3262	1465	...	1797	3360	1193	...	2167	3392	1170	...	2222

	1979				1980			
	TOTAL	Total Private	Public Enterprises	General Government	TOTAL	Total Private	Public Enterprises	General Government
	At constant prices of: 1970								
Increase in stocks, total a	152	24	...	128	-174	...	...	...
Gross Fixed Capital Formation, Total a	3017	1262	...	1755	2565	...	...	...
1 Residential buildings	619	452	...	167	...	...	...	...
2 Non-residential buildings	281	103	...	178	...	...	...	...
3 Other construction	776	31	...	745	...	...	...	...
4 Land improvement and plantation and orchard development	-	-	...	-	...	...	...	...
5 Producers' durable goods	1335	671	...	664	...	...	...	...
a Transport equipment	460	319	...	141	...	...	...	...
b Machinery and equipment	875	352	...	523	...	...	...	...
6 Breeding stock, dairy cattle, etc.	6	5	...	1	...	...	...	...
Total Gross Capital Formation a	3169	1286	...	1883	...	...	...	...

a) Column 'Public Enterprises' is included in column 'General Government'.

2.17 Exports and Imports of Goods and Services, Detail

Million Bolivian pesos

	1970	1971	1972	1973	1974	1975	1976	1977	1978	1979	1980
	Exports of Goods and Services										
1 Exports of merchandise, f.o.b.	2355	2186	2718	5414	11580	9386	11480	13244	12862	15921	...
2 Transport and communication	17	18	20	32	44	82	128	132	224	497	...
a In respect of merchandise imports	-	-	-	-	-	-	-	-	14	422	...
b Other	17	18	20	32	44	82	128	132	210	75	...
3 Insurance service charges	50	36	53	78	130	92	130	142	240	444	...
a In respect of merchandise imports	-	-	-	-	-	-	-	-	-	-	...
b Other	50	36	53	78	130	92	130	142	240	444	...
4 Other commodities	-	2	8	34	260	474	386	334	120	86	...
5 Adjustments of merchandise exports to change-of-ownership basis	...	...	...	...	...	...	...	...	...	...	...
6 Direct purchases in the domestic market by non-residential households	33	76	148	280	406	408	540	620	750	805	...
7 Direct purchases in the domestic market by extraterritorial bodies	39	18	16	40	28	32	34	40	40	41	...
Total Exports of Goods and Services	2494	2336	2963	5878	12448	10474	12698	14512	14236	17794	...
	Imports of Goods and Services										
1 Imports of merchandise, c.i.f.	2302	2504	3041	5414	8586	12066	12712	14694	17556	21289	...

Bolivia

2.17 Exports and Imports of Goods and Services, Detail
(Continued)

Million Bolivian pesos

	1970	1971	1972	1973	1974	1975	1976	1977	1978	1979	1980
a Imports of merchandise, f.o.b.	2000	2182	2652	4710	7362	10652	11178	12998	15246	18138	...
b Transport of services on merchandise imports	264	284	355	640	1128	1300	1412	1560	2116	2896	...
c Insurance service charges on merchandise imports	38	38	34	64	96	114	122	136	194	255	...
2 Adjustments of merchandise imports to change-of-ownership basis	...	...	...	...	...	...	...	...	...	...	...
3 Other transport and communication	36	26	45	82	140	282	210	360	284	222	...
4 Other insurance service charges	39	50	58	82	154	118	116	130	202	310	...
5 Other commodities	36	18	29	54	74	86	102	144	150	133	...
6 Direct purchases abroad by government	35	32	104	190	152	160	172	238	300	315	...
7 Direct purchases abroad by resident households	66	83	153	292	514	530	644	788	850	954	...
Total Imports of Goods and Services	2514	2713	3430	6114	9620	13242	13956	16354	19342	23223	...
Balance of Goods and Services	-20	-377	-467	-236	2828	-2768	-1258	-1842	-5106	-5429	...
Total Imports and Balance of Goods and Services	2494	2336	2963	5878	12448	10474	12698	14512	14236	17794	...

3.11 General Government Production Account: Total and Subsectors

Million Bolivian pesos

	1970					1971				
	Total General Government	Central Government	State or Provincial Government	Local Government	Social Security Funds	Total General Government	Central Government	State or Provincial Government	Local Government	Social Security Funds
Gross Output										
1 Sales	87	11	...	75	1	58	11	...	45	2
2 Services produced for own use	1324	1130	...	89	105	1520	1300	...	100	120
3 Own account capital formation	...	...	...	...	...	...	...	...	...	...
Gross Output	1411	1141	...	164	106	1578	1311	...	145	122
Gross Input										
Intermediate Consumption	425	272	...	100	53	411	295	...	73	43
Subtotal: Value Added	986	869	...	64	53	1167	1016	...	72	79
1 Indirect taxes, net	1	1	...	-	-	1	1	...	-	-
2 Consumption of fixed capital	9	8	...	-	1	11	8	...	-	3
3 Compensation of employees	976	860	...	64	52	1155	1007	...	72	76
4 Net Operating surplus	...	...	...	...	...	...	...	...	...	...
Gross Input	1411	1141	...	164	106	1578	1311	...	145	122
	1972					1973				
	Total General Government	Central Government	State or Provincial Government	Local Government	Social Security Funds	Total General Government	Central Government	State or Provincial Government	Local Government	Social Security Funds
Gross Output										
1 Sales	71	18	...	52	1	64	22	...	41	1
2 Services produced for own use	1920	1705	...	115	100	2814	2489	...	140	185
3 Own account capital formation	...	...	...	...	...	...	...	...	...	...
Gross Output	1991	1723	...	167	101	2878	2511	...	181	186
Gross Input										
Intermediate Consumption	564	462	...	81	21	888	756	...	69	63
Subtotal: Value Added	1427	1261	...	86	80	1990	1755	...	112	123
1 Indirect taxes, net	2	2	...	-	-	1	1	...	-	-
2 Consumption of fixed capital	16	12	...	-	4	21	15	...	-	6
3 Compensation of employees	1409	1247	...	86	76	1968	1739	...	112	117
4 Net Operating surplus	...	...	...	...	...	...	...	...	...	...
Gross Input	1991	1723	...	167	101	2878	2511	...	181	186

Bolivia

3.11 General Government Production Account: Total and Subsectors

Million Bolivian pesos

	1974 Total General Government	Central Government	State or Provincial Government	Local Government	Social Security Funds	1975 Total General Government	Central Government	State or Provincial Government	Local Government	Social Security Funds
					Gross Output					
1 Sales	73	31	...	39	2	86	37	...	47	2
2 Services produced for own use	4461	4038	...	213	210	5699	5041	...	324	334
3 Own account capital formation	...	...	...	...	...	...	...	...	...	...
Gross Output	4534	4070	...	252	212	5785	5078	...	371	336
					Gross Input					
Intermediate Consumption	1270	1140	...	82	48	1522	1295	...	113	114
Subtotal: Value Added	3264	2930	...	170	164	4263	3783	...	258	222
1 Indirect taxes, net	6	6	...	-	-	6	5	...	-	1
2 Consumption of fixed capital	26	20	...	-	6	31	23	...	-	8
3 Compensation of employees	3232	2904	...	170	158	4226	3755	...	258	213
4 Net Operating surplus	...	...	...	...	...	...	...	...	...	...
Gross Input	4534	4070	...	252	212	5785	5078	...	371	336

	1976 Total General Government	Central Government	State or Provincial Government	Local Government	Social Security Funds	1977 Total General Government	Central Government	State or Provincial Government	Local Government	Social Security Funds
					Gross Output					
1 Sales	123	52	...	68	3	187	71	...	87	29
2 Services produced for own use	6700	5707	...	335	658	8559	7441	...	316	802
3 Own account capital formation	...	...	...	...	...	...	...	...	...	...
Gross Output	6823	5759	...	403	661	8746	7512	...	403	831
					Gross Input					
Intermediate Consumption	1745	1357	...	182	206	2760	2365	...	134	261
Subtotal: Value Added	5078	4402	...	221	455	5986	5147	...	269	570
1 Indirect taxes, net	5	5	...	-	-	3	2	...	1	-
2 Consumption of fixed capital	53	41	...	-	12	98	74	...	-	24
3 Compensation of employees	5020	4356	...	221	443	5885	5071	...	268	546
4 Net Operating surplus	...	...	...	...	...	...	...	...	...	...
Gross Input	6823	5759	...	403	661	8746	7512	...	403	831

	1978 Total General Government	Central Government	State or Provincial Government	Local Government	Social Security Funds	1979 Total General Government	Central Government	State or Provincial Government	Local Government	Social Security Funds
					Gross Output					
1 Sales	171	72	...	77	22	222	131	...	62	29
2 Services produced for own use	10781	9147	...	469	1165	12276	10080	...	599	1597
3 Own account capital formation	...	...	...	...	...	...	...	...	...	...
Gross Output	10952	9219	...	546	1187	12498	10211	...	661	1626
					Gross Input					
Intermediate Consumption	3357	2759	...	227	371	2819	2190	...	234	395
Subtotal: Value Added	7595	6460	...	319	816	9679	8021	...	427	1231
1 Indirect taxes, net	3	3	...	-	-	4	4	...	-	-
2 Consumption of fixed capital	162	132	...	-	30	210	166	...	-	440
3 Compensation of employees	7430	6325	...	319	786	9465	7851	...	427	1187
4 Net Operating surplus	...	...	...	...	...	...	...	...	...	...
Gross Input	10952	9219	...	546	1187	12498	10211	...	661	2022

4.3 Derivation of Value Added by Kind of Activity, ISIC Divisions, in Current Prices

Million Bolivian pesos

	1970 Gross Output	Intermediate Consumption	Value Added	1971 Gross Output	Intermediate Consumption	Value Added	1972 Gross Output	Intermediate Consumption	Value Added	1973 Gross Output	Intermediate Consumption	Value Added
						All Producers						
1 Agriculture, hunting, forestry and fishing	2553	313	2240	2861	351	2510	3594	495	3099	5439	701	4738
a Agriculture and hunting	2477	302	2175	2760	336	2424	3465	476	2989	5232	668	4564
b Forestry and logging	75	11	64	99	15	84	127	19	108	204	33	171
c Fishing	1	-	1	2	-	2	2	-	2	3	-	3
2 Mining and quarrying	2193	920	1273	2177	1035	1142	4053	1898	2155	6621	2640	3981

143

Bolivia

4.3 Derivation of Value Added by Kind of Activity, ISIC Divisions, in Current Prices
(Continued)

Million Bolivian pesos

	1970 Gross Output	1970 Intermediate Consumption	1970 Value Added	1971 Gross Output	1971 Intermediate Consumption	1971 Value Added	1972 Gross Output	1972 Intermediate Consumption	1972 Value Added	1973 Gross Output	1973 Intermediate Consumption	1973 Value Added
a Coal mining	...	...	...	...	...	...	...	...	...	...	...	...
b Crude petroleum and natural gas production	153	35	118	283	51	232	679	136	543	1377	335	1042
c Metal ore mining	2040	885	1155	1894	984	910	3374	1762	1612	5244	2305	2939
d Other mining	...	...	...	...	...	...	...	...	...	...	...	...
3 Manufacturing	3988	2198	1790	4620	2653	1967	5628	3225	2403	8819	5194	3625
a Manufacture of food, beverages and tobacco	1637	1046	591	1695	1090	605	2195	1412	783	3587	2315	1272
b Textile, wearing apparel and leather industries	1349	733	616	1381	749	632	1598	875	723	2149	1161	988
c Manufacture of wood and wood products, including furniture	125	71	54	161	92	69	224	130	94	450	258	192
d Manufacture of paper and paper products, printing and publishing	57	35	22	74	44	30	96	57	39	154	93	61
e Manufacture of chemicals and chemical petroleum, coal, rubber and plastic products	501	157	344	565	186	379	655	225	430	936	324	612
f Manufacture of non-metallic mineral products, except products of petroleum and coal	147	60	87	166	67	99	193	80	113	266	108	158
g Basic metal industries	6	4	2	328	283	45	400	321	79	788	656	132
h Manufacture of fabricated metal products, machinery and equipment	50	28	22	115	64	51	155	85	70	232	128	104
i Other manufacturing industries	116	64	52	135	78	57	112	40	72	257	151	106
4 Electricity, gas and water	210	43	167	227	46	181	277	57	220	388	82	306
5 Construction	902	391	511	1001	420	581	1322	621	701	2130	1001	1129
6 Wholesale and retail trade, restaurants and hotels	2920	738	2182	3211	798	2413	3690	887	2803	5397	1379	4018
a Wholesale and retail trade	2870	713	2157	3153	767	2386	3620	847	2773	5277	1306	3971
b Restaurants and hotels	50	25	25	58	31	27	70	40	30	120	73	47
7 Transport, storage and communication	2154	1223	931	2247	1155	1092	2835	1419	1416	3506	1656	1850
a Transport and storage	2103	1206	897	2189	1138	1051	2765	1401	1364	3380	1604	1776
b Communication	51	17	34	58	17	41	70	18	52	126	52	74
8 Finance, insurance, real estate and business services	1533	266	1267	1676	292	1384	2002	355	1647	3107	554	2553
a Financial institutions	198	29	169	231	35	196	327	46	281	498	81	417
b Insurance	24	14	10	26	16	10	46	32	14	72	47	25
c Real estate and business services	1311	223	1088	1419	241	1178	1629	277	1352	2537	426	2111
9 Community, social and personal services	1346	343	1003	1467	377	1090	1855	471	1384	2593	664	1929
a Sanitary and similar services	...	...	...	...	...	...	...	...	...	...	...	...
b Social and related community services	980	250	730	1084	279	805	1313	333	980	1845	472	1373
c Recreational and cultural services	...	...	...	...	...	...	...	...	...	...	...	...
d Personal and household services	366	93	273	383	98	285	542	138	404	748	192	556
Total, Industries	17799	6435	11364	19487	7127	12360	25256	9428	15828	38000	13871	24129
Producers of Government Services	1411	425	986	1578	411	1167	1991	564	1427	2878	888	1990
Other Producers	158	7	151	167	8	159	202	13	189	272	19	253
Total	19368	6867	12501	21232	7546	13686	27449	10005	17444	41150	14778	26372
Imputed bank service charge	-	131	-131	-	143	-143	-	195	-195	-	316	-316
Import duties	...	...	...	...	...	...	...	...	...	...	...	...
Value added tax	...	...	...	...	...	...	...	...	...	...	...	...
Total	19368	6998	12370	21232	7689	13543	27449	10200	17249	41150	15094	26056

	1974 Gross Output	1974 Intermediate Consumption	1974 Value Added	1975 Gross Output	1975 Intermediate Consumption	1975 Value Added	1976 Gross Output	1976 Intermediate Consumption	1976 Value Added	1977 Gross Output	1977 Intermediate Consumption	1977 Value Added
					All Producers							
1 Agriculture, hunting, forestry and fishing	9597	1332	8265	10607	1474	9133	11881	1617	10264	13458	1882	11576
a Agriculture and hunting	9270	1279	7991	10244	1420	8824	11454	1558	9896	13002	1811	11191
b Forestry and logging	322	53	269	358	54	304	418	59	359	438	70	368
c Fishing	5	-	5	5	-	5	9	-	9	18	1	17

Bolivia

4.3 Derivation of Value Added by Kind of Activity, ISIC Divisions, in Current Prices
(Continued)

Million Bolivian pesos

	1974 Gross Output	1974 Intermediate Consumption	1974 Value Added	1975 Gross Output	1975 Intermediate Consumption	1975 Value Added	1976 Gross Output	1976 Intermediate Consumption	1976 Value Added	1977 Gross Output	1977 Intermediate Consumption	1977 Value Added
2 Mining and quarrying	11186	3619	7567	9317	3788	5529	10873	4507	6366	12762	5527	7235
a Coal mining	...	...	...	...	...	...	...	...	...	...	...	...
b Crude petroleum and natural gas production	3937	572	3365	3055	712	2343	3337	773	2564	2734	633	2101
c Metal ore mining	7249	3047	4202	6262	3076	3186	7536	3734	3802	10028	4894	5134
d Other mining	...	...	...	...	...	...	...	...	...	...	...	...
3 Manufacturing	14375	8614	5761	16105	9502	6603	19231	11409	7822	22907	13841	9066
a Manufacture of food, beverages and tobacco	6295	4085	2210	7005	4489	2516	8634	5564	3070	9550	6131	3419
b Textile, wearing apparel and leather industries	3503	1894	1609	3833	2050	1783	4018	2162	1856	4289	2306	1983
c Manufacture of wood and wood products, including furniture	649	372	277	776	439	337	688	396	292	1160	754	406
d Manufacture of paper and paper products, printing and publishing	263	158	105	338	206	132	375	225	150	445	267	178
e Manufacture of chemicals and chemical petroleum, coal, rubber and plastic products	1285	460	825	1597	580	1017	2250	759	1491	2677	906	1771
f Manufacture of non-metallic mineral products, except products of petroleum and coal	378	154	224	467	190	277	507	205	302	615	249	366
g Basic metal industries	1235	1047	188	1027	895	132	1750	1519	231	3131	2719	412
h Manufacture of fabricated metal products, machinery and equipment	348	195	153	492	281	211	631	355	276	702	306	396
i Other manufacturing industries	419	249	170	570	372	198	378	224	154	338	203	135
4 Electricity, gas and water	469	97	372	591	122	469	733	147	586	918	186	732
5 Construction	3130	1565	1565	4034	2017	2017	4745	2372	2373	5879	2940	2939
6 Wholesale and retail trade, restaurants and hotels	9067	2205	6862	12920	3514	9406	13780	3590	10190	15110	3846	11264
a Wholesale and retail trade	8867	2081	6786	12638	3338	9300	13430	3375	10055	14712	3603	11109
b Restaurants and hotels	200	124	76	282	176	106	350	215	135	398	243	155
7 Transport, storage and communication	4536	1753	2783	5975	2355	3620	7046	2696	4350	9646	4187	5459
a Transport and storage	4345	1678	2667	5710	2261	3449	6680	2562	4118	9155	4022	5133
b Communication	191	75	116	265	94	171	366	134	232	491	165	326
8 Finance, insurance, real estate and business services	4777	853	3924	5734	1053	4681	6836	1315	5521	8093	1611	6482
a Financial institutions	834	131	703	1119	191	928	1524	276	1248	1960	402	1558
b Insurance	134	95	39	180	127	53	204	138	66	246	158	88
c Real estate and business services	3809	627	3182	4435	735	3700	5108	901	4207	5887	1051	4836
9 Community, social and personal services	4203	1076	3127	5067	1262	3805	5793	1468	4325	6609	1630	4979
a Sanitary and similar services	...	...	...	...	...	...	...	...	...	...	...	...
b Social and related community services	2765	708	2057	3071	765	2306	3505	894	2611	3978	997	2981
c Recreational and cultural services	...	...	...	...	...	...	...	...	...	...	...	...
d Personal and household services	1438	368	1070	1996	497	1499	2288	574	1714	2631	633	1998
Total, Industries	61340	21114	40226	70350	25087	45263	80918	29121	51797	95382	35650	59732
Producers of Government Services	4534	1270	3264	5785	1522	4263	6823	1745	5078	8746	2760	5986
Other Producers	375	30	345	394	31	363	549	89	460	661	72	589
Total	66249	22414	43835	76529	26640	49889	88290	30955	57335	104789	38482	66307
Imputed bank service charge	-	510	-510	-	688	-688	-	888	-888	-	1087	-1087
Import duties	...	...	...	...	...	...	...	...	...	...	...	...
Value added tax	...	...	...	...	...	...	...	...	...	...	...	...
Total	66249	22924	43325	76529	27328	49201	88290	31843	56447	104789	39569	65220

Bolivia

4.3 Derivation of Value Added by Kind of Activity, ISIC Divisions, in Current Prices

Million Bolivian pesos

		1978			1979			1980		
		Gross Output	Intermediate Consumption	Value Added	Gross Output	Intermediate Consumption	Value Added	Gross Output	Intermediate Consumption	Value Added
		All Producers								
1	Agriculture, hunting, forestry and fishing	15088	2151	12937	17412	2402	15010	...	...	22197
a	Agriculture and hunting	14620	2081	12539	16738	2293	14445	...	...	...
b	Forestry and logging	443	69	374	632	106	526	...	...	...
c	Fishing	25	1	24	42	3	39	...	...	...
2	Mining and quarrying	13818	5327	8491	17730	6965	10765	...	...	13298
a	Coal mining	...	...	...	...	...	...	...	...	...
b	Crude petroleum and natural gas production	2496	546	1950	3041	718	2323	...	...	3270
c	Metal ore mining	11322	4781	6541	14689	6247	8442	...	...	10028
d	Other mining	...	...	...	...	...	...	...	...	...
3	Manufacturing	27091	16693	10398	31948	19601	12347	...	...	18885
a	Manufacture of food, beverages and tobacco	11113	7115	3998	13035	8286	4749	...	...	...
b	Textile, wearing apparel and leather industries	4488	2406	2082	4885	2624	2261	...	...	...
c	Manufacture of wood and wood products, including furniture	961	617	344	1313	839	474	...	...	...
d	Manufacture of paper and paper products, printing and publishing	489	293	196	531	320	211	...	...	...
e	Manufacture of chemicals and chemical petroleum, coal, rubber and plastic products	3301	1152	2149	4091	1443	2648	...	...	...
f	Manufacture of non-metallic mineral products, except products of petroleum and coal	961	417	544	1064	461	603	...	...	...
g	Basic metal industries	4544	4046	498	5497	4857	640	...	...	...
h	Manufacture of fabricated metal products, machinery and equipment	840	411	429	1102	526	576	...	...	...
i	Other manufacturing industries	394	236	158	430	245	185	...	...	...
4	Electricity, gas and water	1042	218	824	1166	237	929	...	...	1286
5	Construction	6923	3600	3323	8017	4169	3848	...	...	5485
6	Wholesale and retail trade, restaurants and hotels	18102	4699	13403	21459	5619	15840	...	...	24003
a	Wholesale and retail trade	17623	4406	13217	20903	5279	15624	...	...	...
b	Restaurants and hotels	479	293	186	556	340	216	...	...	...
7	Transport, storage and communication	11255	4685	6570	14017	6105	7912	...	...	12449
a	Transport and storage	10693	4528	6165	13178	5821	7357	...	...	...
b	Communication	562	157	405	839	284	555	...	...	...
8	Finance, insurance, real estate and business services	9368	1795	7573	10724	2108	8616	...	...	13488
a	Financial institutions	2300	478	1822	2931	612	2319	...	...	4107
b	Insurance	269	161	108	357	232	125	...	...	...
c	Real estate and business services	6799	1156	5643	7436	1264	6172	...	...	9381
9	Community, social and personal services	8057	2041	6016	10642	2773	7869	...	...	11701
a	Sanitary and similar services	...	...	...	...	...	...	...	...	...
b	Social and related community services	4821	1225	3596	6670	1788	4882	...	...	...
c	Recreational and cultural services	...	...	...	...	...	...	...	...	...
d	Personal and household services	3236	816	2420	3972	985	2987	...	...	...
Total, Industries		110744	41209	69535	133115	49979	83136	...	...	122792
Producers of Government Services		10952	3357	7595	12498	2819	9679	...	...	13331
Other Producers		822	115	707	1074	147	927	...	...	1379
Total		122518	44681	77837	146687	52945	93742	...	...	137502
Imputed bank service charge		-	1363	-1363	-	1686	-1686	...	...	-2515
Import duties		...	...	...	...	...	...	...	...	...
Value added tax		...	...	...	...	...	...	...	...	...
Total		122518	46044	76474	146687	54631	92056	...	...	134987

Bolivia

4.4 Derivation of Value Added by Kind of Activity, ISIC Divisions, in Constant Prices

Million Bolivian pesos

At constant prices of: 1970

All Producers

	1970 Gross Output	1970 Intermediate Consumption	1970 Value Added	1971 Gross Output	1971 Intermediate Consumption	1971 Value Added	1972 Gross Output	1972 Intermediate Consumption	1972 Value Added	1973 Gross Output	1973 Intermediate Consumption	1973 Value Added
1 Agriculture, hunting, forestry and fishing	...	...	2240	...	...	2373	...	...	2512	...	...	2628
a Agriculture and hunting	...	...	2175	...	...	2291	...	...	2422	...	...	2528
b Forestry and logging	...	...	64	...	...	81	...	...	89	...	...	99
c Fishing	...	...	1	...	...	1	...	...	1	...	...	1
2 Mining and quarrying	...	...	1273	...	...	1351	...	...	1480	...	...	1842
a Coal mining	...	...	...	...	...	...	...	...	...	...	...	...
b Crude petroleum and natural gas production	...	...	118	...	...	233	...	...	318	...	...	429
c Metal ore mining	...	...	1155	...	...	1118	...	...	1162	...	...	1413
d Other mining	...	...	...	...	...	...	...	...	...	...	...	...
3 Manufacturing	...	...	1790	...	...	1854	...	...	2004	...	...	2104
a Manufacture of food, beverages and tobacco	...	...	591	...	...	584	...	...	665	...	...	701
b Textile, wearing apparel and leather industries	...	...	616	...	...	565	...	...	585	...	...	555
c Manufacture of wood and wood products, including furniture	...	...	54	...	...	68	...	...	65	...	...	88
d Manufacture of paper and paper products, printing and publishing	...	...	22	...	...	27	...	...	28	...	...	34
e Manufacture of chemicals and chemical petroleum, coal, rubber and plastic products	...	...	344	...	...	371	...	...	403	...	...	444
f Manufacture of non-metallic mineral products, except products of petroleum and coal	...	...	87	...	...	95	...	...	104	...	...	114
g Basic metal industries	...	...	2	...	...	45	...	...	44	...	...	59
h Manufacture of fabricated metal products, machinery and equipment	...	...	22	...	...	45	...	...	52	...	...	48
i Other manufacturing industries	...	...	52	...	...	54	...	...	58	...	...	61
4 Electricity, gas and water	...	...	167	...	...	179	...	...	190	...	...	211
5 Construction	...	...	511	...	...	524	...	...	545	...	...	563
6 Wholesale and retail trade, restaurants and hotels	...	...	2182	...	...	2240	...	...	2290	...	...	2362
a Wholesale and retail trade	...	...	2157	...	...	2215	...	...	2266	...	...	2334
b Restaurants and hotels	...	...	25	...	...	25	...	...	24	...	...	28
7 Transport, storage and communication	...	...	931	...	...	1001	...	...	1072	...	...	1141
a Transport and storage	...	...	897	...	...	965	...	...	1037	...	...	1104
b Communication	...	...	34	...	...	36	...	...	35	...	...	37
8 Finance, insurance, real estate and business services	...	...	1267	...	...	1313	...	...	1384	...	...	1441
a Financial institutions	...	...	169	...	...	187	...	...	224	...	...	233
b Insurance	...	...	10	...	...	10	...	...	11	...	...	15
c Real estate and business services	...	...	1088	...	...	1116	...	...	1149	...	...	1193
9 Community, social and personal services	...	...	1003	...	...	1038	...	...	1074	...	...	1123
a Sanitary and similar services	...	...	...	...	...	...	...	...	...	...	...	...
b Social and related community services	...	...	730	...	...	766	...	...	761	...	...	799
c Recreational and cultural services	...	...	...	...	...	...	...	...	...	...	...	...
d Personal and household services	...	...	273	...	...	272	...	...	313	...	...	324
Total, Industries	...	...	11364	...	...	11873	...	...	12551	...	...	13415
Producers of Government Services	...	...	986	...	...	1089	...	...	1186	...	...	1262
Other Producers	...	...	151	...	...	151	...	...	147	...	...	147
Total	...	...	12501	...	...	13113	...	...	13884	...	...	14824
Imputed bank service charge	...	...	-131	...	...	-137	...	...	-155	...	...	-178
Import duties	...	...	...	...	...	...	...	...	...	...	...	...
Value added tax	...	...	...	...	...	...	...	...	...	...	...	...
Total	...	...	12370	...	...	12976	...	...	13729	...	...	14646

Bolivia

4.4 Derivation of Value Added by Kind of Activity, ISIC Divisions, in Constant Prices

Million Bolivian pesos

	1974 Gross Output	1974 Intermediate Consumption	1974 Value Added	1975 Gross Output	1975 Intermediate Consumption	1975 Value Added	1976 Gross Output	1976 Intermediate Consumption	1976 Value Added	1977 Gross Output	1977 Intermediate Consumption	1977 Value Added
						At constant prices of: 1970						
						All Producers						
1 Agriculture, hunting, forestry and fishing	...	...	2725	...	...	2938	...	...	3085	...	...	3065
a Agriculture and hunting	...	...	2618	...	...	2839	...	...	2972	...	...	2942
b Forestry and logging	...	...	106	...	...	97	...	...	111	...	...	120
c Fishing	...	...	1	...	...	2	...	...	2	...	...	3
2 Mining and quarrying	...	...	1705	...	...	1635	...	...	1652	...	...	1609
a Coal mining	...	...	...	...	...	...	...	...	...	...	...	...
b Crude petroleum and natural gas production	...	...	377	...	...	296	...	...	313	...	...	238
c Metal ore mining	...	...	1328	...	...	1339	...	...	1339	...	...	1371
d Other mining	...	...	...	...	...	...	...	...	...	...	...	...
3 Manufacturing	...	...	2342	...	...	2485	...	...	2692	...	...	2879
a Manufacture of food, beverages and tobacco	...	...	779	...	...	859	...	...	1004	...	...	1044
b Textile, wearing apparel and leather industries	...	...	590	...	...	593	...	...	591	...	...	583
c Manufacture of wood and wood products, including furniture	...	...	87	...	...	85	...	...	71	...	...	88
d Manufacture of paper and paper products, printing and publishing	...	...	37	...	...	43	...	...	46	...	...	47
e Manufacture of chemicals and chemical petroleum, coal, rubber and plastic products	...	...	545	...	...	580	...	...	632	...	...	721
f Manufacture of non-metallic mineral products, except products of petroleum and coal	...	...	138	...	...	158	...	...	157	...	...	179
g Basic metal industries	...	...	50	...	...	39	...	...	65	...	...	80
h Manufacture of fabricated metal products, machinery and equipment	...	...	48	...	...	56	...	...	72	...	...	95
i Other manufacturing industries	...	...	68	...	...	72	...	...	54	...	...	42
4 Electricity, gas and water	...	...	232	...	...	237	...	...	256	...	...	285
5 Construction	...	...	605	...	...	679	...	...	713	...	...	791
6 Wholesale and retail trade, restaurants and hotels	...	...	2435	...	...	2634	...	...	2765	...	...	2834
a Wholesale and retail trade	...	...	2408	...	...	2604	...	...	2728	...	...	2795
b Restaurants and hotels	...	...	27	...	...	30	...	...	37	...	...	39
7 Transport, storage and communication	...	...	1311	...	...	1491	...	...	1668	...	...	1891
a Transport and storage	...	...	1268	...	...	1439	...	...	1557	...	...	-1750
b Communication	...	...	43	...	...	52	...	...	111	...	...	141
8 Finance, insurance, real estate and business services	...	...	1501	...	...	1614	...	...	1750	...	...	1858
a Financial institutions	...	...	250	...	...	309	...	...	383	...	...	431
b Insurance	...	...	14	...	...	18	...	...	22	...	...	27
c Real estate and business services	...	...	1237	...	...	1287	...	...	1345	...	...	1400
9 Community, social and personal services	...	...	1207	...	...	1321	...	...	1379	...	...	1432
a Sanitary and similar services	...	...	...	...	...	...	...	...	...	...	...	...
b Social and related community services	...	...	794	...	...	801	...	...	833	...	...	857
c Recreational and cultural services	...	...	...	...	...	...	...	...	...	...	...	...
d Personal and household services	...	...	413	...	...	520	...	...	546	...	...	575
Total, Industries	...	...	14063	...	...	15034	...	...	15960	...	...	16644
Producers of Government Services	...	...	1385	...	...	1487	...	...	1585	...	...	1641
Other Producers	...	...	133	...	...	126	...	...	147	...	...	169
Total	...	...	15581	...	...	16647	...	...	17692	...	...	18454
Imputed bank service charge	...	...	-181	...	...	-230	...	...	-274	...	...	-303
Import duties	...	...	...	...	...	...	...	...	...	...	...	...
Value added tax	...	...	...	...	...	...	...	...	...	...	...	...
Total	...	...	15400	...	...	16417	...	...	17418	...	...	18151

Bolivia

4.4 Derivation of Value Added by Kind of Activity, ISIC Divisions, in Constant Prices

Million Bolivian pesos

At constant prices of: 1970 — All Producers

	1978 Gross Output	1978 Intermediate Consumption	1978 Value Added	1979 Gross Output	1979 Intermediate Consumption	1979 Value Added	1980 Gross Output	1980 Intermediate Consumption	1980 Value Added
1 Agriculture, hunting, forestry and fishing	...	...	3130	...	...	3222	...	...	3286
a Agriculture and hunting	...	...	3008	...	...	3060	...	...	...
b Forestry and logging	...	...	118	...	...	157	...	...	...
c Fishing	...	...	4	...	...	5	...	...	...
2 Mining and quarrying	...	...	1464	...	...	1342	...	...	1315
a Coal mining	...	...	...	...	...	...	...	...	...
b Crude petroleum and natural gas production	...	...	228	...	...	211	...	...	198
c Metal ore mining	...	...	1236	...	...	1131	...	...	1117
d Other mining	...	...	...	...	...	...	...	...	...
3 Manufacturing	...	...	3010	...	...	3094	...	...	3063
a Manufacture of food, beverages and tobacco	...	...	1098	...	...	1150	...	...	...
b Textile, wearing apparel and leather industries	...	...	575	...	...	539	...	...	...
c Manufacture of wood and wood products, including furniture	...	...	72	...	...	95	...	...	...
d Manufacture of paper and paper products, printing and publishing	...	...	48	...	...	50	...	...	...
e Manufacture of chemicals and chemical petroleum, coal, rubber and plastic products	...	...	812	...	...	836	...	...	...
f Manufacture of non-metallic mineral products, except products of petroleum and coal	...	...	182	...	...	177	...	...	...
g Basic metal industries	...	...	87	...	...	88	...	...	...
h Manufacture of fabricated metal products, machinery and equipment	...	...	91	...	...	112	...	...	...
i Other manufacturing industries	...	...	45	...	...	47	...	...	...
4 Electricity, gas and water	...	...	302	...	...	318	...	...	326
5 Construction	...	...	813	...	...	804	...	...	764
6 Wholesale and retail trade, restaurants and hotels	...	...	2899	...	...	2929	...	...	2949
a Wholesale and retail trade	...	...	2859	...	...	2889	...	...	...
b Restaurants and hotels	...	...	40	...	...	40	...	...	...
7 Transport, storage and communication	...	...	2143	...	...	2234	...	...	2279
a Transport and storage	...	...	1950	...	...	1983	...	...	...
b Communication	...	...	193	...	...	251	...	...	...
8 Finance, insurance, real estate and business services	...	...	1981	...	...	2019	...	...	2042
a Financial institutions	...	...	444	...	...	480	...	...	522
b Insurance	...	...	29	...	...	27	...	...	...
c Real estate and business services	...	...	1508	...	...	1512	...	...	1520
9 Community, social and personal services	...	...	1477	...	...	1516	...	...	1553
a Sanitary and similar services	...	...	...	...	...	...	...	...	...
b Social and related community services	...	...	883	...	...	941	...	...	...
c Recreational and cultural services	...	...	...	...	...	...	...	...	...
d Personal and household services	...	...	594	...	...	575	...	...	...
Total, Industries	...	...	17219	...	...	17478	...	...	17577
Producers of Government Services	...	...	1701	...	...	1797	...	...	1820
Other Producers	...	...	174	...	...	179	...	...	183
Total	...	...	19094	...	...	19454	...	...	19580
Imputed bank service charge	...	...	-334	...	...	-350	...	...	-360
Import duties	...	...	...	...	...	...	...	...	...
Value added tax	...	...	...	...	...	...	...	...	...
Total	...	...	18760	...	...	19104	...	...	19220

Bolivia

4.6 Cost Components of Value Added, ISIC Divisions

Million Bolivian pesos

	1970 Compensation of Employees	1970 Capital Consumption	1970 Net Operating Surplus	1970 Indirect Taxes	1970 Less: Subsidies Received	1970 Value Added	1971 Compensation of Employees	1971 Capital Consumption	1971 Net Operating Surplus	1971 Indirect Taxes	1971 Less: Subsidies Received	1971 Value Added
					All Producers							
1 Agriculture, hunting, forestry and fishing	403	...	1830	7	...	2240	452	...	2050	8	...	2510
a Agriculture and hunting	398	...	1773	4	...	2175	447	...	1973	4	...	2424
b Forestry and logging	5	...	56	3	...	64	5	...	75	4	...	84
c Fishing	-	...	1	-	...	1	-	...	2	-	...	2
2 Mining and quarrying	544	...	356	373	...	1273	664	...	193	285	...	1142
a Coal mining	...	...	...	...	...	...	...	...	...	...	...	...
b Crude petroleum and natural gas production	42	...	10	66	...	118	74	...	56	102	...	232
c Metal ore mining	502	...	346	307	...	1155	590	...	137	183	...	910
d Other mining	...	...	...	...	...	...	...	...	...	...	...	...
3 Manufacturing	780	...	854	156	...	1790	851	...	930	186	...	1967
a Manufacture of food, beverages and tobacco	198	...	291	102	...	591	204	...	278	123	...	605
b Textile, wearing apparel and leather industries	357	...	249	10	...	616	365	...	256	11	...	632
c Manufacture of wood and wood products, including furniture	17	...	33	4	...	54	21	...	43	5	...	69
d Manufacture of paper and paper products, printing and publishing	11	...	10	1	...	22	14	...	14	2	...	30
e Manufacture of chemicals and chemical petroleum, coal, rubber and plastic products	128	...	186	30	...	344	157	...	188	34	...	379
f Manufacture of non-metallic mineral products, except products of petroleum and coal	37	...	46	4	...	87	43	...	51	5	...	99
g Basic metal industries	1	...	1	-	...	2	4	...	41	-	...	45
h Manufacture of fabricated metal products, machinery and equipment	8	...	13	1	...	22	17	...	32	2	...	51
i Other manufacturing industries	23	...	25	4	...	52	26	...	27	4	...	57
4 Electricity, gas and water	44	...	115	8	...	167	48	...	124	9	...	181
5 Construction	227	...	274	10	...	511	273	...	296	12	...	581
6 Wholesale and retail trade, restaurants and hotels	297	...	1647	238	...	2182	348	...	1753	312	...	2413
a Wholesale and retail trade	285	...	1635	237	...	2157	337	...	1739	310	...	2386
b Restaurants and hotels	12	...	12	1	...	25	11	...	14	2	...	27
7 Transport, storage and communication	322	...	588	21	...	931	384	...	672	36	...	1092
a Transport and storage	294	...	583	20	...	897	350	...	666	35	...	1051
b Communication	28	...	5	1	...	34	34	...	6	1	...	41
8 Finance, insurance, real estate and business services	204	...	1018	45	...	1267	237	...	1094	53	...	1384
a Financial institutions	84	...	83	2	...	169	104	...	88	4	...	196
b Insurance	4	...	4	2	...	10	5	...	3	2	...	10
c Real estate and business services	116	...	931	41	...	1088	128	...	1003	47	...	1178
9 Community, social and personal services	261	...	659	83	...	1003	301	...	695	94	...	1090
a Sanitary and similar services	...	...	...	...	...	...	...	...	...	...	...	...
b Social and related community services	206	...	496	28	...	730	240	...	518	47	...	805
c Recreational and cultural services	...	...	...	...	...	...	...	...	...	...	...	...
d Personal and household services	55	...	163	55	...	273	61	...	177	47	...	285
Total, Industries	3082	...	7341	941	...	11364	3558	...	7807	995	...	12360
Producers of Government Services	976	...	9	1	...	986	1155	...	11	1	...	1167
Other Producers	151	...	-	-	...	151	159	...	-	-	...	159
Total	4209	...	7350	942	...	12501	4872	...	7818	996	...	13686
Imputed bank service charge	-	...	-131	-	...	-131	-	...	-143	-	...	-143
Import duties	...	...	...	...	...	...	...	...	...	...	...	...
Value added tax	...	...	...	...	...	...	...	...	...	...	...	...
Other adjustments	...	...	...	...	...	...	...	...	...	...	...	...
Total	4209	...	7219	942	...	12370	4872	...	7675	996	...	13543

Bolivia

4.6 Cost Components of Value Added, ISIC Divisions

Million Bolivian pesos

		1972						1973				
	Compensation of Employees	Capital Consumption	Net Operating Surplus	Indirect Taxes	Less: Subsidies Received	Value Added	Compensation of Employees	Capital Consumption	Net Operating Surplus	Indirect Taxes	Less: Subsidies Received	Value Added

All Producers

1 Agriculture, hunting, forestry and fishing	562	...	2526	11	...	3099	862	...	3859	17	...	4738
a Agriculture and hunting	551	...	2432	6	...	2989	845	...	3709	10	...	4564
b Forestry and logging	11	...	92	5	...	108	17	...	147	7	...	171
c Fishing	-	...	2	-	...	2	-	...	3	-	...	3
2 Mining and quarrying	958	...	587	610	...	2155	1002	...	1425	1554	...	3981
a Coal mining	...	...	...	...	...	...	...	...	...	...	...	...
b Crude petroleum and natural gas production	98	...	232	213	...	543	119	...	399	524	...	1042
c Metal ore mining	860	...	355	397	...	1612	883	...	1026	1030	...	2939
d Other mining	...	...	...	...	...	...	...	...	...	...	...	...
3 Manufacturing	1012	...	1176	215	...	2403	1459	...	1829	337	...	3625
a Manufacture of food, beverages and tobacco	268	...	374	141	...	783	441	...	602	229	...	1272
b Textile, wearing apparel and leather industries	417	...	293	13	...	723	565	...	404	19	...	988
c Manufacture of wood and wood products, including furniture	28	...	59	7	...	94	56	...	121	15	...	192
d Manufacture of paper and paper products, printing and publishing	19	...	18	2	...	39	29	...	29	3	...	61
e Manufacture of chemicals and chemical petroleum, coal, rubber and plastic products	164	...	228	38	...	430	202	...	359	51	...	612
f Manufacture of non-metallic mineral products, except products of petroleum and coal	49	...	58	6	...	113	68	...	82	8	...	158
g Basic metal industries	11	...	68	-	...	79	16	...	116	-	...	132
h Manufacture of fabricated metal products, machinery and equipment	23	...	44	3	...	70	34	...	65	5	...	104
i Other manufacturing industries	33	...	34	5	...	72	48	...	51	7	...	106
4 Electricity, gas and water	60	...	150	10	...	220	74	...	219	13	...	306
5 Construction	308	...	372	21	...	701	485	...	610	34	...	1129
6 Wholesale and retail trade, restaurants and hotels	391	...	2062	350	...	2803	581	...	2950	487	...	4018
a Wholesale and retail trade	377	...	2048	348	...	2773	558	...	2929	484	...	3971
b Restaurants and hotels	14	...	14	2	...	30	23	...	21	3	...	47
7 Transport, storage and communication	506	...	871	39	...	1416	672	...	1114	64	...	1850
a Transport and storage	463	...	863	38	...	1364	612	...	1101	63	...	1776
b Communication	43	...	8	1	...	52	60	...	13	1	...	74
8 Finance, insurance, real estate and business services	285	...	1296	66	...	1647	416	...	2058	79	...	2553
a Financial institutions	132	...	141	8	...	281	182	...	225	10	...	417
b Insurance	9	...	3	2	...	14	12	...	9	4	...	25
c Real estate and business services	144	...	1152	56	...	1352	222	...	1824	65	...	2111
9 Community, social and personal services	343	...	928	113	...	1384	494	...	1298	137	...	1929
a Sanitary and similar services	...	...	...	...	...	...	...	...	...	...	...	...
b Social and related community services	255	...	670	55	...	980	371	...	926	76	...	1373
c Recreational and cultural services	...	...	...	...	...	...	...	...	...	...	...	...
d Personal and household services	88	...	258	58	...	404	123	...	372	61	...	556
Total, Industries	4425	...	9968	1435	...	15828	6045	...	15362	2722	...	24129
Producers of Government Services	1409	...	16	2	...	1427	1968	...	21	1	...	1990
Other Producers	189	...	-	-	...	189	253	...	-	-	...	253
Total	6023	...	9984	1437	...	17444	8266	...	15383	2723	...	26372
Imputed bank service charge	-	...	-195	-	...	-195	-	...	-316	-	...	-316
Import duties	...	...	...	...	...	...	...	...	...	...	...	...
Value added tax	...	...	...	...	...	...	...	...	...	...	...	...
Other adjustments	...	...	...	...	...	...	...	...	...	...	...	...
Total	6023	...	9789	1437	...	17249	8266	...	15067	2723	...	26056

Bolivia

4.6 Cost Components of Value Added, ISIC Divisions

Million Bolivian pesos

		1974						1975					
		Compensation of Employees	Capital Consumption	Net Operating Surplus	Indirect Taxes	Less: Subsidies Received	Value Added	Compensation of Employees	Capital Consumption	Net Operating Surplus	Indirect Taxes	Less: Subsidies Received	Value Added
					All Producers								
1	Agriculture, hunting, forestry and fishing	1560	...	6681	24	...	8265	1749	...	7354	30	...	9133
	a Agriculture and hunting	1544	...	6431	16	...	7991	1731	...	7071	22	...	8824
	b Forestry and logging	16	...	245	8	...	269	18	...	278	8	...	304
	c Fishing	-	...	5	-	...	5	-	...	5	-	...	5
2	Mining and quarrying	1567	...	2250	3750	...	7567	1547	...	1001	2981	...	5529
	a Coal mining	...	...	...	...	...	...	...	...	...	...	...	...
	b Crude petroleum and natural gas production	160	...	1253	1952	...	3365	170	...	556	1617	...	2343
	c Metal ore mining	1407	...	997	1798	...	4202	1377	...	445	1364	...	3186
	d Other mining	...	...	...	...	...	...	...	...	...	...	...	...
3	Manufacturing	2437	...	2711	613	...	5761	2780	...	2987	836	...	6603
	a Manufacture of food, beverages and tobacco	756	...	992	462	...	2210	848	...	1038	630	...	2516
	b Textile, wearing apparel and leather industries	921	...	657	31	...	1609	1014	...	732	37	...	1783
	c Manufacture of wood and wood products, including furniture	81	...	174	22	...	277	101	...	211	25	...	337
	d Manufacture of paper and paper products, printing and publishing	51	...	49	5	...	105	63	...	62	7	...	132
	e Manufacture of chemicals and chemical petroleum, coal, rubber and plastic products	380	...	382	63	...	825	448	...	469	100	...	1017
	f Manufacture of non-metallic mineral products, except products of petroleum and coal	98	...	115	11	...	224	123	...	140	14	...	277
	g Basic metal industries	24	...	164	-	...	188	24	...	108	-	...	132
	h Manufacture of fabricated metal products, machinery and equipment	50	...	96	7	...	153	70	...	132	9	...	211
	i Other manufacturing industries	76	...	82	12	...	170	89	...	95	14	...	198
4	Electricity, gas and water	101	...	258	13	...	372	130	...	325	14	...	469
5	Construction	657	...	877	31	...	1565	847	...	1089	81	...	2017
6	Wholesale and retail trade, restaurants and hotels	979	...	5064	819	...	6862	1241	...	6948	1217	...	9406
	a Wholesale and retail trade	939	...	5033	814	...	6786	1185	...	6906	1209	...	9300
	b Restaurants and hotels	40	...	31	5	...	76	56	...	42	8	...	106
7	Transport, storage and communication	1058	...	1622	103	...	2783	1416	...	2040	164	...	3620
	a Transport and storage	975	...	1591	101	...	2667	1302	...	1985	162	...	3449
	b Communication	83	...	31	2	...	116	114	...	55	2	...	171
8	Finance, insurance, real estate and business services	700	...	3120	104	...	3924	870	...	3672	139	...	4681
	a Financial institutions	300	...	391	12	...	703	407	...	510	11	...	928
	b Insurance	19	...	12	8	...	39	27	...	16	10	...	53
	c Real estate and business services	381	...	2717	84	...	3182	436	...	3146	118	...	3700
9	Community, social and personal services	986	...	1933	208	...	3127	1195	...	2287	323	...	3805
	a Sanitary and similar services	...	...	...	...	...	...	...	...	...	...	...	...
	b Social and related community services	751	...	1184	122	...	2057	852	...	1311	143	...	2306
	c Recreational and cultural services	...	...	...	...	...	...	...	...	...	...	...	...
	d Personal and household services	235	...	749	86	...	1070	343	...	976	180	...	1499
Total, Industries		10045	...	24516	5665	...	40226	11775	...	27703	5785	...	45263
Producers of Government Services		3232	...	26	6	...	3264	4226	...	31	6	...	4263
Other Producers		345	...	-	-	...	345	363	...	-	-	...	363
Total		13622	...	24542	5671	...	43835	16364	...	27734	5791	...	49889
Imputed bank service charge		-	...	-510	-	...	-510	-	...	-688	-	...	-688
Import duties		...	...	...	...	...	...	...	...	...	...	...	...
Value added tax		...	...	...	...	...	...	...	...	...	...	...	...
Other adjustments		...	...	...	...	...	...	...	...	...	...	...	...
Total		13622	...	24032	5671	...	43325	16364	...	27046	5791	...	49201

Bolivia

4.6 Cost Components of Value Added, ISIC Divisions

Million Bolivian pesos

	1976 Compensation of Employees	Capital Consumption	Net Operating Surplus	Indirect Taxes	Less: Subsidies Received	Value Added	1977 Compensation of Employees	Capital Consumption	Net Operating Surplus	Indirect Taxes	Less: Subsidies Received	Value Added
					All Producers							
1 Agriculture, hunting, forestry and fishing	1967	...	8263	34	...	10264	2228	...	9310	38	...	11576
a Agriculture and hunting	1947	...	7924	25	...	9896	2209	...	8953	29	...	11191
b Forestry and logging	20	...	330	9	...	359	19	...	340	9	...	368
c Fishing	-	...	9	-	...	9	-	...	17	-	...	17
2 Mining and quarrying	1760	...	1370	3236	...	6366	1988	...	1238	4009	...	7235
a Coal mining	...	...	...	...	...	...	...	...	...	...	...	...
b Crude petroleum and natural gas production	190	...	639	1735	...	2564	227	...	316	1558	...	2101
c Metal ore mining	1570	...	731	1501	...	3802	1761	...	922	2451	...	5134
d Other mining	...	...	...	...	...	...	...	...	...	...	...	...
3 Manufacturing	3079	...	3782	961	...	7822	3500	...	4367	1199	...	9066
a Manufacture of food, beverages and tobacco	1070	...	1424	576	...	3070	1165	...	1604	650	...	3419
b Textile, wearing apparel and leather industries	1052	...	763	41	...	1856	1124	...	804	55	...	1983
c Manufacture of wood and wood products, including furniture	84	...	184	24	...	292	119	...	256	32	...	406
d Manufacture of paper and paper products, printing and publishing	72	...	71	7	...	150	86	...	83	9	...	178
e Manufacture of chemicals and chemical petroleum, coal, rubber and plastic products	463	...	757	271	...	1491	560	...	815	395	...	1771
f Manufacture of non-metallic mineral products, except products of petroleum and coal	134	...	153	15	...	302	161	...	187	18	...	366
g Basic metal industries	42	...	186	3	...	231	95	...	314	3	...	412
h Manufacture of fabricated metal products, machinery and equipment	94	...	170	12	...	276	138	...	239	19	...	396
i Other manufacturing industries	68	...	74	12	...	154	52	...	65	18	...	135
4 Electricity, gas and water	154	...	411	21	...	586	198	...	511	23	...	732
5 Construction	997	...	1281	95	...	2373	1205	...	1616	118	...	2939
6 Wholesale and retail trade, restaurants and hotels	1456	...	7434	1300	...	10190	1584	...	8222	1458	...	11264
a Wholesale and retail trade	1378	...	7390	1287	...	10055	1494	...	8171	1444	...	11109
b Restaurants and hotels	78	...	44	13	...	135	90	...	51	14	...	155
7 Transport, storage and communication	1682	...	2477	191	...	4350	2116	...	3073	270	...	5459
a Transport and storage	1523	...	2412	183	...	4118	1911	...	2956	266	...	5133
b Communication	159	...	65	8	...	232	205	...	117	4	...	326
8 Finance, insurance, real estate and business services	1131	...	4217	173	...	5521	1533	...	4746	203	...	6482
a Financial institutions	586	...	640	22	...	1248	875	...	656	27	...	1558
b Insurance	39	...	14	13	...	66	55	...	19	14	...	88
c Real estate and business services	506	...	3563	138	...	4207	603	...	4071	162	...	4836
9 Community, social and personal services	1422	...	2542	361	...	4325	1751	...	2825	403	...	4979
a Sanitary and similar services	...	...	...	...	...	...	...	...	...	...	...	...
b Social and related community services	916	...	1523	172	...	2611	1009	...	1765	207	...	2981
c Recreational and cultural services	...	...	...	...	...	...	...	...	...	...	...	...
d Personal and household services	506	...	1019	189	...	1714	742	...	1060	196	...	1998
Total, Industries	13648	...	31777	6372	...	51797	16103	...	35908	7721	...	59732
Producers of Government Services	5020	...	53	5	...	5078	5885	...	98	3	...	5986
Other Producers	460	...	-	-	...	460	589	...	-	-	...	589
Total	19128	...	31830	6377	...	57335	22577	...	36006	7724	...	66307
Imputed bank service charge	-	...	-888	-	...	-888	-	...	-1087	-	...	-1087
Import duties	...	...	...	...	...	...	...	...	...	...	...	...
Value added tax	...	...	...	...	...	...	...	...	...	...	...	...
Other adjustments	...	...	...	...	...	...	...	...	...	...	...	...
Total	19128	...	30942	6377	...	56447	22577	...	34919	7724	...	65220

Bolivia

4.6 Cost Components of Value Added, ISIC Divisions

Million Bolivian pesos

			1978						1979			
		Compensation of Employees	Capital Consumption	Net Operating Surplus	Indirect Taxes	Less: Subsidies Received	Value Added	Compensation of Employees	Capital Consumption	Net Operating Surplus	Indirect Taxes	Less: Subsidies Received	Value Added

All Producers

		Comp.	Cap. Cons.	Net Op. Surplus	Ind. Taxes	Subs.	Value Added	Comp.	Cap. Cons.	Net Op. Surplus	Ind. Taxes	Subs.	Value Added
1	Agriculture, hunting, forestry and fishing	2491	...	10403	43	...	12937	2867	...	12090	53	...	15010
	a Agriculture and hunting	2470	...	10035	34	...	12539	2838	...	11568	39	...	14445
	b Forestry and logging	21	...	344	9	...	374	29	...	483	14	...	526
	c Fishing	-	...	24	-	...	24	-	...	39	-	...	39
2	Mining and quarrying	2275	...	2071	4145	...	8491	3126	...	2670	4969	...	10765
	a Coal mining	...	...	...	...	...	...	...	...	...	...	...	...
	b Crude petroleum and natural gas production	189	...	312	1449	...	1950	281	...	606	1436	...	2323
	c Metal ore mining	2086	...	1759	2696	...	6541	...	...	...	...	...	...
	d Other mining	...	...	...	...	...	...	2845	...	2064	3533	...	8442
3	Manufacturing	4055	...	5034	1309	...	10398	4670	...	6144	1533	...	12347
	a Manufacture of food, beverages and tobacco	1373	...	1808	817	...	3998	1603	...	2144	1002	...	4749
	b Textile, wearing apparel and leather industries	1173	...	849	60	...	2082	1280	...	919	62	...	2261
	c Manufacture of wood and wood products, including furniture	98	...	218	28	...	344	134	...	300	40	...	474
	d Manufacture of paper and paper products, printing and publishing	94	...	92	10	...	196	101	...	99	11	...	211
	e Manufacture of chemicals and chemical petroleum, coal, rubber and plastic products	735	...	1092	322	...	2149	830	...	1486	332	...	2648
	f Manufacture of non-metallic mineral products, except products of petroleum and coal	251	...	262	31	...	544	277	...	293	33	...	603
	g Basic metal industries	114	...	382	2	...	498	171	...	465	4	...	640
	h Manufacture of fabricated metal products, machinery and equipment	155	...	255	19	...	429	202	...	349	25	...	576
	i Other manufacturing industries	62	...	76	20	...	158	72	...	89	24	...	185
4	Electricity, gas and water	223	...	570	31	...	824	250	...	645	34	...	929
5	Construction	1495	...	1662	166	...	3323	1732	...	1924	192	...	3848
6	Wholesale and retail trade, restaurants and hotels	1865	...	9829	1709	...	13403	2187	...	11641	2012	...	15840
	a Wholesale and retail trade	1757	...	9768	1692	...	13217	2062	...	11570	1992	...	15624
	b Restaurants and hotels	108	...	61	17	...	186	125	...	71	20	...	216
7	Transport, storage and communication	2574	...	3590	406	...	6570	3211	...	4235	466	...	7912
	a Transport and storage	2301	...	3469	395	...	6165	2838	...	4060	459	...	7357
	b Communication	273	...	121	11	...	405	373	...	175	7	...	555
8	Finance, insurance, real estate and business services	1764	...	5598	211	...	7573	2121	...	6260	235	...	8616
	a Financial institutions	1015	...	783	24	...	1822	1300	...	989	30	...	2319
	b Insurance	72	...	18	18	...	108	80	...	25	20	...	125
	c Real estate and business services	677	...	4797	169	...	5643	741	...	5246	185	...	6172
9	Community, social and personal services	2071	...	3489	456	...	6016	2426	...	4788	655	...	7869
	a Sanitary and similar services	...	...	...	...	...	...	...	...	...	...	...	...
	b Social and related community services	1220	...	2167	209	...	3596	1457	...	3061	364	...	4882
	c Recreational and cultural services	...	...	...	...	...	...	...	...	...	...	...	...
	d Personal and household services	851	...	1322	247	...	2420	969	...	1727	291	...	2987
Total, Industries		18813	...	42246	8476	...	69535	22590	...	50397	10149	...	83136
Producers of Government Services		7430	...	162	3	...	7595	9465	...	210	4	...	9679
Other Producers		707	...	-	-	...	707	927	...	-	-	...	927
Total		26950	...	42408	8479	...	77837	32982	...	50607	10153	...	93742
Imputed bank service charge		-	..	-1363	-	...	-1363	-	...	-1686	-	...	-1686
Import duties		...	...	...	...	...	...	...	...	...	...	...	...
Value added tax		...	...	...	...	...	...	...	...	...	...	...	...
Other adjustments		...	...	...	...	...	...	...	...	...	...	...	...
Total		26950	...	41045	8479	...	76474	32982	...	48921	10153	...	92056

Botswana

General note. The preparation of national accounts statistics in Botswana is undertaken by the Central Statistics Office of the Ministry of Finance and Development Planning, Gaborone. Official estimates together with methodological notes are published in a series of reports entitled 'National Accounts of Botswana'. The most detailed description of the sources and methods used for the national accounts estimation is found in the fifth edition of this report published in July 1976 for the fiscal year 1973/74. The estimates are generally in accordance with the classifications and definitions recommended in the United Nations System of National Acconts (SNA). The following tables have been prepared from successive replies to the United Nations national accounts questionnaire. The estimates relate to fiscal year beginning 1 July. When the scope and coverage of the estimates differ for conceptual or statistical reasons from the definitions and classifications recommended in SNA, a footnote is indicated to the relevant tables.

Sources and methods:

(a) Gross domestic product. Gross domestic product is estimated mainly through the production approach.

(b) Expenditure on the gross domestic product. All components of GDP by expenditure type are estimated through the expenditure approach except private final consumption expenditure which is obtained as a residual. The estimates of government final consumption expenditure are based on annual statements of the accounts of central and local governments. Change in stocks is estimated on the basis of the production census for all sectors. Gross fixed capital formation of the government sector is estimated from the government accounts and of the private sector from the production census figures for sectors covered by the census questionnaire. Included in the capital formation estimates are the cost of land clearings and imputed values of new huts. The estimates of exports and imports of goods and services are based on balance-of-payments data. Exports and imports of goods have to be adjusted for duty content, in accordance with the Southern African customs union agreement. GDP by expenditure type at constant price is not estimated.

(c) Cost-structure of the gross domestic product. Estimates of compensation of employees are obtained from the Census of Production and Distribution (CPD). Data on payment of wages and salaries are distinguished whether paid to residents or to non-residents and are also classified by type. The main source for estimating consumption of fixed capital formation in the private sector is the CPD. For government assets, straight line depreciation is applied, the constant percentage varying for different types of assets. Indirect taxes are extracted from the Accountant-General's annual statement of accounts, the CPD and the Customs Statistics Unit.

(d) Gross domestic product by kind of economic activity. The table of gross domestic product by kind of economic activity is prepared at market prices, i.e. producers' values. The production approach is used to estimate value added of almost all industries. The income approach is used for some sub-groups of private services and for producers of government services. For the traditional farming of the agricultural sector, the main source used for crops is the annual agricultural sample survey and for cattle, the sources used include Rural Income Distribution Survey 1974/75 and annual reports of Botswana Meat Commission and the Ministry of Agriculture. The method has been to obtain quantities of production from the above-mentioned sources and apply unit values. Data from the 1974/75 Rural Income Distribution Survey also provided information on milk production for own use and the value of meat consumed. From this survey, detailed input-output activity analysis of the traditional farming sector is being carried out. For the freehold agriculture, the main source has been an attempted census of the accounts of all freehold farmers. For the non-respondents, a scaling up is made by reference to other farms of the same type. The small firms of the mining sector fill in a questionnaire about their accounts, whereas the two large groups of mining companies are interviewed at length. Manufacturing is dominated by Botswana Meat Commission which contributes more than 40 per cent of the sector's product. The main source is the questionnaire for Census of Production and Distribution (CPD). The CPD is based on the income and outlay accounts and balance sheets of a stratified sample of establishments within Botswana, covering all ISIC sectors. The census gives information for estimating the cost of intermediate consumption. The Government Printer's services are included in manufacturing and valued at cost. For construction, the private contractors and the brigades are covered by the CPD. Estimates of construction outlays for sites and services of low-cost housing are supplied by city and town councils while rural hut construction estimates are derived from the Rural Income Distribution Survey 1974/75. Estimates of construction carried out by government departments are derived from the analysis of government accounts. The main source of information for the trade sector is the CPD. The data obtained from this census are inflated to allow for under-coverage. Gross margins are estimated as the difference between sales and purchases of goods for resale. Taxes levied on imported goods are treated as indirect taxes collected by the trade sector. For transport, the main contributor is the transport service rendered by the Rhodesia Railways. The source of information is a series of returns received from General Manager of the Accounting Branch of Rhodesia Railways. Adjustments are made to convert the data to national accounts framework and significant imputations have to be made on the expenditure side. For other private firms of the transport sector, the financial sector and other services, the main source of information is the CPD. Gross output of financial institutions is made up of the actual sale of services and an imputed service charge. Estimates for producers of government services are based on the Annual Statement of Accounts of the Central Government. For the constant price estimates, the CPD data are deflated by a cost-of-living index.

1.1 Expenditure on the Gross Domestic Product, in Current Prices

Million Botswana pula — Fiscal year beginning 1 July

		1970	1971	1972	1973	1974	1975	1976	1977	1978	1979	1980
1	General government final consumption expenditure	...	16.0	...	28.3	37.0	50.6	71.9	85.2	101.7	122.1	...
2	Private final consumption expenditure	...	58.1	...	105.7	128.1	155.3	193.7	224.6	279.3	339.8	...
	a Households	...	57.1	...	103.7	125.9	152.0	190.0	219.3	275.2	330.9	...
	b Private non-profit institutions serving households	...	1.0	...	2.0	2.2	3.3	3.7	5.3	4.1	8.9	...
3	Gross capital formation	...	55.7	...	97.4	101.7	115.0	98.7	142.5	204.7	287.8	...
	a Increase in stocks	...	1.2	...	17.8	44.4	35.9	20.9	32.4	34.9	50.4	...
	b Gross fixed capital formation	...	54.5	...	79.6	57.3	79.1	77.8	110.1	169.8	237.4	...
	Residential buildings	...	6.4	...	12.7	11.0	13.4	9.6	17.0	20.8	19.2	...
	Non-residential buildings	...	5.8	...	7.9	9.4	10.7	14.0	8.8	19.5	23.4	...
	Other construction and land improvement etc.	...	11.6	...	30.9	21.2	28.6	33.4	55.1	62.5	101.1	...
	Other	...	30.7	...	28.1	15.7	26.4	20.8	29.2	67.0	93.7	...
4	Exports of goods and services [a]	...	39.8	...	76.4	93.8	135.2	155.5	161.1	275.9	357.8	...
5	Less: Imports of goods and services [b]	...	65.7	...	121.8	147.6	187.5	209.0	259.2	355.9	436.6	...
	Statistical discrepancy	...	-1.3	...	-1.1	-4.5	1.2	-	-	-	-	...
	Equals: Gross Domestic Product	...	102.6	...	184.9	208.5	269.8	310.8	354.2	505.7	670.9	...

a) Exports of goods only.
b) Imports of goods plus net imports of services.

1.2 Expenditure on the Gross Domestic Product, in Constant Prices

Million Botswana pula — Fiscal year beginning 1 July

		1970	1971	1972	1973	1974	1975	1976	1977	1978	1979	1980
					At constant prices of: 1974							
1	General government final consumption expenditure	...	...	...	36.6	37.0	44.0	53.8	58.0	59.4	66.0	...
2	Private final consumption expenditure	...	...	...	117.1	128.1	137.1	149.8	159.1	183.0	194.0	...
	a Households	...	...	...	114.9	125.9	134.2	146.9	155.3	180.3	188.9	...
	b Private non-profit institutions serving households	...	...	...	2.2	2.2	2.9	2.9	3.8	2.7	5.1	...
3	Gross capital formation	...	...	...	114.5	101.7	97.7	73.5	101.6	124.7	151.6	...

Botswana

1.2 Expenditure on the Gross Domestic Product, in Constant Prices
(Continued)

Million Botswana pula

	1970	1971	1972	1973	1974	1975	1976	1977	1978	1979	1980
					At constant prices of:1974					Fiscal year beginning 1 July	
a Increase in stocks	...	...	...	20.5	44.4	32.0	18.6	28.0	24.1	29.9	...
b Gross fixed capital formation	...	...	...	94.0	57.3	65.7	54.9	73.6	100.6	121.7	...
Residential buildings	...	...	...	15.0	11.0	11.0	6.6	11.0	12.1	9.3	...
Non-residential buildings	...	...	...	9.4	9.4	8.7	9.7	5.9	11.3	11.3	...
Other construction and land improvement etc.	...	...	...	36.6	21.2	23.6	23.2	35.8	36.1	49.0	...
Other	...	...	...	33.0	15.7	22.4	15.4	20.9	41.1	52.1	...
4 Exports of goods and services [a]	...	...	...	87.0	93.8	127.3	127.8	143.0	167.3	158.4	...
5 Less: Imports of goods and services [b]	...	...	...	143.8	147.6	162.3	156.5	179.8	220.9	235.5	...
Statistical discrepancy	...	...	...	-	-4.5	-	-1.0	0.2	6.2	13.0	...
Equals: Gross Domestic Product	...	138.0	...	211.4	208.5	243.8	247.4	282.1	315.5	347.5	...

a) Exports of goods only.
b) Imports of goods plus net imports of services.

1.3 Cost Components of the Gross Domestic Product

Million Botswana pula

	1970	1971	1972	1973	1974	1975	1976	1977	1978	1979	1980
										Fiscal year beginning 1 July	
1 Indirect taxes, net	...	10.8	...	15.4	18.1	23.1	28.5	40.2	60.6	89.1	...
a Indirect taxes paid	...	10.8	...	15.4	18.1	23.1	30.0	40.5	61.2	90.5	...
b Less: Subsidies received	...	-	...	-	-	-	1.5	0.3	-0.6	1.4	...
2 Consumption of fixed capital	...	5.2	...	17.6	20.0	26.9	29.8	39.2	38.6	59.0	...
3 Compensation of employees paid by resident producers to:	...	30.7	...	65.1	88.4	107.9	129.5	144.5	185.8	230.3	...
4 Net operating surplus	...	55.9	...	84.6	80.0	107.0	112.6	122.6	216.9	292.5	...
a Corporate and quasi-corporate enterprises	...	...	...	30.2	27.2	45.7	44.1	...	...	...	...
b Private unincorporated enterprises	...	...	...	53.7	52.5	60.0	67.5	...	...	...	...
c General government	...	0.5	...	0.7	0.3	1.3	1.0	...	...	...	...
Statistical discrepancy	...	...	...	2.2	2.0	4.9	10.4	7.7	2.3	...	...
Equals: Gross Domestic Product	...	102.6	...	184.9	208.5	269.8	310.8	354.2	505.7	670.9	...

1.4 General Government Current Receipts and Disbursements

Million Botswana pula

	1970	1971	1972	1973	1974	1975	1976	1977	1978	1979	1980
										Fiscal year beginning 1 July	
					Receipts						
1 Property and entrepreneurial income	...	1.8	...	6.3	5.6	19.1	15.3	19.0	42.2	...	...
2 Taxes, fees and contributions	...	16.3	...	29.2	38.5	47.7	56.9	76.6	118.3	...	...
a Indirect taxes	...	11.2	...	15.5	18.6	21.3	29.3	41.1	60.6	...	...
b Direct taxes	...	4.4	...	13.0	18.7	25.1	26.1	33.2	53.8	...	...
c Social security contributions	...	-	...	0.3	0.4	0.4	0.4	0.8	1.1	...	...
d Compulsory fees, fines and penalties	...	0.7	...	0.4	0.8	0.9	1.1	1.5	2.8	...	...
3 Other current receipts	...	7.6	...	11.1	16.5	25.6	27.6	28.2	48.4	...	...
Total Current Receipts of General Government	...	25.7	...	46.6	60.6	92.4	99.8	123.8	208.9	...	...
					Disbursements						
1 General government final consumption expenditure	...	16.0	...	28.3	37.0	50.6	71.9	85.2	101.7	...	...
a Compensation of employees	...	8.3	...	17.4	24.0	34.0	45.5	49.8	70.2	...	...
b Consumption of fixed capital	...	1.4	...	0.8	0.9	2.1	2.5	2.7	3.3	...	...
c Purchases of goods and services, net	...	6.3	...	10.1	12.1	14.5	23.9	32.7	28.2	...	...
d Less: Own account production of fixed assets	...	...	...	...	...	...	...	...	...	...	...
e Indirect taxes paid, net	...	-	...	-	-	-	-	-	-	...	...
2 Property income paid	...	0.9	...	0.7	1.4	3.3	3.0	0.7	5.1	...	...

Botswana

1.4 General Government Current Receipts and Disbursements
(Continued)

Million Botswana pula — Fiscal year beginning 1 July

	1970	1971	1972	1973	1974	1975	1976	1977	1978	1979	1980
a Interest	...	0.9	...	0.7	1.4	3.3	3.0	0.7	5.1	...	...
b Net land rent and royalties	...	...	...	...	...	...	...	...	...	...	...
3 Subsidies	...	...	...	-	-	-	...	...	...	...	...
4 Other current transfers paid	...	3.0	...	3.9	7.2	9.5	7.0	8.2	13.2	...	...
a Social security benefits and social assistance grants	...	0.2	...	0.3	0.4	0.6	0.5	0.8	1.1	...	...
b Other	...	2.8	...	3.6	6.8	8.9	6.5	7.4	12.1	...	...
5 Net saving	...	5.6	...	13.7	15.0	29.0	17.9	29.7	88.9	...	...
Total Current Disbursements and Net Saving of General Government	...	25.7	...	46.6	60.6	92.4	99.8	123.8	208.9	...	...

1.5 Current Income and Outlay of Corporate and Quasi-Corporate Enterprises, Summary

Million Botswana pula — Fiscal year beginning 1 July

	1970	1971	1972	1973	1974	1975	1976	1977	1978	1979	1980
Receipts											
1 Net operating surplus	...	...	...	30.2	27.2	45.7	44.1	51.4	139.8	...	...
2 Other property and entrepreneurial income received	...	...	...	9.9	19.1	22.9	29.7	36.6	53.1	...	...
3 Current transfers received [a]	...	...	...	4.5	5.2	8.9	24.8	34.1	33.8	...	...
Total Current Receipts	...	...	...	44.6	51.5	77.5	98.6	122.1	226.7	...	...
Disbursements											
1 Property and entrepreneurial income paid	...	...	...	36.2	53.3	82.6	86.7	113.2	150.9	...	...
2 Direct taxes and other current payments to general government	...	...	...	12.0	17.9	17.5	19.8	23.1	44.1	...	...
3 Other current transfers paid	...	...	...	4.8	5.7	5.6	21.7	31.2	42.2	...	...
4 Net saving	...	...	...	-8.4	-25.4	-28.2	-29.6	-45.4	-10.5	...	...
Total Current Disbursements and Net Saving	...	...	...	44.6	51.5	77.5	98.6	122.1	226.7	...	...

a) Including imputed intercompany transfers.

1.6 Current Income and Outlay of Households and Non-Profit Institutions

Million Botswana pula — Fiscal year beginning 1 July

	1970	1971	1972	1973	1974	1975	1976	1977	1978	1979	1980
Receipts											
1 Compensation of employees	...	30.7	...	79.9	95.1	117.4	147.4	162.0	201.3	...	...
a From resident producers	...	...	...	65.1	88.4	107.9	127.5	142.4	183.7	...	...
b From rest of the world	...	...	...	14.8	6.7	9.5	19.9	19.6	17.6	...	...
2 Property and entrepreneurial income received	...	...	...	52.5	51.5	69.6	70.0	78.0	82.8	...	...
3 Current transfers received	...	...	...	3.8	4.4	5.6	9.1	13.1	14.3	...	...
a Social security benefits and social assistance grants received	...	...	...	0.3	0.4	0.6	0.5	0.8	1.1	...	...
b Other	...	...	...	3.5	4.0	5.0	8.6	12.3	13.2	...	...
Total Current Receipts	...	...	...	136.2	151.0	192.6	226.5	253.1	298.4	...	...
Disbursements											
1 Private final consumption expenditure	...	58.1	...	105.7	128.1	155.3	193.7	216.1	279.3	...	...
2 Property income paid	...	...	...	-	-	-	-	-	...	...	...
3 Direct taxes and other payments n.e.c. to general government	...	...	...	1.3	1.2	8.0	6.7	10.9	10.8	...	...
a Social security contributions	...	...	...	0.3	0.4	0.4	0.4	0.8	1.1	...	...
b Direct taxes	...	...	...	1.0	0.8	7.6	6.3	10.1	9.7	...	...
c Fees, fines and penalties	...	...	...	...	...	...	...	...	...	...	...
4 Other current transfers paid	...	...	...	2.6	3.3	5.0	7.6	9.5	6.5	...	...
5 Net saving	...	...	...	26.6	18.4	24.3	18.5	16.6	1.8	...	...
Total Current Disbursements and Net Saving	...	...	...	136.2	151.0	192.6	226.5	253.1	298.4	...	...

Botswana

1.7 External Transactions on Current Account, Summary

Million Botswana pula — Fiscal year beginning 1 July

	1970	1971	1972	1973	1974	1975	1976	1977	1978	1979	1980
Payments to the Rest of the World											
1 Imports of goods and services a	...	...	...	124.0	149.6	192.4	219.4	266.9	359.7	...	...
2 Factor income paid to the rest of the world	...	...	...	22.8	31.6	35.4	48.4	56.3	71.6	...	...
a Compensation of employees b	...	...	...	...	...	...	2.0	2.0	2.1	...	...
b Property and entrepreneurial income paid c	...	...	...	22.8	31.6	35.4	46.4	54.3	69.5	...	...
3 Indirect taxes paid to supranational organizations	...	...	...	...	...	...	...	...	...	...	...
4 Current transfers to the rest of the world	...	...	...	1.3	1.8	3.2	10.1	11.9	19.1	...	...
5 Surplus of the nation on current transactions	...	...	...	-48.2	-72.4	-56.9	-61.1	-105.2	-85.9	...	...
Payments to the Rest of the World and Surplus of the Nation on Current Transactions	...	...	...	99.9	110.6	174.1	216.8	229.9	364.5	...	...
Receipts From The Rest of the World											
1 Exports of goods and services d	...	...	...	76.4	93.8	135.2	155.5	161.1	275.9	...	...
2 Factor income received from rest of the world	...	...	...	14.8	6.7	9.5	24.0	24.4	30.7	...	...
a Compensation of employees b	...	...	...	14.8	6.7	9.5	19.9	19.6	17.6	...	...
b Property and entrepreneurial income received c	...	...	...	...	...	...	4.1	4.8	13.1	...	...
3 Subsidies received from supranational organisations	...	...	...	...	...	...	...	...	...	...	...
4 Current transfers from rest of the world e	...	...	...	8.7	10.1	29.4	37.3	44.4	57.9	...	...
Receipts from the Rest of the World on Current Transactions	...	...	...	99.9	110.6	174.1	216.8	229.9	364.5	...	...

a) Imports of goods plus net imports of services.
b) For 1973-75, compensation of employees from the rest of the world is net of compensation paid of employees from the rest of the world.
c) For 1973-75, property and entrepreneurial income paid is net of property and entrepreneurial income received.
d) Exports of goods only.
e) For 1973-75, current and capital transfers are net. Beginning 1976, current and capital transfers are gross, excluding loan waivers and direct grants which are assumed to be capital transfers.

1.8 Capital Transactions of The Nation, Summary

Million Botswana pula — Fiscal year beginning 1 July

	1970	1971	1972	1973	1974	1975	1976	1977	1978	1979	1980
Finance of Gross Capital Formation											
Gross saving	...	36.2	...	49.5	28.0	52.0	36.6	40.0	118.8	...	...
1 Consumption of fixed capital	...	5.2	...	17.6	20.0	26.9	29.8	39.2	38.6	...	...
a General government	...	1.4	...	1.6	1.9	3.2	3.7	3.8	4.5	...	...
b Corporate and quasi-corporate enterprises	...	...	...	14.8	16.9	22.2	22.5	31.0	29.2	...	...
Public	...	...	...	0.9	1.8	2.5	2.9	3.1	3.7	...	...
Private	...	...	...	13.9	15.1	19.7	19.6	27.9	25.5	...	...
c Other	...	...	...	2.4	2.6	3.2	3.6	4.3	4.9	...	...
2 Net saving	...	31.0	...	31.9	8.0	25.1	6.8	0.9	80.2	...	...
a General government	...	5.6	...	13.7	15.0	29.0	17.9	29.7	88.9	...	...
b Corporate and quasi-corporate enterprises	...	...	...	-8.4	-25.4	-28.2	-29.6	-45.4	-10.5	...	...
Public	...	...	...	-0.1	5.2	4.8	1.6	-1.4	10.9	...	...
Private	...	...	...	-8.3	-30.6	-33.0	-31.2	-44.0	-21.4	...	...
c Other	...	...	...	26.6	18.4	24.3	18.5	16.6	1.8	...	...
Less: Surplus of the nation on current transactions	...	...	...	-48.2	-72.4	-56.9	-61.1	-96.7	-85.9	...	...
Statistical discrepancy	...	...	...	-0.3	1.3	6.1	1.0	5.7	-	...	...
Finance of Gross Capital Formation	...	54.4	...	97.4	101.7	115.0	98.7	142.5	204.7	...	...
Gross Capital Formation											
Increase in stocks	...	1.2	...	17.8	44.4	35.9	20.9	32.4	34.9	...	...
Gross fixed capital formation	...	54.5	...	79.6	57.3	79.1	77.8	110.1	169.8	...	...
1 General government	...	5.7	...	17.0	25.7	30.4	33.0	42.4	63.9	...	...
2 Corporate and quasi-corporate enterprises	...	...	...	59.1	26.9	42.6	39.1	59.7	94.7	...	...
a Public a	...	...	...	23.7	8.7	9.8	6.7	10.0	10.8	...	...
b Private	...	...	...	35.4	18.2	32.8	32.4	49.7	83.9	...	...
3 Other	...	...	...	3.5	4.7	6.1	5.7	8.0	11.2	...	...
Gross Capital Formation	...	55.7	...	97.4	101.7	115.0	98.7	142.5	204.7	...	...

a) Non-financial sector only.

Botswana

1.10 Gross Domestic Product by Kind of Activity, in Current Prices

Million Botswana pula — Fiscal year beginning 1 July

	1970	1971	1972	1973	1974	1975	1976	1977	1978	1979	1980
1 Agriculture, hunting, forestry and fishing	...	33.1	...	62.4	61.2	65.7	74.4	71.7	78.1	79.6	...
2 Mining and quarrying	...	11.2	...	16.0	18.0	33.6	42.0	55.8	117.4	217.2	...
3 Manufacturing	...	5.1	...	10.1	15.5	20.9	25.3	24.4	42.8	30.1	...
4 Electricity, gas and water	...	1.3	...	3.3	6.9	11.1	9.2	10.0	11.5	14.0	...
5 Construction	...	10.0	...	20.1	20.1	18.8	15.3	17.1	21.4	28.5	...
6 Wholesale and retail trade, restaurants and hotels a	...	17.5	...	14.5	17.9	23.1	28.0	33.0	44.5	57.7	...
7 Transport, storage and communication	...	3.8	...	7.5	7.5	12.2	11.9	15.0	11.6	13.1	...
8 Finance, insurance, real estate and business services	...	6.1	...	13.3	14.6	18.2	24.6	29.9	46.4	74.0	...
9 Community, social and personal services	...	1.3	...	2.3	2.6	4.3	3.3	3.9	4.3	14.8	...
Total, Industries	...	89.4	...	149.5	164.3	207.9	234.0	260.8	378.0	529.0	...
Producers of Government Services	...	11.8	...	18.2	24.9	36.1	48.0	52.5	73.5	68.3	...
Other Producers	...	2.2	...	4.5	6.2	8.8	9.2	11.3	13.9	17.0	...
Subtotal	...	103.4	...	172.2	195.4	252.8	291.2	324.6	465.4	614.3	...
Less: Imputed bank service charge	...	0.8	...	0.7	3.3	2.7	7.9	9.3	17.6	28.1	...
Plus: Import duties a	...	...	...	13.4	16.4	19.4	27.5	38.9	57.9	84.7	...
Plus: Value added tax	...	...	...	...	...	...	...	...	...	...	...
Equals: Gross Domestic Product b	...	102.6	...	184.9	208.5	269.8	310.8	354.2	505.7	670.9	...

a) Prior to 1973, item 'Imports duties' is included in item 'Wholesale and retail, restaurants and hotels'.
b) For 1976 & 1977, items 'Producers of government services' and 'Other producers' are included in item 'Community, social and personal services'.

1.11 Gross Domestic Product by Kind of Activity, in Constant Prices

Million Botswana pula — Fiscal year beginning 1 July

At constant prices of: 1974

	1970	1971	1972	1973	1974	1975	1976	1977	1978	1979	1980
1 Agriculture, hunting, forestry and fishing	...	...	...	68.9	61.2	62.0	64.6	61.8	58.9	54.9	...
2 Mining and quarrying	...	...	...	17.9	18.0	32.0	33.7	62.7	57.8	81.6	...
3 Manufacturing	...	...	...	11.0	15.5	19.9	21.9	19.3	28.9	14.1	...
4 Electricity, gas and water	...	...	...	2.6	6.9	10.4	8.7	9.5	11.5	10.5	...
5 Construction	...	...	...	24.0	20.1	14.5	9.6	10.2	10.9	12.7	...
6 Wholesale and retail trade, restaurants and hotels	...	...	...	16.4	17.9	21.3	21.0	20.7	26.3	27.3	...
7 Transport, storage and communication	...	...	...	8.6	7.5	9.8	9.6	11.2	9.1	11.8	...
8 Finance, insurance, real estate and business services	...	...	...	15.0	14.6	15.8	17.6	19.4	29.5	47.0	...
9 Community, social and personal services	...	...	...	2.5	2.6	3.9	2.6	3.2	5.2	7.2	...
Total, Industries	...	...	...	166.9	164.3	189.6	189.3	218.0	238.1	267.1	...
Producers of Government Services	...	...	...	25.3	24.9	31.1	35.0	35.1	42.7	41.0	...
Other Producers	...	...	...	5.0	6.2	7.6	7.2	8.0	7.1	6.5	...
Subtotal	...	...	...	197.2	195.4	228.5	231.5	261.1	287.9	314.6	...
Less: Imputed bank service charge	...	...	...	0.8	3.3	2.4	6.2	6.6	11.5	14.9	...
Plus: Import duties	...	...	...	15.0	16.4	17.7	22.1	27.6	39.1	47.8	...
Plus: Value added tax	...	...	...	...	...	...	...	...	...	...	...
Equals: Gross Domestic Product	...	138.0	...	211.4	208.5	243.8	247.4	282.1	315.5	347.5	...

1.12 Relations Among National Accounting Aggregates

Million Botswana pula — Fiscal year beginning 1 July

	1970	1971	1972	1973	1974	1975	1976	1977	1978	1979	1980
Gross Domestic Product	...	...	...	182.7	206.5	264.9	300.4	346.5	501.9	670.9	...
Plus: Net factor income received from abroad	...	...	...	-8.0	-24.9	-25.9	-24.4	-31.9	-40.9	-38.4	...
Factor income received	...	...	...	14.8	6.7	9.5	24.0	24.4	30.7	...	...
Less: Factor income paid	...	...	...	22.8	31.6	35.4	48.4	56.3	71.6	...	...
Equals: Gross National Product	...	...	...	174.7	181.6	239.0	276.0	314.6	461.0	632.5	...

Botswana

1.12 Relations Among National Accounting Aggregates
(Continued)

Million Botswana pula — Fiscal year beginning 1 July

	1970	1971	1972	1973	1974	1975	1976	1977	1978	1979	1980
Less: Consumption of fixed capital	...	...	...	17.6	20.0	26.9	29.8	39.2	38.6	59.0	...
Less: Net indirect taxes paid to supranational organisations	...	...	...	...	...	...	...	...	...	...	...
Equals: National Income at Market Prices	...	...	...	157.1	161.6	212.1	246.2	275.4	422.4	573.5	...
Plus: Net current transfers received from abroad	...	...	...	7.4	8.3	26.2	27.2	32.5	38.8	53.2	...
Current transfers received	...	...	...	8.7	10.1	29.4	37.3	44.4	57.9	...	...
Less: Current transfers paid	...	...	...	1.3	1.8	3.2	10.1	11.9	19.1	...	...
Equals: National Disposable Income at Market Prices	...	...	...	164.5	169.9	238.3	273.4	307.9	461.2	626.7	...
Less: Final consumption	...	...	...	134.0	165.1	205.9	265.6	309.8	381.0	461.9	...
Statistical discrepancy [a]	...	...	...	1.4	3.2	-7.3	-1.0	2.8	...	...	...
Equals: Net Saving	...	...	...	31.9	8.0	25.1	6.8	0.9	80.2	164.8	...
Less: Surplus of the nation on current transactions	...	...	...	-48.2	-72.4	-56.9	-61.1	-105.2	-85.9	-13.6	...
Statistical discrepancy [b]	...	...	...	-0.3	1.3	6.1	1.0	5.7	-	-	...
Equals: Net Capital Formation	...	...	...	79.8	81.7	88.1	68.9	111.8	166.1	178.4	...

a) Refering to statistical discrepancy in income and outlay account.
b) Refering to statistical discrepancy in capital finance account.

2.1 General Government Final Consumption Expenditure by Function, in Current Prices

Million Botswana pula — Fiscal year beginning 1 July

	1970	1971	1972	1973	1974	1975	1976	1977	1978	1979	1980
1 General public services	...	7.8	...	15.2	15.3	...	...	...	...	...	...
2 Defence	...	-	...	...	-	...	...	...	...	...	...
3 Public order and safety	...	-	...	-	-	...	...	...	...	...	...
4 Education	...	1.2	...	1.4	3.3	...	...	...	...	...	...
5 Health	...	1.6	...	1.5	3.0	...	...	...	...	...	...
6 Social security and welfare	...	-	...	-	-	...	...	...	...	...	...
7 Housing and community amenities	...	-	...	-	-	...	...	...	...	...	...
8 Recreational, cultural and religious affairs	...	0.4	...	0.2	0.1	...	...	...	...	...	...
9 Economic services	...	...	...	...	...	...	...	...	...	...	...
a Fuel and energy	...		...			...	...	...	...	...	...
b Agriculture, forestry, fishing and hunting	...		...			...	...	...	...	...	...
c Mining, manufacturing and construction, except fuel and energy	...	5.0	...	8.9	15.3	...	...	...	...	...	...
d Transportation and communication	...		...			...	...	...	...	...	...
e Other economic affairs	...		...			...	...	...	...	...	...
10 Other functions	...	-	...	1.1	-	...	...	...	...	...	...
Total General Government Final Consumption Expenditure	...	16.0	...	28.3	37.0	50.6	71.9	85.2	101.7	...	...

2.7 Gross Capital Formation by Type of Good and Owner, in Current Prices

Million Botswana pula — Fiscal year beginning 1 July

	1971 TOTAL	Total Private	Public Enterprises	General Government	1973 TOTAL	Total Private	Public Enterprises	General Government	1974 TOTAL	Total Private	Public Enterprises	General Government
Increase in stocks, total	1.2	...	...	...	17.8	19.4	-1.6	-	44.4	41.0	3.4	-
1 Goods producing industries	1.2	...	...	...	15.1	...	...	...	24.2	...	...	...
a Materials and supplies	1.9	...	...	...	2.9	...	...	...	-1.8	...	...	...
b Work in progress [a]	-	...	...	...	3.1	...	...	...	12.5	...	...	...
c Livestock, except breeding stocks, dairy cattle, etc.	-0.7	...	...	...	9.1	...	...	...	13.5	...	...	...
d Finished goods [a]	...	...	...	...	...	...	...	...	...	...	...	...
2 Wholesale and retail trade	...	...	...	...	5.0	...	...	...	13.1	...	...	...
3 Other, except government stocks	...	...	...	...	-2.3	...	...	...	7.1	...	...	...
4 Government stocks	...	...	...	...	...	...	...	...	...	...	...	...
Gross Fixed Capital Formation, Total	54.5	...	...	...	79.6	38.9	23.7	17.0	57.3	22.9	8.7	25.7
1 Residential buildings	6.4	...	...	...	12.7	7.2	3.9	1.6	11.0	6.7	2.8	1.5
2 Non-residential buildings	5.8	...	...	...	7.9	4.9	0.2	2.8	9.4	4.8	1.4	3.2

Botswana

2.7 Gross Capital Formation by Type of Good and Owner, in Current Prices
(Continued)

Million Botswana pula — Fiscal year beginning 1 July

	1971 TOTAL	1971 Total Private	1971 Public Enterprises	1971 General Government	1973 TOTAL	1973 Total Private	1973 Public Enterprises	1973 General Government	1974 TOTAL	1974 Total Private	1974 Public Enterprises	1974 General Government
3 Other construction	11.6	...	...	...	30.9	2.7	18.7	9.5	21.2	2.9	2.2	16.1
4 Land improvement and plantation and orchard development	...	...	...	...	-	...	...	...	-	...	...	...
5 Producers' durable goods	30.7	...	...	...	28.1	24.1	0.9	3.1	15.7	8.5	2.3	4.9
a Transport equipment	...	...	...	...	12.0	10.9	0.1	1.0	7.0	5.4	0.1	1.5
b Machinery and equipment	...	...	...	...	16.1	13.2	0.8	2.1	8.7	3.1	2.2	3.4
6 Breeding stock, dairy cattle, etc.	...	...	...	...	...	...	...	...	...	...	...	...
Total Gross Capital Formation	55.7	...	...	7.0	97.4	58.3	22.1	17.0	101.7	63.9	12.1	25.7

	1975 TOTAL	1975 Total Private	1975 Public Enterprises	1975 General Government	1976 TOTAL	1976 Total Private	1976 Public Enterprises	1976 General Government	1977 TOTAL	1977 Total Private	1977 Public Enterprises	1977 General Government
Increase in stocks, total	35.9	30.7	5.0	0.2	20.9	17.1	3.7	0.1	32.4	36.2	-3.8	-
1 Goods producing industries	21.7	...	...	...	14.9	...	...	...	25.8	...	...	...
a Materials and supplies	2.9	...	...	...	-2.6	...	...	...	1.7	...	...	...
b Work in progress a	5.6	...	...	...	1.9	...	...	...	-0.4	...	...	...
c Livestock, except breeding stocks, dairy cattle, etc.	13.2	...	...	...	15.6	...	...	...	24.5	...	...	...
d Finished goods a	...	...	...	...	...	...	...	...	...	...	...	...
2 Wholesale and retail trade	7.5	...	...	...	6.4	...	...	...	6.0	...	...	...
3 Other, except government stocks	6.5	...	...	...	-0.5	...	...	...	0.6	...	...	...
4 Government stocks	0.2	...	...	...	0.1	...	...	...	...	...	...	...
Gross Fixed Capital Formation, Total	79.1	38.9	9.8	30.4	77.8	38.1	6.7	33.0	110.1	57.7	10.0	42.4
1 Residential buildings	13.4	7.6	3.3	2.5	9.6	6.9	1.4	1.3	17.0	9.3	6.2	1.5
2 Non-residential buildings	10.7	5.0	2.5	3.2	14.0	5.5	2.3	6.2	8.8	4.4	1.3	3.1
3 Other construction	28.6	10.5	0.6	17.5	33.4	12.6	2.0	18.8	55.1	26.7	1.1	27.3
4 Land improvement and plantation and orchard development	-	...	...	...	-	...	...	...	...	...	...	...
5 Producers' durable goods	26.4	15.8	3.4	7.2	20.8	13.1	1.0	6.7	29.2	17.3	1.4	10.5
a Transport equipment	6.9	3.9	0.2	2.8	7.8	4.0	0.1	3.7	8.8	4.2	0.1	4.5
b Machinery and equipment	19.5	11.9	3.2	4.4	13.0	9.1	0.9	3.0	20.4	13.1	1.3	6.0
6 Breeding stock, dairy cattle, etc.	...	...	...	...	...	...	...	...	...	...	...	...
Total Gross Capital Formation	115.0	69.6	14.8	30.6	98.7	55.2	10.4	33.1	142.5	93.9	6.2	42.4

	1978 TOTAL	1978 Total Private	1978 Public Enterprises	1978 General Government	1979 TOTAL	1979 Total Private	1979 Public Enterprises	1979 General Government
Increase in stocks, total	34.7	31.1	3.7	-	50.4	...	...	...
1 Goods producing industries	29.2	...	...	...	28.1	...	...	...
a Materials and supplies	4.1	...	...	...	9.1	...	...	...
b Work in progress a	2.8	...	...	...	1.6	...	...	...
c Livestock, except breeding stocks, dairy cattle, etc.	15.7	...	...	...	12.5	...	...	...
d Finished goods a	6.6	...	...	...	4.9	...	...	...
2 Wholesale and retail trade	5.1	...	...	...	17.9	...	...	...
3 Other, except government stocks	0.4	...	...	...	4.4	...	...	...
4 Government stocks	-	...	...	...	...	...	...	...
Gross Fixed Capital Formation, Total	169.8	91.3	10.8	67.7	237.4	...	...	...
1 Residential buildings	20.8	12.0	5.1	3.7	19.2	...	...	...
2 Non-residential buildings	19.5	5.8	1.4	12.3	23.4	...	...	...

Botswana

2.7 Gross Capital Formation by Type of Good and Owner, in Current Prices
(Continued)

Million Botswana pula — Fiscal year beginning 1 July

	1978 TOTAL	1978 Total Private	1978 Public Enterprises	1978 General Government	1979 TOTAL	1979 Total Private	1979 Public Enterprises	1979 General Government
3 Other construction	62.5	29.0	1.2	32.3	101.1	...	...	...
4 Land improvement and plantation and orchard development	...	...	...	...	...	...	...	...
5 Producers' durable goods	67.0	44.5	3.1	19.4	93.7	...	...	...
a Transport equipment	13.7	4.5	0.3	8.9	17.5	...	...	...
b Machinery and equipment	53.3	40.0	2.8	10.5	76.2	...	...	...
6 Breeding stock, dairy cattle, etc.	...	...	...	...	...	...	...	...
Total Gross Capital Formation	204.7	122.4	14.5	67.7	287.8	...	...	...

a) Item 'Finished goods' is included in item 'Work in progress'.

2.9 Gross Capital Formation by Kind of Activity of Owner, ISIC Major Divisions, in Current Prices

Million Botswana pula — Fiscal year beginning 1 July

	1971 Total Gross Capital Formation	1971 Increase in Stocks	1971 Gross Fixed Capital Formation	1973 Total Gross Capital Formation	1973 Increase in Stocks	1973 Gross Fixed Capital Formation	1974 Total Gross Capital Formation	1974 Increase in Stocks	1974 Gross Fixed Capital Formation	1975 Total Gross Capital Formation	1975 Increase in Stocks	1975 Gross Fixed Capital Formation
					All Producers							
1 Agriculture, hunting, fishing and forestry	0.2	-0.6	0.8	13.5	12.0	1.5	14.1	11.7	2.4	17.5	15.0	2.5
2 Mining and quarrying	27.3	0.2	27.1	23.6	4.7	18.9	15.5	8.3	7.2	17.7	3.1	14.6
3 Manufacturing	1.9	0.6	1.3	-0.9	-1.6	0.7	6.8	4.2	2.6	11.2	3.6	7.6
4 Electricity, gas and water	10.9	...	10.9	18.6	...	18.6	2.5	0.2	2.3	3.7	2.8	0.9
5 Construction	1.7	0.6	1.1	3.3	-2.2	5.5	7.5	6.6	0.9	6.3	3.4	2.9
6 Wholesale and retail trade, restaurants and hotels	1.8	0.9	0.9	6.7	5.0	1.7	15.6	13.1	2.5	11.2	7.5	3.7
7 Transport, storage and communication	2.5	1.0	1.5	3.5	...	3.5	2.8	...	2.8	4.3	...	4.3
8 Finance, insurance, real estate and business services	0.8	-2.3	3.1	11.5	...	11.5	9.8	0.1	9.7	10.3	0.1	10.2
9 Community, social and personal services	0.7	...	0.7	0.1	...	0.1	0.5	0.1	0.4	0.6	0.2	0.4
Total Industries	47.8	0.4	47.4	79.9	17.9	62.0	75.1	44.3	30.8	82.8	35.7	47.1
Producers of Government Services	7.0	1.3	5.7	16.2	...	16.2	24.5	...	24.5	29.2	0.2	29.0
Private Non-Profit Institutions Serving Households	0.9	...	0.9	1.3	...	1.3	2.1	0.1	2.0	3.0	...	3.0
Total	55.7	1.7	54.0	97.4	17.9	79.5	101.7	44.4	57.3	115.0	35.9	79.1

	1976 Total Gross Capital Formation	1976 Increase in Stocks	1976 Gross Fixed Capital Formation	1977 Total Gross Capital Formation	1977 Increase in Stocks	1977 Gross Fixed Capital Formation	1978 Total Gross Capital Formation	1978 Increase in Stocks	1978 Gross Fixed Capital Formation	1979 Total Gross Capital Formation	1979 Increase in Stocks	1979 Gross Fixed Capital Formation
					All Producers							
1 Agriculture, hunting, fishing and forestry	17.2	15.2	2.0	26.6	24.5	2.1	15.9	13.6	2.3	17.3	...	...
2 Mining and quarrying	9.0	-4.0	13.0	39.8	4.1	35.7	74.6	9.1	65.5	127.5	...	...
3 Manufacturing	7.3	3.7	3.6	1.2	-2.8	4.0	7.7	4.6	3.1	3.0	...	...
4 Electricity, gas and water	2.2	-2.3	4.5	0.2	0.2	-	3.3	0.3	3.0	6.3	...	...
5 Construction	5.4	1.2	4.2	2.1	0.4	1.7	3.7	1.6	2.1	7.2	...	...
6 Wholesale and retail trade, restaurants and hotels	9.8	6.4	3.4	9.3	6.0	3.3	10.4	5.1	5.3	29.3	...	...
7 Transport, storage and communication	4.5	-	4.5	2.8	-	2.8	5.3	-	5.3	7.3	...	...
8 Finance, insurance, real estate and business services	10.3	0.4	9.9	15.5	0.1	15.4	16.6	0.1	16.5	14.1	...	...
9 Community, social and personal services	0.5	0.1	0.4	0.5	0.1	0.4	0.4	0.4	-	0.8	...	...
Total Industries	66.2	20.7	45.5	98.0	32.6	65.4	137.9	34.8	103.1	212.8	...	...
Producers of Government Services	30.3	0.1	30.2	41.1	-	41.1	63.9	-	63.9	71.2	...	...
Private Non-Profit Institutions Serving Households	2.2	0.1	2.1	3.4	-	3.4	2.9	0.2	2.7	3.8	...	...
Total	98.7	20.9	77.8	142.5	32.6	109.9	204.7	35.0	169.7	287.8	...	...

Botswana

2.10 Gross Capital Formation by Kind of Activity of Owner, ISIC Major Divisions, in Constant Prices

Million Botswana pula — Fiscal year beginning 1 July

	1973 Total Gross Capital Formation	1973 Increase in Stocks	1973 Gross Fixed Capital Formation	1974 Total Gross Capital Formation	1974 Increase in Stocks	1974 Gross Fixed Capital Formation	1975 Total Gross Capital Formation	1975 Increase in Stocks	1975 Gross Fixed Capital Formation	1976 Total Gross Capital Formation	1976 Increase in Stocks	1976 Gross Fixed Capital Formation
				At constant prices of: 1974 All Producers								
1 Agriculture, hunting, fishing and forestry	15.7	...	...	14.1	...	...	16.4	...	...	15.6	...	...
2 Mining and quarrying	27.8	...	...	15.5	...	...	14.6	...	...	6.3	...	...
3 Manufacturing	-1.1	...	...	6.8	...	...	9.3	...	...	5.2	...	...
4 Electricity, gas and water	21.9	...	...	2.5	...	...	3.1	...	...	1.4	...	...
5 Construction	3.9	...	...	7.5	...	...	5.2	...	...	3.8	...	...
6 Wholesale and retail trade, restaurants and hotels	7.6	...	...	15.6	...	...	10.0	...	...	7.5	...	...
7 Transport, storage and communication	3.2	...	...	1.6	...	...	2.4	...	...	1.2	...	...
8 Finance, insurance, real estate and business services	13.7	...	...	9.8	...	...	8.5	...	...	7.2	...	...
9 Community, social and personal services	1.6	...	...	2.6	...	...	3.0	...	...	2.1	...	...
Total Industries	94.3	...	...	76.0	...	...	72.5	...	...	50.3	...	...
Producers of Government Services	20.2	...	...	25.7	...	...	25.2	...	...	23.2	...	...
Private Non-Profit Institutions Serving Households	...	...	...	...	...	...	...	...	...	...	...	...
Total	114.5	...	...	101.7	...	...	97.7	...	...	73.5	...	...

	1977 Total Gross Capital Formation	1977 Increase in Stocks	1977 Gross Fixed Capital Formation	1978 Total Gross Capital Formation	1978 Increase in Stocks	1978 Gross Fixed Capital Formation	1979 Total Gross Capital Formation	1979 Increase in Stocks	1979 Gross Fixed Capital Formation
			At constant prices of: 1974 All Producers						
1 Agriculture, hunting, fishing and forestry	23.7	...	...	12.2	...	...	11.9	...	...
2 Mining and quarrying	25.9	...	...	44.8	...	...	65.6	...	...
3 Manufacturing	0.8	...	...	4.7	...	...	1.4	...	...
4 Electricity, gas and water	0.1	...	...	2.0	...	...	3.5	...	...
5 Construction	1.4	...	...	2.1	...	...	4.1	...	...
6 Wholesale and retail trade, restaurants and hotels	6.9	...	...	6.5	...	...	15.5	...	...
7 Transport, storage and communication	2.0	...	...	3.3	...	...	4.1	...	...
8 Finance, insurance, real estate and business services	10.1	...	...	9.6	...	...	7.0	...	...
9 Community, social and personal services	2.8	...	...	1.9	...	...	2.8	...	...
Total Industries	73.7	...	...	87.1	...	...	115.9	...	...
Producers of Government Services	27.9	...	...	37.6	...	...	35.7	...	...
Private Non-Profit Institutions Serving Households	...	...	...	...	...	...	...	...	...
Total	101.6	...	...	124.7	...	...	151.6	...	...

3.12 General Government Income and Outlay Account: Total and Subsectors

Million Botswana pula — Fiscal year beginning 1 July

	1971 Total General Government	1971 Central Government	1971 State or Provincial Government	1971 Local Government	1971 Social Security Funds	1973 Total General Government	1973 Central Government	1973 State or Provincial Government	1973 Local Government	1973 Social Security Funds
					Receipts					
1 Property and entrepreneurial income	1.8	1.6	...	...	...	6.3	6.1	...	0.2	...
a Net operating surplus	0.5	0.4	...	...	...	0.7	0.6	...	0.1	...
b Withdrawals from public quasi-corporations	-	-	...	...	...	-	-	...	-	...
c Interest			...	...	...	1.5	1.5	...	-	...
d Dividends	1.3	1.2	...	...	...	1.4	1.4	...	-	...
e Net land rent and royalties			...	...	...	2.7	2.6	...	0.1	...
2 Taxes, fees and contributions	16.3	14.7	...	...	...	28.9	26.8	...	2.1	...
a Indirect taxes	11.2	11.0	...	...	...	15.5	15.0	...	0.5	...
b Direct taxes	4.4	3.1	...	...	...	13.0	11.4	...	1.6	...
Income	4.4	3.1	...	...	...	13.0	11.4	...	1.6	...

Botswana

3.12 General Government Income and Outlay Account: Total and Subsectors
(Continued)

Million Botswana pula — Fiscal year beginning 1 July

	1971 Total General Government	1971 Central Government	1971 State or Provincial Government	1971 Local Government	1971 Social Security Funds	1973 Total General Government	1973 Central Government	1973 State or Provincial Government	1973 Local Government	1973 Social Security Funds
Other	-	-	...	...	...	-	-	...	-	...
c Social security contributions	-	-	...	...	...	-	-	...	-	...
d Fees, fines and penalties	0.7	0.6	...	...	...	0.4	0.4	...	-	...
3 Other current transfers received	7.6	7.2	...	...	...	11.4	10.5	...	0.9	...
a Casualty insurance claims	-	-	...	...	...	-	-	...	-	...
b Transfers from other government subsectors	...	-	...	...	...	-	-	...	-	...
c Transfers from abroad	6.6	6.6	...	...	...	9.8	9.8	...	-	...
d Other transfers, except imputed	0.6	0.2	...	...	...	0.4	0.4	...	-	...
e Imputed unfunded employee welfare contributions	0.4	0.4	...	...	...	0.3	0.3	...	-	...
Total Current Receipts	25.7	23.5	...	...	...	46.6	43.4	...	3.2	...

Disbursements

	Total General Government	Central Government	State or Provincial Government	Local Government	Social Security Funds	Total General Government	Central Government	State or Provincial Government	Local Government	Social Security Funds
1 General government final consumption expenditures	15.9	13.8	...	...	...	28.3	25.3	...	3.0	...
a Compensation of employees	...	...	...	...	...	17.4	14.5	2.9	2.9	...
b Consumption of fixed capital	1.4	1.3	...	...	...	0.8	0.6	...	0.2	...
c Goods and services purchased, net	...	...	...	...	...	10.1	10.2	...	-0.1	...
Purchases	...	...	...	...	...	12.5	11.7	...	-	...
Less: Sales	...	...	...	...	...	2.4	1.5	...	-	...
d Less: Own account production of fixed assets	...	...	...	...	...	...	...	...	...	...
e Indirect taxes paid, net	...	...	...	...	...	...	...	...	...	...
2 Property income paid	0.9	0.9	...	...	...	0.7	0.7	...	-	...
a Interest	...	...	...	...	...	0.7	0.7	...	-	...
b Net land rent and royalties	...	...	...	...	...	...	...	...	...	...
3 Subsidies	0.2	0.2	...	...	...	-	-	...	-	...
4 Other current transfers paid	4.3	3.1	...	0.5	...	3.9	3.8	...	0.1	...
a Casualty insurance premiums, net	-	-	...	...	...	-	-	...	-	...
b Transfers to other government subsectors	...	-	...	...	...	-	-	...	-	...
c Transfers to households	2.0	2.1	...	...	...	2.6	2.1	...	0.5	...
Social security benefits	-	-	...	...	...	-	-	...	-	...
Social assistance grants	1.5	1.6	...	...	...	1.8	1.8	...	-	...
Unfunded employee welfare benefits	0.5	0.5	...	...	...	0.8	0.3	...	0.5	...
d Transfers to private non-profit institutions serving households	0.1	0.1	...	...	...	0.9	0.9	...	-	...
e Transfers to the rest of the world	0.9	0.9	...	...	...	0.8	0.8	...	-	...
Net saving	5.6	5.6	...	...	...	13.7	13.6	...	0.1	...
Total Current Disbursements and Net Saving	25.7	23.5	...	...	...	47.0	43.4	...	3.6	...

	1974 Total General Government	1974 Central Government	1974 State or Provincial Government	1974 Local Government	1974 Social Security Funds	1975 Total General Government	1975 Central Government	1975 State or Provincial Government	1975 Local Government	1975 Social Security Funds

Receipts

1 Property and entrepreneurial income	5.6	5.4	...	0.2	...	19.1	18.7	...	0.4	...
a Net operating surplus	0.3	0.1	...	0.2	...	1.3	0.9	...	0.4	...
b Withdrawals from public quasi-corporations	-	-	...	-	...	-	-	...	-	...
c Interest	1.9	1.9	...	-	...	4.0	4.0	...	-	...
d Dividends	1.2	1.2	...	-	...	11.0	11.0	...	-	...
e Net land rent and royalties	2.2	2.2	...	-	...	2.8	2.8	...	-	...
2 Taxes, fees and contributions	38.1	35.6	...	2.5	...	47.3	44.8	...	2.5	...
a Indirect taxes	18.6	18.0	...	0.6	...	21.3	21.1	...	0.2	...
b Direct taxes	18.7	16.8	...	1.9	...	25.1	22.8	...	2.3	...
Income	18.7	16.8	...	1.9	...	25.1	22.8	...	2.3	...

Botswana

3.12 General Government Income and Outlay Account: Total and Subsectors
(Continued)

Million Botswana pula — Fiscal year beginning 1 July

	1974					1975				
	Total General Government	Central Government	State or Provincial Government	Local Government	Social Security Funds	Total General Government	Central Government	State or Provincial Government	Local Government	Social Security Funds
Other	-	-	...	-	...	...	...	...	-	...
c Social security contributions	-	-	...	-	...	-	-	...	-	...
d Fees, fines and penalties	0.8	0.8	...	-	...	0.9	0.9	...	-	...
3 Other current transfers received	16.9	13.0	...	3.9	...	26.0	21.6	...	4.4	...
a Casualty insurance claims	-	-	...	-	...	-	-	...	-	...
b Transfers from other government subsectors	-	-	...	-	...	-	-	...	-	...
c Transfers from abroad	12.6	12.6	...	-	...	21.2	21.2	...	-	...
d Other transfers, except imputed	3.9	-	...	3.9	...	4.4	-	...	4.4	...
e Imputed unfunded employee welfare contributions	0.4	0.4	...	-	...	0.4	0.4	...	-	...
Total Current Receipts	60.6	54.0	...	6.6	...	92.4	85.1	...	7.3	...

Disbursements

	Total General Government	Central Government	State or Provincial Government	Local Government	Social Security Funds	Total General Government	Central Government	State or Provincial Government	Local Government	Social Security Funds
1 General government final consumption expenditures	37.0	32.8	...	4.2	...	50.6	44.6	...	6.0	...
a Compensation of employees	24.0	20.0	...	4.0	...	34.0	27.5	...	6.5	...
b Consumption of fixed capital	0.9	0.7	...	0.2	...	2.1	1.8	...	0.3	...
c Goods and services purchased, net	12.1	12.1	...	-	...	14.5	15.3	...	-0.8	...
Purchases	16.5	15.5	...	1.0	...	21.3	19.7	...	1.6	...
Less: Sales	4.4	3.4	...	1.0	...	6.8	4.4	...	2.4	...
d Less: Own account production of fixed assets	...	...	...	...	...	...	...	...	...	...
e Indirect taxes paid, net	...	...	...	...	...	...	...	...	...	...
2 Property income paid	1.4	1.4	...	-	...	3.3	3.3	...	-	...
a Interest	...	...	...	...	...	...	...	...	...	...
b Net land rent and royalties	...	...	...	...	...	...	...	...	...	...
3 Subsidies	-	-	...	-	...	-	-	...	-	...
4 Other current transfers paid	7.2	7.1	...	0.1	...	9.5	9.3	...	0.2	...
a Casualty insurance premiums, net	0.1	-	...	0.1	...	0.1	-	...	0.1	...
b Transfers to other government subsectors	...	-	...	...	...	...	...	...	...	...
c Transfers to households	4.7	4.7	...	-	...	5.1	5.0	...	0.1	...
Social security benefits	-	-	...	...	...	-	-	...	...	...
Social assistance grants	4.3	4.3	...	...	...	4.5	4.4	...	...	...
Unfunded employee welfare benefits	0.4	0.4	...	...	...	0.6	0.6	...	...	...
d Transfers to private non-profit institutions serving households	1.6	1.6	...	...	...	3.6	3.6	...	...	...
e Transfers to the rest of the world	0.8	0.8	...	...	...	0.7	0.7	...	...	...
Net saving	15.0	12.7	...	2.3	...	29.0	27.9	...	1.1	...
Total Current Disbursements and Net Saving	60.6	54.0	...	6.6	...	92.4	85.1	...	7.3	...

	1976					1977				
	Total General Government	Central Government	State or Provincial Government	Local Government	Social Security Funds	Total General Government	Central Government	State or Provincial Government	Local Government	Social Security Funds

Receipts

	Total General Government	Central Government	State or Provincial Government	Local Government	Social Security Funds	Total General Government	Central Government	State or Provincial Government	Local Government	Social Security Funds
1 Property and entrepreneurial income	15.1	15.1	...	-	...	19.0	18.7	...	0.3	...
a Net operating surplus	1.0	1.0	...	-	...	1.8	1.7	...	0.1	...
b Withdrawals from public quasi-corporations	-	-	...	-	...	-	-	...	...	...
c Interest	4.8	4.8	...	-	...	3.3	3.3	...	-	...
d Dividends	5.0	5.0	...	-	...	7.6	7.6	...	-	...
e Net land rent and royalties	4.3	4.3	...	-	...	6.3	6.1	...	0.2	...
2 Taxes, fees and contributions	56.5	52.9	...	3.6	...	75.8	70.3	...	5.5	...
a Indirect taxes	29.3	29.1	...	0.2	...	41.1	40.8	...	0.3	...
b Direct taxes	26.1	22.7	...	3.4	...	33.2	28.0	...	5.2	...
Income	26.1	22.7	...	3.4	...	33.2	28.0	...	5.2	...

Botswana

3.12 General Government Income and Outlay Account: Total and Subsectors
(Continued)

Million Botswana pula — Fiscal year beginning 1 July

	1976 Total General Government	1976 Central Government	1976 State or Provincial Government	1976 Local Government	1976 Social Security Funds	1977 Total General Government	1977 Central Government	1977 State or Provincial Government	1977 Local Government	1977 Social Security Funds
Other	-	-	...	-	...	-	-	...	-	...
c Social security contributions	-	-	...	-	...	-	-	...	-	...
d Fees, fines and penalties	1.1	1.1	...	-	...	1.5	1.5	...	-	...
3 Other current transfers received	28.0	26.0	...	2.0	...	29.0	26.2	...	2.8	...
a Casualty insurance claims	-	-	...	-	...	-	-	...	-	...
b Transfers from other government subsectors	...	...	...	...	...	...	...	...	...	...
c Transfers from abroad	25.6	25.6	...	-	...	25.4	25.4	...	-	...
d Other transfers, except imputed	2.0	-	...	2.0	...	2.8	-	...	2.8	...
e Imputed unfunded employee welfare contributions	0.4	0.4	...	-	...	0.8	0.8	...	-	...
Total Current Receipts	99.8	94.2	...	5.6	...	123.8	115.2	...	8.6	...

Disbursements

1 General government final consumption expenditures	71.9	66.8	...	5.1	...	85.2	77.5	...	7.7	...
a Compensation of employees	45.5	41.5	...	4.0	...	49.8	44.4	...	5.4	...
b Consumption of fixed capital	2.5	2.1	...	0.4	...	2.7	2.5	...	0.2	...
c Goods and services purchased, net	23.9	23.2	...	0.7	...	32.7	30.6	...	2.1	...
Purchases	30.9	28.4	...	2.5	...	39.1	35.6	...	3.5	...
Less: Sales	7.0	5.2	...	1.8	...	6.4	5.0	...	1.4	...
d Less: Own account production of fixed assets	...	...	...	...	...	...	...	...	...	...
e Indirect taxes paid, net	...	...	...	...	...	...	...	...	...	...
2 Property income paid	3.0	3.0	...	-	...	0.7	0.7	...	-	...
a Interest	3.0	3.0	...	-	...	0.7	0.7	...	-	...
b Net land rent and royalties	-	-	...	-	...	-	-	...	-	...
3 Subsidies	...	-	...	-	...	...	-	...	-	...
4 Other current transfers paid	7.0	7.0	...	-	...	8.2	-	...	7.3	...
a Casualty insurance premiums, net	-	-	...	-	...	0.1	-	...	0.1	...
b Transfers to other government subsectors	-	-	...	-	...	-	-	...	-	...
c Transfers to households	3.7	3.7	...	-	...	5.5	7.2	...	4.7	...
Social security benefits	-	-	...	-	...	...	...	...	...	...
Social assistance grants	3.2	3.2	...	-	...	4.7	3.9	...	0.8	...
Unfunded employee welfare benefits	0.5	0.5	...	-	...	0.8	0.8	...	-	...
d Transfers to private non-profit institutions serving households	2.5	2.5	...	-	...	2.5	2.5	...	-	...
e Transfers to the rest of the world	0.8	0.8	...	-	...	0.1	0.1	...	-	...
Net saving	17.9	17.4	...	0.5	...	29.7	29.7	...	-	...
Total Current Disbursements and Net Saving	99.8	94.2	...	5.6	...	123.8	115.2	...	8.6	...

	1978 Total General Government	1978 Central Government	1978 State or Provincial Government	1978 Local Government	1978 Social Security Funds

Receipts

1 Property and entrepreneurial income	42.2	41.8	...	0.4	...
a Net operating surplus	1.1	0.9	...	0.2	...
b Withdrawals from public quasi-corporations	-	-	...	-	...
c Interest	6.7	6.7	...	-	...
d Dividends	19.3	19.3	...	-	...
e Net land rent and royalties	15.1	14.9	...	0.2	...
2 Taxes, fees and contributions	117.2	110.5	...	6.7	...
a Indirect taxes	60.6	60.3	...	0.3	...
b Direct taxes	53.8	47.4	...	6.4	...
Income	53.8	47.4	...	6.4	...

Botswana

3.12 General Government Income and Outlay Account: Total and Subsectors
(Continued)

Million Botswana pula — Fiscal year beginning 1 July

	1978				
	Total General Government	Central Government	State or Provincial Government	Local Government	Social Security Funds
Other	-	-	...	-	...
c Social security contributions	-	-	...	-	...
d Fees, fines and penalties	2.8	2.8	...	-	...
3 Other current transfers received	49.5	46.1	...	3.4	...
a Casualty insurance claims	-	-	...	-	...
b Transfers from other government subsectors	-	-	...	-	...
c Transfers from abroad	57.9	57.9	...	-	...
d Other transfers, except imputed	-9.5	-12.9	...	3.4	...
e Imputed unfunded employee welfare contributions	1.1	1.1	...	-	...
Total Current Receipts	208.9	198.4	...	10.5	...

Disbursements

1 General government final consumption expenditures	101.7	92.3	...	9.4	...
a Compensation of employees	70.2	63.7	...	6.5	...
b Consumption of fixed capital	3.3	3.0	...	0.3	...
c Goods and services purchased, net	28.2	25.6	...	2.6	...
Purchases	36.5	32.3	...	4.2	...
Less: Sales	8.3	6.7	...	1.6	...
d Less: Own account production of fixed assets	...	...	...	...	...
e Indirect taxes paid, net	...	...	...	...	...
2 Property income paid	5.1	5.1	...	-	...
a Interest	5.1	5.1	...	-	...
b Net land rent and royalties	...	...	...	...	...
3 Subsidies	...	...	...	...	...
4 Other current transfers paid	13.2	12.3	...	0.9	...
a Casualty insurance premiums, net	0.1	-	...	0.1	...
b Transfers to other government subsectors	...	...	...	...	...
c Transfers to households	6.9	6.1	...	0.8	...
Social security benefits	...	...	...	...	...
Social assistance grants	5.0	5.0	...	-	...
Unfunded employee welfare benefits	1.1	1.1	...	-	...
d Transfers to private non-profit institutions serving households	5.4	5.4	...	-	...
e Transfers to the rest of the world	0.8	0.8	...	-	...
Net saving	88.9	88.7	...	0.2	...
Total Current Disbursements and Net Saving	208.9	198.4	...	10.5	...

3.13 General Government Capital Accumulation Account: Total and Subsectors

Million Botswana pula — Fiscal year beginning 1 July

	1971					1973				
	Total General Government	Central Government	State or Provincial Government	Local Government	Social Security Funds	Total General Government	Central Government	State or Provincial Government	Local Government	Social Security Funds

Finance of Gross Accumulation

1 Gross saving	7.0	6.9	...	...	...	15.3	15.0	...	0.3	...
a Consumption of fixed capital	1.4	1.3	...	...	...	1.6	1.4	...	0.2	...
b Net saving	5.6	5.6	...	...	...	13.7	13.6	...	0.1	...
2 Capital transfers received [a]	0.5	0.5	...	...	...	1.6	0.7	...	0.9	...
Statistical discrepancy	...	...	...	...	...	...	...	...	...	...
Finance of Gross Accumulation	7.5	7.4	...	...	...	16.9	15.7	...	1.2	...

Gross Accumulation

1 Gross capital formation	7.0	6.7	...	...	...	17.0	16.6	...	0.4	...

Botswana

3.13 General Government Capital Accumulation Account: Total and Subsectors
(Continued)

Million Botswana pula — Fiscal year beginning 1 July

	1971 Total General Government	1971 Central Government	1971 State or Provincial Government	1971 Local Government	1971 Social Security Funds	1973 Total General Government	1973 Central Government	1973 State or Provincial Government	1973 Local Government	1973 Social Security Funds
a Increase in stocks	...	...	...	...	...	...	...	...	...	...
b Gross fixed capital formation	...	...	...	...	...	17.0	16.6	...	0.4	...
Own account construction	...	...	...	...	...	...	...	...	...	...
Other	...	...	...	...	...	17.0	16.6	...	0.4	...
2 Purchases of land, net	-0.1	-0.1	...	...	...	-0.3	-0.3	...	-	...
3 Purchases of intangible assets, net	-	-	...	...	...	-	-	...	-	...
4 Capital transfers paid	...	...	...	...	...	...	...	...	...	...
Net lending	0.6	0.8	...	...	...	0.2	-0.6	...	0.8	...
Gross Accumulation	7.5	7.4	...	...	...	16.9	15.7	...	1.2	...

	1974 Total General Government	1974 Central Government	1974 State or Provincial Government	1974 Local Government	1974 Social Security Funds	1975 Total General Government	1975 Central Government	1975 State or Provincial Government	1975 Local Government	1975 Social Security Funds
Finance of Gross Accumulation										
1 Gross saving	16.9	14.4	...	2.5	...	32.2	30.8	...	1.4	...
a Consumption of fixed capital	1.9	1.7	...	0.2	...	3.2	2.9	...	0.3	...
b Net saving	15.0	12.7	...	2.3	...	29.0	27.9	...	1.1	...
2 Capital transfers received [a]	3.9	2.1	...	1.8	...	9.0	6.5	...	2.5	...
Statistical discrepancy	...	...	...	...	...	...	...	...	...	...
Finance of Gross Accumulation	20.8	16.5	...	4.3	...	41.2	37.3	...	3.9	...
Gross Accumulation										
1 Gross capital formation	25.7	24.9	...	0.8	...	30.6	27.5	...	3.1	...
a Increase in stocks	-	-	...	-	...	0.2	0.2	...	-	...
b Gross fixed capital formation	25.7	24.9	...	0.8	...	30.4	27.3	...	3.1	...
Own account construction	...	...	...	...	...	...	...	...	...	...
Other	25.7	24.9	...	0.8	...	30.4	27.3	...	3.1	...
2 Purchases of land, net	-0.2	-0.2	...	-	...	-0.9	-0.9	...	-	...
3 Purchases of intangible assets, net	-	-	...	...	...	-	-	...	...	...
4 Capital transfers paid	...	...	...	...	...	...	...	...	...	...
Net lending	-4.7	-8.2	...	3.5	...	11.5	10.7	...	0.8	...
Gross Accumulation	20.8	16.5	...	4.3	...	41.2	37.3	...	3.9	...

	1976 Total General Government	1976 Central Government	1976 State or Provincial Government	1976 Local Government	1976 Social Security Funds	1977 Total General Government	1977 Central Government	1977 State or Provincial Government	1977 Local Government	1977 Social Security Funds
Finance of Gross Accumulation										
1 Gross saving	21.6	20.7	...	0.9	...	33.5	33.3	...	0.2	...
a Consumption of fixed capital	3.7	3.3	...	0.4	...	3.8	3.6	...	0.2	...
b Net saving	17.9	17.4	...	0.5	...	29.7	29.7	...	-	...
2 Capital transfers received [a]	14.0	12.4	...	1.6	...	14.7	14.5	...	0.2	...
Statistical discrepancy	...	...	...	...	...	...	...	...	...	...
Finance of Gross Accumulation	35.6	33.1	...	2.5	...	48.2	47.8	...	0.4	...
Gross Accumulation										
1 Gross capital formation	33.1	29.9	...	3.2	...	42.4	41.3	...	1.1	...
a Increase in stocks	0.1	0.1	...	-	...	-	-	...	-	...
b Gross fixed capital formation	33.0	29.8	...	3.2	...	42.4	41.3	...	1.1	...
Own account construction	...	...	...	...	...	...	...	...	...	...
Other	33.0	29.8	...	3.2	...	42.4	41.3	...	1.1	...
2 Purchases of land, net	...	-	...	...	...	...	...	...	...	...
3 Purchases of intangible assets, net	-	-	...	-	...	-	-	...	-	...
4 Capital transfers paid	...	...	...	...	...	...	...	...	...	...
Net lending	2.5	3.2	...	-0.7	...	5.8	6.5	...	-0.7	...
Gross Accumulation	35.6	33.1	...	2.5	...	48.2	47.8	...	0.4	...

Botswana

3.13 General Government Capital Accumulation Account: Total and Subsectors

Million Botswana pula
Fiscal year beginning 1 July

	\multicolumn{5}{c	}{1978}
	Total General Government	Central Government	State or Provincial Government	Local Government	Social Security Funds

Finance of Gross Accumulation

	Total	Central	State/Prov	Local	SSF
1 Gross saving	93.4	92.9	...	0.5	...
a Consumption of fixed capital	4.5	4.2	...	0.3	...
b Net saving	88.9	88.7	...	0.2	...
2 Capital transfers received [a]	21.4	21.1	...	0.3	...
Statistical discrepancy	-0.1	-	...	-0.1	...
Finance of Gross Accumulation	114.7	114.0	...	0.7	...

Gross Accumulation

	Total	Central	State/Prov	Local	SSF
1 Gross capital formation	67.8	66.6	...	1.2	...
a Increase in stocks	0.1	0.1	...	-	...
b Gross fixed capital formation	67.7	66.5	...	1.2	...
Own account construction	...	...	...	...	...
Other	...	...	...	...	...
2 Purchases of land, net	-0.4	-0.4	...	-	...
3 Purchases of intangible assets, net	...	...	...	...	...
4 Capital transfers paid	...	...	...	...	...
Net lending	47.3	47.8	...	-0.5	...
Gross Accumulation	114.7	114.0	...	0.7	...

a) Net.

3.14 General Government Capital Finance Account, Total and Subsectors

Million Botswana pula
Fiscal year beginning 1 July

	\multicolumn{5}{c	}{1973}	\multicolumn{5}{c	}{1974}
	Total Gen Gov	Central	State/Prov	Local	SSF	Total Gen Gov	Central	State/Prov	Local	SSF

Acquisition of Financial Assets

	1973 T	C	S/P	L	SSF	1974 T	C	S/P	L	SSF
1 Gold and SDRs	...	...	...	...	...	...	...	...	...	...
2 Currency and transferable deposits	...	8.0	...	...	...	...	4.7	...	...	...
3 Other deposits	...	...	...	...	...	...	...	...	...	...
4 Bills and bonds, short term	...	...	...	...	...	...	...	...	...	...
5 Bonds, long term	...	...	...	...	...	...	...	...	...	...
6 Corporate equity securities	...	4.3	...	...	...	...	4.9	...	...	...
7 Short-term loans, n.e.c.	...	0.9	...	...	...	...	...	...	...	...
8 Long-term loans, n.e.c.	...	12.0	...	...	...	...	0.4	...	...	...
9 Other receivables	...	...	...	...	...	...	...	...	...	...
10 Other assets [a]	...	-4.7	...	...	...	...	-5.7	...	...	...
Total Acquisition of Financial Assets	...	20.5	...	...	...	...	4.3	...	...	...

Incurrence of Liabilities

	1973 T	C	S/P	L	SSF	1974 T	C	S/P	L	SSF
1 Currency and transferable deposits	...	...	...	...	...	...	...	...	...	...
2 Other deposits	...	0.3	...	...	...	...	...	...	...	...
3 Bills and bonds, short term	...	...	...	...	...	...	...	...	...	...
4 Bonds, long term	...	...	...	...	...	...	...	...	...	...
5 Short-term loans, n.e.c.	...	...	...	...	...	...	15.5	...	...	...
6 Long-term loans, n.e.c.	...	21.4	...	...	...	...	...	...	...	...
7 Other payables	...	...	...	...	...	...	...	...	...	...
8 Other liabilities [b]	...	-0.6	...	...	...	...	-3.0	...	...	...
Total Incurrence of Liabilities	...	21.1	...	-0.8	...	...	...	...	-3.5	...
Net Lending	...	-0.6	...	0.8	...	-4.7	-8.2	...	3.5	...
Incurrence of Liabilities and Net Worth	...	20.5	...	...	...	...	4.3	...	...	...

	\multicolumn{5}{c	}{1975}	\multicolumn{5}{c	}{1976}
	Total Gen Gov	Central	State/Prov	Local	SSF	Total Gen Gov	Central	State/Prov	Local	SSF

Acquisition of Financial Assets

	1975 T	C	S/P	L	SSF	1976 T	C	S/P	L	SSF
1 Gold and SDRs	...	...	...	...	...	...	...	...	...	...
2 Currency and transferable deposits	...	12.3	...	...	...	...	15.0	...	0.2	...
3 Other deposits	...	...	...	...	...	...	...	...	...	...
4 Bills and bonds, short term	...	...	...	...	...	...	...	...	...	...

Botswana

3.14 General Government Capital Finance Account, Total and Subsectors
(Continued)

Million Botswana pula

Fiscal year beginning 1 July

	1975					1976				
	Total General Government	Central Government	State or Provincial Government	Local Government	Social Security Funds	Total General Government	Central Government	State or Provincial Government	Local Government	Social Security Funds
5 Bonds, long term	...	...	...	...	...	...	...	...	...	...
6 Corporate equity securities	...	1.9	...	...	...	...	...	...	...	...
7 Short-term loans, n.e.c.	...	9.2	...	...	...	...	...	...	...	...
8 Long-term loans, n.e.c.	...	2.7	...	...	...	-5.1	-5.1	...	...	...
9 Other receivables	...	...	...	...	...	...	...	...	...	...
10 Other assets [a]	...	8.0	...	...	...	15.3	15.3	...	...	...
Total Acquisition of Financial Assets	...	34.1	...	...	...	25.2	25.0	...	0.2	...

Incurrence of Liabilities

1 Currency and transferable deposits	...	...	...	...	...	1.0	...	...	1.0	...
2 Other deposits	...	...	...	...	...	...	...	...	...	...
3 Bills and bonds, short term	...	...	...	...	...	...	...	...	...	...
4 Bonds, long term	...	...	...	...	...	...	...	...	...	...
5 Short-term loans, n.e.c.	...	3.4	...	...	...	10.8	10.8	...	...	...
6 Long-term loans, n.e.c.	...	17.1	...	...	...	9.8	9.8	...	...	...
7 Other payables	...	...	...	...	...	...	...	...	...	...
8 Other liabilities [b]	...	2.9	...	...	...	1.1	1.2	...	-0.1	...
Total Incurrence of Liabilities	...	23.4	...	0.8	...	22.7	21.8	...	0.9	...
Net Lending	11.5	10.7	...	0.8	...	2.5	3.2	...	-0.7	...
Incurrence of Liabilities and Net Worth	...	34.1	...	...	...	25.2	25.0	...	0.2	...

	1977					1978				
	Total General Government	Central Government	State or Provincial Government	Local Government	Social Security Funds	Total General Government	Central Government	State or Provincial Government	Local Government	Social Security Funds

Acquisition of Financial Assets

1 Gold and SDRs	...	...	...	...	...	...	...	...	...	...
2 Currency and transferable deposits	6.2	2.9	...	3.3	...	21.4	19.4	...	2.0	...
3 Other deposits	...	...	...	...	...	...	...	...	...	...
4 Bills and bonds, short term	...	...	...	...	...	...	...	...	...	...
5 Bonds, long term	...	...	...	...	...	...	...	...	...	...
6 Corporate equity securities	...	...	...	...	...	...	...	...	...	...
7 Short-term loans, n.e.c.	1.0	...	...	1.0	...	21.1	20.1	...	1.0	...
8 Long-term loans, n.e.c.	-7.7	-7.7	...	...	...	1.5	1.5	...	-	...
9 Other receivables	...	...	...	...	...	17.6	17.6	...	-	...
10 Other assets [a]	13.9	13.9	...	...	...	11.9	11.9	...	-	...
Total Acquisition of Financial Assets	13.4	9.1	...	4.3	...	73.5	70.5	...	3.0	...

Incurrence of Liabilities

1 Currency and transferable deposits	4.2	...	...	4.2	...	3.0	-	...	3.0	...
2 Other deposits	...	...	...	...	...	...	...	...	...	...
3 Bills and bonds, short term	...	...	...	...	...	...	...	...	...	...
4 Bonds, long term	...	...	...	...	...	...	...	...	...	...
5 Short-term loans, n.e.c.	4.9	4.1	...	0.8	...	13.3	12.8	...	0.5	...
6 Long-term loans, n.e.c.	3.8	3.8	...	...	...	9.9	9.9	...	-	...
7 Other payables	...	...	...	...	...	...	...	...	...	...
8 Other liabilities [b]	-5.9	-5.9	...	...	...	...	...	...	...	...
Total Incurrence of Liabilities	7.0	2.0	...	5.0	...	...	...	...	...	...
Net Lending	6.4	7.1	...	-0.7	...	47.3	47.8	...	-0.5	...
Incurrence of Liabilities and Net Worth	13.4	9.1	...	4.3	...	73.5	70.5	...	3.0	...

a) Refering to foreign assets.
b) Refering to statistical discrepancy.

Botswana

3.22 Corporate and Quasi-Corporate Enterprise Income and Outlay Account: Total and Sectors

Fiscal year beginning 1 July
Million Botswana pula

	1973 TOTAL	1973 Non-Financial	1973 Financial	1974 TOTAL	1974 Non-Financial	1974 Financial	1975 TOTAL	1975 Non-Financial	1975 Financial	1976 TOTAL	1976 Non-Financial	1976 Financial
Receipts												
1 Property and entrepreneurial income received	40.1	34.7	5.4	46.3	34.2	12.1	68.6	51.0	17.6	73.8	50.2	23.6
a Net operating surplus	30.2	30.8	-0.6	27.2	29.2	-2.0	45.7	46.8	-1.1	44.1	46.3	-2.2
b Withdrawals from quasi-corporate enterprises	0.7	0.5	0.2	0.2	0.2	-	0.1	0.1	-	0.1	0.1	-
c Interest	7.4	1.7	5.7	17.3	3.5	13.8	21.7	3.2	18.5	28.4	2.9	25.5
d Dividends	1.6	1.5	0.1	1.3	1.0	0.3	0.4	0.2	0.2	0.5	0.2	0.3
e Net land rent and royalties	0.2	0.2	-	0.3	0.3	-	0.7	0.7	-	0.7	0.7	-
2 Other current transfers received [a]	1.6	1.6	-	1.3	1.2	0.1	5.9	5.6	0.3	9.0	6.0	3.0
a Casualty insurance transactions	...	...	...	...	...	...	1.8	1.8	-	3.0	-	3.0
Claims received	...	...	...	...	...	...	1.8	1.8	-	-	-	-
Net premiums received by insurance companies	...	...	...	...	...	...	...	...	...	3.0	-	3.0
b Current transfers received from the rest of the world	...	...	...	...	...	...	...	...	...	...	...	...
c Other transfers received, except imputed	...	...	...	...	...	...	4.1	3.8	0.3	6.0	6.0	-
d Imputed unfunded employee welfare contributions	...	...	...	...	...	...	...	...	...	...	...	...
Total Current Receipts	41.7	36.3	5.4	47.6	35.4	12.2	74.5	56.6	17.9	82.8	56.2	26.6
Disbursements												
1 Property and entrepreneurial income paid out	36.2	32.2	4.0	53.3	42.1	11.2	82.6	63.3	19.3	86.7	62.7	24.0
a Withdrawals from quasi-corporations	2.1	2.1	-	3.0	3.0	-	3.1	3.1	-	2.9	2.9	-
b Interest	17.5	13.7	3.8	34.7	24.0	10.7	51.7	33.0	18.7	57.7	34.4	23.3
c Dividends	14.3	14.1	0.2	13.3	12.8	0.5	23.9	23.3	0.6	20.3	19.6	0.7
d Net land rent and royalties	2.3	2.3	-	2.3	2.3	-	3.9	3.9	-	5.8	5.8	-
2 Direct taxes and other current payments n.e.c. to general government	12.0	11.5	0.5	17.9	17.7	0.2	17.5	17.0	0.5	19.8	19.1	0.7
a Direct taxes	12.0	11.5	0.5	17.9	17.7	0.2	17.5	17.0	0.5	19.8	19.1	0.7
Income	12.0	11.5	0.5	17.9	17.7	0.2	17.5	17.0	0.5	19.8	19.1	0.7
Other	...	...	...	...	...	...	...	...	...	...	...	...
b Fines, fees, penalties and other payments n.e.c.	...	...	...	...	...	...	...	...	...	...	...	...
3 Other current transfers paid	1.9	1.4	0.5	1.8	1.8	...	2.6	2.5	0.1	5.9	2.9	3.0
a Casualty insurance transactions	1.4	1.4	-	1.8	1.8	-	2.5	2.5	...	5.4	2.9	2.5
Casualty insurance premiums paid, net	1.4	1.4	-	1.8	1.8	-	2.5	2.5	...	5.0	2.9	2.1
Claims paid by insurance companies	...	...	...	...	...	...	...	...	...	0.4	-	0.4
b Transfers to private non-profit institutions	...	...	...	...	...	...	0.1	-	0.1	0.5	-	0.5
c Transfers to households	0.5	...	0.5	...	...	...	...	...	...	...	...	...
Unfunded employee welfare benefits	...	...	...	...	...	...	...	...	...	...	...	...
Social assistance grants and other transfers n.e.c.	...	...	...	...	...	...	...	...	...	0.5	-	0.5
d Transfers to the rest of the world	...	...	...	...	...	...	...	...	...	...	...	...
Net saving	-8.4	-8.8	0.4	-25.4	-26.2	0.8	-28.2	-26.2	-2.0	-29.5	-28.5	-1.1
Total Current Disbursements and Net Saving	41.7	36.3	5.4	47.6	35.4	12.2	74.5	56.6	17.9	82.9	56.2	26.6

	1977 TOTAL	1977 Non-Financial	1977 Financial	1978 TOTAL	1978 Non-Financial	1978 Financial
Receipts						
1 Property and entrepreneurial income received	88.0	62.0	26.0	186.1	152.2	33.9
a Net operating surplus	51.4	56.1	-4.7	139.8	143.5	-3.7
b Withdrawals from quasi-corporate enterprises	1.2	1.2	-	4.2	4.2	-
c Interest	34.5	4.3	30.2	34.8	4.0	30.8

Botswana

3.22 Corporate and Quasi-Corporate Enterprise Income and Outlay Account: Total and Sectors
(Continued)

Million Botswana pula — Fiscal year beginning 1 July

	1977 TOTAL	1977 Non-Financial	1977 Financial	1978 TOTAL	1978 Non-Financial	1978 Financial
d Dividends	0.6	0.1	0.5	7.2	0.4	6.8
e Net land rent and royalties	0.3	0.3	-	0.1	0.1	-
2 Other current transfers received [a]	10.8	5.7	5.1	40.6	31.5	9.1
a Casualty insurance transactions	4.3	0.2	4.1	...	...	...
Claims received	0.2	0.2	-	...	...	...
Net premiums received by insurance companies	4.1	-	4.1	6.8	-	6.8
b Current transfers received from the rest of the world	...	...	...	...	...	...
c Other transfers received, except imputed	6.5	5.5	1.0	33.8	31.5	2.3
d Imputed unfunded employee welfare contributions	...	...	...	...	...	...
Total Current Receipts	98.8	67.7	31.1	226.7	183.7	43.0

Disbursements

	1977 TOTAL	1977 Non-Financial	1977 Financial	1978 TOTAL	1978 Non-Financial	1978 Financial
1 Property and entrepreneurial income paid out	113.1	84.6	28.5	145.5	114.0	31.5
a Withdrawals from quasi-corporations	2.9	2.9	-	1.4	1.4	-
b Interest	69.4	41.9	27.5	66.0	35.8	30.2
c Dividends	32.2	31.1	1.1	62.6	61.3	1.3
d Net land rent and royalties	8.7	8.7	-	15.5	15.5	-
2 Direct taxes and other current payments n.e.c. to general government	23.1	22.2	0.9	44.1	43.0	1.1
a Direct taxes	23.1	22.2	0.9	44.1	43.0	1.1
Income	23.1	22.2	0.9	44.1	43.0	1.1
Other	...	...	...	...	...	...
b Fines, fees, penalties and other payments n.e.c.	...	...	...	...	...	...
3 Other current transfers paid	7.9	3.0	4.9	47.6	39.8	7.8
a Casualty insurance transactions	6.6	3.0	3.6	5.4	3.1	2.3
Casualty insurance premiums paid, net	5.2	3.0	2.2	1.1	-	1.1
Claims paid by insurance companies	1.4	-	1.4	4.3	3.1	1.2
b Transfers to private non-profit institutions	...	...	...	...	...	...
c Transfers to households	1.3	-	1.3	42.2	36.7	5.5
Unfunded employee welfare benefits	...	...	...	...	...	...
Social assistance grants and other transfers n.e.c.	...	...	...	...	...	...
d Transfers to the rest of the world	...	...	...	...	...	...
Net saving	-45.4	-42.1	-3.3	-10.5	-13.1	2.6
Total Current Disbursements and Net Saving	98.8	67.7	31.1	226.7	183.7	43.0

a) Net current transfers received.

3.23 Corporate and Quasi-Corporate Enterprise Capital Accumulation Account: Total and Sectors

Million Botswana pula — Fiscal year beginning 1 July

	1973 TOTAL	1973 Non-Financial	1973 Financial	1974 TOTAL	1974 Non-Financial	1974 Financial	1975 TOTAL	1975 Non-Financial	1975 Financial	1976 TOTAL	1976 Non-Financial	1976 Financial
Finance of Gross Accumulation												
1 Gross saving	6.4	5.9	0.5	-8.5	-9.4	0.9	-6.0	-4.2	-1.8	-7.1	-6.4	-0.7
a Consumption of fixed capital	14.8	14.7	0.1	16.9	16.8	0.1	22.2	22.0	0.2	22.5	22.1	0.4
b Net saving	-8.4	-8.8	0.4	-25.4	-26.2	0.8	-28.2	-26.2	-2.0	-29.6	-28.5	-1.1
2 Capital transfers received [a]	0.6	0.6	-	0.4	0.4	-	-0.1	-0.1	-	1.3	1.3	-
Finance of Gross Accumulation	7.0	6.5	0.5	-8.1	-9.0	0.9	-6.1	-4.3	-1.8	-5.8	-5.1	-0.7
Gross Accumulation												
1 Gross capital formation	69.3	68.5	0.8	60.3	59.1	1.2	64.2	63.8	0.4	47.2	44.6	2.6

Botswana

3.23 Corporate and Quasi-Corporate Enterprise Capital Accumulation Account: Total and Sectors
(Continued)

Million Botswana pula — Fiscal year beginning 1 July

	1973 TOTAL	1973 Non-Financial	1973 Financial	1974 TOTAL	1974 Non-Financial	1974 Financial	1975 TOTAL	1975 Non-Financial	1975 Financial	1976 TOTAL	1976 Non-Financial	1976 Financial
a Increase in stocks	10.2	10.2	-	33.4	33.4	-	21.6	21.6	-	8.1	7.9	0.2
b Gross fixed capital formation	59.1	58.3	0.8	26.9	25.7	1.2	42.6	42.2	0.4	39.1	36.7	2.4
Own account	58.3	58.3	...	25.7	25.7	...	42.2	42.2	...	36.7	36.7	...
1- Other	0.8	-	0.8	1.2	-	1.2	0.4	-	0.4	2.4	-	2.4
2 Purchases of land, net	1.2	1.2	-	-0.1	-0.1	-	0.3	0.3	-	0.6	0.6	-
3 Purchases of intangible assets, net	-	-	-	-	-	...	...	...	...	...	...	...
4 Capital transfers paid	...	...	...	...	...	...	...	...	...	...	...	...
Statistical discrepancy	...	...	...	...	...	...	...	...	...	...	...	...
5 Net lending	-63.5	-63.2	-0.3	-68.3	-68.0	-0.3	-70.6	-68.4	-2.2	-53.6	-50.3	-3.3
Gross Accumulation	7.0	6.5	0.5	-8.1	-9.0	0.9	-6.1	-4.3	-1.8	-5.8	-5.1	-0.7

	1977 TOTAL	1977 Non-Financial	1977 Financial	1978 TOTAL	1978 Non-Financial	1978 Financial
Finance of Gross Accumulation						
1 Gross saving	-14.4	-11.9	-2.5	18.7	15.3	3.4
a Consumption of fixed capital	31.0	30.2	0.8	29.2	28.4	0.8
b Net saving	-45.4	-42.1	-3.3	-10.5	-13.1	2.6
2 Capital transfers received [a]	0.5	0.5	-	2.2	2.1	0.1
Finance of Gross Accumulation	-13.9	-11.4	-2.5	20.9	17.4	3.5
Gross Accumulation						
1 Gross capital formation	68.0	66.3	1.7	115.3	114.1	1.2
a Increase in stocks	8.0	8.2	-0.2	20.9	20.9	-
b Gross fixed capital formation	60.0	58.1	1.9	94.4	93.2	1.2
Own account	58.1	58.1	...	...	...	...
1- Other	1.9	-	1.9	...	...	...
2 Purchases of land, net	0.5	0.2	0.3	0.3	0.3	-
3 Purchases of intangible assets, net	...	...	...	...	...	...
4 Capital transfers paid	...	...	...	...	...	...
Statistical discrepancy	...	...	...	0.9	0.9	-
5 Net lending	-82.4	-77.9	-4.5	-95.6	-97.9	2.3
Gross Accumulation	-13.9	-11.4	-2.5	20.9	17.4	3.5

a) Net.

4.3 Derivation of Value Added by Kind of Activity, ISIC Divisions, in Current Prices

Million Botswana pula — Fiscal year beginning 1 July

	1973 Gross Output	1973 Intermediate Consumption	1973 Value Added	1974 Gross Output	1974 Intermediate Consumption	1974 Value Added	1975 Gross Output	1975 Intermediate Consumption	1975 Value Added	1976 Gross Output	1976 Intermediate Consumption	1976 Value Added
All Producers												
1 Agriculture, hunting, forestry and fishing	78.7	16.3	62.4	82.9	21.7	61.2	89.0	23.3	65.7	101.9	27.5	74.4
2 Mining and quarrying	34.8	18.8	16.0	56.6	38.6	18.0	80.5	46.9	33.6	95.9	53.9	42.0
3 Manufacturing	53.4	43.3	10.1	64.4	48.9	15.5	71.7	50.8	20.9	85.2	59.9	25.3
4 Electricity, gas and water	6.3	3.0	3.3	12.3	5.4	6.9	18.4	7.3	11.1	19.8	10.6	9.2
5 Construction	46.2	26.1	20.1	48.1	28.0	20.1	49.0	30.2	18.8	40.7	25.4	15.3
6 Wholesale and retail trade, restaurants and hotels	24.6	10.1	14.5	32.4	14.5	17.9	38.2	15.1	23.1	46.6	18.6	28.0
7 Transport, storage and communication	30.8	23.3	7.5	36.3	28.8	7.5	52.9	40.7	12.2	61.7	49.8	11.9
8 Finance, insurance, real estate and business services	18.3	5.0	13.3	21.8	7.2	14.6	29.4	11.2	18.2	37.5	12.9	24.6
9 Community, social and personal services	5.3	3.0	2.3	5.9	3.3	2.6	9.5	5.2	4.3	6.2	2.9	3.3
Total, Industries	298.4	148.9	149.5	360.7	196.4	164.3	438.6	230.7	207.9	495.5	261.5	234.0
Producers of Government Services	30.7	12.5	18.2	41.4	16.5	24.9	57.4	21.3	36.1	78.9	30.9	48.0
Other Producers	6.3	1.8	4.5	8.1	1.9	6.2	11.1	2.3	8.8	14.5	5.3	9.2
Total	335.4	163.2	172.2	410.2	214.8	195.4	507.1	254.3	252.8	588.9	297.7	291.2
Imputed bank service charge	-	0.7	-0.7	-	3.3	-3.3	-	2.7	-2.7	-	7.9	-7.9
Import duties	13.4	-	13.4	16.4	-	16.4	19.4	-	19.4	27.5	-	27.5
Value added tax	...	...	...	...	...	...	...	...	...	...	...	...
Total	348.8	163.9	184.9	426.6	218.1	208.5	526.5	257.0	269.8	616.4	305.6	310.8

Botswana

4.3 Derivation of Value Added by Kind of Activity, ISIC Divisions, in Current Prices
(Continued)

Million Botswana pula

Fiscal year beginning 1 July

	1973			1974			1975			1976		
	Gross Output	Intermediate Consumption	Value Added	Gross Output	Intermediate Consumption	Value Added	Gross Output	Intermediate Consumption	Value Added	Gross Output	Intermediate Consumption	Value Added

of which General Government:

1 Agriculture, hunting, forestry and fishing	...	...	...	...	...	...	...	...	...	...	...	...
2 Mining and quarrying	...	...	...	...	...	...	...	...	...	...	...	...
3 Manufacturing	...	...	...	...	...	...	...	...	...	0.6	0.5	0.1
4 Electricity, gas and water	...	...	...	...	...	...	...	...	...	1.7	0.6	1.1
5 Construction	...	...	...	...	...	...	...	...	...	7.3	5.5	1.8
6 Wholesale and retail trade, restaurants and hotels	...	...	...	...	...	...	...	...	...	...	...	...
7 Transport and communication	...	...	...	...	...	...	...	...	...	9.3	4.5	4.8
8 Finance, insurance, real estate and business services	...	...	...	...	...	...	...	...	...	...	...	...
9 Community, social and personal services	...	...	...	...	...	...	...	...	...	...	...	...
Total, Industries of General Government	...	...	...	...	...	...	...	...	...	18.9	11.1	7.8
Producers of Government Services	...	...	...	...	...	...	...	...	...	...	...	...
Total, General Government	...	...	...	...	...	...	...	...	...	...	...	...

	1977			1978			1979		
	Gross Output	Intermediate Consumption	Value Added	Gross Output	Intermediate Consumption	Value Added	Gross Output	Intermediate Consumption	Value Added

All Producers

1 Agriculture, hunting, forestry and fishing	98.6	26.9	71.7	103.7	25.6	78.1	105.9	26.3	79.6
2 Mining and quarrying	113.0	57.2	55.8	184.0	66.6	117.4	300.1	82.9	217.2
3 Manufacturing	78.2	53.8	24.4	129.1	86.3	42.8	114.8	84.7	30.1
4 Electricity, gas and water	22.7	12.7	10.0	25.5	14.0	11.5	35.9	21.9	14.0
5 Construction	45.1	28.0	17.1	64.0	42.6	21.4	88.4	59.9	28.5
6 Wholesale and retail trade, restaurants and hotels	53.6	20.6	33.0	74.3	29.8	44.5	93.9	36.2	57.7
7 Transport, storage and communication	60.4	45.4	15.0	56.6	45.0	11.6	72.7	59.6	13.1
8 Finance, insurance, real estate and business services	44.0	14.1	29.9	59.2	12.8	46.4	91.8	17.8	74.0
9 Community, social and personal services	9.4	5.5	3.9	9.6	5.3	4.3	23.0	8.2	14.8
Total, Industries	525.0	264.2	260.8	706.0	328.0	378.0	926.5	397.5	529.0
Producers of Government Services	91.6	39.1	52.5	110.0	36.5	73.5	121.5	53.2	68.3
Other Producers	17.6	6.3	11.3	19.2	5.3	13.9	23.5	6.5	17.0
Total	634.2	309.6	324.6	835.2	369.8	465.4	1071.5	457.2	614.3
Imputed bank service charge	-	9.3	-9.3	-	17.6	-17.6	-	28.1	-28.1
Import duties	38.9	-	38.9	57.9	-	57.9	84.7	-	84.7
Value added tax	...	...	...	...	...	...	...	...	...
Total	673.1	318.9	354.2	893.1	387.4	505.7	1156.2	485.3	670.9

of which General Government:

1 Agriculture, hunting, forestry and fishing	...	...	...	...	...	...	...	...	...
2 Mining and quarrying	...	...	...	...	...	...	...	...	...
3 Manufacturing	0.6	0.4	0.2	0.6	0.4	0.2	...	...	...
4 Electricity, gas and water	2.0	0.9	1.1	2.6	1.0	1.6	...	...	...
5 Construction	3.7	2.0	1.7	3.6	1.4	2.2	...	...	...
6 Wholesale and retail trade, restaurants and hotels	...	...	...	...	...	...	...	...	...
7 Transport and communication	11.7	6.2	5.5	12.3	7.8	4.5	...	...	...
8 Finance, insurance, real estate and business services	...	...	...	...	...	...	...	...	...
9 Community, social and personal services	...	...	...	...	...	...	...	...	...
Total, Industries of General Government	18.0	9.5	8.5	19.1	10.6	8.5	...	...	...
Producers of Government Services	...	...	...	...	...	...	...	...	...
Total, General Government	...	...	...	...	...	...	...	...	...

Botswana

4.4 Derivation of Value Added by Kind of Activity, ISIC Divisions, in Constant Prices

Fiscal year beginning 1 July

Million Botswana pula

	1973 Gross Output	1973 Intermediate Consumption	1973 Value Added	1974 Gross Output	1974 Intermediate Consumption	1974 Value Added	1975 Gross Output	1975 Intermediate Consumption	1975 Value Added	1976 Gross Output	1976 Intermediate Consumption	1976 Value Added
				At constant prices of: 1974								
				All Producers								
1 Agriculture, hunting, forestry and fishing	87.4	18.5	68.9	82.9	21.7	61.2	83.3	21.3	62.0	87.4	22.8	64.6
2 Mining and quarrying	40.1	22.2	17.9	56.6	38.6	18.0	72.0	40.0	32.0	73.2	39.5	33.7
3 Manufacturing	61.4	50.4	11.0	64.4	48.9	15.5	67.1	47.2	19.9	72.5	50.6	21.9
4 Electricity, gas and water	6.1	3.5	2.6	12.3	5.4	6.9	16.7	6.3	10.4	16.5	7.8	8.7
5 Construction	54.8	30.8	24.0	48.1	28.0	20.1	40.2	25.7	14.5	28.2	18.6	9.6
6 Wholesale and retail trade, restaurants and hotels	27.7	11.3	16.4	32.4	14.5	17.9	34.7	13.4	21.3	35.5	14.5	21.0
7 Transport, storage and communication	33.9	25.3	8.6	34.3	26.8	7.5	40.6	30.8	9.8	37.9	28.3	9.6
8 Finance, insurance, real estate and business services	20.6	5.6	15.0	21.8	7.2	14.6	25.7	9.9	15.8	27.7	10.1	17.6
9 Community, social and personal services	5.9	3.4	2.5	5.9	7.3	2.6	8.5	4.6	3.9	5.2	2.6	2.6
Total, Industries	337.9	171.0	166.9	358.7	198.4	164.3	388.8	199.2	189.6	384.1	194.8	189.3
Producers of Government Services	46.3	16.0	30.3	49.5	18.4	31.1	59.8	20.9	38.9	70.5	28.3	42.2
Other Producers												
Total	384.2	187.0	197.2	408.2	216.8	195.4	448.6	220.1	228.5	454.6	223.1	231.5
Imputed bank service charge	-	0.8	-0.8	-	3.3	-3.3	-	2.4	-2.4	-	6.2	-6.2
Import duties	15.0	-	15.0	...	...	...	17.7	-	17.7	22.1	-	22.1
Value added tax	...	...	...	...	...	...	...	...	...	...	...	...
Total	399.2	187.8	211.4	424.6	220.1	208.5	466.3	222.5	243.8	476.7	229.3	247.4

	1977 Gross Output	1977 Intermediate Consumption	1977 Value Added	1978 Gross Output	1978 Intermediate Consumption	1978 Value Added	1979 Gross Output	1979 Intermediate Consumption	1979 Value Added
				At constant prices of: 1974					
				All Producers					
1 Agriculture, hunting, forestry and fishing	82.4	20.6	61.8	77.0	18.1	58.9	...	...	54.9
2 Mining and quarrying	101.8	39.1	62.7	98.5	40.7	57.8	...	...	81.6
3 Manufacturing	61.4	42.1	19.3	89.0	60.1	28.9	...	...	14.1
4 Electricity, gas and water	18.1	8.6	9.5	2.0	8.6	11.5	...	...	10.5
5 Construction	29.3	19.1	10.2	36.9	26.0	10.9	...	...	12.7
6 Wholesale and retail trade, restaurants and hotels	35.3	14.6	20.7	45.8	19.5	26.3	...	...	27.3
7 Transport, storage and communication	35.1	23.9	11.2	32.8	23.7	9.1	...	...	11.8
8 Finance, insurance, real estate and business services	29.4	10.0	19.4	38.4	8.9	29.5	...	...	47.0
9 Community, social and personal services	6.8	3.6	3.2	5.0	4.2	5.2	...	...	7.2
Total, Industries	399.6	181.6	218.0	443.5	205.4	238.1	...	...	267.1
Producers of Government Services	75.1	32.0	43.1	76.7	26.9	49.8	...	...	41.0
Other Producers							...	...	6.5
Total	474.7	213.6	261.1	520.2	232.3	287.9	...	...	314.6
Imputed bank service charge	-	6.6	-6.6	-	11.5	-11.5	...	...	-14.9
Import duties	27.6	-	27.6	39.1	-	39.1	...	...	47.8
Value added tax	...	...	...	...	...	...	...	...	...
Total	502.3	220.2	282.1	559.3	243.8	315.5	...	...	347.5

4.6 Cost Components of Value Added, ISIC Divisions

Fiscal year beginning 1 July

Million Botswana pula

	1971 Compensation of Employees	1971 Capital Consumption	1971 Net Operating Surplus	1971 Indirect Taxes	1971 Less: Subsidies Received	1971 Value Added	1973 Compensation of Employees	1973 Capital Consumption	1973 Net Operating Surplus	1973 Indirect Taxes	1973 Less: Subsidies Received	1973 Value Added
						All Producers						
1 Agriculture, hunting, forestry and fishing	0.8	...	26.1	...	...	33.1	9.3	0.8	52.3	...	...	62.4
2 Mining and quarrying	1.0	...	10.1	...	...	11.2	6.0	5.6	4.4	...	...	16.0
3 Manufacturing	1.8	...	5.4	...	...	5.1	4.0	0.8	4.8	0.5	...	10.1
4 Electricity, gas and water	0.2	...	1.1	...	...	1.3	0.8	0.7	1.8	...	...	3.3

Botswana

4.6 Cost Components of Value Added, ISIC Divisions
(Continued)

Million Botswana pula
Fiscal year beginning 1 July

	1971 Compensation of Employees	Capital Consumption	Net Operating Surplus	Indirect Taxes	Less: Subsidies Received	Value Added	1973 Compensation of Employees	Capital Consumption	Net Operating Surplus	Indirect Taxes	Less: Subsidies Received	Value Added
5 Construction	4.0	...	5.1	...	...	10.0	11.2	2.6	6.3	...	...	20.1
6 Wholesale and retail trade, restaurants and hotels	2.0	...	4.5	...	...	17.5	3.6	0.7	10.1	0.1	...	14.5
7 Transport, storage and communication	2.1	...	1.3	...	...	3.8	3.5	2.5	1.5	...	...	7.5
8 Finance, insurance, real estate and business services	1.7	...	1.3	...	...	6.1	4.0	2.7	6.5	0.1	...	13.3
9 Community, social and personal services	13.4	...	0.1	...	...	3.5	1.0	0.2	1.0	0.1	...	2.3
Statistical discrepancy	-6.1	...	1.7	...	...	...	...	...	...	...	...	...
Total, Industries	20.9	...	56.7	...	...	89.4	43.4	16.6	88.7	0.8	...	149.5
Producers of Government Services	8.3	...	-	...	...	11.8	17.4	0.8	-	-	...	18.2
Other Producers	1.5	...	-	...	...	2.2	4.3	0.2	-	-	...	4.5
Total	30.7	...	56.7	...	...	103.4	69.4	17.6	88.7	0.8	...	172.2
Imputed bank service charge	...	...	0.8	...	...	0.8	...	...	-0.7	...	...	-0.7
Import duties	...	...	...	...	...	...	...	...	...	13.4	...	13.4
Value added tax	...	...	...	...	...	...	...	...	...	...	...	...
Other adjustments	...	...	...	...	...	...	...	...	...	...	...	...
Total	30.7	5.2	55.9	10.8	...	102.6	65.1	17.6	88.0	14.2	...	184.9

of which General Government:

1 Agriculture, hunting, forestry and fishing	...	...	...	...	...	...	...	...	...	...	...	...
2 Mining and quarrying	...	...	...	...	...	...	...	...	...	...	...	...
3 Manufacturing	...	...	...	...	...	...	...	...	...	...	...	...
4 Electricity, gas and water	...	...	...	...	...	...	...	...	...	...	...	...
5 Construction	...	...	...	...	...	...	...	...	...	...	...	...
6 Wholesale and retail trade, restaurants and hotels	...	...	...	...	...	...	...	...	...	...	...	...
7 Transport and communication	...	...	...	...	...	...	...	...	...	...	...	...
8 Finance, insurance, real estate & business services	...	...	...	...	...	...	...	...	...	...	...	...
9 Community, social and personal services	...	...	...	...	...	...	...	...	...	...	...	...
Total, Industries of General Government	...	...	...	...	...	...	...	...	...	...	...	...
Producers of Government Services	...	...	...	...	...	...	...	...	...	...	...	...
Total, General Government	...	...	...	...	...	...	...	...	...	...	...	...

	1974 Compensation of Employees	Capital Consumption	Net Operating Surplus	Indirect Taxes	Less: Subsidies Received	Value Added	1975 Compensation of Employees	Capital Consumption	Net Operating Surplus	Indirect Taxes	Less: Subsidies Received	Value Added

All Producers

1 Agriculture, hunting, forestry and fishing	11.2	1.1	48.8	0.1	...	61.2	12.3	1.2	52.1	0.1	...	65.7
2 Mining and quarrying	7.8	8.1	2.1	-	...	18.0	11.2	9.1	13.3	-	...	33.6
3 Manufacturing	8.0	1.1	5.9	0.5	...	15.5	7.5	1.6	11.4	0.4	...	20.9
4 Electricity, gas and water	2.4	1.0	3.5	-	...	6.9	2.9	1.1	7.1	-	...	11.1
5 Construction	12.7	2.0	5.4	...	...	20.1	12.7	3.4	2.7	-	...	18.8
6 Wholesale and retail trade, restaurants and hotels	5.7	0.8	11.0	0.4	...	17.9	6.2	1.2	14.3	1.4	...	23.1
7 Transport, storage and communication	4.8	1.9	0.6	0.2	...	7.5	6.5	2.9	1.7	1.1	...	12.2
8 Finance, insurance, real estate and business services	4.9	2.7	6.8	0.2	...	14.6	5.7	3.5	8.9	0.1	...	18.2
9 Community, social and personal services	1.1	0.2	1.0	0.3	...	2.6	1.5	0.3	2.2	0.3	...	4.3
Statistical discrepancy	...	...	...	...	...	...	...	...	...	...	...	...
Total, Industries	58.6	18.9	85.1	1.7	...	164.3	66.5	24.3	109.3	3.4	...	207.9
Producers of Government Services	24.0	0.9	-	-	...	24.9	34.0	2.1	-	-	...	36.1
Other Producers	5.9	0.2	0.1	...	...	6.2	7.4	0.5	0.8	0.1	...	8.8
Total	88.5	20.0	85.2	1.7	...	195.4	107.9	26.9	114.5	3.5	...	252.8
Imputed bank service charge	...	...	3.3	...	...	-3.3	...	...	-2.4	...	...	-2.4
Import duties	...	...	...	16.4	...	16.4	...	...	...	19.4	...	19.4
Value added tax	...	...	...	...	...	...	...	...	...	...	...	...
Other adjustments	...	...	...	...	...	...	...	...	...	...	...	...
Total	88.5	...	81.9	...	...	208.5	...	...	112.1	22.9	...	269.8

Botswana

4.6 Cost Components of Value Added, ISIC Divisions
(Continued)

Million Botswana pula — Fiscal year beginning 1 July

1974 / 1975

	Compensation of Employees	Capital Consumption	Net Operating Surplus	Indirect Taxes	Less: Subsidies Received	Value Added	Compensation of Employees	Capital Consumption	Net Operating Surplus	Indirect Taxes	Less: Subsidies Received	Value Added
of which General Government:												
1 Agriculture, hunting, forestry and fishing	...	...	...	...	...	...	...	...	...	...	...	...
2 Mining and quarrying	...	...	...	...	...	...	...	...	...	...	...	...
3 Manufacturing	...	...	...	...	...	...	...	...	...	...	...	...
4 Electricity, gas and water	...	...	...	...	...	...	...	...	...	...	...	...
5 Construction	...	...	...	...	...	...	...	...	...	...	...	...
6 Wholesale and retail trade, restaurants and hotels	...	...	...	...	...	...	...	...	...	...	...	...
7 Transport and communication	...	...	...	...	...	...	...	...	...	...	...	...
8 Finance, insurance, real estate & business services	...	...	...	...	...	...	...	...	...	...	...	...
9 Community, social and personal services	...	...	...	...	...	...	...	...	...	...	...	...
Total, Industries of General Government	...	...	...	...	...	...	...	...	...	...	...	...
Producers of Government Services	...	...	...	...	...	...	...	...	...	...	...	...
Total, General Government	...	...	...	...	...	...	...	...	...	...	...	...

1976 / 1977

	Compensation of Employees	Capital Consumption	Net Operating Surplus	Indirect Taxes	Less: Subsidies Received	Value Added	Compensation of Employees	Capital Consumption	Net Operating Surplus	Indirect Taxes	Less: Subsidies Received	Value Added
All Producers												
1 Agriculture, hunting, forestry and fishing	13.8	1.6	58.9	0.1	...	74.4	14.6	2.4	54.9	-	0.2	71.7
2 Mining and quarrying	15.1	10.5	15.9	0.5	...	42.0	15.3	17.1	23.4	-	...	55.8
3 Manufacturing	8.9	1.7	13.4	1.3	...	25.3	12.3	2.1	9.3	0.7	...	24.4
4 Electricity, gas and water	3.9	1.4	3.9	-	...	9.2	3.3	1.6	5.1	-	...	10.0
5 Construction	9.8	1.8	5.1	0.1	1.5	15.3	9.4	2.0	5.7	-	...	17.1
6 Wholesale and retail trade, restaurants and hotels	8.7	2.7	16.3	0.3	...	28.0	10.7	1.8	20.0	0.5	-	33.0
7 Transport, storage and communication	6.6	2.5	2.1	0.7	...	11.9	7.2	3.0	4.0	0.8	...	15.0
8 Finance, insurance, real estate and business services	7.6	4.6	12.4	-	...	24.6	9.9	5.8	14.0	0.2	...	29.9
9 Community, social and personal services	1.0	0.2	1.9	0.2	...	3.3	1.4	0.4	2.1	-	...	3.9
Statistical discrepancy	...	...	...	...	...	...	...	...	...	...	...	...
Total, Industries	75.4	27.0	130.0	3.2	1.5	234.0	84.1	36.2	138.6	2.2	10.2	260.8
Producers of Government Services	45.5	2.5	-	-	...	48.0	49.8	2.7	-	-	...	52.5
Other Producers	8.6	0.3	0.2	-	...	9.2	10.6	0.3	0.3	-	...	11.3
Total	129.5	29.8	130.2	3.2	1.5	291.2	144.5	39.2	138.9	2.2	10.2	324.6
Imputed bank service charge	...	...	-7.9	...	...	-7.9	...	...	-9.3	...	...	-9.3
Import duties	...	...	...	27.5	...	27.5	...	...	...	38.9	...	38.9
Value added tax	...	...	...	...	...	...	...	...	...	...	...	...
Other adjustments	...	...	...	...	...	...	...	...	...	...	...	...
Total	129.5	29.8	122.3	30.7	1.5	310.8	144.5	39.2	129.6	41.1	-0.2	354.2
of which General Government:												
1 Agriculture, hunting, forestry and fishing	...	...	...	...	...	...	...	...	...	...	...	...
2 Mining and quarrying	...	...	...	...	...	...	...	...	...	...	...	...
3 Manufacturing	0.2	...	...	...	...	0.2	0.2	...	...	...	...	0.2
4 Electricity, gas and water	1.1	...	...	...	...	1.1	1.2	...	...	...	...	1.2
5 Construction	1.8	...	...	...	...	1.8	1.8	...	...	...	...	1.8
6 Wholesale and retail trade, restaurants and hotels	...	...	...	...	...	...	...	...	...	...	...	...
7 Transport and communication	2.4	1.0	1.2	-	...	4.6	2.7	1.1	1.7	...	...	5.5
8 Finance, insurance, real estate & business services	...	...	...	...	...	...	...	...	...	...	...	...
9 Community, social and personal services	...	...	...	...	...	...	...	...	...	...	...	...
Total, Industries of General Government	5.5	1.0	1.2	-	...	7.7	5.9	1.1	1.7	-	...	8.7
Producers of Government Services	...	...	...	...	...	...	...	...	...	...	...	...
Total, General Government	...	...	...	...	...	...	...	...	...	...	...	...

Botswana

4.6 Cost Components of Value Added, ISIC Divisions

Million Botswana pula — Fiscal year beginning 1 July

	Compensation of Employees	Capital Consumption	Net Operating Surplus	Indirect Taxes	Less: Subsidies Received	Value Added	Compensation of Employees	Capital Consumption	Net Operating Surplus	Indirect Taxes	Less: Subsidies Received	Value Added
	\multicolumn{6}{c|}{1978}	\multicolumn{6}{c}{1979}

All Producers

	Comp. Emp.	Cap. Cons.	Net Op. Surp.	Ind. Tax	Subs.	VA	Comp. Emp.	Cap. Cons.	Net Op. Surp.	Ind. Tax	Subs.	VA
1 Agriculture, hunting, forestry and fishing	16.3	1.7	60.6	-	-0.5	78.1	16.6	1.5	57.2	-	-	75.3
2 Mining and quarrying	17.4	17.3	82.7	-	...	117.4	21.5	33.1	163.0	-	-	217.6
3 Manufacturing	12.7	1.7	25.8	2.6	...	42.8	15.6	1.8	11.5	0.3	-	29.2
4 Electricity, gas and water	4.7	1.7	5.1	-	...	11.5	7.3	2.1	5.6	-	-	15.0
5 Construction	13.6	1.3	6.4	0.1	...	21.4	24.0	2.8	9.6	0.1	0.1	36.4
6 Wholesale and retail trade, restaurants and hotels	12.7	1.3	30.5	0.3	...	44.8	15.7	2.6	37.9	16.2	0.1	72.3
7 Transport, storage and communication	7.9	2.9	1.6	1.0	...	13.4	8.6	3.0	1.6	0.4	-	13.6
8 Finance, insurance, real estate and business services	14.6	6.4	25.3	0.1	...	46.4	16.3	7.3	46.7	0.2	-	70.5
9 Community, social and personal services	14.3	0.8	2.7	0.4	...	18.2	15.6	0.6	4.5	0.2	-	20.9
Statistical discrepancy	...	...	...	...	...	...	...	...	...	...	...	...
Total, Industries	114.2	35.1	240.7	4.5	-0.5	394.0	141.2	54.8	337.6	17.4	0.2	550.8
Producers of Government Services	66.9	3.3	-	-	...	70.2	77.1	4.4	-	0.1	-	81.6
Other Producers	...	...	...	...	...	...	...	...	...	...	...	...
Total	181.1	38.4	240.7	4.5	-0.5	464.2	218.3	59.2	337.6	17.5	0.2	632.4
Imputed bank service charge	...	...	-17.6	...	...	-17.6	...	...	-27.7	...	...	-27.7
Import duties	...	...	...	57.6	...	57.6	...	...	...	...	...	...
Value added tax	...	...	...	...	...	...	...	...	...	84.7	...	84.7
Other adjustments	...	...	...	...	...	...	...	...	...	...	...	...
Total	181.1	38.4	223.1	62.1	-0.5	504.2	218.3	59.2	309.9	102.2	0.2	689.4

of which General Government:

	Comp. Emp.	Cap. Cons.	Net Op. Surp.	Ind. Tax	Subs.	VA	Comp. Emp.	Cap. Cons.	Net Op. Surp.	Ind. Tax	Subs.	VA
1 Agriculture, hunting, forestry and fishing	...	...	...	...	...	...	...	...	...	...	...	...
2 Mining and quarrying	...	...	...	...	...	...	...	...	...	...	...	...
3 Manufacturing	0.2	...	...	...	...	0.2	...	...	...	...	...	...
4 Electricity, gas and water	1.9	...	...	...	...	1.9	...	...	...	...	...	...
5 Construction	2.2	...	...	...	...	2.2	...	...	...	...	...	...
6 Wholesale and retail trade, restaurants and hotels	...	...	...	...	...	...	...	...	...	...	...	...
7 Transport and communication	3.6	1.2	0.9	-	...	5.7	...	...	...	...	...	...
8 Finance, insurance, real estate & business services	...	...	...	...	...	...	...	...	...	...	...	...
9 Community, social and personal services	...	...	...	...	...	...	...	...	...	...	...	...
Total, Industries of General Government	7.9	1.2	0.9	-	...	10.0	...	...	...	...	...	...
Producers of Government Services	...	...	...	...	...	...	...	...	...	...	...	...
Total, General Government	...	...	...	...	...	...	...	...	...	...	...	...

4.9 Supply of Goods and Services, in Current Prices

Million Botswana pula — Fiscal year beginning 1 July

	Gross Domestic Output Marketed	Gross Domestic Output Non-Marketed	Imports c.i.f.	Import Duties	Trade & Transport Margins	Value Added Tax	TOTAL SUPPLY

1973

	Marketed	Non-Marketed	Imports c.i.f.	Import Duties	Trade & Transport Margins	VAT	TOTAL SUPPLY
1 Agriculture, hunting, forestry and fishing	31.1	47.6	2.8	0.1	3.3	...	84.9
2 Mining and quarrying	34.7	0.1	1.9	0.4	4.3	...	41.4
3 Manufacturing	51.8	1.6	107.0	12.9	13.9	...	187.2
4 Electricity, gas and water	6.3	...	...	...	...	...	6.3
5 Construction	43.7	2.5	...	...	...	...	46.2
6 Wholesale and retail trade, restaurants and hotels	24.5	0.1	...	...	-21.5	...	3.1
7 Transport and communications	27.7	0.9	13.4	...	...	...	42.0
8 Finance, insurance, real estate and business services	18.3	...	7.0	...	...	...	25.3
9 Community, social and personal services	5.2	0.1	0.7	...	...	...	6.0
Total, Industries	242.6	53.6	132.8	13.4	-	...	442.4
Producers of Government Services	...	...	...	...	...	...	...
Other Producers	...	...	...	...	...	...	...
Total	249.2	84.0	132.8	13.4	-	...	479.4

Botswana

4.9 Supply of Goods and Services, in Current Prices
(Continued)

Fiscal year beginning 1 July

Million Botswana pula

	Gross Domestic Output – Marketed	Gross Domestic Output – Non-Marketed	Imports c.i.f.	Import Duties	Trade & Transport Margins	Value Added Tax	TOTAL SUPPLY
1974							
1 Agriculture, hunting, forestry and fishing	38.6	44.3	2.2	0.2	4.0	...	89.3
2 Mining and quarrying	56.6	...	1.0	0.1	3.6	...	61.3
3 Manufacturing	60.9	3.5	125.0	16.1	22.2	...	227.7
4 Electricity, gas and water	11.8	0.5	...	...	...	...	12.3
5 Construction	45.8	2.3	...	...	...	...	48.1
6 Wholesale and retail trade, restaurants and hotels	32.3	0.1	1.5	...	-29.8	...	4.1
7 Transport and communications	33.8	0.5	15.2	...	...	...	49.5
8 Finance, insurance, real estate and business services	21.5	0.3	23.8	...	...	...	45.6
9 Community, social and personal services	5.8	0.1	0.6	...	...	...	6.5
Total, Industries	307.1	51.6	169.3	16.4	-	...	544.4
Producers of Government Services	...	...	...	...	...	...	...
Other Producers	...	...	...	...	...	...	...
Total	317.3	90.9	169.3	16.4	...	...	593.9
1975							
1 Agriculture, hunting, forestry and fishing	41.6	47.4	2.3	0.3	0.5	...	92.1
2 Mining and quarrying	80.5	-	1.1	0.2	5.6	...	87.4
3 Manufacturing	67.8	3.9	160.8	18.9	28.8	...	280.2
4 Electricity, gas and water	17.3	1.1	...	...	...	...	18.4
5 Construction	45.9	3.1	5.4	...	...	...	54.4
6 Wholesale and retail trade, restaurants and hotels	38.1	0.1	1.8	...	-34.9	...	5.1
7 Transport and communications	47.4	0.9	20.0	...	...	...	68.3
8 Finance, insurance, real estate and business services	29.4	...	15.8	...	...	...	45.2
9 Community, social and personal services	9.5	...	3.4	...	...	...	12.9
Total, Industries	377.5	56.5	210.6	19.4	-	...	664.0
Producers of Government Services	...	...	...	...	...	...	...
Other Producers	...	...	...	...	...	...	...
Total	391.7	110.8	210.6	19.4	-	...	732.5
1976							
1 Agriculture, hunting, forestry and fishing	49.7	52.2	3.6	0.6	0.7	...	106.8
2 Mining and quarrying	95.9	...	1.0	0.1	4.4	...	101.4
3 Manufacturing	80.5	4.7	188.4	26.8	30.6	...	331.0
4 Electricity, gas and water	19.8	...	...	...	...	...	19.8
5 Construction	37.4	3.3	...	...	...	...	40.7
6 Wholesale and retail trade, restaurants and hotels	46.4	0.2	2.0	...	-35.7	...	12.9
7 Transport and communications	51.3	...	31.7	...	...	...	83.0
8 Finance, insurance, real estate and business services	37.0	0.5	30.6	...	...	...	68.1
9 Community, social and personal services	6.2	...	...	...	...	...	6.2
Total, Industries	424.2	60.9	257.3	27.5	-	...	769.9
Producers of Government Services	...	...	...	...	...	...	...
Other Producers	...	...	...	...	...	...	...
Total	441.8	136.7	257.3	27.5	-	...	863.3
1977							
1 Agriculture, hunting, forestry and fishing	36.2	62.4	-	-	0.7	...	99.3
2 Mining and quarrying	113.0	...	...	...	6.5	...	119.5
3 Manufacturing	73.1	5.1	225.8	38.9	32.6	...	375.5
4 Electricity, gas and water	22.7	...	...	...	...	...	22.7
5 Construction	41.4	3.7	...	...	...	...	45.1

Botswana

4.9 Supply of Goods and Services, in Current Prices
(Continued)

Million Botswana pula — Fiscal year beginning 1 July

	Gross Domestic Output – Marketed	Gross Domestic Output – Non-Marketed	Imports c.i.f.	Import Duties	Trade & Transport Margins	Value Added Tax	TOTAL SUPPLY
6 Wholesale and retail trade, restaurants and hotels	53.5	0.1	2.4	-	-39.8	...	16.2
7 Transport and communications	52.7	-	31.6	...	...	...	84.3
8 Finance, insurance, real estate and business services	43.4	0.6	36.7	...	...	...	80.7
9 Community, social and personal services	9.4	...	...	...	...	...	9.4
Total, Industries	445.4	71.9	296.5	38.9	...	...	852.7
Producers of Government Services	...	...	...	...	...	...	...
Other Producers	...	...	...	...	...	...	...
Total	463.9	162.6	296.5	38.9	-	...	961.9
1978							
1 Agriculture, hunting, forestry and fishing	49.7	51.7	...	...	0.3	...	101.7
2 Mining and quarrying	194.0	...	...	...	12.3	...	196.3
3 Manufacturing	123.2	5.9	302.7	57.6	50.1	...	539.5
4 Electricity, gas and water	25.5	...	...	...	...	...	25.5
5 Construction	60.1	3.9	...	...	...	...	64.0
6 Wholesale and retail trade, restaurants and hotels	132.2	...	2.9	-57.6	-62.7	...	14.8
7 Transport and communications	...	...	...	...	...	...	...
8 Finance, insurance, real estate and business services	59.2	...	40.4	...	...	...	99.6
9 Community, social and personal services	28.8	...	...	...	...	...	28.8
Total, Industries	725.5	61.5	374.9	...	...	...	1151.9
Producers of Government Services	...	...	...	...	...	...	...
Other Producers	...	...	...	...	...	...	...
Total	729.1	157.9	374.9	-	-	...	1261.9

Brazil

General note. The preparation of national accounts statistics in Brazil is undertaken by Instituto Brasileiro de Economia, Rio de Janeiro. The official estimates are published in the series 'Conjuntura Economica'. The most detailed description of the sources and methods used for the national accounts estimation is found in 'Contas Nacionais do Brasil, Conceitos e Metodologia', published by Instituto Brasileiro de Economia in 1972. The estimates are generally in accordance with the classifications and definitions recommended in the United Nations System of National Accounts(SNA). The following tables have been prepared from successive replies to the United Nations national accounts questionnaire. When the scope and coverage of the estimates differ for conceptual or statistical reasons from the definitions and classifications recommended in SNA, a footnote is indicated to the relevant tables.

Sources and methods :

(a) Gross domestic product. The main approach used to estimate GDP is the income approach, but the production approach is also used.

(b) Expenditure on the gross domestic product. The expenditure approach is used to estimate government final consumption expenditure, increase in stocks and exports and imports of goods and services. A combination of the commodity-flow method and the expenditure approach is used to estimate gross fixed capital formation, whereas private final consumption expenditure is taken as a residual. Government consumption expenditure is estimated by the Center of Fiscal Studies, based on information from government budgetary and accounting statements. Bench-mark estimates on production and imports of capital goods have been prepared for 1949, 1959 and 1970 based on industrial censuses and foreign trade statistics. These estimates are extrapolated by an index of material purchases and, adjusted for business mark-ups and value added. For urban construction, bench-mark estimates are obtained from the industrial censuses held in 1950, 1960 and 1970. The bench-mark estimates are extrapolated by the use of an indicator made up of data on consumption of construction materials and wholesale prices. Bench-mark estimates for rural construction are based on the censuses of agriculture in 1940 and 1950 and the demographic censuses of 1950, 1960 and 1970. Extrapolation is done by the estimated growth of rural population and a general price index. Data on exports and imports of goods and services are prepared by the Central Bank. To calculate constant prices, government consumption expenditure is deflated by the implicit price index of gross domestic product, whereas value added of private consumption expenditure is calculated as a residual. Gross fixed capital formation of the base-year is extrapolated by different volume indexes. The value of the 1970 exports of goods is extrapolated by a quantum index. In order to include the value of exports of services, the obtained value is expanded by the ratio of total exports to export of goods.

(c) Cost-structure of the gross domestic product. Estimates for wages and salaries are based on the demographic and economic censuses carried out usually at 10-year intervals. For non-census years social security data are used as estimators. Operating surplus is calculated as a residual. Depreciation is estimated for all years at 5 per cent of the gross domestic product. Estimates of indirect taxes and subsidies are obtained from the federal, state and municipal budgets and balance sheets.

(d) Gross domestic product by kind of economic activity. The table of GDP by kind of economic activity is prepared in net factor values. Depreciation and indirect taxes net of subsidies are estimated as aggregates only. Combinations of the income approach and the production approach used to estimate value added of all industries except the agricultural sector, for which only the production approach is used. Factor income data are not available for this sector. The censuses of 1949, 1959 and 1970 provide agricultural bench-mark data. For the years after 1959, estimates of gross product are made by using value indexes. The rates of intermediate consumption found in 1959 and 1970 censuses have been interpolated and extrapolated to apply to other years. For mining and quarrying, manufacturing and construction the census data for 1949, 1959 and 1970 are used as bench-marks. For mining and manufacturing, value indexes for the most important products are used as estimators for the years after 1970. For the estimation of the value of construction after 1970, indicators based on construction inputs are used. In the calculation of value added, data from the demographic census and business income tax files are also used. Bench-mark estimates for the trade sector are based on the censuses of commerce held in 1950, 1960 and 1970. Small units are covered by the industrial or demographic census. For the transport sector, data are provided by the authorities of air transport, railways and maritime transport. For road transportation, special surveys of freight and passenger transport enterprises are held every second year. Data on self-employed carriers are estimated through data from the demographic census. The censuses held in 1950 and 1970 provide the basis for bench-mark estimates for the financial institutions. Estimates for other years are based on accounts data from various sources. Rent estimation is based on the demographic censuses of 1950, 1960 and 1970 and includes imputed rents for owner-occupied dwellings. For non-census years the main indicator is the series of property tax revenues. For the community, social and personal services, government data are obtained from official budgetary and accounting statements. Constant prices for the agricultural sector are obtained through extrapolating the value added of 1970 by quantity indexes of output for each of the three subsectors: farming, livestock production and forestry. For mining and quarrying, a quantity index of output based on the production data for the three most important mineral products is applied to the value added of 1970. Value added of manufacturing is extrapolated by a quantity index of output, based on production data for approximately 400 products. Value added of construction is extrapolated by an index based on the production of principal materials used in the sector. For the trade sector, value added is extrapolated by a quantity index of output. Value added of the transport sector is extrapolated by various output indicators. For financing, insurance, real estate and business services, value added is deflated by the cost of living index. Value added of public administration and defense is deflated by the implicit price index of gross domestic product, whereas value added of other private services is deflated by the cost of living index.

1.1 Expenditure on the Gross Domestic Product, in Current Prices

Million Brazilian cruzeiros

	1970	1971	1972	1973	1974	1975	1976	1977	1978	1979	1980
1 General government final consumption expenditure	22006	28665	37332	50677	69448	106762	170454	240217	347506	584963	1159731
2 Private final consumption expenditure a	141234	187325	245882	328663	483328	698463	1136111	1725125	2648651	4544256	9457451
3 Gross capital formation	47694	68010	90690	135377	229618	287051	412707	574329	776756	1234494	2768850
a Increase in stocks a	2571	6772	9407	21420	52913	24313	21555	36777	-12089	-34680	-
b Gross fixed capital formation	45123	61238	81283	113957	176705	262738	391152	537552	788845	1269174	2768850
4 Exports of goods and services	13660	16679	25203	40152	57174	74815	114593	180623	242101	431639	1121155
5 Less: Imports of goods and services	14476	21164	30706	46123	99064	115029	153632	197193	285216	555950	1402902
Equals: Gross Domestic Product	210118	279515	368401	508746	740504	1052062	1680233	2523101	3729798	6239402	13104285

a) For 1980, item 'Increase in stocks' is included in item 'Private final consumption expenditure'.

1.2 Expenditure on the Gross Domestic Product, in Constant Prices

Million Brazilian cruzeiros

	1970	1971	1972	1973	1974	1975	1976	1977	1978	1979	1980
					At constant prices of:1970						
1 General government final consumption expenditure	22006	24129	26514	29705	30621	34992	38364	37967	38936	41801	42565
2 Private final consumption expenditure a	141234	157547	173170	189326	204755	220788	243432	258708	281644	306113	331558
3 Gross capital formation	47694	58031	65371	82167	105348	100125	104608	104107	101341	104411	113173
a Increase in stocks a	2571	5622	6597	12894	24622	8883	5502	6587	-1574	-2896	-
b Gross fixed capital formation	45123	52409	58774	69273	80726	91242	99106	97520	102915	107307	113173
4 Exports of goods and services	13660	13647	18174	23004	19264	20849	23361	27186	26503	26549	26951
5 Less: Imports of goods and services	14476	18022	21632	26045	33465	31950	31553	29164	30500	33004	33287
Equals: Gross Domestic Product	210118	235332	261597	298157	326523	344804	378212	398804	417924	445870	480960

a) For 1980, item 'Increase in stocks' is included in item 'Private final consumption expenditure'.

Brazil

1.3 Cost Components of the Gross Domestic Product

Million Brazilian cruzeiros

	1970	1971	1972	1973	1974	1975	1976	1977	1978	1979	1980
1 Indirect taxes, net	30937	38313	51454	69471	93400	116871	195090	294066	416514	613930	1365067
a Indirect taxes paid	32532	40396	53847	73452	102716	133251	210937	315248	454978	674265	1512580
b Less: Subsidies received	1595	2083	2393	3981	9316	16380	15847	21182	38464	60335	147513
2 Consumption of fixed capital	10408	13845	18244	25200	36695	51873	82723	124073	182194	303662	634638
3 Compensation of employees paid by resident producers to:	168773	227357	298703	414075	610409	883318	1402420	2104962	3131090	5321810	11104580
4 Net operating surplus											
Equals: Gross Domestic Product	210118	279515	368401	508746	740504	1052062	1680233	2523101	3729798	6239402	13104285

1.8 Capital Transactions of The Nation, Summary

Million Brazilian cruzeiros

	1970	1971	1972	1973	1974	1975	1976	1977	1978	1979	1980
Finance of Gross Capital Formation											
Gross saving	45036	61066	81876	124936	181546	232821	348841	517542	649807	947479	2082817
1 Consumption of fixed capital	10408	13845	18244	25200	36695	51873	82723	124073	182194	303662	634638
2 Net saving	34628	47221	63632	99737	144851	180949	266118	393468	467613	643817	1448179
Less: Surplus of the nation on current transactions	...	...	...	...	...	...	...	...	...	...	...
Statistical discrepancy a	2658	6944	8814	10440	48072	54230	63865	56787	126950	287015	686032
Finance of Gross Capital Formation	47694	68010	90690	135376	229618	287051	412707	574329	776757	1234494	2768849
Gross Capital Formation											
Increase in stocks	2571	6772	9407	21420	52913	24313	21555	36777	-12089	-34680	-
Gross fixed capital formation	45123	61238	81283	113957	176705	262738	391152	537552	788845	1269174	2768850
Gross Capital Formation	47694	68010	90690	135377	229618	287051	412707	574329	776756	1234494	2768850

a) Relating to capital transfers received from the rest of the world.

1.10 Gross Domestic Product by Kind of Activity, in Current Prices

Million Brazilian cruzeiros

	1970	1971	1972	1973	1974	1975	1976	1977	1978	1979	1980
1 Agriculture, hunting, forestry and fishing	17127	23686	31218	46921	70241	97067	179283	314641	421933	708848	1446050
2 Mining and quarrying	1294	1550	1869	1763	3401	5610	7569	9619	12775	20959	56175
3 Manufacturing	45020	61219	81977	116942	179295	254344	390636	563876	823751	1370656	2951922
4 Electricity, gas and water	4301	5832	7323	10001	13658	20491	28885	39159	52139	66269	126339
5 Construction	9934	12555	16649	22944	34988	47398	73078	107286	157625	268277	643624
6 Wholesale and retail trade, restaurants and hotels a	26283	35965	48214	68782	105420	150880	236241	351535	503213	832799	1786281
7 Transport, storage and communication	9583	12480	16851	22654	32688	48442	74215	110743	160835	266860	562328
8 Finance, insurance, real estate and business services b	23131	31827	40490	54076	73006	114488	189697	287418	515363	986030	1876968
9 Community, social and personal services abc	32100	42243	54112	69992	97712	144598	222815	320685	483456	801112	1654892
Total, Industries	168773	227357	298703	414075	610409	883318	1402419	2104962	3131090	5321810	11104579
Producers of Government Services c	...	...	...	...	...	...	...	...	...	...	...
Other Producers c	...	...	...	...	...	...	...	...	...	...	...
Subtotal d	168773	227357	298703	414075	610409	883318	1402419	2104962	3131090	5321810	11104579
Less: Imputed bank service charge	...	...	...	...	...	...	...	...	...	...	...
Plus: Import duties	...	...	...	...	...	...	...	...	...	...	...
Plus: Value added tax	...	...	...	...	...	...	...	...	...	...	...
Plus: Other adjustments e	41345	52158	69698	94671	130095	168744	277814	418139	598708	917592	1999706
Equals: Gross Domestic Product	210118	279515	368401	508746	740504	1052062	1680233	2523101	3729798	6239402	13104285

a) Restaurants and hotels are included in item 'Community, social and personal services'.
b) Business services are included in item 'Community, social and personal services'.
c) Items 'Other producers' and 'Producers of government services' are included in item 'Community, social and personal services'.
d) Net domestic product in factor values.
e) Relating to depreciation and indirect taxes net of subsidies.

1.12 Relations Among National Accounting Aggregates

Million Brazilian cruzeiros

	1970	1971	1972	1973	1974	1975	1976	1977	1978	1979	1980
Gross Domestic Product	210118	279515	368401	508746	740504	1052062	1680233	2523101	3729798	6239402	13104285
Plus: Net factor income received from abroad	-1842	-2459	-3311	-4469	-6183	-14015	-24827	-40217	-83835	-162704	-404285
Equals: Gross National Product	208276	277056	365090	504277	734321	1038047	1655406	2482884	3645963	6076698	12700000
Less: Consumption of fixed capital	10408	13845	18244	25200	36695	51873	82723	124073	182194	303662	634638
Less: Net indirect taxes paid to supranational organisations	...	...	...	...	...	...	...	...	...	...	...

Brazil

1.12 Relations Among National Accounting Aggregates
(Continued)

Million Brazilian cruzeiros

	1970	1971	1972	1973	1974	1975	1976	1977	1978	1979	1980
Equals: National Income at Market Prices	197868	263211	346846	479077	697626	986174	1572683	2358811	3463769	5773036	12065362
Plus: Net current transfers received from abroad	...	...	...	...	...	...	...	...	...	...	...
Equals: National Disposable Income at Market Prices	197868	263211	346846	479077	697626	986174	1572683	2358811	3463769	5773036	12065362
Less: Final consumption	163240	215990	283214	379340	552775	805225	1306564	1965342	2996157	5129219	10617182
Equals: Net Saving	34628	47221	63632	99737	144851	180949	266119	393469	467612	643817	1448180
Less: Surplus of the nation on current transactions	...	...	...	...	...	...	...	...	...	...	...
Statistical discrepancy	2658	6944	8814	10440	48072	54230	63865	56786	126951	287015	686031
Equals: Net Capital Formation	37286	54165	72446	110177	192923	235179	329984	450255	594563	930832	2134211

British Virgin Islands

Source. Statistics Office, Finance Department, Road Town, Tortola.
General note. The estimates shown in the following tables have been prepared in accordance with the United Nations System of National Accounts so far as the existing data would permit.

1.1 Expenditure on the Gross Domestic Product, in Current Prices

Thousand United States dollars

	1970	1971	1972	1973	1974	1975	1976	1977	1978	1979	1980
1 General government final consumption expenditure	2188	2361	2550	2181	2956	2570	3424	3539	3940	...	...
2 Private final consumption expenditure	9032	8188	6348	8534	10465	11367	10687	8727	9841	...	...
3 Gross capital formation [a]	13754	9899	7053	8289	9351	9778	8521	7800	10565	...	...
a Increase in stocks [a]	403	240	276	337	818	209	321	232	-	...	...
b Gross fixed capital formation	13351	9659	6777	7952	8533	9569	8200	7568	10565	...	...
4 Exports of goods and services	6239	7298	8728	10332	11690	14383	17310	20621	24690	...	...
5 Less: Imports of goods and services	13433	12087	10962	13519	15496	17408	18561	18834	21730	...	...
Statistical discrepancy [a,b]	-1833	-1890	658	455	489	683	1918	2235	1204	...	...
Equals: Gross Domestic Product	15947	13769	14375	16272	19455	21373	23299	24088	28510	...	...

a) Including also unrecorded increase in stocks.
b) For 1978, item 'Increase in stocks' is included in item 'Statistical discrepancy'.

1.3 Cost Components of the Gross Domestic Product

Thousand United States dollars

	1970	1971	1972	1973	1974	1975	1976	1977	1978	1979	1980
1 Indirect taxes, net	1804	1327	1740	2150	2219	2363	2340	2632	3280	...	...
a Indirect taxes paid	1900	1423	1821	2258	2346	2538	2537	2835	3500	...	...
b Less: Subsidies received	96	96	81	108	127	175	197	203	220	...	...
2 Consumption of fixed capital [a]	...	...	...	...	...	...	...	...	...	...	...
3 Compensation of employees paid by resident producers to:	8860	8368	8803	9210	11229	11786	13286	13068	14974	...	...
4 Net operating surplus [a]	5283	4074	3832	4912	6007	7224	7673	8388	10256	...	...
Equals: Gross Domestic Product	15947	13769	14375	16272	19455	21373	23299	24088	28510	...	...

a) Item 'Consumption of fixed capital' is included in item 'Net Operating Surplus'.

1.4 General Government Current Receipts and Disbursements

Thousand United States dollars

	1970	1971	1972	1973	1974	1975	1976	1977	1978	1979	1980
Receipts											
1 Property and entrepreneurial income	...	...	...	...	...	...	...	...	...	...	...
2 Taxes, fees and contributions	2499	3358	3906	4141	4173	4233	4748	4846	...	...	...
a Indirect taxes	1900	1423	1821	2258	2346	2538	2537	2835	...	...	...
b Direct taxes	465	607	685	744	891	799	1264	1333	...	...	...
c Social security contributions	84	1266	1325	1069	848	806	855	572	...	...	...
d Compulsory fees, fines and penalties	50	62	75	70	88	90	92	106	...	...	...
3 Other current receipts	...	...	...	...	...	...	...	...	...	...	...
Total Current Receipts of General Government	2499	3358	3906	4141	4173	4233	4748	4846	...	...	...
Disbursements											
1 General government final consumption expenditure	2188	2361	2550	2181	2956	2570	3424	3539	...	...	...
a Compensation of employees	1733	1902	2094	2213	2738	2686	3243	3263	2939	...	...
b Consumption of fixed capital									...	...	...
c Purchases of goods and services, net	455	459	456	-32	218	-116	181	276			
d Less: Own account production of fixed assets									...	...	...
e Indirect taxes paid, net									...	...	...
2 Property income paid	296	433	743	775	779	686	626	588	...	...	...
3 Subsidies	96	96	81	108	127	175	197	203	...	...	...
4 Other current transfers paid	162	276	367	403	547	463	619	614	...	...	...
a Social security benefits and social assistance grants	162	276	367	403	547	463	619	614	...	...	...
b Other	...	...	...	...	...	...	...	...	...	...	...
5 Net saving	-243	192	165	674	-236	339	-118	-98	...	...	...
Total Current Disbursements and Net Saving of General Government	2499	3358	3906	4141	4173	4233	4748	4846	...	...	...

British Virgin Islands

1.7 External Transactions on Current Account, Summary

Thousand United States dollars

	1970	1971	1972	1973	1974	1975	1976	1977	1978	1979	1980
Payments to the Rest of the World											
1 Imports of goods and services	13433	12087	10962	13519	15496	17408	18561	18834	...	...	...
a Imports of merchandise c.i.f.	11658	10162	8867	11139	12766	14350	15102	15149	...	...	...
b Other	1775	1925	2095	2380	2730	3058	3459	3685	...	...	...
2 Factor income paid to the rest of the world	2970	2497	1976	2611	3105	3425	3743	4047	...	...	...
3 Indirect taxes paid to supranational organizations	...	...	...	...	...	...	...	...	...	...	...
4 Current transfers to the rest of the world	23	33	51	102	63	68	74	89	...	...	...
5 Surplus of the nation on current transactions	-9575	-5514	-2392	-4198	-5419	-4944	-3420	-913	...	...	...
Payments to the Rest of the World and Surplus of the Nation on Current Transactions	6851	9103	10597	12034	13245	15957	18958	22057	...	...	...
Receipts From The Rest of the World											
1 Exports of goods and services	6239	7298	8728	10332	11690	14383	17310	20621	...	...	...
a Exports of merchandise f.o.b.	253	406	243	877	690	1137	910	911	...	...	...
b Other	5986	6892	8485	9455	11000	13246	16400	19710	...	...	...
2 Factor income received from rest of the world	602	682	684	736	820	881	931	965	...	...	...
3 Subsidies received from supranational organisations	...	...	...	...	...	...	...	...	...	...	...
4 Current transfers from rest of the world	10	1123	1185	966	735	693	717	471	...	...	...
Receipts from the Rest of the World on Current Transactions	6851	9103	10597	12034	13245	15957	18958	22057	...	...	...

1.10 Gross Domestic Product by Kind of Activity, in Current Prices

Thousand United States dollars

	1970	1971	1972	1973	1974	1975	1976	1977	1978	1979	1980
1 Agriculture, hunting, forestry and fishing	1139	1052	1085	1497	1827	1959	2137	2366	2577	...	...
2 Mining and quarrying	945	738	687	805	919	1258	1206	1271	1700	...	...
3 Manufacturing										...	...
4 Electricity, gas and water	208	245	265	258	364	339	412	469	495	...	...
5 Construction	4813	3146	2458	2285	2872	3434	3071	2388	3340	...	...
6 Wholesale and retail trade, restaurants and hotels [a]	2441	2557	2896	3698	4644	4912	5985	6295	7574	...	...
7 Transport, storage and communication	1306	1192	1385	1483	1530	1729	2002	2253	2737	...	...
8 Finance, insurance, real estate and business services [b]	2413	2575	2578	2948	3636	4002	4036	4394	4800	...	...
9 Community, social and personal services [a,b]	179	189	211	237	257	261	269	303	358	...	...
Total, Industries	13444	11694	11565	13211	16049	17894	19118	19739	23581	...	...
Producers of Government Services	1383	1637	1864	1860	2314	2270	2746	2808	2939	...	...
Other Producers	...	...	...	...	...	...	...	...	...	...	...
Subtotal [c]	14827	13331	13429	15071	18363	20164	21864	22547	26520	...	...
Less: Imputed bank service charge	684	889	794	949	1127	1154	905	1091	1290	...	...
Plus: Import duties	...	...	...	...	...	...	...	...	...	...	...
Plus: Value added tax	...	...	...	...	...	...	...	...	...	...	...
Plus: Other adjustments [d]	1804	1327	1740	2150	2219	2363	2340	2632	3280	...	...
Equals: Gross Domestic Product	15947	13769	14375	16272	19455	21373	23299	24088	28510	...	...

a) Boat charter is included in item 'Restaurants and hotels'.
b) Medical services are included in item 'Finance, insurance, real estate and business services'.
c) Gross domestic product in factor values.
d) Referring to indirect taxes net of subsidies.

1.11 Gross Domestic Product by Kind of Activity, in Constant Prices

Thousand United States dollars

	1970	1971	1972	1973	1974	1975	1976	1977	1978	1979	1980
				At constant prices of:1976							
1 Agriculture, hunting, forestry and fishing	1940	1790	1850	2060	2110	2090	2137	2200	2250	...	...
2 Mining and quarrying	1160	970	900	1020	1090	1310	1206	1220	1450	...	...
3 Manufacturing										...	...
4 Electricity, gas and water	250	300	320	310	370	340	412	440	450	...	...
5 Construction	6340	4450	3480	3160	3700	3980	3071	2310	3230	...	...

British Virgin Islands

1.11 Gross Domestic Product by Kind of Activity, in Constant Prices
(Continued)

Thousand United States dollars

	1970	1971	1972	1973	1974	1975	1976	1977	1978	1979	1980
					At constant prices of:1976						
6 Wholesale and retail trade, restaurants and hotels [a]	2840	3010	3390	4200	4950	5210	5985	6500	7340	...	...
7 Transport, storage and communication	1440	1380	1600	1680	1820	1940	2002	2320	2510	...	...
8 Finance, insurance, real estate and business services [b]	4250	4350	4260	4460	4590	4530	4036	4170	4690		
9 Community, social and personal services [ab]	210	230	260	290	300	310	269	310	300	...	...
Total, Industries	18430	16480	16060	17180	18930	19710	19118	19470	22220	...	...
Producers of Government Services	1760	2080	2370	2370	2490	2580	2746	2860	3020		
Other Producers	...	...	...	...	...	...	...	...	...		
Subtotal [c]	20190	18560	18430	19550	21420	22290	21864	22330	25240	...	...
Less: Imputed bank service charge	910	1200	1060	1220	1300	1260	905	1090	1230		
Plus: Import duties	...	...	...	...	...	...	...	...	...		
Plus: Value added tax	...	...	...	...	...	...	...	...	...		
Plus: Other adjustments [d]	2150	1940	1940	2050	2250	2350	2340	2490	2820		
Equals: Gross Domestic Product	21430	19300	19310	20380	22370	23380	23299	23730	26830	...	...

a) Boat charter is included in item 'Restaurants and hotels'.
b) Medical services are included in item 'Finance, insurance, real estate and business services'.
c) Gross domestic product in factor values.
d) Referring to indirect taxes net of subsidies.

2.1 General Government Final Consumption Expenditure by Function, in Current Prices

Thousand United States dollars

	1970	1971	1972	1973	1974	1975	1976	1977	1978	1979	1980
1 General public services	909	937	1077	856	1176	832	1297	1452	...	...	...
2 Defence	...	...	...	...	...	...	...	...	...	...	...
3 Public order and safety	...	...	...	...	...	...	...	...	...	...	...
4 Education	597	651	665	656	820	802	941	976	...	...	...
5 Health	419	444	421	427	513	544	659	680	...	...	...
6 Social security and welfare	-	-	-	-	-	-	-	-	...		
7 Housing and community amenities	-	-	-	-	-	-	-	-	...		
8 Recreational, cultural and religious affairs	-	-	-	-	-	-	-	-			
9 Economic services	263	329	387	242	447	392	527	431	...	...	...
10 Other functions	-	-	-	-	-	-	-	-			
Total General Government Final Consumption Expenditure	2188	2361	2550	2181	2956	2570	3424	3539	...	...	...

2.3 Total General Government Outlays by Function and Type

Thousand United States dollars

	Final Consumption Expenditures Total	Compensation of Employees	Other	Subsidies	Other Current Transfers & Property Income	Total Current Disbursements	Gross Capital Formation	Other Capital Outlays	Total Outlays
					1970				
1 General public services	909	623	286	...	...	...	...	...	...
2 Defence	...	...	...	...	...	...	...	...	...
3 Public order and safety	...	...	...	...	...	...	...	...	...
4 Education	597	523	74	...	...	...	...	...	...
5 Health	419	307	112	...	...	...	...	...	...
6 Social security and welfare	-	-	-	...	...	...	...	...	...
7 Housing and community amenities	-	-	-	...	...	...	...	...	...
8 Recreation, culture and religion	-	-	-	...	...	...	...	...	...
9 Economic services	263	280	-17	...	...	...	...	...	...
10 Other functions	-	-	-	...	...	...	...	...	...
Total	2188	1733	455	96	458	2742	...	...	...

British Virgin Islands

2.3 Total General Government Outlays by Function and Type
(Continued)

Thousand United States dollars

		Final Consumption Expenditures				Other Current Transfers & Property Income	Total Current Disbursements	Gross Capital Formation	Other Capital Outlays	Total Outlays
		Total	Compensation of Employees	Other	Subsidies					

1971

1	General public services	937	695	242	...	...	...	...	...	...
2	Defence	...	...	...	...	...	...	...	...	...
3	Public order and safety	...	...	...	...	...	...	...	...	...
4	Education	651	579	72	...	...	...	...	...	...
5	Health	444	324	120	...	...	...	...	...	...
6	Social security and welfare	-	-	-	...	...	...	...	...	...
7	Housing and community amenities	-	-	-	...	...	...	...	...	...
8	Recreation, culture and religion	-	-	-	...	...	...	...	...	...
9	Economic services	329	304	25	...	...	...	...	...	...
10	Other functions	-	-	-	...	...	...	...	...	...
	Total	2361	1902	459	96	709	3166	...	...	...

1972

1	General public services	1077	806	271	...	...	...	...	...	...
2	Defence	...	...	...	...	...	...	...	...	...
3	Public order and safety	...	...	...	...	...	...	...	...	...
4	Education	665	598	67	...	...	...	...	...	...
5	Health	421	323	98	...	...	...	...	...	...
6	Social security and welfare	-	-	-	...	...	...	...	...	...
7	Housing and community amenities	-	-	-	...	...	...	...	...	...
8	Recreation, culture and religion	-	-	-	...	...	...	...	...	...
9	Economic services	387	367	20	...	...	...	...	...	...
10	Other functions	-	-	-	...	...	...	...	...	...
	Total	2550	2094	456	81	1110	3741	...	...	...

1973

1	General public services	856	851	5	...	...	...	...	...	...
2	Defence	...	...	...	...	...	...	...	...	...
3	Public order and safety	...	...	...	...	...	...	...	...	...
4	Education	656	603	53	...	...	...	...	...	...
5	Health	427	332	95	...	...	...	...	...	...
6	Social security and welfare	-	-	-	...	...	...	...	...	...
7	Housing and community amenities	-	-	-	...	...	...	...	...	...
8	Recreation, culture and religion	-	-	-	...	...	...	...	...	...
9	Economic services	242	427	-185	...	...	...	...	...	...
10	Other functions	-	-	-	...	...	...	...	...	...
	Total	2181	2213	-32	108	1178	3467	...	...	...

1974

1	General public services	1176	1061	115	...	...	...	...	...	...
2	Defence	...	...	...	...	...	...	...	...	...
3	Public order and safety	...	...	...	...	...	...	...	...	...
4	Education	820	754	66	...	...	...	...	...	...
5	Health	513	413	100	...	...	...	...	...	...
6	Social security and welfare	-	-	-	...	...	...	...	...	...
7	Housing and community amenities	-	-	-	...	...	...	...	...	...
8	Recreation, culture and religion	-	-	-	...	...	...	...	...	...
9	Economic services	447	510	-63	...	...	...	...	...	...
10	Other functions	-	-	-	...	...	...	...	...	...
	Total	2956	2738	218	127	1326	4409	...	...	...

British Virgin Islands

2.3 Total General Government Outlays by Function and Type
(Continued)

Thousand United States dollars

	Final Consumption Expenditures Total	Compensation of Employees	Other	Subsidies	Other Current Transfers & Property Income	Total Current Disbursements	Gross Capital Formation	Other Capital Outlays	Total Outlays
1975									
1 General public services	832	1017	-185	...	...	...	...	...	...
2 Defence	...	...	...	...	...	...	...	...	...
3 Public order and safety	...	...	...	...	...	...	...	...	...
4 Education	802	747	55	...	...	...	...	...	...
5 Health	544	406	138	...	...	...	...	...	...
6 Social security and welfare	-	-	-	...	...	...	...	...	...
7 Housing and community amenities	-	-	-	...	...	...	...	...	...
8 Recreation, culture and religion	-	-	-	...	...	...	...	...	...
9 Economic services	392	516	-124	...	...	...	...	...	...
10 Other functions	-	-	-	...	...	...	...	...	...
Total	2570	2686	-116	175	1149	3894	...	...	...
1976									
1 General public services	1297	1247	50	...	...	...	...	...	...
2 Defence	...	...	...	...	...	...	...	...	...
3 Public order and safety	...	...	...	...	...	...	...	...	...
4 Education	941	871	70	...	...	...	...	...	...
5 Health	659	499	160	...	...	...	...	...	...
6 Social security and welfare	-	-	-	...	...	...	...	...	...
7 Housing and community amenities	-	-	-	...	...	...	...	...	...
8 Recreation, culture and religion	-	-	-	...	...	...	...	...	...
9 Economic services	527	626	-99	...	...	...	...	...	...
10 Other functions	-	-	-	...	...	...	...	...	...
Total	3424	3243	181	197	1245	4866	...	...	...
1977									
1 General public services	1452	1253	199	...	...	...	...	...	...
2 Defence	...	...	...	...	...	...	...	...	...
3 Public order and safety	...	...	...	...	...	...	...	...	...
4 Education	976	909	67	...	...	...	...	...	...
5 Health	680	512	168	...	...	...	...	...	...
6 Social security and welfare	-	-	-	...	...	...	...	...	...
7 Housing and community amenities	-	-	-	...	...	...	...	...	...
8 Recreation, culture and religion	-	-	-	...	...	...	...	...	...
9 Economic services	431	589	-158	...	...	...	...	...	...
10 Other functions	-	-	-	...	...	...	...	...	...
Total	3539	3263	276	203	1202	4944	...	...	...

2.17 Exports and Imports of Goods and Services, Detail

Thousand United States dollars

	1970	1971	1972	1973	1974	1975	1976	1977	1978	1979	1980
Exports of Goods and Services											
1 Exports of merchandise, f.o.b.	253	406	243	877	690	1137	910	911	...	...	...
2 Transport and communication	501	572	530	705	840	991	1215	1395	...	...	...
3 Insurance service charges	...	...	...	...	...	...	...	...	...	...	...
4 Other commodities	615	550	595	490	530	555	625	645	...	...	...
5 Adjustments of merchandise exports to change-of-ownership basis	...	...	...	...	...	...	...	...	...	...	...
6 Direct purchases in the domestic market by non-residential households	4870	5770	7360	8260	9630	11700	14560	17670	...	...	...
7 Direct purchases in the domestic market by extraterritorial bodies	...	...	...	...	...	...	...	...	...	...	...
Total Exports of Goods and Services	6239	7298	8728	10332	11690	14383	17310	20621	...	...	...
Imports of Goods and Services											
1 Imports of merchandise, c.i.f.	11658	10162	8867	11139	12766	14350	15102	15149	...	...	...

British Virgin Islands

2.17 Exports and Imports of Goods and Services, Detail
(Continued)

Thousand United States dollars

	1970	1971	1972	1973	1974	1975	1976	1977	1978	1979	1980
2 Adjustments of merchandise imports to change-of-ownership basis	...	...	...	...	...	...	...	...	...	...	...
3 Other transport and communication	350	425	530	560	580	645	655	725			
4 Other insurance service charges	...	...	...	...	...	...	...	...			
5 Other commodities	715	780	815	1020	1220	1333	1622	1725			
6 Direct purchases abroad by government	710	720	750	800	930	1080	1182	1235	...	...	...
7 Direct purchases abroad by resident households									...	...	...
Total Imports of Goods and Services	13433	12087	10962	13519	15496	17408	18561	18834	...	...	...
Balance of Goods and Services	-7194	-4789	-2234	-3187	-3806	-3025	-1251	1787			
Total Imports and Balance of Goods and Services	6239	7298	8728	10332	11690	14383	17310	20621			

4.6 Cost Components of Value Added, ISIC Divisions

Thousand United States dollars

	1970						1971					
	Compensation of Employees	Capital Consumption	Net Operating Surplus	Indirect Taxes	Less: Subsidies Received	Value Added	Compensation of Employees	Capital Consumption	Net Operating Surplus	Indirect Taxes	Less: Subsidies Received	Value Added
	All Producers												
1 Agriculture, hunting, forestry and fishing	61	...	1078	...	...	1139	60	...	992	...	...	1052
2 Mining and quarrying	538	...	407	...	...	945	471	...	267	...	...	738
3 Manufacturing		...		...	...			...		...	...	
4 Electricity, gas and water	208	...	...	...	...	208	245	...	...	...	...	245
5 Construction	3387	...	1426	...	...	4813	2294	...	852	...	...	3146
6 Wholesale and retail trade, restaurants and hotels	1626	...	815	...	...	2441	1889	...	668	...	...	2557
a Wholesale and retail trade	533	...	730	...	...	1263	658	...	583	...	...	1241
b Restaurants and hotels	1093	...	85	...	...	1178	1231	...	85	...	...	1316
7 Transport, storage and communication	886	...	420	...	...	1306	932	...	260	...	...	1192
8 Finance, insurance, real estate and business services	626	...	1787	...	...	2413	682	...	1893	...	...	2575
a Financial institutions	318	...	264	...	...	582	372	...	336	...	...	708
b Insurance		...		...	...			...		...	...	
c Real estate and business services	308	...	1523	...	...	1831	310	...	1557	...	...	1867
Real estate, except dwellings	45	...	1321	...	...	1366	40	...	1380	...	...	1420
Dwellings		...		...	...			...		...	...	
9 Community, social and personal services	145	...	34	...	...	179	158	...	31	...	...	189
Total, Industries	7477	...	5967	...	...	13444	6731	...	4963	...	...	11694
Producers of Government Services	1383	...	...	...	...	1383	1637	...	...	...	...	1637
Other Producers	...	...	...	...	...	...	...	...	...	...	...	...
Total [a]	8860	...	5967	...	...	14827	8368	...	4963	...	...	13331
Imputed bank service charge	...	...	-684	...	...	-684	...	...	-889	...	...	-889
Import duties	...	...	...	...	...	...	...	...	...	...	...	...
Value added tax	...	...	...	...	...	...	...	...	...	...	...	...
Other adjustments	...	...	...	1804	...	1804	...	...	...	1327	...	1327
Total	8860	...	5283	1804	...	15947	8368	...	4074	1327	...	13769

	1972						1973					
	Compensation of Employees	Capital Consumption	Net Operating Surplus	Indirect Taxes	Less: Subsidies Received	Value Added	Compensation of Employees	Capital Consumption	Net Operating Surplus	Indirect Taxes	Less: Subsidies Received	Value Added
	All Producers												
1 Agriculture, hunting, forestry and fishing	49	...	1036	...	...	1085	80	...	1417	...	...	1497
2 Mining and quarrying	445	...	242	...	...	687	483	...	322	...	...	805
3 Manufacturing		...		...	...			...		...	...	
4 Electricity, gas and water	265	...	...	...	...	265	258	...	...	...	...	258

British Virgin Islands

4.6 Cost Components of Value Added, ISIC Divisions
(Continued)

Thousand United States dollars

	1972						1973					
	Compensation of Employees	Capital Consumption	Net Operating Surplus	Indirect Taxes	Less: Subsidies Received	Value Added	Compensation of Employees	Capital Consumption	Net Operating Surplus	Indirect Taxes	Less: Subsidies Received	Value Added
5 Construction	1847	...	611	...	...	2458	1760	...	525	...	...	2285
6 Wholesale and retail trade, restaurants and hotels	2381	...	515	...	...	2896	2648	...	1050	...	...	3698
a Wholesale and retail trade	693	...	701	...	...	1394	763	...	936	...	...	1699
b Restaurants and hotels	1688	...	-186	...	...	1502	1885	...	114	...	...	1999
7 Transport, storage and communication	1002	...	383	...	...	1385	1007	...	476	...	...	1483
8 Finance, insurance, real estate and business services	771	...	1807	...	...	2578	911	...	2037	...	...	2948
a Financial institutions	451	...	208	...	...	659	534	...	192	...	...	726
b Insurance		...		...	...			...		...	...	
c Real estate and business services	320	...	1599	...	...	1919	377	...	1845	...	...	2222
Real estate, except dwellings	41	...	1457	...	...	1498	38	...	1675	...	...	1713
Dwellings		...		...	...			...		...	...	
9 Community, social and personal services	179	...	32	...	...	211	203	...	34	...	...	237
Total, Industries	6939	...	4626	...	...	11565	7350	...	5861	...	...	13211
Producers of Government Services	1864	...	...	...	...	1864	1860	...	...	...	...	1860
Other Producers	...	...	...	...	...	...	...	...	...	...	...	...
Total [a]	8803	...	4626	...	...	13429	9210	...	5861	...	...	15071
Imputed bank service charge	...	...	-794	...	...	-794	...	...	-949	...	...	-949
Import duties	...	...	...	...	...	...	...	...	...	...	...	...
Value added tax	...	...	...	...	...	...	...	...	...	...	...	...
Other adjustments	...	...	...	1740	...	1740	...	...	...	2150	...	2150
Total	8803	...	3832	1740	...	14375	9210	...	4912	2150	...	16272

	1974						1975					
	Compensation of Employees	Capital Consumption	Net Operating Surplus	Indirect Taxes	Less: Subsidies Received	Value Added	Compensation of Employees	Capital Consumption	Net Operating Surplus	Indirect Taxes	Less: Subsidies Received	Value Added
					All Producers							
1 Agriculture, hunting, forestry and fishing	108	...	1719	...	...	1827	114	...	1845	...	...	1959
2 Mining and quarrying	619	...	300	...	...	919	681	...	577	...	...	1258
3 Manufacturing		...		...	...			...		...	...	
4 Electricity, gas and water	364	...	...	...	...	364	339	...	...	...	...	339
5 Construction	2210	...	662	...	...	2872	2286	...	1148	...	...	3434
6 Wholesale and retail trade, restaurants and hotels	3353	...	1291	...	...	4644	3520	...	1392	...	...	4912
a Wholesale and retail trade	908	...	1253	...	...	2161	932	...	1291	...	...	2223
b Restaurants and hotels	2445	...	38	...	...	2483	2588	...	101	...	...	2689
7 Transport, storage and communication	1079	...	451	...	...	1530	1288	...	441	...	...	1729
8 Finance, insurance, real estate and business services	961	...	2675	...	...	3636	1051	...	2951	...	...	4002
a Financial institutions	575	...	298	...	...	873	631	...	302	...	...	933
b Insurance		...		...	...			...		...	...	
c Real estate and business services	386	...	2377	...	...	2763	420	...	2649	...	...	3069
Real estate, except dwellings	40	...	2173	...	...	2213	41	...	2420	...	...	2461
Dwellings		...		...	...			...		...	...	
9 Community, social and personal services	221	...	36	...	...	257	237	...	24	...	...	261
Total, Industries	8915	...	7134	...	...	16049	9516	...	8378	...	...	17894
Producers of Government Services	2314	...	...	...	...	2314	2270	...	...	...	...	2270
Other Producers	...	...	...	...	...	...	...	...	...	...	...	...
Total [a]	11229	...	7134	...	...	18363	11786	...	8378	...	...	20164
Imputed bank service charge	...	...	-1127	...	...	-1127	...	...	-1154	...	...	-1154
Import duties	...	...	...	...	...	...	...	...	...	...	...	...
Value added tax	...	...	...	...	...	...	...	...	...	...	...	...
Other adjustments	...	...	...	2219	...	2219	...	...	...	2363	...	2363
Total	11229	...	6007	2219	...	19455	11786	...	7224	2363	...	21373

British Virgin Islands

4.6 Cost Components of Value Added, ISIC Divisions

Thousand United States dollars

	1976 Compensation of Employees	Capital Consumption	Net Operating Surplus	Indirect Taxes	Less: Subsidies Received	Value Added	1977 Compensation of Employees	Capital Consumption	Net Operating Surplus	Indirect Taxes	Less: Subsidies Received	Value Added
					All Producers							
1 Agriculture, hunting, forestry and fishing	132	...	2005	...	...	2137	140	...	2226	...	...	2366
2 Mining and quarrying	759	...	447	...	...	1206	786	...	485	...	...	1271
3 Manufacturing		...		...	...			...		...	...	
4 Electricity, gas and water	412	...	...	...	...	412	469	...	...	...	...	469
5 Construction	2515	...	556	...	...	3071	1771	...	617	...	...	2388
6 Wholesale and retail trade, restaurants and hotels	3920	...	2065	...	...	5985	4148	...	2147	...	...	6295
a Wholesale and retail trade	1083	...	1481	...	...	2564	1094	...	1282	...	...	2376
b Restaurants and hotels	2837	...	584	...	...	3421	3054	...	865	...	...	3919
7 Transport, storage and communication	1513	...	489	...	...	2002	1676	...	577	...	...	2253
8 Finance, insurance, real estate and business services	1046	...	2990	...	...	4036	1010	...	3384	...	...	4394
a Financial institutions	630	...	76	...	...	706	660	...	304	...	...	964
b Insurance		...		...	...			...		...	...	
c Real estate and business services	416	...	2914	...	...	3330	35^	...	3080	...	...	3430
Real estate, except dwellings	50	...	2659	...	...	2709	50	...	2883	...	...	2933
Dwellings		...		...	...			...		...	...	
9 Community, social and personal services	243	...	26	...	...	269	260	...	43	...	...	303
Total, Industries	10540	...	8578	...	...	19118	10260	...	9479	...	...	19739
Producers of Government Services	2746	...	...	...	...	2746	2808	...	...	...	...	2808
Other Producers	...	...	...	...	...	...	...	...	...	...	...	...
Total a	13286	...	8578	...	...	21864	13068	...	9479	...	...	22547
Imputed bank service charge	...	...	-905	...	...	-905	...	...	-1091	...	...	-1091
Import duties	...	...	...	...	...	...	...	...	...	...	...	...
Value added tax	...	...	...	...	...	...	...	...	...	...	...	...
Other adjustments	...	...	...	2340	...	2340	...	...	...	2632	...	2632
Total	13286	...	7673	2340	...	23299	13068	...	8388	2632	...	24088

	1978 Compensation of Employees	Capital Consumption	Net Operating Surplus	Indirect Taxes	Less: Subsidies Received	Value Added
				All Producers		
1 Agriculture, hunting, forestry and fishing	150	...	2427	...	...	2577
2 Mining and quarrying	870	...	830	...	...	1700
3 Manufacturing		...		...	...	
4 Electricity, gas and water	495	...	...	...	...	495
5 Construction	2670	...	670	...	...	3340
6 Wholesale and retail trade, restaurants and hotels	4600	...	2974	...	...	7574
a Wholesale and retail trade	1200	...	1474	...	...	2674
b Restaurants and hotels	3400	...	1500	...	...	4900
7 Transport, storage and communication	1850	...	887	...	...	2737
8 Finance, insurance, real estate and business services	1110	...	3690	...	...	4800
a Financial institutions	690	...	450	...	...	1140
b Insurance		...		...	...	
c Real estate and business services	420	...	3240	...	...	3660
Real estate, except dwellings	50	...	2980	...	...	3030
Dwellings		...		...	...	
9 Community, social and personal services	290	...	68	...	...	358
Total, Industries	12035	...	11546	...	...	23581
Producers of Government Services	2939	...	...	...	...	2939

British Virgin Islands

4.6 Cost Components of Value Added, ISIC Divisions
(Continued)

Thousand United States dollars

	1978 Compensation of Employees	Capital Consumption	Net Operating Surplus	Indirect Taxes	Less: Subsidies Received	Value Added
Other Producers	...	...	...	...	...	...
Total [a]	14974	...	11546	...	...	26520
Imputed bank service charge	...	...	-1290	...	...	-1290
Import duties	...	...	...	...	...	...
Value added tax	...	...	...	...	...	...
Other adjustments	...	...	...	3280	...	3280
Total	14974	...	10256	3280	...	28510

a) Gross domestic product in factor values.

Brunei

Source. Reply to the United Nations National Accounts Questionnaire from the British High Commission, Bandar Seri Begawan.
General note. The estimates shown in the following tables have been prepared by the Government of Brunei in accordance with the United Nations System of National Accounts so far as the existing data would permit.

1.10 Gross Domestic Product by Kind of Activity, in Current Prices

Million Brunei dollars

	1970	1971	1972	1973	1974	1975	1976	1977	1978	1979	1980
1 Agriculture, hunting, forestry and fishing	...	...	...	...	35.2	37.4	38.6	42.9	47.5	53.8	59.6
2 Mining and quarrying	...	...	...	...	2100.2	2093.8	2603.1	2983.1	2932.2	4392.6	7246.4
3 Manufacturing	...	...	...	...	227.1	324.1	497.5	505.8	526.0	647.7	1368.8
4 Electricity, gas and water	...	...	...	...	5.9	6.4	8.2	5.7	1.8	2.0	2.8
5 Construction	...	...	...	...	35.1	55.8	72.4	88.1	98.7	109.5	121.6
6 Wholesale and retail trade, restaurants and hotels	...	...	...	...	58.2	70.0	74.3	271.0	430.9	489.4	1069.8
7 Transport, storage and communication	...	...	...	...	14.1	22.5	29.6	39.0	50.3	55.8	64.1
8 Finance, insurance, real estate and business services	...	...	...	...	38.0	56.4	68.5	103.7	120.7	135.1	156.6
9 Community, social and personal services	...	...	...	...	115.7	127.9	152.9	220.5	247.6	274.8	372.2
Total, Industries	...	...	...	...	2629.5	2794.3	3545.1	4259.8	4455.7	6160.7	10461.9
Producers of Government Services	...	...	...	...	...	...	...	...	...	...	...
Other Producers	...	...	...	...	...	...	...	...	...	...	...
Subtotal	...	...	...	...	2629.5	2794.3	3545.1	4259.8	4455.7	6160.7	10461.9
Less: Imputed bank service charge	...	...	...	...	13.3	23.9	29.0	33.0	39.5	43.9	48.7
Plus: Import duties	...	...	...	...	...	...	...	...	...	...	...
Plus: Value added tax	...	...	...	...	...	...	...	...	...	...	...
Equals: Gross Domestic Product	...	...	...	...	2616.2	2770.4	3516.1	4226.8	4416.2	6116.8	10413.2

1.11 Gross Domestic Product by Kind of Activity, in Constant Prices

Million Brunei dollars

	1970	1971	1972	1973	1974	1975	1976	1977	1978	1979	1980
					At constant prices of: 1974						
1 Agriculture, hunting, forestry and fishing	...	...	...	...	35.2	35.3	33.1	33.9	35.8	38.4	39.7
2 Mining and quarrying	...	...	...	...	2100.2	1992.7	2389.1	2542.1	2630.0	3411.0	2820.5
3 Manufacturing	...	...	...	...	227.1	299.3	401.5	376.1	390.2	439.4	455.5
4 Electricity, gas and water	...	...	...	...	5.9	6.2	7.5	4.6	1.4	1.5	1.9
5 Construction	...	...	...	...	35.1	51.2	58.9	67.8	58.4	61.9	65.6
6 Wholesale and retail trade, restaurants and hotels	...	...	...	...	58.2	67.1	70.9	215.0	332.6	349.1	405.7
7 Transport, storage and communication	...	...	...	...	14.1	21.3	25.6	30.6	38.9	41.0	44.9
8 Finance, insurance, real estate and business services	...	...	...	...	38.0	52.5	58.7	81.2	92.3	97.7	103.7
9 Community, social and personal services	...	...	...	...	115.7	122.5	136.7	178.9	194.6	197.6	254.7
Total, Industries	...	...	...	...	2629.5	2648.1	3182.0	3530.2	3774.2	4637.6	4192.2
Producers of Government Services	...	...	...	...	...	...	...	...	...	...	...
Other Producers	...	...	...	...	...	...	...	...	...	...	...
Subtotal	...	...	...	...	2629.5	2648.1	3182.0	3530.2	3774.2	4637.6	4192.2
Less: Imputed bank service charge	...	...	...	...	13.3	22.5	27.2	31.1	37.2	39.4	41.7
Plus: Import duties	...	...	...	...	...	...	...	...	...	...	...
Plus: Value added tax	...	...	...	...	...	...	...	...	...	...	...
Equals: Gross Domestic Product	...	...	...	...	2616.2	2625.6	3154.8	3499.1	3737.0	4598.2	4150.5

Bulgaria

Source. Reply to the United Nations National Accounts Questionnaire from the Committee for Unified System of Social Information to the Council of Ministers, Sofia. Official estimates and descriptions are published annually by the same Committee in 'Statisticheski Godishnik' (Statistical Yearbook).

General note. The estimates shown in the following tables have been prepared in accordance with the System of Material Product Balances. Therefore, these estimates are not comparable in concept and coverage with those conforming to the United Nations System of National Accounts. It should be noted that beginning 1970, all activities relating to transport and communication are included in the sphere of material production.

1a Net Material Product by Use at Current Market Prices

Million Bulgarian leva

	1970	1971	1972	1973	1974	1975	1976	1977	1978	1979	1980
1 Personal consumption [a]	6654.8	...	...	...	...	...	...	...	...	...	...
2 Material consumption in the units of the non-material sphere serving individuals [a]	464.6	...	...	...	...	...	...	...	...	...	...
Consumption of the Population	7119.4	7590.0	8052.0	...	...	...	...	...	...	...	...
3 Material consumption in the units of the non-material sphere serving the community as a whole	296.9	384.0	438.0	...	...	...	...	...	...	...	...
4 Net fixed capital formation	1947.8	1379.0	1774.0	...	...	...	...	...	...	...	...
5 Increase in material circulating assets and in stocks	1111.9	1083.0	1314.0	...	...	...	...	...	...	...	...
6 Losses				...	...	...	...	...	...	...	...
7 Exports of goods and material services	51.4	-25.0	-336.0	...	...	...	...	...	...	...	...
8 Less: Imports of goods and material services				...	...	...	...	...	...	...	...
Net Material Product	10527.4	10411.0	11242.0	12148.0	13093.0	14289.0	15145.1	15486.2	16337.9	17666.0	20508.6

a) Beginning 1970, all activities relating to transport and communication are included in the sphere of material production.

2a Net Material Product by Kind of Activity of the Material Sphere in Current Market Prices

Million Bulgarian leva

	1970	1971	1972	1973	1974	1975	1976	1977	1978	1979	1980
1 Agriculture and forestry [a]	2378.9	2471.0	2640.9	2724.9	2705.4	3141.3	3221.2	2833.0	2986.6	3426.8	3463.4
a Agriculture and livestock	2309.9	2400.0	2568.7	2651.1	2627.7	3062.6	3146.8	2759.5	2912.9	3358.8	3384.0
b Forestry	69.0	71.0	72.2	73.8	77.7	78.7	74.4	73.5	73.7	68.0	79.4
c Other	...	...	...	...	...	...	...	...	...	...	...
2 Industrial activity	5167.5	5284.9	5704.2	6216.8	6853.9	7291.1	7656.8	7970.6	9004.5	9723.7	9938.8
3 Construction	917.2	957.4	993.4	1101.4	1171.2	1256.7	1264.4	1378.8	1429.1	1474.0	1904.5
4 Wholesale and retail trade and restaurants and other eating and drinking places [b]	1040.3	600.8	729.3	839.2	951.3	1119.9	1320.4	1565.7	1024.3	1006.8	2820.5
5 Transport and communication [c]	730.3	761.6	828.3	922.9	1065.7	1172.3	1287.4	1348.3	1508.4	1583.3	1659.2
a Transport [c]	644.6	665.4	723.1	806.3	936.3	1035.3	1149.0	1210.4	1362.9	1419.3	1462.4
b Communication [c]	85.7	96.2	105.2	116.6	129.4	137.0	138.4	137.9	145.5	164.0	196.8
6 Other activities of the material sphere [d]	293.2	335.7	345.6	342.3	345.1	307.3	394.9	389.8	385.0	451.4	722.2
Net material product [e]	10527.4	10411.4	11241.7	12147.5	13092.6	14288.6	15145.1	15486.2	16337.9	17666.0	20508.6

a) Excluding hunting, fishing and logging. When organized, they are included in item 'Industrial activity', when non-organized, they are included in item 'Other activities of the material sphere'.
b) Including material and technical supply.
c) Beginning 1970, all activities relating to transport and communication are included in the sphere of material production.
d) Beginning 1970, including such activities as canning of processed meat, preservation of fruits and vegetables (excluding pickles) etc. by the population. Also included are purchases of second-hand goods disposed by enterprises, offices and organizations.
e) The volume of net material product at current prices is influenced by depreciations, beginning 1977 estimated by new norms and on the basis of replacing value of the fixed assets.

Bulgaria

2b Net Material Product by Kind of Activity of the Material Sphere in Constant Market Prices

Index numbers 1975 = 100

	1970	1971	1972	1973	1974	1975	1976	1977	1978	1979	1980
					At constant prices of: 1957						
1 Agriculture and forestry a	91.9	90.3	97.0	96.2	90.0	100.0	101.5	88.1	88.2	96.7	77.8
a Agriculture and livestock	92.3	90.3	97.2	96.3	89.8	100.0	101.7	88.8	88.1	97.1	77.2
b Forestry	87.7	90.2	91.7	93.8	98.7	100.0	94.5	93.4	93.7	86.5	101.0
c Other	...	...	...	...	...	...	...	...	...	...	...
2 Industrial activity	64.2	70.0	75.3	82.9	92.8	100.0	107.2	117.8	131.2	138.2	138.8
3 Construction	73.2	76.1	79.1	87.7	93.2	100.0	100.6	112.2	116.2	119.8	124.8
4 Wholesale and retail trade and restaurants and other eating and drinking places b	49.0	52.9	61.4	74.8	85.4	100.0	113.0	136.8	98.8	119.9	275.4
5 Transport and communication c	58.9	65.0	70.7	78.7	90.9	100.0	109.8	115.0	122.2	127.3	130.2
a Transport c	58.4	64.3	76.9	85.1	94.4	100.0	101.0	116.3	123.7	127.7	130.0
b Communication c	62.5	70.2	76.9	85.1	94.4	100.0	101.0	104.8	110.6	124.6	132.7
6 Other activities of the material sphere d	90.0	105.4	108.9	109.8	110.9	100.0	119.3	124.5	127.4	142.6	180.2
Net material product	68.6	73.3	79.0	85.4	91.9	100.0	106.5	113.2	119.5	127.4	134.7

a) Excluding hunting, fishing and logging. When organized, they are included in item 'Industrial activity', when non-organized, they are included in item 'Other activities of the material sphere'.
b) Including material and technical supply.
c) Beginning 1970, all activities relating to transport and communication are included in the sphere of material production.
d) Beginning 1970, including such activities as canning of processed meat, preservation of fruits and vegetables (excluding pickles) etc. by the population. Also included are purchases of second-hand goods disposed by enterprises, offices and organizations.

3 Primary Incomes by Kind of Activity of the Material Sphere in Current Market Prices

Million Bulgarian leva

	1970	
	Primary Income of the Population	Primary Income of Enterprises
1 Agriculture and forestry a	1773.4	605.5
a Agriculture and livestock	1743.5	566.4
b Forestry	29.9	39.1
c Other	-	-
2 Industrial activity	1966.1	3201.4
3 Construction	673.7	243.5
4 Wholesale and retail trade and restaurants and other eating and drinking places b	326.2	714.1
5 Transport and communication c	419.8	310.5
a Transport c	377.4	267.2
b Communication c	42.4	43.3
6 Other activities of the material sphere d	255.6	37.6
Total	5414.8	5112.6

a) Excluding hunting, fishing and logging. When organized, they are included in item 'Industrial activity', when non-organized, they are included in item 'Other activities of the material sphere'.
b) Including material and technical supply.
c) Beginning 1970, all activities relating to transport and communication are included in the sphere of material production.
d) Beginning 1970, including such activities as canning of processed meat, preservation of fruits and vegetables (excluding pickles) etc. by the population. Also included are purchases of second-hand goods disposed by enterprises, offices and organizations.

4 Primary Incomes From Net Material Product

Million Bulgarian leva

	1970	1971	1972	1973	1974	1975	1976	1977	1978	1979	1980
					a) Primary Incomes of the Population						
1 Socialist sector	5382.6	...	...	...	...	...	...	...	...	...	...
a State sector	3203.9	...	...	...	...	...	...	...	...	...	...
b Co-operative sector	1337.3	...	...	...	...	...	...	...	...	...	...
c Personal plots of households	841.4	...	...	...	...	...	...	...	...	...	...
2 Private sector	32.2	...	...	...	...	...	...	...	...	...	...
Sub-total	5414.8	...	...	...	...	...	...	...	...	...	...
					b) Primary incomes of the enterprises						
1 Socialist sector	5112.6	...	...	...	...	...	...	...	...	...	...
a State sector	4213.3	...	...	...	...	...	...	...	...	...	...
b Co-operative sector	899.3	...	...	...	...	...	...	...	...	...	...
2 Private sector	-	...	...	...	...	...	...	...	...	...	...
Sub-total	5112.6	...	...	...	...	...	...	...	...	...	...
Total net material product	10527.4	10411.4	11241.7	12147.5	13093.0	14289.0	...	...	...	...	...

Bulgaria

5a Supply and Disposition of Goods and Material Services in Current Market Prices

Million Bulgarian leva

	Supply				Total Supply and Disposition	Disposition				
	Gross Output at Producers Prices	Trade Margins and Transport Charges	Gross Output at Market Prices	Imports		Intermediate Material Consumption including Depreciation	Final Consumption	Net Capital Formation	Losses	Exports
					1970					
1 Agriculture and forestry a	4279.9	209.8	4489.7	42.5	4532.2	3346.4	543.3	231.1	26.5	370.5
a Agriculture and livestock a	4206.9	209.8	4416.7	42.5	4459.2	3304.2	543.3	200.6	26.5	370.5
b Forestry	73.0	-	73.0	-	73.0	42.2	-	30.5	-	-
c Other	-	-	-	-	-	-	-	-	-	-
2 Industrial activity	16379.6	1869.4	18249.0	3311.5	21560.5	11928.4	5662.0	1091.4	51.8	3134.2
3 Construction	2368.2	-	2368.2	-	2368.2	281.6	264.0	1737.2	51.1	-
4 Transport and communication b	475.3	-	475.3	9.3	484.6	37.0	415.6	-	-	25.5
a Transport b	363.8	-	363.8	9.3	373.1	-	341.1	-	-	25.5
b Communication b	111.5	-	111.5	-	111.5	37.0	74.5	-	-	-
5 Other activities of the material sphere c	655.7	5.1	660.8	3.8	664.6	122.2	531.4	-	-	11.8
Total	24158.7	2084.3	26243.0	3367.1	29610.1	15715.6	7416.3	3059.7	129.4	3542.0

a) Excluding hunting, fishing and logging. When organized, they are included in item 'Industrial activity', when non-organized, they are included in item 'Other activities of the material sphere'.
b) Beginning 1970, all activities relating to transport and communication are included in the sphere of material production.
c) Beginning 1970, including such activities as canning of processed meat, preservation of fruits and vegetables (excluding pickles) etc. by the population. Also included are purchases of second-hand goods disposed by enterprises, offices and organizations.

6a Capital Formation by Kind of Activity of the Material and Non-Material Spheres in Current Market Prices

Million Bulgarian leva

	1970	1971	1972	1973	1974	1975	1976	1977	1978	1979	1980
				Net Fixed Capital Formation							
1 Agriculture and forestry a	230.4	226.4	261.9	...	...	...	...	...	...	...	...
2 Industrial activity	848.7	285.6	473.1	...	...	...	...	...	...	...	...
3 Construction	34.0	47.5	71.1	...	...	...	...	...	...	...	...
4 Wholesale and retail trade, restaurants and other eating and drinking places b	81.0	57.5	71.4	...	...	...	...	...	...	...	...
5 Transport and communication	170.0	224.9	259.0	...	...	...	...	...	...	...	...
6 Other activities of the material sphere	0.9	-0.2	-0.9	...	...	...	...	...	...	...	...
Total Material Sphere	1365.0	841.7	1135.6	...	...	...	...	...	...	...	...
7 Housing except owner-occupied, communal and miscellaneous personal services	247.7	199.8	263.8	...	...	...	...	...	...	...	...
8 Education, culture and art	101.3	95.8	106.5	...	...	...	...	...	...	...	...
9 Health and social welfare services and sports	25.8	30.7	33.1	...	...	...	...	...	...	...	...
Total Non-Material Sphere Serving Individuals	374.8	326.3	403.4	...	...	...	...	...	...	...	...
10 Government	...	...	...	...	...	...	...	...	...	...	...
11 Finance, credit and insurance	...	...	...	...	...	...	...	...	...	...	...
12 Research, scientific and technological institutes	...	...	...	...	...	...	...	...	...	...	...
13 Other activities of the non-material sphere	...	...	...	...	...	...	...	...	...	...	...
Total Non-Material Sphere Serving the Community as a Whole	54.8	49.1	95.7	...	...	...	...	...	...	...	...
14 Owner-occupied dwellings	153.2	161.8	138.8	...	...	...	...	...	...	...	...
Total Net Fixed Capital Formation	1947.8	1379.0	1774.0	...	...	...	...	...	...	...	...
				Gross Fixed Capital Formation							
1 Agriculture and forestry a	589.4	625.5	681.2	...	...	...	...	...	...	...	...
2 Industrial activity	1621.8	1139.3	1413.3	...	...	...	...	...	...	...	...
3 Construction	113.0	122.9	154.2	...	...	...	...	...	...	...	...
4 Wholesale and retail trade and restaurants and other eating and drinking places b	125.4	101.6	122.7	...	...	...	...	...	...	...	...
5 Transport and communication	419.4	520.3	570.3	...	...	...	...	...	...	...	...
6 Other activities of the material sphere	1.9	1.2	0.6	...	...	...	...	...	...	...	...

Bulgaria

6a Capital Formation by Kind of Activity of the Material and Non-Material Spheres in Current Market Prices
(Continued)

Million Bulgarian leva

	1970	1971	1972	1973	1974	1975	1976	1977	1978	1979	1980
Total Material Sphere	2870.9	2510.8	2942.3	...	...	...	...	...	...	...	...
7 Housing except owner-occupied, communal and miscellaneous personal services	318.3	278.8	342.8	...	...	...	...	...	...	...	...
8 Education, culture and art	128.1	123.0	135.7	...	...	...	...	...	...	...	...
9 Health and social welfare services and sports	57.7	49.2	51.2	...	...	...	...	...	...	...	...
Total Non-Material Sphere Serving Individuals	504.1	451.0	529.7	...	...	...	...	...	...	...	...
10 Government	...	...	...	...	...	...	...	...	...	...	...
11 Finance, credit and insurance	...	...	...	...	...	...	...	...	...	...	...
12 Research, scientific and technological institutes	...	...	...	...	...	...	...	...	...	...	...
13 Other activities of the non-material sphere	...	...	...	...	...	...	...	...	...	...	...
Total Non-Material Sphere Serving the Community as a Whole	88.0	88.8	139.3	...	...	...	...	...	...	...	...
14 Owner-occupied dwellings	300.8	314.8	296.9	...	...	...	...	...	...	...	...
Total Gross Fixed Capital Formation	3763.8	3365.4	3908.2	...	...	...	...	...	...	...	...

Increases in Material Circulating Assets and Stocks

	1970	1971	1972	1973	1974	1975	1976	1977	1978	1979	1980
1 Agriculture and forestry [a]	165.5	83.1	254.0	...	...	...	...	...	...	...	...
2 Industrial activity	371.2	534.9	460.8	...	...	...	...	...	...	...	...
3 Construction	56.2	13.9	45.7	...	...	...	...	...	...	...	...
4 Wholesale and retail trade and restaurants and other eating and drinking places [b]	188.1	159.3	192.0	...	...	...	...	...	...	...	...
5 Transport and communication	95.7	25.1	115.2	...	...	...	...	...	...	...	...
6 Other activities of the non-material sphere	0.7	3.4	13.8	...	...	...	...	...	...	...	...
Total increase in material circulating assets	877.4	819.7	1081.5	...	...	...	...	...	...	...	...
Statistical discrepancy	...	...	...	...	...	...	...	...	...	...	...
Increase in stocks of the non-material sphere	234.5	264.1	232.2	...	...	...	...	...	...	...	...

Gross Fixed Capital Formation by Socio-economic Sector and Industrial Use

	1970	1971	1972	1973	1974	1975	1976	1977	1978	1979	1980
1 State and co-operative (excluding collective farms)	3046.5	2646.6	3190.8	...	...	...	...	...	...	...	...
a Industry	1606.5	1130.7	1407.8	...	...	...	...	...	...	...	...
b Construction	113.0	122.8	154.0	...	...	...	...	...	...	...	...
c Agriculture and forestry [a]	194.6	231.1	268.5	...	...	...	...	...	...	...	...
d Transport and communication	419.4	520.3	570.1	...	...	...	...	...	...	...	...
e Residential building	316.5	278.8	342.5	...	...	...	...	...	...	...	...
f Trade and other [b]	396.5	362.9	447.9	...	...	...	...	...	...	...	...
2 Collective farms	369.6	341.7	360.5	...	...	...	...	...	...	...	...
a Agriculture	348.9	333.1	354.0	...	...	...	...	...	...	...	...
b Other	20.7	8.6	6.5	...	...	...	...	...	...	...	...
3 Other	347.7	377.1	356.9	...	...	...	...	...	...	...	...
Gross Fixed Capital Formation	3763.8	3365.4	3908.2	...	...	...	...	...	...	...	...

a) Excluding hunting, fishing and logging. When organized, they are included in item 'Industrial activity', when non-organized, they are included in item 'Other activities of the material sphere'.
b) Including stocks.

Bulgaria

7a Final Consumption at Current Market Prices

Million Bulgarian leva

	1970	1971	1972	1973	1974	1975	1976	1977	1978	1979	1980
1 Personal consumption [a]	6654.8	...	...	...	...	...	...	...	...	...	...

a) Material Consumption in the Units of the Non-Material Sphere Serving Individuals

	1970	1971	1972	1973	1974	1975	1976	1977	1978	1979	1980
Housing except owner-occupied, communal and miscellaneous personal services	122.3	...	...	...	...	...	...	...	...	...	...
Education, culture and art	179.5	...	...	...	...	...	...	...	...	...	...
Health and social welfare services and sports	162.8	...	...	...	...	...	...	...	...	...	...
Other	-	...	...	...	...	...	...	...	...	...	...
2 Total non-material sphere serving individuals [a]	464.6	...	...	...	...	...	...	...	...	...	...

b) Material Consumption in the Units of the Non-Material Sphere Serving the Community as a Whole

	1970	1971	1972	1973	1974	1975	1976	1977	1978	1979	1980
3 Total non-material sphere serving the community as a whole	296.9	384.0	438.0	...	...	...	...	...	...	...	...
Final consumption	7416.3	7974.4	8489.7	...	...	...	...	...	...	...	...

a) Beginning 1970, all activities relating to transport and communication are included in the sphere of material production.

8 Personal Consumption According to Source of Supply of Goods and Material Services in Current Market Prices

Million Bulgarian leva

	1970	1971	1972	1973	1974	1975	1976	1977	1978	1979	1980
1 Purchases of goods in state and co-operative retail trade [a]	4759.7	...	...	...	...	...	...	...	...	...	...
2 Purchases of goods in the free market and from private retail trade [a]	229.1	...	...	...	...	...	...	...	...	...	...
3 Goods produced on own account and received in kind [b]	883.7	...	...	...	...	...	...	...	...	...	...
4 Payments for transport and communication services	387.9	...	...	...	...	...	...	...	...	...	...
5 Purchases of electricity, gas and water	65.0	...	...	...	...	...	...	...	...	...	...
6 Purchases directly from handicrafts, repair shops and the like [c]	164.2	...	...	...	...	...	...	...	...	...	...
7 Consumption of fixed assets in respect of all dwellings	165.2	...	...	...	...	...	...	...	...	...	...
8 Other	...	...	...	...	...	...	...	...	...	...	...
Personal consumption	6654.8	...	...	...	...	...	...	...	...	...	...

a) Private retail trade is included in item 'Purchases of goods in state and co-operative retail trade'.
b) Including consumers' goods obtained from enterprises, offices and organizations.
c) Only the cost of manufactures and repairs. Excluding the costs of consumers' materials.

Burma

Source. Reply to the United Nations National Accounts Questionnaire from the Planning Department, Ministry of Planning and Finance, Rangoon. The official estimates and descriptions are published annually in the 'National Income of Burma', by the same Department.

General note. The estimates shown in the following tables have been prepared in accordance with the United Nations System of National Accounts so far as the existing data would permit.

1.1 Expenditure on the Gross Domestic Product, in Current Prices

Fiscal year beginning 1 April

Million Burmese kyats	1970	1971	1972	1973	1974	1975	1976	1977	1978	1979	1980
1 General government final consumption expenditure	9168	9474	9712	10493	12824 / 17452	21389	24805	26132	27318	...	...
2 Private final consumption expenditure										...	...
3 Gross capital formation	1453	1231	1317	1266	1498 / 2000	2339	2836	3845	5778	...	...
a Increase in stocks	293	175	133	155	352 / 475	659	515	92	414	...	...
b Gross fixed capital formation	1160	1056	1184	1111	1146 / 1525	1680	2321	3753	5364	...	...
4 Exports of goods and services	535	584	664	680	953 / 912	1192	1414	1728	1842	...	...
5 Less: Imports of goods and services	896	852	921	704	575 / 1016	1443	1628	2087	3222	...	...
Equals: Gross Domestic Product [a]	10260	10437	10772	11735	14700 / 19348	23477	27427	29618	31716	...	...

a) For 1970-1974, estimates refer to fiscal year ending 30 september.

1.2 Expenditure on the Gross Domestic Product, in Constant Prices

Fiscal year beginning 1 April

At constant prices of: 1970

Million Burmese kyats	1970	1971	1972	1973	1974	1975	1976	1977	1978	1979	1980
1 General government final consumption expenditure	9026	9308	9494	9548	9634 / 9867	10410	11020	11521	12037	...	...
2 Private final consumption expenditure										...	...
3 Gross capital formation	1311	1220	1223	927	1009 / 1101	1158	1208	1470	2033	...	...
a Increase in stocks	158	201	132	32	236 / 321	350	243	40	181	...	...
b Gross fixed capital formation	1153	1019	1091	895	773 / 780	808	965	1430	1852	...	...
4 Exports of goods and services	535	650	681	557	500 / 511	448	491	573	555	...	...
5 Less: Imports of goods and services	896	790	757	494	331 / 378	454	454	568	782	...	...
Equals: Gross Domestic Product [a]	9976	10388	10641	10538	10812 / 11101	11562	12265	12996	13843	...	...

a) For 1970-1974, estimates refer to fiscal year ending 30 september.

1.3 Cost Components of the Gross Domestic Product

Fiscal year beginning 1 April

Million Burmese kyats	1970	1971	1972	1973	1974	1975	1976	1977	1978	1979	1980
1 Indirect taxes, net	974	1010	1033	1098	1409 / 1842	2270	2700	2918	3103	...	...
a Indirect taxes paid	974	1010	1033	1098	1409 / 1842	2270	2700	2918	3103	...	...
b Less: Subsidies received	...	...	...	...	... / ...	...	...	...	...	...	...
2 Consumption of fixed capital	711	729	810	830	982 / 1669	1903	2004	2112	2288	...	...
3 Compensation of employees paid by resident producers to:	4202	4364	4898	5165	6385 / 8153	9494	10509	11111	11998	...	...
4 Net operating surplus	4373	4334	4031	4642	5924 / 7684	9810	12214	13477	14327	...	...
Equals: Gross Domestic Product [a]	10260	10437	10772	11735	14700 / 19348	23477	27427	29618	31716	...	...

a) For 1970-1974, estimates refer to fiscal year ending 30 september.

Burma

1.10 Gross Domestic Product by Kind of Activity, in Current Prices

Million Burmese kyats

Fiscal year beginning 1 April

	1970	1971	1972	1973	1974	1975	1976	1977	1978	1979	1980
1 Agriculture, hunting, forestry and fishing	3899	3997	4073	4531	6159 / 8830	11051	12788	13309	14290	...	...
2 Mining and quarrying	111	145	170	196	154 / 164	136	193	283	316	...	...
3 Manufacturing	1072	1082	1083	1049	1276 / 1564	2106	2656	3084	3172	...	...
4 Electricity, gas and water [a]	61	67	65	72	76 / 59	66	70	94	98	...	...
5 Construction	212	203	200	208	195 / 198	221	237	314	419	...	...
6 Wholesale and retail trade, restaurants and hotels [b]	2611	2595	2712	2972	4070 / 5530	6846	8115	8766	9262	...	...
7 Transport, storage and communication	618	631	640	621	629 / 691	740	797	884	961	...	...
8 Finance, insurance, real estate and business services [c]	112	129	169	204	184 / 242	123	235	359	564	...	...
9 Community, social and personal services [bca]	749	750	757	795	822 / 840	864	900	929	958	...	...
Total, Industries	9445	9599	9869	10648	13565 / 18118	22153	25991	28022	30040	...	...
Producers of Government Services	815	838	903	1087	1135 / 1230	1324	1436	1596	1676	...	...
Other Producers	...	...	...	...	...					...	...
Subtotal [de]	10260	10437	10772	11735	14700 / 19348	23477	27427	29618	31716	...	...
Less: Imputed bank service charge	...	...	...	...	...					...	...
Plus: Import duties	...	...	...	...	...					...	...
Plus: Value added tax	...	...	...	...	...					...	...
Equals: Gross Domestic Product [de]	10260	10437	10772	11735	14700 / 19348	23477	27427	29618	31716	...	...

a) Electricity only. Gas and water are included in item 'Community, social and personal services'.
b) Restaurants and hotels are included in item 'Community, social and personal services'.
c) Insurance, real estate and business services are included in item 'Community, social and personal services'.
d) For 1970-1974, estimates refer to fiscal year ending 30 september.
e) Constant price data are valued at 1969-1970 average market prices, thus, data for current and constant prices do not agree in the base year.

1.11 Gross Domestic Product by Kind of Activity, in Constant Prices

Million Burmese kyats

Fiscal year beginning 1 April

At constant prices of: 1970

	1970	1971	1972	1973	1974	1975	1976	1977	1978	1979	1980
1 Agriculture, hunting, forestry and fishing	3707	3982	4054	3752	4062 / 4029	4219	4447	4670	5033	...	...
2 Mining and quarrying	111	149	137	139	120 / 117	120	134	157	169	...	...
3 Manufacturing	1071	1107	1108	1081	1054 / 1098	1200	1295	1385	1419	...	...
4 Electricity, gas and water [a]	61	67	65	72	89 / 89	97	109	131	136	...	...
5 Construction	212	203	200	204	187 / 191	200	206	237	313	...	...
6 Wholesale and retail trade, restaurants and hotels [b]	2519	2540	2600	2637	2663 / 2760	2863	3010	3119	3250	...	...
7 Transport, storage and communication	619	623	648	622	593 / 613	625	645	679	719	...	...
8 Finance, insurance, real estate and business services [c]	112	129	169	205	184 / 217	146	240	325	436	...	...
9 Community, social and personal services [bca]	749	750	757	795	822 / 840	859	874	898	924	...	...

Burma

1.11 Gross Domestic Product by Kind of Activity, in Constant Prices
(Continued)

Fiscal year beginning 1 April

Million Burmese kyats	1970	1971	1972	1973	1974	1975	1976	1977	1978	1979	1980
					At constant prices of: 1970						
Total, Industries	9161	9550	9738	9507	9774 / 9954	10329	10960	11601	12399	...	...
Producers of Government Services	815	838	903	1031	1038 / 1147	1233	1305	1395	1444	...	...
Other Producers	...	...	...	...	...	...	...	...	...	...	...
Subtotal de	9976	10388	10641	10538	10812 / 11101	11562	12265	12996	13843	...	...
Less: Imputed bank service charge	...	...	...	...	...	...	...	...	...	...	...
Plus: Import duties	...	...	...	...	...	...	...	...	...	...	...
Plus: Value added tax	...	...	...	...	...	...	...	...	...	...	...
Equals: Gross Domestic Product de	9976	10388	10641	10538	10812 / 11101	11562	12265	12996	13843	...	...

a) Electricity only. Gas and water are included in item 'Community, social and personal services'.
b) Restaurants and hotels are included in item 'Community, social and personal services'.
c) Insurance, real estate and business services are included in item 'Community, social and personal services'.
d) For 1970-1974, estimates refer to fiscal year ending 30 september.
e) Constant price data are valued at 1969-1970 average market prices, thus, data for current and constant prices do not agree in the base year.

4.3 Derivation of Value Added by Kind of Activity, ISIC Divisions, in Current Prices

Fiscal year beginning 1 April

Million Burmese kyats	1974 Gross Output	1974 Intermediate Consumption	1974 Value Added	1975 Gross Output	1975 Intermediate Consumption	1975 Value Added	1976 Gross Output	1976 Intermediate Consumption	1976 Value Added	1977 Gross Output	1977 Intermediate Consumption	1977 Value Added
						All Producers						
1 Agriculture, hunting, forestry and fishing	10900	2070	8830	13675	2624	11051	15752	2964	12788	16392	3083	13309
2 Mining and quarrying	367	203	164	302	166	136	390	197	193	483	200	283
3 Manufacturing	8822	7258	1564	11845	9739	2106	14710	12054	2656	17221	14137	3084
4 Electricity, gas and water a	114	55	59	126	60	66	145	75	70	166	72	94
5 Construction	641	443	198	717	496	221	770	533	237	1021	707	314
6 Wholesale and retail trade, restaurants and hotels b	6744	1214	5530	8355	1509	6846	9897	1782	8115	10690	1924	8766
7 Transport, storage and communication	1220	529	691	1306	566	740	1399	602	797	1551	667	884
8 Finance, insurance, real estate and business services c	303	61	242	242	119	123	380	145	235	487	128	359
9 Community, social and personal services abc	993	153	840	1022	158	864	1072	172	900	1116	187	929
Total, Industries d	30104	11986	18118	37590	15437	22153	44515	18524	25991	49127	21105	28022
Producers of Government Services	2196	966	1230	2361	1037	1324	2542	1106	1436	2878	1282	1596
Other Producers	...	...	...	...	...	...	...	...	...	...	...	...
Total ed	32300	12952	19348	39951	16474	23477	47057	19630	27427	52005	22387	29618
Imputed bank service charge	...	...	...	...	...	...	...	...	...	...	...	...
Import duties	...	...	...	...	...	...	...	...	...	...	...	...
Value added tax	...	...	...	...	...	...	...	...	...	...	...	...
Total ed	32300	12952	19348	39951	16474	23477	47057	19630	27427	52005	22387	29618

Million Burmese kyats	1978 Gross Output	1978 Intermediate Consumption	1978 Value Added
		All Producers	
1 Agriculture, hunting, forestry and fishing	17177	2887	14290
2 Mining and quarrying	540	224	316
3 Manufacturing	17860	14688	3172
4 Electricity, gas and water a	173	75	98
5 Construction	1360	941	419
6 Wholesale and retail trade, restaurants and hotels b	11229	1967	9262
7 Transport, storage and communication	1683	722	961
8 Finance, insurance, real estate and business services c	728	164	564
9 Community, social and personal services abc	1180	222	958

Burma

4.3 Derivation of Value Added by Kind of Activity, ISIC Divisions, in Current Prices
(Continued)

Million Burmese kyats — Fiscal year beginning 1 April

	1978 Gross Output	Intermediate Consumption	Value Added
Total, Industries [d]	51930	21890	30040
Producers of Government Services	3115	1439	1676
Other Producers	...	...	...
Total [ed]	55045	23329	31716
Imputed bank service charge	...	...	...
Import duties	...	...	...
Value added tax	...	...	...
Total [ed]	55045	23329	31716

a) Electricity only. Gas and water are included in item 'Community, social and personal services'.
b) Restaurants and hotels are included in item 'Community, social and personal services'.
c) Insurance, real estate and business services are included in item 'Community, social and personal services'.
d) Constant price data are valued at 1969-1970 average market prices, thus, data for current and constant prices do not agree in the base year.
e) For 1970-1974, estimates refer to fiscal year ending 30 september.

4.4 Derivation of Value Added by Kind of Activity, ISIC Divisions, in Constant Prices

Million Burmese kyats — Fiscal year beginning 1 April

At constant prices of: 1970 — All Producers

	1974 GO	1974 IC	1974 VA	1975 GO	1975 IC	1975 VA	1976 GO	1976 IC	1976 VA	1977 GO	1977 IC	1977 VA
1 Agriculture, hunting, forestry and fishing	5008	979	4029	5206	987	4219	5432	985	4447	5680	1010	4670
2 Mining and quarrying	210	93	117	215	95	120	233	99	134	268	111	157
3 Manufacturing	5116	4018	1098	5583	4383	1200	6003	4708	1295	6437	5052	1385
4 Electricity, gas and water [a]	114	25	89	126	29	97	145	36	109	166	35	131
5 Construction	609	418	191	627	427	200	644	438	206	730	493	237
6 Wholesale and retail trade, restaurants and hotels [b]	3366	606	2760	3494	631	2863	3671	661	3010	3804	685	3119
7 Transport, storage and communication	1075	462	613	1093	468	625	1114	469	645	1166	487	679
8 Finance, insurance, real estate and business services [c]	252	35	217	215	69	146	315	75	240	403	78	325
9 Community, social and personal services [abc]	993	153	840	1014	155	859	1034	160	874	1072	174	898
Total, Industries [d]	16743	6789	9954	17573	7244	10329	18591	7631	10960	19726	8125	11601
Producers of Government Services	1911	764	1147	2045	812	1233	2189	884	1305	2377	982	1395
Other Producers	...	...	...	...	...	...	...	...	...	...	...	...
Total [ed]	18654	7553	11101	19618	8056	11562	20780	8515	12265	22103	9107	12996
Imputed bank service charge	...	...	...	...	...	...	...	...	...	...	...	...
Import duties	...	...	...	...	...	...	...	...	...	...	...	...
Value added tax	...	...	...	...	...	...	...	...	...	...	...	...
Total [ed]	18654	7553	11101	19618	8056	11562	20780	8515	12265	22103	9107	12996

At constant prices of: 1970 — All Producers

	1978 Gross Output	Intermediate Consumption	Value Added
1 Agriculture, hunting, forestry and fishing	6078	1045	5033
2 Mining and quarrying	288	119	169
3 Manufacturing	6608	5189	1419
4 Electricity, gas and water [a]	173	37	136
5 Construction	926	613	313
6 Wholesale and retail trade, restaurants and hotels [b]	3941	691	3250
7 Transport, storage and communication	1233	514	719
8 Finance, insurance, real estate and business services [c]	551	115	436
9 Community, social and personal services [abc]	1129	205	924

Burma

4.4 Derivation of Value Added by Kind of Activity, ISIC Divisions, in Constant Prices
(Continued)

Million Burmese kyats — Fiscal year beginning 1 April

	1978 Gross Output	1978 Intermediate Consumption	1978 Value Added
At constant prices of: 1970			
Total, Industries [d]	20927	8528	12399
Producers of Government Services	2503	1059	1444
Other Producers	...	...	...
Total [ed]	23430	9587	13843
Imputed bank service charge	...	...	...
Import duties	...	...	...
Value added tax	...	...	...
Total [ed]	23430	9587	13843

a) Electricity only. Gas and water are included in item 'Community, social and personal services'.
b) Restaurants and hotels are included in item 'Community, social and personal services'.
c) Insurance, real estate and business services are included in item 'Community, social and personal services'.
d) Constant price data are valued at 1969-1970 average market prices, thus, data for current and constant prices do not agree in the base year.
e) For 1970-1974, estimates refer to fiscal year ending 30 september.

Burundi

Source. Reply to the United Nations National Accounts Questionnaire from the Departement des Etudes et Statistiques, Bujumbura.
General note. The estimates shown in the following tables have been prepared in accordance with the United Nations System of National Accounts so far as the existing data would permit.

1.1 Expenditure on the Gross Domestic Product, in Current Prices

Million Burundi francs

	1970	1971	1972	1973	1974	1975	1976	1977	1978	1979	1980
1 General government final consumption expenditure	2075.4	2341.7	2790.9	2821.0	3425.7	3827.8	5372.5	5495.0	7571.0	9048.8	10059.1
2 Private final consumption expenditure	18636.0	19339.4	18799.9	20896.8	22989.1	29886.9	31698.3	37729.4	44624.1	59089.7	70281.2
3 Gross capital formation	962.3	1683.1	687.1	1293.7	2434.0	2513.0	3515.0	5517.4	7709.1	10504.7	11493.5
a Increase in stocks	113.4	561.6	-450.0	-98.1	666.1	-556.0	.	.	.	.	.
b Gross fixed capital formation	848.9	1121.5	1137.1	1391.8	1767.9	3069.0	3515.0	5517.4	7709.1	10504.7	11493.5
4 Exports of goods and services	2270.2	1866.3	2534.1	2683.0	2651.9	2743.6	5308.8	8670.8	6429.9	10068.5	6640.6
5 Less: Imports of goods and services	2468.2	3135.3	3255.0	3247.2	4223.6	6299.6	6449.6	8520.9	11108.4	17356.6	18443.7
Equals: Gross Domestic Product	21475.7	22095.2	21556.0	24447.3	27277.1	32671.3	39445.0	48891.7	55225.7	71355.1	80030.7

1.2 Expenditure on the Gross Domestic Product, in Constant Prices

Million Burundi francs

At constant prices of: 1970

	1970	1971	1972	1973	1974	1975	1976	1977	1978	1979	1980
1 General government final consumption expenditure	2075.4	2211.2	2343.3	2271.3	2308.4	2328.4	2905.6	2792.2	3102.9	2922.7	2659.7
2 Private final consumption expenditure	18636.0	18904.6	17887.6	18979.8	18304.0	19436.6	20238.2	23136.9	22927.3	24024.3	24775.3
3 Gross capital formation	962.3	1733.0	533.1	1086.6	1835.2	1326.6	1981.4	2910.0	3347.1	3481.8	3329.5
a Increase in stocks	113.4	663.8	-487.6	-90.8	578.7	-551.6	.	.	.	...	...
b Gross fixed capital formation	848.9	1069.2	1020.7	1177.4	1256.5	1878.2	1981.4	2910.0	3347.1	3481.8	3329.5
4 Exports of goods and services	2270.2	2212.2	2742.4	2483.0	2303.6	2721.8	2330.5	1990.5	2713.0	3161.2	2014.7
5 Less: Imports of goods and services	2468.1	2960.6	2833.3	2659.5	2832.7	3626.7	3389.2	4156.5	4477.4	5240.7	4618.6
Equals: Gross Domestic Product	21475.7	22100.4	20673.1	22161.2	21918.5	22186.7	24066.5	26673.1	27612.9	28349.3	28160.6

1.3 Cost Components of the Gross Domestic Product

Million Burundi francs

	1970	1971	1972	1973	1974	1975	1976	1977	1978	1979	1980
1 Indirect taxes, net	1593.8	1437.1	1504.7	1664.2	1995.3	2204.6	3172.8	6378.5	6106.2	7887.7	7980.2
2 Consumption of fixed capital	316.9	...	...	...	...	480.0	...	...	...	...	...
3 Compensation of employees paid by resident producers to:	13309.1	...	...	...	...	5316.6	...	...	...	...	...
a Resident households	12718.1	...	...	...	...	4704.0	...	...	...	...	...
b Rest of the world	591.0	715.2	883.3	658.5	664.7	612.6	949.4	1308.9	1528.7	...	...
4 Net operating surplus	6255.9	...	...	...	...	24670.5	...	...	...	...	...
Equals: Gross Domestic Product	21475.7	22095.2	21556.0	24447.3	27277.1	32671.3	39445.0	48891.7	55225.7	71355.1	80030.7

1.7 External Transactions on Current Account, Summary

Million Burundi francs

	1970	1971	1972	1973	1974	1975	1976	1977	1978	1979	1980

Payments to the Rest of the World

	1970	1971	1972	1973	1974	1975	1976	1977	1978	1979	1980
1 Imports of goods and services	2468.1	3135.3	3255.5	3247.2	4223.6	6299.6	6449.6	8520.9	11108.4	17356.6	18443.7
a Imports of merchandise c.i.f.	2024.4	2680.2	2812.8	2574.8	3475.5	5025.4	5152.0	7008.0	8887.9	...	...
b Other	443.7	455.1	442.7	672.4	748.1	1274.2	1297.6	1512.9	2220.5	...	...
2 Factor income paid to the rest of the world	701.0	859.3	1055.2	754.2	805.7	765.0	1085.8	1467.2	1730.4	1536.6	1620.1
a Compensation of employees	591.0	715.2	883.3	658.5	664.7	612.6	949.4	1308.9	1528.7	1287.7	1443.2
b Property and entrepreneurial income paid	110.0	144.1	171.9	95.7	141.0	152.0	136.4	158.3	201.7	248.9	176.9
3 Indirect taxes paid to supranational organizations	...	...	...	...	...	...	...	...	...	...	...
4 Current transfers to the rest of the world	11.9	27.2	34.0	57.6	60.8	80.6	87.5	190.1	321.9	...	...
5 Surplus of the nation on current transactions	203.3	-805.1	-366.0	-47.1	-842.8	-2575.7	594.9	1525.0	-3041.2	...	...
Payments to the Rest of the World and Surplus of the Nation on Current Transactions	3384.3	3216.7	3978.7	4011.9	4247.3	4569.5	8217.8	11703.2	10119.5	...	...

Receipts From The Rest of the World

	1970	1971	1972	1973	1974	1975	1976	1977	1978	1979	1980
1 Exports of goods and services	2270.2	1866.3	2534.1	2683.0	2651.9	2743.6	5308.8	8670.8	6429.9	10068.5	6640.6

Burundi

1.7 External Transactions on Current Account, Summary
(Continued)

Million Burundi francs

	1970	1971	1972	1973	1974	1975	1976	1977	1978	1979	1980
a Exports of merchandise f.o.b.	2148.5	1718.9	2323.5	2472.7	2466.9	2542.3	4908.9	8389.0	6028.4	...	...
b Other	121.7	147.4	210.6	210.3	185.0	201.3	399.9	281.8	401.5	...	...
2 Factor income received from rest of the world	49.2	65.2	57.9	85.4	97.7	84.2	114.4	236.0	429.0	622.3	985.6
a Compensation of employees	...	...	...	...	...	...	...	...	1.6	...	...
b Property and entrepreneurial income received	49.2	65.2	57.9	85.4	97.7	84.2	114.4	236.0	427.4	622.3	985.6
3 Subsidies received from supranational organisations	...	...	...	...	...	...	...	...	...	...	...
4 Current transfers from rest of the world	1064.9	1285.2	1386.7	1243.5	1497.7	1741.7	2794.4	2796.4	3260.6	...	...
Receipts from the Rest of the World on Current Transactions	3384.3	3216.7	3978.7	4011.9	4247.3	4569.5	8217.8	11703.2	10119.5	...	...

1.10 Gross Domestic Product by Kind of Activity, in Current Prices

Million Burundi francs

	1970	1971	1972	1973	1974	1975	1976	1977	1978	1979	1980
1 Agriculture, hunting, forestry and fishing	13568.0	13938.8	12782.1	15050.2	16178.9	19754.1	22443.0	26348.9	27985.3	35932.3	40467.3
2 Mining and quarrying a	63.9	68.1	79.4	88.8	99.8	126.6	135.0	119.6	199.6	301.2	418.8
3 Manufacturing	1345.5	1517.4	1628.9	1924.2	2232.1	2227.6	3449.3	3023.3	4659.2	5951.6	6714.7
4 Electricity, gas and water a	...	...	...	...	...	...	...	...	...	...	...
5 Construction	449.5	408.4	429.7	417.5	528.7	987.4	1006.0	1727.7	2858.9	3480.7	4373.2
6 Wholesale and retail trade, restaurants and hotels	1581.8	1763.4	1984.4	1949.5	2328.1	2932.1	2932.1	3885.4	4040.7	5551.3	6098.9
7 Transport, storage and communication	238.4	277.4	375.0	313.9	393.9	439.3	679.4	1028.8	1113.5	1770.3	1794.7
8 Finance, insurance, real estate and business services	736.0	686.6	710.4	697.0	831.9	1067.5	1127.3	1590.1	1644.0	2324.3	2671.0
9 Community, social and personal services											
Total, Industries	17983.1	18660.1	17989.9	20441.1	22593.3	27534.6	31772.0	37723.8	42501.2	55311.7	62538.6
Producers of Government Services	1445.6	1525.4	1578.3	1835.6	2162.3	2303.8	3441.2	3717.8	4771.7	5529.3	...
Other Producers	453.2	471.6	483.1	506.4	526.2	628.3	1058.9	1071.6	1846.6	2626.4	...
Subtotal b	19881.9	20658.1	20051.3	22783.1	25281.8	30466.7	36272.2	42513.2	49119.5	63467.4	72050.5
Less: Imputed bank service charge	...	...	...	...	...	...	...	...	...	...	...
Plus: Import duties	...	...	...	...	...	...	...	...	...	...	...
Plus: Value added tax	...	...	...	...	...	...	...	...	...	...	...
Plus: Other adjustments c	1593.8	1437.1	1504.7	1664.2	1995.3	2204.6	3172.8	6378.5	6106.2	7887.7	7980.2
Equals: Gross Domestic Product	21475.7	22095.2	21556.0	24447.3	27277.1	32671.7	39445.0	48891.7	55225.7	71355.1	80030.7

a) Item 'Electricity, gas and water' is included in item 'Mining and Quarrying'.
b) Gross domestic product in factor values.
c) Referring to indirect taxes net of subsidies.

1.11 Gross Domestic Product by Kind of Activity, in Constant Prices

Million Burundi francs

	1970	1971	1972	1973	1974	1975	1976	1977	1978	1979	1980
					At constant prices of:1970						
1 Agriculture, hunting, forestry and fishing	13568.0	14047.1	12589.9	14142.2	13563.9	14224.5	14770.3	14921.8	15336.6	15717.9	15628.1
2 Mining and quarrying a	63.9	67.0	72.0	74.0	74.0	69.4	71.3	77.5	87.6	102.1	131.3
3 Manufacturing	1345.5	1493.4	1476.7	1603.5	1647.3	1653.4	1824.6	1866.7	2045.0	2239.6	2518.9
4 Electricity, gas and water a	...	...	...	...	...	...	...	...	...	...	...
5 Construction	449.5	402.0	389.6	347.9	392.2	410.2	534.6	1046.2	1255.0	1179.9	1370.9
6 Wholesale and retail trade, restaurants and hotels	1581.8	1735.6	1799.1	1624.6	1727.8	1560.1	1559.5	1630.9	1723.8	1881.8	1911.9
7 Transport, storage and communication	238.4	273.0	340.0	261.0	292.1	381.0	361.4	427.1	488.8	600.1	562.6
8 Finance, insurance, real estate and business services	736.0	675.8	644.1	580.8	617.9	607.0	599.1	663.2	721.7	787.9	800.5
9 Community, social and personal services											
Statistical discrepancy	...	...	...	...	8.5	3.7	16.9	22.1	23.7	15.2	...
Total, Industries	17983.1	18693.9	17311.4	18634.0	18323.7	18909.3	19737.7	20655.5	21682.2	22524.5	22924.2
Producers of Government Services	1445.6	1504.0	1431.4	1529.7	1604.9	1371.6	1861.1	1889.1	1955.6	...	...

Burundi

1.11 Gross Domestic Product by Kind of Activity, in Constant Prices
(Continued)

Million Burundi francs

	1970	1971	1972	1973	1974	1975	1976	1977	1978	1979	1980
				At constant prices of: 1970							
Other Producers	453.2	453.2	438.0	422.0	391.1	468.9	562.7	675.2	776.5	...	...
Subtotal [b]	19881.9	20663.1	19180.8	20585.7	20319.7	20749.8	22161.5	23219.8	24414.3	25199.0	25659.0
Less: Imputed bank service charge	...	...	...	...	...	...	...	...	...	...	...
Plus: Import duties	...	...	...	...	...	...	...	...	...	...	...
Plus: Value added tax	...	...	...	...	...	...	...	...	...	...	...
Plus: Other adjustments [c]	1593.8	1437.3	1492.3	1575.5	1598.8	1436.9	1905.0	3453.3	3198.6	3150.3	2081.3
Equals: Gross Domestic Product	21475.7	22100.4	20673.1	22161.2	21918.5	22186.7	24066.5	26673.1	27612.9	28349.3	27740.3

a) Item 'Electricity, gas and water' is included in item 'Mining and Quarrying'.
b) Gross domestic product in factor values.
c) Referring to indirect taxes net of subsidies.

1.12 Relations Among National Accounting Aggregates

Million Burundi francs

	1970	1971	1972	1973	1974	1975	1976	1977	1978	1979	1980
Gross Domestic Product	21475.7	22095.2	21556.0	24447.3	27277.1	32671.7	39445.0	48891.7	55225.7	71355.1	80030.7
Plus: Net factor income received from abroad	-651.8	-794.1	-997.3	-668.8	-708.0	-680.8	-971.4	-1231.2	-1301.4	-914.3	-634.5
Factor income received	49.2	65.2	57.9	85.4	97.7	84.2	114.4	236.0	429.0	622.3	985.6
Less: Factor income paid	701.0	859.3	1055.2	754.2	805.7	765.0	1085.8	1467.2	1730.4	1536.6	1620.1
Equals: Gross National Product	20823.9	21301.1	20558.7	23778.5	26569.1	31990.9	38473.6	47660.5	53924.3	70440.8	79396.2
Less: Consumption of fixed capital	...	...	...	...	...	...	...	...	...	...	...
Less: Net indirect taxes paid to supranational organisations	...	...	...	...	...	...	...	...	...	...	...
Equals: National Income at Market Prices	...	...	...	...	...	...	...	...	...	...	...
Plus: Net current transfers received from abroad	...	...	...	...	...	...	...	...	...	...	...
Equals: National Disposable Income at Market Prices	...	...	...	...	...	...	...	...	...	...	...
Less: Final consumption	20711.4	21681.1	21590.8	23717.8	26414.8	33714.7	37070.8	43224.4	52195.1	68138.5	80340.3
Equals: Net Saving	...	...	...	...	...	...	...	...	...	...	...
Less: Surplus of the nation on current transactions	...	...	...	...	...	...	...	...	...	...	...
Equals: Net Capital Formation	...	...	...	...	...	...	...	...	...	...	...

2.9 Gross Capital Formation by Kind of Activity of Owner, ISIC Major Divisions, in Current Prices

Million Burundi francs

	1970 TGCF	1970 IS	1970 GFCF	1971 TGCF	1971 IS	1971 GFCF	1972 TGCF	1972 IS	1972 GFCF	1973 TGCF	1973 IS	1973 GFCF
					All Producers							
1 Agriculture, hunting, fishing and forestry	...	...	13.4	...	...	14.0	...	...	-	...	...	15.6
2 Mining and quarrying [a]	...	...	62.1	...	...	49.5	...	...	39.3	...	...	43.9
3 Manufacturing	...	...	103.9	...	...	144.4	...	...	112.0	...	...	108.0
4 Electricity, gas and water [a]	...	...	...	...	...	...	...	...	...	...	...	...
5 Construction	...	...	-	...	...	-	...	...	-	...	...	...
6 Wholesale and retail trade, restaurants and hotels	...	...	...	...	...	...	...	...	...	...	...	...
7 Transport, storage and communication	...	...	51.5	...	...	66.3	...	...	75.6	...	...	78.3
8 Finance, insurance, real estate and business services	...	...	...	...	...	...	...	...	...	...	...	...
9 Community, social and personal services	...	...	...	...	...	...	...	...	...	...	...	...
Total Industries	...	...	230.9	...	...	274.2	...	...	226.9	...	...	245.8
Producers of Government Services	...	...	453.5	...	...	644.0	...	...	731.4	...	...	965.1
Private Non-Profit Institutions Serving Households	...	...	164.5	...	...	203.3	...	...	178.8	...	...	180.8
Total	...	...	848.9	...	...	1121.5	...	...	1137.1	...	...	1391.8

	1974 TGCF	1974 IS	1974 GFCF	1975 TGCF	1975 IS	1975 GFCF	1976 TGCF	1976 IS	1976 GFCF	1977 TGCF	1977 IS	1977 GFCF
					All Producers							
1 Agriculture, hunting, fishing and forestry	...	...	20.8	...	...	93.8	...	...	69.3	...	...	10.0
2 Mining and quarrying [a]	...	...	104.9	...	...	477.2	...	...	200.8	...	...	967.7
3 Manufacturing	...	...	123.0	...	...	123.0	...	...	140.9	...	...	375.7
4 Electricity, gas and water [a]	...	...	...	...	...	...	...	...	...	...	...	...

Burundi

2.9 Gross Capital Formation by Kind of Activity of Owner, ISIC Major Divisions, in Current Prices
(Continued)

Million Burundi francs

	1974 Total Gross Capital Formation	1974 Increase in Stocks	1974 Gross Fixed Capital Formation	1975 Total Gross Capital Formation	1975 Increase in Stocks	1975 Gross Fixed Capital Formation	1976 Total Gross Capital Formation	1976 Increase in Stocks	1976 Gross Fixed Capital Formation	1977 Total Gross Capital Formation	1977 Increase in Stocks	1977 Gross Fixed Capital Formation
5 Construction	...	...	-	...	...	21.7	...	...	18.1	...	...	117.9
6 Wholesale and retail trade, restaurants and hotels	...	...	...	...	...	228.5	...	...	...	...	...	...
7 Transport, storage and communication	...	...	33.5	...	...	235.2	...	...	249.1	...	...	686.8
8 Finance, insurance, real estate and business services	...	...	...	...	...	...	...	...	...	...	...	73.8
9 Community, social and personal services	...	...	...	...	...	...	...	...	...	...	...	...
Total Industries	...	...	282.2	...	...	1197.3	...	...	913.0	...	...	2562.2
Producers of Government Services	...	...	1279.7	...	...	1463.5	...	...	1845.6	...	...	2443.0
Private Non-Profit Institutions Serving Households	...	...	206.0	...	...	274.5	...	...	340.1	...	...	354.2
Total	...	...	1767.9	...	...	3069.0	...	...	3515.0	...	...	5517.4

	1978 Total Gross Capital Formation	1978 Increase in Stocks	1978 Gross Fixed Capital Formation
All Producers			
1 Agriculture, hunting, fishing and forestry	...	...	-
2 Mining and quarrying [a]	...	...	1265.4
3 Manufacturing	...	...	706.0
4 Electricity, gas and water [a]	...	...	...
5 Construction	...	...	486.7
6 Wholesale and retail trade, restaurants and hotels	...	...	152.5
7 Transport, storage and communication	...	...	731.9
8 Finance, insurance, real estate and business services	...	...	57.5
9 Community, social and personal services	...	...	...
Total Industries	...	...	3240.0
Producers of Government Services	...	...	3699.1
Private Non-Profit Institutions Serving Households	...	...	-
Total	...	...	7709.1

a) Item 'Electricity, gas and water' is included in item 'Mining and Quarrying'.

2.17 Exports and Imports of Goods and Services, Detail

Million Burundi francs

	1970	1971	1972	1973	1974	1975	1976	1977	1978	1979	1980
Exports of Goods and Services											
1 Exports of merchandise, f.o.b.	2148.5	1718.9	2323.5	2472.7	2466.9	2542.3	4908.9	8389.0	6028.4	...	...
2 Transport and communication	53.8	67.1	95.0	87.9	59.5	60.0	71.9	30.5	50.8	...	...
3 Insurance service charges	...	...	...	...	...	...	...	...	...	...	...
4 Other commodities	4.2	4.1	5.9	1.9	1.4	13.6	15.9	63.4	14.2	...	...
5 Adjustments of merchandise exports to change-of-ownership basis	...	...	...	...	...	...	...	...	...	...	...
6 Direct purchases in the domestic market by non-residential households	63.7	76.2	109.7	120.5	124.1	127.7	212.1	187.9	336.5	...	...
7 Direct purchases in the domestic market by extraterritorial bodies										...	...
Total Exports of Goods and Services	2270.2	1866.3	2534.1	2683.0	2651.9	2743.6	5308.8	8670.8	6429.9	...	...
Imports of Goods and Services											
1 Imports of merchandise, c.i.f.	2024.4	2680.2	2812.8	2574.8	3475.5	5025.4	5152.0	7008.0	8887.9	...	...

Burundi

2.17 Exports and Imports of Goods and Services, Detail
(Continued)

Million Burundi francs

		1970	1971	1972	1973	1974	1975	1976	1977	1978	1979	1980
	a Imports of merchandise, f.o.b.	1956.1	2618.9	2736.4	2495.6	3395.6	4855.6	5023.0	6866.2	8681.6	...	...
	b Transport of services on merchandise imports	67.2	59.9	72.3	77.2	77.8	167.7	121.4	126.1	131.6	...	...
	c Insurance service charges on merchandise imports	1.1	1.4	4.1	2.0	2.1	2.1	7.6	15.7	74.7	...	...
2	Adjustments of merchandise imports to change-of-ownership basis	...	...	...	...	...	...	...	...	...	...	...
3	Other transport and communication	...	...	...	...	...	...	...	...	...	...	...
4	Other insurance service charges	...	...	...	...	...	...	...	...	...	...	...
5	Other commodities	...	...	...	...	...	...	...	...	...	...	...
6	Direct purchases abroad by government	443.7	455.1	447.2	672.9	748.1	1274.2	1297.6	1512.8	2220.5	...	...
7	Direct purchases abroad by resident households										...	...
	Total Imports of Goods and Services	2468.1	3135.3	3255.5	3247.2	4223.6	6299.6	6449.6	8520.9	11108.4	...	...
	Balance of Goods and Services	-197.9	-1269.0	-721.4	-564.2	-1571.7	-3556.0	-1140.8	149.9	-4678.5	...	...
	Total Imports and Balance of Goods and Services	2270.2	1866.3	2534.1	2683.0	2651.9	2743.6	5308.8	8670.8	6429.9	...	...

Byelorussian SSR

Source. The Central Statistical Administration, Minsk.
General note. The estimates shown in the following tables have been prepared in accordance with the System of Material Product Balances. Therefore, these estimates are not comparable in concept and coverage with those conforming to the United Nations System of National Accounts.

2a Net Material Product by Kind of Activity of the Material Sphere in Current Market Prices

Percentages

	1970	1971	1972	1973	1974	1975	1976	1977	1978	1979	1980
1 Agriculture and forestry	31.9	29.2	...	...	...	...	...	...	...	...	...
2 Industrial activity [a]	42.8	44.6	...	...	...	...	...	...	...	...	...
3 Construction	9.6	10.3	...	...	...	...	...	...	...	...	...
4 Wholesale and retail trade and restaurants and other eating and drinking places [b]	...	...	...	...	...	...	...	...	...	...	...
5 Transport and communication [c]	3.8	3.9	...	...	...	...	...	...	...	...	...
6 Other activities of the material sphere [b]	11.9	12.0	...	...	...	...	...	...	...	...	...
Net material product	100.0	100.0	...	...	...	...	...	...	...	...	...

a) Mining, quarrying, manufacturing and production of electricity and gas.
b) Item 'Wholesale and retail trade and restaurants and other eating and drinking places' is included in item 'Other activities of the material sphere'.
c) Transport of goods and communications for 'productive' enterprises only.

2b Net Material Product by Kind of Activity of the Material Sphere in Constant Market Prices

Index numbers 1960 = 100

	1970	1971	1972	1973	1974	1975	1976	1977	1978	1979	1980
					At constant prices of: 1975						
1 Agriculture and forestry	108	110	105	111	101	90	...	...	...	...	...
2 Industrial activity	329	381	418	461	510	578	...	...	...	...	...
3 Construction	238	253	271	288	324	434	...	...	...	...	...
4 Wholesale and retail trade and restaurants and other eating and drinking places	...	...	...	...	...	...	...	...	...	...	...
5 Transport and communication	278	305	340	369	398	418	...	...	...	...	...
6 Other activities of the material sphere	217	224	267	286	296	332	...	...	...	...	...
Net material product	219	241	259	281	298	326	344	361	389	402	418

6b Capital Formation by Kind of Activity of the Material and Non-Material Spheres in Constant Market Prices

Million USSR roubles

	1970	1971	1972	1973	1974	1975	1976	1977	1978	1979	1980
					At constant prices of: 1969						
				Gross Fixed Capital Formation by Socio-economic Sector and Industrial Use							
1 State and co-operative (excluding collective farms)	2660	2809	3050	3242	3491	3638	3909	4124	4323	4312	4300
a Industry [a]	957	923	999	1084	1146	1159	1325	1431	1475	1372	1352
b Construction	75	114	117	97	102	101	125	127	132	149	158
c Agriculture and forestry	644	756	848	906	956	1058	1055	1077	1125	1131	1149
d Transport and communication	193	174	188	220	289	273	332	382	428	435	405
e Residential building	450	449	482	515	529	557	559	582	612	626	642
f Trade and other	341	393	416	420	469	490	513	525	551	599	594
2 Collective farms	...	...	...	...	...	...	...	...	...	...	...
3 Other	...	...	...	...	...	...	...	...	...	...	...
Gross Fixed Capital Formation [b]	2660	2809	3050	3242	3491	3638	3909	4124	4323	4312	4300

a) Mining, quarrying, manufacturing and production of electricity and gas.
b) The estimates for this table are at constant prices of 1 January 1969, with adjustment for wholesale prices of equipment as of 1 January 1973 and coefficients of building and installation work as of 1 January 1976.

Canada

General note. The preparation of national accounts statistics in Canada is undertaken by Statistics Canada, Ottawa. Official estimates are published quarterly and annually in 'National Income and Expenditure Accounts'. A detailed description of the sources and methods used for the national accounts estimation is found in volume 3 of the above-mentioned publication published in September 1975. The estimates are generally in accordance with the classifications and definitions recommended in the United Nations System of National Accounts (SNA). Annual input-output tables at constant and current prices are published in 'The Input-Output Structure of the Canadian Economy'. The following tables have been prepared from successive replies to the United Nations national accounts questionnaire. When the scope and coverage of the estimates differ for conceptual or statistical reasons from the definitions and classifications recommended in SNA, a footnote is indicated to the relevant tables.

Sources and methods:

(a) Gross domestic product. Gross domestic product is estimated mainly through the income approach.

(b) Expenditure on the gross domestic product. All components of GDP by expenditure type are estimated through the expenditure approach. Government final consumption expenditure is based on public accounts and financial records and statements of the government bodies. At the federal and provincial levels, the figures are derived by eliminating from total government budgetary expenditures all outlays that are not made directly to purchases new goods and services. At the local level, the estimates are built up directly on a gross basis from the data sources subtracting revenues from sales of goods and services. Bench-mark estimates of consumption expenditure are based on the censuses of merchandising and services held in 1951, 1961, and 1966. These estimates are first adjusted to include commodities purchased through non-retail trade outlets and then broken down into trade groupings. For the non-census years, the bench-mark estimates of each trade group are interpolated or projected by using the movement of sales of equivalent kind-of-business groupings. For non-retail trade groups, surveys of wholesale and service trade, surveys of direct selling and surveys of vending machine sales are used. Estimates of consumer expenditure on services such as transport, health care and education are based on annual surveys or published reports. Estimates for other services are based on decennial censuses of merchandising and services with projections to other years being made on directly related series. Comprehensive figures on the quantities of physical stocks held on farms and grains in commercial channels are available from the Agriculture Division of Statistics Canada. Inventories held by Government agencies are obtained from government records. Estimates of inventory book values of non-farm business are based on annual censuses or sample surveys. The estimates of gross fixed capital investment are based on the results of annual surveys which are published in the 'Private and Public Investment in Canada: Outlook' reports. Data are available separately for residential and non-residential construction and machinery and equipment. The estimates of exports and imports of goods and services are based on information available in the balance of payments. For merchandise, the import and export figures are obtained from the customs entries while for services, the estimates draw upon a number of sources such as surveys of business firms and Department of Manpower and Immigration. Constant values of government consumption expenditure are obtained through extrapolating base-year wages and salaries by employment data and through deflating other current expenditure by base-weighted price indexes. Price deflation is also used for private final consumption expenditure, non-farm stocks, non-residential construction and machinery and equipment and part of exports and imports of goods and services. The constant price series of farm inventories is derived by valuing the physical quantities of stocks in prices relevant to the base period chosen. For residential construction, the estimates are derived by multiplying the quantity of work put in place by the base-year average unit value. Exports and imports of merchandise are each revalued by specially constructed current-weighted indexes.

(c) Cost-structure of the gross domestic product. The general method used in the preparation of the labour income estimates consists in calculating the payments made on labour account by the various industrial groups and summing the results. The estimates are based on monthly and annual samples of full-coverage surveys conducted by Statistics Canada, decennial or quinquennial censuses and published statements of governments. Another source of information is the tabulation of total wages and salaries submitted by employers with respect to employees' earnings, undertaken by the Department of National Revenue in connexion with the administration of the Canada Pension Plan. The estimates of corporation profits are obtained from two publications: 'Corporation Financial Statistics' and 'Corporation Taxation Statistics'. Estimates of interest and miscellaneous investment income are based on information obtained from various sources such as Department of National Revenue, Bank of Canada, accounts and financial statements of governments and others. For unincorporated business, estimates are obtained either through direct inquiry, projections from bench-mark data, subtracting expenses from gross income or through applying the ratio of net of gross income based on survey or income-tax data. The estimates of depreciation are calculated on an original cost valuation basis with a close link to the figures of book depreciation reported in the accounting records of business firms. For the government sector, capital consumption allowances are imputed while for the agricultural and housing sectors, replacement cost estimates of capital consumption are prepared from estimates of fixed reproducible capital at market values. The estimates of indirect taxes are based on accounting records of the various levels of government. Subsidies consist of federal production and consumption subsidies.

(d) Gross domestic product by kind of economic activity. The table of GDP by kind of economic activity is prepared in factor values. The income approach is used to estimate the value added of the various industries, except in the case of agriculture, for which the income approach is combined with the production approach through the use of an operating account for agricultural activity. The components of GDP at factor cost are classified by industry on the basis of establishment data. Wages, salaries and supplementary labour income as well as net incomes of farms and non-farm unincorporated businesses, corporation profits and capital consumption allowances are essentially built up by assembling data on an industry-by-industry basis. Certain imputations are made to include non-market activities. They are allocated to their appropriate industry of origin. For the estimates in constant prices, double deflation is used for agriculture, manufacturing, electricity and railway and air transports. Price deflation is used for non-residential and other engineering construction, road transport and advertising services. For producers of government services and producers of private non-profit services to households, various indicators are used to extrapolate or deflate value added. For the remaining industries, value added is exprapolated by various quantity indicators or indexes.

1.1 Expenditure on the Gross Domestic Product, in Current Prices

Million Canadian dollars

	1970	1971	1972	1973	1974	1975	1976	1977	1978	1979	1980
1 General government final consumption expenditure	16587	18329	20249	22980	27728	33302	38252	43276	47544	51887	57813
2 Private final consumption expenditure	49753	54986	61470	70457	82484	95814	109537	121069	133630	149056	166520
3 Gross capital formation [a]	18120	21192	23595	29436	37711	39805	46458	48567	52651	64760	67333
a Increase in stocks [a]	105	392	544	1588	3451	-239	1563	374	361	4165	-1192
b Gross fixed capital formation [b]	18015	20800	23051	27848	34260	40044	44895	48193	52290	60595	68525
Residential buildings	3515	4834	5844	7411	8799	9257	12347	12838	13589	14123	13889
Non-residential buildings	3470	3764	3744	4461	5806	6953	6660	6901	7079	8892	10723
Other construction and land improvement etc.	4738	5498	5936	6563	8022	10112	10779	12329	13575	15616	18116
Other [c]	6292	6704	7527	9413	11633	13722	15109	16125	18047	21964	25797
4 Exports of goods and services [d]	20184	21265	23637	29562	37649	38832	44044	50897	60790	74696	86856
5 Less: Imports of goods and services [d]	17845	19516	22756	27974	37311	41302	45077	51059	59826	72953	81938
Statistical discrepancy	-345	-891	-190	45	630	300	-266	-889	-260	189	-348
Equals: Gross Domestic Product	86454	95365	106005	124506	148891	166751	192948	211861	234529	267635	296236

a) Including increases in stocks of breeding stocks, draught animals, dairy cattle, etc. Stocks of commodities internally processed are valued at cost.
b) Outlays on embassies, consulates and military establishments abroad are included under government current expenditure and imports.
c) Including work put in place on uncompleted heavy machinery and equipment.
d) Exports and imports of merchandise are recorded on the basis of the crossing of frontiers. No data are available on the basis of changes in the ownership of the goods.

1.2 Expenditure on the Gross Domestic Product, in Constant Prices

Million Canadian dollars

	1970	1971	1972	1973	1974	1975	1976	1977	1978	1979	1980
	At constant prices of: 1971										
1 General government final consumption expenditure	17604	18329	18887	19746	20527	21350	21648	22329	22674	22827	22709
2 Private final consumption expenditure	50907	54986	59068	63177	66579	69908	74487	76479	78524	80242	81090
3 Gross capital formation	18988	21192	22470	25730	28336	26409	28385	27255	27520	30634	29095
a Increase in stocks [a]	84	392	515	1346	2642	-252	988	82	260	1898	-735
b Gross fixed capital formation [b]	18904	20800	21955	24384	25694	26661	27397	27173	27260	28736	29830

Canada

1.2 Expenditure on the Gross Domestic Product, in Constant Prices
(Continued)

Million Canadian dollars	1970	1971	1972	1973	1974	1975	1976	1977	1978	1979	1980
				At constant prices of:1971							
Residential buildings	3734	4834	5455	5986	5950	5518	6578	6167	5964	5528	4943
Non-residential buildings	3654	3764	3552	3938	4421	4818	4265	4121	3989	4487	4952
Other construction and land improvement etc.	5061	5498	5611	5667	5768	6425	6320	6691	6904	7327	7944
Other [c]	6455	6704	7337	8793	9555	9900	10234	10194	10403	11394	11991
4 Exports of goods and services [d]	20250	21265	22736	25108	24617	22942	25223	27103	29826	30717	30802
5 Less: Imports of goods and services [d]	18165	19516	22077	25309	28202	27221	29383	29564	30392	32477	31582
Statistical discrepancy	-435	-891	-159	76	516	243	-135	-503	-130	119	-124
Equals: Gross Domestic Product	89149	95365	100925	108528	112373	113631	120225	123099	128022	132062	131990

a) Including increases in stocks of breeding stocks, draught animals, dairy cattle, etc. Stocks of commodities internally processed are valued at cost.
b) Outlays on embassies, consulates and military establishments abroad are included under government current expenditure and imports.
c) Including work put in place on uncompleted heavy machinery and equipment.
d) Exports and imports of merchandise are recorded on the basis of the crossing of frontiers. No data are available on the basis of changes in the ownership of the goods.

1.3 Cost Components of the Gross Domestic Product

Million Canadian dollars	1970	1971	1972	1973	1974	1975	1976	1977	1978	1979	1980
1 Indirect taxes, net	11299	12276	13876	15598	18257	17584	21520	23907	25854	27925	29191
a Indirect taxes paid	12055	13048	14760	16686	20876	21442	24864	27227	29314	32537	36134
b Less: Subsidies received	756	772	884	1088	2619	3858	3344	3320	3460	4612	6943
2 Consumption of fixed capital	9806	10500	11474	13355	16046	18270	20738	23043	25662	28854	32174
3 Compensation of employees paid by resident producers to:	47620	52436	58549	67849	81289	94625	109375	120523	131382	146639	164036
a Resident households	47620	52436	58549	67849	81289	94625	109375	120523	131382	146639	164036
b Rest of the world	...	...	...	...	...	...	...	...	...	...	...
4 Net operating surplus	17384	19262	21916	27748	33928	36572	41049	43499	51370	64405	70486
Statistical discrepancy	345	891	190	-44	-629	-300	266	889	261	-188	349
Equals: Gross Domestic Product	86454	95365	106005	124506	148891	166751	192948	211861	234529	267635	296236

1.4 General Government Current Receipts and Disbursements

Million Canadian dollars	1970	1971	1972	1973	1974	1975	1976	1977	1978	1979	1980
					Receipts						
1 Property and entrepreneurial income	2662	3141	3648	4329	5828	7034	8284	9829	12344	14315	16585
2 Taxes, fees and contributions	27752	30542	34404	39996	50501	54446	62166	68087	73465	82305	93366
a Indirect taxes	12055	13048	14760	16686	20876	21442	24864	27227	29314	32537	36134
b Direct taxes	12309	13941	15785	18898	23864	26214	28931	31766	34011	39011	45315
c Social security contributions	2470	2620	3016	3551	4864	5895	7158	7743	8633	9114	10169
d Compulsory fees, fines and penalties	918	933	843	861	897	895	1213	1351	1507	1643	1748
3 Other current receipts	...	...	...	...	...	...	...	...	...	...	...
Total Current Receipts of General Government	30414	33683	38052	44325	56329	61480	70450	77916	85809	96620	109951
					Disbursements						
1 General government final consumption expenditure	16587	18329	20249	22980	27728	33302	38252	43276	47544	51887	57813
a Compensation of employees	11017	12444	13896	15771	19129	23070	27234	30441	33326	36307	41013
b Consumption of fixed capital	1231	1334	1495	1710	2161	2525	2825	3157	3510	3984	4624
c Purchases of goods and services, net	...	...	...	...	...	...	...	...	...	...	...
d Less: Own account production of fixed assets	...	...	...	...	...	...	...	...	...	...	...
e Indirect taxes paid, net	3250	3622	4137	4788	5425	6538	8101	9268	11406	13575	15719
2 Property income paid	756	772	884	1088	2619	3858	3344	3320	3460	4612	6943
3 Subsidies	7229	8504	10197	11516	14287	17672	20025	22858	26071	27104	31125
4 Other current transfers paid	6985	8255	9918	11198	13880	17080	19483	22220	25058	26337	30308
a Social security benefits and social assistance grants	244	249	279	318	407	592	542	638	1013	767	817
b Other	2592	2456	2585	3953	6270	110	728	-806	-2672	-558	-1649
5 Net saving											
Total Current Disbursements and Net Saving of General Government	30414	33683	38052	44325	56329	61480	70450	77916	85809	96620	109951

Canada

1.5 Current Income and Outlay of Corporate and Quasi-Corporate Enterprises, Summary

Million Canadian dollars

	1970	1971	1972	1973	1974	1975	1976	1977	1978	1979	1980
					Receipts						
1 Net operating surplus	15242	17031	20198	26557	34819	36550	41235	45639	56038	73104	82441
2 Other property and entrepreneurial income received											
3 Current transfers received	...	...	...	...	...	...	...	...	...	...	...
Statistical discrepancy	-195	-665	-1032	-2362	-4244	-2938	-2064	-3419	-4577	-6718	-6841
Total Current Receipts	15047	16366	19166	24195	30575	33612	39171	42220	51461	66386	75600
					Disbursements						
1 Property and entrepreneurial income paid	9101	10050	11735	14337	18658	21077	24274	28233	35866	42458	50019
2 Direct taxes and other current payments to general government	3070	3346	3920	5080	7051	7486	7113	7256	8241	10027	11608
3 Other current transfers paid	148	163	172	192	224	264	281	323	369	439	469
Statistical discrepancy	-195	-665	-1032	-2362	-4244	-2938	-2064	-3419	-4577	-6718	-6841
4 Net saving	2923	3472	4371	6948	8886	7723	9567	9827	11562	20180	20345
Total Current Disbursements and Net Saving	15047	16366	19166	24195	30575	33612	39171	42220	51461	66386	75600

1.6 Current Income and Outlay of Households and Non-Profit Institutions

Million Canadian dollars

	1970	1971	1972	1973	1974	1975	1976	1977	1978	1979	1980
					Receipts						
1 Compensation of employees	47620	52436	58549	67849	81289	94625	109375	120523	131382	146639	164036
a From resident producers	47620	52436	58549	67849	81289	94625	109375	120523	131382	146639	164036
b From rest of the world	...	...	...	...	...	...	...	...	...	...	...
2 Property and entrepreneurial income received	11281	12491	14122	17511	20770	22490	24438	26327	31261	36006	40604
3 Current transfers received	7240	8578	10263	11605	14333	17602	20042	22874	25821	27224	31284
a Social security benefits and social assistance grants received	6985	8255	9918	11198	13880	17080	19483	22220	25058	26337	30308
b Other	255	323	345	407	453	522	559	654	763	887	976
Total Current Receipts	66141	73505	82934	96965	116392	134717	153855	169724	188464	209869	235924
					Disbursements						
1 Private final consumption expenditure	49753	54986	61470	70457	82484	95814	109537	121069	133630	149056	166520
2 Property income paid	641	648	699	986	1517	1616	1808	1928	2373	3596	4668
3 Direct taxes and other payments n.e.c. to general government	12358	13870	15437	17908	22144	25053	29685	33070	35328	38987	44629
a Social security contributions	2470	2620	3016	3551	4864	5895	7158	7743	8633	9114	10169
b Direct taxes	8970	10317	11578	13496	16383	18263	21314	25327	26695	29873	34460
c Fees, fines and penalties	918	933	843	861	897	895	1213				
4 Other current transfers paid	169	170	178	225	234	246	256	269	277	289	299
5 Net saving	3220	3831	5150	7389	10013	11988	12569	13388	16856	17941	19808
Total Current Disbursements and Net Saving	66141	73505	82934	96965	116392	134717	153855	169724	188464	209869	235924

1.7 External Transactions on Current Account, Summary

Million Canadian dollars

	1970	1971	1972	1973	1974	1975	1976	1977	1978	1979	1980
				Payments to the Rest of the World							
1 Imports of goods and services	17845	19516	22756	27974	37311	41302	45077	51059	59826	72953	81938
a Imports of merchandise c.i.f.	14788	16352	19427	24051	32559	35811	38566	43648	51309	63886	71481
b Other	3057	3164	3329	3923	4752	5491	6511	7411	8517	9067	10457
2 Factor income paid to the rest of the world	2397	2537	2528	3012	3741	4338	4940	6248	8188	9761	11561
a Compensation of employees	...	...	...	...	...	...	...	...	...	...	...
b Property and entrepreneurial income paid	2397	2537	2528	3012	3741	4338	4940	6248	8188	9761	11561
By general government	456	481	553	650	713	946	1364	1905	2368	2764	2942
By corporate and quasi-corporate enterprises	1941	2056	1975	2362	3028	3392	3576	4343	5820	6997	8619

Canada

1.7 External Transactions on Current Account, Summary
(Continued)

Million Canadian dollars	1970	1971	1972	1973	1974	1975	1976	1977	1978	1979	1980
By other	...	...	...	...	...	...	...	...	...	...	...
3 Indirect taxes paid to supranational organizations	...	...	...	...	...	...	...	...	...	...	...
4 Current transfers to the rest of the world	413	419	457	543	641	838	798	907	1290	1056	1116
5 Surplus of the nation on current transactions	916	184	-667	-242	-1999	-5252	-4388	-4756	-5299	-5438	-2799
Payments to the Rest of the World and Surplus of the Nation on Current Transactions	21571	22656	25074	31287	39694	41226	46427	53458	64005	78332	91816

Receipts From The Rest of the World

	1970	1971	1972	1973	1974	1975	1976	1977	1978	1979	1980
1 Exports of goods and services	20184	21265	23637	29562	37649	38832	44044	50897	60790	74696	86856
a Exports of merchandise f.o.b.	17597	18595	20901	26367	33572	34499	39274	45715	54681	67219	78323
b Other	2587	2670	2736	3195	4077	4333	4770	5182	6109	7477	8533
2 Factor income received from rest of the world	1011	953	977	1188	1386	1671	1601	1696	2239	2434	3458
a Compensation of employees	...	...	...	...	...	...	...	...	...	...	...
b Property and entrepreneurial income received	1011	953	977	1188	1386	1671	1601	1696	2239	2434	3458
By general government	38	32	35	44	51	57	89	111	88	92	80
By corporate and quasi-corporate enterprises	863	819	799	988	1178	1445	1332	1374	1909	2060	3076
By other	110	102	143	156	157	169	180	211	242	282	302
3 Subsidies received from supranational organisations	...	...	...	...	...	...	...	...	...	...	...
4 Current transfers from rest of the world	376	438	460	537	659	723	782	865	976	1202	1502
Receipts from the Rest of the World on Current Transactions	21571	22656	25074	31287	39694	41226	46427	53458	64005	78332	91816

1.8 Capital Transactions of The Nation, Summary

Million Canadian dollars	1970	1971	1972	1973	1974	1975	1976	1977	1978	1979	1980

Finance of Gross Capital Formation

	1970	1971	1972	1973	1974	1975	1976	1977	1978	1979	1980
Gross saving	18346	19594	22548	29283	36971	35153	41538	42033	46831	59699	63837
1 Consumption of fixed capital	9806	10500	11474	13355	16046	18270	20738	23043	25662	28854	32174
a General government	1231	1334	1495	1710	2161	2525	2825	3157	3510	3984	4624
b Corporate and quasi-corporate enterprises	5684	6080	6577	7632	9169	10359	11865	13306	14958	16927	18892
Public	647	685	770	835	955	1058	1206	1397	1642	1923	2075
Private	5037	5395	5807	6797	8214	9301	10659	11909	13316	15004	16817
c Other	2891	3086	3402	4013	4716	5386	6048	6580	7194	7943	8658
2 Net saving	8540	9094	11074	15928	20925	16883	20800	18990	21169	30845	31663
a General government	2592	2456	2585	3953	6270	110	728	-806	-2672	-558	-1649
b Corporate and quasi-corporate enterprises	2923	3472	4371	6948	8886	7723	9567	9827	11562	20180	20345
Public	249	215	217	217	302	-67	307	588	745	1583	1540
Private	2674	3257	4154	6731	8584	7790	9260	9239	10817	18597	18805
c Other	3025	3166	4118	5027	5769	9050	10505	9969	12279	11223	12967
Less: Surplus of the nation on current transactions	916	184	-667	-242	-1999	-5252	-4388	-4756	-5299	-5438	-2799
Statistical discrepancy	345	891	190	-44	-629	-300	266	889	261	-188	349
Finance of Gross Capital Formation	18120	21192	23595	29436	37711	39805	46458	48567	52651	64760	67333

Gross Capital Formation

	1970	1971	1972	1973	1974	1975	1976	1977	1978	1979	1980
Increase in stocks	105	392	544	1588	3451	-239	1563	374	361	4165	-1192
Gross fixed capital formation	18015	20800	23051	27848	34260	40044	44895	48193	52290	60595	68525
1 General government	3173	3754	3968	4305	5462	6323	6318	6790	7140	7397	8015
2 Corporate and quasi-corporate enterprises	11428	12561	13835	16844	20741	24484	27326	29822	32660	38308	45568
3 Other	3414	4485	5248	6699	8057	9237	11251	11581	12490	14890	14942
Gross Capital Formation	18120	21192	23595	29436	37711	39805	46458	48567	52651	64760	67333

Canada

1.10 Gross Domestic Product by Kind of Activity, in Current Prices

Million Canadian dollars

	1970	1971	1972	1973	1974	1975	1976	1977	1978	1979	1980
1 Agriculture, hunting, forestry and fishing	3175	3451	3675	5670	7087	7311	7336	7580	9157	10706	11591
2 Mining and quarrying	3040	2840	3160	4713	5864	6157	7170	8625	9533	14100	17459
3 Manufacturing	17600	19006	21376	25119	30133	32018	36011	38580	43655	52412	57815
4 Electricity, gas and water	2065	2241	2497	2831	3347	3829	4762	5887	6870	8189	9072
5 Construction	4687	5589	6123	7642	9546	11579	12514	13183	13067	14189	15482
6 Wholesale and retail trade, restaurants and hotels	9348	9869	11310	12890	15614	18190	20588	20816	23064	26914	29466
7 Transport, storage and communication	6350	6997	7894	8745	10124	11303	13033	14725	16810	19160	21353
8 Finance, insurance, real estate and business services	8492	9657	10712	12273	14445	17291	20739	23039	25986	26947	28364
9 Community, social and personal services	6705	7441	8346	9977	11881	14041	16266	18005	20018	22932	25799
Total, Industries	61462	67091	75093	89860	108041	121719	138419	150440	168160	195549	216401
Producers of Government Services	12248	13778	15391	17481	21290	25595	30059	33598	36836	40291	45637
Other Producers	1717	1998	2235	2489	2924	3412	4106	4586	5191	5711	6384
Subtotal a	75427	82867	92719	109830	132255	150726	172584	188624	210187	241551	268422
Less: Imputed bank service charge	617	669	780	878	992	1259	1422	1559	1773	1653	1726
Plus: Import duties b	11299	12276	13876	15598	18257	17584	21520	23907	25854	27925	29191
Plus: Value added tax	...	...	...	...	...	...	...	...	...	...	...
Plus: Other adjustments	345	891	190	-44	-629	-300	266	889	261	-188	349
Equals: Gross Domestic Product	86454	95365	106005	124506	148891	166751	192948	211861	234529	267635	296236

a) Gross domestic product in factor values.
b) Referring to indirect taxes net of subsidies.

1.11 Gross Domestic Product by Kind of Activity, in Constant Prices

Million Canadian dollars

At constant prices of: 1971

	1970	1971	1972	1973	1974	1975	1976	1977	1978	1979	1980
1 Agriculture, hunting, forestry and fishing	3272	3513	3239	3523	3296	3557	3798	3974	3953	3664	3771
2 Mining and quarrying	2873	2979	3092	3475	3392	3000	3049	3118	2837	3090	3110
3 Manufacturing	18103	19042	20517	22674	23497	22124	23433	23903	25109	26286	25460
4 Electricity, gas and water a	1852	1990	2223	2420	2621	2626	2873	3063	3200	3385	3479
5 Construction	5522	6014	6215	6433	6641	6955	7187	7076	6942	7082	7003
6 Wholesale and retail trade, restaurants and hotels	11204	11951	13083	14237	15320	15645	16409	16699	17317	17861	17893
7 Transport, storage and communication b	6812	7177	7743	8448	8956	9044	9509	10045	10498	11337	11614
8 Finance, insurance, real estate and business services	11496	12246	13064	14166	15272	16078	17065	18164	19326	20332	20794
9 Community, social and personal services c	2984	3096	3329	3512	3775	4079	4344	4402	4594	4765	4943
Total, Industries	64111	68006	72504	78889	82771	83107	87664	90443	93774	97801	98067
Producers of Government Services	13875	14446	14818	15270	15660	16215	16592	16881	17119	17117	17238
Other Producers	769	808	821	870	916	960	993	1017	1048	1103	1120
Subtotal d	78755	83260	88143	95028	99347	100283	105249	108341	111941	116021	116425
Less: Imputed bank service charge	...	...	...	...	...	...	...	...	...	...	...
Plus: Import duties e	...	...	...	...	...	...	...	...	...	...	...
Plus: Value added tax	...	...	...	...	...	...	...	...	...	...	...
Equals: Gross Domestic Product	89149	95365	100925	108528	112373	113631	120225	123099	128022	132062	131990

a) Electricity and gas only.
b) Excluding highway and bridge maintenance, radio and television broadcasting.
c) Including radio and television broadcasting.
d) Gross domestic product in factor values.
e) Referring to indirect taxes net of subsidies.

1.12 Relations Among National Accounting Aggregates

Million Canadian dollars

	1970	1971	1972	1973	1974	1975	1976	1977	1978	1979	1980
Gross Domestic Product	86454	95365	106005	124506	148891	166751	192948	211861	234529	267635	296236
Plus: Net factor income received from abroad	-1386	-1584	-1551	-1824	-2355	-2667	-3339	-4552	-5949	-7327	-8103
Factor income received	1011	953	977	1188	1386	1671	1601	1696	2239	2434	3458
Less: Factor income paid	2397	2537	2528	3012	3741	4338	4940	6248	8188	9761	11561
Equals: Gross National Product	85068	93781	104454	122682	146536	164084	189609	207309	228580	260308	288133

Canada

1.12 Relations Among National Accounting Aggregates
(Continued)

Million Canadian dollars

	1970	1971	1972	1973	1974	1975	1976	1977	1978	1979	1980
Less: Consumption of fixed capital	9806	10500	11474	13355	16046	18270	20738	23043	25662	28854	32174
Less: Net indirect taxes paid to supranational organisations	345	891	190	-44	-629	-300	266	889	261	-188	349
Equals: National Income at Market Prices	74917	82390	92790	109371	131119	146114	168605	183377	202657	231642	255610
Plus: Net current transfers received from abroad	-37	19	3	-6	18	-115	-16	-42	-314	146	386
Current transfers received	376	438	460	537	659	723	782	865	976	1202	1502
Less: Current transfers paid	413	419	457	543	641	838	798	907	1290	1056	1116
Equals: National Disposable Income at Market Prices	74880	82409	92793	109365	131137	145999	168589	183335	202343	231788	255996
Less: Final consumption	66340	73315	81719	93437	110212	129116	147789	164345	181174	200943	224333
Equals: Net Saving	8540	9094	11074	15928	20925	16883	20800	18990	21169	30845	31663
Less: Surplus of the nation on current transactions	916	184	-667	-242	-1999	-5252	-4388	-4756	-5299	-5438	-2799
Statistical discrepancy	690	1782	380	-89	-1259	-600	532	1778	521	-377	697
Equals: Net Capital Formation [a][b]	8314	10692	12121	16081	21665	21535	25720	25524	26989	35906	35159

a) Including increases in stocks of breeding stocks, draught animals, dairy cattle, etc. Stocks of commodities internally processed are valued at cost.
b) Outlays on embassies, consulates and military establishments abroad are included under government current expenditure and imports.

2.5 Private Final Consumption Expenditure by Type, in Current Prices

Million Canadian dollars

	1970	1971	1972	1973	1974	1975	1976	1977	1978	1979	1980
Final Consumption Expenditure of Resident Households											
1 Food, beverages and tobacco	11217	12148	13437	15395	17762	20757	22679	24756	27655	30782	34381
a Food	7923	8554	9499	11078	12936	15206	16567	18041	20358	22862	25339
b Non-alcoholic beverages											
c Alcoholic beverages	1898	2139	2391	2653	3027	3501	3779	4133	4487	4838	5518
d Tobacco	1396	1455	1547	1664	1799	2050	2333	2582	2810	3082	3524
2 Clothing and footwear	4276	4381	4822	5433	6846	7621	8670	9330	10107	11272	12313
3 Gross rent, fuel and power	10039	10808	11674	12804	14709	16885	19649	22414	24990	27912	31767
4 Furniture, furnishings and household equipment and operation	4195	4651	5381	6435	7453	8539	9570	10314	11147	12312	13363
a Household operation	1340	1382	1495	1680	1912	2242	2560	2833	3086	3418	3749
b Other	2855	3269	3886	4755	5541	6297	7010	7481	8061	8894	9614
5 Medical care and health expenses	1758	1618	1804	2054	2466	2896	3465	3829	4272	4755	5266
6 Transport and communication	7025	8207	9278	10854	12561	14836	17040	18660	20376	23281	25808
a Personal transport equipment	2416	3050	3563	4260	4623	5676	6161	6646	7314	8414	8764
b Other	4609	5157	5715	6594	7938	9160	10879	12014	13062	14867	17044
7 Recreational, entertainment, education and cultural services	4225	5000	5869	6793	8127	9343	10793	11898	12967	14338	15903
a Education	1402	1682	1822	2001	2302	2723	3081	3475	3832	4190	4575
b Other	2823	3318	4047	4792	5825	6620	7712	8423	9135	10148	11328
8 Miscellaneous goods and services	6892	8077	9076	10518	12421	14405	16731	18518	20726	23629	26841
a Personal care	1465	1482	1660	1906	2268	2574	2957	3236	3554	4084	4639
b Expenditures in restaurants, cafes and hotels	2746	3446	3925	4610	5354	6345	7493	8439	9460	10609	11830
c Other	2681	3149	3491	4002	4799	5486	6281	6843	7712	8936	10372
Total Final Consumption Expenditure in the Domestic Market by Households, of which	49627	54890	61341	70286	82345	95282	108597	119719	132240	148281	165642
a Durable goods	6799	7883	9440	11481	13139	15320	17021	18335	19998	22593	24154
b Semi-durable goods	6645	7133	7962	9059	11184	12428	14176	15374	16710	18709	20554
c Non-durable goods	16186	17521	19432	22302	26218	30422	33967	37383	41689	46451	52422

Canada

2.5 Private Final Consumption Expenditure by Type, in Current Prices
(Continued)

Million Canadian dollars

	1970	1971	1972	1973	1974	1975	1976	1977	1978	1979	1980
d Services	19997	22353	24507	27444	31804	37112	43433	48627	53843	60528	68512
Plus: Direct purchases abroad by resident households	1332	1342	1359	1617	1833	2347	2870	3375	3768	3662	4227
Less: Direct purchases in the domestic market by non-resident households	1206	1246	1230	1446	1694	1815	1930	2025	2378	2887	3349
Equals: Final Consumption Expenditure of Resident Households	49753	54986	61470	70457	82484	95814	109537	121069	133630	149056	166520

Final Consumption Expenditure of Private Non-profit Institutions Serving Households

	1970	1971	1972	1973	1974	1975	1976	1977	1978	1979	1980
Equals: Final Consumption Expenditure of Private Non-profit Organisations Serving Households	...	...	...	...	...	...	...	...	...	...	...
Private Final Consumption Expenditure	49753	54986	61470	70457	82484	95814	109537	121069	133630	149056	166520

2.6 Private Final Consumption Expenditure by Type, in Constant Prices

Million Canadian dollars

	1970	1971	1972	1973	1974	1975	1976	1977	1978	1979	1980

At constant prices of: 1971

Final Consumption Expenditure of Resident Households

	1970	1971	1972	1973	1974	1975	1976	1977	1978	1979	1980
1 Food, beverages and tobacco	11291	12148	12601	12885	13195	13781	14622	14684	14605	14693	14753
a Food	7954	8554	8779	8825	8895	9350	10063	9983	9826	9827	9789
b Non-alcoholic beverages											
c Alcoholic beverages	1918	2139	2314	2497	2692	2782	2843	2943	3030	3044	3087
d Tobacco	1426	1455	1508	1563	1608	1649	1716	1758	1749	1822	1877
2 Clothing and footwear	4304	4381	4722	5079	5911	6325	6831	6956	7310	7469	7456
3 Gross rent, fuel and power	10518	10808	11256	11603	12191	12656	13220	13682	14193	14644	15117
4 Furniture, furnishings and household equipment and operation	4249	4651	5236	5950	6102	6311	6601	6703	6896	7007	6962
a Household operation	1373	1382	1439	1527	1515	1547	1621	1665	1704	1733	1689
b Other	2876	3269	3797	4423	4587	4764	4980	5038	5192	5274	5273
5 Medical care and health expenses	1741	1618	1743	1880	2082	2169	2352	2431	2534	2587	2611
6 Transport and communication	7193	8207	9041	10262	10779	11533	12174	12481	12857	13476	13339
a Personal transport equipment	2501	3050	3489	4115	4151	4694	4834	4913	4972	5117	4775
b Other	4756	5157	5552	6147	6628	6839	7340	7568	7885	8359	8564
7 Recreational, entertainment, education and cultural services	4344	5000	5639	6225	6877	7047	7568	7723	8018	8320	8561
a Education	1483	1682	1706	1689	1711	1715	1727	1610	1600	1570	1562
b Other	2872	3318	3933	4536	5166	5332	5841	6113	6418	6750	6999
8 Miscellaneous goods and services	7206	8077	8663	9061	9164	9523	10185	10805	11300	11710	11947
a Personal care	1502	1482	1598	1751	1877	1943	2131	2205	2262	2262	2180
b Expenditures in restaurants, cafes and hotels	2838	3446	3680	3864	3857	3992	4372	4604	4825	4876	4947
c Other	2866	3149	3385	3446	3430	3588	3682	3996	4213	4572	4820
Total Final Consumption Expenditure in the Domestic Market by Households, of which	50801	54890	58901	62945	66301	69345	73553	75465	77713	79906	80746
a Durable goods	6865	7883	9285	11051	11606	12377	13025	13385	13892	14502	14271
b Semi-durable goods	6784	7133	7731	8318	9306	9778	10543	10779	11210	11314	11178
c Non-durable goods	16414	17521	18464	19210	20070	20735	21943	22187	22375	22637	22766
d Services	20738	22353	23421	24366	25319	26455	28042	29114	30236	31453	32531
Plus: Direct purchases abroad by resident households	1348	1342	1340	1502	1585	1796	2136	2198	2128	1799	1835
Less: Direct purchases in the domestic market by non-resident households	1246	1246	1173	1270	1307	1233	1202	1184	1317	1463	1491
Equals: Final Consumption Expenditure of Resident Households	50903	54986	59068	63177	66579	69908	74487	76479	78524	80242	81090

Final Consumption Expenditure of Private Non-profit Institutions Serving Households

	1970	1971	1972	1973	1974	1975	1976	1977	1978	1979	1980
Equals: Final Consumption Expenditure of Private Non-profit Organisations Serving Households	...	...	...	...	...	...	...	...	...	...	...
Private Final Consumption Expenditure	50907	54986	59068	63177	66579	69908	74487	76479	78524	80242	81090

Canada

2.7 Gross Capital Formation by Type of Good and Owner, in Current Prices

Million Canadian dollars

	1970 TOTAL	1970 Total Private	1970 Public Enterprises	1970 General Government	1971 TOTAL	1971 Total Private	1971 Public Enterprises	1971 General Government	1972 TOTAL	1972 Total Private	1972 Public Enterprises	1972 General Government
Increase in stocks, total [ab]	105	118	...	-13	392	432	...	-40	544	528	...	16
1 Goods producing industries	134	134	...	...	249	249	...	...	-91	-91	...	...
2 Wholesale and retail trade	-51	-51	...	...	184	184	...	...	632	632	...	...
3 Other, except government stocks	35	35	...	...	-1	-1	...	...	-13	-13	...	...
4 Government stocks	-13	...	...	-13	-40	...	...	-40	16	...	...	16
Gross Fixed Capital Formation, Total [cb]	18015	14842	...	3173	20800	17046	...	3754	23051	19083	...	3968
1 Residential buildings	3515	3500	...	15	4834	4816	...	18	5844	5820	...	24
2 Non-residential buildings	3470	2304	...	1166	3764	2401	...	1363	3744	2479	...	1265
3 Other construction	4720	3063	...	1657	5480	3533	...	1947	5913	3703	...	2210
4 Land improvement and plantation and orchard development [d]	18	18	...	...	18	18	...	...	23	23	...	...
5 Producers' durable goods [e]	6292	5957	...	335	6704	6278	...	426	7527	7058	...	469
a Transport equipment	1452	...	...	...	1650	...	...	...	2110	...	...	...
b Machinery and equipment [e]	4840	...	...	...	5054	...	...	...	5417	...	...	...
6 Breeding stock, dairy cattle, etc. [a]	...	...	...	...	...	...	...	...	...	...	...	...
Total Gross Capital Formation [cb]	18120	14960	...	3160	21192	17478	...	3714	23595	19611	...	3984

	1973 TOTAL	1973 Total Private	1973 Public Enterprises	1973 General Government	1974 TOTAL	1974 Total Private	1974 Public Enterprises	1974 General Government	1975 TOTAL	1975 Total Private	1975 Public Enterprises	1975 General Government
Increase in stocks, total [ab]	1588	1603	...	-15	3451	3425	...	26	-239	-270	...	31
1 Goods producing industries	1035	1035	...	...	1817	1817	...	...	79	79	...	...
2 Wholesale and retail trade	535	535	...	...	1581	1581	...	...	-404	-404	...	...
3 Other, except government stocks	33	33	...	...	27	27	...	...	55	55	...	...
4 Government stocks	-15	...	...	-15	26	...	...	26	31	...	...	31
Gross Fixed Capital Formation, Total [cb]	27848	23543	...	4305	34260	28798	...	5462	40044	33721	...	6323
1 Residential buildings	7411	7387	...	24	8799	8776	...	23	9257	9232	...	25
2 Non-residential buildings	4461	3133	...	1328	5806	4203	...	1603	6953	5091	...	1862
3 Other construction	6535	4166	...	2369	7987	4940	...	3047	10074	6562	...	3512
4 Land improvement and plantation and orchard development [d]	28	28	...	...	35	35	...	...	38	38	...	...
5 Producers' durable goods [e]	9413	8829	...	584	11633	10844	...	789	13722	12798	...	924
a Transport equipment	2870	...	...	...	3295	...	...	...	3976	...	...	...
b Machinery and equipment [e]	6543	...	...	...	8338	...	...	...	9746	...	...	...
6 Breeding stock, dairy cattle, etc. [a]	...	...	...	...	...	...	...	...	...	...	...	...
Total Gross Capital Formation [cb]	29436	25146	...	4290	37711	32223	...	5488	39805	33451	...	6354

	1976 TOTAL	1976 Total Private	1976 Public Enterprises	1976 General Government	1977 TOTAL	1977 Total Private	1977 Public Enterprises	1977 General Government	1978 TOTAL	1978 Total Private	1978 Public Enterprises	1978 General Government
Increase in stocks, total [ab]	1563	1522	...	41	374	331	...	43	361	303	...	58
1 Goods producing industries	829	829	...	...	553	553	...	...	-98	-98	...	...
2 Wholesale and retail trade	669	669	...	...	-233	-233	...	...	441	441	...	...
3 Other, except government stocks	24	24	...	...	11	11	...	...	-40	-40	...	...
4 Government stocks	41	...	...	41	43	...	...	43	58	...	...	58
Gross Fixed Capital Formation, Total [cb]	44895	38577	...	6318	48193	41403	...	6790	52290	45150	...	7140
1 Residential buildings	12347	12321	...	26	12838	12806	...	32	13589	13552	...	37
2 Non-residential buildings	6660	4837	...	1823	6901	5053	...	1848	7079	5260	...	1819

Canada

2.7 Gross Capital Formation by Type of Good and Owner, in Current Prices
(Continued)

Million Canadian dollars

	1976				1977				1978			
	TOTAL	Total Private	Public Enterprises	General Government	TOTAL	Total Private	Public Enterprises	General Government	TOTAL	Total Private	Public Enterprises	General Government
3 Other construction	10737	7226	...	3511	12281	8371	...	3910	13519	9274	...	4245
4 Land improvement and plantation and orchard development [d]	42	42	...	...	48	48	...	...	56	56	...	...
5 Producers' durable goods [e]	15109	14151	...	958	16125	15125	...	1000	18047	17008	...	1039
a Transport equipment	4049	...	...	...	4413	...	...	...	5445	...	...	...
b Machinery and equipment [e]	11060	...	...	...	11712	...	...	...	12602	...	...	...
6 Breeding stock, dairy cattle, etc. [a]	...	...	...	...	...	...	...	...	...	...	...	...
Total Gross Capital Formation [cb]	46458	40099	...	6359	48567	41734	...	6833	52651	45453	...	7198

	1979				1980			
	TOTAL	Total Private	Public Enterprises	General Government	TOTAL	Total Private	Public Enterprises	General Government
Increase in stocks, total [ab]	4165	4105	...	60	-1192	-1261	...	69
1 Goods producing industries	2042	2042	...	...	-725	-725	...	...
2 Wholesale and retail trade	1813	1813	...	...	-891	-891	...	...
3 Other, except government stocks	250	250	...	...	355	355	...	...
4 Government stocks	60	...	...	60	69	...	...	69
Gross Fixed Capital Formation, Total [cb]	60595	53198	...	7397	68525	60510	...	8015
1 Residential buildings	14123	14085	...	38	13889	13843	...	46
2 Non-residential buildings	8892	6976	...	1916	10723	8497	...	2226
3 Other construction	15550	11085	...	4465	18044	13368	...	4676
4 Land improvement and plantation and orchard development [d]	66	66	...	...	72	72	...	...
5 Producers' durable goods [e]	21964	20986	...	978	25797	24730	...	1067
a Transport equipment	7046	...	...	...	6991	...	...	...
b Machinery and equipment [e]	14918	...	...	...	18806	...	...	...
6 Breeding stock, dairy cattle, etc. [a]	...	...	...	...	...	...	...	...
Total Gross Capital Formation [cb]	64760	57303	...	7457	67333	59249	...	8084

a) Item 'Breeding stocks, dairy cattle, etc.' is included in item 'Increase in stocks'.
b) Column 'Public enterprises' is included in Column 'Total private'.
c) Outlays on embassies, consulates and military establishments abroad are included under government current expenditure and imports.
d) Comprising construction outlays on dams and reservoirs along with irrigation and land reclamation projects for primary industries.
e) Including work put in place on uncompleted heavy machinery and equipment.

2.8 Gross Capital Formation by Type of Good and Owner, in Constant Prices

Million Canadian dollars

	1970				1971				1972			
	TOTAL	Total Private	Public Enterprises	General Government	TOTAL	Total Private	Public Enterprises	General Government	TOTAL	Total Private	Public Enterprises	General Government
	At constant prices of:1971											
Increase in stocks, total [ab]	84	103	...	-19	392	432	...	-40	515	500	...	15
1 Goods producing industries	137	137	...	...	249	249	...	...	-111	-111	...	...
2 Wholesale and retail trade	-74	-74	...	...	184	184	...	...	624	624	...	...
3 Other, except government stocks	40	40	...	...	-1	-1	...	...	-13	-13	...	...
4 Government stocks	-19	...	...	-19	-40	...	...	-40	15	...	...	15
Gross Fixed Capital Formation, Total [cb]	18910	15581	...	3329	20800	17046	...	3754	21955	18183	...	3772
1 Residential buildings	3735	3718	...	17	4834	4816	...	18	5455	5432	...	23
2 Non-residential buildings	3654	2427	...	1227	3764	2401	...	1363	3552	2350	...	1202
3 Other construction	5023	3274	...	1749	5498	3551	...	1947	5611	3519	...	2092
4 Land improvement and plantation and orchard development [d]	35	44	...	-9	...	...	...	...	...	...	...	...
5 Producers' durable goods [e]	6463	6118	...	345	6704	6278	...	426	7337	6882	...	455
6 Breeding stock, dairy cattle, etc. [a]	...	...	...	...	...	...	...	...	...	...	...	...
Total Gross Capital Formation [cb]	18994	15684	...	3310	21192	17478	...	3714	22470	18683	...	3787

Canada

2.8 Gross Capital Formation by Type of Good and Owner, in Constant Prices

Million Canadian dollars

	1973				1974				1975			
	TOTAL	Total Private	Public Enterprises	General Government	TOTAL	Total Private	Public Enterprises	General Government	TOTAL	Total Private	Public Enterprises	General Government
At constant prices of: 1971												
Increase in stocks, total ab	1346	1362	...	-16	2642	2624	...	18	-252	-268	...	16
1 Goods producing industries	834	834	...	...	1449	1449	...	...	-81	-81	...	...
2 Wholesale and retail trade	498	498	...	...	1152	1152	...	...	-228	-228	...	...
3 Other, except government stocks	30	30	...	...	23	23	...	...	41	41	...	...
4 Government stocks	-16	...	...	-16	18	...	...	18	16	...	...	16
Gross Fixed Capital Formation, Total cb	24384	20633	...	3751	25694	21737	...	3957	26661	22534	...	4127
1 Residential buildings	5986	5966	...	20	5950	5935	...	15	5518	5503	...	15
2 Non-residential buildings	3938	2763	...	1175	4421	3187	...	1234	4818	3514	...	1304
3 Other construction	5667	3648	...	2019	5768	3711	...	2057	6425	4308	...	2117
4 Land improvement and plantation and orchard development d	...	...	...	...	...	...	...	...	...	...	...	...
5 Producers' durable goods e	8793	8256	...	537	9555	8904	...	651	9900	9209	...	691
6 Breeding stock, dairy cattle, etc. a	...	...	...	...	...	...	...	...	...	...	...	...
Total Gross Capital Formation cb	25730	21995	...	3735	28336	24361	...	3975	26409	22266	...	4143

	1976				1977				1978			
	TOTAL	Total Private	Public Enterprises	General Government	TOTAL	Total Private	Public Enterprises	General Government	TOTAL	Total Private	Public Enterprises	General Government
At constant prices of: 1971												
Increase in stocks, total ab	988	966	...	22	82	60	...	22	260	232	...	28
1 Goods producing industries	453	453	...	...	151	151	...	...	-42	-42	...	...
2 Wholesale and retail trade	495	495	...	...	-100	-100	...	...	288	288	...	...
3 Other, except government stocks	18	18	...	...	9	9	...	...	-14	-14	...	...
4 Government stocks	22	...	...	22	22	...	...	22	28	...	...	28
Gross Fixed Capital Formation, Total cb	27397	23537	...	3860	27173	23314	...	3859	27260	23481	...	3779
1 Residential buildings	6578	6564	...	14	6167	6152	...	15	5964	5947	...	17
2 Non-residential buildings	4265	3088	...	1177	4121	3009	...	1112	3989	2958	...	1031
3 Other construction	6320	4334	...	1986	6691	4638	...	2053	6904	4833	...	2071
4 Land improvement and plantation and orchard development d	...	...	...	...	...	...	...	...	...	...	...	...
5 Producers' durable goods e	10234	9551	...	683	10194	9515	...	679	10403	9743	...	660
6 Breeding stock, dairy cattle, etc. a	...	...	...	...	...	...	...	...	...	...	...	...
Total Gross Capital Formation cb	28385	24503	...	3882	27255	23374	...	3881	27520	23713	...	3807

	1979				1980			
	TOTAL	Total Private	Public Enterprises	General Government	TOTAL	Total Private	Public Enterprises	General Government
At constant prices of: 1971								
Increase in stocks, total ab	1898	1872	...	26	-735	-762	...	27
1 Goods producing industries	886	886	...	...	-332	-332	...	...
2 Wholesale and retail trade	944	944	...	...	-475	-475	...	...
3 Other, except government stocks	42	42	...	...	45	45	...	...
4 Government stocks	26	...	...	26	27	...	...	27
Gross Fixed Capital Formation, Total cb	28736	25168	...	3568	29830	26277	...	3553
1 Residential buildings	5528	5513	...	15	4943	4926	...	17
2 Non-residential buildings	4487	3508	...	979	4952	3912	...	1040
3 Other construction	7327	5316	...	2011	7944	6005	...	1939
4 Land improvement and plantation and orchard development d	...	...	...	...	...	...	...	...
5 Producers' durable goods e	11394	10831	...	563	11991	11434	...	557
6 Breeding stock, dairy cattle, etc. a	...	...	...	...	...	...	...	...
Total Gross Capital Formation cb	30634	27040	...	3594	29095	25515	...	3580

a) Item 'Breeding stocks, dairy cattle, etc.' is included in item 'Increase in stocks'.
b) Column 'Public enterprises' is included in Column 'Total private'.
c) Outlays on embassies, consulates and military establishments abroad are included under government current expenditure and imports.
d) Comprising construction outlays on dams and reservoirs along with irrigation and land reclamation projects for primary industries.
e) Including work put in place on uncompleted heavy machinery and equipment.

Canada

2.9 Gross Capital Formation by Kind of Activity of Owner, ISIC Major Divisions, in Current Prices

Million Canadian dollars

	1970 Total Gross Capital Formation	1970 Increase in Stocks	1970 Gross Fixed Capital Formation	1971 Total Gross Capital Formation	1971 Increase in Stocks	1971 Gross Fixed Capital Formation	1972 Total Gross Capital Formation	1972 Increase in Stocks	1972 Gross Fixed Capital Formation	1973 Total Gross Capital Formation	1973 Increase in Stocks	1973 Gross Fixed Capital Formation
All Producers												
1 Agriculture, hunting, fishing and forestry	968	57	911	1120	96	1024	944	-381	1325	2062	314	1748
2 Mining and quarrying	1378	37	1341	1826	77	1749	1638	34	1604	1575	-87	1662
3 Manufacturing	3057	-19	3076	2934	95	2839	3077	257	2820	4282	784	3498
4 Electricity, gas and water	1794	39	1755	1887	-	1887	1945	22	1923	2413	12	2401
5 Construction	294	20	274	288	-19	307	323	-23	346	416	12	404
6 Wholesale and retail trade, restaurants and hotels	483	-51	534	686	184	502	1275	632	643	1318	535	783
7 Transport, storage and communication	1854	37	1817	2039	2	2037	2225	-14	2239	2710	28	2682
8 Finance, insurance, real estate and business services [a]	4112	-2	4114	5474	-3	5477	6787	1	6786	8729	5	8724
9 Community, social and personal services [a]	1020	...	1020	1224	...	1224	1397	...	1397	1641	...	1641
Total Industries	14960	118	14842	17478	432	17046	19611	528	19083	25146	1603	23543
Producers of Government Services	3160	-13	3173	3714	-40	3754	3984	16	3968	4290	-15	4305
Private Non-Profit Institutions Serving Households	...	...	...	...	...	...	...	...	...	...	...	...
Total [bc]	18120	105	18015	21192	392	20800	23595	544	23051	29436	1588	27848

	1974 Total Gross Capital Formation	1974 Increase in Stocks	1974 Gross Fixed Capital Formation	1975 Total Gross Capital Formation	1975 Increase in Stocks	1975 Gross Fixed Capital Formation	1976 Total Gross Capital Formation	1976 Increase in Stocks	1976 Gross Fixed Capital Formation	1977 Total Gross Capital Formation	1977 Increase in Stocks	1977 Gross Fixed Capital Formation
All Producers												
1 Agriculture, hunting, fishing and forestry	1941	-223	2164	2871	272	2599	3399	375	3024	3347	165	3182
2 Mining and quarrying	1983	-	1983	2686	123	2563	3516	119	3397	4035	189	3846
3 Manufacturing	6631	1979	4652	4690	-542	5232	5641	381	5260	6001	150	5851
4 Electricity, gas and water	3046	127	2919	4368	229	4139	4409	-7	4416	5174	70	5104
5 Construction	401	-66	467	565	-3	568	720	-39	759	799	-21	820
6 Wholesale and retail trade, restaurants and hotels	2542	1581	961	528	-404	932	1678	669	1009	789	-233	1022
7 Transport, storage and communication	3193	17	3176	3811	48	3763	3734	14	3720	3983	1	3982
8 Finance, insurance, real estate and business services [a]	10460	10	10450	11182	7	11175	14536	10	14526	15193	10	15183
9 Community, social and personal services [a]	2026	...	2026	2750	...	2750	2466	...	2466	2413	...	2413
Total Industries	32223	3425	28798	33451	-270	33721	40099	1522	38577	41734	331	41403
Producers of Government Services	5488	26	5462	6354	31	6323	6359	41	6318	6833	43	6790
Private Non-Profit Institutions Serving Households	...	...	...	...	...	...	...	...	...	...	...	...
Total [bc]	37711	3451	34260	39805	-239	40044	46458	1563	44895	48567	374	48193

	1978 Total Gross Capital Formation	1978 Increase in Stocks	1978 Gross Fixed Capital Formation	1979 Total Gross Capital Formation	1979 Increase in Stocks	1979 Gross Fixed Capital Formation	1980 Total Gross Capital Formation	1980 Increase in Stocks	1980 Gross Fixed Capital Formation
All Producers									
1 Agriculture, hunting, fishing and forestry	3873	194	3679	4678	64	4614	4518	-272	4790
2 Mining and quarrying	3609	-250	3859	5560	-47	5607	8354	201	8153
3 Manufacturing	5916	35	5881	9036	1888	7148	8790	-547	9337
4 Electricity, gas and water	6238	16	6222	6810	143	6667	6825	-96	6921
5 Construction	782	-93	875	979	-6	985	1089	-11	1100
6 Wholesale and retail trade, restaurants and hotels	1619	441	1178	3359	1813	1546	747	-891	1638
7 Transport, storage and communication	4136	-47	4183	4945	16	4929	6138	49	6089
8 Finance, insurance, real estate and business services [a]	16361	7	16354	17899	234	17665	18280	306	17974
9 Community, social and personal services [a]	2919	...	2919	4037	...	4037	4508	...	4508
Total Industries	45453	303	45150	57303	4105	53198	59249	-1261	60510
Producers of Government Services	7198	58	7140	7457	60	7397	8084	69	8015
Private Non-Profit Institutions Serving Households	...	...	...	...	...	...	...	...	...
Total [bc]	52651	361	52290	64760	4165	60595	67333	-1192	68525

a) For column 'Increase in stocks', item 'Community, social and personal services' is included in item 'Finance, insurance, real estate and business services'.
b) Outlays on embassies, consulates and military establishments abroad are included under government current expenditure and imports.
c) Item 'Breeding stocks, dairy cattle, etc.' is included in item 'Increase in stocks'.

Canada

2.17 Exports and Imports of Goods and Services, Detail

Million Canadian dollars

	1970	1971	1972	1973	1974	1975	1976	1977	1978	1979	1980
Exports of Goods and Services											
1 Exports of merchandise, f.o.b. [ab]	17597	18595	20901	26367	33572	34499	39274	45715	54681	67219	78323
2 Transport and communication	478	503	503	620	874	777	847	954	1131	1568	1797
a In respect of merchandise imports	28	37	34	32	43	51	44	45	44	43	56
b Other	450	466	469	588	831	726	803	909	1087	1525	1741
3 Insurance service charges	...	...	...	...	...	...	...	...	...	...	...
4 Other commodities	903	921	1003	1129	1509	1741	1993	2203	2600	3022	3387
5 Adjustments of merchandise exports to change-of-ownership basis	...	...	...	...	...	...	...	...	...	...	...
6 Direct purchases in the domestic market by non-residential households [c]	1206	1246	1230	1446	1694	1815	1930	2025	2378	2887	3349
7 Direct purchases in the domestic market by extraterritorial bodies	...	...	...	...	...	...	...	...	...	...	...
Total Exports of Goods and Services	20184	21265	23637	29562	37649	38832	44044	50897	60790	74696	86856
Imports of Goods and Services											
1 Imports of merchandise, c.i.f. [a]	14788	16352	19427	24051	32559	35811	38566	43648	51309	63886	71481
a Imports of merchandise, f.o.b. [d]	14318	15786	18833	23375	31677	34874	37595	42586	50218	62593	70069
b Transport of services on merchandise imports	470	566	594	676	882	937	971	1062	1091	1293	1412
By residents	28	37	34	32	43	51	44	45	44	43	56
By non-residents	442	529	560	644	839	886	927	1017	1047	1250	1356
c Insurance service charges on merchandise imports	...	...	...	...	...	...	...	...	...	...	...
2 Adjustments of merchandise imports to change-of-ownership basis	...	...	...	...	...	...	...	...	...	...	...
3 Other transport and communication	215	195	194	267	422	349	317	317	365	442	461
4 Other insurance service charges	1342	1458	1588	1816	2215	2479	2921	3199	3766	4314	4986
5 Other commodities											
6 Direct purchases abroad by government	168	169	188	223	282	316	403	520	618	649	783
7 Direct purchases abroad by resident households	1332	1342	1359	1617	1833	2347	2870	3375	3768	3662	4227
Total Imports of Goods and Services	17845	19516	22756	27974	37311	41302	45077	51059	59826	72953	81938
Balance of Goods and Services	2339	1749	881	1588	338	-2470	-1033	-162	964	1743	4918
Total Imports and Balance of Goods and Services	20184	21265	23637	29562	37649	38832	44044	50897	60790	74696	86856

a) Exports and imports of merchandise are recorded on the basis of the crossing of frontiers. No data are available on the basis of changes in the ownership of the goods.
b) Exports of Canadian produce and re-exports of foreign produce are valued f.o.b. point of shipment in Canada plus inland freight and gold.
c) Excluding crew expenditures included in transport and communication. Diplomatic and military personnel expenditures are included in other commodities.
d) Imports are valued f.o.b. point of shipment in the foreign country plus inland freight payments.

3.12 General Government Income and Outlay Account: Total and Subsectors

Million Canadian dollars

	1970					1971				
	Total General Government	Central Government	State or Provincial Government	Local Government	Social Security Funds	Total General Government	Central Government	State or Provincial Government	Local Government	Social Security Funds
Receipts											
1 Property and entrepreneurial income	2662	1259	1009	121	273	3141	1438	1183	145	375
a Net operating surplus	...	...	...	...	...	...	...	...	...	...
b Withdrawals from public quasi-corporations	...	...	...	...	...	...	...	...	...	...
c Interest	1904	932	642	57	273	2291	1099	746	71	375
d Dividends [a]	420	320	36	64	...	463	338	51	74	...
e Net land rent and royalties [b]	338	7	331	-	...	387	1	386	-	...
2 Taxes, fees and contributions	27752	13906	8966	3826	1054	30542	15402	9963	4074	1103
a Indirect taxes	12055	4034	4263	3758	...	13048	4480	4566	4002	...
b Direct taxes	12309	8847	3462	-	...	13941	9836	4105	-	...
Income	12150	8847	3303	...	...	13767	9836	3931	...	...

Canada

3.12 General Government Income and Outlay Account: Total and Subsectors
(Continued)

Million Canadian dollars

		1970					1971			
		Total General Government	Central Government	State or Provincial Government	Local Government	Social Security Funds	Total General Government	Central Government	State or Provincial Government	Local Government	Social Security Funds
	Other	159	-	159	-	...	174	-	174	-	...
c	Social security contributions	2470	1023	393	-	1054	2620	1082	435	-	1103
d	Fees, fines and penalties	918	2	848	68	...	933	4	857	72	...
3	Other current transfers received	...	...	3347	5500	...	...	...	4274	6092	...
a	Casualty insurance claims	...	...	...	...	...	...	...	...	...	...
b	Transfers from other government subsectors	...	-	3347	5500	...	...	-	4274	6092	...
c	Transfers from abroad	269	-	...	...	...	278	-	...	...	...
d	Other transfers, except imputed										
e	Imputed unfunded employee welfare contributions	...	...	...	...	...	...	...	...	...	...
	Total Current Receipts cd	30414	15165	13322	9447	1327	33683	16840	15420	10311	1478

Disbursements

1	General government final consumption expenditures	16587	4531	4086	7940	30	18329	4938	4689	8674	28
a	Compensation of employees	10907	2893	2056	5958	...	12325	3158	2587	6580	...
b	Consumption of fixed capital	1231	232	395	604	-	1334	245	436	653	-
c	Goods and services purchased, net	4449	1406	1635	1378	30	4670	1535	1666	1441	28
d	Less: Own account production of fixed assets	...	...	...	...	...	...	...	...	...	...
e	Indirect taxes paid, net	...	...	...	...	...	...	...	...	...	...
2	Property income paid	3250	1862	759	629	...	3622	1974	920	728	...
a	Interest	3250	1862	759	629	...	3622	1974	920	728	...
b	Net land rent and royalties	...	...	...	...	...	...	...	...	...	...
3	Subsidies	756	589	167	-	...	772	513	259	-	...
4	Other current transfers paid	7229	7698	8017	257	104	8504	9256	9138	304	172
a	Casualty insurance premiums, net	...	...	...	...	...	...	...	...	...	...
b	Transfers to other government subsectors	...	3397	5406	44	...	...	4323	5999	44	...
c	Transfers to households e	6985	4057	2611	213	104	8255	4684	3139	260	172
	Social security benefits	3185	2773	308	-	104	3751	3254	325	-	172
	Social assistance grants	3800	1284	2303	213	...	4504	1430	2814	260	...
	Unfunded employee welfare benefits										
d	Transfers to private non-profit institutions serving households e	...	...	...	...	...	...	...	...	...	...
e	Transfers to the rest of the world	244	244	...	...	...	249	249	...	...	...
	Net saving	2592	485	293	621	1193	2456	159	414	605	1278
	Total Current Disbursements and Net Saving cd	30414	15165	13322	9447	1327	33683	16840	15420	10311	1478

		1972					1973				
		Total General Government	Central Government	State or Provincial Government	Local Government	Social Security Funds	Total General Government	Central Government	State or Provincial Government	Local Government	Social Security Funds

Receipts

1	Property and entrepreneurial income	3648	1662	1360	159	467	4329	1795	1787	177	570
a	Net operating surplus	...	...	...	...	...	...	...	...	...	...
b	Withdrawals from public quasi-corporations	...	...	...	...	...	...	...	...	...	...
c	Interest	2590	1229	818	76	467	3066	1427	982	87	570
d	Dividends a	574	432	59	83	...	525	365	70	90	...
e	Net land rent and royalties b	484	1	483	-	...	738	3	735	-	...
2	Taxes, fees and contributions	34404	17519	11242	4453	1190	39996	20648	13310	4733	1305
a	Indirect taxes	14760	5121	5261	4378	...	16686	5837	6198	4651	...
b	Direct taxes	15785	11077	4708	-	...	18898	13194	5704	-	...
	Income	15592	11077	4515	...	...	18687	13194	5493	...	...

Canada

3.12 General Government Income and Outlay Account: Total and Subsectors
(Continued)

Million Canadian dollars

	1972					1973				
	Total General Government	Central Government	State or Provincial Government	Local Government	Social Security Funds	Total General Government	Central Government	State or Provincial Government	Local Government	Social Security Funds
Other	193	-	193	-	...	211	-	211	-	...
c Social security contributions	3016	1316	510	-	1190	3551	1611	635	-	1305
d Fees, fines and penalties	843	5	763	75	...	861	6	773	82	...
3 Other current transfers received	...	...	4449	6981	...	...	...	4734	7653	...
a Casualty insurance claims	...	...	...	...	...	...	...	...	...	...
b Transfers from other government subsectors	...	-	4449	6981	...	...	-	4734	7653	...
c Transfers from abroad	287	-	...	...	...	322	-	...	...	...
d Other transfers, except imputed	...	...	...	...	...	...	...	...	...	...
e Imputed unfunded employee welfare contributions	...	...	...	...	...	...	...	...	...	...
Total Current Receipts cd	38052	19181	17051	11593	1657	44325	22443	19831	12563	1875

Disbursements

	1972					1973				
1 General government final consumption expenditures	20249	5430	5277	9508	34	22980	6055	6087	10801	37
a Compensation of employees	13734	3539	2962	7233	...	15605	3933	3415	8257	...
b Consumption of fixed capital	1495	277	481	737	-	1710	312	575	823	-
c Goods and services purchased, net	5020	1614	1834	1538	34	5665	1810	2097	1721	37
d Less: Own account production of fixed assets	...	...	...	...	...	...	...	...	...	...
e Indirect taxes paid, net	...	...	...	...	...	...	...	...	...	...
2 Property income paid	4137	2253	1127	757	...	4788	2518	1404	866	...
a Interest	4137	2253	1127	757	...	4788	2518	1404	866	...
b Net land rent and royalties	...	...	...	...	...	...	...	...	...	...
3 Subsidies	884	596	288	-	...	1088	738	350	-	...
4 Other current transfers paid	10197	11021	10061	295	250	11516	12130	11114	290	369
a Casualty insurance premiums, net	...	...	...	...	...	...	...	...	...	...
b Transfers to other government subsectors	...	4558	6823	49	...	...	4807	7540	40	...
c Transfers to households e	9918	6186	3238	246	248	11198	7008	3574	250	366
Social security benefits	5235	4607	380	-	248	5973	5160	447	-	366
Social assistance grants	4683	1579	2858	246	...	5225	1848	3127	250	...
Unfunded employee welfare benefits	...	...	...	...	...	...	...	...	...	...
d Transfers to private non-profit institutions serving households e	...	...	...	...	...	...	...	...	...	...
e Transfers to the rest of the world	279	277	...	...	2	318	315	...	...	3
Net saving	2585	-119	298	1033	1373	3953	1002	876	606	1469
Total Current Disbursements and Net Saving cd	38052	19181	17051	11593	1657	44325	22443	19831	12563	1875

	1974					1975				
	Total General Government	Central Government	State or Provincial Government	Local Government	Social Security Funds	Total General Government	Central Government	State or Provincial Government	Local Government	Social Security Funds

Receipts

1 Property and entrepreneurial income	5828	2070	2855	198	705	7034	2262	3665	233	874
a Net operating surplus	...	...	...	...	...	...	...	...	...	...
b Withdrawals from public quasi-corporations	...	...	...	...	...	...	...	...	...	...
c Interest	3707	1681	1227	94	705	4461	2012	1470	105	874
d Dividends a	576	382	90	104	...	656	237	291	128	...
e Net land rent and royalties b	1545	7	1538	-	...	1917	13	1904	-	...
2 Taxes, fees and contributions	50501	27474	16195	5224	1608	54446	28952	17490	6098	1906
a Indirect taxes	20876	8495	7236	5145	...	21442	7882	7547	6013	...
b Direct taxes	23864	16563	7301	-	...	26214	18115	8099	-	...
Income	23636	16563	7073	...	...	25970	18115	7855	...	...

223

Canada

3.12 General Government Income and Outlay Account: Total and Subsectors
(Continued)

Million Canadian dollars

	1974					1975				
	Total General Government	Central Government	State or Provincial Government	Local Government	Social Security Funds	Total General Government	Central Government	State or Provincial Government	Local Government	Social Security Funds
Other	228	-	228	-	...	244	-	244	-	...
c Social security contributions	4864	2408	848	-	1608	5895	2947	1042	-	1906
d Fees, fines and penalties	897	8	810	79		895	8	802	85	...
3 Other current transfers received	...	...	6054	9284	...	...	...	7577	11483	...
a Casualty insurance claims	...	...	...	...	...	...	...	...	...	...
b Transfers from other government subsectors	...	-	6054	9284	...	...	-	7577	11483	...
c Transfers from abroad	430	-	...	...	...	465	-	...	...	...
d Other transfers, except imputed	...	...	...	...	...	...	...	...	...	...
e Imputed unfunded employee welfare contributions	...	...	...	...	...	...	...	...	...	...
Total Current Receipts [cd]	56329	29544	25104	14706	2313	61480	31214	28732	17814	2780

Disbursements

	1974					1975				
1 General government final consumption expenditures	27728	7362	7497	12826	43	33302	8287	9598	15365	52
a Compensation of employees	18927	4704	4230	9993	...	22868	5491	5311	12066	...
b Consumption of fixed capital	2161	379	778	1004	-	2525	441	912	1172	-
c Goods and services purchased, net	6640	2279	2489	1829	43	7909	2355	3375	2127	52
d Less: Own account production of fixed assets	...	...	...	...	...	...	...	...	...	...
e Indirect taxes paid, net	...	...	...	...	...	...	...	...	...	...
2 Property income paid	5425	2961	1545	919	...	6538	3705	1839	994	...
a Interest	5425	2961	1545	919	...	6538	3705	1839	994	...
b Net land rent and royalties	...	...	...	...	...	...	...	...	...	...
3 Subsidies	2619	2060	559	-	...	3858	3183	675	-	...
4 Other current transfers paid	14287	15273	13596	257	499	17672	18878	16822	307	725
a Casualty insurance premiums, net	...	...	...	...	...	...	...	...	...	...
b Transfers to other government subsectors	...	6165	9132	41	...	...	7670	11340	50	...
c Transfers to households [e]	13880	8705	4464	216	495	17080	10620	5482	257	721
Social security benefits	6832	5775	562	-	495	8741	7298	722	-	721
Social assistance grants	7048	2930	3902	216	...	8339	3322	4760	257	...
Unfunded employee welfare benefits	...	...	...	...	...	...	...	...	...	...
d Transfers to private non-profit institutions serving households [e]	...	...	...	...	...	...	...	...	...	...
e Transfers to the rest of the world	407	403	...	...	4	592	588	...	...	4
Net saving	6270	1888	1907	704	1771	110	-2839	-202	1148	2003
Total Current Disbursements and Net Saving [cd]	56329	29544	25104	14706	2313	61480	31214	28732	17814	2780

	1976					1977				
	Total General Government	Central Government	State or Provincial Government	Local Government	Social Security Funds	Total General Government	Central Government	State or Provincial Government	Local Government	Social Security Funds

Receipts

	1976					1977				
1 Property and entrepreneurial income	8284	2565	4345	297	1077	9829	3068	5158	350	1253
a Net operating surplus	...	...	...	...	...	...	...	...	...	...
b Withdrawals from public quasi-corporations	...	...	...	...	...	...	...	...	...	...
c Interest	5320	2365	1739	139	1077	6157	2684	2054	166	1253
d Dividends [a]	681	190	333	158	...	1012	374	454	184	...
e Net land rent and royalties [b]	2283	10	2273	-	...	2660	10	2650	-	...
2 Taxes, fees and contributions	62166	32192	20462	7307	2205	68087	32809	24625	8240	2413
a Indirect taxes	24864	8601	9077	7186	...	27227	9085	10039	8103	...
b Direct taxes	28931	20027	8904	-	...	31766	19974	11792	-	...
Income	28664	20027	8637	...	...	31446	19974	11472	...	...

Canada

3.12 General Government Income and Outlay Account: Total and Subsectors
(Continued)

Million Canadian dollars

	1976 Total General Government	1976 Central Government	1976 State or Provincial Government	1976 Local Government	1976 Social Security Funds	1977 Total General Government	1977 Central Government	1977 State or Provincial Government	1977 Local Government	1977 Social Security Funds
Other	267	-	267	-	...	320	-	320	-	...
c Social security contributions	7158	3553	1400	-	2205	7743	3737	1593	-	2413
d Fees, fines and penalties	1213	11	1081	121	...	1351	13	1201	137	...
3 Other current transfers received	...	...	8369	13000	...	...	...	9665	15552	...
a Casualty insurance claims	...	...	...	...	...	...	...	...	...	...
b Transfers from other government subsectors	...	-	8369	13000	...	...	-	9665	15552	...
c Transfers from abroad	504	-	...	...	...	534	-	...	...	...
d Other transfers, except imputed	...	...	...	...	...	...	...	...	...	...
e Imputed unfunded employee welfare contributions	...	...	...	...	...	...	...	...	...	...
Total Current Receipts cd	70450	34757	33176	20604	3282	77916	35877	39448	24142	3666

Disbursements

1 General governement final consumption expenditures	38252	9627	10766	17801	58	43276	11087	12368	19757	64
a Compensation of employees	27015	6225	6285	14505	...	30182	6858	6980	16344	...
b Consumption of fixed capital	2825	501	1001	1323	-	3157	554	1113	1490	-
c Goods and services purchased, net	8412	2901	3480	1973	58	9937	3675	4275	1923	64
d Less: Own account production of fixed assets	...	...	...	...	...	...	...	...	...	...
e Indirect taxes paid, net	...	...	...	...	...	...	...	...	...	...
2 Property income paid	8101	4519	2327	1255	...	9268	5101	2690	1477	...
a Interest	8101	4519	2327	1255	...	9268	5101	2690	1477	...
b Net land rent and royalties	...	...	...	...	...	...	...	...	...	...
3 Subsidies	3344	2398	946	-	...	3320	2222	1098	-	...
4 Other current transfers paid	20025	20592	19438	323	1041	22858	23686	22707	318	1364
a Casualty insurance premiums, net	...	...	...	...	...	...	...	...	...	...
b Transfers to other government subsectors	...	8522	12796	51	...	...	9967	15200	50	...
c Transfers to households e	19483	11533	6642	272	1036	22220	13089	7507	268	1356
Social security benefits	10088	8145	907	-	1036	11543	9200	987	-	1356
Social assistance grants	9395	3388	5735	272	...	10677	3889	6520	268	...
Unfunded employee welfare benefits	...	...	...	...	...	...	...	...	...	...
d Transfers to private non-profit institutions serving households e	...	...	...	...	...	...	...	...	...	...
e Transfers to the rest of the world	542	537	...	...	5	638	630	...	...	8
Net saving	728	-2379	-301	1225	2183	-806	-6219	585	2590	2238
Total Current Disbursements and Net Saving cd	70450	34757	33176	20604	3282	77916	35877	39448	24142	3666

	1978 Total General Government	1978 Central Government	1978 State or Provincial Government	1978 Local Government	1978 Social Security Funds	1979 Total General Government	1979 Central Government	1979 State or Provincial Government	1979 Local Government	1979 Social Security Funds

Receipts

1 Property and entrepreneurial income	12344	3804	6643	392	1505	14315	4145	7954	436	1780
a Net operating surplus	...	...	...	...	...	...	...	...	...	...
b Withdrawals from public quasi-corporations	...	...	...	...	...	...	...	...	...	...
c Interest	7424	3114	2617	188	1505	8345	3352	3007	206	1780
d Dividends a	1299	680	415	204	...	1557	782	545	230	...
e Net land rent and royalties b	3621	10	3611	-	...	4413	11	4402	-	...
2 Taxes, fees and contributions	73465	33822	27736	9181	2726	82305	38561	30615	10042	3087
a Indirect taxes	29314	9750	10536	9028	...	32537	10661	12009	9867	...
b Direct taxes	34011	20056	13955	-	...	39011	23967	15044	-	...
Income	33492	20056	13436	...	...	38451	23967	14484	...	...

Canada

3.12 General Government Income and Outlay Account: Total and Subsectors
(Continued)

Million Canadian dollars

	1978					1979				
	Total General Government	Central Government	State or Provincial Government	Local Government	Social Security Funds	Total General Government	Central Government	State or Provincial Government	Local Government	Social Security Funds
Other	519	-	519	-	...	560	-	560	-	...
c Social security contributions	8633	4001	1906	-	2726	9114	3916	2111	-	3087
d Fees, fines and penalties	1507	15	1339	153	...	1643	17	1451	175	...
3 Other current transfers received	...	...	10574	16060	...	...	...	11467	18456	...
a Casualty insurance claims	...	...	...	...	...	...	...	...	...	...
b Transfers from other government subsectors	...	-	10574	16060	...	...	-	11467	18456	...
c Transfers from abroad	582	-	...	...	...	754	...	...	...	...
d Other transfers, except imputed	...	...	...	...	...	...	...	...	...	...
e Imputed unfunded employee welfare contributions	...	...	...	...	...	...	...	...	...	...
Total Current Receipts cd	85809	37626	44953	25633	4231	96620	42706	50036	28934	4867

Disbursements

	1978					1979				
1 General government final consumption expenditures	47544	11906	13810	21757	71	51887	12696	15124	23993	74
a Compensation of employees	33036	7373	7751	17912	...	36008	7786	8502	19720	...
b Consumption of fixed capital	3510	606	1248	1656	-	3984	686	1405	1893	...
c Goods and services purchased, net	10998	3927	4811	2189	71	11895	4224	5217	2380	74
d Less: Own account production of fixed assets	...	...	...	...	...	...	...	...	...	...
e Indirect taxes paid, net	...	...	...	...	...	...	...	...	...	...
2 Property income paid	11406	6410	3343	1653	...	13575	8080	3712	1783	...
a Interest	11406	6410	3343	1653	...	13575	8080	3712	1783	...
b Net land rent and royalties	...	...	...	...	...	...	...	...	...	...
3 Subsidies	3460	2301	1159	...	...	4612	3220	1392	...	...
4 Other current transfers paid	26071	26525	24131	338	1711	27104	27167	27372	388	2100
a Casualty insurance premiums, net	...	...	...	...	...	...	...	...	...	...
b Transfers to other government subsectors	...	10875	15712	47	...	...	11754	18121	48	...
c Transfers to households [e]	25058	14647	8419	291	1701	26337	14657	9251	340	2089
Social security benefits	13389	10486	1202	...	1701	14474	11039	1346	...	2089
Social assistance grants	11669	4161	7217	291	...	11863	3618	7905	340	...
Unfunded employee welfare benefits	...	...	...	...	...	...	...	...	...	...
d Transfers to private non-profit institutions serving households [e]	...	...	...	...	...	...	...	...	...	...
e Transfers to the rest of the world	1013	1003	...	...	10	767	756	...	...	11
Net saving	-2672	-9516	2510	1885	2449	-558	-8457	2436	2770	2693
Total Current Disbursements and Net Saving cd	85809	37626	44953	25633	4231	96620	42706	50036	28934	4867

	1980				
	Total General Government	Central Government	State or Provincial Government	Local Government	Social Security Funds

Receipts

1 Property and entrepreneurial income	16585	4659	9328	470	2128
a Net operating surplus	...	...	...	...	...
b Withdrawals from public quasi-corporations	...	...	...	...	...
c Interest	9628	3750	3531	219	2128
d Dividends [a]	1671	895	525	251	...
e Net land rent and royalties [b]	5286	14	5272	-	...
2 Taxes, fees and contributions	93366	44581	34165	11079	3541
a Indirect taxes	36134	12131	13109	10894	...
b Direct taxes	45315	28134	17181	-	...
Income	44729	28134	16595	-	...

Canada

3.12 General Government Income and Outlay Account: Total and Subsectors
(Continued)

Million Canadian dollars

		1980			
	Total General Government	Central Government	State or Provincial Government	Local Government	Social Security Funds
Other	586	-	586	-	...
c Social security contributions	10169	4296	2332	-	3541
d Fees, fines and penalties	1748	20	1543	185	...
3 Other current transfers received	...	-	12592	19899	...
a Casualty insurance claims	...	...	...	...	...
b Transfers from other government subsectors	...	-	12592	19899	...
c Transfers from abroad	995	...	...	...	...
d Other transfers, except imputed	...	...	...	...	...
e Imputed unfunded employee welfare contributions	...	...	...	...	...
Total Current Receipts cd	109951	49240	56085	31448	5669

Disbursements

1 General government final consumption expenditures	57813	13648	16894	27184	87
a Compensation of employees	40669	8362	9945	22362	-
b Consumption of fixed capital	4624	776	1656	2192	-
c Goods and services purchased, net	12520	4510	5293	2630	87
d Less: Own account production of fixed assets	...	...	...	...	...
e Indirect taxes paid, net	...	...	...	...	...
2 Property income paid	15719	9653	4107	1959	-
a Interest	15719	9653	4107	1959	-
b Net land rent and royalties	...	...	...	...	...
3 Subsidies	6943	5486	1457	...	...
4 Other current transfers paid	31125	30206	30387	443	2580
a Casualty insurance premiums, net	...	...	...	...	...
b Transfers to other government subsectors	...	12828	19604	59	...
c Transfers to households e	30308	16574	10783	384	2567
Social security benefits	16607	12546	1494	...	2567
Social assistance grants	13701	4028	9289	384	...
Unfunded employee welfare benefits	...	...	...	...	...
d Transfers to private non-profit institutions serving households e	...	...	...	...	...
e Transfers to the rest of the world	817	804	...	...	13
Net saving	-1649	-9753	3240	1862	3002
Total Current Disbursements and Net Saving cd	109951	49240	56085	31448	5669

a) Remitted profits of government business enterprises.
b) Royalties only.
c) Column 'Local governemnt' includes hospitals.
d) Column 'Social security funds' refers to Canada and Quebec pension plans only.
e) Item 'Transfers to private non-profit institutions servicing household' is included in item 'Transfers to households'.

3.13 General Government Capital Accumulation Account: Total and Subsectors

Million Canadian dollars

	1970					1971				
	Total General Government	Central Government	State or Provincial Government	Local Government	Social Security Funds	Total General Government	Central Government	State or Provincial Government	Local Government	Social Security Funds

Finance of Gross Accumulation

1 Gross saving	3823	717	688	1225	1193	3790	404	850	1258	1278
a Consumption of fixed capital	1231	232	395	604	-	1334	245	436	653	-
b Net saving	2592	485	293	621	1193	2456	159	414	605	1278
2 Capital transfers received	266	111	155	-	...	279	136	143	-	...
a From other government subsectors	...	...	...	...	...	...	...	...	...	...
b From other resident sectors	266	111	155	-	...	279	136	143	-	...
c From rest of the world	...	...	...	...	...	...	...	...	...	...
Finance of Gross Accumulation ab	4089	828	843	1225	1193	4069	540	993	1258	1278

Canada

3.13 General Government Capital Accumulation Account: Total and Subsectors
(Continued)

Million Canadian dollars

	1970 Total General Government	1970 Central Government	1970 State or Provincial Government	1970 Local Government	1970 Social Security Funds	1971 Total General Government	1971 Central Government	1971 State or Provincial Government	1971 Local Government	1971 Social Security Funds
Gross Accumulation										
1 Gross capital formation	3160	465	1046	1649	...	3714	514	1409	1791	...
a Increase in stocks	-13	-13	-	-	...	-40	-40	-	-	...
b Gross fixed capital formation	3173	478	1046	1649	-	3754	554	1409	1791	-
2 Purchases of land, net	...	...	...	...	...	...	...	...	...	...
3 Purchases of intangible assets, net										
4 Capital transfers paid	123	97	26	-	...	225	171	54	-	...
a To other government subsectors	...	...	...	...	...	...	...	...	...	...
b To other resident sectors	123	97	26	-	...	225	171	54	-	...
c To rest of the world	...	...	...	...	...	...	...	...	...	...
Net lending c	806	266	-229	-424	1193	130	-145	-470	-533	1278
Gross Accumulation ab	4089	828	843	1225	1193	4069	540	993	1258	1278

	1972 Total General Government	1972 Central Government	1972 State or Provincial Government	1972 Local Government	1972 Social Security Funds	1973 Total General Government	1973 Central Government	1973 State or Provincial Government	1973 Local Government	1973 Social Security Funds
Finance of Gross Accumulation										
1 Gross saving	4080	158	779	1770	1373	5663	1314	1451	1429	1469
a Consumption of fixed capital	1495	277	481	737	-	1710	312	575	823	-
b Net saving	2585	-119	298	1033	1373	3953	1002	876	606	1469
2 Capital transfers received	230	80	150	-	...	205	22	183	-	...
a From other government subsectors	...	...	...	...	...	...	...	...	...	...
b From other resident sectors	230	80	150	-	...	205	22	183	-	...
c From rest of the world	...	...	...	...	...	...	...	...	...	...
Finance of Gross Accumulation ab	4310	238	929	1770	1373	5868	1336	1634	1429	1469
Gross Accumulation										
1 Gross capital formation	3984	623	1556	1805	...	4290	722	1637	1931	...
a Increase in stocks	16	16	-	-	...	-15	-15	-	-	...
b Gross fixed capital formation	3968	607	1556	1805	-	4305	737	1637	1931	-
2 Purchases of land, net	...	...	...	...	-	...	...	...	...	-
3 Purchases of intangible assets, net										
4 Capital transfers paid	245	181	64	-	...	326	227	99	-	...
a To other government subsectors	...	...	...	...	...	...	...	...	...	...
b To other resident sectors	245	181	64	-	...	326	227	99	-	...
c To rest of the world	...	...	...	...	...	...	...	...	...	...
Net lending c	81	-566	-691	-35	1373	1252	387	-102	-502	1469
Gross Accumulation ab	4310	238	929	1770	1373	5868	1336	1634	1429	1469

	1974 Total General Government	1974 Central Government	1974 State or Provincial Government	1974 Local Government	1974 Social Security Funds	1975 Total General Government	1975 Central Government	1975 State or Provincial Government	1975 Local Government	1975 Social Security Funds
Finance of Gross Accumulation										
1 Gross saving	8431	2267	2685	1708	1771	2635	-2398	710	2320	2003
a Consumption of fixed capital	2161	379	778	1004	-	2525	441	912	1172	-
b Net saving	6270	1888	1907	704	1771	110	-2839	-202	1148	2003
2 Capital transfers received	178	9	169	-	...	156	6	150	-	...
a From other government subsectors	...	...	...	...	...	...	...	...	...	...
b From other resident sectors	178	9	169	-	...	156	6	150	-	...
c From rest of the world	...	...	...	...	...	...	...	...	...	...
Finance of Gross Accumulation ab	8609	2276	2854	1708	1771	2791	-2392	860	2320	2003
Gross Accumulation										
1 Gross capital formation	5488	974	2069	2445	...	6354	1125	2418	2811	...
a Increase in stocks	26	26	-	-	...	31	31	-	-	...
b Gross fixed capital formation	5462	948	2069	2445	-	6323	1094	2418	2811	-

Canada

3.13 General Government Capital Accumulation Account: Total and Subsectors
(Continued)

Million Canadian dollars

	1974					1975				
	Total General Government	Central Government	State or Provincial Government	Local Government	Social Security Funds	Total General Government	Central Government	State or Provincial Government	Local Government	Social Security Funds
2 Purchases of land, net	...	...	...	...	-	...	...	...	...	-
3 Purchases of intangible assets, net	...	...	...	...	...	...	...	...	...	...
4 Capital transfers paid	326	193	133	-	...	486	288	198	-	...
a To other government subsectors	...	...	...	...	...	...	...	...	...	...
b To other resident sectors	326	193	133	-	...	486	288	198	-	...
c To rest of the world	...	...	...	...	...	...	...	...	...	...
Net lending c	2795	1109	652	-737	1771	-4049	-3805	-1756	-491	2003
Gross Accumulation ab	8609	2276	2854	1708	1771	2791	-2392	860	2320	2003

	1976					1977				
	Total General Government	Central Government	State or Provincial Government	Local Government	Social Security Funds	Total General Government	Central Government	State or Provincial Government	Local Government	Social Security Funds

Finance of Gross Accumulation

1 Gross saving	3553	-1878	700	2548	2183	2351	-5665	1698	4080	2238
a Consumption of fixed capital	2825	501	1001	1323	-	3157	554	1113	1490	-
b Net saving	728	-2379	-301	1225	2183	-806	-6219	585	2590	2238
2 Capital transfers received	148	12	136	-	...	139	22	117	-	...
a From other government subsectors	...	...	...	...	...	...	...	...	...	...
b From other resident sectors	148	12	136	-	...	139	22	117	-	...
c From rest of the world	...	...	...	...	...	...	...	...	...	...
Finance of Gross Accumulation ab	3701	-1866	836	2548	2183	2490	-5643	1815	4080	2238

Gross Accumulation

1 Gross capital formation	6359	1158	2182	3019	...	6833	1163	2384	3286	...
a Increase in stocks	41	41	-	-	...	43	43	-	-	...
b Gross fixed capital formation	6318	1117	2182	3019	-	6790	1120	2384	3286	-
2 Purchases of land, net	...	...	...	...	-	...	...	...	...	-
3 Purchases of intangible assets, net	...	...	...	...	...	...	...	...	...	...
4 Capital transfers paid	564	367	197	-	...	662	497	165	-	...
a To other government subsectors	...	...	...	...	...	...	...	...	...	...
b To other resident sectors	564	367	197	-	...	662	497	165	-	...
c To rest of the world	...	...	...	...	...	...	...	...	...	...
Net lending c	-3222	-3391	-1543	-471	2183	-5005	-7303	-734	794	2238
Gross Accumulation ab	3701	-1866	836	2548	2183	2490	-5643	1815	4080	2238

	1978					1979				
	Total General Government	Central Government	State or Provincial Government	Local Government	Social Security Funds	Total General Government	Central Government	State or Provincial Government	Local Government	Social Security Funds

Finance of Gross Accumulation

1 Gross saving	838	-8910	3758	3541	2449	3426	-7771	3841	4663	2693
a Consumption of fixed capital	3510	606	1248	1656	-	3984	686	1405	1893	-
b Net saving	-2672	-9516	2510	1885	2449	-558	-8457	2436	2770	2693
2 Capital transfers received	116	18	98	-	...	99	15	84	-	...
a From other government subsectors	...	...	...	...	...	...	...	...	...	...
b From other resident sectors	116	18	98	-	...	99	15	84	-	...
c From rest of the world	...	...	...	...	...	...	...	...	...	...
Finance of Gross Accumulation ab	954	-8892	3856	3541	2449	3525	-7756	3925	4663	2693

Gross Accumulation

1 Gross capital formation	7198	1206	2653	3339	...	7457	911	2940	3606	...
a Increase in stocks	58	58	...	...	...	60	60	...	...	...
b Gross fixed capital formation	7140	1148	2653	3339	-	7397	851	2940	3606	...

Canada

3.13 General Government Capital Accumulation Account: Total and Subsectors
(Continued)

Million Canadian dollars

		1978					1979			
		Total General Government	Central Government	State or Provincial Government	Local Government	Social Security Funds	Total General Government	Central Government	State or Provincial Government	Local Government	Social Security Funds
2	Purchases of land, net	...	...	...	...	...	...	...	...	...
3	Purchases of intangible assets, net	...	...	...	...	...	...	...	...	...
4	Capital transfers paid	710	556	154	-	...	759	546	213	-	...
	a To other government subsectors	...	...	...	...	...	...	...	...	...
	b To other resident sectors	710	556	154	-	...	759	546	213	-	...
	c To rest of the world	...	...	...	...	...	...	...	...	...
	Net lending c	-6954	-10654	1049	202	2449	-4691	-9213	772	1057	2693
	Gross Accumulation ab	954	-8892	3856	3541	2449	3525	-7756	3925	4663	2693

		1980				
		Total General Government	Central Government	State or Provincial Government	Local Government	Social Security Funds

Finance of Gross Accumulation

1	Gross saving	2975	-8977	4896	4054	3002
	a Consumption of fixed capital	4624	776	1656	2192	...
	b Net saving	-1649	-9753	3240	1862	3002
2	Capital transfers received	71	1	70	...	...
	a From other government subsectors	...	...	...	...	...
	b From other resident sectors	71	1	70	...	...
	c From rest of the world	...	...	...	...	...
	Finance of Gross Accumulation ab	3046	-8976	4966	4054	3002

Gross Accumulation

1	Gross capital formation	8084	1014	3163	3907	...
	a Increase in stocks	69	69	...	...	...
	b Gross fixed capital formation	8015	945	3163	3907	...
2	Purchases of land, net	...	...	...	...	...
3	Purchases of intangible assets, net	...	...	...	...	...
4	Capital transfers paid	945	707	238	...	...
	a To other government subsectors	...	...	...	...	...
	b To other resident sectors	945	707	238	-	...
	c To rest of the world	...	...	...	...	...
	Net lending c	-5983	-10697	1565	147	3002
	Gross Accumulation ab	3046	-8976	4966	4054	3002

a) Column 'Local governemnt' includes hospitals.
b) Column 'Social security funds' refers to Canada and Quebec pension plans only.
c) Net lending of the Capital Accumulation Account and the Capital Finance Account have not been reconciled and are different due to different statistical sources.

3.14 General Government Capital Finance Account, Total and Subsectors

Million Canadian dollars

		1970					1971				
		Total General Government	Central Government	State or Provincial Government	Local Government	Social Security Funds	Total General Government	Central Government	State or Provincial Government	Local Government	Social Security Funds

Acquisition of Financial Assets

1	Gold and SDRs	...	...	...	...	...	...	...	...	...	...
2	Currency and transferable deposits	362	89	258	15	...	703	761	-23	-35	-
3	Other deposits					...					
4	Bills and bonds, short term	11	-3	-	14	...	15	6	-2	11	...
5	Bonds, long term	1328	-48	416	93	867	860	-479	351	66	922
	a Corporations	182	4	142	36	-	78	2	61	15	-
	b Other government subsectors	1146	-52	274	57	867	782	-481	290	51	922
	c Rest of the world	-	-	-	-	-	-	-	-	-	-
6	Corporate equity securities a	26	-6	19	13	...	4	-1	-3	8	...
7	Short-term loans, n.e.c. b	259	195	64	-	...	726	437	286	3	...
8	Long-term loans, n.e.c. b	221	23	198	-	...	272	8	264	-	...
	a Mortgages	221	23	198	-	...	272	8	264	-	...
	b Other	...	...	...	...	...	...	...	...	...	...
9	Other receivables	28	-	9	19	...	17	1	-2	18	...
10	Other assets c	3064	2254	421	63	326	3265	2288	568	53	356
	Total Acquisition of Financial Assets c	5299	2504	1385	217	1193	5862	3021	1439	124	1278

Canada

3.14 General Government Capital Finance Account, Total and Subsectors
(Continued)

Million Canadian dollars

	1970					1971				
	Total General Government	Central Government	State or Provincial Government	Local Government	Social Security Funds	Total General Government	Central Government	State or Provincial Government	Local Government	Social Security Funds

Incurrence of Liabilities

1 Currency and transferable deposits	24	24	-	-	...	25	25	-	-	...
2 Other deposits					...					...
3 Bills and bonds, short term	786	730	11	45	...	344	205	175	-36	...
4 Bonds, long term	3171	1129	1451	591	...	4721	2571	1566	584	...
5 Short-term loans, n.e.c. [b]	55	-54	86	23	...	196	48	166	-18	...
6 Long-term loans, n.e.c. [b]	15	-	12	3	...	2	-	8	-6	...
7. Other payables	163	12	131	20	...	5	2	-15	18	...
8 Other liabilities	659	445	191	23	...	407	278	123	6	...
Total Incurrence of Liabilities	4873	2286	1882	705	...	5700	3129	2023	548	-
Net Lending [d]	426	218	-497	-488	1193	162	-108	-584	-424	1278
Incurrence of Liabilities and Net Worth	5299	2504	1385	217	1193	5862	3021	1439	124	1278

	1972					1973				
	Total General Government	Central Government	State or Provincial Government	Local Government	Social Security Funds	Total General Government	Central Government	State or Provincial Government	Local Government	Social Security Funds

Acquisition of Financial Assets

1 Gold and SDRs	...	...	...	...	...	...	...	...	...	...
2 Currency and transferable deposits	921	281	553	87	-	-285	-474	206	-17	-
3 Other deposits										
4 Bills and bonds, short term	29	5	-	24	...	3	-6	-2	11	...
5 Bonds, long term	1342	5	322	55	960	1344	-10	253	56	1045
a Corporations	-7	2	-13	4	-	-46	2	-51	3	-
b Other government subsectors	1349	3	335	51	960	1390	-12	304	53	1045
c Rest of the world	-	-	-	-	-	-	-	-	-	-
6 Corporate equity securities [a]	12	26	-17	3	...	-7	28	18	-53	...
7 Short-term loans, n.e.c. [b]	530	327	217	-14	...	865	664	208	-7	...
8 Long-term loans, n.e.c. [b]	176	-3	179	-	...	187	-1	188	-	...
a Mortgages	176	-3	179	-	...	187	-1	188	-	...
b Other	...	...	...	...	...	...	...	...	...	...
9 Other receivables	63	9	46	8	...	7	1	-24	30	...
10 Other assets [c]	2141	1129	568	31	413	1330	350	489	67	424
Total Acquisition of Financial Assets [c]	5214	1779	1868	194	1373	3444	552	1336	87	1469

Incurrence of Liabilities

1 Currency and transferable deposits	26	26	-	-	...	65	65	-	-	...
2 Other deposits					...					...
3 Bills and bonds, short term	452	330	129	-7	...	438	530	-90	-2	...
4 Bonds, long term	3970	1260	2086	624	...	1488	-636	1583	541	...
5 Short-term loans, n.e.c. [b]	375	26	226	123	...	757	62	341	354	...
6 Long-term loans, n.e.c. [b]	21	-	3	18	...	-19	-	-	-19	...
7 Other payables	158	59	81	18	...	29	-7	18	18	...
8 Other liabilities	980	750	151	79	...	48	136	-100	12	...
Total Incurrence of Liabilities	5982	2451	2676	855	-	2806	150	1752	904	-
Net Lending [d]	-768	-672	-808	-661	1373	638	402	-416	-817	1469
Incurrence of Liabilities and Net Worth	5214	1779	1868	194	1373	3444	552	1336	87	1469

	1974					1975				
	Total General Government	Central Government	State or Provincial Government	Local Government	Social Security Funds	Total General Government	Central Government	State or Provincial Government	Local Government	Social Security Funds

Acquisition of Financial Assets

1 Gold and SDRs	...	...	...	...	...	...	...	...	...	...
2 Currency and transferable deposits	2695	2559	27	109	-	-1377	-752	-775	150	-
3 Other deposits										
4 Bills and bonds, short term	4	-	-	4	...	9	6	-	3	...
5 Bonds, long term	1734	6	423	64	1241	2828	4	1340	84	1400
a Corporations	40	6	28	6	-	199	4	171	24	-
b Other government subsectors	1694	-	395	58	1241	2629	-	1169	60	1400

Canada

3.14 General Government Capital Finance Account, Total and Subsectors
(Continued)

Million Canadian dollars

	1974					1975				
	Total General Government	Central Government	State or Provincial Government	Local Government	Social Security Funds	Total General Government	Central Government	State or Provincial Government	Local Government	Social Security Funds
c Rest of the world	-	-	-	-	...	-	-	-	-	...
6 Corporate equity securities [a]	260	35	225	-	...	-96	55	-158	7	...
7 Short-term loans, n.e.c. [b]	746	489	239	18	...	788	518	228	42	...
8 Long-term loans, n.e.c. [b]	277	17	260	-	...	327	-15	342	-	...
a Mortgages	277	17	260	-	...	327	-15	342	-	...
b Other	...	...	...	...	...	...	...	...	...	...
9 Other receivables	139	9	35	95	...	190	22	34	134	...
10 Other assets [c]	5440	2793	1887	230	530	3352	1339	884	526	603
Total Acquisition of Financial Assets [c]	11295	5908	3096	520	1771	6021	1177	1895	946	2003

Incurrence of Liabilities

1 Currency and transferable deposits	86	86	-	-	...	69	69	-	-	...
2 Other deposits					...					...
3 Bills and bonds, short term	800	940	-219	79	...	999	570	332	97	...
4 Bonds, long term	6753	3439	2453	861	...	8693	3416	3722	1555	...
5 Short-term loans, n.e.c. [b]	784	60	367	357	...	562	56	113	393	...
6 Long-term loans, n.e.c. [b]	9	-	-	9	...	19	-	...	19	...
7 Other payables	119	31	70	18	...	157	11	128	18	...
8 Other liabilities	1002	778	92	132	...	689	529	35	125	...
Total Incurrence of Liabilities	9553	5334	2763	1456	-	11188	4651	4330	2207	-
Net Lending [d]	1742	574	333	-936	1771	-5167	-3474	-2435	-1261	2003
Incurrence of Liabilities and Net Worth	11295	5908	3096	520	1771	6021	1177	1895	946	2003

	1976					1977				
	Total General Government	Central Government	State or Provincial Government	Local Government	Social Security Funds	Total General Government	Central Government	State or Provincial Government	Local Government	Social Security Funds

Acquisition of Financial Assets

1 Gold and SDRs	...	...	...	...	...	...	...	...	...	...
2 Currency and transferable deposits	3	-823	405	421	-	2593	1344	904	345	-
3 Other deposits										
4 Bills and bonds, short term	178	-	99	79	...	145	8	58	79	...
5 Bonds, long term	3217	9	1642	47	1519	3603	-6	1845	110	1654
a Corporations	259	-2	219	42	-	274	-1	177	98	-
b Other government subsectors	2958	11	1423	5	1519	3329	-5	1668	12	1654
c Rest of the world	-	-	-	-	...	-	-	-	-	...
6 Corporate equity securities [a]	-30	-54	3	21	...	-2	-7	-16	21	...
7 Short-term loans, n.e.c. [b]	618	410	233	-25	...	714	602	119	-7	...
8 Long-term loans, n.e.c. [b]	419	-36	455	-	...	233	-40	273	-	...
a Mortgages	419	-36	455	-	...	233	-40	273	-	...
b Other	...	...	...	...	...	...	...	...	...	...
9 Other receivables	141	3	21	117	...	112	22	-27	117	...
10 Other assets [c]	2355	1854	57	-220	664	2792	-78	2054	232	584
Total Acquisition of Financial Assets [c]	6901	1363	2915	440	2183	10190	1845	5210	897	2238

Incurrence of Liabilities

1 Currency and transferable deposits	47	47	-	-	...	61	61	-	-	...
2 Other deposits					...					...
3 Bills and bonds, short term	1555	1645	-39	-51	...	2401	2470	70	-139	...
4 Bonds, long term	8140	2543	3790	1807	...	11353	5664	3960	1729	...
5 Short-term loans, n.e.c. [b]	191	-12	130	73	...	-77	3	495	-575	...
6 Long-term loans, n.e.c. [b]	-51	-	-	-51	...	-51	-	-	-51	...
7 Other payables	137	-24	143	18	...	356	51	287	18	...
8 Other liabilities	931	58	525	348	...	48	-405	131	322	...
Total Incurrence of Liabilities	10950	4257	4549	2144	-	14091	7844	4943	1304	-
Net Lending [d]	-4049	-2894	-1634	-1704	2183	-3901	-5999	267	-407	2238
Incurrence of Liabilities and Net Worth	6901	1363	2915	440	2183	10190	1845	5210	897	2238

Canada

3.14 General Government Capital Finance Account, Total and Subsectors

Million Canadian dollars

	1978 Total General Government	1978 Central Government	1978 State or Provincial Government	1978 Local Government	1978 Social Security Funds	1979 Total General Government	1979 Central Government	1979 State or Provincial Government	1979 Local Government	1979 Social Security Funds
Acquisition of Financial Assets										
1 Gold and SDRs	...	...	...	...	...	...	...	...	...	...
2 Currency and transferable deposits	2983	1946	778	259	-	-1627	-4277	2322	328	...
3 Other deposits										...
4 Bills and bonds, short term	325	-8	328	5	...	120	-12	133	-1	...
5 Bonds, long term	3931	-12	2267	2	1674	2999	144	842	99	1914
a Corporations	89	-8	108	-11	-	132	1	101	30	-
b Other government subsectors	3842	-4	2159	13	1674	2867	143	741	69	1914
c Rest of the world	-	-	-	-	-	-	-	-	-	-
6 Corporate equity securities [a]	-12	-1	-20	9	...	20	-1	10	11	...
7 Short-term loans, n.e.c. [b]	590	473	121	-4	...	802	678	116	8	...
8 Long-term loans, n.e.c. [b]	62	-52	114	-	...	-46	-49	3	-	...
a Mortgages	62	-52	114	-	...	-46	-49	3	-	...
b Other	...	...	...	...	...	...	...	...	...	...
9 Other receivables	3	28	-7	-18	...	34	48	-	-14	...
10 Other assets [c]	5513	1681	2681	376	775	4874	1250	2411	434	779
Total Acquisition of Financial Assets [c]	13395	4055	6262	629	2449	7176	-2219	5837	865	2693
Incurrence of Liabilities										
1 Currency and transferable deposits	80	80	-	-	...	88	88	-	-	...
2 Other deposits					...					...
3 Bills and bonds, short term	3029	2820	210	-1	...	1900	2125	-225	-	...
4 Bonds, long term	13635	7747	4652	1236	...	10204	5903	3750	551	...
5 Short-term loans, n.e.c. [b]	4097	3554	637	-94	...	-1325	-1647	1	321	...
6 Long-term loans, n.e.c. [b]	-19	-	-	-19	...	-23	-	-	-23	...
7 Other payables	280	55	207	18	...	823	-6	811	18	...
8 Other liabilities	1278	895	274	109	...	904	562	305	37	...
Total Incurrence of Liabilities	22380	15151	5980	1249	-	12571	7025	4642	904	...
Net Lending [d]	-8985	-11096	282	-620	2449	-5395	-9244	1195	-39	2693
Incurrence of Liabilities and Net Worth	13395	4055	6262	629	2449	7176	-2219	5837	865	2693

	1980 Total General Government	1980 Central Government	1980 State or Provincial Government	1980 Local Government	1980 Social Security Funds
Acquisition of Financial Assets					
1 Gold and SDRs	...	...	...	...	...
2 Currency and transferable deposits	1632	1744	-384	272	-
3 Other deposits					
4 Bills and bonds, short term	576	5	571	-	-
5 Bonds, long term	5989	-148	4060	153	1924
a Corporations	180	4	84	92	-
b Other government subsectors	5809	-152	3976	61	1924
c Rest of the world	-	-	-	-	-
6 Corporate equity securities [a]	29	6	12	11	...
7 Short-term loans, n.e.c. [b]	571	458	114	-1	...
8 Long-term loans, n.e.c. [b]	146	-39	185	-	...
a Mortgages	146	-39	185	-	...
b Other	...	...	...	...	...
9 Other receivables	24	38	-	-14	...
10 Other assets [c]	5000	814	2871	237	1078
Total Acquisition of Financial Assets [c]	13967	2878	7429	658	3002
Incurrence of Liabilities					
1 Currency and transferable deposits	61	61	-	-	...
2 Other deposits					...
3 Bills and bonds, short term	5806	5475	333	-2	...

Canada

3.14 General Government Capital Finance Account, Total and Subsectors
(Continued)

Million Canadian dollars

	1980				
	Total General Government	Central Government	State or Provincial Government	Local Government	Social Security Funds
4 Bonds, long term	12628	6460	5228	940	...
5 Short-term loans, n.e.c. b	1646	763	710	173	...
6 Long-term loans, n.e.c. b	-23	-	-	-23	...
7 Other payables	59	8	33	18	...
8 Other liabilities	1296	1407	-148	37	...
Total Incurrence of Liabilities	21473	14174	6156	1143	...
Net Lending d	-7506	-11296	1273	-485	3002
Incurrence of Liabilities and Net Worth	13967	2878	7429	658	3002

a) Investment in short-term papers, bonds and corporate equity securities of the rest of the world cannot be split between long-term and short-term by purchasers, the total investment has been allocated to the item.
b) Loans other than mortgages are included in item 'Short-term loans, n.e.c.'.
c) Column 'Social security funds' refers to Canada and Quebec pension plans only.
d) Net lending of the Capital Accumulation Account and the Capital Finance Account have not been reconciled and are different due to different statistical sources.

3.15 General Government Balance Sheet, Total and Subsectors

Million Canadian dollars

	1970					1971				
	Total General Government	Central Government	State or Provincial Government	Local Government	Social Security Funds	Total General Government	Central Government	State or Provincial Government	Local Government	Social Security Funds
Assets										
Non-financial assets	...	...	...	...	...	...	...	...	...	...
Financial assets	45054	21888	14446	3813	4907	50958	24857	16141	3775	6185
1 Gold and SDRs	...	...	...	...	...	...	...	...	...	...
2 Currency and transferable deposits	2672	1143	1093	436	...	3327	1905	1070	352	...
3 Other deposits					...					...
4 Bills and bonds, short term	53	15	4	34	...	63	15	2	46	...
5 Bonds, long term	9329	548	4533	728	3520	10189	69	4884	794	4442
a Corporate	261	23	141	97	-	339	25	202	112	-
b Other government subsectors	9068	525	4392	631	3520	9850	44	4682	682	4442
c Rest of the world	-	-	-	-	-	-	-	-	-	-
6 Corporate equity securities	249	81	49	119	...	252	79	46	127	...
7 Short term loans, n.e.c.	4106	2648	1447	11	...	4831	3085	1733	13	...
8 Long term loans, n.e.c.	1208	548	660	-	...	1480	556	924	-	...
a Mortgages	1208	548	660	-	...	1480	556	924	-	...
b Other	-	-	-	-	...	-	-	-	-	...
9 Other receivables	233	9	42	182	...	250	10	40	200	...
10 Other assets	27204	16896	6618	2303	1387	30566	19138	7442	2243	1743
Total Assets	...	...	...	...	...	...	...	...	...	...
Liabilities and Net Worth										
Liabilities	55306	28222	14296	12788	...	61067	31353	16319	13395	...
1 Currency and transferable deposits	504	504	-	-	...	529	529	-	-	...
2 Other deposits					...					...
3 Other deposits	3799	3625	99	75	...	4143	3830	274	39	...
4 Bonds, long term	42847	21030	12208	9609	...	47800	23601	13774	10425	...
5 Short term loans, n.e.c. a	2209	11	658	1540	...	2217	59	824	1334	...
6 Long term loans, n.e.c. a	159	-	60	99	...	157	-	68	89	...
7 Other payables	715	62	481	172	...	721	65	466	190	...
8 Other liabilities	5073	2990	790	1293	...	5500	3269	913	1318	...
Net worth	...	...	...	...	...	...	...	...	...	...
Total Liabilities and Net Worth	...	...	...	...	...	...	...	...	...	...

	1972					1973				
	Total General Government	Central Government	State or Provincial Government	Local Government	Social Security Funds	Total General Government	Central Government	State or Provincial Government	Local Government	Social Security Funds
Assets										
Non-financial assets	...	...	...	...	...	...	...	...	...	...
Financial assets	55997	26848	18042	3549	7558	61209	27655	19802	4725	9027
1 Gold and SDRs	...	...	...	...	...	...	...	...	...	...
2 Currency and transferable deposits	4286	2163	1623	500	...	4048	1687	1829	532	...
3 Other deposits					...					...
4 Bills and bonds, short term	92	20	2	70	...	93	14	-	79	...

Canada

3.15 General Government Balance Sheet, Total and Subsectors
(Continued)

Million Canadian dollars

	1972					1973				
	Total General Government	Central Government	State or Provincial Government	Local Government	Social Security Funds	Total General Government	Central Government	State or Provincial Government	Local Government	Social Security Funds
5 Bonds, long term	11531	74	5206	849	5402	12888	64	5459	918	6447
a Corporate	330	27	189	114	-	289	29	138	122	-
b Other government subsectors	11201	47	5017	735	5402	12599	35	5321	796	6447
c Rest of the world	-	-	-	-	-	-	-	-	-	-
6 Corporate equity securities	264	105	29	130	...	256	132	47	77	...
7 Short term loans, n.e.c.	5362	3412	1950	-	...	6259	4076	2158	25	...
8 Long term loans, n.e.c.	1656	553	1103	-	...	1843	552	1291	-	...
a Mortgages	1656	553	1103	-	...	1843	552	1291	-	...
b Other	-	-	-	-	...	-	-	-	-	...
9 Other receivables	314	19	86	209	...	321	20	62	239	...
10 Other assets	32492	20502	8043	1791	2156	35501	21110	8956	2855	2580
Total Assets	...	...	...	...	...	...	...	...	...	...

Liabilities and Net Worth

Liabilities	66643	33707	18995	13941	...	70358	33855	20747	15756	...
1 Currency and transferable deposits	554	554	-	-	...	618	618	-	-	...
2 Other deposits					...					...
3 Other deposits	4595	4160	403	32	...	5033	4690	313	30	...
4 Bonds, long term	51808	24861	15860	11087	...	53452	24225	17443	11784	...
5 Short term loans, n.e.c. [a]	2605	85	1050	1470	...	3392	147	1391	1854	...
6 Long term loans, n.e.c. [a]	177	-	71	106	...	158	-	71	87	...
7 Other payables	812	57	547	208	...	841	50	565	226	...
8 Other liabilities	6092	3990	1064	1038	...	6864	4125	964	1775	...
Net worth	...	...	...	...	...	...	...	...	...	...
Total Liabilities and Net Worth	...	...	...	...	...	...	...	...	...	...

	1974					1975				
	Total General Government	Central Government	State or Provincial Government	Local Government	Social Security Funds	Total General Government	Central Government	State or Provincial Government	Local Government	Social Security Funds

Assets

Non-financial assets	...	...	...	...	...	...	...	...	...	...
Financial assets	72871	33610	23347	5121	10793	78758	34677	25400	5894	12787
1 Gold and SDRs	...	...	...	...	...	...	...	...	...	...
2 Currency and transferable deposits	6843	4246	1956	641	...	5447	3494	1181	772	...
3 Other deposits					...					...
4 Bills and bonds, short term	95	12	-	83	...	103	18	-	85	...
5 Bonds, long term	15010	70	6267	985	7688	17946	73	7725	1060	9088
a Corporate	321	35	156	130	-	515	39	327	149	-
b Other government subsectors	14689	35	6111	855	7688	17431	34	7398	911	9088
c Rest of the world	-	-	-	-	-	-	-	-	-	-
6 Corporate equity securities	380	167	136	77	...	422	193	145	84	...
7 Short term loans, n.e.c.	6881	4565	2274	42	...	7650	5083	2502	65	...
8 Long term loans, n.e.c.	2149	569	1580	-	...	2476	554	1922	-	...
a Mortgages	2149	569	1580	-	...	2476	554	1922	-	...
b Other	-	-	-	-	...	-	-	-	-	...
9 Other receivables	388	30	24	334	...	577	52	58	467	...
10 Other assets	41125	23951	11110	2959	3105	44137	25210	11867	3361	3699
Total Assets	...	...	...	...	...	...	...	...	...	...

Liabilities and Net Worth

Liabilities	80251	39189	23694	17368	...	91392	43777	27952	19663	...
1 Currency and transferable deposits	704	704	-	-	...	773	773	-	-	...
2 Other deposits					...					...
3 Other deposits	5860	5630	94	136	...	6834	6200	426	208	...
4 Bonds, long term	60119	27664	19729	12726	...	68883	31080	23451	14352	...
5 Short term loans, n.e.c. [a]	4346	207	1869	2270	...	4888	262	1911	2715	...
6 Long term loans, n.e.c. [a]	168	-	71	97	...	187	-	71	116	...
7 Other payables	1093	81	768	244	...	1250	92	896	262	...
8 Other liabilities	7961	4903	1163	1895	...	8577	5370	1197	2010	...
Net worth	...	...	...	...	...	...	...	...	...	...
Total Liabilities and Net Worth	...	...	...	...	...	...	...	...	...	...

Canada

3.15 General Government Balance Sheet, Total and Subsectors

Million Canadian dollars

	1976					1977				
	Total General Government	Central Government	State or Provincial Government	Local Government	Social Security Funds	Total General Government	Central Government	State or Provincial Government	Local Government	Social Security Funds
Assets											
Non-financial assets	...	...	...	...	...	...	...	...	...	...
Financial assets	85640	35335	29130	6205	14970	96519	37638	34706	6946	17229
1 Gold and SDRs	...	...	...	...	...	...	...	...	...	...
2 Currency and transferable deposits	5468	2671	1586	1211	...	7955	4020	2379	1556	...
3 Other deposits					...					...
4 Bills and bonds, short term	280	18	99	163	...	476	26	208	242	...
5 Bonds, long term	21027	80	9225	1115	10607	24747	75	11189	1222	12261
a Corporate	781	37	546	198	-	1085	36	757	292	-
b Other government subsectors	20246	43	8679	917	10607	23662	39	10432	930	12261
c Rest of the world	-	-	-	-	-	-	-	-	-	-
6 Corporate equity securities	321	69	148	104	...	342	62	155	125	...
7 Short term loans, n.e.c.	8303	5493	2756	54	...	9047	6095	2906	46	...
8 Long term loans, n.e.c.	2800	519	2281	-	...	3024	479	2545	-	...
a Mortgages	2800	519	2281	-	...	3024	479	2545	-	...
b Other	-	-	-	-	...	-	-	-	-	...
9 Other receivables	714	55	79	580	...	827	77	53	697	...
10 Other assets	46727	26430	12956	2978	4363	50101	26804	15271	3058	4968
Total Assets	...	...	...	...	...	...	...	...	...	...
Liabilities and Net Worth											
Liabilities	101588	48076	32406	21106	...	117132	55962	38128	23042	...
1 Currency and transferable deposits	821	821	-	-	...	882	882	-	-	...
2 Other deposits					...					...
3 Other deposits	8163	7845	303	15	...	10599	10315	279	5	...
4 Bonds, long term	76570	33623	27219	15728	...	88838	39286	31738	17814	...
5 Short term loans, n.e.c. a	4980	250	2052	2678	...	5199	253	2697	2249	...
6 Long term loans, n.e.c. a	136	-	71	65	...	85	-	71	14	...
7 Other payables	1387	68	1039	280	...	2122	119	1705	298	...
8 Other liabilities	9531	5469	1722	2340	...	9407	5107	1638	2662	...
Net worth	...	...	...	...	...	...	...	...	...	...
Total Liabilities and Net Worth	...	...	...	...	...	...	...	...	...	...

	1978					1979				
	Total General Government	Central Government	State or Provincial Government	Local Government	Social Security Funds	Total General Government	Central Government	State or Provincial Government	Local Government	Social Security Funds
Assets											
Non-financial assets	...	...	...	...	...	...	...	...	...	...
Financial assets	111367	42351	41827	7511	19678	119204	40501	47971	8320	22412
1 Gold and SDRs	...	...	...	...	...	...	...	...	...	...
2 Currency and transferable deposits	10968	5985	3157	1826	...	10244	1709	6505	2030	...
3 Other deposits					...					...
4 Bills and bonds, short term	1024	18	814	192	...	423	6	226	191	...
5 Bonds, long term	28685	64	13456	1230	13935	31602	209	14265	1279	15849
a Corporate	1182	29	865	288	-	1319	30	1023	266	-
b Other government subsectors	27503	35	12591	942	13935	30283	179	13242	1013	15849
c Rest of the world	-	-	-	-	-	-	-	-	-	-
6 Corporate equity securities	315	61	135	119	...	330	59	141	130	...
7 Short term loans, n.e.c.	9320	6570	2749	1	...	10311	7243	3060	8	...
8 Long term loans, n.e.c.	3208	427	2781	-	...	2964	377	2587	-	...
a Mortgages	3208	427	2781	-	...	2964	377	2587	-	...
b Other	-	-	-	-	...	-	-	-	-	...
9 Other receivables	698	105	46	547	...	743	153	57	533	...
10 Other assets	57149	29121	18689	3596	5743	62587	30745	21130	4149	6563
Total Assets	...	...	...	...	...	...	...	...	...	...
Liabilities and Net Worth											
Liabilities	139016	71119	44110	23787	...	151928	78173	49029	24726	...

Canada

3.15 General Government Balance Sheet, Total and Subsectors
(Continued)

Million Canadian dollars

	1978 Total General Government	1978 Central Government	1978 State or Provincial Government	1978 Local Government	1978 Social Security Funds	1979 Total General Government	1979 Central Government	1979 State or Provincial Government	1979 Local Government	1979 Social Security Funds
1 Currency and transferable deposits	962	962	-	-	...	1050	1050	-	-	...
2 Other deposits					...					...
3 Other deposits	13640	13135	489	16	...	15572	15260	296	16	...
4 Bonds, long term	102477	47073	36390	19014	...	113319	53074	40246	19990	...
5 Short term loans, n.e.c. [a]	9369	3832	3405	2132	...	8000	2104	3443	2453	...
6 Long term loans, n.e.c. [a]	38	-	-	38	...	15	-	-	15	...
7 Other payables	2401	173	1912	316	...	3430	167	2929	334	...
8 Other liabilities	10129	5944	1914	2271	...	10542	6518	2115	1909	...
Net worth	...	...	...	...	...	...	...	...	...	...
Total Liabilities and Net Worth	...	...	...	...	...	...	...	...	...	...

	1980 Total General Government	1980 Central Government	1980 State or Provincial Government	1980 Local Government	1980 Social Security Funds
Assets					
Non-financial assets	...	...	...	...	...
Financial assets	135205	44363	56616	8806	25420
1 Gold and SDRs	...	...			
2 Currency and transferable deposits	12143	3453	6584	2106	...
3 Other deposits					...
4 Bills and bonds, short term	535	11	334	190	...
5 Bonds, long term	37569	133	18325	1338	17773
a Corporate	1422	34	1107	281	...
b Other government subsectors	36147	99	17218	1057	17773
c Rest of the world	-	-	-	-	-
6 Corporate equity securities	348	64	143	141	...
7 Short term loans, n.e.c.	10878	7701	3174	3	...
8 Long term loans, n.e.c.	3109	337	2772	-	...
a Mortgages	3109	337	2772	-	...
b Other	-	-	-	-	...
9 Other receivables	768	192	57	519	...
10 Other assets	69855	32472	25227	4509	7647
Total Assets	...	...	...	...	
Liabilities and Net Worth					
Liabilities	173638	92583	55185	25870	...
1 Currency and transferable deposits	1111	1111	-	-	...
2 Other deposits					...
3 Other deposits	21374	20735	629	10	...
4 Bonds, long term	126093	59560	45466	21067	...
5 Short term loans, n.e.c. [a]	9463	2797	4109	2557	...
6 Long term loans, n.e.c. [a]	-	-	-	-	...
7 Other payables	3489	175	2962	352	...
8 Other liabilities	12108	8205	2019	1884	...
Net worth	...	...	...	...	...
Total Liabilities and Net Worth	...	...	...	...	...

a) Loans other than mortgages are included in item 'Short-term loans, n.e.c.'

3.22 Corporate and Quasi-Corporate Enterprise Income and Outlay Account: Total and Sectors

Million Canadian dollars

	1970 TOTAL	1970 Non-Financial	1970 Financial	1971 TOTAL	1971 Non-Financial	1971 Financial	1972 TOTAL	1972 Non-Financial	1972 Financial	1973 TOTAL	1973 Non-Financial	1973 Financial
Receipts												
1 Property and entrepreneurial income received	15242	...	...	17031	...	...	20198	...	...	26557	...	...
2 Other current transfers received	...	...	...	...	...	...	...	...	...	...	...	...
Statistical discrepancy [a]	-195			-665			-1032			-2362		
Total Current Receipts [b]	15047	...	...	16366	...	...	19166	...	...	24195	...	...

Canada

3.22 Corporate and Quasi-Corporate Enterprise Income and Outlay Account: Total and Sectors
(Continued)

Million Canadian dollars

	1970 TOTAL	1970 Non-Financial	1970 Financial	1971 TOTAL	1971 Non-Financial	1971 Financial	1972 TOTAL	1972 Non-Financial	1972 Financial	1973 TOTAL	1973 Non-Financial	1973 Financial
Disbursements												
1 Property and entrepreneurial income paid out	9101	...	...	10050	...	...	11735	...	...	14337	...	...
2 Direct taxes and other current payments n.e.c. to general government	3070	...	...	3346	...	...	3920	...	...	5080	...	...
a Direct taxes	3070	...	...	3346	...	...	3920	...	...	5080	...	...
Income	3070	...	...	3346	...	...	3920	...	...	5080	...	...
Other	...	...	...	...	...	...	-	...	...	-	...	...
b Fines, fees, penalties and other payments n.e.c.	...	...	...	-	...	...	-	...	...	...	...	...
3 Other current transfers paid	148	...	...	163	...	...	172	...	...	192	...	...
a Casualty insurance transactions	...	...	...	...	...	...	...	...	...	...	...	...
b Transfers to private non-profit institutions	148	...	...	163	...	...	172	...	...	192	...	...
c Transfers to households		...	...		...	...		...	...		...	...
d Transfers to the rest of the world	...	...	...	...	...	...	...	...	...	...	...	...
Statistical discrepancy [a]	-195	...	...	-665	...	...	-1032	...	...	-2362	...	...
Net saving	2923	...	...	3472	...	...	4371	...	...	6948	...	...
Total Current Disbursements and Net Saving [b]	15047	...	...	16366	...	...	19166	...	...	24195	...	...

	1974 TOTAL	1974 Non-Financial	1974 Financial	1975 TOTAL	1975 Non-Financial	1975 Financial	1976 TOTAL	1976 Non-Financial	1976 Financial	1977 TOTAL	1977 Non-Financial	1977 Financial
Receipts												
1 Property and entrepreneurial income received	34819	...	...	36550	...	...	41235	...	...	45639	...	...
2 Other current transfers received	...	...	...	...	...	...	...	...	...	...	...	...
Statistical discrepancy [a]	-4244	...	...	-2938	...	...	-2064	...	...	-3419	...	...
Total Current Receipts [b]	30575	...	...	33612	...	...	39171	...	...	42220	...	...
Disbursements												
1 Property and entrepreneurial income paid out	18658	...	...	21077	...	...	24274	...	...	28233	...	...
2 Direct taxes and other current payments n.e.c. to general government	7051	...	...	7486	...	...	7113	...	...	7256	...	...
a Direct taxes	7051	...	...	7486	...	...	7113	...	...	7256	...	...
Income	7051	...	...	7486	...	...	7113	...	...	7256	...	...
Other	-	...	...	-	...	...	-	...	...	-	...	...
b Fines, fees, penalties and other payments n.e.c.	-	...	...	-	...	...	-	...	...	-	...	...
3 Other current transfers paid	224	...	...	264	...	...	281	...	...	323	...	...
a Casualty insurance transactions	...	...	...	...	...	...	...	...	...	...	...	...
b Transfers to private non-profit institutions	224	...	...	264	...	...	281	...	...	323	...	...
c Transfers to households		...	...		...	...		...	...		...	...
d Transfers to the rest of the world	...	...	...	...	...	...	...	...	...	...	...	...
Statistical discrepancy [a]	-4244	...	...	-2938	...	...	-2064	...	...	-3419	...	...
Net saving	8886	...	...	7723	...	...	9567	...	...	9827	...	...
Total Current Disbursements and Net Saving [b]	30575	...	...	33612	...	...	39171	...	...	42220	...	...

	1978 TOTAL	1978 Non-Financial	1978 Financial	1979 TOTAL	1979 Non-Financial	1979 Financial	1980 TOTAL	1980 Non-Financial	1980 Financial
Receipts									
1 Property and entrepreneurial income received	56038	...	...	73104	...	...	82441	...	...
2 Other current transfers received	...	...	...	...	...	...	...	...	...
Statistical discrepancy [a]	-4577	...	...	-6718	...	...	-6841	...	...
Total Current Receipts [b]	51461	...	...	66386	...	...	75600	...	...
Disbursements									
1 Property and entrepreneurial income paid out	35866	...	...	42458	...	...	50019	...	...

Canada

3.22 Corporate and Quasi-Corporate Enterprise Income and Outlay Account: Total and Sectors
(Continued)

Million Canadian dollars

	1978 TOTAL	1978 Non-Financial	1978 Financial	1979 TOTAL	1979 Non-Financial	1979 Financial	1980 TOTAL	1980 Non-Financial	1980 Financial
2 Direct taxes and other current payments n.e.c. to general government	8241	...	...	10027	...	...	11608	...	...
a Direct taxes	8241	...	...	10027	...	...	11608	...	...
Income	8241	...	...	10027	...	...	11608	...	...
Other	-	...	...	-	...	...	-	...	...
b Fines, fees, penalties and other payments n.e.c.	-	...	...	-	...	...	-	...	...
3 Other current transfers paid	369	...	...	439	...	...	469	...	...
a Casualty insurance transactions	...	...	...	...	...	...	...	...	...
b Transfers to private non-profit institutions	369	...	...	439	...	...	469	...	...
c Transfers to households		...	...		...	...		...	...
d Transfers to the rest of the world	...	...	...	...	...	...	...	...	...
Statistical discrepancy [a]	-4577	...	...	-6718	...	...	-6841	...	...
Net saving	11562	...	...	20180	...	...	20345	...	...
Total Current Disbursements and Net Saving [b]	51461	...	...	66386	...	...	75600	...	...

a) Relating to inventory valuation adjustment.
b) This table covers corporate and governemnt business enterprises only.

3.23 Corporate and Quasi-Corporate Enterprise Capital Accumulation Account: Total and Sectors

Million Canadian dollars

	1970 TOTAL	1970 Non-Financial	1970 Financial	1971 TOTAL	1971 Non-Financial	1971 Financial	1972 TOTAL	1972 Non-Financial	1972 Financial	1973 TOTAL	1973 Non-Financial	1973 Financial
Finance of Gross Accumulation												
1 Gross saving	8412	...	...	8887	...	...	9916	...	...	12218	...	...
a Consumption of fixed capital	5684	...	...	6080	...	...	6577	...	...	7632	...	...
b Net saving	2923	...	...	3472	...	...	4371	...	...	6948	...	...
2 Capital transfers received	113	...	...	203	...	...	199	...	...	267	...	...
a From resident sectors	113	...	...	203	...	...	199	...	...	267	...	...
b From the rest of the world	...	...	...	...	...	...	...	...	...	...	...	...
Finance of Gross Accumulation [a]	8525	...	...	9090	...	...	10115	...	...	12485	...	...
Gross Accumulation												
1 Gross capital formation	11683	...	...	12967	...	...	14636	...	...	18328	...	...
a Increase in stocks	255	...	...	406	...	...	801	...	...	1484	...	...
b Gross fixed capital formation	11428	...	...	12561	...	...	13835	...	...	16844	...	...
2 Purchases of land, net	...	...	...	...	...	...	...	...	...	...	...	...
3 Purchases of intangible assets, net	...	...	...	...	...	...	...	...	...	...	...	...
4 Capital transfers paid	...	...	...	...	...	...	...	...	...	...	...	...
5 Net lending	-3158	...	...	-3877	...	...	-4521	...	...	-5843	...	...
Gross Accumulation [a]	8525	...	...	9090	...	...	10115	...	...	12485	...	...

	1974 TOTAL	1974 Non-Financial	1974 Financial	1975 TOTAL	1975 Non-Financial	1975 Financial	1976 TOTAL	1976 Non-Financial	1976 Financial	1977 TOTAL	1977 Non-Financial	1977 Financial
Finance of Gross Accumulation												
1 Gross saving	13811	...	...	15144	...	...	19368	...	...	19714	...	...
a Consumption of fixed capital	9169	...	...	10359	...	...	11865	...	...	13306	...	...
b Net saving	8886	...	...	7723	...	...	9567	...	...	9827	...	...
2 Capital transfers received	255	...	...	293	...	...	392	...	...	510	...	...
a From resident sectors	255	...	...	293	...	...	392	...	...	510	...	...
b From the rest of the world	...	...	...	...	...	...	...	...	...	...	...	...
Finance of Gross Accumulation [a]	14066	...	...	15437	...	...	19760	...	...	20224	...	...
Gross Accumulation												
1 Gross capital formation	24471	...	...	23973	...	...	28375	...	...	30116	...	...

Canada

3.23 Corporate and Quasi-Corporate Enterprise Capital Accumulation Account: Total and Sectors
(Continued)

Million Canadian dollars

	1974 TOTAL	1974 Non-Financial	1974 Financial	1975 TOTAL	1975 Non-Financial	1975 Financial	1976 TOTAL	1976 Non-Financial	1976 Financial	1977 TOTAL	1977 Non-Financial	1977 Financial
a Increase in stocks	3730	...	...	-511	...	...	1049	...	...	294	...	...
b Gross fixed capital formation	20741	...	...	24484	...	...	27326	...	...	29822	...	...
2 Purchases of land, net	...	...	...	...	...	...	...	...	...	...	...	...
3 Purchases of intangible assets, net	...	...	...	...	...	...	...	...	...	...	...	...
4 Capital transfers paid	...	...	...	...	...	...	...	...	...	...	...	...
5 Net lending	-10405	...	...	-8536	...	...	-8615	...	...	-9892	...	...
Gross Accumulation a	14066	...	...	15437	...	...	19760	...	...	20224	...	...

	1978 TOTAL	1978 Non-Financial	1978 Financial	1979 TOTAL	1979 Non-Financial	1979 Financial	1980 TOTAL	1980 Non-Financial	1980 Financial
				Finance of Gross Accumulation					
1 Gross saving	21943	...	...	30389	...	...	32396	...	...
a Consumption of fixed capital	14958	...	...	16927	...	...	18892	...	...
b Net saving	11562	...	...	20180	...	...	20345	...	...
2 Capital transfers received	528	...	...	502	...	...	517	...	...
a From resident sectors	528	...	...	502	...	...	517	...	...
b From the rest of the world	...	...	...	...	...	...	...	...	...
Finance of Gross Accumulation a	22471	...	...	30891	...	...	32913	...	...
				Gross Accumulation					
1 Gross capital formation	32594	...	...	42296	...	...	44798	...	...
a Increase in stocks	-66	...	...	3988	...	...	-770	...	...
b Gross fixed capital formation	32660	...	...	38308	...	...	45568	...	...
2 Purchases of land, net	...	...	...	...	...	...	...	...	...
3 Purchases of intangible assets, net	...	...	...	...	...	...	...	...	...
4 Capital transfers paid	...	...	...	...	...	...	...	...	...
5 Net lending	-10123	...	...	-11405	...	...	-11885	...	...
Gross Accumulation a	22471	...	...	30891	...	...	32913	...	...

a) This table covers corporate and government business enterprises only.

3.24 Corporate and Quasi-Corporate Enterprise Capital Finance Account: Total and Sectors

Million Canadian dollars

	1970 TOTAL	1970 Non-Financial	1970 Financial	1971 TOTAL	1971 Non-Financial	1971 Financial	1972 TOTAL	1972 Non-Financial	1972 Financial	1973 TOTAL	1973 Non-Financial	1973 Financial
				Acquisition of Financial Assets								
1 Gold and SDRs	1662	-	1662	896	-	896	336	-	336	-467	-	-467
2 Currency and transferable deposits	1773	46	1727	451	545	-94	2463	412	2051	5373	544	4829
3 Other deposits												
4 Bills and bonds, short term	1284	19	1265	414	-10	424	928	147	781	715	526	189
5 Bonds, long term	2700	23	2677	3829	49	3780	2174	-32	2206	2154	-74	2228
a Corporate, resident	778	-23	801	1448	-10	1458	1185	18	1167	994	-31	1025
b Government	1922	46	1876	2381	59	2322	989	-50	1039	1160	-43	1203
c Rest of the world	-	-	-	-	-	-	-	-	-	-	-	-
6 Corporate equity securities a	516	-69	585	1076	120	956	742	189	553	942	105	837
7 Short term loans, n.e.c. b	318	-113	431	2950	79	2871	3904	100	3804	6624	213	6411
8 Long term loans, n.e.c. b	2064	-25	2089	3136	70	3066	4573	103	4470	6786	24	6762
a Mortgages	2064	-25	2089	3136	70	3066	4573	103	4470	6786	24	6762
b Other	-	-	-	-	-	-	-	-	-	-	-	-
9 Trade credits and advances	1785	1142	643	3090	1824	1266	3505	1480	2025	6033	3387	2646
a Consumer credit	679	50	629	1313	98	1215	2001	17	1984	2751	109	2642
b Other	1106	1092	14	1777	1726	51	1504	1463	41	3282	3278	4
10 Other receivables	...	...	...	...	...	...	...	...	...	...	...	...
11 Other assets	1539	1105	434	2122	1531	591	2369	1497	872	3419	1912	1507
Total Acquisition of Financial Assets	13641	2128	11513	17964	4208	13756	20994	3896	17098	31579	6637	24942
				Incurrence of Liabilities								
1 Currency and transferable deposits	6251	-	6251	8088	-	8088	10410	-	10410	17342	-	17342
2 Other deposits												

Canada

3.24 Corporate and Quasi-Corporate Enterprise Capital Finance Account: Total and Sectors
(Continued)

Million Canadian dollars

	1970 TOTAL	1970 Non-Financial	1970 Financial	1971 TOTAL	1971 Non-Financial	1971 Financial	1972 TOTAL	1972 Non-Financial	1972 Financial	1973 TOTAL	1973 Non-Financial	1973 Financial
3 Bills and bonds, short term	-112	36	-148	129	256	-127	57	-330	387	782	-160	942
4 Bonds, long term	2178	1980	198	2635	2393	242	2584	1972	612	2797	1948	849
5 Corporate equity securities	872	846	26	625	704	-79	362	484	-122	1228	1118	110
6 Short-term loans, n.e.c. [b]	343	175	168	2033	1520	513	2580	2149	431	3834	3797	37
7 Long-term loans, n.e.c. [b]	604	596	8	682	674	8	446	428	18	384	426	-42
8 Net equity of households in life insurance and pension fund reserves	1813	-	1813	2278	-	2278	2898	-	2898	3691	-	3691
9 Proprietors' net additions to the accumulation of quasi-corporations [c]	4018	1288	2730	2959	1016	1943	2343	805	1538	1529	629	900
10 Trade credit and advances	364	340	24	1248	1246	2	1862	1821	41	2741	2684	57
11 Other accounts payable	...	...	...	...	...	607	832	230	602	2156	1382	774
12 Other liabilities	361	112	249	1282	675	607						
Total Incurrence of Liabilities	16692	5373	11319	21959	8484	13475	24374	7559	16815	36484	11824	24660
Net Lending	-3051	-3245	194	-3995	-4276	281	-3380	-3663	283	-4905	-5187	282
Incurrence of Liabilities and Net Lending	13641	2128	11513	17964	4208	13756	20994	3896	17098	31579	6637	24942

	1974 TOTAL	1974 Non-Financial	1974 Financial	1975 TOTAL	1975 Non-Financial	1975 Financial	1976 TOTAL	1976 Non-Financial	1976 Financial	1977 TOTAL	1977 Non-Financial	1977 Financial
Acquisition of Financial Assets												
1 Gold and SDRs	24	-	24	-405	-	-405	522	...	522	-1421	-	-1421
2 Currency and transferable deposits	2695	618	2077	1495	584	911	7732	3244	4488	2936	902	2034
3 Other deposits	2383	-157	2540	1082	451	631	1216	-244	1460	2669	320	2349
4 Bills and bonds, short term	2883	-75	2958	4877	131	4746	5713	-63	5776	8014	26	7988
5 Bonds, long term	967	-74	1041	2173	19	2154	1994	19	1975	2341	-46	2387
a Corporate, resident	1916	-1	1917	2704	112	2592	3719	-82	3801	5673	72	5601
b Government	-	-	-	-	-	-	-	-	-	2313	89	2224
c Rest of the world												
6 Corporate equity securities [a]	741	255	486	1053	89	964	1671	465	1206	7293	418	6875
7 Short term loans, n.e.c. [b]	8921	343	8578	6622	240	6382	8783	-276	9059	13395	77	13318
8 Long term loans, n.e.c. [b]	7409	42	7367	8200	24	8176	10044	184	9860	13395	77	13318
a Mortgages	7409	42	7367	8200	24	8176	10044	184	9860	-	-	-
b Other	-	-	-	-	-	-	-	-	-	7553	4119	3434
9 Trade credits and advances	8513	5739	2774	6952	3749	3203	6620	2502	4118	3291	17	3274
a Consumer credit	2831	133	2698	3138	96	3042	3850	-38	3888	4262	4102	160
b Other	5682	5606	76	3814	3653	161	2770	2540	230			
10 Other receivables	...	...	...	...	...	...	...	...	...	...	...	...
11 Other assets	5282	3466	1816	2590	1886	704	4495	2506	1989	5848	3780	2068
Total Acquisition of Financial Assets	38851	10231	28620	32466	7154	25312	46796	8318	38478	48600	9731	38869
Incurrence of Liabilities												
1 Currency and transferable deposits	17457	-	17457	14659	-	14659	22681	-	22681	24005	-	24005
2 Other deposits												
3 Bills and bonds, short term	2867	1547	1320	179	81	98	1090	351	739	406	-570	976
4 Bonds, long term	3439	2787	652	6384	5414	970	9681	7570	2111	6858	5201	1657
5 Corporate equity securities	1170	855	315	1931	1172	759	1679	998	681	3506	2706	800
6 Short-term loans, n.e.c. [b]	4562	3880	682	4584	4141	443	5120	4893	227	2987	2528	459
7 Long-term loans, n.e.c. [b]	608	578	30	511	511	-	935	908	27	544	491	53
8 Net equity of households in life insurance and pension fund reserves	4153	-	4153	5111	-	5111	6631	-	6631	7637	-	7637
9 Proprietors' net additions to the accumulation of quasi-corporations [c]	5111	2243	2868	4342	2632	1710	4804	1951	2853	4927	3754	1173
10 Trade credit and advances	6106	6069	37	2250	2177	73	1424	1381	43	2295	2227	68
11 Other accounts payable	...	...	...	...	...	...	3055	1371	1684	3973	2362	1611
12 Other liabilities	3693	2622	1071	1837	770	1067						
Total Incurrence of Liabilities	49166	20581	28585	41788	16898	24890	57100	19423	37677	57138	18699	38439
Net Lending	-10315	-10350	35	-9322	-9744	422	-10304	-11105	801	-8538	-8968	430
Incurrence of Liabilities and Net Lending	38851	10231	28620	32466	7154	25312	46796	8318	38478	48600	9731	38869

Canada

3.24 Corporate and Quasi-Corporate Enterprise Capital Finance Account: Total and Sectors

Million Canadian dollars

	1978 TOTAL	1978 Non-Financial	1978 Financial	1979 TOTAL	1979 Non-Financial	1979 Financial	1980 TOTAL	1980 Non-Financial	1980 Financial
Acquisition of Financial Assets									
1 Gold and SDRs	-185	-	-185	-858	-	-858	-542	-	-542
2 Currency and transferable deposits	8228	3653	4575	4853	-1256	6109	6010	1067	4943
3 Other deposits									
4 Bills and bonds, short term	3284	273	3011	4519	1116	3403	4732	1269	3463
5 Bonds, long term	8410	72	8338	7367	164	7203	9203	-105	9308
a Corporate, resident	2925	49	2876	1293	83	1210	1488	-159	1647
b Government	5485	23	5462	6074	81	5993	7715	54	7661
c Rest of the world	-	-	-	-	-	-	-	-	-
6 Corporate equity securities a	7579	1358	6221	3290	1468	1822	4524	1012	3512
7 Short term loans, n.e.c. b	10619	933	9686	19577	542	19035	21789	707	21082
8 Long term loans, n.e.c. b	14244	651	13593	13812	-71	13883	10772	79	10693
a Mortgages	14244	651	13593	13812	-71	13883	10772	79	10693
b Other	-	-	-	-	-	-	-	-	-
9 Trade credits and advances	13370	8658	4712	12730	7570	5160	11945	6940	5005
a Consumer credit	4504	30	4474	4860	-60	4920	4690	-92	4782
b Other	8866	8628	238	7870	7630	240	7255	7032	223
10 Other receivables	...	...	...	...	...	...	...	...	...
11 Other assets	10306	5705	4601	14334	10205	4129	22819	10529	12290
Total Acquisition of Financial Assets	75855	21303	54552	79624	19738	59886	91252	21498	69754
Incurrence of Liabilities									
1 Currency and transferable deposits	34427	-	34427	35390	-	35390	38762	-	38762
2 Other deposits									
3 Bills and bonds, short term	2419	511	1908	3298	1195	2103	2848	-38	2886
4 Bonds, long term	5806	4334	1472	5493	3425	2068	7860	5707	2153
5 Corporate equity securities	8674	6888	1786	6840	5230	1610	7697	5528	2169
6 Short-term loans, n.e.c. b	6690	5584	1106	9631	7437	2194	9378	8769	609
7 Long-term loans, n.e.c. b	1286	1315	-29	961	894	67	1887	1813	74
8 Net equity of households in life insurance and pension fund reserves	9095	-	9095	11721	-	11721	13663	-	13663
9 Proprietors' net additions to the accumulation of quasi-corporations c	4378	2703	1675	6642	3378	3264	8835	3748	5087
10 Trade credit and advances	6390	6296	94	7600	7477	123	7126	7167	-41
11 Other accounts payable	...	...	...	...	...	...	...	...	...
12 Other liabilities	6729	4575	2154	6547	5224	1323	8160	4475	3685
Total Incurrence of Liabilities	85894	32206	53688	94123	34260	59863	106216	37169	69047
Net Lending	-10039	-10903	864	-14499	-14522	23	-14964	-15671	707
Incurrence of Liabilities and Net Lending	75855	21303	54552	79624	19738	59886	91252	21498	69754

a) Investment in short-term papers, bonds and corporate equity securities of the rest of the world   b) Loans other than mortgages are included in item 'Short-term loans, n.e.c.' cannot be split between long-term and short-term by purchasers, the total investment has been c) Consisting of corporate and government claims on their associated enterprises. allocated to the item.

3.25 Corporate and Quasi-Corporate Enterprise Balance Sheet: Total and Sectors

Million Canadian dollars

	1970 TOTAL	1970 Non-Financial	1970 Financial	1971 TOTAL	1971 Non-Financial	1971 Financial	1972 TOTAL	1972 Non-Financial	1972 Financial	1973 TOTAL	1973 Non-Financial	1973 Financial
Assets												
Non-financial assets	...	...	...	...	...	...	...	...	...	...	...	...
Financial assets	159621	42338	117283	178046	46734	131312	203504	51622	151882	237573	59234	178339
1 Gold and SDRs	4731	-	4731	5582	-	5582	6018	-	6018	5745	-	5745
2 Currency and transferable deposits	15354	4015	11339	15878	4751	11127	18600	5372	13228	24463	6354	18109
3 Other deposits												
4 Bills and bonds, short term	5955	762	5193	6427	809	5618	7362	620	6742	8644	1373	7271
a Corporate and quasi-corporate, resident	...	...	...	...	...	...	...	...	...	...	...	...
b Government	...	...	...	...	...	...	...	...	...	...	...	...
c Rest of the world	...	...	...	...	...	...	...	...	...	...	...	...
5 Bonds, long term	28372	1423	26949	32242	1483	30759	34554	1775	32779	36080	1267	34813
a Corporate, resident	7651	712	6939	9082	709	8373	10204	883	9321	10873	415	10458
b Government	20721	711	20010	23160	774	22386	24350	892	23458	25207	852	24355

Canada

3.25 Corporate and Quasi-Corporate Enterprise Balance Sheet: Total and Sectors
(Continued)

Million Canadian dollars

	1970 TOTAL	1970 Non-Financial	1970 Financial	1971 TOTAL	1971 Non-Financial	1971 Financial	1972 TOTAL	1972 Non-Financial	1972 Financial	1973 TOTAL	1973 Non-Financial	1973 Financial
c Rest of the world	-	-	-	-	-	-	-	-	-	-	-	-
6 Corporate equity securities a	10548	1806	8742	11887	1899	9988	12923	1673	11250	13459	1551	11908
7 Short-term loans, n.e.c. b	20437	475	19962	23472	622	22850	27760	803	26957	34368	1396	32972
8 Long-term loans, n.e.c. b	25040	1067	23973	28704	1125	27579	33764	1519	32245	40883	1793	39090
a Mortgages	25040	1067	23973	28704	1125	27579	33764	1519	32245	40883	1793	39090
b Other	-	-	-	-	-	-	-	-	-	-	-	-
9 Trade credits and allowances	28674	18296	10378	31338	20047	11291	36134	22081	14053	42145	25453	16692
a Consumer credit	11337	1433	9904	12213	1448	10765	14369	892	13477	17116	1001	16115
b Other	17337	16863	474	19125	18599	526	21765	21189	576	25029	24452	577
10 Other receivables	...	...	...	...	...	...	...	...	...	...	...	...
11 Other assets	20510	14494	6016	22516	15998	6518	26389	17779	8610	31786	20047	11739
Total Assets	...	...	...	...	...	...	...	...	...	...	...	...

Liabilities and Net Worth

	1970 TOTAL	1970 Non-Financial	1970 Financial	1971 TOTAL	1971 Non-Financial	1971 Financial	1972 TOTAL	1972 Non-Financial	1972 Financial	1973 TOTAL	1973 Non-Financial	1973 Financial
Liabilities	255542	136271	119271	282561	149038	133523	316044	161755	154289	364295	183063	181232
1 Currency and transferable deposits	56566	-	56566	64577	-	64577	74553	-	74553	91957	-	91957
2 Other deposits												
3 Bills and bonds, short term	3157	1379	1778	3292	1642	1650	3412	1210	2202	4330	1044	3286
4 Bonds, long term	25345	23268	2077	28060	25825	2235	30440	26689	3751	32807	28244	4563
5 Corporate equity securities	64065	53037	11028	69026	57232	11794	75452	61435	14017	84681	68718	15963
6 Short-term loans, n.e.c. b	13869	11974	1895	15925	13552	2373	19540	16669	2871	23789	20534	3255
7 Long-term loans, n.e.c. b	7297	7258	39	7989	7941	48	8995	8922	73	10826	10762	64
8 Net equity of households in life insurance and pension fund reserves	26659	-	26659	28958	-	28958	32082	-	32082	35879	-	35879
9 Proprietors' net equity in quasi-corporations c	34986	19889	15097	38121	21048	17073	41229	22124	19105	43947	23418	20529
1 Trade credit and advances	11661	11587	74	12824	12737	87	15630	15513	117	19354	19208	146
1 Other accounts payable	...	...	...	...	...	...	...	...	...	...	...	...
12 Other liabilities	11937	7879	4058	13789	9061	4728	14711	9193	5518	16725	11135	5590
Net worth	...	...	...	...	...	...	...	...	...	...	...	...
Total Liabilities and Net Worth	...	...	...	...	...	...	...	...	...	...	...	...

	1974 TOTAL	1974 Non-Financial	1974 Financial	1975 TOTAL	1975 Non-Financial	1975 Financial	1976 TOTAL	1976 Non-Financial	1976 Financial	1977 TOTAL	1977 Non-Financial	1977 Financial

Assets

	1974 TOTAL	1974 Non-Financial	1974 Financial	1975 TOTAL	1975 Non-Financial	1975 Financial	1976 TOTAL	1976 Non-Financial	1976 Financial	1977 TOTAL	1977 Non-Financial	1977 Financial
Non-financial assets	...	...	...	...	...	...	...	...	...	...	...	...
Financial assets	276590	70619	205971	312721	76727	235994	361389	83760	277629	422948	102023	320925
1 Gold and SDRs	5770	-	5770	5410	-	5410	5894	-	5894	5040	-	5040
2 Currency and transferable deposits	27305	7115	20190	29111	7468	21643	37095	10695	26400	43387	13351	30036
3 Other deposits												
4 Bills and bonds, short term	11258	1410	9848	12507	1918	10589	13934	1722	12212	16363	2069	14294
a Corporate and quasi-corporate, resident	...	...	...	...	...	...	...	...	...	...	...	...
b Government	...	...	...	...	...	...	...	...	...	...	...	...
c Rest of the world	...	...	...	...	...	...	...	...	...	...	...	...
5 Bonds, long term	39015	1193	37822	43650	1183	42467	49321	1115	48206	57519	1193	56326
a Corporate, resident	12646	321	12325	14043	316	13727	16052	334	15718	18094	392	17702
b Government	26369	872	25497	29607	867	28740	33269	781	32488	39425	801	38624
c Rest of the world	-	-	-	-	-	-	-	-	-	-	-	-
6 Corporate equity securities a	13861	1775	12086	15064	1656	13408	16612	1826	14786	20164	2082	18082
7 Short-term loans, n.e.c. b	43329	1932	41397	51573	2092	49481	60567	1825	58742	68717	1940	66777
8 Long-term loans, n.e.c. b	48620	2105	46515	57155	2138	55017	68100	2325	65775	81045	2838	78207
a Mortgages	48620	2105	46515	57155	2138	55017	68100	2325	65775	81045	2838	78207
b Other	-	-	-	-	-	-	-	-	-	-	-	-
9 Trade credits and allowances	50524	31024	19500	56962	34255	22707	63120	36331	26789	74060	43241	30819
a Consumer credit	19960	1134	18826	23102	1229	21873	26916	1189	25727	30232	1206	29026
b Other	30564	29890	674	33860	33026	834	36204	35142	1062	43828	42035	1793
10 Other receivables	...	...	...	...	...	...	...	...	...	...	...	...

243

Canada

3.25 Corporate and Quasi-Corporate Enterprise Balance Sheet: Total and Sectors
(Continued)

Million Canadian dollars

	1974 TOTAL	1974 Non-Financial	1974 Financial	1975 TOTAL	1975 Non-Financial	1975 Financial	1976 TOTAL	1976 Non-Financial	1976 Financial	1977 TOTAL	1977 Non-Financial	1977 Financial
11 Other assets	36908	24065	12843	41289	26017	15272	46746	27921	18825	56653	35309	21344
Total Assets	...	...	...	...	...	...	...	...	...	...	...	...

Liabilities and Net Worth

	1974 TOTAL	1974 Non-Financial	1974 Financial	1975 TOTAL	1975 Non-Financial	1975 Financial	1976 TOTAL	1976 Non-Financial	1976 Financial	1977 TOTAL	1977 Non-Financial	1977 Financial
Liabilities	425214	215736	209478	478577	238520	240057	545654	263877	281777	635958	309043	326915
1 Currency and transferable deposits	109454	-	109454	124495	-	124495	147359	-	147359	173438	-	173438
2 Other deposits												
3 Bills and bonds, short term	6905	2698	4207	7592	2859	4733	9024	3252	5772	10144	3323	6821
4 Bonds, long term	36274	31083	5191	42426	36166	6260	51884	43494	8390	59544	49447	10097
5 Corporate equity securities	94645	78340	16305	107058	85853	21205	117322	92857	24465	138563	112385	26178
6 Short-term loans, n.e.c. [b]	28729	24654	4075	34427	28932	5495	39987	34026	5961	41851	35143	6708
7 Long-term loans, n.e.c. [b]	12986	12906	80	13611	13431	180	14673	14346	327	17370	16951	419
8 Net equity of households in life insurance and pension fund reserves	39614	-	39614	44887	-	44887	51448	-	51448	57491	-	57491
9 Proprietors' net equity in quasi-corporations [c]	49878	26330	23548	53849	29404	24445	59221	30869	28352	71373	40073	31300
1 Trade credit and advances	25910	25642	268	27235	26873	362	29601	29183	418	35579	34712	867
1 Other accounts payable	...	...	...	...	...	...	...	...	...	...	...	...
12 Other liabilities	20819	14083	6736	22997	15002	7995	25135	15850	9285	30605	17009	13596
Net worth	...	...	...	...	...	...	...	...	...	...	...	...
Total Liabilities and Net Worth	...	...	...	...	...	...	...	...	...	...	...	...

	1978 TOTAL	1978 Non-Financial	1978 Financial	1979 TOTAL	1979 Non-Financial	1979 Financial	1980 TOTAL	1980 Non-Financial	1980 Financial

Assets

	1978 TOTAL	1978 Non-Financial	1978 Financial	1979 TOTAL	1979 Non-Financial	1979 Financial	1980 TOTAL	1980 Non-Financial	1980 Financial
Non-financial assets	...	...	...	...	...	...	...	...	...
Financial assets	504205	124170	380035	594263	151240	443023	687331	173482	513849
1 Gold and SDRs	5413	-	5413	4535	-	4535	4811	-	4811
2 Currency and transferable deposits	47875	16891	30984	59508	22643	36865	67116	25169	41947
3 Other deposits									
4 Bills and bonds, short term	19863	2401	17462	24635	3544	21091	29442	4551	24891
a Corporate and quasi-corporate, resident	...	...	...	...	...	...	...	...	...
b Government	...	...	...	...	...	...	...	...	...
c Rest of the world	...	...	...	...	...	...	...	...	...
5 Bonds, long term	66041	1260	64781	72977	1227	71750	82085	1510	80575
a Corporate, resident	21191	460	20731	22128	358	21770	23929	519	23410
b Government	44850	800	44050	50849	869	49980	58156	991	57165
c Rest of the world	-	-	-	-	-	-	-	-	-
6 Corporate equity securities [a]	27442	2506	24936	31159	3100	28059	36442	4024	32418
7 Short-term loans, n.e.c. [b]	79383	2554	76829	99405	3462	95943	121203	4194	117009
8 Long-term loans, n.e.c. [b]	95045	3128	91917	109194	3407	105787	119541	3381	116160
a Mortgages	95045	3128	91917	109194	3407	105787	119541	3381	116160
b Other	-	-	-	-	-	-	-	-	-
9 Trade credits and allowances	89952	54140	35812	103194	62226	40968	115313	69409	45904
a Consumer credit	34999	1236	33763	39819	1176	38643	44348	1084	43264
b Other	54953	52904	2049	63375	61050	2325	70965	68325	2640
10 Other receivables	...	...	...	...	...	...	...	...	...
11 Other assets	73191	41290	31901	89656	51631	38025	111378	61244	50134
Total Assets	...	...	...	...	...	...	...	...	...

Liabilities and Net Worth

	1978 TOTAL	1978 Non-Financial	1978 Financial	1979 TOTAL	1979 Non-Financial	1979 Financial	1980 TOTAL	1980 Non-Financial	1980 Financial
Liabilities	743355	356427	386928	892530	441451	451079	1023808	501350	522458
1 Currency and transferable deposits	209058	-	209058	243939	-	243939	283723	-	283723
2 Other deposits									
3 Bills and bonds, short term	11890	3233	8657	15354	4556	10798	18302	4976	13326

Canada

3.25 Corporate and Quasi-Corporate Enterprise Balance Sheet: Total and Sectors
(Continued)

Million Canadian dollars

	1978 TOTAL	1978 Non-Financial	1978 Financial	1979 TOTAL	1979 Non-Financial	1979 Financial	1980 TOTAL	1980 Non-Financial	1980 Financial
4 Bonds, long term	64911	53313	11598	70909	57189	13720	77986	62075	15911
5 Corporate equity securities	156883	127090	29793	198789	163923	34866	227900	189039	38861
6 Short-term loans, n.e.c. b	52137	44578	7559	68945	59097	9848	79437	69005	10432
7 Long-term loans, n.e.c. b	19654	19239	415	25556	25089	467	27329	26781	548
8 Net equity of households in life insurance and pension fund reserves	68662	-	68662	80739	-	80739	93842	-	93842
9 Proprietors' net equity in quasi-corporations c	81163	44754	36409	90791	50592	40199	102572	57110	45462
1 Trade credit and advances	43184	42551	633	53389	52556	833	60486	59842	644
1 Other accounts payable	...	...	...	...	...	...	...	...	...
12 Other liabilities	35813	21669	14144	44119	28449	15670	52231	32522	19709
Net worth	...	...	...	...	...	...	...	...	...
Total Liabilities and Net Worth	...	...	...	...	...	...	...	...	...

a) Investment in short-term papers, bonds and corporate equity securities of the rest of the world   b) Loans other than mortgages are included in item 'Short-term loans, n.e.c.'. cannot be split between long-term and short-term by purchasers, the total investment has been   c) Consisting of corporate and government claims on their associated enterprises. allocated to the item.

3.26 Financial Transactions of Financial Institutions: Detail

Million Canadian dollars

	1970 ALL FINANCIAL INSTITUTIONS	1970 Central Bank	1970 Other Monetary Institutions	1970 Insurance	1970 Other Financial Institutions	1971 ALL FINANCIAL INSTITUTIONS	1971 Central Bank	1971 Other Monetary Institutions	1971 Insurance	1971 Other Financial Institutions
Acquisition of Financial Assets										
1 Gold and SDRs a	1662	1662	-	-	-	896	896	-	-	-
a Gold	1270	1270	-	-	-	1045	1045	-	-	-
b Net acquisitions of SDRs	193	193	-	-	-	192	192	-	-	-
2 Currency and transferable deposits b	1727	-	1658	145	-76	-94	-	-220	-54	180
a Liability of resident institutions	444	-	290	146	8	818	-	682	-53	189
b Liability of rest of the world	1283	-	1368	-1	-84	-912	-	-902	-1	-9
3 Other deposits b	...	...	...	...	...	...	...	...	...	...
4 Bills and bonds, short term	1265	141	720	106	298	424	264	135	9	16
5 Bonds, long term	2677	40	1283	947	407	3780	311	1895	1146	428
6 Corporate equity securities c	585	-	-29	462	152	956	-	29	904	23
7 Short-term loans, n.e.c. d	431	-1	525	-4	-89	2871	3	2301	9	558
8 Long-term loans, n.e.c. d	2089	-	1171	304	614	3066	-	2111	298	657
a Mortgages	2089	-	1171	304	614	3066	-	2111	298	657
b Other	-	-	-	-	-	-	-	-	-	-
9 Trade credit and advances	643	-	597	89	-43	1266	-	1314	90	-138
a Consumer credit	629	-	597	100	-68	1215	-	1314	25	-124
b Other	14	-	-	-11	25	51	-	-	65	-14
10 Other assets	434	89	85	33	227	591	53	231	26	281
Total Acquisition of Financial Assets	11513	1931	6010	2082	1490	13756	1527	7796	2428	2005
Incurrence of Liabilities										
1 Currency and transferable deposits	6251	282	5964	-	5	8088	678	7347	-	63
2 Other deposits										
3 Bills and bonds, short term	-148	-	-	-	-148	-127	-	-	-	-127
4 Bonds, long term	198	-	-	-	198	242	-	150	-	92
5 Corporate equity securities	26	-	87	13	-74	-79	-	37	23	-139
6 Short-term loans, n.e.c. d	168	-	-58	-	226	513	-	-41	-	554
7 Long-term loans, n.e.c. d	8	-	-	-	8	8	-	-	-	8
9 Net equity of households in life insurance and pension fund reserves	1813	-	-	1813	-	2278	-	-	2278	-
10 Other liabilities	3003	1645	-60	244	1174	2552	846	96	139	1471
Total Incurrence of liabilities	11319	1927	5933	2070	1389	13475	1524	7589	2440	1922
Net Lending	194	4	77	12	101	281	3	207	-12	83
Incurrence of Liabilities and Net Lending	11513	1931	6010	2082	1490	13756	1527	7796	2428	2005

Canada

3.26 Financial Transactions of Financial Institutions: Detail

Million Canadian dollars

	1972					1973				
	ALL FINANCIAL INSTITUTIONS	Central Bank	Other Monetary Institutions	Insurance	Other Financial Institutions	ALL FINANCIAL INSTITUTIONS	Central Bank	Other Monetary Institutions	Insurance	Other Financial Institutions

Acquisition of Financial Assets

1 Gold and SDRs [a]	336	336	-	-	-	-467	-467	-	-	-
a Gold	262	262	-	-	-	-428	-428	-	-	-
b Net acquisitions of SDRs	92	92	-	-	-	2	2	-	-	-
2 Currency and transferable deposits [b]	2051	-	1711	212	128	4829	-	4339	177	313
a Liability of resident institutions	1039	-	717	211	111	1102	-	725	154	223
b Liability of rest of the world	1012	-	994	1	17	3727	-	3614	23	90
3 Other deposits [b]	...	...	...	...	...	...	...	...	...	...
4 Bills and bonds, short term	781	45	182	122	432	189	188	363	89	-451
5 Bonds, long term	2206	545	43	1204	414	2228	420	-237	1661	384
6 Corporate equity securities [c]	553	-	10	1036	-493	837	-	61	862	-86
7 Short-term loans, n.e.c. [d]	3804	-	3164	-6	646	6411	-2	5217	12	1184
8 Long-term loans, n.e.c. [d]	4470	-	3370	445	655	6762	-	4850	963	949
a Mortgages	4470	-	3370	445	655	6762	-	4850	963	949
b Other	-	-	-	-	-	-	-	-	-	-
9 Trade credit and advances	2025	-	1679	54	292	2646	-	2201	66	379
a Consumer credit	1984	-	1679	19	286	2642	-	2201	73	368
b Other	41	-	-	35	6	4	-	-	-7	11
10 Other assets	872	92	90	106	584	1507	148	274	178	907
Total Acquisition of Financial Assets	17098	1018	10249	3173	2658	24942	287	17068	4008	3579

Incurrence of Liabilities

1 Currency and transferable deposits	10410	877	9458	-	75	17342	1134	15995	-	213
2 Other deposits										
3 Bills and bonds, short term	387	-	-	-	387	942	-	65	-	877
4 Bonds, long term	612	-	308	-	304	849	-	344	-	505
5 Corporate equity securities	-122	-	99	34	-255	110	-	78	69	-37
6 Short-term loans, n.e.c. [d]	431	-	46	-	385	37	-	100	-	-63
7 Long-term loans, n.e.c. [d]	18	-	-	-	18	-42	-	-	-	-42
9 Net equity of households in life insurance and pension fund reserves	2898	-	-	2898	-	3691	-	-	3691	-
10 Other liabilities	2181	141	77	211	1752	1731	-840	232	287	2052
Total Incurrence of liabilities	16815	1018	9988	3143	2666	24660	294	16814	4047	3505
Net Lending	283	-	261	30	-8	282	-7	254	-39	74
Incurrence of Liabilities and Net Lending	17098	1018	10249	3173	2658	24942	287	17068	4008	3579

	1974					1975				
	ALL FINANCIAL INSTITUTIONS	Central Bank	Other Monetary Institutions	Insurance	Other Financial Institutions	ALL FINANCIAL INSTITUTIONS	Central Bank	Other Monetary Institutions	Insurance	Other Financial Institutions

Acquisition of Financial Assets

1 Gold and SDRs [a]	24	24	-	-	-	-405	-405	-	-	-
a Gold	-157	-157	-	-	-	-566	-566	-	-	-
b Net acquisitions of SDRs	2	2	-	-	-	7	7	-	-	-
2 Currency and transferable deposits [b]	2077	-	2005	334	-262	911	-	299	101	511
a Liability of resident institutions	1152	-	922	347	-117	1391	-	843	111	437
b Liability of rest of the world	925	-	1083	-13	-145	-480	-	-544	-10	74
3 Other deposits [b]	...	...	...	...	...	...	...	...	...	...
4 Bills and bonds, short term	2540	612	919	352	657	631	389	-431	244	429
5 Bonds, long term	2958	499	369	1745	345	4746	331	900	3043	472
6 Corporate equity securities [c]	486	-	87	537	-138	964	-	110	856	-2
7 Short-term loans, n.e.c. [d]	8578	-1	6072	25	2482	6382	28	5068	-16	1302
8 Long-term loans, n.e.c. [d]	7367	-	4743	1210	1414	8176	-	5456	1341	1379
a Mortgages	7367	-	4743	1210	1414	8176	-	5456	1341	1379
b Other	-	-	-	-	-	-	-	-	-	-
9 Trade credit and advances	2774	-	2361	245	168	3203	-	2877	207	119
a Consumer credit	2698	-	2361	178	159	3042	-	2877	95	70
b Other	76	-	-	67	9	161	-	-	112	49
10 Other assets	1816	273	382	106	1055	704	63	74	77	490
Total Acquisition of Financial Assets	28620	1407	16938	4554	5721	25312	406	14353	5853	4700

Canada

3.26 Financial Transactions of Financial Institutions: Detail
(Continued)

Million Canadian dollars

1974 / 1975

	1974 ALL FINANCIAL INSTITUTIONS	Central Bank	Other Monetary Institutions	Insurance	Other Financial Institutions	1975 ALL FINANCIAL INSTITUTIONS	Central Bank	Other Monetary Institutions	Insurance	Other Financial Institutions
Incurrence of Liabilities										
1 Currency and transferable deposits	17457	1188	16126	-	143	14659	1273	13093	-	293
2 Other deposits			82	-	1238	98	-	-85	-	183
3 Bills and bonds, short term	1320	-	82	-	389	970	-	307	-	663
4 Bonds, long term	652	-	263	-	93	759	-	307	73	379
5 Corporate equity securities	315	-	181	41	752	443	-	6	-	437
6 Short-term loans, n.e.c. d	682	-	-70	-	30	-	-	-	-	-
7 Long-term loans, n.e.c. d	30	-	-	-	30	-	-	-	-	-
9 Net equity of households in life insurance and pension fund reserves	4153	-	-	4153	-	5111	-	-	5111	-
10 Other liabilities	3976	235	294	500	2947	2850	-859	364	662	2683
Total Incurrence of liabilities	28585	1423	16876	4694	5592	24890	414	13992	5846	4638
Net Lending	35	-16	62	-140	129	422	-8	361	7	62
Incurrence of Liabilities and Net Lending	28620	1407	16938	4554	5721	25312	406	14353	5853	4700

1976 / 1977

	1976 ALL FINANCIAL INSTITUTIONS	Central Bank	Other Monetary Institutions	Insurance	Other Financial Institutions	1977 ALL FINANCIAL INSTITUTIONS	Central Bank	Other Monetary Institutions	Insurance	Other Financial Institutions
Acquisition of Financial Assets										
1 Gold and SDRs a	522	522	-	-	-	-1421	-1421	-	-	-
a Gold	224	224	-	-	-	-1198	-1198	-	-	-
b Net acquisitions of SDRs	6	6	-	-	-	-80	-80	-	-	-
2 Currency and transferable deposits b	4488	-	3758	203	527	2034	-	1560	406	68
a Liability of resident institutions	1651	-	1019	234	398	1741	-	1335	395	11
b Liability of rest of the world	2837	-	2739	-31	129	293	-	225	11	57
3 Other deposits b	...	...	...	...	...	...	277	1176	798	98
4 Bills and bonds, short term	1460	-3	1082	46	335	2349	1501	1556	4281	650
5 Bonds, long term	5776	551	843	3506	876	7988	-	2021	459	-256
6 Corporate equity securities c	1206	-	106	1297	-197	2224	-182	4956	-25	2126
7 Short-term loans, n.e.c. d	9059	-60	7554	38	1527	6875	-	9115	2540	1663
8 Long-term loans, n.e.c. d	9860	-	6361	2034	1465	13318	-	9115	2540	1663
a Mortgages	9860	-	6361	2034	1465	133 3	-	-	-	-
b Other	-	-	-	-	-	-	-	-	-	-
9 Trade credit and advances	4118	-	3741	284	93	34.1	-	3221	188	25
a Consumer credit	3888	-	3741	85	62	3274	-	3221	65	-12
b Other	230	-	-	199	31	160	-	-	123	37
10 Other assets	1989	6	5	212	1766	2068	34	528	277	1229
Total Acquisition of Financial Assets	38478	1016	23450	7620	6392	38869	209	24133	8924	5603
Incurrence of Liabilities										
1 Currency and transferable deposits	22681	799	21687	-	195	24005	1481	22239	-	285
2 Other deposits			91	-	648	976	-	52	-	924
3 Bills and bonds, short term	739	-	91	-	648	976	-	293	-	1364
4 Bonds, long term	2111	-	515	-	1596	1657	-	274	56	470
5 Corporate equity securities	681	-	268	55	358	800	-	328	9	122
6 Short-term loans, n.e.c. d	227	-	136	-7	98	459	-	21	-	32
7 Long-term loans, n.e.c. d	27	-	-	1	26	53	-	-	-	-
9 Net equity of households in life insurance and pension fund reserves	6631	-	-	6631	-	7637	-	-	7637	-
10 Other liabilities	4580	225	395	821	3139	2852	-1267	331	1005	2783
Total Incurrence of liabilities	37677	1024	23092	7501	6060	38439	214	23538	8707	5980
Net Lending	801	-8	358	119	332	430	-5	595	217	-377
Incurrence of Liabilities and Net Lending	38478	1016	23450	7620	6392	38869	209	24133	8924	5603

Canada

3.26 Financial Transactions of Financial Institutions: Detail

Million Canadian dollars

	1978 ALL FINANCIAL INSTITUTIONS	Central Bank	Other Monetary Institutions	Insurance	Other Financial Institutions	1979 ALL FINANCIAL INSTITUTIONS	Central Bank	Other Monetary Institutions	Insurance	Other Financial Institutions
Acquisition of Financial Assets									
1 Gold and SDRs [a]	-185	-185	-	-	-	-858	-858	-	-	-
a Gold	227	227	-	-	-	-734	-734	-	-	-
b Net acquisitions of SDRs	-21	-21	-	-	-	74	74	-	-	-
2 Currency and transferable deposits [b]	4575	-	3511	275	789	6109	-	4064	539	1506
a Liability of resident institutions	1990	-	980	191	819	2886	-	1171	553	1162
b Liability of rest of the world	2585	-	2531	84	-30	3223	-	2893	-14	344
3 Other deposits [b]	...	...	...	...	...	...	...	...	...	...
4 Bills and bonds, short term	3011	1080	137	823	971	3403	728	1388	1491	-204
5 Bonds, long term	8338	627	2030	5177	504	7203	877	-439	5853	912
6 Corporate equity securities [c]	6221	-	5801	711	-291	1822	-	356	1503	-37
7 Short-term loans, n.e.c. [d]	9686	-211	7418	-16	2495	19035	-54	15295	80	3714
8 Long-term loans, n.e.c. [d]	13593	-	10021	2278	1294	13883	-	10913	2368	602
a Mortgages	13593	-	10021	2278	1294	13883	-	10913	2368	602
b Other	-	-	-	-	-	-	-	-	-	-
9 Trade credit and advances	4712	-	4106	306	300	5160	-	4607	370	183
a Consumer credit	4474	-	4106	86	282	4920	-	4607	196	117
b Other	238	-	-	220	18	240	-	-	174	66
10 Other assets	4601	11	2478	467	1645	4129	51	1972	42	2064
Total Acquisition of Financial Assets	54552	1322	35502	10021	7707	59886	744	38156	12246	8740
Incurrence of Liabilities									
1 Currency and transferable deposits	34427	1477	32666	-	284	35390	1300	33667	-	423
2 Other deposits										
3 Bills and bonds, short term	1908	-	79	-	1829	2103	-	74	-	2029
4 Bonds, long term	1472	-	304	-	1168	2068	-	657	-	1411
5 Corporate equity securities	1786	-	502	107	1177	1610	-	463	20	1127
6 Short-term loans, n.e.c. [d]	1106	-	249	14	843	2194	-	1039	10	1145
7 Long-term loans, n.e.c. [d]	-29	-	-32	-13	16	67	-	8	36	23
9 Net equity of households in life insurance and pension fund reserves	9095	-	-	9095	-	11721	-	-	11721	-
10 Other liabilities	3923	-147	945	660	2465	4710	-557	1887	533	2847
Total Incurrence of liabilities	53688	1330	34713	9863	7782	59863	743	37795	12320	9005
Net Lending	864	-8	789	158	-75	23	1	361	-74	-265
Incurrence of Liabilities and Net Lending	54552	1322	35502	10021	7707	59886	744	38156	12246	8740

	1980 ALL FINANCIAL INSTITUTIONS	Central Bank	Other Monetary Institutions	Insurance	Other Financial Institutions
Acquisition of Financial Assets					
1 Gold and SDRs [a]	-542	-542	-	-	-
a Gold	-648	-648	-	-	-
b Net acquisitions of SDRs	237	237	-	-	-
2 Currency and transferable deposits [b]	4943	-	4474	757	-288
a Liability of resident institutions	1499	-	1079	755	-335
b Liability of rest of the world	3444	-	3395	2	47
3 Other deposits [b]	...	...	...	...	...
4 Bills and bonds, short term	3463	1012	1863	-13	601
5 Bonds, long term	9308	1230	-8	6807	1279
6 Corporate equity securities [c]	3512	-	40	3168	304
7 Short-term loans, n.e.c. [d]	21082	-274	16396	159	4801
8 Long-term loans, n.e.c. [d]	10693	-	7584	2125	984
a Mortgages	10693	-	7584	2125	984
b Other	-	-	-	-	-
9 Trade credit and advances	5005	-	4427	533	45
a Consumer credit	4782	-	4427	300	55
b Other	223	-	-	233	-10
10 Other assets	12290	13	9542	476	2259
Total Acquisition of Financial Assets	69754	1439	44318	14012	9985

Canada

3.26 Financial Transactions of Financial Institutions: Detail
(Continued)

Million Canadian dollars

1980

	ALL FINANCIAL INSTITUTIONS	Central Bank	Other Monetary Institutions	Insurance	Other Financial Institutions
Incurrence of Liabilities					
1 Currency and transferable deposits	38762	1470	36746	-	546
2 Other deposits					
3 Bills and bonds, short term	2886	-	46	-	2840
4 Bonds, long term	2153	-	391	-	1762
5 Corporate equity securities	2169	-	776	68	1325
6 Short-term loans, n.e.c. [d]	609	-	510	48	51
7 Long-term loans, n.e.c. [d]	74	-	20	30	24
9 Net equity of households in life insurance and pension fund reserves	13663	-	-	13663	-
10 Other liabilities	8731	-31	5007	618	3137
Total Incurrence of liabilities	69047	1439	43496	14427	9685
Net Lending	707	-	822	-415	300
Incurrence of Liabilities and Net Lending	69754	1439	44318	14012	9985

a) Referring to official international reserves, components do not add up to total because I.M.F. general account of -249, 293, 199, -341, -18, -41, 179, 154, 292, -143, -391 and -198 are included for the years 1968 to 1979 respectively.
b) Item 'Other deposits' is included in item 'Currency and transferable deposits'.
c) Investment in short-term papers, bonds and corporate equity securities of the rest of the world cannot be split between long-term and short-term by purchasers, the total investment has been allocated to the item.
d) Relating to inventory valuation adjustment.

3.32 Household and Private Unincorporated Enterprise Income and Outlay Account

Million Canadian dollars

	1970	1971	1972	1973	1974	1975	1976	1977	1978	1979	1980
Receipts											
1 Compensation of employees	47620	52436	58549	67849	81289	94625	109375	120523	131382	146639	164036
a Wages and salaries	44935	49329	54863	63443	75636	87983	101468	111571	121314	135796	152049
b Employers' contributions for social security	1475	1551	1846	2244	3009	3609	4479	4779	5211	5594	6161
c Employers' contributions for private pension & welfare plans	1210	1556	1840	2162	2644	3033	3428	4173	4857	5249	5826
2 Property and entrepreneurial income received	11281	12491	14122	17511	20770	22490	24438	26327	31261	36006	40604
a Operating surplus of private unincorporated enterprises [a]	6635	7504	7832	9665	10760	11613	11755	11944	13229	14486	15407
b Withdrawals from private quasi-corporations	-	-	-	-	-	-	-	-	-	-	-
c Interest	3772	4137	4752	5693	7433	8567	11036	12310	14598	18565	22041
d Dividends	874	850	1538	2153	2577	2310	1647	2073	3434	2955	3156
e Net land rent and royalties	-	-	-	-	-	-	-	-	-	-	-
3 Other current transfers received	7240	8578	10263	11605	14333	17602	20042	22874	25821	27224	31284
a Casualty insurance claims	-	-	-	-	-	-	-	-	-	-	-
b Social security benefits	3185	3751	5235	5973	6832	8741	10088	11543	13389	14474	16607
c Social assistance grants	3800	4504	4683	5225	7048	8339	9395	10677	11669	11863	13701
d Unfunded employee welfare benefits	-	-	-	-	-	-	-	-	-	-	-
e Other current transfers received	255	323	345	407	453	522	559	654	763	887	976
From general government	-	-	-	-	-	-	-	-	-	-	-
From the rest fo the world	107	160	173	215	229	258	278	331	394	448	507
Other	148	163	172	192	224	264	281	323	369	439	469
Total Current Receipts	66141	73505	82934	96965	116392	134717	153855	169724	188464	209869	235924
Disbursements											
1 Final consumption expenditures	49753	54986	61470	70457	82484	95814	109537	121069	133630	149056	166520
2 Property income paid	641	648	699	986	1517	1616	1808	1928	2373	3596	4668
a Interest	641	648	699	986	1517	1616	1808	1928	2373	3596	4668
Consumer debt	641	648	699	986	1517	1616	1808	1928	2373	3596	4668
Mortgage	-	-	-	-	-	-	-	-	-	-	-

Canada

3.32 Household and Private Unincorporated Enterprise Income and Outlay Account
(Continued)

Million Canadian dollars

	1970	1971	1972	1973	1974	1975	1976	1977	1978	1979	1980
Other	-	-	-	-	-	-	-	-	-	-	-
b Net land rent and royalties	-	-	-	-	-	-	-	-	-	-	-
3 Direct taxes, fees, fines & other payments n.e.c. to government	12358	13870	15437	17908	22144	25053	29685	33070	35328	38987	44629
a Social security contributions	2470	2620	3016	3551	4864	5895	7158	7743	8633	9114	10169
b Direct taxes	8970	10317	11578	13496	16383	18263	21314	23656	24669	27670	32126
Income taxes	8811	10143	11385	13285	16155	18019	21047	23656	24669	27670	32126
Other	159	174	193	211	228	244	267	...	...	...	...
c Fees, fines and penalties	918	933	843	861	897	895	1203	1671	2026	2203	2334
4 Other current transfers paid	169	170	178	225	234	246	256	269	277	289	299
a Net casualty insurance premiums	-	-	-	-	-	-	-	-	-	-	-
b Transfers to private non-profit institutions serving households	-	-	-	-	-	-	-	-	-	-	-
c Transfers to the rest of the world	169	170	178	225	234	246	256	269	277	289	299
d Other current transfers, except imputed	-	-	-	-	-	-	-	-	-	-	-
e Imputed employee welfare contributions	-	-	-	-	-	-	-	-	-	-	-
Net saving	3220	3831	5150	7389	10013	11988	12569	13388	16856	17941	19808
Total Current Disbursements and Net Saving	66141	73505	82934	96965	116392	134717	153855	169724	188464	209869	235924

a) Net income of unincorporated business including net rent.

3.33 Household and Private Unincorporated Enterprise Capital Accumulation Account

Million Canadian dollars

	1970	1971	1972	1973	1974	1975	1976	1977	1978	1979	1980
Finance of Gross Accumulation											
1 Gross saving	6111	6917	8552	11402	14729	17374	18617	19968	24050	25884	28466
a Consumption of fixed capital	2891	3086	3402	4013	4716	5386	6048	6580	7194	7943	8658
b Net saving	3220	3831	5150	7389	10013	11988	12569	13388	16856	17941	19808
2 Capital transfers received	399	454	489	580	772	858	899	842	798	1056	1589
a From resident sectors	10	22	46	59	71	193	172	152	182	257	428
b From the rest of the world	389	432	443	521	701	665	727	690	616	799	1161
Total Finance of Gross Accumulation	6510	7371	9041	11982	15501	18232	19516	20810	24848	26940	30055
Gross Accumulation											
1 Gross Capital Formation	3277	4511	4975	6818	7752	9478	11724	11618	12859	15007	14451
a Increase in stocks	-137	26	-273	119	-305	241	473	37	369	117	-491
b Gross fixed capital formation	3414	4485	5248	6699	8057	9237	11251	11581	12490	14890	14942
2 Purchases of land, net	...	...	...	...	...	...	...	...	...	...	...
3 Purchases of intangibles, net	...	...	...	...	...	...	...	...	...	...	...
4 Capital transfers paid	465	464	392	376	340	326	329	374	368	354	337
a To resident sectors	266	279	230	205	178	156	148	139	116	99	71
b To the rest of the world	199	185	162	171	162	170	181	235	252	255	266
5 Net lending	2768	2396	3674	4788	7409	8428	7463	8818	11621	11579	15267
Total Gross Accumulation	6510	7371	9041	11982	15501	18232	19516	20810	24848	26940	30055

3.34 Household and Private Unincorporated Enterprise Capital Finance Account

Million Canadian dollars

	1970	1971	1972	1973	1974	1975	1976	1977	1978	1979	1980
Acquisition of Financial Assets											
1 Gold	...	...	...	...	...	...	...	...	...	...	...
2 Currency and transferable deposits	4174	5771	6411	12282	10935	13289	15333	16764	19219	26957	23625
3 Other deposits											
4 Bills and bonds, short term	-840	34	-319	533	952	-299	328	-428	1796	105	2229
5 Bonds, long term	827	2470	1726	250	3749	3037	270	1696	2024	1967	1324
a Corporate	378	490	253	666	920	62	-1052	-595	-1317	-208	-240
b Government	449	1980	1473	-416	2829	2975	1322	2291	3341	2175	1564
c Rest of the world	-	-	-	-	-	-	-	-	-	-	-
6 Corporate equity securities [a]	-574	-1775	-1741	-1195	-1438	2	-562	-785	-684	-418	-1460
7 Short term loans, n.e.c.	...	...	...	...	...	...	...	...	...	...	...
8 Long term loans, n.e.c.	926	141	531	1017	1109	1416	2438	-371	1832	160	160

Canada

3.34 Household and Private Unincorporated Enterprise Capital Finance Account
(Continued)

Million Canadian dollars

	1970	1971	1972	1973	1974	1975	1976	1977	1978	1979	1980
a Mortgages	926	141	531	1017	1109	1416	2438	-371	1832	160	160
b Other	-	-	-	-	-	-	-	-	-	-	-
9 Trade credit and advances of unincorporated enterprises	...	...	...	...	...	...	...	...	...	...	...
10 Net equity of households in life insurance and pension fund reserves	1807	2267	2896	3665	4133	5089	6607	7651	9070	11708	13650
11 Proprietors' net additions to the accumulation of quasi-corporations	...	...	...	...	...	...	...	...	...	...	...
12 Other	886	-261	452	910	747	1581	3217	3470	1632	-225	766
Total Acquisition of Financial Assets	7206	8647	9956	17462	20187	24115	27631	27997	34889	40254	40294

Incurrence of Liabilities

	1970	1971	1972	1973	1974	1975	1976	1977	1978	1979	1980
1 Short term loans, n.e.c. [b]	531	2257	3257	5520	6082	4409	7331	7374	6332	15214	12453
a Consumer credit	684	1322	2031	2789	2864	3175	3866	3309	4530	4888	4682
b Other	-153	935	1226	2731	3218	1234	3465	4065	1802	10326	7771
2 Long term loans, n.e.c. [b]	2646	2895	4780	7661	8218	9498	12085	12765	14955	12792	9126
a Mortgages	2646	2895	4780	7661	8218	9498	12085	12765	14955	12792	9126
b Consumer credit	-	-	-	-	-	-	-	-	-	-	-
c Other	-	-	-	-	-	-	-	-	-	-	-
3 Trade credit and advances of unincorporated enterprises	607	541	-453	519	-404	1597	1350	1723	2199	-519	94
4 Other accounts payable	...	...	...	...	...	...	...	12	32	-4	35	66
5 Other liabilities	78	38	65	37	44	82	12	32	-4	35	66
Total Incurrence of Liabilities	3862	5731	7649	13737	13940	15586	20778	21894	23482	27522	21739
Net Lending	3344	2916	2307	3725	6247	8529	6853	6103	11407	12732	18555
Incurrence of Liabilities and Net Lending	7206	8647	9956	17462	20187	24115	27631	27997	34889	40254	40294

a) Investment in short-term papers, bonds and corporate equity securities of the rest of the world cannot be split between long-term and short-term by purchasers, the total investment has been allocated to the item. b) Loans other than mortgages are included in item 'Short-term loans, n.e.c.'.

3.35 Household and Private Unincorporated Enterprise Balance Sheet

Million Canadian dollars

	1970	1971	1972	1973	1974	1975	1976	1977	1978	1979	1980
					Assets						
Non-financial assets	...	...	...	...	...	...	...	...	...	...	...
Financial assets	126488	139556	153135	174112	200530	231475	262985	308881	354523	415786	475623
1 Gold	...	...	...	...	...	...	...	...	...	...	...
2 Currency and transferable deposits	41289	46968	52641	64544	75303	88605	104063	119809	139320	158778	181240
3 Other deposits											
4 Bills and bonds, short term	260	248	-17	78	536	573	774	1211	3053	2737	5466
5 Bonds, long term	19169	21736	22966	23500	26819	29800	30002	33644	36100	37992	38719
a Corporate	4950	5242	5220	5614	6449	6389	5487	6374	4761	4089	2913
b Government	14219	16494	17746	17886	20370	23411	24515	27270	31339	33903	35806
c Rest of the world	-	-	...	...	-	-	-	-	-	-	-
6 Corporate equity securities [a]	28073	29782	31929	35322	41360	46775	50584	67180	71722	105072	121213
7 Short-term loans, n.e.c.	...	...	...	...	...	...	...	...	...	...	...
8 Long-term loans, n.e.c.	6924	7065	7596	8613	9722	11138	13576	13205	16992	14998	15158
a Mortgages	6924	7065	7596	8613	9722	11138	13576	13205	16992	14998	15158
b Other	-	-	...	...	-	-	-	-	-	-	-
9 Trade credit and advances of unincorporated enterprises	...	...	...	...	...	...	...	...	...	...	...
1 Net equity in life insurance and pension fund reserves	27936	30224	33347	37117	40832	46084	52621	58678	67751	81888	94978
1 Proprietors' equity in quasi-corporations	...	...	...	...	...	...	...	...	...	...	...
12 Other	2837	3533	4673	4938	5958	8500	11365	15154	19585	14321	18849
Total Assets	...	...	...	...	...	...	...	...	...	...	...

Liabilities and Net Worth

	1970	1971	1972	1973	1974	1975	1976	1977	1978	1979	1980
Liabilities	50126	56406	63661	74702	85596	102132	122080	142333	166982	175319	195747
1 Short-term loans, n.e.c. [b]	18099	20265	22955	27877	32948	37715	44837	53907	60546	64535	75512
a Consumer credit	11637	12515	14700	17484	20362	23541	27371	30704	35375	40345	44866
b Other	6462	7750	8255	10393	12586	14174	17466	23203	25171	24190	30646
2 Long-term loans, n.e.c. [b]	26622	30053	34761	41310	48332	57976	70817	80939	97125	103033	111993
a Mortgages	26622	30053	34761	41310	48332	57976	70817	80939	97125	103033	111993

Canada

3.35 Household and Private Unincorporated Enterprise Balance Sheet
(Continued)

Million Canadian dollars

	1970	1971	1972	1973	1974	1975	1976	1977	1978	1979	1980
b Consumer credit	-	-	-	-	-	-	-	-	-	-	-
c Other	-	-	-	-	-	-	-	-	-	-	-
3 Trade credit and advances	5194	5830	5637	5155	3949	5952	5930	6954	8828	7299	7758
4 Other accounts payable	-	-	-	-	-	-	-	-	-	-	-
5 Other liabilities	211	258	308	360	367	489	496	533	483	452	484
Net worth	...	...	...	...	...	...	...	...	...	...	...
Total Liabilities and Net Worth	...	...	...	...	...	...	...	...	...	...	...

a) Investment in short-term papers, bonds and corporate equity securities of the rest of the world allocated to the item. cannot be split between long-term and short-term by purchasers, the total investment has been b) Loans other than mortgages are included in item 'Short-term loans, n.e.c.'.

3.51 External Transactions: Current Account: Detail

Million Canadian dollars

	1970	1971	1972	1973	1974	1975	1976	1977	1978	1979	1980
Payments to the Rest of the World											
1 Imports of goods and services	17845	19516	22756	27974	37311	41302	45077	51059	59826	72953	81938
a Imports of merchandise c.i.f.	14788	16352	19427	24051	32559	35811	38566	43648	51309	63886	71481
b Other	3057	3164	3329	3923	4752	5491	6511	7411	8517	9067	10457
2 Factor income paid to the rest of the world	2397	2537	2528	3012	3741	4338	4940	6248	8188	9761	11561
a Compensation of employees	-	-	-	-	-	-	-	-	-	-	-
b Property and entrepreneurial income paid	2397	2537	2528	3012	3741	4338	4940	6248	8188	9761	11561
By general government	456	481	553	650	713	946	1364	1905	2368	2764	2942
By corporate and quasi-cororate enterprises	1941	2056	1975	2362	3028	3392	3576	4343	5820	6997	8619
By other	-	-	-	-	-	-	-	-	-	-	-
3 Indirect taxes paid to supranational organizations	-	-	-	-	-	-	-	-	-	-	-
4 Other current transfers to the rest of the world	413	419	457	543	641	838	798	907	1290	1056	1116
a By general government	244	249	279	318	407	592	542	638	1013	767	817
b By other resident sectors	169	170	178	225	234	246	256	269	277	289	299
5 Surplus of the nation on current transactions	916	184	-667	-242	-1999	-5252	-4388	-4756	-5299	-5438	-2799
Payments to the Rest of the World, and Surplus of the Nation on Current Transfers	21571	22656	25074	31287	39694	41226	46427	53458	64005	78332	91816
Receipts From The Rest of the World											
1 Exports of goods and services	20184	21265	23637	29562	37649	38832	44044	50897	60790	74696	86856
a Exports of merchandise f.o.b.	17597	18595	20901	26367	33572	34499	39274	45715	54681	67219	78323
b Other	2587	2670	2736	3195	4077	4333	4770	5182	6109	7477	8533
2 Factor income received from the rest of the world	1011	953	977	1188	1386	1671	1601	1696	2239	2434	3458
a Compensation of employees	-	-	-	-	-	-	-	-	-	-	-
b Property and entrepreneurial income received	1011	953	977	1188	1386	1671	1601	1696	2239	2434	3458
By general government	38	32	35	44	51	57	89	111	88	92	80
By corporate and quasi-corporate enterprises	863	819	799	988	1178	1445	1332	1374	1909	2060	3076
By other	110	102	143	156	157	169	180	211	242	282	302
3 Subsidies received from supranational organizations	-	-	-	-	-	-	-	-	-	-	-
4 Other current transfers from the rest of the world	376	438	460	537	659	723	782	865	976	1202	1502
a To general government	269	278	287	322	430	465	504	534	582	754	995
b To other resident sectors	107	160	173	215	229	258	278	331	394	448	507
Receipts from the Rest of the World on Current Transfers	21571	22656	25074	31287	39694	41226	46427	53458	64005	78332	91816

Canada

3.52 External Transactions: Capital Accumulation Account

Million Canadian dollars

	1970	1971	1972	1973	1974	1975	1976	1977	1978	1979	1980
Finance of Gross Accumulation											
1 Surplus of the nation on current transactions	916	184	-667	-242	-1999	-5252	-4388	-4756	-5299	-5438	-2799
2 Capital transfers received from the rest of the world	389	432	443	521	701	665	727	690	616	799	1161
a By general government	-	-	-	-	-	-	-	-	-	-	-
b By other resident sectors	389	432	443	521	701	665	727	690	616	799	1161
Total Finance of Gross Accumulation	1305	616	-224	279	-1298	-4587	-3661	-4066	-4683	-4639	-1638
Gross Accumulation											
1 Capital transfers paid to the rest of the world	199	185	162	171	162	170	181	235	252	255	266
a By general government	-	-	-	-	-	-	-	-	-	-	-
b By other resident sectors	199	185	162	171	162	170	181	235	252	255	266
2 Purchases of intangible assets, n.e.c., net, from the rest of the world	-	-	-	-	-	-	-	-	-	-	-
3 Net lending to the rest of the world	1106	431	-386	108	-1460	-4757	-3842	-4301	-4935	-4894	-1904
Total Gross Accumulation	1305	616	-224	279	-1298	-4587	-3661	-4066	-4683	-4639	-1638

3.53 External Transactions: Capital Finance Account

Million Canadian dollars

	1970	1971	1972	1973	1974	1975	1976	1977	1978	1979	1980
Acquisitions of Foreign Financial Assets											
1 Gold and SDR's [a]	1662	896	336	-467	24	-405	522	-1421	-185	-858	-542
2 Currency and transferable deposits	1300	-270	1330	3637	-776	-474	2701	827	2637	2487	3435
3 Other deposits											
4 Bills and bonds, short term	...	...	...	...	...	...	...	...	...	...	...
5 Bonds, long term	...	...	...	...	...	...	...	...	...	...	...
6 Corporate equity securities	...	...	...	...	...	...	...	...	...	...	...
7 Short-term loans, n.e.c.	337	750	606	755	1478	1363	1384	1599	1527	2429	4138
8 Long-term loans											
9 Proprietors' net additions to accumulation of quasi-corporate, non-resident enterprises [b]	351	291	421	826	798	726	347	1010	3663	3233	9214
10 Trade credit and advances	...	...	...	...	...	...	...	...	...	...	...
11 Other	-81	-202	-246	88	153	192	180	10	186	802	736
Total Acquisitions of Foreign Financial Assets	3569	1465	2447	4839	1677	1402	5134	2025	7828	8124	16978
Incurrence of Foreign Liabilities											
1 Currency and transferable deposits	1266	918	1971	3674	442	847	2361	2600	6714	7782	10991
2 Other deposits											
3 Bills and bonds, short term	219	11	-127	-34	334	395	929	434	44	466	1111
4 Bonds, long term	572	234	1375	577	1864	4408	8627	4917	5071	3387	4044
5 Corporate equity securities	-79	-126	-23	13	-139	86	-52	-105	-271	525	1450
6 Short-term loans, n.e.c. [c]	5	238	353	588	375	333	759	567	2907	682	573
7 Long-term loans [c]	54	30	-33	36	40	85	68	1	84	-165	-91
8 Non-resident proprietors' net additions to accumulation of resident quasi-corporate enterprises [d]	824	903	604	823	905	695	-229	407	163	1921	2943
9 Trade credit and advances	...	...	...	...	...	...	...	...	...	...	...
10 Other	-11	174	168	-296	182	513	171	-460	733	688	-128
Total Incurrence of Liabilities	2850	2382	4288	5381	4003	7362	12634	8361	15445	15286	20893
Statistical discrepancy	-387	-1348	-1455	-650	-866	-1203	-3658	-2035	-2682	-2268	-2011
Net Lending	1106	431	-386	108	-1460	-4757	-3842	-4301	-4935	-4894	-1904
Total Incurrence of Liabilities and Net Lending	3569	1465	2447	4839	1677	1402	5134	2025	7828	8124	16978

a) Referring to official international reserves.
b) Relating to claims on associated enterprises aboard.
c) Relating to inventory valuation adjustment.
d) Relating to liabilities to associated enterprises abroad.

Canada

4.4 Derivation of Value Added by Kind of Activity, ISIC Divisions, in Constant Prices

Million Canadian dollars

	1970 Gross Output	1970 Intermediate Consumption	1970 Value Added	1971 Gross Output	1971 Intermediate Consumption	1971 Value Added	1972 Gross Output	1972 Intermediate Consumption	1972 Value Added	1973 Gross Output	1973 Intermediate Consumption	1973 Value Added
At constant prices of: 1971 — All Producers												
1 Agriculture, hunting, forestry and fishing	...	...	3272	7062	3549	3513	6961	3722	3239	7527	4004	3523
a Agriculture and hunting	...	...	2415	5027	2320	2706	4864	2463	2401	5161	2537	2624
b Forestry and logging	...	...	713	1831	1162	670	1903	1195	708	2160	1399	761
c Fishing	...	...	144	204	67	137	194	64	130	206	68	138
2 Mining and quarrying	...	...	2873	5479	2500	2979	5715	2623	3092	6463	2988	3475
a Coal mining	...	...	56	155	66	89	165	71	94	174	71	103
b Crude petroleum and natural gas production	...	...	1099	2067	878	1189	2379	1007	1372	2689	1129	1560
c Metal ore mining	...	...	1360	2644	1327	1317	2549	1308	1241	2914	1522	1392
d Other mining	...	...	358	613	229	384	622	237	385	686	266	420
3 Manufacturing	...	...	18103	57738	38696	19042	62356	41839	20517	68188	45514	22674
a Manufacture of food, beverages and tobacco	...	...	2746	11018	8197	2821	11465	8493	2972	11702	8642	3060
b Textile, wearing apparel and leather industries	...	...	1507	4271	2659	1613	4676	2926	1750	4967	3121	1846
c Manufacture of wood and wood products, including furniture	...	...	1066	3289	2108	1181	3648	2363	1285	4018	2583	1435
d Manufacture of paper and paper products, printing and publishing	...	...	2460	5969	3503	2466	6471	3765	2706	6931	4023	2908
e Manufacture of chemicals and chemical petroleum, coal, rubber and plastic products	...	...	1845	6947	4994	1953	7642	5503	2139	8601	6168	2433
f Manufacture of non-metallic mineral products, except products of petroleum and coal	...	...	658	1664	918	746	1810	996	814	1985	1094	891
g Basic metal industries	...	...	1666	4491	2834	1657	4659	2981	1679	5001	3143	1858
h Manufacture of fabricated metal products, machinery and equipment [a]	...	...	5627	18719	12657	6061	20500	13918	6581	23381	15773	7608
i Other manufacturing industries [a]	...	...	528	1370	826	544	1485	894	591	1602	967	635
4 Electricity, gas and water	...	...	1852	...	...	1990	...	...	2223	...	...	2420
5 Construction	...	...	5522	13355	7341	6014	13777	7561	6215	14245	7811	6433
6 Wholesale and retail trade, restaurants and hotels	...	...	11204	65402	53451	11951	71484	58401	13083	77974	63737	14237
a Wholesale and retail trade	...	...	9185	61157	51351	9806	66911	56137	10774	73055	61304	11751
b Restaurants and hotels	...	...	2019	4245	2100	2145	4573	2264	2309	4919	2433	2486
7 Transport, storage and communication	...	...	6812	...	...	7177	...	...	7743	...	...	8448
8 Finance, insurance, real estate and business services	...	...	11496	...	...	12246	...	...	13064	...	...	14166
9 Community, social and personal services	...	...	2984	...	...	3096	...	...	3329	...	...	3512
Total, Industries	...	...	64111	188120	120114	68006	202214	129710	72504	219790	140901	78889
Producers of Government Services	...	...	13875	16114	1668	14446	16510	1692	14818	16993	1723	15270
Other Producers	...	...	769	855	47	808	870	49	821	919	50	870
Total [bc]	...	...	78755	205089	121829	83260	219594	131451	88143	237703	142673	95028
Imputed bank service charge	...	...	...	...	...	...	...	...	...	...	...	...
Import duties	...	...	...	...	...	...	...	...	...	...	...	...
Value added tax	...	...	...	...	...	...	...	...	...	...	...	...
Total	...	...	...	...	...	...	...	...	...	...	...	...

	1974 Gross Output	1974 Intermediate Consumption	1974 Value Added	1975 Gross Output	1975 Intermediate Consumption	1975 Value Added	1976 Gross Output	1976 Intermediate Consumption	1976 Value Added	1977 Gross Output	1977 Intermediate Consumption	1977 Value Added
At constant prices of: 1971 — All Producers												
1 Agriculture, hunting, forestry and fishing	7369	4073	3296	7446	3889	3557	7940	4142	3798	8141	4167	3974
a Agriculture and hunting	4999	2576	2423	5398	2612	2786	5646	2687	2959	5816	2734	3082
b Forestry and logging	2188	1437	751	1875	1220	655	2096	1390	706	2101	1359	742
c Fishing	182	60	122	173	57	116	198	65	133	224	74	150
2 Mining and quarrying	6470	3078	3392	5952	2952	3000	6024	2975	3049	6261	3143	3118
a Coal mining	184	80	104	230	107	123	221	106	115	238	126	112
b Crude petroleum and natural gas production	2571	1081	1490	2307	992	1315	2208	949	1259	2250	974	1276
c Metal ore mining	2971	1631	1340	2762	1562	1200	2896	1623	1273	3045	1735	1310

Canada

4.4 Derivation of Value Added by Kind of Activity, ISIC Divisions, in Constant Prices
(Continued)

Million Canadian dollars

	1974 Gross Output	1974 Intermediate Consumption	1974 Value Added	1975 Gross Output	1975 Intermediate Consumption	1975 Value Added	1976 Gross Output	1976 Intermediate Consumption	1976 Value Added	1977 Gross Output	1977 Intermediate Consumption	1977 Value Added
				At constant prices of: 1971								
d Other mining	744	286	458	653	291	362	699	297	402	728	308	420
3 Manufacturing	71055	47558	23497	68086	45962	22124	71533	48100	23433	73285	49382	23903
a Manufacture of food, beverages and tobacco	11844	8807	3037	12017	8984	3033	12644	9438	3206	12932	9680	3252
b Textile, wearing apparel and leather industries	4900	3087	1812	4824	3024	1800	5012	3149	1863	4948	3101	1847
c Manufacture of wood and wood products, including furniture	3919	2497	1422	3600	2295	1305	4178	2658	1520	4279	2722	1557
d Manufacture of paper and paper products, printing and publishing	7324	4257	3068	6374	3718	2656	7097	4134	2963	7131	4130	3001
e Manufacture of chemicals and chemical petroleum, coal, rubber and plastic products	8984	6471	2513	8545	6199	2346	8912	6410	2502	9463	6844	2619
f Manufacture of non-metallic mineral products, except products of petroleum and coal	2079	1146	934	1973	1095	878	2016	1117	899	1986	1096	890
g Basic metal industries	5384	3417	1967	4866	3093	1773	4724	2973	1751	5059	3183	1876
h Manufacture of fabricated metal products, machinery and equipment [a]	24904	16840	8064	24236	16555	7681	25211	17168	8043	25784	17592	8192
i Other manufacturing industries [a]	1717	1036	680	1651	999	652	1739	1053	686	1703	1034	669
4 Electricity, gas and water	...	...	2621	...	...	2626	...	...	2873	...	...	3063
5 Construction	14750	8110	6641	15447	8492	6955	15966	8779	7187	15716	8640	7076
6 Wholesale and retail trade, restaurants and hotels	83998	68678	15320	85735	70090	15645	89080	72671	16409	89822	73123	16699
a Wholesale and retail trade	78814	66114	12700	80489	67496	12993	83389	69858	13531	83915	70205	13710
b Restaurants and hotels	5184	2564	2620	5246	2594	2652	5691	2813	2878	5907	2918	2989
7 Transport, storage and communication	...	...	8956	...	...	9044	...	...	9509	...	...	10045
8 Finance, insurance, real estate and business services	...	...	15272	...	...	16078	...	...	17065	...	...	18164
9 Community, social and personal services	...	...	3775	...	...	4079	...	...	4344	...	...	4402
Total, Industries	232167	149396	82771	233330	150222	83107	244339	156676	87664	249891	159449	90443
Producers of Government Services	17424	1764	15660	18025	1810	16215	18446	1855	16592	18765	1883	16881
Other Producers	966	50	916	1013	52	960	1047	54	993	1071	55	1017
Total [bc]	250556	151210	99347	252368	152085	100283	263833	158584	105249	269727	161387	108341
Imputed bank service charge	...	...	...	...	...	...	...	...	...	...	...	...
Import duties	...	...	...	...	...	...	...	...	...	...	...	...
Value added tax	...	...	...	...	...	...	...	...	...	...	...	...
Total	...	...	...	...	...	...	...	...	...			

	1978 Gross Output	1978 Intermediate Consumption	1978 Value Added	1979 Gross Output	1979 Intermediate Consumption	1979 Value Added	1980 Gross Output	1980 Intermediate Consumption	1980 Value Added
	At constant prices of: 1971								
	All Producers								
1 Agriculture, hunting, forestry and fishing	8461	4508	3953	8412	4748	3664	8635	4864	3771
a Agriculture and hunting	5966	2958	3008	5827	3113	2714	6143	3283	2860
b Forestry and logging	2246	1468	778	2333	1552	781	2262	1505	757
c Fishing	249	82	167	252	83	169	230	76	154
2 Mining and quarrying	5725	2888	2837	6314	3224	3090	6296	3186	3110
a Coal mining	267	117	150	273	114	159	297	124	173
b Crude petroleum and natural gas production	2294	1018	1276	2623	1190	1433	2499	1134	1365
c Metal ore mining	2459	1451	1008	2664	1594	1070	2737	1601	1136
d Other mining	705	302	403	754	326	428	763	327	436

255

Canada

4.4 Derivation of Value Added by Kind of Activity, ISIC Divisions, in Constant Prices
(Continued)

Million Canadian dollars

		1978			1979			1980	
	Gross Output	Intermediate Consumption	Value Added	Gross Output	Intermediate Consumption	Value Added	Gross Output	Intermediate Consumption	Value Added
				At constant prices of:1971					
3 Manufacturing	77128	52019	25109	80899	54613	26286	78058	52598	25460
a Manufacture of food, beverages and tobacco	13218	9936	3282	13561	10187	3374	13823	10422	3401
b Textile, wearing apparel and leather industries	5259	3290	1969	5600	3509	2091	5274	3306	1968
c Manufacture of wood and wood products, including furniture	4478	2847	1631	4557	2895	1662	4442	2821	1621
d Manufacture of paper and paper products, printing and publishing	7774	4444	3330	8192	4669	3523	8237	4687	3550
e Manufacture of chemicals and chemical petroleum, coal, rubber and plastic products	10021	7285	2736	10948	7964	2984	10754	7846	2908
f Manufacture of non-metallic mineral products, except products of petroleum and coal	2123	1171	952	2282	1263	1019	2137	1184	953
g Basic metal industries	5417	3443	1974	5789	3763	2026	6057	3957	2100
h Manufacture of fabricated metal products, machinery and equipment [a]	26996	18483	8513	27980	19157	8823	25434	17223	8211
i Other manufacturing industries [a]	1842	1120	722	1990	1206	784	1900	1152	748
4 Electricity, gas and water	...	...	3200	...	...	3385	...	...	3479
5 Construction	15420	8477	6942	15727	8645	7082	15549	8547	7003
6 Wholesale and retail trade, restaurants and hotels	92976	75659	17317	95949	78088	17861	95830	77937	17893
a Wholesale and retail trade	86828	72624	14204	89671	74991	14680	89460	74794	14666
b Restaurants and hotels	6148	3035	3113	6278	3097	3181	6370	3143	3227
7 Transport, storage and communication	...	...	10498	...	...	11337	...	...	11614
8 Finance, insurance, real estate and business services	...	...	19326	...	...	20332	...	...	20794
9 Community, social and personal services	...	...	4594	...	...	4765	...	...	4943
Total, Industries	259579	165805	93774	270472	172670	97801	269066	170999	98067
Producers of Government Services	19013	1894	17119	19030	1913	17117	19161	1924	17238
Other Producers	1106	58	1048	1161	58	1103	1179	59	1120
Total [bc]	279698	167757	111941	290663	174641	116021	289406	172981	116425
Imputed bank service charge	...	...	...	...	...	...	...	...	...
Import duties	...	...	...	...	...	...	...	...	...
Value added tax	...	...	...	...	...	...	...	...	...
Total	...	...	...	...	...	...	...	...	...

a) Scientific and professional equipment manufacturers are included in item 'Other manufacturing industries'.
b) Components do not add up to total.
c) Indexes based on 1961 were used to deflate the period 1961 to 1970, while indexes based on 1971 were used to deflate the period from 1971. The series were then linked at the component and total levels, producing a residual difference.

4.6 Cost Components of Value Added, ISIC Divisions

Million Canadian dollars

			1970						1971			
	Compensation of Employees	Capital Consumption	Net Operating Surplus	Indirect Taxes	Less: Subsidies Received	Value Added	Compensation of Employees	Capital Consumption	Net Operating Surplus	Indirect Taxes	Less: Subsidies Received	Value Added
					All Producers							
1 Agriculture, hunting, forestry and fishing	893	...	...	...	...	3175	947	...	...	...	...	3451
2 Mining and quarrying	1233	...	...	...	...	3040	1328	...	...	...	...	2840
3 Manufacturing	12292	...	...	...	...	17600	13080	...	...	...	...	19006
4 Electricity, gas and water	744	...	...	...	...	2065	700	...	...	...	...	2241
5 Construction	3509	...	...	...	...	4687	4269	...	...	...	...	5589
6 Wholesale and retail trade, restaurants and hotels	6268	...	...	...	...	9348	6801	...	...	...	...	9869
7 Transport, storage and communication	4077	...	...	...	...	6350	4449	...	...	...	...	6997
8 Finance, insurance, real estate and business services	2547	...	...	...	...	8492	2762	...	...	...	...	9657
9 Community, social and personal services	3323	...	...	...	...	6705	3658	...	...	...	...	7441
Total, Industries	34886	...	...	...	...	61462	37994	...	...	...	...	67091
Producers of Government Services	11017	1231	...	...	...	12248	12444	1334	...	...	...	13778

Canada

4.6 Cost Components of Value Added, ISIC Divisions
(Continued)

Million Canadian dollars

	1970						1971					
	Compensation of Employees	Capital Consumption	Net Operating Surplus	Indirect Taxes	Less: Subsidies Received	Value Added	Compensation of Employees	Capital Consumption	Net Operating Surplus	Indirect Taxes	Less: Subsidies Received	Value Added
Other Producers	1717	...	...	...	...	1717	1998	...	...	...	...	1998
Total	47620	...	...	...	...	75427	52436	...	...	...	...	82867
Imputed bank service charge	...	...	...	...	...	-617	...	...	...	...	...	-669
Import duties	...	...	...	...	...	11299	...	...	...	...	...	12276
Value added tax	...	...	...	...	...	...	...	...	...	...	...	...
Other adjustments	...	...	...	...	...	345	...	...	...	...	...	891
Total	...	...	...	...	...	86454	...	...	...	...	...	95365

	1972						1973					
	Compensation of Employees	Capital Consumption	Net Operating Surplus	Indirect Taxes	Less: Subsidies Received	Value Added	Compensation of Employees	Capital Consumption	Net Operating Surplus	Indirect Taxes	Less: Subsidies Received	Value Added
	All Producers											
1 Agriculture, hunting, forestry and fishing	1008	...	...	...	...	3675	1282	...	...	...	...	5670
2 Mining and quarrying	1395	...	...	...	...	3160	1643	...	...	...	...	4713
3 Manufacturing	14470	...	...	...	...	21376	16589	...	...	...	...	25119
4 Electricity, gas and water	742	...	...	...	...	2497	880	...	...	...	...	2831
5 Construction	4652	...	...	...	...	6123	5739	...	...	...	...	7642
6 Wholesale and retail trade, restaurants and hotels	7694	...	...	...	...	11310	8860	...	...	...	...	12890
7 Transport, storage and communication	4953	...	...	...	...	7894	5608	...	...	...	...	8745
8 Finance, insurance, real estate and business services	3258	...	...	...	...	10712	4008	...	...	...	...	12273
9 Community, social and personal services	4246	...	...	...	...	8346	4980	...	...	...	...	9977
Total, Industries	42418	...	...	...	...	75093	49589	...	...	...	...	89860
Producers of Government Services	13896	1495	...	...	...	15391	15771	1710	...	...	...	17481
Other Producers	2235	...	...	...	...	2235	2489	...	...	...	...	2489
Total	58549	...	...	...	...	92719	67849	...	...	...	...	109830
Imputed bank service charge	...	...	...	...	...	-780	...	...	...	...	...	-878
Import duties	...	...	...	...	...	13876	...	...	...	...	...	15598
Value added tax	...	...	...	...	...	...	...	...	...	...	...	...
Other adjustments	...	...	...	...	...	190	...	...	...	...	...	-44
Total	...	...	...	...	...	106005	...	...	...	...	...	124506

	1974						1975					
	Compensation of Employees	Capital Consumption	Net Operating Surplus	Indirect Taxes	Less: Subsidies Received	Value Added	Compensation of Employees	Capital Consumption	Net Operating Surplus	Indirect Taxes	Less: Subsidies Received	Value Added
	All Producers											
1 Agriculture, hunting, forestry and fishing	1503	...	...	...	...	7087	1627	...	...	...	...	7311
2 Mining and quarrying	2062	...	...	...	...	5864	2426	...	...	...	...	6157
3 Manufacturing	19495	...	...	...	...	30133	21507	...	...	...	...	32018
4 Electricity, gas and water	1065	...	...	...	...	3347	1223	...	...	...	...	3829
5 Construction	6954	...	...	...	...	9546	8421	...	...	...	...	11579
6 Wholesale and retail trade, restaurants and hotels	10621	...	...	...	...	15614	12488	...	...	...	...	18190
7 Transport, storage and communication	6806	...	...	...	...	10124	7756	...	...	...	...	11303
8 Finance, insurance, real estate and business services	4769	...	...	...	...	14445	5601	...	...	...	...	17291
9 Community, social and personal services	5961	...	...	...	...	11881	7094	...	...	...	...	14041
Total, Industries	59236	...	...	...	...	108041	68143	...	...	...	...	121719
Producers of Government Services	19129	2161	...	...	...	21290	23070	2525	...	...	...	25595
Other Producers	2924	...	...	...	...	2924	3412	...	...	...	...	3412
Total	81289	...	...	...	...	132255	94625	...	...	...	...	150726
Imputed bank service charge	...	...	...	...	...	-992	...	...	...	...	...	-1259
Import duties	...	...	...	...	...	18257	...	...	...	...	...	17584
Value added tax	...	...	...	...	...	...	...	...	...	...	...	...
Other adjustments	...	...	...	...	...	-629	...	...	...	...	...	-300
Total	...	...	...	...	...	148891	...	...	...	...	...	166751

Canada

4.6 Cost Components of Value Added, ISIC Divisions

Million Canadian dollars

1976

	Compensation of Employees	Capital Consumption	Net Operating Surplus	Indirect Taxes	Less: Subsidies Received	Value Added
All Producers						
1 Agriculture, hunting, forestry and fishing	2014	...	...	...	...	7336
2 Mining and quarrying	2845	...	...	...	...	7170
3 Manufacturing	24722	...	...	...	...	36011
4 Electricity, gas and water	1433	...	...	...	...	4762
5 Construction	8923	...	...	...	...	12514
6 Wholesale and retail trade, restaurants and hotels	14238	...	...	...	...	20588
7 Transport, storage and communication	9092	...	...	...	...	13033
8 Finance, insurance, real estate and business services	6508	...	...	...	...	20739
9 Community, social and personal services	8260	...	...	...	...	16266
Total, Industries	78035	...	...	...	...	138419
Producers of Government Services	27234	2825	...	...	...	30059
Other Producers	4106	...	...	...	...	4106
Total	109375	...	...	...	...	172584
Imputed bank service charge	...	...	...	...	...	-1422
Import duties	...	...	...	...	...	21520
Value added tax	...	...	...	...	...	...
Other adjustments	...	...	...	...	...	266
Total	...	...	...	...	...	192948

1977

	Compensation of Employees	Capital Consumption	Net Operating Surplus	Indirect Taxes	Less: Subsidies Received	Value Added
1 Agriculture, hunting, forestry and fishing	2286	...	...	...	...	7580
2 Mining and quarrying	3247	...	...	...	...	8625
3 Manufacturing	26912	...	...	...	...	38580
4 Electricity, gas and water	1595	...	...	...	...	5887
5 Construction	9695	...	...	...	...	13183
6 Wholesale and retail trade, restaurants and hotels	15104	...	...	...	...	20816
7 Transport, storage and communication	10081	...	...	...	...	14725
8 Finance, insurance, real estate and business services	7389	...	...	...	...	23039
9 Community, social and personal services	9187	...	...	...	...	18005
Total, Industries	85496	...	...	...	...	150440
Producers of Government Services	30441	3157	...	...	...	33598
Other Producers	4586	...	...	...	...	4586
Total	120523	...	...	...	...	188624
Imputed bank service charge	...	...	...	...	...	-1559
Import duties	...	...	...	...	...	23907
Value added tax	...	...	...	...	...	...
Other adjustments	...	...	...	...	...	889
Total	...	...	...	...	...	211861

1978

	Compensation of Employees	Capital Consumption	Net Operating Surplus	Indirect Taxes	Less: Subsidies Received	Value Added
All Producers						
1 Agriculture, hunting, forestry and fishing	2588	...	...	...	...	9157
2 Mining and quarrying	3442	...	...	...	...	9533
3 Manufacturing	29673	...	...	...	...	43655
4 Electricity, gas and water	1774	...	...	...	...	6870
5 Construction	9432	...	...	...	...	13067
6 Wholesale and retail trade, restaurants and hotels	16318	...	...	...	...	23064
7 Transport, storage and communication	11137	...	...	...	...	16810
8 Finance, insurance, real estate and business services	8338	...	...	...	...	25986
9 Community, social and personal services	10163	...	...	...	...	20018
Total, Industries	92865	...	...	...	...	168160
Producers of Government Services	33326	3510	...	...	...	36836
Other Producers	5191	...	...	...	...	5191
Total	131382	...	...	...	...	210187
Imputed bank service charge	...	...	...	...	...	-1773
Import duties	...	...	...	...	...	25854
Value added tax	...	...	...	...	...	...
Other adjustments	...	...	...	...	...	261
Total	...	...	...	...	...	234529

1979

	Compensation of Employees	Capital Consumption	Net Operating Surplus	Indirect Taxes	Less: Subsidies Received	Value Added
1 Agriculture, hunting, forestry and fishing	2894	...	...	...	...	10706
2 Mining and quarrying	4109	...	...	...	...	14100
3 Manufacturing	33644	...	...	...	...	52412
4 Electricity, gas and water	2005	...	...	...	...	8189
5 Construction	9987	...	...	...	...	14189
6 Wholesale and retail trade, restaurants and hotels	18332	...	...	...	...	26914
7 Transport, storage and communication	12544	...	...	...	...	19160
8 Finance, insurance, real estate and business services	9607	...	...	...	...	26947
9 Community, social and personal services	11499	...	...	...	...	22932
Total, Industries	104621	...	...	...	...	195549
Producers of Government Services	36307	3984	...	...	...	40291
Other Producers	5711	...	...	...	...	5711
Total	146639	...	...	...	...	241551
Imputed bank service charge	...	...	...	...	...	-1653
Import duties	...	...	...	...	...	27925
Value added tax	...	...	...	...	...	...
Other adjustments	...	...	...	...	...	-188
Total	...	...	...	...	...	267635

1980

	Compensation of Employees	Capital Consumption	Net Operating Surplus	Indirect Taxes	Less: Subsidies Received	Value Added
All Producers						
1 Agriculture, hunting, forestry and fishing	3099	...	...	...	...	11591
2 Mining and quarrying	5066	...	...	...	...	17459
3 Manufacturing	36611	...	...	...	...	57815
4 Electricity, gas and water	2302	...	...	...	...	9072

Canada

4.6 Cost Components of Value Added, ISIC Divisions
(Continued)

Million Canadian dollars

	Compensation of Employees	Capital Consumption	Net Operating Surplus	Indirect Taxes	Less: Subsidies Received	Value Added
	1980					
5 Construction	10752	...	...	...	...	15482
6 Wholesale and retail trade, restaurants and hotels	20470	...	...	...	...	29466
7 Transport, storage and communication	14396	...	...	...	...	21353
8 Finance, insurance, real estate and business services	10934	...	...	...	...	28364
9 Community, social and personal services	13009	...	...	...	...	25799
Total, Industries	116639	...	...	...	...	216401
Producers of Government Services	41013	4624	...	...	...	45637
Other Producers	6384	...	...	...	...	6384
Total	164036	...	...	...	...	268422
Imputed bank service charge	...	...	...	...	...	-1726
Import duties	...	...	...	...	...	29191
Value added tax	...	...	...	...	...	...
Other adjustments	...	...	...	...	...	349
Total	...	...	...	...	...	296236

Central African Rep.

Source. Reply to the United Nations National Accounts Questionnaire from the Ministere du Plan, de la Cooperation International et des Statistiques, Bangui.
General note. The estimates shown in the following tables have been prepared and adjusted by the Ministere Francais de la Cooperationto conform to the United Nations System of National Accounts so far as the existing data would permit.

1.1 Expenditure on the Gross Domestic Product, in Current Prices

Million CFA francs

	1970	1971	1972	1973	1974	1975	1976	1977	1978	1979	1980
1 General government final consumption expenditure	10892	...	...	...	...	...	...	...	...	...	...
2 Private final consumption expenditure	39632	...	...	...	...	...	...	...	...	...	...
3 Gross capital formation	10323	...	...	...	...	...	...	...	...	...	...
a Increase in stocks	2137	...	...	...	...	...	...	...	...	...	...
b Gross fixed capital formation	8186	...	...	...	...	...	...	...	...	...	...
4 Exports of goods and services	11069	...	...	...	...	...	...	...	...	...	...
5 Less: Imports of goods and services	14933	...	...	...	...	...	...	...	...	...	...
Equals: Gross Domestic Product	56983	...	...	...	...	...	...	...	...	...	...

1.3 Cost Components of the Gross Domestic Product

Million CFA francs

	1970	1971	1972	1973	1974	1975	1976	1977	1978	1979	1980
1 Indirect taxes, net	6674	...	...	...	...	...	...	...	...	...	...
a Indirect taxes paid	6867	...	...	...	...	...	...	...	...	...	...
b Less: Subsidies received	193	...	...	...	...	...	...	...	...	...	...
2 Consumption of fixed capital	...	...	...	...	...	...	...	...	...	...	...
3 Compensation of employees paid by resident producers to:	13586	...	...	...	...	...	...	...	...	...	...
4 Net operating surplus [a]	36723	...	...	...	...	...	...	...	...	...	...
Equals: Gross Domestic Product	56983	...	...	...	...	...	...	...	...	...	...

a) Item 'Consumption of fixed capital' is included in item 'Operating surplus'.

1.10 Gross Domestic Product by Kind of Activity, in Current Prices

Million CFA francs

	1970	1971	1972	1973	1974	1975	1976	1977	1978	1979	1980
1 Agriculture, hunting, forestry and fishing	17676	...	...	...	...	...	...	...	...	...	...
2 Mining and quarrying [a]	2360	...	...	...	...	...	...	...	...	...	...
3 Manufacturing [a]	7687	...	...	...	...	...	...	...	...	...	...
4 Electricity, gas and water		...	...	...	...	...	...	...	...	...	...
5 Construction	2200	...	...	...	...	...	...	...	...	...	...
6 Wholesale and retail trade, restaurants and hotels [b]	11352	...	...	...	...	...	...	...	...	...	...
7 Transport, storage and communication	1500	...	...	...	...	...	...	...	...	...	...
8 Finance, insurance, real estate and business services	3101	...	...	...	...	...	...	...	...	...	...
9 Community, social and personal services		...	...	...	...	...	...	...	...	...	...
Total, Industries	45876	...	...	...	...	...	...	...	...	...	...
Producers of Government Services	7484	...	...	...	...	...	...	...	...	...	...
Other Producers	...	...	...	...	...	...	...	...	...	...	...
Subtotal	53360	...	...	...	...	...	...	...	...	...	...
Less: Imputed bank service charge	...	...	...	...	...	...	...	...	...	...	...
Plus: Import duties	3623	...	...	...	...	...	...	...	...	...	...
Plus: Value added tax	...	...	...	...	...	...	...	...	...	...	...
Equals: Gross Domestic Product [c]	56983	...	...	...	...	...	...	...	...	...	...

a) Diamond cutting is included in item 'Manufacturing'.
b) Restaurants and hotels are included in item 'Community, social and personal services'.
c) Gross domestic production. This differs from domestic product, primarily in the exclusion of the product originating in general government agencies and in public establishments of administrative nature.

1.11 Gross Domestic Product by Kind of Activity, in Constant Prices

Million CFA francs

	1970	1971	1972	1973	1974	1975	1976	1977	1978	1979	1980
	At constant prices of: 1967										
1 Agriculture, hunting, forestry and fishing	16461	16090	16116	17937	17825	18545	19089	19812	...	...	...
2 Mining and quarrying	2065	1958	2194	1592	1411	1417	1196	1241	...	...	...
3 Manufacturing	4504	4521	4424	4643	4678	4432	4544	5243	...	...	...
4 Electricity, gas and water	620	632	644	673	696	697	717	760	...	...	...
5 Construction	2719	2646	2007	2437	1896	2118	2408	3088	...	...	...

Central African Rep.

1.11 Gross Domestic Product by Kind of Activity, in Constant Prices
(Continued)

Million CFA francs

	1970	1971	1972	1973	1974	1975	1976	1977	1978	1979	1980
	\multicolumn{11}{c}{At constant prices of:1967}											
6 Wholesale and retail trade, restaurants and hotels	13229	12413	12022	11931	11365	11344	12252	13448	...	...	...
7 Transport, storage and communication	1170	1106	1044	1082	1032	1045	1173	1277	...	...	...
8 Finance, insurance, real estate and business services	3635	3690	3755	3822	3898	3982	4136	4306	...	...	...
9 Community, social and personal services									...	...	...
Total, Industries	...	...	...	...	...	...	...	...	...	...	...
Producers of Government Services	...	...	...	...	...	...	...	...	...	...	...
Other Producers	...	...	...	...	...	...	...	...	...	...	...
Subtotal	...	...	...	...	...	...	...	...	...	...	...
Less: Imputed bank service charge	...	...	...	...	...	...	...	...	...	...	...
Plus: Import duties	...	...	...	...	...	...	...	...	...	...	...
Plus: Value added tax	...	...	...	...	...	...	...	...	...	...	...
Equals: Gross Domestic Product	44403	43055	42206	44117	42801	43580	45515	49175	...	...	...

Chad

Source. Reply to the United Nations National Accounts Questionnaire from the Sous-Direction de la Statistique, Direction du Plan et du Developpement, Ministere des Finances, de L'Economie et du Plan, Ndjamena.

General note. The official estimates have been adjusted by the Sous-Direction de la Statistique to conform to the United Nations System of National Accounts so far as the existing data would permit.

1.1 Expenditure on the Gross Domestic Product, in Current Prices

Thousand Million CFA francs

	1970	1971	1972	1973	1974	1975	1976	1977	1978	1979	1980
1 General government final consumption expenditure	10.25	11.47	11.51	11.45	12.43	12.97	12.59	15.10	...	...	...
2 Private final consumption expenditure	77.01	83.24	77.92	80.10	97.62	133.25	135.50	134.92	...	...	...
3 Gross capital formation	9.62	10.80	11.60	11.71	18.42	27.75	28.75	29.34	...	...	...
a Increase in stocks	0.52	1.20	2.10	0.61	0.92	2.17	2.25	2.55	...	...	...
b Gross fixed capital formation	9.10	9.60	9.50	11.10	17.50	25.58	26.50	26.79	...	...	...
4 Exports of goods and services	21.11	21.98	21.52	21.96	29.14	25.26	33.31	35.89	...	...	...
5 Less: Imports of goods and services	27.48	29.09	28.95	33.43	42.10	50.65	54.62	53.49	...	...	...
Equals: Gross Domestic Product	90.50	98.40	93.60	91.80	115.50	148.57	155.53	161.76	...	...	...

1.2 Expenditure on the Gross Domestic Product, in Constant Prices

Thousand Million CFA francs

At constant prices of: 1970

	1970	1971	1972	1973	1974	1975	1976	1977	1978	1979	1980
1 General government final consumption expenditure	10.25	10.82	10.55	9.89	9.72	8.77	8.24	8.76	...	...	...
2 Private final consumption expenditure	77.01	78.53	71.42	69.17	76.32	90.09	88.62	84.05	...	...	...
3 Gross capital formation	9.62	10.24	10.59	10.24	14.25	20.37	19.07	16.66	...	...	...
4 Exports of goods and services	21.11	21.13	20.90	20.53	21.44	21.55	21.19	20.82	...	...	...
5 Less: Imports of goods and services	27.48	28.52	27.57	28.09	28.82	31.86	29.83	31.03	...	...	...
Equals: Gross Domestic Product	90.50	92.20	85.89	81.73	92.91	108.93	107.28	99.26	...	...	...

1.3 Cost Components of the Gross Domestic Product

Thousand Million CFA francs

	1970	1971	1972	1973	1974	1975	1976	1977	1978	1979	1980
1 Indirect taxes, net	...	...	...	...	...	7.32	9.03	8.96	...	...	...
a Indirect taxes paid	...	...	...	...	...	7.46	...	...	...	...	...
b Less: Subsidies received	...	...	...	...	...	0.14	...	...	...	...	...
2 Consumption of fixed capital	...	...	...	...	...	5.32	11.26	10.51	...	...	...
3 Compensation of employees paid by resident producers to:	...	...	...	...	...	19.41	18.75	21.42	...	...	...
a Resident households	...	...	...	...	...	19.21	...	...	...	...	...
b Rest of the world	0.29	0.20	0.11	0.16	0.14	0.20	...	...	...	...	...
4 Net operating surplus	...	...	...	...	...	116.52	116.51	120.86	...	...	...
Equals: Gross Domestic Product	90.50	98.40	93.60	91.80	115.50	148.57	155.53	161.76	...	...	...

1.7 External Transactions on Current Account, Summary

Thousand Million CFA francs

	1970	1971	1972	1973	1974	1975	1976	1977	1978	1979	1980
Payments to the Rest of the World											
1 Imports of goods and services	27.48	29.09	28.95	33.43	42.10	50.65	54.62	53.49	...	...	...
a Imports of merchandise c.i.f.	19.38	20.81	19.80	24.08	30.08	38.64	38.84	...	...	...	...
b Other	8.11	8.27	9.14	9.35	12.02	12.02	15.78	...	...	...	...
2 Factor income paid to the rest of the world	0.92	0.89	0.80	0.97	1.01	0.82	0.89	0.97	...	...	...
a Compensation of employees	0.29	0.20	0.11	0.16	0.14	0.20	0.32	0.35	...	...	...
b Property and entrepreneurial income paid	0.63	0.69	0.69	0.81	0.87	0.62	0.57	0.62	...	...	...
3 Indirect taxes paid to supranational organizations	...	...	...	...	...	...	...	...	...	...	...
4 Current transfers to the rest of the world	1.79	2.79	2.32	2.37	2.06	2.42	2.81	4.57	...	...	...
5 Surplus of the nation on current transactions	-4.10	-2.82	-3.71	-2.29	-5.91	-18.36	-11.68	-10.92	...	...	...
Payments to the Rest of the World and Surplus of the Nation on Current Transactions	26.09	29.95	28.36	34.48	39.26	35.54	46.64	48.11	...	...	...
Receipts From The Rest of the World											
1 Exports of goods and services	21.11	21.98	21.52	21.96	29.14	25.26	33.31	35.89	...	...	...

Chad

1.7 External Transactions on Current Account, Summary
(Continued)

Thousand Million CFA francs

	1970	1971	1972	1973	1974	1975	1976	1977	1978	1979	1980
a Exports of merchandise f.o.b.	12.24	11.72	10.06	10.87	16.94	12.42	24.08	...	...	...	...
b Other	8.87	10.26	11.46	11.09	12.20	12.84	9.23	...	...	...	...
2 Factor income received from rest of the world	0.15	0.24	0.34	0.39	0.44	0.13	0.09	0.40	...	...	...
a Compensation of employees	0.05	0.19	0.18	0.24	0.34	-	-	-	...	...	...
b Property and entrepreneurial income received	0.10	0.05	0.16	0.15	0.10	0.13	0.09	0.40	...	...	...
3 Subsidies received from supranational organisations	...	...	...	...	...	...	...	...	...	...	...
4 Current transfers from rest of the world	4.84	7.73	6.50	12.13	9.69	10.14	13.24	11.82	...	...	...
Receipts from the Rest of the World on Current Transactions	26.09	29.94	28.36	34.48	39.26	35.53	46.64	48.11	...	...	...

1.10 Gross Domestic Product by Kind of Activity, in Current Prices

Thousand Million CFA francs

	1970	1971	1972	1973	1974	1975	1976	1977	1978	1979	1980
1 Agriculture, hunting, forestry and fishing	...	...	...	...	...	60.93	59.78	66.99	...	...	...
2 Mining and quarrying	...	...	...	...	...	1.21	0.86	0.35	...	...	...
3 Manufacturing	...	...	...	...	...	16.53	20.07	26.28	...	...	...
4 Electricity, gas and water	...	...	...	...	...	0.97	1.20	0.91	...	...	...
5 Construction	...	...	...	...	...	4.18	2.07	1.70	...	...	...
6 Wholesale and retail trade, restaurants and hotels	...	...	...	...	...	42.20	48.02	48.71	...	...	...
7 Transport, storage and communication	...	...	...	...	...	3.55	4.68	3.87	...	...	...
8 Finance, insurance, real estate and business services	...	...	...	...	...	7.66	9.26	8.23	...	...	...
9 Community, social and personal services	...	...	...	...	...	9.97	8.36	3.44	...	...	...
Total, Industries	...	...	...	...	...	...	...	...	...	...	...
Producers of Government Services	...	...	...	...	...	...	...	...	...	...	...
Other Producers	...	...	...	...	...	...	...	...	...	...	...
Subtotal	...	...	...	...	...	147.18	154.30	160.48	...	...	...
Less: Imputed bank service charge	...	...	...	...	...	1.25	-	-	...	...	...
Plus: Import duties	...	...	...	...	...	2.64	1.23	1.28	...	...	...
Plus: Value added tax	...	...	...	...	...	...	...	...	...	...	...
Equals: Gross Domestic Product	...	...	...	...	...	148.57	155.53	161.76	...	...	...

1.12 Relations Among National Accounting Aggregates

Thousand Million CFA francs

	1970	1971	1972	1973	1974	1975	1976	1977	1978	1979	1980
Gross Domestic Product	90.50	98.40	93.60	91.80	115.50	148.57	155.53	161.76	...	...	...
Plus: Net factor income received from abroad	-0.77	-0.65	-0.46	-0.58	-0.57	-0.70	-0.80	-0.57	...	...	...
Factor income received	0.15	0.24	0.34	0.39	0.44	0.13	0.09	...	...	...	...
Less: Factor income paid	0.92	0.89	0.80	0.97	1.01	0.82	0.89	...	...	...	...
Equals: Gross National Product	89.73	97.75	93.14	91.22	114.93	147.87	154.73	161.19	...	...	...
Less: Consumption of fixed capital	...	...	...	...	...	5.32	11.26	10.50	...	...	...
Less: Net indirect taxes paid to supranational organisations	...	...	...	...	...	...	...	...	...	...	...
Equals: National Income at Market Prices	...	...	...	...	...	142.55	143.47	150.69	...	...	...
Plus: Net current transfers received from abroad	3.05	4.94	4.18	9.76	7.63	7.73	10.43	7.23	...	...	...
Current transfers received	4.84	7.73	6.50	12.13	9.69	10.14	13.24	...	...	...	...
Less: Current transfers paid	1.79	2.79	2.32	2.37	2.06	2.42	2.81	...	...	...	...
Equals: National Disposable Income at Market Prices	...	...	...	...	...	150.28	153.90	157.92	...	...	...
Less: Final consumption	87.26	94.71	89.43	91.55	110.05	146.22	148.09	150.02	...	...	...
Equals: Net Saving	...	...	...	...	...	4.07	5.81	7.90	...	...	...
Less: Surplus of the nation on current transactions	-4.10	-2.82	-3.71	-2.29	-5.91	-18.36	-11.68	...	...	...	...
Equals: Net Capital Formation	...	...	...	...	...	22.43	17.49	...	...	...	...

Chad

2.1 General Government Final Consumption Expenditure by Function, in Current Prices

Thousand Million CFA francs

	1970	1971	1972	1973	1974	1975	1976	1977	1978	1979	1980
1 General public services	...	...	...	...	...	5.18	...	...	...	...	...
2 Defence	...	...	...	...	...	...	...	...	...	...	...
3 Public order and safety	...	...	...	...	...	...	...	...	...	...	...
4 Education	...	...	...	...	...	1.81	...	...	...	...	...
5 Health	...	...	...	...	...	0.80	...	...	...	...	...
6 Social security and welfare	...	...	...	...	...	0.07	...	...	...	...	...
7 Housing and community amenities	...	...	...	...	...	-	...	...	...	...	...
8 Recreational, cultural and religious affairs	...	...	...	...	...	0.08	...	...	...	...	...
9 Economic services	...	...	...	...	...	5.77	...	...	...	...	...
10 Other functions	...	...	...	...	...	-0.74	...	...	...	...	...
Total General Government Final Consumption Expenditure	...	...	...	...	...	12.97	...	...	...	...	...

2.17 Exports and Imports of Goods and Services, Detail

Thousand Million CFA francs

	1970	1971	1972	1973	1974	1975	1976	1977	1978	1979	1980
Exports of Goods and Services											
1 Exports of merchandise, f.o.b.	12.24	11.72	10.06	10.87	16.94	12.42	24.08	...	...	...	...
2 Transport and communication	0.74	1.76	2.02	1.82	2.20	2.30	2.86	...	...	...	...
a In respect of merchandise imports	0.27	1.22	1.26	1.48	1.89	2.00	2.01	...	...	...	...
b Other	0.47	0.54	0.76	0.34	0.31	0.30	0.85	...	...	...	...
3 Insurance service charges	0.25	0.15	0.22	0.26	0.29	0.65	0.12	...	...	...	...
a In respect of merchandise imports	-	-	-	-	-	-	-	...	...	...	...
b Other	0.25	0.15	0.22	0.26	0.29	0.65	0.12	...	...	...	...
4 Other commodities	1.43	0.79	0.95	0.31	1.67	1.94	1.97	...	...	...	...
5 Adjustments of merchandise exports to change-of-ownership basis	-	-	-	-	-	-	-	...	...	...	...
6 Direct purchases in the domestic market by non-residential households	6.46	7.56	8.28	8.70	8.03	7.95	4.29	...	...	...	...
7 Direct purchases in the domestic market by extraterritorial bodies	...	...	...	...	...	...	...	...	...	...	...
Total Exports of Goods and Services	21.11	21.98	21.52	21.96	29.14	25.26	33.31	...	...	...	...
Imports of Goods and Services											
1 Imports of merchandise, c.i.f.	19.38	20.81	19.80	24.08	30.08	38.64	38.84	...	...	...	...
a Imports of merchandise, f.o.b.	14.07	14.71	14.74	16.37	19.94	25.66	27.57	...	...	...	...
b Transport of services on merchandise imports	5.31	6.10	5.06	7.71	10.14	12.98	11.27	...	...	...	...
c Insurance service charges on merchandise imports	...	...	...	...	...	...	...	...	...	...	...
2 Adjustments of merchandise imports to change-of-ownership basis	...	...	...	...	...	...	...	...	...	...	...
3 Other transport and communication	0.93	0.95	1.12	1.25	2.61	1.39	1.55	...	...	...	...
4 Other insurance service charges	0.41	0.44	0.42	0.43	0.54	0.80	0.15	...	...	...	...
5 Other commodities	2.09	2.08	2.36	2.35	3.03	2.36	5.69	...	...	...	...
6 Direct purchases abroad by government	4.68	4.80	5.24	5.32	5.84	7.47	8.39	...	...	...	...
7 Direct purchases abroad by resident households								...	...	...	...
Total Imports of Goods and Services	27.48	29.09	28.95	33.43	42.10	50.65	54.62	...	...	...	...
Balance of Goods and Services	-6.37	-7.11	-7.43	-11.47	-12.96	-25.39	-21.31	...	...	...	...
Total Imports and Balance of Goods and Services	21.11	21.98	21.52	21.96	29.14	25.26	33.31	...	...	...	...

Chad

4.3 Derivation of Value Added by Kind of Activity, ISIC Divisions, in Current Prices

Thousand Million CFA francs

		1975	
	Gross Output	Intermediate Consumption	Value Added

All Producers

1	Agriculture, hunting, forestry and fishing	...	...	60.93
	a Agriculture and hunting	...	...	50.70
	b Forestry and logging	...	...	2.18
	c Fishing	...	...	8.05
2	Mining and quarrying	...	...	1.21
	a Coal mining	...	...	...
	b Crude petroleum and natural gas production	...	...	0.80
	c Metal ore mining	...	...	...
	d Other mining	...	...	...
3	Manufacturing	...	...	16.53
	a Manufacture of food, beverages and tobacco	...	...	7.42
	b Textile, wearing apparel and leather industries	...	...	6.57
	c Manufacture of wood and wood products, including furniture	...	...	0.37
	d Manufacture of paper and paper products, printing and publishing	...	...	0.23
	e Manufacture of chemicals and chemical petroleum, coal, rubber and plastic products	...	...	0.05
	f Manufacture of non-metallic mineral products, except products of petroleum and coal	...	...	0.94
	g Basic metal industries	...	...	...
	h Manufacture of fabricated metal products, machinery and equipment	...	...	...
	i Other manufacturing industries	...	...	...
4	Electricity, gas and water	...	...	0.97
5	Construction	...	...	4.18
6	Wholesale and retail trade, restaurants and hotels	...	...	42.20
	a Wholesale and retail trade	...	...	41.07
	b Restaurants and hotels	...	...	1.13
7	Transport, storage and communication	...	...	3.55
8	Finance, insurance, real estate and business services	...	...	7.66
9	Community, social and personal services	...	...	9.97
	Total, Industries	...	...	147.18
	Producers of Government Services	...	...	1.25
	Other Producers	...	...	2.65
	Total	...	...	148.57
	Imputed bank service charge	...	...	...
	Import duties	...	...	...
	Value added tax	...	...	...
	Total	...	...	...

4.6 Cost Components of Value Added, ISIC Divisions

Thousand Million CFA francs

		1975				
	Compensation of Employees	Capital Consumption	Net Operating Surplus	Indirect Taxes	Less: Subsidies Received	Value Added

All Producers

1	Agriculture, hunting, forestry and fishing	1.52	...	58.49	...	...	60.93
	a Agriculture and hunting	...	...	49.21	...	...	50.70
	b Forestry and logging	-	...	2.17	...	...	2.18
	c Fishing	0.62	...	7.11	...	...	8.05
2	Mining and quarrying	0.30	...	0.16	...	...	1.21

Chad

4.6 Cost Components of Value Added, ISIC Divisions
(Continued)

Thousand Million CFA francs

	Compensation of Employees	Capital Consumption	Net Operating Surplus	Indirect Taxes	Less: Subsidies Received	Value Added
1975						
a Coal mining	...	...	...	...	...	...
b Crude petroleum and natural gas production	...	...	...	...	...	0.80
c Metal ore mining	...	...	...	...	...	...
d Other mining	...	...	...	...	...	...
3 Manufacturing	2.11	...	11.64	...	...	16.53
a Manufacture of food, beverages and tobacco	0.59	...	6.01	...	...	7.42
b Textile, wearing apparel and leather industries	1.23	...	3.51	...	...	6.57
c Manufacture of wood and wood products, including furniture	0.08	...	0.24	...	...	0.37
d Manufacture of paper and paper products, printing and publishing	0.06	...	0.16	...	...	0.23
e Manufacture of chemicals and chemical petroleum, coal, rubber and plastic products	0.01	...	0.02	...	...	0.05
f Manufacture of non-metallic mineral products, except products of petroleum and coal	-	...	0.93	...	...	0.94
g Basic metal industries	...	...	...	...	...	...
h Manufacture of fabricated metal products, machinery and equipment	...	...	...	...	...	...
i Other manufacturing industries	...	...	...	...	...	...
4 Electricity, gas and water	0.17	...	0.73	...	...	0.97
5 Construction	1.63	...	2.31	...	...	4.18
6 Wholesale and retail trade, restaurants and hotels	1.89	...	36.72	...	...	42.20
a Wholesale and retail trade	...	...	...	...	...	41.07
b Restaurants and hotels	...	...	...	...	...	1.13
7 Transport, storage and communication	1.43	...	1.48	...	...	3.55
8 Finance, insurance, real estate and business services	0.59	...	6.31	...	...	7.66
9 Community, social and personal services	0.02	...	0.16	...	...	9.97
Total, Industries	9.66	...	118.00	...	...	147.18
Producers of Government Services	9.73	...	-	...	...	9.49
Other Producers	0.26	...	-	...	...	0.28
Total	19.41	...	117.77	...	...	147.18
Imputed bank service charge	...	...	-1.25	...	...	-1.25
Import duties	...	...	...	...	...	2.64
Value added tax	...	...	...	...	...	...
Other adjustments	...	...	...	...	...	...
Total	...	...	...	...	...	148.57

Chile

General note. The preparation of national accounts statistics in Chile is undertaken by Oficina de Planificacion Nacional (ODEPLAN), Santiago. The official estimates are published in 'Cuentas Nacionales de Chile'. The following presentation of sources and methods is mainly based on a detailed description received by the United Nations from ODEPLAN. However, descriptions can also be found in 'Cuentas Nacionales de Chile, 1960-1975', published in 1976. The estimates are generally in accordance with the classifications and definitions recommended in the United Nations System of National Accounts (SNA). The following tables have been prepared from successive replies to the United Nations national accounts questionnaire. When the scope and coverage of the estimates differ for conceptual or statistical reasons from the definitions and classifications recommended in SNA, a footnote is indicated to the relevant tables.

Sources and methods:

(a) Gross domestic product. The main approach used to estimate GDP is the production approach.

(b) Expenditure on the gross domestic product. The expenditure approach is used to estimate government final consumption expenditure, increase in stocks, exports and imports of goods and services and capital formation in new construction. The commodity-flow approach is used to estimate other construction. Private final consumption expenditure is estimated as a residual. Data on government consumption expenditure is obtained i.a. through special inquiries and direct information from the concerned authorities. Values of locally produced and imported capital goods are adjusted by coefficients by type of capital goods to arrive at purchasers' values. Estimates of exports and imports of goods and services are obtained from the balance of payments statements prepared by the Central Bank. To arrive at constant prices, value added of government services is deflated by index of wages and salaries. Purchases of goods and services are deflated by the wholesale price index and the price index of intermediate imported goods. For private consumption expenditure most domestically produced items are deflated by appropriate components of the consumer price index. Imported goods are deflated by the price index of imported consumer goods. For gross fixed capital formation, buildings and other construction are devalued using double deflation. Base year estimates of transport equipment, machinery and equipment are extrapolated by a quantity index for each industrial group, except for imports which are deflated by price indexes of imported capital goods. Price deflation is used for exports and imports of goods and services.

(c) Cost-structure of the gross domestic product. Wages and salaries are in most cases estimated from company accounts and/or direct information from the enterprises. Employers' contributions to social security schemes as well as wages and salaries in kind are included in the estimates. Operating surplus is obtained as a residual. Depreciation data are obtained from accounting statements of enterprises or computed from data of fixed assets by type of capital and useful life time. For indirect taxes, published fiscal statements by type of tax, are used.

(d) Gross domestic product by kind of economic activity. This table is prepared at market prices, i.e. producers' values. The production approach is used to estimate value added of most industries. The income approach is however used for government services, business services and domestic services. The general method of estimating gross value of agricultural production involves the use of physical quantities of production together with the respective wholesale or producers' prices. Quantities of livestock production are obtained from published data and directly from Instituto Nacional de Estadistica (INE). The estimates include both marketed and non-marketed production. The inputs into agriculture and forestry are based on information from the suppliers of input products. The estimates for the mining and quarrying sector are mainly based on data on sales and change in stocks, but in some cases on physical production valued at average sales price or on expenditure data in the construction and industrial sectors. For manufacturing, the required statistics for companies with 1 to 49 employees are found in their annual industrial declarations. For units with 50 or more employees, the industrial yearbook of INE is used. The gross value of construction in the public sector is obtained from accounts of the respective institutions. For the private sector the construction expenditure on all buildings is calculated on the basis of the municipal building permits. In order to estimate intermediate consumption and the components of value added, cost-structure by type of construction are applied to the gross value of production. Estimates of private sector trade is made on the basis of a continuous survey. For public enterprises, information provided in their accounting statements and in their budget statements is used. For transport, information is based on accounts, sales data and on the stock of motor vehicles. The production and input estimates for financial institutions and corporations, real estate and insurance are made possible through data from the Superintendencia de Bancos. Bench-mark estimates for actual rents paid and imputed rent for owner-occupied dwellings have been made on the basis of the housing censuses in 1960 and 1970. These estimates are projected annually by a value index which combines the increase in physical stock with a price index for rent. For public administration and defense, budgets and accounts provide the required basic data. For the constant price estimates, double deflation is used in the agricultural sector, the output value is extrapolated by quantity indexes by product, whereas intermediate inputs are deflated by an index of input prices. Value added of fishing, mining and quarrying, manufacturing and electricity is extrapolated by quantity indexes of production. Double deflation is used for construction, current gross values are deflated by price indexes for each type of construction. For intermediate consumption, input-structures are used. For trade, value added of the base year is extrapolated by a quantity index. Double deflation is used for the transport and financing, insurance, real estate and business services sector. For transport, current output is deflated separately for different uses and types of transport. For financial institutions, output is deflated by an implicit price index for expenditure. Output of ownership of dwellings is extrapolated by an index based on the change in the housing stock, whereas inputs are deflated by the value index for repairs. For community, social and personal services, double deflation is used.

1.1 Expenditure on the Gross Domestic Product, in Current Prices

Million Chilean pesos

	1970	1971	1972	1973	1974	1975	1976	1977	1978	1979	1980
1 General government final consumption expenditure	13	19	38	151	1271 / 1448	5560	17990	41939	66586	95590	135363
2 Private final consumption expenditure	69	93	179	915	7049 / 5743	25942	88669	209507	346627	528140	789974
a Households	...	...	...	...	... / 5607	25333	86692	205154	339666	518381	...
b Private non-profit institutions serving households	...	...	...	...	... / 136	609	1977	4353	6961	9759	...
3 Gross capital formation	15	18	30	169	1304 / 1946	4645	16447	41509	86835	162162	196787
a Increase in stocks	2	1	1	7	102 / 387	-1626	-621	3163	15241	45693	8922
b Gross fixed capital formation	13	17	29	162	1202 / 1559	6271	17068	38346	71594	116469	187865
Residential buildings	2	4	7	34	255 / 508	1606	4435	9487	13494	25716	...
Non-residential buildings	1	2	4	16	124 / 138	399	1347	3752	6761	11093	...
Other construction and land improvement etc.	4	5	9	40	429 / 424	1313	3205	5635	13590	22429	...
Other	6	6	9	72	394 / 489	2953	8081	19472	37749	57231	...
4 Exports of goods and services	15	14	22	155	1633 / 1877	9026	32322	59338	100352	177842	231663
5 Less: Imports of goods and services	14	15	30	176	1596 / 1815	9726	26752	64523	112894	201605	258609
Equals: Gross Domestic Product	97	129	239	1213	9661 / 9199	35447	128676	287770	487506	762129	1095178

Chile

1.2 Expenditure on the Gross Domestic Product, in Constant Prices

Million Chilean pesos

	1970	1971	1972	1973	1974	1975	1976	1977	1978	1979	1980
				At constant prices of:							
			1965					1977			
1 General government final consumption expenditure	3	3	3	3	3 45067	40428	40385	41939	42390	41595	40627
2 Private final consumption expenditure	17	19	20	19	19 203367	180139	180596	209507	225279	243665	261964
a Households	...	...	...	...	... 198995	175661	176234	205154	220871	239191	...
b Private non-profit institutions serving households	...	...	...	...	... 4372	4478	4362	4353	4408	4474	...
3 Gross capital formation	4	4	3	3	3 64218	35479	35536	41509	51235	67772	67052
a Increase in stocks	-	-	-	-	- 13731	-3513	2321	3163	6226	15227	2903
b Gross fixed capital formation	3	3	3	3	3 50487	38992	33215	38346	45009	52545	64149
Residential buildings	1	1	1	1	1 15528	11645	9395	9487	8123	11685	...
Non-residential buildings	1	1	1	1	1a 4137	2650	2742	3752	4338	5227	...
Other construction and land improvement etc.					... 14102	8372	6398	5635	8661	9731	...
Other	1	1	1	1	1 16720	16325	14680	19472	23887	25902	...
4 Exports of goods and services	3	3	3	3	4 41666	42645	53037	59338	65979	73948	82047
5 Less: Imports of goods and services	4	4	4	4	4 63764	45648	47609	64523	73466	89800	92593
Equals: Gross Domestic Product	23	24	24	24	25 290554	253043	261945	287770	311417	337180	359097

a) Including item 'Other construction and land improvement etc.

1.3 Cost Components of the Gross Domestic Product

Million Chilean pesos

	1970	1971	1972	1973	1974	1975	1976	1977	1978	1979	1980
1 Indirect taxes, net	10	12	20	120	1208 1434	4961	17674	41321	67389	97419	...
a Indirect taxes paid	13	17	30	193	1626 1607	5569	19925	45827	76876	114111	...
b Less: Subsidies received	2	5	10	73	418 173	608	2251	4506	9487	16692	...
2 Consumption of fixed capital	8	11	19	129	851 1041	5200	17048	33697	55633	79734	...
3 Compensation of employees paid by resident producers to:	41	65	125	454	3205 3425	13817	49335	113492	187713	287326	...
4 Net operating surplus	37	40	74	509	4397 3299	11469	44619	99260	176771	297650	...
Equals: Gross Domestic Product	97	129	239	1213	9660 9199	35447	128676	287770	487506	762129	1095178

1.4 General Government Current Receipts and Disbursements

Million Chilean pesos

	1970	1971	1972	1973	1974	1975	1976	1977	1978	1979	1980
					Receipts						
1 Property and entrepreneurial income	4.0	0.6	-3.5	-84.1	-46.5	228.3	525.8	...	...	...	...
2 Taxes, fees and contributions	27.2	38.3	66.0	331.0	2924.0	11249.4	38747.8	...	...	...	...
a Indirect taxes	12.8	17.2	30.4	193.2	1626.4	5617.3	20284.0	...	...	...	...
b Direct taxes	5.2	6.6	8.3	54.6	568.2	2546.6	8521.5	...	...	...	...
c Social security contributions	9.2	14.5	27.3	83.2	729.4	3085.5	9942.3	...	...	...	...
d Compulsory fees, fines and penalties	...	...	...	...	...	...	...	...	...	...	...
3 Other current receipts	0.8	1.1	2.1	6.9	63.1	377.1	1061.9	...	...	...	...
Total Current Receipts of General Government	32.0	40.0	64.6	253.8	2940.6	11854.8	40335.5	...	...	...	...
					Disbursements						
1 General government final consumption expenditure	12.6	19.4	38.0	150.7	1271.0	5529.3	18928.0	...	...	...	...
2 Property income paid	0.5	0.7	0.4	1.6	82.3	1419.3	3093.0	...	...	...	...

Chile

1.4 General Government Current Receipts and Disbursements
(Continued)

Million Chilean pesos	1970	1971	1972	1973	1974	1975	1976	1977	1978	1979	1980
a Interest	0.5	0.7	1.4	1.6	82.3	1419.3	3093.0	...	...	...	...
b Net land rent and royalties	...	...	...	...	...	...	...	...	...	...	...
3 Subsidies	2.3	4.8	10.5	72.8	418.4	947.9	2835.0	...	...	...	...
4 Other current transfers paid	8.7	15.8	27.4	82.0	603.3	3049.2	9313.3	...	...	...	...
a Social security benefits and social assistance grants	8.7	15.6	27.3	81.5	600.0	3033.4	9219.1	...	...	...	...
b Other	...	0.2	0.1	0.5	3.3	15.8	94.2	...	...	...	...
5 Net saving	7.7	-0.6	-11.4	-53.3	565.8	909.2	6165.9	...	...	...	...
Total Current Disbursements and Net Saving of General Government	31.9	40.0	64.6	253.8	2940.6	11854.9	40335.5	...	...	...	...

1.6 Current Income and Outlay of Households and Non-Profit Institutions

Million Chilean pesos	1970	1971	1972	1973	1974	1975	1976	1977	1978	1979	1980
Receipts											
1 Compensation of employees	41	65	125	454	3205	13994	47830	...	...	...	...
2 Property and entrepreneurial income received	27	34	76	514	3416	18722	59942	...	...	...	...
3 Current transfers received	9	16	27	82	607	3080	9350	...	...	...	...
a Social security benefits and social assistance grants received	9	16	27	81	600	3033	9219	...	...	...	...
b Other				1	7	47	131	...	...	...	...
Total Current Receipts	77	115	229	1052	7228	35797	117122	...	...	...	...
Disbursements											
1 Private final consumption expenditure	69	93	179	915	7049	35360	113774	...	...	...	...
2 Property income paid	...	...	...	...	...	...	...	...	...	...	...
3 Direct taxes and other payments n.e.c. to general government	11	18	33	114	1025	4333	14392	...	...	...	...
a Social security contributions	9	15	27	83	729	3086	9942	...	...	...	...
b Direct taxes	2	3	6	31	296	1247	4450	...	...	...	...
c Fees, fines and penalties	...	...	...	...	...	...	...	...	...	...	...
4 Other current transfers paid	1	1	2	5	40	224	596	...	...	...	...
5 Net saving	-4	3	15	18	-886	-4138	-11690	...	...	...	...
Total Current Disbursements and Net Saving	77	115	229	1052	7228	35797	117122	...	...	...	...

1.7 External Transactions on Current Account, Summary

Million Chilean pesos	1970	1971	1972	1973	1974	1975	1976	1977	1978	1979	1980
Payments to the Rest of the World											
1 Imports of goods and services	13.9	15.2	30.0	175.9	1596.0 / 1815.0	9726.0	26752.0	64523.0	12894.0	01605.0	...
2 Factor income paid to the rest of the world	2.6	1.6	1.4	12.4	142.6 / 163.0	1429.0	4438.0	8323.0	15377.0	29960.0	...
3 Indirect taxes paid to supranational organizations	...	...	...	...	...	...	...	...	...	...	...
4 Current transfers to the rest of the world	-	0.2	0.1	0.5	3.3 / 8.0	64.0	117.0	885.0	125.0	3635.0	...

Chile

1.7 External Transactions on Current Account, Summary
(Continued)

Million Chilean pesos

	1970	1971	1972	1973	1974	1975	1976	1977	1978	1979	1980
5 Surplus of the nation on current transactions	-1.2	-2.6	-9.1	-30.4	-62.8 / -41.0	-1841.0	2244.0	10737.0	21677.0	45990.0	...
Payments to the Rest of the World and Surplus of the Nation on Current Transactions	15.4	14.4	23.1	158.3	1679.1 / 1945.0	9378.0	33551.0	62994.0	06719.0	89210.0	...

Receipts From The Rest of the World

	1970	1971	1972	1973	1974	1975	1976	1977	1978	1979	1980
1 Exports of goods and services	14.5	13.9	22.5	154.6	1632.9 / 1877.0	9026.0	32322.0	59338.0	00352.0	77842.0	...
2 Factor income received from rest of the world	0.3	0.1	-	-	16.2 / 20.0	41.0	234.0	710.0	2034.0	4701.0	...
3 Subsidies received from supranational organisations	...	...	...	...	... / ...	...	...	...	...	...	...
4 Current transfers from rest of the world	0.5	0.3	0.6	3.7	30.1 / 48.0	311.0	996.0	2946.0	4333.0	6667.0	...
Receipts from the Rest of the World on Current Transactions	15.4	14.4	23.1	158.3	1679.1 / 1945.0	9378.0	33551.0	62994.0	06719.0	89210.0	...

1.8 Capital Transactions of The Nation, Summary

Million Chilean pesos

	1970	1971	1972	1973	1974	1975	1976	1977	1978	1979	1980

Finance of Gross Capital Formation

	1970	1971	1972	1973	1974	1975	1976	1977	1978	1979	1980
Gross saving	13.9	15.6	21.1	138.6	1241.2 / 1905.0	2805.0	18691.0	30772.0	65159.0	16171.0	...
1 Consumption of fixed capital	8.2	11.4	19.4	129.4	851.2 / 1041.0	5200.0	17048.0	33697.0	55633.0	79734.0	...
2 Net saving	5.7	4.2	1.7	9.2	390.0 / 864.0	-2395.0	1643.0	-2925.0	9526.0	36437.0	...
a General government	7.7	-0.6	-11.4	-53.3	565.8 / 871.0	1190.0	9517.0	15358.0	19275.0	58636.0	...
b Corporate and quasi-corporate enterprises	...	...	...	...	... / -7.0	-3585.0	-7874.0	18283.0	-9749.0	22199.0	...
c Other	...	...	...	...	... / ...	...	...	...	...	...	...
Less: Surplus of the nation on current transactions	-1.2	-2.6	-9.1	-30.4	-62.8 / -41.0	-1841.0	2244.0	10737.0	21676.0	45991.0	...
Finance of Gross Capital Formation	15.1	18.2	30.3	169.0	1304.0 / 1946.0	4646.0	16447.0	41509.0	86835.0	62162.0	...

Gross Capital Formation

	1970	1971	1972	1973	1974	1975	1976	1977	1978	1979	1980
Increase in stocks	1.8	1.5	1.3	7.0	102.0 / 387.0	-1625.0	-621.0	3163.0	15241.0	45693.0	...
Gross fixed capital formation	13.0	17.0	29.0	162.0	1202.0 / 1560.0	6271.0	17068.0	38346.0	71594.0	16469.0	...
Gross Capital Formation	15.1	18.2	30.0	169.0	1304.0 / 1946.0	4645.0	16447.0	41509.0	86835.0	62162.0	...

1.10 Gross Domestic Product by Kind of Activity, in Current Prices

Million Chilean pesos

	1970	1971	1972	1973	1974	1975	1976	1977	1978	1979	1980
1 Agriculture, hunting, forestry and fishing	7	10	17	80	536 / 524	2333	10859	28289	37054	56656	78957
2 Mining and quarrying	10	9	19	111	922 / 1100	3683	13089	23161	36280	78028	98115
3 Manufacturing	26	33	59	316	2244 / 2718	7187	29934	62574	109175	155142	226511
4 Electricity, gas and water	1	2	3	6	87 / 104	739	2903	6477	9629	15241	22983
5 Construction	4	6	12	39	325 / 560	1907	5508	11706	20423	33641	55379

Chile

1.10 Gross Domestic Product by Kind of Activity, in Current Prices
(Continued)

Million Chilean pesos	1970	1971	1972	1973	1974	1975	1976	1977	1978	1979	1980
6 Wholesale and retail trade, restaurants and hotels [a]	19	25	53	306	2782 / 1298	6121	19442	44844	80311	133812	199272
7 Transport, storage and communication	4	6	11	54	374 / 529	2023	6362	15377	26707	38318	53467
8 Finance, insurance, real estate and business services [b]	9	13	17	101	835 / 824	5161	17470	38699	72672	109827	166022
9 Community, social and personal services [ab]	...	...	...	...	1555 / ...	...	...	...	...	...	...
Total, Industries	91	121	222	1144	9660 / 8495	32984	119354	264657	448582	708282	1025573
Producers of Government Services	6	8	17	70	... / 600	2207	7723	18275	28067	41100	60309
Other Producers	...	...	...	...	...	...	...	...	...	...	...
Subtotal	97	129	239	1214	9660 / 9095	35191	127077	282932	476649	749382	1085882
Less: Imputed bank service charge	...	...	...	...	... / 223	1047	3343	9152	14267	29472	52283
Plus: Import duties	...	...	...	...	... / 327	1303	4942	13990	25124	42219	61579
Plus: Value added tax	...	...	...	...	...	...	...	...	...	...	...
Equals: Gross Domestic Product	97	129	239	1213	9660 / 9199	35447	128676	287770	487506	762129	1095178

a) Restaurants and hotels are included in item 'Community, social and personal services'.
b) Business services are included in item 'Community, social and personal services'.

1.11 Gross Domestic Product by Kind of Activity, in Constant Prices

Million Chilean pesos	1970	1971	1972	1973	1974	1975	1976	1977	1978	1979	1980
		At constant prices of: 1965						1977			
1 Agriculture, hunting, forestry and fishing	2	2	2	2	2 / 24904	25993	25573	28290	27241	29489	30376
2 Mining and quarrying	2	2	2	2	3 / 22642	20094	22544	23161	23529	24785	25752
3 Manufacturing	5	6	6	6	6 / 72994	54406	57678	62574	68374	73120	76776
4 Electricity, gas and water	-	-	-	-	1 / 6013	5786	6124	6477	6913	7383	7856
5 Construction	1	1	1	1	1 / 19128	14147	11809	11706	12650	15636	18294
6 Wholesale and retail trade, restaurants and hotels	5[a]	5[a]	5[a]	5[a]	5[a] / 42297	35060	35933	44844	53820	58727	64305
7 Transport, storage and communication	1	1	1	1	1 / 14363	13262	13879	15375	16665	18075	19377
8 Finance, insurance, real estate and business services	3[b]	3[b]	3[b]	3[b]	3[b] / 35059	34783	36280	38698	42539	48328	110025
9 Community, social and personal services	...	...	...	...	... / 32358	31966	32376	33530	34744	36390	...
Total, Industries	22	23	23	22	24 / 269758	235497	242196	264656	286475	311933	...
Producers of Government Services	1	1	1	1	1 / 16646	16957	17953	18275	17714	17527	...
Other Producers	...	...	...	...	...	...	...	...	...	...	...
Subtotal	23	24	24	24	25 / 286404	252454	260149	282931	304189	329460	352761
Less: Imputed bank service charge	...	...	...	...	... / 7027	7530	6849	9157	9123	13004	16398
Plus: Import duties	...	...	...	...	... / 11177	8119	8645	13990	16351	20724	22734
Plus: Value added tax	...	...	...	...	...	...	...	...	...	...	...
Equals: Gross Domestic Product	23	24	24	24	25 / 290554	253043	261945	287770	311417	337180	359097

a) Restaurants and hotels are included in item 'Community, social and personal services'.
b) Business services are included in item 'Community, social and personal services'.

Chile

1.12 Relations Among National Accounting Aggregates

Million Chilean pesos

	1970	1971	1972	1973	1974	1975	1976	1977	1978	1979	1980
Gross Domestic Product	97	129	239	1213	9660 / 9199	35447	128676	287770	487506	762129	...
Plus: Net factor income received from abroad	-2	-1	-1	-12	-127 / -144	-1389	-4204	-7613	-13343	-25260	...
Factor income received	...	...	...	...	16 / 20	40	234	710	2034	4701	...
Less: Factor income paid	2	1	1	12	143 / 164	1429	4438	8323	15377	29961	...
Equals: Gross National Product	95	128	238	1201	9533 / 9055	34058	124472	280157	474163	736869	...
Less: Consumption of fixed capital	8	11	19	129	851 / 1041	5200	17048	33697	55633	79734	...
Less: Net indirect taxes paid to supranational organisations	...	...	...	...	...	...	...	...	...	...	...
Equals: National Income at Market Prices	86	116	218	1071	8683 / 8014	28858	107424	246460	418530	657135	...
Plus: Net current transfers received from abroad	-	-	-	3	27 / 41	248	879	2061	4209	3032	...
Current transfers received	1	-	1	4	30 / 48	311	996	2946	4333	6668	...
Less: Current transfers paid	-	-	-	-	3 / 7	63	117	885	124	3636	...
Equals: National Disposable Income at Market Prices	87	116	219	1075	8713 / 8055	29106	108303	248521	422739	660167	...
Less: Final consumption	81	112	217	1065	8320 / 7191	31501	106659	251446	413213	623730	...
Equals: Net Saving	6	4	2	9	393 / 864	-2395	1644	-2925	9526	36437	...
Less: Surplus of the nation on current transactions	-1	-3	-9	-30	-63 / -41	-1840	2244	-10737	-21676	-45990	...
Equals: Net Capital Formation	7	7	11	40	453 / 905	-555	-600	7812	31202	82427	...

4.3 Derivation of Value Added by Kind of Activity, ISIC Divisions, in Current Prices

Million Chilean pesos

	1974 Gross Output	1974 Intermediate Consumption	1974 Value Added	1975 Gross Output	1975 Intermediate Consumption	1975 Value Added	1976 Gross Output	1976 Intermediate Consumption	1976 Value Added	1977 Gross Output	1977 Intermediate Consumption	1977 Value Added
						All Producers						
1 Agriculture, hunting, forestry and fishing	1042	518	524	4876	2543	2333	19023	8164	10859	42512	14223	28289
2 Mining and quarrying	1835	735	1100	7099	3416	3683	25115	12026	13089	42551	19390	23161
3 Manufacturing	6242	3524	2718	24338	17151	7187	86128	56194	29934	176082	113508	62574
4 Electricity, gas and water	201	97	104	1249	510	739	5237	2334	2903	11215	4738	6477
5 Construction	1275	715	560	4169	2262	1907	11501	5993	5508	23737	12031	11706
6 Wholesale and retail trade, restaurants and hotels	1755	457	1298	8109	1988	6121	25659	6217	19442	60113	15269	44844
7 Transport, storage and communication	1089	560	529	5137	3114	2023	15788	9426	6362	34500	19123	15377
8 Finance, insurance, real estate and business services	1061	242	819	6232	1098	5134	21234	3849	17385	47172	8643	38529
9 Community, social and personal services	638	246	392	3123	1148	1975	11937	4459	7478	29390	11251	18139
Total, Industries	15138	7094	8044	64332	33230	31102	221622	108662	112960	467272	218176	249096
Producers of Government Services	1481	532	949	5767	2111	3656	19033	6323	12710	43473	12928	30545
Other Producers	147	46	101	663	230	433	2198	791	1407	5081	1790	3291
Total	16766	7672	9094	70762	35571	35191	242853	115776	127077	515826	232894	282932
Imputed bank service charge	-	223	-223	-	1047	-1047	-	3343	-3343	-	9152	-9152
Import duties	327	...	327	1303	...	1303	4942	...	4942	13990	...	13990
Value added tax	...	...	...	...	...	...	...	...	...	...	...	...
Total	17094	7895	9199	72065	36618	35447	247795	119119	128676	529816	242046	287770

	1978 Gross Output	1978 Intermediate Consumption	1978 Value Added	1979 Gross Output	1979 Intermediate Consumption	1979 Value Added
			All Producers			
1 Agriculture, hunting, forestry and fishing	59709	22655	37054	91105	34449	56656
2 Mining and quarrying	68363	32083	36280	124703	46675	78028
3 Manufacturing	290318	181143	109175	447542	292400	155142
4 Electricity, gas and water	17738	8109	9629	27316	12075	15241

Chile

4.3 Derivation of Value Added by Kind of Activity, ISIC Divisions, in Current Prices
(Continued)

Million Chilean pesos

	1978 Gross Output	1978 Intermediate Consumption	1978 Value Added	1979 Gross Output	1979 Intermediate Consumption	1979 Value Added
5 Construction	41233	20810	20423	69517	35876	33641
6 Wholesale and retail trade, restaurants and hotels	108675	28364	80311	179747	45935	133812
7 Transport, storage and communication	60451	33744	26707	92508	54190	38318
8 Finance, insurance, real estate and business services	85818	13446	72372	129804	20470	109334
9 Community, social and personal services	52605	20348	32257	85806	33266	52540
Total, Industries	784910	360702	424208	1248048	575336	672712
Producers of Government Services	69843	22589	47254	100414	31228	69186
Other Producers	8088	2901	5187	11611	4127	7484
Total	862841	386192	476649	1360073	610691	749382
Imputed bank service charge	-	14267	-14267	-	29472	-29472
Import duties	25124	...	25124	42219	...	42219
Value added tax	...	...	...	...	...	...
Total	887965	400459	487506	1402292	640163	762129

4.4 Derivation of Value Added by Kind of Activity, ISIC Divisions, in Constant Prices

Million Chilean pesos

At constant prices of: 1977 — All Producers

	1974 GO	1974 IC	1974 VA	1975 GO	1975 IC	1975 VA	1976 GO	1976 IC	1976 VA	1977 GO	1977 IC	1977 VA
1 Agriculture, hunting, forestry and fishing	41900	16996	24904	40764	14771	25993	39857	14284	25573	42512	14222	28290
2 Mining and quarrying	40710	18068	22642	38169	18075	20094	42092	19548	22544	42551	19390	23161
3 Manufacturing	200108	127114	72994	154801	100395	54406	163956	106278	57678	176082	113508	62574
4 Electricity, gas and water	10387	4374	6013	10011	4225	5786	10583	4459	6124	11215	4738	6477
5 Construction	39048	19920	19128	27954	13807	14147	23489	11680	11809	23737	12031	11706
6 Wholesale and retail trade, restaurants and hotels	56723	14426	42297	47074	12014	35060	48165	12232	35933	60113	15269	44844
7 Transport, storage and communication	32325	17962	14363	29516	16254	13262	30699	16820	13879	34499	19124	15375
8 Finance, insurance, real estate and business services	42334	7411	34923	42007	7396	34611	43909	7796	36113	47172	8643	38529
9 Community, social and personal services	28678	11043	17635	27078	10327	16751	27569	10397	17172	29390	11251	18139
Total, Industries	492213	237314	254899	417374	197264	220110	430319	203494	226825	467271	218176	249095
Producers of Government Services	46703	18030	28673	42097	12836	29261	42725	12456	30269	43474	12929	30545
Other Producers	4484	1652	2832	4753	1670	3083	4777	1722	3055	5081	1790	3291
Total	543400	256996	286404	464224	211770	252454	477821	217672	260149	515826	232895	282931
Imputed bank service charge	-	7027	-7027	-	7530	-7530	-	6849	-6849	-	9151	-9151
Import duties	11177	-	11177	8119	-	8119	8645	-	8645	13990	-	13990
Value added tax	...	...	...	...	...	...	...	...	...	...	...	...
Total	554577	264023	290554	472343	219300	253043	486466	224521	261945	529816	242046	287770

	1978 Gross Output	1978 Intermediate Consumption	1978 Value Added	1979 Gross Output	1979 Intermediate Consumption	1979 Value Added
	At constant prices of: 1977 — All Producers					
1 Agriculture, hunting, forestry and fishing	42446	15205	27241	45686	16197	29489
2 Mining and quarrying	42999	19470	23529	45620	20835	24785
3 Manufacturing	192091	123717	68374	202603	129483	73120
4 Electricity, gas and water	11955	5042	6913	12724	5341	7383
5 Construction	25978	13328	12650	31445	15809	15636
6 Wholesale and retail trade, restaurants and hotels	72149	18329	53820	79352	20625	58727
7 Transport, storage and communication	37533	20868	16665	40879	22804	18075
8 Finance, insurance, real estate and business services	51919	9566	42353	59519	11402	48117
9 Community, social and personal services	31427	11954	19473	33562	12788	20774

Chile

4.4 Derivation of Value Added by Kind of Activity, ISIC Divisions, in Constant Prices
(Continued)

Million Chilean pesos

	1978 Gross Output	1978 Intermediate Consumption	1978 Value Added	1979 Gross Output	1979 Intermediate Consumption	1979 Value Added
				At constant prices of: 1977		
Total, Industries	508497	237479	271018	551390	255284	296106
Producers of Government Services	44279	14384	29895	43841	13821	30020
Other Producers	5155	1879	3276	5305	1971	3334
Total	557931	253742	304189	600536	271076	329460
Imputed bank service charge	-	9123	-9123	-	13004	-13004
Import duties	16351	-	16351	20724	-	20724
Value added tax	...	...	...	...	...	...
Total	574282	262865	311417	621260	284080	337180

Colombia

General note. The preparation of national accounts statistics in Colombia is undertaken following the classifications and definitions recommended in the United Nations System of National Accounts (SNA). Work has been done by the Banco de la Republica, Departamento de Investigaciones Economicas, according to SNA, Revision 2. At the same time, the Departamento Administrativo Nacional de Estadistica (DANE), is working on the establishment of a new system of accounts according to SNA, Revision 3. The official estimates of the Bank have been included in various publications entitled 'Cuentas Nacionales de Colombia'. These estimates were first calculated having 1958 as bench-mark year but in 1975 revised series were calculated with 1970 as a basis year. Estimates included in the questionnaire have 1970 as bench-mark year. DANE has already published some methodological reports among which are worth mentioning: 'Cuentas Nacionales e Insumo Producto', 'Analisis Preliminar de la Oferta y Utilizacion de Bienes y Servicios a Disposicion de la Economia Nacional durante el Periodo 1967-69', and more recently 'Metodologia de las Cuentas Nacionales de Colombia segun el Nuevo SCN'. The following tables have been prepared from successive replies to the United Nations national accounts questionnaire. When the scope and coverage of the estimates differ for conceptual or statistical reasons from the definitions and classifications recommended in SNA, a footnote is indicated to the relevant tables.

(a) Gross domestic product. Gross domestic product is estimated mainly through the production approach.

(b) Expenditure on the gross domestic product. The expenditure approach is used to estimate government final consumption expenditure, exports and imports of goods and services, part of increase in stocks and gross fixed capital formation in construction. For other gross fixed capital formation, the commodity-flow approach is used. Private final consumption expenditure and part of increase in stocks are obtained as a residual. The estimates of government final consumption expenditures are based on official sources such as Informe Financiero de la Contraloria General de la Republica. The estimates of private consumption expenditure are obtained as a residual except for the bench-mark year 1970 which were based on results from the family budget survey conducted that year. The estimates for changes in stocks are based on information obtained from various sources such as manufacturing surveys, commercial census, and the Federacion Nacional de Cafeteros. For gross fixed capital formation, the c.i.f. values of imported capital goods in the foreign trade statistics are adjusted to include customs duties, other taxes and transport and insurance costs. Adjustments are also made for trade margins and installation costs on goods passing through trade channels. For domestic production, estimates are based on manufacturing surveys. Estimates of capital formation in construction are obtained as by-product in the calculation of the construction sector's contribution to GDP whereas investments in the government sector is obtained from the government accounts. The estimates of exports and imports of goods and services are derived from the balance of payments. For the constant price estimates, current values of government expenditure and gross fixed capital formation estimates are deflated by appropriate price indexes. Estimates of private consumption expenditure at constant prices are obtained as a residual. No specific information is available for the remaining expenditure items.

(c) Cost-structure of the gross domestic product. The estimates of compensation of employees are obtained in the process of estimating value added by industrial origin. The estimates are obtained from the statistical surveys held in 1970 and from accounting data. In the case of agriculture, hunting, forestry and fishing, the estimates are based on projections from census data on employment and statistics of average wages and salaries. Depreciation of assets owned by general government are not included in the estimates. Operating surplus is obtained as a residual and no information is available for the estimates of consumption of fixed capital and of net indirect taxes.

(d) Gross domestic product by kind of economic activity. The table of gross domestic product by kind of economic activity is prepared at market prices, i.e. producers' values. The production approach is used to estimate value added of almost all industries. The income approach is used to estimate the value added of producers of government services and some private services, while the expenditure approach is used for ownership of dwellings. Gross output of the trade sector is estimated by the commodity-flow approach. For agriculture, the gross value of production is obtained by multiplying the output of each commodity by the price paid to producers. The production and price data are derived from agricultural sample surveys and from various concerned institutions. The Federacion Nacional de Cafeteros supplies information on data for coffee. For livestock, the estimates are based on statistics of government controlled slaughterings and net exports with rough estimates made for uncontrolled slaughterings. Data for the petroleum industry are obtained directly from the oil companies. Information on the output and value of minerals is available from censuses of mines and concerned institutions. For manufacturing, results of surveys carried out by the Departamento Administrativo Nacional de Estadistica are used. The estimates are projected by applying volume and price indexes to both output and input. The basic data for electricity, gas and water are obtained from concerned enterprises and surveys. Coefficients calculated from these surveys are used to estimate value added of plants not covered. For urban construction, estimates are derived from building permits issued while rural construction estimates are based on an estimation of economic life of existing constructions and on demographic data. Estimates of public construction are obtained from the government records. For the trade sector, value added is based on estimates of the flow of goods through trade channels. The gross margins are based on data provided by the Banco de la Republica or recalculated from the Commercial Census 1967. The mark-ups are kept constant over the period of analysis. For transport, estimates are based on indormation provided by the Banco de la Republica. Data to measure the contribution of the communication sector are obtained by direct inquiries. Estimates for the financial institutions are obtained directly from the enterprises concerned through the Superintendencia Bancaria. The contribution of the government sector is measured by the wages and salaries paid to employees. Value added of other private services is estimated by the Banco de la Republica using the results of the Census of services in 1970. Constant input-output ratios have been assumed. For the constant price estimates, value added of the majority of industries is extrapolated by quantity index for output. For ownership of dwellings and producers of government services, value added is deflated by an index of rents and an index of wages and salaries, respectively.

1.1 Expenditure on the Gross Domestic Product, in Current Prices

Million Colombian pesos

		1970	1971	1972	1973	1974	1975	1976	1977	1978	1979	1980
1	General government final consumption expenditure	9962	13429	14649	19014	23158	30425	38730	48154	65724	91120	123692
2	Private final consumption expenditure	93863	110031	134849	180201	237438	306614	373652	474943	615724	805146	1083481
3	Gross capital formation	28660	34585	37739	40765	74279	73600	111353	169140	208942	269192	379551
	a Increase in stocks	2219	2981	3219	-1770	10419	-3972	14272	34356	21221	26151	23399
	b Gross fixed capital formation	26441	31604	34520	42535	63860	77572	97081	134784	187721	243041	356152
	Residential buildings	4475	5107	4978	7882	10509	9378	12162	19331	29991	33914	44267
	Non-residential buildings	745	950	1558	2133	4069	2883	3641	5761	6674	9181	13291
	Other construction and land improvement etc.	10840	12618	14835	18544	25795	33045	33554	43164	61020	81258	116856
	Other	10381	12929	13149	13976	23487	32266	47724	66528	90036	118688	181738
4	Exports of goods and services	18516	19151	25217	36186	46795	62243	88048	124727	155181	193133	258161
5	Less: Imports of goods and services	20640	24933	26362	32930	52515	60053	77768	98489	129011	163211	260611
	Equals: Gross Domestic Product	130361	152263	186092	243236	329155	412829	534015	718475	916560	1195380	1584274

1.2 Expenditure on the Gross Domestic Product, in Constant Prices

Million Colombian pesos

		1970	1971	1972	1973	1974	1975	1976	1977	1978	1979	1980
		At constant prices of:1970										
1	General government final consumption expenditure	9962	11806	11333	12231	11986	12719	13505	13987	15345	16502	17675
2	Private final consumption expenditure	93863	99585	108717	119679	126388	130234	133896	140800	153277	159720	166011
3	Gross capital formation	28661	30768	30193	26837	35652	29461	36857	42020	42647	43814	48888
	a Increase in stocks	2220	2701	2407	-2315	3952	-2383	4055	7533	3910	4094	3028
	b Gross fixed capital formation	26441	28067	27786	29152	31700	31844	32802	34487	38737	39719	45860

Colombia

1.2 Expenditure on the Gross Domestic Product, in Constant Prices
(Continued)

Million Colombian pesos

	1970	1971	1972	1973	1974	1975	1976	1977	1978	1979	1980
					At constant prices of:1970						
Residential buildings	4475	4449	3826	5157	5151	3729	4044	5001	5770	4781	4618
Non-residential buildings	745	824	1187	1393	2000	1149	1219	1517	1297	1304	1386
Other construction and land improvement etc.	10840	11465	12132	12788	13129	13964	11665	11438	12429	12580	14109
Other	10381	11328	10641	9814	11420	13002	15874	16531	19241	21054	25747
4 Exports of goods and services	18516	18834	19592	20205	18978	24646	22590	21583	28102	31334	36131
5 Less: Imports of goods and services	20640	23104	21205	19757	24217	21833	23552	26202	30002	31279	39411
Equals: Gross Domestic Product	130361	137889	148630	159195	168787	175226	183296	192187	209368	220091	229294

1.3 Cost Components of the Gross Domestic Product

Million Colombian pesos

	1970	1971	1972	1973	1974	1975	1976	1977	1978	1979	1980
1 Indirect taxes, net	10565	11731	13861	16851	21358	26457	39743	55861	75404	112741	159196
a Indirect taxes paid	11395	13199	15489	19673	25777	32262	43963	60276	83384	121521	169754
b Less: Subsidies received	830	1468	1628	2822	4419	5805	4220	4415	7980	8780	10558
2 Consumption of fixed capital	10109	11894	13796	16651	26574	36751	45413	60822	80181	109114	142968
3 Compensation of employees paid by resident producers to:	49325	58380	68511	85025	111663	140091	171338	231626	311365	408665	551546
4 Net operating surplus	60363	70258	89925	124709	169560	209530	277521	370166	449610	564860	730564
a Corporate and quasi-corporate enterprises	10260	13265	13475	17111	20985	28826	36599	43043	59872	69863	86104
b Private unincorporated enterprises	49505	56227	75356	107835	148550	181608	238240	324451	386724	492155	644129
c General government	598	766	1094	-237	25	-904	2682	2672	3014	2842	331
Equals: Gross Domestic Product	130361	152263	186092	243236	329155	412829	534015	718475	916560	1195380	1584274

1.4 General Government Current Receipts and Disbursements

Million Colombian pesos

	1970	1971	1972	1973	1974	1975	1976	1977	1978	1979	1980
					Receipts						
1 Property and entrepreneurial income	598	766	1094	-237	25	-904	2682	2672	3014	2842	331
2 Taxes, fees and contributions	19682	24281	26996	35319	46635	60088	79265	97208	146247	180575	253001
a Indirect taxes	11395	13199	15489	19673	25777	32262	43963	60276	83384	121521	169754
b Direct taxes	6175	8342	8161	10942	14911	20143	25555	24311	48669	34149	50878
c Social security contributions	2112	2740	3346	4704	5947	7683	9747	12621	14194	24905	32369
d Compulsory fees, fines and penalties	...	...	...	...	...	...	...	...	...	...	...
3 Other current receipts	870	820	824	888	1273	1085	976	1384	1856	946	2055
Total Current Receipts of General Government	21150	25867	28914	35970	47933	60269	82923	101264	151117	184363	255387
					Disbursements						
1 General government final consumption expenditure	9962	13429	14649	19014	23158	30425	38730	48154	65724	91120	123692
2 Property income paid	...	...	...	...	...	...	...	...	...	...	...
3 Subsidies	830	1468	1628	2822	4419	5805	4220	4415	7980	8780	10558
4 Other current transfers paid	2698	3241	3942	5052	6091	7940	9379	11305	12577	20229	27953
a Social security benefits and social assistance grants	...	...	...	...	...	...	...	...	...	...	...
b Other	2698	3241	3942	5052	6091	7940	9379	11305	12577	20229	27953
5 Net saving	7661	7730	8695	9083	14264	16100	30593	37390	64836	64234	93184
Total Current Disbursements and Net Saving of General Government	21151	25868	28914	35971	47932	60270	82922	101264	151117	184363	255387

1.6 Current Income and Outlay of Households and Non-Profit Institutions

Million Colombian pesos

	1970	1971	1972	1973	1974	1975	1976	1977	1978	1979	1980
					Receipts						
1 Compensation of employees	49325	58380	68511	85025	111663	140091	171338	231626	311365	408665	551546
2 Property and entrepreneurial income received	49505	56227	75356	107835	148550	181608	238240	324451	386724	492155	644129
3 Current transfers received	2906	3581	4515	5681	7157	9416	11362	13618	15066	24330	33861
a Social security benefits and social assistance grants received	...	...	...	...	...	...	...	...	...	...	...
b Other	2906	3581	4515	5681	7157	9416	11362	13618	15066	24330	33861

Colombia

1.6 Current Income and Outlay of Households and Non-Profit Institutions
(Continued)

Million Colombian pesos	1970	1971	1972	1973	1974	1975	1976	1977	1978	1979	1980
Total Current Receipts	101736	118188	148382	198541	267370	331114	420939	569695	713155	925150	1229536

Disbursements

	1970	1971	1972	1973	1974	1975	1976	1977	1978	1979	1980
1 Private final consumption expenditure	93863	110031	134849	180201	237438	306614	373652	474943	615724	805146	1083481
2 Property income paid	...	...	...	...	...	...	...	...	...	...	...
3 Direct taxes and other payments n.e.c. to general government	5038	6695	7234	9905	13030	17901	22675	24247	37125	41149	56825
a Social security contributions	2112	2740	3346	4704	5947	7683	9747	12621	14194	24905	32369
b Direct taxes	2926	3955	3888	5201	7083	10218	12928	11626	22931	16244	24456
c Fees, fines and penalties	...	...	...	...	...	...	...	...	...	...	...
4 Other current transfers paid	592	505	647	709	928	1141	1242	2053	1605	830	2054
5 Net saving	2242	958	5654	7727	15975	5459	23372	68452	58701	78025	87176
Total Current Disbursements and Net Saving	101735	118189	148384	198542	267370	331115	420941	569695	713155	925150	1229536

1.7 External Transactions on Current Account, Summary

Million Colombian pesos	1970	1971	1972	1973	1974	1975	1976	1977	1978	1979	1980

Payments to the Rest of the World

	1970	1971	1972	1973	1974	1975	1976	1977	1978	1979	1980
1 Imports of goods and services	20640	24933	26362	32930	52515	60053	77768	98489	129011	163211	260611
2 Factor income paid to the rest of the world	...	...	...	...	...	...	...	...	...	...	...
3 Indirect taxes paid to supranational organizations	...	...	...	...	...	...	...	...	...	...	...
4 Current transfers to the rest of the world	510	418	491	567	711	939	1091	1368	1383	523	2017
5 Surplus of the nation on current transactions	-5229	-8816	-4844	-1200	-9511	-4433	1087	17732	17130	23307	-9366
Payments to the Rest of the World and Surplus of the Nation on Current Transactions	15921	16534	22009	32297	43715	56558	79946	117589	147525	187041	253262

Receipts From The Rest of the World

	1970	1971	1972	1973	1974	1975	1976	1977	1978	1979	1980
1 Exports of goods and services	18516	19151	25217	36186	46795	62243	88048	124727	155181	193133	258161
2 Factor income received from rest of the world	-3591	-3690	-4448	-5264	-5201	-8043	-10910	-10149	-11779	-10832	-12824
3 Subsidies received from supranational organisations	...	...	...	...	...	...	...	...	...	...	...
4 Current transfers from rest of the world	996	1073	1240	1375	2121	2358	2808	3011	4123	4739	7925
Receipts from the Rest of the World on Current Transactions	15921	16534	22009	32297	43715	56558	79946	117589	147525	187041	253262

1.8 Capital Transactions of The Nation, Summary

Million Colombian pesos	1970	1971	1972	1973	1974	1975	1976	1977	1978	1979	1980

Finance of Gross Capital Formation

	1970	1971	1972	1973	1974	1975	1976	1977	1978	1979	1980
Gross saving	23431	25770	32895	39565	64769	69168	112441	186872	226073	292498	370184
1 Consumption of fixed capital	10109	11894	13796	16651	26574	36751	45413	60822	80181	109114	142968
2 Net saving	13322	13876	19099	22914	38195	32417	67028	126050	145892	183384	227216
a General government	7661	7730	8695	9083	14264	16100	30593	37390	64836	64234	93184
b Corporate and quasi-corporate enterprises	5661	6146	10404	13831	23931	16317	36435	88660	81056	119150	134032
c Other											
Less: Surplus of the nation on current transactions	-5229	-8816	-4844	-1200	-9511	-4433	1087	17732	17130	23307	-9366
Finance of Gross Capital Formation	28660	34586	37739	40765	74279	73600	111353	169140	208942	269192	379551

Gross Capital Formation

	1970	1971	1972	1973	1974	1975	1976	1977	1978	1979	1980
Increase in stocks	2219	2982	3219	-1770	10419	-3972	14272	34356	21221	26151	23399
Gross fixed capital formation	26441	31604	34520	42535	63860	77572	97081	134784	187721	243041	356152
Gross Capital Formation	28660	34586	37739	40765	74279	73600	111353	169140	208942	269192	379551

Colombia

1.10 Gross Domestic Product by Kind of Activity, in Current Prices

Million Colombian pesos

	1970	1971	1972	1973	1974	1975	1976	1977	1978	1979	1980
1 Agriculture, hunting, forestry and fishing	34306	38881	49465	66746	88478	113485	148560	212327	256406	311521	394172
2 Mining and quarrying	2546	2989	2949	3326	4001	4898	6032	7631	11264	14940	28101
3 Manufacturing	24211	29522	36551	49570	70894	88160	116259	147415	192793	264722	346043
4 Electricity, gas and water	1831	2245	2755	3330	3931	4901	6773	8817	11581	16060	24309
5 Construction	6566	8084	8976	12285	17196	19846	20575	27838	38233	52422	75517
6 Wholesale and retail trade, restaurants and hotels [a]	22393	24784	30581	41150	57132	72155	97372	132485	169153	216093	282563
7 Transport, storage and communication	8884	10164	11375	13520	19453	22400	30775	42997	54566	76952	104913
8 Finance, insurance, real estate and business services [b]	11818	14064	17113	20506	26798	33744	41098	52863	70175	93913	133075
9 Community, social and personal services [ab]	9523	11305	13613	16348	20423	26482	34113	46000	58327	74295	95023
Total, Industries	122078	142038	173378	226781	308306	386071	501557	678371	862498	1120918	1483716
Producers of Government Services	8283	10225	12714	16455	20849	26758	32458	40103	54062	74462	100559
Other Producers	...	...	...	...	...	...	...	...	...	...	...
Subtotal	130361	152263	186092	243236	329155	412829	534015	718476	916560	1195380	1584275
Less: Imputed bank service charge	...	...	...	...	...	...	...	...	...	...	...
Plus: Import duties	...	...	...	...	...	...	...	...	...	...	...
Plus: Value added tax	...	...	...	...	...	...	...	...	...	...	...
Equals: Gross Domestic Product	130361	152263	186092	243236	329155	412829	534015	718474	916560	1195380	1584275

a) Restaurants and hotels are included in item 'Community, social and personal services'.
b) Business services are included in item 'Community, social and personal services'.

1.11 Gross Domestic Product by Kind of Activity, in Constant Prices

Million Colombian pesos

At constant prices of: 1970

	1970	1971	1972	1973	1974	1975	1976	1977	1978	1979	1980
1 Agriculture, hunting, forestry and fishing	34306	34935	37970	39214	41661	44123	45062	46178	50719	52780	54123
2 Mining and quarrying	2546	2565	2376	2507	2332	2204	2162	2079	2171	2145	2449
3 Manufacturing	24211	26276	28699	31251	32996	33214	35587	37047	40192	42087	43036
4 Electricity, gas and water	1831	1996	2244	2483	2644	2783	3069	3130	3434	3737	4009
5 Construction	6566	6898	7032	7884	8190	7836	6724	7109	7379	7277	7981
6 Wholesale and retail trade, restaurants and hotels [a]	22393	23804	25393	27588	28954	29335	31193	32895	36346	38454	39416
7 Transport, storage and communication	8884	9378	10115	11065	12262	13148	14333	15599	17292	18847	20091
8 Finance, insurance, real estate and business services [b]	11818	13016	14081	14959	16536	18252	19605	21099	22909	24088	25846
9 Community, social and personal services [ab]	9523	10162	10961	11714	12437	13142	14190	15266	16247	17113	17828
Total, Industries	122078	129030	138871	148665	158012	164037	171925	180401	196690	206525	214778
Producers of Government Services	8283	8859	9757	10530	10775	11189	11371	11786	12678	13567	14516
Other Producers	...	...	...	...	...	...	...	...	...	...	...
Subtotal	130361	137889	148628	159195	168787	175226	183296	192188	209368	220092	229294
Less: Imputed bank service charge	...	...	...	...	...	...	...	...	...	...	...
Plus: Import duties	...	...	...	...	...	...	...	...	...	...	...
Plus: Value added tax	...	...	...	...	...	...	...	...	...	...	...
Equals: Gross Domestic Product	130361	137889	148630	159195	168787	175226	183296	192187	209368	220092	229294

a) Restaurants and hotels are included in item 'Community, social and personal services'.
b) Business services are included in item 'Community, social and personal services'.

1.12 Relations Among National Accounting Aggregates

Million Colombian pesos

	1970	1971	1972	1973	1974	1975	1976	1977	1978	1979	1980
Gross Domestic Product	130361	152263	186092	243236	329155	412829	534015	718475	916560	1195380	1584274
Plus: Net factor income received from abroad	-3592	-3690	-4448	-5266	-5200	-8043	-10909	-10149	-11779	-10832	-12824
Factor income received	-3592	-3690	-4448	-5266	-5200	-8043	-10909	-10149	-11779	-10832	-12824
Less: Factor income paid	...	...	...	...	...	...	...	...	...	...	...
Equals: Gross National Product	126769	148573	181644	237970	323955	404786	523106	708326	904781	1184548	1571450

Colombia

1.12 Relations Among National Accounting Aggregates
(Continued)

Million Colombian pesos

	1970	1971	1972	1973	1974	1975	1976	1977	1978	1979	1980
Less: Consumption of fixed capital	10109	11894	13796	16651	26574	36751	45413	60822	80181	109114	142968
Less: Net indirect taxes paid to supranational organisations	...	...	...	...	...	...	...	...	...	...	...
Equals: National Income at Market Prices	116660	136679	167848	221319	297381	368035	477693	647504	824600	1075434	1428482
Plus: Net current transfers received from abroad	486	656	749	809	1410	1420	1717	1643	2740	4216	5908
Current transfers received	996	1073	1240	1375	2121	2358	2808	3011	4123	4739	7925
Less: Current transfers paid	510	418	491	567	711	939	1091	1368	1383	523	2017
Equals: National Disposable Income at Market Prices	117147	137335	168597	222128	298791	369455	479410	649147	827340	1079650	1434390
Less: Final consumption	103825	123460	149498	199215	260596	337039	412382	523097	681448	896266	1207174
Equals: Net Saving	13322	13876	19099	22914	38195	32417	67028	126050	145892	183384	227216
Less: Surplus of the nation on current transactions	-5229	-8816	-4844	-1200	-9511	-4433	1087	17732	17130	23307	-9366
Equals: Net Capital Formation	18551	22691	23943	24114	47705	36849	65940	108318	128761	160078	236583

3.12 General Government Income and Outlay Account: Total and Subsectors

Million Colombian pesos

	\multicolumn{4}{c}{1970}		\multicolumn{4}{c}{1971}	
	Total General Government	Central Government	State or Provincial Government	Local Government	Social Security Funds	Total General Government	Central Government	State or Provincial Government	Local Government	Social Security Funds

Receipts

1 Property and entrepreneurial income	598	-677	...	1275	...	766	-857	...	1624	...
a Net operating surplus	598	-677	...	1275	...	766	-857	...	1624	...
b Withdrawals from public quasi-corporations	...	...	...	...	...	...	...	...	...	...
c Interest	...	...	...	...	...	...	...	...	...	...
d Dividends	...	...	...	...	...	...	...	...	...	...
e Net land rent and royalties	...	...	...	...	...	...	...	...	...	...
2 Taxes, fees and contributions	19682	12747	...	6935	...	24281	16064	...	8217	...
a Indirect taxes	11395	6608	...	4787	...	13199	7768	...	5431	...
b Direct taxes	6175	6139	...	36	...	8342	8296	...	46	...
Income	6175	6139	...	36	...	8342	8296	...	46	...
Other	-	-	...	-	...	-	-	...	-	...
c Social security contributions	2112	-	...	2112	...	2740	-	...	2740	...
d Fees, fines and penalties	...	...	...	...	...	...	...	...	...	...
3 Other current transfers received	870	759	...	111	...	820	703	...	117	...
a Casualty insurance claims	...	...	...	...	...	...	...	...	...	...
b Transfers from other government subsectors	...	...	...	...	...	...	...	...	...	...
c Transfers from abroad	729	729	...	-	...	666	666	...	-	...
d Other transfers, except imputed	141	30	...	111	...	154	37	...	117	...
e Imputed unfunded employee welfare contributions	...	...	...	...	...	...	...	...	...	...
Total Current Receipts	21150	12829	...	8321	...	25867	15910	...	9957	...

Disbursements

1 General governement final consumption expenditures	9962	5310	...	4652	...	13429	7572	...	5857	...
a Compensation of employees	...	...	...	...	...	...	...	...	...	...
b Consumption of fixed capital	...	...	...	...	...	...	...	...	...	...
c Goods and services purchased, net	...	...	...	...	...	...	...	...	...	...
d Less: Own account production of fixed assets	...	...	...	...	...	...	...	...	...	...
e Indirect taxes paid, net	...	...	...	...	...	...	...	...	...	...
2 Property income paid	...	...	...	...	...	...	...	...	...	...

Colombia

3.12 General Government Income and Outlay Account: Total and Subsectors
(Continued)

Million Colombian pesos

	1970					1971				
	Total General Government	Central Government	State or Provincial Government	Local Government	Social Security Funds	Total General Government	Central Government	State or Provincial Government	Local Government	Social Security Funds
3 Subsidies	830	500	...	330	...	1468	680	...	788	...
4 Other current transfers paid	2698	522	...	2176	...	3241	634	...	2607	...
a Casualty insurance premiums, net	...	...	...	...	...	...	...	...	...	...
b Transfers to other government subsectors	...	...	...	...	...	...	...	...	...	...
c Transfers to households	...	...	...	...	...	...	...	...	...	...
d Transfers to private non-profit institutions serving households	2639	463	...	2176	...	3174	568	...	2606	...
e Transfers to the rest of the world	59	59	...	...	...	67	67	...	...	...
Net saving	7661	6497	...	1164	...	7730	7024	...	706	...
Total Current Disbursements and Net Saving	21151	12829	...	8322	...	25868	15910	...	9958	...

	1972					1973				
	Total General Government	Central Government	State or Provincial Government	Local Government	Social Security Funds	Total General Government	Central Government	State or Provincial Government	Local Government	Social Security Funds

Receipts

1 Property and entrepreneurial income	1094	-915	...	2009	...	-237	-1585	...	1348	...
a Net operating surplus	1094	-915	...	2009	...	-237	-1585	...	1348	...
b Withdrawals from public quasi-corporations	...	...	...	...	...	...	...	...	...	...
c Interest	...	...	...	...	...	...	...	...	...	...
d Dividends	...	...	...	...	...	...	...	...	...	...
e Net land rent and royalties	...	...	...	...	...	...	...	...	...	...
2 Taxes, fees and contributions	26996	16980	...	10016	...	35319	23164	...	12155	...
a Indirect taxes	15489	8873	...	6616	...	19673	12279	...	7394	...
b Direct taxes	8161	8107	...	54	...	10942	10885	...	57	...
Income	8161	8107	...	54	...	10942	10885	...	57	...
Other	-	-	...	-	...	-	-	...	-	...
c Social security contributions	3346	-	...	3346	...	4704	-	...	4704	...
d Fees, fines and penalties	...	...	...	...	...	...	...	...	...	...
3 Other current transfers received	823	636	...	187	...	888	688	...	200	...
a Casualty insurance claims	...	...	...	...	...	...	...	...	...	...
b Transfers from other government subsectors	...	...	...	...	...	...	...	...	...	...
c Transfers from abroad	594	594	...	-	...	641	641	...	-	...
d Other transfers, except imputed	229	42	...	187	...	247	47	...	200	...
e Imputed unfunded employee welfare contributions	...	...	...	...	...	...	...	...	...	...
Total Current Receipts	28914	16701	...	12213	...	35970	22267	...	13703	...

Disbursements

1 General government final consumption expenditures	14649	6902	...	7747	...	19014	7577	...	11437	...
a Compensation of employees	...	...	...	...	...	...	...	...	...	...
b Consumption of fixed capital	...	...	...	...	...	...	...	...	...	...
c Goods and services purchased, net	...	...	...	...	...	...	...	...	...	...
d Less: Own account production of fixed assets	...	...	...	...	...	...	...	...	...	...
e Indirect taxes paid, net	...	...	...	...	...	...	...	...	...	...
2 Property income paid	...	...	...	...	...	...	...	...	...	...

Colombia

3.12 General Government Income and Outlay Account: Total and Subsectors
(Continued)

Million Colombian pesos

	1972					1973				
	Total General Government	Central Government	State or Provincial Government	Local Government	Social Security Funds	Total General Government	Central Government	State or Provincial Government	Local Government	Social Security Funds
3 Subsidies	1628	713	...	915	...	2822	1006	...	1816	...
4 Other current transfers paid	3942	849	...	3093	...	5052	853	...	4199	...
a Casualty insurance premiums, net	...	...	...	...	...	...	...	...	...	...
b Transfers to other government subsectors	...	...	...	...	...	...	...	...	...	...
c Transfers to households	...	...	...	...	...	...	...	...	...	...
d Transfers to private non-profit institutions serving households	3869	776	...	3093	...	4947	748	...	4199	...
e Transfers to the rest of the world	73	73	...	-	...	105	105	...	-	...
Net saving	8695	8237	...	458	...	9083	12831	...	-3748	...
Total Current Disbursements and Net Saving	28914	16701	...	12213	...	35971	22267	...	13704	...

	1974					1975				
	Total General Government	Central Government	State or Provincial Government	Local Government	Social Security Funds	Total General Government	Central Government	State or Provincial Government	Local Government	Social Security Funds

Receipts

1 Property and entrepreneurial income	25	-1716	...	1741	...	-904	-2829	...	1925	...
a Net operating surplus	25	-1716	...	1741	...	-904	-2829	...	1925	...
b Withdrawals from public quasi-corporations	...	...	...	...	...	...	...	...	...	...
c Interest	...	...	...	...	...	...	...	...	...	...
d Dividends	...	...	...	...	...	...	...	...	...	...
e Net land rent and royalties	...	...	...	...	...	...	...	...	...	...
2 Taxes, fees and contributions	46635	31643	...	14992	...	60088	41737	...	18351	...
a Indirect taxes	25777	16809	...	8968	...	32262	21674	...	10588	...
b Direct taxes	14911	14834	...	77	...	20143	20063	...	80	...
Income	14911	14834	...	77	...	20143	20063	...	80	...
Other	-	-	...	-	...	-	-	...	-	...
c Social security contributions	5947	-	...	5947	...	7683	-	...	7683	...
d Fees, fines and penalties	...	...	...	...	...	...	...	...	...	...
3 Other current transfers received	1272	1001	...	271	...	1084	777	...	307	...
a Casualty insurance claims	...	...	...	...	...	...	...	...	...	...
b Transfers from other government subsectors	...	...	...	...	...	...	...	...	...	...
c Transfers from abroad	943	943	...	-	...	704	704	...	-	...
d Other transfers, except imputed	329	58	...	271	...	380	73	...	307	...
e Imputed unfunded employee welfare contributions	...	...	...	...	...	...	...	...	...	...
Total Current Receipts	47933	30928	...	17005	...	60269	39685	...	20584	...

Disbursements

1 General government final consumption expenditures	23158	9560	...	13598	...	30425	12528	...	17897	...
a Compensation of employees	...	...	...	...	...	...	...	...	...	...
b Consumption of fixed capital	...	...	...	...	...	...	...	...	...	...
c Goods and services purchased, net	...	...	...	...	...	...	...	...	...	...
d Less: Own account production of fixed assets	...	...	...	...	...	...	...	...	...	...
e Indirect taxes paid, net	...	...	...	...	...	...	...	...	...	...
2 Property income paid	...	...	...	...	...	...	...	...	...	...

Colombia

3.12 General Government Income and Outlay Account: Total and Subsectors
(Continued)

Million Colombian pesos

	1974					1975				
	Total General Government	Central Government	State or Provincial Government	Local Government	Social Security Funds	Total General Government	Central Government	State or Provincial Government	Local Government	Social Security Funds
3 Subsidies	4419	878	...	3541	...	5805	2294	...	3511	...
4 Other current transfers paid	6091	937	...	5154	...	7940	1220	...	6720	...
a Casualty insurance premiums, net	...	...	...	...	...	...	...	...	...	...
b Transfers to other government subsectors	...	...	...	...	...	...	...	...	...	...
c Transfers to households	...	...	...	...	...	...	...	...	...	...
d Transfers to private non-profit institutions serving households	5979	825	...	5154	...	7762	1042	...	6720	...
e Transfers to the rest of the world	112	112	...	-	...	178	178	...	-	...
Net saving	14264	19553	...	-5289	...	16100	23643	...	-7543	...
Total Current Disbursements and Net Saving	47932	30928	...	17004	...	60270	39685	...	20585	...

	1976					1977				
	Total General Government	Central Government	State or Provincial Government	Local Government	Social Security Funds	Total General Government	Central Government	State or Provincial Government	Local Government	Social Security Funds

Receipts

1 Property and entrepreneurial income	2682	-2793	...	5475	...	2672	-3781	...	6453	...
a Net operating surplus	2682	-2793	...	5475	...	2672	-3781	...	6453	...
b Withdrawals from public quasi-corporations	...	...	...	...	...	...	...	...	...	...
c Interest	...	...	...	...	...	...	...	...	...	...
d Dividends	...	...	...	...	...	...	...	...	...	...
e Net land rent and royalties	...	...	...	...	...	...	...	...	...	...
2 Taxes, fees and contributions	79265	55072	...	24193	...	97208	64338	...	32870	...
a Indirect taxes	43963	29592	...	14371	...	60276	40117	...	20159	...
b Direct taxes	25555	25480	...	75	...	24311	24221	...	90	...
Income	25555	25480	...	75	...	24311	24221	...	90	...
Other	-	-	...	-	...	-	-	...	-	...
c Social security contributions	9747	-	...	9747	...	12621	-	...	12621	...
d Fees, fines and penalties	...	...	...	...	...	...	...	...	...	...
3 Other current transfers received	976	711	...	265	...	1384	762	...	622	...
a Casualty insurance claims	...	...	...	...	...	...	...	...	...	...
b Transfers from other government subsectors	...	...	...	...	...	...	...	...	...	...
c Transfers from abroad	613	613	...	-	...	458	458	...	-	...
d Other transfers, except imputed	363	98	...	265	...	926	304	...	622	...
e Imputed unfunded employee welfare contributions	...	...	...	...	...	...	...	...	...	...
Total Current Receipts	82923	52990	...	29933	...	101264	61319	...	39945	...

Disbursements

1 General government final consumption expenditures	38730	16747	...	21983	...	48154	21366	...	26788	...
a Compensation of employees	...	...	...	...	...	...	...	...	...	...
b Consumption of fixed capital	...	...	...	...	...	...	...	...	...	...
c Goods and services purchased, net	...	...	...	...	...	...	...	...	...	...
d Less: Own account production of fixed assets	...	...	...	...	...	...	...	...	...	...
e Indirect taxes paid, net	...	...	...	...	...	...	...	...	...	...
2 Property income paid	...	...	...	...	...	...	...	...	...	...

Colombia

3.12 General Government Income and Outlay Account: Total and Subsectors
(Continued)

Million Colombian pesos

		1976				1977			
	Total General Government	Central Government	State or Provincial Government	Local Government	Social Security Funds	Total General Government	Central Government	State or Provincial Government	Local Government	Social Security Funds
3 Subsidies	4220	1034	...	3186	...	4415	958	...	3457	...
4 Other current transfers paid	9379	875	...	8504	...	11305	1100	...	10205	...
a Casualty insurance premiums, net	...	...	...	...	...	...	...	...	...	...
b Transfers to other government subsectors	...	...	...	...	...	...	...	...	...	...
c Transfers to households	...	...	...	...	...	...	...	...	...	...
d Transfers to private non-profit institutions serving households	9167	663	...	8504	...	11065	860	...	10205	...
e Transfers to the rest of the world	212	212	...	-	...	240	240	...	-	...
Net saving	30593	34334	...	-3741	...	37390	37895	...	-505	...
Total Current Disbursements and Net Saving	82922	52990	...	29932	...	101264	61319	...	39945	...

		1978				1979			
	Total General Government	Central Government	State or Provincial Government	Local Government	Social Security Funds	Total General Government	Central Government	State or Provincial Government	Local Government	Social Security Funds

Receipts

1 Property and entrepreneurial income	3014	-856	531	3339	-	2842	-1556	769	3629	-
a Net operating surplus	3014	-856	531	3339	-	2842	-1556	769	3629	-
b Withdrawals from public quasi-corporations	...	...	...	...	...	...	...	...	...	...
c Interest	...	...	...	...	...	...	...	...	...	...
d Dividends	...	...	...	...	...	...	...	...	...	...
e Net land rent and royalties	...	...	...	...	...	...	...	...	...	...
2 Taxes, fees and contributions	146247	123675	16142	6430	-	180575	150069	21973	8533	-
a Indirect taxes	83384	62006	15366	6012	-	121521	92675	21014	7832	-
b Direct taxes	48669	48602	21	46	-	34149	33829	27	293	-
Income	48562	48562	-	-	-	33785	33785	-	-	-
Other	107	40	21	46	-	364	44	27	293	-
c Social security contributions	14194	13067	755	372	-	24905	23565	932	408	-
d Fees, fines and penalties	...	...	...	...	...	...	...	...	...	...
3 Other current transfers received	1855	1674	80	101	-	947	742	92	113	-
a Casualty insurance claims	...	...	...	...	...	...	...	...	...	...
b Transfers from other government subsectors	...	...	...	...	...	...	...	...	...	...
c Transfers from abroad	1357	1357	-	-	-	386	386	-	-	-
d Other transfers, except imputed	498	317	80	101	-	561	356	92	113	-
e Imputed unfunded employee welfare contributions	...	...	...	...	...	...	...	...	...	...
Total Current Receipts	151116	124493	16753	9870	-	184364	149255	22834	12275	-

Disbursements

1 General government final consumption expenditures	65724	40597	18113	7014	-	91120	56051	26976	8093	-
a Compensation of employees	54061	33850	14514	5697	-	74462	46232	21817	6413	-
b Consumption of fixed capital	...	...	...	...	...	...	...	...	...	...
c Goods and services purchased, net	11663	6747	3599	1317	-	16658	9819	5159	1680	-
d Less: Own account production of fixed assets	...	...	...	...	...	...	...	...	...	...
e Indirect taxes paid, net	...	...	...	...	...	...	...	...	...	...
2 Property income paid	...	...	...	...	...	...	...	...	...	...

Colombia

3.12 General Government Income and Outlay Account: Total and Subsectors
(Continued)

Million Colombian pesos

	1978					1979				
	Total General Government	Central Government	State or Provincial Government	Local Government	Social Security Funds	Total General Government	Central Government	State or Provincial Government	Local Government	Social Security Funds
3 Subsidies	7980	7955	-	25	-	8780	8747	-	33	-
4 Other current transfers paid	12576	11330	974	272	-	20229	18399	1465	365	-
a Casualty insurance premiums, net	...	...	...	...	...	...	...	...	...	...
b Transfers to other government subsectors	...	...	...	...	...	...	...	...	...	...
c Transfers to households	12300	11054	974	272	-	19976	18146	1465	365	-
d Transfers to private non-profit institutions serving households	...	...	...	...	...	...	...	...	...	...
e Transfers to the rest of the world	276	276	-	-	-	253	253	-	-	-
Net saving	64836	64611	-2334	2559	-	64235	66058	-5607	3784	-
Total Current Disbursements and Net Saving	151116	124493	16753	9870	-	184364	149255	22834	12275	-

	1980				
	Total General Government	Central Government	State or Provincial Government	Local Government	Social Security Funds

Receipts

1 Property and entrepreneurial income	331	-4491	606	4216	-
a Net operating surplus	331	-4491	606	4216	-
b Withdrawals from public quasi-corporations	...	...	...	...	...
c Interest	...	...	...	...	...
d Dividends	...	...	...	...	...
e Net land rent and royalties	...	...	...	...	...
2 Taxes, fees and contributions	253000	213448	28560	10992	-
a Indirect taxes	169754	132666	27107	9981	-
b Direct taxes	50877	50489	31	357	-
Income	50432	50432	-	-	-
Other	445	57	31	357	-
c Social security contributions	32369	30293	1422	654	-
d Fees, fines and penalties	...	...	...	...	...
3 Other current transfers received	2054	1818	106	130	-
a Casualty insurance claims	...	...	...	...	...
b Transfers from other government subsectors	...	...	...	...	...
c Transfers from abroad	1633	1633	-	-	-
d Other transfers, except imputed	421	185	106	130	-
e Imputed unfunded employee welfare contributions	...	...	...	...	...
Total Current Receipts	255385	210775	29272	15338	-

Disbursements

1 General government final consumption expenditures	123692	78479	32738	12475	-
a Compensation of employees	100559	63908	26844	9807	-
b Consumption of fixed capital	...	...	...	...	...
c Goods and services purchased, net	23133	14571	5894	2668	-
d Less: Own account production of fixed assets	...	...	...	...	...
e Indirect taxes paid, net	...	...	...	...	...
2 Property income paid	...	...	...	...	...

Colombia

3.12 General Government Income and Outlay Account: Total and Subsectors
(Continued)

Million Colombian pesos

	1980				
	Total General Government	Central Government	State or Provincial Government	Local Government	Social Security Funds
3 Subsidies	10558	10403	-	155	-
4 Other current transfers paid	27952	26131	1469	352	-
a Casualty insurance premiums, net	...	...	...	...	...
b Transfers to other government subsectors	...	...	...	...	...
c Transfers to households	27568	25747	1469	352	-
d Transfers to private non-profit institutions serving households	...	...	...	...	...
e Transfers to the rest of the world	384	384	-	-	-
Net saving	93183	95762	-4935	2356	-
Total Current Disbursements and Net Saving	255385	210775	29272	15338	-

Congo

Source. Reply to the United Nations National Accounts Questionnaire from the Centre National de la Statistique et des Etudes Economique, Brazzaville.
General note. The estimates shown in the following tables have been prepared by the Centre National in accordance with the United Nations System of National Accounts so far as the existing data would permit.

1.1 Expenditure on the Gross Domestic Product, in Current Prices

Million CFA francs

	1970	1971	1972	1973	1974	1975	1976	1977	1978	1979	1980
1 General government final consumption expenditure	...	...	...	...	...	...	37057	...	45505	...	...
2 Private final consumption expenditure	...	...	...	...	...	...	98808	...	117888	...	...
a Households	...	...	...	...	...	...	98228	...	117438	...	...
b Private non-profit institutions serving households	...	...	...	...	...	...	580	...	450	...	...
3 Gross capital formation	...	...	...	...	...	...	55895	...	54294	...	...
a Increase in stocks	...	...	...	...	...	...	2325	...	7934	...	...
b Gross fixed capital formation	...	...	...	...	...	...	53570	...	46360	...	...
4 Exports of goods and services	...	...	...	...	...	...	71177	...	78562	...	...
5 Less: Imports of goods and services	...	...	...	...	...	...	82635	...	97936	...	...
Equals: Gross Domestic Product	...	...	...	...	...	...	180302	...	198313	...	...

1.3 Cost Components of the Gross Domestic Product

Million CFA francs

	1970	1971	1972	1973	1974	1975	1976	1977	1978	1979	1980
1 Indirect taxes, net	...	...	...	...	...	...	26806	...	31941	...	...
a Indirect taxes paid	...	...	...	...	...	...	27080	...	32223	...	...
b Less: Subsidies received	...	...	...	...	...	...	274	...	282	...	...
2 Consumption of fixed capital	...	...	...	...	...	...	39437	...	36464	...	...
3 Compensation of employees paid by resident producers to:	...	...	...	...	...	...	72355	...	83024	...	...
4 Net operating surplus	...	...	...	...	...	...	41704	...	46884	...	...
a Corporate and quasi-corporate enterprises	...	...	...	...	...	...	20561	...	10868	...	...
b Private unincorporated enterprises	...	...	...	...	...	...	21143	...	36016	...	...
c General government	...	...	...	...	...	...	...	...	...	...	...
Equals: Gross Domestic Product	...	...	...	...	...	...	180302	...	198313	...	...

1.4 General Government Current Receipts and Disbursements

Million CFA francs

	1970	1971	1972	1973	1974	1975	1976	1977	1978	1979	1980
Receipts											
1 Property and entrepreneurial income	...	...	...	...	...	...	8634	...	189	...	...
2 Taxes, fees and contributions	...	...	...	...	...	...	46981	...	55148	...	...
a Indirect taxes	...	...	...	...	...	...	27081	...	32224	...	...
b Direct taxes	...	...	...	...	...	...	16327	...	19025	...	...
c Social security contributions	...	...	...	...	...	...	2864	...	3152	...	...
d Compulsory fees, fines and penalties	...	...	...	...	...	...	709	...	747	...	...
3 Other current receipts	...	...	...	...	...	...	1211	...	3920	...	...
Statistical discrepancy	...	...	...	...	...	...	981	...	...	...	...
Total Current Receipts of General Government	...	...	...	...	...	...	57807	...	59257	...	...
Disbursements											
1 General government final consumption expenditure	...	...	...	...	...	...	37057	...	45505	...	...
2 Property income paid	...	...	...	...	...	...	4609	...	5000	...	...
a Interest	...	...	...	...	...	...	4609	...	5000	...	...
b Net land rent and royalties	...	...	...	...	...	...	...	...	...	...	...
3 Subsidies	...	...	...	...	...	...	274	...	281	...	...
4 Other current transfers paid	...	...	...	...	...	...	13749	...	8737	...	...
a Social security benefits and social assistance grants	...	...	...	...	...	...	6891	...	3308	...	...
b Other	...	...	...	...	...	...	6858	...	5429	...	...
5 Net saving	...	...	...	...	...	...	2118	...	-266	...	...
Total Current Disbursements and Net Saving of General Government	...	...	...	...	...	...	57807	...	59257	...	...

Congo

1.7 External Transactions on Current Account, Summary

Million CFA francs

	1970	1971	1972	1973	1974	1975	1976	1977	1978	1979	1980
Payments to the Rest of the World											
1 Imports of goods and services	...	...	...	...	...	...	82635	...	97936	...	...
a Imports of merchandise c.i.f.	...	...	...	...	...	...	52140	...	74701	...	...
b Other	...	...	...	...	...	...	30495	...	23235	...	...
2 Factor income paid to the rest of the world	...	...	...	...	...	...	13712	...	13422	...	...
a Compensation of employees	...	...	...	...	...	...	1754	...	329	...	...
b Property and entrepreneurial income paid	...	...	...	...	...	...	11958	...	13093	...	...
3 Indirect taxes paid to supranational organizations	...	...	...	...	...	...	...	...	...	...	...
4 Current transfers to the rest of the world	...	...	...	...	...	...	11228	...	4259	...	...
5 Surplus of the nation on current transactions	...	...	...	...	...	...	-29584	...	-31315	...	...
Payments to the Rest of the World and Surplus of the Nation on Current Transactions	...	...	...	...	...	...	77991	...	84302	...	...
Receipts From The Rest of the World											
1 Exports of goods and services	...	...	...	...	...	...	71177	...	78562	...	...
a Exports of merchandise f.o.b.	...	...	...	...	...	...	52935	...	69545	...	...
b Other	...	...	...	...	...	...	18242	...	9017	...	...
2 Factor income received from rest of the world	...	...	...	...	...	...	1413	...	770	...	...
a Compensation of employees	...	...	...	...	...	...	432	...	564	...	...
b Property and entrepreneurial income received	...	...	...	...	...	...	981	...	206	...	...
3 Subsidies received from supranational organisations	...	...	...	...	...	...	...	...	...	...	...
4 Current transfers from rest of the world	...	...	...	...	...	...	5401	...	4970	...	...
Receipts from the Rest of the World on Current Transactions	...	...	...	...	...	...	77991	...	84302	...	...

1.8 Capital Transactions of The Nation, Summary

Million CFA francs

	1970	1971	1972	1973	1974	1975	1976	1977	1978	1979	1980
Finance of Gross Capital Formation											
Gross saving	...	...	...	...	...	...	26310	...	22979	...	...
1 Consumption of fixed capital	...	...	...	...	...	...	39436	...	36464	...	...
a General government	...	...	...	...	...	...	...	...	...	...	...
b Corporate and quasi-corporate enterprises	...	...	...	...	...	...	37170	...	30971	...	...
c Other	...	...	...	...	...	...	2266	...	5493	...	...
2 Net saving	...	...	...	...	...	...	-13126	...	-13485	...	...
a General government	...	...	...	...	...	...	2112	...	-266	...	...
b Corporate and quasi-corporate enterprises	...	...	...	...	...	...	-19168	...	-14867	...	...
c Other	...	...	...	...	...	...	3930	...	1648	...	...
Less: Surplus of the nation on current transactions	...	...	...	...	...	...	-29584	...	-31315	...	...
Finance of Gross Capital Formation	...	...	...	...	...	...	55894	...	54294	...	...
Gross Capital Formation											
Increase in stocks	...	...	...	...	...	...	2325	...	7934	...	...
Gross fixed capital formation	...	...	...	...	...	...	53570	...	46360	...	...
1 General government	...	...	...	...	...	...	5865	...	4400	...	...
2 Corporate and quasi-corporate enterprises	...	...	...	...	...	...	44922	...	35660	...	...
3 Other	...	...	...	...	...	...	2782	...	6300	...	...
Gross Capital Formation	...	...	...	...	...	...	55895	...	54294	...	...

Congo

1.9 Gross Domestic Product by Institutional Sectors of Origin

Million CFA francs

	1970	1971	1972	1973	1974	1975	1976	1977	1978	1979	1980
					Domestic Factor Incomes Originating						
1 General government	...	...	...	...	...	...	27294	...	36064	...	...
2 Corporate and quasi-corporate enterprises	...	...	...	...	...	...	...	...	...	...	...
3 Households and private unincorporated enterprises	...	...	...	...	...	...	...	...	...	...	...
4 Non-profit institutions serving households	...	...	...	...	...	...	...	...	...	...	...
Subtotal: Domestic Factor Incomes	...	...	...	...	...	...	114059	...	129908	...	...
Indirect taxes paid, net	...	...	...	...	...	...	26806	...	31941	...	...
Consumption of fixed capital	...	...	...	...	...	...	39437	...	36464	...	...
Gross Domestic Product	...	...	...	...	...	...	180302	...	198313	...	...

1.10 Gross Domestic Product by Kind of Activity, in Current Prices

Million CFA francs

	1970	1971	1972	1973	1974	1975	1976	1977	1978	1979	1980
1 Agriculture, hunting, forestry and fishing	...	...	...	...	...	...	24285	...	31793	...	...
2 Mining and quarrying	...	...	...	...	...	...	43868	...	31937	...	...
3 Manufacturing	...	...	...	...	...	...	14053	...	19363	...	...
4 Electricity, gas and water	...	...	...	...	...	...	2908	...	3250	...	...
5 Construction	...	...	...	...	...	...	6945	...	6020	...	...
6 Wholesale and retail trade, restaurants and hotels	...	...	...	...	...	...	19416	...	28700	...	...
7 Transport, storage and communication	...	...	...	...	...	...	16302	...	17699	...	...
8 Finance, insurance, real estate and business services	...	...	...	...	...	...	9885	...	14584	...	...
9 Community, social and personal services	...	...	...	...	...	...		...		...	...
Total, Industries	...	...	...	...	...	...	137662	...	153346	...	...
Producers of Government Services	...	...	...	...	...	...	27294	...	36063	...	...
Other Producers	...	...	...	...	...	...	421	...	500	...	...
Subtotal	...	...	...	...	...	...	165377	...	189910	...	...
Less: Imputed bank service charge	...	...	...	...	...	...	2968	...	2024	...	...
Plus: Import duties	...	...	...	...	...	...	17893	...	10427	...	...
Plus: Value added tax	...	...	...	...	...	...	...	...	...	...	...
Equals: Gross Domestic Product	...	...	...	...	...	...	180302	...	198313	...	...

1.12 Relations Among National Accounting Aggregates

Million CFA francs

	1970	1971	1972	1973	1974	1975	1976	1977	1978	1979	1980
Gross Domestic Product	...	...	...	...	...	...	180302	...	198313	...	...
Plus: Net factor income received from abroad	...	...	...	...	...	...	-12299	...	-12652	...	...
Factor income received	...	...	...	...	...	...	1413	...	770	...	...
Less: Factor income paid	...	...	...	...	...	...	13712	...	13422	...	...
Equals: Gross National Product	...	...	...	...	...	...	168003	...	185661	...	...
Less: Consumption of fixed capital	...	...	...	...	...	...	39436	...	36464	...	...
Less: Net indirect taxes paid to supranational organisations	...	...	...	...	...	...	...	...	...	...	...
Equals: National Income at Market Prices	...	...	...	...	...	...	128567	...	149197	...	...
Plus: Net current transfers received from abroad	...	...	...	...	...	...	-5828	...	711	...	...
Current transfers received	...	...	...	...	...	...	5401	...	4970	...	...
Less: Current transfers paid	...	...	...	...	...	...	11228	...	4259	...	...
Equals: National Disposable Income at Market Prices	...	...	...	...	...	...	122739	...	149908	...	...
Less: Final consumption	...	...	...	...	...	...	135865	...	163393	...	...
Equals: Net Saving	...	...	...	...	...	...	-13126	...	-13485	...	...
Less: Surplus of the nation on current transactions	...	...	...	...	...	...	-29584	...	-31315	...	...
Equals: Net Capital Formation	...	...	...	...	...	...	16458	...	17831	...	...

Cook Islands

Source. Reply to the United Nations National Accounts Questionnaire from the Statistical Office of the Cook Islands, Rarotonga. Official estimates are published by the same Office in 'Gross Domestic Product Estimates of the Cook Islands for 1976 and 1977.'

General note. The estimates shown in the following tables have been prepared by the Statistical Office in accordance with the United Nations System of National Accounts so far as the existing data would permit.

1.1 Expenditure on the Gross Domestic Product, in Current Prices

Thousand New Zealand dollars

	1970	1971	1972	1973	1974	1975	1976	1977	1978	1979	1980
1 General government final consumption expenditure	2654.1	...	2936.5	...	...	...	...	...	...	...	...
2 Private final consumption expenditure	6667.2	...	...	...	...	...	...	...	...	...	...
3 Gross capital formation	2170.7	...	...	...	...	...	...	...	...	...	...
a Increase in stocks	852.7	...	...	...	...	...	...	...	...	...	...
b Gross fixed capital formation	1318.0	...	1007.8	...	...	...	...	...	...	...	...
4 Exports of goods and services	2691.6	...	...	...	...	...	...	...	...	...	...
5 Less: Imports of goods and services	5863.6	...	...	...	...	...	...	...	...	...	...
Statistical discrepancy	-20.0	...	...	...	...	...	...	...	...	...	...
Equals: Gross Domestic Product	8300.0	...	8110.7	...	...	...	13730.8	16371.8	17818.0	...	...

1.2 Expenditure on the Gross Domestic Product, in Constant Prices

Thousand New Zealand dollars

	1970	1971	1972	1973	1974	1975	1976	1977	1978	1979	1980
				At constant prices of:1970							
1 General government final consumption expenditure	...	...	...	...	...	...	...	...	...	...	...
2 Private final consumption expenditure	...	...	...	...	...	...	...	...	...	...	...
3 Gross capital formation	...	...	...	...	...	...	...	...	...	...	...
4 Exports of goods and services	...	...	...	...	...	...	...	...	...	...	...
5 Less: Imports of goods and services	...	...	...	...	...	...	...	...	...	...	...
Equals: Gross Domestic Product	8300.0	...	6585.0	...	...	...	6297.0	6269.0	6098.0	...	...

1.10 Gross Domestic Product by Kind of Activity, in Current Prices

Thousand New Zealand dollars

	1970	1971	1972	1973	1974	1975	1976	1977	1978	1979	1980
1 Agriculture, hunting, forestry and fishing	2189.0	...	1951.7	...	...	...	2211.0	2860.0	3093.0	...	...
2 Mining and quarrying	16.6	...	12.0	...	...	...	...	...	...	...	...
3 Manufacturing	907.0	...	776.2	...	...	...	740.0	740.0	905.0	...	...
4 Electricity, gas and water	157.8	...	166.8	...	...	...	83.0	80.0	81.0	...	...
5 Construction	763.9	...	653.0	...	...	...	487.0	560.0	763.0	...	...
6 Wholesale and retail trade, restaurants and hotels	1135.6	...	1130.1	...	...	...	4090.0	5202.0	5890.0	...	...
7 Transport, storage and communication	599.4	...	520.2	...	...	...	1178.0	1413.0	1140.0	...	...
8 Finance, insurance, real estate and business services	268.8	...	358.3	...	...	...	637.0	697.0	910.0	...	...
9 Community, social and personal services	2262.0	...	2542.0	...	...	...	4307.0	4820.0	564.0	...	...
Total, Industries	8300.0	...	8110.0	...	...	...	13733.0	16372.0	13346.0	...	...
Producers of Government Services	...	...	...	...	...	...	...	...	4472.0	...	...
Other Producers	...	...	...	...	...	...	...	...	...	...	...
Subtotal	8300.0	...	8110.7	...	...	...	13730.0	16372.0	17818.0	...	...
Less: Imputed bank service charge	...	...	...	...	...	...	...	...	...	...	...
Plus: Import duties	...	...	...	...	...	...	...	...	...	...	...
Plus: Value added tax	...	...	...	...	...	...	...	...	...	...	...
Equals: Gross Domestic Product	8300.0	...	8110.7	...	...	...	13730.8	16371.8	17818.0	...	...

1.11 Gross Domestic Product by Kind of Activity, in Constant Prices

Thousand New Zealand dollars

	1970	1971	1972	1973	1974	1975	1976	1977	1978	1979	1980
				At constant prices of:1980							
1 Agriculture, hunting, forestry and fishing	8089.0	...	5853.0	...	...	...	3762.0	4046.0	3912.0	...	...
2 Mining and quarrying	...	...	...	...	...	...	...	...	...	...	...
3 Manufacturing	3377.0	...	2328.0	...	...	...	1259.0	1047.0	1145.0	...	...
4 Electricity, gas and water	621.0	...	537.0	...	...	...	141.0	113.0	102.0	...	...
5 Construction	2823.0	...	1959.0	...	...	...	829.0	792.0	965.0	...	...

Cook Islands

1.11 Gross Domestic Product by Kind of Activity, in Constant Prices
(Continued)

Thousand New Zealand dollars

	1970	1971	1972	1973	1974	1975	1976	1977	1978	1979	1980
					At constant prices of:1980						
6 Wholesale and retail trade, restaurants and hotels	4198.0	...	3390.0	...	...	...	6960.0	7360.0	7450.0	...	...
7 Transport, storage and communication	2213.0	...	1560.0	...	...	...	2005.0	1999.0	1442.0	...	...
8 Finance, insurance, real estate and business services	994.0	...	1074.0	...	...	...	1084.0	986.0	1151.0	...	...
9 Community, social and personal services	8358.0	...	7636.0	...	...	...	7330.0	6820.0	6369.0	...	...
Total, Industries	30673.0	...	24337.0	...	...	...	23370.0	23163.0	22536.0	...	...
Producers of Government Services	...	...	...	...	...	...	...	...	...	...	...
Other Producers	...	...	...	...	...	...	...	...	...	...	...
Subtotal	30669.0	...	24333.0	...	...	...	23366.0	23165.0	22534.0	...	...
Less: Imputed bank service charge	...	...	...	...	...	...	...	...	...	...	...
Plus: Import duties	...	...	...	...	...	...	...	...	...	...	...
Plus: Value added tax	...	...	...	...	...	...	...	...	...	...	...
Equals: Gross Domestic Product	...	...	...	...	...	...	...	...	...	...	...

Costa Rica

Source. Reply to the United Nations National Accounts Questionnaire from the Banco Central de Costa Rica, Departamento de Estudios Economicos, Seccion Ingreso Nacional, San Jose. Official estimates are published in 'Cifras de Cuentas Nacionales de Costa Rica'.

General note. The estimates shown in the tables below have been prepared in accordance with the United Nations System of National Accounts so far as the existing data would permit.

1.1 Expenditure on the Gross Domestic Product, in Current Prices

Million Costa Rican colones

		1970	1971	1972	1973	1974	1975	1976	1977	1978	1979	1980
1	General government final consumption expenditure	819.8	990.0	1182.0	1417.1	1889.0	2557.9	3306.4	4208.1	5068.6	6243.2	7544.3
2	Private final consumption expenditure	4806.5	5151.5	5752.9	6927.0	9750.3	12014.4	13690.0	17142.6	20387.9	23136.9	27674.2
3	Gross capital formation	1339.9	1736.9	1809.7	2438.3	3533.7	3636.7	4892.3	6390.4	7083.9	8754.7	10448.1
	a Increase in stocks	70.1	158.4	9.5	186.7	358.9	-58.1	46.3	501.6	131.5	-295.2	716.2
	b Gross fixed capital formation	1269.8	1578.5	1800.2	2251.6	3174.8	3694.8	4846.0	5888.8	6952.4	9049.9	9731.9
4	Exports of goods and services	1841.2	1945.0	2519.7	3162.6	4431.3	5107.0	6081.5	8198.0	8589.0	9353.6	10758.5
5	Less: Imports of goods and services	2282.9	2686.4	3048.5	3782.6	6388.6	6511.4	7294.6	9608.4	10935.5	12904.0	14890.2
	Equals: Gross Domestic Product	6524.5	7137.0	8215.8	10162.4	13215.7	16804.6	20675.6	26330.7	30193.9	34584.4	41534.9

1.2 Expenditure on the Gross Domestic Product, in Constant Prices

Million Costa Rican colones

		1970	1971	1972	1973	1974	1975	1976	1977	1978	1979	1980
						At constant prices of: 1966						
1	General government final consumption expenditure	659.6	738.8	790.8	838.7	909.5	961.0	1036.0	1126.7	1168.0	1258.1	1257.2
2	Private final consumption expenditure	4089.1	4129.8	4324.1	4502.6	4734.6	4837.4	5039.0	5726.2	6204.7	6352.6	6457.6
3	Gross capital formation	1128.6	1399.9	1297.4	1539.5	1671.6	1522.7	1926.5	2365.0	2355.2	2573.1	2519.8
	a Increase in stocks	50.7	145.5	-15.8	115.1	108.4	-21.2	16.8	217.9	33.5	-103.5	123.6
	b Gross fixed capital formation	1077.9	1254.4	1313.2	1424.4	1563.2	1543.9	1909.7	2147.1	2321.7	2676.6	2396.2
4	Exports of goods and services	1904.2	2059.3	2410.7	2586.4	2774.2	2719.5	2866.9	3100.7	3408.9	3520.0	3425.7
5	Less: Imports of goods and services	2208.0	2376.5	2385.0	2532.9	2771.1	2568.1	2983.6	3731.7	4011.7	4128.0	3965.7
	Equals: Gross Domestic Product	5573.5	5951.3	6438.0	6934.3	7318.8	7472.5	7884.8	8586.9	9125.1	9575.8	9694.6

1.3 Cost Components of the Gross Domestic Product

Million Costa Rican colones

		1970	1971	1972	1973	1974	1975	1976	1977	1978	1979	1980
1	Indirect taxes, net	725.2	769.8	883.1	1167.0	1661.7	2117.4	2565.1	3409.6	3999.9	4215.2	4910.2
	a Indirect taxes paid	750.7	801.1	919.1	1213.8	1688.1	2153.4	2678.4	3474.6	4086.9	4430.4	5161.7
	b Less: Subsidies received	25.5	31.3	36.0	46.8	26.4	36.0	113.3	65.0	87.0	215.1	251.5
2	Consumption of fixed capital	415.5	449.7	503.6	567.1	697.8	891.9	1123.2	1352.0	1584.3	1845.8	2132.9
3	Compensation of employees paid by resident producers to:	3057.5	3423.6	3912.7	4596.8	5991.7	7693.4	9620.3	11801.2	14339.8	17148.2	20857.1
	a Resident households	3053.2	3418.5	3905.0	4589.0	5965.4	7650.2	9563.3	...	...	...	...
	b Rest of the world	4.3	5.1	7.7	7.8	26.3	43.2	57.0	...	...	...	...
4	Net operating surplus	2326.3	2449.1	2770.3	3520.3	4716.2	6101.9	7367.0	9767.9	10269.9	11375.2	13634.7
	Statistical discrepancy [a]	-	44.8	146.1	311.2	148.3	-	-	-	-	-	-
	Equals: Gross Domestic Product	6524.5	7137.0	8215.8	10162.4	13215.7	16804.6	20675.6	26330.7	30193.9	34584.4	41534.9

a) Relating to adjustment for changes in exchange rate.

1.4 General Government Current Receipts and Disbursements

Million Costa Rican colones

		1970	1971	1972	1973	1974	1975	1976	1977	1978	1979	1980
						Receipts						
1	Property and entrepreneurial income	27.7	33.8	36.5	44.3	78.7	90.5	110.5	149.5	214.2	286.2	504.8
2	Taxes, fees and contributions	1150.6	1279.2	1554.1	2023.3	2707.1	3413.7	4365.4	5597.6	6617.9	7436.6	8606.8
	a Indirect taxes	750.7	801.1	919.1	1213.8	1688.1	2153.4	2678.4	3474.6	4086.9	4430.4	5245.3
	b Direct taxes	176.0	192.0	233.1	324.5	398.7	447.4	624.9	784.8	925.9	945.4	1013.7
	c Social security contributions	206.4	267.9	378.3	459.2	585.3	776.3	1028.7	1296.8	1564.2	1989.9	2274.4
	d Compulsory fees, fines and penalties	17.5	18.2	23.6	25.8	35.0	36.6	33.4	41.4	40.9	70.9	73.4
3	Other current receipts	14.0	31.1	27.0	25.4	35.5	40.2	51.4	46.2	53.5	81.1	105.5
	Total Current Receipts of General Government	1192.3	1344.1	1617.6	2093.0	2821.3	3544.4	4527.3	5793.3	6885.6	7803.9	9217.1
						Disbursements						
1	General government final consumption expenditure	819.8	990.0	1182.0	1417.1	1889.0	2557.9	3306.4	4208.1	5068.6	6243.2	7544.3

Costa Rica

1.4 General Government Current Receipts and Disbursements
(Continued)

Million Costa Rican colones

	1970	1971	1972	1973	1974	1975	1976	1977	1978	1979	1980
a Compensation of employees	693.2	813.6	998.0	1196.6	1576.4	2083.7	2682.2	3402.0	4218.3	5200.4	6288.4
b Consumption of fixed capital	...	...	...	...	...	...	...	...	...	...	...
c Purchases of goods and services, net	...	...	...	...	...	...	...	...	...	...	...
d Less: Own account production of fixed assets	...	...	...	...	...	...	...	...	...	...	...
e Indirect taxes paid, net	...	...	...	...	...	...	...	...	...	...	...
2 Property income paid	71.7	86.4	95.9	122.3	175.2	201.8	245.0	334.4	549.6	764.6	1211.6
a Interest	71.7	86.4	95.9	122.3	175.2	201.8	245.0	334.4	549.6	764.6	1211.6
b Net land rent and royalties	...	...	...	...	...	...	...	...	...	...	...
3 Subsidies	25.5	31.3	36.0	46.8	26.4	36.0	113.3	65.0	87.0	215.1	383.0
4 Other current transfers paid	106.6	125.6	189.6	281.8	202.1	242.5	359.8	501.9	592.4	753.7	752.1
a Social security benefits and social assistance grants	53.1	56.9	91.3	164.7	131.2	207.1	316.6	430.4	552.1	649.6	414.1
b Other	52.9	68.7	98.3	117.1	70.9	35.4	43.2	71.5	40.3	104.1	338.0
5 Net saving	168.7	110.8	114.1	225.0	528.6	506.2	502.8	683.9	588.0	-172.7	-673.9
Total Current Disbursements and Net Saving of General Government	1192.3	1344.1	1617.6	2093.0	2821.3	3544.4	4527.3	5793.3	6885.6	7803.9	9217.1

1.7 External Transactions on Current Account, Summary

Million Costa Rican colones

	1970	1971	1972	1973	1974	1975	1976	1977	1978	1979	1980
Payments to the Rest of the World											
1 Imports of goods and services	2282.9	2686.4	3048.5	3782.6	6388.6	6511.4	7294.6	9608.4	10935.5	12904.0	14890.2
a Imports of merchandise c.i.f.	2073.0	2378.3	2694.1	3440.9	5909.1	5906.6	6554.1	8718.4	9897.2	11863.8	13684.1
b Other	209.9	308.1	354.4	341.7	479.5	604.8	740.5	890.0	1038.3	1040.2	1206.1
2 Factor income paid to the rest of the world	101.1	111.0	272.7	316.3	380.5	601.3	697.6	791.0	1136.8	1414.2	2118.1
a Compensation of employees	4.3	5.1	7.7	7.8	26.3	43.2	57.0	50.8	51.2	62.2	66.8
b Property and entrepreneurial income paid	96.8	105.9	265.0	308.5	354.2	558.1	640.6	740.2	1085.6	1352.0	2051.3
3 Indirect taxes paid to supranational organizations	...	...	...	...	...	...	...	...	...	...	...
4 Current transfers to the rest of the world	35.1	33.0	40.5	44.3	46.7	81.4	86.2	93.8	102.4	153.1	126.4
5 Surplus of the nation on current transactions	-506.2	-801.6	-749.6	-853.3	-2204.9	-1865.2	-1726.6	-1933.3	-3112.5	-4725.3	-5900.0
Payments to the Rest of the World and Surplus of the Nation on Current Transactions	1912.9	2028.8	2612.1	3289.9	4610.9	5328.9	6351.8	8559.9	9062.2	9746.0	11234.7
Receipts From The Rest of the World											
1 Exports of goods and services	1841.2	1945.0	2519.7	3162.6	4431.3	5107.0	6081.5	8198.0	8589.0	9353.6	10758.5
a Exports of merchandise f.o.b.	1529.9	1551.7	2044.1	2620.3	3645.5	4225.2	5076.7	7094.6	7403.8	8074.0	9184.6
b Other	311.3	393.3	475.6	542.3	785.8	881.8	1004.8	1103.4	1185.2	1279.6	1573.9
2 Factor income received from rest of the world	13.5	12.7	19.6	31.5	52.6	57.7	70.7	135.8	233.6	135.2	195.6
a Compensation of employees	7.0	8.1	10.3	11.8	18.1	21.2	22.2	25.4	33.6	34.7	37.9
b Property and entrepreneurial income received	6.5	4.6	9.3	19.7	34.5	36.5	48.5	110.4	200.0	100.5	157.7
3 Subsidies received from supranational organisations	...	...	...	...	...	...	...	...	...	...	...
4 Current transfers from rest of the world	58.2	71.1	72.8	95.8	127.0	164.2	199.6	226.1	239.6	257.2	280.6
Receipts from the Rest of the World on Current Transactions	1912.9	2028.8	2612.1	3289.9	4610.9	5328.9	6351.8	8559.9	9062.2	9746.0	11234.7

1.8 Capital Transactions of The Nation, Summary

Million Costa Rican colones

	1970	1971	1972	1973	1974	1975	1976	1977	1978	1979	1980
Finance of Gross Capital Formation											
Gross saving	833.7	935.3	1060.1	1585.0	1328.8	1771.5	3165.7	4457.1	3971.4	4029.4	4548.1
1 Consumption of fixed capital	415.5	449.7	503.6	567.1	697.8	891.9	1123.2	1352.0	1584.3	1845.8	2132.9
2 Net saving	418.2	485.6	556.5	1017.9	631.0	879.6	2042.5	3105.1	2387.1	2183.6	2415.2
a General government	168.7	110.8	114.1	225.0	528.6	506.2	502.8	683.9	588.0	-172.7	...

Costa Rica

1.8 Capital Transactions of The Nation, Summary
(Continued)

Million Costa Rican colones

	1970	1971	1972	1973	1974	1975	1976	1977	1978	1979	1980
b Corporate and quasi-corporate enterprises [a]	...	79.3	124.8	144.9	175.4	285.3	383.1	434.8	443.9	286.7	...
Public	...	79.3	124.8	144.9	175.4	285.3	383.1	434.8	443.9	286.7	...
Private [a]	...	...	...	...	...	...	...	...	...	...	...
c Other [a]	...	295.5	317.6	648.0	-73.0	88.1	1156.6	1986.4	1355.2	2069.6	...
Less: Surplus of the nation on current transactions	-506.2	-801.6	-749.6	-853.3	-2204.9	-1865.2	-1726.6	-1933.3	-3112.5	-4725.3	-5900.0
Finance of Gross Capital Formation	1339.9	1736.9	1809.7	2438.3	3533.7	3636.7	4892.3	6390.4	7083.9	8754.7	10448.1
Gross Capital Formation											
Increase in stocks	70.1	158.4	9.5	186.7	358.9	-58.1	46.3	501.6	131.5	-295.2	716.2
Gross fixed capital formation	1269.8	1578.5	1800.2	2251.6	3174.8	3694.8	4846.0	5888.8	6952.4	9049.9	9731.9
1 General government	151.4	230.2	325.0	345.2	487.1	533.1	887.8	1112.9	1035.1	1565.2	...
2 Corporate and quasi-corporate enterprises	...	...	...	...	...	...	...	...	...	...	...
3 Other	...	...	...	...	...	...	...	...	...	...	...
Gross Capital Formation	1339.9	1736.9	1809.7	2438.3	3533.7	3636.7	4892.3	6390.4	7083.9	8754.7	10448.1

a) Private corporate and quasi-corporate enterprises are included in item 'Other'.

1.10 Gross Domestic Product by Kind of Activity, in Current Prices

Million Costa Rican colones

	1970	1971	1972	1973	1974	1975	1976	1977	1978	1979	1980
1 Agriculture, hunting, forestry and fishing	1469.3	1443.4	1601.6	1962.9	2522.4	3417.8	4212.9	5762.6	6163.7	6398.6	7204.8
2 Mining and quarrying	7.2	9.4	16.0	19.0	24.5	38.6	40.6	53.2	5657.8	6331.5	8123.3
3 Manufacturing	1185.0	1315.6	1491.1	1884.3	2653.4	3388.7	4031.5	4947.1			
4 Electricity, gas and water	109.8	127.8	147.9	160.3	205.9	303.7	409.6	521.4	549.7	602.8	730.5
5 Construction	277.4	343.3	423.8	507.1	692.6	868.9	1193.4	1367.1	1663.3	2215.6	2675.2
6 Wholesale and retail trade, restaurants and hotels	1371.3	1502.0	1651.3	2054.5	2754.7	3203.6	3832.2	5134.6	5949.9	7056.4	8313.2
7 Transport, storage and communication	274.2	316.0	362.0	435.6	590.7	788.6	954.7	1091.2	1277.0	1444.6	1792.7
8 Finance, insurance, real estate and business services	801.4	845.9	957.9	1135.0	1420.1	1940.4	2411.9	2953.4	3407.0	3781.0	4456.6
9 Community, social and personal services	245.9	280.4	319.3	384.4	470.3	572.5	684.5	850.0	5525.5	6753.9	8238.6
Total, Industries	5741.5	6183.8	6970.9	8543.1	11334.6	14522.8	17771.3	22680.6	...	...	...
Producers of Government Services	693.2	813.6	998.0	1196.6	1576.4	2083.7	2682.2	3402.0	...	...	...
Other Producers	89.8	94.8	100.8	111.5	156.4	198.1	222.1	248.1	...	...	...
Subtotal	6524.5	7092.2	8069.7	9851.2	13067.4	16804.6	20675.6	26330.7	30193.9	34584.4	41534.9
Less: Imputed bank service charge	...	...	...	...	...	...	...	...	...	...	...
Plus: Import duties	...	...	...	...	...	...	...	...	...	...	...
Plus: Value added tax	...	...	...	...	...	...	...	...	...	...	...
Plus: Other adjustments [a]	-	44.8	146.1	311.2	148.3	-	-	-	-	-	-
Equals: Gross Domestic Product	6524.5	7137.0	8215.8	10162.4	13215.7	16804.6	20675.6	26330.7	30193.9	34584.4	41534.9

a) Relating to adjustment for changes in exchange rate.

1.11 Gross Domestic Product by Kind of Activity, in Constant Prices

Million Costa Rican colones

	1970	1971	1972	1973	1974	1975	1976	1977	1978	1979	1980
	At constant prices of:1966										
1 Agriculture, hunting, forestry and fishing	1343.6	1405.6	1481.8	1565.5	1539.0	1585.7	1593.6	1628.7	1736.2	1744.8	1729.1
2 Mining and quarrying	1036.3	1120.3	1238.3	1364.8	1538.4	1587.1	1679.2	1893.0	2048.2	2102.8	2142.3
3 Manufacturing											
4 Electricity, gas and water	106.4	120.3	131.6	139.6	152.6	156.1	169.8	181.6	191.4	201.2	224.9
5 Construction	229.1	268.6	327.6	337.7	364.0	384.7	464.7	482.8	510.8	609.4	607.1
6 Wholesale and retail trade, restaurants and hotels	1109.5	1159.3	1248.0	1354.8	1345.0	1288.0	1402.0	1653.2	1722.6	1794.0	1745.3
7 Transport, storage and communication	247.7	275.6	307.5	356.7	407.0	432.2	457.3	512.2	572.1	643.0	672.1
8 Finance, insurance, real estate and business services	663.8	705.8	742.1	803.2	875.6	924.3	963.1	1013.2	1067.7	1135.5	1177.3
9 Community, social and personal services	287.9	301.4	318.5	333.5	351.1	346.6	356.0	383.1	395.0	1345.1	1396.5

Costa Rica

1.11 Gross Domestic Product by Kind of Activity, in Constant Prices
(Continued)

Million Costa Rican colones

	1970	1971	1972	1973	1974	1975	1976	1977	1978	1979	1980
					At constant prices of:1966						
Total, Industries	5024.3	5356.9	5795.4	6255.8	6572.7	6702.7	7085.7	7747.8	8244.0	...	...
Producers of Government Services	549.2	594.4	642.6	678.5	746.1	769.8	799.1	839.1	881.1	...	...
Other Producers	...	...	...	...	...	...	...	...	...	...	...
Subtotal	5573.5	5951.3	6438.0	6934.3	7318.8	7472.5	7884.8	8586.9	9125.1	9575.8	9694.6
Less: Imputed bank service charge	...	...	...	...	...	...	...	...	...	...	...
Plus: Import duties	...	...	...	...	...	...	...	...	...	...	...
Plus: Value added tax	...	...	...	...	...	...	...	...	...	...	...
Equals: Gross Domestic Product	5573.5	5951.3	6438.0	6934.3	7318.8	7472.5	7884.8	8586.9	9125.1	9575.8	9694.6

1.12 Relations Among National Accounting Aggregates

Million Costa Rican colones

	1970	1971	1972	1973	1974	1975	1976	1977	1978	1979	1980
Gross Domestic Product	6524.5	7137.0	8215.8	10162.4	13215.7	16804.6	20675.6	26330.7	30193.9	34584.4	41534.9
Plus: Net factor income received from abroad	-87.6	-98.3	-253.1	-284.8	-327.9	-543.6	-626.9	-655.2	-903.2	-1279.0	-1922.5
Factor income received	13.5	12.7	19.6	31.5	52.6	57.7	70.7	135.8	233.6	135.2	195.6
Less: Factor income paid	101.1	111.0	272.7	316.3	380.5	601.3	697.6	791.0	1136.8	1414.2	2118.1
Equals: Gross National Product	6436.9	7038.7	7962.7	9877.6	12887.8	16261.0	20048.7	25675.5	29290.7	33305.4	39612.4
Less: Consumption of fixed capital	415.5	449.7	503.6	567.1	697.8	891.9	1123.2	1352.0	1584.3	1845.8	2132.9
Less: Net indirect taxes paid to supranational organisations	...	...	...	...	...	...	...	...	...	...	...
Equals: National Income at Market Prices	6021.4	6589.0	7459.1	9310.5	12190.0	15369.1	18925.5	24323.5	27706.4	31459.6	37479.5
Plus: Net current transfers received from abroad	23.1	38.1	32.3	51.5	80.3	82.8	113.4	132.3	137.2	104.1	154.2
Current transfers received	58.2	71.1	72.8	95.8	127.0	164.2	199.6	226.1	239.6	257.2	280.6
Less: Current transfers paid	35.1	33.0	40.5	44.3	46.7	81.4	86.2	93.8	102.4	153.1	126.4
Equals: National Disposable Income at Market Prices	6044.5	6627.1	7491.4	9362.0	12270.3	15451.9	19038.9	24455.8	27843.6	31563.7	37633.7
Less: Final consumption	5626.3	6141.5	6934.9	8344.1	11639.3	14572.3	16996.4	21350.7	25456.5	29380.1	35218.5
Equals: Net Saving	418.2	485.6	556.5	1017.9	631.0	879.6	2042.5	3105.1	2387.1	2183.6	2415.2
Less: Surplus of the nation on current transactions	-506.2	-801.6	-749.6	-853.3	-2204.9	-1865.2	-1726.6	-1933.3	-3112.5	-4725.3	-5900.0
Equals: Net Capital Formation	924.4	1287.2	1306.1	1871.2	2835.9	2744.8	3769.1	5038.4	5499.6	6908.9	8315.2

2.7 Gross Capital Formation by Type of Good and Owner, in Current Prices

Million Costa Rican colones

	1970 TOTAL	1970 Total Private	1970 Public Enterprises	1970 General Government	1971 TOTAL	1971 Total Private	1971 Public Enterprises	1971 General Government	1972 TOTAL	1972 Total Private	1972 Public Enterprises	1972 General Government
Increase in stocks, total [a]	70.1	...	...	...	158.4	124.7	35.9	-2.2	9.5	1.6	3.3	4.6
1 Goods producing industries	...	...	...	...	...	...	...	...	...	...	...	...
2 Wholesale and retail trade	...	...	...	...	...	...	...	...	...	...	...	...
3 Other, except government stocks	...	...	...	...	...	...	...	...	...	...	...	...
4 Government stocks	1.1	...	...	...	-2.2	...	...	...	4.6	...	...	...
Gross Fixed Capital Formation, Total	1269.8	...	...	...	1578.5	1170.3	178.0	230.2	1800.2	1237.8	237.4	325.0
1 Residential buildings	...	...	...	...	...	...	...	...	...	...	...	...
2 Non-residential buildings	...	...	...	...	...	...	...	...	...	...	...	...
3 Other construction	...	...	...	...	...	...	...	...	...	...	...	...
4 Land improvement and plantation and orchard development	...	...	...	...	...	...	...	...	...	...	...	...
5 Producers' durable goods	...	...	...	22.5	824.5	720.5	33.9	70.1	984.8	852.7	29.0	103.1
6 Breeding stock, dairy cattle, etc.	...	...	...	...	...	...	...	...	...	...	...	...
Total Gross Capital Formation	1339.9	...	...	...	1736.9	1295.0	213.9	228.0	1809.7	1239.4	240.7	329.6

	1973 TOTAL	1973 Total Private	1973 Public Enterprises	1973 General Government	1974 TOTAL	1974 Total Private	1974 Public Enterprises	1974 General Government	1975 TOTAL	1975 Total Private	1975 Public Enterprises	1975 General Government
Increase in stocks, total [a]	186.7	152.8	23.8	10.1	358.9	258.9	81.0	19.0	-58.1	-305.5	208.4	39.0
1 Goods producing industries	...	...	...	...	...	...	...	...	...	...	...	...
2 Wholesale and retail trade	...	...	...	...	...	...	...	...	...	...	...	...
3 Other, except government stocks	...	...	...	...	...	...	...	...	...	...	...	...
4 Government stocks	10.1	...	...	...	19.0	...	...	...	39.0	...	...	...

Costa Rica

2.7 Gross Capital Formation by Type of Good and Owner, in Current Prices
(Continued)

Million Costa Rican colones

	1973 TOTAL	1973 Total Private	1973 Public Enterprises	1973 General Government	1974 TOTAL	1974 Total Private	1974 Public Enterprises	1974 General Government	1975 TOTAL	1975 Total Private	1975 Public Enterprises	1975 General Government
Gross Fixed Capital Formation, Total	2251.6	1615.6	290.8	345.2	3174.8	2301.4	386.3	487.1	3694.8	2527.2	634.5	533.1
1 Residential buildings	...	...	...	...	...	...	...	...	...	...	...	...
2 Non-residential buildings	...	...	...	...	...	...	...	...	...	...	...	...
3 Other construction	...	...	...	...	...	...	...	...	...	...	...	...
4 Land improvement and plantation and orchard development	...	...	...	...	...	...	...	...	...	...	...	...
5 Producers' durable goods	1237.5	1113.6	52.7	71.2	1611.7	1483.4	31.5	96.8	1819.1	1599.9	112.5	106.7
6 Breeding stock, dairy cattle, etc.	...	...	...	...	...	...	...	...	...	...	...	...
Total Gross Capital Formation	2438.3	1768.4	314.6	355.3	3533.7	2560.3	467.3	506.1	3636.7	2221.7	842.9	572.1

	1976 TOTAL	1976 Total Private	1976 Public Enterprises	1976 General Government	1977 TOTAL	1977 Total Private	1977 Public Enterprises	1977 General Government	1978 TOTAL	1978 Total Private	1978 Public Enterprises	1978 General Government
Increase in stocks, total [a]	46.3	9.0	13.6	23.7	501.6	541.1	-78.2	38.7	131.5	-27.1	57.4	101.2
1 Goods producing industries	...	...	...	...	...	...	...	...	...	...	...	...
2 Wholesale and retail trade	...	...	...	...	...	...	...	...	...	...	...	...
3 Other, except government stocks	...	...	...	...	...	...	...	...	...	...	...	...
4 Government stocks	23.7	...	...	...	38.7	...	...	...	...	...	...	...
Gross Fixed Capital Formation, Total	4846.0	3113.4	844.8	887.8	5888.8	3741.8	1034.1	1112.9	6952.4	4705.4	1211.9	1035.1
1 Residential buildings	...	...	...	...	...	...	...	...	...	...	...	...
2 Non-residential buildings	...	...	...	...	...	...	...	...	...	...	...	...
3 Other construction	...	...	...	...	...	...	...	...	...	...	...	...
4 Land improvement and plantation and orchard development	...	...	...	...	...	...	...	...	...	...	...	...
5 Producers' durable goods	2293.4	2086.8	74.9	131.7	2945.6	2519.9	105.3	320.4	3617.0	3214.2	217.1	185.7
6 Breeding stock, dairy cattle, etc.	...	...	...	...	...	...	...	...	...	...	...	...
Total Gross Capital Formation	4892.3	3122.4	858.4	911.5	6390.4	4282.9	955.9	1151.6	7083.9	4678.3	1269.3	1136.3

	1979 TOTAL	1979 Total Private	1979 Public Enterprises	1979 General Government
Increase in stocks, total [a]	-295.2	-311.8	-48.4	65.0
1 Goods producing industries	...	...	...	...
2 Wholesale and retail trade	...	...	...	...
3 Other, except government stocks	...	...	...	...
4 Government stocks	...	...	...	...
Gross Fixed Capital Formation, Total	9049.9	5975.9	1508.8	1565.2
1 Residential buildings	...	...	...	...
2 Non-residential buildings	...	...	...	...
3 Other construction	...	...	...	...
4 Land improvement and plantation and orchard development	...	...	...	...
5 Producers' durable goods	4322.4	3769.5	184.9	368.0
6 Breeding stock, dairy cattle, etc.	...	...	...	...
Total Gross Capital Formation	8754.7	5664.1	1460.4	1630.2

a) Representing cattle and pig stocks, coffee, basic grains in silos and materials in the public sector.

Costa Rica

2.8 Gross Capital Formation by Type of Good and Owner, in Constant Prices

Million Costa Rican colones

	1970 TOTAL	Total Private	Public Enterprises	General Government	1971 TOTAL	Total Private	Public Enterprises	General Government	1972 TOTAL	Total Private	Public Enterprises	General Government
	At constant prices of: 1966												
Increase in stocks, total	50.7	40.3	9.5	0.9	145.5	119.2	28.0	-1.7	-15.8	-21.7	2.5	3.4
Gross Fixed Capital Formation, Total	1077.9	843.3	113.9	120.7	1254.4	946.8	137.1	170.5	1313.2	915.4	172.4	225.4
1 Residential buildings	...	...	...	...	...	...	...	...	...	...	...	...
2 Non-residential buildings	...	...	...	...	...	...	...	...	...	...	...	...
3 Other construction	...	...	...	...	...	...	...	...	...	...	...	...
4 Land improvement and plantation and orchard development	...	...	...	...	...	...	...	...	...	...	...	...
5 Producers' durable goods	563.5	512.0	29.0	22.5	677.8	600.4	28.2	49.2	711.7	627.0	21.3	63.4
6 Breeding stock, dairy cattle, etc.	...	...	...	...	...	...	...	...	...	...	...	...
Total Gross Capital Formation	1128.6	883.6	123.4	121.6	1399.9	1066.0	165.1	168.8	1297.4	893.7	174.9	228.8

	1973 TOTAL	Total Private	Public Enterprises	General Government	1974 TOTAL	Total Private	Public Enterprises	General Government	1975 TOTAL	Total Private	Public Enterprises	General Government
	At constant prices of: 1966												
Increase in stocks, total	115.1	93.5	15.2	6.4	108.4	75.7	24.0	8.7	-21.2	-122.8	87.0	14.6
Gross Fixed Capital Formation, Total	1424.4	1036.7	177.5	210.2	1563.2	1159.0	175.0	229.2	1543.9	1076.5	249.8	217.6
1 Residential buildings	...	...	...	...	...	...	...	...	...	...	...	...
2 Non-residential buildings	...	...	...	...	...	...	...	...	...	...	...	...
3 Other construction	...	...	...	...	...	...	...	...	...	...	...	...
4 Land improvement and plantation and orchard development	...	...	...	...	...	...	...	...	...	...	...	...
5 Producers' durable goods	800.8	723.1	34.2	43.5	857.7	786.7	16.7	54.3	818.7	715.1	50.3	53.3
6 Breeding stock, dairy cattle, etc.	...	...	...	...	...	...	...	...	...	...	...	...
Total Gross Capital Formation	1539.5	1130.2	192.7	216.6	1671.6	1234.7	199.0	237.9	1522.7	953.7	336.8	232.2

	1976 TOTAL	Total Private	Public Enterprises	General Government	1977 TOTAL	Total Private	Public Enterprises	General Government	1978 TOTAL	Total Private	Public Enterprises	General Government
	At constant prices of: 1966												
Increase in stocks, total	16.8	3.3	5.4	8.1	217.9	236.5	-28.2	9.6	33.5	-5.8	12.9	26.4
Gross Fixed Capital Formation, Total	1909.7	1275.6	301.1	333.0	2147.1	1408.1	343.3	395.7	2321.7	1632.6	363.9	325.2
1 Residential buildings	...	...	...	...	...	...	...	...	...	...	...	...
2 Non-residential buildings	...	...	...	...	...	...	...	...	...	...	...	...
3 Other construction	...	...	...	...	...	...	...	...	...	...	...	...
4 Land improvement and plantation and orchard development	...	...	...	...	...	...	...	...	...	...	...	...
5 Producers' durable goods	997.7	902.7	32.4	62.6	1168.1	991.8	41.4	134.9	1321.3	1167.9	78.9	74.5
6 Breeding stock, dairy cattle, etc.	...	...	...	...	...	...	...	...	...	...	...	...
Total Gross Capital Formation	1926.5	1278.9	306.5	341.1	2365.0	1644.6	315.1	405.3	2355.2	1626.8	376.8	351.6

	1979 TOTAL	Total Private	Public Enterprises	General Government
	At constant prices of: 1966			
Increase in stocks, total	-103.5	-74.0	-34.6	5.1
Gross Fixed Capital Formation, Total	2676.6	1824.2	385.8	466.6
1 Residential buildings	...	...	...	...
2 Non-residential buildings	...	...	...	...
3 Other construction	...	...	...	...
4 Land improvement and plantation and orchard development	...	...	...	...
5 Producers' durable goods	1487.4	1264.1	62.0	161.3
6 Breeding stock, dairy cattle, etc.	...	...	...	...
Total Gross Capital Formation	2573.1	1750.2	351.2	471.7

Costa Rica

2.9 Gross Capital Formation by Kind of Activity of Owner, ISIC Major Divisions, in Current Prices

Million Costa Rican colones

	1970 TGCF	1970 IS	1970 GFCF	1971 TGCF	1971 IS	1971 GFCF	1972 TGCF	1972 IS	1972 GFCF	1973 TGCF	1973 IS	1973 GFCF
					All Producers							
1 Agriculture, hunting, fishing and forestry	...	...	191.0	264.9	68.3	196.6	202.3	44.4	157.9	269.2	112.9	156.3
2 Mining and quarrying	...	...	245.6	324.9	73.7	251.2	257.3	-50.2	307.5	549.2	64.0	485.2
3 Manufacturing	...	...										
4 Electricity, gas and water	...	...	79.1	148.8	6.3	142.5	182.2	10.0	172.2	171.7	2.3	169.4
5 Construction	...	...	81.2	116.5	-	116.5	142.3	-	142.3	131.3	-	131.3
6 Wholesale and retail trade, restaurants and hotels	...	...	86.1	93.0	-	93.0	88.6	-	88.6	116.4	-	116.4
7 Transport, storage and communication	...	...	190.7	244.7	12.5	232.2	304.3	0.2	304.1	433.7	-3.6	437.3
8 Finance, insurance, real estate and business services	...	...	197.8	264.6	-0.2	264.8	249.6	0.6	249.0	362.4	0.9	361.5
9 Community, social and personal services	...	...	46.9	51.6	-	51.6	53.9	-	53.9	49.0	-	49.0
Total Industries	...	...	1118.4	1509.0	160.6	1348.4	1480.1	5.0	1475.1	2082.9	176.5	1906.4
Producers of Government Services	152.5	1.1	151.4	227.9	-2.2	230.1	329.6	4.5	325.1	355.4	10.2	345.2
Private Non-Profit Institutions Serving Households	...	...	...	...	...	...	...	...	...	...	...	...
Total	1339.9	70.1	1269.8	1736.9	158.4	1578.5	1809.7	9.5	1800.2	2438.3	186.7	2251.6

	1974 TGCF	1974 IS	1974 GFCF	1975 TGCF	1975 IS	1975 GFCF	1976 TGCF	1976 IS	1976 GFCF	1977 TGCF	1977 IS	1977 GFCF
					All Producers							
1 Agriculture, hunting, fishing and forestry	353.0	127.6	225.4	341.5	87.6	253.9	283.7	9.3	274.4	275.9	-115.2	391.1
2 Mining and quarrying	763.2	158.2	605.0	328.4	-307.7	636.1	794.0	-5.3	799.3	1346.9	303.2	1043.7
3 Manufacturing												
4 Electricity, gas and water	219.1	24.8	194.3	382.7	78.0	304.7	531.5	-20.1	551.6	671.7	46.8	624.9
5 Construction	201.8	-	201.8	226.4	-	226.4	326.7	-	326.7	328.5	-	328.5
6 Wholesale and retail trade, restaurants and hotels	219.5	-	219.5	134.1	-	134.1	249.4	-	249.4	535.6	236.3	299.3
7 Transport, storage and communication	641.6	24.5	617.1	779.1	39.9	739.2	876.7	36.4	840.3	948.9	-6.8	955.7
8 Finance, insurance, real estate and business services	509.6	4.8	504.8	792.4	5.0	787.4	827.3	2.3	825.0	1016.5	-1.4	1017.9
9 Community, social and personal services	119.9	-	119.9	80.0	-	80.0	91.4	-	91.4	114.8	-	114.8
Total Industries	3027.7	339.9	2687.8	3064.5	-97.2	3161.7	3980.7	22.6	3958.1	5238.8	462.9	4775.9
Producers of Government Services	506.0	19.0	487.0	572.1	39.0	533.1	911.6	23.7	887.9	1151.6	38.7	1112.9
Private Non-Profit Institutions Serving Households	...	...	...	...	...	...	...	...	...	...	...	...
Total	3533.7	358.9	3174.8	3636.7	-58.2	3694.9	4892.3	46.3	4846.0	6390.4	501.6	5888.8

	1978 TGCF	1978 IS	1978 GFCF	1979 TGCF	1979 IS	1979 GFCF
			All Producers			
1 Agriculture, hunting, fishing and forestry	450.0	2.5	447.5	669.6	4.2	665.4
2 Mining and quarrying	1260.3	-29.2	1289.5	1371.3	-315.8	1687.1
3 Manufacturing						
4 Electricity, gas and water	788.6	40.6	748.0	864.5	40.1	824.4
5 Construction	443.8	-	443.8	526.7	-	526.7
6 Wholesale and retail trade, restaurants and hotels	306.9	-	306.9	400.4	-	400.4
7 Transport, storage and communication	1272.3	13.5	1258.8	1382.4	-90.9	1473.3
8 Finance, insurance, real estate and business services	1274.3	2.9	1271.4	1731.4	2.2	1729.2
9 Community, social and personal services	151.4	-	151.4	178.1	-	178.1
Total Industries	5947.6	30.3	5917.3	7124.4	-360.2	7484.6
Producers of Government Services	1136.3	101.2	1035.1	1630.3	65.0	1565.3
Private Non-Profit Institutions Serving Households	...	...	...	...	...	...
Total	7083.9	131.5	6952.4	8754.7	-295.2	9049.9

Costa Rica

2.17 Exports and Imports of Goods and Services, Detail

Million Costa Rican colones

	1970	1971	1972	1973	1974	1975	1976	1977	1978	1979	1980
Exports of Goods and Services											
1 Exports of merchandise, f.o.b.	1529.9	1551.7	2044.1	2620.3	3645.5	4225.2	5076.7	7094.6	7403.8	8074.0	9184.6
2 Transport and communication	70.7	110.5	108.3	114.3	166.3	194.5	238.6	250.3	202.2	195.7	241.8
3 Insurance service charges	0.9	1.0	1.0	0.8	-	-	-	-	-	-	-
4 Other commodities	75.8	91.7	115.8	120.5	173.8	193.8	238.3	251.4	287.8	366.8	454.0
5 Adjustments of merchandise exports to change-of-ownership basis	...	...	...	...	...	...	...	...	...	...	...
6 Direct purchases in the domestic market by non-residential households	163.9	190.1	250.5	306.7	445.7	493.5	527.9	601.7	695.2	717.1	878.1
7 Direct purchases in the domestic market by extraterritorial bodies	...	...	...	...	...	...	...	...	...	...	...
Total Exports of Goods and Services	1841.2	1945.0	2519.7	3162.6	4431.3	5107.0	6081.5	8198.0	8589.0	9353.6	10758.5
Imports of Goods and Services											
1 Imports of merchandise, c.i.f.	2073.0	2378.3	2694.1	3440.9	5909.1	5906.6	6554.1	8718.4	9897.2	11863.8	13684.1
a Imports of merchandise, f.o.b.	1899.3	2185.4	2470.9	3132.2	5374.8	5375.7	5960.2	7928.4	8993.8	10774.2	12423.5
b Transport of services on merchandise imports	159.9	177.0	205.2	286.1	495.3	492.0	550.7	732.8	838.7	1011.4	1170.3
By residents	...	...	...	...	...	...	...	...	...	...	...
By non-residents	159.9	177.0	205.2	286.1	495.3	492.0	550.7	732.8	838.7	1011.4	1170.3
c Insurance service charges on merchandise imports	13.8	15.9	18.0	22.6	39.0	38.9	43.2	57.2	64.7	78.2	90.3
By residents	...	...	...	...	...	...	...	...	...	...	...
By non-residents	13.8	15.9	18.0	22.6	39.0	38.9	43.2	57.2	64.7	78.2	90.3
2 Adjustments of merchandise imports to change-of-ownership basis	...	...	...	...	...	...	...	...	...	...	...
3 Other transport and communication	35.8	74.9	84.3	48.9	77.0	92.7	123.3	138.2	164.9	201.1	224.6
4 Other insurance service charges	...	...	...	...	...	...	...	...	...	...	...
5 Other commodities [a]	69.5	85.7	104.8	91.7	111.5	137.5	159.3	192.4	221.7	257.3	377.6
6 Direct purchases abroad by government	104.6	147.5	165.3	201.1	291.0	374.6	457.9	559.4	651.7	581.8	603.9
7 Direct purchases abroad by resident households											
Total Imports of Goods and Services	2282.9	2686.4	3048.5	3782.6	6388.6	6511.4	7294.6	9608.4	10935.5	12904.0	14890.2
Balance of Goods and Services	-441.7	-741.4	-528.8	-620.0	-1957.3	-1404.4	-1213.1	-1410.4	-2346.5	-3550.4	-4131.7
Total Imports and Balance of Goods and Services	1841.2	1945.0	2519.7	3162.6	4431.3	5107.0	6081.5	8198.0	8589.0	9353.6	10758.5

a) Relating to non-factor services.

3.12 General Government Income and Outlay Account: Total and Subsectors

Million Costa Rican colones

	1970					1971				
	Total General Government	Central Government	State or Provincial Government	Local Government	Social Security Funds	Total General Government	Central Government	State or Provincial Government	Local Government	Social Security Funds
Receipts										
1 Property and entrepreneurial income	27.7	6.3	...	...	...	33.8	4.5	...	...	...
a Net operating surplus	...	...	...	...	...	6.0	...	...	...	...
b Withdrawals from public quasi-corporations	...	...	...	...	...		...	...	...	...
c Interest	...	...	...	...	...	...	...	...	...	...
d Dividends	...	...	...	...	...	...	...	...	...	...
e Net land rent and royalties	...	...	...	...	...	...	...	...	...	...
2 Taxes, fees and contributions	1150.6	850.0	...	...	...	1279.2	890.8	...	...	...
a Indirect taxes	750.7	667.0	...	...	...	801.1	692.0	...	...	...
b Direct taxes	176.0	176.0	...	...	...	192.0	192.0	...	...	...
Income	176.0	176.0	...	...	...	192.0	192.0	...	...	...

Costa Rica

3.12 General Government Income and Outlay Account: Total and Subsectors
(Continued)

Million Costa Rican colones

	1970 Total General Government	1970 Central Government	1970 State or Provincial Government	1970 Local Government	1970 Social Security Funds	1971 Total General Government	1971 Central Government	1971 State or Provincial Government	1971 Local Government	1971 Social Security Funds
Other	-	-	...	...	...	-	-	...	...	...
c Social security contributions	206.4	...	...	...	...	267.9	...	...	...	...
d Fees, fines and penalties	17.5	7.0	...	...	...	18.2	6.8	...	...	...
3 Other current transfers received	14.0	6.5	...	...	...	31.1	21.5	...	...	...
a Casualty insurance claims	...	...	...	...	...	...	...	...	...	...
b Transfers from other government subsectors	...	...	...	...	...	...	...	...	...	...
c Transfers from abroad	4.4	2.9	...	...	...	19.1	17.6	...	...	...
d Other transfers, except imputed	9.6	3.6	...	...	...	12.0	3.9	...	...	...
e Imputed unfunded employee welfare contributions	...	...	...	...	...	...	...	...	...	...
Total Current Receipts	1192.3	862.8	...	...	...	1344.1	916.8	...	...	...

Disbursements

1 General government final consumption expenditures	819.8	544.9	...	...	...	990.0	667.0	...	...	...
a Compensation of employees	...	...	...	...	...	...	...	...	...	...
b Consumption of fixed capital	...	...	...	...	...	...	...	...	...	...
c Goods and services purchased, net	...	...	...	...	...	...	...	...	...	...
Purchases	...	...	...	...	...	...	...	...	...	...
Less: Sales	...	...	...	...	...	...	...	...	...	...
d Less: Own account production of fixed assets	...	...	...	...	...	...	...	...	...	...
e Indirect taxes paid, net	...	...	...	...	...	...	...	...	...	...
2 Property income paid	71.7	69.8	...	...	...	86.4	84.3	...	...	...
a Interest	...	...	...	...	...	86.4	...	...	...	...
b Net land rent and royalties	...	...	...	...	...	...	...	...	...	...
3 Subsidies	25.5	25.5	...	...	...	31.3	31.3	...	...	...
4 Other current transfers paid	106.6	79.5	...	...	...	125.6	87.5	...	...	...
a Casualty insurance premiums, net	...	...	...	...	...	...	...	...	...	...
b Transfers to other government subsectors	...	...	...	...	...	...	...	...	...	...
c Transfers to households	102.5	75.9	...	...	...	120.0	82.3	...	...	...
Social security benefits	19.6	...	...	...	...	25.4	...	...	...	...
Social assistance grants	34.1	27.1	...	...	...	31.5	19.2	...	...	...
Unfunded employee welfare benefits [a]	48.8	48.8	...	...	...	63.1	63.1	...	...	...
d Transfers to private non-profit institutions serving households	...	...	...	...	...	...	...	...	...	...
e Transfers to the rest of the world	4.1	3.6	...	...	...	5.6	5.2	...	...	...
Net saving	168.7	143.1	...	...	...	110.8	46.7	...	...	...
Total Current Disbursements and Net Saving	1192.3	862.8	...	...	...	1344.1	916.8	...	...	...

	1972 Total General Government	1972 Central Government	1972 State or Provincial Government	1972 Local Government	1972 Social Security Funds	1973 Total General Government	1973 Central Government	1973 State or Provincial Government	1973 Local Government	1973 Social Security Funds

Receipts

1 Property and entrepreneurial income	36.5	3.7	...	...	...	44.3	6.9	...	...	...
a Net operating surplus	5.0		...	...	...	9.7		...	...	...
b Withdrawals from public quasi-corporations			...	...	...			...	...	...
c Interest	...	...	...	...	...	...	...	...	...	...
d Dividends	...	...	...	...	...	...	...	...	...	...
e Net land rent and royalties	...	...	...	...	...	...	...	...	...	...
2 Taxes, fees and contributions	1554.1	1032.6	...	...	...	2023.3	1399.9	...	...	...
a Indirect taxes	919.1	793.4	...	...	...	1213.8	1067.4	...	...	...
b Direct taxes	233.1	233.1	...	...	...	324.5	324.5	...	...	...
Income	233.1	233.1	...	...	...	324.5	324.5	...	...	...

Costa Rica

3.12 General Government Income and Outlay Account: Total and Subsectors
(Continued)

Million Costa Rican colones

	1972					1973				
	Total General Government	Central Government	State or Provincial Government	Local Government	Social Security Funds	Total General Government	Central Government	State or Provincial Government	Local Government	Social Security Funds
Other	-	-	...	...	...	-	-	...	...	...
c Social security contributions	378.3	...	...	...	...	459.2	...	...	...	...
d Fees, fines and penalties	23.6	6.1	...	...	...	25.8	8.0	...	...	...
3 Other current transfers received	27.0	15.1	...	...	...	25.4	9.7	...	...	...
a Casualty insurance claims	...	...	...	...	...	...	...	...	...	...
b Transfers from other government subsectors	...	...	...	...	...	...	...	...	...	...
c Transfers from abroad	12.3	11.6	...	...	...	8.4	6.8	...	...	...
d Other transfers, except imputed	14.7	3.5	...	...	...	17.0	2.9	...	...	...
e Imputed unfunded employee welfare contributions	...	...	...	...	...	...	...	...	...	...
Total Current Receipts	1617.6	1051.4	...	...	...	2093.0	1416.5	...	...	...

Disbursements

1 General government final consumption expenditures	1182.0	750.5	...	...	...	1417.1	893.9	...	...	...
a Compensation of employees	...	...	...	...	...	...	...	...	...	...
b Consumption of fixed capital	...	...	...	...	...	...	...	...	...	...
c Goods and services purchased, net	...	...	...	...	...	...	...	...	...	...
Purchases	...	...	...	...	...	...	...	...	...	...
Less: Sales	...	...	...	...	...	...	...	...	...	...
d Less: Own account production of fixed assets	...	...	...	...	...	...	...	...	...	...
e Indirect taxes paid, net	...	...	...	...	...	...	...	...	...	...
2 Property income paid	95.9	93.2	...	...	...	122.3	118.5	...	...	...
a Interest	95.9	...	...	...	...	122.3	...	...	...	...
b Net land rent and royalties	...	...	...	...	...	...	...	...	...	...
3 Subsidies	36.0	36.0	...	...	...	46.8	46.8	...	...	...
4 Other current transfers paid	189.6	129.1	...	...	...	281.8	203.3	...	...	...
a Casualty insurance premiums, net	...	...	...	...	...	...	...	...	...	...
b Transfers to other government subsectors	...	...	...	...	...	...	...	...	...	...
c Transfers to households	179.8	120.4	...	...	...	271.4	193.6	...	...	...
Social security benefits	41.6	...	...	...	...	56.7	...	...	...	...
Social assistance grants	49.7	31.9	...	...	...	108.0	86.9	...	...	...
Unfunded employee welfare benefits [a]	88.5	88.5	...	...	...	106.7	106.7	...	...	...
d Transfers to private non-profit institutions serving households	...	...	...	...	...	...	...	...	...	...
e Transfers to the rest of the world	9.8	8.7	...	...	...	10.4	9.7	...	...	...
Net saving	114.1	42.6	...	...	...	225.0	154.0	...	...	...
Total Current Disbursements and Net Saving	1617.6	1051.4	...	...	...	2093.0	1416.5	...	...	...

	1974					1975				
	Total General Government	Central Government	State or Provincial Government	Local Government	Social Security Funds	Total General Government	Central Government	State or Provincial Government	Local Government	Social Security Funds

Receipts

1 Property and entrepreneurial income	78.7	35.9	...	...	...	90.5	32.9	...	...	...
a Net operating surplus	17.2	...	...	...	...	9.0	...	...	...	...
b Withdrawals from public quasi-corporations		...	...	...	...		...	...	...	...
c Interest	...	...	...	...	...	...	...	...	...	...
d Dividends	...	...	...	...	...	...	...	...	...	...
e Net land rent and royalties	...	...	...	...	...	...	...	...	...	...
2 Taxes, fees and contributions	2707.1	1930.4	...	...	...	3413.7	2206.1	...	...	...
a Indirect taxes	1688.1	1521.7	...	...	...	2153.4	1746.5	...	...	...
b Direct taxes	398.7	398.7	...	...	...	447.4	447.4	...	...	...
Income	398.7	398.7	...	...	...	447.4	447.4	...	...	...

Costa Rica

3.12 General Government Income and Outlay Account: Total and Subsectors
(Continued)

Million Costa Rican colones

		1974				1975				
	Total General Government	Central Government	State or Provincial Government	Local Government	Social Security Funds	Total General Government	Central Government	State or Provincial Government	Local Government	Social Security Funds
Other	-	-	...	...	...	-	-	...	...	...
c Social security contributions	585.3	...	...	...	...	776.3	...	...	...	...
d Fees, fines and penalties	35.0	10.0	...	...	...	36.6	12.2	...	...	...
3 Other current transfers received	35.5	16.6	...	...	...	40.2	18.3	...	...	...
a Casualty insurance claims	...	...	...	...	...	...	...	...	...	...
b Transfers from other government subsectors	...	...	...	...	...	...	...	...	...	...
c Transfers from abroad	15.0	14.7	...	...	...	14.8	12.8	...	...	...
d Other transfers, except imputed	20.5	1.9	...	...	...	25.4	5.5	...	...	...
e Imputed unfunded employee welfare contributions	...	...	...	...	...	...	...	...	...	...
Total Current Receipts	2821.3	1982.9	...	...	...	3544.4	2257.3	...	...	...

Disbursements

1 General governement final consumption expenditures	1889.0	1187.6	...	...	...	2557.9	1507.4	...	...	...
a Compensation of employees	...	...	...	...	...	...	...	...	...	...
b Consumption of fixed capital	...	...	...	...	...	...	...	...	...	...
c Goods and services purchased, net	...	...	...	...	...	...	...	...	...	...
Purchases	...	...	...	...	...	...	...	...	...	...
Less: Sales	...	...	...	...	...	...	...	...	...	...
d Less: Own account production of fixed assets	...	...	...	...	...	...	...	...	...	...
e Indirect taxes paid, net	...	...	...	...	...	...	...	...	...	...
2 Property income paid	175.2	170.4	...	...	...	201.8	195.0	...	...	...
a Interest	175.2	...	...	...	...	201.8	...	...	...	...
b Net land rent and royalties	...	...	...	...	...	...	...	...	...	...
3 Subsidies	26.4	26.4	...	...	...	36.0	36.0	...	...	...
4 Other current transfers paid	202.1	101.0	...	...	...	242.5	90.3	...	...	...
a Casualty insurance premiums, net	...	...	...	...	...	...	...	...	...	...
b Transfers to other government subsectors	...	...	...	...	...	...	...	...	...	...
c Transfers to households	195.0	94.6	...	...	...	229.4	77.7	...	...	...
Social security benefits	79.0	...	...	...	...	105.6	...	...	...	...
Social assistance grants	52.2	30.8	...	...	...	101.5	56.1	...	...	...
Unfunded employee welfare benefits [a]	63.8	63.8	...	...	...	22.3	21.6	...	...	...
d Transfers to private non-profit institutions serving households	...	...	...	...	...	...	...	...	...	...
e Transfers to the rest of the world	7.1	6.4	...	...	...	13.1	12.6	...	...	...
Net saving	528.6	497.5	...	...	...	506.2	428.6	...	...	...
Total Current Disbursements and Net Saving	2821.3	1982.9	...	...	...	3544.4	2257.3	...	...	...

		1976				1977				
	Total General Government	Central Government	State or Provincial Government	Local Government	Social Security Funds	Total General Government	Central Government	State or Provincial Government	Local Government	Social Security Funds

Receipts

1 Property and entrepreneurial income	110.5	36.5	...	...	...	149.5	61.2	...	...	...
a Net operating surplus	17.0	...	...	...	...	31.9	...	...	...	...
b Withdrawals from public quasi-corporations		...	...	...	...		...	...	...	...
c Interest	...	...	...	...	...	...	...	...	...	...
d Dividends	...	...	...	...	...	...	...	...	...	...
e Net land rent and royalties	...	...	...	...	...	...	...	...	...	...
2 Taxes, fees and contributions	4365.4	2708.6	...	...	...	5597.6	3473.1	...	...	...
a Indirect taxes	2678.4	2067.9	...	...	...	3474.6	2670.4	...	...	...
b Direct taxes	624.9	624.9	...	...	...	784.8	784.8	...	...	...
Income	624.9	624.9	...	...	...	784.8	784.8	...	...	...

Costa Rica

3.12 General Government Income and Outlay Account: Total and Subsectors
(Continued)

Million Costa Rican colones

	1976					1977				
	Total General Government	Central Government	State or Provincial Government	Local Government	Social Security Funds	Total General Government	Central Government	State or Provincial Government	Local Government	Social Security Funds
Other	...	...	...	...	...	...	...	...	...	...
c Social security contributions	1028.7	...	...	...	...	1296.8	...	...	...	...
d Fees, fines and penalties	33.4	15.8	...	...	...	41.4	17.9	...	...	...
3 Other current transfers received	51.4	18.6	...	...	...	46.2	3.7	...	...	...
a Casualty insurance claims	...	...	...	...	...	...	...	...	...	...
b Transfers from other government subsectors	...	...	...	...	...	...	...	...	...	...
c Transfers from abroad	25.2	16.2	...	...	...	15.2	0.2	...	...	...
d Other transfers, except imputed	26.2	2.4	...	...	...	31.0	3.5	...	...	...
e Imputed unfunded employee welfare contributions	...	...	...	...	...	...	...	...	...	...
Total Current Receipts	4527.3	2763.7	...	...	...	5793.3	3538.0	...	...	...

Disbursements

1 General government final consumption expenditures	3306.4	1848.5	...	...	...	4208.1	2350.7	...	...	...
a Compensation of employees	...	...	...	...	...	...	...	...	...	...
b Consumption of fixed capital	...	...	...	...	...	...	...	...	...	...
c Goods and services purchased, net	...	...	...	...	...	...	...	...	...	...
Purchases	...	...	...	...	...	...	...	...	...	...
Less: Sales	...	...	...	...	...	...	...	...	...	...
d Less: Own account production of fixed assets	...	...	...	...	...	...	...	...	...	...
e Indirect taxes paid, net	...	...	...	...	...	...	...	...	...	...
2 Property income paid	245.0	226.7	...	...	...	334.4	316.0	...	...	...
a Interest	245.0	...	...	...	...	334.4	...	...	...	...
b Net land rent and royalties	...	...	...	...	...	...	...	...	...	...
3 Subsidies	113.3	113.3	...	...	...	65.0	72.2	...	...	...
4 Other current transfers paid	359.8	107.2	...	...	...	501.9	162.9	...	...	...
a Casualty insurance premiums, net	...	...	...	...	...	...	...	...	...	...
b Transfers to other government subsectors	...	...	...	...	...	...	...	...	...	...
c Transfers to households	352.0	101.4	...	...	...	490.1	149.2	...	...	...
Social security benefits	146.4	...	...	...	...	192.4	...	...	...	...
Social assistance grants	170.2	71.0	...	...	...	238.0	112.1	...	...	...
Unfunded employee welfare benefits [a]	35.4	30.4	...	...	...	59.7	37.1	...	...	...
d Transfers to private non-profit institutions serving households	...	...	...	...	...	...	...	...	...	...
e Transfers to the rest of the world	7.8	5.8	...	...	...	11.8	13.7	...	...	...
Net saving	502.6	468.0	...	...	...	683.0	636.2	...	...	...
Total Current Disbursements and Net Saving	4527.3	2763.7	...	...	...	5793.3	3538.0	...	...	...

	1978					1979				
	Total General Government	Central Government	State or Provincial Government	Local Government	Social Security Funds	Total General Government	Central Government	State or Provincial Government	Local Government	Social Security Funds

Receipts

1 Property and entrepreneurial income	214.2	...	...	...	...	286.2	...	...	...	...
a Net operating surplus	29.9	...	...	...	...	25.2	...	...	...	...
b Withdrawals from public quasi-corporations		...	...	...	...		...	...	...	...
c Interest	...	...	...	...	...	...	...	...	...	...
d Dividends	...	...	...	...	...	...	...	...	...	...
e Net land rent and royalties	...	...	...	...	...	...	...	...	...	...
2 Taxes, fees and contributions	6617.9	3941.1	...	...	...	7436.6	4165.0	...	...	...
a Indirect taxes	4086.9	2990.8	...	...	...	4430.4	3172.9	...	...	...
b Direct taxes	925.9	925.9	...	...	...	945.4	945.4	...	...	...
Income	925.9	925.9	...	...	...	...	...	...	...	...

Costa Rica

3.12 General Government Income and Outlay Account: Total and Subsectors
(Continued)

Million Costa Rican colones

	1978 Total General Government	1978 Central Government	1978 State or Provincial Government	1978 Local Government	1978 Social Security Funds	1979 Total General Government	1979 Central Government	1979 State or Provincial Government	1979 Local Government	1979 Social Security Funds
Other	...	...	...	...	...	...	...	...	...	...
c Social security contributions	1564.2	...	...	...	...	1989.9	...	...	...	...
d Fees, fines and penalties	40.9	24.4	...	...	...	70.9	46.7	...	...	...
3 Other current transfers received	53.5	6.0	...	...	...	81.1	...	...	...	...
a Casualty insurance claims	...	...	...	...	...	...	...	...	...	...
b Transfers from other government subsectors	...	...	...	...	...	...	...	...	...	...
c Transfers from abroad	16.2	0.7	...	...	...	19.2	...	...	...	...
d Other transfers, except imputed	37.3	5.3	...	...	...	61.9	8.6	...	...	...
e Imputed unfunded employee welfare contributions	...	...	...	...	...	...	...	...	...	...
Total Current Receipts	6885.6	4060.8	...	...	...	7803.9	4305.0	...	...	...

Disbursements

1 General government final consumption expenditures	5068.6	2808.0	...	...	...	6243.2	3211.3	...	...	...
a Compensation of employees	...	...	...	...	...	...	...	...	...	...
b Consumption of fixed capital	...	...	...	...	...	...	...	...	...	...
c Goods and services purchased, net	...	...	...	...	...	...	...	...	...	...
Purchases	...	...	...	...	...	...	...	...	...	...
Less: Sales	...	...	...	...	...	...	...	...	...	...
d Less: Own account production of fixed assets	...	...	...	...	...	...	...	...	...	...
e Indirect taxes paid, net	...	...	...	...	...	...	...	...	...	...
2 Property income paid	549.6	530.8	...	...	...	764.6	727.0	...	...	...
a Interest	549.6	530.8	...	...	...	764.6	...	...	...	...
b Net land rent and royalties	...	...	...	...	...	...	...	...	...	...
3 Subsidies	87.0	100.4	...	...	...	215.1	248.9	...	...	...
4 Other current transfers paid	592.4	170.5	...	...	...	753.7	...	...	...	...
a Casualty insurance premiums, net	...	...	...	...	...	...	...	...	...	...
b Transfers to other government subsectors	...	...	...	...	...	...	...	...	...	...
c Transfers to households	582.6	155.2	...	...	...	697.2	...	...	...	...
Social security benefits	283.0	...	...	...	...	268.5	...	...	...	...
Social assistance grants	269.1	114.0	...	...	...	381.1	145.8	...	...	...
Unfunded employee welfare benefits [a]	30.5	41.2	...	...	...	47.6	...	...	...	...
d Transfers to private non-profit institutions serving households	...	...	...	...	...	...	...	...	...	...
e Transfers to the rest of the world	9.8	15.3	...	...	...	56.5	19.7	...	...	...
Net saving	588.0	451.0	...	...	...	-172.7	-95.2	...	...	...
Total Current Disbursements and Net Saving	6885.6	4060.8	...	...	...	7803.9	4305.0	...	...	...

	1980 Total General Government	1980 Central Government	1980 State or Provincial Government	1980 Local Government	1980 Social Security Funds

Receipts

1 Property and entrepreneurial income	504.8	...	...	...	...
a Net operating surplus	...	...	...	...	...
b Withdrawals from public quasi-corporations	459.9	...	...	...	...
c Interest	...	...	...	...	...
d Dividends	...	...	...	...	...
e Net land rent and royalties	44.9	...	...	...	...
2 Taxes, fees and contributions	8606.8	...	...	...	...
a Indirect taxes	5245.3	...	...	...	...
b Direct taxes	1013.7	...	...	...	...
Income	1013.7	...	...	...	...

Costa Rica

3.12 General Government Income and Outlay Account: Total and Subsectors
(Continued)

Million Costa Rican colones

	1980 Total General Government	Central Government	State or Provincial Government	Local Government	Social Security Funds
Other	-	...	...	...	...
c Social security contributions	2274.4	...	...	...	...
d Fees, fines and penalties	73.4	...	...	...	...
3 Other current transfers received	105.5	...	...	...	...
a Casualty insurance claims	...	...	...	...	...
b Transfers from other government subsectors	...	...	...	...	...
c Transfers from abroad	25.3	...	...	...	...
d Other transfers, except imputed	80.2	...	...	...	...
e Imputed unfunded employee welfare contributions	...	...	...	...	...
Total Current Receipts	9217.1	...	...	...	...

Disbursements

1 General governement final consumption expenditures	7544.3	...	...	...	...
a Compensation of employees	6474.6	...	...	...	...
b Consumption of fixed capital	-	...	...	...	...
c Goods and services purchased, net	1069.7	...	...	...	...
Purchases	1638.6	...	...	...	...
Less: Sales	568.9	...	...	...	...
d Less: Own account production of fixed assets	...	...	...	...	...
e Indirect taxes paid, net	...	...	...	...	...
2 Property income paid	1211.6	...	...	...	...
a Interest	1211.6	...	...	...	...
b Net land rent and royalties	-	...	...	...	...
3 Subsidies	383.0	...	...	...	...
4 Other current transfers paid	752.1	...	...	...	...
a Casualty insurance premiums, net	...	...	...	...	...
b Transfers to other government subsectors	...	...	...	...	...
c Transfers to households	450.8	...	...	...	...
Social security benefits	357.9	...	...	...	...
Social assistance grants	56.2	...	...	...	...
Unfunded employee welfare benefits [a]	36.7	...	...	...	...
d Transfers to private non-profit institutions serving households	225.6	...	...	...	...
e Transfers to the rest of the world	75.7	...	...	...	...
Net saving	-673.9	...	...	...	...
Total Current Disbursements and Net Saving	9217.1	...	...	...	...

a) Relating to social security contributions rather than unfunded employee welfare benefits.

4.3 Derivation of Value Added by Kind of Activity, ISIC Divisions, in Current Prices

Million Costa Rican colones

	1970 Gross Output	1970 Intermediate Consumption	1970 Value Added	1971 Gross Output	1971 Intermediate Consumption	1971 Value Added	1972 Gross Output	1972 Intermediate Consumption	1972 Value Added	1973 Gross Output	1973 Intermediate Consumption	1973 Value Added
All Producers												
1 Agriculture, hunting, forestry and fishing	...	...	1469.3	...	...	1443.4	...	...	1601.6	...	...	1962.9
a Agriculture and hunting	...	...	1407.3	...	...	1370.0	...	...	1520.5	...	...	1867.1
b Forestry and logging	...	...	53.7	...	...	62.9	...	...	69.8	...	...	81.6
c Fishing	...	...	8.3	...	...	10.5	...	...	11.3	...	...	14.2
2 Mining and quarrying	...	...	7.2	...	...	9.4	...	...	16.0	...	...	19.0

Costa Rica

4.3 Derivation of Value Added by Kind of Activity, ISIC Divisions, in Current Prices
(Continued)

Million Costa Rican colones

	1970 Gross Output	1970 Intermediate Consumption	1970 Value Added	1971 Gross Output	1971 Intermediate Consumption	1971 Value Added	1972 Gross Output	1972 Intermediate Consumption	1972 Value Added	1973 Gross Output	1973 Intermediate Consumption	1973 Value Added
3 Manufacturing	...	...	1185.0	...	...	1315.6	...	...	1491.1	...	...	1884.3
a Manufacture of food, beverages and tobacco	...	...	564.7	...	...	606.6	...	...	684.6	...	...	881.8
b Textile, wearing apparel and leather industries	...	...	146.2	...	...	164.7	...	...	179.4	...	...	220.4
c Manufacture of wood and wood products, including furniture	...	...	80.0	...	...	88.9	...	...	102.9	...	...	128.6
d Manufacture of paper and paper products, printing and publishing	...	...	56.8	...	...	61.4	...	...	70.1	...	...	104.6
e Manufacture of chemicals and chemical petroleum, coal, rubber and plastic products	...	...	152.8	...	...	182.6	...	...	213.7	...	...	272.1
f Manufacture of non-metallic mineral products, except products of petroleum and coal	...	...	61.5	...	...	68.1	...	...	81.2	...	...	77.5
g Basic metal industries	...	...	4.0	...	...	4.9	...	...	6.1	...	...	12.8
h Manufacture of fabricated metal products, machinery and equipment	...	...	108.6	...	...	127.8	...	...	143.3	...	...	176.0
i Other manufacturing industries	...	...	10.4	...	...	10.6	...	...	9.8	...	...	10.5
4 Electricity, gas and water	...	...	109.8	...	...	127.8	...	...	147.9	...	...	160.3
a Electricity, gas and steam	...	...	100.8	...	...	117.8	...	...	138.6	...	...	149.3
b Water works and supply	...	...	9.0	...	...	10.0	...	...	9.3	...	...	11.0
5 Construction	...	...	277.4	...	...	343.3	...	...	423.8	...	...	507.1
6 Wholesale and retail trade, restaurants and hotels	...	...	1371.3	...	...	1502.0	...	...	1651.3	...	...	2054.5
a Wholesale and retail trade	...	...	1261.5	...	...	1378.8	...	...	1512.0	...	...	1882.1
b Restaurants and hotels	...	...	109.8	...	...	123.2	...	...	139.3	...	...	172.4
7 Transport, storage and communication	...	...	274.2	...	...	316.0	...	...	362.0	...	...	435.6
a Transport and storage	...	...	...	...	...	...	...	...	...	...	...	...
b Communication	...	...	...	...	...	...	...	...	...	...	...	...
8 Finance, insurance, real estate and business services	...	...	801.4	...	...	845.9	...	...	957.9	...	...	1135.0
a Financial institutions	...	...	...	...	...	...	...	...	...	...	...	...
b Insurance	...	...	...	...	...	...	...	...	...	...	...	...
c Real estate and business services	...	...	...	...	...	...	...	...	...	...	...	...
9 Community, social and personal services	...	...	245.9	...	...	280.4	...	...	319.3	...	...	384.4
Total, Industries	...	...	5741.5	...	...	6183.8	...	...	6970.9	...	...	8543.1
Producers of Government Services	...	...	693.2	...	...	813.6	...	...	998.0	...	...	1196.6
Other Producers	...	...	89.8	...	...	94.8	...	...	100.8	...	...	111.5
Total	...	...	6524.5	...	...	7092.2	...	...	8069.7	...	...	9851.2
Imputed bank service charge	...	...	...	...	...	...	...	...	...	...	...	...
Import duties	...	...	...	...	...	...	...	...	...	...	...	...
Value added tax	...	...	...	...	...	...	...	...	...	...	...	...
Other adjustments	...	...	.	...	...	44.8	...	...	146.1	...	...	311.2
Total	...	...	6524.5	...	...	7137.0	...	...	8215.8	...	...	10162.4

	1974 Gross Output	1974 Intermediate Consumption	1974 Value Added	1975 Gross Output	1975 Intermediate Consumption	1975 Value Added	1976 Gross Output	1976 Intermediate Consumption	1976 Value Added	1977 Gross Output	1977 Intermediate Consumption	1977 Value Added
					All Producers							
1 Agriculture, hunting, forestry and fishing	...	...	2522.4	...	...	3417.8	...	...	4212.9	...	...	5762.6
a Agriculture and hunting	...	...	2384.9	...	...	3230.8	...	...	3976.1	...	...	5545.3
b Forestry and logging	...	...	116.2	...	...	160.5	...	...	198.7	...	...	191.8
c Fishing	...	...	21.3	...	...	26.5	...	...	38.1	...	...	25.5
2 Mining and quarrying	...	...	24.5	...	...	38.6	...	...	40.6	...	...	53.2

Costa Rica

4.3 Derivation of Value Added by Kind of Activity, ISIC Divisions, in Current Prices
(Continued)

Million Costa Rican colones

	1974 Gross Output	1974 Intermediate Consumption	1974 Value Added	1975 Gross Output	1975 Intermediate Consumption	1975 Value Added	1976 Gross Output	1976 Intermediate Consumption	1976 Value Added	1977 Gross Output	1977 Intermediate Consumption	1977 Value Added
3 Manufacturing	...	...	2653.4	...	...	3388.7	...	...	4031.5	...	...	4947.1
a Manufacture of food, beverages and tobacco	...	...	1206.0	...	...	1514.3	...	...	1826.2	...	...	2341.3
b Textile, wearing apparel and leather industries	...	...	308.7	...	...	400.7	...	...	476.0	...	...	560.2
c Manufacture of wood and wood products, including furniture	...	...	227.5	...	...	320.4	...	...	405.1	...	...	391.7
d Manufacture of paper and paper products, printing and publishing	...	...	122.6	...	...	132.8	...	...	170.2	...	...	213.8
e Manufacture of chemicals and chemical petroleum, coal, rubber and plastic products	...	...	414.5	...	...	579.0	...	...	603.5	...	...	740.7
f Manufacture of non-metallic mineral products, except products of petroleum and coal	...	...	90.4	...	...	123.8	...	...	152.2	...	...	203.7
g Basic metal industries	...	...	14.0	...	...	14.6	...	...	20.7	...	...	13.3
h Manufacture of fabricated metal products, machinery and equipment	...	...	251.6	...	...	288.7	...	...	359.8	...	...	462.5
i Other manufacturing industries	...	...	18.1	...	...	14.4	...	...	17.8	...	...	19.9
4 Electricity, gas and water	...	...	205.9	...	...	303.7	...	...	409.6	...	...	521.4
a Electricity, gas and steam	...	...	186.5	...	...	272.4	...	...	363.3	...	...	456.3
b Water works and supply	...	...	19.4	...	...	31.3	...	...	46.3	...	...	65.1
5 Construction	...	...	692.6	...	...	868.9	...	...	1193.4	...	...	1367.1
6 Wholesale and retail trade, restaurants and hotels	...	...	2754.7	...	...	3203.6	...	...	3832.2	...	...	5134.6
a Wholesale and retail trade	...	...	2560.9	...	...	2954.4	...	...	3537.7	...	...	4748.1
b Restaurants and hotels	...	...	193.8	...	...	249.2	...	...	294.5	...	...	386.5
7 Transport, storage and communication	...	...	590.7	...	...	788.6	...	...	954.7	...	...	1091.2
a Transport and storage	...	...	...	...	...	...	...	...	...	...	...	...
b Communication	...	...	...	...	...	...	...	...	...	...	...	...
8 Finance, insurance, real estate and business services	...	...	1420.1	...	...	1940.4	...	...	2411.9	...	...	2953.4
a Financial institutions	...	...	...	...	...	...	...	...	...	...	...	...
b Insurance	...	...	...	...	...	...	...	...	...	...	...	...
c Real estate and business services	...	...	...	...	...	...	...	...	...	...	...	...
9 Community, social and personal services	...	...	470.3	...	...	572.5	...	...	684.5	...	...	850.0
Total, Industries	...	...	11334.6	...	...	14522.8	...	...	17771.3	...	...	22680.6
Producers of Government Services	...	...	1576.4	...	...	2083.7	...	...	2682.2	...	...	3402.0
Other Producers	...	...	156.4	...	...	198.1	...	...	222.1	...	...	248.1
Total	...	...	13067.4	...	...	16804.6	...	...	20675.6	...	...	26330.7
Imputed bank service charge	...	...	...	...	...	...	...	...	...	...	...	...
Import duties	...	...	...	...	...	...	...	...	...	...	...	...
Value added tax	...	...	...	...	...	...	...	...	...	...	...	...
Other adjustments	...	...	148.3	...	...	-	...	...	-	...	...	-
Total	...	...	13215.7	...	...	16804.6	...	...	20675.6	...	...	26330.7

	1978 Gross Output	1978 Intermediate Consumption	1978 Value Added	1979 Gross Output	1979 Intermediate Consumption	1979 Value Added	1980 Gross Output	1980 Intermediate Consumption	1980 Value Added

All Producers

1 Agriculture, hunting, forestry and fishing	...	...	6163.7	...	...	6398.6	...	...	7204.8
a Agriculture and hunting	...	...	5909.8	...	...	6068.4	...	...	...
b Forestry and logging	...	...	188.8	...	...	244.5	...	...	...
c Fishing	...	...	65.1	...	...	85.7	...	...	...

Costa Rica

4.3 Derivation of Value Added by Kind of Activity, ISIC Divisions, in Current Prices
(Continued)

Million Costa Rican colones

	1978 Gross Output	1978 Intermediate Consumption	1978 Value Added	1979 Gross Output	1979 Intermediate Consumption	1979 Value Added	1980 Gross Output	1980 Intermediate Consumption	1980 Value Added
2 Mining and quarrying	...	...	5657.8	...	...	6331.5	...	...	8123.3
3 Manufacturing	...	...		...	...		...	...	
a Manufacture of food, beverages and tobacco	...	...	...	...	...	2704.4	...	...	...
b Textile, wearing apparel and leather industries	...	...	...	...	...	572.4	...	...	...
c Manufacture of wood and wood products, including furniture	...	...	...	...	...	414.4	...	...	...
d Manufacture of paper and paper products, printing and publishing	...	...	...	...	...	264.0	...	...	...
e Manufacture of chemicals and chemical petroleum, coal, rubber and plastic products	...	...	...	...	...	887.3	...	...	...
f Manufacture of non-metallic mineral products, except products of petroleum and coal	...	...	...	...	...	240.7	...	...	...
g Basic metal industries	...	...	...	...	...	19.1	...	...	...
h Manufacture of fabricated metal products, machinery and equipment	...	...	...	...	...	561.8	...	...	...
i Other manufacturing industries	...	...	...	...	...	16.9	...	...	...
4 Electricity, gas and water	...	...	549.7	...	...	602.8	...	...	730.5
a Electricity, gas and steam	...	...	...	...	...	...	...	...	...
b Water works and supply	...	...	...	...	...	...	...	...	...
5 Construction	...	...	1663.3	...	...	2215.6	...	...	2675.2
6 Wholesale and retail trade, restaurants and hotels	...	...	5949.9	...	...	7056.4	...	...	8313.2
a Wholesale and retail trade	...	...	5949.9	...	...	7056.4	...	...	...
b Restaurants and hotels	...	...		...	...		...	...	
7 Transport, storage and communication	...	...	1277.0	...	...	1444.6	...	...	1792.7
a Transport and storage	...	...	1277.0	...	...	1444.6	...	...	...
b Communication	...	...	...	...	...	...	...	...	...
8 Finance, insurance, real estate and business services	...	...	3407.0	...	...	3781.0	...	...	4456.6
a Financial institutions	...	...	1574.1	...	...	1714.5	...	...	...
b Insurance	...	...	...	...	...	...	...	...	...
c Real estate and business services	...	...	1832.9	...	...	2066.5	...	...	...
9 Community, social and personal services	...	...	5525.5	...	...	6753.9	...	...	8238.6
Total, Industries	...	...	...	...	...	...	...	...	...
Producers of Government Services	...	...	...	...	...	...	...	...	...
Other Producers	...	...	...	...	...	...	...	...	...
Total	...	...	30193.9	...	...	34584.4	...	...	41534.9
Imputed bank service charge	...	...	...	...	...	...	...	...	...
Import duties	...	...	...	...	...	...	...	...	...
Value added tax	...	...	...	...	...	...	...	...	...
Other adjustments	...	...	...	...	...	...	...	...	...
Total	...	...	30193.9	...	...	34584.4	...	...	41534.9

4.6 Cost Components of Value Added, ISIC Divisions

Million Costa Rican colones

	1970 Compensation of Employees	1970 Capital Consumption	1970 Net Operating Surplus	1970 Indirect Taxes	1970 Less: Subsidies Received	1970 Value Added	1971 Compensation of Employees	1971 Capital Consumption	1971 Net Operating Surplus	1971 Indirect Taxes	1971 Less: Subsidies Received	1971 Value Added
					All Producers							
1 Agriculture, hunting, forestry and fishing	622.4	...	846.9	...	...	1469.3	587.5	...	855.9	...	...	1443.4
a Agriculture and hunting	...	...	...	...	...	1407.3	...	...	...	...	...	1370.0
b Forestry and logging	...	...	...	...	...	53.7	...	...	...	...	...	62.9
c Fishing	...	...	...	...	...	8.3	...	...	...	...	...	10.5
2 Mining and quarrying	3.3	...	3.9	...	...	7.2	4.3	...	5.1	...	...	9.4

Costa Rica

4.6 Cost Components of Value Added, ISIC Divisions
(Continued)

Million Costa Rican colones

	1970						1971					
	Compensation of Employees	Capital Consumption	Net Operating Surplus	Indirect Taxes	Less: Subsidies Received	Value Added	Compensation of Employees	Capital Consumption	Net Operating Surplus	Indirect Taxes	Less: Subsidies Received	Value Added
3 Manufacturing	464.4	...	720.6	...	...	1185.0	526.2	...	789.4	...	...	1315.6
a Manufacture of food, beverages and tobacco	162.1	...	402.6	...	...	564.7	179.3	...	427.3	...	...	606.6
b Textile, wearing apparel and leather industries	79.7	...	66.5	...	...	146.2	90.2	...	74.5	...	...	164.7
c Manufacture of wood and wood products, including furniture	43.4	...	36.6	...	...	80.0	48.5	...	40.4	...	...	88.9
d Manufacture of paper and paper products, printing and publishing	27.7	...	29.1	...	...	56.8	30.0	...	31.4	...	...	61.4
e Manufacture of chemicals and chemical petroleum, coal, rubber and plastic products	63.3	...	89.5	...	...	152.8	75.2	...	107.4	...	...	182.6
f Manufacture of non-metallic mineral products, except products of petroleum and coal	28.2	...	33.3	...	...	61.5	31.5	...	36.6	...	...	68.1
g Basic metal industries	...	...	...	...	...	4.0	...	...	...	...	...	4.9
h Manufacture of fabricated metal products, machinery and equipment	...	...	...	...	...	108.6	...	...	...	...	...	127.8
i Other manufacturing industries	4.8	...	5.6	...	...	10.4	5.0	...	5.6	...	...	10.6
4 Electricity, gas and water	43.4	...	66.4	...	...	109.8	55.6	...	72.2	...	...	127.8
a Electricity, gas and steam	...	...	...	...	...	100.8	...	...	...	...	...	117.8
b Water works and supply	...	...	...	...	...	9.0	...	...	...	...	...	10.0
5 Construction	204.8	...	72.6	...	...	277.4	257.5	...	85.8	...	...	343.3
6 Wholesale and retail trade, restaurants and hotels	491.5	...	879.8	...	...	1371.3	552.8	...	949.2	...	...	1502.0
a Wholesale and retail trade	...	...	...	...	...	1261.5	...	...	...	...	...	1378.8
b Restaurants and hotels	...	...	...	...	...	109.8	...	...	...	...	...	123.2
7 Transport, storage and communication	169.2	...	105.0	...	...	274.2	203.8	...	112.2	...	...	316.0
8 Finance, insurance, real estate and business services	165.4	...	636.0	...	...	801.4	187.8	...	658.1	...	...	845.9
9 Community, social and personal services	110.1	...	135.8	...	...	245.9	139.7	...	140.7	...	...	280.4
Total, Industries	2274.5	...	3467.0	...	...	5741.5	2515.2	...	3668.6	...	...	6183.8
Producers of Government Services	693.2	...	...	...	...	693.2	813.6	...	...	...	...	813.6
Other Producers	89.8	...	...	...	...	89.8	94.8	...	...	...	...	94.8
Total	3057.5	...	3467.0	...	...	6524.5	3423.6	...	3668.6	...	...	7092.2
Imputed bank service charge	...	...	...	...	...	...	...	...	...	...	...	...
Import duties	...	...	...	...	...	...	...	...	...	...	...	...
Value added tax	...	...	...	...	...	...	...	...	...	...	...	...
Other adjustments	...	...	...	...	...	·	...	...	...	...	...	44.8
Total	...	...	...	...	...	6524.5	...	...	...	...	...	7137.0

	1972						1973					
	Compensation of Employees	Capital Consumption	Net Operating Surplus	Indirect Taxes	Less: Subsidies Received	Value Added	Compensation of Employees	Capital Consumption	Net Operating Surplus	Indirect Taxes	Less: Subsidies Received	Value Added
						All Producers						
1 Agriculture, hunting, forestry and fishing	626.4	...	975.2	...	...	1601.6	712.6	...	1250.3	...	...	1962.9
a Agriculture and hunting	...	...	...	...	...	1520.5	...	...	...	...	...	1867.1
b Forestry and logging	...	...	...	...	...	69.8	...	...	...	...	...	81.6
c Fishing	...	...	...	...	...	11.3	...	...	...	...	...	14.2
2 Mining and quarrying	7.3	...	8.7	...	...	16.0	8.6	...	10.4	...	...	19.0

Costa Rica

4.6 Cost Components of Value Added, ISIC Divisions
(Continued)

Million Costa Rican colones

	1972						1973					
	Compensation of Employees	Capital Consumption	Net Operating Surplus	Indirect Taxes	Less: Subsidies Received	Value Added	Compensation of Employees	Capital Consumption	Net Operating Surplus	Indirect Taxes	Less: Subsidies Received	Value Added
3 Manufacturing	580.8	...	910.3	...	...	1491.1	703.8	...	1180.5	...	...	1884.3
a Manufacture of food, beverages and tobacco	196.1	...	488.5	...	...	684.6	271.0	...	610.8	...	...	881.8
b Textile, wearing apparel and leather industries	96.2	...	83.2	...	...	179.4	110.9	...	109.5	...	...	220.4
c Manufacture of wood and wood products, including furniture	54.9	...	48.0	...	...	102.9	63.8	...	64.8	...	...	128.6
d Manufacture of paper and paper products, printing and publishing	33.4	...	36.7	...	...	70.1	42.8	...	61.8	...	...	104.6
e Manufacture of chemicals and chemical petroleum, coal, rubber and plastic products	86.7	...	127.0	...	...	213.7	110.6	...	161.5	...	...	272.1
f Manufacture of non-metallic mineral products, except products of petroleum and coal	36.9	...	44.3	...	...	81.2	37.2	...	40.3	...	...	77.5
g Basic metal industries	...	...	...	...	...	6.1	...	...	...	...	...	12.8
h Manufacture of fabricated metal products, machinery and equipment	...	...	...	...	...	143.3	...	...	...	...	...	176.0
i Other manufacturing industries	4.5	...	5.3	...	...	9.8	3.7	...	6.8	...	...	10.5
4 Electricity, gas and water	52.8	...	95.1	...	...	147.9	53.7	...	106.6	...	...	160.3
a Electricity, gas and steam	...	...	...	...	...	138.6	...	...	...	...	...	149.3
b Water works and supply	...	...	...	...	...	9.3	...	...	...	...	...	11.0
5 Construction	324.1	...	99.7	...	...	423.8	384.4	...	122.7	...	...	507.1
6 Wholesale and retail trade, restaurants and hotels	611.0	...	1040.3	...	...	1651.3	711.4	...	1343.1	...	...	2054.5
a Wholesale and retail trade	...	...	...	...	...	1512.0	...	...	...	...	...	1882.1
b Restaurants and hotels	...	...	...	...	...	139.3	...	...	...	...	...	172.4
7 Transport, storage and communication	224.6	...	137.4	...	...	362.0	261.5	...	174.1	...	...	435.6
8 Finance, insurance, real estate and business services	222.2	...	735.7	...	...	957.9	255.5	...	879.5	...	...	1135.0
9 Community, social and personal services	164.7	...	154.6	...	...	319.3	197.2	...	187.2	...	...	384.4
Total, Industries	2813.9	...	4157.0	...	...	6970.9	3288.7	...	5254.4	...	...	8543.1
Producers of Government Services	998.0	...	...	...	...	998.0	1196.6	...	...	...	...	1196.6
Other Producers	100.8	...	...	...	...	100.8	111.5	...	...	...	...	111.5
Total	3912.7	...	4157.0	...	...	8069.7	4596.8	...	5254.4	...	...	9851.2
Imputed bank service charge	...	...	...	...	...	...	...	...	...	...	...	...
Import duties	...	...	...	...	...	...	...	...	...	...	...	...
Value added tax	...	...	...	...	...	...	...	...	...	...	...	...
Other adjustments	...	...	...	...	...	146.1	...	...	...	...	...	311.2
Total	...	...	...	...	...	8215.8	...	...	...	...	...	10162.4

	1974						1975					
	Compensation of Employees	Capital Consumption	Net Operating Surplus	Indirect Taxes	Less: Subsidies Received	Value Added	Compensation of Employees	Capital Consumption	Net Operating Surplus	Indirect Taxes	Less: Subsidies Received	Value Added
					All Producers							
1 Agriculture, hunting, forestry and fishing	906.4	...	1616.0	...	...	2522.4	1197.3	...	2220.5	...	...	3417.8
a Agriculture and hunting	...	...	...	...	...	2384.9	...	...	...	...	...	3230.8
b Forestry and logging	...	...	...	...	...	116.2	...	...	...	...	...	160.5
c Fishing	...	...	...	...	...	21.3	...	...	...	...	...	26.5
2 Mining and quarrying	11.1	...	13.4	...	...	24.5	17.5	...	21.1	...	...	38.6

Costa Rica

4.6 Cost Components of Value Added, ISIC Divisions
(Continued)

Million Costa Rican colones

	1974						1975					
	Compensation of Employees	Capital Consumption	Net Operating Surplus	Indirect Taxes	Less: Subsidies Received	Value Added	Compensation of Employees	Capital Consumption	Net Operating Surplus	Indirect Taxes	Less: Subsidies Received	Value Added
3 Manufacturing	944.5	...	1708.9	...	...	2653.4	1222.0	...	2166.7	...	...	3388.7
a Manufacture of food, beverages and tobacco	380.0	...	826.0	...	...	1206.0	463.9	...	1050.4	...	...	1514.3
b Textile, wearing apparel and leather industries	148.4	...	160.3	...	...	308.7	227.9	...	172.8	...	...	400.7
c Manufacture of wood and wood products, including furniture	92.0	...	135.5	...	...	227.5	128.9	...	191.5	...	...	320.4
d Manufacture of paper and paper products, printing and publishing	54.5	...	68.1	...	...	122.6	54.7	...	78.1	...	...	132.8
e Manufacture of chemicals and chemical petroleum, coal, rubber and plastic products	118.9	...	295.6	...	...	414.5	160.0	...	419.0	...	...	579.0
f Manufacture of non-metallic mineral products, except products of petroleum and coal	34.7	...	55.7	...	...	90.4	54.2	...	69.6	...	...	123.8
g Basic metal industries	...	...	...	...	...	14.0	...	...	...	...	...	14.6
h Manufacture of fabricated metal products, machinery and equipment	...	...	...	...	...	251.6	...	...	...	...	...	288.7
i Other manufacturing industries	4.9	...	13.2	...	...	18.1	3.9	...	10.5	...	...	14.4
4 Electricity, gas and water	67.7	...	138.2	...	...	205.9	103.7	...	200.0	...	...	303.7
a Electricity, gas and steam	...	...	...	...	...	186.5	...	...	...	...	...	272.4
b Water works and supply	...	...	...	...	...	19.4	...	...	...	...	...	31.3
5 Construction	513.9	...	178.7	...	...	692.6	641.3	...	227.6	...	...	868.9
6 Wholesale and retail trade, restaurants and hotels	896.2	...	1858.5	...	...	2754.7	1062.9	...	2140.7	...	...	3203.6
a Wholesale and retail trade	...	...	...	...	...	2560.9	...	...	...	...	...	2954.4
b Restaurants and hotels	...	...	...	...	...	193.8	...	...	...	...	...	249.2
7 Transport, storage and communication	352.7	...	238.0	...	...	590.7	470.1	...	318.5	...	...	788.6
8 Finance, insurance, real estate and business services	327.0	...	1093.1	...	...	1420.1	412.5	...	1527.9	...	...	1940.4
9 Community, social and personal services	239.4	...	230.9	...	...	470.3	284.3	...	288.2	...	...	572.5
Total, Industries	4258.9	...	7075.7	...	...	11334.6	5411.6	...	9111.2	...	...	14522.8
Producers of Government Services	1576.4	...	...	...	...	1576.4	2083.7	...	...	...	...	2083.7
Other Producers	156.4	...	...	...	...	156.4	198.1	...	...	...	...	198.1
Total	5991.7	...	7075.7	...	...	13067.4	7693.4	...	9111.2	...	...	16804.6
Imputed bank service charge	...	...	...	...	...	...	...	...	...	...	...	...
Import duties	...	...	...	...	...	...	...	...	...	...	...	...
Value added tax	...	...	...	...	...	...	...	...	...	...	...	...
Other adjustments	...	...	...	...	...	148.3	...	...	...	...	...	-
Total	...	...	...	...	...	13215.7	...	...	...	...	...	16804.6

	1976						1977					
	Compensation of Employees	Capital Consumption	Net Operating Surplus	Indirect Taxes	Less: Subsidies Received	Value Added	Compensation of Employees	Capital Consumption	Net Operating Surplus	Indirect Taxes	Less: Subsidies Received	Value Added
	All Producers											
1 Agriculture, hunting, forestry and fishing	1476.6	...	2736.3	...	...	4212.9	1737.3	...	4025.3	...	...	5762.6
a Agriculture and hunting	...	...	...	...	...	3976.1	...	...	...	...	...	5545.3
b Forestry and logging	...	...	...	...	...	198.7	...	...	...	...	...	191.8
c Fishing	...	...	...	...	...	38.1	...	...	...	...	...	25.5
2 Mining and quarrying	18.8	...	21.8	...	...	40.6	24.3	...	28.9	...	...	53.2

…

Costa Rica

4.6 Cost Components of Value Added, ISIC Divisions
(Continued)

Million Costa Rican colones

1976 / 1977

	Compensation of Employees	Capital Consumption	Net Operating Surplus	Indirect Taxes	Less: Subsidies Received	Value Added	Compensation of Employees	Capital Consumption	Net Operating Surplus	Indirect Taxes	Less: Subsidies Received	Value Added
3 Manufacturing	1458.7	...	2572.8	...	...	4031.5	1676.1	...	3271.0	...	...	4947.1
a Manufacture of food, beverages and tobacco	549.2	...	1277.0	...	...	1826.2	...	...	...	...	...	2341.3
b Textile, wearing apparel and leather industries	273.7	...	202.3	...	...	476.0	...	...	...	...	...	560.2
c Manufacture of wood and wood products, including furniture	164.5	...	240.6	...	...	405.1	...	...	...	...	...	391.7
d Manufacture of paper and paper products, printing and publishing	65.3	...	104.9	...	...	170.2	...	...	...	...	...	213.8
e Manufacture of chemicals and chemical petroleum, coal, rubber and plastic products	193.1	...	410.4	...	...	603.5	...	...	...	...	...	740.7
f Manufacture of non-metallic mineral products, except products of petroleum and coal	60.2	...	92.0	...	...	152.2	...	...	...	...	...	203.7
g Basic metal industries	...	...	...	...	...	20.7	...	...	...	...	...	13.3
h Manufacture of fabricated metal products, machinery and equipment	...	...	...	...	...	359.8	...	...	...	...	...	462.5
i Other manufacturing industries	4.7	...	13.1	...	...	17.8	...	...	...	...	...	19.9
4 Electricity, gas and water	123.5	...	286.1	...	...	409.6	155.4	...	366.0	...	...	521.4
a Electricity, gas and steam	...	...	...	...	...	363.3	...	...	...	...	...	456.3
b Water works and supply	...	...	...	...	...	46.3	...	...	...	...	...	65.1
5 Construction	878.7	...	314.7	...	...	1193.4	980.4	...	386.7	...	...	1367.1
6 Wholesale and retail trade, restaurants and hotels	1323.5	...	2508.7	...	...	3832.2	1832.7	...	3301.9	...	...	5134.6
a Wholesale and retail trade	...	...	...	...	...	3537.7	...	...	...	...	...	4748.1
b Restaurants and hotels	...	...	...	...	...	294.5	...	...	...	...	...	386.5
7 Transport, storage and communication	550.5	...	404.2	...	...	954.7	616.0	...	475.2	...	...	1091.2
8 Finance, insurance, real estate and business services	529.4	...	1882.5	...	...	2411.9	615.8	...	2337.6	...	...	2953.4
9 Community, social and personal services	356.3	...	328.2	...	...	684.5	468.6	...	381.4	...	...	850.0
Total, Industries	6716.0	...	11055.3	...	...	17771.3	8106.6	...	14574.0	...	...	22680.6
Producers of Government Services	2682.2	...	...	...	...	2682.2	3402.0	...	...	...	...	3402.0
Other Producers	222.1	...	...	...	...	222.1	248.1	...	...	...	...	248.1
Total	9620.3	...	11055.3	...	...	20675.6	11756.7	...	14574.0	...	...	26330.7
Imputed bank service charge	...	...	...	...	...	...	...	...	...	...	...	...
Import duties	...	...	...	...	...	...	...	...	...	...	...	...
Value added tax	...	...	...	...	...	...	...	...	...	...	...	...
Other adjustments	...	...	...	...	...	...	...	...	...	...	...	-
Total	...	...	...	...	...	20675.6	...	...	...	...	...	26330.7

1978 / 1979

	Compensation of Employees	Capital Consumption	Net Operating Surplus	Indirect Taxes	Less: Subsidies Received	Value Added	Compensation of Employees	Capital Consumption	Net Operating Surplus	Indirect Taxes	Less: Subsidies Received	Value Added
					All Producers							
1 Agriculture, hunting, forestry and fishing	...	...	...	...	...	6163.7	...	...	...	...	...	6398.6
a Agriculture and hunting	...	...	...	...	...	...	...	...	...	...	...	...
b Forestry and logging	...	...	...	...	...	...	...	...	...	...	...	...
c Fishing	...	...	...	...	...	...	...	...	...	...	...	...

311

Costa Rica

4.6 Cost Components of Value Added, ISIC Divisions
(Continued)

Million Costa Rican colones

	1978						1979					
	Compensation of Employees	Capital Consumption	Net Operating Surplus	Indirect Taxes	Less: Subsidies Received	Value Added	Compensation of Employees	Capital Consumption	Net Operating Surplus	Indirect Taxes	Less: Subsidies Received	Value Added
2 Mining and quarrying	...	...	...	...	...	5657.8	...	...	...	...	...	6331.5
3 Manufacturing	...	...	...	...	...		...	...	...	...	...	
a Manufacture of food, beverages and tobacco	...	...	...	...	...	...	...	...	...	...	...	...
b Textile, wearing apparel and leather industries	...	...	...	...	...	...	...	...	...	...	...	...
c Manufacture of wood and wood products, including furniture	...	...	...	...	...	...	...	...	...	...	...	...
d Manufacture of paper and paper products, printing and publishing	...	...	...	...	...	...	...	...	...	...	...	...
e Manufacture of chemicals and chemical petroleum, coal, rubber and plastic products	...	...	...	...	...	...	...	...	...	...	...	...
f Manufacture of non-metallic mineral products, except products of petroleum and coal	...	...	...	...	...	...	...	...	...	...	...	...
g Basic metal industries	...	...	...	...	...	...	...	...	...	...	...	...
h Manufacture of fabricated metal products, machinery and equipment	...	...	...	...	...	...	...	...	...	...	...	...
i Other manufacturing industries	...	...	...	...	...	...	...	...	...	...	...	...
4 Electricity, gas and water	...	...	...	...	...	549.7	...	...	...	...	...	602.8
a Electricity, gas and steam	...	...	...	...	...	...	...	...	...	...	...	...
b Water works and supply	...	...	...	...	...	...	...	...	...	...	...	...
5 Construction	...	...	...	...	...	1663.3	...	...	...	...	...	2215.6
6 Wholesale and retail trade, restaurants and hotels	...	...	...	...	...	5949.9	...	...	...	...	...	7056.4
a Wholesale and retail trade	...	...	...	...	...	...	...	...	...	...	...	...
b Restaurants and hotels	...	...	...	...	...	...	...	...	...	...	...	...
7 Transport, storage and communication	...	...	...	...	...	1277.0	...	...	...	...	...	1444.6
8 Finance, insurance, real estate and business services	...	...	...	...	...	3407.0	...	...	...	...	...	3781.0
9 Community, social and personal services	...	...	...	...	...	5525.5	...	...	...	...	...	6753.9
Total, Industries	...	...	...	...	...	...	...	...	...	...	...	...
Producers of Government Services	...	...	...	...	...	...	...	...	...	...	...	...
Other Producers	...	...	...	...	...	...	...	...	...	...	...	...
Total	...	...	...	...	...	30193.9	...	...	...	...	...	34584.4
Imputed bank service charge	...	...	...	...	...	...	...	...	...	...	...	...
Import duties	...	...	...	...	...	...	...	...	...	...	...	...
Value added tax	...	...	...	...	...	...	...	...	...	...	...	...
Other adjustments	...	...	...	...	...	-	...	...	...	...	...	-
Total	...	...	...	...	...	30193.9	...	...	...	...	...	34584.4

	1980					
	Compensation of Employees	Capital Consumption	Net Operating Surplus	Indirect Taxes	Less: Subsidies Received	Value Added
All Producers							
1 Agriculture, hunting, forestry and fishing	2895.3	257.5	3485.5	595.7	29.2	7204.8
a Agriculture and hunting	...	...	...	...	...	...
b Forestry and logging	...	...	...	...	...	...
c Fishing	...	...	...	...	...	...

Costa Rica

4.6 Cost Components of Value Added, ISIC Divisions
(Continued)

Million Costa Rican colones

1980

	Compensation of Employees	Capital Consumption	Net Operating Surplus	Indirect Taxes	Less: Subsidies Received	Value Added
2 Mining and quarrying	2782.8	465.0	3074.6	1861.1	60.2	8123.3
3 Manufacturing						
a Manufacture of food, beverages and tobacco	...	...	...	...	...	...
b Textile, wearing apparel and leather industries	...	...	...	...	...	...
c Manufacture of wood and wood products, including furniture	...	...	...	...	...	...
d Manufacture of paper and paper products, printing and publishing	...	...	...	...	...	...
e Manufacture of chemicals and chemical petroleum, coal, rubber and plastic products	...	...	...	...	...	...
f Manufacture of non-metallic mineral products, except products of petroleum and coal	...	...	...	...	...	...
g Basic metal industries	...	...	...	...	...	...
h Manufacture of fabricated metal products, machinery and equipment	...	...	...	...	...	...
i Other manufacturing industries	...	...	...	...	...	...
4 Electricity, gas and water	249.2	124.9	397.5	17.0	58.1	730.5
a Electricity, gas and steam	...	...	...	...	...	...
b Water works and supply	...	...	...	...	...	...
5 Construction	1977.0	181.8	465.0	51.4	-	2675.2
6 Wholesale and retail trade, restaurants and hotels	3313.9	172.4	2531.9	2298.0	3.0	8313.2
a Wholesale and retail trade	...	...	...	...	...	...
b Restaurants and hotels	...	...	...	...	...	...
7 Transport, storage and communication	971.9	259.4	537.2	71.8	47.6	1792.7
8 Finance, insurance, real estate and business services	1046.1	56.0	885.0	63.8	53.5	4456.6
9 Community, social and personal services	7621.0	132.6	364.7	120.3	-	8238.6
Total, Industries	20857.2	1649.6	11741.4	5079.1	251.6	...
Producers of Government Services	...	...	...	...	...	...
Other Producers	...	...	...	...	...	...
Total	...	...	...	...	...	41534.9
Imputed bank service charge	...	...	...	...	...	...
Import duties	...	...	...	...	...	...
Value added tax	...	...	...	...	...	-
Other adjustments	...	...	...	...	...	
Total	...	...	...	...	...	41534.9

Cuba

Source. Correspondence from the Direccion Central de Estadistica, Junta Central de Planificacion, Habana. The official estimates are published in 'Anuario Estadistico de Cuba'.

General note. The estimates shown in the following tables have been prepared in accordance with the System of Material Product Balances. Therefore, these estimates are not comparable in concept and coverage with those conforming to the United Nations System of National Accounts.

1a Net Material Product by Use at Current Market Prices

Million Cuban pesos

	1970	1971	1972	1973	1974	1975	1976	1977	1978	1979	1980
1 Personal consumption	3372.0	4076.8	5009.1	5184.7	5218.9	...	...	...	...	...	...
2 Material consumption in the units of the non-material sphere serving individuals	263.1	288.0	299.1	314.4	308.1	...	...	...	...	...	...
Consumption of the Population	3635.1	4364.8	5308.2	5499.1	5527.0	...	...	...	...	...	...
3 Material consumption in the units of the non-material sphere serving the community as a whole	150.0	138.7	137.6	134.7	154.5	...	...	...	...	...	...
4 Net fixed capital formation [a]	668.5	830.3	980.8	1314.9	1664.8	...	...	...	...	...	...
5 Increase in material circulating assets and in stocks	...	...	...	...	...	...	...	...	...	...	...
6 Losses	...	...	...	...	...	...	...	...	...	...	...
7 Exports of goods and material services	1088.4	906.8	810.6	1199.6	2328.3	...	...	...	...	...	...
8 Less: Imports of goods and material services	1338.1	1422.4	1210.3	1437.9	2260.5	...	...	...	...	...	...
Net Material Product [b]	4203.9	4818.2	6026.9	6710.4	7414.1	...	...	...	...	...	...

a) Gross fixed capital formation.
b) Gross material product rather than Net material product.

Cyprus

Source. Reply to the United Nations National Accounts Questionnaire from the Department of Statistics and Research, Ministry of Finance, Nicosia. Official estimates are published annually in the 'Economic Report', issued by the same Department. Information on concepts, sources and methods of estimation utilized can be found in 'History and Analysis of the Methodology of National Accounts in Cyprus', October 1977.

General note. The preparation of national accounts statistics in Cyprus is undertaken by the Statistics and Research Department of the Ministry of Finance, Nicosia. The official estimates are published annually in the 'Economic Report'. A decription of the sources and methods used for the national accounts estimation is found in 'History and Analysis of the Methodology of National Accounts in Cyprus' published in 1977. The estimates are generally in accordance with the classifications and definitions recommended in the United Nations System of National Accounts (SNA). The following tables have been prepared from successive replies to the United Nations national accounts questionnaire. When the scope and coverage of the estimates differ for conceptual or statistical reasons from the definitions and classifications recommended in SNA, a footnote is indicated to the relevant tables.

Sources and methods:

(a) Gross domestic product. Gross domestic product is estimated mainly through the production approach.

(b) Expenditure on the gross domestic product. The expenditure approach is used to estimate government final consumption expenditure and exports and imports of goods and services. This approach, in combination with the commodity-flow approach, is also used to estimate gross capital formation. Private final consumption expenditure is mainly estimated by the commodity-flow approach. Details of actual expenditure of the central government are published in the Accountant-General's Financial Report. Estimates for the local government are derived from the final accounts of all town municipalities. For private consumption expenditure, the sources used are agricultural surveys, industrial production surveys, services surveys, exports and imports data and financial reports from the Treasury department - all these are available annually. Household expenditure surveys are conducted occasionally on a sample basis. The estimates of changes in stocks are derived from agricultural surveys and annual industrial surveys. Estimates of gross fixed capital formation are made by user and not by owner sector as recommended in the SNA. From 1972, the estimates are made by sector and type of capital assets. Data on fixed capital formation are obtained through censuses of industrial production, industrial surveys, construction surveys, import and export data and direct information from organizations. A special manufacturing survey was undertaken in 1971 based on import licences for plant and machinery. Data on exports and imports of goods and services are obtained from the balance of payments prepared by the Central Bank of Cyprus. For the constant price estimates, government expenditure on wages and salaries are derived by using total allowance index as deflator for the current years values. Private consumption expenditure is estimated at constant prices by using general retail price index as deflator. For the other expenditure items, price deflation is used.

(c) Cost-structure of the gross domestic product. Separate estimates for compensation of employees and operating surplus are not available. Data on compensation of employees for the industrial activity sector are collected regularly. For the trade and transport sectors, only total value added is available. The estimate of consumption of fixed capital is based on a fixed percentage (10.0) of the gross national product. All the data on net indirect taxes are available in the Financial Report.

(d) Gross domestic product by kind of economic activity. The table of gross domestic product by kind of economic activity is prepared in factor values. The production approach is used to estimate value added of most industries. The income approach is used for part of the transport sector, community services and part of the social and personal services. The commodity-flow approach is used for wholesale and retail trade. For the agricultural sector, up to the year 1969, estimates were derived mainly from reports submitted by Agricultural Beat Officers based upon their local knowledge. From 1969 to 1974, area sample surveys were conducted twice a year. From 1975, a new procedure was introduced which consists of establishing a frame of agricultural holders, from which a stratified random sample of 1,600 holders are selected and interviewed annually. Livestock statistics are collected through sample surveys conducted twice a year and through information from the town and village authorities. Data on output of fishing are supplied by the Fisheries Department. Data for mining and quarrying, manufacturing and water sectors are derived from the annual industrial production surveys and the censuses of industrial production held every five years. Gross output, production expenses, employment, labour costs, sales, expenditure on fixed assets and stocks are obtained from the surveys while data on administrative and other non industrial expenses, plant capacity, and exports are obtained from the censuses. Estimates of public construction are extracted from annual financial reports and balance sheets. For the private sector, data are collected through construction surveys using building permits as a frame. For repairs and maintenance, estimates are based on rental value of the premises. The value added of the trade sector is estimated as the sum of gross trade margins, wages and salaries of Cyprus Grain Commission, certain rents a grain price subsidy minus 20 per cent representing inputs and indirect taxes. For the transport sector, 1967 bench-mark estimates of bus passenger transport are extrapolated by the indexes of the number of buses in use and the bus fares. The bench-mark estimates of the taxi-cab operation are obtained by multiplying the number of vehicles in circulation by daily earnings per vehicle and by working days. For other years, the index of vehicles in circulation is used to extrapolate the base-year value added. Since 1980 a Survey on Land Transport is conducted. For the financial sector, data are collected by the Central Bank of Cyprus. Data on insurance activities are extracted from the records of the Office of the Supervisor of Insurance Companies. The rental value of residential buildings is estimated on the basis of the total dwelling stock and the prevailing rents. The main source of information for public services is the Treasury's Annual Financial Report and annual returns submitted by the local authorities. Estimates for the private services are derived from the annual services survey. For the constant price estimates, double deflation is used for the agricultural sector. For mining and quarrying, manufacturing and construction, value added is extrapolated by quantity indexes. Output of electricity is computed at constant prices by valuing the sales of electricity at base-year average prices. Value added of the remaining trade sector is deflated by retail and wholesale prices indexes. Price deflators and employment indices are used to estimate the value added of the transport and services sectors.

1.1 Expenditure on the Gross Domestic Product, in Current Prices

Million Cyprus pounds

		1970	1971	1972	1973	1974	1975	1976	1977	1978	1979	1980
1	General government final consumption expenditure	21.6	25.5	29.6	35.8	43.1	44.9	53.6	62.2	68.1	87.8	107.6
2	Private final consumption expenditure	171.5	194.0	218.9	238.4	240.7	208.4	240.7	305.0	357.7	418.8	497.4
3	Gross capital formation	55.2	61.8	70.0	99.7	80.1	56.3	79.7	141.9	188.1	237.5	269.5
	a Increase in stocks	1.9	3.3	2.8	5.4	0.1	7.4	10.6	19.3	17.2	17.7	14.1
	b Gross fixed capital formation	53.3	58.5	67.2	94.3	80.0	48.9	69.1	122.6	170.9	219.8	255.4
	Residential buildings	17.4	19.5	21.9	38.7	30.6	13.5	26.8	46.4	69.6	96.9	109.8
	Non-residential buildings	6.2	8.1	10.9	17.9	13.8	8.3	7.9	14.9	20.5	26.4	40.9
	Other construction and land improvement etc.	7.0	8.8	9.3	10.8	8.2	10.1	10.4	13.2	17.3	24.8	29.0
	Other	22.7	22.1	25.1	26.9	27.4	17.0	24.0	48.1	63.5	71.7	75.7
4	Exports of goods and services	85.9	99.0	115.3	131.6	115.8	91.2	166.1	202.3	214.4	281.4	343.6
5	Less: Imports of goods and services	107.6	118.8	136.7	176.1	176.5	145.7	209.1	286.7	318.7	401.6	475.7
	Equals: Gross Domestic Product	226.6	261.5	297.1	329.4	303.2	255.1	331.0	424.7	509.6	623.9	742.4

1.2 Expenditure on the Gross Domestic Product, in Constant Prices

Million Cyprus pounds

		1970	1971	1972	1973	1974	1975	1976	1977	1978	1979	1980
		\multicolumn{3}{At constant prices of:}									
		1967				1973						
1	General government final consumption expenditure	16.5	17.0	18.3	20.4 / 35.8	38.1	38.6	45.5	48.5	47.1	51.6	54.2
2	Private final consumption expenditure	158.1	175.7	192.8	212.3 / 238.4	207.3	171.5	190.8	225.6	246.2	264.4	275.6
3	Gross capital formation	44.6	46.6	47.2	48.2 / 99.7	66.4	45.9	59.4	94.4	108.0	118.2	115.2
	a Increase in stocks	1.6	3.1	1.8	3.5 / 5.4	-0.2	5.7	7.4	12.1	9.5	9.9	7.2
	b Gross fixed capital formation	43.0	43.5	45.4	44.7 / 94.3	66.6	40.2	52.0	82.3	98.5	108.3	108.0

Cyprus

1.2 Expenditure on the Gross Domestic Product, in Constant Prices
(Continued)

Million Cyprus pounds

	1970	1971	1972	1973	1974	1975	1976	1977	1978	1979	1980
				At constant prices of:							
		1967					1973				
Residential buildings	14.1	15.0	15.4	15.8 / 38.7	24.8	11.2	21.3	33.9	42.9	50.3	47.0
Non-residential buildings	5.0	6.2	7.7	8.1 / 17.9	11.2	6.9	6.3	10.9	12.6	13.6	17.3
Other construction and land improvement etc.	5.6	6.7	6.5	6.0 / 10.8	6.7	8.4	8.3	9.6	10.6	12.8	12.3
Other	18.3	15.6	15.8	14.8 / 26.9	23.9	13.7	16.1	27.9	32.4	31.6	31.4
4 Exports of goods and services	74.0	85.3	93.9	99.4 / 131.6	100.4	69.9	120.2	142.7	147.9	179.9	199.1
5 Less: Imports of goods and services	91.9	97.2	109.1	131.0 / 176.1	131.6	98.4	138.8	180.8	199.9	227.5	235.6
Statistical discrepancy	...	...	...	...	-5.8	-5.0	-11.3	-16.1	-5.4	-13.9	-20.8
Equals: Gross Domestic Product	201.3	227.4	243.1	249.3 / 329.4	274.8	222.5	265.8	314.3	343.9	371.7	387.7

1.3 Cost Components of the Gross Domestic Product

Million Cyprus pounds

	1970	1971	1972	1973	1974	1975	1976	1977	1978	1979	1980
1 Indirect taxes, net	17.6	19.9	22.9	19.1	18.7	16.5	18.9	34.5	44.8	47.9	47.4
a Indirect taxes paid	19.4	22.4	25.9	31.9	25.1	20.3	24.6	37.8	49.4	59.6	68.3
b Less: Subsidies received	1.8	2.5	3.0	12.8	6.4	3.8	5.7	3.3	4.6	11.7	20.9
2 Consumption of fixed capital	10.5	12.1	13.8	34.1	31.5	26.9	34.5	44.4	53.0	64.6	76.8
3 Compensation of employees paid by resident producers to:	198.5	229.5	260.4	276.2	253.0	211.7	277.6	345.8	411.8	511.4	618.2
4 Net operating surplus											
Equals: Gross Domestic Product	226.6	261.5	297.1	329.4	303.2	255.1	331.0	424.7	509.6	623.9	742.4

1.8 Capital Transactions of The Nation, Summary

Million Cyprus pounds

	1970	1971	1972	1973	1974	1975	1976	1977	1978	1979	1980
				Finance of Gross Capital Formation							
Gross saving	48.0	58.0	64.7	71.5	53.5	42.6	75.5	106.0	129.5	164.9	188.6
1 Consumption of fixed capital	10.5	12.1	13.8	34.1	31.5	26.9	34.5	44.4	53.0	64.6	76.8
2 Net saving	37.5	45.9	50.9	37.4	22.0	15.7	41.0	61.6	76.5	100.3	111.8
Less: Surplus of the nation on current transactions	-7.2	-3.8	-5.3	-28.2	-26.5	-13.7	-4.2	-35.9	-58.6	-72.6	-80.9
Finance of Gross Capital Formation	55.2	61.8	70.0	99.7	80.1	56.3	79.7	141.9	188.1	237.5	269.5
				Gross Capital Formation							
Increase in stocks	1.9	3.3	2.8	5.4	0.1	7.4	10.6	19.3	17.2	17.7	14.1
Gross fixed capital formation	53.3	58.5	67.2	94.3	80.0	48.9	69.1	122.6	170.9	219.8	255.4
Gross Capital Formation	55.2	61.8	70.0	99.7	80.1	56.3	79.7	141.9	188.1	237.5	269.5

1.10 Gross Domestic Product by Kind of Activity, in Current Prices

Million Cyprus pounds

	1970	1971	1972	1973	1974	1975	1976	1977	1978	1979	1980
1 Agriculture, hunting, forestry and fishing	36.0	46.7	49.2	41.1	50.5	40.4	53.6	56.4	56.2	65.7	74.3
2 Mining and quarrying	12.7	10.5	9.2	11.6	9.3	6.1	7.3	8.6	8.8	9.6	10.1
3 Manufacturing	25.5	29.9	37.9	43.3	38.4	36.8	53.7	70.3	85.4	102.0	124.6
4 Electricity, gas and water	4.3	4.6	5.0	5.6	5.1	4.0	5.1	5.7	7.0	7.8	10.0
5 Construction	16.9	19.8	23.0	36.7	28.9	17.8	25.7	41.5	59.4	81.5	100.1
6 Wholesale and retail trade, restaurants and hotels	36.8	43.1	50.8	62.0	51.3	41.3	58.0	76.3	89.5	112.3	132.2
7 Transport, storage and communication	19.8	23.2	25.4	20.8	16.1	16.9	23.5	29.2	35.5	44.0	55.1
8 Finance, insurance, real estate and business services	29.9	32.8	36.1	44.1	37.9	29.6	36.1	43.9	55.0	67.3	80.6
9 Community, social and personal services	9.4	11.0	13.2	26.2	24.7	20.7	22.8	30.5	37.2	47.9	58.1
Total, Industries	191.3	221.6	249.8	291.4	262.1	213.6	286.0	362.4	433.6	537.1	645.1
Producers of Government Services [a]	17.7	20.0	24.4	18.9	22.4	25.0	26.1	27.8	31.2	38.9	49.9

Cyprus

1.10 Gross Domestic Product by Kind of Activity, in Current Prices
(Continued)

Million Cyprus pounds	1970	1971	1972	1973	1974	1975	1976	1977	1978	1979	1980
Other Producers	...	...	...	...	...	...	...	...	...	...	...
Subtotal [b]	209.0	241.6	274.2	310.3	284.5	238.6	312.1	390.2	464.8	576.0	695.0
Less: Imputed bank service charge	...	...	...	...	...	...	...	...	...	...	...
Plus: Import duties	...	...	...	...	...	...	...	...	...	...	...
Plus: Value added tax	...	...	...	...	...	...	...	...	...	...	...
Plus: Other adjustments [c]	17.6	19.9	22.9	19.1	18.7	16.5	18.9	34.5	44.8	47.9	47.4
Equals: Gross Domestic Product	226.6	261.5	297.1	329.4	303.2	255.1	331.0	424.7	509.6	623.9	742.4

a) Public administration and defence only. All other activities of government are included in the corresponding industries. b) Gross domestic product in factor values. c) Referring to indirect taxes net of subsidies.

1.11 Gross Domestic Product by Kind of Activity, in Constant Prices

Million Cyprus pounds	1970	1971	1972	1973	1974	1975	1976	1977	1978	1979	1980
	At constant prices of: 1967				1973						
1 Agriculture, hunting, forestry and fishing	33.8	42.2	39.8	27.7 / 41.1	48.2	37.0	40.1	40.2	39.8	42.0	44.1
2 Mining and quarrying	9.8	10.6	11.1	11.3 / 11.6	8.4	6.3	6.8	7.2	7.4	7.6	7.5
3 Manufacturing	22.9	25.6	30.4	32.2 / 43.3	33.0	28.9	37.4	43.6	48.0	51.8	55.5
4 Electricity, gas and water	4.4	4.8	5.6	6.1 / 5.6	4.8	3.9	4.6	5.0	5.4	5.8	6.0
5 Construction	13.5	15.3	16.2	16.4 / 36.7	23.6	14.9	20.4	30.3	36.5	42.1	42.8
6 Wholesale and retail trade, restaurants and hotels	33.2	37.7	42.7	46.7 / 62.0	44.1	32.8	44.1	54.0	59.3	66.9	68.5
7 Transport, storage and communication	17.3	19.4	20.9	23.7 / 20.8	16.0	15.0	18.8	22.2	23.5	25.9	28.6
8 Finance, insurance, real estate and business services	27.5	29.0	30.3	31.5 / 44.1	35.0	28.0	32.4	36.1	40.5	43.4	44.9
9 Community, social and personal services	7.5	8.1	8.8	9.5 / 26.2	23.9	19.1	20.3	22.4	23.7	25.0	26.1
Total, Industries	169.9	192.7	205.8	205.1 / 291.4	237.0	185.9	224.9	261.0	284.1	310.5	324.0
Producers of Government Services [a]	13.7	14.4	14.9	17.4 / 18.9	20.1	21.9	22.8	22.3	21.9	22.7	25.1
Other Producers	...	...	...	...	...	...	...	...	...	...	...
Subtotal [b]	183.6	207.1	220.7	222.5 / 310.3	257.1	207.8	247.7	283.3	306.0	333.2	349.1
Less: Imputed bank service charge	...	...	...	...	...	...	...	...	...	...	...
Plus: Import duties	...	...	...	...	...	...	...	...	...	...	...
Plus: Value added tax	...	...	...	...	...	...	...	...	...	...	...
Plus: Other adjustments [c]	17.7	20.3	22.4	26.8 / 19.1	17.7	14.7	18.1	31.0	37.9	38.5	38.6
Equals: Gross Domestic Product	201.3	227.4	243.1	249.3 / 329.4	274.8	222.5	265.8	314.3	343.9	371.7	387.7

a) Public administration and defence only. All other activities of government are included in the corresponding industries. b) Gross domestic product in factor values. c) Referring to indirect taxes net of subsidies.

1.12 Relations Among National Accounting Aggregates

Million Cyprus pounds	1970	1971	1972	1973	1974	1975	1976	1977	1978	1979	1980
Gross Domestic Product	226.6	261.5	297.1	329.4	303.2	255.1	331.0	424.7	509.6	623.9	742.4
Plus: Net factor income received from abroad	7.4	8.1	8.9	11.1	11.9	14.2	13.9	18.8	20.5	22.2	25.3
Equals: Gross National Product	234.0	269.6	306.0	340.5	315.1	269.3	344.9	443.5	530.1	646.1	767.7
Less: Consumption of fixed capital	10.5	12.1	13.8	34.1	31.5	26.9	34.5	44.4	53.0	64.6	76.8
Less: Net indirect taxes paid to supranational organisations	...	...	...	...	...	...	...	...	...	...	...

Cyprus

1.12 Relations Among National Accounting Aggregates
(Continued)

Million Cyprus pounds

	1970	1971	1972	1973	1974	1975	1976	1977	1978	1979	1980
Equals: National Income at Market Prices	223.5	257.5	292.2	306.4	283.6	242.4	310.4	399.1	477.1	581.5	690.9
Plus: Net current transfers received from abroad	7.1	7.9	7.2	5.2	22.2	26.6	24.9	29.7	25.2	25.4	25.9
Current transfers received	...	...	...	6.0	23.0	27.7	26.2	31.0	26.4	26.8	27.3
Less: Current transfers paid	...	...	...	0.8	0.8	1.1	1.3	1.3	1.2	1.4	1.4
Equals: National Disposable Income at Market Prices	230.6	265.4	299.4	311.6	305.8	269.0	335.3	428.8	502.3	606.9	716.8
Less: Final consumption	193.1	219.5	248.5	274.2	283.8	253.3	294.3	367.2	425.8	506.6	605.0
Equals: Net Saving	37.5	45.9	50.9	37.4	22.0	15.7	41.0	61.6	76.5	100.3	111.8
Less: Surplus of the nation on current transactions	-7.2	-3.8	-5.3	-28.2	-26.5	-13.7	-4.2	-35.9	-58.6	-72.6	-80.9
Equals: Net Capital Formation	44.7	49.7	56.2	65.6	48.5	29.4	45.2	97.5	135.1	172.9	192.7

2.1 General Government Final Consumption Expenditure by Function, in Current Prices

Million Cyprus pounds

	1970	1971	1972	1973	1974	1975	1976	1977	1978	1979	1980
1 General public services	9.4	11.4	13.1	16.3	18.2	19.3	20.3	16.8	19.5	25.1	33.0
2 Defence	3.0	3.6	3.7	3.6	6.5	7.1	7.2	10.2	8.3	12.2	10.5
3 Public order and safety	...	...	...	...	...	...	...	...	...	...	...
4 Education	4.4	4.9	6.4	8.0	9.0	8.9	9.9	11.7	14.1	17.5	21.8
5 Health	2.1	2.6	3.2	4.1	4.9	5.1	5.2	5.5	5.8	8.3	11.1
6 Social security and welfare								6.1	6.2	6.8	9.2
7 Housing and community amenities								2.7	2.9	3.8	5.0
8 Recreational, cultural and religious affairs								2.2	2.8	3.4	4.3
9 Economic services								6.7	8.2	10.3	12.2
a Fuel and energy	2.7	3.0	3.2	3.8	4.5	4.5	11.0	0.8	0.8	1.2	1.8
b Agriculture, forestry, fishing and hunting								2.1	3.0	3.5	4.6
c Mining, manufacturing and construction, except fuel and energy								0.9	1.0	1.2	1.6
d Transportation and communication								0.7	0.8	1.4	0.5
e Other economic affairs								2.2	2.6	3.0	3.7
10 Other functions								0.3	0.3	0.4	0.5
Total General Government Final Consumption Expenditure	21.6	25.5	29.6	35.8	43.1	44.9	53.6	62.2	68.1	87.8	107.6

2.5 Private Final Consumption Expenditure by Type, in Current Prices

Million Cyprus pounds

	1970	1971	1972	1973	1974	1975	1976	1977	1978	1979	1980
Final Consumption Expenditure of Resident Households											
1 Food, beverages and tobacco	...	86.6	93.5	109.1	104.1	90.9	111.7	121.3	139.9	164.7	...
a Food	...	71.3	76.4	88.7	80.7	70.4	85.5	95.2	112.3	132.3	...
b Non-alcoholic beverages	...	3.1	3.4	4.2	3.8	3.4	8.3	4.7	5.4	8.0	...
c Alcoholic beverages	...	5.5	6.4	7.6	11.2	8.9	10.0	11.7	11.6	15.2	...
d Tobacco	...	6.7	7.4	8.7	8.4	8.2	7.9	9.7	10.6	11.2	...
2 Clothing and footwear	...	20.4	24.8	28.0	23.1	21.0	22.6	39.4	49.6	58.8	...
3 Gross rent, fuel and power	...	25.1	26.1	31.2	29.9	24.4	26.0	28.2	32.8	39.5	...
a Fuel and power	...	...	...	...	...	...	...	6.4	7.2	8.8	...
b Other	...	...	...	...	...	...	...	21.8	25.6	30.7	...
4 Furniture, furnishings and household equipment and operation	...	19.1	23.2	29.6	24.0	17.3	28.2	45.0	56.1	77.5	...
a Household operation	...	4.7	5.6	6.9	6.5	5.9	8.2	12.7	14.6	19.0	...
b Other	...	14.4	17.6	22.7	17.5	11.4	20.0	32.3	41.5	58.5	...
5 Medical care and health expenses	...	3.7	4.2	5.1	4.2	3.9	4.5	6.2	6.8	8.5	...
6 Transport and communication	...	34.8	45.7	55.2	43.4	42.0	59.7	85.4	86.1	107.7	...
a Personal transport equipment	...	10.1	15.7	19.5	9.3	4.8	9.1	24.0	31.5	37.7	...
b Other	...	24.7	30.0	35.7	34.1	37.2	50.6	61.4	54.6	70.0	...
7 Recreational, entertainment, education and cultural services	...	13.1	15.1	17.6	13.0	12.7	16.2	20.2	25.2	32.7	...
a Education	...	1.8	1.8	2.1	2.1	1.4	1.6	1.9	2.3	2.9	...

Cyprus

2.5 Private Final Consumption Expenditure by Type, in Current Prices
(Continued)

Million Cyprus pounds

	1970	1971	1972	1973	1974	1975	1976	1977	1978	1979	1980
b Other	...	11.3	13.3	15.5	10.9	11.3	14.6	18.3	22.9	29.8	...
8 Miscellaneous goods and services	...	18.2	23.8	28.6	22.1	18.7	26.0	33.1	40.3	57.4	...
a Personal care	...	5.6	6.3	7.7	5.9	5.8	9.4	11.6	12.1	17.5	...
b Expenditures in restaurants, cafes and hotels	...	11.1	14.4	16.6	12.7	9.5	12.2	15.9	21.2	30.5	...
c Other	...	1.5	3.1	4.2	3.5	3.4	4.4	5.6	7.0	9.4	...
Statistical discrepancy	...	10.0	1.1	-21.3	13.1	-1.9	-23.3	-36.9	-31.2	-70.7	...
Total Final Consumption Expenditure in the Domestic Market by Households, of which	...	231.0	257.5	283.1	276.9	229.0	271.6	341.9	405.6	476.1	...
Plus: Direct purchases abroad by resident households	...	5.8	6.5	7.9	8.7	8.4	8.5	10.2	12.0	14.2	...
Less: Direct purchases in the domestic market by non-resident households	...	42.8	45.1	52.6	44.9	29.0	39.4	47.1	59.9	71.5	...
Equals: Final Consumption Expenditure of Resident Households [a]	171.5	194.0	218.9	238.4	240.7	208.4	240.7	305.0	357.7	418.8	...

Final Consumption Expenditure of Private Non-profit Institutions Serving Households

| Equals: Final Consumption Expenditure of Private Non-profit Organisations Serving Households | ... | ... | ... | ... | ... | ... | ... | ... | ... | ... | ... |
| Private Final Consumption Expenditure | 171.5 | 194.0 | 218.9 | 238.4 | 240.7 | 208.4 | 240.7 | 305.0 | 357.7 | 418.8 | ... |

a) Including consumption expenditure of private non-profit institutions.

2.6 Private Final Consumption Expenditure by Type, in Constant Prices

Million Cyprus pounds

	1970	1971	1972	1973	1974	1975	1976	1977	1978	1979	1980
		At constant prices of:									
		1967				1973					

Final Consumption Expenditure of Resident Households

	1970	1971	1972	1973	1974	1975	1976	1977	1978	1979	1980
1 Food, beverages and tobacco	...	78.1	80.1	85.5	...	...	...	...	...	...	...
a Food	...	63.8	64.7	68.9	...	...	...	...	...	...	...
b Non-alcoholic beverages	...	2.9	2.8	3.2	...	...	...	...	...	...	...
c Alcoholic beverages	...	5.0	5.8	6.5	...	...	...	...	...	...	...
d Tobacco	...	6.4	6.8	6.9	...	...	...	...	...	...	...
2 Clothing and footwear	...	19.1	22.3	23.3	...	...	...	...	...	...	...
3 Gross rent, fuel and power	...	22.6	22.7	25.5	...	...	...	...	...	...	...
4 Furniture, furnishings and household equipment and operation	...	16.1	19.0	22.0	...	...	...	...	...	...	...
a Household operation	...	4.1	4.7	5.5	...	...	...	...	...	...	...
b Other	...	12.0	14.3	16.5	...	...	...	...	...	...	...
5 Medical care and health expenses	...	2.6	2.9	3.4	...	...	...	...	...	...	...
6 Transport and communication	...	28.5	35.9	38.6	...	...	...	...	...	...	...
a Personal transport equipment	...	7.3	10.9	11.3	...	...	...	...	...	...	...
b Other	...	21.2	25.0	27.3	...	...	...	...	...	...	...
7 Recreational, entertainment, education and cultural services	...	10.6	11.4	12.0	...	...	...	...	...	...	...
a Education	...	1.5	1.3	1.3	...	...	...	...	...	...	...
b Other	...	9.1	10.1	10.7	...	...	...	...	...	...	...
8 Miscellaneous goods and services	...	15.1	17.9	19.6	...	...	...	...	...	...	...

Cyprus

2.6 Private Final Consumption Expenditure by Type, in Constant Prices
(Continued)

Million Cyprus pounds

	1970	1971	1972	1973	1974	1975	1976	1977	1978	1979	1980
		1967			At constant prices of:		1973				
a Personal care	...	5.1	5.4	5.9							
				...	...	...	...	...	...	...	...
b Expenditures in restaurants, cafes and hotels	...	8.8	10.3	11.0							
				...	...	...	...	...	...	...	...
c Other	...	1.2	2.2	2.7							
				...	...	...	...	...	...	...	...
Statistical discrepancy	...	16.0	13.4	19.1							
				...	...	...	...	...	...	...	...
Total Final Consumption Expenditure in the Domestic Market by Households, of which	...	208.7	225.6	249.0							
				...	...	...	...	...	...	...	...
Plus: Direct purchases abroad by resident households	...	4.8	5.2	5.9							
				...	...	...	...	...	...	...	...
Less: Direct purchases in the domestic market by non-resident households	...	37.8	38.0	42.6							
				...	...	...	...	...	...	...	...
Equals: Final Consumption Expenditure of Resident Households [a]	158.1	175.7	192.8	212.3							
				238.4	207.3	171.5	190.8	225.6	246.2	263.4	...

Final Consumption Expenditure of Private Non-profit Institutions Serving Households

Equals: Final Consumption Expenditure of Private Non-profit Organisations Serving Households	...	...	...	...							
				...	...	...	...	...	...	...	...
Private Final Consumption Expenditure	158.1	175.7	192.8	212.3							
				238.4	207.3	171.5	190.8	225.6	246.2	263.4	...

a) Including consumption expenditure of private non-profit institutions.

2.9 Gross Capital Formation by Kind of Activity of Owner, ISIC Major Divisions, in Current Prices

Million Cyprus pounds

	1970			1971			1972			1973		
	Total Gross Capital Formation	Increase in Stocks	Gross Fixed Capital Formation	Total Gross Capital Formation	Increase in Stocks	Gross Fixed Capital Formation	Total Gross Capital Formation	Increase in Stocks	Gross Fixed Capital Formation	Total Gross Capital Formation	Increase in Stocks	Gross Fixed Capital Formation
					All Producers							
1 Agriculture, hunting, fishing and forestry	...	...	4.2	...	...	4.5	...	...	6.0	...	...	5.9
2 Mining and quarrying	...	...	0.8	...	...	1.0	...	...	0.7	...	...	0.7
3 Manufacturing	...	...	9.7	...	...	7.5	...	...	7.5	...	...	8.0
4 Electricity, gas and water	...	...	2.5	...	...	3.9	...	...	3.9	...	...	5.2
5 Construction	...	...	1.6	...	...	1.4	...	...	2.1	...	...	1.8
6 Wholesale and retail trade, restaurants and hotels [a]	...	...	2.7	...	...	3.0	...	...	3.8	...	...	5.3
7 Transport, storage and communication	...	...	10.3	...	...	11.2	...	...	11.8	...	...	12.4
8 Finance, insurance, real estate and business services [b]	...	...	17.7	...	...	19.9	...	...	22.3	...	...	39.4
9 Community, social and personal services [ab]	...	...	3.3	...	...	5.5	...	...	8.5	...	...	14.4
Total Industries	...	...	52.8	...	...	57.9	...	...	66.6	...	...	93.7
Producers of Government Services	...	...	0.5	...	...	0.6	...	...	0.6	...	...	0.6
Private Non-Profit Institutions Serving Households	...	...	...	...	...	...	...	...	...	...	...	...
Total	55.2	1.9	53.3	61.8	3.3	58.5	70.0	2.8	67.2	99.7	5.4	94.3

	1974			1975			1976			1977		
	Total Gross Capital Formation	Increase in Stocks	Gross Fixed Capital Formation	Total Gross Capital Formation	Increase in Stocks	Gross Fixed Capital Formation	Total Gross Capital Formation	Increase in Stocks	Gross Fixed Capital Formation	Total Gross Capital Formation	Increase in Stocks	Gross Fixed Capital Formation
					All Producers							
1 Agriculture, hunting, fishing and forestry	...	...	5.0	...	...	5.5	...	...	6.3	...	...	8.5
2 Mining and quarrying	...	...	0.6	...	...	1.2	...	...	1.0	...	...	1.1
3 Manufacturing	...	...	10.0	...	...	6.6	...	...	9.6	...	...	20.0
4 Electricity, gas and water	...	...	4.7	...	...	2.5	...	...	3.3	...	...	4.4

Cyprus

2.9 Gross Capital Formation by Kind of Activity of Owner, ISIC Major Divisions, in Current Prices
(Continued)

Million Cyprus pounds

	1974 TGCF	1974 IS	1974 GFCF	1975 TGCF	1975 IS	1975 GFCF	1976 TGCF	1976 IS	1976 GFCF	1977 TGCF	1977 IS	1977 GFCF
5 Construction	...	...	2.0	...	...	1.5	...	...	0.9	...	...	3.6
6 Wholesale and retail trade, restaurants and hotels [a]	...	...	4.9	...	...	3.1	...	...	3.7	...	...	7.1
7 Transport, storage and communication	...	...	11.8	...	...	14.0	...	...	10.7	...	...	21.3
8 Finance, insurance, real estate and business services [b]	...	...	31.0	...	...	5.6	...	...	27.2	...	...	50.0
9 Community, social and personal services [a,b]	...	...	9.3	...	...	8.0	...	...	5.1	...	...	8.4
Total Industries	...	...	79.3	...	...	48.0	...	...	67.8	...	...	121.4
Producers of Government Services	...	...	0.7	...	...	0.9	...	...	1.3	...	...	1.2
Private Non-Profit Institutions Serving Households	...	...	...	...	...	...	...	...	...	...	...	...
Total	80.1	0.1	80.0	56.3	7.4	48.9	79.7	10.6	69.1	141.9	19.3	122.6

	1978 TGCF	1978 IS	1978 GFCF	1979 TGCF	1979 IS	1979 GFCF	1980 TGCF	1980 IS	1980 GFCF

All Producers

	1978 TGCF	1978 IS	1978 GFCF	1979 TGCF	1979 IS	1979 GFCF	1980 TGCF	1980 IS	1980 GFCF
1 Agriculture, hunting, fishing and forestry	...	...	11.9	...	...	16.0	...	...	14.8
2 Mining and quarrying	...	...	1.4	...	...	1.7	...	...	1.4
3 Manufacturing	...	...	23.7	...	...	26.2	...	...	24.6
4 Electricity, gas and water	...	...	3.8	...	...	3.8	...	...	10.0
5 Construction	...	...	5.6	...	...	9.3	...	...	11.1
6 Wholesale and retail trade, restaurants and hotels [a]	...	...	10.9	...	...	14.1	...	...	16.0
7 Transport, storage and communication	...	...	32.7	...	...	36.1	...	...	40.2
8 Finance, insurance, real estate and business services [b]	...	...	70.4	...	...	98.1	...	...	111.3
9 Community, social and personal services [a,b]	...	...	9.6	...	...	13.5	...	...	24.6
Total Industries	...	...	170.0	...	...	218.8	...	...	254.0
Producers of Government Services	...	...	0.9	...	...	1.0	...	...	1.4
Private Non-Profit Institutions Serving Households	...	...	...	...	...	...	...	...	...
Total	188.1	17.2	170.9	237.5	17.7	219.8	269.5	14.1	255.4

a) Restaurants and hotels are included in item 'Community, social and personal services'.
b) Business services are included in item 'Community, social and personal services'.

2.10 Gross Capital Formation by Kind of Activity of Owner, ISIC Major Divisions, in Constant Prices

Million Cyprus pounds

	1973 TGCF	1973 IS	1973 GFCF	1974 TGCF	1974 IS	1974 GFCF	1975 TGCF	1975 IS	1975 GFCF	1976 TGCF	1976 IS	1976 GFCF

At constant prices of: 1973
All Producers

	1973 TGCF	1973 IS	1973 GFCF	1974 TGCF	1974 IS	1974 GFCF	1975 TGCF	1975 IS	1975 GFCF	1976 TGCF	1976 IS	1976 GFCF
1 Agriculture, hunting, fishing and forestry	...	...	5.9	...	...	4.4	...	...	4.6	...	...	4.8
2 Mining and quarrying	...	...	0.7	...	...	0.5	...	...	1.0	...	...	0.7
3 Manufacturing	...	...	8.0	...	...	8.5	...	...	5.3	...	...	6.6
4 Electricity, gas and water	...	...	5.2	...	...	4.0	...	...	2.0	...	...	2.5
5 Construction	...	...	1.8	...	...	1.7	...	...	1.2	...	...	0.6
6 Wholesale and retail trade, restaurants and hotels [a]	...	...	5.9	...	...	4.0	...	...	2.5	...	...	2.7
7 Transport, storage and communication	...	...	12.4	...	...	10.0	...	...	6.6	...	...	7.8
8 Finance, insurance, real estate and business services [b]	...	...	39.4	...	...	25.1	...	...	11.6	...	...	21.6
9 Community, social and personal services [a,b]	...	...	14.4	...	...	7.7	...	...	4.6	...	...	3.8
Total Industries	...	...	93.7	...	...	65.9	...	...	39.4	...	...	51.1
Producers of Government Services	...	...	0.6	...	...	0.7	...	...	0.8	...	...	0.9
Private Non-Profit Institutions Serving Households	...	...	...	...	...	...	...	...	...	...	...	...
Total	99.7	5.4	94.3	66.4	-0.2	66.6	45.9	5.7	40.2	59.4	7.4	52.0

Cyprus

2.10 Gross Capital Formation by Kind of Activity of Owner, ISIC Major Divisions, in Constant Prices

Million Cyprus pounds

	1977 Total Gross Capital Formation	1977 Increase in Stocks	1977 Gross Fixed Capital Formation	1978 Total Gross Capital Formation	1978 Increase in Stocks	1978 Gross Fixed Capital Formation	1979 Total Gross Capital Formation	1979 Increase in Stocks	1979 Gross Fixed Capital Formation	1980 Total Gross Capital Formation	1980 Increase in Stocks	1980 Gross Fixed Capital Formation
At constant prices of: 1973											
All Producers											
1 Agriculture, hunting, fishing and forestry	...	...	5.7	...	...	7.1	...	...	8.1	...	...	6.5
2 Mining and quarrying	...	...	0.6	...	...	0.7	...	...	0.7	...	...	0.6
3 Manufacturing	...	...	12.3	...	...	12.5	...	...	12.0	...	...	10.2
4 Electricity, gas and water	...	...	2.8	...	...	2.2	...	...	1.8	...	...	4.2
5 Construction	...	...	2.1	...	...	2.8	...	...	4.1	...	...	4.6
6 Wholesale and retail trade, restaurants and hotels [a]	...	...	4.7	...	...	6.3	...	...	6.9	...	...	6.6
7 Transport, storage and communication	...	...	13.4	...	...	17.4	...	...	16.6	...	...	16.6
8 Finance, insurance, real estate and business services [b]	...	...	34.2	...	...	43.3	...	...	50.9	...	...	47.6
9 Community, social and personal services [ab]	...	...	5.7	...	...	5.7	...	...	6.7	...	...	10.5
Total Industries	...	...	81.5	...	...	98.0	...	...	107.8	...	...	107.4
Producers of Government Services	...	...	0.8	...	...	0.5	...	...	0.5	...	...	0.6
Private Non-Profit Institutions Serving Households	...	...	...	...	...	...	...	...	...	...	...	...
Total	94.4	12.1	82.3	108.0	9.5	98.5	118.2	9.9	108.3	115.2	7.2	108.0

a) Restaurants and hotels are included in item 'Community, social and personal services'.
b) Business services are included in item 'Community, social and personal services'.

4.3 Derivation of Value Added by Kind of Activity, ISIC Divisions, in Current Prices

Million Cyprus pounds

	1970 Gross Output	1970 Intermediate Consumption	1970 Value Added	1971 Gross Output	1971 Intermediate Consumption	1971 Value Added	1972 Gross Output	1972 Intermediate Consumption	1972 Value Added	1973 Gross Output	1973 Intermediate Consumption	1973 Value Added
All Producers											
1 Agriculture, hunting, forestry and fishing	...	...	36.0	...	...	46.7	...	...	49.2	...	...	41.1
a Agriculture and hunting	...	...	35.4	...	...	45.9	...	...	48.3	...	...	40.0
b Forestry and logging	...	...	0.2	...	...	0.2	...	...	0.2	...	...	0.2
c Fishing	...	...	0.4	...	...	0.6	...	...	0.7	...	...	0.9
2 Mining and quarrying	...	...	12.7	...	...	10.5	...	...	9.2	...	...	11.6
a Coal mining	...	...	-	...	...	-	...	...	-	...	...	-
b Crude petroleum and natural gas production	...	...	-	...	...	-	...	...	-	...	...	-
c Metal ore mining	...	...	9.0	...	...	5.7	...	...	4.2	...	...	6.0
d Other mining	...	...	3.7	...	...	4.8	...	...	5.0	...	...	5.6
3 Manufacturing	...	...	25.5	...	...	29.9	...	...	37.9	...	...	43.3
a Manufacture of food, beverages and tobacco	...	...	7.9	...	...	9.1	...	...	10.9	...	...	12.0
b Textile, wearing apparel and leather industries	...	...	5.2	...	...	6.2	...	...	7.0	...	...	7.9
c Manufacture of wood and wood products, including furniture	...	...	2.1	...	...	2.4	...	...	3.0	...	...	3.5
d Manufacture of paper and paper products, printing and publishing	...	...	1.4	...	...	1.7	...	...	1.9	...	...	2.2
e Manufacture of chemicals and chemical petroleum, coal, rubber and plastic products	...	...	1.3	...	...	1.6	...	...	3.6	...	...	4.4
f Manufacture of non-metallic mineral products, except products of petroleum and coal	...	...	2.8	...	...	3.0	...	...	3.7	...	...	4.4
g Basic metal industries	...	...	-	...	...	-	...	...	-	...	...	...
h Manufacture of fabricated metal products, machinery and equipment	...	...	4.4	...	...	5.4	...	...	7.0	...	...	8.0
i Other manufacturing industries	...	...	0.4	...	...	0.5	...	...	0.8	...	...	0.9
4 Electricity, gas and water	...	...	4.3	...	...	4.6	...	...	5.0	...	...	5.6
a Electricity, gas and steam	...	...	3.9	...	...	4.2	...	...	4.5	...	...	5.1
b Water works and supply	...	...	0.4	...	...	0.4	...	...	0.5	...	...	0.5

Cyprus

4.3 Derivation of Value Added by Kind of Activity, ISIC Divisions, in Current Prices
(Continued)

Million Cyprus pounds

	1970 Gross Output	1970 Intermediate Consumption	1970 Value Added	1971 Gross Output	1971 Intermediate Consumption	1971 Value Added	1972 Gross Output	1972 Intermediate Consumption	1972 Value Added	1973 Gross Output	1973 Intermediate Consumption	1973 Value Added
5 Construction	...	...	16.9	...	...	19.8	...	...	23.0	...	...	36.7
6 Wholesale and retail trade, restaurants and hotels	...	...	36.8	...	...	43.1	...	...	50.8	...	...	62.0
a Wholesale and retail trade	...	...	31.9	...	...	36.6	...	...	42.2	...	...	52.0
b Restaurants and hotels	...	...	4.9	...	...	6.5	...	...	8.6	...	...	10.0
Restaurants	...	...	...	...	...	...	...	...	...	...	...	5.3
Hotels and other lodging places	...	...	...	...	...	...	...	...	...	...	...	4.7
7 Transport, storage and communication	...	...	19.8	...	...	23.2	...	...	25.4	...	...	20.8
a Transport and storage	...	...	...	...	...	...	...	...	...	...	...	16.0
b Communication	...	...	...	...	...	...	...	...	...	...	...	4.8
8 Finance, insurance, real estate and business services	...	...	29.9	...	...	32.8	...	...	36.1	...	...	44.1
a Financial institutions	...	...	...	...	...	...	...	...	...	...	...	9.7
b Insurance	...	...	...	...	...	...	...	...	...	...	...	2.8
c Real estate and business services	...	...	...	...	...	...	...	...	...	...	...	31.6
Real estate, except dwellings	...	...	...	...	...	...	...	...	...	...	...	7.9
Dwellings	...	...	...	...	...	...	...	...	...	...	...	23.7
9 Community, social and personal services	...	...	9.4	...	...	11.0	...	...	13.2	...	...	26.2
a Sanitary and similar services	...	...	...	...	...	...	...	...	...	...	...	0.4
b Social and related community services [a]	...	...	...	...	...	...	...	...	...	...	...	15.3
Educational services	...	...	...	...	...	...	...	...	...	...	...	8.5
Medical, dental, other health and veterinary services	...	...	...	...	...	...	...	...	...	...	...	5.1
c Recreational and cultural services	...	...	...	...	...	...	...	...	...	...	...	2.9
d Personal and household services	...	...	...	...	...	...	...	...	...	...	...	7.5
Total, Industries	...	...	191.3	...	...	221.6	...	...	249.8	...	...	291.4
Producers of Government Services [b]	...	...	17.7	...	...	20.0	...	...	24.4	...	...	18.9
Other Producers	...	...	...	...	...	...	...	...	...	...	...	...
Total [c]	...	...	209.0	...	...	241.6	...	...	274.2	...	...	310.3
Imputed bank service charge	...	...	...	...	...	...	...	...	...	...	...	...
Import duties	...	...	...	...	...	...	...	...	...	...	...	...
Value added tax	...	...	...	...	...	...	...	...	...	...	...	...
Other adjustments [d]	...	...	17.6	...	...	19.9	...	...	22.9	...	...	19.1
Total	...	...	226.6	...	...	261.5	...	...	297.1	...	...	329.4

	1974 Gross Output	1974 Intermediate Consumption	1974 Value Added	1975 Gross Output	1975 Intermediate Consumption	1975 Value Added	1976 Gross Output	1976 Intermediate Consumption	1976 Value Added	1977 Gross Output	1977 Intermediate Consumption	1977 Value Added
						All Producers						
1 Agriculture, hunting, forestry and fishing	...	...	50.5	...	...	40.4	...	...	53.6	...	...	56.4
a Agriculture and hunting	...	...	49.6	...	...	39.5	...	...	52.0	...	...	54.7
b Forestry and logging	...	...	0.2	...	...	0.3	...	...	0.9	...	...	0.8
c Fishing	...	...	0.7	...	...	0.6	...	...	0.7	...	...	0.9
2 Mining and quarrying	...	...	9.3	...	...	6.1	...	...	7.3	...	...	8.6
a Coal mining	...	...	-	...	...	-	...	...	-	...	...	-
b Crude petroleum and natural gas production	...	...	-	...	...	-	...	...	-	...	...	-
c Metal ore mining	...	...	5.5	...	...	2.8	...	...	2.8	...	...	2.0
d Other mining	...	...	3.8	...	...	3.3	...	...	4.5	...	...	6.6

Cyprus

4.3 Derivation of Value Added by Kind of Activity, ISIC Divisions, in Current Prices
(Continued)

Million Cyprus pounds

		1974 Gross Output	1974 Intermediate Consumption	1974 Value Added	1975 Gross Output	1975 Intermediate Consumption	1975 Value Added	1976 Gross Output	1976 Intermediate Consumption	1976 Value Added	1977 Gross Output	1977 Intermediate Consumption	1977 Value Added
3	Manufacturing	...	...	38.4	...	...	36.8	...	...	53.7	...	...	70.3
a	Manufacture of food, beverages and tobacco	...	...	12.0	...	...	10.1	...	...	13.3	...	...	16.1
b	Textile, wearing apparel and leather industries	...	...	7.1	...	...	8.2	...	...	12.9	...	...	18.3
c	Manufacture of wood and wood products, including furniture	...	...	2.6	...	...	2.6	...	...	4.0	...	...	4.7
d	Manufacture of paper and paper products, printing and publishing	...	...	2.2	...	...	2.1	...	...	3.0	...	...	3.7
e	Manufacture of chemicals and chemical petroleum, coal, rubber and plastic products	...	...	4.0	...	...	3.5	...	...	4.7	...	...	7.0
f	Manufacture of non-metallic mineral products, except products of petroleum and coal	...	...	3.6	...	...	4.4	...	...	6.4	...	...	8.4
g	Basic metal industries	...	...	-	...	...	-	...	...	-	...	...	
h	Manufacture of fabricated metal products, machinery and equipment	...	...	6.2	...	...	5.2	...	...	8.3	...	...	10.8
i	Other manufacturing industries	...	...	0.7	...	...	0.7	...	...	1.1	...	...	1.3
4	Electricity, gas and water	...	...	5.1	...	...	4.0	...	...	5.1	...	...	5.7
a	Electricity, gas and steam	...	...	4.7	...	...	3.7	...	...	4.6	...	...	5.2
b	Water works and supply	...	...	0.4	...	...	0.3	...	...	0.5	...	...	0.5
5	Construction	...	...	28.9	...	...	17.8	...	...	25.7	...	...	41.5
6	Wholesale and retail trade, restaurants and hotels	...	...	51.3	...	...	41.3	...	...	58.0	...	...	76.3
a	Wholesale and retail trade	...	...	44.0	...	...	35.8	...	...	50.8	...	...	66.3
b	Restaurants and hotels	...	...	7.3	...	...	5.4	...	...	7.2	...	...	10.0
	Restaurants	...	...	4.0	...	...	4.1	...	...	4.3	...	...	6.3
	Hotels and other lodging places	...	...	3.3	...	...	1.3	...	...	2.9	...	...	3.7
7	Transport, storage and communication	...	...	16.1	...	...	16.9	...	...	23.5	...	...	29.2
a	Transport and storage	...	...	11.4	...	...	12.1	...	...	16.1	...	...	20.5
b	Communication	...	...	4.7	...	...	4.8	...	...	7.4	...	...	8.7
8	Finance, insurance, real estate and business services	...	...	37.9	...	...	29.6	...	...	36.1	...	...	43.9
a	Financial institutions	...	...	9.0	...	...	6.6	...	...	9.9	...	...	12.5
b	Insurance	...	...	2.8	...	...	0.7	...	...	1.9	...	...	2.6
c	Real estate and business services	...	...	26.1	...	...	22.3	...	...	24.3	...	...	28.8
	Real estate, except dwellings	...	...	4.2	...	...	3.7	...	...	5.4	...	...	8.5
	Dwellings	...	...	21.9	...	...	18.6	...	...	18.9	...	...	20.3
9	Community, social and personal services	...	...	24.7	...	...	20.7	...	...	22.8	...	...	30.5
a	Sanitary and similar services	...	...	0.5	...	...	0.5	...	...	0.5	...	...	0.6
b	Social and related community services [a]	...	...	16.0	...	...	15.6	...	...	17.0	...	...	23.1
	Educational services	...	...	9.4	...	...	8.9	...	...	9.8	...	...	13.8
	Medical, dental, other health and veterinary services	...	...	5.1	...	...	5.1	...	...	5.5	...	...	6.4
c	Recreational and cultural services	...	...	2.7	...	...	2.4	...	...	2.8	...	...	3.3
d	Personal and household services	...	...	5.4	...	...	2.3	...	...	2.7	...	...	3.4
Total, Industries		...	...	262.1	...	...	213.6	...	...	286.0	...	...	362.4
Producers of Government Services [b]		...	...	22.4	...	...	25.0	...	...	26.1	...	...	27.8
Other Producers		...	...	...	...	...	...	...	...	...	...	...	...
Total [c]		...	...	284.5	...	...	238.6	...	...	312.1	...	...	390.2
Imputed bank service charge		...	...	...	...	...	...	...	...	...	...	...	...
Import duties		...	...	...	...	...	...	...	...	...	...	...	...
Value added tax		...	...	...	...	...	...	...	...	...	...	...	...
Other adjustments [d]		...	...	18.7	...	...	16.5	...	...	18.9	...	...	34.5
Total		...	...	303.2	...	...	255.1	...	...	331.0	...	...	424.7

Cyprus

4.3 Derivation of Value Added by Kind of Activity, ISIC Divisions, in Current Prices

Million Cyprus pounds

	1978 Gross Output	1978 Intermediate Consumption	1978 Value Added	1979 Gross Output	1979 Intermediate Consumption	1979 Value Added	1980 Gross Output	1980 Intermediate Consumption	1980 Value Added
				All Producers					
1 Agriculture, hunting, forestry and fishing	...	...	56.2	...	...	65.7	...	...	74.3
a Agriculture and hunting	...	...	54.7	...	...	63.9	...	...	71.8
b Forestry and logging	...	...	0.4	...	...	0.5	...	...	0.7
c Fishing	...	...	1.1	...	...	1.3	...	...	1.8
2 Mining and quarrying	...	...	8.8	...	...	9.6	...	...	10.1
a Coal mining	...	...	-	...	...	-	...	...	-
b Crude petroleum and natural gas production	...	...	-	...	...	-	...	...	-
c Metal ore mining	...	...	1.6	...	...	2.0	...	...	1.8
d Other mining	...	...	7.2	...	...	7.6	...	...	8.3
3 Manufacturing	...	...	85.4	...	...	102.0	...	...	124.6
a Manufacture of food, beverages and tobacco	...	...	18.3	...	...	20.9	...	...	24.7
b Textile, wearing apparel and leather industries	...	...	21.9	...	...	26.5	...	...	32.4
c Manufacture of wood and wood products, including furniture	...	...	5.4	...	...	6.4	...	...	7.5
d Manufacture of paper and paper products, printing and publishing	...	...	5.2	...	...	6.5	...	...	9.0
e Manufacture of chemicals and chemical petroleum, coal, rubber and plastic products	...	...	7.5	...	...	8.8	...	...	11.2
f Manufacture of non-metallic mineral products, except products of petroleum and coal	...	...	10.5	...	...	12.8	...	...	16.3
g Basic metal industries	...	...	-	...	...	-	...	...	-
h Manufacture of fabricated metal products, machinery and equipment	...	...	13.9	...	...	17.1	...	...	19.9
i Other manufacturing industries	...	...	2.7	...	...	3.0	...	...	3.6
4 Electricity, gas and water	...	...	7.0	...	...	7.8	...	...	10.0
a Electricity, gas and steam	...	...	6.4	...	...	7.2	...	...	9.2
b Water works and supply	...	...	0.6	...	...	0.6	...	...	0.8
5 Construction	...	...	59.4	...	...	81.5	...	...	100.1
6 Wholesale and retail trade, restaurants and hotels	...	...	89.5	...	...	112.3	...	...	132.2
a Wholesale and retail trade	...	...	76.1	...	...	91.6	...	...	105.5
b Restaurants and hotels	...	...	13.4	...	...	20.7	...	...	26.6
Restaurants	...	...	8.1	...	...	10.8	...	...	13.0
Hotels and other lodging places	...	...	5.3	...	...	9.9	...	...	13.6
7 Transport, storage and communication	...	...	35.5	...	...	44.0	...	...	55.1
a Transport and storage	...	...	25.5	...	...	32.1	...	...	39.5
b Communication	...	...	10.0	...	...	11.9	...	...	15.6
8 Finance, insurance, real estate and business services	...	...	55.0	...	...	67.3	...	...	80.6
a Financial institutions	...	...	15.8	...	...	19.7	...	...	25.0
b Insurance	...	...	3.4	...	...	4.8	...	...	5.5
c Real estate and business services	...	...	35.8	...	...	42.8	...	...	50.1
Real estate, except dwellings	...	...	12.5	...	...	15.2	...	...	17.3
Dwellings	...	...	23.3	...	...	27.6	...	...	32.8
9 Community, social and personal services	...	...	37.2	...	...	47.9	...	...	58.1
a Sanitary and similar services	...	...	0.7	...	...	0.9	...	...	1.0
b Social and related community services [a]	...	...	27.8	...	...	35.5	...	...	44.3
Educational services	...	...	16.8	...	...	20.9	...	...	25.6
Medical, dental, other health and veterinary services	...	...	7.3	...	...	10.1	...	...	13.1
c Recreational and cultural services	...	...	4.2	...	...	5.4	...	...	6.4
d Personal and household services	...	...	4.1	...	...	5.2	...	...	6.3

Cyprus

4.3 Derivation of Value Added by Kind of Activity, ISIC Divisions, in Current Prices
(Continued)

Million Cyprus pounds

	1978 Gross Output	1978 Intermediate Consumption	1978 Value Added	1979 Gross Output	1979 Intermediate Consumption	1979 Value Added	1980 Gross Output	1980 Intermediate Consumption	1980 Value Added
Total, Industries	...	...	433.6	...	...	537.1	...	...	645.1
Producers of Government Services [b]	...	...	31.2	...	...	38.9	...	...	49.9
Other Producers	...	...	...	...	...	...	...	...	...
Total [c]	...	...	464.8	...	...	576.0	...	...	695.0
Imputed bank service charge	...	...	...	...	...	...	...	...	...
Import duties	...	...	...	...	...	...	...	...	...
Value added tax	...	...	...	...	...	...	...	...	...
Other adjustments [d]	...	...	44.8	...	...	47.9	...	...	47.4
Total	...	...	509.6	...	...	623.9	...	...	742.4

a) Social and related community services include in addition to educational and health services (items 33 and 34) also the services of commercial and professional associations, welfare institutions and other social and related community services.
b) Public administration and defence only. All other activities of government are included in the corresponding industries.
c) Gross domestic product in factor values.
d) Referring to indirect taxes net of subsidies.

4.4 Derivation of Value Added by Kind of Activity, ISIC Divisions, in Constant Prices

Million Cyprus pounds

		1973 Gross Output	1973 Intermediate Consumption	1973 Value Added	1974 Gross Output	1974 Intermediate Consumption	1974 Value Added	1975 Gross Output	1975 Intermediate Consumption	1975 Value Added	1976 Gross Output	1976 Intermediate Consumption	1976 Value Added
		At constant prices of: 1973 — All Producers												
1	Agriculture, hunting, forestry and fishing	...	...	41.1	...	...	48.2	...	...	37.0	...	...	40.1
a	Agriculture and hunting	...	...	40.0	...	...	47.3	...	...	36.2	...	...	38.8
b	Forestry and logging	...	...	...	...	...	...	...	...	...	...	...	0.7
c	Fishing	...	...	0.9	...	...	0.7	...	...	0.5	...	...	0.6
2	Mining and quarrying	...	...	11.6	...	...	8.4	...	...	6.3	...	...	6.8
a	Coal mining	...	...	...	...	...	...	...	...	...	...	...	...
b	Crude petroleum and natural gas production	...	...	...	...	...	...	...	...	...	...	...	...
c	Metal ore mining	...	...	6.0	...	...	...	...	...	...	...	...	...
d	Other mining	...	...	5.6	...	...	...	...	...	...	...	...	...
3	Manufacturing	...	...	43.3	...	...	33.0	...	...	28.9	...	...	37.4
a	Manufacture of food, beverages and tobacco	...	...	12.0	...	...	...	...	...	...	...	...	...
b	Textile, wearing apparel and leather industries	...	...	7.9	...	...	...	...	...	...	...	...	...
c	Manufacture of wood and wood products, including furniture	...	...	3.5	...	...	...	...	...	...	...	...	...
d	Manufacture of paper and paper products, printing and publishing	...	...	2.2	...	...	...	...	...	...	...	...	...
e	Manufacture of chemicals and chemical petroleum, coal, rubber and plastic products	...	...	4.4	...	...	...	...	...	...	...	...	...
f	Manufacture of non-metallic mineral products, except products of petroleum and coal	...	...	4.4	...	...	...	...	...	...	...	...	...
g	Basic metal industries	...	...	-	...	...	...	...	...	...	...	...	...
h	Manufacture of fabricated metal products, machinery and equipment	...	...	8.0	...	...	...	...	...	...	...	...	...
i	Other manufacturing industries	...	...	0.9	...	...	...	...	...	...	...	...	...
4	Electricity, gas and water	...	...	5.6	...	...	4.8	...	...	3.9	...	...	4.6
a	Electricity, gas and steam	...	...	5.1	...	...	...	...	...	...	...	...	...
b	Water works and supply	...	...	0.5	...	...	...	...	...	...	...	...	...
5	Construction	...	...	36.7	...	...	23.6	...	...	14.9	...	...	20.4
6	Wholesale and retail trade, restaurants and hotels	...	...	62.0	...	...	44.1	...	...	32.8	...	...	44.1
a	Wholesale and retail trade	...	...	52.0	...	...	37.5	...	...	28.6	...	...	38.6
b	Restaurants and hotels	...	...	10.0	...	...	6.6	...	...	4.2	...	...	5.5
	Restaurants	...	...	5.3	...	...	3.4	...	...	3.0	...	...	3.0
	Hotels and other lodging places	...	...	4.7	...	...	3.2	...	...	1.2	...	...	2.5
7	Transport, storage and communication	...	...	20.8	...	...	16.0	...	...	15.0	...	...	18.8
a	Transport and storage	...	...	16.0	...	...	11.4	...	...	10.7	...	...	13.4

Cyprus

4.4 Derivation of Value Added by Kind of Activity, ISIC Divisions, in Constant Prices
(Continued)

Million Cyprus pounds

	1973 GO	1973 IC	1973 VA	1974 GO	1974 IC	1974 VA	1975 GO	1975 IC	1975 VA	1976 GO	1976 IC	1976 VA
				At constant prices of:1973								
b Communication	...	...	4.8	...	...	4.6	...	...	4.3	...	...	5.4
8 Finance, insurance, real estate and business services	...	...	44.1	...	...	35.0	...	...	28.0	...	...	32.4
a Financial institutions	...	...	9.2	...	...	7.5	...	...	4.8	...	...	7.3
b Insurance	...	...	2.8	...	...	2.3	...	...	0.7	...	...	1.5
c Real estate and business services	...	...	30.8	...	...	24.3	...	...	21.9	...	...	22.7
Real estate, except dwellings	...	...	7.1	...	...	3.1	...	...	3.5	...	...	4.0
Dwellings	...	...	2.3	...	...	21.2	...	...	18.4	...	...	18.7
9 Community, social and personal services	...	...	26.2	...	...	23.9	...	...	19.1	...	...	20.3
a Sanitary and similar services	...	...	0.4	...	...	0.5	...	...	0.4	...	...	0.5
b Social and related community services [a]	...	...	15.3	...	...	15.6	...	...	14.1	...	...	14.8
Educational services	...	...	8.5	...	...	8.8	...	...	7.7	...	...	8.3
Medical, dental, other health and veterinary services	...	...	5.1	...	...	5.2	...	...	4.9	...	...	4.9
c Recreational and cultural services	...	...	2.9	...	...	2.7	...	...	2.5	...	...	2.7
d Personal and household services	...	...	7.5	...	...	5.3	...	...	2.2	...	...	2.4
Total, Industries	...	...	291.4	...	...	237.0	...	...	185.9	...	...	224.9
Producers of Government Services [b]	...	...	18.9	...	...	20.1	...	...	21.9	...	...	22.8
Other Producers	...	...		...	...		...	...		...	...	
Total [c]	...	...	310.3	...	...	257.1	...	...	207.8	...	...	247.7
Imputed bank service charge	...	...		...	...		...	...		...	...	
Import duties	...	...		...	...		...	...		...	...	
Value added tax	...	...		...	...		...	...		...	...	
Other adjustments [d]	...	...	19.1	...	...	17.7	...	...	14.7	...	...	18.1
Total	...	...	329.4	...	...	274.8	...	...	222.5	...	...	265.8

	1977 GO	1977 IC	1977 VA	1978 GO	1978 IC	1978 VA	1979 GO	1979 IC	1979 VA	1980 GO	1980 IC	1980 VA
				At constant prices of:1973								
				All Producers								
1 Agriculture, hunting, forestry and fishing	...	...	40.2	...	...	39.8	...	...	42.0	...	...	44.1
a Agriculture and hunting	...	...	38.8	...	...	38.8	...	...	40.9	...	...	42.9
b Forestry and logging	...	...	0.7	...	...	0.3	...	...	0.4	...	...	0.4
c Fishing	...	...	0.7	...	...	0.7	...	...	0.7	...	...	0.8
2 Mining and quarrying	...	...	7.2	...	...	7.4	...	...	7.6	...	...	7.5
a Coal mining	...	...	...	...	...	...	...	...		...	...	
b Crude petroleum and natural gas production	...	...	...	...	...	...	...	...	7.6	...	...	7.5
c Metal ore mining	...	...	...	...	...	...	...	...		...	...	
d Other mining	...	...	...	...	...	...	...	...		...	...	

Cyprus

4.4 Derivation of Value Added by Kind of Activity, ISIC Divisions, in Constant Prices
(Continued)

Million Cyprus pounds

	1977 Gross Output	1977 Intermediate Consumption	1977 Value Added	1978 Gross Output	1978 Intermediate Consumption	1978 Value Added	1979 Gross Output	1979 Intermediate Consumption	1979 Value Added	1980 Gross Output	1980 Intermediate Consumption	1980 Value Added
				At constant prices of: 1973								
3 Manufacturing	...	...	43.6	...	...	48.0	...	...	51.8	...	...	55.5
a Manufacture of food, beverages and tobacco	...	...	...	...	...	...	...	...	...	...	...	...
b Textile, wearing apparel and leather industries	...	...	...	...	...	...	...	...	...	...	...	...
c Manufacture of wood and wood products, including furniture	...	...	...	...	...	...	...	...	...	...	...	...
d Manufacture of paper and paper products, printing and publishing	...	...	...	...	...	...	...	...	...	...	...	...
e Manufacture of chemicals and chemical petroleum, coal, rubber and plastic products	...	...	...	...	...	...	...	...	...	...	...	...
f Manufacture of non-metallic mineral products, except products of petroleum and coal	...	...	...	...	...	...	...	...	...	...	...	...
g Basic metal industries	...	...	...	...	...	...	...	...	...	...	...	...
h Manufacture of fabricated metal products, machinery and equipment	...	...	...	...	...	...	...	...	...	...	...	...
i Other manufacturing industries	...	...	...	...	...	...	...	...	...	...	...	...
4 Electricity, gas and water	...	...	5.0	...	...	5.4	...	...	5.8	...	...	6.0
a Electricity, gas and steam	...	...	...	...	...	...	...	...	...	...	...	...
b Water works and supply	...	...	...	...	...	...	...	...	...	...	...	...
5 Construction	...	...	30.3	...	...	36.5	...	...	42.1	...	...	42.8
6 Wholesale and retail trade, restaurants and hotels	...	...	54.0	...	...	59.3	...	...	66.9	...	...	68.5
a Wholesale and retail trade	...	...	47.2	...	...	51.3	...	...	56.5	...	...	57.2
b Restaurants and hotels	...	...	6.8	...	...	8.0	...	...	10.4	...	...	11.3
Restaurants	...	...	3.8	...	...	4.7	...	...	5.5	...	...	5.5
Hotels and other lodging places	...	...	2.9	...	...	3.3	...	...	4.9	...	...	5.8
7 Transport, storage and communication	...	...	22.2	...	...	23.5	...	...	25.9	...	...	28.6
a Transport and storage	...	...	16.2	...	...	16.6	...	...	18.4	...	...	19.5
b Communication	...	...	6.0	...	...	6.9	...	...	7.5	...	...	9.1
8 Finance, insurance, real estate and business services	...	...	36.1	...	...	40.5	...	...	43.4	...	...	44.9
a Financial institutions	...	...	8.5	...	...	9.5	...	...	10.2	...	...	10.8
b Insurance	...	...	1.7	...	...	2.1	...	...	2.5	...	...	2.4
c Real estate and business services	...	...	26.5	...	...	28.4	...	...	30.7	...	...	31.7
Real estate, except dwellings	...	...	7.0	...	...	7.8	...	...	8.7	...	...	8.1
Dwellings	...	...	19.5	...	...	20.6	...	...	22.0	...	...	23.6
9 Community, social and personal services	...	...	22.4	...	...	23.7	...	...	25.0	...	...	26.1
a Sanitary and similar services	...	...	0.4	...	...	0.4	...	...	0.5	...	...	0.5
b Social and related community services [a]	...	...	16.5	...	...	17.5	...	...	18.5	...	...	19.1
Educational services	...	...	8.9	...	...	9.3	...	...	9.7	...	...	...
Medical, dental, other health and veterinary services	...	...	5.3	...	...	5.7	...	...	6.1	...	...	...
c Recreational and cultural services	...	...	3.0	...	...	3.2	...	...	3.2	...	...	3.2
d Personal and household services	...	...	2.6	...	...	2.6	...	...	2.8	...	...	2.9
Total, Industries	...	...	261.0	...	...	284.1	...	...	310.5	...	...	324.0
Producers of Government Services [b]	...	...	22.3	...	...	21.9	...	...	22.7	...	...	25.1

Cyprus

4.4 Derivation of Value Added by Kind of Activity, ISIC Divisions, in Constant Prices
(Continued)

Million Cyprus pounds

	1977 Gross Output	1977 Intermediate Consumption	1977 Value Added	1978 Gross Output	1978 Intermediate Consumption	1978 Value Added	1979 Gross Output	1979 Intermediate Consumption	1979 Value Added	1980 Gross Output	1980 Intermediate Consumption	1980 Value Added
					At constant prices of: 1973							
Other Producers	...	...	...	...	...	...	...	...	...	...	...	...
Total c	...	...	283.3	...	...	306.0	...	...	333.2	...	...	349.1
Imputed bank service charge	...	...	...	...	...	...	...	...	...	...	...	...
Import duties	...	...	...	...	...	...	...	...	...	...	...	...
Value added tax	...	...	...	...	...	...	...	...	...	...	...	...
Other adjustments d	...	...	31.0	...	...	37.9	...	...	38.5	...	...	38.6
Total	...	...	314.3	...	...	343.9	...	...	371.7	...	...	387.7

a) Social and related community services include in addtion to educational and health services (items 33 and 34) also the services of commercial and professional associations, welfare institutions and other social and related community services.
b) Public administration and defence only. All other activities of government are included in the corresponding industries.
c) Gross domestic product in factor values.
d) Referring to indirect taxes net of subsidies.

Czechoslovakia

Source. Reply to the United Nations Material Balances Questionnaire from the Federal Statistical Office, Prague. The official estimates and descriptions are published annually in 'Statisticka Rocenka' (Statistical Yearbook), issued by the same Office.

General note. The estimates shown in the following tables have been prepared in accordance with the System of Material Product Balances. Therefore, these estimates are not comparable in concept and coverage with those conforming to the United Nations System of National Accounts.

1a Net Material Product by Use at Current Market Prices

Million Czechoslovak koruny

		1970	1971	1972	1973	1974	1975	1976	1977	1978	1979	1980
1	Personal consumption [a]	175815	184033	192246	202438	216230	223547	231479	239868	252496	261111	268771
2	Material consumption in the units of the non-material sphere serving individuals	23477	25755	27453	29514	32019	34671	37124	38808	41036	43508	46175
	Consumption of the Population	199292	209788	219699	231952	248249	258218	268603	278676	293532	304619	314946
3	Material consumption in the units of the non-material sphere serving the community as a whole	19521	21136	22787	24156	25179	26727	28838	29894	31120	33026	34955
4	Net fixed capital formation	49854	54926	58194	67751	71745	80426	88437	65658	75588	71857	76279
5	Increase in material circulating assets and in stocks	30969	24750	26794	26312	37472	37349	31132	37681	32062	40106	47908
6	Losses	5300	6407	5791	5221	6403	7033	5384	4378	4457	4721	5116
7	Exports of goods and material services	6204	8345	8952	2304	-4300	-5755	-10160	-6233	-4007	1268	3248
8	Less: Imports of goods and material services											
	Net Material Product	311140	325352	342217	357696	384748	403998	412234	410054	432752	455597	482452

a) In personal consumption there is included wear and tear of the buildings in ownership of population only. That of residential buildings in ownership of enterprises, state and co-operative organizations is included in the material consumption of units of non-material sphere serving the population.

1b Net Material Product by Use at Constant Market Prices

Million Czechoslovak koruny

		1970	1971	1972	1973	1974	1975	1976	1977	1978	1979	1980
						At constant prices of: 1967			1977			
1	Personal consumption	165002	173580	181226	190258	202650	208184	214035 / 231625	237950	245993	245205	245781
2	Material consumption in the units of the non-material sphere serving individuals	22967	25275	26574	28184	30326	32577	34646 / 36423	39251	41388	43212	44846
	Consumption of the Population	187969	198855	207800	218442	232976	240761	248681 / 268048	277201	287381	288417	290627
3	Material consumption in the units of the non-material sphere serving the community as a whole	18523	19987	21041	22366	22965	23112	24480 / 27620	29929	31134	32579	33596
4	Net fixed capital formation	41443	44486	47091	55449	59778	68519	75098 / 74939	61949	71299	67403	71379
5	Increase in material circulating assets and in stocks	21661	18246	20454	20330	26837	26093	21104 / 29430	37681	27814	33491	37805
6	Losses	4982	5816	4942	4498	5517	6009	4695 / 5426	4404	4372	4723	4974
7	Exports of goods and material services	4774	6052	7675	2572	-4980	574	4731 / -16969	-5723	-	8041	9199
8	Less: Imports of goods and material services											
	Net Material Product [a]	279352	293442	309003	323657	343093	365068	378789 / 388494	405441	422000	434654	447580

a) For this table, the estimates for the first series are at constant prices of 24 April 1960, the second series are at constant prices of 1 January 1967 and the third series are at constant prices of 1 January 1977.

2a Net Material Product by Kind of Activity of the Material Sphere in Current Market Prices

Million Czechoslovak koruny

		1970	1971	1972	1973	1974	1975	1976	1977	1978	1979	1980
1	Agriculture and forestry	35180	37750	38409	40329	40255	37848	34460	40642	39897	33779	40597
	a Agriculture and livestock	...	...	...	...	...	...	...	...	...	...	...
	b Forestry	3641	3830	3769	3802	3920	4032	4155	4617	4804	5218	5795
	c Other	31539	33920	34640	36527	36335	33816	30305	36025	35093	28561	34802
2	Industrial activity	190583	199943	207845	220636	243764	262922	278427	247344	261128	291716	309066

Czechoslovakia

2a Net Material Product by Kind of Activity of the Material Sphere in Current Market Prices
(Continued)

Million Czechoslovak koruny

	1970	1971	1972	1973	1974	1975	1976	1977	1978	1979	1980
3 Construction	35032	37889	43279	45607	48984	51486	52504	47484	49591	50272	50983
4 Wholesale and retail trade and restaurants and other eating and drinking places	35135	34881	38120	37566	36970	36365	32352	59203	65462	60421	59379
5 Transport and communication	12009	11843	11282	10267	11174	11614	12462	13391	14616	17090	20542
a Transport	8841	8429	7886	6777	7242	7497	8443	9005	9689	10985	12286
b Communication	3168	3414	3396	3490	3932	4117	4019	4386	4927	6105	8256
6 Other activities of the material sphere	3201	3046	3282	3291	3601	3763	2029	1990	2058	2319	1885
Net material product	311140	325352	342217	357696	384748	403998	412234	410054	432752	455597	482452

2b Net Material Product by Kind of Activity of the Material Sphere in Constant Market Prices

Million Czechoslovak koruny

	1970	1971	1972	1973	1974	1975	1976	1977	1978	1979	1980
				At constant prices of: 1967				1977			
1 Agriculture and forestry	30589	31765	32039	32988	33187	32859	31055 / 35151	40005	37994	36436	38813
a Agriculture and livestock	...	...	...	...	...	...	...	...	...	...	...
b Forestry	3574	3701	3767	3706	3566	3770	3931 / 4107	4583	4441	4410	4707
c Other	27015	28064	28272	29282	29621	29089	27124 / 31044	35422	33553	32026	34106
2 Industrial activity	172918	182633	190641	200372	214303	232592	246507 / 237696	241234	252451	261344	267799
3 Construction	30498	33480	37953	39606	42143	44257	45241 / 48760	47392	48874	49519	51436
4 Wholesale and retail trade and restaurants and other eating and drinking places	33273	33950	37324	40773	42624	43128	44786 / 53605	61905	66372	70552	72617
5 Transport and communication	8656	8304	7697	6264	6984	8109	8769 / 11168	12923	14260	14508	15148
a Transport	6158	5565	5042	3485	3821	4870	5628 / 7154	8618	9416	9865	10885
b Communication	2498	2739	2655	2779	3163	3239	3141 / 4014	4305	4844	4643	4263
6 Other activities of the material sphere	3418	3310	3349	3654	3852	4123	2431 / 2114	1982	2049	2295	1767
Net material product [a]	279352	293442	309003	323657	343093	365068	378789 / 388494	405441	422000	434654	447580

a) For this table, the estimates for the first series are at constant prices of 24 April 1960, the second series are at constant prices of 1 January 1967 and the third series are at constant prices of 1 January 1977.

3 Primary Incomes by Kind of Activity of the Material Sphere in Current Market Prices

Million Czechoslovak koruny

	1970 Primary Income of the Population	1970 Primary Income of Enterprises	1971 Primary Income of the Population	1971 Primary Income of Enterprises	1972 Primary Income of the Population	1972 Primary Income of Enterprises	1973 Primary Income of the Population	1973 Primary Income of Enterprises	1974 Primary Income of the Population	1974 Primary Income of Enterprises	1975 Primary Income of the Population	1975 Primary Income of Enterprises
1 Agriculture and forestry	32932	2248	33828	3922	34269	4140	35783	4546	35225	5030	35276	2572
a Agriculture and livestock	...	...	...	...	...	...	...	...	...	...	...	...
b Forestry	2591	1050	2635	1195	2629	1140	2761	1041	2828	1092	2888	1144
c Other	30341	1198	31193	2727	31640	3000	33022	3505	32397	3938	32388	1428
2 Industrial activity	62278	128305	65209	134734	68554	139291	71464	149172	74359	169405	77696	185226
3 Construction	19108	15924	20220	17669	22534	20745	23745	21862	25093	23891	26180	25306
4 Wholesale and retail trade and restaurants and other eating and drinking places	12790	22345	13465	21416	14580	23540	15415	22151	16312	20658	17006	19359
5 Transport and communication	12245	-236	12619	-776	13167	-1885	13457	-3190	13824	-2650	14283	-2669
a Transport	10117	-1276	10441	-2012	10883	-2997	11133	-4356	11376	-4134	11749	-4252
b Communication	2128	1040	2178	1236	2284	1112	2324	1166	2448	1484	2534	1583
6 Other activities of the material sphere	1039	2162	1027	2019	1227	2055	1406	1885	1443	2158	1565	2198
Total [a]	140392	170748	146368	178984	154331	187886	161270	196426	166256	218492	172006	231992

Czechoslovakia

3 Primary Incomes by Kind of Activity of the Material Sphere in Current Market Prices

Million Czechoslovak koruny

	1976 Primary Income of the Population	1976 Primary Income of Enterprises	1977 Primary Income of the Population	1977 Primary Income of Enterprises	1978 Primary Income of the Population	1978 Primary Income of Enterprises	1979 Primary Income of the Population	1979 Primary Income of Enterprises	1980 Primary Income of the Population	1980 Primary Income of Enterprises
1 Agriculture and forestry	35129	-669	36408	4234	36847	3050	35339	-1560	37473	3124
a Agriculture and livestock	...	...	...	...	...	...	...	...	...	...
b Forestry	3005	1150	3103	1514	3279	1525	3319	1899	3309	2486
c Other	32124	-1819	33305	2720	33568	1525	32020	-3459	34164	638
2 Industrial activity	80401	198026	84109	163235	87413	173715	91715	200001	94664	214402
3 Construction	27723	24781	28337	19147	29415	20176	30467	19805	31178	19805
4 Wholesale and retail trade and restaurants and other eating and drinking places	17802	14550	18761	40442	19630	45832	20514	39907	21140	38239
5 Transport and communication	14985	-2523	15656	-2265	16313	-1697	17509	-419	17908	2634
a Transport	12261	-3818	12808	-3803	13387	-3698	14501	-3516	14824	-2538
b Communication	2724	1295	2848	1538	2926	2001	3008	3097	3084	5172
6 Other activities of the material sphere	1297	732	1153	837	1352	706	1481	838	1156	729
Total [a]	177337	234897	184424	225630	190970	241782	197025	258572	203519	278933

a) Reimbursement of the travelling and similar expenses for the state and co-operative organizations in the productive sphere is included in 'primary income of enterprises', and not in 'primary income of the population'.

4 Primary Incomes From Net Material Product

Million Czechoslovak koruny

	1970	1971	1972	1973	1974	1975	1976	1977	1978	1979	1980
a) Primary Incomes of the Population
1 Socialist sector	137955	143808	151845	158687	164043	169948	175369	182360	188951	195115	201040
a State sector	107059	111949	117993	123429	128620	133829	139339	145455	151215	156385	160862
b Co-operative sector	20718	21558	23072	24092	25076	25607	26133	27269	28245	29023	30101
c Personal plots of households	10178	10301	10780	11166	10347	10512	9897	9636	9491	9707	10077
2 Private sector	2437	2560	2486	2583	2213	2058	1968	2064	2019	1910	2479
Sub-total	140392	146368	154331	161270	166256	172006	177337	184424	190970	197025	203519
b) Primary incomes of the enterprises
1 Socialist sector	170748	178984	187886	196426	218492	231992	234897	225630	241782	258572	278933
a State sector	161131	167496	175376	181937	202475	216840	221712	208518	224609	243308	260950
b Co-operative sector	9617	11488	12510	14489	16017	15152	13185	17112	17173	15264	17983
2 Private sector	-	-	-	-	-	-	-	-	-	-	...
Sub-total	170748	178984	187886	196426	218492	231992	234897	225630	241782	258572	278933
Total net material product [a]	311140	325352	342217	357696	384748	403998	412234	410054	432752	455597	482452

a) Reimbursement of the travelling and similar expenses for the state and co-operative organizations in the productive sphere is included in 'primary income of enterprises', and not in 'primary income of the population'.

5a Supply and Disposition of Goods and Material Services in Current Market Prices

Million Czechoslovak koruny

	Supply: Gross Output at Producers Prices	Supply: Trade Margins and Transport Charges	Supply: Gross Output at Market Prices	Imports	Total Supply and Disposition	Disposition: Intermediate Material Consumption including Depreciation	Disposition: Final Consumption	Disposition: Net Capital Formation	Losses	Exports
1970
1 Agriculture and forestry	94725	9706	104431	4430	108861	86547	19844	293	2177	...
2 Industrial activity	483170	62443	545613	-10686	534927	312598	184444	36017	1868	...
3 Construction	76836	60	76896	1	76897	16111	15018	44513	1255	...
4 Transport and communication	10066	-	10066	-	10066	-	10066	-	-	...
a Transport	7540	-	7540	-	7540	-	7540	-	-	...
b Communication	2526	-	2526	-	2526	-	2526	-	-	...
5 Other activities of the material sphere	5948	200	6148	51	6199	5487	712	-	-	...
Total [a]	670745	72409	743154	-6204	736950	420743	230084	80823	5300	...

Czechoslovakia

5a Supply and Disposition of Goods and Material Services in Current Market Prices
(Continued)

Million Czechoslovak koruny

	Gross Output at Producers Prices	Trade Margins and Transport Charges	Gross Output at Market Prices	Imports	Total Supply and Disposition	Intermediate Material Consumption including Depreciation	Final Consumption	Net Capital Formation	Losses	Exports
1971										
1 Agriculture and forestry	99052	8945	107997	5030	113027	87838	20403	2325	2461	...
2 Industrial activity	512771	65871	578642	-13520	565122	336907	196407	29177	2631	...
3 Construction	83297	38	83335	97	83432	17973	15970	48174	1315	...
4 Transport and communication	10565	-	10565	-	10565	-	10565	-	-	...
a Transport	7854	-	7854	-	7854	-	7854	-	-	...
b Communication	2711	-	2711	-	2711	-	2711	-	-	...
5 Other activities of the material sphere	5987	208	6195	48	6243	5536	707	-	-	...
Total [a]	711672	75062	786734	-8345	778389	448254	244052	79676	6407	...
1972										
1 Agriculture and forestry	102598	9691	112289	4951	117240	92804	20930	720	2786	...
2 Industrial activity	538444	72037	610481	-14560	595921	357451	207585	28836	2049	...
3 Construction	92733	291	93024	610	93634	20003	17243	55432	956	...
4 Transport and communication	10711	-	10711	-	10711	-	10711	-	-	...
a Transport	7918	-	7918	-	7918	-	7918	-	-	...
b Communication	2793	-	2793	-	2793	-	2793	-	-	...
5 Other activities of the material sphere	6582	229	6811	47	6858	6014	844	-	-	...
Total [a]	751068	82248	833316	-8952	824364	476272	257313	84988	5791	...
1973										
1 Agriculture and forestry	109565	9038	118603	5767	124370	97780	21515	2623	2452	...
2 Industrial activity	571139	73765	644904	-8483	636421	381224	221523	31725	1949	...
3 Construction	97995	165	98160	374	98534	20265	17734	59715	820	...
4 Transport and communication	10962	-	10962	-	10962	-	10962	-	-	...
a Transport	7995	-	7995	-	7995	-	7995	-	-	...
b Communication	2967	-	2967	-	2967	-	2967	-	-	...
5 Other activities of the material sphere	6631	235	6866	38	6904	6060	844	-	-	...
Total [a]	796292	83203	879495	-2304	877191	505329	272578	94063	5221	...
1974										
1 Agriculture and forestry	112798	8318	121116	6179	127295	99943	22570	1515	3267	...
2 Industrial activity	617956	77569	695525	-4199	691326	410874	235777	42302	2373	...
3 Construction	105814	151	105965	2291	108256	22147	19946	65400	763	...
4 Transport and communication	11790	-	11790	-	11790	-	11790	-	-	...
a Transport	8564	-	8564	-	8564	-	8564	-	-	...
b Communication	3226	-	3226	-	3226	-	3226	-	-	...
5 Other activities of the material sphere	7375	241	7616	29	7645	6818	827	-	-	...
Total [a]	855733	86279	942012	4300	946312	539782	290910	109217	6403	...
1975										
1 Agriculture and forestry	113500	9406	122906	6426	129332	104366	22287	-696	3375	...
2 Industrial activity	664956	78574	743530	-3350	740180	442330	246415	48769	2666	...
3 Construction	113246	251	113497	2664	116161	24146	21321	69702	992	...
4 Transport and communication	12229	-	12229	-	12229	-	12229	-	-	...
a Transport	8860	-	8860	-	8860	-	8860	-	-	...
b Communication	3369	-	3369	-	3369	-	3369	-	-	...
5 Other activities of the material sphere	7319	259	7578	15	7593	6699	894	-	-	...
Total [a]	911250	88490	999740	5755	1005495	577541	303146	117775	7033	...

Czechoslovakia

5a Supply and Disposition of Goods and Material Services in Current Market Prices
(Continued)

Million Czechoslovak koruny

	Gross Output at Producers Prices	Trade Margins and Transport Charges	Gross Output at Market Prices	Imports	Total Supply and Disposition	Intermediate Material Consumption including Depreciation	Final Consumption	Net Capital Formation	Losses	Exports
1976										
1 Agriculture and forestry	111878	8521	120399	9697	130096	104038	22629	1419	2010	...
2 Industrial activity	703862	77904	781766	-2667	779099	473384	256260	47250	2205	...
3 Construction	118037	200	118237	3096	121333	25703	23561	70900	1169	...
4 Transport and communication	12395	-	12395	-	12395	-	12395	-	-	...
a Transport	9069	-	9069	-	9069	-	9069	-	-	...
b Communication	3326	-	3326	-	3326	-	3326	-	-	...
5 Other activities of the material sphere	4621	270	4891	34	4925	3986	939	-	-	...
Total a	950793	86895	1037688	10160	1047848	607111	315784	119569	5384	...
1977										
1 Agriculture and forestry	122298	8678	130976	7780	138756	111321	23219	3155	1061	...
2 Industrial activity	715525	104270	819795	-3791	816004	513964	267178	32507	2355	...
3 Construction	111775	126	111901	2211	114112	23137	22336	67677	962	...
4 Transport and communication	12680	-	12680	-	12680	-	12680	-	-	...
a Transport	9196	-	9196	-	9196	-	9196	-	-	...
b Communication	3484	-	3484	-	3484	-	3484	-	-	...
5 Other activities of the material sphere	4772	266	5038	33	5071	4298	773	-	-	...
Total a	967050	113340	1080390	6233	1086623	652720	326186	103339	4378	...
1978										
1 Agriculture and forestry	127747	11918	139665	5989	145654	119506	23190	1995	963	...
2 Industrial activity	751709	111532	863241	-3291	859950	538094	282283	37591	1982	...
3 Construction	115847	120	115967	1271	117238	24200	23462	68064	1512	...
4 Transport and communication	13014	-	13014	-	13014	-	13014	-	-	...
a Transport	9140	-	9140	-	9140	-	9140	-	-	...
b Communication	3874	-	3874	-	3874	-	3874	-	-	...
5 Other activities of the material sphere	5011	295	5306	38	5344	4364	980	-	-	...
Total a	1013328	123865	1137193	4007	1141200	686164	342929	107650	4457	...
1979										
1 Agriculture and forestry	112237	11312	123549	8298	131847	104066	22569	3179	2033	...
2 Industrial activity	806608	110273	916881	-4599	912282	568676	294151	47784	1671	...
3 Construction	117461	169	117630	-4988	112642	25927	24698	61000	1017	...
4 Transport and communication	13886	-	13886	-	13886	-	13886	-	-	...
a Transport	9419	-	9419	-	9419	-	9419	-	-	...
b Communication	4467	-	4467	-	4467	-	4467	-	-	...
5 Other activities of the material sphere	5263	343	5606	21	5627	4330	1297	-	-	...
Total a	1055455	122097	1177552	-1268	1176284	702999	356601	111963	4721	...
1980										
1 Agriculture and forestry	127074	14592	141666	9372	151038	118646	25117	5158	2117	...
2 Industrial activity	856436	110897	967333	-14368	952965	595570	300425	55114	1856	...
3 Construction	120417	321	120738	1716	122454	29917	27479	63915	1143	...
4 Transport and communication	15397	-	15397	-	15397	-	15397	-	-	...
a Transport	9767	-	9767	-	9767	-	9767	-	-	...
b Communication	5630	-	5630	-	5630	-	5630	-	-	...
5 Other activities of the material sphere	5029	293	5322	32	5354	4645	709	-	-	...
Total a	1124353	126103	1250456	-3248	1247208	748778	369127	124187	5116	...

a) Column 'Imports' is net of column 'Exports'.

# Czechoslovakia

5b Supply and Disposition of Goods and Material Services in Constant Market Prices

Million Czechoslovak koruny

	Gross Output at Producers Prices	Trade Margins and Transport Charges	Gross Output at Market Prices	Imports	Total Supply and Disposition	Intermediate Material Consumption including Depreciation	Final Consumption	Net Capital Formation	Losses	Exports
At constant prices of: 1967										
1970										
1 Agriculture and forestry	82300	9763	92063	4430	96493	77136	18254	-610	1713	...
2 Industrial activity	452748	57184	509932	-9256	500676	296349	173021	29438	1868	...
3 Construction	69861	60	69921	1	69922	18671	16139	33875	1237	...
4 Transport and communication	9731	-	9731	-	9731	-	9731	-	-	...
a Transport	7540	-	7540	-	7540	-	7540	-	-	...
b Communication	2191	-	2191	-	2191	-	2191	-	-	...
5 Other activities of the material sphere	5638	178	5816	51	5867	5152	715	-	-	...
Total ab	620278	67185	687463	-4774	682689	397308	217860	62703	4818	...
1971										
1 Agriculture and forestry	85234	9004	94238	5030	99268	76865	18539	1921	1943	...
2 Industrial activity	480526	60489	541015	-11227	529788	320559	185691	21139	2399	...
3 Construction	76226	38	76264	97	76361	18516	16699	39672	1474	...
4 Transport and communication	10207	-	10207	-	10207	-	10207	-	-	...
a Transport	7854	-	7854	-	7854	-	7854	-	-	...
b Communication	2353	-	2353	-	2353	-	2353	-	-	...
5 Other activities of the material sphere	5674	185	5859	48	5907	5197	710	-	-	...
Total ab	657867	69716	727583	-6052	721531	421137	231846	62732	5816	...
1972										
1 Agriculture and forestry	88535	9686	98221	4951	103172	81380	19035	560	2197	...
2 Industrial activity	507249	65877	573126	-13283	559843	341838	195353	20983	1669	...
3 Construction	84621	291	84912	610	85522	20574	17870	46002	1076	...
4 Transport and communication	10340	-	10340	-	10340	-	10340	-	-	...
a Transport	7918	-	7918	-	7918	-	7918	-	-	...
b Communication	2422	-	2422	-	2422	-	2422	-	-	...
5 Other activities of the material sphere	6038	205	6243	47	6290	5441	849	-	-	...
Total ab	696783	76059	772842	-7675	765167	449233	243447	67545	4942	...
1973										
1 Agriculture and forestry	92841	10018	102859	5767	108626	85022	19475	2250	1879	...
2 Industrial activity	535070	70675	605745	-8751	596994	363569	207710	23992	1723	...
3 Construction	89214	165	89379	374	89753	20649	18671	49537	896	...
4 Transport and communication	10588	-	10588	-	10588	-	10588	-	-	...
a Transport	7995	-	7995	-	7995	-	7995	-	-	...
b Communication	2593	-	2593	-	2593	-	2593	-	-	...
5 Other activities of the material sphere	6311	213	6524	38	6562	5710	852	-	-	...
Total ab	734024	81071	815095	-2572	812523	474950	257296	75779	4498	...
1974										
1 Agriculture and forestry	95029	9301	104330	6179	110509	86034	20661	1193	2621	...
2 Industrial activity	565482	74634	640116	-3519	636597	384143	219551	30784	2119	...
3 Construction	96235	151	96386	2291	98677	22429	20833	54638	777	...
4 Transport and communication	11371	-	11371	-	11371	-	11371	-	-	...
a Transport	8564	-	8564	-	8564	-	8564	-	-	...
b Communication	2807	-	2807	-	2807	-	2807	-	-	...
5 Other activities of the material sphere	6931	216	7147	29	7176	6342	834	-	-	...
Total ab	775048	84302	859350	4980	864330	498948	273250	86615	5517	...

Czechoslovakia

5b Supply and Disposition of Goods and Material Services in Constant Market Prices
(Continued)

Million Czechoslovak koruny

	Gross Output at Producers Prices	Trade Margins and Transport Charges	Gross Output at Market Prices	Imports	Total Supply and Disposition	Intermediate Material Consumption Including Depreciation	Final Consumption	Net Capital Formation	Losses	Exports
At constant prices of:1967										
1975										
1 Agriculture and forestry	96045	10352	106397	6426	112823	90092	20212	-172	2691	...
2 Industrial activity	603220	76385	679605	-9679	669926	405064	226529	35982	2351	...
3 Construction	103006	251	103257	2664	105921	24190	21962	58802	967	...
4 Transport and communication	11785	-	11785	-	11785	-	11785	-	-	
a Transport	8860	-	8860	-	8860	-	8860	-	-	...
b Communication	2925	-	2925	-	2925	-	2925	-	-	...
5 Other activities of the material sphere	6872	234	7106	15	7121	6219	902	-	-	
Total ab	820928	87222	908150	-574	907576	525565	281390	94612	6009	...
1976										
1 Agriculture and forestry	94989	9503	104492	9697	114189	90410	20686	1650	1443	...
2 Industrial activity	633543	80669	714212	-17558	696654	427482	232427	34210	2535	...
3 Construction	107966	200	108166	3096	111262	25533	24154	60342	1233	...
4 Transport and communication	11952	-	11952	-	11952	-	11952	-	-	
a Transport	9069	-	9069	-	9069	-	9069	-	-	...
b Communication	2883	-	2883	-	2883	-	2883	-	-	...
5 Other activities of the material sphere	4339	242	4581	34	4615	3669	946	-	-	
Total ab	852789	90614	943403	-4731	938672	547094	290165	96202	5211	...

a) Column 'Imports' is net of column 'Exports'.
b) At constant prices of 1 January 1967.

5b Supply and Disposition of Goods and Material Services in Constant Market Prices

Million Czechoslovak koruny

	Gross Output at Producers Prices	Trade Margins and Transport Charges	Gross Output at Market Prices	Imports	Total Supply and Disposition	Intermediate Material Consumption Including Depreciation	Final Consumption	Net Capital Formation	Losses	Exports
At constant prices of:1977										
1976										
1 Agriculture and forestry	111002	9864	120866	9447	130313	105246	21676	1497	1894	...
2 Industrial activity	688204	93540	781744	4405	786149	487576	255236	41080	2257	...
3 Construction	108712	200	108912	3096	112008	25546	23395	61792	1275	...
4 Transport and communication	12347	-	12347	-	12347	-	12347	-	-	
a Transport	9069	-	9069	-	9069	-	9069	-	-	...
b Communication	3278	-	3278	-	3278	-	3278	-	-	...
5 Other activities of the material sphere	4700	274	4974	21	4995	4052	943	-	-	
Total ab	924965	103878	1028843	16969	1045812	622420	313597	104369	5426	...
1977										
1 Agriculture and forestry	122298	8678	130976	7780	138756	111321	23219	3155	1061	...
2 Industrial activity	710609	107125	817734	-4301	813433	515253	265162	30660	2358	...
3 Construction	111775	126	111901	2211	114112	24165	23147	65815	985	...
4 Transport and communication	12683	-	12683	-	12683	-	12683	-	-	
a Transport	9196	-	9196	-	9196	-	9196	-	-	...
b Communication	3487	-	3487	-	3487	-	3487	-	-	...
5 Other activities of the material sphere	4772	266	5038	33	5071	4298	773	-	-	
Total ab	962137	116195	1078332	5723	1084055	655037	324984	99630	4404	...
1978										
1 Agriculture and forestry	125105	10904	136009	5964	141973	116334	22791	1996	852	...
2 Industrial activity	742375	113867	856242	-7273	848969	539049	275906	32029	1985	...
3 Construction	115847	120	115967	1271	117238	26293	24322	65088	1535	...
4 Transport and communication	13014	-	13014	-	13014	-	13014	-	-	
a Transport	9140	-	9140	-	9140	-	9140	-	-	...
b Communication	3874	-	3874	-	3874	-	3874	-	-	...
5 Other activities of the material sphere	5006	295	5301	38	5339	4359	980	-	-	
Total ab	1001347	125186	1126533	-	1126533	686035	337013	99113	4372	...

Czechoslovakia

5b Supply and Disposition of Goods and Material Services in Constant Market Prices
(Continued)

Million Czechoslovak koruny

	Gross Output at Producers Prices	Trade Margins and Transport Charges	Gross Output at Market Prices	Imports	Total Supply and Disposition	Intermediate Material Consumption including Depreciation	Final Consumption	Net Capital Formation	Losses	Exports
At constant prices of: 1977										
1979										
1 Agriculture and forestry	123075	10019	133094	8449	141543	114479	21899	3163	2002	...
2 Industrial activity	767764	119916	887680	-11523	876157	556330	278169	39987	1671	...
3 Construction	117344	169	117513	-4988	112525	28206	25525	57744	1050	...
4 Transport and communication	13189	-	13189	-	13189	-	13189	-	-	...
a Transport	9419	-	9419	-	9419	-	9419	-	-	...
b Communication	3770	-	3770	-	3770	-	3770	-	-	...
5 Other activities of the material sphere	5243	329	5572	21	5593	4310	1283	-	-	...
Total ab	1026615	130433	1157048	-8041	1149007	703325	340065	100894	4723	...
1980										
1 Agriculture and forestry	133263	12325	145588	10281	155869	124861	23839	5171	1998	...
2 Industrial activity	783890	121693	905583	-21228	884355	561939	277211	43387	1818	...
3 Construction	120211	321	120532	1716	122248	32197	28267	60626	1158	...
4 Transport and communication	13411	-	13411	-	13411	-	13411	-	-	...
a Transport	9767	-	9767	-	9767	-	9767	-	-	...
b Communication	3644	-	3644	-	3644	-	3644	-	-	...
5 Other activities of the material sphere	4913	292	5205	32	5237	4529	708	-	-	...
Total ab	1055688	134631	1190319	-9199	1181120	723526	343436	109184	4974	...

a) Column 'Imports' is net of column 'Exports'.
b) At constant prices of 1 January 1977.

6a Capital Formation by Kind of Activity of the Material and Non-Material Spheres in Current Market Prices

Million Czechoslovak koruny

	1970	1971	1972	1973	1974	1975	1976	1977	1978	1979	1980
Net Fixed Capital Formation											
1 Agriculture and forestry	3512	5702	6288	6691	8068	8263	10216	8471	10092	9366	9164
2 Industrial activity	17675	16854	16807	21968	22337	26414	33564	22573	22422	24442	26748
3 Construction	1559	1328	1568	2242	2413	3040	2656	2170	3448	2482	2836
4 Wholesale and retail trade, restaurants and other eating and drinking places	3325	3891	3326	3280	3972	5549	4427	4539	4638	3434	3390
5 Transport and communication	5882	7197	5371	9308	8266	7276	8503	4417	8918	6578	9815
6 Other activities of the material sphere	275	192	115	119	24	65	86	329	22	53	12
Total Material Sphere	32228	35164	33475	43608	45080	50607	59452	42499	49540	46355	51965
7 Housing except owner-occupied, communal and miscellaneous personal services	10444	11533	13693	13800	13980	14712	14451	9627	11896	12156	11737
8 Education, culture and art	1860	2049	3264	2661	3016	4053	3663	3173	3973	3547	2944
9 Health and social welfare services and sports	935	1002	910	1436	1390	2026	1946	891	1731	1179	1843
Total Non-Material Sphere Serving Individuals	13239	14584	17867	17897	18386	20791	20060	13691	17600	16882	16524
10 Government	...	...	...	...	...	...	...	...	...	...	...
11 Finance, credit and insurance	...	...	...	...	...	...	...	...	...	...	...
12 Research, scientific and technological institutes	...	...	...	...	...	...	...	...	...	...	...
13 Other activities of the non-material sphere	...	...	...	...	...	...	...	...	...	...	...
Total Non-Material Sphere Serving the Community as a Whole	1499	2251	2770	2217	3675	3951	3790	4577	4149	4320	4123
14 Owner-occupied dwellings	2888	2927	4082	4029	4604	5077	5135	4891	4299	4300	3667
Total Net Fixed Capital Formation	49854	54926	58194	67751	71745	80426	88437	65658	75588	71857	76279
Gross Fixed Capital Formation											
1 Agriculture and forestry	8192	10659	10987	11615	13226	14058	16297	14145	16306	16075	16462
2 Industrial activity	34266	35056	36548	42558	44462	50454	59307	47486	48814	52775	57239

Czechoslovakia

6a Capital Formation by Kind of Activity of the Material and Non-Material Spheres in Current Market Prices
(Continued)

Million Czechoslovak koruny

	1970	1971	1972	1973	1974	1975	1976	1977	1978	1979	1980
3 Construction	2867	2762	3155	4171	4738	5640	5889	4852	6273	5625	6290
4 Wholesale and retail trade and restaurants and other eating and drinking places	4709	5444	4988	5120	5960	7764	6898	6784	7124	6089	6273
5 Transport and communication	11503	13288	11884	16162	15866	15211	17202	12441	17902	16194	20089
6 Other activities of the material sphere	353	281	212	236	160	212	140	449	94	131	94
Total Material Sphere	61890	67490	67774	79862	84412	93339	105733	86157	96513	96889	106447
7 Housing except owner-occupied, communal and miscellaneous personal services	13463	14853	16993	17077	17346	18262	18398	14038	16501	17149	16871
8 Education, culture and art	2976	3270	4486	4009	4401	5568	5564	5132	6029	5737	5240
9 Health and social welfare services and sports	1456	1604	1489	2069	2081	2780	2812	1724	2601	2061	2780
Total Non-Material Sphere Serving Individuals	17895	19727	22968	23155	23828	26610	26774	20894	25131	24947	24891
10 Government	...	...	...	...	...	...	...	...	...	...	...
11 Finance, credit and insurance	...	...	...	...	...	...	...	...	...	...	...
12 Research, scientific and technological institutes	...	...	...	...	...	...	...	...	...	...	...
13 Other activities of the non-material sphere	...	...	...	...	...	...	...	...	...	...	...
Total Non-Material Sphere Serving the Community as a Whole	3086	4235	4774	4562	5919	6366	6764	7232	7081	7497	7449
14 Owner-occupied dwellings	4408	4495	5710	5659	6298	6889	7033	6866	6391	6487	5943
Total Gross Fixed Capital Formation	87279	95947	101226	113238	120457	133204	146304	121149	135116	135820	144730

Increases in Material Circulating Assets and Stocks

	1970	1971	1972	1973	1974	1975	1976	1977	1978	1979	1980
1 Agriculture and forestry	2871	2130	679	1973	2444	1728	886	4677	1990	3598	3542
2 Industrial activity	11165	9315	7692	7748	14790	13791	11254	9486	7587	19415	23092
3 Construction	2030	2055	9871	5371	7784	5051	867	16189	8744	12670	4926
4 Wholesale and retail trade and restaurants and other eating and drinking places	8529	6024	3433	7153	7626	10071	9454	770	4316	5880	10138
5 Transport and communication	427	1164	1578	844	1102	3130	4564	4448	3517	-5090	73
6 Other activities of the non-material sphere	343	161	-42	-61	61	226	57	21	60	77	169
Total increase in material circulating assets	25365	20849	23211	23028	33807	33997	27082	35591	26214	36550	41940
Statistical discrepancy	...	...	...	...	...	...	...	...	...	...	...
Increase in stocks of the non-material sphere	5604	3901	3583	3284	3665	3352	4050	2090	5848	3556	5968

Gross Fixed Capital Formation by Socio-economic Sector and Industrial Use

	1970	1971	1972	1973	1974	1975	1976	1977	1978	1979	1980
1 State and co-operative (excluding collective farms)	79349	85688	89435	101168	106686	118502	129537	105185	118391	119321	128619
a Industry	34266	35056	36548	42558	44462	50454	59307	47486	48814	52775	57239
b Construction	2867	2762	3155	4171	4738	5640	5889	4852	6273	5625	6290
c Agriculture and forestry	4740	4975	4986	5204	5736	6245	6563	5047	5972	6063	6294
d Transport and communication	11503	13288	11884	16162	15866	15211	17202	12441	17902	16194	20089
e Residential building	25973	29607	32862	33073	35884	40952	40576	35359	39430	38664	38707
f Trade and other											
2 Collective farms	3716	6007	6440	6827	7875	8223	10030	9307	10483	10098	10257
a Agriculture	3646	5927	6360	6827	7875	8223	10030	9307	10483	10098	10257
b Other	70	80	80	-	-	-	-	-	-	-	...
3 Other	4214	4252	5351	5243	5896	6479	6737	6657	6242	6401	5854
Gross Fixed Capital Formation	87279	95947	101226	113238	120457	133204	146304	121149	135116	135820	144730

Czechoslovakia

6b Capital Formation by Kind of Activity of the Material and Non-Material Spheres in Constant Market Prices

Million Czechoslovak koruny

	1970	1971	1972	1973	1974	1975	1976	1977	1978	1979	1980
				At constant prices of: 1967				1977			

Net Fixed Capital Formation

	1970	1971	1972	1973	1974	1975	1976	1977	1978	1979	1980
1 Agriculture and forestry	2860	4632	6174	5610	6932	7243	8974 / 8788	7802	9311	8546	8435
2 Industrial activity [a]	14252	13000	12057	17224	17889	21749	27848 / 27368	21110	20713	22640	24551
3 Construction [a]	1379	1103	1210	1876	1965	2698	2188 / 2083	2006	3257	2270	2618
4 Wholesale and retail trade, restaurants and other eating and drinking places	2944	3392	2716	2767	3517	5010	3868 / 3917	4386	4452	3248	3195
5 Transport and communication	4595	5605	3692	7382	6304	5618	6950 / 6979	3912	8307	5948	9124
6 Other activities of the material sphere	249	168	89	97	8	52	72 / 76	321	18	47	8
Total Material Sphere [a]	26279	27900	25938	34956	36615	42370	49900 / 49211	39537	46058	42699	47931
7 Housing except owner-occupied, communal and miscellaneous personal services [a]	9280	9354	12048	12265	12450	13341	12984 / 13219	9298	11548	11814	11406
8 Education, culture and art	1547	1664	2740	2144	2620	3653	3228 / 3278	3029	3816	3392	2788
9 Health and social welfare services and sports	796	821	715	1239	1220	1810	1779 / 1782	828	1660	1110	1769
Total Non-Material Sphere Serving Individuals	11623	11839	15503	15648	16290	18804	17991 / 18279	13155	17024	16316	15963
10 Government	...	...	...	...	...	...	... / ...	...	...	...	...
11 Finance, credit and insurance	...	...	...	...	...	...	... / ...	...	...	...	...
12 Research, scientific and technological institutes	...	...	...	...	...	...	... / ...	...	...	...	...
13 Other activities of the non-material sphere	...	...	...	...	...	...	... / ...	...	...	...	...
Total Non-Material Sphere Serving the Community as a Whole	1190	1820	2269	1568	3030	3059	2854 / 2956	4518	4079	4251	3966
14 Owner-occupied dwellings	2351	2927	3381	3277	3843	4286	4353 / 4493	4739	4138	4137	3519
Total Net Fixed Capital Formation	41443	44486	47091	55449	59778	68519	75098 / 74939	61949	71299	67403	71379

Gross Fixed Capital Formation

	1970	1971	1972	1973	1974	1975	1976	1977	1978	1979	1980
1 Agriculture and forestry	7776	9825	11091	10739	12344	13073	15046 / 14793	14145	16259	16006	16315
2 Industrial activity	32221	32378	33470	39314	41477	46970	54320 / 52149	47486	48651	52397	56427
3 Construction	2705	2550	2825	3827	4312	5235	5305 / 5044	4852	6250	5576	6189
4 Wholesale and retail trade and restaurants and other eating and drinking places	4431	5026	4465	4726	5605	7268	6353 / 6253	6784	7109	6064	6223
5 Transport and communciation	10815	12268	10742	15243	14890	14054	16082 / 15687	12441	17858	16098	19906
6 Other activities of the material sphere	331	262	193	219	149	201	126 / 124	449	94	129	92
Total Material Sphere [a]	58279	62309	62786	74068	78777	86801	97232 / 94050	86157	96221	96270	105152
7 Housing except owner-occupied, communal and miscellaneous personal services	12707	13707	15711	15860	16072	17174	17196 / 17497	14038	16498	17142	16860
8 Education, culture and art	2802	3013	4072	3646	4136	5274	5229 / 5227	5132	6024	5727	5217
9 Health and social welfare services and sports	1374	1477	1334	1928	1959	2605	2683 / 2638	1724	2598	2053	2762
Total Non-Material Sphere Serving Individuals [a]	16883	18197	21117	21434	22167	25053	25108 / 25362	20894	25120	24922	24839

339

Czechoslovakia

6b Capital Formation by Kind of Activity of the Material and Non-Material Spheres in Constant Market Prices
(Continued)

Million Czechoslovak koruny

	1970	1971	1972	1973	1974	1975	1976	1977	1978	1979	1980
					At constant prices of: 1967			1977			
10 Government	...	...	...	...	...	...	...	...	...	...	...
11 Finance, credit and insurance	...	...	...	...	...	...	...	...	...	...	...
12 Research, scientific and technological institutes	...	...	...	...	...	...	...	...	...	...	...
13 Other activities of the non-material sphere	...	...	...	...	...	...	...	...	...	...	...
Total Non-Material Sphere Serving the Community as a Whole [a]	2898	3923	4351	4066	5460	5565	5882 / 5662	7232	7064	7459	7365
14 Owner-occupied dwellings	4137	4127	5271	5151	5786	6335	6478 / 6615	6866	6391	6487	5943
Total Gross Fixed Capital Formation [a]	82197	88556	93525	104719	112190	123754	134700 / 131689	121149	134796	135138	143299

Increases in Material Circulating Assets and Stocks

	1970	1971	1972	1973	1974	1975	1976	1977	1978	1979	1980
1 Agriculture and forestry	2215	1496	467	1523	1750	1207	601 / 838	4677	1726	3004	3599
2 Industrial activity	7866	7079	5911	5985	10593	9635	7628 / 10638	9486	6582	16213	17787
3 Construction	1494	1600	7793	4142	5575	3529	588 / 820	16189	7586	10580	4161
4 Wholesale and retail trade and restaurants and other eating and drinking places	5946	3940	2414	5535	5462	7036	6409 / 8937	770	3744	4910	6332
5 Transport and communication	-24	973	1234	654	789	2186	3094 / 4314	4448	3051	-4250	-167
6 Other activities of the non-material sphere	230	109	-33	-43	44	158	39 / 54	21	52	64	420
Total increase in material circulating assets	17727	15197	17786	17796	24213	23751	18359 / 25601	35591	22741	30521	32132
Statistical discrepancy	...	...	...	...	...	...	...	...	...	...	...
Increase in stocks of the non-material sphere [a]	3934	3049	2668	2534	2624	2342	2745 / 3829	2090	5073	2970	5673

Gross Fixed Capital Formation by Socio-economic Sector and Industrial Use

	1970	1971	1972	1973	1974	1975	1976	1977	1978	1979	1980
1 State and co-operative (excluding collective farms)	74663	79096	81621	93623	99410	110163	119193 / 116192	105185	118105	118679	127084
a Industry	32221	32378	33470	39314	41477	46970	54320 / 52149	47486	48651	52397	56427
b Construction	2705	2550	2825	3827	4312	5235	5305 / 5044	4852	6250	5576	6189
c Agriculture and forestry	4445	4572	4530	4794	5350	5817	6017 / 5911	5047	5959	6034	6043
d Transport and communication	10815	12268	10742	15243	14890	14054	16082 / 15687	12441	17858	16098	19906
e Residential building	24477	27328	30054	30445	33381	38087	37469 / 37401	35359	39387	38574	38519
f Trade and other											
2 Collective farms	3495	5465	6684	6178	7214	7488	9190 / 9042	9307	10431	10044	10337
a Agriculture	3429	5385	6612	6178	7214	7488	9190 / 9042	9307	10431	10044	10337
b Other	66	80	72	-	-	-	-	-	-	-	...
3 Other	4039	3995	5220	4918	5566	6103	6317 / 6455	6657	6260	6415	5878
Gross Fixed Capital Formation [a]	82197	88556	93525	104719	112190	123754	134700 / 131689	121149	134796	135138	143299

a) For this table, the estimates for the first series are at constant prices of 24 April 1960, the second series are at constant prices of 1 January 1967 and the third series are at constant prices of 1 January 1977.

Czechoslovakia

7a Final Consumption at Current Market Prices

Million Czechoslovak koruny	1970	1971	1972	1973	1974	1975	1976	1977	1978	1979	1980
1 Personal consumption [a]	175815	184033	192246	202438	216230	223547	231479	239868	252496	261111	268771

a) Material Consumption in the Units of the Non-Material Sphere Serving Individuals

	1970	1971	1972	1973	1974	1975	1976	1977	1978	1979	1980
Housing except owner-occupied, communal and miscellaneous personal services [a]	8069	9009	9338	10019	11064	12137	14273	14664	15287	16804	17702
Education, culture and art	8480	9126	9885	10707	11428	12289	13081	13721	14659	15197	16151
Health and social welfare services and sports	6928	7620	8230	8788	9527	10245	9770	10423	11090	11507	12322
Other	...	...	...	...	...	...	...	...	...	...	...
2 Total non-material sphere serving individuals [a]	23477	25755	27453	29514	32019	34671	37124	38808	41036	43508	46175

b) Material Consumption in the Units of the Non-Material Sphere Serving the Community as a Whole

	1970	1971	1972	1973	1974	1975	1976	1977	1978	1979	1980
3 Total non-material sphere serving the community as a whole	19521	21136	22787	24156	25179	26727	28838	29894	31120	33026	34955
Final consumption	218813	230924	242486	256108	273428	284945	297441	308570	324652	337645	349901

a) In personal consumption there is included wear and tear of the buildings in ownership of population only. That of residential buildings in ownership of enterprises, state and co-operative organizations is included in the material consumption of units of non-material sphere serving the population.

7b Final Consumption at Constant Market Prices

Million Czechoslovak koruny	1970	1971	1972	1973	1974	1975	1976	1977	1978	1979	1980
At constant prices of:				1967				1977			
1 Personal consumption [a]	165002	173580	181226	190258	202650	208184	214035 / 231625	237950	245993	245205	245781

a) Material Consumption in the Units of the Non-Material Sphere Serving Individuals

	1970	1971	1972	1973	1974	1975	1976	1977	1978	1979	1980
Housing except owner-occupied, communal and miscellaneous personal services	7845[a]	8829[a]	9038[a]	9525[a]	10364[a]	11269[a]	13211[a] / 14221	14965	15577	16945	17625
Education, culture and art	8262	8897	9474	10112	10680	11313	11942 / 12748	13821	14706	14872	15224
Health and social welfare services and sports	6860	7549	8062	8547	9282	9995	9493 / 9454	10465	11105	11395	11997
Other	...	...	...	...	...	...	...	...	...	...	...
2 Total non-material sphere serving individuals	22967[ab]	25275[ab]	26574[ab]	28184[ab]	30326[ab]	32577[ab]	34646[ab] / 36423	39251	41388	43212	44846

b) Material Consumption in the Units of the Non-Material Sphere Serving the Community as a Whole

	1970	1971	1972	1973	1974	1975	1976	1977	1978	1979	1980
3 Total non-material sphere serving the community as a whole	18523	19987	21041	22366	22965	23112	24480 / 27620	29929	31134	32579	33596
Final consumption [b]	206492	218842	228841	240808	255941	263873	273161 / 295668	307130	318515	320996	324223

a) In personal consumption there is included wear and tear of the buildings in ownership of population only. That of residential buildings in ownership of enterprises, state and co-operative organizations is included in the material consumption of units of non-material sphere serving the population.
b) For this table, the estimates for the first series are at constant prices of 24 April 1960, the second series are at constant prices of 1 January 1967 and the third series are at constant prices of 1 January 1977.

8 Personal Consumption According to Source of Supply of Goods and Material Services in Current Market Prices

Million Czechoslovak koruny	1970	1971	1972	1973	1974	1975	1976	1977	1978	1979	1980
1 Purchases of goods in state and co-operative retail trade	151025	158781	166209	175880	189319	195798	203447	211211	223543	231291	235078
2 Purchases of goods in the free market and from private retail trade	1556	1759	1784	2226	1910	1961	1949	2060	2015	1667	1745
3 Goods produced on own account and received in kind	9145	8778	8765	8216	7964	7724	7112	7080	7034	6837	7455
4 Payments for transport and communication services	8144	8538	8649	8740	9330	9720	9956	10122	10095	10700	11569
5 Purchases of electricity, gas and water	2516	2712	3158	3363	3505	3805	4092	4276	4544	5059	6855
6 Purchases directly from handicrafts, repair shops and the like	1909	1897	2053	2383	2508	2727	3025	3144	3173	3370	3793
7 Consumption of fixed assets in respect of all dwellings	1520	1568	1628	1630	1694	1812	1898	1975	2092	2187	2276
8 Other	...	...	...	...	...	...	...	...	...	...	...
Personal consumption [a]	175815	184033	192246	202438	216230	223547	231479	239868	252496	261111	268771

a) In personal consumption there is included wear and tear of the buildings in ownership of population only. That of residential buildings in ownership of enterprises, state and co-operative organizations is included in the material consumption of units of non-material sphere serving the population.

Democratic Yemen

Source. Reply to the United Nations National Accounts Questionnaire from the Central Board of Statistics, Tawahi.
General note. The estimates shown in the following tables have been prepared by the Central Board of Statistics in accordance with the United Nations System of National Accounts so far as the existing data would permit.

1.3 Cost Components of the Gross Domestic Product

Thousand Yemeni dinars

	1970	1971	1972	1973	1974	1975	1976	1977	1978	1979	1980
1 Indirect taxes, net	...	...	...	8517	10933	11593	15299	20198	25114	29887	...
2 Consumption of fixed capital	...	...	...	4943	5785	6864	7735	11356	20112	18717	...
3 Compensation of employees paid by resident producers to:	...	...	...	45975	47919	54600	63454	77075	97786	116806	...
4 Net operating surplus	...	...	...	24594	33447	27729	41143	51550	36917	44485	...
Equals: Gross Domestic Product	...	...	...	84029	98084	100786	127631	160179	179929	209895	...

1.10 Gross Domestic Product by Kind of Activity, in Current Prices

Thousand Yemeni dinars

	1970	1971	1972	1973	1974	1975	1976	1977	1978	1979	1980
1 Agriculture, hunting, forestry and fishing	13165	14590	15264	17823	18874	19189	26910	27892	22696	27250	...
2 Mining and quarrying	47	48	55	77	152	152	178	341	297	209	...
3 Manufacturing	17059	9703	10271	9018	16135	10113	13778	19817	24262	24032	...
4 Electricity, gas and water	1097	1122	997	1305	1045	1962	2041	2768	3161	3252	...
5 Construction	680	1475	3163	4293	5644	8684	10368	15253	25561	24015	...
6 Wholesale and retail trade, restaurants and hotels	14324	13292	11898	15205	18198	19919	23845	28638	26005	32628	...
7 Transport, storage and communication	4644	4496	4447	6322	8958	10305	14641	19504	22862	28801	...
8 Finance, insurance, real estate and business services	2882	2717	2652	5269	6860	7442	8412	11072	11401	17253	...
9 Community, social and personal services	...	...	...	2640	3442	4016	4207	4489	1460	1526	...
Total, Industries	53898	47443	48747	61952	79308	81782	104380	129774	137705	158965	...
Producers of Government Services	13478	13929	14613	18559	16541	18273	21472	25660	34714	43157	...
Other Producers	...	...	...	...	...	...	...	...	...	...	...
Subtotal [a]	67376	61372	63360	80511	95849	100055	125852	155434	172419	202122	...
Less: Imputed bank service charge	...	...	...	1550	3283	4406	4525	6235	6542	10633	...
Plus: Import duties [b]	1064	1201	1401	5068	5518	5137	6304	10980	14052	18406	...
Plus: Value added tax	...	...	...	...	...	...	...	...	...	...	...
Plus: Other adjustments [c]	2333	2482	2468	...	...	...	...	...	...	...	...
Equals: Gross Domestic Product	70773	65055	67229	68042 / 84029	98084	100786	127631	160179	179929	209895	...

a) For the first series, net domestic product in factor values.
b) For the first series, referring to indirect taxes net of subsidies.
c) For the first series, referring to consumption of fixed capital.

Denmark

General note. The preparation of national accounts statistics in Denmark is undertaken by the Danmarks Statistik, Copenhagen. The official estimates are published annually in 'Statistiske Efterretninger'. The following presentation of sources and methods is mainly based on a report prepared by the Statistical Office of the European Communities in 1976 entitled 'Base statistics needed for the ESA accounts and tables: present situation and prospects for improvements' and on 'Input-output tabeller for Danmark 1966' published by Danmarks Statistik in 1973. The estimates are generally in accordance with the classifications and definitions recommended in the United Nations System of National Accounts (SNA). The following tables have been prepared from successive replies to the United Nations national accounts questionnaire. When the scope and coverage of the estimates differ for conceptual or statistical reasons from the definitions and classifications recommended in SNA, a footnote is indicated to the relevant tables.

Sources and methods:

(a) Gross domestic product. Gross domestic product is estimated mainly through the production approach.

(b) Expenditure on the gross domestic product. The expenditure approach is used to estimate government final consumption expenditure, increase in stocks and exports and imports of goods and services. The commodity-flow approach is used for private final consumption expenditure and gross fixed capital formation. The estimates of government consumption expenditure are mainly based on the accounts of the central and local government and on social secutiry funds. The estimates of private consumption expenditure, using the commodity-flow method, have a time-lag of two years. Therefore, short-term estimates are made, using turnover statistics for the retail trade. This is supplemented by family budget surveys which are conducted every five years. Changes in stocks are estimated on the basis of inventory statistics. For gross fixed capital formation, information is primarily classified by product and breakdown by ownership branch is only partially provided. The valuation is made net of deductible value added tax. Estimates of investments in buildings are based partly on data available on construction starts, work under construction and work completed and partly on information from accounting data. Estimates of investments in machinery and equipment are based on production and foreign trade statistics adjusted to include gross margins, duties etc. Exports and imports of goods and services are estimated mainly form the balance-of-payments and foreign trade statistics. Special surveys are available for shipping and for payments to and receipts from the rest of the world by Danish enterprises. For the constant price estimates, price indexes arrived at for the supply of goods and services, broken down into 4,000 groups, are used for all components of GDP by expenditure type except that of exports for which the indexes for domestic output are used.

(c) Cost-structure of the gross domestic product. Data on the compensation of employees are taken directly from the annual surveys on current transactions. For consumption of fixed capital, only rough estimates are made. Total indirect taxes and subsidies are obtained from government accounts. Operating surplus is estimated as a residual.

(d) Gross domestic product by kind of economic activity. The table of GDP by kind of economic activity is prepared in factor values. The production approach is used to estimate the value added of almost all industries. The income approach is used to estimate the value added of producers of government services, parts of business services and other private services. The gross output of the trade sector is primarily estimated by means of the commodity-flow approach. The estimates of agricultural production are based on product-by-product data in terms of volume and prices which are obtained from the annual agricultural statistics. The estimates of gross output are supplemented by survey data on total costs and cost structure. For forestry and fishing, the main sources used are the annual agricultural reports and the annual reports of the Ministry of Fisheries. For manufacturing, estimates are based on an annual survey covering all enterprises employing 20 or more persons and on a quarterly survey on the turnover of 4,000 products. Censuses taken in 1966 and 1975 provide a product-by-product breakdown of intermediate inputs. The value-added tax returns of enterprises are used to make estimates for small enterprises and services not covered by direct surveys. For electricity, gas and water, the estimates are based on annual electricity statistics, accunting statistics of the municipalities and on local government reports, respectively. For private construction, various sources are used such as an annual accounting survey and investment statistics. Construction in the public sector is estimated from government accounts. The estimates of gross trade and trasnport margins are based on data obtained from a sample survey of trade enterprises adjusted for under-coverage, mark-ups and other non-available margins. Another method used is to estimate the size of the gross margins of each commodity and its share in the distributive channel. These estimates are partly based on information from the Price Directorate. For restaurants and hotels, value-added tax statistics are used. For the transport sector, the information is taken from the accounts of the exterprises concerned except road transport which makes use of the vaue-added tax returns. For the finanacial sector, the balance-sheets and complete accounts of the companies' current transactions are used. A bench-mark survey of housing rents is carried out every five years. For intervening years, changes in the average rent and total stock of residential buildings are used. Rents of rented dwellings are used for the imputation of rents of owner-occupied dwellings. Value-added tax statistics, population census and accouting data of advertising services are used for the business services sector. The main sources for the producers of government services are the account of the central and local government and social secutiry funds. For other services, value-added tax statistics are used except for professions like doctors and dentists, for which social security data are used. For the constant price estimates, double deflation is used. The data are deflated by means of a price index related to each of the 4,000 groups of goods and services. The price indexes are applied to domestic output as well as imports.

1.1 Expenditure on the Gross Domestic Product, in Current Prices

Million Danish kroner

		1970	1971	1972	1973	1974	1975	1976	1977	1978	1979	1980
1	General government final consumption expenditure	23675	27865	32075	36808	45254	53182	60523	67124	76407	87163	100432
2	Private final consumption expenditure	68078	73165	80437	94202	105224	119942	142133	158684	173792	195578	209889
	a Households	67800	72802	79976	93679	104585	119184	141217	157640	172604	194246	208412
	b Private non-profit institutions serving households	278	363	461	523	639	758	916	1044	1188	1332	1477
3	Gross capital formation	30431	32511	37324	45140	48826	45164	60247	63063	68117	73355	68033
	a Increase in stocks	1148	759	318	2332	2365	-424	2569	2091	1200	2300	-300
	b Gross fixed capital formation	29283	31752	37006	42808	46461	45588	57678	60972	66917	71055	68333
	Residential buildings	9538	9985	13806	16608	15273	14462	18522	17648	19846	21023	18833
	Non-residential buildings	6738	7514	7733	9089	10920	10247	11938	12702	23621	25784	24954
	Other construction and land improvement etc.	3562	3919	4148	4100	4972	5635	6332	7953			
	Other	9445	10334	11319	13011	15296	15244	20886	22669	23450	24248	24546
4	Exports of goods and services	33104	36184	40835	49314	61481	65049	72455	80463	86515	102525	124503
5	Less: Imports of goods and services	36661	38604	39943	52605	67157	67080	84144	90656	93246	112701	128762
	Equals: Gross Domestic Product	118627	131120	150729	172860	193629	216256	251214	278679	311585	345920	374095

1.2 Expenditure on the Gross Domestic Product, in Constant Prices

Million Danish kroner

		1970	1971	1972	1973	1974	1975	1976	1977	1978	1979	1980
		At constant prices of:1975										
1	General government final consumption expenditure	43426	45798	48430	50363	52132	53182	55272	56821	59600	62617	65900
2	Private final consumption expenditure	111236	110530	112299	118721	115768	119942	130450	132270	132308	135795	130293
	a Households	110696	109899	111576	117988	115022	119184	129612	131394	131428	134895	129398
	b Private non-profit institutions serving households	540	631	723	733	746	758	838	876	880	900	895
3	Gross capital formation	51374	51507	55466	60240	54430	45164	55784	53510	53932	53768	44692

Denmark

1.2 Expenditure on the Gross Domestic Product, in Constant Prices
(Continued)

Million Danish kroner

	1970	1971	1972	1973	1974	1975	1976	1977	1978	1979	1980
					At constant prices of: 1975						
a Increase in stocks	1907	1196	833	3232	2530	-424	2385	1797	990	1735	-195
b Gross fixed capital formation	49467	50311	54633	57008	51900	45588	53399	51713	52942	52033	44887
Residential buildings	16917	16617	21757	22299	16782	14462	17376	15175	15801	15401	12277
Non-residential buildings	11157	11831	11545	11960	12192	10247	11122	11112	18670	18580	15940
Other construction and land improvement etc.	6624	6659	6483	5893	5793	5635	5832	6507			
Other	14769	15204	14848	16856	17133	15244	19069	18919	18471	18052	16670
4 Exports of goods and services	53005	55704	58878	63390	66191	65049	68059	70645	72462	78467	83108
5 Less: Imports of goods and services	62871	62565	63148	72669	70095	67080	78466	77707	79589	84667	78551
Equals: Gross Domestic Product	196170	200974	211925	220045	218426	216256	231099	235539	238713	245980	245442

1.3 Cost Components of the Gross Domestic Product

Million Danish kroner

	1970	1971	1972	1973	1974	1975	1976	1977	1978	1979	1980
1 Indirect taxes, net	17295	19246	21890	23757	23976	27543	33130	38569	46474	54721	57222
a Indirect taxes paid	20484	22935	26222	29133	30833	33560	40833	47651	56815	65845	69843
b Less: Subsidies received	3189	3689	4332	5376	6857	6017	7703	9082	10341	11124	12621
2 Consumption of fixed capital	8161	9137	10477	12169	15379	17859	20259	23015	26122	29748	34300
3 Compensation of employees paid by resident producers to:	63859	72120	80223	92318	109094	122742	140460	156173	170971	189778	204960
a Resident households	63790	72041	80129	92218	108970	122593	140269	155960	170743	189519	204662
b Rest of the world	69	79	94	100	124	149	191	213	228	259	298
4 Net operating surplus	29312	30616	38140	44616	45180	48112	57365	60922	68018	71673	77613
Equals: Gross Domestic Product	118627	131120	150729	172860	193629	216256	251214	278679	311585	345920	374095

1.4 General Government Current Receipts and Disbursements

Million Danish kroner

	1970	1971	1972	1973	1974	1975	1976	1977	1978	1979	1980
					Receipts						
1 Property and entrepreneurial income	1667	1595	1925	2350	2995	3570	4425	...	...	...	...
2 Taxes, fees and contributions	46992	55925	63570	72960	85825	88790	103770	...	...	...	...
a Indirect taxes	19910	21832	24826	28160	30175	32797	39890	...	...	...	...
b Direct taxes	24759	30998	35069	42970	53325	53113	61795	...	...	...	...
c Social security contributions	2156	2475	2995	1760	1425	1505	1640	...	...	...	...
d Compulsory fees, fines and penalties	167	620	680	70	900	1375	445	...	...	...	...
3 Other current receipts	...	...	...	...	...	...	...	...	...	...	...
Total Current Receipts of General Government	48659	57520	65495	75310	88820	92360	108195	...	...	...	...
					Disbursements						
1 General government final consumption expenditure	23137	27349	30777	34657	42182	50199	56377	...	...	...	...
a Compensation of employees	...	...	...	...	...	...	...	...	...	...	...
b Consumption of fixed capital	669	734	782	877	937	999	1067	...	...	...	...
c Purchases of goods and services, net	...	...	...	...	...	...	...	...	...	...	...
d Less: Own account production of fixed assets	...	...	...	...	...	...	...	...	...	...	...
e Indirect taxes paid, net	...	...	...	...	...	...	...	...	...	...	...
2 Property income paid	1284	1470	1645	1760	1985	1915	2495	...	...	...	...
3 Subsidies	1726	1857	2125	1025	3135	2306	3078	...	...	...	...
4 Other current transfers paid	14247	16475	19080	21690	25885	33035	37725	...	...	...	...
a Social security benefits and social assistance grants	13539	15600	18035	20100	24125	30510	34870	...	...	...	...
b Other	708	875	1045	1590	1760	2525	2855	...	...	...	...
5 Net saving	8265	10369	11868	16178	15633	4905	8520	...	...	...	...
Total Current Disbursements and Net Saving of General Government	48659	57520	65495	75310	88820	92360	108195	...	...	...	...

Denmark

1.7 External Transactions on Current Account, Summary

Million Danish kroner

	1970	1971	1972	1973	1974	1975	1976	1977	1978	1979	1980
Payments to the Rest of the World											
1 Imports of goods and services	36661	38604	39943	52605	67157	67080	84144	90656	93246	112701	128762
a Imports of merchandise c.i.f.	33101	34264	35434	47031	60543	59805	75086	79662	81435	98429	111295
b Other	3560	4340	4509	5574	6614	7275	9058	10994	11811	14272	17467
2 Factor income paid to the rest of the world	1051	1271	1663	2122	3307	3501	3987	5789	8188	11504	15768
a Compensation of employees	69	79	94	100	124	149	191	213	228	259	298
b Property and entrepreneurial income paid	982	1192	1569	2022	3183	3352	3796	5576	7960	11245	15470
3 Indirect taxes paid to supranational organizations	...	...	...	...	...	...	...	...	...	...	...
4 Current transfers to the rest of the world	1028	660	954	1760	1762	2475	2890	3920	4219	5628	6551
5 Surplus of the nation on current transactions	-4569	-3188	-523	-2986	-6050	-3327	-12305	-11089	-8531	-15524	-14208
Payments to the Rest of the World and Surplus of the Nation on Current Transactions	34171	37347	42037	53501	66176	69729	78716	89276	97122	114309	136873
Receipts From The Rest of the World											
1 Exports of goods and services	33104	36184	40835	49314	61481	65049	72455	80463	86515	102525	124503
a Exports of merchandise f.o.b.	25254	27450	30931	37846	47280	50201	55223	60690	65575	78516	95889
b Other	7850	8734	9904	11468	14201	14848	17232	19773	20940	24009	28614
2 Factor income received from rest of the world	785	790	872	1209	1916	1712	1898	2591	3430	4759	5935
a Compensation of employees	137	141	141	143	196	220	272	294	330	359	415
b Property and entrepreneurial income received	648	649	731	1066	1720	1492	1626	2297	3100	4400	5520
3 Subsidies received from supranational organisations	...	...	...	...	...	...	...	...	...	...	...
4 Current transfers from rest of the world	282	373	330	2978	2779	2968	4363	6222	7177	7025	6435
Receipts from the Rest of the World on Current Transactions	34171	37347	42037	53501	66176	69729	78716	89276	97122	114309	136873

1.8 Capital Transactions of The Nation, Summary

Million Danish kroner

	1970	1971	1972	1973	1974	1975	1976	1977	1978	1979	1980
Finance of Gross Capital Formation											
Gross saving	25862	29322	36802	42155	42777	41836	47942	51975	59586	57831	53825
1 Consumption of fixed capital	8161	9137	10477	12169	15379	17859	20259	23015	26122	29748	34300
2 Net saving	17701	20185	26325	29986	27398	23977	27683	28960	33464	28083	19525
Less: Surplus of the nation on current transactions	-4569	-3188	-523	-2986	-6050	-3327	-12305	-11089	-8531	-15524	-14208
Finance of Gross Capital Formation	30431	32511	37324	45140	48826	45164	60247	63063	68117	73355	68033
Gross Capital Formation											
Increase in stocks	1148	759	318	2332	2365	-424	2569	2091	1200	2300	-300
Gross fixed capital formation	29283	31752	37006	42808	46461	45588	57678	60972	66917	71055	68333
Gross Capital Formation	30431	32511	37324	45140	48826	45164	60247	63063	68117	73355	68033

1.10 Gross Domestic Product by Kind of Activity, in Current Prices

Million Danish kroner

	1970	1971	1972	1973	1974	1975	1976	1977	1978	1979	1980
1 Agriculture, hunting, forestry and fishing	6612	7163	8564	10525	11442	10927	12301	14623	...	...	...
2 Mining and quarrying	152	140	182	141	156	163	163	451	...	...	...
3 Manufacturing	21967	23555	26651	30912	34959	39046	43966	47656	...	...	...
4 Electricity, gas and water	1814	1949	2069	2125	2651	3110	3290	3155	...	...	...
5 Construction	11129	12276	14432	15336	16063	16670	18870	19510	...	...	...
6 Wholesale and retail trade, restaurants and hotels	17993	18948	21609	25471	28070	31169	37493	40414	...	...	...
7 Transport, storage and communication	9329	9692	10858	12503	14375	15814	17624	19613	...	...	...
8 Finance, insurance, real estate and business services	12908	15098	18145	22194	25323	28475	34340	38481	...	...	...
9 Community, social and personal services	5454	6114	6699	7525	8923	10041	11200	12474	...	...	...

Denmark

1.10 Gross Domestic Product by Kind of Activity, in Current Prices
(Continued)

Million Danish kroner

	1970	1971	1972	1973	1974	1975	1976	1977	1978	1979	1980
Total, Industries	87358	94935	109209	126732	141962	155415	179247	196377	...	...	...
Producers of Government Services	16218	19451	22640	26435	32504	38683	44561	50051	...	...	...
Other Producers	659	740	831	915	1090	1242	1443	1577	...	...	...
Subtotal [a]	104235	115126	132680	154082	175556	195340	225251	248005	...	...	...
Less: Imputed bank service charge	2903	3252	3841	4979	5903	6627	7167	7895	...	...	...
Plus: Import duties	...	...	...	...	...	...	...	...	...	...	...
Plus: Value added tax	...	...	...	...	...	...	...	...	...	...	...
Plus: Other adjustments	17295	19246	21890	23757	23976	27543	33130	38569	46474	54721	57222
Equals: Gross Domestic Product	118627	131120	150729	172860	193629	216256	251214	278679	311585	345920	374095
Memorandum Item: Mineral fuels and power	1715	1818	1956	2072	2614	3107	3311	3292	...	...	...

a) Gross domestic product in factor values.

1.11 Gross Domestic Product by Kind of Activity, in Constant Prices

Million Danish kroner

	1970	1971	1972	1973	1974	1975	1976	1977	1978	1979	1980
					At constant prices of:1975						
1 Agriculture, hunting, forestry and fishing	9430	10483	10579	9829	11969	10927	10858	11762	...	...	...
2 Mining and quarrying	183	150	242	227	176	163	169	343	...	...	...
3 Manufacturing	33661	34160	37135	39289	39878	39046	42480	43389	...	...	...
4 Electricity, gas and water	2539	2684	2803	2696	2894	3110	3279	3540	...	...	...
5 Construction	19877	20365	22093	20376	18849	16670	18108	17219	...	...	...
6 Wholesale and retail trade, restaurants and hotels	28217	27997	28761	32003	31174	31169	34389	33973	...	...	...
7 Transport, storage and communication	16915	16510	16849	17630	16469	15814	16623	17231	...	...	...
8 Finance, insurance, real estate and business services	22188	23546	25505	27996	28350	28475	29432	30088	...	...	...
9 Community, social and personal services	9309	9597	9714	9763	10134	10041	10278	10430	...	...	...
Total, Industries	142319	145492	153681	159809	159893	155415	165616	167975	...	...	...
Producers of Government Services	31101	33050	34935	36775	38051	38683	40527	42449	...	...	...
Other Producers	1413	1344	1300	1279	1264	1242	1293	1285	...	...	...
Subtotal [a]	174833	179886	189916	197863	199208	195340	207436	211709	...	...	...
Less: Imputed bank service charge	5092	5224	5755	6662	6703	6627	6559	6695	...	...	...
Plus: Import duties	...	...	...	...	...	...	...	...	...	...	...
Plus: Value added tax	...	...	...	...	...	...	...	...	...	...	...
Plus: Other adjustments	26429	26312	27764	28844	25921	27543	30222	30525	30309	30913	28578
Equals: Gross Domestic Product	196170	200974	211925	220045	218426	216256	231099	235539	238713	245980	245442
Memorandum Item: Mineral fuels and power	2488	2501	2706	2668	2685	3107	3292	3672	...	...	...

a) Gross domestic product in factor values.

1.12 Relations Among National Accounting Aggregates

Million Danish kroner

	1970	1971	1972	1973	1974	1975	1976	1977	1978	1979	1980
Gross Domestic Product	118627	131120	150729	172860	193629	216256	251214	278679	311585	345920	374095
Plus: Net factor income received from abroad	-266	-481	-791	-913	-1391	-1789	-2089	-3198	-4758	-6745	-9833
Factor income received	785	790	872	1209	1916	1712	1898	2591	3430	4759	5935
Less: Factor income paid	1051	1271	1663	2122	3307	3501	3987	5789	8188	11504	15768
Equals: Gross National Product	118361	130639	149938	171947	192238	214467	249125	275481	306827	339175	364262
Less: Consumption of fixed capital	8161	9137	10477	12169	15379	17859	20259	23015	26122	29748	34300
Less: Net indirect taxes paid to supranational organisations	...	...	...	...	...	...	...	...	...	...	...
Equals: National Income at Market Prices	110200	121502	139461	159778	176859	196608	228866	252466	280705	309427	329962
Plus: Net current transfers received from abroad	-746	-287	-624	1218	1017	493	1473	2302	2958	1397	-116
Current transfers received	282	373	330	2978	2779	2968	4363	6222	7177	7025	6435
Less: Current transfers paid	1028	660	954	1760	1762	2475	2890	3920	4219	5628	6551
Equals: National Disposable Income at Market Prices	109454	121215	138837	160996	177876	197101	230339	254768	283663	310824	329846
Less: Final consumption	91753	101030	112512	131010	150478	173124	202656	225808	250199	282741	310321
Equals: Net Saving	17701	20185	26325	29986	27398	23977	27683	28960	33464	28083	19525
Less: Surplus of the nation on current transactions	-4569	-3188	-523	-2986	-6050	-3327	-12305	-11089	-8531	-15524	-14208
Equals: Net Capital Formation	22270	23374	26847	32971	33447	27305	39988	40048	41995	43607	33733

Denmark

2.1 General Government Final Consumption Expenditure by Function, in Current Prices

Million Danish kroner

		1970	1971	1972	1973	1974	1975	1976	1977	1978	1979	1980
1	General public services	...	3562	3879	4541	5491	6474	...	...	...	...	...
2	Defence	2716	3046	3229	3476	4245	4926	...	...	...	...	...
3	Public order and safety							...	...	...	...	...
4	Education	5536	7062	8020	9014	11008	13187	...	...	...	...	...
5	Health	4495	6086	6887	7223	8680	10239	...	...	...	...	...
6	Social security and welfare	...	4331	5269	6423	7841	9381	...	...	...	...	...
7	Housing and community amenities	...	308	349	406	503	600	...	...	...	...	...
8	Recreational, cultural and religious affairs	...	1052	1190	1379	1636	1976	...	...	...	...	...
9	Economic services	...	1920	1954	2195	2778	3416	...	...	...	...	...
10	Other functions	...	-	-	-	-	-	...	...	...	...	...
	Total General Government Final Consumption Expenditure	23137	27349	30777	34657	42182	50199	...	...	...	...	...

2.2 General Government Final Consumption Expenditure by Function, in Constant Prices

Million Danish kroner

		1970	1971	1972	1973	1974	1975	1976	1977	1978	1979	1980
					At constant prices of: 1970							
1	General public services	...	3260	3155	3222	3298	3463	...	...	...	...	...
2	Defence	2716	2787	2627	2466	2549	2635	...	...	...	...	...
3	Public order and safety							...	...	...	...	...
4	Education	5536	6462	6523	6396	6611	7055	...	...	...	...	...
5	Health	4495	5569	5602	5125	5213	5478	...	...	...	...	...
6	Social security and welfare	...	3963	4286	4557	4709	5019	...	...	...	...	...
7	Housing and community amenities	...	282	284	288	302	321	...	...	...	...	...
8	Recreational, cultural and religious affairs	...	963	968	979	982	1057	...	...	...	...	...
9	Economic services	...	1740	1589	1557	1668	1827	...	...	...	...	...
10	Other functions	...	-	-	-	-	-	...	...	...	...	...
	Total General Government Final Consumption Expenditure	23137	25026	25034	24590	25332	26855	...	...	...	...	...

2.5 Private Final Consumption Expenditure by Type, in Current Prices

Million Danish kroner

		1970	1971	1972	1973	1974	1975	1976	1977	1978	1979	1980
					Final Consumption Expenditure of Resident Households							
1	Food, beverages and tobacco	20530	21804	23481	27215	29838	32337	37607	42066	45963	49515	54118
	a Food	14001	14716	15782	18606	20340	21928	25774	28711	31521	33827	37116
	b Non-alcoholic beverages	463	515	562	636	686	778	912	1046			
	c Alcoholic beverages	2819	3251	3527	4005	4553	5237	5854	6477	14442	15688	17002
	d Tobacco	3247	3322	3610	3968	4259	4394	5067	5832			
2	Clothing and footwear	5266	5201	5628	6452	7178	7682	9419	10186	10713	11594	12143
3	Gross rent, fuel and power	12432	14378	16196	19229	23543	27138	32036	36395	41327	49124	55806
	a Fuel and power	3124	3450	3536	4405	6309	6856	7701	8197	9564	13656	16312
	b Other	9307	10929	12660	14824	17234	20282	24335	28198	31763	35468	39494
4	Furniture, furnishings and household equipment and operation	6576	6757	7607	8766	9303	10823	12408	13366	13739	15863	16666
	a Household operation	1827	1868	1970	2153	2431	2724	2867	3146	...	...	...
	b Other	4748	4889	5636	6613	6872	8099	9541	10220	...	...	...
5	Medical care and health expenses	1382	1548	1735	2022	2218	2417	2497	2805	2961	3214	3466
6	Transport and communication	10208	11007	12279	14540	14939	18318	22720	24634	26907	29721	28191
	a Personal transport equipment	3332	3357	3916	4992	3665	5613	8324	8714	...	...	...
	b Other	6876	7650	8363	9548	11274	12705	14396	15920	...	...	...
7	Recreational, entertainment, education and cultural services	5610	6220	6781	8146	9653	11473	13431	15243	16342	17903	18940
	a Education	421	523	624	727	908	1126	1219	1465	...	...	...
	b Other	5189	5696	6157	7419	8745	10347	12212	13778	...	...	...
8	Miscellaneous goods and services	6596	6931	7604	8466	9562	10542	12523	14104	15778	17605	19421
	a Personal care	1098	1128	1164	1333	1494	1636	1891	2151	...	...	...
	b Expenditures in restaurants, cafes and hotels	3562	3767	4189	4565	4971	5619	6532	7611	...	...	...

Denmark

2.5 Private Final Consumption Expenditure by Type, in Current Prices
(Continued)

Million Danish kroner

	1970	1971	1972	1973	1974	1975	1976	1977	1978	1979	1980
c Other	1935	2036	2251	2568	3097	3287	4100	4342	...	...	...
Total Final Consumption Expenditure in the Domestic Market by Households, of which	68600	73846	81311	94836	106234	120730	142641	158799	173730	194539	208751
a Durable goods	8158	8494	9810	12343	11524	14870	19849	21088	...	...	...
b Semi-durable goods	11518	11789	12874	14777	16721	18597	22182	24225	...	...	...
c Non-durable goods	28237	30385	32587	37986	43790	47633	54510	60684	...	...	...
d Services	20685	23178	26039	29730	34198	39630	46100	52802	...	...	...
Plus: Direct purchases abroad by resident households	2009	2250	2526	2938	3142	3661	4433	5511	6126	7784	8361
Less: Direct purchases in the domestic market by non-resident households	2809	3294	3861	4095	4791	5207	5857	6670	7252	8077	8700
Equals: Final Consumption Expenditure of Resident Households	67800	72802	79976	93679	104585	119184	141217	157640	172604	194246	208412

Final Consumption Expenditure of Private Non-profit Institutions Serving Households

	1970	1971	1972	1973	1974	1975	1976	1977	1978	1979	1980
Equals: Final Consumption Expenditure of Private Non-profit Organisations Serving Households	278	363	461	523	639	758	916	1044	1188	1332	1477
Private Final Consumption Expenditure	68078	73165	80437	94202	105224	119942	142133	158684	173792	195578	209889

2.6 Private Final Consumption Expenditure by Type, in Constant Prices

Million Danish kroner

At constant prices of: 1975

Final Consumption Expenditure of Resident Households

	1970	1971	1972	1973	1974	1975	1976	1977	1978	1979	1980
1 Food, beverages and tobacco	31558	31889	31802	32525	32571	32337	34260	33772	33643	34234	34227
a Food	22606	22689	22181	22349	22432	21928	23122	22650	22875	23284	23168
b Non-alcoholic beverages	710	758	781	827	747	778	856	887			
c Alcoholic beverages	3984	4403	4580	4969	4946	5237	5569	5452	10768	10950	11059
d Tobacco	4258	4039	4260	4380	4446	4394	4713	4783			
2 Clothing and footwear	8024	7363	7516	7892	7679	7682	8945	8909	8472	8540	8412
3 Gross rent, fuel and power	22356	22935	24162	25182	26061	27138	28175	28896	30171	31185	30817
a Fuel and power	6993	6673	6996	6829	6578	6856	7217	7144	7494	7734	6497
b Other	15363	16262	17166	18353	19483	20282	20958	21752	22677	23451	24320
4 Furniture, furnishings and household equipment and operation	10988	10498	11023	11780	10418	10823	11798	11665	11163	11665	11054
a Household operation	3363	3124	2998	3044	2792	2724	2690	2634	...	...	...
b Other	7625	7374	8025	8736	7626	8099	9108	9031	...	...	...
5 Medical care and health expenses	2342	2374	2460	2720	2564	2417	2303	2417	2367	2423	2381
6 Transport and communication	17541	17229	17085	18611	16390	18318	21099	21276	21261	21272	17918
a Personal transport equipment	5981	5302	4954	5984	3960	5613	7622	7466	...	...	...
b Other	11560	11927	12131	12627	12430	12705	13477	13810	...	...	...
7 Recreational, entertainment, education and cultural services	8637	8904	9015	10116	10598	11473	12608	13382	12950	13274	12926
a Education	777	849	912	961	1031	1126	1160	1324	...	...	...
b Other	7860	8055	8103	9155	9567	10347	11448	12058	...	...	...
8 Miscellaneous goods and services	10765	10613	10713	10852	10622	10542	11648	11809	11707	11998	11838
a Personal care	1721	1678	1578	1738	1712	1636	1769	1795	...	...	...
b Expenditures in restaurants, cafes and hotels	5560	5603	5771	5681	5459	5619	6045	6276	...	...	...

Denmark

2.6 Private Final Consumption Expenditure by Type, in Constant Prices
(Continued)

Million Danish kroner

	1970	1971	1972	1973	1974	1975	1976	1977	1978	1979	1980
					At constant prices of:1975						
c Other	3484	3332	3364	3433	3451	3287	3834	3738	...	...	...
Total Final Consumption Expenditure in the Domestic Market by Households, of which	112211	111805	113776	119678	116903	120730	130836	132126	131734	134591	129573
Plus: Direct purchases abroad by resident households	2829	2935	3128	3477	3362	3661	4125	4683	4964	5707	5098
Less: Direct purchases in the domestic market by non-resident households	4344	4841	5328	5167	5243	5207	5349	5415	5270	5403	5273
Equals: Final Consumption Expenditure of Resident Households	110696	109899	111576	117988	115022	119184	129612	131394	131428	134895	129398

Final Consumption Expenditure of Private Non-profit Institutions Serving Households

	1970	1971	1972	1973	1974	1975	1976	1977	1978	1979	1980
Equals: Final Consumption Expenditure of Private Non-profit Organisations Serving Households	540	631	723	733	746	758	838	876	880	900	895
Private Final Consumption Expenditure	111236	110530	112299	118721	115768	119942	130450	132270	132308	135795	130293

2.9 Gross Capital Formation by Kind of Activity of Owner, ISIC Major Divisions, in Current Prices

Million Danish kroner

	1970			1971			1972			1973		
	Total Gross Capital Formation	Increase in Stocks	Gross Fixed Capital Formation	Total Gross Capital Formation	Increase in Stocks	Gross Fixed Capital Formation	Total Gross Capital Formation	Increase in Stocks	Gross Fixed Capital Formation	Total Gross Capital Formation	Increase in Stocks	Gross Fixed Capital Formation
						All Producers						
1 Agriculture, hunting, fishing and forestry	...	...	1179	...	...	1371	...	...	1965	...	...	2720
2 Mining and quarrying	...	...	-	...	...	-	...	...	-	...	...	-
3 Manufacturing	...	...	2950	...	...	2975	...	...	3075	...	...	3870
4 Electricity, gas and water	...	...	1314	...	...	1425	...	...	1574	...	...	1601
5 Construction	...	...	...	...	...	...	...	...	...	...	...	...
6 Wholesale and retail trade, restaurants and hotels	...	...	...	...	...	...	...	...	...	...	...	...
7 Transport, storage and communication	...	...	3907	...	...	4797	...	...	5436	...	...	4912
8 Finance, insurance, real estate and business services	...	...	5870	...	...	6090	...	...	8330	...	...	10775
9 Community, social and personal services	...	...	9442	...	...	10166	...	...	10587	...	...	13319
Total Industries	...	...	24662	...	...	26824	...	...	30967	...	...	37197
Producers of Government Services	...	...	720	...	...	735	...	...	784	...	...	692
Private Non-Profit Institutions Serving Households	...	...	...	...	...	...	...	...	...	...	...	...
Total	...	...	25382	...	...	27559	...	...	31751	...	...	37889

	1974			1975		
	Total Gross Capital Formation	Increase in Stocks	Gross Fixed Capital Formation	Total Gross Capital Formation	Increase in Stocks	Gross Fixed Capital Formation
			All Producers			
1 Agriculture, hunting, fishing and forestry	...	...	3233	...	...	3469
2 Mining and quarrying	...	...	-	...	...	-
3 Manufacturing	...	...	4930	...	...	4050
4 Electricity, gas and water	...	...	2016	...	...	2101
5 Construction	...	...	...	...	...	...
6 Wholesale and retail trade, restaurants and hotels	...	...	...	...	...	...
7 Transport, storage and communication	...	...	6260	...	...	7026
8 Finance, insurance, real estate and business services	...	...	10040	...	...	9355
9 Community, social and personal services	...	...	13726	...	...	13495
Total Industries	...	...	40205	...	...	39496
Producers of Government Services	...	...	649	...	...	850
Private Non-Profit Institutions Serving Households	...	...	...	...	...	...
Total	...	...	40854	...	...	40346

Denmark

2.10 Gross Capital Formation by Kind of Activity of Owner, ISIC Major Divisions, in Constant Prices

Million Danish kroner

	1970 TGCF	1970 IS	1970 GFCF	1971 TGCF	1971 IS	1971 GFCF	1972 TGCF	1972 IS	1972 GFCF	1973 TGCF	1973 IS	1973 GFCF
					At constant prices of:1970 — All Producers							
1 Agriculture, hunting, fishing and forestry	...	...	1179	...	...	1256	...	...	1674	...	...	2025
2 Mining and quarrying	...	...	-	...	...	-	...	...	-	...	...	-
3 Manufacturing	...	...	2950	...	...	2852	...	...	2753	...	...	3220
4 Electricity, gas and water	...	...	1314	...	...	1339	...	...	1376	...	...	1284
5 Construction	...	...	...	...	...	...	...	...	...	...	...	...
6 Wholesale and retail trade, restaurants and hotels	...	...	...	...	...	...	...	...	...	...	...	...
7 Transport, storage and communication	...	...	3907	...	...	4576	...	...	4992	...	...	4072
8 Finance, insurance, real estate and business services	...	...	5870	...	...	5750	...	...	7307	...	...	7841
9 Community, social and personal services	...	...	9442	...	...	9654	...	...	9491	...	...	11005
Total Industries	...	...	24662	...	...	25427	...	...	27593	...	...	29447
Producers of Government Services	...	...	720	...	...	693	...	...	688	...	...	553
Private Non-Profit Institutions Serving Households	...	...	...	...	...	...	...	...	...	...	...	...
Total	...	...	25382	...	...	26120	...	...	28281	...	...	30000

	1974 TGCF	1974 IS	1974 GFCF	1975 TGCF	1975 IS	1975 GFCF
		At constant prices of:1970 — All Producers				
1 Agriculture, hunting, fishing and forestry	...	...	2051	...	...	1913
2 Mining and quarrying	...	...	-	...	...	-
3 Manufacturing	...	...	3481	...	...	1909
4 Electricity, gas and water	...	...	1367	...	...	1260
5 Construction	...	...	...	...	...	...
6 Wholesale and retail trade, restaurants and hotels	...	...	...	...	...	...
7 Transport, storage and communication	...	...	4783	...	...	4778
8 Finance, insurance, real estate and business services	...	...	5740	...	...	4799
9 Community, social and personal services	...	...	9508	...	...	8517
Total Industries	...	...	26930	...	...	23176
Producers of Government Services	...	...	437	...	...	517
Private Non-Profit Institutions Serving Households	...	...	...	...	...	...
Total	...	...	27367	...	...	23693

2.17 Exports and Imports of Goods and Services, Detail

Million Danish kroner

	1970	1971	1972	1973	1974	1975	1976	1977	1978	1979	1980
					Exports of Goods and Services						
1 Exports of merchandise, f.o.b.	25254	27450	30931	37846	47280	50201	55223	60690	65575	78516	95889
2 Transport and communication	4617	5037	5428	6614	8526	8681	10071	11754	12113	14124	...
a In respect of merchandise imports	185	172	162	185	120	120	150	160	165	170	200
b Other	4432	4865	5266	6429	8406	8561	9921	11594	11948	13954	...
3 Insurance service charges	19	21	23	26	29	17	8	15	-50	-10	...
4 Other commodities	405	382	592	733	855	943	1296	1334	1625	1818	...
5 Adjustments of merchandise exports to change-of-ownership basis	...	...	...	...	...	...	...	...	...	...	...
6 Direct purchases in the domestic market by non-residential households	2809	3294	3861	4095	4791	5207	5857	6670	7252	8077	8700
7 Direct purchases in the domestic market by extraterritorial bodies	...	...	...	...	...	...	...	...	...	...	...
Total Exports of Goods and Services	33104	36184	40835	49314	61481	65049	72455	80463	86515	102525	124503

Denmark

2.17 Exports and Imports of Goods and Services, Detail
(Continued)

Million Danish kroner

	1970	1971	1972	1973	1974	1975	1976	1977	1978	1979	1980
					Imports of Goods and Services						
1 Imports of merchandise, c.i.f.	33101	34264	35434	47031	60543	59805	75086	79662	81435	98429	111295
a Imports of merchandise, f.o.b. [a]	31051	32394	33544	44606	58033	57335	72196	76462	77885	93709	106095
b Transport of services on merchandise imports	2050	1870	1890	2425	2510	2470	2890	3200	3550	4720	5200
By residents	185	172	162	185	120	120	150	160	165	170	200
By non-residents	1865	1698	1728	2240	2390	2350	2740	3040	3385	4550	5000
c Insurance service charges on merchandise imports [a]	...	...	...	...	...	...	...	...	...	...	...
2 Adjustments of merchandise imports to change-of-ownership basis	...	...	...	...	...	...	...	...	...	...	...
3 Other transport and communication	1510	2016	1887	2521	3339	3360	4324	5254	5515	6153	8375
4 Other insurance service charges	·	·	·	·	·	·	·	·	·	...	...
5 Other commodities	41	74	96	115	133	254	301	229	170	335	731
6 Direct purchases abroad by government	...	...	...	...	...	...	...	...	...	...	...
7 Direct purchases abroad by resident households	2009	2250	2526	2938	3142	3661	4433	5511	6126	7784	8361
Total Imports of Goods and Services	36661	38604	39943	52605	67157	67080	84144	90656	93246	112701	128762
Balance of Goods and Services	-3557	-2420	892	-3291	-5676	-2031	-11689	-10193	-6731	-10176	-4259
Total Imports and Balance of Goods and Services	33104	36184	40835	49314	61481	65049	72455	80463	86515	102525	124503

a) Item 'Insurance service charges in respect of merchandise imports' is included in item 'Import of merchandise, f.o.b.'.

3.12 General Government Income and Outlay Account: Total and Subsectors

Million Danish kroner

	1970					1971				
	Total General Government	Central Government	State or Provincial Government	Local Government	Social Security Funds	Total General Government	Central Government	State or Provincial Government	Local Government	Social Security Funds
					Receipts					
1 Property and entrepreneurial income	1667	...	...	...	...	1595	...	...	...	...
2 Taxes, fees and contributions	46992	...	...	...	...	55925	...	...	...	...
a Indirect taxes	19910	...	...	...	...	21832	...	...	...	...
b Direct taxes	24759	...	...	...	...	30998	...	...	...	...
Income	23956	...	...	...	...	30155	...	...	...	...
Other	803	...	...	...	...	843	...	...	...	...
c Social security contributions	2156	...	...	...	...	2475	...	...	...	...
d Fees, fines and penalties	167	...	...	...	...	620	...	...	...	...
3 Other current transfers received	·					·				
a Casualty insurance claims	...	...	...	...	...	...	...	...	...	...
b Transfers from other government subsectors	...	...	...	...	...	...	...	...	...	...
c Transfers from abroad	·					·				
d Other transfers, except imputed	·	...	...	...	...	·	...	...	...	...
e Imputed unfunded employee welfare contributions	·	...	...	...	...	·	...	...	...	...
Total Current Receipts	48659	...	...	...	...	57520	...	...	...	...
					Disbursements					
1 General governement final consumption expenditures	23137	...	...	...	...	27349	...	...	...	...
a Compensation of employees	...	...	...	...	...	...	...	...	...	...
b Consumption of fixed capital	669	...	...	...	...	734	...	...	...	...
c Goods and services purchased, net	...	...	...	...	...	...	...	...	...	...
d Less: Own account production of fixed assets	...	...	...	...	...	...	...	...	...	...
e Indirect taxes paid, net	...	...	...	...	...	...	...	...	...	...
2 Property income paid	1284	...	...	...	...	1470	...	...	...	...

Denmark

3.12 General Government Income and Outlay Account: Total and Subsectors
(Continued)

Million Danish kroner

	1970					1971				
	Total General Government	Central Government	State or Provincial Government	Local Government	Social Security Funds	Total General Government	Central Government	State or Provincial Government	Local Government	Social Security Funds
3 Subsidies	1726	...	...	...	...	1857	...	...	...	...
4 Other current transfers paid	14247	...	...	...	...	16475	...	...	...	...
a Casualty insurance premiums, net	...	...	...	...	...	...	...	...	...	...
b Transfers to other government subsectors	...	...	...	...	...	...	...	...	...	...
c Transfers to households	...	...	...	...	...	...	...	...	...	...
Social security benefits	...	...	...	...	...	...	...	...	...	...
Social assistance grants	...	...	...	...	...	...	...	...	...	...
Unfunded employee welfare benefits	-	...	...	...	...	-	...	...	...	...
d Transfers to private non-profit institutions serving households	...	...	...	...	...	...	...	...	...	...
e Transfers to the rest of the world	708	...	...	...	...	875	...	...	...	...
Net saving	8265	...	...	...	...	10369	...	...	...	...
Total Current Disbursements and Net Saving	48659	...	...	...	...	57520	...	...	...	...

	1972					1973				
	Total General Government	Central Government	State or Provincial Government	Local Government	Social Security Funds	Total General Government	Central Government	State or Provincial Government	Local Government	Social Security Funds

Receipts

1 Property and entrepreneurial income	1925	...	...	...	...	2350	...	...	...	...
2 Taxes, fees and contributions	63570	...	...	...	...	72960	...	...	...	...
a Indirect taxes	24826	...	...	...	...	28160	...	...	...	...
b Direct taxes	35069	...	...	...	...	42970	...	...	...	...
Income	34165	...	...	...	...	41926	...	...	...	...
Other	904	...	...	...	...	1044	...	...	...	...
c Social security contributions	2995	...	...	...	...	1760	...	...	...	...
d Fees, fines and penalties	680	...	...	...	...	70	...	...	...	...
3 Other current transfers received	-	...	...	...	...	-	...	...	...	...
a Casualty insurance claims	...	...	...	...	...	...	...	...	...	...
b Transfers from other government subsectors	...	...	...	...	...	...	...	...	...	...
c Transfers from abroad	-	...	...	...	...	-	...	...	...	...
d Other transfers, except imputed	-	...	...	...	...	-	...	...	...	...
e Imputed unfunded employee welfare contributions	-	...	...	...	...	-	...	...	...	...
Total Current Receipts	65495	...	...	...	...	75310	...	...	...	...

Disbursements

1 General governement final consumption expenditures	30777	...	...	...	...	34657	...	...	...	...
a Compensation of employees	...	...	...	...	...	...	...	...	...	...
b Consumption of fixed capital	782	...	...	...	...	877	...	...	...	...
c Goods and services purchased, net	...	...	...	...	...	...	...	...	...	...
d Less: Own account production of fixed assets	...	...	...	...	...	...	...	...	...	...
e Indirect taxes paid, net	...	...	...	...	...	...	...	...	...	...
2 Property income paid	1645	...	...	...	...	1760	...	...	...	...

Denmark

3.12 General Government Income and Outlay Account: Total and Subsectors
(Continued)

Million Danish kroner

	1972					1973				
	Total General Government	Central Government	State or Provincial Government	Local Government	Social Security Funds	Total General Government	Central Government	State or Provincial Government	Local Government	Social Security Funds
3 Subsidies	2125	...	...	...	...	1025	...	...	...	...
4 Other current transfers paid	19080	...	...	...	...	21690	...	...	...	...
a Casualty insurance premiums, net	...	...	...	...	...	...	...	...	...	...
b Transfers to other government subsectors	...	...	...	...	...	...	...	...	...	...
c Transfers to households	...	...	...	...	...	...	...	...	...	...
Social security benefits	...	...	...	...	...	...	...	...	...	...
Social assistance grants	...	...	...	...	...	...	...	...	...	...
Unfunded employee welfare benefits	-	...	...	...	...	-	...	...	...	...
d Transfers to private non-profit institutions serving households	...	...	...	...	...	...	...	...	...	...
e Transfers to the rest of the world	1045	...	...	...	...	1590	...	...	...	...
Net saving	11868	...	...	...	...	16178	...	...	...	...
Total Current Disbursements and Net Saving	65495	...	...	...	...	75310	...	...	...	...

	1974					1975				
	Total General Government	Central Government	State or Provincial Government	Local Government	Social Security Funds	Total General Government	Central Government	State or Provincial Government	Local Government	Social Security Funds

Receipts

1 Property and entrepreneurial income	2995	...	...	...	...	3570	...	...	...	...
2 Taxes, fees and contributions	85825	...	...	...	...	88790	...	...	...	...
a Indirect taxes	30175	...	...	...	...	32797	...	...	...	...
b Direct taxes	53325	...	...	...	...	53113	...	...	...	...
Income	52012	...	...	...	...	51541	...	...	...	...
Other	1313	...	...	...	...	1572	...	...	...	...
c Social security contributions	1425	...	...	...	...	1505	...	...	...	...
d Fees, fines and penalties	900	...	...	...	...	1375	...	...	...	...
3 Other current transfers received	-	...	...	...	...	-	...	...	...	...
a Casualty insurance claims	...	...	...	...	...	...	...	...	...	...
b Transfers from other government subsectors	...	...	...	...	...	...	...	...	...	...
c Transfers from abroad	-	...	...	...	...	-	...	...	...	...
d Other transfers, except imputed	-	...	...	...	...	-	...	...	...	...
e Imputed unfunded employee welfare contributions	-	...	...	...	...	-	...	...	...	...
Total Current Receipts	88820	...	...	...	...	92360	...	...	...	...

Disbursements

1 General government final consumption expenditures	42182	...	...	...	...	50199	...	...	...	...
a Compensation of employees	...	...	...	...	...	...	...	...	...	...
b Consumption of fixed capital	937	...	...	...	...	999	...	...	...	...
c Goods and services purchased, net	...	...	...	...	...	...	...	...	...	...
d Less: Own account production of fixed assets	...	...	...	...	...	...	...	...	...	...
e Indirect taxes paid, net	...	...	...	...	...	...	...	...	...	...
2 Property income paid	1985	...	...	...	...	1915	...	...	...	...

Denmark

3.12 General Government Income and Outlay Account: Total and Subsectors
(Continued)

Million Danish kroner

		1974					1975			
		Total General Government	Central Government	State or Provincial Government	Local Government	Social Security Funds	Total General Government	Central Government	State or Provincial Government	Local Government	Social Security Funds
3	Subsidies	3135	...	...	...	...	2306	...	...	...	...
4	Other current transfers paid	25885	...	...	...	...	33035	...	...	...	...
	a Casualty insurance premiums, net	...	...	...	...	...	...	...	...	...	...
	b Transfers to other government subsectors		...	...	...	...		...	...	...	...
	c Transfers to households	...	...	...	...	...	...	...	...	...	...
	Social security benefits	...	...	...	...	...	...	...	...	...	...
	Social assistance grants	...	...	...	...	...	...	...	...	...	...
	Unfunded employee welfare benefits	-	...	...	...	...	-	...	...	...	...
	d Transfers to private non-profit institutions serving households	...	...	...	...	...	...	...	...	...	...
	e Transfers to the rest of the world	1760	...	...	...	...	2525	...	...	...	...
Net saving		15633	...	...	...	...	4905	...	...	...	...
Total Current Disbursements and Net Saving		88820	...	...	...	...	92360	...	...	...	...

		1976				
		Total General Government	Central Government	State or Provincial Government	Local Government	Social Security Funds

Receipts

1	Property and entrepreneurial income	4425	...	...	...	...
2	Taxes, fees and contributions	103770	...	...	...	...
	a Indirect taxes	39890	...	...	...	...
	b Direct taxes	61795	...	...	...	...
	Income	...	...	...	...	...
	Other	...	...	...	...	...
	c Social security contributions	1640	...	...	...	...
	d Fees, fines and penalties	445	...	...	...	...
3	Other current transfers received	-	...	...	...	...
	a Casualty insurance claims	...	...	...	...	...
	b Transfers from other government subsectors	...	...	...	...	...
	c Transfers from abroad	-	...	...	...	...
	d Other transfers, except imputed	...	...	...	...	...
	e Imputed unfunded employee welfare contributions	-	...	...	...	...
Total Current Receipts		108195	...	...	...	...

Disbursements

1	General government final consumption expenditures	56377	...	...	...	...
	a Compensation of employees	...	...	...	...	...
	b Consumption of fixed capital	1067	...	...	...	...
	c Goods and services purchased, net	...	...	...	...	...
	d Less: Own account production of fixed assets	...	...	...	...	...
	e Indirect taxes paid, net	...	...	...	...	...
2	Property income paid	2495	...	...	...	...

Denmark

3.12 General Government Income and Outlay Account: Total and Subsectors
(Continued)

Million Danish kroner

	1976				
	Total General Government	Central Government	State or Provincial Government	Local Government	Social Security Funds
3 Subsidies	3078	...	...	...	...
4 Other current transfers paid	37725	...	...	...	...
a Casualty insurance premiums, net	...	...	...	...	...
b Transfers to other government subsectors	...	...	...	...	...
c Transfers to households	...	...	...	...	...
Social security benefits	...	...	...	...	...
Social assistance grants	...	...	...	...	...
Unfunded employee welfare benefits	-	...	...	...	...
d Transfers to private non-profit institutions serving households	...	...	...	...	...
e Transfers to the rest of the world	2855	...	...	...	...
Net saving	8520	...	...	...	...
Total Current Disbursements and Net Saving	108195	...	...	...	...

3.13 General Government Capital Accumulation Account: Total and Subsectors

Million Danish kroner

	1970					1971				
	Total General Government	Central Government	State or Provincial Government	Local Government	Social Security Funds	Total General Government	Central Government	State or Provincial Government	Local Government	Social Security Funds
	Finance of Gross Accumulation									
1 Gross saving	8934	...	...	...	...	11103	...	...	...	...
a Consumption of fixed capital	669	...	...	...	...	734	...	...	...	...
b Net saving	8265	...	...	...	...	10369	...	...	...	...
2 Capital transfers received	-151	...	...	...	...	-173	...	...	...	...
a From other government subsectors	...	...	...	...	...	...	...	...	...	...
b From other resident sectors	131	...	...	...	...	112	...	...	...	...
c From rest of the world	-282	...	...	...	...	-285	...	...	...	...
Finance of Gross Accumulation	8783	...	...	...	...	10930	...	...	...	...
	Gross Accumulation									
1 Gross capital formation	6354	...	...	...	...	7058	...	...	...	...
2 Purchases of land, net	...	...	...	...	...	...	...	...	...	...
3 Purchases of intangible assets, net	...	...	...	...	...	...	...	...	...	...
4 Capital transfers paid	...	...	...	...	...	...	...	...	...	...
Net lending	2429	...	...	...	...	3872	...	...	...	...
Gross Accumulation	8783	...	...	...	...	10930	...	...	...	...

	1972					1973				
	Total General Government	Central Government	State or Provincial Government	Local Government	Social Security Funds	Total General Government	Central Government	State or Provincial Government	Local Government	Social Security Funds
	Finance of Gross Accumulation									
1 Gross saving	12650	...	...	...	...	17055	...	...	...	...
a Consumption of fixed capital	782	...	...	...	...	877	...	...	...	...
b Net saving	11868	...	...	...	...	16178	...	...	...	...
2 Capital transfers received	-70	...	...	...	...	-45	...	...	...	...
a From other government subsectors	...	...	...	...	...	...	...	...	...	...
b From other resident sectors	220	...	...	...	...	220	...	...	...	...
c From rest of the world	-290	...	...	...	...	-265	...	...	...	...
Finance of Gross Accumulation	12580	...	...	...	...	17010	...	...	...	...
	Gross Accumulation									
1 Gross capital formation	7268	...	...	...	...	7197	...	...	...	...
2 Purchases of land, net	...	...	...	...	...	...	...	...	...	...
3 Purchases of intangible assets, net	...	...	...	...	...	...	...	...	...	...
4 Capital transfers paid	...	...	...	...	...	...	...	...	...	...
Net lending	5312	...	...	...	...	9813	...	...	...	...
Gross Accumulation	12580	...	...	...	...	17010	...	...	...	...

Denmark

3.13 General Government Capital Accumulation Account: Total and Subsectors

Million Danish kroner

	1974 Total General Government	1974 Central Government	1974 State or Provincial Government	1974 Local Government	1974 Social Security Funds	1975 Total General Government	1975 Central Government	1975 State or Provincial Government	1975 Local Government	1975 Social Security Funds
Finance of Gross Accumulation										
1 Gross saving	16570	...	...	...	...	5904	...	...	...	...
a Consumption of fixed capital	937	...	...	...	...	999	...	...	...	...
b Net saving	15633	...	...	...	...	4905	...	...	...	...
2 Capital transfers received	-25	...	...	...	...	-209	...	...	...	...
a From other government subsectors	...	...	...	...	...	...	...	...	...	...
b From other resident sectors	265	...	...	...	...	96	...	...	...	...
c From rest of the world	-290	...	...	...	...	-305	...	...	...	...
Finance of Gross Accumulation	16545	...	...	...	...	5695	...	...	...	...
Gross Accumulation										
1 Gross capital formation	8184	...	...	...	...	9158	...	...	...	...
2 Purchases of land, net	...	...	...	...	...	...	...	...	...	...
3 Purchases of intangible assets, net	...	...	...	...	...	...	...	...	...	...
4 Capital transfers paid	...	...	...	...	...	...	...	...	...	...
Net lending	8361	...	...	...	...	-3463	...	...	...	...
Gross Accumulation	16545	...	...	...	...	5695	...	...	...	...

	1976 Total General Government	1976 Central Government	1976 State or Provincial Government	1976 Local Government	1976 Social Security Funds
Finance of Gross Accumulation					
1 Gross saving	9587	...	...	...	...
a Consumption of fixed capital	1067	...	...	...	...
b Net saving	8520	...	...	...	...
2 Capital transfers received	-1087	...	...	...	...
a From other government subsectors	...	...	...	...	...
b From other resident sectors	-757	...	...	...	...
c From rest of the world	-330	...	...	...	...
Finance of Gross Accumulation	8500	...	...	...	...
Gross Accumulation					
1 Gross capital formation	10084	...	...	...	...
2 Purchases of land, net	...	...	...	...	...
3 Purchases of intangible assets, net	...	...	...	...	...
4 Capital transfers paid	...	...	...	...	...
Net lending	-1584	...	...	...	...
Gross Accumulation	8500	...	...	...	...

3.32 Household and Private Unincorporated Enterprise Income and Outlay Account

Million Danish kroner

	1970	1971	1972	1973	1974	1975	1976	1977	1978	1979	1980
Receipts											
1 Compensation of employees	61547	68700	77418	89117	105629	120268	...	...	...	...	...
a Wages and salaries	60752	67840	76313	88157	104654	119263	...	...	...	...	...
b Employers' contributions for social security	795	860	1105	960	975	1005	...	...	...	...	...
c Employers' contributions for private pension & welfare plans	...	...	...	...	...	...	...	...	...	...	...

Denmark

3.32 Household and Private Unincorporated Enterprise Income and Outlay Account
(Continued)

Million Danish kroner

	1970	1971	1972	1973	1974	1975	1976	1977	1978	1979	1980
2 Property and entrepreneurial income received	25860	27391	30974	33370	30718	29231	...	...	...	...	...
3 Other current transfers received	13539	15600	18035	20100	24125	30510	34870	...	...	...	...
a Casualty insurance claims	-	-	-	-	-	-	-	...	...	...	...
b Social security benefits	13539	15600	18035	20100	24125	30510	34870	...	...	...	...
c Social assistance grants	...	...	...	...	...	...	...	...	...	...	...
d Unfunded employee welfare benefits	...	...	...	...	...	...	...	...	...	...	...
e Other current transfers received	-	-	-	-	-	-	-	...	...	...	...
From general government	...	...	...	...	...	...	...	...	...	...	...
From the rest fo the world	-	-	-	-	-	-	-	...	...	...	...
Other	...	...	...	...	...	...	...	...	...	...	...
Total Current Receipts	100946	111691	126427	142587	160472	180009	204434	...	...	...	...
					Disbursements						
1 Final consumption expenditures	70228	74879	81334	93045	103738	117883	135975	...	...	...	...
2 Property income paid	...	...	...	...	...	...	...	...	...	...	...
3 Direct taxes, fees, fines & other payments n.e.c. to government	25912	32833	37404	42600	52995	53508	...	...	...	...	...
a Social security contributions	2156	2475	2995	1760	1425	1505	1640	...	...	...	...
b Direct taxes	23756	30358	34409	40840	51570	52003	...	...	...	...	...
Income taxes	22786	28895	32825	39726	49357	49056	...	...	...	...	...
Other	970	1463	1584	1114	2213	2947	...	...	...	...	...
c Fees, fines and penalties	...	...	...	...	...	...	...	...	...	...	...
4 Other current transfers paid	...	...	...	...	...	...	...	...	...	...	...
a Net casualty insurance premiums	-	-	-	-	-	-	-	...	...	...	...
b Transfers to private non-profit institutions serving households	...	...	...	...	...	...	...	...	...	...	...
c Transfers to the rest of the world	-	-	-	-	-	-	-	...	...	...	...
d Other current transfers, except imputed	...	...	...	...	...	...	...	...	...	...	...
e Imputed employee welfare contributions	...	...	...	...	...	...	...	...	...	...	...
Net saving	4806	3979	7689	6942	3739	8618	8179	...	...	...	...
Total Current Disbursements and Net Saving	100946	111691	126427	142587	160472	180009	204434	...	...	...	...

3.33 Household and Private Unincorporated Enterprise Capital Accumulation Account

Million Danish kroner

	1970	1971	1972	1973	1974	1975	1976	1977	1978	1979	1980
				Finance of Gross Accumulation							
1 Gross saving	13460	13651	18788	19933	20291	27784	29530	...	...	...	...
a Consumption of fixed capital	8654	9672	11099	12991	16552	19166	21351	...	...	...	...
b Net saving	4806	3979	7689	6942	3739	8618	8179	...	...	...	...
2 Capital transfers received	-131	-112	-220	-220	-265	-96	757	...	...	...	...
Total Finance of Gross Accumulation	13329	13539	18568	19713	20026	27688	30287	...	...	...	...
				Gross Accumulation							
1 Gross Capital Formation	20266	21010	24666	32975	34628	27762	41009	...	...	...	...
2 Purchases of land, net	...	...	...	...	...	...	...	...	...	...	...
3 Purchases of intangibles, net	...	...	...	...	...	...	...	...	...	...	...
4 Capital transfers paid	...	...	...	...	...	...	...	...	...	...	...
5 Net lending	-6937	-7471	-6098	-13262	-14602	-74	-10722	...	...	...	...
Total Gross Accumulation	13329	13539	18568	19713	20026	27688	30287	...	...	...	...

Denmark

3.51 External Transactions: Current Account: Detail

Million Danish kroner

	1970	1971	1972	1973	1974	1975	1976	1977	1978	1979	1980
	\multicolumn{11}{c}{Payments to the Rest of the World}
1 Imports of goods and services	36661	38604	39943	52605	67157	67080	84144	90656	93246	112701	128762
a Imports of merchandise c.i.f.	33101	34264	35434	47031	60543	59805	75086	79662	81435	98429	111295
b Other	3560	4340	4509	5574	6614	7275	9058	10994	11811	14272	17467
2 Factor income paid to the rest of the world	1051	1271	1663	2122	3307	3501	3987	5789	8188	11504	15768
a Compensation of employees	69	79	94	100	124	149	191	213	228	259	298
b Property and entrepreneurial income paid	982	1192	1569	2022	3183	3352	3796	5576	7960	11245	15470
3 Indirect taxes paid to supranational organizations	...	...	...	...	...	...	...	...	...	...	...
4 Other current transfers to the rest of the world	1028	660	954	1760	1762	2475	2890	3920	4219	5628	6551
5 Surplus of the nation on current transactions	-4569	-3188	-523	-2986	-6050	-3327	-12305	-11089	-8531	-15524	-14208
Payments to the Rest of the World, and Surplus of the Nation on Current Transfers	34171	37347	42037	53501	66176	69729	78716	89276	97122	114309	136873
	\multicolumn{11}{c}{Receipts From The Rest of the World}
1 Exports of goods and services	33104	36184	40835	49314	61481	65049	72455	80463	86515	102525	124503
a Exports of merchandise f.o.b.	25254	27450	30931	37846	47280	50201	55223	60690	65575	78516	95889
b Other	7850	8734	9904	11468	14201	14848	17232	19773	20940	24009	28614
2 Factor income received from the rest of the world	785	790	872	1209	1916	1712	1898	2591	3430	4759	5935
a Compensation of employees	137	141	141	143	196	220	272	294	330	359	415
b Property and entrepreneurial income received	648	649	731	1066	1720	1492	1626	2297	3100	4400	5520
3 Subsidies received from supranational organizations	...	...	...	...	...	...	...	...	...	...	...
4 Other current transfers from the rest of the world	282	373	330	2978	2779	2968	4363	6222	7177	7025	6435
Receipts from the Rest of the World on Current Transfers	34171	37347	42037	53501	66176	69729	78716	89276	97122	114309	136873

3.52 External Transactions: Capital Accumulation Account

Million Danish kroner

	1970	1971	1972	1973	1974	1975	1976	1977	1978	1979	1980
	\multicolumn{11}{c}{Finance of Gross Accumulation}
1 Surplus of the nation on current transactions	-4569	-3188	-523	-2986	-6050	-3327	-12305	-11089	-8531	-15524	-14208
2 Capital transfers received from the rest of the world	-	-	1	1	1	46	83	112	84	94	119
Total Finance of Gross Accumulation	-4569	-3188	-522	-2985	-6049	-3281	-12222	-10977	-8447	-15430	-14089
	\multicolumn{11}{c}{Gross Accumulation}
1 Capital transfers paid to the rest of the world	282	313	308	297	384	369	388	429	508	599	553
2 Purchases of intangible assets, n.e.c., net, from the rest of the world	...	...	...	...	...	...	...	...	...	...	...
3 Net lending to the rest of the world	-4851	-3501	-830	-3282	-6433	-3650	-12610	-11406	-8955	-16029	-14642
Total Gross Accumulation	-4569	-3188	-522	-2985	-6049	-3281	-12222	-10977	-8447	-15430	-14089

3.53 External Transactions: Capital Finance Account

Million Danish kroner

	1970	1971	1972	1973	1974	1975	1976	1977	1978	1979	1980
	\multicolumn{11}{c}{Acquisitions of Foreign Financial Assets}
1 Gold and SDR's	-257	-11	-2	357	-210	-64	-1	206	...	...	...
2 Currency and transferable deposits	958	1394	670	1846	-845	-1912	1261	713	...	...	...
3 Other deposits			-238	-9	2238	822	1855	6955	...	...	...
4 Bills and bonds, short term	...	...	542	906	-1084	546	-122	1953	...	...	...
5 Bonds, long term	25	18	155	95	-84	1563	136	190	...	...	...
6 Corporate equity securities	177	229	500	450	473	594	217	635	...	...	...
a Subsidiaries abroad	205	245	511	411	388	583	117	545	...	...	...
b Other	-28	-16	-11	39	85	11	100	90	...	...	...
7 Short-term loans, n.e.c.	6	-	-280	230	329	-163	117	461	...	...	...

Denmark

3.53 External Transactions: Capital Finance Account
(Continued)

Million Danish kroner

	1970	1971	1972	1973	1974	1975	1976	1977	1978	1979	1980
8 Long-term loans	840	1322	712	552	758	429	574	2291	...	...	...
9 Proprietors' net additions to accumulation of quasi-corporate, non-resident enterprises									...	...	...
10 Trade credit and advances	192	-38	1244	2000	1498	-113	739	812	...	...	...
11 Other	-	-	327	1200	-226	-325	290	-19	...	...	...
Total Acquisitions of Foreign Financial Assets [a]	1941	2914	3630	7627	2847	1377	5066	14197	...	...	...

Incurrence of Foreign Liabilities

	1970	1971	1972	1973	1974	1975	1976	1977	1978	1979	1980
1 Currency and transferable deposits	1309	1040	42	19	59	249	732	-183	...	...	...
2 Other deposits			191	296	154	5	79	185	...	...	...
3 Bills and bonds, short term	...	...	...	...	...	...	...	...	...	...	...
4 Bonds, long term	689	2097	848	1071	349	1092	6716	5241	...	...	...
5 Corporate equity securities	673	470	903	1045	950	1137	194	121	...	...	...
a Subsidiaries of non-resident incorporated units	678	445	914	700	1036	1161	334	292	...	...	...
b Other	-5	25	-11	345	-86	-24	-140	-171	...	...	...
6 Short-term loans, n.e.c.	96	9	-1176	2041	1736	1494	1924	5268	...	...	...
7 Long-term loans	489	1467	1868	1423	2901	237	5880	12077	...	...	...
8 Non-resident proprietors' net additions to accumulation of resident quasi-corporate enterprises									...	...	...
9 Trade credit and advances	2143	470	582	3654	1511	667	1097	2156	...	...	...
10 Other	-	-	281	330	140	-156	184	-1	...	...	...
Total Incurrence of Liabilities [a]	5399	5553	3539	9879	7800	4725	16806	24864	...	...	...
Statistical discrepancy [a]	1393	862	921	1030	1480	302	870	739	...	...	...
Net Lending	-4851	-3501	-830	-3282	-6433	-3650	-12610	-11406	...	...	...
Total Incurrence of Liabilities and Net Lending [a]	1941	2914	3630	7627	2847	1377	5066	14197	...	...	...

a) Data taken from balance of payments records which include the Faroe Islands and Greenland. Consequently, the statistical discrepancy comprise both errors and omissions and an adjustment for the difference in geographical coverage.

4.6 Cost Components of Value Added, ISIC Divisions

Million Danish kroner

	1970						1971					
	Compensation of Employees	Capital Consumption	Net Operating Surplus	Indirect Taxes	Less: Subsidies Received	Value Added	Compensation of Employees	Capital Consumption	Net Operating Surplus	Indirect Taxes	Less: Subsidies Received	Value Added

All Producers

	CE	CC	NOS	IT	Sub	VA	CE	CC	NOS	IT	Sub	VA
1 Agriculture, hunting, forestry and fishing	1210	...	5401	...	...	6612	1321	...	5842	...	...	7163
a Agriculture and hunting	895	...	4977	...	...	5873	977	...	5349	...	...	6326
b Forestry and logging	138	...	43	...	...	181	158	...	21	...	...	179
c Fishing	177	...	381	...	...	558	186	...	471	...	...	658
2 Mining and quarrying	78	...	74	...	...	152	86	...	54	...	...	140
a Coal mining	...	...	...	...	...	...	...	...	...	...	...	...
b Crude petroleum and natural gas production	6	...	-29	...	...	-23	1	...	-31	...	...	-30
c Metal ore mining	...	...	...	...	...	...	...	...	...	...	...	...
d Other mining	72	...	103	...	...	175	85	...	85	...	...	170

Denmark

4.6 Cost Components of Value Added, ISIC Divisions
(Continued)

Million Danish kroner

	1970						1971					
	Compensation of Employees	Capital Consumption	Net Operating Surplus	Indirect Taxes	Less: Subsidies Received	Value Added	Compensation of Employees	Capital Consumption	Net Operating Surplus	Indirect Taxes	Less: Subsidies Received	Value Added
3 Manufacturing	16250	...	5718	...	...	21967	17854	...	5701	...	...	23555
a Manufacture of food, beverages and tobacco	3131	...	1475	...	...	4605	3567	...	1557	...	...	5124
b Textile, wearing apparel and leather industries	1466	...	486	...	...	1952	1519	...	446	...	...	1965
c Manufacture of wood and wood products, including furniture	962	...	348	...	...	1310	1002	...	376	...	...	1378
d Manufacture of paper and paper products, printing and publishing	1942	...	563	...	...	2505	2152	...	479	...	...	2631
e Manufacture of chemicals and chemical petroleum, coal, rubber and plastic products	1365	...	813	...	...	2178	1515	...	735	...	...	2250
f Manufacture of non-metallic mineral products, except products of petroleum and coal	1034	...	602	...	...	1636	1170	...	571	...	...	1741
g Basic metal industries	296	...	102	...	...	399	320	...	88	...	...	408
h Manufacture of fabricated metal products, machinery and equipment	5803	...	1233	...	...	7036	6339	...	1366	...	...	7705
i Other manufacturing industries	251	...	96	...	...	346	270	...	83	...	...	353
4 Electricity, gas and water	534	...	1280	...	...	1814	597	...	1352	...	...	1949
a Electricity, gas and steam	464	...	1178	...	...	1641	521	...	1237	...	...	1758
b Water works and supply	70	...	102	...	...	172	76	...	115	...	...	191
5 Construction	7733	...	3396	...	...	11129	8324	...	3952	...	...	12276
6 Wholesale and retail trade, restaurants and hotels	9720	...	8273	...	...	17993	10776	...	8172	...	...	18948
a Wholesale and retail trade	8730	...	7951	...	...	16681	9678	...	7876	...	...	17554
b Restaurants and hotels	990	...	322	...	...	1312	1098	...	296	...	...	1394
7 Transport, storage and communication	4929	...	4400	...	...	9329	5543	...	4149	...	...	9692
a Transport and storage	3878	...	3738	...	...	7616	4410	...	3503	...	...	7913
b Communication	1051	...	662	...	...	1713	1133	...	646	...	...	1779
8 Finance, insurance, real estate and business services	4397	...	8511	...	...	12908	5076	...	10022	...	...	15098
a Financial institutions	1498	...	1261	...	...	2759	1785	...	1319	...	...	3104
b Insurance	737	...	-154	...	...	583	833	...	-105	...	...	728
c Real estate and business services	2162	...	7404	...	...	9566	2458	...	8808	...	...	11266
Real estate, except dwellings	1832	...	1344	...	...	3176	2070	...	1497	...	...	3567
Dwellings	330	...	6060	...	...	6390	388	...	7311	...	...	7699
9 Community, social and personal services	2697	...	2757	...	...	5454	3020	...	3094	...	...	6114
a Sanitary and similar services	...	...	...	...	...	...	...	...	...	...	...	...
b Social and related community services	384	...	1257	...	...	1640	421	...	1477	...	...	1898
Educational services	16	...	141	...	...	156	17	...	153	...	...	170
Medical, dental, other health and veterinary services	368	...	1116	...	...	1484	404	...	1324	...	...	1728
c Recreational and cultural services	531	...	292	...	...	823	612	...	315	...	...	927
d Personal and household services	1782	...	1208	...	...	2991	1987	...	1302	...	...	3289
Total, Industries [a]	47548	...	39810	...	...	87358	52597	...	42337	...	...	94935
Producers of Government Services	15664	...	554	...	...	16218	18798	...	653	...	...	19451
Other Producers [a]	647	...	12	...	...	659	725	...	15	...	...	740
Total [b]	63859	...	40376	...	...	104235	72120	...	43005	...	...	115126
Imputed bank service charge	...	...	-2903	...	...	-2903	...	...	-3252	...	...	-3252
Import duties	...	...	...	...	...	...	...	...	...	...	...	...
Value added tax	...	...	...	...	...	...	...	...	...	...	...	...
Other adjustments	...	...	...	20484	3189	17295	...	...	...	22935	3689	19246
Total	63859	...	37473	20484	3189	118627	72120	...	39753	22935	3689	131120

Denmark

4.6 Cost Components of Value Added, ISIC Divisions

Million Danish kroner

	1972 Compensation of Employees	1972 Capital Consumption	1972 Net Operating Surplus	1972 Indirect Taxes	1972 Less: Subsidies Received	1972 Value Added	1973 Compensation of Employees	1973 Capital Consumption	1973 Net Operating Surplus	1973 Indirect Taxes	1973 Less: Subsidies Received	1973 Value Added
						All Producers						
1 Agriculture, hunting, forestry and fishing	1364	...	7200	...	...	8564	1497	...	9027	...	...	10525
a Agriculture and hunting	1001	...	6597	...	...	7598	1083	...	8198	...	...	9282
b Forestry and logging	175	...	21	...	...	196	198	...	22	...	...	219
c Fishing	188	...	582	...	...	770	216	...	807	...	...	1024
2 Mining and quarrying	114	...	68	...	...	182	122	...	19	...	...	141
a Coal mining	...	...	...	...	...	...	...	...	...	...	...	...
b Crude petroleum and natural gas production	13	...	-38	...	...	-25	13	...	-89	...	...	-75
c Metal ore mining	...	...	...	...	...	...	...	...	...	...	...	...
d Other mining	101	...	106	...	...	207	109	...	108	...	...	216
3 Manufacturing	19852	...	6800	...	...	26651	23115	...	7797	...	...	30912
a Manufacture of food, beverages and tobacco	3915	...	1815	...	...	5730	4535	...	2253	...	...	6788
b Textile, wearing apparel and leather industries	1721	...	485	...	...	2206	1880	...	520	...	...	2399
c Manufacture of wood and wood products, including furniture	1128	...	410	...	...	1537	1327	...	486	...	...	1813
d Manufacture of paper and paper products, printing and publishing	2353	...	579	...	...	2932	2650	...	699	...	...	3349
e Manufacture of chemicals and chemical petroleum, coal, rubber and plastic products	1702	...	882	...	...	2584	1963	...	1158	...	...	3120
f Manufacture of non-metallic mineral products, except products of petroleum and coal	1334	...	750	...	...	2084	1559	...	776	...	...	2335
g Basic metal industries	373	...	95	...	...	468	435	...	125	...	...	560
h Manufacture of fabricated metal products, machinery and equipment	7013	...	1659	...	...	8672	8406	...	1611	...	...	10018
i Other manufacturing industries	313	...	125	...	...	438	360	...	170	...	...	530
4 Electricity, gas and water	660	...	1410	...	...	2069	761	...	1364	...	...	2125
a Electricity, gas and steam	573	...	1275	...	...	1847	658	...	1212	...	...	1870
b Water works and supply	87	...	135	...	...	222	103	...	152	...	...	255
5 Construction	8576	...	5856	...	...	14432	9593	...	5743	...	...	15336
6 Wholesale and retail trade, restaurants and hotels	11720	...	9888	...	...	21609	13589	...	11883	...	...	25471
a Wholesale and retail trade	10545	...	9479	...	...	20025	12234	...	11480	...	...	23714
b Restaurants and hotels	1175	...	409	...	...	1584	1355	...	403	...	...	1757
7 Transport, storage and communication	6073	...	4784	...	...	10858	6812	...	5690	...	...	12503
a Transport and storage	4838	...	4094	...	...	8933	5335	...	5002	...	...	10338
b Communication	1235	...	690	...	...	1925	1477	...	688	...	...	2165
8 Finance, insurance, real estate and business services	5866	...	12280	...	...	18145	6745	...	15449	...	...	22194
a Financial institutions	2040	...	1566	...	...	3605	2401	...	2285	...	...	4686
b Insurance	934	...	-55	...	...	879	1034	...	49	...	...	1083
c Real estate and business services	2893	...	10769	...	...	13661	3310	...	13115	...	...	16425
Real estate, except dwellings	2453	...	1773	...	...	4226	2785	...	2103	...	...	4888
Dwellings	440	...	8996	...	...	9435	525	...	11012	...	...	11537
9 Community, social and personal services	3323	...	3376	...	...	6699	3695	...	3830	...	...	7525
a Sanitary and similar services	...	...	...	...	...	...	...	...	...	...	...	...
b Social and related community services	463	...	1661	...	...	2124	544	...	1880	...	...	2424
Educational services	17	...	166	...	...	182	21	...	188	...	...	209
Medical, dental, other health and veterinary services	446	...	1495	...	...	1942	523	...	1692	...	...	2215
c Recreational and cultural services	677	...	326	...	...	1004	752	...	341	...	...	1093
d Personal and household services	2183	...	1389	...	...	3571	2399	...	1609	...	...	4008

Denmark

4.6 Cost Components of Value Added, ISIC Divisions
(Continued)

Million Danish kroner

	1972						1973					
	Compensation of Employees	Capital Consumption	Net Operating Surplus	Indirect Taxes	Less: Subsidies Received	Value Added	Compensation of Employees	Capital Consumption	Net Operating Surplus	Indirect Taxes	Less: Subsidies Received	Value Added
Total, Industries [a]	57548	...	51662	...	...	109209	65929	...	60803	...	...	126732
Producers of Government Services	21863	...	777	...	...	22640	25496	...	939	...	...	26435
Other Producers [a]	811	...	19	...	...	831	89	...	22	...	...	915
Total [b]	80223	...	52458	...	...	132680	92318	...	61764	...	...	154082
Imputed bank service charge	...	...	-3841	...	...	-3841	...	...	-4979	...	...	-4979
Import duties	...	...	...	...	...	...	...	...	...	...	...	...
Value added tax	...	...	...	...	...	...	...	...	...	...	...	...
Other adjustments	...	...	...	26222	4332	21890	...	...	...	29133	5376	23757
Total	80223	...	48617	26222	4332	150729	92318	...	56785	29133	5376	172860

	1974						1975					
	Compensation of Employees	Capital Consumption	Net Operating Surplus	Indirect Taxes	Less: Subsidies Received	Value Added	Compensation of Employees	Capital Consumption	Net Operating Surplus	Indirect Taxes	Less: Subsidies Received	Value Added

All Producers

1 Agriculture, hunting, forestry and fishing	1746	...	9696	...	...	11442	1975	...	8951	...	...	10927
a Agriculture and hunting	1258	...	8739	...	...	9997	1418	...	8393	...	...	9812
b Forestry and logging	234	...	64	...	...	298	266	...	73	...	...	339
c Fishing	254	...	893	...	...	1147	291	...	485	...	...	776
2 Mining and quarrying	124	...	32	...	...	156	124	...	39	...	...	163
a Coal mining	...	...	...	...	...	...	...	...	...	...	...	...
b Crude petroleum and natural gas production	15	...	-67	...	...	-52	16	...	-93	...	...	-77
c Metal ore mining	...	...	...	...	...	...	...	...	...	...	...	...
d Other mining	109	...	99	...	...	208	108	...	132	...	...	240
3 Manufacturing	27484	...	7476	...	...	34959	29071	...	9976	...	...	39046
a Manufacture of food, beverages and tobacco	5300	...	2138	...	...	7438	5777	...	2863	...	...	8640
b Textile, wearing apparel and leather industries	1999	...	548	...	...	2547	2110	...	710	...	...	2820
c Manufacture of wood and wood products, including furniture	1497	...	439	...	...	1936	1491	...	525	...	...	2015
d Manufacture of paper and paper products, printing and publishing	3247	...	587	...	...	3834	3407	...	683	...	...	4090
e Manufacture of chemicals and chemical petroleum, coal, rubber and plastic products	2390	...	1042	...	...	3431	2622	...	1408	...	...	4029
f Manufacture of non-metallic mineral products, except products of petroleum and coal	1756	...	434	...	...	2190	1757	...	685	...	...	2442
g Basic metal industries	580	...	172	...	...	752	601	...	53	...	...	654
h Manufacture of fabricated metal products, machinery and equipment	10288	...	1961	...	...	12249	10840	...	2822	...	...	13662
i Other manufacturing industries	427	...	155	...	...	582	466	...	227	...	...	694
4 Electricity, gas and water	915	...	1736	...	...	2651	1070	...	2040	...	...	3110
a Electricity, gas and steam	787	...	1602	...	...	2389	918	...	1896	...	...	2814
b Water works and supply	128	...	134	...	...	262	152	...	144	...	...	296
5 Construction	10158	...	5904	...	...	16063	10453	...	6217	...	...	16670
6 Wholesale and retail trade, restaurants and hotels	15835	...	12234	...	...	28070	18075	...	13094	...	...	31169
a Wholesale and retail trade	14250	...	11872	...	...	26122	16285	...	12665	...	...	28950
b Restaurants and hotels	1585	...	362	...	...	1948	1790	...	429	...	...	2219
7 Transport, storage and communication	8060	...	6315	...	...	14375	9237	...	6578	...	...	15814
a Transport and storage	6326	...	5690	...	...	12016	7256	...	5927	...	...	13182
b Communication	1734	...	626	...	...	2359	1981	...	651	...	...	2632
8 Finance, insurance, real estate and business services	8142	...	17181	...	...	25323	9458	...	19017	...	...	28475
a Financial institutions	3042	...	2494	...	...	5536	3757	...	2449	...	...	6206
b Insurance	1201	...	13	...	...	1214	1335	...	-217	...	...	1118
c Real estate and business services	3899	...	14674	...	...	18573	4366	...	16785	...	...	21151
Real estate, except dwellings	3264	...	2227	...	...	5491	3621	...	2690	...	...	6311

Denmark

4.6 Cost Components of Value Added, ISIC Divisions
(Continued)

Million Danish kroner

	1974						1975				
	Compensation of Employees	Capital Consumption	Net Operating Surplus	Indirect Taxes	Less: Subsidies Received	Value Added	Compensation of Employees	Capital Consumption	Net Operating Surplus	Indirect Taxes	Less: Subsidies Received	Value Added
Dwellings	635	...	12447	...	...	13082	745	...	14095	...	...	14840
9 Community, social and personal services	4293	...	4629	...	...	8923	4836	...	5204	...	...	10041
a Sanitary and similar services	...	...	...	...	...	...	...	...	...	...	...	...
b Social and related community services	654	...	2259	...	...	2913	792	...	2418	...	...	3211
Educational services	22	...	205	...	...	227	23	...	232	...	...	255
Medical, dental, other health and veterinary services	632	...	2054	...	...	2686	769	...	2186	...	...	2956
c Recreational and cultural services	890	...	422	...	...	1312	1020	...	499	...	...	1519
d Personal and household services	2749	...	1948	...	...	4698	3024	...	2287	...	...	5311
Total, Industries a	76757	...	65204	...	...	141962	84299	...	71116	...	...	155415
Producers of Government Services	31283	...	1221	...	...	32504	37233	...	1450	...	...	38683
Other Producers a	1054	...	37	...	...	1090	1210	...	32	...	...	1242
Total b	109094	...	66462	...	...	175556	122742	...	72598	...	...	195340
Imputed bank service charge	...	...	-5903	...	...	-5903	...	...	-6627	...	...	-6627
Import duties	...	...	...	...	...	...	...	...	...	...	...	...
Value added tax	...	...	...	...	...	...	...	...	...	...	...	...
Other adjustments	...	...	...	30833	6857	23976	...	...	...	33560	6017	27543
Total	109094	...	60559	30833	6857	193629	122742	...	65971	33560	6017	216256

	1976						1977				
	Compensation of Employees	Capital Consumption	Net Operating Surplus	Indirect Taxes	Less: Subsidies Received	Value Added	Compensation of Employees	Capital Consumption	Net Operating Surplus	Indirect Taxes	Less: Subsidies Received	Value Added

All Producers

1 Agriculture, hunting, forestry and fishing	2230	...	10071	...	...	12301	2438	...	12185	...	...	14623
a Agriculture and hunting	1541	...	9161	...	...	10702	1649	...	11020	...	...	12669
b Forestry and logging	321	...	43	...	...	364	368	...	54	...	...	422
c Fishing	368	...	867	...	...	1235	421	...	1111	...	...	1532
2 Mining and quarrying	132	...	30	...	...	163	152	...	298	...	...	451
a Coal mining	...	...	...	...	...	...	...	...	...	...	...	...
b Crude petroleum and natural gas production	25	...	-93	...	...	-67	29	...	94	...	...	123
c Metal ore mining	...	...	...	...	...	...	...	...	...	...	...	...
d Other mining	107	...	123	...	...	230	123	...	204	...	...	328
3 Manufacturing	32788	...	11178	...	...	43966	36105	...	11551	...	...	47656
a Manufacture of food, beverages and tobacco	6348	...	2655	...	...	9003	7616	...	2904	...	...	10519
b Textile, wearing apparel and leather industries	2494	...	804	...	...	3298	2564	...	711	...	...	3275
c Manufacture of wood and wood products, including furniture	1808	...	636	...	...	2444	1908	...	649	...	...	2557
d Manufacture of paper and paper products, printing and publishing	3852	...	925	...	...	4777	4150	...	844	...	...	4994
e Manufacture of chemicals and chemical petroleum, coal, rubber and plastic products	2937	...	1668	...	...	4605	3227	...	1655	...	...	4882
f Manufacture of non-metallic mineral products, except products of petroleum and coal	2010	...	787	...	...	2797	2201	...	886	...	...	3087
g Basic metal industries	697	...	9	...	...	706	693	...	97	...	...	790
h Manufacture of fabricated metal products, machinery and equipment	12141	...	3409	...	...	15550	13202	...	3517	...	...	16719
i Other manufacturing industries	501	...	285	...	...	786	544	...	288	...	...	833
4 Electricity, gas and water	1200	...	2089	...	...	3290	1327	...	1828	...	...	3155
a Electricity, gas and steam	1022	...	1922	...	...	2944	1134	...	1616	...	...	2750
b Water works and supply	178	...	168	...	...	346	193	...	212	...	...	405

Denmark

4.6 Cost Components of Value Added, ISIC Divisions
(Continued)

Million Danish kroner

	1976						1977					
	Compensation of Employees	Capital Consumption	Net Operating Surplus	Indirect Taxes	Less: Subsidies Received	Value Added	Compensation of Employees	Capital Consumption	Net Operating Surplus	Indirect Taxes	Less: Subsidies Received	Value Added
5 Construction	12589	...	6281	...	...	18870	13274	...	6236	...	...	19510
6 Wholesale and retail trade, restaurants and hotels	20645	...	16849	...	...	37493	23376	...	17038	...	...	40414
a Wholesale and retail trade	18577	...	16227	...	...	34804	21225	...	16080	...	...	37305
b Restaurants and hotels	2068	...	622	...	...	2689	2151	...	958	...	...	3109
7 Transport, storage and communication	10505	...	7119	...	...	17624	11505	...	8107	...	...	19613
a Transport and storage	8251	...	6296	...	...	14547	9097	...	7114	...	...	16212
b Communication	2254	...	823	...	...	3077	2408	...	993	...	...	3401
8 Finance, insurance, real estate and business services	10532	...	23808	...	...	34340	12043	...	26439	...	...	38481
a Financial institutions	4017	...	2778	...	...	6795	4499	...	2825	...	...	7324
b Insurance	1472	...	-111	...	...	1361	1676	...	-594	...	...	1082
c Real estate and business services	5043	...	21141	...	...	26184	5868	...	24208	...	...	30075
Real estate, except dwellings	4181	...	3241	...	...	7422	4914	...	3608	...	...	8522
Dwellings	862	...	17900	...	...	18762	954	...	20600	...	...	21553
9 Community, social and personal services	5532	...	5668	...	...	11200	6261	...	6213	...	...	12474
a Sanitary and similar services	...	...	...	...	...	...	...	...	...	...	...	...
b Social and related community services	822	...	2543	...	...	3366	892	...	2634	...	...	3526
Educational services	24	...	257	...	...	282	25	...	265	...	...	290
Medical, dental, other health and veterinary services	798	...	2286	...	...	3084	867	...	2369	...	...	3236
c Recreational and cultural services	1143	...	575	...	...	1717	1320	...	834	...	...	2154
d Personal and household services	3567	...	2550	...	...	6117	4049	...	2745	...	...	6794
Total, Industries [a]	96154	...	83093	...	...	179247	106481	...	89895	...	...	196377
Producers of Government Services	42909	...	1652	...	...	44561	48157	...	1894	...	...	50051
Other Producers [a]	1397	...	46	...	...	1443	1535	...	43	...	...	1577
Total [b]	140460	...	84791	...	...	225251	156173	...	91832	...	...	248005
Imputed bank service charge	...	...	-7167	...	...	-7167	...	...	-7895	...	...	-7895
Import duties	...	...	...	...	...	...	...	...	...	...	...	...
Value added tax	...	...	...	...	...	...	...	...	...	...	...	...
Other adjustments	...	...	...	40833	7703	33130	...	...	...	47651	9082	38569
Total	140460	...	77624	40833	7703	251214	156173	...	83937	47651	9082	278679

a)
b) Gross domestic product in factor values.

Djibouti

Source. Reply to the United Nations National Accounts Questionnaire from le Directeur Direction de la Statistique, Djibouti.

General note. The estimates shown in the following tables have been prepared in accordance with the United Nations System of National Accounts so far as the existing data would permit.

1.1 Expenditure on the Gross Domestic Product, in Current Prices

Million Djibouti francs	1970	1971	1972	1973	1974	1975	1976	1977	1978	1979	1980
1 General government final consumption expenditure	...	...	...	...	...	...	...	...	...	...	...
2 Private final consumption expenditure	...	...	...	...	...	...	...	...	...	...	...
3 Gross capital formation	...	...	...	...	...	...	...	...	...	...	...
4 Exports of goods and services	...	...	...	...	...	...	...	...	...	...	...
5 Less: Imports of goods and services	...	...	...	...	...	...	...	...	...	...	...
Equals: Gross Domestic Product	15300	17200	19100	21800	27100	30100	35900	38700	42400	50700	60313

1.2 Expenditure on the Gross Domestic Product, in Constant Prices

Million Djibouti francs	1970	1971	1972	1973	1974	1975	1976	1977	1978	1979	1980
					At constant prices of:1970						
1 General government final consumption expenditure	...	...	...	...	...	...	...	...	...	...	...
2 Private final consumption expenditure	...	...	...	...	...	...	...	...	...	...	...
3 Gross capital formation	...	...	...	...	...	...	...	...	...	...	...
4 Exports of goods and services	...	...	...	...	...	...	...	...	...	...	...
5 Less: Imports of goods and services	...	...	...	...	...	...	...	...	...	...	...
Equals: Gross Domestic Product	15300	16900	18000	19300	19300	20100	21900	19200	...	...	...

1.10 Gross Domestic Product by Kind of Activity, in Current Prices

Million Djibouti francs	1970	1971	1972	1973	1974	1975	1976	1977	1978	1979	1980
1 Agriculture, hunting, forestry and fishing	...	...	...	...	...	...	...	...	...	2974	3165
2 Mining and quarrying	...	...	...	...	...	...	...	...	...	...	...
3 Manufacturing	...	...	...	...	...	...	...	...	...	3874	4581
4 Electricity, gas and water	...	...	...	...	...	...	...	...	...	1469	1384
5 Construction	...	...	...	...	...	...	...	...	...	2155	2994
6 Wholesale and retail trade, restaurants and hotels	...	...	...	...	...	...	...	...	...	13210	15271
7 Transport, storage and communication	...	...	...	...	...	...	...	...	...	4175	4931
8 Finance, insurance, real estate and business services	...	...	...	...	...	...	...	...	...	3837	6306
9 Community, social and personal services	...	...	...	...	...	...	...	...	...	782	835
Total, Industries	...	...	...	...	...	...	...	...	...	32476	39467
Producers of Government Services	...	...	...	...	...	...	...	...	...	12332	13745
Other Producers	...	...	...	...	...	...	...	...	...	...	...
Subtotal	...	...	...	...	...	...	...	...	...	44808	53212
Less: Imputed bank service charge	...	...	...	...	...	...	...	...	...	555	1903
Plus: Import duties	...	...	...	...	...	...	...	...	...	6463	9004
Plus: Value added tax	...	...	...	...	...	...	...	...	...	...	...
Equals: Gross Domestic Product	15300	17200	19100	21800	27100	30100	35900	38700	42400	50700	60313

Dominica

Source. Reply to the United Nations National Accounts Questionnaire from the Ministry of Finance, Trade and Industry, Roseau.

General note. The estimates shown in the following tables have been prepared in accordance with the United Nations System of National Accounts so far as the existing data would permit.

1.1 Expenditure on the Gross Domestic Product, in Current Prices

Thousand East Caribbean dollars

	1970	1971	1972	1973	1974	1975	1976	1977	1978	1979	1980
1 General government final consumption expenditure	...	14530	...	15743	... 14907	18147	19750	21210	...	...	...
2 Private final consumption expenditure	...	34453	...	43377	... 43086	43153	50917	63561	...	...	...
3 Gross capital formation	...	19202	...	12649	... 10622	...	...	...	...	...	...
a Increase in stocks	...	2650	...	1185	... 1907	...	...	...	...	...	...
b Gross fixed capital formation	...	16552	...	11464	... 8715	16009	16859	19349	...	...	...
Residential buildings	...	781	...	2577	...	...	...	...	...	...	...
Non-residential buildings	...	4248	...	1132	...	...	...	...	...	...	...
Other construction and land improvement etc.	...	4471	...	4076	...	...	...	...	...	...	...
Other	...	7052	...	3679	...	...	...	...	...	...	...
4 Exports of goods and services	...	16416	...	24058	... 29387	30800	36500	40300	...	...	...
5 Less: Imports of goods and services	...	33681	...	33148	... 41833	45200	50100	59400	...	...	...
Statistical discrepancy	...	-64	...	-374	... 326	-	-	-	...	...	...
Equals: Gross Domestic Product	...	50857	...	62304	... 56495	62909	73926	85020	...	...	...

1.2 Expenditure on the Gross Domestic Product, in Constant Prices

Thousand East Caribbean dollars

	1970	1971	1972	1973	1974	1975	1976	1977	1978	1979	1980
	At constant prices of: 1977									
1 General government final consumption expenditure	...	...	...	...	...	20060	20047	21210	...	...	...
2 Private final consumption expenditure	...	...	...	...	...	63150	62685	63561	...	...	...
3 Gross capital formation	...	...	...	...	...	...	...	...	...	...	...
4 Exports of goods and services	...	...	...	...	...	35402	41011	40300	...	...	...
5 Less: Imports of goods and services	...	...	...	...	...	61081	58941	59400	...	...	...
Equals: Gross Domestic Product	...	...	...	...	...	77473	82854	85020	...	...	...

1.3 Cost Components of the Gross Domestic Product

Thousand East Caribbean dollars

	1970	1971	1972	1973	1974	1975	1976	1977	1978	1979	1980
1 Indirect taxes, net	...	8217	...	7874	...	...	...	...	...	...	...
a Indirect taxes paid	...	8217	...	7875	...	...	...	...	...	...	...
b Less: Subsidies received	...	-	...	1	...	...	...	...	...	...	...
2 Consumption of fixed capital	...	2190	...	2007	...	...	...	...	...	...	...
3 Compensation of employees paid by resident producers to:	...	20242	...	23126	...	...	...	...	...	...	...
4 Net operating surplus	...	20207	...	29298	...	...	...	...	...	...	...
Equals: Gross Domestic Product	...	50857	...	62304	... 56495	62909	73926	85020	...	...	...

Dominica

1.8 Capital Transactions of The Nation, Summary

Thousand East Caribbean dollars	1970	1971	1972	1973	1974	1975	1976	1977	1978	1979	1980
Finance of Gross Capital Formation											
Gross saving	...	14702	...	17851	...	...	...	...	...	...	...
1 Consumption of fixed capital	...	2190	...	2007	...	...	...	...	...	...	...
2 Net saving	...	12512	...	15844	...	...	...	...	...	...	...
Less: Surplus of the nation on current transactions	...	-4500	...	5202	...	...	...	...	...	...	...
Finance of Gross Capital Formation	...	19202	...	12649	...	...	...	...	...	...	...
Gross Capital Formation											
Increase in stocks	...	2650	...	1185	...	...	...	...	...	...	...
Gross fixed capital formation	...	16552	...	11464	...	...	...	...	...	...	...
1 General government	...	8096	...	5474	...	...	...	...	...	...	...
2 Corporate and quasi-corporate enterprises	...	...	...	...	...	...	...	...	...	...	...
3 Other	...	...	...	...	...	...	...	...	...	...	...
Gross Capital Formation	...	19202	...	12649	...	...	...	...	...	...	...

1.10 Gross Domestic Product by Kind of Activity, in Current Prices

Thousand East Caribbean dollars	1970	1971	1972	1973	1974	1975	1976	1977	1978	1979	1980
1 Agriculture, hunting, forestry and fishing	...	15963	...	24159	...	19876	24694	33100 / 33877	41354	...	...
2 Mining and quarrying	...	15	...	30	...	628	835	1022 / 4734[a]	5823	...	...
3 Manufacturing	...	656	...	1000	...	2396	3163	3409		...	...
4 Electricity, gas and water	...	499	...	635	...	902	962	1026 / 1627	1817	...	...
5 Construction	...	1735	...	2288	...	3842	4458	4115 / 4480	5465	...	...
6 Wholesale and retail trade, restaurants and hotels	...	4480	...	4778	...	5901	7353	7527 / 8006	10138	...	...
7 Transport, storage and communication	...	519	...	537	...	5359	6246	6961 / 5804	6380	...	...
8 Finance, insurance, real estate and business services	...	5812	...	7107	...	7190	8061	8731 / 8479	9407	...	...
9 Community, social and personal services	...	1330	...	1439	...	696	821	865 / 866	905	...	...
Total, Industries	...	31009	...	41973	...	46789	56592	66755 / 67873	81289	...	...
Producers of Government Services	...	11629	...	12459	...	16120	17333	18265 / 17345	19273	...	...
Other Producers	...	...	...	...	...	...	...	...	...	...	...
Subtotal [b]	...	42638	...	54432	...	62910	73926	85021 / 85218	100562	...	...
Less: Imputed bank service charge	...	...	...	...	...	...	...	...	...	...	...
Plus: Import duties	...	...	...	...	...	...	...	...	...	...	...
Plus: Value added tax	...	...	...	...	...	...	...	...	...	...	...
Plus: Other adjustments [c]	...	8217	...	7873	...	...	...	...	...	...	...
Equals: Gross Domestic Product	...	50857	...	62304	...	62909	73926	85020 / 85218	100562	...	...

a) Including item 'Manufacturing'.
b) Gross domestic product in factor values.
c) Referring to indirect taxes net of subsidies.

Dominica

1.11 Gross Domestic Product by Kind of Activity, in Constant Prices

Thousand East Caribbean dollars

	1970	1971	1972	1973	1974	1975	1976	1977	1978	1979	1980
					At constant prices of:1977						
1 Agriculture, hunting, forestry and fishing	...	...	...	...	...	29119	32199	33100	...	...	...
2 Mining and quarrying	...	...	...	...	...	739	854	1022	...	...	...
3 Manufacturing	...	...	...	...	...	2957	3392	3409	...	...	...
4 Electricity, gas and water	...	...	...	...	...	947	999	1026	...	...	...
5 Construction	...	...	...	...	...	4390	4692	4115	...	...	...
6 Wholesale and retail trade, restaurants and hotels	...	...	...	...	...	6872	7791	7527	...	...	...
7 Transport, storage and communication	...	...	...	...	...	5665	6326	6961	...	...	...
8 Finance, insurance, real estate and business services	...	...	...	...	...	8347	8351	8731	...	...	...
9 Community, social and personal services	...	...	...	...	...	763	825	865	...	...	...
Total, Industries	...	...	...	...	...	59798	65434	66755	...	...	...
Producers of Government Services	...	...	...	...	...	17675	17420	18265	...	...	...
Other Producers	...	...	...	...	...	...	...	...	...	...	...
Subtotal	...	...	...	...	...	77474	82849	85021	...	...	...
Less: Imputed bank service charge	...	...	...	...	...	...	...	...	...	...	...
Plus: Import duties	...	...	...	...	...	...	...	...	...	...	...
Plus: Value added tax	...	...	...	...	...	...	...	...	...	...	...
Equals: Gross Domestic Product	...	...	...	...	...	77473	82854	85020	...	...	...

1.12 Relations Among National Accounting Aggregates

Thousand East Caribbean dollars

	1970	1971	1972	1973	1974	1975	1976	1977	1978	1979	1980
Gross Domestic Product	...	50857	...	62304	56495	62909	73926	85020	...	...	...
Plus: Net factor income received from abroad	...	1124	...	367	...	...	...	...	...	...	...
Equals: Gross National Product	...	51981	...	62671	...	...	...	...	...	...	...
Less: Consumption of fixed capital	...	2190	...	2007	...	...	...	...	...	...	...
Less: Net indirect taxes paid to supranational organisations	...	...	...	...	...	...	...	...	...	...	...
Equals: National Income at Market Prices	...	49790	...	60664	...	...	...	...	...	...	...
Plus: Net current transfers received from abroad	...	4743	...	4176	...	...	...	...	...	...	...
Equals: National Disposable Income at Market Prices	...	54533	...	64840	...	...	...	...	...	...	...
Less: Final consumption	...	48983	...	59120	57993	61300	70667	84771	...	...	...
Statistical discrepancy	...	6962	...	10124	...	...	...	...	...	...	...
Equals: Net Saving	...	12512	...	15844	...	...	...	...	...	...	...
Less: Surplus of the nation on current transactions	...	-4500	...	5202	...	...	...	...	...	...	...
Equals: Net Capital Formation	...	17012	...	10642	...	...	...	...	...	...	...

2.9 Gross Capital Formation by Kind of Activity of Owner, ISIC Major Divisions, in Current Prices

Thousand East Caribbean dollars

	1971			1973		
	Total Gross Capital Formation	Increase in Stocks	Gross Fixed Capital Formation	Total Gross Capital Formation	Increase in Stocks	Gross Fixed Capital Formation
			All Producers			
1 Agriculture, hunting, fishing and forestry	1656	...	...	1044	...	...
2 Mining and quarrying	36	...	...	-	...	...
3 Manufacturing	173	...	...	59	...	...
4 Electricity, gas and water	2713	...	...	1720	...	...

Dominica

2.9 Gross Capital Formation by Kind of Activity of Owner, ISIC Major Divisions, in Current Prices
(Continued)

Thousand East Caribbean dollars

	1971 Total Gross Capital Formation	1971 Increase in Stocks	1971 Gross Fixed Capital Formation	1973 Total Gross Capital Formation	1973 Increase in Stocks	1973 Gross Fixed Capital Formation
5 Construction	1040	...	...	2482	...	...
6 Wholesale and retail trade, restaurants and hotels	2718	...	...	892	...	...
7 Transport, storage and communication	1366	...	...	341	...	...
8 Finance, insurance, real estate and business services	1000	...	...	268	...	...
9 Community, social and personal services	404	...	...	369	...	...
Total Industries	11107	...	...	7174	...	...
Producers of Government Services	...	...	...	...	...	...
Private Non-Profit Institutions Serving Households	...	...	...	...	...	...
Total	19202	2650	16552	12649	1185	11464

Dominican Republic

General note. The preparation of national accounts statistics in Dominican Republic is undertaken by Banco Central de la Republica Dominicana, Santo Domingo. The official estimates are published in the series 'Cuentas Nacionales, Producto Nacional Bruto', which also includes a detailed description of the sources and methods used for the national accounts estimation. The estimates are generally in accordance with the classifications and definitions recommended in the United Nations System of National Accounts (SNA). The following tables have been prepared from successive replies to the United Nations national accounts questionnaire. When the scope and coverage of the estimates differ for conceptual or statistical reasons from the definitions and classifications recommended in SNA a footnote is indicated to the relevant tables.

Sources and methods:

(a) *Gross domestic product.* The main approach used to estimate GDP is the production approach.

(b) *Expenditure on the gross domestic product.* The expenditure approach is used to estimate government final consumption expenditure, increase in stocks and exports and imports of goods and services. Gross fixed capital formation is mainly estimated by the commodity-flow method, whereas private final consumption expenditure is taken as a residual, which also includes changes in stocks which could not be computed directly. Government consumption expenditure data for the central government is obtained from the Ministry of Finance and the National Budget Office. For gross fixed capital formation, import statistics are utilized for capital goods such as machinery, equipment and transport and communication equipment, since no such products are produced locally. To the import values are added customs duties, surcharges, mark-ups, etc. The data on exports and imports of goods and services are taken from the publication on balance of payments, prepared by the Central Bank. For the calculation of constant prices, price deflation is used for government consumption expenditure. Compensation of employees is deflated by means of the cost of living index, whereas for government purchases and sales general price indexes are used. Constant value of private consumption expenditure is obtained as a residual. The value of construction is deflated by a construction costs index. In the case of rural dwellings base-year prices are multiplied by number of dwellings built. The import price index is used as a deflator for exports and imports of goods and services.

(c) *Cost-structure of the gross domestic product.* The data on indirect taxes and subsidies are based on the annual reports of the Ministry of Finance and on information from the Treasury and the National Budget Office.

(d) *Gross domestic product by kind of economic activity.* The production approach is the basic method of estimation used for most sectors. The income approach is used for trade, transport and communication, finance, general government and other services. In agriculture gross output is estimated by multiplying the quantities harvested by the average price paid to the producers. Quantity data are available from the agricultural censuses of 1950, 1960 and 1970 and from estimates by the Banco Agricola, the Ministry of Agriculture and others. Own account consumption is included in the production series. Data on the volume of livestock production is provided by the Ministry of Agriculture, which also estimates the quantity of unreported slaughter and herd changes in livestock. The basic information for calculating gross output of the mining and quarrying sector is obtained directly from the reports on production and sales of enterprises. For manufacturing the main source of information is the series of annual bulletins of industrial statistics. The value of construction for 1960, which is taken as a bench-mark, is extrapolated by means of a value index. This index is a combination of a price index of construction costs and an index of main materials used. Value added is obtained by applying to gross output a coefficient representing the ratio of gross factor income. Data for the trade sector are available from the first national trade census carried out in 1955, and from total wholesale and retail sales figures published periodically by the National Statistical Office. Wages and salaries are calculated by combining average remunerations series with sectoral employment series. The Dominican merchant marine and the Dominican airline provide the data needed to estimate incomes, inputs and value added for shipping and air transport. For land transport the information obtained include data from transport enterprises and surveys among owners of trucks and taxis. For financial institutions the estimates are based on complete accounting information which is available for all banks and finance companies and most insurance companies. Value added of ownership of dwellings is taken as the difference between gross rents paid or imputed based on census data and the inputs for maintenance, upkeep and management and property taxes. For public administration and defence, data are obtained from Government Authorities, publications and from independent institutions. For other private services, data on the number of persons employed and mean income are used. The bench-mark data are extrapolated according to a specially constructed income index. For the computation of constant prices, the value added for agriculture is estimated by a revaluation at base-year prices of the harvested quantities. In the case of livestock products, estimates of annual changes in average meat yield per animal are utilized. For mining and quarrying value added is estimated by revaluating the different minerals at their respective 1962 prices. Value added of manufacturing is extrapolated by a quantity index of output. Current values of public and private construction are deflated by means of an index of construction costs. Wholesale and retail sales of locally produced and imported goods are deflated using the respective price indexes. For transport, storage and communication, value added is extrapolated by quantity index of output. For financial institutions value added is extrapolated by quantity indicators of personnel employed. For ownership of dwellings the indicator used is the number of urban and rural dwellings. Value added for public administration, defence and other services is extrapolated by an indicator of the number of personnel employed.

1.1 Expenditure on the Gross Domestic Product, in Current Prices

Million Dominican pesos

	1970	1971	1972	1973	1974	1975	1976	1977	1978	1979	1980
1 General government final consumption expenditure	172.0	169.1	177.7	193.6	291.5	222.1	151.9	189.4	271.1	420.3	...
2 Private final consumption expenditure	1137.8	1317.5	1449.3	1684.7	2138.6	2495.6	3082.5	3540.8	3618.7	4058.0	...
3 Gross capital formation [a]	284.3	297.6	391.7	518.1	683.1	882.1	881.7	999.5	1130.2	1300.8	...
a Increase in stocks [a]	38.4	3.9	-35.0	20.3	39.5	79.4	101.4	60.3	98.4	48.0	...
b Gross fixed capital formation	245.9	293.7	426.7	497.8	643.6	802.7	780.3	939.2	1031.8	1252.8	...
Residential buildings	...	...	...	...	...	...	...	...	...	...	...
Non-residential buildings	147.0	203.6	259.1	311.2	400.9	502.7	518.5	619.1	706.1	792.3	...
Other construction and land improvement etc. [b]											...
Other [c]	98.9	90.1	167.6	186.6	242.7	300.0	261.8	320.1	325.7	460.5	...
4 Exports of goods and services	255.9	292.2	410.8	513.0	729.5	1009.1	840.4	917.9	822.7	1128.7	...
5 Less: Imports of goods and services	364.5	409.9	442.1	564.6	917.0	1009.8	1005.0	1108.9	1144.2	1411.5	...
Equals: Gross Domestic Product	1485.5	1666.5	1987.4	2344.8	2925.7	3599.1	3951.5	4538.7	4698.5	5496.3	...

a) Including only mining, manufacturing, peanuts, raw tobacco and beans.
b) Including item 'Residential buildings'.
c) For agricultural sector only.

1.2 Expenditure on the Gross Domestic Product, in Constant Prices

Million Dominican pesos

	1970	1971	1972	1973	1974	1975	1976	1977	1978	1979	1980
	\multicolumn{11}{c}{At constant prices of: 1970}										
1 General government final consumption expenditure	172.0	159.7	158.9	162.7	223.2	179.3	134.7	151.5	175.3	215.7	...
2 Private final consumption expenditure	1137.8	1252.2	1306.5	1431.2	1580.4	1699.5	1838.7	1896.5	1879.9	1866.1	...
3 Gross capital formation [a]	284.3	333.2	374.7	475.4	566.2	612.1	572.7	618.9	635.6	680.3	...
a Increase in stocks [a]	38.4	3.8	-16.6	11.4	56.8	40.4	46.4	41.0	60.8	31.0	...
b Gross fixed capital formation	245.9	329.4	391.3	464.0	509.4	571.7	526.3	577.9	574.8	649.3	...

Dominican Republic

1.2 Expenditure on the Gross Domestic Product, in Constant Prices
(Continued)

Million Dominican pesos	1970	1971	1972	1973	1974	1975	1976	1977	1978	1979	1980
					At constant prices of:1970						
Residential buildings	...	...	...	...	...	...	...	...	...	372.2	...
Non-residential buildings	147.0	209.1	228.0	278.1	285.4	308.7	310.1	341.4	353.2		
Other construction and land improvement etc. [b]											
Other [c]	98.9	120.3	163.3	185.9	224.0	263.0	216.2	236.5	221.6	277.1	...
4 Exports of goods and services	255.9	299.1	389.0	436.9	415.0	430.3	515.6	550.0	545.0	683.8	...
5 Less: Imports of goods and services	364.5	397.2	410.9	453.5	608.9	632.3	618.8	652.3	615.8	699.8	...
Equals: Gross Domestic Product	1485.5	1647.0	1818.2	2052.7	2175.9	2288.9	2442.9	2564.6	2620.0	2746.1	...

a) Including only mining, manufacturing, peanuts, raw tobacco and beans.
b) Including item 'Residential buildings'.
c) For agricultural sector only.

1.3 Cost Components of the Gross Domestic Product

Million Dominican pesos	1970	1971	1972	1973	1974	1975	1976	1977	1978	1979	1980
1 Indirect taxes, net	160.2	180.5	205.1	228.6	397.6	432.1	386.7	449.5	402.5	455.6	...
2 Consumption of fixed capital	89.1	100.0	119.2	140.7	175.4	216.0	237.1	272.7	280.0	327.5	...
3 Compensation of employees paid by resident producers to:	1236.2	1386.0	1663.1	1975.5	2352.7	2951.0	3327.7	3816.6	4016.0	4713.1	...
4 Net operating surplus											...
Equals: Gross Domestic Product	1485.5	1666.5	1987.4	2344.8	2925.7	3599.1	3951.5	4538.7	4698.5	5496.3	...

1.8 Capital Transactions of The Nation, Summary

Million Dominican pesos	1970	1971	1972	1973	1974	1975	1976	1977	1978	1979	1980
				Finance of Gross Capital Formation							
Gross saving	175.8	179.9	360.4	466.5	495.5	881.5	717.1	808.6	808.7	1018.0	...
1 Consumption of fixed capital	89.1	100.0	119.2	140.7	175.4	216.0	237.1	272.7	280.0	327.5	...
2 Net saving	86.7	79.9	241.2	325.8	320.1	665.5	480.0	535.9	528.7	690.5	...
Less: Surplus of the nation on current transactions	...	...	...	...	...	...	...	...	...	...	...
Finance of Gross Capital Formation	284.3	297.6	391.7	518.1	683.1	882.1	881.8	999.5	1130.2	1300.8	...
				Gross Capital Formation							
Increase in stocks	38.4	3.9	-35.0	20.3	39.5	79.4	101.5	60.3	98.4	48.0	...
Gross fixed capital formation	245.9	293.7	426.7	497.8	643.6	802.7	780.3	939.2	1031.8	1252.8	...
Gross Capital Formation	284.3	297.6	391.7	518.1	683.1	882.1	881.8	999.5	1130.2	1300.8	...

1.10 Gross Domestic Product by Kind of Activity, in Current Prices

Million Dominican pesos	1970	1971	1972	1973	1974	1975	1976	1977	1978	1979	1980
1 Agriculture, hunting, forestry and fishing	345.1	370.6	409.0	521.2	648.1	772.8	752.7	920.4	886.3	1026.2	...
2 Mining and quarrying	22.7	23.6	51.4	81.3	78.0	107.8	139.6	144.0	118.0	227.8	...
3 Manufacturing	275.4	306.2	347.3	398.9	544.8	752.1	814.8	822.3	726.5	852.8	...
4 Electricity, gas and water	17.6	19.3	22.4	23.8	11.8	30.1	27.9	32.9	42.6	31.3	...
5 Construction	72.7	100.6	128.0	153.8	198.1	248.5	256.2	305.9	348.9	391.6	...
6 Wholesale and retail trade, restaurants and hotels [a]	237.6	272.9	332.2	384.6	505.2	586.0	675.0	787.1	850.1	955.5	...
7 Transport, storage and communication	114.8	125.7	144.7	168.5	196.7	217.8	238.4	282.9	322.3	354.9	...
8 Finance, insurance, real estate and business services [b]	127.2	142.1	179.7	210.6	248.7	308.9	401.5	506.2	557.7	647.0	...
9 Community, social and personal services [ab]	120.3	138.3	197.4	215.7	282.8	346.5	389.9	463.5	521.1	...	...
Total, Industries	1333.4	1499.3	1812.1	2158.4	2714.2	3370.5	3696.0	4264.5	4373.5	...	...
Producers of Government Services	152.1	167.1	175.3	186.4	211.5	228.6	255.5	273.5	325.0	...	...
Other Producers	...	...	...	...	...	...	...	...	...	...	...
Subtotal	1485.5	1666.4	1987.4	2344.8	2925.7	3599.1	3951.5	4538.7	4698.5	5496.3	...
Less: Imputed bank service charge	...	...	...	...	...	...	...	...	...	...	...
Plus: Import duties	...	...	...	...	...	...	...	...	...	...	...
Plus: Value added tax	...	...	...	...	...	...	...	...	...	...	...
Equals: Gross Domestic Product	1485.5	1666.4	1987.4	2344.8	2925.7	3599.1	3951.5	4538.7	4698.5	5496.3	...

a) Restaurants and hotels are included in item 'Community, social and personal services'.
b) Business services are included in item 'Community, social and personal services'.

Dominican Republic

1.11 Gross Domestic Product by Kind of Activity, in Constant Prices

Million Dominican pesos

	1970	1971	1972	1973	1974	1975	1976	1977	1978	1979	1980
					At constant prices of:1970						
1 Agriculture, hunting, forestry and fishing	345.1	363.6	377.6	410.1	410.2	399.9	429.2	436.8	456.9	461.7	...
2 Mining and quarrying	22.7	23.5	63.4	100.2	109.9	121.7	146.7	142.9	114.3	146.5	...
3 Manufacturing	275.4	311.0	336.5	381.3	399.4	428.5	457.4	483.4	480.3	504.8	...
4 Electricity, gas and water	17.5	19.8	22.4	26.2	28.1	30.0	30.9	39.3	42.9	43.7	...
5 Construction	72.7	103.3	112.7	137.5	141.0	152.6	153.2	168.7	174.5	184.0	...
6 Wholesale and retail trade, restaurants and hotels [a]	237.6	269.9	308.9	340.2	369.0	385.9	414.0	429.8	441.4	455.5	...
7 Transport, storage and communication	114.8	127.7	138.1	156.9	175.1	182.6	190.8	211.8	218.9	225.4	...
8 Finance, insurance, real estate and business services [b]	127.2	136.7	147.3	162.6	181.5	197.7	215.0	233.3	243.6	253.9	...
9 Community, social and personal services [a,b]	120.3	133.7	154.5	180.6	193.1	206.9	215.4	227.4	246.8	234.5	...
Total, Industries	1333.4	1489.2	1661.4	1895.6	2007.3	2105.8	2253.0	2373.4	2419.0	2510.0	...
Producers of Government Services	152.1	157.8	156.8	157.1	168.6	183.1	189.9	191.2	200.4	236.1	...
Other Producers	...	...	...	...	...	...	...	...	...	...	...
Subtotal	1485.4	1647.0	1818.2	2052.7	2175.9	2288.9	2442.9	2564.6	2620.0	2746.1	...
Less: Imputed bank service charge	...	...	...	...	...	...	...	...	...	...	...
Plus: Import duties	...	...	...	...	...	...	...	...	...	...	...
Plus: Value added tax	...	...	...	...	...	...	...	...	...	...	...
Equals: Gross Domestic Product	1485.5	1647.0	1818.2	2052.7	2175.9	2288.9	2442.9	2564.6	2620.0	2746.1	...

a) Restaurants and hotels are included in item 'Community, social and personal services'.
b) Business services are included in item 'Community, social and personal services'.

1.12 Relations Among National Accounting Aggregates

Million Dominican pesos

	1970	1971	1972	1973	1974	1975	1976	1977	1978	1979	1980
Gross Domestic Product	1485.5	1666.5	1987.4	2344.8	2925.7	3599.1	3951.5	4538.7	4698.5	5496.3	...
Plus: Net factor income received from abroad	-25.9	-28.8	-46.9	-76.8	-89.9	-112.8	-123.8	-123.4	-107.7	-174.9	...
Equals: Gross National Product	1459.6	1637.7	1940.5	2268.0	2835.8	3486.3	3827.7	4415.3	4590.8	5321.4	...
Less: Consumption of fixed capital	89.1	100.0	119.2	140.7	175.4	216.0	237.1	272.7	280.0	327.5	...
Less: Net indirect taxes paid to supranational organisations	...	...	...	...	...	...	...	...	...	...	...
Equals: National Income at Market Prices	1370.5	1537.7	1821.3	2127.3	2660.4	3270.3	3590.6	4142.6	4310.8	4993.9	...
Plus: Net current transfers received from abroad	...	...	...	...	...	...	...	...	...	...	...
Equals: National Disposable Income at Market Prices	...	...	...	...	...	...	...	...	...	...	...
Less: Final consumption	1309.8	1486.6	1627.0	1878.2	2430.1	2717.7	3234.4	3730.2	3889.8	4478.3	...
Equals: Net Saving	86.7	79.9	241.2	325.8	320.1	665.5	480.0	535.9	528.7	690.5	...
Less: Surplus of the nation on current transactions	...	...	...	...	...	...	...	...	...	...	...
Equals: Net Capital Formation [a]	195.2	197.6	272.4	377.4	507.7	666.1	644.6	728.4	850.2	973.3	...

a) Including only mining, manufacturing, peanuts, raw tobacco and beans.

4.3 Derivation of Value Added by Kind of Activity, ISIC Divisions, in Current Prices

Million Dominican pesos

	1970			1971			1972			1973		
	Gross Output	Intermediate Consumption	Value Added	Gross Output	Intermediate Consumption	Value Added	Gross Output	Intermediate Consumption	Value Added	Gross Output	Intermediate Consumption	Value Added
						All Producers						
1 Agriculture, hunting, forestry and fishing	...	...	345.1	...	...	370.6	...	...	409.0	...	...	521.2
a Agriculture and hunting	...	...	335.9	...	...	361.1	...	...	397.6	...	...	505.6
b Forestry and logging	...	...	6.0	...	...	6.3	...	...	6.9	...	...	7.2
c Fishing	...	...	3.2	...	...	3.2	...	...	4.5	...	...	8.4
2 Mining and quarrying	...	...	22.7	...	...	23.6	...	...	51.4	...	...	81.3
a Coal mining	...	...		...	...		...	...		...	...	
b Crude petroleum and natural gas production	...	...	22.7	...	...	23.6	...	...	51.4	...	...	81.3
c Metal ore mining	...	...		...	...		...	...		...	...	
d Other mining	...	...		...	...		...	...		...	...	

Dominican Republic

4.3 Derivation of Value Added by Kind of Activity, ISIC Divisions, in Current Prices
(Continued)

Million Dominican pesos

	1970 Gross Output	1970 Intermediate Consumption	1970 Value Added	1971 Gross Output	1971 Intermediate Consumption	1971 Value Added	1972 Gross Output	1972 Intermediate Consumption	1972 Value Added	1973 Gross Output	1973 Intermediate Consumption	1973 Value Added
3 Manufacturing	...	...	275.4	...	...	306.2	...	...	347.3	...	...	398.9
a Manufacture of food, beverages and tobacco	...	...	199.8	...	...	217.3	...	...	242.5	...	...	277.0
b Textile, wearing apparel and leather industries	...	...	14.8	...	...	15.0	...	...	15.2	...	...	18.3
c Manufacture of wood and wood products, including furniture	...	...	2.4	...	...	3.3	...	...	3.8	...	...	4.5
d Manufacture of paper and paper products, printing and publishing	...	...	7.8	...	...	8.8	...	...	15.5	...	...	15.0
e Manufacture of chemicals and chemical petroleum, coal, rubber and plastic products	...	...	23.7	...	...	26.9	...	...	28.5	...	...	32.9
f Manufacture of non-metallic mineral products, except products of petroleum and coal	...	...	13.1	...	...	17.0	...	...	19.7	...	...	23.8
g Basic metal industries	...	...	3.6	...	...	4.9	...	...	4.2	...	...	8.0
h Manufacture of fabricated metal products, machinery and equipment	...	...	5.6	...	...	7.6	...	...	11.9	...	...	11.4
i Other manufacturing industries	...	...	0.1	...	...	0.4	...	...	0.3	...	...	0.6
4 Electricity, gas and water	...	...	17.6	...	...	19.3	...	...	22.4	...	...	23.8
a Electricity, gas and steam	...	...	...	...	...	...	...	...	...	...	...	...
b Water works and supply	...	...	...	...	...	...	...	...	...	...	...	...
5 Construction	...	...	72.7	...	...	100.6	...	...	128.0	...	...	153.8
6 Wholesale and retail trade, restaurants and hotels	...	...	237.6	...	...	272.9	...	...	332.2	...	...	384.6
7 Transport, storage and communication	...	...	114.8	...	...	125.7	...	...	144.7	...	...	168.5
8 Finance, insurance, real estate and business services	...	...	127.2	...	...	142.1	...	...	179.7	...	...	210.6
9 Community, social and personal services	...	...	120.3	...	...	138.3	...	...	197.4	...	...	215.7
Total, Industries	...	...	1333.4	...	...	1499.3	...	...	1812.1	...	...	2158.4
Producers of Government Services	...	...	152.1	...	...	167.1	...	...	175.3	...	...	186.4
Other Producers	...	...	...	...	...	...	...	...	...	...	...	...
Total	...	...	1485.5	...	...	1666.4	...	...	1987.4	...	...	2344.8
Imputed bank service charge	...	...	...	...	...	...	...	...	...	...	...	...
Import duties	...	...	...	...	...	...	...	...	...	...	...	...
Value added tax	...	...	...	...	...	...	...	...	...	...	...	...
Total	...	...	...	...	...	...	...	...	...	...	...	...
Memorandum Item: Mineral fuels and power	...	...	1485.5	...	...	1666.4	...	...	1987.4	...	...	2344.8

	1974 Gross Output	1974 Intermediate Consumption	1974 Value Added	1975 Gross Output	1975 Intermediate Consumption	1975 Value Added	1976 Gross Output	1976 Intermediate Consumption	1976 Value Added	1977 Gross Output	1977 Intermediate Consumption	1977 Value Added
					All Producers							
1 Agriculture, hunting, forestry and fishing	...	...	648.1	...	...	772.8	...	...	752.7	...	...	920.4
a Agriculture and hunting	...	...	628.6	...	...	753.6	...	...	732.9	...	...	902.3
b Forestry and logging	...	...	8.3	...	...	9.3	...	...	10.2	...	...	11.4
c Fishing	...	...	11.2	...	...	9.9	...	...	9.6	...	...	6.7
2 Mining and quarrying	...	...	78.0	...	...	107.8	...	...	139.6	...	...	144.0
a Coal mining	...	...		...	...		...	...		...	...	
b Crude petroleum and natural gas production	...	...	78.0	...	...	107.8	...	...	139.6	...	...	144.0
c Metal ore mining	...	...		...	...		...	...		...	...	
d Other mining	...	...		...	...		...	...		...	...	

Dominican Republic

4.3 Derivation of Value Added by Kind of Activity, ISIC Divisions, in Current Prices
(Continued)

Million Dominican pesos

	1974 Gross Output	1974 Intermediate Consumption	1974 Value Added	1975 Gross Output	1975 Intermediate Consumption	1975 Value Added	1976 Gross Output	1976 Intermediate Consumption	1976 Value Added	1977 Gross Output	1977 Intermediate Consumption	1977 Value Added
3 Manufacturing	...	...	544.8	...	...	752.1	...	...	814.8	...	...	822.3
a Manufacture of food, beverages and tobacco	...	...	387.6	...	...	561.0	...	...	593.4	...	...	567.8
b Textile, wearing apparel and leather industries	...	...	26.0	...	...	27.0	...	...	38.1	...	...	37.3
c Manufacture of wood and wood products, including furniture	...	...	5.7	...	...	5.4	...	...	6.4	...	...	10.2
d Manufacture of paper and paper products, printing and publishing	...	...	16.1	...	...	19.1	...	...	24.3	...	...	32.8
e Manufacture of chemicals and chemical petroleum, coal, rubber and plastic products	...	...	52.2	...	...	75.9	...	...	89.7	...	...	105.9
f Manufacture of non-metallic mineral products, except products of petroleum and coal	...	...	30.9	...	...	27.9	...	...	24.9	...	...	31.6
g Basic metal industries	...	...	4.6	...	...	6.8	...	...	1.6	...	...	2.0
h Manufacture of fabricated metal products, machinery and equipment	...	...	14.3	...	...	21.3	...	...	26.9	...	...	27.1
i Other manufacturing industries	...	...	1.1	...	...	0.5	...	...	0.2	...	...	0.4
4 Electricity, gas and water	...	...	11.8	...	...	30.1	...	...	27.9	...	...	32.9
a Electricity, gas and steam	...	...	...	...	...	30.1	...	...	27.9	...	...	32.9
b Water works and supply	...	...	...	...	...	...	...	...	...	...	...	...
5 Construction	...	...	198.1	...	...	248.5	...	...	256.2	...	...	305.9
6 Wholesale and retail trade, restaurants and hotels	...	...	505.2	...	...	586.0	...	...	675.0	...	...	787.1
7 Transport, storage and communication	...	...	196.7	...	...	217.8	...	...	238.4	...	...	282.9
8 Finance, insurance, real estate and business services	...	...	248.7	...	...	308.9	...	...	401.5	...	...	506.2
9 Community, social and personal services	...	...	282.8	...	...	346.5	...	...	389.9	...	...	463.5
Total, Industries	...	...	2714.2	...	...	3370.5	...	...	3696.0	...	...	4264.5
Producers of Government Services	...	...	211.5	...	...	228.6	...	...	255.5	...	...	273.5
Other Producers	...	...	...	...	...	...	...	...	...	...	...	...
Total	...	...	2925.7	...	...	3599.1	...	...	3951.5	...	...	4538.7
Imputed bank service charge	...	...	...	...	...	...	...	...	...	...	...	...
Import duties	...	...	...	...	...	...	...	...	...	...	...	...
Value added tax	...	...	...	...	...	...	...	...	...	...	...	...
Total	...	...	...	...	...	...	...	...	...	...	...	...
Memorandum Item: Mineral fuels and power	...	...	2925.7	...	...	3599.1	...	...	3951.5	...	...	4538.0

4.4 Derivation of Value Added by Kind of Activity, ISIC Divisions, in Constant Prices

Million Dominican pesos

At constant prices of: 1970 — All Producers

	1970 Gross Output	1970 Intermediate Consumption	1970 Value Added	1971 Gross Output	1971 Intermediate Consumption	1971 Value Added	1972 Gross Output	1972 Intermediate Consumption	1972 Value Added	1973 Gross Output	1973 Intermediate Consumption	1973 Value Added
1 Agriculture, hunting, forestry and fishing	...	...	345.1	...	...	363.6	...	...	377.6	...	...	410.1
a Agriculture and hunting	...	...	335.9	...	...	354.6	...	...	367.7	...	...	397.6
b Forestry and logging	...	...	6.0	...	...	6.3	...	...	6.4	...	...	6.7
c Fishing	...	...	3.2	...	...	2.7	...	...	3.5	...	...	5.8
2 Mining and quarrying	...	...	22.7	...	...	23.5	...	...	63.4	...	...	100.2
a Coal mining	...	...		...	...		...	...		...	...	
b Crude petroleum and natural gas production	...	...	22.7	...	...	23.5	...	...	63.4	...	...	100.2
c Metal ore mining	...	...		...	...		...	...		...	...	
d Other mining	...	...		...	...		...	...		...	...	

Dominican Republic

4.4 Derivation of Value Added by Kind of Activity, ISIC Divisions, in Constant Prices
(Continued)

Million Dominican pesos

	1970 Gross Output	1970 Intermediate Consumption	1970 Value Added	1971 Gross Output	1971 Intermediate Consumption	1971 Value Added	1972 Gross Output	1972 Intermediate Consumption	1972 Value Added	1973 Gross Output	1973 Intermediate Consumption	1973 Value Added
					At constant prices of:1970							
3 Manufacturing	...	...	275.4	...	...	311.0	...	...	336.5	...	...	381.3
a Manufacture of food, beverages and tobacco	...	...	199.8	...	...	216.4	...	...	230.2	...	...	245.7
b Textile, wearing apparel and leather industries	...	...	14.8	...	...	17.0	...	...	17.0	...	...	21.0
c Manufacture of wood and wood products, including furniture	...	...	2.4	...	...	3.6	...	...	4.8	...	...	6.0
d Manufacture of paper and paper products, printing and publishing	...	...	7.8	...	...	8.0	...	...	10.8	...	...	12.5
e Manufacture of chemicals and chemical petroleum, coal, rubber and plastic products	...	...	23.7	...	...	28.9	...	...	29.8	...	...	38.0
f Manufacture of non-metallic mineral products, except products of petroleum and coal	...	...	13.1	...	...	16.4	...	...	20.5	...	...	30.3
g Basic metal industries	...	...	3.6	...	...	5.6	...	...	4.3	...	...	5.1
h Manufacture of fabricated metal products, machinery and equipment	...	...	5.6	...	...	9.9	...	...	12.8	...	...	15.2
i Other manufacturing industries	...	...	0.1	...	...	0.3	...	...	0.7	...	...	0.5
4 Electricity, gas and water	...	...	17.5	...	...	19.8	...	...	22.4	...	...	26.2
a Electricity, gas and steam	...	...	...	...	...	...	...	...	22.4	...	...	26.2
b Water works and supply	...	...	...	...	...	...	...	...	...	...	...	...
5 Construction	...	...	72.7	...	...	103.3	...	...	112.7	...	...	137.5
6 Wholesale and retail trade, restaurants and hotels	...	...	237.6	...	...	269.9	...	...	308.9	...	...	340.2
7 Transport, storage and communication	...	...	114.8	...	...	127.7	...	...	138.1	...	...	156.9
8 Finance, insurance, real estate and business services	...	...	127.2	...	...	136.7	...	...	147.3	...	...	162.6
9 Community, social and personal services	...	...	120.3	...	...	133.7	...	...	154.5	...	...	180.6
Total, Industries	...	...	1333.4	...	...	1489.2	...	...	1661.4	...	...	1895.6
Producers of Government Services	...	...	152.1	...	...	157.8	...	...	156.8	...	...	157.1
Other Producers	...	...	...	...	...	...	...	...	...	...	...	...
Total	...	...	1485.5	...	...	1647.0	...	...	1818.2	...	...	2052.7
Imputed bank service charge	...	...	...	...	...	...	...	...	...	...	...	...
Import duties	...	...	...	...	...	...	...	...	...	...	...	...
Value added tax	...	...	...	...	...	...	...	...	...	...	...	...
Total	...	...	...	...	...	...	...	...	...	...	...	...
Memorandum Item: Mineral fuels and power	...	...	1485.5	...	...	1647.0	...	...	1818.2	...	...	2052.7

of which General Government:

1 Agriculture, hunting, forestry and fishing	...	...	...	...	...	...	...	...	...	...	...	...
2 Mining and quarrying	...	...	...	...	...	...	...	...	...	...	...	...
3 Manufacturing	...	...	...	...	...	...	...	...	...	...	...	...
4 Electricity, gas and water	...	...	...	...	...	...	...	...	...	...	...	...
5 Construction	...	...	...	...	...	...	...	...	...	...	...	...
6 Wholesale and retail trade, restaurants and hotels	...	...	...	...	...	269.9	...	...	308.9	...	...	340.2
7 Transport and communication	...	...	...	...	...	127.7	...	...	138.1	...	...	156.9
8 Finance, insurance, real estate and business services	...	...	...	...	...	136.7	...	...	147.3	...	...	162.6
9 Community, social and personal services	...	...	...	...	...	133.7	...	...	154.5	...	...	180.6
Total, Industries of General Government	...	...	...	...	...	668.0	...	...	758.8	...	...	840.3
Producers of Government Services	...	...	152.1	...	...	157.8	...	...	156.8	...	...	157.1
Total, General Government	...	...	...	...	...	825.8	...	...	905.6	...	...	497.4

Dominican Republic

4.4 Derivation of Value Added by Kind of Activity, ISIC Divisions, in Constant Prices

Million Dominican pesos

	1974 Gross Output	1974 Intermediate Consumption	1974 Value Added	1975 Gross Output	1975 Intermediate Consumption	1975 Value Added	1976 Gross Output	1976 Intermediate Consumption	1976 Value Added	1977 Gross Output	1977 Intermediate Consumption	1977 Value Added
				At constant prices of: 1970								
				All Producers								
1 Agriculture, hunting, forestry and fishing	...	...	410.2	...	...	399.9	...	...	429.2	...	...	436.8
a Agriculture and hunting	...	...	397.9	...	...	388.3	...	...	417.4	...	...	426.3
b Forestry and logging	...	...	7.1	...	...	7.3	...	...	7.5	...	...	7.7
c Fishing	...	...	5.2	...	...	4.3	...	...	4.3	...	...	2.8
2 Mining and quarrying	...	...	109.9	...	...	121.7	...	...	146.7	...	...	142.9
a Coal mining	...	...		...	...		...	...		...	...	
b Crude petroleum and natural gas production	...	...	109.9	...	...	121.7	...	...	146.7	...	...	142.9
c Metal ore mining	...	...		...	...		...	...		...	...	
d Other mining	...	...		...	...		...	...		...	...	
3 Manufacturing	...	...	399.4	...	...	428.5	...	...	457.4	...	...	483.4
a Manufacture of food, beverages and tobacco	...	...	261.9	...	...	264.0	...	...	278.4	...	...	285.3
b Textile, wearing apparel and leather industries	...	...	24.3	...	...	30.5	...	...	32.6	...	...	34.4
c Manufacture of wood and wood products, including furniture	...	...	7.1	...	...	6.3	...	...	6.3	...	...	6.3
d Manufacture of paper and paper products, printing and publishing	...	...	10.2	...	...	11.9	...	...	12.6	...	...	13.4
e Manufacture of chemicals and chemical petroleum, coal, rubber and plastic products	...	...	40.4	...	...	41.6	...	...	44.2	...	...	46.7
f Manufacture of non-metallic mineral products, except products of petroleum and coal	...	...	32.3	...	...	44.3	...	...	47.1	...	...	49.7
g Basic metal industries	...	...	3.6	...	...	5.3	...	...	5.6	...	...	5.9
h Manufacture of fabricated metal products, machinery and equipment	...	...	13.6	...	...	17.8	...	...	19.0	...	...	20.0
i Other manufacturing industries	...	...	0.9	...	...	0.9	...	...	1.1	...	...	1.2
4 Electricity, gas and water	...	...	28.1	...	...	30.9	...	...	30.9	...	...	39.3
a Electricity, gas and steam	...	...	28.1	...	...	30.0	...	...	30.9	...	...	39.3
b Water works and supply	...	...	...	...	...	...	...	...	...	...	...	...
5 Construction	...	...	141.0	...	...	152.6	...	...	153.2	...	...	168.7
6 Wholesale and retail trade, restaurants and hotels	...	...	369.0	...	...	385.9	...	...	414.0	...	...	429.8
7 Transport, storage and communication	...	...	175.1	...	...	182.6	...	...	190.8	...	...	211.8
8 Finance, insurance, real estate and business services	...	...	181.5	...	...	197.7	...	...	215.0	...	...	233.3
9 Community, social and personal services	...	...	193.1	...	...	206.9	...	...	215.8	...	...	227.4
Total, Industries	...	...	2007.3	...	...	2105.8	...	...	2253.0	...	...	2373.4
Producers of Government Services	...	...	168.6	...	...	183.1	...	...	189.9	...	...	191.2
Other Producers	...	...	...	...	...	...	...	...	...	...	...	...
Total	...	...	2175.9	...	...	2288.9	...	...	2442.9	...	...	2564.6
Imputed bank service charge	...	...	...	...	...	...	...	...	...	...	...	...
Import duties	...	...	...	...	...	...	...	...	...	...	...	...
Value added tax	...	...	...	...	...	...	...	...	...	...	...	...
Total	...	...	...	...	...	...	...	...	...	...	...	...
Memorandum Item: Mineral fuels and power	...	...	2175.9	...	...	2288.9	...	...	2442.9	...	...	2564.6
				of which General Government:								
1 Agriculture, hunting, forestry and fishing	...	...	...	...	...	...	...	...	...	...	...	...
2 Mining and quarrying	...	...	...	...	...	...	...	...	...	...	...	...
3 Manufacturing	...	...	...	...	...	...	...	...	...	...	...	...
4 Electricity, gas and water	...	...	...	...	...	...	...	...	...	...	...	...

Dominican Republic

4.4 Derivation of Value Added by Kind of Activity, ISIC Divisions, in Constant Prices
(Continued)

Million Dominican pesos

	1974			1975			1976			1977		
	Gross Output	Intermediate Consumption	Value Added	Gross Output	Intermediate Consumption	Value Added	Gross Output	Intermediate Consumption	Value Added	Gross Output	Intermediate Consumption	Value Added
				At constant prices of:1970								
5 Construction	...	...	...	...	...	...	...	...	...	...	...	...
6 Wholesale and retail trade, restaurants and hotels	...	...	...	...	...	...	...	...	...	...	...	...
7 Transport and communication	...	...	...	...	...	...	...	...	...	...	...	...
8 Finance, insurance, real estate and business services	...	...	...	...	...	...	...	...	...	...	...	...
9 Community, social and personal services	...	...	...	...	...	...	...	...	...	...	...	...
Total, Industries of General Government	...	...	...	...	...	...	...	...	...	...	...	...
Producers of Government Services	...	...	168.6	...	...	183.1	...	...	189.9	...	...	191.2
Total, General Government	...	...	...	...	...	...	...	...	...	...	...	...

Ecuador

Source. Reply to the United Nations National Accounts Questionnaire from the Departamento de Investigaciones Economicas, Banco Central del Ecuador, Quito. The official estimates are published annually in 'Memoria del Gerente General del Banco Central del Ecuador'.

General note. The estimates shown in the following tables have been prepared in accordance with the United Nations System of National Accounts so far as the existing data would permit.

1.1 Expenditure on the Gross Domestic Product, in Current Prices

Million Ecuadoran sucres

	1970	1971	1972	1973	1974	1975	1976	1977	1978	1979	1980
1 General government final consumption expenditure	3864	4117	4744	6394	11646	15624	18629	24656	26450	30084	40053
2 Private final consumption expenditure	26375	30436	34429	41711	55506	70298	84517	102578	121244	143332	170679
3 Gross capital formation	6371	9278	9377	12115	20850	28797	31579	44137	54432	60193	79353
a Increase in stocks	529	574	936	1230	3991	3890	2109	4852	4347	4403	9637
b Gross fixed capital formation	5842	8704	8441	10885	16859	24907	29470	39285	50085	55790	69716
Residential buildings	850	996	1045	1555	2642	3921	4580	6031	7244	7454	...
Non-residential buildings	958	1243	1623	2066	2665	3127	3526	4758	4833	7158	36630
Other construction and land improvement etc.	2018	3638	2586	2536	4152	5435	7981	10139	14837	15387	
Other	2016	2827	3187	4728	7400	12424	13383	18357	23171	25791	33086
4 Exports of goods and services	4909	5986	8808	15506	33589	28242	34171	41315	40831	60122	69485
5 Less: Imports of goods and services	6500	9769	10499	13497	28828	35221	35983	46310	51612	57831	75372
Equals: Gross Domestic Product	35019	40048	46859	62229	92763	107740	132913	166376	191345	235900	284198

1.2 Expenditure on the Gross Domestic Product, in Constant Prices

Million Ecuadoran sucres

	1970	1971	1972	1973	1974	1975	1976	1977	1978	1979	1980
	\multicolumn{11}{c}{At constant prices of:1975}										
1 General government final consumption expenditure	7600	7429	7853	8590	13158	15624	17098	20572	20613	21658	23308
2 Private final consumption expenditure	49468	52286	54223	58127	63666	70298	76810	82724	87408	92555	99074
a Households	49468	52286	54223	58127	63666	70298	76810	82724	87408	92555	99074
b Private non-profit institutions serving households	...	...	...	...	...	...	...	...	...	...	...
3 Gross capital formation	14549	18399	16034	17749	24574	28797	27297	33153	37097	36186	41828
a Increase in stocks	973	1209	1932	1797	4380	3890	2029	3972	4039	3332	6632
b Gross fixed capital formation	13576	17190	14102	15952	20194	24907	25268	29181	33058	32854	35196
Residential buildings	...	...	...	...	...	...	...	...	...	...	...
Non-residential buildings a	8902	12058	9401	9842	11515	12483	13269	14842	16134	15850	16332
Other construction and land improvement etc.											
Other	4674	5132	4701	6110	8679	12424	11999	14339	16924	17004	18864
4 Exports of goods and services	8333	9293	18294	32370	30837	28242	30629	29095	30032	31602	30015
5 Less: Imports of goods and services	17038	20555	19911	20969	30189	35221	34155	40175	41518	41581	47023
Equals: Gross Domestic Product	62912	66852	76493	95867	102046	107740	117679	125369	133632	140420	147202

a) Including item 'Residential buildings'.

1.3 Cost Components of the Gross Domestic Product

Million Ecuadoran sucres

	1970	1971	1972	1973	1974	1975	1976	1977	1978	1979	1980
1 Indirect taxes, net	3766	4607	5499	7727	10394	10740	10551	13427	16481	18417	21873
a Indirect taxes paid	3881	4804	5713	8294	11829	11681	11605	14679	17554	19889	24346
b Less: Subsidies received	115	197	214	567	1435	941	1054	1252	1073	1472	2473
2 Consumption of fixed capital a	...	...	...	...	...	...	...	...	...	...	...
3 Compensation of employees paid by resident producers to:	10764	12672	14086	17188	24044	32047	40635	47450	54331	64755	93057
a Resident households	10755	12660	14086	17158	23746	31364	40045	46767	53768	63965	92109
b Rest of the world	9	12	-	30	298	683	590	683	563	790	948
4 Net operating surplus a	20489	22769	27274	37314	58325	64953	81727	105499	120533	152728	169268
a Corporate and quasi-corporate enterprises b	2029	2003	3072	7982	17673	15399	20152	26052	27255	38873	54668
b Private unincorporated enterprises c	18505	20820	24241	29309	40638	49536	61539	79461	93171	113544	114300
c General government	-45	-54	-39	23	14	18	36	-14	107	311	300
Equals: Gross Domestic Product	35019	40048	46859	62229	92763	107740	132913	166376	191345	235900	284198

a) Item 'Consumption of fixed capital' is included in item 'Operating surplus'.
b) Beginning 1976, including quasi-corporate enterprises that up to 1975 were included with households.
c) Relating to households.

Ecuador

1.4 General Government Current Receipts and Disbursements

Million Ecuadoran sucres

	1970	1971	1972	1973	1974	1975	1976	1977	1978	1979	1980
Receipts											
1 Property and entrepreneurial income	534	658	917	1584	3436	3775	3685	4249	6227	10061	13850
2 Taxes, fees and contributions	5771	6900	8537	13254	20932	21502	25464	29239	34054	43381	58134
a Indirect taxes	3881	4804	5713	8294	11829	11681	11605	14679	17554	19889	24346
b Direct taxes	772	1016	1462	2939	6923	6895	9828	10273	11374	16987	24614
c Social security contributions	1035	968	1160	1759	1912	2584	3668	3770	4491	5822	7977
d Compulsory fees, fines and penalties	83	112	202	262	268	342	363	517	635	683	1197
3 Other current receipts	561	884	1347	1848	2800	3269	4233	6971	6457	9887	10875
Total Current Receipts of General Government	6866	8442	10801	16686	27168	28546	33382	40459	46738	63329	82859
Disbursements											
1 General government final consumption expenditure	3864	4117	4744	6394	11646	15624	18629	24656	26450	30084	40053
2 Property income paid	600	680	699	733	977	983	1581	2664	3245	5619	6799
a Interest	600	680	699	733	977	983	1581	2664	3245	5619	6799
b Net land rent and royalties	...	...	...	...	...	...	...	...	...	...	...
3 Subsidies	115	197	214	567	1435	941	1054	1252	1073	1472	2473
4 Other current transfers paid	1227	1720	2508	3094	4512	5010	6024	8891	9150	13558	16380
a Social security benefits and social assistance grants [a]	778	955	1084	1201	1713	1835	2129	2845	3307	4305	6543
b Other	449	765	1424	1893	2799	3175	3895	6046	5843	9253	9837
5 Net saving	1060	1728	2636	5898	8598	5988	6094	2996	6820	12596	17154
Total Current Disbursements and Net Saving of General Government	6866	8442	10801	16686	27168	28546	33382	40459	46738	63329	82859

a) Excluding social assistance grants.

1.5 Current Income and Outlay of Corporate and Quasi-Corporate Enterprises, Summary

Million Ecuadoran sucres

	1970	1971	1972	1973	1974	1975	1976	1977	1978	1979	1980
Receipts											
1 Net operating surplus	2029	2003	3072	7982	17673	15399	20152	26052	27255	38873	54668
2 Other property and entrepreneurial income received	1047	1304	1550	2016	2913	3654	5041	6828	8706	11046	12665
3 Current transfers received	215	288	349	432	678	884	1433	965	1403	1555	1844
Total Current Receipts	3291	3595	4971	10430	21264	19937	26626	33845	37364	51474	69177
Disbursements											
1 Property and entrepreneurial income paid	1732	2307	3598	6588	11564	8071	10693	12716	17430	23257	30777
2 Direct taxes and other current payments to general government	256	357	598	1900	5971	5904	8887	9038	9322	14764	22443
3 Other current transfers paid	277	370	410	579	920	1330	1830	2370	2466	2937	3220
4 Net saving	1026	561	365	1363	2809	4632	5216	9721	8146	10516	12737
Total Current Disbursements and Net Saving	3291	3595	4971	10430	21264	19937	26626	33845	37364	51474	69177

1.6 Current Income and Outlay of Households and Non-Profit Institutions

Million Ecuadoran sucres

	1970	1971	1972	1973	1974	1975	1976	1977	1978	1979	1980
Receipts											
1 Compensation of employees	10755	12660	14086	17159	23806	31369	40066	46793	53778	63983	92132
a From resident producers	10755	12660	14086	17158	23746	31364	40045	46767	53768	63965	92109
b From rest of the world	-	-	-	1	60	5	21	26	10	18	23
2 Property and entrepreneurial income received	18775	21159	24843	30147	42147	50634	62840	81694	95918	117126	118378
3 Current transfers received	1460	1775	2143	2468	3742	4312	5310	6161	7526	8984	11618
a Social security benefits and social assistance grants received	778	955	1083	1199	1571	1818	2112	2806	3283	4248	6441
b Other	682	820	1060	1269	2171	2494	3198	3355	4243	4736	5177
Total Current Receipts	30990	35594	41072	49774	69695	86315	108216	134648	157222	190093	222128
Disbursements											
1 Private final consumption expenditure	26375	30436	34429	41711	55506	70298	84517	102578	121244	143332	170679

Ecuador

1.6 Current Income and Outlay of Households and Non-Profit Institutions
(Continued)

Million Ecuadoran sucres

	1970	1971	1972	1973	1974	1975	1976	1977	1978	1979	1980
2 Property income paid	360	458	785	1042	1440	1895	2168	2931	3562	5453	6955
3 Direct taxes and other payments n.e.c. to general government	1634	1739	2226	3060	3132	3917	4972	5522	7178	8728	11345
a Social security contributions	1035	968	1160	1759	1912	2584	3668	3770	4491	5822	7977
b Direct taxes	541	690	905	1112	1116	1146	1093	1407	2274	2447	2665
c Fees, fines and penalties	58	81	161	189	104	187	211	345	413	459	703
4 Other current transfers paid	231	279	333	428	654	967	1561	1105	1310	1600	2036
5 Net saving	2390	2682	3299	3533	8963	9238	14998	22512	23928	30980	31113
Total Current Disbursements and Net Saving	30990	35594	41072	49774	69695	86315	108216	134648	157222	190093	222128

1.7 External Transactions on Current Account, Summary

Million Ecuadoran sucres

	1970	1971	1972	1973	1974	1975	1976	1977	1978	1979	1980
Payments to the Rest of the World											
1 Imports of goods and services	6500	9769	10499	13497	28828	35221	35983	46310	51612	57831	75372
a Imports of merchandise c.i.f.	5507	8464	9004	11625	26522	32527	33124	42253	46804	51090	66439
b Other	993	1305	1495	1872	2306	2694	2859	4057	4808	6741	8933
2 Factor income paid to the rest of the world	694	948	1731	3695	6360	2898	4519	5377	6725	10820	15200
a Compensation of employees	9	12	-	30	298	683	590	683	563	790	948
b Property and entrepreneurial income paid	685	936	1731	3665	6062	2215	3929	4694	6162	10030	14252
3 Indirect taxes paid to supranational organizations	...	...	...	...	...	...	...	...	...	...	...
4 Current transfers to the rest of the world	71	76	109	219	271	313	583	604	1037	966	970
5 Surplus of the nation on current transactions	-1895	-4307	-3077	-1321	-480	-8939	-5271	-8908	-15538	-6101	-18349
Payments to the Rest of the World and Surplus of the Nation on Current Transactions	5370	6486	9262	16090	34979	29493	35814	43383	43836	63516	73193
Receipts From The Rest of the World											
1 Exports of goods and services	4909	5986	8808	15506	33589	28242	34171	41315	40831	60122	69485
a Exports of merchandise f.o.b.	4533	5488	8195	14788	31993	26058	31933	37725	36632	53691	62485
b Other	376	498	613	718	1596	2184	2238	3590	4199	6431	7000
2 Factor income received from rest of the world	22	26	53	153	695	430	458	899	1202	1779	2048
a Compensation of employees	-	-	-	1	60	5	21	26	10	18	23
b Property and entrepreneurial income received	22	26	53	152	635	425	437	873	1192	1761	2025
3 Subsidies received from supranational organisations	...	...	...	...	...	...	...	...	...	...	...
4 Current transfers from rest of the world	439	474	401	431	695	821	1185	1169	1803	1615	1660
Receipts from the Rest of the World on Current Transactions	5370	6486	9262	16090	34979	29493	35814	43383	43836	63516	73193

1.8 Capital Transactions of The Nation, Summary

Million Ecuadoran sucres

	1970	1971	1972	1973	1974	1975	1976	1977	1978	1979	1980
Finance of Gross Capital Formation											
Gross saving	4476	4971	6300	10794	20370	19858	26308	35229	38894	54092	61004
Less: Surplus of the nation on current transactions	-1895	-4307	-3077	-1321	-480	-8939	-5271	-8908	-15538	-6101	-18349
Finance of Gross Capital Formation	6371	9278	9377	12115	20850	28797	31579	44137	54432	60193	79353
Gross Capital Formation											
Increase in stocks	529	574	936	1230	3991	3890	2109	4852	4347	4403	9637

Ecuador

1.8 Capital Transactions of The Nation, Summary
(Continued)

Million Ecuadoran sucres

	1970	1971	1972	1973	1974	1975	1976	1977	1978	1979	1980
Gross fixed capital formation	5842	8704	8441	10885	16859	24907	29470	39285	50085	55790	69716
1 General government	1790	2331	1974	3264	5233	6308	8741	9881	11855	12323	18208
2 Corporate and quasi-corporate enterprises	2378	4226	4180	4376	6623	10459	13840	20559	25525	30085	36115
a Public	531	463	1078	878	3091	2888	3422	6961	5823	7274	9186
b Private	1847	3763	3102	3498	3532	7571	10418	13598	19702	22811	26929
3 Other	1674	2147	2287	3245	5003	8140	6889	8845	12705	13382	15393
Gross Capital Formation	6371	9278	9377	12115	20850	28797	31579	44137	54432	60193	79353

1.9 Gross Domestic Product by Institutional Sectors of Origin

Million Ecuadoran sucres

	1970	1971	1972	1973	1974	1975	1976	1977	1978	1979	1980
Domestic Factor Incomes Originating											
1 General government	3254	3502	4050	5317	7920	10545	13041	15035	17034	19576	27384
2 Corporate and quasi-corporate enterprises	6382	7731	9995	17533	31636	29919	39620	48994	57461	77774	103055
a Non-financial	5643	6887	9014	16178	29375	27348	36354	44397	51393	70316	94492
Public	680	871	1071	1291	2970	5163	6446	12300	14337	18531	30640
Private	4963	6016	7943	14887	26405	22185	29908	32097	37056	51785	63852
b Financial	739	844	981	1355	2261	2571	3266	4597	6068	7458	8563
Public	310	314	386	526	1119	1082	1246	1932	2537	3367	3532
Private	429	530	595	829	1142	1489	2020	2665	3531	4091	5031
3 Households and private unincorporated enterprises	24095	27581	31287	36947	51277	64419	77714	97702	112625	134792	148322
4 Non-profit institutions serving households	...	...	...	...	...	...	...	...	...	...	...
Subtotal: Domestic Factor Incomes [a,b]	33731	38814	45332	59797	90833	104883	130375	161731	187120	232142	278761
Indirect taxes paid, net [c]	1921	1972	2369	3522	3772	4920	5141	8287	9081	9685	12133
Consumption of fixed capital [a]	...	...	...	...	...	...	...	...	...	...	...
Statistical discrepancy [d]	-633	-738	-842	-1090	-1842	-2063	-2603	-3642	-4856	-5927	-6696
Gross Domestic Product	35019	40048	46859	62229	92763	107740	132913	166376	191345	235900	284198

a) Item 'Consumption of fixed capital' is included in item 'Domestic factor income'.
b) Including net indirect taxes other than import duties.
c) Import duties only.
d) Relating to imputed bank service charges.

1.10 Gross Domestic Product by Kind of Activity, in Current Prices

Million Ecuadoran sucres

	1970	1971	1972	1973	1974	1975	1976	1977	1978	1979	1980
1 Agriculture, hunting, forestry and fishing	8386	9180	10535	12241	17377	19333	22614	27671	28499	31637	34823
2 Mining and quarrying	74	63	937	6071	21629	15746	17809	21648	17297	40976	58780
3 Manufacturing	6841	8105	9369	10929	8983	13945	19341	23963	32694	31006	25097
4 Electricity, gas and water	333	405	550	608	647	809	1009	1269	1491	1768	2619
5 Construction	1377	2157	2221	2519	4145	5988	8822	10402	14591	16300	20612
6 Wholesale and retail trade, restaurants and hotels	5099	5969	7176	9600	13402	16949	20404	26107	29415	33549	39329
7 Transport, storage and communication	2359	2689	3211	3719	4683	6169	8260	10602	15563	20876	25949
8 Finance, insurance, real estate and business services	3799	4296	4815	5932	8386	11237	13973	18394	22082	26317	32042
9 Community, social and personal services	2189	2432	2581	3017	3847	4509	5634	7301	9339	11362	13493
Total, Industries	30457	35296	41395	54636	83099	94685	117866	147357	170971	213791	252744
Producers of Government Services	3008	3173	3581	4789	7266	9640	11794	13631	15348	17388	24568
Other Producers	266	345	356	372	468	558	715	743	801	963	1449
Subtotal	33731	38814	45332	59797	90833	104883	130375	161731	187120	232142	278761
Less: Imputed bank service charge	633	738	842	1090	1842	2063	2603	3642	4856	5927	6696
Plus: Import duties	1921	1972	2369	3522	3772	4920	5141	8287	9081	9685	12133
Plus: Value added tax	...	...	...	...	...	...	...	...	...	...	...
Equals: Gross Domestic Product	35019	40048	46859	62229	92763	107740	132913	166376	191345	235900	284198

Ecuador

1.11 Gross Domestic Product by Kind of Activity, in Constant Prices

Million Ecuadoran sucres

	1970	1971	1972	1973	1974	1975	1976	1977	1978	1979	1980
	\multicolumn{11}{c}{At constant prices of:1975}
1 Agriculture, hunting, forestry and fishing	15710	16497	17160	17340	18894	19333	19892	20360	19575	20279	21338
2 Mining and quarrying	429	408	7659	21451	18859	15746	18647	18039	20148	21651	19708
3 Manufacturing	8060	8661	9798	10651	11674	13945	15956	17267	19034	20486	21800
4 Electricity, gas and water	477	512	595	644	693	809	915	927	915	1019	1202
5 Construction	3940	5076	4402	4856	5585	5988	6415	6573	6903	6825	6943
6 Wholesale and retail trade, restaurants and hotels	10731	11682	12620	13665	14959	16949	17929	20066	21504	22552	24159
7 Transport, storage and communication	3765	3992	4352	4773	5326	6169	6944	8003	8616	9257	10087
8 Finance, insurance, real estate and business services	7536	7882	8275	9521	10610	11237	12108	13703	14622	15760	16466
9 Community, social and personal services	3629	3727	3705	4072	4371	4509	5129	5809	6445	7059	7507
Total, Industries	54277	58437	68566	86973	90971	94685	103935	110747	117762	124888	129210
Producers of Government Services	6005	5867	6178	6446	8320	9640	10914	11056	11926	12487	13811
Other Producers	458	475	490	512	537	558	579	602	627	650	674
Subtotal	60740	64779	75234	93931	99828	104883	115428	122405	130315	138025	143695
Less: Imputed bank service charge	1258	1351	1476	1606	2028	2063	2304	2781	3161	3724	3845
Plus: Import duties	3430	3424	2735	3542	4247	4920	4555	5745	6478	6119	7352
Plus: Value added tax	...	...	...	...	...	...	...	...	...	...	...
Equals: Gross Domestic Product	62912	66852	76493	95867	102046	107740	117679	125369	133632	140420	147202

1.12 Relations Among National Accounting Aggregates

Million Ecuadoran sucres

	1970	1971	1972	1973	1974	1975	1976	1977	1978	1979	1980
Gross Domestic Product	35019	40048	46859	62229	92763	107740	132913	166376	191345	235900	284198
Plus: Net factor income received from abroad	-672	-922	-1678	-3542	-5665	-2468	-4061	-4478	-5523	-9041	-13152
Factor income received	22	26	53	153	695	430	458	899	1202	1779	2048
Less: Factor income paid	694	948	1731	3695	6360	2898	4519	5377	6725	10820	15200
Equals: Gross National Product	34347	39126	45181	58687	87098	105272	128852	161898	185822	226859	271046
Less: Consumption of fixed capital	...	...	...	...	...	...	...	...	...	...	...
Less: Net indirect taxes paid to supranational organisations	...	...	...	...	...	...	...	...	...	...	...
Equals: National Income at Market Prices	34347	39126	45181	58687	87098	105272	128852	161898	185822	226859	271046
Plus: Net current transfers received from abroad	368	398	292	212	424	508	602	565	766	649	690
Current transfers received	439	474	401	431	695	821	1185	1169	1803	1615	1660
Less: Current transfers paid	71	76	109	219	271	313	583	604	1037	966	970
Equals: National Disposable Income at Market Prices [a]	34715	39524	45473	58899	87522	105780	129454	162463	186588	227508	271736
Less: Final consumption	30239	34553	39173	48105	67152	85922	103146	127234	147694	173416	210732
Equals: Net Saving [a]	4476	4971	6300	10794	20370	19858	26308	35229	38894	54092	61004
Less: Surplus of the nation on current transactions	-1895	-4307	-3077	-1321	-480	-8939	-5271	-8908	-15538	-6101	-18349
Equals: Net Capital Formation	6371	9278	9377	12115	20850	28797	31579	44137	54432	60193	79353

a) Including consumption of fixed capital.

2.7 Gross Capital Formation by Type of Good and Owner, in Current Prices

Million Ecuadoran sucres

	\multicolumn{4}{c}{1970}	\multicolumn{4}{c}{1971}	\multicolumn{4}{c}{1972}
	TOTAL	Total Private	Public Enterprises	General Government	TOTAL	Total Private	Public Enterprises	General Government	TOTAL	Total Private	Public Enterprises	General Government
Increase in stocks, total	529	429	59	41	574	509	-	65	936	600	132	204
Gross Fixed Capital Formation, Total	5842	3521	531	1790	8704	5910	463	2331	8441	5389	1078	1974
1 Residential buildings	850	850	...	...	996	996	...	...	1045	1045	...	...
2 Non-residential buildings	958	547	36	375	1243	722	80	441	1623	1042	56	525
3 Other construction	2018	650	348	1020	3638	1991	199	1448	2586	971	637	978
4 Land improvement and plantation and orchard development	...	...	...	...	...	...	...	...	...	...	...	...
5 Producers' durable goods	1871	1329	147	395	2667	2041	184	442	3009	2155	385	469
6 Breeding stock, dairy cattle, etc.	145	145	...	...	160	160	...	...	178	176	...	2
Total Gross Capital Formation	6371	3950	590	1831	9278	6419	463	2396	9377	5989	1210	2178

Ecuador

2.7 Gross Capital Formation by Type of Good and Owner, in Current Prices

Million Ecuadoran sucres

	1973 TOTAL	Total Private	Public Enterprises	General Government	1974 TOTAL	Total Private	Public Enterprises	General Government	1975 TOTAL	Total Private	Public Enterprises	General Government
Increase in stocks, total	1230	959	88	183	3991	3369	491	131	3890	3476	339	75
Gross Fixed Capital Formation, Total	10885	6743	878	3264	16859	8535	3091	5233	24907	15711	2888	6308
1 Residential buildings	1555	1555	...	...	2642	2642	...	...	3921	3921	...	...
2 Non-residential buildings	2066	1313	114	639	2665	1643	154	868	3127	1723	145	1259
3 Other construction	2536	362	471	1703	4152	314	791	3047	5435	276	1202	3957
4 Land improvement and plantation and orchard development	...	...	...	...	...	...	...	...	...	...	...	...
5 Producers' durable goods	4522	3312	293	917	7114	3652	2146	1316	12008	9396	1539	1073
6 Breeding stock, dairy cattle, etc.	206	201	...	5	286	284	...	2	416	395	2	19
Total Gross Capital Formation	12115	7702	966	3447	20850	11904	3582	5364	28797	19187	3227	6383

	1976 TOTAL	Total Private	Public Enterprises	General Government	1977 TOTAL	Total Private	Public Enterprises	General Government	1978 TOTAL	Total Private	Public Enterprises	General Government
Increase in stocks, total	2109	1906	69	134	4852	4171	525	156	4347	3218	979	150
Gross Fixed Capital Formation, Total	29470	17307	3422	8741	39285	22443	6961	9881	50085	32407	5823	11855
1 Residential buildings	4580	4580	...	...	6031	6019	...	12	7244	7190	...	54
2 Non-residential buildings	3526	2255	203	1068	4758	2919	572	1267	4833	3100	408	1325
3 Other construction	7981	495	1267	6219	10139	-892	3713	7318	14837	1987	3783	9067
4 Land improvement and plantation and orchard development	...	...	...	...	...	...	...	...	...	...	...	...
5 Producers' durable goods	12999	9593	1952	1454	17949	14058	2676	1215	22671	19646	1632	1393
6 Breeding stock, dairy cattle, etc.	384	384	...	-	408	339	...	69	500	484	...	16
Total Gross Capital Formation	31579	19213	3491	8875	44137	26614	7486	10037	54432	35625	6802	12005

	1979 TOTAL	Total Private	Public Enterprises	General Government	1980 TOTAL	Total Private	Public Enterprises	General Government
Increase in stocks, total	4403	3912	199	292	9637	8718	440	479
Gross Fixed Capital Formation, Total	55790	36193	7274	12323	69716	42322	9186	18208
1 Residential buildings	7454	7448	...	6	...	...	...	...
2 Non-residential buildings	7158	4872	500	1786	...	...	...	...
3 Other construction	15387	2036	4539	8812	...	...	...	...
4 Land improvement and plantation and orchard development	...	...	...	...	...	...	...	...
5 Producers' durable goods	25223	21295	2235	1693	...	...	...	...
6 Breeding stock, dairy cattle, etc.	568	542	...	26	...	...	...	...
Total Gross Capital Formation	60193	40105	7473	12615	79353	51040	9626	18687

2.8 Gross Capital Formation by Type of Good and Owner, in Constant Prices

Million Ecuadoran sucres

	1970 TOTAL	Total Private	Public Enterprises	General Government	1971 TOTAL	Total Private	Public Enterprises	General Government	1972 TOTAL	Total Private	Public Enterprises	General Government
At constant prices of: 1975												
Increase in stocks, total	973	...	...	...	1209	...	...	...	1932	...	...	...
Gross Fixed Capital Formation, Total	13576	...	...	...	17190	...	...	...	14102	...	...	...
1 Residential buildings												
2 Non-residential buildings	8902	...	...	...	12058	...	...	...	9401	...	...	...
3 Other construction												
4 Land improvement and plantation and orchard development	...	...	...	...	...	...	...	...	...	...	...	...
5 Producers' durable goods	4379	...	...	...	4828	...	...	...	4388	...	...	...
6 Breeding stock, dairy cattle, etc.	295	...	...	...	304	...	...	...	313	...	...	...
Total Gross Capital Formation	14549	...	...	...	18399	...	...	...	16034	...	...	...

Ecuador

2.8 Gross Capital Formation by Type of Good and Owner, in Constant Prices

Million Ecuadoran sucres

	1973 TOTAL	1973 Total Private	1973 Public Enterprises	1973 General Government	1974 TOTAL	1974 Total Private	1974 Public Enterprises	1974 General Government	1975 TOTAL	1975 Total Private	1975 Public Enterprises	1975 General Government
					At constant prices of: 1975							
Increase in stocks, total	1797	...	...	...	4380	...	...	...	3890	...	...	...
Gross Fixed Capital Formation, Total	15952	...	...	...	20194	...	...	...	24907	...	...	...
1 Residential buildings		...	...	...		...	...	...		...	...	...
2 Non-residential buildings	9842	...	...	...	11515	...	...	...	12483	...	...	...
3 Other construction		...	...	...		...	...	...		...	...	...
4 Land improvement and plantation and orchard development	...	...	...	...	...	...	...	...	...	...	...	...
5 Producers' durable goods	5784	...	...	...	8339	...	...	...	12008	...	...	...
6 Breeding stock, dairy cattle, etc.	326	...	...	...	340	...	...	...	416	...	...	...
Total Gross Capital Formation	17749	...	...	...	24574	...	...	...	28797	...	...	...

	1976 TOTAL	1976 Total Private	1976 Public Enterprises	1976 General Government	1977 TOTAL	1977 Total Private	1977 Public Enterprises	1977 General Government	1978 TOTAL	1978 Total Private	1978 Public Enterprises	1978 General Government
					At constant prices of: 1975							
Increase in stocks, total	2029	...	...	...	3972	...	...	...	4039	...	...	...
Gross Fixed Capital Formation, Total	25268	...	...	...	29181	...	...	...	33058	...	...	...
1 Residential buildings		...	...	...		...	...	...		...	...	...
2 Non-residential buildings	13269	...	...	...	14842	...	...	...	16134	...	...	...
3 Other construction		...	...	...		...	...	...		...	...	...
4 Land improvement and plantation and orchard development	...	...	...	...	...	...	...	...	...	...	...	...
5 Producers' durable goods	11636	...	...	...	13994	...	...	...	16558	...	...	...
6 Breeding stock, dairy cattle, etc.	363	...	...	...	345	...	...	...	366	...	...	...
Total Gross Capital Formation	27297	...	...	...	33153	...	...	...	37097	...	...	...

	1979 TOTAL	1979 Total Private	1979 Public Enterprises	1979 General Government	1980 TOTAL	1980 Total Private	1980 Public Enterprises	1980 General Government
					At constant prices of: 1975			
Increase in stocks, total	3332	...	...	...	6632	...	...	...
Gross Fixed Capital Formation, Total	32854	...	...	...	35196	...	...	...
1 Residential buildings		...	...	...		...	...	...
2 Non-residential buildings	15850	...	...	...	16332	...	...	...
3 Other construction		...	...	...		...	...	...
4 Land improvement and plantation and orchard development	...	...	...	...	...	...	...	...
5 Producers' durable goods	16627	...	...	...	18479	...	...	...
6 Breeding stock, dairy cattle, etc.	377	...	...	...	385	...	...	...
Total Gross Capital Formation	36186	...	...	...	41828	...	...	...

2.17 Exports and Imports of Goods and Services, Detail

Million Ecuadoran sucres

	1970	1971	1972	1973	1974	1975	1976	1977	1978	1979	1980
	Exports of Goods and Services										
1 Exports of merchandise, f.o.b.	4533	5488	8195	14788	31993	26058	31933	37725	36632	53691	62485
2 Transport and communication	95	110	184	215	868	1263	1414	1882	2195	3579	3822
a In respect of merchandise imports	38	51	65	76	251	359	421	578	625	1365	1447
b Other	57	59	119	139	617	904	993	1304	1570	2214	2375
3 Insurance service charges	3	12	11	5	13	34	51	35	56	20	28
a In respect of merchandise imports	2	5	5	2	7	20	17	25	55	20	28
b Other	1	7	6	3	6	14	34	10	1	-	-

Ecuador

2.17 Exports and Imports of Goods and Services, Detail
(Continued)

Million Ecuadoran sucres

	1970	1971	1972	1973	1974	1975	1976	1977	1978	1979	1980
4 Other commodities	9	15	33	18	20	8	5	263	28	464	450
5 Adjustments of merchandise exports to change-of-ownership basis	-	-	-	-	-	-	-	-	-	-	-
6 Direct purchases in the domestic market by non-residential households	206	254	382	470	652	871	623	1199	1604	1941	2213
7 Direct purchases in the domestic market by extraterritorial bodies	63	107	3	10	43	8	145	211	316	427	487
Total Exports of Goods and Services	4909	5986	8808	15506	33589	28242	34171	41315	40831	60122	69485

Imports of Goods and Services

	1970	1971	1972	1973	1974	1975	1976	1977	1978	1979	1980
1 Imports of merchandise, c.i.f.	5507	8464	9004	11625	26522	32527	33124	42253	46804	51090	66439
a Imports of merchandise, f.o.b.	4943	7636	8101	10416	23980	29189	29692	37834	41681	45757	59501
b Transport of services on merchandise imports	562	823	898	1207	2535	3318	3415	4394	4868	5313	6910
By residents	38	51	65	76	251	359	421	578	625	1365	1447
By non-residents	524	772	833	1131	2284	2959	2994	3816	4243	3948	5463
c Insurance service charges on merchandise imports	2	5	5	2	7	20	17	25	55	20	28
By residents	2	5	5	2	7	20	17	25	55	20	28
By non-residents	...	...	...	...	...	...	...	...	...	...	...
2 Adjustments of merchandise imports to change-of-ownership basis	...	...	...	...	...	...	...	...	...	...	...
3 Other transport and communication	199	232	247	280	669	696	673	826	1113	2073	2744
4 Other insurance service charges	50	89	81	108	89	118	3	230	68	367	839
5 Other commodities	486	616	719	931	868	836	938	773	912	941	1135
6 Direct purchases abroad by government	56	100	23	25	33	40	178	363	565	712	819
7 Direct purchases abroad by resident households	202	268	425	528	647	1004	1067	1865	2150	2953	3396
Total Imports of Goods and Services	6500	9769	10499	13497	28828	35221	35983	46310	51612	57831	75372
Balance of Goods and Services	-1591	-3783	-1691	2009	4761	-6979	-1812	-4995	-10781	2291	-5887
Total Imports and Balance of Goods and Services	4909	5986	8808	15506	33589	28242	34171	41315	40831	60122	69485

3.12 General Government Income and Outlay Account: Total and Subsectors

Million Ecuadoran sucres

	1970					1971				
	Total General Government	Central Government	State or Provincial Government	Local Government	Social Security Funds	Total General Government	Central Government	State or Provincial Government	Local Government	Social Security Funds

Receipts

1 Property and entrepreneurial income	534	158	...	-12	388	658	179	...	-8	487
a Net operating surplus	-45	-	...	-45	-	-54	-	...	-54	-
b Withdrawals from public quasi-corporations	...	...	...	...	...	...	...	...	...	...
c Interest	383	4	...	12	367	445	6	...	16	423
d Dividends	25	-	...	4	21	67	-	...	3	64
e Net land rent and royalties	171	154	...	17	-	200	173	...	27	-
2 Taxes, fees and contributions	5771	3999	...	733	1039	6900	5182	...	748	970
a Indirect taxes	3881	3309	...	572	-	4804	4266	...	538	-
b Direct taxes	772	659	...	113	-	1016	890	...	126	-
Income	743	644	...	99	-	975	872	...	103	-
Other	29	15	...	14	-	41	18	...	23	-
c Social security contributions	1035	-	...	-	1035	968	-	...	-	968
d Fees, fines and penalties	83	31	...	48	4	112	26	...	84	2
3 Other current transfers received	561	311	...	241	9	884	343	...	530	11
a Casualty insurance claims	...	...	...	...	...	...	...	...	...	...
b Transfers from other government subsectors	231	13	...	217	1	514	15	...	496	3

Ecuador

3.12 General Government Income and Outlay Account: Total and Subsectors
(Continued)

Million Ecuadoran sucres

	1970					1971				
	Total General Government	Central Government	State or Provincial Government	Local Government	Social Security Funds	Total General Government	Central Government	State or Provincial Government	Local Government	Social Security Funds
c Transfers from abroad	215	213	...	2	-	225	225	...	-	-
d Other transfers, except imputed	65	54	...	11	-	93	71	...	22	-
e Imputed unfunded employee welfare contributions	50	31	...	11	8	52	32	...	12	8
Total Current Receipts [a]	6866	4468	...	962	1436	8442	5704	...	1270	1468

Disbursements

1 General governement final consumption expenditures	3864	3301	...	455	108	4117	3405	...	597	115
2 Property income paid	600	515	...	34	51	680	452	...	84	144
a Interest	600	515	...	34	51	680	452	...	84	144
b Net land rent and royalties	-	-	...	-	-	-	-	...	-	-
3 Subsidies	115	115	...	-	-	197	197	...	-	-
4 Other current transfers paid	1227	301	...	130	796	1720	614	...	140	966
a Casualty insurance premiums, net	...	...	...	...	...	...	...	...	...	...
b Transfers to other government subsectors	231	218	...	13	-	514	499	...	15	-
c Transfers to households	828	31	...	11	786	1007	32	...	12	963
Social security benefits	778	-	...	-	778	955	-	...	-	955
Social assistance grants	-	-	...	-	-	-	-	...	-	-
Unfunded employee welfare benefits	50	31	...	11	8	52	32	...	12	8
d Transfers to private non-profit institutions serving households	155	39	...	106	10	175	59	...	113	3
e Transfers to the rest of the world	13	13	...	-	-	24	24	...	-	-
Net saving	1060	236	...	343	481	1728	1036	...	449	243
Total Current Disbursements and Net Saving [a]	6866	4468	...	962	1436	8442	5704	...	1270	1468

	1972					1973				
	Total General Government	Central Government	State or Provincial Government	Local Government	Social Security Funds	Total General Government	Central Government	State or Provincial Government	Local Government	Social Security Funds

Receipts

1 Property and entrepreneurial income	917	260	...	25	632	1584	887	...	87	610
a Net operating surplus	-39	-12	...	-27	-	23	-4	...	27	-
b Withdrawals from public quasi-corporations	...	...	...	...	...	...	...	...	...	...
c Interest	674	66	...	26	582	695	84	...	22	589
d Dividends	56	-	...	6	50	30	1	...	8	21
e Net land rent and royalties	226	206	...	20	-	836	806	...	30	-
2 Taxes, fees and contributions	8537	6764	...	610	1163	13254	10694	...	799	1761
a Indirect taxes	5713	5330	...	383	-	8294	7808	...	486	-
b Direct taxes	1462	1383	...	79	-	2939	2824	...	115	-
Income	1401	1358	...	43	-	2851	2801	...	50	-
Other	61	25	...	36	-	88	23	...	65	-
c Social security contributions	1160	-	...	-	1160	1759	-	...	-	1759
d Fees, fines and penalties	202	51	...	148	3	262	62	...	198	2
3 Other current transfers received	1347	288	...	1036	23	1848	377	...	1454	17
a Casualty insurance claims	...	...	...	...	...	...	...	...	...	...
b Transfers from other government subsectors	1094	55	...	1032	7	1499	59	...	1436	4
c Transfers from abroad	139	139	...	-	-	146	146	...	-	-
d Other transfers, except imputed	61	55	...	3	3	132	125	...	7	-
e Imputed unfunded employee welfare contributions	53	39	...	1	13	71	47	...	11	13
Total Current Receipts [a]	10801	7312	...	1671	1818	16686	11958	...	2340	2388

Disbursements

1 General governement final consumption expenditures	4744	3975	...	636	133	6394	5297	...	953	144
2 Property income paid	699	618	...	31	50	733	557	...	26	150

Ecuador

3.12 General Government Income and Outlay Account: Total and Subsectors
(Continued)

Million Ecuadoran sucres

	1972					1973				
	Total General Government	Central Government	State or Provincial Government	Local Government	Social Security Funds	Total General Government	Central Government	State or Provincial Government	Local Government	Social Security Funds
a Interest	699	618	...	31	50	733	557	...	26	150
b Net land rent and royalties	-	-	...	-	-	-	-	...	-	-
3 Subsidies	214	214	...	-	-	567	567	...	-	-
4 Other current transfers paid	2508	1244	...	166	1098	3094	1724	...	155	1215
a Casualty insurance premiums, net	...	...	...	...	...	...	...	...	...	...
b Transfers to other government subsectors	1094	1039	...	55	-	1499	1440	...	59	-
c Transfers to households	1137	40	...	1	1096	1272	49	...	11	1212
Social security benefits	1083	-	...	-	1083	1199	-	...	-	1199
Social assistance grants	1	1	...	-	-	2	2	...	-	-
Unfunded employee welfare benefits	53	39	...	1	13	71	47	...	11	13
d Transfers to private non-profit institutions serving households	235	123	...	110	2	184	96	...	85	3
e Transfers to the rest of the world	42	42	...	-	-	139	139	...	-	-
Net saving	2636	1261	...	838	537	5898	3813	...	1206	879
Total Current Disbursements and Net Saving [a]	10801	7312	...	1671	1818	16686	11958	...	2340	2388

	1974					1975				
	Total General Government	Central Government	State or Provincial Government	Local Government	Social Security Funds	Total General Government	Central Government	State or Provincial Government	Local Government	Social Security Funds

Receipts

1 Property and entrepreneurial income	3436	2649	...	94	693	3775	2826	...	123	826
a Net operating surplus	14	26	...	-12	-	18	23	...	-5	-
b Withdrawals from public quasi-corporations	...	...	...	...	...	...	...	...	...	...
c Interest	701	10	...	25	666	860	66	...	17	777
d Dividends	32	-	...	5	27	56	-	...	7	49
e Net land rent and royalties	2689	2613	...	76	-	2841	2737	...	104	-
2 Taxes, fees and contributions	20932	18138	...	877	1917	21502	17876	...	1037	2589
a Indirect taxes	11829	11287	...	542	-	11681	10964	...	717	-
b Direct taxes	6923	6811	...	112	-	6895	6729	...	166	-
Income	6830	6768	...	62	-	6804	6695	...	109	-
Other	93	43	...	50	-	91	34	...	57	-
c Social security contributions	1912	-	...	-	1912	2584	-	...	-	2584
d Fees, fines and penalties	268	40	...	223	5	342	183	...	154	5
3 Other current transfers received	2800	722	...	2012	66	3269	1143	...	2067	59
a Casualty insurance claims	...	...	...	...	...	...	...	...	...	...
b Transfers from other government subsectors	2073	62	...	1974	37	2145	80	...	2022	43
c Transfers from abroad	212	212	...	-	-	372	372	...	-	-
d Other transfers, except imputed	389	384	...	5	-	439	436	...	3	-
e Imputed unfunded employee welfare contributions	126	64	...	33	29	313	255	...	42	16
Total Current Receipts [a]	27168	21509	...	2983	2676	28546	21845	...	3227	3474

Disbursements

1 General governement final consumption expenditures	11646	10199	...	1286	161	15624	13599	...	1770	255
2 Property income paid	977	752	...	40	185	983	651	...	81	251
a Interest	977	752	...	40	185	983	651	...	81	251
b Net land rent and royalties	-	-	...	-	-	-	-	...	-	-

Ecuador

3.12 General Government Income and Outlay Account: Total and Subsectors
(Continued)

Million Ecuadoran sucres

	1974					1975				
	Total General Government	Central Government	State or Provincial Government	Local Government	Social Security Funds	Total General Government	Central Government	State or Provincial Government	Local Government	Social Security Funds
3 Subsidies	1435	1435	...	-	-	941	941	...	-	-
4 Other current transfers paid	4512	2652	...	238	1622	5010	2884	...	274	1852
a Casualty insurance premiums, net	...	...	...	...	...	...	...	...	...	...
b Transfers to other government subsectors	2073	2011	...	62	-	2145	2065	...	78	2
c Transfers to households	1839	206	...	33	1600	2148	272	...	42	1834
Social security benefits	1571	-	...	-	1571	1818	-	...	-	1818
Social assistance grants	142	142	...	-	-	17	17	...	-	-
Unfunded employee welfare benefits	126	64	...	33	29	313	255	...	42	16
d Transfers to private non-profit institutions serving households	542	377	...	143	22	645	475	...	154	16
e Transfers to the rest of the world	58	58	...	-	-	72	72	...	-	-
Net saving	8598	6471	...	1419	708	5988	3770	...	1102	1116
Total Current Disbursements and Net Saving [a]	27168	21509	...	2983	2676	28546	21845	...	3227	3474

	1976					1977				
	Total General Government	Central Government	State or Provincial Government	Local Government	Social Security Funds	Total General Government	Central Government	State or Provincial Government	Local Government	Social Security Funds

Receipts

1 Property and entrepreneurial income	3685	2294	...	148	1243	4249	2831	...	106	1312
a Net operating surplus	36	40	...	-4	-	-14	23	...	-37	-
b Withdrawals from public quasi-corporations	...	...	...	...	...	...	...	...	...	...
c Interest	1261	27	...	41	1193	1352	57	...	45	1250
d Dividends	54	1	...	3	50	76	2	...	12	62
e Net land rent and royalties	2334	2226	...	108	-	2835	2749	...	86	-
2 Taxes, fees and contributions	25464	20605	...	1181	3678	29239	24063	...	1397	3779
a Indirect taxes	11605	10847	...	758	-	14679	13815	...	864	-
b Direct taxes	9828	9582	...	246	-	10273	9987	...	286	-
Income	9694	9543	...	151	-	10076	9890	...	186	-
Other	134	39	...	95	-	197	97	...	100	-
c Social security contributions	3668	-	...	-	3668	3770	-	...	-	3770
d Fees, fines and penalties	363	176	...	177	10	517	261	...	247	9
3 Other current transfers received	4233	1282	...	2895	56	6971	2274	...	3380	1317
a Casualty insurance claims	...	...	...	...	...	...	...	...	...	...
b Transfers from other government subsectors	2950	89	...	2831	30	4661	66	...	3307	1288
c Transfers from abroad	524	524	...	-	-	505	504	...	1	-
d Other transfers, except imputed	396	380	...	9	7	1357	1340	...	17	-
e Imputed unfunded employee welfare contributions	363	289	...	55	19	448	364	...	55	29
Total Current Receipts [a]	33382	24181	...	4224	4977	40459	29168	...	4883	6408

Disbursements

1 General governement final consumption expenditures	18629	16257	...	2036	336	24656	22015	...	2208	433
2 Property income paid	1581	1446	...	92	43	2664	2307	...	30	327
a Interest	1580	1445	...	92	43	2664	2307	...	30	327
b Net land rent and royalties	1	1	...	-	-	-	-	...	-	-

Ecuador

3.12 General Government Income and Outlay Account: Total and Subsectors
(Continued)

Million Ecuadoran sucres

		1976				1977				
		Total General Government	Central Government	State or Provincial Government	Local Government	Social Security Funds	Total General Government	Central Government	State or Provincial Government	Local Government	Social Security Funds
3	Subsidies	1054	1054	...	-	-	1252	1252	...	-	-
4	Other current transfers paid	6024	3541	...	322	2161	8891	5631	...	414	2846
	a Casualty insurance premiums, net	...	...	...	...	...	...	...	...	...	...
	b Transfers to other government subsectors	2950	2861	...	89	-	4661	4595	...	66	-
	c Transfers to households	2492	306	...	55	2131	3293	403	...	55	2835
	Social security benefits	2112	-	...	-	2112	2806	-	...	-	2806
	Social assistance grants	17	17	...	-	-	39	39	...	-	-
	Unfunded employee welfare benefits	363	289	...	55	19	448	364	...	55	29
	d Transfers to private non-profit institutions serving households	497	290	...	177	30	824	520	...	293	11
	e Transfers to the rest of the world	85	84	...	1	-	113	113	...	-	-
	Net saving	6094	1883	...	1774	2437	2996	-2037	...	2231	2802
	Total Current Disbursements and Net Saving [a]	33382	24181	...	4224	4977	40459	29168	...	4883	6408

		1978				1979				
		Total General Government	Central Government	State or Provincial Government	Local Government	Social Security Funds	Total General Government	Central Government	State or Provincial Government	Local Government	Social Security Funds

Receipts

1	Property and entrepreneurial income	6227	4413	...	145	1669	10061	7112	...	238	2711
	a Net operating surplus	107	141	...	-34	-	311	347	...	-36	-
	b Withdrawals from public quasi-corporations	...	...	...	...	...	...	...	...	...	...
	c Interest	1825	231	...	46	1548	3107	442	...	53	2612
	d Dividends	133	-	...	12	121	110	-	...	11	99
	e Net land rent and royalties	4162	4041	...	121	...	6533	6323	...	210	-
2	Taxes, fees and contributions	34054	27782	...	1767	4505	43381	35501	...	2036	5844
	a Indirect taxes	17554	16424	...	1130	-	19889	18624	...	1265	-
	b Direct taxes	11374	11006	...	368	-	16987	16529	...	458	-
	Income	11091	10884	...	207	-	16662	16410	...	252	-
	Other	283	122	...	161	-	325	119	...	206	-
	c Social security contributions	4491	-	...	-	4491	5822	-	...	-	5822
	d Fees, fines and penalties	635	352	...	269	14	683	348	...	313	22
3	Other current transfers received	6457	2153	...	4237	67	9887	2412	...	4913	2562
	a Casualty insurance claims	...	...	...	...	...	...	...	...	...	...
	b Transfers from other government subsectors	4329	146	...	4146	37	7485	191	...	4767	2527
	c Transfers from abroad	625	625	...	-	...	759	759	...	-	-
	d Other transfers, except imputed	1044	1019	...	25	...	1125	1064	...	61	-
	e Imputed unfunded employee welfare contributions	459	363	...	66	30	518	398	...	85	35
	Total Current Receipts [a]	46738	34348	...	6149	6241	63329	45025	...	7187	11117

Disbursements

1	General governement final consumption expenditures	26450	23181	...	2640	629	30084	26213	...	3161	710
2	Property income paid	3245	2737	...	41	467	5619	4668	...	127	824
	a Interest	3245	2737	...	41	467	5619	4668	...	127	824
	b Net land rent and royalties	-	-	...	-	-	-	-	...	-	-

Ecuador

3.12 General Government Income and Outlay Account: Total and Subsectors
(Continued)

Million Ecuadoran sucres

	1978					1979				
	Total General Government	Central Government	State or Provincial Government	Local Government	Social Security Funds	Total General Government	Central Government	State or Provincial Government	Local Government	Social Security Funds
3 Subsidies	1073	1073	...	-	-	1472	1472	...	-	-
4 Other current transfers paid	9150	5274	...	549	3327	13558	8583	...	675	4300
a Casualty insurance premiums, net	...	...	...	...	...	...	...	...	...	...
b Transfers to other government subsectors	4329	4183	...	146	-	7485	7294	...	191	-
c Transfers to households	3766	387	...	66	3313	4823	455	...	85	4283
Social security benefits	3283	-	...	-	3283	4248	-	...	-	4248
Social assistance grants	24	24	...	-	-	57	57	...	-	-
Unfunded employee welfare benefits	459	363	...	66	30	518	398	...	85	35
d Transfers to private non-profit institutions serving households	907	556	...	337	14	1140	724	...	399	17
e Transfers to the rest of the world	148	148	...	-	-	110	110	...	-	-
Net saving	6820	2083	...	2919	1818	12596	4089	...	3224	5283
Total Current Disbursements and Net Saving [a]	46738	34348	...	6149	6241	63329	45025	...	7187	11117

	1980				
	Total General Government	Central Government	State or Provincial Government	Local Government	Social Security Funds

Receipts

1 Property and entrepreneurial income	13850	8223	...	238	5389
a Net operating surplus	300	404	...	-104	-
b Withdrawals from public quasi-corporations	...	...	...	...	...
c Interest	5405	69	...	34	5302
d Dividends	105	-	...	18	87
e Net land rent and royalties	8040	7750	...	290	-
2 Taxes, fees and contributions	58134	45799	...	4316	8019
a Indirect taxes	24346	22837	...	1509	-
b Direct taxes	24614	22135	...	2479	-
Income	24254	21999	...	2255	-
Other	360	136	...	224	-
c Social security contributions	7977	-	...	-	7977
d Fees, fines and penalties	1197	827	...	328	42
3 Other current transfers received	10875	2862	...	7932	81
a Casualty insurance claims	...	...	...	...	...
b Transfers from other government subsectors	8092	259	...	7793	40
c Transfers from abroad	791	791	...	-	-
d Other transfers, except imputed	1381	1354	...	27	-
e Imputed unfunded employee welfare contributions	611	458	...	112	41
Total Current Receipts [a]	82859	56884	...	12486	13489

Disbursements

1 General governement final consumption expenditures	40053	34132	...	4732	1189
2 Property income paid	6799	6509	...	219	71
a Interest	6799	6509	...	219	71
b Net land rent and royalties	-	-	...	-	-

Ecuador

3.12 General Government Income and Outlay Account: Total and Subsectors
(Continued)

Million Ecuadoran sucres

	1980 Total General Government	Central Government	State or Provincial Government	Local Government	Social Security Funds
3 Subsidies	2473	2473	...	-	-
4 Other current transfers paid	16380	9146	...	713	6521
a Casualty insurance premiums, net	...	...	...	...	...
b Transfers to other government subsectors	8092	7833	...	246	13
c Transfers to households	7154	560	...	112	6482
Social security benefits	6441	-	...	-	6441
Social assistance grants	102	102	...	-	-
Unfunded employee welfare benefits	611	458	...	112	41
d Transfers to private non-profit institutions serving households	1036	655	...	355	26
e Transfers to the rest of the world	98	98	...	-	-
Net saving	17154	4624	...	6822	5708
Total Current Disbursements and Net Saving [a]	82859	56884	...	12486	13489

a) Column 'State or Provincial government' is included in column 'Local government'.

3.13 General Government Capital Accumulation Account: Total and Subsectors

Million Ecuadoran sucres

	1970 Total General Gov.	Central Gov.	State or Provincial Gov.	Local Gov.	Social Security Funds	1971 Total General Gov.	Central Gov.	State or Provincial Gov.	Local Gov.	Social Security Funds
Finance of Gross Accumulation										
1 Gross saving	1060	236	...	343	481	1728	1036	...	449	243
2 Capital transfers received	225	225	...	...	...	225	225	...	...	...
a From other government subsectors	...	...	...	...	...	...	...	...	...	...
b From other resident sectors	225	225	...	...	...	225	225	...	...	...
c From rest of the world	...	...	...	...	...	...	...	...	...	...
Finance of Gross Accumulation [a]	1285	461	...	343	481	1953	1261	...	449	243
Gross Accumulation										
1 Gross capital formation	1831	1439	...	341	51	2396	1765	...	525	106
a Increase in stocks	41	...	...	...	41	65	...	...	...	65
b Gross fixed capital formation	1790	1439	...	341	10	2331	1765	...	525	41
2 Purchases of land, net	-	...	...	-22	22	-14	...	...	-32	18
3 Purchases of intangible assets, net	...	...	...	...	...	...	...	...	...	...
4 Capital transfers paid	146	86	...	60	...	184	119	...	65	...
a To other government subsectors	...	...	...	...	...	...	...	...	...	...
b To other resident sectors	146	86	...	60	...	184	119	...	65	...
c To rest of the world	...	...	...	...	...	...	...	...	...	...
Net lending	-692	-1064	...	-36	408	-613	-623	...	-109	119
Gross Accumulation [a]	1285	461	...	343	481	1953	1261	...	449	243

	1972 Total General Gov.	Central Gov.	State or Provincial Gov.	Local Gov.	Social Security Funds	1973 Total General Gov.	Central Gov.	State or Provincial Gov.	Local Gov.	Social Security Funds
Finance of Gross Accumulation										
1 Gross saving	2636	1261	...	838	537	5898	3813	...	1206	879
2 Capital transfers received	...	...	...	...	...	...	...	...	...	...
a From other government subsectors	...	...	...	...	...	...	...	...	...	...
b From other resident sectors	...	...	...	...	...	...	...	...	...	...
c From rest of the world	...	...	...	...	...	...	...	...	...	...
Finance of Gross Accumulation [a]	2636	1261	...	838	537	5898	3813	...	1206	879
Gross Accumulation										
1 Gross capital formation	2178	1364	...	528	286	3447	2571	...	674	202
a Increase in stocks	204	...	...	...	204	183	...	...	...	183
b Gross fixed capital formation	1974	1364	...	528	82	3264	2571	...	674	19

Ecuador

3.13 General Government Capital Accumulation Account: Total and Subsectors
(Continued)

Million Ecuadoran sucres

	1972					1973				
	Total General Government	Central Government	State or Provincial Government	Local Government	Social Security Funds	Total General Government	Central Government	State or Provincial Government	Local Government	Social Security Funds
2 Purchases of land, net	39	25	...	-2	16	73	48	...	-17	42
3 Purchases of intangible assets, net	...	...	...	...	...	...	...	...	...	...
4 Capital transfers paid	320	206	...	114	...	399	256	...	143	...
a To other government subsectors	...	...	...	...	...	...	...	...	...	...
b To other resident sectors	320	206	...	114	...	399	256	...	143	...
c To rest of the world	...	...	...	...	...	...	...	...	...	...
Net lending	99	-334	...	198	235	1979	938	...	406	635
Gross Accumulation [a]	2636	1261	...	838	537	5898	3813	...	1206	879

	1974					1975				
	Total General Government	Central Government	State or Provincial Government	Local Government	Social Security Funds	Total General Government	Central Government	State or Provincial Government	Local Government	Social Security Funds

Finance of Gross Accumulation

1 Gross saving	8598	6471	...	1419	708	5988	3770	...	1102	1116
2 Capital transfers received	...	...	...	...	...	...	...	...	...	...
a From other government subsectors	...	...	...	...	...	...	...	...	...	...
b From other resident sectors	...	...	...	...	...	...	...	...	...	...
c From rest of the world	...	...	...	...	...	...	...	...	...	...
Finance of Gross Accumulation [a]	8598	6471	...	1419	708	5988	3770	...	1102	1116

Gross Accumulation

1 Gross capital formation	5364	4075	...	1116	173	6383	4733	...	1418	232
a Increase in stocks	131	...	...	...	131	75	...	...	...	75
b Gross fixed capital formation	5233	4075	...	1116	42	6308	4733	...	1418	157
2 Purchases of land, net	-35	35	...	-119	49	45	26	...	-19	38
3 Purchases of intangible assets, net	...	...	...	...	...	...	...	...	...	...
4 Capital transfers paid	443	258	...	185	...	545	338	...	207	...
a To other government subsectors	...	...	...	...	...	...	...	...	...	...
b To other resident sectors	443	258	...	185	...	545	338	...	207	...
c To rest of the world	...	...	...	...	...	...	...	...	...	...
Net lending	2826	2103	...	237	486	-985	-1327	...	-504	846
Gross Accumulation [a]	8598	6471	...	1419	708	5988	3770	...	1102	1116

	1976					1977				
	Total General Government	Central Government	State or Provincial Government	Local Government	Social Security Funds	Total General Government	Central Government	State or Provincial Government	Local Government	Social Security Funds

Finance of Gross Accumulation

1 Gross saving	6094	1883	...	1774	2437	2996	-2037	...	2231	2802
2 Capital transfers received	...	...	...	...	...	...	...	...	...	...
a From other government subsectors	...	...	...	...	...	...	...	...	...	...
b From other resident sectors	...	...	...	...	...	...	...	...	...	...
c From rest of the world	...	...	...	...	...	...	...	...	...	...
Finance of Gross Accumulation [a]	6094	1883	...	1774	2437	2996	-2037	...	2231	2802

Gross Accumulation

1 Gross capital formation	8875	6991	...	1684	200	10037	7436	...	2392	209
a Increase in stocks	134	...	...	...	134	156	...	...	...	156
b Gross fixed capital formation	8741	6991	...	1684	66	9881	7436	...	2392	53
2 Purchases of land, net	-58	25	...	-83	...	-33	4	...	-201	164
3 Purchases of intangible assets, net	...	...	...	...	...	...	...	...	...	...
4 Capital transfers paid	698	456	...	242	...	514	187	...	327	...
a To other government subsectors	...	...	...	...	...	...	...	...	...	...
b To other resident sectors	698	456	...	242	...	514	187	...	327	...
c To rest of the world	...	...	...	...	...	...	...	...	...	...
Net lending	-3421	-5589	...	-69	2237	-7522	-9664	...	-287	2429
Gross Accumulation [a]	6094	1883	...	1774	2437	2996	-2037	...	2231	2802

Ecuador

3.13 General Government Capital Accumulation Account: Total and Subsectors

Million Ecuadoran sucres

	1978 Total General Government	1978 Central Government	1978 State or Provincial Government	1978 Local Government	1978 Social Security Funds	1979 Total General Government	1979 Central Government	1979 State or Provincial Government	1979 Local Government	1979 Social Security Funds
Finance of Gross Accumulation										
1 Gross saving	6820	2083	...	2919	1818	12596	4084	...	3229	5283
2 Capital transfers received	217	217	...	...	...	...	...	...	...	...
a From other government subsectors	...	...	...	...	...	...	...	...	...	...
b From other resident sectors	217	217	...	...	...	...	...	...	...	...
c From rest of the world	...	...	...	...	...	...	...	...	...	...
Finance of Gross Accumulation [a]	7037	2300	...	2919	1818	12596	4084	...	3229	5283
Gross Accumulation										
1 Gross capital formation	12005	8654	...	3111	240	12615	9114	...	3009	492
a Increase in stocks	150	...	...	...	150	292	...	...	...	292
b Gross fixed capital formation	11855	8654	...	3111	90	12323	9114	...	3009	200
2 Purchases of land, net	24	83	...	-76	17	-86	2	...	-122	34
3 Purchases of intangible assets, net	...	...	...	...	...	...	...	...	...	...
4 Capital transfers paid	539	186	...	353	...	623	281	...	342	...
a To other government subsectors	...	...	...	...	...	...	...	...	...	...
b To other resident sectors	539	186	...	353	...	623	281	...	342	...
c To rest of the world	...	...	...	...	...	...	...	...	...	...
Net lending	-5531	-6623	...	-469	1561	-556	-5313	...	-	4757
Gross Accumulation [a]	7037	2300	...	2919	1818	12596	4084	...	3229	5283

	1980 Total General Government	1980 Central Government	1980 State or Provincial Government	1980 Local Government	1980 Social Security Funds
Finance of Gross Accumulation					
1 Gross saving	17154	4624	...	6822	5708
2 Capital transfers received	1	1	...	...	...
a From other government subsectors	...	...	...	...	...
b From other resident sectors	...	...	...	...	...
c From rest of the world	...	...	...	...	...
Finance of Gross Accumulation [a]	17155	4625	...	6822	5708
Gross Accumulation					
1 Gross capital formation	18687	12219	...	5833	635
a Increase in stocks	479	...	...	...	479
b Gross fixed capital formation	18208	12219	...	5833	156
2 Purchases of land, net	65	35	...	-40	70
3 Purchases of intangible assets, net	...	...	...	...	...
4 Capital transfers paid	789	354	...	435	...
a To other government subsectors	...	...	...	...	...
b To other resident sectors	789	354	...	435	...
c To rest of the world	...	...	...	...	...
Net lending	-2386	-7983	...	594	5003
Gross Accumulation [a]	17155	4625	...	6822	5708

a) Column 'State or Provincial Government' is included in column 'Local Government'.

3.22 Corporate and Quasi-Corporate Enterprise Income and Outlay Account: Total and Sectors

Million Ecuadoran sucres

	1970 TOTAL	1970 Non-Financial	1970 Financial	1971 TOTAL	1971 Non-Financial	1971 Financial	1972 TOTAL	1972 Non-Financial	1972 Financial	1973 TOTAL	1973 Non-Financial	1973 Financial
Receipts												
1 Property and entrepreneurial income received	3076	2616	460	3307	2733	574	4622	3887	735	9998	8925	1073
a Net operating surplus [a]	2029	2447	-418	2003	2515	-512	3072	3600	-528	7982	8556	-574
b Withdrawals from quasi-corporate enterprises	...	...	...	...	...	...	...	...	...	...	...	...
c Interest	1011	141	870	1258	182	1076	1490	239	1251	1930	301	1629

Ecuador

3.22 Corporate and Quasi-Corporate Enterprise Income and Outlay Account: Total and Sectors
(Continued)

Million Ecuadoran sucres

	1970 TOTAL	1970 Non-Financial	1970 Financial	1971 TOTAL	1971 Non-Financial	1971 Financial	1972 TOTAL	1972 Non-Financial	1972 Financial	1973 TOTAL	1973 Non-Financial	1973 Financial
d Dividends	36	28	8	46	36	10	60	48	12	56	38	18
e Net land rent and royalties	...	...	...	...	...	...	...	...	...	30	30	...
2 Other current transfers received	215	184	31	288	246	42	349	298	51	432	373	59
a Casualty insurance transactions	58	44	14	87	61	26	100	71	29	107	71	36
Claims received	44	44	...	61	61	...	73	71	2	73	71	2
Net premiums received by insurance companies	14	...	14	26	...	26	27	...	27	34	...	34
b Current transfers received from the rest of the world	...	...	...	...	...	...	...	...	...	...	...	...
c Other transfers received, except imputed	...	...	...	...	...	...	...	...	...	...	...	...
d Imputed unfunded employee welfare contributions	157	140	17	201	185	16	249	227	22	325	302	23
Total Current Receipts	3291	2800	491	3595	2979	616	4971	4185	786	10430	9298	1132

Disbursements

	1970 TOTAL	1970 Non-Financial	1970 Financial	1971 TOTAL	1971 Non-Financial	1971 Financial	1972 TOTAL	1972 Non-Financial	1972 Financial	1973 TOTAL	1973 Non-Financial	1973 Financial
1 Property and entrepreneurial income paid out	1732	1439	293	2307	1928	379	3598	3088	510	6588	5920	668
a Withdrawals from quasi-corporations	8	3	5	9	4	5	26	4	22	27	-	27
Public	...	...	...	...	...	...	...	...	...	...	...	...
Private	8	3	5	9	4	5	26	4	22	27	-	27
b Interest	749	511	238	1041	700	341	1260	847	413	1754	1208	546
c Dividends [b]	796	746	50	1044	1011	33	2071	1996	75	3862	3767	95
d Net land rent and royalties	179	179	...	213	213	...	241	241	...	945	945	...
2 Direct taxes and other current payments n.e.c. to general government	256	242	14	357	344	13	598	570	28	1900	1873	27
a Direct taxes	231	217	14	326	313	13	557	529	28	1827	1800	27
Income	220	206	14	310	297	13	542	514	28	1809	1782	27
Other	11	11	...	16	16	...	15	15	...	18	18	...
b Fines, fees, penalties and other payments n.e.c.	25	25	...	31	31	...	41	41	...	73	73	...
3 Other current transfers paid	277	216	61	370	283	87	410	313	97	579	407	172
a Casualty insurance transactions	62	48	14	93	67	26	102	73	29	113	76	37
Casualty insurance premiums paid, net	48	48	...	67	67	...	75	73	2	79	76	3
Claims paid by insurance companies	14	...	14	26	...	26	27	...	27	34	...	34
b Transfers to private non-profit institutions	...	...	...	...	...	...	...	...	...	...	...	...
c Transfers to households	215	168	47	276	216	60	308	240	68	466	331	135
Unfunded employee welfare benefits	157	140	17	201	185	16	249	227	22	325	302	23
Social assistance grants and other transfers n.e.c.	58	28	30	75	31	44	59	13	46	141	29	112
d Transfers to the rest of the world	...	...	...	1	...	1	...	...	...	...	...	...
Net saving	1026	903	123	561	424	137	365	214	151	1363	1098	265
Total Current Disbursements and Net Saving	3291	2800	491	3595	2979	616	4971	4185	786	10430	9298	1132

	1974 TOTAL	1974 Non-Financial	1974 Financial	1975 TOTAL	1975 Non-Financial	1975 Financial	1976 TOTAL	1976 Non-Financial	1976 Financial	1977 TOTAL	1977 Non-Financial	1977 Financial

Receipts

	1974 TOTAL	1974 Non-Financial	1974 Financial	1975 TOTAL	1975 Non-Financial	1975 Financial	1976 TOTAL	1976 Non-Financial	1976 Financial	1977 TOTAL	1977 Non-Financial	1977 Financial
1 Property and entrepreneurial income received	20586	18595	1991	19053	16737	2316	25193	22189	3004	32880	28723	4157
a Net operating surplus [a]	17673	18313	-640	15399	16283	-884	20152	21225	-1073	26052	27392	-1340
b Withdrawals from quasi-corporate enterprises	...	...	...	...	...	...	...	...	...	...	...	...
c Interest	2847	234	2613	3475	355	3120	4687	685	4002	6420	1012	5408

Ecuador

3.22 Corporate and Quasi-Corporate Enterprise Income and Outlay Account: Total and Sectors
(Continued)

Million Ecuadoran sucres

	1974 TOTAL	1974 Non-Financial	1974 Financial	1975 TOTAL	1975 Non-Financial	1975 Financial	1976 TOTAL	1976 Non-Financial	1976 Financial	1977 TOTAL	1977 Non-Financial	1977 Financial
d Dividends	66	48	18	169	89	80	354	279	75	408	319	89
e Net land rent and royalties	...	...	...	10	10	...	...	...	...	...	...	...
2 Other current transfers received	678	609	69	884	748	136	1433	1321	112	965	771	194
a Casualty insurance transactions	224	179	45	334	225	109	414	346	68	481	341	140
Claims received	184	179	5	236	225	11	353	346	7	350	341	9
Net premiums received by insurance companies	40	...	40	98	...	98	61	...	61	131	...	131
b Current transfers received from the rest of the world	...	...	...	...	...	...	...	...	...	...	...	...
c Other transfers received, except imputed	...	...	...	...	...	...	...	...	...	...	...	...
d Imputed unfunded employee welfare contributions	454	430	24	550	523	27	1019	975	44	484	430	54
Total Current Receipts	21264	19204	2060	19937	17485	2452	26626	23510	3116	33845	29494	4351

Disbursements

	1974 TOTAL	1974 Non-Financial	1974 Financial	1975 TOTAL	1975 Non-Financial	1975 Financial	1976 TOTAL	1976 Non-Financial	1976 Financial	1977 TOTAL	1977 Non-Financial	1977 Financial
1 Property and entrepreneurial income paid out	11564	10635	929	8071	6780	1291	10693	8919	1774	12716	10571	2145
a Withdrawals from quasi-corporations	20	-	20	22	2	20	116	6	110	36	23	13
Public	...	...	...	...	...	...	...	...	...	...	...	...
Private	20	-	20	22	2	20	116	6	110	36	23	13
b Interest	2132	1361	771	2599	1489	1110	4131	2691	1440	5359	3552	1807
c Dividends [b]	6432	6294	138	2526	2365	161	3967	3743	224	4231	3906	325
d Net land rent and royalties	2980	2980	...	2924	2924	...	2479	2479	...	3090	3090	...
2 Direct taxes and other current payments n.e.c. to general government	5971	5934	37	5904	5847	57	8887	8807	80	9038	8869	169
a Direct taxes	5807	5770	37	5749	5692	57	8735	8655	80	8866	8697	169
Income	5782	5745	37	5725	5668	57	8694	8614	80	8816	8647	169
Other	25	25	...	24	24	...	41	41	...	50	50	...
b Fines, fees, penalties and other payments n.e.c.	164	164	...	155	155	...	152	152	...	172	172	...
3 Other current transfers paid	920	531	389	1330	774	556	1830	1407	423	2370	1206	1164
a Casualty insurance transactions	219	174	45	322	213	109	409	341	68	509	369	140
Casualty insurance premiums paid, net	179	174	5	224	213	11	348	341	7	378	369	9
Claims paid by insurance companies	40	...	40	98	...	98	61	...	61	131	...	131
b Transfers to private non-profit institutions	...	...	...	...	...	...	...	...	...	...	...	...
c Transfers to households	701	357	344	1008	561	447	1421	1066	355	1856	833	1023
Unfunded employee welfare benefits	454	430	24	550	523	27	1019	975	44	484	430	54
Social assistance grants and other transfers n.e.c.	247	-73	320	458	38	420	402	91	311	1372	403	969
d Transfers to the rest of the world	...	...	...	...	...	...	...	...	...	5	4	1
Net saving	2809	2104	705	4632	4084	548	5216	4377	839	9721	8848	873
Total Current Disbursements and Net Saving	21264	19204	2060	19937	17485	2452	26626	23510	3116	33845	29494	4351

	1978 TOTAL	1978 Non-Financial	1978 Financial	1979 TOTAL	1979 Non-Financial	1979 Financial	1980 TOTAL	1980 Non-Financial	1980 Financial

Receipts

	1978 TOTAL	1978 Non-Financial	1978 Financial	1979 TOTAL	1979 Non-Financial	1979 Financial	1980 TOTAL	1980 Non-Financial	1980 Financial
1 Property and entrepreneurial income received	35961	30493	5468	49919	43435	6484	67333	59859	7474
a Net operating surplus [a]	27255	29029	-1774	38873	41259	-2386	54668	57155	-2487
b Withdrawals from quasi-corporate enterprises	...	...	...	...	...	...	...	...	...
c Interest	8185	1100	7085	10729	1986	8743	12096	2377	9719

395

Ecuador

3.22 Corporate and Quasi-Corporate Enterprise Income and Outlay Account: Total and Sectors
(Continued)

Million Ecuadoran sucres

	1978 TOTAL	1978 Non-Financial	1978 Financial	1979 TOTAL	1979 Non-Financial	1979 Financial	1980 TOTAL	1980 Non-Financial	1980 Financial
d Dividends	521	364	157	311	184	127	564	322	242
e Net land rent and royalties	-	-	-	6	6	-	5	5	-
2 Other current transfers received	1403	1143	260	1555	1263	292	1844	1531	313
a Casualty insurance transactions	835	629	206	743	518	225	777	558	219
Claims received	652	629	23	546	518	28	584	558	26
Net premiums received by insurance companies	183	...	183	197	...	197	193	...	193
b Current transfers received from the rest of the world	...	...	...	...	...	...	...	...	...
c Other transfers received, except imputed	...	...	...	...	...	...	...	...	...
d Imputed unfunded employee welfare contributions	568	514	54	812	745	67	1067	973	94
Total Current Receipts	37364	31636	5728	51474	44698	6776	69177	61390	7787

Disbursements

1 Property and entrepreneurial income paid out	17430	14520	2910	23257	19818	3439	30777	26881	3896
a Withdrawals from quasi-corporations	149	24	125	83	30	53	138	27	111
Public	...	...	...	...	...	...	...	...	...
Private	149	24	125	83	30	53	138	27	111
b Interest	7498	5182	2316	10777	7948	2829	15432	12299	3133
c Dividends [b]	5205	4736	469	5336	4779	557	6503	5851	652
d Net land rent and royalties	4578	4578	...	7061	7061	...	8704	8704	...
2 Direct taxes and other current payments n.e.c. to general government	9322	9079	243	14764	14443	321	22443	22060	383
a Direct taxes	9100	8857	243	14540	14219	321	21949	21566	383
Income	9029	8786	243	14459	14138	321	21856	21473	383
Other	71	71	...	81	81	...	93	93	...
b Fines, fees, penalties and other payments n.e.c.	222	222	...	224	224	...	494	494	...
3 Other current transfers paid	2466	1471	995	2937	1744	1193	3220	1928	1292
a Casualty insurance transactions	790	584	206	792	567	225	722	502	220
Casualty insurance premiums paid, net	607	584	23	595	567	28	529	502	27
Claims paid by insurance companies	183	...	183	197	...	197	193	...	193
b Transfers to private non-profit institutions	...	...	...	...	...	...	...	...	...
c Transfers to households	1664	878	786	2131	1177	954	2491	1421	1070
Unfunded employee welfare benefits	568	514	54	812	745	67	1067	973	94
Social assistance grants and other transfers n.e.c.	1096	364	732	1319	432	887	1424	448	976
d Transfers to the rest of the world	12	9	3	14	...	14	7	5	2
Net saving	8146	6566	1580	10516	8693	1823	12737	10521	2216
Total Current Disbursements and Net Saving	37364	31636	5728	51474	44698	6776	69177	61390	7787

a) Gross.
b) Including profit participation.

3.23 Corporate and Quasi-Corporate Enterprise Capital Accumulation Account: Total and Sectors

Million Ecuadoran sucres

	1970 TOTAL	1970 Non-Financial	1970 Financial	1971 TOTAL	1971 Non-Financial	1971 Financial	1972 TOTAL	1972 Non-Financial	1972 Financial	1973 TOTAL	1973 Non-Financial	1973 Financial
				Finance of Gross Accumulation								
1 Gross saving	1026	903	123	561	424	137	365	214	151	1363	1098	265
2 Capital transfers received	158	146	12	94	84	10	302	302	...	374	374	...
a From resident sectors	158	146	12	94	84	10	302	302	...	374	374	...
b From the rest of the world	...	...	...	...	...	...	...	...	...	...	...	...
Finance of Gross Accumulation	1184	1049	135	655	508	147	667	516	151	1737	1472	265

Ecuador

3.23 Corporate and Quasi-Corporate Enterprise Capital Accumulation Account: Total and Sectors
(Continued)

Million Ecuadoran sucres

	1970 TOTAL	1970 Non-Financial	1970 Financial	1971 TOTAL	1971 Non-Financial	1971 Financial	1972 TOTAL	1972 Non-Financial	1972 Financial	1973 TOTAL	1973 Non-Financial	1973 Financial
Gross Accumulation												
1 Gross capital formation	2902	2790	112	4872	4658	214	4846	4625	221	5467	5109	358
a Increase in stocks	437	412	25	475	432	43	538	445	93	858	733	125
b Gross fixed capital formation	2465	2378	87	4397	4226	171	4308	4180	128	4609	4376	233
2 Purchases of land, net	133	63	70	90	89	1	4	-12	16	210	188	22
3 Purchases of intangible assets, net	17	17	...	10	10	...	...	...	...	...	...	...
4 Capital transfers paid	257	243	14	251	243	8	8	...	8	9	...	9
a To resident sectors	257	243	14	251	243	8	8	...	8	9	...	9
b To the rest of the world	...	...	...	...	...	...	...	...	...	...	...	...
5 Net lending	-2125	-2064	-61	-4568	-4492	-76	-4191	-4097	-94	-3949	-3825	-124
Gross Accumulation	1184	1049	135	655	508	147	667	516	151	1737	1472	265

	1974 TOTAL	1974 Non-Financial	1974 Financial	1975 TOTAL	1975 Non-Financial	1975 Financial	1976 TOTAL	1976 Non-Financial	1976 Financial	1977 TOTAL	1977 Non-Financial	1977 Financial
Finance of Gross Accumulation												
1 Gross saving	2809	2104	705	4632	4084	548	5216	4377	839	9721	8848	873
2 Capital transfers received	414	414	...	443	427	16	540	501	39	545	492	53
a From resident sectors	414	414	...	443	427	16	540	501	39	534	492	42
b From the rest of the world	...	...	...	...	...	...	...	...	...	11	...	11
Finance of Gross Accumulation	3223	2518	705	5075	4511	564	5756	4878	878	10266	9340	926
Gross Accumulation												
1 Gross capital formation	9723	8738	985	13986	13193	793	16667	15315	1352	25474	24903	571
a Increase in stocks	2730	2115	615	3249	2734	515	2210	1475	735	4416	4344	72
b Gross fixed capital formation	6993	6623	370	10737	10459	278	14457	13840	617	21058	20559	499
2 Purchases of land, net	241	248	-7	162	105	57	659	670	-11	1249	1186	63
3 Purchases of intangible assets, net	73	73	...	-39	-39	...	106	106	...	-68	-68	...
4 Capital transfers paid	42	...	42	...	...	...	...	...	...	213	116	97
a To resident sectors	42	...	42	...	...	...	...	...	...	213	116	97
b To the rest of the world	...	...	...	...	...	...	...	...	...	...	...	...
5 Net lending	-6856	-6541	-315	-9034	-8748	-286	-11676	-11213	-463	-16602	-16797	195
Gross Accumulation	3223	2518	705	5075	4511	564	5756	4878	878	10266	9340	926

	1978 TOTAL	1978 Non-Financial	1978 Financial	1979 TOTAL	1979 Non-Financial	1979 Financial	1980 TOTAL	1980 Non-Financial	1980 Financial
Finance of Gross Accumulation									
1 Gross saving	8146	6566	1580	10516	8693	1823	12737	10521	2216
2 Capital transfers received	602	509	93	709	619	90	951	809	142
a From resident sectors	590	509	81	698	608	90	951	809	142
b From the rest of the world	12	...	12	11	11	...	...	...	...
Finance of Gross Accumulation	8748	7075	1673	11225	9312	1913	13688	11330	2358
Gross Accumulation									
1 Gross capital formation	29789	28733	1056	34644	32999	1645	45204	43091	2113
a Increase in stocks	3318	3208	110	3524	2914	610	7526	6976	550
b Gross fixed capital formation	26471	25525	946	31120	30085	1035	37678	36115	1563
2 Purchases of land, net	1271	1183	88	1554	1309	245	1460	1079	381
3 Purchases of intangible assets, net	1	1	...	216	216	...	79	79	...
4 Capital transfers paid	348	243	105	106	...	106	201	20	181
a To resident sectors	348	243	105	106	...	106	201	20	181
b To the rest of the world	...	...	...	...	...	...	...	...	...
5 Net lending	-22661	-23085	424	-25295	-25212	-83	-33256	-32939	-317
Gross Accumulation	8748	7075	1673	11225	9312	1913	13688	11330	2358

Ecuador

3.32 Household and Private Unincorporated Enterprise Income and Outlay Account

Million Ecuadoran sucres

	1970	1971	1972	1973	1974	1975	1976	1977	1978	1979	1980
Receipts											
1 Compensation of employees	10755	12660	14086	17159	23806	31369	40066	46793	53778	63983	92132
a Wages and salaries	10010	11911	13225	15918	22303	29250	36710	44073	50622	59666	86656
b Employers' contributions for social security	538	496	559	845	923	1256	1974	1788	2129	2987	3798
c Employers' contributions for private pension & welfare plans	207	253	302	396	580	863	1382	932	1027	1330	1678
2 Property and entrepreneurial income received	18908	21339	25139	30582	42857	51284	63799	82860	97612	118808	120389
a Operating surplus of private unincorporated enterprises	18505	20820	24241	29309	40638	49536	61539	79461	93171	113544	114300
b Withdrawals from private quasi-corporations	...	...	...	...	...	...	...	...	...	...	...
c Interest	134	202	311	571	918	862	946	1646	2086	2585	2900
d Dividends [a]	267	313	582	678	1214	864	1270	1677	2213	2482	2885
e Net land rent and royalties	2	4	5	24	87	22	44	76	142	197	304
3 Other current transfers received	1339	1625	1857	2043	3034	3662	4367	5012	5844	7302	9607
a Casualty insurance claims	28	32	33	38	69	92	174	201	238	293	241
b Social security benefits	778	955	1083	1199	1571	1818	2112	2806	3283	4248	6441
c Social assistance grants	...	...	...	...	...	...	...	...	...	...	...
d Unfunded employee welfare benefits	207	253	302	396	580	863	1382	932	1027	1330	1678
e Other current transfers received	326	385	439	410	814	889	699	1073	1296	1431	1247
From general government	155	175	235	184	542	645	497	824	907	1140	1036
From the rest fo the world	166	198	195	208	270	208	170	175	300	31	48
Other	5	12	9	18	2	36	32	74	89	260	163
Total Current Receipts	31002	35624	41082	49784	69697	86315	108232	134665	157234	190093	222128
Disbursements											
1 Final consumption expenditures	26375	30436	34429	41711	55506	70298	84517	102578	121244	143332	170679
2 Property income paid	360	458	785	1042	1440	1895	2168	2931	3562	5453	6955
a Interest	360	458	785	1042	1440	1895	2168	2931	3562	5453	6955
b Net land rent and royalties	...	...	...	...	...	...	...	...	...	...	...
3 Direct taxes, fees, fines & other payments n.e.c. to government	1634	1739	2226	3060	3132	3917	4972	5522	7178	8728	11345
a Social security contributions	1035	968	1160	1759	1912	2584	3668	3770	4491	5822	7977
b Direct taxes	541	690	905	1112	1116	1146	1093	1407	2274	2447	2665
Income taxes	523	665	859	1042	1048	1079	1000	1260	2062	2203	2398
Other	18	25	46	70	68	67	93	147	212	244	267
c Fees, fines and penalties	58	81	161	189	104	187	211	345	413	459	703
4 Other current transfers paid	243	309	343	438	656	967	1577	1122	1322	1600	2036
a Net casualty insurance premiums	24	26	31	32	74	104	179	173	283	244	296
b Transfers to private non-profit institutions serving households	...	...	...	...	...	...	...	...	...	...	...
c Transfers to the rest of the world	...	...	-	3	-	-	3	-	-	20	45
d Other current transfers, except imputed	12	30	10	7	2	-	13	17	12	6	17
e Imputed employee welfare contributions	207	253	302	396	580	863	1382	932	1027	1330	1678
Net saving [b]	2390	2682	3299	3533	8963	9238	14998	22512	23928	30980	31113
Total Current Disbursements and Net Saving	31002	35624	41082	49784	69697	86315	108232	134665	157234	190093	222128

a) Including profit participation.
b) Gross.

Ecuador

3.33 Household and Private Unincorporated Enterprise Capital Accumulation Account

Million Ecuadoran sucres	1970	1971	1972	1973	1974	1975	1976	1977	1978	1979	1980
Finance of Gross Accumulation											
1 Gross saving	2390	2682	3299	3533	8963	9238	14998	22512	23928	30980	31113
2 Capital transfers received	32	26	26	34	71	102	158	193	80	31	38
a From resident sectors	32	26	26	34	71	102	158	193	80	31	38
b From the rest of the world	...	...	...	...	...	...	...	...	...	...	...
Total Finance of Gross Accumulation	2422	2708	3325	3567	9034	9340	15156	22705	24008	31011	31151
Gross Accumulation											
1 Gross Capital Formation	1638	2010	2353	3201	5763	8428	6037	8626	12638	12934	15462
a Increase in stocks	51	34	194	189	1130	566	-235	280	879	587	1632
b Gross fixed capital formation	1587	1976	2159	3012	4633	7862	6272	8346	11759	12347	13830
Owner-occupied housing	850	996	1045	1555	2642	3921	4580	6019	...	...	...
Other gross fixed capital formation	737	980	1114	1457	1991	3941	1692	2327	...	...	...
2 Purchases of land, net	-133	-76	-43	-283	-206	-207	-601	-1216	-1295	-1468	-1525
3 Purchases of intangibles, net	...	...	...	...	...	47	2	...	...	...	...
4 Capital transfers paid	12	10	...	...	...	...	...	...	...	...	...
a To resident sectors	12	10	...	...	...	...	...	...	...	...	...
b To the rest of the world	...	...	...	...	...	...	...	...	...	...	...
5 Net lending	905	764	1015	649	3477	1072	9718	15295	12665	19545	17214
Total Gross Accumulation	2422	2708	3325	3567	9034	9340	15156	22705	24008	31011	31151

3.51 External Transactions: Current Account: Detail

Million Ecuadoran sucres	1970	1971	1972	1973	1974	1975	1976	1977	1978	1979	1980
Payments to the Rest of the World											
1 Imports of goods and services	6500	9769	10499	13497	28828	35221	35983	46310	51612	57831	75372
2 Factor income paid to the rest of the world	694	948	1731	3695	6360	2898	4519	5377	6725	10820	15200
a Compensation of employees	9	12		30	298	683	590	683	563	790	948
b Property and entrepreneurial income paid	685	936	1731	3665	6062	2215	3929	4694	6162	10030	14252
3 Indirect taxes paid to supranational organizations	...	...	...	...	...	...	...	...	...	...	...
4 Other current transfers to the rest of the world	71	76	109	219	271	313	583	604	1037	966	970
a By general government	13	24	42	139	58	72	85	113	148	110	98
b By other resident sectors	58	52	67	80	213	241	498	491	889	856	872
5 Surplus of the nation on current transactions	-1895	-4307	-3077	-1321	-480	-8939	-5271	-8908	-15538	-6101	-18349
Payments to the Rest of the World, and Surplus of the Nation on Current Transfers	5370	6486	9262	16090	34979	29493	35814	43383	43836	63516	73193
Receipts From The Rest of the World											
1 Exports of goods and services	4909	5986	8808	15506	33589	28242	34171	41315	40831	60122	69485
2 Factor income received from the rest of the world	22	26	53	153	695	430	458	899	1202	1779	2048
a Compensation of employees	·	·	·	1	60	5	21	26	10	18	23
b Property and entrepreneurial income received	22	26	53	152	635	425	437	873	1192	1761	2025
3 Subsidies received from supranational organizations	...	...	...	...	...	...	...	...	...	...	...
4 Other current transfers from the rest of the world	439	474	401	431	695	821	1185	1169	1803	1615	1660
a To general government	215	225	139	146	212	372	524	505	625	759	791
b To other resident sectors	224	249	262	285	483	449	661	664	1178	856	869
Receipts from the Rest of the World on Current Transfers	5370	6486	9262	16090	34979	29493	35814	43383	43836	63516	73193

Ecuador

3.52 External Transactions: Capital Accumulation Account

Million Ecuadoran sucres

	1970	1971	1972	1973	1974	1975	1976	1977	1978	1979	1980
					Finance of Gross Accumulation						
1 Surplus of the nation on current transactions	-1895	-4307	-3077	-1321	-480	-8939	-5271	-8908	-15538	-6101	-18349
2 Capital transfers received from the rest of the world	...	...	...	...	...	...	...	11	12	11	-
a By general government	...	...	...	...	...	...	...	...	...	...	...
b By other resident sectors	...	...	...	...	...	...	...	11	12	11	-
Total Finance of Gross Accumulation	-1895	-4307	-3077	-1321	-480	-8939	-5271	-8897	-15526	-6090	-18349
					Gross Accumulation						
1 Capital transfers paid to the rest of the world	...	...	...	...	...	...	...	...	...	...	...
2 Purchases of intangible assets, n.e.c., net, from the rest of the world	17	10	-	-	73	8	108	-68	1	216	79
3 Net lending to the rest of the world	-1912	-4317	-3077	-1321	-553	-8947	-5379	-8829	-15527	-6306	-18428
Total Gross Accumulation	-1895	-4307	-3077	-1321	-480	-8939	-5271	-8897	-15526	-6090	-18349

4.3 Derivation of Value Added by Kind of Activity, ISIC Divisions, in Current Prices

Million Ecuadoran sucres

	1970 Gross Output	1970 Intermediate Consumption	1970 Value Added	1971 Gross Output	1971 Intermediate Consumption	1971 Value Added	1972 Gross Output	1972 Intermediate Consumption	1972 Value Added	1973 Gross Output	1973 Intermediate Consumption	1973 Value Added
						All Producers						
1 Agriculture, hunting, forestry and fishing	9742	1356	8386	10599	1419	9180	12180	1645	10535	14202	1961	12241
a Agriculture and hunting	9176	1274	7902	9785	1297	8488	11143	1493	9650	12932	1771	11161
b Forestry and logging	331	45	286	404	58	346	496	70	426	627	92	535
c Fishing	235	37	198	410	64	346	541	82	459	643	98	545
2 Mining and quarrying	208	134	74	228	165	63	1896	959	937	7599	1528	6071
a Coal mining [a]	...	...	...	...	...	...	...	...	...	...	...	...
b Crude petroleum and natural gas production	86	98	-12	71	116	-45	1729	905	824	7346	1465	5881
c Metal ore mining [a]	...	...	...	...	...	...	...	...	...	...	...	...
d Other mining	122	36	86	157	49	108	167	54	113	253	63	190
3 Manufacturing	17797	10956	6841	20715	12610	8105	24220	14851	9369	30119	19190	10929
a Manufacture of food, beverages and tobacco	9707	6418	3289	10637	6901	3736	12355	8152	4203	15001	10013	4988
b Textile, wearing apparel and leather industries	2587	1460	1127	3362	1937	1425	4089	2273	1816	5281	3065	2216
c Manufacture of wood and wood products, including furniture	832	539	293	1014	662	352	1294	816	478	1651	1036	615
d Manufacture of paper and paper products, printing and publishing	1157	779	378	1370	924	446	1439	935	504	1710	1121	589
e Manufacture of chemicals and chemical petroleum, coal, rubber and plastic products	2029	1007	1022	2474	1211	1263	2664	1414	1250	3315	2346	969
f Manufacture of non-metallic mineral products, except products of petroleum and coal	1036	484	552	1287	624	663	1645	806	839	2058	1029	1029
g Basic metal industries												
h Manufacture of fabricated metal products, machinery and equipment	449	269	180	571	351	220	734	455	279	1103	580	523
i Other manufacturing industries												
4 Electricity, gas and water	569	236	333	698	293	405	933	383	550	1074	466	608
5 Construction	4156	2779	1377	6275	4118	2157	6266	4045	2221	7294	4775	2519
6 Wholesale and retail trade, restaurants and hotels	8814	3715	5099	10305	4336	5969	12065	4889	7176	15181	5581	9600
a Wholesale and retail trade	7440	2923	4517	8722	3424	5298	10126	3775	6351	12806	4248	8558
b Restaurants and hotels	1374	792	582	1583	912	671	1939	1114	825	2375	1333	1042
7 Transport, storage and communication	3781	1422	2359	4406	1717	2689	5142	1931	3211	6037	2318	3719
a Transport and storage	3511	1379	2132	4045	1659	2386	4721	1858	2863	5539	2229	3310

Ecuador

4.3 Derivation of Value Added by Kind of Activity, ISIC Divisions, in Current Prices
(Continued)

Million Ecuadoran sucres

	1970 Gross Output	1970 Intermediate Consumption	1970 Value Added	1971 Gross Output	1971 Intermediate Consumption	1971 Value Added	1972 Gross Output	1972 Intermediate Consumption	1972 Value Added	1973 Gross Output	1973 Intermediate Consumption	1973 Value Added
b Communication	270	43	227	361	58	303	421	73	348	498	89	409
8 Finance, insurance, real estate and business services	4467	668	3799	5095	798	4296	5736	921	4815	7027	1095	5932
a Financial institutions	978	239	739	1131	287	844	1351	323	1028	1792	381	1411
b Insurance												
c Real estate and business services	3489	429	3060	3963	511	3452	4385	598	3787	5235	714	4521
9 Community, social and personal services	2678	489	2189	3006	574	2432	3190	609	2581	3764	747	3017
a Sanitary and similar services	...	...	...	...	...	...	...	...	...	...	...	...
b Social and related community services	...	...	...	...	...	...	...	...	...	...	...	...
c Recreational and cultural services	...	...	...	...	...	...	...	...	...	...	...	...
d Personal and household services	2678	489	2189	3006	574	2432	3190	609	2581	3764	747	3017
Total, Industries	52212	21755	30457	61326	26030	35296	71628	30233	41395	92297	37661	54636
Producers of Government Services	4318	1310	3008	4584	1411	3173	5230	1649	3581	7035	2246	4789
Other Producers	266	-	266	345	-	345	356	-	356	372	-	372
Total	56796	23065	33731	66255	27441	38814	77214	31882	45332	99704	39907	59797
Imputed bank service charge	...	633	-633	...	738	-738	...	842	-842	...	1090	-1090
Import duties	1921	...	1921	1972	...	1972	2369	...	2369	3522	...	3522
Value added tax	...	...	...	...	...	...	...	...	...	...	...	...
Total	58717	23698	35019	68227	28179	40048	79583	32724	46859	103226	40997	62229

	1974 Gross Output	1974 Intermediate Consumption	1974 Value Added	1975 Gross Output	1975 Intermediate Consumption	1975 Value Added	1976 Gross Output	1976 Intermediate Consumption	1976 Value Added	1977 Gross Output	1977 Intermediate Consumption	1977 Value Added
All Producers												
1 Agriculture, hunting, forestry and fishing	19947	2570	17377	22741	3408	19333	26134	3520	22614	31365	3694	27671
a Agriculture and hunting	18232	2319	15913	20591	3112	17479	23514	3180	20334	28080	3282	24798
b Forestry and logging	931	130	801	1172	153	1019	1439	175	1264	1910	221	1689
c Fishing	784	121	663	978	143	835	1181	165	1016	1375	191	1184
2 Mining and quarrying	23174	1545	21629	18133	2387	15746	20865	3056	17809	25027	3379	21648
a Coal mining [a]	...	...	...	...	...	...	...	...	...	...	...	...
b Crude petroleum and natural gas production	22832	1459	21373	17685	2271	15414	20347	2915	17432	24333	3196	21137
c Metal ore mining [a]	...	...	...	...	...	...	...	...	...	...	...	...
d Other mining	342	86	256	448	116	332	518	141	377	694	183	511
3 Manufacturing	41992	33009	8983	51583	37638	13945	65648	46307	19341	84317	60354	23963
a Manufacture of food, beverages and tobacco	20557	14006	6551	25072	17390	7682	33411	22681	10730	41733	27338	14395
b Textile, wearing apparel and leather industries	7507	4669	2838	9021	5272	3749	10764	6110	4654	13951	7737	6214
c Manufacture of wood and wood products, including furniture	2444	1491	953	3016	1986	1030	3793	2486	1307	5247	3614	1633
d Manufacture of paper and paper products, printing and publishing	2292	1525	767	3036	1986	1050	3546	2147	1399	4017	2401	1616
e Manufacture of chemicals and chemical petroleum, coal, rubber and plastic products	4269	8604	-4335	5176	7326	-2150	6206	8350	-2144	9038	13199	-4161
f Manufacture of non-metallic mineral products, except products of petroleum and coal	3246	1761	1485	4058	2289	1769	4892	2694	2198	6384	3392	2992
g Basic metal industries												
h Manufacture of fabricated metal products, machinery and equipment	1677	953	724	2204	1389	815	3036	1839	1197	3947	2673	1274
i Other manufacturing industries	1278	631	647	1600	791	809	1989	980	1009	2854	1585	1269
4 Electricity, gas and water	11580	7435	4145	15231	9243	5988	19848	11026	8822	23763	13361	10402
5 Construction	21218	7816	13402	27187	10238	16949	32337	11933	20404	40802	14695	26107
6 Wholesale and retail trade, restaurants and hotels	17948	6035	11913	23064	8093	14971	27545	9489	18056	34668	11612	23056
a Wholesale and retail trade	17948	6035	11913	23064	8093	14971	27545	9489	18056	34668	11612	23056
b Restaurants and hotels	3270	1781	1489	4123	2145	1978	4792	2444	2348	6134	3083	3051
7 Transport, storage and communication	7967	3284	4683	10383	4214	6169	13446	5186	8260	17195	6593	10602

Ecuador

4.3 Derivation of Value Added by Kind of Activity, ISIC Divisions, in Current Prices
(Continued)

Million Ecuadoran sucres

	1974 Gross Output	1974 Intermediate Consumption	1974 Value Added	1975 Gross Output	1975 Intermediate Consumption	1975 Value Added	1976 Gross Output	1976 Intermediate Consumption	1976 Value Added	1977 Gross Output	1977 Intermediate Consumption	1977 Value Added
a Transport and storage	7363	3161	4202	9587	4033	5554	12499	4947	7552	16033	6298	9735
b Communication	604	123	481	796	181	615	947	239	708	1162	295	867
8 Finance, insurance, real estate and business services	10052	1666	8386	13301	2064	11237	16568	2595	13973	21785	3391	18394
a Financial institutions	2972	619	2353	3437	749	2688	4447	1013	3434	5860	1283	4577
b Insurance												
c Real estate and business services	7080	1047	6033	9864	1315	8549	12121	1582	10539	15925	2108	13817
9 Community, social and personal services	4927	1080	3847	5778	1269	4509	7214	1580	5634	9296	1995	7301
a Sanitary and similar services	...	...	...	...	...	...	...	...	...	...	...	...
b Social and related community services	...	...	...	...	...	...	...	...	...	...	...	...
c Recreational and cultural services	...	...	...	...	...	...	...	...	...	...	...	...
d Personal and household services	4927	1080	3847	5778	1269	4509	7214	1580	5634	9296	1995	7301
Total, Industries	142135	59036	83099	165937	71252	94685	204049	86183	117866	256404	109047	147357
Producers of Government Services	12657	5391	7266	16965	7325	9640	20028	8234	11794	25929	12298	13631
Other Producers	468	-	468	558	-	558	715	-	715	743	-	743
Total	155260	64427	90833	183460	78577	104883	224792	94417	130375	283076	121345	161731
Imputed bank service charge	...	1842	-1842	...	2063	-2063	...	2603	-2603	...	3642	-3642
Import duties	3772	...	3772	4920	...	4920	5141	...	5141	8287	...	8287
Value added tax	...	...	...	...	...	...	...	...	...	...	...	...
Total	159032	66269	92763	188380	80640	107740	229933	97020	132913	291363	124987	166376

	1978 Gross Output	1978 Intermediate Consumption	1978 Value Added	1979 Gross Output	1979 Intermediate Consumption	1979 Value Added	1980 Gross Output	1980 Intermediate Consumption	1980 Value Added
				All Producers					
1 Agriculture, hunting, forestry and fishing	32773	4274	28499	36496	4859	31637	40676	5853	34823
a Agriculture and hunting	29112	3813	25299	32151	4310	27841	34962	5142	29820
b Forestry and logging	2164	246	1918	2531	300	2231	2949	367	2582
c Fishing	1497	215	1282	1814	249	1565	2765	344	2421
2 Mining and quarrying	21042	3745	17297	45336	4360	40976	64949	6169	58780
a Coal mining [a]	...	...	...	...	...	...	...	...	...
b Crude petroleum and natural gas production	20253	3555	16698	44373	4131	40242	63674	5894	57780
c Metal ore mining [a]	...	...	...	...	...	...	...	...	...
d Other mining	789	190	599	963	229	734	1275	275	1000
3 Manufacturing	98408	65714	32694	117128	86122	31006	133921	108824	25097
a Manufacture of food, beverages and tobacco	47033	29177	17856	55100	33080	22020	59369	35691	23678
b Textile, wearing apparel and leather industries	15049	8144	6905	17090	9245	7845	19199	10529	8670
c Manufacture of wood and wood products, including furniture	5884	4066	1818	7348	4923	2425	8889	5960	2929
d Manufacture of paper and paper products, printing and publishing	4697	2826	1871	5442	3160	2282	6545	3793	2752
e Manufacture of chemicals and chemical petroleum, coal, rubber and plastic products	12375	13693	-1318	15312	26076	-10764	19885	40955	-21070
f Manufacture of non-metallic mineral products, except products of petroleum and coal	8443	4463	3980	10902	5584	5318	12758	6860	5898
g Basic metal industries									
h Manufacture of fabricated metal products, machinery and equipment	4927	3345	1582	4496	3534	962	5623	4420	1203
i Other manufacturing industries				1438	520	918	1653	616	1037
4 Electricity, gas and water	3455	1964	1491	4141	2373	1768	5651	3032	2619

Ecuador

4.3 Derivation of Value Added by Kind of Activity, ISIC Divisions, in Current Prices
(Continued)

Million Ecuadoran sucres

	1978 Gross Output	1978 Intermediate Consumption	1978 Value Added	1979 Gross Output	1979 Intermediate Consumption	1979 Value Added	1980 Gross Output	1980 Intermediate Consumption	1980 Value Added
5 Construction	29772	15181	14591	33756	17456	16300	41023	20411	20612
6 Wholesale and retail trade, restaurants and hotels	47882	18467	29415	55304	21755	33549	65983	26654	39329
a Wholesale and retail trade	40201	14807	25394	46202	17500	28702	55169	21679	33490
b Restaurants and hotels	7681	3660	4021	9102	4255	4847	10814	4975	5839
7 Transport, storage and communication	23469	7906	15563	30523	9647	20876	38129	12180	25949
a Transport and storage	21896	7546	14350	28766	9242	19524	35857	11592	24265
b Communication	1573	360	1213	1757	405	1352	2272	588	1684
8 Finance, insurance, real estate and business services	26273	4191	22082	31607	5290	26317	38628	6586	32042
a Financial institutions	7704	1636	6068	9454	2034	7420	10993	2470	8523
b Insurance									
c Real estate and business services	18569	2555	16014	22153	3256	18897	27635	4116	23519
9 Community, social and personal services	11826	2487	9339	14267	2905	11362	17069	3576	13493
a Sanitary and similar services	...	...	...	...	...	...	...	...	...
b Social and related community services	...	...	...	...	...	...	...	...	...
c Recreational and cultural services	...	...	...	...	...	...	...	...	...
d Personal and household services	11826	2487	9339	14267	2905	11362	17069	3576	13493
Total, Industries	294900	123929	170971	368558	154767	213791	446029	193285	252744
Producers of Government Services	27996	12648	15348	32242	14854	17388	42468	17900	24568
Other Producers	801		801	963	-	963	1449	-	1449
Total	323697	136577	187120	401763	169621	232142	489946	211185	278761
Imputed bank service charge	...	4856	-4856	...	5927	-5927	...	6696	-6696
Import duties	9081	...	9081	9685	...	9685	12133	...	12133
Value added tax	...	...	...	...	...	...	...	...	...
Total	332778	141433	191345	411448	175548	235900	502079	217881	284198

a) Item 'Coal mining' is included in item 'Metal ore mining'.

4.4 Derivation of Value Added by Kind of Activity, ISIC Divisions, in Constant Prices

Million Ecuadoran sucres

	1970 Gross Output	1970 Intermediate Consumption	1970 Value Added	1971 Gross Output	1971 Intermediate Consumption	1971 Value Added	1972 Gross Output	1972 Intermediate Consumption	1972 Value Added	1973 Gross Output	1973 Intermediate Consumption	1973 Value Added

At constant prices of: 1975

All Producers

1 Agriculture, hunting, forestry and fishing	18434	2724	15710	19204	2707	16497	20038	2878	17160	20266	2926	17340
a Agriculture and hunting	17309	2609	14700	17803	2539	15264	18456	2692	15764	18462	2706	15756
b Forestry and logging	625	55	570	714	83	631	841	96	745	974	113	861
c Fishing	500	60	440	687	85	602	741	90	651	830	107	723
2 Mining and quarrying	674	245	429	677	269	408	9136	1477	7659	23540	2089	21451
a Coal mining	...	...	...	...	...	...	...	...	...	...	...	...
b Crude petroleum and natural gas production	446	190	256	416	207	209	8878	1416	7462	23230	2013	21217
c Metal ore mining	...	...	...	...	...	...	...	...	...	...	...	...
d Other mining	228	55	173	261	62	199	258	61	197	310	76	234

Ecuador

4.4 Derivation of Value Added by Kind of Activity, ISIC Divisions, in Constant Prices
(Continued)

Million Ecuadoran sucres

	1970 Gross Output	1970 Intermediate Consumption	1970 Value Added	1971 Gross Output	1971 Intermediate Consumption	1971 Value Added	1972 Gross Output	1972 Intermediate Consumption	1972 Value Added	1973 Gross Output	1973 Intermediate Consumption	1973 Value Added
				At constant prices of: 1975								
3 Manufacturing	31142	23082	8060	33418	24757	8661	36357	26559	9798	39927	29276	10651
a Manufacture of food, beverages and tobacco	16941	11622	5319	17450	11932	5518	18585	12846	5739	19886	14014	5872
b Textile, wearing apparel and leather industries	4967	2762	2205	5541	3344	2197	6367	3631	2736	6951	4003	2948
c Manufacture of wood and wood products, including furniture	1501	849	652	1725	988	737	1937	1199	738	2284	1465	819
d Manufacture of paper and paper products, printing and publishing	2226	1507	719	2366	1592	774	2400	1518	882	2421	1621	800
e Manufacture of chemicals and chemical petroleum, coal, rubber and plastic products	2794	4852	-2058	3236	5127	-1891	3357	5236	-1879	4093	5935	-1842
f Manufacture of non-metallic mineral products, except products of petroleum and coal	1897	970	927	2130	1165	965	2531	1400	1131	2756	1364	1392
g Basic metal industries												
h Manufacture of fabricated metal products, machinery and equipment	816	520	296	970	609	361	1180	729	451	1536	874	662
i Other manufacturing industries												
4 Electricity, gas and water	774	297	477	841	329	512	985	390	595	1100	456	644
5 Construction	9646	5706	3940	12847	7771	5076	11066	6664	4402	11534	6678	4856
6 Wholesale and retail trade, restaurants and hotels	17331	6600	10731	18620	6938	11682	19976	7356	12620	21332	7667	13665
a Wholesale and retail trade	14458	5140	9318	15538	5386	10152	16544	5614	10930	17736	5860	11876
b Restaurants and hotels	2873	1460	1413	3082	1552	1530	3432	1742	1690	3596	1807	1789
7 Transport, storage and communication	5819	2054	3765	6238	2246	3992	6783	2431	4352	7606	2833	4773
a Transport and storage	5342	1968	3374	5742	2155	3587	6275	2327	3948	7067	2720	4347
b Communication	477	86	391	496	91	405	508	104	404	539	113	426
8 Finance, insurance, real estate and business services	8743	1207	7536	9182	1300	7882	9631	1356	8275	11025	1504	9521
a Financial institutions	1941	393	1548	2075	430	1645	2280	450	1830	2638	514	2124
b Insurance												
c Real estate and business services	6802	814	5988	7107	870	6237	7351	906	6445	8387	990	7397
9 Community, social and personal services	4620	991	3629	4727	1000	3727	4677	972	3705	5141	1069	4072
a Sanitary and similar services	...	...	...	...	...	...	...	...	...	...	...	...
b Social and related community services	...	...	...	...	...	...	...	...	...	...	...	...
c Recreational and cultural services	...	...	...	...	...	...	...	...	...	...	...	...
d Personal and household services	4620	991	3629	4727	1000	3727	4677	972	3705	5141	1069	4072
Total, Industries	97183	42906	54277	105754	47317	58437	118649	50083	68566	141471	54498	86973
Producers of Government Services	8364	2359	6005	8182	2315	5867	8619	2441	6178	9465	3019	6446
Other Producers	458	-	458	475	-	475	490	-	490	512	-	512
Total	106005	45265	60740	114411	49632	64779	127758	52524	75234	151448	57517	93931
Imputed bank service charge	...	1258	-1258	...	1351	-1351	...	1476	-1476	...	1606	-1606
Import duties	3430	...	3430	3424	...	3424	2735	...	2735	3542	...	3542
Value added tax	...	...	...	...	...	...	...	...	...	...	...	...
Total	109435	46523	62912	117835	50983	66852	130493	54000	76493	154990	59123	95867

	1974 Gross Output	1974 Intermediate Consumption	1974 Value Added	1975 Gross Output	1975 Intermediate Consumption	1975 Value Added	1976 Gross Output	1976 Intermediate Consumption	1976 Value Added	1977 Gross Output	1977 Intermediate Consumption	1977 Value Added
				At constant prices of: 1975								
				All Producers								
1 Agriculture, hunting, forestry and fishing	22268	3374	18894	22741	3408	19333	23189	3297	19892	23663	3303	20360
a Agriculture and hunting	20312	3113	17199	20591	3112	17479	20870	2976	17894	21062	2947	18115
b Forestry and logging	1076	135	941	1172	153	1019	1255	165	1090	1440	188	1252
c Fishing	880	126	754	978	143	835	1064	156	908	1161	168	993
2 Mining and quarrying	20591	1732	18859	18133	2387	15746	21390	2743	18647	20704	2665	18039
a Coal mining	...	...	...	...	...	...	...	...	...	...	...	...
b Crude petroleum and natural gas production	20207	1637	18570	17685	2271	15414	20903	2614	18289	20129	2513	17616

Ecuador

4.4 Derivation of Value Added by Kind of Activity, ISIC Divisions, in Constant Prices
(Continued)

Million Ecuadoran sucres

		1974			1975			1976			1977		
		Gross Output	Intermediate Consumption	Value Added	Gross Output	Intermediate Consumption	Value Added	Gross Output	Intermediate Consumption	Value Added	Gross Output	Intermediate Consumption	Value Added

At constant prices of: 1975

		1974			1975			1976			1977		
	c Metal ore mining	...	...	...	448	116	332	487	129	358	575	152	423
	d Other mining	384	95	289	51583	37638	13945	57869	41913	15956	64983	47716	17267
3	Manufacturing	45581	33907	11674									
	a Manufacture of food, beverages and tobacco	21895	15231	6664	25072	17390	7682	28406	19663	8743	30123	20799	9324
	b Textile, wearing apparel and leather industries	8106	5034	3072	9021	5272	3749	10020	5735	4285	11661	6524	5137
	c Manufacture of wood and wood products, including furniture	2766	1774	992	3016	1986	1030	3362	2225	1137	3993	2712	1281
	d Manufacture of paper and paper products, printing and publishing	2626	1734	892	3036	1986	1050	3210	1982	1228	3176	1867	1309
	e Manufacture of chemicals and chemical petroleum, coal, rubber and plastic products	4673	6937	-2264	5176	7326	-2150	5759	8176	-2417	8051	11167	-3116
	f Manufacture of non-metallic mineral products, except products of petroleum and coal	3646	2025	1621	4058	2289	1769	4481	2461	2020	4770	2599	2171
	g Basic metal industries												
	h Manufacture of fabricated metal products, machinery and equipment	1869	1172	697	2204	1389	815	2631	1671	960	3209	2048	1161
	i Other manufacturing industries												
4	Electricity, gas and water	1316	623	693	1600	791	809	1828	913	915	2386	1459	927
5	Construction	13945	8360	5585	15231	9243	5988	16472	10057	6415	16926	10353	6573
6	Wholesale and retail trade, restaurants and hotels	24097	9138	14959	27187	10238	16949	28656	10727	17929	31885	11819	20066
	a Wholesale and retail trade	20303	7120	13183	23064	8093	14971	24292	8464	15828	26989	9237	17752
	b Restaurants and hotels	3794	2018	1776	4123	2145	1978	4364	2263	2101	4896	2582	2314
7	Transport, storage and communication	8827	3501	5326	10383	4214	6169	11769	4825	6944	13581	5578	8003
	a Transport and storage	8212	3364	4848	9587	4033	5554	10827	4610	6217	12538	5341	7197
	b Communication	615	137	478	796	181	615	942	215	727	1043	237	806
8	Finance, insurance, real estate and business services	12483	1873	10610	13301	2064	11237	14457	2349	12108	16459	2756	13703
	a Financial institutions	3277	686	2591	3437	749	2688	3966	926	3040	4494	1044	3450
	b Insurance												
	c Real estate and business services	9206	1187	8019	9864	1315	8549	10491	1423	9068	11965	1712	10253
9	Community, social and personal services	5610	1239	4371	5778	1269	4509	6566	1437	5129	7452	1643	5809
	a Sanitary and similar services	...	...	...	...	...	...	...	...	...	...	...	...
	b Social and related community services	...	...	...	...	...	...	...	...	...	...	...	...
	c Recreational and cultural services	...	...	...	...	...	...	...	...	...	...	...	...
	d Personal and household services	5610	1239	4371	5778	1269	4509	6566	1437	5129	7452	1643	5809
	Total, Industries	154718	63747	90971	165937	71252	94685	182196	78261	103935	198039	87292	110747
	Producers of Government Services	14309	5989	8320	16965	7325	9640	18390	7476	10914	21609	10553	11056
	Other Producers	537	-	537	558	-	558	579	-	579	602	-	602
	Total	169564	69736	99828	183460	78577	104883	201165	85737	115428	220250	97845	122405
	Imputed bank service charge	...	2028	-2028	...	2063	-2063	...	2304	-2304	...	2781	-2781
	Import duties	4247	...	4247	4920	...	4920	4555	...	4555	5745	...	5745
	Value added tax	...	...	...	...	...	...	...	...	...	...	...	...
	Total	173811	71764	102046	188380	80640	107740	205720	88041	117679	225995	100626	125369

		1978			1979			1980		
		Gross Output	Intermediate Consumption	Value Added	Gross Output	Intermediate Consumption	Value Added	Gross Output	Intermediate Consumption	Value Added

At constant prices of: 1975

All Producers

		Gross Output	Intermediate Consumption	Value Added	Gross Output	Intermediate Consumption	Value Added	Gross Output	Intermediate Consumption	Value Added
1	Agriculture, hunting, forestry and fishing	23187	3612	19575	24038	3759	20279	25359	4021	21338
	a Agriculture and hunting	20409	3223	17186	21019	3333	17686	21840	3521	18319
	b Forestry and logging	1540	204	1336	1679	224	1455	1844	247	1597
	c Fishing	1238	185	1053	1340	202	1138	1675	253	1422
2	Mining and quarrying	22840	2692	20148	24398	2747	21651	23154	3446	19708

Ecuador

4.4 Derivation of Value Added by Kind of Activity, ISIC Divisions, in Constant Prices
(Continued)

Million Ecuadoran sucres

	1978 Gross Output	1978 Intermediate Consumption	1978 Value Added	1979 Gross Output	1979 Intermediate Consumption	1979 Value Added	1980 Gross Output	1980 Intermediate Consumption	1980 Value Added
				At constant prices of: 1975					
a Coal mining	...	...	...	...	...	...	...	...	...
b Crude petroleum and natural gas production	22297	2547	19750	23807	2589	21218	22462	3260	19202
c Metal ore mining	...	...	...	...	...	...	...	...	...
d Other mining	543	145	398	591	158	433	692	186	506
3 Manufacturing	71252	52218	19034	76078	55592	20486	81257	59457	21800
a Manufacture of food, beverages and tobacco	31689	21452	10237	33841	22600	11241	35319	23347	11972
b Textile, wearing apparel and leather industries	11650	6602	5048	12209	6811	5398	12731	7136	5595
c Manufacture of wood and wood products, including furniture	4202	2873	1329	4733	3170	1563	5252	3542	1710
d Manufacture of paper and paper products, printing and publishing	3523	2145	1378	3624	2122	1502	3888	2287	1601
e Manufacture of chemicals and chemical petroleum, coal, rubber and plastic products	10690	13595	-2905	11332	14692	-3360	12834	16370	-3536
f Manufacture of non-metallic mineral products, except products of petroleum and coal	5758	3155	2603	6358	3597	2761	6805	3859	2946
g Basic metal industries									
h Manufacture of fabricated metal products, machinery and equipment	3740	2396	1344	3126	2277	849	3538	2579	959
i Other manufacturing industries				855	323	532	890	337	553
4 Electricity, gas and water	2589	1674	915	2944	1925	1019	3418	2216	1202
5 Construction	17947	11044	6903	17896	11071	6825	18351	11408	6943
6 Wholesale and retail trade, restaurants and hotels	34451	12947	21504	36028	13476	22552	38663	14504	24159
a Wholesale and retail trade	29020	10145	18875	30237	10437	19800	32498	11294	21204
b Restaurants and hotels	5431	2802	2629	5791	3039	2752	6165	3210	2955
7 Transport, storage and communication	14806	6190	8616	16054	6797	9257	17487	7400	10087
a Transport and storage	13681	5927	7754	14893	6526	8367	16136	7087	9049
b Communication	1125	263	862	1161	271	890	1351	313	1038
8 Finance, insurance, real estate and business services	17641	3019	14622	19121	3361	15760	20090	3624	16466
a Financial institutions	5215	1205	4010	5770	1350	4420	5911	1459	4452
b Insurance									
c Real estate and business services	12426	1814	10612	13351	2011	11340	14179	2165	12014
9 Community, social and personal services	8279	1834	6445	9082	2023	7059	9669	2162	7507
a Sanitary and similar services	...	...	...	...	...	...	...	...	...
b Social and related community services	...	...	...	...	...	...	...	...	...
c Recreational and cultural services	...	...	...	...	...	...	...	...	...
d Personal and household services	8279	1834	6445	9082	2023	7059	9669	2162	7507
Total, Industries	212992	95230	117762	225639	100751	124888	237448	108238	129210
Producers of Government Services	21798	9872	11926	22932	10445	12487	24758	10947	13811
Other Producers	627	-	627	650	-	650	674	-	674
Total	235417	105102	130315	249221	111196	138025	262880	119185	143695
Imputed bank service charge	...	3161	-3161	...	3724	-3724	...	3845	-3845
Import duties	6478	...	6478	6119	...	6119	7352	...	7352
Value added tax	...	...	...	...	...	...	...	...	...
Total	241895	108263	133632	255340	114920	140420	270232	123030	147202

Ecuador

4.6 Cost Components of Value Added, ISIC Divisions

Million Ecuadoran sucres

	1970						1971					
	Compensation of Employees	Capital Consumption	Net Operating Surplus	Indirect Taxes	Less: Subsidies Received	Value Added	Compensation of Employees	Capital Consumption	Net Operating Surplus	Indirect Taxes	Less: Subsidies Received	Value Added

All Producers

1 Agriculture, hunting, forestry and fishing	1173	...	6731	482	...	8386	1244	...	7303	633	...	9180
a Agriculture and hunting	1128	...	6296	478	...	7902	1180	...	6683	625	...	8488
b Forestry and logging	11	...	272	3	...	286	12	...	330	4	...	346
c Fishing	34	...	163	1	...	198	52	...	290	4	...	346
2 Mining and quarrying	114	...	-40	-	...	74	145	...	-83	1	...	63
a Coal mining [a]	...	...	...	...	...	...	...	...	...	...	...	...
b Crude petroleum and natural gas production	77	...	-89	-	...	-12	98	...	-143	-	...	-45
c Metal ore mining [a]	...	...	...	...	...	...	...	...	...	...	...	...
d Other mining	37	...	49	-	...	84	47	...	60	1	...	108
3 Manufacturing	1508	...	4203	1130	...	6841	1805	...	4765	1535	...	8105
a Manufacture of food, beverages and tobacco	480	...	2190	619	...	3289	560	...	2399	777	...	3736
b Textile, wearing apparel and leather industries	293	...	785	49	...	1127	387	...	929	109	...	1425
c Manufacture of wood and wood products, including furniture	144	...	136	13	...	293	177	...	155	20	...	352
d Manufacture of paper and paper products, printing and publishing	142	...	216	20	...	378	165	...	245	36	...	446
e Manufacture of chemicals and chemical petroleum, coal, rubber and plastic products	239	...	436	347	...	1022	271	...	556	436	...	1263
f Manufacture of non-metallic mineral products, except products of petroleum and coal	148	...	362	42	...	552	166	...	396	101	...	663
g Basic metal industries		...			...			...			...	
h Manufacture of fabricated metal products, machinery and equipment	62	...	78	40	...	180	79	...	85	56	...	220
i Other manufacturing industries		...			...			...			...	
4 Electricity, gas and water	173	...	116	44	...	333	217	...	136	52	...	405
5 Construction	1047	...	304	26	...	1377	1653	...	444	60	...	2157
6 Wholesale and retail trade, restaurants and hotels	1091	...	3919	89	...	5099	1279	...	4558	132	...	5969
a Wholesale and retail trade	967	...	3489	61	...	4517	1132	...	4074	92	...	5298
b Restaurants and hotels	124	...	430	28	...	582	147	...	484	40	...	671
7 Transport, storage and communication	1052	...	1339	-32	...	2359	1276	...	1333	80	...	2689
a Transport and storage	959	...	1210	-37	...	2132	1176	...	1157	53	...	2386
b Communication	93	...	129	5	...	227	100	...	176	27	...	303
8 Finance, insurance, real estate and business services	675	...	3053	71	...	3799	807	...	3398	91	...	4296
a Financial institutions	475	...	215	49	...	739	568	...	226	50	...	844
b Insurance		...			...			...			...	
c Real estate and business services	200	...	2838	22	...	3060	239	...	3172	41	...	3452
9 Community, social and personal services	657	...	1497	35	...	2189	728	...	1653	51	...	2432
Total, Industries	7490	...	21122	1845	...	30457	9154	...	23507	2635	...	35296
Producers of Government Services	3008	...	...	...	...	3008	3173	...	...	...	...	3173
Other Producers	266	...	...	...	...	266	345	...	...	...	...	345
Total	10764	...	21122	1845	...	33731	12672	...	23507	2635	...	38814
Imputed bank service charge	...	...	-633	...	...	-633	...	...	-738	...	...	-738
Import duties	...	...	...	1921	...	1921	...	...	...	1972	...	1972
Value added tax	...	...	...	...	...	...	...	...	...	...	...	...
Other adjustments	...	...	...	...	...	...	...	...	...	...	...	...
Total	10764	...	20489	3766	...	35019	12672	...	22769	4607	...	40048

Ecuador

4.6 Cost Components of Value Added, ISIC Divisions

Million Ecuadoran sucres

	1972 Compensation of Employees	1972 Capital Consumption	1972 Net Operating Surplus	1972 Indirect Taxes	1972 Less: Subsidies Received	1972 Value Added	1973 Compensation of Employees	1973 Capital Consumption	1973 Net Operating Surplus	1973 Indirect Taxes	1973 Less: Subsidies Received	1973 Value Added
All Producers												
1 Agriculture, hunting, forestry and fishing	1351	...	8595	589	...	10535	1590	...	10096	555	...	12241
a Agriculture and hunting	1270	...	7798	582	...	9650	1498	...	9119	544	...	11161
b Forestry and logging	15	...	407	4	...	426	18	...	510	7	...	535
c Fishing	66	...	390	3	...	459	74	...	467	4	...	545
2 Mining and quarrying	104	...	553	280	...	937	218	...	3984	1869	...	6071
a Coal mining a	...	...	...	...	...	...	...	...	...	...	...	...
b Crude petroleum and natural gas production	55	...	491	278	...	824	159	...	3855	1867	...	5881
c Metal ore mining a	...	...	...	...	...	...	...	...	...	...	...	...
d Other mining	49	...	62	2	...	113	59	...	129	2	...	190
3 Manufacturing	2147	...	5606	1616	...	9369	2700	...	7099	1130	...	10929
a Manufacture of food, beverages and tobacco	632	...	2792	779	...	4203	807	...	3144	1037	...	4988
b Textile, wearing apparel and leather industries	466	...	1228	122	...	1816	596	...	1475	145	...	2216
c Manufacture of wood and wood products, including furniture	228	...	244	6	...	478	282	...	329	4	...	615
d Manufacture of paper and paper products, printing and publishing	195	...	285	24	...	504	225	...	342	22	...	589
e Manufacture of chemicals and chemical petroleum, coal, rubber and plastic products	328	...	405	517	...	1250	387	...	866	-284	...	969
f Manufacture of non-metallic mineral products, except products of petroleum and coal	200	...	533	106	...	839	268	...	637	124	...	1029
g Basic metal industries		...			...			...			...	
h Manufacture of fabricated metal products, machinery and equipment	98	...	119	62	...	279	135	...	306	82	...	523
i Other manufacturing industries		...			...			...			...	
4 Electricity, gas and water	295	...	192	63	...	550	322	...	209	77	...	608
5 Construction	1726	...	451	44	...	2221	1912	...	554	53	...	2519
6 Wholesale and retail trade, restaurants and hotels	1443	...	5536	197	...	7176	1678	...	7769	153	...	9600
a Wholesale and retail trade	1264	...	4929	158	...	6351	1467	...	6986	105	...	8558
b Restaurants and hotels	179	...	607	39	...	825	211	...	783	48	...	1042
7 Transport, storage and communication	1381	...	1753	77	...	3211	1533	...	2148	38	...	3719
a Transport and storage	1273	...	1547	43	...	2863	1348	...	1956	6	...	3310
b Communication	108	...	206	34	...	348	185	...	192	32	...	409
8 Finance, insurance, real estate and business services	899	...	3709	207	...	4815	1122	...	4544	266	...	5932
a Financial institutions	620	...	361	47	...	1028	773	...	572	66	...	1411
b Insurance		...			...			...			...	
c Real estate and business services	279	...	3348	160	...	3787	349	...	3972	200	...	4521
9 Community, social and personal services	803	...	1721	57	...	2581	952	...	2001	64	...	3017
Total, Industries	10149	...	28116	3130	...	41395	12027	...	38404	4205	...	54636
Producers of Government Services	3581	...	...	...	...	3581	4789	...	...	...	...	4789
Other Producers	356	...	...	...	...	356	372	...	...	...	...	372
Total	14086	...	28116	3130	...	45332	17188	...	38404	4205	...	59797
Imputed bank service charge	...	...	-842	...	...	-842	...	...	-1090	...	...	-1090
Import duties	...	...	...	2369	...	2369	...	...	...	3522	...	3522
Value added tax	...	...	...	...	...	...	...	...	...	...	...	...
Other adjustments	...	...	...	...	...	...	...	...	...	...	...	...
Total	14086	...	27274	5499	...	46859	17188	...	37314	7727	...	62229

Ecuador

4.6 Cost Components of Value Added, ISIC Divisions

Million Ecuadoran sucres

		1974					1975				
	Compensation of Employees	Capital Consumption	Net Operating Surplus	Indirect Taxes	Less: Subsidies Received	Value Added	Compensation of Employees	Capital Consumption	Net Operating Surplus	Indirect Taxes	Less: Subsidies Received	Value Added

All Producers

	Comp. Emp.	Cap. Cons.	Net Op. Surp.	Ind. Taxes	Subs. Rec.	Value Added	Comp. Emp.	Cap. Cons.	Net Op. Surp.	Ind. Taxes	Subs. Rec.	Value Added
1 Agriculture, hunting, forestry and fishing	2268	...	14289	820	...	17377	2708	...	16074	551	...	19333
a Agriculture and hunting	2149	...	12953	811	...	15913	2582	...	14361	536	...	17479
b Forestry and logging	24	...	771	6	...	801	25	...	984	10	...	1019
c Fishing	95	...	565	3	...	663	101	...	729	5	...	835
2 Mining and quarrying	255	...	12341	9033	...	21629	350	...	8936	6460	...	15746
a Coal mining [a]	...	...	...	...	...	...	...	...	...	...	...	...
b Crude petroleum and natural gas production	188	...	12152	9033	...	21373	268	...	8688	6458	...	15414
c Metal ore mining [a]	...	...	...	...	...	...	...	...	...	...	...	...
d Other mining	67	...	189	-	...	256	82	...	248	2	...	332
3 Manufacturing	3611	...	9309	-3937	...	8983	4834	...	11234	-2123	...	13945
a Manufacture of food, beverages and tobacco	1090	...	4364	1097	...	6551	1458	...	5328	896	...	7682
b Textile, wearing apparel and leather industries	807	...	1862	169	...	2838	1085	...	2475	189	...	3749
c Manufacture of wood and wood products, including furniture	384		560	9		953	560		465	5		1030
d Manufacture of paper and paper products, printing and publishing	282		455	30		767	361		646	43		1050
e Manufacture of chemicals and chemical petroleum, coal, rubber and plastic products	467		670	-5472		-4335	585		766	-3501		-2150
f Manufacture of non-metallic mineral products, except products of petroleum and coal	372	...	967	146	...	1485	526	...	1107	136	...	1769
g Basic metal industries		...			...			...			...	
h Manufacture of fabricated metal products, machinery and equipment	209	...	431	84	...	724	259	...	447	109	...	815
i Other manufacturing industries		...			...			...			...	
4 Electricity, gas and water	381	...	217	49	...	647	525	...	229	55	...	809
5 Construction	2893	...	1201	51	...	4145	4044	...	1857	87	...	5988
6 Wholesale and retail trade, restaurants and hotels	2449	...	10772	181	...	13402	3651	...	13076	222	...	16949
a Wholesale and retail trade	2138	...	9654	121	...	11913	3269	...	11563	139	...	14971
b Restaurants and hotels	311	...	1118	60	...	1489	382	...	1513	83	...	1978
7 Transport, storage and communication	1815	...	2833	35	...	4683	2199	...	3892	78	...	6169
a Transport and storage	1600	...	2607	-5	...	4202	1872	...	3643	39	...	5554
b Communication	215	...	226	40	...	481	327	...	249	39	...	615
8 Finance, insurance, real estate and business services	1411	...	6643	332	...	8386	1898	...	8921	418	...	11237
a Financial institutions	977	...	1294	82	...	2353	1298	...	1296	94	...	2688
b Insurance		...			...			...			...	
c Real estate and business services	434	...	5349	250	...	6033	600	...	7625	324	...	8549
9 Community, social and personal services	1227	...	2562	58	...	3847	1640	...	2797	72	...	4509
Total, Industries	16310	...	60167	6622	...	83099	21849	...	67016	5820	...	94685
Producers of Government Services	7266	...	...	...	...	7266	9640	...	...	...	...	9640
Other Producers	468	...	...	...	...	468	558	...	...	...	...	558
Total	24044	...	60167	6622	...	90833	32047	...	67016	5820	...	104883
Imputed bank service charge	...	...	-1842	...	...	-1842	...	...	-2063	...	...	-2063
Import duties	...	...	...	3772	...	3772	...	...	...	4920	...	4920
Value added tax	...	...	...	...	...	...	...	...	...	...	...	...
Other adjustments	...	...	...	...	...	...	...	...	...	...	...	...
Total	24044	...	58325	10394	...	92763	32047	...	64953	10740	...	107740

Ecuador

4.6 Cost Components of Value Added, ISIC Divisions

Million Ecuadoran sucres

	1976						1977					
	Compensation of Employees	Capital Consumption	Net Operating Surplus	Indirect Taxes	Less: Subsidies Received	Value Added	Compensation of Employees	Capital Consumption	Net Operating Surplus	Indirect Taxes	Less: Subsidies Received	Value Added
All Producers												
1 Agriculture, hunting, forestry and fishing	3256	...	18882	476	...	22614	3509	...	23657	505	...	27671
a Agriculture and hunting	3110	...	16753	471	...	20334	3354	...	20947	497	...	24798
b Forestry and logging	29	...	1224	11	...	1264	31	...	1649	9	...	1689
c Fishing	117	...	905	-6	...	1016	124	...	1061	-1	...	1184
2 Mining and quarrying	394	...	11487	5928	...	17809	611	...	12235	8802	...	21648
a Coal mining [a]	...	...	...	...	...	...	...	...	...	...	...	...
b Crude petroleum and natural gas production	292	...	11215	5925	...	17432	461	...	11876	8800	...	21137
c Metal ore mining [a]	...	...	...	...	...	...	...	...	...	...	...	...
d Other mining	102	...	272	3	...	377	150	...	359	2	...	511
3 Manufacturing	6069	...	15391	-2119	...	19341	7494	...	21948	-5479	...	23963
a Manufacture of food, beverages and tobacco	1691	...	6933	2106	...	10730	2233	...	10411	1751	...	14395
b Textile, wearing apparel and leather industries	1340	...	3108	206	...	4654	1644	...	4327	243	...	6214
c Manufacture of wood and wood products, including furniture	648	...	645	14	...	1307	720	...	901	12	...	1633
d Manufacture of paper and paper products, printing and publishing	460	...	884	55	...	1399	602	...	964	50	...	1616
e Manufacture of chemicals and chemical petroleum, coal, rubber and plastic products	765	...	1865	-4774	...	-2144	903	...	2856	-7920	...	-4161
f Manufacture of non-metallic mineral products, except products of petroleum and coal	787	...	1260	151	...	2198	869	...	1909	214	...	2992
g Basic metal industries		...			...			...			...	
h Manufacture of fabricated metal products, machinery and equipment	378	...	696	123	...	1197	523	...	580	171	...	1274
i Other manufacturing industries		...			...			...			...	
4 Electricity, gas and water	609	...	331	69	...	1009	723	...	444	103	...	1269
5 Construction	5977	...	2735	110	...	8822	6651	...	3652	99	...	10402
6 Wholesale and retail trade, restaurants and hotels	4523	...	15596	285	...	20404	5663	...	20191	253	...	26107
a Wholesale and retail trade	4044	...	13826	186	...	18056	5112	...	17801	143	...	23056
b Restaurants and hotels	479	...	1770	99	...	2348	551	...	2390	110	...	3051
7 Transport, storage and communication	2781	...	5386	93	...	8260	3039	...	7354	209	...	10602
a Transport and storage	2340	...	5174	38	...	7552	2540	...	7066	129	...	9735
b Communication	441	...	212	55	...	708	499	...	288	80	...	867
8 Finance, insurance, real estate and business services	2359	...	11123	491	...	13973	3003	...	14836	555	...	18394
a Financial institutions	1603	...	1698	133	...	3434	2147	...	2265	165	...	4577
b Insurance		...			...			...			...	
c Real estate and business services	756	...	9425	358	...	10539	856	...	12571	390	...	13817
9 Community, social and personal services	2158	...	3399	77	...	5634	2384	...	4824	93	...	7301
Total, Industries	28126	...	84330	5410	...	117866	33076	...	109141	5140	...	147357
Producers of Government Services	11794	...	...	...	...	11794	13631	...	...	...	...	13631
Other Producers	715	...	...	...	...	715	743	...	...	...	...	743
Total	40635	...	84330	5410	...	130375	47450	...	109141	5140	...	161731
Imputed bank service charge	...	...	-2603	...	...	-2603	...	...	-3642	...	...	-3642
Import duties	...	...	...	5141	...	5141	...	...	...	8287	...	8287
Value added tax	...	...	...	...	...	...	...	...	...	...	...	...
Other adjustments	...	...	...	...	...	...	...	...	...	...	...	...
Total	40635	...	81727	10551	...	132913	47450	...	105499	13427	...	166376

Ecuador

4.6 Cost Components of Value Added, ISIC Divisions

Million Ecuadoran sucres

	1978						1979					
	Compensation of Employees	Capital Consumption	Net Operating Surplus	Indirect Taxes	Less: Subsidies Received	Value Added	Compensation of Employees	Capital Consumption	Net Operating Surplus	Indirect Taxes	Less: Subsidies Received	Value Added
All Producers												
1 Agriculture, hunting, forestry and fishing	3744	...	24246	509	...	28499	5800	...	25408	429	...	31637
a Agriculture and hunting	3580	...	21224	495	...	25299	5580	...	21830	431	...	27841
b Forestry and logging	33	...	1875	10	...	1918	43	...	2176	12	...	2231
c Fishing	131	...	1147	4	...	1282	177	...	1402	-14	...	1565
2 Mining and quarrying	894	...	8538	7865	...	17297	1129	...	20224	19623	...	40976
a Coal mining [a]	...	...	...	...	...	...	...	...	...	...	...	...
b Crude petroleum and natural gas production	726	...	8109	7863	...	16698	939	...	19682	19621	...	40242
c Metal ore mining [a]	...	...	...	...	...	...	...	...	...	...	...	...
d Other mining	168	...	429	2	...	599	190	...	542	2	...	734
3 Manufacturing	8642	...	26722	-2670	...	32694	9971	...	34418	-13383	...	31006
a Manufacture of food, beverages and tobacco	2603	...	12247	3006	...	17856	2957	...	15494	3569	...	22020
b Textile, wearing apparel and leather industries	1774	...	4839	292	...	6905	1985	...	5541	319	...	7845
c Manufacture of wood and wood products, including furniture	802	...	1013	3	...	1818	917	...	1509	-1	...	2425
d Manufacture of paper and paper products, printing and publishing	677	...	1133	61	...	1871	804	...	1408	70	...	2282
e Manufacture of chemicals and chemical petroleum, coal, rubber and plastic products	1101	...	4104	-6523	...	-1318	1309	...	5849	-17922	...	-10764
f Manufacture of non-metallic mineral products, except products of petroleum and coal	1058	...	2628	294	...	3980	1247	...	3746	325	...	5318
g Basic metal industries					...							
h Manufacture of fabricated metal products, machinery and equipment	627	...	758	197	...	1582	602	...	134	226	...	962
i Other manufacturing industries		...			...		150	...	737	31	...	918
4 Electricity, gas and water	949	...	420	122	...	1491	1250	...	388	130	...	1768
5 Construction	7412	...	7068	111	...	14591	8096	...	8078	126	...	16300
6 Wholesale and retail trade, restaurants and hotels	6778	...	22370	267	...	29415	8109	...	25097	343	...	33549
a Wholesale and retail trade	6102	...	19126	166	...	25394	7301	...	21159	242	...	28702
b Restaurants and hotels	676	...	3244	101	...	4021	808	...	3938	101	...	4847
7 Transport, storage and communication	3326	...	11831	406	...	15563	3849	...	16541	486	...	20876
a Transport and storage	2794	...	11252	304	...	14350	3229	...	15905	390	...	19524
b Communication	532	...	579	102	...	1213	620	...	636	96	...	1352
8 Finance, insurance, real estate and business services	3767	...	17602	713	...	22082	5031	...	20400	886	...	26317
a Financial institutions	2803	...	3082	183	...	6068	3676	...	3472	272	...	7420
b Insurance		...			...			...			...	
c Real estate and business services	964	...	14520	530	...	16014	1355	...	16928	614	...	18897
9 Community, social and personal services	2670	...	6592	77	...	9339	3169	...	8101	92	...	11362
Total, Industries	38182	...	125389	7400	...	170971	46404	...	158655	8732	...	213791
Producers of Government Services	15348	...	...	...	...	15348	17388	...	...	...	...	17388
Other Producers	801	...	...	...	...	801	963	...	...	...	...	963
Total	54331	...	125389	7400	...	187120	64755	...	158655	8732	...	232142
Imputed bank service charge	...	...	-4856	...	...	-4856	...	...	-5927	...	...	-5927
Import duties	...	...	...	9081	...	9081	...	...	...	9685	...	9685
Value added tax	...	...	...	...	...	...	...	...	...	...	...	...
Other adjustments	...	...	...	...	...	...	...	...	...	...	...	...
Total	54331	...	120533	16481	...	191345	64755	...	152728	18417	...	235900

Ecuador

4.6 Cost Components of Value Added, ISIC Divisions

Million Ecuadoran sucres

1980

All Producers

	Compensation of Employees	Capital Consumption	Net Operating Surplus	Indirect Taxes	Less: Subsidies Received	Value Added
1 Agriculture, hunting, forestry and fishing	7955	...	26412	456	...	34823
a Agriculture and hunting	7654	...	21732	434	...	29820
b Forestry and logging	60	...	2507	15	...	2582
c Fishing	241	...	2173	7	...	2421
2 Mining and quarrying	1639	...	23766	33375	...	58780
a Coal mining [a]	...	...	...	...	...	...
b Crude petroleum and natural gas production	1361	...	23050	33369	...	57780
c Metal ore mining [a]	...	...	...	...	...	...
d Other mining	278	...	716	6	...	1000
3 Manufacturing	14753	...	36604	-26260	...	25097
a Manufacture of food, beverages and tobacco	4395	...	16652	2631	...	23678
b Textile, wearing apparel and leather industries	2978	...	5241	451	...	8670
c Manufacture of wood and wood products, including furniture	1375	...	1550	4	...	2929
d Manufacture of paper and paper products, printing and publishing	1206	...	1457	89	...	2752
e Manufacture of chemicals and chemical petroleum, coal, rubber and plastic products	1925	...	7223	-30218	...	-21070
f Manufacture of non-metallic mineral products, except products of petroleum and coal	1866	...	3602	430	...	5898
g Basic metal industries		...			...	
h Manufacture of fabricated metal products, machinery and equipment	783	...	115	305	...	1203
i Other manufacturing industries	225	...	764	48	...	1037
4 Electricity, gas and water	1875	...	566	178	...	2619
5 Construction	12144	...	8330	138	...	20612
6 Wholesale and retail trade, restaurants and hotels	12160	...	26834	335	...	39329
a Wholesale and retail trade	10951	...	22345	194	...	33490
b Restaurants and hotels	1209	...	4489	141	...	5839
7 Transport, storage and communication	5678	...	19880	391	...	25949
a Transport and storage	4682	...	19316	267	...	24265
b Communication	996	...	564	124	...	1684
8 Finance, insurance, real estate and business services	6082	...	24945	1015	...	32042
a Financial institutions	4117	...	4126	280	...	8523
b Insurance		...			...	
c Real estate and business services	1965	...	20819	735	...	23519
9 Community, social and personal services	4754	...	8627	112	...	13493
Total, Industries	67040	...	175964	9740	...	252744
Producers of Government Services	24568	...	...	...	...	24568
Other Producers	1449	...	...	...	...	1449
Total	93057	...	175964	9740	...	278761
Imputed bank service charge	...	...	-6696	...	...	-6696
Import duties	...	...	...	12133	...	12133
Value added tax	...	...	...	...	...	...
Other adjustments	...	...	...	...	...	...
Total	93057	...	169268	21873	...	284198

a) Item 'Coal mining' is included in item 'Metal ore mining'.

Egypt

General note. The preparation of national accounts statistics in Egypt is undertaken by the Central Agency for Public Mobilisation and Statistics (CAPMAS), Cairo. Official estimates are published in the annual 'Statistical Yearbook' published by the same agency. The estimates are generally in accordance with the classifications and definitions recommended in the United Nations System of National Accounts (SNA). An input-output table for the year 1966-67 has been completed by CAPMAS. The following tables have been prepared from successive replies to the United Nations national accounts questionnaire. Estimates up to the year 1971 relate to fiscal year beginning 1 July. When the scope and coverage of the estimates differ for conceptual or statistical reasons from the definitions and classifications recommended in SNA, a footnote is indicated to the relevant tables.

Sources and methods:

(a) Gross domestic product. Gross domestic product is estimated mainly through the production approach.

(b) Expenditure on the gross domestic product. All components of GDP by expenditure type are estimated through the expenditure approach. The estimates of government final consumption expenditure are based on government budgets and accounts. For private consumption expenditures, the estimates are based on family budgets and household expenditure surveys. The Department of Statistics prepares data on inventories of cotton, covering both commercial stocks and stocks of spinning industry. Other sources of information for changes in stocks include data collected regularly by the Ministry of Supply. For gross fixed capital formation, the government sector is estimated directly together with government consumption expenditure. The private sector estimate is obtained by deducting the government estimate from total capital formation. Capital formation in machinery and equipment is estimated through the commodity-flow approach using information on domestic production, imports and exports of capital goods. The estimates of exports and imports of merchandise are generally based on foreign trade statistics. The estimates of GDP by expenditure type in constant prices are prepared by the CAPMAS on the basis of official index numbers of prices and quantities.

(c) Cost-structure of the gross domestic product. The estimates of wages and salaries are based on government accounts and on various sectoral surveys. No specific information is available for operating surplus, which is computed as a gross estimate, i.e., including consumption of fixed capital. Indirect taxes and subsidies are seperately available for all economic units in the compulsory standard accounts for public enterprises and in the economic surveys for the private sector.

(d) Gross domestic product by kind of economic activity. The table of gross domestic product by kind of economic activity is prepared in factor values. The production approach is used to estimate value added of most industries. The income approach is used to estimate value added of community, social and personal services. The Ministry of Agriculture collects, through annual sample surveys, data on crop area, yield and crop-cutting. Livestock data are obtained through special censuses every two years and prices received by farmers are collected annually. The estimated acreage of each of the main crops is multiplied by average productivity of the basic area of measurement. The gross output is evaluated at farm-gate prices and estimates of intermediate consumption are based on data collected from the co-operative societies and from censuses. For the industrial activity sector, annual statistics on industrial production, capital formation, employment, wages and salaries are available for industrial establishments with ten workers or more which form the organized sector of the economy. For the non-organized sector, estimates are made by using data from industrial censuses and by studying the cost-structure of each industry, productivity and degree of mechanization. The output of construction is estimated indirectly from the input side by means of employment data and data on intermediate consumption. The value of gross output and components of value added are obtained by using the relationship between available data on intermediate consumption and primary inputs in organized enterprises and applying this relationship on the estimated intermediate consumption of this industry. For trade, annual basic statistics are available for establishments with five or more workers, while those with less than five workers are covered by sample surveys conducted every three years. Estimates for restaurants are made by using data on establishments, wages and salaries, working hours and data from sample surveys. Estimates for hotels are obtained through annual questionnaires. Data on input, output and other elements of large-scale transport are available through annual accounts. For unorganized transport, estimates are based on information on the number of establishments and workers, on wages and salaries and on other sources. Indicators such as input-ratios are used to estimate value added. Gross output and input of public financial institutions and insurance companies are based on data collected annually. The estimates of real estate, business services, and imputed rents of owner-occupied dwellings are based on family budget surveys. The government accounts provide information to estimate government services. Annual data are available for non-profit institutions serving households. For the service activities of unincorporated enterprises, gross output and inputs are estimated by using available censuses of establishments, wages and salaries statistics. The constant prices of GDP by kind of economic activity are estimated by CAPMAS on the basis of official index numbers of prices and quantities such as wholesale prices, consumer prices and quantities of imported and exported merchandise.

1.1 Expenditure on the Gross Domestic Product, in Current Prices

Million Egyptian pounds

		1970	1971	1972	1973	1974	1975	1976	1977	1978	1979	1980
1	General government final consumption expenditure	794.2	883.1	... 905.0	974.5	1117.3	1344.1	1505.7	1696.8	1840.6	2058.7	...
2	Private final consumption expenditure	2065.8	2207.6	... 2237.0	2482.8	2839.7	3100.9	4030.8	4916.9	6278.5	8622.8	...
3	Gross capital formation	437.0	420.4	... 467.0	698.7	970.1	1723.8	1888.9	2398.8	3033.9	3795.6	...
	a Increase in stocks	82.0	50.0	... 62.0	235.2	290.0	458.5	438.8	560.5	416.1	450.0	...
	b Gross fixed capital formation	355.0	370.4	... 405.0	463.5	680.1	1265.3	1450.1	1838.3	2617.8	3345.6	...
	Residential buildings	...	...	...	...	...	...	...	...	...	...	...
	Non-residential buildings a	162.2	202.5	... 188.5	238.9	350.4	652.1	748.5	975.6	1361.2	1705.1	...
	Other construction and land improvement etc. a											...
	Other	192.8	167.9	... 216.5	224.6	329.7	613.2	701.6	862.7	1256.6	1640.5	...
4	Exports of goods and services	442.1	451.9	... 457.0	541.0	905.0	964.1	1151.0	1772.5	1945.0	3251.6	...
5	Less: Imports of goods and services	599.9	624.6	... 649.0	725.9	1390.2	1886.3	1871.8	2575.1	3315.5	5254.1	...
	Statistical discrepancy	6.3	-1.7	...	-	-	-	-	-	-0.1	-	...
	Equals: Gross Domestic Product b	3145.5	3336.7	... 3417.0	3971.1	4441.9	5246.6	6704.6	8209.9	9782.4	12474.6	...

a) Including item 'Residential buildings'.
b) For 1960-1971, fiscal year beginning 1 July.

Egypt

1.2 Expenditure on the Gross Domestic Product, in Constant Prices

Million Egyptian pounds

	1970	1971	1972	1973	1974	1975	1976	1977	1978	1979	1980
				At constant prices of:							
			1969			1975					
1 General government final consumption expenditure	782.3	865.4	...	1026.3	1201.2	1344.1	1286.3	1362.4	1312.6	1335.3	...
2 Private final consumption expenditure	1999.4	2078.6	...	2897.9	3026.0	3100.9	3225.3	3271.1	3524.9	3750.5	...
3 Gross capital formation	428.4	400.3	...	920.4	1075.6	1723.8	1691.8	1872.0	2272.0	2580.7	...
a Increase in stocks	78.5	47.6	...	286.2	307.1	458.5	397.9	460.5	292.8	245.0	...
b Gross fixed capital formation	349.9	352.7	...	634.2	768.5	1265.3	1293.9	1411.5	1979.2	2335.7	...
4 Exports of goods and services	451.5	447.8	...	858.3	888.8	964.1	1083.5	1523.9	1564.8	1731.0	...
5 Less: Imports of goods and services	555.3	557.7	...	1312.2	1577.5	1886.3	1631.8	1927.0	1954.3	2094.7	...
Statistical discrepancy	9.3	1.3	...	...	...	...	...	...	...	...	...
Equals: Gross Domestic Product [a]	3115.6	3235.7	...	4390.7	4614.1	5246.6	5655.1	6102.4	6720.0	7302.8	...

a) For 1960-1971, fiscal year beginning 1 July.

1.3 Cost Components of the Gross Domestic Product

Million Egyptian pounds

	1970	1971	1972	1973	1974	1975	1976	1977	1978	1979	1980
1 Indirect taxes, net	445.0	452.7	460.0	445.0	242.3	185.3	540.4	810.0	774.3	538.1	...
2 Consumption of fixed capital	...	...	...	...	...	...	...	...	...	...	...
3 Compensation of employees paid by resident producers to:	1337.6	1414.7	1460.0	1696.9	1887.7	2401.2	2583.3	2828.0	3222.6	3596.1	...
4 Net operating surplus [a]	1362.9	1469.3	1497.0	1829.2	2311.9	2660.1	3580.9	4571.9	5785.5	8340.4	...
Equals: Gross Domestic Product [b]	3145.5	3336.7	3417.0	3971.1	4441.9	5246.6	6704.6	8209.9	9782.4	12474.6	...

a) Including consumption of fixed capital.
b) For 1960-1971, fiscal year beginning 1 July.

1.7 External Transactions on Current Account, Summary

Million Egyptian pounds

	1970	1971	1972	1973	1974	1975	1976	1977	1978	1979	1980
			Payments to the Rest of the World								
1 Imports of goods and services	599.9	624.6	649.0	725.9	1390.2	1886.3	1871.8	2575.1	3315.5	5254.1	...
a Imports of merchandise c.i.f.	599.9	624.6	649.0	725.9	1390.2	1886.3	1871.8	2575.1	3315.5	5254.1	...
b Other	...	...	...	...	...	...	...	...	...	...	...
2 Factor income paid to the rest of the world	69.6	72.3	58.3	67.8	129.6	161.9	166.6	213.9	266.5	699.6	...
a Compensation of employees [a]	...	...	...	...	...	...	...	...	...	...	...
b Property and entrepreneurial income paid [a]	69.6	72.3	58.3	67.8	129.6	161.9	166.6	213.9	266.5	699.6	...
3 Indirect taxes paid to supranational organizations	...	...	...	...	...	...	...	...	...	...	...
4 Current transfers to the rest of the world	0.3	0.6	1.0	8.4	12.7	22.3	18.0	32.3	22.1	30.2	...
5 Surplus of the nation on current transactions	-94.1	-106.2	-75.0	31.4	-126.0	-524.4	-314.8	-205.8	-226.1	-1072.7	...
Payments to the Rest of the World and Surplus of the Nation on Current Transactions	575.7	591.3	633.3	833.5	1406.5	1546.1	1741.6	2615.5	3378.0	4911.2	...
			Receipts From The Rest of the World								
1 Exports of goods and services	442.1	451.9	457.0	541.0	905.0	964.1	1151.0	1772.5	1945.0	3251.6	...

Egypt

1.7 External Transactions on Current Account, Summary
(Continued)

Million Egyptian pounds

	1970	1971	1972	1973	1974	1975	1976	1977	1978	1979	1980
a Exports of merchandise f.o.b.	381.7	383.8	371.0	541.0	905.0	964.1	1151.0	1772.5	1945.0	3251.6	...
b Other	60.4	68.1	86.0	...	...	...	...	...	...	...	...
2 Factor income received from rest of the world	10.4	10.1	44.3	35.3	77.0	145.8	299.6	647.1	1249.2	1484.2	...
a Compensation of employees [a]	...	...	...	...	...	...	...	...	...	...	...
b Property and entrepreneurial income received [a]	10.4	10.1	44.3	35.3	77.0	145.8	299.6	647.1	1249.2	1484.2	...
3 Subsidies received from supranational organisations	...	...	...	...	...	...	...	...	...	...	...
4 Current transfers from rest of the world	123.2	129.3	132.0	257.2	424.5	436.2	291.0	195.9	183.8	175.4	...
Receipts from the Rest of the World on Current Transactions [b]	575.7	591.3	633.3	833.5	1406.5	1546.1	1741.6	2615.5	3378.0	4911.2	...

a) Item 'Compensation of employees' is included in item 'Property and entrepreneurial income'.
b) For 1960-1971, fiscal year beginning 1 July.

1.8 Capital Transactions of The Nation, Summary

Million Egyptian pounds

	1970	1971	1972	1973	1974	1975	1976	1977	1978	1979	1980
Finance of Gross Capital Formation											
Gross saving	342.9	314.2	392.0	730.1	844.1	1199.4	1574.1	2193.0	2807.7	2722.9	...
Less: Surplus of the nation on current transactions	-94.1	-106.2	-75.0	31.4	-126.0	-524.4	-314.8	-205.8	-226.1	-1072.7	...
Finance of Gross Capital Formation	437.0	420.4	467.0	698.7	970.1	1723.8	1888.9	2398.8	3033.9	3795.6	...
Gross Capital Formation											
Increase in stocks	82.0	50.0	62.0	235.2	290.0	458.5	438.8	560.5	416.1	450.0	...
Gross fixed capital formation	355.0	370.4	405.0	463.5	680.1	1265.3	1450.1	1838.3	2617.8	3345.6	...
Gross Capital Formation [a]	437.0	420.4	467.0	698.7	970.1	1723.8	1888.9	2398.8	3033.9	3795.6	...

a) For 1960-1971, fiscal year beginning 1 July.

1.10 Gross Domestic Product by Kind of Activity, in Current Prices

Million Egyptian pounds

	1970	1971	1972	1973	1974	1975	1976	1977	1978	1979	1980
1 Agriculture, hunting, forestry and fishing	774.1	854.6	933.6	1062.2	1279.6	1468.1	1744.2	2037.6	2285.8	2687.6	...
2 Mining and quarrying	52.7	45.2	32.8	47.3	111.0	149.0	246.9	467.8	626.1	1907.7	...
3 Manufacturing	558.5	591.3	556.5	640.3	746.2	887.6	993.1	1119.6	1318.9	1478.4	...
4 Electricity, gas and water	40.0	47.8	45.8	44.3	48.0	69.2	75.0	83.1	98.0	102.3	...
5 Construction	121.4	117.3	121.2	87.3	128.7	242.5	279.0	357.5	509.1	651.0	...
6 Wholesale and retail trade, restaurants and hotels [a]	239.5	263.1	280.0	487.3	634.1	777.3	959.3	1188.2	1544.0	1953.8	...
7 Transport, storage and communication	143.6	147.8	154.5	165.7	179.1	258.4	400.6	490.8	688.8	894.9	...
8 Finance, insurance, real estate and business services [a]	120.2	121.1	121.6	196.0	202.8	208.7	222.1	243.5	261.8	287.0	...
9 Community, social and personal services [b]	650.5	695.8	711.0	795.7	870.1	1000.5	1244.0	1411.8	1675.6	1973.8	...
Total, Industries	...	...	...	...	...	...	...	...	...	...	...
Producers of Government Services [b]	...	...	...	...	...	...	...	...	...	...	...

Egypt

1.10 Gross Domestic Product by Kind of Activity, in Current Prices
(Continued)

Million Egyptian pounds

	1970	1971	1972	1973	1974	1975	1976	1977	1978	1979	1980
Other Producers [b]	...	...	...	...	...	...	...	...	...	...	...
Subtotal [c]	2700.5	2884.0	2957.0	3526.1	4199.6	5061.3	6164.2	7399.9	9008.1	11936.5	...
Less: Imputed bank service charge	...	...	...	...	...	...	...	...	...	...	...
Plus: Import duties	...	...	...	...	...	...	...	...	...	...	...
Plus: Value added tax	...	...	...	...	...	...	...	...	...	...	...
Plus: Other adjustments [d]	445.0	452.7	460.0	445.0	242.3	185.3	540.4	810.0	774.3	538.1	...
Equals: Gross Domestic Product [e]	3145.5	3336.7	3417.0	3971.1	4441.9	5246.6	6704.6	8209.9	9782.4	12474.6	...

a) Prior to 1973, finance and insurance are included in item 'Wholesale and retail trade, restaurants and hotels'.
b) Items 'Other producers' and 'Producers of government services' are included in item 'Community, social and personal services'.
c) Gross domestic product in factor values.
d) Referring to indirect taxes net of subsidies.
e) For 1960-1971, fiscal year beginning 1 July.

1.11 Gross Domestic Product by Kind of Activity, in Constant Prices

Million Egyptian pounds

	1970	1971	1972	1973	1974	1975	1976	1977	1978	1979	1980
	At constant prices of:										
		1969				1975					
1 Agriculture, hunting, forestry and fishing	761.5	791.6	...	1339.0	1417.2	1468.1	1490.9	1447.2	1528.0	1587.4	...
2 Mining and quarrying	53.2	42.7	...	117.2	72.6	149.0	265.4	350.1	426.8	470.6	...
3 Manufacturing	547.0	573.2	...	775.1	810.4	887.6	947.9	1012.4	1067.8	1179.6	...
4 Electricity, gas and water	44.6	49.0	...	39.4	48.1	69.2	76.7	86.0	102.9	107.5	...
5 Construction	115.2	117.3	...	120.8	146.0	242.5	233.1	263.1	336.1	346.7	...
6 Wholesale and retail trade, restaurants and hotels [a]	237.5	253.1	...	628.4	669.2	720.1	788.8	823.8	905.2	978.6	...
7 Transport, storage and communication	145.0	148.5	...	169.4	186.4	258.4	391.4	459.5	533.5	619.8	...
8 Finance, insurance, real estate and business services [a]	120.1	121.0	...	303.5	331.1	360.0	384.4	445.4	537.1	605.4	...
9 Community, social and personal services [b]	646.5	686.6	...	849.4	872.0	906.4	942.2	1019.5	1094.2	1169.3	...
Total, Industries	...	...	...	...	...	...	...	...	...	...	...
Producers of Government Services [b]	...	...	...	...	...	...	...	...	...	...	...
Other Producers [b]	...	...	...	...	...	...	...	...	...	...	...
Subtotal [c]	2670.6	2783.0	...	4342.2	4553.0	5061.3	5520.8	5907.0	6531.6	7064.9	...
Less: Imputed bank service charge	...	...	...	...	...	...	...	...	...	...	...
Plus: Import duties	...	...	...	...	...	...	...	...	...	...	...
Plus: Value added tax	...	...	...	...	...	...	...	...	...	...	...
Plus: Other adjustments [d]	445.0	452.7	...	48.5	61.1	185.3	134.3	195.4	188.4	237.9	...
Equals: Gross Domestic Product [e]	3115.6	3235.7	...	4390.7	4614.1	5246.6	5655.1	6102.4	6720.0	7302.8	...

a) Prior to 1973, finance and insurance are included in item 'Wholesale and retail trade, restaurants and hotels'.
b) Items 'Other producers' and 'Producers of government services' are included in item 'Community, social and personal services'.
c) Gross domestic product in factor values.
d) Referring to indirect taxes net of subsidies.
e) For 1960-1971, fiscal year beginning 1 July.

Egypt

1.12 Relations Among National Accounting Aggregates

Million Egyptian pounds

	1970	1971	1972	1973	1974	1975	1976	1977	1978	1979	1980
Gross Domestic Product [a]	3145.5	3336.7	3417.0	3971.1	4441.9	5246.6	6704.6	8209.9	9782.4	12474.6	...
Plus: Net factor income received from abroad	-59.2	-62.2	-14.0	-32.5	-52.6	-16.1	133.0	433.2	982.7	784.6	...
Factor income received	10.4	10.1	44.3	35.3	77.0	145.8	299.6	647.1	1249.2	1484.2	...
Less: Factor income paid	69.6	72.3	58.3	67.8	129.6	161.9	166.6	213.9	266.5	699.6	...
Equals: Gross National Product [a]	3086.3	3274.5	3403.0	3938.5	4389.3	5230.5	6837.6	8643.1	10765.1	13259.2	...
Less: Consumption of fixed capital	...	...	...	...	...	...	...	...	...	...	...
Less: Net indirect taxes paid to supranational organisations	...	...	...	...	...	...	...	...	...	...	...
Equals: National Income at Market Prices [b]	3086.3	3274.5	3403.0	3938.5	4389.3	5230.5	6837.6	8643.1	10765.1	13259.2	...
Plus: Net current transfers received from abroad	122.9	128.7	131.0	248.8	411.8	413.9	273.0	163.6	161.7	145.2	...
Current transfers received	123.2	129.3	132.0	257.2	424.5	436.2	291.0	195.9	183.8	175.4	...
Less: Current transfers paid	0.3	0.6	1.0	8.4	12.7	22.3	18.0	32.3	22.1	30.2	...
Equals: National Disposable Income at Market Prices [a]	3209.2	3403.2	3534.0	4187.4	4801.1	5644.4	7110.6	8806.7	10926.8	13404.4	...
Less: Final consumption	2860.0	3090.7	3142.0	3457.3	3957.0	4445.0	5536.5	6613.7	8119.1	10681.5	...
Statistical discrepancy	-6.3	1.7	...	...	...	...	...	...	...	...	...
Equals: Net Saving [b]	342.9	314.2	392.0	730.1	844.1	1199.4	1574.1	2193.0	2807.7	2722.9	...
Less: Surplus of the nation on current transactions	-94.1	-106.2	-75.0	31.4	-126.0	-524.4	-314.8	-205.8	-226.1	-1072.7	...
Equals: Net Capital Formation [a]	437.0	420.4	467.0	698.7	970.1	1723.8	1888.9	2398.8	3033.8	3795.6	...

a) For 1960-1971, fiscal year beginning 1 July.
b) Including consumption of fixed capital.

2.9 Gross Capital Formation by Kind of Activity of Owner, ISIC Major Divisions, in Current Prices

Million Egyptian pounds

	1972 TGCF	1972 IS	1972 GFCF	1973 TGCF	1973 IS	1973 GFCF	1974 TGCF	1974 IS	1974 GFCF	1975 TGCF	1975 IS	1975 GFCF
All Producers												
1 Agriculture, hunting, fishing and forestry	...	...	55.1	...	...	57.6	...	...	54.2	...	...	94.6
2 Mining and quarrying	...	...	24.7	...	...	28.3	...	...	73.6	...	...	121.9
3 Manufacturing	...	...	128.2	...	...	126.0	...	...	193.2	...	...	286.8
4 Electricity, gas and water	...	...	25.8	...	...	30.3	...	...	30.0	...	...	53.3
5 Construction	...	...	5.5	...	...	5.0	...	...	10.6	...	...	30.6
6 Wholesale and retail trade, restaurants and hotels [a]	...	...	2.9	...	...	3.2	...	...	7.7	...	...	15.7
7 Transport, storage and communication	...	...	75.6	...	...	123.0	...	...	190.0	...	...	383.5
8 Finance, insurance, real estate and business services [a]	...	...	37.1	...	...	38.1	...	...	47.9	...	...	159.8
9 Community, social and personal services	...	...	50.1	...	...	52.0	...	...	72.9	...	...	119.1
Total Industries	...	...	405.0	...	...	463.5	...	...	680.1	...	...	1265.3
Producers of Government Services	...	...	...	...	...	...	...	...	...	...	...	...
Private Non-Profit Institutions Serving Households	...	...	...	...	...	...	...	...	...	...	...	...
Total [b]	467.0	62.0	405.0	698.7	235.2	463.5	970.1	290.0	680.1	1723.8	458.5	1265.3

	1976 TGCF	1976 IS	1976 GFCF	1977 TGCF	1977 IS	1977 GFCF	1978 TGCF	1978 IS	1978 GFCF	1979 TGCF	1979 IS	1979 GFCF
All Producers												
1 Agriculture, hunting, fishing and forestry	...	...	98.5	...	...	146.4	...	...	191.3	...	...	268.0
2 Mining and quarrying	...	...	185.9	...	...	205.7	...	...	201.0	...	...	450.0
3 Manufacturing	...	...	378.7	...	...	561.0	...	...	765.0	...	...	817.2
4 Electricity, gas and water	...	...	59.4	...	...	109.0	...	...	202.7	...	...	229.0

Egypt

2.9 Gross Capital Formation by Kind of Activity of Owner, ISIC Major Divisions, in Current Prices
(Continued)

Million Egyptian pounds

	1976 Total Gross Capital Formation	1976 Increase in Stocks	1976 Gross Fixed Capital Formation	1977 Total Gross Capital Formation	1977 Increase in Stocks	1977 Gross Fixed Capital Formation	1978 Total Gross Capital Formation	1978 Increase in Stocks	1978 Gross Fixed Capital Formation	1979 Total Gross Capital Formation	1979 Increase in Stocks	1979 Gross Fixed Capital Formation
5 Construction	...	...	80.3	...	...	48.4	...	...	132.3	...	...	76.0
6 Wholesale and retail trade, restaurants and hotels [a]	...	...	25.9	...	...	29.8	...	...	36.8	...	...	70.0
7 Transport, storage and communication	...	...	372.9	...	...	443.3	...	...	691.8	...	...	882.4
8 Finance, insurance, real estate and business services [a]	...	...	106.8	...	...	90.5	...	...	89.4	...	...	86.0
9 Community, social and personal services	...	...	141.7	...	...	204.2	...	...	307.5	...	...	467.0
Total Industries	...	...	1450.1	...	...	1838.3	...	...	2617.8	...	...	3345.6
Producers of Government Services	...	...	...	...	...	...	...	...	...	...	...	...
Private Non-Profit Institutions Serving Households	...	...	...	...	...	...	...	...	...	...	...	...
Total [b]	1888.9	438.8	1450.1	2398.8	560.5	1838.3	3033.9	416.1	2617.8	3795.6	450.0	3345.6

a) Prior to 1973, finance and insurance are included in item 'Wholesale and retail trade, restaurants and hotels'.
b) For 1960-1971, fiscal year beginning 1 July.

2.17 Exports and Imports of Goods and Services, Detail

Million Egyptian pounds

	1970	1971	1972	1973	1974	1975	1976	1977	1978	1979	1980
Exports of Goods and Services											
1 Exports of merchandise, f.o.b.	381.7	383.8	371.0	541.0	905.0	964.1	1151.0	1772.5	1945.0	3251.6	...
2 Transport and communication	60.4	68.1	86.0	...	...	...	...	...	...	...	...
3 Insurance service charges	...	...	...	...	...	...	...	...	...	...	...
4 Other commodities	...	...	...	...	...	...	...	...	...	...	...
5 Adjustments of merchandise exports to change-of-ownership basis	...	...	...	...	...	...	...	...	...	...	...
6 Direct purchases in the domestic market by non-residential households	...	...	...	...	...	...	...	...	...	...	...
7 Direct purchases in the domestic market by extraterritorial bodies	...	...	...	...	...	...	...	...	...	...	...
Total Exports of Goods and Services	442.1	451.9	457.0	541.0	905.0	964.1	1151.0	1772.5	1945.0	3251.6	...
Imports of Goods and Services											
1 Imports of merchandise, c.i.f.	599.9	624.6	649.0	725.9	1390.2	1886.3	1871.8	2575.1	3315.5	5254.1	...
2 Adjustments of merchandise imports to change-of-ownership basis	...	...	...	...	...	...	...	...	...	...	...
3 Other transport and communication	...	...	...	...	...	...	...	...	...	...	...
4 Other insurance service charges	...	...	...	...	...	...	...	...	...	...	...
5 Other commodities	...	...	...	...	...	...	...	...	...	...	...
6 Direct purchases abroad by government	...	...	...	...	...	...	...	...	...	...	...
7 Direct purchases abroad by resident households	...	...	...	...	...	...	...	...	...	...	...
Total Imports of Goods and Services	599.9	624.6	649.0	725.9	1390.2	1886.3	1871.8	2575.1	3315.5	5254.1	...
Balance of Goods and Services	-157.8	-172.7	-192.0	-184.9	-485.2	-922.2	-720.8	-802.6	-1370.5	-2002.5	...
Total Imports and Balance of Goods and Services	442.1	451.9	457.0	541.0	905.0	964.1	1151.0	1772.5	1945.0	3251.6	...

Egypt

4.6 Cost Components of Value Added, ISIC Divisions

Million Egyptian pounds

1972 / 1973

	Compensation of Employees	Capital Consumption	Net Operating Surplus	Indirect Taxes	Less: Subsidies Received	Value Added	Compensation of Employees	Capital Consumption	Net Operating Surplus	Indirect Taxes	Less: Subsidies Received	Value Added
					All Producers							
1 Agriculture, hunting, forestry and fishing	236.9	...	696.7	...	...	933.6	252.1	...	810.1	...	...	1062.2
2 Mining and quarrying	10.2	...	22.6	...	...	32.8	10.5	...	36.8	...	...	47.3
3 Manufacturing	269.2	...	287.3	...	...	556.5	380.6	...	259.7	...	...	640.3
4 Electricity, gas and water	10.2	...	35.6	...	...	45.8	11.4	...	32.9	...	...	44.3
5 Construction	69.2	...	52.0	...	...	121.2	75.6	...	11.7	...	...	87.3
6 Wholesale and retail trade, restaurants and hotels [a]	150.9	...	129.1	...	...	280.0	164.3	...	323.0	...	...	487.3
7 Transport, storage and communication	102.8	...	51.7	...	...	154.5	136.9	...	28.8	...	...	165.7
8 Finance, insurance, real estate and business services [a]	...	...	...	...	...	121.6	10.9	...	185.1	...	...	196.0
9 Community, social and personal services [b]	610.0	...	222.6	...	...	711.0	654.6	...	141.1	...	...	795.7
Total, Industries [c]	1459.4	...	1497.6	...	...	2957.0	1696.9	...	1829.2	...	...	3526.1
Producers of Government Services [b]	...	...	...	...	...	...	...	...	...	...	...	...
Other Producers [b]	...	...	...	...	...	...	...	...	...	...	...	...
Total [dce]	1459.4	...	1497.6	...	...	2957.0	1696.9	...	1829.2	...	...	3526.1
Imputed bank service charge	...	...	...	...	...	...	...	...	...	...	...	...
Import duties	...	...	...	...	...	...	...	...	...	...	...	...
Value added tax	...	...	...	...	...	...	...	...	...	...	...	...
Other adjustments [f]	...	...	...	...	...	460.0	...	...	...	...	...	445.0
Total [c]	...	...	...	...	...	3417.0	...	...	...	...	...	3971.1

1974 / 1975

	Compensation of Employees	Capital Consumption	Net Operating Surplus	Indirect Taxes	Less: Subsidies Received	Value Added	Compensation of Employees	Capital Consumption	Net Operating Surplus	Indirect Taxes	Less: Subsidies Received	Value Added
					All Producers							
1 Agriculture, hunting, forestry and fishing	303.4	...	976.2	...	...	1279.6	449.1	...	1019.0	...	...	1468.1
2 Mining and quarrying	10.9	...	100.1	...	...	111.0	13.6	...	135.4	...	...	149.0
3 Manufacturing	409.9	...	336.3	...	...	746.2	440.4	...	447.2	...	...	887.6
4 Electricity, gas and water	15.5	...	32.5	...	...	48.0	14.7	...	54.5	...	...	69.2
5 Construction	82.2	...	46.5	...	...	128.7	135.0	...	107.5	...	...	242.5
6 Wholesale and retail trade, restaurants and hotels [a]	172.7	...	461.4	...	...	634.1	270.6	...	506.7	...	...	777.3
7 Transport, storage and communication	145.7	...	33.4	...	...	179.1	153.1	...	105.3	...	...	258.4
8 Finance, insurance, real estate and business services [a]	11.1	...	191.7	...	...	202.8	13.5	...	195.2	...	...	208.7
9 Community, social and personal services [b]	736.3	...	133.8	...	...	870.1	911.2	...	89.3	...	...	1000.5
Total, Industries [c]	1887.7	...	2311.9	...	...	4199.6	2401.2	...	2660.1	...	...	5061.3
Producers of Government Services [b]	...	...	...	...	...	...	...	...	...	...	...	...
Other Producers [b]	...	...	...	...	...	...	...	...	...	...	...	...
Total [dce]	1887.7	...	2311.9	...	...	4199.6	2401.2	...	2660.1	...	...	5061.3
Imputed bank service charge	...	...	...	...	...	...	...	...	...	...	...	...
Import duties	...	...	...	...	...	...	...	...	...	...	...	...
Value added tax	...	...	...	...	...	...	...	...	...	...	...	...
Other adjustments [f]	...	...	...	...	...	242.3	...	...	...	...	...	185.3
Total [c]	...	...	...	...	...	4441.9	...	...	...	...	...	5246.6

1976 / 1977

	Compensation of Employees	Capital Consumption	Net Operating Surplus	Indirect Taxes	Less: Subsidies Received	Value Added	Compensation of Employees	Capital Consumption	Net Operating Surplus	Indirect Taxes	Less: Subsidies Received	Value Added
					All Producers							
1 Agriculture, hunting, forestry and fishing	440.1	...	1304.1	...	...	1744.2	483.0	...	1554.6	...	...	2037.6
2 Mining and quarrying	18.9	...	228.0	...	...	246.9	24.9	...	442.9	...	...	467.8
3 Manufacturing	465.7	...	527.4	...	...	993.1	499.0	...	620.6	...	...	1119.6
4 Electricity, gas and water	17.8	...	57.2	...	...	75.0	21.2	...	61.9	...	...	83.1

Egypt

4.6 Cost Components of Value Added, ISIC Divisions
(Continued)

Million Egyptian pounds

	1976						1977					
	Compensation of Employees	Capital Consumption	Net Operating Surplus	Indirect Taxes	Less: Subsidies Received	Value Added	Compensation of Employees	Capital Consumption	Net Operating Surplus	Indirect Taxes	Less: Subsidies Received	Value Added
5 Construction	152.8	...	126.2	...	...	279.0	153.7	...	203.8	...	...	357.5
6 Wholesale and retail trade, restaurants and hotels [a]	297.7	...	661.6	...	...	959.3	322.7	...	865.5	...	...	1188.2
7 Transport, storage and communication	162.9	...	237.7	...	...	400.6	185.5	...	305.3	...	...	490.8
8 Finance, insurance, real estate and business services [a]	14.5	...	207.6	...	...	222.1	15.2	...	228.3	...	...	243.5
9 Community, social and personal services [b]	1012.9	...	231.1	...	...	1244.0	1122.8	...	289.0	...	...	1411.8
Total, Industries [c]	2583.3	...	3580.9	...	...	6164.2	2828.0	...	4571.9	...	...	7399.9
Producers of Government Services [b]	...	...	...	...	...	...	...	...	...	...	...	...
Other Producers [b]	...	...	...	...	...	...	...	...	...	...	...	...
Total [dce]	2583.3	...	3580.9	...	...	6164.2	2828.0	...	4571.9	...	...	7399.9
Imputed bank service charge	...	...	...	...	...	...	...	...	...	...	...	...
Import duties	...	...	...	...	...	...	...	...	...	...	...	...
Value added tax	...	...	...	...	...	...	...	...	...	...	...	...
Other adjustments [f]	...	...	...	...	...	540.4	...	...	...	...	...	810.0
Total [c]	...	...	...	...	...	6704.6	...	...	...	...	...	8209.9

	1978						1979					
	Compensation of Employees	Capital Consumption	Net Operating Surplus	Indirect Taxes	Less: Subsidies Received	Value Added	Compensation of Employees	Capital Consumption	Net Operating Surplus	Indirect Taxes	Less: Subsidies Received	Value Added

All Producers

1 Agriculture, hunting, forestry and fishing	530.9	...	1754.9	...	...	2285.8	588.0	...	2099.6	...	...	2687.6
2 Mining and quarrying	30.3	...	595.8	...	...	626.1	34.6	...	1873.1	...	...	1907.7
3 Manufacturing	579.2	...	739.7	...	...	1318.9	626.4	...	852.0	...	...	1478.4
4 Electricity, gas and water	24.7	...	73.3	...	...	98.0	32.1	...	70.2	...	...	102.3
5 Construction	201.0	...	308.1	...	...	509.1	244.4	...	406.6	...	...	651.0
6 Wholesale and retail trade, restaurants and hotels [a]	367.4	...	1176.6	...	...	1544.0	410.5	...	1543.3	...	...	1953.8
7 Transport, storage and communication	212.6	...	476.2	...	...	688.8	239.1	...	655.8	...	...	894.9
8 Finance, insurance, real estate and business services [a]	15.9	...	245.9	...	...	261.8	18.1	...	268.9	...	...	287.0
9 Community, social and personal services [b]	1260.6	...	415.0	...	...	1675.6	1402.9	...	570.9	...	...	1973.8
Total, Industries [c]	3222.6	...	5785.5	...	...	9008.1	3596.1	...	8340.4	...	...	11936.5
Producers of Government Services [b]	...	...	...	...	...	...	...	...	...	...	...	...
Other Producers [b]	...	...	...	...	...	...	...	...	...	...	...	...
Total [dce]	3222.6	...	5785.5	...	...	9008.1	3596.1	...	8340.4	...	...	11936.5
Imputed bank service charge	...	...	...	...	...	...	...	...	...	...	...	...
Import duties	...	...	...	...	...	...	...	...	...	...	...	...
Value added tax	...	...	...	...	...	...	...	...	...	...	...	...
Other adjustments [f]	...	...	...	...	...	774.3	...	...	...	...	...	538.1
Total [c]	...	...	...	...	...	9782.4	...	...	...	...	...	12474.6

a) Prior to 1973, finance and insurance are included in item 'Wholesale and retail trade, restaurants and hotels'.
b) Items 'Other producers' and 'Producers of government services' are included in item 'Community, social and personal services'.
c) For 1960-1971, fiscal year beginning 1 July.
d) Gross domestic product in factor values.
e) For column 3, gross rather than net.
f) Referring to indirect taxes net of subsidies.

El Salvador

General note. The preparation of national accounts statistics in El Salvador is undertaken by the Departamento de Investigaciones Economicas del Banco Central, San Salvador. The official estimates are published monthly in 'Revista Mensual'. A detailed description of the sources and methods used for the national accounts estimation is contained in 'Metodologia de Cuentas Nacionales de los Paises Centroamericanos' published by the Consejo Monetario Centroamericano Secretaria Ejecutiva in October 1976. The estimates are generally in accordance with the classifications and definitions recommended in the United Nations System of National Accounts (SNA). The following tables have been prepared from successive replies to the United Nations national accounts questionnaire. When the scope and coverage of the estimates differ for conceptual or statistical reasons from the definitions and classifications recommended in SNA, a footnote is indicated to the relevant tables.

Sources and methods:

(a) *Gross domestic product.* Gross domestic product is estimated mainly through the production approach.

(b) *Expenditure on the gross domestic product.* The expenditure approach is used to estimate government final consumption expenditure, increase in stocks, and exports and imports of goods and services. The commodity-flow approach supplemented by the expenditure approach is used for private final consumption expenditure and gross fixed capital formation. The estimates of government consumption expenditure are obtained directly from government sources. For private consumption expenditure, the commodity-flow approach is used with adjustments made for distribution and other costs which are included in the retail value. The estimates of increase in stocks are based on information on stored agricultural products, the stocks of the manufacturing and trade industries and the stocks of public construction. Private capital formation is estimated on the basis of data on domestically produced and imported capital goods and on statistics of construction and repair work. The imports data are adjusted to include import duties, trade margins and installation costs. For public expenditure on capital formation, data are obtained directly from official sources. Data on exports and imports of goods and services are obtained from the balance of payments. Export data on coffee are obtained from the Compania Salvadorena de Cafe, while other merchandise data are furnished by the Direccion General de Estadistica y Censos. GDP by expenditure at constant prices is not estimated.

(c) *Cost-structure of the gross domestic product.* Compensation of employees, combined with operating surplus, is obtained as a residual. The estimates of net indirect taxes are derived from the government accounts. No specific information is available on how consumption of fixed capital is estimated.

(d) *Gross domestic product by kind of economic activity.* The table of gross domestic product by kind of economic activity is prepared at market prices, i.e. producers' values. The production approach is used to estimate value added of most industries. The income approach is used for domestic services and public administration and defence while an indirect method is used for the trade sector. The agricultural data, which are provided by Ministerio de Agricultura y Ganaderia, are obtained through various periodic surveys. Data on the coffee harvest are supplied by the Compania Salvadorena de Cafe while coffee prices are taken from the Compania de Cafe's export prices. Information on the production of cotton is provided by the Cooperative Algodonera Salvadorena Ltda. The gross value of production is calculated by applying producers' prices to the quantity of each commodity produced. For the livestock sector, information is obtained from the Direccion General de Estadistica y Censos, external trade data and through direct studies on prices. Value added of forestry and logging is estimated by means of indirect methods. For the mining and quarrying sector, the estimates are based on 1961 census figures combined with a volume index constructed from square-metre construction data and on price index. The gross value of production in manufacturing is based on the results of annual surveys and industrial censuses held every five years. Estimates for small-scale manufacturing is extrapolated from census data. The estimates for electricity are based on industrial census results and on information furnished by the concerned agencies. For private construction, the information is obtained from the Direccion General de Estadistica y Censos. The basic sources include permits issued for urban construction. Rural population figures are used to determine the number of new dwellings in rural areas. The estimates for public construction are obtained from concerned institutions. For both public and private constructions, intermediate consumption is determined by using a fixed percentage of gross value of production. Gross output of the trade sector is determined on the basis of the values of domestic and imported goods marketed. The gross value of production of domestic goods and the c.i.f. values of imported goods are adjusted for changes in stocks and trade margin are added. An estimate of inputs, which is made from survey based on percentages for electricity, transport, etc., is deducted from the total gross value of production to arrive at value added. Estimates of restaurants and hotels are inter-and extrapolated on the basis of census figures. The enterprises concerned with road transport are classified into international, interdepartamental, urban and interurban transport. A sample from each category is taken in order to obtain average figures for estimating receipts per ton, which are multiplied by quantity figures to arrive at gross value of production and value added. For railways, air transport and communication, information is obtained directly from concerned companies. The estimates of the financial sector are based on financial statements furnished by the banks and insurance companies. Imputation is made for service charges by deducting interest from investment income. The estimate of ownership of dwellings are based on the number of urban and rural dwellings obtained from the population censuses and rents data from surveys, and using the cost of living index as an inflator. Ten percent of the gross value of production are deducted for inputs. The estimates of government services are based on information published by the Ministerio de Hacienda. For other services such as education, hospitals, religion, the estimates are obtained from concerned institutions or from publications such as Indicadores Economicas and Boletin Estadistico. For domestic services, the annual average wages for four regional areas of the country are applied to an estimate of the number of persons engaged. The latter is based on the 1961 census figures and average growth rates while the wage is estimated annually, applying the cost of living index. For the constant price estimates, value added for the agricultural, electricity, trade, transport and financial sectors is estimated by using volume or quantity indexes. Double deflation is used for the manufacturing sector. Price deflation is used for mining and quarrying, construction, restaurants and hotels and government services. For domestic services, wages paid in the base-year are applied to the number employed in the current year.

1.1 Expenditure on the Gross Domestic Product, in Current Prices

Million Salvadoran colones

		1970	1971	1972	1973	1974	1975	1976	1977	1978	1979	1980
1	General government final consumption expenditure	276	275	307	349	429	501	686	805	969	1106	1262
2	Private final consumption expenditure	1935	2064	2175	2464	2946	3283	4016	4607	5414	5895	6381
3	Gross capital formation	341	422	408	609	892	991	1119	1679	1968	1359	999
	a Increase in stocks	33	62	-66	88	174	-40	-26	158	182	-203	-170
	b Gross fixed capital formation	308	359	474	521	718	1031	1145	1521	1786	1561	1170
	Residential buildings	55	61	64	72	96	88	...	...	...	...	...
	Non-residential buildings	49	72	101	115	177	250	...	...	...	...	...
	Other construction and land improvement etc.	28	19	25	11	14	70	...	...	...	...	...
	Other	176	207	284	323	431	623	739	891	1037	828	609
4	Exports of goods and services	639	666	838	998	1278	1480	2028	2735	2446	3412	2697
5	Less: Imports of goods and services	631	720	811	1099	1610	1711	2101	2686	3043	3153	2870
	Statistical discrepancy	13	-3	-37	11	8	-66	-41	27	-61	-	-
	Equals: Gross Domestic Product	2571	2704	2882	3332	3944	4478	5705	7167	7692	8619	8469

1.3 Cost Components of the Gross Domestic Product

Million Salvadoran colones

		1970	1971	1972	1973	1974	1975	1976	1977	1978	1979	1980
1	Indirect taxes, net	197	199	223	268	329	353	562	848	661	855	642
	a Indirect taxes paid	200	209	229	283	344	386	581	876	687	885	677
	b Less: Subsidies received	3	10	6	15	15	33	19	28	26	30	36
2	Consumption of fixed capital	125	134	137	148	176	198	230	269	318	349	339
3	Compensation of employees paid by resident producers to: a	2249	2371	2522	2916	3438	3926	4913	6050	6713	7415	7488
4	Net operating surplus											
	Equals: Gross Domestic Product	2571	2704	2882	3332	3944	4478	5706	7167	7692	8619	8469

a) Obtained as a residual.

El Salvador

1.8 Capital Transactions of The Nation, Summary

Million Salvadoran colones

	1970	1971	1972	1973	1974	1975	1976	1977	1978	1979	1980
Finance of Gross Capital Formation											
Gross saving	376	383	402	515	561	695	1061	1782	1307	1687	785
1 Consumption of fixed capital	125	134	137	148	176	198	230	269	318	349	339
2 Net saving	251	249	265	367	385	497	831	1513	989	1338	446
Less: Surplus of the nation on current transactions	35	-38	-6	-94	-331	-296	-58	103	-661	328	-214
Finance of Gross Capital Formation	341	421	408	609	892	991	1119	1679	1968	1359	999
Gross Capital Formation											
Increase in stocks	33	62	-66	88	174	-40	-26	158	182	-203	-170
Gross fixed capital formation	308	359	474	521	718	1031	1145	1521	1786	1561	1170
1 General government	8	14	23	40	56	70	93	104	114	177	165
2 Corporate and quasi-corporate enterprises	...	...	...	...	...	...	...	...	...	...	...
3 Other	...	...	...	...	...	...	...	...	...	...	...
Gross Capital Formation	341	421	408	609	892	990	1120	1679	1968	1358	999

1.10 Gross Domestic Product by Kind of Activity, in Current Prices

Million Salvadoran colones

	1970	1971	1972	1973	1974	1975	1976	1977	1978	1979	1980
1 Agriculture, hunting, forestry and fishing	731	729	728	922	999	1028	1614	2374	2110	2589	2250
2 Mining and quarrying	4	4	4	6	7	7	8	8	8	10	11
3 Manufacturing	485	519	563	610	707	831	933	1047	1205	1311	1295
4 Electricity, gas and water	39	40	43	49	54	57	90	107	131	149	163
5 Construction	72	80	102	104	146	219	216	327	382	367	280
6 Wholesale and retail trade, restaurants and hotels	581	629	691	794	1023	1178	1486	1683	1925	2104	2132
7 Transport, storage and communication	128	132	140	146	173	188	211	243	291	292	313
8 Finance, insurance, real estate and business services	152	162	172	203	246	300	349	462	544	616	698
9 Community, social and personal services	109	118	126	137	151	166	182	194	222	420	444
Total, Industries	2302	2414	2569	2972	3508	3973	5089	6444	6818	7858	7586
Producers of Government Services	200	219	239	279	338	384	486	571	697	761	883
Other Producers	69	71	74	81	98	120	132	152	177	...	...
Subtotal	2571	2704	2882	3332	3944	4477	5707	7167	7692	8619	8469
Less: Imputed bank service charge	...	...	...	...	...	...	...	...	...	...	...
Plus: Import duties	...	...	...	...	...	...	...	...	...	...	...
Plus: Value added tax	...	...	...	...	...	...	...	...	...	...	...
Equals: Gross Domestic Product	2571	2704	2882	3332	3944	4478	5707	7167	7692	8619	8469

1.11 Gross Domestic Product by Kind of Activity, in Constant Prices

Million Salvadoran colones

	1970	1971	1972	1973	1974	1975	1976	1977	1978	1979	1980
At constant prices of:1962											
1 Agriculture, hunting, forestry and fishing	627	651	660	672	741	789	725	751	828	840	790
2 Mining and quarrying	4	4	4	4	5	5	4	4	4	4	4
3 Manufacturing	438	469	487	522	552	566	629	663	691	671	567
4 Electricity, gas and water	45	49	54	61	64	71	78	88	97	103	102
5 Construction	64	72	94	81	86	122	116	157	165	141	93
6 Wholesale and retail trade, restaurants and hotels	600	614	655	702	724	724	794	847	874	855	741
7 Transport, storage and communication	128	130	136	142	164	173	196	210	223	209	195
8 Finance, insurance, real estate and business services	141	148	159	171	182	188	203	220	226	233	228
9 Community, social and personal services	103	113	119	125	130	132	139	146	145	216	196

… El Salvador

1.11 Gross Domestic Product by Kind of Activity, in Constant Prices
(Continued)

Million Salvadoran colones

	1970	1971	1972	1973	1974	1975	1976	1977	1978	1979	1980
				At constant prices of:1962							
Total, Industries	2151	2249	2369	2481	2648	2769	2884	3086	3253	3272	2916
Producers of Government Services	183	199	214	234	243	244	273	288	311	323	334
Other Producers	60	61	63	65	67	69	71	74	86	...	...
Subtotal	2394	2509	2646	2780	2958	3082	3227	3448	3650	3595	3250
Less: Imputed bank service charge	...	...	...	...	...	...	...	...	...	...	...
Plus: Import duties	...	...	...	...	...	...	...	...	...	...	...
Plus: Value added tax	...	...	...	...	...	...	...	...	...	...	...
Equals: Gross Domestic Product	2394	2509	2646	2780	2958	3082	3228	3448	3650	3595	3250

1.12 Relations Among National Accounting Aggregates

Million Salvadoran colones

	1970	1971	1972	1973	1974	1975	1976	1977	1978	1979	1980
Gross Domestic Product	2571	2704	2882	3332	3944	4478	5706	7167	7692	8619	8469
Plus: Net factor income received from abroad	-21	-25	-27	-38	-54	-70	-17	-72	-130	-60	-163
Equals: Gross National Product	2550	2679	2855	3294	3890	4408	5689	7095	7562	8559	8306
Less: Consumption of fixed capital	125	134	137	148	176	198	230	269	318	349	339
Less: Net indirect taxes paid to supranational organisations	...	...	...	...	...	...	...	...	...	...	...
Equals: National Income at Market Prices	2425	2545	2718	3146	3714	4210	5458	6826	7244	8210	7967
Plus: Net current transfers received from abroad	36	43	30	34	46	71	75	99	128	129	122
Equals: National Disposable Income at Market Prices	2461	2588	2748	3180	3760	4281	5533	6925	7372	8339	8089
Less: Final consumption	2210	2339	2483	2813	3375	3784	4702	5412	6383	7001	7643
Equals: Net Saving	251	249	265	367	385	497	831	1513	989	1338	446
Less: Surplus of the nation on current transactions	35	-38	-6	-94	-331	-296	-58	103	-661	328	-214
Equals: Net Capital Formation	216	288	271	461	716	793	889	1410	1650	1010	660

2.5 Private Final Consumption Expenditure by Type, in Current Prices

Million Salvadoran colones

	1970	1971	1972	1973	1974	1975	1976	1977	1978	1979	1980
Final Consumption Expenditure of Resident Households											
1 Food, beverages and tobacco	827	860	907	1006	1200	1331	1671	1923	2211	...	...
a Food	696	715	750	853	1027	1128	1420	1648	1893	...	...
b Non-alcoholic beverages	18	20	24	22	27	33	44	53	69	...	...
c Alcoholic beverages	78	85	90	86	107	118	136	149	166	...	...
d Tobacco	35	41	43	45	40	51	71	73	83	...	...
2 Clothing and footwear	197	227	247	272	313	348	425	449	509	...	...
3 Gross rent, fuel and power	144	153	162	179	205	266	300	348	423	...	...
a Fuel and power	...	...	...	...	...	...	...	...	109	...	...
b Other	...	...	...	...	...	...	...	...	314	...	...
4 Furniture, furnishings and household equipment and operation	236	227	245	279	338	402	492	585	684	...	...
a Household operation	130	127	131	149	186	220	270	296	352	...	...
b Other	106	100	114	130	152	182	222	289	332	...	...
5 Medical care and health expenses	85	94	98	108	130	145	156	178	214	...	...
6 Transport and communication	160	191	200	243	327	341	411	501	585	...	...
a Personal transport equipment	33	36	36	55	44	37	53	95	104	...	...
b Other	127	155	164	188	283	304	358	406	481	...	...
7 Recreational, entertainment, education and cultural services	113	130	140	151	188	205	236	216	239	...	...
a Education	24	31	32	29	31	42	49	54	63	...	...
b Other	89	99	109	121	157	164	187	162	176	...	...
8 Miscellaneous goods and services	109	119	133	150	180	190	238	301	336	...	...
a Personal care	39	45	49	51	59	50	77	96	107	...	...
b Expenditures in restaurants, cafes and hotels	38	42	47	52	59	66	74	82	92	...	...

El Salvador

2.5 Private Final Consumption Expenditure by Type, in Current Prices
(Continued)

Million Salvadoran colones

	1970	1971	1972	1973	1974	1975	1976	1977	1978	1979	1980
c Other	32	32	37	46	62	74	87	123	137	...	...
Total Final Consumption Expenditure in the Domestic Market by Households, of which [a]	1871	2002	2131	2388	2880	3227	3929	4501	5201	...	...
Plus: Direct purchases abroad by resident households	68	72	65	104	108	105	135	175	292	...	...
Less: Direct purchases in the domestic market by non-resident households	25	32	41	47	64	77	81	104	120	...	...
Equals: Final Consumption Expenditure of Resident Households [a]	1914	2042	2155	2445	2924	3255	3983	4572	5373	...	...

Final Consumption Expenditure of Private Non-profit Institutions Serving Households

	1970	1971	1972	1973	1974	1975	1976	1977	1978	1979	1980
1 Research and science	...	...	...	...	...	...	...	...	...	...	...
2 Education	21	22	20	19	22	28	33	33	41	...	...
3 Medical and other health services	...	...	...	...	...	...	...	...	...	...	...
4 Welfare services	...	...	...	...	...	...	...	...	...	...	...
5 Recreational and related cultural services	...	...	...	...	...	...	...	...	...	...	...
6 Religious organisations	...	...	...	...	...	...	...	...	...	...	...
7 Professional and labour organisations serving households	...	...	...	...	...	...	...	...	...	...	...
8 Miscellaneous	...	...	...	...	...	...	...	...	...	...	...
Equals: Final Consumption Expenditure of Private Non-profit Organisations Serving Households	21	22	20	19	22	28	33	33	41	...	...
Private Final Consumption Expenditure	1935	2064	2175	2464	2946	3283	4016	4607	5414	...	...

a) Including consumption expenditure of private non-profit institutions.

2.9 Gross Capital Formation by Kind of Activity of Owner, ISIC Major Divisions, in Current Prices

Million Salvadoran colones

	1970 TGCF	1970 IS	1970 GFCF	1971 TGCF	1971 IS	1971 GFCF	1972 TGCF	1972 IS	1972 GFCF	1973 TGCF	1973 IS	1973 GFCF
						All Producers						
1 Agriculture, hunting, fishing and forestry	...	...	13	...	...	16	...	...	20	...	...	26
2 Mining and quarrying	...	...	-	...	...	-	...	...	-	...	...	...
3 Manufacturing	...	...	68	...	...	72	...	...	107	...	...	...
4 Electricity, gas and water	...	...	10	...	...	10	...	...	28	...	...	...
5 Construction	...	...	20	...	...	19	...	...	23	...	...	...
6 Wholesale and retail trade, restaurants and hotels [a]	21	4	16	17	5	12	24	5	18	...	12	...
7 Transport, storage and communication	...	...	76	...	...	105	...	...	138	...	...	...
8 Finance, insurance, real estate and business services [b]	...	...	56	...	...	61	...	...	64	...	...	...
9 Community, social and personal services [ab]	...	...	41	...	...	50	...	...	53	...	...	...
Total Industries	...	...	300	...	...	346	...	...	452	...	...	481
Producers of Government Services	4	-4	8	19	5	14	23	-	23	40	-	40
Private Non-Profit Institutions Serving Households	...	...	...	...	...	...	...	...	...	...	...	...
Total	341	33	308	422	62	359	408	-66	474	609	88	521

	1974 TGCF	1974 IS	1974 GFCF	1975 TGCF	1975 IS	1975 GFCF	1976 TGCF	1976 IS	1976 GFCF	1977 TGCF	1977 IS	1977 GFCF
						All Producers						
1 Agriculture, hunting, fishing and forestry	...	...	34	...	...	48	...	...	40	...	...	60
2 Mining and quarrying	...	...	...	...	...	...	...	...	...	...	...	...
3 Manufacturing	...	...	...	...	...	...	...	...	...	...	...	...
4 Electricity, gas and water	...	...	...	...	...	...	...	...	...	...	...	...

El Salvador

2.9 Gross Capital Formation by Kind of Activity of Owner, ISIC Major Divisions, in Current Prices
(Continued)

Million Salvadoran colones

	1974 Total Gross Capital Formation	1974 Increase in Stocks	1974 Gross Fixed Capital Formation	1975 Total Gross Capital Formation	1975 Increase in Stocks	1975 Gross Fixed Capital Formation	1976 Total Gross Capital Formation	1976 Increase in Stocks	1976 Gross Fixed Capital Formation	1977 Total Gross Capital Formation	1977 Increase in Stocks	1977 Gross Fixed Capital Formation
5 Construction	...	...	...	...	...	...	...	...	...	...	...	...
6 Wholesale and retail trade, restaurants and hotels a	...	-15	...	...	5	...	...	25	...	...	71	...
7 Transport, storage and communication	...	...	...	...	...	...	...	...	...	...	...	...
8 Finance, insurance, real estate and business services b	...	...	...	...	...	...	...	...	...	...	...	...
9 Community, social and personal services ab	...	...	...	...	...	...	...	...	...	...	...	...
Total Industries	...	...	663	...	...	961	...	...	1053	...	...	1416
Producers of Government Services	81	25	56	111	43	68	105	12	93	105	3	104
Private Non-Profit Institutions Serving Households	...	...	...	...	...	...	...	...	...	...	...	...
Total	892	174	718	991	-40	1031	1119	-26	1145	1679	158	1521

	1978 Total Gross Capital Formation	1978 Increase in Stocks	1978 Gross Fixed Capital Formation

All Producers

	Total Gross Capital Formation	Increase in Stocks	Gross Fixed Capital Formation
1 Agriculture, hunting, fishing and forestry	...	...	73
2 Mining and quarrying	...	...	...
3 Manufacturing	...	...	...
4 Electricity, gas and water	...	...	...
5 Construction	...	...	...
6 Wholesale and retail trade, restaurants and hotels a	...	63	...
7 Transport, storage and communication	...	...	...
8 Finance, insurance, real estate and business services b	...	...	...
9 Community, social and personal services ab	...	...	...
Total Industries	...	...	1672
Producers of Government Services	124	10	114
Private Non-Profit Institutions Serving Households	...	...	...
Total	1968	182	1786

a) Restaurants and hotels are included in item 'Community, social and personal services'.
b) Business services are included in item 'Community, social and personal services'.

4.3 Derivation of Value Added by Kind of Activity, ISIC Divisions, in Current Prices

Million Salvadoran colones

	1970 Gross Output	1970 Intermediate Consumption	1970 Value Added	1971 Gross Output	1971 Intermediate Consumption	1971 Value Added	1972 Gross Output	1972 Intermediate Consumption	1972 Value Added	1973 Gross Output	1973 Intermediate Consumption	1973 Value Added

All Producers

	1970 GO	1970 IC	1970 VA	1971 GO	1971 IC	1971 VA	1972 GO	1972 IC	1972 VA	1973 GO	1973 IC	1973 VA
1 Agriculture, hunting, forestry and fishing	...	...	731	...	...	729	...	...	728	...	...	922
a Agriculture and hunting	...	...	692	...	...	687	...	...	685	...	...	873
b Forestry and logging	...	...	24	...	...	25	...	...	23	...	...	24
c Fishing	...	...	16	...	...	17	...	...	20	...	...	25
2 Mining and quarrying	...	...	4	...	...	4	...	...	4	...	...	6
a Coal mining	...	...	...	...	...	...	...	...	...	...	...	...
b Crude petroleum and natural gas production	...	...	...	...	...	...	...	...	...	...	...	...
c Metal ore mining	...	...	...	...	...	...	...	...	...	...	...	...
d Other mining	...	...	4	...	...	4	...	...	4	...	...	6

El Salvador

4.3 Derivation of Value Added by Kind of Activity, ISIC Divisions, in Current Prices
(Continued)

Million Salvadoran colones

	1970 Gross Output	1970 Intermediate Consumption	1970 Value Added	1971 Gross Output	1971 Intermediate Consumption	1971 Value Added	1972 Gross Output	1972 Intermediate Consumption	1972 Value Added	1973 Gross Output	1973 Intermediate Consumption	1973 Value Added
3 Manufacturing	...	...	485	...	...	519	...	...	563	...	...	610
a Manufacture of food, beverages and tobacco	...	...	206	...	...	223	...	...	242	...	...	258
b Textile, wearing apparel and leather industries	...	...	119	...	...	121	...	...	129	...	...	140
c Manufacture of wood and wood products, including furniture	...	...	12	...	...	11	...	...	11	...	...	13
d Manufacture of paper and paper products, printing and publishing	...	...	16	...	...	16	...	...	16	...	...	20
e Manufacture of chemicals and chemical petroleum, coal, rubber and plastic products	...	...	61	...	...	71	...	...	79	...	...	86
f Manufacture of non-metallic mineral products, except products of petroleum and coal	...	...	17	...	...	20	...	...	24	...	...	26
g Basic metal industries	...	...	5	...	...	5	...	...	8	...	...	8
h Manufacture of fabricated metal products, machinery and equipment	...	...	33	...	...	35	...	...	38	...	...	41
i Other manufacturing industries	...	...	17	...	...	17	...	...	17	...	...	18
4 Electricity, gas and water	...	...	39	...	...	40	...	...	43	...	...	49
a Electricity, gas and steam	...	...	35	...	...	37	...	...	39	...	...	42
b Water works and supply	...	...	4	...	...	4	...	...	4	...	...	6
5 Construction	...	...	72	...	...	80	...	...	102	...	...	104
6 Wholesale and retail trade, restaurants and hotels	...	...	581	...	...	629	...	...	691	...	...	794
a Wholesale and retail trade	...	...	544	...	...	587	...	...	644	...	...	742
b Restaurants and hotels	...	...	38	...	...	42	...	...	47	...	...	52
Restaurants	...	...	...	...	...	...	...	...	...	...	...	...
Hotels and other lodging places	...	...	...	...	...	...	...	...	...	...	...	...
7 Transport, storage and communication	...	...	128	...	...	132	...	...	140	...	...	146
8 Finance, insurance, real estate and business services	...	...	152	...	...	162	...	...	172	...	...	203
9 Community, social and personal services	...	...	109	...	...	118	...	...	126	...	...	137
Total, Industries	...	...	2302	...	...	2414	...	...	2569	...	...	2972
Producers of Government Services	...	...	200	...	...	219	...	...	239	...	...	279
Other Producers	...	...	69	...	...	71	...	...	74	...	...	81
Total	...	...	2571	...	...	2704	...	...	2882	...	...	3332
Imputed bank service charge	...	...	...	...	...	...	...	...	...	...	...	...
Import duties	...	...	...	...	...	...	...	...	...	...	...	...
Value added tax	...	...	...	...	...	...	...	...	...	...	...	...
Total	...	...	...	...	...	...	...	...	...	...	...	...

	1974 Gross Output	1974 Intermediate Consumption	1974 Value Added	1975 Gross Output	1975 Intermediate Consumption	1975 Value Added	1976 Gross Output	1976 Intermediate Consumption	1976 Value Added	1977 Gross Output	1977 Intermediate Consumption	1977 Value Added

All Producers

	1974 GO	1974 IC	1974 VA	1975 GO	1975 IC	1975 VA	1976 GO	1976 IC	1976 VA	1977 GO	1977 IC	1977 VA
1 Agriculture, hunting, forestry and fishing	...	...	999	...	...	1028	...	...	1614	...	...	2374
a Agriculture and hunting	...	...	948	...	...	970	...	...	1552	...	...	2312
b Forestry and logging	...	...	27	...	...	31	...	...	31	...	...	33
c Fishing	...	...	25	...	...	27	...	...	31	...	...	29
2 Mining and quarrying	...	...	7	...	...	7	...	...	8	...	...	8
a Coal mining	...	...	...	...	...	...	...	...	...	...	...	...
b Crude petroleum and natural gas production	...	...	...	...	...	...	...	...	...	...	...	...
c Metal ore mining	...	...	...	...	...	...	...	...	...	...	...	...
d Other mining	...	...	7	...	...	7	...	...	8	...	...	8

El Salvador

4.3 Derivation of Value Added by Kind of Activity, ISIC Divisions, in Current Prices
(Continued)

Million Salvadoran colones

	1974 Gross Output	1974 Intermediate Consumption	1974 Value Added	1975 Gross Output	1975 Intermediate Consumption	1975 Value Added	1976 Gross Output	1976 Intermediate Consumption	1976 Value Added	1977 Gross Output	1977 Intermediate Consumption	1977 Value Added
3 Manufacturing	...	...	707	...	...	831	...	...	933	...	...	1047
a Manufacture of food, beverages and tobacco	...	...	293	...	...	385	...	...	419	...	...	456
b Textile, wearing apparel and leather industries	...	...	156	...	...	165	...	...	187	...	...	213
c Manufacture of wood and wood products, including furniture	...	...	17	...	...	19	...	...	23	...	...	27
d Manufacture of paper and paper products, printing and publishing	...	...	24	...	...	25	...	...	29	...	...	34
e Manufacture of chemicals and chemical petroleum, coal, rubber and plastic products	...	...	109	...	...	120	...	...	139	...	...	160
f Manufacture of non-metallic mineral products, except products of petroleum and coal	...	...	31	...	...	35	...	...	41	...	...	49
g Basic metal industries	...	...	11	...	...	13	...	...	14	...	...	15
h Manufacture of fabricated metal products, machinery and equipment	...	...	47	...	...	49	...	...	57	...	...	65
i Other manufacturing industries	...	...	18	...	...	21	...	...	24	...	...	29
4 Electricity, gas and water	...	...	54	...	...	57	...	...	90	...	...	107
a Electricity, gas and steam	...	...	49	...	...	48	...	...	80	...	...	94
b Water works and supply	...	...	5	...	...	9	...	...	9	...	...	12
5 Construction	...	...	146	...	...	219	...	...	216	...	...	327
6 Wholesale and retail trade, restaurants and hotels	...	...	1023	...	...	1178	...	...	1486	...	...	1683
a Wholesale and retail trade	...	...	965	...	...	1112	...	...	1412	...	...	1600
b Restaurants and hotels	...	...	59	...	...	66	...	...	74	...	...	82
Restaurants	...	...	...	...	...	...	...	...	...	...	...	...
Hotels and other lodging places	...	...	...	...	...	...	...	...	...	...	...	...
7 Transport, storage and communication	...	...	173	...	...	188	...	...	211	...	...	243
8 Finance, insurance, real estate and business services	...	...	246	...	...	300	...	...	349	...	...	462
9 Community, social and personal services	...	...	151	...	...	166	...	...	182	...	...	194
Total, Industries	...	...	3508	...	...	3974	...	...	5089	...	...	6444
Producers of Government Services	...	...	338	...	...	384	...	...	486	...	...	571
Other Producers	...	...	98	...	...	120	...	...	132	...	...	152
Total	...	...	3944	...	...	4478	...	...	5707	...	...	7167
Imputed bank service charge	...	...	...	...	...	...	...	...	...	...	...	...
Import duties	...	...	...	...	...	...	...	...	...	...	...	...
Value added tax	...	...	...	...	...	...	...	...	...	...	...	...
Total	...	...	...	...	...	...	...	...	...	...	...	...

	1978 Gross Output	1978 Intermediate Consumption	1978 Value Added	1979 Gross Output	1979 Intermediate Consumption	1979 Value Added	1980 Gross Output	1980 Intermediate Consumption	1980 Value Added

All Producers

	1978 GO	1978 IC	1978 VA	1979 GO	1979 IC	1979 VA	1980 GO	1980 IC	1980 VA
1 Agriculture, hunting, forestry and fishing	...	...	2110	...	...	2589	...	...	2250
a Agriculture and hunting	...	...	2046	...	...	2523	...	...	2174
b Forestry and logging	...	...	33	...	...	32	...	...	34
c Fishing	...	...	31	...	...	34	...	...	42
2 Mining and quarrying	...	...	8	...	...	10	...	...	11
a Coal mining	...	...	...	...	...	...	...	...	...
b Crude petroleum and natural gas production	...	...	...	...	...	...	...	...	...
c Metal ore mining	...	...	...	...	...	...	...	...	...
d Other mining	...	...	8	...	...	10	...	...	11

El Salvador

4.3 Derivation of Value Added by Kind of Activity, ISIC Divisions, in Current Prices
(Continued)

Million Salvadoran colones

	1978 Gross Output	1978 Intermediate Consumption	1978 Value Added	1979 Gross Output	1979 Intermediate Consumption	1979 Value Added	1980 Gross Output	1980 Intermediate Consumption	1980 Value Added
3 Manufacturing	...	...	1205	...	...	1311	...	...	1295
a Manufacture of food, beverages and tobacco	...	...	510	...	...	532	...	...	538
b Textile, wearing apparel and leather industries	...	...	248	...	...	284	...	...	269
c Manufacture of wood and wood products, including furniture	...	...	31	...	...	33	...	...	30
d Manufacture of paper and paper products, printing and publishing	...	...	40	...	...	46	...	...	43
e Manufacture of chemicals and chemical petroleum, coal, rubber and plastic products	...	...	188	...	...	211	...	...	233
f Manufacture of non-metallic mineral products, except products of petroleum and coal	...	...	58	...	...	60	...	...	48
g Basic metal industries	...	...	17	...	...	20	...	...	18
h Manufacture of fabricated metal products, machinery and equipment	...	...	75	...	...	87	...	...	81
i Other manufacturing industries	...	...	38	...	...	38	...	...	35
4 Electricity, gas and water	...	...	131	...	...	149	...	...	163
a Electricity, gas and steam	...	...	119	...	...	137	...	...	150
b Water works and supply	...	...	12	...	...	12	...	...	13
5 Construction	...	...	382	...	...	367	...	...	280
6 Wholesale and retail trade, restaurants and hotels	...	...	1925	...	...	2104	...	...	2132
a Wholesale and retail trade	...	...	1833	...	...	2000	...	...	2015
b Restaurants and hotels	...	...	92	...	...	104	...	...	117
Restaurants	...	...	...	...	...	89	...	...	101
Hotels and other lodging places	...	...	...	...	...	15	...	...	16
7 Transport, storage and communication	...	...	291	...	...	292	...	...	313
8 Finance, insurance, real estate and business services	...	...	544	...	...	616	...	...	698
9 Community, social and personal services	...	...	222	...	...	420	...	...	444
Total, Industries	...	...	6818	...	...	7858	...	...	7586
Producers of Government Services	...	...	697	...	...	761	...	...	883
Other Producers	...	...	177	...	...	...	...	...	...
Total	...	...	7692	...	...	8619	...	...	8469
Imputed bank service charge	...	...	...	...	...	...	...	...	...
Import duties	...	...	...	...	...	...	...	...	...
Value added tax	...	...	...	...	...	...	...	...	...
Total	...	...	...	...	...	...	...	...	...

4.4 Derivation of Value Added by Kind of Activity, ISIC Divisions, in Constant Prices

Million Salvadoran colones

	1970 Gross Output	1970 Intermediate Consumption	1970 Value Added	1971 Gross Output	1971 Intermediate Consumption	1971 Value Added	1972 Gross Output	1972 Intermediate Consumption	1972 Value Added	1973 Gross Output	1973 Intermediate Consumption	1973 Value Added
	\multicolumn{12}{c}{At constant prices of:1962}
	\multicolumn{12}{c}{All Producers}
1 Agriculture, hunting, forestry and fishing	...	...	627	...	...	651	...	...	660	...	...	672
a Agriculture and hunting	...	...	591	...	...	615	...	...	624	...	...	633
b Forestry and logging	...	...	22	...	...	22	...	...	22	...	...	24
c Fishing	...	...	15	...	...	14	...	...	14	...	...	15
2 Mining and quarrying	...	...	4	...	...	4	...	...	4	...	...	4
a Coal mining	...	...	...	...	...	...	...	...	...	...	...	...
b Crude petroleum and natural gas production	...	...	...	...	...	...	...	...	...	...	...	...
c Metal ore mining	...	...	...	...	...	...	...	...	...	...	...	...
d Other mining	...	...	4	...	...	4	...	...	4	...	...	4

El Salvador

4.4 Derivation of Value Added by Kind of Activity, ISIC Divisions, in Constant Prices
(Continued)

Million Salvadoran colones

	1970 Gross Output	1970 Intermediate Consumption	1970 Value Added	1971 Gross Output	1971 Intermediate Consumption	1971 Value Added	1972 Gross Output	1972 Intermediate Consumption	1972 Value Added	1973 Gross Output	1973 Intermediate Consumption	1973 Value Added
				At constant prices of:1962								
3 Manufacturing	...	...	438	...	...	469	...	...	487	...	...	522
a Manufacture of food, beverages and tobacco	...	...	218	...	...	236	...	...	242	...	...	269
b Textile, wearing apparel and leather industries	...	...	86	...	...	76	...	...	82	...	...	64
c Manufacture of wood and wood products, including furniture	...	...	13	...	...	10	...	...	9	...	...	12
d Manufacture of paper and paper products, printing and publishing	...	...	16	...	...	17	...	...	17	...	...	23
e Manufacture of chemicals and chemical petroleum, coal, rubber and plastic products	...	...	43	...	...	60	...	...	63	...	...	70
f Manufacture of non-metallic mineral products, except products of petroleum and coal	...	...	15	...	...	20	...	...	23	...	...	23
g Basic metal industries	...	...	2	...	...	2	...	...	4	...	...	7
h Manufacture of fabricated metal products, machinery and equipment	...	...	28	...	...	31	...	...	32	...	...	35
i Other manufacturing industries	...	...	17	...	...	17	...	...	14	...	...	18
4 Electricity, gas and water	...	...	45	...	...	49	...	...	54	...	...	61
a Electricity, gas and steam	...	...	41	...	...	45	...	...	51	...	...	56
b Water works and supply	...	...	4	...	...	3	...	...	3	...	...	5
5 Construction	...	...	64	...	...	72	...	...	94	...	...	81
6 Wholesale and retail trade, restaurants and hotels	...	...	600	...	...	614	...	...	655	...	...	702
a Wholesale and retail trade	...	...	566	...	...	576	...	...	613	...	...	658
b Restaurants and hotels	...	...	34	...	...	38	...	...	42	...	...	44
Restaurants	...	...	...	...	...	...	...	...	...	...	...	...
Hotels and other lodging places	...	...	...	...	...	...	...	...	...	...	...	...
7 Transport, storage and communication	...	...	128	...	...	130	...	...	136	...	...	142
8 Finance, insurance, real estate and business services	...	...	141	...	...	148	...	...	159	...	...	171
9 Community, social and personal services	...	...	103	...	...	113	...	...	119	...	...	125
Total, Industries	...	...	2151	...	...	2248	...	...	2369	...	...	2481
Producers of Government Services	...	...	183	...	...	199	...	...	214	...	...	234
Other Producers	...	...	60	...	...	61	...	...	63	...	...	65
Total	...	...	2394	...	...	2509	...	...	2646	...	...	2780
Imputed bank service charge	...	...	...	...	...	...	...	...	...	...	...	...
Import duties	...	...	...	...	...	...	...	...	...	...	...	...
Value added tax	...	...	...	...	...	...	...	...	...	...	...	...
Total	...	...	...	...	...	...	...	...	...	...	...	...

	1974 Gross Output	1974 Intermediate Consumption	1974 Value Added	1975 Gross Output	1975 Intermediate Consumption	1975 Value Added	1976 Gross Output	1976 Intermediate Consumption	1976 Value Added	1977 Gross Output	1977 Intermediate Consumption	1977 Value Added
				At constant prices of:1962								
				All Producers								
1 Agriculture, hunting, forestry and fishing	...	...	741	...	...	789	...	...	725	...	...	751
a Agriculture and hunting	...	...	702	...	...	748	...	...	687	...	...	712
b Forestry and logging	...	...	24	...	...	26	...	...	26	...	...	27
c Fishing	...	...	14	...	...	16	...	...	12	...	...	12
2 Mining and quarrying	...	...	5	...	...	5	...	...	4	...	...	4
a Coal mining	...	...	...	...	...	...	...	...	...	...	...	...
b Crude petroleum and natural gas production	...	...	...	...	...	...	...	...	...	...	...	...
c Metal ore mining	...	...	...	...	...	...	...	...	...	...	...	...
d Other mining	...	...	5	...	...	5	...	...	4	...	...	4

El Salvador

4.4 Derivation of Value Added by Kind of Activity, ISIC Divisions, in Constant Prices
(Continued)

Million Salvadoran colones

	1974 Gross Output	1974 Intermediate Consumption	1974 Value Added	1975 Gross Output	1975 Intermediate Consumption	1975 Value Added	1976 Gross Output	1976 Intermediate Consumption	1976 Value Added	1977 Gross Output	1977 Intermediate Consumption	1977 Value Added
					At constant prices of: 1962							
3 Manufacturing	...	...	552	...	...	566	...	...	629	...	...	663
a Manufacture of food, beverages and tobacco	...	...	292	...	...	319	...	...	340	...	...	355
b Textile, wearing apparel and leather industries	...	...	72	...	...	62	...	...	70	...	...	75
c Manufacture of wood and wood products, including furniture	...	...	8	...	...	12	...	...	15	...	...	16
d Manufacture of paper and paper products, printing and publishing	...	...	31	...	...	19	...	...	23	...	...	26
e Manufacture of chemicals and chemical petroleum, coal, rubber and plastic products	...	...	59	...	...	73	...	...	79	...	...	83
f Manufacture of non-metallic mineral products, except products of petroleum and coal	...	...	27	...	...	26	...	...	26	...	...	26
g Basic metal industries	...	...	7	...	...	9	...	...	9	...	...	10
h Manufacture of fabricated metal products, machinery and equipment	...	...	38	...	...	40	...	...	45	...	...	47
i Other manufacturing industries	...	...	18	...	...	18	...	...	21	...	...	23
4 Electricity, gas and water	...	...	64	...	...	71	...	...	78	...	...	88
a Electricity, gas and steam	...	...	60	...	...	65	...	...	72	...	...	82
b Water works and supply	...	...	4	...	...	5	...	...	6	...	...	6
5 Construction	...	...	86	...	...	122	...	...	116	...	...	157
6 Wholesale and retail trade, restaurants and hotels	...	...	724	...	...	724	...	...	794	...	...	847
a Wholesale and retail trade	...	...	682	...	...	684	...	...	752	...	...	803
b Restaurants and hotels	...	...	42	...	...	40	...	...	42	...	...	44
Restaurants	...	...	...	...	...	...	...	...	...	...	...	...
Hotels and other lodging places	...	...	...	...	...	...	...	...	...	...	...	...
7 Transport, storage and communication	...	...	164	...	...	173	...	...	196	...	...	210
8 Finance, insurance, real estate and business services	...	...	182	...	...	188	...	...	203	...	...	220
9 Community, social and personal services	...	...	130	...	...	132	...	...	139	...	...	146
Total, Industries	...	...	2648	...	...	2770	...	...	2884	...	...	3086
Producers of Government Services	...	...	243	...	...	244	...	...	273	...	...	288
Other Producers	...	...	67	...	...	69	...	...	71	...	...	74
Total	...	...	2958	...	...	3082	...	...	3228	...	...	3448
Imputed bank service charge	...	...	...	...	...	...	...	...	...	...	...	...
Import duties	...	...	...	...	...	...	...	...	...	...	...	...
Value added tax	...	...	...	...	...	...	...	...	...	...	...	...
Total	...	...	...	...	...	...	...	...	...	...	...	...

	1978 Gross Output	1978 Intermediate Consumption	1978 Value Added	1979 Gross Output	1979 Intermediate Consumption	1979 Value Added	1980 Gross Output	1980 Intermediate Consumption	1980 Value Added
				At constant prices of: 1962					
				All Producers					
1 Agriculture, hunting, forestry and fishing	...	...	828	...	...	840	...	...	790
a Agriculture and hunting	...	...	788	...	...	798	...	...	750
b Forestry and logging	...	...	28	...	...	29	...	...	27
c Fishing	...	...	12	...	...	13	...	...	13
2 Mining and quarrying	...	...	3	...	...	4	...	...	4
a Coal mining	...	...	...	...	...	...	...	...	...
b Crude petroleum and natural gas production	...	...	...	...	...	...	...	...	...
c Metal ore mining	...	...	...	...	...	...	...	...	...
d Other mining	...	...	4	...	...	4	...	...	4

4.4 Derivation of Value Added by Kind of Activity, ISIC Divisions, in Constant Prices
(Continued)

El Salvador

Million Salvadoran colones

	1978 Gross Output	1978 Intermediate Consumption	1978 Value Added	1979 Gross Output	1979 Intermediate Consumption	1979 Value Added	1980 Gross Output	1980 Intermediate Consumption	1980 Value Added
				At constant prices of:1962					
3 Manufacturing	...	...	691	...	...	671	...	...	567
a Manufacture of food, beverages and tobacco	...	...	372	...	...	355	...	...	307
b Textile, wearing apparel and leather industries	...	...	77	...	...	80	...	...	66
c Manufacture of wood and wood products, including furniture	...	...	17	...	...	16	...	...	13
d Manufacture of paper and paper products, printing and publishing	...	...	27	...	...	27	...	...	22
e Manufacture of chemicals and chemical petroleum, coal, rubber and plastic products	...	...	87	...	...	83	...	...	69
f Manufacture of non-metallic mineral products, except products of petroleum and coal	...	...	27	...	...	25	...	...	20
g Basic metal industries	...	...	11	...	...	11	...	...	9
h Manufacture of fabricated metal products, machinery and equipment	...	...	49	...	...	52	...	...	42
i Other manufacturing industries	...	...	24	...	...	22	...	...	19
4 Electricity, gas and water	...	...	97	...	...	103	...	...	102
a Electricity, gas and steam	...	...	...	...	...	96	...	...	94
b Water works and supply	...	...	...	...	...	8	...	...	8
5 Construction	...	...	165	...	...	141	...	...	93
6 Wholesale and retail trade, restaurants and hotels	...	...	874	...	...	855	...	...	741
a Wholesale and retail trade	...	...	834	...	...	813	...	...	700
b Restaurants and hotels	...	...	41	...	...	42	...	...	40
Restaurants	...	...	...	...	...	37	...	...	35
Hotels and other lodging places	...	...	...	...	...	5	...	...	5
7 Transport, storage and communication	...	...	223	...	...	209	...	...	195
8 Finance, insurance, real estate and business services	...	...	226	...	...	233	...	...	228
9 Community, social and personal services	...	...	145	...	...	216	...	...	196
Total, Industries	...	...	3253	...	...	3272	...	...	2916
Producers of Government Services	...	...	311	...	...	323	...	...	334
Other Producers	...	...	86	...	...	...	...	...	...
Total	...	...	3650	...	...	3595	...	...	3250
Imputed bank service charge	...	...	...	...	...	...	...	...	...
Import duties	...	...	...	...	...	...	...	...	...
Value added tax	...	...	...	...	...	...	...	...	...
Total	...	...	...	...	...	...	...	...	...

Ethiopia

General note. The preparation of national accounts statistics in Ethiopia is undertaken by the Central Statistical Office, Addis Ababa. The official estimates with methodological notes are published annually in the 'Statistical Abstract'. The estimates are generally in accordance with the classifications and definitions recommended in the United Nations Systems of National Accounts (SNA). The following tables have been prepared from successive replies to the United Nations national accounts questionnaire. The Ethiopian Fiscal year which is from June to July has been used for all estimates except the 'External Transactions' table. When the scope and coverage of the estimates differ for conceptual or statistical reasons from the definitions and classifications recommended in SNA, a footnote is indicated to the relevant tables.

Sources and methods:

(a) Gross domestic product. Gross domestic product is estimated mainly through the production approach.

(b) Expenditure on the gross domestic product. The expenditure approach is used to estimate government final consumption expenditure and exports and imports of goods and services. This approach, in combination with the commodity-flow approach, is also used for estimating gross fixed capital formation. Private consumption expenditure is obtained as a residual which also includes increase in stocks. Government final consumption expenditure, consisting of compensation of employees and net purchases of goods and services, is obtained from the annual Budgetary Revenue and Expenditure report, from the Ministry of Finance and from municipalities. These sources are also used for estimating the public sector's capital formation in building and construction. The estimates of private construction in urban areas are based on building permits which are adjusted for timing by taking the average of the last two years and adding 5 percent for underreporting. Other urban private construction is estimated by applying the ratio of per capita consumption expenditure in Addis Ababa to the per capita consumption expenditure in other urban areas. Construction in the rural areas is estimated by multiplying the assumed number of tukuls built in a given year by an assumed average cost per tukul. For capital formation in machinery and equipment, import statistics are used. To the import values are added import duties, transport costs, trade margins and installation costs. The data on exports and imports of goods and services are obtained from the external trade statistics. GDP by expenditure type at constant prices is not estimated.

(c) Cost-structure of the gross domestic product. The cost-structure of the gross domestic product is not estimated.

(d) Gross domestic product by kind of economic activity. The table of GDP by kind of economic activity is prepared in factor values. The production approach is used to estimate value added of most industries. The income approach is also used in measuring the output of the modern sectors of the economy such as the industrial activity and the services sectors. The estimates of the value added of agriculture for the bench-mark years 1961-1963 are based on various sources such as population figures, assumed per capita consumption of food grains and wholesale prices. Recent years' estimates are also based on qualitative crop surveys and surveys on cultivated area. The net output by type of plant product is multiplied by wholesale prices adjusted for trade and transport margins. The 1961-1963 bench-mark estimates of livestock production were based on the number of livestock by type, on gross output and on value added. For subsequent years, gross output and value added are derived by applying growth factors linked to the population growth rate. For forestry, the sources include the Forestry Dept., the survey of wood working industries, family budget studies in 1967/68 and the annual surveys of manufacturing industries. Value added is derived by deducting 10 percent from gross value of production of industrial wood and firewood. The Ministry of Mines and the annual budgetary reports provide data for the mining sector. The value of production is estimated by multiplying the quantity produced of each mineral product by its average price. The source of data for large-scale manufacturing is the annual surveys of manufacturing industries. Values added is obtained by deducting the cost of inputs of raw materials, fuel and energy from the gross value of production. For small scale manufacturing and handicraft, value added is derived by assuming that the growth rate is half of the one observed for output of large-scale manufacturing. Data for electricity are obtained from annual returns to questionnaires submitted to concerned enterprises. Data on the number of building permits issued, the 1968 household expenditure survey and population estimates are used to estimate the value of construction in the private sector. The total value of Addis Ababa building permits is adjusted for timing and underreporting. Work done in other towns is estimated by applying the ratio of per capita consumption expenditure in Addis Ababa to the per capita consumption expenditure in other towns. For the public sector, data are obtained from the Budgetary Revenue and Expenditure reports as well as from questionnaires sent to municipalities and public agencies. The gross trade margin of imported goods is estimated at 15 percent of the value of imports based on the 1963 trade inquiry. Similar assumptions are made for locally produced goods. Value added in the transport sector is based on the annual reports of concerned enterprises for the railway, water and air transports. For road transport, data on passenger or ton kilometres, registration statistics, and passenger fares and freight rates are used. For the financial institutions the profit and loss statement and the annual reports of concerned institutions are used. Bench-mark estimates for 1961-1963 are available for ownership of dwellings. The gross rental income of the urban areas is obtained by multiplying the total number of housing units by assumed actual and imputed average annual rental rates, while for the rural areas the total number of tukuls is multiplied by the assumed average value per tukul. Value added of public administration and defence is equal to total wages and salaries paid to government employees, including payment in kind. The sources of data include annual reports and questionnaires sent to different agencies. For other government services such as education and health, value added is based on government reports. Value added per student enrolled in non-governmental schools is estimated as two-thirds of the value added per student in government schools. The value of domestic services is obtained by multiplying the number of employees by assumed average pay rates. For the constant price estimates, the current net output of plant products in the agricultural sector is revalued at base-year producer prices. For livestock, water supply and construction, value added at current factor costs is assumed to be equal to the value added at constant factor costs. Price indexes are used to deflate the current value added of mining and quarrying, small-scale manufacturing, trade, finance and most of the services sectors. For large-scale manufacturing, electricity, transport and domestic services, value added is extrapolated by volume indexes.

1.1 Expenditure on the Gross Domestic Product, in Current Prices

Million Ethiopian birr — Fiscal year ending 7 July

	1970	1971	1972	1973	1974	1975	1976	1977	1978	1979	1980
1 General government final consumption expenditure	443.4	461.2	507.8	537.6	585.8	730.1	866.0	...	...	...	...
2 Private final consumption expenditure	3518.4	3782.5	3719.9	3796.6	4243.8	4406.9	4618.0	...	...	...	...
3 Gross capital formation	512.5	554.4	603.2	569.3	549.0	579.7	578.0	...	...	...	...
a Increase in stocks	...	...	...	...	...	...	...	...	...	...	...
b Gross fixed capital formation	512.5	554.4	603.1	569.3	549.0	579.7	578.0	...	...	...	...
Residential buildings	171.5	165.7	179.0	200.6	219.2	217.1	180.9	...	...	...	...
Non-residential buildings	31.7	34.6	53.3	81.5	85.6	79.2	47.4	...	...	...	...
Other construction and land improvement etc.	141.3	173.0	162.3	104.9	84.1	85.8	131.6	...	...	...	...
Other	168.0	181.1	208.5	182.3	160.1	197.6	218.1	...	...	...	...
4 Exports of goods and services	490.2	468.2	490.6	653.6	827.8	683.1	760.1	...	...	...	...
5 Less: Imports of goods and services	503.9	555.9	577.8	551.9	655.2	875.3	818.1	...	...	...	...
Equals: Gross Domestic Product	4460.6	4710.4	4743.7	5005.2	5551.2	5524.5	6004.0	...	...	...	...

1.7 External Transactions on Current Account, Summary

Million Ethiopian birr — Fiscal year ending 7 July

	1970	1971	1972	1973	1974	1975	1976	1977	1978	1979	1980
				Payments to the Rest of the World							
1 Imports of goods and services	...	...	539.0	563.7	729.2	853.3	981.8	...	...	...	...
a Imports of merchandise c.i.f.	...	...	435.6	448.2	603.3	699.7	851.7	...	...	...	...
b Other	...	...	103.4	115.5	125.9	153.6	130.1	...	...	...	...
2 Factor income paid to the rest of the world	...	...	58.5	66.0	65.7	58.8	38.1	...	...	...	...

Ethiopia

1.7 External Transactions on Current Account, Summary
(Continued)

Fiscal year ending 7 July

Million Ethiopian birr	1970	1971	1972	1973	1974	1975	1976	1977	1978	1979	1980
a Compensation of employees	...	...	6.1	6.0	...	7.5	...	...	...	...	...
b Property and entrepreneurial income paid [a]	...	...	52.4	60.0	...	51.3	38.1	...	...	...	...
3 Indirect taxes paid to supranational organizations	...	...	...	...	...	...	...	...	...	...	...
4 Current transfers to the rest of the world	...	...	25.8	24.6	35.1	23.5	9.4	...	...	...	...
5 Surplus of the nation on current transactions	...	...	19.7	159.2	132.1	-96.1	-68.3	...	...	...	...
Payments to the Rest of the World and Surplus of the Nation on Current Transactions	...	...	643.0	813.5	962.1	839.5	961.0	...	...	...	...

Receipts From The Rest of the World

	1970	1971	1972	1973	1974	1975	1976	1977	1978	1979	1980
1 Exports of goods and services	...	...	568.4	716.8	776.4	703.8	785.7	...	...	...	...
a Exports of merchandise f.o.b.	...	...	385.3	503.7	556.5	497.8	581.1	...	...	...	...
b Other	...	...	183.1	213.1	219.9	206.0	204.6	...	...	...	...
2 Factor income received from rest of the world	...	...	8.2	18.3	42.6	29.5	34.9	...	...	...	...
a Compensation of employees	...	...	-	-	-	-	-	...	...	...	...
b Property and entrepreneurial income received [a]	...	...	8.2	18.3	42.6	29.5	34.9	...	...	...	...
3 Subsidies received from supranational organisations	...	...	...	...	...	...	...	...	...	...	...
4 Current transfers from rest of the world	...	...	66.4	78.4	143.1	106.2	140.4	...	...	...	...
Receipts from the Rest of the World on Current Transactions	...	...	643.0	813.5	962.1	839.5	961.0	...	...	...	...

a) For 1975, including insurance claims.

1.10 Gross Domestic Product by Kind of Activity, in Current Prices

Fiscal year ending 7 July

Million Ethiopian birr	1970	1971	1972	1973	1974	1975	1976	1977	1978	1979	1980
1 Agriculture, hunting, forestry and fishing	2327.2	2404.8	2286.0	2331.4	2605.2	2423.4	2738.9	...	...	...	...
2 Mining and quarrying	9.4	10.4	10.2	11.1	12.5	12.6	11.8	...	...	...	...
3 Manufacturing	372.3	419.7	439.9	464.0	507.6	569.4	582.5	...	...	...	...
4 Electricity, gas and water	29.9	32.2	35.7	39.7	40.5	40.5	38.3	...	...	...	...
5 Construction	190.0	209.2	220.8	233.4	235.7	232.3	221.0	...	...	...	...
6 Wholesale and retail trade, restaurants and hotels [a]	350.6	377.6	391.1	441.6	532.5	522.7	551.6	...	...	...	...
7 Transport, storage and communication	202.1	222.3	243.9	255.9	263.1	272.9	302.5	...	...	...	...
8 Finance, insurance, real estate and business services [b]	214.1	230.3	244.4	256.6	287.8	306.5	330.6	...	...	...	...
9 Community, social and personal services [a,b]	198.3	217.3	241.2	263.0	288.2	310.1	322.2	...	...	...	...
Total, Industries	3893.9	4123.8	4113.2	4296.7	4773.1	4690.4	5099.4	...	...	...	...
Producers of Government Services	219.5	224.4	241.6	269.6	304.2	348.7	365.9	...	...	...	...
Other Producers	59.6	60.7	61.8	62.9	63.5	64.1	64.7	...	...	...	...
Subtotal [c]	4173.0	4408.9	4416.6	4629.2	5140.8	5103.2	5530.0	...	...	...	...
Less: Imputed bank service charge	...	...	...	...	...	...	...	...	...	...	...
Plus: Import duties	...	...	...	...	...	...	...	...	...	...	...
Plus: Value added tax	...	...	...	...	...	...	...	...	...	...	...
Plus: Other adjustments [d]	287.6	301.5	327.1	376.0	410.4	421.3	474.0	...	...	...	...
Equals: Gross Domestic Product	4460.6	4710.4	4743.7	5005.2	5551.2	5524.5	6004.0	...	...	...	...

a) Restaurants and hotels are included in item 'Community, social and personal services'.
b) Business services are included in item 'Community, social and personal services'.
c) Gross domestic product in factor values.
d) Referring to indirect taxes net of subsidies.

1.11 Gross Domestic Product by Kind of Activity, in Constant Prices

Fiscal year ending 7 July

Million Ethiopian birr	1970	1971	1972	1973	1974	1975	1976	1977	1978	1979	1980
	At constant prices of: 1961										
1 Agriculture, hunting, forestry and fishing	1833.3	1870.3	1936.8	1950.8	1940.1	1902.6	1953.7	...	...	...	...
2 Mining and quarrying	9.2	9.6	9.3	10.2	9.7	8.7	7.5	...	...	...	...
3 Manufacturing	308.7	337.1	350.9	368.4	364.7	360.5	355.2	...	...	...	...
4 Electricity, gas and water	33.6	37.9	39.6	41.9	44.4	44.2	42.9	...	...	...	...
5 Construction	190.0	209.2	220.8	216.7	214.9	210.9	192.1	...	...	...	...

Ethiopia

1.11 Gross Domestic Product by Kind of Activity, in Constant Prices
(Continued)

Million Ethiopian birr — Fiscal year ending 7 July

	1970	1971	1972	1973	1974	1975	1976	1977	1978	1979	1980
				At constant prices of:1961							
6 Wholesale and retail trade, restaurants and hotels [a]	296.6	311.7	324.6	335.9	358.6	356.2	362.3	...	...	...	...
7 Transport, storage and communication	195.3	215.4	236.1	249.6	254.1	255.4	285.2	...	...	...	...
8 Finance, insurance, real estate and business services [b]	183.8	195.1	202.5	215.0	231.1	247.2	261.0	...	...	...	...
9 Community, social and personal services [ab]	159.1	173.1	192.1	202.3	209.9	215.3	218.9	...	...	...	...
Total, Industries	3209.6	3359.4	3512.7	3590.8	3627.5	3601.0	3678.8	...	...	...	...
Producers of Government Services	182.2	186.0	203.3	225.9	245.0	274.4	287.9	...	...	...	...
Other Producers	59.6	60.7	61.8	62.9	63.5	64.1	64.7	...	...	...	...
Subtotal [c]	3451.4	3606.1	3777.8	3879.6	3936.0	3939.5	4031.4	...	...	...	...
Less: Imputed bank service charge	...	...	...	...	...	...	...	...	...	...	...
Plus: Import duties	...	...	...	...	...	...	...	...	...	...	...
Plus: Value added tax	...	...	...	...	...	...	...	...	...	...	...
Equals: Gross Domestic Product	3451.4	3606.1	3777.8	3879.6	3936.0	3939.5	4031.4	...	...	...	...

a) Restaurants and hotels are included in item 'Community, social and personal services'.
b) Business services are included in item 'Community, social and personal services'.
c) Gross domestic product in factor values.

1.12 Relations Among National Accounting Aggregates

Million Ethiopian birr — Fiscal year ending 7 July

	1970	1971	1972	1973	1974	1975	1976	1977	1978	1979	1980
Gross Domestic Product	4460.6	4710.4	4743.7	5005.2	5551.2	5524.5	6004.0	...	...	...	...
Plus: Net factor income received from abroad	...	...	-50.3	-47.7	-23.1	-29.3	-3.2	...	...	...	...
Factor income received [a]	...	...	8.2	18.3	42.6	29.5	34.9	...	...	...	...
Less: Factor income paid [a]	...	...	58.5	66.0	65.7	58.8	38.1	...	...	...	...
Equals: Gross National Product	...	...	4693.4	4957.5	5528.1	5495.2	...	...	...	...	...
Less: Consumption of fixed capital	...	...	...	...	...	...	...	...	...	...	...
Less: Net indirect taxes paid to supranational organisations	...	...	...	...	...	...	...	...	...	...	...
Equals: National Income at Market Prices	...	...	...	...	...	...	...	...	...	...	...
Plus: Net current transfers received from abroad	...	...	...	...	...	...	...	...	...	...	...
Equals: National Disposable Income at Market Prices	...	...	...	...	...	...	...	...	...	...	...
Less: Final consumption	...	...	...	...	...	...	...	...	...	...	...
Equals: Net Saving	...	...	...	...	...	...	...	...	...	...	...
Less: Surplus of the nation on current transactions	...	...	...	...	...	...	...	...	...	...	...
Equals: Net Capital Formation	...	...	...	...	...	...	...	...	...	...	...

a) For 1975, including insurance claims.

2.9 Gross Capital Formation by Kind of Activity of Owner, ISIC Major Divisions, in Current Prices

Million Ethiopian birr — Fiscal year ending 7 July

	1970			1971			1972			1973		
	Total Gross Capital Formation	Increase in Stocks	Gross Fixed Capital Formation	Total Gross Capital Formation	Increase in Stocks	Gross Fixed Capital Formation	Total Gross Capital Formation	Increase in Stocks	Gross Fixed Capital Formation	Total Gross Capital Formation	Increase in Stocks	Gross Fixed Capital Formation
						All Producers						
1 Agriculture, hunting, fishing and forestry	...	...	63.2	...	...	69.0	...	...	86.3	...	...	67.0
2 Mining and quarrying	...	...	4.2	...	...	5.0	...	...	2.1	...	...	1.3
3 Manufacturing	...	...	89.7	...	...	95.0	...	...	95.1	...	...	76.9
4 Electricity, gas and water	...	...	25.7	...	...	46.5	...	...	42.8	...	...	19.9
5 Construction	...	...	10.5	...	...	13.7	...	...	20.9	...	...	7.0
6 Wholesale and retail trade, restaurants and hotels	...	...	103.2	...	...	124.7	...	...	132.6	...	...	137.2
7 Transport, storage and communication	...	...		...	...		...	...		...	...	
8 Finance, insurance, real estate and business services	...	...	171.5	...	...	165.7	...	...	179.0	...	...	200.5
9 Community, social and personal services	...	...	38.2	...	...	28.8	...	...	34.5	...	...	50.8
Total Industries	...	...	506.2	...	...	548.4	...	...	593.3	...	...	560.6
Producers of Government Services	...	...	6.3	...	...	6.0	...	...	9.8	...	...	8.7
Private Non-Profit Institutions Serving Households	...	...	...	...	...	...	...	...	...	...	...	...
Total	...	...	512.5	...	...	554.4	...	...	603.1	...	...	569.3

# Ethiopia

2.9 Gross Capital Formation by Kind of Activity of Owner, ISIC Major Divisions, in Current Prices

Million Ethiopian birr — Fiscal year ending 7 July

	1974 Total Gross Capital Formation	1974 Increase in Stocks	1974 Gross Fixed Capital Formation	1975 Total Gross Capital Formation	1975 Increase in Stocks	1975 Gross Fixed Capital Formation	1976 Total Gross Capital Formation	1976 Increase in Stocks	1976 Gross Fixed Capital Formation
All Producers									
1 Agriculture, hunting, fishing and forestry	...	...	64.2	...	...	78.0	...	...	70.5
2 Mining and quarrying	...	...	1.3	...	...	2.4	...	...	1.6
3 Manufacturing	...	...	42.1	...	...	50.6	...	...	47.0
4 Electricity, gas and water	...	...	11.4	...	...	15.9	...	...	15.9
5 Construction	...	...	5.4	...	...	11.6	...	...	5.1
6 Wholesale and retail trade, restaurants and hotels	...	...	119.1	...	...	135.5	...	...	197.2
7 Transport, storage and communication	...	...		...	...		...	...	
8 Finance, insurance, real estate and business services	...	...	219.1	...	...	217.1	...	...	181.0
9 Community, social and personal services	...	...	75.8	...	...	68.0	...	...	47.2
Total Industries	...	...	538.4	...	...	579.1	...	...	565.5
Producers of Government Services	...	...	11.0	...	...	1.6	...	...	12.5
Private Non-Profit Institutions Serving Households	...	...	...	...	...	...	...	...	...
Total	...	...	548.9	...	...	579.7	...	...	578.0

2.17 Exports and Imports of Goods and Services, Detail

Million Ethiopian birr — Fiscal year ending 7 July

	1970	1971	1972	1973	1974	1975	1976	1977	1978	1979	1980
Exports of Goods and Services											
1 Exports of merchandise, f.o.b.	...	...	385.3	503.7	556.5	497.8	581.1	...	...	...	...
2 Transport and communication	...	...	66.0	72.5	57.0	79.4	82.6	...	...	...	...
a In respect of merchandise imports	...	...	...	...	...	...	6.1	...	...	...	...
b Other	...	...	66.0	72.5	57.0	79.4	76.5	...	...	...	...
3 Insurance service charges	...	...	1.9	2.6	4.8	...	4.1	...	...	...	...
a In respect of merchandise imports	...	...	...	...	...	...	...	...	...	...	...
b Other	...	...	1.9	2.6	4.8	...	4.1	...	...	...	...
4 Other commodities	...	...	64.4	78.4	86.1	52.5	39.8	...	...	...	...
5 Adjustments of merchandise exports to change-of-ownership basis	...	...	...	...	...	...	...	...	...	...	...
6 Direct purchases in the domestic market by non-residential households	...	...	50.8	59.6	72.0	74.1	78.1	...	...	...	...
7 Direct purchases in the domestic market by extraterritorial bodies	...	...	...	...	...	...	...	...	...	...	...
Total Exports of Goods and Services	...	...	568.4	716.8	776.4	703.8	785.7	...	...	...	...
Imports of Goods and Services											
1 Imports of merchandise, c.i.f.	...	...	435.6	448.2	603.3	699.7	851.7	...	...	...	...
a Imports of merchandise, f.o.b.	...	...	366.0	376.3	506.9	586.5	713.5	...	...	...	...
b Transport of services on merchandise imports	...	...	69.6	71.9	96.4	113.2	138.2	...	...	...	...
By residents	...	...	4.8	4.9	6.5	7.6	9.4	...	...	...	...
By non-residents	...	...	64.8	67.0	89.9	105.6	128.8	...	...	...	...
c Insurance service charges on merchandise imports	...	...	...	...	...	...	...	...	...	...	...
By residents	...	...	...	...	...	...	...	...	...	...	...

Ethiopia

2.17 Exports and Imports of Goods and Services, Detail
(Continued)

Million Ethiopian birr   Fiscal year ending 7 July

	1970	1971	1972	1973	1974	1975	1976	1977	1978	1979	1980
By non-residents	...	...	4.8	4.9	6.6	7.7	9.4	...	...	...	...
2 Adjustments of merchandise imports to change-of-ownership basis	...	...	...	...	...	...	...	...	...	...	...
3 Other transport and communication	...	...	22.6	25.1	...	...	51.0	...	...	...	...
4 Other insurance service charges	...	...	4.9	6.0	6.3	7.3	4.5	...	...	...	...
5 Other commodities	...	...	54.9	65.3	98.6	112.9	35.2	...	...	...	...
6 Direct purchases abroad by government	...	...	21.0	19.1	21.0	33.4	39.4	...	...	...	...
7 Direct purchases abroad by resident households	...	...						...	...	...	...
Total Imports of Goods and Services	...	...	539.0	563.7	729.2	853.3	981.8	...	...	...	...
Balance of Goods and Services	...	...	29.4	153.1	47.2	-149.5	-196.1	...	...	...	...
Total Imports and Balance of Goods and Services	...	...	568.4	716.8	776.4	703.8	785.7	...	...	...	...

3.12 General Government Income and Outlay Account: Total and Subsectors

Million Ethiopian birr   Fiscal year ending 7 July

	1972					1973				
	Total General Government	Central Government	State or Provincial Government	Local Government	Social Security Funds	Total General Government	Central Government	State or Provincial Government	Local Government	Social Security Funds

Receipts

1 Property and entrepreneurial income	...	21.7	...	...	...	...	27.5	...	...	...
a Net operating surplus	...	...	...	...	...	...	...	...	...	...
b Withdrawals from public quasi-corporations	...	1.2	...	...	...	...	2.0	...	...	...
c Interest	...	...	...	...	...	...	...	...	...	...
d Dividends	...	...	...	...	...	...	...	...	...	...
e Net land rent and royalties	...	...	...	...	...	...	...	...	...	...
2 Taxes, fees and contributions	...	457.1	...	...	...	...	515.3	...	...	...
a Indirect taxes	...	306.7	...	...	...	...	353.1	...	...	...
b Direct taxes	...	133.1	...	...	...	...	142.1	...	...	...
c Social security contributions	...	6.4	...	...	...	...	7.4	...	...	...
d Fees, fines and penalties	...	10.9	...	...	...	...	12.7	...	...	...
3 Other current transfers received	...	86.8	...	...	...	...	90.7	...	...	...
a Casualty insurance claims	...	...	...	...	...	...	...	...	...	...
b Transfers from other government subsectors	...	...	...	...	...	...	...	...	...	...
c Transfers from abroad	...	86.8	...	...	...	...	90.7	...	...	...
d Other transfers, except imputed	...	...	...	...	...	...	...	...	...	...
e Imputed unfunded employee welfare contributions	...	...	...	...	...	...	...	...	...	...
Total Current Receipts	...	565.6	...	...	...	...	633.5	...	...	...

Disbursements

1 General government final consumption expenditures	...	487.9	...	...	...	...	514.2	...	...	...
2 Property income paid	...	16.2	...	...	...	...	17.5	...	...	...

3.12 General Government Income and Outlay Account: Total and Subsectors
(Continued)

Ethiopia

Million Ethiopian birr — Fiscal year ending 7 July

	1972 Total General Government	1972 Central Government	1972 State or Provincial Government	1972 Local Government	1972 Social Security Funds	1973 Total General Government	1973 Central Government	1973 State or Provincial Government	1973 Local Government	1973 Social Security Funds
3 Subsidies	...	0.8	...	...	...	...	0.9	...	...	...
4 Other current transfers paid	...	30.8	...	...	...	...	33.4	...	...	...
a Casualty insurance premiums, net	...	...	...	...	...	...	...	...	...	...
b Transfers to other government subsectors	...	...	...	...	...	...	...	...	...	...
c Transfers to households	...	...	...	...	...	...	28.4	...	...	...
Social security benefits	...	23.9	...	...	...	...	...	...	...	...
Social assistance grants	...	...	...	...	...	...	...	...	...	...
Unfunded employee welfare benefits	...	...	...	...	...	...	...	...	...	...
d Transfers to private non-profit institutions serving households	...	...	...	...	...	...	...	...	...	...
e Transfers to the rest of the world	...	2.0	...	...	...	...	2.1	...	...	...
Net saving	...	29.9	...	...	...	...	67.5	...	...	...
Total Current Disbursements and Net Saving	...	565.6	...	...	...	...	633.5	...	...	...

	1974 Total General Government	1974 Central Government	1974 State or Provincial Government	1974 Local Government	1974 Social Security Funds	1975 Total General Government	1975 Central Government	1975 State or Provincial Government	1975 Local Government	1975 Social Security Funds
Receipts										
1 Property and entrepreneurial income	...	29.4	...	...	...	...	61.0	...	...	...
a Net operating surplus	...	...	...	...	...	...	...	...	...	...
b Withdrawals from public quasi-corporations	...	5.8	...	...	...	...	.	...	...	...
c Interest	...	...	...	...	...	...	...	...	...	...
d Dividends	...	...	...	...	...	...	...	...	...	...
e Net land rent and royalties	...	...	...	...	...	...	...	...	...	...
2 Taxes, fees and contributions	...	570.2	...	...	...	...	630.6	...	...	...
a Indirect taxes	...	396.1	...	...	...	...	426.0	...	...	...
b Direct taxes	...	151.6	...	...	...	...	176.8	...	...	...
c Social security contributions	...	8.1	...	...	...	...	11.4	...	...	...
d Fees, fines and penalties	...	14.4	...	...	...	...	16.4	...	...	...
3 Other current transfers received	...	66.0	...	...	...	...	64.0	...	...	...
a Casualty insurance claims	...	...	...	...	...	...	...	...	...	...
b Transfers from other government subsectors	...	...	...	...	...	...	...	...	...	...
c Transfers from abroad	...	65.8	...	...	...	...	64.0	...	...	...
d Other transfers, except imputed	...	...	...	...	...	...	...	...	...	...
e Imputed unfunded employee welfare contributions	...	...	...	...	...	...	...	...	...	...
Total Current Receipts	...	665.6	...	...	...	...	755.6	...	...	...
Disbursements										
1 General government final consumption expenditures	...	564.2	...	...	...	...	708.4	...	...	...
2 Property income paid	...	17.7	...	...	...	...	20.1	...	...	...

Ethiopia

3.12 General Government Income and Outlay Account: Total and Subsectors
(Continued)

Million Ethiopian birr — Fiscal year ending 7 July

	1974 Total General Government	1974 Central Government	1974 State or Provincial Government	1974 Local Government	1974 Social Security Funds	1975 Total General Government	1975 Central Government	1975 State or Provincial Government	1975 Local Government	1975 Social Security Funds
3 Subsidies	...	13.1	...	...	...	...	36.0	...	...	...
4 Other current transfers paid	...	36.8	...	...	...	...	73.6	...	...	...
a Casualty insurance premiums, net	...	...	...	...	...	...	...	...	...	...
b Transfers to other government subsectors	...	...	...	...	...	...	...	...	...	...
c Transfers to households	...	30.1	...	...	...	...	70.9	...	...	...
Social security benefits	...	28.6	...	...	...	...	44.4	...	...	...
Social assistance grants	...	1.5	...	...	...	...	26.5	...	...	...
Unfunded employee welfare benefits	...	...	...	...	...	...	...	...	...	...
d Transfers to private non-profit institutions serving households	...	4.1	...	...	...	...	1.3	...	...	...
e Transfers to the rest of the world	...	2.7	...	...	...	...	1.4	...	...	...
Net saving	...	33.8	...	...	...	...	-82.6	...	...	...
Total Current Disbursements and Net Saving	...	665.6	...	...	...	...	755.5	...	...	...

	1976 Total General Government	1976 Central Government	1976 State or Provincial Government	1976 Local Government	1976 Social Security Funds

Receipts

1 Property and entrepreneurial income	...	43.0	...	...	...
a Net operating surplus	...	...	...	...	...
b Withdrawals from public quasi-corporations	...	-	...	...	...
c Interest	...	...	...	...	...
d Dividends	...	...	...	...	...
e Net land rent and royalties	...	...	...	...	...
2 Taxes, fees and contributions	...	656.6	...	...	...
a Indirect taxes	...	450.5	...	...	...
b Direct taxes	...	174.4	...	...	...
c Social security contributions	...	13.7	...	...	...
d Fees, fines and penalties	...	18.0	...	...	...
3 Other current transfers received	...	41.7	...	...	...
a Casualty insurance claims	...	...	...	...	...
b Transfers from other government subsectors	...	...	...	...	...
c Transfers from abroad	...	41.7	...	...	...
d Other transfers, except imputed	...	...	...	...	...
e Imputed unfunded employee welfare contributions	...	...	...	...	...
Total Current Receipts	...	741.3	...	...	...

Disbursements

1 General government final consumption expenditures	...	843.8	...	...	...
2 Property income paid	...	32.8	...	...	...

Ethiopia

3.12 General Government Income and Outlay Account: Total and Subsectors
(Continued)

Million Ethiopian birr — Fiscal year ending 7 July

	\multicolumn{5}{c	}{1976}
	Total General Government	Central Government	State or Provincial Government	Local Government	Social Security Funds
3 Subsidies	...	8.9	...	...	...
4 Other current transfers paid	...	71.0	...	...	...
a Casualty insurance premiums, net	...	...	...	...	...
b Transfers to other government subsectors	...	...	...	...	...
c Transfers to households	...	...	...	...	...
Social security benefits	...	48.6	...	...	...
Social assistance grants	...	...	...	...	...
Unfunded employee welfare benefits	...	...	...	...	...
d Transfers to private non-profit institutions serving households	...	...	...	...	...
e Transfers to the rest of the world	...	2.4	...	...	...
Net saving	...	-215.2	...	...	...
Total Current Disbursements and Net Saving	...	741.3	...	...	...

3.13 General Government Capital Accumulation Account: Total and Subsectors

Million Ethiopian birr — Fiscal year ending 7 July

	\multicolumn{5}{c	}{1972}	\multicolumn{5}{c	}{1973}
	Total General Government	Central Government	State or Provincial Government	Local Government	Social Security Funds	Total General Government	Central Government	State or Provincial Government	Local Government	Social Security Funds

Finance of Gross Accumulation

1 Gross saving	...	29.9	...	...	...	...	67.5	...	...	...
a Consumption of fixed capital	...	-	...	...	...	...	-	...	...	...
b Net saving	...	29.9	...	...	...	...	67.5	...	...	...
2 Capital transfers received a	...	-1.5	...	...	...	...	-0.1	...	...	...
a From other government subsectors	...	...	...	...	...	...	...	...	...	...
b From other resident sectors	...	-7.6	...	...	...	...	-1.1	...	...	...
c From rest of the world	...	6.1	...	...	...	...	1.0	...	...	...
Finance of Gross Accumulation	...	28.4	...	...	...	...	67.4	...	...	...

Gross Accumulation

1 Gross capital formation	...	92.8	...	...	...	...	91.9	...	...	...
2 Purchases of land, net	...	-	...	...	...	...	-	...	...	...
3 Purchases of intangible assets, net	...	-	...	...	...	...	-	...	...	...
4 Capital transfers paid	...	...	...	...	...	...	...	...	...	...
Net lending	...	-64.4	...	...	...	...	-24.5	...	...	...
Gross Accumulation	...	28.4	...	...	...	...	67.4	...	...	...

	\multicolumn{5}{c	}{1974}	\multicolumn{5}{c	}{1975}
	Total General Government	Central Government	State or Provincial Government	Local Government	Social Security Funds	Total General Government	Central Government	State or Provincial Government	Local Government	Social Security Funds

Finance of Gross Accumulation

1 Gross saving	...	33.8	...	...	...	...	-82.6	...	...	...
a Consumption of fixed capital	...	-	...	...	...	...	-	...	...	...
b Net saving	...	33.8	...	...	...	...	-82.6	...	...	...
2 Capital transfers received a	...	31.5	...	...	...	...	9.9	...	...	...
a From other government subsectors	...	...	...	...	...	...	...	...	...	...
b From other resident sectors	...	-0.6	...	...	...	...	-22.2	...	...	...
c From rest of the world	...	32.1	...	...	...	...	32.1	...	...	...
Finance of Gross Accumulation	...	65.3	...	...	...	...	-72.7	...	...	...

Gross Accumulation

1 Gross capital formation	...	81.0	...	...	...	...	105.4	...	...	...
2 Purchases of land, net	...	-	...	...	...	...	-	...	...	...
3 Purchases of intangible assets, net	...	-	...	...	...	...	-	...	...	...
4 Capital transfers paid	...	...	...	...	...	...	...	...	...	...
Net lending	...	-15.7	...	...	...	...	-178.1	...	...	...
Gross Accumulation	...	65.3	...	...	...	...	-72.7	...	...	...

Ethiopia

3.13 General Government Capital Accumulation Account: Total and Subsectors

Million Ethiopian birr — Fiscal year ending 7 July

1976

	Total General Government	Central Government	State or Provincial Government	Local Government	Social Security Funds
Finance of Gross Accumulation					
1 Gross saving	...	-215.2	...	...	...
a Consumption of fixed capital	...	.	...	...	...
b Net saving	...	-215.2	...	...	...
2 Capital transfers received [a]	...	25.1	...	...	...
a From other government subsectors	...	...	...	...	...
b From other resident sectors	...	-10.4	...	...	...
c From rest of the world	...	35.5	...	...	...
Finance of Gross Accumulation	...	-190.1	...	...	...
Gross Accumulation					
1 Gross capital formation	...	162.2	...	...	...
2 Purchases of land, net	...	.	...	...	...
3 Purchases of intangible assets, net	...	.	...	...	...
4 Capital transfers paid	...	...	...	...	...
Net lending	...	-352.3	...	...	...
Gross Accumulation	...	-190.1	...	...	...

a) Net.

3.14 General Government Capital Finance Account, Total and Subsectors

Million Ethiopian birr — Fiscal year ending 7 July

1972 / 1973

	1972 Total Gen. Gov.	1972 Central	1972 State/Prov.	1972 Local	1972 SSF	1973 Total Gen. Gov.	1973 Central	1973 State/Prov.	1973 Local	1973 SSF
Acquisition of Financial Assets										
1 Gold and SDRs	...	...	...	...	...	...	...	...	...	...
2 Currency and transferable deposits	...	-1.3	...	...	...	...	-10.8	...	...	...
3 Other deposits	...	...	...	...	...	...	...	...	...	...
4 Bills and bonds, short term	...	...	...	...	...	...	...	...	...	...
5 Bonds, long term	...	.	...	...	...	...	...	...	...	...
6 Corporate equity securities	...	...	...	...	...	...	...	...	...	...
7 Short-term loans, n.e.c.	...	...	...	...	...	...	...	...	...	...
8 Long-term loans, n.e.c.	...	...	...	...	...	...	...	...	...	...
9 Other receivables	...	7.4	...	...	...	...	16.7	...	...	...
10 Other assets	...	-4.2	...	...	...	...	8.9	...	...	...
Total Acquisition of Financial Assets	...	2.0	...	...	...	...	14.9	...	...	...
Incurrence of Liabilities										
1 Currency and transferable deposits	...	...	...	...	...	...	...	...	...	...
2 Other deposits	...	...	...	...	...	...	...	...	...	...
3 Bills and bonds, short term	...	9.0	...	...	...	...	6.5	...	...	...
4 Bonds, long term	...	2.3	...	...	...	...	5.8	...	...	...
5 Short-term loans, n.e.c.	...	9.0	...	...	...	...	-13.0	...	...	...
6 Long-term loans, n.e.c.	...	44.1	...	...	...	...	39.8	...	...	...
7 Other payables	...	...	...	...	...	...	...	...	...	...
8 Other liabilities	...	...	...	...	...	...	...	...	...	...
Total Incurrence of Liabilities	...	64.4	...	...	...	...	39.1	...	...	...
Statistical discrepancy	...	2.0	...	...	...	...	0.3	...	...	...
Net Lending	...	-64.4	...	...	...	...	-24.5	...	...	...
Incurrence of Liabilities and Net Worth	...	.	...	...	...	...	14.6	...	...	...

1974 / 1975

	1974 Total Gen. Gov.	1974 Central	1974 State/Prov.	1974 Local	1974 SSF	1975 Total Gen. Gov.	1975 Central	1975 State/Prov.	1975 Local	1975 SSF
Acquisition of Financial Assets										
1 Gold and SDRs	...	...	...	...	...	...	...	...	...	...
2 Currency and transferable deposits	...	15.9	...	...	...	...	18.9	...	...	...
3 Other deposits	...	...	...	...	...	...	...	...	...	...
4 Bills and bonds, short term	...	...	...	...	...	...	...	...	...	...

Ethiopia

3.14 General Government Capital Finance Account, Total and Subsectors
(Continued)

Million Ethiopian birr — Fiscal year ending 7 July

	1974 Total General Government	1974 Central Government	1974 State or Provincial Government	1974 Local Government	1974 Social Security Funds	1975 Total General Government	1975 Central Government	1975 State or Provincial Government	1975 Local Government	1975 Social Security Funds
5 Bonds, long term	...	...	...	...	...	...	...	...	...	...
6 Corporate equity securities	...	...	...	...	...	...	...	...	...	...
7 Short-term loans, n.e.c.	...	...	...	...	...	...	...	...	...	...
8 Long-term loans, n.e.c.	...	...	...	...	...	...	...	...	...	...
9 Other receivables	...	13.8	...	...	...	...	23.4	...	...	...
10 Other assets	...	15.6	...	...	...	...	23.9	...	...	...
Total Acquisition of Financial Assets	...	45.3	...	...	...	...	66.2	...	...	...

Incurrence of Liabilities

1 Currency and transferable deposits	...	...	...	...	...	...	...	...	...	...
2 Other deposits	...	...	...	...	...	...	...	...	...	...
3 Bills and bonds, short term	...	27.4	...	...	...	...	15.0	...	...	...
4 Bonds, long term	...	8.4	...	...	...	...	101.1	...	...	...
5 Short-term loans, n.e.c.	...	-21.0	...	...	...	...	30.0	...	...	...
6 Long-term loans, n.e.c.	...	46.9	...	...	...	...	98.3	...	...	...
7 Other payables	...	...	...	...	...	...	...	...	...	...
8 Other liabilities	...	...	...	...	...	...	...	...	...	...
Total Incurrence of Liabilities	...	61.7	...	...	...	...	244.4	...	...	...
Statistical discrepancy	...	-0.7	...	...	...	...	-0.1	...	...	...
Net Lending	...	-15.7	...	...	...	...	-178.1	...	...	...
Incurrence of Liabilities and Net Worth	...	46.0	...	...	...	...	66.3	...	...	...

	1976 Total General Government	1976 Central Government	1976 State or Provincial Government	1976 Local Government	1976 Social Security Funds

Acquisition of Financial Assets

1 Gold and SDRs	...	...	...	...	...
2 Currency and transferable deposits	...	-16.5	...	...	...
3 Other deposits	...	...	...	...	...
4 Bills and bonds, short term	...	...	...	...	...
5 Bonds, long term	...	...	...	...	...
6 Corporate equity securities	...	...	...	...	...
7 Short-term loans, n.e.c.	...	...	...	...	...
8 Long-term loans, n.e.c.	...	...	...	...	...
9 Other receivables	...	9.1	...	...	...
10 Other assets	...	26.5	...	...	...
Total Acquisition of Financial Assets	...	-35.1	...	...	...

Incurrence of Liabilities

1 Currency and transferable deposits	...	...	...	...	...
2 Other deposits	...	...	...	...	...
3 Bills and bonds, short term	...	9.0	...	...	...
4 Bonds, long term	...	150.8	...	...	...
5 Short-term loans, n.e.c.	...	44.0	...	...	...
6 Long-term loans, n.e.c.	...	104.3	...	...	...
7 Other payables	...	...	...	...	...
8 Other liabilities	...	...	...	...	...
Total Incurrence of Liabilities	...	308.1	...	...	...
Statistical discrepancy	...	9.1	...	...	...
Net Lending	...	-352.3	...	...	...
Incurrence of Liabilities and Net Worth	...	-44.2	...	...	...

Ethiopia

3.51 External Transactions: Current Account: Detail

Million Ethiopian birr — Fiscal year ending 7 July

	1970	1971	1972	1973	1974	1975	1976	1977	1978	1979	1980
Payments to the Rest of the World											
1 Imports of goods and services	...	...	539.0	563.7	729.2	853.3	981.8	...	...	...	...
a Imports of merchandise c.i.f.	...	...	435.6	448.2	603.3	699.7	851.7	...	...	...	...
b Other	...	...	103.4	115.5	125.9	153.6	130.1	...	...	...	...
2 Factor income paid to the rest of the world	...	...	58.5	66.0	65.7	58.8	38.1	...	...	...	...
a Compensation of employees	...	...	6.1	6.0	...	7.5	...	...	...	...	...
b Property and entrepreneurial income paid [a]	...	...	52.4	60.0	...	51.3	38.1	...	...	...	...
3 Indirect taxes paid to supranational organizations	...	...	...	...	...	...	...	...	...	...	...
4 Other current transfers to the rest of the world	...	...	25.8	24.6	35.1	23.5	9.4	...	...	...	...
a By general government	...	...	.	.	.	.	.	...	...	...	...
b By other resident sectors	...	...	25.8	24.6	35.1	23.5	9.4	...	...	...	...
5 Surplus of the nation on current transactions	...	...	19.7	159.2	132.1	-96.1	-68.3	...	...	...	...
Payments to the Rest of the World, and Surplus of the Nation on Current Transfers	...	...	643.0	813.5	962.1	839.5	961.0	...	...	...	...
Receipts From The Rest of the World											
1 Exports of goods and services	...	...	568.4	716.8	776.4	703.8	785.7	...	...	...	...
a Exports of merchandise f.o.b.	...	...	385.3	503.7	556.5	497.8	581.1	...	...	...	...
b Other	...	...	183.1	213.1	219.9	206.0	204.6	...	...	...	...
2 Factor income received from the rest of the world	...	...	8.2	18.3	42.6	29.5	34.9	...	...	...	...
a Compensation of employees	...	...	.	.	.	.	.	...	...	...	...
b Property and entrepreneurial income received [a]	...	...	8.2	18.3	42.6	29.5	34.9	...	...	...	...
3 Subsidies received from supranational organizations	...	...	...	...	...	...	...	...	...	...	...
4 Other current transfers from the rest of the world	...	...	66.4	78.4	143.1	106.2	140.4	...	...	...	...
a To general government	...	...	34.2	30.0	70.3	52.7	85.7	...	...	...	...
b To other resident sectors	...	...	32.2	48.4	72.8	53.5	54.7	...	...	...	...
Receipts from the Rest of the World on Current Transfers	...	...	643.0	813.5	962.1	839.5	961.0	...	...	...	...

a) For 1975, including insurance claims.

3.52 External Transactions: Capital Accumulation Account

Million Ethiopian birr — Fiscal year ending 7 July

	1970	1971	1972	1973	1974	1975	1976	1977	1978	1979	1980
Finance of Gross Accumulation											
1 Surplus of the nation on current transactions	...	...	19.7	159.2	132.1	-96.1	-68.3	...	...	...	...
2 Capital transfers received from the rest of the world	...	...	...	...	...	...	...	...	...	...	...
Total Finance of Gross Accumulation	...	...	...	...	...	...	...	...	...	...	...
Gross Accumulation											
1 Capital transfers paid to the rest of the world	...	...	...	...	...	...	...	...	...	...	...
2 Purchases of intangible assets, n.e.c., net, from the rest of the world	...	...	...	...	...	...	...	...	...	...	...
3 Net lending to the rest of the world	...	...	10.3	126.9	101.5	-122.9	-81.8	...	...	...	...
Total Gross Accumulation	...	...	...	...	...	...	...	...	...	...	...

3.53 External Transactions: Capital Finance Account

Million Ethiopian birr — Fiscal year ending 7 July

	1970	1971	1972	1973	1974	1975	1976	1977	1978	1979	1980
Acquisitions of Foreign Financial Assets											
1 Gold and SDR's	...	...	1.1	0.5	0.3	...	...	...	...	...	...
2 Currency and transferable deposits	...	...	57.3	172.8	0.4	46.9	32.1	...	...	...	...
3 Other deposits	...	...	4.4	11.6	197.3	-15.8	-1.1	...	...	...	...
4 Bills and bonds, short term	...	...	9.3	28.2	-1.6	-18.5	...	...	...	...	...

Ethiopia

3.53 External Transactions: Capital Finance Account
(Continued)

Million Ethiopian birr — Fiscal year ending 7 July

	1970	1971	1972	1973	1974	1975	1976	1977	1978	1979	1980
5 Bonds, long term	...	...	...	...	...	...	...	...	...	...	...
6 Corporate equity securities	...	...	...	...	...	...	...	...	...	...	...
7 Short-term loans, n.e.c.	...	...	...	...	...	...	...	...	...	...	...
8 Long-term loans	...	...	...	...	...	...	...	...	...	...	...
9 Proprietors' net additions to accumulation of quasi-corporate, non-resident enterprises	...	...		...	...	...	...	...	...	...	...
10 Trade credit and advances	...	...	-	25.3	-	-3.9	21.7	...	...	...	...
11 Other	...	...	-	0.7	0.7	...	-2.0	...	...	...	...
Total Acquisitions of Foreign Financial Assets	...	...	72.1	239.1	197.1	8.7	50.2	...	...	...	...

Incurrence of Foreign Liabilities

	1970	1971	1972	1973	1974	1975	1976	1977	1978	1979	1980
1 Currency and transferable deposits	...	...	-8.9	-	-2.2	1.7	-2.4	...	...	...	...
2 Other deposits	...	...	-	-2.9	2.5	5.5	...	...	...	...	...
3 Bills and bonds, short term	...	...	...	...	...	...	...	...	...	...	...
4 Bonds, long term	...	...	...	...	...	...	...	...	...	...	...
5 Corporate equity securities	...	...	9.9	47.4	-	30.8	-	...	...	...	...
6 Short-term loans, n.e.c.	...	...	...	...	...	...	...	...	...	...	...
7 Long-term loans	...	...	48.5	45.4	44.4	107.3	131.6	...	...	...	...
8 Non-resident proprietors' net additions to accumulation of resident quasi-corporate enterprises	...	...	12.4	17.6	60.3	8.8	8.7	...	...	...	...
9 Trade credit and advances	...	...	-	2.8	-9.3	-22.5	-4.8	...	...	...	...
10 Other	...	...	-0.1	-0.1	-0.1	...	-1.1	...	...	...	...
Total Incurrence of Liabilities	...	...	61.8	110.2	95.6	131.6	132.0	...	...	...	...
Net Lending	...	...	10.3	128.9	101.5	-122.9	-81.8	...	...	...	...
Total Incurrence of Liabilities and Net Lending	...	...	72.1	239.1	197.1	8.7	50.2	...	...	...	...

Fiji

General note. The preparation of national accounts statistics in Fiji is undertaken by the Bureau of Statistics, Suva. The official estimates together with methodological notes are published in a series of reports entitled 'National Accounts Studies'. The third volume of this series, 'The National Accounts of Fiji 1968-1972', contains a detailed description of the sources and methods used for the national accounts estimation. The estimates are generally in accordance with the classifications and definitions recommended in the United Nations System of National Accounts (SNA). Input-output tables have been compiled for the years 1966 and 1967. The 1967 tables were published in 1970 in 'An Input-Output Table for Fiji 1967'. The following tables have been prepared from successive replies to the United Nations national accounts questionnaire. When the scope and coverage of the estimates differ for conceptual or statistical reasons from the definitions and classifications recommended in SNA, a footnote is indicated to the relevant tables.

Sources and methods:
(a) **Gross domestic product.** Gross domestic product is estimated mainly through the production approach.
(b) **Expenditure on the gross domestic product.** All components of GDP by expenditure type are estimated through the expenditure approach except private final consumption expenditure which is mostly based on the commodity-flow approach. The estimates of government final consumption expenditure are based on the annual report 'An Economic and Functional Classification of Government Accounts'. For private consumption expenditure estimates, all imported items valued at landed cost from foreign trade statistics and producers' values from industrial censuses are grossed up by margins established in the 1970 Census of Distribution and Services. Special estimates are made for those items of consumer expenditure, such as food, electricity, gas and water, medical services and recreation, which are not covered by the commodity-flow approach. For these estimates data from the household budget survey in 1972, income tax statistics and the 1970 census of distribution are used. Estimates of gross capital formation for the private industries are based on surveys of capital investment, for government industries and producers of government services the estimates are derived from government accounts and for the producers of private non-profit services to households from the 1970/1971 survey of non-profit making institutions. Value of imports and exports of goods and services are obtained from the balance of payments and annual shipping and aircraft statistics. For the constant price estimates, the current values of the expenditure items are deflated by various price indexes such as consumer price index, index of rural produce prices, implicit price index of value added of building and construction, trade index of exports, etc.
(c) **Cost-structure of the gross domestic product.** Estimates of the cost-structure of GDP are made from the various sectoral surveys and taxation data. Estimates of indirect taxes and subsidies are based on government accounts.
(d) **Gross domestic product by kind of economic activity.** The table of GDP by kind of economic activity is prepared at market price, i.e. producers' values. The production approach is used to estimate value added of most industries, such as agriculture, mining, manufacturing, electricity, gas and water, construction, and for the trade sector in combination with the commodity-flow approach. The income approach is used to estimate value added of restaurants and hotels and most of the sub-sectors of the service industries. For the agricultural sector, the total output of sugar-cane and copra are estimated from material inputs revealed by annual industrial censuses. The bench-mark estimate of subsistence output is based on the 1968 Agricultural Census, the 1965 Rural-Urban Household Expenditure Survey and Bureau of Statistics data. The annual increases are based on estimates of population growth and an index of rural produce prices. For other agricultural produce gross output is based on 1968 and 1972 household budget surveys and intermediate consumption is based on case studies. The gross output and intermediate consumption of the industrial activity sectors are based on annual industrial censuses carried out since 1970. Estimates of gross output, intermediate consumption and compensation of employees of private construction are obtained from annual censuses of building and construction conducted annually since 1970. Government bodies engaged in construction are covered through their annual reports and operating budgets. For the trade sector, the estimates are based on statistics from the Inland Revenue Department and on the Census of Distribution 1970. The producers' values and c.i.f. import values are grossed up by the margin established in the 1970 Census of Distribution. Banking estimates are obtained from income tax statistics while insurance estimates are derived from annual surveys. Imputed rent per urban household is derived from the household budget survey in 1968, grossed up by the consumer price index for rent and the growth in urban population. For rural areas, an estimated rent has been assumed in 1968 and grossed up annually by a rural price factor and growth in rural population. Estimates for producers of government services are based on the operating budgets and government accounts and finance. Other services estimates are derived from income tax statistics, the 1970/71 survey of non-profit institutions and the 1970 Census of Distribution and Services. For the constant price estimates, the general approach used for the major crops of agriculture, industrial activity, transport, insurance and private services is extrapolaton. Value added is extrapolated by production indexes. Price deflation is used for construction, trade, restaurant and hotels, real estate, banking and producers of government services, the current value being deflated by various price indexes such as consumer price index, index of wage rates, etc.

1.1 Expenditure on the Gross Domestic Product, in Current Prices

Million Fiji dollars

	1970	1971	1972	1973	1974	1975	1976	1977	1978	1979	1980
1 General government final consumption expenditure	27	31	38	42	54	67	85	102	115	128	153
2 Private final consumption expenditure	125	147	181	261	334	382	434	417	459	520	590
3 Gross capital formation	43	53	63	76	85	116	135	151	178	265	304
a Increase in stocks	8	7	10	10	11	13	15	24	28	60	57
b Gross fixed capital formation	35	46	53	66	74	103	120	127	150	205	247
Residential buildings	15	19	23	...	...	...	...	...	...	...	...
Non-residential buildings	...	...	...	...	...	...	...	...	...	...	...
Other construction and land improvement etc.	4	5	7	...	...	...	...	...	...	...	...
Other	16	22	23	...	...	...	...	...	...	...	...
4 Exports of goods and services	93	106	120	153	221	242	235	290	299	386	470
5 Less: Imports of goods and services	99	122	144	199	245	245	265	308	330	432	519
Statistical discrepancy	4	-2	5	5	-	-	-	8	-19	-15	
Equals: Gross Domestic Product	192	212	261	338	450	562	624	660	702	852	998

1.2 Expenditure on the Gross Domestic Product, in Constant Prices

Million Fiji dollars

	1970	1971	1972	1973	1974	1975	1976	1977	1978	1979	1980
	\multicolumn{7}{c}{At constant prices of: 1968}		1977		
1 General government final consumption expenditure	25	27	30	30	32	35	42	45 / 102	104	111	...
2 Private final consumption expenditure	113	126	136	173	182	185	189	197 / 415	432	455	...
3 Gross capital formation	36	41	46	50	45	49	49	49 / 153	165	227	...
a Increase in stocks	7	6	7	7	7	7	7	7 / 24	26	52	...
b Gross fixed capital formation	29	35	39	43	38	42	42	42 / 129	...	175	...

Fiji

1.2 Expenditure on the Gross Domestic Product, in Constant Prices
(Continued)

Million Fiji dollars

	1970	1971	1972	1973	1974	1975	1976	1977	1978	1979	1980
	\multicolumn{7}{c}{At constant prices of: 1968}	\multicolumn{4}{c}{1977}
Residential buildings	11	12	13	...	...	...	...	...	...	...	...
Non-residential buildings	...	...	...	...	...	...	...	...	...	...	...
Other construction and land improvement etc.	3	2	5	...	...	...	...	...	...	...	...
Other	15	21	21	...	...	...	...	...	...	...	...
4 Exports of goods and services	79	87	94	105	100	91	87	102 / 290	288	345	...
5 Less: Imports of goods and services	90	105	117	135	136	133	136	150 / 308	308	359	...
Statistical discrepancy	5	4	4	-7	-	-	-	- / 8	-8	-24	...
Equals: Gross Domestic Product	169	180	194	216	222	227	231	243 / 660	673	755	...

1.3 Cost Components of the Gross Domestic Product

Million Fiji dollars

	1970	1971	1972	1973	1974	1975	1976	1977	1978	1979	1980
1 Indirect taxes, net	23	28	31	37	39	46	52	54	59	73	81
a Indirect taxes paid	23	28	31	38	40	47	53	56	62	75	83
b Less: Subsidies received	-	-	-	1	1	1	1	2	3	2	2
2 Consumption of fixed capital	9	10	13	...	...	...	...	35	43	53	63
3 Compensation of employees paid by resident producers to:	73	82	109	...	...	...	...	288	313	359	423
4 Net operating surplus	87	93	109	...	...	...	...	283	287	367	431
Equals: Gross Domestic Product	192	212	261	338	450	562	624	660	702	852	998

1.4 General Government Current Receipts and Disbursements

Thousand Fiji dollars

	1970	1971	1972	1973	1974	1975	1976	1977	1978	1979	1980
\multicolumn{12}{c}{Receipts}
1 Property and entrepreneurial income	...	...	...	...	...	...	...	8555	10029	13205	...
2 Taxes, fees and contributions	...	...	...	...	...	...	...	124883	146778	171749	...
a Indirect taxes	...	...	...	...	...	...	...	56639	61965	75456	...
b Direct taxes	...	...	...	...	...	...	...	63982	77687	88534	...
c Social security contributions	...	...	...	...	...	...	...	148	140	212	...
d Compulsory fees, fines and penalties	...	...	...	...	...	...	...	4114	6986	7547	...
3 Other current receipts	...	...	...	...	...	...	...	21522	7505	14158	...
Total Current Receipts of General Government	...	...	...	...	...	...	...	154960	164312	199112	...
\multicolumn{12}{c}{Disbursements}
1 General government final consumption expenditure	...	...	...	...	...	...	...	100382	114647	130183	...
2 Property income paid	...	...	...	...	...	...	...	9731	12862	17638	...
a Interest	...	...	...	...	...	...	...	9731	12856	17632	...
b Net land rent and royalties	...	...	...	...	...	...	...	-	6	6	...
3 Subsidies	...	...	...	...	...	...	...	2299	2729	2635	...
4 Other current transfers paid	...	...	...	...	...	...	...	18604	22392	24556	...
a Social security benefits and social assistance grants	...	...	...	...	...	...	...	1273	1484	1660	...
b Other	...	...	...	...	...	...	...	17331	20908	22896	...
5 Net saving	...	...	...	...	...	...	...	23944	11682	24100	...
Total Current Disbursements and Net Saving of General Government	...	...	...	...	...	...	...	154960	164312	199112	...

Fiji

1.7 External Transactions on Current Account, Summary

Million Fiji dollars

	1970	1971	1972	1973	1974	1975	1976	1977	1978	1979	1980
Payments to the Rest of the World											
1 Imports of goods and services	...	...	...	...	...	...	...	308	330	432	518
2 Factor income paid to the rest of world	...	...	...	...	...	...	...	17	14	24	33
a Compensation of employees	...	...	...	...	...	...	...	2	2	1	-
b Property and entrepreneurial income paid	...	...	...	...	...	...	...	15	12	23	33
3 Indirect taxes paid to supranational organizations	...	...	...	...	...	...	...	...	...	...	...
4 Current transfers to the rest of the world	...	...	...	...	...	...	...	12	12	13	27
5 Surplus of the nation on current transactions	...	...	...	...	...	...	...	-32	-42	-64	-56
Payments to the Rest of the World and Surplus of the Nation on Current Transactions	...	...	...	...	...	...	...	305	315	405	522
Receipts From The Rest of the World											
1 Exports of goods and services	...	...	...	...	...	...	...	290	299	386	470
2 Factor income received from rest of the world	...	...	...	...	...	...	...	9	10	11	18
a Compensation of employees	...	...	...	...	...	...	...	2	2	2	3
b Property and entrepreneurial income received	...	...	...	...	...	...	...	7	8	9	15
3 Subsidies received from supranational organisations	...	...	...	...	...	...	...	...	...	...	...
4 Current transfers from rest of the world	...	...	...	...	...	...	...	6	6	8	34
Receipts from the Rest of the World on Current Transactions	...	...	...	...	...	...	...	305	315	405	522

1.8 Capital Transactions of The Nation, Summary

Million Fiji dollars

	1970	1971	1972	1973	1974	1975	1976	1977	1978	1979	1980
Finance of Gross Capital Formation											
Gross saving	34	27	41	...	...	...	...	128	118	187	247
1 Consumption of fixed capital	9	10	13	...	...	...	...	35	43	53	63
2 Net saving	25	17	28	...	...	...	...	93	75	134	184
Less: Surplus of the nation on current transactions	...	...	...	...	...	...	...	-32	-42	-64	-56
Finance of Gross Capital Formation	43	53	63	76	85	116	135	160	160	251	303
Gross Capital Formation											
Increase in stocks	8	7	10	10	11	13	15	32	10	45	57
Gross fixed capital formation	35	46	53	66	74	103	120	129	150	205	247
1 General government	7	9	10	...	...	...	...	...	...	...	...
2 Corporate and quasi-corporate enterprises	28	37	43	...	...	...	...	...	...	...	...
3 Other				...	...	...	...	...	...	...	...
Statistical discrepancy	...	...	...	...	...	...	...	-1	4	1	-1
Gross Capital Formation	43	53	63	76	85	116	135	160	160	251	303

1.10 Gross Domestic Product by Kind of Activity, in Current Prices

Million Fiji dollars

	1970	1971	1972	1973	1974	1975	1976	1977	1978	1979	1980
1 Agriculture, hunting, forestry and fishing	47	47	56	72	...	...	...	141	141	168	212
2 Mining and quarrying	3	3	4	5	...	...	...	1	1	1	2
3 Manufacturing	24	22	32	41	...	...	...	69	71	99	118
4 Electricity, gas and water	2	3	3	4	...	...	...	6	7	11	15
5 Construction	11	13	18	25	...	...	...	49	47	57	63
6 Wholesale and retail trade, restaurants and hotels	32	39	47	62	...	...	...	105	113	144	163
7 Transport, storage and communication	10	12	16	21	...	...	...	55	61	67	82
8 Finance, insurance, real estate and business services	21	24	31	41	...	...	...	77	86	101	114
9 Community, social and personal services	3	3	3	3	...	...	...	64	69	82	99

Fiji

1.10 Gross Domestic Product by Kind of Activity, in Current Prices
(Continued)

Million Fiji dollars

	1970	1971	1972	1973	1974	1975	1976	1977	1978	1979	1980
Total, Industries	153	166	210	275	...	...	...	567	596	731	868
Producers of Government Services	16	19	23	30	...	...	...	46	55	57	64
Other Producers	6	6	7	8	...	...	...	9	9	12	14
Subtotal [a]	175	191	240	313	...	...	...	622	660	800	946
Less: Imputed bank service charge	2	2	4	5	...	...	...	16	17	21	29
Plus: Import duties	19	23	25	31	...	...	...	...	...	...	...
Plus: Value added tax	...	...	...	...	...	...	...	...	...	...	...
Plus: Other adjustments [b]	...	...	...	...	...	...	...	54	59	73	81
Equals: Gross Domestic Product	192	212	261	338	450	562	624	660	702	852	998

a) Gross domestic product in factor values.
b) Referring to indirect taxes net of subsidies.

1.11 Gross Domestic Product by Kind of Activity, in Constant Prices

Million Fiji dollars

	1970	1971	1972	1973	1974	1975	1976	1977	1978	1979	1980
	\multicolumn{7}{c}{At constant prices of: 1968}	\multicolumn{4}{c}{1977}
1 Agriculture, hunting, forestry and fishing	40	38	38	40	40	40	41	44 / 141	140	163	153
2 Mining and quarrying	3	2	2	2	2	2	2	1 / 1	-	-	-
3 Manufacturing	19	21	19	19	20	20	22	24 / 69	74	88	81
4 Electricity, gas and water	2	2	3	3	3	3	4	4 / 6	6	7	7
5 Construction	8	9	10	11	10	9	8	9 / 49	44	51	51
6 Wholesale and retail trade, restaurants and hotels	30	34	38	44	45	43	43	45 / 105	109	125	117
7 Transport, storage and communication	10	11	13	15	16	17	17	17 / 55	58	67	67
8 Finance, insurance, real estate and business services	20	21	24	28	30	32	33	33 / 77	80	83	86
9 Community, social and personal services	2	2	2	2	2	2	...	... / 117	121	123	124
Statistical discrepancy	...	...	...	...	...	...	...	... / 2	2	2	1
Total, Industries	133	140	151	167	172	171	...	... / 622	634	709	687
Producers of Government Services	15	16	18	22	24	25	...	...	...	...	...
Other Producers	5	6	6	8	8	8	...	...	...	...	...
Subtotal	153	162	175	197	204	204	...	... / 622	634	709	687
Less: Imputed bank service charge	2	2	2	2	2	2	...	... / 16	17	18	18
Plus: Import duties	17	20	20	21	20	25	...	...	...	...	...
Plus: Value added tax	...	...	...	...	...	...	...	...	...	...	...
Plus: Other adjustments	...	...	...	...	...	...	...	54	56	64	...
Equals: Gross Domestic Product	169	180	194	216	222	227	...	... / 660	673	755	...

1.12 Relations Among National Accounting Aggregates

Million Fiji dollars

	1970	1971	1972	1973	1974	1975	1976	1977	1978	1979	1980
Gross Domestic Product	192	212	261	338	450	562	624	659	702	852	998
Plus: Net factor income received from abroad	-8	-10	-9	...	...	...	...	-9	-5	-12	-15
Equals: Gross National Product	184	202	252	...	...	...	...	650	697	840	983
Less: Consumption of fixed capital	9	10	13	...	...	...	...	35	43	53	63
Less: Net indirect taxes paid to supranational organisations	...	...	...	...	...	...	...	...	...	...	...

Fiji

1.12 Relations Among National Accounting Aggregates
(Continued)

Million Fiji dollars

	1970	1971	1972	1973	1974	1975	1976	1977	1978	1979	1980
Equals: National Income at Market Prices	175	192	240	...	...	...	...	615	654	787	920
Plus: Net current transfers received from abroad	2	3	7	5	1	-	-3	-5	-6	-5	7
Equals: National Disposable Income at Market Prices	177	195	247	...	...	...	...	610	648	782	927
Less: Final consumption	152	178	219	303	388	449	519	517	573	648	743
Equals: Net Saving	25	17	28	...	...	...	...	93	75	134	184
Less: Surplus of the nation on current transactions	-9	-26	-22	...	...	...	...	-32	-43	-64	-57
Equals: Net Capital Formation	34	43	50	...	...	...	...	125	118	218	241

2.1 General Government Final Consumption Expenditure by Function, in Current Prices

Million Fiji dollars

	1970	1971	1972	1973	1974	1975	1976	1977	1978	1979	1980
1 General public services	7	8	11	10	12	14	19	15	19	24	...
2 Defence	-	-	1	1	1	1	2	3	6	7	...
3 Public order and safety	...	...	...	...	...	...	...	8	9	9	...
4 Education	6	6	8	10	13	18	24	30	31	34	...
5 Health	4	4	5	6	7	8	12	14	15	16	...
6 Social security and welfare	-	-	-	-	-	-	-	1	1	1	...
7 Housing and community amenities	1	1	1	1	1	1	2	2	1	2	...
8 Recreational, cultural and religious affairs	1	1	1	1	1	1	1	1	1	1	...
9 Economic services	9	10	13	15	18	20	26	28	32	36	...
a Fuel and energy	...	...	...	...	...	...	...	2	2	3	...
b Agriculture, forestry, fishing and hunting	...	...	...	...	...	...	...	2	2	4	...
c Mining, manufacturing and construction, except fuel and energy	...	...	...	...	...	...	...	8	9	10	...
d Transportation and communication	...	...	...	...	...	...	...	10	11	12	...
e Other economic affairs	...	...	...	...	...	...	...	6	7	7	...
10 Other functions	...	...	...	...	...	...	...	...	...	...	...
Total General Government Final Consumption Expenditure	28	30	40	44	55	63	86	100	115	130	...

2.3 Total General Government Outlays by Function and Type

Million Fiji dollars

	Final Consumption Expenditures Total	Compensation of Employees	Other	Subsidies	Other Current Transfers & Property Income	Total Current Disbursements	Gross Capital Formation	Other Capital Outlays	Total Outlays
					1971				
1 General public services	8	6	2	...	...	...	...	...	...
2 Defence	-	-	-	...	...	...	...	...	...
3 Public order and safety	...	...	...	...	...	...	...	...	...
4 Education	6	6	-	...	...	...	...	...	...
5 Health	4	3	1	...	...	...	...	...	...
6 Social security and welfare	...	-	-	...	...	...	...	...	...
7 Housing and community amenities	1	-	1	...	...	...	...	...	...
8 Recreation, culture and religion	1	-	-	...	...	...	...	...	...
9 Economic services	10	7	3	...	...	...	...	...	...
10 Other functions	...	...	...	...	...	...	...	...	...
Total	30	24	7	...	...	...	...	...	...

Fiji

2.3 Total General Government Outlays by Function and Type
(Continued)

Million Fiji dollars

		Final Consumption Expenditures			Subsidies	Other Current Transfers & Property Income	Total Current Disbursements	Gross Capital Formation	Other Capital Outlays	Total Outlays
		Total	Compensation of Employees	Other						

1972

1	General public services	11	7	4	...	...	...	...	...	...
2	Defence	1	1	-	...	...	...	...	...	...
3	Public order and safety	...	...	...	...	...	...	...	...	...
4	Education	8	7	-	...	...	...	...	...	...
5	Health	5	4	1	...	...	...	...	...	...
6	Social security and welfare	...	-	-	...	...	...	...	...	...
7	Housing and community amenities	1	-	1	...	...	...	...	...	...
8	Recreation, culture and religion	1	1	-	...	...	...	...	...	...
9	Economic services	13	9	4	...	...	...	...	...	...
10	Other functions	...	...	...	...	...	...	...	...	...
	Total	40	29	9	...	...	...	...	...	...

1973

1	General public services	10	8	2	...	...	...	...	...	...
2	Defence	1	1	-	...	...	...	...	...	...
3	Public order and safety	...	...	...	...	...	...	...	...	...
4	Education	10	10	-	...	...	...	...	...	...
5	Health	6	5	1	...	...	...	...	...	...
6	Social security and welfare	...	-	-	...	...	...	...	...	...
7	Housing and community amenities	1	-	1	...	...	...	...	...	...
8	Recreation, culture and religion	1	1	-	...	...	...	...	...	...
9	Economic services	15	10	5	...	...	...	...	...	...
10	Other functions	...	...	...	...	...	...	...	...	...
	Total	42	34	9	...	...	...	...	...	...

1974

1	General public services	10	8	2	...	...	...	...	...	...
2	Defence	1	1	-	...	...	...	...	...	...
3	Public order and safety	...	...	...	...	...	...	...	...	...
4	Education	13	12	1	...	...	...	...	...	...
5	Health	7	5	2	...	...	...	...	...	...
6	Social security and welfare	-	-	-	...	...	...	...	...	...
7	Housing and community amenities	1	-	-	...	...	...	...	...	...
8	Recreation, culture and religion	1	-	-	...	...	...	...	...	...
9	Economic services	17	10	7	...	...	...	...	...	...
10	Other functions	...	...	...	...	...	...	...	...	...
	Total	55	36	12	...	...	...	...	...	...

1975

1	General public services	13	10	3	...	...	...	...	...	...
2	Defence	1	1	-	...	...	...	...	...	...
3	Public order and safety	...	...	...	...	...	...	...	...	...
4	Education	18	17	1	...	...	...	...	...	...
5	Health	8	7	2	...	...	...	...	...	...
6	Social security and welfare	-	-	-	...	...	...	...	...	...
7	Housing and community amenities	1	-	-	...	...	...	...	...	...
8	Recreation, culture and religion	1	-	-	...	...	...	...	...	...
9	Economic services	24	16	8	...	...	...	...	...	...
10	Other functions	...	...	...	...	...	...	...	...	...
	Total	67	51	14	...	...	...	...	...	...

Fiji

2.3 Total General Government Outlays by Function and Type
(Continued)

Million Fiji dollars

	Final Consumption Expenditures Total	Compensation of Employees	Other	Subsidies	Other Current Transfers & Property Income	Total Current Disbursements	Gross Capital Formation	Other Capital Outlays	Total Outlays
1976									
1 General public services	16	13	3	...	...	...	...	...	...
2 Defence	2	1	1	...	...	...	...	...	...
3 Public order and safety	...	...	...	...	...	...	...	...	...
4 Education	24	23	1	...	...	...	...	...	...
5 Health	12	10	2	...	...	...	...	...	...
6 Social security and welfare	-	-	-	...	...	...	...	...	...
7 Housing and community amenities	2	-	-	...	...	...	...	...	...
8 Recreation, culture and religion	1	-	-	...	...	...	...	...	...
9 Economic services	29	19	10	...	...	...	...	...	...
10 Other functions	...	...	...	...	...	...	...	...	...
Total	86	66	17	...	...	...	...	...	...
1977									
1 General public services	23	18	5	...	...	...	3	...	...
2 Defence	3	2	1	...	...	...	1	...	...
3 Public order and safety	...	...	...	...	...	...	1	...	...
4 Education	31	30	1	...	...	...	3	...	...
5 Health	14	12	2	...	...	...	2	...	...
6 Social security and welfare	-	-	-	...	...	...	-	...	...
7 Housing and community amenities	2	1	1	...	...	...	2	...	...
8 Recreation, culture and religion	1	-	-	...	...	...	-	...	...
9 Economic services	29	20	9	...	...	...	26	...	...
10 Other functions	...	...	...	...	...	...	...	...	...
Total	103	83	19	...	...	...	39	...	...
1978									
1 General public services	28	22	6	...	...	...	2	...	...
2 Defence	6	4	2	...	...	...	1	...	...
3 Public order and safety	...	...	...	...	...	...	1	...	...
4 Education	32	31	1	...	...	...	4	...	...
5 Health	15	13	2	...	...	...	2	...	...
6 Social security and welfare	1	1	-	...	...	...	-	...	...
7 Housing and community amenities	1	1	-	...	...	...	2	...	...
8 Recreation, culture and religion	1	-	-	...	...	...	-	...	...
9 Economic services	35	24	11	...	...	...	21	...	...
10 Other functions	...	...	...	...	...	...	...	...	...
Total	119	96	22	...	...	...	33	...	...
1979									
1 General public services	33	20	13	...	...	...	2	...	...
2 Defence	7	6	1	...	...	...	-	...	...
3 Public order and safety	...	...	...	...	...	...	1	...	...
4 Education	34	33	1	...	...	...	4	...	...
5 Health	16	14	2	...	...	...	2	...	...
6 Social security and welfare	1	1	-	...	...	...	-	...	...
7 Housing and community amenities	1	1	-	...	...	...	2	...	...
8 Recreation, culture and religion	1	-	-	...	...	...	-	...	...
9 Economic services	38	26	12	...	...	...	22	...	...
10 Other functions	...	...	...	...	...	...	...	...	...
Total	131	101	29	...	...	...	35	...	...

Fiji

2.5 Private Final Consumption Expenditure by Type, in Current Prices

Million Fiji dollars

	1970	1971	1972	1973	1974	1975	1976	1977	1978	1979	1980
Final Consumption Expenditure of Resident Households											
1 Food, beverages and tobacco	39	47	64	89	118	133	149	140	152	169	...
a Food	30	34	44	62	82	92	103	105	116	128	...
b Non-alcoholic beverages	1	1	1	2	3	3	3	8	9	9	...
c Alcoholic beverages	4	7	11	16	21	24	26	17	17	20	...
d Tobacco	5	5	7	10	13	15	17	10	10	12	...
2 Clothing and footwear	8	10	10	14	18	20	23	27	30	35	...
3 Gross rent, fuel and power	16	17	19	26	35	39	44	58	63	70	...
4 Furniture, furnishings and household equipment and operation	13	15	19	26	34	39	44	35	36	45	...
a Household operation	6	7	9	13	17	19	21	-	-	-	...
b Other	7	8	10	13	17	20	23	-	-	-	...
5 Medical care and health expenses	1	1	1	2	2	3	2	7	8	10	...
6 Transport and communication	14	18	23	32	43	48	53	42	49	61	...
a Personal transport equipment	2	3	3	4	5	6	7	6	7	9	...
b Other	11	14	20	28	38	42	46	36	42	52	...
7 Recreational, entertainment, education and cultural services	17	21	22	30	40	45	51	17	19	21	...
a Education	4	5	5	7	9	10	12	6	6	7	...
b Other	13	17	17	23	31	35	39	11	13	14	...
8 Miscellaneous goods and services	21	29	26	43	54	59	60	25	27	31	...
a Personal care	7	10	11	16	21	23	24	-	-	-	...
b Expenditures in restaurants, cafes and hotels	13	18	15	27	32	34	34	5	6	6	...
c Other	...	...	...	...	...	...	...	20	21	25	...
Statistical discrepancy	19	21	31	43	43	52	72	42	44	46	...
Total Final Consumption Expenditure in the Domestic Market by Households, of which	146	177	214	305	387	438	498	393	428	488	...
a Durable goods	18	25	...	...	...	...	...	22	24	31	...
b Semi-durable goods	16	20	...	...	...	...	...	42	47	56	...
c Non-durable goods	65	75	...	...	...	...	...	213	229	257	...
d Services	47	57	...	...	...	...	...	116	128	144	...
Plus: Direct purchases abroad by resident households	2	3	4	5	8	8	12	12	13	13	...
Less: Direct purchases in the domestic market by non-resident households	23	33	37	49	61	70	76	-	-	-	...
Equals: Final Consumption Expenditure of Resident Households	125	147	181	261	334	376	434	405	441	501	...
Final Consumption Expenditure of Private Non-profit Institutions Serving Households											
1 Research and science	...	...	...	...	...	...	...	...	...	...	...
2 Education	...	...	...	...	...	...	...	...	...	...	...
3 Medical and other health services	...	...	...	...	...	...	...	...	...	...	...
4 Welfare services	...	...	...	...	...	...	...	...	...	...	...
5 Recreational and related cultural services	...	...	...	...	...	...	...	...	...	...	...
6 Religious organisations	...	...	...	...	...	...	...	...	...	...	...
7 Professional and labour organisations serving households	...	...	...	...	...	...	...	...	...	...	...
8 Miscellaneous	...	...	...	...	...	...	...	4	6	5	...
Equals: Final Consumption Expenditure of Private Non-profit Organisations Serving Households	...	...	...	...	...	...	...	8	12	14	...
Statistical discrepancy	...	...	...	...	...	6	...	-65	...	...	...
Private Final Consumption Expenditure	125	147	181	261	334	382	434	417	459	520	...

Fiji

2.7 Gross Capital Formation by Type of Good and Owner, in Current Prices

Thousand Fiji dollars

	1977 TOTAL	1977 Total Private	1977 Public Enterprises	1977 General Government	1978 TOTAL	1978 Total Private	1978 Public Enterprises	1978 General Government	1979 TOTAL	1979 Total Private	1979 Public Enterprises	1979 General Government
Increase in stocks, total	24051	24163	386	-498	27806	23877	3628	301	59644	58132	707	805
1 Goods producing industries	6716	6395	321	-	10922	10924	-2	-	14407	14318	89	-
a Materials and supplies	193	15	178	...	3216	3216	-	-	4438	4367	71	-
b Work in progress	1123	1123	-	...	565	565	-	-	4771	4753	18	-
c Livestock, except breeding stocks, dairy cattle, etc.	1457	1457	...	...	1751	1751	-	-	-824	-824	-	-
d Finished goods	3943	3800	143	...	5390	5392	-2	-	6022	6022	-	-
2 Wholesale and retail trade	21418	21339	79	...	15232	15221	11	-	45086	45077	9	-
3 Other, except government stocks	-3585	-3571	-14	...	1351	-2268	3619	-	-654	-1263	609	-
4 Government stocks	-498	-	-	-498	301	-	-	301	805	-	-	805
Statistical discrepancy	-	-	-	-	-	-	-	-	-	-	-	-
Gross Fixed Capital Formation, Total	126811	69926	20480	36405	149642	85481	31334	32827	204956	110856	47846	46254
Total Gross Capital Formation	150862	94089	20866	35907	177448	109358	34919	33128	264600	168988	48553	47059

2.9 Gross Capital Formation by Kind of Activity of Owner, ISIC Major Divisions, in Current Prices

Million Fiji dollars

	1970 Total Gross Capital Formation	1970 Increase in Stocks	1970 Gross Fixed Capital Formation	1971 Total Gross Capital Formation	1971 Increase in Stocks	1971 Gross Fixed Capital Formation	1972 Total Gross Capital Formation	1972 Increase in Stocks	1972 Gross Fixed Capital Formation	1977 Total Gross Capital Formation	1977 Increase in Stocks	1977 Gross Fixed Capital Formation
All Producers												
1 Agriculture, hunting, fishing and forestry	...	...	3	...	...	5	...	...	2	11	-	11
2 Mining and quarrying	...	...	-	...	...	-	...	...	1	-	-	-
3 Manufacturing	...	...	-	...	...	3	...	...	6	24	7	17
4 Electricity, gas and water	...	...	6	...	...	3	...	...	3	10	-	10
5 Construction	...	...	1	...	...	2	...	...	5	-	-	-
6 Wholesale and retail trade, restaurants and hotels [a]	12	5	7	13	6	7	15	7	8	34	22	13
7 Transport, storage and communication	...	...	5	...	...	10	...	...	8	13	-	13
8 Finance, insurance, real estate and business services [a]	...	...	4	...	...	5	...	...	4	21	-4	25
9 Community, social and personal services [a]	...	...	-	...	...	1	...	...	5	38	-1	38
Total Industries	...	...	27	...	...	35	...	...	40	151	24	127
Producers of Government Services	...	...	7	...	...	9	...	...	10	...	...	...
Private Non-Profit Institutions Serving Households	...	...	2	...	...	3	...	...	3	...	...	...
Total	43	8	35	53	7	46	63	10	53	151	24	127

	1978 Total Gross Capital Formation	1978 Increase in Stocks	1978 Gross Fixed Capital Formation	1979 Total Gross Capital Formation	1979 Increase in Stocks	1979 Gross Fixed Capital Formation
All Producers						
1 Agriculture, hunting, fishing and forestry	13	-	13	15	-	14
2 Mining and quarrying	1	-	-	1	-	1
3 Manufacturing	29	10	19	40	10	30
4 Electricity, gas and water	20	-	20	48	-	48
5 Construction	2	-	2	8	3	5
6 Wholesale and retail trade, restaurants and hotels [a]	34	16	18	67	45	22
7 Transport, storage and communication	20	1	18	19	1	18
8 Finance, insurance, real estate and business services [a]	26	-	26	26	-2	28
9 Community, social and personal services [a]	38	1	33	40	1	39
Total Industries	177	28	150	265	60	205
Producers of Government Services	...	...	...	...	...	...
Private Non-Profit Institutions Serving Households	...	...	...	...	...	...
Total	177	28	150	265	60	205

a) For 1968, including items 'Finance, insurance, real estate, business services' and 'Community, social and personal services'.

Fiji

2.10 Gross Capital Formation by Kind of Activity of Owner, ISIC Major Divisions, in Constant Prices

Million Fiji dollars

	1970			1971			1972		
	Total Gross Capital Formation	Increase in Stocks	Gross Fixed Capital Formation	Total Gross Capital Formation	Increase in Stocks	Gross Fixed Capital Formation	Total Gross Capital Formation	Increase in Stocks	Gross Fixed Capital Formation

At constant prices of: 1968

All Producers

1 Agriculture, hunting, fishing and forestry	...	...	2	...	...	4	...	...	2
2 Mining and quarrying	...	...	3	...	...	2	...	...	5
3 Manufacturing	...	...		...	...		...	...	
4 Electricity, gas and water	...	...	2	...	...	3	...	...	2
5 Construction	...	...	1	...	...	1	...	...	4
6 Wholesale and retail trade, restaurants and hotels [a]	10	4	6	10	5	5	11	6	6
7 Transport, storage and communication	...	...	5	...	...	8	...	...	7
8 Finance, insurance, real estate and business services [a]	...	...	3	...	...	3	...	...	3
9 Community, social and personal services [a]	...	...	-	...	...	-	...	...	4
Total Industries	...	...	23	...	...	28	...	...	30
Producers of Government Services	...	...	5	...	...	6	...	...	7
Private Non-Profit Institutions Serving Households	...	...	1	...	...	2	...	...	2
Total	36	7	29	41	6	35	46	7	39

a) For 1968, including items 'Finance, insurance, real estate, business services' and 'Community, social and personal services'.

4.3 Derivation of Value Added by Kind of Activity, ISIC Divisions, in Current Prices

Million Fiji dollars

	1977			1978			1979			1980		
	Gross Output	Intermediate Consumption	Value Added	Gross Output	Intermediate Consumption	Value Added	Gross Output	Intermediate Consumption	Value Added	Gross Output	Intermediate Consumption	Value Added

All Producers

1 Agriculture, hunting, forestry and fishing	163	22	141	168	27	141	203	35	168	252	40	212
a Agriculture and hunting	150	19	131	150	21	129	184	28	156	...	...	...
b Forestry and logging	7	2	5	9	3	6	8	3	5	...	...	...
c Fishing	6	1	5	9	3	6	11	4	7	...	...	...
2 Mining and quarrying	8	7	-	9	8	1	14	12	2	25	23	2
3 Manufacturing	255	186	69	279	208	71	364	266	98	440	322	118
a Manufacture of food, beverages and tobacco	179	138	41	192	151	41	255	195	60	...	...	...
b Textile, wearing apparel and leather industries	4	2	2	5	3	2	7	5	2	...	...	...
c Manufacture of wood and wood products, including furniture	18	11	7	20	14	6	20	12	8	...	...	...
d Manufacture of paper and paper products, printing and publishing	8	5	3	9	5	4	13	7	6	...	...	...
e Manufacture of chemicals and chemical petroleum, coal, rubber and plastic products	12	9	3	14	10	4	20	15	5	...	...	...
f Manufacture of non-metallic mineral products, except products of petroleum and coal	10	6	4	10	7	3	12	7	5	...	...	...
g Basic metal industries	...	...	...	...	...	...	...	...	...	...	...	...
h Manufacture of fabricated metal products, machinery and equipment	21	14	7	24	17	7	35	24	11	...	...	...
i Other manufacturing industries	3	1	2	4	1	3	4	1	3	...	...	...
4 Electricity, gas and water	17	10	7	21	14	7	28	17	11	39	24	15
a Electricity, gas and steam	15	9	6	19	12	7	...	...	...	...	...	...
b Water works and supply	2	1	1	2	2	-	...	...	...	...	...	...
5 Construction	88	39	49	93	45	48	118	61	57	133	70	63
6 Wholesale and retail trade, restaurants and hotels	157	52	105	174	62	112	221	77	144	249	86	163
a Wholesale and retail trade	115	30	85	125	32	93	161	42	119	...	...	...
b Restaurants and hotels	42	23	19	50	30	20	60	35	25	...	...	...
7 Transport, storage and communication	93	38	55	115	54	61	134	66	68	170	89	81
a Transport and storage	82	37	45	103	52	51	118	64	54	...	...	...

Fiji

4.3 Derivation of Value Added by Kind of Activity, ISIC Divisions, in Current Prices
(Continued)

Million Fiji dollars

	1977 Gross Output	1977 Intermediate Consumption	1977 Value Added	1978 Gross Output	1978 Intermediate Consumption	1978 Value Added	1979 Gross Output	1979 Intermediate Consumption	1979 Value Added	1980 Gross Output	1980 Intermediate Consumption	1980 Value Added
b Communication	11	1	10	12	2	10	16	2	14	...	...	...
8 Finance, insurance, real estate and business services	117	39	77	134	48	86	157	56	99	172	58	114
a Financial institutions	21	5	16	27	7	20	32	6	26	...	...	...
b Insurance	10	1	9	9	2	7	8	2	6	...	...	...
c Real estate and business services	86	33	53	98	39	59	116	49	67	...	...	...
Real estate, except dwellings	49	29	20	44	28	16	54	37	21	...	...	...
Dwellings	37	4	33	54	11	43	54	11	47	...	...	...
9 Community, social and personal services	82	18	64	88	19	69	114	32	82	254	76	99
a Sanitary and similar services	...	...	...	...	...	...	...	...	...	...	...	...
b Social and related community services	59	7	52	64	7	57	69	8	61	...	...	...
Educational services	41	5	36	45	5	40	48	5	43	...	...	...
Medical, dental, other health and veterinary services	18	2	16	19	2	17	21	3	18	...	...	...
c Recreational and cultural services	7	4	3	6	4	2	10	6	4	...	...	...
d Personal and household services	16	7	9	18	8	10	35	18	17	...	...	...
Statistical discrepancy	4	3	1	3	2	1	...	...	...	...	...	...
Total, Industries	980	412	567	1081	485	596	1354	623	731	...	...	...
Producers of Government Services	61	15	46	75	20	55	82	25	57	...	...	...
Other Producers	13	4	9	14	5	9	22	10	12	...	...	...
Total [a]	1054	431	622	1170	510	660	1458	658	800	1734	788	946
Imputed bank service charge	-	16	-16	-	17	-17	-	21	-21	-	29	-29
Import duties	...	...	...	...	...	...	...	...	...	...	...	...
Value added tax	...	...	...	...	...	...	...	...	...	...	...	...
Other adjustments	54	-	54	59	-	59	73	-	73	81	-	81
Total	1108	447	660	1229	527	702	1531	679	852	1815	817	998

a) Column 'Value added' is in factor values.

4.6 Cost Components of Value Added, ISIC Divisions

Million Fiji dollars

	1977 Compensation of Employees	1977 Capital Consumption	1977 Net Operating Surplus	1977 Indirect Taxes	1977 Less: Subsidies Received	1977 Value Added	1978 Compensation of Employees	1978 Capital Consumption	1978 Net Operating Surplus	1978 Indirect Taxes	1978 Less: Subsidies Received	1978 Value Added
				All Producers								
1 Agriculture, hunting, forestry and fishing	19	4	118	...	...	141	21	5	115	...	...	141
a Agriculture and hunting	15	2	114	...	...	131	17	3	111	...	...	131
b Forestry and logging	2	1	2	...	...	5	2	1	3	...	...	4
c Fishing	2	1	2	...	...	5	2	1	1	...	...	6
2 Mining and quarrying	5	-	-4	...	...	1	4	-	-3	...	...	1
a Coal mining	...	...	...	...	...	...	...	...	...	...	...	...
b Crude petroleum and natural gas production	...	...	...	...	...	...	...	...	...	...	...	...
c Metal ore mining	...	...	...	...	...	...	...	...	...	...	...	...
d Other mining	...	...	...	...	...	...	...	...	...	...	...	...

Fiji

4.6 Cost Components of Value Added, ISIC Divisions
(Continued)

Million Fiji dollars

		1977					1978				
	Compensation of Employees	Capital Consumption	Net Operating Surplus	Indirect Taxes	Less: Subsidies Received	Value Added	Compensation of Employees	Capital Consumption	Net Operating Surplus	Indirect Taxes	Less: Subsidies Received	Value Added
3 Manufacturing	34	5	30	...	...	69	38	6	27	...	...	71
a Manufacture of food, beverages and tobacco	19	3	19	...	...	41	22	4	16	...	...	42
b Textile, wearing apparel and leather industries	1	...	1	...	...	2	1	...	1	...	...	2
c Manufacture of wood and wood products, including furniture	5	1	1	...	...	7	5	1	1	...	...	7
d Manufacture of paper and paper products, printing and publishing	2	...	1	...	...	3	2	...	1	...	...	3
e Manufacture of chemicals and chemical petroleum, coal, rubber and plastic products	2	...	2	...	...	4	2	...	2	...	...	4
f Manufacture of non-metallic mineral products, except products of petroleum and coal	1	1	2	...	...	4	1	...	2	...	...	3
g Basic metal industries	...	...	...	...	...	...	...	...	...	...	...	...
h Manufacture of fabricated metal products, machinery and equipment	4	1	2	...	...	7	4	1	2	...	...	7
i Other manufacturing industries	...	...	...	...	...	...	...	...	3	...	...	3
4 Electricity, gas and water	4	2	-	...	...	6	3	3	1	...	...	7
a Electricity, gas and steam	2	1	2	...	...	5	2	1	3	...	...	6
b Water works and supply	2	1	-3	...	...	1	2	1	-3	...	...	...
5 Construction	34	1	14	...	...	49	33	2	12	...	...	47
6 Wholesale and retail trade, restaurants and hotels	37	7	61	...	...	105	41	9	63	...	...	113
a Wholesale and retail trade	28	5	52	...	...	85	31	6	56	...	...	93
b Restaurants and hotels	8	2	9	...	...	19	10	3	7	...	...	20
7 Transport, storage and communication	30	9	16	...	...	55	31	12	18	...	...	61
a Transport and storage	25	7	13	...	...	45	26	10	15	...	...	51
b Communication	6	2	2	...	...	10	6	2	2	...	...	10
8 Finance, insurance, real estate and business services	16	4	57	...	...	77	18	4	64	...	...	86
a Financial institutions	7	1	8	...	...	16	8	1	11	...	...	20
b Insurance	3	...	5	...	...	8	3	...	4	...	...	7
c Real estate and business services	6	4	43	...	...	53	7	3	50	...	...	60
Real estate, except dwellings	6	3	11	...	...	20	7	3	14	...	...	24
Dwellings	...	1	32	...	...	33	...	...	36	...	...	36
9 Community, social and personal services	55	2	7	...	...	64	60	2	7	...	...	69
a Sanitary and similar services	...	...	...	...	...	...	...	...	...	...	...	...
b Social and related community services	47	1	4	...	...	52	52	1	4	...	...	57
Educational services	35	1	...	...	...	36	39	1	...	...	...	40
Medical, dental, other health and veterinary services	12	...	4	...	...	16	13	...	4	...	...	17
c Recreational and cultural services	2	...	1	...	...	3	1	1	...	...	...	2
d Personal and household services	6	1	3	...	...	9	6	1	3	...	...	10
Total, Industries	234	35	299	...	...	567	249	43	304	...	...	596
Producers of Government Services	46	...	...	...	...	46	55	...	...	...	...	55
Other Producers	8	...	1	...	...	9	9	...	-	...	...	9
Total [a]	288	35	299	...	...	622	313	43	304	...	...	660
Imputed bank service charge	...	...	-16	...	...	-16	...	...	-17	...	...	-17
Import duties	...	...	...	...	...	...	...	...	...	...	...	...
Value added tax	...	...	...	...	...	...	...	...	...	...	...	...
Other adjustments	...	...	...	54	...	54	...	...	...	59	...	...
Total	288	35	283	54	...	660	313	43	287	59	...	702

Fiji

4.6 Cost Components of Value Added, ISIC Divisions

Million Fiji dollars

		1979						1980				
	Compensation of Employees	Capital Consumption	Net Operating Surplus	Indirect Taxes	Less: Subsidies Received	Value Added	Compensation of Employees	Capital Consumption	Net Operating Surplus	Indirect Taxes	Less: Subsidies Received	Value Added

All Producers

1 Agriculture, hunting, forestry and fishing	27	6	135	...	...	168	28	7	177	...	...	212
a Agriculture and hunting	22	4	129	...	...	155	...	...	...	...	...	...
b Forestry and logging	3	1	2	...	...	6	...	...	...	...	...	...
c Fishing	2	1	4	...	...	7	...	...	...	...	...	...
2 Mining and quarrying	6	-	-5	...	...	1	8	-	-6	...	...	2
a Coal mining	...		...	...	...	...	...	...	...	...	...	...
b Crude petroleum and natural gas production	...	1	...	...	...	...	...	...	...	...	...	...
c Metal ore mining	...		...	...	...	...	...	...	...	...	...	...
d Other mining	...		...	...	...	...	...	...	...	...	...	...
3 Manufacturing	40	8	51	...	...	99	51	11	56	...	...	118
a Manufacture of food, beverages and tobacco	21	4	35	...	...	60	...	...	...	...	...	...
b Textile, wearing apparel and leather industries	1	-	1	...	...	2	...	...	...	...	...	...
c Manufacture of wood and wood products, including furniture	5	1	2	...	...	8	...	...	...	...	...	...
d Manufacture of paper and paper products, printing and publishing	3	1	2	...	...	6	...	...	...	...	...	...
e Manufacture of chemicals and chemical petroleum, coal, rubber and plastic products	2	1	2	...	...	5	...	...	...	...	...	...
f Manufacture of non-metallic mineral products, except products of petroleum and coal	2	-	2	...	...	4	...	...	...	...	...	...
g Basic metal industries	...	...	...	...	...	...	...	...	...	...	...	...
h Manufacture of fabricated metal products, machinery and equipment	6	1	3	...	...	10	...	...	...	...	...	...
i Other manufacturing industries	-	-	3	...	...	3	...	...	...	...	...	...
4 Electricity, gas and water	4	4	3	...	...	11	5	4	6	...	...	15
a Electricity, gas and steam	...	...	...	...	...	...	...	...	...	...	...	...
b Water works and supply	...	...	...	...	...	...	...	...	...	...	...	...
5 Construction	42	2	13	...	...	57	46	2	15	...	...	63
6 Wholesale and retail trade, restaurants and hotels	51	11	82	...	...	144	59	13	91	...	...	163
a Wholesale and retail trade	40	7	72	...	...	119	...	...	...	...	...	...
b Restaurants and hotels	11	4	10	...	...	25	...	...	...	...	...	...
7 Transport, storage and communication	34	13	20	...	...	67	45	18	19	...	...	82
a Transport and storage	27	11	16	...	...	54	...	...	...	...	...	...
b Communication	7	2	4	...	...	13	...	...	...	...	...	...
8 Finance, insurance, real estate and business services	21	5	75	...	...	101	23	5	86	...	...	114
a Financial institutions	9	1	16	...	...	26	...	...	...	...	...	...
b Insurance	3	1	2	...	...	6	...	...	...	...	...	...
c Real estate and business services	9	4	57	...	...	70	...	...	...	...	...	...
Real estate, except dwellings	9	4	17	...	...	30	...	...	...	...	...	...
Dwellings	...	...	40	...	...	40	...	...	...	...	...	...
9 Community, social and personal services	65	3	13	...	...	82	80	3	6	...	...	99
a Sanitary and similar services	...	...	...	...	...	...	...	...	...	...	...	...
b Social and related community services	56	1	4	...	...	61	...	...	...	...	...	...
Educational services	42	1	...	...	...	43	...	...	...	...	...	...
Medical, dental, other health and veterinary services	14	...	4	...	...	18	...	...	...	...	...	...
c Recreational and cultural services	2	1	1	...	...	4	...	...	...	...	...	...
d Personal and household services	10	1	6	...	...	17	...	...	...	...	...	...

Fiji

4.6 Cost Components of Value Added, ISIC Divisions
(Continued)

Million Fiji dollars

	1979						1980					
	Compensation of Employees	Capital Consumption	Net Operating Surplus	Indirect Taxes	Less: Subsidies Received	Value Added	Compensation of Employees	Capital Consumption	Net Operating Surplus	Indirect Taxes	Less: Subsidies Received	Value Added
Total, Industries	293	52	385	...	...	730	345	63	460	...	...	868
Producers of Government Services	56	...	...	...	...	56	64	-	-	...	...	64
Other Producers	10	1	2	...	...	13	14	-	-	...	...	14
Total [a]	359	53	388	...	...	799	423	63	460	...	...	946
Imputed bank service charge	...	...	-21	...	...	-21	...	...	-29	...	...	-29
Import duties	...	...	...	...	...	...	...	...	...	...	...	...
Value added tax	...	...	...	...	...	...	...	...	...	...	...	...
Other adjustments	...	...	...	73	...	73	...	...	...	81	...	81
Total	359	53	367	73	...	852	423	63	431	81	...	998

a) Column 'Value added' is in factor values.

Finland

Source. Reply to the United Nations National Accounts Questionnaire from the Central Statistical Office, Helsinki. Official estimates are published annually in 'Tilastotiedotus Kansantalouden Tilinpito' (Statistical Report, National Accounting) issued by the same Office. Information on concepts, sources and methods of estimation utilized can be found in 'Heikki Sourama-Olli Saariaho, Kansantalouden tilinipito, Rakenne, Maaritelmat ja luokitukset, Central Statistical office of Finland, Studies No. 63, Helsinki, 1980.'

General note. The estimates shown in the following tables have been prepared by the Central Statistical Office in accordance with the United Nations System of National Accounts so far as the existing data would permit.

1.1 Expenditure on the Gross Domestic Product, in Current Prices

Million Finnish markkaa

	1970	1971	1972	1973	1974	1975	1976	1977	1978	1979	1980
1 General government final consumption expenditure	6610	7627	8967	10700	13676	17790	21296	23969	26252	29755	34538
2 Private final consumption expenditure	25859	28016	32780	39021	47291	56750	64709	71268	78733	89604	101892
3 Gross capital formation	13220	14596	15558	19946	30371	33338	31074	31182	29367	40691	51482
a Increase in stocks	1594	1163	-347	-74	4258	1717	-768	-2596	-3401	3692	5693
b Gross fixed capital formation	11626	13433	15905	20019	26113	31621	31841	33778	32768	36999	45789
Residential buildings	3014	3372	4220	5466	7453	8034	8020	9384	9739	10444	12637
Non-residential buildings	2398	2406	2835	4016	5330	6736	6107	6913	6872	7695	9862
Other construction and land improvement etc.	1785	2173	2380	3067	3838	4721	4916	4943	4968	5227	5907
Other	4430	5481	6470	7470	9492	12129	12799	12538	11189	13634	17383
4 Exports of goods and services	11745	12226	14946	18086	24702	24717	29637	37079	43090	52654	63797
5 Less: Imports of goods and services	12310	13139	14797	18672	28193	31020	32062	34986	37654	50256	65294
Statistical discrepancy	-266	-83	-53	764	297	307	351	-1447	131	-492	-276
Equals: Gross Domestic Product	44858	49243	57401	69845	88143	101882	115003	127065	139918	161957	186139

1.2 Expenditure on the Gross Domestic Product, in Constant Prices

Million Finnish markkaa

	1970	1971	1972	1973	1974	1975	1976	1977	1978	1979	1980
					At constant prices of:1975						
1 General government final consumption expenditure	13144	13922	15039	15909	16651	17790	18792	19562	20313	21060	21934
2 Private final consumption expenditure	46382	47231	50863	53874	55030	56750	57276	56470	57939	61183	62701
3 Gross capital formation	27345	27300	26111	28770	34844	33338	28136	25076	22179	28433	31919
a Increase in stocks	3315	2236	-602	-114	4926	1717	-714	-2219	-2741	2579	3571
b Gross fixed capital formation	24029	25064	26713	28885	29918	31621	28850	27295	24920	25855	28348
Residential buildings	6243	6312	7176	7816	8245	8035	7336	7700	7567	7308	7620
Non-residential buildings	5113	4647	4968	5870	6023	6736	5610	5631	5384	5535	6189
Other construction and land improvement etc.	3805	4217	4204	4636	4536	4721	4364	3984	3799	3745	3748
Other	8868	9888	10365	10563	11114	12129	11540	9980	8170	9267	10791
4 Exports of goods and services	23883	23584	26994	28853	28665	24717	28386	31065	33583	36657	40085
5 Less: Imports of goods and services	24620	24473	25503	28927	30860	31020	29983	28135	27254	31635	35412
Statistical discrepancy	-1986	-1870	-1347	-300	-3039	307	-467	-1526	-1914	-2885	-2735
Equals: Gross Domestic Product	84148	85695	92158	98180	101290	101882	102141	102512	104845	112813	118492

1.3 Cost Components of the Gross Domestic Product

Million Finnish markkaa

	1970	1971	1972	1973	1974	1975	1976	1977	1978	1979	1980
1 Indirect taxes, net	4741	5426	6370	7720	8368	8875	10219	12566	14880	16590	19473
a Indirect taxes paid	6091	6861	7989	9471	11335	13016	15082	17797	20399	23700	27069
b Less: Subsidies received	1350	1435	1619	1751	2967	4141	4863	5231	5520	7110	7596
2 Consumption of fixed capital	6055	6329	7096	8799	11577	12639	13835	15583	17889	21426	24533
3 Compensation of employees paid by resident producers to:	22783	26272	30737	37544	47428	59267	68518	73986	77906	89169	104144
a Resident households	22780	26268	30733	37538	47418	59245	68490	73951	77864	89124	104096
b Rest of the world	4	4	4	6	10	22	28	36	42	45	48
4 Net operating surplus	11279	11216	13197	15782	20771	21101	22432	24930	29244	34772	37988
a Corporate and quasi-corporate enterprises	2999	2849	3286	4104	6542	5466	4283	5202	8018	11875	13382
b Private unincorporated enterprises	8279	8380	9920	11694	14229	15680	18205	19792	21222	22926	24643
c General government	1	-13	-9	-16	-	-45	-56	-64	4	-28	-37
Equals: Gross Domestic Product	44858	49243	57401	69845	88143	101882	115003	127065	139918	161957	186139

Finland

1.4 General Government Current Receipts and Disbursements

Million Finnish markkaa

	1970	1971	1972	1973	1974	1975	1976	1977	1978	1979	1980
Receipts											
1 Property and entrepreneurial income	715	689	702	720	932	994	1239	1404	1789	2018	2085
2 Taxes, fees and contributions	14227	16488	19196	23950	30045	36664	45151	48993	50764	56324	64771
a Indirect taxes	6091	6861	7989	9471	11335	13016	15082	17797	20399	23700	27069
b Direct taxes	6005	7053	8260	10570	13638	17037	22241	22779	21905	23737	27987
c Social security contributions	1977	2411	2761	3675	4781	6249	7359	7857	7825	8153	8972
d Compulsory fees, fines and penalties	154	163	186	234	291	362	469	560	635	734	743
3 Other current receipts	2869	2993	3710	4435	5754	7700	9652	11067	12421	14157	16563
Total Current Receipts of General Government	17811	20170	23608	29105	36731	45358	56042	61464	64974	72499	83419
Disbursements											
1 General government final consumption expenditure	6610	7627	8967	10700	13676	17790	21296	23969	26252	29755	34538
2 Property income paid	467	482	507	537	586	675	761	999	1185	1575	1893
a Interest	466	481	506	536	585	674	760	997	1183	1572	1890
b Net land rent and royalties	1	1	1	1	1	1	1	2	2	3	3
3 Subsidies	1350	1435	1619	1751	2967	4141	4863	5231	5520	7110	7596
4 Other current transfers paid	5980	6747	8232	9608	12580	16044	19671	23118	25943	28713	32619
a Social security benefits and social assistance grants	2665	3177	3781	4242	5607	7007	8476	10197	11436	12087	13367
b Other	3315	3570	4451	5366	6973	9037	11195	12922	14507	16626	19252
5 Net saving	3405	3880	4283	6508	6922	6708	9451	8147	6074	5346	6773
Total Current Disbursements and Net Saving of General Government	17811	20170	23608	29105	36732	45358	56042	61464	64974	72499	83419

1.5 Current Income and Outlay of Corporate and Quasi-Corporate Enterprises, Summary

Million Finnish markkaa

	1970	1971	1972	1973	1974	1975	1976	1977	1978	1979	1980
Receipts											
1 Net operating surplus	2999	2849	3286	4104	6542	5466	4283	5202	8018	11874	13382
2 Other property and entrepreneurial income received	3081	3757	4259	5526	7661	9158	10466	12108	12670	14373	19807
3 Current transfers received	2282	2724	3337	4153	5135	6474	8180	9772	10078	12664	15731
Total Current Receipts	8362	9330	10882	13783	19338	21098	22929	27082	30766	38911	48917
Disbursements											
1 Property and entrepreneurial income paid	3867	4511	5152	6667	9194	11413	13306	15184	16402	18231	24413
2 Direct taxes and other current payments to general government	864	928	967	1192	1500	2004	2574	2351	2580	2936	3466
3 Other current transfers paid	1908	2325	2759	3145	3885	4978	6511	7615	8477	10046	11833
4 Net saving	1723	1565	2003	2779	4759	2703	538	1932	3308	7698	9207
Total Current Disbursements and Net Saving	8362	9329	10882	13783	19338	21098	22929	27082	30766	38911	48917

1.6 Current Income and Outlay of Households and Non-Profit Institutions

Million Finnish markkaa

	1970	1971	1972	1973	1974	1975	1976	1977	1978	1979	1980
Receipts											
1 Compensation of employees	22810	26314	30767	37598	47529	59318	68589	74144	78218	89531	104518
2 Property and entrepreneurial income received	9383	9654	11333	13564	16597	18606	21565	23259	25060	27313	30990
3 Current transfers received	5405	6492	7817	9075	11678	14736	18053	21481	23948	26336	29789
a Social security benefits and social assistance grants received	3321	4034	4914	5609	7349	9324	11612	14228	16192	17610	19850
b Other	2084	2458	2903	3466	4329	5412	6441	7253	7756	8726	9939
Total Current Receipts	37598	42460	49917	60237	75804	92660	108207	118884	127226	143180	165297
Disbursements											
1 Private final consumption expenditure	25859	28016	32780	39021	47291	56750	64709	71268	78733	89604	101892

Finland

1.6 Current Income and Outlay of Households and Non-Profit Institutions
(Continued)

Million Finnish markkaa

	1970	1971	1972	1973	1974	1975	1976	1977	1978	1979	1980
2 Property income paid	1020	1278	1401	1795	2324	2611	2987	3497	3645	4096	5592
3 Direct taxes and other payments n.e.c. to general government [a]	9339	11140	13314	17277	22217	27974	35414	38385	37640	41744	49228
a Social security contributions [a]	3951	4737	5707	7513	9605	12341	14956	17054	17258	19688	23334
b Direct taxes	5228	6234	7417	9523	12313	15257	19958	20753	19721	21289	25110
c Fees, fines and penalties	160	169	190	241	299	376	500	578	661	767	784
4 Other current transfers paid	613	714	851	1000	1190	1680	1952	2242	2375	2640	3028
5 Net saving	768	1310	1572	1144	2781	3645	3146	3493	4833	5096	5557
Total Current Disbursements and Net Saving	37598	42460	49917	60237	75803	92660	108207	118884	127226	143180	165297

a) Including private pensions and welfare plans.

1.7 External Transactions on Current Account, Summary

Million Finnish markkaa

	1970	1971	1972	1973	1974	1975	1976	1977	1978	1979	1980
Payments to the Rest of the World											
1 Imports of goods and services	12310	13139	14797	18672	28193	31020	32062	34986	37654	50256	65294
a Imports of merchandise c.i.f.	11138	11814	13132	16629	25815	28188	28727	30961	32600	44431	58315
b Other	1172	1325	1665	2042	2378	2832	3335	4025	5054	5825	6979
2 Factor income paid to the rest of the world	600	734	902	1143	1611	2037	2402	3085	3636	4227	5265
a Compensation of employees	4	4	4	6	10	22	28	36	42	45	48
b Property and entrepreneurial income paid	596	730	898	1137	1601	2015	2374	3049	3594	4182	5217
3 Indirect taxes paid to supranational organizations	...	...	...	...	...	...	...	...	...	...	...
4 Current transfers to the rest of the world	261	315	352	401	454	611	716	835	926	1253	1632
5 Surplus of the nation on current transactions	-1004	-1429	-550	-1480	-4628	-7950	-4455	-580	2606	-632	-5136
Payments to the Rest of the World and Surplus of the Nation on Current Transactions	12166	12758	15500	18736	25630	25718	30725	38326	44822	55104	67055
Receipts From The Rest of the World											
1 Exports of goods and services	11745	12226	14946	18086	24702	24717	29637	37079	43090	52654	63797
a Exports of merchandise f.o.b.	9640	9846	12012	14530	20611	20209	24417	30805	35068	43302	52860
b Other	2105	2380	2934	3556	4091	4508	5220	6274	8022	9352	10937
2 Factor income received from rest of the world	174	237	254	329	569	512	542	607	1011	1494	2017
a Compensation of employees	31	45	34	60	110	72	99	193	354	408	422
b Property and entrepreneurial income received	143	192	220	269	458	440	443	414	657	1086	1595
3 Subsidies received from supranational organisations	...	...	...	...	...	...	...	...	...	...	...
4 Current transfers from rest of the world	247	295	301	321	359	489	547	640	722	955	1241
Receipts from the Rest of the World on Current Transactions	12166	12758	15500	18736	25630	25718	30725	38326	44822	55104	67055

1.8 Capital Transactions of The Nation, Summary

Million Finnish markkaa

	1970	1971	1972	1973	1974	1975	1976	1977	1978	1979	1980
Finance of Gross Capital Formation											
Gross saving	11950	13084	14954	19229	26039	25694	26970	29155	32104	39567	46070
1 Consumption of fixed capital	6055	6329	7095	8799	11577	12639	13835	15583	17889	21426	24533
a General government	346	406	466	576	761	1014	1093	1305	1444	1659	1964
b Corporate and quasi-corporate enterprises	3482	3448	3829	4887	6546	6619	7164	8108	9783	12233	13853
c Other	2227	2475	2801	3335	4271	5006	5578	6169	6662	7535	8716
2 Net saving	5895	6755	7859	10430	14462	13055	13135	13572	14215	18141	21537
a General government	3405	3880	4283	6508	6922	6708	9451	8147	6074	5346	6773
b Corporate and quasi-corporate enterprises	1722	1565	2004	2779	4759	2703	538	1932	3308	7699	9207

Finland

1.8 Capital Transactions of The Nation, Summary
(Continued)

Million Finnish markkaa

	1970	1971	1972	1973	1974	1975	1976	1977	1978	1979	1980
c Other	768	1310	1572	1143	2781	3644	3146	3493	4833	5097	5557
Less: Surplus of the nation on current transactions	-1004	-1429	-550	-1480	-4628	-7950	-4455	-580	2606	-632	-5136
Statistical discrepancy	266	83	53	-764	-297	-307	-351	1447	-131	492	276
Finance of Gross Capital Formation	13220	14596	15558	19946	30371	33338	31073	31182	29367	40691	51482
Gross Capital Formation											
Increase in stocks	1594	1163	-347	-74	4258	1717	-768	-2596	-3401	3692	5693
Gross fixed capital formation	11626	13433	15905	20019	26113	31621	31841	33778	32768	36999	45789
1 General government	1602	1805	2316	2599	3257	4086	4304	4842	5108	5637	6472
2 Corporate and quasi-corporate enterprises	5854	7140	8081	10141	13259	16572	16451	16428	14517	16923	21669
3 Other	4170	4489	5508	7280	9597	10963	11087	12508	13143	14440	17647
Gross Capital Formation	13220	14596	15558	19946	30371	33338	31074	31182	29367	40691	51482

1.10 Gross Domestic Product by Kind of Activity, in Current Prices

Million Finnish markkaa

	1970	1971	1972	1973	1974	1975	1976	1977	1978	1979	1980
1 Agriculture, hunting, forestry and fishing	5132	5562	5757	6774	8317	9993	10491	11299	11635	13289	15193
2 Mining and quarrying	365	222	264	381	488	364	458	499	539	770	841
3 Manufacturing	10905	11615	13870	17231	23738	25283	28527	30322	34264	41418	47886
4 Electricity, gas and water	1037	1116	1328	1610	2068	2625	2872	3708	4108	4866	5559
5 Construction	3618	3979	4916	6130	7782	9374	9092	9500	9588	10428	12102
6 Wholesale and retail trade, restaurants and hotels	4387	4877	5736	7058	8908	10701	12085	12709	13967	16307	19169
7 Transport, storage and communication	3235	3564	4008	4751	5851	6643	8281	9310	10380	12323	13557
8 Finance, insurance, real estate and business services	4894	5449	6610	8172	10487	12451	14199	16133	17672	19519	22593
9 Community, social and personal services	1252	1436	1654	1996	2463	3003	3561	3978	4316	5024	5750
Total, Industries	34825	37819	44142	54103	70103	80438	89566	97458	106468	123943	142649
Producers of Government Services	5037	5728	6638	7940	10020	13027	15822	17709	19351	22072	25133
Other Producers	987	1098	1222	1370	1628	1835	2028	2176	2328	2638	3013
Subtotal	40849	44644	52002	63413	81751	95300	107416	117342	128146	148653	170796
Less: Imputed bank service charge	656	744	891	1133	1904	2350	2729	3020	3281	3639	4682
Plus: Import duties [a]	4665	5343	6290	7565	8296	8933	10317	12743	15053	16944	20026
Plus: Value added tax	...	...	...	...	...	...	...	...	...	...	...
Equals: Gross Domestic Product	44858	49243	57401	69845	88143	101882	115003	127065	139918	161957	186139

a) Including also commodity indirect taxes net of subsidies.

1.11 Gross Domestic Product by Kind of Activity, in Constant Prices

Million Finnish markkaa

	1970	1971	1972	1973	1974	1975	1976	1977	1978	1979	1980
					At constant prices of:1975						
1 Agriculture, hunting, forestry and fishing	11729	11413	11045	10958	10473	9993	10125	10310	10492	11705	11900
2 Mining and quarrying	363	300	349	366	369	364	399	428	444	477	501
3 Manufacturing	20734	21061	23581	25111	26370	25283	25665	25428	26477	29397	31767
4 Electricity, gas and water	1900	1983	2265	2506	2592	2625	2719	2980	3180	3413	3577
5 Construction	7582	7433	8086	8851	9023	9374	8533	8542	8328	8396	8875
6 Wholesale and retail trade, restaurants and hotels	8032	8430	9245	10115	10421	10701	10689	9970	10159	10898	11242
7 Transport, storage and communication	5368	5499	5956	6436	6772	6643	6507	6561	6746	7477	7901
8 Finance, insurance, real estate and business services	9207	9687	10339	10999	11661	12451	12917	13330	13780	14301	14920
9 Community, social and personal services	2551	2672	2780	2861	2938	3003	3082	2973	2958	3086	3186
Total, Industries	67467	68479	73646	78204	80618	80438	80636	80520	82565	89151	93870
Producers of Government Services	9842	10319	10939	11633	12387	13027	13787	14405	15013	15637	16260
Other Producers	1937	1948	1976	1952	1953	1835	1747	1746	1771	1803	1846
Subtotal	79246	80746	86561	91789	94958	95300	96170	96671	99349	106591	111976
Less: Imputed bank service charge	1613	1724	1867	2056	2155	2350	2337	2387	2480	2512	2571
Plus: Import duties [a]	6515	6673	7464	8447	8487	8933	8308	8229	7976	8733	9088
Plus: Value added tax	...	...	...	...	...	...	...	...	...	...	...
Equals: Gross Domestic Product	84148	85695	92158	98180	101290	101882	102141	102512	104845	112813	118493

a) Including also commodity indirect taxes net of subsidies.

Finland

1.12 Relations Among National Accounting Aggregates

Million Finnish markkaa

	1970	1971	1972	1973	1974	1975	1976	1977	1978	1979	1980
Gross Domestic Product	44858	49243	57401	69845	88143	101882	115003	127065	139918	161957	186139
Plus: Net factor income received from abroad	-426	-496	-648	-814	-1042	-1525	-1860	-2478	-2625	-2733	-3248
Factor income received	174	237	254	329	569	512	542	607	1011	1494	2017
Less: Factor income paid	600	734	902	1143	1611	2037	2402	3085	3636	4227	5265
Equals: Gross National Product	44432	48747	56753	69031	87101	100357	113143	124587	137293	159224	182891
Less: Consumption of fixed capital	6055	6329	7096	8799	11577	12639	13835	15583	17889	21427	24533
Less: Net indirect taxes paid to supranational organisations	...	...	...	...	...	...	...	...	...	...	...
Equals: National Income at Market Prices	38377	42418	49656	60232	75524	87718	99308	109004	119404	137798	158358
Plus: Net current transfers received from abroad	-13	-19	-51	-80	-95	-123	-169	-195	-205	-297	-391
Current transfers received	247	295	301	321	359	489	547	640	722	955	1241
Less: Current transfers paid	261	315	352	401	454	611	716	835	926	1253	1632
Equals: National Disposable Income at Market Prices	38364	42398	49605	60151	75429	87596	99139	108809	119200	137501	157967
Less: Final consumption	32468	35643	41747	49721	60967	74540	86004	95237	104985	119359	136430
Equals: Net Saving	5895	6755	7858	10430	14462	13056	13135	13572	14215	18141	21537
Less: Surplus of the nation on current transactions	-1004	-1429	-550	-1480	-4628	-7950	-4455	-580	2606	-632	-5136
Statistical discrepancy	266	83	53	-764	-297	-307	-351	1447	-131	492	276
Equals: Net Capital Formation	7165	8267	8461	11147	18794	20699	17238	15599	11478	19265	26949

2.1 General Government Final Consumption Expenditure by Function, in Current Prices

Million Finnish markkaa

	1970	1971	1972	1973	1974	1975	1976	1977	1978	1979	1980
1 General public services	...	...	...	...	...	1817	2207	2483	2674	2975	3527
2 Defence	...	...	...	...	...	1386	1489	1739	1967	2233	2704
3 Public order and safety	...	...	...	...	...	1208	1374	1527	1666	1872	2137
4 Education	...	...	...	...	...	4906	5960	6664	7256	8101	9295
5 Health	...	...	...	...	...	3735	4504	5138	5583	6393	7323
6 Social security and welfare	...	...	...	...	...	2012	2492	2786	3165	3685	4345
7 Housing and community amenities	...	...	...	...	...	647	782	863	952	1095	1242
8 Recreational, cultural and religious affairs	...	...	...	...	...	431	556	646	744	882	1047
9 Economic services	...	...	...	...	...	1615	1898	2060	2087	2360	2750
a Fuel and energy	...	...	...	...	...	...	...	...	...	...	...
b Agriculture, forestry, fishing and hunting	...	...	...	...	...	...	...	...	...	...	...
c Mining, manufacturing and construction, except fuel and energy	...	...	...	...	...	...	...	...	...	...	...
d Transportation and communication	...	...	...	...	...	1172	1379	1465	1447	1626	1846
e Other economic affairs [a]	...	...	...	...	...	443	519	595	640	734	904
10 Other functions	...	...	...	...	...	35	35	65	159	160	168
Total General Government Final Consumption Expenditure	...	...	...	...	...	17790	21296	23969	26252	29755	34538

a) Item 'Fuel and energy' through 'Mining (except fuels), manufacturing and construction' are included in item 'Other economic affairs'.

2.2 General Government Final Consumption Expenditure by Function, in Constant Prices

Million Finnish markkaa

	1970	1971	1972	1973	1974	1975	1976	1977	1978	1979	1980
					At constant prices of:1975						
1 General public services	...	...	...	...	...	1817	1952	2022	2050	2111	2239
2 Defence	...	...	...	...	...	1386	1318	1419	1499	1556	1694
3 Public order and safety	...	...	...	...	...	1208	1200	1240	1287	1340	1385
4 Education	...	...	...	...	...	4906	5249	5433	5643	5734	5914
5 Health	...	...	...	...	...	3735	4049	4270	4424	4614	4744
6 Social security and welfare	...	...	...	...	...	2012	2150	2231	2373	2507	2645
7 Housing and community amenities	...	...	...	...	...	647	679	691	721	777	795
8 Recreational, cultural and religious affairs	...	...	...	...	...	431	489	526	578	623	662
9 Economic services	...	...	...	...	...	1615	1675	1677	1617	1687	1753

Finland

2.2 General Government Final Consumption Expenditure by Function, in Constant Prices
(Continued)

Million Finnish markkaa

	1970	1971	1972	1973	1974	1975	1976	1977	1978	1979	1980
					At constant prices of:1975						
a Fuel and energy	...	...	...	...	...	...	...	...	...	...	...
b Agriculture, forestry, fishing and hunting	...	...	...	...	...	...	...	...	...	...	...
c Mining, manufacturing and construction, except fuel and energy	...	...	...	...	...	...	...	...	...	...	...
d Transportation and communication	...	...	...	...	...	1172	1216	1189	1119	1164	1172
e Other economic affairs	...	...	...	...	...	443	459	488	498	523	581
10 Other functions	...	...	...	...	...	35	32	54	123	112	103
Total General Government Final Consumption Expenditure	...	...	...	...	...	17790	18792	19562	20313	21060	21934

2.3 Total General Government Outlays by Function and Type

Million Finnish markkaa

	Final Consumption Expenditures Total	Compensation of Employees	Other	Subsidies	Other Current Transfers & Property Income	Total Current Disbursements	Gross Capital Formation	Other Capital Outlays	Total Outlays
1975									
1 General public services	1817	1139	679	...	...	...	...	...	...
2 Defence	1386	767	619	...	...	...	...	...	...
3 Public order and safety	1208	1013	195	...	...	...	...	...	...
4 Education	4906	3506	1400	...	...	...	...	...	...
5 Health	3735	2853	882	...	...	...	...	...	...
6 Social security and welfare	2012	1445	566	...	...	...	...	...	...
7 Housing and community amenities	647	493	154	...	...	...	...	...	...
8 Recreation, culture and religion	431	273	159	...	...	...	...	...	...
9 Economic services	1615	633	982	...	...	...	...	...	...
a Fuel and energy	...	...	...	...	...	...	...	...	...
b Agriculture, forestry, fishing and hunting	...	...	...	...	...	...	...	...	...
c Mining (except fuels), manufacturing and construction	...	...	...	...	...	...	...	...	...
d Transportation and communication	1172	308	864	...	...	...	...	...	...
e Other economic affairs [a]	443	325	118	...	...	...	...	...	...
10 Other functions	35	7	28	...	...	...	...	...	...
Total	17790	12126	5664	4141	16719	38650	...	...	...
1976									
1 General public services	2207	1424	783	...	...	...	...	...	...
2 Defence	1489	903	586	...	...	...	...	...	...
3 Public order and safety	1374	1169	205	...	...	...	...	...	...
4 Education	5960	4221	1739	...	...	...	...	...	...
5 Health	4504	3482	1022	...	...	...	...	...	...
6 Social security and welfare	2492	1848	644	...	...	...	...	...	...
7 Housing and community amenities	782	606	176	...	...	...	...	...	...
8 Recreation, culture and religion	556	352	204	...	...	...	...	...	...
9 Economic services	1898	772	1126	...	...	...	...	...	...
a Fuel and energy	...	...	...	...	...	...	...	...	...
b Agriculture, forestry, fishing and hunting	...	...	...	...	...	...	...	...	...
c Mining (except fuels), manufacturing and construction	...	...	...	...	...	...	...	...	...
d Transportation and communication	1379	364	1015	...	...	...	...	...	...
e Other economic affairs [a]	519	408	111	...	...	...	...	...	...
10 Other functions	35	6	30	...	...	...	...	...	...
Total	21296	14783	6513	4863	20432	46591	...	...	...
1977									
1 General public services	2483	1618	865	...	...	...	...	...	...
2 Defence	1739	976	763	...	...	...	...	...	...
3 Public order and safety	1527	1281	246	...	...	...	...	...	...
4 Education	6664	4684	1980	...	...	...	...	...	...
5 Health	5138	3888	1250	...	...	...	...	...	...

Finland

2.3 Total General Government Outlays by Function and Type
(Continued)

Million Finnish markkaa

		Final Consumption Expenditures			Subsidies	Other Current Transfers & Property Income	Total Current Disbursements	Gross Capital Formation	Other Capital Outlays	Total Outlays
		Total	Compensation of Employees	Other						
6	Social security and welfare	2786	2091	695	...	...	...	...	...	...
7	Housing and community amenities	863	668	195	...	...	...	...	...	...
8	Recreation, culture and religion	646	402	244	...	...	...	...	...	...
9	Economic services	2060	848	1212	...	...	...	...	...	...
	a Fuel and energy	...	...	...	...	...	...	...	...	...
	b Agriculture, forestry, fishing and hunting				...	...	...	...	...	...
	c Mining (except fuels), manufacturing and construction	...	...	...	...	...	...	...	...	...
	d Transportation and communication	1465	385	1080	...	...	...	...	...	...
	e Other economic affairs [a]	595	463	132	...	...	...	...	...	...
10	Other functions	65	5	61	...	...	...	...	...	...
	Total	23969	16460	7509	5231	24117	53317	...	...	...

1978

1	General public services	2674	1726	948	...	...	...	...	...	...
2	Defence	1967	1008	960	...	...	...	...	...	...
3	Public order and safety	1666	1374	291	...	...	...	...	...	...
4	Education	7256	5065	2191	...	...	...	...	...	...
5	Health	5583	4256	1327	...	...	...	...	...	...
6	Social security and welfare	3165	2381	785	...	...	...	...	...	...
7	Housing and community amenities	952	748	204	...	...	...	...	...	...
8	Recreation, culture and religion	744	465	280	...	...	...	...	...	...
9	Economic services	2087	931	1156	...	...	...	...	...	...
	a Fuel and energy	...	...	...	...	...	...	...	...	...
	b Agriculture, forestry, fishing and hunting	...	...	...	...	...	...	...	...	...
	c Mining (except fuels), manufacturing and construction	...	...	...	...	...	...	...	...	...
	d Transportation and communication	1447	404	1043	...	...	...	...	...	...
	e Other economic affairs [a]	640	527	113	...	...	...	...	...	...
10	Other functions	159	8	151	...	...	...	...	...	...
	Total	26252	17961	8291	5520	27128	58900	...	...	...

1979

1	General public services	2975	1947	1028	...	...	...	...	...	...
2	Defence	2233	1121	1112	...	...	...	...	...	...
3	Public order and safety	1872	1543	329	...	...	...	...	...	...
4	Education	8101	5701	2400	...	...	...	...	...	...
5	Health	6393	4880	1513	...	...	...	...	...	...
6	Social security and welfare	3685	2781	904	...	...	...	...	...	...
7	Housing and community amenities	1095	877	218	...	...	...	...	...	...
8	Recreation, culture and religion	882	563	319	...	...	...	...	...	...
9	Economic services	2360	1070	1290	...	...	...	...	...	...
	a Fuel and energy	...	...	...	...	...	...	...	...	...
	b Agriculture, forestry, fishing and hunting	...	...	...	...	...	...	...	...	...
	c Mining (except fuels), manufacturing and construction	...	...	...	...	...	...	...	...	...
	d Transportation and communication	1626	454	1172	...	...	...	...	...	...
	e Other economic affairs [a]	734	616	118	...	...	...	...	...	...
10	Other functions	160	22	138	...	...	...	...	...	...
	Total	29755	20505	9250	7110	30288	67153	...	...	...

1980

1	General public services	3527	2251	1276	...	...	...	...	...	...
2	Defence	2704	1206	1498	...	...	...	...	...	...
3	Public order and safety	2137	1747	390	...	...	...	...	...	...
4	Education	9295	6445	2850	...	...	...	...	...	...
5	Health	7323	5505	1818	...	...	...	...	...	...

Finland

2.3 Total General Government Outlays by Function and Type
(Continued)

Million Finnish markkaa

		Final Consumption Expenditures		Subsidies	Other Current Transfers & Property Income	Total Current Disbursements	Gross Capital Formation	Other Capital Outlays	Total Outlays
		Total	Compensation of Employees	Other						
6	Social security and welfare	4345	3202	1143	...	...	...	...	...	
7	Housing and community amenities	1242	987	255	...	...	...	...	...	
8	Recreation, culture and religion	1047	648	399	...	...	...	...	...	
9	Economic services	2750	1259	1491	...	...	...	...	...	
	a Fuel and energy	...	...	...	...	...	...	...	...	
	b Agriculture, forestry, fishing and hunting	...	...	...	...	...	...	...	...	
	c Mining (except fuels), manufacturing and construction	...	...	...	...	...	...	...	...	
	d Transportation and communication	1846	504	1342	...	...	...	...	...	
	e Other economic affairs [a]	904	755	149	...	...	...	...	...	
10	Other functions	168	34	134	...	...	...	...	...	
	Total	34538	23283	11255	7596	34512	76646	...	...	...

[a] Item 'Fuel and energy' through 'Mining (except fuels), manufacturing and construction' are included in item 'Other economic affairs'.

2.5 Private Final Consumption Expenditure by Type, in Current Prices

Million Finnish markkaa

	1970	1971	1972	1973	1974	1975	1976	1977	1978	1979	1980
Final Consumption Expenditure of Resident Households											
1 Food, beverages and tobacco	8171	8896	10198	11421	13274	16549	18814	20916	22768	25203	28183
a Food	6206	6683	7665	8545	10013	12619	14354	16089	17322	19096	21400
b Non-alcoholic beverages	156	162	188	216	256	300	330	379	401	447	556
c Alcoholic beverages	1097	1254	1447	1705	1994	2469	2742	2916	3331	3666	4072
d Tobacco	714	797	898	955	1010	1160	1387	1532	1714	1994	2155
2 Clothing and footwear	2069	1965	2291	2711	3131	3145	3561	3707	3803	4422	5029
3 Gross rent, fuel and power	4483	4983	5734	6929	9206	10395	11936	13341	14696	16218	18215
a Fuel and power	679	812	878	1043	1610	1823	2160	2362	2546	2825	3210
b Other	3804	4171	4856	5886	7596	8572	9776	10979	12150	13393	15004
4 Furniture, furnishings and household equipment and operation	1699	1849	2209	2808	3589	4121	4400	4594	5052	6022	6980
a Household operation	238	245	263	272	304	316	336	376	374	441	474
b Other	1461	1604	1946	2536	3285	3805	4064	4218	4678	5581	6506
5 Medical care and health expenses	699	778	856	1003	1171	1448	1699	1844	2068	2197	2490
6 Transport and communication	3810	4019	5022	6265	7146	8905	9990	11115	12412	14750	17001
a Personal transport equipment	1253	1095	1664	2094	1877	2715	2674	2894	3103	4308	4839
b Other	2557	2924	3358	4171	5269	6190	7316	8221	9309	10442	12162
7 Recreational, entertainment, education and cultural services	1470	1683	2037	2598	3193	4042	4743	5314	6207	7179	8299
8 Miscellaneous goods and services	2699	3068	3627	4316	5351	6472	7629	8287	9555	11179	13033
a Personal care	339	381	449	529	648	728	866	956	1105	1257	1421
b Expenditures in restaurants, cafes and hotels	1281	1522	1844	2192	2797	3391	3844	4107	4782	5600	6495
c Other	1079	1165	1334	1594	1905	2353	2919	3225	3668	4322	5117
Total Final Consumption Expenditure in the Domestic Market by Households, of which	25099	27240	31974	38050	46060	55075	62772	69117	76561	87168	99229
a Durable goods	2414	2368	3269	4225	4757	6235	6423	6724	7279	9170	10529
b Semi-durable goods	3834	3883	4561	5523	6668	7206	8310	8855	9864	11510	13064
c Non-durable goods	10608	11728	13374	15302	18386	22709	26154	29243	32045	35610	40644
d Services	8243	9261	10770	13001	16249	18925	21885	24295	27373	30878	34992
Plus: Direct purchases abroad by resident households	418	498	672	849	885	1151	1339	1583	1720	2050	2290
Less: Direct purchases in the domestic market by non-resident households	560	746	1011	1193	1206	1250	1346	1560	1861	2207	2614
Equals: Final Consumption Expenditure of Resident Households	24957	26992	31635	37706	45739	54977	62764	69140	76420	87011	98905
Final Consumption Expenditure of Private Non-profit Institutions Serving Households											
1 Research and science	400	452	482	522	559	19	22	22	26	31	35
2 Education						515	465	433	456	511	548

Finland

2.5 Private Final Consumption Expenditure by Type, in Current Prices
(Continued)

Million Finnish markkaa

	1970	1971	1972	1973	1974	1975	1976	1977	1978	1979	1980
3 Medical and other health services	60	69	81	95	110	148	166	187	202	214	253
4 Welfare services	49	56	67	79	100	130	151	166	190	233	286
5 Recreational and related cultural services						131	153	172	193	209	257
6 Religious organisations	393	448	516	619	784	491	606	674	747	832	930
7 Professional and labour organisations serving households						145	182	242	252	288	334
8 Miscellaneous						194	200	233	247	277	337
Equals: Final Consumption Expenditure of Private Non-profit Organisations Serving Households	901	1024	1145	1315	1552	1773	1945	2128	2313	2594	2987
Private Final Consumption Expenditure	25859	28016	32780	39021	47291	56750	64709	71268	78733	89604	101892

2.6 Private Final Consumption Expenditure by Type, in Constant Prices

Million Finnish markkaa

	1970	1971	1972	1973	1974	1975	1976	1977	1978	1979	1980

At constant prices of: 1975

Final Consumption Expenditure of Resident Households

	1970	1971	1972	1973	1974	1975	1976	1977	1978	1979	1980
1 Food, beverages and tobacco	14459	14898	15726	15719	16222	16549	16360	15777	16150	16889	16993
a Food	11382	11625	12211	12009	12159	12619	12578	11918	12334	13074	13155
b Non-alcoholic beverages	298	297	319	338	321	300	269	256	261	265	278
c Alcoholic beverages	1751	1899	2046	2243	2582	2469	2518	2579	2535	2484	2513
d Tobacco	1029	1077	1149	1128	1161	1160	996	1024	1020	1066	1047
2 Clothing and footwear	3512	3283	3575	3704	3663	3145	3216	3084	2988	3138	3208
3 Gross rent, fuel and power	8008	8423	8900	9412	9821	10395	10973	11423	11868	12292	12628
a Fuel and power	1598	1672	1740	1827	1727	1823	1986	2014	2071	2142	2121
b Other	6410	6751	7160	7585	8094	8572	8987	9409	9797	10150	10507
4 Furniture, furnishings and household equipment and operation	2970	3018	3373	3887	4160	4121	4053	3834	4014	4395	4565
a Household operation	529	476	458	408	369	316	290	301	291	295	276
b Other	2441	2542	2915	3479	3791	3805	3762	3533	3723	4100	4289
5 Medical care and health expenses	1228	1316	1357	1378	1398	1448	1517	1510	1556	1544	1599
6 Transport and communication	6753	6622	7549	8529	8037	8905	8307	8252	8230	9008	9077
a Personal transport equipment	2092	1727	2283	2738	2224	2715	2152	2174	1927	2390	2517
b Other	4661	4895	5266	5791	5813	6190	6155	6078	6303	6618	6560
7 Recreational, entertainment, education and cultural services	2684	2778	3125	3617	3849	4042	4328	4306	4642	5012	5314
8 Miscellaneous goods and services	5386	5589	6068	6374	6492	6472	6741	6482	6873	7292	7659
a Personal care	644	662	719	751	756	728	781	766	827	873	884
b Expenditures in restaurants, cafes and hotels	2519	2745	3016	3217	3418	3391	3380	3095	3254	3457	3703
c Other	2223	2182	2333	2406	2318	2353	2581	2621	2792	2962	3072
Total Final Consumption Expenditure in the Domestic Market by Households, of which:	44999	45927	49672	52619	53641	55075	55494	54668	56322	59568	61043
a Durable goods	4002	3658	4636	5586	5466	6235	5730	5594	5498	6315	6732
b Semi-durable goods	6598	6462	7059	7620	7798	7206	7572	7306	7572	8037	8174
c Non-durable goods	19270	20010	21158	21640	21905	22709	22684	22112	22702	23710	23798
d Services	15129	15797	16819	17773	18472	18925	19507	19657	20551	21505	22340
Plus: Direct purchases abroad by resident households	704	775	932	1075	1006	1151	1261	1299	1198	1285	1339
Less: Direct purchases in the domestic market by non-resident households	988	1236	1562	1650	1427	1250	1178	1211	1340	1478	1570
Equals: Final Consumption Expenditure of Resident Households	44714	45466	49042	52044	53220	54977	55578	54756	56181	59375	60812

Final Consumption Expenditure of Private Non-profit Institutions Serving Households

	1970	1971	1972	1973	1974	1975	1976	1977	1978	1979	1980
1 Research and science	732	764	758	722	654	19	19	18	19	20	20
2 Education						515	409	354	353	361	359
3 Medical and other health services	111	120	127	132	130	148	144	149	154	151	161

Finland

2.6 Private Final Consumption Expenditure by Type, in Constant Prices
(Continued)

Million Finnish markkaa

	1970	1971	1972	1973	1974	1975	1976	1977	1978	1979	1980
				At constant prices of:1975							
4 Welfare services	90	94	103	108	117	130	133	135	143	163	177
5 Recreational and related cultural services						131	138	138	146	143	156
6 Religious organisations	735	787	833	868	908	491	519	546	571	583	604
7 Professional and labour organisations serving households						145	153	182	181	189	195
8 Miscellaneous						194	182	192	192	197	215
Equals: Final Consumption Expenditure of Private Non-profit Organisations Serving Households	1668	1765	1821	1830	1809	1773	1698	1714	1759	1807	1889
Private Final Consumption Expenditure	46382	47231	50863	53874	55030	56750	57276	56470	57939	61183	62701

2.9 Gross Capital Formation by Kind of Activity of Owner, ISIC Major Divisions, in Current Prices

Million Finnish markkaa

	1970			1971			1972			1973		
	Total Gross Capital Formation	Increase in Stocks	Gross Fixed Capital Formation	Total Gross Capital Formation	Increase in Stocks	Gross Fixed Capital Formation	Total Gross Capital Formation	Increase in Stocks	Gross Fixed Capital Formation	Total Gross Capital Formation	Increase in Stocks	Gross Fixed Capital Formation
						All Producers						
1 Agriculture, hunting, fishing and forestry	...	...	917	...	...	1083	...	...	1148	...	...	1433
2 Mining and quarrying	...	...	49	...	...	94	...	...	108	...	...	75
3 Manufacturing	...	...	2491	...	...	3005	...	...	3208	...	...	3390
4 Electricity, gas and water	...	...	567	...	...	904	...	...	952	...	...	1531
5 Construction	...	...	296	...	...	325	...	...	371	...	...	448
6 Wholesale and retail trade, restaurants and hotels	...	...	827	...	...	888	...	...	1014	...	...	1613
7 Transport, storage and communication	...	...	1225	...	...	1359	...	...	1892	...	...	1990
8 Finance, insurance, real estate and business services	...	...	3377	...	...	3833	...	...	4707	...	...	6389
9 Community, social and personal services	...	...	252	...	...	241	...	...	299	...	...	505
Total Industries	...	...	10001	...	...	11731	...	...	13698	...	...	17374
Producers of Government Services	...	...	1486	...	...	1645	...	...	2122	...	...	2323
Private Non-Profit Institutions Serving Households	...	...	140	...	...	57	...	...	84	...	...	322
Total	13220	1594	11627	14596	1163	13433	15558	-347	15905	19946	-74	20019

	1974			1975			1976			1977		
	Total Gross Capital Formation	Increase in Stocks	Gross Fixed Capital Formation	Total Gross Capital Formation	Increase in Stocks	Gross Fixed Capital Formation	Total Gross Capital Formation	Increase in Stocks	Gross Fixed Capital Formation	Total Gross Capital Formation	Increase in Stocks	Gross Fixed Capital Formation
						All Producers						
1 Agriculture, hunting, fishing and forestry	...	...	1722	...	...	2284	...	...	2532	...	...	2674
2 Mining and quarrying	...	...	156	...	...	181	...	...	143	...	...	116
3 Manufacturing	...	...	5521	...	...	6471	...	...	6297	...	...	5874
4 Electricity, gas and water	...	...	2138	...	...	3186	...	...	3412	...	...	3110
5 Construction	...	...	637	...	...	645	...	...	442	...	...	695
6 Wholesale and retail trade, restaurants and hotels	...	...	1250	...	...	1509	...	...	1448	...	...	1478
7 Transport, storage and communication	...	...	2623	...	...	3621	...	...	3795	...	...	3953
8 Finance, insurance, real estate and business services	...	...	8242	...	...	9028	...	...	8969	...	...	10493
9 Community, social and personal services	...	...	613	...	...	708	...	...	663	...	...	694
Total Industries	...	...	22900	...	...	27634	...	...	27701	...	...	29086
Producers of Government Services	...	...	2896	...	...	3635	...	...	3846	...	...	4312
Private Non-Profit Institutions Serving Households	...	...	317	...	...	352	...	...	295	...	...	380
Total	30371	4258	26113	33338	1717	31621	31074	-768	31841	31182	-2596	33778

Finland

2.9 Gross Capital Formation by Kind of Activity of Owner, ISIC Major Divisions, in Current Prices

Million Finnish markkaa

	1978 Total Gross Capital Formation	1978 Increase in Stocks	1978 Gross Fixed Capital Formation	1979 Total Gross Capital Formation	1979 Increase in Stocks	1979 Gross Fixed Capital Formation	1980 Total Gross Capital Formation	1980 Increase in Stocks	1980 Gross Fixed Capital Formation
				All Producers					
1 Agriculture, hunting, fishing and forestry	...	...	2836	...	...	3278	...	...	4024
2 Mining and quarrying	...	...	116	...	...	263	...	...	125
3 Manufacturing	...	...	4852	...	...	5772	...	...	8725
4 Electricity, gas and water	...	...	2119	...	...	2890	...	...	3046
5 Construction	...	...	617	...	...	701	...	...	814
6 Wholesale and retail trade, restaurants and hotels	...	...	1630	...	...	1985	...	...	2389
7 Transport, storage and communication	...	...	3732	...	...	3818	...	...	4577
8 Finance, insurance, real estate and business services	...	...	11080	...	...	11937	...	...	14657
9 Community, social and personal services	...	...	800	...	...	855	...	...	975
Total Industries	...	...	27784	...	...	31498	...	...	39332
Producers of Government Services	...	...	4578	...	...	5051	...	...	5865
Private Non-Profit Institutions Serving Households	...	...	406	...	...	450	...	...	592
Total	29367	-3401	32768	40691	3692	36999	51482	5693	45789

2.10 Gross Capital Formation by Kind of Activity of Owner, ISIC Major Divisions, in Constant Prices

Million Finnish markkaa

	1970 Total Gross Capital Formation	1970 Increase in Stocks	1970 Gross Fixed Capital Formation	1971 Total Gross Capital Formation	1971 Increase in Stocks	1971 Gross Fixed Capital Formation	1972 Total Gross Capital Formation	1972 Increase in Stocks	1972 Gross Fixed Capital Formation	1973 Total Gross Capital Formation	1973 Increase in Stocks	1973 Gross Fixed Capital Formation
					At constant prices of:1975							
					All Producers							
1 Agriculture, hunting, fishing and forestry	...	...	1947	...	...	2101	...	...	1996	...	...	2198
2 Mining and quarrying	...	...	97	...	...	167	...	...	175	...	...	107
3 Manufacturing	...	...	5220	...	...	5641	...	...	5330	...	...	4798
4 Electricity, gas and water	...	...	1168	...	...	1686	...	...	1618	...	...	2222
5 Construction	...	...	602	...	...	584	...	...	602	...	...	641
6 Wholesale and retail trade, restaurants and hotels	...	...	1698	...	...	1620	...	...	1671	...	...	2321
7 Transport, storage and communication	...	...	2381	...	...	2416	...	...	2985	...	...	2619
8 Finance, insurance, real estate and business services	...	...	6982	...	...	7160	...	...	7997	...	...	9146
9 Community, social and personal services	...	...	527	...	...	452	...	...	511	...	...	741
Total Industries	...	...	20622	...	...	21827	...	...	22886	...	...	24992
Producers of Government Services	...	...	3120	...	...	3136	...	...	3687	...	...	3426
Private Non-Profit Institutions Serving Households	...	...	287	...	...	102	...	...	140	...	...	466
Total	27345	3315	24029	27300	2236	25064	26111	-602	26713	28770	-114	28885

	1974 Total Gross Capital Formation	1974 Increase in Stocks	1974 Gross Fixed Capital Formation	1975 Total Gross Capital Formation	1975 Increase in Stocks	1975 Gross Fixed Capital Formation	1976 Total Gross Capital Formation	1976 Increase in Stocks	1976 Gross Fixed Capital Formation	1977 Total Gross Capital Formation	1977 Increase in Stocks	1977 Gross Fixed Capital Formation
					At constant prices of:1975							
					All Producers							
1 Agriculture, hunting, fishing and forestry	...	...	2100	...	...	2284	...	...	2240	...	...	2092
2 Mining and quarrying	...	...	182	...	...	181	...	...	130	...	...	93
3 Manufacturing	...	...	6326	...	...	6471	...	...	5703	...	...	4744
4 Electricity, gas and water	...	...	2468	...	...	3186	...	...	3137	...	...	2513

Finland

2.10 Gross Capital Formation by Kind of Activity of Owner, ISIC Major Divisions, in Constant Prices
(Continued)

Million Finnish markkaa

	1974 Total Gross Capital Formation	1974 Increase in Stocks	1974 Gross Fixed Capital Formation	1975 Total Gross Capital Formation	1975 Increase in Stocks	1975 Gross Fixed Capital Formation	1976 Total Gross Capital Formation	1976 Increase in Stocks	1976 Gross Fixed Capital Formation	1977 Total Gross Capital Formation	1977 Increase in Stocks	1977 Gross Fixed Capital Formation
				At constant prices of: 1975								
5 Construction	...	...	752	...	...	645	...	...	399	...	...	555
6 Wholesale and retail trade, restaurants and hotels	...	...	1461	...	...	1509	...	...	1315	...	...	1182
7 Transport, storage and communication	...	...	3097	...	...	3621	...	...	3376	...	...	3148
8 Finance, insurance, real estate and business services	...	...	9138	...	...	9028	...	...	8206	...	...	8595
9 Community, social and personal services	...	...	713	...	...	708	...	...	592	...	...	562
Total Industries	...	...	26239	...	...	27634	...	...	25099	...	...	23483
Producers of Government Services	...	...	3324	...	...	3635	...	...	3481	...	...	3504
Private Non-Profit Institutions Serving Households	...	...	355	...	...	352	...	...	270	...	...	308
Total	34844	4926	29918	33338	1717	31621	28136	-714	28850	25076	-2219	27295

	1978 Total Gross Capital Formation	1978 Increase in Stocks	1978 Gross Fixed Capital Formation	1979 Total Gross Capital Formation	1979 Increase in Stocks	1979 Gross Fixed Capital Formation	1980 Total Gross Capital Formation	1980 Increase in Stocks	1980 Gross Fixed Capital Formation
			At constant prices of: 1975						
			All Producers						
1 Agriculture, hunting, fishing and forestry	...	...	2052	...	...	2160	...	...	2357
2 Mining and quarrying	...	...	86	...	...	183	...	...	82
3 Manufacturing	...	...	3834	...	...	4282	...	...	5835
4 Electricity, gas and water	...	...	1602	...	...	2039	...	...	1932
5 Construction	...	...	451	...	...	463	...	...	478
6 Wholesale and retail trade, restaurants and hotels	...	...	1191	...	...	1322	...	...	1412
7 Transport, storage and communication	...	...	2670	...	...	2569	...	...	2765
8 Finance, insurance, real estate and business services	...	...	8586	...	...	8345	...	...	8851
9 Community, social and personal services	...	...	612	...	...	599	...	...	604
Total Industries	...	...	21081	...	...	21961	...	...	24315
Producers of Government Services	...	...	3530	...	...	3582	...	...	3677
Private Non-Profit Institutions Serving Households	...	...	308	...	...	311	...	...	356
Total	22179	-2741	24920	28433	2579	25855	31919	3571	28348

2.17 Exports and Imports of Goods and Services, Detail

Million Finnish markkaa

	1970	1971	1972	1973	1974	1975	1976	1977	1978	1979	1980
				Exports of Goods and Services							
1 Exports of merchandise, f.o.b. [a]	9640	9846	12012	14530	20611	20209	24417	30805	35068	43302	52860
2 Transport and communication	1115	1122	1257	1648	1953	1844	2203	2673	3201	4322	4723
a In respect of merchandise imports [b]	249	244	287	350	521	498	446	457	514	756	914
b Other	867	878	969	1298	1432	1345	1757	2216	2687	3567	3809
3 Insurance service charges	29	46	106	97	34	39	75	134	295	343	308
a In respect of merchandise imports [b]	...	...	...	...	...	...	...	...	...	...	...
b Other	29	46	106	97	34	39	75	134	295	343	308
4 Other commodities	380	445	528	586	871	1315	1488	1801	2556	2367	3165
5 Adjustments of merchandise exports to change-of-ownership basis	...	...	...	...	...	...	...	...	...	...	...
6 Direct purchases in the domestic market by non-residential households	560	746	1011	1193	1206	1250	1346	1560	1861	2207	2614
7 Direct purchases in the domestic market by extraterritorial bodies	21	21	31	33	27	61	107	107	109	113	128
Total Exports of Goods and Services	11745	12226	14945	18086	24702	24717	29637	37079	43090	52654	63797
				Imports of Goods and Services							
1 Imports of merchandise, c.i.f. [a]	11138	11814	13132	16629	25815	28188	28727	30961	32600	44431	58315

Finland

2.17 Exports and Imports of Goods and Services, Detail
(Continued)

Million Finnish markkaa

	1970	1971	1972	1973	1974	1975	1976	1977	1978	1979	1980
2 Adjustments of merchandise imports to change-of-ownership basis	...	...	...	...	...	...	...	...	...	...	...
3 Other transport and communication	347	378	452	562	596	574	713	926	1177	1312	1695
4 Other insurance service charges	26	40	63	60	87	69	68	82	161	183	205
5 Other commodities	367	396	463	551	779	1000	1163	1373	1831	2152	2654
6 Direct purchases abroad by government	14	14	14	21	31	38	52	61	166	129	136
7 Direct purchases abroad by resident households	418	498	672	849	885	1151	1339	1583	1720	2050	2290
Total Imports of Goods and Services	12310	13139	14797	18672	28193	31020	32062	34986	37654	50256	65294
Balance of Goods and Services	-565	-913	149	-585	-3491	-6302	-2426	2094	5436	2398	-1497
Total Imports and Balance of Goods and Services	11745	12226	14946	18086	24702	24717	29637	37079	43090	52654	63797

a) Exports and imports of merchandise are recorded on the basis of the crossing of the customs frontiers of Finland. b) Insurance service charges in respect of merchandise imports are included in transport and communication in respect of merchandise imports.

3.12 General Government Income and Outlay Account: Total and Subsectors

Million Finnish markkaa

	1970 Total General Government	1970 Central Government	1970 State or Provincial Government	1970 Local Government	1970 Social Security Funds	1971 Total General Government	1971 Central Government	1971 State or Provincial Government	1971 Local Government	1971 Social Security Funds
Receipts										
1 Property and entrepreneurial income	715	202	...	357	156	689	177	...	359	154
a Net operating surplus	1	2	...	-1	...	-13	-8	...	-5	...
b Withdrawals from public quasi-corporations	241	-2	...	243	...	147	-80	...	227	...
c Interest	375	155	...	64	156	446	210	...	82	154
d Dividends	47	47	...	-	...	54	54	...	-	...
e Net land rent and royalties	51	-	...	51	...	55	-	...	55	...
2 Taxes, fees and contributions	14227	9522	...	3394	1311	16488	10566	...	3926	1996
a Indirect taxes	6091	6084	...	6	...	6861	6855	...	6	...
b Direct taxes	6005	2624	...	3381	...	7053	3140	...	3913	...
Income	6005	2624	...	3381	...	7053	3140	...	3913	...
Other	-	-	...	-	-	-	-	...	-	-
c Social security contributions	1977	666	...	-	1311	2411	415	...	-	1996
d Fees, fines and penalties	154	147	...	7	-	163	156	...	7	-
3 Other current transfers received	2869	345	...	1804	720	2993	377	...	2077	539
a Casualty insurance claims	...	...	...	...	...	...	...	...	...	...
b Transfers from other government subsectors	2164	84	...	1456	624	2185	86	...	1679	420
c Transfers from abroad	...	...	...	...	...	...	...	...	...	...
d Other transfers, except imputed	93	5	...	-	88	115	5	...	-	110
e Imputed unfunded employee welfare contributions	612	256	...	348	8	692	286	...	397	9
Total Current Receipts a	17811	10069	...	5555	2187	20170	11120	...	6361	2690
Disbursements										
1 General government final consumption expenditures	6610	2665	...	3764	181	7627	3031	...	4373	224
a Compensation of employees	4696	1768	...	2862	67	5328	1974	...	3276	78
b Consumption of fixed capital	341	150	...	183	8	400	176	...	212	12
c Goods and services purchased, net	1573	747	...	719	107	1899	881	...	885	133
Purchases	2387	928	...	1352	107	2779	1066	...	1579	134
Less: Sales	814	181	...	633	-	880	185	...	694	-
d Less: Own account production of fixed assets	...	...	...	...	...	...	...	...	...	...
e Indirect taxes paid, net	...	...	...	...	...	...	...	...	...	...
2 Property income paid	467	291	...	175	1	482	298	...	183	1
a Interest	466	290	...	175	1	481	297	...	183	1
b Net land rent and royalties	1	1	...	-	-	1	1	...	-	-

Finland

3.12 General Government Income and Outlay Account: Total and Subsectors
(Continued)

Million Finnish markkaa

	1970					1971				
	Total General Government	Central Government	State or Provincial Government	Local Government	Social Security Funds	Total General Government	Central Government	State or Provincial Government	Local Government	Social Security Funds
3 Subsidies	1350	1308	...	42	...	1435	1374	...	61	...
4 Other current transfers paid	5980	3508	...	539	1934	6747	3754	...	621	2372
a Casualty insurance premiums, net	...	...	...	...	...	...	...	...	...	...
b Transfers to other government subsectors	2185	1957	...	202	26	2216	1966	...	220	30
c Transfers to households	3249	1060	...	282	1907	3868	1195	...	333	2340
Social security benefits	2146	304	...	-	1842	2584	337	...	-	2248
Social assistance grants	519	341	...	115	64	592	370	...	131	91
Unfunded employee welfare benefits	583	415	...	167	1	691	488	...	202	2
d Transfers to private non-profit institutions serving households	517	461	...	55	1	612	543	...	68	2
e Transfers to the rest of the world	30	30	...	-	-	51	51	...	-	-
Net saving	3405	2297	...	1037	71	3880	2663	...	1124	94
Total Current Disbursements and Net Saving [a]	17811	10069	...	5555	2187	20170	11120	...	6361	2690

	1972					1973				
	Total General Government	Central Government	State or Provincial Government	Local Government	Social Security Funds	Total General Government	Central Government	State or Provincial Government	Local Government	Social Security Funds

Receipts

1 Property and entrepreneurial income	702	132	...	427	144	720	222	...	362	136
a Net operating surplus	-9	-12	...	3	...	-16	1	...	-17	...
b Withdrawals from public quasi-corporations	122	-154	...	275	...	49	-175	...	224	...
c Interest	461	232	...	86	144	556	333	...	87	136
d Dividends	65	65	...	-	...	73	62	...	11	...
e Net land rent and royalties	63	-	...	63	...	58	-	...	57	...
2 Taxes, fees and contributions	19195	12570	...	4311	2314	23950	15363	...	5439	3147
a Indirect taxes	7989	7982	...	7	...	9471	9453	...	19	...
b Direct taxes	8260	3963	...	4297	...	10570	5167	...	5403	...
Income	8260	3963	...	4297	...	10570	5167	...	5403	...
Other	-	-	...	-	...	-	-	...	-	-
c Social security contributions	2761	447	...	-	2314	3675	527	...	-	3147
d Fees, fines and penalties	186	178	...	8	-	234	216	...	18	-
3 Other current transfers received	3710	425	...	2559	726	4435	481	...	3222	732
a Casualty insurance claims	2	-	...	2	...	1	-	...	1	...
b Transfers from other government subsectors	2781	100	...	2090	591	3318	112	...	2634	573
c Transfers from abroad	...	...	...	...	...	...	...	...	...	...
d Other transfers, except imputed	128	4	...	-	125	152	6	...	-	146
e Imputed unfunded employee welfare contributions	800	322	...	467	11	963	363	...	587	13
Total Current Receipts [a]	23608	13127	...	7297	3184	29105	16066	...	9023	4016

Disbursements

1 General government final consumption expenditures	8967	3453	...	5255	259	10700	3950	...	6437	313
a Compensation of employees	6176	2240	...	3845	91	7373	2551	...	4707	115
b Consumption of fixed capital	462	206	...	242	14	567	254	...	301	12
c Goods and services purchased, net	2329	1007	...	1169	154	2760	1145	...	1429	186
Purchases	3236	1205	...	1878	154	3852	1389	...	2277	186
Less: Sales	907	198	...	709	-	1093	244	...	848	-
d Less: Own account production of fixed assets	...	...	...	...	...	...	...	...	...	...
e Indirect taxes paid, net	...	...	...	...	...	...	...	...	...	...
2 Property income paid	507	296	...	211	1	537	287	...	248	2
a Interest	506	295	...	211	1	536	286	...	248	2
b Net land rent and royalties	1	1	...	-	-	1	1	...	-	-

Finland

3.12 General Government Income and Outlay Account: Total and Subsectors
(Continued)

Million Finnish markkaa

	1972					1973				
	Total General Government	Central Government	State or Provincial Government	Local Government	Social Security Funds	Total General Government	Central Government	State or Provincial Government	Local Government	Social Security Funds
3 Subsidies	1619	1540	...	79	...	1751	1648	...	103	...
4 Other current transfers paid	8232	4680	...	739	2814	9608	5428	...	850	3330
a Casualty insurance premiums, net	1	-	...	1	-	2	-	...	2	-
b Transfers to other government subsectors	2830	2511	...	249	70	3389	3003	...	284	102
c Transfers to households	4645	1496	...	407	2742	5284	1641	...	418	3225
Social security benefits	2931	354	...	-	2577	3398	358	...	-	3040
Social assistance grants	850	540	...	147	163	844	564	...	-	-
Unfunded employee welfare benefits	864	602	...	261	2	1042	719	...	98	182
d Transfers to private non-profit institutions serving households	690	607	...	81	2	839	690	...	320	3
e Transfers to the rest of the world	66	66	...	-	-	95	95	...	146	4
Net saving	4283	3159	...	1014	110	6508	4753	...	-	-
Total Current Disbursements and Net Saving a	23608	13127	...	7297	3184	29105	16066	...	1385	371
									9023	4016

	1974					1975				
	Total General Government	Central Government	State or Provincial Government	Local Government	Social Security Funds	Total General Government	Central Government	State or Provincial Government	Local Government	Social Security Funds

Receipts

1 Property and entrepreneurial income	932	317	...	451	164	994	238	...	589	168
a Net operating surplus	-	-12	...	11	...	-45	-37	...	-7	...
b Withdrawals from public quasi-corporations	88	-165	...	252	...	135	-258	...	393	...
c Interest	692	412	...	116	164	703	421	...	122	160
d Dividends	86	82	...	4	...	123	112	...	4	8
e Net land rent and royalties	68	-	...	67	...	78	1	...	77	...
2 Taxes, fees and contributions	30045	19164	...	6779	4103	36664	22250	...	9075	5339
a Indirect taxes	11335	11314	...	21	...	13016	12993	...	23	...
b Direct taxes	13638	6900	...	6738	...	17037	8014	...	9023	...
Income	13638	6900	...	6738	...	17037	8014	...	9023	...
Other	-	-	...	-	...	-	-	...	-	...
c Social security contributions	4781	678	...	-	4103	6249	911	...	-	5339
d Fees, fines and penalties	291	272	...	20	-	362	333	...	29	-
3 Other current transfers received	5754	585	...	4257	913	7700	769	...	5814	1117
a Casualty insurance claims	2	-	...	2	...	1	-	...	1	...
b Transfers from other government subsectors	4360	132	...	3509	719	5883	182	...	4829	872
c Transfers from abroad	...	...	...	...	...	...	...	...	...	...
d Other transfers, except imputed	184	7	...	-	176	238	13	...	-	225
e Imputed unfunded employee welfare contributions	1209	446	...	746	17	1578	574	...	984	20
Total Current Receipts a	36731	20066	...	11487	5180	45358	23257	...	15477	6624

Disbursements

1 General government final consumption expenditures	13676	4925	...	8378	373	17790	6364	...	10955	472
a Compensation of employees	9268	3159	...	5963	146	12122	4056	...	7891	175
b Consumption of fixed capital	748	336	...	408	4	901	407	...	484	11
c Goods and services purchased, net	3656	1431	...	2002	223	4763	1901	...	2576	286
Purchases	4980	1754	...	3003	223	6428	2310	...	3831	287
Less: Sales	1324	323	...	1001	-	1665	409	...	1255	-
d Less: Own account production of fixed assets	...	...	...	...	...	...	...	...	...	...
e Indirect taxes paid, net	5	-	...	5	...	4	-	...	4	...
2 Property income paid	586	263	...	322	1	675	265	...	409	2
a Interest	585	262	...	322	1	674	264	...	409	2
b Net land rent and royalties	1	1	...	-	-	1	1	...	-	-

Finland

3.12 General Government Income and Outlay Account: Total and Subsectors
(Continued)

Million Finnish markkaa

	1974					1975				
	Total General Government	Central Government	State or Provincial Government	Local Government	Social Security Funds	Total General Government	Central Government	State or Provincial Government	Local Government	Social Security Funds
3 Subsidies	2967	2831	...	137	-	4141	3966	...	175	...
4 Other current transfers paid	12580	7095	...	1095	4391	16044	9283	...	1372	5388
a Casualty insurance premiums, net	3	-	...	3	-	4	-	...	4	-
b Transfers to other government subsectors	4459	3979	...	363	118	6055	5447	...	459	149
c Transfers to households	6902	2084	...	550	4267	8661	2742	...	686	5233
Social security benefits	4513	499	...	-	4014	5642	706	...	-	4936
Social assistance grants	1094	683	...	164	247	1365	928	...	152	285
Unfunded employee welfare benefits	1295	903	...	386	6	1654	1108	...	534	12
d Transfers to private non-profit institutions serving households	1100	916	...	179	5	1206	977	...	223	6
e Transfers to the rest of the world	116	116	...	-	-	118	118	...	-	-
Net saving	6922	4952	...	1555	415	6708	3379	...	2566	763
Total Current Disbursements and Net Saving [a]	36732	20066	...	11487	5180	45358	23257	...	15477	6624

	1976					1977				
	Total General Government	Central Government	State or Provincial Government	Local Government	Social Security Funds	Total General Government	Central Government	State or Provincial Government	Local Government	Social Security Funds

Receipts

1 Property and entrepreneurial income	1239	477	...	583	180	1404	528	...	632	244
a Net operating surplus	-56	-38	...	-18	...	-64	-42	...	-21	...
b Withdrawals from public quasi-corporations	234	-110	...	344	...	233	-96	...	330	...
c Interest	829	492	...	163	175	982	540	...	204	239
d Dividends	142	132	...	5	5	138	126	...	6	5
e Net land rent and royalties	91	1	...	90	...	115	-	...	114	...
2 Taxes, fees and contributions	45150	28344	...	10682	6125	48994	30194	...	12224	6576
a Indirect taxes	15082	15057	...	24	...	17797	17769	...	28	...
b Direct taxes	22241	11612	...	10629	...	22779	10614	...	12165	...
Income	22241	11612	...	10629	...	22779	10614	...	12165	...
Other	-	-	...	-	...	-	-	...	-	...
c Social security contributions	7359	1234	...	-	6125	7857	1281	...	-	6576
d Fees, fines and penalties	469	441	...	28	-	560	529	...	31	-
3 Other current transfers received	9652	911	...	7346	1395	11067	996	...	8473	1598
a Casualty insurance claims	6	-	...	6	-	1	-	...	1	-
b Transfers from other government subsectors	7418	223	...	6118	1078	8595	260	...	7088	1247
c Transfers from abroad	...	...	...	...	...	...	...	...	...	...
d Other transfers, except imputed	322	29	...	-	293	342	17	...	-	325
e Imputed unfunded employee welfare contributions	1906	659	...	1222	24	2128	718	...	1384	26
Total Current Receipts [a]	56042	29732	...	18611	7700	61464	31718	...	21328	8418

Disbursements

1 General governement final consumption expenditures	21296	7306	...	13405	584	23969	7972	...	15352	645
a Compensation of employees	14778	4729	...	9836	213	16456	5088	...	11141	228
b Consumption of fixed capital	1040	471	...	565	4	1248	565	...	676	8
c Goods and services purchased, net	5473	2106	...	3000	367	6261	2320	...	3532	410
Purchases	7674	2649	...	4658	367	8776	2906	...	5460	410
Less: Sales	2200	542	...	1658	-	2515	586	...	1929	1
d Less: Own account production of fixed assets	...	...	...	...	...	...	...	...	...	...
e Indirect taxes paid, net	5	-	...	5	-	4	-	...	4	-
2 Property income paid	761	287	...	473	2	999	469	...	526	3
a Interest	760	286	...	472	2	997	468	...	525	3
b Net land rent and royalties	1	1	...	-	-	2	1	...	1	-

Finland

3.12 General Government Income and Outlay Account: Total and Subsectors
(Continued)

Million Finnish markkaa

	1976					1977				
	Total General Government	Central Government	State or Provincial Government	Local Government	Social Security Funds	Total General Government	Central Government	State or Provincial Government	Local Government	Social Security Funds
3 Subsidies	4863	4631	...	232	...	5231	5004	...	226	...
4 Other current transfers paid	19671	11443	...	1713	6515	23118	13548	...	2098	7473
a Casualty insurance premiums, net	5	-	...	5	-	7	-	...	7	-
b Transfers to other government subsectors	7696	6885	...	540	270	8962	7986	...	639	336
c Transfers to households	10567	3407	...	923	6237	12718	4430	...	1162	7126
Social security benefits	6719	818	...	-	5901	7794	1055	...	-	6738
Social assistance grants	1757	1192	...	246	318	2403	1703	...	337	363
Unfunded employee welfare benefits	2091	1397	...	677	17	2521	1671	...	825	25
d Transfers to private non-profit institutions serving households	1262	1009	...	244	8	1281	982	...	289	10
e Transfers to the rest of the world	141	141	...	-	-	151	151	...	-	-
Net saving	9451	6065	...	2787	599	8147	4724	...	3126	297
Total Current Disbursements and Net Saving [a]	56042	29732	...	18611	7700	61464	31718	...	21328	8418

	1978					1979				
	Total General Government	Central Government	State or Provincial Government	Local Government	Social Security Funds	Total General Government	Central Government	State or Provincial Government	Local Government	Social Security Funds

Receipts

1 Property and entrepreneurial income	1789	691	...	819	280	2018	1021	...	748	248
a Net operating surplus	4	-13	...	17	...	-28	-25	...	-4	...
b Withdrawals from public quasi-corporations	329	-105	...	434	...	385	23	...	363	...
c Interest	1170	671	...	225	274	1365	876	...	248	241
d Dividends	150	138	...	6	6	161	146	...	8	7
e Net land rent and royalties	136	1	...	136	...	135	1	...	133	...
2 Taxes, fees and contributions	50764	31628	...	12559	6577	56323	34502	...	14168	7654
a Indirect taxes	20399	20374	...	26	...	23700	23668	...	32	...
b Direct taxes	21905	9411	...	12494	...	23737	9642	...	14095	...
Income	21905	9411	...	12494	...	23737	9642	...	14095	...
Other	-	-	...	-	...	-	-	...	-	...
c Social security contributions	7825	1248	...	-	6577	8153	499	...	-	7654
d Fees, fines and penalties	635	595	...	40	-	734	693	...	41	-
3 Other current transfers received	12421	1110	...	9367	1944	14157	1321	...	10845	1992
a Casualty insurance claims	4	...	...	4	...	5	...	...	5	...
b Transfers from other government subsectors	9672	311	...	7843	1518	10949	413	...	9064	1472
c Transfers from abroad	...	...	...	...	...	...	...	...	...	...
d Other transfers, except imputed	423	24	...	-	398	520	31	...	-	489
e Imputed unfunded employee welfare contributions	2322	774	...	1520	28	2683	877	...	1776	31
Total Current Receipts [a]	64974	33428	...	22746	8801	72499	36844	...	25761	9894

Disbursements

1 General government final consumption expenditures	26252	8777	...	16724	752	29755	9867	...	19017	871
a Compensation of employees	17954	5505	...	12200	249	20497	6195	...	14028	274
b Consumption of fixed capital	1390	621	...	759	10	1568	690	...	875	3
c Goods and services purchased, net	6902	2650	...	3758	494	7683	2982	...	4108	594
Purchases	9966	3365	...	6107	495	11189	3802	...	6793	595
Less: Sales	3065	715	...	2349	1	3506	820	...	2685	1
d Less: Own account production of fixed assets	...	...	...	...	...	...	...	...	...	...
e Indirect taxes paid, net	7	-	...	7	-	7	-	...	7	-
2 Property income paid	1185	658	...	522	5	1575	1001	...	564	9
a Interest	1183	657	...	521	5	1572	1000	...	563	9
b Net land rent and royalties	2	1	...	1	-	3	1	...	1	-

Finland

3.12 General Government Income and Outlay Account: Total and Subsectors
(Continued)

Million Finnish markkaa

	1978					1979				
	Total General Government	Central Government	State or Provincial Government	Local Government	Social Security Funds	Total General Government	Central Government	State or Provincial Government	Local Government	Social Security Funds
3 Subsidies	5520	5266	...	254	...	7110	6860	...	250	...
4 Other current transfers paid	25943	15221	...	2426	8296	28713	17211	...	2778	8724
a Casualty insurance premiums, net	9	-	...	9	-	10	-	...	10	-
b Transfers to other government subsectors	10204	9016	...	726	463	11747	10350	...	841	556
c Transfers to households	14307	5097	...	1388	7822	15280	5534	...	1588	8157
Social security benefits	8487	1146	...	-	7342	8927	1276	...	-	7651
Social assistance grants	2949	2102	...	393	454	3160	2239	...	445	475
Unfunded employee welfare benefits	2871	1849	...	995	27	3193	2019	...	1142	31
d Transfers to private non-profit institutions serving households	1273	958	...	304	11	1436	1086	...	339	11
e Transfers to the rest of the world	151	151	...	-	-	241	241	...	-	-
Net saving	6074	3506	...	2820	-252	5346	1903	...	3152	290
Total Current Disbursements and Net Saving [a]	64974	33428	...	22746	8801	72499	36844	...	25761	9894

	1980				
	Total General Government	Central Government	State or Provincial Government	Local Government	Social Security Funds

Receipts

1 Property and entrepreneurial income	2085	909	...	888	290
a Net operating surplus	-36	-42	...	5	-
b Withdrawals from public quasi-corporations	357	-64	...	421	-
c Interest	1532	947	...	305	280
d Dividends	85	66	...	10	10
e Net land rent and royalties	148	1	...	147	-
2 Taxes, fees and contributions	64770	40248	...	15680	8844
a Indirect taxes	27069	27033	...	37	-
b Direct taxes	27987	12387	...	15600	-
Income	27987	12387	...	15600	-
Other	-	-	...	-	-
c Social security contributions	8972	128	...	-	8844
d Fees, fines and penalties	743	700	...	43	-
3 Other current transfers received	16563	1381	...	12875	2306
a Casualty insurance claims	7	-	...	7	-
b Transfers from other government subsectors	12883	350	...	10851	1681
c Transfers from abroad	-	-	...	-	-
d Other transfers, except imputed	629	38	...	-	591
e Imputed unfunded employee welfare contributions	3043	992	...	2017	34
Total Current Receipts [a]	83419	42538	...	29441	11440

Disbursements

1 General governement final consumption expenditures	34538	11469	...	22015	1054
a Compensation of employees	23275	7014	...	15959	303
b Consumption of fixed capital	1850	795	...	1040	16
c Goods and services purchased, net	9405	3661	...	5008	735
Purchases	13463	4607	...	8119	736
Less: Sales	4058	946	...	3111	1
d Less: Own account production of fixed assets	-	-	...	-	-
e Indirect taxes paid, net	8	-	...	8	-
2 Property income paid	1893	1222	...	668	4
a Interest	1890	1221	...	666	4
b Net land rent and royalties	3	1	...	2	-

Finland

3.12 General Government Income and Outlay Account: Total and Subsectors
(Continued)

Million Finnish markkaa

	1980 Total General Government	Central Government	State or Provincial Government	Local Government	Social Security Funds
3 Subsidies	7596	7333	...	263	-
4 Other current transfers paid	32619	19996	...	3059	9562
a Casualty insurance premiums, net	11	-	...	11	-
b Transfers to other government subsectors	13654	12336	...	837	480
c Transfers to households	16947	6050	...	1827	9069
Social security benefits	9963	1453	...	-	8510
Social assistance grants	3403	2353	...	517	532
Unfunded employee welfare benefits	3581	2244	...	1310	27
d Transfers to private non-profit institutions serving households	1677	1280	...	384	13
e Transfers to the rest of the world	330	330	...	-	-
Net saving	6773	2518	...	3436	820
Total Current Disbursements and Net Saving [a]	83419	42538	...	29441	11440

a) Column 'Total general government' is shown non-consolidated.

3.13 General Government Capital Accumulation Account: Total and Subsectors

Million Finnish markkaa

	1970 Total General Government	Central Government	State or Provincial Government	Local Government	Social Security Funds	1971 Total General Government	Central Government	State or Provincial Government	Local Government	Social Security Funds
				Finance of Gross Accumulation						
1 Gross saving	3751	2452	...	1220	79	4286	2845	...	1335	106
a Consumption of fixed capital	346	155	...	183	8	406	182	...	212	12
b Net saving	3405	2297	...	1037	71	3880	2663	...	1124	94
2 Capital transfers received [a]	-76	-159	...	84	...	-68	-158	...	89	...
a From other government subsectors	-	-83	...	83	...	-	-88	...	88	...
b From other resident sectors	-76	-77	...	1	...	-73	-74	...	1	...
c From rest of the world	-	-	...	-	...	5	5	...	-	...
Finance of Gross Accumulation [b]	3675	2293	...	1303	79	4217	2687	...	1425	106
				Gross Accumulation						
1 Gross capital formation	1599	835	...	757	8	1844	978	...	855	11
a Increase in stocks	-3	-3	...	-	...	39	39	...	-	...
b Gross fixed capital formation	1602	838	...	757	8	1805	939	...	855	11
2 Purchases of land, net	113	37	...	76	...	123	45	...	78	...
3 Purchases of intangible assets, net	...	...	...	...	...	...	...	...	...	...
4 Capital transfers paid	...	...	...	...	...	...	...	...	...	...
Net lending	1963	1421	...	471	72	2251	1665	...	491	95
Gross Accumulation [b]	3675	2293	...	1303	79	4217	2687	...	1425	106

	1972 Total General Government	Central Government	State or Provincial Government	Local Government	Social Security Funds	1973 Total General Government	Central Government	State or Provincial Government	Local Government	Social Security Funds
				Finance of Gross Accumulation						
1 Gross saving	4749	3369	...	1255	125	7084	5012	...	1689	383
a Consumption of fixed capital	466	210	...	242	14	576	260	...	304	12
b Net saving	4283	3159	...	1014	110	6508	4753	...	1385	371
2 Capital transfers received [a]	16	-103	...	119	...	-94	-240	...	146	...
a From other government subsectors	-	-118	...	118	...	-	-145	...	145	...
b From other resident sectors	-72	-73	...	1	...	-93	-95	...	1	...
c From rest of the world	89	89	...	-	-	-1	-1	...	-	-
Finance of Gross Accumulation [b]	4765	3266	...	1374	125	6990	4772	...	1835	383
				Gross Accumulation						
1 Gross capital formation	2362	1254	...	1094	15	2700	1427	...	1266	8

Finland

3.13 General Government Capital Accumulation Account: Total and Subsectors
(Continued)

Million Finnish markkaa

	1972 Total General Government	1972 Central Government	1972 State or Provincial Government	1972 Local Government	1972 Social Security Funds	1973 Total General Government	1973 Central Government	1973 State or Provincial Government	1973 Local Government	1973 Social Security Funds
a Increase in stocks	46	46	...	-	...	101	101	...	-	...
b Gross fixed capital formation	2316	1207	...	1094	15	2599	1326	...	1266	8
2 Purchases of land, net	142	64	...	78	...	210	63	...	147	...
3 Purchases of intangible assets, net	...	...	...	...	...	...	...	...	...	...
4 Capital transfers paid	...	...	...	...	...	...	...	...	...	...
Net lending	2261	1949	...	202	110	4079	3282	...	422	375
Gross Accumulation b	4765	3266	...	1374	125	6990	4772	...	1835	383

	1974 Total General Government	1974 Central Government	1974 State or Provincial Government	1974 Local Government	1974 Social Security Funds	1975 Total General Government	1975 Central Government	1975 State or Provincial Government	1975 Local Government	1975 Social Security Funds
Finance of Gross Accumulation										
1 Gross saving	7683	5295	...	1968	419	7722	3804	...	3144	774
a Consumption of fixed capital	761	343	...	413	4	1014	426	...	578	11
b Net saving	6922	4952	...	1555	415	6708	3379	...	2566	763
2 Capital transfers received a	-114	-384	...	270	...	-461	-896	...	434	...
a From other government subsectors	-	-269	...	269	...	-	-425	...	425	...
b From other resident sectors	-114	-114	...	-	...	-459	-469	...	10	...
c From rest of the world	-	-	...	-	...	-2	-2	...	-	...
Finance of Gross Accumulation b	7569	4912	...	2238	419	7261	2909	...	3578	774
Gross Accumulation										
1 Gross capital formation	3277	1505	...	1764	8	4247	1919	...	2307	21
a Increase in stocks	20	20	...	-	...	161	161	...	-	...
b Gross fixed capital formation	3257	1486	...	1764	8	4086	1758	...	2307	21
2 Purchases of land, net	167	79	...	89	...	279	139	...	140	...
3 Purchases of intangible assets, net	...	...	...	...	...	...	...	...	...	...
4 Capital transfers paid	...	...	...	...	...	...	...	...	...	...
Net lending	4124	3328	...	385	411	2735	851	...	1132	753
Gross Accumulation b	7569	4912	...	2238	419	7261	2909	...	3578	774

	1976 Total General Government	1976 Central Government	1976 State or Provincial Government	1976 Local Government	1976 Social Security Funds	1977 Total General Government	1977 Central Government	1977 State or Provincial Government	1977 Local Government	1977 Social Security Funds
Finance of Gross Accumulation										
1 Gross saving	10545	6567	...	3375	603	9453	5317	...	3831	305
a Consumption of fixed capital	1093	501	...	588	4	1305	593	...	705	8
b Net saving	9451	6065	...	2787	599	8147	4724	...	3126	297
2 Capital transfers received a	-155	-493	...	338	...	-146	-497	...	351	...
a From other government subsectors	-	-338	...	338	...	-	-353	...	353	...
b From other resident sectors	-155	-155	...	-	...	-146	-144	...	-2	...
c From rest of the world	-	-	...	-	...	-	-	...	-	-
Finance of Gross Accumulation b	10390	6074	...	3712	603	9306	4820	...	4181	305
Gross Accumulation										
1 Gross capital formation	4373	1919	...	2436	19	4948	2001	...	2939	8
a Increase in stocks	70	70	...	-	-	106	106	...	-	-
b Gross fixed capital formation	4304	1849	...	2436	19	4842	1895	...	2939	8
2 Purchases of land, net	312	179	...	134	...	320	122	...	199	...
3 Purchases of intangible assets, net	...	...	...	...	...	...	...	...	...	...
4 Capital transfers paid	...	...	...	...	...	...	...	...	...	...
Net lending	5704	3977	...	1143	584	4038	2698	...	1043	298
Gross Accumulation b	10390	6074	...	3712	603	9306	4820	...	4181	305

Finland

3.13 General Government Capital Accumulation Account: Total and Subsectors

Million Finnish markkaa

	1978					1979				
	Total General Government	Central Government	State or Provincial Government	Local Government	Social Security Funds	Total General Government	Central Government	State or Provincial Government	Local Government	Social Security Funds
	Finance of Gross Accumulation									
1 Gross saving	7518	4161	...	3599	-243	7005	2629	...	4082	293
a Consumption of fixed capital	1444	655	...	779	10	1659	726	...	930	3
b Net saving	6074	3506	...	2820	-252	5346	1903	...	3152	290
2 Capital transfers received a	-162	-609	...	447	...	-395	-809	...	414	-
a From other government subsectors	-	-447	...	447	...	-	-416	...	416	-
b From other resident sectors	-162	-162	...	-	...	-267	-265	...	-2	-
c From rest of the world	-	-	...	-	-	-128	-128	...	-	-
Finance of Gross Accumulation b	7355	3552	...	4046	-243	6609	1820	...	4496	293
	Gross Accumulation									
1 Gross capital formation	5057	2051	...	2996	10	5492	2196	...	3294	2
a Increase in stocks	-52	-52	...	-	-	-145	-145	...	-	-
b Gross fixed capital formation	5108	2102	...	2996	10	5637	2341	...	3294	2
2 Purchases of land, net	304	90	...	214	...	331	95	...	236	...
3 Purchases of intangible assets, net	...	...	...	...	...	...	...	...	...	...
4 Capital transfers paid	...	...	...	...	...	...	...	...	...	...
Net lending	1994	1411	...	836	-253	787	-470	...	966	291
Gross Accumulation b	7355	3552	...	4046	-243	6609	1820	...	4496	293

	1980			
	Total General Government	Central Government	State or Provincial Government	Local Government	Social Security Funds
	Finance of Gross Accumulation				
1 Gross saving	8738	3362	...	4541	836
a Consumption of fixed capital	1965	844	...	1105	16
b Net saving	6773	2518	...	3436	820
2 Capital transfers received a	-473	-937	...	464	-
a From other government subsectors	-	-467	...	467	-
b From other resident sectors	-423	-420	...	-3	-
c From rest of the world	-50	-50	...	-	-
Finance of Gross Accumulation b	8264	2424	...	5005	836
	Gross Accumulation				
1 Gross capital formation	6482	2598	...	3867	18
a Increase in stocks	10	10	...	-	-
b Gross fixed capital formation	6472	2588	...	3867	18
2 Purchases of land, net	379	144	...	235	-
3 Purchases of intangible assets, net	...	...	...	...	...
4 Capital transfers paid	...	...	...	...	...
Net lending	1403	-318	...	903	818
Gross Accumulation b	8264	2424	...	5005	836

a) Net.
b) Column 'Total general government' is shown non-consolidated.

3.14 General Government Capital Finance Account, Total and Subsectors

Million Finnish markkaa

	1970					1971				
	Total General Government	Central Government	State or Provincial Government	Local Government	Social Security Funds	Total General Government	Central Government	State or Provincial Government	Local Government	Social Security Funds
	Acquisition of Financial Assets									
1 Gold and SDRs	...	...	...	...	...	...	...	...	...	...
2 Currency and transferable deposits	82	11	...	61	10	272	157	...	33	83
3 Other deposits	537	261	...	276	-	363	143	...	220	-
4 Bills and bonds, short term	...	...	...	...	...	...	...	...	...	...
5 Bonds, long term	101	89	...	3	9	51	46	...	-	5
a Corporations	..	39	...	-	..	..	46	...	-	-
b Other government subsectors	..	-	...	3	..	..	-	...	-	-

Finland

3.14 General Government Capital Finance Account, Total and Subsectors
(Continued)

Million Finnish markkaa

	1970 Total General Government	1970 Central Government	1970 State or Provincial Government	1970 Local Government	1970 Social Security Funds	1971 Total General Government	1971 Central Government	1971 State or Provincial Government	1971 Local Government	1971 Social Security Funds
c Rest of the world	50	50	...	-	-	383	262	...	119	2
6 Corporate equity securities	199	88	...	105	5	68	11	...	54	3
7 Short-term loans, n.e.c.	91	5	...	80	6	604	562	...	109	-67
8 Long-term loans, n.e.c.	544	447	...	117	-20	370	370	...	-	-
a Mortgages	333	333	...	-	-	234	192	...	109	-67
b Other	211	114	...	117	-20	294	10	...	168	116
9 Other receivables	101	24	...	29	48	499	266	...	233	-
10 Other assets	389	208	...	181	-	2534	1457	...	937	141
Total Acquisition of Financial Assets	2044	1133	...	852	59					

Incurrence of Liabilities

1 Currency and transferable deposits	...	...	...	...	...	...	...	...	...	...
2 Other deposits	...	...	...	...	...	...	...	...	...	...
3 Bills and bonds, short term	-139	-138	...	-1	-	-209	-203	...	-6	-
4 Bonds, long term	156	162	...	-6	-	79	14	...	65	-
5 Short-term loans, n.e.c.	26	5	...	21	-	73	32	...	41	-
6 Long-term loans, n.e.c.	-46	-249	...	202	1	188	-100	...	287	1
7 Other payables	46	-72	...	115	3	179	25	...	109	45
8 Other liabilities	85	-	...	85	-	57	-	...	57	-
Total Incurrence of Liabilities	127	-292	...	416	3	367	-233	...	554	46
Statistical discrepancy	-47	4	...	-34	-16	-84	25	...	-108	-
Net Lending	1963	1421	...	471	72	2251	1665	...	491	95
Incurrence of Liabilities and Net Worth	2044	1133	...	852	59	2534	1457	...	937	141

	1972 Total General Government	1972 Central Government	1972 State or Provincial Government	1972 Local Government	1972 Social Security Funds	1973 Total General Government	1973 Central Government	1973 State or Provincial Government	1973 Local Government	1973 Social Security Funds

Acquisition of Financial Assets

1 Gold and SDRs	...	...	...	...	...	...	...	...	...	...
2 Currency and transferable deposits	454	273	...	54	128	856	540	...	168	149
3 Other deposits	-34	-93	...	59	-	686	649	...	37	1
4 Bills and bonds, short term	...	...	...	...	...	...	...	...	...	...
5 Bonds, long term	197	207	...	-1	-9	-11	-12	...	-9	9
a Corporations	..	86	...	12	..	..	27	...	-9	..
b Other government subsectors	..	-	...	-13	..	-39	-39	...	-	-
c Rest of the world	121	121	...	-	-	329	147	...	171	11
6 Corporate equity securities	308	163	...	144	2	134	28	...	103	3
7 Short-term loans, n.e.c.	45	20	...	23	2	1353	1044	...	273	36
8 Long-term loans, n.e.c.	909	705	...	265	-60	677	677	...	-	-
a Mortgages	547	547	...	-	-	676	367	...	273	36
b Other	362	158	...	265	-60	481	21	...	300	160
9 Other receivables	323	21	...	212	90	816	275	...	541	-
10 Other assets	745	440	...	305	-	4644	2692	...	1584	368
Total Acquisition of Financial Assets	2948	1735	...	1060	153					

Incurrence of Liabilities

1 Currency and transferable deposits	...	...	...	...	...	...	...	...	...	...
2 Other deposits	...	...	...	...	...	...	...	...	...	...
3 Bills and bonds, short term	19	-	...	19	-	5	-	...	5	-
4 Bonds, long term	-121	-103	...	-18	-	-410	-402	...	-8	-
5 Short-term loans, n.e.c.	81	44	...	37	-	83	34	...	49	-
6 Long-term loans, n.e.c.	432	-220	...	651	1	440	-270	...	711	-
7 Other payables	249	50	...	154	45	365	138	...	237	-10
8 Other liabilities	87	-	...	87	-	108	-	...	108	-
Total Incurrence of Liabilities	748	-228	...	929	46	590	-501	...	1101	-10
Statistical discrepancy	-60	14	...	-71	-3	-25	-89	...	61	3
Net Lending	2261	1949	...	202	110	4079	3282	...	422	375
Incurrence of Liabilities and Net Worth	2948	1735	...	1060	153	4644	2692	...	1584	368

Finland

3.14 General Government Capital Finance Account, Total and Subsectors

Million Finnish markkaa

	1974					1975				
	Total General Government	Central Government	State or Provincial Government	Local Government	Social Security Funds	Total General Government	Central Government	State or Provincial Government	Local Government	Social Security Funds

Acquisition of Financial Assets

1 Gold and SDRs	...	...	...	...	...	...	...	...	...	...
2 Currency and transferable deposits	526	327	...	62	137	-676	-1206	...	157	372
3 Other deposits	126	198	...	-72	-	-185	-561	...	376	-
4 Bills and bonds, short term	...	...	...	...	...	...	...	...	...	...
5 Bonds, long term	133	114	...	7	12	98	109	...	-2	-9
a Corporations	..	112	...	7	..	..	126	...	-2	..
b Other government subsectors	..	-	...	..	..	..	-	...	..	..
c Rest of the world	2	2	...	-	-	-17	-17	...	-	..
6 Corporate equity securities	605	331	...	265	9	952	439	...	481	32
7 Short-term loans, n.e.c.	103	49	...	50	4	196	-21	...	214	3
8 Long-term loans, n.e.c.	1590	1089	...	476	26	2606	1954	...	595	57
a Mortgages	782	782	...	-	-	1158	1158	...	-	-
b Other	808	307	...	476	26	1448	796	...	595	57
9 Other receivables	919	452	...	290	177	445	-142	...	253	334
10 Other assets	1735	944	...	791	-	2487	1435	...	1052	-
Total Acquisition of Financial Assets	5737	3504	...	1868	365	5923	2007	...	3126	790

Incurrence of Liabilities

1 Currency and transferable deposits	...	...	...	...	...	...	...	...	...	...
2 Other deposits	...	...	...	...	...	...	...	...	...	...
3 Bills and bonds, short term	34	-	...	34	-	-10	-	...	-10	-
4 Bonds, long term	-340	-339	...	-1	-	598	531	...	67	-
5 Short-term loans, n.e.c.	71	16	...	55	-	166	149	...	12	5
6 Long-term loans, n.e.c.	917	-58	...	968	7	1317	281	...	1040	-4
7 Other payables	931	654	...	318	-42	720	156	...	515	48
8 Other liabilities	133	-	...	133	-	321	-	...	321	-
Total Incurrence of Liabilities	1745	273	...	1507	-35	3110	1116	...	1945	49
Statistical discrepancy	-133	-97	...	-24	-12	78	40	...	50	-12
Net Lending	4124	3328	...	385	411	2735	851	...	1131	753
Incurrence of Liabilities and Net Worth	5737	3504	...	1868	365	5923	2007	...	3126	790

	1976					1977				
	Total General Government	Central Government	State or Provincial Government	Local Government	Social Security Funds	Total General Government	Central Government	State or Provincial Government	Local Government	Social Security Funds

Acquisition of Financial Assets

1 Gold and SDRs	...	...	...	...	...	...	...	...	...	...
2 Currency and transferable deposits	965	728	...	101	136	-161	-159	...	78	-80
3 Other deposits	-135	-208	...	71	1	371	-292	...	665	-1
4 Bills and bonds, short term	...	...	...	...	...	...	...	...	...	...
5 Bonds, long term	-40	-16	...	1	-26	61	121	...	-4	-56
a Corporations	..	101	...	1	..	..	121	...	-4	..
b Other government subsectors	..	-	...	..	..	..	-	...	..	..
c Rest of the world	-117	-117	...	-	-	-	-	...	-	-
6 Corporate equity securities	1925	477	...	1438	11	1434	532	...	898	4
7 Short-term loans, n.e.c.	551	436	...	110	5	85	62	...	19	4
8 Long-term loans, n.e.c.	3985	2472	...	1004	509	4240	2478	...	1064	698
a Mortgages	2228	2228	...	-	-	1734	1734	...	-	-
b Other	1757	244	...	1004	509	2506	744	...	1064	698
9 Other receivables	698	-276	...	1034	-61	-400	-70	...	-151	-178
10 Other assets	2432	1467	...	965	-	2345	1261	...	1084	-
Total Acquisition of Financial Assets	10380	5080	...	4725	575	7975	3933	...	3652	391

Incurrence of Liabilities

1 Currency and transferable deposits	...	...	...	...	...	...	...	...	...	...
2 Other deposits	...	...	...	...	...	...	...	...	...	...
3 Bills and bonds, short term	-25	-	...	-25	-	-18	-	...	-18	-
4 Bonds, long term	1127	1132	...	-5	-	1242	1260	...	-18	-
5 Short-term loans, n.e.c.	201	215	...	-14	-	-333	-186	...	-147	-

Finland

3.14 General Government Capital Finance Account, Total and Subsectors
(Continued)

Million Finnish markkaa

	1976 Total General Government	Central Government	State or Provincial Government	Local Government	Social Security Funds	1977 Total General Government	Central Government	State or Provincial Government	Local Government	Social Security Funds
6 Long-term loans, n.e.c.	1291	-96	...	1388	-2	1692	72	...	1578	42
7 Other payables	965	90	...	881	-5	398	100	...	257	41
8 Other liabilities	1244	-	...	1244	-	647	-	...	647	-
Total Incurrence of Liabilities	4804	1342	...	3469	-7	3628	1246	...	2299	83
Statistical discrepancy	-128	-238	...	113	584	309	-11	...	310	10
Net Lending	5704	3977	...	1143	-3	4038	2698	...	1043	298
Incurrence of Liabilities and Net Worth	10380	5080	...	4725	575	7975	3933	...	3652	391

	1978 Total General Government	Central Government	State or Provincial Government	Local Government	Social Security Funds	1979 Total General Government	Central Government	State or Provincial Government	Local Government	Social Security Funds
Acquisition of Financial Assets										
1 Gold and SDRs	...	...	...	...	...	...	...	...	...	...
2 Currency and transferable deposits	843	1193	...	-124	-226	-518	-1161	...	258	385
3 Other deposits	1412	1120	...	223	69	1411	742	...	759	-90
4 Bills and bonds, short term	...	...	...	...	...	...	...	...	...	...
5 Bonds, long term	136	144	...	-2	-6	420	105	...	121	194
a Corporations	..	144	...	-2	..	297	105	...	-	192
b Other government subsectors	..	-	...	..	..	123	-	...	121	2
c Rest of the world	-	-	...	-	-	...	...	...	...	...
6 Corporate equity securities	1094	351	...	728	15	1144	425	...	718	1
7 Short-term loans, n.e.c.	362	257	...	104	1	32	-120	...	147	5
8 Long-term loans, n.e.c.	3179	2140	...	1234	-195	3111	2026	...	1259	-174
a Mortgages	1745	1745	...	-	-	1749	1749	...	-	-
b Other	1434	395	...	1234	-195	1362	277	...	1259	-174
9 Other receivables	688	154	...	319	215	238	-129	...	393	-26
10 Other assets	1391	831	...	560	1	1543	764	...	779	-
Total Acquisition of Financial Assets	9103	6188	...	3042	-127	7381	2652	...	4434	295
Incurrence of Liabilities										
1 Currency and transferable deposits	...	...	...	...	...	...	...	...	...	...
2 Other deposits	...	...	...	...	...	...	...	...	...	...
3 Bills and bonds, short term	18	-	...	18	-	4	-	...	4	-
4 Bonds, long term	3718	3765	...	-47	-	2769	2738	...	31	-
5 Short-term loans, n.e.c.	47	122	...	46	-	359	220	...	143	-4
6 Long-term loans, n.e.c.	2222	835	...	1357	30	2361	700	...	1700	-39
7 Other payables	341	173	...	80	88	528	-404	...	902	30
8 Other liabilities	631	-	...	509	-	467	-	...	467	-
Total Incurrence of Liabilities	6976	4895	...	1964	118	6488	3254	...	3247	-13
Statistical discrepancy	133	-118	...	243	8	105	-132	...	220	17
Net Lending	1994	1411	...	836	-253	787	-470	...	967	291
Incurrence of Liabilities and Net Worth	9103	6188	...	3042	-127	7381	2652	...	4434	295

3.22 Corporate and Quasi-Corporate Enterprise Income and Outlay Account: Total and Sectors

Million Finnish markkaa

	1970 TOTAL	Non-Financial	Financial	1971 TOTAL	Non-Financial	Financial	1972 TOTAL	Non-Financial	Financial	1973 TOTAL	Non-Financial	Financial
Receipts												
1 Property and entrepreneurial income received	6080	4132	1948	6606	4125	2481	7545	4669	2876	9630	5675	3955
a Net operating surplus	2999	3357	-358	2849	3247	-398	3286	3667	-381	4104	4470	-365
b Withdrawals from quasi-corporate enterprises	-	-	-	-	-	-	-	-	-	-	-	-
c Interest	2901	623	2278	3574	731	2844	4080	866	3213	5309	1051	4259
d Dividends	163	135	28	162	126	36	158	114	43	191	130	61
e Net land rent and royalties	18	18	-	21	21	-	22	22	-	25	25	-
2 Other current transfers received	2282	354	1928	2724	416	2308	3337	467	2871	4153	541	3612
a Casualty insurance transactions	1014	179	836	1205	219	986	1293	241	1052	1400	276	1124

Finland

3.22 Corporate and Quasi-Corporate Enterprise Income and Outlay Account: Total and Sectors
(Continued)

Million Finnish markkaa

	1970 TOTAL	1970 Non-Financial	1970 Financial	1971 TOTAL	1971 Non-Financial	1971 Financial	1972 TOTAL	1972 Non-Financial	1972 Financial	1973 TOTAL	1973 Non-Financial	1973 Financial
Claims received	357	179	179	422	219	203	421	241	180	482	276	206
Net premiums received by insurance companies	657	-	657	783	-	783	872	-	872	918	-	918
b Current transfers received from the rest of the world	-	-	-	-	-	-	-	-	-	-	-	-
c Other transfers received, except imputed	1094	10	1083	1324	12	1312	1822	16	1806	2494	21	2473
d Imputed unfunded employee welfare contributions	174	165	9	196	186	10	221	209	12	260	244	15
Total Current Receipts a	8362	4486	3876	9330	4540	4789	10882	5136	5747	13783	6217	7567

Disbursements

	1970 TOTAL	1970 Non-Financial	1970 Financial	1971 TOTAL	1971 Non-Financial	1971 Financial	1972 TOTAL	1972 Non-Financial	1972 Financial	1973 TOTAL	1973 Non-Financial	1973 Financial
1 Property and entrepreneurial income paid out	3867	2402	1464	4511	2753	1758	5152	3117	2035	6667	3831	2837
a Withdrawals from quasi-corporations	241	241	-	147	147	-	122	122	-	49	49	-
Public	241	241	-	147	147	-	122	122	-	49	49	-
Private	-	-	-	-	-	-	-	-	-	-	-	-
b Interest	3144	1755	1389	3829	2153	1676	4437	2506	1931	5934	3215	2719
c Dividends	374	299	76	414	332	82	444	339	104	503	386	118
d Net land rent and royalties	108	108	-	121	121	-	150	150	-	181	181	-
2 Direct taxes and other current payments n.e.c. to general government	864	693	171	928	738	190	967	742	226	1192	924	269
a Direct taxes	777	693	84	818	738	81	843	742	101	1047	924	123
b Fines, fees, penalties and other payments n.e.c.	87	-	87	110	-	110	124	-	124	146	-	146
3 Other current transfers paid	1908	431	1478	2325	512	1814	2759	594	2166	3145	693	2452
a Casualty insurance transactions	1010	173	837	1200	212	988	1289	235	1054	1390	264	1126
Casualty insurance premiums paid, net	353	173	180	417	212	205	417	235	182	472	264	208
Claims paid by insurance companies	657	-	657	783	-	783	872	-	872	918	-	918
b Transfers to private non-profit institutions	37	23	14	40	25	15	41	24	18	52	31	21
c Transfers to households	862	235	626	1085	275	810	1429	335	1094	1703	398	1305
Unfunded employee welfare benefits	238	235	3	279	275	4	339	335	4	403	398	6
Social assistance grants and other transfers n.e.c.	623	-	623	806	-	807	1089	-	1089	1300	-	1300
d Transfers to the rest of the world	-	-	-	-	-	-	-	-	-	-	-	-
Net saving	1723	960	763	1565	538	1027	2003	683	1321	2779	769	2010
Total Current Disbursements and Net Saving a	8362	4486	3876	9330	4540	4789	10882	5136	5747	13783	6217	7567

	1974 TOTAL	1974 Non-Financial	1974 Financial	1975 TOTAL	1975 Non-Financial	1975 Financial	1976 TOTAL	1976 Non-Financial	1976 Financial	1977 TOTAL	1977 Non-Financial	1977 Financial

Receipts

	1974 TOTAL	1974 Non-Financial	1974 Financial	1975 TOTAL	1975 Non-Financial	1975 Financial	1976 TOTAL	1976 Non-Financial	1976 Financial	1977 TOTAL	1977 Non-Financial	1977 Financial
1 Property and entrepreneurial income received	14203	8652	5551	14624	8179	6446	14749	7444	7305	17310	8596	8714
a Net operating surplus	6542	7263	-722	5466	6628	-1162	4283	5673	-1391	5202	6500	-1298
b Withdrawals from quasi-corporate enterprises	-	-	-	-	-	-	-	-	-	-	-	-
c Interest	7383	1183	6200	8747	1242	7505	10165	1580	8585	11790	1892	9898
d Dividends	248	175	73	344	243	101	234	127	107	247	134	113
e Net land rent and royalties	30	31	-	67	66	1	67	64	3	72	70	1
2 Other current transfers received	5135	663	4472	6474	814	5660	8180	950	7231	9772	1051	8721
a Casualty insurance transactions	1632	330	1302	2012	406	1607	2487	479	2008	2634	526	2107

Finland

3.22 Corporate and Quasi-Corporate Enterprise Income and Outlay Account: Total and Sectors
(Continued)

Million Finnish markkaa

	1974 TOTAL	1974 Non-Financial	1974 Financial	1975 TOTAL	1975 Non-Financial	1975 Financial	1976 TOTAL	1976 Non-Financial	1976 Financial	1977 TOTAL	1977 Non-Financial	1977 Financial
Claims received	573	330	243	701	406	296	889	479	411	917	526	390
Net premiums received by insurance companies	1059	-	1059	1311	-	1311	1598	-	1598	1717	-	1717
b Current transfers received from the rest of the world	-	-	-	-	-	-	-	-	-	-	-	-
c Other transfers received, except imputed	3184	34	3150	4080	55	4025	5261	71	5190	6645	67	6578
d Imputed unfunded employee welfare contributions	319	299	20	381	354	27	432	400	32	494	458	36
Total Current Receipts [a]	19338	9315	10024	21098	8993	12105	22929	8394	14535	27082	9648	17435

Disbursements

	1974 TOTAL	1974 Non-Financial	1974 Financial	1975 TOTAL	1975 Non-Financial	1975 Financial	1976 TOTAL	1976 Non-Financial	1976 Financial	1977 TOTAL	1977 Non-Financial	1977 Financial
1 Property and entrepreneurial income paid out	9194	5199	3996	11413	7072	4341	13306	8282	5024	15184	9382	5802
a Withdrawals from quasi-corporations	88	88	-	752	752	-	807	807	-	566	566	-
Public	88	88	-	135	135	-	234	234	-	233	233	-
Private	-	-	-	617	617	-	573	573	-	332	332	-
b Interest	8272	4414	3858	9552	5407	4145	11329	6537	4793	13421	7867	5554
c Dividends	618	481	137	824	629	196	822	590	232	811	564	247
d Net land rent and royalties	216	216	-	285	285	-	348	348	-	387	386	-
2 Direct taxes and other current payments n.e.c. to general government	1500	1175	325	2004	1563	440	2574	2026	549	2351	1813	538
a Direct taxes	1324	1175	149	1780	1563	216	2283	2026	257	2026	1813	213
b Fines, fees, penalties and other payments n.e.c.	176	-	176	224	-	224	291	-	291	325	-	325
3 Other current transfers paid	3885	873	3012	4978	1067	3912	6511	1384	5127	7615	1494	6122
a Casualty insurance transactions	1627	325	1302	1994	386	1609	2512	502	2010	2623	515	2108
Casualty insurance premiums paid, net	568	325	243	683	386	297	914	502	412	906	515	391
Claims paid by insurance companies	1059	-	1059	1311	-	1311	1598	-	1598	1717	-	1717
b Transfers to private non-profit institutions	62	38	23	88	49	39	96	57	39	114	71	43
c Transfers to households	2196	510	1686	2896	632	2264	3904	825	3079	4878	907	3971
Unfunded employee welfare benefits	518	510	8	645	632	13	840	825	15	927	907	20
Social assistance grants and other transfers n.e.c.	1678	-	1678	2251	-	2252	3064	-	3064	3951	-	3952
d Transfers to the rest of the world	-	-	-	-	-	-	-	-	-	-	-	-
Net saving	4759	2068	2691	2703	-709	3412	538	-3298	3835	1932	-3042	4974
Total Current Disbursements and Net Saving [a]	19338	9315	10024	21098	8993	12105	22929	8394	14535	27082	9648	17435

	1978 TOTAL	1978 Non-Financial	1978 Financial	1979 TOTAL	1979 Non-Financial	1979 Financial	1980 TOTAL	1980 Non-Financial	1980 Financial

Receipts

	1978 TOTAL	1978 Non-Financial	1978 Financial	1979 TOTAL	1979 Non-Financial	1979 Financial	1980 TOTAL	1980 Non-Financial	1980 Financial
1 Property and entrepreneurial income received	20689	11870	8819	26247	16205	10042	33189	18557	14632
a Net operating surplus	8018	9544	-1526	11874	13616	-1742	13382	15464	-2082
b Withdrawals from quasi-corporate enterprises	-	-	-	-	-	-	-	-	-
c Interest	12419	2179	10239	14064	2424	11640	19434	2899	16535
d Dividends	196	92	104	250	108	142	308	131	177
e Net land rent and royalties	57	55	1	59	57	2	65	63	2
2 Other current transfers received	10078	1166	8912	12664	1355	11309	15731	1550	14181
a Casualty insurance transactions	2772	563	2210	3395	679	2716	4075	849	3226

Finland

3.22 Corporate and Quasi-Corporate Enterprise Income and Outlay Account: Total and Sectors
(Continued)

Million Finnish markkaa

	1978 TOTAL	1978 Non-Financial	1978 Financial	1979 TOTAL	1979 Non-Financial	1979 Financial	1980 TOTAL	1980 Non-Financial	1980 Financial
Claims received	914	563	352	1122	679	443	1324	849	475
Net premiums received by insurance companies	1858	-	1858	2273	-	2273	2751	-	2751
b Current transfers received from the rest of the world	-	-	-	-	-	-	-	-	-
c Other transfers received, except imputed	6781	120	6662	8651	105	8546	10961	60	10901
d Imputed unfunded employee welfare contributions	524	484	41	618	571	47	695	641	54
Total Current Receipts [a]	30766	13036	17731	38911	17561	21350	48917	20106	28811

Disbursements

	1978 TOTAL	1978 Non-Financial	1978 Financial	1979 TOTAL	1979 Non-Financial	1979 Financial	1980 TOTAL	1980 Non-Financial	1980 Financial
1 Property and entrepreneurial income paid out	16402	10436	5966	18231	11518	6713	24413	14177	10236
a Withdrawals from quasi-corporations	871	871	-	1068	1068	-	1131	1131	-
Public	329	329	-	385	385	-	357	357	-
Private	542	542	-	683	683	-	774	774	-
b Interest	14334	8616	5719	15716	9253	6463	21683	11663	10020
c Dividends	802	555	247	1007	757	250	1082	866	216
d Net land rent and royalties	395	395	-	440	440	-	517	517	-
2 Direct taxes and other current payments n.e.c. to general government	2580	1933	647	2936	2184	752	3466	2614	852
a Direct taxes	2183	1933	250	2449	2184	265	2877	2614	263
b Fines, fees, penalties and other payments n.e.c.	397	-	397	487	-	487	589	-	589
3 Other current transfers paid	8477	1534	6943	10046	1833	8213	11833	2151	9682
a Casualty insurance transactions	2701	488	2213	3395	679	2716	4070	844	3226
Casualty insurance premiums paid, net	843	488	355	1122	679	443	1319	844	475
Claims paid by insurance companies	1858	-	1858	2273	-	2273	2751	-	2751
b Transfers to private non-profit institutions	104	61	44	124	75	49	169	108	61
c Transfers to households	5672	986	4686	6527	1079	5448	7594	1199	6395
Unfunded employee welfare benefits	1009	986	24	1107	1079	28	1232	1199	33
Social assistance grants and other transfers n.e.c.	4662	-	4662	5420	-	5420	6362	-	6362
d Transfers to the rest of the world	-	-	-	-	-	-	-	-	-
Net saving	3308	-868	4175	7698	2025	5673	9207	1165	8042
Total Current Disbursements and Net Saving [a]	30766	13036	17731	38911	17561	21350	48917	20106	28811

a) Column 'Total' is shown non-consolidated.

3.23 Corporate and Quasi-Corporate Enterprise Capital Accumulation Account: Total and Sectors

Million Finnish markkaa

	1970 TOTAL	1970 Non-Financial	1970 Financial	1971 TOTAL	1971 Non-Financial	1971 Financial	1972 TOTAL	1972 Non-Financial	1972 Financial	1973 TOTAL	1973 Non-Financial	1973 Financial

Finance of Gross Accumulation

	1970 TOTAL	1970 Non-Financial	1970 Financial	1971 TOTAL	1971 Non-Financial	1971 Financial	1972 TOTAL	1972 Non-Financial	1972 Financial	1973 TOTAL	1973 Non-Financial	1973 Financial
1 Gross saving	5205	4366	838	5013	3885	1129	5832	4397	1435	7666	5503	2163
a Consumption of fixed capital	3482	3407	75	3448	3347	101	3829	3714	115	4887	4734	154
b Net saving	1723	960	763	1565	538	1027	2003	683	1321	2779	769	2010
2 Capital transfers received [a]	-2	-2	-	-5	-5	-	-9	-9	-	-1	-1	-
Finance of Gross Accumulation [b]	5202	4364	838	5008	3879	1129	5824	4389	1435	7665	5502	2163

Gross Accumulation

	1970 TOTAL	1970 Non-Financial	1970 Financial	1971 TOTAL	1971 Non-Financial	1971 Financial	1972 TOTAL	1972 Non-Financial	1972 Financial	1973 TOTAL	1973 Non-Financial	1973 Financial
1 Gross capital formation	7491	7277	214	8187	7883	304	7718	7445	272	10019	9601	418

Finland

3.23 Corporate and Quasi-Corporate Enterprise Capital Accumulation Account: Total and Sectors
(Continued)

Million Finnish markkaa

	1970 TOTAL	1970 Non-Financial	1970 Financial	1971 TOTAL	1971 Non-Financial	1971 Financial	1972 TOTAL	1972 Non-Financial	1972 Financial	1973 TOTAL	1973 Non-Financial	1973 Financial
a Increase in stocks	1637	1637	-	1047	1047	-	-363	-363	-	-122	-122	-
b Gross fixed capital formation	5854	5641	214	7140	6836	304	8081	7808	272	10141	9723	418
2 Purchases of land, net	230	230	-	391	391	-	315	315	-	487	487	-
3 Purchases of intangible assets, net	...	...	...	...	...	...	...	...	...	...	...	...
4 Capital transfers paid	...	...	...	...	...	...	...	...	...	...	...	...
5 Net lending	-2518	-3143	625	-3569	-4394	825	-2209	-3372	1163	-2840	-4586	1745
Gross Accumulation b	5202	4364	838	5008	3879	1129	5824	4389	1435	7665	5502	2163

	1974 TOTAL	1974 Non-Financial	1974 Financial	1975 TOTAL	1975 Non-Financial	1975 Financial	1976 TOTAL	1976 Non-Financial	1976 Financial	1977 TOTAL	1977 Non-Financial	1977 Financial
Finance of Gross Accumulation												
1 Gross saving	11305	8468	2836	9322	5697	3624	7701	3594	4107	10040	4647	5394
a Consumption of fixed capital	6546	6401	145	6618	6406	213	7164	6892	272	8108	7689	420
b Net saving	4759	2068	2691	2703	-709	3412	538	-3298	3835	1932	-3042	4974
2 Capital transfers received a	-1	-1	-	64	64	-	12	12	-	28	28	-
Finance of Gross Accumulation b	11304	8468	2836	9385	5761	3624	7713	3606	4107	10068	4675	5394
Gross Accumulation												
1 Gross capital formation	17464	17021	443	17873	17053	821	15556	14786	770	14154	13063	1091
a Increase in stocks	4205	4205	-	1302	1302	-	-895	-875	-20	-2274	-2278	3
b Gross fixed capital formation	13259	12816	443	16572	15751	821	16451	15661	790	16428	15340	1088
2 Purchases of land, net	360	360	-	456	436	20	600	576	24	277	75	202
3 Purchases of intangible assets, net	...	...	...	...	...	...	...	...	...	...	...	...
4 Capital transfers paid	...	...	...	...	...	...	...	...	...	...	...	...
5 Net lending	-6519	-8913	2394	-8944	-11728	2784	-8443	-11757	3313	-4362	-8463	4101
Gross Accumulation b	11304	8468	2836	9385	5761	3624	7713	3606	4107	10068	4675	5394

	1978 TOTAL	1978 Non-Financial	1978 Financial	1979 TOTAL	1979 Non-Financial	1979 Financial	1980 TOTAL	1980 Non-Financial	1980 Financial
Finance of Gross Accumulation									
1 Gross saving	13090	8431	4659	19931	13704	6227	23060	14420	8640
a Consumption of fixed capital	9783	9299	484	12233	11679	554	13853	13255	598
b Net saving	3308	-868	4175	7698	2025	5673	9207	1165	8042
2 Capital transfers received a	17	17	-	73	73	-	80	80	-
Finance of Gross Accumulation b	13107	8448	4659	20004	13777	6227	23140	14500	8640
Gross Accumulation									
1 Gross capital formation	11184	10162	1022	20669	19340	1329	27203	25623	1580
a Increase in stocks	-3333	-3332	-1	3747	3748	-1	5534	5534	-
b Gross fixed capital formation	14517	13494	1023	16923	15592	1330	21669	20089	1580
2 Purchases of land, net	233	205	28	282	146	136	255	170	85
3 Purchases of intangible assets, net	...	...	...	...	...	...	...	...	...
4 Capital transfers paid	...	...	...	...	...	...	...	...	...
5 Net lending	1690	-1919	3609	-947	-5709	4762	-4318	-11293	6975
Gross Accumulation b	13107	8448	4659	20004	13777	6227	23140	14500	8640

a) Net.
b) Column 'Total' is shown non-consolidated.

3.24 Corporate and Quasi-Corporate Enterprise Capital Finance Account: Total and Sectors

Million Finnish markkaa

	1970 TOTAL	1970 Non-Financial	1970 Financial	1971 TOTAL	1971 Non-Financial	1971 Financial	1972 TOTAL	1972 Non-Financial	1972 Financial	1973 TOTAL	1973 Non-Financial	1973 Financial
Acquisition of Financial Assets												
1 Gold and SDRs	49	-	49	85	-	85	1	-	1	-83	-	-83
2 Currency and transferable deposits	822	130	692	1213	234	979	1349	668	681	540	508	33
3 Other deposits	227	232	-5	716	79	637	472	-133	605	551	-15	566
4 Bills and bonds, short term	524	-	524	549	-	549	-141	-	-141	2885	-	2885

Finland

3.24 Corporate and Quasi-Corporate Enterprise Capital Finance Account: Total and Sectors
(Continued)

Million Finnish markkaa

	1970 TOTAL	1970 Non-Financial	1970 Financial	1971 TOTAL	1971 Non-Financial	1971 Financial	1972 TOTAL	1972 Non-Financial	1972 Financial	1973 TOTAL	1973 Non-Financial	1973 Financial
a Corporate and quasi-corporate, resident	672	-	672	683	-	683	-144	-	-144	2898	-	2898
b Government	-139	-	-139	-209	-	-209	19	-	19	5	-	5
c Rest of the world	-9	-	-9	75	-	75	-17	-	-17	-18	-	-18
5 Bonds, long term	304	-	304	350	-	350	568	-	568	550	-	550
a Corporate, resident	282	-	282	364	-	364	411	-	411	482	-	482
b Government	41	-	41	10	-	10	-27	-	-27	-108	-	-108
c Rest of the world	-19	-	-19	-24	-	-24	184	-	184	176	-	176
6 Corporate equity securities	655	474	180	882	754	128	1019	858	161	1364	1130	235
7 Short term loans, n.e.c.	70	-	70	16	-	16	99	-	99	193	-	193
8 Long term loans, n.e.c.	3808	181	3627	3706	185	3522	5184	59	5125	7112	14	7099
a Mortgages	902	-	902	873	-	873	1465	-	1465	1812	-	1812
b Other	2906	181	2725	2833	185	2649	3719	59	3660	5300	14	5287
9 Trade credits and advances	1479	1463	16	529	508	22	1585	1577	8	4083	4109	-26
10 Other receivables	-50	-	-50	895	303	592	401	-	401	996	-	996
11 Other assets	...	...	...	...	...	...	...	...	...	...	...	...
Total Acquisition of Financial Assets	7885	2480	5405	8942	2062	6880	10537	3029	7508	18192	5745	12447

Incurrence of Liabilities

	1970 TOTAL	1970 Non-Financial	1970 Financial	1971 TOTAL	1971 Non-Financial	1971 Financial	1972 TOTAL	1972 Non-Financial	1972 Financial	1973 TOTAL	1973 Non-Financial	1973 Financial
1 Currency and transferable deposits	769	-	769	1153	-	1153	1394	-	1394	2317	-	2317
2 Other deposits	2546	53	2493	2718	68	2650	3589	78	3511	4139	85	4054
3 Bills and bonds, short term	536	157	379	619	558	61	-337	-238	-99	2685	780	1905
4 Bonds, long term	453	163	291	795	195	600	1095	425	670	695	279	417
5 Corporate equity securities	505	444	62	1022	868	154	1014	833	181	1364	1138	225
6 Short-term loans, n.e.c.	76	81	-6	-61	-47	-15	8	-9	17	227	108	120
7 Long-term loans, n.e.c.	2712	2560	152	3480	3314	166	3734	3077	657	4515	4210	305
8 Net equity of households in life insurance and pension fund reserves	223	-	223	195	-	195	293	-	293	432	-	432
9 Proprietors' net additions to the accumulation of quasi-corporations	389	389	-	499	499	-	745	745	-	816	816	-
10 Trade credit and advances	2341	2302	39	1212	1154	58	1203	1173	30	3644	3618	26
11 Other accounts payable	-57	-156	99	910	-	910	207	548	-341	895	74	821
12 Other liabilities	-	-	-	-	-	-	-	-	-	-	-	-
Total Incurrence of Liabilities	10492	5992	4499	12541	6610	5932	12945	6631	6314	21728	11108	10620
Statistical discrepancy	-88	-369	281	-30	-153	123	-199	-231	31	-696	-777	82
Net Lending	-2518	-3143	625	-3569	-4394	825	-2209	-3372	1163	-2840	-4586	1745
Incurrence of Liabilities and Net Lending	7885	2480	5405	8942	2062	6880	10537	3029	7508	18192	5745	12447

	1974 TOTAL	1974 Non-Financial	1974 Financial	1975 TOTAL	1975 Non-Financial	1975 Financial	1976 TOTAL	1976 Non-Financial	1976 Financial	1977 TOTAL	1977 Non-Financial	1977 Financial

Acquisition of Financial Assets

	1974 TOTAL	1974 Non-Financial	1974 Financial	1975 TOTAL	1975 Non-Financial	1975 Financial	1976 TOTAL	1976 Non-Financial	1976 Financial	1977 TOTAL	1977 Non-Financial	1977 Financial
1 Gold and SDRs	1	-	1	-276	-	-276	-42	-	-42	-62	-	-62
2 Currency and transferable deposits	1265	742	524	1051	1100	-49	919	-202	1121	1208	43	1165
3 Other deposits	-125	195	-320	1938	1496	442	199	-109	308	-79	-547	469
4 Bills and bonds, short term	1886	-	1886	3043	-	3043	1379	-	1379	1994	-	1994
a Corporate and quasi-corporate, resident	1693	-	1693	2912	-	2912	1273	-	1273	1824	-	1824
b Government	34	-	34	10	-	10	-24	-	-24	-18	-	-18
c Rest of the world	159	-	159	121	-	121	130	-	130	188	-	188
5 Bonds, long term	720	-	720	560	-33	593	510	3	506	645	-2	647
a Corporate, resident	791	-	791	708	-33	741	287	3	283	231	-2	233
b Government	-69	-	-69	4	-	4	-29	-	-29	131	-	131
c Rest of the world	-2	-	-2	-152	-	-152	252	-	252	283	-	283
6 Corporate equity securities	1637	1286	350	1733	1094	640	1746	1126	620	1215	962	253
7 Short term loans, n.e.c.	176	-	176	1570	1191	379	1663	778	886	2373	1112	1261
8 Long term loans, n.e.c.	8898	49	8849	9670	465	9206	8236	113	8122	9663	137	9526
a Mortgages	2032	-	2032	2068	-	2068	1938	-	1938	2051	-	2051
b Other	6866	49	6817	7602	465	7138	6298	113	6184	7612	137	7475
9 Trade credits and advances	3211	3155	56	3258	3196	62	5604	5399	205	2964	3085	-122
10 Other receivables	1978	-	1978	1704	678	1026	944	553	392	1218	512	706

Finland

3.24 Corporate and Quasi-Corporate Enterprise Capital Finance Account: Total and Sectors
(Continued)

Million Finnish markkaa

	1974 TOTAL	1974 Non-Financial	1974 Financial	1975 TOTAL	1975 Non-Financial	1975 Financial	1976 TOTAL	1976 Non-Financial	1976 Financial	1977 TOTAL	1977 Non-Financial	1977 Financial
11 Other assets	...	...	...	...	...	...	...	...	...	...	...	...
Total Acquisition of Financial Assets	19647	5427	14220	24251	9185	15066	21158	7661	13497	21139	5301	15838

Incurrence of Liabilities

	1974 TOTAL	1974 Non-Financial	1974 Financial	1975 TOTAL	1975 Non-Financial	1975 Financial	1976 TOTAL	1976 Non-Financial	1976 Financial	1977 TOTAL	1977 Non-Financial	1977 Financial
1 Currency and transferable deposits	3271	-	3271	1956	-	1956	1927	-	1927	1474	-	1474
2 Other deposits	4194	116	4078	5911	146	5765	3844	162	3682	5035	96	4939
3 Bills and bonds, short term	1363	721	643	2679	2258	421	918	1061	-143	1425	1334	90
4 Bonds, long term	1362	34	1328	2217	716	1501	965	282	683	1307	501	806
5 Corporate equity securities	1435	1225	211	1952	1722	230	1535	1409	126	1310	1146	164
6 Short-term loans, n.e.c.	209	208	1	1600	1007	594	2369	1661	709	2387	1544	843
7 Long-term loans, n.e.c.	6277	5454	823	8206	7239	967	7887	5641	2246	8944	6251	2693
8 Net equity of households in life insurance and pension fund reserves	573	-	573	194	-	194	399	-	399	462	-	462
9 Proprietors' net additions to the accumulation of quasi-corporations	1735	1735	-	2487	2487	-	2431	2431	-	2344	2344	-
10 Trade credit and advances	4244	4203	41	5821	5878	-57	5838	5721	117	1349	1338	11
11 Other accounts payable	1575	598	977	865	183	682	1357	1048	309	154	-274	429
12 Other liabilities	-	-	-	-	-	-	-	-	-	-	-	-
Total Incurrence of Liabilities	26238	14293	11945	33889	21635	12253	29471	19416	10054	26191	14280	11911
Statistical discrepancy	-72	47	-119	-693	-722	29	130	1	129	-690	-516	-175
Net Lending	-6519	-8913	2394	-8944	-11728	2784	-8443	-11757	3313	-4362	-8463	4101
Incurrence of Liabilities and Net Lending	19647	5427	14220	24251	9185	15066	21158	7661	13497	21139	5301	15838

	1978 TOTAL	1978 Non-Financial	1978 Financial	1979 TOTAL	1979 Non-Financial	1979 Financial

Acquisition of Financial Assets

	1978 TOTAL	1978 Non-Financial	1978 Financial	1979 TOTAL	1979 Non-Financial	1979 Financial
1 Gold and SDRs	350	-	350	-12	-	-12
2 Currency and transferable deposits	4854	953	3901	2435	1361	1074
3 Other deposits	1840	913	927	1938	119	1819
4 Bills and bonds, short term	-2262	-	-2262	1059	-	1059
a Corporate and quasi-corporate, resident	-2247	-	-2247	1041	-	1041
b Government	18	-	18	4	-	4
c Rest of the world	-33	-	-33	14	-	14
5 Bonds, long term	1411	127	1284	2393	-5	2398
a Corporate, resident	667	127	540	1055	-5	1060
b Government	440	-	440	137	-	137
c Rest of the world	304	-	304	1201	-	1201
6 Corporate equity securities	1727	890	837	2125	1404	721
7 Short term loans, n.e.c.	2743	1888	855	3350	1038	2312
8 Long term loans, n.e.c.	10209	124	10085	14757	130	14627
a Mortgages	2492	-	2492	3635	-	3635
b Other	7717	124	7593	11122	130	10992
9 Trade credits and advances	5111	5078	33	8370	8352	18
10 Other receivables	1365	793	572	2949	1032	1917
11 Other assets	...	...	...	-	-	-
Total Acquisition of Financial Assets	27347	10766	16581	39364	13431	25933

Incurrence of Liabilities

	1978 TOTAL	1978 Non-Financial	1978 Financial	1979 TOTAL	1979 Non-Financial	1979 Financial
1 Currency and transferable deposits	3414	-	3414	4574	-	4574
2 Other deposits	8536	-6	8542	10022	-244	10266
3 Bills and bonds, short term	-2553	-454	-2099	849	1131	-282
4 Bonds, long term	1576	824	752	632	-11	643
5 Corporate equity securities	1576	1316	260	1622	1215	407
6 Short-term loans, n.e.c.	2523	1354	1169	3585	1007	2578

Finland

3.24 Corporate and Quasi-Corporate Enterprise Capital Finance Account: Total and Sectors
(Continued)

Million Finnish markkaa

	1978 TOTAL	1978 Non-Financial	1978 Financial	1979 TOTAL	1979 Non-Financial	1979 Financial
7 Long-term loans, n.e.c.	5375	5961	-586	7405	6465	940
8 Net equity of households in life insurance and pension fund reserves	801	-	801	751	-	751
9 Proprietors' net additions to the accumulation of quasi-corporations	1391	1391	-	1543	1543	-
10 Trade credit and advances	2080	2101	-21	6565	6405	160
11 Other accounts payable	1395	648	747	2547	1231	1316
12 Other liabilities	-	-	-	-	-	-
Total Incurrence of Liabilities	26114	13136	12978	40095	18742	21353
Statistical discrepancy	-457	-451	-6	216	398	-182
Net Lending	1690	-1919	3609	-947	-5709	4762
Incurrence of Liabilities and Net Lending	27347	10766	16581	39364	13431	25933

3.26 Financial Transactions of Financial Institutions: Detail

Million Finnish markkaa

	1970 ALL FINANCIAL INSTITUTIONS	1970 Central Bank	1970 Other Monetary Institutions	1970 Insurance	1970 Other Financial Institutions	1971 ALL FINANCIAL INSTITUTIONS	1971 Central Bank	1971 Other Monetary Institutions	1971 Insurance	1971 Other Financial Institutions
Acquisition of Financial Assets										
1 Gold and SDRs	49	49	-	-	-	85	85	-	-	-
a Gold	39	39	-	-	-	71	71	-	-	-
b Net acquisitions of SDRs	10	10	-	-	-	14	14	-	-	-
2 Currency and transferable deposits	692	441	305	3	-57	979	654	250	27	48
a Liability of resident institutions	-86	-	-39	4	-51	73	-	-11	26	58
b Liability of rest of the world	778	441	344	-1	-6	906	654	261	1	-10
3 Other deposits	-5	-	-31	25	-	637	-	483	51	103
a Liability of resident institutions	-8	-	-31	22	-	633	-	483	46	104
b Liability of rest of the world	3	-	-	3	-	4	-	-	5	-1
4 Bills and bonds, short term	524	63	461	-	-	549	51	498	-	-
a Corporate and quasi-corporate, resident	672	88	583	-	-	683	11	673	-	-
b Government	-139	-	-139	-	-	-209	-	-209	-	-
c Rest of the world	-9	-25	17	-	-	75	41	35	-	-
5 Bonds, long term	304	-27	252	79	1	350	66	224	79	-18
6 Corporate equity securities	180	12	165	12	-9	128	11	85	21	12
7 Short-term loans, n.e.c.	70	-35	-8	91	22	16	-38	-3	56	1
a Liability of: resident sectors	46	-35	-8	67	22	-12	-38	-3	28	1
b Liability of: rest of the world	24	-	-	24	-	28	-	-	28	-
8 Long-term loans, n.e.c.	3627	21	2374	720	512	3522	60	2056	836	570
a Mortgages	902	..	..	..	..	873	..	..	..	..
b Other	2725	..	..	..	..	2649	..	..	..	..
9 Trade credit and advances	16	3	-	13	-	22	-3	-	25	-
a Consumer credit	..	..	.	..	.	..	..	.	..	.
b Other	..	..	.	..	.	..	..	.	..	.
10 Other assets	-50	1	-170	45	74	592	-	381	76	135
Total Acquisition of Financial Assets [a]	5405	528	3347	988	542	6880	885	3973	1170	852
Incurrence of Liabilities										
1 Currency and transferable deposits	769	64	705	-	-1	1153	386	767	-	-
2 Other deposits	2493	312	2181	-	-	2650	291	2359	-	-
3 Bills and bonds, short term	379	-	335	-	44	61	-	54	2	5
4 Bonds, long term	291	-8	-12	-	310	600	-	-10	-	611
5 Corporate equity securities	62	-	57	5	-	154	-	47	3	104
6 Short-term loans, n.e.c.	33	1	-29	54	7	43	5	-67	112	-7

Finland

3.26 Financial Transactions of Financial Institutions: Detail
(Continued)

Million Finnish markkaa

	1970					1971				
	ALL FINANCIAL INSTITUTIONS	Central Bank	Other Monetary Institutions	Insurance	Other Financial Institutions	ALL FINANCIAL INSTITUTIONS	Central Bank	Other Monetary Institutions	Insurance	Other Financial Institutions
7 Long-term loans, n.e.c.	152	-	89	14	48	166	-	70	-4	100
9 Net equity of households in life insurance and pension fund reserves	223	-	-	223	-	195	-	-	195	-
10 Other liabilities	99	-1	-68	30	139	910	-	876	14	21
Total Incurrence of liabilities [a]	4499	368	3258	326	547	5932	682	4096	321	833
Statistical discrepancy	281	124	123	46	-13	124	151	-50	6	16
Net Lending [a]	625	36	-35	615	9	825	52	-73	843	3
Incurrence of Liabilities and Net Lending	5405	528	3347	988	542	6880	885	3973	1170	852

	1972					1973				
	ALL FINANCIAL INSTITUTIONS	Central Bank	Other Monetary Institutions	Insurance	Other Financial Institutions	ALL FINANCIAL INSTITUTIONS	Central Bank	Other Monetary Institutions	Insurance	Other Financial Institutions

Acquisition of Financial Assets

1 Gold and SDRs	1	1	-	-	-	-83	-83	-	-	-
a Gold	-	-	-	-	-	-84	-84	-	-	-
b Net acquisitions of SDRs	1	1	-	-	-	1	1	-	-	-
2 Currency and transferable deposits	681	12	585	32	52	33	-409	470	6	-35
a Liability of resident institutions	189	-	136	31	22	92	-	91	9	-9
b Liability of rest of the world	492	12	449	1	30	-59	-409	379	-2	-27
3 Other deposits	605	-	563	72	-30	566	-	519	90	-43
a Liability of resident institutions	589	-	563	69	-43	552	-	519	81	-48
b Liability of rest of the world	16	-	-	3	13	14	-	-	9	5
4 Bills and bonds, short term	-141	-172	31	-	-	2885	1850	1035	-	-
a Corporate and quasi-corporate, resident	-144	-161	18	-	-	2898	1867	1031	-	-
b Government	19	-	19	-	-	5	-	5	-	-
c Rest of the world	-17	-10	-6	-	-	-18	-17	-1	-	-
5 Bonds, long term	568	110	325	100	33	550	283	199	77	-8
6 Corporate equity securities	161	4	96	58	4	235	19	107	68	41
7 Short-term loans, n.e.c.	99	26	-9	15	66	193	26	-3	99	71
a Liability of: resident sectors	57	26	-9	-27	66	153	26	-3	59	71
b Liability of: rest of the world	42	-	-	42	-	40	-	-	40	-
8 Long-term loans, n.e.c.	5125	53	3038	1085	949	7099	32	4962	1416	689
a Mortgages	1465	..	..	..	..	1812	..	..	..	..
b Other	3660	..	..	..	..	5287	..	..	..	..
9 Trade credit and advances	8	-	-	8	-	-26	1	-	-27	-
a Consumer credit	..	-	-	..	-	..	-	-	..	-
b Other	..	-	-	..	-	..	-	-	..	-
10 Other assets	401	-	157	167	77	996	-	468	509	19
Total Acquisition of Financial Assets [a]	7508	34	4785	1537	1152	12447	1719	7757	2237	734

Incurrence of Liabilities

1 Currency and transferable deposits	1394	48	1346	-	-	2317	236	2080	-	-
2 Other deposits	3511	-6	3517	-	-	4054	1322	2732	-	-
3 Bills and bonds, short term	-99	-	-48	-4	-47	1905	-	1918	-10	-3
4 Bonds, long term	670	-	-8	-	678	417	-	24	-	393
5 Corporate equity securities	181	-	126	9	46	225	-	151	22	53
6 Short-term loans, n.e.c.	48	-4	-	50	2	144	2	-	140	2
7 Long-term loans, n.e.c.	657	-	249	13	395	305	-	230	6	69
9 Net equity of households in life insurance and pension fund reserves	293	-	-	293	-	432	-	-	432	-
10 Other liabilities	-341	-	-402	25	36	821	-	597	62	162
Total Incurrence of liabilities [a]	6314	38	4779	386	1111	10620	1560	7731	652	677
Statistical discrepancy	31	-41	-7	67	12	82	100	9	-16	-12
Net Lending [a]	1163	38	13	1084	29	1745	59	16	1602	70
Incurrence of Liabilities and Net Lending	7508	34	4785	1537	1152	12447	1719	7757	2237	734

Finland

3.26 Financial Transactions of Financial Institutions: Detail

Million Finnish markkaa

	1974					1975				
	ALL FINANCIAL INSTITUTIONS	Central Bank	Other Monetary Institutions	Insurance	Other Financial Institutions	ALL FINANCIAL INSTITUTIONS	Central Bank	Other Monetary Institutions	Insurance	Other Financial Institutions

Acquisition of Financial Assets

1 Gold and SDRs	1	1	-	-	-	-276	-276	-	-	-
a Gold	-	-	-	-	-	-268	-268	-	-	-
b Net acquisitions of SDRs	1	1	-	-	-	-8	-8	-	-	-
2 Currency and transferable deposits	524	-410	884	55	-6	-49	576	-659	19	16
a Liability of resident institutions	757	-	698	51	7	-361	-	-394	19	15
b Liability of rest of the world	-233	-410	186	4	-13	312	576	-265	1	1
3 Other deposits	-320	-	-480	86	74	442	-	90	52	301
a Liability of resident institutions	-304	-	-480	86	90	419	-	90	50	280
b Liability of rest of the world	-16	-	-	..	-16	23	-	-	2	21
4 Bills and bonds, short term	1886	772	1114	-	-	3043	584	2360	100	-
a Corporate and quasi-corporate, resident	1688	610	1077	-	-	2912	562	2250	100	-
b Government	34	-	34	-	-	10	-	10	-	-
c Rest of the world	164	162	3	-	-	121	22	100	-	-
5 Bonds, long term	720	108	529	84	-1	593	-42	557	60	18
6 Corporate equity securities	350	16	203	101	30	640	30	261	298	51
7 Short-term loans, n.e.c.	176	55	20	-11	113	379	404	-51	-19	45
a Liability of: resident sectors	188	55	20	1	113	349	404	-51	-49	45
b Liability of: rest of the world	-12	-	-	-12	-	30	-	-	30	-
8 Long-term loans, n.e.c.	8849	-	5929	1862	1057	9206	125	5663	2172	1245
a Mortgages	2032	..	..	..	..	2068	..	..	..	..
b Other	6817	..	..	..	..	7138	..	..	..	..
9 Trade credit and advances	56	-1	-	56	-	62	2	15	32	13
a Consumer credit	..	..	-	..	-	..	..	..	..	..
b Other	..	..	-	..	-	..	..	..	..	..
10 Other assets	1978	-	1290	508	180	1026	-1	816	183	28
Total Acquisition of Financial Assets a	14220	542	9488	2741	1449	15066	1402	9052	2896	1717

Incurrence of Liabilities

1 Currency and transferable deposits	3271	685	2587	-	-	1956	195	1761	-	-
2 Other deposits	4078	-408	4486	-	-	5765	482	5283	-	-
3 Bills and bonds, short term	643	-	629	14	-	421	-	440	-15	-4
4 Bonds, long term	1328	-	32	-	1296	1501	-	-4	-	1505
5 Corporate equity securities	211	-	140	31	40	230	-	157	-3	76
6 Short-term loans, n.e.c.	42	4	-	57	-19	538	-4	491	-34	85
7 Long-term loans, n.e.c.	823	-	713	36	74	967	329	610	48	-20
9 Net equity of households in life insurance and pension fund reserves	573	-	-	573	-	194	-	-	194	-
10 Other liabilities	977	-	827	95	55	682	-	423	243	16
Total Incurrence of liabilities a	11945	281	9413	806	1445	12253	1001	9162	433	1658
Statistical discrepancy	-119	-34	1	-38	-47	29	51	26	-38	-11
Net Lending a	2394	296	74	1974	50	2784	349	-136	2501	70
Incurrence of Liabilities and Net Lending	14220	542	9488	2741	1449	15066	1402	9052	2896	1717

	1976					1977				
	ALL FINANCIAL INSTITUTIONS	Central Bank	Other Monetary Institutions	Insurance	Other Financial Institutions	ALL FINANCIAL INSTITUTIONS	Central Bank	Other Monetary Institutions	Insurance	Other Financial Institutions

Acquisition of Financial Assets

1 Gold and SDRs	-42	-42	-	-	-	-62	-62	-	-	-
a Gold	-	-	-	-	-	12	12	-	-	-
b Net acquisitions of SDRs	-42	-42	-	-	-	-74	-74	-	-	-
2 Currency and transferable deposits	1121	16	1041	-40	104	1165	30	1221	-11	-76
a Liability of resident institutions	813	-	750	-41	103	-170	-	-70	-24	-76
b Liability of rest of the world	308	16	291	1	1	1335	30	1292	13	-

Finland

3.26 Financial Transactions of Financial Institutions: Detail
(Continued)

Million Finnish markkaa

	1976 ALL FINANCIAL INSTITUTIONS	Central Bank	Other Monetary Institutions	Insurance	Other Financial Institutions	1977 ALL FINANCIAL INSTITUTIONS	Central Bank	Other Monetary Institutions	Insurance	Other Financial Institutions
3 Other deposits	308	-	87	117	103	469	-	357	69	43
a Liability of resident institutions	294	-	87	117	90	475	-	357	79	39
b Liability of rest of the world	14	-	-	-	14	-6	-	-	-10	4
4 Bills and bonds, short term	1379	89	1253	37	-	1994	21	1970	2	-
a Corporate and quasi-corporate, resident	1273	-89	1326	37	-	1824	-36	1857	2	-
b Government	-24	-	-25	1	-	-18	-	-18	-	-
c Rest of the world	130	178	-48	-	-	188	57	131	-	-
5 Bonds, long term	506	187	231	68	21	647	158	319	167	3
6 Corporate equity securities	620	14	238	314	53	253	12	193	249	-201
7 Short-term loans, n.e.c.	886	855	-19	-83	133	1261	664	223	128	246
a Liability of: resident sectors	842	855	-19	-127	133	954	664	11	34	246
b Liability of: rest of the world	44	-	-	44	-	307	-	212	94	-
8 Long-term loans, n.e.c.	8122	162	4484	2522	955	9526	164	5035	3415	912
a Mortgages	1938	..	..	..	..	2051	..	..	..	..
b Other	6184	..	..	..	..	7475	..	..	..	..
9 Trade credit and advances	205	76	69	60	-	-122	-43	-101	156	-134
a Consumer credit	..	..	..	..	..	..	..	..	..	..
b Other	..	..	..	..	..	..	..	..	..	..
10 Other assets	392	1	-151	470	72	706	-1	17	598	92
Total Acquisition of Financial Assets a	13497	1357	7233	3465	1442	15838	944	9234	4773	886

Incurrence of Liabilities

1 Currency and transferable deposits	1927	985	942	-	-	1474	75	1399	-	-
2 Other deposits	3682	-490	4172	-	-	4939	-655	5594	-	-
3 Bills and bonds, short term	-143	-	-166	13	10	90	-	99	-7	-2
4 Bonds, long term	683	-	54	-	630	806	-	272	-	534
5 Corporate equity securities	126	-	52	14	60	164	-	32	62	70
6 Short-term loans, n.e.c.	826	-2	748	47	32	855	-	955	158	-257
7 Long-term loans, n.e.c.	2246	509	1137	33	567	2693	1262	962	43	426
9 Net equity of households in life insurance and pension fund reserves	399	-	-	399	-	462	-	-	462	-
10 Other liabilities	309	1	230	20	59	429	1	224	145	58
Total Incurrence of liabilities a	10054	1003	7168	526	1358	11911	683	9535	864	830
Statistical discrepancy	129	16	21	70	22	-175	13	-60	-108	-20
Net Lending a	3313	339	43	2870	62	4101	249	-242	4018	76
Incurrence of Liabilities and Net Lending	13497	1357	7233	3465	1442	15838	944	9234	4773	886

	1978 ALL FINANCIAL INSTITUTIONS	Central Bank	Other Monetary Institutions	Insurance	Other Financial Institutions	1979 ALL FINANCIAL INSTITUTIONS	Central Bank	Other Monetary Institutions	Insurance	Other Financial Institutions

Acquisition of Financial Assets

1 Gold and SDRs	350	350	-	-	-	-12	-12	-	-	-
a Gold	253	253	-	-	-	-8	-8	-	-	-
b Net acquisitions of SDRs	97	97	-	-	-	-4	-4	-	-	-
2 Currency and transferable deposits	3901	2050	1927	2	-78	1074	-224	917	153	228
a Liability of resident institutions	1090	-	1174	-6	-78	-425	-	-755	103	227
b Liability of rest of the world	2811	2050	753	8	-	1499	-224	1672	50	1
3 Other deposits	927	-	611	113	202	1819	-	2221	-3	-399
a Liability of resident institutions	930	-	611	102	216	1820	-	2221	-2	-399
b Liability of rest of the world	-3	-	-	11	-14	-1	-	-	-1	-
4 Bills and bonds, short term	-2262	-2146	-266	150	-	1059	-601	1579	81	-
a Corporate and quasi-corporate, resident	-2247	-2146	-251	150	-	1042	-601	1562	81	-
b Government	18	-	18	-	-	3	-	3	-	-
c Rest of the world	-33	-	-33	-	-	14	-	14	-	-

Finland

3.26 Financial Transactions of Financial Institutions: Detail
(Continued)

Million Finnish markkaa

	1978					1979				
	ALL FINANCIAL INSTITUTIONS	Central Bank	Other Monetary Institutions	Insurance	Other Financial Institutions	ALL FINANCIAL INSTITUTIONS	Central Bank	Other Monetary Institutions	Insurance	Other Financial Institutions
5 Bonds, long term	1284	362	711	210	1	2398	1205	1109	96	-12
6 Corporate equity securities	837	7	442	305	84	721	7	267	459	-12
7 Short-term loans, n.e.c.	855	417	174	178	86	2312	1696	203	52	361
a Liability of: resident sectors	761	417	175	84	85	2277	1696	214	5	362
b Liability of: rest of the world	94	-	-1	94	1	35	-	-11	47	-1
8 Long-term loans, n.e.c.	10085	220	5814	2984	1067	14627	394	9206	3978	1049
a Mortgages	2492	..	..	..	..	3635	..	..	..	..
b Other	7593	..	..	..	..	10992	..	..	..	..
9 Trade credit and advances	33	-7	-3	73	-30	18	3	-84	-13	112
a Consumer credit	..	..	..	..	..	..	..	..	..	..
b Other	..	..	..	..	..	..	..	..	..	..
10 Other assets	572	-	496	11	65	1917	-	1316	620	-19
Total Acquisition of Financial Assets [a]	16581	1253	9907	4025	1397	25933	2468	16734	5423	1308
Incurrence of Liabilities											
1 Currency and transferable deposits	3414	1790	1623	-	-	4574	568	4006	-	-
2 Other deposits	8542	822	7720	-	-	10266	2209	8057	-	-
3 Bills and bonds, short term	-2099	-	-2125	29	-4	-282	-	-573	-3	294
4 Bonds, long term	752	-	110	-	641	643	-	40	-	603
5 Corporate equity securities	260	-	113	75	72	407	-	309	17	81
6 Short-term loans, n.e.c.	1148	-	851	31	266	2738	-	2421	103	214
7 Long-term loans, n.e.c.	-586	-1434	640	-18	226	940	-433	1190	4	179
9 Net equity of households in life insurance and pension fund reserves	801	-	-	801	-	752	-	-	752	-
10 Other liabilities	747	-1	646	67	35	1315	-	1213	63	39
Total Incurrence of liabilities [a]	12978	1178	9578	986	1237	21353	2344	16663	936	1410
Statistical discrepancy	-6	-53	20	-23	49	-182	-103	-26	-28	-25
Net Lending [a]	3609	128	308	3063	110	4762	227	97	4515	-77
Incurrence of Liabilities and Net Lending	16581	1253	9907	4025	1397	25933	2468	16734	5423	1308

a) The data in this table are compiled on the basis of financial statistics which are not integrated with other tables.

3.32 Household and Private Unincorporated Enterprise Income and Outlay Account

Million Finnish markkaa

	1970	1971	1972	1973	1974	1975	1976	1977	1978	1979	1980
Receipts												
1 Compensation of employees	22810	26314	30767	37598	47529	59318	68589	74144	78218	89531	104518
a Wages and salaries	19646	22514	26134	31473	39673	49310	56373	60113	63670	73016	84746
b Employers' contributions for social security	3164	3800	4633	6124	7856	10008	12216	14031	14548	16515	19772
c Employers' contributions for private pension & welfare plans											
2 Property and entrepreneurial income received	9489	9799	11468	13608	16694	18811	21900	23684	25455	27879	32055
a Operating surplus of private unincorporated enterprises	8423	8579	10107	11818	14421	16003	18669	20370	21785	23672	25912
b Withdrawals from private quasi-corporations	..	..	..	..	..	617	573	332	542	683	774
c Interest	913	1052	1185	1583	2028	1883	2315	2619	2695	3013	4780

Finland

3.32 Household and Private Unincorporated Enterprise Income and Outlay Account
(Continued)

Million Finnish markkaa

	1970	1971	1972	1973	1974	1975	1976	1977	1978	1979	1980
d Dividends	107	119	120	146	171	223	243	247	307	352	412
e Net land rent and royalties	46	49	55	62	74	85	101	116	126	159	177
3 Other current transfers received	4458	5380	6553	7524	9688	12357	15425	18581	21061	23055	25988
a Casualty insurance claims	256	297	355	377	416	566	681	680	707	808	907
b Social security benefits	2769	3391	4020	4698	6191	7893	9783	11745	13149	14346	16326
c Social assistance grants	552	643	894	911	1158	1431	1829	2483	3043	3264	3524
d Unfunded employee welfare benefits	800	945	1178	1414	1769	2267	2903	3401	3831	4269	4815
e Other current transfers received	81	104	105	125	154	200	229	272	331	368	416
From general government	35	41	47	57	76	73	95	124	136	129	108
From the rest fo the world	36	51	44	51	58	102	106	117	153	192	251
Other	10	11	14	18	20	25	28	31	42	47	58
Total Current Receipts	36757	41493	48787	58731	73911	90486	105913	116409	124734	140467	162559

Disbursements

	1970	1971	1972	1973	1974	1975	1976	1977	1978	1979	1980
1 Final consumption expenditures	24957	26992	31635	37706	45739	54977	62764	69140	76420	87011	98905
2 Property income paid	671	853	941	1219	1607	1839	2135	2534	2620	2991	4252
a Interest	632	812	896	1169	1547	1768	2070	2456	2535	2893	4146
b Net land rent and royalties	39	41	45	50	60	71	65	78	85	97	105
3 Direct taxes, fees, fines & other payments n.e.c. to government	8386	10051	12087	15807	20422	25714	32670	35383	34362	37963	44940
a Social security contributions	3050	3704	4534	6098	7865	10145	12337	14131	14073	16007	19162
b Direct taxes	5182	6184	7368	9474	12266	15207	19864	20692	19653	21222	25035
Income taxes	5182	6184	7368	9474	12266	15207	19864	20692	19653	21222	25035
Other	...	...	...	...	...	...	...	...	...	...	...
c Fees, fines and penalties	154	163	186	234	291	362	469	560	635	734	743
4 Other current transfers paid	1452	1663	1939	2301	2809	3736	4394	4968	5327	6054	6893
a Net casualty insurance premiums	256	297	355	377	416	578	654	681	767	808	907
b Transfers to private non-profit institutions serving households	320	377	444	562	712	965	1129	1360	1352	1531	1746
c Transfers to the rest of the world	20	22	32	41	38	105	131	160	203	235	297
d Other current transfers, except imputed	-	-	-	-	-	-	-	-	-	-	...
e Imputed employee welfare contributions	856	967	1108	1322	1644	2088	2480	2767	3004	3480	3943
Net saving	1292	1934	2186	1698	3333	4220	3951	4385	6004	6449	7570
Total Current Disbursements and Net Saving	36757	41493	48787	58731	73911	90486	105914	116409	124734	140467	162559

3.33 Household and Private Unincorporated Enterprise Capital Accumulation Account

Million Finnish markkaa

	1970	1971	1972	1973	1974	1975	1976	1977	1978	1979	1980

Finance of Gross Accumulation

	1970	1971	1972	1973	1974	1975	1976	1977	1978	1979	1980
1 Gross saving	3064	3880	4369	4266	6566	8002	8150	8931	10934	12032	14009
a Consumption of fixed capital	1772	1946	2183	2569	3233	3782	4199	4546	4929	5583	6439
b Net saving	1292	1934	2186	1698	3333	4220	3951	4385	6004	6449	7570
2 Capital transfers received [a]	30	15	24	21	13	306	45	19	38	63	162
Total Finance of Gross Accumulation	3094	3895	4393	4287	6579	8308	8195	8950	10972	12095	14171

Gross Accumulation

	1970	1971	1972	1973	1974	1975	1976	1977	1978	1979	1980
1 Gross Capital Formation	2483	2826	3105	4078	5367	6920	7192	7755	8660	9649	12310
a Increase in stocks	-40	77	-30	-53	33	254	58	-428	-17	90	149
b Gross fixed capital formation	2523	2748	3135	4131	5334	6666	7135	8183	8676	9559	12160
2 Purchases of land, net	-389	-565	-528	-784	-649	-849	-1005	-698	-688	-776	-817
3 Purchases of intangibles, net	-	-	-	-	-	-	-	-	-	-	-
4 Capital transfers paid	...	...	...	...	...	...	...	...	...	...	...
5 Net lending	1000	1634	1816	994	1861	2238	2008	1893	3002	3222	2678
Total Gross Accumulation	3094	3895	4393	4287	6579	8309	8195	8950	10972	12095	14171

a) Net.

Finland

3.34 Household and Private Unincorporated Enterprise Capital Finance Account

Million Finnish markkaa

	1970	1971	1972	1973	1974	1975	1976	1977	1978	1979	1980
Acquisition of Financial Assets											
1 Gold	...	...	...	...	...	...	...	...	...	...	...
2 Currency and transferable deposits	117	184	148	383	304	391	-122	175	622	642	...
3 Other deposits	1896	1778	3114	2749	4127	4338	3637	3720	5361	6585	...
4 Bills and bonds, short term	...	...	...	...	...	...	...	...	...	...	...
5 Bonds, long term	120	73	-23	-69	-49	424	498	622	588	735	...
6 Corporate equity securities	732	1116	1410	1681	2134	2216	1411	2709	2693	2786	...
7 Short term loans, n.e.c.	-	-	-	-	-	-	567	-	-	-	...
8 Long term loans, n.e.c.	-	-	-	-	-	-	-	149	-5	-144	...
a Mortgages	...	...	...	...	...	...	...	...	...	...	...
b Other	...	...	...	...	...	...	...	...	...	-144	...
9 Trade credit and advances of unincorporated enterprises	-	-	-	-	-	-	25	-	-	37	...
10 Net equity of households in life insurance and pension fund reserves	223	195	293	432	573	194	399	462	801	751	...
11 Proprietors' net additions to the accumulation of quasi-corporations	-	-	-	-	-	-	-	-	-	-	...
12 Other	-	-	-	-	-	519	595	277	-	127	...
Total Acquisition of Financial Assets	3089	3346	4943	5174	7089	8082	7008	8113	10060	11519	...
Incurrence of Liabilities											
1 Short term loans, n.e.c.	128	62	180	223	313	314	262	384	320	453	...
2 Long term loans, n.e.c.	1306	1197	2126	2847	3189	4015	3393	3893	5189	7264	...
a Mortgages	662	744	1219	1558	1742	1900	2212	2592	3277	4308	...
b Consumer credit	644	453	907	1289	1447	2115	1181	1301	1912	1259	...
c Other										1697	...
3 Trade credit and advances of unincorporated enterprises	156	26	265	548	520	500	24	300	215	355	...
4 Other accounts payable	60	90	263	181	397	1002	-	606	246	156	...
5 Other liabilities											...
Total Incurrence of Liabilities	1650	1374	2834	3800	4419	5831	3679	5183	5970	8228	...
Statistical discrepancy	439	338	293	380	809	13	1321	1037	1090	69	...
Net Lending	1000	1634	1816	994	1861	2238	2008	1893	3002	3222	...
Incurrence of Liabilities and Net Lending	3089	3346	4943	5174	7089	8082	7008	8113	10060	11519	...

3.42 Private Non-Profit Institutions Serving Households: Income and Outlay Account

Million Finnish markkaa

	1970	1971	1972	1973	1974	1975	1976	1977	1978	1979	1980
Receipts											
1 Property and entrepreneurial income received	-106	-145	-135	-44	-97	-205	-335	-425	-395	-566	-1064
a Withdrawals from quasi-corporations	-145	-199	-188	-124	-192	-324	-464	-578	-563	-746	-1269
b Interest	24	32	33	48	57	67	73	89	103	108	122
c Dividends	9	13	13	20	23	35	37	41	40	44	51
d Net land rent and royalties	6	8	7	12	15	17	19	23	25	28	32
2 Other current transfers received	947	1112	1264	1550	1990	2379	2628	2900	2887	3279	3802
a Casualty insurance claims	13	14	15	14	16	22	28	30	33	45	51
b Other Current transfers received from resident sectors, except imputed	863	1019	1162	1437	1858	2227	2457	2723	2695	3053	3544
General government	517	612	690	839	1100	1206	1262	1281	1273	1436	1677
Corporations and quasi-corporations	26	29	28	36	45	56	66	82	70	87	122
Households and unincorporated enterprises	320	377	444	562	712	965	1129	1360	1352	1530	1746
c Current transfers received from the rest of the world	1	1	1	1	1	1	1	2	1	2	2
d Imputed unfunded employee welfare contributions	70	79	87	99	115	129	142	146	158	179	205
Total Current Receipts	841	967	1130	1506	1893	2173	2293	2475	2492	2713	2738

Finland

3.42 Private Non-Profit Institutions Serving Households: Income and Outlay Account
(Continued)

Million Finnish markkaa

	1970	1971	1972	1973	1974	1975	1976	1977	1978	1979	1980
	\multicolumn{11}{c}{Disbursements}
1 Final consumption expenditures	901	1024	1145	1315	1552	1773	1945	2128	2313	2594	2987
a Compensation of employees	...	...	...	...	...	...	...	...	...	...	...
b Consumption of fixed capital	...	...	...	...	...	...	...	...	...	...	...
c Purchases of goods and services, net	901	1024	1145	1315	1552	1773	1945	2128	2313	2594	2987
Purchases	901	1024	1145	1315	1552	1773	1945	2128	2313	2594	2987
Less: Sales	-	-	-	-	-	-	-	-	-	-	-
2 Property income paid	349	425	460	576	717	772	852	963	1024	1105	1341
a Interest	312	386	415	537	671	714	791	884	936	1010	1232
b Net land rent and royalties	37	39	45	39	46	58	61	79	88	95	109
3 Direct taxes and other payments to general government	46	50	49	49	48	50	94	61	68	67	75
a Direct taxes	46	50	49	49	47	50	94	61	68	67	75
b Fees, fines and penalties	-	-	-	-	-	-	-	-	-	-	-
4 Other current transfers paid	68	91	90	120	128	154	208	215	258	300	348
a Net casualty insurance premiums	13	13	15	14	16	22	28	31	34	36	41
b Current transfers to household	46	66	65	93	96	108	139	156	180	202	230
Social assistance grants	33	50	44	67	64	66	72	80	94	104	121
Unfunded employee welfare benefits	13	16	21	26	32	42	67	76	86	98	109
c Current transfers to the rest of the world	4	4	5	6	5	6	7	6	11	20	26
d Other current transfers n.e.c.	6	6	5	9	10	18	35	22	34	42	51
Net saving	-523	-624	-614	-554	-552	-576	-805	-892	-1171	-1353	-2013
Total Current Disbursements	841	967	1130	1506	1892	2173	2293	2475	2492	2713	2738

3.43 Private Non-Profit Institutions Serving Households: Capital Accumulation Account

Million Finnish markkaa

	1970	1971	1972	1973	1974	1975	1976	1977	1978	1979	1980
	\multicolumn{11}{c}{Finance of Gross Accumulation}
1 Gross saving	-69	-95	4	213	485	648	574	731	562	599	265
a Consumption of fixed capital	455	529	618	767	1037	1224	1379	1623	1733	1952	2278
b Net saving	-524	-624	-614	-554	-552	-576	-805	-892	-1171	-1353	-2013
2 Capital transfers received [a]	48	64	57	74	102	89	98	99	108	131	181
a From resident sectors	48	64	57	74	102	89	98	99	108	131	181
Private	...	...	...	...	...	...	...	...	-	-	-
Public	...	...	...	...	...	...	...	...	108	131	181
b From the rest of the world	-	-	-	-	-	-	-	-	-	-	-
Finance of Gross Accumulation	-21	-31	61	287	587	737	672	830	670	730	445
	\multicolumn{11}{c}{Gross Accumulation}
1 Gross capital formation	1647	1740	2373	3149	4263	4297	3952	4325	4467	4881	5487
a Increase in stocks	-	-	-	-	-	-	-	-	-	-	-
b Gross fixed capital formation	1647	1740	2373	3149	4263	4297	3952	4325	4467	4881	5487
2 Purchases of land, net	47	52	71	87	122	115	93	102	151	164	183
3 Purchases of intangible assets, net	...	...	...	...	...	...	...	...	...	...	...
4 Capital transfers paid	...	...	...	...	...	...	...	...	...	...	...
5 Net lending	-1715	-1823	-2383	-2950	-3798	-3674	-3373	-3597	-3948	-4314	-5225
Gross Accumulation	-21	-31	61	287	587	738	672	830	670	730	445

a) Net.

3.44 Private Non-Profit Institutions Serving Households: Capital Finance Account

Million Finnish markkaa

	1970	1971	1972	1973	1974	1975	1976	1977	1978	1979	1980
	\multicolumn{11}{c}{Acquisition of Financial Assets}
1 Gold	...	...	...	...	...	...	...	...	...	...	...
2 Currency and transferable deposits	7	6	8	13	26	118	59	58	70	66	...
3 Other deposits	22	25	13	64	64	181	278	340	68	133	...
4 Bills and bonds, short term	...	...	...	...	...	...	...	...	...	...	...

Finland

3.44 Private Non-Profit Institutions Serving Households: Capital Finance Account
(Continued)

Million Finnish markkaa

	1970	1971	1972	1973	1974	1975	1976	1977	1978	1979	1980
5 Bonds, long term	4	5	5	8	6	22	29	29	25	30	...
a Corporate, resident	4	5	5	8	6	22	29	29	25	30	...
b Government											...
c Rest of the world	-	-	-	-	-	-	-	-	-	-	...
6 Corporate equity securities	66	57	61	121	104	139	180	163	168	254	...
7 Short-term loans, n.e.c.	13	11	12	18	17	41	16	21	36	37	...
8 Long-term loans, n.e.c.	41	34	34	53	45	28	42	43	66	143	...
9 Other receivables	14	-6	4	-25	17	40	54	55	13	65	...
10 Proprietors' net additions to the accumulation of quasi-corporations	.	.	.	.	.	.	.	.	.	.	...
11 Other assets	.	.	.	.	.	.	.	.	.	.	...
Total Acquisition of Financial Assets	167	132	136	252	277	569	658	708	446	728	...

Incurrence of Liabilities

	1970	1971	1972	1973	1974	1975	1976	1977	1978	1979	1980
1 Short-term loans	37	19	34	20	43	44	-	50	18	92	...
2 Long-term loans	653	569	868	1078	1163	1464	1536	1179	1012	1090	...
3 Other liabilities	1075	1387	1656	1953	2903	2735	2483	3092	3364	3860	...
Total Incurrence of Liabilities	1765	1975	2559	3051	4109	4243	4019	4321	4394	5042	...
Statistical discrepancy	117	-20	-40	150	-34	-	13	-16	.	.	...
Net Lending	-1715	-1823	-2383	-2950	-3798	-3674	-3373	-3597	-3948	-4314	...
Incurrence of Liabilities and Net Lending	167	132	136	252	277	569	658	708	446	728	...

3.51 External Transactions: Current Account: Detail

Million Finnish markkaa

	1970	1971	1972	1973	1974	1975	1976	1977	1978	1979	1980

Payments to the Rest of the World

	1970	1971	1972	1973	1974	1975	1976	1977	1978	1979	1980
1 Imports of goods and services	12310	13139	14797	18672	28193	31020	32062	34986	37654	50256	65294
2 Factor income paid to the rest of the world	600	734	902	1143	1611	2037	2402	3085	3636	4227	5265
a Compensation of employees	4	4	4	6	10	22	28	36	42	45	48
b Property and entrepreneurial income paid	596	730	898	1137	1601	2015	2374	3049	3594	4182	5217
3 Indirect taxes paid to supranational organizations	...	...	...	...	...	...	...	...	...	...	...
4 Other current transfers to the rest of the world	261	315	352	401	454	611	716	835	926	1253	1632
a By general government	30	51	66	94	116	118	141	150	151	241	330
b By other resident sectors	231	264	286	307	338	493	575	685	775	1012	1302
5 Surplus of the nation on current transactions	-1004	-1429	-550	-1480	-4628	-7950	-4455	-580	2606	-632	-5136
Payments to the Rest of the World, and Surplus of the Nation on Current Transfers	12166	12758	15500	18736	25630	25718	30725	38326	44822	55104	67055

Receipts From The Rest of the World

	1970	1971	1972	1973	1974	1975	1976	1977	1978	1979	1980
1 Exports of goods and services	11745	12226	14946	18086	24702	24717	29637	37079	43090	52654	63797
2 Factor income received from the rest of the world	174	237	254	329	569	512	542	607	1011	1494	2017
a Compensation of employees	30	46	34	60	111	73	99	193	354	408	422
b Property and entrepreneurial income received	143	192	220	269	458	440	443	414	657	1086	1595
3 Subsidies received from supranational organizations	...	...	...	...	...	...	...	...	...	...	...
4 Other current transfers from the rest of the world	247	295	301	321	359	489	547	640	722	955	1241
a To general government	-	-	-	-	-	-	-	-	-	-	-
b To other resident sectors	247	295	301	321	359	489	547	640	722	955	1241
Receipts from the Rest of the World on Current Transfers	12166	12758	15500	18736	25630	25718	30725	38326	44822	55104	67055

Finland

3.52 External Transactions: Capital Accumulation Account

Million Finnish markkaa

	1970	1971	1972	1973	1974	1975	1976	1977	1978	1979	1980
Finance of Gross Accumulation											
1 Surplus of the nation on current transactions	-1004	-1429	-550	-1480	-4628	-7950	-4455	-580	2606	-632	-5136
2 Capital transfers received from the rest of the world [a]	-	5	89	-1	-	-2	-	-	-	-128	-50
Total Finance of Gross Accumulation	-1004	-1424	-461	-1481	-4628	-7952	-4455	-580	2606	-761	-5186
Gross Accumulation											
1 Capital transfers paid to the rest of the world	...	...	...	...	...	...	...	...	...	...	...
2 Purchases of intangible assets, n.e.c., net, from the rest of the world	...	...	...	...	...	...	...	...	...	...	...
3 Net lending to the rest of the world	-1004	-1424	-461	-1481	-4628	-7952	-4455	-580	2606	-761	-5186
Total Gross Accumulation	-1004	-1424	-461	-1481	-4628	-7952	-4455	-580	2606	-761	-5186

a) Net.

3.53 External Transactions: Capital Finance Account

Million Finnish markkaa

	1970	1971	1972	1973	1974	1975	1976	1977	1978	1979	1980
Acquisitions of Foreign Financial Assets											
1 Gold and SDR's	49	85	1	-83	1	-276	-42	-62	350	-12	...
2 Currency and transferable deposits	776	903	516	-34	-148	276	383	1266	2813	1455	...
3 Other deposits	136	163	-23	-90	-2	362	135	-563	25	45	...
4 Bills and bonds, short term	-9	75	-17	-18	159	121	130	188	143	14	...
5 Bonds, long term	34	-7	289	140	-6	-169	135	283	304	1357	...
6 Corporate equity securities	47	70	154	67	109	197	154	542	359	562	...
a Subsidiaries abroad	37	60	129	19	61	170	99	457	241	423	...
b Other	10	10	25	48	48	295	55	186	118	139	...
7 Short-term loans, n.e.c.	24	28	42	40	-12	37	52	305	105	80	...
a Subsidiaries abroad	-1004	-	-	-	-	-	-	-	-	-	...
b Other	24	28	42	40	-12	37	52	305	105	80	...
8 Long-term loans	182	135	61	44	64	-84	46	-90	49	229	...
a Subsidiaries abroad	182	135	86	38	51	-68	19	-164	16	58	...
b Other	-	-	-26	6	13	-16	27	74	33	171	...
9 Proprietors' net additions to accumulation of quasi-corporate, non-resident enterprises	-	-	-	-	-	-	-	-	-	-	...
10 Trade credit and advances	209	-122	983	960	1751	-561	1033	1051	1443	1329	...
11 Other	-	-	-	-	-	135	45	67	161	168	...
Total Acquisitions of Foreign Financial Assets	1448	1330	2006	1025	1914	38	2071	2987	5751	5227	...
Incurrence of Foreign Liabilities											
1 Currency and transferable deposits	517	381	-51	490	1003	1348	489	1460	-162	3404	...
2 Other deposits	-	-	-	-	-	-	-	119	-119	-	...
3 Bills and bonds, short term	-	-	-	-	-	76	-106	-117	12	24	...
4 Bonds, long term	115	388	517	-53	205	1543	1230	1475	3438	1180	...
5 Corporate equity securities	60	97	113	-3	101	165	154	70	126	186	...
a Subsidiaries of non-resident incorporated units	60	97	113	-3	101	162	154	70	126	145	...
b Other	-	-	-	-	-	3	-	-	-	41	...
6 Short-term loans, n.e.c.	15	6	13	26	18	-1	-15	42	-15	624	...
a Subsidiaries of non-residents	-	-	-	-	-	-	-	-	-	-	...
b Other	15	6	13	26	18	-1	-15	42	-15	624	...
7 Long-term loans	414	1225	1095	406	1077	2614	1890	1524	398	482	...
a Subsidiaries of non-residents	36	39	23	60	49	911	68	80	15	145	...

Finland

3.53 External Transactions: Capital Finance Account
(Continued)

Million Finnish markkaa

	1970	1971	1972	1973	1974	1975	1976	1977	1978	1979	1980
b Other	378	1186	1072	346	1029	2503	1822	1444	383	337	...
8 Non-resident proprietors' net additions to accumulation of resident quasi-corporate enterprises	-	-	-	-	-	-	-	-	-	-	...
9 Trade credit and advances	1177	536	840	1066	3272	2499	1107	-326	-1524	95	...
10 Other	-	-	-	-	-	42	89	126	95	77	...
Total Incurrence of Liabilities	2296	2633	2527	1932	5675	8286	4838	4373	2249	6072	...
Statistical discrepancy	156	121	-60	574	867	-296	1688	-806	896	-84	...
Net Lending	-1004	-1424	-461	-1481	-4628	-7952	-4455	-580	2606	-761	...
Total Incurrence of Liabilities and Net Lending a	1448	1330	2006	1025	1914	38	2071	2987	5751	5227	...

a) Beginning 1970, including allocated Special Drawing Rights.

4.3 Derivation of Value Added by Kind of Activity, ISIC Divisions, in Current Prices

Million Finnish markkaa

	1970 Gross Output	1970 Intermediate Consumption	1970 Value Added	1971 Gross Output	1971 Intermediate Consumption	1971 Value Added	1972 Gross Output	1972 Intermediate Consumption	1972 Value Added	1973 Gross Output	1973 Intermediate Consumption	1973 Value Added
All Producers												
1 Agriculture, hunting, forestry and fishing	...	...	5132	...	...	5562	...	...	5757	...	...	6774
a Agriculture and hunting a	...	...	2407	...	...	2721	...	...	2971	...	...	3154
b Forestry and logging	...	...	2626	...	...	2721	...	...	2652	...	...	3448
c Fishing a	...	...	100	...	...	120	...	...	134	...	...	172
2 Mining and quarrying	...	...	365	...	...	222	...	...	264	...	...	381
a Coal mining	...	...	...	...	...	...	...	...	...	...	...	...
b Crude petroleum and natural gas production	...	...	...	...	...	...	...	...	...	...	...	...
c Metal ore mining	...	...	365	...	...	222	...	...	264	...	...	381
d Other mining	...	...		...	...		...	...		...	...	
3 Manufacturing	...	...	10905	...	...	11615	...	...	13870	...	...	17231
a Manufacture of food, beverages and tobacco	...	...	1436	...	...	1617	...	...	1946	...	...	2154
b Textile, wearing apparel and leather industries	...	...	1059	...	...	1153	...	...	1388	...	...	1568
c Manufacture of wood and wood products, including furniture	...	...	1011	...	...	1056	...	...	1194	...	...	1951
d Manufacture of paper and paper products, printing and publishing	...	...	2402	...	...	2229	...	...	2517	...	...	3216
e Manufacture of chemicals and chemical petroleum, coal, rubber and plastic products	...	...	1120	...	...	1330	...	...	1555	...	...	1868
f Manufacture of non-metallic mineral products, except products of petroleum and coal	...	...	459	...	...	485	...	...	619	...	...	737
g Basic metal industries	...	...	481	...	...	441	...	...	650	...	...	951
h Manufacture of fabricated metal products, machinery and equipment	...	...	2842	...	...	3208	...	...	3880	...	...	4649
i Other manufacturing industries	...	...	97	...	...	96	...	...	121	...	...	138
4 Electricity, gas and water	...	...	1037	...	...	1116	...	...	1328	...	...	1610
a Electricity, gas and steam	...	...	1037	...	...	1116	...	...	1328	...	...	1610
b Water works and supply	...	...		...	...		...	...		...	...	
5 Construction	...	...	3618	...	...	3979	...	...	4916	...	...	6130
6 Wholesale and retail trade, restaurants and hotels	...	...	4387	...	...	4877	...	...	5736	...	...	7058
a Wholesale and retail trade	...	...	3762	...	...	4135	...	...	4838	...	...	5991
b Restaurants and hotels	...	...	625	...	...	741	...	...	898	...	...	1067
7 Transport, storage and communication	...	...	3235	...	...	3564	...	...	4008	...	...	4751
a Transport and storage	...	...	2570	...	...	2841	...	...	3229	...	...	3786
b Communication	...	...	665	...	...	723	...	...	779	...	...	965
8 Finance, insurance, real estate and business services	...	...	4894	...	...	5449	...	...	6610	...	...	8172
a Financial institutions	...	...	955	...	...	1136	...	...	1441	...	...	1920
b Insurance	...	...		...	...		...	...		...	...	
c Real estate and business services	...	...	3939	...	...	4313	...	...	5169	...	...	6252
Real estate, except dwellings	...	...	742	...	...	873	...	...	1079	...	...	1371

Finland

4.3 Derivation of Value Added by Kind of Activity, ISIC Divisions, in Current Prices
(Continued)

Million Finnish markkaa

	1970 GO	1970 IC	1970 VA	1971 GO	1971 IC	1971 VA	1972 GO	1972 IC	1972 VA	1973 GO	1973 IC	1973 VA
Dwellings	...	...	3197	...	...	3440	...	...	4090	...	...	4881
9 Community, social and personal services	...	...	1252	...	...	1436	...	...	1654	...	...	1996
a Sanitary and similar services	...	...	50	...	...	66	...	...	91	...	...	130
b Social and related community services [b]	...	...	283	...	...	312	...	...	327	...	...	358
Educational services	...	...	31	...	...	34	...	...	37	...	...	48
Medical, dental, other health and veterinary services	...	...	253	...	...	278	...	...	290	...	...	310
c Recreational and cultural services [b]	...	...	302	...	...	345	...	...	400	...	...	491
d Personal and household services	...	...	617	...	...	713	...	...	836	...	...	1017
Total, Industries	...	...	34825	...	...	37819	...	...	44142	...	...	54103
Producers of Government Services	...	...	5037	...	...	5728	...	...	6638	...	...	7940
Other Producers	...	...	987	...	...	1098	...	...	1222	...	...	1370
Total	...	...	40849	...	...	44644	...	...	52002	...	...	63413
Imputed bank service charge	...	...	...	...	...	...	...	...	...	...	...	...
Import duties	...	...	...	...	...	...	...	...	...	...	...	...
Value added tax	...	...	...	...	...	...	...	...	...	...	...	...
Total	...	...	...	...	...	...	...	...	...	...	...	...

	1974 GO	1974 IC	1974 VA	1975 GO	1975 IC	1975 VA	1976 GO	1976 IC	1976 VA	1977 GO	1977 IC	1977 VA
All Producers												
1 Agriculture, hunting, forestry and fishing	...	...	8317	...	...	9993	...	...	10491	...	...	11299
a Agriculture and hunting [a]	...	...	3414	...	...	5058	...	...	5461	...	...	5596
b Forestry and logging	...	...	4678	...	...	4678	...	...	4728	...	...	5359
c Fishing [a]	...	...	226	...	...	257	...	...	301	...	...	344
2 Mining and quarrying	...	...	488	...	...	364	...	...	458	...	...	499
a Coal mining	...	...	...	...	...	...	...	...	...	...	...	...
b Crude petroleum and natural gas production	...	...	...	...	...	...	...	...	...	...	...	...
c Metal ore mining	...	...	488	...	...	364	...	...	458	...	...	499
d Other mining	...	...		...	...		...	...		...	...	
3 Manufacturing	...	...	23738	...	...	25283	...	...	28527	...	...	30322
a Manufacture of food, beverages and tobacco	...	...	2533	...	...	3229	...	...	3722	...	...	4349
b Textile, wearing apparel and leather industries	...	...	2041	...	...	2280	...	...	2606	...	...	2671
c Manufacture of wood and wood products, including furniture	...	...	2312	...	...	1492	...	...	2055	...	...	2528
d Manufacture of paper and paper products, printing and publishing	...	...	5097	...	...	4892	...	...	4627	...	...	5104
e Manufacture of chemicals and chemical petroleum, coal, rubber and plastic products	...	...	2862	...	...	2716	...	...	3013	...	...	3467
f Manufacture of non-metallic mineral products, except products of petroleum and coal	...	...	996	...	...	1081	...	...	1228	...	...	1351
g Basic metal industries	...	...	1195	...	...	1231	...	...	1143	...	...	1251
h Manufacture of fabricated metal products, machinery and equipment	...	...	6549	...	...	8171	...	...	9890	...	...	9314
i Other manufacturing industries	...	...	155	...	...	192	...	...	245	...	...	288
4 Electricity, gas and water	...	...	2068	...	...	2625	...	...	2872	...	...	3708
a Electricity, gas and steam	...	...	2068	...	...	2625	...	...	2872	...	...	3708
b Water works and supply	...	...		...	...		...	...		...	...	
5 Construction	...	...	7782	...	...	9374	...	...	9092	...	...	9500
6 Wholesale and retail trade, restaurants and hotels	...	...	8908	...	...	10701	...	...	12085	...	...	12709
a Wholesale and retail trade	...	...	7597	...	...	9094	...	...	10276	...	...	10776
b Restaurants and hotels	...	...	1310	...	...	1607	...	...	1809	...	...	1933
7 Transport, storage and communication	...	...	5851	...	...	6643	...	...	8281	...	...	9310

Finland

4.3 Derivation of Value Added by Kind of Activity, ISIC Divisions, in Current Prices
(Continued)

Million Finnish markkaa

	1974 Gross Output	1974 Intermediate Consumption	1974 Value Added	1975 Gross Output	1975 Intermediate Consumption	1975 Value Added	1976 Gross Output	1976 Intermediate Consumption	1976 Value Added	1977 Gross Output	1977 Intermediate Consumption	1977 Value Added
a Transport and storage	...	...	4662	...	...	5128	...	...	6074	...	...	6777
b Communication	...	...	1189	...	...	1515	...	...	2207	...	...	2533
8 Finance, insurance, real estate and business services	...	...	10487	...	...	12451	...	...	14199	...	...	16133
a Financial institutions	...	...	2686	...	...	3186	...	...	3735	...	...	4508
b Insurance	...	...		...	...		...	...		...	...	
c Real estate and business services	...	...	7801	...	...	9265	...	...	10464	...	...	11625
Real estate, except dwellings	...	...	1848	...	...	2392	...	...	2731	...	...	3057
Dwellings	...	...	5953	...	...	6873	...	...	7733	...	...	8567
9 Community, social and personal services	...	...	2463	...	...	3003	...	...	3561	...	...	3978
a Sanitary and similar services	...	...	173	...	...	239	...	...	305	...	...	360
b Social and related community services [b]	...	...	429	...	...	541	...	...	622	...	...	673
Educational services	...	...	62	...	...	95	...	...	104	...	...	114
Medical, dental, other health and veterinary services	...	...	367	...	...	446	...	...	517	...	...	559
c Recreational and cultural services [b]	...	...	576	...	...	708	...	...	842	...	...	992
d Personal and household services	...	...	1285	...	...	1516	...	...	1792	...	...	1954
Total, Industries	...	...	70103	...	...	80438	...	...	89566	...	...	97458
Producers of Government Services	...	...	10020	...	...	13027	...	...	15822	...	...	17709
Other Producers	...	...	1628	...	...	1835	...	...	2028	...	...	2176
Total	...	...	81751	...	...	95300	...	...	107416	...	...	117342
Imputed bank service charge	...	...	...	...	...	...	...	...	...	...	...	...
Import duties	...	...	...	...	...	...	...	...	...	...	...	...
Value added tax	...	...	...	...	...	...	...	...	...	...	...	...
Total	...	...	...	...	...	...	...	...	...	...	...	...

	1978 Gross Output	1978 Intermediate Consumption	1978 Value Added	1979 Gross Output	1979 Intermediate Consumption	1979 Value Added	1980 Gross Output	1980 Intermediate Consumption	1980 Value Added
All Producers									
1 Agriculture, hunting, forestry and fishing	...	...	11635	...	...	13289	...	...	15193
a Agriculture and hunting [a]	...	...	5888	...	...	6146	...	...	6863
b Forestry and logging	...	...	5299	...	...	6647	...	...	7787
c Fishing [a]	...	...	448	...	...	496	...	...	543
2 Mining and quarrying	...	...	539	...	...	770	...	...	841
a Coal mining	...	...	...	...	...	...	...	...	...
b Crude petroleum and natural gas production	...	...	...	...	...	...	...	...	...
c Metal ore mining	...	...	539	...	...	770	...	...	841
d Other mining	...	...		...	...		...	...	

Finland

4.3 Derivation of Value Added by Kind of Activity, ISIC Divisions, in Current Prices
(Continued)

Million Finnish markkaa

		1978			1979			1980	
	Gross Output	Intermediate Consumption	Value Added	Gross Output	Intermediate Consumption	Value Added	Gross Output	Intermediate Consumption	Value Added
3 Manufacturing	...	...	34264	...	...	41418	...	...	47886
a Manufacture of food, beverages and tobacco	...	...	4333	...	...	4481	...	...	5140
b Textile, wearing apparel and leather industries	...	...	2789	...	...	3348	...	...	3926
c Manufacture of wood and wood products, including furniture	...	...	2893	...	...	3849	...	...	4974
d Manufacture of paper and paper products, printing and publishing	...	...	6698	...	...	8775	...	...	10148
e Manufacture of chemicals and chemical petroleum, coal, rubber and plastic products	...	...	4258	...	...	5396	...	...	5883
f Manufacture of non-metallic mineral products, except products of petroleum and coal	...	...	1344	...	...	1713	...	...	1963
g Basic metal industries	...	...	1783	...	...	2294	...	...	2361
h Manufacture of fabricated metal products, machinery and equipment	...	...	9848	...	...	11227	...	...	13062
i Other manufacturing industries	...	...	318	...	...	334	...	...	409
4 Electricity, gas and water	...	...	4108	...	...	4866	...	...	5559
a Electricity, gas and steam	...	...	4108	...	...	4866	...	...	5559
b Water works and supply	...	...		...	...		...	...	
5 Construction	...	...	9588	...	...	10428	...	...	12102
6 Wholesale and retail trade, restaurants and hotels	...	...	13967	...	...	16307	...	...	19169
a Wholesale and retail trade	...	...	11772	...	...	13738	...	...	16197
b Restaurants and hotels	...	...	2195	...	...	2569	...	...	2972
7 Transport, storage and communication	...	...	10380	...	...	12323	...	...	13557
a Transport and storage	...	...	7521	...	...	9154	...	...	10141
b Communication	...	...	2859	...	...	3168	...	...	3417
8 Finance, insurance, real estate and business services	...	...	17672	6647	...	19519	...	...	22593
a Financial institutions	...	...	4790	...	...	5312	...	...	6613
b Insurance	...	...		...	...		...	...	
c Real estate and business services	...	...	12881	...	...	14208	...	...	15980
Real estate, except dwellings	...	...	3377	...	...	3991	...	...	4932
Dwellings	...	...	9504	...	...	10217	...	...	11048
9 Community, social and personal services	...	...	4316	...	...	5024	...	...	5750
a Sanitary and similar services	...	...	395	...	...	483	...	...	573
b Social and related community services [b]	...	...	716	...	...	814	...	...	927
Educational services	...	...	122	...	...	154	...	...	164
Medical, dental, other health and veterinary services	...	...	594	...	...	660	...	...	763
c Recreational and cultural services [b]	...	...	1142	...	...	1367	...	...	1545
d Personal and household services	...	...	2063	...	...	2360	...	...	2705
Total, Industries	...	...	106468	...	...	123943	...	...	142649
Producers of Government Services	...	...	19351	...	...	22072	...	...	25133
Other Producers	...	...	2328	...	...	2638	...	...	3013
Total	...	...	128146	...	...	148652	...	...	170796
Imputed bank service charge	...	...	...	...	...	...	...	...	...
Import duties	...	...	...	...	...	...	...	...	...
Value added tax	...	...	...	...	...	...	...	...	...
Total	...	...	...	...	...	...	...	...	...

a) Hunting is included in item 'Fishing'.
b) ISIC groups 935 and 939 are included in item 'Recreational and cultural services'.

Finland

4.4 Derivation of Value Added by Kind of Activity, ISIC Divisions, in Constant Prices

Million Finnish markkaa

At constant prices of: 1975 — All Producers

	1970 GO	1970 IC	1970 VA	1971 GO	1971 IC	1971 VA	1972 GO	1972 IC	1972 VA	1973 GO	1973 IC	1973 VA
1 Agriculture, hunting, forestry and fishing	...	...	11729	...	...	11413	...	...	11045	...	...	10958
a Agriculture and hunting [a]	...	...	5038	...	...	5234	...	...	5079	...	...	4922
b Forestry and logging	...	...	6511	...	...	5981	...	...	5761	...	...	5818
c Fishing [a]	...	...	180	...	...	199	...	...	205	...	...	218
2 Mining and quarrying	...	...	363	...	...	300	...	...	349	...	...	366
a Coal mining	...	...	...	...	...	...	...	...	...	...	...	...
b Crude petroleum and natural gas production	...	...	...	...	...	...	...	...	...	...	...	...
c Metal ore mining	...	...	363	...	...	300	...	...	349	...	...	366
d Other mining	...	...		...	...		...	...		...	...	
3 Manufacturing	...	...	20734	...	...	21061	...	...	23581	...	...	25111
a Manufacture of food, beverages and tobacco	...	...	2868	...	...	2951	...	...	3134	...	...	3161
b Textile, wearing apparel and leather industries	...	...	1926	...	...	1940	...	...	2081	...	...	2096
c Manufacture of wood and wood products, including furniture	...	...	1629	...	...	1679	...	...	1792	...	...	2027
d Manufacture of paper and paper products, printing and publishing	...	...	4693	...	...	4713	...	...	5234	...	...	5570
e Manufacture of chemicals and chemical petroleum, coal, rubber and plastic products	...	...	2264	...	...	2390	...	...	2768	...	...	2987
f Manufacture of non-metallic mineral products, except products of petroleum and coal	...	...	882	...	...	912	...	...	975	...	...	1080
g Basic metal industries	...	...	964	...	...	845	...	...	1112	...	...	1246
h Manufacture of fabricated metal products, machinery and equipment	...	...	5315	...	...	5431	...	...	6272	...	...	6732
i Other manufacturing industries	...	...	194	...	...	199	...	...	213	...	...	213
4 Electricity, gas and water	...	...	1900	...	...	1983	...	...	2265	...	...	2506
a Electricity, gas and steam	...	...	1900	...	...	1983	...	...	2265	...	...	2506
b Water works and supply	...	...		...	...		...	...		...	...	
5 Construction	...	...	7582	...	...	7433	...	...	8086	...	...	8851
6 Wholesale and retail trade, restaurants and hotels	...	...	8032	...	...	8430	...	...	9245	...	...	10115
a Wholesale and retail trade	...	...	6805	...	...	7103	...	...	7790	...	...	8564
b Restaurants and hotels	...	...	1227	...	...	1327	...	...	1455	...	...	1551
7 Transport, storage and communication	...	...	5368	...	...	5499	...	...	5956	...	...	6436
a Transport and storage	...	...	4356	...	...	4410	...	...	4757	...	...	5159
b Communication	...	...	1012	...	...	1089	...	...	1199	...	...	1277
8 Finance, insurance, real estate and business services	...	...	9207	...	...	9687	...	...	10339	...	...	10999
a Financial institutions	...	...	2509	...	...	2627	...	...	2777	...	...	2929
b Insurance	...	...		...	...		...	...		...	...	
c Real estate and business services	...	...	6698	...	...	7061	...	...	7562	...	...	8070
Real estate, except dwellings	...	...	1415	...	...	1528	...	...	1732	...	...	1927
Dwellings	...	...	5284	...	...	5532	...	...	5830	...	...	6143
9 Community, social and personal services	...	...	2551	...	...	2672	...	...	2780	...	...	2861
a Sanitary and similar services	...	...	105	...	...	124	...	...	152	...	...	186
b Social and related community services [b]	...	...	520	...	...	547	...	...	547	...	...	530
Educational services	...	...	80	...	...	78	...	...	76	...	...	85
Medical, dental, other health and veterinary services	...	...	440	...	...	469	...	...	471	...	...	445
c Recreational and cultural services [b]	...	...	573	...	...	584	...	...	605	...	...	659
d Personal and household services	...	...	1353	...	...	1418	...	...	1477	...	...	1486

Finland

4.4 Derivation of Value Added by Kind of Activity, ISIC Divisions, in Constant Prices
(Continued)

Million Finnish markkaa

	1970 Gross Output	1970 Intermediate Consumption	1970 Value Added	1971 Gross Output	1971 Intermediate Consumption	1971 Value Added	1972 Gross Output	1972 Intermediate Consumption	1972 Value Added	1973 Gross Output	1973 Intermediate Consumption	1973 Value Added
				At constant prices of: 1975								
Total, Industries	...	...	67467	...	...	68479	...	...	73646	...	...	78204
Producers of Government Services	...	...	9842	...	...	10319	...	...	10939	...	...	11633
Other Producers	...	...	1937	...	...	1948	...	...	1976	...	...	1952
Total	...	...	79246	...	...	80746	...	...	86561	...	...	91789
Imputed bank service charge	...	...	...	...	...	...	...	...	...	...	...	...
Import duties	...	...	...	...	...	...	...	...	...	...	...	...
Value added tax	...	...	...	...	...	...	...	...	...	...	...	...
Total	...	...	...	...	...	...	...	...	...	...	...	...

	1974 Gross Output	1974 Intermediate Consumption	1974 Value Added	1975 Gross Output	1975 Intermediate Consumption	1975 Value Added	1976 Gross Output	1976 Intermediate Consumption	1976 Value Added	1977 Gross Output	1977 Intermediate Consumption	1977 Value Added
				At constant prices of: 1975								
				All Producers								
1 Agriculture, hunting, forestry and fishing	...	...	10473	...	...	9993	...	...	10125	...	...	10310
a Agriculture and hunting a	...	...	4851	...	...	5058	...	...	5275	...	...	5089
b Forestry and logging	...	...	5378	...	...	4678	...	...	4577	...	...	4927
c Fishing a	...	...	245	...	...	257	...	...	273	...	...	295
2 Mining and quarrying	...	...	369	...	...	364	...	...	399	...	...	428
a Coal mining	...	...	...	...	...	...	...	...	...	...	...	...
b Crude petroleum and natural gas production	...	...	...	...	...	...	...	...	...	...	...	...
c Metal ore mining	...	...	369	...	...	364	...	...	399	...	...	428
d Other mining	...	...		...	...		...	...		...	...	
3 Manufacturing	...	...	26370	...	...	25283	...	...	25665	...	...	25426
a Manufacture of food, beverages and tobacco	...	...	3194	...	...	3229	...	...	3147	...	...	3071
b Textile, wearing apparel and leather industries	...	...	2210	...	...	2280	...	...	2310	...	...	2192
c Manufacture of wood and wood products, including furniture	...	...	1932	...	...	1492	...	...	1565	...	...	1618
d Manufacture of paper and paper products, printing and publishing	...	...	5836	...	...	4892	...	...	5048	...	...	4995
e Manufacture of chemicals and chemical petroleum, coal, rubber and plastic products	...	...	2973	...	...	2716	...	...	2893	...	...	2913
f Manufacture of non-metallic mineral products, except products of petroleum and coal	...	...	1147	...	...	1081	...	...	1031	...	...	1048
g Basic metal industries	...	...	1292	...	...	1231	...	...	1223	...	...	1500
h Manufacture of fabricated metal products, machinery and equipment	...	...	7583	...	...	8171	...	...	8252	...	...	7880
i Other manufacturing industries	...	...	202	...	...	192	...	...	195	...	...	211
4 Electricity, gas and water	...	...	2592	...	...	2625	...	...	2719	...	...	2980
a Electricity, gas and steam	...	...	2592	...	...	2625	...	...	2719	...	...	2980
b Water works and supply	...	...		...	...		...	...		...	...	
5 Construction	...	...	9023	...	...	9374	...	...	8533	...	...	8542
6 Wholesale and retail trade, restaurants and hotels	...	...	10421	...	...	10701	...	...	10689	...	...	9970
a Wholesale and retail trade	...	...	8814	...	...	9094	...	...	9092	...	...	8452
b Restaurants and hotels	...	...	1607	...	...	1607	...	...	1597	...	...	1518
7 Transport, storage and communication	...	...	6772	...	...	6643	...	...	6507	...	...	6561
a Transport and storage	...	...	5353	...	...	5128	...	...	4999	...	...	4986
b Communication	...	...	1419	...	...	1515	...	...	1508	...	...	1575
8 Finance, insurance, real estate and business services	...	...	11661	...	...	12451	...	...	12917	...	...	13330
a Financial institutions	...	...	2988	...	...	3186	...	...	3292	...	...	3341
b Insurance	...	...		...	...		...	...		...	...	
c Real estate and business services	...	...	8673	...	...	9265	...	...	9624	...	...	9989
Real estate, except dwellings	...	...	2157	...	...	2392	...	...	2418	...	...	2444

Finland

4.4 Derivation of Value Added by Kind of Activity, ISIC Divisions, in Constant Prices
(Continued)

Million Finnish markkaa

	1974 Gross Output	1974 Intermediate Consumption	1974 Value Added	1975 Gross Output	1975 Intermediate Consumption	1975 Value Added	1976 Gross Output	1976 Intermediate Consumption	1976 Value Added	1977 Gross Output	1977 Intermediate Consumption	1977 Value Added
				At constant prices of: 1975								
Dwellings	...	...	6516	...	...	6873	...	...	7206	...	...	7545
9 Community, social and personal services	...	...	2938	...	...	3003	...	...	3082	...	...	2973
a Sanitary and similar services	...	...	206	...	...	239	...	...	265	...	...	287
b Social and related community services b	...	...	545	...	...	541	...	...	535	...	...	514
Educational services	...	...	84	...	...	95	...	...	89	...	...	85
Medical, dental, other health and veterinary services	...	...	461	...	...	446	...	...	446	...	...	428
c Recreational and cultural services b	...	...	688	...	...	708	...	...	712	...	...	731
d Personal and household services	...	...	1499	...	...	1516	...	...	1570	...	...	1441
Total, Industries	...	...	80618	...	...	80438	...	...	80636	...	...	80520
Producers of Government Services	...	...	12387	...	...	13027	...	...	13787	...	...	14405
Other Producers	...	...	1953	...	...	1835	...	...	1747	...	...	1746
Total	...	...	94958	...	...	95300	...	...	96170	...	...	96671
Imputed bank service charge	...	...	...	...	...	...	...	...	...	...	...	...
Import duties	...	...	...	...	...	...	...	...	...	...	...	...
Value added tax	...	...	...	...	...	...	...	...	...	...	...	...
Total	...	...	...	...	...	...	...	...	...	...	...	...

	1978 Gross Output	1978 Intermediate Consumption	1978 Value Added	1979 Gross Output	1979 Intermediate Consumption	1979 Value Added	1980 Gross Output	1980 Intermediate Consumption	1980 Value Added
			At constant prices of: 1975						
			All Producers						
1 Agriculture, hunting, forestry and fishing	...	...	10492	...	...	11705	...	...	11900
a Agriculture and hunting a	...	...	4971	...	...	5090	...	...	5345
b Forestry and logging	...	...	5150	...	...	6210	...	...	6132
c Fishing a	...	...	371	...	...	405	...	...	424
2 Mining and quarrying	...	...	444	...	...	477	...	...	501
a Coal mining	...	...	...	...	...	...	...	...	...
b Crude petroleum and natural gas production	...	...	...	...	...	...	...	...	...
c Metal ore mining	...	...	444	...	...	477	...	...	501
d Other mining	...	...		...	...		...	...	
3 Manufacturing	...	...	26477	...	...	29397	...	...	31767
a Manufacture of food, beverages and tobacco	...	...	3255	...	...	3458	...	...	3694
b Textile, wearing apparel and leather industries	...	...	2178	...	...	2406	...	...	2512
c Manufacture of wood and wood products, including furniture	...	...	1745	...	...	2060	...	...	2230
d Manufacture of paper and paper products, printing and publishing	...	...	5478	...	...	6137	...	...	6435
e Manufacture of chemicals and chemical petroleum, coal, rubber and plastic products	...	...	3176	...	...	3522	...	...	3850
f Manufacture of non-metallic mineral products, except products of petroleum and coal	...	...	1034	...	...	1181	...	...	1251
g Basic metal industries	...	...	1836	...	...	2042	...	...	2146
h Manufacture of fabricated metal products, machinery and equipment	...	...	7554	...	...	8355	...	...	9400
i Other manufacturing industries	...	...	223	...	...	235	...	...	249
4 Electricity, gas and water	...	...	3180	...	...	3413	...	...	3577
a Electricity, gas and steam	...	...	3180	...	...	3413	...	...	3577
b Water works and supply	...	...		...	...		...	...	

Finland

4.4 Derivation of Value Added by Kind of Activity, ISIC Divisions, in Constant Prices
(Continued)

Million Finnish markkaa

	1978 Gross Output	1978 Intermediate Consumption	1978 Value Added	1979 Gross Output	1979 Intermediate Consumption	1979 Value Added	1980 Gross Output	1980 Intermediate Consumption	1980 Value Added
			At constant prices of: 1975						
5 Construction	...	...	8328	...	...	8396	...	...	8875
6 Wholesale and retail trade, restaurants and hotels	...	...	10159	...	...	10898	...	...	11242
a Wholesale and retail trade	...	...	8606	...	...	9249	...	...	9534
b Restaurants and hotels	...	...	1553	...	...	1649	...	...	1708
7 Transport, storage and communication	...	...	6746	...	...	7483	...	...	7901
a Transport and storage	...	...	5108	...	...	5704	...	...	5993
b Communication	...	...	1638	...	...	1779	...	...	1908
8 Finance, insurance, real estate and business services	...	...	13780	...	...	14301	...	...	14920
a Financial institutions	...	...	3389	...	...	3426	...	...	3502
b Insurance	...	...		...	...		...	...	
c Real estate and business services	...	...	10392	...	...	10875	...	...	11418
Real estate, except dwellings	...	...	2511	...	...	2718	...	...	2978
Dwellings	...	...	7881	...	...	8157	...	...	8440
9 Community, social and personal services	...	...	2958	...	...	3086	...	...	3186
a Sanitary and similar services	...	...	294	...	...	326	...	...	348
b Social and related community services b	...	...	481	...	...	487	...	...	488
Educational services	...	...	82	...	...	95	...	...	95
Medical, dental, other health and veterinary services	...	...	399	...	...	392	...	...	394
c Recreational and cultural services b	...	...	775	...	...	823	...	...	869
d Personal and household services	...	...	1408	...	...	1450	...	...	1481
Total, Industries	...	...	82565	...	...	89151	...	...	93870
Producers of Government Services	...	...	15013	...	...	15637	...	...	16260
Other Producers	...	...	1771	...	...	1803	...	...	1846
Total	...	...	99349	...	...	106591	...	...	111976
Imputed bank service charge	...	...	...	...	...	...	...	...	...
Import duties	...	...	...	...	...	...	...	...	...
Value added tax	...	...	...	...	...	...	...	...	...
Total	...	...	...	...	...	...	...	...	...

a) Hunting is included in item 'Fishing'.
b) ISIC groups 935 and 939 are included in item 'Recreational and cultural services'.

4.6 Cost Components of Value Added, ISIC Divisions

Million Finnish markkaa

	1970 Compensation of Employees	1970 Capital Consumption	1970 Net Operating Surplus	1970 Indirect Taxes	1970 Less: Subsidies Received	1970 Value Added	1971 Compensation of Employees	1971 Capital Consumption	1971 Net Operating Surplus	1971 Indirect Taxes	1971 Less: Subsidies Received	1971 Value Added
						All Producers						
1 Agriculture, hunting, forestry and fishing	1026	...	3507	...	...	5132	1101	...	3764	...	...	5562
a Agriculture and hunting a	202	...	1808	...	...	2407	217	...	2035	...	...	2721
b Forestry and logging	820	...	1622	...	...	2626	880	...	1637	...	...	2721
c Fishing a	3	...	77	...	...	100	4	...	92	...	...	120
2 Mining and quarrying	99	...	259	...	...	365	113	...	104	...	...	222
a Coal mining	...	...	...	...	...	...	...	...	...	...	...	...
b Crude petroleum and natural gas production	...	...	...	...	...	...	...	...	...	...	...	...
c Metal ore mining	99	...	259	...	...	365	113	...	104	...	...	222
d Other mining												

Finland

4.6 Cost Components of Value Added, ISIC Divisions
(Continued)

Million Finnish markkaa

	1970 Compensation of Employees	1970 Capital Consumption	1970 Net Operating Surplus	1970 Indirect Taxes	1970 Less: Subsidies Received	1970 Value Added	1971 Compensation of Employees	1971 Capital Consumption	1971 Net Operating Surplus	1971 Indirect Taxes	1971 Less: Subsidies Received	1971 Value Added
3 Manufacturing	6432	...	2565	...	...	10905	7444	...	2514	...	...	11615
a Manufacture of food, beverages and tobacco	746	...	578	...	...	1436	859	...	653	...	...	1617
b Textile, wearing apparel and leather industries	712	...	232	...	...	1058	815	...	229	...	...	1153
c Manufacture of wood and wood products, including furniture	689	...	145	...	...	1011	792	...	120	...	...	1056
d Manufacture of paper and paper products, printing and publishing	1200	...	620	...	...	2402	1420	...	391	...	...	2229
e Manufacture of chemicals and chemical petroleum, coal, rubber and plastic products	477	...	310	...	...	1120	589	...	383	...	...	1330
f Manufacture of non-metallic mineral products, except products of petroleum and coal	292	...	95	...	...	459	331	...	64	...	...	485
g Basic metal industries	221	...	50	...	...	481	265	...	48	...	...	441
h Manufacture of fabricated metal products, machinery and equipment	2038	...	502	...	...	2842	2303	...	608	...	...	3208
i Other manufacturing industries	57	...	33	...	...	96	71	...	18	...	...	96
4 Electricity, gas and water	328	...	364	...	...	1037	384	...	380	...	...	1116
a Electricity, gas and steam	328	...	364	...	...	1037	384	...	380	...	...	1116
b Water works and supply		...		...	...			...		...	...	
5 Construction	3027	...	416	...	...	3618	3244	...	526	...	...	3979
6 Wholesale and retail trade, restaurants and hotels	3160	...	839	...	...	4387	3581	...	837	...	...	4877
a Wholesale and retail trade	2683	...	731	...	...	3762	3002	...	719	...	...	4135
b Restaurants and hotels	477	...	108	...	...	625	579	...	118	...	...	742
7 Transport, storage and communication	1745	...	770	...	...	3235	1991	...	759	...	...	3564
a Transport and storage	1253	...	744	...	...	2570	1411	...	775	...	...	2841
b Communication	492	...	26	...	...	665	580	...	-16	...	...	723
8 Finance, insurance, real estate and business services	1140	...	2514	...	...	4894	1369	...	2694	...	...	5449
a Financial institutions	619	...	264	...	...	955	726	...	311	...	...	1136
b Insurance		...		...	...			...		...	...	
c Real estate and business services	521	...	2250	...	...	3939	643	...	2383	...	...	4313
Real estate, except dwellings	341	...	328	...	...	742	428	...	362	...	...	873
Dwellings	180	...	1922	...	...	3197	215	...	2021	...	...	3440
9 Community, social and personal services	713	...	439	...	...	1252	838	...	485	...	...	1436
a Sanitary and similar services	33	...	15	...	...	50	43	...	20	...	...	66
b Social and related community services [b]	61	...	214	...	...	283	74	...	229	...	...	312
Educational services	18	...	9	...	...	31	20	...	11	...	...	34
Medical, dental, other health and veterinary services	43	...	205	...	...	253	54	...	218	...	...	278
c Recreational and cultural services [b]	195	...	86	...	...	302	220	...	105	...	...	345
d Personal and household services	424	...	124	...	...	617	502	...	131	...	...	713
Total, Industries	17669	...	11670	...	...	34825	20065	...	12064	...	...	37820
Producers of Government Services	4696	...	...	...	...	5037	5328	...	...	...	...	5728
Other Producers	419	...	265	...	...	987	879	...	-104	...	...	1098
Total	22783	6055	11935	227	151	40849	26272	6329	11960	244	160	44644
Imputed bank service charge	...	...	...	...	...	...	...	...	...	...	...	...
Import duties	...	...	...	...	...	...	...	...	...	...	...	...
Value added tax	...	...	...	...	...	...	...	...	...	...	...	...
Other adjustments	...	...	...	...	...	...	...	...	...	...	...	...

Finland

4.6 Cost Components of Value Added, ISIC Divisions

Million Finnish markkaa

		1972					1973				
	Compensation of Employees	Capital Consumption	Net Operating Surplus	Indirect Taxes	Less: Subsidies Received	Value Added	Compensation of Employees	Capital Consumption	Net Operating Surplus	Indirect Taxes	Less: Subsidies Received	Value Added

All Producers

1 Agriculture, hunting, forestry and fishing	1116	...	3863	...	...	5757	1301	...	4499	...	...	6774
a Agriculture and hunting [a]	259	...	2197	...	...	2971	321	...	2172	...	...	3154
b Forestry and logging	853	...	1565	...	...	2652	975	...	2194	...	...	3448
c Fishing [a]	4	...	101	...	...	134	5	...	134	...	...	172
2 Mining and quarrying	134	...	128	...	...	264	160	...	213	...	...	381
a Coal mining	...	...	...	...	...	...	...	...	...	...	...	...
b Crude petroleum and natural gas production	...	...	...	...	...	...	...	...	...	...	...	...
c Metal ore mining	134	...	128	...	...	264	160	...	213	...	...	381
d Other mining		...		...	...			...		...	...	
3 Manufacturing	8890	...	3233	...	...	13870	10836	...	3982	...	...	17231
a Manufacture of food, beverages and tobacco	998	...	836	...	...	1946	1204	...	786	...	...	2154
b Textile, wearing apparel and leather industries	966	...	310	...	...	1388	1167	...	273	...	...	1568
c Manufacture of wood and wood products, including furniture	903	...	138	...	...	1194	1117	...	592	...	...	1951
d Manufacture of paper and paper products, printing and publishing	1635	...	455	...	...	2517	2026	...	657	...	...	3216
e Manufacture of chemicals and chemical petroleum, coal, rubber and plastic products	717	...	419	...	...	1555	865	...	531	...	...	1868
f Manufacture of non-metallic mineral products, except products of petroleum and coal	392	...	126	...	...	619	475	...	135	...	...	737
g Basic metal industries	328	...	235	...	...	650	393	...	227	...	...	951
h Manufacture of fabricated metal products, machinery and equipment	2861	...	691	...	...	3880	3484	...	759	...	...	4648
i Other manufacturing industries	90	...	23	...	...	121	105	...	22	...	...	138
4 Electricity, gas and water	446	...	370	...	...	1328	547	...	580	...	...	1610
a Electricity, gas and steam	446	...	370	...	...	1328	547	...	580	...	...	1610
b Water works and supply		...		...	...			...		...	...	
5 Construction	3934	...	739	...	...	4916	4808	...	1004	...	...	6130
6 Wholesale and retail trade, restaurants and hotels	4132	...	1097	...	...	5736	5066	...	1367	...	...	7058
a Wholesale and retail trade	3437	...	940	...	...	4838	4222	...	1200	...	...	5991
b Restaurants and hotels	695	...	157	...	...	898	844	...	167	...	...	1067
7 Transport, storage and communication	2332	...	811	...	...	4008	2823	...	865	...	...	4751
a Transport and storage	1653	...	887	...	...	3229	2012	...	928	...	...	3786
b Communication	679	...	-76	...	...	779	811	...	-63	...	...	965
8 Finance, insurance, real estate and business services	1652	...	3405	...	...	6610	2041	...	4240	...	...	8172
a Financial institutions	861	...	469	...	...	1441	1047	...	725	...	...	1920
b Insurance		...		...	...			...		...	...	
c Real estate and business services	791	...	2936	...	...	5169	994	...	3515	...	...	6252
Real estate, except dwellings	548	...	429	...	...	1079	709	...	533	...	...	1371
Dwellings	242	...	2507	...	...	4090	286	...	2982	...	...	4881
9 Community, social and personal services	975	...	544	...	...	1654	1195	...	632	...	...	1996
a Sanitary and similar services	61	...	27	...	...	91	77	...	48	...	...	129
b Social and related community services [b]	81	...	236	...	...	327	96	...	251	...	...	358
Educational services	22	...	11	...	...	37	28	...	15	...	...	48
Medical, dental, other health and veterinary services	59	...	225	...	...	290	68	...	236	...	...	310
c Recreational and cultural services [b]	253	...	119	...	...	400	310	...	142	...	...	491
d Personal and household services	581	...	162	...	...	836	712	...	191	...	...	1017

Finland

4.6 Cost Components of Value Added, ISIC Divisions
(Continued)

Million Finnish markkaa

	1972						1973					
	Compensation of Employees	Capital Consumption	Net Operating Surplus	Indirect Taxes	Less: Subsidies Received	Value Added	Compensation of Employees	Capital Consumption	Net Operating Surplus	Indirect Taxes	Less: Subsidies Received	Value Added
Total, Industries	23611	...	14190	...	...	44143	28777	...	17382	...	...	54103
Producers of Government Services	6175	...	...	...	...	6638	7373	...	...	...	...	7940
Other Producers	952	...	-102	...	...	1222	1394	...	-467	...	...	1370
Total	30738	7097	14088	278	196	52002	37544	8799	16915	335	180	63413
Imputed bank service charge	...	...	...	...	...	...	...	...	...	...	...	...
Import duties	...	...	...	...	...	...	...	...	...	...	...	...
Value added tax	...	...	...	...	...	...	...	...	...	...	...	...
Other adjustments	...	...	...	...	...	...	...	...	...	...	...	...

	1974						1975					
	Compensation of Employees	Capital Consumption	Net Operating Surplus	Indirect Taxes	Less: Subsidies Received	Value Added	Compensation of Employees	Capital Consumption	Net Operating Surplus	Indirect Taxes	Less: Subsidies Received	Value Added

All Producers

1 Agriculture, hunting, forestry and fishing	1574	...	5577	...	...	8317	1874	...	6721	...	...	9993
a Agriculture and hunting [a]	442	...	2213	...	...	3414	567	...	3595	...	...	5058
b Forestry and logging	1125	...	3181	...	...	4677	1298	...	2922	...	...	4678
c Fishing [a]	7	...	183	...	...	226	9	...	204	...	...	257
2 Mining and quarrying	206	...	271	...	...	488	257	...	95	...	...	364
a Coal mining	...	...	...	...	...	...	...	...	...	...	...	...
b Crude petroleum and natural gas production	...	...	...	...	...	...	...	...	...	...	...	...
c Metal ore mining	206	...	271	...	...	488	257	...	95	...	...	364
d Other mining												
3 Manufacturing	13767	...	6503	...	...	23738	16871	...	5361	...	...	25283
a Manufacture of food, beverages and tobacco	1471	...	848	...	...	2533	1806	...	1058	...	...	3229
b Textile, wearing apparel and leather industries	1431	...	444	...	...	2041	1731	...	381	...	...	2280
c Manufacture of wood and wood products, including furniture	1408	...	571	...	...	2312	1433	...	-183	...	...	1492
d Manufacture of paper and paper products, printing and publishing	2574	...	1600	...	...	5097	3196	...	950	...	...	4892
e Manufacture of chemicals and chemical petroleum, coal, rubber and plastic products	1086	...	1104	...	...	2862	1335	...	827	...	...	2715
f Manufacture of non-metallic mineral products, except products of petroleum and coal	616	...	205	...	...	996	731	...	179	...	...	1081
g Basic metal industries	504	...	257	...	...	1194	709	...	343	...	...	1231
h Manufacture of fabricated metal products, machinery and equipment	4552	...	1457	...	...	6548	5785	...	1771	...	...	8171
i Other manufacturing industries	125	...	17	...	...	155	145	...	37	...	...	192
4 Electricity, gas and water	697	...	669	...	...	2068	900	...	683	...	...	2625
a Electricity, gas and steam	697	...	669	...	...	2068	900	...	683	...	...	2625
b Water works and supply												
5 Construction	6075	...	1300	...	...	7782	7374	...	1482	...	...	9374
6 Wholesale and retail trade, restaurants and hotels	6367	...	1909	...	...	8908	8122	...	1824	...	...	10701
a Wholesale and retail trade	5279	...	1759	...	...	7597	6760	...	1666	...	...	9094
b Restaurants and hotels	1088	...	150	...	...	1311	1362	...	158	...	...	1607
7 Transport, storage and communication	3468	...	1034	...	...	5851	4279	...	982	...	...	6643
a Transport and storage	2448	...	1121	...	...	4662	2967	...	1123	...	...	5128
b Communication	1020	...	-87	...	...	1189	1312	...	-141	...	...	1515
8 Finance, insurance, real estate and business services	2713	...	5340	...	...	10487	3551	...	6034	...	...	12451
a Financial institutions	1404	...	1140	...	...	2686	1846	...	1136	...	...	3186
b Insurance												
c Real estate and business services	1309	...	4200	...	...	7801	1705	...	4898	...	...	9265
Real estate, except dwellings	964	...	690	...	...	1848	1271	...	871	...	...	2392

Finland

4.6 Cost Components of Value Added, ISIC Divisions
(Continued)

Million Finnish markkaa

	1974						1975					
	Compensation of Employees	Capital Consumption	Net Operating Surplus	Indirect Taxes	Less: Subsidies Received	Value Added	Compensation of Employees	Capital Consumption	Net Operating Surplus	Indirect Taxes	Less: Subsidies Received	Value Added
Dwellings	345	...	3510	...	...	5953	434	...	4027	...	...	6873
9 Community, social and personal services	1519	...	744	...	...	2463	1871	...	898	...	...	3003
a Sanitary and similar services	101	...	67	...	...	173	134	...	98	...	...	239
b Social and related community services [b]	122	...	293	...	...	429	158	...	364	...	...	541
Educational services	38	...	19	...	...	62	56	...	30	...	...	95
Medical, dental, other health and veterinary services	85	...	274	...	...	367	102	...	334	...	...	446
c Recreational and cultural services [b]	389	...	151	...	...	576	472	...	200	...	...	706
d Personal and household services	907	...	233	...	...	1285	1108	...	236	...	...	1516
Total, Industries	36386	...	23345	...	...	70103	45099	...	24081	...	...	80437
Producers of Government Services	9267	...	...	...	...	10020	12122	...	...	...	...	13027
Other Producers	1775	...	-671	...	...	1628	2047	...	-629	...	...	1835
Total	47428	11577	22674	386	313	81751	59267	12639	23452	451	509	95300
Imputed bank service charge	...	...	...	...	...	...	...	...	...	...	...	...
Import duties	...	...	...	...	...	...	...	...	...	...	...	...
Value added tax	...	...	...	...	...	...	...	...	...	...	...	...
Other adjustments	...	...	...	...	...	...	...	...	...	...	...	...

	1976						1977					
	Compensation of Employees	Capital Consumption	Net Operating Surplus	Indirect Taxes	Less: Subsidies Received	Value Added	Compensation of Employees	Capital Consumption	Net Operating Surplus	Indirect Taxes	Less: Subsidies Received	Value Added

All Producers

1 Agriculture, hunting, forestry and fishing	2115	...	6710	...	...	10491	2277	...	7063	...	...	11299
a Agriculture and hunting [a]	644	...	3733	...	...	5461	687	...	3645	...	...	5596
b Forestry and logging	1459	...	2730	...	...	4728	1578	...	3137	...	...	5359
c Fishing [a]	11	...	247	...	...	301	12	...	281	...	...	344
2 Mining and quarrying	327	...	118	...	...	458	364	...	123	...	...	499
a Coal mining	...	...	...	...	...	...	...	...	...	...	...	...
b Crude petroleum and natural gas production	...	...	...	...	...	...	...	...	...	...	...	...
c Metal ore mining	327	...	118	...	...	458	364	...	123	...	...	499
d Other mining		...		...	...			...		...	...	
3 Manufacturing	19857	...	5409	...	...	28527	21139	...	5929	...	...	30322
a Manufacture of food, beverages and tobacco	2159	...	1094	...	...	3722	2414	...	1451	...	...	4349
b Textile, wearing apparel and leather industries	1972	...	454	...	...	2606	1987	...	514	...	...	2671
c Manufacture of wood and wood products, including furniture	1811	...	1	...	...	2055	2006	...	308	...	...	2528
d Manufacture of paper and paper products, printing and publishing	3774	...	194	...	...	4627	4064	...	455	...	...	5104
e Manufacture of chemicals and chemical petroleum, coal, rubber and plastic products	1569	...	887	...	...	3012	1677	...	1195	...	...	3467
f Manufacture of non-metallic mineral products, except products of petroleum and coal	831	...	238	...	...	1228	858	...	345	...	...	1351
g Basic metal industries	857	...	71	...	...	1143	911	...	144	...	...	1251
h Manufacture of fabricated metal products, machinery and equipment	6707	...	2411	...	...	9689	7018	...	1447	...	...	9314
i Other manufacturing industries	177	...	59	...	...	245	204	...	70	...	...	288
4 Electricity, gas and water	1112	...	873	...	...	2872	1211	...	1452	...	...	3706
a Electricity, gas and steam	1112	...	873	...	...	2872	1211	...	1452	...	...	3706
b Water works and supply		...		...	...			...		...	...	

Finland

4.6 Cost Components of Value Added, ISIC Divisions
(Continued)

Million Finnish markkaa

	1976						1977					
	Compensation of Employees	Capital Consumption	Net Operating Surplus	Indirect Taxes	Less: Subsidies Received	Value Added	Compensation of Employees	Capital Consumption	Net Operating Surplus	Indirect Taxes	Less: Subsidies Received	Value Added
5 Construction	7162	...	1388	...	...	9092	7436	...	1488	...	...	9500
6 Wholesale and retail trade, restaurants and hotels	9515	...	1772	...	...	12085	10272	...	1558	...	...	12709
a Wholesale and retail trade	7943	...	1629	...	...	10276	8483	...	1503	...	...	10776
b Restaurants and hotels	1572	...	143	...	...	1809	1789	...	55	...	...	1933
7 Transport, storage and communication	5034	...	1528	...	...	8261	5404	...	1846	...	...	9310
a Transport and storage	3466	...	1416	...	...	6074	3720	...	1683	...	...	6777
b Communication	1568	...	112	...	...	2207	1684	...	163	...	...	2533
8 Finance, insurance, real estate and business services	4194	...	6773	...	...	14199	4752	...	7610	...	...	16133
a Financial institutions	2192	...	1277	...	...	3735	2514	...	1660	...	...	4508
b Insurance a		...		...	...			...		...	...	
c Real estate and business services	2002	...	5496	...	...	10464	2238	...	5950	...	...	11625
Real estate, except dwellings	1494	...	965	...	...	2731	1669	...	1079	...	...	3057
Dwellings	508	...	4531	...	...	7733	569	...	4871	...	...	8567
9 Community, social and personal services	2187	...	1095	...	...	3561	2326	...	1333	...	...	3978
a Sanitary and similar services	161	...	134	...	...	305	186	...	163	...	...	360
b Social and related community services b	180	...	422	...	...	621	199	...	453	...	...	673
Educational services	62	...	33	...	...	104	68	...	36	...	...	114
Medical, dental, other health and veterinary services	118	...	389	...	...	517	131	...	417	...	...	559
c Recreational and cultural services b	554	...	236	...	...	842	622	...	295	...	...	992
d Personal and household services	1292	...	303	...	...	1793	1319	...	422	...	...	1953
Total, Industries	51503	...	25666	...	...	89566	55181	...	28402	...	...	97458
Producers of Government Services	14778	...	...	...	...	15822	16456	...	...	...	...	17709
Other Producers	2240	...	-504	...	...	2028	2350	...	-452	...	...	2176
Total	68518	13835	25161	567	665	107416	73986	15583	27950	637	813	117342
Imputed bank service charge	...	...	...	...	...	...	...	...	...	...	...	...
Import duties	...	...	...	...	...	...	...	...	...	...	...	...
Value added tax	...	...	...	...	...	...	...	...	...	...	...	...
Other adjustments	...	...	...	...	...	...	...	...	...	...	...	...

	1978						1979					
	Compensation of Employees	Capital Consumption	Net Operating Surplus	Indirect Taxes	Less: Subsidies Received	Value Added	Compensation of Employees	Capital Consumption	Net Operating Surplus	Indirect Taxes	Less: Subsidies Received	Value Added
					All Producers							
1 Agriculture, hunting, forestry and fishing	2313	...	7151	...	...	11635	2659	...	8229	...	...	13289
a Agriculture and hunting a	757	...	3714	...	...	5888	876	...	3703	...	...	6146
b Forestry and logging	1543	...	3060	...	...	5299	1769	...	4108	...	...	6647
c Fishing a	13	...	377	...	...	448	14	...	418	...	...	496
2 Mining and quarrying	373	...	150	...	...	539	418	...	307	...	...	770
a Coal mining	...	...	...	...	...	...	...	...	...	...	...	...
b Crude petroleum and natural gas production	...	...	...	...	...	...	...	...	...	...	...	...
c Metal ore mining	373	...	150	...	...	539	418	...	307	...	...	770
d Other mining		...		...	...			...		...	...	

Finland

4.6 Cost Components of Value Added, ISIC Divisions
(Continued)

Million Finnish markkaa

	1978 Compensation of Employees	1978 Capital Consumption	1978 Net Operating Surplus	1978 Indirect Taxes	1978 Less: Subsidies Received	1978 Value Added	1979 Compensation of Employees	1979 Capital Consumption	1979 Net Operating Surplus	1979 Indirect Taxes	1979 Less: Subsidies Received	1979 Value Added
3 Manufacturing	21932	...	8510	...	...	34264	25436	...	10826	...	...	41418
a Manufacture of food, beverages and tobacco	2498	...	1391	...	...	4333	2852	...	1101	...	...	4481
b Textile, wearing apparel and leather industries	2032	...	536	...	...	2789	2385	...	667	...	...	3348
c Manufacture of wood and wood products, including furniture	2147	...	497	...	...	2893	2627	...	782	...	...	3849
d Manufacture of paper and paper products, printing and publishing	4269	...	1742	...	...	6698	4908	...	2670	...	...	8775
e Manufacture of chemicals and chemical petroleum, coal, rubber and plastic products	1774	...	1811	...	...	4258	2051	...	2394	...	...	5396
f Manufacture of non-metallic mineral products, except products of petroleum and coal	867	...	294	...	...	1344	981	...	555	...	...	1713
g Basic metal industries	946	...	486	...	...	1783	1076	...	707	...	...	2294
h Manufacture of fabricated metal products, machinery and equipment	7186	...	1661	...	...	9848	8332	...	1870	...	...	11227
i Other manufacturing industries	212	...	92	...	...	318	225	...	81	...	...	334
4 Electricity, gas and water	1307	...	1550	...	...	4108	1480	...	1976	...	...	4866
a Electricity, gas and steam	1307	...	1550	...	...	4108	1480	...	1976	...	...	4866
b Water works and supply	...	...	...	...	...	...	...	...	...	...	...	...
5 Construction	7461	...	1510	...	...	9588	8114	...	1625	...	...	10428
6 Wholesale and retail trade, restaurants and hotels	10717	...	2293	...	...	13967	12234	...	2841	...	...	16307
a Wholesale and retail trade	8792	...	2124	...	...	11772	10148	...	2481	...	...	13738
b Restaurants and hotels	1925	...	169	...	...	2195	2086	...	360	...	...	2569
7 Transport, storage and communication	5799	...	2070	...	...	10380	6687	...	2688	...	...	12323
a Transport and storage	4000	...	1812	...	...	7521	4650	...	2376	...	...	9154
b Communication	1799	...	258	...	...	2859	2037	...	312	...	...	3168
8 Finance, insurance, real estate and business services	5125	...	8424	...	...	17672	5861	...	9008	...	...	19519
a Financial institutions	2726	...	1676	...	...	4791	3090	...	1793	...	...	5312
b Insurance	...	...	...	...	...	...	...	...	...	...	...	...
c Real estate and business services	2399	...	6748	...	...	12881	2770	...	7215	...	...	14208
Real estate, except dwellings	1777	...	1252	...	...	3377	2084	...	1495	...	...	3991
Dwellings	622	...	5496	...	...	9504	686	...	5720	...	...	10217
9 Community, social and personal services	2459	...	1487	...	...	4316	2813	...	1794	...	...	5024
a Sanitary and similar services	200	...	184	...	...	395	243	...	226	...	...	483
b Social and related community services [b]	207	...	486	...	...	716	237	...	551	...	...	814
Educational services	69	...	42	...	...	122	83	...	58	...	...	154
Medical, dental, other health and veterinary services	138	...	444	...	...	594	154	...	493	...	...	660
c Recreational and cultural services [b]	697	...	334	...	...	1142	806	...	439	...	...	1367
d Personal and household services	1356	...	483	...	...	2063	1528	...	579	...	...	2360
Total, Industries	57487	...	33144	...	...	106468	65662	...	39293	...	...	123943
Producers of Government Services	17954	...	...	...	...	19351	20496	...	*	...	...	22072
Other Producers	2465	...	-618	...	...	2328	3011	...	-882	...	...	2638
Total	77906	17889	32525	804	977	128146	89169	21426	38411	865	1220	148652
Imputed bank service charge	...	...	...	...	...	...	...	...	...	...	...	...
Import duties	...	...	...	...	...	...	...	...	...	...	...	...
Value added tax	...	...	...	...	...	...	...	...	...	...	...	...
Other adjustments	...	...	...	...	...	...	...	...	...	...	...	...

Finland

4.6 Cost Components of Value Added, ISIC Divisions

Million Finnish markkaa

		1980				
		Compensation of Employees	Capital Consumption	Net Operating Surplus	Indirect Taxes	Less: Subsidies Received	Value Added

All Producers

		Comp.	Cap. Cons.	Net Op. Surplus	Ind. Taxes	Less: Subs.	Value Added
1	Agriculture, hunting, forestry and fishing	3046	...	9407	...	...	15193
	a Agriculture and hunting [a]	1001	...	4080	...	...	6863
	b Forestry and logging	2029	...	4874	...	...	7787
	c Fishing [a]	16	...	452	...	...	543
2	Mining and quarrying	469	...	321	...	...	841
	a Coal mining	...	...	...	...	...	...
	b Crude petroleum and natural gas production	...	...	...	...	...	...
	c Metal ore mining	469	...	321	...	...	841
	d Other mining						
3	Manufacturing	30388	...	11812	...	...	47886
	a Manufacture of food, beverages and tobacco	3350	...	1196	...	...	5140
	b Textile, wearing apparel and leather industries	2775	...	829	...	...	3926
	c Manufacture of wood and wood products, including furniture	3135	...	1276	...	...	4974
	d Manufacture of paper and paper products, printing and publishing	5778	...	3080	...	...	10148
	e Manufacture of chemicals and chemical petroleum, coal, rubber and plastic products	2475	...	2423	...	...	5883
	f Manufacture of non-metallic mineral products, except products of petroleum and coal	1168	...	609	...	...	1983
	g Basic metal industries	1269	...	567	...	...	2361
	h Manufacture of fabricated metal products, machinery and equipment	10184	...	1712	...	...	13062
	i Other manufacturing industries	255	...	120	...	...	409
4	Electricity, gas and water	1684	...	1997	...	...	5559
	a Electricity, gas and steam	1684	...	1997	...	...	5559
	b Water works and supply						
5	Construction	9068	...	2248	...	...	12102
6	Wholesale and retail trade, restaurants and hotels	14330	...	3377	...	...	19169
	a Wholesale and retail trade	11850	...	3028	...	...	16197
	b Restaurants and hotels	2480	...	349	...	...	2972
7	Transport, storage and communication	7501	...	2901	...	...	13557
	a Transport and storage	5286	...	2594	...	...	10141
	b Communication	2215	...	307	...	...	3417
8	Finance, insurance, real estate and business services	7062	...	10130	...	...	22593
	a Financial institutions	3670	...	2493	...	...	6613
	b Insurance						
	c Real estate and business services	3392	...	7636	...	...	15980
	Real estate, except dwellings	2604	...	1828	...	...	4932
	Dwellings	788	...	5808	...	...	11048
9	Community, social and personal services	3217	...	2067	...	...	5750
	a Sanitary and similar services	286	...	269	...	...	573
	b Social and related community services [b]	268	...	630	...	...	927
	Educational services	94	...	55	...	...	164
	Medical, dental, other health and veterinary services	174	...	575	...	...	763
	c Recreational and cultural services [b]	935	...	472	...	...	1545
	d Personal and household services	1728	...	696	...	...	2705

Finland

4.6 Cost Components of Value Added, ISIC Divisions
(Continued)

Million Finnish markkaa

	1980					
	Compensation of Employees	Capital Consumption	Net Operating Surplus	Indirect Taxes	Less: Subsidies Received	Value Added
Total, Industries	76765	...	44258	...	...	142649
Producers of Government Services	23276	...	.	...	...	25133
Other Producers	4104	...	-1588	...	...	3013
Total	104144	24533	42670	998	1551	170795
Imputed bank service charge	...	...	...	...	...	...
Import duties	...	...	...	...	...	...
Value added tax	...	...	...	...	...	...
Other adjustments	...	...	...	...	...	...

a) Hunting is included in item 'Fishing'.
b) ISIC groups 935 and 939 are included in item 'Recreational and cultural services'.

France

General note. The preparation of national accounts statistics in France is undertaken by the Institut national de la statistique et des etudes economiques, Paris. The official estimates are published annually in 'Rapport sur les comptes de la nation'. The following presentation of sources and methods is mainly based on a report prepared by the Statistical Office of the European Communities in 1976 entitled 'Basic statistics needed for the ESA accounts and tables: present situation and prospects for improvements' and on information contained in 'Presentation de la comptabilite nationale francaise'. The estimates are generally in accordance with the classifications and definitions recommended in the United Nations System of national accounts (SNA). 'Le Systeme elargi de comptabilite nationale' which is an adaptation by France of the European System of Integrated Economic Accounts (ESA) and closely resembles the present SNA, was introduced in 1976, and its concepts were described in 'Le Systeme elargi de comptabilite nationale-methodes'. Input-output tables have been published by the Institut national de la statistique et des etudes economiques. The following tables have been prepared from sucessive replies to the United Nations national accounts questionnaire. When the scope and coverage of the estimates differ for conceptual or statistical reasons from the definitions and classifications recommended in SNA, a footnote is indicated to the relevant tables.

Sources and methods:

(a) Gross domestic product. GDP is estimated mainly through the production approach.

(b) Expenditure on the gross domestic product. The expenditure approach is used to estimate government final consumption expenditure, gross fixed capital formation and exports and imports of goods and services. This approach, in combination with the commodity-flow approach is used to estimated private final consumption expenditure and increase in stocks. Government final consumption expenditure estimates referring to central government are based on budgetary accounts and on an accounting plan for enterprises. For local government, the centralized accounting scheme is used while for social security funds, an accounting plan is adopted for the general scheme and various sets of accounts are used for special schemes. Private consumption estimates are based on the annual input-output tables, results of expenditure surveys, estimates of fiscal revenues and statistics of retail sales derived from periodic surveys of large retail stores. Increase in stocks is estimated for producers, users and trade. For petroleum products and products of the iron and steel industry, the changes in quantity and value are available from specific sources. For other products, changes are valued on the basis of tax returns excluding stock assessment. Data for gross fixed capital formation in enterprises are available from the accounts of the large national enterprises, annual surveys, surveys of business cycles and income tax returns. Exports and imports of goods and services are estimated from customs returns and balance-of-payments statements. The constant price estimates of government consumption expenditure are obtained by using the implicit price index for producers of government services. For private consumption expenditure, estimates are obtained by extrapolation, use of quantum indexes, and price deflation. Price deflation is also used for the remaining expenditure items, except dwellings, for which the value of construction is extrapolated.

(c) Cost-structure of the gross domestic product. Wages and salaries of the private sector are calculated from various sources such as income and revenue statements of enterprises, quarterly surveys and statistics based on wage declarations of employees. Compensation of government employees is estimated from government accounts. Estimates of the income of enterprises are based on fiscal statistics of industrial and commercial profits and other sources. The enterprises are required to follow an accounting plan for taxation. The data from the plan are merged with information obtained from the annual survey of enterprises. Statistical information on agriculture is obtained from the Ministere de l'agriculture and on general government from an accounting plan, budgetary accounts and other sources. The depreciation estimates are based on information on the value of capital stock derived from various sources such as financial statements, sample surveys and accounts. Indirect taxes and subsidies are estimated on the basis of government accounts.

(d) Gross domestic product by kind of economic activity. The table of GDP by kind of economic activity is prepared at market prices. The production approach is used to estimate the value added of almost all industries. This is done within the framework of annual input-output tables, using the commodity-flow approach. For the agricultural sector, the Ministere de l'agriculture provides all output figures for quantities and prices while figures on intermediate consumption are derived indirectly from the suppliers of products used. Bench-mark information is derived from censuses and surveys held in 1955, 1963/64, 1970 and 1975. Agricultural output estimated on the basis of the total area of land used and yield per hectare for the different crops. For livestock, a survey on the structure of bovine herds is undertaken every 12-18 months supplemented every 3 or 4 years by a detailed survey. For the industrial activity and construction sector, the main sources of information consist of the branch surveys carried out by the employers' associations and the annual surveys of enterprises. The branch surveys record annual or quarterly output or sales in values and/or quantities, producers' stocks in terms of physical quantity and productive capital and intermediate consumption. The annual survey of enterprises covers all large enterprises and a representative sample of small enterprises. Gross fixed capital formation is broken down into transport equipment, building and construction, tools, land and buildings, etc. For government construction, information is obtained by analysing tax records. For the trade sector, bench-mark information is provided by the 1967 census of distribution and services. Annual fiscal information on turnover is provided by the tax authorities. Trade margins and distribution channels are based on estimates provided by professional organizations. The estimates for restaurants and hotels are mainly based on tax statistics. For the transport sector, the transport surveys and the accounts of nationalized enterprises or the structural surveys are used for the estimation of gross output and intermediate consumption, respectively. For the financial sector and insurance, information is obtained from sources such as the Banque de France, the accounting plans, the Direction des assurances du Ministere de l'economie and annual surveys. The value added of real estate is estimated on the basis of fiscal statistics and special surveys. For government services an accounting plan and the budgetary accounts are the main sources. The value of services by non-profit institutions are based on a detailed study conducted by the Centre de recherche et de documentation sur la consommation for 1971 and extrapolated for other years by growth rates. For other community and social services, estimates are classified by type of producer. Remuneration of domestic services is obtained by multiplying the number of persons on the work force by the wage-rates and adding social assessments. Constant price estimates of all industrial sectors are obtained by using double deflation and the commodity-flow method based on annual input-output tables. The estimates are calculated at the previous years's prices, the current value series being deflated by price indexes or extrapolated by a volume index using the preceding year as a base. The constant-price estimates are subsequently converted to the base year by a process of chaining.

1.1 Expenditure on the Gross Domestic Product, in Current Prices

Million French francs

		1970	1971	1972	1973	1974	1975	1976	1977	1978	1979	1980
1	General government final consumption expenditure	105138	117326	129094	146713	173905	209142	245023	277711	320331	362291	421134
2	Private final consumption expenditure	469338	527872	592243	668980	781334	898751	1041901	1171464	1326746	1516561	1745141
	a Households	467231	525499	589580	665934	777851	894798	1037398	1166384	1321046	1510166	1737742
	b Private non-profit institutions serving households	2107	2373	2663	3046	3483	3953	4503	5080	5700	6395	7399
3	Gross capital formation	204098	218701	250427	291859	341438	334249	410401	440714	472228	558355	635476
	a Increase in stocks	21057	12772	18379	26878	30536	-3640	19730	20815	13282	37184	41679
	b Gross fixed capital formation	183041	205929	232048	264981	310902	337889	390671	419899	458946	521171	593797
	Residential buildings	52409	59437	67316	79610	97741	105666	117931	125457	135139	155188	173199
	Non-residential buildings	55480	59674	67246	74250	86426	98190	110963	116351	124891	138774	160608
	Other construction and land improvement etc.											
	Other	75152	86818	97486	111121	126735	134033	161777	178091	198916	227209	259990
4	Exports of goods and services	127894	148812	169140	203222	275084	283851	338244	401900	455881	534569	617530
5	Less: Imports of goods and services	123908	140278	159789	196574	293459	273674	357596	407204	434440	532372	664391
	Equals: Gross Domestic Product	782560	872433	981115	1114200	1278302	1452319	1677973	1884585	2140746	2439404	2754890

France

1.2 Expenditure on the Gross Domestic Product, in Constant Prices

Million French francs

	1970	1971	1972	1973	1974	1975	1976	1977	1978	1979	1980
					At constant prices of: 1970						
1 General government final consumption expenditure	105138	108777	111669	115234	116560	122071	129658	131492	137130	139422	142988
2 Private final consumption expenditure	469338	500344	530732	561288	577625	597229	630678	650494	678314	702732	717074
a Households	467231	498118	528460	558865	575167	594752	628027	647785	675457	699935	714242
b Private non-profit institutions serving households	2107	2226	2272	2423	2458	2477	2651	2709	2857	2797	2832
3 Gross capital formation	204098	208998	227638	245193	248023	215098	238721	234452	234155	253792	259910
a Increase in stocks	21057	12943	17403	22069	22820	-2876	12606	10144	7054	18314	19690
b Gross fixed capital formation	183041	196055	210235	223124	225203	217974	226115	224308	227101	235478	240220
Residential buildings	52409	56864	60685	64872	67986	66465	65382	63505	62237	64870	62481
Non-residential buildings	55480	55959	59395	59177	59086	59433	60016	57854	56878	56496	57181
Other construction and land improvement etc.											
Other	75152	83232	90155	99075	98131	92076	100717	102949	107986	114112	120558
4 Exports of goods and services	127894	141976	160320	179297	197871	194994	215591	234937	251695	267736	276985
5 Less: Imports of goods and services	123908	135215	156809	180586	189903	177446	213481	219635	231324	256700	277172
Equals: Gross Domestic Product	782560	824880	873550	920426	950176	951946	1001167	1031740	1069970	1106982	1119785

1.3 Cost Components of the Gross Domestic Product

Million French francs

	1970	1971	1972	1973	1974	1975	1976	1977	1978	1979	1980
1 Indirect taxes, net	103659	114057	128647	142670	159699	176123	207759	219843	259485	309984	352970
a Indirect taxes paid	119091	131256	148163	167621	187056	211619	252715	271771	316064	373796	422020
b Less: Subsidies received	15432	17199	19516	24951	27357	35496	44956	51928	56579	63812	69050
2 Consumption of fixed capital	80565	83171	93291	106490	132198	157633	197862	211579	240005	271558	314243
3 Compensation of employees paid by resident producers to:	382291	432107	483793	558116	665700	783732	909686	1036356	1174000	1325341	1523282
a Resident households	381120	430911	482002	556247	663264	780723	905872	1032044	1167967	1317220	1514818
b Rest of the world	1171	1196	1791	1869	2436	3009	3814	4312	6033	8121	8464
4 Net operating surplus	216045	243098	275384	306924	320705	334831	362666	416807	467256	532521	564395
a Corporate and quasi-corporate enterprises	58678	65350	75731	84504	82418	69973	65144	88401	97974	118624	108660
b Private unincorporated enterprises [a]	158101	177579	199254	222418	239141	264845	295655	327545	367974	412888	455776
c General government	-734	169	399	2	-854	13	1867	861	1308	1009	-41
Equals: Gross Domestic Product	782560	872433	981115	1114200	1278302	1452319	1677973	1884585	2140746	2439404	2754890

a) Including households.

1.4 General Government Current Receipts and Disbursements

Million French francs

	1970	1971	1972	1973	1974	1975	1976	1977	1978	1979	1980
					Receipts						
1 Property and entrepreneurial income	7390	8995	9172	11066	14401	15775	17650	19988	21354	23154	23055
2 Taxes, fees and contributions	277581	304272	343573	393986	459824	533260	650064	730031	826907	979397	1150632
a Indirect taxes [a]	119046	129845	146031	165066	183871	203813	243347	260689	299942	355454	404177
b Direct taxes	56138	58078	66205	77739	94670	105157	138048	154993	167865	192452	235967
c Social security contributions	100926	114662	129601	149223	179340	221950	265826	311301	355917	427885	505007
d Compulsory fees, fines and penalties	1471	1687	1736	1958	1943	2340	2843	3048	3183	3606	5481
3 Other current receipts	20036	20666	22453	25024	29674	36150	45644	48852	57028	62434	77578
Total Current Receipts of General Government [b]	305007	333933	375198	430076	503899	585185	713358	798871	905289	1064985	1251265
					Disbursements						
1 General government final consumption expenditure	105138	117326	129094	146713	173905	209142	245023	277711	320331	362291	421134
a Compensation of employees	71941	81016	90247	102691	122340	147681	173784	200016	230618	258231	298050
b Consumption of fixed capital	5308	5935	6633	7519	9446	11615	13960	16226	18751	22202	26948
c Purchases of goods and services, net	26457	28697	30343	34377	39578	46571	53374	56827	65844	76004	89625
d Less: Own account production of fixed assets	...	...	...	...	...	...	...	...	...	...	...
e Indirect taxes paid, net	1432	1678	1871	2126	2541	3275	3905	4642	5118	5854	6511
2 Property income paid	8946	9111	8667	9387	12053	18588	20829	25502	30926	37621	45385

France

1.4 General Government Current Receipts and Disbursements
(Continued)

Million French francs

	1970	1971	1972	1973	1974	1975	1976	1977	1978	1979	1980
a Interest	8944	9109	8664	9382	12045	18579	20819	25488	30904	37598	45358
b Net land rent and royalties	2	2	3	5	8	9	10	14	22	23	27
3 Subsidies [a]	15407	13580	14650	18285	22981	28685	35806	41037	43230	49046	52416
4 Other current transfers paid	142023	159623	183344	213148	249527	313037	364766	424004	504901	580658	667897
a Social security benefits and social assistance grants	118891	133298	152162	176360	209818	268426	313849	330521	434467	503192	580789
b Other	23132	26325	31182	36788	39709	44611	50917	93483	70434	77466	87108
5 Net saving	33493	34293	39443	42543	45433	15733	46934	30617	5901	35369	64433
Total Current Disbursements and Net Saving of General Government [b]	305007	333933	375198	430076	503899	585185	713358	798871	905289	1064985	1251265

[a] Indirect taxes paid to and subsidies received from supranational organizations are not included in the receipts and disbursements respectively of the general government. [b] Data for this table have not been revised, therefore, data for some years are not comparable with those of other tables.

1.5 Current Income and Outlay of Corporate and Quasi-Corporate Enterprises, Summary

Million French francs

	1970	1971	1972	1973	1974	1975	1976	1977	1978	1979	1980
Receipts											
1 Net operating surplus	58678	65350	75731	84504	82418	69973	65144	88401	97974	118624	108660
2 Other property and entrepreneurial income received	69162	76701	86029	121890	178339	181229	211626	255788	295553	363419	466930
3 Current transfers received	26503	31128	37176	42657	47682	59228	68486	76823	90421	108133	126036
Total Current Receipts	154343	173179	198936	249051	308439	310430	345256	421012	483948	590176	701626
Disbursements											
1 Property and entrepreneurial income paid	83749	94778	108186	145739	209395	213322	241988	285850	325068	392863	488481
2 Direct taxes and other current payments to general government	18459	18618	20952	25472	37464	30926	41236	44288	43019	51132	68173
3 Other current transfers paid	31397	36709	41917	47653	55471	68879	77662	84589	96999	114280	134687
4 Net saving	20738	23074	27881	30187	6109	-2697	-15630	6285	18862	31901	10285
Total Current Disbursements and Net Saving	154343	173179	198936	249051	308439	310430	345256	421012	483948	590176	701626

1.6 Current Income and Outlay of Households and Non-Profit Institutions

Million French francs

	1970	1971	1972	1973	1974	1975	1976	1977	1978	1979	1980
Receipts											
1 Compensation of employees	381801	431750	482884	557271	664687	782384	907859	1034563	1170841	1320685	1518852
a From resident producers	381120	430911	482002	556247	663264	780723	905872	1032044	1167967	1317220	1514818
b From rest of the world	681	839	882	1024	1423	1661	1987	2519	2874	3465	4034
2 Property and entrepreneurial income received	191180	216083	243394	271748	289181	314620	350387	423717	475740	536479	601085
3 Current transfers received	159805	180150	204247	235432	296521	380665	442427	476348	563691	649602	747177
a Social security benefits and social assistance grants received	118366	132617	151478	175449	208828	267522	312752	364061	432970	501599	578416
b Other	41439	47533	52769	59983	87693	113143	129675	112287	130721	148003	168761
Total Current Receipts [a]	732786	827983	930525	1064451	1250389	1477669	1700673	1934628	2210272	2506766	2867114
Disbursements											
1 Private final consumption expenditure	469338	527872	592243	668980	781334	898751	1041901	1171464	1326746	1516561	1745141
2 Property income paid	12839	14583	17166	23285	23292	35340	42042	50207	54662	62318	79643
3 Direct taxes and other payments n.e.c. to general government	160430	178584	202254	232801	273440	340181	414195	480917	548779	643439	757882
a Social security contributions	121791	138007	155858	179468	215095	264584	315822	368612	422325	500273	588200
b Direct taxes	38639	40577	46396	53333	58345	75597	98373	112305	126454	143166	169682
c Fees, fines and penalties	...	...	...	...	...	...	...	...	...	...	...
4 Other current transfers paid	20171	23770	24530	28430	43486	40230	46344	52933	59362	66752	75113
5 Net saving	70008	83174	94332	110955	128837	163167	156191	179107	220723	217696	209329
Total Current Disbursements and Net Saving [a]	732786	827983	930525	1064451	1250389	1477669	1700673	1934628	2210272	2506766	2867114

[a] Data for this table have not been revised, therefore, data for some years are not comparable with those of other tables.

France

1.7 External Transactions on Current Account, Summary

Million French francs

		1970	1971	1972	1973	1974	1975	1976	1977	1978	1979	1980
		\multicolumn{11}{c}{Payments to the Rest of the World}
1	Imports of goods and services	123908	140278	159789	196574	293459	273674	357596	407204	434440	532372	664391
2	Factor income paid to the rest of the world	8962	9533	11263	15215	23645	24698	29007	32831	41914	58931	84551
	a Compensation of employees	1171	1196	1791	1869	2436	3009	3814	4312	6033	8121	8464
	b Property and entrepreneurial income paid	7791	8337	9472	13346	21209	21689	25193	28519	35881	50810	76087
3	Indirect taxes paid to supranational organizations	30	1398	2109	2532	3136	7763	9304	11024	16060	18342	17843
4	Current transfers to the rest of the world	14727	17841	19047	22732	25976	27972	26846	32129	35182	39075	46160
5	Surplus of the nation on current transactions	706	5011	4520	-1684	-28861	-413	-25044	-13126	13263	-1831	-37186
	Payments to the Rest of the World and Surplus of the Nation on Current Transactions	148333	174061	196728	235369	317355	333694	397709	470062	540859	646889	775759
		\multicolumn{11}{c}{Receipts From The Rest of the World}
1	Exports of goods and services	127894	148812	169140	203222	275084	283851	338244	401900	455881	534569	617530
2	Factor income received from rest of the world	13303	14735	15277	18243	28577	28570	35272	40566	51504	70628	101947
	a Compensation of employees	681	839	882	1024	1423	1661	1987	2519	2874	3465	4034
	b Property and entrepreneurial income received	12622	13896	14395	17219	27154	26909	33285	38047	48630	67163	97913
3	Subsidies received from supranational organisations	10	3606	4843	6643	4327	6768	9086	10833	13287	14766	16634
4	Current transfers from rest of the world	7126	6908	7468	7261	9367	14505	15107	16763	20187	26926	39648
	Receipts from the Rest of the World on Current Transactions	148333	174061	196728	235369	317355	333694	397709	470062	540859	646889	775759

1.8 Capital Transactions of The Nation, Summary

Million French francs

	1970	1971	1972	1973	1974	1975	1976	1977	1978	1979	1980
\multicolumn{12}{c}{Finance of Gross Capital Formation}
Gross saving	204804	223712	254947	290175	312577	333836	385357	427588	485491	556524	598290
1 Consumption of fixed capital	80565	83171	93291	106490	132198	157633	197862	211579	240005	271558	314243
a General government	6719	7017	7877	8990	11294	13858	16751	19318	22235	26276	31828
b Corporate and quasi-corporate enterprises	49108	52488	59174	67443	84043	100820	131352	136336	155246	174928	202265
c Other	24738	23666	26240	30057	36861	42955	49759	55925	62524	70354	80150
2 Net saving	130325	140541	161656	183685	180379	176203	187495	216009	245486	284966	284047
a General government	33959	34293	39443	42543	45433	15733	46934	30617	5901	35369	64433
b Corporate and quasi-corporate enterprises	23045	23074	27881	30187	6109	-2697	-15630	6285	18862	31901	10285
c Other	73321	83174	94332	110955	128837	163167	156191	179107	220723	217696	209329
Less: Surplus of the nation on current transactions	706	5011	4520	-1684	-28861	-413	-25044	-13126	13263	-1831	-37186
Finance of Gross Capital Formation	204098	218701	250427	291859	341438	334249	410401	440714	472228	558355	635476
\multicolumn{12}{c}{Gross Capital Formation}
Increase in stocks	21057	12772	18379	26878	30536	-3640	19730	20815	13282	37184	41679
Gross fixed capital formation	183041	205929	232048	264981	310902	337889	390671	419899	458946	521171	593797
1 General government	28208	29984	31881	35644	42028	51761	56985	57842	60530	68308	79003
2 Corporate and quasi-corporate enterprises	91949	101818	115728	130648	150210	159773	189677	209274	230192	258073	300733
3 Other	62884	74127	84439	98689	118664	126355	144009	152783	168224	194790	214061
Gross Capital Formation	204098	218701	250427	291859	341438	334249	410401	440714	472228	558355	635476

1.9 Gross Domestic Product by Institutional Sectors of Origin

Million French francs

		1970	1971	1972	1973	1974	1975	1976	1977	1978	1979	1980
		\multicolumn{11}{c}{Domestic Factor Incomes Originating}
1	General government	74692	85164	95050	107842	127604	154886	184044	210125	242655	271083	311497
2	Corporate and quasi-corporate enterprises	322127	365205	412902	478086	553930	623571	708612	820963	925618	1055009	1183839
	a Non-financial	320488	364505	410174	473801	549958	620562	704191	817141	921786	1050801	1180191
	b Financial	1639	700	2728	4285	3972	3009	4421	3822	3832	4208	3648

France

1.9 Gross Domestic Product by Institutional Sectors of Origin
(Continued)

Million French francs

	1970	1971	1972	1973	1974	1975	1976	1977	1978	1979	1980
3 Households and private unincorporated enterprises	199456	222515	248621	276135	301478	336284	375325	417175	467544	525725	585411
4 Non-profit institutions serving households	2061	2321	2604	2977	3393	3822	4371	4900	5439	6045	6930
Subtotal: Domestic Factor Incomes	598336	675205	759177	865040	986405	1118563	1272352	1453163	1641256	1857862	2087677
Indirect taxes paid, net	103659	114057	128647	142670	159699	176123	207759	219843	259485	309984	352970
Consumption of fixed capital	80565	83171	93291	106490	132198	157633	197862	211579	240005	271558	314243
Gross Domestic Product	782560	872433	981115	1114200	1278302	1452319	1677973	1884585	2140746	2439404	2754890

1.10 Gross Domestic Product by Kind of Activity, in Current Prices

Million French francs

	1970	1971	1972	1973	1974	1975	1976	1977	1978	1979	1980
1 Agriculture, hunting, forestry and fishing	50542	53185	63352	74853	72903	73247	80558	88647	99997	114033	114383
2 Mining and quarrying	6652	7234	7450	7733	10288	12334	13061	14969	15945	17614	21896
3 Manufacturing	224957	249073	276959	315717	356777	397391	459366	517370	581413	661382	722545
4 Electricity, gas and water	13603	15016	17329	19842	21148	26097	29104	34501	39972	46254	58203
5 Construction	58315	64016	72831	80687	93757	110558	123583	136325	146165	160936	182935
6 Wholesale and retail trade, restaurants and hotels	98300	112673	122933	138742	167687	186761	204185	233503	260515	290523	331591
7 Transport, storage and communication	42766	47984	52297	59449	66100	75722	89656	100851	117690	135212	152573
8 Finance, insurance, real estate and business services	105033	118768	135042	161849	192170	214153	248639	289688	332521	386464	457603
9 Community, social and personal services	46284	52186	60620	69910	80877	100577	119799	136156	162344	188148	217834
Total, Industries	646452	720135	808813	928782	1061707	1196840	1367951	1552010	1756562	2000566	2259563
Producers of Government Services	78681	88629	98751	112336	134327	162560	191536	220797	253800	285390	351761
Other Producers	5944	6538	7205	8070	9585	11260	12971	14429	16582	18646	
Subtotal	731077	815302	914769	1049188	1205619	1370660	1572458	1787236	2026944	2304602	2611324
Less: Imputed bank service charge	21848	24838	26314	33377	44918	46755	52990	62518	71487	84321	107600
Plus: Import duties a	73331	81969	92660	98389	117601	128414	158505	159867	185289	219123	251166
Plus: Value added tax	...	...	...	...	...	...	...	...	...	...	...
Equals: Gross Domestic Product	782560	872433	981115	1114200	1278302	1452319	1677973	1884585	2140746	2439404	2754890

a) Including also value added tax.

1.11 Gross Domestic Product by Kind of Activity, in Constant Prices

Million French francs

	1970	1971	1972	1973	1974	1975	1976	1977	1978	1979	1980
	At constant prices of: 1970										
1 Agriculture, hunting, forestry and fishing	50542	51418	51669	54546	54419	50474	48458	48584	51576	56054	56279
2 Mining and quarrying	6652	6183	6055	6001	5891	5542	5614	5569	5452	5351	4899
3 Manufacturing	224957	239399	254473	272204	280963	275188	294607	305574	313928	323807	320033
4 Electricity, gas and water	13603	14474	15852	17675	18879	19714	20886	22693	24091	24976	26083
5 Construction	58315	59922	63092	61756	64077	65277	63370	62632	59895	59132	58605
6 Wholesale and retail trade, restaurants and hotels	98300	105487	110167	114700	118361	117417	124356	126387	131396	134912	136107
7 Transport, storage and communication	42766	44740	48664	51821	53076	52952	56853	59673	63925	68072	70440
8 Finance, insurance, real estate and business services	105033	111268	118631	129671	139693	140862	147518	156076	163873	171427	181094
9 Community, social and personal services	46284	48732	52994	56431	59765	63331	67428	70109	74678	79019	81996
Total, Industries	646452	681623	721597	764805	795124	790757	829090	857297	888814	922750	935536
Producers of Government Services	78681	81745	84433	86030	87133	89163	94587	96697	99650	100525	109074
Other Producers	5944	5967	6002	6037	5995	5907	6065	5867	6044	6097	
Subtotal	731077	769335	812032	856872	888252	885827	929742	959861	994508	1029372	1044610
Less: Imputed bank service charge	21848	22398	22701	26327	30592	27896	28283	30098	31161	32700	36851
Plus: Import duties a	73331	77943	84219	89881	92516	94015	99708	101977	106623	110310	112026
Plus: Value added tax	...	...	...	...	...	...	...	...	...	...	...
Equals: Gross Domestic Product	782560	824880	873550	920426	950176	951946	1001167	1031740	1069970	1106982	1119785

a) Including also value added tax.

France

1.12 Relations Among National Accounting Aggregates

Million French francs

	1970	1971	1972	1973	1974	1975	1976	1977	1978	1979	1980
Gross Domestic Product	782560	872433	981115	1114200	1278302	1452319	1677973	1884585	2140746	2439404	2754890
Plus: Net factor income received from abroad	4341	5202	4014	3028	4932	3872	6265	7735	9590	11697	17396
Factor income received	13303	14735	15277	18243	28577	28570	35272	40566	51504	70628	101947
Less: Factor income paid	8962	9533	11263	15215	23645	24698	29007	32831	41914	58931	84551
Equals: Gross National Product	786901	877635	985129	1117228	1283234	1456191	1684238	1892320	2150336	2451101	2772286
Less: Consumption of fixed capital	74479	83171	93291	106490	132198	157633	197862	211579	240005	271558	314243
Less: Net indirect taxes paid to supranational organisations	20	-2208	-2734	-4111	-1191	995	218	191	2773	3576	1209
Indirect taxes paid	30	1398	2109	2532	3136	7763	9304	11024	16060	18342	17843
Less: Subsidies received	10	3606	4843	6643	4327	6768	9086	10833	13287	14766	16634
Equals: National Income at Market Prices	712402	796672	894572	1014849	1152227	1297563	1486158	1680550	1907558	2175967	2456834
Plus: Net current transfers received from abroad [a]	-7601	-10933	-11579	-15471	-16609	-13467	-11739	-15366	-14995	-12149	-6512
Current transfers received	7126	6908	7468	7261	9367	14505	15107	16763	20187	26926	39648
Less: Current transfers paid	14727	17841	19047	22732	25976	27972	26846	32129	35182	39075	46160
Equals: National Disposable Income at Market Prices	704801	785739	882993	999378	1135618	1284096	1474419	1665184	1892563	2163818	2450322
Less: Final consumption	574476	645198	721337	815693	955239	1107893	1286924	1449175	1647077	1878852	2166275
Equals: Net Saving	130325	140541	161656	183685	180379	176203	187495	216009	245486	284966	284047
Less: Surplus of the nation on current transactions	706	5011	4520	-1684	-28861	-413	-25044	-13126	13263	-1831	-37186
Equals: Net Capital Formation	129619	135530	157136	185369	209240	176616	212539	229135	232223	286797	321233

a) Including also insurance against damages received from the rest of the world, net.

2.5 Private Final Consumption Expenditure by Type, in Current Prices

Million French francs

	1970	1971	1972	1973	1974	1975	1976	1977	1978	1979	1980
Final Consumption Expenditure of Resident Households											
1 Food, beverages and tobacco	127042	136949	151339	168224	191495	216302	243643	274754	303455	336810	376381
a Food	103037	111366	123512	136420	157189	178634	201663	229275	253502	280090	313558
b Non-alcoholic beverages	2568	3011	3353	3800	4039	4639	5501	5528	6099	7153	8106
c Alcoholic beverages	14420	15444	16788	19361	20939	23024	25505	27567	30321	33946	36688
d Tobacco	7017	7128	7686	8643	9328	10005	10974	12384	13533	15621	18029
2 Clothing and footwear [a]	40278	44810	49676	54076	61625	70637	77905	84733	93904	104287	114217
3 Gross rent, fuel and power	68221	77234	86544	99721	118509	135246	159110	181105	207069	241725	293029
4 Furniture, furnishings and household equipment and operation	46740	54073	60971	69158	84508	93645	106476	116958	130400	147486	166480
a Household operation	13196	14603	16236	17666	21634	24434	27458	30337	33595	37637	44282
b Other	33544	39470	44735	51492	62874	69211	79018	86621	96805	109849	122198
5 Medical care and health expenses	46159	52867	60306	69448	82000	101984	119711	135023	160573	186841	218568
6 Transport and communication	54494	62755	72061	81103	92885	108107	133543	148726	174671	203868	234844
a Personal transport equipment	12780	15697	19283	22137	21121	25301	37144	37011	45369	52768	55366
b Other	41714	47058	52778	58966	71764	82806	96399	111715	129302	151100	179478
7 Recreational, entertainment, education and cultural services	28818	32899	37596	42571	51148	58621	67188	76882	88630	100011	113935
a Education	1392	1577	1869	2057	2371	2882	2709	3262	3837	4479	5320
b Other	27426	31322	35727	40514	48777	55739	64479	73620	84793	95532	108615
8 Miscellaneous goods and services	57338	64417	72268	81890	96199	110469	129593	148127	169279	195869	229225
a Personal care [a]	15928	18290	20275	23046	28305	32110	37341	42133	48376	56591	66776
b Expenditures in restaurants, cafes and hotels	32290	35515	39169	43664	50860	58547	68877	80327	91416	104379	120889
c Other	9120	10612	12824	15180	17034	19812	23375	25667	29487	34899	41560
Statistical discrepancy	2107	2373	2663	3046	3483	3953	4503	5080	5700	6395	7399
Total Final Consumption Expenditure in the Domestic Market by Households, of which	471197	528377	593424	669237	781852	898964	1041672	1171388	1333681	1523292	1754078
a Durable goods	46280	55055	64348	75292	87426	100182	123600	133280	155407	178702	198436
b Semi-durable goods	79460	89726	99568	109718	128631	146576	165462	180798	202803	228096	256550
c Non-durable goods	185056	203182	225792	252098	296713	335329	379849	428421	481106	542323	627113

France

2.5 Private Final Consumption Expenditure by Type, in Current Prices
(Continued)

Million French francs

	1970	1971	1972	1973	1974	1975	1976	1977	1978	1979	1980
d Services	160401	180414	203716	232129	269082	316877	372761	428889	494365	574171	671979
Plus: Direct purchases abroad by resident households	6323	8855	9295	11077	12679	14509	17716	22537	21431	24597	27811
Less: Direct purchases in the domestic market by non-resident households	8182	9360	10476	11334	13197	14722	17487	22461	28366	31328	36748
Equals: Final Consumption Expenditure of Resident Households [b]	469338	527872	592243	668980	781334	898751	1041901	1171464	1326746	1516561	1745141

Final Consumption Expenditure of Private Non-profit Institutions Serving Households

| Equals: Final Consumption Expenditure of Private Non-profit Organisations Serving Households | ... | ... | ... | ... | ... | ... | ... | ... | ... | ... | ... |
| Private Final Consumption Expenditure | 469338 | 527872 | 592243 | 668980 | 781334 | 898751 | 1041901 | 1171464 | 1326746 | 1516561 | 1745141 |

a) Personal effects are included in item 'Clothing and footwear'.
b) Including consumption expenditure of private non-profit institutions.

2.6 Private Final Consumption Expenditure by Type, in Constant Prices

Million French francs

	1970	1971	1972	1973	1974	1975	1976	1977	1978	1979	1980

At constant prices of: 1970

Final Consumption Expenditure of Resident Households

1 Food, beverages and tobacco	127042	130225	133740	136760	139580	142227	145063	146499	149436	152533	155318
a Food	103037	105351	108216	110757	113117	114900	116933	118353	121526	123908	126610
b Non-alcoholic beverages	2568	2867	3060	3305	3220	3289	3602	3351	3388	3508	3476
c Alcoholic beverages	14420	14918	15258	15182	15163	15465	15847	15680	15425	15492	15366
d Tobacco	7017	7089	7206	7516	8080	8573	8681	9115	9097	9625	9866
2 Clothing and footwear [a]	40278	42973	45307	45678	45864	46527	47117	47334	48234	48148	47235
3 Gross rent, fuel and power	68221	72225	76424	82181	85289	88450	93979	98628	104286	108897	112937
4 Furniture, furnishings and household equipment and operation	46740	51622	55802	60423	64049	63092	67232	68790	70550	72246	72244
a Household operation	13196	13636	14319	14633	15224	14989	15401	15719	15963	16021	16351
b Other	33544	37986	41483	45790	48825	48103	51831	53071	54587	56225	55893
5 Medical care and health expenses	46159	50509	54723	59815	64045	70386	74448	78047	84934	90978	96173
6 Transport and communication	54494	58768	64751	69552	66686	69259	76789	77860	83572	87161	87941
a Personal transport equipment	12780	14469	16725	18209	15554	15466	20067	18746	21269	22248	20723
b Other	41714	44299	48026	51343	51132	53793	56722	59114	62303	64913	67218
7 Recreational, entertainment, education and cultural services	28818	31075	33439	36018	38991	40496	43717	47012	50274	52416	54474
a Education	1392	1507	1684	1732	1799	1867	1546	1672	1794	1903	1987
b Other	27426	29568	31755	34286	37192	38629	42171	45340	48480	50513	52487
8 Miscellaneous goods and services	57338	61103	64672	67950	71800	74405	79338	83418	87011	89949	90973
a Personal care [a]	15928	17578	18655	19516	20987	21207	22983	24382	25042	25311	23815
b Expenditures in restaurants, cafes and hotels	32290	33347	34066	34611	35673	36366	37900	39625	40910	41858	42400
c Other	9120	10178	11951	13823	15140	16832	18455	19411	21059	22780	24758
Statistical discrepancy	2107	2226	2272	2423	2458	2477	2651	2709	2857	2797	2832
Total Final Consumption Expenditure in the Domestic Market by Households, of which	471197	500726	531130	560800	578762	597319	630334	650297	681154	705125	720127
Plus: Direct purchases abroad by resident households	6323	8490	8981	9988	8631	9692	10929	12668	11647	12111	12039
Less: Direct purchases in the domestic market by non-resident households	8182	8872	9379	9500	9768	9782	10585	12471	14487	14504	15092
Equals: Final Consumption Expenditure of Resident Households [b]	469338	500344	530732	561288	577625	597229	630678	650494	678314	702732	717074

Final Consumption Expenditure of Private Non-profit Institutions Serving Households

| Equals: Final Consumption Expenditure of Private Non-profit Organisations Serving Households | ... | ... | ... | ... | ... | ... | ... | ... | ... | ... | ... |
| Private Final Consumption Expenditure | 469338 | 500344 | 530732 | 561288 | 577625 | 597229 | 630678 | 650494 | 678314 | 702732 | 717074 |

a) Personal effects are included in item 'Clothing and footwear'.
b) Including consumption expenditure of private non-profit institutions.

France

2.9 Gross Capital Formation by Kind of Activity of Owner, ISIC Major Divisions, in Current Prices

Million French francs

	1970 TGCF	Incr. Stocks	GFCF	1971 TGCF	Incr. Stocks	GFCF	1972 TGCF	Incr. Stocks	GFCF	1973 TGCF	Incr. Stocks	GFCF
					All Producers							
1 Agriculture, hunting, fishing and forestry [a]	...	...	8061	...	...	10186	...	...	11662	...	...	13399
2 Mining and quarrying [b]	...	...	} 48494	...	...	} 51724	...	...	} 56593	...	...	} 62100
3 Manufacturing [bc]												
4 Electricity, gas and water	...	...		...	...		...	...		...	...	
5 Construction	...	...	5516	...	...	6330	...	...	6053	...	...	6477
6 Wholesale and retail trade, restaurants and hotels [d]												
7 Transport, storage and communication	...	...	} 95205	...	...	} 110682	...	...	} 128806	...	...	} 150740
8 Finance, insurance, real estate and business services												
9 Community, social and personal services [d]												
Total Industries	...	...	157276	...	...	178922	...	...	203114	...	...	232716
Producers of Government Services	...	...	25386	...	...	27007	...	...	28934	...	...	31702
Private Non-Profit Institutions Serving Households	...	...	379	...	...	...	...	...	...	...	...	563
Total	204098	21057	183041	218701	12772	205929	250427	18379	232048	291859	26878	264981

	1974 TGCF	Incr. Stocks	GFCF	1975 TGCF	Incr. Stocks	GFCF	1976 TGCF	Incr. Stocks	GFCF
				All Producers					
1 Agriculture, hunting, fishing and forestry [a]	...	...	15999	...	...	15815	...	...	17836
2 Mining and quarrying [b]	...	...	} 71649	...	...	} 75270	...	...	} 88642
3 Manufacturing [bc]									
4 Electricity, gas and water	...	...		...	...		...	...	
5 Construction	...	...	7389	...	...	7691	...	...	10220
6 Wholesale and retail trade, restaurants and hotels [d]									
7 Transport, storage and communication	...	...	} 178144	...	...	} 192382	...	...	} 222596
8 Finance, insurance, real estate and business services									
9 Community, social and personal services [d]									
Total Industries	...	...	273181	...	...	291158	...	...	339294
Producers of Government Services	...	...	37040	...	...	45958	...	...	50497
Private Non-Profit Institutions Serving Households	...	...	681	...	...	773	...	...	880
Total	341438	30536	310902	334249	-3640	337889	410401	19730	390671

a) Including production of wine, but excluding fishing.
b) Quarrying of building materials is included in item 'Manufacturing'.
c) Including fishing, but excluding production of wine.
d) Restaurants and hotels are included in item 'Community, social and personal services'.

2.10 Gross Capital Formation by Kind of Activity of Owner, ISIC Major Divisions, in Constant Prices

Million French francs

	1970 TGCF	Incr. Stocks	GFCF	1971 TGCF	Incr. Stocks	GFCF	1972 TGCF	Incr. Stocks	GFCF	1973 TGCF	Incr. Stocks	GFCF
				At constant prices of:1970								
					All Producers							
1 Agriculture, hunting, fishing and forestry [a]	...	...	8061	...	...	9502	...	...	10238	...	...	10730
2 Mining and quarrying	...	...	} 48494	...	...	} 49835	...	...	} 52815	...	...	} 54357
3 Manufacturing [b]												
4 Electricity, gas and water	...	...		...	...		...	...		...	...	

France

2.10 Gross Capital Formation by Kind of Activity of Owner, ISIC Major Divisions, in Constant Prices
(Continued)

Million French francs

	1970 Total Gross Capital Formation	1970 Increase in Stocks	1970 Gross Fixed Capital Formation	1971 Total Gross Capital Formation	1971 Increase in Stocks	1971 Gross Fixed Capital Formation	1972 Total Gross Capital Formation	1972 Increase in Stocks	1972 Gross Fixed Capital Formation	1973 Total Gross Capital Formation	1973 Increase in Stocks	1973 Gross Fixed Capital Formation
						At constant prices of:1970						
5 Construction	...	...	5516	...	...	6205	...	...	5689	...	...	5590
6 Wholesale and retail trade, restaurants and hotels c	...	...	{	...	...	{	...	...	{	...	...	{
7 Transport, storage and communication	...	...	95205	...	...	105333	...	...	115881	...	...	126263
8 Finance, insurance, real estate and business services	...	...		...	...		...	...		...	...	
9 Community, social and personal services c	...	...		...	...		...	...		...	...	
Total Industries	...	...	157276	...	...	170875	...	...	184623	...	...	196940
Producers of Government Services	...	...	25386	...	...	24768	...	...	25141	...	...	25665
Private Non-Profit Institutions Serving Households	...	...	379	...	...	412	...	...	471	...	...	519
Total	204098	21057	183041	208998	12943	196055	227638	17403	210235	245193	22069	223124

	1974 Total Gross Capital Formation	1974 Increase in Stocks	1974 Gross Fixed Capital Formation	1975 Total Gross Capital Formation	1975 Increase in Stocks	1975 Gross Fixed Capital Formation	1976 Total Gross Capital Formation	1976 Increase in Stocks	1976 Gross Fixed Capital Formation
				At constant prices of:1970					
				All Producers					
1 Agriculture, hunting, fishing and forestry a	...	...	10997	...	...	9696	...	...	9798
2 Mining and quarrying	...	...	{	...	...	{	...	...	{
3 Manufacturing b	...	...	53601	...	...	50292	...	...	54663
4 Electricity, gas and water	...	...		...	...		...	...	
5 Construction	...	...	5354	...	...	5197	...	...	6310
6 Wholesale and retail trade, restaurants and hotels c	...	...	{	...	...	{	...	...	{
7 Transport, storage and communication	...	...	129222	...	...	123978	...	...	126874
8 Finance, insurance, real estate and business services	...	...		...	...		...	...	
9 Community, social and personal services c	...	...		...	...		...	...	
Total Industries	...	...	199174	...	...	189163	...	...	197645
Producers of Government Services	...	...	25515	...	...	28289	...	...	27930
Private Non-Profit Institutions Serving Households	...	...	514	...	...	522	...	...	540
Total	248023	22820	225203	215098	-2876	217974	238721	12606	226115

a) Including production of wine, but excluding fishing.
b) Quarrying of building materials is included in item 'Manufacturing'.
c) Restaurants and hotels are included in item 'Community, social and personal services'.

3.11 General Government Production Account: Total and Subsectors

Million French francs

	1970 Total General Government	1970 Central Government	1970 State or Provincial Government	1970 Local Government	1970 Social Security Funds	1971 Total General Government	1971 Central Government	1971 State or Provincial Government	1971 Local Government	1971 Social Security Funds
					Gross Output					
1 Sales	...	...	...	...	...	...	...	...	...	...
2 Services produced for own use	105138	79511	...	19475	6152	117326	88692	...	21749	6885
3 Own account capital formation	21006	14591	...	6266	149	24158	16513	...	7404	241
Gross Output	126144	94102	...	25741	6301	141484	105205	...	29153	7126
					Gross Input					
Intermediate Consumption	43649	30833	...	11215	1601	47966	34020	...	12143	1803
Subtotal: Value Added	82495	63269	...	14526	4700	93518	71185	...	17010	5323
1 Indirect taxes, net	1084	1043	...	-117	158	1337	1206	...	-65	196
a Indirect taxes paid	1565	1239	...	168	158	1859	1424	...	239	196
b Less: Subsidies received	481	196	...	285	-	522	218	...	304	-
2 Consumption of fixed capital	6719	2424	...	4111	184	7017	2811	...	4000	206
3 Compensation of employees	75426	60391	...	10677	4358	84995	67472	...	12602	4921
a Paid to residents	74255	...	...	...	...	83799	...	...	...	...
b Paid to the rest of the world	1171	...	...	...	...	1196	...	...	...	...
4 Net Operating surplus	-734	-589	...	-145	...	169	-304	...	473	-
Gross Input	126144	94102	...	25741	6301	141484	105205	...	29153	7126

France

3.11 General Government Production Account: Total and Subsectors

Million French francs

	1972 Total General Government	1972 Central Government	1972 State or Provincial Government	1972 Local Government	1972 Social Security Funds	1973 Total General Government	1973 Central Government	1973 State or Provincial Government	1973 Local Government	1973 Social Security Funds
Gross Output										
1 Sales	...	...	...	...	...	...	...	...	...	...
2 Services produced for own use	129094	96938	...	24449	7707	146713	109352	...	28153	9208
3 Own account capital formation	27117	18201	...	8697	219	28435	18176	...	9925	334
Gross Output	156211	115139	...	33146	7926	175148	127528	...	38078	9542
Gross Input										
Intermediate Consumption	51924	36111	...	13807	2006	57989	39487	...	15746	2756
Subtotal: Value Added	104287	79028	...	19339	5920	117159	88041	...	22332	6786
1 Indirect taxes, net	1360	1264	...	-119	215	327	229	...	-140	238
a Indirect taxes paid	2094	1611	...	268	215	2397	1857	...	302	238
b Less: Subsidies received	734	347	...	387	-	2070	1628	...	442	-
2 Consumption of fixed capital	7877	3129	...	4516	232	8990	3529	...	5198	263
3 Compensation of employees	94651	74854	...	14324	5473	107840	84921	...	16634	6285
a Paid to residents	92860	...	...	...	...	105971	...	...	...	...
b Paid to the rest of the world	1791	...	...	...	...	1869	...	...	...	...
4 Net Operating surplus	399	-219	...	618	-	2	-638	...	640	-
Gross Input	156211	115139	...	33146	7926	175148	127528	...	38078	9542

	1974 Total General Government	1974 Central Government	1974 State or Provincial Government	1974 Local Government	1974 Social Security Funds	1975 Total General Government	1975 Central Government	1975 State or Provincial Government	1975 Local Government	1975 Social Security Funds
Gross Output										
1 Sales	...	...	...	...	...	...	...	...	...	...
2 Services produced for own use	173905	128443	...	34746	10716	209142	153971	...	41168	14003
3 Own account capital formation	33828	22080	...	11237	511	40563	26951	...	13107	505
Gross Output	207733	150523	...	45983	11227	249705	180922	...	54275	14508
Gross Input										
Intermediate Consumption	67189	45914	...	18524	2751	79276	54695	...	20788	3793
Subtotal: Value Added	140544	104609	...	27459	8476	170429	126227	...	33487	10715
1 Indirect taxes, net	1646	1575	...	-251	322	1685	1688	...	-447	444
a Indirect taxes paid	2818	2197	...	299	322	3611	2849	...	318	444
b Less: Subsidies received	1172	622	...	550	-	1926	1161	...	765	-
2 Consumption of fixed capital	11294	4213	...	6738	343	13858	5133	...	8293	432
3 Compensation of employees	128458	100398	...	20249	7811	154873	120098	...	24936	9839
a Paid to residents	126022	...	...	...	...	151864	...	...	...	...
b Paid to the rest of the world	2436	...	...	...	...	3009	...	...	...	...
4 Net Operating surplus	-854	-1577	...	723	-	13	-692	...	705	-
Gross Input	207733	150523	...	45983	11227	249705	180922	...	54275	14508

	1976 Total General Government	1976 Central Government	1976 State or Provincial Government	1976 Local Government	1976 Social Security Funds	1977 Total General Government	1977 Central Government	1977 State or Provincial Government	1977 Local Government	1977 Social Security Funds
Gross Output										
1 Sales	...	...	...	...	...	...	...	...	...	...
2 Services produced for own use	245023	180076	...	48756	16191	277711	202429	...	56730	18552
3 Own account capital formation	44817	28618	...	15540	659	48176	30424	...	17055	697
Gross Output	289840	208694	...	64296	16850	325887	232853	...	73785	19249
Gross Input										
Intermediate Consumption	87488	59140	...	24055	4293	93465	61212	...	27481	4772
Subtotal: Value Added	202352	149554	...	40241	12557	232422	171641	...	46304	14477
1 Indirect taxes, net	1557	1590	...	-564	531	2979	2890	...	-569	658

France

3.11 General Government Production Account: Total and Subsectors
(Continued)

Million French francs

		1976				1977				
		Total General Government	Central Government	State or Provincial Government	Local Government	Social Security Funds	Total General Government	Central Government	State or Provincial Government	Local Government	Social Security Funds
	a Indirect taxes paid	4299	3385	...	383	531	5060	4003	...	399	658
	b Less: Subsidies received	2742	1795	...	947	-	2081	1113	...	968	-
2	Consumption of fixed capital	16751	5998	...	10234	519	19318	6690	...	12033	595
3	Compensation of employees	182177	141093	...	29577	11507	209264	161876	...	34164	13224
	a Paid to residents	178363	...	...	...	...	204952	...	...	...	...
	b Paid to the rest of the world	3814	...	...	...	...	4312	...	...	...	...
4	Net Operating surplus	1867	873	...	994	-	861	185	...	676	-
	Gross Input	289840	208694	...	64296	16850	325887	232853	...	73785	19249

		1978					1979				
		Total General Government	Central Government	State or Provincial Government	Local Government	Social Security Funds	Total General Government	Central Government	State or Provincial Government	Local Government	Social Security Funds

Gross Output

1	Sales	...	...	...	...	...	...	...	...	...	...
2	Services produced for own use	320331	231807	...	66550	21974	362291	261600	...	76052	24639
3	Own account capital formation	55018	35080	...	19165	773	60239	36853	...	22375	1011
	Gross Output	375349	266887	...	85715	22747	422530	298453	...	98427	25650

Gross Input

	Intermediate Consumption	106950	69784	...	31425	5741	121196	79037	...	35940	6219
	Subtotal: Value Added	268399	197103	...	54290	17006	301334	219416	...	62487	19431
1	Indirect taxes, net	3509	3528	...	-837	818	3975	3914	...	-875	936
	a Indirect taxes paid	5586	4302	...	466	818	6386	4901	...	549	936
	b Less: Subsidies received	2077	774	...	1303	-	2411	987	...	1424	-
2	Consumption of fixed capital	22235	7378	...	14153	704	26276	8496	...	16937	843
3	Compensation of employees	241347	185558	...	40305	15484	270074	206684	...	45738	17652
	a Paid to residents	235314	...	...	...	...	261953	...	...	...	...
	b Paid to the rest of the world	6033	...	...	...	...	8121	...	...	...	...
4	Net Operating surplus	1308	639	...	669	-	1009	322	...	687	-
	Gross Input	375349	266887	...	85715	22747	422530	298453	...	98427	25650

		1980				
		Total General Government	Central Government	State or Provincial Government	Local Government	Social Security Funds

Gross Output

1	Sales	...	...	...	...	...
2	Services produced for own use	421134	303489	...	88532	29113
3	Own account capital formation	67567	39769	...	26873	925
	Gross Output	488701	343258	...	115405	30038

Gross Input

	Intermediate Consumption	140755	90615	...	42987	7153
	Subtotal: Value Added	347946	252643	...	72418	22885
1	Indirect taxes, net	4621	4503	...	-909	1027
	a Indirect taxes paid	7129	5461	...	641	1027
	b Less: Subsidies received	2508	958	...	1550	-
2	Consumption of fixed capital	31828	10212	...	20592	1024
3	Compensation of employees	311538	239009	...	51695	20834
	a Paid to residents	303074	...	...	...	...
	b Paid to the rest of the world	8464	...	...	...	...
4	Net Operating surplus	-41	-1081	...	1040	-
	Gross Input	488701	343258	...	115405	30038

France

3.12 General Government Income and Outlay Account: Total and Subsectors

Million French francs

	1970 Total General Government	1970 Central Government	1970 State or Provincial Government	1970 Local Government	1970 Social Security Funds	1971 Total General Government	1971 Central Government	1971 State or Provincial Government	1971 Local Government	1971 Social Security Funds
Receipts										
1 Property and entrepreneurial income	7444	4618	...	1068	1758	9058	5428	...	1744	1886
a Net operating surplus	-734	-589	...	-145	-	169	-304	...	473	-
b Withdrawals from public quasi-corporations	-	-	...	-	-	313	313	...	-	-
c Interest	4996	3162	...	379	1455	5273	3307	...	430	1536
d Dividends	2771	1977	...	491	303	2849	2040	...	459	350
e Net land rent and royalties	411	68	...	343	-	454	72	...	382	-
2 Taxes, fees and contributions	277939	160680	...	17423	99836	304617	172851	...	18275	113491
a Indirect taxes	119046	109375	...	9303	368	129845	119463	...	9972	410
b Direct taxes	56496	48395	...	8101	-	58423	50137	...	8286	-
Income	43561	43561	...	-	-	45482	45482	...	-	-
Other	12935	4834	...	8101	-	12941	4655	...	8286	-
c Social security contributions	100926	1458	...	-	99468	114662	1581	...	-	113081
d Fees, fines and penalties	1471	1452	...	19	-	1687	1670	...	17	-
3 Other current transfers received	39230	6498	...	19223	13509	41876	4480	...	22265	15131
a Casualty insurance claims	20	-	...	16	4	24	-	...	20	4
b Transfers from other government subsectors	19194	-9956	...	16327	12823	21210	-12210	...	19023	14397
c Transfers from abroad	3118	3118	...	-	-	2189	2189	...	-	-
d Other transfers, except imputed	3846	1166	...	1998	682	3962	957	...	2275	730
e Imputed unfunded employee welfare contributions	13052	12170	...	882	-	14491	13544	...	947	-
Total Current Receipts	324613	171796	...	37714	115103	355551	182759	...	42284	130508
Disbursements										
1 General government final consumption expenditures	105138	79511	...	19475	6152	117326	88692	...	21749	6885
a Compensation of employees	71941	57771	...	9812	4358	81016	64492	...	11603	4921
b Consumption of fixed capital	5308	2293	...	2831	184	5935	2564	...	3165	206
c Goods and services purchased, net	26457	18260	...	6745	1452	28697	20277	...	6858	1562
Purchases	35002	23679	...	9722	1601	37907	25696	...	10408	1803
Less: Sales	8545	5419	...	2977	149	9210	5419	...	3550	241
d Less: Own account production of fixed assets	...	...	...	...	...	...	...	...	...	...
e Indirect taxes paid, net	1432	1187	...	87	158	1678	1359	...	123	196
2 Property income paid	9000	5886	...	3091	23	9174	5734	...	3416	24
a Interest	8998	5884	...	3091	23	9172	5732	...	3416	24
b Net land rent and royalties	2	2	...	-	-	2	2	...	-	-
3 Subsidies	15407	14201	...	1060	146	13580	12155	...	1291	134
4 Other current transfers paid	161575	49323	...	9268	102984	181178	55026	...	10010	116142
a Casualty insurance premiums, net	84	8	...	73	3	119	10	...	106	3
b Transfers to other government subsectors	19194	18286	...	703	205	21210	20202	...	722	285
c Transfers to households	133366	24674	...	7027	101665	149351	27227	...	7478	114646
Social security benefits	101670	10	...	-	101660	114595	2	...	-	114593
Social assistance grants	17221	11071	...	6145	5	18703	12119	...	6531	53
Unfunded employee welfare benefits	14475	13593	...	882	-	16053	15106	...	947	-
d Transfers to private non-profit institutions serving households	893	252	...	407	234	1005	241	...	489	275
e Transfers to the rest of the world	8038	6103	...	1058	877	9493	7346	...	1215	933
Net saving	33493	22875	...	4820	5798	34293	21152	...	5818	7323
Total Current Disbursements and Net Saving	324613	171796	...	37714	115103	355551	182759	...	42284	130508

France

3.12 General Government Income and Outlay Account: Total and Subsectors

Million French francs

	\multicolumn{5}{c	}{1972}	\multicolumn{5}{c	}{1973}
	Total General Government	Central Government	State or Provincial Government	Local Government	Social Security Funds	Total General Government	Central Government	State or Provincial Government	Local Government	Social Security Funds

Receipts

1 Property and entrepreneurial income	9228	5174	...	1977	2077	11113	6317	...	2332	2464
a Net operating surplus	399	-219	...	618	-	2	-638	...	640	-
b Withdrawals from public quasi-corporations	-	-	...	-	-	-	-	...	-	-
c Interest	5632	3460	...	493	1679	7182	4703	...	486	1993
d Dividends	2648	1814	...	436	398	3289	2154	...	664	471
e Net land rent and royalties	549	119	...	430	-	640	98	...	542	-
2 Taxes, fees and contributions	344025	194664	...	21154	128207	394485	212343	...	33452	148690
a Indirect taxes	146031	133727	...	11837	467	165066	145262	...	18359	1445
b Direct taxes	66657	57380	...	9277	-	78238	63162	...	15076	-
Income	52134	52134	...	-	-	57145	57145	...	-	-
Other	14523	5246	...	9277	-	21093	6017	...	15076	-
c Social security contributions	129601	1861	...	-	127740	149223	1978	...	-	147245
d Fees, fines and penalties	1736	1696	...	40	-	1958	1941	...	17	-
3 Other current transfers received	45572	2424	...	26684	16464	51719	11083	...	21689	18947
a Casualty insurance claims	26	-	...	21	5	31	-	...	26	5
b Transfers from other government subsectors	23119	-15613	...	23171	15561	26695	-8813	...	17681	17827
c Transfers from abroad	1819	1815	...	-	4	1749	1749	...	-	-
d Other transfers, except imputed	4290	1030	...	2366	894	4863	1073	...	2675	1115
e Imputed unfunded employee welfare contributions	16318	15192	...	1126	-	18381	17074	...	1307	-
Total Current Receipts	398825	202262	...	49815	146748	457317	229743	...	57473	170101

Disbursements

1 General governement final consumption expenditures	129094	96938	...	24449	7707	146713	109352	...	28153	9208
a Compensation of employees	90247	71629	...	13145	5473	102691	81135	...	15271	6285
b Consumption of fixed capital	6633	2857	...	3544	232	7519	3232	...	4024	263
c Goods and services purchased, net	30343	20911	...	7645	1787	34377	23231	...	8724	2422
Purchases	41297	27496	...	11795	2006	46890	30644	...	13490	2756
Less: Sales	10954	6585	...	4150	219	12513	7413	...	4766	334
d Less: Own account production of fixed assets	...	...	...	...	...	...	...	...	...	...
e Indirect taxes paid, net	1871	1541	...	115	215	2126	1754	...	134	238
2 Property income paid	8723	4503	...	4123	97	9434	4168	...	5165	101
a Interest	8720	4500	...	4123	97	9429	4163	...	5165	101
b Net land rent and royalties	3	3	...	-	-	5	5	...	-	-
3 Subsidies	14650	13322	...	1209	119	18285	16705	...	1396	184
4 Other current transfers paid	206915	62565	...	12489	131861	240342	71806	...	14523	154013
a Casualty insurance premiums, net	125	13	...	110	2	176	16	...	156	4
b Transfers to other government subsectors	23119	22051	...	807	261	26695	25181	...	1018	496
c Transfers to households	170223	30328	...	9058	130837	196694	33707	...	10664	152323
Social security benefits	130791	-	...	-	130791	152320	-	...	-	152320
Social assistance grants	21371	13393	...	7932	46	24040	14680	...	9357	3
Unfunded employee welfare benefits	18061	16935	...	1126	-	20334	19027	...	1307	-
d Transfers to private non-profit institutions serving households	1136	286	...	743	107	1312	365	...	800	147
e Transfers to the rest of the world	12312	9887	...	1771	654	15465	12537	...	1885	1043
Net saving	39443	24934	...	7545	6964	42543	27712	...	8236	6595
Total Current Disbursements and Net Saving	398825	202262	...	49815	146748	457317	229743	...	57473	170101

France

3.12 General Government Income and Outlay Account: Total and Subsectors

Million French francs

		1974				1975			
	Total General Government	Central Government	State or Provincial Government	Local Government	Social Security Funds	Total General Government	Central Government	State or Provincial Government	Local Government	Social Security Funds

Receipts

1 Property and entrepreneurial income	14437	8610	...	2697	3130	15810	8831	...	3107	3872
a Net operating surplus	-854	-1577	...	723	-	13	-692	...	705	-
b Withdrawals from public quasi-corporations	-	-	...	-	-	-	-	...	-	-
c Interest	8760	5645	...	615	2500	9341	5524	...	769	3048
d Dividends	5822	4437	...	755	630	5596	3856	...	916	824
e Net land rent and royalties	709	105	...	604	-	860	143	...	717	-
2 Taxes, fees and contributions	460387	260829	...	20682	178876	534014	271581	...	41324	221109
a Indirect taxes	183871	166551	...	15516	1804	203813	178286	...	23551	1976
b Direct taxes	95233	90288	...	4945	-	105911	88381	...	17530	-
Income	82225	82225	...	-	-	77974	77974	...	-	-
Other	13008	8063	...	4945	-	27937	10407	...	17530	-
c Social security contributions	179340	2268	...	-	177072	221950	2817	...	-	219133
d Fees, fines and penalties	1943	1722	...	221	-	2340	2097	...	243	-
3 Other current transfers received	59985	-6058	...	44091	21952	78198	4730	...	38152	35316
a Casualty insurance claims	37	-	...	31	6	42	-	...	35	7
b Transfers from other government subsectors	30311	-29448	...	39514	20245	42048	-23118	...	32142	33024
c Transfers from abroad	1765	1765	...	-	-	2209	2209	...	-	-
d Other transfers, except imputed	6012	1442	...	2869	1701	8022	1824	...	3913	2285
e Imputed unfunded employee welfare contributions	21860	20183	...	1677	-	25877	23815	...	2062	-
Total Current Receipts	534809	263381	...	67470	203958	628022	285142	...	82583	260297

Disbursements

1 General government final consumption expenditures	173905	128443	...	34746	10716	209142	153971	...	41168	14003
a Compensation of employees	122340	95789	...	18740	7811	147681	114877	...	22965	9839
b Consumption of fixed capital	9446	3853	...	5250	343	11615	4701	...	6482	432
c Goods and services purchased, net	39578	26722	...	10616	2240	46571	31697	...	11586	3288
Purchases	54122	35442	...	15929	2751	63809	42382	...	17634	3793
Less: Sales	14544	8720	...	5313	511	17238	10685	...	6048	505
d Less: Own account production of fixed assets	...	...	...	...	...	...	...	...	...	...
e Indirect taxes paid, net	2541	2079	...	140	322	3275	2696	...	135	444
2 Property income paid	12089	5783	...	6203	103	18623	11089	...	7430	104
a Interest	12081	5775	...	6203	103	18614	11080	...	7430	104
b Net land rent and royalties	8	8	...	-	-	9	9	...	-	-
3 Subsidies	22981	21090	...	1590	301	28685	26152	...	2126	407
4 Other current transfers paid	280401	78949	...	17265	184187	355839	97097	...	22350	236392
a Casualty insurance premiums, net	190	15	...	172	3	217	2	...	212	3
b Transfers to other government subsectors	30311	28512	...	1347	452	42048	39658	...	1848	542
c Transfers to households	233547	38739	...	13161	181647	296811	47391	...	15867	233553
Social security benefits	181639	-	...	-	181639	233553	-	...	-	233553
Social assistance grants	28179	16687	...	11484	8	34873	21068	...	13805	-
Unfunded employee welfare benefits	23729	22052	...	1677	-	28385	26323	...	2062	-
d Transfers to private non-profit institutions serving households	1518	459	...	921	138	1647	441	...	1005	201
e Transfers to the rest of the world	14835	11224	...	1664	1947	15116	9605	...	3418	2093
Net saving	45433	29116	...	7666	8651	15733	-3167	...	9509	9391
Total Current Disbursements and Net Saving	534809	263381	...	67470	203958	628022	285142	...	82583	260297

France

3.12 General Government Income and Outlay Account: Total and Subsectors

Million French francs

	1976					1977				
	Total General Government	Central Government	State or Provincial Government	Local Government	Social Security Funds	Total General Government	Central Government	State or Provincial Government	Local Government	Social Security Funds

Receipts

1 Property and entrepreneurial income	17690	9441	...	3844	4405	20035	10273	...	3978	5784
a Net operating surplus	1867	873	...	994	-	861	185	...	676	-
b Withdrawals from public quasi-corporations	-	-	...	-	-	-	-	...	-	-
c Interest	10207	5659	...	1007	3541	12638	6800	...	1169	4669
d Dividends	4626	2735	...	1027	864	5339	3012	...	1212	1115
e Net land rent and royalties	990	174	...	816	-	1197	276	...	921	-
2 Taxes, fees and contributions	650983	335828	...	50365	264790	731121	366796	...	54153	310172
a Indirect taxes	243347	213351	...	27685	2311	260689	227007	...	30830	2852
b Direct taxes	138967	116588	...	22379	-	156083	133081	...	23002	-
Income	103400	103400	...	-	-	118511	118511	...	-	-
Other	35567	13188	...	22379	-	37572	14570	...	23002	-
c Social security contributions	265826	3347	...	-	262479	311301	3981	...	-	307320
d Fees, fines and penalties	2843	2542	...	301	-	3048	2727	...	321	-
3 Other current transfers received	88220	9581	...	42259	36380	100565	8049	...	53028	39488
a Casualty insurance claims	48	-	...	42	6	52	-	...	45	7
b Transfers from other government subsectors	42576	-26121	...	35275	33422	51713	-29211	...	44497	36427
c Transfers from abroad	2356	2356	...	-	...	2907	2598	...	-	309
d Other transfers, except imputed	12268	4903	...	4413	2952	10375	2006	...	5624	2745
e Imputed unfunded employee welfare contributions	30972	28443	...	2529	-	35518	32656	...	2862	-
Total Current Receipts	756893	354850	...	96468	305575	851721	385118	...	111159	355444

Disbursements

1 General governement final consumption expenditures	245023	180076	...	48756	16191	277711	202429	...	56730	18552
a Compensation of employees	173784	135104	...	27173	11507	200016	155418	...	31374	13224
b Consumption of fixed capital	13960	5452	...	7989	519	16226	6138	...	9493	595
c Goods and services purchased, net	53374	36335	...	13405	3634	56827	37062	...	15690	4075
Purchases	70624	45689	...	20642	4293	76149	47830	...	23547	4772
Less: Sales	17250	9354	...	7237	659	19322	10768	...	7857	697
d Less: Own account production of fixed assets	...	...	...	...	...	...	...	...	...	...
e Indirect taxes paid, net	3905	3185	...	189	531	4642	3811	...	173	658
2 Property income paid	20869	11475	...	9262	132	25549	13897	...	11400	252
a Interest	20859	11465	...	9262	132	25535	13883	...	11400	252
b Net land rent and royalties	10	10	...	-	-	14	14	...	-	-
3 Subsidies	35806	32654	...	2628	524	41037	37152	...	3347	538
4 Other current transfers paid	408261	105232	...	27165	275864	476807	125328	...	30208	321271
a Casualty insurance premiums, net	272	3	...	259	10	326	5	...	308	13
b Transfers to other government subsectors	42576	39668	...	2200	708	51713	48777	...	2160	776
c Transfers to households	346884	54456	...	19548	272880	403458	62908	...	22514	318036
Social security benefits	272880	-	...	-	272880	318036	-	...	-	318036
Social assistance grants	40969	23950	...	17019	-	47415	27763	...	19652	-
Unfunded employee welfare benefits	33035	30506	...	2529	-	38007	35145	...	2862	-
d Transfers to private non-profit institutions serving households	1892	601	...	1009	282	2070	579	...	1182	309
e Transfers to the rest of the world	16637	10504	...	4149	1984	19240	13059	...	4044	2137
Net saving	46934	25413	...	8657	12864	30617	6312	...	9474	14831
Total Current Disbursements and Net Saving	756893	354850	...	96468	305575	851721	385118	...	111159	355444

France

3.12 General Government Income and Outlay Account: Total and Subsectors

Million French francs

	1978					1979				
	Total General Government	Central Government	State or Provincial Government	Local Government	Social Security Funds	Total General Government	Central Government	State or Provincial Government	Local Government	Social Security Funds
Receipts										
1 Property and entrepreneurial income	21420	11063	...	4334	6023	23207	11448	...	4857	6902
a Net operating surplus	1308	639	...	669	-	1009	322	...	687	-
b Withdrawals from public quasi-corporations	49	49	...	-	-	-	-	...	-	-
c Interest	13561	7251	...	1463	4847	13951	6812	...	1664	5475
d Dividends	5237	2839	...	1236	1162	6826	3992	...	1407	1427
e Net land rent and royalties	1265	285	...	966	14	1421	322	...	1099	-
2 Taxes, fees and contributions	828111	413462	...	60371	354278	980789	483644	...	70929	426216
a Indirect taxes	299942	263503	...	33503	2936	355454	311596	...	40281	3577
b Direct taxes	169069	142563	...	26506	-	193844	163578	...	30266	-
Income	126716	126716	...	-	-	146184	146184	...	-	-
Other	42353	15847	...	26506	-	47660	17394	...	30266	-
c Social security contributions	355917	4575	...	-	351342	427885	5246	...	-	422639
d Fees, fines and penalties	3183	2821	...	362	-	3606	3224	...	382	-
3 Other current transfers received	121491	9048	...	63029	49414	142518	12171	...	70827	59520
a Casualty insurance claims	59	2	...	48	9	67	5	...	52	10
b Transfers from other government subsectors	64463	-34881	...	52707	46637	80084	-37075	...	60366	56793
c Transfers from abroad	3106	3106	...	-	-	3701	3701	...	-	...
d Other transfers, except imputed	11481	1747	...	6966	2768	13009	2335	...	7957	2717
e Imputed unfunded employee welfare contributions	42382	39074	...	3308	-	45657	43205	...	2452	-
Total Current Receipts	971022	433573	...	127734	409715	1146514	507263	...	146613	492638
Disbursements										
1 General governement final consumption expenditures	320331	231807	...	66550	21974	362291	261600	...	76052	24639
a Compensation of employees	230618	177999	...	37135	15484	258231	198475	...	42104	17652
b Consumption of fixed capital	18751	6837	...	11210	704	22202	7863	...	13496	843
c Goods and services purchased, net	65844	42881	...	17995	4968	76004	50590	...	20206	5208
Purchases	87931	55182	...	27008	5741	99979	62945	...	30815	6219
Less: Sales	22087	12301	...	9013	773	23975	12355	...	10609	1011
d Less: Own account production of fixed assets	...	...	...	...	...	...	...	...	...	...
e Indirect taxes paid, net	5118	4090	...	210	818	5854	4672	...	246	936
2 Property income paid	30992	17264	...	13527	201	37674	21541	...	15948	185
a Interest	30970	17242	...	13527	201	37651	21518	...	15948	185
b Net land rent and royalties	22	22	...	-	-	23	23	...	-	-
3 Subsidies	43230	38488	...	4096	646	49046	43762	...	4560	724
4 Other current transfers paid	570568	153302	...	34827	382439	662134	177207	...	37196	447731
a Casualty insurance premiums, net	367	4	...	350	13	438	9	...	413	16
b Transfers to other government subsectors	64463	61125	...	2374	964	80084	76662	...	2339	1083
c Transfers to households	478016	73528	...	25743	378745	551452	81007	...	26995	443450
Social security benefits	378745	-	...	-	378745	443450	-	...	-	443450
Social assistance grants	55722	33287	...	22435	-	59742	35199	...	24543	-
Unfunded employee welfare benefits	43549	40241	...	3308	-	48260	45808	...	2452	-
d Transfers to private non-profit institutions serving households	2346	1374	...	583	389	2801	1826	...	564	411
e Transfers to the rest of the world	25376	17271	...	5777	2328	27359	17703	...	6885	2771
Net saving	5901	-7288	...	8734	4455	35369	3153	...	12857	19359
Total Current Disbursements and Net Saving	971022	433573	...	127734	409715	1146514	507263	...	146613	492638

France

3.12 General Government Income and Outlay Account: Total and Subsectors

Million French francs

	Total General Government	Central Government	State or Provincial Government	Local Government	Social Security Funds
	1980				

Receipts

	Total General Government	Central Government	State or Provincial Government	Local Government	Social Security Funds
1 Property and entrepreneurial income	23110	9200	...	5883	8027
a Net operating surplus	-41	-1081	...	1040	-
b Withdrawals from public quasi-corporations	-	-	...	-	-
c Interest	14207	5790	...	1986	6431
d Dividends	7374	4174	...	1604	1596
e Net land rent and royalties	1570	317	...	1253	-
2 Taxes, fees and contributions	1152359	569268	...	80120	502971
a Indirect taxes	404177	355531	...	44641	4005
b Direct taxes	237694	202796	...	34898	-
Income	176775	176775	...	-	-
Other	60919	26021	...	34898	-
c Social security contributions	505007	6041	...	-	498966
d Fees, fines and penalties	5481	4900	...	581	-
3 Other current transfers received	172634	20093	...	82334	70207
a Casualty insurance claims	60	4	...	47	9
b Transfers from other government subsectors	95056	-44396	...	71490	67962
c Transfers from abroad	5721	5721	...	-	-
d Other transfers, except imputed	19767	8639	...	8892	2236
e Imputed unfunded employee welfare contributions	52030	50125	...	1905	-
Total Current Receipts	1348103	598561	...	168337	581205

Disbursements

	Total General Government	Central Government	State or Provincial Government	Local Government	Social Security Funds
1 General governement final consumption expenditures	421134	303489	...	88532	29113
a Compensation of employees	298050	229653	...	47563	20834
b Consumption of fixed capital	26948	9429	...	16495	1024
c Goods and services purchased, net	89625	59208	...	24189	6228
Purchases	117314	73496	...	36665	7153
Less: Sales	27689	14288	...	12476	925
d Less: Own account production of fixed assets	...	...	...	...	...
e Indirect taxes paid, net	6511	5199	...	285	1027
2 Property income paid	45440	26057	...	19138	245
a Interest	45413	26030	...	19138	245
b Net land rent and royalties	27	27	...	-	-
3 Subsidies	52416	46250	...	4974	1192
4 Other current transfers paid	764680	200935	...	41867	521878
a Casualty insurance premiums, net	564	10	...	543	11
b Transfers to other government subsectors	95056	91347	...	2882	827
c Transfers to households	635578	87956	...	30289	517333
Social security benefits	517333	-	...	-	517333
Social assistance grants	63456	35072	...	28384	-
Unfunded employee welfare benefits	54789	52884	...	1905	-
d Transfers to private non-profit institutions serving households	3057	1878	...	603	576
e Transfers to the rest of the world	30425	19744	...	7550	3131
Net saving	64433	21830	...	13826	28777
Total Current Disbursements and Net Saving	1348103	598561	...	168337	581205

3.13 General Government Capital Accumulation Account: Total and Subsectors

Million French francs

	1970					1971				
	Total General Government	Central Government	State or Provincial Government	Local Government	Social Security Funds	Total General Government	Central Government	State or Provincial Government	Local Government	Social Security Funds
	Finance of Gross Accumulation									
1 Gross saving	40212	25299	...	8931	5982	41310	23963	...	9818	7529
a Consumption of fixed capital	6719	2424	...	4111	184	7017	2811	...	4000	206
b Net saving	33493	22875	...	4820	5798	34293	21152	...	5818	7323
2 Capital transfers received	7877	2521	...	5066	290	7793	2483	...	5150	160
a From other government subsectors	6796	2366	...	4140	290	...	...	...	...	...
b From other resident sectors	1081	155	...	926	-	...	...	...	...	...
c From rest of the world	-	-	...	-	-	...	...	...	...	...
Finance of Gross Accumulation	48089	27820	...	13997	6272	49103	26446	...	14968	7689
	Gross Accumulation									
1 Gross capital formation	30104	10435	...	19252	417	32341	11452	...	20312	577
a Increase in stocks	1896	1886	...	10	-	2357	2350	...	7	-
b Gross fixed capital formation	28208	8549	...	19242	417	29984	9102	...	20305	577
2 Purchases of land, net	555	617	...	-92	30	481	742	...	-297	36
3 Purchases of intangible assets, net	-	-	...	-	-	3	-	...	3	-
4 Capital transfers paid	10273	8709	...	1202	362	9838	8550	...	1016	272
a To other government subsectors	4562	4087	...	422	53	...	...	...	...	...
b To other resident sectors	4784	3695	...	780	309	...	...	...	...	...
c To rest of the world	927	927	...	-	-	...	...	...	...	...
Net lending [a]	7157	8059	...	-6365	5463	6440	5702	...	-6066	6804
Gross Accumulation	48089	27820	...	13997	6272	49103	26446	...	14968	7689

	1972					1973				
	Total General Government	Central Government	State or Provincial Government	Local Government	Social Security Funds	Total General Government	Central Government	State or Provincial Government	Local Government	Social Security Funds
	Finance of Gross Accumulation									
1 Gross saving	47320	28063	...	12061	7196	51533	31241	...	13434	6858
a Consumption of fixed capital	7877	3129	...	4516	232	8990	3529	...	5198	263
b Net saving	39443	24934	...	7545	6964	42543	27712	...	8236	6595
2 Capital transfers received	8029	2667	...	5351	11	9032	3313	...	5665	54
a From other government subsectors	6843	2470	...	4373	-	7572	2981	...	4537	54
b From other resident sectors	1186	197	...	978	11	1460	332	...	1128	-
c From rest of the world	-	-	...	-	-	-	-	...	-	-
Finance of Gross Accumulation	55349	30730	...	17412	7207	60565	34554	...	19099	6912
	Gross Accumulation									
1 Gross capital formation	35757	13256	...	22031	470	36979	10956	...	25516	507
a Increase in stocks	3876	3858	...	18	-	1335	1335	...	-	-
b Gross fixed capital formation	31881	9398	...	22013	470	35644	9621	...	25516	507
2 Purchases of land, net	1460	787	...	597	76	1263	878	...	314	71
3 Purchases of intangible assets, net	3	-	...	3	-	-4	-4	...	-	-
4 Capital transfers paid	10422	8712	...	1448	262	11825	9877	...	1667	281
a To other government subsectors	4895	4274	...	582	39	5236	4495	...	699	42
b To other resident sectors	4622	3533	...	866	223	5540	4333	...	968	239
c To rest of the world	905	905	...	-	-	1049	1049	...	-	-
Net lending [a]	7707	7975	...	-6667	6399	10502	12847	...	-8398	6053
Gross Accumulation	55349	30730	...	17412	7207	60565	34554	...	19099	6912

	1974					1975				
	Total General Government	Central Government	State or Provincial Government	Local Government	Social Security Funds	Total General Government	Central Government	State or Provincial Government	Local Government	Social Security Funds
	Finance of Gross Accumulation									
1 Gross saving	56727	33329	...	14404	8994	29591	1966	...	17802	9823
a Consumption of fixed capital	11294	4213	...	6738	343	13858	5133	...	8293	432
b Net saving	45433	29116	...	7666	8651	15733	-3167	...	9509	9391
2 Capital transfers received	10587	3666	...	6912	9	14233	5429	...	8788	16

France

3.13 General Government Capital Accumulation Account: Total and Subsectors
(Continued)

Million French francs

	1974					1975				
	Total General Government	Central Government	State or Provincial Government	Local Government	Social Security Funds	Total General Government	Central Government	State or Provincial Government	Local Government	Social Security Funds
a From other government subsectors	8897	3483	...	5414	-	12575	5255	...	7320	-
b From other resident sectors	1690	183	...	1498	9	1658	174	...	1468	16
c From rest of the world	-	-	...	-	-	-	-	...	-	-
Finance of Gross Accumulation	67314	36995	...	21316	9003	43824	7395	...	26590	9839

Gross Accumulation

	Total General Government	Central Government	State or Provincial Government	Local Government	Social Security Funds	Total General Government	Central Government	State or Provincial Government	Local Government	Social Security Funds
1 Gross capital formation	42940	11431	...	30409	1100	55158	17019	...	36937	1202
a Increase in stocks	912	882	...	30	-	3397	3375	...	22	-
b Gross fixed capital formation	42028	10549	...	30379	1100	51761	13644	...	36915	1202
2 Purchases of land, net	1361	889	...	404	68	1645	1054	...	517	74
3 Purchases of intangible assets, net	51	54	...	2	-5	60	59	...	1	-
4 Capital transfers paid	14946	12805	...	1808	333	19423	16485	...	2617	321
a To other government subsectors	6105	5393	...	691	21	8610	7275	...	1290	45
b To other resident sectors	6920	5491	...	1117	312	9362	7759	...	1327	276
c To rest of the world	1921	1921	...	-	-	1451	1451	...	-	-
Net lending a	8016	11816	...	-11307	7507	-32462	-27222	...	-13482	8242
Gross Accumulation	67314	36995	...	21316	9003	43824	7395	...	26590	9839

	1976					1977				
	Total General Government	Central Government	State or Provincial Government	Local Government	Social Security Funds	Total General Government	Central Government	State or Provincial Government	Local Government	Social Security Funds

Finance of Gross Accumulation

	Total General Government	Central Government	State or Provincial Government	Local Government	Social Security Funds	Total General Government	Central Government	State or Provincial Government	Local Government	Social Security Funds
1 Gross saving	63685	31411	...	18891	13383	49935	13002	...	21507	15426
a Consumption of fixed capital	16751	5998	...	10234	519	19318	6690	...	12033	595
b Net saving	46934	25413	...	8657	12864	30617	6312	...	9474	14831
2 Capital transfers received	14384	4831	...	8808	745	14423	5245	...	9170	8
a From other government subsectors	11574	4552	...	7022	-	12812	4992	...	7820	-
b From other resident sectors	2793	262	...	1786	745	1609	251	...	1350	8
c From rest of the world	17	17	...	-	-	2	2	...	-	-
Finance of Gross Accumulation	78069	36242	...	27699	14128	64358	18247	...	30677	15434

Gross Accumulation

	Total General Government	Central Government	State or Provincial Government	Local Government	Social Security Funds	Total General Government	Central Government	State or Provincial Government	Local Government	Social Security Funds
1 Gross capital formation	55347	10846	...	43327	1174	57487	12970	...	43447	1070
a Increase in stocks	-1638	-1644	...	6	-	-355	-362	...	7	-
b Gross fixed capital formation	56985	12490	...	43321	1174	57842	13332	...	43440	1070
2 Purchases of land, net	1393	1013	...	314	66	1363	992	...	276	95
3 Purchases of intangible assets, net	-165	-165	...	-	-	57	56	...	1	-
4 Capital transfers paid	29586	26079	...	3034	473	21154	17252	...	3434	468
a To other government subsectors	8515	6963	...	1485	67	9089	7784	...	1251	54
b To other resident sectors	18749	16794	...	1549	406	10731	8134	...	2183	414
c To rest of the world	2322	2322	...	-	-	1334	1334	...	-	-
Net lending a	-8092	-1531	...	-18976	12415	-15703	-13023	...	-16481	13801
Gross Accumulation	78069	36242	...	27699	14128	64358	18247	...	30677	15434

	1978					1979				
	Total General Government	Central Government	State or Provincial Government	Local Government	Social Security Funds	Total General Government	Central Government	State or Provincial Government	Local Government	Social Security Funds

Finance of Gross Accumulation

	Total General Government	Central Government	State or Provincial Government	Local Government	Social Security Funds	Total General Government	Central Government	State or Provincial Government	Local Government	Social Security Funds
1 Gross saving	28136	90	...	22887	5159	61645	11649	...	29794	20202
a Consumption of fixed capital	22235	7378	...	14153	704	26276	8496	...	16937	843
b Net saving	5901	-7288	...	8734	4455	35369	3153	...	12857	19359
2 Capital transfers received	16949	6372	...	10576	1	19784	7624	...	12080	80
a From other government subsectors	15141	6090	...	9050	1	11935	1523	...	10341	71
b From other resident sectors	1806	280	...	1526	-	7842	6094	...	1739	9
c From rest of the world	2	2	...	-	-	7	7	...	-	-
Finance of Gross Accumulation	45085	6462	...	33463	5160	81429	19273	...	41874	20282

France

3.13 General Government Capital Accumulation Account: Total and Subsectors
(Continued)

Million French francs

		1978				1979			
	Total General Government	Central Government	State or Provincial Government	Local Government	Social Security Funds	Total General Government	Central Government	State or Provincial Government	Local Government	Social Security Funds

Gross Accumulation

1 Gross capital formation	61167	14692	...	44783	1692	70739	18093	...	50854	1792
a Increase in stocks	637	630	...	7	-	2431	2423	...	8	-
b Gross fixed capital formation	60530	14062	...	44776	1692	68308	15670	...	50846	1792
2 Purchases of land, net	1422	967	...	296	159	1341	907	...	337	97
3 Purchases of intangible assets, net	84	75	...	9	-	85	72	...	13	-
4 Capital transfers paid	21954	17861	...	3646	447	25068	20816	...	3785	467
a To other government subsectors	10528	9041	...	1475	12	11935	10352	...	1577	6
b To other resident sectors	10154	7548	...	2171	435	11578	8909	...	2208	461
c To rest of the world	1272	1272	...	-	-	1555	1555	...	-	-
Net lending [a]	-39542	-27133	...	-15271	2862	-15804	-20615	...	-13115	17926
Gross Accumulation	45085	6462	...	33463	5160	81429	19273	...	41874	20282

	1980				
	Total General Government	Central Government	State or Provincial Government	Local Government	Social Security Funds

Finance of Gross Accumulation

1 Gross saving	96261	32042	...	34418	29801
a Consumption of fixed capital	31828	10212	...	20592	1024
b Net saving	64433	21830	...	13826	28777
2 Capital transfers received	24337	10208	...	14119	10
a From other government subsectors	14212	2011	...	12201	-
b From other resident sectors	10125	8197	...	1918	10
c From rest of the world	-	-	...	-	-
Finance of Gross Accumulation	120598	42250	...	48537	29811

Gross Accumulation

1 Gross capital formation	79393	17967	...	59464	1962
a Increase in stocks	390	381	...	9	-
b Gross fixed capital formation	79003	17586	...	59455	1962
2 Purchases of land, net	1434	784	...	650	-
3 Purchases of intangible assets, net	86	71	...	15	-
4 Capital transfers paid	29315	24299	...	4511	505
a To other government subsectors	14212	12196	...	1995	21
b To other resident sectors	13481	10481	...	2516	484
c To rest of the world	1622	1622	...	-	-
Net lending [a]	10370	-871	...	-16103	27344
Gross Accumulation	120598	42250	...	48537	29811

a) Net lending of the Capital Accumulation Account and the Capital Finance Account have not been reconciled and are different due to different statistical sources.

3.14 General Government Capital Finance Account, Total and Subsectors

Million French francs

		1970				1971			
	Total General Government	Central Government	State or Provincial Government	Local Government	Social Security Funds	Total General Government	Central Government	State or Provincial Government	Local Government	Social Security Funds

Acquisition of Financial Assets

1 Gold and SDRs	-	-	...	-	-	-	-	...	-	-
2 Currency and transferable deposits	1818	298	...	48	1472	4827	695	...	480	3652
3 Other deposits	1436	-263	...	394	1305	1508	99	...	436	973
4 Bills and bonds, short term	-2	-	...	-	-2	4	-	...	-	4
5 Bonds, long term	1211	-17	...	79	1149	1017	34	...	38	945
6 Corporate equity securities	5209	4497	...	-	712	5194	4944	...	3	247
7 Short-term loans, n.e.c.	4220	3512	...	180	528	1393	-198	...	1267	324
8 Long-term loans, n.e.c.	3244	2438	...	386	420	3807	2814	...	501	492
9 Other receivables	6	-	...	6	-	6	-	...	6	-
10 Other assets	653	205	...	231	217	937	929	...	-17	25
Total Acquisition of Financial Assets	17795	10670	...	1324	5801	18693	9317	...	2714	6662

France

3.14 General Government Capital Finance Account, Total and Subsectors
(Continued)

Million French francs

	1970					1971				
	Total General Government	Central Government	State or Provincial Government	Local Government	Social Security Funds	Total General Government	Central Government	State or Provincial Government	Local Government	Social Security Funds

Incurrence of Liabilities

1 Currency and transferable deposits	2742	2742	...	-	-	6464	6464	...	-	-
2 Other deposits	1822	1772	...	-	50	3063	3063	...	-	-
3 Bills and bonds, short term	-1971	-1971	...	-	-	-1614	-1614	...	-	-
4 Bonds, long term	-1987	-2522	...	535	-	-456	-1300	...	844	-
5 Short-term loans, n.e.c.	4230	3051	...	975	204	-2020	-2687	...	781	-114
6 Long-term loans, n.e.c.	5460	-641	...	6101	-	6305	-769	...	6692	382
7 Other payables	...	...	...	...	...	...	...	...	...	...
8 Other liabilities	990	233	...	372	385	1269	536	...	619	114
Total Incurrence of Liabilities	11286	2664	...	7983	639	13011	3693	...	8936	382
Net Lending a	6509	8006	...	-6659	5162	5682	5624	...	-6222	6280
Incurrence of Liabilities and Net Worth	17795	10670	...	1324	5801	18693	9317	...	2714	6662

	1972					1973				
	Total General Government	Central Government	State or Provincial Government	Local Government	Social Security Funds	Total General Government	Central Government	State or Provincial Government	Local Government	Social Security Funds

Acquisition of Financial Assets

1 Gold and SDRs	-	-	...	-	-	-	-	...	-	-
2 Currency and transferable deposits	12029	3118	...	4960	3951	6203	2731	...	2430	1042
3 Other deposits	2184	218	...	936	1030	3333	397	...	1316	1620
4 Bills and bonds, short term	-	-	...	-	-	-	-	...	-	-
5 Bonds, long term	719	-32	...	61	690	1904	44	...	195	1665
6 Corporate equity securities	5763	5585	...	-	178	5645	5078	...	-	567
7 Short-term loans, n.e.c.	4946	2553	...	1254	1139	12126	5793	...	2004	4329
8 Long-term loans, n.e.c.	1862	835	...	506	521	2469	964	...	864	641
9 Other receivables	9	-	...	9	-	34	-	...	34	-
10 Other assets	1298	1601	...	-66	-237	2764	1699	...	146	919
Total Acquisition of Financial Assets	28810	13878	...	7660	7272	34478	16706	...	6989	10783

Incurrence of Liabilities

1 Currency and transferable deposits	9002	9002	...	-	-	10147	10147	...	-	-
2 Other deposits	2696	2685	...	11	-	2172	2206	...	-34	-
3 Bills and bonds, short term	-10842	-10842	...	-	-	-16060	-16060	...	-	-
4 Bonds, long term	844	-814	...	1658	-	5592	5033	...	559	-
5 Short-term loans, n.e.c.	6747	3681	...	1624	1442	17535	12044	...	2683	2808
6 Long-term loans, n.e.c.	11593	1134	...	10459	-	3094	-8610	...	11704	-
7 Other payables	...	...	...	...	...	...	...	...	...	...
8 Other liabilities	1570	1176	...	732	-338	690	-353	...	459	584
Total Incurrence of Liabilities	21610	6022	...	14484	1104	23170	4407	...	15371	3392
Net Lending a	7200	7856	...	-6824	6168	11308	12299	...	-8382	7391
Incurrence of Liabilities and Net Worth	28810	13878	...	7660	7272	34478	16706	...	6989	10783

	1974					1975				
	Total General Government	Central Government	State or Provincial Government	Local Government	Social Security Funds	Total General Government	Central Government	State or Provincial Government	Local Government	Social Security Funds

Acquisition of Financial Assets

1 Gold and SDRs	-	-	...	-	-	-	-	...	-	-
2 Currency and transferable deposits	-4232	-1682	...	-1227	-1323	8613	2561	...	2937	3115
3 Other deposits	4454	1010	...	815	2629	4180	62	...	910	3208
4 Bills and bonds, short term	-41	-	...	-	-41	-	-	...	-	-
5 Bonds, long term	2052	-15	...	230	1837	748	-5	...	316	437
6 Corporate equity securities	5769	4949	...	28	792	8106	7397	...	1	708
7 Short-term loans, n.e.c.	15844	5495	...	4043	6306	12656	4471	...	4663	3522
8 Long-term loans, n.e.c.	1758	792	...	366	600	7492	5012	...	787	1693
9 Other receivables	48	-	...	48	-	257	-	...	257	-
10 Other assets	9610	8136	...	168	1306	-3188	-5172	...	26	1958
Total Acquisition of Financial Assets	35262	18685	...	4471	12106	38864	14326	...	9897	14641

Incurrence of Liabilities

1 Currency and transferable deposits	11875	11875	...	-	-	5465	5465	...	-	-

France

3.14 General Government Capital Finance Account, Total and Subsectors
(Continued)

Million French francs

		1974					1975			
		Total General Government	Central Government	State or Provincial Government	Local Government	Social Security Funds	Total General Government	Central Government	State or Provincial Government	Local Government	Social Security Funds
2	Other deposits	-3356	-3593	...	237	-	-698	-796	...	98	-
3	Bills and bonds, short term	-510	-510	...	-	-	40304	40304	...	-	-
4	Bonds, long term	-4147	-5235	...	1088	-	-6101	-6858	...	757	-
5	Short-term loans, n.e.c.	11122	3110	...	3004	5008	8231	-23	...	3623	4631
6	Long-term loans, n.e.c.	11176	-156	...	11332	-	19467	667	...	18800	-
7	Other payables	5	-	...	5	-	3	-	...	3	-
8	Other liabilities	2148	1736	...	55	357	4504	2648	...	99	1757
	Total Incurrence of Liabilities	28313	7227	...	15721	5365	71175	41407	...	23380	6388
	Net Lending [a]	6949	11458	...	-11250	6741	-32311	-27081	...	-13483	8253
	Incurrence of Liabilities and Net Worth	35262	18685	...	4471	12106	38864	14326	...	9897	14641

		1976					1977			
		Total General Government	Central Government	State or Provincial Government	Local Government	Social Security Funds	Total General Government	Central Government	State or Provincial Government	Local Government	Social Security Funds

Acquisition of Financial Assets

1	Gold and SDRs	-	-	...	-	-	-	-	...	-	-
2	Currency and transferable deposits	2308	-666	...	795	2179	12317	5006	...	3013	4298
3	Other deposits	5147	1838	...	976	2333	2906	-1868	...	875	3899
4	Bills and bonds, short term	-	-	...	-	-	2167	6	...	214	1947
5	Bonds, long term	1895	130	...	201	1564	7542	6660	...	11	871
6	Corporate equity securities	12151	11347	...	3	801	9522	6785	...	391	2346
7	Short-term loans, n.e.c.	14502	8239	...	1047	5216	4691	904	...	1548	2239
8	Long-term loans, n.e.c.	6705	3817	...	1506	1382	19	-	...	19	-
9	Other receivables	11	-	...	11	-	6361	4900	...	1085	376
10	Other assets	7009	5580	...	-553	1982					
	Total Acquisition of Financial Assets	49728	30285	...	3986	15457	45525	22393	...	7156	15976

Incurrence of Liabilities

1	Currency and transferable deposits	10939	10939	...	-	-	14063	14063	...	-	-
2	Other deposits	5666	5719	...	-66	13	8682	8462	...	207	13
3	Bills and bonds, short term	8351	8351	...	-	-	5820	5820	...	-	-
4	Bonds, long term	-3267	-3930	...	663	-	6646	5125	...	1521	-
5	Short-term loans, n.e.c.	14263	6823	...	5488	1952	7525	1503	...	3148	2874
6	Long-term loans, n.e.c.	18763	1772	...	16991	-	21079	2344	...	18735	-
7	Other payables	7	-	...	7	-	-	-	...	-	-
8	Other liabilities	3704	2184	...	138	1382	-2262	-1789	...	26	-499
	Total Incurrence of Liabilities	58426	31858	...	23221	3347	61553	35528	...	23637	2388
	Net Lending [a]	-8698	-1573	...	-19235	12110	-16028	-13135	...	-16481	13588
	Incurrence of Liabilities and Net Worth	49728	30285	...	3986	15457	45525	22393	...	7156	15976

		1978					1979			
		Total General Government	Central Government	State or Provincial Government	Local Government	Social Security Funds	Total General Government	Central Government	State or Provincial Government	Local Government	Social Security Funds

Acquisition of Financial Assets

1	Gold and SDRs	-	-	...	-	-	-	-	...	-	-
2	Currency and transferable deposits	26995	24257	...	3371	-633	2588	-8428	...	3947	7069
3	Other deposits	4479	74	...	1898	2507	6453	546	...	2012	3895
4	Bills and bonds, short term	-	-	...	-	-	...	...	...	320	2254
5	Bonds, long term	1844	172	...	198	1474	2730	156	...	28	933
6	Corporate equity securities	8194	7582	...	27	585	6767	5806	...	4713	57
7	Short-term loans, n.e.c.	6031	-1711	...	3879	3863	7538	2768	...	776	1651
8	Long-term loans, n.e.c.	4761	1765	...	1561	1435	10600	8173	...	27	-
9	Other receivables	22	-	...	22	-	27	-	...	178	762
10	Other assets	2494	853	...	121	1520	14073	13133	...		
	Total Acquisition of Financial Assets	54820	32992	...	11077	10751	50776	22154	...	12001	16621

Incurrence of Liabilities

1	Currency and transferable deposits	13134	13134	...	-	-	15547	15547	...	-	-
2	Other deposits	1524	1305	...	219	-	1314	1185	...	127	2
3	Bills and bonds, short term	22741	22741	...	-	-	8112	8112	...	-	-

France

3.14 General Government Capital Finance Account, Total and Subsectors
(Continued)

Million French francs

	1978					1979				
	Total General Government	Central Government	State or Provincial Government	Local Government	Social Security Funds	Total General Government	Central Government	State or Provincial Government	Local Government	Social Security Funds
4 Bonds, long term	12659	9789	...	2870	-	15221	12578	...	2643	-
5 Short-term loans, n.e.c.	22166	11871	...	4231	6064	8853	7238	...	3061	-1446
6 Long-term loans, n.e.c.	19275	381	...	18894	...	18146	-1071	...	19167	50
7 Other payables	2873	847	...	140	1886	30	-625	...	118	537
8 Other liabilities	...	...	...	...	...	...	...	...	...	...
Total Incurrence of Liabilities	94372	60068	...	26354	7950	67223	42964	...	25116	-857
Net Lending a	-39552	-27076	...	-15277	2801	-16447	-20810	...	-13115	17478
Incurrence of Liabilities and Net Worth	54820	32992	...	11077	10751	50776	22154	...	12001	16621

	1980				
	Total General Government	Central Government	State or Provincial Government	Local Government	Social Security Funds

Acquisition of Financial Assets

1 Gold and SDRs	-	-	...		
2 Currency and transferable deposits	22962	11081	...	360	11521
3 Other deposits	3249	400	...	2000	849
4 Bills and bonds, short term	-	-	...	-	
5 Bonds, long term	4322	250	...	500	3572
6 Corporate equity securities	18376	17674	...	-	702
7 Short-term loans, n.e.c.	4407	681	...	670	3056
8 Long-term loans, n.e.c.	1005	-1931	...	650	2286
9 Other receivables	28	-	...	28	-
10 Other assets	...	...	...	...	...
Total Acquisition of Financial Assets	54349	28155	...	4208	21986

Incurrence of Liabilities

1 Currency and transferable deposits	12475	12475	...	-	-
2 Other deposits	1411	1411	...	-	-
3 Bills and bonds, short term	-6210	-6210	...	-	-
4 Bonds, long term	29066	27620	...	1446	-
5 Short-term loans, n.e.c.	-11597	-6239	...	-	-5358
6 Long-term loans, n.e.c.	18834	-31	...	18865	-
7 Other payables	...	...	...	...	...
8 Other liabilities	...	...	...	...	...
Total Incurrence of Liabilities	43979	29026	...	20311	-5358
Net Lending a	10370	-871	...	-16103	27344
Incurrence of Liabilities and Net Worth	54349	28155	...	4208	21986

a) Net lending of the Capital Accumulation Account and the Capital Finance Account have not been reconciled and are different due to different statistical sources.

3.21 Corporate and Quasi-Corporate Enterprise Production Account: Total and Sectors

Million French francs

	1970				1971				1972			
	Corporate and Quasi-Corporate Enterprises			ADDENDUM: Total, including Unincorporated	Corporate and Quasi-Corporate Enterprises			ADDENDUM: Total, including Unincorporated	Corporate and Quasi-Corporate Enterprises			ADDENDUM: Total, including Unincorporated
	TOTAL	Non-Financial	Financial		TOTAL	Non-Financial	Financial		TOTAL	Non-Financial	Financial	

Gross Output

1 Output for sale	801869	786067	15802	1138945	897541	880571	16970	1265859	1015708	993878	21830	1418388
2 Imputed bank service charge	21848	-	21848	21848	24838	-	24838	24838	26314	-	26314	26314
3 Own-account capital formation	...	...	...	...	...	...	...	...	...	...	...	...
Gross Output	823717	786067	37650	1160793	922379	880571	41808	1290697	1042022	993878	48144	1444702

Gross Input

Intermediate consumption	427490	396297	31193	536212	478328	441791	36537	596178	540496	500136	40360	663258
1 Imputed banking service charge	21848	-	21848	21848	24838	-	24838	24838	26314	-	26314	26314
2 Other intermediate consumption	405642	396297	9345	514364	453490	441791	11699	571340	514182	500136	14046	636944
Subtotal: Value Added	396227	389770	6457	624581	444051	438780	5271	694519	501526	493742	7784	781444

France

3.21 Corporate and Quasi-Corporate Enterprise Production Account: Total and Sectors
(Continued)

Million French francs

1970–1972

	1970 Corp. TOTAL	1970 Non-Financial	1970 Financial	1970 ADDENDUM: Total, including Unincorporated	1971 Corp. TOTAL	1971 Non-Financial	1971 Financial	1971 ADDENDUM	1972 Corp. TOTAL	1972 Non-Financial	1972 Financial	1972 ADDENDUM
1 Indirect taxes, net	24992	22485	2507	29232	26358	24466	1892	30735	29450	27697	1753	34609
a Indirect taxes paid	38548	34264	4284	44168	41320	36690	4630	47399	46359	41211	5148	53368
b Less: Subsidies received	13556	11779	1777	14936	14962	12224	2738	16664	16909	13514	3395	18759
2 Consumption of fixed capital	49108	46797	2311	73766	52488	49809	2679	76064	59174	55871	3303	85312
3 Compensation of employees	263449	251266	12183	304804	299855	285598	14257	344791	337171	320699	16472	386538
4 Net operating surplus	58678	69222	-10544	216779	65350	78907	-13557	242929	75731	89475	-13744	274985
Gross Input	823717	786067	37650	1160793	922379	880571	41808	1290697	1042022	993878	48144	1444702

1973–1975

	1973 TOTAL	1973 Non-Fin.	1973 Financial	1973 ADDENDUM	1974 TOTAL	1974 Non-Fin.	1974 Financial	1974 ADDENDUM	1975 TOTAL	1975 Non-Fin.	1975 Financial	1975 ADDENDUM
Gross Output												
1 Output for sale	1173430	1145457	27973	1643210	1465709	1433572	32137	1990945	1566718	1531684	35034	2143727
2 Imputed bank service charge	33377	-	33377	33377	44918	-	44918	44918	46755	-	46755	46755
3 Own-account capital formation	...	...	...	...	...	...	...	...	...	...	...	...
Gross Output	1206807	1145457	61350	1676587	1510627	1433572	77055	2035863	1613473	1531684	81789	2190482
Gross Input												
Intermediate consumption	622867	572280	50587	812729	834135	768485	65650	1019267	846533	776612	69921	1041018
1 Imputed banking service charge	33377	-	33377	33377	44918	-	44918	44918	46755	-	46755	46755
2 Other intermediate consumption	589490	572280	17210	779352	789217	768485	20732	974349	799778	776612	23166	994263
Subtotal: Value Added	583940	573177	10763	863858	676492	665087	11405	1016596	766940	755072	11868	1149464
1 Indirect taxes, net	38411	36055	2356	43570	38519	36505	2014	40428	42549	40303	2246	45997
a Indirect taxes paid	58612	52343	6269	65621	58716	52463	6253	66564	69725	61795	7930	79524
b Less: Subsidies received	20201	16288	3913	22051	20197	15958	4239	26136	27176	21492	5684	33527
2 Consumption of fixed capital	67443	63321	4122	93581	84043	78624	5419	120760	100820	94207	6613	143612
3 Compensation of employees	393582	373839	19743	442949	471512	446722	24790	533849	553598	523415	30183	625037
4 Net operating surplus	84504	99962	-15458	283758	82418	103236	-20818	321559	69973	97147	-27174	334818
Gross Input	1206807	1145457	61350	1676587	1510627	1433572	77055	2035863	1613473	1531684	81789	2190482

1976–1978

	1976 TOTAL	1976 Non-Fin.	1976 Financial	1976 ADDENDUM	1977 TOTAL	1977 Non-Fin.	1977 Financial	1977 ADDENDUM	1978 TOTAL	1978 Non-Fin.	1978 Financial	1978 ADDENDUM
Gross Output												
1 Output for sale	1811920	1770999	40921	2472500	2026932	1980211	46721	2767862	2259473	2206722	52751	3083717
2 Imputed bank service charge	52990	-	52990	52990	62518	-	62518	62518	71487	-	71487	71487
3 Own-account capital formation	...	...	...	...	...	...	...	...	...	...	...	...
Gross Output	1864910	1770999	93911	2525490	2089450	1980211	109239	2830380	2330960	2206722	124238	3155204
Gross Input												
Intermediate consumption	981310	901121	80189	1212962	1079964	986957	93007	1343229	1187992	1081570	106422	1473859
1 Imputed banking service charge	52990	-	52990	52990	62518	-	62518	62518	71487	-	71487	71487
2 Other intermediate consumption	928320	901121	27199	1159972	1017446	986957	30489	1280711	1116505	1081570	34935	1402372
Subtotal: Value Added	883600	869878	13722	1312528	1009486	993254	16232	1487151	1142968	1125152	17816	1681345
1 Indirect taxes, net	43636	42532	1104	47666	52187	49289	2898	56962	62104	58948	3156	70649
a Indirect taxes paid	78763	69652	9111	89816	94386	83710	10676	106751	110294	97691	12603	125089
b Less: Subsidies received	35127	27120	8007	42150	42199	34421	7778	49789	48190	38743	9447	54440
2 Consumption of fixed capital	131352	123155	8197	180925	136336	126824	9512	192051	155246	144418	10828	217534
3 Compensation of employees	643468	607783	35685	723138	732562	692240	40322	822192	827644	781033	46611	927214
4 Net operating surplus	65144	96408	-31264	360799	88401	124901	-36500	415946	97974	140753	-42779	465948
Gross Input	1864910	1770999	93911	2525490	2089450	1980211	109239	2830380	2330960	2206722	124238	3155204

France

3.21 Corporate and Quasi-Corporate Enterprise Production Account: Total and Sectors

Million French francs

	1979			1979 ADDENDUM	1980			1980 ADDENDUM
	Corporate and Quasi-Corporate Enterprises TOTAL	Non-Financial	Financial	Total, Including Unincorporated	Corporate and Quasi-Corporate Enterprises TOTAL	Non-Financial	Financial	Total, Including Unincorporated
Gross Output								
1 Output for sale	2623558	2564803	58755	3556936	...	...	70104	4083684
2 Imputed bank service charge	84321	-	84321	84321	107600	-	107600	107600
3 Own-account capital formation	...	...	...	...	...	...	...	...
Gross Output	2707879	2564803	143076	3641257	...	...	177704	4191284
Gross Input								
Intermediate consumption	1402563	1278056	124507	1728662	...	...	154137	2042791
1 Imputed banking service charge	84321	-	84321	84321	107600	-	107600	107600
2 Other intermediate consumption	1318242	1278056	40186	1644341	...	...	46537	1935191
Subtotal: Value Added	1305316	1286747	18569	1912595	1472775	1449208	23567	2148493
1 Indirect taxes, net	75379	73792	1587	86844	86671	81967	4704	97135
a Indirect taxed paid	130336	116901	13435	148245	144609	129658	14951	163677
b Less: Subsidies received	54957	43109	11848	61401	57938	47691	10247	66542
2 Consumption of fixed capital	174928	162154	12774	245017	202265	187050	15215	282108
3 Compensation of employees	936385	882537	53848	1049222	1075179	1012391	62788	1204814
4 Net operating surplus	118624	168264	-49640	531512	108660	167800	-59140	564436
Gross Input	2707879	2564803	143076	3641257	...	...	177704	4191284

3.22 Corporate and Quasi-Corporate Enterprise Income and Outlay Account: Total and Sectors

Million French francs

	1970 TOTAL	1970 Non-Financial	1970 Financial	1971 TOTAL	1971 Non-Financial	1971 Financial	1972 TOTAL	1972 Non-Financial	1972 Financial	1973 TOTAL	1973 Non-Financial	1973 Financial
Receipts												
1 Property and entrepreneurial income received	127840	78625	49215	142051	90126	51925	161760	100772	60988	206394	115779	90615
a Net operating surplus	58678	69222	-10544	65350	78907	-13557	75731	89475	-13744	84504	99962	-15458
b Withdrawals from quasi-corporate enterprises	62847	4308	58539	68237	4254	63983	76992	4362	72630	111700	8093	103607
c Interest	3794	2577	1217	4820	3324	1496	5692	3592	2100	7762	5297	2465
d Dividends	528	525	3	544	541	3	609	607	2	736	735	1
e Net land rent and royalties	1993	1993	-	3100	3100	-	2736	2736	-	1692	1692	-
2 Other current transfers received	26503	10134	16369	31128	11515	19613	37176	13723	23453	42657	15353	27304
a Casualty insurance transactions	17139	2993	14146	20894	3725	17169	23008	4138	18870	25393	4234	21159
Claims received	3006	2993	13	3739	3725	14	4155	4138	17	4255	4234	21
Net premiums received by insurance companies	14133	-	14133	17155	-	17155	18853	-	18853	21138	-	21138
b Current transfers received from the rest of the world	1720	1448	272	1604	1310	294	4336	2376	1960	5542	2519	3023
c Other transfers received, except imputed	5649	5430	219	6467	6191	276	7202	6885	317	8641	8238	403
d Imputed unfunded employee welfare contributions	1995	263	1732	2163	289	1874	2630	324	2306	3081	362	2719
Total Current Receipts	154343	88759	65584	173179	101641	71538	198936	114495	84441	249051	131132	117919
Disbursements												
1 Property and entrepreneurial income paid out [a]	83749	44964	38785	94778	52847	41931	108186	58336	49850	145739	71593	74146
a Withdrawals from quasi-corporations	583	583	-	834	834	-	482	482	-	577	577	-
b Interest	60857	25544	35313	67712	30107	37605	78188	33204	44984	110070	41553	68517
c Dividends [a]	21000	17528	3472	24735	20409	4326	27787	22921	4866	33361	27732	5629
d Net land rent and royalties	1309	1309	-	1497	1497	-	1729	1729	-	1731	1731	-
2 Direct taxes and other current payments n.e.c. to general government	18459	13681	4778	18618	14558	4060	20952	16901	4051	25472	21383	4089

France

3.22 Corporate and Quasi-Corporate Enterprise Income and Outlay Account: Total and Sectors
(Continued)

Million French francs

	1970 TOTAL	1970 Non-Financial	1970 Financial	1971 TOTAL	1971 Non-Financial	1971 Financial	1972 TOTAL	1972 Non-Financial	1972 Financial	1973 TOTAL	1973 Non-Financial	1973 Financial
a Direct taxes	18459	13681	4778	5298	1238	4060	1938	1278	660	2727	1911	816
b Fines, fees, penalties and other payments n.e.c.	...	...	-	13320	13320	-	19014	15623	3391	22745	19472	3273
3 Other current transfers paid	31397	14316	17081	36709	16256	20453	41917	19259	22658	47653	22093	25560
a Casualty insurance transactions	18870	4723	14147	22887	5711	17176	24950	6073	18877	27637	6476	21161
Casualty insurance premiums paid, net	4737	4723	14	5732	5711	21	6097	6073	24	6499	6476	23
Claims paid by insurance companies	14133	...	14133	17155	-	17155	18853	-	18853	21138	-	21138
b Transfers to private non-profit institutions	1576	1460	116	1776	1649	127	2007	1860	147	2348	2157	191
c Transfers to households	10951	8133	2818	12046	8896	3150	14960	11326	3634	17668	13460	4208
Unfunded employee welfare benefits	7767	5693	2074	8783	6480	2303	10050	7209	2841	11926	8600	3326
Social assistance grants and other transfers n.e.c.	3184	2440	744	3263	2416	847	4910	4117	793	5742	4860	882
d Transfers to the rest of the world	...	...	...	...	...	...	...	...	...	...	...	...
Net saving	20738	15798	4940	23074	17980	5094	27881	19999	7882	30187	16063	14124
Total Current Disbursements and Net Saving	154343	88759	65584	173179	101641	71538	198936	114495	84441	249051	131132	117919

	1974 TOTAL	1974 Non-Financial	1974 Financial	1975 TOTAL	1975 Non-Financial	1975 Financial	1976 TOTAL	1976 Non-Financial	1976 Financial	1977 TOTAL	1977 Non-Financial	1977 Financial
Receipts												
1 Property and entrepreneurial income received	260757	124767	135990	251202	121155	130047	276770	129453	147317	344189	167902	176287
a Net operating surplus	82418	103236	-20818	69973	97147	-27174	65144	96408	-31264	88401	124901	-36500
b Withdrawals from quasi-corporate enterprises	165322	11631	153691	165425	11846	153579	190731	16613	174118	229344	21533	207811
c Interest	9855	6739	3116	10812	7172	3640	13312	8877	4435	17070	12136	4934
d Dividends	918	917	1	1088	1086	2	1261	1233	28	1743	1701	42
e Net land rent and royalties	2244	2244	-	3904	3904	-	6322	6322	-	7631	7631	-
2 Other current transfers received	47682	19146	28536	59228	24050	35178	68486	26798	41688	76823	28969	47854
a Casualty insurance transactions	29443	5132	24311	36450	6619	29831	43400	8239	35161	47755	8763	38992
Claims received	5154	5132	22	6644	6619	25	8269	8239	30	8797	8763	34
Net premiums received by insurance companies	24289	-	24289	29806	-	29806	35131	-	35131	38958	-	38958
b Current transfers received from the rest of the world	4430	3815	615	6002	5249	753	5816	5122	694	7012	5098	1914
c Other transfers received, except imputed	10144	9778	366	12095	11672	423	13276	12825	451	14960	14378	582
d Imputed unfunded employee welfare contributions	3665	421	3244	4681	510	4171	5994	612	5382	7096	730	6366
Total Current Receipts	308439	143913	164526	310430	145205	165225	345256	156251	189005	421012	196871	224141
Disbursements												
1 Property and entrepreneurial income paid out [a]	209395	94095	115300	213322	100425	112897	241988	114265	127723	285850	134056	151794
a Withdrawals from quasi-corporations	773	773	-	1297	1297	-	1850	1850	-	2274	2274	-
b Interest	164114	57836	106278	163935	59694	104241	186766	68585	118181	221886	80108	141778
c Dividends [a]	42667	33645	9022	45462	36808	8654	50053	40513	9540	58337	48336	10001
d Net land rent and royalties	1841	1841	-	2628	2628	-	3319	3317	2	3353	3338	15
2 Direct taxes and other current payments n.e.c. to general government	37464	29135	8329	30926	23442	7484	41229	32678	8551	44288	37551	6737

France

3.22 Corporate and Quasi-Corporate Enterprise Income and Outlay Account: Total and Sectors
(Continued)

Million French francs

	1974 TOTAL	1974 Non-Financial	1974 Financial	1975 TOTAL	1975 Non-Financial	1975 Financial	1976 TOTAL	1976 Non-Financial	1976 Financial	1977 TOTAL	1977 Non-Financial	1977 Financial
a Direct taxes	1989	983	1006	3585	2355	1230	10399	3367	7032	4868	3148	1720
b Fines, fees, penalties and other payments n.e.c.	35475	28152	7323	27341	21087	6254	30830	29311	1519	39420	34403	5017
3 Other current transfers paid	55471	25617	29854	68879	33371	35508	77662	33084	44578	84589	37492	47097
a Casualty insurance transactions	31912	7585	24327	39244	9390	29854	46298	11112	35186	51276	12259	39017
Casualty insurance premiums paid, net	7623	7585	38	9438	9390	48	11167	11112	55	12318	12259	59
Claims paid by insurance companies	24289	-	24289	29806	-	29806	35131	-	35131	38958	-	38958
b Transfers to private non-profit institutions	2817	2598	219	3274	2956	318	3713	3287	426	4252	3696	556
c Transfers to households	20742	15434	5308	26361	21025	5336	27651	18685	8966	29064	21537	7524
Unfunded employee welfare benefits	13709	10199	3510	16569	12182	4387	18369	13437	4932	20709	15108	5601
Social assistance grants and other transfers n.e.c.	7033	5235	1798	9792	8843	949	9282	5248	4034	8355	6429	1923
d Transfers to the rest of the world	...	...	...	...	...	...	...	...	...	...	...	...
Net saving	6109	-4934	11043	-2697	-12033	9336	-15630	-23776	8146	6285	-12228	18513
Total Current Disbursements and Net Saving	308439	143913	164526	310430	145205	165225	345256	156251	189005	421012	196871	224141

	1978 TOTAL	1978 Non-Financial	1978 Financial	1979 TOTAL	1979 Non-Financial	1979 Financial	1980 TOTAL	1980 Non-Financial	1980 Financial
Receipts									
1 Property and entrepreneurial income received	393527	189352	204175	482043	224346	257697	575590	238679	336911
a Net operating surplus	97974	140753	-42779	118624	168264	-49640	108660	167800	-59140
b Withdrawals from quasi-corporate enterprises	264994	23591	241403	328122	28094	300028	423822	35857	387965
c Interest	19597	14069	5528	24047	16760	7287	29841	21780	8061
d Dividends	1846	1823	23	2149	2127	22	2829	2804	25
e Net land rent and royalties	9116	9116	-	9101	9101	-	10438	10438	-
2 Other current transfers received	90421	33134	57287	108133	43233	64900	126036	55481	70555
a Casualty insurance transactions	54245	9839	44406	65797	12689	53108	71392	12856	58536
Claims received	9877	9839	38	12738	12689	49	12913	12856	57
Net premiums received by insurance companies	44368	-	44368	53059	-	53059	58479	-	58479
b Current transfers received from the rest of the world	11419	6330	5089	14235	11536	2699	22205	20713	1492
c Other transfers received, except imputed	16759	16127	632	18931	18198	733	21840	20968	872
d Imputed unfunded employee welfare contributions	7998	838	7160	9170	810	8360	10599	944	9655
Total Current Receipts	483948	222486	261462	590176	267579	322597	701626	294160	407466
Disbursements									
1 Property and entrepreneurial income paid out [a]	325068	148410	176658	392863	167547	225316	488481	198596	289885
a Withdrawals from quasi-corporations	2631	2631	-	2721	2721	-	3127	3127	-
b Interest	252721	87069	165652	309176	97356	211820	390791	115561	275230
c Dividends [a]	66008	55023	10985	76736	63280	13456	89372	74762	14610
d Net land rent and royalties	3708	3687	21	4230	4190	40	5191	5146	45
2 Direct taxes and other current payments n.e.c. to general government	43019	35077	7942	51132	42621	8511	68173	55034	13139

France

3.22 Corporate and Quasi-Corporate Enterprise Income and Outlay Account: Total and Sectors
(Continued)

Million French francs

	1978 TOTAL	1978 Non-Financial	1978 Financial	1979 TOTAL	1979 Non-Financial	1979 Financial	1980 TOTAL	1980 Non-Financial	1980 Financial
a Direct taxes	5773	3696	2077	6527	4102	2425	8906	5252	3654
b Fines, fees, penalties and other payments n.e.c.	37246	31381	5865	44605	38519	6086	59267	49782	9485
3 Other current transfers paid	96999	42237	54762	114280	49594	64706	134687	56902	77785
a Casualty insurance transactions	58236	13802	44434	71465	18332	53133	76988	18425	58563
Casualty insurance premiums paid, net	13868	13802	66	18406	18332	74	18509	18425	84
Claims paid by insurance companies	44368	-	44368	53059	-	53059	58479	-	58479
b Transfers to private non-profit institutions	4748	4153	595	5165	4647	518	6151	5564	587
c Transfers to households	34015	24282	9733	37650	26615	11055	51548	32913	18635
Unfunded employee welfare benefits	23815	16965	6850	26973	19008	7965	31007	21912	9095
Social assistance grants and other transfers n.e.c.	10200	7317	2883	10677	7607	3090	20541	11001	9540
d Transfers to the rest of the world	...	...	...	...	...	...	...	...	...
Net saving	18862	-3238	22100	31901	7817	24084	10285	-16372	26657
Total Current Disbursements and Net Saving	483948	222486	261462	590176	267579	322597	701626	294160	407466

a) Including profit-sharing by employees.

3.23 Corporate and Quasi-Corporate Enterprise Capital Accumulation Account: Total and Sectors

Million French francs

	1970 TOTAL	1970 Non-Financial	1970 Financial	1971 TOTAL	1971 Non-Financial	1971 Financial	1972 TOTAL	1972 Non-Financial	1972 Financial	1973 TOTAL	1973 Non-Financial	1973 Financial
					Finance of Gross Accumulation							
1 Gross saving	69846	62595	7251	75562	67789	7773	87055	75870	11185	97630	79384	18246
a Consumption of fixed capital	49108	46797	2311	52488	49809	2679	59174	55871	3303	67443	63321	4122
b Net saving	20738	15798	4940	23074	17980	5094	27881	19999	7882	30187	16063	14124
2 Capital transfers received	3445	3064	381	3723	2984	739	4111	3513	598	4793	4135	658
Finance of Gross Accumulation	73291	65659	7632	79285	70773	8512	91166	79383	11783	102423	83519	18904
					Gross Accumulation							
1 Gross capital formation	108182	100518	7664	111590	103714	7876	127281	115719	11562	151766	137432	14334
a Increase in stocks	16233	16233	-	9772	9772	-	11553	11553	-	21118	21118	-
b Gross fixed capital formation	91949	84285	7664	101818	93942	7876	115728	104166	11562	130648	116314	14334
2 Purchases of land, net	579	160	419	406	103	303	287	146	141	822	210	612
3 Purchases of intangible assets, net	-72	-77	5	153	9	144	11	2	9	14	3	11
4 Capital transfers paid	1562	1555	7	2276	2076	200	2009	1985	24	2197	2189	8
5 Net lending a	-36960	-36497	-463	-35140	-35129	-11	-38422	-38469	47	-52376	-56315	3939
Gross Accumulation	73291	65659	7632	79285	70773	8512	91166	79383	11783	102423	83519	18904

	1974 TOTAL	1974 Non-Financial	1974 Financial	1975 TOTAL	1975 Non-Financial	1975 Financial	1976 TOTAL	1976 Non-Financial	1976 Financial	1977 TOTAL	1977 Non-Financial	1977 Financial
					Finance of Gross Accumulation							
1 Gross saving	90152	73690	16462	98123	82174	15949	115722	99379	16343	142621	114596	28025
a Consumption of fixed capital	84043	78624	5419	100820	94207	6613	131352	123155	8197	136336	126824	9512
b Net saving	6109	-4934	11043	-2697	-12033	9336	-15630	-23776	8146	6285	-12228	18513
2 Capital transfers received	6585	5583	1002	8895	7422	1473	16495	14796	1699	11965	9539	2426
Finance of Gross Accumulation	96737	79273	17464	107018	89596	17422	132217	114175	18042	154586	124135	30451
					Gross Accumulation							
1 Gross capital formation	179985	163761	16224	154975	139670	15305	210660	192124	18536	228897	208115	20782
a Increase in stocks	29775	29768	7	-4798	-4838	40	20983	20965	18	19623	19616	7
b Gross fixed capital formation	150210	133993	16217	159773	144508	15265	189677	171159	18518	209274	188499	20775
2 Purchases of land, net	869	231	638	678	233	445	641	162	479	822	198	624
3 Purchases of intangible assets, net	18	3	15	22	5	17	211	191	20	35	10	25
4 Capital transfers paid	3263	2852	411	4131	3441	690	5169	4261	908	5692	4573	1119
5 Net lending a	-87398	-87574	176	-52788	-53753	965	-84464	-82563	-1901	-80860	-88761	7901
Gross Accumulation	96737	79273	17464	107018	89596	17422	132217	114175	18042	154586	124135	30451

France

3.23 Corporate and Quasi-Corporate Enterprise Capital Accumulation Account: Total and Sectors
Million French francs

	1978 TOTAL	1978 Non-Financial	1978 Financial	1979 TOTAL	1979 Non-Financial	1979 Financial	1980 TOTAL	1980 Non-Financial	1980 Financial
				Finance of Gross Accumulation					
1 Gross saving	174108	141180	32928	206829	169971	36858	212550	170678	41872
a Consumption of fixed capital	155246	144418	10828	174928	162154	12774	202265	187050	15215
b Net saving	18862	-3238	22100	31901	7817	24084	10285	-16372	26657
2 Capital transfers received	12001	9951	2050	12936	10578	2358	15033	12289	2744
Finance of Gross Accumulation	186109	151131	34978	219765	180549	39216	227583	182967	44616
				Gross Accumulation					
1 Gross capital formation	240113	218524	21589	287931	262607	25324	340745	312182	28563
a Increase in stocks	9921	9882	39	29858	29839	19	40012	39992	20
b Gross fixed capital formation	230192	208642	21550	258073	232768	25305	300733	272190	28543
2 Purchases of land, net	966	231	735	1053	46	1007	1282	163	1119
3 Purchases of intangible assets, net	27	1	26	68	18	50	62	23	39
4 Capital transfers paid	6431	4884	1547	7099	5406	1693	8117	7018	1099
5 Net lending a	-61428	-72509	11081	-76386	-87528	11142	-122623	-136419	13796
Gross Accumulation	186109	151131	34978	219765	180549	39216	227583	182967	44616

a) Net lending of the Capital Accumulation Account and the Capital Finance Account have not been reconciled and are different due to different statistical sources.

3.24 Corporate and Quasi-Corporate Enterprise Capital Finance Account: Total and Sectors
Million French francs

	1970 TOTAL	1970 Non-Financial	1970 Financial	1971 TOTAL	1971 Non-Financial	1971 Financial	1972 TOTAL	1972 Non-Financial	1972 Financial	1973 TOTAL	1973 Non-Financial	1973 Financial
					Acquisition of Financial Assets							
1 Gold and SDRs	-41	-	-41	37	-	37	425	-	425	-467	-	-467
2 Currency and transferable deposits	19160	9669	9491	36088	9062	27026	51096	11842	39254	26373	10977	15396
3 Other deposits	8290	5335	2955	27442	7441	20001	33045	6439	26606	44720	5125	39595
4 Bills and bonds, short term	-1268	-949	-319	725	607	118	-9879	-576	-9303	-16045	-543	-15502
5 Bonds, long term	7131	110	7021	11265	700	10565	16124	716	15408	18972	934	18038
6 Corporate equity securities	6507	978	5529	6276	1551	4725	8760	2258	6502	12910	2597	10313
7 Short term loans, n.e.c.	37456	3621	33835	24344	-9796	34140	90264	3254	87010	80745	-4771	85516
8 Long term loans, n.e.c.	50547	2973	47574	62124	2982	59142	94827	4700	90127	99707	5258	94449
9 Trade credits and advances	6648	5855	793	8129	6606	1523	8655	7943	712	9611	7724	1887
10 Other receivables	684	684	-	852	852	-	891	891	-	1102	1102	-
11 Other assets	...	...	...	...	...	...	...	...	...	...	...	...
Total Acquisition of Financial Assets	135114	28276	106838	177282	20005	157277	294208	37467	256741	277628	28403	249225
					Incurrence of Liabilities							
1 Currency and transferable deposits	20376	-	20376	33999	-	33999	72628	-	72628	44963	-	44963
2 Other deposits	53742	596	53146	85455	861	84594	95647	1167	94480	107904	2316	105588
3 Bills and bonds, short term	726	-	726	2187	-	2187	823	-	823	39	-	39
4 Bonds, long term	11987	3834	8153	19871	7359	12512	21424	6786	14638	24526	6047	18479
5 Corporate equity securities	16397	8575	7822	16260	8573	7687	20246	11467	8779	21878	12805	9073
6 Short-term loans, n.e.c.	28224	25764	2460	19712	18831	881	75877	27518	48359	68078	25904	42174
7 Long-term loans, n.e.c.	31842	23416	8426	32532	23714	8818	39169	30171	8998	49433	36248	13185
8 Net equity of households in life insurance and pension fund reserves	2691	-	2691	3056	-	3056	3545	-	3545	4120	-	4120
9 Proprietors' net additions to the accumulation of quasi-corporations	...	...	...	...	...	...	...	...	...	...	...	...
10 Trade credit and advances	4898	4825	73	5557	5111	446	8000	7279	721	12306	11257	1049
11 Other accounts payable	4479	-	4479	5182	-	5182	5514	-	5514	6063	-	6063
12 Other liabilities	...	...	...	...	...	...	...	...	...	2289		2289
Total Incurrence of Liabilities	175362	67010	108352	223811	64449	159362	342873	84388	258485	341599	94577	247022
Net Lending a	-40248	-38734	-1514	-46529	-44444	-2085	-48665	-46921	-1744	-63971	-66174	2203
Incurrence of Liabilities and Net Lending	135114	28276	106838	177282	20005	157277	294208	37467	256741	277628	28403	249225

France

3.24 Corporate and Quasi-Corporate Enterprise Capital Finance Account: Total and Sectors

Million French francs

	1974 TOTAL	1974 Non-Financial	1974 Financial	1975 TOTAL	1975 Non-Financial	1975 Financial	1976 TOTAL	1976 Non-Financial	1976 Financial	1977 TOTAL	1977 Non-Financial	1977 Financial
Acquisition of Financial Assets												
1 Gold and SDRs	68	-	68	-56	-	-56	51	-	51	136	-	136
2 Currency and transferable deposits	13671	15554	-1883	1706	18468	-16762	-1043	5219	-6262	30523	19024	11499
3 Other deposits	5305	9348	-4043	38467	11870	26597	36979	10437	26542	75717	16325	59392
4 Bills and bonds, short term	-283	-308	25	41715	-23	41738	9813	123	9690	8610	-1	8611
5 Bonds, long term	12262	-153	12415	21951	259	21692	19639	639	19000	24720	1007	23713
6 Corporate equity securities	8725	4036	4689	11143	4662	6481	15864	8441	7423	13081	6857	6224
7 Short term loans, n.e.c.	70522	-1599	72121	-44582	-16537	-28045	51952	-8470	60422	86749	4542	82207
8 Long term loans, n.e.c.	108283	5592	102691	149051	10386	138665	182160	8029	174131	188324	10642	177682
9 Trade credits and advances	18921	15271	3650	5797	4990	807	25817	23750	2067	11793	10622	1171
10 Other receivables	1527	1527	-	1641	1641	-	1737	1737	-	2111	2102	9
11 Other assets	...	...	...	...	...	...	...	...	...	...	...	...
Total Acquisition of Financial Assets	239001	49268	189733	226833	35716	191117	342969	49905	293064	441764	71120	370644
Incurrence of Liabilities												
1 Currency and transferable deposits	27995	-	27995	19943	-	19943	38963	-	38963	54141	-	54141
2 Other deposits	94245	2109	92136	149698	709	148989	156481	2797	153684	192859	4803	188056
3 Bills and bonds, short term	366	-	366	426	-	426	2215	-	2215	2712	-	2712
4 Bonds, long term	17926	4071	13855	41362	14410	26952	43176	12482	30694	35772	12256	23516
5 Corporate equity securities	19416	13515	5901	22015	15346	6669	26682	19942	6740	27096	19063	8033
6 Short-term loans, n.e.c.	71587	55688	15899	-27812	13378	-41190	26541	10701	15840	85430	50009	35421
7 Long-term loans, n.e.c.	61442	43657	17785	81355	63812	17543	95755	68220	27535	103405	70002	33403
8 Net equity of households in life insurance and pension fund reserves	4455	-	4455	5566	-	5566	6704	-	6704	7732	-	7732
9 Proprietors' net additions to the accumulation of quasi-corporations	...	...	...	...	...	...	...	...	...	...	...	...
10 Trade credit and advances	27051	26316	735	-6399	-7282	883	28179	26152	2027	9383	9245	138
11 Other accounts payable	7486	-	7486	7901	-	7901	8322	-	8322	9127	-	9127
12 Other liabilities	-719	-	-719	-122	-	-122	80	-	80	-39	-	-39
Total Incurrence of Liabilities	331250	145356	185894	293933	100373	193560	433098	140294	292804	527618	165378	362240
Net Lending a	-92249	-96088	3839	-67100	-64657	-2443	-90129	-90389	260	-85854	-94258	8404
Incurrence of Liabilities and Net Lending	239001	49268	189733	226833	35716	191117	342969	49905	293064	441764	71120	370644

	1978 TOTAL	1978 Non-Financial	1978 Financial	1979 TOTAL	1979 Non-Financial	1979 Financial	1980 TOTAL	1980 Non-Financial	1980 Financial
Acquisition of Financial Assets									
1 Gold and SDRs	53	-	53	100	-	100	-	-	-
2 Currency and transferable deposits	24490	14127	10363	41268	20303	20965	59543	6797	52746
3 Other deposits	73599	10248	63351	70458	21301	49157	31190	18424	12766
4 Bills and bonds, short term	24223	-10	24233	11603	-7	11610	-5880	-	-5880
5 Bonds, long term	26501	727	25774	36158	1655	34503	42929	2100	40829
6 Corporate equity securities	18954	6066	12888	22740	6014	16726	26982	7567	19415
7 Short term loans, n.e.c.	58398	-10059	68457	76390	5713	70677	58090	-12756	70846
8 Long term loans, n.e.c.	214761	9738	205023	262210	9044	253166	266735	13072	253663
9 Trade credits and advances	15319	13069	2250	16187	11944	4243	...	...	...
10 Other receivables	2376	2365	11	3378	3364	14	3565	3550	15
11 Other assets	...	...	...	...	...	...	...	...	...
Total Acquisition of Financial Assets	458674	46271	412403	540492	79331	461161	483154	38754	444400
Incurrence of Liabilities									
1 Currency and transferable deposits	83661	-	83661	52570	-	52570	75872	-	75872
2 Other deposits	177772	1912	175860	249822	3014	246808	225376	1260	224116
3 Bills and bonds, short term	1524	-	1524	3755	-	3755	330	-	330
4 Bonds, long term	34170	9863	24307	36675	12508	24167	61767	13078	48689
5 Corporate equity securities	36397	26290	10107	40023	25280	14743	57285	42635	14650
6 Short-term loans, n.e.c.	60409	30194	30215	73361	47392	25969	70489	63034	7455

France

3.24 Corporate and Quasi-Corporate Enterprise Capital Finance Account: Total and Sectors
(Continued)

Million French francs

	1978 TOTAL	1978 Non-Financial	1978 Financial	1979 TOTAL	1979 Non-Financial	1979 Financial	1980 TOTAL	1980 Non-Financial	1980 Financial
7 Long-term loans, n.e.c.	107717	59863	47854	120299	72445	47854	89343	57198	32145
8 Net equity of households in life insurance and pension fund reserves	9187	-	9187	11108	-	11108	...	...	...
9 Proprietors' net additions to the accumulation of quasi-corporations	...	...	...	...	...	...	...	...	...
10 Trade credit and advances	12190	11388	802	16838	15713	1125	...	...	...
11 Other accounts payable	10376	-	10376	13624	-	13624	27044	-	27044
12 Other liabilities	-297	-	-297	-874	-	-874	.	.	.
Total Incurrence of Liabilities	533106	139510	393596	617201	176352	440849	607506	177205	430301
Net Lending a	-74432	-93239	18807	-76709	-97021	20312	-124352	-138451	14099
Incurrence of Liabilities and Net Lending	458674	46271	412403	540492	79331	461161	483154	38754	444400

a) Net lending of the Capital Accumulation Account and the Capital Finance Account have not been reconciled and are different due to different statistical sources.

3.26 Financial Transactions of Financial Institutions: Detail

Million French francs

	1970 ALL FINANCIAL INSTITUTIONS	1970 Central Bank	1970 Other Monetary Institutions	1970 Insurance	1970 Other Financial Institutions	1971 ALL FINANCIAL INSTITUTIONS	1971 Central Bank	1971 Other Monetary Institutions	1971 Insurance	1971 Other Financial Institutions
Acquisition of Financial Assets										
1 Gold and SDRs	-41	-37	-4	-	-	37	39	-2	-	-
a Gold	-74	-70	-4	-	-	-52	-50	-2	-	-
b Net acquisitions of SDRs	33	33	-	-	-	89	89	-	-	-
2 Currency and transferable deposits	9491	5195	2724	365	1207	27026	15517	9475	206	1828
3 Other deposits	2955	337	1203	631	784	20001	-168	16376	605	3188
4 Bills and bonds, short term	-319	-1638	395	195	729	118	1593	-384	138	-1229
5 Bonds, long term	7021	21	45	3321	3634	10565	-3	867	4346	5355
6 Corporate equity securities	5529	12	1287	1708	2522	4725	3	1097	1020	2605
7 Short-term loans, n.e.c.	33835	-6344	33761	723	5695	34140	-12185	33914	714	11697
8 Long-term loans, n.e.c.	47574	-203	15756	692	31329	59142	-213	25792	1109	32454
9 Trade credit and advances	793	-	7	588	198	1523	-	49	1009	465
10 Other assets	...	...	...	...	...	...	...	...	...	...
Total Acquisition of Financial Assets	106838	-2657	55174	8223	46098	157277	4583	87184	9147	56363
Incurrence of Liabilities										
1 Currency and transferable deposits	20376	522	18348	-	1506	33999	6009	23994	-	3996
2 Other deposits	53146	-3216	36445	829	19088	84594	-	61441	545	22608
3 Bills and bonds, short term	726	-	-	-	726	2187	-	-	...	2187
4 Bonds, long term	8153	-	2261	-	5892	12512	-	4555	-	7957
5 Corporate equity securities	7822	-	1579	98	6145	7687	-	1494	15	6178
6 Short-term loans, n.e.c.	2460	578	-2506	4	4384	881	-747	-3208	297	4539
7 Long-term loans, n.e.c.	8426	-	239	2	8185	8818	-	631	2	8185
9 Net equity of households in life insurance and pension fund reserves	2691	-	-	2691	-	3056	-	-	3056	-
10 Other liabilities	4552	-	4517	35	5628	-	47	5639	-58	
Total Incurrence of liabilities a	108352	-2116	56366	8141	45961	159362	5262	88954	9554	55592
Net Lending	-1514	-541	-1192	82	137	-2085	-679	-1770	-407	771
Incurrence of Liabilities and Net Lending	106838	-2657	55174	8223	46098	157277	4583	87184	9147	56363

	1972 ALL FINANCIAL INSTITUTIONS	1972 Central Bank	1972 Other Monetary Institutions	1972 Insurance	1972 Other Financial Institutions	1973 ALL FINANCIAL INSTITUTIONS	1973 Central Bank	1973 Other Monetary Institutions	1973 Insurance	1973 Other Financial Institutions
Acquisition of Financial Assets										
1 Gold and SDRs	425	414	11	-	-	-467	-488	21	-	-
a Gold	16	5	11	-	-	64	43	21	-	-
b Net acquisitions of SDRs	409	409	-	-	-	-531	-531	-	-	-
2 Currency and transferable deposits	39254	7421	25330	1090	5413	15396	-4617	16990	718	2305
3 Other deposits	26606	57	24331	332	1886	39595	-169	35040	830	3894
4 Bills and bonds, short term	-9303	-3168	-774	-111	-5250	-15502	-2669	-6500	-121	-6212

France

3.26 Financial Transactions of Financial Institutions: Detail
(Continued)

Million French francs

	1972					1973				
	ALL FINANCIAL INSTITUTIONS	Central Bank	Other Monetary Institutions	Insurance	Other Financial Institutions	ALL FINANCIAL INSTITUTIONS	Central Bank	Other Monetary Institutions	Insurance	Other Financial Institutions
5 Bonds, long term	15408	184	3262	5175	6787	18038	-3	1183	5831	11027
6 Corporate equity securities	6502	42	1811	1366	3283	10313	-2	3937	3168	3210
7 Short-term loans, n.e.c.	87010	30426	40205	585	15794	85516	43134	26817	690	14875
8 Long-term loans, n.e.c.	90127	1398	48052	751	39926	94449	-7196	51649	541	49455
9 Trade credit and advances	712	-	1	875	-164	1887	-	-	1519	368
10 Other assets	...	...	...	...	...	...	...	...	...	...
Total Acquisition of Financial Assets	256741	36774	142229	10063	67675	249225	27990	129137	13176	78922

Incurrence of Liabilities

1 Currency and transferable deposits	72628	34948	30706	-	6974	44963	19422	20890	-	4651
2 Other deposits	94480	-	68466	555	25459	105588	-	75430	851	29307
3 Bills and bonds, short term	823	-	-	-	823	39	-	-	-	39
4 Bonds, long term	14638	-	4117	-	10521	18479	-	6260	-	12219
5 Corporate equity securities	8779	-	1762	67	6950	9073	-	1889	88	7096
6 Short-term loans, n.e.c.	48359	593	38495	88	9183	42174	-116	29337	310	12643
7 Long-term loans, n.e.c.	8998	-	1366	8	7624	13185	-	1577	2	11606
9 Net equity of households in life insurance and pension fund reserves	3545	-	-	3545	-	4120	-	-	4120	-
10 Other liabilities	6235	-	-49	5721	563	7112	-	-112	6566	658
Total Incurrence of liabilities [a]	258485	35541	144863	9984	68097	247022	21595	135271	11937	78219
Net Lending	-1744	1233	-2634	79	-422	2203	6395	-6134	1239	703
Incurrence of Liabilities and Net Lending	256741	36774	142227	10063	67675	249225	27990	129137	13176	78922

	1974					1975				
	ALL FINANCIAL INSTITUTIONS	Central Bank	Other Monetary Institutions	Insurance	Other Financial Institutions	ALL FINANCIAL INSTITUTIONS	Central Bank	Other Monetary Institutions	Insurance	Other Financial Institutions

Acquisition of Financial Assets

1 Gold and SDRs	68	-7	75	-	-	-56	-	-56	-	-
a Gold	68	-7	75	-	-	-56	-	-56	-	-
b Net acquisitions of SDRs	...	-	-	-	-	-	-	-	-	-
2 Currency and transferable deposits	-1883	-2035	-4507	2250	2409	-16762	16734	-33869	-146	519
3 Other deposits	-4043	-	-3986	123	-180	26597	-	27691	1277	-2371
4 Bills and bonds, short term	25	2554	-1904	-17	-608	41738	13947	15379	86	12326
5 Bonds, long term	12415	17	-1141	4481	9058	21692	-1	1877	8101	11715
6 Corporate equity securities	4689	-1	1033	2715	942	6481	16	17	4149	2299
7 Short-term loans, n.e.c.	72121	-702	60632	821	11370	-28045	-54054	19107	798	6104
8 Long-term loans, n.e.c.	102691	2080	42431	703	57477	138665	-48	53241	1075	84397
9 Trade credit and advances	3650	-	5	2685	960	807	-	-	18	789
10 Other assets	...	...	...	...	...	...	...	...	...	...
Total Acquisition of Financial Assets	189733	1906	92638	13761	81428	191117	-23406	83387	15358	115778

Incurrence of Liabilities

1 Currency and transferable deposits	27995	220	28184	-	-409	19943	-24783	41954	-	2772
2 Other deposits	92136	1381	51610	1442	37703	148989	1814	85778	1561	59836
3 Bills and bonds, short term	366	-	-	-	366	426	-	-	-	426
4 Bonds, long term	13855	-	4125	-	9730	26952	-	8665	-	18287
5 Corporate equity securities	5901	-	1387	87	4427	6669	-	1411	104	5154
6 Short-term loans, n.e.c.	15899	-20	5381	39	10499	-41190	2870	-53661	198	9403
7 Long-term loans, n.e.c.	17785	-	2528	19	15238	17543	-	1290	4	16249
9 Net equity of households in life insurance and pension fund reserves	4455	-	-	4455	-	5566	-	-	5566	-
10 Other liabilities	8221	-	-42	7950	313	8784	-	-	8332	452
Total Incurrence of liabilities [a]	185894	862	93173	13992	77867	193560	-20221	85437	15765	112579
Net Lending	3839	1044	-535	-231	3561	-2443	-3185	-2050	-407	3199
Incurrence of Liabilities and Net Lending	189733	1906	92638	13761	81428	191117	-23406	83387	15358	115778

France

3.26 Financial Transactions of Financial Institutions: Detail

Million French francs

		1976				1977				
		ALL FINANCIAL INSTITUTIONS	Central Bank	Other Monetary Institutions	Insurance	Other Financial Institutions	ALL FINANCIAL INSTITUTIONS	Central Bank	Other Monetary Institutions	Insurance	Other Financial Institutions

Acquisition of Financial Assets

1	Gold and SDRs	51	52	-1	.	.	136	132	4	.	.
	a Gold	51	52	-1	.	.	136	132	4	.	.
	b Net acquisitions of SDRs	...	...	...	...	...	...	...	...	...	...
2	Currency and transferable deposits	-6262	-12769	7884	966	-2343	11499	672	8339	775	1713
3	Other deposits	26542	.	25565	715	262	59392	.	54083	505	4804
4	Bills and bonds, short term	9690	6531	-6446	263	9342	8611	-9336	10624	-25	7348
5	Bonds, long term	19000	411	1450	7379	9760	23713	94	1451	10173	11995
6	Corporate equity securities	7423	19	2025	3463	1916	6224	-5	2470	4696	-937
7	Short-term loans, n.e.c.	60422	7257	35191	2131	15843	82207	19280	48495	1219	13213
8	Long-term loans, n.e.c.	174131	205	73826	1003	99097	177682	-73	70916	904	105935
9	Trade credit and advances	2067	.	.	1188	879	1171	.	.	1347	-167
10	Other assets	...	...	...	...	...	...	...	...	...	...
	Total Acquisition of Financial Assets	293064	1706	139494	17108	134756	370644	10764	196382	19594	143904

Incurrence of Liabilities

1	Currency and transferable deposits	38963	7025	27648	-	4290	54141	13162	35000	-	5979
2	Other deposits	153684	696	92617	765	59606	188056	-2550	127643	1925	61038
3	Bills and bonds, short term	2215	.	1613	.	602	2712	.	1674	.	1038
4	Bonds, long term	30694	.	10717	.	19977	23516	.	9475	.	14041
5	Corporate equity securities	6740	.	2035	18	4687	8033	.	2004	812	5217
6	Short-term loans, n.e.c.	15840	-2498	1562	470	16306	35421	-1052	17666	-222	19029
7	Long-term loans, n.e.c.	27535	.	2108	48	25379	33403	.	3671	64	29668
9	Net equity of households in life insurance and pension fund reserves	6704	.	.	6704	.	7732	.	.	7732	.
10	Other liabilities	10349	.	.	8791	1558	9265	.	.	9089	176
	Total Incurrence of liabilities a	292804	5303	138300	16796	132405	362240	9521	197133	19400	136186
	Net Lending	260	-3597	1194	312	2351	8404	1243	-751	194	7718
	Incurrence of Liabilities and Net Lending	293064	1706	139494	17108	134756	370644	10764	196382	19594	143904

		1978					1979				
		ALL FINANCIAL INSTITUTIONS	Central Bank	Other Monetary Institutions	Insurance	Other Financial Institutions	ALL FINANCIAL INSTITUTIONS	Central Bank	Other Monetary Institutions	Insurance	Other Financial Institutions

Acquisition of Financial Assets

1	Gold and SDRs	53	62	-9	.	.	100	60	40	.	.
	a Gold	53	62	-9	.	.	100	60	40	.	.
	b Net acquisitions of SDRs	.	.	.	.	.	.	.	.	.	.
2	Currency and transferable deposits	10363	14680	-8230	916	2997	20965	6136	6932	2053	5844
3	Other deposits	63351	.	60167	2045	1139	49157	.	45277	1381	2499
4	Bills and bonds, short term	24233	4318	12119	10	7786	11610	-2289	2432	-35	11502
5	Bonds, long term	25774	53	-47	10663	15105	34503	-64	6390	9077	19100
6	Corporate equity securities	12888	46	4195	5686	2961	16726	18	3982	7062	5664
7	Short-term loans, n.e.c.	68457	27780	23717	1649	15311	70677	-534	52313	2427	16471
8	Long-term loans, n.e.c.	205023	-2023	87450	1304	118292	253166	-3	122519	1510	129140
9	Trade credit and advances	2250	.	.	1764	486	4243	.	.	3020	1223
10	Other assets	11	.	.	.	11	14	.	.	.	14
	Total Acquisition of Financial Assets	412403	44916	179362	24037	164088	461161	3324	239885	26495	191457

Incurrence of Liabilities

1	Currency and transferable deposits	83661	41277	38684	-	3700	52570	1931	36654	-	13985
2	Other deposits	175860	-57	100869	1608	73440	246808	-1216	168084	1418	78522
3	Bills and bonds, short term	1524	.	-16	.	1540	3755	.	2024	.	1731

France

3.26 Financial Transactions of Financial Institutions: Detail
(Continued)

Million French francs

	1978 ALL FINANCIAL INSTITUTIONS	Central Bank	Other Monetary Institutions	Insurance	Other Financial Institutions	1979 ALL FINANCIAL INSTITUTIONS	Central Bank	Other Monetary Institutions	Insurance	Other Financial Institutions
4 Bonds, long term	24307	-	8773	-	15534	24167	-	10110	-	14057
5 Corporate equity securities	10107	-	1395	122	8590	14743	-	3053	118	11572
6 Short-term loans, n.e.c.	30215	691	8238	474	20812	25969	965	-780	50	25734
7 Long-term loans, n.e.c.	47854	-	11275	129	36450	47854	-	9334	40	38480
9 Net equity of households in life insurance and pension fund reserves	9187	-	-	9187	-	11108	-	-	11108	-
10 Other liabilities	11178	-	-	11188	-10	14749	-	-	14600	149
Total Incurrence of liabilities a	393596	41614	169218	22708	160056	440849	806	228479	27334	184230
Net Lending	18807	3302	10144	1329	4032	20312	2518	11406	-839	7227
Incurrence of Liabilities and Net Lending	412403	44916	179362	24037	164088	461161	3324	239885	26495	191457

	1980 ALL FINANCIAL INSTITUTIONS	Central Bank	Other Monetary Institutions	Insurance	Other Financial Institutions
Acquisition of Financial Assets					
1 Gold and SDRs					
a Gold	52746	28757	13764	885	9340
b Net acquisitions of SDRs					
2 Currency and transferable deposits					
3 Other deposits	12766	920	7160	2265	2421
4 Bills and bonds, short term	-5880	-5762	-4426	-	4308
5 Bonds, long term	40829	-	9700	12750	18379
6 Corporate equity securities	19415	-	4597	7553	7265
7 Short-term loans, n.e.c.	70846	8240	61130	2920	-1444
8 Long-term loans, n.e.c.	253663	-	111490	1665	140508
9 Trade credit and advances	...	...	...	...	...
10 Other assets	15	-	-	-	15
Total Acquisition of Financial Assets	444400	32155	203415	28038	180792
Incurrence of Liabilities					
1 Currency and transferable deposits	75872	39808	29400	-	6664
2 Other deposits	224116	5720	144187	1550	72659
3 Bills and bonds, short term	330	-	-140	-	470
4 Bonds, long term	48689	-	20690	-	27999
5 Corporate equity securities	14650	-	3980	355	10315
6 Short-term loans, n.e.c.	7455	-	-14670	1135	20990
7 Long-term loans, n.e.c.	32145	-	9880	45	22220
9 Net equity of households in life insurance and pension fund reserves	...	...	...	...	...
10 Other liabilities	27044	-	-	27044	-
Total Incurrence of liabilities a	430301	45528	193327	30129	161317
Net Lending	14099	-13373	10088	-2091	19475
Incurrence of Liabilities and Net Lending	444400	32155	203415	28038	180792

a) Beginning 1973, item 'Total incurrence of liability' includes IMF SDRs.

3.31 Household and Private Unincorporated Enterprise Production Account

Million French francs

	1970	1971	1972	1973	1974	1975	1976	1977	1978	1979	1980
Gross Output											
1 Marketed output (Sales)	332481	363301	397182	463664	517887	568297	650612	729848	812007	919733	...
2 Non-marketed output	4595	5017	5498	6116	7349	8712	9968	11082	12237	13645	...
Gross Output	337076	368318	402680	469780	525236	577009	660580	740930	824244	933378	...
Gross Input											
Intermediate consumption	108722	117850	122762	158184	185132	194485	231652	263265	285867	326099	...

France

3.31 Household and Private Unincorporated Enterprise Production Account
(Continued)

Million French francs

	1970	1971	1972	1973	1974	1975	1976	1977	1978	1979	1980
Subtotal: Value Added	228354	250468	279918	311596	340104	382524	428928	477665	538377	607279	675718
1 Indirect taxes paid by unincorporated enterprises	4240	4377	5159	5522	1909	3448	4030	4775	8545	11465	10464
a Indirect taxes paid	5620	6079	7009	8179	7848	9799	11053	12365	14795	17909	19068
b Less: Subsidies received	1380	1702	1850	2657	5939	6351	7023	7590	6250	6444	8604
2 Consumption of fixed capital	24658	23576	26138	29939	36717	42792	49573	55715	62288	70089	79843
3 Compensation of employees	41355	44936	49367	53717	62337	71439	79670	89630	99570	112837	129635
4 Net operating surplus	158101	177579	199254	222418	239141	264845	295655	327545	367974	412888	455776
Gross Input	337076	368318	402680	469780	525236	577009	660580	740930	824244	933378	...

3.32 Household and Private Unincorporated Enterprise Income and Outlay Account

Million French francs

	1970	1971	1972	1973	1974	1975	1976	1977	1978	1979	1980
Receipts											
1 Compensation of employees	381801	431750	482884	557271	664687	782384	907859	1034563	1170841	1320685	1518852
a Wages and salaries	289551	327053	366027	422474	502986	583427	673576	764026	860182	963155	...
b Employers' contributions for social security	73072	83205	92757	107136	128953	160156	189163	219071	250431	291721	...
c Employers' contributions for private pension & welfare plans	19178	21492	24100	27661	32748	38801	45120	51466	60228	65809	...
2 Property and entrepreneurial income received	190967	215849	243127	271434	305523	339868	380681	423134	475088	535748	600251
a Operating surplus of private unincorporated enterprises	158101	177579	199254	222418	239141	264845	295655	327545	367974	412888	...
b Withdrawals from private quasi-corporations	-	-	-	-	-	-	-	-	-	-	...
c Interest	12961	15894	19183	22552	32843	40586	46528	52311	58537	68283	...
d Dividends	17648	19837	21873	23823	29912	31200	35470	40230	44749	50505	...
e Net land rent and royalties	2257	2539	2817	2641	3627	3237	3028	3048	3828	4072	...
3 Other current transfers received	156402	176360	200055	230564	274015	348397	404141	467917	554232	638979	734896
a Casualty insurance claims	11837	14367	15750	17575	19958	24012	27736	31293	36034	41821	47342
b Social security benefits	102833	115742	132361	154092	183391	236015	275616	321042	382682	448139	522018
c Social assistance grants	17388	18902	21641	24280	28581	35471	41617	48047	56506	60692	64621
d Unfunded employee welfare benefits	20769	23246	26077	29719	34904	41765	47582	54444	61946	68972	78712
e Other current transfers received	3575	4103	4226	4898	7181	11134	11590	13091	17064	19355	22203
Total Current Receipts	729170	823959	926066	1059269	1244225	1470649	1692681	1925614	2200161	2495412	2853999
Disbursements											
1 Final consumption expenditures	467231	525499	589580	665934	777851	894798	1037398	1166384	1321046	1510166	1737742
2 Property income paid	12822	14564	17145	23262	32934	35306	42004	50164	54574	62264	79583
a Interest	10245	11687	13939	19822	28373	31454	38268	46319	49881	57208	74287
b Net land rent and royalties	2577	2877	3206	3440	4561	3852	3736	3845	4693	5056	5296
3 Direct taxes, fees, fines & other payments n.e.c. to government	141252	156998	178099	205111	240685	301380	369075	429452	488551	577636	683775
a Social security contributions	102613	116515	131758	151807	182347	225783	270702	317146	362097	434464	512919
b Direct taxes	38639	40483	46341	53304	58338	75597	98373	112306	126454	143172	170856
Income taxes	27164	28734	33120	34400	46750	50633	67050	79091	89470	101579	117508
Other	11475	11749	13221	18904	11588	24964	31323	33215	36984	41593	53348
c Fees, fines and penalties	...	...	...	...	...	...	...	...	...	...	...
4 Other current transfers paid	38680	44604	47886	55180	65486	77736	89884	102669	117715	130393	146739
a Net casualty insurance premiums	9521	11645	12881	14321	16283	19938	23543	26206	29998	33842	39130
b Transfers to private non-profit institutions serving households	910	979	1016	1175	1408	1597	1819	2052	2302	2583	2989
c Transfers to the rest of the world	4255	4747	5133	5602	6571	7170	7749	8568	10085	11100	12774
d Other current transfers, except imputed	4339	5207	4176	5782	7732	9401	10781	13389	14015	15838	15154
e Imputed employee welfare contributions	19655	22026	24680	28300	33492	39630	45992	52454	61315	67030	76692
Net saving	69185	82294	93356	109782	127269	161429	154320	176945	218275	214953	206160
Total Current Disbursements and Net Saving	729170	823959	926066	1059269	1244225	1470649	1692681	1925614	2200161	2495412	2853999

France

3.33 Household and Private Unincorporated Enterprise Capital Accumulation Account

Million French francs

	1970	1971	1972	1973	1974	1975	1976	1977	1978	1979	1980
Finance of Gross Accumulation											
1 Gross saving	93843	105870	119494	139721	163986	204221	203893	232660	280563	285042	286003
a Consumption of fixed capital	24658	23576	26138	29939	36717	42792	49573	55715	62288	70089	79843
b Net saving	69185	82294	93356	109782	127269	161429	154320	176945	218275	214953	206160
2 Capital transfers received	1793	1908	2084	2481	2406	3833	5470	3662	3440	4547	5208
Total Finance of Gross Accumulation	95636	107778	121578	142202	166392	208054	209363	236322	284003	289589	291211
Gross Accumulation											
1 Gross Capital Formation	65264	74154	86691	102301	117529	122999	143122	152895	169338	197879	213249
a Increase in stocks	2928	643	2950	4425	-151	-2239	385	1547	2724	4895	1277
b Gross fixed capital formation	62336	73511	83741	97876	117680	125238	142737	151348	166614	192984	211972
2 Purchases of land, net	-1143	-897	-1747	-2098	-2246	-2341	-2054	-2208	-2514	-2423	-2750
3 Purchases of intangibles, net	72	-156	-14	-10	-69	-82	-46	-92	-11	-153	-148
4 Capital transfers paid	2455	2521	2878	3508	3521	4857	4028	4700	5445	6816	8831
5 Net lending [a]	28988	32156	33770	38501	47657	82621	64313	81027	111745	87470	72029
Total Gross Accumulation	95636	107778	121578	142202	166392	208054	209363	236322	284003	289589	291211

a) Net lending of the Capital Accumulation Account and the Capital Finance Account have not been reconciled and are different due to different statistical sources.

3.34 Household and Private Unincorporated Enterprise Capital Finance Account

Million French francs

	1970	1971	1972	1973	1974	1975	1976	1977	1978	1979	1980
Acquisition of Financial Assets											
1 Gold	.	.	.	.	.	.	.	.	.	.	.
2 Currency and transferable deposits	11384	17535	24379	18494	28422	31788	30981	30337	44212	52428	30280
3 Other deposits	38256	49066	57761	62968	67380	102756	111075	113927	122045	137958	122098
4 Bills and bonds, short term	...	...	.	.	.	-3	6	.	.	.	.
a Corporate and quasi-corporate	.	.	...	...	...	...	...	...	...	...	...
b Government	...	...	...	...	...	...	...	...	...	...	...
c Rest of the world	...	...	...	...	...	...	...	...	...	...	...
5 Bonds, long term	439	5347	5042	9725	-3051	6445	10190	10777	18187	17105	41698
6 Corporate equity securities	2703	4151	5243	5258	3382	3405	4255	4276	7709	10657	12530
7 Short term loans, n.e.c.	3921	-475	4285	4190	13638	4294	3752	7701	-382	10692	...
8 Long term loans, n.e.c.	-69	-28	-20	-74	...	...	43	24	53	-907	...
9 Trade credit and advances of unincorporated enterprises	559	687	1167	1473	977	2246	3082	-1395	2042	823	...
10 Net equity of households in life insurance and pension fund reserves	2691	3056	3545	4120	4455	5566	6704	7732	9187	11108	23431
11 Proprietors' net additions to the accumulation of quasi-corporations	...	...	...	...	...	...	...	...	...	...	...
12 Other	3778	4312	4596	4894	5863	5746	6486	6934	7913	10129	...
Total Acquisition of Financial Assets	63662	83651	105998	111048	121066	162243	176574	180313	210966	249993	230037
Incurrence of Liabilities											
1 Short term loans, n.e.c.	13195	11666	20421	19446	24360	6727	25228	13179	6299	23441	18880
2 Long term loans, n.e.c.	15447	26916	41972	43250	34006	48915	68819	70079	78057	119589	120277
3 Trade credit and advances of unincorporated enterprises	319	491	-593	1454	1737	915	5439	3512	234	8768	...
4 Other accounts payable	...	...	...	...	...	...	...	...	...	...	...
5 Other liabilities	...	...	...	...	...	...	...	...	...	...	...
Total Incurrence of Liabilities	28961	39073	61800	64150	60103	56557	99486	86770	84590	151798	139157
Net Lending [a]	34701	44578	44198	46898	60963	105686	77088	93543	126376	98195	90880
Incurrence of Liabilities and Net Lending	63662	83651	105998	111048	121066	162243	176574	180313	210966	249993	230037

a) Net lending of the Capital Accumulation Account and the Capital Finance Account have not been reconciled and are different due to different statistical sources.

France

3.41 Private Non-Profit Institutions Serving Households: Production Account

Million French francs

	1970	1971	1972	1973	1974	1975	1976	1977	1978	1979	1980
Gross Output											
1 Sales	2534	2856	3205	3663	4177	4657	5355	5972	6527	7157	8093
2 Non-marketed output	2629	2964	3326	3804	4347	4933	5619	6338	7111	7978	9231
Gross Output	5163	5820	6531	7467	8524	9590	10974	12310	13638	15135	17324
Gross Input											
Intermediate consumption	3010	3393	3807	4351	4963	5578	6386	7165	7925	8783	10039
Subtotal: Value Added	2153	2427	2724	3116	3561	4012	4588	5145	5713	6352	7285
1 Indirect taxes, net	12	16	18	21	24	27	31	35	38	42	48
2 Consumption of fixed capital	80	90	102	118	144	163	186	210	236	265	307
3 Compensation of employees	2061	2321	2604	2977	3393	3822	4371	4900	5439	6045	6930
Gross Input	5163	5820	6531	7467	8524	9590	10974	12310	13638	15135	17324

3.42 Private Non-Profit Institutions Serving Households: Income and Outlay Account

Million French francs

	1970	1971	1972	1973	1974	1975	1976	1977	1978	1979	1980
Receipts											
1 Property and entrepreneurial income received	213	234	267	314	381	456	516	583	652	731	834
a Withdrawals from quasi-corporations	-	-	-	-	-	-	-	-	-	-	-
b Interest	111	119	137	163	198	225	253	285	319	357	401
c Dividends	102	115	130	151	183	231	263	298	333	374	433
d Net land rent and royalties	-	-	-	-	-	-	-	-	-	-	-
2 Other current transfers received	3403	3790	4192	4868	5783	6564	7476	8431	9459	10623	12281
a Casualty insurance claims	24	30	33	33	40	46	52	57	63	74	84
b Other Current transfers received from resident sectors, except imputed	3379	3760	4159	4835	5743	6518	7424	8374	9396	10549	12197
c Current transfers received from the rest of the world	...	...	...	...	...	...	...	...	...	...	...
d Imputed unfunded employee welfare contributions	...	...	...	...	...	...	...	...	...	...	...
Total Current Receipts	3616	4024	4459	5182	6164	7020	7992	9014	10111	11354	13115
Disbursements											
1 Final consumption expenditures	2107	2373	2663	3046	3483	3953	4503	5080	5700	6395	7399
2 Property income paid	17	19	21	23	30	34	38	43	48	54	60
a Interest	17	19	21	23	30	34	38	43	48	54	60
b Net land rent and royalties	-	-	-	-	-	-	-	-	-	-	-
3 Direct taxes and other payments to general government	47	53	61	83	30	95	154	148	165	189	222
a Direct taxes	47	53	61	83	30	95	154	148	165	189	222
b Fees, fines and penalties	-	-	-	-	-	-	-	-	-	-	-
4 Other current transfers paid	622	699	738	857	1053	1200	1426	1581	1750	1973	2265
a Net casualty insurance premiums	47	52	54	66	72	83	96	105	118	133	151
b Current transfers to household	473	532	603	699	846	960	1093	1233	1383	1552	1796
Social assistance grants	...	...	...	...	...	...	...	...	...	...	...
Unfunded employee welfare benefits	473	532	603	699	846	960	1093	1233	1383	1552	1796
c Current transfers to the rest of the world	...	...	...	...	...	...	...	...	...	...	...
d Other current transfers n.e.c.	102	115	81	92	135	157	237	243	249	288	318
Net saving	823	880	976	1173	1568	1738	1871	2162	2448	2743	3169
Total Current Disbursements	3616	4024	4459	5182	6164	7020	7992	9014	10111	11354	13115

France

3.43 Private Non-Profit Institutions Serving Households: Capital Accumulation Account

Million French francs

		1970	1971	1972	1973	1974	1975	1976	1977	1978	1979	1980
		\multicolumn{11}{c}{Finance of Gross Accumulation}
1	Gross saving	903	970	1078	1291	1712	1901	2057	2372	2684	3008	3476
	a Consumption of fixed capital	80	90	102	118	144	163	186	210	236	265	307
	b Net saving	823	880	976	1173	1568	1738	1871	2162	2448	2743	3169
2	Capital transfers received	300	183	309	377	480	319	399	513	476	487	514
	Finance of Gross Accumulation	1203	1153	1387	1668	2192	2220	2456	2885	3160	3495	3990
		\multicolumn{11}{c}{Gross Accumulation}
1	Gross capital formation	548	616	698	813	984	1117	1272	1435	1610	1806	2089
	a Increase in stocks	-	-	-	-	-	-	-	-	-	-	-
	b Gross fixed capital formation	548	616	698	813	984	1117	1272	1435	1610	1806	2089
2	Purchases of land, net	9	10	-	13	16	18	20	23	26	29	34
3	Purchases of intangible assets, net	-	-	-	-	-	-	-	-	...	...	...
4	Capital transfers paid	52	60	58	70	99	96	111	125	140	157	182
5	Net lending	594	467	631	772	1093	989	1053	1302	1384	1503	1685
	Gross Accumulation	1203	1153	1387	1668	2192	2220	2456	2885	3160	3495	3990

3.44 Private Non-Profit Institutions Serving Households: Capital Finance Account

Million French francs

		1970	1971	1972	1973	1974	1975	1976	1977	1978	1979	1980
		\multicolumn{11}{c}{Acquisition of Financial Assets}
1	Gold	-	-	-	-	-	-	-	-	-	-	-
2	Currency and transferable deposits	-15	315	318	347	448	288	212	215	562	532	605
3	Other deposits	411	53	66	76	16	-174	265	306	-268	71	80
4	Bills and bonds, short term	-	-	-	-	-	-	-	-	-	-	-
5	Bonds, long term	6	9	11	17	11	-14	-	11	20	25	30
6	Corporate equity securities	12	15	15	15	16	-	-	-	-	-	-
7	Short-term loans, n.e.c.	27	-49	77	12	74	-97	9	-29	313	36	5
8	Long-term loans, n.e.c.	255	282	290	450	774	986	556	972	784	914	1050
9	Other receivables	...	...	...	...	...	...	...	12	14	16	20
10	Proprietors' net additions to the accumulation of quasi-corporations	...	...	...	...	...	...	...	...	...	...	...
11	Other assets	...	...	...	...	...	...	...	...	...	...	...
	Total Acquisition of Financial Assets	696	625	777	917	1338	989	1042	1487	1425	1594	1790
		\multicolumn{11}{c}{Incurrence of Liabilities}
1	Short-term loans	1	-5	-5	-3	63	2	-38	59	68	53	60
2	Long-term loans	101	163	151	148	181	-2	27	126	-27	38	45
3	Other liabilities	-	-	-	-	-	-	-	-	-	-	-
	Total Incurrence of Liabilities	102	158	146	145	245	-	-11	185	41	91	105
	Net Lending	594	467	631	772	1093	989	1053	1302	1384	1503	1685
	Incurrence of Liabilities and Net Lending	696	625	777	917	1338	989	1042	1487	1425	1594	1790

3.51 External Transactions: Current Account: Detail

Million French francs

		1970	1971	1972	1973	1974	1975	1976	1977	1978	1979	1980
		\multicolumn{11}{c}{Payments to the Rest of the World}
1	Imports of goods and services	123908	140278	159789	196574	293459	273674	357596	407204	434440	532372	664391
2	Factor income paid to the rest of the world	8962	9533	11263	15215	23645	24698	29007	32831	41914	58931	84551
	a Compensation of employees	1171	1196	1791	1869	2436	3009	3814	4312	6033	8121	8464
	b Property and entrepreneurial income paid	7791	8337	9472	13346	21209	21689	25193	28519	35881	50810	76087
3	Indirect taxes paid to supranational organizations	30	1398	2109	2532	3136	7763	9304	11024	16060	18342	17843
4	Other current transfers to the rest of the world	14727	17841	19047	22732	25976	27972	26846	32129	35182	39075	46160
5	Surplus of the nation on current transactions	706	5011	4520	-1684	-28861	-413	-25044	-13126	13263	-1831	-37186
	Payments to the Rest of the World, and Surplus of the Nation on Current Transfers	148333	174061	196728	235369	317355	333694	397709	470062	540859	646889	775759

France

3.51 External Transactions: Current Account: Detail
(Continued)

Million French francs

	1970	1971	1972	1973	1974	1975	1976	1977	1978	1979	1980
Receipts From The Rest of the World
1 Exports of goods and services	127894	148812	169140	203222	275084	283851	338244	401900	455881	534569	617530
2 Factor income received from the rest of the world	13303	14735	15277	18243	28577	28570	35272	40566	51504	70628	101947
a Compensation of employees	681	839	882	1024	1423	1661	1987	2519	2874	3465	4034
b Property and entrepreneurial income received	12622	13896	14395	17219	27154	26909	33285	38047	48630	67163	97913
3 Subsidies received from supranational organizations	10	3606	4843	6643	4327	6768	9086	10833	13287	14766	16634
4 Other current transfers from the rest of the world	7126	6908	7468	7261	9367	14505	15107	16763	20187	26926	39648
Receipts from the Rest of the World on Current Transfers	148333	174061	196728	235369	317355	333694	397709	470062	540859	646889	775759

3.52 External Transactions: Capital Accumulation Account

Million French francs

	1970	1971	1972	1973	1974	1975	1976	1977	1978	1979	1980
Finance of Gross Accumulation
1 Surplus of the nation on current transactions	706	5011	4520	-1684	-28861	-413	-25044	-13126	13263	-1831	-37186
2 Capital transfers received from the rest of the world	-	35	71	132	150	224	176	226	168	169	269
Total Finance of Gross Accumulation	706	5046	4591	-1552	-28711	-189	-24868	-12900	13431	-1662	-36917
Gross Accumulation
1 Capital transfers paid to the rest of the world	927	1123	905	1049	1921	1451	2322	1334	1272	1555	1622
2 Purchases of intangible assets, n.e.c., net, from the rest of the world	-	-	-	-	-	-	-	-	-	-	-
3 Net lending to the rest of the world	-221	3923	3686	-2601	-30632	-1640	-27190	-14234	12159	-3217	-38539
Total Gross Accumulation	706	5046	4591	-1552	-28711	-189	-24868	-12900	13431	-1662	-36917

3.53 External Transactions: Capital Finance Account

Million French francs

	1970	1971	1972	1973	1974	1975	1976	1977	1978	1979	1980
Acquisitions of Foreign Financial Assets
1 Gold and SDR's	-41	37	425	-467	68	-56	51	136	53	100	28441
2 Currency and transferable deposits	5737	17722	9264	83	-761	17600	-6866	4568	-651	9935	
3 Other deposits	3799	16388	24044	33902	-4944	27878	24573	48173	57072	50450	529
4 Bills and bonds, short term	-	49	125	-24	-180	982	-747	78	-42	-264	-
5 Bonds, long term	425	269	1342	632	849	561	3227	2431	4239	6093	6166
6 Corporate equity securities	2288	2806	5086	6931	4363	6801	8629	6238	9157	10873	13248
7 Short-term loans, n.e.c.	-201	-8447	-4170	-7209	-8988	-21259	-18687	4805	-16026	-480	5730
8 Long-term loans	4342	2526	6261	9886	14912	15208	21233	17212	33698	31391	49164
9 Proprietors' net additions to accumulation of quasi-corporate, non-resident enterprises	-	-	-	-	-	-	-	-	-	-	-
10 Trade credit and advances	5086	5558	5520	6309	11850	2141	18567	10693	8623	8773	-
11 Other	...	...	...	...	...	...	...	...	...	...	...
Total Acquisitions of Foreign Financial Assets	21435	36908	47897	50043	17169	49856	49980	94334	96123	116871	103278
Incurrence of Foreign Liabilities
1 Currency and transferable deposits	-3492	-580	3072	6065	81	491	10658	-659	-412	-19638	3398
2 Other deposits	10970	26837	29331	32881	8790	31649	33254	56804	36549	86697	70699
3 Bills and bonds, short term	25	-107	-15	-	-	-	-	-	-	-	-
4 Bonds, long term	1638	2041	1709	126	3354	6692	11412	7174	4516	1971	8050
5 Corporate equity securities	4254	3430	5551	4981	5894	6166	3048	8446	10727	10763	12645
6 Short-term loans, n.e.c.	-175	-4302	-697	780	-1935	-6383	-22908	7098	8490	10490	21030

France

3.53 External Transactions: Capital Finance Account
(Continued)

Million French francs

		1970	1971	1972	1973	1974	1975	1976	1977	1978	1979	1980
7	Long-term loans	3215	2257	2187	3259	10902	7414	15133	17890	18361	16646	8873
8	Non-resident proprietors' net additions to accumulation of resident quasi-corporate enterprises	...	...	...	...	...	...	...	...	...	...	...
9	Trade credit and advances	3433	3122	3377	6911	13279	-3694	19981	4567	4065	3326	...
10	Other	11	12	18	33	48	257	88	51	51	74	-
	Total Incurrence of Liabilities	19879	32710	44533	55036	40413	42592	70666	101371	82347	110329	124695
	Statistical discrepancy	1777	275	-322	-2392	7388	8904	6504	7197	1617	9759	17122
	Net Lending	-221	3923	3686	-2601	-30632	-1640	-27190	-14234	12159	-3217	-38539
	Total Incurrence of Liabilities and Net Lending	21435	36908	47897	50043	17169	49856	49980	94334	96123	116871	103278

4.3 Derivation of Value Added by Kind of Activity, ISIC Divisions, in Current Prices

Million French francs

		1970 Gross Output	1970 Intermediate Consumption	1970 Value Added	1971 Gross Output	1971 Intermediate Consumption	1971 Value Added	1972 Gross Output	1972 Intermediate Consumption	1972 Value Added	1973 Gross Output	1973 Intermediate Consumption	1973 Value Added
					All Producers								
1	Agriculture, hunting, forestry and fishing	...	...	50542	...	...	53185	...	...	63352	...	...	74853
	a Agriculture and hunting	...	...	46154	...	...	48470	...	...	58254	...	...	68294
	b Forestry and logging	...	...	3161	...	...	3515	...	...	3593	...	...	4995
	c Fishing	...	...	1227	...	...	1200	...	...	1505	...	...	1564
2	Mining and quarrying	...	...	6652	...	...	7234	...	...	7450	...	...	7733
	a Coal mining	...	...	2778	...	...	3133	...	...	3067	...	...	2747
	b Crude petroleum and natural gas production	...	...	700	...	...	773	...	...	814	...	...	832
	c Metal ore mining	...	...	582	...	...	576	...	...	543	...	...	612
	d Other mining	...	...	2592	...	...	2752	...	...	3026	...	...	3542
3	Manufacturing	...	...	224957	...	...	249073	...	...	276959	...	...	315717
	a Manufacture of food, beverages and tobacco	...	...	31765	...	...	35861	...	...	39611	...	...	45559
	b Textile, wearing apparel and leather industries	...	...	21291	...	...	23619	...	...	26780	...	...	29215
	c Manufacture of wood and wood products, including furniture	...	...	5742	...	...	6785	...	...	8017	...	...	8360
	d Manufacture of paper and paper products, printing and publishing	...	...	11163	...	...	12594	...	...	14108	...	...	15311
	e Manufacture of chemicals and chemical petroleum, coal, rubber and plastic products	...	...	44147	...	...	48945	...	...	52883	...	...	59371
	f Manufacture of non-metallic mineral products, except products of petroleum and coal	...	...	8255	...	...	9258	...	...	10553	...	...	12408
	g Basic metal industries	...	...	20171	...	...	18889	...	...	20525	...	...	26260
	h Manufacture of fabricated metal products, machinery and equipment	...	...	79507	...	...	89696	...	...	100664	...	...	114654
	i Other manufacturing industries	...	...	2916	...	...	3426	...	...	3818	...	...	4579
4	Electricity, gas and water	...	...	13603	...	...	15016	...	...	17329	...	...	19842
	a Electricity, gas and steam	...	...	10920	...	...	...	...	...	13577	...	...	15255
	b Water works and supply	...	...	2683	...	...	...	...	...	3752	...	...	4587
5	Construction	...	...	58315	...	...	64016	...	...	72831	...	...	80687
6	Wholesale and retail trade, restaurants and hotels	...	...	98300	...	...	112673	...	...	122933	...	...	138742
	a Wholesale and retail trade	...	...	83540	...	...	96309	...	...	105936	...	...	120649
	b Restaurants and hotels	...	...	14760	...	...	16364	...	...	16997	...	...	18093
7	Transport, storage and communication	...	...	42766	...	...	47984	...	...	52297	...	...	59449
8	Finance, insurance, real estate and business services	...	...	105033	...	...	118768	...	...	135042	...	...	161849
9	Community, social and personal services	...	...	46284	...	...	52186	...	...	60620	...	...	69910

France

4.3 Derivation of Value Added by Kind of Activity, ISIC Divisions, in Current Prices
(Continued)

Million French francs

	1970 Gross Output	1970 Intermediate Consumption	1970 Value Added	1971 Gross Output	1971 Intermediate Consumption	1971 Value Added	1972 Gross Output	1972 Intermediate Consumption	1972 Value Added	1973 Gross Output	1973 Intermediate Consumption	1973 Value Added
Total, Industries	...	...	646452	...	...	720135	...	...	808813	...	...	928782
Producers of Government Services	...	...	78681	...	...	88629	...	...	98751	...	...	112336
Other Producers	...	...	5944	...	...	6538	...	...	7205	...	...	8070
Total	...	...	731077	...	...	815302	...	...	914769	...	...	1049188
Imputed bank service charge	...	...	-21848	...	...	-24838	...	...	-26314	...	...	-33377
Import duties [a]	...	...	73331	...	...	81969	...	...	92660	...	...	98389
Value added tax	...	...	...	...	...	...	...	...	...	...	...	...
Total	...	...	782560	...	...	872433	...	...	981115	...	...	1114200

	1974 Gross Output	1974 Intermediate Consumption	1974 Value Added	1975 Gross Output	1975 Intermediate Consumption	1975 Value Added	1976 Gross Output	1976 Intermediate Consumption	1976 Value Added	1977 Gross Output	1977 Intermediate Consumption	1977 Value Added
All Producers												
1 Agriculture, hunting, forestry and fishing	...	...	72903	...	...	73247	...	...	80558	...	...	88647
a Agriculture and hunting	...	...	63863	...	...	66449	...	...	73690	...	...	80034
b Forestry and logging	...	...	7254	...	...	5117	...	...	5067	...	...	6369
c Fishing	...	...	1786	...	...	1681	...	...	1801	...	...	2244
2 Mining and quarrying	...	...	10288	...	...	12334	...	...	13061	...	...	14969
a Coal mining	...	...	4055	...	...	4942	...	...	4987	...	...	6161
b Crude petroleum and natural gas production	...	...	1484	...	...	2005	...	...	2130	...	...	2561
c Metal ore mining	...	...	709	...	...	946	...	...	920	...	...	921
d Other mining	...	...	4040	...	...	4441	...	...	5024	...	...	5326
3 Manufacturing	...	...	356777	...	...	397391	...	...	459366	...	...	517370
a Manufacture of food, beverages and tobacco	...	...	50463	...	...	61054	...	...	67928	...	...	74595
b Textile, wearing apparel and leather industries	...	...	31713	...	...	35446	...	...	37443	...	...	41238
c Manufacture of wood and wood products, including furniture	...	...	8836	...	...	10293	...	...	11493	...	...	12262
d Manufacture of paper and paper products, printing and publishing	...	...	19347	...	...	20968	...	...	23141	...	...	25131
e Manufacture of chemicals and chemical petroleum, coal, rubber and plastic products	...	...	66463	...	...	66851	...	...	76842	...	...	92891
f Manufacture of non-metallic mineral products, except products of petroleum and coal	...	...	14009	...	...	14947	...	...	18341	...	...	19509
g Basic metal industries	...	...	35612	...	...	31062	...	...	35230	...	...	37587
h Manufacture of fabricated metal products, machinery and equipment	...	...	125456	...	...	150969	...	...	182294	...	...	206924
i Other manufacturing industries	...	...	4878	...	...	5801	...	...	6654	...	...	7233
4 Electricity, gas and water	...	...	21148	...	...	26097	...	...	29104	...	...	34501
a Electricity, gas and steam	...	...	15804	...	...	...	...	...	...	...	...	...
b Water works and supply	...	...	5344	...	...	...	...	...	...	...	...	...
5 Construction	...	...	93757	...	...	110558	...	...	123583	...	...	136325
6 Wholesale and retail trade, restaurants and hotels	...	...	167687	...	...	186761	...	...	204185	...	...	233503
a Wholesale and retail trade	...	...	146331	...	...	161215	...	...	174960	...	...	196924
b Restaurants and hotels	...	...	21356	...	...	25546	...	...	29225	...	...	36579
7 Transport, storage and communication	...	...	66100	...	...	75722	...	...	89656	...	...	100851
8 Finance, insurance, real estate and business services	...	...	192170	...	...	214153	...	...	248639	...	...	289688
9 Community, social and personal services	...	...	80877	...	...	100577	...	...	119799	...	...	136156
Total, Industries	...	...	1061707	...	...	1196840	...	...	1367951	...	...	1552010
Producers of Government Services	...	...	134327	...	...	162560	...	...	191536	...	...	220797
Other Producers	...	...	9585	...	...	11260	...	...	12971	...	...	14429
Total	...	...	1205619	...	...	1370660	...	...	1572458	...	...	1787236
Imputed bank service charge	...	...	-44918	...	...	-46755	...	...	-52990	...	...	-62518
Import duties [a]	...	...	117601	...	...	128414	...	...	158505	...	...	159867
Value added tax	...	...	...	...	...	...	...	...	...	...	...	...
Total	...	...	1278302	...	...	1452319	...	...	1677973	...	...	1884585

France

4.3 Derivation of Value Added by Kind of Activity, ISIC Divisions, in Current Prices

Million French francs

	1978 Gross Output	1978 Intermediate Consumption	1978 Value Added	1979 Gross Output	1979 Intermediate Consumption	1979 Value Added
			All Producers			
1 Agriculture, hunting, forestry and fishing	...	...	99997	...	...	114033
a Agriculture and hunting	...	...	90632	...	...	102739
b Forestry and logging	...	...	7117	...	...	8814
c Fishing	...	...	2248	...	...	2480
2 Mining and quarrying	...	...	15945	...	...	17614
a Coal mining	...	...	6254	...	...	6621
b Crude petroleum and natural gas production	...	...	2843	...	...	3173
c Metal ore mining	...	...	952	...	...	990
d Other mining	...	...	5886	...	...	6830
3 Manufacturing	...	...	581413	...	...	661382
a Manufacture of food, beverages and tobacco	...	...	88289	...	...	95942
b Textile, wearing apparel and leather industries	...	...	44677	...	...	48862
c Manufacture of wood and wood products, including furniture	...	...	13326	...	...	14981
d Manufacture of paper and paper products, printing and publishing	...	...	28464	...	...	30824
e Manufacture of chemicals and chemical petroleum, coal, rubber and plastic products	...	...	109816	...	...	136587
f Manufacture of non-metallic mineral products, except products of petroleum and coal	...	...	21102	...	...	24358
g Basic metal industries	...	...	41919	...	...	46150
h Manufacture of fabricated metal products, machinery and equipment	...	...	225765	...	...	254740
i Other manufacturing industries	...	...	8055	...	...	8938
4 Electricity, gas and water	...	...	39972	...	...	46254
a Electricity, gas and steam	...	...	...	...	...	...
b Water works and supply	...	...	...	...	...	...
5 Construction	...	...	146165	...	...	160936
6 Wholesale and retail trade, restaurants and hotels	...	...	260515	...	...	290523
a Wholesale and retail trade	...	...	216586	...	...	239978
b Restaurants and hotels	...	...	43929	...	...	50545
7 Transport, storage and communication	...	...	117690	...	...	135212
8 Finance, insurance, real estate and business services	...	...	332521	...	...	386464
9 Community, social and personal services	...	...	162344	...	...	188148
Total, Industries	...	...	1756562	...	...	2000566
Producers of Government Services	...	...	253800	...	...	285390
Other Producers	...	...	16582	...	...	18646
Total	...	...	2026944	...	...	2304602
Imputed bank service charge	...	...	-71487	...	...	-84321
Import duties [a]	...	...	185289	...	...	219123
Value added tax	...	...	...	...	...	...
Total	...	...	2140746	...	...	2439404

a) Including also value added tax.

France

4.4 Derivation of Value Added by Kind of Activity, ISIC Divisions, in Constant Prices

Million French francs

	1970 GO	1970 IC	1970 VA	1971 GO	1971 IC	1971 VA	1972 GO	1972 IC	1972 VA	1973 GO	1973 IC	1973 VA
					At constant prices of: 1970 — All Producers							
1 Agriculture, hunting, forestry and fishing	...	...	50542	...	...	51418	...	...	51669	...	...	54546
a Agriculture and hunting	...	...	46154	...	...	47002	...	...	47152	...	...	49925
b Forestry and logging	...	...	3161	...	...	3318	...	...	3267	...	...	3413
c Fishing	...	...	1227	...	...	1098	...	...	1250	...	...	1208
2 Mining and quarrying	...	...	6652	...	...	6183	...	...	6055	...	...	6001
a Coal mining	...	...	2778	...	...	2338	...	...	2167	...	...	1888
b Crude petroleum and natural gas production	...	...	700	...	...	675	...	...	674	...	...	649
c Metal ore mining	...	...	582	...	...	556	...	...	537	...	...	539
d Other mining	...	...	2592	...	...	2614	...	...	2677	...	...	2955
3 Manufacturing	...	...	224957	...	...	239399	...	...	254473	...	...	272204
a Manufacture of food, beverages and tobacco	...	...	31765	...	...	34095	...	...	35910	...	...	37554
b Textile, wearing apparel and leather industries	...	...	21291	...	...	22579	...	...	24605	...	...	23860
c Manufacture of wood and wood products, including furniture	...	...	5742	...	...	6414	...	...	7150	...	...	6967
d Manufacture of paper and paper products, printing and publishing	...	...	11163	...	...	11688	...	...	11351	...	...	11722
e Manufacture of chemicals and chemical petroleum, coal, rubber and plastic products	...	...	44147	...	...	46938	...	...	49412	...	...	54552
f Manufacture of non-metallic mineral products, except products of petroleum and coal	...	...	8255	...	...	8651	...	...	9426	...	...	10618
g Basic metal industries	...	...	20171	...	...	19288	...	...	20662	...	...	23390
h Manufacture of fabricated metal products, machinery and equipment	...	...	79507	...	...	86388	...	...	92450	...	...	99788
i Other manufacturing industries	...	...	2916	...	...	3358	...	...	3507	...	...	3753
4 Electricity, gas and water	...	...	13603	...	...	14474	...	...	15852	...	...	17675
a Electricity, gas and steam	...	...	...	...	...	...	...	...	12769	...	...	14229
b Water works and supply	...	...	...	...	...	...	...	...	3083	...	...	3446
5 Construction	...	...	58315	...	...	59922	...	...	63092	...	...	61756
6 Wholesale and retail trade, restaurants and hotels	...	...	98300	...	...	105487	...	...	110167	...	...	114700
a Wholesale and retail trade	...	...	83540	...	...	90398	...	...	95435	...	...	100137
b Restaurants and hotels	...	...	14760	...	...	15089	...	...	14732	...	...	14563
7 Transport, storage and communication	...	...	42766	...	...	44740	...	...	48664	...	...	51821
8 Finance, insurance, real estate and business services	...	...	105033	...	...	111268	...	...	118631	...	...	129671
9 Community, social and personal services	...	...	46284	...	...	48732	...	...	52994	...	...	56431
Total, Industries	...	...	646452	...	...	681623	...	...	721597	...	...	764805
Producers of Government Services	...	...	78681	...	...	81745	...	...	84433	...	...	86030
Other Producers	...	...	5944	...	...	5967	...	...	6002	...	...	6037
Total	...	...	731077	...	...	769335	...	...	812032	...	...	856872
Imputed bank service charge	...	...	-21848	...	...	-22398	...	...	-22701	...	...	-26327
Import duties [a]	...	...	73331	...	...	77943	...	...	84219	...	...	89881
Value added tax	...	...	...	...	...	...	...	...	...	...	...	...
Total	...	...	782560	...	...	824880	...	...	873550	...	...	920426

	1974 GO	1974 IC	1974 VA	1975 GO	1975 IC	1975 VA	1976 GO	1976 IC	1976 VA	1977 GO	1977 IC	1977 VA
					At constant prices of: 1970 — All Producers							
1 Agriculture, hunting, forestry and fishing	...	...	54419	...	...	50474	...	...	48458	...	...	48584
a Agriculture and hunting	...	...	49830	...	...	46315	...	...	44354	...	...	44317
b Forestry and logging	...	...	3399	...	...	3014	...	...	2917	...	...	3040
c Fishing	...	...	1190	...	...	1145	...	...	1187	...	...	1227
2 Mining and quarrying	...	...	5891	...	...	5542	...	...	5614	...	...	5569

France

4.4 Derivation of Value Added by Kind of Activity, ISIC Divisions, in Constant Prices
(Continued)

Million French francs

	1974 Gross Output	1974 Intermediate Consumption	1974 Value Added	1975 Gross Output	1975 Intermediate Consumption	1975 Value Added	1976 Gross Output	1976 Intermediate Consumption	1976 Value Added	1977 Gross Output	1977 Intermediate Consumption	1977 Value Added
				At constant prices of: 1970								
a Coal mining	...	...	1696	...	...	1518	...	...	1561	...	...	1568
b Crude petroleum and natural gas production	...	...	666	...	...	696	...	...	656	...	...	706
c Metal ore mining	...	...	553	...	...	518	...	...	500	...	...	440
d Other mining	...	...	2976	...	...	2810	...	...	2897	...	...	2855
3 Manufacturing	...	...	280963	...	...	275188	...	...	294607	...	...	305574
a Manufacture of food, beverages and tobacco	...	...	38987	...	...	41613	...	...	42368	...	...	43809
b Textile, wearing apparel and leather industries	...	...	24369	...	...	22771	...	...	22787	...	...	22752
c Manufacture of wood and wood products, including furniture	...	...	7409	...	...	7362	...	...	7807	...	...	8097
d Manufacture of paper and paper products, printing and publishing	...	...	11979	...	...	11340	...	...	12241	...	...	12715
e Manufacture of chemicals and chemical petroleum, coal, rubber and plastic products	...	...	56267	...	...	51999	...	...	57710	...	...	59660
f Manufacture of non-metallic mineral products, except products of petroleum and coal	...	...	11043	...	...	9948	...	...	11174	...	...	11053
g Basic metal industries	...	...	23550	...	...	19793	...	...	22171	...	...	22813
h Manufacture of fabricated metal products, machinery and equipment	...	...	103247	...	...	106404	...	...	114049	...	...	120011
i Other manufacturing industries	...	...	4112	...	...	3958	...	...	4300	...	...	4664
4 Electricity, gas and water	...	...	18879	...	...	19714	...	...	20886	...	...	22693
a Electricity, gas and steam	...	...	15158	...	...	15797	...	...	...	...	...	...
b Water works and supply	...	...	3721	...	...	3917	...	...	...	...	...	...
5 Construction	...	...	64077	...	...	65277	...	...	63370	...	...	62632
6 Wholesale and retail trade, restaurants and hotels	...	...	118361	...	...	117417	...	...	124356	...	...	126387
a Wholesale and retail trade	...	...	103207	...	...	108419	...	...	108419	...	...	109499
b Restaurants and hotels	...	...	15154	...	...	8998	...	...	15937	...	...	16888
7 Transport, storage and communication	...	...	53076	...	...	52952	...	...	56853	...	...	59673
8 Finance, insurance, real estate and business services	...	...	139693	...	...	140862	...	...	147518	...	...	156076
9 Community, social and personal services	...	...	59765	...	...	63331	...	...	67428	...	...	70109
Total, Industries	...	...	795124	...	...	790757	...	...	829090	...	...	857297
Producers of Government Services	...	...	87133	...	...	89163	...	...	94587	...	...	96697
Other Producers	...	...	5995	...	...	5907	...	...	6065	...	...	5867
Total	...	...	888252	...	...	885827	...	...	929742	...	...	959861
Imputed bank service charge	...	...	-30592	...	...	-27896	...	...	-28283	...	...	-30098
Import duties [a]	...	...	92516	...	...	94015	...	...	99708	...	...	101977
Value added tax	...	...	...	...	...	...	...	...	...	...	...	...
Total	...	...	950176	...	...	951946	...	...	1001167	...	...	1031740

	1978 Gross Output	1978 Intermediate Consumption	1978 Value Added	1979 Gross Output	1979 Intermediate Consumption	1979 Value Added
	At constant prices of: 1970					
	All Producers					
1 Agriculture, hunting, forestry and fishing	...	...	51576	...	...	56054
a Agriculture and hunting	...	...	47359	...	...	51691
b Forestry and logging	...	...	3073	...	...	3158
c Fishing	...	...	1144	...	...	1205
2 Mining and quarrying	...	...	5452	...	...	5351
a Coal mining	...	...	1402	...	...	1200
b Crude petroleum and natural gas production	...	...	668	...	...	607
c Metal ore mining	...	...	412	...	...	383
d Other mining	...	...	2970	...	...	3161

France

4.4 Derivation of Value Added by Kind of Activity, ISIC Divisions, in Constant Prices
(Continued)

Million French francs

	1978 Gross Output	1978 Intermediate Consumption	1978 Value Added	1979 Gross Output	1979 Intermediate Consumption	1979 Value Added
				At constant prices of: 1970		
3 Manufacturing	...	...	313928	...	...	323807
a Manufacture of food, beverages and tobacco	...	...	45077	...	...	45888
b Textile, wearing apparel and leather industries	...	...	21586	...	...	22214
c Manufacture of wood and wood products, including furniture	...	...	8027	...	...	8407
d Manufacture of paper and paper products, printing and publishing	...	...	13124	...	...	13358
e Manufacture of chemicals and chemical petroleum, coal, rubber and plastic products	...	...	61189	...	...	65709
f Manufacture of non-metallic mineral products, except products of petroleum and coal	...	...	10901	...	...	11331
g Basic metal industries	...	...	24210	...	...	23960
h Manufacture of fabricated metal products, machinery and equipment	...	...	125147	...	...	128394
i Other manufacturing industries	...	...	4667	...	...	4546
4 Electricity, gas and water	...	...	24091	...	...	24976
a Electricity, gas and steam	...	...	...	...	...	...
b Water works and supply	...	...	...	...	...	...
5 Construction	...	...	59895	...	...	59132
6 Wholesale and retail trade, restaurants and hotels	...	...	131396	...	...	134912
a Wholesale and retail trade	...	...	114030	...	...	116808
b Restaurants and hotels	...	...	17366	...	...	18104
7 Transport, storage and communication	...	...	63925	...	...	68072
8 Finance, insurance, real estate and business services	...	...	163873	...	...	171427
9 Community, social and personal services	...	...	74678	...	...	79019
Total, Industries	...	...	888814	...	...	922750
Producers of Government Services	...	...	99650	...	...	100525
Other Producers	...	...	6044	...	...	6097
Total	...	...	994508	...	...	1029372
Imputed bank service charge	...	...	-31161	...	...	-32700
Import duties [a]	...	...	106623	...	...	110310
Value added tax	...	...	...	...	...	...
Total	...	...	1069970	...	...	1106982

a) Including also value added tax.

French Polynesia

Source. Reply to the United Nations National Accounts Questionnaire from the Institute National de la Statistique et des Etudes Economiques (INSEE), Paris. Official estimates and descriptions are published by the same Institute in 'Comptes Economiques de la Polynesie Francaise'.

General note. The estimates shown in the following tables have been adjusted by the INSEE to conform to the United Nations System of National Accounts so far as the existing data would permit.

1.1 Expenditure on the Gross Domestic Product, in Current Prices

Million CFP francs

		1970	1971	1972	1973	1974	1975	1976	1977	1978	1979	1980
1	General government final consumption expenditure	10012	12449	12331	14358	16387	18738	21349	...	...	...	...
2	Private final consumption expenditure	17288	18882	19576	21293	27665	29963	34390	...	...	...	...
3	Gross capital formation	4948	5541	5358	7288	16090	13477	15767	...	...	...	...
	a Increase in stocks	...	...	...	...	565	296	172	...	...	...	...
	b Gross fixed capital formation	4948	5541	5358	7288	15525	13181	15595	...	...	...	...
	Residential buildings	...	...	...	...	...	...	2816	...	...	...	...
	Non-residential buildings [a]	2106	2469	2497	3142	4754	5704	4400	...	...	...	...
	Other construction and land improvement etc.								...	...	...	...
	Other	2842	3072	2861	4146	10771	7477	8379	...	...	...	...
4	Exports of goods and services	2800	2997	2714	3227	5686	5159	5797	...	...	...	...
5	Less: Imports of goods and services	13580	14855	14944	16916	25151	22317	25576	...	...	...	...
	Equals: Gross Domestic Product	21468	25014	25035	29250	40677	45020	51727	...	...	...	...

a) Including item 'Residential buildings'.

1.3 Cost Components of the Gross Domestic Product

Million CFP francs

		1970	1971	1972	1973	1974	1975	1976	1977	1978	1979	1980
1	Indirect taxes, net	2209	2151	2319	3095	3445	2862	3868	...	...	...	...
	a Indirect taxes paid	2642	2675	2771	3636	3910	4029	4927	...	...	...	...
	b Less: Subsidies received	433	524	452	541	465	1167	1059	...	...	...	...
2	Consumption of fixed capital	3523	3875	3800	5466	14008	10771	9859	...	...	...	...
3	Compensation of employees paid by resident producers to:	10938	13726	13533	15375	19507	22488	26977	...	...	...	...
4	Net operating surplus	4798	5262	5383	5314	3717	8899	11023	...	...	...	...
	Equals: Gross Domestic Product	21468	25014	25035	29250	40677	45020	51727	...	...	...	...

1.7 External Transactions on Current Account, Summary

Million CFP francs

		1970	1971	1972	1973	1974	1975	1976	1977	1978	1979	1980
	Payments to the Rest of the World											
1	Imports of goods and services	13580	14855	14944	16916	25151	22317	25576	...	...	...	...
2	Factor income paid to the rest of the world	...	...	...	...	...	...	...	...	...	...	...
3	Indirect taxes paid to supranational organizations											
4	Current transfers to the rest of the world	...	...	...	...	...	...	...	...	...	...	...
5	Surplus of the nation on current transactions	-1067	403	-162	961	-3592	1087	1376	...	...	...	...
	Payments to the Rest of the World and Surplus of the Nation on Current Transactions	12513	15258	14782	17877	21559	23404	26952	...	...	...	...
	Receipts From The Rest of the World											
1	Exports of goods and services	2800	2997	2714	3227	5686	5159	5797	...	...	...	...
2	Factor income received from rest of the world	...	...	...	...	...	...	...	...	...	...	...
3	Subsidies received from supranational organisations	...	...	...	...	...	...	...	...	...	...	...
4	Current transfers from rest of the world	9713	12261	12068	14650	15873	18245	21155	...	...	...	...
	Receipts from the Rest of the World on Current Transactions	12513	15258	14782	17877	21559	23404	26952	...	...	...	...

1.10 Gross Domestic Product by Kind of Activity, in Current Prices

Million CFP francs

		1970	1971	1972	1973	1974	1975	1976	1977	1978	1979	1980
1	Agriculture, hunting, forestry and fishing	1488	1273	1404	1448	1891	2089	2265	...	...	...	...
2	Mining and quarrying	-	-	-	-	-	-	-	...	...	...	...
3	Manufacturing	1340	1414	1414	2039	2851	2769	3031	...	...	...	...
4	Electricity, gas and water [a]	319	415	445	374	428	498	540	...	...	...	...
5	Construction	1310	1617	1676	2630	3553	4442	4939	...	...	...	...

French Polynesia

1.10 Gross Domestic Product by Kind of Activity, in Current Prices
(Continued)

Million CFP francs

	1970	1971	1972	1973	1974	1975	1976	1977	1978	1979	1980
6 Wholesale and retail trade, restaurants and hotels	5106	5558	5647	8065	13100	13203	14994	...	...	...	...
7 Transport, storage and communication				1744	2198	2308	2589	...	...	...	...
8 Finance, insurance, real estate and business services [b]	5287	5763	6096	3275	4088	5232	6138	...	...	...	...
9 Community, social and personal services [b]					471	513	480	...	...	...	...
Total, Industries	14850	16040	16682	19575	28580	31054	34976	...	...	...	...
Producers of Government Services	6548	8897	8268	9575	11959	13807	16568	...	...	...	...
Other Producers	70	77	85	100	138	159	183	...	...	...	...
Subtotal	21468	25014	25035	29250	40677	45020	51727	...	...	...	...
Less: Imputed bank service charge	...	...	...	...	...	...	...	...	...	...	...
Plus: Import duties	...	...	...	...	...	...	...	...	...	...	...
Plus: Value added tax	...	...	...	...	...	...	...	...	...	...	...
Equals: Gross Domestic Product	21468	25014	25035	29250	40677	45020	51727	...	...	...	...

a) Electricity only.
b) Business services and real estate except dwellings are included in item 'Community, social and personal services'.

Gabon

Source. Reply to the United Nations National Accounts Questionnaire from the Direction de la Statistique et des Etudes Economiques, Libreville. The official estimates which conform to the present United Nations System of National Accounts are published annually by the same office in 'Comptes Economiques'.

General note. The estimates shown in the following tables have been prepared by the Direction de la Statistique et des Etudes Economiques to conform to the United Nations System of National Accounts so far as the existing data would permit.

1.1 Expenditure on the Gross Domestic Product, in Current Prices

Million CFA francs

	1970	1971	1972	1973	1974	1975	1976	1977	1978	1979	1980
1 General government final consumption expenditure	17600	...	19217	25127	34412	56531	76008	124926	73817	77922	...
2 Private final consumption expenditure	37400	...	36273	73602	91791	108706	118297	162123	196600	213038	...
3 Gross capital formation	27600	...	52125	60385	192359	289760	528576	400872	188829	188655	...
a Increase in stocks	1400	...	650	8076	36082	31614	93030	62827	-35201	6833	...
b Gross fixed capital formation	26200	...	51475	52309	156277	258146	435546	338045	224030	181822	...
Residential buildings	...	...	...	...	1451	...	116802	...	...	...	...
Non-residential buildings	...	...	...	...	4562	...	...	...	...	...	...
Other construction and land improvement etc.	...	...	...	22871	92847	...	...	...	...	...	...
Other	...	...	22333	22001	57417	72101	111911	80581	...	...	...
4 Exports of goods and services	44500	...	79277	94828	213918	228955	327754	356104	332992	...	...
5 Less: Imports of goods and services	34000	...	78440	92885	160796	221511	331543	353854	253032	...	...
Equals: Gross Domestic Product	93100	...	108452	161057	371684	462441	719092	690171	539206	...	...

1.3 Cost Components of the Gross Domestic Product

Million CFA francs

	1970	1971	1972	1973	1974	1975	1976	1977	1978	1979	1980
1 Indirect taxes, net	15400	...	18556	23143	67415	90185	115234	138333	104621	113835	...
a Indirect taxes paid	16300	...	19047	...	68413	93013	116607	140976	107545	117923	...
b Less: Subsidies received	900	...	491	...	998	2828	1373	2643	2924	4088	...
2 Consumption of fixed capital	21600	...	23789	22743	46013	66536	88307	94105	85430	90079	...
3 Compensation of employees paid by resident producers to:	36800	...	42108	50169	78035	113981	163711	199749	182835	186774	...
a Resident households	...	...	39702	47256	71377	101794	149429	178072	175239	...	...
b Rest of the world	...	...	2406	2913	6658	12187	14282	21677	7596	...	...
4 Net operating surplus	19300	...	23999	65002	180221	191739	351840	257984	166302	231527	...
a Corporate and quasi-corporate enterprises	...	...	...	...	...	...	...	...	...	...	...
b Private unincorporated enterprises	...	...	...	...	...	...	...	...	...	...	...
c General government	...	...	...	...	175	300	372	590	954	...	...
Equals: Gross Domestic Product	93100	...	108452	161057	371684	462441	719092	690171	539206	622215	...

1.4 General Government Current Receipts and Disbursements

Million CFA francs

	1970	1971	1972	1973	1974	1975	1976	1977	1978	1979	1980
Receipts											
1 Property and entrepreneurial income	...	...	...	...	1053	4083	16091	20686	17795	...	...
2 Taxes, fees and contributions	...	...	...	...	147411	214527	228919	284997	229850	...	...
a Indirect taxes	...	...	...	...	68413	121448	115901	141630	109058	...	...
b Direct taxes	...	...	...	...	74332	86530	98327	123534	101373	...	...
c Social security contributions	...	...	...	...	4666	6549	14691	19833	19419	...	...
d Compulsory fees, fines and penalties	...	...	...	...	...	...	...	...	...	...	...

Gabon

1.4 General Government Current Receipts and Disbursements
(Continued)

Million CFA francs

	1970	1971	1972	1973	1974	1975	1976	1977	1978	1979	1980
3 Other current receipts	...	...	...	...	11109	44914	40018	44598	47073	...	...
Total Current Receipts of General Government	...	...	...	...	159573	263524	285028	350281	294718	...	...

Disbursements

	1970	1971	1972	1973	1974	1975	1976	1977	1978	1979	1980
1 General government final consumption expenditure	...	...	...	...	34412	56531	76008	124926	73817	...	...
a Compensation of employees	...	...	10485	13018	16944	23046	28811	39612	39013	...	...
b Consumption of fixed capital	...	...	...	...	77	94	144	260	538	...	...
c Purchases of goods and services, net	...	...	...	...	...	...	...	...	...	...	•
d Less: Own account production of fixed assets	...	...	...	...	...	...	...	...	...	...	...
e Indirect taxes paid, net	...	...	...	...	...	...	...	...	...	...	...
2 Property income paid	...	...	...	...	5219	6461	9775	15234	25461	...	...
3 Subsidies	...	...	...	...	998	2828	1856	23043	21766	...	...
4 Other current transfers paid	...	...	...	...	8122	7591	13633	13611	...	...	...
a Social security benefits and social assistance grants	...	...	...	...	4200	5152	5988	6406	...	...	...
b Other	...	...	...	...	3922	2439	7645	7205	...	...	...
5 Net saving	...	...	...	...	110645	189885	183481	173088	140292	...	...
Total Current Disbursements and Net Saving of General Government	...	...	...	...	159574	263524	285028	350281	294718	...	...

1.7 External Transactions on Current Account, Summary

Million CFA francs

	1970	1971	1972	1973	1974	1975	1976	1977	1978	1979	1980

Payments to the Rest of the World

	1970	1971	1972	1973	1974	1975	1976	1977	1978	1979	1980
1 Imports of goods and services	...	...	78440	92885	160796	221511	274633	289562	257382	...	...
a Imports of merchandise c.i.f.	...	...	47977	47977	59403	109434	146741	176352	192031	...	...
b Other	...	...	30463	33482	51362	74770	98281	97531	89809	130501	...
2 Factor income paid to the rest of the world	...	...	10408	15269	30359	35198	43469	47974	52223	...	...
a Compensation of employees	...	...	2406	2913	6658	12187	14282	21677	7596	...	...
b Property and entrepreneurial income paid	...	...	8002	12356	23701	23011	29187	26297	44627	...	...
3 Indirect taxes paid to supranational organizations	...	...	...	...	...	...	...	...	...	...	...
4 Current transfers to the rest of the world	...	...	4198	6156	8012	11850	16753	20430	17467	...	...
5 Surplus of the nation on current transactions [a]	...	...	-6297	-8796	25128	-23008	6590	10400	24798	47087	...
Payments to the Rest of the World and Surplus of the Nation on Current Transactions [a]	...	...	86749	105513	224784	245551	341445	368366	351870	377000	...

Receipts From The Rest of the World

	1970	1971	1972	1973	1974	1975	1976	1977	1978	1979	1980
1 Exports of goods and services [a]	...	...	79277	94828	213918	228955	316990	345438	332992	...	...
a Exports of merchandise f.o.b.	...	...	347374	67594	84741	204227	210736	290928	307401	...	...
b Other	...	...	11683	10087	9691	18219	26062	38037	36620	37842	...
2 Factor income received from rest of the world	...	...	773	738	3177	5586	9630	9169	5488	...	...
a Compensation of employees	...	...	379	412	1382	3919	6741	5843	4515	...	...
b Property and entrepreneurial income received	...	...	394	326	1795	1667	2889	3326	973	...	...
3 Subsidies received from supranational organisations	...	...	...	...	...	...	...	...	...	...	...
4 Current transfers from rest of the world	...	...	6699	9946	7689	11010	14825	13759	13390	...	...
Receipts from the Rest of the World on Current Transactions	...	...	86749	105513	224784	245551	341445	368366	351870	377000	...

a) Beginning 1976, estimates are not strictly comparable with those of other tables.

Gabon

1.8 Capital Transactions of The Nation, Summary

Million CFA francs

	1970	1971	1972	1973	1974	1975	1976	1977	1978	1979	1980
Finance of Gross Capital Formation										
Gross saving	...	...	45828	51588	217487	266752	489021	357646	205432	229797	...
1 Consumption of fixed capital	...	...	23789	22743	46013	66536	88307	94105	85430	90079	...
a General government	...	...	...	...	77	94	144	260	538	...	...
b Corporate and quasi-corporate enterprises	...	...	...	...	...	...	...	...	...	...	...
c Other	...	...	...	...	...	...	...	...	...	...	...
2 Net saving	...	...	22039	28845	171474	200216	400714	263541	120002	139718	...
a General government	...	...	...	...	110645	189885	183481	173088	140262	...	...
b Corporate and quasi-corporate enterprises	...	...	...	...	...	...	...	...	...	...	...
c Other	...	...	...	...	...	...	...	...	...	...	...
Less: Surplus of the nation on current transactions a	...	...	-6297	-8796	25128	-23008	6590	10400	24798	142600	...
Finance of Gross Capital Formation	...	...	52125	60385	192359	289760	528576	400872	188829	188655	...
Gross Capital Formation										
Increase in stocks	...	...	650	8076	36082	31614	93030	62827	-35201	6833	...
Gross fixed capital formation	...	...	51475	52309	156277	258146	435546	338045	224030	181822	...
1 General government	...	...	...	...	55007	129582	268951	160486	82432	72125	...
2 Corporate and quasi-corporate enterprises	...	...	...	...	...	...	...	...	...	...	...
3 Other	...	...	...	...	...	...	...	...	...	...	...
Gross Capital Formation	...	...	52125	60385	192359	289760	528576	400872	188829	188655	...

a) Beginning 1976, estimates are not strictly comparable with those of other tables.

1.10 Gross Domestic Product by Kind of Activity, in Current Prices

Million CFA francs

	1970	1971	1972	1973	1974	1975	1976	1977	1978	1979	1980
1 Agriculture, hunting, forestry and fishing	...	...	13474	18756	33937	40772	36912	39373	36100	33980	...
2 Mining and quarrying	...	...	35178	49729	178085	187163	227461	242839	206269	260917	...
3 Manufacturing a	...	...	8660	10671	15328	22998	34911	45711	39572	41278	...
4 Electricity, gas and water	...	...	2221	2883	3920	4909	6026	5311	9379	9695	...
5 Construction	...	...	12342	16710	42452	79826	193579	96951	44309	48021	...
6 Wholesale and retail trade, restaurants and hotels	...	...	17264	13478	23342	32152	67743	55867	37221	44879	...
7 Transport, storage and communication	...	...	4715	7153	10452	18423	28728	30095	23896	28967	...
8 Finance, insurance, real estate and business services	...	...	2907	15772	28263	26951	58811	83175	64625	73203	...
9 Community, social and personal services	...	...	113	149	1367	1627	3183	4639	47799	52706	...
Total, Industries	...	...	96874	135302	337146	414821	657354	603961	...	...	...
Producers of Government Services	...	...	10556	13080	17022	23142	28924	39809	53044	...	...
Other Producers	...	...	1021	800	1230	1648	3312	4166	...	...	...
Subtotal	...	...	108451	149182	355398	439611	689590	647936	509170	593646	...
Less: Imputed bank service charge	...	...	...	1584	4001	9007	8982	8595	8721	9282	...
Plus: Import duties	...	...	...	13459	20287	31837	38484	50830	38757	37851	...
Plus: Value added tax	...	...	...	...	...	...	...	...	...	...	...
Equals: Gross Domestic Product	...	...	108452	161057	371684	462441	719092	690171	539206	622215	...

a) Including repair services.

1.12 Relations Among National Accounting Aggregates

Million CFA francs

	1970	1971	1972	1973	1974	1975	1976	1977	1978	1979	1980
Gross Domestic Product	...	...	108452	161057	371684	462441	719092	690171	539206	622215	...
Plus: Net factor income received from abroad	...	...	-9635	-14530	-27183	-29612	-33838	-38805	-59280	-76902	...
Factor income received	...	...	773	738	3177	5586	9630	9169	5488	1561	...
Less: Factor income paid	...	...	10408	15269	30359	35198	43469	47974	64768	78463	...
Equals: Gross National Product	...	...	98817	146527	344501	432829	685254	651366	479926	545313	...

Gabon

1.12 Relations Among National Accounting Aggregates
(Continued)

Million CFA francs

	1970	1971	1972	1973	1974	1975	1976	1977	1978	1979	1980
Less: Consumption of fixed capital	...	...	23789	22743	46013	66536	88307	94105	85430	90079	...
Less: Net indirect taxes paid to supranational organisations	...	...	...	...	...	...	...	...	...	...	...
Equals: National Income at Market Prices	...	...	75028	123784	298488	366293	596947	557261	394496	455234	...
Plus: Net current transfers received from abroad	...	...	2501	3790	-811	-840	-1928	-6671	-4077	-24556	...
Current transfers received	...	...	6699	9946	7689	11010	14825	13759	13390	15365	...
Less: Current transfers paid	...	...	4198	6156	8012	11850	16753	20430	17467	39921	...
Equals: National Disposable Income at Market Prices	...	...	77529	127574	297677	365453	595019	550590	390419	430678	...
Less: Final consumption	...	...	55490	98729	126203	165237	194305	287049	270417	290960	...
Equals: Net Saving	...	...	22039	28845	171474	200216	400714	263541	120002	139718	...
Less: Surplus of the nation on current transactions [a]	...	...	-6297	-8796	25128	-23008	6590	10400	24798	142600	...
Statistical discrepancy	...	...	...	...	...	...	46145	53626	8195	101458	...
Equals: Net Capital Formation	...	...	28336	37642	146346	223224	440269	306767	103399	98576	...

a) Beginning 1976, estimates are not strictly comparable with those of other tables.

2.1 General Government Final Consumption Expenditure by Function, in Current Prices

Million CFA francs

	1970	1971	1972	1973	1974	1975	1976	1977	1978	1979	1980
1 General public services	...	...	8564	...	...	...	...	...	...	...	...
2 Defence	...	...	1138	...	...	...	...	...	...	...	...
3 Public order and safety	...	...		...	...	...	...	...	...	...	...
4 Education	...	...	2040	...	...	...	...	...	...	...	...
5 Health	...	...	1259	...	...	...	...	...	...	...	...
6 Social security and welfare	...	...	419	...	...	...	...	...	...	...	...
7 Housing and community amenities	...	...	35	...	...	...	...	...	...	...	...
8 Recreational, cultural and religious affairs	...	...	96	...	...	...	...	...	...	...	...
9 Economic services	...	...	1606	...	...	...	...	...	...	...	...
10 Other functions	...	...	4060	...	...	...	...	...	...	...	...
Total General Government Final Consumption Expenditure	...	...	19217	...	...	...	...	...	...	...	...

2.9 Gross Capital Formation by Kind of Activity of Owner, ISIC Major Divisions, in Current Prices

Million CFA francs

	1974 Total Gross Capital Formation	1974 Increase in Stocks	1974 Gross Fixed Capital Formation	1975 Total Gross Capital Formation	1975 Increase in Stocks	1975 Gross Fixed Capital Formation	1976 Total Gross Capital Formation	1976 Increase in Stocks	1976 Gross Fixed Capital Formation	1977 Total Gross Capital Formation	1977 Increase in Stocks	1977 Gross Fixed Capital Formation
					All Producers							
1 Agriculture, hunting, fishing and forestry	...	...	4300	...	...	2811	...	...	4528	...	...	5095
2 Mining and quarrying	...	...	38564	...	...	37658	...	...	36697	...	...	29705
3 Manufacturing	...	...	4494	...	...	14394	...	...	25793	...	...	13934
4 Electricity, gas and water	...	...	1227	...	...	3203	...	...	4056	...	...	4050
5 Construction	...	...	31426	...	...	20721	...	...	34774	...	...	73337
6 Wholesale and retail trade, restaurants and hotels	...	...	4873	...	...	8562	...	...	8576	...	...	12180
7 Transport, storage and communication	...	...	11429	...	...	32012	...	...	39986	...	...	10222
8 Finance, insurance, real estate and business services	...	...	4597	...	...	8778	...	...	9422	...	...	15321
9 Community, social and personal services	...	...	239	...	...	425	...	...	344	...	...	880
Statistical discrepancy	...	...	...	...	...	...	...	...	390	...	...	...
Total Industries	...	...	101150	...	...	128564	...	...	164566	...	...	164724
Producers of Government Services	...	...	55007	...	...	129582	...	...	268951	...	...	160486
Private Non-Profit Institutions Serving Households	...	...	120	...	...	...	...	...	2029	...	...	12835
Total	192359	36082	156277	289760	31614	258146	528576	93030	435546	400872	62827	338045

Gabon

2.9 Gross Capital Formation by Kind of Activity of Owner, ISIC Major Divisions, in Current Prices

Million CFA francs

		1978	
	Total Gross Capital Formation	Increase in Stocks	Gross Fixed Capital Formation

All Producers

1	Agriculture, hunting, fishing and forestry	4664	151	4513
2	Mining and quarrying	24183	2394	21789
3	Manufacturing	19712	1402	18310
4	Electricity, gas and water	1	-1906	1907
5	Construction	-15760	-29734	13974
6	Wholesale and retail trade, restaurants and hotels	309	-7756	8065
7	Transport, storage and communication	54047	254	53793
8	Finance, insurance, real estate and business services	12731	51	12680
9	Community, social and personal services	938	-29	967
	Statistical discrepancy	...	...	...
	Total Industries	100825	-35173	135998
	Producers of Government Services	82432	...	82432
	Private Non-Profit Institutions Serving Households	5600	...	5600
	Total	188829	-35173	224030

2.17 Exports and Imports of Goods and Services, Detail

Million CFA francs

		1970	1971	1972	1973	1974	1975	1976	1977	1978	1979	1980

Exports of Goods and Services

1	Exports of merchandise, f.o.b.	...	...	67594	84741	204227	210736	290928	307401	296372	382292	...
2	Transport and communication	...	...	2087	2159	3248	4162	4905	4272	3444	7819	...
	a In respect of merchandise imports	...	...	1553	1538	...	...	...	...	...	...	...
	b Other	...	...	534	621	...	...	...	...	...	...	...
3	Insurance service charges	...	...	800	722	882	2291	1593	3420	3459	4278	...
4	Other commodities	...	...	5508	5542	3070	7931	15946	26130	25644	23145	...
5	Adjustments of merchandise exports to change-of-ownership basis	...	...	...	...	...	...	...	...	...	...	...
6	Direct purchases in the domestic market by non-residential households	...	...	3288	1664	2491	3835	3618	4215	4073	2600	...
7	Direct purchases in the domestic market by extraterritorial bodies	...	...	...	...	...	...	...	...	...	...	...
	Total Exports of Goods and Services [a]	...	...	79277	94828	213918	228955	316990	345438	332992	420134	...

Imports of Goods and Services

1	Imports of merchandise, c.i.f.	...	...	47977	59403	109434	146741	176352	192031	155028	143244	...
2	Adjustments of merchandise imports to change-of-ownership basis	...	...	...	...	...	...	...	...	...	...	...
3	Other transport and communication	...	...	...	3039	4944	5625	7381	8154	6250	7903	...
4	Other insurance service charges	...	...	1684	2035	2297	4072	4083	6511	5963	6150	...
5	Other commodities	...	...	23195	24254	36868	54173	72566	64964	62206	97894	...
6	Direct purchases abroad by government	...	...	5584	4154	7253	10900	14251	17902	15390	18554	...
7	Direct purchases abroad by resident households	...	...									...
	Total Imports of Goods and Services	...	...	78440	92885	160796	221511	274633	289562	253032	273745	...
	Balance of Goods and Services	...	...	837	1943	53122	7444	42357	55876	88155	146389	...
	Total Imports and Balance of Goods and Services	...	...	79277	94828	213918	228955	316990	345438	332992	420134	...

a) Beginning 1976, estimates are not strictly comparable with those of other tables.

Gabon

3.12 General Government Income and Outlay Account: Total and Subsectors

Million CFA francs

	1974 Total General Government	1974 Central Government	1974 State or Provincial Government	1974 Local Government	1974 Social Security Funds	1975 Total General Government	1975 Central Government	1975 State or Provincial Government	1975 Local Government	1975 Social Security Funds
Receipts										
1 Property and entrepreneurial income	1053	896	...	...	...	4083	3706	...	...	...
a Net operating surplus	175	175	...	...	...	300	223	...	...	...
b Withdrawals from public quasi-corporations	-	-	...	...	...	-	-	...	...	...
c Interest	...	...	...	...	...	...	...	...	...	...
d Dividends	...	...	...	...	...	...	...	...	...	...
e Net land rent and royalties	...	...	...	...	...	...	...	...	...	...
2 Taxes, fees and contributions	147411	142185	...	...	...	214527	210815	...	...	...
a Indirect taxes	68413	68413	...	...	...	121448	124850	...	...	...
b Direct taxes	74332	73772	...	...	...	86530	85965	...	...	...
Income	3184	2624	...	...	...	4777	4211	...	...	...
Other	71149	71149	...	...	...	81753	81754	...	...	...
c Social security contributions	4666	...	...	...	...	6549	...	...	...	...
d Fees, fines and penalties	...	...	...	...	...	...	...	...	...	...
3 Other current transfers received	11108	8142	...	...	...	32324	11984	...	...	...
a Casualty insurance claims	11108	8142	...	...	...	19865	11984	...	...	...
b Transfers from other government subsectors	...	...	...	...	...	...	...	...	...	...
c Transfers from abroad	-	...	...	...	...	9940	...	...	...	...
d Other transfers, except imputed	...	...	...	...	...	2519	...	...	...	...
e Imputed unfunded employee welfare contributions	...	...	...	...	...	...	...	...	...	...
Statistical discrepancy	...	...	...	...	...	12590	...	...	...	...
Total Current Receipts	159573	151223	...	...	...	263524	226505	...	...	...
Disbursements										
1 General governement final consumption expenditures	34412	31004	...	...	...	56531	51684	...	...	...
a Compensation of employees	...	...	...	...	...	...	...	...	...	...
b Consumption of fixed capital	77	-	...	...	...	94	-	...	...	...
c Goods and services purchased, net	...	...	...	...	...	...	...	...	...	...
d Less: Own account production of fixed assets	...	...	...	...	...	...	...	...	...	...
e Indirect taxes paid, net	...	...	...	...	...	...	...	...	...	...
2 Property income paid	5219	5191	...	...	...	6461	6288	...	...	...
3 Subsidies	998	912	...	...	...	2828	2546	...	...	...
4 Other current transfers paid	8300	6011	...	...	...	7819	7223	...	...	...
a Casualty insurance premiums, net	178	126	...	...	...	228	157	...	...	...
b Transfers to other government subsectors	...	121	...	...	...	...	237	...	...	...
c Transfers to households	...	4002	...	...	...	...	3711	...	...	...
Social security benefits	4200	2077	...	...	...	5152	2837	...	...	...
Social assistance grants	...	...	...	...	...	...	...	...	...	...
Unfunded employee welfare benefits	...	...	...	...	...	...	...	...	...	...
d Transfers to private non-profit institutions serving households	856	856	...	...	...	949	1670	...	...	...
e Transfers to the rest of the world	...	906	...	...	...	...	1448	...	...	...
Net saving	110645	108105	...	...	...	189885	158764	...	...	...
Total Current Disbursements and Net Saving	159574	151223	...	...	...	263524	226505	...	...	...

Gabon

3.12 General Government Income and Outlay Account: Total and Subsectors

Million CFA francs

	1976 Total General Government	1976 Central Government	1976 State or Provincial Government	1976 Local Government	1976 Social Security Funds	1977 Total General Government	1977 Central Government	1977 State or Provincial Government	1977 Local Government	1977 Social Security Funds
Receipts										
1 Property and entrepreneurial income	16091	15405	...	...	...	21866	19689	...	...	...
a Net operating surplus	372	202	...	...	...	590	73	...	...	...
b Withdrawals from public quasi-corporations	...	...	...	...	...	...	...	...	...	...
c Interest	...	...	...	...	...	...	...	...	...	...
d Dividends	...	...	...	...	...	...	...	...	...	...
e Net land rent and royalties	...	...	...	...	...	...	...	...	...	...
2 Taxes, fees and contributions	228919	212544	...	...	...	284997	263001	...	...	...
a Indirect taxes	115901	115369	...	...	...	141630	140849	...	...	...
b Direct taxes	98327	97175	...	...	...	123534	122152	...	...	...
Income	7394	6242	...	...	...	6114	4732	...	...	...
Other	90933	90933	...	...	...	117420	117420	...	...	...
c Social security contributions	14691	...	...	...	...	19833	...	...	...	...
d Fees, fines and penalties	...	...	...	...	...	...	...	...	...	...
3 Other current transfers received	18020	...	...	...	...	16950	25416	...	...	...
a Casualty insurance claims	...	20873	...	...	...	...	25416	...	...	...
b Transfers from other government subsectors	...	...	...	...	...	...	...	...	...	...
c Transfers from abroad	13691	...	...	...	...	12262	...	...	...	...
d Other transfers, except imputed	4329	...	...	...	...	4688	...	...	...	...
e Imputed unfunded employee welfare contributions	...	...	...	...	...	...	...	...	...	...
Statistical discrepancy	21998	...	...	...	...	26468	...	...	...	...
Total Current Receipts	285028	248822	...	...	...	350281	308106	...	...	...
Disbursements										
1 General government final consumption expenditures	76008	68378	...	...	...	124926	116658	...	...	...
a Compensation of employees	...	...	...	...	...	...	...	...	...	...
b Consumption of fixed capital	144	...	...	...	...	260	...	...	...	...
c Goods and services purchased, net	...	...	...	...	...	...	...	...	...	...
d Less: Own account production of fixed assets	...	...	...	...	...	...	...	...	...	...
e Indirect taxes paid, net	...	...	...	...	...	...	...	...	...	...
2 Property income paid	9775	9573	...	...	...	15234	15130	...	...	...
3 Subsidies	1856	1773	...	...	...	23043	23020	...	...	...
4 Other current transfers paid	13908	10895	...	...	...	13990	9989	...	...	...
a Casualty insurance premiums, net	275	222	...	...	...	379	260	...	...	...
b Transfers to other government subsectors	...	295	...	...	...	...	963	...	...	...
c Transfers to households	...	5330	...	...	...	...	5563	...	...	...
Social security benefits	5988	3196	...	...	...	6406	2260	...	...	...
Social assistance grants	...	...	...	...	...	...	...	...	...	...
Unfunded employee welfare benefits	...	...	...	...	...	...	...	...	...	...
d Transfers to private non-profit institutions serving households	1736	1736	...	...	...	2083	2083	...	...	...
e Transfers to the rest of the world	3313	3312	...	...	...	1120	1120	...	...	...
Net saving	183481	158203	...	...	...	173088	143309	...	...	...
Total Current Disbursements and Net Saving	285028	248822	...	...	...	350281	308106	...	...	...

Gabon

3.12 General Government Income and Outlay Account: Total and Subsectors

Million CFA francs

	1978 Total General Government	Central Government	State or Provincial Government	Local Government	Social Security Funds
Receipts					
1 Property and entrepreneurial income	17826	16728	...	...	...
a Net operating surplus	290	255	...	35	...
b Withdrawals from public quasi-corporations	...	...	...	...	...
c Interest	12164	11101	...	...	1063
d Dividends	5372	5372	...	...	...
e Net land rent and royalties	...	...	...	...	...
2 Taxes, fees and contributions	...	...	...	...	...
a Indirect taxes	109058	107545	...	1513	...
b Direct taxes	100209	100209	...	...	...
Income	...	...	...	...	...
Other	...	...	...	...	...
c Social security contributions	...	...	...	...	...
d Fees, fines and penalties	...	...	...	...	...
3 Other current transfers received	44352	20841	...	4092	19419
a Casualty insurance claims	...	...	...	...	...
b Transfers from other government subsectors	3796	...	...	3796	...
c Transfers from abroad	...	...	...	...	...
d Other transfers, except imputed	296	...	...	296	...
e Imputed unfunded employee welfare contributions	...	...	...	...	...
Statistical discrepancy	...	...	...	...	...
Total Current Receipts	271983	245323	...	5640	21020
Disbursements					
1 General government final consumption expenditures	80595	63005	...	2255	15335
a Compensation of employees	39013	34987	...	1519	2507
b Consumption of fixed capital	538	...	...	...	538
c Goods and services purchased, net	...	...	...	...	...
d Less: Own account production of fixed assets	...	...	...	...	...
e Indirect taxes paid, net	...	...	...	...	...
2 Property income paid	25443	25376	...	67	...
3 Subsidies	21766	21718	...	3	45
4 Other current transfers paid	267795	7453	...	159	...
a Casualty insurance premiums, net	459	244	...	54	161
b Transfers to other government subsectors	907	907	...	...	...
c Transfers to households	...	3492	...	...	...
Social security benefits	7626	2131	...	38	5457
Social assistance grants	...	...	...	...	...
Unfunded employee welfare benefits	...	...	...	...	...
d Transfers to private non-profit institutions serving households	1755	1755	...	...	...
e Transfers to the rest of the world	1055	1055	...	...	...
Net saving	140262	127771	...	3156	9335
Total Current Disbursements and Net Saving	271983	245323	...	5640	21020

Gabon

3.13 General Government Capital Accumulation Account: Total and Subsectors

Million CFA francs

	1974					1975				
	Total General Government	Central Government	State or Provincial Government	Local Government	Social Security Funds	Total General Government	Central Government	State or Provincial Government	Local Government	Social Security Funds
Finance of Gross Accumulation
1 Gross saving	110722	108105	...	...	...	189979	158764	...	...	...
a Consumption of fixed capital	77	-	...	...	...	94	-	...	...	...
b Net saving	110645	108105	...	...	...	189885	158764	...	...	...
2 Capital transfers received [a]	-10096	-10096	...	...	...	-21502	-21502	...	...	...
Finance of Gross Accumulation	100626	98008	...	...	...	141517	137262	...	...	...
Gross Accumulation
1 Gross capital formation	55127	53078	...	...	...	129582	126650	...	...	...
a Increase in stocks	...	...	...	...	...	...	...	...	...	...
b Gross fixed capital formation	...	...	...	...	...	...	...	...	...	...
2 Purchases of land, net	16	16	...	...	...	23	23	...	...	...
3 Purchases of intangible assets, net	659	659	...	...	...	2722	2722	...	...	...
4 Capital transfers paid	...	...	...	...	...	...	...	...	...	...
Net lending	44824	44255	...	...	...	9190	7867	...	...	...
Gross Accumulation	100626	98008	...	...	...	141517	137262	...	...	...

	1976					1977				
	Total General Government	Central Government	State or Provincial Government	Local Government	Social Security Funds	Total General Government	Central Government	State or Provincial Government	Local Government	Social Security Funds
Finance of Gross Accumulation
1 Gross saving	183625	158203	...	...	...	173348	143309	...	...	...
a Consumption of fixed capital	144	...	...	...	...	260	...	...	...	...
b Net saving	183481	158203	...	...	...	173088	143309	...	...	...
2 Capital transfers received [a]	-30000	-30000	...	...	...	-30312	-30312	...	...	...
Finance of Gross Accumulation	141396	129939	...	...	...	131044	115080	...	...	...
Gross Accumulation
1 Gross capital formation	268951	262213	...	...	...	160486	152092	...	...	...
a Increase in stocks	...	...	...	...	...	...	...	...	...	...
b Gross fixed capital formation	...	...	...	...	...	...	...	...	...	...
2 Purchases of land, net	226	208	...	...	...	591	591	...	...	...
3 Purchases of intangible assets, net	21745	21745	...	...	...	6571	6571	...	...	...
4 Capital transfers paid	...	...	...	...	...	...	...	...	...	...
Net lending	-149526	-154227	...	...	...	-36604	-44174	...	...	...
Gross Accumulation	141396	129939	...	...	...	131044	115080	...	...	...

	1978				
	Total General Government	Central Government	State or Provincial Government	Local Government	Social Security Funds
Finance of Gross Accumulation
1 Gross saving	140800	127771	...	3156	9873
a Consumption of fixed capital	538	...	...	...	538
b Net saving	140262	127771	...	3156	9335
2 Capital transfers received [a]	-23925	-23925	...	...	...
Finance of Gross Accumulation	116875	103478	...	...	...
Gross Accumulation
1 Gross capital formation	82663	79654	...	1794	1215
a Increase in stocks	368	...	...	...	368
b Gross fixed capital formation	82295	79654	...	1794	847
2 Purchases of land, net	9508	482	...	...	9026
3 Purchases of intangible assets, net	2287	2287	...	...	...
4 Capital transfers paid	...	...	...	...	...
Net lending	22417	21055	...	1362	...
Gross Accumulation	116875	103478	...	...	...

a) Net.

Gabon

3.51 External Transactions: Current Account: Detail

Million CFA francs

	1970	1971	1972	1973	1974	1975	1976	1977	1978	1979	1980
Payments to the Rest of the World											
1 Imports of goods and services	...	...	78440	92885	160796	221511	274633	289562	253032	273745	...
2 Factor income paid to the rest of the world	...	...	10408	15269	30359	35198	43469	47974	52223	78463	...
a Compensation of employees	...	...	2406	2913	6658	12187	14282	21677	7596	-	...
b Property and entrepreneurial income paid	...	...	8002	12356	23701	23011	29187	26297	44627	78463	...
3 Indirect taxes paid to supranational organizations	...	...	...	...	...	...	...	...	...	...	...
4 Other current transfers to the rest of the world	...	...	4198	6156	8012	11850	16753	20430	17467	39921	...
a By general government	...	...	713	946	1255	1449	3312	4122	3529	5247	...
b By other resident sectors	...	...	3485	5210	6757	10401	13441	16308	13938	34674	...
5 Surplus of the nation on current transactions [a]	...	...	-6297	-8796	25128	-23008	6590	10400	24798	47087	...
Payments to the Rest of the World, and Surplus of the Nation on Current Transfers [a]	...	...	86749	105513	224784	245551	341445	368366	347374	439216	...
Receipts From The Rest of the World											
1 Exports of goods and services [a]	...	...	79277	94828	213918	228955	316990	345438	332992	420134	...
2 Factor income received from the rest of the world	...	...	773	738	3177	5586	9630	9169	992	1561	...
a Compensation of employees	...	...	379	412	1382	3919	6741	5843	19	-	...
b Property and entrepreneurial income received	...	...	394	326	1795	1667	2889	3326	973	1561	...
3 Subsidies received from supranational organizations	...	...	...	...	...	...	...	...	...	...	...
4 Other current transfers from the rest of the world	...	...	6699	9946	7689	11010	14825	13759	13390	15365	...
a To general government	...	...	5384	8624	6706	9940	13691	12262	11940	14651	...
b To other resident sectors	...	...	1315	1323	983	1070	1134	1497	1450	714	...
Receipts from the Rest of the World on Current Transfers [a]	...	...	86749	105513	224784	245551	341445	368366	351870	377000	...

a) Beginning 1976, estimates are not strictly comparable with those of other tables.

3.52 External Transactions: Capital Accumulation Account

Million CFA francs

	1970	1971	1972	1973	1974	1975	1976	1977	1978	1979	1980
Finance of Gross Accumulation											
1 Surplus of the nation on current transactions [a]	...	...	-6297	-8796	25128	-23008	6590	10400	24798	...	...
2 Capital transfers received from the rest of the world [b]	...	...	6448	7053	-18054	52535	47208	-4320	-3055	...	...
a By general government	...	...	5003	7206	...	...	...	...	...	...	...
b By other resident sectors	...	...	1445	-153	...	...	...	...	...	...	...
Total Finance of Gross Accumulation	...	...	151	-1743	7074	29527	53798	6080	21743	...	...
Gross Accumulation											
1 Capital transfers paid to the rest of the world	...	...	...	...	...	...	...	...	...	...	...
2 Purchases of intangible assets, n.e.c., net, from the rest of the world	...	...	...	...	...	...	...	...	...	...	...
3 Net lending to the rest of the world [a]	...	...	151	-1743	7074	29527	53798	6080	21743	...	...
Total Gross Accumulation	...	...	151	-1743	7074	29527	53798	6080	21743	...	...

a) Beginning 1976, estimates are not strictly comparable with those of other tables.
b) Net.

4.6 Cost Components of Value Added, ISIC Divisions

Million CFA francs

	1972						1973					
	Compensation of Employees	Capital Consumption	Net Operating Surplus	Indirect Taxes	Less: Subsidies Received	Value Added	Compensation of Employees	Capital Consumption	Net Operating Surplus	Indirect Taxes	Less: Subsidies Received	Value Added
All Producers												
1 Agriculture, hunting, forestry and fishing	4343	...	6300	...	...	13474	4985	...	9901	...	...	18756
a Agriculture and hunting [a]	1227	...	3309	...	...	4668	987	...	5883	...	...	7038
b Forestry and logging	2945	...	2909	...	...	8541	3748	...	3891	...	...	11314
c Fishing [a]	171	...	82	...	...	266	250	...	127	...	...	405
2 Mining and quarrying	5923	...	9399	...	...	35178	6858	...	30634	...	...	49729

Gabon

4.6 Cost Components of Value Added, ISIC Divisions
(Continued)

Million CFA francs

	1972						1973					
	Compensation of Employees	Capital Consumption	Net Operating Surplus	Indirect Taxes	Less: Subsidies Received	Value Added	Compensation of Employees	Capital Consumption	Net Operating Surplus	Indirect Taxes	Less: Subsidies Received	Value Added
a Coal mining	...	...	...	...	...	...	...	...	...	...	...	...
b Crude petroleum and natural gas production	...	...	...	...	...	25712	...	...	...	...	...	39330
c Metal ore mining	...	...	...	...	...	...	...	...	...	...	...	...
d Other mining	...	...	...	...	...	...	...	...	...	...	...	...
3 Manufacturing	3469	...	1772	...	...	8660	4243	...	3306	...	...	10671
a Manufacture of food, beverages and tobacco	494	...	792	...	...	3208	532	...	1039	...	...	2990
b Textile, wearing apparel and leather industries	207	...	201	...	...	618	264	...	320	...	...	702
c Manufacture of wood and wood products, including furniture	1322	...	197	...	...	2070	1639	...	607	...	...	2917
d Manufacture of paper and paper products, printing and publishing	75	...	92	...	...	198	56	...	57	...	...	123
e Manufacture of chemicals and chemical petroleum, coal, rubber and plastic products	668	...	378	...	...	1485	711	...	409	...	...	1566
f Manufacture of non-metallic mineral products, except products of petroleum and coal	46	...	63	...	...	166	121	...	67	...	...	243
g Basic metal industries	...	...	...	...	...	...	...	...	...	...	...	...
h Manufacture of fabricated metal products, machinery and equipment	...	...	...	...	...	915	...	...	...	...	...	2130
i Other manufacturing industries	...	...	...	...	...	...	...	...	...	...	...	...
4 Electricity, gas and water	689	...	65	...	...	2221	855	...	1295	...	...	2883
a Electricity, gas and steam	...	...	...	...	...	...	...	...	...	...	...	...
b Water works and supply	...	...	...	...	...	...	...	...	...	...	...	...
5 Construction	5779	...	2690	...	...	12342	8257	...	4358	...	...	16710
6 Wholesale and retail trade, restaurants and hotels	5654	...	2902	...	...	17264	5484	...	4646	...	...	13478
a Wholesale and retail trade	...	...	...	...	...	15689	...	...	...	...	...	12493
b Restaurants and hotels	...	...	...	...	...	1575	...	...	...	...	...	985
7 Transport, storage and communication	3372	...	202	...	...	4715	3262	...	2376	...	...	7153
a Transport and storage	...	...	...	...	...	...	...	...	...	...	...	...
b Communication	...	...	...	...	...	...	...	...	...	...	...	...
8 Finance, insurance, real estate and business services	1424	...	635	...	...	2907	2381	...	10030	...	...	15772
a Financial institutions	...	...	...	...	...	...	...	...	...	...	...	...
b Insurance	...	...	...	...	...	...	...	...	...	...	...	...
c Real estate and business services	...	...	...	...	...	...	...	...	...	...	...	...
9 Community, social and personal services	50	...	34	...	...	113	76	...	40	...	...	149
a Sanitary and similar services	...	...	...	...	...	...	...	...	...	...	...	...
b Social and related community services	...	...	...	...	...	...	...	...	...	...	...	...
Educational services	...	...	...	...	...	...	...	...	...	...	...	...
Medical, dental, other health and veterinary services	...	...	...	...	...	...	...	...	...	...	...	...
c Recreational and cultural services	...	...	...	...	...	...	...	...	...	...	...	...
d Personal and household services	...	...	...	...	...	...	...	...	...	...	...	...
Total, Industries	30704	...	23999	...	...	96875	36402	...	66586	...	...	135302
Producers of Government Services	10485	...	...	...	...	10556	13018	...	...	...	...	13080
Other Producers	920	...	...	...	...	1021	750	...	...	...	...	800
Total	42108	...	23999	...	...	108452	50169	...	66586	...	...	149182
Imputed bank service charge	...	...	...	...	...	...	...	...	1584	...	...	1587
Import duties	...	...	...	...	...	...	...	...	...	...	...	13459
Value added tax	...	...	...	...	...	...	...	...	...	...	...	...
Other adjustments	...	...	...	...	...	...	...	...	...	...	...	...
Total	...	...	...	...	...	108452	...	...	...	...	...	161057

Gabon

4.6 Cost Components of Value Added, ISIC Divisions

Million CFA francs

	1974 Compensation of Employees	1974 Capital Consumption	1974 Net Operating Surplus	1974 Indirect Taxes	1974 Less: Subsidies Received	1974 Value Added	1975 Compensation of Employees	1975 Capital Consumption	1975 Net Operating Surplus	1975 Indirect Taxes	1975 Less: Subsidies Received	1975 Value Added
All Producers												
1 Agriculture, hunting, forestry and fishing	5974	...	17772	...	...	33937	4238	...	20274	...	...	40772
a Agriculture and hunting a	44	...	14947	...	...	15003	72	...	19266	...	...	19441
b Forestry and logging	5743	...	1855	...	...	17710	3980	...	-392	...	...	19674
c Fishing a	187	...	970	...	...	1225	186	...	1400	...	...	1657
2 Mining and quarrying	8100	...	126361	...	...	178085	9024	...	118988	...	...	187163
a Coal mining	...	...	...	...	...	...	...	...	...	...	...	...
b Crude petroleum and natural gas production	...	...	...	...	...	162188	...	...	...	...	...	161547
c Metal ore mining	...	...	...	...	...	15657	...	...	...	...	...	25249
d Other mining	...	...	...	...	...	240	...	...	...	...	...	367
3 Manufacturing	7323	...	2861	...	...	15328	12007	...	5269	...	...	22998
a Manufacture of food, beverages and tobacco	1045	...	1074	...	...	4170	1428	...	1180	...	...	5199
b Textile, wearing apparel and leather industries	324	...	188	...	...	613	475	...	496	...	...	1115
c Manufacture of wood and wood products, including furniture	2506	...	522	...	...	4062	3731	...	477	...	...	5921
d Manufacture of paper and paper products, printing and publishing	141	...	74	...	...	248	205	...	167	...	...	377
e Manufacture of chemicals and chemical petroleum, coal, rubber and plastic products	894	...	-627	...	...	1053	1253	...	57	...	...	1011
f Manufacture of non-metallic mineral products, except products of petroleum and coal	180	...	156	...	...	495	466	...	246	...	...	873
g Basic metal industries	...	...	...	...	...	-	...	...	...	...	...	-
h Manufacture of fabricated metal products, machinery and equipment	...	...	...	...	...	4631	...	...	...	...	...	8501
i Other manufacturing industries	10	...	43	...	...	56	...	...	...	...	...	...
4 Electricity, gas and water	1084	...	2285	...	...	3920	1459	...	2665	...	...	4909
a Electricity, gas and steam	...	...	...	...	...	...	...	...	...	...	...	...
b Water works and supply	...	...	...	...	...	...	...	...	...	...	...	...
5 Construction	18446	...	721	...	...	42452	33675	...	8719	...	...	79826
6 Wholesale and retail trade, restaurants and hotels	9093	...	10983	...	...	23342	12406	...	15268	...	...	32152
a Wholesale and retail trade	...	...	...	...	...	21967	...	...	...	...	...	29138
b Restaurants and hotels	...	...	...	...	...	1375	...	...	...	...	...	3014
7 Transport, storage and communication	5918	...	2628	...	...	10452	8807	...	4885	...	...	18423
a Transport and storage	...	...	...	...	...	...	...	...	...	...	...	...
b Communication	...	...	...	...	...	...	...	...	...	...	...	...
8 Finance, insurance, real estate and business services	3015	...	19774	...	...	28263	6966	...	15050	...	...	26951
a Financial institutions	...	...	...	...	...	...	...	...	...	...	...	...
b Insurance	...	...	...	...	...	...	...	...	...	...	...	...
c Real estate and business services	...	...	...	...	...	...	...	...	...	...	...	...
9 Community, social and personal services	708	...	210	...	...	1367	701	...	619	...	...	1627
a Sanitary and similar services	...	...	...	...	...	...	...	...	...	...	...	...
b Social and related community services	...	...	...	...	...	...	...	...	...	...	...	...
Educational services	...	...	...	...	...	...	...	...	...	...	...	...
Medical, dental, other health and veterinary services	...	...	...	...	...	...	...	...	...	...	...	...
c Recreational and cultural services	...	...	...	...	...	...	...	...	...	...	...	...
d Personal and household services	...	...	...	...	...	...	...	...	...	...	...	...
Total, Industries	59861	...	184047	...	...	337146	89286	...	200446	...	...	414821
Producers of Government Services	16944	...	175	...	...	17022	23046	...	300	...	...	23142

Gabon

4.6 Cost Components of Value Added, ISIC Divisions
(Continued)

Million CFA francs

	1974						1975					
	Compensation of Employees	Capital Consumption	Net Operating Surplus	Indirect Taxes	Less: Subsidies Received	Value Added	Compensation of Employees	Capital Consumption	Net Operating Surplus	Indirect Taxes	Less: Subsidies Received	Value Added
Other Producers	1230	...	-	...	...	1230	1649	...	-	...	...	1648
Total	78035	...	184222	...	...	355398	113981	...	200746	...	...	439611
Imputed bank service charge	...	...	4001	...	...	4001	...	...	9007	...	...	9007
Import duties	...	...	...	...	...	20287	...	...	...	...	...	31837
Value added tax	...	...	...	...	...	...	...	...	...	...	...	...
Other adjustments	...	...	...	...	...	...	...	...	...	...	...	...
Total	...	...	...	...	...	371684	...	...	...	...	...	462441

	1976						1977					
	Compensation of Employees	Capital Consumption	Net Operating Surplus	Indirect Taxes	Less: Subsidies Received	Value Added	Compensation of Employees	Capital Consumption	Net Operating Surplus	Indirect Taxes	Less: Subsidies Received	Value Added

All Producers

1 Agriculture, hunting, forestry and fishing	5137	...	26885	...	...	36912	8868	...	26239	...	...	39373
a Agriculture and hunting [a]	104	...	21692	...	...	21925	...	...	...	...	...	...
b Forestry and logging	4999	...	3411	...	...	13124	6271	...	1425	...	...	11277
c Fishing [a]	34	...	1782	...	...	1863	...	...	...	...	...	...
2 Mining and quarrying	12542	...	128769	...	...	227461	15434	...	124500	...	...	242839
a Coal mining	...	...	...	...	...	...	...	...	...	...	...	...
b Crude petroleum and natural gas production	...	...	...	...	...	195603	...	...	...	...	...	209225
c Metal ore mining	...	...	...	...	...	30787	...	...	...	...	...	33364
d Other mining	...	...	...	...	...	1071	...	...	...	...	...	250
3 Manufacturing	15893	...	11679	...	...	34911	19758	...	14483	...	...	45711
a Manufacture of food, beverages and tobacco	2453	...	2636	...	...	8329	3107	...	1115	...	...	7801
b Textile, wearing apparel and leather industries	798	...	458	...	...	1418	639	...	339	...	...	1160
c Manufacture of wood and wood products, including furniture	5656	...	1002	...	...	8763	6753	...	-806	...	...	8384
d Manufacture of paper and paper products, printing and publishing	657	...	-260	...	...	484	610	...	-808	...	...	296
e Manufacture of chemicals and chemical petroleum, coal, rubber and plastic products	1609	...	1700	...	...	3487	1673	...	4504	...	...	8486
f Manufacture of non-metallic mineral products, except products of petroleum and coal	701	...	1344	...	...	2190	1476	...	783	...	...	2602
g Basic metal industries	...	...	...	...	...	...	...	...	...	...	...	...
h Manufacture of fabricated metal products, machinery and equipment	...	...	...	...	...	10240	...	...	...	...	...	16982
i Other manufacturing industries	...	...	...	...	...	...	...	...	...	...	...	...
4 Electricity, gas and water	1872	...	3254	...	...	6026	2425	...	1512	...	...	5311
a Electricity, gas and steam	...	...	...	...	...	6026	...	...	...	...	...	5311
b Water works and supply	...	...	...	...	...	...	...	...	...	...	...	...
5 Construction	55805	...	95894	...	...	193579	50867	...	24246	...	...	96951
6 Wholesale and retail trade, restaurants and hotels	17509	...	43676	...	...	67743	20317	...	21435	...	...	55867
a Wholesale and retail trade	...	...	...	...	...	64232	...	...	...	...	...	51524
b Restaurants and hotels	...	...	...	...	...	3511	...	...	...	...	...	4343
7 Transport, storage and communication	12944	...	8458	...	...	28728	16158	...	6939	...	...	30095
a Transport and storage	...	...	...	...	...	...	...	...	...	...	...	...
b Communication	...	...	...	...	...	...	...	...	...	...	...	...
8 Finance, insurance, real estate and business services	9023	...	40283	...	...	58811	20320	...	44649	...	...	83175
a Financial institutions	...	...	...	...	...	...	...	...	...	...	...	...
b Insurance	...	...	...	...	...	...	...	...	...	...	...	...
c Real estate and business services	...	...	...	...	...	...	...	...	...	...	...	...
9 Community, social and personal services	994	...	1700	...	...	3183	1974	...	2490	...	...	4639
a Sanitary and similar services	...	...	...	...	...	...	...	...	...	...	...	...
b Social and related community services	...	...	...	...	...	...	...	...	...	...	...	...

Gabon

4.6 Cost Components of Value Added, ISIC Divisions
(Continued)

Million CFA francs

	1976						1977					
	Compensation of Employees	Capital Consumption	Net Operating Surplus	Indirect Taxes	Less: Subsidies Received	Value Added	Compensation of Employees	Capital Consumption	Net Operating Surplus	Indirect Taxes	Less: Subsidies Received	Value Added
Educational services	...	...	...	...	...	...	...	...	...	...	...	...
Medical, dental, other health and veterinary services	...	...	...	...	...	...	...	...	...	...	...	...
c Recreational and cultural services	...	...	...	...	...	...	...	...	...	...	...	...
d Personal and household services	...	...	...	...	...	...	...	...	...	...	...	...
Total, Industries	131719	...	360580	...	...	657354	156121	...	266494	...	...	603961
Producers of Government Services	28811	...	117	...	...	28924	39612	...	85	...	...	39809
Other Producers	3182	...	126	...	...	3312	4016	...	150	...	...	4166
Total	163712	...	360822	...	...	689590	199749	...	266579	...	...	647936
Imputed bank service charge	...	...	8982	...	...	8982	...	...	8595	...	...	8595
Import duties	...	...	...	...	...	38484	...	...	...	...	...	50830
Value added tax	...	...	...	...	...	...	...	...	...	...	...	...
Other adjustments	...	...	...	...	...	...	...	...	...	...	...	...
Total	...	...	...	...	...	719092	...	...	...	...	...	690171

	1978					
	Compensation of Employees	Capital Consumption	Net Operating Surplus	Indirect Taxes	Less: Subsidies Received	Value Added
	All Producers					
1 Agriculture, hunting, forestry and fishing	9319	3309	22664	...	...	36100
a Agriculture and hunting [a]	2292	351	23106	...	...	26097
b Forestry and logging	7027	2958	-442	...	...	10003
c Fishing [a]	...	...	...	...	...	...
2 Mining and quarrying	15620	42908	100649	...	...	206269
a Coal mining	...	...	...	...	...	...
b Crude petroleum and natural gas production	4844	36202	88755	...	...	171905
c Metal ore mining	10518	6631	12115	...	...	34192
d Other mining	258	75	-221	...	...	172
3 Manufacturing	17787	7932	11753	...	...	39572
a Manufacture of food, beverages and tobacco	2708	857	2308	...	...	6908
b Textile, wearing apparel and leather industries	576	63	357	...	...	1108
c Manufacture of wood and wood products, including furniture	5237	2134	-1007	...	...	6360
d Manufacture of paper and paper products, printing and publishing	525	93	73	...	...	519
e Manufacture of chemicals and chemical petroleum, coal, rubber and plastic products	2112	3297	4072	...	...	9720
f Manufacture of non-metallic mineral products, except products of petroleum and coal	1188	832	-291	...	...	1821
g Basic metal industries	...	...	...	...	...	...
h Manufacture of fabricated metal products, machinery and equipment	4127	599	104	...	...	5318
i Other manufacturing industries	1314	57	6137	...	...	7818
4 Electricity, gas and water	3378	1538	4040	...	...	9379
a Electricity, gas and steam	3378	1538	4040	...	...	9379
b Water works and supply	...	...	...	...	...	...
5 Construction	43689	15309	7271	...	...	72501
6 Wholesale and retail trade, restaurants and hotels	17672	2681	12220	...	...	37221
a Wholesale and retail trade	15968	2572	10875	...	...	33376
b Restaurants and hotels	1704	109	1345	...	...	3845
7 Transport, storage and communication	16863	2952	-179	...	...	23896
a Transport and storage	15073	2282	-3202	...	...	18655

Gabon

4.6 Cost Components of Value Added, ISIC Divisions
(Continued)

Million CFA francs

	1978					
	Compensation of Employees	Capital Consumption	Net Operating Surplus	Indirect Taxes	Less: Subsidies Received	Value Added
b Communication	1790	670	3023	...	...	5241
8 Finance, insurance, real estate and business services	13873	6315	5316	...	...	27712
a Financial institutions	5513	1353	-1719	...	...	11503
b Insurance	526	40	535	...	...	1204
c Real estate and business services	7834	4922	9206	...	...	23726
9 Community, social and personal services	1961	1118	2267	...	...	4398
a Sanitary and similar services	...	...	...	...	...	...
b Social and related community services	...	...	...	...	...	...
Educational services	...	...	...	...	...	...
Medical, dental, other health and veterinary services	1366	964	1467	...	...	2696
c Recreational and cultural services	...	...	...	...	...	...
d Personal and household services	595	154	800	...	...	1702
Total, Industries	140162	84062	166001	...	...	465769
Producers of Government Services	41033	538	418	...	...	41739
Other Producers				...	...	
Total	194307	85430	225301	...	...	509170
Imputed bank service charge	...	...	8721	...	...	8721
Import duties	...	...	...	...	...	38757
Value added tax	...	...	...	...	...	...
Other adjustments	...	...	...	...	...	...
Total	...	...	...	...	...	539206

a) Beginning 1977, item 'Agricultural services, hunting, etc.' and item 'Fishing' are included in item 'Agricultural and livestock production'.

German Democratic Rep.

Source. Reply to the United Nations Material Balances Questionnaire from the State Central Administration for Statistics, Berlin. The official estimates are published in the 'Statistisches Jahrbuch Der Deutschen Demokratishen Republik' (Statistical Yearbook of the German Democratic Republic). The methodological explanations used in the compilation of the National Accounts can be found in 'Statistik Des Nationaleinkommens, Planung Und Leitung Der Volkswirtschaft, Heft 36'.

General note. The estimates shown in the following tables have been prepared in accordance with the System of Material Product Balances. Therefore, these estimates are not comparable in concept and coverage with those conforming to the United Nations System of National Accounts. The estimates include the relevant data relating to Berlin for which separate data have not been supplied. This is without prejudice to any question of status which may be involved.

1b Net Material Product by Use at Constant Market Prices

Percentages

At constant prices of: 1975

	1970	1971	1972	1973	1974	1975	1976	1977	1978	1979	1980
1 Personal consumption	66.4	67.1	67.5	66.7	66.5	67.0	66.2	65.9	67.3	68.8	68.2
2 Material consumption in the units of the non-material sphere serving individuals	3.6	3.7	3.9	3.9	4.2	4.4	4.5	4.5	4.5	4.6	4.5
Consumption of the Population	70.0	70.8	71.3	70.6	70.7	71.4	70.6	70.4	71.9	73.4	72.7
3 Material consumption in the units of the non-material sphere serving the community as a whole	5.6	6.1	6.2	6.1	6.2	6.4	6.5	6.6	6.7	6.6	6.2
4 Net fixed capital formation	24.4	23.1	22.5	23.3	23.1	22.3	22.9	23.0	21.4	20.0	21.1
5 Increase in material circulating assets and in stocks											
6 Losses	...	...	...	...	...	...	...	...	...	...	...
7 Exports of goods and material services	...	...	...	...	...	...	...	...	...	...	...
8 Less: Imports of goods and material services	...	...	...	...	...	...	...	...	...	...	...
Net Material Product	100.0	100.0	100.0	100.0	100.0	100.0	100.0	100.0	100.0	100.0	100.0

1b Net Material Product by Use at Constant Market Prices

Index numbers 1960 = 100

At constant prices of: 1975

	1970	1971	1972	1973	1974	1975	1976	1977	1978	1979	1980
1 Personal consumption	137.4	143.0	151.5	159.7	169.0	175.1	182.7	190.7	197.1	204.8	212.7
2 Material consumption in the units of the non-material sphere serving individuals	164.8	175.2	192.0	206.0	232.0	251.6	270.4	284.4	292.2	298.8	308.8
Consumption of the Population	138.6	144.4	153.3	161.7	171.7	178.4	186.5	194.8	201.3	208.9	216.9
3 Material consumption in the units of the non-material sphere serving the community as a whole	174.9	196.4	209.9	222.7	239.2	252.8	271.0	290.9	298.8	297.2	293.1
4 Net fixed capital formation	203.5	199.1	204.0	225.1	237.1	234.7	255.3	268.1	253.2	240.6	265.9
5 Increase in material circulating assets and in stocks											
6 Losses	...	...	...	...	...	...	...	...	...	...	...
7 Exports of goods and material services	...	...	...	...	...	...	...	...	...	...	...
8 Less: Imports of goods and material services	...	...	...	...	...	...	...	...	...	...	...
Net Material Product	152.2	156.9	165.3	176.2	186.9	192.3	203.1	212.8	215.5	219.0	229.5

2b Net Material Product by Kind of Activity of the Material Sphere in Constant Market Prices

Million Marks der DDR

At constant prices of: 1975

	1970	1971	1972	1973	1974	1975	1976	1977	1978	1979	1980
1 Agriculture and forestry [a]	14462	13889	15304	15377	16418	16002	14228	15877	15351	16163	16120
2 Industrial activity [a]	64536	67920	71397	75711	80495	85492	90500	94533	98921	103611	109360
3 Construction	8511	8920	9251	9658	10110	10705	11287	11778	12036	11956	12125
4 Wholesale and retail trade and restaurants and other eating and drinking places	15978	17039	18059	19086	20464	21158	21871	22984	23826	24401	25017
5 Transport and communication	5611	6013	6134	6412	6743	7266	7604	7830	8142	8252	8510
6 Other activities of the material sphere	3072	3209	3275	3546	3730	4087	4390	4638	5028	5157	5430
Statistical discrepancy [b]	-2700	-2540	-2490	-2140	-2180	-2340	-2360	-2430	-2544	-2640	-2692
Net material product	109470	114450	120930	127650	135780	142370	147520	155210	160760	166900	173870

a) Deep-sea fishery is included in item 'Industrial activity'.
b) Relating to price supports.

Germany, Fed. Rep. of

General note. The preparation of national accounts statistics in the Federal Republic of Germany is undertaken by the Federal Statistical Office, Wiesbaden. The official estimates are published in the monthly bulletin 'Wirtschaft und Statistik'. Detailed data as well as description of the sources and methods used for the national accounts estimation are published annually in Fachserie 18 'Volkswirtschaftliche Gesamtrechnungen', Reihe 1 'Konten und Standardtabellen'. The estimates are in close accordance with the classifications and definitions recommended in the United Nations System of National Accounts (SNA). Input-output tables for 1970 and 1974 have been published in 'Input-Output-Tabellen 1974' and for 1975 in 'Input-Output Tabellen 1975' in Reihe 2 of Fachserie 18. The 1978 tables will be issued in 1983. The following tables have been prepared from successive replies to the United Nations national accounts questionnaire. Estimates shown include the relevant data relating to Berlin, for which separate data have not been supplied. This is without prejudice to any question of status which may be involved. When the scope and coverage of the estimates differ for conceptual or statistical reasons from the definitions and classifications recommended in SNA, a footnote is indicated to the relevant tables. As a general principle, the statistical units in the case of the data provided in the ISIC classification are institutional units (e.g. enterprises). Only the ownership of dwellings (including owner-occupied housing) is shown in a functional delimitation and fully allocated to the enterprise sector. The enterprise sector comprises all enterprises, i.e. also those which according to SNA should be shown in the sector of private households or general government, respectively.

Sources and methods:

(a) Gross domestic product. The main approach used to estimate GDP is the production approach.

(b) Expenditure on the gross domestic product. The expenditure approach is used to estimate all components of GDP by expenditure type except gross fixed capital formation which is calculated mainly by the commodity-flow approach. Government final consumption expenditure is based on records from all sectors of general government. Private final consumption expenditure is estimated mainly from data on retail sales. Data for certain base-years are derived mainly from censuses (trade census 1967/69, crafts census 1977, industrial production census 1967). Annual data are linked with these base-year data by means of current turnover and other supply statistics. The estimates of gross fixed capital formation are based on quarterly production reports, monthly construction reports, statistics on building activity and the previously mentioned censuses. Exports and imports of goods are based on foreign trade statistics, while exports and imports of services are obtained mainly from the Central Bank. For the calculation of constant prices, price deflation is used for all expenditure groups.

(c) Cost-structure of the gross domestic product. Compensation of employees is calculated from three sources - social security statistics, census data extrapolated by current data and taxation statistics. Capital consumption is calculated at constant prices and at current replacement costs according to the perpetual inventory method. Indirect taxes and subsidies are taken directly from the general government accounts. Operating surplus is then obtained as a residual.

(d) Gross domestic product by kind of economic activity. The table of GDP by kind of economic activity is prepared at market prices, i.e. producers' values. The production approach is used to estimate value added of most industries. The income approach is used to estimate value added of domestic services, private non-profit institutions and producers of government services. The value of agricultural production is defined as the difference between primary gross production and internally used quantities, times average prices, or, as the sum of sales, change in livestock and other stocks, own account consumption, investment and exports. The basic statistics used are mainly data on utilization of agricultural production. Inputs are derived from book-keeping records, foreign trade statistics and production and sales statistics from suppliers of agricultural input goods. The main sources for estimating mining and quarrying, manufacturing, electricity, gas and water and construction are the censuses of production industries, which provide bench-mark data, and annual data taken from several sources. Data on intermediate consumption for these sectors are taken from the censuses and cost-structure statistics. For trade, the bench-mark estimates are mainly based on the trade censuses 1967/69. Output is extrapolated by turnover data, while input is estimated from the trade censuses, cost-structure statistics and annual trade reports. For the transport sector, cost-structure statistics are used to estimate parts of output and intermediate consumption for most sub-sectors. Turnover tax statistics are utilized for preparing the current output estimates. Banking statistics, collected by Central Bank, and insurance statistics, collected by Federal Supervisory Board, provide the basis for estimating output of financial institutions including insurance. Input is estimated on the basis of bank company reports and insurance company reports. Rents are estimated separately for three different categories - old, medium and new buildings. The rents are based on data from censuses of buildings and dwellings, which include owner-occupied dwellings. The data are extrapolated by quantity and price indexes. The data used to estimate value added of government services, are mainly based on receipts and expenditure statistics of general government. For private non-profit institutions output is estimated as the sum of costs for wages and salaries, estimated capital consumption and indirect taxes. Double deflation is used in the calculations of constant prices, for all sectors except transport and real estate and business services. Output of most sectors is deflated by producer price indexes. However, for most agricultural products, current quantities are multiplied by base year prices, for some transport and communication services output is extrapolated by quantity indexes, and for insurance and business services extrapolation is used. Deflation by purchase price indexes or specially constructed input indexes is done for almost all sectors. For trade, and partly for transportation and communication, however, constant input-ouput ratios are assumed.

1.1 Expenditure on the Gross Domestic Product, in Current Prices

Million Deutsche marks

		1970	1971	1972	1973	1974	1975	1976	1977	1978	1979	1980
1	General government final consumption expenditure	108110	129240	144030	166700	194020	215290	227190	239380	257130	278580	303520
2	Private final consumption expenditure	367550	407830	447750	491680	527550	577420	623590	669560	713910	766360	821590
	a Households	362520	402260	442170	485670	521540	571160	616850	661900	705250	756560	810640
	b Private non-profit institutions serving households	5030	5570	5580	6010	6010	6260	6740	7660	8660	9800	10950
3	Gross capital formation	189090	203400	216940	232640	221890	213240	245590	262160	282410	339990	369890
	a Increase in stocks	15400	3800	2600	7200	5500	-1300	13700	13200	9400	25600	18900
	b Gross fixed capital formation	173690	199600	214340	225440	216390	214540	231890	248960	273010	314390	350990
	Residential buildings	44860	55050	66890	72610	64470	59190	64980	70080	76190	89320	101940
	Non-residential buildings	60400	68180	70700	73070	75450	73030	76230	78990	86440	101350	116880
	Other construction and land improvement etc.	...	...	...	...	...	...	...	...	...	...	...
	Other	68430	76370	76750	79760	76470	82320	90680	99890	110380	123720	132170
4	Exports of goods and services	142920	156690	170920	200820	259840	256390	293890	311330	326390	357710	401590
5	Less: Imports of goods and services	128920	142280	153650	173240	216170	228310	267440	281940	293460	348700	407670
	Equals: Gross Domestic Product	678750	754880	825990	918600	987130	1034030	1122820	1200490	1286380	1393940	1488920

1.2 Expenditure on the Gross Domestic Product, in Constant Prices

Million Deutsche marks

		1970	1971	1972	1973	1974	1975	1976	1977	1978	1979	1980
		At constant prices of: 1970										
1	General government final consumption expenditure	108110	114950	120270	126850	132310	138250	141010	141760	147770	152600	156500
2	Private final consumption expenditure	367550	386800	402240	412480	413790	426550	441010	456300	474380	490130	498620
	a Households	362520	381910	397690	408140	409840	422790	437190	452260	470030	485470	493720
	b Private non-profit institutions serving households	5030	4890	4550	4340	3950	3760	3820	4040	4350	4660	4900
3	Gross capital formation	189090	188770	193700	197770	177010	164370	183400	189440	195650	222330	224680

Germany, Fed. Rep. of

1.2 Expenditure on the Gross Domestic Product, in Constant Prices
(Continued)

Million Deutsche marks

	1970	1971	1972	1973	1974	1975	1976	1977	1978	1979	1980
					At constant prices of: 1970						
a Increase in stocks	15400	3900	2400	6100	4400	-1000	10200	9500	6600	17400	12100
b Gross fixed capital formation	173690	184870	191300	191670	172610	165370	173200	179940	189050	204930	212580
Residential buildings	44860	49690	56680	57410	47750	42780	45500	46830	48020	51680	53420
Non-residential buildings	60400	62740	62870	61960	59960	57460	58350	58400	60220	64760	68110
Other construction and land improvement etc.	...	...	...	...	...	...	...	...	...	...	...
Other	68430	72440	71750	72300	64900	65130	69350	74710	80810	88490	91050
4 Exports of goods and services	142920	151200	161450	180730	202550	190590	212910	222380	230710	243140	257070
5 Less: Imports of goods and services	128920	141040	151380	155990	159710	167960	187740	195300	207670	229880	241730
Equals: Gross Domestic Product	678750	700680	726280	761840	765950	751800	790590	814580	840840	878320	895140

1.3 Cost Components of the Gross Domestic Product

Million Deutsche marks

	1970	1971	1972	1973	1974	1975	1976	1977	1978	1979	1980
1 Indirect taxes, net	77540	86480	95380	103440	107280	111320	121540	129810	139980	155000	166280
a Indirect taxes paid	87240	96440	107630	118480	122300	126780	138250	149130	163920	179840	189960
b Less: Subsidies received	9700	9960	12250	15040	15020	15460	16710	19320	23940	24840	23680
2 Consumption of fixed capital	68350	78450	86330	95740	107260	117030	125490	134250	144770	158340	175850
3 Compensation of employees paid by resident producers to:	360110	407080	447790	508530	559680	582350	625230	668610	713640	768200	828760
a Resident households	359280	405980	446400	506920	557880	580400	623140	666370	711280	765720	826080
b Rest of the world	830	1100	1390	1610	1800	1950	2090	2240	2360	2480	2680
4 Net operating surplus	172750	182870	196490	210890	212910	223330	250560	267820	287990	312400	318030
a Corporate and quasi-corporate enterprises	172750	182870	196490	210890	212910	223330	250560	267820	287990	312400	318030
b Private unincorporated enterprises	...	...	...	...	...	...	...	...	...	...	...
c General government	...	...	...	...	...	...	...	...	...	...	...
Equals: Gross Domestic Product	678750	754880	825990	918600	987130	1034030	1122820	1200490	1286380	1393940	1488920

1.4 General Government Current Receipts and Disbursements

Million Deutsche marks

	1970	1971	1972	1973	1974	1975	1976	1977	1978	1979	1980
					Receipts						
1 Property and entrepreneurial income	8630	9150	8560	10670	10620	9600	10150	10270	11850	13690	14340
2 Taxes, fees and contributions	235820	268100	298290	352270	381160	392900	443410	487140	517070	555220	593450
a Indirect taxes [a]	87180	96370	107560	118400	122210	126700	138170	149050	163850	179770	189930
b Direct taxes	72840	84960	91070	115810	128380	123820	143830	164650	167490	175510	187750
c Social security contributions	73740	84330	96820	114870	126890	138340	156860	168410	180150	193930	209430
d Compulsory fees, fines and penalties	2060	2440	2840	3190	3680	4040	4550	5030	5580	6010	6340
3 Other current receipts	9810	11650	13160	15820	18050	19290	21140	24670	27910	28900	30070
Total Current Receipts of General Government	254260	288900	320010	378760	409830	421790	474700	522080	556830	597810	637860
					Disbursements						
1 General government final consumption expenditure	108110	129240	144030	166700	194020	215290	227190	239380	257130	278580	303520
a Compensation of employees	60140	71890	80760	94030	109160	118530	124980	133380	141840	151930	164130
b Consumption of fixed capital	3250	3740	4150	4640	5230	5740	6240	6800	7460	8270	9340
c Purchases of goods and services, net	44720	53620	59120	68000	79610	91010	95960	99210	107830	118410	130100
d Less: Own account production of fixed assets	90	120	130	120	140	170	190	220	220	260	300
e Indirect taxes paid, net	90	110	130	150	160	180	200	210	220	230	250
2 Property income paid	6600	7430	8480	10220	12200	14230	17500	20470	21520	24210	28730

Germany, Fed. Rep. of

1.4 General Government Current Receipts and Disbursements
(Continued)

Million Deutsche marks

	1970	1971	1972	1973	1974	1975	1976	1977	1978	1979	1980
a Interest	6600	7430	8480	10220	12200	14230	17500	20470	21520	24210	28730
b Net land rent and royalties	...	...	...	...	...	...	...	...	...	...	...
3 Subsidies [a]	9630	9830	12130	14850	14800	15230	16640	19230	23840	24770	23680
4 Other current transfers paid	90160	101070	116360	130900	149640	184840	198690	215000	228360	242790	256960
a Social security benefits and social assistance grants	68560	76020	87430	97690	113180	143850	154490	165970	175790	186070	197110
b Other	21600	25050	28930	33210	36460	40990	44200	49030	52570	56720	59850
5 Net saving	39760	41330	39010	56090	39170	-7800	14680	28000	25980	27460	24970
Total Current Disbursements and Net Saving of General Government	254260	288900	320010	378760	409830	421790	474700	522080	556830	597810	637860

a) Indirect taxes paid to and subsidies received from supranational organizations are not included in the receipts and disbursements respectively of the general government.

1.5 Current Income and Outlay of Corporate and Quasi-Corporate Enterprises, Summary

Million Deutsche marks

	1970	1971	1972	1973	1974	1975	1976	1977	1978	1979	1980
					Receipts						
1 Net operating surplus	172750	182870	196490	210890	212910	223330	250560	267820	287990	312400	318030
2 Other property and entrepreneurial income received	16390	19290	20980	25650	30670	31180	35450	39360	43420	50500	61440
3 Current transfers received [a]	22210	24510	28230	31370	35200	37450	41650	43190	48420	53950	57890
Total Current Receipts [a]	211350	226670	245700	267910	278780	291960	327660	350370	379830	416850	437360
					Disbursements						
1 Property and entrepreneurial income paid	174610	189840	194460	211810	223770	234660	255010	281070	292970	321380	...
2 Direct taxes and other current payments to general government [a]	12310	11290	11680	15370	15400	14260	18410	24430	25340	28000	26380
3 Other current transfers paid [a]	19770	22750	25280	27870	29580	32350	35400	37900	40918	44310	48410
4 Net saving [a]	4660	2790	12770	12860	10030	10690	18840	6970	20610	23160	...
Total Current Disbursements and Net Saving [a]	211350	226670	244190	267910	278780	291960	327660	350370	379830	416850	...

a) Corporate enterprises only.

1.6 Current Income and Outlay of Households and Non-Profit Institutions

Million Deutsche marks

	1970	1971	1972	1973	1974	1975	1976	1977	1978	1979	1980
					Receipts						
1 Compensation of employees	361320	408300	448790	509470	560600	583400	626320	669680	714720	769410	829980
a From resident producers	359280	405980	446400	506920	557880	580400	623140	666370	711280	765720	826080
b From rest of the world	2040	2320	2390	2550	2720	3000	3180	3310	3440	3690	3900
2 Property and entrepreneurial income received [a]	158900	173000	179920	193000	201170	214930	235060	258460	270680	294240	...
3 Current transfers received	103050	115540	131310	146520	166660	202070	217460	232980	247780	263610	281550
a Social security benefits and social assistance grants received [b]	70330	77980	89630	100140	115980	146980	157750	169590	179610	189910	201180
b Other	32720	37560	41680	46380	50680	55090	59710	63390	68170	73700	80370
Total Current Receipts [c]	623270	696840	760020	848990	928430	1000400	1078840	1161120	1233180	1327260	...
					Disbursements						
1 Private final consumption expenditure	367550	407830	447750	491680	527550	577420	623590	669560	713910	766360	821590
2 Property income paid	3670	4270	4780	6730	7640	7000	7060	7510	8220	9790	13140
3 Direct taxes and other payments n.e.c. to general government	138050	162240	181130	220630	246660	255080	290090	317350	331880	351830	381570
a Social security contributions	75960	86780	99620	117900	130460	142320	161070	172960	185100	199100	214940
b Direct taxes	60440	73520	79210	100170	113180	109400	125190	140170	...	...	...
c Fees, fines and penalties	1650	1940	2300	2560	3020	3360	3830	4220	...	76650	82860
4 Other current transfers paid	33820	38690	43980	49890	55160	57820	62040	63330	69470	76650	...
5 Net saving	80180	83810	82380	80060	91420	103080	96060	103370	109700	122630	...
Total Current Disbursements and Net Saving [ac]	623270	696840	760020	848990	928430	1000400	1078840	1161120	1233180	1327260	...

a) Including undistributed profits of enterprises having no legal personality of their own.
b) Including transfers to and by enterprises having no legal personality of yheir own.
c) Including private non-profit organizations.

Germany, Fed. Rep. of

1.7 External Transactions on Current Account, Summary

Million Deutsche marks

	1970	1971	1972	1973	1974	1975	1976	1977	1978	1979	1980
Payments to the Rest of the World											
1 Imports of goods and services [a]	128920	142280	153650	173240	216170	228310	267440	281940	293460	348700	407670
a Imports of merchandise c.i.f.	118190	129350	138530	155300	197150	205800	243860	255870	264100	315820	369490
b Other	10730	12930	15120	17940	19020	22510	23580	26070	29360	32880	38180
2 Factor income paid to the rest of the world	9520	10510	11200	12400	16580	15420	15980	19130	17360	21020	26040
a Compensation of employees	830	1100	1390	1610	1800	1950	2090	2240	2360	2480	2680
b Property and entrepreneurial income paid	8690	9410	9810	10790	14780	13470	13890	16890	15000	18540	23360
By general government	60	70	150	220	260	220	270	420	470	560	770
By corporate and quasi-corporate enterprises	8630	9340	9660	10570	14520	13250	13620	16470	14530	17980	22590
By other	-	-	-	-	-	-	-	-	-	-	-
3 Indirect taxes paid to supranational organizations	60	70	70	80	90	80	80	80	70	70	30
4 Current transfers to the rest of the world	12740	15400	18320	21320	21750	23820	24710	26950	28620	31150	32930
5 Surplus of the nation on current transactions	3860	2980	3550	12110	25990	9760	9480	10430	18650	-8400	-26280
Payments to the Rest of the World and Surplus of the Nation on Current Transactions	155100	171240	186790	219150	280580	277390	317690	338530	358160	392540	440390
Receipts From The Rest of the World											
1 Exports of goods and services [a]	142920	156690	170920	200820	259840	256390	293890	311330	326390	357710	401590
a Exports of merchandise f.o.b.	122780	133090	145780	174190	228160	219640	252720	268430	278480	307250	343240
b Other	20140	23600	25140	26630	31680	36750	41170	42900	47910	50460	58350
2 Factor income received from rest of the world	9770	11630	12410	13900	16350	16290	18160	19240	21680	25280	29020
a Compensation of employees	2040	2320	2390	2550	2720	3000	3180	3310	3440	3690	3900
b Property and entrepreneurial income received	7730	9310	10020	11350	13630	13290	14980	15930	18240	21590	25120
By general government	140	130	260	190	60	90	270	150	100	90	50
By corporate and quasi-corporate enterprises	7560	9140	9710	11110	13510	13150	14650	15710	18070	21420	24980
By other	30	40	50	50	60	50	60	70	70	80	90
3 Subsidies received from supranational organisations	70	130	120	190	220	230	70	90	100	70	-
4 Current transfers from rest of the world	2340	2790	3340	4240	4170	4480	5570	7870	9990	9480	9780
Receipts from the Rest of the World on Current Transactions	155100	171240	186790	219150	280580	277390	317690	338530	358160	392540	440390

a) Exports and imports of goods for purposes of repair and improvement are reduced to the value of these services.

1.8 Capital Transactions of The Nation, Summary

Million Deutsche marks

	1970	1971	1972	1973	1974	1975	1976	1977	1978	1979	1980
Finance of Gross Capital Formation											
Gross saving	192950	206380	220490	244750	247880	223000	255070	272590	301060	331590	343610
1 Consumption of fixed capital	68350	78450	86330	95740	107260	117030	125490	134250	144770	158340	175850
a General government	3250	3740	4150	4640	5230	5740	6240	6800	7460	8270	9340
b Corporate and quasi-corporate enterprises	64170	73640	80990	89780	100550	109710	117580	125640	135370	147930	164130
c Other	930	1070	1190	1320	1480	1580	1670	1810	1940	2140	2380
2 Net saving	124600	127930	134160	149010	140620	105970	129580	138340	156290	173250	167760
a General government	39760	41330	39010	56090	39170	-7800	14680	28000	25980	27460	24970
b Corporate and quasi-corporate enterprises	26460	22950	18530	12690	8750	9480	17350	13870	28130	29430	16370
c Other	58380	63650	76620	80230	92700	104290	97550	96470	102180	116360	126420
Less: Surplus of the nation on current transactions	3860	2980	3550	12110	25990	9760	9480	10430	18650	-8400	-26280
Finance of Gross Capital Formation	189090	203400	216940	232640	221890	213240	245590	262160	282410	339990	369890

Germany, Fed. Rep. of

1.8 Capital Transactions of The Nation, Summary
(Continued)

Million Deutsche marks

	1970	1971	1972	1973	1974	1975	1976	1977	1978	1979	1980
Gross Capital Formation											
Increase in stocks	15400	3800	2600	7200	5500	-1300	13700	13200	9400	25600	18900
Gross fixed capital formation	173690	199600	214340	225440	216390	214540	231890	248960	273010	314390	350990
1 General government	29280	31710	32080	33200	38100	37960	37840	37450	41630	48380	55450
2 Corporate and quasi-corporate enterprises [a]	144410	167890	182260	192240	178290	176580	194050	211510	231380	266010	295540
3 Other	...	...	...	...	...	...	...	...	...	...	...
Gross Capital Formation	189090	203400	216940	232640	221890	213240	245590	262160	282410	339990	369890

a) Referring to gross fixed capital formation of all public and private unincorporated enterprises.

1.9 Gross Domestic Product by Institutional Sectors of Origin

Million Deutsche marks

	1970	1971	1972	1973	1974	1975	1976	1977	1978	1979	1980
Domestic Factor Incomes Originating											
1 General government	60140	71890	80760	94030	109160	118530	124980	133380	141840	151930	164130
2 Corporate and quasi-corporate enterprises	464620	508490	552910	613200	649790	672070	734480	785240	840490	907780	959810
a Non-financial	461490	504480	547780	606880	643690	665090	727410	778120	832970	900060	1009570
b Financial [a]	3130	4010	5130	6320	6100	6980	7070	7120	7520	7720	-49760
3 Households and private unincorporated enterprises	1100	1140	1200	1240	1380	1470	1530	1600	1660	1750	1840
4 Non-profit institutions serving households	7000	8430	9410	10950	12260	13610	14800	16210	17640	19140	21010
Subtotal: Domestic Factor Incomes	532860	589950	644280	719420	772590	805680	875790	936430	1001630	1080600	1146790
Indirect taxes paid, net	77540	86480	95380	103440	107280	111320	121540	129810	139980	155000	166280
Consumption of fixed capital	68350	78450	86330	95740	107260	117030	125490	134250	144770	158340	175850
Gross Domestic Product	678750	754880	825990	918600	987130	1034030	1122820	1200490	1286380	1393940	1488920

a) Net of imputed output of bank services.

1.10 Gross Domestic Product by Kind of Activity, in Current Prices

Million Deutsche marks

	1970	1971	1972	1973	1974	1975	1976	1977	1978	1979	1980
1 Agriculture, hunting, forestry and fishing	23070	24460	26810	29070	27030	30780	32770	33480	34410	32590	32220
2 Mining and quarrying [a]	9060	9500	8930	9500	11420	12690	13150	11180	11550	...	...
3 Manufacturing [abc]	280010	301270	320900	357880	384620	385610	422160	452740	484110	524310	542310
4 Electricity, gas and water	16050	17310	20230	22860	25160	28560	31710	32900	35930	...	...
5 Construction [b]	55590	65260	72850	76770	73870	70560	74310	79370	86480	100590	115940
6 Wholesale and retail trade, restaurants and hotels	79370	89000	96630	102600	104050	114020	123590	132470	141460	152930	140360
7 Transport, storage and communication	38700	42300	47540	53300	58920	61200	66790	71480	75540	82420	86440
8 Finance, insurance, real estate and business services [d]	55820	63380	72500	82800	93370	103110	110310	117260	124510	131200	142160
9 Community, social and personal services [dc]	53130	63040	71870	82040	92150	101410	112910	125900	139670	155400	193610
Total, Industries	610800	675520	738260	816820	870590	907940	987700	1056780	1133660	1230460	1308460
Producers of Government Services	63480	75740	85040	98820	114550	124450	131420	140390	149520	160430	173720
Other Producers	9060	10650	11810	13520	15130	16670	18010	19630	21250	23050	25250
Subtotal	683340	761910	835110	929160	1000270	1049060	1137130	1216800	1304430	1413940	1507430
Less: Imputed bank service charge	15590	18130	20790	23270	29650	32610	34910	38280	41760	45650	49760
Plus: Import duties	18600	19700	21270	23510	26910	28180	32800	34970	38610	45150	53050
Plus: Value added tax	...	...	...	...	...	...	...	...	...	...	...
Plus: Other adjustments [e]	-7600	-8600	-9600	-10800	-10400	-10600	-12200	-13000	-14900	-19500	-21800
Equals: Gross Domestic Product	678750	754880	825990	918600	987130	1034030	1122820	1200490	1286380	1393940	1488920

a) Quarrying is included in item 'Manufacturing'.
b) Structural steel erection is included in item 'Manufacturing'.
c) Publishing is included in item 'Community, social and personal services'.
d) Business services and real estate except dwellings are included in item 'Community, social and personal services'.
e) Relating to adjustment for double accounting of turnover taxes on investment goods.

1.11 Gross Domestic Product by Kind of Activity, in Constant Prices

Million Deutsche marks

	1970	1971	1972	1973	1974	1975	1976	1977	1978	1979	1980
At constant prices of: 1970											
1 Agriculture, hunting, forestry and fishing	23070	23790	23240	25790	26060	24960	24230	25790	27060	26050	26470
2 Mining and quarrying [a]	9060	8470	7580	7780	7780	6760	6360	5520	5600	...	...
3 Manufacturing [abc]	280010	283810	291850	309720	310560	294300	315440	324250	330000	346010	346880
4 Electricity, gas and water	16050	17230	18950	21160	22490	22260	23840	24980	26320	-	...
5 Construction [b]	55590	60180	63920	64380	59120	55660	57000	57930	59360	63310	66120

Germany, Fed. Rep. of

1.11 Gross Domestic Product by Kind of Activity, in Constant Prices
(Continued)

Million Deutsche marks

	1970	1971	1972	1973	1974	1975	1976	1977	1978	1979	1980
					At constant prices of: 1970						
6 Wholesale and retail trade, restaurants and hotels	78370	81610	83490	85080	83420	83720	87170	89910	93380	96750	85480
7 Transport, storage and communication	38700	39090	39960	41800	42910	41940	45040	47490	50030	54190	56680
8 Finance, insurance, real estate and business services d	55820	57870	62200	65230	66930	69040	71810	74350	77010	80280	82650
9 Community, social and personal services dc	53130	56840	60000	62660	65230	68220	72200	76720	81870	86970	102280
Total, Industries	610800	628890	651190	683600	684500	666860	703090	726940	750630	787150	800450
Producers of Government Services	63480	66270	69470	72760	76070	78290	79270	80290	82590	85110	87190
Other Producers	9060	9190	9350	9460	9560	9790	10010	10190	10550	10900	11230
Subtotal	683340	704350	730010	765820	770130	754940	792370	817420	843770	883160	898870
Less: Imputed bank service charge	15590	16310	18170	18970	19310	19820	21210	23530	25600	27460	28070
Plus: Import duties	18600	19950	21830	22430	21830	23200	26760	28320	30710	32550	34180
Plus: Value added tax	...	...	...	...	...	...	...	...	...	...	...
Plus: Other adjustments e	-7600	-7310	-7390	-7440	-6700	-6520	-7330	-7630	-8040	-9930	-9840
Equals: Gross Domestic Product	678750	700680	726280	761840	765950	751800	790590	814580	840840	878320	895140

a) Quarrying is included in item 'Manufacturing'.
b) Structural steel erection is included in item 'Manufacturing'.
c) Publishing is included in item 'Community, social and personal services'.
d) Business services and real estate except dwellings are included in item 'Community, social and personal services'.
e) Relating to adjustment for double accounting of turnover taxes on investment goods.

1.12 Relations Among National Accounting Aggregates

Million Deutsche marks

	1970	1971	1972	1973	1974	1975	1976	1977	1978	1979	1980
Gross Domestic Product	678750	754880	825990	918600	987130	1034030	1122820	1200490	1286380	1393940	1488920
Plus: Net factor income received from abroad	250	1120	1210	1500	-230	870	2180	110	4320	4260	2980
Factor income received	9770	11630	12410	13900	16350	16290	18160	19240	21680	25280	29020
Less: Factor income paid	9520	10510	11200	12400	16580	15420	15980	19130	17360	21020	26040
Equals: Gross National Product	679000	756000	827200	920100	986900	1034900	1125000	1200600	1290700	1398200	1491900
Less: Consumption of fixed capital	68350	78450	86330	95740	107260	117030	125490	134250	144770	158340	175850
Less: Net indirect taxes paid to supranational organisations a	-10	-60	-50	-110	-130	-150	10	-10	-30	-	30
Indirect taxes paid	60	70	70	80	90	80	80	80	70	70	30
Less: Subsidies received	70	130	120	190	220	230	70	90	100	70	-
Equals: National Income at Market Prices	610660	677610	740920	824470	879770	918020	999500	1066360	1145960	1239860	1316020
Plus: Net current transfers received from abroad	-10400	-12610	-14980	-17080	-17580	-19340	-19140	-19080	-18630	-21670	-23150
Current transfers received	2340	2790	3340	4240	4170	4480	5570	7870	9990	9480	9780
Less: Current transfers paid	12740	15400	18320	21320	21750	23820	24710	26950	28620	31150	32930
Equals: National Disposable Income at Market Prices	600260	665000	725940	807390	862190	898680	980360	1047280	1127330	1218190	1292870
Less: Final consumption	475660	537070	591780	658380	721570	792710	850780	908940	971040	1044940	1125110
Equals: Net Saving	124600	127930	134160	149010	140620	105970	129580	138340	156290	173250	167760
Less: Surplus of the nation on current transactions	3860	2980	3550	12110	25990	9760	9480	10430	18650	-8400	-26280
Equals: Net Capital Formation	120740	124950	130610	136900	114630	96210	120100	127910	137640	181650	194040

a) Indirect taxes paid to and subsidies received from supranational organizations are not included in the receipts and disbursements respectively of the general government.

2.1 General Government Final Consumption Expenditure by Function, in Current Prices

Million Deutsche marks

	1970	1971	1972	1973	1974	1975	1976	1977	1978	1979	1980
1 General public services	13070	15350	17360	19770	22860	24510	24800	26980	28730	31540	...
2 Defence	19900	23470	24450	26780	30000	32520	34370	33950	36430	38670	...
3 Public order and safety	8760	10320	11340	12970	15050	16360	17340	18820	20150	21850	...
4 Education	19690	24050	27120	31960	37250	41700	44570	47490	51270	55770	...
5 Health	26620	32980	38350	46040	54680	63550	68020	71530	76170	82150	...
6 Social security and welfare	8110	9750	11130	12730	15610	17250	18730	20300	21850	23710	...
7 Housing and community amenities	2270	2500	2650	3250	3970	3790	3500	3460	4010	4330	...
8 Recreational, cultural and religious affairs	2030	2450	2790	3210	3540	4070	4390	4750	5270	5840	...
9 Economic services	7660	8370	8840	9990	11060	11540	11470	12080	13240	14720	...

Germany, Fed. Rep. of

2.1 General Government Final Consumption Expenditure by Function, in Current Prices
(Continued)

Million Deutsche marks

	1970	1971	1972	1973	1974	1975	1976	1977	1978	1979	1980
a Fuel and energy	...	...	...	...	...	...	...	...	...	...	...
b Agriculture, forestry, fishing and hunting	1010	990	1270	1560	1780	1850	1850	1940	2110	2180	...
c Mining, manufacturing and construction, except fuel and energy [a]	1120	1310	1450	1490	1590	1420	1240	1230	1440	1610	...
d Transportation and communication	5530	6070	6120	6940	7690	8270	8380	8910	9690	10930	...
e Other economic affairs	...	...	...	...	...	...	...	...	...	...	...
10 Other functions	-	-	-	-	-	-	-	20	10	-	...
Total General Government Final Consumption Expenditure	108110	129240	144030	166700	194020	215290	227190	239380	257130	278580	303520

a) Including fuel, energy and other economic affairs.

2.3 Total General Government Outlays by Function and Type

Million Deutsche marks

	Final Consumption Expenditures Total	Compensation of Employees	Other	Subsidies	Other Current Transfers & Property Income	Total Current Disbursements	Gross Capital Formation	Other Capital Outlays	Total Outlays
1970									
1 General public services	13070	...	...	...	4170	17240	780	...	18020
2 Defence	19900	...	...	...	520	20420	200	...	20620
3 Public order and safety	8760	...	...	...	10	8770	580	...	9350
4 Education	19690	...	...	...	1130	20820	6440	...	27260
5 Health	26620	...	...	...	360	26980	1790	...	28770
6 Social security and welfare	8110	...	...	...	90170	98280	480	...	98760
7 Housing and community amenities	2270	...	...	...	1240	3510	3980	...	7490
8 Recreation, culture and religion	2030	...	...	...	750	2780	1100	...	3880
9 Economic services	7660	...	...	...	13870	21530	12430	...	33960
a Fuel and energy	...	...	...	...	...	...	...	...	...
b Agriculture, forestry, fishing and hunting	1010	...	...	...	6250	7260	220	...	7480
c Mining (except fuels), manufacturing and construction	1120	...	...	...	2910	4030	690	...	4720
d Transportation and communication	5530	...	...	...	4710	10240	11520	...	21760
e Other economic affairs	...	...	...	...	...	...	...	...	...
10 Other functions	-	...	...	...	6600	6600	-	...	6600
Total	108110	60140	47970	...	118820	226930	27780	...	254710
1971									
1 General public services	15350	...	...	...	5170	20520	960	...	21480
2 Defence	23470	...	...	...	590	24060	200	...	24260
3 Public order and safety	10320	...	...	...	10	10330	710	...	11040
4 Education	24050	...	...	...	1590	25640	8250	...	33890
5 Health	32980	...	...	...	420	33400	2070	...	35470
6 Social security and welfare	9750	...	...	...	102260	112010	710	...	112720
7 Housing and community amenities	2500	...	...	...	1250	3750	4690	...	8440
8 Recreation, culture and religion	2450	...	...	...	1110	3560	1450	...	5010
9 Economic services	8370	...	...	...	13890	22260	13970	...	36230
a Fuel and energy	...	...	...	...	...	...	...	...	...
b Agriculture, forestry, fishing and hunting	990	...	...	...	5120	6110	240	...	6350
c Mining (except fuels), manufacturing and construction	1310	...	...	...	3340	4650	760	...	5410
d Transportation and communication	6070	...	...	...	5430	11500	12970	...	24470
e Other economic affairs	...	...	...	...	...	...	...	...	...
10 Other functions	-	...	...	...	7430	7430	-	...	7430
Total	129240	71890	57350	...	133720	262960	33010	...	295970
1972									
1 General public services	17360	...	...	...	7410	24770	1050	...	25820
2 Defence	24450	...	...	...	630	25080	230	...	25310
3 Public order and safety	11340	...	...	...	10	11350	860	...	12210
4 Education	27120	...	...	...	2990	30110	8500	...	38610
5 Health	38350	...	...	...	460	38810	2210	...	41020

Germany, Fed. Rep. of

2.3 Total General Government Outlays by Function and Type
(Continued)

Million Deutsche marks

		Final Consumption Expenditures Total	Compensation of Employees	Other	Subsidies	Other Current Transfers & Property Income	Total Current Disbursements	Gross Capital Formation	Other Capital Outlays	Total Outlays
6	Social security and welfare	11130	...	...	...	114700	125830	890	...	126720
7	Housing and community amenities	2650	...	...	...	1660	4310	4860	...	9170
8	Recreation, culture and religion	2790	...	...	...	1220	4010	1740	...	5750
9	Economic services	8840	...	...	...	16830	25670	14220	...	39890
	a Fuel and energy	...	...	...	...	...	...	...	...	...
	b Agriculture, forestry, fishing and hunting	1270	...	...	...	4620	5890	270	...	6160
	c Mining (except fuels), manufacturing and construction	1450	...	...	...	4090	5540	630	...	6170
	d Transportation and communication	6120	...	...	...	8120	14240	13320	...	27560
	e Other economic affairs	...	...	...	...	...	...	...	...	...
10	Other functions	-	...	...	...	8480	8480	-	...	8480
	Total	144030	80760	63270	...	154390	298420	34560	...	332980

1973

1	General public services	19770	...	...	...	8780	28550	1140	...	29690
2	Defence	26780	...	...	...	750	27530	190	...	27720
3	Public order and safety	12970	...	...	...	30	13000	990	...	13990
4	Education	31960	...	...	...	3400	35360	8920	...	44280
5	Health	46040	...	...	...	1320	47360	2420	...	49780
6	Social security and welfare	12730	...	...	...	127320	140050	1090	...	141140
7	Housing and community amenities	3250	...	...	...	1970	5220	5420	...	10640
8	Recreation, culture and religion	3210	...	...	...	820	4030	1980	...	6010
9	Economic services	9990	...	...	...	20320	30310	14290	...	44600
	a Fuel and energy	...	...	...	...	...	...	...	...	...
	b Agriculture, forestry, fishing and hunting	1560	...	...	...	5560	7120	280	...	7400
	c Mining (except fuels), manufacturing and construction	1490	...	...	...	5090	6580	670	...	7250
	d Transportation and communication	6940	...	...	...	9670	16610	13340	...	29950
	e Other economic affairs	...	...	...	...	...	...	...	...	...
10	Other functions	-	...	...	...	10220	10220	-	...	10220
	Total	166700	94030	72670	...	174930	341630	36440	...	378070

1974

1	General public services	22860	...	...	...	9070	31930	1260	...	33190
2	Defence	30000	...	...	...	770	30770	270	...	31040
3	Public order and safety	15050	...	...	...	40	15090	1330	...	16420
4	Education	37250	...	...	...	3960	41210	9890	...	51100
5	Health	54680	...	...	...	1520	56200	2880	...	59080
6	Social security and welfare	15610	...	...	...	147060	162670	1340	...	164010
7	Housing and community amenities	3970	...	...	...	2470	6440	6340	...	12780
8	Recreation, culture and religion	3540	...	...	...	1000	4540	2470	...	7010
9	Economic services	11060	...	...	...	20800	31860	15170	...	47030
	a Fuel and energy	...	...	...	...	...	...	...	...	...
	b Agriculture, forestry, fishing and hunting	1780	...	...	...	4940	6720	280	...	7000
	c Mining (except fuels), manufacturing and construction	1590	...	...	...	5820	7410	750	...	8160
	d Transportation and communication	7690	...	...	...	10040	17730	14140	...	31870
	e Other economic affairs	...	...	...	...	...	...	...	...	...
10	Other functions	-	...	...	...	12220	12220	-	...	12220
	Total	194020	109160	84860	...	198910	392930	40950	...	433880

1975

1	General public services	24510	...	...	...	10560	35070	1260	...	36330
2	Defence	32520	...	...	...	830	33350	230	...	33580
3	Public order and safety	16360	...	...	...	50	16410	1480	...	17890
4	Education	41700	...	...	...	4660	46360	9720	...	56080
5	Health	63550	...	...	...	1500	65050	3090	...	68140

Germany, Fed. Rep. of

2.3 Total General Government Outlays by Function and Type
(Continued)

Million Deutsche marks

		Final Consumption Expenditures Total	Compensation of Employees	Other	Subsidies	Other Current Transfers & Property Income	Total Current Disbursements	Gross Capital Formation	Other Capital Outlays	Total Outlays
6	Social security and welfare	17250	...	...	...	180390	197640	1320	...	198960
7	Housing and community amenities	3790	...	...	...	2000	5790	6240	...	12030
8	Recreation, culture and religion	4070	...	...	...	1150	5220	2450	...	7670
9	Economic services	11540	...	...	...	21720	33260	15670	...	48930
	a Fuel and energy	...	...	...	...	...	...	...	...	...
	b Agriculture, forestry, fishing and hunting	1850	...	...	...	4990	6840	260	...	7100
	c Mining (except fuels), manufacturing and construction	1420	...	...	...	6250	7670	1310	...	8980
	d Transportation and communication	8270	...	...	...	10480	18750	14100	...	32850
	e Other economic affairs	...	...	...	...	...	...	...	...	...
10	Other functions	-	...	...	...	14280	14280	-	...	14280
	Total	215290	118530	96760	...	237140	452430	41460	...	493890

1976

1	General public services	24800	...	...	...	11790	36590	1420	...	38010
2	Defence	34370	...	...	...	910	35280	220	...	35500
3	Public order and safety	17340	...	...	...	50	17390	1400	...	18790
4	Education	44570	...	...	...	4230	48800	8720	...	57520
5	Health	68020	...	...	...	1670	69690	2850	...	72540
6	Social security and welfare	18730	...	...	...	194130	212860	1160	...	214020
7	Housing and community amenities	3500	...	...	...	2830	6330	6950	...	13280
8	Recreation, culture and religion	4390	...	...	...	1150	5540	2360	...	7900
9	Economic services	11470	...	...	...	26730	38200	14410	...	52610
	a Fuel and energy	...	...	...	...	...	...	...	...	...
	b Agriculture, forestry, fishing and hunting	1850	...	...	...	5510	7360	260	...	7620
	c Mining (except fuels), manufacturing and construction	1240	...	...	...	10830	12070	880	...	12950
	d Transportation and communication	8380	...	...	...	10390	18770	13270	...	32040
	e Other economic affairs	...	...	...	...	...	...	...	...	...
10	Other functions	-	...	...	...	17630	17630	10	...	17640
	Total	227190	124980	102210	...	261120	488310	39500	...	527810

1977

1	General public services	26980	...	...	...	14230	41210	1350	...	42560
2	Defence	33950	...	...	...	910	34860	180	...	35040
3	Public order and safety	18820	...	...	...	40	18860	1470	...	20330
4	Education	47490	...	...	...	4900	52390	7610	...	60000
5	Health	71530	...	...	...	1660	73190	3000	...	76190
6	Social security and welfare	20300	...	...	...	208960	229260	980	...	230240
7	Housing and community amenities	3460	...	...	...	3010	6470	6380	...	12850
8	Recreation, culture and religion	4750	...	...	...	1260	6010	2060	...	8070
9	Economic services	12080	...	...	...	29520	41600	15150	...	56750
	a Fuel and energy	...	...	...	...	...	...	...	...	...
	b Agriculture, forestry, fishing and hunting	1940	...	...	...	6960	8900	260	...	9160
	c Mining (except fuels), manufacturing and construction	1230	...	...	...	11140	12370	980	...	13350
	d Transportation and communication	8910	...	...	...	11420	20330	13910	...	34240
	e Other economic affairs	...	...	...	...	...	...	...	...	...
10	Other functions	20	...	...	...	20580	20600	-	...	20600
	Total	239380	133380	106000	...	285070	524450	38180	...	562630

1978

1	General public services	28730	...	...	...	15570	44300	1660	...	45960
2	Defence	36430	...	...	...	1030	37460	200	...	37660
3	Public order and safety	20150	...	...	...	50	20200	1660	...	21860
4	Education	51270	...	...	...	5150	56420	7400	...	63820
5	Health	76170	...	...	...	1830	78000	3170	...	81170

Germany, Fed. Rep. of

2.3 Total General Government Outlays by Function and Type
(Continued)

Million Deutsche marks

		Final Consumption Expenditures			Subsidies	Other Current Transfers & Property Income	Total Current Disbursements	Gross Capital Formation	Other Capital Outlays	Total Outlays
		Total	Compensation of Employees	Other						
6	Social security and welfare	21850	...	...	...	218790	240640	920	...	241560
7	Housing and community amenities	4010	...	...	...	4290	8300	7560	...	15860
8	Recreation, culture and religion	5270	...	...	...	1420	6690	2330	...	9020
9	Economic services	13240	...	...	...	33640	46880	16590	...	63470
	a Fuel and energy	...	...	...	...	...	...	...	...	...
	b Agriculture, forestry, fishing and hunting	2110	...	...	...	8880	10990	310	...	11300
	c Mining (except fuels), manufacturing and construction	1440	...	...	...	11050	12490	910	...	13400
	d Transportation and communication	9690	...	...	...	13710	23400	15370	...	38770
	e Other economic affairs	...	...	...	...	...	...	...	...	...
10	Other functions	10	...	...	...	21550	21560	-	...	21560
	Total	257130	141840	115290	...	303320	560450	41490	...	601940
	1979									
1	General public services	31540	...	...	...	19120	50660	1880	...	52540
2	Defence	38670	...	...	...	1060	39730	300	...	40030
3	Public order and safety	21850	...	...	...	60	21910	1870	...	23780
4	Education	55770	...	...	...	5770	61540	7680	...	69220
5	Health	82150	...	...	...	1690	83840	3470	...	87310
6	Social security and welfare	23710	...	...	...	229700	253410	950	...	254360
7	Housing and community amenities	4330	...	...	...	4640	8970	8870	...	17840
8	Recreation, culture and religion	5840	...	...	...	1590	7430	2530	...	9960
9	Economic services	14720	...	...	...	35680	50400	17990	...	68390
	a Fuel and energy	...	...	...	...	...	...	...	...	...
	b Agriculture, forestry, fishing and hunting	2180	...	...	...	9130	11310	380	...	11690
	c Mining (except fuels), manufacturing and construction	1610	...	...	...	12080	13690	940	...	14630
	d Transportation and communication	10930	...	...	...	14470	25400	16670	...	42070
	e Other economic affairs	...	...	...	...	...	...	...	...	...
10	Other functions	-	...	...	...	24230	24230	-	...	24230
	Total	278580	151930	126650	...	323540	602120	45540	...	647660

2.5 Private Final Consumption Expenditure by Type, in Current Prices

Million Deutsche marks

		1970	1971	1972	1973	1974	1975	1976	1977	1978	1979	1980
	Final Consumption Expenditure of Resident Households											
1	Food, beverages and tobacco [a]	110260	119070	128500	139260	146980	157840	169650	179780	188770	197710	211750
	a Food											
	b Non-alcoholic beverages	100400	108650	117120	126810	134310	144870	156140	165500	173770	182000	195400
	c Alcoholic beverages											
	d Tobacco	9860	10420	11380	12450	12670	12970	13510	14280	15000	15710	16350
2	Clothing and footwear	38320	42400	46980	49830	53140	57570	60060	64430	68450	71440	76910
3	Gross rent, fuel and power [b]	58160	63320	70050	79720	88090	97170	106040	110640	118050	130890	140370
	a Fuel and power	13190	13920	15550	19410	22250	25080	28570	29050	32060	40110	42670
	b Other	44970	49400	54500	60310	65840	72090	77470	81590	85990	90780	97700
4	Furniture, furnishings and household equipment and operation [b]	44210	50420	56100	60570	64150	66940	70840	76760	80250	85420	91810
5	Medical care and health expenses	9650	11410	12880	14780	16950	18580	19660	21670	23460	25130	27320
6	Transport and communication	49190	55680	60390	64640	67610	79370	90870	100450	109230	116890	121900
	a Personal transport equipment	14020	16000	16750	16510	14370	19960	24570	28920	30930	31050	28800

Germany, Fed. Rep. of

2.5 Private Final Consumption Expenditure by Type, in Current Prices
(Continued)

Million Deutsche marks

	1970	1971	1972	1973	1974	1975	1976	1977	1978	1979	1980
b Other	35170	39680	43640	48130	53240	59410	66300	71530	78300	85840	93100
7 Recreational, entertainment, education and cultural services	26450	29220	32290	35980	39650	42910	45320	48240	51480	56110	58390
8 Miscellaneous goods and services [a]	24290	27600	30550	33840	37130	40830	44630	48310	52130	56760	62760
Total Final Consumption Expenditure in the Domestic Market by Households, of which	360530	399120	437740	478620	513700	561210	607070	650280	691820	740350	791210
Plus: Direct purchases abroad by resident households	10730	12930	15120	17940	19020	22510	23580	26070	29360	32880	38180
Less: Direct purchases in the domestic market by non-resident households	8740	9790	10690	10890	11180	12560	13800	14450	15930	16670	18750
Equals: Final Consumption Expenditure of Resident Households	362520	402260	442170	485670	521540	571160	616850	661900	705250	756560	810640

Final Consumption Expenditure of Private Non-profit Institutions Serving Households

	1970	1971	1972	1973	1974	1975	1976	1977	1978	1979	1980
Equals: Final Consumption Expenditure of Private Non-profit Organisations Serving Households	5030	5570	5580	6010	6010	6260	6740	7660	8660	9800	10950
Private Final Consumption Expenditure	367550	407830	447750	491680	527550	577420	623590	669560	713910	766360	821590

a) Expenditure in restaurants and cafes is included in item 'Food, beverages and tobacco', expenditure in hotels, etc., is included in item 'Miscellaneous goods and services'. b) Indoor repairs and upkeep paid for by tenants are included in household equipment and operation.

2.6 Private Final Consumption Expenditure by Type, in Constant Prices

Million Deutsche marks

	1970	1971	1972	1973	1974	1975	1976	1977	1978	1979	1980

At constant prices of: 1970

Final Consumption Expenditure of Resident Households

	1970	1971	1972	1973	1974	1975	1976	1977	1978	1979	1980
1 Food, beverages and tobacco [a]	110260	114900	117360	118080	119710	121900	125160	126190	131350	135250	139030
a Food											
b Non-alcoholic beverages	100400	104480	106660	107630	109070	111390	114540	116430	121090	124760	128370
c Alcoholic beverages											
d Tobacco	9860	10420	10700	10450	10640	10510	10620	9760	10260	10490	10660
2 Clothing and footwear	38320	40060	41900	41140	41150	42540	42780	43630	44680	44700	45450
3 Gross rent, fuel and power [b]	58160	59860	62790	65970	68370	70430	72910	74130	77040	79640	81000
a Fuel and power	13190	13280	14270	15230	15480	15820	16880	16980	18480	19670	19600
b Other	44970	46580	48520	50740	52890	54610	56030	57150	58560	59970	61400
4 Furniture, furnishings and household equipment and operation [b]	44210	48110	51590	53330	53180	52590	53730	56260	57210	59120	60120
5 Medical care and health expenses	9650	10480	10970	11910	12480	12660	12670	13400	13980	14340	14710
6 Transport and communication	49190	51670	52330	51900	49260	55130	60230	64720	68720	70230	68610
a Personal transport equipment	14020	15050	14990	14210	11470	14750	17570	19950	20520	19810	17550
b Other	35170	36620	37340	37690	37790	40380	42660	44770	48200	50420	51060
7 Recreational, entertainment, education and cultural services	26450	27880	29680	31260	32060	32640	33450	34830	36420	38210	39260
8 Miscellaneous goods and services [a]	24290	25660	26970	27360	27600	28400	29660	31270	32700	34410	35500
Total Final Consumption Expenditure in the Domestic Market by Households, of which	360530	378620	393590	400950	403810	416290	430590	444430	462100	475900	483680
Plus: Direct purchases abroad by resident households	10730	12520	13620	16270	14770	15760	16350	17550	18250	19930	21060
Less: Direct purchases in the domestic market by non-resident households	8740	9230	9520	9080	8740	9260	9750	9720	10320	10360	11020
Equals: Final Consumption Expenditure of Resident Households	362520	381910	397690	408140	409840	422790	437190	452260	470030	485470	493720

Final Consumption Expenditure of Private Non-profit Institutions Serving Households

	1970	1971	1972	1973	1974	1975	1976	1977	1978	1979	1980
Equals: Final Consumption Expenditure of Private Non-profit Organisations Serving Households	5030	4890	4550	4340	3950	3760	3820	4040	4350	4660	4900
Private Final Consumption Expenditure	367550	386800	402240	412480	413790	426550	441010	456300	474380	490130	498620

a) Expenditure in restaurants and cafes is included in item 'Food, beverages and tobacco', expenditure in hotels, etc., is included in item 'Miscellaneous goods and services'. b) Indoor repairs and upkeep paid for by tenants are included in household equipment and operation.

Germany, Fed. Rep. of

2.7 Gross Capital Formation by Type of Good and Owner, in Current Prices

Million Deutsche marks

	1970 TOTAL	1970 Total Private	1970 Public Enterprises	1970 General Government	1971 TOTAL	1971 Total Private	1971 Public Enterprises	1971 General Government	1972 TOTAL	1972 Total Private	1972 Public Enterprises	1972 General Government
Increase in stocks, total [a]	15400	...	...	...	3800	...	...	...	2600	...	...	...
1 Goods producing industries [b]	12800	...	...	...	1800	...	...	...	1000	...	...	...
a Materials and supplies	5500	...	...	...	-1100	...	...	...	-200	...	...	...
b Work in progress		...	...	...		...	...	...		...	...	...
c Livestock, except breeding stocks, dairy cattle, etc. [c]	-300	...	...	...	-200	...	...	...	100	...	...	...
d Finished goods	7600	...	...	...	3100	...	...	...	1100	...	...	...
2 Wholesale and retail trade	2400	...	...	...	1800	...	...	...	1600	...	...	...
3 Other, except government stocks [b]	...	...	...	...	...	...	...	...	...	...	...	...
4 Government stocks	200	...	...	...	200	...	...	...	-	...	...	...
Gross Fixed Capital Formation, Total	173690	...	...	...	199600	...	...	...	214340	...	...	...
1 Residential buildings	44860	...	...	...	55050	...	...	...	66890	...	...	...
2 Non-residential buildings	60400	...	...	...	68180	...	...	...	70700	...	...	...
3 Other construction	...	...	...	...	...	...	...	...	...	...	...	...
4 Land improvement and plantation and orchard development	...	...	...	...	...	...	...	...	...	...	...	...
5 Producers' durable goods	70460	...	...	...	78700	...	...	...	79390	...	...	...
a Transport equipment	14470	...	...	...	16200	...	...	...	16020	...	...	...
b Machinery and equipment	55990	...	...	...	62500	...	...	...	63370	...	...	...
6 Breeding stock, dairy cattle, etc. [a]	...	...	...	...	...	...	...	...	...	...	...	...
Statistical discrepancy [d]	-2030	...	...	...	-2330	...	...	...	-2640	...	...	...
Total Gross Capital Formation [d]	189090	...	...	29480	203400	...	...	31910	216940	...	...	32080

	1973 TOTAL	1973 Total Private	1973 Public Enterprises	1973 General Government	1974 TOTAL	1974 Total Private	1974 Public Enterprises	1974 General Government	1975 TOTAL	1975 Total Private	1975 Public Enterprises	1975 General Government
Increase in stocks, total [a]	7200	...	...	...	5500	...	...	...	-1300	...	...	...
1 Goods producing industries [b]	5700	...	...	...	7700	...	...	...	-2500	...	...	...
a Materials and supplies	3000	...	...	...	5100	...	...	...	-3100	...	...	...
b Work in progress		...	...	...		...	...	...		...	...	...
c Livestock, except breeding stocks, dairy cattle, etc. [c]	-	...	...	...	-100	...	...	...	-	...	...	...
d Finished goods	2700	...	...	...	2700	...	...	...	600	...	...	...
2 Wholesale and retail trade	1500	...	...	...	-2300	...	...	...	600	...	...	...
3 Other, except government stocks [b]	...	...	...	...	...	...	...	...	...	...	...	...
4 Government stocks	-	...	...	...	100	...	...	...	600	...	...	...
Gross Fixed Capital Formation, Total	225440	...	...	...	216390	...	...	...	214540	...	...	...
1 Residential buildings	72610	...	...	...	64470	...	...	...	59190	...	...	...
2 Non-residential buildings	73070	...	...	...	75450	...	...	...	73030	...	...	...
3 Other construction	...	...	...	...	...	...	...	...	...	...	...	...
4 Land improvement and plantation and orchard development	...	...	...	...	...	...	...	...	...	...	...	...
5 Producers' durable goods	82340	...	...	...	79760	...	...	...	85850	...	...	...
a Transport equipment	15910	...	...	...	14200	...	...	...	16890	...	...	...
b Machinery and equipment	66430	...	...	...	65560	...	...	...	68960	...	...	...
6 Breeding stock, dairy cattle, etc. [a]	...	...	...	...	...	...	...	...	...	...	...	...
Statistical discrepancy [d]	-2580	...	...	...	-3290	...	...	...	-3530	...	...	...
Total Gross Capital Formation [d]	232640	...	...	33200	221890	...	...	38200	213240	...	...	38560

Germany, Fed. Rep. of

2.7 Gross Capital Formation by Type of Good and Owner, in Current Prices

Million Deutsche marks

	1976 TOTAL	1976 Total Private	1976 Public Enterprises	1976 General Government	1977 TOTAL	1977 Total Private	1977 Public Enterprises	1977 General Government	1978 TOTAL	1978 Total Private	1978 Public Enterprises	1978 General Government
Increase in stocks, total [a]	13700	...	...	...	13200	...	...	...	9400	...	...	...
1 Goods producing industries [b]	8200	...	...	...	9700	...	...	...	5800	...	...	...
a Materials and supplies	4800	...	...	...	5400	...	...	...	5900	...	...	...
b Work in progress		...	...	...		...	...	...		...	...	...
c Livestock, except breeding stocks, dairy cattle, etc. [c]	-	...	...	...	200	...	...	...	200	...	...	...
d Finished goods	3400	...	...	...	4100	...	...	...	-300	...	...	...
2 Wholesale and retail trade	5300	...	...	...	3200	...	...	...	3400	...	...	...
3 Other, except government stocks [b]	...	...	...	...	...	...	...	...	...	...	...	...
4 Government stocks	200	...	...	...	300	...	...	...	200	...	...	...
Gross Fixed Capital Formation, Total	231890	...	...	...	248960	...	...	...	273010	...	...	...
1 Residential buildings	64980	...	...	...	70080	...	...	...	76190	...	...	...
2 Non-residential buildings	76230	...	...	...	78990	...	...	...	86440	...	...	...
3 Other construction	...	...	...	...	...	...	...	...	...	...	...	...
4 Land improvement and plantation and orchard development	...	...	...	...	...	...	...	...	...	...	...	...
5 Producers' durable goods	94120	...	...	...	103460	...	...	...	114210	...	...	...
a Transport equipment	19610	...	...	...	22850	...	...	...	25110	...	...	...
b Machinery and equipment	74510	...	...	...	80610	...	...	...	89100	...	...	...
6 Breeding stock, dairy cattle, etc. [a]	...	...	...	...	...	...	...	...	...	...	...	...
Statistical discrepancy [d]	-3440	...	...	...	-3570	...	...	...	-3830	...	...	...
Total Gross Capital Formation [d]	245590	...	...	38040	262160	...	...	37750	282410	...	...	41830

	1979 TOTAL	1979 Total Private	1979 Public Enterprises	1979 General Government	1980 TOTAL	1980 Total Private	1980 Public Enterprises	1980 General Government
Increase in stocks, total [a]	25600	...	...	...	18900	...	...	...
1 Goods producing industries [b]	...	...	...	...	...	...	...	...
a Materials and supplies	...	...	...	...	...	...	...	...
b Work in progress	...	...	...	...	...	...	...	...
c Livestock, except breeding stocks, dairy cattle, etc. [c]	...	...	...	...	...	...	...	...
d Finished goods	...	...	...	...	...	...	...	...
2 Wholesale and retail trade	...	...	...	...	...	...	...	...
3 Other, except government stocks [b]	...	...	...	...	...	...	...	...
4 Government stocks	...	...	...	...	...	...	...	...
Gross Fixed Capital Formation, Total	314390	...	...	...	350990	...	...	...
1 Residential buildings	89320	...	...	...	101940	...	...	...
2 Non-residential buildings	101350	...	...	...	116880	...	...	...
3 Other construction	...	...	...	...	...	...	...	...
4 Land improvement and plantation and orchard development	...	...	...	...	...	...	...	...
5 Producers' durable goods	127490	...	...	...	136500	...	...	...
a Transport equipment	25920	...	...	...	27510	...	...	...
b Machinery and equipment	101570	...	...	...	108990	...	...	...
6 Breeding stock, dairy cattle, etc. [a]	...	...	...	...	...	...	...	...
Statistical discrepancy [d]	-3770	...	...	...	-4330	...	...	...
Total Gross Capital Formation [d]	339990	...	...	48380	369890	...	...	55950

a) Item 'Breeding stocks, dairy cattle, etc.' is included in item 'Increase in stocks'.
b) Item 'Other, except government stocks' is included in item 'Goods producing industries'.
c) Expenditure in restaurants and cafes is included in item 'Food, beverages and tobacco', expenditure in hotels, etc., is included in item 'Miscellaneous goods and services'.
d) Relating to adjustment for net sales of used capital goods.

Germany, Fed. Rep. of

2.8 Gross Capital Formation by Type of Good and Owner, in Constant Prices

Million Deutsche marks

	1970 TOTAL	Total Private	Public Enterprises	General Government	1971 TOTAL	Total Private	Public Enterprises	General Government	1972 TOTAL	Total Private	Public Enterprises	General Government
	\multicolumn{12}{c}{At constant prices of:1970}
Increase in stocks, total [a]	15400	...	...	...	3900	...	...	...	2400	...	...	...
1 Goods producing industries [bc]	15200	...	...	...	3700	...	...	...	2400	...	...	...
a Materials and supplies [d]	15500	...	...	...	3900	...	...	...	2300	...	...	...
b Work in progress	...	...	...	...	...	...	...	...	...	...	...	...
c Livestock, except breeding stocks, dairy cattle, etc. [a]	-300	...	...	...	-200	...	...	...	100	...	...	...
d Finished goods [d]	...	...	...	...	...	...	...	...	...	...	...	...
2 Wholesale and retail trade [b]	...	...	...	...	...	...	...	...	...	...	...	...
3 Other, except government stocks [c]	...	...	...	...	...	...	...	...	...	...	...	...
4 Government stocks	200	...	...	...	200	...	...	...	-	...	...	...
Gross Fixed Capital Formation, Total	173690	...	...	...	184870	...	...	...	191300	...	...	...
1 Residential buildings	44860	...	...	...	49690	...	...	...	56680	...	...	...
2 Non-residential buildings	60400	...	...	...	62740	...	...	...	62870	...	...	...
3 Other construction	...	...	...	...	...	...	...	...	...	...	...	...
4 Land improvement and plantation and orchard development	...	...	...	...	...	...	...	...	...	...	...	...
5 Producers' durable goods	70460	...	...	...	74640	...	...	...	74160	...	...	...
a Transport equipment	14470	...	...	...	15310	...	...	...	14800	...	...	...
b Machinery and equipment	55990	...	...	...	59330	...	...	...	59360	...	...	...
6 Breeding stock, dairy cattle, etc. [a]	...	...	...	...	...	...	...	...	...	...	...	...
Statistical discrepancy [e]	-2030	...	...	...	-2200	...	...	...	-2410	...	...	...
Total Gross Capital Formation [e]	189090	...	...	...	188770	...	...	...	193700	...	...	...

	1973 TOTAL	Total Private	Public Enterprises	General Government	1974 TOTAL	Total Private	Public Enterprises	General Government	1975 TOTAL	Total Private	Public Enterprises	General Government
	\multicolumn{12}{c}{At constant prices of:1970}
Increase in stocks, total [a]	6100	...	...	...	4400	...	...	...	-1000	...	...	...
1 Goods producing industries [bc]	6100	...	...	...	4300	...	...	...	-1200	...	...	...
a Materials and supplies [d]	6100	...	...	...	4400	...	...	...	-1200	...	...	...
b Work in progress	...	...	...	...	...	...	...	...	...	...	...	...
c Livestock, except breeding stocks, dairy cattle, etc. [a]	-	...	...	...	-100	...	...	...	-	...	...	...
d Finished goods [d]	...	...	...	...	...	...	...	...	...	...	...	...
2 Wholesale and retail trade [b]	...	...	...	...	...	...	...	...	...	...	...	...
3 Other, except government stocks [c]	...	...	...	...	...	...	...	...	...	...	...	...
4 Government stocks	-	...	...	...	100	...	...	...	200	...	...	...
Gross Fixed Capital Formation, Total	191670	...	...	...	172610	...	...	...	165370	...	...	...
1 Residential buildings	57410	...	...	...	47750	...	...	...	42780	...	...	...
2 Non-residential buildings	61960	...	...	...	59960	...	...	...	57460	...	...	...
3 Other construction	...	...	...	...	...	...	...	...	...	...	...	...
4 Land improvement and plantation and orchard development	...	...	...	...	...	...	...	...	...	...	...	...
5 Producers' durable goods	74550	...	...	...	67540	...	...	...	67730	...	...	...
a Transport equipment	14110	...	...	...	11740	...	...	...	12880	...	...	...
b Machinery and equipment	60440	...	...	...	55800	...	...	...	54850	...	...	...
6 Breeding stock, dairy cattle, etc. [a]	...	...	...	...	...	...	...	...	...	...	...	...
Statistical discrepancy [e]	-2250	...	...	...	-2640	...	...	...	-2600	...	...	...
Total Gross Capital Formation [e]	197770	...	...	...	177010	...	...	...	164370	...	...	...

Germany, Fed. Rep. of

2.8 Gross Capital Formation by Type of Good and Owner, in Constant Prices

Million Deutsche marks

	1976 TOTAL	1976 Total Private	1976 Public Enterprises	1976 General Government	1977 TOTAL	1977 Total Private	1977 Public Enterprises	1977 General Government	1978 TOTAL	1978 Total Private	1978 Public Enterprises	1978 General Government
At constant prices of: 1970												
Increase in stocks, total [a]	10200	...	...	...	9500	...	...	...	6600	...	...	...
1 Goods producing industries [bc]	10100	...	...	...	9400	...	...	...	6500	...	...	...
a Materials and supplies [d]	10100	...	...	...	9300	...	...	...	6400	...	...	...
b Work in progress	...	...	...	...	...	...	...	...	...	...	...	...
c Livestock, except breeding stocks, dairy cattle, etc. [a]	-	...	...	...	100	...	...	...	100	...	...	...
d Finished goods [d]	...	...	...	...	...	...	...	...	...	...	...	...
2 Wholesale and retail trade [b]	...	...	...	...	...	...	...	...	...	...	...	...
3 Other, except government stocks [c]	...	...	...	...	...	...	...	...	...	...	...	...
4 Government stocks	100	...	...	...	100	...	...	...	100	...	...	...
Gross Fixed Capital Formation, Total	173200	...	...	...	179940	...	...	...	189050	...	...	...
1 Residential buildings	45500	...	...	...	46830	...	...	...	48020	...	...	...
2 Non-residential buildings	58350	...	...	...	58400	...	...	...	60220	...	...	...
3 Other construction	...	...	...	...	...	...	...	...	...	...	...	...
4 Land improvement and plantation and orchard development	...	...	...	...	...	...	...	...	...	...	...	...
5 Producers' durable goods	71780	...	...	...	77110	...	...	...	83310	...	...	...
a Transport equipment	14470	...	...	...	16260	...	...	...	17100	...	...	...
b Machinery and equipment	57310	...	...	...	60850	...	...	...	66210	...	...	...
6 Breeding stock, dairy cattle, etc. [a]	...	...	...	...	...	...	...	...	...	...	...	...
Statistical discrepancy [e]	-2430	...	...	...	-2400	...	...	...	-2500	...	...	...
Total Gross Capital Formation [e]	183400	...	...	...	189440	...	...	...	195650	...	...	...

	1979 TOTAL	1979 Total Private	1979 Public Enterprises	1979 General Government	1980 TOTAL	1980 Total Private	1980 Public Enterprises	1980 General Government
At constant prices of: 1970								
Increase in stocks, total [a]	17400	...	...	...	12100	...	...	...
1 Goods producing industries [bc]	...	...	...	...	...	...	...	...
a Materials and supplies [d]	...	...	...	...	...	...	...	...
b Work in progress	...	...	...	...	...	...	...	...
c Livestock, except breeding stocks, dairy cattle, etc. [a]	...	...	...	...	...	...	...	...
d Finished goods [d]	...	...	...	...	...	...	...	...
2 Wholesale and retail trade [b]	...	...	...	...	...	...	...	...
3 Other, except government stocks [c]	...	...	...	...	...	...	...	...
4 Government stocks	...	...	...	...	...	...	...	...
Gross Fixed Capital Formation, Total	204930	...	...	...	212580	...	...	...
1 Residential buildings	51680	...	...	...	53420	...	...	...
2 Non-residential buildings	64760	...	...	...	68110	...	...	...
3 Other construction	...	...	...	...	...	...	...	...
4 Land improvement and plantation and orchard development	...	...	...	...	...	...	...	...
5 Producers' durable goods	90860	...	...	...	93700	...	...	...
a Transport equipment	17150	...	...	...	17370	...	...	...
b Machinery and equipment	73710	...	...	...	76330	...	...	...
6 Breeding stock, dairy cattle, etc. [a]	...	...	...	...	...	...	...	...
Statistical discrepancy [e]	-2370	...	...	...	-2650	...	...	...
Total Gross Capital Formation [e]	222330	...	...	...	224680	...	...	...

a) Item 'Breeding stocks, dairy cattle, etc.' is included in item 'Increase in stocks'.
b) Items 'Wholesale and retail trade' is included in item 'Goods producing industries'.
c) Item 'Other, except government stocks' is included in item 'Goods producing industries'.
d) Item 'Finished goods' is included in item 'Materials and supplies' through 'Work-in-progress'.
e) Relating to adjustment for net sales of used capital goods.

Germany, Fed. Rep. of

2.9 Gross Capital Formation by Kind of Activity of Owner, ISIC Major Divisions, in Current Prices

Million Deutsche marks

	1970 TGCF	1970 IS	1970 GFCF	1971 TGCF	1971 IS	1971 GFCF	1972 TGCF	1972 IS	1972 GFCF	1973 TGCF	1973 IS	1973 GFCF
					All Producers							
1 Agriculture, hunting, fishing and forestry	5330	-200	5530	4970	-100	5070	5460	200	5260	8360	1900	6460
2 Mining and quarrying a	...	...	1010	...	...	1620	...	...	1380	...	...	1210
3 Manufacturing abc	...	...	45900	...	...	49140	...	...	44830	...	...	43280
4 Electricity, gas and water	...	...	7170	...	...	9530	...	...	11440	...	...	11900
5 Construction c	...	...	4770	...	...	5420	...	...	5810	...	...	5200
6 Wholesale and retail trade, restaurants and hotels d	10550	2400	8150	10970	1800	9170	11850	1600	10250	12180	1500	10680
7 Transport, storage and communication	...	...	14210	...	...	17150	...	...	18530	...	...	18770
8 Finance, insurance, real estate and business services e	...	...	45400	...	...	55400	...	...	67050	...	...	72460
9 Community, social and personal services bde	...	...	10990	...	...	14240	...	...	16950	...	...	21450
Total Industries	158330	15200	143130	170340	3600	166740	184100	2600	181500	198610	7200	191410
Producers of Government Services	30860	200	30660	33550	200	33350	33800	-	33800	35150	-	35150
Private Non-Profit Institutions Serving Households	3240	-	3240	3400	-	3400	3320	-	3320	3320	-	3320
Statistical discrepancy f	-3340		-3340	-3890		-3890	-4280		-4280	-4440		-4440
Total	189090	15400	173690	203400	3800	199600	216940	2600	214340	232640	7200	225440

	1974 TGCF	1974 IS	1974 GFCF	1975 TGCF	1975 IS	1975 GFCF	1976 TGCF	1976 IS	1976 GFCF	1977 TGCF	1977 IS	1977 GFCF
					All Producers							
1 Agriculture, hunting, fishing and forestry	6410	100	6310	6120	-1000	7120	7830	-300	8130	10740	1400	9340
2 Mining and quarrying a	...	...	1290	...	...	2050	...	...	2420	...	...	2160
3 Manufacturing abc	...	...	42020	...	...	40790	...	...	44110	...	...	46760
4 Electricity, gas and water	...	...	13640	...	...	14710	...	...	13670	...	...	12890
5 Construction c	...	...	3340	...	...	3450	...	...	3550	...	...	4070
6 Wholesale and retail trade, restaurants and hotels d	6120	-2300	8420	9180	600	8580	16150	5300	10850	14830	3200	11630
7 Transport, storage and communication	...	...	18820	...	...	18930	...	...	19370	...	...	20780
8 Finance, insurance, real estate and business services e	...	...	65250	...	...	60370	...	...	65960	...	...	70340
9 Community, social and personal services bde	...	...	19320	...	...	21160	...	...	26280	...	...	33860
Total Industries	183610	5200	178410	175260	-1900	177160	207840	13500	194340	224730	12900	211830
Producers of Government Services	40850	300	40550	40920	600	40320	40330	200	40130	39860	300	39560
Private Non-Profit Institutions Serving Households	3090	-	3090	2890	-	2890	3080	-	3080	3160	-	3160
Statistical discrepancy f	-5660	...	-5660	-5830		-5830	-5660		-5660	-5590	...	-5590
Total	221890	5500	216390	213240	-1300	214540	245590	13700	231890	262160	13200	248960

	1978 TGCF	1978 IS	1978 GFCF	1979 TGCF	1979 IS	1979 GFCF	1980 TGCF	1980 IS	1980 GFCF
				All Producers					
1 Agriculture, hunting, fishing and forestry	10340	500	9840	10720	-	10720	...	...	...
2 Mining and quarrying a	...	...	1960	...	...	...	...	...	...
3 Manufacturing abc	...	...	48000	...	...	...	...	...	...
4 Electricity, gas and water	...	...	14170	...	...	...	...	...	...

Germany, Fed. Rep. of

2.9 Gross Capital Formation by Kind of Activity of Owner, ISIC Major Divisions, in Current Prices
(Continued)

Million Deutsche marks

	1978 Total Gross Capital Formation	1978 Increase in Stocks	1978 Gross Fixed Capital Formation	1979 Total Gross Capital Formation	1979 Increase in Stocks	1979 Gross Fixed Capital Formation	1980 Total Gross Capital Formation	1980 Increase in Stocks	1980 Gross Fixed Capital Formation
5 Construction c	...	...	4910	...	...	...	...	...	...
6 Wholesale and retail trade, restaurants and hotels d	14820	3400	11420	...	...	...	...	...	...
7 Transport, storage and communication	...	...	22950	...	...	...	...	...	...
8 Finance, insurance, real estate and business services e	...	...	75280	...	...	87250	...	...	94300
9 Community, social and personal services bde	...	...	43150	...	...	...	...	...	...
Total Industries	240980	9300	231680	291350	25600	265750	314300	18900	295400
Producers of Government Services	44040	100	43940	50920	-	50920	58130	...	58130
Private Non-Profit Institutions Serving Households	3440	-	3440	3940	-	3940	4370	-	4370
Statistical discrepancy f	-6050	...	-6050	-6220	...	-6220	-6910	...	-6910
Total	282410	9400	273010	339990	25600	314390	369890	18900	350990

a) Quarrying is included in item 'Manufacturing'.
b) Publishing is included in item 'Community, social and personal services'.
c) Structural steel erection is included in item 'Manufacturing'.
d) Restaurants and hotels are included in item 'Community, social and personal services'.
e) Business services and real estate except dwellings are included in item 'Community, social and personal services'.
f) Relating to adjustment for net purchases of used capital goods.

2.10 Gross Capital Formation by Kind of Activity of Owner, ISIC Major Divisions, in Constant Prices

Million Deutsche marks

	1970 Total Gross Capital Formation	1970 Increase in Stocks	1970 Gross Fixed Capital Formation	1971 Total Gross Capital Formation	1971 Increase in Stocks	1971 Gross Fixed Capital Formation	1972 Total Gross Capital Formation	1972 Increase in Stocks	1972 Gross Fixed Capital Formation	1973 Total Gross Capital Formation	1973 Increase in Stocks	1973 Gross Fixed Capital Formation
					At constant prices of: 1970 All Producers							
1 Agriculture, hunting, fishing and forestry	5330	-200	5530	4540	-200	4740	4930	200	4730	7080	1600	5480
2 Mining and quarrying a	...	...	1010	...	...	1490	...	...	1230	...	...	1030
3 Manufacturing abc	...	...	45900	...	...	46290	...	...	41580	...	...	38970
4 Electricity, gas and water	...	...	7170	...	...	8920	...	...	10390	...	...	10390
5 Construction	...	...	4770	...	...	5110	...	...	5350	...	...	4600
6 Wholesale and retail trade, restaurants and hotels d	...	...	8150	...	...	8560	...	...	9230	...	...	9240
7 Transport, storage and communication	...	...	14210	...	...	16140	...	...	17190	...	...	16700
8 Finance, insurance, real estate and business services e	...	...	45400	...	...	50080	...	...	56990	...	...	57510
9 Community, social and personal services bde	...	...	10990	...	...	13370	...	...	15410	...	...	18820
Total Industries	158330	15200	143130	158400	3700	154700	164500	2400	162100	168840	6100	162740
Producers of Government Services	30860	200	30660	30890	200	30690	30180	-	30180	30030	-	30030
Private Non-Profit Institutions Serving Households	3240	-	3240	3110	-	3110	2880	-	2880	2710	-	2710
Statistical discrepancy f	-3340		-3340	-3630	-	-3630	-3860	-	-3860	-3810	-	-3810
Total	189090	15400	173690	188770	3900	184870	193700	2400	191300	197770	6100	191670

	1974 Total Gross Capital Formation	1974 Increase in Stocks	1974 Gross Fixed Capital Formation	1975 Total Gross Capital Formation	1975 Increase in Stocks	1975 Gross Fixed Capital Formation	1976 Total Gross Capital Formation	1976 Increase in Stocks	1976 Gross Fixed Capital Formation	1977 Total Gross Capital Formation	1977 Increase in Stocks	1977 Gross Fixed Capital Formation
					At constant prices of: 1970 All Producers							
1 Agriculture, hunting, fishing and forestry	5080	100	4980	4610	-600	5210	5540	-200	5740	7330	1000	6330
2 Mining and quarrying a	...	...	990	...	...	1470	...	...	1690	...	...	1420
3 Manufacturing abc	...	...	35520	...	...	32420	...	...	33780	...	...	34680
4 Electricity, gas and water	...	...	10980	...	...	11280	...	...	10200	...	...	9360

593

Germany, Fed. Rep. of

2.10 Gross Capital Formation by Kind of Activity of Owner, ISIC Major Divisions, in Constant Prices
(Continued)

Million Deutsche marks

	1974			1975			1976			1977		
	Total Gross Capital Formation	Increase in Stocks	Gross Fixed Capital Formation	Total Gross Capital Formation	Increase in Stocks	Gross Fixed Capital Formation	Total Gross Capital Formation	Increase in Stocks	Gross Fixed Capital Formation	Total Gross Capital Formation	Increase in Stocks	Gross Fixed Capital Formation
	At constant prices of:1970											
5 Construction	...	...	2770	...	...	2690	...	...	2680	...	...	2940
6 Wholesale and retail trade, restaurants and hotels [d]	...	...	6860	...	...	6700	...	...	8170	...	...	8380
7 Transport, storage and communication	...	...	15750	...	...	15240	...	...	15150	...	...	15870
8 Finance, insurance, real estate and business services [e]	...	...	48580	...	...	43930	...	...	46500	...	...	47380
9 Community, social and personal services [bde]	...	...	16090	...	...	17310	...	...	20740	...	...	26290
Total Industries	146820	4300	142520	135050	-1200	136250	154750	10100	144650	162050	9400	152650
Producers of Government Services	32360	100	32260	31590	200	31390	30550	100	30450	29100	100	29000
Private Non-Profit Institutions Serving Households	2360	-	2360	2150	-	2150	2220	-	2220	2170	-	2170
Statistical discrepancy [f]	-4530	-	-4530	-4420	-	-4420	-4120	-	-4120	-3880	-	-3880
Total	177010	4400	172610	164370	-1000	165370	183400	10200	173200	189440	9500	179940

	1978			1979			1980		
	Total Gross Capital Formation	Increase in Stocks	Gross Fixed Capital Formation	Total Gross Capital Formation	Increase in Stocks	Gross Fixed Capital Formation	Total Gross Capital Formation	Increase in Stocks	Gross Fixed Capital Formation
	At constant prices of:1970								
	All Producers								
1 Agriculture, hunting, fishing and forestry	6700	200	6500	6850	-	6850	...	...	...
2 Mining and quarrying [a]	...	...	1240	...	...	...	...	...	...
3 Manufacturing [abc]	...	...	34380	...	...	...	...	...	...
4 Electricity, gas and water	...	...	9900	...	...	...	...	...	...
5 Construction	...	...	3430	...	...	...	...	...	...
6 Wholesale and retail trade, restaurants and hotels [d]	...	...	7890	...	...	...	...	...	...
7 Transport, storage and communication	...	...	16690	...	...	...	...	...	...
8 Finance, insurance, real estate and business services [e]	...	...	47880	...	...	51050	...	...	49420
9 Community, social and personal services [bde]	...	...	32490	...	...	...	...	...	...
Total Industries	166900	6500	160400	191580	17400	174180	192930	12100	180830
Producers of Government Services	30540	100	30440	32290	-	32290	33480	...	33480
Private Non-Profit Institutions Serving Households	2240	-	2240	2380	-	2380	2420	-	2420
Statistical discrepancy [f]	-4030	-	-4030	-3920	-	-3920	-4150	...	-4150
Total	195650	6600	189050	222330	17400	204930	224680	12100	212580

a) Quarrying is included in item 'Manufacturing'.
b) Publishing is included in item 'Community, social and personal services'.
c) Structural steel erection is included in item 'Manufacturing'.
d) Restaurants and hotels are included in item 'Community, social and personal services'.
e) Business services and real estate except dwellings are included in item 'Community, social and personal services'.
f) Relating to adjustment for net purchases of used capital goods.

2.11 Gross Fixed Capital Formation by Kind of Activity of Owner, ISIC Divisions, in Current Prices

Million Deutsche marks

	1970	1971	1972	1973	1974	1975	1976	1977	1978	1979	1980
	All Producers										
1 Agriculture, hunting, forestry and fishing	5530	5070	5260	6460	6310	7120	8130	9340	9840	10720	...
a Agriculture and hunting	5280	4800	4900	6050	6050	6770	7770	8920	9400	10210	...
b Forestry and logging	250	270	360	410	260	350	360	420	440	510	...
c Fishing											...
2 Mining and quarrying [a]	1010	1620	1380	1210	1290	2050	2420	2160	1960	...	...

Germany, Fed. Rep. of

2.11 Gross Fixed Capital Formation by Kind of Activity of Owner, ISIC Divisions, in Current Prices
(Continued)

Million Deutsche marks

	1970	1971	1972	1973	1974	1975	1976	1977	1978	1979	1980
3 Manufacturing	45900	49140	44830	43280	42020	40790	44110	46760	48000	...	...
a Manufacturing of food, beverages and tobacco	4690	5440	5310	5110	4410	4670	5180	5450	5180	...	...
b Textile, wearing apparel and leather industries	2430	2410	2170	1980	1600	1650	1900	1860	1890	...	...
c Manufacture of wood, and wood products, including furniture	1420	1620	1800	1910	1290	1090	1410	1630	1730	...	...
d Manufacture of paper and paper products, printing and publishing [b]	2530	2180	1990	2000	1880	1780	2140	2370	2650	...	...
e Manufacture of chemicals and chemical petroleum, coal, rubber and plastic products	9910	9840	8460	8210	9720	9370	9360	10140	9680	...	...
f Manufacture of non-metallic mineral products except products of petroleum and coal [a]	2780	3390	3330	3560	2600	1810	2310	2670	2840	...	...
g Basic metal industries	5490	6910	6340	4990	4840	5080	6190	4720	3960	...	...
h Manufacture of fabricated metal products, machinery and equipment [c]	16450	17150	15230	15320	15470	15150	15420	17640	19780	...	...
i Other manufacturing industries	200	200	200	200	210	190	200	280	290	...	...
4 Electricity, gas and water	7170	9530	11440	11900	13640	14710	13670	12890	14170	...	...
5 Construction [c]	4770	5420	5810	5200	3340	3450	3550	4070	4910	...	...
6 Wholesale and retail trade, restaurants and hotels	8150	9170	10250	10680	8420	8580	10850	11630	11420	...	...
a Wholesale and retail trade	8150	9170	10250	10680	8420	8580	10850	11630	11420	...	...
b Restaurants and hotels	...	...	...	...	...	...	...	...	...	...	...
7 Transport, storage and communication	14210	17150	18530	18770	18820	18930	19370	20780	22950	...	...
8 Finance, insurance, real estate and business services	45400	55400	67050	72460	65250	60370	65960	70340	75280	87250	94300
a Financial institutions	1990	2210	2570	2640	3080	3430	3480	3350	2820	2880	...
b Insurance	790	830	1010	1060	1310	1120	1390	1320	1530	1750	...
c Real estate and business services	42620	52360	63470	68760	60860	55820	61090	65670	70930	82620	...
Real estate except dwellings	...	...	...	...	...	...	...	...	...	...	...
Dwellings	42620	52360	63470	68760	60860	55820	61090	65670	70930	82620	94300
9 Community, social and personal services [de]	10990	14240	16950	21450	19320	21160	26280	33860	43150	...	...
Total Industries [f]	143130	166740	181500	191410	178410	177160	194340	211830	231680	265750	295400
Producers of Government Services	30660	33350	33800	35150	40550	40320	40130	39560	43940	50920	58130
Private Non-Profit Institutions Serving Households [f]	3240	3400	3320	3320	3090	2890	3080	3160	3440	3940	4370
Statistical discrepancy [g]	-3340	-3890	-4280	-4440	-5660	-5830	-5660	-5590	-6050	-6220	-6910
Total	173690	199600	214340	225440	216390	214540	231890	248960	273010	314390	350990

a) Quarrying is included in item 'Manufacture of non-metalic mineral products except products of petroleum and coal'.
b) Publishing is included in item 'Community, social and personal services'.
c) Structural steel erection is included in item 'Manufacture of fabricated metal products, machinery and equipment'.
d) Item 'Breeding stocks, dairy cattle, etc.' is included in item 'Increase in stocks'.
e) Item 'Forestry and logging' is included in item 'Agricultural and livestock production'.
f) Item 'Gross fixed capital formation of producers of private non-profit services to households' is included in item 'Gross fixed capital formation of industries'.
g) Relating to adjustment for net purchases of used capital goods.

2.12 Gross Fixed Capital Formation by Kind of Activity of Owner, ISIC Divisions, in Constant Prices

Million Deutsche marks

	1970	1971	1972	1973	1974	1975	1976	1977	1978	1979	1980
	\multicolumn{11}{c}{At constant prices of: 1970}
	\multicolumn{11}{c}{All Producers}
1 Agriculture, hunting, forestry and fishing	5530	4740	4730	5480	4980	5210	5740	6330	6500	6850	...
a Agriculture and hunting	5280	4500	4400	5110	4750	4950	5490	6040	6190	6510	...
b Forestry and logging	250	240	330	370	230	260	250	290	310	340	...
c Fishing											...
2 Mining and quarrying [a]	1010	1490	1230	1030	990	1470	1690	1420	1240	...	...

Germany, Fed. Rep. of

2.12 Gross Fixed Capital Formation by Kind of Activity of Owner, ISIC Divisions, in Constant Prices
(Continued)

Million Deutsche marks

		1970	1971	1972	1973	1974	1975	1976	1977	1978	1979	1980
						At constant prices of:1970						
3	Manufacturing	45900	46290	41580	38970	35520	32420	33780	34680	34380	...	...
	a Manufacturing of food, beverages and tobacco	4690	5110	4870	4510	3630	3590	3850	3890	3530	...	...
	b Textile, wearing apparel and leather industries	2430	2270	2000	1790	1370	1330	1480	1400	1360	...	...
	c Manufacture of wood, and wood products, including furniture	1420	1510	1640	1690	1060	840	1050	1160	1180	...	...
	d Manufacture of paper and paper products, printing and publishing [b]	2530	2020	1790	1730	1480	1300	1490	1560	1650	...	...
	e Manufacture of chemicals and chemical petroleum, coal, rubber and plastic products	9910	9350	7980	7530	8280	7560	7230	7630	7040	...	...
	f Manufacture of non-metalic mineral products except products of petroleum and coal [a]	2780	3150	3010	3090	2090	1370	1730	1870	1880	...	...
	g Basic metal industries	5490	6480	5870	4490	4050	3920	4590	3430	2850	...	...
	h Manufacture of fabricated metal products, machinery and equipment [c]	16450	16210	14240	13960	13380	12360	12210	13530	14680	...	...
	i Other manufacturing industries	200	190	180	180	180	150	150	210	210	...	...
4	Electricity, gas and water	7170	8920	10390	10390	10980	11280	10200	9360	9900	...	...
	a Electricity, gas and steam	...	...	...	...	...	...	...	...	9900	...	...
	b Water works and supply	...	...	...	...	...	...	...	...	...	...	...
5	Construction [c]	4770	5110	5350	4600	2770	2690	2680	2940	3430	...	...
6	Wholesale and retail trade, restaurants and hotels	8150	8560	9230	9240	6860	6700	8170	8380	7890	...	...
	a Wholesale and retail trade	8150	8560	9230	9240	6860	6700	8170	8380	7890	...	...
	b Restaurants and hotels	...	...	...	...	...	...	...	...	...	...	...
7	Transport, storage and communication	14210	16140	17190	16700	15750	15240	15150	15870	16690	...	...
8	Finance, insurance, real estate and business services	45400	50080	56990	57510	48580	43930	46500	47380	47880	51050	...
	a Financial institutions	1990	2060	2320	2270	2490	2730	2700	2560	2150	2140	...
	b Insurance	790	760	880	870	1010	860	1030	940	1030	1100	...
	c Real estate and business services	42620	47260	53790	54370	45080	40340	42770	43880	44700	47810	49420
	Real estate except dwellings	...	...	...	...	...	...	...	...	...	...	...
	Dwellings	42620	47260	53790	54370	45080	40340	42770	43880	44700	47810	49420
9	Community, social and personal services [de]	10990	13370	15410	18820	16090	17310	20740	26290	32490	...	...
	a Sanitary and similar services	...	...	...	...	...	...	...	...	...	...	...
	b Social and related community services	...	...	...	...	...	...	...	...	32490	...	...
	c Recreational and cultural services	...	...	...	...	...	...	...	...	...	...	...
	d Personal and household services	...	...	...	...	...	...	...	...	...	...	...
Total Industries [f]		143130	154700	162100	162740	142520	136250	144650	152650	160400	174180	180830
Producers of Government Services		30660	30690	30180	30030	32260	31390	30450	29000	30440	32290	33480
Private Non-Profit Institutions Serving Households [f]		3240	3110	2880	2710	2360	2150	2220	2170	2240	2380	2420
Statistical discrepancy [g]		-3340	-3630	-3860	-3810	-4530	-4420	-4120	-3880	-4030	-3920	-4150
Total		173690	184870	191300	191670	172610	165370	173200	179940	189050	204930	212580

a) Quarrying is included in item 'Manufacture of non-metalic mineral products except products of petroleum and coal'.
b) Publishing is included in item 'Community, social and personal services'.
c) Structural steel erection is included in item 'Manufacture of fabricated metal products, machinery and equipment'.
d) Item 'Breeding stocks, dairy cattle, etc.' is included in item 'Increase in stocks'.
e) Item 'Forestry and logging' is included in item 'Agricultural and livestock production'.
f) Item 'Gross fixed capital formation of producers of private non-profit services to households' is included in item 'Gross fixed capital formation of industries'.
g) Relating to adjustment for net purchases of used capital goods.

Germany, Fed. Rep. of

2.13 Stocks of Reproducible Fixed Assets, by Type of Good and Owner, in Current Prices

Thousand Million Deutsche marks

		TOTAL Gross	TOTAL Net	Total Private Gross	Total Private Net	Public Enterprises Gross	Public Enterprises Net	General Government Gross	General Government Net
					1970				
1	Residential buildings	883.0	656.6	...	...	...	...	883.0	656.6
2	Non-residential buildings	711.3	505.0	136.7	98.7	...	...	574.6	406.3
3	Other construction	...	...	...	...	...	...	...	...
4	Land improvement and plantation and orchard development	...	...	...	...	...	...	...	...
5	Producers' durable goods	554.9	317.0	21.8	13.0	...	...	533.1	304.0
6	Breeding stock, dairy cattle, etc.	...	...	...	...	...	...	...	...
	Total [a]	2149.2	1478.6	158.5	111.7	...	...	1990.7	1366.9
					1971				
1	Residential buildings	1033.4	768.8	...	...	...	...	1033.4	768.8
2	Non-residential buildings	834.9	593.7	161.7	117.4	...	...	673.2	476.3
3	Other construction	...	...	...	...	...	...	...	...
4	Land improvement and plantation and orchard development	...	...	...	...	...	...	...	...
5	Producers' durable goods	632.4	364.4	24.5	14.5	...	...	607.9	349.9
6	Breeding stock, dairy cattle, etc.	...	...	...	...	...	...	...	...
	Total [a]	2500.7	1726.9	186.2	131.9	...	...	2314.5	1595.0
					1972				
1	Residential buildings	1178.4	877.7	...	...	...	...	1178.4	877.7
2	Non-residential buildings	942.6	671.1	184.2	134.3	...	...	758.4	536.8
3	Other construction	...	...	...	...	...	...	...	...
4	Land improvement and plantation and orchard development	...	...	...	...	...	...	...	...
5	Producers' durable goods	696.7	403.8	27.1	16.2	...	...	669.6	387.6
6	Breeding stock, dairy cattle, etc.	...	...	...	...	...	...	...	...
	Total [a]	2817.7	1952.6	211.3	150.5	...	...	2606.4	1802.1
					1973				
1	Residential buildings	1314.8	981.6	...	...	...	...	1314.8	981.6
2	Non-residential buildings	1037.4	738.5	204.0	149.1	...	...	833.4	589.4
3	Other construction	...	...	...	...	...	...	...	...
4	Land improvement and plantation and orchard development	...	...	...	...	...	...	...	...
5	Producers' durable goods	752.3	435.6	29.6	17.8	...	...	722.7	417.8
6	Breeding stock, dairy cattle, etc.	...	...	...	...	...	...	...	...
	Total [a]	3104.5	2155.7	233.6	166.9	...	...	2870.9	1988.8
					1974				
1	Residential buildings	1472.9	1101.2	...	...	...	...	1472.9	1101.2
2	Non-residential buildings	1155.5	821.7	226.1	165.3	...	...	929.4	656.4
3	Other construction	...	...	...	...	...	...	...	...
4	Land improvement and plantation and orchard development	...	...	...	...	...	...	...	...
5	Producers' durable goods	834.2	480.5	33.2	20.0	...	...	801.0	460.5
6	Breeding stock, dairy cattle, etc.	...	...	...	...	...	...	...	...
	Total [a]	3462.6	2403.4	259.3	185.3	...	...	3203.3	2218.1
					1975				
1	Residential buildings	1617.3	1206.7	...	...	...	...	1617.3	1206.7
2	Non-residential buildings	1253.0	888.0	249.2	182.6	...	...	1003.8	705.4
3	Other construction	...	...	...	...	...	...	...	...
4	Land improvement and plantation and orchard development	...	...	...	...	...	...	...	...
5	Producers' durable goods	936.2	531.3	38.5	23.3	...	...	897.7	508.0
6	Breeding stock, dairy cattle, etc.	...	...	...	...	...	...	...	...
	Total [a]	3806.5	2626.0	287.7	205.9	...	...	3518.8	2420.1

Germany, Fed. Rep. of

2.13 Stocks of Reproducible Fixed Assets, by Type of Good and Owner, in Current Prices
(Continued)

Thousand Million Deutsche marks

		TOTAL Gross	TOTAL Net	Total Private Gross	Total Private Net	Public Enterprises Gross	Public Enterprises Net	General Government Gross	General Government Net
					1976				
1	Residential buildings	1703.8	1266.5	...	...	...	...	1703.8	1266.5
2	Non-residential buildings	1316.7	928.6	264.8	194.2	...	...	1051.9	734.4
3	Other construction	...	...	...	...	...	...	...	...
4	Land improvement and plantation and orchard development	...	...	...	...	...	...	...	...
5	Producers' durable goods	1022.2	571.6	42.4	25.6	...	...	979.8	546.0
6	Breeding stock, dairy cattle, etc.	...	...	...	...	...	...	...	...
	Total a	4042.7	2766.7	307.2	219.8	...	...	3735.5	2546.9
					1977				
1	Residential buildings	1833.7	1358.3	...	...	...	...	1833.7	1358.3
2	Non-residential buildings	1425.1	1000.1	288.2	211.4	...	...	1136.9	788.7
3	Other construction	...	...	...	...	...	...	...	...
4	Land improvement and plantation and orchard development	...	...	...	...	...	...	...	...
5	Producers' durable goods	1087.2	601.4	45.9	27.3	...	...	1041.3	574.1
6	Breeding stock, dairy cattle, etc.	...	...	...	...	...	...	...	...
	Total a	4346.0	2959.8	334.1	238.7	...	...	4011.9	2721.1
					1978				
1	Residential buildings	1997.1	1474.1	...	...	...	...	1997.1	1474.1
2	Non-residential buildings	1552.5	1084.1	315.3	230.9	...	...	1237.2	853.2
3	Other construction	...	...	...	...	...	...	...	...
4	Land improvement and plantation and orchard development	...	...	...	...	...	...	...	...
5	Producers' durable goods	1149.5	632.2	49.6	29.3	...	...	1099.9	602.9
6	Breeding stock, dairy cattle, etc.	...	...	...	...	...	...	...	...
	Total a	4699.1	3190.4	364.9	260.2	...	...	4334.2	2930.2
					1979				
1	Residential buildings	2192.4	1612.3	...	...	...	...	2192.4	1612.3
2	Non-residential buildings	1715.3	1191.7	347.4	254.0	...	...	1367.9	937.7
3	Other construction	...	...	...	...	...	...	...	...
4	Land improvement and plantation and orchard development	...	...	...	...	...	...	...	...
5	Producers' durable goods	1222.3	671.3	53.4	31.3	...	...	1168.9	640.0
6	Breeding stock, dairy cattle, etc.	...	...	...	...	...	...	...	...
	Total a	5130.0	3475.3	400.8	285.3	...	...	4729.2	3190.0
					1980				
1	Residential buildings	2505.0	1836.4	...	...	...	...	2505.0	1836.4
2	Non-residential buildings	1955.6	1353.1	396.5	289.3	...	...	1559.1	1063.8
3	Other construction	...	...	...	...	...	...	...	...
4	Land improvement and plantation and orchard development	...	...	...	...	...	...	...	...
5	Producers' durable goods	1315.2	724.5	58.5	34.1	...	...	1256.7	690.4
6	Breeding stock, dairy cattle, etc.	...	...	...	...	...	...	...	...
	Total a	5775.8	3914.0	455.0	323.4	...	...	5320.8	3590.6

a) Public underground construction is not contained in the data of this table.

Germany, Fed. Rep. of

2.14 Stocks of Reproducible Fixed Assets, by Type of Good and Owner, in Constant Prices

Thousand Million Deutsche marks

		TOTAL Gross	TOTAL Net	Total Private Gross	Total Private Net	Public Enterprises Gross	Public Enterprises Net	General Government Gross	General Government Net
		\multicolumn{8}{c}{At constant prices of: 1970}

1970

		Gross	Net	Gross	Net	Gross	Net	Gross	Net
1	Residential buildings	953.6	708.9	...	...	...	...	953.6	708.9
2	Non-residential buildings	769.3	546.3	147.9	106.7	...	...	621.4	439.6
3	Other construction	...	...	...	...	...	...	...	...
4	Land improvement and plantation and orchard development	...	...	...	...	...	...	...	...
5	Producers' durable goods	570.2	325.7	22.5	13.4	...	...	547.7	312.3
6	Breeding stock, dairy cattle, etc.	...	...	...	...	...	...	...	...
	Total [a]	2293.1	1580.9	170.4	120.1	...	...	2122.7	1460.8

1971

1	Residential buildings	993.6	739.0	...	...	...	...	993.6	739.0
2	Non-residential buildings	809.4	575.6	155.5	112.9	...	...	653.9	462.7
3	Other construction	...	...	...	...	...	...	...	...
4	Land improvement and plantation and orchard development	...	...	...	...	...	...	...	...
5	Producers' durable goods	612.0	352.6	24.0	14.2	...	...	588.0	338.4
6	Breeding stock, dairy cattle, etc.	...	...	...	...	...	...	...	...
	Total [a]	2415.0	1667.2	179.5	127.1	...	...	2235.5	1540.1

1972

1	Residential buildings	1038.2	773.1	...	...	...	...	1038.2	773.1
2	Non-residential buildings	852.3	607.0	163.0	118.9	...	...	689.3	488.1
3	Other construction	...	...	...	...	...	...	...	...
4	Land improvement and plantation and orchard development	...	...	...	...	...	...	...	...
5	Producers' durable goods	655.9	380.1	25.7	15.2	...	...	630.2	364.9
6	Breeding stock, dairy cattle, etc.	...	...	...	...	...	...	...	...
	Total [a]	2546.4	1760.2	188.7	134.1	...	...	2357.7	1626.1

1973

1	Residential buildings	1089.3	813.0	...	...	...	...	1089.3	813.0
2	Non-residential buildings	896.0	638.4	170.1	124.3	...	...	725.9	514.1
3	Other construction	...	...	...	...	...	...	...	...
4	Land improvement and plantation and orchard development	...	...	...	...	...	...	...	...
5	Producers' durable goods	697.0	403.5	27.5	16.4	...	...	669.5	387.1
6	Breeding stock, dairy cattle, etc.	...	...	...	...	...	...	...	...
	Total [a]	2682.3	1854.9	197.6	140.7	...	...	2484.7	1714.2

1974

1	Residential buildings	1140.9	852.8	...	...	...	...	1140.9	852.8
2	Non-residential buildings	938.8	668.1	176.8	129.2	...	...	762.0	538.9
3	Other construction	...	...	...	...	...	...	...	...
4	Land improvement and plantation and orchard development	...	...	...	...	...	...	...	...
5	Producers' durable goods	736.7	424.3	29.5	17.7	...	...	707.2	406.6
6	Breeding stock, dairy cattle, etc.	...	...	...	...	...	...	...	...
	Total [a]	2816.4	1945.2	206.3	146.9	...	...	2610.1	1798.3

1975

1	Residential buildings	1183.1	882.6	...	...	...	...	1183.1	882.6
2	Non-residential buildings	978.6	694.1	184.8	135.3	...	...	793.8	558.8
3	Other construction	...	...	...	...	...	...	...	...
4	Land improvement and plantation and orchard development	...	...	...	...	...	...	...	...
5	Producers' durable goods	766.6	435.0	31.6	19.1	...	...	735.0	415.9
6	Breeding stock, dairy cattle, etc.	...	...	...	...	...	...	...	...
	Total [a]	2928.3	2011.7	216.4	154.4	...	...	2711.9	1857.3

Germany, Fed. Rep. of

2.14 Stocks of Reproducible Fixed Assets, by Type of Good and Owner, in Constant Prices
(Continued)

Thousand Million Deutsche marks

		TOTAL Gross	TOTAL Net	Total Private Gross	Total Private Net	Public Enterprises Gross	Public Enterprises Net	General Government Gross	General Government Net
		At constant prices of: 1970							
		1976							
1	Residential buildings	1220.5	907.0	...	...	...	...	1220.5	907.0
2	Non-residential buildings	1016.1	717.1	192.8	141.3	...	...	823.3	575.8
3	Other construction	...	...	...	...	...	...	...	...
4	Land improvement and plantation and orchard development	...	...	...	...	...	...	...	...
5	Producers' durable goods	794.1	444.0	33.5	20.1	...	...	760.6	423.9
6	Breeding stock, dairy cattle, etc.	...	...	...	...	...	...	...	...
	Total a	3030.7	2068.1	226.3	161.4	...	...	2804.4	1906.7
		1977							
1	Residential buildings	1260.3	933.3	...	...	...	...	1260.3	933.3
2	Non-residential buildings	1055.2	741.1	200.8	147.2	...	...	854.4	593.9
3	Other construction	...	...	...	...	...	...	...	...
4	Land improvement and plantation and orchard development	...	...	...	...	...	...	...	...
5	Producers' durable goods	822.8	455.1	35.1	20.8	...	...	787.7	434.3
6	Breeding stock, dairy cattle, etc.	...	...	...	...	...	...	...	...
	Total a	3138.3	2129.5	235.9	168.0	...	...	2902.4	1961.5
		1978							
1	Residential buildings	1301.1	960.1	...	...	...	...	1301.1	960.1
2	Non-residential buildings	1094.9	765.2	207.9	152.2	...	...	887.0	613.0
3	Other construction	...	...	...	...	...	...	...	...
4	Land improvement and plantation and orchard development	...	...	...	...	...	...	...	...
5	Producers' durable goods	853.9	469.5	36.9	21.7	...	...	817.0	447.8
6	Breeding stock, dairy cattle, etc.	...	...	...	...	...	...	...	...
	Total a	3249.9	2194.8	244.8	173.9	...	...	3005.1	2020.9
		1979							
1	Residential buildings	1342.6	987.1	...	...	...	...	1342.6	987.1
2	Non-residential buildings	1135.4	789.4	215.0	157.1	...	...	920.4	632.3
3	Other construction	...	...	...	...	...	...	...	...
4	Land improvement and plantation and orchard development	...	...	...	...	...	...	...	...
5	Producers' durable goods	888.1	487.6	38.8	22.7	...	...	849.3	464.9
6	Breeding stock, dairy cattle, etc.	...	...	...	...	...	...	...	...
	Total a	3366.1	2264.1	253.8	179.8	...	...	3112.3	2084.3
		1980							
1	Residential buildings	1387.1	1016.6	...	...	...	...	1387.1	1016.6
2	Non-residential buildings	1179.5	816.5	222.5	162.3	...	...	957.0	654.2
3	Other construction	...	...	...	...	...	...	...	...
4	Land improvement and plantation and orchard development	...	...	...	...	...	...	...	...
5	Producers' durable goods	927.4	510.7	40.8	23.7	...	...	886.6	487.0
6	Breeding stock, dairy cattle, etc.	...	...	...	...	...	...	...	...
	Total a	3494.0	2343.8	263.3	186.0	...	...	3230.7	2157.8

a) Public underground construction is not contained in the data of this table.

2.15 Stocks of Reproducible Fixed Assets by Kind of Activity, in Current Prices

Thousand Million Deutsche marks

		1970 Gross	1970 Net	1971 Gross	1971 Net	1972 Gross	1972 Net	1973 Gross	1973 Net	1974 Gross	1974 Net	1975 Gross	1975 Net
a	Residential buildings	883.0	656.6	1033.4	768.8	1178.4	877.7	1314.8	981.6	1472.9	1101.2	1617.3	1206.7
b	Other structures	711.3	505.0	834.9	593.7	942.6	671.1	1037.4	738.5	1155.5	821.7	1253.0	888.0
	Industries	537.8	378.0	629.4	442.4	707.9	497.7	777.4	546.0	867.1	608.2	935.9	653.2
	1 Agriculture	68.0	38.6	77.5	44.0	85.3	48.3	90.9	51.2	97.7	54.8	103.1	57.6
	2 Mining and quarrying a	10.2	6.3	11.1	6.9	11.9	7.3	12.4	7.6	13.0	7.8	13.3	7.9

Germany, Fed. Rep. of

2.15 Stocks of Reproducible Fixed Assets by Kind of Activity, in Current Prices
(Continued)

Thousand Million Deutsche marks

	1970 Gross	1970 Net	1971 Gross	1971 Net	1972 Gross	1972 Net	1973 Gross	1973 Net	1974 Gross	1974 Net	1975 Gross	1975 Net
3 Manufacturing [a]	156.9	105.7	184.8	124.1	207.4	138.4	225.1	148.1	246.9	160.1	258.5	164.4
4 Electricity, gas and water	60.1	47.1	69.6	54.3	78.1	60.9	86.2	67.2	97.0	75.4	106.8	82.7
5 Construction	9.5	7.7	11.3	9.1	13.0	10.4	14.7	11.7	17.0	13.4	18.5	14.4
6 Wholesale and retail trade	48.4	37.8	57.9	45.1	65.8	51.2	73.1	56.9	82.0	63.6	88.5	68.0
7 Transport and communication	82.8	54.3	95.5	63.0	106.0	70.4	115.3	76.9	128.9	86.3	141.3	94.6
8 Finance, etc.	26.3	20.9	31.6	25.1	36.4	28.9	41.2	32.7	46.5	37.0	51.6	41.0
9 Community, social and personal services	75.6	59.6	90.1	70.8	104.0	81.9	118.5	93.7	138.1	109.8	154.3	122.6
Statistical discrepancy	...	...	...	...	...	...	...	...	...	...	...	...
Producers of government services	136.7	98.7	161.7	117.4	184.2	134.3	204.0	149.1	226.1	165.3	249.2	182.6
Other producers	36.8	28.3	43.8	33.9	50.5	39.1	56.0	43.4	62.3	48.2	67.9	52.2
c Land improvement and development and plantation and orchard development	...	...	...	...	...	...	...	...	...	...	...	...
d Producers' durable goods	554.9	317.0	632.4	364.4	696.7	403.8	752.3	435.6	834.2	480.5	936.2	531.3
Industries	526.7	300.1	600.7	345.6	661.6	382.8	714.0	412.7	791.3	454.8	886.8	501.7
1 Agriculture	54.4	30.0	58.3	31.7	62.7	33.4	66.9	35.1	73.4	38.4	80.9	41.8
2 Mining and quarrying [a]	14.1	6.6	15.2	7.1	15.9	7.7	16.3	7.9	17.5	8.4	19.2	9.2
3 Manufacturing [a]	247.6	143.4	286.7	168.4	317.2	187.1	339.8	198.9	372.2	214.7	415.4	234.3
4 Electricity, gas and water	42.2	24.3	47.5	27.3	52.4	30.2	57.8	33.8	66.0	39.0	79.1	47.3
5 Construction	25.7	13.5	29.1	15.5	31.6	17.1	33.8	18.5	36.5	19.6	38.6	19.7
6 Wholesale and retail trade	32.8	18.2	36.7	20.4	39.8	22.2	43.0	24.0	47.4	26.5	51.4	28.0
7 Transport and communication	80.4	44.5	90.8	50.9	98.9	56.3	106.7	61.5	118.5	68.5	131.9	75.7
8 Finance, etc.	5.5	3.3	6.4	3.8	7.1	4.2	7.9	4.7	8.8	5.3	10.1	6.0
9 Community, social and personal services	24.0	16.3	30.0	20.5	36.0	24.6	41.8	28.3	51.0	34.4	60.2	39.7
Statistical discrepancy	...	...	...	...	...	...	...	...	...	...	...	...
Producers of government services	21.8	13.0	24.5	14.5	27.1	16.2	29.6	17.8	33.2	20.0	38.5	23.3
Other producers	6.4	3.9	7.2	4.3	8.0	4.8	8.7	5.1	9.7	5.7	10.9	6.3
e Breeding stock, dairy cattle, etc.	...	...	...	...	...	...	...	...	...	...	...	...
Total [c]	2149.2	1478.6	2500.7	1726.9	2817.7	1952.6	3104.5	2155.7	3462.6	2403.4	3806.5	2626.0

	1976 Gross	1976 Net	1977 Gross	1977 Net	1978 Gross	1978 Net	1979 Gross	1979 Net	1980 Gross	1980 Net
a Residential buildings	1703.8	1266.5	1833.7	1358.3	1997.1	1474.1	2192.4	1612.3	2505.0	1836.4
b Other structures	1316.7	928.6	1425.1	1000.1	1552.5	1084.1	1715.3	1191.7	1955.6	1353.1
Industries	980.9	680.0	1060.3	730.4	1153.9	790.2	1276.5	869.0	1455.7	986.5
1 Agriculture	106.1	59.1	113.5	63.1	121.1	67.1	130.9	72.4	144.3	79.5
2 Mining and quarrying [a]	13.5	7.9	14.2	8.3	15.2	8.8	16.7	9.6	...	...
3 Manufacturing [a]	268.5	167.2	285.8	173.8	305.6	182.0	332.2	193.1	...	...
4 Electricity, gas and water	114.1	88.2	124.5	96.4	136.2	104.9	151.5	116.3	...	...
5 Construction	19.1	14.6	20.2	15.1	22.1	16.3	24.6	17.8	...	...
6 Wholesale and retail trade	91.9	70.2	100.5	76.2	110.8	83.5	122.7	91.8	...	...
7 Transport and communication	148.0	98.8	157.2	104.4	168.5	111.3	183.8	120.6	...	...
8 Finance, etc.	55.6	44.1	61.5	48.8	67.8	53.5	75.0	58.8	...	...
9 Community, social and personal services	164.1	129.9	182.9	144.3	206.6	162.8	239.1	188.6	...	...
Statistical discrepancy	...	...	...	...	...	...	...	...	...	...
Producers of government services	264.8	194.2	288.2	211.4	315.3	230.9	347.4	254.0	396.5	289.3
Other producers	71.0	54.4	76.6	58.3	83.3	63.0	91.4	68.7	103.4	77.3
c Land improvement and development and plantation and orchard development	...	...	...	...	...	...	...	...	...	...
d Producers' durable goods	1022.2	571.6	1087.2	601.4	1149.5	632.2	1222.3	671.3	1315.2	724.5
Industries	968.1	539.4	1028.9	567.2	1086.8	595.7	1155.1	632.5	1242.0	682.5
1 Agriculture	87.0	44.6	91.8	47.0	96.9	49.9	101.5	52.6	107.3	56.1
2 Mining and quarrying [a]	20.7	10.2	22.2	11.2	23.4	11.9	24.2	12.2	...	...

Germany, Fed. Rep. of

2.15 Stocks of Reproducible Fixed Assets by Kind of Activity, in Current Prices
(Continued)

Thousand Million Deutsche marks

	1976 Gross	1976 Net	1977 Gross	1977 Net	1978 Gross	1978 Net	1979 Gross	1979 Net	1980 Gross	1980 Net
3 Manufacturing [a]	448.7	247.0	470.0	253.8	485.2	257.9	502.4	264.3	...	...
4 Electricity, gas and water	89.8	53.5	96.3	56.4	101.5	58.1	106.4	59.6	...	...
5 Construction	39.9	19.4	40.0	18.8	40.2	18.5	40.7	18.9	...	...
6 Wholesale and retail trade	54.5	28.8	57.8	30.4	61.0	32.0	64.3	33.6	...	...
7 Transport and communication	144.1	81.9	152.7	86.1	162.1	90.8	176.0	98.2	...	...
8 Finance, etc.	11.2	6.7	12.4	7.3	13.7	8.1	14.8	8.7	...	...
9 Community, social and personal services	72.2	47.3	85.7	56.2	102.8	68.5	124.8	84.4	...	...
Statistical discrepancy	...	...	...	...	...	...	...	...	...	...
Producers of government services	42.4	25.6	45.9	27.3	49.6	29.3	53.4	31.3	58.5	34.1
Other producers	11.7	6.6	12.4	6.9	13.1	7.2	13.8	7.5	14.7	7.9
e Breeding stock, dairy cattle, etc.	...	...	...	...	...	...	...	...	...	...
Total [c]	4042.7	2766.7	4346.0	2959.8	4699.1	3190.4	5130.0	3475.3	5775.8	3914.0

a) Quarrying is included in item 'Manufacturing'.
b) Including fuel, energy and other economic affairs.
c) Public underground construction is not contained in the data of this table.

2.16 Stocks of Reproducible Fixed Assets by Kind of Activity, in Constant Prices

Thousand Million Deutsche marks

	1970 Gross	1970 Net	1971 Gross	1971 Net	1972 Gross	1972 Net	1973 Gross	1973 Net	1974 Gross	1974 Net	1975 Gross	1975 Net
					At constant prices of:1970							
a Residential buildings	953.6	708.9	993.6	739.0	1038.2	773.1	1089.3	813.0	1140.9	852.8	1183.1	882.6
b Other structures	769.3	546.3	809.4	575.6	852.3	607.0	896.0	638.4	938.8	668.1	978.6	694.1
Industries	581.6	408.7	611.6	429.7	644.7	453.3	679.2	4.8	713.3	501.1	743.4	519.9
1 Agriculture	74.7	42.7	75.3	43.0	75.7	43.1	75.9	43.0	76.2	43.0	76.6	43.1
2 Mining and quarrying [a]	10.9	6.9	10.8	6.8	10.9	6.8	10.9	6.7	10.9	6.6	10.9	6.5
3 Manufacturing [a]	168.8	113.5	179.2	120.1	189.4	126.4	197.9	131.0	204.9	133.9	210.7	135.3
4 Electricity, gas and water	64.6	50.5	68.2	53.1	72.6	56.4	77.4	60.1	81.9	63.5	86.3	66.7
5 Construction	10.3	8.3	11.0	8.8	11.8	9.4	12.9	10.2	14.0	11.0	14.6	11.3
6 Wholesale and retail trade	52.9	41.3	56.1	43.7	59.4	46.2	63.0	48.9	66.4	51.4	68.9	53.0
7 Transport and communication	88.4	58.0	93.3	61.6	99.0	65.8	104.9	70.0	111.0	74.3	116.9	78.2
8 Finance, etc.	28.4	22.7	30.3	24.2	32.0	25.6	34.0	27.2	36.0	28.7	38.2	30.5
9 Community, social and personal services	82.6	64.8	87.4	68.4	93.9	73.6	102.3	80.6	112.0	88.7	120.3	95.3
Statistical discrepancy	...	...	...	...	...	...	...	...	...	...	...	...
Producers of government services	581.6	106.7	611.6	112.9	644.7	118.9	679.2	124.3	713.3	129.2	743.4	135.3
Other producers	-393.9	30.9	-413.8	33.0	-437.1	34.8	-462.4	36.4	-487.8	37.8	-508.2	38.9
c Land improvement and development and plantation and orchard development	...	...	...	...	...	...	...	...	...	...	...	...
d Producers' durable goods	570.2	325.7	612.0	352.6	655.9	380.1	697.0	403.5	736.7	424.3	766.6	435.0
Industries	541.2	308.6	581.1	334.5	622.8	360.7	661.6	382.6	699.0	401.9	726.5	411.1
1 Agriculture	55.0	30.2	57.0	30.9	58.1	30.9	59.2	31.0	60.8	31.7	61.6	31.8
2 Mining and quarrying [a]	14.6	6.6	14.3	6.4	14.4	6.7	14.3	6.8	14.1	6.7	13.9	6.6
3 Manufacturing [a]	254.7	148.4	277.4	163.6	299.9	177.5	318.2	186.4	334.3	192.7	346.5	195.3
4 Electricity, gas and water	43.7	25.1	45.7	26.1	48.6	28.0	52.4	30.6	56.3	33.2	60.8	36.2
5 Construction	26.3	13.7	28.0	14.9	29.7	16.1	31.2	17.1	31.9	17.2	31.2	16.0
6 Wholesale and retail trade	33.6	18.6	35.4	19.6	37.3	20.7	39.4	22.0	41.6	23.3	42.1	22.9
7 Transport and communication	83.1	46.0	87.6	49.1	93.0	52.9	98.9	57.0	104.1	60.2	108.1	62.1
8 Finance, etc.	5.8	3.3	6.4	3.7	7.1	4.1	7.9	4.6	8.6	5.0	9.4	5.4
9 Community, social and personal services	24.4	16.7	29.3	20.2	34.7	23.8	40.1	27.1	47.3	31.9	52.9	34.8
Statistical discrepancy	...	...	...	...	...	...	...	...	...	...	...	...
Producers of government services	22.5	13.4	24.0	14.2	25.7	15.2	27.5	16.4	29.5	17.7	31.6	19.1
Other producers	6.5	3.7	6.9	3.9	7.4	4.2	7.9	4.5	8.2	4.7	8.5	4.8
e Breeding stock, dairy cattle, etc.	...	...	...	...	...	...	...	...	...	...	...	...
Total [b]	2293.1	1580.9	2415.0	1667.2	2546.4	1760.2	2682.3	1854.9	2816.4	1945.2	2928.3	2011.7

Germany, Fed. Rep. of

2.16 Stocks of Reproducible Fixed Assets by Kind of Activity, in Constant Prices

Thousand Million Deutsche marks

	1976 Gross	1976 Net	1977 Gross	1977 Net	1978 Gross	1978 Net	1979 Gross	1979 Net	1980 Gross	1980 Net
	\multicolumn{10}{c}{At constant prices of: 1970}
a Residential buildings	1220.5	907.0	1260.3	933.3	1301.1	960.1	1342.6	987.1	1387.1	1016.6
b Other structures	1016.1	717.1	1055.2	741.1	1094.9	765.2	1135.4	789.4	1179.5	816.5
Industries	771.4	536.0	800.9	553.1	832.0	571.4	863.8	589.8	898.7	610.7
1 Agriculture	77.0	43.2	77.5	43.4	78.1	43.7	78.6	43.8	79.1	43.9
2 Mining and quarrying [a]	10.9	6.4	11.0	6.4	11.1	6.4	11.2	6.4	...	...
3 Manufacturing [a]	215.4	135.4	219.9	135.3	225.2	135.9	229.7	135.6	...	...
4 Electricity, gas and water	91.7	70.8	97.3	75.0	102.6	78.8	108.3	82.9	...	...
5 Construction	14.9	11.4	15.3	11.5	15.8	11.7	16.2	11.8	...	...
6 Wholesale and retail trade	71.3	54.4	74.3	56.4	77.3	58.3	80.0	59.9	...	...
7 Transport and communication	122.3	81.5	127.3	84.4	132.4	87.4	137.4	90.1	...	...
8 Finance, etc.	40.4	32.3	42.7	34.0	44.6	35.4	46.1	36.4	...	...
9 Community, social and personal services	127.5	100.6	135.6	106.7	144.9	113.8	156.3	122.9	...	...
Statistical discrepancy	...	...	...	...	...	...	...	...	...	...
Producers of government services	771.4	141.3	800.9	147.2	832.0	152.2	863.8	157.1	898.7	162.3
Other producers	-526.7	39.8	-546.6	40.8	-569.1	41.6	-592.2	42.5	-617.9	43.5
c Land improvement and development and plantation and orchard development	...	...	...	...	...	...	...	...	...	...
d Producers' durable goods	794.1	444.0	822.8	455.1	853.9	469.5	888.1	487.6	927.4	510.7
Industries	751.8	419.0	778.7	429.4	807.7	442.8	839.9	459.9	877.0	481.9
1 Agriculture	62.5	32.0	63.6	32.5	65.1	33.4	66.8	34.5	68.7	35.9
2 Mining and quarrying [a]	14.2	7.0	14.6	7.4	14.7	7.5	14.6	7.4	...	...
3 Manufacturing [a]	355.1	195.3	363.7	196.1	370.7	196.5	376.5	196.8	...	...
4 Electricity, gas and water	64.5	38.3	66.8	39.0	68.4	39.0	70.0	39.1	...	...
5 Construction	30.6	15.0	29.8	14.1	28.9	13.4	28.5	13.4	...	...
6 Wholesale and retail trade	42.3	22.4	43.2	22.7	44.2	23.2	44.9	23.4	...	...
7 Transport and communication	111.9	63.7	115.8	65.3	120.0	67.2	124.8	69.7	...	...
8 Finance, etc.	10.2	5.8	11.0	6.3	11.9	6.8	12.8	7.3	...	...
9 Community, social and personal services	60.5	39.5	70.2	46.0	83.8	55.8	101.0	68.3	...	...
Statistical discrepancy	...	...	...	...	...	...	...	...	...	...
Producers of government services	33.5	20.1	35.1	20.8	36.9	21.7	38.8	22.7	40.8	23.7
Other producers	8.8	4.9	9.0	4.9	9.3	5.0	9.4	5.0	9.6	5.1
e Breeding stock, dairy cattle, etc.	...	...	...	...	...	...	...	...	...	...
Total [b]	3030.7	2068.1	3138.3	2129.5	3249.9	2194.8	3366.1	2264.1	3494.0	2343.8

a) Quarrying is included in item 'Manufacturing'.
b) Public underground construction is not contained in the data of this table.

2.17 Exports and Imports of Goods and Services, Detail

Million Deutsche marks

	1970	1971	1972	1973	1974	1975	1976	1977	1978	1979	1980
	\multicolumn{11}{c}{Exports of Goods and Services}
1 Exports of merchandise, f.o.b.	122780	133090	145780	174190	228160	219640	252720	268430	278480	307250	343240
2 Transport and communication [a]	11400	13810	14450	15740	20500	24190	27370	28450	31980	33790	39500
3 Insurance service charges	...	...	...	...	...	...	...	...	...	...	...
4 Other commodities	...	...	...	...	...	...	...	...	...	...	...
5 Adjustments of merchandise exports to change-of-ownership basis	...	...	...	...	...	...	...	...	...	...	...
6 Direct purchases in the domestic market by non-residential households	8740	9790	10690	10890	11180	12560	13800	14450	15930	16670	18750
7 Direct purchases in the domestic market by extraterritorial bodies											...
Total Exports of Goods and Services [b]	142920	156690	170920	200820	259840	256390	293890	311330	326390	357710	401590
	\multicolumn{11}{c}{Imports of Goods and Services}
1 Imports of merchandise, c.i.f.	118190	129350	138530	155300	197150	205800	243860	255870	264100	315820	369490

Germany, Fed. Rep. of

2.17 Exports and Imports of Goods and Services, Detail
(Continued)

Million Deutsche marks

	1970	1971	1972	1973	1974	1975	1976	1977	1978	1979	1980
a Imports of merchandise, f.o.b.	100820	109590	119090	134440	173100	178660	213220	224740	230290	277890	327630
b Transport of services on merchandise imports [a]	17370	19760	19440	20860	24050	27140	30640	31130	33810	37930	41860
c Insurance service charges on merchandise imports	...	...	...	...	...	...	...	...	...	...	...
2 Adjustments of merchandise imports to change-of-ownership basis	...	...	...	...	...	...	...	...	...	...	...
3 Other transport and communication	...	...	...	...	...	...	...	...	...	...	...
4 Other insurance service charges	...	...	...	...	...	...	...	...	...	...	...
5 Other commodities	...	...	...	...	...	...	...	...	...	...	...
6 Direct purchases abroad by government	...	...	...	...	...	...	...	...	...	...	...
7 Direct purchases abroad by resident households	10730	12930	15120	17940	19020	22510	23580	26070	29360	32880	38180
Total Imports of Goods and Services [b]	128920	142280	153650	173240	216170	228310	267440	281940	293460	348700	407670
Balance of Goods and Services	14000	14410	17270	27580	43670	28080	26450	29390	32930	9010	-6080
Total Imports and Balance of Goods and Services	142920	156690	170920	200820	259840	256390	293890	311330	326390	357710	401590

a) Including insurance service charges and other commodities.
b) Exports and imports of goods for purposes of repair and improvement are reduced to the value of these services.

3.11 General Government Production Account: Total and Subsectors

Million Deutsche marks

	\multicolumn{5}{c	}{1970}	\multicolumn{5}{c	}{1971}
	Total General Government	Central Government	State or Provincial Government	Local Government	Social Security Funds	Total General Government	Central Government	State or Provincial Government	Local Government	Social Security Funds

Gross Output

1 Sales	11650	310	2690	8600	50	14020	540	3070	10380	30
2 Services produced for own use	108110	27100	35410	19380	26220	129240	32050	42250	22790	32150
3 Own account capital formation	90	-	60	30	-	120	-	70	50	-
Gross Output	119850	27410	38160	28010	26270	143380	32590	45390	33220	32180

Gross Input

Intermediate Consumption	56370	14620	7260	11430	23060	67640	17710	8080	13390	28460
Subtotal: Value Added	63480	12790	30900	16580	3210	75740	14880	37310	19830	3720
1 Indirect taxes, net	90	10	40	30	10	110	10	50	40	10
a Indirect taxes paid	90	10	40	30	10	110	10	50	40	10
b Less: Subsidies received	-	-	-	-	-	-	-	-	-	-
2 Consumption of fixed capital	3250	230	950	1970	100	3740	270	1100	2260	110
3 Compensation of employees	60140	12550	29910	14580	3100	71890	14600	36160	17530	3600
4 Net Operating surplus	-	-	-	-	-	-	-	-	-	-
Gross Input	119850	27410	38160	28010	26270	143380	32590	45390	33220	32180

	\multicolumn{5}{c	}{1972}	\multicolumn{5}{c	}{1973}
	Total General Government	Central Government	State or Provincial Government	Local Government	Social Security Funds	Total General Government	Central Government	State or Provincial Government	Local Government	Social Security Funds

Gross Output

1 Sales	16550	670	3620	12210	50	19740	800	4370	14500	70
2 Services produced for own use	144030	33920	47210	25220	37680	166700	37360	54880	29340	45120
3 Own account capital formation	130	-	70	60	-	120	-	70	50	-
Gross Output	160710	34590	50900	37490	37730	186560	38160	59320	43890	45190

Gross Input

Intermediate Consumption	75670	17850	9170	15160	33490	87740	19270	10690	17620	40160
Subtotal: Value Added	85040	16740	41730	22330	4240	98820	18890	48630	26270	5030
1 Indirect taxes, net	130	10	60	50	10	150	10	70	60	10
a Indirect taxes paid	130	10	60	50	10	150	10	70	60	10
b Less: Subsidies received	-	-	-	-	-	-	-	-	-	-
2 Consumption of fixed capital	4150	280	1240	2510	120	4640	310	1400	2800	130
3 Compensation of employees	80760	16450	40430	19770	4110	94030	18570	47160	23410	4890
4 Net Operating surplus	-	-	-	-	-	-	-	-	-	-
Gross Input	160710	34590	50900	37490	37730	186560	38160	59320	43890	45190

Germany, Fed. Rep. of

3.11 General Government Production Account: Total and Subsectors

Million Deutsche marks

	\multicolumn{5}{c	}{1974}	\multicolumn{5}{c	}{1975}
	Total General Government	Central Government	State or Provincial Government	Local Government	Social Security Funds	Total General Government	Central Government	State or Provincial Government	Local Government	Social Security Funds
\multicolumn{11}{c	}{**Gross Output**}
1 Sales	22960	930	5570	16440	20	26450	1360	6510	18560	20
2 Services produced for own use	194020	42030	63420	33660	54910	215290	45560	69470	36160	64100
3 Own account capital formation	140	-	80	60	-	170	-	100	70	-
Gross Output	217120	42960	69070	50160	54930	241910	46920	76080	54790	64120
\multicolumn{11}{c	}{**Gross Input**}
Intermediate Consumption	102570	21320	12350	19990	48910	117460	24120	13970	21910	57460
Subtotal: Value Added	114550	21640	56720	30170	6020	124450	22800	62110	32880	6660
1 Indirect taxes, net	160	10	70	70	10	180	10	80	80	10
a Indirect taxes paid	160	10	70	70	10	180	10	80	80	10
b Less: Subsidies received	-	-	-	-	-	-	-	-	-	-
2 Consumption of fixed capital	5230	350	1580	3170	130	5740	380	1760	3460	140
3 Compensation of employees	109160	21280	55070	26930	5880	118530	22410	60270	29340	6510
4 Net Operating surplus	-	-	-	-	-	-	-	-	-	-
Gross Input	217120	42960	69070	50160	54930	241910	46920	76080	54790	64120

	\multicolumn{5}{c	}{1976}	\multicolumn{5}{c	}{1977}
	Total General Government	Central Government	State or Provincial Government	Local Government	Social Security Funds	Total General Government	Central Government	State or Provincial Government	Local Government	Social Security Funds
\multicolumn{11}{c	}{**Gross Output**}
1 Sales	30280	1810	7290	21160	20	32140	1660	8000	22470	10
2 Services produced for own use	227190	47340	73430	37310	69110	239380	47900	78590	40400	72490
3 Own account capital formation	190	-	110	80	-	220	-	110	110	-
Gross Output	257660	49150	80830	58550	69130	271740	49560	86700	62980	72500
\multicolumn{11}{c	}{**Gross Input**}
Intermediate Consumption	126240	25580	14680	23840	62140	131350	24930	15590	25670	65160
Subtotal: Value Added	131420	23570	66150	34710	6990	140390	24630	71110	37310	7340
1 Indirect taxes, net	200	10	90	90	10	210	10	90	100	10
a Indirect taxes paid	200	10	90	90	10	210	10	90	100	10
b Less: Subsidies received	-	-	-	-	-	-	-	-	-	-
2 Consumption of fixed capital	6240	410	1930	3750	150	6800	440	2090	4100	170
3 Compensation of employees	124980	23150	64130	30870	6830	133380	24180	68930	33110	7160
4 Net Operating surplus	-	-	-	-	-	-	-	-	-	-
Gross Input	257660	49150	80830	58550	69130	271740	49560	86700	62980	72500

	\multicolumn{5}{c	}{1978}	\multicolumn{5}{c	}{1979}
	Total General Government	Central Government	State or Provincial Government	Local Government	Social Security Funds	Total General Government	Central Government	State or Provincial Government	Local Government	Social Security Funds
\multicolumn{11}{c	}{**Gross Output**}
1 Sales	34870	1820	8930	24110	10	37160	2040	9520	25600	-
2 Services produced for own use	257130	51490	84360	43660	77620	278580	55220	91470	48200	83690
3 Own account capital formation	220	-	110	110	-	260	-	120	140	-
Gross Output	292220	53310	93400	67880	77630	316000	57260	101110	73940	83690
\multicolumn{11}{c	}{**Gross Input**}
Intermediate Consumption	142700	27400	17420	27980	69900	155570	30140	19410	30650	75370
Subtotal: Value Added	149520	25910	75980	39900	7730	160430	27120	81700	43290	8320
1 Indirect taxes, net	220	10	90	110	10	230	10	100	110	10
a Indirect taxes paid	220	10	90	110	10	230	10	100	110	10
b Less: Subsidies received	-	-	-	-	-	-	-	-	-	-
2 Consumption of fixed capital	7460	470	2290	4510	190	8270	520	2540	4990	220
3 Compensation of employees	141840	25430	73600	35280	7530	151930	26590	79060	38190	8090
4 Net Operating surplus	-	-	-	-	-	-	-	-	-	-
Gross Input	292220	53310	93400	67880	77630	316000	57260	101110	73940	83690

Germany, Fed. Rep. of

3.11 General Government Production Account: Total and Subsectors

Million Deutsche marks

			1980		
		Total General Government	Central Government	State or Provincial Government	Local Government	Social Security Funds

Gross Output

		Total	Central	State/Prov	Local	Social Sec
1	Sales	40300	2010	10390	27900	-
2	Services produced for own use	303520	59200	99590	53490	91240
3	Own account capital formation	300	-	140	160	-
	Gross Output	344120	61210	110120	81550	91240

Gross Input

		Total	Central	State/Prov	Local	Social Sec
	Intermediate Consumption	170400	32240	21480	34200	82480
	Subtotal: Value Added	173720	28970	88640	47350	8760
1	Indirect taxes, net	250	10	110	120	10
a	Indirect taxes paid	250	10	110	120	10
b	Less: Subsidies received	-	-	-	-	-
2	Consumption of fixed capital	9340	590	2870	5640	240
3	Compensation of employees	164130	28370	85660	41590	8510
4	Net Operating surplus	-	-	-	-	-
	Gross Input	344120	61210	110120	81550	91240

3.12 General Government Income and Outlay Account: Total and Subsectors

Million Deutsche marks

		1970					1971				
		Total Gen Gov	Central Gov	State/Prov Gov	Local Gov	Social Sec Funds	Total Gen Gov	Central Gov	State/Prov Gov	Local Gov	Social Sec Funds

Receipts

		1970 Total	Central	State/Prov	Local	Soc Sec	1971 Total	Central	State/Prov	Local	Soc Sec
1	Property and entrepreneurial income	8630	5460	...	...	3170	9150	5600	...	...	3550
2	Taxes, fees and contributions	235820	162060	...	...	73760	268100	183750	...	...	84350
a	Indirect taxes	87180	87180	...	...	...	96370	96370	...	...	...
b	Direct taxes	72840	72840	...	...	...	84960	84960	...	...	...
	Income	67640	67640	...	...	...	79470	79470	...	...	...
	Other	5200	5200	...	...	...	5490	5490	...	...	...
c	Social security contributions	73740	-	...	...	73740	84330	-	...	...	84330
d	Fees, fines and penalties	2060	2040	...	...	20	2440	2420	...	...	20
3	Other current transfers received	9810	9230	...	...	12370	11650	10980	...	...	13390
a	Casualty insurance claims	440	70	...	...	370	550	110	...	...	440
b	Transfers from other government subsectors	...	...	...	...	11790	...	...	...	...	12720
c	Transfers from abroad	1580	1580	...	...	...	1890	1890	...	...	...
d	Other transfers, except imputed	-	-	...	...	...	-	-	...	...	...
e	Imputed unfunded employee welfare contributions	7790	7580	...	...	210	9210	8980	...	...	230
	Total Current Receipts	254260	176750	...	...	89300	288900	200330	...	...	101290

Disbursements

		1970 Total	Central	State/Prov	Local	Soc Sec	1971 Total	Central	State/Prov	Local	Soc Sec
1	General government final consumption expenditures	108110	81890	...	...	26220	129240	97090	...	...	32150
a	Compensation of employees	60140	57040	...	...	3100	71890	68290	...	...	3600
b	Consumption of fixed capital	3250	3150	...	...	100	3740	3630	...	...	110
c	Goods and services purchased, net	44720	21710	...	...	23010	53620	25190	...	...	28430
	Purchases	56370	33310	...	...	23060	67640	39180	...	...	28460
	Less: Sales	11650	11600	...	...	50	14020	13990	...	...	30
d	Less: Own account production of fixed assets	90	90	...	...	-	120	120	...	...	-
e	Indirect taxes paid, net	90	80	...	...	10	110	100	...	...	10
2	Property income paid	6600	6600	...	...	-	7430	7430	...	...	-
a	Interest	6600	6600	...	...	-	7430	7430	...	...	-
b	Net land rent and royalties	...	...	...	...	...	...	...	...	...	...

Germany, Fed. Rep. of

3.12 General Government Income and Outlay Account: Total and Subsectors
(Continued)

Million Deutsche marks

	1970 Total General Government	1970 Central Government	1970 State or Provincial Government	1970 Local Government	1970 Social Security Funds	1971 Total General Government	1971 Central Government	1971 State or Provincial Government	1971 Local Government	1971 Social Security Funds
3 Subsidies	9630	9590	...	...	40	9830	9760	...	...	70
4 Other current transfers paid	90160	46230	...	...	55720	101070	52370	...	...	61420
a Casualty insurance premiums, net	1450	1450	...	...	-	1560	1560	...	...	-
b Transfers to other government subsectors	...	11790	...	...	...	...	12720	...	...	...
c Transfers to households	80380	25330	...	...	55050	89860	29140	...	...	60720
Social security benefits	54730	-	...	...	54730	60370	-	...	...	60370
Social assistance grants	13830	13830	...	...	-	15650	15650	...	...	...
Unfunded employee welfare benefits	11820	11500	...	...	320	13840	13490	...	...	350
d Transfers to private non-profit institutions serving households	2400	2400	...	...	-	2820	2820	...	...	-
e Transfers to the rest of the world	5930	5260	...	...	670	6830	6130	...	...	700
Net saving [a]	39760	32440	...	...	7320	41330	33680	...	...	7650
Total Current Disbursements and Net Saving	254260	176750	...	...	89300	288900	200330	...	...	101290

	1972 Total General Government	1972 Central Government	1972 State or Provincial Government	1972 Local Government	1972 Social Security Funds	1973 Total General Government	1973 Central Government	1973 State or Provincial Government	1973 Local Government	1973 Social Security Funds
Receipts										
1 Property and entrepreneurial income	8560	4600	...	...	3960	10670	4900	...	...	5770
2 Taxes, fees and contributions	298290	201440	...	...	96850	352270	237370	...	...	114900
a Indirect taxes	107560	107560	...	...	-	118400	118400	...	...	-
b Direct taxes	91070	91070	...	...	-	115810	115810	...	...	-
Income	85320	85320	...	...	-	109830	109830	...	...	-
Other	5750	5750	...	...	-	5980	5980	...	...	-
c Social security contributions	96820	-	...	...	96820	114870	-	...	...	114870
d Fees, fines and penalties	2840	2810	...	...	30	3190	3160	...	...	30
3 Other current transfers received	13160	12380	...	...	16430	15820	14930	...	...	18740
a Casualty insurance claims	650	130	...	...	520	710	160	...	...	550
b Transfers from other government subsectors	...	...	...	...	15650	...	...	...	...	17850
c Transfers from abroad	2290	2290	...	...	-	3010	3010	...	...	-
d Other transfers, except imputed	-	-	...	...	...	-	-	...	...	...
e Imputed unfunded employee welfare contributions	10220	9960	...	...	260	12100	11760	...	...	340
Total Current Receipts	320010	218420	...	...	117240	378760	257200	...	...	139410
Disbursements										
1 General government final consumption expenditures	144030	106350	...	...	37680	166700	121580	...	...	45120
a Compensation of employees	80760	76650	...	...	4110	94030	89140	...	...	4890
b Consumption of fixed capital	4150	4030	...	...	120	4640	4510	...	...	130
c Goods and services purchased, net	59120	25680	...	...	33440	68000	27910	...	...	40090
Purchases	75670	42180	...	...	33490	87740	47580	...	...	40160
Less: Sales	16550	16500	...	...	50	19740	19670	...	...	70
d Less: Own account production of fixed assets	130	130	...	...	-	120	120	...	...	-
e Indirect taxes paid, net	130	120	...	...	10	150	140	...	...	10
2 Property income paid	8480	8480	...	...	-	10220	10220	...	...	-
a Interest	8480	8480	...	...	-	10220	10220	...	...	-
b Net land rent and royalties	...	...	...	...	...	...	...	...	...	...

Germany, Fed. Rep. of

3.12 General Government Income and Outlay Account: Total and Subsectors
(Continued)

Million Deutsche marks

	1972					1973				
	Total General Government	Central Government	State or Provincial Government	Local Government	Social Security Funds	Total General Government	Central Government	State or Provincial Government	Local Government	Social Security Funds
3 Subsidies	12130	12100	...	...	30	14850	14830	...	...	20
4 Other current transfers paid	116360	61460	...	...	70550	130900	68320	...	...	80430
a Casualty insurance premiums, net	1730	1730	...	...	-	1900	1900	...	...	-
b Transfers to other government subsectors	...	15650	...	...	...	...	17850	...	...	...
c Transfers to households	102470	32760	...	...	69710	114480	35060	...	...	79420
Social security benefits	69330	-	...	...	69330	78980	-	...	...	78980
Social assistance grants	18100	18100	...	...	-	18710	18710	...	...	-
Unfunded employee welfare benefits	15040	14660	...	...	380	16790	16350	...	...	440
d Transfers to private non-profit institutions serving households	3110	3110	...	...	-	3570	3570	...	...	-
e Transfers to the rest of the world	9050	8210	...	...	840	10950	9940	...	...	1010
Net saving [a]	39010	30030	...	...	8980	56090	42250	...	...	13840
Total Current Disbursements and Net Saving	320010	218420	...	...	117240	378760	257200	...	...	139410

	1974					1975				
	Total General Government	Central Government	State or Provincial Government	Local Government	Social Security Funds	Total General Government	Central Government	State or Provincial Government	Local Government	Social Security Funds

Receipts

1 Property and entrepreneurial income	10620	5250	...	...	5370	9600	4460	...	...	5140
2 Taxes, fees and contributions	381160	254250	...	...	126910	392900	254560	...	...	138340
a Indirect taxes	122210	122210	...	...	-	126700	126700	...	...	-
b Direct taxes	128380	128380	...	...	-	123820	123820	...	...	-
Income	121890	121890	...	...	-	117480	117480	...	...	-
Other	6490	6490	...	...	-	6340	6340	...	...	...
c Social security contributions	126890	-	...	...	126890	138340	-	...	...	138340
d Fees, fines and penalties	3680	3660	...	...	20	4040	4040	...	...	-
3 Other current transfers received	18050	16960	...	...	21350	19290	18060	...	...	28580
a Casualty insurance claims	800	110	...	...	690	920	140	...	...	780
b Transfers from other government subsectors	...	...	...	...	20260	...	...	...	...	27350
c Transfers from abroad	3250	3250	...	...	-	3110	3110	...	...	-
d Other transfers, except imputed	-	-	...	...	-	-	-	...	...	...
e Imputed unfunded employee welfare contributions	14000	13600	...	...	400	15260	14810	...	...	450
Total Current Receipts	409830	276460	...	...	153630	421790	277080	...	...	172060

Disbursements

1 General government final consumption expenditures	194020	139110	...	...	54910	215290	151190	...	...	64100
a Compensation of employees	109160	103280	...	...	5880	118530	112020	...	...	6510
b Consumption of fixed capital	5230	5100	...	...	130	5740	5600	...	...	140
c Goods and services purchased, net	79610	30720	...	...	48890	91010	33570	...	...	57440
Purchases	102570	53660	...	...	48910	117460	60000	...	...	57460
Less: Sales	22960	22940	...	...	20	26450	26430	...	...	20
d Less: Own account production of fixed assets	140	140	...	...	-	170	170	...	...	-
e Indirect taxes paid, net	160	150	...	...	10	180	170	...	...	10
2 Property income paid	12200	12200	...	...	-	14230	14230	...	...	-
a Interest	12200	12200	...	...	-	14230	14230	...	...	-
b Net land rent and royalties	...	...	...	...	...	...	...	...	...	...

Germany, Fed. Rep. of

3.12 General Government Income and Outlay Account: Total and Subsectors
(Continued)

Million Deutsche marks

	1974					1975				
	Total General Government	Central Government	State or Provincial Government	Local Government	Social Security Funds	Total General Government	Central Government	State or Provincial Government	Local Government	Social Security Funds
3 Subsidies	14800	14780	...	...	20	15230	15180	...	...	50
4 Other current transfers paid	149640	75660	...	...	94240	184840	100340	...	...	111850
a Casualty insurance premiums, net	2050	2050	...	...	-	2260	2260	...	...	-
b Transfers to other government subsectors	...	20260	...	...	...	...	27350	...	...	...
c Transfers to households	132040	39240	...	...	92800	164380	54170	...	...	110210
Social security benefits	92270	-	...	...	92270	109650	-	...	...	109650
Social assistance grants	20910	20910	...	...	...	34200	34200	...	...	...
Unfunded employee welfare benefits	18860	18330	...	...	530	20530	19970	...	...	560
d Transfers to private non-profit institutions serving households	4140	4140	...	...	-	4640	4640	...	...	-
e Transfers to the rest of the world	11410	9970	...	...	1440	13560	11920	...	...	1640
Net saving [a]	39170	34710	...	...	4460	-7800	-3860	...	...	-3940
Total Current Disbursements and Net Saving	409830	276460	...	...	153630	421790	277080	...	...	172060

	1976					1977				
	Total General Government	Central Government	State or Provincial Government	Local Government	Social Security Funds	Total General Government	Central Government	State or Provincial Government	Local Government	Social Security Funds

Receipts

1 Property and entrepreneurial income	10150	5380	...	...	4770	10270	5790	...	...	4480
2 Taxes, fees and contributions	443410	286550	...	...	156860	487140	318730	...	...	168410
a Indirect taxes	138170	138170	...	...	-	149050	149050	...	...	-
b Direct taxes	143830	143830	...	...	-	164650	164650	...	...	-
Income	136880	136880	...	...	-	156610	156610	...	...	-
Other	6950	6950	...	...	-	8040	8040	...	...	-
c Social security contributions	156860	-	...	...	156860	168410	-	...	...	168410
d Fees, fines and penalties	4550	4550	...	...	-	5030	5030	...	...	-
3 Other current transfers received	21140	19750	...	...	29700	24670	23140	...	...	29410
a Casualty insurance claims	1080	170	...	...	910	1180	160	...	...	1020
b Transfers from other government subsectors	...	...	...	...	28310	...	...	...	...	27880
c Transfers from abroad	3950	3950	...	...	...	6280	6280	...	...	...
d Other transfers, except imputed	-	-	...	...	...	-	-	...	...	...
e Imputed unfunded employee welfare contributions	16110	15630	...	...	480	17210	16700	...	...	510
Total Current Receipts	474700	311680	...	...	191330	522080	347660	...	...	202300

Disbursements

1 General government final consumption expenditures	227190	158080	...	...	69110	239380	166890	...	...	72490
a Compensation of employees	124980	118150	...	...	6830	133380	126220	...	...	7160
b Consumption of fixed capital	6240	6090	...	...	150	6800	6630	...	...	170
c Goods and services purchased, net	95960	33840	...	...	62120	99210	34060	...	...	65150
Purchases	126240	64100	...	...	62140	131350	66190	...	...	65160
Less: Sales	30280	30260	...	...	20	32140	32130	...	...	10
d Less: Own account production of fixed assets	190	190	...	...	-	220	220	...	...	-
e Indirect taxes paid, net	200	190	...	...	10	210	200	...	...	10
2 Property income paid	17500	17500	...	...	-	20470	20470	...	...	-
a Interest	17500	17500	...	...	-	20470	20470	...	...	-
b Net land rent and royalties	...	...	...	...	...	...	...	...	...	...

Germany, Fed. Rep. of

3.12 General Government Income and Outlay Account: Total and Subsectors
(Continued)

Million Deutsche marks

	1976					1977				
	Total General Government	Central Government	State or Provincial Government	Local Government	Social Security Funds	Total General Government	Central Government	State or Provincial Government	Local Government	Social Security Funds
3 Subsidies	16640	16600	...	...	40	19230	19140	...	...	90
4 Other current transfers paid	198690	104440	...	...	122560	215000	109330	...	...	133550
a Casualty insurance premiums, net	2490	2490	...	...	-	2860	2860	...	...	-
b Transfers to other government subsectors	...	28310	...	...	...	...	27880	...	...	...
c Transfers to households	176170	55810	...	...	120360	188890	57930	...	...	130960
Social security benefits	119730	-	...	...	119730	130320	-	...	...	130320
Social assistance grants	34760	34760	...	...	-	35650	35650	...	...	-
Unfunded employee welfare benefits	21680	21050	...	...	630	22920	22280	...	...	640
d Transfers to private non-profit institutions serving households	5070	5070	...	...	...	5610	5610	...	...	...
e Transfers to the rest of the world	14960	12760	...	...	2200	17640	15050	...	...	2590
Net saving [a]	14680	15060	...	...	-380	28000	31830	...	...	-3830
Total Current Disbursements and Net Saving	474700	311680	...	...	191330	522080	347660	...	...	202300

	1978					1979				
	Total General Government	Central Government	State or Provincial Government	Local Government	Social Security Funds	Total General Government	Central Government	State or Provincial Government	Local Government	Social Security Funds

Receipts

1 Property and entrepreneurial income	11850	7900	...	...	3950	13690	9750	...	...	3940
2 Taxes, fees and contributions	517070	336920	...	...	180150	555220	361290	...	...	193930
a Indirect taxes	163850	163850	...	...	-	179770	179770	...	...	-
b Direct taxes	167490	167490	...	...	-	175510	175510	...	...	-
Income	159830	159830	...	...	-	167260	167260	...	...	-
Other	7660	7660	...	...	-	8250	8250	...	...	-
c Social security contributions	180150	-	...	...	180150	193930	-	...	...	193930
d Fees, fines and penalties	5580	5580	...	...	-	6010	6010	...	...	...
3 Other current transfers received	27910	26330	...	...	33180	28900	27210	...	...	34140
a Casualty insurance claims	1210	180	...	...	1030	1330	200	...	...	1130
b Transfers from other government subsectors	...	...	...	...	31600	...	...	...	...	32450
c Transfers from abroad	8250	8250	...	...	-	7970	7970	...	...	-
d Other transfers, except imputed	-	-	...	...	-	...	...	...	...	-
e Imputed unfunded employee welfare contributions	18450	17900	...	...	550	19600	19040	...	...	560
Total Current Receipts	556830	371150	...	...	217280	597810	398250	...	...	232010

Disbursements

1 General government final consumption expenditures	257130	179510	...	...	77620	278580	194890	...	...	83690
a Compensation of employees	141840	134310	...	...	7530	151930	143840	...	...	8090
b Consumption of fixed capital	7460	7270	...	...	190	8270	8050	...	...	220
c Goods and services purchased, net	107830	37940	...	...	69890	118410	43040	...	...	75370
Purchases	142700	72800	...	...	69900	155570	80200	...	...	75370
Less: Sales	34870	34860	...	...	10	37160	37160	...	...	-
d Less: Own account production of fixed assets	220	220	...	...	-	260	260	...	...	-
e Indirect taxes paid, net	220	210	...	...	10	230	220	...	...	10
2 Property income paid	21520	21520	...	...	-	24210	24210	...	...	-
a Interest	21520	21520	...	...	-	24210	24210	...	...	-
b Net land rent and royalties	...	...	...	...	...	...	...	...	...	...

Germany, Fed. Rep. of

3.12 General Government Income and Outlay Account: Total and Subsectors
(Continued)

Million Deutsche marks

		1978				1979			
	Total General Government	Central Government	State or Provincial Government	Local Government	Social Security Funds	Total General Government	Central Government	State or Provincial Government	Local Government	Social Security Funds
3 Subsidies	23840	23750	...	...	90	24770	24620	...	...	150
4 Other current transfers paid	228360	118460	...	...	141500	242790	126370	...	...	148870
a Casualty insurance premiums, net	3060	3060	...	...	-	3420	3420	...	...	-
b Transfers to other government subsectors	...	31600	...	...	...	...	32450	...	...	...
c Transfers to households	199950	61290	...	...	138660	211550	65560	...	...	145990
Social security benefits	137990	-	...	...	137990	145310	-	...	...	145310
Social assistance grants	37800	37800	...	...	-	40760	40760	...	...	-
Unfunded employee welfare benefits	24160	23490	...	...	670	25480	24800	...	...	680
d Transfers to private non-profit institutions serving households	6380	6380	...	...	-	7170	7170	...	...	-
e Transfers to the rest of the world	18970	16130	...	...	2840	20650	17770	...	...	2880
Net saving a	25980	27910	...	...	-1930	27460	28160	...	...	-700
Total Current Disbursements and Net Saving	556830	371150	...	...	217280	597810	398250	...	...	232010

		1980			
	Total General Government	Central Government	State or Provincial Government	Local Government	Social Security Funds

Receipts

1 Property and entrepreneurial income	14340	10270	...	...	4070
2 Taxes, fees and contributions	593450	384020	...	...	209430
a Indirect taxes	189930	189930	...	...	-
b Direct taxes	187750	187750	...	...	-
Income	179970	179970	...	...	-
Other	7780	7780	...	...	-
c Social security contributions	209430	-	...	...	209430
d Fees, fines and penalties	6340	6340	...	...	-
3 Other current transfers received	30070	28410	...	...	38990
a Casualty insurance claims	1270	220	...	...	1050
b Transfers from other government subsectors	...	...	...	...	37330
c Transfers from abroad	7670	7670	...	...	...
d Other transfers, except imputed	-	-	...	...	-
e Imputed unfunded employee welfare contributions	21130	20520	...	...	610
Total Current Receipts	637860	422700	...	...	252490

Disbursements

1 General government final consumption expenditures	303520	212280	...	...	91240
a Compensation of employees	164130	155620	...	...	8510
b Consumption of fixed capital	9340	9100	...	...	240
c Goods and services purchased, net	130100	47620	...	...	82480
Purchases	170400	87920	...	...	82480
Less: Sales	40300	40300	...	...	-
d Less: Own account production of fixed assets	300	300	...	...	-
e Indirect taxes paid, net	250	240	...	...	10
2 Property income paid	28730	28730	...	...	-
a Interest	28730	28730	...	...	-
b Net land rent and royalties	...	...	...	...	...

Germany, Fed. Rep. of

3.12 General Government Income and Outlay Account: Total and Subsectors
(Continued)

Million Deutsche marks

		1980				
		Total General Government	Central Government	State or Provincial Government	Local Government	Social Security Funds
3	Subsidies	23680	23420	...	...	260
4	Other current transfers paid	256960	135890	...	...	158400
	a Casualty insurance premiums, net	3630	3630	...	...	-
	b Transfers to other government subsectors	...	37330	...	...	-
	c Transfers to households	224350	68980	...	...	155370
	Social security benefits	154660	-	...	...	154660
	Social assistance grants	42450	42450	...	...	-
	Unfunded employee welfare benefits	27240	26530	...	...	710
	d Transfers to private non-profit institutions serving households	7890	7890	...	...	-
	e Transfers to the rest of the world	21090	18060	...	...	3030
	Net saving [a]	24970	22380	...	...	2590
	Total Current Disbursements and Net Saving	637860	422700	...	...	252490

a) Columns 'State or provincial government' and 'Local government' are included in column 'Central government'.

3.13 General Government Capital Accumulation Account: Total and Subsectors

Million Deutsche marks

		1970					1971				
		Total General Government	Central Government	State or Provincial Government	Local Government	Social Security Funds	Total General Government	Central Government	State or Provincial Government	Local Government	Social Security Funds
					Finance of Gross Accumulation						
1	Gross saving	43010	35590	...	...	7420	45070	37310	...	...	7760
	a Consumption of fixed capital	3250	3150	...	...	100	3740	3630	...	...	110
	b Net saving	39760	32440	...	...	7320	41330	33680	...	...	7650
2	Capital transfers received	2470	2470	...	...	-	2720	2720	...	...	-
	a From other government subsectors	...	...	...	...	...	...	...	...	...	...
	b From other resident sectors	2470	2470	...	...	-	2720	2720	...	...	-
	c From rest of the world	...	...	...	...	...	...	...	...	...	...
	Finance of Gross Accumulation [a]	45480	38060	...	...	7420	47790	40030	...	...	7760
					Gross Accumulation						
1	Gross capital formation	29480	29310	...	...	170	31910	31660	...	...	250
	a Increase in stocks	200	200	...	...	-	200	200	...	...	-
	b Gross fixed capital formation	29280	29110	...	...	170	31710	31460	...	...	250
	Own account construction	90	90	...	...	-	120	120	...	...	...
	Other	29190	29020	...	...	170	31590	31340	...	...	250
2	Purchases of land, net	1380	1380	...	...	-	1640	1640	...	...	-
3	Purchases of intangible assets, net	...	...	...	...	...	...	...	...	...	...
4	Capital transfers paid	12430	12390	...	...	40	15390	15340	...	...	50
	a To other government subsectors	-	-	...	...	-	-	-	...	...	-
	b To other resident sectors	11950	11910	...	...	40	14930	14880	...	...	50
	c To rest of the world	480	480	...	...	-	460	460	...	...	-
	Net lending [b]	2190	-5020	...	...	7210	-1150	-8610	...	...	7460
	Gross Accumulation [a]	45480	38060	...	...	7420	47790	40030	...	...	7760
		1972					1973				
		Total General Government	Central Government	State or Provincial Government	Local Government	Social Security Funds	Total General Government	Central Government	State or Provincial Government	Local Government	Social Security Funds
					Finance of Gross Accumulation						
1	Gross saving	43160	34060	...	...	9100	60730	46760	...	...	13970
	a Consumption of fixed capital	4150	4030	...	...	120	4640	4510	...	...	130
	b Net saving	39010	30030	...	...	8980	56090	42250	...	...	13840
2	Capital transfers received	4040	3080	...	...	960	4310	3300	...	...	1010

Germany, Fed. Rep. of

3.13 General Government Capital Accumulation Account: Total and Subsectors
(Continued)

Million Deutsche marks

	1972 Total General Government	1972 Central Government	1972 State or Provincial Government	1972 Local Government	1972 Social Security Funds	1973 Total General Government	1973 Central Government	1973 State or Provincial Government	1973 Local Government	1973 Social Security Funds
a From other government subsectors	...	...	...	...	...	...	...	...	...	...
b From other resident sectors	4040	3080	...	...	960	4310	3300	...	...	1010
c From rest of the world	...	...	...	...	...	...	...	...	...	...
Finance of Gross Accumulation [a]	47200	37140	...	...	10060	65040	50060	...	...	14980
Gross Accumulation										
1 Gross capital formation	32080	31800	...	...	280	33200	32810	...	...	390
a Increase in stocks	-	-	...	...	-	-	-	...	...	-
b Gross fixed capital formation	32080	31800	...	...	280	33200	32810	...	...	390
Own account construction	130	130	...	...	-	120	120	...	...	-
Other	31950	31670	...	...	280	33080	32690	...	...	390
2 Purchases of land, net	1720	1720	...	...	-	1950	1950	...	...	-
3 Purchases of intangible assets, net	...	...	...	...	...	...	...	...	...	...
4 Capital transfers paid	17420	17350	...	...	70	18960	18830	...	...	130
a To other government subsectors	-	-	...	...	-	-	-	...	...	-
b To other resident sectors	16990	16920	...	...	70	18520	18390	...	...	130
c To rest of the world	430	430	...	...	-	440	440	...	...	-
Net lending [b]	-4020	-13730	...	...	9710	10930	-3530	...	...	14460
Gross Accumulation [a]	47200	37140	...	...	10060	65040	50060	...	...	14980

	1974 Total General Government	1974 Central Government	1974 State or Provincial Government	1974 Local Government	1974 Social Security Funds	1975 Total General Government	1975 Central Government	1975 State or Provincial Government	1975 Local Government	1975 Social Security Funds
Finance of Gross Accumulation										
1 Gross saving	44400	39810	...	...	4590	-2060	1740	...	...	-3800
a Consumption of fixed capital	5230	5100	...	...	130	5740	5600	...	...	140
b Net saving	39170	34710	...	...	4460	-7800	-3860	...	...	-3940
2 Capital transfers received	4960	3780	...	...	1180	6030	4090	...	...	1940
a From other government subsectors	...	...	...	...	...	...	...	...	...	...
b From other resident sectors	4960	3780	...	...	1180	6030	4090	...	...	1940
c From rest of the world	...	...	...	...	...	...	...	...	...	...
Finance of Gross Accumulation [a]	49360	43590	...	...	5770	3970	5830	...	...	-1860
Gross Accumulation										
1 Gross capital formation	38200	37610	...	...	590	38560	37960	...	...	600
a Increase in stocks	100	100	...	...	-	600	600	...	...	-
b Gross fixed capital formation	38100	37510	...	...	590	37960	37360	...	...	600
Own account construction	140	140	...	...	-	170	170	...	...	-
Other	37960	37370	...	...	590	37790	37190	...	...	600
2 Purchases of land, net	2450	2400	...	...	50	2360	2310	...	...	50
3 Purchases of intangible assets, net	...	...	...	...	...	...	...	...	...	...
4 Capital transfers paid	22270	22070	...	...	200	22840	22620	...	...	220
a To other government subsectors	-	-	...	...	-	-	-	...	...	-
b To other resident sectors	21770	21570	...	...	200	22270	22050	...	...	220
c To rest of the world	500	500	...	...	-	570	570	...	...	-
Net lending [b]	-13560	-18490	...	...	4930	-59790	-57060	...	...	-2730
Gross Accumulation [a]	49360	43590	...	...	5770	3970	5830	...	...	-1860

	1976 Total General Government	1976 Central Government	1976 State or Provincial Government	1976 Local Government	1976 Social Security Funds	1977 Total General Government	1977 Central Government	1977 State or Provincial Government	1977 Local Government	1977 Social Security Funds
Finance of Gross Accumulation										
1 Gross saving	20920	21150	...	...	-230	34800	38460	...	...	-3660
a Consumption of fixed capital	6240	6090	...	...	150	6800	6630	...	...	170
b Net saving	14680	15060	...	...	-380	28000	31830	...	...	-3830
2 Capital transfers received	7550	4990	...	...	2560	6210	4760	...	...	1560

Germany, Fed. Rep. of

3.13 General Government Capital Accumulation Account: Total and Subsectors
(Continued)

Million Deutsche marks

	1976					1977				
	Total General Government	Central Government	State or Provincial Government	Local Government	Social Security Funds	Total General Government	Central Government	State or Provincial Government	Local Government	Social Security Funds
a From other government subsectors	...	...	...	...	-	-	110	...	...	-
b From other resident sectors	7500	4940	...	...	2560	6090	4530	...	...	1560
c From rest of the world	50	50	...	...	-	120	120	...	...	-
Finance of Gross Accumulation a	28470	26140	...	...	2330	41010	43220	...	...	-2100
Gross Accumulation										
1 Gross capital formation	38040	37500	...	...	540	37750	37190	...	...	560
a Increase in stocks	200	200	...	...	-	300	300	...	...	-
b Gross fixed capital formation	37840	37300	...	...	540	37450	36890	...	...	560
Own account construction	190	190	...	...	-	220	220	...	...	-
Other	37650	37110	...	...	540	37230	36670	...	...	560
2 Purchases of land, net	2290	2280	...	...	10	2110	2070	...	...	40
3 Purchases of intangible assets, net	...	...	...	...	...	...	...	...	...	...
4 Capital transfers paid	28290	27600	...	...	690	30370	29450	...	...	1030
a To other government subsectors	-		...	...	-		-	...	...	110
b To other resident sectors	27150	26900	...	...	250	29250	28760	...	...	490
c To rest of the world	1140	700	...	...	440	1120	690	...	...	430
Net lending b	-40150	-41240	...	...	1090	-29220	-25490	...	...	-3730
Gross Accumulation a	28470	26140	...	...	2330	41010	43220	...	...	-2100

	1978					1979				
	Total General Government	Central Government	State or Provincial Government	Local Government	Social Security Funds	Total General Government	Central Government	State or Provincial Government	Local Government	Social Security Funds
Finance of Gross Accumulation										
1 Gross saving	33440	35180	...	...	-1740	35730	36210	...	...	-480
a Consumption of fixed capital	7460	7270	...	...	190	8270	8050	...	...	220
b Net saving	25980	27910	...	...	-1930	27460	28160	...	...	-700
2 Capital transfers received	5840	4820	...	...	1140	6010	5100	...	...	1030
a From other government subsectors	-	120	...	...	-		120	...	...	-
b From other resident sectors	5780	4640	...	...	1140	5950	4920	...	...	1030
c From rest of the world	60	60	...	...	-	60	60	...	...	-
Finance of Gross Accumulation a	39280	40000	...	...	-600	41740	41310	...	...	550
Gross Accumulation										
1 Gross capital formation	41830	41380	...	...	450	48380	47960	...	...	420
a Increase in stocks	200	200	...	...	-			...	...	-
b Gross fixed capital formation	41630	41180	...	...	450	48380	47960	...	...	420
Own account construction	220	220	...	...	-	260	260	...	...	-
Other	41410	40960	...	...	450	48120	47700	...	...	420
2 Purchases of land, net	2310	2270	...	...	40	2540	2440	...	...	100
3 Purchases of intangible assets, net	...	...	...	...	...	...	...	...	...	...
4 Capital transfers paid	29600	28470	...	...	1250	31770	30590	...	...	1300
a To other government subsectors	-	-	...	...	120	-	-	...	...	120
b To other resident sectors	28570	27870	...	...	700	29890	28710	...	...	1180
c To rest of the world	1030	600	...	...	430	1880	1880	...	...	-
Net lending b	-34460	-32120	...	...	-2340	-40950	-39680	...	...	-1270
Gross Accumulation a	39280	40000	...	...	-600	41740	41310	...	...	550

	1980				
	Total General Government	Central Government	State or Provincial Government	Local Government	Social Security Funds
Finance of Gross Accumulation					
1 Gross saving	34310	31480	...	...	2830
a Consumption of fixed capital	9340	9100	...	...	240
b Net saving	24970	22380	...	...	2590
2 Capital transfers received	7090	5660	...	...	1550

Germany, Fed. Rep. of

3.13 General Government Capital Accumulation Account: Total and Subsectors
(Continued)

Million Deutsche marks

	\multicolumn{5}{c	}{1980}
	Total General Government	Central Government	State or Provincial Government	Local Government	Social Security Funds
a From other government subsectors	-	120	...	...	-
b From other resident sectors	7050	5500	...	...	1550
c From rest of the world	40	40	...	...	-
Finance of Gross Accumulation [a]	41400	37140	...	...	4380
\multicolumn{6}{c	}{Gross Accumulation}
1 Gross capital formation	55950	55550	...	...	400
a Increase in stocks	500	500	...	...	-
b Gross fixed capital formation	55450	55050	...	...	400
Own account construction	300	300	...	...	-
Other	55150	54750	...	...	400
2 Purchases of land, net	2680	2600	...	...	80
3 Purchases of intangible assets, net	...	...	...	...	...
4 Capital transfers paid	34200	33080	...	...	1240
a To other government subsectors	-	-	...	...	120
b To other resident sectors	30710	29590	...	...	1120
c To rest of the world	3490	3490	...	...	-
Net lending [b]	-51430	-54090	...	...	2660
Gross Accumulation [a]	41400	37140	...	...	4380

a) Columns 'State or provincial government' and 'Local government' are included in column 'Central government'.   b) Net lending of the Capital Accumulation Account and the Capital Finance Account have not been reconciled and are different due to different statistical sources.

3.14 General Government Capital Finance Account, Total and Subsectors

Million Deutsche marks

	\multicolumn{5}{c	}{1970}	\multicolumn{5}{c	}{1971}
	Total General Government	Central Government	State or Provincial Government	Local Government	Social Security Funds	Total General Government	Central Government	State or Provincial Government	Local Government	Social Security Funds
\multicolumn{11}{c	}{Acquisition of Financial Assets}
1 Gold and SDRs	-	-	...	...	-	-	-	...	...	-
2 Currency and transferable deposits	3790	3780	...	...	10	4450	4350	...	...	100
3 Other deposits	3800	-140	...	...	3950	4520	1170	...	...	3350
4 Bills and bonds, short term	1150	40	...	...	1100	-540	-70	...	...	-470
5 Bonds, long term	-130	-350	...	...	220	1230	90	...	...	1140
6 Corporate equity securities	230	230	...	...	...	640	640	...	...	...
7 Short-term loans, n.e.c.	300	-320	...	...	620	-640	-1300	...	...	660
8 Long-term loans, n.e.c.	1670	1010	...	...	1040	2550	1970	...	...	2600
9 Other receivables	-	-	...	...	-	-	-	...	...	-
10 Other assets	...	...	...	...	...	...	...	...	...	...
Total Acquisition of Financial Assets [a]	10800	4240	...	...	6940	12200	6850	...	...	7380
\multicolumn{11}{c	}{Incurrence of Liabilities}
1 Currency and transferable deposits	-	-	...	...	-	-	-	...	...	-
2 Other deposits	-	-	...	...	-	-	-	...	...	-
3 Bills and bonds, short term	-660	-660	...	...	-	-	-	...	...	-
4 Bonds, long term	740	740	...	...	-	1910	1910	...	...	-
5 Short-term loans, n.e.c.	540	560	...	...	-20	1350	1310	...	...	40
6 Long-term loans, n.e.c.	7980	8350	...	...	...	9990	11990	...	...	30
7 Other payables	-	-	...	...	-	-	-	...	...	-
8 Other liabilities	-	-	...	...	-	-	-	...	...	-
Total Incurrence of Liabilities	8600	9000	...	...	-20	13250	15200	...	...	80
Net Lending [b]	2200	-4760	...	...	6960	-1050	-8350	...	...	7300
Incurrence of Liabilities and Net Worth [a]	10800	4240	...	...	6940	12200	6850	...	...	7380

Germany, Fed. Rep. of

3.14 General Government Capital Finance Account, Total and Subsectors

Million Deutsche marks

	1972 Total General Government	1972 Central Government	1972 State or Provincial Government	1972 Local Government	1972 Social Security Funds	1973 Total General Government	1973 Central Government	1973 State or Provincial Government	1973 Local Government	1973 Social Security Funds
Acquisition of Financial Assets										
1 Gold and SDRs	-	-	...	...	-	-	-	...	...	-
2 Currency and transferable deposits	-2120	-2690	...	...	570	6750	6080	...	...	660
3 Other deposits	8330	4540	...	...	3780	6710	5010	...	...	1700
4 Bills and bonds, short term	-500	-50	...	...	-450	4570	80	...	...	4490
5 Bonds, long term	160	-300	...	...	460	-210	-100	...	...	-110
6 Corporate equity securities	370	370	...	...	...	160	160	...	...	...
7 Short-term loans, n.e.c.	1050	180	...	...	870	1250	260	...	...	990
8 Long-term loans, n.e.c.	3650	1240	...	...	4370	7720	5450	...	...	6200
9 Other receivables	-	-	...	...	-	-	-	...	...	-
10 Other assets	...	...	...	...	...	...	...	...	...	...
Total Acquisition of Financial Assets [a]	10920	3290	...	...	9600	26940	16940	...	...	13930
Incurrence of Liabilities										
1 Currency and transferable deposits	-	-	...	...	-	-	-	...	...	-
2 Other deposits	-	-	...	...	-	-	-	...	...	-
3 Bills and bonds, short term	-320	-320	...	...	...	-370	-370	...	...	...
4 Bonds, long term	4560	4560	...	...	...	2130	2130	...	...	...
5 Short-term loans, n.e.c.	-540	-590	...	...	50	3310	3400	...	...	-90
6 Long-term loans, n.e.c.	11270	13200	...	...	20	10940	14910	...	...	-40
7 Other payables	-	-	...	...	-	-	-	...	...	-
8 Other liabilities	...	...	...	...	...	...	...	...	...	...
Total Incurrence of Liabilities	14970	16860	...	...	80	16000	20060	...	...	-130
Net Lending [b]	-4050	-13570	...	...	9520	10940	-3120	...	...	14060
Incurrence of Liabilities and Net Worth [a]	10920	3290	...	...	9600	26940	16940	...	...	13930

	1974 Total General Government	1974 Central Government	1974 State or Provincial Government	1974 Local Government	1974 Social Security Funds	1975 Total General Government	1975 Central Government	1975 State or Provincial Government	1975 Local Government	1975 Social Security Funds
Acquisition of Financial Assets										
1 Gold and SDRs	-	-	...	...	-	-	-	...	...	-
2 Currency and transferable deposits	-60	-240	...	...	180	570	520	...	...	50
3 Other deposits	2700	970	...	...	1730	-350	2930	...	...	-3280
4 Bills and bonds, short term	-1290	-70	...	...	-1220	-2140	-10	...	...	-2120
5 Bonds, long term	-820	-500	...	...	-320	10	-90	...	...	100
6 Corporate equity securities	510	510	...	...	...	600	600	...	...	...
7 Short-term loans, n.e.c.	1550	490	...	...	1060	80	-60	...	...	140
8 Long-term loans, n.e.c.	7760	5880	...	...	3400	6460	8860	...	...	4790
9 Other receivables	-	-	...	...	-	-	-	...	...	-
10 Other assets	-	-	...	...	-	-	-	...	...	-
Total Acquisition of Financial Assets [a]	10360	7040	...	...	4830	5230	12740	...	...	-320
Incurrence of Liabilities										
1 Currency and transferable deposits	-	-	...	...	-	-	-	...	...	-
2 Other deposits	-	-	...	...	-	-	-	...	...	-
3 Bills and bonds, short term	4270	4270	...	...	...	6950	6950	...	...	...
4 Bonds, long term	3470	3470	...	...	...	13700	13700	...	...	...
5 Short-term loans, n.e.c.	-1210	-1230	...	...	20	2240	2180	...	...	60
6 Long-term loans, n.e.c.	17280	18800	...	...	...	41840	46590	...	...	2450
7 Other payables	-	-	...	...	-	-	-	...	...	-
8 Other liabilities	-	-	...	...	-	-	-	...	...	-
Total Incurrence of Liabilities	23820	25310	...	...	20	64730	69410	...	...	2510
Net Lending [b]	-13460	-18270	...	...	4810	-59500	-56670	...	...	-2830
Incurrence of Liabilities and Net Worth [a]	10360	7040	...	...	4830	5230	12740	...	...	-320

Germany, Fed. Rep. of

3.14 General Government Capital Finance Account, Total and Subsectors

Million Deutsche marks

	1976					1977				
	Total General Government	Central Government	State or Provincial Government	Local Government	Social Security Funds	Total General Government	Central Government	State or Provincial Government	Local Government	Social Security Funds

Acquisition of Financial Assets

1 Gold and SDRs	-	-	...	...	-	-	-	...	...	-
2 Currency and transferable deposits	-8410	-9110	...	...	700	-630	-470	...	...	-160
3 Other deposits	8090	5850	...	...	2240	3990	4370	...	...	-380
4 Bills and bonds, short term	-430	-20	...	...	-410	-1570	30	...	...	-1600
5 Bonds, long term	930	-20	...	...	950	100	-240	...	...	340
6 Corporate equity securities	300	300	...	...	...	490	490	...	...	...
7 Short-term loans, n.e.c.	340	160	...	...	180	170	50	...	...	120
8 Long-term loans, n.e.c.	5570	3240	...	...	-2700	3480	3860	...	...	-2480
9 Other receivables	-	-	...	...	-	-	-	...	...	-
10 Other assets	-	-	...	...	-	-	-	...	...	-
Total Acquisition of Financial Assets [a]	6390	400	...	...	950	6020	8080	...	...	-4160

Incurrence of Liabilities

1 Currency and transferable deposits	-	-	...	...	-	-	-	...	...	-
2 Other deposits	-	-	...	...	-	-	-	...	...	-
3 Bills and bonds, short term	-3860	-3860	...	...	...	130	130	...	...	...
4 Bonds, long term	15540	15540	...	...	...	19950	19950	...	...	...
5 Short-term loans, n.e.c.	490	560	...	...	-70	-110	-140	...	...	30
6 Long-term loans, n.e.c.	34590	29520	...	...	30	16610	14510	...	...	-
7 Other payables	-	-	...	...	-	-	-	...	...	-
8 Other liabilities	-	-	...	...	-	-	-	...	...	-
Total Incurrence of Liabilities	46770	41770	...	...	-40	36580	34450	...	...	30
Net Lending [b]	-40380	-41370	...	...	990	-30560	-26370	...	...	-4190
Incurrence of Liabilities and Net Worth [a]	6390	400	...	...	950	6020	8080	...	...	-4160

	1978					1979				
	Total General Government	Central Government	State or Provincial Government	Local Government	Social Security Funds	Total General Government	Central Government	State or Provincial Government	Local Government	Social Security Funds

Acquisition of Financial Assets

1 Gold and SDRs	-	-	...	...	...	...	...	...	...	...
2 Currency and transferable deposits	4150	3070	...	...	1080	110	-1010	...	...	1120
3 Other deposits	3130	5280	...	...	-2150	2130	4720	...	...	-2590
4 Bills and bonds, short term	-30	-30	...	...	-	-70	-70	...	...	-
5 Bonds, long term	1430	500	...	...	930	1030	620	...	...	410
6 Corporate equity securities	860	860	...	...	...	1140	1140	...	...	...
7 Short-term loans, n.e.c.	830	-140	...	...	970	870	-20	...	...	890
8 Long-term loans, n.e.c.	-450	630	...	...	-3270	-3020	-2000	...	...	-1020
9 Other receivables	-	-	...	...	-	-	-	...	...	-
10 Other assets	-	-	...	...	-	-	-	...	...	-
Total Acquisition of Financial Assets [a]	9910	10170	...	...	-2450	2210	3390	...	...	-1180

Incurrence of Liabilities

1 Currency and transferable deposits	-	-	...	...	-	-	-	...	...	-
2 Other deposits	-	-	...	...	-	-	-	...	...	-
3 Bills and bonds, short term	20	20	...	...	...	-450	-450	...	...	...
4 Bonds, long term	11650	11650	...	...	...	7600	7600	...	...	...
5 Short-term loans, n.e.c.	-750	-830	...	...	90	-420	-360	...	...	-60
6 Long-term loans, n.e.c.	34260	32100	...	...	-20	35330	35330	...	...	-
7 Other payables	-	-	...	...	-	-	-	...	...	-
8 Other liabilities	-	-	...	...	-	-	-	...	...	-
Total Incurrence of Liabilities	45180	42930	...	...	60	42070	42120	...	...	-50
Net Lending [b]	-35270	-32760	...	...	-2510	-39860	-38730	...	...	-1130
Incurrence of Liabilities and Net Worth [a]	9910	10170	...	...	-2450	2210	3390	...	...	-1180

Germany, Fed. Rep. of

3.14 General Government Capital Finance Account, Total and Subsectors

Million Deutsche marks

	1980				
	Total General Government	Central Government	State or Provincial Government	Local Government	Social Security Funds
Acquisition of Financial Assets					
1 Gold and SDRs	-	-	...	...	-
2 Currency and transferable deposits	-3230	-2900	...	...	-330
3 Other deposits	9740	6640	...	...	3100
4 Bills and bonds, short term	10	10	...	...	-
5 Bonds, long term	-20	100	...	...	-120
6 Corporate equity securities	1110	1110	...	...	-
7 Short-term loans, n.e.c.	770	50	...	...	720
8 Long-term loans, n.e.c.	-3480	-3370	...	...	-110
9 Other receivables	-	-	...	...	-
10 Other assets	-	-	...	...	-
Total Acquisition of Financial Assets [a]	4900	1650	...	...	3250
Incurrence of Liabilities					
1 Currency and transferable deposits	-	-	...	...	-
2 Other deposits	-	-	...	...	-
3 Bills and bonds, short term	-2160	-2160	...	...	-
4 Bonds, long term	2140	2140	...	...	-
5 Short-term loans, n.e.c.	5240	5160	...	...	80
6 Long-term loans, n.e.c.	49490	49480	...	...	10
7 Other payables	-	-	...	...	-
8 Other liabilities	-	-	...	...	-
Total Incurrence of Liabilities	54710	54620	...	...	90
Net Lending [b]	-49810	-52970	...	...	3160
Incurrence of Liabilities and Net Worth [a]	4900	1650	...	...	3250

a) Columns 'State or provincial government' and 'Local government' are included in column 'Central government'.
b) Net lending of the Capital Accumulation Account and the Capital Finance Account have not been reconciled and are different due to different statistical sources.

3.21 Corporate and Quasi-Corporate Enterprise Production Account: Total and Sectors

Million Deutsche marks

	1970				1971				1972			
	Corporate and Quasi-Corporate Enterprises			ADDENDUM: Total, including Unincorporated	Corporate and Quasi-Corporate Enterprises			ADDENDUM: Total, including Unincorporated	Corporate and Quasi-Corporate Enterprises			ADDENDUM: Total, including Unincorporated
	TOTAL	Non-Financial	Financial		TOTAL	Non-Financial	Financial		TOTAL	Non-Financial	Financial	
Gross Output												
1 Output for sale	...	...	...	...	...	...	...	...	...	...	...	...
2 Imputed bank service charge	15590	-	15590	...	18130	-	18130	...	20790	-	20790	...
3 Own-account capital formation	...	...	...	...	...	...	...	...	...	...	...	...
Gross Output [a]	1680230	1648570	31660	...	1829720	1791320	38400	...	1969400	1925590	43810	...
Gross Input												
Intermediate consumption	1092620	1066590	26030	...	1180930	1149680	31250	...	1261530	1226620	34910	...
1 Imputed banking service charge	15590	-	15590	...	18130	-	18130	...	20790	-	20790	...
2 Other intermediate consumption	...	...	...	...	...	...	...	...	...	...	...	...
Subtotal: Value Added	587610	581980	5630	...	648790	641640	7150	...	707870	698970	8900	...
1 Indirect taxes, net	58820	57210	1610	...	66660	64550	2110	...	73970	71360	2610	...
a Indirect taxed paid	68520	66910	1610	...	76620	74510	2110	...	86220	83610	2610	...
b Less: Subsidies received	9700	9700	-	...	9960	9960	-	...	12250	12250	-	...
2 Consumption of fixed capital	64170	63280	890	...	73640	72610	1030	...	80990	79830	1160	...
3 Compensation of employees	291870	279960	11910	...	325620	311350	14270	...	356420	340160	16260	...
a Paid to residents	291060	279150	11910	...	324540	310270	14270	...	355050	338790	16260	...
b Paid to the rest of the world	810	810	-	...	1080	1080	-	...	1370	1370	...	...
4 Net operating surplus	172750	181530	-8780	...	182870	193130	-10260	...	196490	207620	-11130	...
Gross Input [a]	1680230	1648570	31660	...	1829720	1791320	38400	...	1969400	1925590	43810	...

Germany, Fed. Rep. of

3.21 Corporate and Quasi-Corporate Enterprise Production Account: Total and Sectors

Million Deutsche marks

	1973				1974				1975			
	\multicolumn{3}{c}{Corporate and Quasi-Corporate Enterprises}	ADDENDUM: Total, including Unincorporated	\multicolumn{3}{c}{Corporate and Quasi-Corporate Enterprises}	ADDENDUM: Total, including Unincorporated	\multicolumn{3}{c}{Corporate and Quasi-Corporate Enterprises}	ADDENDUM: Total, including Unincorporated
	TOTAL	Non-Financial	Financial		TOTAL	Non-Financial	Financial		TOTAL	Non-Financial	Financial	
Gross Output												
1 Output for sale	...	...	...	...	...	...	...	...	...	...	...	...
2 Imputed bank service charge	23270	-	23270	...	29650	-	29650	...	32610	-	32610	...
3 Own-account capital formation	...	...	...	...	...	...	...	...	...	...	...	...
Gross Output a	2203180	2153300	49880	...	2433640	2373850	59790	...	2492300	2426570	65730	...
Gross Input												
Intermediate consumption	1420430	1380920	39510	...	1603100	1554220	48880	...	1627570	1574460	53110	...
1 Imputed banking service charge	23270	-	23270	...	29650	-	29650	...	32610	-	32610	...
2 Other intermediate consumption	...	...	...	...	...	...	...	...	...	...	...	...
Subtotal: Value Added	782750	772380	10370	...	830540	819630	10910	...	864730	852110	12620	...
1 Indirect taxes, net	79770	77010	2760	...	80200	76910	3290	...	82950	79000	3950	...
a Indirect taxed paid	94810	92050	2760	...	95220	91930	3290	...	98410	94460	3950	...
b Less: Subsidies received	15040	15040	-	...	15020	15020	-	...	15460	15460	-	...
2 Consumption of fixed capital	89780	88490	1290	...	100550	99030	1520	...	109710	108020	1690	...
3 Compensation of employees	402310	383710	18600	...	436880	415080	21800	...	448740	424800	23940	...
a Paid to residents	400710	382110	18600	...	435090	413290	21800	...	446810	422870	23940	...
b Paid to the rest of the world	1600	1600	...	...	1790	1790	-	...	1930	1930	-	...
4 Net operating surplus	210890	223170	-12280	...	212910	228610	-15700	...	223330	240290	-16960	...
Gross Input a	2203180	2153300	49880	...	2433640	2373850	59790	...	2492300	2426570	65730	...

	1976				1977				1978			
	\multicolumn{3}{c}{Corporate and Quasi-Corporate Enterprises}	ADDENDUM: Total, including Unincorporated	\multicolumn{3}{c}{Corporate and Quasi-Corporate Enterprises}	ADDENDUM: Total, including Unincorporated	\multicolumn{3}{c}{Corporate and Quasi-Corporate Enterprises}	ADDENDUM: Total, including Unincorporated
	TOTAL	Non-Financial	Financial		TOTAL	Non-Financial	Financial		TOTAL	Non-Financial	Financial	
Gross Output												
1 Output for sale	...	...	...	...	...	...	...	...	...	...	...	...
2 Imputed bank service charge	34910	-	34910	...	38280	-	38280	...	41760	-	41760	...
3 Own-account capital formation	...	...	...	...	...	...	...	...	...	...	...	...
Gross Output a	2746880	2675740	71140	...	2906680	2828380	78300	...	3084360	2999840	84520	...
Gross Input												
Intermediate consumption	1806290	1748450	57840	...	1901180	1837070	64110	...	2007360	1937590	69770	...
1 Imputed banking service charge	34910	-	34910	...	38280	-	38280	...	41760	-	41760	...
2 Other intermediate consumption	...	...	...	...	...	...	...	...	...	...	...	...
Subtotal: Value Added	940590	927290	13300	...	1005500	991310	14190	...	1077000	1062250	14750	...
1 Indirect taxes, net	88530	84170	4360	...	94620	89600	5020	...	101140	96180	4960	...
a Indirect taxed paid	105240	100880	4360	...	113940	108920	5020	...	125080	120120	4960	...
b Less: Subsidies received	16710	16710	-	...	19320	19320	-	...	23940	23940	-	...
2 Consumption of fixed capital	117580	115710	1870	...	125640	123590	2050	...	135370	133100	2270	...
3 Compensation of employees	483920	458680	25240	...	517420	490600	26820	...	552500	523910	28590	...
a Paid to residents	481850	456610	25240	...	515200	488380	26820	...	550160	521570	28590	...
b Paid to the rest of the world	2070	2070	-	...	2220	2220	-	...	2340	2340	-	...
4 Net operating surplus	250560	268730	-18170	...	267820	287520	-19700	...	287990	309060	-21070	...
Gross Input a	2746880	2675740	71140	...	2906680	2828380	78300	...	3084360	2999840	84520	...

	1979				1980			
	\multicolumn{3}{c}{Corporate and Quasi-Corporate Enterprises}	ADDENDUM: Total, including Unincorporated	\multicolumn{3}{c}{Corporate and Quasi-Corporate Enterprises}	ADDENDUM: Total, including Unincorporated
	TOTAL	Non-Financial	Financial		TOTAL	Non-Financial	Financial	
Gross Output								
1 Output for sale	...	...	...	...	...	...	...	...
2 Imputed bank service charge	45650	-	45650	...	49760	-	49760	...
3 Own-account capital formation	...	...	...	...	...	...	...	...
Gross Output a	3403380	3312050	91330	...	3613750	...	...	...
Gross Input								
Intermediate consumption	2238070	2161760	76310	...	2376850	...	...	...

Germany, Fed. Rep. of

3.21 Corporate and Quasi-Corporate Enterprise Production Account: Total and Sectors
(Continued)

Million Deutsche marks

	1979				1980			
	\multicolumn{3}{c	}{Corporate and Quasi-Corporate Enterprises}	ADDENDUM: Total, including Unincorporated	\multicolumn{3}{c	}{Corporate and Quasi-Corporate Enterprises}	ADDENDUM: Total, including Unincorporated
	TOTAL	Non-Financial	Financial		TOTAL	Non-Financial	Financial	
1 Imputed banking service charge	45650	-	45650	...	49760	-	49760	...
2 Other intermediate consumption	...	...	...	...	...	...	...	...
Subtotal: Value Added	1165310	1150290	15020	...	1236900	...	...	...
1 Indirect taxes, net	109600	104780	4820	...	112860	...	...	...
a Indirect taxed paid	134440	129620	4820	...	136640	...	...	...
b Less: Subsidies received	24840	24840	-	...	23680	23680	-	...
2 Consumption of fixed capital	147930	145450	2480	...	164130	...	...	...
3 Compensation of employees	595380	564580	30800	...	641780	...	...	...
a Paid to residents	592920	562120	30800	...	...	...	...	...
b Paid to the rest of the world	2460	2460	-	...	2660	2660	-	...
4 Net operating surplus	312400	335480	-23080	...	318030	...	...	...
Gross Input [a]	3403380	3312050	91330	...	3613750	...	...	...

a) Corporate and quasi-corporate enterprises include unincorporated enterprises.

3.22 Corporate and Quasi-Corporate Enterprise Income and Outlay Account: Total and Sectors

Million Deutsche marks

	1970			1971			1972			1973		
	TOTAL	Non-Financial	Financial	TOTAL	Non-Financial	Financial	TOTAL	Non-Financial	Financial	TOTAL	Non-Financial	Financial

Receipts

1 Property and entrepreneurial income received	239340	192250	47090	258390	205760	52630	277650	219600	58050	321580	240750	80830
a Net operating surplus	172750	181530	-8780	182870	193130	-10260	196490	207620	-11130	210890	223170	-12280
b Withdrawals from quasi-corporate enterprises	1650	1400	250	1870	1590	280	1850	1500	350	2200	1820	380
c Interest	58830	3960	54870	66910	5090	61820	73280	5350	67930	101630	9870	91760
d Dividends	6110	5360	750	6740	5950	790	6030	5130	900	6860	5890	970
e Net land rent and royalties	...	...	...	...	...	...	...	...	...	...	...	...
2 Other current transfers received	26300	10560	15740	29410	11270	18140	34240	12930	21310	37730	14590	23140
a Casualty insurance transactions	16640	1830	14810	19250	2220	17030	22760	2710	20050	24590	2840	21750
Claims received	1880	1830	50	2270	2220	50	2780	2710	70	2940	2840	100
Net premiums received by insurance companies	14760	-	14760	16980	-	16980	19980	-	19980	21650	-	21650
b Current transfers received from the rest of the world	220	60	160	250	60	190	290	80	210	290	80	210
c Other transfers received, except imputed	1380	1340	40	1450	1400	50	1600	1550	50	1740	1680	60
d Imputed unfunded employee welfare contributions	8060	7330	730	8460	7590	870	9590	8590	1000	11110	9990	1120
Total Current Receipts [a]	265640	202810	62830	287800	217030	70770	311890	232530	79360	359310	255340	103970

Disbursements

1 Property and entrepreneurial income paid out	224810	184310	40500	246070	200700	45370	256170	206950	49220	296850	226340	70510
a Withdrawals from quasi-corporations	137520	137520	-	148810	148810	-	152850	152850	-	158760	158760	-
b Interest	73070	33490	39580	82450	38470	43980	90430	43010	47420	123850	55240	68610
c Dividends	14220	13300	920	14810	13420	1390	12890	11090	1800	14240	12340	1900
d Net land rent and royalties	...	...	...	...	...	...	...	...	...	...	...	...
2 Direct taxes and other current payments n.e.c. to general government	12720	11440	1280	11790	10130	1660	12220	10130	2090	16000	14020	1980

Germany, Fed. Rep. of

3.22 Corporate and Quasi-Corporate Enterprise Income and Outlay Account: Total and Sectors
(Continued)

Million Deutsche marks

	1970 TOTAL	1970 Non-Financial	1970 Financial	1971 TOTAL	1971 Non-Financial	1971 Financial	1972 TOTAL	1972 Non-Financial	1972 Financial	1973 TOTAL	1973 Non-Financial	1973 Financial
a Direct taxes	12310	11030	1280	11290	9630	1660	11680	9590	2090	15370	13390	1980
b Fines, fees, penalties and other payments n.e.c.	410	410	-	500	500	-	540	540	-	630	630	-
3 Other current transfers paid	23450	8690	14760	27150	10200	16950	30730	10890	19840	33600	12010	21590
a Casualty insurance transactions	14550	2160	12390	16900	2580	14320	20050	3140	16910	21640	3320	18320
Casualty insurance premiums paid, net	2210	2160	50	2630	2580	50	3210	3140	70	3420	3320	100
Claims paid by insurance companies	12340	-	12340	14270	-	14270	16840	-	16840	18220	-	18220
b Transfers to private non-profit institutions	...	...	...	...	...	...	...	...	...	...	...	...
c Transfers to households	8420	6290	2130	9450	7080	2370	10210	7570	2640	11480	8490	2990
Unfunded employee welfare benefits	8420	6290	2130	9450	7080	2370	10210	7570	2640	11480	8490	2990
Social assistance grants and other transfers n.e.c.	...	...	...	...	...	...	...	...	...	...	...	...
d Transfers to the rest of the world	480	240	240	800	540	260	470	180	290	480	200	280
Net saving	4660	-1630	6290	2790	-4000	6790	12770	4560	8210	12860	2970	9890
Total Current Disbursements and Net Saving [a]	265640	202810	62830	287800	217030	70770	311890	232530	79360	359310	255340	103970

	1974 TOTAL	1974 Non-Financial	1974 Financial	1975 TOTAL	1975 Non-Financial	1975 Financial	1976 TOTAL	1976 Non-Financial	1976 Financial	1977 TOTAL	1977 Non-Financial	1977 Financial
Receipts												
1 Property and entrepreneurial income received	346200	250830	95370	347520	255920	91600	387130	288550	98580	418600	310670	107930
a Net operating surplus	212910	228610	-15700	223330	240290	-16960	250560	268730	-18170	267820	287520	-19700
b Withdrawals from quasi-corporate enterprises	2400	2100	300	2310	1970	340	2770	2440	330	2910	2490	420
c Interest	122960	13210	109750	113700	6660	107040	125630	10770	114860	136630	11140	125490
d Dividends	7930	6910	1020	8180	7000	1180	8170	6610	1560	11240	9520	1720
e Net land rent and royalties	...	...	...	...	...	...	...	...	...	...	...	...
2 Other current transfers received	41920	17160	24760	44170	17000	27170	49300	19480	29820	51020	19620	31400
a Casualty insurance transactions	25830	2980	22850	27820	2960	24860	31120	3400	27720	32810	3490	29320
Claims received	3130	2980	150	3110	2960	150	3560	3400	160	3640	3490	150
Net premiums received by insurance companies	22700	-	22700	24710	-	24710	27560	-	27560	29170	-	29170
b Current transfers received from the rest of the world	350	90	260	370	120	250	420	160	260	500	170	330
c Other transfers received, except imputed	1940	1880	60	2120	2050	70	2320	2250	70	2700	2630	70
d Imputed unfunded employee welfare contributions	13800	12210	1590	13860	11870	1990	15440	13670	1770	15010	13330	1680
Total Current Receipts [a]	388120	267990	120130	391690	272920	118770	436430	308030	128400	469620	330290	139330
Disbursements												
1 Property and entrepreneurial income paid out	326390	245290	81100	327670	251910	75760	356130	273900	82230	392490	302980	89510
a Withdrawals from quasi-corporations	163160	163160	-	175210	175210	-	192790	192790	-	210810	210810	-
b Interest	146140	66830	79310	137310	63690	73620	147170	67980	79190	159070	72720	86350
c Dividends	17090	15300	1790	15150	13010	2140	16170	13130	3040	22610	19450	3160
d Net land rent and royalties	...	...	...	...	...	...	...	...	...	...	...	...
2 Direct taxes and other current payments n.e.c. to general government	16060	13490	2570	14940	11410	3530	19130	15140	3990	25240	20100	5140

Germany, Fed. Rep. of

3.22 Corporate and Quasi-Corporate Enterprise Income and Outlay Account: Total and Sectors
(Continued)

Million Deutsche marks

	1974 TOTAL	1974 Non-Financial	1974 Financial	1975 TOTAL	1975 Non-Financial	1975 Financial	1976 TOTAL	1976 Non-Financial	1976 Financial	1977 TOTAL	1977 Non-Financial	1977 Financial
a Direct taxes	15400	12830	2570	14260	10730	3530	18410	14420	3990	24430	19290	5140
b Fines, fees, penalties and other payments n.e.c.	660	660	-	680	680	-	720	720	-	810	810	-
3 Other current transfers paid	35640	13070	22570	38390	13890	24500	42330	15090	27240	44920	16010	28910
a Casualty insurance transactions	22300	3440	18860	23770	3460	20310	26790	3930	22860	28140	4040	24100
Casualty insurance premiums paid, net	3590	3440	150	3610	3460	150	4090	3930	160	4190	4040	150
Claims paid by insurance companies	18710	-	18710	20160	-	20160	22700	-	22700	23950	-	23950
b Transfers to private non-profit institutions	...	...	...	...	...	...	...	...	...	...	...	...
c Transfers to households	12820	9430	3390	13960	10190	3770	14870	10920	3950	16040	11720	4320
Unfunded employee welfare benefits	12820	9430	3390	13960	10190	3770	14870	10920	3950	16040	11720	4320
Social assistance grants and other transfers n.e.c.	...	...	...	...	...	...	...	...	...	...	...	...
d Transfers to the rest of the world	520	200	320	660	240	420	670	240	430	740	250	490
Net saving	10030	-3860	13890	10690	-4290	14980	18840	3900	14940	6970	-8800	15770
Total Current Disbursements and Net Saving [a]	388120	267990	120130	391690	272920	118770	436430	308030	128400	469620	330290	139330

	1978 TOTAL	1978 Non-Financial	1978 Financial	1979 TOTAL	1979 Non-Financial	1979 Financial	1980 TOTAL	1980 Non-Financial	1980 Financial
Receipts									
1 Property and entrepreneurial income received	443060	326740	116320	499250	358980	140270	...	...	...
a Net operating surplus	287990	309060	-21070	312400	335480	-23080	...	...	...
b Withdrawals from quasi-corporate enterprises	3270	2830	440	3670	3170	500	3840	3320	520
c Interest	143130	8310	134820	172380	11820	160560	216510	18630	197880
d Dividends	8670	6540	2130	10800	8510	2290	63590	25830	37760
e Net land rent and royalties	...	...	...	...	...	...	...	...	...
2 Other current transfers received	56940	22730	34210	63590	25830	37760	68550	23710	41430
a Casualty insurance transactions	35830	3820	32010	39580	4290	35290	43670	4740	38930
Claims received	3960	3820	140	4490	4290	200	4960	4740	220
Net premiums received by insurance companies	31870	-	31870	35090	-	35090	38710	-	38710
b Current transfers received from the rest of the world	520	180	340	560	210	350	600	230	370
c Other transfers received, except imputed	2880	2810	70	3220	3150	70	3410	-	-
d Imputed unfunded employee welfare contributions	17710	15920	1790	20230	18180	2050	20870	18740	2130
Total Current Receipts [a]	500000	349470	150530	562840	384810	178030	300120	57550	242570
Disbursements									
1 Property and entrepreneurial income paid out	404620	308980	95640	457730	339970	117760	271150	119970	151180
a Withdrawals from quasi-corporations	223930	223930	-	238480	238480	-	...	...	...
b Interest	161950	69460	92490	195250	80960	114290	246590	98730	147860
c Dividends	18740	15590	3150	24000	20530	3470	24560	21240	3320
d Net land rent and royalties	...	...	...	...	...	...	...	...	...
2 Direct taxes and other current payments n.e.c. to general government	26210	20840	5370	28970	24360	4610	27400	22930	4470

Germany, Fed. Rep. of

3.22 Corporate and Quasi-Corporate Enterprise Income and Outlay Account: Total and Sectors
(Continued)

Million Deutsche marks

	1978 TOTAL	1978 Non-Financial	1978 Financial	1979 TOTAL	1979 Non-Financial	1979 Financial	1980 TOTAL	1980 Non-Financial	1980 Financial
a Direct taxes	25340	19970	5370	28000	23390	4610	26380	21910	4470
b Fines, fees, penalties and other payments n.e.c.	870	870	-	970	970	-	1020	1020	-
3 Other current transfers paid	48560	17120	31440	52980	18400	34580	58050	19910	38140
a Casualty insurance transactions	30690	4420	26270	34220	4950	29270	37990	5480	32510
Casualty insurance premiums paid, net	4560	4420	140	5150	4950	200	5700	5480	220
Claims paid by insurance companies	26130	-	26130	29070	-	29070	32290	-	32290
b Transfers to private non-profit institutions	...	...	...	...	...	...	...	...	...
c Transfers to households	16950	12370	4580	17830	13120	4710	19050	14060	4990
Unfunded employee welfare benefits	16950	12370	4580	17830	13120	4710	19050	14060	4990
Social assistance grants and other transfers n.e.c.	...	...	...	...	...	...	...	...	...
d Transfers to the rest of the world	920	330	590	930	330	600	1010	370	640
Net saving	20610	2530	18080	23160	2080	21080	...	...	...
Total Current Disbursements and Net Saving [a]	500000	349470	150530	562840	384810	178030	...	...	...

a) Column 'Total' refers to the non-consolidated receipts and expenditures which do not coincide with the data presented in Table 1.5 which are consolidated receipts and expenditures.

3.23 Corporate and Quasi-Corporate Enterprise Capital Accumulation Account: Total and Sectors

Million Deutsche marks

	1970 TOTAL	1970 Non-Financial	1970 Financial	1971 TOTAL	1971 Non-Financial	1971 Financial	1972 TOTAL	1972 Non-Financial	1972 Financial	1973 TOTAL	1973 Non-Financial	1973 Financial
Finance of Gross Accumulation												
1 Gross saving	91560	84380	7180	97660	89840	7820	100710	91340	9370	103790	92610	11180
a Consumption of fixed capital	65100	64210	890	74710	73680	1030	82180	81020	1160	91100	89810	1290
b Net saving	26460	20170	6290	22950	16160	6790	18530	10320	8210	12690	2800	9890
2 Capital transfers received	20780	20780	-	24000	24000	-	28390	28390	-	31500	31500	-
a From resident sectors	20780	20780	-	24000	24000	-	28390	28390	-	31500	31500	-
b From the rest of the world	...	...	...	...	...	...	...	...	...	...	...	...
Finance of Gross Accumulation [a]	112340	105160	7180	121660	113840	7820	129100	119730	9370	135290	124110	11180
Gross Accumulation												
1 Gross capital formation	159610	156800	2810	171490	168440	3050	184860	181200	3660	199440	195690	3750
a Increase in stocks	15200	15170	30	3600	3590	10	2600	2520	80	7200	7150	50
b Gross fixed capital formation	144410	141630	2780	167890	164850	3040	182260	178680	3580	192240	188540	3700
2 Purchases of land, net	-1380	-1700	320	-1640	-2130	490	-1720	-2190	470	-1950	-2650	700
3 Purchases of intangible assets, net	...	...	...	...	...	...	...	...	...	...	...	...
4 Capital transfers paid	6990	5240	1750	8000	5170	2830	9080	6200	2880	9860	7150	2710
a To resident sectors	6990	5240	1750	8000	5170	2830	9080	6200	2880	9860	7150	2710
b To the rest of the world	...	...	...	...	...	...	...	...	...	...	...	...
5 Net lending	-52880	-55180	2300	-56190	-57640	1450	-63120	-65480	2360	-72060	-76080	4020
Gross Accumulation [a]	112340	105160	7180	121660	113840	7820	129100	119730	9370	135290	124110	11180

	1974 TOTAL	1974 Non-Financial	1974 Financial	1975 TOTAL	1975 Non-Financial	1975 Financial	1976 TOTAL	1976 Non-Financial	1976 Financial	1977 TOTAL	1977 Non-Financial	1977 Financial
Finance of Gross Accumulation												
1 Gross saving	110780	95370	15410	120770	104100	16670	136600	119790	16810	141320	123500	17820
a Consumption of fixed capital	102030	100510	1520	111290	109600	1690	119250	117380	1870	127450	125400	2050
b Net saving	8750	-5140	13890	9480	-5500	14980	17350	2410	14940	13870	-1900	15770
2 Capital transfers received	37040	37040	-	37300	37250	50	44760	44710	50	48390	48340	50
a From resident sectors	37040	37040	-	37300	37250	50	44760	44710	50	48390	48340	50
b From the rest of the world	...	...	...	...	...	...	...	...	...	...	...	...
Finance of Gross Accumulation [a]	147820	132410	15410	158070	141350	16720	181360	164500	16860	189710	171840	17870
Gross Accumulation												
1 Gross capital formation	183690	179240	4450	174680	170070	4610	207550	202620	4930	224410	219670	4740

Germany, Fed. Rep. of

3.23 Corporate and Quasi-Corporate Enterprise Capital Accumulation Account: Total and Sectors
(Continued)

Million Deutsche marks

	1974 TOTAL	1974 Non-Financial	1974 Financial	1975 TOTAL	1975 Non-Financial	1975 Financial	1976 TOTAL	1976 Non-Financial	1976 Financial	1977 TOTAL	1977 Non-Financial	1977 Financial
a Increase in stocks	5400	5340	60	-1900	-1960	60	13500	13440	60	12900	12830	70
b Gross fixed capital formation	178290	173900	4390	176580	172030	4550	194050	189180	4870	211510	206840	4670
2 Purchases of land, net	-2450	-3200	750	-2360	-3130	770	-2290	-2940	650	-2110	-2700	590
3 Purchases of intangible assets, net	...	...	...	...	...	...	...	...	...	...	...	...
4 Capital transfers paid	12640	9450	3190	13350	8760	4590	15180	10560	4620	14020	9250	4770
a To resident sectors	12640	9450	3190	13350	8760	4590	15180	10560	4620	14020	9250	4770
b To the rest of the world	...	...	...	...	...	...	...	...	...	...	...	...
5 Net lending	-46060	-53080	7020	-27600	-34350	6750	-39080	-45740	6660	-46610	-54380	7770
Gross Accumulation [a]	147820	132410	15410	158070	141350	16720	181360	164500	16860	189710	171840	17870

	1978 TOTAL	1978 Non-Financial	1978 Financial	1979 TOTAL	1979 Non-Financial	1979 Financial	1980 TOTAL	1980 Non-Financial	1980 Financial
Finance of Gross Accumulation									
1 Gross saving	165440	145090	20350	179500	155940	23560	182880	...	...
a Consumption of fixed capital	137310	135040	2270	150070	147590	2480	166510	...	...
b Net saving	28130	10050	18080	29430	8350	21080	16370	...	...
2 Capital transfers received	52430	52370	60	56530	56530	-	58680	58680	-
a From resident sectors	52430	52370	60	56530	56530	-	58680	58680	-
b From the rest of the world	...	...	...	...	...	...	...	...	...
Finance of Gross Accumulation [a]	217870	197460	20410	236030	212470	23560	241560	14250	4000
Gross Accumulation									
1 Gross capital formation	240580	236160	4420	291610	287160	4450	313940	...	...
a Increase in stocks	9200	9130	70	25600	25530	70	18400	...	...
b Gross fixed capital formation	231380	227030	4350	266010	261630	4380	295540	...	...
2 Purchases of land, net	-2310	-2680	370	-2540	-2760	220	-2680	...	...
3 Purchases of intangible assets, net	...	...	...	...	...	...	...	...	...
4 Capital transfers paid	16140	11470	4670	17520	13670	3850	18250	14250	4000
a To resident sectors	16140	11470	4670	17520	13670	3850	18250	14250	4000
b To the rest of the world	...	...	...	...	...	...	...	...	...
5 Net lending	-36540	-47490	10950	-70560	-85600	15040	-87950	...	...
Gross Accumulation [a]	217870	197460	20410	236030	212470	23560	241560	14250	4000

a) Including private non-profit organizations.

3.24 Corporate and Quasi-Corporate Enterprise Capital Finance Account: Total and Sectors

Million Deutsche marks

	1970 TOTAL	1970 Non-Financial	1970 Financial	1971 TOTAL	1971 Non-Financial	1971 Financial	1972 TOTAL	1972 Non-Financial	1972 Financial	1973 TOTAL	1973 Non-Financial	1973 Financial
Acquisition of Financial Assets											
1 Gold and SDRs	580	-	580	1070	-	1070	1410	-	1410	1830	-	1830
2 Currency and transferable deposits	15210	6260	8950	13940	5850	8090	28790	11770	17020	5250	-2140	7390
3 Other deposits	7490	2470	5020	11630	9000	2630	13050	10140	2910	26290	15280	11010
4 Bills and bonds, short term	26770	70	26700	14470	-50	14520	13460	90	13370	22510	50	22460
5 Bonds, long term	2410	-10	2420	8640	130	8510	11360	860	10500	7510	780	6730
6 Corporate equity securities	4350	2740	1610	4840	3010	1830	2530	130	2400	3230	1480	1750
7 Short term loans, n.e.c.	20830	8150	12680	22920	5580	17340	33370	5700	27670	11360	4540	6820
8 Long term loans, n.e.c.	56270	2420	53850	65750	3070	62680	81280	2940	78340	73610	2040	71570
9 Trade credits and advances	1200	1200	...	2800	2800	...	3000	3000	...	1800	1800	...
a Consumer credit	-	-	-	-	-	-	-	-	-	-	-	-
b Other	1200	1200	...	2800	2800	...	3000	3000	...	1800	1800	...
10 Other receivables	-	-	-	-	-	-	-	-	-	-	-	-
11 Other assets	-	-	-	-	-	-	-	-	-	-	-	-
Total Acquisition of Financial Assets	135120	23310	111810	146060	29390	116670	188250	34630	153620	153380	23820	129560
Incurrence of Liabilities											
1 Currency and transferable deposits	23210	20	23190	27230	10	27220	34020	30	33990	13100	30	13070
2 Other deposits	50700	-	50700	54320	-	54320	68080	-	68080	74430	-	74430
3 Bills and bonds, short term	...	-240	...	...	-590	...	...	620	...	...	-1230	...

Germany, Fed. Rep. of

3.24 Corporate and Quasi-Corporate Enterprise Capital Finance Account: Total and Sectors
(Continued)

Million Deutsche marks

	1970			1971			1972			1973		
	TOTAL	Non-Financial	Financial	TOTAL	Non-Financial	Financial	TOTAL	Non-Financial	Financial	TOTAL	Non-Financial	Financial
4 Bonds, long term	...	1430	...	...	3720	...	...	3310	...	...	1220	...
5 Corporate equity securities	3590	2860	730	5340	4300	1040	4130	2600	1530	3590	2400	1190
6 Short-term loans, n.e.c.	...	23160	...	...	18350	...	...	18570	...	...	12440	...
7 Long-term loans, n.e.c.	...	45510	...	...	56520	...	...	70330	...	...	73490	...
8 Net equity of households in life insurance and pension fund reserves	9130	3290	5840	10290	2960	7330	12930	3650	9280	13650	4320	9330
9 Proprietors' net additions to the accumulation of quasi-corporations	-	-	-	-	-	-	-	-	-	-	-	-
10 Trade credit and advances	3200	3200	-	4000	4000	...	2400	2400	...	7800	7800	...
11 Other accounts payable												
12 Other liabilities	.	.	.	.	.	.	.	.	.	.	.	.
Total Incurrence of Liabilities	...	79240	109510	...	89270	115220	...	101510	150530	...	100470	124860
Net Lending	...	-55930	2300	...	-59880	1450	...	-66880	3090	...	-76650	4700
Incurrence of Liabilities and Net Lending	...	23310	111810	...	29390	116670	...	34630	153620	...	23820	129560

	1974			1975			1976			1977		
	TOTAL	Non-Financial	Financial	TOTAL	Non-Financial	Financial	TOTAL	Non-Financial	Financial	TOTAL	Non-Financial	Financial

Acquisition of Financial Assets

1 Gold and SDRs	170	-	170	30	-	30	860	-	860	-1480	-	-1480
2 Currency and transferable deposits	5380	9360	-3980	11380	12860	-1480	13780	4020	9760	15000	11910	3090
3 Other deposits	7980	-6330	14310	20700	3640	17060	17080	12360	4720	24800	16480	8320
4 Bills and bonds, short term	-5630	700	-6330	2030	-380	2410	3550	-180	3730	9250	260	8990
5 Bonds, long term	22440	70	22370	44500	2010	42490	25600	4850	20750	40720	3000	37720
6 Corporate equity securities	3940	2980	960	5070	3060	2010	5450	2280	3170	3970	990	2980
7 Short term loans, n.e.c.	24620	3480	21140	-9730	2770	-12500	26200	4710	21490	15350	-1040	16390
8 Long term loans, n.e.c.	69910	3200	66710	110200	3230	106970	110970	4460	106510	101780	4220	97560
9 Trade credits and advances	18640	18640	...	2300	2300	...	10740	10740	...	6550	6550	.
a Consumer credit	-	-	-	-	-	-	-	-	-	-	-	-
b Other	18640	18640	-	2300	2300	-	10740	10740	-	6550	6550	-
10 Other receivables	.	.	.	.	.	.	.	.	.	.	.	.
11 Other assets	.	.	.	.	.	.	.	.	.	.	.	.
Total Acquisition of Financial Assets	147450	32100	115350	186490	29500	156990	214220	43230	170990	215940	42370	173570

Incurrence of Liabilities

1 Currency and transferable deposits	13460	10	13450	19020	40	18980	11700	20	11680	26130	-	26130
2 Other deposits	50450	...	50450	84060	...	84060	87010	...	87010	88640	-	88640
3 Bills and bonds, short term	-320	670	-990	-4550	140	-4690	2160	-140	2300	-2040	-930	-1110
4 Bonds, long term	21210	1820	19390	34060	-850	34910	31990	360	31630	29580	930	28650
5 Corporate equity securities	3530	2290	1240	6010	4110	1900	6070	4400	1670	4370	2990	1380
6 Short-term loans, n.e.c.	30890	17570	13320	-3850	-5150	1300	26520	12600	13920	24960	19860	5100
7 Long-term loans, n.e.c.	51280	51230	50	55520	55520	-	62080	62080	-	66080	66080	-
8 Net equity of households in life insurance and pension fund reserves	17060	6140	10920	17690	5200	12490	20460	6680	13780	20620	5620	15000
9 Proprietors' net additions to the accumulation of quasi-corporations	-	-	-	-	-	-	-	-	-	-	-	-
10 Trade credit and advances	6250	6250	...	6360	6360	...	5090	5090	...	2660	2660	-
11 Other accounts payable	...	...	...	...	...	...	...	...	...	...	...	...
12 Other liabilities	...	...	...	...	...	...	...	...	...	...	...	...
Total Incurrence of Liabilities	193820	85970	107850	214310	65380	148930	253080	91080	162000	261000	97210	163790
Net Lending	-46360	-53870	7510	-27810	-35880	8070	-38860	-47850	8990	-45050	-54840	9790
Incurrence of Liabilities and Net Lending	147460	32100	115360	186490	29500	156990	214220	43230	170990	215940	42370	173570

	1978			1979			1980		
	TOTAL	Non-Financial	Financial	TOTAL	Non-Financial	Financial	TOTAL	Non-Financial	Financial

Acquisition of Financial Assets

1 Gold and SDRs	480	-	480	-2910	-	-2910	-400	-	-400
2 Currency and transferable deposits	27650	15140	12510	17150	-3440	20590	-12000	4430	-16430
3 Other deposits	25230	15450	9780	21240	14520	6720	21550	7380	14170
4 Bills and bonds, short term	33230	50	33180	-22600	-90	-22510	-15530	-400	-15130

Germany, Fed. Rep. of

3.24 Corporate and Quasi-Corporate Enterprise Capital Finance Account: Total and Sectors
(Continued)

Million Deutsche marks

	1978 TOTAL	1978 Non-Financial	1978 Financial	1979 TOTAL	1979 Non-Financial	1979 Financial	1980 TOTAL	1980 Non-Financial	1980 Financial
5 Bonds, long term	32340	2100	30240	12210	5060	7150	26250	530	25720
6 Corporate equity securities	3920	2210	1710	7090	5890	1200	8870	6490	2380
7 Short term loans, n.e.c.	28570	6940	21630	53190	5780	47410	64830	7460	57370
8 Long term loans, n.e.c.	135050	4600	130450	151460	5770	145690	135560	6360	129200
9 Trade credits and advances	5970	5970	-	9510	9510	-	9400	9400	-
a Consumer credit	-	-	-	-	-	-	-	-	-
b Other	5970	5970	-	9510	9510	-	9400	9400	-
10 Other receivables	-	-	-	-	-	-	-	-	-
11 Other assets	-	-	-	-	-	-	-	-	-
Total Acquisition of Financial Assets	292430	52450	239980	246330	42990	203340	238530	41650	196890

Incurrence of Liabilities

	TOTAL	Non-Financial	Financial	TOTAL	Non-Financial	Financial	TOTAL	Non-Financial	Financial
1 Currency and transferable deposits	50370	-	50370	7630	-	7630	8030	-	8030
2 Other deposits	103180	40	103140	106730	-	106730	80350	-	80350
3 Bills and bonds, short term	8140	300	7840	-5820	700	-6520	-1610	880	-2490
4 Bonds, long term	29080	-480	29560	33770	-2660	36430	42450	820	41630
5 Corporate equity securities	5560	3620	1940	5520	3850	1670	6990	5300	1690
6 Short-term loans, n.e.c.	27800	9130	18670	43200	20270	22990	71520	39240	32280
7 Long-term loans, n.e.c.	76870	76990	-120	89960	89910	50	84960	84460	500
8 Net equity of households in life insurance and pension fund reserves	24630	7770	16860	28630	9760	18870	30030	9760	20270
9 Proprietors' net additions to the accumulation of quasi-corporations	...	-	...	-	-	-	-	-	-
10 Trade credit and advances	2100	2100	...	7850	7850	-	4630	4630	-
11 Other accounts payable	...	...	...	...	...	...	...	...	...
12 Other liabilities	...	...	...	...	...	...	...	...	...
Total Incurrence of Liabilities	327720	99450	228270	317460	129620	187840	327340	145080	182260
Net Lending	-35280	-47000	11720	-71140	-86630	15490	-88800	-103430	14630
Incurrence of Liabilities and Net Lending	292440	52450	239990	246320	42990	203330	238530	41650	196890

3.26 Financial Transactions of Financial Institutions: Detail

Million Deutsche marks

	1970 ALL FINANCIAL INSTITUTIONS	1970 Central Bank	1970 Other Monetary Institutions	1970 Insurance	1970 Other Financial Institutions	1971 ALL FINANCIAL INSTITUTIONS	1971 Central Bank	1971 Other Monetary Institutions	1971 Insurance	1971 Other Financial Institutions

Acquisition of Financial Assets

1 Gold and SDRs	580	580	-	-	...	1070	1070	-	-	...
a Gold	-370	-370	-	-	...	350	350	-	-	...
b Net acquisitions of SDRs [a]	950	950	-	-	...	720	720	-	-	...
2 Currency and transferable deposits	8950	-1340	10200	90	...	8090	730	7080	280	...
a Liability of resident institutions	9850	-	9760	90	...	6930	-80	6730	280	...
b Liability of rest of the world	-900	-1340	440	-	...	1160	810	350	-	...
3 Other deposits	5020	1900	1730	1390	...	2630	-10	710	1930	...
a Liability of resident institutions	1390	-	-	1390	...	1930	-	-	1930	...
b Liability of rest of the world	3630	1900	1730	-	...	700	-10	710	-	...
4 Bills and bonds, short term	26700	24230	2470	-	...	14520	14850	-330	-	...
5 Bonds, long term	2420	-1890	2510	1800	...	8510	-100	6010	2600	...
6 Corporate equity securities	1610	-	1130	480	...	1830	-	1040	790	...
7 Short-term loans, n.e.c.	12680	1560	11120	-	...	17340	290	17050	-	...
a Liability of: resident sectors	15050	1520	13530	-	...	19020	280	18740	-	...
b Liability of: rest of the world	-2370	40	-2410	-	...	-1680	10	-1690	-	...
8 Long-term loans, n.e.c.	53850	-280	49910	4220	...	62680	-430	57240	5870	...
a Mortgages	...	...	...	...	...	...	...	...	...	...
b Other	...	-280	...	...	...	...	-430	...	...	...
9 Trade credit and advances	...	...	...	...	...	...	...	...	...	...
10 Other assets	...	...	...	...	...	...	...	...	...	...
Total Acquisition of Financial Assets [b,c]	111810	24760	79070	7980	...	116670	16400	88800	11470	...

Germany, Fed. Rep. of

3.26 Financial Transactions of Financial Institutions: Detail
(Continued)

Million Deutsche marks

	1970 ALL FINANCIAL INSTITUTIONS	Central Bank	Other Monetary Institutions	Insurance	Other Financial Institutions	1971 ALL FINANCIAL INSTITUTIONS	Central Bank	Other Monetary Institutions	Insurance	Other Financial Institutions
				Incurrence of Liabilities						
1 Currency and transferable deposits [d]	23930	16810	7120	-	...	27850	15660	12190	-	...
2 Other deposits	50700	-	50700	-	...	54320	-	54320	-	...
3 Bills and bonds, short term	5500	5500	...	...	...	-1060	-1060	...	...	...
4 Bonds, long term	11800	-	11800	-	...	14790	-	14790	-	...
5 Corporate equity securities	730	-	570	160	...	1040	-	950	90	...
6 Short-term loans, n.e.c.	9960	...	7140	2820	...	8410	...	3680	4730	...
7 Long-term loans, n.e.c.	30	...	10	20	...	40	...	-	40	...
9 Net equity of households in life insurance and pension fund reserves [e]	6140	-	130	6010	...	7700	-	210	7490	...
10 Other liabilities	...	...	...	...	...	...	...	...	...	...
Total Incurrence of liabilities [bc]	108790	22320	77460	9010	...	113080	14600	86130	12350	...
Net Lending	3020	2440	1610	-1030	...	3590	1800	2670	-880	...
Incurrence of Liabilities and Net Lending [bc]	111810	24760	79070	7980	...	116670	16400	88800	11470	...

	1972 ALL FINANCIAL INSTITUTIONS	Central Bank	Other Monetary Institutions	Insurance	Other Financial Institutions	1973 ALL FINANCIAL INSTITUTIONS	Central Bank	Other Monetary Institutions	Insurance	Other Financial Institutions
				Acquisition of Financial Assets						
1 Gold and SDRs	1410	1410	-	-	...	1830	1830	-	-	...
a Gold	110	110	-	-	...	30	30	-	-	...
b Net acquisitions of SDRs [a]	1300	1300	-	-	...	1800	1800	-	-	...
2 Currency and transferable deposits	17020	230	16860	-70	...	7390	40	6990	360	...
a Liability of resident institutions	15150	160	15060	-70	...	5860	-60	5560	360	...
b Liability of rest of the world	1870	70	1800	-	...	1530	100	1430	-	...
3 Other deposits	2910	-40	150	2800	...	11010	780	6800	3430	...
a Liability of resident institutions	2800	-	-	2800	...	3430	-	-	3430	...
b Liability of rest of the world	110	-40	150	-	...	7580	780	6800	-	...
4 Bills and bonds, short term	13370	15620	-2250	-	...	22460	22200	140	120	...
5 Bonds, long term	10500	-260	7500	3260	...	6730	-20	3570	3180	...
6 Corporate equity securities	2400	-	1470	930	...	1750	-	860	890	...
7 Short-term loans, n.e.c.	27670	2450	25220	-	...	6820	-5540	12360	-	...
a Liability of: resident sectors	27350	2300	25050	-	...	7030	-5570	12600	-	...
b Liability of: rest of the world	320	150	170	-	...	-210	30	-240	-	...
8 Long-term loans, n.e.c.	78340	-150	71580	6910	...	71570	-20	64630	6960	...
a Mortgages	...	...	...	...	...	...	...	...	...	...
b Other	...	-150	...	...	...	...	-20	...	...	...
9 Trade credit and advances	...	...	...	...	...	...	...	...	...	...
10 Other assets	...	...	...	...	...	...	...	...	...	...
Total Acquisition of Financial Assets [bc]	153620	19260	120530	13830	...	129560	19270	95350	14940	...
				Incurrence of Liabilities						
1 Currency and transferable deposits [d]	34610	18600	16010	-	...	13070	10400	2670	-	...
2 Other deposits	68080	-	68080	-	...	74430	-	74430	-	...
3 Bills and bonds, short term	-2010	-2010	-	-	...	5390	5390	-	...	...
4 Bonds, long term	26000	-	26000	-	...	21340	-	21340	...	...
5 Corporate equity securities	1530	-	1350	180	...	1190	-	1070	120	...
6 Short-term loans, n.e.c.	11860	-	7020	4840	...	-360	-	-6500	6140	...
7 Long-term loans, n.e.c.	10	-	10	-	...	130	-	120	10	...
9 Net equity of households in life insurance and pension fund reserves [e]	9730	-	190	9540	...	9810	-	220	9590	...
10 Other liabilities	-	-	-	-	...	-	-	-	-	...
Total Incurrence of liabilities [bc]	149810	16590	118660	14560	...	124990	15800	93330	15860	...
Net Lending	3810	2670	1870	-730	...	4570	3470	2020	-920	...
Incurrence of Liabilities and Net Lending [bc]	153620	19260	120530	13830	...	129560	19270	95350	14940	...

Germany, Fed. Rep. of

3.26 Financial Transactions of Financial Institutions: Detail

Million Deutsche marks

	1974					1975				
	ALL FINANCIAL INSTITUTIONS	Central Bank	Other Monetary Institutions	Insurance	Other Financial Institutions	ALL FINANCIAL INSTITUTIONS	Central Bank	Other Monetary Institutions	Insurance	Other Financial Institutions
Acquisition of Financial Assets											
1 Gold and SDRs	170	170	-	-	...	30	30	-	-	-
a Gold	-	-	-	-	...	-	-	-	-	-
b Net acquisitions of SDRs [a]	170	170	-	-	...	30	30	-	-	...
2 Currency and transferable deposits	-3980	420	-4490	90	...	-1480	700	-2060	-120	-
a Liability of resident institutions	-4950	180	-5220	90	...	-1850	-290	-1440	-120	-
b Liability of rest of the world	970	240	730	-	...	370	990	-620	-	-
3 Other deposits	14310	130	10280	3900	...	17060	-	12490	4570	...
a Liability of resident institutions	3900	-	-	3900	...	4570	-	-	4570	...
b Liability of rest of the world	10410	130	10280	-	...	12490	-	12490	-	-
4 Bills and bonds, short term	-6330	-11160	4840	-10	...	2410	-3090	5600	-100	...
5 Bonds, long term	22370	3420	14660	4290	...	42490	8080	28110	6300	...
6 Corporate equity securities	960	-	200	760	...	2010	-	850	1160	...
7 Short-term loans, n.e.c.	21140	5410	15730	-	...	-12500	-6440	-6060	-	...
a Liability of: resident sectors	20290	5400	14890	-	...	-12770	-6580	-6190	-	...
b Liability of: rest of the world	850	10	840	-	...	270	140	130	-	...
8 Long-term loans, n.e.c.	66710	5300	54040	7370	...	106970	-1150	102040	6080	...
a Mortgages	...	-	...	...	...	...	-	...	...	...
b Other	...	5300	...	...	...	...	-1150	...	...	...
9 Trade credit and advances	...	...	...	...	...	...	...	...	...	...
10 Other assets	...	...	...	...	...	...	...	...	...	...
Total Acquisition of Financial Assets [bc]	115350	3690	95260	16400	...	156990	-1870	140970	17890	...
Incurrence of Liabilities											
1 Currency and transferable deposits [d]	13450	-410	13860	-	...	18980	-800	19780	-	...
2 Other deposits	50450	-	50450	-	...	84060	-	84060	-	...
3 Bills and bonds, short term	-990	-990	-	-	...	-4690	-4690	-	-	...
4 Bonds, long term	19390	-	19390	-	...	34910	-	34910	-	...
5 Corporate equity securities	1240	-	950	290	...	1900	-	1810	90	...
6 Short-term loans, n.e.c.	13320	-	7920	5400	...	1300	-	-3820	5140	...
7 Long-term loans, n.e.c.	50	-	50	-	...	-	-	-50	50	...
9 Net equity of households in life insurance and pension fund reserves [e]	10920	-	500	10420	...	12490	-	700	11790	...
10 Other liabilities	-	-	-	-	...	-	-	-	-	...
Total Incurrence of liabilities [bc]	107850	-1400	93120	16130	...	148930	-5500	137380	17050	...
Net Lending	7510	5090	2150	270	...	8070	3630	3600	840	...
Incurrence of Liabilities and Net Lending [bc]	115350	3690	95260	16400	...	156990	-1870	140970	17890	...

	1976					1977				
	ALL FINANCIAL INSTITUTIONS	Central Bank	Other Monetary Institutions	Insurance	Other Financial Institutions	ALL FINANCIAL INSTITUTIONS	Central Bank	Other Monetary Institutions	Insurance	Other Financial Institutions
Acquisition of Financial Assets											
1 Gold and SDRs	860	860	-	-	-	-1480	-1480	-	-	...
a Gold	-	-	-	-	-	60	60	-	-	...
b Net acquisitions of SDRs [a]	860	860	-	-	...	-1540	-1540	-	-	...
2 Currency and transferable deposits	9760	1540	8620	-400	...	3090	780	2170	140	...
a Liability of resident institutions	6420	-90	6910	-400	...	3410	730	2540	140	...
b Liability of rest of the world	3340	1630	1710	-	...	-320	50	-370	-	...
3 Other deposits	4720	-40	-270	5030	...	8320	3280	-1930	6970	...
a Liability of resident institutions	5030	-	-	5030	...	6970	-	-	6970	...
b Liability of rest of the world	-310	-40	-270	-	...	1350	3280	-1930	-	...
4 Bills and bonds, short term	3730	7530	-3800	-	...	8990	8950	40	-	...

Germany, Fed. Rep. of

3.26 Financial Transactions of Financial Institutions: Detail
(Continued)

Million Deutsche marks

		1976					1977			
		ALL FINANCIAL INSTITUTIONS	Central Bank	Other Monetary Institutions	Insurance	Other Financial Institutions	ALL FINANCIAL INSTITUTIONS	Central Bank	Other Monetary Institutions	Insurance	Other Financial Institutions
5	Bonds, long term	20750	-6880	20430	7200	...	37720	-1890	31530	8080	...
6	Corporate equity securities	3170	-	2240	930	...	2980	-	1750	1230	...
7	Short-term loans, n.e.c.	21490	7690	13800	-	-	16390	1800	14590	-	...
	a Liability of: resident sectors	20190	7530	12660	-	-	15430	1860	13570	-	...
	b Liability of: rest of the world	1300	160	1140	-	-	960	-60	1020	-	...
8	Long-term loans, n.e.c.	106510	1450	98210	6850	...	97560	-520	92840	5240	...
	a Mortgages	...	...	...	...	...	...	...	...	...	...
	b Other	...	1450	...	...	...	...	-520	...	...	...
9	Trade credit and advances	...	...	...	...	...	...	...	...	...	...
10	Other assets	...	...	...	...	...	...	...	...	...	...
	Total Acquisition of Financial Assets [bc]	170990	12150	139230	19610	...	173570	10920	140990	21660	...

Incurrence of Liabilities

1	Currency and transferable deposits [d]	11680	5730	5950	-	-	26130	7950	18180	-	...
2	Other deposits	87010	-	87010	-	...	88640	-	88640	-	...
3	Bills and bonds, short term	2300	2300	-	-	...	-1110	-1110	-	-	...
4	Bonds, long term	31630	-	31630	-	...	28650	-	28650	-	...
5	Corporate equity securities	1670	-	1490	180	-	1380	-	1170	210	...
6	Short-term loans, n.e.c.	13920	-	8950	4970	...	5100	-	-500	5600	...
7	Long-term loans, n.e.c.	-	-	-	-	...	-	-	-30	30	...
9	Net equity of households in life insurance and pension fund reserves [e]	13780	-	620	13160	-	15000	-	530	14470	...
10	Other liabilities	-	-	-	-	...	-	-	-	-	...
	Total Incurrence of liabilities [bc]	162000	8030	135650	18320	...	163780	6840	136640	20300	...
	Net Lending	8990	4120	3580	1290	...	9790	4100	4350	1360	...
	Incurrence of Liabilities and Net Lending [bc]	170990	12150	139230	19610	...	173570	10940	140990	21660	...

		1978					1979			
		ALL FINANCIAL INSTITUTIONS	Central Bank	Other Monetary Institutions	Insurance	Other Financial Institutions	ALL FINANCIAL INSTITUTIONS	Central Bank	Other Monetary Institutions	Insurance	Other Financial Institutions

Acquisition of Financial Assets

1	Gold and SDRs	480	480	-	-	...	-2910	-2910	-	-	...
	a Gold	30	30	-	-	...	-3390	-3390	-	-	...
	b Net acquisitions of SDRs [a]	450	450	-	-	...	480	480	-	-	...
2	Currency and transferable deposits	12510	2860	9290	360	...	20590	16840	3820	-70	...
	a Liability of resident institutions	8570	220	7990	360	...	3930	-840	4040	-70	...
	b Liability of rest of the world	3940	2640	1300	-	...	17460	17680	-220	-	...
3	Other deposits	9780	-30	-850	10660	...	6720	-4500	1030	10190	...
	a Liability of resident institutions	10660	-	-	10660	...	10190	-	-	10190	...
	b Liability of rest of the world	-880	-30	-850	-	...	-3470	-4500	1030	-	...
4	Bills and bonds, short term	33180	26360	6820	-	...	-22510	-15340	-7170	-	...
5	Bonds, long term	30240	2490	21880	5870	...	7150	-1860	4450	4560	...
6	Corporate equity securities	1710	-	560	1150	...	1200	-	670	530	...
7	Short-term loans, n.e.c.	21630	7530	14100	-	...	47410	13840	33570	-	...
	a Liability of: resident sectors	19810	7390	12420	-	...	46030	13840	32190	-	...
	b Liability of: rest of the world	1820	140	1680	-	...	1380	-	1385	-	...
8	Long-term loans, n.e.c.	130450	-3500	127470	6480	...	145690	-280	134010	11960	...
	a Mortgages	...	-	...	...	...	...	-	...	...	...
	b Other	...	-3500	...	...	...	...	-280	...	...	...
9	Trade credit and advances	...	...	...	...	...	...	...	...	...	...
10	Other assets	...	...	...	...	...	...	...	...	...	...
	Total Acquisition of Financial Assets [bc]	239980	36190	179270	24520	...	203340	5800	170380	27160	...

Incurrence of Liabilities

1	Currency and transferable deposits [d]	50370	23330	27040	-	...	7630	5430	2200	-	...
2	Other deposits	103140	-	103140	-	...	106730	-	106730	-	...
3	Bills and bonds, short term	7840	7840	-	-	...	-6520	-6520	-	-	...

Germany, Fed. Rep. of

3.26 Financial Transactions of Financial Institutions: Detail
(Continued)

Million Deutsche marks

	1978					1979				
	ALL FINANCIAL INSTITUTIONS	Central Bank	Other Monetary Institutions	Insurance	Other Financial Institutions	ALL FINANCIAL INSTITUTIONS	Central Bank	Other Monetary Institutions	Insurance	Other Financial Institutions
4 Bonds, long term	29560	-	29560	-	...	36430	-	36430	...	...
5 Corporate equity securities	1940	-	1700	240	...	1670	-	1250	420	...
6 Short-term loans, n.e.c.	18670	-	11930	6740	...	22990	-	15810	7180	...
7 Long-term loans, n.e.c.	-120	-	-150	30	...	50	-	20	30	...
9 Net equity of households in life insurance and pension fund reserves [e]	16860	-	560	16300	...	18870	-	710	18160	...
10 Other liabilities	-	-	-	-	...	-	-	-	-	...
Total Incurrence of liabilities [b][c]	228270	31170	173790	23310	...	187840	-1090	163140	25790	...
Net Lending	11720	5020	5490	1210	...	15490	6880	7240	1370	...
Incurrence of Liabilities and Net Lending [b][c]	239990	36190	179280	24520	...	203330	5800	170380	27160	...

	1980				
	ALL FINANCIAL INSTITUTIONS	Central Bank	Other Monetary Institutions	Insurance	Other Financial Institutions

Acquisition of Financial Assets

1 Gold and SDRs	-400	-400	-	-	...
a Gold	-10	-10	-	-	...
b Net acquisitions of SDRs [a]	-390	-390	-	-	...
2 Currency and transferable deposits	-16430	-7660	-9050	280	...
a Liability of resident institutions	-9510	-50	-9740	280	...
b Liability of rest of the world	-6920	-7610	690	-	...
3 Other deposits	14170	560	7260	6350	...
a Liability of resident institutions	6350	-	-	6350	...
b Liability of rest of the world	7820	560	7260	-	...
4 Bills and bonds, short term	-15130	-9990	-5140	-	...
5 Bonds, long term	25720	1860	16170	7690	...
6 Corporate equity securities	2380	-	1300	1080	...
7 Short-term loans, n.e.c.	57370	22890	34480	-	...
a Liability of: resident sectors	57950	22870	35080	-	...
b Liability of: rest of the world	-580	20	-600	...	...
8 Long-term loans, n.e.c.	129200	-	115460	13740	...
a Mortgages	...	...	...	...	...
b Other	...	...	...	...	...
9 Trade credit and advances	...	...	...	...	...
10 Other assets	...	...	...	...	...
Total Acquisition of Financial Assets [b][c]	196890	7270	160480	29140	...

Incurrence of Liabilities

1 Currency and transferable deposits [d]	8030	1500	6530	-	...
2 Other deposits	80350	-	80350	-	...
3 Bills and bonds, short term	-2490	-2490	-	-	...
4 Bonds, long term	41630	-	41630	-	...
5 Corporate equity securities	1690	-	1210	480	...
6 Short-term loans, n.e.c.	32280	-	24670	7610	...
7 Long-term loans, n.e.c.	500	-	60	440	...
9 Net equity of households in life insurance and pension fund reserves [e]	20270	-	710	19560	...
10 Other liabilities	-	-	-	-	...
Total Incurrence of liabilities [b][c]	182260	-990	155160	28090	...
Net Lending	14630	8260	5320	1050	...
Incurrence of Liabilities and Net Lending [b][c]	196890	7270	160480	29140	...

a) Including net allocation of SDRs.
b) Column 'All financial institutions' is nonconsolidated.
c) Column 'Other financial institutions' is included in column 'Other monetary institutions'.
d) Central bank: Including counterpart item for net allocation of SDRs.
e) Including corresponding assets with other insurance companies.

Germany, Fed. Rep. of

3.32 Household and Private Unincorporated Enterprise Income and Outlay Account

Million Deutsche marks

		1970	1971	1972	1973	1974	1975	1976	1977	1978	1979	1980
						Receipts						
1	Compensation of employees	361320	408300	448790	509470	560600	583400	626320	669680	714720	769410	829980
	a Wages and salaries	306400	345000	376240	423800	463600	479600	510600	547100	582300	625800	675500
	b Employers' contributions for social security	36800	43150	49940	59360	65480	70790	79900	85980	91430	98590	107040
	c Employers' contributions for private pension & welfare plans	18120	20150	22610	26310	31520	33010	35820	36600	40990	45020	47440
2	Property and entrepreneurial income received	158900	173000	179920	193000	201170	214930	235060	258460	270680	294240	...
	a Operating surplus of private unincorporated enterprises	21800	20160	5760	-170	-1280	-1210	-1490	6900	7520	6270	...
	b Withdrawals from private quasi-corporations	114070	126780	145240	156730	162040	174110	191510	201000	213140	228540	241340
	c Interest	20220	23070	26530	33740	37360	39040	42480	46530	47420	56050	69330
	d Dividends	2810	2990	2390	2700	3050	2990	2560	4030	2600	3380	3380
	e Net land rent and royalties	...	...	...	...	...	...	...	...	...	...	...
3	Other current transfers received	103050	115540	131310	146520	166660	202070	217460	232980	247780	263610	281550
	a Casualty insurance claims	10020	11450	13410	14570	14780	16130	18060	19130	20960	23250	26060
	b Social security benefits	56360	62170	71340	81260	94850	112540	122730	133640	141500	148890	158440
	c Social assistance grants	13970	15810	18290	18880	21130	34440	35020	35950	38110	41020	42740
	d Unfunded employee welfare benefits	19170	22140	23920	26770	29950	32520	34540	36690	38720	40920	43760
	e Other current transfers received	3530	3970	4350	5040	5950	6440	7110	7570	8490	9530	10550
	From general government	2400	2820	3110	3570	4140	4640	5070	5610	6380	7170	7890
	From the rest fo the world	140	100	70	110	120	110	140	140	190	170	410
	Other	990	1050	1170	1360	1690	1690	1900	1820	1920	2190	2250
	Total Current Receipts [a]	623270	696840	760020	848990	928430	1000400	1078840	1161120	1233180	1327260	...
						Disbursements						
1	Final consumption expenditures	367550	407830	447750	491680	527550	577420	623590	669560	713910	766360	821590
	a Market purchases	362520	402260	442170	485670	521540	571160	616850	661900	705250	756560	810640
	b Gross rents of owner-occupied housing	...	...	...	...	...	...	...	...	...	...	...
	c Consumption from own-account production	5030	5570	5580	6010	6010	6260	6740	7660	8660	9800	10950
2	Property income paid	3670	4270	4780	6730	7640	7000	7060	7510	8220	9790	13140
	a Interest	3670	4270	4780	6730	7640	7000	7060	7510	8220	9790	13140
	Consumer debt	3670	4270	4780	6730	7640	7000	7060	7510	8220	9790	13140
	Mortgage	...	...	...	...	...	...	...	...	...	...	...
	Other	...	...	...	...	...	...	...	...	...	...	...
	b Net land rent and royalties	...	...	...	...	...	...	...	...	...	...	...
3	Direct taxes, fees, fines & other payments n.e.c. to government	138050	162240	181130	220630	246660	255080	290090	317350	331880	351830	381570
	a Social security contributions	75960	86780	99620	117900	130460	142320	161070	172960	185100	199100	214940
	b Direct taxes	60440	73520	79210	100170	113180	109400	125190	140170	...	...	...
	Income taxes	58300	71200	76610	97440	110350	106470	122070	136870	146780	152730	166630
	Other	2140	2320	2600	2730	2830	2930	3120	3300	...	...	...
	c Fees, fines and penalties	1650	1940	2300	2560	3020	3360	3830	4220	...	...	...
4	Other current transfers paid	33820	38690	43980	49890	55160	57820	62040	63330	69470	76650	82860
	a Net casualty insurance premiums	10140	11600	13580	14710	15070	16580	18610	19760	21640	23970	...
	b Transfers to private non-profit institutions serving households	...	...	...	...	...	...	...	...	...	...	...
	c Transfers to the rest of the world	6280	7720	8740	9830	9750	9510	8990	8480	8630	9470	...
	d Other current transfers, except imputed	560	650	680	780	850	920	990	1050	1120	1190	1250
	e Imputed employee welfare contributions	16840	18720	20980	24570	29490	30810	33450	34040	38080	42020	44250
	Net saving	80180	83810	82380	80060	91420	103080	96060	103370	109700	122630	...
	Total Current Disbursements and Net Saving [a]	623270	696840	760020	848990	928430	1000400	1078840	1161120	1233180	1327260	...

a) Including private non-profit organizations.

Germany, Fed. Rep. of

3.33 Household and Private Unincorporated Enterprise Capital Accumulation Account
Million Deutsche marks

	1970	1971	1972	1973	1974	1975	1976	1977	1978	1979	1980
Finance of Gross Accumulation											
1 Gross saving	58380	63650	76620	80230	92700	104290	97550	96470	116360	115250	126420
a Consumption of fixed capital	...	...	...	...	...	...	...	...	...	...	...
b Net saving a	58380	63650	76620	80230	92700	104290	97550	96470	116360	115250	126420
2 Capital transfers received	8240	11100	12570	12660	15960	17490	18910	19230	19920	21030	19770
a From resident sectors	8220	11080	12550	12640	15940	17470	18890	19210	19900	21010	19750
b From the rest of the world	20	20	20	20	20	20	20	20	20	20	20
Total Finance of Gross Accumulation	66620	74750	89190	92890	108660	121780	116460	115700	136280	136280	146190
Gross Accumulation											
1 Gross Capital Formation	...	...	...	...	...	...	...	...	...	...	...
2 Purchases of land, net	...	...	...	...	...	...	...	...	...	...	...
3 Purchases of intangibles, net	...	...	...	...	...	...	...	...	...	...	...
4 Capital transfers paid	12710	15070	19090	20260	23730	25430	29030	30700	33390	35290	36930
a To resident sectors	12530	14870	18910	20070	23530	25180	28820	30420	33110	34970	36520
b To the rest of the world	180	200	180	190	200	250	210	280	280	320	410
5 Net lending b	53910	59680	70100	72630	84930	96350	87430	85000	88420	100990	109260
Total Gross Accumulation	66620	74750	89190	92890	108660	121780	116460	115700	121810	136280	146190

a) Excluding undistributed profits of enterprises having no legal personality of their own.
b) Net lending of the Capital Accumulation Account and the Capital Finance Account have not been reconciled and are different due to different statistical sources.

3.34 Household and Private Unincorporated Enterprise Capital Finance Account
Million Deutsche marks

	1970	1971	1972	1973	1974	1975	1976	1977	1978	1979	1980
Acquisition of Financial Assets											
1 Gold	...	...	...	...	...	...	...	...	...	...	
2 Currency and transferable deposits	2570	7130	7820	1840	6930	9210	5620	11570	13280	5600	4530
3 Other deposits	32580	37440	46150	45590	47800	62920	51710	49930	51340	53360	54730
4 Bills and bonds, short term	-	-	-	440	240	-320	690	220	400	770	390
5 Bonds, long term	10150	7650	10490	10540	9280	8670	18890	11420	9360	27830	25410
6 Corporate equity securities	1440	930	-400	1510	240	1580	-10	1160	1900	-700	-300
7 Short term loans, n.e.c.	1910	2860	2650	3610	3820	3980	4180	4570	4990	5000	6220
8 Long term loans, n.e.c.	80	70	100	60	120	80	50	70	70	60	60
9 Trade credit and advances of unincorporated enterprises	-	-	-	-	-	-	-	-	-	-	...
10 Net equity of households in life insurance and pension fund reserves a	9430	10660	13380	14130	17060	17690	20460	20620	24640	28630	30030
11 Proprietors' net additions to the accumulation of quasi-corporations	-	-	-	-	-	-	-	-	-	-	...
12 Other	...	...	...	...	...	...	...	...	...	...	...
Total Acquisition of Financial Assets	58160	66740	80170	77720	85490	103810	101590	99550	105990	120550	121070
Incurrence of Liabilities											
1 Short term loans, n.e.c.	1110	3140	4640	1410	-630	1210	3210	4070	3700	4620	4660
2 Long term loans, n.e.c.	3140	3930	5440	3680	990	6250	10940	10640	14010	14930	7190
3 Trade credit and advances of unincorporated enterprises	-	-	-	-	-	-	-	-	-	-	...
4 Other accounts payable	...	...	...	...	...	...	...	...	...	...	...
5 Other liabilities	...	...	...	...	...	...	...	...	...	...	...
Total Incurrence of Liabilities	4250	7060	10070	5090	360	7460	14160	14710	17710	19560	11840
Net Lending b	53910	59680	70100	72630	85130	96350	87430	84840	88280	100990	109230
Incurrence of Liabilities and Net Lending	58160	66740	80170	77720	85490	103810	101590	99550	105990	120550	121070

a) Including corresponding assets with other insurance companies.
b) Net lending of the Capital Accumulation Account and the Capital Finance Account have not been reconciled and are different due to different statistical sources.

Germany, Fed. Rep. of

3.41 Private Non-Profit Institutions Serving Households: Production Account

Million Deutsche marks

	1970	1971	1972	1973	1974	1975	1976	1977	1978	1979	1980
Gross Output											
1 Sales	6490	7930	9370	11220	13200	15320	16710	18060	19410	20870	22900
2 Non-marketed output	5030	5570	5580	6010	6010	6260	6740	7660	8660	9800	10950
a Services produced for own use	5030	5570	5580	6010	6010	6260	6740	7660	8660	9800	10950
Gross Output	11520	13500	14950	17230	19210	21580	23450	25720	28070	30670	33850
Gross Input											
Intermediate consumption	3560	3990	4340	4950	5460	6380	6970	7690	8480	9370	10440
Subtotal: Value Added	7960	9510	10610	12280	13750	15200	16480	18030	19590	21300	23410
1 Indirect taxes, net	30	10	10	10	10	10	10	10	10	20	20
2 Consumption of fixed capital	930	1070	1190	1320	1480	1580	1670	1810	1940	2140	2380
3 Compensation of employees	7000	8430	9410	10950	12260	13610	14800	16210	17640	19140	21010
a Paid to residents	7000	8430	9410	10950	12260	13610	14800	16210	17640	19140	21010
Gross Input	11520	13500	14950	17230	19210	21580	23450	25720	28070	30670	33850

3.51 External Transactions: Current Account: Detail

Million Deutsche marks

	1970	1971	1972	1973	1974	1975	1976	1977	1978	1979	1980
Payments to the Rest of the World											
1 Imports of goods and services [a]	128920	142280	153650	173240	216170	228310	267440	281940	293460	348700	407670
a Imports of merchandise c.i.f.	118190	129350	138530	155300	197150	205800	243860	255870	264100	315820	369490
b Other	10730	12930	15120	17940	19020	22510	23580	26070	29360	32880	38180
2 Factor income paid to the rest of the world	9520	10510	11200	12400	16580	15420	15980	19130	17360	21020	26040
a Compensation of employees	830	1100	1390	1610	1800	1950	2090	2240	2360	2480	2680
b Property and entrepreneurial income paid	8690	9410	9810	10790	14780	13470	13890	16890	15000	18540	23360
By general government	60	70	150	220	260	220	270	420	470	560	770
By corporate and quasi-corporate enterprises	8630	9340	9660	10570	14520	13250	13620	16470	14530	17980	22590
By other	...	...	...	...	...	...	...	...	...	...	...
3 Indirect taxes paid to supranational organizations	60	70	70	80	90	80	80	80	70	70	30
4 Other current transfers to the rest of the world	12740	15400	18320	21320	21750	23820	24710	26950	28620	31150	32930
a By general government	5930	6830	9050	10950	11410	13560	14960	17640	18970	20650	21090
b By other resident sectors	6810	8570	9270	10370	10340	10260	9750	9310	9650	10500	11840
5 Surplus of the nation on current transactions	3860	2980	3550	12110	25990	9760	9480	10430	18650	-8400	-26280
Payments to the Rest of the World, and Surplus of the Nation on Current Transfers	155100	171240	186790	219150	280580	277390	317690	338530	358160	392540	440390
Receipts From The Rest of the World											
1 Exports of goods and services [a]	142920	156690	170920	200820	259840	256390	293890	311330	326390	357710	401590
a Exports of merchandise f.o.b.	122780	133090	145780	174190	228160	219640	252720	268430	278480	307250	343240
b Other	20140	23600	25140	26630	31680	36750	41170	42900	47910	50460	58350
2 Factor income received from the rest of the world	9770	11630	12410	13900	16350	16290	18160	19240	21680	25280	29020
a Compensation of employees	2040	2320	2390	2550	2720	3000	3180	3310	3440	3690	3900
b Property and entrepreneurial income received	7730	9310	10020	11350	13630	13290	14980	15930	18240	21590	25120
By general government	140	130	260	190	60	90	270	150	100	90	50
By corporate and quasi-corporate enterprises	7560	9140	9710	11110	13510	13150	14650	15710	18070	21420	24980
By other	30	40	50	50	60	50	60	70	70	80	90
3 Subsidies received from supranational organizations	70	130	120	190	220	230	70	90	100	70	-
4 Other current transfers from the rest of the world	2340	2790	3340	4240	4170	4480	5570	7870	9990	9480	9780
a To general government	1840	2280	2790	3670	3480	3760	4750	6930	8970	8490	8480
b To other resident sectors	500	510	550	570	690	720	820	940	1020	990	1300
Receipts from the Rest of the World on Current Transfers	155100	171240	186790	219150	280580	277390	317690	338530	358160	392540	440390

a) Exports and imports of goods for purposes of repair and improvement are reduced to the value of these services.

Germany, Fed. Rep. of

3.52 External Transactions: Capital Accumulation Account

Million Deutsche marks

	1970	1971	1972	1973	1974	1975	1976	1977	1978	1979	1980
Finance of Gross Accumulation											
1 Surplus of the nation on current transactions	3860	2980	3550	12110	25990	9760	9480	10430	18650	-8400	-26280
2 Capital transfers received from the rest of the world	20	20	20	20	20	20	70	140	80	80	60
a By general government	-	-	-	-	-	-	50	120	60	60	40
b By other resident sectors	20	20	20	20	20	20	20	20	20	20	20
Total Finance of Gross Accumulation	3880	3000	3570	12130	26010	9780	9550	10570	18730	-8320	-26220
Gross Accumulation											
1 Capital transfers paid to the rest of the world	660	660	610	630	700	820	1350	1400	1310	2200	3900
a By general government	480	460	430	440	500	570	1140	1120	1030	1880	3490
b By other resident sectors	180	200	180	190	200	250	210	280	280	320	410
2 Purchases of intangible assets, n.e.c., net, from the rest of the world	...	...	...	...	...	...	...	...	...	...	...
3 Net lending to the rest of the world	3220	2340	2960	11500	25310	8960	8200	9170	17420	-10520	-30120
Total Gross Accumulation	3880	3000	3570	12130	26010	9780	9550	10570	18730	-8320	-26220

3.53 External Transactions: Capital Finance Account

Million Deutsche marks

	1970	1971	1972	1973	1974	1975	1976	1977	1978	1979	1980
Acquisitions of Foreign Financial Assets											
1 Gold and SDR's	...	...	...	...	...	...	...	...	...	-2910	-390
2 Currency and transferable deposits	...	...	...	...	...	...	...	...	...	17460	-5680
3 Other deposits	...	...	...	...	...	...	...	...	...	-3510	8970
4 Bills and bonds, short term	...	...	...	...	...	...	...	...	...	-16270	-10540
5 Bonds, long term	...	...	...	...	...	...	...	...	...	3730	7340
6 Corporate equity securities	...	...	...	...	...	...	...	...	...	3460	3560
7 Short-term loans, n.e.c.	...	...	...	...	...	...	...	...	...	2910	-50
8 Long-term loans	...	...	...	...	...	...	...	...	...	13250	17980
9 Proprietors' net additions to accumulation of quasi-corporate, non-resident enterprises	...	...	...	...	...	...	...	...	...	...	...
10 Trade credit and advances	...	...	...	...	...	...	...	...	...	9510	9400
11 Other	...	...	...	...	...	...	...	...	...	...	...
Total Acquisitions of Foreign Financial Assets	...	...	...	...	...	...	...	...	...	27620	30580
Incurrence of Foreign Liabilities											
1 Currency and transferable deposits	...	...	...	...	...	...	...	...	...	1690	12530
2 Other deposits	...	...	...	...	...	...	...	...	...	26490	3300
3 Bills and bonds, short term	...	...	...	...	...	...	...	...	...	-640	810
4 Bonds, long term	...	...	...	...	...	...	...	...	...	4030	290
5 Corporate equity securities	...	...	...	...	...	...	...	...	...	1440	880
6 Short-term loans, n.e.c.	...	...	...	...	...	...	...	...	...	-8730	9530
7 Long-term loans	...	...	...	...	...	...	...	...	...	4970	27480
8 Non-resident proprietors' net additions to accumulation of resident quasi-corporate enterprises	...	...	...	...	...	...	...	...	...	...	...
9 Trade credit and advances	...	...	...	...	...	...	...	...	...	7850	4630
10 Other	...	...	...	...	...	...	...	...	...	530	510
Total Incurrence of Liabilities	...	...	...	...	...	...	...	...	...	37630	59960
Net Lending	...	...	...	...	...	...	...	...	...	-10010	-29380
Total Incurrence of Liabilities and Net Lending	...	...	...	...	...	...	...	...	...	27620	30580

Germany, Fed. Rep. of

4.3 Derivation of Value Added by Kind of Activity, ISIC Divisions, in Current Prices

Million Deutsche marks

		1970			1971			1972			1973		
		Gross Output	Intermediate Consumption	Value Added	Gross Output	Intermediate Consumption	Value Added	Gross Output	Intermediate Consumption	Value Added	Gross Output	Intermediate Consumption	Value Added

All Producers

		1970 GO	1970 IC	1970 VA	1971 GO	1971 IC	1971 VA	1972 GO	1972 IC	1972 VA	1973 GO	1973 IC	1973 VA
1	Agriculture, hunting, forestry and fishing	42630	19560	23070	44740	20280	24460	48090	21280	26810	53830	24760	29070
	a Agriculture and hunting	37490	17590	19900	39530	18220	21310	42880	19100	23780	47540	22240	25300
	b Forestry and logging [a]	5140	1970	3170	5210	2060	3150	5210	2180	3030	6290	2520	3770
	c Fishing	...	...	...	...	...	...	...	...	...	...	...	...
2	Mining and quarrying [b]	16850	7790	9060	17520	8020	9500	16670	7740	8930	17930	8430	9500
	a Coal mining	13790	6060	7730	15290	6770	8520	14070	6370	7700	15110	6980	8130
	b Crude petroleum and natural gas production												
	c Metal ore mining	3060	1730	1330	2230	1250	980	2600	1370	1230	2820	1450	1370
	d Other mining												
3	Manufacturing	703650	423640	280010	750380	449110	301270	794550	473650	320900	895180	537300	357880
	a Manufacture of food, beverages and tobacco	110780	74010	36770	117980	79150	38830	127150	85550	41600	140350	93520	46830
	b Textile, wearing apparel and leather industries	54810	32130	22680	57780	34120	23660	60770	36740	24030	61490	37400	24090
	c Manufacture of wood and wood products, including furniture	24920	14870	10050	28590	16790	11800	32460	18870	13590	36960	21780	15180
	d Manufacture of paper and paper products, printing and publishing [c]	28350	15380	12970	29630	15860	13770	31100	16690	14410	34680	18820	15860
	e Manufacture of chemicals and chemical petroleum, coal, rubber and plastic products	114380	68940	45440	124320	74620	49700	131000	77840	53160	155300	93100	62200
	f Manufacture of non-metallic mineral products, except products of petroleum and coal [b]	28840	14600	14240	33480	16970	16510	36790	18650	18140	38990	19990	19000
	g Basic metal industries	80540	53060	27480	74530	48850	25680	75000	49080	25920	89990	59600	30390
	h Manufacture of fabricated metal products, machinery and equipment [d]	257050	148680	108370	279840	160650	119190	295680	167880	127800	332500	190540	141960
	i Other manufacturing industries	3980	1970	2010	4230	2100	2130	4600	2350	2250	4920	2550	2370
4	Electricity, gas and water	34490	18440	16050	38480	21170	17310	45000	24770	20230	50680	27820	22860
5	Construction [d]	103110	47520	55590	121920	56660	65260	137280	64430	72850	146410	69640	76770
6	Wholesale and retail trade, restaurants and hotels	562780	483410	79370	608540	519540	89000	649710	553080	96630	725660	623060	102600
	a Wholesale and retail trade	537100	467100	70000	580420	501770	78650	619220	533930	85290	693290	602850	90440
	b Restaurants and hotels	25680	16310	9370	28120	17770	10350	30490	19150	11340	32370	20210	12160
7	Transport, storage and communication	70030	31330	38700	76500	34200	42300	83800	36260	47540	93840	40540	53300
	a Transport and storage	55460	28490	26970	59980	30830	29150	64030	32620	31410	71480	36730	34750
	b Communication	14570	2840	11730	16520	3370	13150	19770	3640	16130	22360	3810	18550
8	Finance, insurance, real estate and business services	77230	21410	55820	88450	25070	63380	99060	26560	72500	111040	28240	82800
	a Financial institutions	23430	6760	16670	26940	7560	19380	30780	8260	22520	34880	9420	25460
	b Insurance	8230	3680	4550	11460	5560	5900	13030	5860	7170	15000	6820	8180
	c Real estate and business services [e]	45570	10970	34600	50050	11950	38100	55250	12440	42810	61160	12000	49160
	Real estate, except dwellings	...	...	...	...	...	...	...	...	...	...	...	...
	Dwellings	45570	10970	34600	50050	11950	38100	55250	12440	42810	61160	12000	49160
9	Community, social and personal services [e]	77060	23930	53130	91790	28750	63040	104840	32970	71870	119410	37370	82040
	a Sanitary and similar services	63710	20770	42940	75240	24760	50480	86010	28420	57590	97550	32120	65430
	b Social and related community services [c]												
	c Recreational and cultural services	13350	3160	10190	16550	3990	12560	18830	4550	14280	21860	5250	16610
	d Personal and household services												
	Total, Industries	1687830	1077030	610800	1838320	1162800	675520	1979000	1240740	738260	2213980	1397160	816820
	Producers of Government Services	119850	56370	63480	143380	67640	75740	160710	75670	85040	186560	87740	98820

Germany, Fed. Rep. of

4.3 Derivation of Value Added by Kind of Activity, ISIC Divisions, in Current Prices
(Continued)

Million Deutsche marks

	1970 Gross Output	1970 Intermediate Consumption	1970 Value Added	1971 Gross Output	1971 Intermediate Consumption	1971 Value Added	1972 Gross Output	1972 Intermediate Consumption	1972 Value Added	1973 Gross Output	1973 Intermediate Consumption	1973 Value Added
Other Producers	12620	3560	9060	14640	3990	10650	16150	4340	11810	18470	4950	13520
Total	1820300	1136960	683340	1996340	1234430	761910	2155860	1320750	835110	2419010	1489850	929160
Imputed bank service charge	...	15590	-15590	...	18130	-18130	...	20790	-20790	...	23270	-23270
Import duties	18600	...	18600	19700	...	19700	21270	...	21270	23510	...	23510
Value added tax	...	...	...	...	...	...	...	...	...	...	...	...
Other adjustments	-7600	...	-7600	-8600	...	-8600	-9600	...	-9600	-10800	...	-10800
Total	1831300	1152550	678750	2007440	1252560	754880	2167530	1341540	825990	2431720	1513120	918600

	1974 Gross Output	1974 Intermediate Consumption	1974 Value Added	1975 Gross Output	1975 Intermediate Consumption	1975 Value Added	1976 Gross Output	1976 Intermediate Consumption	1976 Value Added	1977 Gross Output	1977 Intermediate Consumption	1977 Value Added
						All Producers						
1 Agriculture, hunting, forestry and fishing	53300	26270	27030	57800	27020	30780	63860	31090	32770	65700	32220	33480
a Agriculture and hunting	46160	23420	22740	50960	24060	26900	56310	27810	28500	57980	29330	28650
b Forestry and logging [a]	7140	2850	4290	6840	2960	3880	7550	3280	4270	7720	2890	4830
c Fishing	...	...	...	...	...	...	...	...	...	...	...	...
2 Mining and quarrying [b]	22550	11130	11420	24980	12290	12690	26470	13320	13150	23150	11970	11180
a Coal mining	19140	9370	9770	20960	10430	10530	23030	11600	11430	20920	10880	10040
b Crude petroleum and natural gas production												
c Metal ore mining	3410	1760	1650	4020	1860	2160	3440	1720	1720	2230	1090	1140
d Other mining												
3 Manufacturing	1007990	623370	384620	1005570	619960	385610	1117270	695110	422160	1180650	727910	452740
a Manufacture of food, beverages and tobacco	151480	103770	47710	155160	107120	48040	167650	116900	50750	177050	123400	53650
b Textile, wearing apparel and leather industries	63600	38650	24950	63290	38800	24490	67580	42390	25190	69200	43050	26150
c Manufacture of wood and wood products, including furniture	38220	22650	15570	36860	21730	15130	40080	23930	16150	44970	26410	18560
d Manufacture of paper and paper products, printing and publishing [c]	40420	23180	17240	39420	22030	17390	42410	23920	18490	45100	25280	19820
e Manufacture of chemicals and chemical petroleum, coal, rubber and plastic products	202640	130120	72520	188280	121390	66890	217360	141600	75760	222970	145910	77060
f Manufacture of non-metallic mineral products, except products of petroleum and coal [b]	39760	21230	18530	37960	20320	17640	43580	23990	19590	44710	24750	19960
g Basic metal industries	111050	73580	37470	103880	67860	36020	106400	70380	36020	106990	68940	38050
h Manufacture of fabricated metal products, machinery and equipment [d]	355540	207280	148260	375380	217970	157410	426090	248900	177190	462510	266520	195990
i Other manufacturing industries	5280	2910	2370	5340	2740	2600	6120	3100	3020	7150	3650	3500
4 Electricity, gas and water	58210	33050	25160	68510	39950	28560	78250	46540	31710	83160	50260	32900
5 Construction [d]	143250	69380	73870	138760	68200	70560	147290	72980	74310	157100	77730	79370
6 Wholesale and retail trade, restaurants and hotels	791730	687680	104050	807250	693230	114020	886890	763300	123590	931290	798820	132470
a Wholesale and retail trade	757540	666240	91300	770250	670250	100000	847410	738810	108600	888460	772440	116020
b Restaurants and hotels	34190	21440	12750	37000	22980	14020	39480	24490	14990	42830	26380	16450
7 Transport, storage and communication	104700	45780	58920	108090	46890	61200	118150	51360	66790	126490	55010	71480
a Transport and storage	79560	41770	37790	79890	42800	37090	88150	47080	41070	94110	50740	43370
b Communication	25140	4010	21130	28200	4090	24110	30000	4280	25720	32380	4270	28110
8 Finance, insurance, real estate and business services	126430	33060	93370	138670	35560	103110	149590	39280	110310	160740	43480	117260
a Financial institutions	42100	10990	31110	46110	11470	34640	50730	13620	37110	54890	15140	39750
b Insurance	17690	8240	9450	19620	9030	10590	20410	9310	11100	23410	10690	12720
c Real estate and business services [e]	66640	13830	52810	72940	15060	57880	78450	16350	62100	82440	17650	64790
Real estate, except dwellings	...	...	...	...	...	...	...	...	...	...	...	...

Germany, Fed. Rep. of

4.3 Derivation of Value Added by Kind of Activity, ISIC Divisions, in Current Prices
(Continued)

Million Deutsche marks

	1974 Gross Output	1974 Intermediate Consumption	1974 Value Added	1975 Gross Output	1975 Intermediate Consumption	1975 Value Added	1976 Gross Output	1976 Intermediate Consumption	1976 Value Added	1977 Gross Output	1977 Intermediate Consumption	1977 Value Added
Dwellings	66640	13830	52810	72940	15060	57880	78450	16350	62100	82440	17650	64790
9 Community, social and personal services [e]	135880	43730	92150	153270	51860	101410	171310	58400	112910	191400	65500	125900
a Sanitary and similar services	110830	37770	73060	121650	43220	78430	136530	49150	87380	154740	55710	99030
b Social and related community services [c]												
c Recreational and cultural services	25050	5960	19090	31620	8640	22980	34780	9250	25530	36660	9790	26870
d Personal and household services												
Total, Industries	2444040	1573450	870590	2502900	1594960	907940	2759080	1771380	987700	2919680	1862900	1056780
Producers of Government Services	217120	102570	114550	241910	117460	124450	257660	126240	131420	271740	131350	140390
Other Producers	20590	5460	15130	23050	6380	16670	24980	6970	18010	27320	7690	19630
Total	2681750	1681480	1000270	2767860	1718800	1049060	3041720	1904590	1137130	3218740	2001940	1216800
Imputed bank service charge	...	29650	-29650	...	32610	-32610	...	34910	-34910	...	38280	-38280
Import duties	26910	...	26910	28180	...	28180	32800	...	32800	34970	...	34970
Value added tax	...	...	...	...	...	...	...	...	...	...	...	...
Other adjustments	-10400	...	-10400	-10600	...	-10600	-12200	...	-12200	-13000	...	-13000
Total	2698260	1711130	987130	2785440	1751410	1034030	3062320	1939500	1122820	3240710	2040220	1200490

	1978 Gross Output	1978 Intermediate Consumption	1978 Value Added	1979 Gross Output	1979 Intermediate Consumption	1979 Value Added	1980 Gross Output	1980 Intermediate Consumption	1980 Value Added
All Producers									
1 Agriculture, hunting, forestry and fishing	67110	32700	34410	68430	35840	32590	70360	38140	32220
a Agriculture and hunting	59020	29670	29350	59900	32600	27300	...	...	...
b Forestry and logging [a]	8090	3030	5060	8530	3240	5290	...	...	...
c Fishing	...	...	...	...	...	...	...	...	...
2 Mining and quarrying [b]	24940	13390	11550	...	...	...	...	...	...
a Coal mining	21910	11630	10280	...	...	...	...	...	...
b Crude petroleum and natural gas production									
c Metal ore mining	3030	1760	1270	...	...	...	...	...	...
d Other mining									
3 Manufacturing	1241230	757120	484110	1381380	857070	524310	...	...	542310
a Manufacture of food, beverages and tobacco	187150	129950	57200	...	...	...	...	...	...
b Textile, wearing apparel and leather industries	71290	44180	27110	...	...	...	...	...	...
c Manufacture of wood and wood products, including furniture	46430	27470	18960	...	...	...	...	...	...
d Manufacture of paper and paper products, printing and publishing [c]	47430	25860	21570	...	...	...	...	...	...
e Manufacture of chemicals and chemical petroleum, coal, rubber and plastic products	230000	147830	82170	...	...	...	...	...	...
f Manufacture of non-metallic mineral products, except products of petroleum and coal [b]	48170	26980	21190	...	...	...	...	...	...
g Basic metal industries	109400	69790	39610	...	...	...	...	...	...
h Manufacture of fabricated metal products, machinery and equipment [d]	493700	280990	212710	...	...	...	...	...	...
i Other manufacturing industries	7660	4070	3590	...	...	...	...	...	...
4 Electricity, gas and water	91210	55280	35930	...	...	...	...	...	35930
5 Construction [d]	171130	84650	86480	198990	98400	100590	...	...	115940
6 Wholesale and retail trade, restaurants and hotels	985340	843880	141460	1081560	928630	152930	...	...	140360
a Wholesale and retail trade	939850	816090	123760	1032870	898880	133990	...	...	140360
b Restaurants and hotels	45490	27790	17700	48690	29750	18940	...	...	...
7 Transport, storage and communication	133290	57750	75540	146270	63850	82420	...	...	86440
a Transport and storage	98450	53140	45310	108780	58800	49980	...	...	...
b Communication	34840	4610	30230	37490	5050	32440	...	...	...
8 Finance, insurance, real estate and business services	171490	46980	124510	183200	52000	131200	...	...	142160
a Financial institutions	58990	16180	42810	63980	17460	46520	...	...	...

Germany, Fed. Rep. of

4.3 Derivation of Value Added by Kind of Activity, ISIC Divisions, in Current Prices
(Continued)

Million Deutsche marks

	1978 Gross Output	1978 Intermediate Consumption	1978 Value Added	1979 Gross Output	1979 Intermediate Consumption	1979 Value Added	1980 Gross Output	1980 Intermediate Consumption	1980 Value Added
b Insurance	25530	11830	13700	27350	13200	14150	...	...	...
c Real estate and business services e	86970	18970	68000	91870	21340	70530	...	...	75510
Real estate, except dwellings	...	...	...	...	...	...	...	...	...
Dwellings	86970	18970	68000	91870	21340	70530	...	...	75510
9 Community, social and personal services e	213520	73850	139670	237740	82340	155400	...	...	193610
a Sanitary and similar services	174350	63360	110990	195430	71000	124430	...	...	...
b Social and related community services c							...		...
c Recreational and cultural services	39170	10490	28680	42310	11340	30970			
d Personal and household services							...	...	...
Total, Industries	3099260	1965600	1133660	3422880	2192420	1230460	3635550	2327090	1308460
Producers of Government Services	292220	142700	149520	316000	155570	160430	344120	170400	173720
Other Producers	29730	8480	21250	32420	9370	23050	35690	10440	25250
Total	3421210	2116780	1304430	3771300	2357360	1413940	4015360	2507930	1507430
Imputed bank service charge	...	41760	-41760	...	45650	-45650	...	49760	-49760
Import duties	38610	...	38610	45150	...	45150	53050	...	53050
Value added tax	...	...	...	...	...	...	...	...	...
Other adjustments	-14900	...	-14900	-19500	...	-19500	-21800	...	-21800
Total	3444920	2158540	1286380	3796950	2403010	1393940	4046610	2557690	1488920

a) including hunting and fishing.
b) Gross input and intermediate consumption of electricity, gas and water are included in item 'Mining and quarrying'.
c) Publishing is included in item 'Community, social and personal services'.
d) Structural steel erection is included in item 'Manufacture of fabricated metal products, machinery and equipment'.
e) Business services and real estate except dwellings are included in item 'Community, social and personal services'.

4.4 Derivation of Value Added by Kind of Activity, ISIC Divisions, in Constant Prices

Million Deutsche marks

	1970 Gross Output	1970 Intermediate Consumption	1970 Value Added	1971 Gross Output	1971 Intermediate Consumption	1971 Value Added	1972 Gross Output	1972 Intermediate Consumption	1972 Value Added	1973 Gross Output	1973 Intermediate Consumption	1973 Value Added
					At constant prices of:1970 All Producers							
1 Agriculture, hunting, forestry and fishing	42630	19560	23070	43550	19760	23790	43000	19760	23240	45970	20180	25790
a Agriculture and hunting	...	...	19900	...	...	20700	...	...	20330	...	...	22310
b Forestry and logging a	...	...	3170	...	...	3090	...	...	2910	...	...	3480
c Fishing	...	...	...	...	...	...	...	...	...	...	...	...
2 Mining and quarrying b	51340	26230	9060	53950	28250	8470	56850	30320	7580	61990	33050	7780
a Coal mining	...	...	7730	...	...	7540	...	...	6500	...	...	6610
b Crude petroleum and natural gas production	...	...		...	...		...	...		...	...	
c Metal ore mining	...	...	1330	...	...	930	...	...	1080	...	...	1170
d Other mining	...	...		...	...		...	...		...	...	
3 Manufacturing	703650	423640	280010	720060	436250	283810	745800	453950	291850	790720	481000	309720
a Manufacture of food, beverages and tobacco	...	...	36770	...	...	37570	...	...	37670	...	...	39150
b Textile, wearing apparel and leather industries	...	...	22680	...	...	22710	...	...	22690	...	...	21220
c Manufacture of wood and wood products, including furniture	...	...	10050	...	...	10840	...	...	11800	...	...	12480
d Manufacture of paper and paper products, printing and publishing c	...	...	12970	...	...	12760	...	...	12930	...	...	13690
e Manufacture of chemicals and chemical petroleum, coal, rubber and plastic products	...	...	45440	...	...	48060	...	...	51470	...	...	55940
f Manufacture of non-metallic mineral products, except products of petroleum and coal b	...	...	14240	...	...	15080	...	...	15900	...	...	16280
g Basic metal industries	...	...	27480	...	...	25550	...	...	25710	...	...	27530
h Manufacture of fabricated metal products, machinery and equipment d	...	...	108370	...	...	109230	...	...	111690	...	...	121500
i Other manufacturing industries	...	...	2010	...	...	2010	...	...	1990	...	...	1930
4 Electricity, gas and water b	...	...	16050	...	...	17230	...	...	18950	...	...	21160

Germany, Fed. Rep. of

4.4 Derivation of Value Added by Kind of Activity, ISIC Divisions, in Constant Prices
(Continued)

Million Deutsche marks

	1970 Gross Output	1970 Intermediate Consumption	1970 Value Added	1971 Gross Output	1971 Intermediate Consumption	1971 Value Added	1972 Gross Output	1972 Intermediate Consumption	1972 Value Added	1973 Gross Output	1973 Intermediate Consumption	1973 Value Added
					At constant prices of:1970							
5 Construction	103110	47520	55590	111860	51680	60180	119730	55810	63920	120280	55900	64380
6 Wholesale and retail trade, restaurants and hotels	537100	457100	79370	555300	483200	81610	569240	495350	83490	591990	516430	85080
a Wholesale and retail trade	...	...	70000	...	...	72100	...	...	73890	...	...	75560
b Restaurants and hotels	...	...	9370	...	...	9510	...	...	9600	...	...	9520
7 Transport, storage and communication	70030	31330	38700	70920	31830	39090	72710	32750	39960	76140	34340	41800
a Transport and storage	...	...	26970	...	...	26520	...	...	26880	...	...	28020
b Communication	...	...	11730	...	...	12570	...	...	13080	...	...	13780
8 Finance, insurance, real estate and business services	77230	21410	55820	81620	23750	57870	86800	24600	62200	91300	26070	65230
a Financial institutions	31660	10440	16670	34420	12350	17300	37610	12560	19440	39840	13360	20520
b Insurance	...	...	4550	...	...	4770	...	...	5610	...	...	5960
c Real estate and business services [e]	45570	10970	34600	47200	11400	35800	49190	12040	37150	51460	12710	38750
Real estate, except dwellings	...	...	...	...	...	...	...	...	...	...	...	...
Dwellings	45570	10970	34600	47200	11400	35800	49190	12040	37150	51460	12710	38750
9 Community, social and personal services [e]	102740	40240	53130	109420	43070	56840	115150	45550	60000	118730	46550	62660
Educational services	...	...	...	...	...	...	...	...	...	...	...	...
Medical, dental, other health and veterinary services	...	...	10190	...	...	10820	...	...	11280	...	...	12140
Total, Industries	1687830	1077030	610800	1746680	1117790	628890	1809280	1158090	651190	1897120	1213520	683600
Producers of Government Services	132470	58930	63480	140000	64540	66270	145990	67170	69470	153220	71000	72760
Other Producers	...	...	9060	...	...	9190	...	...	9350	...	...	9460
Total	1820300	1136960	683340	1886680	1182330	704350	1955270	1225260	730010	2050340	1284520	765820
Imputed bank service charge	...	15590	-15590	...	16310	-16310	...	18170	-18170	...	18970	-18970
Import duties	18600	...	18600	19950	...	19950	21830	...	21830	22430	...	22430
Value added tax	...	...	...	...	...	...	...	...	...	...	...	...
Other adjustments [f]	-7600	...	-7600	-7310	...	-7310	-7390	...	-7390	-7440	...	-7440
Total	1831300	1152550	678750	1899320	1198640	700680	1969710	1243430	726280	2065330	1303490	761840

	1974 Gross Output	1974 Intermediate Consumption	1974 Value Added	1975 Gross Output	1975 Intermediate Consumption	1975 Value Added	1976 Gross Output	1976 Intermediate Consumption	1976 Value Added	1977 Gross Output	1977 Intermediate Consumption	1977 Value Added
				At constant prices of:1970								
				All Producers								
1 Agriculture, hunting, forestry and fishing	45940	19880	26060	45030	20070	24960	45660	21430	24230	47700	21910	25790
a Agriculture and hunting	...	...	22420	...	...	21630	...	...	20720	...	...	22280
b Forestry and logging [a]	...	...	3640	...	...	3330	...	...	3510	...	...	3510
c Fishing	...	...	...	...	...	...	...	...	...	...	...	...
2 Mining and quarrying [b]	64980	34710	7780	62520	33500	6760	66130	35930	6360	66740	36240	5520
a Coal mining	...	...	6730	...	...	5560	...	...	5590	...	...	5050
b Crude petroleum and natural gas production	...	...	} 1050	...	...	} 1200	...	...	} 770	...	...	} 470
c Metal ore mining	...	...		...	...		...	...		...	...	
d Other mining	...	...		...	...		...	...		...	...	

Germany, Fed. Rep. of

4.4 Derivation of Value Added by Kind of Activity, ISIC Divisions, in Constant Prices
(Continued)

Million Deutsche marks

	1974 Gross Output	1974 Intermediate Consumption	1974 Value Added	1975 Gross Output	1975 Intermediate Consumption	1975 Value Added	1976 Gross Output	1976 Intermediate Consumption	1976 Value Added	1977 Gross Output	1977 Intermediate Consumption	1977 Value Added
				\multicolumn{3}{c	}{At constant prices of: 1970}						
3 Manufacturing	786070	475510	310560	759070	464770	294300	817040	501600	315440	842560	518310	324250
a Manufacture of food, beverages and tobacco	...	...	39290	...	...	38030	...	...	38460	...	...	37870
b Textile, wearing apparel and leather industries	...	...	20550	...	...	20020	...	...	20490	...	...	20380
c Manufacture of wood and wood products, including furniture	...	...	12120	...	...	11620	...	...	12080	...	...	12510
d Manufacture of paper and paper products, printing and publishing [c]	...	...	13330	...	...	12200	...	...	13010	...	...	13320
e Manufacture of chemicals and chemical petroleum, coal, rubber and plastic products	...	...	55780	...	...	49040	...	...	55910	...	...	57110
f Manufacture of non-metallic mineral products, except products of petroleum and coal [b]	...	...	15620	...	...	14260	...	...	15760	...	...	15690
g Basic metal industries	...	...	28650	...	...	28390	...	...	28080	...	...	29140
h Manufacture of fabricated metal products, machinery and equipment [d]	...	...	123430	...	...	119020	...	...	129680	...	...	136020
i Other manufacturing industries	...	...	1790	...	...	1720	...	...	1970	...	...	2210
4 Electricity, gas and water [b]	...	...	22490	...	...	22260	...	...	23840	...	...	24980
5 Construction	110210	51090	59120	104790	49130	55660	107930	50930	57000	110240	52310	57930
6 Wholesale and retail trade, restaurants and hotels	577380	503460	83420	565560	491580	83720	592840	515670	87170	607130	527500	89910
a Wholesale and retail trade	...	...	73920	...	...	73980	...	...	77170	...	...	79630
b Restaurants and hotels	...	...	9500	...	...	9740	...	...	10000	...	...	10280
7 Transport, storage and communication	77030	34120	42910	75620	33680	41940	81290	36250	45040	85510	38020	47490
a Transport and storage	...	...	28240	...	...	26740	...	...	28560	...	...	29400
b Communication	...	...	14670	...	...	15200	...	...	16480	...	...	18090
8 Finance, insurance, real estate and business services	94090	27160	66930	96570	27530	69040	101030	29220	71810	105400	31050	74350
a Financial institutions	40510	14120	20750	41240	13960	21330	44250	15290	22730	47600	16810	24420
b Insurance	...	...	5640	...	...	5950	...	...	6230	...	...	6370
c Real estate and business services [e]	53580	13040	40540	55330	13570	41760	56780	13930	42850	57800	14240	43560
Real estate, except dwellings	...	...	...	...	...	...	...	...	...	...	...	...
Dwellings	53580	13040	40540	55330	13570	41760	56780	13930	42850	57800	14240	43560
9 Community, social and personal services [e]	121570	46840	65230	126430	48470	68220	133050	50850	72200	140750	53750	76720
Educational services	...	...	...	...	...	...	...	...	...	...	...	...
Medical, dental, other health and veterinary services	...	...	13120	...	...	14610	...	...	15170	...	...	15320
Total, Industries	1877270	1192770	684500	1835590	1168730	666860	1944970	1241880	703090	2006030	1279090	726940
Producers of Government Services	158830	73200	76070	165600	77520	78290	169660	80380	79270	170950	80470	80290
Other Producers	...	...	9560	...	...	9790	...	...	10010	...	...	10190
Total	2036100	1265970	770130	2001190	1246250	754940	2114630	1322260	792370	2176980	1359560	817420
Imputed bank service charge	...	19310	-19310	...	19820	-19820	...	21210	-21210	...	23530	-23530
Import duties	21830	...	21830	23200	...	23200	26760	...	26760	28320	...	28320
Value added tax	...	...	...	...	...	...	...	...	...	...	...	...
Other adjustments [f]	-6700	...	-6700	-6520	...	-6520	-7330	...	-7330	-7630	...	-7630
Total	2051230	1285280	765950	2017870	1266070	751800	2134060	1343470	790590	2197670	1383090	814580

	1978 Gross Output	1978 Intermediate Consumption	1978 Value Added	1979 Gross Output	1979 Intermediate Consumption	1979 Value Added	1980 Gross Output	1980 Intermediate Consumption	1980 Value Added
	\multicolumn{9}{c	}{At constant prices of: 1970}
	\multicolumn{9}{c	}{All Producers}
1 Agriculture, hunting, forestry and fishing	49900	22840	27060	50080	24030	26050	50660	24190	26470
a Agriculture and hunting	...	...	23550	...	...	22510	...	...	...
b Forestry and logging [a]	...	...	3510	...	...	3540	...	...	...
c Fishing	...	...	...	...	...	...	...	...	...
2 Mining and quarrying [b]	70580	38660	5600	74610	41020	33590	...	...	...

Germany, Fed. Rep. of

4.4 Derivation of Value Added by Kind of Activity, ISIC Divisions, in Constant Prices
(Continued)

Million Deutsche marks

		1978 Gross Output	1978 Intermediate Consumption	1978 Value Added	1979 Gross Output	1979 Intermediate Consumption	1979 Value Added	1980 Gross Output	1980 Intermediate Consumption	1980 Value Added
					At constant prices of:1970					
	a Coal mining	...	...	4930	...	...	...	...	...	...
	b Crude petroleum and natural gas production	...	...		...	...		...	...	
	c Metal ore mining	...	...	670	...	...		...	...	
	d Other mining	...	...		...	...	...	...	...	...
3	Manufacturing	869200	539200	330000	913300	567290	346010	...	...	346880
	a Manufacture of food, beverages and tobacco	...	...	39250	...	...	...	...	...	...
	b Textile, wearing apparel and leather industries	...	...	19960	...	...	...	...	...	...
	c Manufacture of wood and wood products, including furniture	...	...	12360	...	...	...	...	...	...
	d Manufacture of paper and paper products, printing and publishing c	...	...	13480	...	...	...	...	...	...
	e Manufacture of chemicals and chemical petroleum, coal, rubber and plastic products	...	...	58750	...	...	...	...	...	...
	f Manufacture of non-metallic mineral products, except products of petroleum and coal b	...	...	16370	...	...	...	...	...	...
	g Basic metal industries	...	...	28910	...	...	...	...	...	...
	h Manufacture of fabricated metal products, machinery and equipment d	...	...	138730	...	...	...	...	...	...
	i Other manufacturing industries	...	...	2190	...	...	...	...	...	...
4	Electricity, gas and water b	...	...	26320	...	...	...	...	...	...
5	Construction	113060	53700	59360	120750	57440	63310	...	...	66120
6	Wholesale and retail trade, restaurants and hotels	634920	551860	93380	659500	573240	96750	...	...	85480
	a Wholesale and retail trade	...	...	83060	...	...	86260	...	...	...
	b Restaurants and hotels	...	...	10320	...	...	10490	...	...	...
7	Transport, storage and communication	88990	38960	50030	95420	41230	54190	...	...	56680
	a Transport and storage	...	...	29970	...	...	32220	...	...	...
	b Communication	...	...	20060	...	...	21970	...	...	...
8	Finance, insurance, real estate and business services	109910	32900	77010	114370	34090	80280	...	...	82650
	a Financial institutions	50620	18060	26080	53610	18840	27930	...	...	...
	b Insurance	...	...	6480	...	...	6840	...	...	...
	c Real estate and business services e	59290	14840	44450	60760	15250	45510	...	...	46650
	Real estate, except dwellings	...	...	...	...	...	...	...	...	...
	Dwellings	59290	14840	44450	60760	15250	45510	...	...	46650
9	Community, social and personal services e	148620	56430	81870	156760	59300	86970	...	...	102280
	Educational services	...	...	...	...	...	...	...	...	...
	Medical, dental, other health and veterinary services	...	...	15670	...	...	16180	...	...	...
Total, Industries		2085180	1334550	750630	2184790	1397640	787150	2200950	1400500	800450
Producers of Government Services		177960	84820	82590	183690	87680	85110	188170	89750	87190
Other Producers		...	...	10550	...	...	10900	...	...	11230
Total		2263140	1419370	843770	2368480	1485320	883160	2389120	1490250	898870
Imputed bank service charge		...	25600	-25600	...	27460	-27460	...	28070	-28070
Import duties		30710	...	30710	32550	...	32550	34180	...	34180
Value added tax		...	...	...	...	...	...	...	...	...
Other adjustments f		-8040	...	-8040	-9930	...	-9930	-9840	...	-9840
Total		2285810	1444970	840840	2391100	1512780	878320	2413460	1518320	895140

a) including hunting and fishing.
b) Gross input and intermediate consumption of electricity, gas and water are included in item 'Mining and quarrying'.
c) Publishing is included in item 'Community, social and personal services'.
d) Structural steel erection is included in 'Manufacture of fabricated metal products, machinery and equipment'.
e) Business services and real estate except dwellings are included in item 'Community, social and personal services'.
f) Relating to adjustment for double accounting of turnover taxes on investment goods.

Germany, Fed. Rep. of

4.6 Cost Components of Value Added, ISIC Divisions

Million Deutsche marks

		1970					1971				
	Compensation of Employees	Capital Consumption	Net Operating Surplus	Indirect Taxes	Less: Subsidies Received	Value Added	Compensation of Employees	Capital Consumption	Net Operating Surplus	Indirect Taxes	Less: Subsidies Received	Value Added

All Producers

	Comp. Emp. 1970	Cap. Cons. 1970	Net Op. Surp. 1970	Ind. Tax 1970	Subs. 1970	V.A. 1970	Comp. Emp. 1971	Cap. Cons. 1971	Net Op. Surp. 1971	Ind. Tax 1971	Subs. 1971	V.A. 1971
1 Agriculture, hunting, forestry and fishing	3530	4470	15670	-600	...	23070	3830	4900	16620	-890	...	24460
a Agriculture and hunting	...	4220	...	-870	...	19900	...	4610	...	-1110	...	21310
b Forestry and logging	...	250	...	270	...	3170	...	290	...	220	...	3150
c Fishing	...	...	...	...	...	...	...	...	...	...	...	...
2 Mining and quarrying	6250	1250	800	760	...	9060	6830	1350	550	770	...	9500
a Coal mining	5750	960	510	510	...	7730	6320	1050	560	590	...	8520
b Crude petroleum and natural gas production					...						...	
c Metal ore mining	500	290	290	250	...	1330	510	300	-10	180	...	980
d Other mining					...						...	
3 Manufacturing	155600	23600	57390	43420	...	280010	170650	27230	56130	47260	...	301270
a Manufacture of food, beverages and tobacco	12070	3020	8630	13050	...	36770	13290	3450	8430	13660	...	38830
b Textile, wearing apparel and leather industries	13290	1570	5470	2350	...	22680	14110	1750	5260	2540	...	23660
c Manufacture of wood and wood products, including furniture	5750	690	2010	1600	...	10050	6510	860	2520	1910	...	11800
d Manufacture of paper and paper products, printing and publishing	8010	1080	2530	1350	...	12970	8710	1220	2370	1470	...	13770
e Manufacture of chemicals and chemical petroleum, coal, rubber and plastic products	19840	4690	7740	13170	...	45440	21640	5420	8450	14190	...	49700
f Manufacture of non-metallic mineral products, except products of petroleum and coal	7390	1670	3390	1790	...	14240	8290	2070	3980	2170	...	16510
g Basic metal industries	16500	2660	5760	2560	...	27480	17190	2860	3140	2490	...	25680
h Manufacture of fabricated metal products, machinery and equipment [a]	71580	8130	21300	7360	...	108370	79680	9500	21390	8620	...	119190
i Other manufacturing industries	1170	90	560	190	...	2010	1230	100	590	210	...	2130
4 Electricity, gas and water	4580	3500	5900	2070	...	16050	5150	3970	5690	2500	...	17310
5 Construction	32340	3040	14490	5720	...	55590	36850	3430	17750	7230	...	65260
6 Wholesale and retail trade, restaurants and hotels	33000	4940	33230	8200	...	79370	37040	5570	35500	10890	...	89000
a Wholesale and retail trade	33000	4150	26230	6620	...	70000	37040	4660	27860	9090	...	78650
b Restaurants and hotels	-	790	7000	1580	...	9370	...	910	7640	1800	...	10350
7 Transport, storage and communication	25360	7120	6110	110	...	38700	29570	8100	5090	-460	...	42300
a Transport and storage	17230	5060	4460	220	...	26970	19860	5690	3910	-310	...	29150
b Communication	8130	2060	1650	-110	...	11730	9710	2410	1180	-150	...	13150
8 Finance, insurance, real estate and business services	11910	13430	27810	2670	...	55820	14270	15610	30120	3380	...	63380
a Financial institutions	8050	650	7290	680	...	16670	9850	760	7900	870	...	19380
b Insurance	3860	240	-480	930	...	4550	4420	270	-30	1240	...	5900
c Real estate and business services	-	12540	21000	1060	...	34600	-	14580	22250	1270	...	38100
Real estate, except dwellings	...	...	...	...	...	...	...	...	...	...	...	...
Dwellings	-	12540	21000	1060	...	34600	-	14580	22250	1270	...	38100
9 Community, social and personal services	19300	2820	26940	4070	...	53130	21430	3480	33550	4580	...	63040
a Sanitary and similar services	19300	2260	17380	4000	...	42940	21430	2760	21780	4510	...	50480
b Social and related community services	...	560	9560	70	...	10190	...	720	11770	70	...	12560
Educational services	...	...	...	...	...	...	...	...	...	...	...	...
Medical, dental, other health and veterinary services	-	560	9560	70	...	10190	-	720	11770	70	...	12560
c Recreational and cultural services	...	...	...	...	...	...	...	...	...	...	...	...
d Personal and household services	...	...	...	...	...	...	...	...	...	...	...	...
Total, Industries [b]	291870	64170	188340	66420	...	610800	325620	73640	201000	75260	...	675520
Producers of Government Services	60140	3250	-	90	...	63480	71890	3740	-	110	...	75740

Germany, Fed. Rep. of

4.6 Cost Components of Value Added, ISIC Divisions
(Continued)

Million Deutsche marks

	1970						1971					
	Compensation of Employees	Capital Consumption	Net Operating Surplus	Indirect Taxes	Less: Subsidies Received	Value Added	Compensation of Employees	Capital Consumption	Net Operating Surplus	Indirect Taxes	Less: Subsidies Received	Value Added
Other Producers	8100	930	-	30	...	9060	9570	1070	-	10	...	10650
Total	360110	68350	188340	66540	...	683340	407080	78450	201000	75380	...	761910
Imputed bank service charge	...	...	-15590	...	...	-15590	...	...	-18130	...	...	-18130
Import duties	...	...	...	18600	...	18600	...	...	...	19700	...	19700
Value added tax	...	...	...	...	...	...	...	...	...	...	...	...
Other adjustments	...	...	...	-7600	...	-7600	...	...	...	-8600	...	-8600
Total	360110	68350	172750	77540	...	678750	407080	78450	182870	86480	...	754880

	1972						1973					
	Compensation of Employees	Capital Consumption	Net Operating Surplus	Indirect Taxes	Less: Subsidies Received	Value Added	Compensation of Employees	Capital Consumption	Net Operating Surplus	Indirect Taxes	Less: Subsidies Received	Value Added
						All Producers						
1 Agriculture, hunting, forestry and fishing	3960	5190	18000	-340	...	26810	4220	5620	19480	-250	...	29070
a Agriculture and hunting	...	4900	...	-590	...	23780	...	5320	...	-560	...	25300
b Forestry and logging	...	290	...	250	...	3030	...	300	...	310	...	3770
c Fishing	...	...	...	...	...	...	...	...	...	...	...	...
2 Mining and quarrying	6790	1400	110	630	...	8930	7040	1450	760	250	...	9500
a Coal mining	6230	1080	-20	410	...	7700	6440	1100	580	10	...	8130
b Crude petroleum and natural gas production	⎱	⎱	⎱	⎱	...	⎱	⎱	⎱	⎱	⎱	...	⎱
c Metal ore mining	560	320	130	220	...	1230	600	350	180	240	...	1370
d Other mining	⎰	⎰	⎰	⎰	...	⎰	⎰	⎰	⎰	⎰	...	⎰
3 Manufacturing	184680	29780	53590	52850	...	320900	210090	32560	56910	58320	...	357880
a Manufacture of food, beverages and tobacco	14480	3650	7820	15650	...	41600	16160	3920	9580	17170	...	46830
b Textile, wearing apparel and leather industries	15190	1760	4410	2670	...	24030	16000	1750	3590	2750	...	24090
c Manufacture of wood and wood products, including furniture	7360	1010	2980	2240	...	13590	8400	1140	3120	2520	...	15180
d Manufacture of paper and paper products, printing and publishing	9240	1300	2300	1570	...	14410	10360	1430	2360	1710	...	15860
e Manufacture of chemicals and chemical petroleum, coal, rubber and plastic products	23520	5830	7990	15820	...	53160	26630	6520	10480	18570	...	62200
f Manufacture of non-metallic mineral products, except products of petroleum and coal	9120	2170	4400	2450	...	18140	10110	2240	4130	2520	...	19000
g Basic metal industries	18260	3030	2170	2460	...	25920	20870	3400	3410	2710	...	30390
h Manufacture of fabricated metal products, machinery and equipment [a]	86190	10920	20940	9750	...	127800	100140	12040	19660	10120	...	141960
i Other manufacturing industries	1320	110	580	240	...	2250	1420	120	580	250	...	2370
4 Electricity, gas and water	5870	4410	6900	3050	...	20230	6710	4940	7560	3650	...	22860
5 Construction	40970	3700	19470	8710	...	72850	44980	4010	18170	9610	...	76770
6 Wholesale and retail trade, restaurants and hotels	41360	6100	37190	11980	...	96630	46620	6710	37250	12020	...	102600
a Wholesale and retail trade	41360	5070	28870	9990	...	85290	46620	5560	28410	9850	...	90440
b Restaurants and hotels	-	1030	8320	1990	...	11340	-	1150	8840	2170	...	12160
7 Transport, storage and communication	32940	8800	8320	-2520	...	47540	37440	9810	9560	-3510	...	53300
a Transport and storage	22030	6010	5730	-2360	...	31410	24900	6470	6730	-3350	...	34750
b Communication	10910	2790	2590	-160	...	16130	12540	3340	2830	-160	...	18550
8 Finance, insurance, real estate and business services	16260	17510	34720	4010	...	72500	18600	19770	39670	4760	...	82800
a Financial institutions	11160	860	9450	1050	...	22520	12820	940	10730	970	...	25460
b Insurance	5100	300	210	1560	...	7170	5780	350	260	1790	...	8180
c Real estate and business services	-	16350	25060	1400	...	42810	-	18480	28680	2000	...	49160
Real estate, except dwellings	...	...	...	...	...	...	...	...	...	...	...	...
Dwellings	-	16350	25060	1400	...	42810	-	18480	28680	2000	...	49160
9 Community, social and personal services	23590	4100	38980	5200	...	71870	26610	4910	44800	5720	...	82040
a Sanitary and similar services	23590	3250	25640	5110	...	57590	26610	3890	29320	5610	...	65430
b Social and related community services	...	850	13340	90	...	14280	...	1020	15480	110	...	16610

Germany, Fed. Rep. of

4.6 Cost Components of Value Added, ISIC Divisions
(Continued)

Million Deutsche marks

	1972						1973					
	Compensation of Employees	Capital Consumption	Net Operating Surplus	Indirect Taxes	Less: Subsidies Received	Value Added	Compensation of Employees	Capital Consumption	Net Operating Surplus	Indirect Taxes	Less: Subsidies Received	Value Added
Educational services	...	...	...	...	...	...	...	...	...	...	...	...
Medical, dental, other health and veterinary services	-	850	13340	90	...	14280	-	1020	15480	110	...	16610
c Recreational and cultural services	...	...	...	...	...	...	...	...	...	...	...	...
d Personal and household services	...	...	...	...	...	...	...	...	...	...	...	...
Total, Industries [b]	356420	80990	217280	83570	...	738260	402310	89780	234160	90570	...	816820
Producers of Government Services	80760	4150	-	130	...	85040	94030	4640	-	150	...	98820
Other Producers	10610	1190	-	10	...	11810	12190	1320	-	10	...	13520
Total	447790	86330	217280	83710	...	835110	508530	95740	234160	90730	...	929160
Imputed bank service charge	...	...	-20790	...	...	-20790	...	...	-23270	...	...	-23270
Import duties	...	...	...	21270	...	21270	...	...	...	23510	...	23510
Value added tax	...	...	...	...	...	...	...	...	...	...	...	...
Other adjustments	...	...	...	-9600	...	-9600	...	...	...	-10800	...	-10800
Total	447790	86330	196490	95380	...	825990	508530	95740	210890	103440	...	918600

	1974						1975					
	Compensation of Employees	Capital Consumption	Net Operating Surplus	Indirect Taxes	Less: Subsidies Received	Value Added	Compensation of Employees	Capital Consumption	Net Operating Surplus	Indirect Taxes	Less: Subsidies Received	Value Added
	All Producers											
1 Agriculture, hunting, forestry and fishing	4660	6160	16120	90	...	27030	5010	6730	18800	240	...	30780
a Agriculture and hunting	...	5850	...	-250	...	22740	...	6360	...	-70	...	26900
b Forestry and logging	...	310	...	340	...	4290	...	370	...	310	...	3880
c Fishing	...	...	...	...	...	...	...	...	...	...	...	...
2 Mining and quarrying	8050	1590	1030	750	...	11420	8930	1690	1450	620	...	12690
a Coal mining	7370	1200	730	470	...	9770	8210	1280	750	290	...	10530
b Crude petroleum and natural gas production					...						...	
c Metal ore mining	680	390	300	280	...	1650	720	410	700	330	...	2160
d Other mining					...						...	
3 Manufacturing	229090	36310	61610	57610	...	384620	233350	39720	55500	57040	...	385610
a Manufacture of food, beverages and tobacco	17500	4260	8930	17020	...	47710	18280	4820	8820	16120	...	48040
b Textile, wearing apparel and leather industries	15930	1830	4550	2640	...	24950	15990	1820	4170	2510	...	24490
c Manufacture of wood and wood products, including furniture	8760	1180	3310	2320	...	15570	8650	1270	3310	1900	...	15130
d Manufacture of paper and paper products, printing and publishing	11060	1630	2730	1820	...	17240	11080	1740	2740	1830	...	17390
e Manufacture of chemicals and chemical petroleum, coal, rubber and plastic products	30060	7480	16430	18550	...	72520	31160	8340	8780	18610	...	66890
f Manufacture of non-metallic mineral products, except products of petroleum and coal	10380	2450	3390	2310	...	18530	9970	2550	3050	2070	...	17640
g Basic metal industries	23320	4010	7140	3000	...	37470	23220	4570	4990	3240	...	36020
h Manufacture of fabricated metal products, machinery and equipment [a]	110560	13330	14650	9720	...	148260	113470	14460	18970	10510	...	157410
i Other manufacturing industries	1520	140	480	230	...	2370	1530	150	670	250	...	2600
4 Electricity, gas and water	7580	5790	7830	3960	...	25160	8090	6640	8120	5710	...	28560
5 Construction	44370	4300	16030	9170	...	73870	41750	4500	15400	8910	...	70560
6 Wholesale and retail trade, restaurants and hotels	49410	7320	35700	11620	...	104050	52140	7880	41370	12630	...	114020
a Wholesale and retail trade	49410	6070	26400	9420	...	91300	52140	6420	31170	10270	...	100000
b Restaurants and hotels	-	1250	9300	2200	...	12750	-	1460	10200	2360	...	14020
7 Transport, storage and communication	41900	10980	9630	-3590	...	58920	43220	12070	9270	-3360	...	61200
a Transport and storage	27880	7070	6290	-3450	...	37790	28580	7860	4050	-3400	...	37090
b Communication	14020	3910	3340	-140	...	21130	14640	4210	5220	40	...	24110
8 Finance, insurance, real estate and business services	21800	22180	44350	5040	...	93370	23940	23690	49970	5510	...	103110
a Financial institutions	15120	1120	13610	1260	...	31110	16540	1250	15110	1740	...	34640

Germany, Fed. Rep. of

4.6 Cost Components of Value Added, ISIC Divisions
(Continued)

Million Deutsche marks

1974 / 1975

		Compensation of Employees	Capital Consumption	Net Operating Surplus	Indirect Taxes	Less: Subsidies Received	Value Added	Compensation of Employees	Capital Consumption	Net Operating Surplus	Indirect Taxes	Less: Subsidies Received	Value Added
	b Insurance	6680	400	340	2030	...	9450	7400	440	540	2210	...	10590
	c Real estate and business services	-	20660	30400	1750	...	52810	-	22000	34320	1560	...	57880
	Real estate, except dwellings	...	...	...	...	...	...	...	...	...	...	...	...
	Dwellings	-	20660	30400	1750	...	52810	-	22000	34320	1560	...	57880
9	Community, social and personal services	30020	5920	50260	5950	...	92150	32310	6790	56060	6250	...	101410
	a Sanitary and similar services	30020	4720	32470	5850	...	73060	32310	5200	34770	6150	...	78430
	b Social and related community services	...	1200	17790	100	...	19090		1590	21290	100	...	22980
	Educational services	...	...	...	...	...	...	...	...	...	...	...	...
	Medical, dental, other health and veterinary services	-	1200	17790	100	...	19090	-	1590	21290	100	...	22980
	c Recreational and cultural services	...	...	...	...	...	...	...	...	...	...	...	...
	d Personal and household services	...	...	...	...	...	...	...	...	...	...	...	...
	Total, Industries b	436880	100550	242560	90600	...	870590	448740	109710	255940	93550	...	907940
	Producers of Government Services	109160	5230	-	160	...	114550	118530	5740	-	180	...	124450
	Other Producers	13640	1480	-	10	...	15130	15080	1580	-	10	...	16670
	Total	559680	107260	242560	90770	...	1000270	582350	117030	255940	93740	...	1049060
	Imputed bank service charge	...	...	-29650	...	...	-29650	...	...	-32610	...	...	-32610
	Import duties	...	...	...	26910	...	26910	...	...	...	28180	...	28180
	Value added tax	...	...	...	...	...	...	...	...	...	...	...	...
	Other adjustments	...	...	...	-10400	...	-10400	...	...	...	-10600	...	-10600
	Total	559680	107260	212910	107280	...	987130	582350	117030	223330	111320	...	1034030

1976 / 1977

		Compensation of Employees	Capital Consumption	Net Operating Surplus	Indirect Taxes	Less: Subsidies Received	Value Added	Compensation of Employees	Capital Consumption	Net Operating Surplus	Indirect Taxes	Less: Subsidies Received	Value Added
						All Producers							
1	Agriculture, hunting, forestry and fishing	5560	7090	19830	290	...	32770	6050	7550	19240	640	...	33480
	a Agriculture and hunting	...	6690	...	10	...	28500	...	7140	...	330	...	28650
	b Forestry and logging	...	400	...	280	...	4270	...	410	...	310	...	4830
	c Fishing	...	...	...	...	...	...	...	...	...	...	...	...
2	Mining and quarrying	9160	1790	1480	720	...	13150	9400	1950	-230	60	...	11180
	a Coal mining	8470	1370	1110	480	...	11430	8680	1710	-250	-100	...	10040
	b Crude petroleum and natural gas production					...						...	
	c Metal ore mining	690	420	370	240		1720	720	240	20	160		1140
	d Other mining					...						...	
3	Manufacturing	252360	42160	65790	61850	...	422160	270720	43890	72000	66130	...	452740
	a Manufacture of food, beverages and tobacco	19440	4980	10110	16220	...	50750	20510	5170	10900	17070	...	53650
	b Textile, wearing apparel and leather industries	17050	1860	3690	2590	...	25190	17280	1890	4360	2620	...	26150
	c Manufacture of wood and wood products, including furniture	9460	1360	3380	1950	...	16150	10460	1440	4470	2190	...	18560
	d Manufacture of paper and paper products, printing and publishing	12200	1840	2580	1870	...	18490	12840	1940	3080	1960	...	19820
	e Manufacture of chemicals and chemical petroleum, coal, rubber and plastic products	33760	8790	12900	20310	...	75760	36050	9280	10530	21200	...	77060
	f Manufacture of non-metallic mineral products, except products of petroleum and coal	11150	2670	3520	2250	...	19590	11480	2740	3420	2320	...	19960
	g Basic metal industries	24700	5000	2690	3630	...	36020	25870	5260	3200	3720	...	38050
	h Manufacture of fabricated metal products, machinery and equipment a	122880	15500	26060	12750	...	177190	134260	16000	31010	14720	...	195990
	i Other manufacturing industries	1720	160	860	280	...	3020	1970	170	1030	330	...	3500
4	Electricity, gas and water	8920	7260	9210	6320	...	31710	9440	7800	9020	6640	...	32900

Germany, Fed. Rep. of

4.6 Cost Components of Value Added, ISIC Divisions
(Continued)

Million Deutsche marks

	1976						1977					
	Compensation of Employees	Capital Consumption	Net Operating Surplus	Indirect Taxes	Less: Subsidies Received	Value Added	Compensation of Employees	Capital Consumption	Net Operating Surplus	Indirect Taxes	Less: Subsidies Received	Value Added
5 Construction	43970	4510	17100	8730	...	74310	45640	4560	18990	10180	...	79370
6 Wholesale and retail trade, restaurants and hotels	57460	8420	44900	12810	...	123590	62170	9210	48940	12150	...	132470
a Wholesale and retail trade	57460	6790	33930	10420	...	108600	62170	7230	36990	9630	...	116020
b Restaurants and hotels	-	1630	10970	2390	...	14990	-	1980	11950	2520	...	16450
7 Transport, storage and communication	44560	12930	12120	-2820	...	66790	46290	13770	13880	-2460	...	71480
a Transport and storage	29540	8160	6230	-2860	...	41070	30400	8730	6750	-2510	...	43370
b Communication	15020	4770	5890	40	...	25720	15890	5040	7130	50	...	28110
8 Finance, insurance, real estate and business services	25240	25390	53770	5910	...	110310	26820	27600	56350	6490	...	117260
a Financial institutions	17530	1390	16240	1950	...	37110	18620	1520	17110	2500	...	39750
b Insurance	7710	480	500	2410	...	11100	8200	530	1470	2520	...	12720
c Real estate and business services	-	23520	37030	1550	...	62100	-	25550	37770	1470	...	64790
Real estate, except dwellings	...	...	...	...	...	...	...	...	...	...	...	...
Dwellings	-	23520	37030	1550	...	62100	-	25550	37770	1470	...	64790
9 Community, social and personal services	36690	8030	61270	6920	...	112910	40890	9310	67910	7790	...	125900
a Sanitary and similar services	36690	6200	37690	6800	...	87380	40890	7140	43300	7700	...	99030
b Social and related community services	...	1830	23580	120	...	25530	...	2170	24610	90	...	26870
Educational services	...	...	...	...	...	...	...	...	...	...	...	...
Medical, dental, other health and veterinary services	-	1830	23580	120	...	25530	-	2170	24610	90	...	26870
c Recreational and cultural services	...	...	...	...	...	...	...	...	...	...	...	...
d Personal and household services	...	...	...	...	...	...	...	...	...	...	...	...
Total, Industries [b]	483920	117580	285470	100730	...	987700	517420	125640	306100	107620	...	1056780
Producers of Government Services	124980	6240	-	200	...	131420	133380	6800	-	210	...	140390
Other Producers	16330	1670	-	10	...	18010	17810	1810	-	10	...	19630
Total	625230	125490	285470	100940	...	1137130	668610	134250	306100	107840	...	1216800
Imputed bank service charge	...	...	-34910	...	...	-34910	...	...	-38280	...	...	-38280
Import duties	...	...	...	32800	...	32800	...	...	...	34970	...	34970
Value added tax	...	...	...	...	...	...	...	...	...	...	...	...
Other adjustments	...	...	...	-12200	...	-12200	...	...	...	-13000	...	-13000
Total	625230	125490	250560	121540	...	1122820	668610	134250	267820	129810	...	1200490

	1978						1979					
	Compensation of Employees	Capital Consumption	Net Operating Surplus	Indirect Taxes	Less: Subsidies Received	Value Added	Compensation of Employees	Capital Consumption	Net Operating Surplus	Indirect Taxes	Less: Subsidies Received	Value Added
				All Producers								
1 Agriculture, hunting, forestry and fishing	6450	7930	19130	900	...	34410	7080	8470	16080	960	...	32590
a Agriculture and hunting	...	7520	...	580	...	29350	...	...	...	...	...	...
b Forestry and logging	...	410	...	320	...	5060	...	...	...	...	...	...
c Fishing	...	...	...	...	...	...	...	...	...	...	...	...
2 Mining and quarrying	9600	2130	220	-400	...	11550	...	...	...	...	...	...
a Coal mining	8860	1850	110	-540	...	10280	...	...	...	...	...	...
b Crude petroleum and natural gas production					...		...	...	...	...	...	...
c Metal ore mining	740	280	110	140	...	1270	...	...	...	...	...	...
d Other mining					...		...	...	...	...	...	...

Germany, Fed. Rep. of

4.6 Cost Components of Value Added, ISIC Divisions
(Continued)

Million Deutsche marks

		1978						1979				
		Compensation of Employees	Capital Consumption	Net Operating Surplus	Indirect Taxes	Less: Subsidies Received	Value Added	Compensation of Employees	Capital Consumption	Net Operating Surplus	Indirect Taxes	Less: Subsidies Received	Value Added
3	Manufacturing	288080	46210	76120	73700	...	484110	310470	48720	84560	80560	...	524310
	a Manufacture of food, beverages and tobacco	22250	5400	11160	18390	...	57200	...	...	...	...	...	...
	b Textile, wearing apparel and leather industries	18120	1910	4230	2850	...	27110	...	...	...	...	...	...
	c Manufacture of wood and wood products, including furniture	11320	1510	3710	2420	...	18960	...	...	...	...	...	...
	d Manufacture of paper and paper products, printing and publishing	14150	2140	2920	2360	...	21570	...	...	...	...	...	...
	e Manufacture of chemicals and chemical petroleum, coal, rubber and plastic products	38250	9730	11090	23100	...	82170	...	...	...	...	...	...
	f Manufacture of non-metallic mineral products, except products of petroleum and coal	12310	2800	3410	2670	...	21190	...	...	...	...	...	...
	g Basic metal industries	26620	5510	3050	4430	...	39610	...	...	...	...	...	...
	h Manufacture of fabricated metal products, machinery and equipment [a]	142950	17030	35620	17110	...	212710	...	...	...	...	...	...
	i Other manufacturing industries	2110	180	930	370	...	3590	...	...	...	...	...	...
4	Electricity, gas and water	9870	8500	10180	7380	...	35930	...	...	...	...	...	...
5	Construction	48540	4570	23470	9900	...	86480	53400	4620	30820	11750	...	100590
6	Wholesale and retail trade, restaurants and hotels	67700	9750	51670	12340	...	141460	...	...	...	...	...	152930
	a Wholesale and retail trade	67700	7750	38810	9500	...	123760	72500	8310	42120	11060	...	133990
	b Restaurants and hotels	-	2000	12860	2840	...	17700	...	...	...	...	...	18940
7	Transport, storage and communication	48530	14800	15860	-3650	...	75540	51010	16330	17680	-2600	...	82420
	a Transport and storage	31750	9350	7920	-3710	...	45310	...	...	...	...	...	...
	b Communication	16780	5450	7940	60	...	30230	...	...	...	...	...	...
8	Finance, insurance, real estate and business services	28590	30370	59040	6510	...	124510	30800	34160	59330	6910	...	131200
	a Financial institutions	19770	1680	18970	2390	...	42810	...	...	...	...	...	...
	b Insurance	8820	590	1720	2570	...	13700	...	...	...	...	...	...
	c Real estate and business services	-	28100	38350	1550	...	68000	...	...	...	...	...	...
	Real estate, except dwellings	...	...	...	...	...	...	...	...	...	...	...	...
	Dwellings	-	28100	38350	1550	...	68000	...	...	...	...	...	...
9	Community, social and personal services	45140	11110	74060	9360	...	139670	...	...	...	...	...	155400
	a Sanitary and similar services	45140	8870	47720	9260	...	110990	...	...	...	...	...	...
	b Social and related community services	...	2240	26340	100	...	28680	...	...	...	...	...	...
	Educational services	...	...	...	...	...	...	...	...	...	...	...	...
	Medical, dental, other health and veterinary services	...	2240	26340	100	...	28680	...	...	...	...	...	...
	c Recreational and cultural services	...	...	...	...	...	...	...	...	...	...	...	...
	d Personal and household services	...	...	...	...	...	...	...	...	...	...	...	...
Total, Industries [b]		552500	135370	329750	116040	...	1133660	595380	147930	358050	129100	...	1230460
Producers of Government Services		141840	7460	-	220	...	149520	...	...	...	...	...	160430
Other Producers		19300	1940	-	10	...	21250	...	...	...	...	...	23050
Total		713640	144770	329750	116270	...	1304430	768200	158340	358050	129350	...	1413940
Imputed bank service charge		...	...	-41760	...	...	-41760	...	...	-45650	...	...	-45650
Import duties		...	...	...	38610	...	38610	...	...	...	45150	...	45150
Value added tax		...	...	...	...	...	...	...	...	...	...	...	...
Other adjustments		...	...	...	-14900	...	-14900	...	...	...	-19500	...	-19500
Total		713640	144770	287990	139980	...	1286380	768200	158340	312400	155000	...	1393940

a) Including steel construction.
b) Column 'Indirect taxes' is net of column 'Less: Subsidies received'.

Germany, Fed. Rep. of

4.9 Supply of Goods and Services, in Current Prices

Million Deutsche marks

	Gross Domestic Output - Marketed	Gross Domestic Output - Non-Marketed	Imports c.i.f.	Import Duties	Trade & Transport Margins	Value Added Tax	TOTAL SUPPLY
1970							
1 Agriculture, hunting, forestry and fishing	54838	...	17809	...	...	...	72647
2 Mining and quarrying	21720	...	11169	...	...	...	32889
3 Manufacturing	714139	...	99097	...	...	...	813236
4 Electricity, gas and water	30510	...	456	...	...	...	30966
5 Construction	113037	...	1533	...	...	...	114570
6 Wholesale and retail trade, restaurants and hotels	144204	...	2196	...	...	...	146400
7 Transport and communications	59522	...	4203	...	...	...	63725
8 Finance, insurance, real estate and business services	80661	...	-124	...	...	...	80537
9 Community, social and personal services	213746	...	3932	...	...	...	217678
Total, Industries [a,b]	1432377	...	140271	...	...	...	1572648
Producers of Government Services	...	...	...	...	...	...	...
Other Producers	...	...	...	...	...	...	...
Total	...	...	...	...	...	...	...
1974							
1 Agriculture, hunting, forestry and fishing	68091	...	22310	...	...	...	90401
2 Mining and quarrying	29911	...	32650	...	...	...	62561
3 Manufacturing	1025259	...	151612	...	...	...	1176871
4 Electricity, gas and water	47271	...	572	...	...	...	47843
5 Construction	156566	...	1721	...	...	...	158287
6 Wholesale and retail trade, restaurants and hotels	190449	...	3449	...	...	...	193898
7 Transport and communications	89287	...	5752	...	...	...	95039
8 Finance, insurance, real estate and business services	131660	...	291	...	...	...	131951
9 Community, social and personal services	380579	...	6184	...	...	...	386763
Total, Industries [a,b]	2119073	...	224541	...	...	...	2343614
Producers of Government Services	...	...	...	...	...	...	...
Other Producers	...	...	...	...	...	...	...
Total	...	...	...	...	...	...	...
1975							
1 Agriculture, hunting, forestry and fishing	76357	...	24332	...	...	...	100689
2 Mining and quarrying	33714	...	29888	...	...	...	63602
3 Manufacturing	1019923	...	160257	...	...	...	1180180
4 Electricity, gas and water	53220	...	599	...	...	...	53819
5 Construction	150695	...	3092	...	...	...	153787
6 Wholesale and retail trade, restaurants and hotels	200480	...	3917	...	...	...	204397
7 Transport and communications	91911	...	6208	...	...	...	98119
8 Finance, insurance, real estate and business services	146996	...	225	...	...	...	147221
9 Community, social and personal services	425314	...	7505	...	...	...	432819
Total, Industries [a,b]	2198610	...	236023	...	...	...	2434633
Producers of Government Services	...	...	...	...	...	...	...
Other Producers	...	...	...	...	...	...	...
Total	...	...	...	...	...	...	...

a) Column 'Nonmarketed' is included in column 'Marketed'.
b) Column 'Import duties' is included in column 'Imports c.i.f.'.

# Germany, Fed. Rep. of

4.11 Disposition of Goods and Services, in Current Prices

Million Deutsche marks

	Intermediate Consumption: General Government	Intermediate Consumption: Public Enterprises	Intermediate Consumption: Private	Final Consumption	Gross Capital Formation: General Government	Gross Capital Formation: Public Enterprises	Gross Capital Formation: Private	Exports	TOTAL DISPOSITION
1970									
1 Agriculture, hunting, forestry and fishing	59363	...	...	11834	-118	...	...	1568	72647
2 Mining and quarrying	27697	...	...	2049	487	...	...	2656	32889
3 Manufacturing	449704	...	...	166459	85219	...	...	111854	813236
4 Electricity, gas and water	23848	...	...	7009	12	...	...	97	30966
5 Construction	4380	...	...	1399	107680	...	...	1111	114570
6 Wholesale and retail trade, restaurants and hotels	60638	...	...	75898	2121	...	...	7743	146400
7 Transport and communications	36870	...	...	16105	1289	...	...	9461	63725
8 Finance, insurance, real estate and business services	28279	...	...	51104	-	...	...	1154	80537
9 Community, social and personal services	73848	...	...	141813	-	...	...	2017	217678
Total, Industries	764627	...	...	473670	196690	...	...	137661	1572648
Producers of Government Services	...	...	...	...	...	...	...	...	...
Other Producers	...	...	...	...	...	...	...	...	...
Total	...	...	...	...	...	...	...	...	...
1974									
1 Agriculture, hunting, forestry and fishing	74462	...	...	13845	24	...	...	2070	90401
2 Mining and quarrying	55240	...	...	2779	-318	...	...	4860	62561
3 Manufacturing	650567	...	...	234149	87785	...	...	204370	1176871
4 Electricity, gas and water	34950	...	...	12683	-11	...	...	221	47843
5 Construction	10966	...	...	2179	143600	...	...	1542	158287
6 Wholesale and retail trade, restaurants and hotels	78423	...	...	99387	38	...	...	16050	193898
7 Transport and communications	52776	...	...	26493	1172	...	...	14598	95039
8 Finance, insurance, real estate and business services	52092	...	...	77796	...	...	...	2063	131951
9 Community, social and personal services	138977	...	...	244419	...	...	...	3369	386763
Total, Industries	1148453	...	...	713730	232290	...	...	249141	2343614
Producers of Government Services	...	...	...	...	...	...	...	...	...
Other Producers	...	...	...	...	...	...	...	...	...
Total	...	...	...	...	...	...	...	...	...
1975									
1 Agriculture, hunting, forestry and fishing	84406	...	...	15267	-1177	...	...	2193	100689
2 Mining and quarrying	56167	...	...	1622	818	...	...	4995	63602
3 Manufacturing	638754	...	...	255479	87182	...	...	198765	1180180
4 Electricity, gas and water	39809	...	...	13739	-	...	...	271	53819
5 Construction	13668	...	...	1293	135710	...	...	3116	153787
6 Wholesale and retail trade, restaurants and hotels	78696	...	...	110925	240	...	...	14536	204397
7 Transport and communications	55488	...	...	26711	1067	...	...	14853	98119
8 Finance, insurance, real estate and business services	58209	...	...	86451	-	...	...	2561	147221
9 Community, social and personal services	156963	...	...	271273	-	...	...	4583	432819
Total, Industries	1182160	...	...	782760	223840	...	...	245873	2434633
Producers of Government Services	...	...	...	...	...	...	...	...	...
Other Producers	...	...	...	...	...	...	...	...	...
Total	...	...	...	...	...	...	...	...	...

Germany, Fed. Rep. of

4.13 Gross Output of Goods and Services by Kind of Activity of Producer (Make Matrix), at Current Prices

Million Deutsche marks

CHARACTERISTIC PRODUCTS OF:

	Agriculture, Hunting, Forestry, Fishing	Mining & Quarrying	Manu-facturing	Electricity, Gas & Water	Construction	Wholesale & Retail Trade, Restaurants & Hotels	Transport & Communi-cations	Finance Insurance, Real Estate & Business Services	Community Social & Personal Services	TOTAL
					1974					
1 Agriculture, hunting, forestry and fishing	68091	...	...	...	...	...	...	...	...	
2 Mining and quarrying	...	23709	3749	2431	...	22	...	...	...	
3 Manufacturing	632	1403	982582	780	19502	18266	1282	...	812	
4 Electricity, gas and water	...	1479	3176	42132	...	...	484	...	...	
5 Construction	72	202	6036	1171	146764	36	1295	850	140	
6 Wholesale and retail trade, restaurants and hotels	...	672	22072	109	2275	163230	542	503	1046	
7 Transport and communications	246	...	301	1295	...	226	87219	...	...	
8 Finance, insurance, real estate and business services	737	136	...	...	...	113	833	122760	7081	
9 Community, social and personal services	245	...	11382	210	2297	2367	669	...	363409	
Statistical discrepancy	...	...	...	...	...	...	...	...	...	
Total, Industries	70023	27601	1029298	48128	170838	184260	92324	124113	372488	
Producers of Government Services	...	...	...	...	...	...	...	...	...	
Other Producers	...	...	...	...	...	...	...	...	...	
Total	...	...	...	...	...	...	...	...	...	
					1975					
1 Agriculture, hunting, forestry and fishing	68091	...	...	...	...	...	...	...	...	
2 Mining and quarrying	...	23709	3749	2431	...	22	...	...	...	
3 Manufacturing	632	1403	982582	780	19502	18266	1282	...	812	
4 Electricity, gas and water	...	1479	3176	42132	...	...	484	...	...	
5 Construction	72	202	6036	1171	146764	36	1295	850	140	
6 Wholesale and retail trade, restaurants and hotels	...	672	22072	109	2275	163230	542	503	1046	
7 Transport and communications	246	...	301	1295	...	226	87219	...	...	
8 Finance, insurance, real estate and business services	737	136	...	...	...	113	833	122760	7081	
9 Community, social and personal services	245	...	11382	210	2297	2367	669	...	363409	
Statistical discrepancy	...	...	...	...	...	...	...	...	...	
Total, Industries	70023	27601	1029298	48128	170838	184260	92324	124113	372488	
Producers of Government Services	...	...	...	...	...	...	...	...	...	
Other Producers	...	...	...	...	...	...	...	...	...	
Total	...	...	...	...	...	...	...	...	...	

4.15 Intermediate Consumption by Kind of Activity of User (Use Matrix), in Current Prices

Million Deutsche marks

KIND OF ACTIVITY OF USER:

	Agriculture, Hunting, Forestry, Fishing	Mining & Quarrying	Manu-facturing	Electricity, Gas & Water	Construction	Wholesale & Retail Trade, Restaurants & Hotels	Transport & Communi-cations	Finance Insurance, Real Estate & Business Services	Community Social & Personal Services	TOTAL
					1970					
1 Agriculture, hunting, forestry and fishing	13934	148	40211	-	192	1887	25	1309	1657	59363
2 Mining and quarrying	47	5051	16451	5521	47	90	179	20	291	27697
3 Manufacturing	11889	3449	305835	4768	47741	24272	12350	2074	37326	449704
4 Electricity, gas and water	655	1031	13014	2109	723	1705	801	1435	2375	23848
4 Construction	283	463	408	81	390	433	438	720	1164	4380
6 Wholesale and retail trade, restaurants and hotels	2437	375	33230	469	4170	9201	1830	777	8149	60638
7 Transport and communications	1880	1561	18614	409	2749	3550	3892	824	3391	36870
8 Finance, insurance, real estate and business services	236	87	1844	89	349	4967	844	17387	2476	28279
9 Community, social and personal services	1380	685	13032	424	6249	11274	1615	11481	27708	73848
Statistical discrepancy	...	...	...	...	...	...	...	...	...	...
Total	32741	12850	442639	13870	62610	57379	21974	36027	84537	764627

Germany, Fed. Rep. of

4.15 Intermediate Consumption by Kind of Activity of User (Use Matrix), in Current Prices
(Continued)

Million Deutsche marks

	Agriculture, Hunting, Forestry, Fishing	Mining & Quarrying	Manu-facturing	Electricity, Gas & Water	Construction	Wholesale & Retail Trade, Restaurants & Hotels	Transport & Communi-cations	Finance Insurance, Real Estate & Business Services	Community Social & Personal Services	TOTAL
					1974					
1 Agriculture, hunting, forestry and fishing	17719	166	51151	-	263	1834	26	834	2473	74462
2 Mining and quarrying	66	6973	38415	9092	58	111	133	22	370	55240
3 Manufacturing	15109	4166	445334	6973	68420	30682	17551	2760	59572	650567
4 Electricity, gas and water	993	2385	18237	3308	1056	2373	1049	2392	3157	34950
4 Construction	664	907	846	106	1206	896	922	2176	3243	10966
6 Wholesale and retail trade, restaurants and hotels	3020	417	43684	925	5159	10242	2182	742	12052	78423
7 Transport and communications	2298	1805	26696	493	3734	4723	5173	1439	6415	52776
8 Finance, insurance, real estate and business services	542	123	3285	132	799	6902	2154	33278	4877	52092
9 Community, social and personal services	1825	1099	25159	615	9239	18775	2775	17971	61519	138977
Statistical discrepancy	...	...	...	...	...	...	...	...	...	...
Total	42232	18041	652807	21644	89934	76538	31965	61614	153678	1148453
					1975					
1 Agriculture, hunting, forestry and fishing	20428	166	55985	2	264	3006	32	1019	3504	84406
2 Mining and quarrying	93	8770	36355	10171	56	128	109	24	461	56167
3 Manufacturing	15607	4776	435002	6781	62497	30798	16660	2809	63824	638754
4 Electricity, gas and water	658	1468	19993	4561	1261	2783	1614	3090	4381	39809
4 Construction	623	1268	858	338	3727	888	878	2329	2759	13668
6 Wholesale and retail trade, restaurants and hotels	3578	395	39146	1081	4791	11108	2611	854	15132	78698
7 Transport and communications	3136	1712	26615	726	3459	5113	5483	1526	7718	55488
8 Finance, insurance, real estate and business services	564	152	3330	96	803	7361	3702	36657	5544	58209
9 Community, social and personal services	2145	1455	27648	436	9722	19207	2594	19483	74273	156963
Statistical discrepancy	...	...	...	...	...	...	...	...	...	...
Total	46832	20162	644932	24192	86580	80392	33683	67791	177596	1182160

Ghana

General note. The preparation of national accounts statistics in Ghana is undertaken by the Central Bureau of Statistics, Accra. The official estimates are published by the bureau in the 'Economic Survey'. A detailed description of the sources and methods used for the national accounts estimation is contained in the publications 'Sources and Methods of Estimation of National Income at Current Prices in Ghana' and 'National Income of Ghana at Constant Prices'. The estimates are generally in accordance with the classifications and definitions recommended in the United Nations System of National Accounts (SNA). Work relating to input-output analysis is being done at present. The following tables have been prepared from successive replies to the United Nations national accounts questionnaire. When the scope and coverage of the estimates differ for conceptual or statistical reasons from the definitions and classifications recommended in SNA, a footnote is indicated to the relevant tables.

(a) Gross domestic product. Gross domestic product is estimated mainly through the production approach.

(b) Expenditure on the gross domestic product. Gross fixed capital formation is estimated by using the commodity-flow approach. A combination of commodity-flow and expenditure approach is used for increase in stock. Private consumption expenditure is treated as a residual. Gross fixed capital formation is classified according to type of capital goods and not according to kind of economic activity. The estimates of increase in stocks are mainly based on special inquiries into the stocks held by selected kinds of producers and distributors. Adjustment is made to arrive at estimates on the equivalent of physical changes in the stocks, valued at average market prices during the period of account. Government consumption expenditure is estimated on a cash basis from government records. These records are reclassified according to government purposes. It is feasible to distinguish between acquisition for military purposes and for civilian purposes which exclude durable goods. Sales of goods and services by government to the public is subtracted from total expenditure. Exports and imports of goods and services are mainly estimated from foreign trade statistics of merchandise trade supplemented by information from the Central Bank. For the constant price estimates, no specific information is available for government consumption expenditure, but wages and salaries paid by government are extrapolated by index numbers of employment. For gross capital formation, current values are deflated by appropriate price indexes. In the case of commodity trade, current values are deflated by Paasche indexes of prices specially prepared for this purpose. Private consumption expenditure is obtained as a residual.

(c) Cost-structure of the gross domestic product. In estimating the cost structure components of GDP, the perpetual inventory method is used for estimating consumption of fixed capital. Indirect taxes net of subsidies are obtained by analysing the taxes on production and expenditure in the revenue account of the government. The domestic factor income is obtained as a residual.

(d) Gross domestic product by kind of economic activity. The table of GDP by kind of economic activity is prepared at market prices i.e., producers values. The value added of the majority of industries is estimated through the production approach. A combination of the commodity-flow approach and the expenditure approach is used for the construction sector. For the agricultural sector, statistics of the Ghana Cocoa Marketing Board is the main source of information for the estimation of cocoa, which is the most important crop in Ghana. For other principal crops, information is collected through annual sample surveys. The production of crop is estimated as the product of area sown and yield per acre. The intermediate consumption is estimated on the basis of a small-scale survey in 1969 and projected on the basis of movements in acreage and prices of the crops. Data on gross output of forestry and logging are obtained from the Forestry Department while for intermediate consumption, a small-scale sample survey has been carried out in a bench-mark year and a constant input ratio applied for subsequent years. Annual establishment surveys are undertaken on a census basis for mining, large-scale manufacturing and electricity and water supply. In the case of manufacturing, the surveys provide detailed information on inputs and outputs for commodity-flow purposes. A sample survey was carried out in 1963 for small-scale and medium-scale manufacturing. The data collected formed the basis for the estimates in the subsequent years by using per worker input and output in the bench-mark year and projected employment data, extrapolated from population census. For the construction sector, data on works undertaken by the government are obtained by analysing the government accounts. Information on domestic production, imports and exports of construction materials, trade and transport margins and cost-composition of the total expenditure are available to prepare estimates of gross output. The gross margins of wholesale and retail trade estimates are based partly on spotchecks in a bench-mark year and partly on sample survey, while gross receipts and intermediate consumption estimates are based on income tax records and annual surveys. For the services sectors, information is generally obtained from the institutions concerned. The rental value of residential dwellings are imputed on the basis of cost components, estimated from the record of the Ministry of Local Government. For the constant price estimates, the general approach used for agriculture, industrial activity, electricity, gas and water and construction sectors is double deflation. The value added of the trade, transport and financial services is extrapolated by quantity indexes. Different kinds of price indexes are used to deflate the value added of restaurants and hotels as well as the education and recreational services.

1.1 Expenditure on the Gross Domestic Product, in Current Prices

Million Ghanaian cedis

		1970	1971	1972	1973	1974	1975	1976	1977	1978	1979	1980
1	General government final consumption expenditure	290.3	324.5	355.0	382.3	569.3	688.5	799.0	1409.4	2370.7	...	...
2	Private final consumption expenditure	1664.0	1915.7	2095.3	2626.6	3645.3	3873.1	5170.5	8637.8	17766.2	...	...
3	Gross capital formation [a]	319.7	353.2	200.9	316.0	607.8	672.5	578.8	1235.1	1128.0	...	...
	a Increase in stocks [a]	48.3	42.5	-43.5	48.2	53.3	58.5	-62.0	186.2	-227.3	...	...
	b Gross fixed capital formation	271.4	310.7	244.4	267.8	554.5	613.8	640.8	1048.9	1355.3	...	...
	Residential buildings [b]	117.8	147.1	105.9	156.6	312.2	296.4	245.5	458.5	592.6	...	...
	Non-residential buildings [b]	...	...	...	...	...	...	...	...	...	...	...
	Other construction and land improvement etc. [c]	36.7	49.3	49.4	50.0	44.1	99.7	157.8	242.3	229.5	...	...
	Other	116.9	114.4	89.1	61.2	198.2	217.7	237.5	348.1	533.2	...	...
4	Exports of goods and services	523.2	536.7	581.5	750.5	853.5	1022.6	1025.2	1170.5	1754.2	...	...
5	Less: Imports of goods and services	538.6	688.7	427.7	574.2	1015.8	973.5	1047.3	1289.4	2033.0	...	...
	Statistical discrepancy	-	59.1	10.4	-	-	-	-	-	...	...	...
	Equals: Gross Domestic Product	2258.6	2500.5	2815.4	3501.2	4660.1	5283.0	6526.2	11163.4	20986.1	...	...

a) Cocoa is valued at cost to the Ghana Cocoa Marketing Board. Stocks of other export commodities, including minerals, are valued at export prices.
b) Item 'Non-residential buildings' is included in item 'Residential buildings'.
c) Including expenditure on mining development but excluding minor engineering construction done by the private sector.

1.2 Expenditure on the Gross Domestic Product, in Constant Prices

Million Ghanaian cedis

		1970	1971	1972	1973	1974	1975	1976	1977	1978	1979	1980
		\multicolumn{11}{c}{At constant prices of:}
		\multicolumn{3}{c}{1968}		\multicolumn{6}{c}{1975}		
1	General government final consumption expenditure	259.9	282.3	266.7	263.3 / 553.9	683.8	688.5	704.5	906.7	1066.0	...	...
2	Private final consumption expenditure	1459.4	1483.9	1392.3	1549.6 / 4218.4	4642.0	3873.1	3714.3	3710.7	4210.9	...	...
3	Gross capital formation [a]	275.6	301.6	150.3	203.3 / 543.9	788.9	672.3	530.2	772.4	517.5	...	...
	a Increase in stocks [a]	44.8	39.2	-22.4	31.0 / 76.5	66.4	58.5	-46.0	81.8	-67.7	...	...
	b Gross fixed capital formation	230.8	262.4	172.7	172.3 / 467.4	722.5	613.8	576.2	690.6	585.2	...	...

Ghana

1.2 Expenditure on the Gross Domestic Product, in Constant Prices
(Continued)

Million Ghanaian cedis

	1970	1971	1972	1973	1974	1975	1976	1977	1978	1979	1980
				At constant prices of:							
		1968				1975					
Residential buildings	...	...	...	292.7[b]	433.0[b]	296.4[b]	225.2[b]	301.8[b]	250.6[b]	...	...
Non-residential buildings	137.5[c]	171.1[c]	118.2[c]	139.2[c]	...	...	...	...	...	...	...
Other construction and land improvement etc.					61.1[d]	99.7[d]	144.8[d]	159.6[d]	97.1[d]	...	...
Other	93.3	91.3	54.5	33.1 / 81.2	228.4	217.7	206.2	229.2	237.5	...	...
4 Exports of goods and services	398.4	414.5	481.5	462.9 / 1341.7	1048.2	1022.6	1073.5	806.1	771.1	...	...
5 Less: Imports of goods and services	471.6	453.0	312.4	391.0 / 1011.8	1129.9	973.5	926.0	983.5	911.3	...	...
Equals: Gross Domestic Product	1921.7	2029.3	1978.4	2088.1 / 5646.1	6033.0	5283.0	5096.5	5212.4	5654.2	...	...

a) Cocoa is valued at cost to the Ghana Cocoa Marketing Board. Stocks of other export commodities, including minerals, are valued at export prices.
b) Item 'Non-residential buildings' is included in item 'Residential buildings'.
c) Including item 'Residential buildings'.
d) Including expenditure on mining development but excluding minor engineering construction done by the private sector.

1.3 Cost Components of the Gross Domestic Product

Million Ghanaian cedis

	1970	1971	1972	1973	1974	1975	1976	1977	1978	1979	1980
1 Indirect taxes, net	308.4	241.1	326.9	348.2	475.7	631.2	589.5	815.4	1074.9	...	...
2 Consumption of fixed capital	134.3	145.2	170.7	216.4	256.1	322.9	378.2	524.6	731.9	...	...
3 Compensation of employees paid by resident producers to: [a]	1815.9	2055.1	2307.4	2903.0	3847.0	4328.9	5558.5	9823.4	19179.3	...	...
4 Net operating surplus	...	...	...	...	...	...	...	...	...	...	...
Statistical discrepancy	-	59.1	10.4	33.6	81.3	-	-	-	...	...	...
Equals: Gross Domestic Product	2258.6	2500.5	2815.4	3501.2	4660.1	5283.0	6526.2	11163.4	20986.1	...	...

a) Including net operating surplus.

1.7 External Transactions on Current Account, Summary

Million Ghanaian cedis

	1970	1971	1972	1973	1974	1975	1976	1977	1978	1979	1980
				Payments to the Rest of the World							
1 Imports of goods and services	538.6	688.7	427.7	574.2	1015.8	973.5	1047.3	1289.4	2033.0	...	...
a Imports of merchandise c.i.f.	463.0	583.0	337.5	467.4	889.1	813.0	860.4	1070.0	1626.0	...	...
b Other	75.6	105.7	90.2	106.8	126.7	160.5	186.9	219.4	407.0	...	...
2 Factor income paid to the rest of the world	52.0	54.5	33.0	26.3	30.9	46.9	51.0	43.0	50.7	...	...
3 Indirect taxes paid to supranational organizations	...	...	...	...	...	...	...	...	...	...	...
4 Current transfers to the rest of the world	18.1	21.5	14.7	16.4	13.3	13.9	15.5	14.8	20.2	...	...
5 Surplus of the nation on current transactions	-67.2	-202.2	143.0	172.4	-160.5	58.5	-39.4	-91.7	-204.8	...	...
Payments to the Rest of the World and Surplus of the Nation on Current Transactions	541.5	562.5	618.4	789.3	899.5	1092.8	1074.4	1255.5	1899.1	...	...
				Receipts From The Rest of the World							
1 Exports of goods and services	523.2	536.7	581.5	750.5	853.5	1022.6	1025.2	1170.5	1754.2	...	...
a Exports of merchandise f.o.b.	487.6	464.5	508.8	678.5	780.8	921.1	895.9	1023.0	1574.5	...	...
b Other	35.6	72.2	72.7	72.0	72.7	101.5	129.3	147.5	179.7	...	...
2 Factor income received from rest of the world	4.2	3.9	4.7	7.9	4.9	5.1	2.9	2.9	2.3	...	...
3 Subsidies received from supranational organisations	...	...	...	...	...	...	...	...	...	...	...
4 Current transfers from rest of the world	14.1	21.9	32.2	30.9	41.1	65.1	46.3	82.1	142.6	...	...
Receipts from the Rest of the World on Current Transactions	541.5	562.5	618.4	789.3	899.5	1092.8	1074.4	1255.5	1899.1	...	...

Ghana

1.8 Capital Transactions of The Nation, Summary

Million Ghanaian cedis

	1970	1971	1972	1973	1974	1975	1976	1977	1978	1979	1980
Finance of Gross Capital Formation										
Gross saving	252.5	206.9	339.6	488.4	447.3	730.8	539.5	1143.4	923.2	...	...
1 Consumption of fixed capital	134.3	145.2	170.7	216.4	256.1	322.9	378.2	524.6	731.9	...	...
2 Net saving	118.2	61.7	168.9	272.0	191.2	407.9	161.3	618.8	191.3	...	...
Less: Surplus of the nation on current transactions	-67.2	-202.2	143.0	172.4	-160.5	58.5	-39.4	-91.7	-204.8	...	...
Statistical discrepancy	-	-55.9	4.3	-	-	-	-0.1	-	-	...	...
Finance of Gross Capital Formation	319.7	353.2	200.9	316.0	607.8	672.3	578.8	1235.1	1128.0	...	...
Gross Capital Formation										
Increase in stocks	48.3	42.5	-43.5	48.2	53.3	58.5	-62.0	186.2	-227.3	...	...
Gross fixed capital formation	271.4	310.7	244.4	267.8	554.5	613.8	640.8	1048.9	1355.3	...	...
Gross Capital Formation	319.7	353.2	200.9	316.0	607.8	672.3	578.8	1235.1	1128.0	...	...

1.9 Gross Domestic Product by Institutional Sectors of Origin

Million Ghanaian cedis

	1970	1971	1972	1973	1974	1975	1976	1977	1978	1979	1980
Domestic Factor Incomes Originating										
1 General government	201.3	216.9	246.1	250.0	331.7	433.0	466.5	771.7	1331.0	...	...
2 Corporate and quasi-corporate enterprises	...	...	...	...	...	...	...	...	...	...	...
3 Households and private unincorporated enterprises	...	...	...	...	...	...	...	...	...	...	...
4 Non-profit institutions serving households	11.1	11.9	13.3	16.0	19.3	24.5	32.7	33.0	46.8	...	...
Subtotal: Domestic Factor Incomes	1815.9	2055.1	2307.4	2903.0	3847.0	4328.9	5558.5	9823.4	19179.2	...	...
Indirect taxes paid, net	308.4	241.1	326.9	348.2	475.7	631.2	589.5	815.4	1074.9	...	...
Consumption of fixed capital	134.3	145.2	170.7	216.4	256.1	322.9	378.2	524.6	731.9	...	...
Statistical discrepancy	-	59.1	10.4	33.6	81.3	-	-	-	0.1	...	...
Gross Domestic Product	2258.6	2500.5	2815.4	3501.2	4660.1	5283.0	6526.2	11163.4	20986.1	...	...

1.10 Gross Domestic Product by Kind of Activity, in Current Prices

Million Ghanaian cedis

	1970	1971	1972	1973	1974	1975	1976	1977	1978	1979	1980
1 Agriculture, hunting, forestry and fishing	1060.0	1103.9	1313.2	1714.7	2383.1	2518.3	3300.1	6274.4	12741.5	...	...
2 Mining and quarrying	37.3	40.6	63.4	81.5	100.0	104.5	87.4	89.5	119.2	...	...
3 Manufacturing	247.6	275.1	305.9	409.3	501.8	735.9	857.5	1203.7	1813.3	...	...
4 Electricity, gas and water	23.2	23.5	25.6	29.5	30.4	32.6	47.6	52.9	74.3	...	...
5 Construction	93.8	117.9	104.0	130.9	213.2	235.6	261.8	422.3	517.0	...	...
6 Wholesale and retail trade, restaurants and hotels	280.9	325.6	340.6	434.8	590.7	642.4	856.1	1293.7	2785.8	...	...
7 Transport, storage and communication	96.9	112.1	124.1	126.8	163.4	206.0	258.9	330.6	552.6	...	...
8 Finance, insurance, real estate and business services	159.8	195.9	240.7	263.4	249.3	275.8	314.3	470.8	648.0	...	...
9 Community, social and personal services	12.2	16.4	21.4	28.5	32.9	55.3	74.6	96.2	132.4	...	...
Total, Industries	2011.7	2211.0	2538.9	3219.4	4264.8	4806.4	6058.3	10234.1	19384.1	...	...
Producers of Government Services	201.3	216.9	246.1	250.0	331.7	433.0	466.5	899.2	1551.0	...	...
Other Producers	11.1	11.9	13.3	16.0	19.3	24.5	32.7	33.3	47.1	...	...
Subtotal	2224.1	2439.8	2798.3	3485.4	4615.8	5263.9	6557.5	11166.6	20982.2	...	...
Less: Imputed bank service charge	26.9	28.0	41.9	58.9	66.5	76.5	127.8	188.3	303.7	...	...
Plus: Import duties	61.4	88.7	59.0	74.6	110.7	95.6	96.5	185.1	307.6	...	...
Plus: Value added tax	...	...	...	...	...	...	...	...	...	...	...
Equals: Gross Domestic Product	2258.6	2500.5	2815.4	3501.2	4660.1	5283.0	6526.2	11163.4	20986.1	...	...

Ghana

1.11 Gross Domestic Product by Kind of Activity, in Constant Prices

Million Ghanaian cedis

	1970	1971	1972	1973	1974	1975	1976	1977	1978	1979	1980
	\multicolumn{4}{c}{At constant prices of: 1968}		\multicolumn{5}{c}{1975}		
1 Agriculture, hunting, forestry and fishing	817.1	859.5	894.7	900.1 / 2890.3	3145.1	2518.3	2476.6	2362.6	2788.9	...	...
2 Mining and quarrying	42.9	43.9	45.6	40.9 / 127.3	110.9	104.5	100.1	97.2	84.0	...	...
3 Manufacturing	264.8	248.5	225.8	274.4 / 715.2	674.5	735.9	703.6	723.6	701.1	...	...
4 Electricity, gas and water	19.6	20.6	29.0	42.8 / 41.7	34.5	32.6	36.9	36.7	32.4	...	...
5 Construction	88.6	110.6	85.3	99.9 / 241.5	299.4	235.6	239.3	270.2	222.2	...	...
6 Wholesale and retail trade, restaurants and hotels	233.0	247.3	233.1	253.8 / 724.0	775.8	642.4	595.0	606.7	587.7	...	...
7 Transport, storage and communication	79.3	90.0	93.0	97.8 / 174.0	203.4	206.0	167.9	190.8	180.5	...	...
8 Finance, insurance, real estate and business services	126.8	130.5	133.2	133.8 / 311.0	325.4	275.8	293.9	329.7	360.4	...	...
9 Community, social and personal services	8.9	10.6	12.3	14.2 / 41.8	42.6	55.3	47.7	51.3	48.2	...	...
Total, Industries	1681.0	1761.5	1752.0	1857.7 / 5266.8	5611.6	4806.4	4661.0	4668.8	5005.4	...	...
Producers of Government Services	179.3	187.3	180.7	180.1 / 333.0	352.8	433.0	438.5	578.0	710.4	...	...
Other Producers	10.0	9.8	10.2	10.5 / 22.7	23.1	24.5	24.5	21.7	22.5	...	...
Subtotal	1870.3	1958.6	1942.9	2048.3 / 5622.5	5987.5	5263.9	5124.0	5268.5	5738.3	...	...
Less: Imputed bank service charge	...	...	...	... / 98.3	88.9	76.5	112.3	137.4	175.8	...	...
Plus: Import duties	51.4	70.6	35.4	39.9 / 121.9	134.4	95.6	84.8	81.3	91.7	...	...
Plus: Value added tax	...	...	...	...	...	...	...	...	...	...	...
Equals: Gross Domestic Product	1921.7	2029.3	1978.4	2088.1 / 5646.1	6033.0	5283.0	5096.5	5212.4	5654.2	...	...

1.12 Relations Among National Accounting Aggregates

Million Ghanaian cedis

	1970	1971	1972	1973	1974	1975	1976	1977	1978	1979	1980
Gross Domestic Product	2258.6	2500.5	2815.4	3501.2	4660.1	5283.0	6526.3	11163.4	20986.1	...	...
Plus: Net factor income received from abroad	-47.8	-64.8	-40.2	-18.4	-26.0	-41.8	-48.1	-40.1	-48.4	...	...
Factor income received	...	...	...	7.9	4.9	5.1	2.9	2.9	2.3	...	...
Less: Factor income paid	...	...	...	26.3	30.9	46.9	51.0	43.0	50.7	...	...
Equals: Gross National Product	2210.8	2435.7	2775.2	3482.8	4634.1	5241.2	6478.1	11123.3	20937.7	...	...
Less: Consumption of fixed capital	134.3	145.2	170.7	216.4	256.1	322.9	378.2	524.6	731.9	...	...
Less: Net indirect taxes paid to supranational organisations	...	...	...	...	...	...	...	...	...	...	...
Equals: National Income at Market Prices	2076.5	2290.5	2604.5	3266.4	4378.0	4918.3	6100.0	10598.7	20205.8	...	...
Plus: Net current transfers received from abroad	-4.0	-1.7	14.6	14.5	27.8	51.2	30.8	67.3	122.4	...	...
Current transfers received	14.1	21.9	32.2	30.9	41.1	65.1	46.3	82.1	142.6	...	...
Less: Current transfers paid	18.1	21.5	14.7	16.4	13.3	13.9	15.5	14.8	20.2	...	...
Equals: National Disposable Income at Market Prices	2072.5	2288.8	2619.1	3280.9	4405.8	4969.5	6130.8	10666.0	20328.2	...	...
Less: Final consumption	1954.3	2240.2	2450.3	3008.9	4214.6	4561.6	5969.5	10047.2	20136.9	...	...
Statistical discrepancy	...	13.1	0.1	...	...	...	...	...	...	...	...
Equals: Net Saving	118.2	61.7	168.9	272.0	191.2	407.9	161.3	618.8	191.3	...	...
Less: Surplus of the nation on current transactions	-67.2	-202.2	143.0	172.4	-160.5	58.5	-39.4	-91.7	-204.8	...	...
Statistical discrepancy	...	-55.9	4.3	...	...	...	-0.1	-	-	...	...
Equals: Net Capital Formation	185.4	208.0	30.2	99.6	351.7	349.4	200.6	710.5	396.1	...	...

Ghana

2.1 General Government Final Consumption Expenditure by Function, in Current Prices

Million Ghanaian cedis

		1970	1971	1972	1973	1974	1975	1976	1977	1978	1979	1980
1	General public services	144.6	165.2	187.1	189.7	312.8	264.3	302.2	635.0	1099.2	...	...
2	Defence										...	...
3	Public order and safety	...	...	...	...	...	...	...	...	...	...	...
4	Education	83.7	88.8	97.4	103.3	140.3	176.3	227.2	322.4	489.8	...	...
5	Health	19.4	20.9	18.0	31.1	40.6	76.1	87.3	108.7	170.5	...	...
6	Social security and welfare	16.9	19.8	21.9	26.2	34.8	69.2	76.5	181.1	266.5	...	...
7	Housing and community amenities										...	...
8	Recreational, cultural and religious affairs	...	...	...	...	...	...	...	...	...	...	...
9	Economic services	25.7	29.8	30.6	32.0	40.8	102.5	105.9	162.2	344.5	...	...
10	Other functions	...	...	...	...	...	...	...	...	...	...	...
	Total General Government Final Consumption Expenditure	290.3	324.5	355.0	382.3	569.3	688.5	799.0	1409.4	2370.7	...	...

2.2 General Government Final Consumption Expenditure by Function, in Constant Prices

Million Ghanaian cedis

		1970	1971	1972	1973	1974	1975	1976	1977	1978	1979	1980
						At constant prices of: 1975						
1	General public services	...	...	...	...	...	264.3	...	410.2	481.1	...	...
2	Defence	...	...	...	...	...		...			...	...
3	Public order and safety	...	...	...	...	...	...	...	...	...	...	...
4	Education	...	...	...	...	...	176.3	...	207.0	226.6	...	...
5	Health	...	...	...	...	...	76.1	...	69.9	76.8	...	...
6	Social security and welfare	...	...	...	...	...	69.2	...	115.6	121.6	...	...
7	Housing and community amenities	...	...	...	...	...		...			...	...
8	Recreational, cultural and religious affairs	...	...	...	...	...	...	...	...	...	...	...
9	Economic services	...	...	...	...	...	102.5	...	104.1	159.9	...	...
10	Other functions	...	...	...	...	...	...	...	...	...	...	...
	Total General Government Final Consumption Expenditure	...	...	...	...	...	688.5	...	906.7	1066.0	...	...

2.5 Private Final Consumption Expenditure by Type, in Current Prices

Million Ghanaian cedis

		1970	1971	1972	1973	1974	1975	1976	1977	1978	1979	1980
					Final Consumption Expenditure of Resident Households							
1	Food, beverages and tobacco	...	...	...	1539.2	2136.1	2269.6	3029.9	5061.7	10410.8	...	...
	a Food	...	...	...	1407.9	1953.9	2076.0	2771.4	4629.9	9522.8	...	...
	b Non-alcoholic beverages	...	...	...	21.0	29.2	31.0	41.4	69.1	142.2	...	...
	c Alcoholic beverages	...	...	...	78.8	109.4	116.2	155.1	259.1	533.0	...	...
	d Tobacco	...	...	...	31.5	43.8	46.5	62.1	103.7	213.3	...	...

Ghana

2.5 Private Final Consumption Expenditure by Type, in Current Prices
(Continued)

Million Ghanaian cedis

	1970	1971	1972	1973	1974	1975	1976	1977	1978	1979	1980
2 Clothing and footwear	...	...	...	375.6	521.3	553.9	739.4	1235.3	2540.8	...	...
3 Gross rent, fuel and power	...	...	...	302.1	419.2	445.4	594.6	993.3	2043.1	...	...
4 Furniture, furnishings and household equipment and operation	...	...	...	99.8	138.5	147.2	196.5	328.3	675.2	...	...
5 Medical care and health expenses	...	...	...	34.2	47.4	50.4	67.3	112.4	231.2	...	...
6 Transport and communication	...	...	...	86.7	120.2	127.8	170.6	285.0	586.2	...	...
7 Recreational, entertainment, education and cultural services	...	...	...	102.4	142.2	151.1	201.7	337.0	693.1	...	...
8 Miscellaneous goods and services	...	...	...	86.7	120.3	127.8	170.6	285.0	586.2	...	...
Total Final Consumption Expenditure in the Domestic Market by Households, of which	1664.0	1915.7	2095.3	2626.6	3645.3	3873.1	5170.5	8637.8	17766.2	...	...
Plus: Direct purchases abroad by resident households	...	...	...	...	...	...	...	...	...	...	...
Less: Direct purchases in the domestic market by non-resident households	...	...	...	...	...	...	...	...	...	...	...
Equals: Final Consumption Expenditure of Resident Households a	1664.0	1915.7	2095.3	2626.6	3645.3	3873.1	5170.5	8637.8	17766.2	...	...

Final Consumption Expenditure of Private Non-profit Institutions Serving Households

	1970	1971	1972	1973	1974	1975	1976	1977	1978	1979	1980
Equals: Final Consumption Expenditure of Private Non-profit Organisations Serving Households	...	...	...	...	...	...	...	...	...	...	...
Private Final Consumption Expenditure	1664.0	1915.7	2095.3	2626.6	3645.3	3873.1	5170.5	8637.8	17766.2	...	...

a) Including consumption expenditure of private non-profit institutions.

2.6 Private Final Consumption Expenditure by Type, in Constant Prices

Million Ghanaian cedis

	1970	1971	1972	1973	1974	1975	1976	1977	1978	1979	1980

At constant prices of: 1975

Final Consumption Expenditure of Resident Households

	1970	1971	1972	1973	1974	1975	1976	1977	1978	1979	1980
1 Food, beverages and tobacco	...	...	...	2335.8	2796.6	2269.6	1824.0	1305.1	1595.3	...	...
a Food	...	...	...	2133.2	2554.1	2076.0	1653.6	1101.8	1421.7	...	...
b Non-alcoholic beverages	...	...	...	32.4	38.8	31.0	27.3	32.5	27.8	...	...
c Alcoholic beverages	...	...	...	121.6	145.5	116.2	102.2	122.0	104.1	...	...
d Tobacco	...	...	...	48.6	58.2	46.5	40.9	48.8	41.7	...	...
2 Clothing and footwear	...	...	...	610.7	689.6	553.9	518.5	577.0	619.1	...	...
3 Gross rent, fuel and power	...	...	...	463.3	517.5	445.4	429.9	448.6	624.8	...	...
4 Furniture, furnishings and household equipment and operation	...	...	...	...	...	...	...	...	...	...	...
5 Medical care and health expenses	...	...	...	50.8	57.6	50.4	65.8	78.6	95.9	...	...
6 Transport and communication	...	...	...	149.0	150.6	127.8	141.0	198.9	256.8	...	...
7 Recreational, entertainment, education and cultural services	...	...	...	...	...	...	...	...	...	...	...
8 Miscellaneous goods and services	...	...	...	135.9	159.5	127.8	126.7	170.4	192.8	...	...
Total Final Consumption Expenditure in the Domestic Market by Households, of which	...	...	...	...	...	...	...	...	...	...	...
Plus: Direct purchases abroad by resident households	...	...	...	...	...	...	...	...	...	...	...
Less: Direct purchases in the domestic market by non-resident households	...	...	...	...	...	...	...	...	...	...	...
Equals: Final Consumption Expenditure of Resident Households a	...	...	...	4218.4	4642.0	3873.1	3714.3	3710.7	4210.9	...	...

Final Consumption Expenditure of Private Non-profit Institutions Serving Households

	1970	1971	1972	1973	1974	1975	1976	1977	1978	1979	1980
Equals: Final Consumption Expenditure of Private Non-profit Organisations Serving Households	...	...	...	...	...	...	...	...	...	...	...
Private Final Consumption Expenditure	...	...	...	4218.4	4642.0	3873.1	3714.3	3710.7	4210.9	...	...

a) Including consumption expenditure of private non-profit institutions.

Ghana

2.17 Exports and Imports of Goods and Services, Detail

Million Ghanaian cedis

	1970	1971	1972	1973	1974	1975	1976	1977	1978	1979	1980
Exports of Goods and Services											
1 Exports of merchandise, f.o.b.	487.6	464.5	508.8	678.5	780.8	921.1	895.9	1023.0	1574.5	...	...
2 Transport and communication	30.0	52.8	53.9	47.4	39.6	71.1	87.7	92.0	122.4	...	...
3 Insurance service charges	...	...	...	...	...	...	...	...	...	...	...
4 Other commodities	5.6	19.4	18.8	24.6	33.1	30.4	41.6	55.5	57.2	...	...
5 Adjustments of merchandise exports to change-of-ownership basis	...	...	...	...	...	...	...	...	...	...	...
6 Direct purchases in the domestic market by non-residential households	...	...	...	...	...	...	...	...	...	...	...
7 Direct purchases in the domestic market by extraterritorial bodies	...	...	...	...	...	...	...	...	...	...	...
Total Exports of Goods and Services	523.2	536.7	581.5	750.5	853.5	1022.6	1025.2	1170.5	1754.2	...	...
Imports of Goods and Services											
1 Imports of merchandise, c.i.f.	463.0	583.0	337.5	467.4	889.1	813.0	860.4	1070.0	1626.0	...	...
a Imports of merchandise, f.o.b.	408.6	511.0	295.3	431.6	814.3	748.1	793.8	989.2	1478.5	...	...
b Transport of services on merchandise imports [a]	54.4	72.0	42.2	35.8	74.8	64.9	66.6	80.8	147.5	...	...
c Insurance service charges on merchandise imports [a]	...	...	...	...	...	...	...	...	...	...	...
2 Adjustments of merchandise imports to change-of-ownership basis	...	...	...	...	...	...	...	...	...	...	...
3 Other transport and communication	40.3	57.7	45.4	58.0	64.2	79.2	90.3	103.6	224.4	...	...
4 Other insurance service charges	...	...	...	...	...	...	...	...	...	...	...
5 Other commodities	35.3	48.0	44.8	48.8	62.5	81.3	96.6	115.8	182.5	...	...
6 Direct purchases abroad by government	...	...	...	...	...	...	...	...	...	...	...
7 Direct purchases abroad by resident households	...	...	...	...	...	...	...	...	...	...	...
Total Imports of Goods and Services	538.6	688.7	427.7	574.2	1015.8	973.5	1047.3	1289.4	2033.0	...	...
Balance of Goods and Services	-15.4	-152.0	153.8	176.3	-162.3	49.1	-22.1	-118.9	-278.8	...	...
Total Imports and Balance of Goods and Services	523.2	536.7	581.5	750.5	853.5	1022.6	1025.2	1170.5	1754.2	...	...

a) Item 'Insurance service charges on merchandise imports' is included in item 'Transport of services on merchandise imports'.

3.51 External Transactions: Current Account: Detail

Million Ghanaian cedis

	1970	1971	1972	1973	1974	1975	1976	1977	1978	1979	1980
Payments to the Rest of the World											
1 Imports of goods and services	538.6	688.7	427.7	574.2	1015.8	973.5	1047.3	1289.4	2033.0	...	...
a Imports of merchandise c.i.f.	463.0	583.0	337.5	467.4	889.1	813.0	860.4	1070.0	1626.0	...	...
b Other	75.6	105.7	90.2	106.8	126.7	160.5	186.9	219.4	407.0	...	...
2 Factor income paid to the rest of the world	52.0	54.5	33.0	26.3	30.9	46.9	51.0	43.0	50.7	...	...
3 Indirect taxes paid to supranational organizations	...	...	...	...	...	...	...	...	...	...	...
4 Other current transfers to the rest of the world	18.1	21.5	14.7	16.4	13.3	13.9	15.5	14.8	20.2	...	...
a By general government	3.1	4.3	4.2	4.7	2.6	3.2	3.8	3.0	6.3	...	...
b By other resident sectors	15.0	17.2	10.5	11.7	10.7	10.7	11.7	11.8	13.9	...	...
5 Surplus of the nation on current transactions	-67.2	-202.2	143.0	172.4	-160.5	58.5	-39.4	-91.7	-204.8	...	...
Payments to the Rest of the World, and Surplus of the Nation on Current Transfers	541.5	562.5	618.4	789.3	899.5	1092.8	1074.4	1255.5	1899.1	...	...
Receipts From The Rest of the World											
1 Exports of goods and services	523.2	536.7	581.5	750.5	853.5	1022.6	1025.2	1170.5	1754.2	...	...
a Exports of merchandise f.o.b.	487.6	464.5	508.8	678.5	780.8	921.1	895.9	1023.0	1574.5	...	...

Ghana

3.51 External Transactions: Current Account: Detail
(Continued)

Million Ghanaian cedis	1970	1971	1972	1973	1974	1975	1976	1977	1978	1979	1980
b Other	35.6	72.2	72.7	72.0	72.7	101.5	129.3	147.5	179.7	...	...
2 Factor income received from the rest of the world	4.2	3.9	4.7	7.9	4.9	5.1	2.9	2.9	2.3	...	...
3 Subsidies received from supranational organizations	...	...	...	...	...	...	...	...	...	...	...
4 Other current transfers from the rest of the world	14.1	21.9	32.2	30.9	41.1	65.1	46.3	82.1	142.6	...	...
a To general government	11.6	16.8	25.7	26.5	34.6	26.5	39.5	77.3	137.7	...	...
b To other resident sectors	2.5	5.1	6.5	4.4	6.5	38.6	6.8	4.8	4.9	...	...
Receipts from the Rest of the World on Current Transfers	541.5	562.5	618.4	789.3	899.5	1092.8	1074.4	1255.5	1899.1	...	...

3.52 External Transactions: Capital Accumulation Account

Million Ghanaian cedis	1970	1971	1972	1973	1974	1975	1976	1977	1978	1979	1980
Finance of Gross Accumulation											
1 Surplus of the nation on current transactions	-67.2	-202.2	143.0	172.4	-160.5	58.5	-39.4	-91.7	-204.8	...	...
2 Capital transfers received from the rest of the world	-	-	-	-	-	-	-	-	-	...	...
Total Finance of Gross Accumulation	-67.2	-202.2	143.0	172.4	-160.5	58.5	-39.4	-91.7	-204.8	...	...
Gross Accumulation											
1 Capital transfers paid to the rest of the world	-	-	-	-	-	-	-	-	-	...	...
2 Purchases of intangible assets, n.e.c., net, from the rest of the world	-	-	-	-	-	-	-	-	-	...	...
3 Net lending to the rest of the world	-67.2	-202.2	143.0	172.4	-160.5	58.5	-39.4	-91.7	-204.8	...	...
Total Gross Accumulation	-67.2	-202.2	143.0	172.4	-160.5	58.5	-39.4	-91.7	-204.8	...	...

3.53 External Transactions: Capital Finance Account

Million Ghanaian cedis	1970	1971	1972	1973	1974	1975	1976	1977	1978	1979	1980
Acquisitions of Foreign Financial Assets											
1 Gold and SDR's	-	10.8	5.2	-0.4	-0.1	-0.2	-0.5	4.7	26.1	...	...
2 Currency and transferable deposits	15.3	31.6	133.9	93.8	-	170.7	-	13.6	100.9	...	...
3 Other deposits										...	...
4 Bills and bonds, short term	...	...	...	...	...	...	...	...	...	...	...
5 Bonds, long term [a]	...	...	...	...	...	...	...	...	...	...	...
6 Corporate equity securities	...	...	...	...	...	...	...	...	...	...	...
7 Short-term loans, n.e.c.	...	...	...	...	...	...	...	...	...	...	...
8 Long-term loans [a]	6.5	5.6	5.7	5.5	6.8	8.2	9.2	9.9	20.1	...	...
9 Proprietors' net additions to accumulation of quasi-corporate, non-resident enterprises	...	...	...	...	...	...	...	...	...	...	...
10 Trade credit and advances	8.0	9.5	60.5	70.7	3.2	28.9	15.5	20.7	-257.7	...	...
11 Other	...	...	...	...	...	...	...	...	...	...	...
Total Acquisitions of Foreign Financial Assets	115.2	96.7	247.8	185.4	30.8	232.4	37.5	62.5	178.5	...	...
Incurrence of Foreign Liabilities											
1 Currency and transferable deposits	...	...	...	...	...	...	...	...	...	...	...
2 Other deposits	...	...	...	...	...	...	...	...	...	...	...
3 Bills and bonds, short term	...	...	...	...	...	...	...	...	...	...	...
4 Bonds, long term	...	...	...	...	...	...	...	...	...	...	...
5 Corporate equity securities	...	...	...	...	...	...	...	...	...	...	...
6 Short-term loans, n.e.c.	...	...	...	...	...	...	...	...	...	...	...
7 Long-term loans	...	...	...	...	...	...	...	...	...	...	...
8 Non-resident proprietors' net additions to accumulation of resident quasi-corporate enterprises	...	...	...	...	...	...	...	...	...	...	...
9 Trade credit and advances	...	...	...	...	...	...	...	...	...	...	...
10 Other	...	...	...	...	...	...	...	...	...	...	...
Total Incurrence of Liabilities	...	...	...	...	...	...	...	...	...	...	...
Net Lending	-67.2	-202.2	143.0	172.4	-160.5	58.5	-39.4	-91.7	-204.8	...	...
Total Incurrence of Liabilities and Net Lending	...	...	...	...	...	...	...	...	...	...	...

a) Item 'Bonds, long term' is included in item 'Long term loans'.

Ghana

4.3 Derivation of Value Added by Kind of Activity, ISIC Divisions, in Current Prices

Million Ghanaian cedis

	1970 Gross Output	1970 Intermediate Consumption	1970 Value Added	1971 Gross Output	1971 Intermediate Consumption	1971 Value Added	1972 Gross Output	1972 Intermediate Consumption	1972 Value Added	1973 Gross Output	1973 Intermediate Consumption	1973 Value Added
					All Producers							
1 Agriculture, hunting, forestry and fishing	...	...	1060.0	...	...	1103.9	...	...	1313.2	1819.2	104.5	1714.7
a Agriculture and hunting	...	...	960.5	...	...	1009.6	...	...	1190.4	1615.1	75.9	1539.2
b Forestry and logging	...	...	74.1	...	...	71.4	...	...	85.6	136.0	8.2	127.8
c Fishing	...	...	25.4	...	...	22.9	...	...	37.2	68.1	20.4	47.7
2 Mining and quarrying	...	...	37.3	...	...	40.6	...	...	63.4	107.7	26.2	81.5
3 Manufacturing	...	...	247.6	...	...	275.1	...	...	305.9	971.1	561.8	409.3
4 Electricity, gas and water	...	...	23.2	...	...	23.5	...	...	25.6	39.4	9.9	29.5
a Electricity, gas and steam	...	...	...	...	...	...	...	...	...	29.9	4.9	25.0
b Water works and supply	...	...	...	...	...	...	...	...	...	9.5	5.0	4.5
5 Construction	...	...	93.8	...	...	117.9	186.5	82.6	104.0	239.5	108.6	130.9
6 Wholesale and retail trade, restaurants and hotels	...	...	280.9	...	...	325.6	...	...	340.6	648.9	214.1	434.8
a Wholesale and retail trade	...	...	270.3	...	...	314.0	...	...	326.2	568.5	151.0	417.5
b Restaurants and hotels	...	...	10.6	...	...	11.6	63.7	49.3	14.4	80.4	63.1	17.3
7 Transport, storage and communication	...	...	96.9	...	...	112.1	269.0	144.9	124.1	286.6	159.8	126.8
a Transport and storage	...	...	...	...	...	...	254.9	139.8	114.9	272.2	151.7	120.5
b Communication	...	...	...	...	...	...	14.1	5.1	9.0	14.4	8.1	6.3
8 Finance, insurance, real estate and business services	...	...	159.8	...	...	195.9	259.6	18.9	240.7	295.7	32.3	263.4
a Financial institutions	...	...	...	...	...	...	57.3	...	57.3	86.8	13.1	73.7
b Insurance	...	...	...	...	...	...	4.8	1.0	3.8	6.0	1.2	4.8
c Real estate and business services	...	...	...	...	...	...	197.5	17.9	179.6	202.9	18.0	184.9
9 Community, social and personal services	...	...	12.2	...	...	16.4	23.8	2.4	21.5	32.8	4.3	28.5
Total, Industries	...	...	2011.7	...	...	2211.0	...	...	2538.9	4440.9	1221.5	3219.4
Producers of Government Services	302.3	101.0	201.3	337.6	120.7	216.9	368.0	121.9	246.1	395.2	145.2	250.0
Other Producers	...	...	11.1	...	...	11.9	...	...	13.3	18.9	2.9	16.0
Total	...	...	2224.1	...	...	2439.8	...	...	2798.3	4855.0	1369.6	3485.4
Imputed bank service charge	...	...	-26.9	...	...	-28.0	...	...	-41.9	...	58.9	-58.9
Import duties	...	...	61.4	...	...	88.7	...	...	59.0	74.6	...	74.6
Value added tax	...	...	...	...	...	...	...	...	...	...	...	...
Total	...	...	2258.6	...	...	2500.5	...	...	2815.4	4929.6	1428.5	3501.2

	1974 Gross Output	1974 Intermediate Consumption	1974 Value Added	1975 Gross Output	1975 Intermediate Consumption	1975 Value Added	1976 Gross Output	1976 Intermediate Consumption	1976 Value Added	1977 Gross Output	1977 Intermediate Consumption	1977 Value Added
					All Producers							
1 Agriculture, hunting, forestry and fishing	2510.1	127.0	2383.1	2665.1	146.6	2518.3	3507.5	207.4	3300.1	6782.7	508.3	6274.4
a Agriculture and hunting	2260.1	93.7	2166.4	2236.7	92.6	2144.1	2987.0	146.1	2840.9	6111.4	419.4	5692.0
b Forestry and logging	175.3	10.9	164.4	312.9	19.4	293.4	398.7	24.8	373.9	468.8	29.1	439.7
c Fishing	74.7	22.4	52.3	115.5	34.6	80.8	121.8	36.5	85.3	202.5	59.8	142.7
2 Mining and quarrying	132.1	32.1	100.0	137.3	32.8	104.5	114.1	26.7	87.4	120.2	30.7	89.5
3 Manufacturing	1298.9	797.1	501.8	1620.1	884.2	735.9	1740.7	883.2	857.5	2544.9	1341.3	1203.7
4 Electricity, gas and water	43.2	12.8	30.4	55.8	23.2	32.6	65.7	18.1	47.6	80.1	27.1	52.9
a Electricity, gas and steam	32.4	7.2	25.2	41.4	15.1	26.3	49.5	8.5	41.0	60.3	15.2	45.1
b Water works and supply	10.8	5.6	5.2	14.4	8.1	6.3	16.2	9.6	6.6	19.8	11.9	7.8
5 Construction	403.9	190.7	213.2	444.1	208.5	235.6	444.3	182.5	261.8	728.0	305.6	422.3
6 Wholesale and retail trade, restaurants and hotels	896.8	306.1	590.7	1000.3	357.9	642.4	1368.0	511.9	856.0	2080.2	786.6	1293.7
a Wholesale and retail trade	799.3	229.8	569.5	866.1	252.8	613.3	1138.6	332.3	806.3	1795.8	563.6	1232.2
b Restaurants and hotels	97.5	76.3	21.2	134.2	105.1	29.1	229.4	179.6	49.7	284.4	223.0	61.5
7 Transport, storage and communication	371.0	207.6	163.4	455.6	249.7	206.0	567.5	308.6	258.9	741.0	410.4	330.6
a Transport and storage	354.9	197.7	157.2	439.5	239.8	199.8	539.2	296.6	242.6	709.0	399.4	309.5
b Communication	16.1	9.9	6.2	16.1	9.9	6.2	28.3	12.0	16.3	32.0	11.0	21.1
8 Finance, insurance, real estate and business services	302.7	53.4	249.3	337.6	61.8	275.8	406.5	92.2	314.3	625.3	154.5	470.8
a Financial institutions	109.6	35.0	74.6	120.2	38.3	82.0	168.4	62.7	105.7	239.0	89.0	150.0

Ghana

4.3 Derivation of Value Added by Kind of Activity, ISIC Divisions, in Current Prices
(Continued)

Million Ghanaian cedis

	1974 Gross Output	1974 Intermediate Consumption	1974 Value Added	1975 Gross Output	1975 Intermediate Consumption	1975 Value Added	1976 Gross Output	1976 Intermediate Consumption	1976 Value Added	1977 Gross Output	1977 Intermediate Consumption	1977 Value Added
b Insurance	7.2	1.5	5.7	21.4	6.6	14.8	31.6	10.7	20.9	29.5	10.4	19.2
c Real estate and business services	185.9	16.9	169.0	196.0	16.9	179.0	206.5	18.8	187.7	356.8	55.1	301.6
9 Community, social and personal services	39.6	6.7	32.9	66.6	11.3	55.3	89.9	15.3	74.6	120.6	24.4	96.2
Total, Industries	5998.3	1733.5	4264.8	6782.4	1976.0	4806.4	8304.2	2246.0	6058.3	13823.0	3588.8	10234.1
Producers of Government Services	584.2	252.5	331.7	708.1	275.2	433.0	832.2	365.6	466.5	1469.7	570.5	899.2
Other Producers	22.8	3.5	19.3	28.7	4.3	24.5	38.6	5.9	32.7	41.2	7.9	33.3
Total	6605.3	1989.5	4615.8	7519.2	2255.5	5263.9	9175.0	2617.5	6557.5	15333.9	4167.2	11166.6
Imputed bank service charge	...	66.5	-66.5	...	76.5	-76.5	...	127.8	-127.8	...	188.3	-188.3
Import duties	110.7	...	110.7	95.6	...	95.6	96.5	...	96.5	185.1	...	185.1
Value added tax	...	...	...	...	...	...	...	...	...	...	...	...
Total	6716.0	2056.0	4660.1	7614.8	2332.0	5283.0	9271.5	2745.3	6526.2	15519.0	4355.5	11163.4

	1978 Gross Output	1978 Intermediate Consumption	1978 Value Added
	All Producers		
1 Agriculture, hunting, forestry and fishing	13716.6	975.0	12741.5
a Agriculture and hunting	12287.6	808.2	11479.4
b Forestry and logging	1068.2	66.3	1001.8
c Fishing	360.8	100.5	260.3
2 Mining and quarrying	187.9	68.7	119.2
3 Manufacturing	3472.6	1659.3	1813.3
4 Electricity, gas and water	113.4	39.2	74.3
a Electricity, gas and steam	82.4	21.5	61.0
b Water works and supply	31.0	17.7	13.3
5 Construction	873.9	356.9	517.0
6 Wholesale and retail trade, restaurants and hotels	4302.6	1516.7	2785.8
a Wholesale and retail trade	3967.4	1258.6	2708.8
b Restaurants and hotels	335.2	258.1	77.0
7 Transport, storage and communication	1208.6	656.0	552.6
a Transport and storage	1170.5	640.3	530.2
b Communication	38.1	15.7	22.4
8 Finance, insurance, real estate and business services	800.5	152.5	648.0
a Financial institutions	382.0	65.0	317.0
b Insurance	23.5	9.2	14.3
c Real estate and business services	395.0	78.3	316.7
9 Community, social and personal services	170.5	38.1	132.4
Total, Industries	24846.6	5462.4	19384.1
Producers of Government Services	2441.1	890.1	1551.0
Other Producers	59.3	12.3	47.1
Total	27347.0	6364.8	20982.2
Imputed bank service charge	...	303.7	-303.7
Import duties	307.6	...	307.6
Value added tax	...	...	...
Total	27654.6	6668.5	20986.1

4.4 Derivation of Value Added by Kind of Activity, ISIC Divisions, in Constant Prices

Million Ghanaian cedis

	1973 Gross Output	1973 Intermediate Consumption	1973 Value Added	1974 Gross Output	1974 Intermediate Consumption	1974 Value Added	1975 Gross Output	1975 Intermediate Consumption	1975 Value Added	1976 Gross Output	1976 Intermediate Consumption	1976 Value Added
	At constant prices of: 1975											
	All Producers											
1 Agriculture, hunting, forestry and fishing	3101.2	210.8	2890.3	3364.3	219.2	3145.1	2665.1	146.6	2518.3	2673.8	197.1	2476.7
a Agriculture and hunting	2710.6	177.7	2532.9	2954.6	183.3	2771.3	2236.7	92.6	2144.1	2243.6	151.2	2092.4
b Forestry and logging	303.2	11.9	291.3	310.4	11.8	298.6	312.9	19.4	293.4	323.8	20.1	303.7
c Fishing	87.4	21.2	66.2	99.3	24.1	75.2	115.5	34.6	80.8	106.4	25.8	80.6
2 Mining and quarrying	169.1	41.8	127.3	147.3	36.4	110.9	137.3	32.8	104.5	133.0	32.9	100.1

Ghana

4.4 Derivation of Value Added by Kind of Activity, ISIC Divisions, in Constant Prices
(Continued)

Million Ghanaian cedis

	1973 Gross Output	1973 Intermediate Consumption	1973 Value Added	1974 Gross Output	1974 Intermediate Consumption	1974 Value Added	1975 Gross Output	1975 Intermediate Consumption	1975 Value Added	1976 Gross Output	1976 Intermediate Consumption	1976 Value Added
				At constant prices of:1975								
3 Manufacturing	1704.5	989.3	715.2	1736.7	1062.2	674.5	1620.1	884.2	735.9	1430.6	727.0	703.6
4 Electricity, gas and water	53.8	12.1	41.7	60.2	25.7	34.5	55.8	23.2	32.6	60.9	24.0	36.9
a Electricity, gas and steam	44.3	3.8	40.5	49.4	17.8	31.6	41.4	15.1	26.3	44.7	16.1	28.6
b Water works and supply	9.5	8.3	1.2	10.8	7.9	2.9	14.4	8.1	6.3	16.2	7.9	8.3
5 Construction	447.7	206.1	241.5	560.3	260.9	299.4	444.1	208.5	235.6	407.6	168.4	239.3
6 Wholesale and retail trade, restaurants and hotels	1429.8	705.7	724.0	1537.0	761.2	775.8	1000.3	357.9	642.4	1229.5	634.6	595.0
a Wholesale and retail trade	1313.6	615.5	698.1	1416.3	667.7	748.6	866.1	252.8	613.3	1090.7	526.1	564.7
b Restaurants and hotels	116.2	90.2	25.9	120.7	93.5	27.2	134.2	105.1	29.1	138.8	108.5	30.3
7 Transport, storage and communication	434.2	260.2	173.9	482.2	278.7	203.4	455.6	249.7	206.0	382.7	214.8	167.9
a Transport and storage	416.5	249.4	167.1	465.5	268.5	197.0	439.5	239.8	199.8	363.9	203.3	160.6
b Communication	17.7	10.8	6.8	16.7	10.2	6.4	16.1	9.9	6.2	18.8	11.5	7.3
8 Finance, insurance, real estate and business services	388.6	77.6	311.0	409.2	83.8	325.4	337.6	61.8	275.8	375.0	81.1	293.9
a Financial institutions	110.8	35.4	75.5	144.8	46.2	98.6	120.2	38.3	82.0	148.0	47.2	100.8
b Insurance	9.9	4.2	5.7	23.9	8.0	15.9	21.4	6.6	14.8	22.3	8.7	13.6
c Real estate and business services	267.9	38.0	229.9	240.5	29.6	210.9	196.0	16.9	179.0	204.7	25.2	179.6
9 Community, social and personal services	50.3	8.5	41.8	51.4	8.8	42.6	66.6	11.3	55.3	57.5	9.8	47.7
Total, Industries	7779.1	2512.3	5266.8	8348.6	2736.8	5611.6	6782.4	1976.0	4806.4	6750.7	2089.7	4661.0
Producers of Government Services	575.3	242.3	333.0	703.7	350.8	352.8	708.1	275.2	433.0	735.8	297.3	438.5
Other Producers	26.5	3.8	22.7	26.9	3.9	23.1	28.7	4.3	24.5	28.7	4.1	24.5
Total	8380.9	2758.4	5622.5	9079.2	3091.5	5987.5	7519.2	2255.5	5263.9	7515.2	2391.1	5124.0
Imputed bank service charge	...	98.3	-98.3	...	88.9	-88.9	...	76.5	-76.5	...	112.3	-112.3
Import duties	121.9	...	121.9	134.4	...	134.4	95.6	...	95.6	84.8	...	84.8
Value added tax	...	...	...	...	...	...	...	...	...	...	...	...
Total	8502.8	2856.7	5646.1	9213.6	3180.4	6033.0	7614.8	2332.0	5283.0	7600.0	2503.4	5096.5

	1977 Gross Output	1977 Intermediate Consumption	1977 Value Added	1978 Gross Output	1978 Intermediate Consumption	1978 Value Added
	At constant prices of:1975					
	All Producers					
1 Agriculture, hunting, forestry and fishing	2559.5	196.9	2362.6	3013.1	224.1	2788.9
a Agriculture and hunting	2110.9	145.8	1965.1	2557.5	172.9	2384.5
b Forestry and logging	319.3	19.8	299.5	328.7	20.4	308.3
c Fishing	129.3	31.3	98.0	126.9	30.8	96.1
2 Mining and quarrying	129.1	31.9	97.2	111.5	27.5	84.0
3 Manufacturing	1540.1	816.5	723.6	1366.9	665.8	701.1
4 Electricity, gas and water	62.6	25.9	36.7	55.9	23.5	32.4
a Electricity, gas and steam	46.9	17.1	29.8	39.7	14.4	25.3
b Water works and supply	15.7	8.8	6.9	16.2	9.1	7.1
5 Construction	479.2	209.0	270.2	369.5	147.3	222.2
6 Wholesale and retail trade, restaurants and hotels	967.5	360.8	606.7	922.2	334.5	587.7
a Wholesale and retail trade	818.6	243.9	574.7	819.2	253.7	565.5
b Restaurants and hotels	148.9	116.9	32.0	103.0	80.8	22.2
7 Transport, storage and communication	419.6	228.8	190.8	398.7	218.2	180.5
a Transport and storage	400.2	219.0	181.2	385.9	211.8	174.1
b Communication	19.4	9.8	9.6	12.8	6.4	6.4
8 Finance, insurance, real estate and business services	422.9	93.2	329.7	467.8	107.5	360.4
a Financial institutions	174.3	55.6	118.7	221.2	70.6	150.6
b Insurance	15.3	6.7	8.6	8.3	4.0	4.3
c Real estate and business services	233.3	30.9	202.4	238.3	32.9	205.5
9 Community, social and personal services	65.8	14.5	51.3	62.0	13.9	48.2

4.4 Derivation of Value Added by Kind of Activity, ISIC Divisions, in Constant Prices
(Continued)

Million Ghanaian cedis

	1977 Gross Output	1977 Intermediate Consumption	1977 Value Added	1978 Gross Output	1978 Intermediate Consumption	1978 Value Added
	\multicolumn{6}{c}{At constant prices of:1975}
Total, Industries	6646.3	1977.5	4668.8	6767.6	1762.3	5005.4
Producers of Government Services	945.6	367.6	578.0	1096.6	386.2	710.4
Other Producers	26.2	4.5	21.7	27.0	4.6	22.5
Total	7618.1	2349.6	5268.5	7891.2	2153.1	5738.3
Imputed bank service charge	...	137.4	-137.4	...	175.8	-175.8
Import duties	81.3	...	81.3	91.7	...	91.7
Value added tax	...	...	...	...	...	...
Total	7699.4	2487.0	5212.4	7982.9	2328.9	5654.2

Ghana

Greece

General note. The preparation of national accounts statistics in Greece is undertaken by the National Accounts Service, Ministry of Co-ordination, Athens. Official estimates are published in a series of reports entitled 'National Accounts of Greece'. The estimates are generally in accordance with the classifications and definitions recommended in the United Nations System of National Accounts (SNA). Input-output tables have been published for the years 1958 and 1970 in 'National Accounts of Greece 1970-1976'. The following tables have been prepared from successive replies to the United Nations national accounts questionnaire. When the scope and coverage of the estimates differ for conceptual or statistical reasons from the definitions and classifications recommended in SNA, a footnote is indicated to the relevant tables.

Sources and methods:

(a) Gross domestic product. Gross domestic product is estimated mainly through the production approach.

(b) Expenditure on the gross domestic product. The expenditure approach is used to estimate government final consumption expenditure and exports and imports of goods and services. This approach, in combination with the commodity-flow approach, is also used to estimate gross capital formation. Private final consumption expenditure is estimated on the basis of the direct expenditure approach. The estimates of government final consumption expenditure are obtained from the accounts of the different government units. For private consumption expenditure, sources include the household budget surveys, tax statistics and other statistical sources. In estimating increase in stocks, delayed information from the manufacturing and mining surveys is used to supplement the commodity-flow method. Estimates of investments in private buildings are based on building permits that have been issued, while for the public sector construction, estimates are derived from government budgetary accounts and replies from public enterprises and public funds. Information from the annual manufacturing and mining surveys as well as investments by large industrial units, public enterprises and public funds are used for machinery and equipment. Own-account construction is covered by information on loans granted for such construction works. For exports and imports of goods and services, foreign trade statistics based on the special trade principle are used. For the constant price estimates, price indices are used to deflate the wages and salaries of government employees. For the private expenditure, the annual quantities of food, fuel, light and water charges are multiplied by average base-year prices. Expenditure on other private goods and services are deflated by appropriate price indexes. Value added of residential and non-residential buildings is extrapolated by specially constructed indicators. For other components of gross capital formation, price deflation is used. The base-year values of exports and imports of merchandise are extrapolated by volume indexes while other goods and services are deflated by mean value index of exports and imports.

(c) Cost-structure of the gross domestic product. Estimates of compensation of employees for various services such as finance, insurance and transport are estimated by using data derived from questionnaires sent to them by the National Accounts Service. For manufacturing and mining, data are derived from the annual industrial surveys. The employers' contributions are estimated by using data derived from statements of the social insurance funds. Capital consumption is estimated as a percentage of the corresponding capital stock figure for each industry and type of assests. The current-price estimates of capital stock and depreciation are calculated on a replacement cost basis. The estimates of indirect taxes and subsidies are obtained from government accounts. Operating surplus is calculated as a residual.

(d) Gross domestic product by kind of economic activity. The table of gross domestic product by kind of economic activity is prepared in factor values. The production approach is used to estimate value added of most industries. The income approach is used for lignite mining, electricity, gas and water and parts of the service sectors such as transportation, communication, health and education, and miscellaneous services. For agricultural and animal breeding, the estimate of production is based on annual surveys conducted by the National Statistical Office of Greece. Intermediate consumption estimates are based on data taken from various sources such as Ministry of Agriculture and the Pubic Power Corporation. Agricultural product prices refer to prices obtained by farmers. The estimates of mining and quarrying and manufacturing are based on the annual survey of industrial establishments. The information from the survey is available within 2-3 years, meanwhile, value added is extrapolated by the index of industrial production and the wholesale price index. Value added of electricity, gas and water is estimated on the basis of annual questionnaires sent to the concerned enterprises. For construction, gross value is obtained from investment data of buildings and other construction to which values of military construction and repairs are added. The estimates of gross trade margins for agricultural products are based on traded quantities valued at the difference between consumers' and producers' prices. For industrial and imported products, percentages of gross trade margins are applied to the traded values at current prices. Intermediate consumption estimates are based on a survey conducted in 1970 for the compilation of the input-output table. Value added of transport and communication and finance and insurance services is based on data compiled through questionnaires sent to the concerned enterprises. For ownership of dwellings, the estimation of real or imputed rent is carried out at constant prices, based on the number of dwelling rooms existing and the average annual rent expenditure in a bench-mark year. These data are obtained from dwelling censuses and household budget surveys. Estimates concerning government services are obtained from general government accounts. For private health and educational services, only wages and salaries data are available. Value added of hotel is based on surveys conducted every three years by the National Accounts Service, while that of restaurants is based on data obtained from household budget surveys. For other services, employment data as well as data on average remuneration per person employed or data derived from taxation returns are used. For the constant price estimates, double deflation is used for agriculture and electricity. For water, construction, transport and hotels, value added is extrapolated by quantity indicators. For the remaining sectors of the industries, price deflation is used.

1.1 Expenditure on the Gross Domestic Product, in Current Prices

Million Greek drachmas

		1970	1971	1972	1973	1974	1975	1976	1977	1978	1979	1980
1	General government final consumption expenditure	37742	41362	45943	55444	78071	102007	124332	153840	185150	233530	276140
2	Private final consumption expenditure	205888	223445	246835	305475	379840	451573	539816	632700	754630	904322	1107585
3	Gross capital formation	84009	92248	111679	173202	165380	181350	219700	264120	321170	429600	482300
	a Increase in stocks	13346	8950	6846	37525	39904	41400	44700	42700	43170	63435	82030
	b Gross fixed capital formation	70663	83298	104833	135677	125476	139950	175000	221420	278000	366165	400270
	Residential buildings	19740	23603	32565	41544	27771	37983	47477	69188	96778	131057	137517
	Non-residential buildings	9579	10483	13556	18956	21670	18865	24396	31952	40266	57652	58274
	Other construction and land improvement etc.	16169	19312	22232	26737	25392	29380	34985	40521	44595	53925	57624
	Other	25175	29900	36480	48440	50643	53722	68142	79759	96361	123531	146855
4	Exports of goods and services [a]	29988	34111	44300	68904	87865	109815	139537	154957	193635	235083	336115
5	Less: Imports of goods and services	54996	60912	75723	122095	144695	180562	213068	243291	286071	360847	451820
	Statistical discrepancy	-3714	46	4692	3221	-2256	7975	14615	1402	-7122	-12742	-39766
	Equals: Gross Domestic Product	298917	330300	377726	484151	564205	672158	824932	963728	1161392	1428946	1710554

a) Excluding income from ocean-going cargo ships under Greek flag or ownership. However, remittances actually received by the bank of Greece from persons engaged in these enterprises are included in factor income from the rest of the world.

1.2 Expenditure on the Gross Domestic Product, in Constant Prices

Million Greek drachmas

		1970	1971	1972	1973	1974	1975	1976	1977	1978	1979	1980
		\multicolumn{11}{c}{At constant prices of:1970}										
1	General government final consumption expenditure	37742	39607	41851	44698	50096	56075	58953	62800	65000	68800	68280
2	Private final consumption expenditure	205888	217242	232324	250057	251650	265242	279343	292500	310250	317131	318614
3	Gross capital formation	84009	89273	99464	126603	97050	95760	99150	102650	106760	117030	110500
	a Increase in stocks	13346	8715	6487	26510	22550	21100	19400	16700	15660	18760	20770
	b Gross fixed capital formation	70663	80558	92977	100093	74500	74660	79750	85950	91100	98270	89730

664

Greece

1.2 Expenditure on the Gross Domestic Product, in Constant Prices
(Continued)

Million Greek drachmas

	1970	1971	1972	1973	1974	1975	1976	1977	1978	1979	1980
					At constant prices of:1970						
Residential buildings	19740	23641	29964	30576	15869	20476	21909	26428	30074	31572	27290
Non-residential buildings	9579	10504	12472	13951	12381	10170	11258	12205	12513	13889	11565
Other construction and land improvement etc.	16167	19424	21139	20426	15076	16010	16078	15886	15028	14765	12719
Other	25175	26989	29402	35140	31174	28004	30505	31431	33485	38044	38156
4 Exports of goods and services [a]	29988	33545	41222	50849	49427	54808	63397	64007	74104	78807	83995
5 Less: Imports of goods and services	54996	59199	68325	90354	75633	80398	85341	92145	98734	105810	98812
Statistical discrepancy	-3714	-270	2095	-7693	-12043	-9125	-8823	-9190	-8587	-10579	-9941
Equals: Gross Domestic Product	298917	320198	348631	374160	360547	382362	406679	420622	448793	465379	472636

a) Excluding income from ocean-going cargo ships under Greek flag or ownership. However, remittances actually received by the bank of Greece from persons engaged in these enterprises are included in factor income from the rest of the world.

1.3 Cost Components of the Gross Domestic Product

Million Greek drachmas

	1970	1971	1972	1973	1974	1975	1976	1977	1978	1979	1980
1 Indirect taxes, net	40917	42878	47749	55935	56877	78977	96197	119100	144683	183570	193470
a Indirect taxes paid	43406	46833	52526	64826	71562	95961	119254	147600	178219	216690	232470
b Less: Subsidies received	2489	3955	4777	8891	14685	16984	23057	28500	33536	33120	39000
2 Consumption of fixed capital	16860	19635	23738	30566	39284	47457	59200	72430	89470	112286	141890
3 Compensation of employees paid by resident producers to: [a]	93913	104392	120549	145548	177373	217793	276599	346534	432380	538853	648838
a Resident households [a]	93451	103796	119706	144240	176041	216254	274855	344369	430210	536496	646167
b Rest of the world	462	596	843	1308	1332	1539	1744	2165	2170	2357	2671
4 Net operating surplus [a]	147227	163395	185690	252102	290671	327931	392936	425664	494859	594237	726356
Equals: Gross Domestic Product	298917	330300	377726	484151	564205	672158	824932	963728	1161392	1428946	1710554

a) Excluding wages paid to agricultural workers which are included in item 'Operating surplus'.

1.4 General Government Current Receipts and Disbursements

Million Greek drachmas

	1970	1971	1972	1973	1974	1975	1976	1977	1978	1979	1980
						Receipts					
1 Property and entrepreneurial income	5678	5300	6719	8636	13802	15851	17610	18660	18462	28580	37880
2 Taxes, fees and contributions	73545	81624	92550	112804	135585	166283	223270	266392	328969	405560	478630
a Indirect taxes	43406	46833	52526	64826	71562	95961	119254	147600	178219	216690	232470
b Direct taxes [a]	30139	34791	40024	47978	64023	70322	104016	118792	150750	188870	246160
c Social security contributions [a]	...	...	...	...	...	...	...	...	...	...	...
d Compulsory fees, fines and penalties [a]	...	...	...	...	...	...	...	...	...	...	...
3 Other current receipts	975	1040	1213	1593	3110	1979	2232	2788	2177	3548	4417
Total Current Receipts of General Government	80198	87964	100482	123033	152497	184113	243112	287840	349608	437688	520927
						Disbursements					
1 General government final consumption expenditure	37742	41362	45943	55444	78071	102007	124332	153840	185150	233530	276140
2 Property income paid	2815	3270	3746	4852	7139	9261	12940	14066	19690	30790	41247
3 Subsidies	2489	3955	4777	8891	14685	16984	23057	28500	33536	33120	39000
4 Other current transfers paid	23950	26568	28767	33064	41324	51314	65331	83510	108985	127583	161468
a Social security benefits and social assistance grants	...	...	...	...	...	...	...	...	...	...	...
b Other	23950	26568	28767	33064	41324	51314	65331	83510	108985	127583	161468
5 Net saving	13202	12809	17249	20782	11278	4547	17452	7924	2247	12665	3072
Total Current Disbursements and Net Saving of General Government	80198	87964	100482	123033	152497	184113	243112	287840	349608	437688	520927

a) Items 'Social security contributions' and 'Fees, fines and other n.e.c.' are included in item 'Direct taxes'.

1.6 Current Income and Outlay of Households and Non-Profit Institutions

Million Greek drachmas

	1970	1971	1972	1973	1974	1975	1976	1977	1978	1979	1980
						Receipts					
1 Compensation of employees	95913	107713	124814	150675	184078	226740	287193	358698	445370	556773	672507
a From resident producers	93451	103796	119706	144240	176041	216254	274855	344369	430210	536496	646167
b From rest of the world	2462	3917	5108	6435	8037	10486	12338	14329	15160	20277	26340
2 Property and entrepreneurial income received [a]	140318	158689	178157	241007	280482	324560	383288	429185	501976	606238	742169

Greece

1.6 Current Income and Outlay of Households and Non-Profit Institutions
(Continued)

Million Greek drachmas

	1970	1971	1972	1973	1974	1975	1976	1977	1978	1979	1980
3 Current transfers received	33178	39487	44680	53100	58869	72777	90501	112999	140483	165208	200799
a Social security benefits and social assistance grants received	-	-	-	-	-	-	-	-	-	-	-
b Other	33178	39487	44680	53100	58869	72777	90501	112999	140483	165208	200799
Total Current Receipts	269409	305889	347651	444782	523429	624077	760982	900882	1087829	1328219	1615475

Disbursements

	1970	1971	1972	1973	1974	1975	1976	1977	1978	1979	1980
1 Private final consumption expenditure	205888	223445	246835	305475	379840	451573	539816	632700	754630	904322	1107585
2 Property income paid	-	-	-	-	-	-	-	-	-	-	-
3 Direct taxes and other payments n.e.c. to general government	28585	32756	36176	44057	55725	63281	84690	108792	137188	173120	225172
4 Other current transfers paid	-	-	-	-	330	100	-	-	-	-	-
5 Net saving a b	34936	49688	64640	95250	87534	109123	136476	159390	196011	250777	282718
Total Current Disbursements and Net Saving	269409	305889	347651	444782	523429	624077	760982	900882	1087829	1328219	1615475

a) Beginning 1975, including savings of corporations.
b) Including a statistical discrepancy.

1.7 External Transactions on Current Account, Summary

Million Greek drachmas

	1970	1971	1972	1973	1974	1975	1976	1977	1978	1979	1980

Payments to the Rest of the World

	1970	1971	1972	1973	1974	1975	1976	1977	1978	1979	1980
1 Imports of goods and services	54996	60912	75723	122095	144695	180562	213068	243291	286071	360847	451820
a Imports of merchandise c.i.f.	49262	54293	67115	109751	130724	164227	194399	221595	260568	326652	407888
b Other	5734	6619	8608	12344	13971	16335	18669	21696	25503	34195	43932
2 Factor income paid to the rest of the world	2274	2897	3450	4519	6876	7554	9964	10323	12260	16097	22701
a Compensation of employees	462	596	843	1308	1332	1539	1744	2165	2170	2357	2671
b Property and entrepreneurial income paid	1812	2301	2607	3211	5544	6015	8220	8158	10090	13740	20030
3 Indirect taxes paid to supranational organizations	...	...	...	...	...	...	...	...	...	...	...
4 Current transfers to the rest of the world	134	131	133	153	1329	1479	1634	1450	2121	1653	1988
5 Surplus of the nation on current transactions	-9302	-4965	-4720	-18477	-18637	-28198	-21187	-25778	-26320	-41130	-14854
Payments to the Rest of the World and Surplus of the Nation on Current Transactions	48102	58975	74586	108290	134263	161397	203479	229286	274132	337467	461655

Receipts From The Rest of the World

	1970	1971	1972	1973	1974	1975	1976	1977	1978	1979	1980
1 Exports of goods and services	29988	34111	44300	68904	87865	109815	139537	154957	193635	235083	336115
a Exports of merchandise f.o.b.	19276	19874	26125	42812	60891	74441	93812	101331	123727	144238	221171
b Other	10712	14237	18175	26092	26974	35374	45725	53626	69909	90845	114944
2 Factor income received from rest of the world	7777	10774	13027	17604	24744	26761	34906	40602	44701	59558	79804
a Compensation of employees	2462	3917	5108	6435	8037	10486	12338	14329	15160	20277	26340
b Property and entrepreneurial income received	5315	6857	7919	11169	16707	16275	22568	26273	29541	39281	53464
3 Subsidies received from supranational organisations	...	...	...	...	...	...	...	...	...	...	...
4 Current transfers from rest of the world	10337	14090	17259	21782	21654	24821	29036	33727	35796	42826	45736
Receipts from the Rest of the World on Current Transactions	48102	58975	74586	108290	134263	161397	203479	229286	274132	337467	461655

1.8 Capital Transactions of The Nation, Summary

Million Greek drachmas

	1970	1971	1972	1973	1974	1975	1976	1977	1978	1979	1980

Finance of Gross Capital Formation

	1970	1971	1972	1973	1974	1975	1976	1977	1978	1979	1980
Gross saving	74707	87283	106959	154725	146743	153152	198513	238342	294850	388470	467446
1 Consumption of fixed capital	16860	19635	23738	30566	39284	47457	59200	72430	89470	112286	141890
2 Net saving	57847	67648	83221	124159	107459	105695	139313	165912	205380	276184	325556
a General government	13202	12809	17249	20782	11278	4547	17452	7924	2247	12665	3072
b Corporate and quasi-corporate enterprises a	5995	5197	6024	11348	6391	...	...	...	...	...	...

Greece

1.8 Capital Transactions of The Nation, Summary
(Continued)

Million Greek drachmas	1970	1971	1972	1973	1974	1975	1976	1977	1978	1979	1980
c Other	38650	49642	59948	92029	89790	101148	121861	157988	203133	263519	322484
Less: Surplus of the nation on current transactions	-9302	-4965	-4720	-18477	-18637	-28198	-21187	-25778	-26320	-41130	-14854
Finance of Gross Capital Formation	84009	92248	111679	173202	165380	181350	219700	264120	321170	429600	482300
Gross Capital Formation												
Increase in stocks	13346	8950	6846	37525	39904	41400	44700	42700	43170	63435	82030
Gross fixed capital formation	70663	83298	104833	135677	125476	139950	175000	221420	278000	366165	400270
1 General government	13386	15093	18217	21300	18908	24599	30645	33635	37440	45122	43427
2 Corporate and quasi-corporate enterprises [b]	6540	10954	13573	16367	18903	14221	16255	15435	24160	36278	52393
a Public	6540	10954	13573	16367	18903	14221	16255	15435	24160	36278	52393
b Private	...	...	...	...	...	...	...	...	...	...	...
3 Other	50737	57251	73043	98010	87665	101130	128100	172350	216400	284765	304450
Gross Capital Formation	84009	92248	111679	173202	165380	181350	219700	264120	321170	429600	482300

a) Beginning 1975, item 'Corporate and quasi-corporate enterprises' is included in item 'Other'.
b) Private corporate and quasi-corporate enterprises are included in item 'Other'.

1.10 Gross Domestic Product by Kind of Activity, in Current Prices

Million Greek drachmas	1970	1971	1972	1973	1974	1975	1976	1977	1978	1979	1980
1 Agriculture, hunting, forestry and fishing	47058	52334	61467	87311	100365	110971	136204	141543	177074	198166	264552
2 Mining and quarrying	3541	4220	4915	6047	6739	8460	10606	12670	14276	19226	23859
3 Manufacturing	49266	55571	61938	86151	102616	118078	146522	165348	191254	238509	296955
4 Electricity, gas and water	5152	5649	6274	7109	8071	9312	12037	13895	16184	20649	23870
5 Construction	23017	26258	33574	42740	37761	43011	53606	71839	91192	123078	130093
6 Wholesale and retail trade, restaurants and hotels [a]	31050	34093	40117	55486	71694	82221	99108	113997	131825	160217	196266
7 Transport, storage and communication [b]	19761	22029	25304	29070	35319	47955	60081	69920	82643	100177	115704
8 Finance, insurance, real estate and business services [c]	27187	29732	32928	38344	46805	54875	64772	76300	92799	109432	132473
9 Community, social and personal services [acd]	29409	32665	36339	43808	54358	66008	82234	101751	124253	153922	186602
Total, Industries	235441	262551	302856	396066	463728	540891	665170	767263	921500	1123376	1370374
Producers of Government Services	22559	24871	27121	32150	43600	52290	63565	77365	95209	122000	146710
Other Producers [d]	...	...	...	...	...	...	...	...	...	...	...
Subtotal [e]	258000	287422	329977	428216	507328	593181	728735	844628	1016709	1245376	1517084
Less: Imputed bank service charge	...	...	...	...	...	...	...	...	...	...	...
Plus: Import duties	...	...	...	...	...	...	...	...	...	...	...
Plus: Value added tax	...	...	...	...	...	...	...	...	...	...	...
Plus: Other adjustments [f]	40917	42878	47749	55935	56877	78977	96197	119100	144683	183570	193470
Equals: Gross Domestic Product	298917	330300	377726	484151	564205	672158	824932	963728	1161392	1428946	1710554

a) Restaurants and hotels are included in item 'Community, social and personal services'.
b) Excluding income from ocean-going cargo ships under Greek flag or ownership. However, remittances actually received by the bank of Greece from persons engaged in these enterprises are included in factor income from the rest of the world.
c) Business services are included in item 'Community, social and personal services'.
d) Item 'Other producers' is included in item 'Community, social and personal services'.
e) Gross domestic product in factor values.
f) Referring to indirect taxes net of subsidies.

1.11 Gross Domestic Product by Kind of Activity, in Constant Prices

Million Greek drachmas	1970	1971	1972	1973	1974	1975	1976	1977	1978	1979	1980
At constant prices of: 1970												
1 Agriculture, hunting, forestry and fishing	47058	48662	51543	51204	53672	56733	55971	51830	57214	53616	59621
2 Mining and quarrying	3541	4031	4495	5082	4774	4885	5242	5797	5723	6329	6215
3 Manufacturing	49266	54586	58892	69228	67266	70944	78029	79143	84341	88998	89125
4 Electricity, gas and water	5152	5911	7389	8133	7701	8596	9753	10726	12156	12996	13724
5 Construction	23017	26274	31179	31924	21967	23147	24576	27558	28751	30548	26577
6 Wholesale and retail trade, restaurants and hotels [a]	31050	32634	36080	41452	41172	42823	45198	46878	49507	51144	50633
7 Transport, storage and communication [b]	19761	21864	24447	27191	27430	28616	31270	32936	35151	37892	39749
8 Finance, insurance, real estate and business services [c]	27187	29320	31675	33966	36309	37892	40122	42147	44273	46643	49132
9 Community, social and personal services [ac]	29409	31547	33614	35255	34584	36855	39361	41461	43837	45433	45180
Total, Industries	235441	254829	279314	303435	294875	310491	329522	338476	360953	373599	379956
Producers of Government Services	22559	23722	24659	25834	28432	29342	30877	32546	33850	35500	36680

Greece

1.11 Gross Domestic Product by Kind of Activity, in Constant Prices
(Continued)

Million Greek drachmas

	1970	1971	1972	1973	1974	1975	1976	1977	1978	1979	1980
					At constant prices of: 1970						
Other Producers	...	...	...	...	...	...	...	...	...	...	...
Subtotal [d]	258000	278551	303973	329269	323307	339833	360399	371022	394803	409099	416636
Less: Imputed bank service charge	...	...	...	...	...	...	...	...	...	...	...
Plus: Import duties	...	...	...	...	...	...	...	...	...	...	...
Plus: Value added tax	...	...	...	...	...	...	...	...	...	...	...
Plus: Other adjustments [e]	40917	41647	44658	44891	37240	42529	46280	49600	53990	56280	56000
Equals: Gross Domestic Product	298917	320198	348631	374160	360547	382362	406679	420622	448793	465379	472636

a) Restaurants and hotels are included in item 'Community, social and personal services'.
b) Excluding income from ocean-going cargo ships under Greek flag or ownership. However, remittances actually received by the bank of Greece from persons engaged in these enterprises are included in factor income from the rest of the world.
c) Business services are included in item 'Community, social and personal services'.
d) Gross domestic product in factor values.
e) Referring to indirect taxes net of subsidies.

1.12 Relations Among National Accounting Aggregates

Million Greek drachmas

	1970	1971	1972	1973	1974	1975	1976	1977	1978	1979	1980
Gross Domestic Product	298917	330300	377726	484151	564205	672158	824932	963728	1161392	1428946	1710554
Plus: Net factor income received from abroad	5503	7877	9577	13085	17868	19207	24942	30279	32441	43461	57103
Factor income received	7777	10774	13027	17604	24744	26761	34906	40602	44701	59558	79804
Less: Factor income paid	2274	2897	3450	4519	6876	7554	9964	10323	12260	16097	22701
Equals: Gross National Product	304420	338177	387303	497236	582073	691365	849874	994007	1193833	1472407	1767657
Less: Consumption of fixed capital	16860	19635	23738	30566	39284	47457	59200	72430	89470	112286	141890
Less: Net indirect taxes paid to supranational organisations	...	...	...	...	...	...	...	...	...	...	...
Equals: National Income at Market Prices	287560	318542	363565	466670	542789	643908	790674	921577	1104363	1360121	1625767
Plus: Net current transfers received from abroad	10203	13959	17126	21629	20325	23342	27402	32277	33675	41173	43748
Current transfers received	10337	14090	17259	21782	21654	24821	29036	33727	35796	42826	45736
Less: Current transfers paid	134	131	133	153	1329	1479	1634	1450	2121	1653	1988
Equals: National Disposable Income at Market Prices	297763	332501	380691	488299	563114	667250	818076	953854	1138038	1401294	1669515
Less: Final consumption	243630	264807	292778	360919	457911	553580	664148	786540	939780	1137852	1383725
Statistical discrepancy	3714	-46	-4692	-3221	2256	-7975	-14615	-1402	7122	12742	39766
Equals: Net Saving	57847	67648	83221	124159	107459	105695	139313	165912	205380	276184	325556
Less: Surplus of the nation on current transactions	-9302	-4965	-4720	-18477	-18637	-28198	-21187	-25778	-26320	-41130	-14854
Equals: Net Capital Formation	67149	72613	87941	142636	126096	133893	160500	191690	231700	317314	340410

2.1 General Government Final Consumption Expenditure by Function, in Current Prices

Million Greek drachmas

	1970	1971	1972	1973	1974	1975	1976	1977	1978	1979	1980
1 General public services	13990	15521	17141	21343	27170	33472	41941	49646	60185	80629	98712
2 Defence	13836	14893	16703	19385	31796	45422	52357	65808	76106	91510	100000
3 Public order and safety	...	...	...	...	...	...	...	...	...	...	...
4 Education	5648	6272	6807	8394	10738	12987	16423	21362	27657	33128	40664
5 Health	3030	3411	3960	4812	6328	7659	10365	12986	16098	21761	27768
6 Social security and welfare											
7 Housing and community amenities	495	519	543	674	824	1011	1423	1813	2306	3054	3791
8 Recreational, cultural and religious affairs											
9 Economic services [a]	743	746	789	836	1215	1456	1823	2225	2798	3448	5205
10 Other functions	...	...	...	...	...	...	...	...	...	...	...
Total General Government Final Consumption Expenditure	37742	41362	45943	55444	78071	102007	124332	153840	185150	233530	276140

a) Including item 'Other functions'.

2.5 Private Final Consumption Expenditure by Type, in Current Prices

Million Greek drachmas

	1970	1971	1972	1973	1974	1975	1976	1977	1978	1979	1980
					Final Consumption Expenditure of Resident Households						
1 Food, beverages and tobacco	87322	94474	102320	130681	162972	190519	227206	258328	310609	376522	484295
a Food	73420	80000	86652	112378	140292	164654	194241	219009	262968	322502	421101
b Non-alcoholic beverages	913	998	840	1287	2575	2696	3580	6014	7008	9261	10386
c Alcoholic beverages	5712	5830	6440	7874	9674	10243	14099	16215	20638	21591	24925
d Tobacco	7277	7646	8388	9142	10431	12926	15286	17090	20035	23168	27433
2 Clothing and footwear	26212	28911	31793	37814	44286	52941	63939	72490	84011	105692	111996
3 Gross rent, fuel and power	29503	31923	35397	41733	49911	57098	65902	77369	94726	113256	146854

Greece

2.5 Private Final Consumption Expenditure by Type, in Current Prices
(Continued)

Million Greek drachmas

	1970	1971	1972	1973	1974	1975	1976	1977	1978	1979	1980
a Fuel and power	4948	5257	6024	7510	9132	11030	12927	14754	17034	20053	31839
b Other	24555	26666	29373	34223	40779	46068	52975	62615	77692	93203	115015
4 Furniture, furnishings and household equipment and operation	15597	17457	20241	27115	33148	40355	49612	58325	66214	78542	101121
a Household operation	4961	5743	6556	8582	10790	13192	14979	17177	20061	23661	29479
b Other	10636	11714	13685	18533	22358	27163	34633	41148	46153	54881	71642
5 Medical care and health expenses	7806	8460	9025	10912	12749	15907	18255	21101	25049	30284	35053
6 Transport and communication	17604	20116	23921	28153	38618	50211	65450	85038	105374	122787	133320
a Personal transport equipment	953	1117	1630	2581	2565	5414	9911	21000	27974	22641	10452
b Other	16651	18999	22291	25572	36053	44797	55539	64038	77400	100146	122868
7 Recreational, entertainment, education and cultural services	10143	11139	12701	16117	18343	22190	27069	33375	41499	43231	52168
a Education	2652	3027	3304	3736	5180	6376	7594	9112	9591	10458	10847
b Other	7491	8112	9397	12381	13163	15814	19475	24263	31908	32773	41321
8 Miscellaneous goods and services	15848	17914	20344	25040	29909	38000	46631	56336	67074	83636	102693
a Personal care	2213	2443	2758	3840	4738	7217	7856	8592	10621	13114	15734
b Expenditures in restaurants, cafes and hotels	9409	10785	12162	14801	17129	21138	27549	34810	41321	52311	64662
c Other	4227	4686	5424	6399	8042	9645	11226	12934	15132	18211	22297
Total Final Consumption Expenditure in the Domestic Market by Households, of which	210036	230394	255742	317565	389936	467221	564064	662362	794556	953950	1167500
a Durable goods	8342	9086	11624	17853	19470	26575	38033	53369	65434	66150	68248
b Semi-durable goods a	32602	36113	40072	48587	58726	70820	84168	97423	111627	137919	149990
c Non-durable goods	104766	114088	124637	157998	197792	233439	277111	316993	381796	464484	600452
d Services	64326	71107	79409	93127	113948	136387	164752	194577	235699	285397	348811
Plus: Direct purchases abroad by resident households	1659	2210	2874	3356	3873	4985	5558	6101	8302	11312	13292
Less: Direct purchases in the domestic market by non-resident households	5807	9159	11781	15446	13969	20533	29806	35763	48228	60940	73207
Equals: Final Consumption Expenditure of Resident Households b	205888	223445	246835	305475	379840	451673	539816	632700	754630	904322	1107585

Final Consumption Expenditure of Private Non-profit Institutions Serving Households

	1970	1971	1972	1973	1974	1975	1976	1977	1978	1979	1980
Equals: Final Consumption Expenditure of Private Non-profit Organisations Serving Households	...	...	...	...	...	...	...	...	...	...	...
Private Final Consumption Expenditure	205888	223445	246835	305475	379840	451673	539816	632700	754630	904322	1107585

a) Jewelries, watches, rings and precious stones are included.
b) Including consumption expenditure of private non-profit institutions.

2.6 Private Final Consumption Expenditure by Type, in Constant Prices

Million Greek drachmas

	1970	1971	1972	1973	1974	1975	1976	1977	1978	1979	1980

At constant prices of: 1970

Final Consumption Expenditure of Resident Households

	1970	1971	1972	1973	1974	1975	1976	1977	1978	1979	1980
1 Food, beverages and tobacco	87322	89801	93596	99494	100733	103980	108022	110200	118100	119770	122577
a Food	73420	75327	78028	82602	82982	86113	87809	87767	93260	94196	96900
b Non-alcoholic beverages	913	999	840	1103	1628	1549	1869	2506	2560	2924	2658
c Alcoholic beverages	5712	5829	6340	6647	6273	6172	7323	8133	9518	9381	9227
d Tobacco	7277	7646	8388	9142	9850	10146	11021	11794	12762	13269	13792
2 Clothing and footwear	26212	28689	30790	32727	31485	33953	36418	36899	37333	38668	34795
3 Gross rent, fuel and power	29503	31771	34452	37896	39185	40573	42716	45012	48287	50909	53870
a Fuel and power	4948	5479	5985	6819	6376	6725	7309	7571	8394	8552	8975
b Other	24555	26292	28467	31077	32809	33848	35407	37441	39893	42357	44895
4 Furniture, furnishings and household equipment and operation	15597	17165	19325	22111	21586	24136	26119	27266	28040	28737	30012
a Household operation	4961	5585	6121	6979	6939	7365	7410	7492	7648	7696	7556
b Other	10636	11580	13204	15132	14647	16771	18709	19774	20392	21041	22456
5 Medical care and health expenses	7806	8368	8314	8469	8023	8280	7771	8085	8294	8914	8815
6 Transport and communication	17604	19861	22692	25175	25701	28092	32367	38450	42669	42638	40546
a Personal transport equipment	953	1078	1453	2084	2016	3398	5309	9409	10767	7889	3121

Greece

2.6 Private Final Consumption Expenditure by Type, in Constant Prices
(Continued)

Million Greek drachmas

	1970	1971	1972	1973	1974	1975	1976	1977	1978	1979	1980
					At constant prices of:1970						
b Other	16651	18783	21239	23091	23685	24694	27058	29041	31902	34749	37425
7 Recreational, entertainment, education and cultural services	10143	10816	11751	12494	11551	12008	12740	13825	15140	13762	13864
a Education	2652	2809	2880	2978	3109	3150	3022	3088	2837	2629	2257
b Other	7491	8007	8871	9516	8442	8858	9718	10737	12303	11133	11607
8 Miscellaneous goods and services	15849	17419	19107	20698	19034	21925	23842	24385	26114	27618	27129
a Personal care	2213	2363	2480	3139	3351	4223	4057	3834	4073	4235	4096
b Expenditures in restaurants, cafes and hotels	9409	10526	11598	12454	10883	12621	14405	15091	16256	17495	17264
c Other	4227	4530	5029	5105	4800	5081	5380	5460	5785	5888	5769
Total Final Consumption Expenditure in the Domestic Market by Households, of which	210036	223890	240027	259064	257298	272947	289995	304122	323977	331016	331608
a Durable goods	8342	8993	11218	14607	13337	16712	20742	25268	27668	25106	21996
b Semi-durable goods	32602	35754	38611	41465	40389	44234	46938	48481	48976	50650	46571
c Non-durable goods	104766	109317	114735	123025	123828	128749	133847	137627	148818	151528	154822
d Services	64326	69826	75463	79967	79744	83252	88468	92746	98515	103732	108219
Plus: Direct purchases abroad by resident households	1659	2201	2760	2468	2530	2895	2927	2915	3683	4604	4788
Less: Direct purchases in the domestic market by non-resident households	5807	8849	10463	11475	8178	10600	13579	14537	17410	18489	17782
Equals: Final Consumption Expenditure of Resident Households [a]	205888	217242	232324	250057	251650	265242	279343	292500	310250	317131	318614

Final Consumption Expenditure of Private Non-profit Institutions Serving Households

Equals: Final Consumption Expenditure of Private Non-profit Organisations Serving Households	...	...	...	...	...	...	...	...	...	...	...
Private Final Consumption Expenditure	205888	217242	232324	250057	251650	265242	279343	292500	310250	317131	318614

a) Including consumption expenditure of private non-profit institutions.

2.7 Gross Capital Formation by Type of Good and Owner, in Current Prices

Million Greek drachmas

	1970				1971				1972			
	TOTAL	Total Private	Public Enterprises	General Government	TOTAL	Total Private	Public Enterprises	General Government	TOTAL	Total Private	Public Enterprises	General Government
Increase in stocks, total	13346	12760	368	218	8950	9955	468	-1473	6846	6294	814	-262
1 Goods producing industries	12752	12681	71	-	9687	9472	215	-	8951	8503	448	-
2 Wholesale and retail trade	-134	-73	-61	-	313	312	1	-	-1679	-1713	34	-
3 Other, except government stocks	510	152	358	-	423	171	252	-	-164	-496	332	-
4 Government stocks	218	-	-	218	-1473	-	-	-1473	-262	-	-	-262
Gross Fixed Capital Formation, Total	70663	50737	6540	13386	83298	57251	10954	15093	104833	73043	13573	18217
1 Residential buildings [a]	19740	19443	297	...	23603	22906	697	...	32565	31832	733	...
2 Non-residential buildings [a]	9579	7309	2270	...	10483	7983	2500	...	13556	8999	4557	...
3 Other construction [a]	13475	1884	11591	...	16478	2000	14478	...	18876	2182	16694	...
4 Land improvement and plantation and orchard development [ab]	2694	270	2424	...	2834	308	2526	...	3356	392	2964	...
5 Producers' durable goods [a]	25175	21831	3344	...	29900	24054	5846	...	36480	29638	6842	...
a Transport equipment [a]	6548	6472	76	...	7492	7467	25	...	7990	7804	186	...
b Machinery and equipment [a]	18627	15359	3268	...	22408	16587	5821	...	28490	21834	6656	...
6 Breeding stock, dairy cattle, etc.	...	...	...	...	...	...	...	...	...	...	...	...
Total Gross Capital Formation	84009	63497	6908	13604	92248	67206	11422	13620	111679	79337	14387	17955

	1973				1974				1975			
	TOTAL	Total Private	Public Enterprises	General Government	TOTAL	Total Private	Public Enterprises	General Government	TOTAL	Total Private	Public Enterprises	General Government
Increase in stocks, total	37525	35972	1275	278	39904	36911	1261	1732	41400	36537	1507	3356
1 Goods producing industries	25801	25821	-20	-	36285	35652	633	-	33977	32756	1221	-
2 Wholesale and retail trade	9525	9576	-51	-	1562	1446	116	-	5304	5096	208	-
3 Other, except government stocks	1921	575	1346	-	325	-187	512	-	-1237	-1315	78	-
4 Government stocks	278	-	-	278	1732	-	-	1732	3356	-	-	3356

Greece

2.7 Gross Capital Formation by Type of Good and Owner, in Current Prices
(Continued)

Million Greek drachmas

	1973 TOTAL	1973 Total Private	1973 Public Enterprises	1973 General Government	1974 TOTAL	1974 Total Private	1974 Public Enterprises	1974 General Government	1975 TOTAL	1975 Total Private	1975 Public Enterprises	1975 General Government
Gross Fixed Capital Formation, Total	135677	98010	16367	21300	125476	87665	18903	18908	139950	101130	14221	24599
1 Residential buildings [a]	41544	41071	473	...	27771	27438	333	...	37983	37437	546	...
2 Non-residential buildings [a]	18956	13491	5465	...	21670	16183	5487	...	18865	13290	5575	...
3 Other construction [a]	23087	4116	18971	...	21845	4095	17750	...	25007	4626	20981	...
4 Land improvement and plantation and orchard development [a,b]	3650	518	3132	...	3547	381	3166	...	3773	486	3287	...
5 Producers' durable goods [a]	48440	38814	9626	...	50643	39568	11075	...	53722	45291	8431	...
a Transport equipment [a]	12746	12496	250	...	9752	8813	939	...	11012	10117	895	...
b Machinery and equipment [a]	35694	26318	9376	...	40891	30755	10136	...	42710	35174	7536	...
6 Breeding stock, dairy cattle, etc.	...	...	...	...	...	...	...	...	...	...	...	...
Total Gross Capital Formation	173202	133982	17642	21578	165380	124576	20164	20640	181350	137667	15728	27955

	1976 TOTAL	1976 Total Private	1976 Public Enterprises	1976 General Government	1977 TOTAL	1977 Total Private	1977 Public Enterprises	1977 General Government	1978 TOTAL	1978 Total Private	1978 Public Enterprises	1978 General Government
Increase in stocks, total	44700	44308	649	-257	42700	39387	475	2838	43170	41010	2073	87
1 Goods producing industries	46966	47098	-132	-	38257	37820	437	-	45460	44076	1384	-
2 Wholesale and retail trade	-4674	-4675	1	-	1092	1290	-198	-	-325	-296	-29	-
3 Other, except government stocks	2665	1885	780	-	513	277	236	-	-2052	-2770	718	-
4 Government stocks	-257	-	-	-257	2838	-	-	2838	87	-	-	87
Gross Fixed Capital Formation, Total	175000	128100	16255	30645	221420	172350	15435	33635	278000	216400	24160	37440
1 Residential buildings [a]	47477	46800	677	...	69188	68487	701	...	96778	96005	773	...
2 Non-residential buildings [a]	24396	18277	6119	...	31952	25324	6628	...	40266	30632	9634	...
3 Other construction [a]	30794	5290	25504	...	35268	6563	28705	...	39844	8708	31136	...
4 Land improvement and plantation and orchard development [a,b]	4191	672	3519	...	5253	909	4344	...	4751	723	4028	...
5 Producers' durable goods [a]	68142	57061	11081	...	79759	71068	8691	...	96361	80332	16029	...
a Transport equipment [a]	17484	15644	1840	...	24133	23066	1067	...	34834	33678	1156	...
b Machinery and equipment [a]	50658	41417	9241	...	55626	48002	7624	...	61527	46654	14873	...
6 Breeding stock, dairy cattle, etc.	...	...	...	...	...	...	...	...	...	...	...	...
Total Gross Capital Formation	219700	172408	16904	30388	264120	211737	15910	36473	321170	257410	26233	37527

	1979 TOTAL	1979 Total Private	1979 Public Enterprises	1979 General Government	1980 TOTAL	1980 Total Private	1980 Public Enterprises	1980 General Government
Increase in stocks, total	63435	59773	2428	1234	82030	72970	6625	2435
1 Goods producing industries	59205	57415	1790	-	69835	65302	4533	-
2 Wholesale and retail trade	-731	-711	-20	-	4280	4158	122	-
3 Other, except government stocks	3727	3069	658	-	5480	3510	1970	-
4 Government stocks	1234	-	-	1234	2435	-	-	2435
Gross Fixed Capital Formation, Total	366165	284765	36278	45122	400270	304450	52393	43427
1 Residential buildings [a]	131057	129710	1100	247	137517	135694	1676	147
2 Non-residential buildings [a]	57652	47091	2597	7964	58274	48541	2529	7204
3 Other construction [a]	48556	8910	11299	28347	51302	7465	17164	26673
4 Land improvement and plantation and orchard development [a,b]	5369	518	-	4851	6322	752	-	5570
5 Producers' durable goods [a]	123531	98536	21282	3713	146855	111999	31024	3832
a Transport equipment [a]	41958	37920	4022	16	46810	38246	8340	224
b Machinery and equipment [a]	81573	60616	17260	3697	100045	73753	22684	3608
6 Breeding stock, dairy cattle, etc.	...	...	...	...	...	...	...	...
Total Gross Capital Formation	429600	344538	38706	46356	482300	377420	59018	45862

a) For the years 1970-1978, column 'General government' is included in column 'Public enterprises'.
b) Outlays on land improvement and transfer costs on purchases and sale of agricultural land only.

Greece

2.8 Gross Capital Formation by Type of Good and Owner, in Constant Prices

Million Greek drachmas

	1970				1971				1972			
	TOTAL	Total Private	Public Enterprises	General Government	TOTAL	Total Private	Public Enterprises	General Government	TOTAL	Total Private	Public Enterprises	General Government
	\multicolumn{12}{c}{At constant prices of: 1970}
Increase in stocks, total	13346	12760	368	218	8715	9690	452	-1427	6487	6082	738	-333
1 Goods producing industries	12752	12681	71	-	9439	9231	208	-	7951	7543	408	-
2 Wholesale and retail trade	-134	-73	-61	-	288	287	1	-	-1004	-1033	29	-
3 Other, except government stocks	510	152	358	-	415	172	243	-	-127	-428	301	-
4 Government stocks	218	-	-	218	-1427	-	-	-1427	-333	-	-	-333
Gross Fixed Capital Formation, Total	70663	50737	6540	13386	80558	55112	11268	14178	92977	64122	11988	16867
1 Residential buildings [a]	19740	19443	297	...	23641	22943	698	...	29964	29290	674	...
2 Non-residential buildings [a]	9579	7309	2270	...	10504	7998	2506	...	12472	8279	4193	...
3 Other construction [a]	13473	1882	11591	...	16637	2019	14618	...	18009	2063	15946	...
4 Land improvement and plantation and orchard development [ab]	2694	270	2424	...	2787	299	2488	...	3130	365	2765	...
5 Producers' durable goods [a]	25175	21831	3344	...	26989	21853	5136	...	29402	24125	5277	...
a Transport equipment [a]	6548	6472	76	...	7083	7059	24	...	7021	6855	166	...
b Machinery and equipment	18627	15359	3268	...	19906	14794	5112	...	22381	17270	5111	...
6 Breeding stock, dairy cattle, etc.	...	...	...	...	...	...	...	...	...	...	...	...
Total Gross Capital Formation	84009	63497	6908	13604	89273	64802	11720	12751	99464	70204	12726	16534

	1973				1974				1975			
	TOTAL	Total Private	Public Enterprises	General Government	TOTAL	Total Private	Public Enterprises	General Government	TOTAL	Total Private	Public Enterprises	General Government
	\multicolumn{12}{c}{At constant prices of: 1970}
Increase in stocks, total	26510	25787	927	-204	22550	20765	754	1031	21100	18210	759	2131
1 Goods producing industries	18584	18589	-5	-	20337	19979	358	-	17215	16584	631	-
2 Wholesale and retail trade	6716	6774	-58	-	662	552	110	-	2747	2661	86	-
3 Other, except government stocks	1414	424	990	-	520	234	286	-	-993	-1035	42	-
4 Government stocks	-204	-	-	-204	1031	-	-	1031	2131	-	-	2131
Gross Fixed Capital Formation, Total	100093	72187	11893	16013	74500	52211	11036	11253	74660	53702	7560	13398
1 Residential buildings [a]	30576	30228	348	...	15869	15679	190	...	20476	20182	294	...
2 Non-residential buildings [a]	13951	9929	4022	...	12381	9245	3136	...	10170	7164	3006	...
3 Other construction [a]	17623	3102	14521	...	12976	2425	10551	...	14001	2427	11574	...
4 Land improvement and plantation and orchard development [ab]	2803	417	2386	...	2100	213	1887	...	2009	252	1757	...
5 Producers' durable goods [a]	35140	28511	6629	...	31174	24649	6525	...	28004	23677	4327	...
a Transport equipment [a]	10236	10035	201	...	7418	6690	728	...	7050	6476	574	...
b Machinery and equipment	24904	18476	6428	...	23756	17959	5797	...	20954	17201	3753	...
6 Breeding stock, dairy cattle, etc.	...	...	...	...	...	...	...	...	...	...	...	...
Total Gross Capital Formation	126603	97974	12820	15809	97050	72976	11790	12284	95760	71912	8319	15529

	1976				1977				1978			
	TOTAL	Total Private	Public Enterprises	General Government	TOTAL	Total Private	Public Enterprises	General Government	TOTAL	Total Private	Public Enterprises	General Government
	\multicolumn{12}{c}{At constant prices of: 1970}
Increase in stocks, total	19400	19680	302	-582	16700	15548	179	973	15660	14990	742	-72
1 Goods producing industries	20279	20339	-60	-	15250	15075	175	-	16416	15914	502	-
2 Wholesale and retail trade	-1581	-1588	7	-	421	512	-91	-	-62	-42	-20	-
3 Other, except government stocks	1284	929	355	-	56	-39	95	-	-622	-882	260	-
4 Government stocks	-582	-	-	-582	973	-	-	973	-72	-	-	-72
Gross Fixed Capital Formation, Total	79750	58380	7241	14129	85950	66750	6030	13170	91100	70600	8494	12006
1 Residential buildings [a]	21909	21597	312	...	26428	26160	268	...	30074	29834	240	...
2 Non-residential buildings [a]	11258	8434	2824	...	12205	9673	2532	...	12513	9519	2994	...

Greece

2.8 Gross Capital Formation by Type of Good and Owner, in Constant Prices
(Continued)

Million Greek drachmas

	1976 TOTAL	1976 Total Private	1976 Public Enterprises	1976 General Government	1977 TOTAL	1977 Total Private	1977 Public Enterprises	1977 General Government	1978 TOTAL	1978 Total Private	1978 Public Enterprises	1978 General Government
					At constant prices of:1970							
3 Other construction [a]	14177	2360	11817	...	13870	2465	11405	...	13458	2795	10663	...
4 Land improvement and plantation and orchard development [ab]	1901	294	1607	...	2016	333	1683	...	1570	225	1345	...
5 Producers' durable goods [a]	30505	25695	4810	...	31431	28119	3312	...	33485	28227	5258	...
a Transport equipment [a]	9345	8360	985	...	10788	10312	476	...	13395	12953	442	...
b Machinery and equipment	21160	17335	3825	...	20643	17807	2836	...	20090	15274	4816	...
6 Breeding stock, dairy cattle, etc.	...	...	...	...	...	...	...	...	...	...	...	...
Total Gross Capital Formation	99150	78060	7543	13547	102650	82298	6209	14143	106760	85590	9236	11934

	1979 TOTAL	1979 Total Private	1979 Public Enterprises	1979 General Government	1980 TOTAL	1980 Total Private	1980 Public Enterprises	1980 General Government
	At constant prices of:1970							
Increase in stocks, total	18760	17717	740	303	20770	18124	1538	1108
1 Goods producing industries	17699	17162	537	-	16354	15295	1059	-
2 Wholesale and retail trade	-437	-442	5	-	1769	1750	19	-
3 Other, except government stocks	1195	997	198	-	1539	1079	460	-
4 Government stocks	303	-	-	303	1108	-	-	1108
Gross Fixed Capital Formation, Total	98270	75536	11049	11685	89730	67490	13231	9009
1 Residential buildings [a]	31572	31248	265	59	27290	26929	332	29
2 Non-residential buildings [a]	13889	11344	626	1919	11565	9633	502	1430
3 Other construction [a]	13312	2319	3654	7339	11318	1537	4410	5371
4 Land improvement and plantation and orchard development [ab]	1453	131	-	1322	1401	150	-	1251
5 Producers' durable goods [a]	38044	30494	6504	1046	38156	29241	7987	928
a Transport equipment [a]	14527	13120	1401	6	13891	11343	2482	66
b Machinery and equipment	23517	17374	5103	1040	24265	17898	5505	862
6 Breeding stock, dairy cattle, etc.	...	...	...	...	...	...	...	...
Total Gross Capital Formation	117030	93253	11789	11987	110500	85614	14769	10117

a) For the years 1970-1978, column 'General government' is included in column 'Public enterprises'.
b) Outlays on land improvement and transfer costs on purchases and sale of agricultural land only.

2.9 Gross Capital Formation by Kind of Activity of Owner, ISIC Major Divisions, in Current Prices

Million Greek drachmas

	1970 Total Gross Capital Formation	1970 Increase in Stocks	1970 Gross Fixed Capital Formation	1971 Total Gross Capital Formation	1971 Increase in Stocks	1971 Gross Fixed Capital Formation	1972 Total Gross Capital Formation	1972 Increase in Stocks	1972 Gross Fixed Capital Formation	1973 Total Gross Capital Formation	1973 Increase in Stocks	1973 Gross Fixed Capital Formation
						All Producers						
1 Agriculture, hunting, fishing and forestry	4513	458	4055	6247	1619	4628	5434	91	5343	12148	4553	7595
2 Mining and quarrying	1157	90	1067	2107	215	1892	1494	199	1295	1893	188	1705
3 Manufacturing	22046	12030	10016	19746	7461	12285	24708	8087	16621	41295	20495	20800
4 Electricity, gas and water	271	174	97	594	392	202	767	574	193	1000	565	435
5 Construction	...	...	...	...	...	...	...	...	...	...	...	...
6 Wholesale and retail trade, restaurants and hotels [a]	-134	-134	...	313	313	...	-1679	-1679	...	9525	9525	...
7 Transport, storage and communication	7142	612	6530	8059	525	7534	7784	-87	7871	14568	1952	12616
8 Finance, insurance, real estate and business services [b]	19341	-102	19443	22804	-102	22906	31755	-77	31832	41040	-31	41071
9 Community, social and personal services [ab]	9529	...	9529	7804	...	7804	9888	...	9888	13788	...	13788
Total Industries [cd]	63865	13128	50737	67674	10423	57251	80151	7108	73043	135257	37247	98010
Producers of Government Services [e]	20144	218	19926	24574	-1473	26047	31528	-262	31790	37945	278	37667
Private Non-Profit Institutions Serving Households	...	...	...	...	...	...	...	...	...	...	...	...
Total	84009	13346	70663	92248	8950	83298	111679	6846	104833	173202	37525	135677

Greece

2.9 Gross Capital Formation by Kind of Activity of Owner, ISIC Major Divisions, in Current Prices

Million Greek drachmas

	1974 TGCF	1974 IS	1974 GFCF	1975 TGCF	1975 IS	1975 GFCF	1976 TGCF	1976 IS	1976 GFCF	1977 TGCF	1977 IS	1977 GFCF
					All Producers							
1 Agriculture, hunting, fishing and forestry	7286	-33	7319	10719	1017	9702	11984	798	11186	13983	-855	14838
2 Mining and quarrying	2621	441	2180	3057	880	2177	3468	449	3019	3427	1145	2282
3 Manufacturing	60805	34934	25871	57084	30682	26402	75961	45641	30320	70551	37226	33325
4 Electricity, gas and water	1284	943	341	1821	1400	421	698	78	620	1870	741	1129
5 Construction	...	...	...	...	...	...	...	...	...	...	...	...
6 Wholesale and retail trade, restaurants and hotels [a]	1562	1562	...	5304	5304	...	-4674	-4674	...	1092	1092	...
7 Transport, storage and communication	10015	1032	8983	9030	-1089	10119	18445	2801	15644	23725	659	23066
8 Finance, insurance, real estate and business services [b]	26731	-707	27438	37287	-150	37437	46664	-136	46800	68341	-146	68487
9 Community, social and personal services [ab]	15533	...	15533	14872	...	14872	20511	...	20511	29223	...	29223
Total Industries [cd]	125837	38172	87665	139174	38044	101130	173057	44957	128100	212212	39862	172350
Producers of Government Services [e]	39543	1732	37811	42176	3356	38820	46643	-257	46900	51908	2838	49070
Private Non-Profit Institutions Serving Households	...	...	...	...	...	...	...	...	...	...	...	...
Total	165380	39904	125476	181350	41400	139950	219700	44700	175000	264120	42700	221420

	1978 TGCF	1978 IS	1978 GFCF	1979 TGCF	1979 IS	1979 GFCF	1980 TGCF	1980 IS	1980 GFCF
				All Producers					
1 Agriculture, hunting, fishing and forestry	15541	729	14812	13893	-5204	19097	14288	-3641	17929
2 Mining and quarrying	3699	232	3467	6528	290	6238	8497	300	8197
3 Manufacturing	77618	42828	34790	112920	61978	50942	133882	68385	65497
4 Electricity, gas and water	2806	1671	1135	20271	2141	18130	28644	4790	23854
5 Construction	...	...	...	...	...	...	...	...	...
6 Wholesale and retail trade, restaurants and hotels [a]	-325	-325	...	-731	-731	-	4280	4280	-
7 Transport, storage and communication	31715	-1964	33679	54917	3853	51064	65133	6284	58849
8 Finance, insurance, real estate and business services [b]	95917	-88	96005	130684	-126	130810	136567	-803	137370
9 Community, social and personal services [ab]	32512	...	32512	44761	-	44761	45147	-	45147
Total Industries [cd]	259483	43083	216400	383243	62201	321042	436438	79595	356843
Producers of Government Services [e]	61687	87	61600	46357	1234	45123	45862	2435	43427
Private Non-Profit Institutions Serving Households	...	...	...	...	...	...	...	...	...
Total	321170	43170	278000	429600	63435	366165	482300	82030	400270

a) Gross fixed capital formation of item 'Wholesale and retail trade, restaurants and hotels' is included in item 'Community, social and personal services'.
b) Ownership of dwellings is included in Gross fixed capital formation only, all other items are included in item 'Community, social and personal services'.
c) Public enterprises are included in column 'Increase in stocks' and are not included in column 'Gross fixed capital formation'.
d) Beginning 1979, gross fixed capital formation and increase in stocks of public enterprises are included in industries.
e) For the years prior to 1979, public enterprises are included in Gross fixed capital formation and not in Increase in stocks.

2.10 Gross Capital Formation by Kind of Activity of Owner, ISIC Major Divisions, in Constant Prices

Million Greek drachmas

	1970 TGCF	1970 IS	1970 GFCF	1971 TGCF	1971 IS	1971 GFCF	1972 TGCF	1972 IS	1972 GFCF	1973 TGCF	1973 IS	1973 GFCF
				At constant prices of: 1970								
				All Producers								
1 Agriculture, hunting, fishing and forestry	4513	458	4055	6148	1644	4504	4709	-107	4816	8641	2950	5691
2 Mining and quarrying	1157	90	1067	1949	208	1741	1259	181	1078	1373	138	1235
3 Manufacturing	22046	12030	10016	18278	7209	11069	20530	7355	13175	29446	15080	14366
4 Electricity, gas and water	271	174	97	579	378	201	694	522	172	721	416	305

Greece

2.10 Gross Capital Formation by Kind of Activity of Owner, ISIC Major Divisions, in Constant Prices
(Continued)

Million Greek drachmas

	1970 TGCF	1970 IS	1970 GFCF	1971 TGCF	1971 IS	1971 GFCF	1972 TGCF	1972 IS	1972 GFCF	1973 TGCF	1973 IS	1973 GFCF
				At constant prices of:1970								
5 Construction	...	...	...	...	...	...	...	...	...	...	...	...
6 Wholesale and retail trade, restaurants and hotels [a]	-134	-134	...	288	288	...	-1004	-1004	...	6716	6716	...
7 Transport, storage and communication	7142	612	6530	7633	507	7126	6844	-74	6918	11559	1433	10126
8 Finance, insurance, real estate and business services [b]	19341	-102	19443	22851	-92	22943	29237	-53	29290	30219	-9	30228
9 Community, social and personal services [ab]	9529	...	9529	7528	...	7528	8673	...	8673	10236	...	10236
Total Industries [cd]	63865	13128	50737	65254	10142	55112	70942	6820	64122	98911	26724	72187
Producers of Government Services [e]	20144	218	19926	24019	-1427	25446	28522	-333	28855	27692	-214	27906
Private Non-Profit Institutions Serving Households	...	...	...	...	...	...	...	...	...	...	...	...
Total	84009	13346	70663	89273	8715	80558	99464	6487	92977	126603	26510	100093

	1974 TGCF	1974 IS	1974 GFCF	1975 TGCF	1975 IS	1975 GFCF	1976 TGCF	1976 IS	1976 GFCF	1977 TGCF	1977 IS	1977 GFCF
				At constant prices of:1970								
				All Producers								
1 Agriculture, hunting, fishing and forestry	4267	-95	4362	5163	139	5024	4193	-745	4938	5251	-406	5657
2 Mining and quarrying	1533	248	1285	1584	457	1127	1544	205	1339	1347	460	887
3 Manufacturing	34503	19654	14849	28925	15892	13033	33596	20783	12813	27291	14899	12392
4 Electricity, gas and water	730	530	200	950	727	223	316	36	280	720	297	423
5 Construction	...	...	...	...	...	...	...	...	...	...	...	...
6 Wholesale and retail trade, restaurants and hotels [a]	662	662	...	2747	2747	...	-1581	-1581	...	421	421	...
7 Transport, storage and communication	7438	649	6789	5514	-963	6477	9668	1309	8359	10393	80	10313
8 Finance, insurance, real estate and business services [b]	15550	-129	15679	20152	-30	20182	21572	-25	21597	26136	-24	26160
9 Community, social and personal services [ab]	9047	...	9047	7636	...	7636	9054	...	9054	10918	...	10918
Total Industries [cd]	73730	21519	52211	72671	18969	53702	78362	19982	58380	82477	15727	66750
Producers of Government Services [e]	23320	1031	22289	23089	2131	20958	20788	-582	21370	20173	973	19200
Private Non-Profit Institutions Serving Households	...	...	...	...	...	...	...	...	...	...	...	...
Total	97050	22550	74500	95760	21100	74660	99150	19400	79750	102650	16700	85950

	1978 TGCF	1978 IS	1978 GFCF	1979 TGCF	1979 IS	1979 GFCF	1980 TGCF	1980 IS	1980 GFCF
				At constant prices of:1970					
				All Producers					
1 Agriculture, hunting, fishing and forestry	4959	174	4785	3616	-1625	5241	3300	-822	4122
2 Mining and quarrying	1263	84	1179	1878	87	1791	2037	70	1967
3 Manufacturing	26684	15551	11133	32333	18595	13738	30805	15986	14819
4 Electricity, gas and water	965	607	358	6091	643	5448	7026	1119	5907
5 Construction	...	...	...	...	...	...	...	...	...
6 Wholesale and retail trade, restaurants and hotels [a]	-62	-62	...	-437	-437	-	1769	1769	-
7 Transport, storage and communication	12343	-610	12953	18484	1205	17279	18376	1572	16804
8 Finance, insurance, real estate and business services [b]	29822	-12	29834	31502	-11	31513	27230	-32	27262
9 Community, social and personal services [ab]	10358	...	10358	11574	-	11574	9842	-	9842
Total Industries [cd]	86332	15732	70600	105041	18457	86584	100385	19662	80723
Producers of Government Services [e]	20428	-72	20500	11989	303	11686	10115	1108	9007
Private Non-Profit Institutions Serving Households	...	...	...	...	...	...	...	...	...
Total	106760	15660	91100	117030	18760	98270	110500	20770	89730

a) Gross fixed capital formation of item 'Wholesale and retail trade, restaurants and hotels' is included in item 'Community, social and personal services'.
b) Ownership of dwellings is included in Gross fixed capital formation only, all other items are included in item 'Community, social and personal services'.
c) Public enterprises are included in column 'Increase in stocks' and are not included in column 'Gross fixed capital formation'.
d) Beginning 1979, gross fixed capital formation and increase in stocks of public enterprises are included in industries.
e) For the years prior to 1979, public enterprises are included in Gross fixed capital formation and not in Increase in stocks.

Greece

2.17 Exports and Imports of Goods and Services, Detail

Million Greek drachmas

	1970	1971	1972	1973	1974	1975	1976	1977	1978	1979	1980
					Exports of Goods and Services						
1 Exports of merchandise, f.o.b.	19276	19874	26125	42812	60891	74441	93812	101331	123727	144238	221171
2 Transport and communication [a]	10712	14237	18175	26092	26974	35374	45725	53626	69909	90845	114944
3 Insurance service charges [a]	...	...	...	...	...	...	...	...	...	...	...
4 Other commodities [a]	...	...	...	...	...	...	...	...	...	...	...
5 Adjustments of merchandise exports to change-of-ownership basis											
6 Direct purchases in the domestic market by non-residential households											
7 Direct purchases in the domestic market by extraterritorial bodies	...	...	...	...	...	...	...	...	...	...	...
Total Exports of Goods and Services	29988	34111	44300	68904	87865	109815	139537	154957	193635	235083	336115
					Imports of Goods and Services						
1 Imports of merchandise, c.i.f.	49262	54293	67115	109751	130724	164227	194399	221595	260568	326652	407888
a Imports of merchandise, f.o.b.	44828	49407	61074	99874	118959	149447	176903	201651	237117	297253	371178
b Transport of services on merchandise imports	...	...	...	...	...	...	...	...	...	...	...
c Insurance service charges on merchandise imports	...	...	...	...	...	...	...	...	...	...	...
2 Adjustments of merchandise imports to change-of-ownership basis											
3 Other transport and communication											
4 Other insurance service charges	5734	6619	8608	12344	13971	16335	18669	21696	25503	34195	43932
5 Other commodities											
6 Direct purchases abroad by government											
7 Direct purchases abroad by resident households											
Total Imports of Goods and Services	54996	60912	75723	122095	144695	180562	213068	243291	286071	360847	451820
Balance of Goods and Services	-25008	-26801	-31423	-53191	-56830	-70747	-73531	-88334	-92436	-125764	-115705
Total Imports and Balance of Goods and Services	29988	34111	44300	68904	87865	109815	139537	154957	193635	235083	336115

a) Items 'Insurance service charges' and 'Other commodities' are included in item 'Transport and communication'.

3.12 General Government Income and Outlay Account: Total and Subsectors

Million Greek drachmas

	1970					1971				
	Total General Government	Central Government	State or Provincial Government	Local Government	Social Security Funds	Total General Government	Central Government	State or Provincial Government	Local Government	Social Security Funds
					Receipts					
1 Property and entrepreneurial income	5678	862	...	3070	1746	5300	217	...	3214	1869
2 Taxes, fees and contributions	73545	46065	...	4438	23042	81624	51676	...	4681	25267
a Indirect taxes	43406	37236	...	2783	...	46833	40700	...	2782	...
b Direct taxes [a]	30139	8829	...	1655	...	34791	10976	...	1899	...
c Social security contributions [a]	...	...	...	...	23042	...	...	...	...	25267
d Fees, fines and penalties [a]	...	...	...	...	...	...	...	...	...	...
3 Other current transfers received	975	1308	...	4810	1376	1040	1264	...	5702	1398
a Casualty insurance claims	...	...	...	...	...	...	...	...	...	...
b Transfers from other government subsectors	...	462	...	4681	1376	...	397	...	5529	1398
c Transfers from abroad	-	-	...	-	...	-	-	...	-	...
d Other transfers, except imputed	975	846	...	129	...	1040	867	...	173	...
e Imputed unfunded employee welfare contributions	...	...	...	...	...	...	...	...	...	...
Total Current Receipts	80198	48235	...	12318	26164	87964	53157	...	13597	28534
					Disbursements					
1 General governement final consumption expenditures	37742	29322	...	6446	1974	41362	32132	...	7024	2206

Greece

3.12 General Government Income and Outlay Account: Total and Subsectors
(Continued)

Million Greek drachmas

	1970					1971				
	Total General Government	Central Government	State or Provincial Government	Local Government	Social Security Funds	Total General Government	Central Government	State or Provincial Government	Local Government	Social Security Funds
2 Property income paid	2815	2815	...	...	...	3270	3270	...	...	...
3 Subsidies	2489	2489	...	...	...	3955	3955	...	...	...
4 Other current transfers paid	23950	8114	...	1259	21096	26568	9124	...	1360	23408
a Casualty insurance premiums, net	...	...	...	...	...	...	...	...	...	...
b Transfers to other government subsectors	...	6057	...	236	...	...	6927	...	170	...
c Transfers to households [b]	23816	1923	...	1023	21096	26437	2066	...	1190	23408
Social security benefits	...	...	...	...	20870	...	...	...	...	23181
Social assistance grants	...	...	...	...	...	...	...	...	...	...
Unfunded employee welfare benefits [c]	...	...	...	...	226	...	...	...	...	227
d Transfers to private non-profit institutions serving households	...	...	...	...	...	...	...	...	...	...
e Transfers to the rest of the world	134	134	...	...	...	131	131	...	...	...
Net saving [d]	13202	5495	...	4613	3094	12809	4676	...	5213	2920
Total Current Disbursements and Net Saving	80198	48235	...	12318	26164	87964	53157	...	13597	28534

	1972					1973				
	Total General Government	Central Government	State or Provincial Government	Local Government	Social Security Funds	Total General Government	Central Government	State or Provincial Government	Local Government	Social Security Funds

Receipts

1 Property and entrepreneurial income	6719	749	...	3662	2308	8636	1555	...	4161	2920
2 Taxes, fees and contributions	92550	58183	...	5121	29246	112804	72701	...	5733	34370
a Indirect taxes	52526	45758	...	3189	...	64826	57676	...	3330	...
b Direct taxes [a]	40024	12425	...	1932	...	47978	15025	...	2403	...
c Social security contributions [a]	...	...	...	...	29246	...	...	...	...	34370
d Fees, fines and penalties [a]	...	...	...	...	...	...	...	...	...	...
3 Other current transfers received	1213	1287	...	6341	1426	1593	1684	...	8294	1225
a Casualty insurance claims	...	...	...	...	...	...	...	...	...	...
b Transfers from other government subsectors	...	328	...	6087	1426	...	399	...	7986	1225
c Transfers from abroad	-	-	...	-	...	-	-	...	-	...
d Other transfers, except imputed	1213	959	...	254	...	1593	1285	...	308	...
e Imputed unfunded employee welfare contributions	...	...	...	...	...	...	...	...	...	...
Total Current Receipts	100482	60219	...	15124	32980	123033	75940	...	18188	38515

Disbursements

1 General governement final consumption expenditures	45943	35912	...	7520	2511	55444	43456	...	8930	3058
2 Property income paid	3746	3746	...	...	...	4852	4852	...	...	...
3 Subsidies	4777	4777	...	...	...	8891	8891	...	...	...
4 Other current transfers paid	28767	10050	...	1510	25048	33064	12172	...	1911	28591
a Casualty insurance premiums, net	...	...	...	...	...	...	...	...	...	...
b Transfers to other government subsectors	...	7513	...	102	...	...	9211	...	173	...
c Transfers to households [b]	28634	2404	...	1408	25048	32911	2808	...	1738	28591
Social security benefits	...	...	...	...	24822	...	...	...	...	28365
Social assistance grants	...	...	...	...	...	...	...	...	...	...
Unfunded employee welfare benefits [c]	...	...	...	...	226	...	...	...	...	226
d Transfers to private non-profit institutions serving households	...	...	...	...	...	...	...	...	...	...
e Transfers to the rest of the world	133	133	...	...	...	153	153	...	...	...
Net saving [d]	17249	5734	...	6094	5421	20782	6569	...	7347	6866
Total Current Disbursements and Net Saving	100482	60219	...	15124	32980	123033	75940	...	18188	38515

Greece

3.12 General Government Income and Outlay Account: Total and Subsectors

Million Greek drachmas

	1974					1975				
	Total General Government	Central Government	State or Provincial Government	Local Government	Social Security Funds	Total General Government	Central Government	State or Provincial Government	Local Government	Social Security Funds

Receipts

1 Property and entrepreneurial income	13802	5874	...	4930	2998	15851	5931	...	6530	3390
2 Taxes, fees and contributions	135585	88486	...	6292	40807	166263	108593	...	6520	51170
a Indirect taxes	71562	63147	...	3905	...	95961	85846	...	3965	...
b Direct taxes [a]	64023	25339	...	2487	...	70322	22747	...	2555	...
c Social security contributions [a]	...	...	...	...	40807	...	...	...	...	51170
d Fees, fines and penalties [a]	...	...	...	...	...	...	...	...	...	...
3 Other current transfers received	3110	3271	...	10399	1378	1979	2170	...	13250	2550
a Casualty insurance claims	...	...	...	...	...	...	...	...	...	...
b Transfers from other government subsectors	...	424	...	10136	1378	...	453	...	12988	2550
c Transfers from abroad	1449	1449	...	.	...	.	.	...	.	...
d Other transfers, except imputed	1661	1398	...	263	...	1979	1717	...	262	...
e Imputed unfunded employee welfare contributions	...	...	...	...	...	...	...	...	...	...
Total Current Receipts	152497	97633	...	21621	45183	184113	116693	...	26300	57110

Disbursements

1 General government final consumption expenditures	78071	62843	...	11276	3952	102007	83637	...	13220	5150
2 Property income paid	7139	7139	...	...	...	9261	9261	...	...	...
3 Subsidies	14685	14685	...	...	...	16984	16984	...	...	...
4 Other current transfers paid	41324	15946	...	2247	35069	51314	20786	...	2522	43997
a Casualty insurance premiums, net	...	...	...	...	...	...	...	...	...	...
b Transfers to other government subsectors	...	11514	...	198	...	...	15537	...	226	...
c Transfers to households [b]	40325	3433	...	2049	35069	49935	3870	...	2296	43997
Social security benefits	...	...	...	...	34843	...	...	...	...	43770
Social assistance grants	...	...	...	...	...	...	...	...	...	...
Unfunded employee welfare benefits [c]	...	...	...	...	226	...	...	...	...	227
d Transfers to private non-profit institutions serving households	...	...	...	...	...	...	...	...	...	...
e Transfers to the rest of the world	999	999	...	...	...	1379	1379	...	...	...
Net saving [d]	11278	-2962	...	8098	6162	4547	-13975	...	10559	7963
Total Current Disbursements and Net Saving	152497	97633	...	21621	45183	184113	116693	...	26300	57110

	1976					1977				
	Total General Government	Central Government	State or Provincial Government	Local Government	Social Security Funds	Total General Government	Central Government	State or Provincial Government	Local Government	Social Security Funds

Receipts

1 Property and entrepreneurial income	17610	6330	...	7080	4200	18660	5780	...	8420	4460
2 Taxes, fees and contributions	223270	147208	...	7140	68922	266392	171620	...	8170	86602
a Indirect taxes	119254	107184	...	4970	...	147600	133000	...	5850	...
b Direct taxes [a]	104016	40024	...	2170	...	118792	38620	...	2320	...
c Social security contributions [a]	...	...	...	...	68922	...	...	...	...	86602
d Fees, fines and penalties [a]	...	...	...	...	...	...	...	...	...	...
3 Other current transfers received	2232	2351	...	20764	2630	2788	2898	...	21840	3110
a Casualty insurance claims	...	...	...	...	...	...	...	...	...	...
b Transfers from other government subsectors	...	419	...	20464	2630	...	440	...	21510	3110
c Transfers from abroad	.	.	...	.	...	.	.	...	.	...
d Other transfers, except imputed	2232	1932	...	300	...	2788	2458	...	330	...
e Imputed unfunded employee welfare contributions	...	...	...	...	...	...	...	...	...	...
Total Current Receipts	243112	155886	...	34984	75752	287840	180298	...	38430	94172

Greece

3.12 General Government Income and Outlay Account: Total and Subsectors
(Continued)

Million Greek drachmas

1976 / 1977

	Total General Government	Central Government	State or Provincial Government	Local Government	Social Security Funds	Total General Government	Central Government	State or Provincial Government	Local Government	Social Security Funds
Disbursements										
1 General government final consumption expenditures	124332	99832	...	17960	6540	153840	123620	...	21940	8280
2 Property income paid	12940	12940	...	...	...	14066	14066	...	...	...
3 Subsidies	23057	23057	...	...	...	28500	28500	...	...	...
4 Other current transfers paid	65331	29365	...	3569	55910	83510	31870	...	4360	72340
a Casualty insurance premiums, net	...	...	...	...	...	...	...	...	...	...
b Transfers to other government subsectors	...	23094	...	189	...	...	24620	...	200	...
c Transfers to households [b]	63697	4637	...	3380	55910	82060	5800	...	4160	72340
Social security benefits	...	...	...	...	55680	...	...	...	...	72100
Social assistance grants	...	...	...	...	...	...	...	...	...	...
Unfunded employee welfare benefits [c]	...	...	...	...	230	...	...	...	...	240
d Transfers to private non-profit institutions serving households	...	...	...	...	...	...	...	...	...	...
e Transfers to the rest of the world	1634	1634	...	...	...	1450	1450	...	...	...
Net saving [d]	17452	-9305	...	13455	13302	7924	-17758	...	12130	13552
Total Current Disbursements and Net Saving	243112	155886	...	34984	75752	287840	180298	...	38430	94172

1978 / 1979

	Total General Government	Central Government	State or Provincial Government	Local Government	Social Security Funds	Total General Government	Central Government	State or Provincial Government	Local Government	Social Security Funds
Receipts										
1 Property and entrepreneurial income	18462	3182	...	9900	5380	28580	6340	...	12800	9440
2 Taxes, fees and contributions	328969	209149	...	9940	109880	405560	258700	...	13080	133780
a Indirect taxes	178219	159569	...	7210	...	216690	195500	...	7760	...
b Direct taxes [a]	150750	49580	...	2730	...	188870	63200	...	5320	...
c Social security contributions [a]	...	...	...	...	109880	...	...	...	...	133780
d Fees, fines and penalties [a]	...	...	...	...	...	...	...	...	...	...
3 Other current transfers received	2177	2187	...	26705	3870	3548	2678	...	34340	830
a Casualty insurance claims	...	...	...	...	...	...	...	...	...	...
b Transfers from other government subsectors	...	400	...	26315	3870	...	440	...	34340	830
c Transfers from abroad	-	-	...	-	...	...	...	...	...	...
d Other transfers, except imputed	2177	1787	...	390	...	3548	2238	...	...	...
e Imputed unfunded employee welfare contributions	...	...	...	...	...	...	...	...	...	...
Total Current Receipts	349608	214518	...	46545	119130	437688	267718	...	60220	144050
Disbursements										
1 General government final consumption expenditures	185150	147700	...	26490	10960	233530	180000	...	39200	14330
2 Property income paid	19690	19690	...	...	...	30790	30790	...	...	...
3 Subsidies	33536	33536	...	...	...	33120	33120	...	...	...
4 Other current transfers paid	108985	40440	...	5040	94090	127583	45873	...	3700	112310
a Casualty insurance premiums, net	...	...	...	...	...	...	...	...	...	...
b Transfers to other government subsectors	...	30185	...	170	...	...	35170	...	210	...
c Transfers to households [b]	106864	8134	...	4870	94090	125930	9050	...	3490	112310
Social security benefits	...	...	...	...	93860	...	...	...	...	112080
Social assistance grants	...	...	...	...	...	...	...	...	...	...
Unfunded employee welfare benefits [c]	...	...	...	...	230	...	...	...	...	230
d Transfers to private non-profit institutions serving households	...	...	...	...	...	...	...	...	...	...
e Transfers to the rest of the world	2121	2121	...	...	...	1653	1653	...	...	...
Net saving [d]	2247	-26848	...	15015	14080	12665	-22065	...	17320	17410
Total Current Disbursements and Net Saving	349608	214518	...	46545	119130	437688	267718	...	60220	144050

Greece

3.12 General Government Income and Outlay Account: Total and Subsectors

Million Greek drachmas

	1980				
	Total General Government	Central Government	State or Provincial Government	Local Government	Social Security Funds

Receipts

1 Property and entrepreneurial income	37880	9380	...	17950	10550
2 Taxes, fees and contributions	478630	296720	...	14160	167750
a Indirect taxes	232470	208300	...	7670	...
b Direct taxes [a]	246160	88420	...	6490	...
c Social security contributions [a]	...	...	...	...	167750
d Fees, fines and penalties [a]	...	...	...	...	...
3 Other current transfers received	4417	3777	...	42230	3070
a Casualty insurance claims	...	...	...	...	...
b Transfers from other government subsectors	...	610	...	42230	3070
c Transfers from abroad	...	...	...	...	...
d Other transfers, except imputed	4417	3167	...	...	...
e Imputed unfunded employee welfare contributions	...	...	...	...	...
Total Current Receipts	520927	309877	...	74340	181370

Disbursements

1 General government final consumption expenditures	276140	207600	...	50340	18200
2 Property income paid	41247	41247	...	...	...
3 Subsidies	39000	39000	...	...	...
4 Other current transfers paid	161468	58468	...	3723	143937
a Casualty insurance premiums, net	...	...	...	...	...
b Transfers to other government subsectors	...	45300	...	373	...
c Transfers to households [b]	159480	11180	...	3350	143937
Social security benefits	...	...	...	...	143700
Social assistance grants	...	...	...	...	...
Unfunded employee welfare benefits [c]	...	...	...	...	237
d Transfers to private non-profit institutions serving households	...	...	...	...	...
e Transfers to the rest of the world	1988	1988	...	...	...
Net saving [d]	3072	-36438	...	20277	19233
Total Current Disbursements and Net Saving	520927	309877	...	74340	181370

a) Items 'Social security contributions' and 'Fees, fines and other n.e.c.' are included in item 'Direct taxes'.
b) For 1979, it is 'net' for column 4.
c) Relating to current transfers to other sub-sectors of general government.
d) Column 'Local government' includes all public funds.

4.3 Derivation of Value Added by Kind of Activity, ISIC Divisions, in Current Prices

Million Greek drachmas

	1970			1971			1972			1973		
	Gross Output	Intermediate Consumption	Value Added	Gross Output	Intermediate Consumption	Value Added	Gross Output	Intermediate Consumption	Value Added	Gross Output	Intermediate Consumption	Value Added

All Producers

1 Agriculture, hunting, forestry and fishing	...	...	47058	...	...	52334	...	...	61467	...	...	87311
a Agriculture and hunting	...	...	44555	...	...	49540	...	...	58614	...	...	83527
b Forestry and logging	...	...	1128	...	...	1352	...	...	1376	...	...	2091
c Fishing	...	...	1375	...	...	1442	...	...	1477	...	...	1693
2 Mining and quarrying	...	...	3541	...	...	4220	...	...	4915	...	...	6047

Greece

4.3 Derivation of Value Added by Kind of Activity, ISIC Divisions, in Current Prices
(Continued)

Million Greek drachmas

	1970 Gross Output	1970 Intermediate Consumption	1970 Value Added	1971 Gross Output	1971 Intermediate Consumption	1971 Value Added	1972 Gross Output	1972 Intermediate Consumption	1972 Value Added	1973 Gross Output	1973 Intermediate Consumption	1973 Value Added
3 Manufacturing	...	...	49266	...	...	55571	...	...	61938	...	...	86151
a Manufacture of food, beverages and tobacco	...	...	9317	...	...	10173	...	...	11177	...	...	14139
b Textile, wearing apparel and leather industries	...	...	11564	...	...	13528	...	...	15765	...	...	21541
c Manufacture of wood and wood products, including furniture	...	...	3051	...	...	3483	...	...	3936	...	...	5649
d Manufacture of paper and paper products, printing and publishing	...	...	2268	...	...	2335	...	...	2685	...	...	3508
e Manufacture of chemicals and chemical petroleum, coal, rubber and plastic products	...	...	5495	...	...	6535	...	...	6997	...	...	10726
f Manufacture of non-metallic mineral products, except products of petroleum and coal	...	...	3736	...	...	4082	...	...	4146	...	...	5495
g Basic metal industries	...	...	3638	...	...	3160	...	...	3165	...	...	5983
h Manufacture of fabricated metal products, machinery and equipment	...	...	8893	...	...	10760	...	...	12327	...	...	16805
i Other manufacturing industries	...	...	1304	...	...	1515	...	...	1740	...	...	2305
4 Electricity, gas and water	...	...	5152	...	...	5649	...	...	6274	...	...	7109
5 Construction	...	...	23017	...	...	26258	...	...	33574	...	...	42740
6 Wholesale and retail trade, restaurants and hotels [a]	...	...	31050	...	...	34093	...	...	40117	...	...	55486
a Wholesale and retail trade	...	...	31050	...	...	34093	...	...	40117	...	...	55486
b Restaurants and hotels	...	...	...	...	...	...	...	...	...	...	...	...
7 Transport, storage and communication [b]	...	...	19761	...	...	22029	...	...	25304	...	...	29070
8 Finance, insurance, real estate and business services [c]	...	...	27187	...	...	29732	...	...	32928	...	...	38344
9 Community, social and personal services [ac]	...	...	29409	...	...	32665	...	...	36339	...	...	43808
Total, Industries	...	...	235441	...	...	262551	...	...	302856	...	...	396066
Producers of Government Services	...	...	22559	...	...	24871	...	...	27121	...	...	32150
Other Producers	...	...	...	...	...	...	...	...	...	...	...	...
Total [d]	...	...	258000	...	...	287422	...	...	329977	...	...	428216
Imputed bank service charge	...	...	...	...	...	...	...	...	...	...	...	...
Import duties	...	...	...	...	...	...	...	...	...	...	...	...
Value added tax	...	...	...	...	...	...	...	...	...	...	...	...
Other adjustments [e]	...	...	40917	...	...	42878	...	...	47749	...	...	55935
Total	...	...	298917	...	...	330300	...	...	377726	...	...	484151

	1974 Gross Output	1974 Intermediate Consumption	1974 Value Added	1975 Gross Output	1975 Intermediate Consumption	1975 Value Added	1976 Gross Output	1976 Intermediate Consumption	1976 Value Added	1977 Gross Output	1977 Intermediate Consumption	1977 Value Added
						All Producers						
1 Agriculture, hunting, forestry and fishing	...	...	100365	...	...	110971	...	...	136204	...	...	141543
a Agriculture and hunting	...	...	96180	...	...	106490	...	...	131078	...	...	135586
b Forestry and logging	...	...	2276	...	...	2576	...	...	2952	...	...	3393
c Fishing	...	...	1909	...	...	1905	...	...	2174	...	...	2564
2 Mining and quarrying	...	...	6739	...	...	8460	...	...	10606	...	...	12670

Greece

4.3 Derivation of Value Added by Kind of Activity, ISIC Divisions, in Current Prices
(Continued)

Million Greek drachmas

	1974 Gross Output	1974 Intermediate Consumption	1974 Value Added	1975 Gross Output	1975 Intermediate Consumption	1975 Value Added	1976 Gross Output	1976 Intermediate Consumption	1976 Value Added	1977 Gross Output	1977 Intermediate Consumption	1977 Value Added
3 Manufacturing	...	...	102616	...	...	118078	...	...	146522	...	...	165348
a Manufacture of food, beverages and tobacco	...	...	17154	...	...	20596	...	...	25604	...	...	30595
b Textile, wearing apparel and leather industries	...	...	25729	...	...	30931	...	...	41779	...	...	45579
c Manufacture of wood and wood products, including furniture	...	...	5645	...	...	7161	...	...	8240	...	...	9341
d Manufacture of paper and paper products, printing and publishing	...	...	4760	...	...	5323	...	...	5816	...	...	6650
e Manufacture of chemicals and chemical petroleum, coal, rubber and plastic products	...	...	12626	...	...	15572	...	...	17275	...	...	18770
f Manufacture of non-metallic mineral products, except products of petroleum and coal	...	...	7050	...	...	7961	...	...	9934	...	...	12728
g Basic metal industries	...	...	6836	...	...	6964	...	...	8484	...	...	7690
h Manufacture of fabricated metal products, machinery and equipment	...	...	19978	...	...	20178	...	...	25247	...	...	29419
i Other manufacturing industries	...	...	2838	...	...	3392	...	...	4143	...	...	4576
4 Electricity, gas and water	...	...	8071	...	...	9312	...	...	12037	...	...	13895
5 Construction	...	...	37761	...	...	43011	...	...	53606	...	...	71839
6 Wholesale and retail trade, restaurants and hotels [a]	...	...	71694	...	...	82221	...	...	99108	...	...	113997
a Wholesale and retail trade	...	...	71694	...	...	82221	...	...	99108	...	...	113997
b Restaurants and hotels	...	...	...	...	...	...	...	...	...	...	...	...
7 Transport, storage and communication [b]	...	...	35319	...	...	47955	...	...	60081	...	...	69920
8 Finance, insurance, real estate and business services [c]	...	...	46805	...	...	54875	...	...	64772	...	...	76300
9 Community, social and personal services [ac]	...	...	54358	...	...	66008	...	...	82234	...	...	101751
Total, Industries	...	...	463728	...	...	540891	...	...	665170	...	...	767263
Producers of Government Services	...	...	43600	...	...	52290	...	...	63565	...	...	77365
Other Producers	...	...	...	...	...	...	...	...	...	...	...	...
Total [d]	...	...	507328	...	...	593181	...	...	728735	...	...	844628
Imputed bank service charge	...	...	...	...	...	...	...	...	...	...	...	...
Import duties	...	...	...	...	...	...	...	...	...	...	...	...
Value added tax	...	...	...	...	...	...	...	...	...	...	...	...
Other adjustments [e]	...	...	56877	...	...	78977	...	...	96197	...	...	119100
Total	...	...	564205	...	...	672158	...	...	824932	...	...	963728

	1978 Gross Output	1978 Intermediate Consumption	1978 Value Added	1979 Gross Output	1979 Intermediate Consumption	1979 Value Added	1980 Gross Output	1980 Intermediate Consumption	1980 Value Added
				All Producers					
1 Agriculture, hunting, forestry and fishing	...	...	177074	...	...	198166	...	...	264552
a Agriculture and hunting	...	...	170690	...	...	190148	...	...	254169
b Forestry and logging	...	...	3019	...	...	3715	...	...	5206
c Fishing	...	...	3365	...	...	4303	...	...	5177
2 Mining and quarrying	...	...	14276	...	...	19226	...	...	23859

Greece

4.3 Derivation of Value Added by Kind of Activity, ISIC Divisions, in Current Prices
(Continued)

Million Greek drachmas

	1978 Gross Output	1978 Intermediate Consumption	1978 Value Added	1979 Gross Output	1979 Intermediate Consumption	1979 Value Added	1980 Gross Output	1980 Intermediate Consumption	1980 Value Added
3 Manufacturing	...	...	191254	...	...	238509	...	...	296955
a Manufacture of food, beverages and tobacco	...	...	37143	...	...	44647	...	...	54737
b Textile, wearing apparel and leather industries	...	...	50939	...	...	64045	...	...	74785
c Manufacture of wood and wood products, including furniture	...	...	10758	...	...	13751	...	...	16089
d Manufacture of paper and paper products, printing and publishing	...	...	8133	...	...	10944	...	...	14688
e Manufacture of chemicals and chemical petroleum, coal, rubber and plastic products	...	...	21971	...	...	26971	...	...	34927
f Manufacture of non-metallic mineral products, except products of petroleum and coal	...	...	15010	...	...	19612	...	...	26395
g Basic metal industries	...	...	9977	...	...	12507	...	...	16622
h Manufacture of fabricated metal products, machinery and equipment	...	...	32563	...	...	40837	...	...	52947
i Other manufacturing industries	...	...	4760	...	...	5195	...	...	5762
4 Electricity, gas and water	...	...	16184	...	...	20649	...	...	23870
5 Construction	...	...	91192	...	...	123078	...	...	130093
6 Wholesale and retail trade, restaurants and hotels [a]	...	...	131825	...	...	160217	...	...	196266
a Wholesale and retail trade	...	...	131825	...	...	160217	...	...	196266
b Restaurants and hotels	...	...	...	...	...	...	...	...	...
7 Transport, storage and communication [b]	...	...	82643	...	...	100177	...	...	115704
8 Finance, insurance, real estate and business services [c]	...	...	92799	...	...	109432	...	...	132473
9 Community, social and personal services [ac]	...	...	124253	...	...	153922	...	...	186602
Total, Industries	...	...	921500	...	...	1123376	...	...	1370374
Producers of Government Services	...	...	95209	...	...	122000	...	...	146710
Other Producers	...	...	...	...	...	...	...	...	...
Total [d]	...	...	1016709	...	...	1245376	...	...	1517084
Imputed bank service charge	...	...		...	...		...	...	
Import duties	...	...		...	...		...	...	
Value added tax	...	...		...	...		...	...	
Other adjustments [e]	...	...	144683	...	...	183570	...	...	193470
Total	...	...	1161392	...	...	1428946	...	...	1710554

a) Restaurants and hotels are included in item 'Community, social and personal services'.
b) Excluding income from ocean-going cargo ships under Greek flag or ownership. However, remittances actually received by the bank of Greece from persons engaged in these enterprises are included in factor income from the rest of the world.
c) Business services are included in item 'Community, social and personal services'.
d) Gross domestic product in factor values.
e) Referring to indirect taxes net of subsidies.

4.4 Derivation of Value Added by Kind of Activity, ISIC Divisions, in Constant Prices

Million Greek drachmas

	1970 Gross Output	1970 Intermediate Consumption	1970 Value Added	1971 Gross Output	1971 Intermediate Consumption	1971 Value Added	1972 Gross Output	1972 Intermediate Consumption	1972 Value Added	1973 Gross Output	1973 Intermediate Consumption	1973 Value Added
					At constant prices of: 1970							
					All Producers							
1 Agriculture, hunting, forestry and fishing	...	...	47058	...	...	48662	...	...	51543	...	...	51204
a Agriculture and hunting	...	...	44555	...	...	46147	...	...	49030	...	...	48639
b Forestry and logging	...	...	1128	...	...	1113	...	...	1099	...	...	1122
c Fishing	...	...	1375	...	...	1402	...	...	1414	...	...	1443
2 Mining and quarrying	...	...	3541	...	...	4031	...	...	4495	...	...	5082

Greece

4.4 Derivation of Value Added by Kind of Activity, ISIC Divisions, in Constant Prices
(Continued)

Million Greek drachmas

	1970 GO	1970 IC	1970 VA	1971 GO	1971 IC	1971 VA	1972 GO	1972 IC	1972 VA	1973 GO	1973 IC	1973 VA
					At constant prices of:1970							
3 Manufacturing	...	...	49266	...	...	54586	...	...	58892	...	...	69228
a Manufacture of food, beverages and tobacco	...	...	9317	...	...	10312	...	...	11008	...	...	12370
b Textile, wearing apparel and leather industries	...	...	11564	...	...	13178	...	...	14641	...	...	16920
c Manufacture of wood and wood products, including furniture	...	...	3051	...	...	3321	...	...	3668	...	...	4142
d Manufacture of paper and paper products, printing and publishing	...	...	2268	...	...	2272	...	...	2527	...	...	2865
e Manufacture of chemicals and chemical petroleum, coal, rubber and plastic products	...	...	5495	...	...	6114	...	...	6446	...	...	8648
f Manufacture of non-metallic mineral products, except products of petroleum and coal	...	...	3736	...	...	4037	...	...	4023	...	...	4935
g Basic metal industries	...	...	3638	...	...	3247	...	...	3222	...	...	4612
h Manufacture of fabricated metal products, machinery and equipment	...	...	8893	...	...	10637	...	...	11783	...	...	12975
i Other manufacturing industries	...	...	1304	...	...	1468	...	...	1574	...	...	1761
4 Electricity, gas and water	...	...	5152	...	...	5911	...	...	7389	...	...	8133
5 Construction	...	...	23017	...	...	26274	...	...	31179	...	...	31924
6 Wholesale and retail trade, restaurants and hotels [a]	...	...	31050	...	...	32634	...	...	36080	...	...	41452
a Wholesale and retail trade	...	...	31050	...	...	32634	...	...	36080	...	...	41452
b Restaurants and hotels	...	...	...	...	...	...	...	...	...	...	...	...
7 Transport, storage and communication [b]	...	...	19761	...	...	21864	...	...	24447	...	...	27191
8 Finance, insurance, real estate and business services [c]	...	...	27187	...	...	29320	...	...	31675	...	...	33966
9 Community, social and personal services [ac]	...	...	29409	...	...	31547	...	...	33614	...	...	35255
Total, Industries	...	...	235441	...	...	254829	...	...	279314	...	...	303435
Producers of Government Services	...	...	22559	...	...	23722	...	...	24659	...	...	25834
Other Producers	...	...	...	...	...	...	...	...	...	...	...	...
Total [d]	...	...	258000	...	...	278551	...	...	303973	...	...	329269
Imputed bank service charge	...	...	...	...	...	...	...	...	...	...	...	...
Import duties	...	...	...	...	...	...	...	...	...	...	...	...
Value added tax	...	...	...	...	...	...	...	...	...	...	...	...
Other adjustments [e]	...	...	40917	...	...	41647	...	...	44658	...	...	44891
Total	...	...	298917	...	...	320198	...	...	348631	...	...	374160

	1974 GO	1974 IC	1974 VA	1975 GO	1975 IC	1975 VA	1976 GO	1976 IC	1976 VA	1977 GO	1977 IC	1977 VA
				At constant prices of:1970 All Producers								
1 Agriculture, hunting, forestry and fishing	...	...	53672	...	...	56733	...	...	55971	...	...	51830
a Agriculture and hunting	...	...	51210	...	...	54229	...	...	53473	...	...	49173
b Forestry and logging	...	...	1135	...	...	1241	...	...	1264	...	...	1366
c Fishing	...	...	1327	...	...	1263	...	...	1234	...	...	1291
2 Mining and quarrying	...	...	4774	...	...	4885	...	...	5242	...	...	5797

Greece

4.4 Derivation of Value Added by Kind of Activity, ISIC Divisions, in Constant Prices
(Continued)

Million Greek drachmas

At constant prices of: 1970

	1974 Gross Output	1974 Intermediate Consumption	1974 Value Added	1975 Gross Output	1975 Intermediate Consumption	1975 Value Added	1976 Gross Output	1976 Intermediate Consumption	1976 Value Added	1977 Gross Output	1977 Intermediate Consumption	1977 Value Added
3 Manufacturing	...	...	67266	...	...	70944	...	...	78029	...	...	79143
a Manufacture of food, beverages and tobacco	...	...	11995	...	...	12420	...	...	13895	...	...	14490
b Textile, wearing apparel and leather industries	...	...	17084	...	...	19368	...	...	21815	...	...	21696
c Manufacture of wood and wood products, including furniture	...	...	3389	...	...	3980	...	...	3981	...	...	4013
d Manufacture of paper and paper products, printing and publishing	...	...	2728	...	...	2667	...	...	2757	...	...	2821
e Manufacture of chemicals and chemical petroleum, coal, rubber and plastic products	...	...	8385	...	...	9260	...	...	9789	...	...	10118
f Manufacture of non-metallic mineral products, except products of petroleum and coal	...	...	5041	...	...	5218	...	...	5956	...	...	6668
g Basic metal industries	...	...	4656	...	...	4554	...	...	4870	...	...	4043
h Manufacture of fabricated metal products, machinery and equipment	...	...	12147	...	...	11397	...	...	12645	...	...	12943
i Other manufacturing industries	...	...	1841	...	...	2080	...	...	2321	...	...	2351
4 Electricity, gas and water	...	...	7701	...	...	8596	...	...	9753	...	...	10726
5 Construction	...	...	21967	...	...	23147	...	...	24576	...	...	27558
6 Wholesale and retail trade, restaurants and hotels [a]	...	...	41172	...	...	42823	...	...	45198	...	...	46878
a Wholesale and retail trade	...	...	41172	...	...	42823	...	...	45198	...	...	46878
b Restaurants and hotels	...	...	...	...	...	...	...	...	...	...	...	...
7 Transport, storage and communication [b]	...	...	27430	...	...	28616	...	...	31270	...	...	32936
8 Finance, insurance, real estate and business services [c]	...	...	36309	...	...	37892	...	...	40122	...	...	42147
9 Community, social and personal services [ac]	...	...	34584	...	...	36855	...	...	39361	...	...	41461
Total, Industries	...	...	294875	...	...	310491	...	...	329522	...	...	338476
Producers of Government Services	...	...	28432	...	...	29342	...	...	30877	...	...	32546
Other Producers	...	...	...	...	...	...	...	...	...	...	...	...
Total [d]	...	...	323307	...	...	339833	...	...	360399	...	...	371022
Imputed bank service charge	...	...	...	...	...	...	...	...	...	...	...	...
Import duties	...	...	...	...	...	...	...	...	...	...	...	...
Value added tax	...	...	...	...	...	...	...	...	...	...	...	...
Other adjustments [e]	...	...	37240	...	...	42529	...	...	46280	...	...	49600
Total	...	...	360547	...	...	382362	...	...	406679	...	...	420622

At constant prices of: 1970

All Producers

	1978 Gross Output	1978 Intermediate Consumption	1978 Value Added	1979 Gross Output	1979 Intermediate Consumption	1979 Value Added	1980 Gross Output	1980 Intermediate Consumption	1980 Value Added
1 Agriculture, hunting, forestry and fishing	...	...	57214	...	...	53616	...	...	59621
a Agriculture and hunting	...	...	54800	...	...	51082	...	...	57150
b Forestry and logging	...	...	1203	...	...	1244	...	...	1203
c Fishing	...	...	1211	...	...	1290	...	...	1268
2 Mining and quarrying	...	...	5723	...	...	6329	...	...	6215

Greece

4.4 Derivation of Value Added by Kind of Activity, ISIC Divisions, in Constant Prices
(Continued)

Million Greek drachmas

	1978 Gross Output	1978 Intermediate Consumption	1978 Value Added	1979 Gross Output	1979 Intermediate Consumption	1979 Value Added	1980 Gross Output	1980 Intermediate Consumption	1980 Value Added
				At constant prices of:1970					
3 Manufacturing	...	...	84341	...	...	88998	...	...	89125
a Manufacture of food, beverages and tobacco	...	...	15911	...	...	16743	...	...	16977
b Textile, wearing apparel and leather industries	...	...	22521	...	...	24205	...	...	23697
c Manufacture of wood and wood products, including furniture	...	...	4044	...	...	4095	...	...	3583
d Manufacture of paper and paper products, printing and publishing	...	...	3279	...	...	3611	...	...	3568
e Manufacture of chemicals and chemical petroleum, coal, rubber and plastic products	...	...	11169	...	...	11593	...	...	11384
f Manufacture of non-metallic mineral products, except products of petroleum and coal	...	...	7088	...	...	7566	...	...	7823
g Basic metal industries	...	...	5093	...	...	5306	...	...	5396
h Manufacture of fabricated metal products, machinery and equipment	...	...	12932	...	...	13687	...	...	14558
i Other manufacturing industries	...	...	2304	...	...	2192	...	...	2139
4 Electricity, gas and water	...	...	12156	...	...	12996	...	...	13724
5 Construction	...	...	28751	...	...	30548	...	...	26577
6 Wholesale and retail trade, restaurants and hotels [a]	...	...	49507	...	...	51144	...	...	50633
a Wholesale and retail trade	...	...	49507	...	...	51144	...	...	50633
b Restaurants and hotels	...	...	...	...	...	...	...	...	...
7 Transport, storage and communication [b]	...	...	35151	...	...	37892	...	...	39749
8 Finance, insurance, real estate and business services [c]	...	...	44273	...	...	46643	...	...	49132
9 Community, social and personal services [a,c]	...	...	43837	...	...	45433	...	...	45180
Total, Industries	...	...	360953	...	...	373599	...	...	379956
Producers of Government Services	...	...	33850	...	...	35500	...	...	36680
Other Producers	...	...	...	...	...	...	...	...	...
Total [d]	...	...	394803	...	...	409099	...	...	416636
Imputed bank service charge	...	...	...	...	...	...	...	...	...
Import duties	...	...	...	...	...	...	...	...	...
Value added tax	...	...	...	...	...	...	...	...	...
Other adjustments [e]	...	...	53990	...	...	56280	...	...	56000
Total	...	...	448793	...	...	465379	...	...	472636

a) Restaurants and hotels are included in item 'Community, social and personal services'.
b) Excluding income from ocean-going cargo ships under Greek flag or ownership. However, remittances actually received by the bank of Greece from persons engaged in these enterprises are included in factor income from the rest of the world.
c) Business services are included in item 'Community, social and personal services'.
d) Gross domestic product in factor values.
e) Referring to indirect taxes net of subsidies.

4.15 Intermediate Consumption by Kind of Activity of User (Use Matrix), in Current Prices

Million Greek drachmas

	Agriculture, Hunting, Forestry, Fishing	Mining & Quarrying	Manufacturing	Electricity, Gas & Water	Construction	Wholesale & Retail Trade, Restaurants & Hotels	Transport & Communications	Finance Insurance, Real Estate & Business Services	Community Social & Personal Services	TOTAL
					1970					
1 Agriculture, hunting, forestry and fishing	86265	...	263555	-	2971	4530	252	5	-	357578
2 Mining and quarrying	412	342	48187	5583	21973	100	-	-	-	76596
3 Manufacturing	65023	8550	607725	5264	217796	47126	75042	1982	20471	1048979
4 Electricity, gas and water	2204	1866	21248	919	1507	11974	2993	350	4420	47483
4 Construction	1739	274	2198	627	-	2164	330	8350	1750	17432
6 Wholesale and retail trade, restaurants and hotels	2347	363	45978	252	16075	6250	8432	225	1931	81853
7 Transport and communications	14867	1095	38692	710	12807	14974	7317	2249	4653	97364
8 Finance, insurance, real estate and business services	9825	84	40151	4466	3500	4680	5299	9612	170	77787
9 Community, social and personal services	127	791	20991	109	1696	11384	7387	2103	8500	53088
Statistical discrepancy	...	...	...	...	...	...	...	...	...	...
Total	182809	13365	1088725	17930	278325	103182	107052	24876	41895	1858160

Grenada

Source. 'National Income Estimates of Grenada', St. George's.
General note. The estimates shown in the following tables have been prepared in accordance with the United Nations System of National Accounts so far as the existing data would permit.

1.10 Gross Domestic Product by Kind of Activity, in Current Prices

Thousand East Caribbean dollars	1970	1971	1972	1973	1974	1975	1976	1977	1978	1979	1980
1 Agriculture, hunting, forestry and fishing	11977	11362	13153	12735	16346	23122	25761	...	...	...	...
2 Mining and quarrying	124	120	110	82	182	89	89	...	...	...	...
3 Manufacturing	2676	2473	2622	3165	2987	3614	4313	...	...	...	...
4 Electricity, gas and water	588	809	806	1133	1161	1363	1377	...	...	...	...
5 Construction	8506	5817	6019	5478	2871	5713	3348	...	...	...	...
6 Wholesale and retail trade, restaurants and hotels	10930	11926	12988	13936	11532	14576	16677	...	...	...	...
7 Transport, storage and communication	5558	6118	5817	7191	7154	7771	8160	...	...	...	...
8 Finance, insurance, real estate and business services	7331	7911	8906	8131	8647	9010	8950	...	...	...	...
9 Community, social and personal services	6306	6547	7065	7449	7693	7999	8296	...	...	...	...
Total, Industries	53996	53083	57486	59300	58573	73257	76971	...	...	...	...
Producers of Government Services	6017	6647	6678	6515	6792	7207	7016	...	...	...	...
Other Producers	...	...	...	...	...	...	...	...	...	...	...
Subtotal	60013	59730	64164	65815	65365	80464	83987	...	...	...	...
Less: Imputed bank service charge	...	...	...	...	...	...	...	...	...	...	...
Plus: Import duties	...	...	...	...	...	...	...	...	...	...	...
Plus: Value added tax	...	...	...	...	...	...	...	...	...	...	...
Equals: Gross Domestic Product [a]	60013	59730	64164	65815	65365	80464	83987	...	...	...	...

a) Gross domestic product in factor values.

Guadeloupe

Source. Reply to the United Nations National Accounts Questionnaire from the Institute national de la statistique et des etudes economiques (INSEE), Paris. Official estimates and descriptions are published by the same Institute in 'Comptes Economiques de la Guadeloupe'.

General note. The estimates shown in the following tables have been adjusted by the INSEE to conform to the United Nations System of National Accounts so far as the existing data would permit.

1.1 Expenditure on the Gross Domestic Product, in Current Prices

Million French francs

	1970	1971	1972	1973	1974	1975	1976	1977	1978	1979	1980
1 General government final consumption expenditure	355.2	429.7	495.4	576.1	690.3	804.3	959.1	1155.9	1378.1	...	...
2 Private final consumption expenditure	1208.8	1297.0	1434.2	1706.7	2053.3	2458.9	2831.8	3291.7	3561.1	...	...
3 Gross capital formation	274.7	289.6	351.1	389.4	550.9	537.9	578.8	747.8	745.1	...	...
a Increase in stocks	10.4	8.4	3.1	-1.1	28.5	-5.9	58.1	73.3	-1.2	...	...
b Gross fixed capital formation	264.3	281.2	348.0	390.5	522.4	543.8	520.7	674.5	746.3	...	...
4 Exports of goods and services	209.0	232.4	203.4	288.0	282.5	359.8	439.4	404.9	519.6	...	...
5 Less: Imports of goods and services	717.7	703.0	758.8	908.7	1120.2	1335.1	1537.8	1869.8	1940.9	...	...
Equals: Gross Domestic Product	1330.0	1545.7	1725.3	2051.5	2456.8	2825.8	3271.3	3730.5	4263.0	5221.2	5716.4

1.3 Cost Components of the Gross Domestic Product

Million French francs

	1970	1971	1972	1973	1974	1975	1976	1977	1978	1979	1980
1 Indirect taxes, net	183.1	178.7	191.0	224.4	260.8	292.6	357.7	412.1	511.2	...	...
a Indirect taxes paid	200.9	202.7	209.3	243.1	283.9	334.3	395.3	441.7	541.1	...	...
b Less: Subsidies received	17.8	24.0	18.3	18.7	23.1	41.7	37.6	29.6	29.9	...	...
2 Consumption of fixed capital	...	...	...	...	...	...	...	...	...	...	...
3 Compensation of employees paid by resident producers to:	737.8	870.6	1006.3	1199.5	1456.6	1710.0	2088.5	2385.9	2762.4		
4 Net operating surplus [a]	409.1	496.4	528.0	627.6	739.3	823.1	825.0	932.5	989.3		
Equals: Gross Domestic Product	1330.0	1545.7	1725.3	2051.5	2456.8	2825.8	3271.3	3730.5	4263.0	5222.2	5716.4

a) Including consumption of fixed capital.

1.7 External Transactions on Current Account, Summary

Million French francs

	1970	1971	1972	1973	1974	1975	1976	1977	1978	1979	1980
Payments to the Rest of the World											
1 Imports of goods and services	717.7	703.0	758.8	908.7	1120.2	1335.1	1537.8	1869.8	1940.9	...	...
2 Factor income paid to the rest of the world	28.1	36.3	44.3	45.6	60.7	63.3	78.6	96.5	119.5	...	...
a Compensation of employees	-	-	-	-	-	-	-	-	-	...	...
b Property and entrepreneurial income paid	28.1	36.3	44.3	45.6	60.7	63.3	78.6	96.5	119.5		
3 Indirect taxes paid to supranational organizations	26.6	21.1	16.3	12.4	9.7	14.3	18.9	18.8	24.4		
4 Current transfers to the rest of the world	-	-	-	-	-	-	-	-	-	...	...
5 Surplus of the nation on current transactions	-142.0	-33.0	-58.0	5.5	-81.4	-51.8	10.8	-163.1	-22.4		
Payments to the Rest of the World and Surplus of the Nation on Current Transactions	630.4	727.4	761.4	972.2	1109.2	1360.9	1646.1	1822.0	2062.4		
Receipts From The Rest of the World											
1 Exports of goods and services	209.0	232.4	203.4	288.0	282.5	359.8	439.4	404.9	519.6	...	...
2 Factor income received from rest of the world	7.4	6.8	6.5	10.7	18.5	13.3	18.1	28.3	40.4	...	...
a Compensation of employees	-	-	-	-	-	-	-	-	-	...	...
b Property and entrepreneurial income received	7.4	6.8	6.5	10.7	18.5	13.3	18.1	28.3	40.4		
3 Subsidies received from supranational organisations	3.2	2.1	2.0	-	1.2	8.0	6.2	7.3	1.5	...	...
4 Current transfers from rest of the world	410.8	486.1	549.5	673.5	807.0	979.8	1182.4	1381.5	1500.9	...	...
Receipts from the Rest of the World on Current Transactions	630.4	727.4	761.4	972.2	1109.2	1360.9	1646.1	1822.0	2062.4	...	...

Guadeloupe

1.10 Gross Domestic Product by Kind of Activity, in Current Prices

Million French francs

	1970	1971	1972	1973	1974	1975	1976	1977	1978	1979	1980
1 Agriculture, hunting, forestry and fishing	260.5	252.5	239.7	277.1	314.4	373.0	366.6	358.8	398.7	...	...
2 Mining and quarrying	20.3	24.4	29.0	33.7	38.6	35.5	53.0	62.1		...	...
3 Manufacturing										...	...
4 Electricity, gas and water	20.5	27.0	31.0	34.6	40.6	42.7	46.5	50.1	...	...	...
5 Construction	55.4	65.9	97.9	102.9	169.4	133.1	111.2	106.8	...	...	...
6 Wholesale and retail trade, restaurants and hotels	293.2	361.2	473.2	599.7	727.4	832.6	1102.9	1282.9	...	...	...
7 Transport, storage and communication	23.0	29.5	43.1	55.9	68.1	80.5	98.9	115.1	...	...	...
8 Finance, insurance, real estate and business services	129.1	133.9	159.6	170.4	215.8	256.4	293.8	374.1	...	...	...
9 Community, social and personal services	99.9	171.3	97.6	123.8	123.6	147.0	118.1	119.1	...	...	...
Total, Industries	901.9	1065.7	1171.1	1398.1	1697.9	1900.8	2191.0	2471.0	2786.4	...	...
Producers of Government Services	303.4	362.3	438.0	526.2	626.5	747.4	885.6	1054.0	1242.2	...	...
Other Producers	27.7	31.1	35.4	41.9	47.7	58.2	68.6	83.1	94.5	...	...
Subtotal	1233.0	1459.1	1644.5	1966.2	2372.1	2706.4	3145.2	3608.1	4123.1	...	...
Less: Imputed bank service charge	32.7	38.3	49.2	60.5	81.7	93.8	114.1	170.2	186.6	...	...
Plus: Import duties	73.4	63.9	61.4	65.8	73.6	89.7	113.8	141.4	154.0	...	...
Plus: Value added tax	56.3	61.0	68.6	80.0	92.8	123.5	126.4	151.2	172.5	...	...
Equals: Gross Domestic Product	1330.0	1545.7	1725.3	2051.5	2456.8	2825.8	3271.3	3730.5	4263.0	...	...

1.12 Relations Among National Accounting Aggregates

Million French francs

	1970	1971	1972	1973	1974	1975	1976	1977	1978	1979	1980
Gross Domestic Product	1330.0	1545.7	1725.3	2051.5	2456.8	2825.8	3271.3	3730.5	4263.0	5222.2	5716.4
Plus: Net factor income received from abroad	-20.7	-29.5	-37.8	-34.9	-42.2	-50.0	-60.5	-68.2	-79.1	...	...
Factor income received	7.4	6.8	6.5	10.7	18.5	13.3	18.1	28.3	40.4	...	...
Less: Factor income paid	28.1	36.3	44.3	45.6	60.7	63.3	78.6	96.5	119.5	...	...
Equals: Gross National Product	1309.3	1516.2	1687.5	2016.6	2414.6	2775.8	3210.8	3662.3	4183.9	...	...
Less: Consumption of fixed capital	...	...	...	...	...	...	...	...	...	...	...
Less: Net indirect taxes paid to supranational organisations	23.4	19.0	14.3	12.4	8.5	6.3	12.7	11.5	22.9	...	...
Indirect taxes paid	26.6	21.1	16.3	12.4	9.7	14.3	18.9	18.8	24.4	...	...
Less: Subsidies received	3.2	2.1	2.0	-	1.2	8.0	6.2	7.3	1.5	...	...
Equals: National Income at Market Prices	1285.9	1497.2	1673.2	2004.2	2406.1	2769.5	3198.1	3650.8	4161.0	...	...
Plus: Net current transfers received from abroad	410.8	486.1	549.5	673.5	807.0	979.8	1182.4	1381.5	1500.9	...	...
Current transfers received	410.8	486.1	549.5	673.5	807.0	979.8	1182.4	1381.5	1500.9	...	...
Less: Current transfers paid	-	-	-	-	-	-	-	-	-	...	...
Equals: National Disposable Income at Market Prices	1696.7	1983.3	2222.7	2677.7	3213.1	3749.3	4380.5	5032.3	5661.9	...	...
Less: Final consumption	1564.0	1726.7	1929.6	2282.8	2743.6	3263.2	3790.9	4447.6	4939.2	...	...
Equals: Net Saving	132.7	256.6	293.1	394.9	469.5	486.1	589.6	584.7	722.7	...	...
Less: Surplus of the nation on current transactions	-142.0	-33.0	-58.0	5.5	-81.4	-51.8	10.8	-163.1	-22.4	...	...
Equals: Net Capital Formation	274.7	289.6	351.1	389.4	550.9	537.9	578.8	747.8	745.1	...	...

Guatemala

Source. Reply to the United Nations National Accounts Questionnaire from the Banco de Guatemala, Guatemala City. The official estimates are published in 'Boletin Estadistico del Banco de Guatemala'.

General note. The estimates shown in the following tables have been prepared in accordance with the United Nations System of National Accounts so far as the existing data would permit.

1.1 Expenditure on the Gross Domestic Product, in Current Prices

Million Guatemalan quetzales

	1970	1971	1972	1973	1974	1975	1976	1977	1978	1979	1980
1 General government final consumption expenditure	151.4	139.3	156.7	166.6	206.6	250.3	297.3	354.5	434.6	488.0	610.0
2 Private final consumption expenditure	1493.3	1588.0	1682.2	2033.6	2469.9	2874.9	3396.0	4126.5	4674.9	5431.5	6216.8
3 Gross capital formation	244.2	285.5	254.8	351.7	588.0	586.8	934.4	1098.2	1312.4	1294.2	1240.3
a Increase in stocks	5.6	21.9	-17.7	-4.9	120.1	16.0	34.2	59.6	94.7	8.0	-34.7
b Gross fixed capital formation	238.6	263.6	272.5	356.6	467.9	570.8	900.2	1038.6	1217.7	1286.2	1275.0
Residential buildings a	28.1	26.9	22.8	32.2	50.0	54.7	113.7	144.2	186.9	204.2	147.4
Non-residential buildings	...	...	...	...	...	...	...	...	...	...	...
Other construction and land improvement etc.	52.8	55.1	67.8	91.6	102.1	127.6	208.1	249.3	270.2	331.9	423.3
Other	157.7	181.6	181.9	232.8	315.8	388.5	578.4	645.1	760.6	750.0	704.3
4 Exports of goods and services b	353.6	343.0	397.3	536.5	708.4	792.0	941.7	1340.3	1303.7	1473.6	1757.2
5 Less: Imports of goods and services	338.5	371.0	389.3	519.1	811.4	858.0	1204.1	1439.0	1655.0	1784.3	1971.4
Equals: Gross Domestic Product	1904.0	1984.8	2101.6	2569.3	3161.5	3646.0	4365.3	5480.5	6070.5	6903.0	7852.9

a) Non-residential buildings are included in item 'Residential construction'.
b) For 1976, not including 51.2 million quetzales for insurance service charges.

1.2 Expenditure on the Gross Domestic Product, in Constant Prices

Million Guatemalan quetzales

	1970	1971	1972	1973	1974	1975	1976	1977	1978	1979	1980
					At constant prices of:1958						
1 General government final consumption expenditure	125.6	116.2	128.6	128.7	134.8	148.5	165.0	176.1	187.2	198.9	216.4
2 Private final consumption expenditure	1399.5	1480.0	1576.6	1665.6	1727.2	1777.9	1897.1	2048.9	2151.4	2242.6	2318.8
3 Gross capital formation	214.9	248.3	209.0	247.7	334.8	280.9	391.2	435.4	480.2	416.8	352.4
a Increase in stocks	5.3	20.9	-17.1	-4.2	87.6	10.3	19.8	29.6	44.6	3.4	-13.7
b Gross fixed capital formation	209.6	227.4	226.1	251.9	247.2	270.6	371.4	405.8	435.6	413.4	366.1
Residential buildings a	25.8	24.7	21.4	24.5	25.1	27.3	49.0	53.0	63.7	61.6	39.4
Non-residential buildings	...	...	...	...	...	...	...	...	...	...	...
Other construction and land improvement etc.	46.2	47.8	59.4	71.0	61.8	69.0	99.2	115.0	113.5	126.6	142.6
Other	137.6	154.9	145.3	156.4	160.3	174.3	223.2	237.8	258.4	225.2	184.2
4 Exports of goods and services	346.0	360.4	412.1	451.6	481.6	497.5	530.3	563.2	562.7	619.1	654.7
5 Less: Imports of goods and services	293.3	312.1	294.7	324.2	370.7	352.1	457.1	499.8	521.6	482.8	443.0
Equals: Gross Domestic Product	1792.7	1892.8	2031.6	2169.4	2307.7	2352.7	2526.5	2723.8	2859.9	2994.6	3099.3

a) Non-residential buildings are included in item 'Residential construction'.

1.7 External Transactions on Current Account, Summary

Million Guatemalan quetzales

	1970	1971	1972	1973	1974	1975	1976	1977	1978	1979	1980
					Payments to the Rest of the World						
1 Imports of goods and services	338.5	371.0	389.3	519.1	811.4	858.0	1204.1	1439.0	1655.0	1784.3	1971.4
a Imports of merchandise c.i.f.	293.9	315.8	328.3	431.0	704.1	734.9	1048.6	1221.8	1390.6	1503.9	1598.2
b Other	44.6	55.2	61.0	88.1	107.3	123.1	155.5	217.1	264.4	280.4	373.2
2 Factor income paid to the rest of the world	46.5	47.6	51.3	57.8	68.4	83.5	96.0	66.3	77.8	90.7	135.7
a Compensation of employees	...	...	...	...	...	...	...	...	...	...	...
b Property and entrepreneurial income paid	46.5	47.6	51.3	57.8	68.4	83.5	96.0	66.3	77.8	90.7	135.7
By general government	8.1	10.2	10.2	9.3	8.7	10.7	13.5	18.2	25.1	28.0	39.3
By corporate and quasi-corporate enterprises	33.3	31.7	34.1	38.9	49.2	60.0	64.4	39.7	43.0	45.6	52.3
By other	5.1	5.7	7.0	9.6	10.5	12.8	18.1	8.4	9.7	17.1	44.1
3 Indirect taxes paid to supranational organizations	...	...	...	...	...	...	...	...	...	...	...
4 Current transfers to the rest of the world	2.2	1.7	2.3	8.9	11.1	11.3	18.1	20.6	23.8	22.9	15.4
5 Surplus of the nation on current transactions	-11.1	-45.9	-9.5	11.0	-99.4	-62.3	-86.1	-35.4	-262.1	-196.4	-162.9
Payments to the Rest of the World and Surplus of the Nation on Current Transactions	376.1	374.4	433.4	596.8	791.5	890.5	1232.1	1490.5	1494.5	1701.5	1959.6

Guatemala

1.7 External Transactions on Current Account, Summary
(Continued)

Million Guatemalan quetzales

	1970	1971	1972	1973	1974	1975	1976	1977	1978	1979	1980
	\multicolumn{11}{c}{Receipts From The Rest of the World}										
1 Exports of goods and services [a]	353.6	343.0	397.3	536.5	708.4	792.0	992.9	1340.3	1303.7	1473.6	1757.2
a Exports of merchandise f.o.b.	297.1	286.9	335.9	442.0	582.2	640.9	784.4	1160.1	1092.4	1221.4	1519.8
b Other	56.5	56.1	61.4	94.5	126.2	151.1	208.5	180.2	211.3	252.2	237.4
2 Factor income received from rest of the world	4.3	3.6	3.7	9.8	18.1	14.5	22.3	33.8	51.3	78.3	76.8
a Compensation of employees	...	...	...	...	...	...	...	...	...	...	...
b Property and entrepreneurial income received	4.3	3.6	3.7	9.8	18.1	14.5	22.3	33.8	51.3	78.3	76.8
By general government	4.0	3.4	3.3	9.3	16.6	13.6	21.3	32.8	50.0	77.9	73.5
By corporate and quasi-corporate enterprises	0.1	0.1	0.2	0.4	0.9	0.5	0.5	0.9	0.3	0.2	2.0
By other	0.2	0.1	0.2	0.1	0.6	0.4	0.5	0.1	1.0	0.2	1.3
3 Subsidies received from supranational organisations	...	...	...	...	...	...	...	...	...	...	...
4 Current transfers from rest of the world [b]	18.2	27.9	32.4	50.5	65.0	84.0	216.9	116.4	139.5	149.6	125.6
Receipts from the Rest of the World on Current Transactions	376.1	374.4	433.4	596.8	791.5	890.5	1232.1	1490.5	1494.5	1701.5	1959.6

a) For 1976, including 51.2 million quetzales for insurance service charges.
b) For 1976, including gifts in kind received after the earthquake.

1.8 Capital Transactions of The Nation, Summary

Million Guatemalan quetzales

	1970	1971	1972	1973	1974	1975	1976	1977	1978	1979	1980
	\multicolumn{11}{c}{Finance of Gross Capital Formation}										
Gross saving	233.1	239.6	245.3	362.7	488.6	524.5	797.1	1062.8	1050.3	1097.8	1077.4
Less: Surplus of the nation on current transactions	-11.1	-45.9	-9.5	11.0	-99.4	-62.3	-86.1	-35.4	-262.1	-196.4	-162.9
Finance of Gross Capital Formation [a]	244.2	285.5	254.8	351.7	588.0	586.8	883.2	1098.2	1312.4	1294.2	1240.3
	\multicolumn{11}{c}{Gross Capital Formation}										
Increase in stocks	5.6	21.9	-17.7	-4.9	120.1	16.0	34.2	59.6	94.7	8.0	-34.7
Gross fixed capital formation	238.6	263.6	272.5	356.6	467.9	570.8	900.2	1038.6	1217.7	1286.2	1275.0
1 General government	42.7	44.6	55.4	76.4	81.6	105.1	182.0	218.8	235.0	294.0	380.4
2 Corporate and quasi-corporate enterprises	...	...	...	...	...	...	...	...	...	...	...
3 Other	...	...	...	...	...	...	...	...	...	...	...
Gross Capital Formation [a]	244.2	285.5	254.8	351.7	588.0	586.8	934.4	1098.2	1312.4	1294.2	1240.3

a) For 1976, not including 51.2 million quetzales for insurance service charges.

1.11 Gross Domestic Product by Kind of Activity, in Constant Prices

Million Guatemalan quetzales

	1970	1971	1972	1973	1974	1975	1976	1977	1978	1979	1980
	\multicolumn{11}{c}{At constant prices of:1958}										
1 Agriculture, hunting, forestry and fishing	489.7	524.3	574.7	605.1	643.8	659.9	689.6	716.5	739.1	760.0	773.3
2 Mining and quarrying	1.7	1.7	1.5	1.6	2.0	2.1	2.7	3.1	4.8	8.6	13.4
3 Manufacturing	282.9	303.2	319.8	345.9	361.6	356.3	393.5	435.6	463.7	489.6	519.3
4 Electricity, gas and water	21.5	22.7	25.7	28.3	30.4	32.8	35.4	44.3	49.0	52.0	53.7
5 Construction	28.4	28.5	34.2	40.8	38.1	43.9	76.3	85.8	88.6	94.4	94.6
6 Wholesale and retail trade, restaurants and hotels	518.0	542.1	569.6	609.1	655.5	648.7	704.1	768.5	802.4	824.7	844.5
7 Transport, storage and communication	98.2	105.5	118.3	130.5	147.5	150.8	164.9	177.0	189.5	199.5	213.8
8 Finance, insurance, real estate and business services	167.1	171.0	176.6	185.7	192.5	200.0	177.1	200.7	215.2	236.2	245.0
9 Community, social and personal services	98.3	105.7	113.7	122.6	129.9	140.0	150.5	161.3	169.4	182.2	137.7
Total, Industries	1705.8	1804.7	1934.1	2069.6	2201.3	2234.5	2394.1	2592.8	2721.7	2847.2	2945.3
Producers of Government Services	86.9	88.1	97.5	99.8	106.4	118.2	132.4	131.1	138.2	147.4	154.0
Other Producers	...	...	...	...	...	...	...	...	...	...	...
Subtotal	1792.7	1892.8	2031.6	2169.4	2307.7	2352.7	2526.5	2723.8	2859.9	2994.6	3099.3
Less: Imputed bank service charge	...	...	...	...	...	...	...	...	...	...	...
Plus: Import duties	...	...	...	...	...	...	...	...	...	...	...
Plus: Value added tax	...	...	...	...	...	...	...	...	...	...	...
Equals: Gross Domestic Product	1792.7	1892.8	2031.6	2169.4	2307.7	2352.7	2526.5	2723.8	2859.9	2994.6	3099.3

Guatemala

1.12 Relations Among National Accounting Aggregates

Million Guatemalan quetzales

	1970	1971	1972	1973	1974	1975	1976	1977	1978	1979	1980
Gross Domestic Product	1904.0	1984.8	2101.6	2569.3	3161.5	3646.0	4365.3	5480.5	6070.5	6903.0	7853.0
Plus: Net factor income received from abroad	-42.2	-44.0	-47.6	-48.0	-50.3	-69.0	-73.7	-32.5	-26.5	-13.0	-59.0
Factor income received	4.3	3.6	3.7	9.8	18.1	14.5	22.3	33.8	51.3	78.0	77.0
Less: Factor income paid	46.5	47.6	51.3	57.8	68.4	83.5	96.0	66.8	77.8	91.0	136.0
Equals: Gross National Product	1861.8	1940.8	2054.0	2521.3	3111.2	3577.0	4291.6	5448.0	6044.0	6890.0	7794.0
Less: Consumption of fixed capital	...	...	...	...	...	...	...	...	...	...	...
Less: Net indirect taxes paid to supranational organisations	...	...	...	...	...	...	...	...	...	...	...
Equals: National Income at Market Prices [a]	1861.8	1940.8	2054.0	2521.3	3111.2	3577.0	4291.6	5448.0	6044.0	6890.0	7794.0
Plus: Net current transfers received from abroad	16.0	26.2	30.1	41.6	53.9	72.7	198.8	95.8	115.7	127.0	110.0
Current transfers received [b]	18.2	27.9	32.4	50.5	65.0	84.0	216.9	116.4	139.5	150.0	125.0
Less: Current transfers paid	2.2	1.7	2.3	8.9	11.1	11.3	18.1	20.6	23.8	23.0	15.0
Equals: National Disposable Income at Market Prices [a]	1877.8	1967.0	2084.1	2562.9	3165.1	3649.9	4490.4	5543.8	6159.7	7017.0	7904.0
Less: Final consumption	1644.7	1727.3	1838.9	2200.2	2676.5	3125.2	3693.3	4481.0	5109.5	5919.0	6827.0
Equals: Net Saving [a]	233.1	239.7	245.2	362.7	488.6	524.5	797.1	1062.8	1050.2	1098.0	1077.0
Less: Surplus of the nation on current transactions	-11.1	-45.9	-9.5	11.0	-99.4	-62.3	-86.1	-35.4	-262.1	-196.0	-163.0
Equals: Net Capital Formation [c]	244.2	285.6	254.7	351.7	588.0	586.8	883.2	1098.2	1312.3	1294.0	1240.0

a) Including consumption of fixed capital.
b) For 1976, including gifts in kind received after the earthquake.
c) For 1976, not including 51.2 million quetzales for insurance service charges.

2.9 Gross Capital Formation by Kind of Activity of Owner, ISIC Major Divisions, in Current Prices

Million Guatemalan quetzales

	1970 TGCF	1970 Inc. Stocks	1970 GFCF	1971 TGCF	1971 Inc. Stocks	1971 GFCF	1972 TGCF	1972 Inc. Stocks	1972 GFCF	1973 TGCF	1973 Inc. Stocks	1973 GFCF
All Producers												
1 Agriculture, hunting, fishing and forestry	...	...	19.5	...	...	21.3	...	...	24.9	...	...	30.5
2 Mining and quarrying	...	...	...	...	...	...	...	...	...	...	...	...
3 Manufacturing	...	...	127.4	...	...	129.7	...	...	140.2	...	...	176.2
4 Electricity, gas and water	...	...	...	...	...	...	...	...	...	...	...	...
5 Construction	...	...	28.1	...	...	26.9	...	...	22.8	...	...	32.2
6 Wholesale and retail trade, restaurants and hotels	...	...	...	...	...	...	...	...	...	...	...	...
7 Transport, storage and communication	...	...	20.9	...	...	41.1	...	...	29.2	...	...	41.3
8 Finance, insurance, real estate and business services	...	...	...	...	...	...	...	...	...	...	...	...
9 Community, social and personal services	...	...	...	...	...	...	...	...	...	...	...	...
Total Industries	...	...	195.9	...	...	219.0	...	...	217.1	...	...	280.2
Producers of Government Services	...	...	42.7	...	...	44.6	...	...	55.4	...	...	76.4
Private Non-Profit Institutions Serving Households	...	...	...	...	...	...	...	...	...	...	...	...
Total	244.2	5.6	238.6	285.5	21.9	263.6	254.8	-17.7	272.5	351.7	-4.9	356.6

	1974 TGCF	1974 Inc. Stocks	1974 GFCF	1975 TGCF	1975 Inc. Stocks	1975 GFCF	1976 TGCF	1976 Inc. Stocks	1976 GFCF	1977 TGCF	1977 Inc. Stocks	1977 GFCF
All Producers												
1 Agriculture, hunting, fishing and forestry	...	...	45.6	...	...	54.4	...	...	67.7	...	...	85.7
2 Mining and quarrying	...	...	...	...	...	...	...	...	...	...	...	...
3 Manufacturing	...	...	234.9	...	...	270.1	...	...	423.1	...	...	442.4
4 Electricity, gas and water	...	...	...	...	...	...	...	...	...	...	...	...

Guatemala

2.9 Gross Capital Formation by Kind of Activity of Owner, ISIC Major Divisions, in Current Prices
(Continued)

Million Guatemalan quetzales

	1974 TGCF	1974 IS	1974 GFCF	1975 TGCF	1975 IS	1975 GFCF	1976 TGCF	1976 IS	1976 GFCF	1977 TGCF	1977 IS	1977 GFCF
5 Construction	...	...	50.0	...	...	54.7	...	...	113.7	...	...	144.3
6 Wholesale and retail trade, restaurants and hotels	...	...	...	...	...	...	...	...	...	...	...	...
7 Transport, storage and communication	...	...	55.8	...	...	86.5	...	...	113.6	...	...	147.4
8 Finance, insurance, real estate and business services	...	...	...	...	...	...	...	...	...	...	...	...
9 Community, social and personal services	...	...	...	...	...	...	...	...	...	...	...	...
Total Industries	...	...	386.3	...	...	465.7	...	...	718.1	...	...	819.8
Producers of Government Services	...	...	81.6	...	...	105.1	...	...	182.0	...	...	218.8
Private Non-Profit Institutions Serving Households	...	...	...	...	...	...	...	...	...	...	...	...
Total	588.0	120.1	467.9	586.8	16.0	570.8	934.4	34.2	900.2	1098.2	59.6	1038.6

	1978 TGCF	1978 IS	1978 GFCF	1979 TGCF	1979 IS	1979 GFCF	1980 TGCF	1980 IS	1980 GFCF
All Producers									
1 Agriculture, hunting, fishing and forestry	...	...	90.0	...	...	76.4	...	...	73.5
2 Mining and quarrying	...	...	...	...	...	...	...	...	...
3 Manufacturing	...	...	541.6	...	...	565.8	...	...	552.0
4 Electricity, gas and water	...	...	...	...	...	...	...	...	...
5 Construction	...	...	186.9	...	...	204.2	...	...	147.4
6 Wholesale and retail trade, restaurants and hotels	...	...	...	...	...	...	...	...	...
7 Transport, storage and communication	...	...	164.2	...	...	145.8	...	...	121.7
8 Finance, insurance, real estate and business services	...	...	...	...	...	...	...	...	...
9 Community, social and personal services	...	...	...	...	...	...	...	...	...
Total Industries	...	...	982.7	...	...	992.2	...	...	894.6
Producers of Government Services	...	...	235.0	...	...	294.0	...	...	380.4
Private Non-Profit Institutions Serving Households	...	...	...	...	...	...	...	...	...
Total	1312.4	94.7	1217.7	1294.2	8.0	1286.2	1240.3	-34.7	1275.0

2.10 Gross Capital Formation by Kind of Activity of Owner, ISIC Major Divisions, in Constant Prices

Million Guatemalan quetzales

	1970 TGCF	1970 IS	1970 GFCF	1971 TGCF	1971 IS	1971 GFCF	1972 TGCF	1972 IS	1972 GFCF	1973 TGCF	1973 IS	1973 GFCF
At constant prices of: 1958												
All Producers												
1 Agriculture, hunting, fishing and forestry	...	...	17.4	...	...	18.7	...	...	21.0	...	...	21.9
2 Mining and quarrying	...	...	...	...	...	...	...	...	...	...	...	...
3 Manufacturing	...	...	111.8	...	...	112.0	...	...	114.1	...	...	121.6
4 Electricity, gas and water	...	...	...	...	...	...	...	...	...	...	...	...
5 Construction	...	...	25.8	...	...	24.7	...	...	21.4	...	...	24.5
6 Wholesale and retail trade, restaurants and hotels	...	...	...	...	...	...	...	...	...	...	...	...
7 Transport, storage and communication	...	...	17.8	...	...	34.0	...	...	21.8	...	...	25.4
8 Finance, insurance, real estate and business services	...	...	...	...	...	...	...	...	...	...	...	...
9 Community, social and personal services	...	...	...	...	...	...	...	...	...	...	...	...
Total Industries	...	...	172.8	...	...	189.4	...	...	178.3	...	...	193.4
Producers of Government Services	...	...	36.8	...	...	38.0	...	...	47.8	...	...	58.5
Private Non-Profit Institutions Serving Households	...	...	...	...	...	...	...	...	...	...	...	...
Total	214.9	5.3	209.6	248.3	20.9	227.4	209.0	-17.1	226.1	247.7	-4.2	251.9

Guatemala

2.10 Gross Capital Formation by Kind of Activity of Owner, ISIC Major Divisions, in Constant Prices

Million Guatemalan quetzales

	1974 TGCF	1974 IS	1974 GFCF	1975 TGCF	1975 IS	1975 GFCF	1976 TGCF	1976 IS	1976 GFCF	1977 TGCF	1977 IS	1977 GFCF
					At constant prices of: 1958 — All Producers							
1 Agriculture, hunting, fishing and forestry	...	...	25.8	...	...	27.0	...	...	29.3	...	...	34.2
2 Mining and quarrying	...	...	...	...	...	...	...	...	...	...	...	...
3 Manufacturing	...	...	123.8	...	...	126.4	...	...	168.7	...	...	168.2
4 Electricity, gas and water	...	...	...	...	...	...	...	...	...	...	...	...
5 Construction	...	...	25.1	...	...	27.3	...	...	49.0	...	...	53.0
6 Wholesale and retail trade, restaurants and hotels	...	...	...	...	...	...	...	...	...	...	...	...
7 Transport, storage and communication	...	...	25.2	...	...	35.0	...	...	39.9	...	...	50.7
8 Finance, insurance, real estate and business services	...	...	...	...	...	...	...	...	...	...	...	...
9 Community, social and personal services	...	...	...	...	...	...	...	...	...	...	...	...
Total Industries	...	...	199.9	...	...	215.7	...	...	286.9	...	...	306.1
Producers of Government Services	...	...	47.3	...	...	54.9	...	...	84.5	...	...	99.7
Private Non-Profit Institutions Serving Households	...	...	...	...	...	...	...	...	...	...	...	...
Total	334.8	87.6	247.2	280.9	10.3	270.6	391.2	19.8	371.4	435.4	29.6	405.8

	1978 TGCF	1978 IS	1978 GFCF	1979 TGCF	1979 IS	1979 GFCF	1980 TGCF	1980 IS	1980 GFCF
			At constant prices of: 1958 — All Producers						
1 Agriculture, hunting, fishing and forestry	...	...	33.1	...	...	26.0	...	...	23.0
2 Mining and quarrying	...	...	...	...	...	...	...	...	...
3 Manufacturing	...	...	189.5	...	...	176.0	...	...	150.3
4 Electricity, gas and water	...	...	...	...	...	...	...	...	...
5 Construction	...	...	63.7	...	...	61.6	...	...	39.4
6 Wholesale and retail trade, restaurants and hotels	...	...	...	...	...	...	...	...	...
7 Transport, storage and communication	...	...	51.1	...	...	39.0	...	...	27.0
8 Finance, insurance, real estate and business services	...	...	...	...	...	...	...	...	...
9 Community, social and personal services	...	...	...	...	...	...	...	...	...
Total Industries	...	...	337.4	...	...	302.6	...	...	239.7
Producers of Government Services	...	...	98.2	...	...	110.8	...	...	126.4
Private Non-Profit Institutions Serving Households	...	...	...	...	...	...	...	...	...
Total	480.2	44.6	435.6	416.8	3.4	413.4	352.4	-13.7	366.1

2.17 Exports and Imports of Goods and Services, Detail

Million Guatemalan quetzales

	1970	1971	1972	1973	1974	1975	1976	1977	1978	1979	1980
					Exports of Goods and Services						
1 Exports of merchandise, f.o.b.	297.1	286.9	335.9	442.0	582.2	640.9	784.4	1160.1	1092.4	1221.4	1519.8
2 Transport and communication	10.3	10.6	10.9	15.8	17.6	19.8	23.2	25.4	31.4	38.7	39.8
a In respect of merchandise imports	0.3	0.5	0.6	1.1	2.2	1.5	3.0	3.4	4.5	3.9	4.4
b Other	10.0	10.1	10.3	14.7	15.4	18.3	20.2	22.0	26.9	34.8	35.4
3 Insurance service charges	3.5	2.3	2.7	3.9	3.7	4.5	56.1	10.5	10.6	9.3	11.4
a In respect of merchandise imports	0.6	0.8	0.9	0.9	1.5	2.5	2.8	2.9	2.1	1.6	3.3
b Other	2.9	1.5	1.8	3.0	2.2	2.0	53.3	7.6	8.5	7.7	8.1

Guatemala

2.17 Exports and Imports of Goods and Services, Detail
(Continued)

Million Guatemalan quetzales

	1970	1971	1972	1973	1974	1975	1976	1977	1978	1979	1980
4 Other commodities	17.5	15.7	18.5	22.1	28.8	33.1	40.0	51.6	64.3	83.0	82.3
5 Adjustments of merchandise exports to change-of-ownership basis	...	...	...	...	...	...	...	...	...	...	...
6 Direct purchases in the domestic market by non-residential households	12.1	13.7	16.9	37.0	56.7	78.0	65.6	66.2	67.5	81.6	61.6
7 Direct purchases in the domestic market by extraterritorial bodies	13.1	13.8	12.4	15.7	19.4	15.7	23.6	26.5	37.5	39.5	42.3
Total Exports of Goods and Services [a]	353.6	343.0	397.3	536.5	708.4	792.0	992.9	1340.3	1303.7	1473.6	1757.2

Imports of Goods and Services

	1970	1971	1972	1973	1974	1975	1976	1977	1978	1979	1980
1 Imports of merchandise, c.i.f.	293.9	315.8	328.3	431.0	704.1	734.9	1048.6	1221.8	1390.6	1503.9	1598.2
a Imports of merchandise, f.o.b.	269.9	289.9	294.7	391.4	631.5	672.4	964.9	1086.9	1283.8	1394.7	1472.6
b Transport of services on merchandise imports	21.8	23.6	30.6	36.0	66.0	56.8	76.2	122.8	101.1	103.4	118.7
By residents	...	...	...	...	...	...	...	...	...	...	...
By non-residents	21.8	23.6	30.6	36.0	66.0	56.8	76.2	122.8	101.1	103.4	118.7
c Insurance service charges on merchandise imports	2.2	2.3	3.0	3.6	6.6	5.7	7.5	12.1	5.7	5.8	6.9
By residents	...	...	...	...	...	...	...	...	...	...	...
By non-residents	2.2	2.3	3.0	3.6	6.6	5.7	7.5	12.1	5.7	5.8	6.9
2 Adjustments of merchandise imports to change-of-ownership basis	...	...	...	...	...	...	...	...	...	...	...
3 Other transport and communication	10.6	12.1	11.3	14.6	16.4	19.9	21.0	27.9	34.7	50.0	61.6
4 Other insurance service charges	1.3	1.6	2.0	3.3	3.4	3.5	3.4	5.5	6.1	8.2	9.4
5 Other commodities	14.8	14.6	16.2	26.8	29.6	36.9	42.8	73.2	102.8	77.6	114.5
6 Direct purchases abroad by government	3.4	5.5	7.2	5.1	6.1	8.0	6.6	10.9	13.1	24.5	23.7
7 Direct purchases abroad by resident households	14.4	21.4	24.3	38.3	51.8	54.8	81.7	99.7	107.7	120.1	164.0
Total Imports of Goods and Services	338.4	371.0	389.3	519.1	811.4	858.0	1204.1	1439.0	1655.0	1784.3	1971.4
Balance of Goods and Services	15.2	-28.1	8.0	17.5	-102.9	-66.0	-211.2	-98.7	-351.3	-310.8	-214.2
Total Imports and Balance of Goods and Services	353.6	343.0	397.3	536.5	708.4	792.0	992.9	1340.3	1303.7	1473.5	1757.2

a) For 1976, including 51.2 million quetzales for insurance service charges.

Guyana

Source. Reply to the United Nations National Accounts Questionnaire from the Statistical Bureau, Georgetown. Official estimates have been published by the Statistical Bureau in 'Annual Statistical Abstract'.

General note. The estimates shown in the following tables have been prepared in accordance with the United Nations System of National Accounts so far as the existing data would permit.

1.1 Expenditure on the Gross Domestic Product, in Current Prices

Thousand Guyana dollars

	1970	1971	1972	1973	1974	1975	1976	1977	1978	1979	1980
1 General government final consumption expenditure	90938	101653	116901	159666	162239	232912	330000	...	...	...	...
2 Private final consumption expenditure	322041	336000	363100	418564	512545	562469	639300	...	...	...	...
3 Gross capital formation	121863	105100	118924	175500	252094	392548	425200	...	...	...	...
a Increase in stocks	9223	2300	10624	20717	54011	42275	44200	...	...	...	...
b Gross fixed capital formation	112640	102800	108300	154783	198083	350273	381000	...	...	...	...
4 Exports of goods and services	302367	329446	344358	336479	651696	890658	750000	...	...	...	...
5 Less: Imports of goods and services	305368	308496	352141	444264	633841	881625	1027000	...	...	...	...
Statistical discrepancy	3709	415	8141	-1148	10053	-9095	-	...	...	...	...
Equals: Gross Domestic Product	535550	564118	599283	644797	954786	1187867	1117500	...	...	...	...

1.2 Expenditure on the Gross Domestic Product, in Constant Prices

Thousand Guyana dollars

	1970	1971	1972	1973	1974	1975	1976	1977	1978	1979	1980
				At constant prices of: 1970							
1 General government final consumption expenditure	90938	93924	98464	112669	110609	155206	209163	...	...	...	...
2 Private final consumption expenditure	322041	330383	340300	357137	365320	378258	395400	...	...	...	...
3 Gross capital formation	121863	104080	86899	129826	117033	204173	169663	...	...	...	...
a Increase in stocks	9223	2142	7847	17958	32791	28869	24426	...	...	...	...
b Gross fixed capital formation	112640	101938	79052	111868	84242	175304	145237	...	...	...	...
4 Exports of goods and services	302367	312567	289864	272386	273822	269406	258264	...	...	...	...
5 Less: Imports of goods and services	305368	290650	283368	321930	286417	352227	364831	...	...	...	...
Statistical discrepancy	3709	408	7630	-980	7165	-6116	-	...	...	...	...
Equals: Gross Domestic Product	535550	550712	539789	549108	587532	648700	667659	...	...	...	...

1.3 Cost Components of the Gross Domestic Product

Thousand Guyana dollars

	1970	1971	1972	1973	1974	1975	1976	1977	1978	1979	1980
1 Indirect taxes, net	65565	65717	68616	68389	84980	90049	92500	...	...	...	...
a Indirect taxes paid	69778	70007	72865	78092	107732	122900	139400	...	...	...	...
b Less: Subsidies received	4213	4290	4249	9703	22752	32851	46900	...	...	...	...
2 Consumption of fixed capital	33785	33371	33368	35948	39976	46465	55000	...	...	...	...
3 Compensation of employees paid by resident producers to:	262173	282931	310982	364558	417934	491803	550000	...	...	...	...
4 Net operating surplus	174027	182099	186317	175902	411896	559550	420000	...	...	...	...
Equals: Gross Domestic Product	535550	564118	599283	644797	954786	1187867	1117500	...	...	...	...

1.8 Capital Transactions of The Nation, Summary

Thousand Guyana dollars

	1970	1971	1972	1973	1974	1975	1976	1977	1978	1979	1980
				Finance of Gross Capital Formation							
Gross saving	80187	89578	96096	39685	223801	350470	74806	...	...	...	...
1 Consumption of fixed capital	33785	33371	33368	35948	39976	46465	55000	...	...	...	...
2 Net saving	46402	56207	62728	3737	183825	304005	19806	...	...	...	...
Less: Surplus of the nation on current transactions	-45385	-15937	-30969	-134667	-38346	-32983	-350394	...	...	...	...
Statistical discrepancy	-3709	-415	-8141	1148	-10053	9095	-	...	...	...	...
Finance of Gross Capital Formation	121863	105100	118924	175500	252094	392548	425200	...	...	...	...
				Gross Capital Formation							
Increase in stocks	9223	2300	10624	20717	54011	42275	44200	...	...	...	...
Gross fixed capital formation	112640	102800	108300	154783	198083	350273	381000	...	...	...	...
Gross Capital Formation	121863	105100	118924	175500	252094	392548	425200	...	...	...	...

Guyana

1.10 Gross Domestic Product by Kind of Activity, in Current Prices

Thousand Guyana dollars

	1970	1971	1972	1973	1974	1975	1976	1977	1978	1979	1980
1 Agriculture, hunting, forestry and fishing	90158	101643	104211	106277	264056	341528	236000	...	...	...	...
2 Mining and quarrying	95495	90668	89744	80458	114828	140990	145000	...	...	...	...
3 Manufacturing	56965	61221	63959	64314	120353	161640	134900	...	...	...	...
4 Electricity, gas and water								...	...	...	...
5 Construction [a,b]	36849	38619	42746	46961	52709	74382	85000	...	...	...	...
6 Wholesale and retail trade, restaurants and hotels [c]	53506	54540	58651	64377	80797	94217	108100	...	...	...	...
7 Transport, storage and communication	27726	29753	32817	36796	46321	49870	55000	...	...	...	...
8 Finance, insurance, real estate and business services [d]	27083	29715	31040	34448	40689	49710	54000	...	...	...	...
9 Community, social and personal services [c,d]	17734	19123	19698	21555	23476	25647	27000	...	...	...	...
Total, Industries	405516	425282	442866	455186	743229	937984	845000	...	...	...	...
Producers of Government Services	64469	73119	87801	121222	126577	159834	180000	...	...	...	...
Other Producers	...	...	...	...	...	...	...	...	...	...	...
Subtotal [e]	469985	498401	530667	576408	869806	1097818	1025000	...	...	...	...
Less: Imputed bank service charge	...	...	...	...	...	...	...	...	...	...	...
Plus: Import duties	...	...	...	...	...	...	...	...	...	...	...
Plus: Value added tax	...	...	...	...	...	...	...	...	...	...	...
Plus: Other adjustments [f]	65565	65717	68616	68389	84980	90049	92500	...	...	...	...
Equals: Gross Domestic Product	535550	564118	599283	644797	954786	1187867	1117500	...	...	...	...

a) Including engineering.
b) Including sewage services.
c) Restaurants and hotels are included in item 'Community, social and personal services'.
d) Business services are included in item 'Community, social and personal services'.
e) Gross domestic product in factor values.
f) Referring to indirect taxes net of subsidies.

1.11 Gross Domestic Product by Kind of Activity, in Constant Prices

Thousand Guyana dollars

	1970	1971	1972	1973	1974	1975	1976	1977	1978	1979	1980
					At constant prices of: 1970						
1 Agriculture, hunting, forestry and fishing	90158	96429	88058	87531	100464	97161	101215	...	...	...	...
2 Mining and quarrying	95495	92706	82325	79677	85239	85120	75020	...	...	...	...
3 Manufacturing	56965	64033	64960	65319	79004	89627	96443	...	...	...	...
4 Electricity, gas and water								...	...	...	...
5 Construction	36849	38324	40471	41467	38539	51289	55250	...	...	...	...
6 Wholesale and retail trade, restaurants and hotels [a]	53506	52909	52777	57864	58441	73049	76998	...	...	...	...
7 Transport, storage and communication	27726	28120	27568	29526	31035	33803	35434	...	...	...	...
8 Finance, insurance, real estate and business services [b]	27083	28902	29670	31113	32316	35220	37000	...	...	...	...
9 Community, social and personal services [a,b]	17734	18803	18461	18392	16733	16812	16700	...	...	...	...
Total, Industries	405516	420226	404290	410889	441771	482081	494060	...	...	...	...
Producers of Government Services	64469	65867	71191	79867	85191	106061	116399	...	...	...	...
Other Producers	...	...	...	...	...	...	...	...	...	...	...
Subtotal [c]	469985	486093	475481	490756	526962	588142	610459	...	...	...	...
Less: Imputed bank service charge	...	...	...	...	...	...	...	...	...	...	...
Plus: Import duties	...	...	...	...	...	...	...	...	...	...	...
Plus: Value added tax	...	...	...	...	...	...	...	...	...	...	...
Plus: Other adjustments [d]	65565	64619	64308	58352	60570	60558	57200	...	...	...	...
Equals: Gross Domestic Product	535550	550712	539789	549108	587532	648700	667659	...	...	...	...

a) Restaurants and hotels are included in item 'Community, social and personal services'.
b) Business services are included in item 'Community, social and personal services'.
c) Gross domestic product in factor values.
d) Referring to indirect taxes net of subsidies.

1.12 Relations Among National Accounting Aggregates

Thousand Guyana dollars

	1970	1971	1972	1973	1974	1975	1976	1977	1978	1979	1980
Gross Domestic Product	535550	564118	599283	644797	954786	1187867	1117500	...	...	...	...
Plus: Net factor income received from abroad	-42483	-36014	-22240	-25601	-48201	-33016	-57000	...	...	...	...
Equals: Gross National Product	493067	528104	577043	619196	906585	1154851	1060500	...	...	...	...
Less: Consumption of fixed capital	33785	33371	33368	35948	39976	46465	55000	...	...	...	...
Less: Net indirect taxes paid to supranational organisations	...	...	...	...	...	...	...	...	...	...	...

Guyana

1.12 Relations Among National Accounting Aggregates
(Continued)

Thousand Guyana dollars

	1970	1971	1972	1973	1974	1975	1976	1977	1978	1979	1980
Equals: National Income at Market Prices	459282	494733	543675	583248	866609	1108386	1005500	...	...	...	...
Plus: Net current transfers received from abroad	99	-873	-946	-1347	-8000	-9000	-16000	...	...	...	...
Equals: National Disposable Income at Market Prices	459381	493860	542729	581901	858609	1099386	989500	...	...	...	...
Less: Final consumption	412979	437653	480001	578230	674784	795381	969300	...	...	...	...
Statistical discrepancy	...	...	...	66	...	...	...	...	...	...	...
Equals: Net Saving	46402	56207	62728	3737	183825	304005	19806	...	...	...	...
Less: Surplus of the nation on current transactions	-45385	-15937	-30969	-134667	-38346	-32983	-350394	...	...	...	...
Statistical discrepancy	-3709	-415	-8141	1148	-10053	9095	-	...	...	...	...
Equals: Net Capital Formation	88078	71729	85556	139552	212118	346083	370200	...	...	...	...

Haiti

Source. Reply to the United Nations National Accounts Questionnaire from the Institut Haitien de Statistique, Port-au-prince. The official estimates are published by the Institut in 'Guide Economique de la Republique d'Haiti'.

General note. The estimates shown in the following tables have been prepared in accordance with the United Nations System of National Accounts so far as the existing data would permit.

1.1 Expenditure on the Gross Domestic Product, in Current Prices

Thousand Haitian gourdes — Fiscal year ending 30 September

	1970	1971	1972	1973	1974	1975	1976	1977	1978	1979	1980
1 General government final consumption expenditure	1571000	1679000	1735000	2133000	2615000	3165000	4100000	4617000	4790000	5226000	6205000
2 Private final consumption expenditure											
3 Gross capital formation	167000	192000	214000	306000	418000	540000	678000	767000	950000	1045000	1409000
4 Exports of goods and services	261000	369000	401000	516000	662000	784000	1046000	1287000	1400000	1413000	1962000
5 Less: Imports of goods and services	343000	426000	490000	621000	868000	1082000	1430000	1730000	1886000	2086000	2481000
Equals: Gross Domestic Product	1656000	1814000	1860000	2334000	2827000	3407000	4394000	4943000	5255000	5599000	7095000

1.2 Expenditure on the Gross Domestic Product, in Constant Prices

Thousand Haitian gourdes — Fiscal year ending 30 September

At constant prices of: 1976

	1970	1971	1972	1973	1974	1975	1976	1977	1978	1979	1980
1 General government final consumption expenditure	3108000	3115000	3087000	3163000	3372000	3460000	4101000	4340000	4477000	4686000	4799000
2 Private final consumption expenditure											
3 Gross capital formation	307000	314000	370000	457000	564000	595000	678000	704000	781000	892000	948000
4 Exports of goods and services	548000	835000	899000	1022000	976000	961000	1046000	1034000	1097000	1094000	1312000
5 Less: Imports of goods and services	599000	682000	739000	853000	904000	963000	1430000	1631000	1717000	1686000	1782000
Equals: Gross Domestic Product	3364000	3582000	3617000	3789000	4008000	4053000	4395000	4442000	4638000	4986000	5277000

1.3 Cost Components of the Gross Domestic Product

Thousand Haitian gourdes — Fiscal year ending 30 September

	1970	1971	1972	1973	1974	1975	1976	1977	1978	1979	1980
1 Indirect taxes, net	...	...	...	...	...	...	354414	...	...	...	...
a Indirect taxes paid	...	...	...	...	...	...	356364	...	...	...	...
b Less: Subsidies received	...	...	...	...	...	...	1950	...	...	...	...
2 Consumption of fixed capital	...	...	...	...	...	...	192962	...	...	...	...
3 Compensation of employees paid by resident producers to:	...	...	...	...	...	...	816245	...	...	...	...
4 Net operating surplus	...	...	...	...	...	...	3029404	...	...	...	...
Equals: Gross Domestic Product	1656000	1814000	1860000	2334000	2827000	3407000	4394000	4943000	5255000	5599000	...

1.4 General Government Current Receipts and Disbursements

Thousand Haitian gourdes — Fiscal year ending 30 September

	1970	1971	1972	1973	1974	1975	1976	1977	1978	1979	1980
Receipts											
1 Property and entrepreneurial income	...	...	...	...	...	...	4503	...	...	...	...
2 Taxes, fees and contributions	...	...	...	...	...	...	486183	...	...	...	...
a Indirect taxes	...	...	...	...	...	...	356364	...	...	...	...
b Direct taxes	...	...	...	...	...	...	69602	...	...	...	...
c Social security contributions	...	...	...	...	...	...	30522	...	...	...	...
d Compulsory fees, fines and penalties	...	...	...	...	...	...	29695	...	...	...	...
3 Other current receipts	...	...	...	...	...	...	121739	...	...	...	...
Total Current Receipts of General Government	...	...	...	...	...	...	612425	...	...	...	...
Disbursements											
1 General government final consumption expenditure	...	...	...	...	...	...	311270	...	...	...	...
a Compensation of employees	...	...	...	...	...	...	247086	...	...	...	...
b Consumption of fixed capital	...	...	...	...	...	...	8200	...	...	...	...
c Purchases of goods and services, net	...	...	...	...	...	...	55984	...	...	...	...
d Less: Own account production of fixed assets	...	...	...	...	...	...	...	...	...	...	...
e Indirect taxes paid, net	...	...	...	...	...	...	5560	...	...	...	...
2 Property income paid	...	...	...	...	...	...	5568	...	...	...	...

Haiti

1.4 General Government Current Receipts and Disbursements
(Continued)

Thousand Haitian gourdes — Fiscal year ending 30 September

	1970	1971	1972	1973	1974	1975	1976	1977	1978	1979	1980
a Interest	...	...	...	...	...	...	5556	...	...	...	...
b Net land rent and royalties	...	...	...	...	...	...	12	...	...	...	...
3 Subsidies	...	...	...	...	...	...	1950	...	...	...	...
4 Other current transfers paid	...	...	...	...	...	...	44771	...	...	...	...
a Social security benefits and social assistance grants	...	...	...	...	...	...	18169	...	...	...	...
b Other	...	...	...	...	...	...	26602	...	...	...	...
5 Net saving	...	...	...	...	...	...	248870	...	...	...	...
Total Current Disbursements and Net Saving of General Government	...	...	...	...	...	...	612425	...	...	...	...

1.10 Gross Domestic Product by Kind of Activity, in Current Prices

Thousand Haitian gourdes — Fiscal year ending 30 September

	1970	1971	1972	1973	1974	1975	1976	1977	1978	1979	1980
1 Agriculture, hunting, forestry and fishing	...	...	...	...	...	...	1675233	...	...	...	...
2 Mining and quarrying	...	...	...	...	...	...	83400	...	...	...	...
3 Manufacturing	...	...	...	...	...	...	663650	...	...	...	...
4 Electricity, gas and water	...	...	...	...	...	...	22865	...	...	...	...
5 Construction	...	...	...	...	...	...	226076	...	...	...	...
6 Wholesale and retail trade, restaurants and hotels	...	...	...	...	...	...	778663	...	...	...	...
7 Transport, storage and communication	...	...	...	...	...	...	88262	...	...	...	...
8 Finance, insurance, real estate and business services	...	...	...	...	...	...	241976	...	...	...	...
9 Community, social and personal services	...	...	...	...	...	...	102914	...	...	...	...
Total, Industries	...	...	...	...	...	...	3883038	...	...	...	...
Producers of Government Services	...	...	...	...	...	...	326715	...	...	...	...
Other Producers	...	...	...	...	...	...	...	...	...	...	...
Subtotal	...	...	...	...	...	...	4209754	...	...	...	...
Less: Imputed bank service charge	...	...	...	...	...	...	...	...	...	...	...
Plus: Import duties	...	...	...	...	...	...	185270	...	...	...	...
Plus: Value added tax	...	...	...	...	...	...	...	...	...	...	...
Equals: Gross Domestic Product	...	...	...	...	...	...	4395024	...	...	...	...

1.11 Gross Domestic Product by Kind of Activity, in Constant Prices

Thousand Haitian gourdes — Fiscal year ending 30 September

At constant prices of: 1976

	1970	1971	1972	1973	1974	1975	1976	1977	1978	1979	1980
1 Agriculture, hunting, forestry and fishing	1482466	1527700	1523660	1558904	1597353	1658446	1675233	1574878	1604393	1708539	1692185
2 Mining and quarrying	72202	84132	72246	83387	88153	62059	83400	80681	72333	69822	66728
3 Manufacturing	438466	501660	539325	536435	605746	555762	663650	738397	777605	863940	977597
4 Electricity, gas and water	9929	11575	12913	15578	17322	18770	22865	24788	29622	33264	35772
5 Construction	87738	100599	116866	154343	197363	205308	226076	234124	254290	280357	288337
6 Wholesale and retail trade, restaurants and hotels	549397	607026	597964	640979	670125	680426	778662	796277	837625	915745	972207
7 Transport, storage and communication	59041	67447	73118	70302	74121	80026	88262	109533	104070	101369	106347
8 Finance, insurance, real estate and business services	209712	212283	216345	221190	229949	239475	241976	246813	251891	257443	261771
9 Community, social and personal services	93812	96801	102211	96896	94664	104484	102914	110282	130197	143689	152323
Total, Industries	3002763	3209223	3254647	3378014	3574796	3604756	3883038	3915773	4062026	4374168	4553267
Producers of Government Services	158597	173147	166180	206647	273462	302194	326715	344782	390163	413687	515230
Other Producers	...	...	...	...	...	...	...	...	...	...	...
Subtotal	3161360	3382370	3420828	3584661	3848258	3906950	4209754	4260555	4452189	4787855	5068497
Less: Imputed bank service charge	...	...	...	...	...	...	...	...	...	...	...
Plus: Import duties	203920	200974	196093	204484	160827	146582	185270	181416	185159	198239	213153
Plus: Value added tax	...	...	...	...	...	...	...	...	...	...	...
Plus: Other adjustments	...	...	...	...	...	...	...	...	1032	...	4440
Equals: Gross Domestic Product	3365280	3583344	3616921	3789145	4009085	4053532	4395024	4441971	4638380	4986094	5277210

Haiti

1.12 Relations Among National Accounting Aggregates

Thousand Haitian gourdes — Fiscal year ending 30 September

	1970	1971	1972	1973	1974	1975	1976	1977	1978	1979	1980
Gross Domestic Product	1656000	1814000	1860000	2334000	2827000	3407000	4394000	4943000	5255000	5599000	...
Plus: Net factor income received from abroad	-14000	-17000	-20000	-21000	-28000	-34000	-43000	-62000	-76000	-69000	
Equals: Gross National Product	1642000	1797000	1839000	2314000	2800000	3374000	4351000	4881000	5179000	5530000	
Less: Consumption of fixed capital	48000	56000	55000	64000	71000	89000	108000	123000	152000	141000	...
Less: Net indirect taxes paid to supranational organisations	...	...	...	...	...	...	...	...	...	...	
Equals: National Income at Market Prices	1594000	1741000	1784000	2250000	2729000	3285000	4243000	4758000	5027000	5389000	
Plus: Net current transfers received from abroad	109000	94000	142000	120000	124000	197000	325000	317000	339000	450000	
Equals: National Disposable Income at Market Prices	1703000	1835000	1926000	2370000	2853000	3482000	4568000	5075000	5366000	5839000	...
Less: Final consumption	1571000	1679000	1735000	2133000	2615000	3165000	4100000	4617000	4790000	5226000	
Equals: Net Saving	132000	156000	191000	237000	238000	317000	468000	458000	576000	614000	
Less: Surplus of the nation on current transactions	12000	20000	32000	-5000	-110000	-135	-101000	-187000	-223000	-292000	
Equals: Net Capital Formation	120000	136000	159000	242000	348000	452000	569000	645000	799000	906000	...

4.3 Derivation of Value Added by Kind of Activity, ISIC Divisions, in Current Prices

Thousand Haitian gourdes — Fiscal year ending 30 September

All Producers

		1976	
	Gross Output	Intermediate Consumption	Value Added
1 Agriculture, hunting, forestry and fishing	1796233	121000	1675233
a Agriculture and hunting	1464052	50587	1413465
b Forestry and logging	332181	70413	261768
c Fishing			
2 Mining and quarrying	98592	15192	83400
3 Manufacturing	1925489	1261838	663651
a Manufacture of food, beverages and tobacco	940310	687184	253126
b Textile, wearing apparel and leather industries	318496	182922	135574
c Manufacture of wood and wood products, including furniture	...	...	...
d Manufacture of paper and paper products, printing and publishing	...	...	...
e Manufacture of chemicals and chemical petroleum, coal, rubber and plastic products	150253	97594	52659
f Manufacture of non-metallic mineral products, except products of petroleum and coal	68433	35678	32755
g Basic metal industries	...	...	...
h Manufacture of fabricated metal products, machinery and equipment	218659	132621	86038
i Other manufacturing industries	229338	125839	103499
4 Electricity, gas and water	48823	25958	22865
a Electricity, gas and steam	48823	25958	22865
b Water works and supply	...	...	...

Haiti

4.3 Derivation of Value Added by Kind of Activity, ISIC Divisions, in Current Prices
(Continued)

Thousand Haitian gourdes — Fiscal year ending 30 September

		1976	
	Gross Output	Intermediate Consumption	Value Added
5 Construction	493195	267119	226076
6 Wholesale and retail trade, restaurants and hotels	901849	123186	778663
a Wholesale and retail trade	869438	106111	763327
b Restaurants and hotels	32411	17075	15336
7 Transport, storage and communication	152091	63829	88262
8 Finance, insurance, real estate and business services	319373	77397	241976
a Financial institutions	67987	58670	9317
b Insurance			
c Real estate and business services	251386	18727	232659
9 Community, social and personal services	142997	40083	102914
a Sanitary and similar services			
b Social and related community services	142997	40083	102914
c Recreational and cultural services			
d Personal and household services			
Total, Industries	5878642	1995602	3883038
Producers of Government Services	438532	111817	326715
Other Producers	...	...	...
Total	6317174	2107419	4209755
Imputed bank service charge	...	...	...
Import duties	...	...	...
Value added tax	...	...	...
Total	...	...	...

4.4 Derivation of Value Added by Kind of Activity, ISIC Divisions, in Constant Prices

Thousand Haitian gourdes — Fiscal year ending 30 September

At constant prices of: 1976 — All Producers

	1970 GO	1970 IC	1970 VA	1971 GO	1971 IC	1971 VA	1972 GO	1972 IC	1972 VA	1973 GO	1973 IC	1973 VA
1 Agriculture, hunting, forestry and fishing	...	...	1482466	...	...	1527700	...	...	1523660	...	...	1558904
a Agriculture and hunting	...	...	1254196	...	...	1294124	...	...	1284295	...	...	1314971
b Forestry and logging	...	...	228270	...	...	233576	...	...	239365	...	...	243933
c Fishing	...	...		...	...		...	...		...	...	
2 Mining and quarrying	...	...	72202	...	...	84132	...	...	72246	...	...	83387
3 Manufacturing	...	...	438466	...	...	501660	...	...	539325	...	...	536435
a Manufacture of food, beverages and tobacco	...	...	146311	...	...	171279	...	...	198263	...	...	197762
b Textile, wearing apparel and leather industries	...	...	138730	...	...	133842	...	...	172633	...	...	108831
c Manufacture of wood and wood products, including furniture												
d Manufacture of paper and paper products, printing and publishing	...	...	...	...	...	...	...	...	...	...	...	...
e Manufacture of chemicals and chemical petroleum, coal, rubber and plastic products	...	...	29851	...	...	40278	...	...	41827	...	...	44930
f Manufacture of non-metallic mineral products, except products of petroleum and coal	...	...	9845	...	...	11334	...	...	13173	...	...	17609
g Basic metal industries	...	...	...	...	...	...	...	...	...	...	...	...
h Manufacture of fabricated metal products, machinery and equipment	...	...	52832	...	...	125518	...	...	85911	...	...	110517
i Other manufacturing industries	...	...	60897	...	...	19409	...	...	27518	...	...	56786
4 Electricity, gas and water	...	...	9929	...	...	11575	...	...	12913	...	...	15578

Haiti

4.4 Derivation of Value Added by Kind of Activity, ISIC Divisions, in Constant Prices
(Continued)

Thousand Haitian gourdes — Fiscal year ending 30 September

	1970 G.O.	1970 I.C.	1970 V.A.	1971 G.O.	1971 I.C.	1971 V.A.	1972 G.O.	1972 I.C.	1972 V.A.	1973 G.O.	1973 I.C.	1973 V.A.
				At constant prices of: 1976								
5 Construction	...	...	87738	...	...	100599	...	...	116866	...	...	154343
6 Wholesale and retail trade, restaurants and hotels	...	...	549397	...	...	607026	...	...	597964	...	...	640979
a Wholesale and retail trade	...	...	545458	...	...	599281	...	...	590635	...	...	632975
b Restaurants and hotels	...	...	3939	...	...	7745	...	...	7329	...	...	8004
7 Transport, storage and communication	...	...	59041	...	...	67447	...	...	73118	...	...	70302
8 Finance, insurance, real estate and business services	...	...	209712	...	...	212283	...	...	216345	...	...	221190
a Financial institutions	...	...	4462	...	...	4776	...	...	5660	...	...	5681
b Insurance	...	...		...	...		...	...		...	...	
c Real estate and business services	...	...	205250	...	...	207507	...	...	210685	...	...	215509
9 Community, social and personal services	...	...	93812	...	...	96801	...	...	102211	...	...	96896
Total, Industries	...	...	3002763	...	...	3209223	...	...	3254647	...	...	3378014
Producers of Government Services	...	...	158597	...	...	173147	...	...	166180	...	...	206647
Other Producers	...	...	...	...	...	...	...	...	...	...	...	...
Total	...	...	3161360	...	...	3382370	...	...	3420827	...	...	3584661
Imputed bank service charge	...	...	...	...	...	...	...	...	...	...	...	...
Import duties	...	...	...	...	...	...	...	...	...	...	...	...
Value added tax	...	...	...	...	...	...	...	...	...	...	...	...
Total	...	...	...	...	...	...	...	...	...	...	...	...

	1974 G.O.	1974 I.C.	1974 V.A.	1975 G.O.	1975 I.C.	1975 V.A.	1976 G.O.	1976 I.C.	1976 V.A.	1977 G.O.	1977 I.C.	1977 V.A.
				At constant prices of: 1976								
				All Producers								
1 Agriculture, hunting, forestry and fishing	...	...	1597353	...	...	1658446	1796233	121000	1675233	...	...	1574878
a Agriculture and hunting	...	...	1346039	...	...	1398997	1464052	50587	1413465	...	...	1321590
b Forestry and logging	...	...	251314	...	...	259449	332181	70413	261768	...	...	253288
c Fishing	...	...		...	...		...	...		...	...	
2 Mining and quarrying	...	...	88153	...	...	62059	98592	15192	83400	...	...	80681
3 Manufacturing	...	...	605746	...	...	555762	1925489	1261838	663651	...	...	738397
a Manufacture of food, beverages and tobacco	...	...	216273	...	...	240067	940310	687184	253126	...	...	267666
b Textile, wearing apparel and leather industries	...	...	125979	...	...	76717	318496	182922	135574	...	...	130449
c Manufacture of wood and wood products, including furniture	...	...	...	...	...	...	...	...	...	...	...	...
d Manufacture of paper and paper products, printing and publishing	...	...	...	...	...	...	...	...	...	...	...	...
e Manufacture of chemicals and chemical petroleum, coal, rubber and plastic products	...	...	56786	...	...	39243	150253	97594	52659	...	...	47641
f Manufacture of non-metallic mineral products, except products of petroleum and coal	...	...	22416	...	...	23631	68433	35678	32755	...	...	36237
g Basic metal industries	...	...	...	...	...	...	...	...	...	...	...	...
h Manufacture of fabricated metal products, machinery and equipment	...	...	131022	...	...	87702	218659	132621	86038	...	...	122233
i Other manufacturing industries	...	...	53270	...	...	88402	229338	125839	103499	...	...	134171
4 Electricity, gas and water	...	...	17322	...	...	18770	48823	25958	22865	...	...	24788

Haiti

4.4 Derivation of Value Added by Kind of Activity, ISIC Divisions, in Constant Prices
(Continued)

Thousand Haitian gourdes — Fiscal year ending 30 September

	1974 Gross Output	1974 Intermediate Consumption	1974 Value Added	1975 Gross Output	1975 Intermediate Consumption	1975 Value Added	1976 Gross Output	1976 Intermediate Consumption	1976 Value Added	1977 Gross Output	1977 Intermediate Consumption	1977 Value Added
					At constant prices of:1976							
5 Construction	...	...	197363	...	...	205308	493195	267119	226076	...	...	234124
6 Wholesale and retail trade, restaurants and hotels	...	...	670125	...	...	680426	901848	123186	778662	...	...	796277
a Wholesale and retail trade	...	...	661225	...	...	669355	869437	106111	763326	...	...	779052
b Restaurants and hotels	...	...	8900	...	...	11071	32411	17075	15336	...	...	17225
7 Transport, storage and communication	...	...	74121	...	...	80026	152091	63829	88262	...	...	109533
8 Finance, insurance, real estate and business services	...	...	229949	...	...	239475	314373	72397	241976	...	...	246813
a Financial institutions	...	...	7445	...	...	7663	62987	53670	9317	...	...	10129
b Insurance	...	...		...	...					...	...	
c Real estate and business services	...	...	222504	...	...	231812	251386	18727	232659	...	...	236684
9 Community, social and personal services	...	...	94664	...	...	104484	142997	40083	102914	...	...	110282
Total, Industries	...	...	3574796	...	...	3604756	5878642	1995602	3883040	...	...	3930190
Producers of Government Services	...	...	273462	...	...	302194	438532	111817	326715	...	...	344782
Other Producers	...	...	...	...	...	...	...	...	...	...	...	...
Total	...	...	3848258	...	...	3906950	6317174	2107419	4209754	...	...	4260555
Imputed bank service charge	...	...	...	...	...	...	...	...	...	...	...	...
Import duties	...	...	...	...	...	...	...	...	...	...	...	...
Value added tax	...	...	...	...	...	...	...	...	...	...	...	...
Total	...	...	...	...	...	...	...	...	...	...	...	...

	1978 Gross Output	1978 Intermediate Consumption	1978 Value Added	1979 Gross Output	1979 Intermediate Consumption	1979 Value Added	1980 Gross Output	1980 Intermediate Consumption	1980 Value Added
		At constant prices of:1976							
		All Producers							
1 Agriculture, hunting, forestry and fishing	...	...	1604393	...	...	1708539	...	...	1692185
a Agriculture and hunting	...	...	1334170	...	...	1433393	...	...	1414030
b Forestry and logging	...	...	270223	...	...	275144	...	...	278155
c Fishing	...	...		...	...		...	...	
2 Mining and quarrying	...	...	72333	...	...	69822	...	...	66728
3 Manufacturing	...	...	777605	...	...	863940	...	...	977597
a Manufacture of food, beverages and tobacco	...	...	253540	...	...	229227	...	...	343299
b Textile, wearing apparel and leather industries	...	...	133740	...	...	124054	...	...	139533
c Manufacture of wood and wood products, including furniture									
d Manufacture of paper and paper products, printing and publishing	...	...							
e Manufacture of chemicals and chemical petroleum, coal, rubber and plastic products	...	...	58159	...	...	65229	...	...	64946
f Manufacture of non-metallic mineral products, except products of petroleum and coal	...	...	36221	...	...	35271	...	...	35936
g Basic metal industries	...	...	...						
h Manufacture of fabricated metal products, machinery and equipment	...	...	193073	...	...	275828	...	...	272651
i Other manufacturing industries	...	...	102289	...	...	134331	...	...	121226
4 Electricity, gas and water	...	...	29622	...	...	33264	...	...	35772

Haiti

4.4 Derivation of Value Added by Kind of Activity, ISIC Divisions, in Constant Prices
(Continued)

Thousand Haitian gourdes — Fiscal year ending 30 September

At constant prices of: 1976

	1978 Gross Output	1978 Intermediate Consumption	1978 Value Added	1979 Gross Output	1979 Intermediate Consumption	1979 Value Added	1980 Gross Output	1980 Intermediate Consumption	1980 Value Added
5 Construction	...	...	254290	...	...	280357	...	...	288337
6 Wholesale and retail trade, restaurants and hotels	...	...	837625	...	...	876528	...	...	941793
a Wholesale and retail trade	...	...	806073	...	...	837311	...	...	911379
b Restaurants and hotels	...	...	31552	...	...	39217	...	...	30414
7 Transport, storage and communication	...	...	104070	...	...	101369	...	...	106347
8 Finance, insurance, real estate and business services	...	...	251891	...	...	257443	...	...	261771
a Financial institutions	...	...	11042	...	...	12290	...	...	12151
b Insurance	...	...		...	...		...	...	
c Real estate and business services	...	...	240849	...	...	245153	...	...	249620
9 Community, social and personal services	...	...	130197	...	...	143689	...	...	152323
Total, Industries	...	...	4081877	...	...	2644113	...	...	2847051
Producers of Government Services	...	...	390163	...	...	413687	...	...	515230
Other Producers	...	...	...	...	...	...	...	...	...
Total	...	...	4452189	...	...	4787855	...	...	5068498
Imputed bank service charge	...	...	...	...	...	...	...	...	...
Import duties	...	...	...	...	...	...	...	...	...
Value added tax	...	...	...	...	...	...	...	...	...
Total	...	...	...	...	...	...	...	...	...

Honduras

General note. The preparation of national accounts statistics in Honduras is undertaken by the Departmento de Estudios Economicos, Banco Central de Honduras, Tegucigalpa, D.C. The official estimates are published in 'Cuentas Nacionales'. A detailed description of sources and methods used for the national accounts estimation is found in 'Metodologia de cuentas nacionales de los paises centroamericanos' issued by the Consejo Monetario Centroamericano in October 1976. The estimates are generally in accordance with the classifications and definitions recommended in the United Nations System of National Accounts (SNA). The following tables have been prepared from successive replies to the United Nations national accounts questionnaire. When the scope and coverage of the estimates differ for conceptual or statistical reasons from the definitions and classifications recommended in SNA, a footnote is indicated to the relevant tables.

Sources and methods:

(a) Gross domestic product. Gross domestic product is estimated mainly through the production approach.

(b) Expenditure on the gross domestic product. The expenditure approach is used to estimate government final consumption expenditure and exports and imports of goods and services. The commodity-flow approach is used for private final consumption expenditure and for gross capital formation. Government final consumption expenditure is estimated on the basis of government accounts. Changes in stocks are estimated on the basis of information obtained from various sectors such as the banana industry, the mines, the petroleum sector and the trade enterprises. Private investment consists of gross value of production in the construction sector, plus industrial production of capital goods which are adjusted to purchasers' values. Public investment is estimated from public sector data on settlements by type of construction and classes of machinery and equipment. The estimates of exports and imports of goods and services are based on the balance of payment data. Private consumption expenditure is estimated as a residual. For the constant price estimates, private final consumption expenditure is estimated as a residual while all other items of GDP by expenditure type are deflated by various price indexes.

(c) Cost-structure of the gross domestic product. Estimates of labour income are derived from sources such as censuses and surveys, supplemented by information on wages and salaries paid by various government agencies and other public bodies. Estimates of profits of enterprises and professional incomes are obtained from the Direccion General del Impuesto sobre la Renta. Estimates of interest and dividend payments received by household and private non-profit institutions are derived as a residual. Indirect taxes and subsidies are estimated on the basis of government sources. For consumption of fixed capital, no specific information is available.

(d) Gross domestic product by kind of economic activity. The table of gross domestic product by kind of economic activity is prepared in factor values. The production approach is used to estimate value added of most industries. The income approach is, however, used to estimate value added of producers of government services, part of the transport sectors and other private services. For the agricultural crop production, information is obtained directly from the most important export enterprises while for other products, estimates are obtained from consumption per capita data adjusted for exports and imports. Surveys are conducted to obtain information on basic production of grains. Agricultural censuses were held in 1953, 1965 and 1974. The Instituto Hondureno del Cafe provides complete information for coffee production. The banana companies in the northern zone are visited annually while for the rest of the country, consumption per capita data are taken into account together with prices collected from native producers. Livestock production information is gathered from the most important producers with adjustments made for clandestine or uncontrolled transaction. Inputs are estimated as 30 percent of the gross value of production. The production in the forestry sector is calculated as a function of household and industrial consumption of firewood, and extrapolated by an index. The estimates of fishing are calculated on the basis of information from the Direccion General de Pesca, the foreign trade statistics and per capita consumption data. For metal mining, the statistical information is obtained directly while estimates for non-metallic mineral are based on inputs used in the construction sector using certain coefficients derived from analysis of construction costs. The estimates of manufacturing are based on censuses, surveys and sample data provided by the Direccion General de Industrias and the Departmento de Estudios Industriales. Information on electricity, gas and water is obtained directly from concerned enterprises. The data available cover gross values of production, aggregated values, physical production, installed capacity and personal occupation. Information on public construction is taken directly from the municipalities. Based on the information obtained from them, a sample is taken from which the growth of private construction can be measured. The population and housing censuses are also taken into account for dwellings. For the trade sector, the estimates are based on the gross value of agricultural and industrial production by item. The value of imports and exports are estimated from foreign trade statistics and information received from the Direccion de Tributacion Directa. In estimating road transport, inforamtion on registered vehicles for rental is used. Data on income and expenditure by type of vehicle, depreciation and profits are obtained. Information for financial institutions is obtained from the Superintendencia de Bancos, which provides financial statements for all banks in the system and insurance companies. The estimates of ownership of dwellings are based on census information for 1949, 1961 and 1974 covering the number of dwellings and the average rents paid and imputed. For producers of government services, information is obtained directly from the Contaduria General de la Nacion and the Asesoria Tecnica Municipal. For private services, use is made of employment data, classified by type of service rendered and data on average wages and salaries from other information sources. For domestic services, data on employment and wages are basis for estimating the value added with 75 percent added to the cash figures for board and lodging as wages and salaries in kind. For the constant price estimates, value added of the agricultural sector is either extrapolated by quantity indexes for output or deflated by price indexes. For the industrial activity sector, trade, transport and storage, financial institutions and insurance and private services, value added is extrapolated by quantity index. For the remaining sectors, current values are deflated by various price indexes.

1.1 Expenditure on the Gross Domestic Product, in Current Prices

Million Honduran lempiras

	1970	1971	1972	1973	1974	1975	1976	1977	1978	1979	1980
1 General government final consumption expenditure	166	175	193	186	242	278	348	417	461	530	682
2 Private final consumption expenditure	1073	1142	1228	1352	1540	1743	1914	2084	2358	2788	3396
3 Gross capital formation	302	250	256	348	542	401	449	750	987	1093	1316
a Increase in stocks	34	-3	11	23	109	-75	-101	39	46	89	81
b Gross fixed capital formation	268	253	245	325	433	476	550	711	941	1004	1235
4 Exports of goods and services	395	426	461	579	656	680	898	1149	1366	1648	1858
5 Less: Imports of goods and services	490	442	449	600	907	890	1032	1311	1555	1863	2274
Equals: Gross Domestic Product [a]	1446	1551	1689	1865	2073	2212	2577	3089	3617	4196	4978

a) Data in this table have been revised, therefore they are not strictly comparable with the unrevised data in the other tables.

1.2 Expenditure on the Gross Domestic Product, in Constant Prices

Million Honduran lempiras

	1970	1971	1972	1973	1974	1975	1976	1977	1978	1979	1980
	\multicolumn{11}{c}{At constant prices of:1966}										
1 General government final consumption expenditure	152	157	167	154	177	189	225	248	260	274	297
2 Private final consumption expenditure	984	1023	1064	1119	1129	1182	1237	1291	1338	1449	1489
3 Gross capital formation	234	193	199	251	326	228	231	356	430	434	472
a Increase in stocks	27	-2	7	15	69	-45	-58	22	25	41	35
b Gross fixed capital formation	207	195	192	236	257	273	289	334	405	393	437
4 Exports of goods and services	383	435	417	441	401	376	426	433	490	587	563
5 Less: Imports of goods and services	441	390	379	457	512	485	525	654	759	790	816
Equals: Gross Domestic Product [a]	1312	1418	1468	1508	1521	1490	1594	1674	1759	1954	2005

a) Data in this table have been revised, therefore they are not strictly comparable with the unrevised data in the other tables.

Honduras

1.3 Cost Components of the Gross Domestic Product

Million Honduran lempiras

	1970	1971	1972	1973	1974	1975	1976	1977	1978	1979	1980
1 Indirect taxes, net	139	143	151	169	199	220	286	414	413	496	545
a Indirect taxes paid	141	145	153	171	201	222	290	415	417	499	548
b Less: Subsidies received	2	2	2	2	2	2	4	1	4	3	3
2 Consumption of fixed capital	53	55	57	61	118	95	115	136	166	200	261
3 Compensation of employees paid by resident producers to:	1254	1353	1481	1635	1756	1897	2176	2539	3038	3500	4172
4 Net operating surplus											
Equals: Gross Domestic Product a	1446	1551	1689	1865	2073	2212	2577	3089	3617	4196	4978

a) Data in this table have been revised, therefore they are not strictly comparable with the unrevised data in the other tables.

1.4 General Government Current Receipts and Disbursements

Million Honduran lempiras

	1970	1971	1972	1973	1974	1975	1976	1977	1978	1979	1980
Receipts											
1 Property and entrepreneurial income	7	8	9	15	32	36	...	...	...	...	...
2 Taxes, fees and contributions	176	178	190	220	266	293	...	...	...	...	...
a Indirect taxes [a]	124	127	136	158	174	183	...	...	...	...	...
b Direct taxes	44	44	45	48	83	94	...	...	...	...	...
c Social security contributions	6	5	7	10	7	9	...	...	...	...	...
d Compulsory fees, fines and penalties	2	2	2	4	2	7	...	...	...	...	...
3 Other current receipts	9	9	10	10	42	29	...	...	...	...	...
Total Current Receipts of General Government	192	195	209	245	340	358	...	...	...	...	...
Disbursements											
1 General government final consumption expenditure	166	175	193	186	242	278	...	...	...	...	...
a Compensation of employees	...	...	...	...	...	...	...	...	...	...	...
b Consumption of fixed capital	13	14	15	15	18	18	...	...	...	...	...
c Purchases of goods and services, net	...	...	...	...	...	...	...	...	...	...	...
d Less: Own account production of fixed assets	...	...	...	...	...	...	...	...	...	...	...
e Indirect taxes paid, net	...	...	...	...	...	...	...	...	...	...	...
2 Property income paid	8	11	13	14	13	20	...	...	...	...	...
3 Subsidies [b]	-15	-16	-15	-11	-25	-36	...	...	...	...	...
4 Other current transfers paid	9	7	14	15	20	14	...	...	...	...	...
a Social security benefits and social assistance grants	...	...	...	...	...	...	...	...	...	...	...
b Other	9	7	14	15	20	14	...	...	...	...	...
5 Net saving	24	18	4	41	90	82	...	...	...	...	...
Total Current Disbursements and Net Saving of General Government	192	195	209	245	340	358	...	...	...	...	...

a) Including profits of government enterprises.
b) Including losses of government enterprises.

1.6 Current Income and Outlay of Households and Non-Profit Institutions

Million Honduran lempiras

	1970	1971	1972	1973	1974	1975	1976	1977	1978	1979	1980
Receipts											
1 Compensation of employees	572	640	688	754	826	911	...	...	...	...	...
2 Property and entrepreneurial income received	554	582	603	662	713	742	...	...	...	...	...
3 Current transfers received	18	16	22	24	49	27	...	...	...	...	...
a Social security benefits and social assistance grants received	7	5	10	12	16	10	...	...	...	...	...
b Other	11	11	12	12	33	17	...	...	...	...	...
Total Current Receipts	1144	1238	1313	1440	1588	1680	...	...	...	...	...

Honduras

1.6 Current Income and Outlay of Households and Non-Profit Institutions
(Continued)

Million Honduran lempiras

	1970	1971	1972	1973	1974	1975	1976	1977	1978	1979	1980
Disbursements											
1 Private final consumption expenditure	1061	1136	1187	1307	1489	1614	...	...	...	...	...
2 Property income paid	...	...	...	...	...	...	...	...	...	...	...
3 Direct taxes and other payments n.e.c. to general government	31	34	37	45	55	72	...	...	...	...	...
4 Other current transfers paid	5	5	6	5	6	7	...	...	...	...	...
5 Net saving	47	63	83	83	38	-13	...	...	...	...	...
Total Current Disbursements and Net Saving	1144	1238	1313	1440	1588	1680	...	...	...	...	...

1.7 External Transactions on Current Account, Summary

Million Honduran lempiras

	1970	1971	1972	1973	1974	1975	1976	1977	1978	1979	1980
Payments to the Rest of the World											
1 Imports of goods and services	485	436	449	600	908	900	...	...	...	...	...
2 Factor income paid to the rest of the world	53	58	64	79	40	71	...	...	...	...	...
3 Indirect taxes paid to supranational organizations	...	...	...	...	...	...	...	...	...	...	...
4 Current transfers to the rest of the world	7	7	9	8	10	11	...	...	...	...	...
5 Surplus of the nation on current transactions	-127	-51	-25	-71	-212	-241	...	...	...	...	...
Payments to the Rest of the World and Surplus of the Nation on Current Transactions	409	425	497	616	746	742	...	...	...	...	...
Receipts From The Rest of the World											
1 Exports of goods and services	376	391	461	577	653	675	...	...	...	...	...
a Exports of merchandise f.o.b.	350	364	430	537	603	619	...	...	...	...	...
b Other	26	27	31	40	50	56	...	...	...	...	...
2 Factor income received from rest of the world	13	13	14	17	18	21	...	...	...	...	...
3 Subsidies received from supranational organisations	...	...	...	...	...	...	...	...	...	...	...
4 Current transfers from rest of the world	20	21	22	22	75	46	...	...	...	...	...
Receipts from the Rest of the World on Current Transactions	409	425	497	616	746	742	...	...	...	...	...

1.8 Capital Transactions of The Nation, Summary

Million Honduran lempiras

	1970	1971	1972	1973	1974	1975	1976	1977	1978	1979	1980
Finance of Gross Capital Formation											
Gross saving	185	199	231	272	307	204	...	...	...	...	...
1 Consumption of fixed capital	53	55	57	61	118	95	...	...	...	...	...
a General government	13	14	15	15	18	18	...	...	...	...	...
b Corporate and quasi-corporate enterprises	17	20	21	24	65	47	...	...	...	...	...
c Other	23	21	21	22	35	30	...	...	...	...	...
2 Net saving	132	144	174	211	189	109	...	...	...	...	...
a General government	24	18	4	41	90	82	...	...	...	...	...
b Corporate and quasi-corporate enterprises	61	63	87	87	61	40	...	...	...	...	...
c Other	47	63	83	83	38	-13	...	...	...	...	...
Less: Surplus of the nation on current transactions	-127	-51	-25	-71	-212	-241	...	...	...	...	...
Finance of Gross Capital Formation	312	250	256	343	519	445	...	...	...	...	...
Gross Capital Formation											
Increase in stocks	39	-6	7	20	119	-11	...	...	...	...	...
Gross fixed capital formation	273	256	249	323	400	456	...	...	...	...	...
1 General government	4	2	2	9	17	20	...	...	...	...	...
2 Corporate and quasi-corporate enterprises	...	...	...	...	...	...	...	...	...	...	...
3 Other	...	...	...	...	...	...	...	...	...	...	...
Gross Capital Formation	312	250	256	343	519	445	...	...	...	...	...

Honduras

1.10 Gross Domestic Product by Kind of Activity, in Current Prices

Million Honduran lempiras

	1970	1971	1972	1973	1974	1975	1976	1977	1978	1979	1980
1 Agriculture, hunting, forestry and fishing	425	454	496	560	573	571	698	867	1002	1197	1384
2 Mining and quarrying	30	28	30	43	64	53	50	55	60	67	80
3 Manufacturing	181	198	218	245	280	314	361	435	540	648	778
4 Electricity, gas and water	18	20	23	27	27	36	39	45	51	60	73
5 Construction	63	63	66	73	96	108	118	140	169	200	220
6 Wholesale and retail trade, restaurants and hotels [a]	171	183	189	197	216	242	280	300	390	477	582
7 Transport, storage and communication	102	117	125	133	149	166	185	206	256	316	386
8 Finance, insurance, real estate and business services	134	143	159	177	200	218	244	283	315	362	428
9 Community, social and personal services [a]	139	153	170	183	207	216	232	240	280	336	398
Total, Industries	1263	1359	1476	1638	1812	1924	2207	2571	3063	3663	4329
Producers of Government Services	44	49	62	58	62	68	84	100	115	134	159
Other Producers	...	...	...	...	...	...	...	...	...	...	...
Subtotal [b]	1307	1408	1538	1696	1874	1992	2291	2671	3178	3797	4488
Less: Imputed bank service charge	...	...	...	...	...	...	...	...	...	...	...
Plus: Import duties	...	...	...	...	...	...	...	...	...	...	...
Plus: Value added tax	...	...	...	...	...	...	...	...	...	...	...
Plus: Other adjustments [c]	139	143	151	169	199	220	286	418	460	535	620
Equals: Gross Domestic Product [d]	1446	1551	1689	1865	2073	2212	2577	3089	3638	4332	5108

a) Restaurants and hotels are included in item 'Community, social and personal services'.
b) Gross domestic product in factor values.
c) Referring to indirect taxes net of subsidies.
d) Data in this table have been revised, therefore they are not strictly comparable with the unrevised data in the other tables.

1.11 Gross Domestic Product by Kind of Activity, in Constant Prices

Million Honduran lempiras

	1970	1971	1972	1973	1974	1975	1976	1977	1978	1979	1980
At constant prices of: 1966											
1 Agriculture, hunting, forestry and fishing	405	438	446	462	417	378	416	448	469	505	591
2 Mining and quarrying	26	24	26	34	45	33	28	27	28	29	30
3 Manufacturing	170	178	185	192	190	195	215	236	260	281	297
4 Electricity, gas and water	13	13	14	15	16	17	18	19	20	21	22
5 Construction	44	43	46	50	50	52	54	57	63	68	66
6 Wholesale and retail trade, restaurants and hotels [a]	153	158	147	147	145	147	155	158	179	194	201
7 Transport, storage and communication	94	105	108	111	120	125	132	137	151	163	169
8 Finance, insurance, real estate and business services	113	119	127	135	144	151	161	174	182	191	97
9 Community, social and personal services [a]	133	140	151	157	167	168	171	175	187	193	197
Total, Industries	1151	1218	1250	1303	1294	1266	1350	1431	1539	1645	1670
Producers of Government Services	42	46	57	51	48	49	57	63	67	71	74
Other Producers	...	...	...	...	...	...	...	...	...	...	...
Subtotal [b]	1193	1264	1307	1354	1342	1315	1407	1489	1606	1716	1744
Less: Imputed bank service charge	...	...	...	...	...	...	...	...	...	...	...
Plus: Import duties	...	...	...	...	...	...	...	...	...	...	...
Plus: Value added tax	...	...	...	...	...	...	...	...	...	...	...
Plus: Other adjustments [c]	127	128	128	135	143	145	176	232	236	250	272
Equals: Gross Domestic Product	1320	1392	1435	1489	1485	1460	1583	1721	1842	1966	2016

a) Restaurants and hotels are included in item 'Community, social and personal services'.
b) Gross domestic product in factor values.
c) Referring to indirect taxes net of subsidies.

1.12 Relations Among National Accounting Aggregates

Million Honduran lempiras

	1970	1971	1972	1973	1974	1975	1976	1977	1978	1979	1980
Gross Domestic Product	1446	1551	1689	1865	2073	2212	2577	3089	3617	4196	4978
Plus: Net factor income received from abroad	-40	-45	-50	-62	-22	-50	-102	-124	-157	-210	-268
Factor income received	13	13	14	17	18	21	29	38	50	70	78
Less: Factor income paid	53	58	64	79	40	71	131	162	207	280	346
Equals: Gross National Product [a]	1406	1506	1639	1803	2051	2162	2475	2965	3460	3986	4710

Honduras

1.12 Relations Among National Accounting Aggregates
(Continued)

Million Honduran lempiras

	1970	1971	1972	1973	1974	1975	1976	1977	1978	1979	1980
Less: Consumption of fixed capital	53	55	57	61	118	95	115	136	166	200	261
Less: Net indirect taxes paid to supranational organisations	...	...	...	...	...	...	...	...	...	...	...
Equals: National Income at Market Prices [a]	1353	1451	1582	1742	1933	2067	2360	2829	3294	3786	4449
Plus: Net current transfers received from abroad	13	14	13	14	65	35	...	...	...	...	...
Current transfers received	20	21	22	22	75	46	...	...	...	...	...
Less: Current transfers paid	7	7	9	8	10	11	...	...	...	...	...
Equals: National Disposable Income at Market Prices	1366	1464	1595	1756	1998	2102	...	...	...	...	...
Less: Final consumption	1239	1317	1421	1538	1782	2021	2262	2501	2819	3318	4078
Statistical discrepancy	5	-3	...	-7	-27	28	...	...	...	...	...
Equals: Net Saving	132	144	174	211	189	109	...	...	...	...	...
Less: Surplus of the nation on current transactions	-127	-51	-25	-71	-212	-241	...	...	...	...	...
Equals: Net Capital Formation	249	195	199	282	401	315	...	...	...	...	...

a) Data in this table have been revised, therefore they are not strictly comparable with the unrevised data in the other tables.

2.1 General Government Final Consumption Expenditure by Function, in Current Prices

Million Honduran lempiras

		1970	1971	1972	1973	1974	1975	1976	1977	1978	1979	1980
1	General public services	45	47	48	45	65	68	...	...	...	...	...
2	Defence	21	25	32	32	34	43	...	...	...	...	...
3	Public order and safety							...	...	...	...	...
4	Education	48	50	53	51	65	77	...	...	...	...	...
5	Health	28	25	31	30	41	46	...	...	...	...	...
6	Social security and welfare							...	...	...	...	...
7	Housing and community amenities	4	5	5	7	9	11	...	...	...	...	...
8	Recreational, cultural and religious affairs							...	...	...	...	...
9	Economic services							...	...	...	...	...
10	Other functions	20	23	24	21	28	33	...	...	...	...	...
	Total General Government Final Consumption Expenditure	166	175	193	186	242	278	...	...	...	...	...

2.5 Private Final Consumption Expenditure by Type, in Current Prices

Million Honduran lempiras

		1970	1971	1972	1973	1974	1975	1976	1977	1978	1979	1980
	Final Consumption Expenditure of Resident Households											
1	Food, beverages and tobacco	507	552	570	649	804	865	...	...	...	...	...
	a Food	417	455	466	530	658	712	...	...	...	...	...
	b Non-alcoholic beverages	...	...	...	...	...	...	...	...	...	...	...
	c Alcoholic beverages	...	...	...	...	...	...	...	...	...	...	...
	d Tobacco	22	21	23	28	33	41	...	...	...	...	...
2	Clothing and footwear	143	150	157	164	173	182	...	...	...	...	...
3	Gross rent, fuel and power	150	161	168	181	199	216	...	...	...	...	...
4	Furniture, furnishings and household equipment and operation	67	71	76	93	99	106	...	...	...	...	...
	a Household operation	36	38	41	43	46	50	...	...	...	...	...

Honduras

2.5 Private Final Consumption Expenditure by Type, in Current Prices
(Continued)

Million Honduran lempiras

	1970	1971	1972	1973	1974	1975	1976	1977	1978	1979	1980
b Other	31	33	35	50	53	56	...	...	...	...	...
5 Medical care and health expenses	70	73	78	83	90	95	...	...	...	...	...
6 Transport and communication	34	36	38	40	45	50	...	...	...	...	...
7 Recreational, entertainment, education and cultural services	64	68	71	74	78	82	...	...	...	...	...
8 Miscellaneous goods and services	16	16	17	18	18	19	...	...	...	...	...
Total Final Consumption Expenditure in the Domestic Market by Households, of which	1051	1127	1175	1302	1506	1615	...	...	...	...	...
Plus: Direct purchases abroad by resident households	24	24	28	29	30	31	...	...	...	...	...
Less: Direct purchases in the domestic market by non-resident households	8	9	10	17	20	21	...	...	...	...	...
Equals: Final Consumption Expenditure of Resident Households	1067	1142	1193	1314	1516	1625	...	...	...	...	...

Final Consumption Expenditure of Private Non-profit Institutions Serving Households

	1970	1971	1972	1973	1974	1975	1976	1977	1978	1979	1980
Equals: Final Consumption Expenditure of Private Non-profit Organisations Serving Households	-6	-6	-6	-7	-27	-11	...	...	...	...	...
Private Final Consumption Expenditure	1061	1136	1187	1307	1489	1614	...	...	...	...	...

2.6 Private Final Consumption Expenditure by Type, in Constant Prices

Million Honduran lempiras

	1970	1971	1972	1973	1974	1975	1976	1977	1978	1979	1980

At constant prices of:1966

Final Consumption Expenditure of Resident Households

	1970	1971	1972	1973	1974	1975	1976	1977	1978	1979	1980
1 Food, beverages and tobacco	432	484	486	522	549	594	...	...	...	...	...
a Food	352	402	400	424	432	467	...	...	...	...	...
b Non-alcoholic beverages	...	...	...	...	...	...	...	...	...	...	...
c Alcoholic beverages	...	...	...	...	...	...	...	...	...	...	...
d Tobacco	20	19	21	25	28	33	...	...	...	...	...
2 Clothing and footwear	130	135	137	132	129	134	...	...	...	...	...
3 Gross rent, fuel and power	143	140	141	148	152	159	...	...	...	...	...
4 Furniture, furnishings and household equipment and operation	63	67	70	80	78	82	...	...	...	...	...
a Household operation	33	35	36	35	31	33	...	...	...	...	...
b Other	30	32	34	45	47	49	...	...	...	...	...
5 Medical care and health expenses	64	63	65	69	70	74	...	...	...	...	...
6 Transport and communication	32	34	35	37	29	31	...	...	...	...	...
7 Recreational, entertainment, education and cultural services	61	64	67	71	74	78	...	...	...	...	...
8 Miscellaneous goods and services	15	15	16	18	17	19	...	...	...	...	...
Total Final Consumption Expenditure in the Domestic Market by Households, of which	940	1002	1017	1077	1098	1171	...	...	...	...	...
Plus: Direct purchases abroad by resident households	22	21	24	25	22	21	...	...	...	...	...
Less: Direct purchases in the domestic market by non-resident households	7	8	9	14	15	14	...	...	...	...	...
Equals: Final Consumption Expenditure of Resident Households	955	1015	1032	1088	1105	1178	...	...	...	...	...

Final Consumption Expenditure of Private Non-profit Institutions Serving Households

	1970	1971	1972	1973	1974	1975	1976	1977	1978	1979	1980
Equals: Final Consumption Expenditure of Private Non-profit Organisations Serving Households	-6	-5	-5	-6	-20	-8	...	...	...	...	...
Private Final Consumption Expenditure	949	1010	1027	1082	1085	1170	...	...	...	...	...

Honduras

2.9 Gross Capital Formation by Kind of Activity of Owner, ISIC Major Divisions, in Current Prices

Million Honduran lempiras

	1970 Total Gross Capital Formation	1970 Increase in Stocks	1970 Gross Fixed Capital Formation	1971 Total Gross Capital Formation	1971 Increase in Stocks	1971 Gross Fixed Capital Formation	1972 Total Gross Capital Formation	1972 Increase in Stocks	1972 Gross Fixed Capital Formation	1973 Total Gross Capital Formation	1973 Increase in Stocks	1973 Gross Fixed Capital Formation
						All Producers						
1 Agriculture, hunting, fishing and forestry	...	...	77	...	...	74	...	...	77	...	...	93
2 Mining and quarrying	...	...	5	...	...	4	...	...	2	...	...	3
3 Manufacturing	...	...	34	...	...	34	...	...	32	...	...	44
4 Electricity, gas and water	...	...	25	...	...	10	...	...	11	...	...	31
5 Construction	...	...	7	...	...	6	...	...	5	...	...	9
6 Wholesale and retail trade, restaurants and hotels [a]	...	...	18	...	...	18	...	...	19	...	...	27
7 Transport, storage and communication	...	...	52	...	...	50	...	...	39	...	...	42
8 Finance, insurance, real estate and business services	...	...	34	...	...	41	...	...	48	...	...	46
9 Community, social and personal services [ab]	...	...	19	...	...	17	...	...	14	...	...	20
Total Industries	...	...	269	...	...	254	...	...	247	...	...	314
Producers of Government Services	...	...	4	...	...	2	...	...	2	...	...	9
Private Non-Profit Institutions Serving Households	...	...	...	...	...	...	...	...	...	...	...	...
Total	312	39	273	250	-6	256	256	7	249	343	20	323

	1974 Total Gross Capital Formation	1974 Increase in Stocks	1974 Gross Fixed Capital Formation	1975 Total Gross Capital Formation	1975 Increase in Stocks	1975 Gross Fixed Capital Formation
			All Producers			
1 Agriculture, hunting, fishing and forestry	...	...	108	...	...	120
2 Mining and quarrying	...	...	8	...	...	10
3 Manufacturing	...	...	47	...	...	57
4 Electricity, gas and water	...	...	31	...	...	35
5 Construction	...	...	13	...	...	15
6 Wholesale and retail trade, restaurants and hotels [a]	...	...	33	...	...	37
7 Transport, storage and communication	...	...	54	...	...	62
8 Finance, insurance, real estate and business services	...	...	57	...	...	65
9 Community, social and personal services [ab]	...	...	32	...	...	36
Total Industries	...	...	383	...	...	436
Producers of Government Services	...	...	17	...	...	20
Private Non-Profit Institutions Serving Households	...	...	...	...	...	...
Total	519	119	400	445	-11	456

a) Restaurants and hotels are included in item 'Community, social and personal services'.
b) Item 'Private non-profit institutions serving households' is included in item 'Community, social and personal services'.

2.17 Exports and Imports of Goods and Services, Detail

Million Honduran lempiras

	1970	1971	1972	1973	1974	1975	1976	1977	1978	1979	1980
					Exports of Goods and Services						
1 Exports of merchandise, f.o.b.	350	364	430	537	603	619	...	...	...	...	...
2 Transport and communication							...	...	...	...	...
3 Insurance service charges	26	27	31	40	50	56	...	...	...	...	...
4 Other commodities							...	...	...	...	...
5 Adjustments of merchandise exports to change-of-ownership basis	...	...	...	...	...	...	...	...	...	...	...
6 Direct purchases in the domestic market by non-residential households	...	...	...	...	...	...	...	...	...	...	...
7 Direct purchases in the domestic market by extraterritorial bodies	...	...	...	...	...	...	...	...	...	...	...
Total Exports of Goods and Services	376	391	461	577	653	675	...	...	...	...	...
					Imports of Goods and Services						
1 Imports of merchandise, c.i.f.	485	436	449	600	908	900	...	...	...	...	...

Honduras

2.17 Exports and Imports of Goods and Services, Detail
(Continued)

Million Honduran lempiras

	1970	1971	1972	1973	1974	1975	1976	1977	1978	1979	1980
a Imports of merchandise, f.o.b.	407	355	353	487	776	755	...	...	...	...	...
b Transport of services on merchandise imports	...	...	...	...	...	...	...	...	...	...	...
c Insurance service charges on merchandise imports	...	...	...	...	...	...	...	...	...	...	...
2 Adjustments of merchandise imports to change-of-ownership basis	...	...	...	...	...	...	...	...	...	...	...
3 Other transport and communication	...	...	...	...	...	...	...	...	...	...	...
4 Other insurance service charges	...	...	...	...	...	...	...	...	...	...	...
5 Other commodities	...	...	...	...	...	...	...	...	...	...	...
6 Direct purchases abroad by government	...	...	...	...	...	...	...	...	...	...	...
7 Direct purchases abroad by resident households	...	...	...	...	...	...	...	...	...	...	...
Total Imports of Goods and Services	485	436	449	600	908	900	...	...	...	...	...
Balance of Goods and Services	-109	-45	12	-23	-255	-225	...	...	...	...	...
Total Imports and Balance of Goods and Services	376	391	461	577	653	675	...	...	...	...	...

3.12 General Government Income and Outlay Account: Total and Subsectors

Million Honduran lempiras

	1970					1971				
	Total General Government	Central Government	State or Provincial Government	Local Government	Social Security Funds	Total General Government	Central Government	State or Provincial Government	Local Government	Social Security Funds

Receipts

1 Property and entrepreneurial income	7	6	...	...	...	8	7	...	...	...
2 Taxes, fees and contributions [a]	176	168	...	...	...	178	170	...	...	...
a Indirect taxes [a]	124	118	...	...	...	127	121	...	...	...
b Direct taxes	44	48	...	...	...	44	47	...	...	...
Income	23	27	...	...	...	27	30	...	...	...
Other	21	21	...	...	...	17	17	...	...	...
c Social security contributions	6	...	...	...	...	5	...	...	...	...
d Fees, fines and penalties	2	1	...	...	...	2	2	...	...	...
3 Other current transfers received	9	9	...	...	...	9	10	...	...	...
a Casualty insurance claims	...	...	...	...	...	...	...	...	...	...
b Transfers from other government subsectors	...	...	...	...	...	...	...	...	...	...
c Transfers from abroad	9	9	...	...	...	9	10	...	...	...
d Other transfers, except imputed	...	...	...	...	...	...	...	...	...	...
e Imputed unfunded employee welfare contributions	...	...	...	...	...	...	...	...	...	...
Total Current Receipts	192	182	...	...	...	195	187	...	...	...

Disbursements

1 General governement final consumption expenditures	166	156	...	...	...	175	167	...	...	...
a Compensation of employees	...	...	...	...	...	...	...	...	...	...
b Consumption of fixed capital	13	12	...	...	...	14	13	...	...	...
c Goods and services purchased, net	...	...	...	...	...	...	...	...	...	...
d Less: Own account production of fixed assets	...	...	...	...	...	...	...	...	...	...
e Indirect taxes paid, net	...	...	...	...	...	...	...	...	...	...
2 Property income paid	8	7	...	...	...	11	10	...	...	...

Honduras

3.12 General Government Income and Outlay Account: Total and Subsectors
(Continued)

Million Honduran lempiras

	1970					1971				
	Total General Government	Central Government	State or Provincial Government	Local Government	Social Security Funds	Total General Government	Central Government	State or Provincial Government	Local Government	Social Security Funds
3 Subsidies [b]	-15	-14	...	...	...	-16	-15	...	...	...
4 Other current transfers paid	9	10	...	...	...	7	7	...	...	...
a Casualty insurance premiums, net	...	...	...	...	...	...	...	...	...	...
b Transfers to other government subsectors	...	2	...	...	...	...	1	...	...	...
c Transfers to households	...	...	...	...	...	...	...	...	...	...
d Transfers to private non-profit institutions serving households	7	6	...	...	...	5	4	...	...	...
e Transfers to the rest of the world	2	2	...	...	...	2	2	...	...	...
Net saving	24	23	...	...	...	18	18	...	...	...
Total Current Disbursements and Net Saving	192	182	...	...	...	195	187	...	...	...

	1972					1973				
	Total General Government	Central Government	State or Provincial Government	Local Government	Social Security Funds	Total General Government	Central Government	State or Provincial Government	Local Government	Social Security Funds

Receipts

1 Property and entrepreneurial income	9	8	...	...	...	15	14	...	...	...
2 Taxes, fees and contributions [a]	190	182	...	...	...	220	210	...	...	...
a Indirect taxes [a]	136	130	...	...	...	158	150	...	...	...
b Direct taxes	45	50	...	...	...	48	56	...	...	...
Income	28	33	...	...	...	31	39	...	...	...
Other	17	17	...	...	...	17	17	...	...	...
c Social security contributions	7	...	...	...	...	10	...	...	...	...
d Fees, fines and penalties	2	2	...	...	...	4	4	...	...	...
3 Other current transfers received	10	10	...	...	...	10	10	...	...	...
a Casualty insurance claims	...	...	...	...	...	...	...	...	...	...
b Transfers from other government subsectors	...	...	...	...	...	...	...	...	...	...
c Transfers from abroad	10	10	...	...	...	10	10	...	...	...
d Other transfers, except imputed	...	...	...	...	...	...	...	...	...	...
e Imputed unfunded employee welfare contributions	...	...	...	...	...	...	...	...	...	...
Total Current Receipts	209	200	...	...	...	245	234	...	...	...

Disbursements

1 General governement final consumption expenditures	193	185	...	...	...	186	179	...	...	...
a Compensation of employees	...	...	...	...	...	...	...	...	...	...
b Consumption of fixed capital	15	15	...	...	...	15	15	...	...	...
c Goods and services purchased, net	...	...	...	...	...	...	...	...	...	...
d Less: Own account production of fixed assets	...	...	...	...	...	...	...	...	...	...
e Indirect taxes paid, net	...	...	...	...	...	...	...	...	...	...
2 Property income paid	13	13	...	...	...	14	14	...	...	...
3 Subsidies [b]	-15	-13	...	...	...	-11	-10	...	...	...
4 Other current transfers paid	14	15	...	...	...	15	15	...	...	...
a Casualty insurance premiums, net	...	...	...	...	...	...	...	...	...	...
b Transfers to other government subsectors	...	1	...	...	...	...	1	...	...	...
c Transfers to households	...	...	...	...	...	...	...	...	...	...
d Transfers to private non-profit institutions serving households	10	10	...	...	...	12	11	...	...	...
e Transfers to the rest of the world	4	4	...	...	...	3	3	...	...	...
Net saving	4	-	...	...	...	41	36	...	...	...
Total Current Disbursements and Net Saving	209	200	...	...	...	245	234	...	...	...

Honduras

3.12 General Government Income and Outlay Account: Total and Subsectors

Million Honduran lempiras

		1974					1975			
	Total General Government	Central Government	State or Provincial Government	Local Government	Social Security Funds	Total General Government	Central Government	State or Provincial Government	Local Government	Social Security Funds

Receipts

1 Property and entrepreneurial income	32	30	...	...	...	36	34	...	...	...
2 Taxes, fees and contributions [a]	266	255	...	...	...	293	281	...	...	...
a Indirect taxes [a]	174	166	...	...	...	183	175	...	...	...
b Direct taxes	83	87	...	...	...	94	99	...	...	...
Income	46	65	...	...	...	56	78	...	...	...
Other	37	22	...	...	...	38	21	...	...	...
c Social security contributions	7	...	...	...	...	9	...	...	...	...
d Fees, fines and penalties	2	2	...	...	...	7	7	...	...	...
3 Other current transfers received	42	42	...	...	...	29	29	...	...	...
a Casualty insurance claims	...	...	...	...	...	...	...	...	...	...
b Transfers from other government subsectors	...	...	...	...	...	...	...	...	...	...
c Transfers from abroad	42	42	...	...	...	29	29	...	...	...
d Other transfers, except imputed	...	...	...	...	...	...	...	...	...	...
e Imputed unfunded employee welfare contributions	...	...	...	...	...	...	...	...	...	...
Total Current Receipts	340	327	...	...	...	358	344	...	...	...

Disbursements

1 General government final consumption expenditures	242	231	...	...	...	278	267	...	...	...
a Compensation of employees	...	...	...	...	...	...	...	...	...	...
b Consumption of fixed capital	18	17	...	...	...	18	21	...	...	...
c Goods and services purchased, net	...	...	...	...	...	...	...	...	...	...
d Less: Own account production of fixed assets	...	...	...	...	...	...	...	...	...	...
e Indirect taxes paid, net	...	...	...	...	...	...	...	...	...	...
2 Property income paid	13	13	...	...	...	20	20	...	...	...
3 Subsidies [b]	-25	-24	...	...	...	-36	-35	...	...	...
4 Other current transfers paid	20	21	...	...	...	14	19	...	...	...
a Casualty insurance premiums, net	...	...	...	...	...	...	...	...	...	...
b Transfers to other government subsectors	...	1	...	...	...	...	5	...	...	...
c Transfers to households	...	...	...	...	...	...	...	...	...	...
d Transfers to private non-profit institutions serving households	16	16	...	...	...	10	10	...	...	...
e Transfers to the rest of the world	4	4	...	...	...	4	4	...	...	...
Net saving	90	86	...	...	...	82	73	...	...	...
Total Current Disbursements and Net Saving	340	327	...	...	...	358	344	...	...	...

a) Including profits of government enterprises.
b) Including losses of government enterprises.

3.13 General Government Capital Accumulation Account: Total and Subsectors

Million Honduran lempiras

		1970					1971			
	Total General Government	Central Government	State or Provincial Government	Local Government	Social Security Funds	Total General Government	Central Government	State or Provincial Government	Local Government	Social Security Funds

Finance of Gross Accumulation

1 Gross saving	37	35	...	...	...	32	31	...	...	...
a Consumption of fixed capital	13	12	...	...	...	14	13	...	...	...
b Net saving	24	23	...	...	...	18	18	...	...	...
2 Capital transfers received	-7	-8	...	...	...	-8	-8	...	...	...
Finance of Gross Accumulation	30	27	...	...	...	24	23	...	...	...

Honduras

3.13 General Government Capital Accumulation Account: Total and Subsectors
(Continued)

Million Honduran lempiras

	1970					1971				
	Total General Government	Central Government	State or Provincial Government	Local Government	Social Security Funds	Total General Government	Central Government	State or Provincial Government	Local Government	Social Security Funds
	Gross Accumulation									
1 Gross capital formation	96	93	...	...	...	73	68	...	...	...
2 Purchases of land, net	...	...	...	...	...	...	...	...	...	...
3 Purchases of intangible assets, net	...	...	...	...	...	...	...	...	...	...
4 Capital transfers paid	...	...	...	...	...	...	...	...	...	...
Net lending	-66	-66	...	...	...	-49	-45	...	...	...
Gross Accumulation	30	27	...	...	...	24	23	...	...	...

	1972					1973				
	Total General Government	Central Government	State or Provincial Government	Local Government	Social Security Funds	Total General Government	Central Government	State or Provincial Government	Local Government	Social Security Funds
	Finance of Gross Accumulation									
1 Gross saving	19	15	...	...	...	56	51	...	...	...
a Consumption of fixed capital	15	15	...	...	...	15	15	...	...	...
b Net saving	4	-	...	...	...	41	36	...	...	...
2 Capital transfers received	-2	-2	...	...	...	-8	-8	...	...	...
Finance of Gross Accumulation	17	13	...	...	...	48	43	...	...	...
	Gross Accumulation									
1 Gross capital formation	60	56	...	...	...	90	85	...	...	...
2 Purchases of land, net	...	...	...	...	...	...	...	...	...	...
3 Purchases of intangible assets, net	...	...	...	...	...	...	...	...	...	...
4 Capital transfers paid	...	...	...	...	...	...	...	...	...	...
Net lending	-43	-43	...	...	...	-42	-42	...	...	...
Gross Accumulation	17	13	...	...	...	48	43	...	...	...

	1974					1975				
	Total General Government	Central Government	State or Provincial Government	Local Government	Social Security Funds	Total General Government	Central Government	State or Provincial Government	Local Government	Social Security Funds
	Finance of Gross Accumulation									
1 Gross saving	108	103	...	...	...	100	94	...	...	...
a Consumption of fixed capital	18	17	...	...	...	18	21	...	...	...
b Net saving	90	86	...	...	...	82	73	...	...	...
2 Capital transfers received	-9	-8	...	...	...	-28	-28	...	...	...
Finance of Gross Accumulation	99	95	...	...	...	72	66	...	...	...
	Gross Accumulation									
1 Gross capital formation	135	134	...	...	...	154	144	...	...	...
2 Purchases of land, net	...	...	...	...	...	...	...	...	...	...
3 Purchases of intangible assets, net	...	...	...	...	...	...	...	...	...	...
4 Capital transfers paid	...	...	...	...	...	...	...	...	...	...
Net lending	-36	-39	...	...	...	-82	-78	...	...	...
Gross Accumulation	99	95	...	...	...	72	66	...	...	...

4.3 Derivation of Value Added by Kind of Activity, ISIC Divisions, in Current Prices

Million Honduran lempiras

	1970			1971			1972			1973		
	Gross Output	Intermediate Consumption	Value Added	Gross Output	Intermediate Consumption	Value Added	Gross Output	Intermediate Consumption	Value Added	Gross Output	Intermediate Consumption	Value Added
	All Producers											
1 Agriculture, hunting, forestry and fishing	...	...	425	...	...	454	...	...	496	...	...	560
2 Mining and quarrying	...	...	30	...	...	28	...	...	30	...	...	43
3 Manufacturing	...	...	181	...	...	198	...	...	218	...	...	245
a Manufacture of food, beverages and tobacco	...	...	89	...	...	94	...	...	106	...	...	111

Honduras

4.3 Derivation of Value Added by Kind of Activity, ISIC Divisions, in Current Prices
(Continued)

Million Honduran lempiras

	1970 Gross Output	1970 Intermediate Consumption	1970 Value Added	1971 Gross Output	1971 Intermediate Consumption	1971 Value Added	1972 Gross Output	1972 Intermediate Consumption	1972 Value Added	1973 Gross Output	1973 Intermediate Consumption	1973 Value Added
b Textile, wearing apparel and leather industries	...	...	27	...	...	30	...	...	32	...	...	36
c Manufacture of wood and wood products, including furniture	...	...	19	...	...	22	...	...	24	...	...	34
d Manufacture of paper and paper products, printing and publishing	...	...	7	...	...	9	...	...	10	...	...	11
e Manufacture of chemicals and chemical petroleum, coal, rubber and plastic products	...	...	18	...	...	20	...	...	21	...	...	22
f Manufacture of non-metallic mineral products, except products of petroleum and coal	...	...	11	...	...	12	...	...	12	...	...	15
g Basic metal industries	...	...	8	...	...	9	...	...	11	...	...	15
h Manufacture of fabricated metal products, machinery and equipment	...	...		...	...		...	...		...	...	
i Other manufacturing industries	...	...	2	...	...	2	...	...	2	...	...	2
4 Electricity, gas and water	...	...	18	...	...	20	...	...	23	...	...	27
5 Construction	...	...	63	...	...	63	...	...	66	...	...	73
6 Wholesale and retail trade, restaurants and hotels	...	...	171	...	...	183	...	...	189	...	...	197
a Wholesale and retail trade	...	...	171	...	...	183	...	...	189	...	...	197
b Restaurants and hotels	...	...	...	...	...	...	...	...	...	...	...	...
7 Transport, storage and communication	...	...	102	...	...	117	...	...	125	...	...	133
8 Finance, insurance, real estate and business services	...	...	134	...	...	143	...	...	159	...	...	177
9 Community, social and personal services	...	...	139	...	...	153	...	...	170	...	...	183
Total, Industries	...	...	1263	...	...	1359	...	...	1476	...	...	1638
Producers of Government Services	...	...	44	...	...	49	...	...	62	...	...	58
Other Producers	...	...	...	...	...	...	...	...	...	...	...	...
Total	...	...	1307	...	...	1408	...	...	1538	...	...	1696
Imputed bank service charge	...	...	...	...	...	...	...	...	...	...	...	...
Import duties	...	...	...	...	...	...	...	...	...	...	...	...
Value added tax	...	...	...	...	...	...	...	...	...	...	...	...
Other adjustments	...	...	139	...	...	143	...	...	151	...	...	169
Total	...	...	1446	...	...	1551	...	...	1689	...	...	1865

	1974 Gross Output	1974 Intermediate Consumption	1974 Value Added	1975 Gross Output	1975 Intermediate Consumption	1975 Value Added
			All Producers			
1 Agriculture, hunting, forestry and fishing	...	...	573	...	...	571
2 Mining and quarrying	...	...	64	...	...	53
3 Manufacturing	...	...	280	...	...	314
a Manufacture of food, beverages and tobacco	...	...	126	...	...	151
b Textile, wearing apparel and leather industries	...	...	41	...	...	43
c Manufacture of wood and wood products, including furniture	...	...	34	...	...	36
d Manufacture of paper and paper products, printing and publishing	...	...	12	...	...	14
e Manufacture of chemicals and chemical petroleum, coal, rubber and plastic products	...	...	33	...	...	34
f Manufacture of non-metallic mineral products, except products of petroleum and coal	...	...	15	...	...	16
g Basic metal industries	...	...	17	...	...	17
h Manufacture of fabricated metal products, machinery and equipment	...	...		...	...	
i Other manufacturing industries	...	...	2	...	...	2
4 Electricity, gas and water	...	...	27	...	...	36

Honduras

4.3 Derivation of Value Added by Kind of Activity, ISIC Divisions, in Current Prices
(Continued)

Million Honduran lempiras

	1974 Gross Output	1974 Intermediate Consumption	1974 Value Added	1975 Gross Output	1975 Intermediate Consumption	1975 Value Added
5 Construction	...	...	96	...	...	108
6 Wholesale and retail trade, restaurants and hotels	...	...	216	...	...	242
a Wholesale and retail trade	...	...	216	...	...	242
b Restaurants and hotels	...	...	...	...	...	...
7 Transport, storage and communication	...	...	149	...	...	166
8 Finance, insurance, real estate and business services	...	...	200	...	...	218
9 Community, social and personal services	...	...	207	...	...	216
Total, Industries	...	...	1812	...	...	1924
Producers of Government Services	...	...	62	...	...	68
Other Producers	...	...	...	...	...	...
Total	...	...	1874	...	...	1992
Imputed bank service charge	...	...	...	...	...	...
Import duties	...	...	...	...	...	...
Value added tax	...	...	...	...	...	...
Other adjustments	...	...	199	...	...	220
Total	...	...	2073	...	...	2212

4.4 Derivation of Value Added by Kind of Activity, ISIC Divisions, in Constant Prices

Million Honduran lempiras

At constant prices of: 1966 — All Producers

	1970 GO	1970 IC	1970 VA	1971 GO	1971 IC	1971 VA	1972 GO	1972 IC	1972 VA	1973 GO	1973 IC	1973 VA
1 Agriculture, hunting, forestry and fishing	...	...	405	...	...	438	...	...	446	...	...	462
2 Mining and quarrying	...	...	26	...	...	24	...	...	26	...	...	34
3 Manufacturing	...	...	170	...	...	178	...	...	185	...	...	192
a Manufacture of food, beverages and tobacco	...	...	78	...	...	85	...	...	88	...	...	90
b Textile, wearing apparel and leather industries	...	...	27	...	...	28	...	...	29	...	...	30
c Manufacture of wood and wood products, including furniture	...	...	20	...	...	21	...	...	23	...	...	25
d Manufacture of paper and paper products, printing and publishing	...	...	7	...	...	7	...	...	7	...	...	8
e Manufacture of chemicals and chemical petroleum, coal, rubber and plastic products	...	...	19	...	...	18	...	...	17	...	...	19
f Manufacture of non-metallic mineral products, except products of petroleum and coal	...	...	11	...	...	11	...	...	12	...	...	13
g Basic metal industries	...	...	8	...	...	7	...	...	6	...	...	6
h Manufacture of fabricated metal products, machinery and equipment	...	...	-	...	...		...	...		...	...	
i Other manufacturing industries	...	...	1	...	...	1	...	...	1	...	...	1
4 Electricity, gas and water	...	...	13	...	...	13	...	...	14	...	...	15
5 Construction	...	...	44	...	...	43	...	...	46	...	...	50
6 Wholesale and retail trade, restaurants and hotels	...	...	153	...	...	158	...	...	147	...	...	147
a Wholesale and retail trade	...	...	153	...	...	158	...	...	147	...	...	147
b Restaurants and hotels	...	...	...	...	...	...	...	...	...	...	...	...
7 Transport, storage and communication	...	...	94	...	...	105	...	...	108	...	...	111
8 Finance, insurance, real estate and business services	...	...	113	...	...	119	...	...	127	...	...	135
9 Community, social and personal services	...	...	133	...	...	140	...	...	151	...	...	157
Total, Industries	...	...	1151	...	...	1218	...	...	1250	...	...	1303
Producers of Government Services	...	...	42	...	...	46	...	...	57	...	...	51

Honduras

4.4 Derivation of Value Added by Kind of Activity, ISIC Divisions, in Constant Prices
(Continued)

Million Honduran lempiras

	1970			1971			1972			1973		
	Gross Output	Intermediate Consumption	Value Added	Gross Output	Intermediate Consumption	Value Added	Gross Output	Intermediate Consumption	Value Added	Gross Output	Intermediate Consumption	Value Added
At constant prices of: 1966													
Other Producers	...	...	...	...	...	...	...	...	...	...	...	...
Total	...	...	1193	...	...	1264	...	...	1307	...	...	1354
Imputed bank service charge	...	...	...	...	...	...	...	...	...	...	...	...
Import duties	...	...	...	...	...	...	...	...	...	...	...	...
Value added tax	...	...	...	...	...	...	...	...	...	...	...	...
Other adjustments	...	...	127	...	...	128	...	...	128	...	...	135
Total	...	...	1320	...	...	1392	...	...	1435	...	...	1489

	1974			1975		
	Gross Output	Intermediate Consumption	Value Added	Gross Output	Intermediate Consumption	Value Added
At constant prices of: 1966						
All Producers						
1 Agriculture, hunting, forestry and fishing	...	...	417	...	...	378
2 Mining and quarrying	...	...	45	...	...	33
3 Manufacturing	...	...	190	...	...	195
a Manufacture of food, beverages and tobacco	...	...	89	...	...	94
b Textile, wearing apparel and leather industries	...	...	29	...	...	30
c Manufacture of wood and wood products, including furniture	...	...	24	...	...	20
d Manufacture of paper and paper products, printing and publishing	...	...	9	...	...	8
e Manufacture of chemicals and chemical petroleum, coal, rubber and plastic products	...	...	19	...	...	20
f Manufacture of non-metallic mineral products, except products of petroleum and coal	...	...	13	...	...	14
g Basic metal industries	...	...	7	...	...	7
h Manufacture of fabricated metal products, machinery and equipment	...	...		...	...	
i Other manufacturing industries	...	...	1	...	...	1
4 Electricity, gas and water	...	...	16	...	...	17
5 Construction	...	...	50	...	...	52
6 Wholesale and retail trade, restaurants and hotels	...	...	145	...	...	147
a Wholesale and retail trade	...	...	145	...	...	147
b Restaurants and hotels	...	...	...	...	...	...
7 Transport, storage and communication	...	...	120	...	...	125
8 Finance, insurance, real estate and business services	...	...	144	...	...	151
9 Community, social and personal services	...	...	167	...	...	168
Total, Industries	...	...	1294	...	...	1266
Producers of Government Services	...	...	48	...	...	49
Other Producers	...	...	...	...	...	...
Total	...	...	1342	...	...	1315
Imputed bank service charge	...	...	...	...	...	...
Import duties	...	...	...	...	...	...
Value added tax	...	...	...	...	...	...
Other adjustments	...	...	143	...	...	145
Total	...	...	1485	...	...	1460

Hong Kong

General note. The preparation of national accounts statistics in Hong Kong is undertaken by the Census and Statistics Department, Hong Kong. The official estimates together with methodological notes of the estimates are published in a series of publications entitled 'Estimates of Gross Domestic Product', issued annually since 1973. The estimates are generally in accordance with the definitions and classifications recommended in the United Nations System of National Accounts (SNA). The following tables have been prepared from successive replies to the United Nations national accounts questionnaire received from the Overseas Development Administration, Foreign and Commonwealth Office, London. When the scope and coverage of the estimates differ for conceptual or statistical reasons from the definitions and classifications recommended in SNA, a footnote is indicated to the relevant tables.

Sources and methods:

(a) Gross domestic product. Gross domestic product is estimated mainly through the expenditure approach.

(b) Expenditure on the gross domestic product. The expenditure approach is used to estimate government final consumption expenditure and exports and imports of goods and services. The commodity-flow approach is used for private final consumption expenditure and gross capital formation supplemented by the expenditure approach. Government consumption expenditure data up to 1972 were obtained from the Annual Reports of the Accountant-General which provide data on the actual expenditure of each department by financial year ending 31 March. Since 1973, quarterly figures are available from the Treasury and adjustment to a calendar year basis is no longer required. The estimates relate to current expenditure on goods and services by government departments not engaged in trading activities. For the large proportion of the commodities included in private consumption expenditure which is imported, adequate and detailed trade statistics are available. Trade statistics of retained imports are supported and complemented by data from the household expenditure surveys, the 1970 Census of Manufacturing Establishments, sample surveys on sales of business establishments, administrative statistics and other sources. Commodities produced domestically for local consumption are mainly foodstuffs for which annual output is regularly made known by the Agriculture and Fisheries Department and other government departments concerned. Imported and domestically produced commodities are reported in importers' and wholesalers' values, respectively, and the retail value is arrived at by adding transport expenses and distributors' profit margins. The change in stocks of consumer goods and capital goods held by wholesalers and retailers were, prior to 1973, included implicitly in the estimation of private consumption expenditure and gross domestic fixed capital formation. Estimates for the year 1973 and onward have been made through a survey of establishments. Information on quantities of hydrocarbon oils kept in stock by oil companies are obtained from the Commerce and Industry Department. Increase in stocks of intermediate goods held by wholesalers and retailers are not yet estimated because of lack of data. For gross fixed capital formation, investment in plant, machinery and equipment is based mainly on the value of retained imports of capital goods, adding 30 per cent to allow for profit, transport, assembly charges and installation expenses. An estimate of domestically manufactured plant, machinery and equipment locally purchased was calculated for 1970 from the Census of Manufacturing Establishments and projected by the number of employees engaged for other years' estimates. Private sector investment in new buildings and construction is based on the monthly statistical returns of the Building Ordinance Office while investment in the government sector is obtained from an analysis of the accounts of government departments. The estimates of exports and imports of merchandise are obtained from detailed external trade statistics. For travel, port and airport charges and expenditure by non-residents, the main sources of data are the surveys conducted by the Hong Kong Tourist Association and government accounts. For the constant price estimates, price deflation is used for most of the expenditure items. The current values are deflated by various price indexes such as specially constructed salary rate index, consumer price indexes, tourist price index, cost index of building and construction, overall index of unit values of exports and imports, etc. For increase in stocks, a special index is constructed based on unit value index of imports of raw material and domestic exports.

(c) Cost-structure of the gross domestic product. The estimates of wages and salaries are obtained mainly from wage surveys conducted by the Census and Statistics Department, the Hong Kong Productivity Center, the Agriculture and Fisheries Department and official publications. For each economic category except the agriculture and fishing sector, the number of employees is multiplied by the estimated average annual income to give the total wage and salary bill. For the agriculture and fishing sector, the estimation is based on the total value of production published in the annual reports of the Agriculture and Fisheries Department. The estimates of gross operating surplus are based on up-to-date tax statistics provided by the Inland Revenue Department. A lag of one year is assumed when calculating profits from tax assesments but no such adjustment is made for interest and property income. The estimates for net indirect taxes are based on information obtained from the annual reports of Accountant-General or directly from the Treasury.

(d) Gross domestic product by kind of economic activity. The table of gross domestic product by kind of economic activity is prepared at factor costs. The estimates are made by using the income approach with the intention of making an independent check on the order of magnitude of the expenditure estimates. An exercise was carried out to compile a commodity-flow table for 1973, showing the sources of all commodities as well as their uses. The estimates of this table have been based on the 1973 and 1976 Census of Industrial Productions as well as information from ad hoc surveys and special exercises carried out by the Census and Statistics Department. GDP by kind of economic activity at constant prices is not estimated.

1.1 Expenditure on the Gross Domestic Product, in Current Prices

Million Hong Kong dollars

	1970	1971	1972	1973	1974	1975	1976	1977	1978	1979	1980
1 General government final consumption expenditure	1157	1230	1534	1912	2438	2646	3047	3675	4454	5568	7294
2 Private final consumption expenditure	13462	15622	17525	23785	27216	28427	31857	39126	48541	58902	75188
a Households	13068	15145	16918	22949	26180	27199	30381	37354	46453	56606	72172
b Private non-profit institutions serving households	394	477	607	836	1036	1228	1476	1772	2088	2296	3016
3 Gross capital formation	...	...	...	7001	8421	8581	12677	14718	18905	27470	34077
a Increase in stocks	...	...	...	303	678	731	2979	1702	2067	3252	3035
b Gross fixed capital formation	3565	4777	5365	6698	7743	7850	9698	13016	16838	24218	31042
Residential buildings [a]	529	842	1106	1354	1738	1467	1550	2176	3080	4780	6595
Non-residential buildings	478	639	624	728	924	1037	1298	1866	2000	3090	4022
Other construction and land improvement etc. [b]	381	541	696	989	1217	1361	1794	2723	3518	4256	4816
Other	2177	2755	2939	3627	3864	3985	5056	6251	8240	12092	15609
4 Exports of goods and services [c]	18665	20531	23218	30315	34853	34452	47912	50892	60920	83872	106349
5 Less: Imports of goods and services [d]	17635	20287	21788	29049	34142	33532	43520	48796	63263	86339	111794
Equals: Gross Domestic Product	19214	21873	25854	33964	38786	40574	51973	59615	69557	89473	111114

a) Including also combined residential and non-residential buildings.
b) Including transfer costs of land and buildings. Beginning 1975, including Mass Transit Railways.
c) Exports of goods and net exports of services.
d) Imports of goods only.

1.2 Expenditure on the Gross Domestic Product, in Constant Prices

Million Hong Kong dollars

	1970	1971	1972	1973	1974	1975	1976	1977	1978	1979	1980
	At constant prices of:1973										
1 General government final consumption expenditure	1547	1571	1707	1912	2106	2213	2392	2690	3033	3356	3612
2 Private final consumption expenditure	16851	19001	20188	23785	23527	24005	26119	30626	35984	39389	44273
a Households	16320	18377	19511	22949	22628	22980	24992	29383	34632	38049	42849
b Private non-profit institutions serving households	531	624	677	836	899	1025	1127	1243	1352	1340	1424
3 Gross capital formation	...	...	...	7001	6959	7291	10096	11014	12859	15346	17527

Hong Kong

1.2 Expenditure on the Gross Domestic Product, in Constant Prices
(Continued)

Million Hong Kong dollars

	1970	1971	1972	1973	1974	1975	1976	1977	1978	1979	1980
				At constant prices of:1973							
a Increase in stocks	...	...	...	303	469	713	2415	1331	1572	1974	1957
b Gross fixed capital formation	4582	5513	5788	6698	6490	6578	7681	9683	11287	13372	15570
Residential buildings	802	1102	1287	1354	1483	1351	1374	1760	2175	2461	2912
Non-residential buildings	725	836	727	728	789	954	1151	1509	1413	1595	1776
Other construction and land improvement etc. [a]	536	672	780	989	1051	1231	1545	2162	2490	2357	2436
Other	2519	2903	2994	3627	3167	3042	3611	4252	5209	6959	8446
4 Exports of goods and services [b]	24683	25882	27754	30315	28050	28886	37141	38375	43420	50755	58599
5 Less: Imports of goods and services [c]	22319	25355	26247	29049	26068	27046	33743	36424	44244	51281	60832
Equals: Gross Domestic Product	25344	26612	29190	33964	34574	35349	42005	46281	51052	57565	63179

a) Including transfer costs of land and buildings. Beginning 1975, including Mass Transit Railways.
b) Exports of goods and net exports of services.
c) Imports of goods only.

1.3 Cost Components of the Gross Domestic Product

Million Hong Kong dollars

	1970	1971	1972	1973	1974	1975	1976	1977	1978	1979	1980
1 Indirect taxes, net	1055	1184	1505	1684	1562	1905	2400	2835	3499	4011	5153
2 Consumption of fixed capital	...	...	...	...	...	...	...	...	...	...	...
3 Compensation of employees paid by resident producers to:	10920	12948	14738	17270	19485	22172	25681	28771	35194	43577	...
4 Net operating surplus [a]	8199	9992	12990	16694	15786	14802	20916	26613	30451	43152	...
Statistical discrepancy [b]	-960	-2251	-3379	-1684	1953	1695	2976	1396	413	-1267	...
Equals: Gross Domestic Product	19214	21873	25854	33964	38786	40574	51973	59615	69557	89473	111114

a) Including consumption of fixed capital.
b) Referring to difference between income estimate and expenditure estimate.

1.10 Gross Domestic Product by Kind of Activity, in Current Prices

Million Hong Kong dollars

	1970	1971	1972	1973	1974	1975	1976	1977	1978	1979	1980
1 Agriculture, hunting, forestry and fishing	377	407	442	530	538	533	645	724	856	826	...
2 Mining and quarrying	27	36	32	27	21	20	28	25	25	28	...
3 Manufacturing	5913	6455	7444	9018	9087	9954	13197	15067	17647	23898	...
4 Electricity, gas and water	378	418	478	541	646	668	793	806	952	1112	...
5 Construction	806	1129	1472	1877	2150	2107	2512	3293	4612	6368	...
6 Wholesale and retail trade, restaurants and hotels	3755	4465	5583	7297	7323	7663	9850	11960	13989	18807	...
7 Transport, storage and communication	1458	1564	1728	2166	2433	2657	3166	3299	3900	4716	...
8 Finance, insurance, real estate and business services	2855	4004	5682	6519	6221	6283	8319	10877	13576	18596	...
9 Community, social and personal services [ab]	3550	4462	4867	5989	6852	7089	8087	9333	10088	12378	...
Total, Industries	...	...	...	...	...	...	...	...	...	...	...
Producers of Government Services [b]	...	...	...	...	...	...	...	...	...	...	...
Other Producers [b]	...	...	...	...	...	...	...	...	...	...	...
Subtotal [c]	19119	22940	27728	33964	35271	36974	46597	55384	65645	86729	...
Less: Imputed bank service charge	...	...	...	...	...	...	...	...	...	...	...
Plus: Import duties [d]	1055	1184	1505	1684	1562	1905	2400	2835	3499	4011	...
Plus: Value added tax	...	...	...	...	...	...	...	...	...	...	...
Plus: Other adjustments [f]	-960	-2251	-3379	-1684	1953	1695	2976	1396	413	-1267	...
Equals: Gross Domestic Product	19214	21873	25854	33964	38786	40574	51973	59615	69557	89473	...

a) Including activities not adequately defined.
b) Items 'Other producers' and 'Producers of government services' are included in item 'Community, social and personal services'.
c) Gross domestic product in factor values.
d) Referring to indirect taxes net of subsidies.
e) Exports of goods and net exports of services.
f) Referring to difference between income estimate and expenditure estimate.

2.5 Private Final Consumption Expenditure by Type, in Current Prices

Million Hong Kong dollars

	1970	1971	1972	1973	1974	1975	1976	1977	1978	1979	1980
				Final Consumption Expenditure of Resident Households							
1 Food, beverages and tobacco	5476	6155	6929	8677	10355	10221	10913	12119	14262	16302	19523
a Food	4744	5330	6006	7669	9309	9052	9606	10687	12575	14238	17322
b Non-alcoholic beverages	...	...	...	...	...	...	...	...	...	...	...
c Alcoholic beverages	395	485	551	635	603	650	738	820	1007	1199	1176
d Tobacco	337	340	372	373	443	519	569	612	680	865	1025

Hong Kong

2.5 Private Final Consumption Expenditure by Type, in Current Prices
(Continued)

Million Hong Kong dollars

	1970	1971	1972	1973	1974	1975	1976	1977	1978	1979	1980
2 Clothing and footwear [a]	2244	2706	2910	4243	4089	3722	3972	5824	8888	10094	12483
3 Gross rent, fuel and power	1972	2140	2318	2795	3619	4213	4647	5279	5957	7091	8700
4 Furniture, furnishings and household equipment and operation	1371	1473	1631	2163	2439	2390	3316	4169	5294	7373	8996
a Household operation	245	292	343	496	578	591	712	871	1068	1418	1871
b Other	1126	1181	1288	1667	1861	1799	2604	3298	4226	5955	7125
5 Medical care and health expenses	690	759	817	1241	1456	1546	1706	2321	2749	3358	3896
6 Transport and communication	1258	1410	1523	1893	1980	2234	2726	3130	3873	4912	6772
7 Recreational, entertainment, education and cultural services	1278	1340	1467	1783	1950	2219	2631	3143	3754	4779	5858
a Education	285	291	326	400	444	513	569	608	682	812	987
b Other	993	1049	1141	1383	1506	1706	2062	2535	3072	3967	4871
8 Miscellaneous goods and services	689	786	1179	1849	1840	2069	2481	3015	3894	4965	6908
Total Final Consumption Expenditure in the Domestic Market by Households, of which	14978	16769	18774	24644	27728	28614	32392	39000	48671	58874	73136
Plus: Direct purchases abroad by resident households	515	616	818	1076	1438	1735	2056	2599	3095	4344	5835
Less: Direct purchases in the domestic market by non-resident households	2425	2240	2674	2771	2986	3150	4067	4245	5313	6612	6799
Equals: Final Consumption Expenditure of Resident Households	13068	15145	16918	22949	26180	27199	30381	37354	46453	56606	72172

Final Consumption Expenditure of Private Non-profit Institutions Serving Households

	1970	1971	1972	1973	1974	1975	1976	1977	1978	1979	1980
Equals: Final Consumption Expenditure of Private Non-profit Organisations Serving Households	394	477	607	836	1036	1228	1476	1772	2088	2296	3016
Private Final Consumption Expenditure	13462	15622	17525	23785	27216	28427	31857	39126	48541	58902	75188

a) Personal effects are included in item 'Clothing and footwear'.

2.6 Private Final Consumption Expenditure by Type, in Constant Prices

Million Hong Kong dollars

At constant prices of: 1973

Final Consumption Expenditure of Resident Households

	1970	1971	1972	1973	1974	1975	1976	1977	1978	1979	1980
1 Food, beverages and tobacco	7277	7800	8267	8677	8783	8787	9033	9547	10629	11026	11782
a Food	6444	6897	7294	7669	7874	7885	8063	8509	9476	9781	10574
b Non-alcoholic beverages	...	...	...	...	...	...	...	...	...	...	...
c Alcoholic beverages	487	558	591	635	521	525	591	660	761	809	761
d Tobacco	346	345	382	373	388	377	379	378	392	436	447
2 Clothing and footwear	2992	3522	3397	4243	3483	3213	3625	5078	6853	7016	7390
3 Gross rent, fuel and power	2277	2396	2475	2795	3208	3488	3699	3937	4271	4508	4844
4 Furniture, furnishings and household equipment and operation	1697	1789	1897	2163	2186	2155	2982	3636	4393	5519	6291
a Household operation	392	422	447	496	529	561	613	665	723	761	814
b Other	1305	1367	1450	1667	1657	1594	2369	2971	3670	4758	5477
5 Medical care and health expenses	816	871	893	1241	1284	1290	1317	1656	1803	1982	1988
6 Transport and communication	1442	1566	1629	1893	1755	1864	2159	2430	2868	2983	3504
7 Recreational, entertainment, education and cultural services	1529	1558	1682	1783	1760	1869	2178	2530	2887	3401	3684
a Education	331	328	391	400	415	445	470	483	523	611	652

Hong Kong

2.6 Private Final Consumption Expenditure by Type, in Constant Prices
(Continued)

Million Hong Kong dollars

At constant prices of: 1973

	1970	1971	1972	1973	1974	1975	1976	1977	1978	1979	1980
b Other	1198	1230	1291	1383	1345	1424	1708	2047	2364	2790	3032
8 Miscellaneous goods and services	954	1043	1591	1849	1600	1749	2051	2309	2833	3168	3855
Total Final Consumption Expenditure in the Domestic Market by Households, of which	18984	20545	21831	24644	24059	24415	27044	31123	36537	39603	43338
Plus: Direct purchases abroad by resident households	591	679	868	1076	1192	1281	1404	1670	1890	2434	2833
Less: Direct purchases in the domestic market by non-resident households	3255	2847	3188	2771	2623	2716	3456	3410	3795	3988	3322
Equals: Final Consumption Expenditure of Resident Households	16320	18377	19511	22949	22628	22980	24992	29383	34632	38049	42849

Final Consumption Expenditure of Private Non-profit Institutions Serving Households

	1970	1971	1972	1973	1974	1975	1976	1977	1978	1979	1980
Equals: Final Consumption Expenditure of Private Non-profit Organisations Serving Households	531	624	677	836	899	1025	1127	1243	1352	1340	1424
Private Final Consumption Expenditure	16851	19001	20188	23785	23527	24005	26119	30626	35984	39389	44273

2.7 Gross Capital Formation by Type of Good and Owner, in Current Prices

Million Hong Kong dollars

	1970				1971				1972			
	TOTAL	Total Private	Public Enterprises	General Government	TOTAL	Total Private	Public Enterprises	General Government	TOTAL	Total Private	Public Enterprises	General Government
Increase in stocks, total	...	...	...	...	...	...	...	...	...	...	...	...
Gross Fixed Capital Formation, Total	3565	3182	...	...	4777	4208	...	...	5365	4679	...	...
1 Residential buildings a	529	425	...	...	842	730	...	...	1106	1016	...	...
2 Non-residential buildings	478	416	...	...	639	531	...	...	624	523	...	...
3 Other construction b	304	124	...	...	442	134	...	...	535	99	...	...
4 Land improvement and plantation and orchard development c	77	77	...	...	99	99	...	...	161	161	...	...
5 Producers' durable goods	2177	2140	...	...	2755	2714	...	...	2939	2880	...	...
a Transport equipment	443	434	...	...	478	466	...	...	471	452	...	...
b Machinery and equipment	1734	1706	...	...	2277	2248	...	...	2468	2428	...	...
6 Breeding stock, dairy cattle, etc.	...	...	...	...	...	...	...	...	...	...	...	...
Total Gross Capital Formation	...	...	...	...	...	...	...	...	...	...	...	...

	1973				1974				1975			
	TOTAL	Total Private	Public Enterprises	General Government	TOTAL	Total Private	Public Enterprises	General Government	TOTAL	Total Private	Public Enterprises	General Government
Increase in stocks, total	303	303	...	...	678	678	...	...	731	731	...	...
Gross Fixed Capital Formation, Total	6698	5641	...	...	7743	6129	...	...	7850	6247	...	...
1 Residential buildings a	1354	1237	...	...	1738	1425	...	...	1467	1173	...	...
2 Non-residential buildings	728	632	...	...	924	800	...	...	1037	967	...	...
3 Other construction b	773	22	...	...	1072	17	...	...	1175	24	...	...
4 Land improvement and plantation and orchard development c	216	216	...	...	145	145	...	...	186	186	...	...
5 Producers' durable goods	3627	3534	...	...	3864	3742	...	...	3985	3897	...	...
a Transport equipment	571	555	...	...	533	500	...	...	846	826	...	...
b Machinery and equipment	3056	2979	...	...	3331	3242	...	...	3139	3071	...	...
6 Breeding stock, dairy cattle, etc.	...	...	...	...	...	...	...	...	...	...	...	...
Total Gross Capital Formation	7001	5944	...	...	8421	6807	...	...	8581	6978	...	...

Hong Kong

2.7 Gross Capital Formation by Type of Good and Owner, in Current Prices

Million Hong Kong dollars

	1976 TOTAL	1976 Total Private	1976 Public Enterprises	1976 General Government	1977 TOTAL	1977 Total Private	1977 Public Enterprises	1977 General Government	1978 TOTAL	1978 Total Private	1978 Public Enterprises	1978 General Government
Increase in stocks, total	2979	2979	...	...	1702	1702	...	...	2067	2067	...	...
Gross Fixed Capital Formation, Total	9698	7803	...	...	13016	10086	...	...	16838	12494	...	...
1 Residential buildings [a]	1550	1300	...	...	2176	1764	...	...	3080	2160	...	...
2 Non-residential buildings	1298	1202	...	...	1866	1756	...	...	2000	1787	...	...
3 Other construction [b]	1515	46	...	...	2351	51	...	...	2955	36	...	...
4 Land improvement and plantation and orchard development [c]	279	279	...	...	372	372	...	...	563	563	...	...
5 Producers' durable goods	5056	4976	...	...	6251	6143	...	...	8240	7948	...	...
a Transport equipment	799	783	...	...	1279	1249	...	...	1221	1059	...	...
b Machinery and equipment	4257	4193	...	...	4972	4894	...	...	7019	6889	...	...
6 Breeding stock, dairy cattle, etc.	...	...	...	...	...	...	...	...	...	...	...	...
Total Gross Capital Formation	12677	10782	...	...	14718	11788	...	...	18905	14561	...	...

	1979 TOTAL	1979 Total Private	1979 Public Enterprises	1979 General Government	1980 TOTAL	1980 Total Private	1980 Public Enterprises	1980 General Government
Increase in stocks, total	3252	3252	...	...	3035	3035	...	...
Gross Fixed Capital Formation, Total	24218	18135	...	...	31042	24049	...	...
1 Residential buildings [a]	4780	3253	...	...	6595	4306	...	...
2 Non-residential buildings	3090	2701	...	...	4022	3611	...	...
3 Other construction [b]	3587	32	...	...	3706	39	...	...
4 Land improvement and plantation and orchard development [c]	669	669	...	...	1110	1110	...	...
5 Producers' durable goods	12092	11480	...	...	15609	14983	...	...
a Transport equipment	2326	1885	...	...	3682	3213	...	...
b Machinery and equipment	9766	9595	...	...	11927	11770	...	...
6 Breeding stock, dairy cattle, etc.	...	...	...	...	...	...	...	...
Total Gross Capital Formation	27470	21387	...	...	34077	27084	...	...

a) Including also combined residential and non-residential buildings.
b) Beginning 1975, including Mass Transit Railway.
c) Referring only to net expenditure incurred in connection with the transfer of ownership of land and of the existing buildings.

2.8 Gross Capital Formation by Type of Good and Owner, in Constant Prices

Million Hong Kong dollars

At constant prices of: 1973

	1970 TOTAL	1970 Total Private	1970 Public Enterprises	1970 General Government	1971 TOTAL	1971 Total Private	1971 Public Enterprises	1971 General Government	1972 TOTAL	1972 Total Private	1972 Public Enterprises	1972 General Government
Increase in stocks, total	...	...	...	...	...	...	...	...	...	...	...	...
Gross Fixed Capital Formation, Total	4582	4015	...	...	5513	4778	...	...	5788	4996	...	...
1 Residential buildings	802	644	...	...	1102	955	...	...	1287	1182	...	...
2 Non-residential buildings	725	631	...	...	836	695	...	...	727	609	...	...
3 Other construction	461	188	...	...	578	175	...	...	623	115	...	...
4 Land improvement and plantation and orchard development	75	75	...	...	94	94	...	...	157	157	...	...
5 Producers' durable goods	2519	2477	...	...	2903	2859	...	...	2994	2933	...	...
a Transport equipment	512	502	...	...	535	522	...	...	545	525	...	...
b Machinery and equipment	2007	1975	...	...	2368	2337	...	...	2449	2408	...	...
6 Breeding stock, dairy cattle, etc.	...	...	...	...	...	...	...	...	...	...	...	...
Total Gross Capital Formation	...	...	...	...	...	...	...	...	...	...	...	...

Hong Kong

2.8 Gross Capital Formation by Type of Good and Owner, in Constant Prices

Million Hong Kong dollars

	1973 TOTAL	1973 Total Private	1973 Public Enterprises	1973 General Government	1974 TOTAL	1974 Total Private	1974 Public Enterprises	1974 General Government	1975 TOTAL	1975 Total Private	1975 Public Enterprises	1975 General Government
					At constant prices of: 1973							
Increase in stocks, total	303	303	...	...	469	469	...	...	713	713	...	...
Gross Fixed Capital Formation, Total	6698	5641	...	...	6490	5117	...	...	6578	5116	...	...
1 Residential buildings	1354	1237	...	...	1483	1216	...	...	1351	1080	...	...
2 Non-residential buildings	728	632	...	...	789	683	...	...	954	890	...	...
3 Other construction	773	22	...	...	915	15	...	...	1082	22	...	...
4 Land improvement and plantation and orchard development	216	216	...	...	136	136	...	...	149	149	...	...
5 Producers' durable goods	3627	3534	...	...	3167	3067	...	...	3042	2975	...	...
a Transport equipment	571	555	...	...	437	410	...	...	646	631	...	...
b Machinery and equipment	3056	2979	...	...	2730	2657	...	...	2396	2344	...	...
6 Breeding stock, dairy cattle, etc.	...	...	...	...	...	...	...	...	...	...	...	...
Total Gross Capital Formation	7001	5944	...	...	6959	5586	...	...	7291	5829	...	...

	1976 TOTAL	1976 Total Private	1976 Public Enterprises	1976 General Government	1977 TOTAL	1977 Total Private	1977 Public Enterprises	1977 General Government	1978 TOTAL	1978 Total Private	1978 Public Enterprises	1978 General Government
					At constant prices of: 1973							
Increase in stocks, total	2415	2415	...	...	1331	1331	...	...	1572	1572	...	...
Gross Fixed Capital Formation, Total	7681	6015	...	...	9683	7327	...	...	11287	8236	...	...
1 Residential buildings	1374	1152	...	...	1760	1427	...	...	2175	1524	...	...
2 Non-residential buildings	1151	1066	...	...	1509	1420	...	...	1413	1262	...	...
3 Other construction	1343	41	...	...	1902	41	...	...	2091	27	...	...
4 Land improvement and plantation and orchard development	202	202	...	...	260	260	...	...	399	399	...	...
5 Producers' durable goods	3611	3554	...	...	4252	4179	...	...	5209	5024	...	...
a Transport equipment	570	559	...	...	870	850	...	...	776	673	...	...
b Machinery and equipment	3041	2995	...	...	3382	3329	...	...	4433	4351	...	...
6 Breeding stock, dairy cattle, etc.	...	...	...	...	...	...	...	...	...	...	...	...
Total Gross Capital Formation	10096	8430	...	...	11014	8658	...	...	12859	9808	...	...

	1979 TOTAL	1979 Total Private	1979 Public Enterprises	1979 General Government	1980 TOTAL	1980 Total Private	1980 Public Enterprises	1980 General Government
				At constant prices of: 1973				
Increase in stocks, total	1974	1974	...	...	1957	1957	...	...
Gross Fixed Capital Formation, Total	13372	10170	...	...	15570	12412	...	...
1 Residential buildings	2461	1670	...	...	2912	1903	...	...
2 Non-residential buildings	1595	1394	...	...	1776	1595	...	...
3 Other construction	1876	18	...	...	1645	16	...	...
4 Land improvement and plantation and orchard development	481	481	...	...	791	791	...	...
5 Producers' durable goods	6959	6607	...	...	8446	8107	...	...
a Transport equipment	1336	1083	...	...	1988	1735	...	...
b Machinery and equipment	5623	5524	...	...	6458	6372	...	...
6 Breeding stock, dairy cattle, etc.	...	...	...	...	...	...	...	...
Total Gross Capital Formation	15346	12144	...	...	17527	14369	...	...

Hungary

Source. Reply to the United Nations Material Balances Questionnaire from the Hungarian Central Statistical Office, Budapest. The estimates are published annually in 'Statisztikai Evkonyv' (Statistical Yearbook). Concepts, definitions and methods of estimation are described in 'Nepgazdasagi Merlegek 1970-1977 & 1978' (Balances of the National Economy 1970-1977 and 1978) issued by the Central Statistical Office.

General note. The estimates shown in the following tables have been prepared in accordance with the System of Material Product Balances. Therefore, these estimates are not comparable in concept and coverage with those conforming to the United Nations System of National Accounts. It should be noted that in the case of some aggregates the current and constant price estimates are not strictly comparable. In the computations at current price, the depreciation is based on the book value of the assets, while in constant price is based on the replacement value of the assets.

1a Net Material Product by Use at Current Market Prices

Thousand Million Hungarian forint

	1970	1971	1972	1973	1974	1975	1976	1977	1978	1979	1980
1 Personal consumption	162.2	173.4	184.1	199.7	216.7	235.7	253.1	273.7	293.5	325.2	355.6
2 Material consumption in the units of the non-material sphere serving individuals	16.0	17.4	18.2	19.8	22.6	25.9	28.9	32.8	38.5	42.1	49.6
Consumption of the Population	178.2	190.8	202.3	219.5	239.3	261.6	282.0	306.5	332.0	367.3	405.2
3 Material consumption in the units of the non-material sphere serving the community as a whole	22.9	24.2	24.5	26.2	29.1	32.1	34.1	38.1	42.8	46.9	51.4
4 Net fixed capital formation	54.7	56.6	64.7	72.0	70.2	101.1	93.1	98.1	112.3	120.1	119.1
5 Increase in material circulating assets and in stocks [a]	22.6	42.1	19.4	11.5	44.6	30.1	40.9	54.1	79.2	38.3	24.7
6 Losses	4.2	4.4	5.1	5.6	5.7	6.9	7.2	8.2	8.6	10.3	10.8
7 Exports of goods and material services	100.2	108.4	133.4	163.8	186.8	198.4	201.9	238.6	241.4	279.8	278.8
8 Less: Imports of goods and material services	107.9	130.9	128.6	144.2	206.7	234.1	224.3	264.4	298.7	303.2	294.6
Net Material Product	274.9	295.6	320.8	354.4	369.0	396.1	434.9	479.2	517.6	559.5	586.4

a) Including changes in incompleted capital formation.

1b Net Material Product by Use at Constant Market Prices

Thousand Million Hungarian forint

	1970	1971	1972	1973	1974	1975	1976	1977	1978	1979	1980
					At constant prices of:1976						
1 Personal consumption	200.8	210.9	218.5	228.0	242.2	253.6	257.0	268.2	277.7	283.4	285.4
2 Material consumption in the units of the non-material sphere serving individuals	19.3	20.7	21.7	22.4	24.8	27.4	29.0	31.6	34.4	36.7	39.0
Consumption of the Population	220.1	231.6	240.2	250.4	267.0	281.0	286.0	299.8	312.1	320.1	324.4
3 Material consumption in the units of the non-material sphere serving the community as a whole	26.0	27.7	27.5	28.9	31.4	33.5	34.5	36.4	39.6	42.3	44.7
4 Net fixed capital formation	66.2	67.4	73.3	77.5	73.1	102.1	89.2	89.1	98.5	102.1	92.2
5 Increase in material circulating assets and in stocks [a]	15.6	39.0	11.4	3.2	36.0	18.2	30.5	42.7	66.3	23.7	18.8
6 Losses	5.4	5.4	6.1	6.6	6.5	7.3	7.3	8.2	8.3	9.9	9.7
7 Exports of goods and material services	119.5	128.2	152.8	175.1	181.2	189.1	201.9	230.7	234.8	261.0	263.0
8 Less: Imports of goods and material services	151.8	180.5	171.4	176.8	207.8	218.5	224.4	246.9	278.9	267.2	264.1
Net Material Product	301.0	318.8	339.9	364.9	387.4	412.7	425.0	460.0	480.7	491.9	488.7

a) Including changes in incompleted capital formation.

2a Net Material Product by Kind of Activity of the Material Sphere in Current Market Prices

Thousand Million Hungarian forint

	1970	1971	1972	1973	1974	1975	1976	1977	1978	1979	1980
1 Agriculture and forestry [a]	48.9	55.7	56.5	66.2	66.2	65.1	69.0	77.1	76.7	73.8	84.0
2 Industrial activity [ab]	120.5	125.2	138.9	152.1	164.6	185.5	210.1	222.9	243.6	268.0	287.0
3 Construction	30.7	33.7	36.2	38.6	43.0	45.8	49.1	57.3	64.0	67.9	58.2
4 Wholesale and retail trade and restaurants and other eating and drinking places [bc]	54.6	59.7	66.9	72.4	67.9	69.8	74.2	86.4	95.8	111.6	118.4
5 Transport and communication	17.0	17.7	18.5	20.5	21.9	24.0	25.7	28.2	31.3	31.8	31.5
a Transport	13.7	14.3	14.9	16.5	17.7	19.5	20.7	22.9	25.1	25.4	24.9
b Communication	3.3	3.4	3.6	4.0	4.2	4.5	5.0	5.3	6.2	6.4	6.7
6 Other activities of the material sphere [c]	3.2	3.6	3.8	4.6	5.4	5.9	6.8	7.3	7.0	6.4	7.3
Net material product	274.9	295.6	320.8	354.4	369.0	396.1	434.9	479.2	518.4	559.5	586.4

a) For 1960-1970, including 'logging and fishing'. Beginning 1970, 'logging' is included in industrial activity.
b) For 1968-1970, the institutional changes of taxation caused great changes in the current value of industry and trade.
c) Import duties are included mostly in the current value of trade, and the rest in other branches except for 1968-1970 of the first series where import duties are included in other activities of the material sphere.

Hungary

2b Net Material Product by Kind of Activity of the Material Sphere in Constant Market Prices

Thousand Million Hungarian forint

	1970	1971	1972	1973	1974	1975	1976	1977	1978	1979	1980
					At constant prices of:1976						
1 Agriculture and forestry [a]	65.3	68.6	69.9	73.2	73.4	73.8	68.5	79.4	77.8	74.5	78.3
2 Industrial activity [b]	132.7	140.8	151.6	165.3	179.0	190.5	200.6	212.8	224.8	239.1	248.6
3 Construction	34.6	36.5	37.1	38.9	41.9	45.8	48.1	51.1	53.9	55.7	52.7
4 Wholesale and retail trade and restaurants and other eating and drinking places	45.2	49.1	56.2	60.3	64.7	71.6	76.4	82.8	89.7	87.6	74.7
5 Transport and communication	18.1	18.6	19.8	21.5	22.1	24.0	24.0	25.8	27.2	27.7	26.7
a Transport	14.7	15.2	16.2	17.6	18.0	19.6	19.3	20.7	21.9	22.3	21.1
b Communication	3.4	3.4	3.6	3.9	4.1	4.4	4.7	5.1	5.3	5.4	5.6
6 Other activities of the material sphere [a]	5.1	5.2	5.3	5.7	6.3	7.0	7.4	8.1	7.3	7.3	7.7
Net material product	301.0	318.8	339.9	364.9	387.4	412.7	425.0	460.0	480.7	491.9	488.7

a) Item 'Logging' is included in item 'Industrial activity'.
b) For 1960-1970, including 'logging and fishing'. Beginning 1970, 'logging' is included in industrial activity.

3 Primary Incomes by Kind of Activity of the Material Sphere in Current Market Prices

Thousand Million Hungarian forint

	1970 Pop.	1970 Ent.	1971 Pop.	1971 Ent.	1972 Pop.	1972 Ent.	1973 Pop.	1973 Ent.	1974 Pop.	1974 Ent.	1975 Pop.	1975 Ent.
1 Agriculture and forestry	43.7	5.2	46.4	9.3	48.1	8.4	49.9	16.3	50.7	15.5	52.3	12.8
2 Industrial activity	50.2	70.3	52.3	72.9	55.6	83.3	62.5	89.6	68.1	96.5	73.2	112.3
3 Construction	17.5	13.2	18.5	15.2	19.0	17.2	20.7	17.9	22.6	20.4	24.6	21.2
4 Wholesale and retail trade and restaurants and other eating and drinking places	11.3	43.3	12.1	47.6	13.2	53.7	14.3	58.1	15.9	52.0	17.9	51.9
5 Transport and communication	9.9	7.1	10.9	6.8	11.6	6.9	12.5	8.0	13.9	8.0	15.2	8.8
6 Other activities of the material sphere	1.6	1.6	1.6	2.0	1.7	2.1	2.0	2.6	2.3	3.1	2.4	3.5
Total	134.2	140.7	141.8	153.8	149.2	171.6	161.9	192.5	173.5	195.5	185.6	210.5

	1976 Pop.	1976 Ent.	1977 Pop.	1977 Ent.
1 Agriculture and forestry	54.5	14.5	60.3	16.8
2 Industrial activity	75.7	134.4	82.7	140.2
3 Construction	25.6	23.5	28.8	28.5
4 Wholesale and retail trade and restaurants and other eating and drinking places	18.5	55.7	20.8	65.6
5 Transport and communication	16.2	9.5	17.6	10.6
6 Other activities of the material sphere	2.6	4.2	2.6	4.7
Total	193.1	241.8	212.8	266.4

4 Primary Incomes From Net Material Product

Thousand Million Hungarian forint

	1970	1971	1972	1973	1974	1975	1976	1977	1978	1979	1980
					a) Primary Incomes of the Population						
1 Socialist sector	128.1	135.4	142.8	155.5	166.9	178.9	186.2	204.6	...	...	...
a State sector	74.7	78.7	84.3	93.2	101.7	110.1	114.3	124.9	...	...	...
b Co-operative sector	45.6	48.7	49.7	52.4	55.1	56.9	57.5	62.5	...	...	...
c Personal plots of households	7.8	8.0	8.8	9.9	10.1	11.9	14.4	17.2	...	...	...
2 Private sector	6.1	6.4	6.4	6.4	6.6	6.7	6.9	8.2	...	...	...
Sub-total	134.2	141.8	149.2	161.9	173.5	185.6	193.1	212.8	...	...	...
					b) Primary incomes of the enterprises						
1 Socialist sector	140.0	153.1	170.8	191.4	194.4	209.3	240.6	265.3	...	...	...
a State sector	121.8	128.7	146.2	158.7	161.3	175.7	204.6	224.8	...	...	...
b Co-operative sector	18.2	24.4	24.6	32.7	33.1	33.6	36.0	40.5	...	...	...
2 Private sector	0.7	0.7	0.8	1.1	1.1	1.2	1.2	1.1	...	...	...
Sub-total	140.7	153.8	171.6	192.5	195.5	210.5	241.8	266.4	...	...	...
Total net material product	274.9	295.6	320.8	354.4	369.0	396.1	434.9	479.2	...	...	...

Hungary

5a Supply and Disposition of Goods and Material Services in Current Market Prices

Thousand Million Hungarian forint

	Gross Output at Producers Prices	Trade Margins and Transport Charges	Gross Output at Market Prices	Imports	Total Supply and Disposition	Intermediate Material Consumption including Depreciation	Final Consumption	Net Capital Formation	Losses	Exports
1970										
1 Agriculture and forestry	117.6	...	117.6	7.9	125.5	73.1	37.2	4.2	...	11.0
a Agriculture and livestock	108.0	...	108.0	6.6	114.6	66.3	34.6	3.3	...	10.4
b Forestry	4.8	...	4.8	1.3	6.1	4.1	0.7	0.7	...	0.6
c Other [a]	4.8	...	4.8	...	4.8	2.7	1.9	0.2	...	...
2 Industrial activity	382.6	...	382.6	97.9	480.5	250.1	100.7	46.7	...	83.0
3 Construction	74.5	...	74.5	-	74.5	9.2	8.1	56.9	...	0.3
4 Transport and communication	39.6	...	39.6	1.3	40.9	25.0	11.1	1.3	...	3.5
5 Other activities of the material sphere [b]	-	51.7	51.7	0.8	52.5	20.1	29.4	0.6	...	2.4
Total	614.3	51.7	666.0	107.9	773.9	377.5	186.5	109.7	...	100.2
1971										
1 Agriculture and forestry	131.2	...	131.2	7.6	138.8	81.0	35.9	8.4	...	13.5
a Agriculture and livestock	121.5	...	121.5	6.2	127.7	74.3	33.5	7.0	...	12.9
b Forestry	5.1	...	5.1	1.4	6.5	4.1	0.7	1.1	...	0.6
c Other [a]	4.6	...	4.6	...	4.6	2.6	1.7	0.3	...	...
2 Industrial activity	415.9	...	415.9	120.7	536.6	272.8	115.8	59.8	...	88.2
3 Construction	82.5	...	82.5	-	82.5	10.3	9.3	62.4	...	0.5
4 Transport and communication	42.8	...	42.8	1.6	44.4	27.1	12.4	1.4	...	3.5
5 Other activities of the material sphere [b]	-	58.3	58.3	1.0	59.3	23.3	32.3	1.0	...	2.7
Total	672.4	58.3	730.7	130.9	861.6	414.5	205.7	133.0	...	108.4
1972										
1 Agriculture and forestry	135.7	...	135.7	9.0	144.7	88.3	32.0	7.8	...	16.6
a Agriculture and livestock	125.2	...	125.2	7.5	132.7	80.4	29.6	6.9	...	15.8
b Forestry	5.8	...	5.8	1.5	7.3	5.1	0.8	0.6	...	0.8
c Other [a]	4.7	...	4.7	...	4.7	2.8	1.6	0.3	...	...
2 Industrial activity	449.3	...	449.3	116.0	565.3	285.2	126.9	44.2	...	109.0
3 Construction	87.8	...	87.8	-	87.8	11.7	10.5	64.9	...	0.7
4 Transport and communication	44.4	...	44.4	1.8	46.2	26.6	13.5	1.9	...	4.2
5 Other activities of the material sphere [b]	-	63.7	63.7	1.8	65.5	27.4	33.6	1.5	...	3.0
Total	717.2	63.7	780.9	128.6	909.5	439.2	216.5	120.3	...	133.5
1973										
1 Agriculture and forestry	153.0	...	153.0	9.4	162.4	95.9	36.6	6.4	...	23.5
a Agriculture and livestock	141.9	...	141.9	7.6	149.5	87.8	33.9	5.3	...	22.5
b Forestry	6.2	...	6.2	1.8	8.0	5.6	0.7	0.7	...	1.0
c Other [a]	4.9	...	4.9	...	4.9	2.5	2.0	0.4	...	...
2 Industrial activity	498.2	...	498.2	131.5	629.7	317.4	136.8	45.1	...	130.4
3 Construction	93.4	...	93.4	-	93.4	12.9	11.0	68.1	...	1.4
4 Transport and communication	48.1	...	48.1	1.6	49.7	29.2	14.3	1.6	...	4.6
5 Other activities of the material sphere [b]	-	68.9	68.9	1.7	70.6	27.3	36.6	2.7	...	4.0
Total	792.7	68.9	861.6	144.2	1005.8	482.7	235.3	123.9	...	163.9
1974										
1 Agriculture and forestry	161.2	...	161.2	15.8	177.0	107.3	34.0	7.7	...	28.0
a Agriculture and livestock	149.3	...	149.3	13.2	162.5	98.0	31.1	6.6	...	26.8
b Forestry	6.3	...	6.3	2.6	8.9	6.3	0.7	0.7	...	1.2
c Other [a]	5.6	...	5.6	...	5.6	3.0	2.2	0.4	...	...
2 Industrial activity	557.1	...	557.1	186.6	743.7	375.6	157.4	66.5	...	144.2
3 Construction	104.4	...	104.4	-	104.4	13.7	11.4	77.0	...	2.3
4 Transport and communication	52.3	...	52.3	2.2	54.5	31.7	15.1	1.7	...	6.0
5 Other activities of the material sphere [b]	-	80.4	80.4	2.0	82.4	31.5	41.1	3.5	...	6.3
Total	875.0	80.4	955.4	206.6	1162.0	559.8	259.0	156.4	...	186.8

Hungary

5a Supply and Disposition of Goods and Material Services in Current Market Prices
(Continued)

Thousand Million Hungarian forint

		Supply				Disposition				
		Gross Output at Producers Prices	Trade Margins and Transport Charges	Gross Output at Market Prices	Imports	Total Supply and Disposition	Intermediate Material Consumption including Depreciation	Final Consumption	Net Capital Formation	Losses	Exports

1975

1	Agriculture and forestry	169.7	...	169.7	8.4	178.1	101.8	36.9	10.8	...	28.6
	a Agriculture and livestock	156.9	...	156.9	6.4	163.3	92.6	33.9	9.4	...	27.4
	b Forestry	6.6	...	6.6	2.0	8.6	5.8	0.8	0.9	...	1.1
	c Other [a]	6.2	...	6.2	...	6.2	3.4	2.2	0.5	...	0.1
2	Industrial activity	638.6	...	638.6	220.9	859.5	448.9	180.5	75.3	...	154.8
3	Construction	116.1	...	116.1	-	116.1	15.6	12.9	85.1		2.5
4	Transport and communication	57.6	...	57.6	2.7	60.3	34.9	16.1	3.0	...	6.3
5	Other activities of the material sphere [b]	-	84.3	84.3	2.1	86.4	33.7	43.6	3.1	...	6.0
	Total	982.0	84.3	1066.3	234.1	1300.4	634.9	290.0	177.3	...	198.2

1976

1	Agriculture and forestry	188.1	...	188.1	10.1	198.2	128.3	43.0	5.1	...	21.8
	a Agriculture and livestock	173.5	...	173.5	8.3	181.8	117.3	39.5	4.4	...	20.6
	b Forestry	7.7	...	7.7	1.8	9.5	7.0	1.0	0.4	...	1.1
	c Other [a]	6.9	...	6.9	...	6.9	4.0	2.5	0.3	...	0.1
2	Industrial activity	695.2	...	695.2	207.7	902.9	458.0	194.5	81.6	...	168.8
3	Construction	127.4	...	127.4	-	127.4	16.6	15.0	95.2	...	0.6
4	Transport and communication	65.0	...	65.0	2.8	67.8	42.5	19.3	0.3	...	5.7
5	Other activities of the material sphere [b]	-	87.4	87.4	3.7	91.1	36.3	45.1	5.1	...	4.6
	Total	1075.7	87.4	1163.1	224.3	1387.4	681.7	316.9	187.3	...	201.5

1977

1	Agriculture and forestry	213.2	...	213.2	14.3	227.5	150.8	40.0	7.0	...	29.7
	a Agriculture and livestock	197.1	...	197.1	12.3	209.4	138.4	36.2	6.2	...	28.6
	b Forestry	8.6	...	8.6	2.0	10.6	8.0	1.0	0.5	...	1.1
	c Other [a]	7.5	...	7.5	...	7.5	4.4	2.8	0.3	...	...
2	Industrial activity	757.2	...	757.2	241.0	998.2	500.4	213.0	90.5	...	194.3
3	Construction	143.6	...	143.6	1.3	144.9	17.4	16.5	109.9	...	1.1
4	Transport and communication	71.2	...	71.2	3.6	74.8	48.4	19.4	0.3	...	6.7
5	Other activities of the material sphere [b]	-	98.9	98.9	4.2	103.1	42.7	50.1	4.0	...	6.3
	Total	1185.2	98.9	1284.1	264.4	1548.5	759.7	339.0	211.7	...	238.1

1978

1	Agriculture and forestry	223.0	...	223.0	13.3	236.3	151.7	45.9	8.4	...	30.6
	a Agriculture and livestock	205.5	...	205.5	11.1	216.6	138.5	41.7	6.9	...	29.5
	b Forestry	9.3	...	9.3	2.2	11.5	8.3	1.1	1.0	...	1.1
	c Other [a]	8.2	...	8.2	...	8.2	4.9	3.1	0.2	...	...
2	Industrial activity	826.2	...	826.2	274.4	1100.6	551.7	230.6	123.8	...	194.5
3	Construction	159.6	...	159.6	1.5	161.1	21.8	20.6	117.7	...	1.0
4	Transport and communication	78.2	...	78.2	4.3	82.5	53.9	20.4	0.3	...	7.9
5	Other activities of the material sphere [b]	-	107.5	107.5	5.3	112.8	47.1	54.2	4.5	...	7.0
	Total	1287.0	107.5	1394.5	298.8	1693.3	826.2	371.7	254.4	...	241.0

1979

1	Agriculture and forestry	225.2	...	225.2	11.5	236.7	151.7	46.7	7.6	...	30.7
	a Agriculture and livestock	206.1	...	206.1	9.8	215.9	137.6	42.2	6.8	...	29.3
	b Forestry	10.1	...	10.1	1.7	11.8	8.8	1.3	0.3	...	1.4
	c Other [a]	9.0	...	9.0	...	9.0	5.3	3.2	0.5	...	...
2	Industrial activity	876.5	...	876.5	279.9	1156.4	590.2	241.3	93.9	...	231.0
3	Construction	170.6	...	170.6	1.6	172.2	23.7	21.6	125.9	...	1.0
4	Transport and communication	82.3	...	82.3	4.2	86.5	55.2	22.3	0.9	...	8.1
5	Other activities of the material sphere [b]	-	110.7	110.7	6.1	116.8	47.7	59.9	1.1	...	8.1
	Total	1354.6	110.7	1465.3	303.3	1768.6	868.5	391.8	229.4	...	278.9

a) Referring to water managements.
b) Referring to trade margins.

Hungary

5b Supply and Disposition of Goods and Material Services in Constant Market Prices

Thousand Million Hungarian forint

	Gross Output at Producers Prices	Trade Margins and Transport Charges	Gross Output at Market Prices	Imports	Total Supply and Disposition	Intermediate Material Consumption including Depreciation	Final Consumption	Net Capital Formation	Losses	Exports
					At constant prices of:1976					
					1970					
1 Agriculture and forestry	149.9	...	149.9	10.7	160.6	103.3	38.1	4.3	...	14.8
a Agriculture and livestock	137.6	...	137.6	9.0	146.6	93.7	35.2	3.5	...	14.2
b Forestry	6.7	...	6.7	1.7	8.4	6.3	0.9	0.6	...	0.6
c Other [a]	5.6	...	5.6	...	5.6	3.3	2.0	0.3	...	...
2 Industrial activity	484.0	...	484.0	138.0	622.0	289.3	188.6	46.7	...	97.4
3 Construction	94.9	...	94.9	-	94.9	15.3	12.5	66.7	...	0.4
4 Transport and communication	47.8	...	47.8	1.9	49.7	29.9	14.3	1.4	...	4.1
5 Other activities of the material sphere [b]	-	58.7	58.7	1.2	59.9	19.7	36.5	0.9	...	2.8
Total	776.6	58.7	835.3	151.8	987.1	457.5	290.0	120.1	...	119.5
					1971					
1 Agriculture and forestry	159.7	...	159.7	11.1	170.8	109.2	37.6	7.1	...	16.9
a Agriculture and livestock	147.5	...	147.5	9.3	156.8	99.7	34.7	6.1	...	16.3
b Forestry	6.9	...	6.9	1.8	8.7	6.5	0.9	0.7	...	0.6
c Other [a]	5.3	...	5.3	...	5.3	3.0	2.0	0.3	...	...
2 Industrial activity	516.2	...	516.2	165.8	682.0	357.9	156.2	64.5	...	103.4
3 Construction	101.2	...	101.2	-	101.2	16.5	13.2	71.0	...	0.5
4 Transport and communication	50.7	...	50.7	2.2	52.9	31.6	15.7	1.4	...	4.2
5 Other activities of the material sphere [b]	-	63.1	63.1	1.5	64.6	23.1	36.9	1.4	...	3.2
Total	827.8	63.1	890.9	180.6	1071.5	538.3	259.6	145.4	...	128.2
					1972					
1 Agriculture and forestry	164.6	...	164.6	13.4	178.0	115.4	38.4	5.7	...	18.5
a Agriculture and livestock	152.2	...	152.2	11.6	163.8	105.8	35.6	4.8	...	17.6
b Forestry	7.0	...	7.0	1.8	8.8	6.5	0.8	0.6	...	0.9
c Other [a]	5.4	...	5.4	...	5.4	3.1	2.0	0.3	...	...
2 Industrial activity	544.0	...	544.0	153.9	697.9	365.1	160.0	46.7	...	126.1
3 Construction	102.7	...	102.7	-	102.7	18.0	13.8	70.2	...	0.7
4 Transport and communication	52.2	...	52.2	2.1	54.3	32.2	16.0	1.7	...	4.4
5 Other activities of the material sphere [b]	-	66.3	66.3	2.0	68.3	25.7	37.9	1.6	...	3.1
Total	863.5	66.3	929.8	171.4	1101.2	556.4	266.1	125.9	...	152.8
					1973					
1 Agriculture and forestry	174.7	...	174.7	12.6	187.3	119.8	39.6	4.2	...	23.7
a Agriculture and livestock	161.8	...	161.8	10.2	172.0	109.6	36.6	3.3	...	22.5
b Forestry	7.3	...	7.3	2.4	9.7	7.1	0.8	0.6	...	1.2
c Other [a]	5.6	...	5.6	...	5.6	3.1	2.2	0.3	...	...
2 Industrial activity	584.1	...	584.1	160.2	744.3	392.2	166.2	44.5	...	141.4
3 Construction	105.6	...	105.6	-	105.6	16.6	13.4	74.1	...	1.5
4 Transport and communication	55.1	...	55.1	2.0	57.1	34.4	16.5	1.7	...	4.5
5 Other activities of the material sphere [b]	-	70.8	70.8	2.0	72.8	27.3	39.3	2.2	...	4.0
Total	919.5	70.8	990.3	176.8	1167.1	590.3	275.0	126.7	...	175.1
					1974					
1 Agriculture and forestry	181.6	...	181.6	16.2	197.8	125.7	39.8	6.3	...	26.0
a Agriculture and livestock	168.4	...	168.4	13.7	182.1	115.2	36.8	5.3	...	24.8
b Forestry	7.1	...	7.1	2.5	9.6	7.1	0.8	0.6	...	1.1
c Other [a]	6.1	...	6.1	...	6.1	3.4	2.2	0.4	...	0.1
2 Industrial activity	633.7	...	633.7	187.5	821.2	431.0	182.4	65.5	...	142.3
3 Construction	113.6	...	113.6	-	113.6	17.1	13.1	81.1	...	2.3
4 Transport and communication	59.7	...	59.7	2.1	61.8	37.5	17.3	1.7	...	5.3
5 Other activities of the material sphere [b]	-	78.4	78.4	2.0	80.4	30.9	41.8	2.4	...	5.3
Total	988.6	78.4	1067.0	207.8	1274.8	642.2	294.4	157.0	...	181.2

Hungary

5b Supply and Disposition of Goods and Material Services in Constant Market Prices
(Continued)

Thousand Million Hungarian forint

	Supply				Total Supply and Disposition	Disposition				
	Gross Output at Producers Prices	Trade Margins and Transport Charges	Gross Output at Market Prices	Imports		Intermediate Material Consumption Including Depreciation	Final Consumption	Net Capital Formation	Losses	Exports

At constant prices of: 1976

1975

1 Agriculture and forestry	190.7	...	190.7	8.7	199.4	123.1	40.8	8.3	...	27.2
a Agriculture and livestock	177.0	...	177.0	6.9	183.9	113.2	37.6	6.9	...	26.2
b Forestry	7.2	...	7.2	1.8	9.0	6.3	0.9	0.9	...	0.8
c Other [a]	6.5	...	6.5	...	6.5	3.6	2.3	0.5	...	0.1
2 Industrial activity	664.2	...	664.2	205.2	869.4	456.2	192.7	70.9	...	149.6
3 Construction	122.8	...	122.8	-	122.8	17.2	13.8	89.4	...	2.4
4 Transport and communication	63.3	...	63.3	2.7	66.0	40.9	18.0	2.4	...	4.7
5 Other activities of the material sphere [b]	-	84.9	84.9	2.0	86.9	34.5	44.8	2.6	...	5.0
Total	1041.0	84.9	1125.9	218.6	1344.5	671.9	310.1	173.6	...	188.9

1976

1 Agriculture and forestry	188.1	...	188.1	10.1	198.2	129.9	42.6	4.0	...	21.7
a Agriculture and livestock	173.5	...	173.5	8.3	181.8	118.9	39.0	3.3	...	20.6
b Forestry	7.7	...	7.7	1.8	9.5	7.0	1.0	0.4	...	1.1
c Other [a]	6.9	...	6.9	...	6.9	4.0	2.6	0.3	...	...
2 Industrial activity	695.2	...	695.2	207.7	902.9	462.0	196.8	75.2	...	168.9
3 Construction	127.4	...	127.4	-	127.4	17.0	15.1	94.7	...	0.6
4 Transport and communication	65.0	...	65.0	2.8	67.8	42.5	19.3	0.3	...	5.7
5 Other activities of the material sphere [b]	-	87.4	87.4	3.7	91.1	36.6	45.2	4.7	...	4.6
Total	1075.7	87.4	1163.1	224.3	1387.4	688.0	319.0	178.9	...	201.5

1977

1 Agriculture and forestry	212.6	...	212.6	10.0	222.6	148.1	44.1	0.6	...	29.8
a Agriculture and livestock	196.7	...	196.7	8.2	204.9	135.9	40.3	-0.1	...	28.8
b Forestry	8.4	...	8.4	1.8	10.2	7.7	1.0	0.5	...	1.0
c Other [a]	7.5	...	7.5	...	7.5	4.5	2.8	0.2	...	...
2 Industrial activity	742.7	...	742.7	228.4	971.1	492.8	202.3	88.9	...	187.1
3 Construction	136.4	...	136.4	1.3	137.7	17.9	15.9	102.8	...	1.1
4 Transport and communication	68.5	...	68.5	3.3	71.8	46.6	18.7	0.2	...	6.3
5 Other activities of the material sphere [b]	-	93.4	93.4	3.9	97.3	39.8	48.3	3.3	...	5.9
Total	1160.2	93.4	1253.6	246.9	1500.5	745.2	329.3	195.8	...	230.2

1978

1 Agriculture and forestry	218.1	...	218.1	12.4	230.5	147.1	44.1	8.0	...	31.3
a Agriculture and livestock	201.4	...	201.4	10.4	211.8	134.5	40.3	6.8	...	30.2
b Forestry	8.9	...	8.9	2.0	10.9	7.8	1.0	1.0	...	1.1
c Other [a]	7.8	...	7.8	...	7.8	4.8	2.8	0.2	...	...
2 Industrial activity	781.1	...	781.1	256.1	1037.2	519.1	217.0	113.0	...	188.1
3 Construction	143.7	...	143.7	1.4	145.1	20.4	18.3	105.5	...	0.9
4 Transport and communication	72.2	...	72.2	4.0	76.2	50.2	18.3	0.3	...	7.4
5 Other activities of the material sphere [b]	-	98.1	98.1	5.0	103.1	44.5	48.3	3.7	...	6.6
Total	1215.1	98.1	1313.2	278.9	1592.1	781.3	346.0	230.5	...	234.3

1979

1 Agriculture and forestry	216.1	...	216.1	8.8	224.6	146.9	45.1	4.0	...	28.9
a Agriculture and livestock	198.3	...	198.3	7.5	205.8	133.7	40.9	3.5	...	27.7
b Forestry	9.3	...	9.3	1.3	10.6	8.0	1.2	0.2	...	1.2
c Other [a]	8.5	...	8.5	...	8.5	5.2	3.0	0.3	...	...
2 Industrial activity	808.2	...	808.2	248.0	1056.2	536.1	221.4	83.3	...	215.4
3 Construction	148.7	...	148.7	1.4	150.1	21.2	18.5	109.4	...	1.0
4 Transport and communication	74.9	...	74.9	3.6	78.5	50.5	20.0	0.5	...	7.5
5 Other activities of the material sphere [b]	-	98.7	98.7	5.3	104.0	44.1	51.4	1.0	...	7.5
Total	1247.9	98.7	1346.6	267.1	1613.7	798.8	356.4	198.2	...	260.3

a) Referring to water managements.
b) Referring to trade margins.

Hungary

6a Capital Formation by Kind of Activity of the Material and Non-Material Spheres in Current Market Prices

Thousand Million Hungarian forint

	1970	1971	1972	1973	1974	1975	1976	1977	1978	1979	1980
Net Fixed Capital Formation											
1 Agriculture and forestry	11.1	10.2	12.3	14.0	11.5	12.6	9.4	10.1	11.7	12.1	7.9
2 Industrial activity	16.5	17.2	18.2	19.4	19.4	37.7	24.1	28.4	42.9	41.4	26.8
3 Construction	0.6	1.9	0.7	0.6	0.4	1.0	0.8	1.5	2.6	1.0	-0.3
4 Wholesale and retail trade, restaurants and other eating and drinking places	1.9	3.0	2.2	2.5	4.1	3.3	6.3	6.0	4.7	4.6	4.8
5 Transport and communication	7.6	4.3	6.3	6.3	5.1	9.5	13.7	8.4	7.3	14.1	15.1
6 Other activities of the material sphere	0.5	0.4	0.8	1.5	0.5	1.0	0.8	1.0	2.3	1.9	0.6
Total Material Sphere	38.2	37.0	40.5	44.3	41.0	65.1	55.1	55.4	71.5	75.1	54.9
7 Housing except owner-occupied, communal and miscellaneous personal services [a]	9.7	12.0	15.6	17.0	17.3	23.2	23.2	25.6	25.6	29.0	31.2
8 Education, culture and art	1.3	2.0	1.7	2.3	3.4	3.6	4.5	4.7	5.1	4.9	5.9
9 Health and social welfare services and sports	2.1	1.9	2.7	2.8	2.7	2.7	3.2	4.6	4.6	4.6	7.1
Total Non-Material Sphere Serving Individuals	13.1	15.9	20.0	22.1	23.4	29.5	30.9	34.9	35.3	38.5	44.2
10 Government	...	...	...	...	...	...	...	...	...	...	...
11 Finance, credit and insurance	...	...	...	...	...	...	...	...	...	...	...
12 Research, scientific and technological institutes	...	...	...	...	...	...	...	...	...	...	...
13 Other activities of the non-material sphere	...	...	...	...	...	...	...	...	...	...	...
Total Non-Material Sphere Serving the Community as a Whole	3.4	3.7	4.2	5.6	5.8	6.5	7.1	7.8	5.5	6.5	11.0
14 Owner-occupied dwellings [a]	...	...	...	...	...	...	...	...	...	...	...
Total Net Fixed Capital Formation	54.7	56.6	64.7	72.0	70.2	101.1	93.1	98.1	112.3	120.1	110.1
Gross Fixed Capital Formation											
1 Agriculture and forestry	16.3	16.1	18.8	21.4	19.8	22.0	20.7	22.7	25.3	25.7	23.6
2 Industrial activity	31.5	34.0	36.1	38.1	39.7	59.5	48.7	56.0	74.6	75.7	66.3
3 Construction	1.9	3.3	2.3	2.3	2.4	3.1	3.2	4.3	5.9	5.0	4.1
4 Wholesale and retail trade and restaurants and other eating and drinking places	2.8	4.0	3.4	3.8	5.6	4.9	8.1	8.1	7.1	7.3	7.7
5 Transport and communication	14.2	11.1	13.4	13.7	13.0	18.0	22.7	18.3	17.9	25.8	28.2
6 Other activities of the material sphere	0.9	1.0	1.4	2.2	1.2	1.8	1.6	1.8	4.8	2.9	1.7
Total Material Sphere	67.6	69.5	75.4	81.5	81.7	109.3	105.0	111.2	135.6	142.4	131.6
7 Housing except owner-occupied, communal and miscellaneous personal services [a]	13.9	16.4	20.4	22.1	22.7	29.1	29.8	32.7	33.0	36.2	39.7
8 Education, culture and art	2.6	3.4	3.2	3.9	5.1	5.5	6.6	7.0	7.6	7.6	8.9
9 Health and social welfare services and sports	2.7	2.5	3.3	3.5	3.4	3.5	4.1	5.6	5.6	5.7	8.4
Total Non-Material Sphere Serving Individuals	19.2	22.3	26.9	29.5	31.2	38.1	40.5	45.3	46.2	49.5	57.0
10 Government	...	...	...	...	...	...	...	...	...	...	...
11 Finance, credit and insurance	...	...	...	...	...	...	...	...	...	...	...
12 Research, scientific and technological institutes	...	...	...	...	...	...	...	...	...	...	...
13 Other activities of the non-material sphere	...	...	...	...	...	...	...	...	...	...	...
Total Non-Material Sphere Serving the Community as a Whole	4.5	5.0	5.6	7.1	7.4	8.5	9.4	10.2	6.6	11.6	14.2
14 Owner-occupied dwellings [a]	...	...	...	...	...	...	...	...	...	...	...
Total Gross Fixed Capital Formation	91.3	96.8	107.9	118.1	120.3	155.9	154.9	166.7	188.4	203.5	202.8
Gross Fixed Capital Formation by Socio-economic Sector and Industrial Use											
1 State and co-operative (excluding collective farms)	55.5	57.0	61.1	66.3	66.7	92.2	89.2	94.8	113.5	124.1	115.4
a Industry	31.5	34.0	36.1	38.1	39.7	59.5	48.7	56.0	74.6	75.7	66.3
b Construction	1.9	3.3	2.3	2.3	2.4	3.1	3.2	4.3	5.9	5.0	4.1
c Agriculture and forestry	4.2	3.6	4.5	6.2	4.8	4.9	4.9	6.3	6.0	7.4	7.4
d Transport and communication	14.2	11.1	13.4	13.7	13.0	18.0	22.7	18.3	17.9	25.8	28.2
e Residential building [b]	...	...	...	...	...	...	...	...	...	...	...

Hungary

6a Capital Formation by Kind of Activity of the Material and Non-Material Spheres in Current Market Prices
(Continued)

Thousand Million Hungarian forint

	1970	1971	1972	1973	1974	1975	1976	1977	1978	1979	1980
f Trade and other	3.7	5.0	4.8	6.0	6.8	6.7	9.7	9.9	9.1	10.2	9.4
2 Collective farms	11.5	11.8	13.6	14.4	14.2	16.3	14.8	15.4	17.5	17.3	16.2
a Agriculture	11.5	11.8	13.6	14.4	14.2	16.3	14.8	15.4	17.5	17.3	16.2
b Other	-	-	-	-	-	-	-	-	...	...	...
3 Other [b]	24.3	28.0	33.2	37.4	39.4	47.4	50.9	56.5	57.4	62.1	71.2
Gross Fixed Capital Formation	91.3	96.8	107.9	118.1	120.3	155.9	154.9	166.7	188.4	203.5	202.8

a) Item 'Owner-occupied dwellings' is included in item 'Housing except owner-occupied, communal, and miscellaneous personal services'.
b) Item 'Residential buildings' is included in item 'Other'.

6b Capital Formation by Kind of Activity of the Material and Non-Material Spheres in Constant Market Prices

Thousand Million Hungarian forint

	1970	1971	1972	1973	1974	1975	1976	1977	1978	1979	1980
At constant prices of: 1976											
Net Fixed Capital Formation											
1 Agriculture and forestry	13.3	11.8	13.4	14.6	11.5	12.3	8.4	8.6	9.5	8.7	5.0
2 Industrial activity	18.6	20.1	20.0	19.9	19.2	36.9	21.9	25.4	38.9	35.9	23.6
3 Construction	0.7	2.1	0.7	0.6	0.3	0.8	0.6	1.3	2.3	0.8	-0.4
4 Wholesale and retail trade, restaurants and other eating and drinking places	2.3	3.2	2.4	2.6	4.3	3.3	6.2	5.8	4.3	4.1	4.2
5 Transport and communication	9.8	5.4	7.5	6.6	5.3	9.5	12.9	7.0	5.1	11.8	13.0
6 Other activities of the material sphere	0.4	0.4	0.7	1.5	0.4	0.9	0.5	0.5	1.6	1.6	0.4
Total Material Sphere	45.1	43.0	44.7	45.8	41.0	63.7	50.5	48.6	61.7	62.9	45.8
7 Housing except owner-occupied, communal and miscellaneous personal services [a]	12.5	15.1	18.7	19.7	19.4	25.0	23.9	24.7	24.4	25.5	26.9
8 Education, culture and art	1.7	2.5	2.0	2.6	3.6	3.7	4.3	4.1	3.6	4.4	5.2
9 Health and social welfare services and sports	2.8	2.4	3.2	3.2	3.0	2.9	3.2	4.4	1.6	1.5	3.7
Total Non-Material Sphere Serving Individuals	17.0	20.0	23.9	25.5	26.0	31.6	31.4	33.2	29.6	31.4	35.8
10 Government	...	...	...	...	...	...	...	...	...	...	...
11 Finance, credit and insurance	...	...	...	...	...	...	...	...	...	...	...
12 Research, scientific and technological institutes	...	...	...	...	...	...	...	...	...	...	...
13 Other activities of the non-material sphere	...	...	...	...	...	...	...	...	...	...	...
Total Non-Material Sphere Serving the Community as a Whole	4.1	4.4	4.7	6.2	6.1	6.8	7.3	7.3	7.2	7.8	...
14 Owner-occupied dwellings [a]	...	...	...	...	...	...	...	...	...	...	10.6
Total Net Fixed Capital Formation	66.2	67.4	73.3	77.5	73.1	102.1	89.2	89.1	98.5	102.1	92.2
Gross Fixed Capital Formation											
1 Agriculture and forestry	19.7	19.0	21.5	23.6	21.5	23.5	20.9	22.2	24.0	24.0	21.1
2 Industrial activity	37.4	40.0	41.1	42.3	42.9	62.5	49.6	54.8	71.0	70.1	60.7
3 Construction	2.2	3.7	2.5	2.5	2.6	3.2	3.2	4.2	5.7	4.6	3.7
4 Wholesale and retail trade and restaurants and other eating and drinking places	3.4	4.5	3.8	4.1	6.0	5.1	8.2	8.0	6.8	6.8	7.1
5 Transport and communication	17.6	13.6	16.1	15.6	14.7	19.4	23.3	17.9	16.5	23.9	26.0
6 Other activities of the material sphere	1.0	1.1	1.5	2.4	1.3	1.9	1.6	1.8	3.8	2.6	1.6
Total Material Sphere	81.3	81.9	86.5	90.5	89.0	115.6	106.8	108.9	127.8	132.0	120.2
7 Housing except owner-occupied, communal and miscellaneous personal services [a]	17.4	20.2	24.1	25.3	25.3	31.3	30.5	31.8	31.9	33.4	35.2
8 Education, culture and art	3.3	4.2	3.8	4.5	5.7	5.9	6.7	6.8	6.4	7.5	8.5
9 Health and social welfare services and sports	3.4	3.1	3.9	4.0	3.8	3.8	4.2	5.5	2.8	2.8	5.1
Total Non-Material Sphere Serving Individuals	24.1	27.5	31.8	33.8	34.8	41.0	41.4	44.1	41.1	43.7	48.8

Hungary

6b Capital Formation by Kind of Activity of the Material and Non-Material Spheres in Constant Market Prices
(Continued)

Thousand Million Hungarian forint

	1970	1971	1972	1973	1974	1975	1976	1977	1978	1979	1980
					At constant prices of:1976						
10 Government	...	...	...	...	...	...	...	...	...	...	...
11 Finance, credit and insurance	...	...	...	...	...	...	...	...	...	...	...
12 Research, scientific and technological institutes	...	...	...	...	...	...	...	...	...	...	...
13 Other activities of the non-material sphere	...	...	...	...	...	...	...	...	...	...	...
Total Non-Material Sphere Serving the Community as a Whole	5.6	6.1	6.5	8.1	8.1	9.0	9.7	9.9	8.9	11.6	14.1
14 Owner-occupied dwellings [a]	...	...	...	...	...	...	...	...	...	...	...
Total Gross Fixed Capital Formation	111.0	115.5	124.8	132.4	131.9	165.6	157.9	162.9	177.8	187.3	183.1

a) Item 'Owner-occupied dwellings' is included in item 'Housing except owner-occupied, communal, and miscellaneous personal services'.

7a Final Consumption at Current Market Prices

Thousand Million Hungarian forint

	1970	1971	1972	1973	1974	1975	1976	1977	1978	1979	1980
1 Personal consumption	162.2	173.4	184.1	199.7	216.7	235.7	253.1	273.7	293.5	325.2	355.6

a) Material Consumption in the Units of the Non-Material Sphere Serving Individuals

	1970	1971	1972	1973	1974	1975	1976	1977	1978	1979	1980
Housing except owner-occupied, communal and miscellaneous personal services	5.7	5.8	5.7	6.7	8.2	9.3	10.8	12.8	16.0	18.5	22.0
Education, culture and art	6.2	7.4	7.9	8.1	8.9	10.3	11.4	12.3	13.5	13.9	16.3
Health and social welfare services and sports	4.1	4.2	4.6	5.0	5.5	6.3	6.7	7.7	9.0	9.7	11.3
Other	...	...	...	...	...	...	...	...	...	...	...
2 Total non-material sphere serving individuals	16.0	17.4	18.2	19.8	22.6	25.9	28.9	32.8	38.5	42.1	49.6

b) Material Consumption in the Units of the Non-Material Sphere Serving the Community as a Whole

	1970	1971	1972	1973	1974	1975	1976	1977	1978	1979	1980
3 Total non-material sphere serving the community as a whole	22.9	24.2	24.5	26.2	29.1	32.1	34.1	38.1	42.8	47.0	51.4
Final consumption	201.1	215.0	226.8	245.7	268.4	293.7	316.1	344.6	374.8	414.3	456.6

7b Final Consumption at Constant Market Prices

Thousand Million Hungarian forint

	1970	1971	1972	1973	1974	1975	1976	1977	1978	1979	1980
					At constant prices of:1976						
1 Personal consumption	200.8	210.9	218.5	228.0	242.2	253.6	257.0	268.2	277.7	283.4	285.4

a) Material Consumption in the Units of the Non-Material Sphere Serving Individuals

	1970	1971	1972	1973	1974	1975	1976	1977	1978	1979	1980
Housing except owner-occupied, communal and miscellaneous personal services	6.8	7.6	7.9	8.0	9.0	10.4	10.8	12.2	14.2	16.2	16.0
Education, culture and art	7.4	8.0	8.5	8.8	9.8	10.5	11.5	12.0	12.5	12.5	14.5
Health and social welfare services and sports	5.1	5.1	5.3	5.6	6.0	6.5	6.7	7.4	7.7	8.0	8.5
Other	...	...	...	...	...	...	...	...	...	...	...
2 Total non-material sphere serving individuals	19.3	20.7	21.7	22.4	24.8	27.4	29.0	31.6	34.4	36.7	39.0

b) Material Consumption in the Units of the Non-Material Sphere Serving the Community as a Whole

	1970	1971	1972	1973	1974	1975	1976	1977	1978	1979	1980
3 Total non-material sphere serving the community as a whole	26.0	27.7	27.5	28.9	31.4	33.5	34.5	36.4	39.6	42.3	44.7
Final consumption	246.1	259.3	267.7	279.3	298.4	314.5	320.5	336.2	351.7	362.4	369.1

Hungary

8 Personal Consumption According to Source of Supply of Goods and Material Services in Current Market Prices

Thousand Million Hungarian forint

	1970	1971	1972	1973	1974	1975	1976	1977	1978	1979	1980
1 Purchases of goods in state and co-operative retail trade [a]	112.4	122.4	132.0	144.3	159.7	175.3	186.3	202.5	219.4	246.3	267.9
2 Purchases of goods in the free market and from private retail trade [a]	7.2	7.1	7.1	7.8	7.7	8.3	9.6	9.8	9.8	10.6	11.5
3 Goods produced on own account and received in kind	17.2	16.8	16.5	16.6	16.0	16.3	18.5	18.7	19.1	19.3	21.7
4 Payments for transport and communication services	6.0	6.4	7.0	7.4	8.0	8.4	8.8	9.2	9.5	10.2	10.8
5 Purchases of electricity, gas and water	2.7	2.9	3.3	3.6	4.0	4.5	5.1	5.6	6.1	6.9	9.1
6 Purchases directly from handicrafts, repair shops and the like	16.7	17.8	18.2	20.0	21.3	22.9	24.8	27.9	29.6	31.9	34.6
7 Consumption of fixed assets in respect of all dwellings	...	...	...	...	...	...	...	...	...	...	...
8 Other	...	...	...	...	...	...	...	...	...	...	...
Personal consumption	162.2	173.4	184.1	199.7	216.7	235.7	253.1	273.7	293.5	325.2	355.6

a) Private retail trade is included in item 'Purchases of goods in state and co-operative retail trade'.

9a Total Consumption of the Population in Current Market Prices

Thousand Million Hungarian forint

	1970	1971	1972	1973	1974	1975	1976	1977	1978	1979	1980
By Object											
1 Housing except owner-occupied, communal and miscellaneous personal services	8.8	10.2	10.8	12.0	13.1	14.3	15.5	18.2	20.3	22.8	25.3
2 Education, culture and art	12.8	14.5	15.7	16.8	18.0	20.4	22.0	23.6	27.9	30.0	34.1
3 Health and social welfare services and sport	8.8	9.7	10.7	11.4	12.4	14.2	15.4	17.0	19.4	21.7	24.7
Total consumption of non-material services	30.4	34.4	37.2	40.2	43.5	48.9	52.9	58.8	67.6	74.5	84.1
4 Personal consumption of goods and material services excluding depreciation of dwellings	162.2	173.4	184.1	199.7	216.7	235.7	253.1	273.7	293.5	325.2	355.6
Total consumption of the population	192.6	207.8	221.3	239.9	260.2	284.6	306.0	332.5	361.1	399.7	439.7
By Commodity and Service											
1 Food	64.2	66.5	68.7	74.4	77.3	81.8	90.2	95.8	101.4	110.2	123.1
2 Beverages, coffee and tea	21.4	24.0	26.5	28.0	30.4	34.6	38.7	43.5	47.2	51.3	55.3
3 Tobacco	4.1	4.4	4.7	5.4	5.9	6.3	6.6	7.0	7.5	9.8	10.4
4 Clothing and footwear	23.2	24.3	25.5	27.2	29.4	31.3	31.1	33.0	35.3	38.3	40.0
5 Gross rent	6.8	8.0	8.9	9.2	10.0	11.2	12.0	13.5	14.4	15.9	17.2
6 Fuel, electricity, water and gas	6.3	6.4	6.8	7.4	8.0	9.0	10.1	10.4	11.3	12.9	16.2
7 Furniture and household equipment	15.6	17.0	18.5	19.8	22.9	25.0	25.8	27.7	29.7	34.2	35.3
8 Health	11.4	12.8	13.5	14.6	16.3	18.4	19.8	22.3	25.2	27.6	30.6
9 Transport and communication	12.3	13.8	15.4	17.7	20.1	22.0	22.7	25.0	27.6	31.6	35.9
10	20.3	22.7	24.3	26.2	29.1	33.0	35.3	38.9	44.5	48.8	54.5
11 Other	7.0	7.9	8.5	9.9	10.8	12.0	13.7	15.4	17.0	19.1	21.2
Total consumption of the population	192.6	207.8	221.3	239.9	260.2	284.6	306.0	332.5	361.1	399.7	439.7
By Mode of Acquisition											
1 Purchased	147.6	160.4	172.0	187.1	205.2	224.8	240.1	260.9	281.9	315.4	345.9
2 Free of charge	25.5	28.1	30.1	33.2	35.8	39.9	43.4	48.6	55.6	60.3	67.1
3 From own production [a]	19.5	19.3	19.2	19.6	19.2	19.9	22.5	23.0	23.6	24.0	26.7
Total consumption of the population	192.6	207.8	221.3	239.9	260.2	284.6	306.0	332.5	361.1	399.7	439.7

a) For 1960-1970, including the difference between the consumer and producer price of the own-consumption of agricultural products.

Hungary

9b Total Consumption of the Population in Constant Market Prices

Thousand Million Hungarian forint

	1970	1971	1972	1973	1974	1975	1976	1977	1978	1979	1980
	\multicolumn{11}{c}{At constant prices of: 1976}											
	\multicolumn{11}{c}{By Object}											
1 Housing except owner-occupied, communal and miscellaneous personal services	...	...	...	...	...	...	...	...	...	...	...
2 Education, culture and art	...	...	...	...	...	...	...	...	...	...	...
3 Health and social welfare services and sport	...	...	...	...	...	...	...	...	...	...	...
Total consumption of non-material services	37.4	40.2	42.2	44.2	46.9	50.5	53.1	56.2	60.0	62.7	65.6
4 Personal consumption of goods and material services excluding depreciation of dwellings	200.8	210.9	218.5	228.0	242.2	253.6	257.0	268.2	277.7	283.4	285.4
Total consumption of the population	238.2	251.1	260.7	272.2	289.1	304.1	310.1	324.4	337.7	346.1	351.0
	\multicolumn{11}{c}{By Commodity and Service}											
1 Food	82.0	83.8	85.9	88.5	91.3	94.7	93.4	95.5	98.6	98.5	97.8
2 Beverages, coffee and tea	28.0	30.3	30.8	31.2	32.6	35.8	39.4	42.1	42.0	41.8	44.0
3 Tobacco	5.1	5.5	5.9	5.4	5.9	6.3	6.6	7.0	7.5	7.6	8.0
4 Clothing and footwear	29.1	29.8	29.7	30.8	32.6	32.9	31.1	31.5	32.0	31.9	32.0
5 Gross rent	9.1	9.8	10.0	10.1	10.8	11.7	12.0	13.0	13.6	14.7	15.0
6 Fuel, electricity, water and gas	6.9	7.1	7.6	8.5	8.5	8.9	10.1	10.5	11.3	12.1	12.6
7 Furniture and household equipment	18.8	20.3	21.4	22.5	25.5	25.9	25.8	26.8	27.4	29.7	27.4
8 Health	13.6	14.4	15.1	16.1	17.5	18.8	19.9	20.8	22.3	23.5	25.3
9 Transport and communication	12.7	14.5	16.3	19.2	21.4	22.6	22.7	24.8	27.0	27.9	28.6
10	23.7	25.7	27.1	28.4	31.2	33.9	35.5	37.5	40.2	41.7	43.7
11 Other	9.2	9.9	10.9	11.5	11.8	12.6	13.6	14.9	15.8	16.7	16.6
Total consumption of the population	238.2	251.1	260.7	272.2	289.1	304.1	310.1	324.4	337.7	346.1	351.0
	\multicolumn{11}{c}{By Mode of Acquisition}											
1 Purchased	180.9	192.5	200.7	210.9	226.3	239.0	242.7	254.3	263.9	270.9	273.2
2 Free of charge	30.8	32.4	34.4	36.8	38.9	41.6	43.9	46.0	49.1	50.6	53.2
3 From own production	26.5	26.2	25.6	24.5	23.9	23.5	23.5	24.1	24.7	24.6	24.6
Total consumption of the population	238.2	251.1	260.7	272.2	289.1	304.1	310.1	324.4	337.7	346.1	351.0

Iceland

Source. Reply to the United Nations National Accounts Questionnaire from the Statistical Bureau of Iceland, Reykjavik. The official estimates have been prepared by the Economic Institute. The sources and methods of estimation utilized are described in an article in the June 1962 issue of 'Ur Pjodarbuskapnum', a journal on economic matters published by the Iceland Bank of Development. This publication also contains a summary of the article in English.

General note. The estimates shown in the following tables have been prepared in accordance with the United Nations System of National Accounts so far as the existing data would permit.

1.1 Expenditure on the Gross Domestic Product, in Current Prices

Million Icelandic kronur

	1970	1971	1972	1973	1974	1975	1976	1977	1978	1979	1980
1 General government final consumption expenditure	4230	5519	7225	9924	15670	21968	29938	42978	68360	102200	159000
2 Private final consumption expenditure	28183	35667	44685	60919	93210	124990	164110	232380	354550	531610	830000
3 Gross capital formation	10118	17630	18260	28421	47728	67240	76300	115780	146820	218740	371600
a Increase in stocks [a]	-289	1413	-1040	-315	2534	3713	-1779	6601	-3857	5100	7986
b Gross fixed capital formation	10407	16217	19300	28736	45194	63527	78079	109179	150677	213640	363614
Residential buildings	2138	2700	4120	7740	10200	13460	16940	23270	34270	49370	74520
Non-residential buildings	2582	3324	4696	5644	9942	11963	15222	22560	33560	45890	64060
Other construction and land improvement etc.	2934	4078	4945	6389	11590	21694	30002	33817	43310	64290	121617
Other	2753	6115	5539	8963	13462	16410	15915	29532	39537	54090	103417
4 Exports of goods and services	20806	22034	25895	36930	47475	71831	104824	144299	248212	380890	574630
5 Less: Imports of goods and services	19674	25385	26760	38385	61090	88348	101931	145124	224242	363030	565360
Equals: Gross Domestic Product	43663	55465	69305	97809	142993	197681	273241	390313	593700	870410	1369870

a) Stocks of export products only.

1.2 Expenditure on the Gross Domestic Product, in Constant Prices

Million Icelandic kronur

	1970	1971	1972	1973	1974	1975	1976	1977	1978	1979	1980
					At constant prices of: 1969						
1 General government final consumption expenditure	3551	3791	4078	4463	4736	4964	5311	5353	5554	5750	5865
2 Private final consumption expenditure	25311	29459	32292	35101	37558	33802	34140	36871	39083	39865	39865
3 Gross capital formation	9017	14522	12256	15320	18312	17143	14720	17840	15893	15870	18196
a Increase in stocks [a]	-170	1225	-912	-414	935	1250	-782	511	-143	17	394
b Gross fixed capital formation	9187	13297	13168	15734	17377	15893	15502	17329	16036	15853	17802
Residential buildings	1825	2057	2569	3775	3270	3040	3100	3275	3280	3210	3115
Non-residential buildings	2228	2562	2988	2764	3193	2731	2812	3250	3310	3080	2735
Other construction and land improvement etc.	2502	3185	3210	3329	4099	5090	5813	4787	4130	4240	5260
Other	2632	5493	4401	5866	6815	5032	3777	6017	5316	5323	6692
4 Exports of goods and services	18763	18027	19957	21651	21473	22035	24591	27114	31079	32462	32526
5 Less: Imports of goods and services	19119	23508	23547	27937	31520	27632	26671	32052	33609	34529	35288
Equals: Gross Domestic Product	37523	42291	45036	48598	50559	50312	52091	55126	58000	59418	61164

a) Stocks of export products only.

1.3 Cost Components of the Gross Domestic Product

Million Icelandic kronur

	1970	1971	1972	1973	1974	1975	1976	1977	1978	1979	1980
1 Indirect taxes, net	7689	9784	12380	18683	28738	39649	57375	81001	115100	163100	276500
a Indirect taxes paid	9357	12798	15697	23063	36247	52080	69989	97839	146200	217300	354000
b Less: Subsidies received	1668	3014	3317	4380	7509	12431	12614	16838	31100	54200	77500
2 Consumption of fixed capital	6061	6703	8458	11353	17175	28332	37133	48929	75269	113750	180140
3 Compensation of employees paid by resident producers to:	29913	38978	48467	67773	97080	129700	178733	260383	403331	593560	913230
4 Net operating surplus											
Equals: Gross Domestic Product	43663	55465	69305	97809	142993	197681	273241	390313	593700	870410	1369870

1.4 General Government Current Receipts and Disbursements

Million Icelandic kronur

	1970	1971	1972	1973	1974	1975	1976	1977	1978	1979	1980
					Receipts						
1 Property and entrepreneurial income	527	544	591	856	751	2142	3296	4950	...	...	...
2 Taxes, fees and contributions	13365	18316	23296	33185	48168	68172	93316	127817	...	...	...
a Indirect taxes	9357	12798	15697	23063	36247	52080	69989	97839	...	...	...
b Direct taxes	2979	4074	6994	9393	10723	14261	19931	25518	...	...	...

Iceland

1.4 General Government Current Receipts and Disbursements
(Continued)

Million Icelandic kronur

	1970	1971	1972	1973	1974	1975	1976	1977	1978	1979	1980
c Social security contributions	1029	1444	605	729	1198	1831	3396	4460	...	...	...
d Compulsory fees, fines and penalties	...	...	...	...	...	...	...	...	...	...	...
3 Other current receipts	...	...	...	1536	...	...	...	...	...	...	...
Total Current Receipts of General Government	13892	18860	23887	35577	48919	70314	96612	132767	...	...	...

Disbursements

	1970	1971	1972	1973	1974	1975	1976	1977	1978	1979	1980
1 General government final consumption expenditure [a]	3795	5017	6578	9064	14295	19758	27102	39062	...	...	...
2 Property income paid	260	301	480	655	1140	2357	3074	4217	...	...	...
3 Subsidies [a]	1516	2841	3100	4105	7068	11661	11602	15423	...	...	...
4 Other current transfers paid	3896	5269	7036	12903	15611	22243	27104	38777	...	...	...
a Social security benefits and social assistance grants	3896	5269	7035	11048	14683	20840	27345	38777	...	...	...
b Other	-	-	1	1855	928	1403	-241	-	...	...	...
5 Net saving	4425	5432	6693	8850	10805	14295	27730	35288	...	...	...
Total Current Disbursements and Net Saving of General Government	13892	18860	23887	35577	48919	70314	96612	132767	...	...	...

a) Estimates have not been adjusted to include imputed depreciation of government assets, therefore they are not strictly comparable to those of other tables.

1.7 External Transactions on Current Account, Summary

Million Icelandic kronur

	1970	1971	1972	1973	1974	1975	1976	1977	1978	1979	1980

Payments to the Rest of the World

	1970	1971	1972	1973	1974	1975	1976	1977	1978	1979	1980
1 Imports of goods and services	19674	25385	26760	38385	61090	88348	101931	145124	224242	363030	565360
a Imports of merchandise c.i.f.	12612	17518	18775	29180	47580	68040	78130	112345	167625	269180	431200
b Other	7062	7867	7985	9205	13510	20308	23801	32779	56617	93850	134160
2 Factor income paid to the rest of the world	813	848	1200	1640	2520	5222	7979	9801	17693	28650	47740
3 Indirect taxes paid to supranational organizations	...	...	...	...	...	...	...	...	...	...	...
4 Current transfers to the rest of the world	32	30	55	64	86	176	155	149	206	514	501
5 Surplus of the nation on current transactions	619	-3890	-1810	-2699	-15616	-21556	-4545	-9804	7664	-7044	-32301
Payments to the Rest of the World and Surplus of the Nation on Current Transactions	21138	22373	26205	37390	48080	72190	105520	145270	249805	385150	581300

Receipts From The Rest of the World

	1970	1971	1972	1973	1974	1975	1976	1977	1978	1979	1980
1 Exports of goods and services	20806	22034	25895	36930	47475	71831	104824	144299	248212	380890	574630
a Exports of merchandise f.o.b.	12850	13178	16700	26020	32880	47440	73500	101890	176285	278450	446000
b Other	7956	8856	9195	10910	14595	24391	31324	42409	71927	102440	128630
2 Factor income received from rest of the world	332	339	310	460	605	359	696	971	1593	4260	6670
3 Subsidies received from supranational organisations	...	...	...	...	...	...	...	...	...	...	...
4 Current transfers from rest of the world	-	-	-	-	-	-	-	-	-	-	-
Receipts from the Rest of the World on Current Transactions	21138	22373	26205	37390	48080	72190	105520	145270	249805	385150	581300

1.8 Capital Transactions of The Nation, Summary

Million Icelandic kronur

	1970	1971	1972	1973	1974	1975	1976	1977	1978	1979	1980

Finance of Gross Capital Formation

	1970	1971	1972	1973	1974	1975	1976	1977	1978	1979	1980
Gross saving [a]	10737	13740	16450	25722	32112	45684	71755	105976	154484	211696	339299
1 Consumption of fixed capital	6061	6703	8458	11353	17175	28332	37133	48929	75269	113750	180140
2 Net saving	4676	7037	7992	14369	14937	17352	34622	57047	79215	97946	159159
a General government	4425	5432	6693	8850	10805	14295	27730	35288	...	...	...
b Corporate and quasi-corporate enterprises	...	...	...	...	...	...	...	...	...	...	...
c Other	...	...	...	...	...	...	...	...	...	...	...
Less: Surplus of the nation on current transactions	619	-3890	-1810	-2699	-15616	-21556	-4545	-9804	7664	-7044	-32301
Finance of Gross Capital Formation	10118	17630	18260	28421	47728	67240	76300	115780	146820	218740	371600

Iceland

1.8 Capital Transactions of The Nation, Summary
(Continued)

Million Icelandic kronur

	1970	1971	1972	1973	1974	1975	1976	1977	1978	1979	1980
					Gross Capital Formation						
Increase in stocks	-289	1413	-1040	-315	2534	3713	-1779	6601	-3857	5100	7986
Gross fixed capital formation	10407	16217	19300	28736	45194	63527	78079	109179	150677	213640	363614
1 General government	2079	2530	3180	4200	6520	8640	10940	15100	19725	...	...
2 Corporate and quasi-corporate enterprises	...	...	...	...	...	...	...	...	...	...	...
3 Other	...	...	...	...	...	...	...	...	...	...	...
Gross Capital Formation	10118	17630	18260	28421	47728	67240	76300	115780	146820	218740	371600

a) Obtained as a residual.

1.12 Relations Among National Accounting Aggregates

Million Icelandic kronur

	1970	1971	1972	1973	1974	1975	1976	1977	1978	1979	1980
Gross Domestic Product	43663	55465	69305	97809	142993	197681	273241	390313	593700	870410	1369870
Plus: Net factor income received from abroad	-481	-509	-890	-1180	-1915	-4863	-7283	-8830	-16100	-24390	-41070
Factor income received	332	339	310	460	605	359	696	971	1593	4260	6670
Less: Factor income paid	813	848	1200	1640	2520	5222	7979	9801	17693	28650	47740
Equals: Gross National Product	43182	54956	68415	96629	141078	192818	265958	381483	577600	846020	1328800
Less: Consumption of fixed capital	6061	6703	8458	11353	17175	28332	37133	48929	75269	113750	180140
Less: Net indirect taxes paid to supranational organisations	...	...	...	...	...	...	...	...	...	...	...
Equals: National Income at Market Prices	37121	48253	59957	85276	123903	164486	228825	332554	502331	732270	1148660
Plus: Net current transfers received from abroad	-32	-30	-55	-64	-86	-176	-155	-149	-206	-514	-501
Current transfers received	-	-	-	-	-	-	-	-	-	-	-
Less: Current transfers paid	32	30	55	64	86	176	155	149	206	514	501
Equals: National Disposable Income at Market Prices	37089	48223	59902	85212	123817	164310	228670	332405	502125	731756	1148159
Less: Final consumption	32413	41186	51910	70843	108880	146958	194048	275358	422910	633810	989000
Equals: Net Saving a	4676	7037	7992	14369	14937	17352	34622	57047	79215	97946	159159
Less: Surplus of the nation on current transactions	619	-3890	-1810	-2699	-15616	-21556	-4545	-9804	7664	-7044	-32301
Equals: Net Capital Formation	4057	10927	9802	17068	30553	38908	39167	66851	71551	104990	191460

a) Obtained as a residual.

2.5 Private Final Consumption Expenditure by Type, in Current Prices

Million Icelandic kronur

	1970	1971	1972	1973	1974	1975	1976	1977	1978	1979	1980
					Final Consumption Expenditure of Resident Households						
1 Food, beverages and tobacco	8783	9959	12450	17193	...	...	...	...	...	...	...
a Food	6664	7391	9003	12429	...	...	...	...	...	...	...
b Non-alcoholic beverages	412	522	615	768	...	...	...	...	...	...	...
c Alcoholic beverages	882	1105	1529	2357	...	...	...	...	...	...	...
d Tobacco	825	941	1303	1639	...	...	...	...	...	...	...
2 Clothing and footwear	2860	3946	4559	5587	...	...	...	...	...	...	...
3 Gross rent, fuel and power	4640	5058	6646	9448	...	...	...	...	...	...	...
4 Furniture, furnishings and household equipment and operation	2895	3939	5060	7105	...	...	...	...	...	...	...
a Household operation	760	836	1072	1346	...	...	...	...	...	...	...
b Other	2135	3103	3988	5759	...	...	...	...	...	...	...
5 Medical care and health expenses	2021	2742	3571	4669	...	...	...	...	...	...	...
6 Transport and communication	3757	5459	6263	8797	...	...	...	...	...	...	...
a Personal transport equipment	2628	4161	4774	6679	...	...	...	...	...	...	...
b Other	1129	1298	1489	2118	...	...	...	...	...	...	...
7 Recreational, entertainment, education and cultural services	1692	2247	2990	4185	...	...	...	...	...	...	...
a Education	122	161	216	286	...	...	...	...	...	...	...
b Other	1570	2086	2774	3899	...	...	...	...	...	...	...
8 Miscellaneous goods and services	1484	2161	2781	3570	...	...	...	...	...	...	...
a Personal care	632	775	931	1198	...	...	...	...	...	...	...
b Expenditures in restaurants, cafes and hotels	428	838	1119	1426	...	...	...	...	...	...	...

Iceland

2.5 Private Final Consumption Expenditure by Type, in Current Prices
(Continued)

Million Icelandic kronur

	1970	1971	1972	1973	1974	1975	1976	1977	1978	1979	1980
c Other	424	548	731	946	...	...	...	...	...	...	...
Total Final Consumption Expenditure in the Domestic Market by Households, of which	28132	35511	44320	60554	...	...	...	...	...	...	...
Plus: Direct purchases abroad by resident households	742	1013	1399	1949	...	...	...	...	...	...	...
Less: Direct purchases in the domestic market by non-resident households	590	717	897	1413	...	...	...	...	...	...	...
Equals: Final Consumption Expenditure of Resident Households	28284	35807	44822	61090	...	...	...	...	...	...	...

Final Consumption Expenditure of Private Non-profit Institutions Serving Households

	1970	1971	1972	1973	1974	1975	1976	1977	1978	1979	1980
Equals: Final Consumption Expenditure of Private Non-profit Organisations Serving Households	-101	-140	-137	-171	...	...	...	...	...	...	...
Private Final Consumption Expenditure	28183	35667	44685	60919	93210	124990	164110	232380	354550	...	...

2.6 Private Final Consumption Expenditure by Type, in Constant Prices

Million Icelandic kronur

	1970	1971	1972	1973	1974	1975	1976	1977	1978	1979	1980

At constant prices of: 1969

Final Consumption Expenditure of Resident Households

	1970	1971	1972	1973	1974	1975	1976	1977	1978	1979	1980
1 Food, beverages and tobacco	7767	8461	8993	9585	...	...	...	...	...	...	...
a Food	5780	6247	6646	7049	...	...	...	...	...	...	...
b Non-alcoholic beverages	388	465	503	527	...	...	...	...	...	...	...
c Alcoholic beverages	842	930	992	1138	...	...	...	...	...	...	...
d Tobacco	757	819	852	871	...	...	...	...	...	...	...
2 Clothing and footwear	2492	3051	3234	3463	...	...	...	...	...	...	...
3 Gross rent, fuel and power	4499	4612	4897	5136	...	...	...	...	...	...	...
4 Furniture, furnishings and household equipment and operation	2567	3176	3795	4448	...	...	...	...	...	...	...
a Household operation	662	673	792	868	...	...	...	...	...	...	...
b Other	1905	2503	3003	3580	...	...	...	...	...	...	...
5 Medical care and health expenses	1703	1895	2421	2470	...	...	...	...	...	...	...
6 Transport and communication	3521	4710	4782	5354	...	...	...	...	...	...	...
a Personal transport equipment	2459	3596	3558	3993	...	...	...	...	...	...	...
b Other	1062	1114	1224	1361	...	...	...	...	...	...	...
7 Recreational, entertainment, education and cultural services	1440	1741	1896	2212	...	...	...	...	...	...	...
a Education	104	104	116	126	...	...	...	...	...	...	...
b Other	1336	1637	1780	2086	...	...	...	...	...	...	...
8 Miscellaneous goods and services	1260	1640	1912	2082	...	...	...	...	...	...	...
a Personal care	531	603	663	723	...	...	...	...	...	...	...
b Expenditures in restaurants, cafes and hotels	338	569	705	714	...	...	...	...	...	...	...
c Other	391	468	544	645	...	...	...	...	...	...	...
Total Final Consumption Expenditure in the Domestic Market by Households, of which	25249	29286	31930	34750	...	...	...	...	...	...	...
Plus: Direct purchases abroad by resident households	741	988	1306	1672	...	...	...	...	...	...	...
Less: Direct purchases in the domestic market by non-resident households	590	702	852	1228	...	...	...	...	...	...	...
Equals: Final Consumption Expenditure of Resident Households	25400	29572	32384	35194	...	...	...	...	...	...	...

Final Consumption Expenditure of Private Non-profit Institutions Serving Households

	1970	1971	1972	1973	1974	1975	1976	1977	1978	1979	1980
Equals: Final Consumption Expenditure of Private Non-profit Organisations Serving Households	-89	-113	-92	-93	...	...	...	...	...	...	...
Private Final Consumption Expenditure	25311	29459	32292	35101	37558	33802	34140	36871	39083	...	...

Iceland

2.9 Gross Capital Formation by Kind of Activity of Owner, ISIC Major Divisions, in Current Prices

Million Icelandic kronur

	1970 TGCF	1970 IS	1970 GFCF	1971 TGCF	1971 IS	1971 GFCF	1972 TGCF	1972 IS	1972 GFCF	1973 TGCF	1973 IS	1973 GFCF
						All Producers						
1 Agriculture, hunting, fishing and forestry	...	...	1329	...	...	1917	...	...	3380	...	...	6626
2 Mining and quarrying	...	...	⎱1602	...	...	⎱2380	...	...	⎱3170	...	...	⎱3070
3 Manufacturing	...	...	⎰	...	...	⎰	...	...	⎰	...	...	⎰
4 Electricity, gas and water	...	...	1391	...	...	1860	...	...	2220	...	...	2450
5 Construction a	...	...	273	...	...	645	...	...	480	...	...	740
6 Wholesale and retail trade, restaurants and hotels b	...	...	668	...	...	825	...	...	1070	...	...	1450
7 Transport, storage and communication	...	...	927	...	...	3360	...	...	1680	...	...	2460
8 Finance, insurance, real estate and business services bc	...	...	2138	...	...	2700	...	...	4120	...	...	7740
9 Community, social and personal services	...	...	...	...	...	...	...	...	...	...	...	...
Total Industries	...	...	8328	...	...	13687	...	...	16120	...	...	24536
Producers of Government Services	...	...	2079	...	...	2530	...	...	3180	...	...	4200
Private Non-Profit Institutions Serving Households	...	...	...	...	...	...	...	...	...	...	...	...
Total d	10118	-289	10407	17630	1413	16217	18260	-1040	19300	28421	-315	28736

	1974 TGCF	1974 IS	1974 GFCF	1975 TGCF	1975 IS	1975 GFCF	1976 TGCF	1976 IS	1976 GFCF	1977 TGCF	1977 IS	1977 GFCF
						All Producers						
1 Agriculture, hunting, fishing and forestry	...	...	7874	...	...	8697	...	...	8339	...	...	17559
2 Mining and quarrying	...	...	⎱4690	...	...	⎱7140	...	...	⎱7810	...	...	⎱13455
3 Manufacturing	...	...	⎰	...	...	⎰	...	...	⎰	...	...	⎰
4 Electricity, gas and water	...	...	5450	...	...	12560	...	...	19070	...	...	20210
5 Construction a	...	...	1510	...	...	2020	...	...	1660	...	...	2210
6 Wholesale and retail trade, restaurants and hotels b	...	...	3120	...	...	3370	...	...	4500	...	...	5915
7 Transport, storage and communication	...	...	5830	...	...	7640	...	...	8820	...	...	11460
8 Finance, insurance, real estate and business services bc	...	...	10200	...	...	13460	...	...	16940	...	...	23270
9 Community, social and personal services	...	...	...	...	...	...	...	...	...	...	...	...
Total Industries	...	...	38674	...	...	54887	...	...	67139	...	...	94079
Producers of Government Services	...	...	6520	...	...	8640	...	...	10940	...	...	15100
Private Non-Profit Institutions Serving Households	...	...	...	...	...	...	...	...	...	...	...	...
Total d	47728	2534	45194	67240	3713	63527	76300	-1779	78079	115780	6601	109179

	1978 TGCF	1978 IS	1978 GFCF	1979 TGCF	1979 IS	1979 GFCF	1980 TGCF	1980 IS	1980 GFCF
					All Producers				
1 Agriculture, hunting, fishing and forestry	...	...	19937	...	...	24460	...	...	40479
2 Mining and quarrying	...	...	⎱25190	...	...	⎱39300	...	...	⎱53300
3 Manufacturing	...	...	⎰	...	...	⎰	...	...	⎰
4 Electricity, gas and water	...	...	24220	...	...	37650	...	...	75250
5 Construction a	...	...	3740	...	...	4160	...	...	10365
6 Wholesale and retail trade, restaurants and hotels b	...	...	9850	...	...	12800	...	...	21080
7 Transport, storage and communication	...	...	13615	...	...	19120	...	...	40260
8 Finance, insurance, real estate and business services bc	...	...	34270	...	...	49370	...	...	74520
9 Community, social and personal services	...	...	...	...	...	...	...	...	...
Total Industries	...	...	130822	...	...	186860	...	...	315254
Producers of Government Services	...	...	19855	...	...	26780	...	...	48360
Private Non-Profit Institutions Serving Households	...	...	...	...	...	...	...	...	...
Total d	146820	-3857	150677	218740	5100	213640	371600	7986	363614

a) Machinery only.
b) Finance, insurance and business services are included in item 'Wholesale and retail trade, restaurants and hotels'.
c) Ownership of dwellings only.
d) Stocks of export products only.

Iceland

2.10 Gross Capital Formation by Kind of Activity of Owner, ISIC Major Divisions, in Constant Prices

Million Icelandic kronur

	1970 TGCF	1970 IS	1970 GFCF	1971 TGCF	1971 IS	1971 GFCF	1972 TGCF	1972 IS	1972 GFCF	1973 TGCF	1973 IS	1973 GFCF
At constant prices of: 1969												
All Producers												
1 Agriculture, hunting, fishing and forestry	...	...	1200	...	...	1530	...	...	2449	...	...	4064
2 Mining and quarrying	...	...	1469	...	...	2016	...	...	2266	...	...	1720
3 Manufacturing	...	...		...	...		...	...		...	...	
4 Electricity, gas and water	...	...	1184	...	...	1474	...	...	1426	...	...	1240
5 Construction a	...	...	261	...	...	589	...	...	403	...	...	501
6 Wholesale and retail trade, restaurants and hotels b	...	...	578	...	...	658	...	...	712	...	...	759
7 Transport, storage and communication	...	...	881	...	...	3036	...	...	1326	...	...	1527
8 Finance, insurance, real estate and business services bc	...	...	1825	...	...	2057	...	...	2569	...	...	3775
9 Community, social and personal services	...	...	...	...	...	...	...	...	...	...	...	...
Total Industries	...	...	7398	...	...	11360	...	...	11151	...	...	13586
Producers of Government Services	...	...	1789	...	...	1937	...	...	2017	...	...	2148
Private Non-Profit Institutions Serving Households	...	...	...	...	...	...	...	...	...	...	...	...
Total d	9017	-170	9187	14522	1225	13297	12256	-912	13168	15320	-414	15734

	1974 TGCF	1974 IS	1974 GFCF	1975 TGCF	1975 IS	1975 GFCF	1976 TGCF	1976 IS	1976 GFCF	1977 TGCF	1977 IS	1977 GFCF
At constant prices of: 1969												
All Producers												
1 Agriculture, hunting, fishing and forestry	...	...	3557	...	...	2423	...	...	1672	...	...	3164
2 Mining and quarrying	...	...	1880	...	...	1950	...	...	1720	...	...	2485
3 Manufacturing	...	...		...	...		...	...		...	...	
4 Electricity, gas and water	...	...	1900	...	...	3080	...	...	3910	...	...	3045
5 Construction a	...	...	800	...	...	630	...	...	410	...	...	445
6 Wholesale and retail trade, restaurants and hotels b	...	...	1105	...	...	810	...	...	880	...	...	920
7 Transport, storage and communication	...	...	2662	...	...	2100	...	...	1925	...	...	2055
8 Finance, insurance, real estate and business services bc	...	...	3270	...	...	3040	...	...	3100	...	...	3275
9 Community, social and personal services	...	...	...	...	...	...	...	...	...	...	...	...
Total Industries	...	...	15174	...	...	14033	...	...	13617	...	...	15389
Producers of Government Services	...	...	2203	...	...	1860	...	...	1885	...	...	1940
Private Non-Profit Institutions Serving Households	...	...	...	...	...	...	...	...	...	...	...	...
Total d	18312	935	17377	17143	1250	15893	14720	-782	15502	17840	511	17329

	1978 TGCF	1978 IS	1978 GFCF	1979 TGCF	1979 IS	1979 GFCF	1980 TGCF	1980 IS	1980 GFCF
At constant prices of: 1969									
All Producers									
1 Agriculture, hunting, fishing and forestry	...	...	2391	...	...	2093	...	...	2182
2 Mining and quarrying	...	...	3105	...	...	3440	...	...	3200
3 Manufacturing	...	...		...	...		...	...	
4 Electricity, gas and water	...	...	2430	...	...	2610	...	...	3460

Iceland

2.10 Gross Capital Formation by Kind of Activity of Owner, ISIC Major Divisions, in Constant Prices
(Continued)

Million Icelandic kronur

	1978 Total Gross Capital Formation	1978 Increase in Stocks	1978 Gross Fixed Capital Formation	1979 Total Gross Capital Formation	1979 Increase in Stocks	1979 Gross Fixed Capital Formation	1980 Total Gross Capital Formation	1980 Increase in Stocks	1980 Gross Fixed Capital Formation
				At constant prices of:1969					
5 Construction [a]	...	...	520	...	...	405	...	...	670
6 Wholesale and retail trade, restaurants and hotels [b]	...	...	1060	...	...	965	...	...	1040
7 Transport, storage and communication	...	...	1510	...	...	1525	...	...	2290
8 Finance, insurance, real estate and business services [bc]	...	...	3280	...	...	3210	...	...	3115
9 Community, social and personal services	...	...	...	...	...	...	...	...	...
Total Industries	...	...	14296	...	...	14248	...	...	15957
Producers of Government Services	...	...	1740	...	...	1605	...	...	1845
Private Non-Profit Institutions Serving Households	...	...	...	...	...	...	...	...	...
Total [d]	15893	-143	16036	15870	17	15853	18196	394	17802

a) Machinery only.
b) Finance, insurance and business services are included in item 'Wholesale and retail trade, restaurants and hotels'.
c) Ownership of dwellings only.
d) Stocks of export products only.

2.17 Exports and Imports of Goods and Services, Detail

Million Icelandic kronur

	1970	1971	1972	1973	1974	1975	1976	1977	1978	1979	1980
				Exports of Goods and Services							
1 Exports of merchandise, f.o.b.	12850	13178	16700	26020	32880	47440	73500	101890	176285	278450	446000
2 Transport and communication											
3 Insurance service charges	7956	8856	9195	10910	14595	24391	31324	42409	71927	102440	128630
4 Other commodities											
5 Adjustments of merchandise exports to change-of-ownership basis	...	...	...	...	...	...	...	...	...	...	...
6 Direct purchases in the domestic market by non-residential households	...	...	...	...	...	...	...	...	...	...	...
7 Direct purchases in the domestic market by extraterritorial bodies	...	...	...	...	...	...	...	...	...	...	...
Total Exports of Goods and Services	20806	22034	25895	36930	47475	71831	104824	144299	248212	380890	574630
				Imports of Goods and Services							
1 Imports of merchandise, c.i.f. [a]	12612	17518	18775	29180	47580	68040	78130	112345	167625	269180	431200
a Imports of merchandise, f.o.b.	12612	17518	18775	29180	47580	68040	78130	112345	167625	269180	431200
b Transport of services on merchandise imports	...	...	...	...	...	...	...	...	...	...	...
c Insurance service charges on merchandise imports	...	...	...	...	...	...	...	...	...	...	...
2 Adjustments of merchandise imports to change-of-ownership basis	...	...	...	...	...	...	...	...	...	...	...
3 Other transport and communication											
4 Other insurance service charges											
5 Other commodities	6320	6854	6586	7256	13510	20308	23801	32779	56617	93850	134160
6 Direct purchases abroad by government											
7 Direct purchases abroad by resident households											
Total Imports of Goods and Services	19674	25385	26760	38385	61090	88348	101931	145124	224242	363030	565360
Balance of Goods and Services	1132	-3351	-865	-1455	-13615	-16517	2893	-825	23970	17860	9270
Total Imports and Balance of Goods and Services	20806	22034	25895	36930	47475	71831	104824	144299	248212	380890	574630

a) Imports of merchandise, f.o.b. rather than c.i.f.

Iceland

3.12 General Government Income and Outlay Account: Total and Subsectors

Million Icelandic kronur

	1970					1971				
	Total General Government	Central Government	State or Provincial Government	Local Government	Social Security Funds	Total General Government	Central Government	State or Provincial Government	Local Government	Social Security Funds

Receipts

1 Property and entrepreneurial income	527	59	...	...	...	544	78	...	...	...
a Net operating surplus	...	...	...	...	...	...	...	...	...	...
b Withdrawals from public quasi-corporations	279	18	...	...	...	248	18	...	...	...
c Interest	...	...	...	...	...	...	...	...	...	...
d Dividends	...	...	...	...	...	...	...	...	...	...
e Net land rent and royalties	...	...	...	...	...	...	...	...	...	...
2 Taxes, fees and contributions	13365	10411	...	...	...	18316	14424	...	...	...
a Indirect taxes	9357	8228	...	...	...	12798	11396	...	...	...
b Direct taxes	2979	1154	...	...	...	4074	1584	...	...	...
Income	2979	1154	...	...	...	4074	1584	...	...	...
Other	-	-	...	...	...	-	-	...	...	...
c Social security contributions	1029	1029	...	...	...	1444	1444	...	...	...
d Fees, fines and penalties	...	...	...	...	...	...	...	...	...	...
3 Other current transfers received										
a Casualty insurance claims	...	...	...	...	...	...	...	...	...	...
b Transfers from other government subsectors	...	-	...	...	...	...	-	...	...	...
c Transfers from abroad	-	-	...	...	...	-	-	...	...	...
d Other transfers, except imputed	...	...	...	...	...	...	-	...	...	...
e Imputed unfunded employee welfare contributions	...	...	...	...	...	...	...	...	...	...
Total Current Receipts	13892	10470	...	...	...	18860	14502	...	...	...

Disbursements

1 General government final consumption expenditures a	3795	2443	...	...	...	5017	3271	...	...	...
2 Property income paid	260	159	...	...	...	301	181	...	...	...
3 Subsidies a	1516	1463	...	...	...	2841	2779	...	...	...
4 Other current transfers paid	3896	3275	...	...	...	5269	4686	...	...	...
a Casualty insurance premiums, net	...	...	...	...	...	...	...	...	...	...
b Transfers to other government subsectors	...	2897	...	...	...	...	4062	...	...	...
c Transfers to households	3896	376	...	...	...	5269	624	...	...	...
d Transfers to private non-profit institutions serving households			...	...	...			...	...	...
e Transfers to the rest of the world	-	-	...	...	...	-	-	...	...	...
Net saving	4425	3130	...	...	...	5432	3585	...	...	...
Total Current Disbursements and Net Saving	13892	10470	...	...	...	18860	14502	...	...	...

	1972					1973				
	Total General Government	Central Government	State or Provincial Government	Local Government	Social Security Funds	Total General Government	Central Government	State or Provincial Government	Local Government	Social Security Funds

Receipts

1 Property and entrepreneurial income	591	119	...	...	...	856	193	...	...	...
a Net operating surplus	...	...	...	...	...	...	...	...	...	...
b Withdrawals from public quasi-corporations	218	42	...	...	...	307	41	...	...	...
c Interest	...	...	...	...	...	...	...	...	...	...
d Dividends	...	...	...	...	...	...	...	...	...	...
e Net land rent and royalties	...	...	...	...	...	...	...	...	...	...
2 Taxes, fees and contributions	23296	18495	...	...	...	33185	27233	...	...	...
a Indirect taxes	15697	13425	...	...	...	23063	20174	...	...	...
b Direct taxes	6994	4465	...	...	...	9393	6330	...	...	...
Income	6994	4465	...	...	...	9393	6330	...	...	...

Iceland

3.12 General Government Income and Outlay Account: Total and Subsectors
(Continued)

Million Icelandic kronur

	1972					1973				
	Total General Government	Central Government	State or Provincial Government	Local Government	Social Security Funds	Total General Government	Central Government	State or Provincial Government	Local Government	Social Security Funds
Other	-	-	...	...	...	-	-	...	...	...
c Social security contributions	605	605	...	...	...	729	729	...	...	...
d Fees, fines and penalties	...	...	...	...	...	...	...	...	...	...
3 Other current transfers received	...	...	...	...	...	1536	1536	...	...	...
a Casualty insurance claims	...	...	...	...	...	...	...	...	...	...
b Transfers from other government subsectors	...	...	...	...	...	...	...	...	...	...
c Transfers from abroad	-	-	...	...	...	1536	1536	...	...	...
d Other transfers, except imputed	-	-	...	...	...	-	-	...	...	...
e Imputed unfunded employee welfare contributions	...	...	...	...	...	...	...	...	...	...
Total Current Receipts	23887	18614	...	...	...	35577	28962	...	...	...

Disbursements

	1972					1973				
1 General government final consumption expenditures [a]	6578	4574	...	...	...	9064	6221	...	...	...
2 Property income paid	480	339	...	...	...	655	462	...	...	...
3 Subsidies [a]	3100	3011	...	...	...	4105	3991	...	...	...
4 Other current transfers paid	7036	6961	...	...	...	12903	12947	...	...	...
a Casualty insurance premiums, net	...	...	...	...	...	...	...	...	...	...
b Transfers to other government subsectors	...	6244	...	...	...	...	8391	...	...	...
c Transfers to households	7035	717	...	...	...	12902	4556	...	...	...
d Transfers to private non-profit institutions serving households			...	...	...			...	...	...
e Transfers to the rest of the world	1	-	...	...	...	1	-	...	...	...
Net saving	6693	3729	...	...	...	8850	5341	...	...	...
Total Current Disbursements and Net Saving	23887	18614	...	...	...	35577	28962	...	...	...

	1974					1975				
	Total General Government	Central Government	State or Provincial Government	Local Government	Social Security Funds	Total General Government	Central Government	State or Provincial Government	Local Government	Social Security Funds

Receipts

	1974					1975				
1 Property and entrepreneurial income	751	307	...	...	...	2142	608	...	...	...
a Net operating surplus	...	...	...	...	...	...	...	...	...	...
b Withdrawals from public quasi-corporations	-51	67	...	...	...	888	128	...	...	...
c Interest	...	...	...	...	...	...	...	...	...	...
d Dividends	...	...	...	...	...	...	...	...	...	...
e Net land rent and royalties	...	...	...	...	...	...	...	...	...	...
2 Taxes, fees and contributions	48168	39404	...	...	...	68172	54080	...	...	...
a Indirect taxes	36247	32014	...	...	...	52080	45760	...	...	...
b Direct taxes	10723	6192	...	...	...	14261	6489	...	...	...
Income	10723	6192	...	...	...	14261	6489	...	...	...
Other	-	-	...	...	...	-	-	...	...	...
c Social security contributions	1198	1198	...	...	...	1831	1831	...	...	...
d Fees, fines and penalties	...	...	...	...	...	...	...	...	...	...
3 Other current transfers received	...	...	...	...	...	...	...	...	...	...
a Casualty insurance claims	...	...	...	...	...	...	...	...	...	...
b Transfers from other government subsectors	...	-	...	...	...	...	-	...	...	...
c Transfers from abroad	-	-	...	...	...	-	-	...	...	...
d Other transfers, except imputed	-	-	...	...	...	-	-	...	...	...
e Imputed unfunded employee welfare contributions	...	...	...	...	...	...	...	...	...	...
Total Current Receipts	48919	39711	...	...	...	70314	54688	...	...	...

Iceland

3.12 General Government Income and Outlay Account: Total and Subsectors
(Continued)

Million Icelandic kronur

	1974					1975				
	Total General Government	Central Government	State or Provincial Government	Local Government	Social Security Funds	Total General Government	Central Government	State or Provincial Government	Local Government	Social Security Funds

Disbursements

1 General governement final consumption expenditures [a]	14295	9874	...	...	...	19758	13430	...	...	...
2 Property income paid	1140	783	...	...	...	2357	1788	...	...	...
3 Subsidies [a]	7068	6939	...	...	...	11661	11414	...	...	...
4 Other current transfers paid	15611	15260	...	...	...	22243	22591	...	...	...
a Casualty insurance premiums, net	...	...	...	...	...	...	...	...	...	...
b Transfers to other government subsectors	...	12252	...	...	...	...	17527	...	...	...
c Transfers to households	15609	3008	...	...	...	22241	5064	...	...	...
d Transfers to private non-profit institutions serving households			...	...	...			...	...	...
e Transfers to the rest of the world	2	-	...	...	...	2	-	...	...	...
Net saving	10805	6855	...	...	...	14295	5465	...	...	...
Total Current Disbursements and Net Saving	48919	39711	...	...	...	70314	54688	...	...	...

	1976					1977				
	Total General Government	Central Government	State or Provincial Government	Local Government	Social Security Funds	Total General Government	Central Government	State or Provincial Government	Local Government	Social Security Funds

Receipts

1 Property and entrepreneurial income	3296	952	...	...	...	4950	1559	...	...	...
a Net operating surplus	...	...	...	...	...	...	...	...	...	...
b Withdrawals from public quasi-corporations	1361	216	...	...	...	1648	230	...	...	...
c Interest	...	...	...	...	...	...	...	...	...	...
d Dividends	...	...	...	...	...	...	...	...	...	...
e Net land rent and royalties	...	...	...	...	...	...	...	...	...	...
2 Taxes, fees and contributions	93316	73463	...	...	...	127817	101714	...	...	...
a Indirect taxes	69989	60265	...	...	...	97839	85397	...	...	...
b Direct taxes	19931	9802	...	...	...	25518	11857	...	...	...
Income	19931	9802	...	...	...	25518	11857	...	...	...
Other	-	-	...	...	...	-	-	...	...	...
c Social security contributions	3396	3396	...	...	...	4460	4460	...	...	...
d Fees, fines and penalties	...	...	...	...	...	...	...	...	...	...
3 Other current transfers received	...	...	...	...	...	...	...	...	...	...
a Casualty insurance claims	...	...	...	...	...	...	...	...	...	...
b Transfers from other government subsectors	...	-	...	...	...	...	...	...	...	...
c Transfers from abroad	-	-	...	...	...	...	...	...	...	...
d Other transfers, except imputed	-	-	...	...	...	-	-	...	...	...
e Imputed unfunded employee welfare contributions	...	...	...	...	...	...	...	...	...	...
Total Current Receipts	96612	74415	...	...	...	132767	103273	...	...	...

Disbursements

1 General governement final consumption expenditures [a]	27102	17830	...	...	...	39062	25996	...	...	...
2 Property income paid	3074	2384	...	...	...	4217	3356	...	...	...

Iceland

3.12 General Government Income and Outlay Account: Total and Subsectors
(Continued)

Million Icelandic kronur

	1976					1977				
	Total General Government	Central Government	State or Provincial Government	Local Government	Social Security Funds	Total General Government	Central Government	State or Provincial Government	Local Government	Social Security Funds
3 Subsidies a	11602	11232	...	...	...	15423	14763	...	...	...
4 Other current transfers paid	27104	26218	...	...	...	38777	37013	...	...	...
a Casualty insurance premiums, net	...	...	...	...	...	...	...	...	...	...
b Transfers to other government subsectors	...	22065	...	...	...	...	32373	...	...	...
c Transfers to households	27104	4153	...	...	...	38777	4640	...	...	...
d Transfers to private non-profit institutions serving households								...	...	...
e Transfers to the rest of the world	-	-				-	-	...	...	...
Net saving	27730	16751	...	...	...	35288	22145	...	...	...
Total Current Disbursements and Net Saving	96612	74415	...	...	...	132767	103273	...	...	...

a) Estimates have not been adjusted to include imputed depreciation of government assets, therefore they are not strictly comparable to those of other tables.

3.13 General Government Capital Accumulation Account: Total and Subsectors

Million Icelandic kronur

	1970					1971				
	Total General Government	Central Government	State or Provincial Government	Local Government	Social Security Funds	Total General Government	Central Government	State or Provincial Government	Local Government	Social Security Funds
Finance of Gross Accumulation											
1 Gross saving	4425	3130	...	...	...	5432	3585	...	...	...
a Consumption of fixed capital	-	-	...	...	...	-	-	...	...	...
b Net saving	4425	3130	...	...	...	5432	3585	...	...	...
2 Capital transfers received a	-1399	-1471	...	...	...	-1552	-1857	...	...	...
a From other government subsectors	...	-570	...	...	...	...	-810	...	...	...
b From other resident sectors	-1399	-901	...	...	...	-1552	-1047	...	...	...
c From rest of the world	...	...	...	...	...	...	...	...	...	...
Finance of Gross Accumulation	3026	1659	...	...	...	3880	1728	...	...	...
Gross Accumulation											
1 Gross capital formation	2077	780	...	...	...	3076	1424	...	...	...
2 Purchases of land, net	...	...	...	...	...	...	...	...	...	...
3 Purchases of intangible assets, net	...	...	...	...	...	...	...	...	...	...
4 Capital transfers paid	...	...	...	...	...	...	...	...	...	...
Net lending	949	879	...	...	...	804	304	...	...	...
Gross Accumulation	3026	1659	...	...	...	3880	1728	...	...	...

	1972					1973				
	Total General Government	Central Government	State or Provincial Government	Local Government	Social Security Funds	Total General Government	Central Government	State or Provincial Government	Local Government	Social Security Funds
Finance of Gross Accumulation											
1 Gross saving	6693	3729	...	...	...	8850	5341	...	...	...
a Consumption of fixed capital	-	-	...	...	...	-	-	...	...	...
b Net saving	6693	3729	...	...	...	8850	5341	...	...	...
2 Capital transfers received a	-2151	-2375	...	...	...	-2664	-2949	...	...	...
a From other government subsectors	...	-804	...	...	...	...	-1124	...	...	...
b From other resident sectors	-2151	-1571	...	...	...	-2664	-1825	...	...	...
c From rest of the world	...	...	...	...	...	...	...	...	...	...
Finance of Gross Accumulation	4542	1354	...	...	...	6186	2392	...	...	...
Gross Accumulation											
1 Gross capital formation	3970	1875	...	...	...	5300	2244	...	...	...
2 Purchases of land, net	...	...	...	...	...	...	...	...	...	...
3 Purchases of intangible assets, net	...	...	...	...	...	...	...	...	...	...
4 Capital transfers paid	...	...	...	...	...	...	...	...	...	...
Net lending	572	-521	...	...	...	886	148	...	...	...
Gross Accumulation	4542	1354	...	...	...	6186	2392	...	...	...

Iceland

3.13 General Government Capital Accumulation Account: Total and Subsectors

Million Icelandic kronur

	1974					1975				
	Total General Government	Central Government	State or Provincial Government	Local Government	Social Security Funds	Total General Government	Central Government	State or Provincial Government	Local Government	Social Security Funds

Finance of Gross Accumulation

1 Gross saving	10805	6855	...	...	...	14295	5465	...	...	...
a Consumption of fixed capital	-	-	...	...	...	-	-	...	...	...
b Net saving	10805	6855	...	...	...	14295	5465	...	...	...
2 Capital transfers received a	-6026	-6872	...	...	...	-8406	-8994	...	...	...
a From other government subsectors	...	-2224	...	...	...	...	-2950	...	...	...
b From other resident sectors	-6026	-4648	...	...	...	-8406	-6044	...	...	...
c From rest of the world	...	...	...	...	...	...	...	...	...	...
Finance of Gross Accumulation	4779	-17	...	...	...	5889	-3529	...	...	...

Gross Accumulation

1 Gross capital formation	8207	2948	...	...	...	12071	5210	...	...	...
2 Purchases of land, net	...	...	...	...	...	...	...	...	...	...
3 Purchases of intangible assets, net	...	...	...	...	...	...	...	...	...	...
4 Capital transfers paid	...	...	...	...	...	...	...	...	...	...
Net lending	-3428	-2965	...	...	...	-6182	-8739	...	...	...
Gross Accumulation	4779	-17	...	...	...	5889	-3529	...	...	...

	1976					1977				
	Total General Government	Central Government	State or Provincial Government	Local Government	Social Security Funds	Total General Government	Central Government	State or Provincial Government	Local Government	Social Security Funds

Finance of Gross Accumulation

1 Gross saving	27730	16751	...	...	...	35288	22145	...	...	...
a Consumption of fixed capital	-	-	...	...	...	-	-	...	...	...
b Net saving	27730	16751	...	...	...	35288	22145	...	...	...
2 Capital transfers received a	-10039	-10663	...	...	...	-15188	-15848	...	...	...
a From other government subsectors	...	-3486	...	...	...	...	-4285	...	...	...
b From other resident sectors	-10039	-7177	...	...	...	-15188	-11563	...	...	...
c From rest of the world	...	...	...	...	...	...	...	...	...	...
Finance of Gross Accumulation	17691	6088	...	...	...	20100	6297	...	...	...

Gross Accumulation

1 Gross capital formation	13797	5254	...	...	...	19993	8529	...	...	...
2 Purchases of land, net	...	...	...	...	...	...	...	...	...	...
3 Purchases of intangible assets, net	...	...	...	...	...	...	...	...	...	...
4 Capital transfers paid	...	...	...	...	...	...	...	...	...	...
Net lending	3894	834	...	...	...	107	-2232	...	...	...
Gross Accumulation	17691	6088	...	...	...	20100	6297	...	...	...

a) Net.

3.51 External Transactions: Current Account: Detail

Million Icelandic kronur

	1970	1971	1972	1973	1974	1975	1976	1977	1978	1979	1980

Payments to the Rest of the World

1 Imports of goods and services	19674	25385	26760	38385	61090	88348	101931	145124	224242	363030	565360
a Imports of merchandise c.i.f.	12612	17518	18775	29180	47580	68040	78130	112345	167625	269180	431200
b Other	7062	7867	7985	9205	13510	20308	23801	32779	56617	93850	134160
2 Factor income paid to the rest of the world	813	848	1200	1640	2520	5222	7979	9801	17693	28650	47740
3 Indirect taxes paid to supranational organizations	...	...	...	...	...	...	...	...	...	...	...
4 Other current transfers to the rest of the world	32	30	55	64	86	176	155	149	206	514	501
a By general government	32	30	55	64	86	176	155	149	206	514	501
b By other resident sectors	-	-	-	-	-	-	-	-	-	-	-
5 Surplus of the nation on current transactions	619	-3890	-1810	-2699	-15616	-21556	-4545	-9804	7664	-7044	-32301
Payments to the Rest of the World, and Surplus of the Nation on Current Transfers	21138	22373	26205	37390	48080	72190	105520	145270	249805	385150	581300

Iceland

3.51 External Transactions: Current Account: Detail
(Continued)

Million Icelandic kronur

	1970	1971	1972	1973	1974	1975	1976	1977	1978	1979	1980
Receipts From The Rest of the World											
1 Exports of goods and services	20806	22034	25895	36930	47475	71831	104824	144299	248212	380890	574630
a Exports of merchandise f.o.b.	12850	13178	16700	26020	32880	47440	73500	101890	176285	278450	446000
b Other	7956	8856	9195	10910	14595	24391	31324	42409	71927	102440	128630
2 Factor income received from the rest of the world	332	339	310	460	605	359	696	971	1593	4260	6670
3 Subsidies received from supranational organizations	...	...	...	...	...	...	...	...	...	...	...
4 Other current transfers from the rest of the world	-	-	-	-	-	-	-	-	-	-	-
Receipts from the Rest of the World on Current Transfers	21138	22373	26205	37390	48080	72190	105520	145270	249805	385150	581300

3.52 External Transactions: Capital Accumulation Account

Million Icelandic kronur

	1970	1971	1972	1973	1974	1975	1976	1977	1978	1979	1980
Finance of Gross Accumulation											
1 Surplus of the nation on current transactions	619	-3890	-1810	-2699	-15616	-21556	-4545	-9804	7664	-7044	-32301
2 Capital transfers received from the rest of the world	-3	20	75	1514	146	81	200	139	-49	-486	-1519
a By general government	-	-	-	1360	66	-	-	-	-	-	-
b By other resident sectors	-3	20	75	154	80	81	200	139	-49	-486	-1519
Total Finance of Gross Accumulation	616	-3870	-1735	-1185	-15470	-21475	-4345	-9665	7615	-7530	-33820
Gross Accumulation											
1 Capital transfers paid to the rest of the world	...	...	...	...	...	...	...	...	...	...	...
2 Purchases of intangible assets, n.e.c., net, from the rest of the world	-	-	-	-	-	-	-	-	-	-	-
3 Net lending to the rest of the world	616	-3870	-1735	-1185	-15470	-21475	-4345	-9665	7615	-7530	-33820
Total Gross Accumulation	616	-3870	-1735	-1185	-15470	-21475	-4345	-9665	7615	-7530	-33820

India

General note. The preparation of national accounts statistics in India is undertaken by the Central Statistical Organization, New Delhi. Official estimates are published annually in 'National Accounts Statistics'. A description of the sources and methods used for the national accounts estimation is found in 'National Accounts Statistics - Sources and Methods' published in Aprial 1980. The estimates are generally in accordance with the classifications and definitions recommended in the United Nations System of National Accounts (SNA). Input-output data and value added by sectors were published in 1975 in 'National Accounts Statistics 1960/61 to 1972/73 - Disaggregated Tables'. The following tables have been prepared from successive replies to the United Nations national accounts questionnaire. Estimates relate to fiscal years beginning 1 April. When the scope and coverage of the estimates differ for conceptual or statistical reasons from the definitions and classifications recommended in SNA, a footnote is indicated to the relevant tables.

Sources and methods:

(a) Gross domestic product. Gross domestic product is estimated mainly through the production approach.

(b) Expenditure on the gross domestic product. The expenditure approach is used to estimate government final consumption expenditure, increase in stocks and exports and imports of goods and services. The commodity-flow approach is used to estimate private final consumption expenditure whereas the estimate of gross fixed capital formation is based on a combination of the commodity-flow and expenditure approaches. Estimates of government consumption expenditure are mainly obtained from budget documents of the government bodies. The estimates of private expenditure on goods are obtained from commodity production data adjusted by stock changes and foreign trade and reduced by intermediate and government consumption and by quantities used for capital formation. Private expenditure on services is estimated as the value of the total output for each kind of service reduced by the estimated service expenditures by government and business. Estimates of increase in stocks for the public sector and organized (i.e. larger or modern) private industries are based on government budget documents and annual accounts and reports of industries. Changes in stocks of agriculture and unorganized private industries are based on sample survey data and data on bank advances and margins as well as on livestock census reports. For gross fixed capital formation, estimates of construction are drawn from a number of sources such as annual surveys of industry, despatches of cement for domestic consumption, sample surveys and government budget documents. Estimates for rural construction are based on the results of the All-India rural debt and investment survey conducted in 1971/72. Bench-mark estimates for rural residential buildings are based on capital and rental values. These estimates are extrapolated by the annual increase in the urban and rural dwellings. For machinery and equipment the estimates are based on the annual survey of industries, foreign trade statistics, customs and excise revenue statements, data on trade, transport and other charges collected from leading manufacturing firms in the country. The estimates of export and imports of goods and services are based on balance of payments statistics supplemented by information supplied by government agencies. For the constant price estimates, private expenditure on goods is extrapolated by quantity and price indexes. Changes in stocks of livestock, mining and foodgrains are valued at base-year values. For government expenditure, private expenditure on services, increase in stock for other sectors and gross fixed capital formation, the current values are deflated by relevant price indexes. Government consumption expenditure and import and export of goods and services are not estimated at constant prices.

(c) Cost-structure of the gross domestic product. Estimates of compensation of employees are based on budget documents, annual reports of enterprises, income and expenditure accounts of institutions and companies and sample surveys. Estimates of operating surplus are based on most of the sources used for compensation of employees. Consumption of fixed capital is estimated for each industry separately. The sources include the All-India rural debt and investment survey of 1971/72, livestock censuses, budget documents and annual accounts. For some industries, depreciation is estimated as a fixed percentage of output. Estimates of indirect taxes and subsidies are based on accounts and records or government bodies.

(d) Gross domestic product by kind of economic activity. The table of GDP by kind of economic activity is prepared in factor values. The production approach is used to estimate value added for all commodity producing sectors, ownership of dwelling and bench-marks for small-scale manufacturing. Value added of construction is based on a combination of the commodity-flow and expenditure approaches. The income approach is used for all other sectors. The production estimates of 36 principal agricultural crops are based on results of the random sample crop-cutting surveys conducted by the respective state government agencies. The wholesale prices in the primary markets are used to evaluate the total production of each commodity. The annual estimates of livestock products are based on the livestock population by type and the corresponding average yield rates. Intermediate consumption is estimated by using a variety of sources such as the National Sample Survey (NSS report), the All-India rural debt and investment survey, and marketing reports. Estimates of the gross output of minerals are based on data available from the Indian Bureau of Mines. For large-scale manufacturing, estimates are prepared for 19 industry groups based on the annual surveys of industries (ASI). Bench-mark 1970/71 estimates for the household and non-household small-scale manufacturing have been prepared using data on value added per worker and estimated working force. Other years' estimates are extrapolated by means of indicators of physical output or input. Estimates of urban type construction are compiled from ASI reports, cement production data, foreign trade statistics, customs and excise revenue, etc. The estimates of rural construction are based on the NSS, debt and investment surveys and other sources. For trade, bench-mark 1970/71 estimates are based on reports of distributive trade surveys for the organized sector and on NSS results for the unorganized sector. Other years' estimates are based on annual reports. For the rest of the distributive trade bench-mark estimates are first extrapolated by volume indexes providing constant price estimates, which are then adjusted by various price indexes. For public transport, estimates are based on analysis of budget documents and annual accounts. Estimates of private passenger and truck transport are prepared by multiplying estimated value added per worker by the estimated number of workers. For the financial sector, estimates are obtained from the Reserve Bank of India and other banks as well as annual accounts of financial corporations. The estimates of gross rents for urban and rural dwellings are based on the number of dwellings and estimated gross rental value per dwelling. For public administration and defense, value added is equivalent to compensation of employees only and is obtained from budget documents. For the service sectors, the estimates of working force and average net earnings per worker are obtained from various sources such as the institutions concerned, the NSS report and population censuses. For the constant price estimates, double deflation is used for the agriculture and mining sectors. Current values of large-scale manufacturing and construction are deflated by price indexes. For small-scale manufacturing, electricity, gas and water, trade, transport, ownership of dwellings and other services, value added is extrapolated by quantity indexes. Current estimates of public administration are adjusted for increase in pay and allowances due to increase in cost of living.

1.1 Expenditure on the Gross Domestic Product, in Current Prices

Thousand Million Indian rupees — Fiscal year beginning 1 April

		1970	1971	1972	1973	1974	1975	1976	1977	1978	1979	1980
1	General government final consumption expenditure	38.01	44.58	47.45	51.00	61.43	73.51	82.06	86.67	96.24	109.24	127.94
2	Private final consumption expenditure	298.03	320.61	350.84	428.65	519.05	527.47	541.70	626.89	669.44	729.67	878.70
3	Gross capital formation	73.44	84.11	85.26	113.52	145.09	164.18	176.91	183.41	229.49	246.83	293.51
	a Increase in stocks	10.39	13.37	4.60	23.23	35.79	31.70	23.63	12.58	37.44	41.63	56.64
	b Gross fixed capital formation [a]	63.05	70.74	80.66	90.29	109.30	132.48	153.28	170.83	192.05	205.20	236.87
	Residential buildings	8.26	9.68	9.48	13.16	15.57	17.55	21.61	21.81	25.73	25.76	30.16
	Non-residential buildings	15.50	13.95	14.82	11.03	17.68	26.22	27.80	34.03	31.95	26.79	28.47
	Other construction and land improvement etc.	15.83	19.01	22.84	25.11	24.29	28.81	35.83	42.19	49.07	54.57	62.50
	Other	23.46	28.10	33.52	40.99	51.76	59.90	68.04	72.80	85.30	98.08	115.74
4	Exports of goods and services	17.71	18.38	22.25	28.30	38.35	48.12	61.39	66.36	71.15	77.65	...
5	Less: Imports of goods and services	18.16	20.06	20.49	31.76	47.79	56.64	56.14	65.22	74.26	95.55	...
	Statistical discrepancy [b]	-6.40	-14.06	-6.66	-0.31	-20.18	-15.80	-2.51	2.85	-17.62	-6.33	...
	Equals: Gross Domestic Product	402.63	433.56	478.65	589.40	695.95	740.84	803.41	900.96	974.44	1061.51	1256.75

a) Data are unadjusted for statistical discrepancy and therefore do not coincide with the data shown in the table 'Gross capital formation by kind of economic activity of owner'. b) The statistical discrepancy is distributed among the individual expenditure items which are shown in tables 1.8, 1.12, 2.7, 2.9, and 3.51.

India

1.2 Expenditure on the Gross Domestic Product, in Constant Prices

Thousand Million Indian rupees — Fiscal year beginning 1 April

	1970	1971	1972	1973	1974	1975	1976	1977	1978	1979	1980
	At constant prices of: 1970										
1 General government final consumption expenditure	38.01	42.60	43.39	43.42	43.50	48.85	52.97	54.76	60.18	65.13	...
2 Private final consumption expenditure	298.38	307.04	300.70	308.80	311.43	334.67	334.22	368.00	380.86	365.89	390.77
3 Gross capital formation	73.44	79.59	74.79	87.39	89.47	93.88	98.59	99.79	116.14	107.53	116.64
a Increase in stocks	10.39	12.73	4.20	16.79	20.91	18.74	13.44	7.01	20.24	18.95	22.76
b Gross fixed capital formation [a]	63.05	66.86	70.59	70.60	68.56	75.14	85.15	92.78	95.90	88.58	93.88
Residential buildings	8.26	9.05	8.23	9.82	9.42	9.76	11.63	11.24	12.21	10.50	10.62
Non-residential buildings	15.50	13.00	12.79	8.25	10.73	15.10	15.39	18.07	15.63	11.53	10.77
Other construction and land improvement etc.	15.83	17.70	19.70	18.96	15.55	16.59	19.81	22.41	23.94	23.30	23.41
Other	23.46	27.11	29.87	33.57	32.86	33.69	38.32	41.06	44.12	43.25	49.08
4 Exports of goods and services	...	...	...	...	...	...	...	...	...	...	...
5 Less: Imports of goods and services	...	...	...	...	...	...	...	...	...	...	...
Equals: Gross Domestic Product	402.63	411.96	409.01	423.70	424.37	465.74	473.46	511.86	543.78	517.90	551.75

a) Data are unadjusted for statistical discrepancy and therefore do not coincide with the data shown in the table 'Gross capital formation by kind of economic activity of owner'.

1.3 Cost Components of the Gross Domestic Product

Thousand Million Indian rupees — Fiscal year beginning 1 April

	1970	1971	1972	1973	1974	1975	1976	1977	1978	1979	1980
1 Indirect taxes, net	35.27	40.93	46.24	51.68	63.32	77.14	85.33	89.17	105.34	121.68	135.88
a Indirect taxes paid	38.64	45.15	51.75	58.76	75.15	88.34	99.26	106.89	127.35	145.94	161.59
b Less: Subsidies received	3.37	4.22	5.51	7.08	11.83	11.20	13.93	17.72	22.01	24.26	25.71
2 Consumption of fixed capital [a]	22.17	23.99	26.69	30.23	35.26	40.46	44.92	50.11	57.62	67.99	79.55
3 Compensation of employees paid by resident producers to:	294.75	311.97	342.99	438.59	511.45	527.44	555.77	636.59	668.85	716.09	...
a Resident households	294.64	311.85	342.88	438.47	511.34	527.33	555.54	636.11	668.31	...	...
b Rest of the world	0.11	0.12	0.11	0.12	0.11	0.11	0.23	0.48	0.54	...	...
4 Net operating surplus	50.44	56.67	62.73	68.90	85.92	95.80	117.39	125.09	142.63	155.75	...
a Corporate and quasi-corporate enterprises	26.43	29.62	30.93	36.52	48.43	53.03	70.95	75.04	87.59	97.88	...
b Private unincorporated enterprises	24.01	27.05	31.80	32.38	37.49	42.77	46.44	50.05	55.04	57.87	...
c General government	...	...	...	...	...	...	...	...	...	...	...
Equals: Gross Domestic Product	402.63	433.56	478.65	589.40	695.95	740.84	803.41	900.96	974.44	1061.51	1256.75

a) Including part of net operating surplus of unincorporated enterprises which cannot be separated from labour income of own-account.

1.4 General Government Current Receipts and Disbursements

Thousand Million Indian rupees — Fiscal year beginning 1 April

	1970	1971	1972	1973	1974	1975	1976	1977	1978	1979	1980
	Receipts										
1 Property and entrepreneurial income	5.74	6.48	6.38	5.45	8.05	9.97	15.98	17.96	18.63	18.29	22.45
2 Taxes, fees and contributions	51.17	60.61	67.91	76.79	96.79	116.74	129.48	138.06	160.74	181.95	201.13
a Indirect taxes	38.64	45.15	51.75	58.76	75.15	88.34	99.26	106.89	127.35	145.94	161.59
b Direct taxes	10.91	12.75	14.70	16.53	19.68	26.43	27.76	28.78	30.57	33.07	36.34
c Social security contributions	...	...	...	...	...	...	...	...	...	...	...
d Compulsory fees, fines and penalties	1.62	2.71	1.46	1.50	1.96	1.97	2.46	2.39	2.82	2.94	3.20
3 Other current receipts	...	...	...	...	...	...	...	...	...	...	...
Total Current Receipts of General Government	56.91	67.09	74.29	82.24	104.84	126.71	145.46	156.02	179.37	200.24	223.58
	Disbursements										
1 General government final consumption expenditure	38.01	44.58	47.45	51.00	61.43	73.51	82.06	86.67	96.24	109.24	127.94
a Compensation of employees	23.69	26.61	28.94	32.69	40.96	46.81	51.30	55.38	61.37	68.27	80.87
b Consumption of fixed capital	...	...	...	...	...	...	...	...	...	...	...
c Purchases of goods and services, net	14.32	17.97	18.51	18.31	20.47	26.70	30.76	31.29	34.87	40.97	47.07
d Less: Own account production of fixed assets	...	...	...	...	...	...	...	...	...	...	...
e Indirect taxes paid, net	...	...	...	...	...	...	...	...	...	...	...
2 Property income paid	2.16	2.69	3.47	4.77	3.40	4.91	6.01	6.99	9.36	9.79	14.81

India

1.4 General Government Current Receipts and Disbursements
(Continued)

Thousand Million Indian rupees — Fiscal year beginning 1 April

	1970	1971	1972	1973	1974	1975	1976	1977	1978	1979	1980
a Interest [a]	2.16	2.69	3.47	4.77	3.40	4.91	6.01	6.99	9.36	9.79	14.81
b Net land rent and royalties	-	-	-	-	-	-	-	-	-	-	-
3 Subsidies	3.37	4.22	5.51	7.08	11.83	11.20	13.93	17.72	22.01	24.26	25.71
4 Other current transfers paid	6.03	8.18	11.08	9.78	11.69	13.60	15.64	17.76	20.19	23.31	28.38
Statistical discrepancy [b]	...	...	...	...	0.97	0.78	2.69	1.23	3.02	6.94	8.27
5 Net saving	7.34	7.42	6.78	9.61	15.52	22.71	25.13	25.65	28.55	26.70	18.47
Total Current Disbursements and Net Saving of General Government	56.91	67.09	74.29	82.24	104.84	126.71	145.46	156.02	179.37	200.24	223.58

a) Interest on the public debt.
b) Relating to inter-governmental accounting adjustments. For years prior to 1973, it is included in item 'Net saving'.

1.7 External Transactions on Current Account, Summary

Thousand Million Indian rupees — Fiscal year beginning 1 April

	1970	1971	1972	1973	1974	1975	1976	1977	1978	1979	1980
Payments to the Rest of the World											
1 Imports of goods and services	18.16	20.06	20.49	31.76	47.79	56.64	56.14	65.22	74.26	...	...
a Imports of merchandise c.i.f.	17.34	20.03	21.57	27.50	41.81	47.73	48.44	55.70	62.58	...	...
b Other	0.82	0.03	-1.08	4.26	5.98	8.91	7.70	9.52	11.68	...	...
2 Factor income paid to the rest of the world	3.41	3.34	3.46	3.70	3.87	3.73	4.25	5.06	5.58	...	...
a Compensation of employees	0.11	0.12	0.11	0.12	0.11	0.11	0.23	0.48	0.54	...	...
b Property and entrepreneurial income paid [a]	3.30	3.22	3.35	3.58	3.76	3.62	4.02	4.58	5.04	...	...
3 Indirect taxes paid to supranational organizations	...	...	...	...	...	...	...	...	...	...	...
4 Current transfers to the rest of the world	0.13	0.12	0.11	0.12	0.06	0.13	0.07	0.07	0.17	...	...
Statistical discrepancy [b]	0.86	1.69	2.79	-2.26	-3.62	-5.21	-2.57	-4.84	5.84	...	...
5 Surplus of the nation on current transactions	-4.24	-5.18	-3.27	-4.25	-7.48	0.77	12.75	14.17	-1.80	...	...
Payments to the Rest of the World and Surplus of the Nation on Current Transactions	18.32	20.03	23.58	29.07	40.62	56.06	70.64	79.68	84.05	...	...
Receipts From The Rest of the World											
1 Exports of goods and services	17.71	18.38	22.25	28.30	38.35	48.12	61.39	66.36	71.15	...	...
a Exports of merchandise f.o.b.	14.03	15.55	18.95	23.51	31.80	41.78	51.33	54.34	55.55	...	...
b Other	3.68	2.83	3.30	4.79	6.55	6.34	10.06	12.02	15.60	...	...
2 Factor income received from rest of the world	0.57	0.43	0.44	0.45	0.96	1.18	1.92	2.73	4.02	...	...
a Compensation of employees	0.08	0.08	0.06	0.03	0.01	0.02	0.04	0.05	0.04	...	...
b Property and entrepreneurial income received	0.49	0.35	0.38	0.42	0.95	1.16	1.88	2.68	3.98	...	...
3 Subsidies received from supranational organisations	...	...	...	...	...	...	...	...	...	...	...
4 Current transfers from rest of the world	1.36	1.75	1.65	2.04	2.80	5.41	7.46	10.29	10.59	...	...
Statistical discrepancy [b]	-1.32	-0.53	-0.76	-1.72	-1.49	1.35	-0.13	0.30	-1.71	...	...
Receipts from the Rest of the World on Current Transactions	18.32	20.03	23.58	29.07	40.62	56.06	70.64	79.68	84.05	...	...

a) Including retained earnings of branches of foreign companies and foreign controlled rupee companies in India.
b) Referring to difference of ownership and payment basis of imports and exports of merchandise.

1.8 Capital Transactions of The Nation, Summary

Thousand Million Indian rupees — Fiscal year beginning 1 April

	1970	1971	1972	1973	1974	1975	1976	1977	1978	1979	1980
Finance of Gross Capital Formation											
Gross saving [a]	67.53	74.58	77.39	113.59	125.58	148.06	176.65	191.87	237.45	237.86	278.06
1 Consumption of fixed capital	22.17	23.99	26.69	30.23	35.26	40.46	44.92	50.11	57.62	67.99	79.55
a General government	...	...	...	...	...	...	...	...	...	...	...
b Corporate and quasi-corporate enterprises	8.83	9.83	11.29	13.07	13.74	15.54	18.33	21.10	23.57	27.17	...
Public	4.49	5.16	5.93	7.26	7.05	8.46	9.79	11.59	13.07	15.49	...
Private	4.34	4.67	5.36	5.81	6.69	7.08	8.54	9.51	10.50	11.68	...
c Other	13.34	14.16	15.40	17.16	21.52	24.92	26.59	29.01	34.05	40.82	...

India

1.8 Capital Transactions of The Nation, Summary
(Continued)

Thousand Million Indian rupees — *Fiscal year beginning 1 April*

	1970	1971	1972	1973	1974	1975	1976	1977	1978	1979	1980
2 Net saving	45.36	50.59	50.70	83.36	90.32	107.60	131.73	141.76	179.83	169.87	...
a General government	7.34	7.42	6.78	9.61	15.52	22.71	25.13	25.65	28.55	26.70	...
b Corporate and quasi-corporate enterprises	2.63	2.66	2.83	5.68	10.96	5.29	9.07	7.20	9.30	11.90	...
Public	0.70	0.20	0.61	1.20	4.19	2.22	6.34	3.55	4.41	4.54	...
Private	1.93	2.46	2.22	4.48	6.77	3.07	2.73	3.65	4.89	7.36	...
c Other	35.39	40.51	41.09	68.07	63.84	79.60	97.53	108.91	141.98	131.27	...
Less: Surplus of the nation on current transactions	-4.24	-5.18	-3.27	-4.25	-7.48	0.77	12.75	14.17	-1.80	-5.08	...
Finance of Gross Capital Formation	71.77	79.76	80.66	117.84	133.06	147.29	163.90	177.70	239.25	242.94	...
Gross Capital Formation											
Increase in stocks	10.39	13.37	4.60	23.23	35.79	31.70	23.63	12.58	37.44	41.63	56.64
Gross fixed capital formation	63.05	70.74	80.66	90.29	109.30	132.48	153.28	170.83	192.05	205.20	236.87
1 General government [b]	6.11	8.42	11.18	12.49	9.95	11.13	13.54	15.62	20.09	23.24	27.25
2 Corporate and quasi-corporate enterprises	24.03	27.42	33.26	38.23	44.36	62.50	70.00	77.88	81.22	91.19	103.37
a Public	17.83	19.60	25.01	27.60	32.77	44.87	57.09	61.29	63.37	73.17	83.57
b Private	6.20	7.82	8.25	10.63	11.59	17.63	12.91	16.59	17.85	18.02	19.80
3 Other	32.91	34.90	36.22	39.57	54.99	58.85	69.74	77.33	90.74	90.77	106.25
Statistical discrepancy	-1.67	-4.35	-4.60	4.32	-12.03	-16.89	-13.01	-5.71	9.76	-3.89	10.02
Gross Capital Formation	71.77	79.76	80.66	117.84	133.06	147.29	163.90	177.70	239.25	242.94	303.53

a) Excluding retained earnings of branches of foreign companies and foreign controlled rupee companies in India.
b) Excluding local authorities.

1.9 Gross Domestic Product by Institutional Sectors of Origin

Thousand Million Indian rupees — *Fiscal year beginning 1 April*

	1970	1971	1972	1973	1974	1975	1976	1977	1978	1979	1980
Domestic Factor Incomes Originating											
1 General government	24.01	26.97	29.31	33.05	41.33	47.20	51.73	55.87	61.94	69.28	...
2 Corporate and quasi-corporate enterprises [a]	70.82	79.44	87.93	100.82	127.48	143.64	170.89	188.16	211.79	237.50	...
a Non-financial	64.47	71.98	79.36	90.16	114.17	126.37	150.57	165.43	187.11	209.89	...
Public	21.84	24.13	26.96	31.54	43.74	53.27	65.48	71.24	79.01	87.89	...
Private	42.63	47.85	52.40	58.62	70.43	73.10	85.09	94.19	108.10	122.00	...
b Financial	6.35	7.46	8.57	10.66	13.31	17.27	20.32	22.73	24.68	27.61	...
Public	4.22	5.11	5.87	7.69	10.19	13.27	16.21	18.21	20.00	23.15	...
Private	2.13	2.35	2.70	2.97	3.12	4.00	4.11	4.52	4.68	4.46	...
3 Households and private unincorporated enterprises [a]	250.36	262.23	288.48	373.62	428.56	432.40	450.54	517.65	537.75	565.06	...
4 Non-profit institutions serving households [a]	...	...	...	...	...	...	...	...	...	...	...
Subtotal: Domestic Factor Incomes	345.19	368.64	405.72	507.49	597.37	623.24	673.16	761.68	811.48	871.84	1041.32
Indirect taxes paid, net	35.27	40.93	46.24	51.68	63.32	77.14	85.33	89.17	105.34	121.68	135.88
Consumption of fixed capital	22.17	23.99	26.69	30.23	35.26	40.46	44.92	50.11	57.62	67.99	79.55
Gross Domestic Product	402.63	433.56	478.65	589.40	695.95	740.84	803.41	900.96	974.44	1061.51	1256.75

a) Item 'Non-profit institutions serving households' is included in items 'Households and private unincorporated enterprises.' and 'Corporate and quasi-corporate enterprises'.

1.10 Gross Domestic Product by Kind of Activity, in Current Prices

Thousand Million Indian rupees — *Fiscal year beginning 1 April*

	1970	1971	1972	1973	1974	1975	1976	1977	1978	1979	1980
1 Agriculture, hunting, forestry and fishing	174.24	180.83	199.35	267.88	290.45	278.45	287.24	329.70	333.66	339.97	417.28
2 Mining and quarrying	3.78	3.96	4.27	4.87	6.95	8.84	10.11	11.17	12.32	15.36	17.18
3 Manufacturing	52.23	57.49	63.75	75.72	98.58	103.75	115.56	129.03	148.38	173.75	199.88
4 Electricity, gas and water	4.19	4.56	4.91	5.25	6.75	8.35	10.95	12.48	15.39	16.24	18.29
5 Construction	19.52	21.42	23.16	24.05	26.37	32.93	39.29	45.08	48.02	46.37	53.79
6 Wholesale and retail trade, restaurants and hotels	40.43	43.92	48.61	60.25	81.05	92.08	96.51	110.44	117.16	132.40	165.94
7 Transport, storage and communication	18.69	20.23	22.32	24.90	31.34	35.24	41.62	45.41	51.80	56.24	65.58
8 Finance, insurance, real estate and business services	21.14	23.50	26.11	30.10	35.23	41.18	47.24	52.30	57.48	64.01	71.64
9 Community, social and personal services	16.79	18.41	20.17	22.49	27.35	30.51	35.03	39.24	44.17	49.77	56.81
Total, Industries	351.01	374.32	412.65	515.51	604.07	631.33	683.55	774.85	828.38	894.11	1066.39
Producers of Government Services	16.35	18.31	19.76	22.21	28.56	32.37	34.53	36.94	40.72	45.72	54.48

India

1.10 Gross Domestic Product by Kind of Activity, in Current Prices
(Continued)

Thousand Million Indian rupees — Fiscal year beginning 1 April

	1970	1971	1972	1973	1974	1975	1976	1977	1978	1979	1980
Other Producers	...	...	...	...	...	...	...	...	...	...	...
Subtotal [a]	367.36	392.63	432.41	537.72	632.63	663.70	718.08	811.79	869.10	939.83	1120.87
Less: Imputed bank service charge [b]	...	...	...	...	...	...	...	...	...	...	...
Plus: Import duties	...	...	...	...	...	...	...	...	...	...	...
Plus: Value added tax	...	...	...	...	...	...	...	...	...	...	...
Plus: Other adjustments [c]	35.27	40.93	46.24	51.68	63.32	77.14	85.33	89.17	105.34	121.68	135.88
Equals: Gross Domestic Product	402.63	433.56	478.65	589.40	695.95	740.84	803.41	900.96	974.44	1061.51	1256.75

a) Gross domestic product in factor values.
b) Imputed bank service charges are adjusted in the respective activity.
c) Referring to indirect taxes net of subsidies.

1.11 Gross Domestic Product by Kind of Activity, in Constant Prices

Thousand Million Indian rupees — Fiscal year beginning 1 April

At constant prices of: 1970

	1970	1971	1972	1973	1974	1975	1976	1977	1978	1979	1980
1 Agriculture, hunting, forestry and fishing	174.24	173.39	162.84	174.83	171.69	193.49	181.38	203.76	207.40	181.44	203.85
2 Mining and quarrying	3.78	3.85	4.06	4.12	4.30	4.80	4.98	5.12	5.21	5.31	5.45
3 Manufacturing	52.23	53.67	55.90	58.61	59.99	61.28	66.90	71.34	79.21	79.04	81.38
4 Electricity, gas and water	4.19	4.51	4.72	4.85	5.07	5.77	6.38	6.63	7.37	7.53	7.92
5 Construction	19.52	19.74	20.05	18.39	17.71	20.27	22.69	24.93	25.09	22.36	22.17
6 Wholesale and retail trade, restaurants and hotels	40.43	41.22	41.38	43.13	45.09	49.32	52.51	55.68	60.36	58.41	61.31
7 Transport, storage and communication	18.69	19.45	20.77	21.42	23.25	25.29	26.96	28.00	29.56	31.06	32.97
8 Finance, insurance, real estate and business services	21.14	22.21	23.03	23.49	23.23	25.01	27.24	28.99	31.46	31.73	32.45
9 Community, social and personal services	16.79	17.24	17.72	17.82	18.60	19.01	19.34	19.68	20.18	21.30	22.37
Total, Industries	351.01	355.28	350.47	366.66	368.93	404.24	408.38	444.13	465.84	438.18	469.87
Producers of Government Services	16.35	17.85	18.63	19.80	20.86	22.38	23.70	25.35	28.19	31.30	35.02
Other Producers	...	...	...	...	...	...	...	...	...	...	...
Subtotal [a]	367.36	373.13	369.10	386.46	389.79	426.62	432.08	469.48	494.03	469.48	504.89
Less: Imputed bank service charge [b]	...	...	...	...	...	...	...	...	...	...	...
Plus: Import duties	...	...	...	...	...	...	...	...	...	...	...
Plus: Value added tax	...	...	...	...	...	...	...	...	...	...	...
Plus: Other adjustments [c]	35.27	38.83	39.91	37.24	34.58	39.12	42.38	42.38	49.75	48.42	46.86
Equals: Gross Domestic Product	402.63	411.96	409.01	423.70	424.37	465.74	474.46	511.86	543.78	517.90	551.75

a) Gross domestic product in factor values.
b) Imputed bank service charges are adjusted in the respective activity.
c) Referring to indirect taxes net of subsidies.

1.12 Relations Among National Accounting Aggregates

Thousand Million Indian rupees — Fiscal year beginning 1 April

	1970	1971	1972	1973	1974	1975	1976	1977	1978	1979	1980
Gross Domestic Product	402.63	433.56	478.65	589.40	695.95	740.84	803.41	900.96	974.44	1061.51	1256.75
Plus: Net factor income received from abroad	-2.84	-2.91	-3.02	-3.25	-2.91	-2.55	-2.33	-2.33	-1.56	0.69	0.69
Factor income received	0.57	0.43	0.44	0.45	0.96	1.18	1.92	2.73	4.02	5.41	5.41
Less: Factor income paid	3.41	3.34	3.46	3.70	3.87	3.73	4.25	5.06	5.58	4.72	4.72
Equals: Gross National Product	399.79	430.65	475.63	586.15	693.04	738.29	801.08	898.63	972.88	1062.20	1257.44
Less: Consumption of fixed capital	22.17	23.99	26.69	30.23	35.26	40.46	44.92	50.11	57.62	67.99	79.55
Less: Net indirect taxes paid to supranational organisations	...	...	...	...	...	...	...	...	...	...	...
Equals: National Income at Market Prices	377.62	406.66	448.94	555.92	657.78	697.83	756.16	848.52	915.26	994.21	1177.89
Plus: Net current transfers received from abroad	1.23	1.63	1.54	1.92	2.74	5.28	7.39	10.22	10.42	12.13	13.84
Current transfers received	1.36	1.75	1.65	2.04	2.80	5.41	7.46	10.29	10.59	12.30	14.01
Less: Current transfers paid	0.13	0.12	0.11	0.12	0.06	0.13	0.07	0.07	0.17	0.17	0.17
Equals: National Disposable Income at Market Prices	378.85	408.29	450.48	557.84	660.52	703.11	763.55	858.74	925.68	1006.34	1191.73
Less: Final consumption	336.04	365.19	398.29	479.65	580.48	600.98	623.76	713.56	765.68	838.91	...
Statistical discrepancy	2.55	7.49	-1.49	5.17	10.28	5.47	-8.06	-3.42	19.83	2.44	...
Equals: Net Saving	45.36	50.59	50.70	83.36	90.32	107.60	131.73	141.76	179.83	169.87	198.51
Less: Surplus of the nation on current transactions	-4.24	-5.18	-3.27	-4.25	-7.48	0.77	12.75	14.17	-1.80	-5.08	-25.47
Equals: Net Capital Formation	49.60	55.77	53.97	87.61	97.80	106.83	118.98	127.59	181.63	174.95	223.98

India

2.1 General Government Final Consumption Expenditure by Function, in Current Prices

Thousand Million Indian rupees — Fiscal year beginning 1 April

		1970	1971	1972	1973	1974	1975	1976	1977	1978	1979	1980
1	General public services [a]	7.74	8.89	9.11	10.60	12.66	14.70	16.48	17.56	19.19	22.16	...
2	Defence	12.31	15.75	16.98	17.41	21.69	25.76	26.87	27.44	29.18	33.74	...
3	Public order and safety [a]	...	...	...	...	...	...	...	...	...	...	...
4	Education	3.14	3.50	4.00	4.55	5.45	6.54	7.55	9.17	10.27	11.93	...
5	Health	1.66	2.04	2.23	2.53	3.13	3.90	4.52	5.12	5.72	6.61	...
6	Social security and welfare	0.85	0.88	0.86	1.00	1.29	1.47	1.82	1.82	2.09	2.41	...
7	Housing and community amenities	0.48	0.54	0.59	0.70	1.00	1.13	1.30	1.39	1.56	1.81	...
8	Recreational, cultural and religious affairs	0.32	0.28	0.53	0.42	0.55	0.55	0.67	0.69	0.86	1.01	...
9	Economic services	4.33	4.48	4.93	5.33	6.52	7.91	9.09	10.01	12.55	14.45	...
	a Fuel and energy	0.22	0.22	0.27	0.33	0.44	0.72	0.81	0.89	1.22	1.41	...
	b Agriculture, forestry, fishing and hunting	1.57	1.68	1.82	2.02	2.55	2.91	3.21	3.84	4.65	5.37	...
	c Mining, manufacturing and construction, except fuel and energy	0.41	0.44	0.50	0.45	0.60	0.68	0.88	0.88	1.19	1.36	...
	d Transportation and communication	1.35	1.25	1.35	1.39	1.68	2.01	2.48	2.57	3.46	4.01	...
	e Other economic affairs	0.78	0.89	0.99	1.14	1.25	1.59	1.71	1.83	2.03	2.30	...
10	Other functions	0.88	1.38	1.00	0.81	0.91	1.62	2.34	2.05	1.85	2.15	...
	Total General Government Final Consumption Expenditure [b]	31.71	37.74	40.23	43.35	53.20	63.58	70.64	75.25	83.27	96.27	...

a) Item 'Public order and safety' is included in item 'General public services'.
b) Excluding local authorities.

2.3 Total General Government Outlays by Function and Type

Thousand Million Indian rupees — Fiscal year beginning 1 April

		Final Consumption Expenditures Total	Compensation of Employees	Other	Subsidies	Other Current Transfers & Property Income	Total Current Disbursements	Gross Capital Formation	Other Capital Outlays	Total Outlays
						1970				
1	General public services [a]	7.74	5.58	2.16	0.22	1.12	9.08	0.57	0.16	9.81
2	Defence	12.31	5.95	6.36	-	0.01	12.32	0.05	-	12.37
3	Public order and safety [a]	...	...	...	...	...	...	...	...	...
4	Education	3.14	2.88	0.26	-	6.68	9.82	0.18	0.03	10.03
5	Health	1.66	1.16	0.50	-	0.24	1.90	0.20	-	2.10
6	Social security and welfare	0.85	0.56	0.29	0.06	0.27	1.18	0.03	-	1.21
7	Housing and community amenities	0.48	0.39	0.09	0.01	0.68	1.17	0.40	0.12	1.69
8	Recreation, culture and religion	0.32	0.25	0.07	0.01	0.11	0.44	0.06	0.01	0.51
9	Economic services	4.33	2.32	2.01	3.06	0.58	7.97	2.81	0.47	11.25
	a Fuel and energy	0.22	0.12	0.10	0.02	0.11	0.35	0.35	0.17	0.87
	b Agriculture, forestry, fishing and hunting	1.57	1.05	0.52	1.60	0.31	3.48	0.32	0.11	3.91
	c Mining (except fuels), manufacturing and construction	0.41	0.32	0.09	0.25	0.04	0.70	0.07	-	0.77
	d Transportation and communication	1.35	0.20	1.15	0.02	0.10	1.47	2.04	0.17	3.68
	e Other economic affairs	0.78	0.63	0.15	1.17	0.02	1.97	0.03	0.02	2.02
10	Other functions	0.88	0.08	0.80	-0.05	0.58	1.41	0.20	0.20	1.81
	Total [b]	31.71	19.17	12.54	3.31	10.27	45.29	4.50	0.99	50.78
						1971				
1	General public services [a]	8.89	6.27	2.62	0.16	2.01	11.06	0.48	0.12	11.66
2	Defence	15.75	6.75	9.00	-	0.03	15.78	0.02	-	15.80
3	Public order and safety [a]	...	...	...	...	...	...	...	...	...
4	Education	3.50	3.20	0.30	-	7.27	10.77	0.18	0.05	11.00
5	Health	2.04	1.35	0.69	-	0.26	2.30	0.17	-	2.47
6	Social security and welfare	0.88	0.57	0.31	0.03	0.40	1.31	-0.08	0.01	1.24
7	Housing and community amenities	0.54	0.44	0.10	0.01	0.57	1.12	0.55	0.09	1.76
8	Recreation, culture and religion	0.28	0.26	0.02	0.01	0.15	0.44	0.11	-	0.55
9	Economic services	4.48	2.52	1.96	3.83	1.01	9.32	3.38	0.81	13.51

India

2.3 Total General Government Outlays by Function and Type
(Continued)

Thousand Million Indian rupees — Fiscal year beginning 1 April

	Final Consumption Expenditures Total	Compensation of Employees	Other	Subsidies	Other Current Transfers & Property Income	Total Current Disbursements	Gross Capital Formation	Other Capital Outlays	Total Outlays
a Fuel and energy	0.22	0.12	0.10	0.13	0.14	0.49	0.91	0.19	1.59
b Agriculture, forestry, fishing and hunting	1.68	1.16	0.52	1.91	0.51	4.10	0.36	0.10	4.56
c Mining (except fuels), manufacturing and construction	0.44	0.33	0.11	0.11	0.05	0.60	0.06	0.23	0.89
d Transportation and communication	1.25	0.21	1.04	0.05	0.09	1.39	2.49	0.24	4.12
e Other economic affairs	0.89	0.70	0.19	1.63	0.22	2.74	-0.44	0.05	2.35
10 Other functions	1.38	0.18	1.20	0.11	1.27	2.76	0.87	0.26	3.89
Total [b]	37.74	21.54	16.20	4.15	12.97	54.86	5.68	1.34	61.88
1972									
1 General public services [a]	9.11	6.94	2.17	0.24	2.91	12.26	0.61	0.15	13.02
2 Defence	16.98	7.11	9.87	-	0.04	17.02	0.02	-	17.04
3 Public order and safety [a]	...	...	...	...	...	...	...	...	...
4 Education	4.00	3.66	0.34	-	8.84	12.84	0.24	0.06	13.14
5 Health	2.23	1.50	0.73	-	0.32	2.55	0.22	-	2.77
6 Social security and welfare	0.86	0.63	0.23	0.05	0.54	1.45	-	0.01	1.46
7 Housing and community amenities	0.59	0.49	0.10	0.02	0.60	1.21	0.70	0.14	2.05
8 Recreation, culture and religion	0.53	0.29	0.24	0.01	0.19	0.73	0.11	0.01	0.85
9 Economic services	4.93	2.83	2.10	5.10	1.35	11.38	5.36	0.69	17.43
a Fuel and energy	0.27	0.14	0.13	0.21	0.15	0.63	1.04	0.16	1.83
b Agriculture, forestry, fishing and hunting	1.82	1.30	0.52	2.13	0.73	4.68	0.65	0.07	5.40
c Mining (except fuels), manufacturing and construction	0.50	0.37	0.13	0.23	0.08	0.81	0.09	0.27	1.17
d Transportation and communication	1.35	0.24	1.11	0.04	0.12	1.51	3.67	0.17	5.35
e Other economic affairs	0.99	0.78	0.21	2.49	0.27	3.75	-0.09	0.02	3.68
10 Other functions	1.00	0.11	0.89	0.01	1.22	2.23	0.69	0.18	3.10
Total [b]	40.23	23.56	16.67	5.43	16.01	61.67	7.95	1.24	70.86
1973									
1 General public services [a]	10.60	8.03	2.57	0.02	1.93	12.55	0.94	0.18	13.67
2 Defence	17.41	7.94	9.47	-	0.04	17.45	0.06	-	17.51
3 Public order and safety [a]	...	...	...	...	...	...	...	...	...
4 Education	4.55	4.27	0.28	-	8.87	13.42	0.28	0.05	13.75
5 Health	2.53	1.76	0.77	-	0.29	2.82	0.17	0.01	3.00
6 Social security and welfare	1.00	0.77	0.23	0.03	0.70	1.73	0.33	-	2.06
7 Housing and community amenities	0.70	0.58	0.12	0.01	0.58	1.29	0.80	0.12	2.21
8 Recreation, culture and religion	0.42	0.33	0.09	-	0.18	0.60	0.12	-	0.72
9 Economic services	5.33	3.27	2.06	6.87	1.29	13.49	8.02	0.82	22.33
a Fuel and energy	0.33	0.18	0.15	0.13	0.24	0.70	1.50	0.23	2.43
b Agriculture, forestry, fishing and hunting	2.02	1.54	0.48	4.61	0.57	7.20	1.74	0.28	9.22
c Mining (except fuels), manufacturing and construction	0.45	0.39	0.06	0.60	0.08	1.13	0.11	0.11	1.35
d Transportation and communication	1.39	0.26	1.13	0.05	0.11	1.55	4.13	0.19	5.87
e Other economic affairs	1.14	0.90	0.24	1.48	0.29	2.91	0.54	0.01	3.46
10 Other functions	0.81	0.11	0.70	0.01	1.11	1.93	0.73	0.16	2.82
Total [b]	43.35	27.06	16.29	6.94	14.99	65.28	11.45	1.34	78.07
1974									
1 General public services [a]	12.66	9.65	3.01	0.01	1.70	14.37	0.67	0.47	15.51
2 Defence	21.69	11.48	10.21	-	0.05	21.74	0.07	-	21.81
3 Public order and safety [a]	...	...	...	...	...	...	...	...	...
4 Education	5.45	5.19	0.26	-	11.47	16.92	0.24	0.02	17.18
5 Health	3.13	2.14	0.99	-	0.33	3.46	0.31	-	3.77
6 Social security and welfare	1.29	0.95	0.34	0.04	0.91	2.24	0.32	0.01	2.57
7 Housing and community amenities	1.00	0.75	0.25	0.01	0.85	1.86	0.85	0.25	2.96
8 Recreation, culture and religion	0.55	0.41	0.14	-	0.19	0.74	0.19	0.03	0.96
9 Economic services	6.52	4.15	2.37	11.71	1.52	19.75	5.88	1.28	26.91

India

2.3 Total General Government Outlays by Function and Type
(Continued)

Thousand Million Indian rupees — Fiscal year beginning 1 April

		Final Consumption Expenditures Total	Compensation of Employees	Other	Subsidies	Other Current Transfers & Property Income	Total Current Disbursements	Gross Capital Formation	Other Capital Outlays	Total Outlays
	a Fuel and energy	0.44	0.30	0.14	0.11	0.31	0.86	0.99	0.38	2.23
	b Agriculture, forestry, fishing and hunting	2.55	1.90	0.65	9.07	0.80	12.42	1.34	0.30	14.06
	c Mining (except fuels), manufacturing and construction	0.60	0.49	0.11	0.45	0.09	1.14	0.18	0.46	1.78
	d Transportation and communication	1.68	0.38	1.30	0.06	0.18	1.92	3.05	0.14	5.11
	e Other economic affairs	1.25	1.08	0.17	2.02	0.14	3.41	0.32	-	3.73
10	Other functions	0.91	0.10	0.81	-	0.50	1.41	0.41	0.11	1.93
	Total b	53.20	34.82	18.38	11.77	17.52	82.49	8.94	2.17	93.60

1975

1	General public services [a]	14.70	10.57	4.13	0.02	1.82	16.54	1.73	0.45	18.72
2	Defence	25.76	12.88	12.88	-	0.03	25.79	0.05	-	25.84
3	Public order and safety [a]	...	...	...	...	...	...	...	...	...
4	Education	6.54	6.16	0.38	-	13.39	19.93	0.31	0.03	20.27
5	Health	3.90	2.46	1.44	-	0.35	4.25	0.39	-	4.64
6	Social security and welfare	1.47	1.06	0.41	0.13	1.11	2.71	-0.97	0.04	1.78
7	Housing and community amenities	1.13	0.86	0.27	0.01	1.00	2.14	0.92	0.40	3.46
8	Recreation, culture and religion	0.55	0.45	0.10	-	0.24	0.79	0.22	0.01	1.02
9	Economic services	7.91	4.81	3.10	10.98	1.98	20.87	7.11	1.91	29.89
	a Fuel and energy	0.72	0.42	0.30	0.32	0.23	1.27	1.31	0.26	2.84
	b Agriculture, forestry, fishing and hunting	2.91	2.18	0.73	7.61	1.18	11.70	2.20	0.32	14.22
	c Mining (except fuels), manufacturing and construction	0.68	0.56	0.12	0.78	0.19	1.65	0.19	1.16	3.00
	d Transportation and communication	2.01	0.38	1.63	0.09	0.26	2.36	3.29	0.16	5.81
	e Other economic affairs	1.59	1.27	0.32	2.18	0.12	3.89	0.12	0.01	4.02
10	Other functions	1.62	0.12	1.50	-	0.36	1.98	0.43	0.14	2.55
	Total b	63.58	39.37	24.21	11.14	20.28	95.00	10.19	2.98	108.17

1976

1	General public services [a]	16.48	11.43	5.05	0.01	2.64	19.13	0.62	0.50	20.25
2	Defence	26.87	12.90	13.97	0.01	0.06	26.94	0.05	-	26.99
3	Public order and safety [a]	...	...	...	...	...	...	...	...	...
4	Education	7.55	7.04	0.51	-	14.52	22.07	0.44	0.05	22.56
5	Health	4.52	2.89	1.63	-	0.41	4.93	0.56	0.01	5.50
6	Social security and welfare	1.82	1.14	0.68	0.17	1.76	3.75	0.11	0.04	3.90
7	Housing and community amenities	1.30	0.92	0.38	0.01	1.15	2.46	1.28	0.48	4.22
8	Recreation, culture and religion	0.67	0.50	0.17	-	0.28	0.95	0.25	0.01	1.21
9	Economic services	9.09	5.26	3.83	13.65	2.51	25.25	6.85	2.46	34.56
	a Fuel and energy	0.81	0.45	0.36	0.33	0.22	1.36	1.31	0.42	3.09
	b Agriculture, forestry, fishing and hunting	3.21	2.46	0.75	9.20	1.53	13.94	1.31	0.51	15.76
	c Mining (except fuels), manufacturing and construction	0.88	0.62	0.26	0.66	0.34	1.88	0.33	1.20	3.41
	d Transportation and communication	2.48	0.41	2.07	0.10	0.25	2.83	3.69	0.28	6.80
	e Other economic affairs	1.71	1.32	0.39	3.36	0.17	5.24	0.21	0.05	5.50
10	Other functions	2.34	0.57	1.77	-	0.22	2.56	0.07	0.23	2.86
	Total b	70.64	42.65	27.99	13.85	23.55	108.04	10.23	3.78	122.05

1977

1	General public services [a]	17.56	12.52	5.04	0.01	2.71	20.28	0.55	0.58	21.41
2	Defence	27.44	13.42	14.02	0.05	0.06	27.55	0.10	-	27.65
3	Public order and safety [a]	...	...	...	...	...	...	...	...	...
4	Education	9.17	8.68	0.49	-	15.82	24.99	0.46	0.06	25.51
5	Health	5.12	3.30	1.82	-	0.50	5.62	0.68	-	6.30
6	Social security and welfare	1.82	1.28	0.54	0.03	1.28	3.13	0.29	0.02	3.44
7	Housing and community amenities	1.39	0.97	0.42	-	1.22	2.61	1.17	0.66	4.44
8	Recreation, culture and religion	0.69	0.55	0.14	0.01	0.31	1.01	0.20	0.01	1.22
9	Economic services	10.01	5.84	4.17	17.54	3.35	30.90	5.01	3.53	39.44

India

2.3 Total General Government Outlays by Function and Type
(Continued)

Thousand Million Indian rupees — Fiscal year beginning 1 April

	Final Consumption Expenditures Total	Compensation of Employees	Other	Subsidies	Other Current Transfers & Property Income	Total Current Disbursements	Gross Capital Formation	Other Capital Outlays	Total Outlays
a Fuel and energy	0.89	0.51	0.38	0.35	0.30	1.54	1.44	0.70	3.68
b Agriculture, forestry, fishing and hunting	3.84	2.83	1.01	11.49	2.10	17.43	-0.77	0.83	17.49
c Mining (except fuels), manufacturing and construction	0.88	0.69	0.19	1.56	0.32	2.76	0.25	1.63	4.64
d Transportation and communication	2.57	0.42	2.15	0.11	0.45	3.13	4.75	0.35	8.23
e Other economic affairs	1.83	1.39	0.44	4.03	0.18	6.04	-0.66	0.02	5.40
10 Other functions	2.05	0.14	1.91	-	0.53	2.58	0.02	0.13	2.73
Total b	75.25	46.70	28.55	17.64	25.78	118.67	8.48	4.99	132.14
1978									
1 General public services a	19.19	14.35	4.84	0.01	3.06	22.26	0.78	0.69	23.73
2 Defence	29.18	13.56	15.62	0.03	0.07	29.28	0.10	-	29.38
3 Public order and safety a	...	...	...	...	...	...	...	...	...
4 Education	10.27	9.57	0.70	-	18.05	28.32	0.55	0.09	28.96
5 Health	5.72	3.78	1.94	-	0.73	6.45	0.69	0.01	7.15
6 Social security and welfare	2.09	1.39	0.70	0.20	1.42	3.71	-0.04	0.14	3.81
7 Housing and community amenities	1.56	1.04	0.52	0.01	1.34	2.91	1.65	1.65	6.21
8 Recreation, culture and religion	0.86	0.62	0.24	-	0.43	1.29	0.22	0.01	1.52
9 Economic services	12.55	7.06	5.49	21.67	3.81	38.03	9.92	3.76	51.71
a Fuel and energy	1.22	0.72	0.50	0.52	0.32	2.06	1.71	0.94	4.71
b Agriculture, forestry, fishing and hunting	4.65	3.31	1.34	13.88	1.80	20.33	1.99	1.41	23.73
c Mining (except fuels), manufacturing and construction	1.19	0.91	0.28	1.91	0.76	3.86	0.24	0.66	4.76
d Transportation and communication	3.46	0.50	2.96	0.03	0.57	4.06	6.01	0.71	10.78
e Other economic affairs	2.03	1.62	0.41	5.33	0.36	7.72	-0.03	0.04	7.73
10 Other functions	1.85	0.15	1.70	-	0.34	2.19	0.10	0.16	2.45
Total b	83.27	51.52	31.75	21.92	29.25	134.44	13.97	6.51	154.92
1979									
1 General public services a	22.16	16.45	5.71	0.01	3.43	25.60	1.40	0.67	27.67
2 Defence	33.74	14.62	19.12	0.04	0.08	33.86	0.12	-	33.98
3 Public order and safety a	...	...	...	...	...	...	...	...	...
4 Education	11.93	11.15	0.78	-	21.00	32.93	0.67	0.11	33.71
5 Health	6.61	4.38	2.23	-	0.83	7.44	0.67	0.02	8.13
6 Social security and welfare	2.41	1.62	0.79	0.22	1.62	4.25	0.28	0.16	4.69
7 Housing and community amenities	1.81	1.21	0.60	0.01	1.53	3.35	1.99	1.94	7.28
8 Recreation, culture and religion	1.01	0.70	0.31	0.01	0.49	1.51	0.24	0.01	1.76
9 Economic services	14.45	8.12	6.33	23.88	4.29	42.62	13.21	6.09	61.92
a Fuel and energy	1.41	0.81	0.60	0.38	0.36	2.15	2.19	1.11	5.45
b Agriculture, forestry, fishing and hunting	5.37	3.84	1.53	14.93	2.02	22.32	3.17	1.75	27.24
c Mining (except fuels), manufacturing and construction	1.36	1.02	0.34	4.06	0.85	6.27	0.29	2.44	9.00
d Transportation and communication	4.01	0.58	3.43	0.07	0.65	4.73	7.23	0.75	12.71
e Other economic affairs	2.30	1.87	0.43	4.44	0.41	7.15	0.33	0.04	7.52
10 Other functions	2.15	0.17	1.98	-	0.40	2.55	0.10	0.19	2.84
Total b	96.27	58.42	37.85	24.17	33.67	154.11	18.68	9.19	181.98

a) Item 'Public order and safety' is included in item 'General public services'.
b) Excluding local authorities.

2.5 Private Final Consumption Expenditure by Type, in Current Prices

Thousand Million Indian rupees — Fiscal year beginning 1 April

	1970	1971	1972	1973	1974	1975	1976	1977	1978	1979	1980
Final Consumption Expenditure of Resident Households											
1 Food, beverages and tobacco	203.97	211.86	233.79	292.13	354.55	347.61	339.04	399.52	411.48	432.99	528.64
a Food	187.79	193.51	214.57	271.38	330.58	321.51	311.98	368.38	376.68	396.56	488.87
b Non-alcoholic beverages	2.39	3.20	3.09	3.37	4.47	5.49	6.12	7.14	8.44	6.92	7.51
c Alcoholic beverages	5.35	5.37	4.95	5.57	7.05	7.07	7.45	8.64	10.01	11.06	12.83
d Tobacco	8.44	9.78	11.18	11.81	12.45	13.54	13.49	15.36	16.35	18.45	19.43

India

2.5 Private Final Consumption Expenditure by Type, in Current Prices
(Continued)

Thousand Million Indian rupees — Fiscal year beginning 1 April

	1970	1971	1972	1973	1974	1975	1976	1977	1978	1979	1980
2 Clothing and footwear	21.21	26.00	27.55	34.98	42.87	45.80	54.17	62.44	72.34	86.02	96.07
3 Gross rent, fuel and power	20.94	23.00	24.86	27.11	29.39	32.71	35.73	41.18	47.98	54.22	59.18
a Fuel and power	10.33	11.54	12.42	13.81	15.36	17.53	18.30	22.05	26.92	31.76	35.23
b Other	10.61	11.46	12.44	13.30	14.03	15.18	17.43	19.13	21.06	22.46	23.95
4 Furniture, furnishings and household equipment and operation	8.90	11.08	12.21	13.18	16.67	19.66	22.19	25.46	27.06	30.87	34.79
a Household operation	4.53	5.25	5.72	5.87	7.66	8.79	10.94	12.94	13.06	14.82	17.20
b Other	4.37	5.83	6.49	7.31	9.01	10.87	11.25	12.52	14.00	16.05	17.59
5 Medical care and health expenses	6.12	7.34	7.99	8.43	10.56	11.87	13.69	14.59	15.10	15.67	17.21
6 Transport and communication	14.81	16.49	17.55	21.44	31.27	34.63	38.39	41.43	46.63	54.11	71.32
a Personal transport equipment	2.86	3.23	3.51	4.83	6.35	6.61	7.93	8.64	10.05	11.81	13.69
b Other	11.95	13.26	14.04	16.61	24.92	28.02	30.46	32.79	36.58	42.30	57.63
7 Recreational, entertainment, education and cultural services	10.88	12.53	13.76	15.95	15.25	16.93	19.11	20.56	24.36	27.56	32.32
a Education	8.96	9.92	10.92	12.80	11.71	12.53	14.40	15.37	18.46	20.92	24.97
b Other	1.92	2.61	2.84	3.15	3.54	4.40	4.71	5.19	5.90	6.64	7.35
8 Miscellaneous goods and services	11.55	12.67	13.60	16.11	19.85	20.71	22.51	27.29	30.37	34.01	39.19
a Personal care	3.70	4.08	4.11	5.03	6.90	6.76	7.63	10.47	12.32	13.21	12.93
b Expenditures in restaurants, cafes and hotels	3.57	3.87	4.44	5.54	5.99	6.39	6.68	7.63	8.05	9.05	13.12
c Other	4.28	4.72	5.05	5.54	6.96	7.56	8.20	9.19	10.00	11.75	13.14
Total Final Consumption Expenditure in the Domestic Market by Households, of which [a]	298.38	320.97	351.31	429.33	520.41	529.92	544.83	632.47	675.32	735.45	878.72
a Durable goods	6.71	8.16	8.78	10.54	12.73	13.20	14.68	17.38	20.36	22.26	23.80
b Semi-durable goods	24.43	30.52	32.09	39.96	49.57	54.44	63.50	73.45	84.60	100.37	111.44
c Non-durable goods	227.97	238.79	262.92	323.83	391.46	386.35	382.55	449.29	466.98	496.27	598.68
d Services	39.27	43.50	47.52	55.00	66.65	75.93	84.10	92.35	103.38	116.55	144.80
Plus: Direct purchases abroad by resident households	0.17	0.19	0.18	0.16	0.14	0.21	0.32	0.41	0.61	1.94	...
Less: Direct purchases in the domestic market by non-resident households	0.52	0.55	0.65	0.84	1.50	2.66	3.45	5.99	6.49	7.72	...
Equals: Final Consumption Expenditure of Resident Households [a]	298.03	320.61	350.84	428.65	519.05	527.47	541.70	626.89	669.44	729.67	...

Final Consumption Expenditure of Private Non-profit Institutions Serving Households

Equals: Final Consumption Expenditure of Private Non-profit Organisations Serving Households	...	...	...	...	...	...	...	...	...	...	...
Private Final Consumption Expenditure [a]	298.03	320.61	350.84	428.65	519.05	527.47	541.70	626.89	669.44	729.67	...

a) Including private non-profit institutions.

2.6 Private Final Consumption Expenditure by Type, in Constant Prices

Thousand Million Indian rupees — Fiscal year beginning 1 April

	1970	1971	1972	1973	1974	1975	1976	1977	1978	1979	1980

At constant prices of: 1970

Final Consumption Expenditure of Resident Households

	1970	1971	1972	1973	1974	1975	1976	1977	1978	1979	1980
1 Food, beverages and tobacco	203.97	204.34	196.34	200.62	203.15	220.40	210.60	236.62	241.02	223.56	244.58
a Food	187.79	187.03	178.77	182.78	186.35	203.55	193.13	217.59	221.18	203.09	223.42
b Non-alcoholic beverages	2.39	3.08	2.99	3.17	2.94	2.90	3.16	3.29	3.82	3.48	3.83
c Alcoholic beverages	5.35	5.30	4.89	5.43	6.26	5.85	5.90	6.88	6.82	6.69	6.73
d Tobacco	8.44	8.93	9.69	9.24	7.60	8.10	8.41	8.86	9.20	10.30	10.60
2 Clothing and footwear	21.21	23.83	24.06	25.62	26.49	28.60	32.32	34.23	37.73	38.95	40.22
3 Gross rent, fuel and power	20.94	21.75	21.99	21.84	22.29	22.96	23.85	24.80	25.70	26.28	27.28
a Fuel and power	10.33	10.89	10.94	10.51	10.70	11.11	11.65	12.27	12.81	13.11	13.83
b Other	10.61	10.86	11.05	11.33	11.59	11.85	12.20	12.53	12.89	13.17	13.45
4 Furniture, furnishings and household equipment and operation	8.90	10.41	10.79	10.58	10.28	10.98	12.52	13.97	13.81	13.60	13.67
a Household operation	4.53	5.11	5.34	4.92	4.70	5.19	6.55	7.51	7.08	7.04	7.26

India

2.6 Private Final Consumption Expenditure by Type, in Constant Prices
(Continued)

Thousand Million Indian rupees   Fiscal year beginning 1 April

	1970	1971	1972	1973	1974	1975	1976	1977	1978	1979	1980
					At constant prices of: 1970						
b Other	4.37	5.30	5.45	5.66	5.58	5.79	5.97	6.46	6.73	6.56	6.41
5 Medical care and health expenses	6.12	7.12	7.52	7.56	9.06	9.32	9.52	9.82	10.02	10.48	10.86
6 Transport and communication	14.81	15.70	15.94	17.40	17.93	19.11	20.64	21.85	23.67	24.06	24.63
a Personal transport equipment	2.86	2.95	3.00	3.37	3.23	3.32	4.09	4.32	4.76	4.86	5.08
b Other	11.95	12.75	12.94	14.03	14.70	15.79	16.55	17.53	18.91	19.20	19.55
7 Recreational, entertainment, education and cultural services	10.88	11.79	12.24	12.94	10.63	11.27	11.70	11.82	12.59	12.75	13.71
a Education	8.96	9.30	9.64	10.36	8.46	8.44	8.66	8.59	8.97	9.08	9.88
b Other	1.92	2.49	2.60	2.58	2.17	2.83	3.04	3.23	3.62	3.67	3.83
8 Miscellaneous goods and services	11.55	12.10	11.82	12.24	11.60	12.03	13.07	14.89	16.32	16.21	15.82
a Personal care	3.70	3.98	3.69	4.17	4.11	4.13	4.68	5.96	7.04	6.47	5.72
b Expenditures in restaurants, cafes and hotels	3.57	3.63	3.65	3.80	3.19	3.49	3.73	3.95	4.29	4.15	4.34
c Other	4.28	4.49	4.48	4.27	4.30	4.41	4.66	4.98	4.99	5.59	5.76
Total Final Consumption Expenditure in the Domestic Market by Households, of which [a]	298.38	307.04	300.70	308.80	311.43	334.67	334.22	368.00	380.86	365.89	390.77
a Durable goods	6.71	7.85	7.97	8.79	7.88	8.32	9.44	10.65	11.82	11.50	11.41
b Semi-durable goods	24.43	27.61	27.68	29.29	30.45	33.08	37.08	39.74	43.45	44.70	45.61
c Non-durable goods	227.97	230.60	223.33	227.54	230.87	246.92	239.44	267.32	272.25	255.35	277.56
d Services	39.27	40.98	41.72	43.18	42.23	46.35	48.26	50.29	53.34	54.34	56.19
Plus: Direct purchases abroad by resident households	...	...	...	...	...	...	...	...	...	...	...
Less: Direct purchases in the domestic market by non-resident households	...	...	...	...	...	...	...	...	...	...	...
Equals: Final Consumption Expenditure of Resident Households	...	...	...	...	...	...	...	...	...	...	...

Final Consumption Expenditure of Private Non-profit Institutions Serving Households

	1970	1971	1972	1973	1974	1975	1976	1977	1978	1979	1980
Equals: Final Consumption Expenditure of Private Non-profit Organisations Serving Households	...	...	...	...	...	...	...	...	...	...	...
Private Final Consumption Expenditure	...	...	...	...	...	...	...	...	...	...	...

a) Including private non-profit institutions.

2.7 Gross Capital Formation by Type of Good and Owner, in Current Prices

Thousand Million Indian rupees   Fiscal year beginning 1 April

	1970				1971				1972			
	TOTAL	Total Private	Public Enterprises	General Government	TOTAL	Total Private	Public Enterprises	General Government	TOTAL	Total Private	Public Enterprises	General Government
Increase in stocks, total [a]	10.39	6.60	4.09	-0.30	13.37	9.74	4.65	-1.02	4.60	4.72	0.92	-1.04
1 Goods producing industries	7.54	...	...	...	10.43	...	...	...	4.87	...	...	...
a Materials and supplies	...	...	...	...	...	...	...	...	...	...	...	...
b Work in progress	...	...	...	...	...	...	...	...	...	...	...	...
c Livestock, except breeding stocks, dairy cattle, etc.	0.10	...	...	...	0.11	...	...	...	0.13	...	...	...
d Finished goods	...	...	...	...	...	...	...	...	...	...	...	...
2 Wholesale and retail trade	2.41	...	...	...	2.83	...	...	...	-0.65	...	...	...
3 Other, except government stocks	0.60	...	...	...	0.95	...	...	...	1.21	...	...	...
4 Government stocks	-0.16	...	...	...	-0.94	...	...	...	-0.83	...	...	...
Gross Fixed Capital Formation, Total [b,a,c]	63.05	39.11	17.83	6.11	70.74	42.72	19.60	8.42	80.66	44.47	25.01	11.18
1 Residential buildings	8.26	7.92	-	0.34	9.68	9.25	-	0.43	9.48	8.98	-	0.50
2 Non-residential buildings [d]	15.50	12.90	1.39	1.21	13.95	11.02	1.41	1.52	14.82	10.54	2.37	1.91

India

2.7 Gross Capital Formation by Type of Good and Owner, in Current Prices
(Continued)

Thousand Million Indian rupees — Fiscal year beginning 1 April

	1970 TOTAL	1970 Total Private	1970 Public Enterprises	1970 General Government	1971 TOTAL	1971 Total Private	1971 Public Enterprises	1971 General Government	1972 TOTAL	1972 Total Private	1972 Public Enterprises	1972 General Government
3 Other construction e	15.83	3.30	8.34	4.19	19.01	3.23	9.88	5.90	22.84	3.35	11.50	7.99
4 Land improvement and plantation and orchard development e	...	...	...	...	...	...	...	...	...	...	...	...
5 Producers' durable goods f	22.94	14.07	8.50	0.37	27.54	18.19	8.78	0.57	32.95	20.36	11.75	0.84
a Transport equipment	6.14	3.95	2.18	0.01	8.01	5.60	2.40	0.01	8.89	6.18	2.69	0.02
b Machinery and equipment	16.80	10.12	6.32	0.36	19.53	12.59	6.38	0.56	24.06	14.18	9.06	0.82
6 Breeding stock, dairy cattle, etc.	0.52	0.52	-	-	0.56	0.56	-	-	0.57	0.57	-	-
Statistical discrepancy	-1.67	...	...	...	-4.35	...	...	...	-4.60	...	...	...
Total Gross Capital Formation	71.77	45.71	21.92	5.81	79.76	52.46	24.25	7.40	80.66	49.19	25.93	10.14

	1973 TOTAL	1973 Total Private	1973 Public Enterprises	1973 General Government	1974 TOTAL	1974 Total Private	1974 Public Enterprises	1974 General Government	1975 TOTAL	1975 Total Private	1975 Public Enterprises	1975 General Government
Increase in stocks, total a	23.23	15.18	7.29	0.76	35.79	21.87	13.07	0.85	31.70	10.93	19.69	1.08
1 Goods producing industries	16.16	...	...	...	28.87	...	...	...	14.45	...	...	...
a Materials and supplies	...	...	...	...	...	...	...	...	...	...	...	...
b Work in progress	...	...	...	...	...	...	...	...	...	...	...	...
c Livestock, except breeding stocks, dairy cattle, etc.	0.15				0.19				0.20			
d Finished goods	...				...				...			
2 Wholesale and retail trade	5.55	...	...	...	5.49	...	...	...	15.88	...	...	...
3 Other, except government stocks	0.73				0.85				0.26			
4 Government stocks	0.79	...	...	...	0.58	...	...	...	1.11	...	...	...
Gross Fixed Capital Formation, Total bac	90.29	50.20	27.60	12.49	109.30	66.58	32.77	9.95	132.48	76.48	44.87	11.13
1 Residential buildings	13.16	12.64	-	0.52	15.57	14.94	-	0.63	17.55	16.78	-	0.77
2 Non-residential buildings d	11.03	7.08	2.02	1.93	17.68	13.41	2.46	1.81	26.22	21.01	3.31	1.90
3 Other construction e	25.11	3.69	12.41	9.01	24.29	4.43	13.32	6.54	28.81	6.07	15.17	7.57
4 Land improvement and plantation and orchard development e	...	...	...	...	...	...	...	...	...	...	...	...
5 Producers' durable goods f	40.30	26.12	13.15	1.03	50.98	33.27	16.64	1.07	59.19	31.23	26.65	1.31
a Transport equipment	8.17	4.19	3.97	0.01	10.73	6.01	4.64	0.08	11.14	4.56	6.56	0.02
b Machinery and equipment	32.13	21.93	9.18	1.02	40.25	27.26	12.00	0.99	48.05	26.67	20.09	1.29
6 Breeding stock, dairy cattle, etc.	0.69	0.69	-	-	0.78	0.78	-	-	0.71	0.71	-	-
Statistical discrepancy	4.32	...	...	...	-12.03	...	...	...	-16.89	...	...	...
Total Gross Capital Formation	117.84	65.38	34.89	13.25	133.06	88.45	45.84	10.80	147.29	87.41	64.56	12.21

	1976 TOTAL	1976 Total Private	1976 Public Enterprises	1976 General Government	1977 TOTAL	1977 Total Private	1977 Public Enterprises	1977 General Government	1978 TOTAL	1978 Total Private	1978 Public Enterprises	1978 General Government
Increase in stocks, total a	23.63	9.16	14.95	-0.48	12.58	15.00	1.38	-3.80	37.44	24.83	14.50	-1.89
1 Goods producing industries	10.62	...	...	...	12.12	...	...	...	24.09	...	...	...
a Materials and supplies	...	...	...	...	...	...	...	...	...	...	...	...
b Work in progress	...	...	...	...	...	...	...	...	...	...	...	...
c Livestock, except breeding stocks, dairy cattle, etc.	0.21				0.23				0.29			
d Finished goods	...				...				...			
2 Wholesale and retail trade	13.38	...	...	...	3.40	...	...	...	13.80	...	...	...
3 Other, except government stocks	-0.27				0.16				0.69			
4 Government stocks	-0.10	...	...	...	-3.10	...	...	...	-1.14	...	...	...
Gross Fixed Capital Formation, Total bac	153.28	82.65	57.09	13.54	170.83	93.92	61.29	15.62	192.05	108.59	63.37	20.09
1 Residential buildings	21.61	20.48	-	1.13	21.81	20.73	-	1.08	25.73	24.48	-	1.25
2 Non-residential buildings d	27.80	21.01	4.32	2.47	34.03	25.75	5.37	2.91	31.95	23.43	4.97	3.55

India

2.7 Gross Capital Formation by Type of Good and Owner, in Current Prices
(Continued)

Thousand Million Indian rupees — Fiscal year beginning 1 April

	1976 TOTAL	Total Private	Public Enterprises	General Government	1977 TOTAL	Total Private	Public Enterprises	General Government	1978 TOTAL	Total Private	Public Enterprises	General Government
3 Other construction e	35.83	6.27	20.58	8.98	42.19	7.40	24.42	10.37	49.07	7.54	27.76	13.77
4 Land improvement and plantation and orchard development e	...	...	...	...	...	...	...	...	...	...	...	...
5 Producers' durable goods f	67.25	33.57	32.20	1.48	71.91	36.81	33.54	1.56	84.32	51.21	31.11	2.00
a Transport equipment	12.91	7.26	5.62	0.03	13.74	8.00	5.70	0.04	17.38	10.67	6.60	0.11
b Machinery and equipment	54.34	26.31	26.58	1.45	58.17	28.81	27.84	1.52	66.94	40.54	24.51	1.89
6 Breeding stock, dairy cattle, etc.	0.79	0.79	-	-	0.89	0.89	-	-	0.98	0.98	-	-
Statistical discrepancy	-13.01	...	...	...	-5.71	...	...	...	9.76	...	...	...
Total Gross Capital Formation	163.90	41.81	72.04	13.06	177.70	108.92	62.67	11.82	239.25	133.42	77.87	18.20

	1979 TOTAL	Total Private	Public Enterprises	General Government	1980 TOTAL	Total Private	Public Enterprises	General Government
Increase in stocks, total a	41.63	24.36	17.60	-0.33	56.64	41.40	15.44	-0.20
1 Goods producing industries	31.08	...	...	...	43.62	...	...	...
a Materials and supplies	...	...	...	...	...	...	...	...
b Work in progress	...	...	...	...	...	...	...	...
c Livestock, except breeding stocks, dairy cattle, etc.	0.39	...	...	...	0.44	...	...	...
d Finished goods	...	...	...	...	...	...	...	...
2 Wholesale and retail trade	8.77	...	...	...	11.45	...	...	...
3 Other, except government stocks	1.48	...	...	...	0.98	...	...	...
4 Government stocks	0.30	...	...	...	0.59	...	...	...
Gross Fixed Capital Formation, Total bac	205.20	108.79	73.17	23.24	236.87	126.05	83.57	27.25
1 Residential buildings	25.76	24.25	-	1.51	30.16	28.65	...	...
2 Non-residential buildings d	26.79	16.88	5.85	4.06	28.47	16.94	6.59	4.94
3 Other construction e	54.57	7.08	31.69	15.80	62.50	8.47	35.87	18.16
4 Land improvement and plantation and orchard development e	...	...	...	...	...	...	...	...
5 Producers' durable goods f	96.94	58.08	36.51	2.35	114.46	69.38	41.93	3.15
a Transport equipment	20.86	14.07	6.64	0.15	24.84	15.60	9.01	0.23
b Machinery and equipment	76.08	44.01	29.87	2.20	89.62	53.78	32.92	2.92
6 Breeding stock, dairy cattle, etc.	1.14	1.14	-	-	1.28	1.28	-	-
Statistical discrepancy	-3.89	...	...	...	10.02	...	...	...
Total Gross Capital Formation	242.94	133.15	90.77	22.91	303.53	167.45	99.01	27.05

a) Data for column 'General government', do not coincide with data shown for general government in table 3.13 because departmental enterprises are included in column 'Public enterprises' instead of column 'General government'.
b) Estimates of gross fixed capital formation by industry of use and by type of assets are prepared independently and therefore, do not always tally.
c) Data are unadjusted for statistical discrepancy and therefore do not coincide with the data shown in the table 'Gross capital formation by kind of economic activity of owner'.
d) Including residential house construction of public enterprises and the private corporate sector.
e) Item 'Land improvement and plantation and orchard development' is included in item 'Other construction'.
f) Unadjusted for purchase and sale of second-hand physical assets.

2.8 Gross Capital Formation by Type of Good and Owner, in Constant Prices

Thousand Million Indian rupees — Fiscal year beginning 1 April

	1970 TOTAL	Total Private	Public Enterprises	General Government	1971 TOTAL	Total Private	Public Enterprises	General Government	1972 TOTAL	Total Private	Public Enterprises	General Government
At constant prices of: 1970												
Increase in stocks, total	10.39	...	...	...	12.73	...	...	...	4.20	...	...	...
1 Goods producing industries	7.54	...	...	...	9.93	...	...	...	4.36	...	...	...
a Materials and supplies	...	...	...	...	...	...	...	...	...	...	...	...
b Work in progress	...	...	...	...	...	...	...	...	...	...	...	...
c Livestock, except breeding stocks, dairy cattle, etc.	0.10	...	...	...	0.11	...	...	...	0.12	...	...	...
d Finished goods	...	...	...	...	...	...	...	...	...	...	...	...
2 Wholesale and retail trade	2.41	...	...	...	2.79	...	...	...	-0.48	...	...	...
3 Other, except government stocks	0.60	...	...	...	0.90	...	...	...	1.04	...	...	...
4 Government stocks	-0.16	...	...	...	-0.89	...	...	...	-0.72	...	...	...
Gross Fixed Capital Formation, Total ab	63.05	...	...	...	66.86	...	...	...	70.59	...	...	...

India

2.8 Gross Capital Formation by Type of Good and Owner, in Constant Prices
(Continued)

Thousand Million Indian rupees — Fiscal year beginning 1 April

	1970 TOTAL	Total Private	Public Enterprises	General Government	1971 TOTAL	Total Private	Public Enterprises	General Government	1972 TOTAL	Total Private	Public Enterprises	General Government
				At constant prices of: 1970								
1 Residential buildings	8.26	...	...	...	9.05	...	...	...	8.23	...	...	...
2 Non-residential buildings c	15.50	...	...	...	13.00	...	...	...	12.79	...	...	...
3 Other construction d	15.83	...	...	...	17.70	...	...	...	19.70	...	...	...
4 Land improvement and plantation and orchard development d	...	...	...	...	...	...	...	...	...	...	...	...
5 Producers' durable goods	22.94	...	...	...	26.56	...	...	...	29.37	...	...	...
a Transport equipment	6.14	...	...	...	7.57	...	...	...	7.69	...	...	...
b Machinery and equipment	16.80	...	...	...	18.99	...	...	...	21.68	...	...	...
6 Breeding stock, dairy cattle, etc.	0.52	...	...	...	0.55	...	...	...	0.50	...	...	...
Statistical discrepancy	-1.67	...	...	...	-4.12	...	...	...	-4.04	...	...	...
Total Gross Capital Formation	71.77	...	...	...	75.47	...	...	...	70.75	...	...	...

	1973 TOTAL	Total Private	Public Enterprises	General Government	1974 TOTAL	Total Private	Public Enterprises	General Government	1975 TOTAL	Total Private	Public Enterprises	General Government
				At constant prices of: 1970								
Increase in stocks, total	16.79	...	...	...	20.91	...	...	...	18.74	...	...	...
1 Goods producing industries	11.65	...	...	...	16.83	...	...	...	8.63	...	...	...
a Materials and supplies	...	...	...	...	...	...	...	...	...	...	...	...
b Work in progress	...	...	...	...	...	...	...	...	...	...	...	...
c Livestock, except breeding stocks, dairy cattle, etc.	0.13	...	...	...	0.16	...	...	...	0.15	...	...	...
d Finished goods	...	...	...	...	...	...	...	...	...	...	...	...
2 Wholesale and retail trade	4.04	...	...	...	3.26	...	...	...	9.31	...	...	...
3 Other, except government stocks	0.53	...	...	...	0.49	...	...	...	0.16	...	...	...
4 Government stocks	0.57	...	...	...	0.33	...	...	...	0.64	...	...	...
Gross Fixed Capital Formation, Total ab	70.60	...	...	...	68.56	...	...	...	75.14	...	...	...
1 Residential buildings	9.82	...	...	...	9.42	...	...	...	9.76	...	...	...
2 Non-residential buildings c	8.25	...	...	...	10.73	...	...	...	15.10	...	...	...
3 Other construction d	18.96	...	...	...	15.55	...	...	...	16.59	...	...	...
4 Land improvement and plantation and orchard development d	...	...	...	...	...	...	...	...	...	...	...	...
5 Producers' durable goods	33.02	...	...	...	32.22	...	...	...	33.18	...	...	...
a Transport equipment	6.57	...	...	...	6.79	...	...	...	6.51	...	...	...
b Machinery and equipment	26.45	...	...	...	25.43	...	...	...	26.67	...	...	...
6 Breeding stock, dairy cattle, etc.	0.55	...	...	...	0.64	...	...	...	0.51	...	...	...
Statistical discrepancy	3.33	...	...	...	-7.42	...	...	...	-9.66	...	...	...
Total Gross Capital Formation	90.72	...	...	...	82.05	...	...	...	84.22	...	...	...

	1976 TOTAL	Total Private	Public Enterprises	General Government	1977 TOTAL	Total Private	Public Enterprises	General Government	1978 TOTAL	Total Private	Public Enterprises	General Government
				At constant prices of: 1970								
Increase in stocks, total	13.44	...	...	...	7.01	...	...	...	20.24	...	...	...
1 Goods producing industries	6.09	...	...	...	6.61	...	...	...	13.04	...	...	...
a Materials and supplies	...	...	...	...	...	...	...	...	...	...	...	...
b Work in progress	...	...	...	...	...	...	...	...	...	...	...	...
c Livestock, except breeding stocks, dairy cattle, etc.	0.17	...	...	...	0.18	...	...	...	0.19	...	...	...
d Finished goods	...	...	...	...	...	...	...	...	...	...	...	...
2 Wholesale and retail trade	7.56	...	...	...	1.98	...	...	...	7.44	...	...	...
3 Other, except government stocks	-0.15	...	...	...	0.09	...	...	...	0.37	...	...	...
4 Government stocks	-0.06	...	...	...	-1.67	...	...	...	-0.61	...	...	...
Gross Fixed Capital Formation, Total ab	85.15	...	...	...	92.78	...	...	...	95.90	...	...	...
1 Residential buildings	11.63	...	...	...	11.24	...	...	...	12.21	...	...	...
2 Non-residential buildings c	15.39	...	...	...	18.07	...	...	...	15.63	...	...	...

763

India

2.8 Gross Capital Formation by Type of Good and Owner, in Constant Prices
(Continued)

Thousand Million Indian rupees — Fiscal year beginning 1 April

	1976 TOTAL	Total Private	Public Enterprises	General Government	1977 TOTAL	Total Private	Public Enterprises	General Government	1978 TOTAL	Total Private	Public Enterprises	General Government
				At constant	prices of:1970							
3 Other construction [d]	19.81	...	...	...	22.41	...	...	...	23.94	...	...	...
4 Land improvement and plantation and orchard development [d]	...	...	...	...	...	...	...	...	...	...	...	...
5 Producers' durable goods	37.78	...	...	...	40.50	...	...	...	43.55	...	...	...
a Transport equipment	7.54	...	...	...	7.58	...	...	...	8.95	...	...	...
b Machinery and equipment	30.24	...	...	...	32.92	...	...	...	34.60	...	...	...
6 Breeding stock, dairy cattle, etc.	0.54	...	...	...	0.56	...	...	...	0.57	...	...	...
Statistical discrepancy	-7.25	...	...	...	-3.11	...	...	...	4.94	...	...	...
Total Gross Capital Formation	91.34	...	...	...	96.68	...	...	...	121.08	...	...	...

	1979 TOTAL	Total Private	Public Enterprises	General Government	1980 TOTAL	Total Private	Public Enterprises	General Government
			At constant prices of:1970					
Increase in stocks, total	18.95	...	...	...	22.76	...	...	...
1 Goods producing industries	14.24	...	...	...	17.51	...	...	...
a Materials and supplies	...	...	...	...	...	...	...	...
b Work in progress	...	...	...	...	...	...	...	...
c Livestock, except breeding stocks, dairy cattle, etc.	0.21	...	...	...	0.22	...	...	...
d Finished goods	...	...	...	...	...	...	...	...
2 Wholesale and retail trade	3.89	...	...	...	4.64	...	...	...
3 Other, except government stocks	0.68	...	...	...	0.38	...	...	...
4 Government stocks	0.14	...	...	...	0.23	...	...	...
Gross Fixed Capital Formation, Total [ab]	88.58	...	...	...	93.88	...	...	...
1 Residential buildings	10.50	...	...	...	10.62	...	...	...
2 Non-residential buildings [c]	11.53	...	...	...	10.77	...	...	...
3 Other construction [d]	23.30	...	...	...	23.41	...	...	...
4 Land improvement and plantation and orchard development [d]	...	...	...	...	...	...	...	...
5 Producers' durable goods	42.65	...	...	...	48.45	...	...	...
a Transport equipment	8.95	...	...	...	9.44	...	...	...
b Machinery and equipment	33.70	...	...	...	39.01	...	...	...
6 Breeding stock, dairy cattle, etc.	0.60	...	...	...	0.63	...	...	...
Statistical discrepancy	-1.69	...	...	...	3.98	...	...	...
Total Gross Capital Formation	105.84	...	...	...	120.62	...	...	...

a) Estimates of gross fixed capital formation by industry of use and by type of assets are prepared independently and therefore, do not always tally.
b) Data are unadjusted for statistical discrepancy and therefore do not coincide with the data shown in the table 'Gross capital formation by kind of economic activity of owner'.
c) Including residential house construction of public enterprises and the private corporate sector.
d) Item 'Land improvement and plantation and orchard development' is included in item 'Other construction'.

2.9 Gross Capital Formation by Kind of Activity of Owner, ISIC Major Divisions, in Current Prices

Thousand Million Indian rupees — Fiscal year beginning 1 April

	1970 Total Gross Capital Formation	Increase in Stocks	Gross Fixed Capital Formation	1971 Total Gross Capital Formation	Increase in Stocks	Gross Fixed Capital Formation	1972 Total Gross Capital Formation	Increase in Stocks	Gross Fixed Capital Formation	1973 Total Gross Capital Formation	Increase in Stocks	Gross Fixed Capital Formation
					All Producers							
1 Agriculture, hunting, fishing and forestry	13.65	0.53	11.61	14.66	0.64	13.14	17.26	1.10	14.96	21.29	1.63	17.18
2 Mining and quarrying	0.92	0.05	0.88	1.50	0.06	1.33	1.31	0.06	1.26	2.30	0.52	1.90
3 Manufacturing	19.76	6.44	12.04	21.43	9.02	11.55	18.98	3.31	14.51	32.27	13.88	15.78
4 Electricity, gas and water	6.50	0.55	5.93	6.66	0.47	6.18	6.90	0.37	6.52	7.07	-0.20	7.32

India

2.9 Gross Capital Formation by Kind of Activity of Owner, ISIC Major Divisions, in Current Prices
(Continued)

Thousand Million Indian rupees — Fiscal year beginning 1 April

	1970 TGCF	1970 IS	1970 GFCF	1971 TGCF	1971 IS	1971 GFCF	1972 TGCF	1972 IS	1972 GFCF	1973 TGCF	1973 IS	1973 GFCF
5 Construction	1.09	-0.04	1.11	1.57	0.22	1.30	1.48	-0.01	1.44	2.01	0.29	1.61
6 Wholesale and retail trade, restaurants and hotels	6.02	2.46	2.91	6.90	3.03	3.30	3.10	-0.37	2.91	11.75	5.81	3.99
7 Transport, storage and communication	8.14	0.51	7.21	9.06	0.87	7.93	11.30	0.98	10.00	12.14	0.37	11.00
8 Finance, insurance, real estate and business services	9.96	0.04	8.56	10.95	0.02	10.08	10.75	-	9.84	16.30	-0.01	13.81
9 Community, social and personal services	1.02	0.01	0.90	1.12	-0.02	1.08	1.55	-0.01	1.48	1.95	0.15	1.66
Total Industries ab	67.06	10.55	51.15	73.85	14.31	55.89	72.63	5.43	62.92	107.08	22.44	74.25
Producers of Government Services	4.71	-0.16	4.87	5.91	-0.94	6.85	8.03	-0.83	8.86	10.76	0.79	9.97
Private Non-Profit Institutions Serving Households	...	...	...	...	...	...	...	...	...	...	...	...
Total ab	71.77	10.39	56.02	79.76	13.37	62.74	80.66	4.60	71.78	117.84	23.23	84.22

	1974 TGCF	1974 IS	1974 GFCF	1975 TGCF	1975 IS	1975 GFCF	1976 TGCF	1976 IS	1976 GFCF	1977 TGCF	1977 IS	1977 GFCF

All Producers

	1974 TGCF	1974 IS	1974 GFCF	1975 TGCF	1975 IS	1975 GFCF	1976 TGCF	1976 IS	1976 GFCF	1977 TGCF	1977 IS	1977 GFCF
1 Agriculture, hunting, fishing and forestry	20.45	1.73	19.16	22.25	2.98	22.25	33.78	4.16	28.79	37.45	2.37	31.40
2 Mining and quarrying	3.37	1.20	2.21	6.41	2.78	4.25	8.01	0.78	7.15	7.54	-0.33	7.49
3 Manufacturing	46.88	24.43	22.97	41.30	7.38	36.28	34.84	5.28	29.03	44.02	8.89	31.75
4 Electricity, gas and water	9.56	0.83	8.73	14.69	0.93	13.79	15.79	-0.14	15.93	19.29	0.45	18.67
5 Construction	2.39	0.67	1.73	2.40	0.37	2.08	3.33	0.54	2.73	3.90	0.74	2.96
6 Wholesale and retail trade, restaurants and hotels	10.62	5.52	5.40	18.59	15.95	4.24	17.63	13.40	4.09	10.23	3.39	4.84
7 Transport, storage and communication	14.15	0.69	13.65	15.04	0.28	15.56	14.98	-0.41	15.25	17.10	0.15	16.03
8 Finance, insurance, real estate and business services	15.69	0.02	16.13	15.40	-0.02	18.23	23.32	0.07	22.49	26.71	0.06	22.81
9 Community, social and personal services	1.95	0.12	1.86	2.05	-0.06	2.35	2.83	0.05	2.73	3.49	-0.04	3.21
Total Industries ab	125.06	35.21	91.84	138.13	30.59	119.03	154.51	23.73	128.19	169.73	15.68	139.16
Producers of Government Services	8.00	0.58	7.42	9.16	1.11	8.05	9.39	-0.10	9.49	7.97	-3.10	11.07
Private Non-Profit Institutions Serving Households	...	...	...	...	...	...	...	...	...	...	...	...
Total ab	133.06	35.79	99.26	147.29	31.70	127.08	163.90	23.63	137.68	177.70	12.58	150.23

	1978 TGCF	1978 IS	1978 GFCF	1979 TGCF	1979 IS	1979 GFCF

All Producers

	1978 TGCF	1978 IS	1978 GFCF	1979 TGCF	1979 IS	1979 GFCF
1 Agriculture, hunting, fishing and forestry	51.54	7.21	37.85	50.43	6.66	44.21
2 Mining and quarrying	6.60	0.54	5.93	8.70	1.64	7.08
3 Manufacturing	61.62	14.00	43.56	68.57	20.74	48.13
4 Electricity, gas and water	21.91	0.77	20.81	25.79	1.63	24.17
5 Construction	5.19	1.57	3.19	3.67	0.41	3.28
6 Wholesale and retail trade, restaurants and hotels	22.62	13.77	5.34	14.75	8.79	6.13
7 Transport, storage and communication	20.14	0.58	18.54	22.88	1.39	21.57
8 Finance, insurance, real estate and business services	31.96	0.07	26.99	27.07	0.06	27.27
9 Community, social and personal services	4.23	0.07	3.81	4.22	0.01	4.24
Total Industries ab	225.81	38.58	166.02	226.08	41.33	186.08
Producers of Government Services	13.44	-1.14	14.58	16.86	0.30	16.56
Private Non-Profit Institutions Serving Households	...	...	...	...	...	...
Total ab	239.25	37.44	180.60	242.94	41.63	202.64

a) Estimates of gross fixed capital formation by industry of use and by type of assets are prepared independently and therefore, do not always tally.
b) Due to the allocation of a statistical discrepancy to column 1 and not to columns 2 and 3, columns 2 and 3 do not add up to column 1.

India

2.10 Gross Capital Formation by Kind of Activity of Owner, ISIC Major Divisions, in Constant Prices

Thousand Million Indian rupees — *Fiscal year beginning 1 April*

At constant prices of: 1970 — All Producers

	1970 TGCF	1970 IS	1970 GFCF	1971 TGCF	1971 IS	1971 GFCF	1972 TGCF	1972 IS	1972 GFCF	1973 TGCF	1973 IS	1973 GFCF
1 Agriculture, hunting, fishing and forestry	13.65	0.53	11.61	13.91	0.65	12.35	15.13	1.08	13.02	15.94	1.21	12.86
2 Mining and quarrying	0.92	0.05	0.88	1.43	0.06	1.26	1.17	0.06	1.11	1.85	0.44	1.52
3 Manufacturing	19.76	6.44	12.04	20.29	8.54	10.84	16.60	2.85	12.73	24.50	9.93	12.31
4 Electricity, gas and water	6.50	0.55	5.93	6.37	0.45	5.91	6.27	0.35	5.91	5.80	-0.18	6.03
5 Construction	1.09	-0.04	1.11	1.48	0.21	1.21	1.30	-0.01	1.26	1.55	0.21	1.24
6 Wholesale and retail trade, restaurants and hotels	6.02	2.46	2.91	6.63	2.89	3.13	2.81	-0.24	2.54	8.95	4.23	3.02
7 Transport, storage and communication	8.14	0.51	7.21	8.45	0.82	7.36	9.84	0.83	8.74	9.95	0.27	8.97
8 Finance, insurance, real estate and business services	9.96	0.04	8.56	10.34	0.02	9.42	9.33	-	8.54	12.48	-	10.32
9 Community, social and personal services	1.02	0.01	0.90	1.06	-0.02	1.02	1.37	-	1.30	1.54	0.11	1.30
Total Industries ab	67.06	10.55	51.15	69.96	13.62	52.50	63.82	4.92	55.15	82.56	16.22	57.57
Producers of Government Services	4.71	-0.16	4.87	5.51	-0.89	6.40	6.93	-0.72	7.65	8.16	0.57	7.59
Private Non-Profit Institutions Serving Households	...	...	...	...	...	...	...	...	...	...	...	...
Total ab	71.77	10.39	56.02	75.47	12.73	58.90	70.75	4.20	62.80	90.72	16.79	65.16

	1974 TGCF	1974 IS	1974 GFCF	1975 TGCF	1975 IS	1975 GFCF	1976 TGCF	1976 IS	1976 GFCF	1977 TGCF	1977 IS	1977 GFCF
1 Agriculture, hunting, fishing and forestry	12.96	1.10	12.06	12.78	2.05	12.71	18.54	2.51	16.00	19.83	1.34	16.79
2 Mining and quarrying	2.14	0.76	1.40	3.54	1.53	2.45	4.52	0.39	4.13	4.31	-0.15	4.24
3 Manufacturing	27.91	13.97	14.21	23.53	4.26	20.93	19.59	2.99	16.57	24.16	4.78	17.57
4 Electricity, gas and water	6.27	0.60	5.67	8.76	0.59	8.19	9.12	-0.08	9.20	10.76	0.25	10.42
5 Construction	1.55	0.40	1.15	1.43	0.20	1.27	1.87	0.29	1.58	2.15	0.39	1.65
6 Wholesale and retail trade, restaurants and hotels	6.33	3.27	3.22	10.68	9.35	2.38	9.90	7.56	2.33	5.66	1.98	2.57
7 Transport, storage and communication	9.22	0.40	8.92	8.91	0.16	9.35	8.85	-0.23	9.07	9.85	0.08	9.25
8 Finance, insurance, real estate and business services	9.51	0.01	9.74	8.20	-0.01	10.16	12.18	0.04	12.10	13.77	0.03	11.79
9 Community, social and personal services	1.22	0.07	1.17	1.16	-0.03	1.35	1.58	0.03	1.55	1.94	-0.02	1.77
Total Industries ab	77.11	20.58	57.54	78.99	18.10	68.79	86.15	13.50	72.53	92.43	8.68	76.05
Producers of Government Services	4.94	0.33	4.61	5.23	0.64	4.59	5.19	-0.06	5.25	4.25	-1.67	5.92
Private Non-Profit Institutions Serving Households	...	...	...	...	...	...	...	...	...	...	...	...
Total ab	82.05	20.91	62.15	84.22	18.74	73.38	91.34	13.44	77.78	96.68	7.01	81.97

	1978 TGCF	1978 IS	1978 GFCF	1979 TGCF	1979 IS	1979 GFCF
1 Agriculture, hunting, fishing and forestry	25.76	4.17	18.91	21.80	3.26	19.31
2 Mining and quarrying	3.44	0.24	3.13	3.72	0.57	3.20
3 Manufacturing	31.98	7.54	22.71	30.46	9.53	21.51
4 Electricity, gas and water	11.33	0.37	10.82	11.69	0.72	11.00

2.10 Gross Capital Formation by Kind of Activity of Owner, ISIC Major Divisions, in Constant Prices
(Continued)

Thousand Million Indian rupees — Fiscal year beginning 1 April

	1978 Total Gross Capital Formation	1978 Increase in Stocks	1978 Gross Fixed Capital Formation	1979 Total Gross Capital Formation	1979 Increase in Stocks	1979 Gross Fixed Capital Formation
	At constant prices of: 1970					
5 Construction	2.57	0.72	1.68	1.69	0.16	1.56
6 Wholesale and retail trade, restaurants and hotels	11.84	7.42	2.84	6.39	3.90	2.80
7 Transport, storage and communication	10.67	0.31	9.90	10.42	0.64	9.93
8 Finance, insurance, real estate and business services	14.84	0.04	12.85	10.68	0.03	11.09
9 Community, social and personal services	2.14	0.04	1.94	1.82	-	1.87
Total Industries [a,b]	114.57	20.85	84.78	98.67	18.81	82.27
Producers of Government Services	6.51	-0.61	7.12	7.17	0.14	7.03
Private Non-Profit Institutions Serving Households	...	...	...	...	...	...
Total [a,b]	121.08	20.24	91.90	105.84	18.95	89.30

a) Estimates of gross fixed capital formation by industry of use and by type of assets are prepared independently and therefore, do not always tally.
b) Due to the allocation of a statistical discrepancy to column 1 and not to columns 2 and 3, columns 2 and 3 do not add up to column 1.

2.11 Gross Fixed Capital Formation by Kind of Activity of Owner, ISIC Divisions, in Current Prices

Thousand Million Indian rupees — Fiscal year beginning 1 April

	1970	1971	1972	1973	1974	1975	1976	1977	1978	1979	1980
	All Producers										
1 Agriculture, hunting, forestry and fishing	11.61	13.14	14.96	17.18	19.16	22.71	29.38	32.09	39.41	...	...
a Agriculture and hunting	11.02	12.48	14.25	16.33	18.13	21.50	27.85	30.48	37.45	...	...
b Forestry and logging	0.23	0.27	0.26	0.29	0.30	0.35	0.55	0.58	0.73	...	...
c Fishing	0.36	0.39	0.45	0.56	0.73	0.86	0.98	1.03	1.23	...	...
2 Mining and quarrying	0.88	1.33	1.26	1.90	2.21	4.25	7.15	7.49	6.36	...	...
3 Manufacturing	12.04	11.55	14.51	15.78	22.97	36.47	29.25	31.98	43.39	...	...
4 Electricity, gas and water	5.93	6.18	6.52	7.32	8.73	13.79	15.94	18.64	20.44	...	...
a Electricity, gas and steam	5.55	5.70	5.81	6.62	7.94	12.80	14.63	17.05	18.70	...	...
b Water works and supply	0.38	0.48	0.71	0.70	0.79	0.99	1.31	1.59	1.74	...	...
5 Construction	1.11	1.30	1.44	1.61	1.73	2.08	2.73	2.97	3.18	...	...
6 Wholesale and retail trade, restaurants and hotels	2.91	3.30	2.91	3.99	5.40	4.67	4.16	5.15	5.33	...	...
a Wholesale and retail trade	1.94	1.89	2.18	2.59	3.54	3.97	3.98	4.63	5.13	...	...
b Restaurants and hotels	0.97	1.41	0.73	1.40	1.86	0.70	0.18	0.52	0.20	...	...
7 Transport, storage and communication	7.21	7.93	10.00	11.00	13.65	15.56	15.28	15.92	18.62	...	...
a Transport and storage	6.66	7.08	8.97	9.96	12.21	13.69	13.13	13.46	15.96	...	...
b Communication	0.55	0.85	1.03	1.04	1.44	1.87	2.15	2.46	2.66	...	...
8 Finance, insurance, real estate and business services	8.56	10.08	9.84	13.81	16.13	18.21	22.45	22.79	26.84	...	...
a Financial institutions	...	...	...	...	...	...	...	...	...	...	...
b Insurance	0.28	0.38	0.34	0.62	...	...	...	...	...	...	...
c Real estate and business services	8.28	9.70	9.50	13.19	15.60	17.79	21.67	21.87	25.79	...	...
Real estate except dwellings	0.02	0.02	0.02	0.03	0.03	0.04	0.06	0.06	0.07	...	...
Dwellings [a]	8.26	9.68	9.48	13.16	15.57	17.75	21.61	21.81	25.72	...	...
9 Community, social and personal services	0.90	1.08	1.48	1.66	1.86	2.37	2.77	3.19	3.89	...	...
Total Industries	51.15	55.89	62.92	74.25	91.84	120.11	129.11	140.23	167.46	...	...
Producers of Government Services	4.87	6.85	8.86	9.97	7.42	8.05	9.49	11.07	13.29	...	...
Private Non-Profit Institutions Serving Households	...	...	...	...	...	...	...	...	...	...	...
Total [b]	56.02	62.74	71.78	84.22	99.26	128.16	138.60	151.30	180.75	...	...

a) Including residential house construction of general government.
b) Data for this table have not been revised, therefore, data for some years are not comparable with those of other tables.

India

2.12 Gross Fixed Capital Formation by Kind of Activity of Owner, ISIC Divisions, in Constant Prices

Thousand Million Indian rupees — Fiscal year beginning 1 April

	1970	1971	1972	1973	1974	1975	1976	1977	1978	1979	1980
At constant prices of: 1970											
All Producers											
1 Agriculture, hunting, forestry and fishing	11.61	12.35	13.02	12.86	12.06	13.03	16.36	17.20	19.72	...	...
a Agriculture and hunting	11.02	11.71	12.39	12.21	11.39	12.29	15.51	16.31	18.74	...	...
b Forestry and logging	0.23	0.26	0.22	0.22	0.19	0.21	0.31	0.32	0.36	...	...
c Fishing	0.36	0.38	0.41	0.43	0.48	0.53	0.54	0.57	0.62	...	...
2 Mining and quarrying	0.88	1.26	1.11	1.52	1.40	2.45	4.13	4.25	3.35	...	...
3 Manufacturing	12.04	10.84	12.73	12.31	14.21	20.93	16.58	17.57	22.48	...	...
4 Electricity, gas and water	5.93	5.91	5.91	6.03	5.67	8.19	9.08	10.26	10.36	...	...
5 Construction	1.11	1.21	1.26	1.24	1.15	1.27	1.58	1.66	1.67	...	...
6 Wholesale and retail trade, restaurants and hotels	2.91	3.13	2.54	3.02	3.22	2.59	2.31	2.75	2.88	...	...
a Wholesale and retail trade	1.94	1.80	1.90	1.92	2.05	2.19	2.21	2.46	2.78	...	...
b Restaurants and hotels	0.97	1.33	0.64	1.10	1.17	0.40	0.10	0.29	0.10	...	...
7 Transport, storage and communication	7.21	7.36	8.74	8.97	8.92	9.35	9.08	9.20	9.93	...	...
a Transport and storage	6.66	6.57	7.81	8.12	7.95	8.20	7.83	7.81	8.55	...	...
b Communication	0.55	0.79	0.93	0.85	0.97	1.15	1.25	1.39	1.38	...	...
8 Finance, insurance, real estate and business services	8.56	9.42	8.54	10.32	9.74	10.15	12.08	11.77	12.78	...	...
a Financial institutions	...	...	...	...	...	...	...	...	...	...	...
b Insurance	0.28	0.35	0.30	0.48	...	...	...	...	...	...	...
c Real estate and business services	8.28	9.07	8.24	9.84	9.44	9.78	11.66	11.27	12.24	...	...
Real estate except dwellings	0.02	0.02	0.01	0.02	0.02	0.02	0.03	0.03	0.04	...	...
Dwellings [a]	8.26	9.05	8.23	9.82	9.42	9.76	11.63	11.24	12.20	...	...
9 Community, social and personal services	0.90	1.02	1.30	1.30	1.17	1.36	1.57	1.76	1.98	...	...
Total Industries	51.15	52.50	55.15	57.57	57.54	69.32	72.77	76.42	85.15	...	...
Producers of Government Services	4.87	6.40	7.65	7.59	4.61	4.59	5.25	5.92	6.49	...	...
Private Non-Profit Institutions Serving Households	...	...	...	...	...	...	...	...	...	...	...
Total [b]	56.02	58.90	62.80	65.16	62.15	73.91	78.02	82.34	91.64	...	...

a) Including residential house construction of general government.
b) Data for this table have not been revised, therefore, data for some years are not comparable with those of other tables.

2.17 Exports and Imports of Goods and Services, Detail

Thousand Million Indian rupees — Fiscal year beginning 1 April

	1970	1971	1972	1973	1974	1975	1976	1977	1978	1979	1980
Exports of Goods and Services											
1 Exports of merchandise, f.o.b.	14.03	15.55	18.95	23.51	31.80	41.78	51.33	54.34	55.55	...	...
2 Transport and communication	1.06	1.12	1.22	1.44	2.16	2.60	3.13	2.81	2.80	...	...
a In respect of merchandise imports	-	-	-	-	-	-	-	-	-	...	...
b Other	1.06	1.12	1.22	1.44	2.16	2.60	3.13	2.81	2.80	...	...
3 Insurance service charges	0.12	0.13	0.17	0.21	0.27	0.38	0.51	0.34	0.35	...	...
a In respect of merchandise imports	-	-	-	-	-	-	-	-	-	...	...
b Other	0.12	0.13	0.17	0.21	0.27	0.38	0.51	0.34	0.35	...	...
4 Other commodities	0.66	0.50	0.50	0.58	1.13	2.05	2.84	3.18	4.25	...	...
5 Adjustments of merchandise exports to change-of-ownership basis	1.32	0.53	0.76	1.72	1.49	-1.35	0.13	-0.30	1.71	...	...
6 Direct purchases in the domestic market by non-residential households	0.51	0.54	0.63	0.82	1.46	2.60	3.43	5.95	6.48	...	...
7 Direct purchases in the domestic market by extraterritorial bodies	0.01	0.01	0.02	0.02	0.04	0.06	0.02	0.04	0.01	...	...
Total Exports of Goods and Services	17.71	18.38	22.25	28.30	38.35	48.12	61.39	66.36	71.15	...	...
Imports of Goods and Services											
1 Imports of merchandise, c.i.f.	17.34	20.03	21.57	27.50	41.81	47.73	48.44	55.70	62.58	...	...

India

2.17 Exports and Imports of Goods and Services, Detail
(Continued)

Thousand Million Indian rupees — Fiscal year beginning 1 April

	1970	1971	1972	1973	1974	1975	1976	1977	1978	1979	1980
2 Adjustments of merchandise imports to change-of-ownership basis	-0.86	-1.69	-2.79	2.26	3.62	5.21	2.57	4.84	5.84	...	...
3 Other transport and communication	0.65	0.60	0.60	0.87	1.09	1.67	2.21	1.86	2.11	...	...
4 Other insurance service charges	0.12	0.18	0.12	0.14	0.14	0.24	0.30	0.31	0.37	...	...
5 Other commodities	0.59	0.58	0.66	0.68	0.80	1.36	1.92	1.80	2.29	...	...
6 Direct purchases abroad by government	0.15	0.17	0.15	0.15	0.19	0.22	0.38	0.30	0.46	...	...
7 Direct purchases abroad by resident households	0.17	0.19	0.18	0.16	0.14	0.21	0.32	0.41	0.61	...	...
Total Imports of Goods and Services	18.16	20.06	20.49	31.76	47.79	56.64	56.14	65.22	74.26	...	...
Balance of Goods and Services	-0.45	-1.68	1.76	-3.46	-9.44	-8.52	5.25	1.14	-3.11	...	...
Total Imports and Balance of Goods and Services	17.71	18.38	22.25	28.30	38.35	48.12	61.39	66.36	71.15	...	...

3.11 General Government Production Account: Total and Subsectors

Thousand Million Indian rupees — Fiscal year beginning 1 April

	1970					1971				
	Total General Government	Central Government	State or Provincial Government	Local Government	Social Security Funds	Total General Government	Central Government	State or Provincial Government	Local Government	Social Security Funds
Gross Output										
1 Sales	3.22	1.16	1.49	0.57	...	3.44	1.20	1.71	0.53	...
2 Services produced for own use	38.01	16.23	15.48	6.30	...	44.58	20.32	17.42	6.84	...
3 Own account capital formation [a]	0.32	0.04	0.28	-	...	0.36	0.05	0.31	-	...
Gross Output	41.55	17.43	17.25	6.87	...	48.38	21.57	19.44	7.37	...
Gross Input										
Intermediate Consumption	17.54	9.16	6.03	2.35	...	21.41	12.20	6.91	2.30	...
Subtotal: Value Added	24.01	8.27	11.22	4.52	...	26.97	9.37	12.53	5.07	...
1 Indirect taxes, net	...	...	...	...	...	...	...	...	...	...
2 Consumption of fixed capital	...	...	...	...	...	...	...	...	...	...
3 Compensation of employees [b]	24.01	8.27	11.22	4.52	...	26.97	9.37	12.53	5.07	...
a Paid to residents	24.01	8.27	11.22	4.52	...	26.97	9.37	12.53	5.07	...
b Paid to the rest of the world	-	-	-	-	...	-	-	-	-	...
4 Net Operating surplus	...	...	...	...	...	...	...	...	...	...
Gross Input	41.55	17.43	17.25	6.87	...	48.38	21.57	19.44	7.37	...

	1972					1973				
	Total General Government	Central Government	State or Provincial Government	Local Government	Social Security Funds	Total General Government	Central Government	State or Provincial Government	Local Government	Social Security Funds
Gross Output										
1 Sales	3.93	1.44	1.89	0.60	...	4.32	1.44	2.22	0.66	...
2 Services produced for own use	47.45	21.45	18.78	7.22	...	51.00	22.06	21.29	7.65	...
3 Own account capital formation [a]	0.37	0.05	0.32	-	...	0.36	0.05	0.31	-	...
Gross Output	51.75	22.94	20.99	7.82	...	55.68	23.55	23.82	8.31	...
Gross Input										
Intermediate Consumption	22.44	12.95	7.05	2.44	...	22.63	12.55	7.40	2.68	...
Subtotal: Value Added	29.31	9.99	13.94	5.38	...	33.05	11.00	16.42	5.63	...
1 Indirect taxes, net	...	...	...	...	...	...	...	...	...	...
2 Consumption of fixed capital	...	...	...	...	...	...	...	...	...	...
3 Compensation of employees [b]	29.31	9.99	13.94	5.38	...	33.05	11.00	16.42	5.63	...
a Paid to residents	29.31	9.99	13.94	5.38	...	33.05	11.00	16.42	5.63	...
b Paid to the rest of the world	-	-	-	-	...	-	-	-	-	...
4 Net Operating surplus	...	...	...	...	...	...	...	...	...	...
Gross Input	51.75	22.94	20.99	7.82	...	55.68	23.55	23.82	8.31	...

India

3.11 General Government Production Account: Total and Subsectors

Thousand Million Indian rupees
Fiscal year beginning 1 April

1974 / 1975

	Total General Government	Central Government	State or Provincial Government	Local Government	Social Security Funds	Total General Government	Central Government	State or Provincial Government	Local Government	Social Security Funds
Gross Output										
1 Sales	5.06	1.79	2.48	0.79	...	6.20	1.96	3.30	0.94	...
2 Services produced for own use	61.43	28.31	24.89	8.23	...	73.51	34.09	29.49	9.93	...
3 Own account capital formation [a]	0.37	0.04	0.33	-	...	0.39	0.05	0.34	-	...
Gross Output	66.86	30.14	27.70	9.02	...	80.10	36.10	33.13	10.87	...
Gross Input										
Intermediate Consumption	25.53	14.27	8.38	2.88	...	32.90	18.15	11.32	3.43	...
Subtotal: Value Added	41.33	15.87	19.32	6.14	...	47.20	17.95	21.81	7.44	...
1 Indirect taxes, net	...	...	...	...	...	...	...	...	...	...
2 Consumption of fixed capital	...	...	...	...	...	...	...	...	...	...
3 Compensation of employees [b]	41.33	15.87	19.32	6.14	...	47.20	17.95	21.81	7.44	...
a Paid to residents	41.33	15.87	19.32	6.14	...	47.20	17.95	21.81	7.44	...
b Paid to the rest of the world	-	-	-	-	...	-	-	-	-	...
4 Net Operating surplus	...	...	...	...	...	...	...	...	...	...
Gross Input	66.86	30.14	27.70	9.02	...	80.10	36.10	33.13	10.87	...

1976 / 1977

	Total General Government	Central Government	State or Provincial Government	Local Government	Social Security Funds	Total General Government	Central Government	State or Provincial Government	Local Government	Social Security Funds
Gross Output										
1 Sales	6.46	2.04	3.31	1.11	...	7.20	2.33	3.75	1.12	...
2 Services produced for own use	82.06	36.12	34.52	11.42	...	86.67	37.64	37.61	11.42	...
3 Own account capital formation [a]	0.43	0.07	0.36	-	...	0.49	0.05	0.44	-	...
Gross Output	88.95	38.23	38.19	12.53	...	94.36	40.02	41.80	12.54	...
Gross Input										
Intermediate Consumption	37.22	20.30	13.04	3.88	...	38.49	21.35	13.28	3.86	...
Subtotal: Value Added	51.73	17.93	25.15	8.65	...	55.87	18.67	28.52	8.68	...
1 Indirect taxes, net	...	...	...	...	...	...	...	...	...	...
2 Consumption of fixed capital	...	...	...	...	...	...	...	...	...	...
3 Compensation of employees [b]	51.73	17.93	25.15	8.65	...	55.87	18.67	28.52	8.68	...
a Paid to residents	51.73	17.93	25.15	8.65	...	55.87	18.67	28.52	8.68	...
b Paid to the rest of the world	-	-	-	-	...	-	-	-	-	...
4 Net Operating surplus	...	...	...	...	...	...	...	...	...	...
Gross Input	88.95	38.23	38.19	12.53	...	94.36	40.02	41.80	12.54	...

1978 / 1979

	Total General Government	Central Government	State or Provincial Government	Local Government	Social Security Funds	Total General Government	Central Government	State or Provincial Government	Local Government	Social Security Funds
Gross Output										
1 Sales	7.94	2.37	4.45	1.12	...	9.03	2.59	5.32	1.12	...
2 Services produced for own use	95.00	40.55	43.03	11.42	...	109.76	45.87	52.47	11.42	...
3 Own account capital formation [a]	0.49	0.06	0.43	-	...	0.55	0.06	0.49	-	...
Gross Output	103.43	42.98	47.91	12.54	...	119.34	48.52	58.28	12.54	...
Gross Input										
Intermediate Consumption	42.14	23.12	15.16	3.86	...	49.74	26.71	19.17	3.86	...
Subtotal: Value Added	61.29	19.86	32.75	8.68	...	69.60	21.81	39.11	8.68	...
1 Indirect taxes, net	...	...	...	...	...	...	...	...	...	...
2 Consumption of fixed capital	...	...	...	...	...	...	...	...	...	...
3 Compensation of employees [b]	61.29	19.86	32.75	8.68	...	69.60	21.81	39.11	8.68	...
a Paid to residents	61.29	19.86	32.75	8.68	...	69.60	21.81	39.11	8.68	...
b Paid to the rest of the world	-	-	-	-	...	-	-	-	-	...
4 Net Operating surplus	...	...	...	...	...	...	...	...	...	...
Gross Input	103.43	42.98	47.91	12.54	...	119.34	48.52	58.28	12.54	...

a) Referring to wages and salaries of regular general government employees engaged in construction.
b) Including labour component of capital expenditure in new construction.

India

3.12 General Government Income and Outlay Account: Total and Subsectors

Thousand Million Indian rupees — Fiscal year beginning 1 April

	1970 Total General Government	1970 Central Government	1970 State or Provincial Government	1970 Local Government	1970 Social Security Funds	1971 Total General Government	1971 Central Government	1971 State or Provincial Government	1971 Local Government	1971 Social Security Funds
Receipts										
1 Property and entrepreneurial income	5.74	5.51	2.81	0.24	...	6.48	6.22	3.15	0.38	...
a Net operating surplus	1.58	0.95	0.72	-0.09	...	2.12	1.47	0.94	-0.29	...
b Withdrawals from public quasi-corporations	...	...	...	...	...	...	...	...	...	...
c Interest	2.95	4.31	1.40	0.06	...	2.73	4.43	1.47	0.10	...
d Dividends	...	...	...	...	...	...	...	...	...	...
e Net land rent and royalties	1.21	0.25	0.69	0.27	...	1.63	0.32	0.74	0.57	...
2 Taxes, fees and contributions	51.17	25.10	23.68	2.39	...	60.61	31.10	27.07	2.44	...
a Indirect taxes	38.64	19.64	17.87	1.13	...	45.15	23.67	20.43	1.05	...
b Direct taxes	10.91	5.04	4.84	1.03	...	12.75	5.77	5.80	1.18	...
c Social security contributions	...	...	...	...	...	...	...	...	...	...
d Fees, fines and penalties	1.62	0.42	0.97	0.23	...	2.71	1.66	0.84	0.21	...
3 Other current transfers received	...	0.02	4.90	4.35	...	...	0.07	6.65	4.75	...
a Casualty insurance claims	...	...	...	...	...	...	...	...	...	...
b Transfers from other government subsectors	...	0.02	4.90	4.35	...	...	0.07	6.65	4.75	...
c Transfers from abroad	...	-	-	-	...	...	-	-	-	...
d Other transfers, except imputed	-	...	...	...	...	-	...	...	...	...
e Imputed unfunded employee welfare contributions	...	...	...	...	...	...	...	...	...	...
Total Current Receipts	56.91	30.63	31.39	6.98	...	67.09	37.39	36.87	7.57	...
Disbursements										
1 General government final consumption expenditures	38.01	16.23	15.48	6.30	...	44.58	20.32	17.42	6.84	...
a Compensation of employees	23.69	8.23	10.94	4.52	...	26.61	9.32	12.22	5.07	...
b Consumption of fixed capital	...	...	...	...	...	...	...	...	...	...
c Goods and services purchased, net	14.32	8.00	4.54	1.78	...	17.97	11.00	5.20	1.77	...
Purchases	17.54	9.16	6.03	2.35	...	21.41	12.20	6.91	2.30	...
Less: Sales	3.22	1.16	1.49	0.57	...	3.44	1.20	1.71	0.53	...
d Less: Own account production of fixed assets	...	...	...	...	...	...	...	...	...	...
e Indirect taxes paid, net	...	...	...	...	...	...	...	...	...	...
2 Property income paid	2.16	2.67	2.25	0.06	...	2.69	2.82	2.96	0.18	...
a Interest	2.16	2.67	2.25	0.06	...	2.69	2.82	2.96	0.18	...
b Net land rent and royalties	...	...	...	...	...	...	...	...	...	...
3 Subsidies	3.37	1.42	1.89	0.06	...	4.22	1.90	2.25	0.07	...
4 Other current transfers paid	6.03	6.63	8.54	0.13	...	8.18	10.17	9.40	0.08	...
a Casualty insurance premiums, net	...	...	...	...	...	...	...	...	...	...
b Transfers to other government subsectors	-	4.87	4.37	0.03	...	-	7.22	4.25	-	...
c Transfers to households [a]	5.78	1.51	4.17	0.10	...	7.28	2.05	5.15	0.08	...
d Transfers to private non-profit institutions serving households [a]	...	...	...	...	...	...	...	...	...	...
e Transfers to the rest of the world	0.25	0.25	-	-	...	0.90	0.90	-	-	...
Statistical discrepancy [b]	...	...	...	...	...	...	...	...	...	...
Net saving	7.34	3.68	3.23	0.43	...	7.42	2.18	4.84	0.40	...
Total Current Disbursements and Net Saving	56.91	30.63	31.39	6.98	...	67.09	37.39	36.87	7.57	...

India

3.12 General Government Income and Outlay Account: Total and Subsectors

Thousand Million Indian rupees
Fiscal year beginning 1 April

	1972 Total General Government	1972 Central Government	1972 State or Provincial Government	1972 Local Government	1972 Social Security Funds	1973 Total General Government	1973 Central Government	1973 State or Provincial Government	1973 Local Government	1973 Social Security Funds
Receipts										
1 Property and entrepreneurial income	6.38	6.93	3.44	0.33	...	5.45	5.41	3.81	0.23	...
a Net operating surplus	1.63	1.07	0.91	-0.35	...	0.24	-0.41	0.97	-0.32	...
b Withdrawals from public quasi-corporations	...	...	...	...	...	...	...	...	...	...
c Interest	3.01	5.54	1.68	0.11	...	3.13	5.47	1.57	0.09	...
d Dividends	...	...	...	...	...	...	...	...	...	...
e Net land rent and royalties	1.74	0.32	0.85	0.57	...	2.08	0.35	1.27	0.46	...
2 Taxes, fees and contributions	67.91	35.05	30.25	2.61	...	76.79	39.67	34.48	2.64	...
a Indirect taxes	51.75	27.24	23.38	1.13	...	58.76	30.80	26.80	1.16	...
b Direct taxes	14.70	7.38	6.05	1.27	...	16.53	8.36	6.90	1.27	...
c Social security contributions	...	...	...	...	...	...	...	...	...	...
d Fees, fines and penalties	1.46	0.43	0.82	0.21	...	1.50	0.51	0.78	0.21	...
3 Other current transfers received	-	0.12	6.56	5.08	...	-	0.01	6.61	5.33	...
a Casualty insurance claims	...	...	...	...	...	...	...	...	...	...
b Transfers from other government subsectors	-	0.12	6.56	5.08	...	-	0.01	6.61	5.33	...
c Transfers from abroad	...	-	-	-	...	...	-	-	-	...
d Other transfers, except imputed	-	...	...	...	...	...	...	...	...	...
e Imputed unfunded employee welfare contributions	...	...	...	...	...	...	...	...	...	...
Total Current Receipts	74.29	42.10	40.25	8.02	...	82.24	45.09	44.90	8.20	...
Disbursements										
1 General government final consumption expenditures	47.45	21.45	18.78	7.22	...	51.00	22.06	21.29	7.65	...
a Compensation of employees	28.94	9.94	13.62	5.38	...	32.69	10.95	16.11	5.63	...
b Consumption of fixed capital	...	...	...	...	...	...	...	...	...	...
c Goods and services purchased, net	18.51	11.51	5.16	1.84	...	18.31	11.11	5.18	2.02	...
Purchases	22.44	12.95	7.05	2.44	...	22.63	12.55	7.40	2.68	...
Less: Sales	3.93	1.44	1.89	0.60	...	4.32	1.44	2.22	0.66	...
d Less: Own account production of fixed assets	...	...	...	...	...	...	...	...	...	...
e Indirect taxes paid, net	...	...	...	...	...	...	...	...	...	...
2 Property income paid	3.47	3.79	3.63	0.38	...	4.77	5.22	3.56	-	...
a Interest	3.47	3.79	3.63	0.38	...	4.77	5.22	3.56	-	...
b Net land rent and royalties	...	...	...	...	...	...	...	...	...	...
3 Subsidies	5.51	2.84	2.59	0.08	...	7.08	4.34	2.60	0.14	...
4 Other current transfers paid	11.08	10.59	12.01	0.23	...	9.78	9.50	12.12	0.10	...
a Casualty insurance premiums, net	...	...	...	...	...	...	...	...	...	...
b Transfers to other government subsectors	-	6.81	4.80	0.14	...	-	6.82	5.12	-	...
c Transfers to households [a]	9.45	2.15	7.21	0.09	...	9.09	1.99	7.00	0.10	...
d Transfers to private non-profit institutions serving households [a]	...	...	...	...	...	...	...	...	...	...
e Transfers to the rest of the world	1.63	1.63	-	-	...	0.69	0.69	-	-	...
Statistical discrepancy [b]	...	...	...	...	...	...	...	...	...	...
Net saving	6.78	3.43	3.24	0.11	...	9.61	3.97	5.33	0.31	...
Total Current Disbursements and Net Saving	74.29	42.10	40.25	8.02	...	82.24	45.09	44.90	8.20	...

India

3.12 General Government Income and Outlay Account: Total and Subsectors

Thousand Million Indian rupees — *Fiscal year beginning 1 April*

		1974					1975			
		Total General Government	Central Government	State or Provincial Government	Local Government	Social Security Funds	Total General Government	Central Government	State or Provincial Government	Local Government	Social Security Funds
	Receipts										
1	Property and entrepreneurial income	8.05	7.64	4.10	0.13	...	9.97	9.01	5.19	0.64	...
a	Net operating surplus	0.77	-0.21	1.21	-0.23	...	1.77	0.36	1.50	-0.09	...
b	Withdrawals from public quasi-corporations	...	...	...	...	...	...	...	...	...	...
c	Interest	3.18	5.68	1.37	-0.05	...	4.04	7.05	1.66	0.20	...
d	Dividends	...	...	...	...	...	...	...	...	...	...
e	Net land rent and royalties	4.10	2.17	1.52	0.41	...	4.16	1.60	2.03	0.53	...
2	Taxes, fees and contributions	96.79	51.49	41.70	3.60	...	116.74	60.68	51.69	4.37	...
a	Indirect taxes	75.15	39.83	33.44	1.88	...	88.34	45.60	40.47	2.27	...
b	Direct taxes	19.68	11.28	7.06	1.34	...	26.43	14.63	10.16	1.64	...
c	Social security contributions	...	...	...	...	...	...	...	...	...	...
d	Fees, fines and penalties	1.96	0.38	1.20	0.38	...	1.97	0.45	1.06	0.46	...
3	Other current transfers received	-	-	8.06	5.17	...	-	-	8.97	6.57	...
a	Casualty insurance claims	...	...	...	...	...	...	...	...	...	...
b	Transfers from other government subsectors	-	-	8.06	5.17	...	-	-	8.97	6.57	...
c	Transfers from abroad	...	...	-	-	...	...	...	-	-	...
d	Other transfers, except imputed	-	...	...	...	...	-	...	...	...	...
e	Imputed unfunded employee welfare contributions	...	...	...	...	...	...	...	...	...	...
	Total Current Receipts	104.84	59.13	53.86	8.90	...	126.71	69.69	65.85	11.58	...
	Disbursements										
1	General government final consumption expenditures	61.43	28.31	24.89	8.23	...	73.51	34.09	29.49	9.93	...
a	Compensation of employees	40.96	15.83	18.99	6.14	...	46.81	17.90	21.47	7.44	...
b	Consumption of fixed capital	...	...	...	...	...	...	...	...	...	...
c	Goods and services purchased, net	20.47	12.48	5.90	2.09	...	26.70	16.19	8.02	2.49	...
	Purchases	25.53	14.27	8.38	2.88	...	32.90	18.15	11.32	3.43	...
	Less: Sales	5.06	1.79	2.48	0.79	...	6.20	1.96	3.30	0.94	...
d	Less: Own account production of fixed assets	...	...	...	...	...	...	...	...	...	...
e	Indirect taxes paid, net	...	...	...	...	...	...	...	...	...	...
2	Property income paid	3.40	3.54	3.61	0.06	...	4.91	5.64	3.88	0.26	...
a	Interest	3.40	3.54	3.61	0.06	...	4.91	5.64	3.88	0.26	...
b	Net land rent and royalties	...	...	...	...	...	...	...	...	...	...
3	Subsidies	11.83	8.99	2.79	0.05	...	11.20	7.93	3.21	0.06	...
4	Other current transfers paid	11.69	11.15	13.67	0.11	...	13.60	12.40	16.51	0.23	...
a	Casualty insurance premiums, net	...	...	...	...	...	...	...	...	...	...
b	Transfers to other government subsectors	-	8.10	5.13	0.01	...	-	9.13	6.39	0.02	...
c	Transfers to households [a]	11.50	2.86	8.54	0.10	...	13.50	3.17	10.12	0.21	...
d	Transfers to private non-profit institutions serving households [a]	...	...	...	...	...	...	...	...	...	...
e	Transfers to the rest of the world	0.19	0.19	-	-	...	0.10	0.10	-	-	...
	Statistical discrepancy [b]	0.97	0.43	0.40	0.14	...	0.78	0.52	0.17	0.09	...
	Net saving	15.52	6.71	8.50	0.31	...	22.71	9.11	12.59	1.01	...
	Total Current Disbursements and Net Saving	104.84	59.13	53.86	8.90	...	126.71	69.69	65.85	11.58	...

India

3.12 General Government Income and Outlay Account: Total and Subsectors

Thousand Million Indian rupees — Fiscal year beginning 1 April

	1976 Total General Government	1976 Central Government	1976 State or Provincial Government	1976 Local Government	1976 Social Security Funds	1977 Total General Government	1977 Central Government	1977 State or Provincial Government	1977 Local Government	1977 Social Security Funds
Receipts										
1 Property and entrepreneurial income	15.98	12.65	7.08	0.77	...	17.96	16.99	7.11	0.57	...
a Net operating surplus	4.54	2.86	1.71	-0.03	...	5.76	4.13	1.90	-0.27	...
b Withdrawals from public quasi-corporations	...	...	...	...	...	...	...	...	...	...
c Interest	6.55	8.28	2.57	0.22	...	6.93	11.39	2.02	0.23	...
d Dividends	...	...	...	...	...	...	...	...	...	...
e Net land rent and royalties	4.89	1.51	2.80	0.58	...	5.27	1.47	3.19	0.61	...
2 Taxes, fees and contributions	129.48	66.21	57.38	5.89	...	138.06	71.01	61.61	5.44	...
a Indirect taxes	99.26	49.29	46.82	3.15	...	106.89	53.39	50.70	2.80	...
b Direct taxes	27.76	16.66	9.17	1.93	...	28.78	17.21	9.62	1.95	...
c Social security contributions	...	...	...	...	...	...	...	...	...	...
d Fees, fines and penalties	2.46	0.26	1.39	0.81	...	2.39	0.41	1.29	0.69	...
3 Other current transfers received	-	-	11.57	7.42	...	-	-	13.33	7.07	...
a Casualty insurance claims	...	...	...	...	...	...	...	...	...	...
b Transfers from other government subsectors	-	-	11.57	7.42	...	-	-	13.33	7.07	...
c Transfers from abroad	...	-	-	-	...	...	-	-	-	...
d Other transfers, except imputed	-	...	...	...	...	-	...	...	...	...
e Imputed unfunded employee welfare contributions	...	...	...	...	...	...	...	...	...	...
Total Current Receipts	145.46	78.86	76.03	14.08	...	156.02	88.00	82.05	13.08	...
Disbursements										
1 General government final consumption expenditures	82.06	36.12	34.52	11.42	...	86.67	37.64	37.61	11.42	...
a Compensation of employees	51.30	17.86	24.79	8.65	...	55.38	18.62	28.08	8.68	...
b Consumption of fixed capital	...	...	...	...	...	...	...	...	...	...
c Goods and services purchased, net	30.76	18.26	9.73	2.77	...	31.29	19.02	9.53	2.74	...
Purchases	37.22	20.30	13.04	3.88	...	38.49	21.35	13.28	3.86	...
Less: Sales	6.46	2.04	3.31	1.11	...	7.20	2.33	3.75	1.12	...
d Less: Own account production of fixed assets	...	...	...	...	...	...	...	...	...	...
e Indirect taxes paid, net	...	...	...	...	...	...	...	...	...	...
2 Property income paid	6.01	6.77	3.29	0.48	...	6.99	6.95	6.16	0.59	...
a Interest	6.01	6.77	3.29	0.48	...	6.99	6.95	6.16	0.59	...
b Net land rent and royalties	...	...	...	...	...	...	...	...	...	...
3 Subsidies	13.93	10.27	3.58	0.08	...	17.72	12.94	4.70	0.08	...
4 Other current transfers paid	15.64	15.99	18.20	0.43	...	17.76	18.28	19.45	0.43	...
a Casualty insurance premiums, net	...	...	...	...	...	...	...	...	...	...
b Transfers to other government subsectors	-	11.77	7.20	0.01	...	-	13.59	6.80	0.01	...
c Transfers to households [a]	15.47	4.05	11.00	0.42	...	17.62	4.55	12.65	0.42	...
d Transfers to private non-profit institutions serving households [a]	...	...	...	...	...	...	...	...	...	...
e Transfers to the rest of the world	0.17	0.17	-	-	...	0.14	0.14	-	-	...
Statistical discrepancy [b]	2.69	0.86	1.85	-0.02	...	1.23	0.99	0.34	-0.10	...
Net saving	25.13	8.85	14.59	1.69	...	25.65	11.20	13.79	0.66	...
Total Current Disbursements and Net Saving	145.46	78.86	76.03	14.08	...	156.02	88.00	82.05	13.08	...

India

3.12 General Government Income and Outlay Account: Total and Subsectors

Thousand Million Indian rupees
Fiscal year beginning 1 April

	1978 Total General Government	1978 Central Government	1978 State or Provincial Government	1978 Local Government	1978 Social Security Funds	1979 Total General Government	1979 Central Government	1979 State or Provincial Government	1979 Local Government	1979 Social Security Funds
Receipts										
1 Property and entrepreneurial income	18.63	16.29	8.33	0.71	...	18.29	14.93	8.70	0.70	...
a Net operating surplus	5.12	3.36	1.94	-0.18	...	3.68	2.50	1.36	-0.18	...
b Withdrawals from public quasi-corporations	...	...	...	...	...	...	...	...	...	...
c Interest	7.79	11.46	2.83	0.20	...	8.10	10.61	3.33	0.20	...
d Dividends	...	...	...	...	...	...	...	...	...	...
e Net land rent and royalties	5.72	1.47	3.56	0.69	...	6.51	1.82	4.01	0.68	...
2 Taxes, fees and contributions	160.74	85.25	69.32	6.17	...	181.95	86.38	89.40	6.17	...
a Indirect taxes	127.35	66.73	57.44	3.18	...	145.94	66.52	76.25	3.17	...
b Direct taxes	30.57	18.11	10.25	2.21	...	33.07	19.42	11.43	2.22	...
c Social security contributions	...	...	...	...	...	...	...	...	...	...
d Fees, fines and penalties	2.82	0.41	1.63	0.78	...	2.94	0.44	1.72	0.78	...
3 Other current transfers received	-	-	16.97	7.47	...	-	-	10.78	7.10	...
a Casualty insurance claims	...	...	...	...	...	...	...	...	...	...
b Transfers from other government subsectors	-	-	16.97	7.47	...	-	-	10.78	7.10	...
c Transfers from abroad	...	-	-	-	...	...	-	-	-	...
d Other transfers, except imputed	-	...	...	...	...	...	...	...	...	...
e Imputed unfunded employee welfare contributions	...	...	...	...	...	...	...	...	...	...
Total Current Receipts	179.37	101.54	94.62	14.35	...	200.24	101.31	108.88	13.97	...
Disbursements										
1 General government final consumption expenditures	96.24	40.59	42.68	12.97	...	109.24	46.78	49.49	12.97	...
a Compensation of employees	61.37	19.83	31.69	9.85	...	68.27	21.37	37.05	9.85	...
b Consumption of fixed capital	...	...	...	...	...	...	...	...	...	...
c Goods and services purchased, net	34.87	20.76	10.99	3.12	...	40.97	25.41	12.44	3.12	...
Purchases	42.73	23.11	15.23	4.39	...	49.70	27.84	17.47	4.39	...
Less: Sales	7.86	2.35	4.24	1.27	...	8.73	2.43	5.03	1.27	...
d Less: Own account production of fixed assets	...	...	...	...	...	...	...	...	...	...
e Indirect taxes paid, net	...	...	...	...	...	...	...	...	...	...
2 Property income paid	9.36	9.22	6.31	0.53	...	9.79	10.30	5.07	0.46	...
a Interest	9.36	9.22	6.31	0.53	...	9.79	10.30	5.07	0.46	...
b Net land rent and royalties	...	...	...	...	...	...	...	...	...	...
3 Subsidies	22.01	16.02	5.90	0.09	...	24.26	17.53	6.64	0.09	...
4 Other current transfers paid	20.19	21.92	22.20	0.51	...	23.31	16.01	24.68	0.50	...
a Casualty insurance premiums, net	...	...	...	...	...	...	...	...	...	...
b Transfers to other government subsectors	-	17.12	7.30	0.02	...	-	10.95	6.92	0.01	...
c Transfers to households [a]	20.05	4.66	14.90	0.49	...	23.15	4.90	17.76	0.49	...
d Transfers to private non-profit institutions serving households [a]	...	...	...	...	...	...	...	...	...	...
e Transfers to the rest of the world	0.14	0.14	-	-	...	0.16	0.16	-	-	...
Statistical discrepancy [b]	3.02	1.33	1.73	-0.04	...	6.94	2.84	4.07	0.03	...
Net saving	28.55	12.46	15.80	0.29	...	26.70	7.85	18.93	-0.08	...
Total Current Disbursements and Net Saving	179.37	101.54	94.62	14.35	...	200.24	101.31	108.88	13.97	...

India

3.12 General Government Income and Outlay Account: Total and Subsectors

Thousand Million Indian rupees — Fiscal year beginning 1 April

	Total General Government	Central Government	State or Provincial Government	Local Government	Social Security Funds
Receipts					
1 Property and entrepreneurial income	22.45	20.25	9.96	0.70	...
a Net operating surplus	4.17	3.04	1.32	-0.19	...
b Withdrawals from public quasi-corporations	...	...	...	...	...
c Interest	11.04	15.18	4.11	0.21	...
d Dividends	...	...	...	...	...
e Net land rent and royalties	7.24	2.03	4.53	0.68	...
2 Taxes, fees and contributions	201.13	94.20	100.76	6.17	...
a Indirect taxes	161.59	72.22	86.20	3.17	...
b Direct taxes	36.34	21.47	12.65	2.22	...
c Social security contributions	...	...	...	...	...
d Fees, fines and penalties	3.20	0.51	1.91	0.78	...
3 Other current transfers received	-	-	14.64	6.46	...
a Casualty insurance claims	...	...	...	...	...
b Transfers from other government subsectors	-	-	14.64	6.46	...
c Transfers from abroad	...	...	...	...	...
d Other transfers, except imputed	...	...	...	...	...
e Imputed unfunded employee welfare contributions	...	...	...	...	...
Total Current Receipts	223.58	114.45	125.36	13.33	...
Disbursements					
1 General governement final consumption expenditures	127.94	52.97	62.00	12.97	...
a Compensation of employees	80.87	25.22	45.80	9.85	...
b Consumption of fixed capital	...	...	...	...	...
c Goods and services purchased, net	47.07	27.75	16.20	3.12	...
Purchases	56.50	30.61	21.50	4.39	...
Less: Sales	9.43	2.86	5.30	1.27	...
d Less: Own account production of fixed assets	...	...	...	...	...
e Indirect taxes paid, net	...	...	...	...	...
2 Property income paid	14.81	14.64	8.10	0.53	...
a Interest	14.81	14.64	8.10	0.53	...
b Net land rent and royalties	...	...	...	...	...
3 Subsidies	25.71	17.29	8.33	0.09	...
4 Other current transfers paid	28.38	20.60	28.38	0.50	...
a Casualty insurance premiums, net	...	...	...	...	...
b Transfers to other government subsectors	-	14.77	6.32	0.01	...
c Transfers to households [a]	28.22	5.67	22.06	0.49	...
d Transfers to private non-profit institutions serving households [a]	...	...	...	...	...
e Transfers to the rest of the world	0.16	0.16	-	-	...
Statistical discrepancy [b]	8.27	2.05	6.26	-0.04	...
Net saving	18.47	6.90	12.29	-0.72	...
Total Current Disbursements and Net Saving	223.58	114.45	125.36	13.33	...

a) Item 'Transfers to private non-profit institutions serving households' is included in item 'Transfers of households'.

b) Relating to inter-governmental accounting adjustments. For years prior to 1973, it is included in item 'Net saving'.

India

3.13 General Government Capital Accumulation Account: Total and Subsectors

Thousand Million Indian rupees — Fiscal year beginning 1 April

1970 / 1971

	Total General Government	Central Government	State or Provincial Government	Local Government	Social Security Funds	Total General Government	Central Government	State or Provincial Government	Local Government	Social Security Funds
Finance of Gross Accumulation										
1 Gross saving	8.57	4.70	3.35	0.52	...	8.64	3.17	4.96	0.51	...
a Consumption of fixed capital	1.23	1.02	0.12	0.09	...	1.22	0.99	0.12	0.11	...
b Net saving	7.34	3.68	3.23	0.43	...	7.42	2.18	4.84	0.40	...
2 Capital transfers received	0.38	0.38	1.26	0.52	...	0.22	0.22	1.98	0.58	...
a From other government subsectors	-	-	1.26	0.52	...	-	-	1.98	0.58	...
b From other resident sectors	-	-	-	-	...	-	-	-	-	...
c From rest of the world	0.38	0.38	-	-	...	0.22	0.22	-	-	...
Finance of Gross Accumulation a	8.95	5.08	4.61	1.04	...	8.86	3.39	6.94	1.09	...
Gross Accumulation										
1 Gross capital formation	14.24	5.07	7.29	1.88	...	17.34	6.21	8.84	2.29	...
a Increase in stocks	0.08	0.28	-0.26	0.06	...	-0.36	0.11	-0.46	-0.01	...
b Gross fixed capital formation	14.16	4.79	7.55	1.82	...	17.70	6.10	9.30	2.30	...
2 Purchases of land, net	-0.06	0.08	-0.10	-0.04	...	-0.17	0.08	-0.15	-0.10	...
3 Purchases of intangible assets, net	-	-	-	-	...	-	-	-	-	...
4 Capital transfers paid	0.36	1.41	0.72	0.01	...	0.69	2.32	0.93	-	...
a To other government subsectors	...	1.26	0.52	-	...	...	1.98	0.58	-	...
b To other resident sectors	0.25	0.04	0.20	0.01	...	0.59	0.24	0.35	-	...
c To rest of the world	0.11	0.11	-	-	...	0.10	0.10	-	-	...
Net lending	-5.59	-1.48	-3.30	-0.81	...	-9.00	-5.22	-2.68	-1.10	...
Gross Accumulation	8.95	5.08	4.61	1.04	...	8.86	3.39	6.94	1.09	...

1972 / 1973

	Total General Government	Central Government	State or Provincial Government	Local Government	Social Security Funds	Total General Government	Central Government	State or Provincial Government	Local Government	Social Security Funds
Finance of Gross Accumulation										
1 Gross saving	8.26	4.71	3.33	0.22	...	11.26	5.37	5.43	0.46	...
a Consumption of fixed capital	1.48	1.28	0.09	0.11	...	1.65	1.40	0.10	0.15	...
b Net saving	6.78	3.43	3.24	0.11	...	9.61	3.97	5.33	0.31	...
2 Capital transfers received	0.25	0.25	3.15	0.50	...	16.74	16.74	3.00	0.63	...
a From other government subsectors	-	-	3.15	0.50	...	-	-	3.00	0.63	...
b From other resident sectors	-	-	-	-	...	-	-	-	-	...
c From rest of the world	0.25	0.25	-	-	...	16.74	16.74	-	-	...
Finance of Gross Accumulation a	8.51	4.96	6.48	0.72	...	28.00	22.11	8.43	1.09	...
Gross Accumulation										
1 Gross capital formation	22.59	7.41	12.08	3.10	...	26.00	8.19	15.25	2.56	...
a Increase in stocks	-0.49	0.19	-0.71	0.03	...	0.71	0.54	0.14	0.03	...
b Gross fixed capital formation	23.08	7.22	12.79	3.07	...	25.29	7.65	15.11	2.53	...
2 Purchases of land, net	-1.30	0.06	-1.21	-0.15	...	-0.21	0.10	-0.20	-0.11	...
3 Purchases of intangible assets, net	-	-	-	-	...	-	-	-	-	...
4 Capital transfers paid	0.74	3.60	0.79	-	...	0.71	3.47	0.87	-	...
a To other government subsectors	...	3.18	0.47	-	...	...	3.01	0.62	-	...
b To other resident sectors	0.63	0.31	0.32	-	...	0.57	0.32	0.25	-	...
c To rest of the world	0.11	0.11	-	-	...	0.14	0.14	-	-	...
Net lending	-13.52	-6.11	-5.18	-2.23	...	1.50	10.35	-7.49	-1.36	...
Gross Accumulation	8.51	4.96	6.48	0.72	...	28.00	22.11	8.43	1.09	...

1974 / 1975

	Total General Government	Central Government	State or Provincial Government	Local Government	Social Security Funds	Total General Government	Central Government	State or Provincial Government	Local Government	Social Security Funds
Finance of Gross Accumulation										
1 Gross saving	17.03	7.97	8.60	0.46	...	24.49	10.57	12.72	1.20	...
a Consumption of fixed capital	1.51	1.26	0.10	0.15	...	1.78	1.46	0.13	0.19	...
b Net saving	15.52	6.71	8.50	0.31	...	22.71	9.11	12.59	1.01	...
2 Capital transfers received	0.18	0.18	2.55	0.70	...	3.03	3.03	3.65	0.72	...

India

3.13 General Government Capital Accumulation Account: Total and Subsectors
(Continued)

Thousand Million Indian rupees — Fiscal year beginning 1 April

	1974					1975				
	Total General Government	Central Government	State or Provincial Government	Local Government	Social Security Funds	Total General Government	Central Government	State or Provincial Government	Local Government	Social Security Funds
a From other government subsectors	-	-	2.55	0.70	...	-	-	3.65	0.72	...
b From other resident sectors	-	-	-	-	...	-	-	-	-	...
c From rest of the world	0.18	0.18	-	-	...	3.03	3.03	-	-	...
Finance of Gross Accumulation [a]	17.21	8.15	11.15	1.16	...	27.52	13.60	16.37	1.92	...
	Gross Accumulation									
1 Gross capital formation	25.91	8.77	13.97	3.17	...	29.96	10.04	16.05	3.87	...
a Increase in stocks	1.36	0.08	1.23	0.05	...	1.51	0.33	1.15	0.03	...
b Gross fixed capital formation	24.55	8.69	12.74	3.12	...	28.45	9.71	14.90	3.84	...
2 Purchases of land, net	-0.11	0.09	-0.07	-0.13	...	-0.29	0.12	-0.21	-0.20	...
3 Purchases of intangible assets, net	-	-	-	-	...	-	-	-	-	...
4 Capital transfers paid	1.48	3.54	1.19	-	...	2.27	5.34	1.29	0.01	...
a To other government subsectors	...	2.61	0.64	...	...	...	3.72	0.65	-	...
b To other resident sectors	1.07	0.52	0.55	-	...	1.86	1.21	0.64	0.01	...
c To rest of the world	0.41	0.41	-	-	...	0.41	0.41	-	-	...
Net lending	-10.07	-4.25	-3.94	-1.88	...	-4.42	-1.90	-0.76	-1.76	...
Gross Accumulation	17.21	8.15	11.15	1.16	...	27.52	13.60	16.37	1.92	...

	1976					1977				
	Total General Government	Central Government	State or Provincial Government	Local Government	Social Security Funds	Total General Government	Central Government	State or Provincial Government	Local Government	Social Security Funds
	Finance of Gross Accumulation									
1 Gross saving	26.99	10.37	14.72	1.90	...	27.55	12.69	13.94	0.92	...
a Consumption of fixed capital	1.86	1.52	0.13	0.21	...	1.90	1.49	0.15	0.26	...
b Net saving	25.13	8.85	14.59	1.69	...	25.65	11.20	13.79	0.66	...
2 Capital transfers received	2.75	2.75	4.12	1.06	...	3.22	3.22	5.67	1.51	...
a From other government subsectors	-	-	4.12	1.06	...	-	-	5.67	1.51	...
b From other resident sectors	-	-	-	-	...	-	-	-	-	...
c From rest of the world	2.75	2.75	-	-	...	3.22	3.22	-	-	...
Finance of Gross Accumulation [a]	29.74	13.12	18.84	2.96	...	30.77	15.91	19.61	2.43	...
	Gross Accumulation									
1 Gross capital formation	34.13	10.87	18.63	4.63	...	35.23	9.14	21.18	4.91	...
a Increase in stocks	-1.00	-0.09	-0.90	-0.01	...	-3.73	-2.42	-1.31	-	...
b Gross fixed capital formation	35.13	10.96	19.53	4.64	...	38.96	11.56	22.49	4.91	...
2 Purchases of land, net	-0.71	-0.29	-0.13	-0.29	...	-0.78	-0.53	0.09	-0.34	...
3 Purchases of intangible assets, net	-	-	-	-	...	-	-	-	-	...
4 Capital transfers paid	2.75	5.96	1.95	0.02	...	3.50	7.96	2.70	0.02	...
a To other government subsectors	...	4.18	1.00	-	...	...	5.71	1.47	-	...
b To other resident sectors	2.32	1.35	0.95	0.02	...	2.99	1.74	1.23	0.02	...
c To rest of the world	0.43	0.43	-	-	...	0.51	0.51	-	-	...
Net lending	-6.43	-3.42	-1.61	-1.40	...	-7.18	-0.66	-4.36	-2.16	...
Gross Accumulation	29.74	13.12	18.84	2.96	...	30.77	15.91	19.61	2.43	...

	1978					1979				
	Total General Government	Central Government	State or Provincial Government	Local Government	Social Security Funds	Total General Government	Central Government	State or Provincial Government	Local Government	Social Security Funds
	Finance of Gross Accumulation									
1 Gross saving	30.76	14.20	15.96	0.60	...	29.36	10.04	19.09	0.23	...
a Consumption of fixed capital	2.21	1.74	0.16	0.31	...	2.66	2.19	0.16	0.31	...
b Net saving	28.55	12.46	15.80	0.29	...	26.70	7.85	18.93	-0.08	...
2 Capital transfers received	2.67	2.67	8.50	2.25	...	3.86	3.86	10.96	2.62	...
a From other government subsectors	-	-	8.50	2.25	...	-	-	10.96	2.62	...
b From other resident sectors	-	-	-	-	...	-	-	-	-	...
c From rest of the world	2.67	2.67	-	-	...	3.86	3.86	-	-	...
Finance of Gross Accumulation [a]	33.43	16.87	24.46	2.85	...	33.22	13.90	30.05	2.85	...

India

3.13 General Government Capital Accumulation Account: Total and Subsectors
(Continued)

Thousand Million Indian rupees — Fiscal year beginning 1 April

	1978 Total General Government	Central Government	State or Provincial Government	Local Government	Social Security Funds	1979 Total General Government	Central Government	State or Provincial Government	Local Government	Social Security Funds
Gross Accumulation										
1 Gross capital formation	44.97	12.41	26.68	5.88	...	53.51	15.36	32.27	5.88	...
a Increase in stocks	-1.29	-0.42	-0.88	0.01	...	0.94	0.71	0.22	0.01	...
b Gross fixed capital formation	46.26	12.83	27.56	5.87	...	52.57	14.65	32.05	5.87	...
2 Purchases of land, net	-0.21	0.14	0.08	-0.43	...	-0.06	0.18	0.19	-0.43	...
3 Purchases of intangible assets, net	-	-	-	-	...	-	-	-	-	...
4 Capital transfers paid	4.29	10.61	4.41	0.02	...	6.59	14.97	5.18	0.02	...
a To other government subsectors	...	8.64	2.11	-	...	...	11.10	2.48	-	...
b To other resident sectors	3.68	1.36	2.30	0.02	...	6.00	3.28	2.70	0.02	...
c To rest of the world	0.61	0.61	-	-	...	0.59	0.59	-	-	...
Net lending	-15.62	-6.29	-6.71	-2.62	...	-26.82	-16.61	-7.59	-2.62	...
Gross Accumulation	33.43	16.87	24.46	2.85	...	33.22	13.90	30.05	2.85	...

	1980 Total General Government	Central Government	State or Provincial Government	Local Government	Social Security Funds
Finance of Gross Accumulation					
1 Gross saving	21.73	9.65	12.49	-0.41	...
a Consumption of fixed capital	3.26	2.75	0.20	0.31	...
b Net saving	18.47	6.90	12.29	-0.72	...
2 Capital transfers received	4.58	4.58	13.00	3.26	...
a From other government subsectors	-	-	13.00	3.26	...
b From other resident sectors	-	-	-	-	...
c From rest of the world	4.58	4.58	-	-	...
Finance of Gross Accumulation a	26.31	14.23	25.49	2.85	...
Gross Accumulation					
1 Gross capital formation	62.15	17.93	38.34	5.88	...
a Increase in stocks	0.44	-0.30	0.73	0.01	...
b Gross fixed capital formation	61.71	18.23	37.61	5.87	...
2 Purchases of land, net	-0.09	0.26	0.08	-0.43	...
3 Purchases of intangible assets, net	...	...	...	...	...
4 Capital transfers paid	6.94	16.43	6.75	0.02	...
a To other government subsectors	-	13.17	3.09	-	...
b To other resident sectors	6.25	2.57	3.66	0.02	...
c To rest of the world	0.69	0.69	-	-	...
Net lending	-42.69	-20.39	-19.68	-2.62	...
Gross Accumulation	26.31	14.23	25.49	2.85	...

a) Including also business services.

3.26 Financial Transactions of Financial Institutions: Detail

Thousand Million Indian rupees — Fiscal year beginning 1 April

	1970 ALL FINANCIAL INSTITUTIONS	Central Bank	Other Monetary Institutions	Insurance	Other Financial Institutions	1971 ALL FINANCIAL INSTITUTIONS	Central Bank	Other Monetary Institutions	Insurance	Other Financial Institutions
Acquisition of Financial Assets										
1 Gold and SDRs	...	...	...	...	...	...	...	...	...	...
2 Currency and transferable deposits	0.64	0.04	0.60	-	-	0.78	0.11	0.68	-0.02	0.01
3 Other deposits	0.38	-	0.16	0.01	0.21	0.40	-	0.40	-0.06	0.06
4 Bills and bonds, short term	2.62	0.13	2.49	-	-	3.32	2.95	0.37	-	-
5 Bonds, long term	...	...	...	...	...	...	...	...	...	...
6 Corporate equity securities	6.37	2.99	2.01	1.05	0.32	5.69	0.25	3.52	1.37	0.55
7 Short-term loans, n.e.c.	7.85	0.25	5.29	1.03	1.28	3.72	-2.35	3.49	1.22	1.36
8 Long-term loans, n.e.c.										
9 Trade credit and advances	...	...	...	...	...	...	...	...	...	...
10 Other assets	0.52	...	0.19	0.11	0.22	2.03	1.11	0.37	0.11	0.44
Total Acquisition of Financial Assets	18.38	3.41	10.74	2.20	2.03	15.94	2.07	8.83	2.62	2.42

India

3.26 Financial Transactions of Financial Institutions: Detail
(Continued)

Thousand Million Indian rupees
Fiscal year beginning 1 April

	1970					1971				
	ALL FINANCIAL INSTITUTIONS	Central Bank	Other Monetary Institutions	Insurance	Other Financial Institutions	ALL FINANCIAL INSTITUTIONS	Central Bank	Other Monetary Institutions	Insurance	Other Financial Institutions
Incurrence of Liabilities											
1 Currency and transferable deposits	9.41	1.30	8.11	...	...	10.70	0.13	10.57	...	...
2 Other deposits	...	...	...	...	...	...	...	...	...	...
3 Bills and bonds, short term	...	...	...	...	...	...	...	...	...	...
4 Bonds, long term	...	...	...	...	...	...	...	...	...	...
5 Corporate equity securities	0.34	-	-	-	0.34	0.50	-	-	0.02	0.48
6 Short-term loans, n.e.c.	3.38	...	2.27	...	1.11	-0.45	...	-1.53	...	1.08
7 Long-term loans, n.e.c.		...		...			...		...	
9 Net equity of households in life insurance and pension fund reserves	...	...	...	...	...	...	...	...	...	...
10 Other liabilities	4.37	1.52	0.40	2.06	0.38	4.17	1.29	-0.15	2.53	0.50
Total Incurrence of liabilities	17.50	2.82	10.78	2.06	1.84	14.92	1.42	8.89	2.55	2.06
Net Lending	0.88	0.59	-0.04	0.14	0.19	1.02	0.65	-0.06	0.07	0.36
Incurrence of Liabilities and Net Lending	18.38	3.41	10.74	2.20	2.03	15.94	2.07	8.83	2.62	2.42

	1972					1973				
	ALL FINANCIAL INSTITUTIONS	Central Bank	Other Monetary Institutions	Insurance	Other Financial Institutions	ALL FINANCIAL INSTITUTIONS	Central Bank	Other Monetary Institutions	Insurance	Other Financial Institutions
Acquisition of Financial Assets											
1 Gold and SDRs	...	...	...	...	...	...	...	...	...	...
2 Currency and transferable deposits	0.10	0.08	0.03	0.01	-0.02	3.88	0.01	3.84	0.03	-
3 Other deposits	2.08	-	1.21	0.55	0.32	0.54	-	-0.94	1.69	-0.21
4 Bills and bonds, short term	0.09	-0.04	0.13	-	-	3.68	0.86	2.82	-	-
5 Bonds, long term	...	...	...	...	...	...	...	...	...	...
6 Corporate equity securities	10.32	0.93	6.67	1.37	1.35	5.19	-3.23	3.21	4.16	1.05
7 Short-term loans, n.e.c.	10.03	2.28	4.51	1.47	1.77	20.67	5.02	11.02	1.86	2.77
8 Long-term loans, n.e.c.										
9 Trade credit and advances	...	...	...	...	...	...	...	...	...	...
10 Other assets	1.52	0.75	0.26	0.26	0.25	5.29	3.92	-0.54	1.36	0.55
Total Acquisition of Financial Assets	24.14	4.00	12.81	3.66	3.67	39.25	6.58	19.41	9.10	4.16
Incurrence of Liabilities											
1 Currency and transferable deposits	16.45	2.73	13.71	...	0.01	19.50	3.24	16.26	...	...
2 Other deposits	...	...	...	...	...	...	...	...	...	...
3 Bills and bonds, short term	...	...	...	...	...	...	...	...	...	...
4 Bonds, long term	...	...	...	...	...	...	...	...	...	...
5 Corporate equity securities	0.72	-	0.02	0.27	0.43	1.00	-	-	0.39	0.61
6 Short-term loans, n.e.c.	0.64	...	-1.08	...	1.72	4.90	...	2.88	...	2.02
7 Long-term loans, n.e.c.		...		...			...		...	
9 Net equity of households in life insurance and pension fund reserves	...	...	...	...	...	...	...	...	...	...
10 Other liabilities	4.62	0.28	0.20	3.15	0.79	12.00	2.21	0.30	8.26	1.23
Total Incurrence of liabilities	22.43	3.01	12.85	3.42	3.15	37.40	5.45	19.44	8.65	3.86
Net Lending	1.71	0.99	-0.04	0.24	0.52	1.85	1.13	-0.03	0.45	0.30
Incurrence of Liabilities and Net Lending	24.14	4.00	12.81	3.66	3.67	39.25	6.58	19.41	9.10	4.16

	1974					1975				
	ALL FINANCIAL INSTITUTIONS	Central Bank	Other Monetary Institutions	Insurance	Other Financial Institutions	ALL FINANCIAL INSTITUTIONS	Central Bank	Other Monetary Institutions	Insurance	Other Financial Institutions
Acquisition of Financial Assets											
1 Gold and SDRs	...	...	...	...	...	...	...	...	...	...
2 Currency and transferable deposits	0.59	-0.21	0.73	0.06	0.01	1.42	0.09	1.35	-	-0.02
3 Other deposits	1.45	-	1.87	-0.44	0.02	1.79	-	1.22	0.20	0.37
4 Bills and bonds, short term	1.75	0.55	1.20	-	-	6.02	-0.44	5.97	-	0.49
5 Bonds, long term	...	...	...	...	...	...	...	...	...	...
6 Corporate equity securities	12.40	4.59	4.60	2.39	0.82	8.41	-1.13	5.69	2.60	1.25
7 Short-term loans, n.e.c.	20.69	5.76	8.75	2.40	3.78	28.75	6.70	14.01	2.26	5.78
8 Long-term loans, n.e.c.										
9 Trade credit and advances	...	...	...	...	...	...	...	...	...	...

India

3.26 Financial Transactions of Financial Institutions: Detail
(Continued)

Thousand Million Indian rupees — Fiscal year beginning 1 April

	1974 ALL FINANCIAL INSTITUTIONS	Central Bank	Other Monetary Institutions	Insurance	Other Financial Institutions	1975 ALL FINANCIAL INSTITUTIONS	Central Bank	Other Monetary Institutions	Insurance	Other Financial Institutions
10 Other assets	0.88	-0.74	0.68	0.24	0.70	10.15	9.20	0.27	0.41	0.27
Total Acquisition of Financial Assets	37.76	9.95	17.83	4.65	5.33	56.54	14.42	28.51	5.47	8.14

Incurrence of Liabilities

	ALL FIN. INST.	Central Bank	Other Monetary Inst.	Insurance	Other Fin. Inst.	ALL FIN. INST.	Central Bank	Other Monetary Inst.	Insurance	Other Fin. Inst.
1 Currency and transferable deposits	22.23	5.35	16.76	...	0.12	36.49	14.40	21.96	...	0.13
2 Other deposits	...	...	...	...	...	...	...	...	...	...
3 Bills and bonds, short term	...	...	...	...	...	...	...	...	...	...
4 Bonds, long term	...	...	...	...	...	...	...	...	...	...
5 Corporate equity securities	0.50	-	-	0.07	0.43	0.65	-	0.01	0.07	0.57
6 Short-term loans, n.e.c.	3.44	...	0.29	...	3.15	8.05	...	4.05	...	4.00
7 Long-term loans, n.e.c.										
9 Net equity of households in life insurance and pension fund reserves	...	...	...	...	...	...	...	...	...	...
10 Other liabilities	8.28	2.40	0.87	3.72	1.29	7.67	-2.19	2.54	4.72	2.60
Total Incurrence of liabilities	34.45	7.75	17.92	3.79	4.99	52.86	12.21	28.56	4.79	7.30
Net Lending	3.31	2.20	-0.09	0.86	0.34	3.68	2.21	-0.05	0.68	0.84
Incurrence of Liabilities and Net Lending	37.76	9.95	17.83	4.65	5.33	56.54	14.42	28.51	5.47	8.14

	1976 ALL FIN. INST.	Central Bank	Other Monetary Inst.	Insurance	Other Fin. Inst.	1977 ALL FIN. INST.	Central Bank	Other Monetary Inst.	Insurance	Other Fin. Inst.

Acquisition of Financial Assets

1 Gold and SDRs	...	...	...	...	...	...	...	...	...	...
2 Currency and transferable deposits	1.32	-0.10	1.44	-0.03	0.01	7.38	-0.02	7.31	0.09	0.01
3 Other deposits	1.77	-	0.97	0.44	0.36	2.45	-	1.95	-0.64	1.14
4 Bills and bonds, short term	0.34	-0.36	0.08	-	0.62	11.14	8.63	2.29	-	0.22
5 Bonds, long term	...	...	...	...	...	...	...	...	...	...
6 Corporate equity securities	14.91	0.84	9.82	3.75	0.50	21.00	4.41	11.38	3.92	1.29
7 Short-term loans, n.e.c.	42.20	5.78	26.19	2.37	7.86	22.71	-0.77	11.28	3.93	8.27
8 Long-term loans, n.e.c.										
9 Trade credit and advances	...	...	...	...	...	...	...	...	...	...
10 Other assets	13.40	8.89	3.73	0.46	0.32	1.79	-4.66	5.59	0.45	0.41
Total Acquisition of Financial Assets	73.94	15.05	42.23	6.99	9.67	66.47	7.59	39.80	7.75	11.33

Incurrence of Liabilities

1 Currency and transferable deposits	47.40	11.00	35.86	...	0.54	40.61	3.68	36.91	...	0.02
2 Other deposits	...	...	...	...	...	...	...	...	...	...
3 Bills and bonds, short term	...	...	...	...	...	...	...	...	...	...
4 Bonds, long term	...	...	...	...	...	...	...	...	...	...
5 Corporate equity securities	0.80	-	0.07	-0.02	0.75	1.27	-	0.08	-0.03	1.22
6 Short-term loans, n.e.c.	9.25	...	5.26	...	3.99	4.20	...	-1.43	...	5.63
7 Long-term loans, n.e.c.										
9 Net equity of households in life insurance and pension fund reserves	...	...	...	...	...	...	...	...	...	...
10 Other liabilities	11.27	1.16	0.79	5.73	3.59	14.59	0.47	4.00	6.66	3.46
Total Incurrence of liabilities	68.72	12.16	41.98	5.71	8.87	60.67	4.15	39.56	6.63	10.33
Net Lending	5.22	2.89	0.25	1.28	0.80	5.80	3.44	0.24	1.12	1.00
Incurrence of Liabilities and Net Lending	73.94	15.05	42.23	6.99	9.67	66.47	7.59	39.80	7.75	11.33

	1978 ALL FIN. INST.	Central Bank	Other Monetary Inst.	Insurance	Other Fin. Inst.	1979 ALL FIN. INST.	Central Bank	Other Monetary Inst.	Insurance	Other Fin. Inst.

Acquisition of Financial Assets

1 Gold and SDRs	...	...	...	...	...	...	...	...	...	...
2 Currency and transferable deposits	6.01	-0.07	6.01	0.06	0.01	11.09	0.04	11.05	-	-
3 Other deposits	1.56	-	-0.42	0.35	1.63	3.07	-	2.20	-0.02	0.89
4 Bills and bonds, short term	12.10	9.55	2.37	-	0.18	23.08	19.99	2.59	-	0.50

India

3.26 Financial Transactions of Financial Institutions: Detail
(Continued)

Thousand Million Indian rupees — Fiscal year beginning 1 April

		1978					1979			
		ALL FINANCIAL INSTITUTIONS	Central Bank	Other Monetary Institutions	Insurance	Other Financial Institutions	ALL FINANCIAL INSTITUTIONS	Central Bank	Other Monetary Institutions	Insurance	Other Financial Institutions
5	Bonds, long term	...	...	...	...	...	...	...	...	...	...
6	Corporate equity securities	19.39	-0.12	14.70	4.34	0.47	20.30	-1.43	15.46	4.87	1.40
7	Short-term loans, n.e.c.	41.76	7.58	20.46	3.21	10.51	42.17	0.21	23.30	3.70	14.96
8	Long-term loans, n.e.c.										
9	Trade credit and advances	...	...	...	...	...	...	...	...	...	...
10	Other assets	19.52	3.45	14.14	0.64	1.29	5.79	-1.12	5.71	0.81	0.39
	Total Acquisition of Financial Assets	100.34	20.39	57.26	8.60	14.09	105.50	17.69	60.31	9.36	18.14

Incurrence of Liabilities

1	Currency and transferable deposits	66.47	15.38	51.06	...	0.03	62.39	7.51	54.88	...	-
2	Other deposits	...	...	...	...	...	...	...	...	...	...
3	Bills and bonds, short term	...	...	...	...	...	...	...	...	...	...
4	Bonds, long term	...	...	...	...	...	...	...	...	...	...
5	Corporate equity securities	1.98	-	0.04	0.07	1.87	1.21	-	0.02	0.06	1.13
6	Short-term loans, n.e.c.	4.00		0.33	...	3.67	11.87	...	4.06	...	7.81
7	Long-term loans, n.e.c.		...					...			
9	Net equity of households in life insurance and pension fund reserves	...	...	...	...	...	...	...	...	...	...
10	Other liabilities	21.38	1.12	5.27	7.45	7.54	22.00	5.64	1.05	8.37	6.94
	Total Incurrence of liabilities	93.83	16.50	56.70	7.52	13.11	97.47	13.15	60.01	8.43	15.88
	Net Lending	6.51	3.89	0.56	1.08	0.98	8.03	4.54	0.30	0.93	2.26
	Incurrence of Liabilities and Net Lending	100.34	20.39	57.26	8.60	14.09	105.50	17.69	60.31	9.36	18.14

3.51 External Transactions: Current Account: Detail

Thousand Million Indian rupees — Fiscal year beginning 1 April

		1970	1971	1972	1973	1974	1975	1976	1977	1978	1979	1980
		Payments to the Rest of the World										
1	Imports of goods and services	18.16	20.06	20.49	31.76	47.79	56.64	56.14	65.22	74.26	...	...
	a Imports of merchandise c.i.f.	17.34	20.03	21.57	27.50	41.81	47.73	48.44	55.70	62.58	...	...
	b Other	0.82	0.03	-1.08	4.26	5.98	8.91	7.70	9.52	11.68	...	...
2	Factor income paid to the rest of the world	3.41	3.34	3.46	3.70	3.87	3.73	4.25	5.06	5.58	...	...
	a Compensation of employees	0.11	0.12	0.11	0.12	0.11	0.11	0.23	0.48	0.54	...	...
	b Property and entrepreneurial income paid [a]	3.30	3.22	3.35	3.58	3.76	3.62	4.02	4.58	5.04	...	...
3	Indirect taxes paid to supranational organizations	...	...	...	...	...	...	...	...	...	...	...
4	Other current transfers to the rest of the world	0.13	0.12	0.11	0.12	0.06	0.13	0.07	0.07	0.17	...	...
	a By general government	-	-	-	-	-	-	-	-	-	...	...
	b By other resident sectors	0.13	0.12	0.11	0.12	0.06	0.13	0.07	0.07	0.17	...	...
	Statistical discrepancy [b]	0.86	1.69	2.79	-2.26	-3.62	-5.21	-2.57	-4.84	5.84	...	...
5	Surplus of the nation on current transactions	-4.24	-5.18	-3.27	-4.25	-7.48	0.77	12.75	14.17	-1.80	...	...
	Payments to the Rest of the World, and Surplus of the Nation on Current Transfers	18.32	20.03	23.58	29.07	40.62	56.06	70.64	79.68	84.05	...	...
		Receipts From The Rest of the World										
1	Exports of goods and services	17.71	18.38	22.25	28.30	38.35	48.12	61.39	66.36	71.15	...	...
	a Exports of merchandise f.o.b.	14.03	15.55	18.95	23.51	31.80	41.78	51.33	54.34	55.55	...	...

India

3.51 External Transactions: Current Account: Detail
(Continued)

Fiscal year beginning 1 April

Thousand Million Indian rupees

	1970	1971	1972	1973	1974	1975	1976	1977	1978	1979	1980
b Other	3.68	2.83	3.30	4.79	6.55	6.34	10.06	12.02	15.60	...	...
2 Factor income received from the rest of the world	0.57	0.43	0.44	0.45	0.96	1.18	1.92	2.73	4.02	...	...
a Compensation of employees	0.08	0.08	0.06	0.03	0.01	0.02	0.04	0.05	0.04	...	...
b Property and entrepreneurial income received	0.49	0.35	0.38	0.42	0.95	1.16	1.88	2.68	3.98	...	...
3 Subsidies received from supranational organizations	...	...	...	...	...	...	...	...	...	...	...
4 Other current transfers from the rest of the world	1.36	1.75	1.65	2.04	2.80	5.41	7.46	10.29	10.59	...	...
a To general government	-	-	-	-	-	-	-	-	-	...	...
b To other resident sectors	1.36	1.75	1.65	2.04	2.80	5.41	7.46	10.29	10.59	...	...
Statistical discrepancy [b]	-1.32	-0.53	-0.76	-1.72	-1.49	1.35	-0.13	0.30	-1.71	...	...
Receipts from the Rest of the World on Current Transfers	18.32	20.03	23.58	29.07	40.62	56.06	70.64	79.68	84.05	...	...

a) Including retained earnings of branches of foreign companies and foreign controlled rupee companies in India.
b) Referring to difference of ownership and payment basis of imports and exports of merchandise.

3.52 External Transactions: Capital Accumulation Account

Fiscal year beginning 1 April

Thousand Million Indian rupees

	1970	1971	1972	1973	1974	1975	1976	1977	1978	1979	1980
Finance of Gross Accumulation											
1 Surplus of the nation on current transactions	-4.24	-5.18	-3.27	-4.25	-7.48	0.77	12.75	14.17	-1.80	...	...
2 Capital transfers received from the rest of the world [a]	0.53	0.75	0.43	16.91	0.08	1.76	2.16	2.70	2.96	...	...
a By general government [a]	0.53	0.75	0.43	16.91	0.08	1.76	2.16	2.70	2.96	...	...
b By other resident sectors	...	...	...	...	...	...	...	...	...	...	...
Total Finance of Gross Accumulation	-3.71	-4.43	-2.84	12.66	-7.40	2.53	14.91	16.87	1.16	...	...
Gross Accumulation											
1 Capital transfers paid to the rest of the world [a]	...	...	...	...	...	...	...	...	...	...	...
2 Purchases of intangible assets, n.e.c., net, from the rest of the world	...	...	...	...	...	...	...	...	...	...	...
3 Net lending to the rest of the world	-3.71	-4.43	-2.84	12.66	-7.40	2.53	14.91	16.87	1.16	...	...
Total Gross Accumulation	...	...	...	...	...	...	...	...	...	...	...

a) Net of item 'Capital transfers paid to the rest of the world'.

4.3 Derivation of Value Added by Kind of Activity, ISIC Divisions, in Current Prices

Fiscal year beginning 1 April

Thousand Million Indian rupees

	1970 Gross Output	1970 Intermediate Consumption	1970 Value Added	1971 Gross Output	1971 Intermediate Consumption	1971 Value Added	1972 Gross Output	1972 Intermediate Consumption	1972 Value Added	1973 Gross Output	1973 Intermediate Consumption	1973 Value Added
All Producers												
1 Agriculture, hunting, forestry and fishing	214.09	39.85	174.24	224.87	44.04	180.83	244.55	45.20	199.35	329.54	61.66	267.88
a Agriculture and hunting	...	...	167.78	...	...	173.80	...	...	191.69	...	...	258.79
b Forestry and logging	...	...	4.01	...	...	4.40	...	...	4.61	...	...	5.16
c Fishing	...	...	2.45	...	...	2.63	...	...	3.05	...	...	3.93
2 Mining and quarrying	4.71	0.93	3.78	4.92	0.96	3.96	5.32	1.05	4.27	5.96	1.09	4.87
a Coal mining	...	...	2.15	...	...	2.13	...	...	2.25	...	...	2.39
b Crude petroleum and natural gas production	...	...	0.47	...	...	0.55	...	...	0.59	...	...	0.82
c Metal ore mining	...	...	0.51	...	...	0.57	...	...	0.62	...	...	0.73
d Other mining	...	...	0.65	...	...	0.71	...	...	0.81	...	...	0.93

India

4.3 Derivation of Value Added by Kind of Activity, ISIC Divisions, in Current Prices
(Continued)

Thousand Million Indian rupees

Fiscal year beginning 1 April

	1970 Gross Output	1970 Intermediate Consumption	1970 Value Added	1971 Gross Output	1971 Intermediate Consumption	1971 Value Added	1972 Gross Output	1972 Intermediate Consumption	1972 Value Added	1973 Gross Output	1973 Intermediate Consumption	1973 Value Added
3 Manufacturing	...	...	52.23	...	...	57.49	...	...	63.75	...	...	75.72
a Manufacture of food, beverages and tobacco	...	...	7.04	...	...	7.41	...	...	8.70	...	...	8.92
b Textile, wearing apparel and leather industries	...	...	11.99	...	...	13.36	...	...	15.04	...	...	20.02
c Manufacture of wood and wood products, including furniture	...	...	2.62	...	...	2.79	...	...	2.96	...	...	2.97
d Manufacture of paper and paper products, printing and publishing	...	...	2.23	...	...	2.32	...	...	2.47	...	...	2.97
e Manufacture of chemicals and chemical petroleum, coal, rubber and plastic products	...	...	6.79	...	...	7.93	...	...	8.34	...	...	9.62
f Manufacture of non-metallic mineral products, except products of petroleum and coal	...	...	2.28	...	...	2.58	...	...	2.83	...	...	3.04
g Basic metal industries	...	...	3.95	...	...	4.12	...	...	3.82	...	...	5.63
h Manufacture of fabricated metal products, machinery and equipment	...	...	10.79	...	...	12.39	...	...	14.39	...	...	16.06
i Other manufacturing industries	...	...	4.54	...	...	4.59	...	...	5.20	...	...	6.49
4 Electricity, gas and water	...	...	4.19	...	...	4.56	...	...	4.91	...	...	5.25
a Electricity, gas and steam	...	...	3.90	...	...	4.22	...	...	4.53	...	...	4.81
b Water works and supply	...	...	0.29	...	...	0.34	...	...	0.38	...	...	0.44
5 Construction	47.51	27.99	19.52	51.53	30.11	21.42	56.49	33.33	23.16	59.54	35.49	24.05
6 Wholesale and retail trade, restaurants and hotels	...	...	40.43	...	...	43.92	...	...	48.61	...	...	60.25
a Wholesale and retail trade	...	...	37.57	...	...	40.82	...	...	45.04	...	...	55.81
b Restaurants and hotels	...	...	2.86	...	...	3.10	...	...	3.57	...	...	4.44
7 Transport, storage and communication	...	...	18.69	...	...	20.23	...	...	22.32	...	...	24.90
a Transport and storage	...	...	16.31	...	...	17.58	...	...	19.56	...	...	21.77
b Communication	...	...	2.38	...	...	2.65	...	...	2.76	...	...	3.13
8 Finance, insurance, real estate and business services	...	...	21.14	...	...	23.50	...	...	26.11	...	...	30.10
a Financial institutions	...	...	4.39	...	...	5.14	...	...	5.80	...	...	7.25
b Insurance	...	...	2.17	...	...	2.56	...	...	3.06	...	...	3.76
c Real estate and business services	...	...	14.58	...	...	15.80	...	...	17.25	...	...	19.09
Real estate, except dwellings [a]	...	...	1.01	...	...	1.13	...	...	1.29	...	...	1.59
Dwellings	...	...	13.57	...	...	14.67	...	...	15.96	...	...	17.50
9 Community, social and personal services	...	...	16.79	...	...	18.41	...	...	20.17	...	...	22.49
a Sanitary and similar services	...	...	0.75	...	...	0.84	...	...	0.96	...	...	1.00
b Social and related community services	...	...	16.04	...	...	17.57	...	...	19.21	...	...	21.49
c Recreational and cultural services	...	...	...	...	...	...	...	...	...	...	...	...
d Personal and household services	...	...	...	...	...	...	...	...	...	...	...	...
Total, Industries	...	...	351.01	...	...	374.32	...	...	412.65	...	...	515.51
Producers of Government Services	...	...	16.35	...	...	18.31	...	...	19.76	...	...	22.21
Other Producers	...	...	...	...	...	...	...	...	...	...	...	...
Total	...	...	367.36	...	...	392.63	...	...	432.41	...	...	537.72
Imputed bank service charge	...	...	...	...	...	...	...	...	...	...	...	...
Import duties	...	...	...	...	...	...	...	...	...	...	...	...
Value added tax	...	...	...	...	...	...	...	...	...	...	...	...
Other adjustments	...	...	35.27	...	...	40.93	...	...	46.24	...	...	51.68
Total	...	...	402.63	...	...	433.56	...	...	478.65	...	...	589.40

India

4.3 Derivation of Value Added by Kind of Activity, ISIC Divisions, in Current Prices

Fiscal year beginning 1 April

Thousand Million Indian rupees

	1974 Gross Output	1974 Intermediate Consumption	1974 Value Added	1975 Gross Output	1975 Intermediate Consumption	1975 Value Added	1976 Gross Output	1976 Intermediate Consumption	1976 Value Added	1977 Gross Output	1977 Intermediate Consumption	1977 Value Added
All Producers												
1 Agriculture, hunting, forestry and fishing	368.62	78.17	290.45	355.34	76.89	278.45	372.68	85.44	287.24	422.64	92.94	329.70
a Agriculture and hunting	...	...	280.29	...	...	266.45	...	...	273.72	...	...	315.29
b Forestry and logging	...	...	5.62	...	...	6.33	...	...	7.51	...	...	8.23
c Fishing	...	...	4.54	...	...	5.67	...	...	6.01	...	...	6.18
2 Mining and quarrying	8.79	1.84	6.95	11.25	2.41	8.84	13.07	2.96	10.11	14.24	3.07	11.17
a Coal mining	...	...	3.30	...	...	4.59	...	...	5.17	...	...	5.15
b Crude petroleum and natural gas production	...	...	1.31	...	...	1.53	...	...	1.90	...	...	2.73
c Metal ore mining	...	...	1.06	...	...	1.37	...	...	1.55	...	...	1.62
d Other mining	...	...	1.28	...	...	1.35	...	...	1.49	...	...	1.67
3 Manufacturing	...	...	98.58	...	...	103.75	...	...	115.56	...	...	129.03
a Manufacture of food, beverages and tobacco	...	...	11.45	...	...	13.31	...	...	15.21	...	...	17.26
b Textile, wearing apparel and leather industries	...	...	23.97	...	...	22.32	...	...	24.14	...	...	28.27
c Manufacture of wood and wood products, including furniture	...	...	4.75	...	...	5.05	...	...	5.13	...	...	5.57
d Manufacture of paper and paper products, printing and publishing	...	...	4.31	...	...	4.26	...	...	4.40	...	...	4.78
e Manufacture of chemicals and chemical petroleum, coal, rubber and plastic products	...	...	13.53	...	...	14.57	...	...	16.84	...	...	18.91
f Manufacture of non-metallic mineral products, except products of petroleum and coal	...	...	4.19	...	...	5.06	...	...	5.67	...	...	6.43
g Basic metal industries	...	...	7.83	...	...	8.63	...	...	9.62	...	...	9.84
h Manufacture of fabricated metal products, machinery and equipment	...	...	20.50	...	...	22.17	...	...	25.01	...	...	26.85
i Other manufacturing industries	...	...	8.05	...	...	8.38	...	...	9.54	...	...	11.12
4 Electricity, gas and water	...	...	6.75	...	...	8.35	...	...	10.95	...	...	12.48
a Electricity, gas and steam	...	...	6.23	...	...	7.76	...	...	10.24	...	...	11.61
b Water works and supply	...	...	0.52	...	...	0.59	...	...	0.71	...	...	0.87
5 Construction	69.44	43.07	26.37	86.37	53.44	32.93	100.51	61.22	39.29	114.98	69.90	45.08
6 Wholesale and retail trade, restaurants and hotels	...	...	81.05	...	...	92.08	...	...	96.51	...	...	110.44
a Wholesale and retail trade	...	...	75.05	...	...	85.67	...	...	89.83	...	...	102.80
b Restaurants and hotels	...	...	6.00	...	...	6.41	...	...	6.68	...	...	7.64
7 Transport, storage and communication	...	...	31.34	...	...	35.24	...	...	41.62	...	...	45.41
a Transport and storage	...	...	27.77	...	...	31.15	...	...	36.18	...	...	39.42
b Communication	...	...	3.57	...	...	4.09	...	...	5.44	...	...	5.99
8 Finance, insurance, real estate and business services	...	...	35.23	...	...	41.18	...	...	47.24	...	...	52.30
a Financial institutions	...	...	9.27	...	...	12.77	...	...	14.92	...	...	17.13
b Insurance	...	...	4.52	...	...	5.00	...	...	6.12	...	...	6.41
c Real estate and business services	...	...	21.44	...	...	23.41	...	...	26.20	...	...	28.76
Real estate, except dwellings [a]	...	...	2.13	...	...	2.38	...	...	2.62	...	...	3.05
Dwellings	...	...	19.31	...	...	21.03	...	...	23.58	...	...	25.71
9 Community, social and personal services	...	...	27.35	...	...	30.51	...	...	35.03	...	...	39.24
a Sanitary and similar services	...	...	1.34	...	...	1.45	...	...	1.70	...	...	2.00
b Social and related community services	...	...	26.01	...	...	29.06	...	...	33.33	...	...	37.24
c Recreational and cultural services	...	...	...	...	...	...	...	...	...	...	...	...
d Personal and household services	...	...	...	...	...	...	...	...	...	...	...	...
Total, industries	...	...	604.07	...	...	631.33	...	...	683.55	...	...	774.85
Producers of Government Services	...	...	28.56	...	...	32.37	...	...	34.53	...	...	36.94

India

4.3 Derivation of Value Added by Kind of Activity, ISIC Divisions, in Current Prices
(Continued)

Thousand Million Indian rupees — Fiscal year beginning 1 April

	1974 Gross Output	1974 Intermediate Consumption	1974 Value Added	1975 Gross Output	1975 Intermediate Consumption	1975 Value Added	1976 Gross Output	1976 Intermediate Consumption	1976 Value Added	1977 Gross Output	1977 Intermediate Consumption	1977 Value Added
Other Producers	...	...	...	...	...	...	...	...	...	...	...	...
Total	...	...	632.63	...	...	663.70	...	...	718.08	...	...	811.79
Imputed bank service charge	...	...	...	...	...	...	...	...	...	...	...	...
Import duties	...	...	...	...	...	...	...	...	...	...	...	...
Value added tax	...	...	...	...	...	...	...	...	...	...	...	...
Other adjustments	...	...	63.32	...	...	77.14	...	...	85.33	...	...	89.17
Total	...	...	695.95	...	...	740.84	...	...	803.41	...	...	900.96

All Producers

	1978 Gross Output	1978 Intermediate Consumption	1978 Value Added	1979 Gross Output	1979 Intermediate Consumption	1979 Value Added	1980 Gross Output	1980 Intermediate Consumption	1980 Value Added
1 Agriculture, hunting, forestry and fishing	431.22	97.56	333.66	449.09	109.12	339.97	556.25	138.97	417.28
a Agriculture and hunting	...	...	316.38	...	...	321.13	...	...	395.61
b Forestry and logging	...	...	10.00	...	...	11.64	...	...	13.48
c Fishing	...	...	7.28	...	...	7.20	...	...	8.19
2 Mining and quarrying	15.66	3.34	12.32	20.06	4.70	15.36	22.85	5.67	17.18
a Coal mining	...	...	5.06	...	...	7.52	...	...	9.47
b Crude petroleum and natural gas production	...	...	3.49	...	...	3.83	...	...	3.61
c Metal ore mining	...	...	1.69	...	...	1.85	...	...	1.90
d Other mining	...	...	2.08	...	...	2.16	...	...	2.20
3 Manufacturing	...	...	148.38	...	...	173.75	...	...	199.88
a Manufacture of food, beverages and tobacco	...	...	16.88	...	...	18.38	...	...	25.38
b Textile, wearing apparel and leather industries	...	...	34.40	...	...	43.17	...	...	46.84
c Manufacture of wood and wood products, including furniture	...	...	6.49	...	...	6.76	...	...	8.05
d Manufacture of paper and paper products, printing and publishing	...	...	5.56	...	...	6.93	...	...	7.54
e Manufacture of chemicals and chemical petroleum, coal, rubber and plastic products	...	...	21.94	...	...	24.67	...	...	29.38
f Manufacture of non-metallic mineral products, except products of petroleum and coal	...	...	7.05	...	...	8.37	...	...	9.66
g Basic metal industries	...	...	11.82	...	...	13.63	...	...	14.65
h Manufacture of fabricated metal products, machinery and equipment	...	...	31.18	...	...	36.44	...	...	41.74
i Other manufacturing industries	...	...	13.06	...	...	15.40	...	...	16.64
4 Electricity, gas and water	...	...	15.39	...	...	16.24	...	...	18.29
a Electricity, gas and steam	...	...	14.28	...	...	14.97	...	...	16.80
b Water works and supply	...	...	1.11	...	...	1.27	...	...	1.49
5 Construction	125.90	77.88	48.02	128.63	82.26	46.37	145.86	92.07	53.79
6 Wholesale and retail trade, restaurants and hotels	...	...	117.16	...	...	132.40	...	...	165.94
a Wholesale and retail trade	...	...	109.11	...	...	123.35	...	...	154.58
b Restaurants and hotels	...	...	8.05	...	...	9.05	...	...	11.36
7 Transport, storage and communication	...	...	51.80	...	...	56.24	...	...	65.58
a Transport and storage	...	...	44.81	...	...	48.64	...	...	56.57
b Communication	...	...	6.99	...	...	7.60	...	...	9.01
8 Finance, insurance, real estate and business services	...	...	57.48	...	...	64.01	...	...	71.64
a Financial institutions	...	...	18.91	...	...	21.83	...	...	25.48
b Insurance	...	...	6.79	...	...	7.09	...	...	7.18
c Real estate and business services	...	...	31.78	...	...	35.09	...	...	38.98
Real estate, except dwellings [a]	...	...	3.42	...	...	3.95	...	...	4.75

India

4.3 Derivation of Value Added by Kind of Activity, ISIC Divisions, in Current Prices
(Continued)

Fiscal year beginning 1 April

Thousand Million Indian rupees

	1978 Gross Output	1978 Intermediate Consumption	1978 Value Added	1979 Gross Output	1979 Intermediate Consumption	1979 Value Added	1980 Gross Output	1980 Intermediate Consumption	1980 Value Added
Dwellings	...	...	28.36	...	...	31.14	...	...	34.23
9 Community, social and personal services	...	...	44.17	...	...	49.77	...	...	56.81
a Sanitary and similar services	...	...	2.13	...	...	2.79	...	...	3.30
b Social and related community services	...	...	42.04	...	...	46.98	...	...	53.51
c Recreational and cultural services	...	...	...	...	...	...	...	...	...
d Personal and household services	...	...	...	...	...	...	...	...	...
Total, industries	...	...	828.38	...	...	894.11	...	...	1066.39
Producers of Government Services	...	...	40.72	...	...	45.72	...	...	54.48
Other Producers	...	...	...	...	...	...	...	...	...
Total	...	...	869.10	...	...	939.83	...	...	1120.87
Imputed bank service charge	...	...	...	...	...	...	...	...	...
Import duties	...	...	...	...	...	...	...	...	...
Value added tax	...	...	...	...	...	...	...	...	...
Other adjustments	...	...	105.34	...	...	121.68	...	...	135.88
Total	...	...	974.44	...	...	1061.51	...	...	1256.75

a) Including also business services.

4.4 Derivation of Value Added by Kind of Activity, ISIC Divisions, in Constant Prices

Fiscal year beginning 1 April

Thousand Million Indian rupees

	1970 Gross Output	1970 Intermediate Consumption	1970 Value Added	1971 Gross Output	1971 Intermediate Consumption	1971 Value Added	1972 Gross Output	1972 Intermediate Consumption	1972 Value Added	1973 Gross Output	1973 Intermediate Consumption	1973 Value Added
At constant prices of: 1970 — All Producers												
1 Agriculture, hunting, forestry and fishing	214.09	39.85	174.24	215.15	41.76	173.39	204.10	41.26	162.84	217.66	42.83	174.83
a Agriculture and hunting	...	...	167.78	...	...	166.61	...	...	156.01	...	...	168.05
b Forestry and logging	...	...	4.01	...	...	4.18	...	...	4.15	...	...	4.03
c Fishing	...	...	2.45	...	...	2.60	...	...	2.68	...	...	2.75
2 Mining and quarrying	4.71	0.93	3.78	4.81	0.96	3.85	5.05	0.99	4.06	5.08	0.96	4.12
a Coal mining	...	...	2.15	...	...	2.13	...	...	2.26	...	...	2.30
b Crude petroleum and natural gas production	...	...	0.47	...	...	0.51	...	...	0.51	...	...	0.50
c Metal ore mining	...	...	0.51	...	...	0.56	...	...	0.58	...	...	0.61
d Other mining	...	...	0.65	...	...	0.65	...	...	0.71	...	...	0.71
3 Manufacturing	...	...	52.23	...	...	53.67	...	...	55.90	...	...	58.61
a Manufacture of food, beverages and tobacco	...	...	7.04	...	...	6.50	...	...	6.67	...	...	6.08
b Textile, wearing apparel and leather industries	...	...	11.99	...	...	12.18	...	...	13.12	...	...	14.61
c Manufacture of wood and wood products, including furniture	...	...	2.62	...	...	2.72	...	...	2.83	...	...	2.65
d Manufacture of paper and paper products, printing and publishing	...	...	2.23	...	...	2.11	...	...	2.15	...	...	2.30
e Manufacture of chemicals and chemical petroleum, coal, rubber and plastic products	...	...	6.79	...	...	7.74	...	...	7.90	...	...	8.17
f Manufacture of non-metallic mineral products, except products of petroleum and coal	...	...	2.28	...	...	2.36	...	...	2.45	...	...	2.47
g Basic metal industries	...	...	3.95	...	...	3.96	...	...	3.35	...	...	3.95
h Manufacture of fabricated metal products, machinery and equipment	...	...	10.79	...	...	11.72	...	...	12.80	...	...	13.04
i Other manufacturing industries	...	...	4.54	...	...	4.38	...	...	4.63	...	...	5.34
4 Electricity, gas and water	...	...	4.19	...	...	4.51	...	...	4.72	...	...	4.85
a Electricity, gas and steam	...	...	3.90	...	...	4.20	...	...	4.39	...	...	4.49
b Water works and supply	...	...	0.29	...	...	0.31	...	...	0.33	...	...	0.36

India

4.4 Derivation of Value Added by Kind of Activity, ISIC Divisions, in Constant Prices
(Continued)

Thousand Million Indian rupees — Fiscal year beginning 1 April

	1970 Gross Output	1970 Intermediate Consumption	1970 Value Added	1971 Gross Output	1971 Intermediate Consumption	1971 Value Added	1972 Gross Output	1972 Intermediate Consumption	1972 Value Added	1973 Gross Output	1973 Intermediate Consumption	1973 Value Added
				At constant prices of: 1970								
5 Construction	47.51	27.99	19.52	48.03	28.29	19.74	48.79	28.74	20.05	44.75	26.36	18.39
6 Wholesale and retail trade, restaurants and hotels	...	...	40.43	...	...	41.22	...	...	41.38	...	...	43.13
a Wholesale and retail trade	...	...	37.57	...	...	38.30	...	...	38.45	...	...	40.07
b Restaurants and hotels	...	...	2.86	...	...	2.92	...	...	2.93	...	...	3.06
7 Transport, storage and communication	...	...	18.69	...	...	19.45	...	...	20.77	...	...	21.42
a Transport and storage	...	...	16.31	...	...	16.93	...	...	18.11	...	...	18.57
b Communication	...	...	2.38	...	...	2.52	...	...	2.66	...	...	2.85
8 Finance, insurance, real estate and business services	...	...	21.14	...	...	22.21	...	...	23.03	...	...	23.49
a Financial institutions	...	...	4.39	...	...	4.87	...	...	5.33	...	...	5.31
b Insurance	...	...	2.17	...	...	2.39	...	...	2.42	...	...	2.48
c Real estate and business services	...	...	14.58	...	...	14.95	...	...	15.28	...	...	15.70
9 Community, social and personal services	...	...	16.79	...	...	17.24	...	...	17.72	...	...	17.82
a Sanitary and similar services	...	...	0.75	...	...	0.78	...	...	0.81	...	...	0.76
b Social and related community services	...	...	16.04	...	...	16.46	...	...	16.91	...	...	17.06
c Recreational and cultural services	...	...	...	...	...	...	...	...	...	...	...	...
d Personal and household services	...	...	...	...	...	...	...	...	...	...	...	...
Total, Industries	...	...	351.01	...	...	355.28	...	...	350.47	...	...	366.66
Producers of Government Services	...	...	16.35	...	...	17.85	...	...	18.63	...	...	19.80
Other Producers	...	...	...	...	...	...	...	...	...	...	...	...
Total	...	...	367.36	...	...	373.13	...	...	369.10	...	...	386.46
Imputed bank service charge	...	...	...	...	...	...	...	...	...	...	...	...
Import duties	...	...	...	...	...	...	...	...	...	...	...	...
Value added tax	...	...	...	...	...	...	...	...	...	...	...	...
Other adjustments	...	...	35.27	...	...	38.83	...	...	39.91	...	...	37.24
Total	...	...	402.63	...	...	411.96	...	...	409.01	...	...	423.70

	1974 Gross Output	1974 Intermediate Consumption	1974 Value Added	1975 Gross Output	1975 Intermediate Consumption	1975 Value Added	1976 Gross Output	1976 Intermediate Consumption	1976 Value Added	1977 Gross Output	1977 Intermediate Consumption	1977 Value Added
				At constant prices of: 1970								
				All Producers								
1 Agriculture, hunting, forestry and fishing	216.07	44.38	171.69	240.20	46.71	193.49	229.80	48.42	181.38	254.19	50.43	203.76
a Agriculture and hunting	...	...	164.62	...	...	186.13	...	...	173.96	...	...	196.55
b Forestry and logging	...	...	4.11	...	...	4.22	...	...	4.38	...	...	4.17
c Fishing	...	...	2.96	...	...	3.14	...	...	3.04	...	...	3.04
2 Mining and quarrying	5.56	1.26	4.30	6.18	1.38	4.80	6.50	1.52	4.98	6.64	1.52	5.12
a Coal mining	...	...	2.35	...	...	2.65	...	...	2.65	...	...	2.64
b Crude petroleum and natural gas production	...	...	0.61	...	...	0.69	...	...	0.73	...	...	0.88
c Metal ore mining	...	...	0.69	...	...	0.78	...	...	0.86	...	...	0.83
d Other mining	...	...	0.65	...	...	0.68	...	...	0.74	...	...	0.77

India

4.4 Derivation of Value Added by Kind of Activity, ISIC Divisions, in Constant Prices
(Continued)

Thousand Million Indian rupees — Fiscal year beginning 1 April

	1974 Gross Output	1974 Intermediate Consumption	1974 Value Added	1975 Gross Output	1975 Intermediate Consumption	1975 Value Added	1976 Gross Output	1976 Intermediate Consumption	1976 Value Added	1977 Gross Output	1977 Intermediate Consumption	1977 Value Added
						At constant prices of: 1970						
3 Manufacturing	...	...	59.99	...	...	61.28	...	...	66.90	...	...	71.34
a Manufacture of food, beverages and tobacco	...	...	6.70	...	...	7.61	...	...	8.24	...	...	9.10
b Textile, wearing apparel and leather industries	...	...	15.11	...	...	15.07	...	...	15.34	...	...	16.18
c Manufacture of wood and wood products, including furniture	...	...	3.08	...	...	3.13	...	...	3.26	...	...	3.13
d Manufacture of paper and paper products, printing and publishing	...	...	2.33	...	...	2.32	...	...	2.44	...	...	2.59
e Manufacture of chemicals and chemical petroleum, coal, rubber and plastic products	...	...	7.89	...	...	7.99	...	...	9.24	...	...	10.36
f Manufacture of non-metallic mineral products, except products of petroleum and coal	...	...	2.57	...	...	2.70	...	...	2.97	...	...	3.30
g Basic metal industries	...	...	4.51	...	...	4.61	...	...	5.00	...	...	5.07
h Manufacture of fabricated metal products, machinery and equipment	...	...	12.89	...	...	12.83	...	...	14.58	...	...	15.28
i Other manufacturing industries	...	...	4.91	...	...	5.02	...	...	5.83	...	...	6.33
4 Electricity, gas and water	...	...	5.07	...	...	5.77	...	...	6.38	...	...	6.63
a Electricity, gas and steam	...	...	4.71	...	...	5.40	...	...	5.97	...	...	6.20
b Water works and supply	...	...	0.36	...	...	0.37	...	...	0.41	...	...	0.43
5 Construction	43.09	25.38	17.71	49.33	29.06	20.27	55.23	32.54	22.69	60.69	35.76	24.93
6 Wholesale and retail trade, restaurants and hotels	...	...	45.09	...	...	49.32	...	...	52.51	...	...	55.68
a Wholesale and retail trade	...	...	41.90	...	...	45.82	...	...	48.77	...	...	51.72
b Restaurants and hotels	...	...	3.19	...	...	3.50	...	...	3.74	...	...	3.96
7 Transport, storage and communication	...	...	23.25	...	...	25.29	...	...	26.96	...	...	28.00
a Transport and storage	...	...	20.27	...	...	22.10	...	...	23.51	...	...	24.35
b Communication	...	...	2.98	...	...	3.19	...	...	3.45	...	...	3.65
8 Finance, insurance, real estate and business services	...	...	23.23	...	...	25.01	...	...	27.24	...	...	28.99
a Financial institutions	...	...	4.91	...	...	5.94	...	...	7.13	...	...	8.37
b Insurance	...	...	2.18	...	...	2.49	...	...	3.00	...	...	2.95
c Real estate and business services	...	...	16.14	...	...	16.58	...	...	17.11	...	...	17.67
9 Community, social and personal services	...	...	18.60	...	...	19.01	...	...	19.34	...	...	19.68
a Sanitary and similar services	...	...	0.84	...	...	0.85	...	...	0.86	...	...	0.91
b Social and related community services	...	...	17.76	...	...	18.16	...	...	18.48	...	...	18.77
c Recreational and cultural services	...	...	...	...	...	...	...	...	...	...	...	...
d Personal and household services	...	...	...	...	...	...	...	...	...	...	...	...
Total, Industries	...	...	368.93	...	...	404.24	...	...	408.38	...	...	444.13
Producers of Government Services	...	...	20.86	...	...	22.38	...	...	23.70	...	...	25.35
Other Producers	...	...	...	...	...	...	...	...	...	...	...	...
Total	...	...	389.79	...	...	426.62	...	...	432.08	...	...	469.48
Imputed bank service charge	...	...	...	...	...	...	...	...	...	...	...	...
Import duties	...	...	...	...	...	...	...	...	...	...	...	...
Value added tax	...	...	...	...	...	...	...	...	...	...	...	...
Other adjustments	...	...	34.58	...	...	39.12	...	...	42.38	...	...	42.38
Total	...	...	424.37	...	...	465.74	...	...	474.46	...	...	511.86

	1978 Gross Output	1978 Intermediate Consumption	1978 Value Added	1979 Gross Output	1979 Intermediate Consumption	1979 Value Added	1980 Gross Output	1980 Intermediate Consumption	1980 Value Added
			At constant prices of: 1970 — All Producers						
1 Agriculture, hunting, forestry and fishing	259.66	52.26	207.40	234.23	52.79	181.44	257.45	53.60	203.85
a Agriculture and hunting	...	...	199.69	...	...	174.31	...	...	196.65
b Forestry and logging	...	...	4.54	...	...	4.14	...	...	4.12
c Fishing	...	...	3.17	...	...	2.99	...	...	3.08

India

4.4 Derivation of Value Added by Kind of Activity, ISIC Divisions, in Constant Prices
(Continued)

Thousand Million Indian rupees — Fiscal year beginning 1 April

At constant prices of: 1970

	1978 Gross Output	1978 Intermediate Consumption	1978 Value Added	1979 Gross Output	1979 Intermediate Consumption	1979 Value Added	1980 Gross Output	1980 Intermediate Consumption	1980 Value Added
2 Mining and quarrying	6.82	1.61	5.21	6.94	1.63	5.31	7.22	1.77	5.45
a Coal mining	...	...	2.57	...	...	2.60	...	...	2.87
b Crude petroleum and natural gas production	...	...	0.95	...	...	0.98	...	...	0.81
c Metal ore mining	...	...	0.74	...	...	0.79	...	...	0.82
d Other mining	...	...	0.95	...	...	0.94	...	...	0.95
3 Manufacturing	...	...	79.21	...	...	79.04	...	...	81.38
a Manufacture of food, beverages and tobacco	...	...	9.83	...	...	8.67	...	...	9.60
b Textile, wearing apparel and leather industries	...	...	18.74	...	...	20.12	...	...	20.93
c Manufacture of wood and wood products, including furniture	...	...	3.39	...	...	3.16	...	...	3.05
d Manufacture of paper and paper products, printing and publishing	...	...	2.83	...	...	2.91	...	...	2.87
e Manufacture of chemicals and chemical petroleum, coal, rubber and plastic products	...	...	11.77	...	...	11.69	...	...	11.68
f Manufacture of non-metallic mineral products, except products of petroleum and coal	...	...	3.30	...	...	3.35	...	...	3.47
g Basic metal industries	...	...	5.53	...	...	5.31	...	...	5.32
h Manufacture of fabricated metal products, machinery and equipment	...	...	16.71	...	...	16.56	...	...	17.28
i Other manufacturing industries	...	...	7.11	...	...	7.27	...	...	7.18
4 Electricity, gas and water	...	...	7.37	...	...	7.53	...	...	7.92
a Electricity, gas and steam	...	...	6.92	...	...	7.06	...	...	7.45
b Water works and supply	...	...	0.45	...	...	0.47	...	...	0.47
5 Construction	61.08	35.99	25.09	54.43	32.07	22.36	53.96	31.79	22.17
6 Wholesale and retail trade, restaurants and hotels	...	...	60.36	...	...	58.41	...	...	61.31
a Wholesale and retail trade	...	...	56.07	...	...	54.26	...	...	56.96
b Restaurants and hotels	...	...	4.29	...	...	4.15	...	...	4.35
7 Transport, storage and communication	...	...	29.56	...	...	31.06	...	...	32.97
a Transport and storage	...	...	25.65	...	...	26.82	...	...	28.42
b Communication	...	...	3.91	...	...	4.24	...	...	4.55
8 Finance, insurance, real estate and business services	...	...	31.46	...	...	31.73	...	...	32.45
a Financial institutions	...	...	10.08	...	...	10.22	...	...	10.51
b Insurance	...	...	3.13	...	...	2.78	...	...	2.72
c Real estate and business services	...	...	18.25	...	...	18.73	...	...	19.22
9 Community, social and personal services	...	...	20.18	...	...	21.30	...	...	22.37
a Sanitary and similar services	...	...	0.94	...	...	0.94	...	...	0.96
b Social and related community services	...	...	19.24	...	...	20.36	...	...	21.41
c Recreational and cultural services	...	...	...	...	...	...	...	...	...
d Personal and household services	...	...	...	...	...	...	...	...	...
Total, Industries	...	...	465.84	...	...	438.18	...	...	469.87
Producers of Government Services	...	...	28.19	...	...	31.30	...	...	35.02
Other Producers	...	...	...	...	...	...	...	...	...
Total	...	...	494.03	...	...	469.48	...	...	504.89
Imputed bank service charge	...	...	...	...	...	...	...	...	...
Import duties	...	...	...	...	...	...	...	...	...
Value added tax	...	...	...	...	...	...	...	...	...
Other adjustments	...	...	49.75	...	...	48.42	...	...	46.86
Total	...	...	543.78	...	...	517.90	...	...	551.75

India

4.6 Cost Components of Value Added, ISIC Divisions

Thousand Million Indian rupees — *Fiscal year beginning 1 April*

1970 / 1971

	Compensation of Employees	Capital Consumption	Net Operating Surplus	Indirect Taxes	Less: Subsidies Received	Value Added	Compensation of Employees	Capital Consumption	Net Operating Surplus	Indirect Taxes	Less: Subsidies Received	Value Added
					All Producers							
1 Agriculture, hunting, forestry and fishing	157.68	4.44	12.12	...	...	174.24	162.21	4.88	13.74	...	...	180.83
2 Mining and quarrying	1.91	0.51	1.36	...	...	3.78	1.97	0.56	1.43	...	...	3.96
3 Manufacturing	34.41	6.04	11.78	...	...	52.23	38.46	6.60	12.43	...	...	57.49
4 Electricity, gas and water	1.25	1.01	1.93	...	...	4.19	1.46	1.15	1.95	...	...	4.56
5 Construction	16.51	0.99	2.02	...	...	19.52	17.67	1.08	2.67	...	...	21.42
6 Wholesale and retail trade, restaurants and hotels	33.45	1.63	5.35	...	...	40.43	35.36	1.74	6.82	...	...	43.92
7 Transport, storage and communication	12.17	2.95	3.57	...	...	18.69	13.21	2.98	4.04	...	...	20.23
8 Finance, insurance, real estate and business services	4.77	4.31	12.06	...	...	21.14	5.53	4.69	13.28	...	...	23.50
9 Community, social and personal services	16.25	0.29	0.25	...	...	16.79	17.79	0.31	0.31	...	...	18.41
Total, Industries [a]	278.40	22.17	50.44	...	...	351.01	293.66	23.99	56.67	...	...	374.32
Producers of Government Services	16.35	...	...	...	...	16.35	18.31	...	...	...	...	18.31
Other Producers	...	...	...	...	...	...	...	...	...	...	...	...
Total	294.75	22.17	50.44	...	...	367.36	311.97	23.99	56.67	...	...	392.63
Imputed bank service charge	...	...	...	...	...	...	...	...	...	...	...	...
Import duties	...	...	...	...	...	...	...	...	...	...	...	...
Value added tax	...	...	...	...	...	...	...	...	...	...	...	...
Other adjustments	...	...	...	...	...	35.27	...	...	...	...	...	40.93
Total	...	...	...	...	...	402.63	...	...	...	...	...	433.56

1972 / 1973

	Compensation of Employees	Capital Consumption	Net Operating Surplus	Indirect Taxes	Less: Subsidies Received	Value Added	Compensation of Employees	Capital Consumption	Net Operating Surplus	Indirect Taxes	Less: Subsidies Received	Value Added
					All Producers							
1 Agriculture, hunting, forestry and fishing	178.84	5.50	15.01	...	...	199.35	246.21	6.26	15.41	...	...	267.88
2 Mining and quarrying	2.25	0.62	1.40	...	...	4.27	2.90	0.70	1.27	...	...	4.87
3 Manufacturing	42.67	7.24	13.84	...	...	63.75	50.06	7.81	17.85	...	...	75.72
4 Electricity, gas and water	1.66	1.21	2.04	...	...	4.91	2.02	1.29	1.94	...	...	5.25
5 Construction	19.57	1.17	2.42	...	...	23.16	19.17	1.22	3.66	...	...	24.05
6 Wholesale and retail trade, restaurants and hotels	37.26	1.92	9.43	...	...	48.61	48.69	2.38	9.18	...	...	60.25
7 Transport, storage and communication	15.09	3.55	3.68	...	...	22.32	17.70	4.06	3.14	...	...	24.90
8 Finance, insurance, real estate and business services	6.40	5.14	14.57	...	...	26.11	7.90	6.13	16.07	...	...	30.10
9 Community, social and personal services	19.49	0.34	0.34	...	...	20.17	21.73	0.38	0.38	...	...	22.49
Total, Industries [a]	323.23	26.69	62.73	...	...	412.65	416.38	30.23	68.90	...	...	515.51
Producers of Government Services	19.76	...	...	...	...	19.76	22.21	...	...	...	...	22.21
Other Producers	...	...	...	...	...	...	...	...	...	...	...	...
Total	342.99	26.69	62.73	...	...	432.41	438.59	30.23	68.90	...	...	537.72
Imputed bank service charge	...	...	...	...	...	...	...	...	...	...	...	...
Import duties	...	...	...	...	...	...	...	...	...	...	...	...
Value added tax	...	...	...	...	...	...	...	...	...	...	...	...
Other adjustments	...	...	...	...	...	46.24	...	...	...	...	...	51.68
Total	...	...	...	...	...	478.65	...	...	...	...	...	589.40

1974 / 1975

	Compensation of Employees	Capital Consumption	Net Operating Surplus	Indirect Taxes	Less: Subsidies Received	Value Added	Compensation of Employees	Capital Consumption	Net Operating Surplus	Indirect Taxes	Less: Subsidies Received	Value Added
					All Producers							
1 Agriculture, hunting, forestry and fishing	264.73	7.63	18.09	...	...	290.45	248.30	8.77	21.38	...	...	278.45
2 Mining and quarrying	4.56	0.88	1.51	...	...	6.95	5.52	1.20	2.12	...	...	8.84
3 Manufacturing	62.68	8.77	27.13	...	...	98.58	68.43	9.73	25.59	...	...	103.75
4 Electricity, gas and water	2.71	1.52	2.52	...	...	6.75	3.20	1.84	3.31	...	...	8.35

India

4.6 Cost Components of Value Added, ISIC Divisions
(Continued)

Thousand Million Indian rupees — Fiscal year beginning 1 April

	1974 Compensation of Employees	Capital Consumption	Net Operating Surplus	Indirect Taxes	Less: Subsidies Received	Value Added	1975 Compensation of Employees	Capital Consumption	Net Operating Surplus	Indirect Taxes	Less: Subsidies Received	Value Added
5 Construction	22.01	1.33	3.03	...	...	26.37	27.53	1.67	3.73	...	...	32.93
6 Wholesale and retail trade, restaurants and hotels	66.92	2.91	11.22	...	...	81.05	75.74	3.58	12.76	...	...	92.08
7 Transport, storage and communication	22.91	4.07	4.36	...	...	31.34	25.31	4.67	5.26	...	...	35.24
8 Finance, insurance, real estate and business services	9.92	7.69	17.62	...	...	35.23	11.49	8.49	21.20	...	...	41.18
9 Community, social and personal services	26.45	0.46	0.44	...	...	27.35	29.55	0.51	0.45	...	...	30.51
Total, Industries [a]	482.89	35.26	85.92	...	...	604.07	495.07	40.46	95.80	...	...	631.33
Producers of Government Services	28.56	...	...	...	...	28.56	32.37	...	...	...	...	32.37
Other Producers	...	...	...	...	...	...	...	...	...	...	...	...
Total	511.45	35.26	85.92	...	...	632.63	527.44	40.46	95.80	...	...	663.70
Imputed bank service charge	...	...	...	...	...	...	...	...	...	...	...	...
Import duties	...	...	...	...	...	...	...	...	...	...	...	...
Value added tax	...	...	...	...	...	...	...	...	...	...	...	...
Other adjustments	...	...	...	...	...	63.32	...	...	...	...	...	77.14
Total	...	...	...	...	...	695.95	...	...	...	...	...	740.84

	1976 Compensation of Employees	Capital Consumption	Net Operating Surplus	Indirect Taxes	Less: Subsidies Received	Value Added	1977 Compensation of Employees	Capital Consumption	Net Operating Surplus	Indirect Taxes	Less: Subsidies Received	Value Added
					All Producers							
1 Agriculture, hunting, forestry and fishing	252.04	9.55	25.65	...	...	287.24	291.58	10.30	27.82	...	...	329.70
2 Mining and quarrying	5.85	1.59	2.67	...	...	10.11	6.76	1.94	2.47	...	...	11.17
3 Manufacturing	71.88	11.01	32.67	...	...	115.56	83.04	12.72	33.27	...	...	129.03
4 Electricity, gas and water	3.98	2.06	4.91	...	...	10.95	4.83	2.36	5.29	...	...	12.48
5 Construction	33.02	1.99	4.28	...	...	39.29	37.07	2.28	5.73	...	...	45.08
6 Wholesale and retail trade, restaurants and hotels	81.00	3.74	11.77	...	...	96.51	94.16	4.28	12.00	...	...	110.44
7 Transport, storage and communication	27.54	5.28	8.80	...	...	41.62	30.50	5.81	9.10	...	...	45.41
8 Finance, insurance, real estate and business services	11.96	9.11	26.17	...	...	47.24	13.61	9.76	28.93	...	...	52.30
9 Community, social and personal services	33.97	0.59	0.47	...	...	35.03	38.10	0.66	0.48	...	...	39.24
Total, Industries [a]	521.24	44.92	117.39	...	...	683.55	599.65	50.11	125.09	...	...	774.85
Producers of Government Services	35.53	...	...	...	...	34.53	36.94	...	...	...	...	36.94
Other Producers	...	...	...	...	...	...	...	...	...	...	...	...
Total	555.77	44.92	117.39	...	...	718.08	636.59	50.11	125.09	...	...	811.79
Imputed bank service charge	...	...	...	...	...	...	...	...	...	...	...	...
Import duties	...	...	...	...	...	...	...	...	...	...	...	...
Value added tax	...	...	...	...	...	...	...	...	...	...	...	...
Other adjustments	...	...	...	...	...	85.33	...	...	...	...	...	89.17
Total	...	...	...	...	...	803.41	...	...	...	...	...	900.96

	1978 Compensation of Employees	Capital Consumption	Net Operating Surplus	Indirect Taxes	Less: Subsidies Received	Value Added	1979 Compensation of Employees	Capital Consumption	Net Operating Surplus	Indirect Taxes	Less: Subsidies Received	Value Added
					All Producers							
1 Agriculture, hunting, forestry and fishing	291.18	11.91	30.57	...	...	333.66	293.30	14.36	32.31	...	...	339.97
2 Mining and quarrying	8.19	2.12	2.01	...	...	12.32	9.31	2.28	3.77	...	...	15.36
3 Manufacturing	88.32	15.32	44.74	...	...	148.38	103.07	18.77	51.91	...	...	173.75
4 Electricity, gas and water	6.12	2.59	6.68	...	...	15.39	6.44	2.86	6.94	...	...	16.24
5 Construction	40.04	2.43	5.55	...	...	48.02	38.67	2.35	5.35	...	...	46.37
6 Wholesale and retail trade, restaurants and hotels	100.36	4.53	12.27	...	...	117.16	114.56	5.11	12.73	...	...	132.40
7 Transport, storage and communication	35.38	7.07	9.35	...	...	51.80	38.11	8.36	9.77	...	...	56.24
8 Finance, insurance, real estate and business services	15.60	10.91	30.97	...	...	57.48	18.48	13.07	32.46	...	...	64.01
9 Community, social and personal services	42.94	0.74	0.49	...	...	44.17	48.43	0.83	0.51	...	...	49.77
Total, Industries [a]	628.13	57.62	142.63	...	...	828.38	670.37	67.99	155.75	...	...	894.11
Producers of Government Services	40.72	...	...	...	...	40.72	45.72	...	...	...	...	45.72

India

4.6 Cost Components of Value Added, ISIC Divisions
(Continued)

Thousand Million Indian rupees
Fiscal year beginning 1 April

	1978							1979						
	Compensation of Employees	Capital Consumption	Net Operating Surplus	Indirect Taxes	Less: Subsidies Received	Value Added	Compensation of Employees	Capital Consumption	Net Operating Surplus	Indirect Taxes	Less: Subsidies Received	Value Added
Other Producers	...	...	...	...	...	...	...	...	...	...	...	...
Total	668.85	57.62	142.63	...	...	869.10	716.09	67.99	155.75	...	...	939.83
Imputed bank service charge	...	...	...	...	...		...	...	...	...	...	
Import duties	...	...	...	...	...		...	...	...	...	...	
Value added tax	...	...	...	...	...		...	...	...	...	...	
Other adjustments						105.34						121.68
Total	...	...	...	...	...	974.44	...	...	...	...	...	1061.51

	1980					
	Compensation of Employees	Capital Consumption	Net Operating Surplus	Indirect Taxes	Less: Subsidies Received	Value Added
			All Producers			
1 Agriculture, hunting, forestry and fishing	...	...	...	...	...	417.28
2 Mining and quarrying	...	...	...	...	...	17.18
3 Manufacturing	...	...	...	...	...	199.88
4 Electricity, gas and water	...	...	...	...	...	18.29
5 Construction	...	...	...	...	...	53.79
6 Wholesale and retail trade, restaurants and hotels	...	...	...	...	...	165.94
7 Transport, storage and communication	...	...	...	...	...	65.58
8 Finance, insurance, real estate and business services	...	...	...	...	...	71.64
9 Community, social and personal services	...	...	...	...	...	56.81
Total, Industries [a]	...	...	...	...	...	1066.39
Producers of Government Services	...	...	...	...	...	54.48
Other Producers	...	...	...	...	...	...
Total	...	...	...	...	...	1120.87
Imputed bank service charge	...	...	...	...	...	...
Import duties	...	...	...	...	...	...
Value added tax	...	...	...	...	...	...
Other adjustments	...	...	...	...	...	135.88
Total	...	...	...	...	...	1256.75

a) Including mixed income of self-employed of unincorporated enterprises consisting of own-account workers.

Indonesia

General note. The preparation of national accounts statistics in Indonesia is undertaken by the Central Bureau of Statistics, Jakarta. The official estimates are generally in accordance with the United Nations System of National Accounts (SNA). The Indonesian Input-output tables were published in 1976 and 1980 for the year 1971 and 1975 respectively, with the title 'Table Input-output Indonesia 1971' and 'Table Input-output Indonesia 1975'. The following tables are prepared for the United Nation's national accounts questionnaire. Whenever the scope and coverage of the estimates differ from those recommended in the SNA, a footnote is indicated to the relevant tables.

Sources and methods:

(a) Gross domestic product. Gross domestic product is estimated mainly through the production approach.

(b) Expenditure on the gross domestic product. The expenditure approach is used to estimate government final consumption expenditure, exports and imports of goods and services. Private final consumption expenditure is derived as residual. The commodity-flow approach is used for gross fixed capital formation. The main sources of data for the estimation of central government consumption expenditure are the budgetary accounts of the Department of Finance, while local governments provide data directly to the Central Bureau of Statistics (CBS). Bench-mark data for capital formation are based on statistics of imports and domestic production of construction materials and machinery and equipment. For other years, import of machineries and equipments are obtained from import statistics, while domestic production is compiled by using production and implicit price indexes to extrapolate the bench-mark estimates. The input-output ratios for buildings and structures have been established for 1971 on the basis of special surveys on construction projects in that year. Other years' estimates are extrapolated by quantity and price indexes of domestic production and imports of construction materials. Estimates of exports and imports of goods and services are obtained from foreign trade and balance of payment statistics. For the constant price estimates, current values of government expenditure items are deflated by the consumer price index and by the wholesale price index. For gross fixed capital formation referring to buildings and structures, the bench-mark values are extrapolated by quantity indicators of domestic production and volume indicators of imports of construction materials. Values of exports and imports are deflated by the corresponding unit value price indexes.

(c) Cost-structure of the gross domestic product. Consumption of fixed capital for manufacturing, electricity, gas and water, is estimated from information available at the CBS. For other sectors the estimates are based on the results of special surveys. The main source of data for net indirect taxes are the budgetary accounts of the central and local governments. Compensation of employees together with operating surplus is obtained as a residual.

(d) Gross domestic product by kind of economic activity. The table on gross domestic product by kind of economic activity is prepared at market prices, i.e. producers' values. The production approach is used to estimate value-added of most of the industries. The income approach is used for government and domestic services while gross output of trade and construction is estimated on the basis of the commodity-flow approach. For agriculture, main food crops production is compiled on the basis of information relating to area harvested and average yield for each crop obtained from the CBS. The prices used are based on farm-gate prices obtained from annual surveys. The consumption of vegetables by households is based on per capita consumption estimates derived from the Household Survey 1969/79 and 1976, extrapolated by population and price changes and adding 1 per cent to cover consumption outside households. For main food crops, commercial and estate crops, the value of intermediate inputs is based on cost-structure surveys. Estimates of livestock, forestry, and fishing are obtained from the departments concerned. For livestock, intermediate inputs are calculated as fixed percentages of gross output. The most important mining commodity is crude petroleum for which production data are available for all enterprises concerned. Estimates of prices and input costs are compiled on the basis of returns furnished by the largest firm. For the base-year 1971, data on output and input structure of manufacturing have been compiled for each industry group from statistics maintained by the CBS and from surveys and other studies undertaken. For other years industrial production indexes are compiled on the basis of output of selected manufactured products. For gross output of construction, the information on imports of construction materials is obtained from commodity imports statistics whereas estimates of domestically produced materials are based on the annual industrial surveys. The average ratios of intermediate inputs to gross output are based on data gathered from surveys. Gross output of the trade sector is calculated by multiplying estimates of the producers' values of the marketed surplus of agricultural products, domestically produced manufactured goods, selected mining and quarrying products and the cost of imported goods by the percentage distribution mark-ups gathered from special surveys undertaken in 1971. Estimates for other years are extrapolated by a quantity index of marketed surplus traded and an implicit price index. For railway transport, the annual reports of the State Railway Company constitute the main source of data for estimating gross output, intermediate input and value added. For road transport, gross output and input values are estimated by multiplying the average earning of each type of vehicle by the corresponding number of vehicles. For other transports, estimates are based on cost-structure surveys and data from concerned authorities and companies. The information of gross output and value added of the banking sector is based on the data compiled annually by the Bank of Indonesia supplemented by special inquiries for other financial intermediaries. Basic data relating to real estate and business services are limited and rough procedures are adopted by using information gathered from the special surveys. For government services, estimates are obtained from current budget expenditure and information furnished by local bodies. Estimates of other services are calculated for the year 1971 as the bench-mark year, and estimates of other years are extrapolated by using employment and price indicators. For the constant price estimates, revaluation is used for the agricultural sector, while value added of public administration and defence, is deflated by a moving average of the consumer price index. In all other sectors value added is extrapolated by various quantity indicators and indexes.

1.1 Expenditure on the Gross Domestic Product, in Current Prices

Thousand Million Indonesian rupiahs

	1970	1971	1972	1973	1974	1975	1976	1977	1978	1979	1980
1 General government final consumption expenditure	293.0	341.0	414.0	716.0	841.0	1253.7	1590.5	2077.3	2658.9	3733.4	5565.1
2 Private final consumption expenditure	2590.0	2832.6	3401.6	4790.7	7258.6	8744.5	10463.8	12458.4	14899.7	18504.6	25045.3
3 Gross capital formation	455.0	580.0	857.0	1208.0	1797.0	2571.7	3204.9	3826.4	4670.7	6704.3	9485.2
a Increase in stocks	...	...	...	...	...	...	...	...	...	...	...
b Gross fixed capital formation	455.0	580.0	857.0	1208.0	1797.0	2571.7	3204.9	3826.4	4670.7	6704.3	9485.2
4 Exports of goods and services	429.0	529.5	753.8	1354.3	3105.1	2850.6	3429.6	4465.8	4787.8	9461.2	13353.1
5 Less: Imports of goods and services	529.0	611.1	862.4	1315.6	2293.7	2778.0	3222.1	3817.2	4558.8	7380.6	9683.7
Equals: Gross Domestic Product	3238.0	3672.0	4564.0	6753.4	10708.0	12642.5	15466.7	19010.7	22458.3	31022.9	43765.0

1.2 Expenditure on the Gross Domestic Product, in Constant Prices

Thousand Million Indonesian rupiahs

	1970	1971	1972	1973	1974	1975	1976	1977	1978	1979	1980
				At constant prices of: 1973							
1 General government final consumption expenditure	483.9	518.3	560.9	716.0	641.0	835.5	896.7	1044.4	1228.2	1345.0	1669.2
2 Private final consumption expenditure	3847.2	3998.4	4276.2	4790.7	5453.6	5678.9	6031.6	6433.2	6895.1	7581.2	8289.0
3 Gross capital formation	715.3	866.9	1032.0	1208.0	1440.0	1650.2	1749.2	2027.5	2332.9	2436.0	2868.5
a Increase in stocks	...	...	...	...	...	...	...	...	...	...	...
b Gross fixed capital formation	715.3	866.9	1032.0	1208.0	1440.0	1650.2	1749.2	2027.5	2332.9	2436.0	2868.5
4 Exports of goods and services	799.6	890.8	1123.4	1354.3	1403.4	1266.8	1425.2	1744.0	1776.3	1758.7	1684.9
5 Less: Imports of goods and services	664.0	729.7	925.3	1315.6	1669.0	1800.6	1946.4	2378.2	2749.2	3131.1	3557.7
Equals: Gross Domestic Product	5182.0	5544.7	6067.2	6753.4	7269.0	7630.8	8156.3	8870.9	9483.3	9989.8	10953.9

Indonesia

1.3 Cost Components of the Gross Domestic Product

Thousand Million Indonesian rupiahs

		1970	1971	1972	1973	1974	1975	1976	1977	1978	1979	1980
1	Indirect taxes, net	188.0	229.0	236.0	328.0	447.0	519.2	690.5	845.6	1028.9	1304.8	1606.5
2	Consumption of fixed capital	219.0	238.7	296.7	439.0	696.0	821.8	1006.3	1235.7	1459.8	2016.5	2844.7
3	Compensation of employees paid by resident producers to:	2831.0	3204.3	4031.3	5986.4	9565.0	11301.5	13769.9	16929.4	19969.6	27701.6	39313.8
4	Net operating surplus											
	Equals: Gross Domestic Product	3238.0	3672.0	4564.0	6753.4	10708.0	12642.5	15466.7	19010.7	22458.3	31022.9	43765.0

1.10 Gross Domestic Product by Kind of Activity, in Current Prices

Thousand Million Indonesian rupiahs

		1970	1971	1972	1973	1974	1975	1976	1977	1978	1979	1980
1	Agriculture, hunting, forestry and fishing	1575.0	1646.0	1837.0	2710.0	3497.0	4003.4	4812.0	5905.7	6706.0	8983.7	11252.5
2	Mining and quarrying	173.0	294.0	491.0	831.0	2374.0	2484.8	2930.0	3599.7	4357.6	6979.8	11672.5
3	Manufacturing	293.0	307.0	448.0	650.0	890.0	1123.7	1453.3	1816.9	2184.7	2614.4	3845.5
4	Electricity, gas and water	15.0	18.0	20.0	30.4	52.0	69.8	98.1	105.6	118.3	148.8	225.1
5	Construction	100.0	128.0	174.0	262.0	406.0	589.6	812.6	1023.3	1242.1	1789.7	2523.8
6	Wholesale and retail trade, restaurants and hotels [a]	536.0	592.0	769.0	1118.0	1775.0	2103.7	2551.9	2959.0	3450.2	4602.6	6167.5
7	Transport, storage and communication	96.0	162.0	182.0	257.0	442.0	521.2	662.6	820.6	979.6	1299.7	1706.1
8	Finance, insurance, real estate and business services	98.0	130.0	156.0	226.0	307.0	409.2	525.4	778.6	1066.2	1569.3	2231.6
9	Community, social and personal services [a]	169.0	181.0	197.0	264.0	380.0	472.8	546.5	607.1	668.2	835.3	995.8
	Total, Industries	3055.0	3458.0	4274.0	6348.4	10123.0	11778.2	14392.4	17616.5	20772.9	28823.3	40620.4
	Producers of Government Services	183.0	214.0	290.0	405.0	585.0	864.3	1074.3	1394.2	1685.4	2199.6	3144.6
	Other Producers	...	...	...	...	...	...	...	...	...	...	...
	Subtotal	3238.0	3672.0	4564.0	6753.4	10708.0	12642.5	15466.7	19010.7	22458.3	31022.9	43765.0
	Less: Imputed bank service charge	...	...	...	...	...	...	...	...	...	...	...
	Plus: Import duties	...	...	...	...	...	...	...	...	...	...	...
	Plus: Value added tax	...	...	...	...	...	...	...	...	...	...	...
	Equals: Gross Domestic Product	3238.0	3672.0	4564.0	6753.4	10708.0	12642.5	15466.7	19010.7	22458.3	31022.9	43765.0

a) Restaurants and hotels are included in item 'Community, social and personal services'.

1.11 Gross Domestic Product by Kind of Activity, in Constant Prices

Thousand Million Indonesian rupiahs

At constant prices of: 1973

		1970	1971	1972	1973	1974	1975	1976	1977	1978	1979	1980
1	Agriculture, hunting, forestry and fishing	2356.2	2441.0	2479.0	2710.0	2811.0	2811.2	2943.7	2981.3	3134.8	3259.9	3438.5
2	Mining and quarrying	521.8	551.0	674.0	831.0	859.0	828.1	952.3	1070.0	1048.8	1046.9	1034.6
3	Manufacturing	434.8	490.0	564.0	650.0	755.0	847.9	930.0	1057.7	1176.5	1295.1	1568.9
4	Electricity, gas and water	22.5	24.7	26.2	30.4	37.0	41.2	46.3	49.0	56.9	68.6	77.9
5	Construction	142.9	171.0	222.0	262.0	320.0	364.8	384.5	463.8	528.9	562.8	628.5
6	Wholesale and retail trade, restaurants and hotels [a]	846.7	924.0	1028.0	1118.0	1224.0	1293.8	1350.7	1438.2	1530.3	1620.3	1789.6
7	Transport, storage and communication	165.4	210.0	229.0	257.0	288.0	302.7	342.6	427.6	490.1	541.4	595.5
8	Finance, insurance, real estate and business services [b]	136.3	157.0	196.0	226.0	262.0	300.0	326.5	403.4	452.2	485.7	536.6
9	Community, social and personal services [ab]	243.7	250.0	256.0	264.0	270.0	277.0	284.2	290.1	296.9	304.0	311.3
	Total, Industries	4870.3	5218.7	5674.2	6348.4	6826.0	7066.7	7560.8	8181.1	8715.4	9184.7	9981.4
	Producers of Government Services	311.7	326.0	393.0	405.0	443.0	564.1	595.5	689.8	767.9	805.1	972.5
	Other Producers	...	...	...	...	...	...	...	...	...	...	...
	Subtotal	5182.0	5544.7	6067.2	6753.4	7269.0	7630.8	8156.3	8870.9	9483.3	9989.8	10953.9
	Less: Imputed bank service charge	...	...	...	...	...	...	...	...	...	...	...
	Plus: Import duties	...	...	...	...	...	...	...	...	...	...	...
	Plus: Value added tax	...	...	...	...	...	...	...	...	...	...	...
	Equals: Gross Domestic Product	5182.0	5544.7	6067.2	6753.4	7269.0	7630.8	8156.3	8870.9	9483.3	9989.8	10953.9

a) Restaurants and hotels are included in item 'Community, social and personal services'.
b) Business services are included in item 'Community, social and personal services'.

Indonesia

1.12 Relations Among National Accounting Aggregates

Thousand Million Indonesian rupiahs

	1970	1971	1972	1973	1974	1975	1976	1977	1978	1979	1980
Gross Domestic Product	3238.0	3672.0	4564.0	6753.4	10708.0	12642.5	15466.7	19010.7	22458.3	31022.9	43765.0
Plus: Net factor income received from abroad	-50.0	-66.7	-159.0	-245.7	-507.1	-555.7	-432.2	-678.5	-852.1	-1489.4	-2169.4
Equals: Gross National Product	3188.0	3605.3	4405.0	6507.7	10200.9	12086.8	15034.5	18332.2	21606.2	29533.5	41595.6
Less: Consumption of fixed capital	219.0	238.7	296.7	439.0	696.0	821.8	1006.3	1235.7	1459.8	2016.5	2844.7
Less: Net indirect taxes paid to supranational organisations	...	...	...	...	...	...	...	...	...	...	...
Equals: National Income at Market Prices	2969.0	3366.6	4108.3	6068.7	9504.9	11265.0	14028.2	17096.5	20146.4	27517.0	38750.9
Plus: Net current transfers received from abroad	...	...	...	...	...	...	...	...	...	...	...
Equals: National Disposable Income at Market Prices	...	...	...	...	...	...	...	...	...	...	...
Less: Final consumption	2883.0	3173.6	3815.6	5506.7	8099.6	9998.2	12054.3	14535.7	17558.6	22238.0	30610.4
Equals: Net Saving	...	...	...	...	...	...	...	...	...	...	...
Less: Surplus of the nation on current transactions	...	...	...	...	...	...	...	...	...	...	...
Equals: Net Capital Formation	...	...	...	...	...	...	...	...	...	...	...

Iran(Islamic Repub.of)

General note. The preparation of national accounts statistics in Iran is undertaken by the Economic Research Department, Bank Markazi Iran, Tehran. The offical estimates are published in 'National Income of Iran'. The following presentation of sources and methods is mainly based on the above-mentioned publication issued in 1969 and 1974. The estimates are generally in accordance with the classifications and definitions recommended in the United Nations System of National Accounts (SNA). Input-output tables have been published for the year 1965 in 'Input-output Tables for Iranian Economy'. The following tables have been prepared from successive replies to the United Nations national accounts questionnaire. When the scope and coverage of the estimates differ for conceptual or statistical reasons from the definitions and classifications recommended in SNA, a footnote is indicated to the relevant tables.

Sources and methods:

(a) Gross domestic product. GDP is estimated mainly through the production approach.

(b) Expenditure on the gross domestic product. The expenditure approach is used to estimate government final consumption expenditure, building and construction of gross fixed capital formation and exports and imports of goods and services. The commodity-flow approach is used to estimate machinery and equipment. The two approaches in combination are used to estimate private final consumption expenditure. Increase in stock is not estimated. Government consumption expenditure is obtained from government accounts. The classification of government expenditure is not fully adapted to national accounts requirements so it is necessary to reallocate items according to an allocation key set up for this purpose. Private consumption expenditure is estimated from the annual household budget surveys and by using the commodity-flow method. For many items, different estimates are yielded by the two approaches and efforts are made to reconcile the conflicting sources. The Ministry of Economy publishes data on the final consumption of goods produced at factor cost. To these data are added indirect taxes and adjustments made for customs duties, profit taxes, transportation costs and other charges. For investment in building and construction, the estimates are based on the annual surveys of urban construction activity and other surveys for the private sector and on economic analysis of government accounts for the public sector. For investment in machinery and equipment, the value of capital goods produced domestically is estimated on the basis of annual industrial statistics, adding 25 per cent to arrive at purchasers' prices. Foreign trade statistics are used to estimate imports of capital goods. To the figures obtained, expenses such as custom duties and commerical profit tax, transportation costs, installation charges and trade mark-ups are added. The estimates of exports and imports of goods services are taken from the balance-of-payments on current accounts and foreign trade statistics. For the constant price estimates, all items of GDP by expenditure type are deflated by appropriate indexes.

(c) Cost-structure of the gross domestic product. Compensation of employees and operating surplus are obtained as a residual, by subtracting depreciation and net indirect taxes from GDP. Depreciation is assumed to be 5 per cent of the GDP. The estimates of indirect taxes and subsidies are made on the basis of the government accounts.

(d) Gross domestic product by kind of economic activity. The tables of GDP by kind of economic activity is prepared in factor values. The production approach is used to estimate the value added of most industries. The income approach is used for producers of government services, the oil sector, the construction sector, communication, banking and insurance and part of other services. The commodity-flow is used for the trade sector. The agricultural estimates are based primarily on the annual surveys of agriculture, supplemented by information obtained from the Ministry of Agriculture and other government agencies. The estimates are checked, using the results of the annual household budget surveys. The estimates are available both at the national and regional levels. Data on the production of red meat are based on information supplied by slaughterhouses in urban areas and on the results of expenditure surveys in rural areas. The data are then converted to current- price estimates by using wholesale price index. Data for white meat production are based on per capita consumption estimates, applying unit prices from the wholesale price index material. Intermediate consumption estimates are based on information supplied by government agencies and from data on domestic production and imports. Statistics concerning forestry and fishing are obtained from the concerned agencies. Mining estimates are compiled at national and regional levels and are based on annual mining surveys and the 1973 census of mining. The information needed to calculate the value added of oil production using the income approach is obtained from the National Iranian Oil Co. The manufacturing estimates for large establishments which employ 10 workers or more are based on the results of the annual surveys of manufacturing. For small establishments, estimates are obtained globally as a function of the output, intermediate consumption and value added of large establishments by region. The estimates of electricity, gas and water are based on information obtained from the concerned establishments and government accounts. Estimates for private new construction in the urban areas are obtained from the results of Bank Markazi's annual surveys with adjustments made to cover contractors' profits which are not included in the surveys. For the rural areas, a 1973 listing of rural construction projects of the Statistical Center of Iran and the average prices from the Bank's surveys are used. Expenditure on the other construction are obtained from household budget data. Public construction estimates are derived from government accounts. For the calculation of the value added of each category of construction, separate ratios are computed for each year on the basis of information on the changes in profit margins and relative to construction costs during 1971-1974. Value added of the trade sector is estimated on the basis of annual changes in the value of traded goods, both domestic production and imports, Bench-mark estimates for wholesale and retail trade in the urban areas have been prepared for 1973. They are based on information such as the number of establishments existing, average sales revenues, operating cost, etc. For the rural areas, estimates are made from the number of retail establishments in these areas, average gross revenue and value added per establishment. For the transport sector, the estimates are generally based on the financial statements of the organizations involved and on data derived from government budgets. The contribution of trucks, buses and taxis is estimated as the product of the number of licensed vehicles operating and estimated gross revenue, intermediate consumption and value added per vehicle. Value added for the organized sector of banking is obtained from the income accounts of banks, while for the unorganized sector, it is assumed to be 30 per cent of the total value added for banking. The estimates of residential housing are based on per capita rent data obtained from the household budget surveys, population data and the rental component of the cost of living index. Government services estimates are derived from government accounts. For private services, estimates are derived from various sources such as the 1973 Urban Establishment Listing, labour force surveys and household budget surveys. GDP by kind of economic activity is estimated at constant price but no information is available on the methods used to derive the constant price estimates.

1.1 Expenditure on the Gross Domestic Product, in Current Prices

Thousand Million Iranian rials — Fiscal year beginning 21 March

	1970	1971	1972	1973	1974	1975	1976	1977	1978	1979	1980
1 General government final consumption expenditure	141.6	189.4	252.6	325.4	628.3	807.4	1003.6	1073.8	...	...	...
2 Private final consumption expenditure	537.3	566.9	686.6	879.7	1127.8	1316.0	1532.5	2160.8	...	...	...
3 Gross capital formation	167.3	216.7	287.4	363.3	562.0	1065.6	1477.9	1831.9	...	...	...
a Increase in stocks	-	-	-	-	-	-	...	...	...	...	...
b Gross fixed capital formation	167.3	216.7	287.4	363.3	562.0	1065.6	1477.9	1831.9	...	...	...
Residential buildings	37.1	46.6	62.2	75.6	128.1	219.2	354.6	438.3	...	...	...
Non-residential buildings	6.1	7.4	11.8	10.6	18.8	20.3	...	...	...	...	...
Other construction and land improvement etc.	61.9	80.6	100.5	137.0	194.3	361.5	...	...	...	...	...
Other	62.2	82.1	112.9	140.1	220.8	464.6	...	...	...	...	...
4 Exports of goods and services	-4.7	41.2	41.8	300.2	818.9	372.1	592.6	326.8	...	...	...
5 Less: Imports of goods and services									...	...	...
Equals: Gross Domestic Product	841.5	1014.3	1268.4	1868.6	3137.0	3561.1	4606.6	5393.3	...	...	...

1.2 Expenditure on the Gross Domestic Product, in Constant Prices

Thousand Million Iranian rials — Fiscal year beginning 21 March

	1970	1971	1972	1973	1974	1975	1976	1977	1978	1979	1980
					At constant prices of:1974						
1 General government final consumption expenditure	216.0	277.1	364.2	427.9	628.3	722.5	796.0	786.0	...	...	...
2 Private final consumption expenditure	774.2	773.4	880.3	1014.6	1127.8	1207.3	1243.9	1422.5	...	...	...
3 Gross capital formation	261.9	331.8	410.5	456.6	562.0	923.6	1114.4	1152.6	...	...	...
a Increase in stocks	...	...	...	...	...	...	...	...	...	...	...
b Gross fixed capital formation	261.9	331.8	410.5	456.6	562.0	923.6	1114.4	1152.6	...	...	...

Iran(Islamic Repub.of)

1.2 Expenditure on the Gross Domestic Product, in Constant Prices
(Continued)

Thousand Million Iranian rials — Fiscal year beginning 21 March

	1970	1971	1972	1973	1974	1975	1976	1977	1978	1979	1980
					At constant prices of:1974						
Residential buildings	64.6	79.3	98.2	93.8	128.1	190.6	251.4	241.5	...	...	...
Non-residential buildings	10.5	12.6	...	...	18.8	...	...	...	...	...	...
Other construction and land improvement etc.	106.6	138.8	...	...	194.3	...	...	...	...	...	...
Other	80.2	101.1	...	...	220.8	...	...	...	...	...	...
4 Exports of goods and services	726.9	845.9	949.3	1010.9	818.9	374.2	418.5	136.9	...	...	...
5 Less: Imports of goods and services									...	...	...
Equals: Gross Domestic Product	1979.0	2228.2	2604.3	2910.0	3137.0	3227.6	3571.8	3498.0	...	...	...

1.3 Cost Components of the Gross Domestic Product

Thousand Million Iranian rials — Fiscal year beginning 21 March

	1970	1971	1972	1973	1974	1975	1976	1977	1978	1979	1980
1 Indirect taxes, net	57.4	65.4	78.2	85.0	65.1	82.1	126.3	185.5	...	...	...
2 Consumption of fixed capital	49.1	56.1	64.8	83.7	114.1	147.2	196.2	248.5	...	...	...
3 Compensation of employees paid by resident producers to:	735.0	892.8	1125.4	1699.9	2957.8	3331.8	4284.1	4959.3	...	...	...
4 Net operating surplus									...	...	...
Equals: Gross Domestic Product	841.5	1014.3	1268.4	1868.6	3137.0	3561.1	4606.6	5393.3	...	...	...

1.10 Gross Domestic Product by Kind of Activity, in Current Prices

Thousand Million Iranian rials — Fiscal year beginning 21 March

	1970	1971	1972	1973	1974	1975	1976	1977	1978	1979	1980
1 Agriculture, hunting, forestry and fishing	160.6	172.7	201.8	234.4	303.3	333.9	426.3	485.0	...	...	...
2 Mining and quarrying [a,b]	140.7	212.6	264.0	587.5	1441.6	1375.8	1678.1	1658.0	...	...	...
3 Manufacturing [b]	113.7	138.1	171.5	231.9	312.9	379.5	496.0	638.1	...	...	...
4 Electricity, gas and water	13.4	15.9	17.3	21.6	25.7	30.0	34.3	37.8	...	...	...
5 Construction	41.0	45.1	58.4	78.9	98.2	208.3	356.9	494.8	...	...	...
6 Wholesale and retail trade, restaurants and hotels [c]	64.2	74.9	90.7	116.1	159.8	199.6	252.6	299.9	...	...	...
7 Transport, storage and communication	43.1	45.6	55.1	77.9	99.2	138.0	159.2	204.5	...	...	...
8 Finance, insurance, real estate and business services [d]	76.3	88.4	137.9	201.4	270.3	366.6	475.8	640.7	...	...	...
9 Community, social and personal services [c,d,e]	131.1	155.6	193.5	233.9	360.9	447.3	601.1	749.0	...	...	...
Total, Industries	...	...	...	...	...	...	...	...	...	...	...
Producers of Government Services [e]	...	...	...	...	...	...	...	...	...	...	...
Other Producers [e]	...	...	...	...	...	...	...	...	...	...	...
Subtotal [f]	784.1	948.9	1190.2	1783.6	3071.9	3479.0	4480.3	5207.8	...	...	...
Less: Imputed bank service charge	...	...	...	...	...	...	...	...	...	...	...
Plus: Import duties	...	...	...	...	...	...	...	...	...	...	...
Plus: Value added tax	...	...	...	...	...	...	...	...	...	...	...
Plus: Other adjustments [g]	57.4	65.4	78.2	85.0	65.1	82.1	126.3	185.5	...	...	...
Equals: Gross Domestic Product	841.5	1014.3	1268.4	1868.6	3137.0	3561.1	4606.6	5393.3	...	...	...

a) Referring only to oil production.
b) Mining is included in item 'Manufacturing'.
c) Restaurants and hotels are included in item 'Community, social and personal services'.
d) Business services are included in item 'Community, social and personal services'.
e) Items 'Other producers' and 'Producers of government services' are included in item 'Community, social and personal services'.
f) Gross domestic product in factor values.
g) Referring to indirect taxes net of subsidies.

1.11 Gross Domestic Product by Kind of Activity, in Constant Prices

Thousand Million Iranian rials — Fiscal year beginning 21 March

	1970	1971	1972	1973	1974	1975	1976	1977	1978	1979	1980
					At constant prices of:1974						
1 Agriculture, hunting, forestry and fishing	264.7	256.9	271.0	286.5	303.3	324.0	341.7	339.0	...	...	...
2 Mining and quarrying [a,b]	1057.9	1168.1	1333.3	1450.6	1441.6	1264.5	1384.6	1284.9	...	...	...
3 Manufacturing	163.1	190.5	224.8	264.4	312.9	360.9	423.0	468.2	...	...	...
4 Electricity, gas and water	13.1	16.7	17.2	21.6	25.7	30.0	33.4	36.6	...	...	...
5 Construction	78.1	83.5	91.4	101.7	98.2	141.6	174.0	179.5	...	...	...
6 Wholesale and retail trade, restaurants and hotels [c]	97.5	107.5	123.7	141.8	159.8	188.2	213.7	228.6	...	...	...
7 Transport, storage and communication	55.5	57.8	65.1	81.8	99.2	131.9	146.3	153.8	...	...	...
8 Finance, insurance, real estate and business services [d]	114.2	123.7	170.4	227.8	270.3	316.2	350.4	377.1	...	...	...
9 Community, social and personal services [c,d,e]	201.4	240.7	270.2	298.2	360.9	392.8	462.8	521.4	...	...	...

Iran(Islamic Repub.of)

1.11 Gross Domestic Product by Kind of Activity, in Constant Prices
(Continued)

Thousand Million Iranian rials — Fiscal year beginning 21 March

	1970	1971	1972	1973	1974	1975	1976	1977	1978	1979	1980
	\multicolumn{11}{c}{At constant prices of: 1974}										
Total, Industries	...	...	...	...	...	...	...	...	...	...	...
Producers of Government Services	...	...	...	...	...	...	...	...	...	...	...
Other Producers	...	...	...	...	...	...	...	...	...	...	...
Subtotal f	2045.5	2245.4	2567.1	2874.4	3071.9	3150.1	3529.9	3589.1	...	...	...
Less: Imputed bank service charge	...	...	...	...	...	...	...	...	...	...	...
Plus: Import duties	...	...	...	...	...	...	...	...	...	...	...
Plus: Value added tax	...	...	...	...	...	...	...	...	...	...	...
Plus: Other adjustments g	-66.5	-17.2	37.2	35.6	65.1	77.5	41.9	-91.1	...	...	...
Equals: Gross Domestic Product	1979.0	2228.2	2604.3	2910.0	3137.0	3227.6	3571.8	3498.0	...	...	...

a) Referring only to oil production.
b) Mining is included in item 'Manufacturing'.
c) Restaurants and hotels are included in item 'Community, social and personal services'.
d) Business services are included in item 'Community, social and personal services'.
e) Items 'Other producers' and 'Producers of government services' are included in item 'Community, social and personal services'.
f) Gross domestic product in factor values.
g) Referring to indirect taxes net of subsidies.

2.9 Gross Capital Formation by Kind of Activity of Owner, ISIC Major Divisions, in Current Prices

Thousand Million Iranian rials — Fiscal year beginning 21 March

	1970 TGCF	1970 IS	1970 GFCF	1971 TGCF	1971 IS	1971 GFCF	1972 TGCF	1972 IS	1972 GFCF	1973 TGCF	1973 IS	1973 GFCF
	\multicolumn{12}{c}{All Producers}											
1 Agriculture, hunting, fishing and forestry	...	...	10.8	...	...	15.1	...	...	25.1	...	...	28.4
2 Mining and quarrying ab	...	...	10.6	...	...	16.7	...	...	28.9	...	...	32.0
3 Manufacturing b	...	...	36.1	...	...	41.2	...	...	44.8	...	...	70.9
4 Electricity, gas and water	...	...	8.0	...	...	16.1	...	...	19.7	...	...	15.9
5 Construction	...	...	43.2	...	...	54.0	...	...	74.0	...	...	86.2
6 Wholesale and retail trade, restaurants and hotels	...	...	...	...	...	...	...	...	...	...	...	...
7 Transport, storage and communication c	...	...	...	...	...	...	...	...	...	...	...	...
8 Finance, insurance, real estate and business services	...	...	15.1	...	...	19.6	...	...	29.2	...	...	66.0
9 Community, social and personal services c	...	...	43.5	...	...	54.0	...	...	65.7	...	...	63.9
Total Industries	...	...	167.3	...	...	216.7	...	...	287.4	...	...	363.3
Producers of Government Services	...	...	...	...	...	...	...	...	...	...	...	...
Private Non-Profit Institutions Serving Households	...	...	...	...	...	...	...	...	...	...	...	...
Total	...	...	167.3	...	...	216.7	...	...	287.4	...	...	363.3

	1974 TGCF	1974 IS	1974 GFCF	1975 TGCF	1975 IS	1975 GFCF	1976 TGCF	1976 IS	1976 GFCF	1977 TGCF	1977 IS	1977 GFCF
	\multicolumn{12}{c}{All Producers}											
1 Agriculture, hunting, fishing and forestry	...	...	42.7	...	...	76.7	...	...	76.0	...	...	71.9
2 Mining and quarrying ab	...	...	63.9	...	...	135.9	...	...	232.5	...	...	239.2
3 Manufacturing b	...	...	89.6	...	...	195.6	...	...	240.3	...	...	300.0
4 Electricity, gas and water	...	...	29.1	...	...	52.9	...	...	153.5	...	...	243.4
5 Construction	...	...	146.9	...	...	239.5	...	...	388.8	...	...	482.7
6 Wholesale and retail trade, restaurants and hotels	...	...	...	...	...	...	...	...	...	...	...	...
7 Transport, storage and communication c	...	...	...	...	...	...	...	...	...	...	...	...
8 Finance, insurance, real estate and business services	...	...	84.6	...	...	131.3	...	...	143.3	...	...	183.0
9 Community, social and personal services c	...	...	105.2	...	...	233.7	...	...	243.5	...	...	311.7
Total Industries	...	...	562.0	...	...	1065.6	...	...	1477.9	...	...	1831.9
Producers of Government Services	...	...	...	...	...	...	...	...	...	...	...	...
Private Non-Profit Institutions Serving Households	...	...	...	...	...	...	...	...	...	...	...	...
Total	...	...	562.0	...	...	1065.6	...	...	1477.9	...	...	1831.9

a) Referring only to oil production.
b) Mining is included in item 'Manufacturing'.
c) Item 'Transport, storage and communication' is included in item 'Community, social and personal services'.

Iran (Islamic Repub.of)

2.10 Gross Capital Formation by Kind of Activity of Owner, ISIC Major Divisions, in Constant Prices

Thousand Million Iranian rials — Fiscal year beginning 21 March

	1970 TGCF	1970 IS	1970 GFCF	1971 TGCF	1971 IS	1971 GFCF	1972 TGCF	1972 IS	1972 GFCF	1973 TGCF	1973 IS	1973 GFCF
At constant prices of: 1974 — All Producers												
1 Agriculture, hunting, fishing and forestry	...	...	16.8	...	...	23.5	...	...	33.3	...	...	34.5
2 Mining and quarrying [a,b]	...	...	18.0	...	...	27.9	...	...	43.8	...	...	41.0
3 Manufacturing [b]	...	...	52.9	...	...	56.4	...	...	61.9	...	...	91.6
4 Electricity, gas and water	...	...	12.0	...	...	24.5	...	...	28.0	...	...	20.3
5 Construction	...	...	75.1	...	...	91.9	...	...	115.0	...	...	110.3
6 Wholesale and retail trade, restaurants and hotels	...	...	...	...	...	...	...	...	...	...	...	...
7 Transport, storage and communication [c]	...	...	...	...	...	...	...	...	...	...	...	...
8 Finance, insurance, real estate and business services	...	...	23.5	...	...	30.0	...	...	41.2	...	...	82.0
9 Community, social and personal services [c]	...	...	63.6	...	...	77.6	...	...	87.3	...	...	76.9
Total Industries	...	...	261.9	...	...	331.8	...	...	410.5	...	...	456.6
Producers of Government Services	...	...	...	...	...	...	...	...	...	...	...	...
Private Non-Profit Institutions Serving Households	...	...	...	...	...	...	...	...	...	...	...	...
Total	...	...	261.9	...	...	331.8	...	...	410.5	...	...	456.6

	1974 TGCF	1974 IS	1974 GFCF	1975 TGCF	1975 IS	1975 GFCF	1976 TGCF	1976 IS	1976 GFCF	1977 TGCF	1977 IS	1977 GFCF
At constant prices of: 1974 — All Producers												
1 Agriculture, hunting, fishing and forestry	...	...	42.7	...	...	66.0	...	...	56.6	...	...	44.8
2 Mining and quarrying [a,b]	...	...	63.9	...	...	118.0	...	...	169.1	...	...	136.0
3 Manufacturing [b]	...	...	89.6	...	...	168.4	...	...	195.0	...	...	220.8
4 Electricity, gas and water	...	...	29.1	...	...	45.9	...	...	117.9	...	...	155.7
5 Construction	...	...	146.9	...	...	208.3	...	...	275.6	...	...	266.0
6 Wholesale and retail trade, restaurants and hotels	...	...	...	...	...	...	...	...	...	...	...	...
7 Transport, storage and communication [c]	...	...	...	...	...	...	...	...	...	...	...	...
8 Finance, insurance, real estate and business services	...	...	84.6	...	...	114.1	...	...	109.5	...	...	119.4
9 Community, social and personal services [c]	...	...	105.2	...	...	202.9	...	...	190.7	...	...	209.9
Total Industries	...	...	562.0	...	...	923.6	...	...	1114.4	...	...	1152.6
Producers of Government Services	...	...	...	...	...	...	...	...	...	...	...	...
Private Non-Profit Institutions Serving Households	...	...	...	...	...	...	...	...	...	...	...	...
Total	...	...	562.0	...	...	923.6	...	...	1114.4	...	...	1152.6

a) Referring only to oil production.
b) Mining is included in item 'Manufacturing'.
c) Item 'Transport, storage and communication' is included in item 'Community, social and personal services'.

Iraq

General note. The preparaton of national accounts statistics in Iraq is undertaken by the Central Statistical Organization, Baghdad. The following presentation of sources and methods is mainly based on information contained in a handbook entitled 'Technical Note on the Estimation of National Income of the Republic of Iraq, 1962-1965'. The estimates are generally in accordance with the classifications and definitions recommended in the United Nations System of National Accounts (SNA). Input-output tables have been published in 'Input-Output and Social Accounts of Iraq 1960-1963'. The following tables have been prepared from successive replies to the United Nations national accounts questionnaire. When the scope and coverage of the estimates differ for conceptual or statistical reasons from the definitions and classifications recommended in SNA, a footnote is indicated to the relevant tables.

Sources and methods:

(a) **Gross domestic product.** GDP is estimated mainly through the production approach.

(b) **Expenditure on the gross domestic product.** The expenditure approach is used to estimate government final consumption expenditure, increase in stocks, and exports and imports of goods and services. This approach, in combination with the commodity-flow approach is used for gross fixed capital formation. The commodity-flow approach is used for private consumption expenditure. The estimates of government final consumption expenditure, consisting of wages, salaries and allowances and intermediate consumption of goods and services are obtained from the final accounts of the concerned bodies. The estimates of private final consumption expenditure is obtained as a residual for some years, while family budget surveys are used for other years. The data used for the estimation of increase in stocks are obtained from the final accounts of the establishments of the trade, transport and communication sectors. The industrial surveys provide data for the manufacturing industries. The gross fixed capital formation is classified according to economic activities and kinds of assets. Data are obtained from various sources such as the ordinary budget, actual expenditure on the development planning budget, reports and surveys. Foreign trade statistics provide data on imports of capital goods in c.i.f. values. Exports and imports of goods and services are estimated from foreign trade statistics and balance-of-payments data. GDP by expenditure type at constant prices is not estimated.

(c) **Cost-structure of the gross domestic product.** The estimates of compensation of employees in the socialist sector are obtained from the final accounts of the government and companies. For the private sector, the data are obtained from family service surveys and internal trade surveys. Operating surplus is obtained as a residual. The depreciation estimates are prepared according to kinds of fixed assets and are based on the estimates of fixed capital formation, taking into consideration the prices of fixed assets and the average age of each kind of asset. The data on indirect taxes and subsidies are obtained from the actual accounts of the government or from the final accounts of the establishments of the socialist sector.

(d) **Gross domestic product by kind of economic activity.** The table of GDP by kind of economic activity is prepared in factor values. The production approach is used to estimate the value added of most industries. The income approach is used for transport and storage, private services and producers of government services. The commodity-flow approach is used to estimate gross output of the trade sector. Data on areas cultivated, average yield, quantity and value of each crop are obtained from the Central Statistical Organization while prices are based on a production survey. The production of various types of vegetables is estimated from data of the Ministry of Agriculture, and the valuation is made by using farm prices collected by the Central Statistical Organization. The results of the 1971 Agricultural census are used for estimating the value of fruit production. Intermediate consumption of these agricultural crops are estimated individually. The estimation of livestock products is based on sample surveys. The quantity of meat is estimated by multiplying the number of animals slaughtered in the abbatoirs by the average weight of the animals. The number of animals slaughtered outside the abbatoirs is estimated on the basis of data on exports of skins and guts. The estimate of the output of crude oil, natural gas and sulphur is based on the final accounts of the producing companies, from which data on the quantity and value of production and other factors of the value added are obtained. The data on manufacturing are obtained from the annual and quarterly industrial surveys which collect data on the number of establishments and employees, wages and salaries, quantity and value of inputs, increase in stocks and capital formation. The data for electricity, gas and water are obtained from the balance sheets and final accounts of the concerned establishments and from the Industrial Department of the Central Statistical Organization. The value added in the construction sector is based on the reports of the Central Statistical Organization and data on fixed capital formation which are based on the national development planning budget. The data used to estimate value added in the trade sector are taken from government final accounts, the internal trade survey and the hotel survey. For restaurants and hotels, a survey of services and hotels comprising the number of employees and establishments, wages and salaries, revenue, purchases, etc. is used. The final accounts of public establishments and the reports issued by the Central Statistical Organization are the basis for estimating transport and communication. The gross value of output is obtained by adding intermediate consumption to value added. Data on banking, insurance and other financing establishments have been obtained directly from concerned establishments. The services survey is used for the value added of real-estate services. For ownership of dwellings, rents are imputed based on the rent survey conducted by the Ministry of Finance and the family budget surveys. For government services, estimates are based on final government accounts and balance-sheets and final accounts of semi-governmental institutions. The services survey and the family budget surveys are used for estimating private services, GDP by kind of economic activity at constant prices is estimated taking 1964, 1969 and 1974 as base year.

1.1 Expenditure on the Gross Domestic Product, in Current Prices

Million Iraqi dinars

		1970	1971	1972	1973	1974	1975	1976	1977	1978	1979	1980
1	General government final consumption expenditure	268.9	308.9	956.1	929.4	1427.1	2060.2	...	...	...	...	...
2	Private final consumption expenditure	578.6	633.2					...	...	...	...	...
3	Gross capital formation	202.8	209.4	273.3	359.2	948.8	1425.2	1447.9	...	...	...	...
a	Increase in stocks	17.7	14.7	56.2	70.6	320.2	357.2	...	...	...	...	...
b	Gross fixed capital formation	185.1	194.7	217.1	288.6	628.6	1068.0	...	...	...	...	...
	Residential buildings	32.8	34.4	39.2	47.5	57.6	116.8	...	...	...	...	...
	Non-residential buildings	28.1	31.6	32.0	42.8	56.7	128.6	...	...	...	...	...
	Other construction and land improvement etc.	42.3	47.0	47.7	93.2	289.3	370.8	...	...	...	...	...
	Other	82.0	81.7	98.1	105.2	224.9	446.2	...	...	...	...	...
4	Exports of goods and services	437.5	596.5	505.7	720.5	2075.9	2329.0	...	...	...	...	...
5	Less: Imports of goods and services	236.6	314.2	294.2	382.7	1073.8	1792.0	...	...	...	...	...
	Equals: Gross Domestic Product	1251.2	1433.8	1440.9	1626.4	3378.0	4022.4	5252.5	5874.1	7040.6	...	...

1.3 Cost Components of the Gross Domestic Product

Million Iraqi dinars

		1970	1971	1972	1973	1974	1975	1976	1977	1978	1979	1980
1	Indirect taxes, net	85.2	90.1	86.2	76.6	30.3	51.9	...	...	...	...	...
a	Indirect taxes paid	86.8	92.4	88.6	94.3	88.0	122.4	...	...	...	...	...
b	Less: Subsidies received	1.6	2.3	2.4	17.7	57.7	70.5	...	...	...	...	...
2	Consumption of fixed capital	74.4	78.8	85.4	93.4	103.2	105.0	...	...	...	...	...
3	Compensation of employees paid by resident producers to:	344.0	363.5	398.7	440.5	633.4	833.6	...	...	...	...	...
4	Net operating surplus	747.6	901.4	870.6	1015.9	2611.1	3031.9	...	...	...	...	...
	Equals: Gross Domestic Product	1251.2	1433.8	1440.9	1626.4	3378.0	4022.4	...	...	...	...	...

Iraq

1.8 Capital Transactions of The Nation, Summary

Million Iraqi dinars

	1970	1971	1972	1973	1974	1975	1976	1977	1978	1979	1980
	\multicolumn{11}{c}{Finance of Gross Capital Formation}										
Gross saving	238.4	277.5	349.3	612.3	1639.6	1712.2	...	...	...	...	...
1 Consumption of fixed capital	74.4	78.8	85.4	93.4	103.2	105.0	...	...	...	...	...
2 Net saving	164.0	198.7	263.9	518.9	1536.4	1607.2	...	...	...	...	...
Less: Surplus of the nation on current transactions	...	...	...	...	...	...	...	...	...	...	...
Finance of Gross Capital Formation	202.8	209.4	273.3	359.2	948.8	1425.2	1447.9	...	...	...	...
	\multicolumn{11}{c}{Gross Capital Formation}										
Increase in stocks	17.7	14.7	...	...	...	...	...	...	...	...	...
Gross fixed capital formation	185.1	194.7	...	...	...	...	...	...	...	...	...
1 General government	5.2	5.4	5.9	12.3	41.1	48.7	...	...	...	...	...
2 Corporate and quasi-corporate enterprises	...	...	...	...	...	...	...	...	...	...	...
3 Other	...	...	...	...	...	...	...	...	...	...	...
Gross Capital Formation	202.8	209.4	273.3	359.2	948.8	1425.2	1447.9	...	...	...	...

1.10 Gross Domestic Product by Kind of Activity, in Current Prices

Million Iraqi dinars

	1970	1971	1972	1973	1974	1975	1976	1977	1978	1979	1980
1 Agriculture, hunting, forestry and fishing [a]	175.6	181.2	235.3	188.2	232.1	297.3				...	...
2 Mining and quarrying	370.5	512.9	407.3	574.3	2030.7	2287.7				...	...
3 Manufacturing [abc]	116.0	118.5	140.0	157.6	176.1	238.5	4054.7	4395.5	5393.8	...	...
4 Electricity, gas and water [c]	12.7	11.9	13.7	16.0	13.7	17.7				...	...
5 Construction	40.6	43.6	45.2	57.6	69.1	91.3				...	...
6 Wholesale and retail trade, restaurants and hotels [bc]	98.6	94.4	102.6	115.2	168.9	194.9				...	...
7 Transport, storage and communication	71.2	79.7	85.9	88.5	124.1	157.6	590.9	690.2	775.1	...	...
8 Finance, insurance, real estate and business services [d]	69.6	75.1	76.3	79.3	118.9	140.7				...	...
9 Community, social and personal services [def]	23.7	22.7	25.2	26.2	28.0	31.1	...	...	...	...	...
Total, Industries	978.5	1140.0	1131.5	1302.9	2961.6	3456.8	...	...	...	...	...
Producers of Government Services	187.5	203.7	223.2	246.9	386.1	513.7	...	...	...	...	...
Other Producers	...	...	...	...	...	...	...	...	...	...	...
Subtotal [g]	1166.0	1343.7	1354.7	1549.8	3347.7	3970.5	...	...	...	...	...
Less: Imputed bank service charge	...	...	...	...	...	...	...	...	...	...	...
Plus: Import duties	...	...	...	...	...	...	...	...	...	...	...
Plus: Value added tax	...	...	...	...	...	...	...	...	...	...	...
Plus: Other adjustments [h]	85.2	90.1	86.2	76.6	30.3	51.9	...	...	...	...	...
Equals: Gross Domestic Product	1251.2	1433.8	1440.9	1626.4	3378.0	4022.4	5252.5	5874.1	7040.6	...	...

a) Agricultural services and related activities such as cotton ginning and pressing are included in item 'Manufacturing'.
b) Prior to 1970, distribution of petroleum products is included in item 'Manufacturing', beginning 1970 it is included in item 'Wholesale and retail trade'.
c) Prior to 1970, gas distribution is included in item 'Manufacturing', beginning 1970, it is included in item 'Wholesale and retail trade'.
d) Business services are included in item 'Community, social and personal services'.
e) Domestic service of households is included in item 'Community, social and personal services'.
f) Prior to 1964, item 'Restaurants and hotels' is included in item 'Community, social and personal services'.
g) Gross domestic product in factor values.
h) Referring to indirect taxes net of subsidies.

1.11 Gross Domestic Product by Kind of Activity, in Constant Prices

Million Iraqi dinars

	1970	1971	1972	1973	1974	1975	1976	1977	1978	1979	1980
	\multicolumn{6}{c}{At constant prices of: 1974}			1975			
1 Agriculture, hunting, forestry and fishing	221.2[a]	213.7[a]	279.1[a]	210.3[a]	232.1[a]	228.5[a]				...	...
2 Mining and quarrying	1617.9	1750.5	1525.5	2096.0	2030.7	2360.9				...	...
3 Manufacturing	120.5[abc]	140.4[abc]	152.0[abc]	164.5[abc]	176.1[abc]	209.0[abc]	3406.0	4119.2	4646.8	...	...
4 Electricity, gas and water	9.4[b]	8.8[b]	10.1[b]	11.8[b]	13.7[b]	17.3[b]				...	...
5 Construction	51.5	52.5	55.5	67.0	69.1	90.8				...	...

Iraq

1.11 Gross Domestic Product by Kind of Activity, in Constant Prices
(Continued)

Million Iraqi dinars

	1970	1971	1972	1973	1974	1975	1976	1977	1978	1979	1980
	\multicolumn{6}{c}{At constant prices of: 1974}			1975			
6 Wholesale and retail trade, restaurants and hotels	122.0cb	112.8cb	116.3cb	124.7cb	168.9cb	177.1cb				...	...
7 Transport, storage and communication	91.5	100.6	100.6	98.4	124.1	163.1	540.4	583.6	613.6		
8 Finance, insurance, real estate and business services	78.3d	81.8d	82.4d	83.5d	118.9d	133.2d				...	...
9 Community, social and personal services	255.0de	270.7de	297.4de	327.3de	414.1de	545.8de	555.6	682.7	675.0		
Total, Industries	2567.3	2731.8	2618.9	3183.5	3347.7	3925.7	...	...	...	...	...
Producers of Government Services	...	...	...	...	...	...	...	...	...	...	...
Other Producers	...	...	...	...	...	...	...	...	...	...	...
Subtotal	2567.3f	2731.8f	2618.9f	3183.5f	3347.7f	3925.7f	4502.0	5385.5	5935.4	...	...
Less: Imputed bank service charge	...	...	...	...	...	...	...	...	...	...	...
Plus: Import duties	...	...	...	...	...	...	...	...	...	...	...
Plus: Value added tax	...	...	...	...	...	...	...	...	...	...	...
Equals: Gross Domestic Product	...	...	...	...	...	...	...	...	...	...	...

a) Agricultural services and related activities such as cotton ginning and pressing are included in item 'Manufacturing'.
b) Prior to 1970, gas distribution is included in item 'Manufacturing', beginning 1970, it is included in item 'Wholesale and retail trade'.
c) Prior to 1970, distribution of petroleum products is included in item 'Manufacturing', beginning 1970 it is included in item 'Wholesale and retail trade'.
d) Business services are included in item 'Community, social and personal services'.
e) Items 'Domestic product of government services' and 'Domestic product of other producers' are included in item 'Community, social and personal services'.
f) Gross domestic product in factor values.

1.12 Relations Among National Accounting Aggregates

Million Iraqi dinars

	1970	1971	1972	1973	1974	1975	1976	1977	1978	1979	1980
Gross Domestic Product	1251.2	1433.8	1440.9	1626.4	3378.0	4022.4	...	...	...	...	...
Plus: Net factor income received from abroad	-166.0	-214.9	-136.5	-82.0	-242.0	-115.0	...	...	...	...	...
Equals: Gross National Product	1085.2	1218.9	1304.4	1544.4	3136.0	3907.4	...	...	...	...	...
Less: Consumption of fixed capital	74.4	78.8	85.4	93.4	103.2	105.0	...	...	...	...	...
Less: Net indirect taxes paid to supranational organisations	...	...	...	...	...	...	...	...	...	...	...
Equals: National Income at Market Prices	1010.8	1140.1	1219.0	1451.0	3032.8	3802.4	4555.0	5484.0	...	...	...
Plus: Net current transfers received from abroad	0.7	0.7	1.0	-2.7	-69.3	-135.0	...	...	...	...	...
Equals: National Disposable Income at Market Prices	1011.5	1140.8	1220.0	1448.3	2963.5	3667.4	...	...	...	...	...
Less: Final consumption	847.5	942.1	956.1	929.4	1427.1	2060.2	...	...	...	...	...
Equals: Net Saving	164.0	198.7	263.9	518.9	1536.4	1607.2	...	...	...	...	...
Less: Surplus of the nation on current transactions	35.6	68.1	76.0	253.1	690.8	287.0	...	...	...	...	...
Equals: Net Capital Formation	128.4	130.6	187.9	265.8	845.6	1320.2	...	...	...	...	...

2.9 Gross Capital Formation by Kind of Activity of Owner, ISIC Major Divisions, in Current Prices

Million Iraqi dinars

	\multicolumn{3}{c}{1970}	\multicolumn{3}{c}{1971}	\multicolumn{3}{c}{1972}	\multicolumn{3}{c}{1973}
	Total Gross Capital Formation	Increase in Stocks	Gross Fixed Capital Formation	Total Gross Capital Formation	Increase in Stocks	Gross Fixed Capital Formation	Total Gross Capital Formation	Increase in Stocks	Gross Fixed Capital Formation	Total Gross Capital Formation	Increase in Stocks	Gross Fixed Capital Formation
	\multicolumn{12}{c}{All Producers}
1 Agriculture, hunting, fishing and forestry	...	...	23.0	...	...	29.0	...	...	31.3	...	...	33.9
2 Mining and quarrying	...	...	7.6	...	...	10.4	...	...	13.2	...	...	30.7
3 Manufacturing	...	...	42.5	...	...	43.4	...	...	50.3	...	...	69.1
4 Electricity, gas and water	...	...	12.1	...	...	11.0	...	...	10.7	...	...	9.8

Iraq

2.9 Gross Capital Formation by Kind of Activity of Owner, ISIC Major Divisions, in Current Prices
(Continued)

Million Iraqi dinars

	1970 TGCF	1970 IS	1970 GFCF	1971 TGCF	1971 IS	1971 GFCF	1972 TGCF	1972 IS	1972 GFCF	1973 TGCF	1973 IS	1973 GFCF
5 Construction	...	...	3.9	...	...	5.1	...	...	5.0	...	...	7.8
6 Wholesale and retail trade, restaurants and hotels a	...	...	7.9	...	...	6.3	...	...	7.1	...	...	22.6
7 Transport, storage and communication	...	...	26.8	...	...	27.7	...	...	31.0	...	...	32.5
8 Finance, insurance, real estate and business services b	...	...	34.3	...	...	36.9	...	...	40.5	...	...	51.2
9 Community, social and personal services ab	...	...	21.9	...	...	19.4	...	...	22.1	...	...	18.7
Total Industries	...	...	179.9	...	...	189.3	...	...	211.2	...	...	276.3
Producers of Government Services	...	...	5.2	...	...	5.4	...	...	5.9	...	...	12.3
Private Non-Profit Institutions Serving Households	...	...	...	...	...	...	...	...	...	...	...	...
Total	202.8	17.7	185.1	209.4	14.7	194.7	273.3	56.2	217.1	359.2	70.6	288.6

	1974 TGCF	1974 IS	1974 GFCF	1975 TGCF	1975 IS	1975 GFCF
All Producers						
1 Agriculture, hunting, fishing and forestry	...	...	47.8	...	...	50.4
2 Mining and quarrying	...	...	79.6	...	...	87.1
3 Manufacturing	...	...	123.7	...	...	242.0
4 Electricity, gas and water	...	...	32.0	...	...	70.0
5 Construction	...	...	21.3	...	...	35.9
6 Wholesale and retail trade, restaurants and hotels a	...	...	25.0	...	...	33.6
7 Transport, storage and communication	...	...	156.6	...	...	320.7
8 Finance, insurance, real estate and business services b	...	...	46.7	...	...	82.9
9 Community, social and personal services ab	...	...	54.7	...	...	65.3
Total Industries	...	...	587.5	...	...	1019.3
Producers of Government Services	...	...	41.1	...	...	48.7
Private Non-Profit Institutions Serving Households	...	...	...	...	...	...
Total	948.8	320.2	628.6	1425.2	357.2	1068.0

a) Restaurants and hotels are included in item 'Community, social and personal services'.
b) Business services are included in item 'Community, social and personal services'.

2.10 Gross Capital Formation by Kind of Activity of Owner, ISIC Major Divisions, in Constant Prices

Million Iraqi dinars

At constant prices of: 1974

All Producers

	1970 TGCF	1970 IS	1970 GFCF	1971 TGCF	1971 IS	1971 GFCF	1972 TGCF	1972 IS	1972 GFCF	1973 TGCF	1973 IS	1973 GFCF
1 Agriculture, hunting, fishing and forestry	...	...	24.4	...	...	30.3	...	...	32.3	...	...	34.5
2 Mining and quarrying	...	...	8.0	...	...	11.0	...	...	13.7	...	...	31.2
3 Manufacturing	...	...	45.2	...	...	45.5	...	...	51.9	...	...	70.2
4 Electricity, gas and water	...	...	12.8	...	...	11.6	...	...	11.0	...	...	9.9
5 Construction	...	...	4.2	...	...	5.3	...	...	5.2	...	...	7.9
6 Wholesale and retail trade, restaurants and hotels a	...	...	8.3	...	...	6.6	...	...	7.3	...	...	23.0
7 Transport, storage and communication	...	...	28.3	...	...	29.2	...	...	32.1	...	...	33.1
8 Finance, insurance, real estate and business services b	...	...	36.3	...	...	38.7	...	...	41.7	...	...	52.0
9 Community, social and personal services ab	...	...	23.1	...	...	20.4	...	...	22.8	...	...	19.0
Total Industries	...	...	190.6	...	...	198.7	...	...	218.0	...	...	280.7
Producers of Government Services	...	...	5.5	...	...	5.6	...	...	6.1	...	...	12.5
Private Non-Profit Institutions Serving Households	...	...	...	...	...	...	...	...	...	...	...	...
Total c	...	...	196.1	...	...	204.3	...	...	224.1	...	...	293.2

Iraq

2.10 Gross Capital Formation by Kind of Activity of Owner, ISIC Major Divisions, in Constant Prices

Million Iraqi dinars

	1974 Total Gross Capital Formation	1974 Increase in Stocks	1974 Gross Fixed Capital Formation	1975 Total Gross Capital Formation	1975 Increase in Stocks	1975 Gross Fixed Capital Formation
			At constant prices of: 1974			
			All Producers			
1 Agriculture, hunting, fishing and forestry	...	...	47.8	...	...	45.5
2 Mining and quarrying	...	...	79.6	...	...	106.2
3 Manufacturing	...	...	123.7	...	...	195.9
4 Electricity, gas and water	...	...	7.2	...	...	11.9
5 Construction	...	...	21.3	...	...	29.0
6 Wholesale and retail trade, restaurants and hotels [a]	...	...	25.0	...	...	38.8
7 Transport, storage and communication	...	...	84.8	...	...	119.9
8 Finance, insurance, real estate and business services [b]	...	...	46.7	...	...	63.0
9 Community, social and personal services [ab]	...	...	54.7	...	...	57.0
Total Industries	...	...	490.9	...	...	667.3
Producers of Government Services	...	...	41.1	...	...	52.2
Private Non-Profit Institutions Serving Households	...	...	...	...	...	...
Total [c]	...	...	532.0	...	...	719.6

a) Restaurants and hotels are included in item 'Community, social and personal services'.
b) Business services are included in item 'Community, social and personal services'.
c) For 1974-1975, estimates not yet revised, therefore not strictly comparable with those of other tables.

4.6 Cost Components of Value Added, ISIC Divisions

Million Iraqi dinars

	1970 Compensation of Employees	1970 Capital Consumption	1970 Net Operating Surplus	1970 Indirect Taxes	1970 Less: Subsidies Received	1970 Value Added	1971 Compensation of Employees	1971 Capital Consumption	1971 Net Operating Surplus	1971 Indirect Taxes	1971 Less: Subsidies Received	1971 Value Added
						All Producers						
1 Agriculture, hunting, forestry and fishing	-	...	175.6	...	...	175.6	-	...	181.2	...	...	181.2
a Agriculture and hunting	...	...	...	...	...	165.5	...	...	...	...	...	170.0
b Forestry and logging	...	...	...	...	...	4.2	...	...	...	...	...	4.3
c Fishing	...	...	...	...	...	5.9	...	...	...	...	...	6.9
2 Mining and quarrying	7.6	...	362.9	...	...	370.5	14.0	...	498.9	...	...	512.9
3 Manufacturing	40.1	...	75.9	...	...	116.0	42.1	...	76.4	...	...	118.5
a Manufacture of food, beverages and tobacco	10.8	...	23.1	...	...	33.9	11.1	...	25.0	...	...	36.1
b Textile, wearing apparel and leather industries	12.3	...	21.4	...	...	33.7	13.5	...	21.2	...	...	34.7
c Manufacture of wood and wood products, including furniture	0.9	...	1.5	...	...	2.4	0.9	...	2.1	...	...	3.0
d Manufacture of paper and paper products, printing and publishing	0.9	...	0.8	...	...	1.7	1.3	...	2.0	...	...	3.3
e Manufacture of chemicals and chemical petroleum, coal, rubber and plastic products	3.8	...	9.8	...	...	13.6	5.1	...	13.5	...	...	18.6
f Manufacture of non-metallic mineral products, except products of petroleum and coal	4.9	...	6.4	...	...	11.3	5.4	...	6.7	...	...	12.1
g Basic metal industries	...	...	...	...	...	...	...	...	...	...	...	...
h Manufacture of fabricated metal products, machinery and equipment	5.9	...	5.7	...	...	11.6	4.6	...	4.2	...	...	8.8
i Other manufacturing industries	0.6	...	7.2	...	...	7.8	0.2	...	1.7	...	...	1.9
4 Electricity, gas and water	5.0	...	7.7	...	...	12.7	5.6	...	6.3	...	...	11.9
5 Construction	22.7	...	17.9	...	...	40.6	23.3	...	20.3	...	...	43.6
6 Wholesale and retail trade, restaurants and hotels	30.1	...	68.5	...	...	98.6	29.3	...	65.1	...	...	94.4
a Wholesale and retail trade	...	...	...	...	...	89.5	...	...	...	...	...	80.1
b Restaurants and hotels	...	...	...	...	...	9.1	...	...	...	...	...	14.3
7 Transport, storage and communication	41.9	...	29.3	...	...	71.2	44.7	...	35.0	...	...	79.7
8 Finance, insurance, real estate and business services	5.3	...	64.3	...	...	69.6	6.3	...	68.8	...	...	75.1
9 Community, social and personal services [a]	188.4	...	22.8	...	...	23.7	198.2	...	28.2	...	...	22.7

Iraq

4.6 Cost Components of Value Added, ISIC Divisions
(Continued)

Million Iraqi dinars

	1970						1971					
	Compensation of Employees	Capital Consumption	Net Operating Surplus	Indirect Taxes	Less: Subsidies Received	Value Added	Compensation of Employees	Capital Consumption	Net Operating Surplus	Indirect Taxes	Less: Subsidies Received	Value Added
Total, Industries	341.1	...	824.9	...	...	978.5	363.5	...	980.2	...	...	1140.0
Producers of Government Services	...	...	...	...	...	187.5	...	...	...	...	...	203.7
Other Producers	...	...	...	...	...	...	...	...	...	...	...	...
Total	341.1	...	824.9	...	...	1166.0	363.5	...	980.2	...	...	1343.7
Imputed bank service charge	...	...	...	...	...	...	...	...	...	...	...	...
Import duties	...	...	...	...	...	...	...	...	...	...	...	...
Value added tax	...	...	...	...	...	...	...	...	...	...	...	...
Other adjustments	...	...	...	...	...	85.2	...	...	...	...	...	90.1
Total	...	...	...	...	...	1251.2	...	...	...	...	...	1433.8

	1972						1973					
	Compensation of Employees	Capital Consumption	Net Operating Surplus	Indirect Taxes	Less: Subsidies Received	Value Added	Compensation of Employees	Capital Consumption	Net Operating Surplus	Indirect Taxes	Less: Subsidies Received	Value Added
						All Producers						
1 Agriculture, hunting, forestry and fishing	-	...	235.3	...	...	235.3	-	...	188.2	...	...	188.2
a Agriculture and hunting	...	...	...	...	...	225.7	...	...	...	...	...	180.4
b Forestry and logging	...	...	...	...	...	4.6	...	...	...	...	...	4.8
c Fishing	...	...	...	...	...	5.0	...	...	...	...	...	3.0
2 Mining and quarrying	16.0	...	391.3	...	...	407.3	17.2	...	557.1	...	...	574.3
3 Manufacturing	47.7	...	92.3	...	...	140.0	49.6	...	108.0	...	...	157.6
a Manufacture of food, beverages and tobacco	12.7	...	32.7	...	...	45.4	12.9	...	32.3	...	...	45.2
b Textile, wearing apparel and leather industries	15.0	...	27.6	...	...	42.6	16.1	...	27.0	...	...	43.1
c Manufacture of wood and wood products, including furniture	0.8	...	1.9	...	...	2.7	0.9	...	2.0	...	...	2.9
d Manufacture of paper and paper products, printing and publishing	1.8	...	0.8	...	...	2.6	1.8	...	2.8	...	...	4.6
e Manufacture of chemicals and chemical petroleum, coal, rubber and plastic products	5.8	...	14.6	...	...	20.4	6.2	...	23.8	...	...	30.0
f Manufacture of non-metallic mineral products, except products of petroleum and coal	6.1	...	5.8	...	...	11.9	6.5	...	7.3	...	...	13.8
g Basic metal industries	...	...	...	...	...	...	...	...	...	...	...	...
h Manufacture of fabricated metal products, machinery and equipment	5.3	...	6.8	...	...	12.1	5.1	...	10.4	...	...	15.5
i Other manufacturing industries	0.2	...	2.1	...	...	2.3	0.1	...	2.4	...	...	2.5
4 Electricity, gas and water	6.1	...	7.6	...	...	13.7	6.5	...	9.5	...	...	16.0
5 Construction	26.4	...	18.8	...	...	45.2	36.0	...	21.6	...	...	57.6
6 Wholesale and retail trade, restaurants and hotels	31.8	...	70.8	...	...	102.6	35.7	...	79.5	...	...	115.2
a Wholesale and retail trade	...	...	...	...	...	87.5	...	...	...	...	...	99.4
b Restaurants and hotels	...	...	...	...	...	15.1	...	...	...	...	...	15.8
7 Transport, storage and communication	46.6	...	39.3	...	...	85.9	50.9	...	37.6	...	...	88.5
8 Finance, insurance, real estate and business services	6.6	...	69.7	...	...	76.3	7.0	...	72.3	...	...	79.3
9 Community, social and personal services [a]	217.5	...	30.9	...	...	25.2	237.7	...	35.4	...	...	26.2
Total, Industries	398.7	...	956.0	...	...	1131.5	440.6	...	1109.2	...	...	1302.9
Producers of Government Services	...	...	...	...	...	223.2	...	...	...	...	...	246.9
Other Producers	...	...	...	...	...	...	...	...	...	...	...	...
Total	398.7	...	956.0	...	...	1354.7	440.6	...	1109.2	...	...	1549.8
Imputed bank service charge	...	...	...	...	...	...	...	...	...	...	...	...
Import duties	...	...	...	...	...	...	...	...	...	...	...	...
Value added tax	...	...	...	...	...	...	...	...	...	...	...	...
Other adjustments	...	...	...	...	...	86.2	...	...	...	...	...	76.6
Total	...	...	...	...	...	1440.9	...	...	...	...	...	1626.4

Iraq

4.6 Cost Components of Value Added, ISIC Divisions

Million Iraqi dinars

	\multicolumn{6}{c	}{1974}	\multicolumn{6}{c}{1975}
	Compensation of Employees	Capital Consumption	Net Operating Surplus	Indirect Taxes	Less: Subsidies Received	Value Added	Compensation of Employees	Capital Consumption	Net Operating Surplus	Indirect Taxes	Less: Subsidies Received	Value Added
\multicolumn{13}{c}{All Producers}
1 Agriculture, hunting, forestry and fishing	-	...	232.1	...	...	232.1	-	...	297.3	...	...	297.3
a Agriculture and hunting	...	...	...	...	...	223.5	...	...	...	...	...	287.4
b Forestry and logging	...	...	...	...	...	5.0	...	...	...	...	...	5.2
c Fishing	...	...	...	...	...	3.6	...	...	...	...	...	4.7
2 Mining and quarrying	18.5	...	2012.2	...	...	2030.7	21.7	...	2266.0	...	...	2287.7
3 Manufacturing	57.5	...	118.6	...	...	176.1	75.4	...	163.1	...	...	238.5
a Manufacture of food, beverages and tobacco	16.8	...	23.5	...	...	40.3	22.3	...	36.2	...	...	58.5
b Textile, wearing apparel and leather industries	15.1	...	48.8	...	...	63.9	18.3	...	55.6	...	...	73.9
c Manufacture of wood and wood products, including furniture	0.8	...	2.8	...	...	3.6	0.8	...	3.2	...	...	4.0
d Manufacture of paper and paper products, printing and publishing	2.4	...	2.7	...	...	5.1	3.1	...	1.6	...	...	4.7
e Manufacture of chemicals and chemical petroleum, coal, rubber and plastic products	7.8	...	20.4	...	...	28.2	10.3	...	31.5	...	...	41.8
f Manufacture of non-metallic mineral products, except products of petroleum and coal	7.6	...	6.0	...	...	13.6	10.2	...	9.0	...	...	19.2
g Basic metal industries	...	...	...	...	...	...	...	...	...	...	...	...
h Manufacture of fabricated metal products, machinery and equipment	6.8	...	12.6	...	...	19.4	10.2	...	24.0	...	...	34.2
i Other manufacturing industries	0.2	...	1.8	...	...	2.0	0.2	...	2.0	...	...	2.2
4 Electricity, gas and water	8.3	...	5.4	...	...	13.7	9.8	...	7.9	...	...	17.7
5 Construction	32.8	...	36.3	...	...	69.1	43.4	...	47.9	...	...	91.3
6 Wholesale and retail trade, restaurants and hotels	55.8	...	113.1	...	...	168.9	70.8	...	124.1	...	...	194.9
a Wholesale and retail trade	...	...	...	...	...	151.5	...	...	...	...	...	176.8
b Restaurants and hotels	...	...	...	...	...	17.4	...	...	...	...	...	18.1
7 Transport, storage and communication	67.8	...	56.3	...	...	124.1	92.3	...	65.3	...	...	157.6
8 Finance, insurance, real estate and business services	8.7	...	110.2	...	...	118.9	9.4	...	131.3	...	...	140.7
9 Community, social and personal services [a]	384.0	...	30.1	...	...	28.0	510.8	...	34.0	...	...	31.1
Total, Industries	633.4	...	2714.3	...	...	2961.6	833.6	...	3136.9	...	...	3456.8
Producers of Government Services	...	...	...	...	...	386.1	...	...	...	...	...	513.7
Other Producers	...	...	...	...	...	...	...	...	...	...	...	...
Total	633.4	...	2714.3	...	...	3347.7	833.6	...	3136.9	...	...	3970.5
Imputed bank service charge	...	...	...	...	...	...	...	...	...	...	...	...
Import duties	...	...	...	...	...	...	...	...	...	...	...	...
Value added tax	...	...	...	...	...	...	...	...	...	...	...	51.9
Other adjustments	...	...	...	...	...	30.3	...	...	...	...	...	...
Total	...	...	...	...	...	3378.0	...	...	...	...	...	4022.4

a) Columnd 1 and 3 include 'Producers of government services'.

Ireland

General note. The preparation of national accounts statistics in Ireland is undertaken by the Central Statistics Office, Dublin. The official estimates are published annually in 'National Income and Expenditure'. The following presentation of sources and methods is mainly based on a report entitled 'Basic statistics needed for the ESA accounts and tables: present situation and prospects for improvements' prepared by the Statistical Office of the European Communities in 1976 and on information received from Ireland's Central Statistics Office. The estimates are generally in accordance with the classifications and definitions recommended in the United Nations System of National Accounts (SNA). Input-output tables have been published for the years 1956, 1960, 1964 and 1969. The following tables have been prepared from successive replies to the United Nations national accounts questionnaire. When the scope and coverage of the estimates differ for conceptual or statistical reasons from the definitions and classifications recommended in SNA, a footnote is indicated to the relevant tables.

Sources and methods:

(a) Gross domestic product. Gross domestic product is estimated mainly through the income approach.

(b) Expenditure on the gross domestic product. The expenditure approach is used to estimate government final consumption expenditure, increase in stocks, and exports and imports of goods and services. The commodity-flow approach is used to estimate private final consumption expenditure and gross fixed capital formation except in the case of building and construction and government capital formation. Government final consumption expenditure is estimated from the accounts of the various government bodies such as the ministries, the local authorities and Health Board, extrabudgetary funds and the Industrial Development Authority. Data on private consumption expenditure are obtained from family budgets. Urban surveys were carried out in 1952/53 and 1955/56 and a national family budget survey was carried out in 1973. For the years between the surveys a small-scale continuous urban survey was introduced in 1974. Estimates of transactions in goods and services are obtained from the censuses of industrial production and the statistics of imports and exports of merchandise. The goods are valued at national average retail prices where volume data are available. Otherwise, they are aggregated at appropriate producers' or import prices and adjusted for distribution costs. In building up the agricultural stock figures, account is taken of changes in distribution stocks from annual sample inquiries, industrial stocks from stocks inquiries and censuses of industrial production, and stockpiles of strategic commodities from the Department of Agriculture. Investment in building and construction is estimated through the use of data from the production surveys. Estimates of locally produced goods are obtained from production census data minus exports plus distribution margins. Estimates of imported goods are obtained from detailed import returns. The estimates of imports and exports of goods and services are obtained from balance-of-payments, special studies and surveys. For the constant price estimates, direct revaluation at base-year prices is used for items of private final consumption expenditure where quantity data are available. For all other components of GDP by expenditure type, price deflation is used.

(c) Cost-structure of the gross domestic product. Estimates of compensation of employees are based on wage rates and number of farm worker for the agricultural sector, censuses of industrial production for the industrial sectors, surveys conducted at intervals and updated by indexes of earnings for the trade sector, annual surveys conducted among the relevant companies for the transport, credit and insurance sectors and salary rates and number of employees for the other market services. Operating surplus is calculated from returns made to the revenue authorities and from government accounts. Depreciation is based on the national farm survey for the agricultural sector. For private enterprises, it is taken as the income tax wear-and-tear and other allowances. Indirect taxes and subsidies are estimated from the government accounts.

(d) Gross domestic product by kind of economic activity. The table of GDP by kind of economic activity is prepared in factor values. The income approach is used to estimate the value added of all industries except agriculture, for which the production approach is used. Annual estimates of agricultural output are calculated on a commodity basis for crops, livestock and livestock products. The data on quantities and values are obtained from various sources such as Department of Agriculture and Central Statistics Office. The total quantities purchased and amounts paid by the purchasers for important agricultural items such as wheat and barley are available from various inquiries and adjusted for marketing margins and transport costs. For live exports, f.o.b. export value less an allowance for marketing margins, is taken as the output value. For the remaining items market prices are used as the basis for evaluation. Input data are obtained through the Department of Agriculture and Fisheries for fertilizers. Data for seeds are compiled indirectly from acreages and seedling rates. Own-account consumption of food and fuel is evaluated at agricultural prices. For mining, quarrying and manufacturing enterprises employing more than three persons, the estimates are based on annual censuses. Quarterly surveys of turnover and employment are conducted for manufacturing. For small-scale manufacturing, the number of persons engaged, which is derived as the difference between population census data and data from the production census, interpolated for intercensal years and projected forward, are multiplied by average income per person. The estimates of electricity, gas and water and of construction are based on annual inquiries. For trade, censuses of distribution provide bench-mark data for turnover, purchase of products, wages and salaries and intermediate inputs. For intervening years, monthly turnover figures from a sample of 2,500 establishments are used together with annual estimates of the number of employees and trends in earnings. For restaurants and hotels, annual surveys and revenue data are used. Transport is mainly provided by public enterprises and data are obtained from published accounts. Data obtained from annual reports, direct surveys on wages and salaries and revenue statistics are used for the estimates of the financial sector. For real estate and business services, data from population census, imputed average income and revenue accounts are used. The imputed rent of owner-occupied dwellings is taken as the average rent paid for similar dwellings in similar locations. Estimates of other private services are based on the results of inquiries into wages and salaries and on trends in operating surplus taken from revenue data. Data on government services are obtained from the government accounts. For the constant price estimates, double deflation is used for agriculture. Value added of all other economic activity sectors of GDP is extrapolated by a quantity index.

1.1 Expenditure on the Gross Domestic Product, in Current Prices

Million Irish pounds

		1970	1971	1972	1973	1974	1975	1976	1977	1978	1979	1980
1	General government final consumption expenditure	237.3	282.5	343.0	422.5	512.8	710.6	841.4	988.1	1179.8	1440.0	1837.0
2	Private final consumption expenditure	1116.0	1260.9	1453.8	1736.3	2041.4	2381.7	2910.2	3407.6	4013.8	4693.0	5519.0
3	Gross capital formation	396.5	444.5	560.6	724.6	866.8	827.1	1137.2	1532.7	1848.1	2499.0	2438.0
a	Increase in stocks	28.0	6.3	30.9	42.4	131.0	-15.7	2.3	113.7	12.1	159.0	-64.0
b	Gross fixed capital formation	368.5	438.2	529.7	682.2	735.8	842.8	1134.9	1419.0	1836.0	2340.0	2502.0
	Residential buildings	61.7	81.9	120.4	150.1	203.4	209.7	251.6	304.0	400.7	541.0	...
	Non-residential buildings	127.7	151.0	149.4	184.5	195.4	250.6	303.6	376.0	474.7	673.0	...
	Other construction and land improvement etc.											...
	Other	179.1	205.3	259.9	347.6	337.0	382.5	579.7	739.0	960.6	1126.0	...
4	Exports of goods and services	598.9	669.1	773.2	1026.4	1271.7	1619.0	2149.5	2813.7	3372.9	3953.0	4669.0
5	Less: Imports of goods and services	728.5	803.9	893.1	1211.0	1708.4	1814.0	2467.2	3256.8	3943.4	5135.0	5800.0
	Equals: Gross Domestic Product	1620.2	1853.1	2237.5	2698.8	2984.3	3724.4	4571.1	5485.3	6471.2	7450.0	8663.0

1.2 Expenditure on the Gross Domestic Product, in Constant Prices

Million Irish pounds

		1970	1971	1972	1973	1974	1975	1976	1977	1978	1979	1980
		\multicolumn{11}{c}{At constant prices of:1975}											
1	General government final consumption expenditure	493.5	536.2	576.5	615.0	661.6	710.6	725.6	749.8	809.8	861.0	894.0
2	Private final consumption expenditure	2115.1	2183.6	2295.9	2457.7	2497.1	2381.7	2449.5	2548.9	2791.7	2877.0	2862.0
3	Gross capital formation	789.1	806.2	892.6	1036.3	1039.8	827.1	953.1	1115.1	1202.9	1416.0	1188.0
a	Increase in stocks	54.6	7.1	34.6	39.6	158.9	-15.7	1.7	91.6	16.2	86.0	-29.0
b	Gross fixed capital formation	734.5	799.1	858.0	996.7	880.9	842.8	951.4	1023.5	1186.7	1330.0	1217.0

Ireland

1.2 Expenditure on the Gross Domestic Product, in Constant Prices
(Continued)

Million Irish pounds

	1970	1971	1972	1973	1974	1975	1976	1977	1978	1979	1980
					At constant prices of:1975						
Residential buildings	125.7	150.5	193.3	219.2	242.3	209.7	212.6	228.8	265.4	294.0	...
Non-residential buildings	280.0	299.7	268.2	291.9	234.0	250.6	260.5	275.1	315.4	386.0	...
Other construction and land improvement etc.											...
Other	328.8	348.9	396.5	485.6	404.6	382.5	478.3	519.6	605.9	650.0	...
4 Exports of goods and services	1253.9	1305.3	1352.3	1499.9	1510.5	1619.0	1748.0	1993.6	2241.7	2402.0	2557.0
5 Less: Imports of goods and services	1610.1	1685.1	1770.3	2107.3	2059.1	1814.0	2074.5	2344.0	2710.1	3114.0	2974.0
Equals: Gross Domestic Product	3041.5	3146.2	3347.0	3501.6	3649.9	3724.4	3801.7	4063.4	4336.0	4442.0	4527.0

1.3 Cost Components of the Gross Domestic Product

Million Irish pounds

	1970	1971	1972	1973	1974	1975	1976	1977	1978	1979	1980
1 Indirect taxes, net	235.6	271.9	319.7	373.7	373.9	386.5	590.0	530.6	479.0	543.0	850.0
a Indirect taxes paid	314.7	358.1	414.5	494.2	532.1	645.8	891.3	1015.5	1111.8	1227.0	1558.0
b Less: Subsidies received	79.1	86.2	94.8	120.5	158.2	259.3	301.3	484.9	632.8	684.0	708.0
2 Consumption of fixed capital	134.9	155.4	184.6	215.1	258.6	297.7	363.9	458.8	588.4	700.0	785.0
3 Compensation of employees paid by resident producers to:	844.8	979.1	1144.3	1393.1	1686.8	2159.2	2575.5	3003.3	3560.0	4318.0	5275.0
a Resident households	844.8	979.1	1144.3	1393.1	1686.8	2159.2	2575.5	3003.3	3560.0	4318.0	5275.0
b Rest of the world	-	-	-	-	-	-	-	-	-	-	-
4 Net operating surplus	404.9	446.7	588.9	716.9	665.0	881.0	1041.7	1492.6	1843.8	1889.0	1753.0
Equals: Gross Domestic Product	1620.2	1853.1	2237.5	2698.8	2984.3	3724.4	4571.1	5485.3	6471.2	7450.0	8663.0

1.4 General Government Current Receipts and Disbursements

Million Irish pounds

	1970	1971	1972	1973	1974	1975	1976	1977	1978	1979	1980
					Receipts						
1 Property and entrepreneurial income	41.3	46.1	57.8	54.8	64.8	77.7	93.8	135.2	177.2	205.6	...
2 Taxes, fees and contributions	530.2	626.1	722.7	874.8	984.0	1233.0	1661.1	1927.1	2190.1	2559.7	...
a Indirect taxes [a]	314.7	358.1	414.5	488.4	524.4	618.2	837.2	941.7	1053.1	1176.4	...
b Direct taxes	146.0	184.0	205.7	257.9	293.0	377.9	519.6	626.6	726.2	889.8	...
c Social security contributions	69.5	84.0	102.5	128.5	166.7	236.8	304.3	358.8	410.8	493.5	...
d Compulsory fees, fines and penalties [a]	...	...	...	...	...	...	...	...	...	...	...
3 Other current receipts	-	-	0.7	0.5	2.1	2.0	4.9	7.3	12.3	84.0	...
Total Current Receipts of General Government	571.5	672.1	781.2	930.1	1050.9	1312.7	1759.8	2069.6	2379.6	2849.3	...
					Disbursements						
1 General government final consumption expenditure [a]	237.3	282.5	343.0	422.5	512.8	710.6	841.4	988.1	1179.8	1440.0	...
a Compensation of employees	...	...	...	...	...	...	...	...	...	...	...
b Consumption of fixed capital	11.4	13.1	15.4	18.4	24.3	30.8	37.1	47.3	55.9	68.9	...
c Purchases of goods and services, net	...	...	...	...	...	...	...	...	...	...	...
d Less: Own account production of fixed assets	...	...	...	...	...	...	...	...	...	...	...
e Indirect taxes paid, net	...	...	...	...	...	...	...	...	...	...	...
2 Property income paid	60.3	66.6	75.0	93.4	109.3	157.9	226.7	286.4	357.0	440.8	...
3 Subsidies	79.1	86.2	94.8	83.3	92.2	140.3	170.5	189.6	244.2	280.0	...
4 Other current transfers paid	176.8	208.7	247.9	324.2	399.7	560.7	687.8	779.6	900.8	1099.7	...
a Social security benefits and social assistance grants	150.1	176.3	208.0	274.4	340.9	480.8	587.0	660.5	755.6	890.0	...
b Other	26.7	32.4	39.9	49.8	58.8	79.9	100.8	119.1	145.2	209.7	...
5 Net saving	18.1	28.1	20.5	6.7	-63.1	-256.8	-166.6	-174.2	-302.3	-410.9	...
Total Current Disbursements and Net Saving of General Government	571.5	672.1	781.2	930.1	1050.9	1312.7	1759.8	2069.6	2379.6	2849.3	...

a) Item 'Compulsory fees, fines and penalties' is included in item 'Indirect taxes' or is offset against item 'Final consumption expenditure'.

Ireland

1.7 External Transactions on Current Account, Summary

Million Irish pounds

	1970	1971	1972	1973	1974	1975	1976	1977	1978	1979	1980
Payments to the Rest of the World											
1 Imports of goods and services	728.5	803.9	893.1	1211.0	1708.4	1814.0	2467.2	3256.8	3943.4	5135.0	5800.0
a Imports of merchandise c.i.f.	667.0	738.6	823.3	1121.5	1601.5	1672.1	2302.0	3042.5	3656.3	4760.4	5340.0
b Other	61.5	65.3	69.8	89.5	106.9	141.9	165.2	214.3	287.1	374.6	460.0
2 Factor income paid to the rest of the world	40.9	47.5	59.5	93.3	121.1	145.7	214.5	259.9	368.0	444.0	...
a Compensation of employees	·	·	·	·	·	·	...	...	...	...	...
b Property and entrepreneurial income paid	40.9	47.5	59.5	93.3	121.1	145.7	214.5	259.9	368.0	444.0	...
3 Indirect taxes paid to supranational organizations	...	...	...	5.8	7.7	27.6	54.1	73.8	66.4	75.5	93.9
4 Current transfers to the rest of the world	2.6	3.1	3.6	4.7	5.3	6.7	8.8	11.3	12.8	16.8	20.6
5 Surplus of the nation on current transactions	-65.3	-71.0	-48.4	-82.3	-280.2	-6.0	-157.1	-155.2	-200.3	-727.0	-725.0
Payments to the Rest of the World and Surplus of the Nation on Current Transactions	706.7	783.5	907.8	1232.5	1562.3	1988.0	2587.5	3446.6	4190.3	4944.0	...
Receipts From The Rest of the World											
1 Exports of goods and services	598.9	669.1	773.2	1026.4	1271.7	1619.0	2149.5	2813.7	3372.9	3953.0	4669.0
a Exports of merchandise f.o.b.	455.0	522.3	632.5	852.8	1060.6	1370.8	1851.1	2424.2	2921.6	3413.0	4050.0
b Other	143.9	146.8	140.7	173.6	211.1	248.2	298.4	389.5	451.3	540.0	619.0
2 Factor income received from rest of the world	69.2	74.1	89.1	116.8	154.6	166.7	216.2	228.4	299.8	375.0	...
a Compensation of employees	1.8	2.0	2.0	2.5	3.3	4.7	4.2	5.1	5.7	7.2	...
b Property and entrepreneurial income received	67.4	72.1	87.1	114.3	151.3	162.0	212.0	223.3	294.1	367.8	368.0
3 Subsidies received from supranational organisations	...	...	...	37.2	66.0	119.1	130.8	295.3	388.6	404.0	381.0
4 Current transfers from rest of the world	38.6	40.3	45.5	52.1	70.0	83.2	91.0	109.2	129.0	212.0	...
Receipts from the Rest of the World on Current Transactions	706.7	783.5	907.8	1232.5	1562.3	1988.0	2587.5	3446.6	4190.3	4944.0	...

1.8 Capital Transactions of The Nation, Summary

Million Irish pounds

	1970	1971	1972	1973	1974	1975	1976	1977	1978	1979	1980
Finance of Gross Capital Formation											
Gross saving	331.2	373.5	512.2	642.3	586.6	821.1	980.1	1377.5	1647.8	1772.0	1713.0
1 Consumption of fixed capital	134.9	155.4	184.6	215.1	258.6	297.7	363.9	458.8	588.4	700.0	785.0
a General government	11.4	13.1	15.4	18.4	24.3	30.8	37.1	47.3	55.9	69.0	...
b Corporate and quasi-corporate enterprises	123.5	142.3	169.2	196.7	234.3	266.9	326.8	411.5	532.5	631.0	...
c Other											...
2 Net saving	196.3	218.1	327.6	427.2	328.0	523.4	616.2	918.7	1059.4	1072.0	928.0
Less: Surplus of the nation on current transactions	-65.3	-71.0	-48.4	-82.3	-280.2	-6.0	-157.1	-155.2	-200.3	-727.0	-725.0
Finance of Gross Capital Formation	396.5	444.5	560.6	724.6	866.8	827.1	1137.2	1532.7	1848.1	2499.0	2438.0
Gross Capital Formation											
Increase in stocks	28.0	6.3	30.9	42.4	131.0	-15.7	2.3	113.7	12.1	159.0	-64.0
Gross fixed capital formation	368.5	438.2	529.7	682.2	735.8	842.8	1134.9	1419.0	1836.0	2340.0	2502.0
Gross Capital Formation	396.5	444.5	560.6	724.6	866.8	827.1	1137.2	1532.7	1848.1	2499.0	2438.0

1.10 Gross Domestic Product by Kind of Activity, in Current Prices

Million Irish pounds

	1970	1971	1972	1973	1974	1975	1976	1977	1978	1979	1980
1 Agriculture, hunting, forestry and fishing	232.9	258.0	349.0	436.1	418.5	585.2	671.6	913.0	1035.9	955.0	...
2 Mining and quarrying	48.8	57.1	70.8	88.7	102.7	123.7	154.0	179.2			...
3 Manufacturing	299.0	333.9	406.3	509.7	613.3	718.4	919.8	1100.2	2205.4	2669.0	...
4 Electricity, gas and water	38.9	45.6	53.4	60.6	76.0	100.1	114.8	136.0			...
5 Construction	121.8	144.7	175.3	213.1	241.0	292.5	337.3	414.5			...

Ireland

1.10 Gross Domestic Product by Kind of Activity, in Current Prices
(Continued)

Million Irish pounds	1970	1971	1972	1973	1974	1975	1976	1977	1978	1979	1980
6 Wholesale and retail trade, restaurants and hotels	183.5	204.7	246.6	305.9	375.6	459.9	553.8	690.1	808.2		...
7 Transport, storage and communication	98.9	113.4	126.0	156.1	191.7	236.0	293.9	351.8	430.3	2577.0	...
8 Finance, insurance, real estate and business services	202.2	236.9	279.2	337.4	391.3	475.6	580.8	736.6	922.2		...
9 Community, social and personal services											...
Total, Industries	1226.0	1394.3	1706.6	2107.6	2410.1	2991.4	3626.0	4521.4	5402.0	6201.0	...
Producers of Government Services	206.1	241.4	288.1	354.2	426.3	581.8	689.2	782.2	913.9	1136.0	
Other Producers											
Subtotal a	1432.1	1635.7	1994.7	2461.8	2836.4	3573.2	4315.2	5303.6	6315.9	7337.0	
Less: Imputed bank service charge	35.0	36.0	43.9	50.6	68.7	102.2	134.8	190.2	206.3	231.0	
Plus: Import duties	...	...	...	...	...	...	...	...	...	...	
Plus: Value added tax	...	...	...	...	...	...	...	...	...	...	
Plus: Other adjustments b	223.1	253.4	286.7	287.6	216.6	253.4	390.7	371.9	361.6	344.0	...
Equals: Gross Domestic Product	1620.2	1853.1	2237.5	2698.8	2984.3	3724.4	4571.1	5485.3	6471.2	7450.0	

a) Gross domestic product in factor values.
b) Referring to indirect taxes net of subsidies.

1.11 Gross Domestic Product by Kind of Activity, in Constant Prices

Million Irish pounds	1970	1971	1972	1973	1974	1975	1976	1977	1978	1979	1980
				At constant prices of:1970							
1 Agriculture, hunting, forestry and fishing	232.9	247.8	260.8	262.0	...	...	...	...	...	...	...
2 Mining and quarrying					...	...	...	...	...	...	...
3 Manufacturing	494.4	521.9	543.2	606.0	...	...	...	...	...	...	...
4 Electricity, gas and water					...	...	...	...	...	...	...
5 Construction					...	...	...	...	...	...	...
6 Wholesale and retail trade, restaurants and hotels	265.6	266.2	276.7	302.0	...	...	...	...	...	...	...
7 Transport, storage and communication					...	...	...	...	...	...	...
8 Finance, insurance, real estate and business services	406.8	438.8	459.5	477.0	...	...	...	...	...	...	...
9 Community, social and personal services					...	...	...	...	...	...	...
Total, Industries	1399.7	1474.7	1540.2	1647.0	...	...	...	...	...	...	...
Producers of Government Services	...	...	...	...	...	...	...	...	...	...	...
Other Producers											
Subtotal a	1399.7	1474.7	1540.2	1647.0	...	...	...	...	...	...	...
Less: Imputed bank service charge	...	...	...	...	...	...	...	...	...	...	...
Plus: Import duties b	247.1	224.4	238.6	227.0	...	...	...	...	...	...	...
Plus: Value added tax	...	...	...	...	...	...	...	...	...	...	...
Plus: Other adjustments	-	-	-	-	...	...	...	...	...	...	...
Equals: Gross Domestic Product	1646.8	1699.1	1778.8	1874.0	...	...	...	...	...	...	...

a) Gross domestic product in factor values.
b) Referring to indirect taxes net of subsidies.

1.12 Relations Among National Accounting Aggregates

Million Irish pounds	1970	1971	1972	1973	1974	1975	1976	1977	1978	1979	1980
Gross Domestic Product	1620.2	1853.1	2237.5	2698.8	2984.3	3724.4	4571.1	5485.3	6471.2	7450.0	8663.0
Plus: Net factor income received from abroad	28.3	26.6	29.6	23.5	33.5	21.0	1.7	-31.5	-68.2	-69.0	-120.0
Factor income received	69.2	74.1	89.1	116.8	154.6	166.7	216.2	228.4	299.8	375.0	...
Less: Factor income paid	40.9	47.5	59.5	93.3	121.1	145.7	214.5	259.9	368.0	444.0	...
Equals: Gross National Product	1648.5	1879.7	2267.1	2722.3	3017.8	3745.4	4572.8	5453.8	6403.0	7381.0	8543.0
Less: Consumption of fixed capital	134.9	155.4	184.6	215.1	258.6	297.7	363.9	458.8	588.4	700.0	785.0
Less: Net indirect taxes paid to supranational organisations	-	-	-	-31.4	-58.3	-91.5	-76.7	-221.5	-329.9	-354.0	-287.0
Indirect taxes paid	-	-	-	5.8	7.7	27.6	54.1	73.8	58.7	50.0	94.0

Ireland

1.12 Relations Among National Accounting Aggregates
(Continued)

Million Irish pounds

	1970	1971	1972	1973	1974	1975	1976	1977	1978	1979	1980
Less: Subsidies received	-	-	-	37.2	66.0	119.1	130.8	295.3	388.6	404.0	381.0
Equals: National Income at Market Prices	1513.6	1724.3	2082.5	2538.6	2817.5	3539.2	4285.6	5216.5	6144.5	7035.0	8045.0
Plus: Net current transfers received from abroad	36.0	37.2	41.9	47.4	64.7	76.5	82.2	97.9	108.5	170.0	239.0
Current transfers received	38.6	40.3	45.5	52.1	70.0	83.2	91.0	109.2	129.0	212.0	...
Less: Current transfers paid	2.6	3.1	3.6	4.7	5.3	6.7	8.8	11.3	20.5	42.0	...
Equals: National Disposable Income at Market Prices	1549.6	1761.5	2124.4	2586.0	2882.2	3615.7	4367.8	5314.4	6253.0	7205.0	8284.0
Less: Final consumption	1353.3	1543.4	1796.8	2158.8	2554.2	3092.3	3751.6	4395.7	5193.6	6133.0	7356.0
Equals: Net Saving	196.3	218.1	327.6	427.2	328.0	523.4	616.2	918.7	1059.4	1072.0	928.0
Less: Surplus of the nation on current transactions	-65.3	-71.0	-48.4	-82.3	-280.2	-6.0	-157.1	-155.2	-200.3	-727.0	-725.0
Equals: Net Capital Formation	261.6	289.1	376.0	509.5	608.2	529.4	773.3	1073.9	1259.7	1799.0	1653.0

2.5 Private Final Consumption Expenditure by Type, in Current Prices

Million Irish pounds

	1970	1971	1972	1973	1974	1975	1976	1977	1978	1979	1980
Final Consumption Expenditure of Resident Households											
1 Food, beverages and tobacco	518.1	571.3	640.6	781.0	918.4	1096.7	1306.4	1511.8	1765.2	2099.0	...
a Food	302.0	332.2	375.5	470.6	557.8	634.1	736.6	890.0	1050.7	1262.0	...
b Non-alcoholic beverages	9.8	13.8	15.4	20.4	22.5	30.4	37.5	48.2	59.3	73.0	...
c Alcoholic beverages	128.3	145.9	165.8	196.5	233.0	303.3	382.2	422.6	485.1	570.0	...
d Tobacco	78.0	79.4	83.9	93.5	105.1	128.9	150.1	151.0	170.1	194.0	...
2 Clothing and footwear	112.8	124.7	139.4	165.9	191.1	193.7	228.3	268.3	331.4	377.0	...
3 Gross rent, fuel and power	130.8	151.4	176.3	188.2	238.8	278.2	336.1	391.9	390.3	467.0	...
a Fuel and power	...	55.9	66.1	70.8	102.1	123.4	150.5	194.0	211.3	248.0	...
b Other	...	95.5	110.2	117.4	136.7	154.8	185.6	197.9	179.0	219.0	...
4 Furniture, furnishings and household equipment and operation	88.5	103.4	122.8	148.4	172.5	192.7	219.8	248.9	287.2	328.0	...
a Household operation	26.9	28.4	32.7	35.9	43.9	49.4	49.7	58.0	68.3	81.0	...
b Other	61.6	75.0	90.1	112.5	128.6	143.3	170.1	190.9	218.9	247.0	...
5 Medical care and health expenses	24.2	33.7	38.3	45.2	47.4	59.5	71.9	84.8	101.8	116.0	...
6 Transport and communication	107.6	123.4	148.1	189.5	214.5	249.7	354.4	450.3	575.9	619.0	...
a Personal transport equipment	37.3	40.0	52.7	76.6	73.8	77.5	134.1	190.5	271.4	271.0	...
b Other	70.3	83.4	95.4	112.9	140.7	172.2	220.3	259.8	304.5	348.0	...
7 Recreational, entertainment, education and cultural services	89.7	102.0	119.8	139.1	164.9	189.9	246.9	288.3	339.0	394.0	...
a Education	...	22.4	27.5	33.9	40.6	50.5	61.9	73.1	86.5	106.0	...
b Other	...	79.6	92.3	105.2	124.3	139.4	185.0	215.2	252.5	288.0	...
8 Miscellaneous goods and services	76.2	87.2	92.0	103.5	123.3	145.1	174.2	212.3	255.1	297.0	...
a Personal care [a]	21.8	11.9	14.1	16.8	19.4	20.8	30.1	36.3	44.0	51.0	...
b Expenditures in restaurants, cafes and hotels	54.4	19.6	20.4	24.1	29.3	33.4	39.0	49.6	62.1	76.0	...
c Other		55.7	57.5	62.6	74.6	90.9	105.1	126.4	149.0	170.0	...
Total Final Consumption Expenditure in the Domestic Market by Households, of which	1147.9	1297.1	1477.3	1760.8	2070.9	2405.5	2938.0	3456.6	4045.9	4697.0	...
Plus: Direct purchases abroad by resident households	40.1	42.8	46.9	60.3	72.8	94.2	109.4	135.6	183.8	253.0	...
Less: Direct purchases in the domestic market by non-resident households	74.3	79.0	70.4	84.8	102.3	118.0	137.2	184.6	215.9	257.0	...
Equals: Final Consumption Expenditure of Resident Households	1113.7	1260.9	1453.8	1736.3	2041.4	2381.7	2910.2	3407.6	4013.8	4693.0	...
Final Consumption Expenditure of Private Non-profit Institutions Serving Households											
Equals: Final Consumption Expenditure of Private Non-profit Organisations Serving Households	...	...	...	...	...	...	...	...	...	...	...
Private Final Consumption Expenditure	1116.0	1260.9	1453.8	1736.3	2041.4	2381.7	2910.2	3407.6	4013.8	4693.0	...

a) Excluding services of barbers, beauty shops etc.

Ireland

2.6 Private Final Consumption Expenditure by Type, in Constant Prices

Million Irish pounds

At constant prices of: 1975

Final Consumption Expenditure of Resident Households

	1970	1971	1972	1973	1974	1975	1976	1977	1978	1979	1980
1 Food, beverages and tobacco	...	987.8	1016.4	1087.1	1146.0	1096.7	1082.6	1136.1	1233.3	1270.0	...
a Food	...	607.8	606.1	652.1	678.6	634.1	616.2	655.3	709.5	733.0	...
b Non-alcoholic beverages	...	24.0	26.4	28.0	29.4	30.4	32.1	35.9	39.8	44.0	...
c Alcoholic beverages	...	240.5	261.6	280.6	299.7	303.3	300.9	317.5	343.9	355.0	...
d Tobacco	...	115.5	122.3	126.4	138.3	128.9	133.4	127.4	140.1	138.0	...
2 Clothing and footwear	...	223.1	226.2	228.5	220.8	193.7	205.5	209.5	231.8	239.0	...
3 Gross rent, fuel and power	...	251.1	262.9	271.4	276.3	278.2	291.4	309.0	323.4	338.0	...
a Fuel and power	...	116.2	123.2	126.1	126.3	123.4	131.5	142.6	151.2	158.0	...
b Other	...	134.9	139.7	145.3	150.0	154.8	159.9	166.4	172.2	180.0	...
4 Furniture, furnishings and household equipment and operation	...	179.6	195.4	211.7	204.5	192.7	192.8	192.1	202.2	210.0	...
a Household operation	...	49.5	52.2	52.3	53.6	49.4	42.0	44.1	47.6	51.0	...
b Other	...	130.1	143.2	159.4	150.9	143.3	150.8	148.0	154.6	159.0	...
5 Medical care and health expenses	...	49.5	52.1	57.1	56.3	59.5	59.9	60.4	64.1	67.0	...
6 Transport and communication	...	215.8	243.5	284.2	269.7	249.7	283.1	311.0	364.0	345.0	...
a Personal transport equipment	...	64.8	79.0	105.0	89.1	77.5	105.6	124.7	159.1	140.0	...
b Other	...	151.0	164.5	179.2	180.6	172.2	177.5	186.3	204.9	205.0	...
7 Recreational, entertainment, education and cultural services	...	183.9	188.4	203.8	208.2	189.9	208.6	210.1	224.2	234.0	...
a Education	...	46.4	47.8	50.0	52.2	50.5	50.6	52.4	54.7	55.0	...
b Other	...	137.5	140.6	153.8	156.0	139.4	158.0	157.7	169.5	179.0	...
8 Miscellaneous goods and services	...	154.8	148.0	148.5	151.0	145.1	149.0	157.3	170.9	177.0	...
a Personal care	...	19.1	21.2	23.5	23.0	20.8	26.3	27.8	30.6	32.0	...
b Expenditures in restaurants, cafes and hotels	...	38.3	36.0	36.1	37.7	33.4	32.9	34.8	38.6	42.0	...
c Other	...	97.4	90.8	88.9	90.3	90.9	90.0	94.7	101.7	103.0	...
Total Final Consumption Expenditure in the Domestic Market by Households, of which	...	2245.6	2332.9	2492.3	2532.8	2405.5	2473.1	2585.5	2813.9	2880.0	...
Plus: Direct purchases abroad by resident households	...	73.3	73.9	85.3	88.0	94.2	92.7	101.1	127.4	155.0	...
Less: Direct purchases in the domestic market by non-resident households	...	135.3	110.9	119.9	123.7	118.0	116.3	137.7	149.6	158.0	...
Equals: Final Consumption Expenditure of Resident Households	...	2183.6	2295.9	2457.7	2497.1	2381.7	2449.5	2548.9	2791.7	2877.0	...

Final Consumption Expenditure of Private Non-profit Institutions Serving Households

Equals: Final Consumption Expenditure of Private Non-profit Organisations Serving Households	...	...	...	...	...	...	...	...	...	...	...
Private Final Consumption Expenditure	...	...	...	...	...	...	...	...	...	...	...

2.7 Gross Capital Formation by Type of Good and Owner, in Current Prices

Million Irish pounds

	1970				1971				1972			
	TOTAL	Total Private	Public Enterprises	General Government	TOTAL	Total Private	Public Enterprises	General Government	TOTAL	Total Private	Public Enterprises	General Government
Increase in stocks, total [a]	28.0	...	...	...	6.3	...	...	...	30.9	...	...	...
1 Goods producing industries	22.9	...	...	...	3.0	...	...	...	17.3	...	...	...
a Materials and supplies	8.3	...	...	...	0.6	...	...	...	3.0	...	...	...
b Work in progress [a]	2.3	...	...	...	-0.2	...	...	...	-2.1	...	...	...
c Livestock, except breeding stocks, dairy cattle, etc.	6.8	...	...	...	-2.2	...	...	...	13.2	...	...	...
d Finished goods	5.5	...	...	...	4.8	...	...	...	3.2	...	...	...
2 Wholesale and retail trade	5.1	...	...	...	3.3	...	...	...	13.6	...	...	...
3 Other, except government stocks	...	...	...	...	...	...	...	...	...	...	...	...
4 Government stocks	...	...	...	...	...	...	...	...	...	...	...	...
Gross Fixed Capital Formation, Total	368.5	...	...	...	438.2	...	...	...	529.7	...	...	...

Ireland

2.7 Gross Capital Formation by Type of Good and Owner, in Current Prices
(Continued)

Million Irish pounds

	1970 TOTAL	1970 Total Private	1970 Public Enterprises	1970 General Government	1971 TOTAL	1971 Total Private	1971 Public Enterprises	1971 General Government	1972 TOTAL	1972 Total Private	1972 Public Enterprises	1972 General Government
1 Residential buildings	61.7	...	...	...	81.9	...	...	...	120.4	...	...	...
2 Non-residential buildings	119.1	...	...	...	141.7	...	...	...	140.8	...	...	...
3 Other construction		...	...	...		...	...	...		...	...	...
4 Land improvement and plantation and orchard development	8.6	...	...	...	9.3	...	...	...	8.6	...	...	...
5 Producers' durable goods	172.2	...	...	...	196.8	...	...	...	226.8	...	...	...
a Transport equipment	53.6	...	...	...	65.8	...	...	...	47.9	...	...	...
Passenger cars	16.0	...	...	...	16.6	...	...	...	22.5	...	...	...
Other	37.6	...	...	...	49.2	...	...	...	25.4	...	...	...
b Machinery and equipment	118.6	...	...	...	131.0	...	...	...	178.9	...	...	...
6 Breeding stock, dairy cattle, etc.	6.9	...	...	...	8.5	...	...	...	33.1	...	...	...
Total Gross Capital Formation	396.5	...	...	...	444.5	...	...	...	560.6	...	...	...

	1973 TOTAL	1973 Total Private	1973 Public Enterprises	1973 General Government	1974 TOTAL	1974 Total Private	1974 Public Enterprises	1974 General Government	1975 TOTAL	1975 Total Private	1975 Public Enterprises	1975 General Government
Increase in stocks, total [a]	42.4	...	...	...	131.0	...	...	...	-15.7	...	...	...
1 Goods producing industries	61.6	...	...	...	44.8	...	...	...	-78.6	...	...	...
a Materials and supplies	4.8	...	...	...	14.3	...	...	...	-7.5	...	...	...
b Work in progress [a]	4.5	...	...	...	-1.2	...	...	...	-4.9	...	...	...
c Livestock, except breeding stocks, dairy cattle, etc.	35.7	...	...	...	15.5	...	...	...	-72.5	...	...	...
d Finished goods	16.6	...	...	...	16.2	...	...	...	6.3	...	...	...
2 Wholesale and retail trade	-19.2	...	...	...	86.3	...	...	...	62.9	...	...	...
3 Other, except government stocks	...	...	...	...	...	...	...	...	...	...	...	...
4 Government stocks	...	...	...	...	...	...	...	...	...	...	...	...
Gross Fixed Capital Formation, Total	682.2	...	...	...	735.8	...	...	...	842.8	...	...	...
1 Residential buildings	150.1	...	...	...	203.4	...	...	...	209.7	...	...	...
2 Non-residential buildings	175.3	...	...	...	184.2	...	...	...	241.4	...	...	...
3 Other construction		...	...	...		...	...	...		...	...	...
4 Land improvement and plantation and orchard development	9.2	...	...	...	11.2	...	...	...	9.2	...	...	...
5 Producers' durable goods	318.9	...	...	...	350.1	...	...	...	406.0	...	...	...
a Transport equipment	86.9	...	...	...	78.5	...	...	...	73.9	...	...	...
Passenger cars	32.1	...	...	...	30.8	...	...	...	33.2	...	...	...
Other	54.8	...	...	...	47.7	...	...	...	40.7	...	...	...
b Machinery and equipment	232.0	...	...	...	271.6	...	...	...	332.1	...	...	...
6 Breeding stock, dairy cattle, etc.	28.7	...	...	...	-13.1	...	...	...	-23.5	...	...	...
Total Gross Capital Formation	724.6	...	...	...	866.8	...	...	...	827.1	...	...	...

	1976 TOTAL	1976 Total Private	1976 Public Enterprises	1976 General Government	1977 TOTAL	1977 Total Private	1977 Public Enterprises	1977 General Government	1978 TOTAL	1978 Total Private	1978 Public Enterprises	1978 General Government
Increase in stocks, total [a]	2.3	...	...	...	113.7	...	...	...	12.1	...	...	...
1 Goods producing industries	40.8	...	...	...	74.0	...	...	...	-10.1	...	...	...
a Materials and supplies	22.7	...	...	...	23.5	...	...	...	8.0	...	...	...
b Work in progress [a]	1.1	...	...	...	1.3	...	...	...	-0.1	...	...	...
c Livestock, except breeding stocks, dairy cattle, etc.	18.5	...	...	...	-10.5	...	...	...	-20.1	...	...	...
d Finished goods	-1.5	...	...	...	59.7	...	...	...	2.1	...	...	...
2 Wholesale and retail trade	-38.4	...	...	...	39.9	...	...	...	22.1	...	...	...
3 Other, except government stocks	...	...	...	...	...	...	...	...	...	...	...	...
4 Government stocks	...	...	...	...	...	...	...	...	...	...	...	...
Gross Fixed Capital Formation, Total	1134.9	...	...	...	1419.0	...	...	...	1836.0	...	...	...

Ireland

2.7 Gross Capital Formation by Type of Good and Owner, in Current Prices
(Continued)

Million Irish pounds

	1976 TOTAL	Total Private	Public Enterprises	General Government	1977 TOTAL	Total Private	Public Enterprises	General Government	1978 TOTAL	Total Private	Public Enterprises	General Government
1 Residential buildings	251.6	...	...	...	304.0	...	...	...	400.7	...	...	...
2 Non-residential buildings	289.4	...	...	...	359.1	...	...	...	453.7	...	...	...
3 Other construction		...	...	...		...	...	...		...	...	...
4 Land improvement and plantation and orchard development	14.2	...	...	...	16.9	...	...	...	21.0	...	...	...
5 Producers' durable goods	574.0	...	...	...	740.9	...	...	...	954.2	...	...	...
a Transport equipment	113.2	...	...	...	171.2	...	...	...	252.6	...	...	...
Passenger cars	61.1	...	...	...	85.1	...	...	...	121.1	...	...	...
Other	52.1	...	...	...	86.1	...	...	...	131.5	...	...	...
b Machinery and equipment	460.8	...	...	...	569.7	...	...	...	701.6	...	...	...
6 Breeding stock, dairy cattle, etc.	5.7	...	...	...	-1.9	...	...	...	6.4	...	...	...
Total Gross Capital Formation	1137.2	...	...	...	1532.7	...	...	...	1848.1	...	...	...

	1979 TOTAL	Total Private	Public Enterprises	General Government
Increase in stocks, total [a]	159.0	...	...	...
1 Goods producing industries	129.0	...	...	...
a Materials and supplies	75.0	...	...	...
b Work in progress [a]	-4.0	...	...	...
c Livestock, except breeding stocks, dairy cattle, etc.	39.0	...	...	...
d Finished goods	19.0	...	...	...
2 Wholesale and retail trade	30.0	...	...	...
3 Other, except government stocks	...	...	...	...
4 Government stocks	...	...	...	...
Gross Fixed Capital Formation, Total	2340.0	...	...	...
1 Residential buildings	541.0	...	...	...
2 Non-residential buildings	648.0	...	...	...
3 Other construction		...	...	...
4 Land improvement and plantation and orchard development	25.0	...	...	...
5 Producers' durable goods	1139.0	...	...	...
a Transport equipment	320.0	...	...	...
Passenger cars	122.0	...	...	...
Other	198.0	...	...	...
b Machinery and equipment	819.0	...	...	...
6 Breeding stock, dairy cattle, etc.	-13.0	...	...	...
Total Gross Capital Formation	2499.0	...	...	...

a) Item 'Breeding stocks, dairy cattle, etc.' is included in item 'Increase in stocks'.

2.8 Gross Capital Formation by Type of Good and Owner, in Constant Prices

Million Irish pounds

	1970 TOTAL	Total Private	Public Enterprises	General Government	1971 TOTAL	Total Private	Public Enterprises	General Government	1972 TOTAL	Total Private	Public Enterprises	General Government
	At constant prices of: 1975											
Increase in stocks, total	54.6	...	...	...	7.1	...	...	...	34.6	...	...	...
1 Goods producing industries	45.5	...	...	...	1.5	...	...	...	12.8	...	...	...
a Materials and supplies	18.0	...	...	...	1.3	...	...	...	5.9	...	...	...
b Work in progress	5.1	...	...	...	-0.4	...	...	...	-4.0	...	...	...
c Livestock, except breeding stocks, dairy cattle, etc.	12.1	...	...	...	-8.0	...	...	...	5.7	...	...	...
d Finished goods	10.3	...	...	...	8.6	...	...	...	5.2	...	...	...
2 Wholesale and retail trade	9.1	...	...	...	5.6	...	...	...	21.8	...	...	...
3 Other, except government stocks	...	...	...	...	...	...	...	...	...	...	...	...
4 Government stocks	...	...	...	...	...	...	...	...	...	...	...	...
Gross Fixed Capital Formation, Total	734.5	...	...	...	799.1	...	...	...	858.0	...	...	...

Ireland

2.8 Gross Capital Formation by Type of Good and Owner, in Constant Prices
(Continued)

Million Irish pounds

	1970 TOTAL	Total Private	Public Enterprises	General Government	1971 TOTAL	Total Private	Public Enterprises	General Government	1972 TOTAL	Total Private	Public Enterprises	General Government
					At constant prices of:1975							
1 Residential buildings	125.7	...	...	...	150.5	...	...	...	193.3	...	...	...
2 Non-residential buildings	261.3	...	...	...	281.2	...	...	...	252.8	...	...	...
3 Other construction		...	...	...		...	...	...		...	...	...
4 Land improvement and plantation and orchard development	18.7	...	...	...	18.5	...	...	...	15.4	...	...	...
5 Producers' durable goods	316.5	...	...	...	333.9	...	...	...	359.6	...	...	...
a Transport equipment	101.9	...	...	...	110.0	...	...	...	75.7	...	...	...
Passenger cars	29.2	...	...	...	26.8	...	...	...	33.6	...	...	...
Other	72.7	...	...	...	83.2	...	...	...	42.1	...	...	...
b Machinery and equipment	214.6	...	...	...	223.9	...	...	...	283.9	...	...	...
6 Breeding stock, dairy cattle, etc.	12.3	...	...	...	15.0	...	...	...	36.9	...	...	...
Total Gross Capital Formation	789.1	...	...	...	806.2	...	...	...	892.6	...	...	...

	1973 TOTAL	Total Private	Public Enterprises	General Government	1974 TOTAL	Total Private	Public Enterprises	General Government	1975 TOTAL	Total Private	Public Enterprises	General Government
					At constant prices of:1975							
Increase in stocks, total	39.6	...	...	...	158.9	...	...	...	-15.7	...	...	...
1 Goods producing industries	67.4	...	...	...	55.8	...	...	...	-78.6	...	...	...
a Materials and supplies	7.8	...	...	...	16.8	...	...	...	-7.5	...	...	...
b Work in progress	7.6	...	...	...	-1.5	...	...	...	-4.9	...	...	...
c Livestock, except breeding stocks, dairy cattle, etc.	28.0	...	...	...	20.3	...	...	...	-72.5	...	...	...
d Finished goods	24.0	...	...	...	20.2	...	...	...	6.3	...	...	...
2 Wholesale and retail trade	-27.8	...	...	...	103.0	...	...	...	62.9	...	...	...
3 Other, except government stocks	...	...	...	...	...	...	...	...	...	...	...	...
4 Government stocks	...	...	...	...	...	...	...	...	...	...	...	...
Gross Fixed Capital Formation, Total	996.7	...	...	...	880.9	...	...	...	842.8	...	...	...
1 Residential buildings	219.2	...	...	...	242.3	...	...	...	209.7	...	...	...
2 Non-residential buildings	277.3	...	...	...	220.6	...	...	...	241.4	...	...	...
3 Other construction		...	...	...		...	...	...		...	...	...
4 Land improvement and plantation and orchard development	14.6	...	...	...	13.4	...	...	...	9.2	...	...	...
5 Producers' durable goods	458.2	...	...	...	419.9	...	...	...	406.0	...	...	...
a Transport equipment	123.0	...	...	...	96.0	...	...	...	73.9	...	...	...
Passenger cars	43.7	...	...	...	37.0	...	...	...	33.2	...	...	...
Other	79.3	...	...	...	59.0	...	...	...	40.7	...	...	...
b Machinery and equipment	335.2	...	...	...	323.9	...	...	...	332.1	...	...	...
6 Breeding stock, dairy cattle, etc.	27.4	...	...	...	-15.3	...	...	...	-23.5	...	...	...
Total Gross Capital Formation	1036.3	...	...	...	1039.8	...	...	...	827.1	...	...	...

	1976 TOTAL	Total Private	Public Enterprises	General Government	1977 TOTAL	Total Private	Public Enterprises	General Government	1978 TOTAL	Total Private	Public Enterprises	General Government
					At constant prices of:1975							
Increase in stocks, total	1.7	...	...	...	91.6	...	...	...	16.2	...	...	...
1 Goods producing industries	34.4	...	...	...	53.5	...	...	...	-0.4	...	...	...
a Materials and supplies	19.4	...	...	...	17.2	...	...	...	5.5	...	...	...
b Work in progress	1.0	...	...	...	1.0	...	...	...	-0.1	...	...	...
c Livestock, except breeding stocks, dairy cattle, etc.	15.3	...	...	...	-7.5	...	...	...	-7.2	...	...	...
d Finished goods	-1.3	...	...	...	42.8	...	...	...	1.4	...	...	...
2 Wholesale and retail trade	-32.7	...	...	...	38.2	...	...	...	16.6	...	...	...
3 Other, except government stocks	...	...	...	...	...	...	...	...	...	...	...	...
4 Government stocks	...	...	...	...	...	...	...	...	...	...	...	...
Gross Fixed Capital Formation, Total	951.4	...	...	...	1023.5	...	...	...	1186.7	...	...	...

Ireland

2.8 Gross Capital Formation by Type of Good and Owner, in Constant Prices
(Continued)

Million Irish pounds

	1976 TOTAL	1976 Total Private	1976 Public Enterprises	1976 General Government	1977 TOTAL	1977 Total Private	1977 Public Enterprises	1977 General Government	1978 TOTAL	1978 Total Private	1978 Public Enterprises	1978 General Government
				At constant prices of:1975								
1 Residential buildings	212.6	...	...	...	228.8	...	...	...	265.4	...	...	...
2 Non-residential buildings	248.3				256.8	...	...	...	301.4	...	...	...
3 Other construction						...	...	...		...	...	...
4 Land improvement and plantation and orchard development	12.2	...	...	...	18.3	...	...	...	14.0	...	...	...
5 Producers' durable goods	474.2	...	...	...	520.8	...	...	...	602.8	...	...	...
a Transport equipment	91.5	...	...	...	116.3	...	...	...	153.1	...	...	...
Passenger cars	17.9	...	...	...	20.8	...	...	...	26.4	...	...	...
Other	73.6	...	...	...	95.5	...	...	...	126.7	...	...	...
b Machinery and equipment	382.7	...	...	...	404.5	...	...	...	449.7	...	...	...
6 Breeding stock, dairy cattle, etc.	4.1	...	...	...	-1.2	...	...	...	3.1	...	...	...
Total Gross Capital Formation	953.1	...	...	...	1115.1	...	...	...	1202.9	...	...	...

	1979 TOTAL	1979 Total Private	1979 Public Enterprises	1979 General Government
		At constant prices of:1975		
Increase in stocks, total	86.0	...	...	...
1 Goods producing industries	73.0	...	...	...
a Materials and supplies	46.0	...	...	...
b Work in progress	-2.0	...	...	...
c Livestock, except breeding stocks, dairy cattle, etc.	18.0	...	...	...
d Finished goods	11.0	...	...	...
2 Wholesale and retail trade	13.0	...	...	...
3 Other, except government stocks	...	...	...	...
4 Government stocks	...	...	...	...
Gross Fixed Capital Formation, Total	1330.0	...	...	...
1 Residential buildings	294.0	...	...	...
2 Non-residential buildings	372.0	...	...	...
3 Other construction		...	...	...
4 Land improvement and plantation and orchard development	14.0	...	...	...
5 Producers' durable goods	656.0	...	...	...
a Transport equipment	175.0	...	...	...
Passenger cars	24.0	...	...	...
Other	151.0	...	...	...
b Machinery and equipment	481.0	...	...	...
6 Breeding stock, dairy cattle, etc.	-6.0	...	...	...
Total Gross Capital Formation	1416.0	...	...	...

2.9 Gross Capital Formation by Kind of Activity of Owner, ISIC Major Divisions, in Current Prices

Million Irish pounds

	1970 Total Gross Capital Formation	1970 Increase in Stocks	1970 Gross Fixed Capital Formation	1971 Total Gross Capital Formation	1971 Increase in Stocks	1971 Gross Fixed Capital Formation	1972 Total Gross Capital Formation	1972 Increase in Stocks	1972 Gross Fixed Capital Formation	1973 Total Gross Capital Formation	1973 Increase in Stocks	1973 Gross Fixed Capital Formation
						All Producers						
1 Agriculture, hunting, fishing and forestry	...	...	54.0	...	...	60.4	...	...	95.2	...	...	104.2
2 Mining and quarrying	...	...	8.9	...	...	6.1	...	...	5.3	...	...	11.2
3 Manufacturing	...	...	71.3	...	...	83.6	...	...	102.7	...	...	115.6
4 Electricity, gas and water	...	...	24.6	...	...	29.7	...	...	25.6	...	...	45.7

Ireland

2.9 Gross Capital Formation by Kind of Activity of Owner, ISIC Major Divisions, in Current Prices
(Continued)

Million Irish pounds

	1970 TGCF	1970 IS	1970 GFCF	1971 TGCF	1971 IS	1971 GFCF	1972 TGCF	1972 IS	1972 GFCF	1973 TGCF	1973 IS	1973 GFCF
5 Construction	...	...	6.3	...	...	7.5	...	...	9.5	...	...	15.3
6 Wholesale and retail trade, restaurants and hotels [a]	...	...	22.9	...	...	23.4	...	...	27.1	...	...	38.0
7 Transport, storage and communication	...	...	57.9	...	...	75.8	...	...	58.8	...	...	94.3
8 Finance, insurance, real estate and business services	...	...	67.4	...	...	89.8	...	...	131.2	...	...	164.9
9 Community, social and personal services [ab]	...	...	47.1	...	...	53.8	...	...	62.1	...	...	74.7
Total Industries	...	...	360.4	...	...	430.1	...	...	517.5	...	...	663.9
Producers of Government Services [b]	...	...	8.1	...	...	8.1	...	...	12.2	...	...	18.3
Private Non-Profit Institutions Serving Households [b]	...	...	...	...	...	...	...	...	...	...	...	...
Total [d]	396.5	28.0	368.5	444.5	6.3	438.2	560.6	30.9	529.7	724.6	42.4	682.2

	1974 TGCF	1974 IS	1974 GFCF	1975 TGCF	1975 IS	1975 GFCF	1976 TGCF	1976 IS	1976 GFCF	1977 TGCF	1977 IS	1977 GFCF

All Producers

	1974 TGCF	1974 IS	1974 GFCF	1975 TGCF	1975 IS	1975 GFCF	1976 TGCF	1976 IS	1976 GFCF	1977 TGCF	1977 IS	1977 GFCF
1 Agriculture, hunting, fishing and forestry	...	...	67.8	...	...	79.4	...	...	177.7	...	...	244.8
2 Mining and quarrying	...	...	14.1	...	...	22.1	...	...	38.8	...	...	48.7
3 Manufacturing	...	...	137.6	...	...	191.7	...	...	242.3	...	...	286.3
4 Electricity, gas and water	...	...	39.3	...	...	28.1	...	...	63.9	...	...	87.3
5 Construction	...	...	17.0	...	...	19.4	...	...	25.4	...	...	37.9
6 Wholesale and retail trade, restaurants and hotels [a]	...	...	38.7	...	...	40.7	...	...	42.6	...	...	55.3
7 Transport, storage and communication	...	...	96.2	...	...	110.2	...	...	113.5	...	...	152.8
8 Finance, insurance, real estate and business services	...	...	218.4	...	...	226.8	...	...	294.1	...	...	334.1
9 Community, social and personal services [ab]	...	...	86.6	...	...	96.9	...	...	115.1	...	...	143.0
Total Industries	...	...	715.7	...	...	815.3	...	...	1113.4	...	...	1390.2
Producers of Government Services [b]	...	...	20.1	...	...	27.5	...	...	21.5	...	...	28.8
Private Non-Profit Institutions Serving Households [b]	...	...	...	...	...	...	...	...	...	...	...	...
Total [d]	866.8	131.0	735.8	827.1	-15.7	842.8	1137.2	2.3	1134.9	1532.7	113.7	1419.0

	1978 TGCF	1978 IS	1978 GFCF	1979 TGCF	1979 IS	1979 GFCF

All Producers

	1978 TGCF	1978 IS	1978 GFCF	1979 TGCF	1979 IS	1979 GFCF
1 Agriculture, hunting, fishing and forestry	...	...	307.3	...	...	336.0
2 Mining and quarrying	...	...	58.2	...	...	64.0
3 Manufacturing	...	...	385.4	...	...	515.0
4 Electricity, gas and water	...	...	91.3	...	...	127.0
5 Construction	...	...	65.7	...	...	73.0
6 Wholesale and retail trade, restaurants and hotels [a]	...	...	77.9	...	...	98.0
7 Transport, storage and communication	...	...	196.3	...	...	283.0
8 Finance, insurance, real estate and business services	...	...	436.6	...	...	580.0
9 Community, social and personal services [ab]	...	...	181.3	...	...	219.0
Total Industries	...	...	1800.0	...	...	2295.0
Producers of Government Services [b]	...	...	36.0	...	...	45.0
Private Non-Profit Institutions Serving Households [b]	...	...	...	...	...	...
Total [d]	1848.1	12.1	1836.0	2499.0	159.0	2340.0

a) Hotels are included in item 'Community, social and personal services'.
b) Items 'Producers of government services' and 'Private non-profit institutions servicing households' are included in item 'Community, social and personal services'.
c) Item 'Private non-profit institutions serving households' is included in item 'Community, social and personal services'.
d) Item 'Breeding stocks, dairy cattle, etc.' is included in item 'Increase in stocks'.

Ireland

2.10 Gross Capital Formation by Kind of Activity of Owner, ISIC Major Divisions, in Constant Prices

Million Irish pounds

At constant prices of: 1975 — All Producers

	1970 Total Gross Capital Formation	1970 Increase in Stocks	1970 Gross Fixed Capital Formation	1971 Total Gross Capital Formation	1971 Increase in Stocks	1971 Gross Fixed Capital Formation	1972 Total Gross Capital Formation	1972 Increase in Stocks	1972 Gross Fixed Capital Formation	1973 Total Gross Capital Formation	1973 Increase in Stocks	1973 Gross Fixed Capital Formation
1 Agriculture, hunting, fishing and forestry	...	...	112.0	...	...	115.6	...	...	142.2	...	...	141.6
2 Mining and quarrying	...	...	17.4	...	...	10.6	...	...	8.3	...	...	15.8
3 Manufacturing	...	...	139.6	...	...	145.5	...	...	166.0	...	...	167.9
4 Electricity, gas and water	...	...	48.1	...	...	56.7	...	...	43.7	...	...	70.4
5 Construction	...	...	12.5	...	...	12.6	...	...	14.8	...	...	21.9
6 Wholesale and retail trade, restaurants and hotels [a]	...	...	44.7	...	...	41.3	...	...	44.1	...	...	55.5
7 Transport, storage and communication	...	...	113.3	...	...	136.2	...	...	102.0	...	...	141.3
8 Finance, insurance, real estate and business services	...	...	136.9	...	...	165.1	...	...	211.6	...	...	241.7
9 Community, social and personal services [ab]	...	...	94.1	...	...	100.9	...	...	105.0	...	...	113.2
Total Industries	...	...	718.6	...	...	784.5	...	...	837.7	...	...	969.3
Producers of Government Services [b]	...	...	15.9	...	...	14.6	...	...	20.3	...	...	27.4
Private Non-Profit Institutions Serving Households [b]	...	...	...	...	...	...	...	...	...	...	...	...
Total	789.1	54.6	734.5	806.2	7.1	799.1	892.6	34.6	858.0	1036.3	39.6	996.7

	1974 Total Gross Capital Formation	1974 Increase in Stocks	1974 Gross Fixed Capital Formation	1975 Total Gross Capital Formation	1975 Increase in Stocks	1975 Gross Fixed Capital Formation	1976 Total Gross Capital Formation	1976 Increase in Stocks	1976 Gross Fixed Capital Formation	1977 Total Gross Capital Formation	1977 Increase in Stocks	1977 Gross Fixed Capital Formation
1 Agriculture, hunting, fishing and forestry	...	...	83.0	...	...	79.4	...	...	142.6	...	...	161.7
2 Mining and quarrying	...	...	17.3	...	...	22.1	...	...	32.5	...	...	34.6
3 Manufacturing	...	...	163.2	...	...	191.7	...	...	204.8	...	...	208.4
4 Electricity, gas and water	...	...	46.8	...	...	28.1	...	...	56.0	...	...	66.2
5 Construction	...	...	20.3	...	...	19.4	...	...	20.7	...	...	26.7
6 Wholesale and retail trade, restaurants and hotels [a]	...	...	46.9	...	...	40.7	...	...	35.4	...	...	38.7
7 Transport, storage and communication	...	...	115.5	...	...	110.2	...	...	94.6	...	...	111.1
8 Finance, insurance, real estate and business services	...	...	260.1	...	...	226.8	...	...	249.1	...	...	251.2
9 Community, social and personal services [ab]	...	...	103.9	...	...	96.9	...	...	97.6	...	...	104.1
Total Industries	...	...	857.0	...	...	815.3	...	...	933.3	...	...	1002.7
Producers of Government Services [b]	...	...	23.9	...	...	27.5	...	...	18.1	...	...	20.8
Private Non-Profit Institutions Serving Households [b]	...	...	...	...	...	...	...	...	...	...	...	...
Total	1039.8	158.9	880.9	827.1	-15.7	842.8	953.1	1.7	951.4	1115.1	91.6	1023.5

	1978 Total Gross Capital Formation	1978 Increase in Stocks	1978 Gross Fixed Capital Formation	1979 Total Gross Capital Formation	1979 Increase in Stocks	1979 Gross Fixed Capital Formation
1 Agriculture, hunting, fishing and forestry	...	...	181.7	...	...	189.0
2 Mining and quarrying	...	...	37.3	...	...	35.0
3 Manufacturing	...	...	253.2	...	...	301.0
4 Electricity, gas and water	...	...	62.1	...	...	75.0

Ireland

2.10 Gross Capital Formation by Kind of Activity of Owner, ISIC Major Divisions, in Constant Prices
(Continued)

Million Irish pounds

	1978 Total Gross Capital Formation	1978 Increase in Stocks	1978 Gross Fixed Capital Formation	1979 Total Gross Capital Formation	1979 Increase in Stocks	1979 Gross Fixed Capital Formation
	\multicolumn{6}{c}{At constant prices of: 1975}
5 Construction	...	...	41.5	...	...	40.0
6 Wholesale and retail trade, restaurants and hotels a	...	...	49.2	...	...	55.0
7 Transport, storage and communication	...	...	128.5	...	...	162.0
8 Finance, insurance, real estate and business services	...	...	290.1	...	...	318.0
9 Community, social and personal services ab	...	...	119.7	...	...	129.0
Total Industries	...	...	1163.3	...	...	1304.0
Producers of Government Services b	...	...	23.4	...	...	26.0
Private Non-Profit Institutions Serving Households b	...	...	...	...	...	...
Total	1202.9	16.2	1186.7	1416.0	86.0	1330.0

a) Hotels are included in item 'Community, social and personal services'.
b) Items 'Producers of government services' and 'Private non-profit institutions servicing households' are included in item 'Community, social and personal services'.

2.11 Gross Fixed Capital Formation by Kind of Activity of Owner, ISIC Divisions, in Current Prices

Million Irish pounds

	1970	1971	1972	1973	1974	1975	1976	1977	1978	1979	1980
	\multicolumn{11}{c}{All Producers}
1 Agriculture, hunting, forestry and fishing	54.0	60.4	95.2	104.2	67.8	79.4	177.7	244.8	307.3	336.0	...
a Agriculture and hunting	50.0	55.8	90.5	98.5	58.7	73.2	170.8	236.8	297.3	327.0	...
b Forestry and logging	2.6	2.8	2.9	3.1	3.7	0.9	0.9	1.1	1.5	1.0	...
c Fishing	1.4	1.8	1.8	2.6	5.4	5.3	6.0	6.9	8.5	8.0	...
2 Mining and quarrying	8.9	6.1	5.3	11.2	14.1	22.1	38.8	48.7	58.2	64.0	...
3 Manufacturing	71.3	83.6	102.7	115.6	137.6	191.7	242.3	286.3	385.4	515.0	...
a Manufacturing of food, beverages and tobacco	20.6	24.4	24.8	47.1	61.0	69.8	49.3	64.6	...	...	...
b Textile, wearing apparel and leather industries	7.6	6.0	5.6	7.2	7.4	12.6	22.8	36.9	...	...	...
c Manufacture of wood, and wood products, including furniture	4.1	4.8	3.7	3.1	5.0	2.6	4.2	5.4	...	...	...
d Manufacture of paper and paper products, printing and publishing	2.8	2.6	3.1	5.7	6.9	9.9	6.6	7.0	...	...	...
e Manufacture of chemicals and chemical petroleum, coal, rubber and plastic products	8.7	19.5	16.3	11.8	15.5	31.7	69.7	63.2	...	...	...
f Manufacture of non-metalic mineral products except products of petroleum and coal	13.4	10.3	22.0	14.2	18.5	23.9	33.0	59.3	...	...	...
g Basic metal industries	2.4	4.5	1.5	12.9	3.3	10.0	25.4	13.9	...	...	...
h Manufacture of fabricated metal products, machinery and equipment	11.7	11.5	25.7	13.6	20.0	31.2	31.3	36.0	...	...	...
i Other manufacturing industries	...	...	...	...	...	...	...	...	...	...	...
4 Electricity, gas and water	24.6	29.7	25.6	45.7	39.3	28.1	63.9	87.3	91.3	127.0	...
5 Construction	6.3	7.5	9.5	15.3	17.0	19.4	25.4	37.9	65.7	73.0	...
6 Wholesale and retail trade, restaurants and hotels	22.9	23.4	27.1	38.0	38.7	40.7	42.6	55.3	77.9	98.0	...
a Wholesale and retail trade	22.9	23.4	27.1	38.0	38.7	40.7	42.6	55.3	77.9	98.0	...
b Restaurants and hotels a	...	...	...	...	...	...	...	...	...	...	...
7 Transport, storage and communication	57.9	75.8	58.8	94.3	96.2	110.2	113.5	152.8	196.3	283.0	...
a Transport and storage	47.3	62.5	39.1	67.4	64.0	58.5	68.8	106.7	138.2	215.0	...
b Communication	10.6	13.3	19.7	26.9	32.2	51.7	44.7	46.1	58.1	68.0	...
8 Finance, insurance, real estate and business services	67.4	89.8	131.2	164.9	218.4	226.8	294.1	334.1	436.6	580.0	...
a Financial institutions	5.7	7.9	10.8	14.8	15.0	17.1	42.5	30.1	35.9	39.0	...
b Insurance											...
c Real estate and business services	61.7	81.9	120.4	150.1	203.4	209.7	251.6	304.0	400.7	541.0	...
Real estate except dwellings	...	...	...	...	...	...	...	...	...	...	...

Ireland

2.11 Gross Fixed Capital Formation by Kind of Activity of Owner, ISIC Divisions, in Current Prices
(Continued)

Million Irish pounds

	1970	1971	1972	1973	1974	1975	1976	1977	1978	1979	1980
Dwellings	61.7	81.9	120.4	150.1	203.4	209.7	251.6	304.0	400.7	541.0	...
9 Community, social and personal services	47.1	53.8	62.1	74.7	86.6	96.9	115.1	143.0	181.3	219.0	...
a Sanitary and similar services [a]	28.6	33.7	36.6	39.9	48.9	51.8	55.6	67.6	83.9	107.0	...
b Social and related community services	18.5	20.1	25.5	34.8	37.7	45.1	59.5	75.4	97.4	112.0	...
Educational services	12.5	13.3	16.3	20.4	24.1	23.6	28.8	37.6	48.7	54.0	...
Medical, dental, other health and veterinary services	6.0	6.8	9.2	14.4	13.6	21.5	30.7	37.8	48.7	58.0	...
c Recreational and cultural services [a]	...	...	...	...	...	...	...	...	...	...	...
d Personal and household services [a]	...	...	...	...	...	...	...	...	...	...	...
Total Industries	360.4	430.1	517.5	663.9	715.7	815.3	1113.4	1390.2	1800.0	2295.0	...
Producers of Government Services	8.1	8.1	12.2	18.3	20.1	27.5	21.5	28.8	36.0	45.0	...
Private Non-Profit Institutions Serving Households	...	...	...	...	...	...	...	...	...	...	...
Total	368.5	438.2	529.7	682.2	735.8	842.8	1134.9	1419.0	1836.0	2340.0	...

a) Items 'Restaurants and hotels', 'Recreational and culture services' and 'Personal and household services' are included in item 'Sanitary and similar services'.

2.12 Gross Fixed Capital Formation by Kind of Activity of Owner, ISIC Divisions, in Constant Prices

Million Irish pounds

At constant prices of: 1975

All Producers

	1970	1971	1972	1973	1974	1975	1976	1977	1978	1979	1980
1 Agriculture, hunting, forestry and fishing	112.0	115.6	142.2	141.6	83.0	79.4	142.6	161.7	181.7	189.0	...
a Agriculture and hunting	104.1	107.0	134.2	133.2	72.0	73.2	136.8	156.0	175.2	184.0	...
b Forestry and logging	5.7	5.5	5.1	4.8	4.5	0.9	0.8	0.8	1.0	1.0	...
c Fishing	2.2	3.1	2.9	3.6	6.5	5.3	5.0	4.9	5.5	4.0	...
2 Mining and quarrying	17.4	10.6	8.3	15.8	17.3	22.1	32.5	34.6	37.3	35.0	...
3 Manufacturing	139.6	145.5	166.0	167.9	163.2	191.7	204.8	208.4	253.2	301.0	
a Manufacturing of food, beverages and tobacco	40.7	43.1	40.1	69.2	72.5	69.8	41.6	47.0	...	...	...
b Textile, wearing apparel and leather industries	14.9	10.4	9.0	10.3	8.9	12.6	19.3	26.9	...	...	
c Manufacture of wood, and wood products, including furniture	8.0	8.5	6.2	4.7	6.0	2.6	3.5	3.9	...	...	
d Manufacture of paper and paper products, printing and publishing	5.4	4.6	5.3	8.2	8.2	9.9	5.6	5.1	...	...	
e Manufacture of chemicals and chemical petroleum, coal, rubber and plastic products	17.0	31.9	25.5	16.9	18.3	31.7	58.6	46.1	...	...	...
f Manufacture of non-metallic mineral products except products of petroleum and coal	26.3	18.6	34.8	20.5	21.8	23.9	27.7	43.0	...	...	
g Basic metal industries	4.7	7.8	2.5	18.3	3.8	10.0	21.9	10.0	...	...	
h Manufacture of fabricated metal products, machinery and equipment	22.6	20.6	42.6	19.8	23.7	31.2	26.6	26.4	...	...	
i Other manufacturing industries	...	...	...	...	...	...	...	...	...	...	...
4 Electricity, gas and water	48.1	56.7	43.7	70.4	46.8	28.1	56.0	66.2	62.1	75.0	...
5 Construction	12.5	12.6	14.8	21.9	20.3	19.4	20.7	26.7	41.5	40.0	
6 Wholesale and retail trade, restaurants and hotels	44.7	41.3	44.1	55.5	46.9	40.7	35.4	38.7	49.2	55.0	
a Wholesale and retail trade	44.7	41.3	44.1	55.5	46.9	40.7	35.4	38.7	49.2	55.0	
b Restaurants and hotels [a]	...	...	...	...	...	...	...	...	...	...	
7 Transport, storage and communication	113.3	136.2	102.0	141.3	115.5	110.2	94.6	111.1	128.5	162.0	...
a Transport and storage	91.3	111.1	68.0	100.0	76.9	58.5	57.3	76.8	89.7	122.0	...
b Communication	22.0	25.1	34.0	41.3	38.6	51.7	37.3	34.3	38.8	40.0	
8 Finance, insurance, real estate and business services	136.9	165.1	211.6	241.7	260.1	226.8	249.1	251.2	290.1	318.0	...
a Financial institutions	11.2	14.6	18.3	22.5	17.8	17.1	36.5	22.4	24.7	24.0	...
b Insurance											...
c Real estate and business services	125.7	150.5	193.3	219.2	242.3	209.7	212.6	228.8	265.4	294.0	
Real estate except dwellings	...	...	...	...	...	...	...	...	...	...	

Ireland

2.12 Gross Fixed Capital Formation by Kind of Activity of Owner, ISIC Divisions, in Constant Prices
(Continued)

Million Irish pounds

	1970	1971	1972	1973	1974	1975	1976	1977	1978	1979	1980
				At constant prices of:1975							
Dwellings	125.7	150.5	193.3	219.2	242.3	209.7	212.6	228.8	265.4	294.0	...
9 Community, social and personal services	94.1	100.9	105.0	113.2	103.9	96.9	97.6	104.1	119.7	129.0	...
a Sanitary and similar services [a]	56.0	62.2	61.2	59.6	58.6	51.8	46.9	49.1	55.0	62.0	...
b Social and related community services	38.1	38.7	43.8	53.6	45.3	45.1	50.7	55.0	64.7	67.0	...
Educational services	26.3	26.1	28.2	32.2	28.9	23.6	24.7	27.5	32.4	32.0	...
Medical, dental, other health and veterinary services	11.8	12.6	15.6	21.4	16.4	21.5	26.0	27.5	32.3	35.0	...
c Recreational and cultural services [a]	...	...	...	...	...	...	...	...	...	...	...
d Personal and household services [a]	...	...	...	...	...	...	...	...	...	...	...
Total Industries	718.6	784.5	837.7	969.3	857.0	815.3	933.3	1002.7	1163.3	1304.0	...
Producers of Government Services	15.9	14.6	20.3	27.4	23.9	27.5	18.1	20.8	23.4	26.0	...
Private Non-Profit Institutions Serving Households	...	...	...	...	...	...	...	...	...	...	...
Total	734.5	799.1	858.0	996.7	880.9	842.8	951.4	1023.5	1186.7	1330.0	...

a) Items 'Restaurants and hotels', 'Recreational and culture services' and 'Personal and household services' are included in item 'Sanitary and similar services'.

2.17 Exports and Imports of Goods and Services, Detail

Million Irish pounds

	1970	1971	1972	1973	1974	1975	1976	1977	1978	1979	1980
					Exports of Goods and Services						
1 Exports of merchandise, f.o.b.	455.0	522.3	632.5	852.8	1060.6	1370.8	1851.1	2424.2	2921.6	3413.0	4050.0
2 Transport and communication	69.6	67.8	70.3	88.8	108.8	130.2	161.2	204.9	235.4	282.4	340.0
a In respect of merchandise imports	4.2	7.8	8.9	9.0	10.4	9.9	13.3	18.4	30.4	35.3	37.0
b Other	62.4	60.0	61.4	79.8	98.4	120.3	147.9	186.5	205.0	247.1	303.0
3 Insurance service charges	...	...	...	...	...	...	...	...	...	...	...
4 Other commodities	...	...	...	...	...	...	...	...	...	...	...
5 Adjustments of merchandise exports to change-of-ownership basis	...	...	...	...	...	...	...	...	...	...	...
6 Direct purchases in the domestic market by non-residential households	74.3	79.0	70.4	84.8	102.3	118.0	137.2	184.6	215.9	257.0	279.0
7 Direct purchases in the domestic market by extraterritorial bodies	...	...	...	...	...	...	...	...	...	...	...
Total Exports of Goods and Services	598.9	669.1	773.2	1026.4	1271.7	1619.0	2149.5	2813.7	3372.9	3953.0	4669.0
					Imports of Goods and Services						
1 Imports of merchandise, c.i.f.	667.0	738.6	823.3	1121.5	1601.5	1672.1	2302.0	3042.5	3656.3	4760.4	5340.0
By residents	...	...	...	...	...	...	...	...	...	3953.0	...
By non-residents	...	...	...	...	...	...	...	...	...	...	...
2 Adjustments of merchandise imports to change-of-ownership basis	...	...	...	...	...	...	...	...	...	...	...
3 Other transport and communication	20.2	21.2	21.6	27.3	32.0	45.9	53.6	76.7	100.3	117.4	156.8
4 Other insurance service charges	...	...	...	...	...	...	...	...	...	...	...
5 Other commodities	1.2	1.3	1.3	1.9	2.1	1.8	2.2	2.0	3.0	3.8	4.2
6 Direct purchases abroad by government	...	...	...	...	...	...	...	...	...	...	...
7 Direct purchases abroad by resident households	40.1	42.8	46.9	60.3	72.8	94.2	109.4	135.6	183.8	253.0	299.0
Total Imports of Goods and Services	728.5	803.9	893.1	1211.0	1708.4	1814.0	2467.2	3256.8	3943.4	5135.0	5800.0
Balance of Goods and Services	-129.6	-134.8	-119.9	-184.6	-436.7	-195.0	-317.7	-443.1	-570.5	-1181.7	-1131.0
Total Imports and Balance of Goods and Services	598.9	669.1	773.2	1026.4	1271.7	1619.0	2149.5	2813.7	3372.9	3953.2	4669.0

Ireland

3.12 General Government Income and Outlay Account: Total and Subsectors

Million Irish pounds

		1970				1971			
	Total General Government	Central Government	State or Provincial Government	Local Government	Social Security Funds	Total General Government	Central Government	State or Provincial Government	Local Government	Social Security Funds

Receipts

1 Property and entrepreneurial income	41.3	44.6	...	11.3	1.0	46.1	50.9	...	12.8	1.3
a Net operating surplus	12.1	4.9	...	7.2	...	11.1	3.1	...	7.9	...
b Withdrawals from public quasi-corporations	27.7	39.7	...	4.2	...	33.7	47.8	...	4.8	...
c Interest	...	...	...	...	...	...	...	...	...	...
d Dividends	...	...	...	...	...	...	...	...	...	...
e Net land rent and royalties	...	...	...	...	...	...	...	...	...	...
2 Taxes, fees and contributions	530.2	430.1	...	58.4	41.7	626.0	506.9	...	69.5	49.7
a Indirect taxes	314.7	263.4	...	51.3	...	358.1	296.6	...	61.5	...
b Direct taxes	146.0	146.1	...	...	...	184.0	184.0	...	...	...
Income	137.0	137.0	...	...	...	173.9	173.9	...	...	...
Other	9.1	9.1	...	...	...	10.1	10.1	...	...	...
c Social security contributions	69.5	20.7	...	7.2	41.7	84.0	26.3	...	8.0	49.7
d Fees, fines and penalties	...	...	...	...	...	...	...	...	...	...
3 Other current transfers received	-	1.6	...	82.1	20.5	-	1.1	...	101.5	26.7
a Casualty insurance claims	...	...	...	...	...	...	...	...	...	...
b Transfers from other government subsectors	...	0.4	...	82.1	20.2	...	0.4	...	101.5	26.1
c Transfers from abroad	1.5	1.2	...	...	0.3	1.0	0.6	...	...	0.6
d Other transfers, except imputed	...	...	...	...	...	...	...	...	...	...
e Imputed unfunded employee welfare contributions	...	...	...	...	...	...	...	...	...	...
Total Current Receipts	571.5	476.4	...	151.9	63.2	672.2	558.9	...	183.7	77.7

Disbursements

1 General governement final consumption expenditures	237.3	-16.5	...	113.7	3.0	282.5	-17.7	...	136.7	3.9
a Compensation of employees	...	...	...	...	...	...	...	...	...	...
b Consumption of fixed capital	11.4	3.4	...	8.0	...	13.1	4.0	...	9.1	...
c Goods and services purchased, net	...	...	...	...	...	...	...	...	...	...
d Less: Own account production of fixed assets	...	...	...	...	...	...	...	...	...	...
e Indirect taxes paid, net	...	...	...	...	...	...	...	...	...	...
2 Property income paid	60.3	58.3	...	19.2	...	66.6	64.4	...	22.3	...
3 Subsidies	79.1	69.3	...	9.8	...	86.2	74.9	...	11.3	...
4 Other current transfers paid	176.8	204.7	...	16.3	58.5	208.7	246.2	...	19.3	71.3
a Casualty insurance premiums, net	...	76.0	...	15.6	...	...	86.9	...	18.2	...
b Transfers to other government subsectors	...	102.3	...	0.4	...	...	127.6	...	0.4	...
c Transfers to households	150.1	...	...	...	...	176.3	...	...	...	...
Social security benefits	58.4	...	...	...	58.5	71.2	...	...	...	71.2
Social assistance grants	91.7	76.0	...	15.6	...	105.1	86.9	...	18.2	...
Unfunded employee welfare benefits	...	...	...	...	...	...	...	...	...	...
d Transfers to private non-profit institutions serving households	25.1	24.9	...	0.3	...	30.6	29.9	...	0.7	...
e Transfers to the rest of the world	1.5	1.5	...	...	...	1.8	1.8	...	...	...
Net saving	18.1	23.6	...	-7.2	1.7	28.1	31.5	...	-5.9	2.5
Total Current Disbursements and Net Saving	571.5	476.4	...	151.9	63.2	672.1	558.9	...	183.7	77.6

Ireland

3.12 General Government Income and Outlay Account: Total and Subsectors

Million Irish pounds

		1972					1973				
		Total General Government	Central Government	State or Provincial Government	Local Government	Social Security Funds	Total General Government	Central Government	State or Provincial Government	Local Government	Social Security Funds
		Receipts									
1	Property and entrepreneurial income	57.8	66.1	...	14.5	1.6	54.8	65.2	...	16.6	1.7
	a Net operating surplus	14.0	4.9	...	9.1	...	13.1	2.9	...	10.2	...
	b Withdrawals from public quasi-corporations	43.8	61.2	...	5.4	...	41.7	62.3	...	6.4	...
	c Interest	...	...	...	...	...	...	...	...	...	...
	d Dividends	...	...	...	...	...	...	...	...	...	...
	e Net land rent and royalties	...	...	...	...	...	...	...	...	...	...
2	Taxes, fees and contributions	721.7	582.8	...	81.0	57.9	873.6	714.0	...	84.0	75.6
	a Indirect taxes	414.5	342.4	...	72.2	...	488.4	414.9	...	73.5	...
	b Direct taxes	205.7	205.7	...	...	...	257.9	257.9	...	...	...
	Income	194.8	194.8	...	...	...	244.4	244.4	...	...	...
	Other	10.9	10.9	...	...	...	13.5	13.5	...	...	...
	c Social security contributions	102.5	34.7	...	8.9	57.9	128.5	41.1	...	10.6	75.6
	d Fees, fines and penalties	...	...	...	...	...	...	...	...	...	...
3	Other current transfers received	0.7	0.6	...	124.6	26.7	0.5	0.6	...	167.4	31.8
	a Casualty insurance claims	...	...	...	...	...	...	...	...	...	...
	b Transfers from other government subsectors	...	0.4	...	124.6	26.3	...	0.4	...	167.4	31.5
	c Transfers from abroad	0.8	0.2	...	...	0.4	0.4	0.1	...	...	0.3
	d Other transfers, except imputed	...	...	...	...	...	...	...	...	...	...
	e Imputed unfunded employee welfare contributions	...	...	...	...	...	...	...	...	...	...
	Total Current Receipts	781.2	649.5	...	220.1	86.3	930.1	779.8	...	268.1	109.1
		Disbursements									
1	General government final consumption expenditures	343.0	-15.7	...	162.1	4.3	422.5	-23.2	...	203.9	5.9
	a Compensation of employees	...	...	...	...	...	...	...	...	...	...
	b Consumption of fixed capital	15.4	4.8	...	10.6	...	18.4	5.9	...	12.6	...
	c Goods and services purchased, net	...	...	...	...	...	...	...	...	...	...
	d Less: Own account production of fixed assets	...	...	...	...	...	...	...	...	...	...
	e Indirect taxes paid, net	...	...	...	...	...	...	...	...	...	...
2	Property income paid	75.0	73.3	...	26.0	...	93.4	91.7	...	30.4	...
3	Subsidies	94.8	82.1	...	12.7	...	83.3	67.7	...	15.6	...
4	Other current transfers paid	247.9	290.7	...	25.9	82.6	324.2	388.2	...	33.8	101.6
	a Casualty insurance premiums, net	...	100.7	...	24.8	...	...	140.5	...	32.5	...
	b Transfers to other government subsectors	...	151.0	...	0.4	...	...	198.9	...	0.4	...
	c Transfers to households	208.0	...	...	...	...	274.4	...	...	...	...
	Social security benefits	82.5	...	...	...	82.5	101.5	...	...	...	101.5
	Social assistance grants	125.5	100.7	...	24.8	...	172.9	140.5	...	32.5	...
	Unfunded employee welfare benefits	...	...	...	...	...	...	...	...	...	...
	d Transfers to private non-profit institutions serving households	37.7	36.9	...	0.7	...	46.9	46.0	...	0.9	...
	e Transfers to the rest of the world	2.2	2.1	...	...	...	2.9	2.9	...	...	...
	Net saving	20.5	27.9	...	-6.7	-0.6	6.7	20.6	...	-15.6	1.7
	Total Current Disbursements and Net Saving	781.2	649.5	...	220.1	86.3	930.1	779.8	...	268.1	109.1

Ireland

3.12 General Government Income and Outlay Account: Total and Subsectors

Million Irish pounds

		1974					1975			
		Total General Government	Central Government	State or Provincial Government	Local Government	Social Security Funds	Total General Government	Central Government	State or Provincial Government	Local Government	Social Security Funds

Receipts

1	Property and entrepreneurial income	64.8	79.4	...	19.1	2.0	77.7	97.2	...	25.1	1.9
	a Net operating surplus	12.7	1.8	...	10.9	...	13.0	-0.2	...	13.2	...
	b Withdrawals from public quasi-corporations	52.1	77.7	...	8.2	...	64.7	97.3	...	11.9	...
	c Interest	...	...	...	...	...	...	...	...	...	...
	d Dividends	...	...	...	...	...	...	...	...	...	...
	e Net land rent and royalties	...	...	...	...	...	...	...	...	...	...
2	Taxes, fees and contributions	984.1	786.4	...	92.9	104.7	1233.0	972.8	...	104.0	156.1
	a Indirect taxes	524.4	444.9	...	79.5	...	618.2	531.4	...	86.8	...
	b Direct taxes	293.0	293.0	...	...	...	377.9	377.9	...	...	...
	Income	278.1	278.1	...	...	...	358.8	358.8	...	...	...
	Other	14.9	14.9	...	...	...	19.1	19.1	...	...	...
	c Social security contributions	166.7	48.5	...	13.4	104.7	236.8	63.5	...	17.2	156.1
	d Fees, fines and penalties	...	...	...	...	...	...	...	...	...	...
3	Other current transfers received	2.1	2.1	...	222.1	28.5	2.0	2.4	...	316.2	46.4
	a Casualty insurance claims	...	...	...	...	...	...	...	...	...	...
	b Transfers from other government subsectors	...	0.4	...	222.1	28.1	...	0.5	...	316.2	46.3
	c Transfers from abroad	1.8	1.7	...	...	0.4	2.1	1.9	...	...	0.1
	d Other transfers, except imputed	...	...	...	...	...	...	...	...	...	...
	e Imputed unfunded employee welfare contributions	...	...	...	...	...	...	...	...	...	...
Total Current Receipts		1050.9	868.0	...	334.1	135.2	1312.7	1072.4	...	445.4	204.4

Disbursements

1	General government final consumption expenditures	-62.8	-96.4	...	251.0	7.1	-259.5	-268.2	...	352.2	10.8
	a Compensation of employees	...	...	...	...	...	...	...	...	...	...
	b Consumption of fixed capital	24.3	8.4	...	15.9	...	30.8	10.9	...	19.9	...
	c Goods and services purchased, net	...	...	...	...	...	...	...	...	...	...
	d Less: Own account production of fixed assets	...	...	...	...	...	...	...	...	...	...
	e Indirect taxes paid, net	...	...	...	...	...	...	...	...	...	...
2	Property income paid	109.3	108.3	...	36.7	...	157.9	153.2	...	51.3	...
3	Subsidies	92.2	71.6	...	20.6	...	140.3	113.2	...	60.3	...
4	Other current transfers paid	399.7	478.5	...	44.9	127.0	560.7	668.0	...	63.0	195.3
	a Casualty insurance premiums, net	...	171.0	...	42.9	...	...	227.9	...	57.6	...
	b Transfers to other government subsectors	...	250.2	...	0.4	...	...	362.5	...	0.5	...
	c Transfers to households	340.9	...	...	...	...	480.8	...	...	...	...
	Social security benefits	127.0	...	...	...	127.0	195.3	...	...	...	195.3
	Social assistance grants	213.9	171.0	...	42.9	...	285.5	227.9	...	57.6	...
	Unfunded employee welfare benefits	...	...	...	...	...	...	...	...	...	...
	d Transfers to private non-profit institutions serving households	55.3	53.8	...	1.5	...	75.4	73.2	...	2.2	...
	e Transfers to the rest of the world	3.5	3.5	...	...	...	4.5	4.5	...	...	...
Net saving		-63.1	-45.1	...	-19.0	1.1	-256.8	-209.8	...	-45.4	-1.7
Total Current Disbursements and Net Saving		1050.9	868.0	...	334.1	135.1	1312.7	1072.4	...	445.4	204.4

Ireland

3.12 General Government Income and Outlay Account: Total and Subsectors

Million Irish pounds

	1976 Total General Government	1976 Central Government	1976 State or Provincial Government	1976 Local Government	1976 Social Security Funds	1977 Total General Government	1977 Central Government	1977 State or Provincial Government	1977 Local Government	1977 Social Security Funds
Receipts										
1 Property and entrepreneurial income	93.8	123.4	...	28.0	2.1	135.2	170.2	...	35.8	2.0
a Net operating surplus	14.3	0.3	...	14.0	...	25.7	4.9	...	20.8	...
b Withdrawals from public quasi-corporations	79.5	123.1	...	14.0	...	109.5	165.3	...	15.0	...
c Interest	...	...	...	...	...	...	...	...	...	...
d Dividends	...	...	...	...	...	...	...	...	...	...
e Net land rent and royalties	...	...	...	...	...	...	...	...	...	...
2 Taxes, fees and contributions	1661.1	1323.6	...	132.9	204.6	1927.1	1544.5	...	139.5	243.0
a Indirect taxes	837.2	724.6	...	112.6	...	941.7	826.4	...	115.3	...
b Direct taxes	519.6	519.6	...	...	...	626.6	626.6	...	...	...
Income	490.1	490.1	...	...	...	600.7	600.7	...	...	...
Other	29.5	29.5	...	...	...	25.8	25.8	...	...	...
c Social security contributions	304.3	79.4	...	20.3	204.6	358.8	91.5	...	24.2	243.0
d Fees, fines and penalties	...	...	...	...	...	...	...	...	...	...
3 Other current transfers received	4.9	5.3	...	395.6	52.8	7.3	7.7	...	487.6	51.9
a Casualty insurance claims	...	...	...	...	...	...	...	...	...	...
b Transfers from other government subsectors	...	0.5	...	395.6	52.7	...	0.5	...	487.6	51.8
c Transfers from abroad	5.0	4.8	...	...	0.1	3.0	7.2	...	...	0.1
d Other transfers, except imputed	...	...	...	...	...	...	...	...	...	...
e Imputed unfunded employee welfare contributions	...	...	...	...	...	...	...	...	...	...
Total Current Receipts	1759.8	1452.2	...	556.5	259.4	2069.6	1722.4	...	662.9	296.8
Disbursements										
1 General government final consumption expenditures	-176.7	-214.2	...	411.0	14.4	-169.6	-238.9	...	497.4	21.1
a Compensation of employees	...	...	...	...	...	...	...	...	...	...
b Consumption of fixed capital	37.1	13.4	...	23.7	...	47.3	16.4	...	30.9	...
c Goods and services purchased, net	...	...	...	...	...	...	...	...	...	...
d Less: Own account production of fixed assets	...	...	...	...	...	...	...	...	...	...
e Indirect taxes paid, net	...	...	...	...	...	...	...	...	...	...
2 Property income paid	226.7	221.1	...	65.2	...	286.5	280.2	...	79.0	...
3 Subsidies	170.5	139.9	...	30.7	...	189.6	155.8	...	33.8	...
4 Other current transfers paid	687.8	816.6	...	74.0	245.9	779.6	961.1	...	79.2	279.1
a Casualty insurance premiums, net	...	271.3	...	69.8	245.9	...	307.0	...	74.4	279.1
b Transfers to other government subsectors	...	448.3	...	0.5	...	...	539.4	...	0.5	...
c Transfers to households	587.0	...	...	...	...	660.5	...	...	...	...
Social security benefits	245.9	...	...	...	245.9	279.1	...	...	...	279.1
Social assistance grants	341.1	271.3	...	69.8	...	381.4	307.0	...	74.4	...
Unfunded employee welfare benefits	...	...	...	...	...	...	...	...	...	...
d Transfers to private non-profit institutions serving households	94.4	90.7	...	3.8	...	110.8	106.5	...	4.3	...
e Transfers to the rest of the world	6.3	6.3	...	...	...	8.2	8.2	...	...	...
Net saving	-166.0	-141.4	...	-24.3	-0.9	-174.2	-144.3	...	-26.5	-3.4
Total Current Disbursements and Net Saving	1759.8	1452.2	...	556.5	259.4	2069.6	1722.4	...	662.9	296.8

3.12 General Government Income and Outlay Account: Total and Subsectors

Ireland

Million Irish pounds

	1978					1979				
	Total General Government	Central Government	State or Provincial Government	Local Government	Social Security Funds	Total General Government	Central Government	State or Provincial Government	Local Government	Social Security Funds
Receipts										
1 Property and entrepreneurial income	177.2	217.6	...	43.3	1.7	205.6	251.2	...	53.8	1.8
a Net operating surplus	41.3	14.9	...	26.4	...	52.0	18.7	...	33.3	...
b Withdrawals from public quasi-corporations	135.9	202.7	...	16.9	...	153.6	232.5	...	20.5	...
c Interest	...	...	...	...	...	...	...	...	...	...
d Dividends	...	...	...	...	...	...	...	...	...	...
e Net land rent and royalties	...	...	...	...	...	...	...	...	...	...
2 Taxes, fees and contributions	2190.1	1799.0	...	116.0	275.1	2559.7	2105.8	...	131.6	322.3
a Indirect taxes	1053.1	966.5	...	86.6	...	1176.4	1080.2	...	96.2	...
b Direct taxes	726.2	726.2	...	...	...	889.8	889.8	...	...	...
Income	710.5	710.5	...	...	...	862.5	862.5	...	...	...
Other	15.6	15.6	...	...	...	27.3	27.3	...	...	...
c Social security contributions	410.8	106.3	...	29.5	275.1	493.5	135.8	...	35.4	322.3
d Fees, fines and penalties	...	...	...	...	...	...	...	...	...	...
3 Other current transfers received	12.3	12.8	...	642.0	64.9	84.0	84.4	...	781.9	80.8
a Casualty insurance claims	...	...	...	...	...	...	...	...	...	...
b Transfers from other government subsectors	...	0.5	...	642.0	64.9	...	0.5	...	781.9	80.7
c Transfers from abroad	9.5	12.3	...	...	-	81.8	83.9	...	...	0.1
d Other transfers, except imputed	...	...	...	...	...	...	...	...	...	...
e Imputed unfunded employee welfare contributions	...	...	...	...	...	...	...	...	...	...
Total Current Receipts	2379.6	2029.3	...	801.3	341.7	2849.3	2441.4	...	967.3	404.9
Disbursements										
1 General government final consumption expenditures	-313.2	-388.3	...	610.0	17.4	-427.4	-512.8	...	737.9	22.9
a Compensation of employees	...	...	...	...	...	...	...	...	...	...
b Consumption of fixed capital	55.9	19.2	...	36.7	...	68.9	23.9	...	45.0	...
c Goods and services purchased, net	...	...	...	...	...	...	...	...	...	...
d Less: Own account production of fixed assets	...	...	...	...	...	...	...	...	...	...
e Indirect taxes paid, net	...	...	...	...	...	...	...	...	...	...
2 Property income paid	357.0	347.3	...	95.1	...	440.8	429.6	...	112.4	...
3 Subsidies	244.2	198.0	...	46.3	...	280.0	218.7	...	61.3	...
4 Other current transfers paid	900.8	1195.1	...	93.2	320.0	1099.7	1468.8	...	129.0	365.0
a Casualty insurance premiums, net	...	348.1	...	87.6	...	...	405.3	...	119.7	...
b Transfers to other government subsectors	...	706.9	...	0.5	...	...	862.6	...	0.5	...
c Transfers to households	753.5	...	...	...	...	890.0	...	...	...	...
Social security benefits	320.0	...	...	...	320.0	365.0	...	...	...	365.0
Social assistance grants	435.6	348.1	...	87.6	...	525.0	405.3	...	119.7	...
Unfunded employee welfare benefits	...	...	...	...	...	...	...	...	...	...
d Transfers to private non-profit institutions serving households	128.3	123.2	...	5.1	...	170.0	161.2	...	8.8	...
e Transfers to the rest of the world	16.9	16.9	...	...	...	39.7	39.7	...	...	...
Net saving	-302.3	-263.4	...	-43.2	4.3	-411.0	-354.6	...	-73.3	17.0
Total Current Disbursements and Net Saving	2379.6	2029.3	...	801.3	341.7	2849.6	2441.4	...	967.3	404.9

Ireland

3.13 General Government Capital Accumulation Account: Total and Subsectors

Million Irish pounds

	1970					1971				
	Total General Government	Central Government	State or Provincial Government	Local Government	Social Security Funds	Total General Government	Central Government	State or Provincial Government	Local Government	Social Security Funds

Finance of Gross Accumulation

1 Gross saving	29.5	27.0	...	0.8	1.7	41.2	35.5	...	3.2	2.5
a Consumption of fixed capital	11.4	3.4	...	8.0	...	13.1	4.0	...	9.1	...
b Net saving	18.1	23.6	...	-7.2	1.7	28.1	31.5	...	-5.9	2.5
2 Capital transfers received	-28.5	-43.5	...	15.0	...	-34.9	-53.0	...	18.2	...
a From other government subsectors	...	-11.2	...	11.2	...	...	-12.3	...	12.3	...
b From other resident sectors	-28.5	-32.2	...	3.8	...	-34.9	-40.8	...	5.9	...
c From rest of the world	-	-	...	-	...	-	-	...	...	...
Finance of Gross Accumulation	1.0	-16.5	...	15.8	1.7	6.3	-17.7	...	21.4	2.5

Gross Accumulation

1 Gross capital formation	60.2	18.3	...	41.9	...	71.4	19.5	...	52.0	...
2 Purchases of land, net	...	...	...	...	...	...	...	...	...	...
3 Purchases of intangible assets, net	...	...	...	...	...	...	...	...	...	...
4 Capital transfers paid	...	...	...	...	...	...	...	...	...	...
Net lending	-59.2	-34.8	...	-26.1	1.7	-65.1	-37.0	...	-30.6	2.5
Gross Accumulation	1.0	16.5	...	15.8	...	6.3	17.7	...	21.4	...

	1972					1973				
	Total General Government	Central Government	State or Provincial Government	Local Government	Social Security Funds	Total General Government	Central Government	State or Provincial Government	Local Government	Social Security Funds

Finance of Gross Accumulation

1 Gross saving	35.9	32.7	...	3.9	-0.6	25.1	26.5	...	-3.0	1.7
a Consumption of fixed capital	15.4	4.8	...	10.6	...	18.4	5.9	...	12.5	...
b Net saving	20.5	27.9	...	-6.7	-0.6	6.7	20.6	...	-15.5	1.7
2 Capital transfers received	-27.4	-48.4	...	21.0	...	-21.0	-49.7	...	28.7	...
a From other government subsectors	...	-14.4	...	14.4	...	...	-19.5	...	19.5	...
b From other resident sectors	-27.4	-34.0	...	6.6	...	-21.0	-30.2	...	9.2	...
c From rest of the world	-	-	...	-	...	-	-	...	-	...
Finance of Gross Accumulation	8.5	-15.7	...	24.9	-0.6	4.2	-23.2	...	25.7	1.7

Gross Accumulation

1 Gross capital formation	81.1	23.2	...	57.9	...	108.0	31.8	...	76.2	...
2 Purchases of land, net	...	...	...	...	...	...	...	...	...	...
3 Purchases of intangible assets, net	...	...	...	...	...	...	...	...	...	...
4 Capital transfers paid	...	...	...	...	...	...	...	...	...	...
Net lending	-72.2	-38.9	...	-33.0	-0.6	-103.8	-55.0	...	-50.5	1.7
Gross Accumulation	8.5	15.7	...	24.9	...	4.2	23.2	...	25.7	...

	1974					1975				
	Total General Government	Central Government	State or Provincial Government	Local Government	Social Security Funds	Total General Government	Central Government	State or Provincial Government	Local Government	Social Security Funds

Finance of Gross Accumulation

1 Gross saving	-38.8	-36.7	...	-3.1	1.1	-226.0	-198.9	...	-25.5	-1.7
a Consumption of fixed capital	24.3	8.4	...	15.9	...	30.8	10.9	...	19.9	...
b Net saving	-63.1	-45.1	...	-19.0	1.1	-256.8	-209.8	...	-45.4	-1.7
2 Capital transfers received	-24.0	59.7	...	35.6	...	-33.5	-69.3	...	35.8	...
a From other government subsectors	...	-23.3	...	23.3	...	...	-19.0	...	19.0	...
b From other resident sectors	-24.0	-36.3	...	12.3	...	-35.2	-52.0	...	16.8	...
c From rest of the world	-	-	...	-	...	1.8	1.8	...	-	...
Finance of Gross Accumulation	-62.8	-96.4	...	32.5	1.1	-259.5	-268.2	...	10.3	-1.7

Gross Accumulation

1 Gross capital formation	145.9	39.3	...	106.6	...	164.8	46.5	...	118.3	...
2 Purchases of land, net	...	...	...	...	...	...	...	...	...	...
3 Purchases of intangible assets, net	...	...	...	...	...	...	...	...	...	...
4 Capital transfers paid	...	...	...	...	...	...	...	...	...	...
Net lending	-208.7	-135.7	...	-74.1	1.1	-424.3	-314.7	...	-108.0	-1.7
Gross Accumulation	62.8	96.4	...	32.5	...	259.5	268.2	...	10.3	...

Ireland

3.13 General Government Capital Accumulation Account: Total and Subsectors

Million Irish pounds

	1976					1977				
	Total General Government	Central Government	State or Provincial Government	Local Government	Social Security Funds	Total General Government	Central Government	State or Provincial Government	Local Government	Social Security Funds

Finance of Gross Accumulation

	1976					1977				
1 Gross saving	-129.5	-128.0	...	-0.6	-0.9	-126.9	-127.9	...	4.4	-3.4
a Consumption of fixed capital	37.1	13.4	...	23.7	...	47.3	16.4	...	30.9	...
b Net saving	-166.6	-141.4	...	-24.3	-0.9	-174.2	-144.3	...	-26.5	-3.4
2 Capital transfers received	-47.2	-86.3	...	39.0	...	-42.7	-111.0	...	68.3	...
a From other government subsectors	...	-14.0	...	14.0	...	...	-22.1	...	22.1	...
b From other resident sectors	-56.0	-81.1	...	25.0	...	-52.0	-98.2	...	46.2	...
c From rest of the world	8.8	8.8	...	-	...	9.3	9.3	...	-	...
Finance of Gross Accumulation	-176.7	-214.2	...	38.4	-0.9	-169.6	-238.9	...	72.8	-3.4

Gross Accumulation

1 Gross capital formation	165.6	40.8	...	124.9	...	207.7	57.0	...	150.7	...
2 Purchases of land, net	...	...	...	...	...	...	...	...	...	...
3 Purchases of intangible assets, net	...	...	...	...	...	...	...	...	...	...
4 Capital transfers paid	...	...	...	...	...	...	...	...	...	...
Net lending	-342.3	-255.0	...	-86.4	-0.9	-377.3	-295.9	...	-78.0	-3.4
Gross Accumulation	176.7	214.2	...	38.4	...	169.6	238.9	...	72.8	...

	1978					1979				
	Total General Government	Central Government	State or Provincial Government	Local Government	Social Security Funds	Total General Government	Central Government	State or Provincial Government	Local Government	Social Security Funds

Finance of Gross Accumulation

1 Gross saving	-246.4	-244.2	...	-6.5	4.3	-342.0	-330.7	...	-28.3	17.0
a Consumption of fixed capital	55.9	19.2	...	36.7	...	69.0	23.9	...	45.0	...
b Net saving	-302.3	-263.4	...	-43.2	4.3	-411.0	-354.6	...	-73.3	17.0
2 Capital transfers received	-66.7	-144.0	...	77.3	...	-85.4	-182.1	...	96.7	...
a From other government subsectors	...	-31.0	...	31.0	...	...	-47.2	...	47.2	...
b From other resident sectors	-79.4	-125.8	...	46.3	...	-115.1	-164.6	...	49.5	...
c From rest of the world	12.7	12.7	...	-	...	29.7	29.7	...	...	...
Finance of Gross Accumulation	-313.2	-388.3	...	70.8	4.3	-427.4	-512.8	...	68.4	17.0

Gross Accumulation

1 Gross capital formation	252.8	86.3	...	166.5	...	296.9	106.9	...	190.0	...
2 Purchases of land, net	...	...	...	...	...	...	...	...	...	...
3 Purchases of intangible assets, net	...	...	...	...	...	...	...	...	...	...
4 Capital transfers paid	...	...	...	...	...	...	...	...	...	...
Net lending	-566.0	-474.6	...	-95.7	4.3	-724.3	-619.7	...	-121.6	17.0
Gross Accumulation	313.2	388.3	...	70.8	...	427.4	512.8	...	68.4	...

3.51 External Transactions: Current Account: Detail

Million Irish pounds

	1970	1971	1972	1973	1974	1975	1976	1977	1978	1979	1980

Payments to the Rest of the World

	1970	1971	1972	1973	1974	1975	1976	1977	1978	1979	1980
1 Imports of goods and services	728.5	803.9	893.1	1211.0	1708.4	1814.0	2467.2	3256.8	3943.4	5135.0	5800.0
2 Factor income paid to the rest of the world	40.9	47.5	59.5	93.3	121.1	145.7	214.5	259.9	368.0	444.0	...
a Compensation of employees	-	-	-	-	-	-	...	...	...	...	...
b Property and entrepreneurial income paid	40.9	47.5	59.5	93.3	121.1	145.7	214.5	259.9	368.0	444.0	...
3 Indirect taxes paid to supranational organizations	...	...	...	5.8	7.7	27.6	54.1	73.8	66.4	75.5	93.9
4 Other current transfers to the rest of the world	2.6	3.1	3.6	4.7	5.3	6.7	8.8	11.3	12.8	16.8	20.6
a By general government	2.1	2.6	3.0	4.0	4.7	6.1	8.1	10.6	12.0	15.9	19.6
b By other resident sectors	0.5	0.5	0.6	0.7	0.6	0.6	0.7	0.7	0.8	0.9	1.0
5 Surplus of the nation on current transactions	-65.3	-71.0	-48.4	-82.3	-280.2	-6.0	-157.1	-155.2	-200.3	-726.7	-725.0
Payments to the Rest of the World, and Surplus of the Nation on Current Transfers	706.7	783.5	907.8	1232.5	1562.3	1988.0	2587.5	3446.6	4190.3	4944.0	...

Ireland

3.51 External Transactions: Current Account: Detail
(Continued)

Million Irish pounds

	1970	1971	1972	1973	1974	1975	1976	1977	1978	1979	1980
Receipts From The Rest of the World											
1 Exports of goods and services	598.9	669.1	773.2	1026.4	1271.7	1619.0	2149.5	2813.7	3372.9	3953.0	4669.0
2 Factor income received from the rest of the world	69.2	74.1	89.1	116.8	154.6	166.7	216.2	228.4	299.8	375.0	...
a Compensation of employees	1.8	2.0	2.0	2.5	3.3	4.7	4.2	5.1	5.7	7.2	9.4
b Property and entrepreneurial income received	67.4	72.1	87.1	114.3	151.3	162.0	212.0	223.3	294.1	367.9	...
3 Subsidies received from supranational organizations	69.2	74.1	89.1	37.2	66.0	119.1	130.8	295.3	388.6	404.0	381.0
4 Other current transfers from the rest of the world	38.6	40.3	45.5	52.1	70.0	83.2	91.0	109.2	129.0	212.0	267.2
a To general government	1.5	1.0	0.8	0.4	1.8	2.1	5.0	3.0	9.5	81.8	89.1
b To other resident sectors	37.1	39.3	44.7	51.7	68.4	81.2	75.0	106.0	120.7	130.0	178.1
Receipts from the Rest of the World on Current Transfers	706.7	783.5	907.8	1232.5	1562.3	1988.0	2587.5	3446.6	4190.3	4944.0	...

3.52 External Transactions: Capital Accumulation Account

Million Irish pounds

	1970	1971	1972	1973	1974	1975	1976	1977	1978	1979	1980
Finance of Gross Accumulation											
1 Surplus of the nation on current transactions	-65.3	-71.0	-48.4	-82.3	-280.2	-6.0	-157.1	-155.2	-200.3	-726.7	-725.0
2 Capital transfers received from the rest of the world	...	...	...	...	...	1.8	8.8	9.3	15.2	33.0	63.0
Total Finance of Gross Accumulation	...	...	...	...	...	-4.2	-148.3	-145.9	-167.3	-693.7	-662.0
Gross Accumulation											
1 Capital transfers paid to the rest of the world	...	...	...	...	...	...	...	...	...	...	...
2 Purchases of intangible assets, n.e.c., net, from the rest of the world	...	...	...	...	...	...	...	...	...	...	...
3 Net lending to the rest of the world	-65.3	-71.0	-48.4	-82.3	-280.2	-4.2	-148.3	-145.9	-167.3	-693.7	662.0
Total Gross Accumulation	...	...	...	...	...	...	...	...	...	...	...

4.6 Cost Components of Value Added, ISIC Divisions

Million Irish pounds

	1970						1971				
	Compensation of Employees	Capital Consumption	Net Operating Surplus	Indirect Taxes	Less: Subsidies Received	Value Added	Compensation of Employees	Capital Consumption	Net Operating Surplus	Indirect Taxes	Less: Subsidies Received	Value Added
All Producers												
1 Agriculture, hunting, forestry and fishing	26.0	...	206.9	...	...	232.9	28.6	...	229.4	...	...	258.0
2 Mining and quarrying	30.3	...	18.5	...	...	48.8	39.2	...	17.9	...	...	57.1
3 Manufacturing	204.1	...	94.9	...	...	299.0	234.8	...	99.1	...	...	333.9
a Manufacture of food, beverages and tobacco	66.0	...	33.7	...	...	99.7	76.5	...	39.9	...	...	116.4
b Textile, wearing apparel and leather industries	43.0	...	18.1	...	...	61.1	47.2	...	16.9	...	...	64.1
c Manufacture of wood and wood products, including furniture	...	...	...	...	...	...	...	...	...	...	...	...
d Manufacture of paper and paper products, printing and publishing	20.9	...	8.0	...	...	28.9	24.1	...	7.8	...	...	31.9
e Manufacture of chemicals and chemical petroleum, coal, rubber and plastic products		...		...	...			...		...	...	
f Manufacture of non-metallic mineral products, except products of petroleum and coal		...		...	...			...		...	...	
g Basic metal industries	74.2	...	35.1	...	...	109.3	87.0	...	34.5	...	...	121.5
h Manufacture of fabricated metal products, machinery and equipment		...		...	...			...		...	...	
i Other manufacturing industries		...		...	...			...		...	...	
4 Electricity, gas and water	19.0	...	19.9	...	...	38.9	21.0	...	24.6	...	...	45.6

Ireland

4.6 Cost Components of Value Added, ISIC Divisions
(Continued)

Million Irish pounds

	\multicolumn{6}{c	}{1970}	\multicolumn{6}{c	}{1971}
	Compensation of Employees	Capital Consumption	Net Operating Surplus	Indirect Taxes	Less: Subsidies Received	Value Added	Compensation of Employees	Capital Consumption	Net Operating Surplus	Indirect Taxes	Less: Subsidies Received	Value Added
5 Construction	100.2	...	21.6	...	...	121.8	116.1	...	28.6	...	...	144.7
6 Wholesale and retail trade, restaurants and hotels	114.1	...	69.4	...	...	183.5	127.4	...	77.3	...	...	204.7
a Wholesale and retail trade	95.3	...	58.3	...	...	153.6	106.3	...	63.4	...	...	169.7
b Restaurants and hotels	18.8	...	11.1	...	...	29.9	21.1	...	13.9	...	...	35.0
7 Transport, storage and communication	68.7	...	30.2	...	...	98.9	79.3	...	34.1	...	...	113.4
a Transport and storage	50.3	...	22.2	...	...	72.5	56.6	...	24.7	...	...	81.3
b Communication	18.4	...	8.0	...	...	26.4	22.7	...	9.4	...	...	32.1
8 Finance, insurance, real estate and business services	34.6	...	26.6	...	...	61.2	33.9	...	21.0	...	...	54.9
a Financial institutions	34.6	...	26.6	...	...	61.2	33.9	...	21.0	...	...	54.9
b Insurance		...		...	...			...		...	...	
c Real estate and business services	...	...	...	...	...	...	...	...	...	...	...	...
9 Community, social and personal services	49.9	...	91.1	...	...	141.0	67.0	...	115.0	...	...	182.0
Total, Industries	646.9	...	579.1	...	...	1226.0	747.3	...	647.0	...	...	1394.3
Producers of Government Services	197.9	...	8.2	...	...	206.1	231.8	...	9.6	...	...	241.4
Other Producers		...		...	...			...		...	...	
Total [a]	844.8	...	587.3	...	...	1432.1	979.1	...	656.6	...	...	1635.7
Imputed bank service charge	...	...	-35.0	...	...	-35.0	...	...	-36.0	...	...	-36.0
Import duties	...	...	...	...	...	...	...	...	...	...	...	...
Value added tax	...	...	...	...	...	...	...	...	...	...	...	...
Other adjustments	...	...	-12.5	314.7	79.1	223.1	...	...	-18.5	358.1	86.2	253.4
Total	844.8	...	539.8	314.7	79.1	1620.2	979.1	...	602.1	358.1	86.2	1853.1

	\multicolumn{6}{c	}{1972}	\multicolumn{6}{c	}{1973}
	Compensation of Employees	Capital Consumption	Net Operating Surplus	Indirect Taxes	Less: Subsidies Received	Value Added	Compensation of Employees	Capital Consumption	Net Operating Surplus	Indirect Taxes	Less: Subsidies Received	Value Added
\multicolumn{13}{c	}{**All Producers**}
1 Agriculture, hunting, forestry and fishing	31.0	...	318.0	...	...	349.0	33.6	...	402.5	...	...	436.1
2 Mining and quarrying	44.7	...	26.1	...	...	70.8	57.4	...	31.3	...	...	88.7
3 Manufacturing	274.4	...	131.9	...	...	406.3	332.5	...	177.2	...	...	509.7
a Manufacture of food, beverages and tobacco	88.1	...	51.3	...	...	139.4	107.6	...	66.3	...	...	173.9
b Textile, wearing apparel and leather industries	51.4	...	19.6	...	...	71.0	62.8	...	24.8	...	...	87.6
c Manufacture of wood and wood products, including furniture	...	...	...	...	...	...	...	...	...	...	...	...
d Manufacture of paper and paper products, printing and publishing	27.4	...	11.1	...	...	38.5	32.0	...	13.3	...	...	45.3
e Manufacture of chemicals and chemical petroleum, coal, rubber and plastic products		...						...				
f Manufacture of non-metallic mineral products, except products of petroleum and coal		...						...				
g Basic metal industries	107.5	...	49.9	...	...	157.4	130.1	...	72.8	...	...	202.9
h Manufacture of fabricated metal products, machinery and equipment		...						...				
i Other manufacturing industries		...						...				
4 Electricity, gas and water	24.8	...	28.6	...	...	53.4	28.0	...	32.6	...	...	60.6
5 Construction	139.1	...	36.2	...	...	175.3	168.8	...	44.3	...	...	213.1
6 Wholesale and retail trade, restaurants and hotels	146.6	...	100.0	...	...	246.6	177.1	...	128.8	...	...	305.9
a Wholesale and retail trade	123.9	...	83.3	...	...	207.2	151.1	...	109.1	...	...	260.2
b Restaurants and hotels	22.7	...	16.7	...	...	39.4	26.0	...	19.7	...	...	45.7
7 Transport, storage and communication	89.8	...	36.2	...	...	126.0	107.6	...	48.5	...	...	156.1
a Transport and storage	64.1	...	26.2	...	...	90.3	77.0	...	35.2	...	...	112.2

Ireland

4.6 Cost Components of Value Added, ISIC Divisions
(Continued)

Million Irish pounds

	1972						1973					
	Compensation of Employees	Capital Consumption	Net Operating Surplus	Indirect Taxes	Less: Subsidies Received	Value Added	Compensation of Employees	Capital Consumption	Net Operating Surplus	Indirect Taxes	Less: Subsidies Received	Value Added
b Communication	25.7	...	10.0	...	...	35.7	30.6	...	13.3	...	...	43.9
8 Finance, insurance, real estate and business services	39.2	...	31.2	...	...	70.4	47.5	...	37.8	...	...	85.3
a Financial institutions	39.2	...	31.2	...	...	70.4	47.5	...	37.8	...	...	85.3
b Insurance												
c Real estate and business services	...	...	...	...	...	...	...	...	...	...	...	...
9 Community, social and personal services	78.0	...	130.8	...	...	208.8	100.3	...	151.8	...	...	252.1
Total, Industries	867.6	...	839.0	...	...	1706.6	1052.8	...	1054.8	...	...	2107.6
Producers of Government Services	276.7		11.4	...	...	288.1	340.3		13.9	...	...	354.2
Other Producers												
Total a	1144.3	...	850.4	...	...	1994.7	1393.1	...	1068.7	...	...	2461.8
Imputed bank service charge	...	...	-43.9	...	...	-43.9	...	...	-50.6	...	...	-50.6
Import duties	...	...	...	...	...	...	...	...	...	...	...	...
Value added tax	...	...	...	...	...	...	...	...	...	...	...	...
Other adjustments	...	...	-33.0	414.5	94.8	286.7	...	...	-86.1	494.2	120.5	287.6
Total	1144.3	...	773.5	414.5	94.8	2237.5	1393.1	...	932.0	494.2	120.5	2698.8

	1974						1975					
	Compensation of Employees	Capital Consumption	Net Operating Surplus	Indirect Taxes	Less: Subsidies Received	Value Added	Compensation of Employees	Capital Consumption	Net Operating Surplus	Indirect Taxes	Less: Subsidies Received	Value Added

All Producers

1 Agriculture, hunting, forestry and fishing	38.1	...	380.4	...	...	418.5	45.3	...	539.9	...	...	585.2
2 Mining and quarrying	73.3	...	29.4	...	...	102.7	89.7	...	34.0	...	...	123.7
3 Manufacturing	405.9	...	207.4	...	...	613.3	500.3	...	218.1	...	...	718.4
a Manufacture of food, beverages and tobacco	135.1	...	100.2	...	...	235.3	174.0	...	100.6	...	...	274.6
b Textile, wearing apparel and leather industries	72.4	...	16.1	...	...	88.5	83.2	...	21.7	...	...	104.9
c Manufacture of wood and wood products, including furniture	...	...	...	...	...	...	...	...	...	...	...	...
d Manufacture of paper and paper products, printing and publishing	39.8	...	14.4	...	...	54.2	49.6	...	12.3	...	...	61.9
e Manufacture of chemicals and chemical petroleum, coal, rubber and plastic products												
f Manufacture of non-metallic mineral products, except products of petroleum and coal												
g Basic metal industries	158.6	...	76.7	...	...	235.3	193.5	...	83.5	...	...	277.0
h Manufacture of fabricated metal products, machinery and equipment												
i Other manufacturing industries												
4 Electricity, gas and water	36.7	...	39.3	...	...	76.0	49.2	...	50.9	...	...	100.1
5 Construction	199.1	...	41.9	...	...	241.0	241.1	...	51.4	...	...	292.5
6 Wholesale and retail trade, restaurants and hotels	213.3	...	162.3	...	...	375.6	279.0	...	180.9	...	...	459.9
a Wholesale and retail trade	183.3	...	139.7	...	...	323.0	240.4	...	153.6	...	...	394.0
b Restaurants and hotels	30.0	...	22.6	...	...	52.6	38.6	...	27.3	...	...	65.9
7 Transport, storage and communication	128.3	...	63.4	...	...	191.7	169.5	...	66.5	...	...	236.0
a Transport and storage	92.7	...	46.9	...	...	139.6	122.3	...	45.4	...	...	167.7
b Communication	35.6	...	16.5	...	...	52.1	47.2	...	21.1	...	...	68.3
8 Finance, insurance, real estate and business services	59.3	...	42.9	...	...	102.2	78.2	...	38.6	...	...	116.8
a Financial institutions	59.3	...	42.9	...	...	102.2	78.2	...	38.6	...	...	116.8
b Insurance												
c Real estate and business services	...	...	...	...	...	...	...	...	...	...	...	...
9 Community, social and personal services	126.2	...	162.9	...	...	289.1	150.5	...	208.3	...	...	358.8

Ireland

4.6 Cost Components of Value Added, ISIC Divisions
(Continued)

Million Irish pounds

	1974						1975					
	Compensation of Employees	Capital Consumption	Net Operating Surplus	Indirect Taxes	Less: Subsidies Received	Value Added	Compensation of Employees	Capital Consumption	Net Operating Surplus	Indirect Taxes	Less: Subsidies Received	Value Added
Total, Industries	1280.2	...	1129.9	...	...	2410.1	1602.8	...	1388.6	...	...	2991.4
Producers of Government Services	406.6	...	19.7	...	...	426.3	556.4	...	25.4	...	...	581.8
Other Producers		...		...	...			...		...	...	
Total [a]	1686.8	...	1149.6	...	...	2836.4	2159.2	...	1414.0	...	...	3573.2
Imputed bank service charge	...	...	-68.7	...	...	-68.7	...	...	-102.2	...	...	-102.2
Import duties	...	...	...	...	...	...	...	...	...	...	...	...
Value added tax	...	...	...	...	...	...	...	...	...	...	...	...
Other adjustments	...	...	-157.3	532.1	158.2	216.6	...	...	-133.1	645.8	259.3	253.4
Total	1686.8	...	923.6	532.1	158.2	2984.3	2159.2	...	1178.7	645.8	259.3	3724.4

	1976						1977					
	Compensation of Employees	Capital Consumption	Net Operating Surplus	Indirect Taxes	Less: Subsidies Received	Value Added	Compensation of Employees	Capital Consumption	Net Operating Surplus	Indirect Taxes	Less: Subsidies Received	Value Added
All Producers											
1 Agriculture, hunting, forestry and fishing	49.4	...	622.2	...	...	671.6	54.6	...	858.4	...	...	913.0
2 Mining and quarrying	106.6	...	47.4	...	...	154.0	129.2	...	50.0	...	...	179.2
3 Manufacturing	619.1	...	300.7	...	...	919.8	726.8	...	373.4	...	...	1100.2
a Manufacture of food, beverages and tobacco	208.3	...	125.7	...	...	334.0	243.6	...	146.1	...	...	389.7
b Textile, wearing apparel and leather industries	102.3	...	29.2	...	...	131.5	112.6	...	35.1	...	...	147.7
c Manufacture of wood and wood products, including furniture	...	...	...	...	...	...	...	...	...	...	...	...
d Manufacture of paper and paper products, printing and publishing	61.7	...	15.3	...	...	77.0	70.6	...	23.3	...	...	93.9
e Manufacture of chemicals and chemical petroleum, coal, rubber and plastic products		...		...	...			...		...	...	
f Manufacture of non-metallic mineral products, except products of petroleum and coal		...		...	...			...		...	...	
g Basic metal industries	246.8	...	130.5	...	...	377.3	300.0	...	168.9	...	...	468.9
h Manufacture of fabricated metal products, machinery and equipment		...		...	...			...		...	...	
i Other manufacturing industries		...		...	...			...		...	...	
4 Electricity, gas and water	54.4	...	60.4	...	...	114.8	62.6	...	73.4	...	...	136.0
5 Construction	275.0	...	62.3	...	...	337.3	333.2	...	81.3	...	...	414.5
6 Wholesale and retail trade, restaurants and hotels	339.8	...	214.0	...	...	553.8	400.9	...	289.2	...	...	690.1
a Wholesale and retail trade	292.3	...	181.9	...	...	474.2	344.5	...	252.7	...	...	597.2
b Restaurants and hotels	47.5	...	32.1	...	...	79.6	56.4	...	36.5	...	...	92.9
7 Transport, storage and communication	192.9	...	101.0	...	...	293.9	218.4	...	133.4	...	...	351.8
a Transport and storage	136.3	...	73.3	...	...	209.6	152.2	...	98.2	...	...	250.4
b Communication	56.6	...	27.7	...	...	84.3	66.2	...	35.2	...	...	101.4
8 Finance, insurance, real estate and business services	94.0	...	69.0	...	...	163.0	110.6	...	109.4	...	...	220.0
a Financial institutions	94.0	...	69.0	...	...	163.0	110.6	...	109.4	...	...	220.0
b Insurance		...		...	...			...		...	...	
c Real estate and business services	...	...	...	...	...	...	...	...	...	...	...	...
9 Community, social and personal services	186.6	...	231.2	...	...	417.8	223.4	...	293.2	...	...	516.6
Total, Industries	1917.8	...	1708.2	...	...	3626.0	2259.7	...	2261.7	...	...	4521.4
Producers of Government Services	657.7	...	31.5	...	...	689.2	743.6	...	38.6	...	...	782.2
Other Producers		...		...	...			...		...	...	
Total [a]	2575.5	...	1739.7	...	...	4315.2	3003.3	...	2300.3	...	...	5303.6
Imputed bank service charge	...	...	-134.8	...	...	-134.8	...	...	-190.2	...	...	-190.2
Import duties	...	...	...	...	...	...	...	...	...	...	...	...
Value added tax	...	...	...	...	...	...	...	...	...	...	...	...
Other adjustments	...	...	-199.3	891.3	301.3	390.7	...	...	-158.7	1015.5	484.9	371.9
Total	2575.5	...	1905.6	891.3	301.3	4571.1	3003.3	...	1951.4	1015.5	484.9	5485.3

Ireland

4.6 Cost Components of Value Added, ISIC Divisions

Million Irish pounds

			1978						1979			
	Compensation of Employees	Capital Consumption	Net Operating Surplus	Indirect Taxes	Less: Subsidies Received	Value Added	Compensation of Employees	Capital Consumption	Net Operating Surplus	Indirect Taxes	Less: Subsidies Received	Value Added

All Producers

1 Agriculture, hunting, forestry and fishing	58.4	...	977.5	...	...	1035.9	65.0	...	890.0	...	...	955.0
2 Mining and quarrying	...	...	...	...	...	...	...	...	...	...	...	...
3 Manufacturing	...	...	...	...	...	...	...	...	...	...	...	...
a Manufacture of food, beverages and tobacco	...	...	...	...	...	...	...	...	...	...	...	...
b Textile, wearing apparel and leather industries	...	...	...	...	...	...	...	...	...	...	...	...
c Manufacture of wood and wood products, including furniture	...	...	...	...	...	...	...	...	...	...	...	...
d Manufacture of paper and paper products, printing and publishing	...	...	...	...	...	...	...	...	...	...	...	...
e Manufacture of chemicals and chemical petroleum, coal, rubber and plastic products	...	...	...	...	...	...	...	...	...	...	...	...
f Manufacture of non-metallic mineral products, except products of petroleum and coal	...	...	...	...	...	...	...	...	...	...	...	...
g Basic metal industries	...	...	...	...	...	...	...	...	...	...	...	...
h Manufacture of fabricated metal products, machinery and equipment	...	...	...	...	...	...	...	...	...	...	...	...
i Other manufacturing industries	...	...	...	...	...	...	...	...	...	...	...	...
4 Electricity, gas and water	...	...	68.3	...	...	...	...	...	...	...	...	...
5 Construction	...	...	108.8	...	...	...	...	...	...	...	...	...
6 Wholesale and retail trade, restaurants and hotels	460.1	...	348.1	...	...	808.2	...	...	...	...	...	...
a Wholesale and retail trade	396.3	...	304.8	...	...	701.1	...	...	...	...	...	...
b Restaurants and hotels	63.8	...	43.3	...	...	107.1	...	...	...	...	...	...
7 Transport, storage and communication	261.2	...	169.1	...	...	430.3	...	...	...	...	...	...
a Transport and storage	187.6	...	116.1	...	...	303.7	...	...	...	...	...	...
b Communication	73.6	...	53.0	...	...	126.6	...	...	...	...	...	...
8 Finance, insurance, real estate and business services	138.4	...	156.9	...	...	295.3	...	...	...	...	...	...
a Financial institutions	138.4	...	156.9	...	...	295.3	...	...	...	...	...	...
b Insurance		...		...	...		...	...	...	...	...	...
c Real estate and business services	...	...	...	...	...	...	...	...	...	...	...	...
9 Community, social and personal services	272.4	...	354.5	...	...	626.9	1355.0	...	1222.0	...	...	2577.0
Total, Industries	2690.8	...	2711.2	...	...	5402.0	3237.0	...	2964.0	...	...	6201.0
Producers of Government Services	869.2	...	44.7	...	...	913.9	1081.0	...	55.0	...	...	1136.0
Other Producers		...		...	...		...	...		...	...	
Total [a]	3560.0	...	2755.9	...	...	6315.9	4318.0	...	3019.0	...	...	7337.0
Imputed bank service charge	...	...	-206.3	...	...	-206.3	...	...	-231.0	...	...	-231.0
Import duties	...	...	...	...	...	...	...	...	...	...	...	...
Value added tax	...	...	...	...	...	...	...	...	...	...	...	...
Other adjustments	...	...	-117.4	1111.8	632.8	361.6	...	...	-199.0	1227.0	684.0	344.0
Total	3560.0	...	2432.2	1111.8	632.8	6471.2	4318.0	...	2589.0	1227.0	684.0	7450.0

a) Gross domestic product in factor values.

Israel

General note. The preparation of national accounts statistics in Israel is undertaken by the Central Bureau of Statistics, Jerusalem. The official estimates are published annually by the Bureau in the 'Statistical Abstract of Israel'. A detailed description of the sources and methods used for the national accounts estimates is found in 'Israel's National Income and Expenditure 1950-1962' published in 1964. Another edition of this publication for the years 1950-1968 published in 1970 included a description of the principal changes made in the methods of estimation. The estimates are generally in accordance with the classifications and definitions recommended in the United Nations Systems of National Accounts (SNA). Input-output tables have been published in 'Input-ouput Tables 1968/69'. The following tables have been prepared from successive replies to the United Nations national accounts questionnaire. When the scope and coverage of the estimates differ for conceptual or statistical reasons from the definitions and classifications recommended in SNA, a footnote is indicated to the relevant tables.

Sources and methods :

(a) Gross domestic product. Gross domestic product is estimated mainly through the expenditure approach.

(b) Expenditure on the gross domestic product. The expenditure approach is used to estimate government final consumption expenditure and exports and imports of goods and services. This approach, in combination with the commodity-flow approach, is used for private final consumption expenditure and gross capital formation. General government consumption expenditure is estimated on the basis of activity reports of the Accountant-General and the Budget Provision supplemented by data from the Ministry of Finance. Expenditure of the local authorities and national institutions is estimated on the basis of financial statements and budget proposals. Private expenditure estimates on food, beverages and tobacco are based on data concerning quantities produced and marketed and on prices to the consumer, while estimates of expenditure on housing and business services, consumption of industrial products and other food products are based on family expenditure surveys held every five or six years. For the intervening years, estimates are computed by extrapolating year-to-year changes by the commodity-flow approach. Estimates of increase in stocks in agriculture, fuel and government strategic stocks are prepared by multiplying inventory stocks by their average prices. Regular quarterly and annual Surveys are used to estimate inventory changes for industry and wholesale trade. The data obtained are adjusted to approximate the value of the physical change in stocks. Building and construction works are estimated either from reports of large companies, institutions and financial reports of the government bodies or by multiplying data on the area under construction by the average cost per square meter for each type of construction. The estimates of imported machinery and equipment are based on the description found in the customs tariff while estimates of locally produced goods are based on a monthly report of sales by product obtained from the principal producers. Quantitative data and prices of investment assets in agriculture are available separately. The estimates of exports and imports of goods and services are based on foreign trade statistics and balance-of-payments data. Data pertaining to trade with the Administered Territories are a gross evaluation based on a sample enumeration of movement of goods through the official transit points. For the constant price estimates, government wages and salaries are extrapolated by the number of employees. Government purchases of goods and services are deflated by relevant components of the consumer price index. Price deflation is also used for most of the items of private expenditure, gross fixed capital formation and exports and imports of goods and services. For private food consumption and inventory changes in agriculture, fuel supplies, and government strategic stocks, estimates are computed by multiplying current quantities by prices in the base year.

(c) Cost-structure of the gross domestic product. The estimates of wages and salaries are based either on surveys of the industrial and construction branches, surveys of parts of the transportation branch and surveys of government and private non-profit institutions and services or on employers' reports to the National Insurance Institute and estimates of supplementary payments. Profits, interest payments and rents are estimated by industry using the income approach. Net profits are calculated in accordance with methods of inventory evaluation including capital gains of losses caused by price changes. Depreciation estimates are based on income tax assessments using historical cost rather than replacement cost. However, an adjustment is made for the difference between depreciation estimates based on balance sheet data and replacement cost. Estimates of indirect taxes are based on the financial reports of the government and the local authorities.

(d) Gross domestic product by kind of economic activity. The table of GDP by kind of economic activity is prepared in net factor values. Depreciation and net indirect taxes are estimated as totals only and not by industry. The production approach is used to estimate value added of the agricultural sector. For all other sectors, the income approach is used. Estimates for recent years have been extrapolated by using the production approach. For the agricultural sector, data on output and input are based on the agricultural statistics series prepared by the Central Bureau of Statistics. Separate estimates are made for wages, interest and rent while net profit is obtained after deducting these expenses from total income. For mining and quarrying and manufacturing, estimates are based on industrial surveys carried out annually until 1972 and again in 1975 and on income tax files. For intervening years, estimates are interpolated and extrapolated using current production indexes. The Israel Electric Corporation and the Water Authority Commission supply data for their respective utility. Construction estimates have been obtained as the total payments to factors of production and recently, have been extrapolated with changes in output by principal components. A fixed ratio is assumed between input and output at constant prices and differences between the price movements of inputs and outputs are taken into account. A special survey of wage and salary payments in the construction industry is also used. Bench-mark estimates for wholesale and retail trade have been based on a survey held in 1972/73. Extrapolation for other years is based on changes in sales to final users. The value added of the hotel industry is estimated by changes in revenue and inputs using data obtained from special surveys. For transport and communication, estimates are based on annual reports of the concerned establishments and on surveys of the trucking industry. Estimates for the financing and insurance industries are based on consolidated reports prepared by the Supervisor of Banks and the Supervisor of Insurance. Bench-mark estimate for residential rent for 1975 has been based on the family expenditure survey, extrapolated by the change in the value of inventories of dwellings. Estimates of government services are based on reports of the Accountant-General, the national institutions and local authorities as well as on data obtained from the Budget Provisions, and from the Ministry of Finance. For other services, estimates are derived from a sample of income tax files, indirect tax data, manpower data and kibbutz personal services. GDP by kind of economic activity is not estimated at constant prices.

1.1 Expenditure on the Gross Domestic Product, in Current Prices

Million Israeli shegels

		1970	1971	1972	1973	1974	1975	1976	1977	1978	1979	1980
1	General government final consumption expenditure	673	794	924	1640	2207	3394	4027	5101	9022	15307	37593
2	Private final consumption expenditure	1134	1341	1706	2212	3288	4641	6231	8849	14674	27710	61387
	a Households	1018	1201	1522	1977	2962	4190	5623	7887	13117	24709	54934
	b Private non-profit institutions serving households	116	141	183	236	326	451	608	962	1557	3001	6453
3	Gross capital formation	537	743	978	1293	1756	2443	2697	3441	6194	12270	23726
	a Increase in stocks	35	49	54	28	5	146	146	336	655	758	165
	b Gross fixed capital formation	502	694	924	1265	1750	2297	2551	3105	5539	11512	23561
	Residential buildings	174	237	356	470	687	873	931	972	1563	3708	9826
	Non-residential buildings	77	91	127	182	290	368	398	533	790	1374	2598
	Other construction and land improvement etc.	54	72	95	103	142	213	258	320	614	1043	2216
	Other	198	294	347	511	632	843	964	1280	2572	5387	8921
4	Exports of goods and services	488	680	905	1120	1574	2321	3506	5789	11258	19771	47211
5	Less: Imports of goods and services	871	1076	1276	2101	2871	4490	5562	7841	15910	27596	62215
	Equals: Gross Domestic Product	1961	2483	3236	4164	5954	8309	10899	15339	25238	47462	107702

Israel

1.2 Expenditure on the Gross Domestic Product, in Constant Prices

Million Israeli shegels

	1970	1971	1972	1973	1974	1975	1976	1977	1978	1979	1980
	\multicolumn{6}{c	}{At constant prices of: 1970}	\multicolumn{5}{c	}{1975}
1 General government final consumption expenditure	673	682	669	979	999	1099 / 3394	3039	2628	2945	2706	2913
2 Private final consumption expenditure	1134	1200	1319	1427	1535	1544 / 4641	4839	5045	5437	5745	5551
a Households	1018	1071	1181	1279	1383	1386 / 4190	4381	4570	4948	5241	5051
b Private non-profit institutions serving households	116	129	138	148	152	158 / 451	458	475	489	504	500
3 Gross capital formation	537	654	738	777	744	775 / 2443	2135	1941	2021	2304	1920
a Increase in stocks	35	44	44	11	-	36 / 146	93	140	130	158	-24
b Gross fixed capital formation	502	611	694	766	744	739 / 2297	2042	1801	1891	2146	1944
Residential buildings	174	210	270	283	275	284 / 873	763	601	587	676	731
Non-residential buildings	77	80	95	107	114	112 / 368	314	305	289	267	224
Other construction and land improvement etc.	54	64	73	65	59	65 / 213	203	193	218	199	188
Other	198	257	257	311	296	278 / 843	762	702	797	1004	801
4 Exports of goods and services	488	606	682	717	760	773 / 2321	2691	2994	3111	3269	3449
5 Less: Imports of goods and services	871	970	974	1330	1327	1405 / 4490	4383	4304	4674	4681	4486
Equals: Gross Domestic Product	1961	2171	2434	2569	2712	2786 / 8309	8321	8304	8840	9343	9347

1.3 Cost Components of the Gross Domestic Product

Million Israeli shegels

	1970	1971	1972	1973	1974	1975	1976	1977	1978	1979	1980
1 Indirect taxes, net [a]	240	328	454	580	925	803	1125	1265	2718	3376	9435
a Indirect taxes paid	317	457	601	822	1273	1739	2637	3541	5259	10086	21763
b Less: Subsidies received [a]	76	129	147	242	348	936	1512	2276	2541	6710	12328
2 Consumption of fixed capital	184	231	299	409	627	958	1282	1930	3539	6531	15411
3 Compensation of employees paid by resident producers to:	925	1132	1404	1864	2565	3601	4916	7439	12058	23927	53086
4 Net operating surplus	593	770	1034	1262	1721	3039	3947	5378	8695	17037	34099
Statistical discrepancy	19	23	45	49	116	-92	-371	-673	-1772	-3409	-4329
Equals: Gross Domestic Product	1961	2483	3236	4164	5954	8309	10899	15339	25238	47462	107702

a) From 1975, including subsidy component in government loans to industries.

1.4 General Government Current Receipts and Disbursements

Million Israeli shegels

	1970	1971	1972	1973	1974	1975	1976	1977	1978	1979	1980
	\multicolumn{11}{c	}{Receipts}
1 Property and entrepreneurial income	48	59	71	87	142	220	323	326	476	1570	4113
2 Taxes, fees and contributions	652	887	1114	1496	2241	3250	5112	7078	10787	21017	48892
a Indirect taxes	316	457	601	822	1273	1739	2637	3541	5259	10086	21763
b Direct taxes	225	278	331	440	631	1017	1715	2354	3654	7417	18561
c Social security contributions	87	124	148	196	281	408	614	961	1575	2997	7345
d Compulsory fees, fines and penalties [a]	24	28	35	38	56	86	146	222	299	517	1223
3 Other current receipts	...	...	...	...	...	...	...	...	...	...	...
Total Current Receipts of General Government [b]	700	946	1185	1584	2383	3470	5435	7404	11263	22587	53005
	\multicolumn{11}{c	}{Disbursements}
1 General government final consumption expenditure	673	794	924	1640	2207	3394	4027	5101	9022	15307	37593

Israel

1.4 General Government Current Receipts and Disbursements
(Continued)

Million Israeli shegels

	1970	1971	1972	1973	1974	1975	1976	1977	1978	1979	1980
a Compensation of employees	220	276	325	502	667	933	1201	1968	3114	6510	14001
b Consumption of fixed capital	...	...	...	...	...	...	...	...	...	...	...
c Purchases of goods and services, net	453	518	600	1138	1541	2461	2826	3133	5908	8797	23592
d Less: Own account production of fixed assets	...	...	...	...	...	...	...	...	...	...	...
e Indirect taxes paid, net	...	...	...	...	...	...	...	...	...	...	...
2 Property income paid [c]	84	111	159	206	312	458	703	1364	2391	3991	8921
3 Subsidies	76	129	147	242	348	936	1512	2276	2541	6710	12328
4 Other current transfers paid	156	205	264	378	635	993	1402	2107	3345	6224	14818
5 Net saving [b]	-289	-294	-308	-882	-1119	-2311	-2209	-3444	-6036	-9645	-20655
Total Current Disbursements and Net Saving of General Government [b]	700	946	1185	1584	2383	3470	5435	7404	11263	22587	53005

a) Relating to other current transfers from households and private non-profit institutions.
b) This table covers general government, local authorities and national institutions.
c) Relating to interest on public debt only.

1.10 Gross Domestic Product by Kind of Activity, in Current Prices

Million Israeli shegels

	1970	1971	1972	1973	1974	1975	1976	1977	1978	1979	1980
1 Agriculture, hunting, forestry and fishing	103	126	151	186	285	398	568	772	1179	2098	4490
2 Mining and quarrying	385	474	601	763	1126	1557	2153	3316	5498	9648	21217
3 Manufacturing [a]							...	...	...	...	...
4 Electricity, gas and water	31	42	47	64	82	128	157	276	461	796	1974
5 Construction	173	229	323	393	570	724	783	941	1576	3547	9047
6 Wholesale and retail trade, restaurants and hotels [b]	189	234	294	374	571	824	1076	1542	2666	4923	10871
7 Transport, storage and communication	146	188	230	301	408	518	670	990	1574	2869	6542
8 Finance, insurance, real estate and business services	260	330	464	637	964	1381	1898	2689	4456	9790	22009
9 Community, social and personal services [b]	60	71	85	107	146	206	291	414	661	1200	2517
Statistical discrepancy [c]	...	...	...	...	...	407	807	1159	1644	4949	9121
Total, Industries	1348	1695	2195	2825	4152	6143	8403	12099	19715	39820	87788
Producers of Government Services	306	378	460	674	915	1266	1625	2626	4143	8823	18797
Other Producers	...	...	...	...	...	...	...	...	...	...	...
Subtotal [d]	1654	2073	2654	3499	5067	7409	10028	14725	23858	48643	106585
Less: Imputed bank service charge	50	66	87	127	208	310	427	667	1153	2652	7056
Plus: Import duties [e]	-86	-105	-129	-247	-573	-459	-737	-1241	-1952	-5027	-12344
Plus: Value added tax	...	...	...	...	...	...	...	...	...	...	...
Plus: Other adjustments [f]	19	23	45	49	116	-92	-371	-673	-1772	-3409	-4329
Equals: Gross Domestic Product [d]	1537	1924	2483	3175	4402	6548	8493	12144	18981	37555	82856

a) For series 1, including garage and other repairs.
b) For series 1, item 'Restaurants and hotels' is included in item 'Community, social and personal services'
c) Relating to subsidy component in government loans to industries.
d) Net domestic product in factor values.
e) Comprising an adjustment for capital gains and losses and an adjustment for the difference between depreciation estimates based on balance-sheet data and estimates at replacement cost.
f) Including errors and omissions.

1.12 Relations Among National Accounting Aggregates

Million Israeli shegels

	1970	1971	1972	1973	1974	1975	1976	1977	1978	1979	1980
Gross Domestic Product	1961	2483	3236	4164	5954	8309	10899	15339	25238	47462	107702
Plus: Net factor income received from abroad	-35	-43	-57	-111	-158	-275	-349	-378	-731	-1760	-3598
Equals: Gross National Product	1926	2440	3179	4053	5796	8034	10550	14961	24507	45702	104104
Less: Consumption of fixed capital	184	231	299	409	627	958	1282	1930	3539	6531	15411
Less: Net indirect taxes paid to supranational organisations	...	...	...	...	...	...	...	...	...	...	...
Equals: National Income at Market Prices	1742	2209	2880	3644	5169	7076	9268	13031	20968	39171	88693
Plus: Net current transfers received from abroad	...	...	...	...	...	...	...	...	...	...	...
Equals: National Disposable Income at Market Prices	...	...	...	...	...	...	...	...	...	...	...
Less: Final consumption	1807	2135	2630	3852	5495	8035	10258	13950	23696	43017	98980
Equals: Net Saving	...	...	...	...	...	...	...	...	...	...	...
Less: Surplus of the nation on current transactions	...	...	...	...	...	...	...	...	...	...	...
Equals: Net Capital Formation	353	512	679	884	1129	1485	1415	1511	2655	5739	8315

Israel

2.1 General Government Final Consumption Expenditure by Function, in Current Prices

Million Israeli sheqels — Fiscal year beginning 1 April

	1970	1971	1972	1973	1974	1975	1976	1977	1978	1979	1980
1 General public services	35.5	45.1	54.9	75.5	99.2	127.0	176.4	274.6	454.1	875.5	...
2 Defence	524.9	560.6	641.0	1474.0	1923.8	2585.0	3013.2	4168.0	6622.1	11930.7	...
3 Public order and safety	19.4	23.2	23.9	35.2	53.2	75.3	110.2	178.0	304.4	650.1	...
4 Education	60.8	82.3	97.5	139.1	206.8	283.8	404.0	651.1	1136.0	2160.0	...
5 Health	20.5	27.2	32.1	47.3	68.1	91.1	147.0	254.2	404.6	952.0	...
6 Social security and welfare	6.9	8.8	11.0	15.2	23.2	34.4	48.6	80.6	142.6	313.0	...
7 Housing and community amenities	12.6	15.6	20.3	27.6	41.2	53.7	74.5	111.5	191.9	390.4	...
8 Recreational, cultural and religious affairs	13.3	16.3	18.6	30.5	37.5	56.2	85.1	133.0	230.6	443.9	...
9 Economic services	22.8	26.9	31.9	43.5	57.4	73.9	103.4	159.6	260.0	519.7	...
a Fuel and energy	0.4	0.4	0.5	0.7	1.0	1.5	2.1	4.3	12.6	25.3	...
b Agriculture, forestry, fishing and hunting	7.7	8.6	9.9	12.9	17.7	23.1	33.8	56.9	86.3	171.3	...
c Mining, manufacturing and construction, except fuel and energy	1.5	1.8	2.1	3.5	3.8	5.4	7.2	10.5	16.1	35.9	...
d Transportation and communication	7.1	9.2	11.3	14.9	21.5	27.9	35.7	50.4	88.6	179.0	...
e Other economic affairs	6.1	6.9	8.1	11.5	13.4	16.0	24.6	37.5	56.4	108.2	...
10 Other functions	-1.9	-3.6	-4.0	-7.8	-9.2	-6.0	-10.5	-20.4	-26.0	-42.0	...
Total General Government Final Consumption Expenditure	714.8	802.4	927.2	1880.1	2501.2	3374.4	4151.9	5990.2	9720.3	18193.3	...

2.3 Total General Government Outlays by Function and Type

Million Israeli sheqels — Fiscal year beginning 1 April

	Final Consumption Expenditures Total	Compensation of Employees	Other	Subsidies	Other Current Transfers & Property Income	Total Current Disbursements	Gross Capital Formation	Other Capital Outlays	Total Outlays
1976									
1 General public services	176.4	...	...	1.1	78.6	256.1	7.5	4.0	267.6
2 Defence	3013.2	...	...	...	14.3	3027.5	22.2	42.1	3091.8
3 Public order and safety	110.2	...	...	...	4.1	114.3	3.9	0.3	118.5
4 Education	404.0	...	...	...	285.8	689.8	90.4	29.0	809.2
5 Health	147.0	...	...	...	235.4	382.4	44.8	13.6	440.8
6 Social security and welfare	48.6	...	...	...	842.4	891.0	12.8	3.4	907.2
7 Housing and community amenities	74.5	...	...	56.1	2.7	133.3	35.6	16.7	185.6
8 Recreation, culture and religion	85.1	...	...	3.1	34.2	122.4	28.3	11.9	162.6
9 Economic services	103.4	...	...	1433.5	7.1	1544.0	108.6	224.6	1877.2
a Fuel and energy	2.1	...	...	16.7	...	18.8	12.2	...	31.0
b Agriculture, forestry, fishing and hunting	33.8	...	...	212.4	1.2	247.4	34.3	4.4	286.1
c Mining (except fuels), manufacturing and construction	7.2	...	...	308.6	0.6	316.4	0.8	113.9	431.1
d Transportation and communication	35.7	...	...	86.4	1.4	123.5	55.6	100.4	279.5
e Other economic affairs [a]	24.6	...	...	809.4	3.9	837.9	5.7	5.9	849.5
10 Other functions	-10.5	...	...	2.0	785.6	777.1	2.4	2.0	781.5
Total [b]	4151.9	...	...	1495.8	2290.2	7937.9	356.5	347.6	8641.0
1977									
1 General public services	274.6	...	...	0.8	125.1	400.5	12.0	8.8	421.3
2 Defence	4168.0	...	...	...	22.1	4190.1	22.2	52.8	4265.1
3 Public order and safety	178.0	...	...	...	7.0	185.0	6.5	0.6	192.1
4 Education	651.1	...	...	0.1	510.2	1161.4	117.1	38.8	1317.3
5 Health	254.2	...	...	0.1	445.6	699.9	50.1	3.3	753.3
6 Social security and welfare	80.6	...	...	...	1218.4	1299.0	18.9	4.7	1322.6
7 Housing and community amenities	111.5	...	...	98.0	3.7	213.2	36.6	38.9	288.7
8 Recreation, culture and religion	133.0	...	...	4.6	57.2	194.8	42.7	12.8	250.3
9 Economic services	159.6	...	...	2314.4	23.4	2497.4	146.5	262.8	2906.7

Israel

2.3 Total General Government Outlays by Function and Type
(Continued)

Million Israeli shegels — Fiscal year beginning 1 April

	Final Consumption Expenditures Total	Compensation of Employees	Other	Subsidies	Other Current Transfers & Property Income	Total Current Disbursements	Gross Capital Formation	Other Capital Outlays	Total Outlays
a Fuel and energy	4.3	...	...	28.3	...	32.6	18.8	0.6	52.0
b Agriculture, forestry, fishing and hunting	56.9	...	...	264.3	2.0	323.2	41.3	11.5	376.0
c Mining (except fuels), manufacturing and construction	10.5	...	...	433.1	0.7	444.3	0.7	136.7	581.7
d Transportation and communication	50.4	...	...	143.5	2.3	196.2	76.7	97.4	370.3
e Other economic affairs [a]	37.5	...	...	1445.2	18.4	1501.1	9.0	16.6	1526.7
10 Other functions	-20.4	...	...	2.0	1608.3	1589.9	3.9	1.6	1595.4
Total [b]	5990.2			2420.0	4021.0	12431.2	456.5	425.1	13312.8
				1978					
1 General public services	454.1	...	...	0.8	215.5	670.4	26.1	18.9	715.4
2 Defence	6622.1	...	...	...	42.1	6664.2	33.9	87.2	6785.3
3 Public order and safety	304.4	...	...	...	9.4	313.8	15.2	0.6	329.6
4 Education	1136.0	...	...	4.1	755.0	1895.1	187.7	47.2	2130.0
5 Health	404.6	...	...	0.1	760.9	1165.6	80.3	4.7	1250.6
6 Social security and welfare	142.6	...	...	0.1	1789.3	1932.0	27.6	8.6	1968.2
7 Housing and community amenities	191.9	...	...	167.6	7.9	367.4	55.4	53.8	476.6
8 Recreation, culture and religion	230.6	...	...	7.9	90.9	329.4	69.6	20.1	419.1
9 Economic services	260.0	...	...	3014.5	35.7	3310.2	263.1	375.1	3948.4
a Fuel and energy	12.6	...	...	39.1	...	51.7	26.2	0.9	78.8
b Agriculture, forestry, fishing and hunting	86.3	...	...	404.6	2.7	493.6	79.6	25.1	598.3
c Mining (except fuels), manufacturing and construction	16.1	...	...	137.7	1.4	155.2	1.6	184.7	341.5
d Transportation and communication	88.6	...	...	256.3	3.7	348.6	145.1	142.3	636.0
e Other economic affairs [a]	56.4	...	...	2176.8	27.9	2261.1	10.6	22.1	2293.8
10 Other functions	-26.0	...	...	0.9	2708.4	2683.3	5.9	3.8	2693.0
Total [b]	9720.3	...	...	3196.0	6415.1	19331.4	764.8	620.0	20716.2
				1979					
1 General public services	875.5	...	...	1.2	373.7	1250.4	51.0	29.8	1331.2
2 Defence	11930.7	...	...	...	72.3	12003.0	61.0	37.0	12101.0
3 Public order and safety	650.1	...	...	...	18.4	668.5	32.4	1.0	701.9
4 Education	2160.0	...	...	4.3	1631.7	3796.0	341.1	84.2	4221.3
5 Health	952.0	...	...	0.2	1732.6	2684.8	162.5	16.1	2863.4
6 Social security and welfare	313.0	...	...	...	3553.9	3866.9	38.5	12.4	3917.8
7 Housing and community amenities	390.4	...	...	377.6	15.7	783.7	118.1	277.9	1179.7
8 Recreation, culture and religion	443.9	...	...	13.7	179.7	637.3	141.1	30.6	809.0
9 Economic services	519.7	...	...	7544.1	48.1	8111.9	483.7	950.7	9546.3
a Fuel and energy	25.3	...	...	60.2	...	85.5	48.6	1.2	135.3
b Agriculture, forestry, fishing and hunting	171.3	...	...	618.1	5.4	794.8	189.4	93.4	1077.6
c Mining (except fuels), manufacturing and construction	35.9	...	...	197.9	2.8	236.6	4.3	347.0	587.9
d Transportation and communication	179.0	...	...	442.5	8.0	629.5	219.8	456.6	1305.9
e Other economic affairs [a]	108.2	...	...	6225.4	31.9	6365.5	21.6	52.5	6439.6
10 Other functions	-42.0	...	...	0.3	4658.6	4616.9	10.7	1.6	4629.2
Total [b]	18193.3	...	...	7941.4	12284.7	38419.4	1440.1	1441.3	41300.8

a) Beginning 1975, column 'Subsidies' includes the subsidy component in government loans to industries.
b) Beginning 1976, re-classification was compiled based on a more detailed analysis of expenditure. The estimates for 1976 are shown in both classifications for comparison purposes.

2.5 Private Final Consumption Expenditure by Type, in Current Prices

Million Israeli shegels

	1970	1971	1972	1973	1974	1975	1976	1977	1978	1979	1980
Final Consumption Expenditure of Resident Households											
1 Food, beverages and tobacco [a]	334.6	393.6	461.6	586.1	852.3	1286.0	1733.0	2549.0	3929.0	7043.0	17660.0
a Food	288.0	338.9	396.9	501.8	740.3	1105.0	1479.0	2191.0	3384.0	6194.0	15736.0
b Non-alcoholic beverages	11.7	13.5	16.7	21.1	32.0	61.0	81.0	114.0	179.0	244.0	632.0
c Alcoholic beverages	13.6	15.9	17.4	22.4	31.3	50.0	65.0	96.0	152.0	258.0	481.0
d Tobacco	23.0	27.3	32.9	43.7	53.0	76.0	117.0	160.0	234.0	382.0	900.0

Israel

2.5 Private Final Consumption Expenditure by Type, in Current Prices
(Continued)

Million Israeli shegels

	1970	1971	1972	1973	1974	1975	1976	1977	1978	1979	1980
2 Clothing and footwear	89.8	94.7	124.0	160.6	225.6	289.0	444.0	584.0	1047.0	1648.0	2977.0
3 Gross rent, fuel and power	194.9	241.1	332.9	465.0	720.6	1037.0	1347.0	1737.3	2868.0	6277.0	14184.0
a Fuel and power	19.5	23.8	29.9	35.0	59.1	113.0	158.0	214.0	348.0	579.0	1888.0
b Other	175.4	217.3	303.0	430.0	661.5	924.0	1189.0	1523.0	2520.0	5698.0	12296.0
4 Furniture, furnishings and household equipment and operation	135.4	157.8	199.1	263.5	415.5	549.0	717.0	988.0	1763.0	3322.0	6547.0
a Household operation	40.8	48.7	62.6	73.5	114.8	155.0	214.0	322.0	534.0	951.0	1910.0
b Other	94.6	109.1	136.5	190.0	300.7	394.0	503.0	666.0	1229.0	2371.0	4637.0
5 Medical care and health expenses	29.5	37.6	50.0	65.7	97.2	144.0	201.0	299.0	538.0	942.0	1927.0
6 Transport and communication	98.4	132.2	181.3	223.2	315.4	414.0	577.0	860.0	1511.0	2967.0	6211.0
a Personal transport equipment	16.2	27.3	46.6	66.7	84.0	75.0	109.0	174.0	406.0	889.0	885.0
b Other	82.2	104.9	134.7	156.5	231.4	339.0	468.0	686.0	1105.0	2078.0	5326.0
7 Recreational, entertainment, education and cultural services	61.3	71.9	91.3	105.5	158.0	213.0	310.0	472.0	826.0	1491.0	3014.0
a Education	23.4	24.4	31.5	37.1	58.9	80.0	110.0	167.0	284.0	533.0	1073.0
b Other	37.9	47.5	59.8	68.4	99.1	133.0	200.0	305.0	542.0	958.0	1941.0
8 Miscellaneous goods and services	91.7	118.4	144.7	170.3	243.8	342.0	475.0	733.0	1200.0	2149.0	4679.0
a Personal care	37.8	47.4	52.1	63.0	92.6	132.0	180.0	265.0	410.0	692.0	1416.0
b Expenditures in restaurants, cafes and hotels	39.1	51.5	62.3	68.4	90.3	126.0	178.0	286.0	488.0	850.0	1804.0
c Other	14.8	19.5	30.3	38.9	60.9	84.0	117.0	182.0	302.0	607.0	1159.0
Total Final Consumption Expenditure in the Domestic Market by Households, of which	1035.6	1247.3	1584.9	2039.9	3028.4	4274.0	5804.0	8222.0	13682.0	25839.0	57199.0
Plus: Direct purchases abroad by resident households	24.5	30.1	38.7	60.8	81.0	130.0	197.0	333.0	624.0	1121.0	2675.0
Less: Direct purchases in the domestic market by non-resident households	41.8	76.8	101.2	124.1	147.3	214.0	378.0	668.0	1189.0	2251.0	4940.0
Equals: Final Consumption Expenditure of Resident Households	1018.3	1200.6	1522.4	1976.6	2962.1	4190.0	5623.0	7887.0	13117.0	24709.0	54934.0

Final Consumption Expenditure of Private Non-profit Institutions Serving Households

	1970	1971	1972	1973	1974	1975	1976	1977	1978	1979	1980
1 Research and science [b]	...	...	...	...	...	...	252.0	381.0	592.0	1076.0	2464.0
2 Education [b]	47.2	62.5	79.7	106.6	146.4	201.0	...	...	...	...	...
3 Medical and other health services	41.0	46.1	65.4	74.7	109.5	149.0	210.0	353.0	603.0	1279.0	2542.0
4 Welfare services [c]	15.0	17.7	21.8	28.0	40.5	59.0	84.0	130.0	206.0	376.0	859.0
5 Recreational and related cultural services [b]	-	-	-	-	-	-	-	-	-	-	-
6 Religious organisations [c]	...	...	...	...	...	...	...	...	...	...	...
7 Professional and labour organisations serving households	12.4	14.5	16.2	26.3	29.2	42.0	62.0	98.0	156.0	270.0	588.0
8 Miscellaneous	...	...	...	...	...	...	...	...	...	...	...
Equals: Final Consumption Expenditure of Private Non-profit Organisations Serving Households	115.6	140.8	183.1	235.6	325.6	451.0	608.0	962.0	1557.0	3001.0	6453.0
Private Final Consumption Expenditure	1133.9	1341.4	1705.5	2212.2	3287.7	4641.0	6231.0	8849.0	14674.0	27710.0	61387.0

a) The sum of the components is greater than the totals shown because the sum has been adjusted for the expenditure included in other items of the national accounts.
b) Items 'Research and science' and 'Recreational and related cultural services' are included in item 'Education'.
c) Item 'Religious organisations' is included in item 'Welfare and other health services'.

2.6 Private Final Consumption Expenditure by Type, in Constant Prices

Million Israeli shegels

	1970	1971	1972	1973	1974	1975	1976	1977	1978	1979	1980
	\multicolumn{5}{c}{At constant prices of:}						
			1970						1975		

Final Consumption Expenditure of Resident Households

	1970	1971	1972	1973	1974	1975	1976	1977	1978	1979	1980
1 Food, beverages and tobacco [a]	334.6	352.8	379.3	403.3	408.2	414.0 / 1286.0	1373.0	1437.0	1502.0	1529.0	1456.0
a Food	288.0	302.2	323.9	341.2	342.9	349.0 / 1105.0	1171.0	1217.0	1286.0	1313.0	1251.0
b Non-alcoholic beverages	11.7	12.9	14.5	15.2	15.0	15.0 / 61.0	71.0	82.0	73.0	71.0	68.0
c Alcoholic beverages	13.6	14.6	14.6	15.8	16.2	16.0 / 50.0	54.0	60.0	64.0	67.0	60.0
d Tobacco	23.0	24.9	28.2	33.1	36.2	36.0 / 76.0	84.0	85.0	87.0	86.0	84.0

Israel

2.6 Private Final Consumption Expenditure by Type, in Constant Prices
(Continued)

Million Israeli shegels

	1970	1971	1972	1973	1974	1975	1976	1977	1978	1979	1980
	\multicolumn{11}{c}{At constant prices of:}
			1970					1975			
2 Clothing and footwear	89.8	86.8	99.3	110.1	120.1	122.0 / 289.0	323.0	324.0	385.0	368.0	333.0
3 Gross rent, fuel and power	194.9	212.3	234.1	256.3	275.5	299.0 / 1037.0	1121.0	1187.0	1245.0	1295.0	1344.0
a Fuel and power	19.5	21.7	24.4	26.3	26.4	28.0 / 113.0	120.0	125.0	131.0	135.0	138.0
b Other	175.4	190.6	209.7	230.0	249.1	271.0 / 924.0	1001.0	1062.0	1114.0	1160.0	1206.0
4 Furniture, furnishings and household equipment and operation	135.4	143.9	160.6	181.7	205.3	194.0 / 549.0	548.0	551.0	644.0	790.0	776.0
a Household operation	40.8	43.8	50.3	49.9	54.1	53.0 / 155.0	165.0	173.0	185.0	188.0	170.0
b Other	94.6	100.1	110.3	131.8	151.2	141.0 / 394.0	383.0	378.0	459.0	602.0	606.0
5 Medical care and health expenses	29.5	33.7	38.8	42.7	46.3	50.0 / 144.0	149.0	155.0	171.0	172.0	160.0
6 Transport and communication	98.4	114.5	136.4	149.6	160.2	144.0 / 414.0	436.0	481.0	548.0	630.0	542.0
a Personal transport equipment	16.2	21.8	30.8	39.8	41.3	21.0 / 75.0	80.0	84.0	109.0	156.0	71.0
b Other	82.2	92.7	105.6	109.8	118.9	123.0 / 339.0	356.0	397.0	439.0	474.0	471.0
7 Recreational, entertainment, education and cultural services	61.3	64.9	73.9	71.5	80.9	77.0 / 213.0	225.0	235.0	254.0	268.0	243.0
a Education	23.4	21.8	25.0	23.8	27.7	27.0 / 80.0	83.0	89.0	100.0	107.0	97.0
b Other	37.9	43.1	48.9	47.7	53.2	50.0 / 133.0	142.0	146.0	154.0	161.0	146.0
8 Miscellaneous goods and services	91.7	102.0	106.3	104.0	109.9	111.0 / 342.0	361.0	389.0	406.0	424.0	400.0
a Personal care	37.8	41.8	40.3	40.8	42.6	42.0 / 132.0	132.0	147.0	151.0	151.0	132.0
b Expenditures in restaurants, cafes and hotels	39.1	44.0	45.1	41.5	41.2	41.0 / 126.0	140.0	148.0	151.0	159.0	152.0
c Other	14.8	16.2	20.9	21.7	26.1	28.0 / 84.0	89.0	94.0	104.0	114.0	116.0
Total Final Consumption Expenditure in the Domestic Market by Households, of which	1035.6	1110.9	1228.7	1319.2	1406.4	1411.0 / 4274.0	4536.0	4759.0	5155.0	5476.0	5254.0
Plus: Direct purchases abroad by resident households	24.5	25.8	28.0	40.5	46.8	46.0 / 130.0	126.0	149.0	172.0	193.0	200.0
Less: Direct purchases in the domestic market by non-resident households	41.8	65.5	76.0	80.9	70.1	71.0 / 214.0	281.0	338.0	379.0	428.0	403.0
Equals: Final Consumption Expenditure of Resident Households	1018.3	1071.2	1180.7	1278.8	1383.1	1386.0 / 4190.0	4381.0	4570.0	4948.0	5241.0	5051.0
	\multicolumn{11}{c}{Final Consumption Expenditure of Private Non-profit Institutions Serving Households}
1 Research and science [b]	...	...	...	...	...	...	...	...	...	...	...
2 Education [b]	47.2	54.0	58.6	63.3	65.8	66.0 / 201.0	195.0	197.0	199.0	209.0	219.0
3 Medical and other health services	41.0	46.1	49.7	50.0	53.2	58.0 / 149.0	153.0	159.0	170.0	178.0	162.0

Israel

2.6 Private Final Consumption Expenditure by Type, in Constant Prices
(Continued)

Million Israeli shegels

	1970	1971	1972	1973	1974	1975	1976	1977	1978	1979	1980
					At constant prices of:						
			1970					1975			
4 Welfare services [c]	15.0	15.8	16.7	17.3	18.6	20.0 / 59.0	64.0	67.0	69.0	72.0	75.0
5 Recreational and related cultural services [b]	-	-	-	-	-	-	-	-	-	-	-
6 Religious organisations [c]	...	...	...	...	...	... / ...	...	...	...	...	...
7 Professional and labour organisations serving households	12.4	12.6	13.2	17.2	14.2	14.0 / 42.0	46.0	52.0	51.0	45.0	44.0
8 Miscellaneous	...	...	...	...	...	... / ...	...	...	...	...	...
Equals: Final Consumption Expenditure of Private Non-profit Organisations Serving Households	115.6	128.5	138.2	147.8	151.8	158.0 / 451.0	458.0	475.0	489.0	504.0	500.0
Private Final Consumption Expenditure	1133.9	1199.7	1318.9	1426.6	1534.9	1544.0 / 4641.0	4839.0	5045.0	5437.0	5745.0	5551.0

a) The sum of the components is greater than the totals shown because the sum has been adjusted for the expenditure included in other items of the national accounts.
b) Items 'Research and science' and 'Recreational and related cultural services' are included in item 'Education'.
c) Item 'Religious organisations' is included in item 'Welfare and other health services'.

2.9 Gross Capital Formation by Kind of Activity of Owner, ISIC Major Divisions, in Current Prices

Million Israeli shegels

	1970			1971			1972			1973		
	Total Gross Capital Formation	Increase in Stocks	Gross Fixed Capital Formation	Total Gross Capital Formation	Increase in Stocks	Gross Fixed Capital Formation	Total Gross Capital Formation	Increase in Stocks	Gross Fixed Capital Formation	Total Gross Capital Formation	Increase in Stocks	Gross Fixed Capital Formation
						All Producers						
1 Agriculture, hunting, fishing and forestry	...	...	23.9	...	...	26.7	...	...	37.9	...	...	46.0
2 Mining and quarrying	...	...	82.4	...	...	105.9	...	...	136.5	...	...	161.7
3 Manufacturing												
4 Electricity, gas and water [a]	...	...	20.0	...	...	20.7	...	...	41.4	...	...	45.9
5 Construction [b]	...	...	8.2	...	...	11.8	...	...	15.2	...	...	18.9
6 Wholesale and retail trade, restaurants and hotels [c]	...	...	99.9	...	...	124.6	...	...	168.4	...	...	238.2
7 Transport, storage and communication	...	...	94.4	...	...	167.9	...	...	168.4	...	...	284.3
8 Finance, insurance, real estate and business services [c]	...	...	173.6	...	...	236.7	...	...	356.0	...	...	469.7
9 Community, social and personal services	...	...	...	...	...	...	...	...	...	...	...	...
Total Industries	...	...	502.4	...	...	694.3	...	...	923.8	...	...	1264.7
Producers of Government Services	...	...	...	...	...	...	...	...	...	...	...	...
Private Non-Profit Institutions Serving Households	...	...	...	...	...	...	...	...	...	...	...	...
Total	537.3	34.9	502.4	742.9	48.6	694.3	977.8	54.0	923.8	1293.0	28.3	1264.7

	1974			1975			1976			1977		
	Total Gross Capital Formation	Increase in Stocks	Gross Fixed Capital Formation	Total Gross Capital Formation	Increase in Stocks	Gross Fixed Capital Formation	Total Gross Capital Formation	Increase in Stocks	Gross Fixed Capital Formation	Total Gross Capital Formation	Increase in Stocks	Gross Fixed Capital Formation
						All Producers						
1 Agriculture, hunting, fishing and forestry	...	...	68.7	...	...	107.0	...	...	145.0	...	...	183.0
2 Mining and quarrying	...	...	220.5	...	...	369.0	...	...	420.0	...	...	511.0
3 Manufacturing												
4 Electricity, gas and water [a]	...	...	60.5	...	...	100.0	...	...	133.0	...	...	196.0
5 Construction [b]	...	...	33.5	...	...	41.0	...	...	28.0	...	...	20.0
6 Wholesale and retail trade, restaurants and hotels [c]	...	...	364.4	...	...	493.0	...	...	555.0	...	...	744.0
7 Transport, storage and communication	...	...	315.6	...	...	314.0	...	...	339.0	...	...	479.0
8 Finance, insurance, real estate and business services [c]	...	...	687.2	...	...	873.0	...	...	931.0	...	...	972.0
9 Community, social and personal services	...	...	...	...	...	...	...	...	...	...	...	...
Total Industries	...	...	1750.4	...	...	2297.0	...	...	2551.0	...	...	3105.0
Producers of Government Services	...	...	...	...	...	...	...	...	...	...	...	...
Private Non-Profit Institutions Serving Households	...	...	...	...	...	...	...	...	...	...	...	...
Total	1755.8	5.4	1750.4	2443.0	146.0	2297.0	2697.0	146.0	2551.0	3441.0	336.0	3105.0

Israel

2.9 Gross Capital Formation by Kind of Activity of Owner, ISIC Major Divisions, in Current Prices

Million Israeli shegels

		1978			1979			1980		
		Total Gross Capital Formation	Increase in Stocks	Gross Fixed Capital Formation	Total Gross Capital Formation	Increase in Stocks	Gross Fixed Capital Formation	Total Gross Capital Formation	Increase in Stocks	Gross Fixed Capital Formation
					All Producers					
1	Agriculture, hunting, fishing and forestry	...	...	306.0	...	...	540.0	...	...	931.0
2	Mining and quarrying	...	...	1019.0	...	...	1785.0	...	...	3228.0
3	Manufacturing	...	...		...	...		...	...	
4	Electricity, gas and water a	...	...	367.0	...	...	697.0	...	...	1722.0
5	Construction b	...	...	42.0	...	...	261.0	...	...	368.0
6	Wholesale and retail trade, restaurants and hotels c	...	...	1278.0	...	...	2251.0	...	...	4113.0
7	Transport, storage and communication	...	...	964.0	...	...	2270.0	...	...	3373.0
8	Finance, insurance, real estate and business services c	...	...	1563.0	...	...	3708.0	...	...	9826.0
9	Community, social and personal services	...	...	...	...	...	...	...	...	...
	Total Industries	...	...	5539.0	...	...	11512.0	...	...	23561.0
	Producers of Government Services	...	...	...	...	...	...	...	...	...
	Private Non-Profit Institutions Serving Households	...	...	...	...	...	...	...	...	...
	Total	6194.0	655.0	5539.0	12270.0	758.0	11512.0	23726.0	165.0	23561.0

a) Including water projects.
b) Construction equipment only.
c) All services are included in item 'Wholesale and retail trade, restaurants and hotels'.

2.10 Gross Capital Formation by Kind of Activity of Owner, ISIC Major Divisions, in Constant Prices

Million Israeli shegels

		1975			1976			1977			1978		
		Total Gross Capital Formation	Increase in Stocks	Gross Fixed Capital Formation	Total Gross Capital Formation	Increase in Stocks	Gross Fixed Capital Formation	Total Gross Capital Formation	Increase in Stocks	Gross Fixed Capital Formation	Total Gross Capital Formation	Increase in Stocks	Gross Fixed Capital Formation
				At constant prices of:1975									
						All Producers							
1	Agriculture, hunting, fishing and forestry	...	...	107.0	...	...	113.0	...	...	107.0	...	...	111.0
2	Mining and quarrying	...	...	369.0	...	...	338.0	...	...	295.0	...	...	337.0
3	Manufacturing	...	...		...	...		...	...		...	...	
4	Electricity, gas and water a	...	...	100.0	...	...	102.0	...	...	112.0	...	...	128.0
5	Construction b	...	...	41.0	...	...	24.0	...	...	12.0	...	...	15.0
6	Wholesale and retail trade, restaurants and hotels c	...	...	493.0	...	...	435.0	...	...	419.0	...	...	431.0
7	Transport, storage and communication	...	...	314.0	...	...	266.0	...	...	254.0	...	...	282.0
8	Finance, insurance, real estate and business services c	...	...	873.0	...	...	764.0	...	...	602.0	...	...	587.0
9	Community, social and personal services	...	...	...	...	...	...	...	...	...	...	...	...
	Total Industries	...	...	2297.0	...	...	2042.0	...	...	1801.0	...	...	1891.0
	Producers of Government Services	...	...	...	...	...	...	...	...	...	...	...	...
	Private Non-Profit Institutions Serving Households	...	...	...	...	...	...	...	...	...	...	...	...
	Total	2443.0	146.0	2297.0	2135.0	93.0	2042.0	1941.0	140.0	1801.0	2021.0	130.0	1891.0

		1979			1980		
		Total Gross Capital Formation	Increase in Stocks	Gross Fixed Capital Formation	Total Gross Capital Formation	Increase in Stocks	Gross Fixed Capital Formation
				At constant prices of:1975			
				All Producers			
1	Agriculture, hunting, fishing and forestry	...	...	110.0	...	...	90.0
2	Mining and quarrying	...	...	353.0	...	...	301.0
3	Manufacturing	...	...		...	...	
4	Electricity, gas and water a	...	...	137.0	...	...	158.0

Israel

2.10 Gross Capital Formation by Kind of Activity of Owner, ISIC Major Divisions, in Constant Prices
(Continued)

Million Israeli shegels

	1979			1980		
	Total Gross Capital Formation	Increase in Stocks	Gross Fixed Capital Formation	Total Gross Capital Formation	Increase in Stocks	Gross Fixed Capital Formation
At constant prices of:1975							
5 Construction [b]	...	...	50.0	...	...	34.0
6 Wholesale and retail trade, restaurants and hotels [c]	...	...	422.0	...	...	349.0
7 Transport, storage and communication	...	...	398.0	...	...	281.0
8 Finance, insurance, real estate and business services [c]	...	...	676.0	...	...	731.0
9 Community, social and personal services	...	...	...	...	...	...
Total Industries	...	...	2146.0	...	...	1944.0
Producers of Government Services	...	...	...	...	...	...
Private Non-Profit Institutions Serving Households	...	...	...	...	...	...
Total	2304.0	158.0	2146.0	1920.0	-24.0	1944.0

a) Including water projects.
b) Construction equipment only.
c) All services are included in item 'Wholesale and retail trade, restaurants and hotels'.

3.12 General Government Income and Outlay Account: Total and Subsectors

Million Israeli shegels

	1970					1971				
	Total General Government	Central Government	State or Provincial Government	Local Government	Social Security Funds	Total General Government	Central Government	State or Provincial Government	Local Government	Social Security Funds
Receipts										
1 Property and entrepreneurial income	48.1	46.8	...	...	0.8	58.9	56.6	...	...	1.5
2 Taxes, fees and contributions [a]	651.6	510.0	...	...	86.6	887.1	697.2	...	...	124.1
a Indirect taxes	316.4	285.2	...	...	...	456.7	419.2	...	...	...
b Direct taxes	224.8	224.8	...	...	...	278.0	278.0	...	...	...
c Social security contributions	86.6	...	...	...	86.6	124.1	...	...	...	124.1
d Fees, fines and penalties [a]	23.8	...	...	...	...	28.3	...	...	...	...
3 Other current transfers received	...	26.5	...	...	22.1	...	31.4	...	...	32.1
a Casualty insurance claims	...	...	...	...	...	...	...	...	...	...
b Transfers from other government subsectors	...	15.1	...	...	22.1	...	17.8	...	...	32.1
c Transfers from abroad	-	...	...	...	...	-	...	...	...	...
d Other transfers, except imputed	...	11.4	...	...	...	...	13.6	...	...	...
e Imputed unfunded employee welfare contributions	...	...	...	...	...	...	...	...	...	...
Total Current Receipts [b]	699.7	583.3	...	...	109.5	946.0	785.2	...	...	157.7
Disbursements										
1 General governement final consumption expenditures	672.8	606.2	...	...	2.0	794.0	712.0	...	...	2.7
2 Property income paid [c]	84.1	76.0	...	...	...	111.2	101.3	...	...	...
3 Subsidies	76.4	76.4	...	...	...	129.2	129.2	...	...	91.6
4 Other current transfers paid	155.5	147.3	...	...	69.3	205.3	198.2	...	...	...
a Casualty insurance premiums, net	...	...	...	...	...	...	...	...	...	...
b Transfers to other government subsectors	...	62.1	...	...	...	...	87.6	...	...	...
c Transfers to households	...	...	...	...	69.3	...	...	...	...	91.6
Social security benefits	...	...	...	...	56.5	...	...	...	...	76.6
Social assistance grants	...	...	...	...	...	...	...	...	...	...
Unfunded employee welfare benefits	...	...	...	...	12.8	...	...	...	...	15.0
d Transfers to private non-profit institutions serving households [d]	155.5	85.2	...	...	...	205.3	110.6	...	...	...
e Transfers to the rest of the world	-	...	...	...	...	-	...	...	...	...
Net saving	-289.1	-322.6	...	...	38.2	-293.7	-355.5	...	...	63.4
Total Current Disbursements and Net Saving [b]	699.7	583.3	...	...	109.5	946.0	785.2	...	...	157.7

Israel

3.12 General Government Income and Outlay Account: Total and Subsectors

Million Israeli sheqels

	1972					1973				
	Total General Government	Central Government	State or Provincial Government	Local Government	Social Security Funds	Total General Government	Central Government	State or Provincial Government	Local Government	Social Security Funds

Receipts

1 Property and entrepreneurial income	70.6	69.0	...	...	0.5	87.4	85.8	...	...	0.3
2 Taxes, fees and contributions a	1114.3	887.0	...	...	147.9	1496.2	1215.2	...	...	196.1
a Indirect taxes	600.9	556.3	...	...	...	822.2	775.2	...	...	...
b Direct taxes	330.7	330.7	...	...	...	440.0	440.0	...	...	...
c Social security contributions	147.9	...	...	...	147.9	196.1	...	...	...	196.1
d Fees, fines and penalties a	34.8	...	...	...	...	37.9	...	...	...	...
3 Other current transfers received	...	33.2	...	...	43.3	...	44.9	...	...	62.1
a Casualty insurance claims	...	...	...	...	...	...	...	...	...	...
b Transfers from other government subsectors	...	16.1	...	...	43.3	...	27.5	...	...	62.0
c Transfers from abroad	-	...	...	...	...	-	...	...	...	...
d Other transfers, except imputed	-	17.1	...	...	...	-	17.4	...	...	0.1
e Imputed unfunded employee welfare contributions	...	...	...	...	...	...	...	...	...	...
Total Current Receipts b	1184.9	989.2	...	...	191.7	1583.6	1345.9	...	...	258.5

Disbursements

1 General governement final consumption expenditures	924.2	822.4	...	...	3.2	1639.6	1502.4	...	...	4.2
2 Property income paid c	158.6	146.4	...	...	...	205.8	189.5	...	...	...
3 Subsidies	146.5	146.5	...	...	...	242.0	242.0	...	...	...
4 Other current transfers paid	263.5	265.3	...	...	106.8	377.9	354.5	...	...	181.7
a Casualty insurance premiums, net	...	...	...	...	...	...	...	...	...	...
b Transfers to other government subsectors	...	118.9	...	...	...	...	166.0	...	...	...
c Transfers to households	...	...	...	...	106.8	...	...	...	...	181.7
Social security benefits	...	...	...	...	94.0	...	...	...	...	157.9
Social assistance grants	...	...	...	...	...	...	...	...	...	...
Unfunded employee welfare benefits	...	...	...	...	12.8	...	...	...	...	23.8
d Transfers to private non-profit institutions serving households d	263.5	146.4	...	...	...	377.9	188.5	...	...	...
e Transfers to the rest of the world	-	...	...	...	...	...	...	...	...	...
Net saving	-307.9	-391.4	...	...	81.7	-881.7	-942.5	...	...	72.6
Total Current Disbursements and Net Saving b	1184.9	989.2	...	...	191.7	1583.6	1345.9	...	...	258.5

	1974					1975				
	Total General Government	Central Government	State or Provincial Government	Local Government	Social Security Funds	Total General Government	Central Government	State or Provincial Government	Local Government	Social Security Funds

Receipts

1 Property and entrepreneurial income	142.4	140.1	...	...	0.3	220.0	217.4	...	...	0.3
2 Taxes, fees and contributions a	2240.7	1844.8	...	...	280.6	3250.0	2671.9	...	...	407.7
a Indirect taxes	1273.1	1213.6	...	...	...	1739.0	1663.7	...	...	...
b Direct taxes	631.2	631.2	...	...	...	1017.0	1008.2	...	...	...
c Social security contributions	280.6	...	...	...	280.6	408.0	...	...	...	407.7
d Fees, fines and penalties a	55.8	...	...	...	...	86.0	...	...	...	...
3 Other current transfers received	...	89.5	...	...	123.4	...	118.8	...	...	239.4
a Casualty insurance claims	...	...	...	...	...	...	...	...	...	...
b Transfers from other government subsectors	...	63.6	...	...	123.2	...	76.3	...	...	239.0
c Transfers from abroad	-	...	...	...	...	-	...	...	...	...
d Other transfers, except imputed	...	25.9	...	...	0.2	...	42.5	...	...	0.4
e Imputed unfunded employee welfare contributions	...	...	...	...	...	...	...	...	...	...
Total Current Receipts b	2383.1	2074.4	...	...	404.3	3470.0	3008.1	...	...	647.4

Israel

3.12 General Government Income and Outlay Account: Total and Subsectors
(Continued)

Million Israeli shegels

	1974					1975				
	Total General Government	Central Government	State or Provincial Government	Local Government	Social Security Funds	Total General Government	Central Government	State or Provincial Government	Local Government	Social Security Funds

Disbursements

1 General government final consumption expenditures	2207.3	2012.5	...	...	6.3	3394.0	3118.3	...	...	10.2
2 Property income paid c	312.0	285.0	...	...	...	458.0	415.9	...	...	...
3 Subsidies	348.4	348.4	...	...	...	936.0	936.0	...	...	...
4 Other current transfers paid	634.6	602.7	...	...	337.7	993.0	950.6	...	...	549.8
a Casualty insurance premiums, net	...	...	...	...	...	...	...	...	...	...
b Transfers to other government subsectors	...	292.8	...	...	...	...	507.7	...	...	...
c Transfers to households	...	...	...	...	337.7	...	...	...	...	549.8
Social security benefits	...	...	...	...	278.7	...	...	...	...	480.3
Social assistance grants	...	...	...	...	...	...	...	...	...	...
Unfunded employee welfare benefits	...	...	...	...	59.0	...	...	...	...	69.5
d Transfers to private non-profit institutions serving households d	634.6	309.9	...	...	...	993.0	442.9	...	...	...
e Transfers to the rest of the world	-	...	...	...	...	*	...	...	...	...
Net saving	-1119.2	-1174.2	...	...	60.3	-2311.0	-2412.7	...	...	87.4
Total Current Disbursements and Net Saving b	2383.1	2074.4	...	...	404.3	3470.0	3008.1	...	...	647.4

	1976					1977				
	Total General Government	Central Government	State or Provincial Government	Local Government	Social Security Funds	Total General Government	Central Government	State or Provincial Government	Local Government	Social Security Funds

Receipts

1 Property and entrepreneurial income	323.0	318.3	...	...	0.3	326.0	318.4	...	...	1.5
2 Taxes, fees and contributions a	5112.0	4236.7	...	...	614.3	7078.0	5722.6	...	...	960.9
a Indirect taxes	2637.0	2521.6	...	...	...	3541.0	3371.1	...	...	...
b Direct taxes	1715.0	1715.1	...	...	...	2354.0	2351.5	...	...	...
c Social security contributions	614.0	...	...	...	614.3	961.0	...	...	...	960.9
d Fees, fines and penalties a	146.0	...	...	...	...	222.0	...	...	...	...
3 Other current transfers received	...	173.3	...	...	364.1	...	251.4	...	...	586.3
a Casualty insurance claims	...	...	...	...	...	...	...	...	...	...
b Transfers from other government subsectors	...	90.5	...	...	363.9	...	125.5	...	...	585.8
c Transfers from abroad	-	...	...	...	...	*	...	...	...	...
d Other transfers, except imputed	-	82.8	...	...	0.2	-	125.9	...	...	0.5
e Imputed unfunded employee welfare contributions	...	...	...	...	...	...	...	...	...	...
Total Current Receipts b	5435.0	4728.3	...	...	978.7	7404.0	6292.4	...	...	1548.7

Disbursements

1 General government final consumption expenditures	4027.0	3642.6	...	...	14.1	5101.0	4512.4	...	...	23.6
2 Property income paid c	703.0	639.4	...	...	...	1364.0	1272.2	...	...	...
3 Subsidies	1512.0	1511.9	...	...	...	2276.0	2275.1	...	...	...
4 Other current transfers paid	1402.0	1341.7	...	...	820.4	2107.0	2130.8	...	...	1170.7
a Casualty insurance premiums, net	...	...	...	...	...	...	...	...	...	...
b Transfers to other government subsectors	...	761.5	...	...	...	...	1180.6	...	...	...
c Transfers to households	...	...	...	...	820.4	...	...	...	...	1170.7
Social security benefits	...	...	...	...	742.2	...	...	...	...	1059.6
Social assistance grants	...	...	...	...	...	...	...	...	...	...
Unfunded employee welfare benefits	...	...	...	...	78.2	...	...	...	...	111.1
d Transfers to private non-profit institutions serving households d	1402.0	580.2	...	...	...	2107.0	950.2	...	...	...
e Transfers to the rest of the world	-	...	...	...	...	*	...	...	...	...
Net saving	-2209.0	-2407.3	...	...	144.2	-3444.0	-3898.1	...	...	354.4
Total Current Disbursements and Net Saving b	5435.0	4728.3	...	...	978.7	7404.0	6292.4	...	...	1548.7

Israel

3.12 General Government Income and Outlay Account: Total and Subsectors

Million Israeli sheqels

	1978 Total General Government	1978 Central Government	1978 State or Provincial Government	1978 Local Government	1978 Social Security Funds	1979 Total General Government	1979 Central Government	1979 State or Provincial Government	1979 Local Government	1979 Social Security Funds
Receipts										
1 Property and entrepreneurial income	476.0	465.4	...	...	2.7	1570.0	1544.8	...	...	12.1
2 Taxes, fees and contributions [a]	10787.0	8648.5	...	...	1575.2	21017.0	17024.8	...	...	2996.6
a Indirect taxes	5259.0	4994.5	...	...	...	10086.0	9607.0	...	...	...
b Direct taxes	3654.0	3654.0	...	...	...	7417.0	7417.8	...	...	...
c Social security contributions	1575.0	...	...	...	1575.2	2997.0	...	...	...	2996.6
d Fees, fines and penalties [a]	299.0	...	...	...	...	517.0	...	...	...	...
3 Other current transfers received	...	429.5	...	...	824.3	...	823.1	...	...	1433.8
a Casualty insurance claims	...	...	...	...	...	...	...	...	...	...
b Transfers from other government subsectors	...	229.8	...	...	823.1	...	444.5	...	...	1433.8
c Transfers from abroad	-	...	...	...	...	...	...	...	...	...
d Other transfers, except imputed	-	199.7	...	...	1.2	...	378.6	...	...	-
e Imputed unfunded employee welfare contributions	...	...	...	...	...	...	...	...	...	...
Total Current Receipts [b]	11263.0	9543.4	...	...	2402.2	22587.0	19392.7	...	...	4442.5
Disbursements										
1 General government final consumption expenditures	9022.0	8057.4	...	...	42.1	15307.0	13379.2	...	...	83.7
2 Property income paid [c]	2391.0	2221.0	...	...	...	3991.0	3612.5	...	...	...
3 Subsidies	2541.0	2541.9	...	...	...	6710.0	6710.1	...	...	...
4 Other current transfers paid	3345.0	3387.1	...	...	1784.1	6224.0	6410.0	...	...	3393.2
a Casualty insurance premiums, net	...	...	...	...	...	...	...	...	...	...
b Transfers to other government subsectors	...	1866.4	...	...	...	...	3420.2	...	...	...
c Transfers to households	...	...	...	...	1784.1	...	...	...	...	3393.2
Social security benefits	...	...	...	...	1587.1	...	...	...	...	3011.7
Social assistance grants	...	...	...	...	...	...	...	...	...	...
Unfunded employee welfare benefits	...	...	...	...	197.0	...	...	...	...	381.5
d Transfers to private non-profit institutions serving households [d]	3345.0	1520.7	...	...	...	6224.0	2989.8	...	...	...
e Transfers to the rest of the world	-	...	...	...	...	-	...	...	...	...
Net saving	-6036.0	-6664.0	...	...	576.0	-9645.0	10719.1	...	...	965.6
Total Current Disbursements and Net Saving [b]	11263.0	9543.4	...	...	2402.2	22587.0	19392.7	...	...	4442.5

	1980 Total General Government	1980 Central Government	1980 State or Provincial Government	1980 Local Government	1980 Social Security Funds
Receipts					
1 Property and entrepreneurial income	4113.0	...	...	...	...
2 Taxes, fees and contributions [a]	48892.0	...	...	...	...
a Indirect taxes	21763.0	...	...	...	...
b Direct taxes	18561.0	...	...	...	...
c Social security contributions	7345.0	...	...	...	...
d Fees, fines and penalties [a]	1223.0	...	...	...	...
3 Other current transfers received	...	...	...	...	...
a Casualty insurance claims	...	...	...	...	...
b Transfers from other government subsectors	...	...	...	...	...
c Transfers from abroad	...	...	...	...	...
d Other transfers, except imputed	...	...	...	...	...
e Imputed unfunded employee welfare contributions	...	...	...	...	...
Total Current Receipts [b]	53005.0	...	...	...	...

Israel

3.12 General Government Income and Outlay Account: Total and Subsectors
(Continued)

Million Israeli sheqels

	1980 Total General Government	Central Government	State or Provincial Government	Local Government	Social Security Funds
	Disbursements				
1 General government final consumption expenditures	37593.0	...	...	...	...
2 Property income paid [c]	8921.0	...	...	...	...
3 Subsidies	12328.0	...	...	...	...
4 Other current transfers paid	14818.0	...	...	...	...
a Casualty insurance premiums, net	...	...	...	...	...
b Transfers to other government subsectors	...	...	...	...	...
c Transfers to households	...	...	...	...	...
Social security benefits	...	...	...	...	...
Social assistance grants	...	...	...	...	...
Unfunded employee welfare benefits	...	...	...	...	...
d Transfers to private non-profit institutions serving households [d]	14818.0	...	...	...	...
e Transfers to the rest of the world	-	...	...	...	...
Net saving	20655.0	...	...	...	...
Total Current Disbursements and Net Saving [b]	53005.0	...	...	...	...

a) Relating to other current transfers from households and private non-profit institutions.
b) Column 'Central government' includes national institutions.
c) Relating to interest on public debt only.
d) Relating to current transfers to private non-profit institutions and to households.

Italy

General note. The preparation of national accounts statistics in Italy is undertaken by the instituto Central di Statistica, Rome. The official estimates are published in the 'Annuario Statistico Italiano' and in 'Compendio Statistico Italiano'. The latter publication is also published in English under the title 'Italian Statistical Abstract'. The following presentation on sources and method is based mainly on information prepared by the Statistical Office of the European Communities in 1976 in a report entitled 'Basic statistics needed for the ESA accounts and tables: present situation and prospects for improvements'. The estimates are generally in accordance with the definitions and classifications recommended in the United Nations System of National Accounts (SNA). Input-output tables have been published in 'Supplemento Straordinario al Bolletiono Mensile di Statistica'. The following tables have been prepared from successive replies to the United Nations national accounts questionnaire. When the scope and coverage of the estimates differ for conceptual or statistical reasons from the definitions and classifications recommended in SNA, a footnote is indicated to the relevant tables.

Sources and methods:

(a) Gross domestic product. GDP is estimated mainly through the production approach.

(b) Expenditure on the gross domestic product. The expenditure approach is used to estimate government final consumption expenditure, increase in stocks and exports and imports of goods and services. This aproach, in combination with the commodity-flow approach is used to estimate private final consumption expenditure and gross fixed capital formation. For central government, the estimates are based on data obtained from the Bilancio dello Stato. Complete accounts for tHe other bodies of the general government are available after 39 months and for social security funds, after 27 months, Household consumption expenditure is primarily based on the quarterly surveys of family budgets suplemented by estimates based on commodity-flows. The surveys cover 36,000 households by rotation with 9000 new families each quarter. Surveys carried out by the Banco d'Italia provide consumption data for non-resident households on the domestic market and for residents abroad. The main statistical source used for estimating changes in stocks is the value-added surveys conducted for all enterprises in the industrial construction, trade and transport sectors that employ more than 20 persons. The stocks relate to industrial products only. Data for estimating gross fixed capital formation are obtained through a questionnaire attached to the value-added survey. Government capital expenditure are obtained from government accounts. For construction and building, the Istituto Central di Statistico conducts specific surveys such as surveys on residential buildings and on public works. The estimates of exports and imports of goods and services are based mainly on the balance-of-payments and foreign trade statistics. For the constant price estimates, most of the items of GDP by expenditure type are deflated by appropriate price indexes. Government building depreciation is estimated as a certain percentage of the stock value at constant prices. Private consumption of own-produced food and stock increases of agricultural products are revalued at base-year prices. Gross rent is extrapolated by the number of dwelling units.

(c) Cost-structure of the gross domestic product. Compensation of employees is estimated through use of the value-added survey and a survey carried out by the Ministry of Labour and Social Security for the industrial sector, minimum contractual wages and survey of the compensation of permanent employees for the agricultural sector, surveys and inquiries carried out by other institutes for the service sector and other indirect evaluation for sectors not covered by surveys. Information on operating surplus is obtained from the value-added surveys and from actual interest received and paid by the various sectors. Depreciation is valued on the basis of time series of gross fixed capital formation at constant prices by product and by branch of economic activity. Constant prices of 1970 are estimated by using the perpetual inventory method, assuming that the devaluation of the product is constant during its economic life. Estimates of indirect taxes and subsidies are obtained from government sources. Taxes linked to production and imports are broken down by branch according to the type of tax. Data on subsidies are classified by branch on the basis of the recipients indicated in the government budgets.

(d) Gross domestic product by kind of economic activity. The table of GDP by kind of economic activity is prepared at market prices, i.e., producers' values. The production approach is used to estimate the value added of most of the industries. This is supplemented by the income aproach for industries to which the value-added surveys are applied. The income approach alone is used for the producers of government services. Statistics on agricultural production prices, etc. are derived from current agricultural surveys. A new survey was carried out in 1975, covering 6,000 farms with complete accounts which produce about 10 percent of the total output. Crop surveys of major products are conducted annually. Information on gross marketable livestock production is available separately for major items. For forestry, a quarterly survey supplies data on production and prices. Monthly surveys of products unloaded in Italian ports are used for estimating value added of fishing. For the industrial activity sector, the estimates are based on value-added surveys and the product surveys. In addition to these surveys, the rapid surveys of large enterprises are also used for manufacturing. The annual value-added survey, which covers all enterprises employing more than 20 persons and is available after 15 months, includes transactions in goods and services, distributive transactions and employment data. The survey does not allow product-by-product analysis. The product survey which covers all enterprises employing more than 50 persons and is available after 24 months, is used for compiling input-output tables and is linked with the European Community surveys on industrial activity. The annual rapid survey, covering all enterprises employing more than 250 persons is available within 3 months. This survey provides information similar to that obtained in the value-added surveys. The surveys used for the manufacturing sector are also used for construction. In addition construction estimates are based on the results of surveys on the number of residential buildings, surveys of public works and sample surveys of work in progress on bUilding sites. For the trade sector, the main source is the value-added survey. However, to cover enterprises employing less than 20 persons, an indirect method, which consists in constructing an index of traded consumer goods, capital goods and goods for export, is used for estimating gross output of the trade sector. The value-added surveys are also used for the transport sector. Additional information is supplied directly by the relevant firms and public agencies. For the financial institutions, annual surveys are carried out which covers 97 percent of the activity. Special calculations are made for institutions not covered. Estimates of government services are based on surveys conducted by the social security funds and on data compiled by the Ragioneria generale dello Stato and the Istituto Centrale de Statistic. For other services, the Istituto Central di Statistica carries out a single direct survey of public hospitals. Other market services are valued indirectly, mostly on the basis of the results of family budgets surveys. For the constant price estimates, price deflation is used for community, social and personal services. Double deflation is used for all the other sectors. Output is either deflated by apropriate indexes or is extrapolated by quantum indexes while input is deflated by price indexes.

1.1 Expenditure on the Gross Domestic Product, in Current Prices

Thousand Million Italian lire

	1970	1971	1972	1973	1974	1975	1976	1977	1978	1979	1980
1 General government final consumption expenditure	8664	10608	12077	13907	16714	19362	23133	28991	35257	43360	54440
2 Private final consumption expenditure	39371	42772	47061	56061	69571	80571	98427	117979	136815	165226	208469
3 Gross capital formation	14511	14371	15307	21676	29427	25424	37062	40680	44434	57461	83887
a Increase in stocks	1077	424	465	3025	4652	-352	5666	3477	2940	6534	16459
b Gross fixed capital formation	13434	13947	14842	18651	24775	25776	31396	37203	41494	50927	67428
4 Exports of goods and services	11176	12471	14178	16869	24686	28529	38613	49938	59536	75318	85183
5 Less: Imports of goods and services	10839	11712	13499	18767	29679	28508	40578	47505	53788	71708	94577
Equals: Gross Domestic Product	62883	68510	75124	89746	110719	125378	156657	190083	222254	269657	337402

1.2 Expenditure on the Gross Domestic Product, in Constant Prices

Thousand Million Italian lire

	1970	1971	1972	1973	1974	1975	1976	1977	1978	1979	1980
	\multicolumn{11}{c}{At constant prices of: 1970}
1 General government final consumption expenditure	8664	9154	9641	9874	10151	10479	10708	11008	11261	11430	11669
2 Private final consumption expenditure	39371	40526	41904	44365	45535	44822	46363	47014	48295	50676	53145
3 Gross capital formation	14511	13399	13533	16303	16793	12602	14909	13901	13672	15073	18047
a Increase in stocks	1077	398	413	2169	2186	-143	1865	903	687	1331	2936
b Gross fixed capital formation	13434	13001	13120	14134	14607	12745	13044	12998	12985	13742	15111
4 Exports of goods and services	11176	11955	13223	13662	14817	15382	17294	18770	20676	22632	21601
5 Less: Imports of goods and services	10839	11118	12338	13603	13771	12434	14263	14258	15416	17503	18893
Equals: Gross Domestic Product	62883	63916	65963	70601	73525	70851	75011	76435	78488	82308	85569

Italy

1.3 Cost Components of the Gross Domestic Product

Thousand Million Italian lire

	1970	1971	1972	1973	1974	1975	1976	1977	1978	1979	1980
1 Indirect taxes, net	6092	6323	6141	7207	9137	7992	11537	15210	16983	18422	26335
a Indirect taxes paid	7032	7618	7864	9044	11196	11333	15617	20410	23485	27372	36503
b Less: Subsidies received	940	1295	1723	1837	2059	3341	4080	5200	6502	8950	10168
2 Consumption of fixed capital	5128	5551	6103	7525	10171	12919	15793	19442	22364	26434	32431
3 Compensation of employees paid by resident producers to:	30349	34727	38753	47080	58606	71204	86953	106501	124315	148624	182918
a Resident households	30306	34684	38707	47015	58524	71102	86845	106364	124148	148448	182685
b Rest of the world	43	43	46	65	82	102	108	137	167	176	233
4 Net operating surplus	21314	21909	24127	27934	32805	33263	42374	48930	58592	76177	95718
Equals: Gross Domestic Product	62883	68510	75124	89746	110719	125378	156657	190083	222254	269657	337402

1.4 General Government Current Receipts and Disbursements

Thousand Million Italian lire

	1970	1971	1972	1973	1974	1975	1976	1977	1978	1979	1980
Receipts											
1 Property and entrepreneurial income	613	715	740	883	1164	1112	1402	1737	2270	2859	3709
2 Taxes, fees and contributions	17181	18989	20703	24404	30479	35562	46965	59543	72404	86729	114476
a Indirect taxes	7028	7445	7625	8784	10870	10962	15021	19485	22368	25490	34131
b Direct taxes	3439	3896	4711	5398	6635	8367	12015	16326	22264	26292	37671
c Social security contributions	6714	7648	8367	10222	12974	16233	19929	23732	27772	34947	42674
d Compulsory fees, fines and penalties	.	.	.	.	.	.	.	.	.	.	.
3 Other current receipts	1315	1587	1738	2040	2233	2492	3199	3881	5440	6798	8457
Total Current Receipts of General Government	19109	21291	23181	27327	33876	39166	51566	65161	80114	96386	126642
Disbursements											
1 General government final consumption expenditure	8664	10608	12077	13907	16714	19362	23133	28991	35257	43360	54440
2 Property income paid	1112	1392	1715	2272	3406	4989	7090	9368	13053	15612	20785
3 Subsidies	940	1095	1400	1443	1780	2791	3374	4422	5628	7460	7914
4 Other current transfers paid	8277	9577	11102	13249	16187	20886	25976	30495	38797	44319	55462
a Social security benefits and social assistance grants	7844	9083	10598	12578	15504	20080	24950	29486	37118	43133	54223
b Other	433	494	504	671	683	806	1026	1009	1679	1186	1239
5 Net saving	116	-1381	-3113	-3544	-4211	-8862	-8007	-8115	-12621	-14365	-11959
Total Current Disbursements and Net Saving of General Government	19109	21291	23181	27327	33876	39166	51566	65161	80114	96386	126642

1.5 Current Income and Outlay of Corporate and Quasi-Corporate Enterprises, Summary

Thousand Million Italian lire

	1970	1971	1972	1973	1974	1975	1976	1977	1978	1979	1980
Receipts											
1 Net operating surplus	1590	1232	1436	1512	1164	-1607	337	672	1152	4807	7844
2 Other property and entrepreneurial income received	6614	7834	8920	11111	18828	23209	31319	39453	44995	53046	69362
3 Current transfers received	2453	2848	3312	3830	4661	5609	6991	6476	7308	8704	10799
Total Current Receipts	10657	11914	13668	16453	24653	27211	38647	46601	53455	66557	88005
Disbursements											
1 Property and entrepreneurial income paid	6532	7697	8648	10362	18083	21905	30034	38257	42835	48674	63505
2 Direct taxes and other current payments to general government	793	823	1059	1164	1191	1709	2447	3033	4016	4786	6020
3 Other current transfers paid	2632	3101	3544	4215	5086	6118	7529	7052	8278	9730	12289
4 Net saving	700	293	417	712	293	-2521	-1363	-1741	-1674	3367	6191
Total Current Disbursements and Net Saving	10657	11914	13668	16453	24653	27211	38647	46601	53455	66557	88005

Italy

1.6 Current Income and Outlay of Households and Non-Profit Institutions

Thousand Million Italian lire

	1970	1971	1972	1973	1974	1975	1976	1977	1978	1979	1980
Receipts											
1 Compensation of employees	30714	35124	39163	47553	59055	71618	87429	107311	125434	149997	184399
a From resident producers	30306	34684	38707	47015	58524	71102	86845	106364	124148	148448	182685
b From rest of the world	408	440	456	538	531	516	584	947	1286	1549	1714
2 Property and entrepreneurial income received	20012	21074	23216	26774	32488	36464	45333	53407	64735	78649	97553
3 Current transfers received	9737	11395	13150	16026	18948	23830	29757	35133	43656	50769	63274
a Social security benefits and social assistance grants received	6983	8112	9463	11229	13962	18280	22440	26504	33268	38146	48208
b Other	2754	3283	3687	4797	4986	5550	7317	8629	10388	12623	15066
Total Current Receipts	60463	67593	75529	90353	110491	131912	162519	195851	233825	279415	345226
Disbursements											
1 Private final consumption expenditure	39057	42397	46639	55623	69008	79906	97511	117005	135691	163881	206825
2 Property income paid	...	...	...	...	...	...	...	...	...	...	...
3 Direct taxes and other payments n.e.c. to general government	9438	10805	12106	14571	18558	23099	29717	37236	46198	56641	74525
a Social security contributions	6792	7732	8454	10337	13114	16441	20149	23943	27950	35135	42874
b Direct taxes	2646	3073	3652	4234	5444	6658	9568	13293	18248	21506	31651
c Fees, fines and penalties	...	...	...	...	...	...	...	...	...	...	...
4 Other current transfers paid	2680	3281	3703	4758	4914	5327	7059	8381	10347	12578	15285
5 Net saving	9288	11110	13081	15401	18011	23580	28232	33229	41589	46315	48591
Total Current Disbursements and Net Saving	60463	67593	75529	90353	110491	131912	162519	195851	233825	279415	345226

1.7 External Transactions on Current Account, Summary

Thousand Million Italian lire

	1970	1971	1972	1973	1974	1975	1976	1977	1978	1979	1980
Payments to the Rest of the World											
1 Imports of goods and services	10839	11712	13499	18767	29679	28508	40578	47505	53788	71708	94577
a Imports of merchandise c.i.f.	9607	10356	11946	16698	27092	25589	37240	43120	48638	65484	86484
b Other	1232	1356	1553	2069	2587	2919	3338	4385	5150	6224	8093
2 Factor income paid to the rest of the world	756	859	970	1380	2493	2170	2327	2674	3241	4049	5853
a Compensation of employees	43	43	46	65	82	102	108	137	167	176	233
b Property and entrepreneurial income paid	713	816	924	1315	2411	2068	2219	2537	3074	3873	5620
3 Indirect taxes paid to supranational organizations	4	...	239	260	326	371	596	925	1117	1882	2372
4 Current transfers to the rest of the world	417	644	466	686	651	756	838	965	1660	1170	1369
5 Surplus of the nation on current transactions	729	1211	1192	-1570	-5144	-285	-2370	2191	5295	4390	-8494
Payments to the Rest of the World and Surplus of the Nation on Current Transactions	12745	14426	16366	19523	28005	31520	41969	54260	65101	83199	95677
Receipts From The Rest of the World											
1 Exports of goods and services	11176	12471	14178	16869	24686	28529	38613	49938	59536	75318	85183
a Exports of merchandise f.o.b.	8284	9392	10912	13030	19878	22907	31210	40020	47563	59992	66821
b Other	2892	3079	3266	3839	4808	5622	7403	9918	11973	15326	18362
2 Factor income received from rest of the world	1000	1122	1213	1577	2311	1628	1733	2254	3103	4420	5933
a Compensation of employees	408	440	456	538	531	516	584	947	1286	1549	1714
b Property and entrepreneurial income received	592	682	757	1039	1780	1112	1149	1307	1817	2871	4219
3 Subsidies received from supranational organisations	-	...	323	394	279	550	706	778	874	1490	2254
4 Current transfers from rest of the world	569	833	652	683	729	813	917	1290	1588	1971	2307
Receipts from the Rest of the World on Current Transactions	12745	14426	16366	19523	28005	31520	41969	54260	65101	83199	95677

Italy

1.8 Capital Transactions of The Nation, Summary

Thousand Million Italian lire

	1970	1971	1972	1973	1974	1975	1976	1977	1978	1979	1980
					Finance of Gross Capital Formation						
Gross saving	15240	15582	16499	20106	24283	25139	34692	42871	49729	61851	75393
1 Consumption of fixed capital	5128	5551	6103	7525	10171	12919	15793	19442	22364	26434	32431
a General government	211	231	250	291	349	394	454	501	599	720	869
b Corporate and quasi-corporate enterprises	2850	3092	3425	4291	5909	7234	8896	10884	12409	14440	17336
c Other	2067	2228	2428	2943	3913	5291	6443	8057	9356	11274	14226
2 Net saving	10112	10031	10396	12581	14112	12220	18899	23429	27365	35417	42962
a General government	116	-1381	-3113	-3544	-4211	-8862	-8007	-8115	-12621	-14365	-11959
b Corporate and quasi-corporate enterprises	700	293	417	712	293	-2521	-1363	-1741	-1674	3367	6191
c Other	9296	11119	13092	15413	18030	23603	28269	33285	41660	46415	48730
Less: Surplus of the nation on current transactions	729	1211	1192	-1570	-5144	-285	-2370	2191	5295	4390	-8494
Finance of Gross Capital Formation	14511	14371	15307	21676	29427	25424	37062	40680	44434	57461	83887
					Gross Capital Formation						
Increase in stocks	1077	424	465	3025	4652	-352	5666	3477	2940	6534	16459
Gross fixed capital formation	13434	13947	14842	18651	24775	25776	31396	37203	41494	50927	67428
Gross Capital Formation	14511	14371	15307	21676	29427	25424	37062	40680	44434	57461	83887

1.10 Gross Domestic Product by Kind of Activity, in Current Prices

Thousand Million Italian lire

	1970	1971	1972	1973	1974	1975	1976	1977	1978	1979	1980
1 Agriculture, hunting, forestry and fishing	5122	5299	5403	6976	8096	9644	11222	13402	15700	18610	21528
2 Mining and quarrying	20341	21852	23932	29435							
3 Manufacturing					39353	43212	56523	67907	78631	95490	118671
4 Electricity, gas and water	1377	1496	1575	1688							
5 Construction	5250	5372	5707	6752	8820	9993	11850	14351	16461	20081	25904
6 Wholesale and retail trade, restaurants and hotels [a]	9845	10735	11914	13547	16217	18954	23605	28727	33244	40992	51542
7 Transport, storage and communication	3874	4157	4444	5009	5935	6926	8431	10584	12553	15433	21106
8 Finance, insurance, real estate and business services	10485	11909	13560	15842	19937	24495	28817	34016	40560	48403	61809
9 Community, social and personal services											
Total, Industries	56294	60820	66535	79249	98358	113224	140448	168987	197149	239009	300560
Producers of Government Services	6557	7898	8980	10470	12445	14215	17241	21736	26445	32410	40837
Other Producers	496	558	617	668	792	936	1128	1314	1517	1795	2236
Subtotal	63347	69276	76132	90387	111595	128375	158817	192037	225111	273214	343633
Less: Imputed bank service charge	1646	1934	2158	2763	4161	6169	7126	8270	9671	11576	17031
Plus: Import duties	1182	1168	1150	2122	3285	3172	4966	6316	6814	8019	10800
Plus: Value added tax	...	...	...	...	...	...	...	...	...	...	...
Equals: Gross Domestic Product	62883	68510	75124	89746	110719	125378	156657	190083	222254	269657	337402

a) Second series, including recoverable scrap and repairs.

1.11 Gross Domestic Product by Kind of Activity, in Constant Prices

Thousand Million Italian lire

	1970	1971	1972	1973	1974	1975	1976	1977	1978	1979	1980
					At constant prices of: 1970						
1 Agriculture, hunting, forestry and fishing	5122	5148	4767	5101	5196	5369	5149	5123	5303	5620	5786
2 Mining and quarrying	20341	20450	21287	23526							
3 Manufacturing					26542	24081	27031	27475	28118	29845	31323
4 Electricity, gas and water	1377	1457	1574	1712							
5 Construction	5250	5013	5066	5221	5328	4929	4894	4897	4936	5065	5279
6 Wholesale and retail trade, restaurants and hotels [a]	9845	10172	10640	11287	11683	11437	11881	12238	12731	13477	14095
7 Transport, storage and communication	3874	4022	4174	4468	4711	4723	4964	5200	5392	5671	5907
8 Finance, insurance, real estate and business services	7792	8126	8512	8791	12465	12694	13102	13464	13909	14434	14958
9 Community, social and personal services	2693	2739	2854	3062							

Italy

1.11 Gross Domestic Product by Kind of Activity, in Constant Prices
(Continued)

Thousand Million Italian lire

	1970	1971	1972	1973	1974	1975	1976	1977	1978	1979	1980
				At constant prices of:1970							
Total, Industries	56294	57127	58874	63168	65925	63233	67021	68397	70389	74112	77348
Producers of Government Services	6557	6817	7085	7338	7573	7779	8067	8230	8271	8275	8366
Other Producers	496	503	513	525	550	576	563	543	545	557	569
Subtotal	63347	64447	66472	71031	74048	71588	75651	77170	79205	82944	86283
Less: Imputed bank service charge	1646	1728	1821	1910	2034	2085	2204	2286	2400	2558	2732
Plus: Import duties	1182	1197	1312	1480	1511	1348	1564	1551	1683	1922	2018
Plus: Value added tax	...	...	...	...	...	...	...	...	...	...	...
Equals: Gross Domestic Product	62883	63916	65963	70601	73525	70851	75011	76435	78488	82308	85569

a) Second series, including recoverable scrap and repairs.

1.12 Relations Among National Accounting Aggregates

Thousand Million Italian lire

	1970	1971	1972	1973	1974	1975	1976	1977	1978	1979	1980
Gross Domestic Product	62883	68510	75124	89746	110719	125378	156657	190083	222254	269657	337402
Plus: Net factor income received from abroad	244	263	243	197	-182	-542	-594	-420	-138	371	80
Factor income received	1000	1122	1213	1577	2311	1628	1733	2254	3103	4420	5933
Less: Factor income paid	756	859	970	1380	2493	2170	2327	2674	3241	4049	5853
Equals: Gross National Product	63127	68773	75367	89943	110537	124836	156063	189663	222116	270028	337482
Less: Consumption of fixed capital	5128	5551	6103	7525	10171	12919	15793	19442	22364	26434	32431
Less: Net indirect taxes paid to supranational organisations	4	...	-84	-134	47	-179	-110	147	243	392	118
Indirect taxes paid	4	...	239	260	326	371	596	925	1117	1882	2372
Less: Subsidies received	-	...	323	394	279	550	706	778	874	1490	2254
Equals: National Income at Market Prices	57995	63222	69348	82552	100319	112096	140380	170074	199509	243202	304933
Plus: Net current transfers received from abroad	152	189	186	-3	78	57	79	325	-72	801	938
Current transfers received	569	833	652	683	729	813	917	1290	1588	1971	2307
Less: Current transfers paid	417	644	466	686	651	756	838	965	1660	1170	1369
Equals: National Disposable Income at Market Prices	58147	63411	69534	82549	100397	112153	140459	170399	199437	244003	305871
Less: Final consumption	48035	53380	59138	69968	86285	99933	121560	146970	172072	208586	262909
Equals: Net Saving	10112	10031	10396	12581	14112	12220	18899	23429	27365	35417	42962
Less: Surplus of the nation on current transactions	729	1211	1192	-1570	-5144	-285	-2370	2191	5295	4390	-8494
Equals: Net Capital Formation	9383	8820	9204	14151	19256	12505	21269	21238	22070	31027	51456

2.1 General Government Final Consumption Expenditure by Function, in Current Prices

Thousand Million Italian lire

		1970	1971	1972	1973	1974	1975	1976	1977	1978	1979	1980
1	General public services	2011	2469	2809	3048	3707	4505	5268	6662	8759	9902	12734
2	Defence	1156	1414	1506	1782	2293	2364	2706	3356	4145	5360	6544
3	Public order and safety											
4	Education	2228	2703	3131	3776	4266	5066	6382	8275	9656	12320	15806
5	Health	1786	2187	2555	3010	3688	4297	5079	6328	7615	9747	12151
6	Social security and welfare	515	674	761	819	956	1180	1467	1700	1883	2026	2409
7	Housing and community amenities	213	246	314	360	405	521	631	765	887	1217	1486
8	Recreational, cultural and religious affairs	40	67	71	120	184	124	164	192	322	258	323
9	Economic services	668	772	850	924	1079	1179	1317	1573	1903	2298	2722
10	Other functions	47	76	80	68	136	126	119	140	87	232	265
	Total General Government Final Consumption Expenditure	8664	10608	12077	13907	16714	19362	23133	28991	35257	43360	54440

Italy

2.2 General Government Final Consumption Expenditure by Function, in Constant Prices

Thousand Million Italian lire

	1970	1971	1972	1973	1974	1975	1976	1977	1978	1979	1980
					At constant prices of:1970						
1 General public services	2011	2109	2203	2222	2236	2286	2265	2375	2551	2396	2504
2 Defence	1156	1195	1236	1282	1325	1365	1349	1401	1422	1460	1485
3 Public order and safety											
4 Education	2228	2364	2498	2581	2715	2819	2945	3015	3035	3193	3286
5 Health	1786	1894	2012	2047	2083	2146	2237	2281	2333	2460	2516
6 Social security and welfare	515	560	617	622	646	726	756	760	730	669	645
7 Housing and community amenities	213	225	235	240	243	245	256	261	257	296	294
8 Recreational, cultural and religious affairs	40	54	55	80	73	62	69	71	70	69	72
9 Economic services	668	704	734	748	757	765	779	790	805	827	810
10 Other functions	47	49	51	52	73	65	52	54	58	60	57
Total General Government Final Consumption Expenditure	8664	9154	9641	9874	10151	10479	10708	11008	11261	11430	11669

2.5 Private Final Consumption Expenditure by Type, in Current Prices

Thousand Million Italian lire

	1970	1971	1972	1973	1974	1975	1976	1977	1978	1979	1980
				Final Consumption Expenditure of Resident Households							
1 Food, beverages and tobacco	15237	16119	17388	20500	24887	28545	34344	40608	46881	55045	65383
a Food	12673	13456	14581	17194	21025	24286	29612	35216	40767	47778	56724
b Non-alcoholic beverages	158	161	158	181	221	270	331	360	399	503	588
c Alcoholic beverages	1281	1340	1390	1741	2063	2154	2284	2548	2864	3347	4084
d Tobacco	1125	1162	1259	1384	1578	1835	2117	2484	2851	3417	3987
2 Clothing and footwear	3800	4081	4507	5491	6825	7502	8995	11302	13166	16072	20936
3 Gross rent, fuel and power	5116	5782	6520	7530	9383	10669	12577	15061	17757	21422	27449
4 Furniture, furnishings and household equipment and operation	2488	2720	3002	3814	5109	5963	7428	9350	10481	12641	16408
a Household operation	868	960	1045	1348	1910	2463	3040	3586	3927	4623	5802
b Other	1620	1760	1957	2466	3199	3500	4388	5764	6554	8018	10606
5 Medical care and health expenses	1477	1572	1811	2241	2751	3401	4149	4703	5524	6581	8493
6 Transport and communication	4036	4569	5111	5882	7104	8532	11435	13915	15804	20381	27507
a Personal transport equipment	1077	1312	1471	1694	1792	2028	3048	3665	4237	6086	8259
b Other	2959	3257	3640	4188	5312	6504	8387	10250	11567	14295	19248
7 Recreational, entertainment, education and cultural services	3011	3208	3474	4123	5033	5968	7119	9010	10551	12416	15351
a Education	193	186	200	237	277	316	344	427	532	612	760
b Other	2818	3022	3274	3886	4756	5652	6775	8583	10019	11804	14591
8 Miscellaneous goods and services	4675	5198	5772	7003	9105	10866	13457	16380	19738	24838	31236
a Personal care	1611	1731	1943	2458	3366	3979	5021	6158	7934	10293	13290
b Expenditures in restaurants, cafes and hotels	2708	3079	3402	4046	5066	6103	7522	9058	10461	12959	15980
c Other	356	388	427	499	673	784	914	1164	1343	1586	1966
Total Final Consumption Expenditure in the Domestic Market by Households, of which	39840	43249	47585	56584	70197	81446	99504	120329	139902	169396	212763
Plus: Direct purchases abroad by resident households	408	477	520	667	626	676	735	986	1229	1446	1860
Less: Direct purchases in the domestic market by non-resident households	1191	1329	1466	1628	1815	2216	2728	4310	5440	6961	7798
Equals: Final Consumption Expenditure of Resident Households	39057	42397	46639	55623	69008	79906	97511	117005	135691	163881	206825
				Final Consumption Expenditure of Private Non-profit Institutions Serving Households							
Equals: Final Consumption Expenditure of Private Non-profit Organisations Serving Households	314	375	422	438	563	665	916	974	1124	1345	1644
Private Final Consumption Expenditure	39371	42772	47061	56061	69571	80571	98427	117979	136815	165226	208469

Italy

2.6 Private Final Consumption Expenditure by Type, in Constant Prices

Thousand Million Italian lire

At constant prices of: 1970

Final Consumption Expenditure of Resident Households

	1970	1971	1972	1973	1974	1975	1976	1977	1978	1979	1980
1 Food, beverages and tobacco	15237	15482	15655	16388	16955	16726	17067	17222	17642	18209	18703
a Food	12673	12886	12972	13541	13885	13648	13920	14028	14448	14819	15230
b Non-alcoholic beverages	158	156	148	163	170	170	187	180	181	203	202
c Alcoholic beverages	1281	1281	1279	1308	1390	1292	1263	1239	1250	1271	1314
d Tobacco	1125	1159	1256	1376	1510	1616	1697	1775	1763	1916	1957
2 Clothing and footwear	3800	3842	4045	4240	4323	4009	4128	4242	4296	4630	5012
3 Gross rent, fuel and power	5116	5303	5495	5706	5869	5918	6093	6244	6494	6635	6828
4 Furniture, furnishings and household equipment and operation	2488	2592	2757	3182	3281	3035	3197	3277	3327	3572	3839
a Household operation	868	912	963	1156	1243	1204	1269	1267	1282	1351	1416
b Other	1620	1680	1794	2026	2038	1831	1928	2010	2045	2221	2423
5 Medical care and health expenses	1477	1495	1663	1919	2128	2236	2412	2472	2539	2712	2796
6 Transport and communication	4036	4326	4601	4771	4608	4622	4945	5021	5235	5744	6168
a Personal transport equipment	1077	1235	1277	1285	1153	1047	1248	1270	1278	1549	1813
b Other	2959	3091	3324	3486	3455	3575	3697	3751	3957	4195	4355
7 Recreational, entertainment, education and cultural services	3011	3051	3122	3390	3438	3419	3561	3941	4141	4383	4591
a Education	193	178	176	193	198	197	194	203	206	201	210
b Other	2818	2873	2946	3197	3240	3222	3367	3738	3935	4182	4381
8 Miscellaneous goods and services	4675	4910	5061	5252	5418	5430	5573	5652	5839	6244	6469
a Personal care	1611	1622	1671	1762	1822	1751	1822	1860	1926	2043	2142
b Expenditures in restaurants, cafes and hotels	2708	2928	3031	3112	3195	3271	3328	3352	3457	3725	3828
c Other	356	360	359	378	401	408	423	440	456	476	499
Total Final Consumption Expenditure in the Domestic Market by Households, of which	39840	41001	42399	44848	46020	45395	46976	48071	49513	52129	54406
Plus: Direct purchases abroad by resident households	408	439	441	461	346	300	258	275	294	297	332
Less: Direct purchases in the domestic market by non-resident households	1191	1255	1292	1280	1210	1274	1325	1738	1926	2180	2023
Equals: Final Consumption Expenditure of Resident Households	39057	40185	41548	44029	45156	44421	45909	46608	47881	50246	52715

Final Consumption Expenditure of Private Non-profit Institutions Serving Households

	1970	1971	1972	1973	1974	1975	1976	1977	1978	1979	1980
Equals: Final Consumption Expenditure of Private Non-profit Organisations Serving Households	314	341	356	336	379	401	454	406	414	430	430
Private Final Consumption Expenditure	39371	40526	41904	44365	45535	44822	46363	47014	48295	50676	53145

2.9 Gross Capital Formation by Kind of Activity of Owner, ISIC Major Divisions, in Current Prices

Thousand Million Italian lire

	1970			1971			1972			1973		
	Total Gross Capital Formation	Increase in Stocks	Gross Fixed Capital Formation	Total Gross Capital Formation	Increase in Stocks	Gross Fixed Capital Formation	Total Gross Capital Formation	Increase in Stocks	Gross Fixed Capital Formation	Total Gross Capital Formation	Increase in Stocks	Gross Fixed Capital Formation

All Producers

1 Agriculture, hunting, fishing and forestry	...	...	846	...	...	925	...	...	1009	...	...	1129
2 Mining and quarrying	...	...	2708	...	...	2974	...	...	3102	...	...	4335
3 Manufacturing	...	...		...	...		...	...		...	...	
4 Electricity, gas and water	...	...	1064	...	...	1150	...	...	1147	...	...	1337

Italy

2.9 Gross Capital Formation by Kind of Activity of Owner, ISIC Major Divisions, in Current Prices
(Continued)

Thousand Million Italian lire

	1970 TGCF	1970 IS	1970 GFCF	1971 TGCF	1971 IS	1971 GFCF	1972 TGCF	1972 IS	1972 GFCF	1973 TGCF	1973 IS	1973 GFCF
5 Construction	...	...	160	...	...	122	...	...	170	...	...	204
6 Wholesale and retail trade, restaurants and hotels [a,b]	...	...	879	...	...	1062	...	...	1111	...	...	1438
7 Transport, storage and communication	...	...	1151	...	...	1363	...	...	1559	...	...	2020
8 Finance, insurance, real estate and business services [b]	...	...	5191	...	...	4912	...	...	5206	...	...	6440
9 Community, social and personal services [a]	...	...	...	...	...	...	...	...	...	...	...	...
Total Industries	...	...	11999	...	...	12508	...	...	13304	...	...	16903
Producers of Government Services	...	...	1435	...	...	1439	...	...	1538	...	...	1748
Private Non-Profit Institutions Serving Households												
Total	...	...	13434	...	...	13947	...	...	14842	...	...	18651

	1974 TGCF	1974 IS	1974 GFCF	1975 TGCF	1975 IS	1975 GFCF	1976 TGCF	1976 IS	1976 GFCF	1977 TGCF	1977 IS	1977 GFCF

All Producers

1 Agriculture, hunting, fishing and forestry	...	...	1476	...	...	1870	...	...	2420	...	...	2879
2 Mining and quarrying	...	...	5973	...	...	5439	...	...	6372	...	...	7496
3 Manufacturing	...	...		...	...		...	...		...	...	
4 Electricity, gas and water	...	...	1829	...	...	1963	...	...	2400	...	...	2682
5 Construction	...	...	269	...	...	278	...	...	386	...	...	437
6 Wholesale and retail trade, restaurants and hotels [a,b]	...	...	1989	...	...	1825	...	...	2305	...	...	2761
7 Transport, storage and communication	...	...	2441	...	...	2842	...	...	3767	...	...	4637
8 Finance, insurance, real estate and business services [b]	...	...	8747	...	...	9041	...	...	10607	...	...	12954
9 Community, social and personal services [a]	...	...	...	...	...	...	...	...	...	...	...	...
Total Industries	...	...	22724	...	...	23258	...	...	28257	...	...	33846
Producers of Government Services	...	...	2051	...	...	2518	...	...	3139	...	...	3357
Private Non-Profit Institutions Serving Households												
Total	...	...	24775	...	...	25776	...	...	31396	...	...	37203

	1978 TGCF	1978 IS	1978 GFCF	1979 TGCF	1979 IS	1979 GFCF	1980 TGCF	1980 IS	1980 GFCF

All Producers

1 Agriculture, hunting, fishing and forestry	...	...	3363	...	...	3832	...	...	4725
2 Mining and quarrying	...	...	7748	...	...	9579	...	...	...
3 Manufacturing	...	...		...	...		...	...	
4 Electricity, gas and water	...	...	3185	...	...	4211	...	...	...
5 Construction	...	...	514	...	...	609	...	...	...
6 Wholesale and retail trade, restaurants and hotels [a,b]	...	...	2912	...	...	3807	...	...	...
7 Transport, storage and communication	...	...	5234	...	...	5813	...	...	7630
8 Finance, insurance, real estate and business services [b]	...	...	14863	...	...	18525	...	...	...
9 Community, social and personal services [a]	...	...	...	...	...	...	...	...	...
Total Industries	...	...	37819	...	...	46376	...	...	61460
Producers of Government Services	...	...	3675	...	...	4551	...	...	5968
Private Non-Profit Institutions Serving Households									
Total	...	...	41494	...	...	50927	...	...	67428

a) Item 'Community, social and personal services' is included in item 'Wholesale and retail trade'.
b) Financial institutions and business services are included in item 'Wholesale and retail trade'.

Italy

2.10 Gross Capital Formation by Kind of Activity of Owner, ISIC Major Divisions, in Constant Prices

Thousand Million Italian lire

At constant prices of: 1970 — All Producers

	1970 TGCF	1970 IS	1970 GFCF	1971 TGCF	1971 IS	1971 GFCF	1972 TGCF	1972 IS	1972 GFCF	1973 TGCF	1973 IS	1973 GFCF
1 Agriculture, hunting, fishing and forestry	...	...	846	...	...	882	...	...	918	...	...	898
2 Mining and quarrying	...	...	2708	...	...	2688	...	...	2632	...	...	3113
3 Manufacturing	...	...		...	...		...	...		...	...	
4 Electricity, gas and water	...	...	1064	...	...	1068	...	...	1008	...	...	1001
5 Construction	...	...	160	...	...	112	...	...	142	...	...	147
6 Wholesale and retail trade, restaurants and hotels [a]	...	...	879	...	...	981	...	...	973	...	...	1082
7 Transport, storage and communication	...	...	1151	...	...	1274	...	...	1403	...	...	1578
8 Finance, insurance, real estate and business services	...	...	5191	...	...	4650	...	...	4693	...	...	4924
9 Community, social and personal services [a]	...	...		...	...		...	...		...	...	
Total Industries	...	...	11999	...	...	11655	...	...	11769	...	...	12743
Producers of Government Services	...	...	1435	...	...	1346	...	...	1351	...	...	1391
Private Non-Profit Institutions Serving Households	...	...		...	...		...	...		...	...	
Total	...	...	13434	...	...	13001	...	...	13120	...	...	14134

At constant prices of: 1970 — All Producers

	1974 TGCF	1974 IS	1974 GFCF	1975 TGCF	1975 IS	1975 GFCF	1976 TGCF	1976 IS	1976 GFCF	1977 TGCF	1977 IS	1977 GFCF
1 Agriculture, hunting, fishing and forestry	...	...	912	...	...	951	...	...	1029	...	...	1036
2 Mining and quarrying	...	...	3294	...	...	2469	...	...	2401	...	...	2427
3 Manufacturing	...	...		...	...		...	...		...	...	
4 Electricity, gas and water	...	...	1071	...	...	951	...	...	977	...	...	921
5 Construction	...	...	153	...	...	130	...	...	148	...	...	144
6 Wholesale and retail trade, restaurants and hotels [a]	...	...	1180	...	...	921	...	...	972	...	...	981
7 Transport, storage and communication	...	...	1572	...	...	1528	...	...	1739	...	...	1752
8 Finance, insurance, real estate and business services	...	...	5084	...	...	4463	...	...	4434	...	...	4534
9 Community, social and personal services [a]	...	...		...	...		...	...		...	...	
Total Industries	...	...	13266	...	...	11413	...	...	11700	...	...	11795
Producers of Government Services	...	...	1341	...	...	1332	...	...	1344	...	...	1203
Private Non-Profit Institutions Serving Households	...	...		...	...		...	...		...	...	
Total	...	...	14607	...	...	12745	...	...	13044	...	...	12998

At constant prices of: 1970 — All Producers

	1978 TGCF	1978 IS	1978 GFCF	1979 TGCF	1979 IS	1979 GFCF	1980 TGCF	1980 IS	1980 GFCF
1 Agriculture, hunting, fishing and forestry	...	...	1082	...	...	1062	...	...	1074
2 Mining and quarrying	...	...	2234	...	...	2477	...	...	...
3 Manufacturing	...	...		...	...		...	...	...
4 Electricity, gas and water	...	...	973	...	...	1106	...	...	...

Italy

2.10 Gross Capital Formation by Kind of Activity of Owner, ISIC Major Divisions, in Constant Prices
(Continued)

Thousand Million Italian lire

	1978 Total Gross Capital Formation	1978 Increase in Stocks	1978 Gross Fixed Capital Formation	1979 Total Gross Capital Formation	1979 Increase in Stocks	1979 Gross Fixed Capital Formation	1980 Total Gross Capital Formation	1980 Increase in Stocks	1980 Gross Fixed Capital Formation
			At constant prices of: 1970						
5 Construction	...	...	151	...	...	159	...	...	...
6 Wholesale and retail trade, restaurants and hotels [a]	...	...	954	...	...	1083	...	...	...
7 Transport, storage and communication	...	...	1788	...	...	1699	...	...	1862
8 Finance, insurance, real estate and business services	...	...	4643	...	...	4922	...	...	...
9 Community, social and personal services [a]									
Total Industries	...	...	11825	...	...	12507	...	...	13785
Producers of Government Services			1160			1235			1326
Private Non-Profit Institutions Serving Households	...	...		...	...		...	...	
Total	...	...	12985	...	...	13742	...	...	15111

a) Item 'Community, social and personal services' is included in item 'Wholesale and retail trade'.

2.17 Exports and Imports of Goods and Services, Detail

Thousand Million Italian lire

	1970	1971	1972	1973	1974	1975	1976	1977	1978	1979	1980
					Exports of Goods and Services						
1 Exports of merchandise, f.o.b.	8284	9392	10912	13030	19878	22907	31210	40020	47563	59992	66821
2 Transport and communication	1083	1076	1079	1264	1626	1793	...	...	...	...	...
a In respect of merchandise imports	266	244	232	207	358	371	...	...	...	...	...
b Other	817	832	847	1057	1268	1422	...	...	...	...	...
3 Insurance service charges	61	60	70	106	136	136	...	...	...	...	...
a In respect of merchandise imports	11	12	13	20	34	36	...	...	...	...	...
b Other	50	48	57	86	102	100	...	...	...	...	...
4 Other commodities	557	614	651	841	1231	1477	...	...	...	...	...
5 Adjustments of merchandise exports to change-of-ownership basis	...	...	...	...	...	...	...	...	...	...	...
6 Direct purchases in the domestic market by non-residential households	1191	1329	1466	1628	1815	2216	2728	4310	5440	6961	7798
7 Direct purchases in the domestic market by extraterritorial bodies	...	...	...	...	...	...	...	...	...	...	...
Total Exports of Goods and Services	11176	12471	14178	16869	24686	28529	38613	49938	59536	75318	85183
					Imports of Goods and Services						
1 Imports of merchandise, c.i.f.	9607	10356	11946	16698	27092	25589	37240	43120	48638	65484	86484
a Imports of merchandise, f.o.b.	8577	9348	10931	15482	25418	23717	...	...	...	...	...
b Transport of services on merchandise imports	1005	980	986	1176	1614	1810	...	...	...	...	...
By residents	266	244	232	207	358	370	...	...	...	...	...
By non-residents	739	736	754	969	1256	1440	...	...	...	...	...
c Insurance service charges on merchandise imports	25	28	29	40	61	62	...	...	...	...	...
By residents	11	12	13	20	35	35	...	...	...	...	...
By non-residents	14	16	16	20	26	27	...	...	...	...	...
2 Adjustments of merchandise imports to change-of-ownership basis	...	...	...	...	...	...	...	...	...	...	...
3 Other transport and communication	247	266	295	358	455	474	...	...	...	...	...
4 Other insurance service charges	45	49	61	75	92	107	...	...	...	...	...
5 Other commodities	532	564	677	969	1413	1662	...	...	...	...	...
6 Direct purchases abroad by government	...	...	...	...	...	...	...	...	...	...	...
7 Direct purchases abroad by resident households	408	477	520	667	626	676	735	986	1229	1446	1860
Total Imports of Goods and Services	10839	11712	13499	18767	29679	28508	40578	47505	53788	71708	94577
Balance of Goods and Services	337	759	679	-1898	-4993	21	-1965	2433	5748	3610	-9394
Total Imports and Balance of Goods and Services	11176	12471	14178	16869	24686	28529	38613	49938	59536	75318	85183

Italy

3.12 General Government Income and Outlay Account: Total and Subsectors

Thousand Million Italian lire

	1970					1971				
	Total General Government	Central Government	State or Provincial Government	Local Government	Social Security Funds	Total General Government	Central Government	State or Provincial Government	Local Government	Social Security Funds

Receipts

1 Property and entrepreneurial income	613	570	...	188	153	715	661	...	198	183
a Net operating surplus	22	-	...	22	...	35	2	...	28	...
b Withdrawals from public quasi-corporations	14	9	...	5	...	31	16	...	15	...
c Interest			...		...			...		...
d Dividends	577	561	...	161	...	649	643	...	155	...
e Net land rent and royalties			...		...			...		...
2 Taxes, fees and contributions	17181	9129	...	1490	6631	18989	9878	...	1641	7546
a Indirect taxes	7028	6342	...	719	...	7445	6664	...	819	...
b Direct taxes	3439	2711	...	764	...	3896	3127	...	807	...
Income	3439	2711	...	764	...	3896	3127	...	807	...
Other	-	...	...	...	...	-	...	...	...	...
c Social security contributions	6714	76	...	7	6631	7648	87	...	15	7546
d Fees, fines and penalties	-	-	...	...	.	-	-	...	...	.
3 Other current transfers received	1315	1001	...	1915	1227	1587	1128	...	2530	1517
a Casualty insurance claims	1	-	...	1	-	2	-	...	2	-
b Transfers from other government subsectors	...	93	...	1559	1218	...	112	...	2043	1504
c Transfers from abroad	55	55	...	...	...	47	47	...	...	...
d Other transfers, except imputed	467	164	...	261	...	686	242	...	373	...
e Imputed unfunded employee welfare contributions	792	689	...	94	9	852	727	...	112	13
Statistical discrepancy	...	...	...	...	42	...	...	...	...	71
Total Current Receipts	19109	10700	...	3593	8053	21291	11667	...	4369	9317

Disbursements

1 General government final consumption expenditures	8664	4994	...	3125	545	10608	6190	...	3705	713
2 Property income paid	1112	886	...	524	...	1392	1070	...	649	...
3 Subsidies	940	769	...	171	...	1095	907	...	188	...
4 Other current transfers paid	8277	3834	...	441	6941	9577	4413	...	604	8295
a Casualty insurance premiums, net	2	-	...	2	-	4	-	...	4	-
b Transfers to other government subsectors	...	2073	...	97	769	...	2483	...	99	1156
c Transfers to households	7844	1400	...	272	6172	9083	1526	...	415	7139
Social security benefits	7775	1353	...	250	6172	8964	1464	...	361	7139
Social assistance grants	69	47	...	22	...	119	62	...	54	...
Unfunded employee welfare benefits	...	...	...	...	...	...	...	...	...	...
d Transfers to private non-profit institutions serving households	204	134	...	70	...	249	163	...	86	...
e Transfers to the rest of the world	227	227	...	...	...	241	241	...	...	...
Net saving	116	217	...	-668	567	-1381	-913	...	-777	309
Total Current Disbursements and Net Saving	19109	10700	...	3593	8053	21291	11667	...	4369	9317

	1972					1973				
	Total General Government	Central Government	State or Provincial Government	Local Government	Social Security Funds	Total General Government	Central Government	State or Provincial Government	Local Government	Social Security Funds

Receipts

1 Property and entrepreneurial income	740	687	...	207	154	883	831	...	244	176
a Net operating surplus	47	2	...	36	...	65	2	...	49	...
b Withdrawals from public quasi-corporations	39	25	...	14	...	31	25	...	6	...
c Interest			...		...			...		...
d Dividends	654	660	...	157	...	787	804	...	189	...
e Net land rent and royalties			...		...			...		...
2 Taxes, fees and contributions	20703	10685	...	1890	8227	24404	12819	...	1550	10065
a Indirect taxes	7625	6801	...	877	...	8784	8357	...	427	...

Italy

3.12 General Government Income and Outlay Account: Total and Subsectors
(Continued)

Thousand Million Italian lire

	1972					1973				
	Total General Government	Central Government	State or Provincial Government	Local Government	Social Security Funds	Total General Government	Central Government	State or Provincial Government	Local Government	Social Security Funds
b Direct taxes	4711	3764	...	993	...	5398	4327	...	1101	...
Income	4711	993	...	...	...	5398	1101	...	...	...
Other	-	2771	...	...	...	-	3226	...	...	...
c Social security contributions	8367	120	...	20	8227	10222	135	...	22	10065
d Fees, fines and penalties	-	-	...	...	...	-	-	...	...	...
3 Other current transfers received	1738	1214	...	3064	1310	2040	1373	...	4163	2621
a Casualty insurance claims	3	1	...	2	-	3	-	...	3	-
b Transfers from other government subsectors	...	130	...	2518	1296	...	132	...	3503	2604
c Transfers from abroad	39	39	...	...	...	26	26	...	...	...
d Other transfers, except imputed	715	200	...	421	...	892	249	...	521	...
e Imputed unfunded employee welfare contributions	981	844	...	123	14	1119	966	...	136	17
Statistical discrepancy	...	...	...	...	94	...	...	...	...	122
Total Current Receipts	23181	12586	...	5161	9785	27327	15023	...	5957	12984
	Disbursements									
1 General government final consumption expenditures	12077	6788	...	4469	820	13907	7818	...	5161	928
2 Property income paid	1715	1215	...	808	...	2272	1642	...	998	...
3 Subsidies	1400	1146	...	254	...	1443	1197	...	246	...
4 Other current transfers paid	11102	4887	...	666	9592	13249	7300	...	843	11375
a Casualty insurance premiums, net	8	3	...	5	-	12	5	...	6	1
b Transfers to other government subsectors	...	2719	...	112	1215	...	4865	...	121	1287
c Transfers to households	10598	1757	...	461	8377	12578	1901	...	586	10087
Social security benefits	10444	1679	...	388	8377	12348	1807	...	454	10087
Social assistance grants	154	78	...	73	...	230	94	...	132	...
Unfunded employee welfare benefits	...	...	...	...	...	...	...	...	...	...
d Transfers to private non-profit institutions serving households	279	191	...	88	...	265	135	...	130	...
e Transfers to the rest of the world	217	217	...	...	...	394	394	...	...	...
Net saving	-3113	-1450	...	-1036	-627	-3544	-2934	...	-1291	681
Total Current Disbursements and Net Saving	23181	12586	...	5161	9785	27327	15023	...	5957	12984

	1974					1975				
	Total General Government	Central Government	State or Provincial Government	Local Government	Social Security Funds	Total General Government	Central Government	State or Provincial Government	Local Government	Social Security Funds
	Receipts									
1 Property and entrepreneurial income	1164	1025	...	324	242	1112	1037	...	368	363
a Net operating surplus	90	3	...	60	...	110	3	...	68	...
b Withdrawals from public quasi-corporations	48	24	...	24	...	35	23	...	12	...
c Interest			...		...			...		...
d Dividends	1026	998	...	240	...	967	1011	...	288	...
e Net land rent and royalties			...		...			...		...
2 Taxes, fees and contributions	30479	16592	...	1130	12811	35562	18499	...	1119	16020
a Indirect taxes	10870	10489	...	381	...	10962	10534	...	428	...
b Direct taxes	6635	5964	...	725	...	8367	7778	...	665	...
Income	6635	725	...	...	...	8367	665	...	...	...
Other	-	5239	...	...	...	-	7113	...	...	...
c Social security contributions	12974	139	...	24	12811	16233	187	...	26	16020
d Fees, fines and penalties	-	-	...	...	...	-	-	...	...	...
3 Other current transfers received	2233	1835	...	5360	2108	2492	4118	...	6638	1399
a Casualty insurance claims	5	1	...	3	1	4	1	...	2	1
b Transfers from other government subsectors	...	439	...	4667	2089	...	2479	...	6039	1378

860

Italy

3.12 General Government Income and Outlay Account: Total and Subsectors
(Continued)

Thousand Million Italian lire

	1974					1975				
	Total General Government	Central Government	State or Provincial Government	Local Government	Social Security Funds	Total General Government	Central Government	State or Provincial Government	Local Government	Social Security Funds
c Transfers from abroad	34	34	...	...	...	69	69	...	...	...
d Other transfers, except imputed	962	300	...	537	...	1083	430	...	420	...
e Imputed unfunded employee welfare contributions	1232	1061	...	153	18	1336	1139	...	177	20
Statistical discrepancy	...	...	...	...	125	...	...	...	...	233
Total Current Receipts	33876	19452	...	6814	15286	39166	23654	...	8125	18015

Disbursements

1 General governement final consumption expenditures	16714	9489	...	6125	1100	19362	10593	...	7814	955
2 Property income paid	3406	2409	...	1424	...	4989	4048	...	1597	...
3 Subsidies	1780	1414	...	366	...	2791	2160	...	631	...
4 Other current transfers paid	16187	7992	...	1018	14426	20886	10045	...	1374	19439
a Casualty insurance premiums, net	13	5	...	7	1	14	5	...	8	1
b Transfers to other government subsectors	...	5557	...	147	1554	...	7344	...	152	2487
c Transfers to households	15504	1918	...	706	12871	20080	2108	...	1010	16951
Social security benefits	15194	1813	...	510	12871	19616	1964	...	701	16951
Social assistance grants	310	105	...	196	...	464	144	...	309	...
Unfunded employee welfare benefits	...	...	...	...	...	...	...	...	...	...
d Transfers to private non-profit institutions serving households	343	185	...	158	...	393	189	...	204	...
e Transfers to the rest of the world	327	327	...	...	...	399	399	...	...	...
Net saving	-4211	-1852	...	-2119	-240	-8862	-3192	...	-3291	-2379
Total Current Disbursements and Net Saving	33876	19452	...	6814	15286	39166	23654	...	8125	18015

	1976					1977				
	Total General Government	Central Government	State or Provincial Government	Local Government	Social Security Funds	Total General Government	Central Government	State or Provincial Government	Local Government	Social Security Funds

Receipts

1 Property and entrepreneurial income	1402	1278	...	520	149	1737	1550	...	628	482
a Net operating surplus	161	1	...	106	...	192	1	...	124	...
b Withdrawals from public quasi-corporations	39	30	...	9	...	69	50	...	19	...
c Interest			...		...			...		...
d Dividends	1202	1247		405		1476	1499		485	
e Net land rent and royalties			...		...			...		...
2 Taxes, fees and contributions	46965	25848	...	1512	19698	59543	34450	...	1780	23452
a Indirect taxes	15021	14560	...	461	...	19485	18933	...	552	...
b Direct taxes	12015	11088	...	1020	...	16326	15273	...	1192	...
Income	12015	11088	...	1020	...	16326	15273	...	1192	...
Other	-	...	...	...	...	-	...	...	...	...
c Social security contributions	19929	200	...	31	19698	23732	244	...	36	23452
d Fees, fines and penalties	-	-	...	...	-	-	-	...	...	-
3 Other current transfers received	3199	5198	...	8456	2135	3881	6110	...	9410	4264
a Casualty insurance claims	6	1	...	3	2	7	2	...	4	1
b Transfers from other government subsectors	...	2994	...	7769	2111	...	3472	...	8616	4239
c Transfers from abroad	17	17	...	...	...	20	20	...	...	...
d Other transfers, except imputed	1195	425	...	486	...	1395	389	...	582	...
e Imputed unfunded employee welfare contributions	1981	1761	...	198	22	2459	2227	...	208	24
Statistical discrepancy	...	...	...	...	284	...	...	...	...	424
Total Current Receipts	51566	32324	...	10488	22266	65161	42110	...	11818	28622

Disbursements

1 General governement final consumption expenditures	23133	12765	...	9080	1288	28991	16308	...	11080	1603
2 Property income paid	7090	5626	...	2009	...	9368	7794	...	2497	...

Italy

3.12 General Government Income and Outlay Account: Total and Subsectors
(Continued)

Thousand Million Italian lire

	1976 Total General Government	1976 Central Government	1976 State or Provincial Government	1976 Local Government	1976 Social Security Funds	1977 Total General Government	1977 Central Government	1977 State or Provincial Government	1977 Local Government	1977 Social Security Funds
3 Subsidies	3374	2265	...	1109	...	4422	2989	...	1433	...
4 Other current transfers paid	25976	13658	...	1468	23817	30495	17239	...	1560	28162
a Casualty insurance premiums, net	17	6	...	9	2	19	7	...	11	1
b Transfers to other government subsectors	...	9777	...	182	3020	...	12744	...	217	3518
c Transfers to households	24950	3105	...	1038	20795	29486	3684	...	1146	24643
Social security benefits	24421	2920	...	706	20795	28963	3494	...	826	24643
Social assistance grants	529	185	...	332	...	523	190	...	320	...
Unfunded employee welfare benefits	...	...	...	...	...	...	...	...	...	...
d Transfers to private non-profit institutions serving households	633	394	...	239	...	568	382	...	186	...
e Transfers to the rest of the world	376	376	...	...	...	422	422	...	...	...
Net saving	-8007	-1990	...	-3178	-2839	-8115	-2220	...	-4752	-1143
Total Current Disbursements and Net Saving	51566	32324	...	10488	22266	65161	42110	...	11818	28622

	1978 Total General Government	1978 Central Government	1978 State or Provincial Government	1978 Local Government	1978 Social Security Funds	1979 Total General Government	1979 Central Government	1979 State or Provincial Government	1979 Local Government	1979 Social Security Funds
Receipts										
1 Property and entrepreneurial income	2270	1198	...	764	445	2859	1273	...	1187	435
a Net operating surplus	354	106	...	172	...	449	153	...	205	...
b Withdrawals from public quasi-corporations	75	55	...	20	...	108	-	...	108	...
c Interest			...		...			...		...
d Dividends	1841	1037	...	572	...	2302	1120	...	874	...
e Net land rent and royalties			...		...			...		...
2 Taxes, fees and contributions	72404	43377	...	1827	27340	86729	50219	...	2241	34397
a Indirect taxes	22368	21696	...	672	...	25490	24690	...	800	...
b Direct taxes	22264	21290	...	1114	...	26292	25027	...	1393	...
Income	22264	21290	...	1114	...	26292	25027	...	1393	...
Other	...	...	...	...	...	...	...	...	...	...
c Social security contributions	27772	391	...	41	27340	34947	502	...	48	34397
d Fees, fines and penalties	-	-	...	-	-	-	-	...	-	-
3 Other current transfers received	5440	8580	...	18732	9824	6798	12245	...	23652	10937
a Casualty insurance claims	19	4	...	8	7	15	5	...	9	1
b Transfers from other government subsectors	...	4871	...	17618	9792	...	7414	...	22340	10910
c Transfers from abroad	39	39	...	-	...	31	31	...	-	...
d Other transfers, except imputed	2073	621	...	867	...	2472	841	...	1003	...
e Imputed unfunded employee welfare contributions	3309	3045	...	239	25	4280	3954	...	300	26
Statistical discrepancy	...	...	...	...	585	...	...	...	...	628
Total Current Receipts	80114	53155	...	21323	38194	96386	63737	...	27080	46397
Disbursements										
1 General government final consumption expenditures	35257	19947	...	13514	1796	43360	24125	...	17262	1973
2 Property income paid	13053	11370	...	1820	...	15612	13919	...	1729	...

Italy

3.12 General Government Income and Outlay Account: Total and Subsectors
(Continued)

Thousand Million Italian lire

	1978					1979				
	Total General Government	Central Government	State or Provincial Government	Local Government	Social Security Funds	Total General Government	Central Government	State or Provincial Government	Local Government	Social Security Funds
3 Subsidies	5628	3725	...	1903	...	7460	5142	...	2318	...
4 Other current transfers paid	38797	33663	...	1773	35782	44319	37119	...	5590	42402
a Casualty insurance premiums, net	33	9	...	22	2	43	12	...	27	4
b Transfers to other government subsectors	...	27217	...	282	4939	...	30015	...	3542	7251
c Transfers to households	37118	4943	...	1317	30841	43133	6235	...	1735	35147
Social security benefits	36577	4731	...	1005	30841	42426	6030	...	1249	35147
Social assistance grants	541	212	...	312	...	707	205	...	486	...
Unfunded employee welfare benefits	...	...	...	...	...	...	...	...	...	...
d Transfers to private non-profit institutions serving households	596	444	...	152	...	736	450	...	286	...
e Transfers to the rest of the world	1050	1050	...	-	...	407	407	...	-	...
Net saving	-12621	-15550	...	2313	616	-14365	-16568	...	181	2022
Total Current Disbursements and Net Saving	80114	53155	...	21323	38194	96386	63737	...	27080	46397

	1980				
	Total General Government	Central Government	State or Provincial Government	Local Government	Social Security Funds

Receipts

1 Property and entrepreneurial income	3709	1843	...	1435	383
a Net operating surplus	509	153	...	245	...
b Withdrawals from public quasi-corporations	185	60	...	125	...
c Interest			...		...
d Dividends	3015	1630	...	1065	...
e Net land rent and royalties			...		...
2 Taxes, fees and contributions	114476	69776	...	2916	41919
a Indirect taxes	34131	33036	...	1095	...
b Direct taxes	37671	36039	...	1767	...
Income	37671	36039	...	1767	...
Other	...	...	...	...	...
c Social security contributions	42674	701	...	54	41919
d Fees, fines and penalties	-	-	...	-	-
3 Other current transfers received	8457	19648	...	35075	15282
a Casualty insurance claims	20	6	...	13	1
b Transfers from other government subsectors	...	13562	...	33395	15246
c Transfers from abroad	83	83	...	.	...
d Other transfers, except imputed	3129	1264	...	1210	...
e Imputed unfunded employee welfare contributions	5225	4733	...	457	35
Statistical discrepancy	...	...	...	...	655
Total Current Receipts	126642	91267	...	39426	58239

Disbursements

1 General governement final consumption expenditures	54440	30468	...	21545	2427
2 Property income paid	20785	18795	...	1942	...

Italy

3.12 General Government Income and Outlay Account: Total and Subsectors
(Continued)

Thousand Million Italian lire

		1980			
		Total General Government	Central Government	State or Provincial Government	Local Government	Social Security Funds
3	Subsidies	7914	5215	...	2699	...
4	Other current transfers paid	55462	51851	...	8044	57905
	a Casualty insurance premiums, net	52	15	...	33	4
	b Transfers to other government subsectors	...	43634	...	5470	13251
	c Transfers to households	54223	7343	...	2213	44650
	Social security benefits	53433	7111	...	1672	44650
	Social assistance grants	790	232	...	541	...
	Unfunded employee welfare benefits	...	...	...	...	...
	d Transfers to private non-profit institutions serving households	845	517	...	328	...
	e Transfers to the rest of the world	342	342	...	-	...
Net saving		-11959	-15062	...	5196	-2093
Total Current Disbursements and Net Saving		126642	91267	...	39426	58239

3.13 General Government Capital Accumulation Account: Total and Subsectors

Thousand Million Italian lire

		1970					1971				
		Total General Government	Central Government	State or Provincial Government	Local Government	Social Security Funds	Total General Government	Central Government	State or Provincial Government	Local Government	Social Security Funds
		Finance of Gross Accumulation									
1	Gross saving	327	324	...	-575	578	-1150	-797	...	-675	322
	a Consumption of fixed capital	211	107	...	93	11	231	116	...	102	13
	b Net saving	116	217	...	-668	567	-1381	-913	...	-777	309
2	Capital transfers received a	-581	-772	...	151	-43	-325	-590	...	265	-45
	a From other government subsectors	...	...	...	...	-43	...	...	...	...	-45
	b From other resident sectors	-556	...	...	...	...	-299	...	...	...	...
	c From rest of the world	-25	...	...	...	...	-26	...	...	...	...
Finance of Gross Accumulation		-254	-448	...	-424	535	-1475	-1387	...	-410	277
		Gross Accumulation									
1	Gross capital formation	2019	985	...	876	75	2078	996	...	968	69
2	Purchases of land, net	-58	-31	...	-27	-	-20	-5	...	-17	2
3	Purchases of intangible assets, net	-	-	...	-	...	...	-	...	-	...
4	Capital transfers paid	...	...	...	...	...	...	...	...	...	...
Net lending		-2215	-1402	...	-1273	460	-3533	-2378	...	-1361	206
Gross Accumulation		-254	-448	...	-424	535	-1475	-1387	...	-410	277

		1972					1973				
		Total General Government	Central Government	State or Provincial Government	Local Government	Social Security Funds	Total General Government	Central Government	State or Provincial Government	Local Government	Social Security Funds
		Finance of Gross Accumulation									
1	Gross saving	-2863	-1322	...	-928	-613	-3253	-2783	...	-1167	697
	a Consumption of fixed capital	250	128	...	108	14	291	151	...	124	16
	b Net saving	-3113	-1450	...	-1036	-627	-3544	-2934	...	-1291	681
2	Capital transfers received a	-395	-546	...	207	-94	-468	-805	...	393	-56
	a From other government subsectors	...	...	...	...	-94	...	...	...	...	-56
	b From other resident sectors	-378	...	...	...	...	-450	...	...	...	...
	c From rest of the world	-17	...	...	...	...	-18	...	...	...	...
Finance of Gross Accumulation		-3258	-1868	...	-721	-707	-3721	-3588	...	-774	641
		Gross Accumulation									
1	Gross capital formation	2361	1105	...	1120	98	2562	1175	...	1277	110
2	Purchases of land, net	-15	-1	...	-22	8	-8	-1	...	-12	5
3	Purchases of intangible assets, net	-	-	...	-	...	...	-	...	-	...
4	Capital transfers paid	...	...	...	...	...	...	...	...	...	...
Net lending		-5604	-2972	...	-1819	-813	-6275	-4762	...	-2039	526
Gross Accumulation		-3258	-1868	...	-721	-707	-3721	-3588	...	-774	641

Italy

3.13 General Government Capital Accumulation Account: Total and Subsectors

Thousand Million Italian lire

	1974					1975				
	Total General Government	Central Government	State or Provincial Government	Local Government	Social Security Funds	Total General Government	Central Government	State or Provincial Government	Local Government	Social Security Funds

Finance of Gross Accumulation

	1974					1975				
1 Gross saving	-3862	-1671	...	-1970	-221	-8468	-2991	...	-3120	-2357
a Consumption of fixed capital	349	181	...	149	19	394	201	...	171	22
b Net saving	-4211	-1852	...	-2119	-240	-8862	-3192	...	-3291	-2379
2 Capital transfers received [a]	-462	-1145	...	760	-77	-1699	-4218	...	2766	-247
a From other government subsectors	...	...	...	...	-77	...	...	...	...	-247
b From other resident sectors	-408	...	...	...	...	-1626	...	...	...	...
c From rest of the world	-54	...	...	...	...	-73	...	...	...	...
Finance of Gross Accumulation	-4324	-2816	...	-1210	-298	-10167	-7209	...	-354	-2604

Gross Accumulation

1 Gross capital formation	3458	1604	...	1697	157	4466	2023	...	2220	223
2 Purchases of land, net	4	3	...	-5	6	2	3	...	-6	5
3 Purchases of intangible assets, net	-	-	...	-	...	-	-	...	-	...
4 Capital transfers paid	...	...	...	...	...	...	...	...	...	...
Net lending	-7786	-4423	...	-2902	-461	-14635	-9235	...	-2568	-2832
Gross Accumulation	-4324	-2816	...	-1210	-298	-10167	-7209	...	-354	-2604

	1976					1977				
	Total General Government	Central Government	State or Provincial Government	Local Government	Social Security Funds	Total General Government	Central Government	State or Provincial Government	Local Government	Social Security Funds

Finance of Gross Accumulation

1 Gross saving	-7553	-1756	...	-2983	-2814	-7614	-1961	...	-4537	-1116
a Consumption of fixed capital	454	234	...	195	25	501	259	...	215	27
b Net saving	-8007	-1990	...	-3178	-2839	-8115	-2220	...	-4752	-1143
2 Capital transfers received [a]	-1123	-3067	...	2136	-192	-1102	-4452	...	2996	354
a From other government subsectors	-2136	...	...	...	-192	-2008	...	...	...	354
b From other resident sectors	1068	...	...	...	...	1004	...	...	...	...
c From rest of the world	-55	...	...	...	...	-98	...	...	...	...
Finance of Gross Accumulation	-8676	-4823	...	-847	-3006	-8716	-6413	...	-1541	-762

Gross Accumulation

1 Gross capital formation	5380	2409	...	2758	213	6347	2965	...	3198	184
2 Purchases of land, net	33	2	...	22	9	52	5	...	40	7
3 Purchases of intangible assets, net	-	-	...	-	...	-	-	...	-	...
4 Capital transfers paid	...	...	...	...	...	...	...	...	...	...
Net lending	-14089	-7234	...	-3627	-3228	-15115	-9383	...	-4779	-953
Gross Accumulation	-8676	-4778	...	-1196	-3006	-8716	-6413	...	-1541	-762

	1978					1979				
	Total General Government	Central Government	State or Provincial Government	Local Government	Social Security Funds	Total General Government	Central Government	State or Provincial Government	Local Government	Social Security Funds

Finance of Gross Accumulation

1 Gross saving	-12022	-15247	...	2577	648	-13645	-16210	...	508	2057
a Consumption of fixed capital	599	303	...	264	32	720	358	...	327	35
b Net saving	-12621	-15550	...	2313	616	-14365	-16568	...	181	2022
2 Capital transfers received [a]	-2640	-6077	...	2699	738	-3464	-5039	...	1109	466
a From other government subsectors	...	...	...	...	738	...	...	...	...	466
b From other resident sectors	...	...	...	...	...	...	...	...	...	...
c From rest of the world	...	...	...	...	...	...	...	...	...	...
Finance of Gross Accumulation	-14662	-21324	...	5276	1386	-17109	-21249	...	1617	2523

Gross Accumulation

1 Gross capital formation	6901	3111	...	3662	128	8326	3533	...	4643	150
2 Purchases of land, net	91	6	...	80	5	29	2	...	22	5
3 Purchases of intangible assets, net	-	-	...	-	...	-	-	...	-	...
4 Capital transfers paid	...	...	...	...	...	...	...	...	...	...
Net lending	-21654	-24441	...	1534	1253	-25464	-24784	...	-3048	2368
Gross Accumulation	-14662	-21324	...	5276	1386	-17109	-21249	...	1617	2523

Italy

3.13 General Government Capital Accumulation Account: Total and Subsectors

Thousand Million Italian lire

	1980				
	Total General Government	Central Government	State or Provincial Government	Local Government	Social Security Funds
Finance of Gross Accumulation					
1 Gross saving	-11090	-14634	...	5597	-2053
a Consumption of fixed capital	869	428	...	401	40
b Net saving	-11959	-15062	...	5196	-2093
2 Capital transfers received a	-4307	-5646	...	894	445
a From other government subsectors	...	...	...	...	445
b From other resident sectors	...	...	...	...	...
c From rest of the world	...	...	...	...	...
Finance of Gross Accumulation	-15397	-20280	...	6491	-1608
Gross Accumulation					
1 Gross capital formation	10738	4438	...	6120	180
2 Purchases of land, net	46	4	...	37	5
3 Purchases of intangible assets, net	-	-	...	-	...
4 Capital transfers paid	...	...	...	...	...
Net lending	-26181	-24722	...	334	-1793
Gross Accumulation	-15397	-20280	...	6491	-1608

a) Net.

3.22 Corporate and Quasi-Corporate Enterprise Income and Outlay Account: Total and Sectors

Thousand Million Italian lire

	1970			1971			1972			1973		
	TOTAL	Non-Financial	Financial	TOTAL	Non-Financial	Financial	TOTAL	Non-Financial	Financial	TOTAL	Non-Financial	Financial
Receipts												
1 Property and entrepreneurial income received	8204	3506	4698	9066	3455	5611	10356	3920	6436	12623	4612	8011
a Net operating surplus	1590	2669	-1079	1232	2533	-1301	1436	2892	-1456	1512	3406	-1894
b Withdrawals from quasi-corporate enterprises	6614	837	5777	7834	922	6912	8920	1028	7892	11111	1206	9905
c Interest												
d Dividends	...	...	...	...	...	...	...	...	...	...	...	...
e Net land rent and royalties	...	...	...	...	...	...	...	...	...	...	...	...
2 Other current transfers received	2453	1990	463	2848	2240	608	3312	2617	695	3830	2907	923
a Casualty insurance transactions	339	212	127	431	266	165	480	309	171	522	319	203
Claims received	339	212	127	431	266	165	480	309	171	522	319	203
Net premiums received by insurance companies	...	...	...	...	...	...	...	...	...	...	...	...
b Current transfers received from the rest of the world	...	...	...	...	...	...	...	...	...	...	...	...
c Other transfers received, except imputed	...	...	...	...	...	...	...	...	...	...	...	...
d Imputed unfunded employee welfare contributions	2114	1778	336	2417	1974	443	2832	2308	524	3308	2588	720
Total Current Receipts	10657	5496	5161	11914	5695	6219	13668	6537	7131	16453	7519	8934
Disbursements												
1 Property and entrepreneurial income paid out	6532	2525	4007	7697	2853	4844	8648	3056	5592	10362	3403	6959
a Withdrawals from quasi-corporations	99	99	...	127	127	...	144	144	...	154	154	...
b Interest	5784	1857	3927	6964	2219	4745	7851	2365	5486	9492	2648	6844
c Dividends	478	398	80	434	335	99	479	373	106	511	396	115
d Net land rent and royalties	171	171	...	172	172	...	174	174	...	205	205	...
2 Direct taxes and other current payments n.e.c. to general government	793	640	153	823	593	230	1059	757	302	1164	812	352

Italy

3.22 Corporate and Quasi-Corporate Enterprise Income and Outlay Account: Total and Sectors
(Continued)

Thousand Million Italian lire

	1970 TOTAL	1970 Non-Financial	1970 Financial	1971 TOTAL	1971 Non-Financial	1971 Financial	1972 TOTAL	1972 Non-Financial	1972 Financial	1973 TOTAL	1973 Non-Financial	1973 Financial
a Direct taxes	793	640	153	823	593	230	1059	757	302	1164	812	352
b Fines, fees, penalties and other payments n.e.c.	...	...	...	...	...	...	...	...	...	...	...	...
3 Other current transfers paid	2632	2145	487	3101	2468	633	3544	2822	722	4215	3262	953
a Casualty insurance transactions	304	177	127	389	224	165	445	274	171	566	363	203
Casualty insurance premiums paid, net	304	177	127	389	224	165	445	274	171	566	363	203
Claims paid by insurance companies	...	...	...	...	...	...	...	...	...	...	...	...
b Transfers to private non-profit institutions	...	...	...	...	...	...	...	...	...	...	...	...
c Transfers to households	2328	1968	360	2712	2244	468	3099	2548	551	3649	2899	750
Unfunded employee welfare benefits	2114	1778	336	2417	1974	443	2832	2308	524	3308	2588	720
Social assistance grants and other transfers n.e.c.	214	190	24	295	270	25	267	240	27	341	311	30
d Transfers to the rest of the world	...	...	...	...	...	...	...	...	...	...	...	...
Net saving	700	186	514	293	-219	512	417	-98	515	712	42	670
Total Current Disbursements and Net Saving	10657	5496	5161	11914	5695	6219	13668	6537	7131	16453	7519	8934

	1974 TOTAL	1974 Non-Financial	1974 Financial	1975 TOTAL	1975 Non-Financial	1975 Financial	1976 TOTAL	1976 Non-Financial	1976 Financial	1977 TOTAL	1977 Non-Financial	1977 Financial
Receipts												
1 Property and entrepreneurial income received	19992	5615	14377	21602	3989	17613	31656	7473	24183	40125	9190	30935
a Net operating surplus	1164	3868	-2704	-1607	2133	-3740	337	4794	-4457	672	5658	-4986
b Withdrawals from quasi-corporate enterprises	18828	1747	17081	23209	1856	21353	31319	2679	28640	39453	3532	35921
c Interest												
d Dividends	...	...	...	...	...	...	...	...	...	...	...	...
e Net land rent and royalties	...	...	...	...	...	...	...	...	...	...	...	...
2 Other current transfers received	4661	3380	1281	5609	4083	1526	6991	5087	1904	6476	4697	1779
a Casualty insurance transactions	633	367	266	796	477	319	963	576	387	1117	676	441
Claims received	633	367	266	796	477	319	963	576	387	1117	676	441
Net premiums received by insurance companies	...	...	...	...	...	...	...	...	...	...	...	...
b Current transfers received from the rest of the world	...	...	...	...	...	...	...	...	...	...	...	...
c Other transfers received, except imputed	...	...	...	...	...	...	...	...	...	...	...	...
d Imputed unfunded employee welfare contributions	4028	3013	1015	4813	3606	1207	6028	4511	1517	5359	4021	1338
Total Current Receipts	24653	8995	15658	27211	8072	19139	38647	12560	26087	46601	13887	32714
Disbursements												
1 Property and entrepreneurial income paid out	18083	5511	12572	21905	7213	14692	30034	9379	20655	38257	11435	26822
a Withdrawals from quasi-corporations	198	198	...	221	221	...	266	266	...	343	343	...
b Interest	17181	4747	12434	20809	6269	14540	28773	8297	20476	36557	9996	26561
c Dividends	478	340	138	568	416	152	650	471	179	923	663	260
d Net land rent and royalties	226	226	...	307	307	...	345	345	-	434	433	1
2 Direct taxes and other current payments n.e.c. to general government	1191	780	411	1709	1308	401	2447	1898	549	3033	2443	590

Italy

3.22 Corporate and Quasi-Corporate Enterprise Income and Outlay Account: Total and Sectors
(Continued)

Thousand Million Italian lire

	1974 TOTAL	1974 Non-Financial	1974 Financial	1975 TOTAL	1975 Non-Financial	1975 Financial	1976 TOTAL	1976 Non-Financial	1976 Financial	1977 TOTAL	1977 Non-Financial	1977 Financial
a Direct taxes	1191	780	411	1709	1308	401	2447	1898	549	3033	2443	590
b Fines, fees, penalties and other payments n.e.c.	...	...	...	...	...	...	...	...	...	...	...	...
3 Other current transfers paid	5086	3767	1319	6118	4549	1569	7529	5569	1960	7052	5182	1870
a Casualty insurance transactions	693	427	266	815	496	319	983	596	387	1178	711	467
Casualty insurance premiums paid, net	693	427	266	815	496	319	983	596	387	1178	711	467
Claims paid by insurance companies	...	...	...	...	...	...	...	...	...	...	...	...
b Transfers to private non-profit institutions	...	...	...	...	...	...	...	...	...	...	...	...
c Transfers to households	4393	3340	1053	5303	4053	1250	6546	4973	1573	5874	4471	1403
Unfunded employee welfare benefits	4028	3013	1015	4813	3606	1207	6028	4511	1517	5359	4021	1338
Social assistance grants and other transfers n.e.c.	365	327	38	490	447	43	518	462	56	515	450	65
d Transfers to the rest of the world	...	...	...	...	...	...	...	...	...	...	...	...
Net saving	293	-1063	1356	-2521	-4998	2477	-1363	-4286	2923	-1741	-5173	3432
Total Current Disbursements and Net Saving	24653	8995	15658	27211	8072	19139	38647	12560	26087	46601	13887	32714

	1978 TOTAL	1978 Non-Financial	1978 Financial	1979 TOTAL	1979 Non-Financial	1979 Financial	1980 TOTAL	1980 Non-Financial	1980 Financial
Receipts									
1 Property and entrepreneurial income received	46147	10619	35528	57853	16419	41434	77206	23314	53892
a Net operating surplus	1152	6582	-5430	4807	11395	-6588	7844	16683	-8839
b Withdrawals from quasi-corporate enterprises	44995	4037	40958	53046	5024	48022	69362	6631	62731
c Interest									
d Dividends	...	...	...	...	...	...	...	...	...
e Net land rent and royalties	...	...	...	...	...	...	...	...	...
2 Other current transfers received	7308	5319	1989	8704	6393	2311	10799	7866	2933
a Casualty insurance transactions	1343	880	463	1513	907	606	1784	1062	722
Claims received	1343	880	463	1513	907	606	1784	1062	722
Net premiums received by insurance companies	...	...	...	...	...	...	...	...	...
b Current transfers received from the rest of the world	...	...	...	...	...	...	...	...	...
c Other transfers received, except imputed	...	...	...	...	...	...	...	...	...
d Imputed unfunded employee welfare contributions	5965	4439	1526	7191	5486	1705	9015	6804	2211
Total Current Receipts	53455	15938	37517	66557	22812	43745	88005	31180	56825
Disbursements									
1 Property and entrepreneurial income paid out	42835	13092	29743	48674	14235	34439	63505	20167	43338
a Withdrawals from quasi-corporations	365	365	...	489	489	...	655	655	...
b Interest	40516	11108	29408	46075	12035	34040	60246	17345	42901
c Dividends	1498	1165	333	1553	1156	397	1881	1449	432
d Net land rent and royalties	456	454	2	557	555	2	723	718	5
2 Direct taxes and other current payments n.e.c. to general government	4016	3081	935	4786	3930	856	6020	4666	1354

Italy

3.22 Corporate and Quasi-Corporate Enterprise Income and Outlay Account: Total and Sectors
(Continued)

Thousand Million Italian lire

	1978 TOTAL	1978 Non-Financial	1978 Financial	1979 TOTAL	1979 Non-Financial	1979 Financial	1980 TOTAL	1980 Non-Financial	1980 Financial
a Direct taxes	4016	3081	935	4786	3930	856	6020	4666	1354
b Fines, fees, penalties and other payments n.e.c.	...	...	...	...	...	...	...	...	...
3 Other current transfers paid	8278	6178	2100	9730	7284	2446	12289	9177	3112
a Casualty insurance transactions	1421	922	499	1562	913	649	1877	1103	774
Casualty insurance premiums paid, net	1421	922	499	1562	913	649	1877	1103	774
Claims paid by insurance companies	...	...	...	...	...	...	...	...	...
b Transfers to private non-profit institutions	...	...	...	...	...	...	...	...	...
c Transfers to households	6857	5256	1601	8168	6371	1797	10412	8074	2338
Unfunded employee welfare benefits	5965	4439	1526	7191	5486	1705	9015	6804	2211
Social assistance grants and other transfers n.e.c.	892	817	75	977	885	92	1397	1270	127
d Transfers to the rest of the world	...	...	...	...	...	...	...	...	...
Net saving	-1674	-6413	4739	3367	-2637	6004	6191	-2830	9021
Total Current Disbursements and Net Saving	53455	15938	37517	66557	22812	43745	88005	31180	56825

3.23 Corporate and Quasi-Corporate Enterprise Capital Accumulation Account: Total and Sectors

Thousand Million Italian lire

	1970 TOTAL	1970 Non-Financial	1970 Financial	1971 TOTAL	1971 Non-Financial	1971 Financial	1972 TOTAL	1972 Non-Financial	1972 Financial	1973 TOTAL	1973 Non-Financial	1973 Financial
Finance of Gross Accumulation												
1 Gross saving	3550	2955	595	3385	2784	601	3842	3225	617	5003	4214	789
a Consumption of fixed capital	2850	2769	81	3092	3003	89	3425	3323	102	4291	4172	119
b Net saving	700	186	514	293	-219	512	417	-98	515	712	42	670
2 Capital transfers received	373	550	-177	240	240	-	351	351	-	426	426	-
Finance of Gross Accumulation	3923	3505	418	3625	3024	601	4193	3576	617	5429	4640	789
Gross Accumulation												
1 Gross capital formation	7133	6870	263	5935	5652	283	7001	6615	386	11352	11000	352
2 Purchases of land, net	39	32	7	20	17	3	27	19	8	20	12	8
3 Purchases of intangible assets, net	12	12	-	11	11	-	14	14	-	32	32	...
4 Capital transfers paid	...	...	...	...	...	...	...	...	...	...	...	...
5 Net lending	-3261	-3409	148	-2341	-2656	315	-2849	-3072	223	-5975	-6404	429
Gross Accumulation	3923	3505	418	3625	3024	601	4193	3576	617	5429	4640	789

	1974 TOTAL	1974 Non-Financial	1974 Financial	1975 TOTAL	1975 Non-Financial	1975 Financial	1976 TOTAL	1976 Non-Financial	1976 Financial	1977 TOTAL	1977 Non-Financial	1977 Financial
Finance of Gross Accumulation												
1 Gross saving	6202	4691	1511	4713	2041	2672	7533	4364	3169	9143	5365	3778
a Consumption of fixed capital	5909	5754	155	7234	7039	195	8896	8650	246	10884	10538	346
b Net saving	293	-1063	1356	-2521	-4998	2477	-1363	-4286	2923	-1741	-5173	3432
2 Capital transfers received	357	357	-	1340	694	646	1002	1002	-	918	1257	-339
Finance of Gross Accumulation	6559	5048	1511	6053	2735	3318	8535	5366	3169	10061	6622	3439
Gross Accumulation												
1 Gross capital formation	17337	16935	402	13522	12957	565	18125	17566	559	19600	18886	714
2 Purchases of land, net	26	17	9	28	24	4	20	14	6	43	35	8
3 Purchases of intangible assets, net	67	67	...	152	152	...	133	133	-	157	157	-
4 Capital transfers paid	...	...	...	...	...	...	...	...	...	...	...	...
5 Net lending	-10871	-11971	1100	-7649	-10398	2749	-9743	-12347	2604	-9739	-12456	2717
Gross Accumulation	6559	5048	1511	6053	2735	3318	8535	5366	3169	10061	6622	3439

Italy

3.23 Corporate and Quasi-Corporate Enterprise Capital Accumulation Account: Total and Sectors

Thousand Million Italian lire

	1978 TOTAL	1978 Non-Financial	1978 Financial	1979 TOTAL	1979 Non-Financial	1979 Financial	1980 TOTAL	1980 Non-Financial	1980 Financial
Finance of Gross Accumulation									
1 Gross saving	10735	5586	5149	17807	11250	6557	23527	13792	9735
a Consumption of fixed capital	12409	11999	410	14440	13887	553	17336	16622	714
b Net saving	-1674	-6413	4739	3367	-2637	6004	6191	-2830	9021
2 Capital transfers received	2221	2302	-81	2973	2973	-	3669	3742	-73
Finance of Gross Accumulation	12956	7888	5068	20780	14223	6557	27196	17534	9662
Gross Accumulation									
1 Gross capital formation	19677	18839	838	26714	25731	983	41625	40326	1299
2 Purchases of land, net	29	16	13	31	14	17	43	14	29
3 Purchases of intangible assets, net	201	201	-	258	258	-	341	341	-
4 Capital transfers paid	...	...	...	...	...	...	...	...	...
5 Net lending	-6951	-11168	4217	-6223	-11780	5557	-14813	-23147	8334
Gross Accumulation	12956	7888	5068	20780	14223	6557	27196	17534	9662

3.32 Household and Private Unincorporated Enterprise Income and Outlay Account

Thousand Million Italian lire

	1970	1971	1972	1973	1974	1975	1976	1977	1978	1979	1980
Receipts											
1 Compensation of employees	30714	35124	39163	47553	59055	71618	87429	107311	125434	149997	184399
a Wages and salaries	22177	25425	28329	34596	42577	51300	62062	78988	92275	110581	136535
b Employers' contributions for social security	5325	6088	6602	8075	10686	13514	16517	19644	22778	26491	31797
c Employers' contributions for private pension & welfare plans	3212	3611	4232	4882	5792	6804	8850	8679	10381	12925	16067
2 Property and entrepreneurial income received	20012	21074	23216	26774	32488	36464	45333	53407	64735	78649	97553
a Operating surplus of private unincorporated enterprises	19702	20642	22644	26357	31551	34760	41876	48066	57086	70921	87365
b Withdrawals from private quasi-corporations	85	96	105	123	150	186	227	274	290	381	470
c Interest	128	287	386	213	735	1417	3078	4972	7034	7138	9479
d Dividends	200	158	192	193	172	223	267	346	607	494	522
e Net land rent and royalties	-103	-109	-111	-112	-120	-122	-115	-251	-282	-285	-283
3 Other current transfers received	9737	11395	13150	16026	18948	23830	29757	35133	43656	50769	63274
a Casualty insurance claims	411	530	686	906	1026	1156	1362	1592	1737	2164	2713
b Social security benefits	6172	7139	8377	10087	12871	16951	20795	24643	30841	35147	44650
c Social assistance grants	811	973	1086	1142	1091	1329	1645	1861	2427	2999	3558
d Unfunded employee welfare benefits	1992	2331	2558	3373	3365	3687	5171	6053	7484	9044	10770
e Other current transfers received	351	422	443	518	595	707	784	984	1167	1415	1583
From general government	...	...	...	...	...	...	...	...	...	...	...
From the rest fo the world	289	336	340	360	351	338	385	626	785	956	1041
Other	62	86	103	158	244	369	399	358	382	459	542
Total Current Receipts	60463	67593	75529	90353	110491	131912	162519	195851	233825	279415	345226
Disbursements											
1 Final consumption expenditures	39057	42397	46639	55623	69008	79906	97511	117005	135691	163881	206825
2 Property income paid	...	...	...	...	...	...	...	...	...	...	...
3 Direct taxes, fees, fines & other payments n.e.c. to government	9438	10805	12106	14571	18558	23099	29717	37236	46198	56641	74525
a Social security contributions	6792	7732	8454	10337	13114	16441	20149	23943	27950	35135	42874
b Direct taxes	2646	3073	3652	4234	5444	6658	9568	13293	18248	21506	31651
Income taxes	2646	3073	3652	4234	5444	6658	9568	13293	18248	21506	31651

Italy

3.32 Household and Private Unincorporated Enterprise Income and Outlay Account
(Continued)

Thousand Million Italian lire

	1970	1971	1972	1973	1974	1975	1976	1977	1978	1979	1980
Other	...	...	...	...	...	...	...	...	...	...	...
c Fees, fines and penalties	...	...	...	...	...	...	...	...	...	...	...
4 Other current transfers paid	2680	3281	3703	4758	4914	5327	7059	8381	10347	12578	15285
a Net casualty insurance premiums	445	570	716	853	958	1127	1331	1519	1645	2087	2588
b Transfers to private non-profit institutions serving households	...	...	...	...	...	...	...	...	...	...	...
c Transfers to the rest of the world	-	-	-	-	-	-	-	-	-	-	-
d Other current transfers, except imputed	356	484	540	652	751	770	830	1121	1550	1856	2283
e Imputed employee welfare contributions	1879	2227	2447	3253	3205	3430	4898	5741	7152	8635	10414
Net saving	9288	11110	13081	15401	18011	23580	28232	33229	41589	46315	48591
Total Current Disbursements and Net Saving	60463	67593	75529	90353	110491	131912	162519	195851	233825	279415	345226

3.33 Household and Private Unincorporated Enterprise Capital Accumulation Account

Thousand Million Italian lire

	1970	1971	1972	1973	1974	1975	1976	1977	1978	1979	1980
Finance of Gross Accumulation											
1 Gross saving	11345	13326	15496	18329	21905	28848	34643	41251	50905	57546	62768
a Consumption of fixed capital	2057	2216	2415	2928	3894	5268	6411	8022	9316	11231	14177
b Net saving	9288	11110	13081	15401	18011	23580	28232	33229	41589	46315	48591
2 Capital transfers received [a]	186	63	30	51	51	286	164	188	409	459	676
Total Finance of Gross Accumulation	11531	13389	15526	18380	21956	29134	34807	41439	51314	58005	63444
Gross Accumulation											
1 Gross Capital Formation	5341	6341	5921	7733	8607	7411	13525	14690	17804	22347	31427
2 Purchases of land, net	19	-	-12	-12	-30	-30	-53	-95	-120	-60	-89
3 Purchases of intangibles, net	-12	-11	-5	-19	-53	-133	-117	-137	-177	-233	-308
4 Capital transfers paid	...	...	...	...	...	...	...	...	...	...	...
5 Net lending	6183	7059	9622	10678	13432	21886	21452	26981	33807	35951	32414
Total Gross Accumulation	11531	13389	15526	18380	21956	29134	34807	41439	51314	58005	63444

a) Net.

3.51 External Transactions: Current Account: Detail

Thousand Million Italian lire

	1970	1971	1972	1973	1974	1975	1976	1977	1978	1979	1980
Payments to the Rest of the World											
1 Imports of goods and services	10839	11712	13499	18767	29679	28508	40578	47505	53788	71708	94577
2 Factor income paid to the rest of the world	756	859	970	1380	2493	2170	2327	2674	3241	4049	5853
a Compensation of employees	43	43	46	65	82	102	108	137	167	176	233
b Property and entrepreneurial income paid	713	816	924	1315	2411	2068	2219	2537	3074	3873	5620
3 Indirect taxes paid to supranational organizations	4	-	239	260	326	371	596	925	1117	1882	2372
4 Other current transfers to the rest of the world	417	644	466	686	651	756	838	965	1660	1170	1369
5 Surplus of the nation on current transactions	729	1211	1192	-1570	-5144	-285	-2370	2191	5295	4390	-8494
Payments to the Rest of the World, and Surplus of the Nation on Current Transfers	12745	14426	16366	19523	28005	31520	41969	54260	65101	83199	95677
Receipts From The Rest of the World											
1 Exports of goods and services	11176	12471	14178	16869	24686	28529	38613	49938	59536	75318	85183
2 Factor income received from the rest of the world	1000	1122	1213	1577	2311	1628	1733	2254	3103	4420	5933
a Compensation of employees	408	440	456	538	531	516	584	947	1286	1549	1714
b Property and entrepreneurial income received	592	682	757	1039	1780	1112	1149	1307	1817	2871	4219
3 Subsidies received from supranational organizations	-	-	323	394	279	550	706	778	874	1490	2254
4 Other current transfers from the rest of the world	569	833	652	683	729	813	917	1290	1588	1971	2307
Receipts from the Rest of the World on Current Transfers	12745	14426	16366	19523	28005	31520	41969	54260	65101	83199	95677

Italy

3.52 External Transactions: Capital Accumulation Account

Thousand Million Italian lire

	1970	1971	1972	1973	1974	1975	1976	1977	1978	1979	1980
Finance of Gross Accumulation											
1 Surplus of the nation on current transactions	729	1211	1192	-1570	-5144	-285	-2370	2191	5295	4390	-8494
2 Capital transfers received from the rest of the world	-22	-22	-14	10	-54	-73	43	4	-10	-32	38
a By general government	-25	-26	-17	-18	-54	-73	-55	-98	-79	...	...
b By other resident sectors	3	4	3	28	-	-	98	102	69	...	...
Total Finance of Gross Accumulation	707	1189	1178	-1560	-5198	-358	-2327	2195	5285	4358	-8456
Gross Accumulation											
1 Capital transfers paid to the rest of the world	...	...	...	...	...	...	...	...	...	...	...
2 Purchases of intangible assets, n.e.c., net, from the rest of the world	-	-	9	14	14	19	16	20	24	25	33
3 Net lending to the rest of the world	707	1189	1169	-1574	-5212	-377	-2343	2175	5261	4333	-8489
Total Gross Accumulation	707	1189	1178	-1560	-5198	-358	-2327	2195	5285	4358	-8456

Ivory Coast

Source. Communication from the Direction des Etudes de Developpement, Ministere du Plan, Abidjan. The official estimates are published annually in 'Comptes de la Nation'.

General note. The official estimates of Ivory Coast have been adjusted by the Direction des Etudes de Developpement to conform to the present United Nations System of National Accounts so far as the existing data would permit.

1.1 Expenditure on the Gross Domestic Product, in Current Prices

Million CFA francs	1970	1971	1972	1973	1974	1975	1976	1977	1978	1979	1980
1 General government final consumption expenditure	64935	73864	77224	95639	118688	140639	177217	206568	278778	...	...
2 Private final consumption expenditure	246058	267101	287824	340080	418142	517272	633187	839252	964898	...	...
3 Gross capital formation	91311	96002	97378	129723	162805	187392	256099	420750	537651	...	...
a Increase in stocks	7430	3638	3128	7763	19150	3446	8918	23118	7309	...	...
b Gross fixed capital formation	83881	92364	94250	121960	143655	183946	247181	397632	530342	...	...
Residential buildings	...	...	...	...	...	...	...	...	...	...	...
Non-residential buildings	...	...	...	...	...	...	...	...	...	...	...
Other construction and land improvement etc.	...	...	...	...	...	...	...	...	...	...	...
Other	...	...	...	50202	59362	65536	92465	165587	195714	...	...
4 Exports of goods and services	153808	157231	174609	221519	345511	315235	476319	669473	659925	...	...
5 Less: Imports of goods and services	141250	154421	165198	220767	306126	325993	428865	596778	700690	...	...
Equals: Gross Domestic Product	414862	439777	471837	566194	739020	834545	1113957	1539265	1740562	...	...

1.2 Expenditure on the Gross Domestic Product, in Constant Prices

Million CFA francs	1970	1971	1972	1973	1974	1975	1976	1977	1978	1979	1980
					At constant prices of: 1975						
1 General government final consumption expenditure	...	...	...	...	...	140639	163793	175914	186820	...	...
2 Private final consumption expenditure	...	...	...	...	...	517272	566025	622061	694843	...	...
3 Gross capital formation	...	...	...	...	...	187392	233445	332799	387707	...	...
a Increase in stocks	...	...	...	...	...	3446	8293	11507	-1699	...	...
b Gross fixed capital formation	...	...	...	...	...	183946	225152	321292	389406	...	...
4 Exports of goods and services	...	...	...	...	...	315235	346954	319892	343564	...	...
5 Less: Imports of goods and services	...	...	...	...	...	325993	375570	472091	530630	...	...
Equals: Gross Domestic Product	...	...	...	...	...	834545	934647	978575	1082304	...	...

1.3 Cost Components of the Gross Domestic Product

Million CFA francs	1970	1971	1972	1973	1974	1975	1976	1977	1978	1979	1980
1 Indirect taxes, net [a]	83844	78826	84274	110800	164564	149748	299704	501472	468406	...	...
a Indirect taxes paid	75212	82436	92042	111653	126977	145167	209998	277121	323483	...	...
b Less: Subsidies received [a]	-8632	3610	7768	853	-37587	-4581	-89706	-224351	-144923	...	...
2 Consumption of fixed capital	15000	19000	22000	25000	30000	40000	55000	82000	115000	...	...
3 Compensation of employees paid by resident producers to:	142328	158721	173096	203445	236140	285403	364541	442420	565800	...	...
a Resident households	142178	158521	172846	203176	235868	285078	364541	440812	565800	...	...
b Rest of the world	150	200	250	269	272	325	-	1608	-	...	...
4 Net operating surplus	173690	183230	192467	226949	308316	359394	394712	513373	591356	...	...
a Corporate and quasi-corporate enterprises	53240	59736	56646	66411	90684	102905	102987	116783		...	...
b Private unincorporated enterprises	120122	122987	135372	160019	217120	256078	291828	396748		...	...
c General government [b]	328	507	449	519	512	411	-103	-158		...	...
Equals: Gross Domestic Product	414862	439777	471837	566194	739020	834545	1113957	1539265	1740562	...	...

a) Including the profit or loss of the Marketing Board.
b) Including consumption of fixed capital.

1.4 General Government Current Receipts and Disbursements

Million CFA francs	1970	1971	1972	1973	1974	1975	1976	1977	1978	1979	1980
					Receipts						
1 Property and entrepreneurial income [a]	2965	3514	2681	3936	8822	8011	8570	15466	18437	...	...
2 Taxes, fees and contributions	105784	102784	110476	143235	203824	198143	361889	589243	598150	...	...
a Indirect taxes	74339	81767	91429	111101	126491	143139	209998	277121	323483	...	...
b Direct taxes	10277	11282	13375	16482	21202	27156	29947	42737	64974	...	...

Ivory Coast

1.4 General Government Current Receipts and Disbursements
(Continued)

Million CFA francs

	1970	1971	1972	1973	1974	1975	1976	1977	1978	1979	1980
c Social security contributions	3506	3849	4672	5354	6556	9796	13902	14822	19908	...	...
d Compulsory fees, fines and penalties b	17662	5886	1000	10298	49575	18052	108042	254563	189785	...	...
3 Other current receipts	15021	17233	20439	29305	29646	32360	34962	45766	47485	...	...
Total Current Receipts of General Government	123770	123531	133596	176476	242292	238514	405421	650475	664072	...	...

Disbursements

	1970	1971	1972	1973	1974	1975	1976	1977	1978	1979	1980
1 General government final consumption expenditure	64935	73864	77224	95639	118688	140639	177217	206568	278778	...	...
2 Property income paid	2534	3558	4084	4514	5503	7098	11005	15714	25701	...	...
3 Subsidies	9030	9496	8768	11151	11988	13471	18236	30212	44862	...	...
4 Other current transfers paid	15456	17734	20862	21970	29184	39884	45146	61188	66474	...	...
a Social security benefits and social assistance grants	6433	7509	6803	7717	9280	12620	15886	20786	25514	...	...
b Other	9023	10225	14059	14253	19904	27264	29260	40402	40960	...	...
5 Net saving a	31815	18879	22658	43202	76929	37422	153817	336793	248257	...	...
Total Current Disbursements and Net Saving of General Government a	123770	123531	133596	176476	242292	238514	405421	650475	664072	...	...

a) Including consumption of fixed capital.
b) Less deductions of the Marketing Board.

1.7 External Transactions on Current Account, Summary

Million CFA francs

	1970	1971	1972	1973	1974	1975	1976	1977	1978	1979	1980

Payments to the Rest of the World

	1970	1971	1972	1973	1974	1975	1976	1977	1978	1979	1980
1 Imports of goods and services	141250	154421	165198	220767	306126	325993	428865	596778	700690	...	...
a Imports of merchandise c.i.f.	...	...	...	...	252714	260562	336836	469834	554062	...	...
b Other	...	...	...	...	53412	65431	92029	126944	146628	...	...
2 Factor income paid to the rest of the world	14213	17382	14960	13828	22893	33241	43024	56489	72948	...	...
a Compensation of employees	150	200	250	269	272	325	-	1608	-	...	...
b Property and entrepreneurial income paid	14063	17182	14710	13559	22621	32916	43024	54881	72948	...	...
3 Indirect taxes paid to supranational organizations	...	...	...	...	...	...	...	...	...	...	...
4 Current transfers to the rest of the world	19163	21473	30322	34221	46907	54668	69220	88611	100561	...	...
5 Surplus of the nation on current transactions	-6934	-20598	-17473	-22700	-5443	-69514	-34850	-30709	-171795	...	...
Payments to the Rest of the World and Surplus of the Nation on Current Transactions	167692	172678	193007	246116	370483	344388	506259	711169	702404	...	...

Receipts From The Rest of the World

	1970	1971	1972	1973	1974	1975	1976	1977	1978	1979	1980
1 Exports of goods and services	153808	157231	174609	221519	345511	315235	476319	669473	659925	...	...
a Exports of merchandise f.o.b.	...	...	...	...	310580	275397	426124	611544	591571	...	...
b Other	...	...	...	...	34931	39838	50195	57929	68354	...	...
2 Factor income received from rest of the world	2733	2200	2223	1250	2378	6005	1954	6048	3500	...	...
a Compensation of employees	350	350	400	475	500	645	-	3229	-	...	...
b Property and entrepreneurial income received	2383	1850	1823	775	1878	5360	1954	2819	3500	...	...
3 Subsidies received from supranational organisations	...	...	...	...	...	...	...	...	...	...	...
4 Current transfers from rest of the world	11151	13247	16175	23347	22594	23148	27986	35648	38979	...	...
Receipts from the Rest of the World on Current Transactions	167692	172678	193007	246116	370483	344388	506259	711169	702404	...	...

Ivory Coast

1.8 Capital Transactions of The Nation, Summary

Million CFA francs

	1970	1971	1972	1973	1974	1975	1976	1977	1978	1979	1980
Finance of Gross Capital Formation											
Gross saving	84377	75404	79905	107023	157362	117878	221249	390041	365856	...	...
1 Consumption of fixed capital	15000	19000	22000	25000	30000	40000	55000	82000	115000	...	...
2 Net saving	69377	56404	57905	82023	127362	77878	166249	308041	250856	...	...
Less: Surplus of the nation on current transactions	-6934	-20598	-17473	-22700	-5443	-69514	-34850	-30709	-171795	...	...
Finance of Gross Capital Formation	91311	96002	97378	129723	162805	187392	256099	420750	537651	...	...
Gross Capital Formation											
Increase in stocks	7430	3638	3128	7763	19150	3446	8918	23118	7309	...	...
Gross fixed capital formation	83881	92364	94250	121960	143655	183946	247181	397632	530342	...	...
Gross Capital Formation	91311	96002	97378	129723	162805	187392	256099	420750	537651	...	...

1.10 Gross Domestic Product by Kind of Activity, in Current Prices

Million CFA francs

	1970	1971	1972	1973	1974	1975	1976	1977	1978	1979	1980
1 Agriculture, hunting, forestry and fishing	112636	117620	125135	159174	193243	240414	284811	380171	427270	...	...
2 Mining and quarrying	941	1252	1515	1784	1850	1636	1673	3000	4287	...	...
3 Manufacturing	55111	61379	71033	77925	107733	109151	130867	164984	204729	...	...
4 Electricity, gas and water	4594	4834	5685	6291	8902	13439	14453	17455	20393	...	...
5 Construction	27693	33217	32209	34112	38151	54980	73606	108628	153376	...	...
6 Wholesale and retail trade, restaurants and hotels [a]	84943	76889	79135	95972	159914	149078	267946	447551	...	...	...
7 Transport, storage and communication	31616	37312	41668	52471	63576	72210	85957	97714	120887	...	...
8 Finance, insurance, real estate and business services	27991	33109	37804	44064	48617	56175	66847	96904	...	...	...
9 Community, social and personal services	3327	3996	4125	5455	5841	6860	8471	10046	...	...	...
Total, Industries	348852	369608	398309	477248	627827	703943	934631	1326453	1481615	...	...
Producers of Government Services	40039	42967	44954	55322	65582	82238	98355	113481	139658	...	...
Other Producers	3310	4227	4552	4494	5510	5897	8559	9362	11524	...	...
Subtotal	392201	416802	447815	537064	698919	792078	1041545	1449296	1632797	...	...
Less: Imputed bank service charge	5125	6345	8123	10405	11332	14821	16226	27246	34713	...	...
Plus: Import duties	27786	29320	32145	39535	51433	57288	88638	117215	142478	...	...
Plus: Value added tax	...	...	...	...	...	...	...	...	...	...	...
Equals: Gross Domestic Product	414862	439777	471837	566194	739020	834545	1113957	1539265	1740562	...	...

a) Including the profit or loss of the Marketing Board.

1.11 Gross Domestic Product by Kind of Activity, in Constant Prices

Million CFA francs

	1970	1971	1972	1973	1974	1975	1976	1977	1978	1979	1980
At constant prices of: 1975											
1 Agriculture, hunting, forestry and fishing	...	...	...	...	...	240414	247821	240346	260819	...	...
2 Mining and quarrying	...	...	...	...	...	1636	1434	2167	2726	...	...
3 Manufacturing	...	...	...	...	...	109151	124512	134971	154002	...	...
4 Electricity, gas and water	...	...	...	...	...	13439	13562	17183	19571	...	...
5 Construction	...	...	...	...	...	54980	68132	87890	106435	...	...
6 Wholesale and retail trade, restaurants and hotels	...	...	...	...	...	82238	88850	94892	95841	...	...
7 Transport, storage and communication	...	...	...	...	...	72210	81880	86138	92254	...	...
8 Finance, insurance, real estate and business services	...	...	...	...	...	...	...	...	...	...	...
9 Community, social and personal services	...	...	...	...	...	...	...	...	...	...	...
Total, Industries	...	...	...	...	...	777257	851904	878952	965845	...	...
Producers of Government Services	...	...	...	...	...	...	...	...	...	...	...
Other Producers	...	...	...	...	...	...	...	...	...	...	...
Subtotal	...	...	...	...	...	777257	851904	878952	965845	...	...
Less: Imputed bank service charge	...	...	...	...	...	...	...	...	...	...	...
Plus: Import duties	...	...	...	...	...	57288	82743	99623	116459	...	...
Plus: Value added tax	...	...	...	...	...	...	...	...	...	...	...
Equals: Gross Domestic Product	...	...	...	...	...	834545	934647	978575	1082304	...	...

Ivory Coast

1.12 Relations Among National Accounting Aggregates

Million CFA francs

	1970	1971	1972	1973	1974	1975	1976	1977	1978	1979	1980
Gross Domestic Product	414862	439777	471837	566194	739020	834545	1113957	1539265	1740562	...	...
Plus: Net factor income received from abroad	-11480	-15182	-12737	-12578	-20515	-27236	-41070	-50441	-69448	...	...
Factor income received	2733	2200	2223	1250	2378	6005	1954	6048	3500	...	...
Less: Factor income paid	14213	17382	14960	13828	22893	33241	43024	56489	72948	...	...
Equals: Gross National Product	403382	424595	459100	553616	718505	807309	1072887	1488824	1671114	...	...
Less: Consumption of fixed capital	15000	19000	22000	25000	30000	40000	55000	82000	115000	...	...
Less: Net indirect taxes paid to supranational organisations	...	...	...	...	...	...	...	...	...	...	...
Equals: National Income at Market Prices	388382	405595	437100	528616	688505	767309	1017887	1406824	1556114	...	...
Plus: Net current transfers received from abroad	-8012	-8226	-14147	-10874	-24313	-31520	-41234	-52963	-61582	...	...
Current transfers received	11151	13247	16175	23347	22594	23148	27986	35648	38979	...	...
Less: Current transfers paid	19163	21473	30322	34221	46907	54668	69220	88611	100561	...	...
Equals: National Disposable Income at Market Prices	380370	397369	422953	517742	664192	735789	976653	1353861	1494532	...	...
Less: Final consumption	310993	340965	365048	435719	536830	657911	810404	1045820	1243676	...	...
Equals: Net Saving	69377	56404	57905	82023	127362	77878	166249	308041	250856	...	...
Less: Surplus of the nation on current transactions	-6934	-20598	-17473	-22700	-5443	-69514	-34850	-30709	-171795	...	...
Equals: Net Capital Formation	76311	77002	75378	104723	132805	147392	201099	338750	422651	...	...

2.17 Exports and Imports of Goods and Services, Detail

Million CFA francs

	1970	1971	1972	1973	1974	1975	1976	1977	1978	1979	1980
Exports of Goods and Services											
1 Exports of merchandise, f.o.b.	...	...	...	...	310580	275397	426124	611544	591571	...	...
2 Transport and communication	...	...	...	...	23915	27878	35664	40560	47168	...	...
3 Insurance service charges	...	...	...	...	...	...	...	...	...	...	...
4 Other commodities	...	...	...	...	3148	3182	3191	4020	4986	...	...
5 Adjustments of merchandise exports to change-of-ownership basis	...	...	...	...	...	...	...	...	...	...	...
6 Direct purchases in the domestic market by non-residential households	...	...	...	...	7868	8778	11340	13349	16200	...	...
7 Direct purchases in the domestic market by extraterritorial bodies	...	...	...	...	...	...	...	...	...	...	...
Total Exports of Goods and Services	153808	157231	174609	221519	345511	315235	476319	669473	659925	...	...
Imports of Goods and Services											
1 Imports of merchandise, c.i.f.	...	...	...	...	252714	260562	336836	469834	554062	...	...
2 Adjustments of merchandise imports to change-of-ownership basis	...	...	...	...	...	...	...	...	...	...	...
3 Other transport and communication	...	...	...	...	10977	13177	19734	27581	31718	...	...
4 Other insurance service charges	...	...	...	...	...	...	...	...	...	...	...
5 Other commodities	...	...	...	...	19519	20780	25058	37544	45000	...	...
6 Direct purchases abroad by government	...	...	...	...	...	...	...	...	...	...	...
7 Direct purchases abroad by resident households	...	...	...	...	...	...	...	...	...	...	...
Total Imports of Goods and Services	141250	154421	165198	220767	306126	325993	428865	596778	700690	...	...
Balance of Goods and Services	12558	2810	9411	752	39385	-10758	47454	72695	-40765	...	...
Total Imports and Balance of Goods and Services	153808	157231	174609	221519	345511	315235	476319	669473	659925	...	...

Ivory Coast

3.12 General Government Income and Outlay Account: Total and Subsectors

Million CFA francs

	1970 Total General Government	Central Government	State or Provincial Government	Local Government	Social Security Funds	1971 Total General Government	Central Government	State or Provincial Government	Local Government	Social Security Funds
Receipts										
1 Property and entrepreneurial income [a]	2965	...	...	...	...	3514	...	...	...	...
a Net operating surplus [a]	328	...	...	...	...	507	...	...	...	...
b Withdrawals from public quasi-corporations	-	...	...	...	...	-	...	...	...	...
c Interest	...	...	...	...	...	...	...	...	...	...
d Dividends	...	...	...	...	...	...	...	...	...	...
e Net land rent and royalties	...	...	...	...	...	...	...	...	...	...
2 Taxes, fees and contributions [b]	105784	...	...	...	...	102784	...	...	...	...
a Indirect taxes	74339	...	...	...	...	81767	...	...	...	...
b Direct taxes	10277	...	...	...	...	11282	...	...	...	...
Income	...	...	...	...	...	10074	...	...	...	...
Other	...	...	...	...	...	1208	...	...	...	...
c Social security contributions	3506	...	...	...	...	3849	...	...	...	...
d Fees, fines and penalties [b]	17662	...	...	...	...	5886	...	...	...	...
3 Other current transfers received	15021	...	...	...	...	17233	...	...	...	...
a Casualty insurance claims	-	...	...	...	...	-	...	...	...	...
b Transfers from other government subsectors	...	...	...	...	...	...	...	...	...	...
c Transfers from abroad	9238	...	...	...	...	11082	...	...	...	...
d Other transfers, except imputed	2853	...	...	...	...	3135	...	...	...	...
e Imputed unfunded employee welfare contributions	2930	...	...	...	...	3016	...	...	...	...
Total Current Receipts	123770	...	...	...	...	123531	...	...	...	...
Disbursements										
1 General governement final consumption expenditures	64935	...	...	...	...	73864	...	...	...	...
2 Property income paid	2534	...	...	...	...	3558	...	...	...	...
3 Subsidies	9030	...	...	...	...	9496	...	...	...	...
4 Other current transfers paid	15456	...	...	...	...	17734	...	...	...	...
a Casualty insurance premiums, net	-	...	...	...	...	-	...	...	...	...
b Transfers to other government subsectors	...	...	...	...	...	...	...	...	...	...
c Transfers to households	10739	...	...	...	...	12526	...	...	...	...
Social security benefits	3313	...	...	...	...	3633	...	...	...	...
Social assistance grants	4496	...	...	...	...	5877	...	...	...	...
Unfunded employee welfare benefits	2930	...	...	...	...	3016	...	...	...	...
d Transfers to private non-profit institutions serving households	940	...	...	...	...	1187	...	...	...	...
e Transfers to the rest of the world	3777	...	...	...	...	3991	...	...	...	...
Net saving [a]	31815	...	...	...	...	18879	...	...	...	...
Total Current Disbursements and Net Saving [a]	123770	...	...	...	...	123531	...	...	...	...

	1972 Total General Government	Central Government	State or Provincial Government	Local Government	Social Security Funds	1973 Total General Government	Central Government	State or Provincial Government	Local Government	Social Security Funds
Receipts										
1 Property and entrepreneurial income [a]	2681	...	...	...	...	3936	...	...	...	...
a Net operating surplus [a]	449	...	...	...	...	519	...	...	...	...
b Withdrawals from public quasi-corporations	-	...	...	...	...	-	...	...	...	...
c Interest	...	...	...	...	...	...	...	...	...	...
d Dividends	...	...	...	...	...	...	...	...	...	...
e Net land rent and royalties	...	...	...	...	...	...	...	...	...	...
2 Taxes, fees and contributions [b]	110476	...	...	...	...	143235	...	...	...	...
a Indirect taxes	91429	...	...	...	...	111101	...	...	...	...
b Direct taxes	13375	...	...	...	...	16482	...	...	...	...

Ivory Coast

3.12 General Government Income and Outlay Account: Total and Subsectors
(Continued)

Million CFA francs

	1972					1973				
	Total General Government	Central Government	State or Provincial Government	Local Government	Social Security Funds	Total General Government	Central Government	State or Provincial Government	Local Government	Social Security Funds
Income	12651	...	...	...	...	15308	...	...	...	...
Other	724	...	...	...	...	1174	...	...	...	...
c Social security contributions	4672	...	...	...	...	5354	...	...	...	...
d Fees, fines and penalties b	1000	...	...	...	...	10298	...	...	...	...
3 Other current transfers received	20439	...	...	...	...	29305	...	...	...	...
a Casualty insurance claims	-	...	...	...	...	-	...	...	...	...
b Transfers from other government subsectors	...	...	...	...	...	...	...	...	...	...
c Transfers from abroad	13975	...	...	...	...	21629	...	...	...	...
d Other transfers, except imputed	3153	...	...	...	...	3869	...	...	...	...
e Imputed unfunded employee welfare contributions	3311	...	...	...	...	3807	...	...	...	...
Total Current Receipts	133596	...	...	...	...	176476	...	...	...	...

Disbursements

	Total General Government	Central Government	State or Provincial Government	Local Government	Social Security Funds	Total General Government	Central Government	State or Provincial Government	Local Government	Social Security Funds
1 General governement final consumption expenditures	77224	...	...	...	...	95639	...	...	...	...
2 Property income paid	4084	...	...	...	...	4514	...	...	...	...
3 Subsidies	8768	...	...	...	...	11151	...	...	...	...
4 Other current transfers paid	20862	...	...	...	...	21970	...	...	...	...
a Casualty insurance premiums, net	-	...	...	...	...	-	...	...	...	...
b Transfers to other government subsectors	...	...	...	...	...	...	...	...	...	...
c Transfers to households	12476	...	...	...	...	14387	...	...	...	...
Social security benefits	2748	...	...	...	...	2736	...	...	...	...
Social assistance grants	6417	...	...	...	...	7844	...	...	...	...
Unfunded employee welfare benefits	3311	...	...	...	...	3807	...	...	...	...
d Transfers to private non-profit institutions serving households	1513	...	...	...	...	1244	...	...	...	...
e Transfers to the rest of the world	6873	...	...	...	...	6339	...	...	...	...
Net saving a	22658	...	...	...	...	43202	...	...	...	...
Total Current Disbursements and Net Saving a	133596	...	...	...	...	176476	...	...	...	...

	1974					1975				
	Total General Government	Central Government	State or Provincial Government	Local Government	Social Security Funds	Total General Government	Central Government	State or Provincial Government	Local Government	Social Security Funds

Receipts

	Total General Government	Central Government	State or Provincial Government	Local Government	Social Security Funds	Total General Government	Central Government	State or Provincial Government	Local Government	Social Security Funds
1 Property and entrepreneurial income a	8822	...	...	...	...	8011	...	...	...	...
a Net operating surplus a	512	...	...	...	...	411	...	...	...	...
b Withdrawals from public quasi-corporations	-	...	...	...	...	-	...	...	...	...
c Interest	...	...	...	...	...	...	...	...	...	...
d Dividends	...	...	...	...	...	...	...	...	...	...
e Net land rent and royalties	...	...	...	...	...	...	...	...	...	...
2 Taxes, fees and contributions b	203824	...	...	...	...	198143	...	...	...	...
a Indirect taxes	126491	...	...	...	...	143139	...	...	...	...
b Direct taxes	21202	...	...	...	...	27156	...	...	...	...
Income	20225	...	...	...	...	24330	...	...	...	...
Other	977	...	...	...	...	2826	...	...	...	...
c Social security contributions	6556	...	...	...	...	9796	...	...	...	...
d Fees, fines and penalties b	49575	...	...	...	...	18052	...	...	...	...
3 Other current transfers received	29646	...	...	...	...	32360	...	...	...	...
a Casualty insurance claims	-	...	...	...	...	-	...	...	...	...
b Transfers from other government subsectors	...	...	...	...	...	...	...	...	...	...

Ivory Coast

3.12 General Government Income and Outlay Account: Total and Subsectors
(Continued)

Million CFA francs

	1974					1975				
	Total General Government	Central Government	State or Provincial Government	Local Government	Social Security Funds	Total General Government	Central Government	State or Provincial Government	Local Government	Social Security Funds
c Transfers from abroad	20815	...	...	...	...	21653	...	...	...	...
d Other transfers, except imputed	4639	...	...	...	...	4739	...	...	...	...
e Imputed unfunded employee welfare contributions	4192	...	...	...	...	5968	...	...	...	...
Total Current Receipts	242292	...	...	...	...	238514	...	...	...	...

Disbursements

1 General governement final consumption expenditures	118688	...	...	...	...	140639	...	...	...	...
2 Property income paid	5503	...	...	...	...	7098	...	...	...	...
3 Subsidies	11988	...	...	...	...	13471	...	...	...	...
4 Other current transfers paid	29184	...	...	...	...	39884	...	...	...	...
a Casualty insurance premiums, net	-	...	...	...	...	-	...	...	...	...
b Transfers to other government subsectors	...	...	...	...	...	...	...	...	...	...
c Transfers to households	17312	...	...	...	...	24570	...	...	...	...
Social security benefits	2933	...	...	...	...	3470	...	...	...	...
Social assistance grants	10187	...	...	...	...	15132	...	...	...	...
Unfunded employee welfare benefits	4192	...	...	...	...	5968	...	...	...	...
d Transfers to private non-profit institutions serving households	1545	...	...	...	...	1631	...	...	...	...
e Transfers to the rest of the world	10327	...	...	...	...	13683	...	...	...	...
Net saving [a]	76929	...	...	...	...	37422	...	...	...	...
Total Current Disbursements and Net Saving [a]	242292	...	...	...	...	238514	...	...	...	...

	1976					1977				
	Total General Government	Central Government	State or Provincial Government	Local Government	Social Security Funds	Total General Government	Central Government	State or Provincial Government	Local Government	Social Security Funds

Receipts

1 Property and entrepreneurial income [a]	8570	...	...	...	...	15466	...	...	...	...
a Net operating surplus [a]	-103	...	...	...	...	-158	...	...	...	...
b Withdrawals from public quasi-corporations	1075	...	...	...	...	459	...	...	...	...
c Interest	...	...	...	...	...	...	...	...	...	...
d Dividends	...	...	...	...	...	...	...	...	...	...
e Net land rent and royalties	...	...	...	...	...	...	...	...	...	...
2 Taxes, fees and contributions [b]	361889	...	...	...	...	589243	...	...	...	...
a Indirect taxes	209998	...	...	...	...	277121	...	...	...	...
b Direct taxes	29947	...	...	...	...	42737	...	...	...	...
Income	28927	...	...	...	...	40856	...	...	...	...
Other	1020	...	...	...	...	1881	...	...	...	...
c Social security contributions	13902	...	...	...	...	14822	...	...	...	...
d Fees, fines and penalties [b]	108042	...	...	...	...	254563	...	...	...	...
3 Other current transfers received	34962	...	...	...	...	45766	...	...	...	...
a Casualty insurance claims	-	...	...	...	...	-	...	...	...	...
b Transfers from other government subsectors	...	...	...	...	...	...	...	...	...	...
c Transfers from abroad	25566	...	...	...	...	31527	...	...	...	...
d Other transfers, except imputed	5738	...	...	...	...	10225	...	...	...	...
e Imputed unfunded employee welfare contributions	3658	...	...	...	...	4014	...	...	...	...
Total Current Receipts	405421	...	...	...	...	650475	...	...	...	...

Disbursements

1 General governement final consumption expenditures	177217	...	...	...	...	206568	...	...	...	...
2 Property income paid	11005	...	...	...	...	15714	...	...	...	...

Ivory Coast

3.12 General Government Income and Outlay Account: Total and Subsectors
(Continued)

Million CFA francs

	1976					1977				
	Total General Government	Central Government	State or Provincial Government	Local Government	Social Security Funds	Total General Government	Central Government	State or Provincial Government	Local Government	Social Security Funds
3 Subsidies	18236	...	...	...	...	30212	...	...	...	...
4 Other current transfers paid	45146	...	...	...	...	61188	...	...	...	...
a Casualty insurance premiums, net	-	...	...	...	...	107	...	...	...	...
b Transfers to other government subsectors	...	...	...	...	...	...	...	...	...	...
c Transfers to households	26217	...	...	...	...	32775	...	...	...	...
Social security benefits	6942	...	...	...	...	8042	...	...	...	...
Social assistance grants	15617	...	...	...	...	20719	...	...	...	...
Unfunded employee welfare benefits	3658	...	...	...	...	4014	...	...	...	...
d Transfers to private non-profit institutions serving households	2981	...	...	...	...	3299	...	...	...	...
e Transfers to the rest of the world	15948	...	...	...	...	25007	...	...	...	...
Net saving [a]	153817	...	...	...	...	336793	...	...	...	...
Total Current Disbursements and Net Saving [a]	405421	...	...	...	...	650475	...	...	...	...

	1978			
	Total General Government	Central Government	State or Provincial Government	Local Government	Social Security Funds

Receipts

1 Property and entrepreneurial income [a]	18437	...	...	...	...
a Net operating surplus [a]	-174	...	...	...	...
b Withdrawals from public quasi-corporations	884	...	...	...	...
c Interest	...	...	...	...	...
d Dividends	...	...	...	...	...
e Net land rent and royalties	...	...	...	...	...
2 Taxes, fees and contributions [b]	598150	...	...	...	...
a Indirect taxes	323483	...	...	...	...
b Direct taxes	64974	...	...	...	...
Income	63923	...	...	...	...
Other	1051	...	...	...	...
c Social security contributions	19908	...	...	...	...
d Fees, fines and penalties [b]	189785	...	...	...	...
3 Other current transfers received	47485	...	...	...	...
a Casualty insurance claims	-	...	...	...	...
b Transfers from other government subsectors	...	...	...	...	...
c Transfers from abroad	34128	...	...	...	...
d Other transfers, except imputed	9091	...	...	...	...
e Imputed unfunded employee welfare contributions	4266	...	...	...	...
Total Current Receipts	664072	...	...	...	...

Disbursements

1 General governement final consumption expenditures	278778	...	...	...	...
2 Property income paid	25701	...	...	...	...

Ivory Coas

3.12 General Government Income and Outlay Account: Total and Subsectors
(Continued)

Million CFA francs

	1978				
	Total General Government	Central Government	State or Provincial Government	Local Government	Social Security Funds
3 Subsidies	44862	...	...	...	...
4 Other current transfers paid	66474	...	...	...	...
a Casualty insurance premiums, net	157	...	...	...	...
b Transfers to other government subsectors	...	...	...	...	...
c Transfers to households	38698	...	...	...	...
Social security benefits	9279	...	...	...	...
Social assistance grants	25153	...	...	...	...
Unfunded employee welfare benefits	4266	...	...	...	...
d Transfers to private non-profit institutions serving households	3382	...	...	...	...
e Transfers to the rest of the world	24237	...	...	...	...
Net saving [a]	248257	...	...	...	...
Total Current Disbursements and Net Saving [a]	664072	...	...	...	...

a) Including consumption of fixed capital.
b) Less deductions of the Marketing Board.

3.13 General Government Capital Accumulation Account: Total and Subsectors

Million CFA francs

	1970					1971				
	Total General Government	Central Government	State or Provincial Government	Local Government	Social Security Funds	Total General Government	Central Government	State or Provincial Government	Local Government	Social Security Funds
Finance of Gross Accumulation										
1 Gross saving	31815	...	...	...	...	18879	...	...	...	...
2 Capital transfers received [a]	3133	...	...	...	...	1502	...	...	...	...
a From other government subsectors	...	...	...	...	...	...	...	...	...	...
b From other resident sectors	...	...	...	...	...	...	...	...	...	...
c From rest of the world	3133	...	...	...	...	1502	...	...	...	...
Finance of Gross Accumulation	34948	...	...	...	...	20381	...	...	...	...
Gross Accumulation										
1 Gross capital formation	29576	...	...	...	...	33653	...	...	...	...
2 Purchases of land, net	...	...	...	...	...	...	...	...	...	...
3 Purchases of intangible assets, net	...	...	...	...	...	...	...	...	...	...
4 Capital transfers paid	...	...	...	...	...	...	...	...	...	...
Net lending	5372	...	...	...	...	-13272	...	...	...	...
Gross Accumulation	34948	...	...	...	...	20381	...	...	...	...

	1972					1973				
	Total General Government	Central Government	State or Provincial Government	Local Government	Social Security Funds	Total General Government	Central Government	State or Provincial Government	Local Government	Social Security Funds
Finance of Gross Accumulation										
1 Gross saving	22658	...	...	...	...	43202	...	...	...	...
2 Capital transfers received [a]	2040	...	...	...	...	1726	...	...	...	...
a From other government subsectors	...	...	...	...	...	...	...	...	...	...
b From other resident sectors	...	...	...	...	...	...	...	...	...	...
c From rest of the world	2040	...	...	...	...	1726	...	...	...	...
Finance of Gross Accumulation	24698	...	...	...	...	44928	...	...	...	...
Gross Accumulation										
1 Gross capital formation	28083	...	...	...	...	37073	...	...	...	...
2 Purchases of land, net	...	...	...	...	...	...	...	...	...	...
3 Purchases of intangible assets, net	...	...	...	...	...	...	...	...	...	...
4 Capital transfers paid	...	...	...	...	...	...	...	...	...	...
Net lending	-3385	...	...	...	...	7855	...	...	...	...
Gross Accumulation	24698	...	...	...	...	44928	...	...	...	...

Ivory Coast

Million CFA francs

3.13 General Government Capital Accumulation Account: Total and Subsectors

	1974					1975				
	Total General Government	Central Government	State or Provincial Government	Local Government	Social Security Funds	Total General Government	Central Government	State or Provincial Government	Local Government	Social Security Funds

Finance of Gross Accumulation

1 Gross saving	76929	...	...	...	...	37422	...	...	...	...
2 Capital transfers received a	1840	...	...	...	...	1630	...	...	...	...
a From other government subsectors	...	...	...	...	...	...	...	...	...	...
b From other resident sectors	...	...	...	...	...	...	...	...	...	...
c From rest of the world	1840	...	...	...	...	1630	...	...	...	...
Finance of Gross Accumulation	78769	...	...	...	...	39052	...	...	...	...

Gross Accumulation

1 Gross capital formation	46437	...	...	...	...	76478	...	...	...	...
2 Purchases of land, net	...	...	...	...	...	...	...	...	...	...
3 Purchases of intangible assets, net	...	...	...	...	...	...	...	...	...	...
4 Capital transfers paid	...	...	...	...	...	...	...	...	...	...
Net lending	32332	...	...	...	...	-37426	...	...	...	...
Gross Accumulation	78769	...	...	...	...	39052	...	...	...	...

	1976					1977				
	Total General Government	Central Government	State or Provincial Government	Local Government	Social Security Funds	Total General Government	Central Government	State or Provincial Government	Local Government	Social Security Funds

Finance of Gross Accumulation

1 Gross saving	153817	...	...	...	...	336793	...	...	...	...
2 Capital transfers received a	2186	...	...	...	...	-1245	...	...	...	...
a From other government subsectors	...	...	...	...	...	...	...	...	...	...
b From other resident sectors	...	...	...	...	...	...	...	...	...	...
c From rest of the world	3041	...	...	...	...	1523	...	...	...	...
Finance of Gross Accumulation	156003	...	...	...	...	335548	...	...	...	...

Gross Accumulation

1 Gross capital formation	105012	...	...	...	...	165820	...	...	...	...
2 Purchases of land, net	...	...	...	...	...	...	...	...	...	...
3 Purchases of intangible assets, net	...	...	...	...	...	...	...	...	...	...
4 Capital transfers paid	...	...	...	...	...	...	...	...	...	...
Net lending	50991	...	...	...	...	169728	...	...	...	...
Gross Accumulation	156003	...	...	...	...	335548	...	...	...	...

	1978				
	Total General Government	Central Government	State or Provincial Government	Local Government	Social Security Funds

Finance of Gross Accumulation

1 Gross saving	248257	...	...	...	...
2 Capital transfers received a	-22096	...	...	...	...
a From other government subsectors	...	...	...	...	...
b From other resident sectors	...	...	...	...	...
c From rest of the world	1904	...	...	...	...
Finance of Gross Accumulation	226161	...	...	...	...

Gross Accumulation

1 Gross capital formation	245683	...	...	...	...
2 Purchases of land, net	...	...	...	...	...
3 Purchases of intangible assets, net	...	...	...	...	...
4 Capital transfers paid	...	...	...	...	...
Net lending	-19522	...	...	...	...
Gross Accumulation	226161	...	...	...	...

a) Net.

Ivory Coast

3.14 General Government Capital Finance Account, Total and Subsectors

Million CFA francs

	1974					1975				
	Total General Government	Central Government	State or Provincial Government	Local Government	Social Security Funds	Total General Government	Central Government	State or Provincial Government	Local Government	Social Security Funds

Acquisition of Financial Assets

1 Gold and SDRs	-	...	...	...	...	-	...	...	...	...
2 Currency and transferable deposits	23486	...	...	...	...	-23319	...	...	...	...
3 Other deposits	28583	...	...	...	...	96	...	...	...	...
4 Bills and bonds, short term	...	...	...	...	...	...	...	...	...	...
5 Bonds, long term	...	...	...	...	...	...	...	...	...	...
6 Corporate equity securities	...	...	...	...	...	...	...	...	...	...
7 Short-term loans, n.e.c.	...	...	...	...	...	...	...	...	...	...
8 Long-term loans, n.e.c.	...	...	...	...	...	...	...	...	...	...
9 Other receivables	...	...	...	...	...	...	...	...	...	...
10 Other assets	...	...	...	...	...	...	...	...	...	...
Total Acquisition of Financial Assets	52027	...	...	...	...	6672	...	...	...	...

Incurrence of Liabilities

1 Currency and transferable deposits	-15	...	...	...	...	6516	...	...	...	...
2 Other deposits	...	...	...	...	...	...	...	...	...	...
3 Bills and bonds, short term	...	...	...	...	...	...	...	...	...	...
4 Bonds, long term	420	...	...	...	...	-466	...	...	...	...
5 Short-term loans, n.e.c.	4492	...	...	...	...	14326	...	...	...	...
6 Long-term loans, n.e.c.	14798	...	...	...	...	23722	...	...	...	...
7 Other payables	...	...	...	...	...	...	...	...	...	...
8 Other liabilities	...	...	...	...	...	...	...	...	...	...
Total Incurrence of Liabilities	19695	...	...	...	...	44098	...	...	...	...
Net Lending	32332	...	...	...	...	-37426	...	...	...	...
Incurrence of Liabilities and Net Worth	52027	...	...	...	...	6672	...	...	...	...

	1976					1977				
	Total General Government	Central Government	State or Provincial Government	Local Government	Social Security Funds	Total General Government	Central Government	State or Provincial Government	Local Government	Social Security Funds

Acquisition of Financial Assets

1 Gold and SDRs	-	...	...	...	...	-	...	...	...	...
2 Currency and transferable deposits	35363	...	...	...	...	102418	...	...	...	...
3 Other deposits	15054	...	...	...	...	38944	...	...	...	...
4 Bills and bonds, short term	...	...	...	...	...	...	...	...	...	...
5 Bonds, long term	...	...	...	...	...	...	...	...	...	...
6 Corporate equity securities	...	...	...	...	...	...	...	...	...	...
7 Short-term loans, n.e.c.	...	...	...	...	...	...	...	...	...	...
8 Long-term loans, n.e.c.	...	...	...	...	...	...	...	...	...	...
9 Other receivables	...	...	...	...	...	...	...	...	...	...
10 Other assets	...	...	...	...	...	...	...	...	...	...
Total Acquisition of Financial Assets	125220	...	...	...	...	276949	...	...	...	...

Incurrence of Liabilities

1 Currency and transferable deposits	7001	...	...	...	...	6498	...	...	...	...
2 Other deposits	...	...	...	...	...	...	...	...	...	...
3 Bills and bonds, short term	...	...	...	...	...	...	...	...	...	...
4 Bonds, long term	2766	...	...	...	...	3049	...	...	...	...
5 Short-term loans, n.e.c.	20076	...	...	...	...	6057	...	...	...	...
6 Long-term loans, n.e.c.	44386	...	...	...	...	91617	...	...	...	...
7 Other payables	...	...	...	...	...	...	...	...	...	...
8 Other liabilities	...	...	...	...	...	...	...	...	...	...
Total Incurrence of Liabilities	74229	...	...	...	...	107221	...	...	...	...
Net Lending	50991	...	...	...	...	169728	...	...	...	...
Incurrence of Liabilities and Net Worth	125220	...	...	...	...	276949	...	...	...	...

Ivory Coast

3.14 General Government Capital Finance Account, Total and Subsectors

Million CFA francs

	1978 Total General Government	Central Government	State or Provincial Government	Local Government	Social Security Funds
Acquisition of Financial Assets					
1 Gold and SDRs	-	...	...	...	...
2 Currency and transferable deposits	13043	...	...	...	...
3 Other deposits	-8278	...	...	...	...
4 Bills and bonds, short term	...	...	...	...	...
5 Bonds, long term	...	...	...	...	...
6 Corporate equity securities	...	...	...	...	...
7 Short-term loans, n.e.c.	...	...	...	...	...
8 Long-term loans, n.e.c.	...	...	...	...	...
9 Other receivables	...	...	...	...	...
10 Other assets	...	...	...	...	...
Total Acquisition of Financial Assets	153313	...	...	...	...
Incurrence of Liabilities					
1 Currency and transferable deposits	5061	...	...	...	...
2 Other deposits	...	...	...	...	...
3 Bills and bonds, short term	...	...	...	...	...
4 Bonds, long term	4519	...	...	...	...
5 Short-term loans, n.e.c.	14974	...	...	...	...
6 Long-term loans, n.e.c.	148281	...	...	...	...
7 Other payables	...	...	...	...	...
8 Other liabilities	...	...	...	...	...
Total Incurrence of Liabilities	172835	...	...	...	...
Net Lending	-19522	...	...	...	...
Incurrence of Liabilities and Net Worth	153313	...	...	...	...

3.51 External Transactions: Current Account: Detail

Million CFA francs

	1970	1971	1972	1973	1974	1975	1976	1977	1978	1979	1980
Payments to the Rest of the World											
1 Imports of goods and services	141250	154421	165198	220767	306126	325993	428865	596778	700690	...	...
a Imports of merchandise c.i.f.	...	...	...	...	252714	260562	336836	469834	554062		
b Other	...	...	...	...	53412	65431	92029	126944	146628		
2 Factor income paid to the rest of the world	14213	17382	14960	13828	22893	33241	43024	56489	72948	...	...
a Compensation of employees	150	200	250	269	272	325	-	1608	-		
b Property and entrepreneurial income paid	14063	17182	14710	13559	22621	32916	43024	54881	72948		
3 Indirect taxes paid to supranational organizations	...	...	...	...	...	...	...	...	...		
4 Other current transfers to the rest of the world	19163	21473	30322	34221	46907	54668	69220	88611	100561	...	...
a By general government	3832	4031	6873	6494	10327	13683	15948	25007	24237		
b By other resident sectors	15331	17442	23449	27727	36580	40985	53272	63604	76324		
5 Surplus of the nation on current transactions	-6934	-20598	-17473	-22700	-5443	-69514	-34850	-30709	-171795	...	...
Payments to the Rest of the World, and Surplus of the Nation on Current Transfers	167692	172678	193007	246116	370483	344388	506259	711169	702404	...	...
Receipts From The Rest of the World											
1 Exports of goods and services	153808	157231	174609	221519	345511	315235	476319	669473	659925	...	...
a Exports of merchandise f.o.b.	...	...	...	...	310580	275397	426124	611544	591571	...	...

Ivory Coast

3.51 External Transactions: Current Account: Detail
(Continued)

Million CFA francs	1970	1971	1972	1973	1974	1975	1976	1977	1978	1979	1980
b Other	...	...	...	...	34931	39638	50195	57929	68354	...	...
2 Factor income received from the rest of the world	2733	2200	2223	1250	2378	6005	1954	6048	3500	...	...
a Compensation of employees	350	350	400	475	500	645	-	3229	-	...	...
b Property and entrepreneurial income received	2383	1850	1823	775	1878	5360	1954	2819	3500	...	...
3 Subsidies received from supranational organizations	...	...	...	...	...	...	...	...	...	...	...
4 Other current transfers from the rest of the world	11151	13247	16175	23347	22594	23148	27986	35648	38979	...	...
a To general government	9338	11172	14075	21921	20815	21653	25566	31527	34128	...	...
b To other resident sectors	1813	2075	2100	1426	1779	1495	2420	4121	4851	...	...
Receipts from the Rest of the World on Current Transfers	167692	172678	193007	246116	370483	344388	506259	711169	702404	...	...

3.52 External Transactions: Capital Accumulation Account

Million CFA francs	1970	1971	1972	1973	1974	1975	1976	1977	1978	1979	1980
Finance of Gross Accumulation											
1 Surplus of the nation on current transactions	-6934	-20598	-17473	-22700	-5443	-69514	-34850	-30709	-171795	...	...
2 Capital transfers received from the rest of the world	3133	1502	2040	1726	1840	1630	3041	1523	2904	...	...
Total Finance of Gross Accumulation	-3801	-19096	-15433	-20974	-3603	-67884	-31809	-29186	-168891	...	...
Gross Accumulation											
1 Capital transfers paid to the rest of the world	...	...	...	...	...	...	...	...	...	...	...
2 Purchases of intangible assets, n.e.c., net, from the rest of the world	...	...	...	...	...	...	...	...	...	...	...
3 Net lending to the rest of the world	-3801	-19096	-15433	-20974	-3603	-67884	-31809	-29186	-168891	...	...
Total Gross Accumulation	-3801	-19096	-15433	-20974	-3603	-67884	-31809	-29186	-168891	...	...

3.53 External Transactions: Capital Finance Account

Million CFA francs	1970	1971	1972	1973	1974	1975	1976	1977	1978	1979	1980
Acquisitions of Foreign Financial Assets											
1 Gold and SDR's	...	...	...	...	...	...	-558	-687	...	...	...
2 Currency and transferable deposits	...	...	...	...	...	...	...	...	...	...	...
3 Other deposits	...	...	...	...	...	...	...	...	...	...	...
4 Bills and bonds, short term	...	...	...	...	...	...	...	...	...	...	...
5 Bonds, long term	...	...	...	...	70	161	1000	-	...	...	...
6 Corporate equity securities	...	...	...	...	1016	502	239	4391	1323	...	...
7 Short-term loans, n.e.c.	...	...	...	...	20854	553	57291	47772	17516	...	...
8 Long-term loans	...	...	...	...	1562	397	7086	23623	4000	...	...
9 Proprietors' net additions to accumulation of quasi-corporate, non-resident enterprises	...	...	...	...	...	...	...	...	...	...	...
10 Trade credit and advances	...	...	...	...	...	...	...	...	...	...	...
11 Other	...	...	...	...	...	...	...	...	...	...	...
Total Acquisitions of Foreign Financial Assets	...	...	...	...	49542	-14987	79662	130364	55686	...	...
Incurrence of Foreign Liabilities											
1 Currency and transferable deposits	...	...	...	...	...	...	...	...	...	...	...
2 Other deposits	...	...	...	...	...	...	...	...	...	...	...
3 Bills and bonds, short term	...	...	...	...	...	...	...	...	...	...	...
4 Bonds, long term	...	...	...	...	-786	-434	-	-603	...	...	...
5 Corporate equity securities	...	...	...	...	2841	2954	3806	4847	4500	...	...
6 Short-term loans, n.e.c.	...	...	...	...	7678	-5154	16304	8057	15000	...	...

Ivory Coast

3.53 External Transactions: Capital Finance Account
(Continued)

Million CFA francs

	1970	1971	1972	1973	1974	1975	1976	1977	1978	1979	1980
7 Long-term loans	...	...	...	...	38322	49199	68497	153893	173274	...	...
8 Non-resident proprietors' net additions to accumulation of resident quasi-corporate enterprises	...	...	...	...	...	...	...	...	...	...	...
9 Trade credit and advances	...	...	...	...	...	...	...	...	...	...	...
10 Other	...	...	...	...	...	...	...	...	...	...	...
Total Incurrence of Liabilities	...	...	...	...	53145	52897	111471	159550	224577	...	...
Net Lending	...	...	...	...	-3603	-67884	-31809	-29186	-168891	...	...
Total Incurrence of Liabilities and Net Lending	...	...	...	...	49542	-14987	79662	130364	55686	...	...

4.6 Cost Components of Value Added, ISIC Divisions

Million CFA francs

	1976 Compensation of Employees	1976 Capital Consumption	1976 Net Operating Surplus	1976 Indirect Taxes	1976 Less: Subsidies Received	1976 Value Added	1977 Compensation of Employees	1977 Capital Consumption	1977 Net Operating Surplus	1977 Indirect Taxes	1977 Less: Subsidies Received	1977 Value Added
						All Producers						
1 Agriculture, hunting, forestry and fishing	35065	...	237607	...	...	284811	34701	...	338801	...	...	380171
2 Mining and quarrying	1126	...	-91	...	...	1673	1042	...	1084	...	...	3000
3 Manufacturing	46437	...	60405	...	...	130867	59260	...	63732	...	...	164984
4 Electricity, gas and water	5462	...	5835	...	...	14453	6382	...	7513	...	...	17455
5 Construction	41261	...	21975	...	...	73606	56988	...	37835	...	...	108628
6 Wholesale and retail trade, restaurants and hotels	...	...	...	...	...	267946	...	...	...	...	...	447551
7 Transport, storage and communication	48107	...	31413	...	...	85957	55135	...	35128	...	...	97714
8 Finance, insurance, real estate and business services	...	...	...	...	...	66847	...	...	...	...	...	96904
9 Community, social and personal services	...	...	...	...	...	8471	...	...	...	...	...	10046
Total, Industries [a]	260219	...	449612	...	...	934631	323318	...	595372	...	...	1326453
Producers of Government Services	95763	...	...	...	...	98355	109740	...	...	...	...	113481
Other Producers	8559	...	...	...	...	8559	9362	...	...	...	...	9362
Total	364541	...	449612	...	...	1041545	442420	...	595372	...	...	1449296
Imputed bank service charge	...	...	...	...	...	-16226	...	...	...	...	...	-27246
Import duties	...	...	...	...	...	88638	...	...	...	...	...	117215
Value added tax	...	...	...	...	...	...	...	...	...	...	...	...
Other adjustments	...	...	...	...	...	...	...	...	...	...	...	...
Total	...	...	...	...	...	1113957	...	...	...	...	...	1539265

a) Columns 'Domestic factor income' and 'Operating surplus' include consumption of fixed capital'.

Jamaica

Source. Reply to the United Nations National Accounts Questionnaire from the Department of Statistics, Kingston. Official estimates, together with information on concepts, sources and methods of estimation utilized are published annually by the Department in 'National Income and Product'.

General note. The estimates have been prepared in accordance with the United Nations System of National Accounts so far as the existing data would permit.

1.1 Expenditure on the Gross Domestic Product, in Current Prices

Million Jamaican dollars

	1970	1971	1972	1973	1974	1975	1976	1977	1978	1979	1980
1 General government final consumption expenditure	137.3	159.1	197.1	280.2	386.1	477.1	562.1	612.4	749.9	846.3	991.7
2 Private final consumption expenditure	713.1	803.2	967.9	1078.3	1479.6	1736.5	1897.3	2060.2	2395.1	2735.2	3174.0
3 Gross capital formation	369.7	409.1	393.1	541.4	541.6	683.0	508.1	373.4	554.3	775.1	744.4
a Increase in stocks	2.5	53.1	26.3	93.2	63.4	73.0	57.3	24.0	52.2	50.5	45.5
b Gross fixed capital formation	367.2	356.0	366.8	448.2	478.2	610.0	450.8	349.4	502.1	724.6	698.9
Residential buildings	...	...	...	...	230.4	277.7	231.4	204.9	281.4	342.6	334.2
Non-residential buildings	...	...	...	...	...	...	...	...	...	...	...
Other construction and land improvement etc.	...	...	...	...	31.8	23.2	17.5	15.2	20.4	27.5	36.0
Other	...	...	...	...	216.0	309.1	201.9	129.3	200.3	354.5	328.7
4 Exports of goods and services	389.0	433.7	471.7	542.6	759.0	903.8	769.1	914.4	1579.5	2065.0	2348.5
5 Less: Imports of goods and services	438.0	525.0	591.0	707.4	996.7	1186.1	1021.7	971.8	1525.2	2132.6	2527.9
Equals: Gross Domestic Product	1171.1	1280.1	1438.8	1735.1	2169.6	2614.3	2715.0	2988.6	3753.6	4289.0	4730.9

1.3 Cost Components of the Gross Domestic Product

Million Jamaican dollars

	1970	1971	1972	1973	1974	1975	1976	1977	1978	1979	1980
1 Indirect taxes, net	97.8	113.7	125.4	146.3	179.6	238.6	236.7	215.7	271.8	355.0	398.6
a Indirect taxes paid	105.5	122.2	138.6	163.0	205.4	269.9	280.8	373.5	473.7	505.8	491.7
b Less: Subsidies received	7.7	8.5	13.2	16.7	25.8	31.3	44.1	157.9	201.9	150.8	93.1
2 Consumption of fixed capital	117.0	122.0	144.0	172.7	205.0	231.2	248.4	284.1	342.8	393.4	417.9
3 Compensation of employees paid by resident producers to:	587.6	639.8	753.8	933.2	1171.5	1456.4	1533.1	1657.1	1949.0	2206.5	2448.4
4 Net operating surplus	369.3	404.6	415.6	482.9	613.4	688.1	696.8	831.7	1190.0	1334.1	1466.0
Equals: Gross Domestic Product	1171.1	1280.1	1438.8	1735.1	2169.6	2614.3	2715.0	2988.6	3753.6	4289.0	4730.9

1.4 General Government Current Receipts and Disbursements

Million Jamaican dollars

	1970	1971	1972	1973	1974	1975	1976	1977	1978	1979	1980
Receipts											
1 Property and entrepreneurial income	24.6	23.7	24.7	34.3	46.6	43.6	39.2	51.4	45.6	57.7	51.5
2 Taxes, fees and contributions	197.2	240.4	273.8	325.2	550.8	623.0	650.9	784.7	1043.6	1162.6	1275.1
a Indirect taxes	105.5	122.2	138.6	163.0	205.4	269.9	280.8	373.5	473.7	505.8	491.6
b Direct taxes	79.9	102.8	117.1	140.8	318.7	327.1	331.0	370.8	526.1	606.3	724.7
c Social security contributions [a]	9.2	12.6	15.1	17.6	18.4	19.5	33.5	35.2	36.1	38.7	47.9
d Compulsory fees, fines and penalties	2.6	2.8	3.0	3.8	8.3	6.5	5.6	5.2	7.7	11.8	10.9
3 Other current receipts	0.6	0.9	1.0	1.8	1.5	1.5	2.0	5.4	5.2	2.1	2.2
Statistical discrepancy	...	...	...	...	...	...	...	3.9	2.7	...	...
Total Current Receipts of General Government	222.4	265.0	299.5	361.3	598.9	668.1	692.0	845.4	1097.1	1222.4	1328.8
Disbursements											
1 General government final consumption expenditure	137.3	159.1	197.1	280.2	386.1	477.1	562.1	612.4	749.9	846.3	991.7
2 Property income paid	15.8	18.2	23.4	26.1	36.5	58.1	69.7	114.9	187.3	252.6	307.4
3 Subsidies	7.7	8.5	13.2	16.7	25.8	31.3	44.1	157.9	201.9	150.8	93.1
4 Other current transfers paid	11.6	15.2	23.8	20.9	27.8	32.1	40.4	48.8	58.1	62.2	68.7
a Social security benefits and social assistance grants	5.1	7.1	10.8	10.4	14.4	20.3	25.5	29.4	34.9	37.7	44.1
b Other	6.5	8.1	13.1	10.5	13.4	11.8	14.9	19.4	23.2	24.5	24.6
5 Net saving	50.0	64.0	42.0	17.4	122.7	69.5	-24.3	-88.6	-100.1	-89.5	-132.1
Total Current Disbursements and Net Saving of General Government	222.4	265.0	299.5	361.3	598.9	668.1	692.0	845.4	1097.1	1222.4	1328.8

a) Social insurance scheme began in 1966.

Jamaica

1.6 Current Income and Outlay of Households and Non-Profit Institutions

Million Jamaican dollars

		1970	1971	1972	1973	1974	1975	1976	1977	1978	1979	1980
						Receipts						
1	Compensation of employees	508.7	566.1	663.2	823.8	1019.2	...	...	...	...	...	...
2	Property and entrepreneurial income received	228.8	243.7	282.3	303.9	349.4	...	...	...	...	...	...
3	Current transfers received	54.1	65.2	77.8	93.9	100.2	...	...	...	...	...	...
	Total Current Receipts a	791.6	875.0	1023.2	1221.6	1468.8	...	...	...	...	...	...
						Disbursements						
1	Private final consumption expenditure	714.9	822.2	983.7	1141.2	1377.0	...	...	...	...	...	...
2	Property income paid	...	...	...	...	...	...	...	...	...	...	...
3	Direct taxes and other payments n.e.c. to general government	49.0	55.3	68.7	85.7	132.9	...	...	...	...	...	...
	a Social security contributions	4.2	5.8	6.9	8.0	8.3	...	...	...	...	...	...
	b Direct taxes	44.9	49.5	61.8	77.7	124.5	...	...	...	...	...	...
	c Fees, fines and penalties	...	...	...	...	...	...	...	...	...	...	...
4	Other current transfers paid	7.0	14.3	20.7	25.2	24.0	...	...	...	...	...	...
5	Net saving	20.7	-16.8	-49.8	-30.6	-65.0	...	...	...	...	...	...
	Total Current Disbursements and Net Saving a	791.6	875.0	1023.2	1221.6	1468.8	...	...	...	...	...	...

a) Data for this table have not been revised, therefore, data for some years are not comparable with those of other tables.

1.7 External Transactions on Current Account, Summary

Million Jamaican dollars

		1970	1971	1972	1973	1974	1975	1976	1977	1978	1979	1980
					Payments to the Rest of the World							
1	Imports of goods and services	438.0	525.0	591.0	707.4	996.7	1186.1	1021.7	971.8	1525.2	2132.6	2527.7
2	Factor income paid to the rest of the world	80.1	104.7	58.8	75.5	92.5	120.4	123.2	182.0	305.3	396.3	564.8
	a Compensation of employees	1.0	1.1	2.1	3.4	4.7	2.0	2.6	7.8	11.7	12.4	11.0
	b Property and entrepreneurial income paid	79.1	103.6	56.7	72.1	87.8	118.4	120.6	174.2	293.6	383.9	553.8
3	Indirect taxes paid to supranational organizations	...	...	...	...	...	...	...	...	...	...	...
4	Current transfers to the rest of the world	5.2	12.5	18.9	23.4	22.9	35.1	49.6	46.8	63.0	79.0	70.4
5	Surplus of the nation on current transactions	-77.7	-143.8	-116.6	-161.4	-156.4	-243.5	-320.0	-138.0	-144.3	-247.8	-505.0
	Payments to the Rest of the World and Surplus of the Nation on Current Transactions	445.6	498.4	552.1	644.9	955.7	1098.1	874.5	1062.6	1749.2	2360.1	2657.9
					Receipts From The Rest of the World							
1	Exports of goods and services	389.0	433.7	471.7	542.6	759.0	903.8	769.1	914.4	1579.5	2065.0	2348.0
2	Factor income received from rest of the world	29.1	30.4	33.7	48.2	144.2	140.1	54.0	84.1	83.5	92.4	109.2
	a Compensation of employees	15.2	17.7	21.6	31.3	30.9	37.4	38.3	48.4	67.0	75.1	82.7
	b Property and entrepreneurial income received	13.9	12.7	12.1	16.9	113.3	102.7	15.7	35.7	16.5	17.3	26.5
3	Subsidies received from supranational organisations	...	...	...	...	...	...	...	...	...	...	...
4	Current transfers from rest of the world	27.5	34.3	46.7	54.1	52.5	54.2	51.4	64.1	86.2	202.7	200.2
	Receipts from the Rest of the World on Current Transactions	445.6	498.4	552.1	644.9	955.7	1098.1	874.5	1062.6	1749.2	2360.1	2657.9

Jamaica

1.8 Capital Transactions of The Nation, Summary

Million Jamaican dollars

	1970	1971	1972	1973	1974	1975	1976	1977	1978	1979	1980
Finance of Gross Capital Formation											
Gross saving	292.0	265.3	276.5	380.0	385.2	439.6	188.2	235.4	409.9	527.3	239.4
1 Consumption of fixed capital	117.0	122.0	144.0	172.7	205.0	231.2	248.4	284.1	342.8	393.4	417.9
2 Net saving	175.0	143.3	132.5	207.3	180.2	208.4	-60.2	-48.7	67.1	133.9	-178.3
Less: Surplus of the nation on current transactions	-77.7	-143.8	-116.6	-161.4	-156.4	-243.5	-320.0	-138.0	-144.3	-247.8	-505.0
Finance of Gross Capital Formation	369.7	409.1	393.1	541.4	541.6	683.0	508.1	373.4	554.3	775.1	744.4
Gross Capital Formation											
Increase in stocks	2.5	53.1	26.3	93.2	63.4	73.0	57.3	24.0	52.2	50.5	45.5
Gross fixed capital formation	367.2	356.0	366.8	448.2	478.2	610.0	450.8	349.4	502.1	724.6	698.9
Gross Capital Formation	369.7	409.1	393.1	541.4	541.6	683.0	508.1	373.4	554.3	775.1	744.4

1.10 Gross Domestic Product by Kind of Activity, in Current Prices

Million Jamaican dollars

	1970	1971	1972	1973	1974	1975	1976	1977	1978	1979	1980
1 Agriculture, hunting, forestry and fishing	78.4	99.4	106.5	128.1	162.6	202.0	226.3	263.0	313.9	320.0	392.2
2 Mining and quarrying	147.8	137.5	122.2	148.9	197.0	220.8	235.3	308.0	510.4	622.5	678.0
3 Manufacturing	183.8	206.5	241.8	286.4	386.8	443.7	490.0	544.1	636.2	681.6	721.2
4 Electricity, gas and water	11.8	13.5	17.0	18.4	22.2	38.8	54.4	58.5	84.2	89.6	79.4
5 Construction	155.7	152.7	152.1	177.6	213.5	252.4	211.9	181.2	252.1	310.5	269.8
6 Wholesale and retail trade, restaurants and hotels	248.0	282.3	330.4	388.3	457.9	572.0	483.2	527.9	707.4	850.5	1013.2
7 Transport, storage and communication	64.5	77.3	89.3	112.5	137.0	156.9	173.6	192.1	227.8	250.9	252.3
8 Finance, insurance, real estate and business services	154.5	166.9	198.7	240.8	297.9	361.5	391.1	413.9	466.0	534.8	605.6
9 Community, social and personal services	40.2	43.7	53.6	62.1	71.0	77.8	90.6	95.7	100.0	108.2	123.0
Total, Industries	1084.8	1180.2	1311.5	1563.1	1946.0	2326.0	2356.4	2584.5	3298.0	3768.7	4134.7
Producers of Government Services	91.6	107.9	137.1	185.9	251.3	327.8	383.2	436.5	509.2	575.7	693.4
Other Producers	18.9	21.0	26.7	34.4	38.0	40.1	49.5	53.2	50.4	47.1	44.2
Subtotal	1195.3	1309.1	1475.3	1783.4	2235.3	2693.9	2789.1	3074.2	3857.6	4391.5	4872.3
Less: Imputed bank service charge	24.2	29.0	36.5	48.3	65.7	79.6	74.1	85.6	104.0	102.5	141.4
Plus: Import duties	...	...	...	...	...	...	...	...	...	...	...
Plus: Value added tax	...	...	...	...	...	...	...	...	...	...	...
Equals: Gross Domestic Product	1171.1	1280.1	1438.8	1735.1	2169.6	2614.3	2715.0	2988.6	3753.6	4289.0	4730.9

1.11 Gross Domestic Product by Kind of Activity, in Constant Prices

Million Jamaican dollars

	1970	1971	1972	1973	1974	1975	1976	1977	1978	1979	1980
At constant prices of: 1974											
1 Agriculture, hunting, forestry and fishing	149.8	167.5	170.6	160.3	162.7	161.9	166.3	171.0	186.7	166.4	161.5
2 Mining and quarrying	139.7	149.3	158.9	181.6	197.0	157.2	124.9	146.7	150.4	148.0	163.3
3 Manufacturing	348.1	356.1	397.8	400.6	386.8	396.1	376.7	350.1	332.9	314.6	275.5
4 Electricity, gas and water	16.4	18.5	21.0	22.2	22.2	23.1	23.8	23.4	23.7	23.3	23.6
5 Construction	261.7	263.1	255.5	225.7	213.5	210.8	168.6	133.5	138.3	137.2	95.6
6 Wholesale and retail trade, restaurants and hotels	462.3	478.0	555.9	537.5	457.8	469.5	384.7	367.7	356.6	340.8	318.2
7 Transport, storage and communication	109.1	115.6	122.6	124.5	137.0	142.6	137.7	130.0	129.4	129.9	125.5
8 Finance, insurance, real estate and business services	272.7	268.8	283.8	300.5	298.0	306.5	305.0	314.3	308.1	307.6	314.9
9 Community, social and personal services	67.0	68.3	80.0	80.0	71.0	63.1	67.8	63.7	58.2	54.9	56.0
Total, Industries	1826.8	1885.0	2046.1	2032.9	1946.0	1930.8	1755.5	1700.5	1684.2	1622.7	1534.1
Producers of Government Services	180.1	181.7	207.2	250.9	251.3	265.1	307.3	328.3	344.1	366.7	362.4
Other Producers	27.9	29.0	33.1	39.9	38.0	29.7	27.3	28.9	21.7	19.0	18.2
Subtotal	2034.8	2095.7	2286.4	2323.7	2235.3	2225.6	2090.1	2057.7	2050.0	2008.4	1914.7
Less: Imputed bank service charge	52.6	53.5	55.1	60.3	65.7	68.9	64.0	70.4	68.0	55.0	66.7
Plus: Import duties	...	...	...	...	...	...	...	...	...	...	...
Plus: Value added tax	...	...	...	...	...	...	...	...	...	...	...
Equals: Gross Domestic Product	1982.2	2042.2	2231.3	2263.4	2169.6	2156.7	2026.1	1987.3	1982.0	1953.4	1848.0

Jamaica

1.12 Relations Among National Accounting Aggregates

Million Jamaican dollars

	1970	1971	1972	1973	1974	1975	1976	1977	1978	1979	1980
Gross Domestic Product	1171.1	1280.1	1438.8	1735.1	2169.6	2614.3	2715.0	2988.6	3753.6	4289.0	4730.9
Plus: Net factor income received from abroad	-50.9	-74.3	-25.2	-27.4	51.7	19.7	-69.3	-97.9	-222.0	-303.9	-455.7
Factor income received	...	30.4	33.7	48.2	144.2	140.1	54.0	84.1	83.5	92.4	109.2
Less: Factor income paid	...	104.7	58.8	75.5	92.5	120.4	123.2	182.0	305.3	396.3	564.8
Equals: Gross National Product	1120.2	1205.8	1413.6	1707.7	2221.3	2634.0	2645.7	2890.7	3531.6	3985.1	4275.2
Less: Consumption of fixed capital	117.0	122.0	144.0	172.7	205.0	231.2	248.4	284.1	342.8	393.4	417.9
Less: Net indirect taxes paid to supranational organisations	...	...	...	...	...	...	...	...	...	...	...
Equals: National Income at Market Prices	1003.1	1083.8	1269.7	1535.1	2016.3	2402.9	2397.4	2606.6	3188.9	3591.7	3857.3
Plus: Net current transfers received from abroad	22.3	21.8	27.8	30.7	29.6	19.1	1.8	17.3	23.2	123.7	129.9
Current transfers received	...	34.3	46.7	54.1	52.5	54.2	51.4	64.1	86.2	202.7	200.2
Less: Current transfers paid	...	12.5	18.9	23.4	22.9	35.1	49.6	46.8	63.0	79.0	70.4
Equals: National Disposable Income at Market Prices	1025.4	1105.6	1297.5	1565.8	2045.9	2422.0	2399.2	2623.9	3212.1	3715.4	3987.4
Less: Final consumption	850.4	962.3	1165.0	1358.5	1865.7	2213.6	2459.4	2672.6	3145.0	3581.5	4165.7
Equals: Net Saving	172.8	143.3	132.5	207.3	180.2	208.4	-60.2	-48.7	67.1	133.9	-178.3
Less: Surplus of the nation on current transactions	...	-143.8	-116.6	-161.4	-156.4	-243.5	-320.0	-138.0	-144.3	-247.8	-505.0
Equals: Net Capital Formation	252.1	287.1	249.1	368.7	336.6	451.8	259.7	89.3	211.5	381.7	326.5

2.5 Private Final Consumption Expenditure by Type, in Current Prices

Million Jamaican dollars

	1970	1971	1972	1973	1974	1975	1976	1977	1978	1979	1980
Final Consumption Expenditure of Resident Households											
1 Food, beverages and tobacco	...	...	...	...	701.9	781.2	814.5	940.2	1164.8	1292.0	1498.8
a Food	...	...	...	...	549.8	609.9	617.2	717.1	910.1	999.3	1162.6
b Non-alcoholic beverages	...	...	...	...	20.5	23.3	27.5	28.5	30.2	29.4	33.2
c Alcoholic beverages	...	...	...	...	55.5	66.2	75.7	90.4	107.0	118.9	132.9
d Tobacco	...	...	...	...	76.1	81.7	94.1	104.2	117.4	144.4	170.2
2 Clothing and footwear	...	...	...	...	67.3	75.5	76.0	84.0	103.4	91.2	107.5
3 Gross rent, fuel and power	...	...	...	...	156.3	199.5	239.2	260.3	314.7	373.1	425.5
a Fuel and power	...	...	...	...	39.3	48.6	58.9	64.5	97.3	121.8	154.6
b Other	...	...	...	...	117.0	150.9	180.3	195.8	217.4	251.3	270.9
4 Furniture, furnishings and household equipment and operation	...	...	...	...	90.9	108.0	129.9	144.8	158.2	176.3	196.7
a Household operation	...	...	...	...	43.6	54.5	72.2	80.9	81.9	93.2	99.3
b Other	...	...	...	...	47.3	53.5	57.7	63.9	76.3	83.1	97.4
5 Medical care and health expenses	...	...	...	...	27.3	37.1	35.9	36.2	48.6	60.4	65.6
6 Transport and communication	...	...	...	...	191.4	221.5	225.5	242.9	301.1	425.1	495.8
a Personal transport equipment	...	...	...	...	109.5	106.7	95.8	87.8	74.7	83.7	92.4
b Other	...	...	...	...	81.9	114.8	129.7	155.1	226.4	341.4	403.4
7 Recreational, entertainment, education and cultural services	...	...	...	...	59.8	73.4	89.3	98.0	101.3	126.4	162.6
a Education	...	...	...	...	5.2	6.0	7.3	7.8	7.5	7.2	9.1
b Other	...	...	...	...	54.6	67.4	82.0	90.2	93.8	119.2	153.5
8 Miscellaneous goods and services	...	...	...	...	274.2	310.4	330.7	349.3	413.4	490.1	564.4
a Personal care	...	...	...	...	64.5	81.4	88.7	95.6	97.8	99.9	123.1
b Expenditures in restaurants, cafes and hotels	...	...	...	...	126.2	134.8	137.6	146.6	189.2	234.3	262.5

Jamaica

2.5 Private Final Consumption Expenditure by Type, in Current Prices
(Continued)

Million Jamaican dollars

	1970	1971	1972	1973	1974	1975	1976	1977	1978	1979	1980
c Other	...	...	...	...	83.5	94.2	104.4	107.1	126.4	155.9	178.8
Total Final Consumption Expenditure in the Domestic Market by Households, of which	...	...	...	...	1569.1	1806.5	1940.9	2155.9	2605.5	3034.7	3517.1
Plus: Direct purchases abroad by resident households	...	...	...	...	33.8	49.1	55.5	17.0	20.4	24.7	23.0
Less: Direct purchases in the domestic market by non-resident households	...	...	...	...	123.3	119.1	99.1	112.7	230.8	324.2	366.1
Equals: Final Consumption Expenditure of Resident Households	...	...	...	...	1479.6	1736.6	1897.3	2060.2	2395.1	2735.2	3174.0

Final Consumption Expenditure of Private Non-profit Institutions Serving Households

	1970	1971	1972	1973	1974	1975	1976	1977	1978	1979	1980
Equals: Final Consumption Expenditure of Private Non-profit Organisations Serving Households	...	...	...	...	...	...	...	...	...	...	...
Private Final Consumption Expenditure	...	...	...	...	1479.6	1736.6	1897.3	2060.2	2395.1	2735.2	3174.0

2.6 Private Final Consumption Expenditure by Type, in Constant Prices

Million Jamaican dollars

	1970	1971	1972	1973	1974	1975	1976	1977	1978	1979	1980

At constant prices of: 1974

Final Consumption Expenditure of Resident Households

	1970	1971	1972	1973	1974	1975	1976	1977	1978	1979	1980
1 Food, beverages and tobacco	...	...	...	...	701.9	688.7	666.0	701.4	648.7	563.0	512.4
a Food	...	...	...	...	549.8	549.9	525.1	552.3	527.9	440.3	391.9
b Non-alcoholic beverages	...	...	...	...	20.5	17.5	17.9	17.9	13.0	10.4	8.6
c Alcoholic beverages	...	...	...	...	55.5	50.3	49.4	53.0	45.6	45.6	46.9
d Tobacco	...	...	...	...	76.1	71.1	73.6	78.2	62.2	66.8	64.8
2 Clothing and footwear	...	...	...	...	67.3	64.4	58.6	58.1	50.2	35.5	34.7
3 Gross rent, fuel and power	...	...	...	...	156.3	164.9	174.0	180.5	189.4	186.7	184.2
a Fuel and power	...	...	...	...	39.3	40.0	43.8	45.6	49.4	45.1	43.0
b Other	...	...	...	...	117.0	124.9	130.2	134.9	140.0	141.6	141.2
4 Furniture, furnishings and household equipment and operation	...	...	...	...	90.9	91.2	98.2	100.3	82.3	75.5	70.6
a Household operation	...	...	...	...	43.6	50.3	59.8	63.4	54.3	51.6	47.5
b Other	...	...	...	...	47.3	40.9	38.4	36.9	28.0	23.9	23.1
5 Medical care and health expenses	...	...	...	...	27.3	36.2	32.1	29.3	35.1	37.3	35.8
6 Transport and communication	...	...	...	...	191.4	188.1	179.5	170.2	134.9	151.3	154.5
a Personal transport equipment	...	...	...	...	109.5	106.7	95.8	87.8	74.7	83.7	92.4
b Other	...	...	...	...	81.9	81.4	83.7	82.4	60.2	67.6	62.1
7 Recreational, entertainment, education and cultural services	...	...	...	...	59.8	72.7	86.8	54.4	53.8	64.9	78.3
a Education	...	...	...	...	5.2	5.9	6.2	6.3	5.1	4.2	5.1
b Other	...	...	...	...	54.6	66.8	80.6	48.1	48.7	60.7	73.2
8 Miscellaneous goods and services	...	...	...	...	274.2	259.6	238.5	240.2	235.1	234.5	243.5
a Personal care	...	...	...	...	64.5	66.7	64.1	56.9	50.9	41.4	42.1
b Expenditures in restaurants, cafes and hotels	...	...	...	...	126.2	106.4	91.2	87.3	88.0	97.7	89.8
c Other	...	...	...	...	83.5	86.5	83.2	96.0	96.2	95.4	111.6
Total Final Consumption Expenditure in the Domestic Market by Households, of which	...	...	...	...	1569.1	1565.8	1533.8	1534.4	1429.4	1348.8	1314.1
Plus: Direct purchases abroad by resident households	...	...	...	...	33.8	42.4	44.3	11.9	9.6	9.7	7.0
Less: Direct purchases in the domestic market by non-resident households	...	...	...	...	123.3	102.9	79.1	78.9	108.2	127.0	111.4
Equals: Final Consumption Expenditure of Resident Households	...	...	...	...	1479.6	1505.3	1499.0	1467.4	1330.7	1231.5	1209.6

Final Consumption Expenditure of Private Non-profit Institutions Serving Households

	1970	1971	1972	1973	1974	1975	1976	1977	1978	1979	1980
Equals: Final Consumption Expenditure of Private Non-profit Organisations Serving Households	...	...	...	...	...	...	...	...	...	...	...
Private Final Consumption Expenditure	...	...	...	...	1479.6	1505.3	1499.0	1467.4	1330.7	1231.5	1209.6

Jamaica

2.9 Gross Capital Formation by Kind of Activity of Owner, ISIC Major Divisions, in Current Prices

Thousand Jamaican dollars

	1970 Total Gross Capital Formation	1970 Increase in Stocks	1970 Gross Fixed Capital Formation	1971 Total Gross Capital Formation	1971 Increase in Stocks	1971 Gross Fixed Capital Formation	1972 Total Gross Capital Formation	1972 Increase in Stocks	1972 Gross Fixed Capital Formation	1973 Total Gross Capital Formation	1973 Increase in Stocks	1973 Gross Fixed Capital Formation
All Producers												
1 Agriculture, hunting, fishing and forestry	...	...	11699	...	...	13010	...	...	12910	...	...	15460
2 Mining and quarrying	...	...	95449	...	...	106149	...	...	105332	...	...	126135
3 Manufacturing	...	...	26056	...	...	28977	...	...	28754	...	...	34433
4 Electricity, gas and water	...	...	16484	...	...	18332	...	...	18191	...	...	21784
5 Construction	...	...	11698	...	...	13009	...	...	12909	...	...	15458
6 Wholesale and retail trade, restaurants and hotels	...	...	9572	...	...	10645	...	...	10563	...	...	12649
7 Transport, storage and communication	...	...	19941	...	...	22176	...	...	22022	...	...	26371
8 Finance, insurance, real estate and business services	...	...	23929	...	...	26612	...	...	26407	...	...	31643
9 Community, social and personal services	...	...	8242	...	...	9157	...	...	9095	...	...	10891
Total Industries	...	...	223070	...	...	248067	...	...	246183	...	...	294824
Producers of Government Services	...	...	42806	...	...	47605	...	...	47238	...	...	56567
Private Non-Profit Institutions Serving Households	...	...	-	...	...	-	...	...	-	...	...	-
Total	273433	7557	265876	311514	15842	295672	299097	5676	293421	382041	30650	351391

	1974 Total Gross Capital Formation	1974 Increase in Stocks	1974 Gross Fixed Capital Formation
All Producers			
1 Agriculture, hunting, fishing and forestry	...	...	21732
2 Mining and quarrying	...	...	177308
3 Manufacturing	...	...	48403
4 Electricity, gas and water	...	...	30622
5 Construction	...	...	21729
6 Wholesale and retail trade, restaurants and hotels	...	...	17781
7 Transport, storage and communication	...	...	37094
8 Finance, insurance, real estate and business services	...	...	44481
9 Community, social and personal services	...	...	15310
Total Industries	...	...	414460
Producers of Government Services	...	...	79516
Private Non-Profit Institutions Serving Households	...	...	-
Total	501393	7417	493976

2.17 Exports and Imports of Goods and Services, Detail

Thousand Jamaican dollars

	1970	1971	1972	1973	1974	1975	1976	1977	1978	1979	1980
Exports of Goods and Services											
1 Exports of merchandise, f.o.b.	244009	285473	302363	354722	632874	...	...	...	...	...	...
2 Transport and communication						...	...	...	...	...	...
3 Insurance service charges	54617	57740	60760	69883	87753						
4 Other commodities						...	...	...	...	...	...
5 Adjustments of merchandise exports to change-of-ownership basis											
6 Direct purchases in the domestic market by non-residential households	79600	90826	107933	115771	124812	...	...	...	...	...	...
7 Direct purchases in the domestic market by extraterritorial bodies	...	...	...	...	...	...	...	...	...	...	...
Total Exports of Goods and Services	378226	434039	471056	540376	845439	...	...	...	...	...	...
Imports of Goods and Services											
1 Imports of merchandise, c.i.f.	374320	458747	493165	604071	847035	...	...	...	...	...	...

Jamaica

2.17 Exports and Imports of Goods and Services, Detail
(Continued)

Thousand Jamaican dollars

	1970	1971	1972	1973	1974	1975	1976	1977	1978	1979	1980
2 Adjustments of merchandise imports to change-of-ownership basis						...	...	...	...	...	...
3 Other transport and communication	36015	38738	48661	62246	72608	...	...	...	...	...	...
4 Other insurance service charges						...	...	...	...	...	...
5 Other commodities						...	...	...	...	...	...
6 Direct purchases abroad by government	...	...	...	...	...	...	...	...	...	...	...
7 Direct purchases abroad by resident households	12900	13600	16500	18100	18801	...	...	...	...	...	...
Total Imports of Goods and Services	423235	511085	558326	684417	938444	...	...	...	...	...	...
Balance of Goods and Services	-45009	-77046	-87270	-144041	-93005	...	...	...	...	...	...
Total Imports and Balance of Goods and Services	378226	434039	471056	540376	845439	...	...	...	...	...	...

4.6 Cost Components of Value Added, ISIC Divisions

Million Jamaican dollars

	1970 Compensation of Employees	Capital Consumption	Net Operating Surplus	Indirect Taxes	Less: Subsidies Received	Value Added	1971 Compensation of Employees	Capital Consumption	Net Operating Surplus	Indirect Taxes	Less: Subsidies Received	Value Added
						All Producers						
1 Agriculture, hunting, forestry and fishing	32.9	3.7	43.2	2.2	3.6	78.4	38.6	4.2	56.8	2.5	2.8	99.4
a Agriculture and hunting	30.7	...	...	...	...	70.8	35.8	...	...	...	...	89.6
b Forestry and logging	1.4	...	...	...	...	2.1	2.0	...	...	...	...	2.2
c Fishing	0.7	...	...	...	...	5.5	0.8	...	...	...	...	7.6
2 Mining and quarrying	27.1	25.5	94.1	1.0	-	147.8	34.3	23.1	78.2	1.9	-	137.5
a Coal mining	...	...	...	...	...	...	...	...	...	...	...	...
b Crude petroleum and natural gas production	...	...	...	...	...	...	...	...	...	...	...	...
c Metal ore mining	22.9	...	...	...	...	141.3	28.6	...	...	...	...	128.8
d Other mining	4.2	...	...	...	...	6.5	5.8	...	...	...	...	8.8
3 Manufacturing	78.2	13.1	48.5	44.3	0.3	183.8	86.0	15.0	56.7	49.3	0.1	206.5
a Manufacture of food, beverages and tobacco	26.0	...	...	...	...	84.9	29.1	...	...	...	...	93.5
b Textile, wearing apparel and leather industries	9.1	...	...	...	...	13.6	10.4	...	...	...	...	16.5
c Manufacture of wood and wood products, including furniture	7.8	...	...	...	...	10.5	7.0	...	...	...	...	11.2
d Manufacture of paper and paper products, printing and publishing	5.1	...	...	...	...	7.5	5.5	...	...	...	...	8.0
e Manufacture of chemicals and chemical petroleum, coal, rubber and plastic products	8.1	...	...	...	...	28.2	9.4	...	...	...	...	33.8
f Manufacture of non-metallic mineral products, except products of petroleum and coal	5.1	...	...	...	...	10.3	5.4	...	...	...	...	10.6
g Basic metal industries	15.5	...	...	...	...	26.1	17.7	...	...	...	...	30.6
h Manufacture of fabricated metal products, machinery and equipment		...						...			...	
i Other manufacturing industries	1.4	...	...	...	...	2.8	1.5	...	...	...	...	2.9
4 Electricity, gas and water	5.4	2.3	4.1	-	-	11.8	6.7	2.6	4.2	-	-	13.5
a Electricity, gas and steam	2.4	...	...	...	...	8.1	2.8	...	...	...	...	9.0
b Water works and supply	3.0	...	...	...	...	3.7	3.9	...	...	...	...	4.5
5 Construction	130.2	14.9	10.5	-	-	155.7	119.9	12.8	20.0	-	-	152.7
6 Wholesale and retail trade, restaurants and hotels [a]	110.6	8.7	79.4	43.2	0.1	248.0	121.5	9.4	93.9	49.8	0.1	282.3
a Wholesale and retail trade	91.4	...	...	...	...	222.6	99.0	...	...	...	...	252.0
b Restaurants and hotels	19.2	...	...	...	...	25.5	22.5	...	...	...	...	30.3
7 Transport, storage and communication	33.9	16.1	12.8	5.1	3.4	64.5	40.5	18.9	17.4	5.7	5.2	77.3
a Transport and storage	25.4	...	...	...	...	52.6	29.3	...	...	...	...	63.9
b Communication	8.6	...	...	...	...	11.9	11.2	...	...	...	...	13.3
8 Finance, insurance, real estate and business services	41.4	28.2	78.7	6.2	-	154.5	45.4	30.9	81.9	8.7	-	166.9
a Financial institutions	11.5	...	...	...	...	25.5	13.3	...	...	...	...	28.3

Jamaica

4.6 Cost Components of Value Added, ISIC Divisions
(Continued)

Million Jamaican dollars

	1970						1971					
	Compensation of Employees	Capital Consumption	Net Operating Surplus	Indirect Taxes	Less: Subsidies Received	Value Added	Compensation of Employees	Capital Consumption	Net Operating Surplus	Indirect Taxes	Less: Subsidies Received	Value Added
b Insurance	9.7	...	...	...	...	18.6	10.6	...	...	...	...	18.9
c Real estate and business services	20.2	...	...	...	...	110.5	21.4	...	...	...	...	119.6
Real estate, except dwellings	9.2	...	...	...	...	40.5	8.8	...	...	...	...	45.3
Dwellings	2.9	...	...	...	...	52.1	3.2	...	...	...	...	57.9
9 Community, social and personal services [a]	19.1	4.4	19.8	3.4	0.3	40.2	20.6	5.0	22.1	4.1	0.3	43.7
a Sanitary and similar services	...	...	...	...	...	...	...	...	...	...	...	...
b Social and related community services	8.0	...	...	...	...	11.7	8.7	...	...	...	...	12.8
Educational services	5.6	...	...	...	...	6.3	6.1	...	...	...	...	6.9
Medical, dental, other health and veterinary services	2.4	...	...	...	...	5.4	2.6	...	...	...	...	5.9
c Recreational and cultural services	5.3	...	...	...	...	13.5	5.7	...	...	...	...	14.7
d Personal and household services	5.8	...	...	...	...	15.0	6.2	...	...	...	...	16.2
Total, Industries	478.8	116.9	391.3	105.4	7.7	1084.8	513.5	121.9	431.3	122.0	8.5	1180.2
Producers of Government Services	91.6	-	-	-	-	91.6	107.9	-	-	-	-	107.9
Other Producers	16.5	0.1	2.2	0.1	-	18.9	18.4	0.1	2.4	0.1	-	21.0
Total	586.9	117.0	393.5	105.5	7.7	1195.3	639.8	122.0	433.7	122.1	8.5	1309.1
Imputed bank service charge	...	-	-24.2	-	-	-24.2	...	-	-29.1	-	-	-29.1
Import duties	...	...	...	...	...	...	...	...	...	...	...	...
Value added tax	...	...	...	...	...	...	...	...	...	...	...	...
Other adjustments	...	...	...	...	...	...	...	...	...	...	...	...
Total	586.9	117.0	369.3	105.5	7.7	1171.1	639.8	122.1	404.6	122.2	8.5	1280.1

	1972						1973					
	Compensation of Employees	Capital Consumption	Net Operating Surplus	Indirect Taxes	Less: Subsidies Received	Value Added	Compensation of Employees	Capital Consumption	Net Operating Surplus	Indirect Taxes	Less: Subsidies Received	Value Added

All Producers

1 Agriculture, hunting, forestry and fishing	42.5	4.8	59.5	2.8	3.1	106.5	48.3	5.6	76.3	3.4	5.5	128.1
a Agriculture and hunting	39.3	...	...	...	...	93.4	43.5	...	...	...	...	110.4
b Forestry and logging	2.3	...	...	...	...	2.5	3.9	...	...	...	...	2.8
c Fishing	0.9	...	...	...	...	10.6	1.0	...	...	...	...	14.9
2 Mining and quarrying	38.3	30.0	51.6	2.3	-	122.2	53.6	34.5	57.6	3.2	-	148.9
a Coal mining	...	...	...	...	...	...	...	...	...	...	...	...
b Crude petroleum and natural gas production	...	...	...	...	...	...	...	...	...	...	...	...
c Metal ore mining	32.5	...	...	...	...	113.2	47.8	...	...	...	...	139.0
d Other mining	5.8	...	...	...	...	9.0	5.8	...	...	...	...	9.8
3 Manufacturing	106.8	17.9	60.9	56.8	0.8	241.8	133.0	19.9	67.1	67.3	0.8	286.4
a Manufacture of food, beverages and tobacco	32.5	...	...	...	...	102.0	41.1	...	...	...	...	120.0
b Textile, wearing apparel and leather industries	16.2	...	...	...	...	21.4	19.7	...	...	...	...	26.4
c Manufacture of wood and wood products, including furniture	9.5	...	...	...	...	14.5	9.7	...	...	...	...	15.8
d Manufacture of paper and paper products, printing and publishing	7.5	...	...	...	...	11.2	8.9	...	...	...	...	13.7
e Manufacture of chemicals and chemical petroleum, coal, rubber and plastic products	12.5	...	...	...	...	41.4	14.9	...	...	...	...	44.9
f Manufacture of non-metallic mineral products, except products of petroleum and coal	6.0	...	...	...	...	11.5	6.7	...	...	...	...	12.6
g Basic metal industries	21.1	...	...	...	...	36.8	30.1	...	...	...	...	49.5
h Manufacture of fabricated metal products, machinery and equipment												
i Other manufacturing industries	1.5	...	...	...	...	2.9	1.8	...	...	...	...	3.4
4 Electricity, gas and water	9.0	2.8	5.4	-	0.3	17.0	10.9	3.5	4.6	-	0.7	18.4
a Electricity, gas and steam	3.8	...	...	...	...	11.3	5.0	...	...	...	...	12.3
b Water works and supply	5.3	...	...	...	...	5.7	5.9	...	...	...	...	6.1

Jamaica

4.6 Cost Components of Value Added, ISIC Divisions
(Continued)

Million Jamaican dollars

	1972						1973					
	Compensation of Employees	Capital Consumption	Net Operating Surplus	Indirect Taxes	Less: Subsidies Received	Value Added	Compensation of Employees	Capital Consumption	Net Operating Surplus	Indirect Taxes	Less: Subsidies Received	Value Added
5 Construction	121.7	12.2	18.3	-	0.1	152.1	139.2	14.6	23.8	-	-	177.6
6 Wholesale and retail trade, restaurants and hotels [a]	147.4	11.5	109.7	53.2	0.3	330.4	179.2	15.2	129.6	55.2	1.5	388.3
a Wholesale and retail trade	121.3	...	...	...	...	295.4	150.0	...	...	...	...	348.5
b Restaurants and hotels	26.1	...	...	...	...	34.9	29.2	...	...	...	...	39.8
7 Transport, storage and communication	44.9	23.7	22.6	6.1	8.1	89.3	52.5	29.3	31.9	6.5	7.6	112.5
a Transport and storage	32.8	...	...	...	...	73.4	38.2	...	...	...	...	91.3
b Communication	12.1	...	...	...	...	15.9	14.3	...	...	...	...	21.2
8 Finance, insurance, real estate and business services	56.9	35.3	94.1	12.8	0.2	198.7	70.6	43.8	104.8	21.7	0.1	240.8
a Financial institutions	16.8	...	...	...	...	39.5	22.0	...	...	...	...	50.2
b Insurance	16.3	...	...	...	...	23.4	20.1	...	...	...	...	22.6
c Real estate and business services	23.8	...	...	...	...	135.9	28.6	...	...	...	...	167.9
Real estate, except dwellings	10.3	...	...	...	...	46.6	12.1	...	...	...	...	66.1
Dwellings	3.6	...	...	...	...	66.3	4.6	...	...	...	...	82.6
9 Community, social and personal services [a]	25.4	5.8	27.2	4.3	0.4	53.6	28.9	6.3	32.4	5.5	0.5	62.1
a Sanitary and similar services	...	...	...	...	...	...	...	...	...	...	...	...
b Social and related community services	10.3	...	...	...	...	15.4	13.9	...	...	...	...	19.2
Educational services	7.0	...	...	...	...	7.8	8.4	...	...	...	...	9.5
Medical, dental, other health and veterinary services	3.3	...	...	...	...	7.6	5.5	...	...	...	...	9.7
c Recreational and cultural services	8.3	...	...	...	...	20.3	8.1	...	...	...	...	24.4
d Personal and household services	6.8	...	...	...	...	17.8	6.9	...	...	...	...	19.5
Total, Industries	592.9	144.0	449.4	138.3	13.3	1311.5	716.2	172.7	528.1	162.8	16.7	1563.1
Producers of Government Services	137.0	-	-	-	-	137.1	185.9	-	-	-	-	185.9
Other Producers	23.8	0.1	2.7	0.1	-	26.7	31.1	0.1	3.1	0.1	-	34.4
Total	753.8	144.1	452.1	138.4	13.3	1475.3	933.2	172.8	531.2	162.9	16.7	1783.4
Imputed bank service charge	...	-	-36.5	-	-	-36.5	...	-	-48.3	-	-	-48.3
Import duties	...	...	...	...	...	...	...	...	...	...	...	...
Value added tax	...	...	...	...	...	...	...	...	...	...	...	...
Other adjustments	...	...	...	...	...	...	...	...	...	...	...	...
Total	753.8	144.0	415.6	138.6	13.2	1438.8	933.2	172.8	482.9	163.0	16.7	1735.1

	1974						1975					
	Compensation of Employees	Capital Consumption	Net Operating Surplus	Indirect Taxes	Less: Subsidies Received	Value Added	Compensation of Employees	Capital Consumption	Net Operating Surplus	Indirect Taxes	Less: Subsidies Received	Value Added
					All Producers							
1 Agriculture, hunting, forestry and fishing	61.1	6.6	95.8	4.4	5.2	162.6	86.5	7.2	110.1	5.0	6.8	202.0
a Agriculture and hunting	56.0	...	...	...	...	143.8	80.2	...	...	...	...	178.8
b Forestry and logging	4.2	...	...	...	...	2.7	5.2	...	...	...	...	3.0
c Fishing	1.0	...	...	...	...	16.1	1.1	...	...	...	...	20.3
2 Mining and quarrying	61.2	37.0	92.8	5.9	-	197.0	61.9	32.6	118.9	8.1	0.6	220.8
a Coal mining	...	...	...	...	...	...	...	...	...	...	...	...
b Crude petroleum and natural gas production	...	...	...	...	...	...	...	...	...	...	...	...
c Metal ore mining	55.4	...	...	...	...	187.3	57.1	...	...	...	...	213.5
d Other mining	5.9	...	...	...	...	9.7	4.8	...	...	...	...	7.4

Jamaica

4.6 Cost Components of Value Added, ISIC Divisions
(Continued)

Million Jamaican dollars

	1974						1975					
	Compensation of Employees	Capital Consumption	Net Operating Surplus	Indirect Taxes	Less: Subsidies Received	Value Added	Compensation of Employees	Capital Consumption	Net Operating Surplus	Indirect Taxes	Less: Subsidies Received	Value Added
3 Manufacturing	164.5	24.9	101.6	96.2	0.4	386.8	205.3	28.8	95.7	114.9	1.1	443.7
a Manufacture of food, beverages and tobacco	59.3	...	...	...	...	180.2	78.4	...	...	...	...	209.7
b Textile, wearing apparel and leather industries	16.2	...	...	...	...	29.4	20.1	...	...	...	...	36.7
c Manufacture of wood and wood products, including furniture	12.3	...	...	...	...	18.8	12.6	...	...	...	...	20.2
d Manufacture of paper and paper products, printing and publishing	14.6	...	...	...	...	21.7	17.8	...	...	...	...	26.0
e Manufacture of chemicals and chemical petroleum, coal, rubber and plastic products	14.4	...	...	...	...	66.5	17.9	...	...	...	...	67.2
f Manufacture of non-metallic mineral products, except products of petroleum and coal	10.0	...	...	...	...	17.8	13.5	...	...	...	...	18.9
g Basic metal industries	35.7					48.6	42.7					60.6
h Manufacture of fabricated metal products, machinery and equipment			...		...			...				
i Other manufacturing industries	1.9	...	...	...	...	3.7	2.3	...	...	...	...	4.4
4 Electricity, gas and water	12.4	6.0	8.5	-	4.7	22.2	19.1	1.9	23.7	-	6.0	38.8
a Electricity, gas and steam	6.5	...	...	...	...	15.0	9.5	...	...	...	...	26.8
b Water works and supply	5.9	...	...	...	...	7.3	9.7	...	...	...	...	12.1
5 Construction	173.2	16.1	24.2	-	-	213.5	212.8	18.3	21.3	-	-	252.4
6 Wholesale and retail trade, restaurants and hotels [a]	215.2	16.7	165.3	55.6	4.6	457.9	262.2	23.3	198.6	85.5	4.7	572.0
a Wholesale and retail trade	176.2	...	...	...	...	409.3	214.4	...	...	...	...	517.1
b Restaurants and hotels	39.0	...	...	...	...	48.6	47.8	...	...	...	...	54.8
7 Transport, storage and communication	73.3	35.1	31.2	6.8	9.4	137.0	90.5	40.7	28.5	8.1	10.8	156.9
a Transport and storage	54.4	...	...	...	...	111.8	68.5	...	...	...	...	127.4
b Communication	18.9	...	...	...	...	25.2	21.9	...	...	...	...	29.5
8 Finance, insurance, real estate and business services	91.1	54.9	124.0	28.0	-	297.9	110.6	70.1	141.1	39.6	-	361.5
a Financial institutions	30.9	...	...	...	...	63.6	38.4	...	...	...	...	74.5
b Insurance	26.0	...	...	...	...	29.8	29.8	...	...	...	...	34.5
c Real estate and business services	34.3	...	...	...	...	204.6	42.4	...	...	...	...	252.4
Real estate, except dwellings	13.9	...	...	...	...	78.3	15.7	...	...	...	...	88.7
Dwellings	5.7	...	...	...	...	102.0	7.6	...	...	...	...	131.5
9 Community, social and personal services [a]	33.7	7.5	32.7	8.1	1.5	71.0	42.6	8.2	26.8	8.6	1.3	77.8
a Sanitary and similar services	...	...	...	...	...	...	...	...	...	...	...	...
b Social and related community services	17.2	...	...	...	...	23.2	24.5	...	...	...	...	32.1
Educational services	9.9	...	...	...	...	11.3	15.3	...	...	...	...	17.2
Medical, dental, other health and veterinary services	7.3	...	...	...	...	11.9	9.1	...	...	...	...	14.9
c Recreational and cultural services	8.4	...	...	...	...	26.3	8.8	...	...	...	...	21.4
d Personal and household services	8.0	...	...	...	...	21.5	9.4	...	...	...	...	24.4
Total, Industries	885.7	204.8	675.9	205.3	25.8	1946.0	1091.5	231.1	764.7	269.8	31.3	2326.0
Producers of Government Services	251.3	-	-	-	-	251.3	327.8	-	-	-	-	327.8
Other Producers	34.5	0.1	3.3	0.1	-	38.0	37.0	0.1	2.9	0.1	-	40.1
Total	1171.5	204.9	679.2	208.2	25.8	2235.3	1456.3	231.2	767.7	269.9	31.3	2693.9
Imputed bank service charge	...	-	-65.7	-	-	-65.7	...	-	-79.6	-	-	-79.6
Import duties	...	...	...	...	...	...	...	...	...	...	...	...
Value added tax	...	...	...	...	...	...	...	...	...	...	...	...
Other adjustments	...	...	...	...	...	...	...	...	...	...	...	...
Total	1171.5	205.0	613.5	205.4	25.8	2169.6	1456.3	231.2	688.1	269.9	31.3	2614.3

Jamaica

4.6 Cost Components of Value Added, ISIC Divisions

Million Jamaican dollars

		1976					1977				
	Compensation of Employees	Capital Consumption	Net Operating Surplus	Indirect Taxes	Less: Subsidies Received	Value Added	Compensation of Employees	Capital Consumption	Net Operating Surplus	Indirect Taxes	Less: Subsidies Received	Value Added

All Producers

	Comp. 1976	Cap. 1976	Net Op. 1976	Ind. Tax 1976	Subs. 1976	VA 1976	Comp. 1977	Cap. 1977	Net Op. 1977	Ind. Tax 1977	Subs. 1977	VA 1977
1 Agriculture, hunting, forestry and fishing	95.2	8.3	123.8	5.5	6.6	226.3	104.3	10.5	147.3	6.3	5.5	263.0
a Agriculture and hunting	88.0	...	...	...	...	199.8	96.0	...	...	...	...	232.0
b Forestry and logging	2.0	...	...	...	...	3.2	1.3	...	...	...	...	3.5
c Fishing	6.0	...	...	...	...	23.3	7.1	...	...	...	...	27.4
2 Mining and quarrying	61.2	29.8	134.6	10.0	0.2	235.3	70.4	30.6	197.5	9.5	-	308.0
a Coal mining												
b Crude petroleum and natural gas production												
c Metal ore mining	56.3	...	...	...	...	228.5	65.6	...	...	...	...	301.5
d Other mining	4.9	...	...	...	...	6.8	4.8	...	...	...	...	6.5
3 Manufacturing	233.5	32.3	83.4	141.6	0.7	490.0	249.9	34.5	90.8	172.2	3.3	544.1
a Manufacture of food, beverages and tobacco	90.9	...	...	...	...	228.9	95.5	...	...	...	...	251.8
b Textile, wearing apparel and leather industries	22.5	...	...	...	...	36.3	22.1	...	...	...	...	38.9
c Manufacture of wood and wood products, including furniture	14.1	...	...	...	...	23.0	16.1	...	...	...	...	25.3
d Manufacture of paper and paper products, printing and publishing	19.0	...	...	...	...	28.5	21.4	...	...	...	...	28.5
e Manufacture of chemicals and chemical petroleum, coal, rubber and plastic products	22.0	...	...	...	...	82.5	25.9	...	...	...	...	108.6
f Manufacture of non-metallic mineral products, except products of petroleum and coal	15.3	...	...	...	...	20.7	14.7	...	...	...	...	17.8
g Basic metal industries	47.2	...	...	...	...	65.4	51.4	...	...	...	...	67.8
h Manufacture of fabricated metal products, machinery and equipment		...	...	...	...			...	...	...	...	
i Other manufacturing industries	2.5	...	...	...	...	4.8	2.8	...	...	...	...	5.4
4 Electricity, gas and water	22.4	7.8	25.8	-	1.6	54.4	25.7	21.9	11.4	-	0.5	58.5
a Electricity, gas and steam	11.7	...	...	...	...	42.4	15.2	...	...	...	...	48.6
b Water works and supply	10.7	...	...	...	...	12.0	10.5	...	...	...	...	9.9
5 Construction	180.6	15.3	16.0	-	-	211.9	150.7	13.2	17.3	-	-	181.2
6 Wholesale and retail trade, restaurants and hotels [a]	223.7	17.7	191.4	61.0	17.0	483.2	247.6	19.6	170.3	112.0	129.5	527.9
a Wholesale and retail trade	179.3	...	...	...	...	432.3	198.5	...	...	...	...	472.0
b Restaurants and hotels	44.4	...	...	...	...	50.8	49.1	...	...	...	...	56.0
7 Transport, storage and communication	111.7	46.9	20.8	10.1	15.9	173.6	127.7	56.3	3.1	21.0	16.0	192.1
a Transport and storage	86.5	...	...	...	...	137.8	100.0	...	...	...	...	151.0
b Communication	25.2	...	...	...	...	35.8	27.7	...	...	...	...	41.1
8 Finance, insurance, real estate and business services	122.8	82.0	146.9	39.7	0.2	391.1	135.4	88.5	250.8	40.9	0.5	413.9
a Financial institutions	41.8	...	...	...	...	70.8	48.1	...	...	...	...	80.5
b Insurance	35.4	...	...	...	...	41.1	39.0	...	...	...	...	34.4
c Real estate and business services	45.6	...	...	...	...	279.2	48.3	...	...	...	...	299.0
Real estate, except dwellings	17.2	...	...	...	...	90.6	17.3	...	...	...	...	93.6
Dwellings	9.2	...	...	...	...	157.1	10.1	...	...	...	...	170.6
9 Community, social and personal services [a]	49.7	8.3	28.1	12.7	1.8	90.6	56.0	8.9	28.7	11.5	2.5	95.7
a Sanitary and similar services	...	...	...	...	...	...	...	...	...	...	...	...
b Social and related community services	27.5	...	...	...	...	35.3	29.5	...	...	...	...	35.7
Educational services	18.4	...	...	...	...	20.6	19.7	...	...	...	...	21.8
Medical, dental, other health and veterinary services	9.0	...	...	...	...	14.7	9.8	...	...	...	...	13.9
c Recreational and cultural services	10.4	...	...	...	...	24.6	12.8	...	...	...	...	25.0
d Personal and household services	11.9	...	...	...	...	30.7	13.8	...	...	...	...	35.0

Jamaica

4.6 Cost Components of Value Added, ISIC Divisions
(Continued)

Million Jamaican dollars

	1976						1977					
	Compensation of Employees	Capital Consumption	Net Operating Surplus	Indirect Taxes	Less: Subsidies Received	Value Added	Compensation of Employees	Capital Consumption	Net Operating Surplus	Indirect Taxes	Less: Subsidies Received	Value Added
Total, Industries	1100.8	248.4	770.8	280.6	44.0	2356.4	1167.7	284.0	917.2	373.4	157.8	2584.5
Producers of Government Services	383.1	-	-	0.1	-	383.2	436.4	-	-	0.1	-	436.5
Other Producers	49.3	0.1	0.1	-	-	49.5	53.0	0.1	0.1	-	-	53.2
Total	1533.1	248.5	770.9	280.8	44.1	2789.1	1657.1	284.1	917.3	373.5	157.8	3074.2
Imputed bank service charge	...	-	-74.1	-	-	-74.1	...	-	-85.6	-	-	-85.6
Import duties	...	...	...	...	...	...	...	...	...	...	...	...
Value added tax	...	...	...	...	...	...	...	...	...	...	...	...
Other adjustments	...	...	...	...	...	...	...	...	...	...	...	...
Total	1533.1	248.4	696.8	280.8	44.1	2715.0	1657.1	284.1	831.7	373.6	157.9	2988.6

	1978						1979					
	Compensation of Employees	Capital Consumption	Net Operating Surplus	Indirect Taxes	Less: Subsidies Received	Value Added	Compensation of Employees	Capital Consumption	Net Operating Surplus	Indirect Taxes	Less: Subsidies Received	Value Added

All Producers

1 Agriculture, hunting, forestry and fishing	130.3	12.5	168.5	8.4	5.9	313.9	137.2	12.5	175.4	8.0	6.5	320.0
a Agriculture and hunting	118.0	...	...	...	...	275.5	123.5	...	...	...	...	283.9
b Forestry and logging	1.2	...	...	...	...	3.3	1.3	...	...	...	...	3.3
c Fishing	11.1	...	...	...	...	35.0	12.3	...	...	...	...	32.9
2 Mining and quarrying	91.2	52.7	348.4	18.1	-	510.4	98.8	62.0	449.8	11.9	-	622.5
a Coal mining	...	...	...	...	...	...	...	...	...	...	...	...
b Crude petroleum and natural gas production	...					...	...					...
c Metal ore mining	85.8	...	...	...	...	503.7	92.4	...	...	...	...	614.9
d Other mining	5.4	...	...	...	...	6.7	6.3	...	...	...	...	7.6
3 Manufacturing	294.7	39.5	94.5	232.9	25.4	636.2	319.7	46.5	48.4	275.1	8.0	681.6
a Manufacture of food, beverages and tobacco	113.9	...	...	...	...	267.1	131.6	...	...	...	...	312.9
b Textile, wearing apparel and leather industries	29.0	...	...	...	...	46.3	26.1	...	...	...	...	40.7
c Manufacture of wood and wood products, including furniture	17.6	...	...	...	...	27.7	16.8	...	...	...	...	27.1
d Manufacture of paper and paper products, printing and publishing	23.4	...	...	...	...	31.3	25.5	...	...	...	...	34.0
e Manufacture of chemicals and chemical petroleum, coal, rubber and plastic products	26.5	...	...	...	...	150.3	31.4	...	...	...	...	158.2
f Manufacture of non-metallic mineral products, except products of petroleum and coal	16.4	...	...	...	...	19.5	16.0	...	...	...	...	17.1
g Basic metal industries	65.1	...	...	...	...	87.9	69.3	...	...	...	...	85.3
h Manufacture of fabricated metal products, machinery and equipment		...	...	...	...			...	...	...	...	
i Other manufacturing industries	2.8	...	...	...	...	6.0	3.1	...	...	...	...	6.3
4 Electricity, gas and water	27.7	27.7	29.0	-	0.2	84.2	36.6	36.1	16.9	2.6	-	89.6
a Electricity, gas and steam	16.9	...	...	...	...	68.1	18.5	...	...	...	...	65.2
b Water works and supply	10.8	...	...	...	...	16.1	18.1	...	...	...	...	24.5
5 Construction	211.6	19.3	21.2	-	-	252.1	263.4	24.1	23.0	-	-	310.5
6 Wholesale and retail trade, restaurants and hotels [a]	272.6	19.1	418.2	128.0	139.8	707.4	311.2	19.1	499.8	118.2	105.3	850.5
a Wholesale and retail trade	209.5	...	...	...	...	635.0	234.4	...	...	...	...	772.8
b Restaurants and hotels	63.1	...	...	...	...	72.4	76.8	...	...	...	...	77.8
7 Transport, storage and communication	146.3	64.5	17.5	25.0	25.4	227.8	171.8	69.6	17.3	17.6	25.4	250.9
a Transport and storage	113.2	...	...	...	...	172.1	132.2	...	...	...	...	168.8
b Communication	33.1	...	...	...	...	55.7	39.6	...	...	...	...	82.1
8 Finance, insurance, real estate and business services	154.2	96.5	176.5	38.9	0.2	466.0	177.2	111.8	197.2	49.1	0.6	534.8
a Financial institutions	57.3	...	...	...	...	98.8	68.3	...	...	...	...	105.1
b Insurance	42.3	...	...	...	...	47.4	47.1	...	...	...	...	60.9
c Real estate and business services	54.6	...	...	...	...	319.8	61.8	...	...	...	...	368.8
Real estate, except dwellings	17.3	...	...	...	...	96.9	20.4	...	...	...	...	112.7

Jamaica

4.6 Cost Components of Value Added, ISIC Divisions
(Continued)

Million Jamaican dollars

	\multicolumn{6}{c	}{1978}	\multicolumn{6}{c	}{1979}
	Compensation of Employees	Capital Consumption	Net Operating Surplus	Indirect Taxes	Less: Subsidies Received	Value Added	Compensation of Employees	Capital Consumption	Net Operating Surplus	Indirect Taxes	Less: Subsidies Received	Value Added
Dwellings	13.4	...	...	...	...	181.8	15.0	...	...	...	...	210.4
9 Community, social and personal services a	61.1	10.8	20.3	22.3	5.1	100.0	68.3	11.5	8.6	25.8	5.0	108.2
a Sanitary and similar services	...	...	...	...	...	...	...	...	...	...	...	...
b Social and related community services	31.8	...	...	...	...	32.9	36.6	...	...	...	...	33.1
Educational services	20.6	...	...	...	...	21.2	24.2	...	...	...	...	20.1
Medical, dental, other health and veterinary services	11.2	...	...	...	...	11.7	12.4	...	...	...	...	13.0
c Recreational and cultural services	14.4	...	...	...	...	29.3	18.3	...	...	...	...	36.7
d Personal and household services	14.9	...	...	...	...	37.8	13.4	...	...	...	...	38.4
Total, Industries	1389.7	342.6	1294.1	473.6	202.0	3298.0	1584.2	393.2	1436.4	508.3	150.8	3768.7
Producers of Government Services	509.1	-	-	0.1	-	509.2	575.6	-	-	0.1	-	575.7
Other Producers	50.2	0.1	0.1	-	-	50.4	46.8	0.2	0.1	-	-	47.1
Total	1949.0	342.7	1294.2	473.7	202.0	3857.6	2206.6	393.4	1436.5	508.4	150.8	4391.5
Imputed bank service charge	...	-	-104.0	-	-	-104.0	...	-	-102.5	-	-	-102.5
Import duties	...	...	...	...	...	...	...	...	...	...	...	...
Value added tax	...	...	...	...	...	...	...	...	...	...	...	...
Other adjustments	...	...	...	...	...	...	...	...	...	...	...	...
Total	1949.0	342.8	1190.0	473.7	201.9	3753.6	2206.4	393.4	1334.1	505.8	150.8	4289.0

	\multicolumn{6}{c	}{1980}
	Compensation of Employees	Capital Consumption	Net Operating Surplus	Indirect Taxes	Less: Subsidies Received	Value Added
	\multicolumn{6}{c	}{All Producers}
1 Agriculture, hunting, forestry and fishing	155.9	13.8	218.9	10.0	6.3	392.2
a Agriculture and hunting	141.1	...	...	...	...	355.0
b Forestry and logging	1.4	...	...	...	...	3.6
c Fishing	13.3	...	...	...	...	33.6
2 Mining and quarrying	114.1	61.7	497.7	4.4	-	678.0
a Coal mining	...	...	...	...	...	...
b Crude petroleum and natural gas production	...	...	...	...	...	...
c Metal ore mining	108.3	...	...	...	...	671.1
d Other mining	5.8	...	...	...	...	6.9
3 Manufacturing	356.6	47.5	32.6	285.6	1.2	721.2
a Manufacture of food, beverages and tobacco	149.6	...	...	...	...	330.9
b Textile, wearing apparel and leather industries	31.1	...	...	...	...	49.4
c Manufacture of wood and wood products, including furniture	16.7	...	...	...	...	27.8
d Manufacture of paper and paper products, printing and publishing	27.2	...	...	...	...	37.6
e Manufacture of chemicals and chemical petroleum, coal, rubber and plastic products	34.4	...	...	...	...	160.3
f Manufacture of non-metallic mineral products, except products of petroleum and coal	18.4	...	...	...	...	19.8
g Basic metal industries	75.7	...	...	...	...	88.5
h Manufacture of fabricated metal products, machinery and equipment			...			
i Other manufacturing industries	3.3	...	...	...	...	6.8
4 Electricity, gas and water	43.9	42.4	-5.7	-	1.2	79.4
a Electricity, gas and steam	20.6	...	...	...	...	54.4
b Water works and supply	23.3	...	...	...	...	25.0

Jamaica

4.6 Cost Components of Value Added, ISIC Divisions
(Continued)

Million Jamaican dollars

	1980 Compensation of Employees	Capital Consumption	Net Operating Surplus	Indirect Taxes	Less: Subsidies Received	Value Added
5 Construction	228.3	21.1	20.4	-	-	269.8
6 Wholesale and retail trade, restaurants and hotels [a]	328.9	17.5	603.6	114.0	46.7	1013.2
a Wholesale and retail trade	244.2	...	...	...	...	932.7
b Restaurants and hotels	84.7	...	...	...	...	80.5
7 Transport, storage and communication	194.3	76.7	-2.2	15.4	31.9	252.3
a Transport and storage	145.1	...	...	...	...	162.8
b Communication	49.1	...	...	...	...	89.5
8 Finance, insurance, real estate and business services	207.3	123.5	237.9	38.2	1.3	605.6
a Financial institutions	83.8	...	...	...	...	132.3
b Insurance	57.1	...	...	...	...	66.2
c Real estate and business services	66.3	...	...	...	...	407.1
Real estate, except dwellings	22.3	...	...	...	...	132.4
Dwellings	16.3	...	...	...	...	226.9
9 Community, social and personal services [a]	81.9	13.4	4.2	23.9	4.5	123.0
a Sanitary and similar services	...	...	...	...	...	...
b Social and related community services	44.8	...	...	...	...	39.4
Educational services	30.4	...	...	...	...	25.3
Medical, dental, other health and veterinary services	14.5	...	...	...	...	14.1
c Recreational and cultural services	21.6	...	...	...	...	40.7
d Personal and household services	15.4	...	...	...	...	43.0
Total, Industries	1711.2	417.6	1607.4	491.5	93.1	4134.7
Producers of Government Services	693.3	-	-	0.1	-	693.4
Other Producers	-	0.2	0.1	-	-	44.2
Total	2448.4	417.8	1607.5	491.6	93.1	4872.3
Imputed bank service charge	...	-	-141.4	-	-	-141.4
Import duties	...	...	...	...	...	...
Value added tax	...	...	...	...	...	...
Other adjustments	...	...	...	...	...	...
Total	2448.4	417.9	1466.0	491.7	93.1	4730.9

a) Columns 1 through 5 do not add up to column 6 because for column 2 thrugh 5 item 'Restaurant and hotels' is included in item 'Community, social and personal services'.

Japan

General note. The preparation of national accounts statistics in Japan is undertaken by the Economic Research Institute of the Economic Planning Agency, Tokyo. The official estimates are published in 'Annual Report on National Income Statistics'. The following presentation of sources and methods is based on information from the supplement to 'Hundred-year Statistics of the Japanese Economy' published by the Statistics Department of the Bank of Japan. This was supplemented by information received from the Administrative Management Bureau of the Office of Statistical Standards. The estimates are generally in accordance with the classifications and definitions recommended in the United Nations System of Nation Accounts (SNA). Input-output tables have been published by the Bureau of Statistical Standards. The following tables have been prepared from successive replies to the United Nations national accounts questionnaire. When the scope and coverage of the estimates differ for conceptual or statistical reasons from the definitions and classifications recommended in SNA, a footnote is indicated to the relevant tables.

Sources and methods:

(a) Gross domestic product. Gross domestic product is estimated mainly through the expenditure approach.

(b) Expenditure on the gross domestic product. All items of the GDP by expenditure type are estimated through the expenditure approach except gross fixed capital formation which is estimated through the commodity-flow approach supplemented by the expenditure approach to compile estimates by investment sector. The estimates of government expenditure are based on figures from the Settlement Report and other financial statements with adjustments made to reconcile the data with the concept used in national accounts. Private consumption expenditure is estimated from the results of the annual agricultural economy surveys for farm household expenditure, from monthly household economy surveys for non-farm household expenditure and from consumption surveys held every five years for expenditure of one-person households. The national census, the agricultural census and surveys are used to obtain data on population, number of households and its members. Estimates of increase in stocks are based on various sources such as the quarterly and annual reports of corporate enterprises, balance sheets of government enterprises, farm household economy survey, rice, wheat and barley stock-in-hand survey, proprietor economy survey and national wealth census. Investment of capital goods are classified into machinery and tools, construction, and large animals and plants. Estimates of machinery and tools are based on industrial statistics, production statistics, foreign trade statistics, data on freight and margin rates, etc. Construction is treated in a production account, where input and value added are delivered to fixed capital formation. Animals are covered through increase in stocks and estimated from agricultural statistics whereas plants are estimated as increased orchard acreage multiplied by the price of nurturing grown orchard. Data on government capital expenditure are obtained from the financial accounts. The estimates of exports and imports of merchandise and services are based on the balance-of-payments. Foreign trade statistics provide data for goods exported from and imported to Japan. The sources of data include export and re-shipment declarations, export declarations, etc. For the constant price estimates, all items of GDP by expenditure type are deflated by appropriate price indexes.

(c) Cost-structure of the gross domestic product. Wages and salaries are estimated by multiplying average per capita consumption by the number of employees which is obtained by extrapolating population census figures. Average wages are based on sources such as the monthly labour survey, the survey of wages and salaries in private firms and unpublished data of the National Personnel Authority, Ministry of Finance and Ministry of Home Affairs. Salaries of executives are based on annual reports of corporate enterprises. Social insurance contributions by employers are estimated by multiplying total social insurance by the ratio of the employers' share of total contributions. Other sources of compensation of employees include settlement of general accounts and local government, data on tax regulations and housing census data for rent subsidies. Data on tax regulations, which are used for estimating corporate profits, are adjusted by adding other sources of profits and subtracting expenses. Surpluses of government enterprises are estimated from profit-and-loss statements of each enterprise. The estimates of interest received on personal deposits are based on the profit-and-loss statements of financial institutions and/or payments received from government bonds and industrial debentures. Net total rent for personally owned houses is estimated by deducting expenses incurred from gross rent which is estimated by multiplying the total rent of all houses by the ratio of personally owned buildings to the total number of privately owned buildings. For Proprietors' income, the national average income per household of farmers is obtained from the annual farm household economy survey and is multiplied by the number of farmers. Depreciation allowances of dwellings are estimated by multiplying the stock of residential buildings by the average rate of depreciation while that of incorporated enterprises is based on the annual reports of corporate enterprises. The survey of casualty insurance companies and the settlement of general accounts are used to estimate the damage of fixed capital due to accidents. The estimates of indirect taxes and subsidies are based on the settlement of general and local government accounts.

(d) Gross domestic product by kind of economic activity. The table of GDP by kind of economic activity is prepared at market prices, i.e. producers' values. Up until 1975, the production approach had been used to estimate GDP by kind of economic activity. This approach is being used again after the new SNA was adopted in 1978. The income approach is used to estimate the value added of producers of government services. For the agricultural sector, two methods are used simultaneously which supplement each other. The first is based on estimates of national income components, such as income received by unincorporated enterprises and wages and salaries and the second is based on the survey of production cost data of farm products. To derive at the national income components, sources such as the annual farmhousehold economy survey and the population census are used. Additional information on agriculture is obtained from input-output tables. For forestry and fishing, bench-mark estimates are made from production statistics, extrapolated by using the production index and the commodity price index. Estimates of mining are derived from census of establishment 1966, annual surveys of mining trends which cover all enterprises to which the Mining Law applies and other special surveys. The annual census of manufacturing is the main source for manufacturing estimates. A basic survey of smaller enteprises is held every four to five years. Current production on a commodity basis is obtained from monthly samples of establishments which provide data on principal production and shipment stock. The estimates of electricity and gas are based on the same sources as manufacturing and mining. For private construction, the value of newly constructed dwellings is derived from stock figures multiplied by average construction costs per area while factory construction is estimated by multiplying total area by average cost per area. A monthly statistical survey is conducted by the Ministry of Construction. For public construction, the estimates are based on government accounts and balance sheets of public enterprises. No information is available on the sources and methods used in estimating the various services sectors except public administration and defence which are based on government accounts. GDP by kind of economic activity is not estimated at constant prices.

1.1 Expenditure on the Gross Domestic Product, in Current Prices

Thousand Million Japanese yen

	1970	1971	1972	1973	1974	1975	1976	1977	1978	1979	1980
1 General government final consumption expenditure	5455	6421	7537	9336	12240	14890	16417	18243	19753	21486	23532
2 Private final consumption expenditure	38272	43160	49813	60229	72837	84568	95149	105789	115910	127066	136779
a Households	37828	42711	49328	59710	72201	83935	94486	104933	115059	126147	135671
b Private non-profit institutions serving households	445	450	485	520	636	633	663	857	851	919	1108
3 Gross capital formation	28616	28852	32822	42824	50091	48511	52950	57388	63421	72065	76788
a Increase in stocks	2573	1215	1299	1885	3396	494	1073	1211	1037	1817	1595
b Gross fixed capital formation	26043	27637	31524	40938	46695	48017	51877	56177	62384	70248	75193
Residential buildings	5102	5525	6923	9780	10678	11253	12972	13736	14960	16143	16205
Non-residential buildings	4220	4550	5152	6596	7564	8038	8416	9008	9874	12173	13832
Other construction and land improvement etc.	5444	5961	6962	9144	11467	12370	13203	14542	16594	18382	20063
Other	11277	11601	12487	15418	16986	16356	17286	18891	20956	23550	25093
4 Exports of goods and services	7926	9452	9779	11291	18258	18982	22582	24308	22729	25627	32887
5 Less: Imports of goods and services	6985	7254	7645	11261	19257	18919	21247	21267	19174	27629	35036
Equals: Gross Domestic Product	73285	80632	92306	112420	134169	148031	165851	184460	202638	218616	234949

Japan

1.2 Expenditure on the Gross Domestic Product, in Constant Prices

Thousand Million Japanese yen

	1970	1971	1972	1973	1974	1975	1976	1977	1978	1979	1980
					At constant prices of: 1975						
1 General government final consumption expenditure	11418	12031	12661	13290	13751	14680	15283	15878	16680	17392	17783
2 Private final consumption expenditure	64530	68319	74830	81820	81254	84546	87383	90693	94968	100606	101238
a Households	63622	67491	74042	81118	80575	83955	86841	90041	94346	99970	100532
b Private non-profit institutions serving households	908	828	788	702	679	592	542	653	622	636	706
3 Gross capital formation	44576	44350	48843	55884	52102	48534	50513	53011	57714	62132	62287
a Increase in stocks	3745	1782	1849	2449	3528	494	1051	1153	966	1809	1845
b Gross fixed capital formation	40831	42568	46994	53435	48574	48040	49462	51857	56748	60323	60442
Residential buildings	8661	9183	10777	12295	10931	11265	12109	12314	13198	12917	11658
Non-residential buildings	6828	7262	7899	8623	7756	8043	7886	8112	8680	9807	10158
Other construction and land improvement etc.	9799	10319	11456	12927	12412	12380	12384	13108	14308	14535	14332
Other	15543	15804	16862	19590	17475	16352	17083	18323	20562	23064	24294
4 Exports of goods and services	11327	13235	13924	14923	18305	19036	22690	25480	25480	26513	31440
5 Less: Imports of goods and services	14007	14662	16118	19972	20981	18981	20216	21226	22766	25737	23951
Equals: Gross Domestic Product	117844	123272	134140	145945	144430	147815	155653	163836	172076	180906	188797

1.3 Cost Components of the Gross Domestic Product

Thousand Million Japanese yen

	1970	1971	1972	1973	1974	1975	1976	1977	1978	1979	1980
1 Indirect taxes, net	4397	4808	5425	6709	7131	7529	8690	10421	11198	13258	14308
a Indirect taxes paid	5202	5712	6491	7889	9254	9736	10870	12890	13912	16188	17764
b Less: Subsidies received	805	904	1066	1180	2123	2207	2181	2469	2713	2930	3456
2 Consumption of fixed capital	9848	11063	12997	15495	18006	19313	21288	24034	26379	28939	31516
3 Compensation of employees paid by resident producers to:	31225	37096	43035	54081	68411	79648	90292	100867	108819	117682	128271
a Resident households	31201	37067	42997	54041	68379	79592	90220	100781	108689	117514	128027
b Rest of the world	24	29	38	40	32	56	72	86	130	168	244
4 Net operating surplus	27881	27414	31323	37421	40541	40871	45634	47723	54670	57724	60664
a Corporate and quasi-corporate enterprises	12734	11917	13388	14923	14401	14191	16473	17904	21890	21963	24864
b Private unincorporated enterprises	15147	15497	17935	22498	26140	26680	29160	29819	32780	35761	35800
c General government	...	...	...	...	...	...	...	...	...	...	...
Statistical discrepancy	-66	251	-473	-1286	80	670	-53	1415	1571	1012	190
Equals: Gross Domestic Product	73285	80632	92306	112420	134169	148031	165851	184460	202638	218616	234949

1.4 General Government Current Receipts and Disbursements

Thousand Million Japanese yen

	1970	1971	1972	1973	1974	1975	1976	1977	1978	1979	1980
					Receipts						
1 Property and entrepreneurial income	633	793	951	1252	1597	1945	2237	2627	3031	3671	4612
2 Taxes, fees and contributions	14466	16570	18830	23907	31057	33518	36797	42887	46716	54367	61353
a Indirect taxes	5202	5712	6491	7890	9254	9736	10870	12890	13912	16188	17764
b Direct taxes	6016	7044	7926	10664	14728	14092	15033	17114	18688	21885	25876
c Social security contributions	3165	3718	4300	5212	6910	9503	10684	12654	13880	16049	17452
d Compulsory fees, fines and penalties	83	96	112	141	165	188	210	230	236	244	262
3 Other current receipts	44	52	65	73	98	108	146	172	192	204	243
Total Current Receipts of General Government	15143	17416	19846	25232	32752	35571	39180	45686	49939	58243	66208
					Disbursements						
1 General government final consumption expenditure	5455	6421	7537	9336	12240	14890	16417	18243	19753	21486	23532
a Compensation of employees	4311	5105	6045	7539	10046	12446	13770	15245	16451	17702	19086
b Consumption of fixed capital	327	369	416	471	553	668	786	900	1053	1195	1348
c Purchases of goods and services, net	813	942	1069	1317	1630	1762	1845	2077	2224	2561	3068
d Less: Own account production of fixed assets	...	...	...	...	...	...	...	...	...	...	...
e Indirect taxes paid, net	5	6	8	10	12	15	17	21	25	28	30
2 Property income paid	458	540	721	1020	1298	1797	2569	3592	4599	5865	7530

Japan

1.4 General Government Current Receipts and Disbursements
(Continued)

Thousand Million Japanese yen

	1970	1971	1972	1973	1974	1975	1976	1977	1978	1979	1980
a Interest	442	522	688	978	1242	1735	2504	3525	4526	5787	7451
b Net land rent and royalties	16	19	32	42	56	62	65	67	73	78	79
3 Subsidies	805	904	1066	1180	2123	2207	2181	2469	2713	2930	3456
4 Other current transfers paid	3549	4090	4985	6065	8666	11996	14732	17219	20061	22688	25173
a Social security benefits and social assistance grants	3393	3881	4753	5791	8300	11485	14140	16547	19281	21801	24157
b Other	156	209	232	274	366	511	592	672	780	887	1016
5 Net saving	4876	5460	5537	7630	8424	4682	3281	4163	2814	5274	6518
Total Current Disbursements and Net Saving of General Government	15143	17416	19846	25232	32752	35571	39180	45686	49939	58243	66208

1.5 Current Income and Outlay of Corporate and Quasi-Corporate Enterprises, Summary

Thousand Million Japanese yen

	1970	1971	1972	1973	1974	1975	1976	1977	1978	1979	1980
					Receipts						
1 Net operating surplus	12734	11917	13388	14923	14401	14191	16473	17904	21890	21963	24864
2 Other property and entrepreneurial income received	11961	13967	16500	21020	28679	33249	36495	39018	39875	46625	60238
3 Current transfers received	783	872	933	1055	1364	1691	2129	2382	2532	2759	3184
Total Current Receipts	25478	26755	30820	36999	44444	49130	55097	59304	64297	71347	88286
					Disbursements						
1 Property and entrepreneurial income paid	15168	17678	20546	25994	35933	41180	44378	46682	46902	53630	70965
2 Direct taxes and other current payments to general government	3147	3446	3595	4878	7457	6757	6652	7758	8967	9472	11121
3 Other current transfers paid	969	1099	1204	1380	1693	2028	2498	2871	3156	3397	3913
4 Net saving	6194	4531	5475	4746	-639	-835	1569	1993	5272	4848	2287
Total Current Disbursements and Net Saving	25478	26755	30820	36999	44444	49130	55097	59304	64297	71347	88286

1.6 Current Income and Outlay of Households and Non-Profit Institutions

Thousand Million Japanese yen

	1970	1971	1972	1973	1974	1975	1976	1977	1978	1979	1980
					Receipts						
1 Compensation of employees	31272	37147	43078	54137	68489	79745	90393	100970	108904	117741	128241
a From resident producers	31201	37067	42997	54041	68379	79592	90220	100781	108689	117514	128027
b From rest of the world	71	80	81	95	110	154	173	189	215	227	214
2 Property and entrepreneurial income received	19819	20941	24185	30194	36787	39226	42671	44086	47107	51389	57509
3 Current transfers received	7248	8515	10188	12430	16378	21285	25153	29105	33294	37368	41416
a Social security benefits and social assistance grants received	3601	4114	5032	6141	8648	11896	14608	17203	19992	22547	25121
b Other	3648	4400	5157	6289	7730	9389	10545	11903	13302	14821	16295
Total Current Receipts	58339	66602	77452	96760	121654	140257	158217	174161	189304	206498	227166
					Disbursements						
1 Private final consumption expenditure	38272	43160	49813	60229	72837	84568	95149	105789	115910	127066	136779
2 Property income paid	1844	2145	2471	2988	4018	5017	5553	5832	5747	6210	8112
3 Direct taxes and other payments n.e.c. to general government	6117	7413	8743	11140	14345	17025	19274	22239	23837	28708	32469
a Social security contributions	3165	3718	4300	5212	6910	9503	10684	12654	13880	16049	17452
b Direct taxes	2912	3644	4381	5850	7354	7422	8472	9459	9833	12514	14862
c Fees, fines and penalties	40	50	62	77	81	100	118	127	124	145	155
4 Other current transfers paid	3597	4302	5062	6153	7520	9118	10260	11651	12922	14419	16012
5 Net saving	8509	9583	11363	16250	22935	24529	27981	28650	30889	30096	33795
Total Current Disbursements and Net Saving	58339	66602	77452	96760	121654	140257	158217	174161	189304	206498	227166

Japan

1.7 External Transactions on Current Account, Summary

Thousand Million Japanese yen

	1970	1971	1972	1973	1974	1975	1976	1977	1978	1979	1980
Payments to the Rest of the World
1 Imports of goods and services	6985	7254	7645	11261	19257	18919	21247	21267	19174	27629	35036
a Imports of merchandise c.i.f.	6025	6104	6379	9561	16827	16042	17957	17839	15849	23455	30113
b Other	960	1150	1266	1700	2430	2877	3290	3428	3325	4174	4923
2 Factor income paid to the rest of the world	503	552	592	820	1436	1430	1414	1346	1306	1998	2898
a Compensation of employees	23	30	37	39	32	57	72	86	130	168	244
b Property and entrepreneurial income paid	480	523	554	781	1404	1373	1341	1259	1176	1830	2654
3 Indirect taxes paid to supranational organizations	...	...	...	...	...	...	...	...	...	...	...
4 Current transfers to the rest of the world	75	98	106	81	94	115	129	151	183	252	342
5 Surplus of the nation on current transactions	744	2036	2077	11	-1285	-152	1117	2867	3504	-1896	-2481
Payments to the Rest of the World and Surplus of the Nation on Current Transactions	8308	9940	10419	12173	19502	20313	23907	25631	24167	27984	35794
Receipts From The Rest of the World
1 Exports of goods and services	7926	9452	9779	11291	18258	18982	22582	24308	22729	25627	32887
a Exports of merchandise f.o.b.	6873	8273	8542	9889	16190	16579	19800	21436	20144	22555	29022
b Other	1053	1179	1238	1403	2068	2403	2782	2872	2584	3072	3865
2 Factor income received from rest of the world	347	443	598	841	1189	1273	1257	1254	1376	2276	2820
a Compensation of employees	71	80	81	95	110	154	173	189	215	227	214
b Property and entrepreneurial income received	276	363	517	746	1079	1119	1084	1065	1162	2050	2606
3 Subsidies received from supranational organisations	...	...	...	...	...	...	...	...	...	...	...
4 Current transfers from rest of the world	35	45	42	41	55	59	68	70	62	80	87
Receipts from the Rest of the World on Current Transactions	8308	9940	10419	12173	19502	20313	23907	25631	24167	27984	35794

1.8 Capital Transactions of The Nation, Summary

Thousand Million Japanese yen

	1970	1971	1972	1973	1974	1975	1976	1977	1978	1979	1980
Finance of Gross Capital Formation
Gross saving	29426	30637	35372	44120	48726	47689	54120	58840	65354	69158	74116
1 Consumption of fixed capital	9848	11063	12997	15495	18006	19313	21288	24034	26379	28939	31516
a General government	327	369	416	471	553	668	786	900	1053	1197	1348
b Corporate and quasi-corporate enterprises	7146	7959	9353	11122	12617	12812	13582	15135	16197	17504	18731
c Other	2375	2735	3228	3902	4837	5833	6921	7999	9129	10238	11437
2 Net saving	19579	19574	22375	28626	30720	28376	32831	34806	38975	40218	42600
a General government	4876	5460	5537	7630	8424	4682	3281	4163	2814	5274	6518
b Corporate and quasi-corporate enterprises	6194	4531	5475	4746	-639	-835	1569	1993	5272	4848	2287
Public	161	-143	18	229	-432	-1418	-1031	-751	-464	-202	-86
Private	6033	4674	5457	4517	-207	583	2599	2744	5736	5050	2374
c Other	8509	9583	11363	16250	22935	24529	27981	28650	30889	30096	33795
Less: Surplus of the nation on current transactions	744	2036	2077	11	-1285	-152	1117	2867	3504	-1896	-2481
Statistical discrepancy	-66	251	-473	-1286	80	670	-53	1415	1571	1012	190
Finance of Gross Capital Formation	28616	28852	32822	42824	50091	48511	52950	57388	63421	72065	76788
Gross Capital Formation
Increase in stocks	2573	1215	1299	1885	3396	494	1073	1211	1037	1817	1595

Japan

1.8 Capital Transactions of The Nation, Summary (Continued)

Thousand Million Japanese yen

	1970	1971	1972	1973	1974	1975	1976	1977	1978	1979	1980
Gross fixed capital formation	26043	27637	31524	40938	46695	48017	51877	56177	62384	70248	75193
1 General government	3276	4061	5053	6370	7003	7841	8591	10274	12522	14025	14723
2 Corporate and quasi-corporate enterprises	15974	16200	17244	22177	25503	24575	24864	26899	29194	33385	37463
a Public	2614	3138	3820	4460	5078	5577	5966	6564	7577	7980	8196
b Private	13360	13062	13424	17717	20425	18998	18898	20335	21617	25405	29267
3 Other	6793	7376	9226	12392	14189	15601	18422	19004	20668	22838	23007
Gross Capital Formation	28617	28852	32823	42824	50091	48511	52950	57388	63421	72065	76788

1.9 Gross Domestic Product by Institutional Sectors of Origin

Thousand Million Japanese yen

	1970	1971	1972	1973	1974	1975	1976	1977	1978	1979	1980
Domestic Factor Incomes Originating											
1 General government	4311	5105	6045	7539	10046	12446	13770	15245	16451	17702	19086
2 Corporate and quasi-corporate enterprises	54195	58700	67429	82837	97409	105999	119716	130506	143798	154066	165877
3 Households and private unincorporated enterprises											
4 Non-profit institutions serving households	600	706	883	1125	1497	2074	2440	2839	3240	3639	3972
Subtotal: Domestic Factor Incomes	59106	64511	74357	91501	108952	120519	135926	148590	163489	175407	188935
Indirect taxes paid, net	4397	4808	5425	6709	7131	7529	8690	10421	11198	13258	14308
Consumption of fixed capital	9848	11063	12997	15495	18006	19313	21288	24034	26379	28939	31516
Statistical discrepancy	-66	251	-473	-1286	80	670	-53	1415	1571	1012	190
Gross Domestic Product	73285	80632	92306	112420	134169	148031	165851	184460	202638	218616	234949

1.10 Gross Domestic Product by Kind of Activity, in Current Prices

Thousand Million Japanese yen

	1970	1971	1972	1973	1974	1975	1976	1977	1978	1979	1980
1 Agriculture, hunting, forestry and fishing	4463	4253	5032	6667	7499	8130	8822	9310	9338	9508	8935
2 Mining and quarrying	621	635	661	821	945	776	840	963	1129	1267	1379
3 Manufacturing	26340	28357	31851	39457	45038	44250	50732	55286	60773	65847	71079
4 Electricity, gas and water	1557	1690	1790	1937	2151	3002	3585	4331	4858	4796	6825
5 Construction	5662	6514	7751	9830	11699	14324	15016	15806	18069	20148	21480
6 Wholesale and retail trade, restaurants and hotels [a]	10504	11295	13051	16070	20400	21904	24292	25735	26858	28144	29195
7 Transport, storage and communication	5022	5433	5824	6960	8100	9541	11113	13152	14185	15018	16188
8 Finance, insurance, real estate and business services	9309	10936	12788	15645	18224	20549	23121	26316	29728	32995	36967
9 Community, social and personal services [a]	7033	7928	9831	11392	13759	16251	18278	20439	23073	25839	28113
Total, Industries	70511	77042	88578	108779	127815	138727	155799	171338	188011	203562	220161
Producers of Government Services	4642	5480	6468	8020	10611	13128	14573	16166	17528	18927	20464
Other Producers	670	781	966	1221	1611	2210	2593	3001	3436	3874	4228
Subtotal	75822	83302	96012	118020	140037	154065	172965	190506	208975	226363	244854
Less: Imputed bank service charge	2970	3400	3743	4961	6588	7253	7773	8238	8667	9705	11019
Plus: Import duties	498	478	510	647	639	549	711	777	759	946	924
Plus: Value added tax	...	...	...	...	...	...	...	...	...	...	...
Plus: Other adjustments [b]	-66	251	-473	-1286	80	670	-53	1415	1571	1012	190
Equals: Gross Domestic Product	73285	80632	92306	112420	134169	148031	165851	184460	202638	218616	234949

a) Restaurants and hotels are included in item 'Community, social and personal services'.
b) Relating to inventory valuation adjustment.

1.11 Gross Domestic Product by Kind of Activity, in Constant Prices

Thousand Million Japanese yen

	1970	1971	1972	1973	1974	1975	1976	1977	1978	1979	1980
At constant prices of: 1975											
1 Agriculture, hunting, forestry and fishing	7188	6832	7792	8360	8216	8130	7716	7556	7622	7674	7368
2 Mining and quarrying	820	860	894	961	816	776	913	1004	1021	980	1049
3 Manufacturing	35142	37317	41288	47008	46085	44250	50139	53803	57752	63488	69462
4 Electricity, gas and water	2360	2646	2704	2692	2711	3002	3112	2927	3140	3439	3659
5 Construction	10957	11749	12999	14206	13030	14324	13746	13964	15262	15557	15259

Japan

1.11 Gross Domestic Product by Kind of Activity, in Constant Prices
(Continued)

Thousand Million Japanese yen

	1970	1971	1972	1973	1974	1975	1976	1977	1978	1979	1980
	\multicolumn{11}{c}{At constant prices of:1975}										
6 Wholesale and retail trade, restaurants and hotels [a]	15902	17158	19797	21568	21325	21904	23019	23968	25075	26596	27366
7 Transport, storage and communication	7381	7725	7887	8718	9307	9541	9914	9894	9819	10358	11946
8 Finance, insurance, real estate and business services	13649	15349	17878	19507	19027	20549	21459	23440	25227	26399	28119
9 Community, social and personal services [a]	14065	14568	16130	16518	16185	16251	16361	16873	17188	18675	19843
Total, Industries	107463	114203	127369	139537	136701	138727	146378	153430	162103	173165	184071
Producers of Government Services	10537	10885	11248	11686	12176	12955	13566	14023	14617	15171	15605
Other Producers	1609	1633	1759	1881	1934	2213	2319	2494	2691	2912	3020
Subtotal	119609	126721	140375	153104	150810	153894	162263	169947	179412	191247	202695
Less: Imputed bank service charge	4426	5106	6197	6901	6434	7253	7426	8129	8573	8902	9416
Plus: Import duties	1620	1470	1461	1605	703	549	714	857	1036	1068	792
Plus: Value added tax	...	...	...	...	...	...	...	...	...	...	...
Plus: Other adjustments	1041	187	-1499	-1862	-649	625	101	1161	201	-2507	-5274
Equals: Gross Domestic Product	117844	123272	134140	145945	144430	147815	155653	163836	172076	180906	188797

a) Restaurants and hotels are included in item 'Community, social and personal services'.

1.12 Relations Among National Accounting Aggregates

Thousand Million Japanese yen

	1970	1971	1972	1973	1974	1975	1976	1977	1978	1979	1980
Gross Domestic Product	73285	80632	92306	112420	134169	148031	165851	184460	202638	218616	234949
Plus: Net factor income received from abroad	-157	-110	6	21	-247	-157	-156	-92	70	278	-78
Factor income received	347	443	598	841	1189	1273	1257	1254	1376	2276	2820
Less: Factor income paid	503	552	592	820	1436	1430	1414	1346	1306	1998	2898
Equals: Gross National Product	73128	80522	92313	112441	133922	147874	165695	184368	202708	218894	234871
Less: Consumption of fixed capital	9848	11063	12997	15495	18006	19313	21288	24034	26379	28939	31516
Less: Net indirect taxes paid to supranational organisations [a]	-66	251	-473	-1286	80	670	-53	1415	1571	1012	190
Equals: National Income at Market Prices	63346	69209	79789	98232	115836	127891	144459	158919	174758	188943	203165
Plus: Net current transfers received from abroad	-40	-53	-64	-41	-39	-57	-62	-81	-121	-172	-254
Current transfers received	35	45	42	40	55	58	68	70	62	80	87
Less: Current transfers paid	75	98	106	81	94	115	129	151	183	252	342
Equals: National Disposable Income at Market Prices	63306	69156	79725	98191	115797	127834	144397	158838	174637	188771	202911
Less: Final consumption	43728	49582	57350	69566	85077	99458	111566	124032	135662	148553	160311
Equals: Net Saving	19579	19574	22375	28626	30720	28376	32831	34806	38975	40218	42600
Less: Surplus of the nation on current transactions	744	2036	2077	11	-1285	-152	1117	2867	3504	-1896	-2481
Statistical discrepancy	-66	251	-473	-1286	80	670	-53	1415	1571	1012	190
Equals: Net Capital Formation	18769	17789	19826	27329	32085	29198	31662	33354	37042	43126	45271

a) Relating to a statistical discrepancy.

2.1 General Government Final Consumption Expenditure by Function, in Current Prices

Thousand Million Japanese yen — Fiscal year beginning 1 April

	1970	1971	1972	1973	1974	1975	1976	1977	1978	1979	1980
1 General public services [a]	1556	1831	2147	2634	3527	4143	4577	5077	5470	5938	6464
2 Defence	560	654	752	886	1137	1285	1413	1578	1715	1882	2067
3 Public order and safety [a]	...	...	...	...	...	...	...	...	...	...	...
4 Education	2078	2424	2851	3504	4845	5745	6385	7013	7646	8272	8955
5 Health	256	314	335	462	576	628	656	752	717	794	907
6 Social security and welfare	219	265	327	437	629	724	813	903	994	1088	1205
7 Housing and community amenities	217	271	349	471	682	783	855	961	1057	1173	1382
8 Recreational, cultural and religious affairs	74	91	113	148	205	242	274	317	359	410	473
9 Economic services	675	775	900	1116	1508	1672	1817	1993	2140	2300	2537
10 Other functions	12	15	20	25	36	40	46	51	55	79	87
Total General Government Final Consumption Expenditure	5647	6639	7795	9680	13144	15262	16836	18645	20152	21937	24077

a) Item 'Public order and safety' is included in item 'General public services'.

Japan

2.2 General Government Final Consumption Expenditure by Function, in Constant Prices

Thousand Million Japanese yen — Fiscal year beginning 1 April

At constant prices of: 1975

	1970	1971	1972	1973	1974	1975	1976	1977	1978	1979	1980
1 General public services [a]	3210	3382	3547	3695	3763	4046	4205	4376	4595	4743	4856
2 Defence	1069	1143	1199	1205	1208	1264	1300	1370	1455	1504	1538
3 Public order and safety [a]	...	...	...	...	...	...	...	...	...	...	...
4 Education	4464	4600	4736	4836	5191	5617	5867	6061	6399	6614	6710
5 Health	494	553	533	627	604	601	588	634	594	634	678
6 Social security and welfare	433	473	528	595	659	697	738	771	831	862	895
7 Housing and community amenities	441	498	583	667	726	67	788	840	911	947	1020
8 Recreational, cultural and religious affairs	138	158	180	200	216	236	251	275	304	328	351
9 Economic services	1304	1364	1438	1518	1588	1619	1651	1706	1790	1815	1860
10 Other functions	26	29	34	35	38	39	42	44	46	64	66
Total General Government Final Consumption Expenditure	11578	12199	12777	13377	13992	14886	15430	16075	16925	17509	17973

a) Item 'Public order and safety' is included in item 'General public services'.

2.3 Total General Government Outlays by Function and Type

Thousand Million Japanese yen — Fiscal year beginning 1 April

	Final Consumption Expenditures Total	Compensation of Employees	Other	Subsidies	Other Current Transfers & Property Income	Total Current Disbursements	Gross Capital Formation	Other Capital Outlays	Total Outlays
1970									
1 General public services [a]	1556	1263	293	14	...	...	236	...	...
2 Defence	560	301	259	-	...	...	-	...	...
3 Public order and safety [a]	...	...	...	...	...	...	...	...	...
4 Education	2078	1689	389	2	...	...	448	...	...
5 Health	256	376	-120	16	...	...	95	...	...
6 Social security and welfare	219	201	18	2	...	...	76	...	...
7 Housing and community amenities	217	147	70	20	...	...	468	...	...
8 Recreation, culture and religion	74	38	35	4	...	...	75	...	...
9 Economic services	675	439	236	...	...	...	2062	...	...
10 Other functions	12	10	2	...	...	...	2	...	...
Total	5647	4464	1183	881	4172	10700	3462	461	14623
1971									
1 General public services [a]	1831	1488	343	22	...	...	280	...	...
2 Defence	654	351	303	-	...	...	-	...	...
3 Public order and safety [a]	...	...	...	...	...	...	...	...	...
4 Education	2424	1973	451	-	...	...	560	...	...
5 Health	314	448	-134	20	...	...	107	...	...
6 Social security and welfare	265	249	16	2	...	...	94	...	...
7 Housing and community amenities	271	185	86	33	...	...	688	...	...
8 Recreation, culture and religion	91	48	43	5	...	...	99	...	...
9 Economic services	775	513	262	...	...	...	2606	...	...
10 Other functions	15	13	2	...	...	...	2	...	...
Total	6639	5269	1370	930	4800	12370	4435	642	17452
1972									
1 General public services [a]	2147	1751	396	23	...	...	331	...	...
2 Defence	752	402	350	-	...	...	-	...	...
3 Public order and safety [a]	...	...	...	...	...	...	...	...	...
4 Education	2851	2326	525	-	...	...	650	...	...
5 Health	335	534	-199	25	...	...	119	...	...
6 Social security and welfare	327	316	11	2	...	...	109	...	...
7 Housing and community amenities	349	236	113	49	...	...	857	...	...
8 Recreation, culture and religion	113	61	52	6	...	...	117	...	...
9 Economic services	900	601	299	...	...	...	3328	...	...
10 Other functions	20	17	3	...	...	...	3	...	...
Total	7795	6242	1553	1053	6076	14923	5513	844	21280

Japan

2.3 Total General Government Outlays by Function and Type
(Continued)

Thousand Million Japanese yen — Fiscal year beginning 1 April

		Final Consumption Expenditures			Subsidies	Other Current Transfers & Property Income	Total Current Disbursements	Gross Capital Formation	Other Capital Outlays	Total Outlays
		Total	Compensation of Employees	Other						

1973

1	General public services [a]	2634	2155	479	26	...	...	389	...	...
2	Defence	886	490	396	-	...	...	-	...	...
3	Public order and safety [a]	...	...	...	...	...	...	...	...	...
4	Education	3504	2885	619	-	...	...	809	...	...
5	Health	462	664	-202	39	...	...	128	...	...
6	Social security and welfare	437	416	21	2	...	...	154	...	...
7	Housing and community amenities	471	313	158	62	...	...	1026	...	...
8	Recreation, culture and religion	148	81	67	6	...	...	143	...	...
9	Economic services	1116	744	372	...	...	...	3440	...	...
10	Other functions	25	21	4	...	...	...	5	...	...
	Total	9683	7768	1912	1533	7590	18803	6094	803	25700

1974

1	General public services [a]	3527	2939	588	29	...	...	499	...	...
2	Defence	1137	667	470	...	...	...	-	...	...
3	Public order and safety [a]	...	...	...	...	...	...	...	...	...
4	Education	4845	4079	766	-	...	...	1152	...	...
5	Health	576	926	-350	54	...	...	191	...	...
6	Social security and welfare	629	605	24	2	...	...	202	...	...
7	Housing and community amenities	682	446	236	93	...	...	1255	...	...
8	Recreation, culture and religion	205	118	87	10	...	...	172	...	...
9	Economic services	1508	1041	467	...	...	...	4016	...	...
10	Other functions	36	30	6	...	...	...	9	...	...
	Total	13144	10851	2293	2021	10870	26035	7496	1082	34613

1975

1	General public services [a]	4143	3472	671	33	...	...	534	...	...
2	Defence	1285	770	515	-	...	...	-	...	...
3	Public order and safety [a]	...	...	...	...	...	...	...	...	...
4	Education	5745	4853	892	-	...	...	1159	...	...
5	Health	628	1074	-446	69	...	...	217	...	...
6	Social security and welfare	724	717	7	83	...	...	175	...	...
7	Housing and community amenities	783	516	267	123	...	...	1527	...	...
8	Recreation, culture and religion	242	140	102	11	...	...	170	...	...
9	Economic services	1672	1169	503	...	...	...	4314	...	...
10	Other functions	41	34	7	...	...	...	8	...	...
	Total	15262	12746	2516	2111	14291	31663	8103	1088	40854

1976

1	General public services [a]	4577	3823	754	41	...	...	580	...	...
2	Defence	1413	874	539	-	...	...	-	...	...
3	Public order and safety [a]	...	...	...	...	...	...	...	...	...
4	Education	6385	5384	1001	-	...	...	1219	...	...
5	Health	656	1189	-533	92	...	...	221	...	...
6	Social security and welfare	813	813	-	11	...	...	158	...	...
7	Housing and community amenities	855	573	282	183	...	...	1523	...	...
8	Recreation, culture and religion	274	158	116	10	...	...	174	...	...
9	Economic services	1817	1266	551	...	...	...	4941	...	...
10	Other functions	46	38	8	...	...	...	6	...	...
	Total	16836	14119	2717	2315	18044	37194	8822	1144	47160

Japan

2.3 Total General Government Outlays by Function and Type
(Continued)

Thousand Million Japanese yen — Fiscal year beginning 1 April

		Final Consumption Expenditures			Subsidies	Other Current Transfers & Property Income	Total Current Disbursements	Gross Capital Formation	Other Capital Outlays	Total Outlays
		Total	Compensation of Employees	Other						

1977

		Total	Comp.	Other	Subs.	Other	Total Curr.	Gross Cap.	Other Cap.	Total
1	General public services a	5077	4201	876	77	...	...	660	...	...
2	Defence	1578	957	621	-	...	...	-	...	...
3	Public order and safety a	...	...	...	...	...	...	...	...	...
4	Education	7013	5892	1121	-	...	...	1408	...	...
5	Health	752	1322	-570	110	...	...	286	...	...
6	Social security and welfare	903	912	-9	11	...	...	183	...	...
7	Housing and community amenities	961	635	326	229	...	...	1901	...	...
8	Recreation, culture and religion	317	182	135	8	...	...	238	...	...
9	Economic services	1993	1368	625	...	...	...	6164	...	...
10	Other functions	51	43	8	...	...	...	10	...	...
	Total	18645	15511	3134	2562	21392	42601	10849	1528	54978

1978

		Total	Comp.	Other	Subs.	Other	Total Curr.	Gross Cap.	Other Cap.	Total
1	General public services a	5470	4485	985	74	...	...	835	...	...
2	Defence	1715	1025	689	-	...	...	-	...	...
3	Public order and safety a	...	...	...	...	...	...	...	...	...
4	Education	7646	6402	1244	1	...	...	1906	...	...
5	Health	717	1418	-701	125	...	...	375	...	...
6	Social security and welfare	994	993	1	26	...	...	243	...	...
7	Housing and community amenities	1057	697	360	258	...	...	2314	...	...
8	Recreation, culture and religion	359	204	155	10	...	...	351	...	...
9	Economic services	2140	1456	684	2370	...	...	7007	...	...
10	Other functions	55	46	9	...	...	...	13	...	...
	Total	20152	16725	3427	2864	25800	48815	13043	1889	63747

1979

		Total	Comp.	Other	Subs.	Other	Total Curr.	Gross Cap.	Other Cap.	Total
1	General public services a	5938	4862	1076	39	...	...	858	...	...
2	Defence	1882	1063	819	-	...	...	-	...	...
3	Public order and safety a	...	...	...	...	...	...	...	...	...
4	Education	8272	6878	1394	1	...	...	2004	...	...
5	Health	797	1529	-732	126	...	...	384	...	...
6	Social security and welfare	1088	1078	10	43	...	...	251	...	...
7	Housing and community amenities	1173	758	415	294	...	...	2544	...	...
8	Recreation, culture and religion	410	225	185	11	...	...	438	...	...
9	Economic services	2300	1538	762	2657	...	...	7651	...	...
10	Other functions	79	67	12	...	...	...	15	...	...
	Total	21937	17997	3940	3170	32485	54422	14145	2008	70575

1980

		Total	Comp.	Other	Subs.	Other	Total Curr.	Gross Cap.	Other Cap.	Total
1	General public services a	6464	5254	1210	47	...	...	854	...	...
2	Defence	2067	1133	934	-	...	...	-	...	...
3	Public order and safety a	...	...	...	...	...	...	...	...	...
4	Education	8955	7399	1556	1	...	...	1991	...	...
5	Health	907	1637	-730	149	...	...	416	...	...
6	Social security and welfare	1205	1173	32	126	...	...	296	...	...
7	Housing and community amenities	1382	825	557	190	...	...	2712	...	...
8	Recreation, culture and religion	473	250	223	11	...	...	458	...	...
9	Economic services	2537	1647	890	2988	...	...	8241	...	...
10	Other functions	87	74	14	...	...	...	18	...	...
	Total	24077	19392	4685	3512	37447	61525	14986	2483	78994

a) Item 'Public order and safety' is included in item 'General public services'.

Japan

2.5 Private Final Consumption Expenditure by Type, in Current Prices

Thousand Million Japanese yen

	1970	1971	1972	1973	1974	1975	1976	1977	1978	1979	1980
Final Consumption Expenditure of Resident Households											
1 Food, beverages and tobacco	11503	12468	13888	16375	20340	23782	26778	28772	30051	31336	34051
2 Clothing and footwear	2924	3402	3933	5242	6014	6785	7731	8047	8526	9060	9316
3 Gross rent, fuel and power	6134	7102	8134	9530	11104	13020	15067	17473	19654	21871	24719
4 Furniture, furnishings and household equipment and operation	2893	3127	3665	4676	5458	5313	6007	6485	6939	8047	8043
5 Medical care and health expenses	2979	3335	3948	4625	6009	7504	8502	9674	11093	12335	13372
6 Transport and communication	2935	3410	3982	5103	6521	7985	8673	9854	10756	11978	12698
7 Recreational, entertainment, education and cultural services	3484	3987	4749	5476	6425	7328	8428	9266	10172	11065	11945
8 Miscellaneous goods and services	4956	5764	6851	8399	10005	11890	12898	14890	17185	19498	20606
Total Final Consumption Expenditure in the Domestic Market by Households, of which	37807	42595	49150	59425	71875	83606	94084	104461	114376	125190	134750
a Durable goods	2350	2590	3169	3978	4455	4836	5372	5870	6295	7105	6697
b Semi-durable goods	5374	6216	7192	9340	10960	11822	13297	13926	14602	16010	16309
c Non-durable goods	14055	15328	17030	20246	25820	30234	33967	36810	38449	40809	45398
d Services	16029	18461	21759	25861	30640	36714	41448	47855	55030	61266	66347
Plus: Direct purchases abroad by resident households	131	194	253	358	415	425	515	606	798	1099	1089
Less: Direct purchases in the domestic market by non-resident households	110	79	75	73	89	96	113	134	115	141	167
Equals: Final Consumption Expenditure of Resident Households	37828	42711	49328	59710	72201	83935	94486	104933	115059	126147	135671
Final Consumption Expenditure of Private Non-profit Institutions Serving Households											
Equals: Final Consumption Expenditure of Private Non-profit Organisations Serving Households	445	450	485	520	636	633	663	857	851	919	1108
Private Final Consumption Expenditure	38272	43160	49813	60229	72837	84568	95149	105789	115910	127066	136779

2.6 Private Final Consumption Expenditure by Type, in Constant Prices

Thousand Million Japanese yen

	1970	1971	1972	1973	1974	1975	1976	1977	1978	1979	1980
At constant prices of: 1975											
Final Consumption Expenditure of Resident Households											
1 Food, beverages and tobacco	19640	20214	21830	23045	22724	23788	24483	24910	25183	25859	26381
2 Clothing and footwear	5301	5683	6269	6869	6435	6796	7243	7107	7285	7440	7259
3 Gross rent, fuel and power	9179	9873	10526	11441	12214	13021	13668	14405	15197	16067	16856
4 Furniture, furnishings and household equipment and operation	4921	5016	5714	6491	5702	5314	5877	6090	6370	7246	6776
5 Medical care and health expenses	4554	5040	5424	6274	6785	7504	7551	8091	8211	8858	9436
6 Transport and communication	5026	5492	5985	7084	7448	7985	7906	8084	8720	9130	8737
7 Recreational, entertainment, education and cultural services	5878	6331	7164	7661	7404	7328	7924	8264	8611	9160	9403
8 Miscellaneous goods and services	9140	9715	10885	11840	11491	11890	11810	12618	13941	15257	14954
Total Final Consumption Expenditure in the Domestic Market by Households, of which	63639	67363	73798	80705	80203	83626	86461	89568	93519	99017	99802
a Durable goods	3252	3566	4384	5263	4653	4837	5312	5731	6090	6787	6266
b Semi-durable goods	9319	10028	11153	12336	11751	11834	12604	12507	12703	13466	12953
c Non-durable goods	24005	24758	26722	28692	28915	30241	31262	32112	32805	33952	34454

Japan

2.6 Private Final Consumption Expenditure by Type, in Constant Prices
(Continued)

Thousand Million Japanese yen

At constant prices of: 1975

	1970	1971	1972	1973	1974	1975	1976	1977	1978	1979	1980
d Services	27062	29011	31539	34414	34885	36714	37283	39218	41922	44812	46129
Plus: Direct purchases abroad by resident households	174	256	361	514	471	425	483	586	921	1064	853
Less: Direct purchases in the domestic market by non-resident households	190	128	116	101	99	96	103	113	94	111	122
Equals: Final Consumption Expenditure of Resident Households	63622	67491	74042	81118	80575	83955	86841	90041	94346	99970	100532

Final Consumption Expenditure of Private Non-profit Institutions Serving Households

	1970	1971	1972	1973	1974	1975	1976	1977	1978	1979	1980
Equals: Final Consumption Expenditure of Private Non-profit Organisations Serving Households	908	828	788	702	679	592	542	653	622	636	706
Private Final Consumption Expenditure	64530	68319	74830	81820	81254	84546	87383	90693	94968	100606	101238

2.7 Gross Capital Formation by Type of Good and Owner, in Current Prices

Thousand Million Japanese yen

	1970					1971					1972			
	TOTAL	Total Private	Public Enterprises	General Government	TOTAL	Total Private	Public Enterprises	General Government	TOTAL	Total Private	Public Enterprises	General Government
Increase in stocks, total	2573	2634	-61	-	1215	1574	-360	-	1299	1495	-197	...
1 Goods producing industries	1467	...	...	...	852	...	...	...	517	...	...	...
a Materials and supplies	318	...	...	...	94	...	...	...	107	...	...	...
b Work in progress	631	...	...	...	292	...	...	...	429	...	...	...
c Livestock, except breeding stocks, dairy cattle, etc.	...	...	...	...	...	...	...	...	...	...	...	...
d Finished goods	519	...	...	...	466	...	...	...	-19	...	...	...
2 Wholesale and retail trade	1106	...	...	...	363	...	...	...	782	...	...	...
3 Other, except government stocks	...	...	...	...	...	...	...	...	...	...	...	...
4 Government stocks	...	...	...	...	...	...	...	...	...	...	...	...
Gross Fixed Capital Formation, Total	26043	20152	2614	3276	27637	20438	3138	4061	31524	22650	3820	5053
1 Residential buildings	5102	4746	355	...	5525	5079	445	...	6923	6450	474	...
2 Non-residential buildings	4220	...	...	...	4550	...	...	...	5152	...	...	...
3 Other construction	4609	...	...	...	5050	...	...	...	5900	...	...	...
4 Land improvement and plantation and orchard development	835	...	...	...	911	...	...	...	1062	...	...	...
5 Producers' durable goods	11278	...	...	...	11602	...	...	...	12487	...	...	...
a Transport equipment	3338	...	...	...	3354	...	...	...	3815	...	...	...
b Machinery and equipment	7940	...	...	...	8248	...	...	...	8672	...	...	...
6 Breeding stock, dairy cattle, etc.	...	...	...	...	...	...	...	...	...	...	...	...
Total Gross Capital Formation	28616	22787	2553	3276	28852	22012	2779	4061	32822	24146	3624	5053

	1973					1974					1975			
	TOTAL	Total Private	Public Enterprises	General Government	TOTAL	Total Private	Public Enterprises	General Government	TOTAL	Total Private	Public Enterprises	General Government
Increase in stocks, total	1885	2046	-161	...	3396	3275	121	-	494	257	237	-
1 Goods producing industries	1420	...	...	...	2982	...	...	...	54	...	...	...
a Materials and supplies	622	...	...	...	501	...	...	...	33	...	...	...
b Work in progress	686	...	...	...	603	...	...	...	56	...	...	...
c Livestock, except breeding stocks, dairy cattle, etc.	...	...	...	...	...	...	...	...	...	...	...	...
d Finished goods	112	...	...	...	1878	...	...	...	-35	...	...	...
2 Wholesale and retail trade	465	...	...	...	414	...	...	...	440	...	...	...
3 Other, except government stocks	...	...	...	...	...	...	...	...	...	...	...	...
4 Government stocks	...	...	...	...	...	...	...	...	...	...	...	...
Gross Fixed Capital Formation, Total	40938	30108	4460	6370	46695	34614	5078	7003	48017	34599	5577	7841
1 Residential buildings	9780	9294	487	...	10678	9954	724	-	11253	10428	825	-
2 Non-residential buildings	6596	...	...	...	7564	...	...	...	8038	...	...	...

Japan

2.7 Gross Capital Formation by Type of Good and Owner, in Current Prices
(Continued)

Thousand Million Japanese yen

	1973 TOTAL	1973 Total Private	1973 Public Enterprises	1973 General Government	1974 TOTAL	1974 Total Private	1974 Public Enterprises	1974 General Government	1975 TOTAL	1975 Total Private	1975 Public Enterprises	1975 General Government
3 Other construction	7758	...	...	...	9744	...	...	...	10922	...	...	...
4 Land improvement and plantation and orchard development	1386	...	...	...	1723	...	...	...	1448	...	...	...
5 Producers' durable goods	15418	...	...	...	16987	...	...	...	16355	...	...	...
a Transport equipment	4171	...	...	...	3737	...	...	...	3728	...	...	...
b Machinery and equipment	11247	...	...	...	13250	...	...	...	12627	...	...	...
6 Breeding stock, dairy cattle, etc.		...	...	...		...	...	...		...	...	...
Total Gross Capital Formation	42824	32155	4299	6370	50091	37888	5199	7003	48511	34856	5814	7841

	1976 TOTAL	1976 Total Private	1976 Public Enterprises	1976 General Government	1977 TOTAL	1977 Total Private	1977 Public Enterprises	1977 General Government	1978 TOTAL	1978 Total Private	1978 Public Enterprises	1978 General Government
Increase in stocks, total	1073	814	259	-	1211	818	392	-	1037	590	447	-
1 Goods producing industries	692	...	...	...	813	...	...	...	-491	...	...	...
a Materials and supplies	25	...	...	...	231	...	...	...	-148	...	...	...
b Work in progress	326	...	...	...	50	...	...	...	-320	...	...	...
c Livestock, except breeding stocks, dairy cattle, etc.	...	...	...	...	...	...	...	...	...	...	...	...
d Finished goods	341	...	...	...	532	...	...	...	-23	...	...	...
2 Wholesale and retail trade	381	...	...	...	397	...	...	...	1529	...	...	...
3 Other, except government stocks	...	...	...	...	...	...	...	...	...	...	...	...
4 Government stocks	...	...	...	...	...	...	...	...	...	...	...	...
Gross Fixed Capital Formation, Total	51877	37320	5966	8591	56177	39339	6564	10274	62384	42285	7577	12522
1 Residential buildings	12972	12164	808	...	13736	12883	853	...	14960	13945	1016	-
2 Non-residential buildings	8416	...	...	...	9008	...	...	...	9874	...	...	...
3 Other construction	11665	...	...	...	12864	...	...	...	14685	...	...	...
4 Land improvement and plantation and orchard development	1538	...	...	...	1678	...	...	...	1909	...	...	...
5 Producers' durable goods	17286	...	...	...	18891	...	...	...	20956	...	...	...
a Transport equipment	3751	...	...	...	4196	...	...	...	5097	...	...	...
b Machinery and equipment	13535	...	...	...	14695	...	...	...	15859	...	...	...
6 Breeding stock, dairy cattle, etc.		...	...	...		...	...	...		...	...	...
Total Gross Capital Formation	52950	38134	6225	8591	57388	40157	6956	10274	63421	42875	8025	12522

	1979 TOTAL	1979 Total Private	1979 Public Enterprises	1979 General Government	1980 TOTAL	1980 Total Private	1980 Public Enterprises	1980 General Government
Increase in stocks, total	1817	1648	169	-	1595	1896	-300	-
1 Goods producing industries	1272	...	...	...	2173	...	...	...
a Materials and supplies	667	...	...	...	-44	...	...	...
b Work in progress	415	...	...	...	1293	...	...	...
c Livestock, except breeding stocks, dairy cattle, etc.	...	...	...	...	...	...	...	...
d Finished goods	190	...	...	...	923	...	...	...
2 Wholesale and retail trade	545	...	...	...	-578	...	...	...
3 Other, except government stocks	...	...	...	...	...	...	...	...
4 Government stocks	...	...	...	...	...	...	...	...
Gross Fixed Capital Formation, Total	70248	48243	7980	14025	75193	52273	8196	14723
1 Residential buildings	16143	15228	917	-	16205	15318	887	...
2 Non-residential buildings	12173	...	...	...	13832	...	...	...

Japan

2.7 Gross Capital Formation by Type of Good and Owner, in Current Prices
(Continued)

Thousand Million Japanese yen

	1979 TOTAL	1979 Total Private	1979 Public Enterprises	1979 General Government	1980 TOTAL	1980 Total Private	1980 Public Enterprises	1980 General Government
3 Other construction	16276	...	...	...	17770	...	...	...
4 Land improvement and plantation and orchard development	2106	...	...	...	2293	...	...	...
5 Producers' durable goods	23549	...	...	...	25092	...	...	...
a Transport equipment	5902	...	...	...	6045	...	...	...
b Machinery and equipment	17647	...	...	...	19047	...	...	...
6 Breeding stock, dairy cattle, etc.		...	...	...		...	...	...
Total Gross Capital Formation	72065	49891	8149	14025	76788	54169	7896	14723

2.8 Gross Capital Formation by Type of Good and Owner, in Constant Prices

Thousand Million Japanese yen

	1970 TOTAL	1970 Total Private	1970 Public Enterprises	1970 General Government	1971 TOTAL	1971 Total Private	1971 Public Enterprises	1971 General Government	1972 TOTAL	1972 Total Private	1972 Public Enterprises	1972 General Government
				At constant prices of:1975								
Increase in stocks, total	3745	3817	-72	-	1782	2415	-633	-	1849	2190	-341	-
1 Goods producing industries	2143	...	...	...	1347	...	...	...	777	...	...	...
a Materials and supplies	515	...	...	...	184	...	...	...	175	...	...	...
b Work in progress	892	...	...	...	439	...	...	...	637	...	...	...
c Livestock, except breeding stocks, dairy cattle, etc.	...	...	...	...	...	...	...	...	...	...	...	...
d Finished goods	736	...	...	...	725	...	...	...	-35	...	...	...
2 Wholesale and retail trade	1602	...	...	...	434	...	...	...	1072	...	...	...
3 Other, except government stocks	...	...	...	...	...	...	...	...	...	...	...	...
4 Government stocks	...	...	...	...	...	...	...	...	...	...	...	...
Gross Fixed Capital Formation, Total	40831	31084	4365	5382	42569	30974	5102	6493	46994	33271	5974	7749
1 Residential buildings	8661	8068	594	-	9183	8451	732	-	10777	10035	742	-
2 Non-residential buildings	6828	...	...	...	7262	...	...	...	7899	...	...	...
3 Other construction	8323	...	...	...	8757	...	...	...	9716	...	...	...
4 Land improvement and plantation and orchard development	1476	...	...	...	1562	...	...	...	1740	...	...	...
5 Producers' durable goods	15543	...	...	...	15804	...	...	...	16862	...	...	...
a Transport equipment	4435	...	...	...	4407	...	...	...	4921	...	...	...
b Machinery and equipment	11108	...	...	...	11398	...	...	...	11942	...	...	...
6 Breeding stock, dairy cattle, etc.	...	...	...	...	...	...	...	...	...	...	...	...
Total Gross Capital Formation	44576	34901	4293	5382	44350	33389	4469	6493	48843	35461	5633	7749

	1973 TOTAL	1973 Total Private	1973 Public Enterprises	1973 General Government	1974 TOTAL	1974 Total Private	1974 Public Enterprises	1974 General Government	1975 TOTAL	1975 Total Private	1975 Public Enterprises	1975 General Government
				At constant prices of:1975								
Increase in stocks, total	2449	2682	-233	-	3528	3522	6	-	494	257	237	-
1 Goods producing industries	1887	...	...	...	3107	...	...	...	54	...	...	...
a Materials and supplies	942	...	...	...	554	...	...	...	33	...	...	...
b Work in progress	863	...	...	...	676	...	...	...	56	...	...	...
c Livestock, except breeding stocks, dairy cattle, etc.	...	...	...	...	...	...	...	...	...	...	...	...
d Finished goods	81	...	...	...	1877	...	...	...	-35	...	...	...
2 Wholesale and retail trade	562	...	...	...	421	...	...	...	440	...	...	...
3 Other, except government stocks	...	...	...	...	...	...	...	...	...	...	...	...
4 Government stocks	...	...	...	...	...	...	...	...	...	...	...	...
Gross Fixed Capital Formation, Total	53435	38608	6148	8679	48574	35762	5390	7421	48040	34619	5580	7841
1 Residential buildings	12295	11661	633	-	10931	10183	748	-	11265	10439	826	-
2 Non-residential buildings	8623	...	...	...	7756	...	...	...	8043	...	...	...

Japan

2.8 Gross Capital Formation by Type of Good and Owner, in Constant Prices
(Continued)

Thousand Million Japanese yen

	1973				1974				1975			
	TOTAL	Total Private	Public Enterprises	General Government	TOTAL	Total Private	Public Enterprises	General Government	TOTAL	Total Private	Public Enterprises	General Government
				At constant prices of:1975								
3 Other construction	10978	...	...	...	10534	...	...	...	10931	...	...	...
4 Land improvement and plantation and orchard development	1949	...	...	...	1878	...	...	...	1449	...	...	...
5 Producers' durable goods	19590	...	...	...	17476	...	...	...	16351	...	...	...
a Transport equipment	5173	...	...	...	3901	...	...	...	3727	...	...	...
b Machinery and equipment	14418	...	...	...	13575	...	...	...	12624	...	...	...
6 Breeding stock, dairy cattle, etc.	...	...	...	...	...	...	...	...	...	...	...	...
Total Gross Capital Formation	55884	41289	5915	8679	52102	39285	5396	7421	48534	34875	5817	7841

	1976				1977				1978			
	TOTAL	Total Private	Public Enterprises	General Government	TOTAL	Total Private	Public Enterprises	General Government	TOTAL	Total Private	Public Enterprises	General Government
				At constant prices of:1975								
Increase in stocks, total	1051	814	237	-	1153	816	337	-	966	548	417	-
1 Goods producing industries	688	...	...	...	798	...	...	...	-408	...	...	...
a Materials and supplies	23	...	...	...	226	...	...	...	-146	...	...	...
b Work in progress	328	...	...	...	70	...	...	...	-244	...	...	...
c Livestock, except breeding stocks, dairy cattle, etc.	...	...	...	...	...	...	...	...	...	...	...	...
d Finished goods	337	...	...	...	501	...	...	...	-18	...	...	...
2 Wholesale and retail trade	363	...	...	...	355	...	...	...	1373	...	...	...
3 Other, except government stocks	...	...	...	...	...	...	...	...	...	...	...	...
4 Government stocks	...	...	...	...	...	...	...	...	...	...	...	...
Gross Fixed Capital Formation, Total	49462	35695	5646	8121	51857	36492	5982	9383	56748	38906	6765	11077
1 Residential buildings	12109	11356	754	-	12314	11549	765	-	13198	12309	889	-
2 Non-residential buildings	7885	...	...	...	8112	...	...	...	8680	...	...	...
3 Other construction	10939	...	...	...	11600	...	...	...	12660	...	...	...
4 Land improvement and plantation and orchard development	1445	...	...	...	1508	...	...	...	1648	...	...	...
5 Producers' durable goods	17083	...	...	...	18323	...	...	...	20563	...	...	...
a Transport equipment	3679	...	...	...	4115	...	...	...	4967	...	...	...
b Machinery and equipment	13404	...	...	...	14208	...	...	...	15596	...	...	...
6 Breeding stock, dairy cattle, etc.	...	...	...	...	...	...	...	...	...	...	...	...
Total Gross Capital Formation	50513	36509	5883	8121	53011	37308	6319	9383	57714	39455	7182	11077

	1979				1980			
	TOTAL	Total Private	Public Enterprises	General Government	TOTAL	Total Private	Public Enterprises	General Government
				At constant prices of:1975				
Increase in stocks, total	1809	1695	115	-	1845	2074	-228	-
1 Goods producing industries	1241	...	...	...	2200	...	...	...
a Materials and supplies	613	...	...	...	95	...	...	...
b Work in progress	439	...	...	...	1188	...	...	...
c Livestock, except breeding stocks, dairy cattle, etc.	...	...	...	...	...	...	...	...
d Finished goods	188	...	...	...	917	...	...	...
2 Wholesale and retail trade	569	...	...	...	-355	...	...	...
3 Other, except government stocks	...	...	...	...	...	...	...	...
4 Government stocks	...	...	...	...	...	...	...	...
Gross Fixed Capital Formation, Total	60323	41920	6797	11607	60442	42691	6559	11192
1 Residential buildings	12917	12181	736	-	11658	11012	646	-
2 Non-residential buildings	9807	...	...	...	10158	...	...	...

Japan

2.8 Gross Capital Formation by Type of Good and Owner, in Constant Prices
(Continued)

Thousand Million Japanese yen

	1979				1980			
	TOTAL	Total Private	Public Enterprises	General Government	TOTAL	Total Private	Public Enterprises	General Government
				At constant prices of:1975				
3 Other construction	12866	...	...	...	12682	...	...	...
4 Land improvement and plantation and orchard development	1669	...	...	...	1650	...	...	...
5 Producers' durable goods	23064	...	...	...	24294	...	...	...
a Transport equipment	5728	...	...	...	5717	...	...	...
b Machinery and equipment	17335	...	...	...	18578	...	...	...
6 Breeding stock, dairy cattle, etc.	...	...	...	...	...	...	...	...
Total Gross Capital Formation	62132	43614	6911	11607	62287	44764	6331	11192

2.9 Gross Capital Formation by Kind of Activity of Owner, ISIC Major Divisions, in Current Prices

Thousand Million Japanese yen

	1970			1971			1972			1973		
	Total Gross Capital Formation	Increase in Stocks	Gross Fixed Capital Formation	Total Gross Capital Formation	Increase in Stocks	Gross Fixed Capital Formation	Total Gross Capital Formation	Increase in Stocks	Gross Fixed Capital Formation	Total Gross Capital Formation	Increase in Stocks	Gross Fixed Capital Formation
					All Producers							
1 Agriculture, hunting, fishing and forestry	...	...	1266	...	...	1332	...	...	1365	...	...	2289
2 Mining and quarrying	...	...	217	...	...	190	...	...	204	...	...	244
3 Manufacturing	...	...	6481	...	...	6211	...	...	5914	...	...	7862
4 Electricity, gas and water	...	...	913	...	...	1087	...	...	1210	...	...	1560
5 Construction	...	...	604	...	...	726	...	...	889	...	...	1189
6 Wholesale and retail trade, restaurants and hotels [a]	2667	1129	1539	2496	916	1580	3390	1365	2025	5102	2067	3035
7 Transport, storage and communication	...	...	1270	...	...	1449	...	...	1609	...	...	1618
8 Finance, insurance, real estate and business services	...	...	5226	...	...	5631	...	...	7018	...	...	9587
9 Community, social and personal services [a]	...	...	1528	...	...	1699	...	...	2041	...	...	2491
Statistical discrepancy	...	...	-48	...	...	-24	...	...	170	...	...	625
Total Industries	...	...	18995	...	...	19883	...	...	22446	...	...	30500
Producers of Government Services	...	-41	...	7674	-225	7898	9460	-24	9484	10584	-39	10623
Private Non-Profit Institutions Serving Households	...	...	...	...	...	...	...	...	...	...	...	...
Total	...	3041	...	29895	1873	28022	35093	1848	33246	46489	3600	42889

	1974			1975			1976		
	Total Gross Capital Formation	Increase in Stocks	Gross Fixed Capital Formation	Total Gross Capital Formation	Increase in Stocks	Gross Fixed Capital Formation	Total Gross Capital Formation	Increase in Stocks	Gross Fixed Capital Formation
				All Producers					
1 Agriculture, hunting, fishing and forestry	...	...	2153	...	...	2465	...	...	3158
2 Mining and quarrying	...	...	236	...	...	219	...	...	156
3 Manufacturing	...	...	9668	...	...	7116	...	...	7626
4 Electricity, gas and water	...	...	1651	...	...	1820	...	...	2157
5 Construction	...	...	1107	...	...	1041	...	...	1090
6 Wholesale and retail trade, restaurants and hotels [a]	4278	1085	3193	4431	1463	2968	4623	1783	2840
7 Transport, storage and communication	...	...	1763	...	...	1679	...	...	1575
8 Finance, insurance, real estate and business services	...	...	10566	...	...	11377	...	...	13181
9 Community, social and personal services [a]	...	...	2776	...	...	2903	...	...	2990
Statistical discrepancy	...	...	147	...	...	-415	...	...	-540
Total Industries	...	...	33259	...	...	31171	...	...	34231
Producers of Government Services	12981	219	12761	14389	413	13976	15270	345	14926
Private Non-Profit Institutions Serving Households	...	...	...	...	...	...	...	...	...
Total	50310	5201	45109	47953	2242	45711	52979	3093	49886

a) Restaurants and hotels are included in item 'Community, social and personal services'.

Japan

2.13 Stocks of Reproducible Fixed Assets, by Type of Good and Owner, in Current Prices

Thousand Million Japanese yen

	TOTAL Gross	TOTAL Net	Total Private Gross	Total Private Net	Public Enterprises Gross	Public Enterprises Net	General Government Gross	General Government Net
1970								
1 Residential buildings	...	20678	...	...	...	...	...	...
2 Non-residential buildings	...	23631	...	...	...	...	...	...
3 Other construction	...	28412	...	...	...	...	...	...
4 Land improvement and plantation and orchard development [a]	...	...	...	...	...	...	...	...
5 Producers' durable goods	...	25396	...	...	...	...	...	...
a Transport equipment	...	4774	...	...	...	...	...	...
b Machinery and equipment	...	20622	...	...	...	...	...	...
6 Breeding stock, dairy cattle, etc.	...		...	...	...	...	...	...
Total	...	98117	...	64230	...	11891	...	21996
1971								
1 Residential buildings	...	24841	...	...	...	...	...	...
2 Non-residential buildings	...	27296	...	...	...	...	...	...
3 Other construction	...	33500	...	...	...	...	...	...
4 Land improvement and plantation and orchard development [a]	...	...	...	...	...	...	...	...
5 Producers' durable goods	...	30759	...	...	...	...	...	...
a Transport equipment	...	6525	...	...	...	...	...	...
b Machinery and equipment	...	24230	...	...	...	...	...	...
6 Breeding stock, dairy cattle, etc.	...		...	...	...	...	...	...
Total	...	116396	...	76552	...	13979	...	25866
1972								
1 Residential buildings	...	36402	...	...	...	...	...	...
2 Non-residential buildings	...	34611	...	...	...	...	...	...
3 Other construction	...	41269	...	...	...	...	...	...
4 Land improvement and plantation and orchard development [a]	...	...	...	...	...	...	...	...
5 Producers' durable goods	...	36324	...	...	...	...	...	...
a Transport equipment	...	8215	...	...	...	...	...	...
b Machinery and equipment	...	28109	...	...	...	...	...	...
6 Breeding stock, dairy cattle, etc.	...		...	...	...	...	...	...
Total	...	148606	...	98424	...	17647	...	32536
1973								
1 Residential buildings	...	50859	...	...	...	...	...	...
2 Non-residential buildings	...	48139	...	...	...	...	...	...
3 Other construction	...	59533	...	...	...	...	...	...
4 Land improvement and plantation and orchard development [a]	...	...	...	...	...	...	...	...
5 Producers' durable goods	...	48998	...	...	...	...	...	...
a Transport equipment	...	10715	...	...	...	...	...	...
b Machinery and equipment	...	38283	...	...	...	...	...	...
6 Breeding stock, dairy cattle, etc.	...		...	...	...	...	...	...
Total	...	207529	...	136873	...	25166	...	45490
1974								
1 Residential buildings	...	60675	...	...	...	...	...	...
2 Non-residential buildings	...	58935	...	...	...	...	...	...
3 Other construction	...	78212	...	...	...	...	...	...
4 Land improvement and plantation and orchard development [a]	...	...	...	...	...	...	...	...
5 Producers' durable goods	...	62122	...	...	...	...	...	...
a Transport equipment	...	12366	...	...	...	...	...	...
b Machinery and equipment	...	49757	...	...	...	...	...	...
6 Breeding stock, dairy cattle, etc.	...		...	...	...	...	...	...
Total	...	259944	...	169811	...	31846	...	58287

Japan

2.13 Stocks of Reproducible Fixed Assets, by Type of Good and Owner, in Current Prices
(Continued)

Thousand Million Japanese yen

		TOTAL Gross	TOTAL Net	Total Private Gross	Total Private Net	Public Enterprises Gross	Public Enterprises Net	General Government Gross	General Government Net
	1975								
1	Residential buildings	...	68143	...	...	...	...	...	...
2	Non-residential buildings	...	64950	...	...	...	...	...	...
3	Other construction	...	87982	...	...	...	...	...	...
4	Land improvement and plantation and orchard development [a]	...	...	...	...	...	...	...	...
5	Producers' durable goods	...	64598	...	...	...	...	...	...
a	Transport equipment	...	12805	...	...	...	...	...	...
b	Machinery and equipment	...	51792	...	...	...	...	...	...
6	Breeding stock, dairy cattle, etc.	...		...	...	...	...	...	...
	Total	...	285672	...	185540	...	35037	...	65095
	1976								
1	Residential buildings	...	81451	...	...	...	...	...	...
2	Non-residential buildings	...	74852	...	...	...	...	...	...
3	Other construction	...	103020	...	...	...	...	...	...
4	Land improvement and plantation and orchard development [a]	...	...	...	...	...	...	...	...
5	Producers' durable goods	...	69033	...	...	...	...	...	...
a	Transport equipment	...	12851	...	...	...	...	...	...
b	Machinery and equipment	...	56182	...	...	...	...	...	...
6	Breeding stock, dairy cattle, etc.	...		...	...	...	...	...	...
	Total	...	328356	...	211865	...	40593	...	75898
	1977								
1	Residential buildings	...	89929	...	...	...	...	...	...
2	Non-residential buildings	...	81713	...	...	...	...	...	...
3	Other construction	...	117596	...	...	...	...	...	...
4	Land improvement and plantation and orchard development [a]	...	...	...	...	...	...	...	...
5	Producers' durable goods	...	72143	...	...	...	...	...	...
a	Transport equipment	...	13215	...	...	...	...	...	...
b	Machinery and equipment	...	58928	...	...	...	...	...	...
6	Breeding stock, dairy cattle, etc.	...		...	...	...	...	...	...
	Total	...	361381	...	229738	...	44820	...	86823
	1978								
1	Residential buildings	...	100675	...	...	...	...	...	...
2	Non-residential buildings	...	90212	...	...	...	...	...	...
3	Other construction	...	134998	...	...	...	...	...	...
4	Land improvement and plantation and orchard development [a]	...	...	...	...	...	...	...	...
5	Producers' durable goods	...	75653	...	...	...	...	...	...
a	Transport equipment	...	14051	...	...	...	...	...	...
b	Machinery and equipment	...	61601	...	...	...	...	...	...
6	Breeding stock, dairy cattle, etc.	...		...	...	...	...	...	...
	Total	...	401538	...	250571	...	50328	...	100639
	1979								
1	Residential buildings	...	121750	...	...	...	...	...	...
2	Non-residential buildings	...	105894	...	...	...	...	...	...
3	Other construction	...	159958	...	...	...	...	...	...
4	Land improvement and plantation and orchard development [a]	...	...	...	...	...	...	...	...
5	Producers' durable goods	...	81903	...	...	...	...	...	...
a	Transport equipment	...	15565	...	...	...	...	...	...
b	Machinery and equipment	...	66339	...	...	...	...	...	...
6	Breeding stock, dairy cattle, etc.	...		...	...	...	...	...	...
	Total	...	469505	...	291410	...	58517	...	119579

Japan

2.13 Stocks of Reproducible Fixed Assets, by Type of Good and Owner, in Current Prices
(Continued)

Thousand Million Japanese yen

		TOTAL Gross	TOTAL Net	Total Private Gross	Total Private Net	Public Enterprises Gross	Public Enterprises Net	General Government Gross	General Government Net
				1980					
1	Residential buildings	...	132301	...	...	...	...	...	...
2	Non-residential buildings	...	118916	...	...	...	...	...	...
3	Other construction	...	183967	...	...	...	...	...	...
4	Land improvement and plantation and orchard development [a]	...	...	...	...	...	...	...	...
5	Producers' durable goods	...	91793	...	...	...	...	...	...
	a Transport equipment	...	17283	...	...	...	...	...	...
	b Machinery and equipment	...	74511	...	...	...	...	...	...
6	Breeding stock, dairy cattle, etc.	...		...	...	...	...	...	...
	Total	...	526977	...	323314	...	65681	...	137983

a) Item 'Land improvement and plantation and orchard development' is excluded from this table.

2.14 Stocks of Reproducible Fixed Assets, by Type of Good and Owner, in Constant Prices

Thousand Million Japanese yen

		TOTAL Gross	TOTAL Net	Total Private Gross	Total Private Net	Public Enterprises Gross	Public Enterprises Net	General Government Gross	General Government Net
				At constant prices of:1975					
				1970					
1	Residential buildings	...	35514	...	...	...	...	...	...
2	Non-residential buildings	...	40106	...	...	...	...	...	...
3	Other construction	...	50628	...	...	...	...	...	...
4	Land improvement and plantation and orchard development [a]	...	...	...	...	...	...	...	...
5	Producers' durable goods	...	35785	...	...	...	...	...	...
	a Transport equipment	...	6599	...	...	...	...	...	...
	b Machinery and equipment	...	29186	...	...	...	...	...	...
6	Breeding stock, dairy cattle, etc.	...		...	...	...	...	...	...
	Total	...	162033	...	...	...	...	...	38515
				1971					
1	Residential buildings	...	41606	...	...	...	...	...	...
2	Non-residential buildings	...	45052	...	...	...	...	...	...
3	Other construction	...	57181	...	...	...	...	...	...
4	Land improvement and plantation and orchard development [a]	...	...	...	...	...	...	...	...
5	Producers' durable goods	...	43243	...	...	...	...	...	...
	a Transport equipment	...	8830	...	...	...	...	...	...
	b Machinery and equipment	...	34413	...	...	...	...	...	...
6	Breeding stock, dairy cattle, etc.	...		...	...	...	...	...	...
	Total	...	187082	...	...	...	...	...	43335
				1972					
1	Residential buildings	...	48616	...	...	...	...	...	...
2	Non-residential buildings	...	50506	...	...	...	...	...	...
3	Other construction	...	64513	...	...	...	...	...	...
4	Land improvement and plantation and orchard development [a]	...	...	...	...	...	...	...	...
5	Producers' durable goods	...	50409	...	...	...	...	...	...
	a Transport equipment	...	10999	...	...	...	...	...	...
	b Machinery and equipment	...	39409	...	...	...	...	...	...
6	Breeding stock, dairy cattle, etc.	...		...	...	...	...	...	...
	Total	...	214043	...	...	...	...	...	49253

Japan

2.14 Stocks of Reproducible Fixed Assets, by Type of Good and Owner, in Constant Prices
(Continued)

Thousand Million Japanese yen

		TOTAL Gross	TOTAL Net	Total Private Gross	Total Private Net	Public Enterprises Gross	Public Enterprises Net	General Government Gross	General Government Net
				At constant prices of: 1975					
				1973					
1	Residential buildings	...	56111	...	...	...	...	...	...
2	Non-residential buildings	...	56180	...	...	...	...	...	...
3	Other construction	...	72787	...	...	...	...	...	...
4	Land improvement and plantation and orchard development [a]	...	...	...	...	...	...	...	...
5	Producers' durable goods	...	58207	...	...	...	...	...	...
	a Transport equipment	...	12761	...	...	...	...	...	...
	b Machinery and equipment	...	45446	...	...	...	...	...	...
6	Breeding stock, dairy cattle, etc.	...		...	...	...	...	...	...
	Total	...	243285	...	...	...	...	...	55277
				1974					
1	Residential buildings	...	62207	...	...	...	...	...	...
2	Non-residential buildings	...	60598	...	...	...	...	...	...
3	Other construction	...	80301	...	...	...	...	...	...
4	Land improvement and plantation and orchard development [a]	...	...	...	...	...	...	...	...
5	Producers' durable goods	...	62394	...	...	...	...	...	...
	a Transport equipment	...	12908	...	...	...	...	...	...
	b Machinery and equipment	...	49485	...	...	...	...	...	...
6	Breeding stock, dairy cattle, etc.	...		...	...	...	...	...	...
	Total	...	265501	...	...	...	...	...	59988
				1975					
1	Residential buildings	...	68143	...	...	...	...	...	...
2	Non-residential buildings	...	64950	...	...	...	...	...	...
3	Other construction	...	87982	...	...	...	...	...	...
4	Land improvement and plantation and orchard development [a]	...	...	...	...	...	...	...	...
5	Producers' durable goods	...	64598	...	...	...	...	...	...
	a Transport equipment	...	12805	...	...	...	...	...	...
	b Machinery and equipment	...	51792	...	...	...	...	...	...
6	Breeding stock, dairy cattle, etc.	...		...	...	...	...	...	...
	Total	...	285672	...	...	...	...	...	65095
				1976					
1	Residential buildings	...	74413	...	...	...	...	...	...
2	Non-residential buildings	...	68845	...	...	...	...	...	...
3	Other construction	...	95423	...	...	...	...	...	...
4	Land improvement and plantation and orchard development [a]	...	...	...	...	...	...	...	...
5	Producers' durable goods	...	66873	...	...	...	...	...	...
	a Transport equipment	...	12666	...	...	...	...	...	...
	b Machinery and equipment	...	54208	...	...	...	...	...	...
6	Breeding stock, dairy cattle, etc.	...		...	...	...	...	...	...
	Total	...	305554	...	...	...	...	...	70193
				1977					
1	Residential buildings	...	80209	...	...	...	...	...	...
2	Non-residential buildings	...	72602	...	...	...	...	...	...
3	Other construction	...	103108	...	...	...	...	...	...
4	Land improvement and plantation and orchard development [a]	...	...	...	...	...	...	...	...
5	Producers' durable goods	...	69765	...	...	...	...	...	...
	a Transport equipment	...	12900	...	...	...	...	...	...
	b Machinery and equipment	...	56866	...	...	...	...	...	...
6	Breeding stock, dairy cattle, etc.	...		...	...	...	...	...	...
	Total	...	325684	...	...	...	...	...	76197

Japan

2.14 Stocks of Reproducible Fixed Assets, by Type of Good and Owner, in Constant Prices
(Continued)

Thousand Million Japanese yen

	TOTAL Gross	TOTAL Net	Total Private Gross	Total Private Net	Public Enterprises Gross	Public Enterprises Net	General Government Gross	General Government Net
	\multicolumn{8}{c}{At constant prices of: 1975}							
	\multicolumn{8}{c}{**1978**}							
1 Residential buildings	...	86305	...	...	...	...	...	...
2 Non-residential buildings	...	76616	...	...	...	...	...	...
3 Other construction	...	111477	...	...	...	...	...	...
4 Land improvement and plantation and orchard development [a]	...	...	...	...	...	...	...	...
5 Producers' durable goods	...	74057	...	...	...	...	...	...
a Transport equipment	...	13822	...	...	...	...	...	...
b Machinery and equipment	...	60236	...	...	...	...	...	...
6 Breeding stock, dairy cattle, etc.	...		...	...	...	...	...	...
Total	...	348456	...	...	...	...	...	83443
	\multicolumn{8}{c}{**1979**}							
1 Residential buildings	...	91742	...	...	...	...	...	...
2 Non-residential buildings	...	81580	...	...	...	...	...	...
3 Other construction	...	119886	...	...	...	...	...	...
4 Land improvement and plantation and orchard development [a]	...	...	...	...	...	...	...	...
5 Producers' durable goods	...	79873	...	...	...	...	...	...
a Transport equipment	...	15237	...	...	...	...	...	...
b Machinery and equipment	...	64636	...	...	...	...	...	...
6 Breeding stock, dairy cattle, etc.	...		...	...	...	...	...	...
Total	...	373080	...	...	...	...	...	90963
	\multicolumn{8}{c}{**1980**}							
1 Residential buildings	...	95577	...	...	...	...	...	...
2 Non-residential buildings	...	86577	...	...	...	...	...	...
3 Other construction	...	127851	...	...	...	...	...	...
4 Land improvement and plantation and orchard development [a]	...	...	...	...	...	...	...	...
5 Producers' durable goods	...	85228	...	...	...	...	...	...
a Transport equipment	...	16250	...	...	...	...	...	...
b Machinery and equipment	...	68978	...	...	...	...	...	...
6 Breeding stock, dairy cattle, etc.	...		...	...	...	...	...	...
Total	...	395233	...	...	...	...	...	97849

a) Item 'Land improvement and plantation and orchard development' is excluded from this table.

2.17 Exports and Imports of Goods and Services, Detail

Thousand Million Japanese yen

	1970	1971	1972	1973	1974	1975	1976	1977	1978	1979	1980
	\multicolumn{11}{c}{**Exports of Goods and Services**}										
1 Exports of merchandise, f.o.b. [a]	6873	8273	8542	9889	16190	16579	19800	21436	20144	22555	29022
2 Transport and communication	544	681	717	862	1339	1518	1808	1751	1533	1827	2447
a In respect of merchandise imports	343	452	456	524	840	928	1129	1073	913	1122	1619
b Other	202	229	262	339	500	589	680	679	620	705	828
3 Insurance service charges	85	101	115	121	176	233	282	299	271	215	71
a In respect of merchandise imports	19	24	25	23	38	40	50	51	46	64	58
b Other	66	77	91	98	138	192	232	248	225	150	13
4 Other commodities	148	169	184	230	352	433	434	533	513	720	938
5 Adjustments of merchandise exports to change-of-ownership basis [a]	...	...	...	...	...	...	...	...	...	...	...
6 Direct purchases in the domestic market by non-residential households	110	79	75	73	89	96	113	134	115	141	167
7 Direct purchases in the domestic market by extraterritorial bodies	167	150	146	116	111	125	145	154	152	169	241
Total Exports of Goods and Services	7926	9452	9779	11291	18258	18982	22582	24308	22729	25627	32887
	\multicolumn{11}{c}{**Imports of Goods and Services**}										
1 Imports of merchandise, c.i.f.	6025	6104	6379	9561	16827	16042	17957	17839	15849	23455	30113

Japan

2.17 Exports and Imports of Goods and Services, Detail
(Continued)

Thousand Million Japanese yen

	1970	1971	1972	1973	1974	1975	1976	1977	1978	1979	1980
a Imports of merchandise, f.o.b. [a]	5484	5626	5878	8948	15873	15158	17096	17104	15182	22541	29153
b Transport of services on merchandise imports	509	442	463	570	884	809	785	656	601	825	859
By residents	...	...	...	...	...	...	...	...	...	...	...
By non-residents	509	442	463	570	884	809	785	656	601	825	859
c Insurance service charges on merchandise imports	32	36	38	43	70	75	76	79	66	89	101
By residents	...	...	...	...	...	...	...	...	...	...	...
By non-residents	32	36	38	43	70	75	76	79	66	89	101
2 Adjustments of merchandise imports to change-of-ownership basis [a]	...	...	...	...	...	...	...	...	...	...	...
3 Other transport and communication	422	498	512	708	1079	1256	1529	1514	1270	1604	2056
4 Other insurance service charges	73	85	92	98	144	204	231	257	241	173	70
5 Other commodities	323	370	407	536	788	989	1004	1044	1009	1289	1698
6 Direct purchases abroad by government	12	4	3	1	4	4	12	8	7	8	11
7 Direct purchases abroad by resident households	131	194	253	358	415	425	515	606	798	1099	1089
Total Imports of Goods and Services	6985	7254	7645	11261	19257	18919	21247	21267	19174	27629	35036
Balance of Goods and Services	941	2198	2134	30	-999	62	1335	3041	3555	-2002	-2150
Total Imports and Balance of Goods and Services	7926	9452	9779	11291	18258	18982	22582	24308	22729	25627	32887

a) Item 'Adjustment of merchandise export/import to change-of-ownership basis' is included in item 'Exports/Imports of merchandise, f.o.b.'.

3.11 General Government Production Account: Total and Subsectors

Thousand Million Japanese yen

	1970					1971				
	Total General Government	Central Government	State or Provincial Government	Local Government	Social Security Funds	Total General Government	Central Government	State or Provincial Government	Local Government	Social Security Funds

Gross Output

1 Sales	...	...	...	...	...	...	...	...	...	...
2 Services produced for own use	5455	1502	...	4051	94	6416	1738	...	4793	108
3 Own account capital formation	...	...	...	...	...	...	...	...	...	...
Gross Output [a]	6198	...	...	...	...	7272	...	...	...	...

Gross Input

Intermediate Consumption	1556	...	...	...	...	1793	...	...	...	...
Subtotal: Value Added	4642	...	...	...	...	5480	...	...	...	...
1 Indirect taxes, net	5	...	...	...	...	6	...	...	...	...
2 Consumption of fixed capital	327	...	...	...	...	369	...	...	...	...
3 Compensation of employees	4311	...	...	...	...	5105	...	...	...	...
4 Net Operating surplus	...	...	...	...	...	...	...	...	...	...
Gross Input [a]	6198	...	...	...	...	7272	...	...	...	...

	1972					1973				
	Total General Government	Central Government	State or Provincial Government	Local Government	Social Security Funds	Total General Government	Central Government	State or Provincial Government	Local Government	Social Security Funds

Gross Output

1 Sales	...	...	...	...	...	...	...	...	...	...
2 Services produced for own use	7524	1981	...	5690	123	9313	2376	...	7154	150
3 Own account capital formation	...	...	...	...	...	...	...	...	...	...
Gross Output [a]	8582	...	...	...	...	10556	...	...	...	...

Gross Input

Intermediate Consumption	2114	...	...	...	...	2537	...	...	...	...
Subtotal: Value Added	6468	...	...	...	...	8020	...	...	...	...
1 Indirect taxes, net	8	...	...	...	...	10	...	...	...	...
2 Consumption of fixed capital	416	...	...	...	...	471	...	...	...	...
3 Compensation of employees	6045	...	...	...	...	7539	...	...	...	...
4 Net Operating surplus	...	...	...	...	...	...	...	...	...	...
Gross Input [a]	8582	...	...	...	...	10556	...	...	...	...

Japan

3.11 General Government Production Account: Total and Subsectors

Thousand Million Japanese yen

	1974					1975				
	Total General Government	Central Government	State or Provincial Government	Local Government	Social Security Funds	Total General Government	Central Government	State or Provincial Government	Local Government	Social Security Funds
Gross Output											
1 Sales	...	...	...	...	...	...	...	...	...	...
2 Services produced for own use	12201	3102	...	9846	196	14834	3522	...	11512	227
3 Own account capital formation	...	...	...	...	...	...	...	...	...	...
Gross Output [a]	13792	...	...	...	...	16830	...	...	...	...
Gross Input											
Intermediate Consumption	3181	...	...	...	...	3701	...	...	...	...
Subtotal: Value Added	10611	...	...	...	...	13128	...	...	...	...
1 Indirect taxes, net	12	...	...	...	...	15	...	...	...	...
2 Consumption of fixed capital	553	...	...	...	...	668	...	...	...	...
3 Compensation of employees	10046	...	...	...	...	12446	...	...	...	...
4 Net Operating surplus	...	...	...	...	...	...	...	...	...	...
Gross Input [a]	13792	...	...	...	...	16830	...	...	...	...

	1976					1977				
	Total General Government	Central Government	State or Provincial Government	Local Government	Social Security Funds	Total General Government	Central Government	State or Provincial Government	Local Government	Social Security Funds
Gross Output											
1 Sales	...	...	...	...	...	...	...	...	...	...
2 Services produced for own use	16356	3928	...	12652	256	18176	4427	...	13933	286
3 Own account capital formation	...	...	...	...	...	...	...	...	...	...
Gross Output [a]	18770	...	...	...	...	21034	...	...	...	...
Gross Input											
Intermediate Consumption	4197	...	...	...	...	4868	...	...	...	...
Subtotal: Value Added	14573	...	...	...	...	16166	...	...	...	...
1 Indirect taxes, net	17	...	...	...	...	21	...	...	...	...
2 Consumption of fixed capital	786	...	...	...	...	900	...	...	...	...
3 Compensation of employees	13770	...	...	...	...	15245	...	...	...	...
4 Net Operating surplus	...	...	...	...	...	...	...	...	...	...
Gross Input [a]	18770	...	...	...	...	21034	...	...	...	...

	1978					1979				
	Total General Government	Central Government	State or Provincial Government	Local Government	Social Security Funds	Total General Government	Central Government	State or Provincial Government	Local Government	Social Security Funds
Gross Output											
1 Sales	...	...	...	...	...	...	...	...	...	...
2 Services produced for own use	19753	4757	...	15106	289	21519	5214	...	16456	314
3 Own account capital formation	...	...	...	...	...	...	...	...	...	...
Gross Output [a]	23037	...	...	...	...	25175	...	...	...	...
Gross Input											
Intermediate Consumption	5509	...	...	...	...	6248	...	...	...	...
Subtotal: Value Added	17528	...	...	...	...	18928	...	...	...	...
1 Indirect taxes, net	25	...	...	...	...	28	...	...	...	...
2 Consumption of fixed capital	1053	...	...	...	...	1197	...	...	...	...
3 Compensation of employees	16451	...	...	...	...	17702	...	...	...	...
4 Net Operating surplus	...	...	...	...	...	...	...	...	...	...
Gross Input [a]	23037	...	...	...	...	25175	...	...	...	...

	1980			
	Total General Government	Central Government	State or Provincial Government	Local Government	Social Security Funds
Gross Output					
1 Sales	...	...	...	...	...
2 Services produced for own use	...	...	...	...	...
3 Own account capital formation	...	...	...	...	...
Gross Output [a]	27676	...	...	...	...

Japan

3.11 General Government Production Account: Total and Subsectors
(Continued)

Thousand Million Japanese yen

	\multicolumn{5}{c	}{1980}
	Total General Government	Central Government	State or Provincial Government	Local Government	Social Security Funds

Gross Input

Intermediate Consumption	7212	...	...	...	...
Subtotal: Value Added	20464	...	...	...	...
1 Indirect taxes, net	30	...	...	...	...
2 Consumption of fixed capital	1348	...	...	...	...
3 Compensation of employees	19086	...	...	...	...
4 Net Operating surplus	...	...	...	...	...
Gross Input [a]	27676	...	...	...	...

a) Columns 'Central government', 'Local government' and 'Social security funds' refer to fiscal year beginning 1 April.

3.12 General Government Income and Outlay Account: Total and Subsectors

Thousand Million Japanese yen

	\multicolumn{5}{c	}{1970}	\multicolumn{5}{c	}{1971}
	Total General Government	Central Government	State or Provincial Government	Local Government	Social Security Funds	Total General Government	Central Government	State or Provincial Government	Local Government	Social Security Funds

Receipts

1 Property and entrepreneurial income	633	105	...	120	474	793	156	...	142	583
a Net operating surplus	...	...	...	...	...	...	...	...	...	...
b Withdrawals from public quasi-corporations	...	...	...	...	...	...	...	...	...	...
c Interest	575	...	...	...	...	725	...	...	...	...
d Dividends	54	...	...	...	...	63	...	...	...	...
e Net land rent and royalties	4	...	...	...	...	5	...	...	...	...
2 Taxes, fees and contributions	14466	7880	...	3939	3312	16570	8420	...	4492	3903
a Indirect taxes	5202	2699	...	2686	...	5712	2834	...	2964	...
b Direct taxes	6016	5136	...	1253	...	7044	5532	...	1489	...
Income	5860	...	...	...	...	6863	...	...	...	...
Other	156	...	...	...	...	181	...	...	...	...
c Social security contributions	3165	...	...	...	3308	3718	...	...	...	3899
d Fees, fines and penalties	83	46	...	1	4	96	54	...	39	4
3 Other current transfers received	44	61	...	2826	672	52	75	...	3290	779
a Casualty insurance claims	1	1	...	1	...	2	1	...	1	...
b Transfers from other government subsectors	...	28	...	2824	661	...	36	...	3288	765
c Transfers from abroad	2	1	...	...	...	1	1	...	...	...
d Other transfers, except imputed	39	30	...	...	11	48	37	...	...	14
e Imputed unfunded employee welfare contributions	1	1	...	1	...	2	1	...	1	...
Total Current Receipts [a]	15143	8046	...	6923	4458	17416	8652	...	7924	5264

Disbursements

1 General governement final consumption expenditures	5455	1502	...	4051	94	6421	1738	...	4793	108
a Compensation of employees	4311	...	...	...	...	5105	...	...	...	...
b Consumption of fixed capital	327	48	...	288	3	369	53	...	323	3
c Goods and services purchased, net	813	...	...	...	...	942	...	...	...	...
d Less: Own account production of fixed assets	...	...	...	...	...	...	...	...	...	...
e Indirect taxes paid, net	5	...	...	...	...	6	...	...	...	...
2 Property income paid	458	267	...	202	...	540	314	...	242	...
a Interest	442	...	...	...	...	522	...	...	...	...
b Net land rent and royalties	16	...	...	...	...	19	...	...	...	...

Japan

3.12 General Government Income and Outlay Account: Total and Subsectors
(Continued)

Thousand Million Japanese yen

	1970					1971				
	Total General Government	Central Government	State or Provincial Government	Local Government	Social Security Funds	Total General Government	Central Government	State or Provincial Government	Local Government	Social Security Funds
3 Subsidies	805	719	...	163	...	904	730	...	200	...
4 Other current transfers paid [b]	3549	3878	...	718	2626	4090	4489	...	850	2994
a Casualty insurance premiums, net	1	1	...	1	...	2	1	...	1	...
b Transfers to other government subsectors	...	3448	...	30	35	...	4009	...	36	44
c Transfers to households	3395	355	...	593	2590	3883	384	...	691	2949
Social security benefits	2465	...	...	...	2590	2828	...	...	...	2949
Social assistance grants	929	354	...	592	...	1053	383	...	690	...
Unfunded employee welfare benefits	1	1	...	1	...	2	1	...	1	...
d Transfers to private non-profit institutions serving households	88	38	...	94	1	119	51	...	122	1
e Transfers to the rest of the world	29	33	...	...	...	42	44	...	...	...
Net saving	4876	1686	...	1790	1738	5461	1380	...	1839	2162
Total Current Disbursements and Net Saving [a]	15143	8046	...	6923	4458	17416	8652	...	7924	5264

	1972					1973				
	Total General Government	Central Government	State or Provincial Government	Local Government	Social Security Funds	Total General Government	Central Government	State or Provincial Government	Local Government	Social Security Funds

Receipts

1 Property and entrepreneurial income	951	174	...	173	709	1252	326	...	199	856
a Net operating surplus	...	...	...	...	...	...	...	...	...	...
b Withdrawals from public quasi-corporations	...	...	...	...	...	...	...	...	...	...
c Interest	869	...	...	...	...	1156	...	...	...	...
d Dividends	76	...	...	...	...	86	...	...	...	...
e Net land rent and royalties	7	...	...	...	...	10	...	...	...	...
2 Taxes, fees and contributions	18830	10276	...	5299	4567	23907	13996	...	6877	5679
a Indirect taxes	6491	3373	...	3416	...	7890	3911	...	4471	...
b Direct taxes	7926	6833	...	1840	...	10664	9992	...	2352	...
Income	7658	...	...	...	...	10352	...	...	...	...
Other	268	...	...	...	...	312	...	...	...	...
c Social security contributions	4300	...	...	...	4564	5212	...	...	...	5676
d Fees, fines and penalties	112	70	...	43	3	141	93	...	54	3
3 Other current transfers received	65	88	...	4006	991	73	110	...	4950	1340
a Casualty insurance claims	2	1	...	2	...	3	2	...	2	...
b Transfers from other government subsectors	...	42	...	4003	972	...	55	...	4947	1320
c Transfers from abroad	2	2	...	...	...	3	5	...	...	...
d Other transfers, except imputed	59	42	...	...	19	65	47	...	...	20
e Imputed unfunded employee welfare contributions	2	1	...	1	...	2	1	...	1	...
Total Current Receipts [a]	19846	10538	...	1092	6267	25232	14431	...	12026	7875

Disbursements

1 General governement final consumption expenditures	7537	1981	...	5690	123	9336	2376	...	7154	150
a Compensation of employees	6045	...	...	...	...	7539	...	...	...	...
b Consumption of fixed capital	416	62	...	362	3	471	68	...	414	4
c Goods and services purchased, net	1069	...	...	...	...	1317	...	...	...	...
d Less: Own account production of fixed assets	...	...	...	...	...	...	...	...	...	...
e Indirect taxes paid, net	8	...	...	...	...	10	...	...	...	...
2 Property income paid	721	491	...	314	...	1020	635	...	415	...
a Interest	688	...	...	...	...	978	...	...	...	...
b Net land rent and royalties	32	...	...	...	...	42	...	...	...	...

Japan

3.12 General Government Income and Outlay Account: Total and Subsectors
(Continued)

Thousand Million Japanese yen

	1972					1973				
	Total General Government	Central Government	State or Provincial Government	Local Government	Social Security Funds	Total General Government	Central Government	State or Provincial Government	Local Government	Social Security Funds
3 Subsidies	1066	807	...	246	...	1180	1234	...	300	...
4 Other current transfers paid b	4985	5417	...	1132	3739	6065	6831	...	1435	4597
a Casualty insurance premiums, net	3	2	...	2	...	3	2	...	2	...
b Transfers to other government subsectors	...	4909	...	58	50	...	6182	...	75	65
c Transfers to households	4756	422	...	928	3688	5794	537	...	1180	4531
Social security benefits	3474	...	...	...	3688	4151	...	...	...	4531
Social assistance grants	1279	421	...	927	...	1640	536	...	1179	...
Unfunded employee welfare benefits	2	1	...	1	...	2	1	...	1	...
d Transfers to private non-profit institutions serving households	153	67	...	144	1	196	91	...	178	1
e Transfers to the rest of the world	25	17	...	...	...	15	19	...	...	...
Net saving	5537	1842	...	2097	2404	7630	3356	...	2723	3127
Total Current Disbursements and Net Saving a	19846	10538	...	9478	6267	25232	14431	...	12026	7875

	1974					1975				
	Total General Government	Central Government	State or Provincial Government	Local Government	Social Security Funds	Total General Government	Central Government	State or Provincial Government	Local Government	Social Security Funds

Receipts

1 Property and entrepreneurial income	1597	434	...	280	1085	1945	438	...	288	1348
a Net operating surplus	...	...	...	...	...	...	...	...	...	...
b Withdrawals from public quasi-corporations	...	...	...	...	...	...	...	...	...	...
c Interest	1487	...	...	...	...	1816	...	...	...	...
d Dividends	99	...	...	...	...	116	...	...	...	...
e Net land rent and royalties	11	...	...	...	...	12	...	...	...	...
2 Taxes, fees and contributions	31057	16160	...	8695	7841	33518	15009	...	8613	9258
a Indirect taxes	9254	4089	...	5375	...	9736	4569	...	5278	...
b Direct taxes	14728	11972	...	3251	...	14092	10328	...	3259	...
Income	14340	...	...	...	...	13630	...	...	...	...
Other	388	...	...	...	...	461	...	...	...	...
c Social security contributions	6910	...	...	-	7838	9503	...	...	-	9253
d Fees, fines and penalties	165	99	...	69	3	188	112	...	76	5
3 Other current transfers received	98	149	...	6720	2002	109	173	...	7508	2632
a Casualty insurance claims	4	2	...	2	...	5	2	...	2	...
b Transfers from other government subsectors	...	77	...	6716	1975	...	92	...	7504	2605
c Transfers from abroad	8	6	...	...	...	5	7	...	...	...
d Other transfers, except imputed	84	63	...	...	27	95	70	...	...	27
e Imputed unfunded employee welfare contributions	3	1	...	2	...	4	2	...	2	...
Total Current Receipts a	32752	16742	...	15694	10928	35571	15619	...	16408	13237

Disbursements

1 General government final consumption expenditures	12240	3102	...	9846	196	14890	3522	...	11512	227
a Compensation of employees	10046	...	...	...	...	12446	...	...	...	...
b Consumption of fixed capital	553	81	...	490	4	668	100	...	593	5
c Goods and services purchased, net	1630	...	...	...	...	1762	...	...	...	...
d Less: Own account production of fixed assets	...	...	...	...	...	...	...	...	...	...
e Indirect taxes paid, net	12	...	...	...	...	15	...	...	...	...
2 Property income paid	1298	826	...	563	...	1797	1167	...	765	...
a Interest	1242	...	...	...	...	1735	...	...	...	...
b Net land rent and royalties	56	...	...	...	...	62	...	...	...	...

Japan

3.12 General Government Income and Outlay Account: Total and Subsectors
(Continued)

Thousand Million Japanese yen

	1974					1975				
	Total General Government	Central Government	State or Provincial Government	Local Government	Social Security Funds	Total General Government	Central Government	State or Provincial Government	Local Government	Social Security Funds
3 Subsidies	2123	1638	...	383	...	2207	1680	...	431	...
4 Other current transfers paid [b]	8666	9391	...	1936	6920	11996	11006	...	2416	9138
a Casualty insurance premiums, net	4	2	...	2	...	4	2	...	2	...
b Transfers to other government subsectors	...	8562	...	114	92	...	9951	...	139	111
c Transfers to households	8303	673	...	1579	6827	11489	845	...	1955	9026
Social security benefits	6150	...	...	...	6827	8788	...	...	...	9026
Social assistance grants	2151	672	...	1577	...	2697	843	...	1953	...
Unfunded employee welfare benefits	3	1	...	2	...	4	2	...	2	...
d Transfers to private non-profit institutions serving households	262	129	...	241	1	383	173	...	320	1
e Transfers to the rest of the world	22	25	...	...	...	34	35	...	...	...
Net saving	8424	1785	...	2966	3812	4682	-1756	...	1284	3872
Total Current Disbursements and Net Saving [a]	32752	16742	...	15694	10928	35571	15619	...	16408	13237

	1976					1977				
	Total General Government	Central Government	State or Provincial Government	Local Government	Social Security Funds	Total General Government	Central Government	State or Provincial Government	Local Government	Social Security Funds

Receipts

1 Property and entrepreneurial income	2237	485	...	319	1591	2627	551	...	384	1885
a Net operating surplus	...	...	...	...	...	...	...	...	...	...
b Withdrawals from public quasi-corporations	...	...	...	...	...	...	...	...	...	...
c Interest	2080	...	...	...	...	2432	...	...	...	...
d Dividends	142	...	...	...	...	176	...	...	...	...
e Net land rent and royalties	16	...	...	...	...	19	...	...	...	...
2 Taxes, fees and contributions	36797	17320	...	10018	10953	42887	19205	...	11505	13000
a Indirect taxes	10870	5547	...	6020	...	12890	6054	...	6963	...
b Direct taxes	15033	11648	...	3914	...	17114	13019	...	4449	...
Income	14437	...	...	...	...	16423	...	...	...	...
Other	596	...	...	...	...	691	...	...	...	...
c Social security contributions	10684	...	...	...	10947	12654	...	...	...	12993
d Fees, fines and penalties	210	125	...	84	6	230	132	...	93	7
3 Other current transfers received	146	220	...	8697	3219	172	252	...	9658	3784
a Casualty insurance claims	6	3	...	3	...	6	3	...	3	...
b Transfers from other government subsectors	...	114	...	8691	3178	...	124	...	9652	3737
c Transfers from abroad	10	7	...	...	...	4	5	...	...	...
d Other transfers, except imputed	126	94	...	...	41	163	117	...	...	47
e Imputed unfunded employee welfare contributions	5	2	...	3	...	6	3	...	3	...
Total Current Receipts [a]	39180	18025	...	19034	15763	45686	20008	...	21548	18669

Disbursements

1 General government final consumption expenditures	16417	3928	...	12652	256	18243	4427	...	13933	286
a Compensation of employees	13770	...	...	...	...	15245	...	...	...	...
b Consumption of fixed capital	786	117	...	692	6	900	138	...	784	7
c Goods and services purchased, net	1845	...	...	...	...	2077	...	...	...	...
d Less: Own account production of fixed assets	...	...	...	...	...	...	...	...	...	...
e Indirect taxes paid, net	17	...	...	...	...	21	...	...	...	...
2 Property income paid	2569	1796	...	1007	...	3592	2536	...	1269	...
a Interest	2504	...	...	...	...	3525	...	...	...	...
b Net land rent and royalties	65	...	...	...	...	67	...	...	...	...

Japan

3.12 General Government Income and Outlay Account: Total and Subsectors
(Continued)

Thousand Million Japanese yen

	1976					1977				
	Total General Government	Central Government	State or Provincial Government	Local Government	Social Security Funds	Total General Government	Central Government	State or Provincial Government	Local Government	Social Security Funds
3 Subsidies	2181	1783	...	532	...	2469	1911	...	651	...
4 Other current transfers paid [b]	14732	13033	...	2840	11352	17219	14756	...	3231	13116
a Casualty insurance premiums, net	6	3	...	3	...	6	3	...	3	...
b Transfers to other government subsectors	...	11697	...	156	131	...	13197	...	173	143
c Transfers to households	14145	1080	...	2334	11220	16553	1258	...	2668	12971
Social security benefits	10834	...	...	...	11220	12720	...	...	...	12971
Social assistance grants	3306	1078	...	2331	...	3827	1255	...	2665	...
Unfunded employee welfare benefits	5	2	...	3	...	6	3	...	3	...
d Transfers to private non-profit institutions serving households	450	220	...	347	1	515	268	...	386	2
e Transfers to the rest of the world	34	33	...	...	...	33	30	...	...	...
Net saving	3281	-2514	...	2003	4155	4163	-3622	...	2464	5268
Total Current Disbursements and Net Saving [a]	39180	18025	...	19034	15763	45686	20008	...	21548	18669

	1978					1979				
	Total General Government	Central Government	State or Provincial Government	Local Government	Social Security Funds	Total General Government	Central Government	State or Provincial Government	Local Government	Social Security Funds

Receipts

1 Property and entrepreneurial income	3031	712	...	425	2152	3671	941	...	483	2458
a Net operating surplus	...	...	...	...	...	...	...	...	...	...
b Withdrawals from public quasi-corporations	...	...	...	...	...	...	...	...	...	...
c Interest	2801	...	...	...	...	3417	...	...	...	...
d Dividends	201	...	...	...	...	225	...	...	...	...
e Net land rent and royalties	20	...	...	...	...	29	...	...	...	...
2 Taxes, fees and contributions	46716	23974	...	12785	14617	54367	25651	...	14641	16061
a Indirect taxes	13912	7286	...	7582	...	16188	8039	...	8654	...
b Direct taxes	18688	16565	...	5098	...	21885	17491	...	5866	...
Income	17920	...	...	...	...	20999	...	...	...	...
Other	768	...	...	...	...	887	...	...	...	...
c Social security contributions	13880	...	...	...	14610	16049	...	...	...	16051
d Fees, fines and penalties	236	123	...	105	8	244	121	...	121	8
3 Other current transfers received	192	306	...	11506	4464	204	333	...	12607	5283
a Casualty insurance claims	7	3	...	3	...	7	4	...	4	...
b Transfers from other government subsectors	...	134	...	11500	4448	...	157	...	12600	5259
c Transfers from abroad	11	11	...	...	...	7	7	...	...	...
d Other transfers, except imputed	211	154	...	...	16	184	162	...	...	27
e Imputed unfunded employee welfare contributions	6	3	...	3	...	7	4	...	3	...
Total Current Receipts [a]	49939	24992	...	24716	21234	58243	26925	...	27737	23802

Disbursements

1 General government final consumption expenditures	19753	4757	...	15106	289	21486	5178	...	16445	314
a Compensation of employees	16451	...	...	...	...	17702	...	...	...	...
b Consumption of fixed capital	1053	197	...	891	7	1195	214	...	1010	8
c Goods and services purchased, net	2224	...	...	...	...	2561	...	...	...	...
d Less: Own account production of fixed assets	...	...	...	...	...	...	...	...	...	...
e Indirect taxes paid, net	25	...	...	...	...	28	...	...	...	...
2 Property income paid	4599	3352	...	1523	...	5865	4394	...	1805	...
a Interest	4526	...	...	...	...	5787	...	...	...	...
b Net land rent and royalties	73	...	...	...	...	78	...	...	...	...

Japan

3.12 General Government Income and Outlay Account: Total and Subsectors
(Continued)

Thousand Million Japanese yen

	1978					1979				
	Total General Government	Central Government	State or Provincial Government	Local Government	Social Security Funds	Total General Government	Central Government	State or Provincial Government	Local Government	Social Security Funds
3 Subsidies	2713	2091	...	772	...	2930	2401	...	769	...
4 Other current transfers paid b	20061	17568	...	3683	15756	22688	19685	...	4033	17422
a Casualty insurance premiums, net	7	3	...	3	...	7	4	...	4	...
b Transfers to other government subsectors	...	15745	...	185	153	...	17635	...	209	179
c Transfers to households	19287	1453	...	3062	15691	21808	1594	...	3339	17240
Social security benefits	14845	...	...	...	15601	16932	...	...	...	17240
Social assistance grants	4436	1449	...	3059	...	4869	1590	...	3336	...
Unfunded employee welfare benefits	6	3	...	3	...	7	3	...	3	...
d Transfers to private non-profit institutions serving households	597	326	...	432	2	670	372	...	481	3
e Transfers to the rest of the world	40	42	...	...	...	57	80	...	...	...
Net saving	2814	-2776	...	3632	5189	5274	-4732	...	4684	6067
Total Current Disbursements and Net Saving a	49939	24992	...	24716	21234	58243	26925	...	27737	23802

	1980				
	Total General Government	Central Government	State or Provincial Government	Local Government	Social Security Funds

Receipts

1 Property and entrepreneurial income	4612	1310	...	651	2905
a Net operating surplus	...	...	...	...	...
b Withdrawals from public quasi-corporations	...	...	...	...	...
c Interest	4332	...	...	...	...
d Dividends	247	...	...	...	...
e Net land rent and royalties	33	...	...	...	...
2 Taxes, fees and contributions	61353	29118	...	16555	18103
a Indirect taxes	17764	8397	...	9714	-
b Direct taxes	25876	20592	...	6712	-
Income	24954	...	...	...	...
Other	921	...	...	...	...
c Social security contributions	17452	-	...	-	18096
d Fees, fines and penalties	262	129	...	129	7
3 Other current transfers received	243	414	...	13608	5780
a Casualty insurance claims	8	4	...	4	-
b Transfers from other government subsectors	...	198	...	13601	5745
c Transfers from abroad	10	14	...	-	-
d Other transfers, except imputed	219	194	...	-	35
e Imputed unfunded employee welfare contributions	7	4	...	3	-
Total Current Receipts a	66208	30841	...	30813	26789

Disbursements

1 General government final consumption expenditures	23532	5683	...	18055	339
a Compensation of employees	19086	...	...	...	...
b Consumption of fixed capital	1348	...	...	...	...
c Goods and services purchased, net	3068	...	...	...	...
d Less: Own account production of fixed assets	...	...	...	...	...
e Indirect taxes paid, net	30	...	...	...	...
2 Property income paid	7530	5857	...	2165	...
a Interest	7451	...	...	...	...
b Net land rent and royalties	79	...	...	...	...

Japan

3.12 General Government Income and Outlay Account: Total and Subsectors
(Continued)

Thousand Million Japanese yen

	1980				
	Total General Government	Central Government	State or Provincial Government	Local Government	Social Security Funds
3 Subsidies	3456	2708	...	803	-
4 Other current transfers paid [b]	25173	21331	...	4348	19778
a Casualty insurance premiums, net	8	4	...	4	...
b Transfers to other government subsectors	...	19083	...	241	220
c Transfers to households	24164	1754	...	3583	19555
Social security benefits	18908	-	...	3580	19555
Social assistance grants	5250	1750	...	-	-
Unfunded employee welfare benefits	7	4	...	3	-
d Transfers to private non-profit institutions serving households	917	74	...	-	-
e Transfers to the rest of the world	84	416	...	520	3
Net saving	6518	-4738	...	5441	6672
Total Current Disbursements and Net Saving [a]	66208	30841	...	30813	26789

a) Columns 'Central government', 'Local government' and 'Social security funds' refer to fiscal year beginning 1 April.
b) Including current transfers to other resident sectors.

3.13 General Government Capital Accumulation Account: Total and Subsectors

Thousand Million Japanese yen

	1970					1971				
	Total General Government	Central Government	State or Provincial Government	Local Government	Social Security Funds	Total General Government	Central Government	State or Provincial Government	Local Government	Social Security Funds
Finance of Gross Accumulation
1 Gross saving	5202	1734	...	2078	1741	5829	1433	...	2162	2165
a Consumption of fixed capital	327	48	...	288	3	369	53	...	323	3
b Net saving	4876	1685	...	1790	1738	5460	1380	...	1839	2162
2 Capital transfers received [a]	-212	-1035	...	801	-2	-209	-1329	...	1134	-2
a From other government subsectors	...	-1044	...	1045	-1	...	-1378	...	1379	-1
b From other resident sectors	-176	9	...	-244	-1	-175	49	...	-245	-1
c From rest of the world	-35		...			-35		...		
Finance of Gross Accumulation [b]	4991	699	...	2879	1739	5620	105	...	3296	2163
Gross Accumulation
1 Gross capital formation	3276	640	...	2814	9	4061	795	...	3631	9
a Increase in stocks	...	...	...	...	...	...	...	...	...	...
b Gross fixed capital formation	3276	640	...	2814	9	4061	795	...	3631	9
2 Purchases of land, net	434	81	...	380	...	601	110	...	536	1
3 Purchases of intangible assets, net	...	...	...	...	...	...	...	...	...	...
4 Capital transfers paid	...	...	...	...	...	...	...	...	...	...
Net lending [c]	1281	-22	...	-315	1730	958	-800	...	-871	2153
Gross Accumulation [b]	4991	699	...	2879	1739	5620	105	...	3296	2163

	1972					1973				
	Total General Government	Central Government	State or Provincial Government	Local Government	Social Security Funds	Total General Government	Central Government	State or Provincial Government	Local Government	Social Security Funds
Finance of Gross Accumulation
1 Gross saving	5953	1904	...	2459	2408	8101	3424	...	3137	3131
a Consumption of fixed capital	416	62	...	362	3	471	68	...	414	4
b Net saving	5537	1842	...	2097	2404	7630	3356	...	2723	3127
2 Capital transfers received [a]	-190	-1819	...	1652	-3	-290	-1899	...	1535	-3
a From other government subsectors	...	-1919	...	1920	-1	...	-2001	...	2002	-2
b From other resident sectors	-114	100	...	-268	-2	-246	102	...	-467	-2
c From rest of the world	-77		...			-44		...		
Finance of Gross Accumulation [b]	5762	86	...	4111	2405	7811	1525	...	4672	3128
Gross Accumulation
1 Gross capital formation	5053	987	...	4516	10	6370	1000	...	5083	12

Japan

3.13 General Government Capital Accumulation Account: Total and Subsectors
(Continued)

Thousand Million Japanese yen

	1972					1973				
	Total General Government	Central Government	State or Provincial Government	Local Government	Social Security Funds	Total General Government	Central Government	State or Provincial Government	Local Government	Social Security Funds
a Increase in stocks	...	...	...	...	...	...	...	...	...	...
b Gross fixed capital formation	5053	987	...	4516	10	6370	1000	...	5083	12
2 Purchases of land, net	797	156	...	688	1	818	67	...	734	2
3 Purchases of intangible assets, net	...	...	...	...	...	...	...	...	...	...
4 Capital transfers paid	...	...	...	...	...	...	...	...	...	...
Net lending [c]	-88	-1057	...	-458	2393	623	458	...	-1145	3115
Gross Accumulation [b]	5762	86	...	4111	2405	7811	1525	...	4672	3128

	1974					1975				
	Total General Government	Central Government	State or Provincial Government	Local Government	Social Security Funds	Total General Government	Central Government	State or Provincial Government	Local Government	Social Security Funds

Finance of Gross Accumulation

1 Gross saving	8977	1865	...	3455	3816	5350	-1656	...	1878	3877
a Consumption of fixed capital	553	81	...	490	4	668	100	...	593	5
b Net saving	8424	1785	...	2966	3812	4682	-1756	...	1284	3872
2 Capital transfers received [a]	-439	-2493	...	2014	-5	-467	-2857	...	2440	-6
a From other government subsectors	...	-2517	...	2519	-2	...	-2867	...	2870	-3
b From other resident sectors	-395	24	...	-506	-3	-418	11	...	-430	-4
c From rest of the world	-44		...			-49		...		
Finance of Gross Accumulation [b]	8538	-628	...	5469	3811	4883	-4513	...	4318	3871

Gross Accumulation

1 Gross capital formation	7003	1224	...	6252	19	7841	1400	...	6681	22
a Increase in stocks	...	...	...	...	...	...	...	...	...	...
b Gross fixed capital formation	7003	1224	...	6252	19	7841	1400	...	6681	22
2 Purchases of land, net	1006	125	...	953	4	1085	185	...	900	3
3 Purchases of intangible assets, net	...	...	...	...	...	...	...	...	...	...
4 Capital transfers paid	...	...	...	...	...	...	...	...	...	...
Net lending [c]	529	-1978	...	-1735	3788	-4043	-6098	...	-3264	3846
Gross Accumulation [b]	8538	-628	...	5469	3811	4883	-4513	...	4318	3871

	1976					1977				
	Total General Government	Central Government	State or Provincial Government	Local Government	Social Security Funds	Total General Government	Central Government	State or Provincial Government	Local Government	Social Security Funds

Finance of Gross Accumulation

1 Gross saving	4067	-2397	...	2695	4160	5063	-3484	...	3248	5274
a Consumption of fixed capital	786	117	...	692	6	900	138	...	784	7
b Net saving	3281	-2514	...	2003	4155	4163	-3622	...	2464	5268
2 Capital transfers received [a]	-423	-3315	...	2869	-12	-396	-4002	...	3622	-19
a From other government subsectors	...	-3319	...	3322	-3	...	-4187	...	4191	-4
b From other resident sectors	-383	4	...	-453	-9	-372	185	...	-569	-15
c From rest of the world	-39		...			-24		...		
Finance of Gross Accumulation [b]	3645	-5712	...	5563	4148	4667	-7487	...	6870	5255

Gross Accumulation

1 Gross capital formation	8591	1496	...	7303	23	10274	1777	...	9039	33
a Increase in stocks	...	...	...	...	...	...	...	...	...	...
b Gross fixed capital formation	8591	1496	...	7303	23	10274	1777	...	9039	33
2 Purchases of land, net	1129	180	...	961	3	1438	247	...	1279	2
3 Purchases of intangible assets, net	...	...	...	...	...	...	...	...	...	...
4 Capital transfers paid	...	...	...	...	...	...	...	...	...	...
Net lending [c]	-6076	-7388	...	-2702	4123	-7045	-9511	...	-3448	5221
Gross Accumulation [b]	3645	-5712	...	5563	4148	4667	-7487	...	6870	5255

Japan

3.13 General Government Capital Accumulation Account: Total and Subsectors

Thousand Million Japanese yen

	1978					1979				
	Total General Government	Central Government	State or Provincial Government	Local Government	Social Security Funds	Total General Government	Central Government	State or Provincial Government	Local Government	Social Security Funds
Finance of Gross Accumulation											
1 Gross saving	3867	-2580	...	4523	5195	6471	-4518	...	5694	6075
a Consumption of fixed capital	1053	197	...	891	7	1197	214	...	1010	8
b Net saving	2814	-2776	...	3632	5189	5274	-4732	...	4684	6067
2 Capital transfers received [a]	-743	-5064	...	4312	-26	-898	-5669	...	4755	-20
a From other government subsectors	...	-4989	...	4994	-5	...	-5490	...	5497	-6
b From other resident sectors	-723	-75	...	-681	-21	-824	-178	...	-742	-14
c From rest of the world	-20		...			-74		...		
Finance of Gross Accumulation [b]	3123	-7644	...	8835	5169	5574	-10187	...	10449	6055
Gross Accumulation											
1 Gross capital formation	12522	2144	...	10858	40	14025	2236	...	11860	49
a Increase in stocks	...	...	...	...	...	...	...	...	...	...
b Gross fixed capital formation	12522	2144	...	10858	40	14025	2236	...	11860	49
2 Purchases of land, net	1804	306	...	1575	8	1975	345	...	1647	15
3 Purchases of intangible assets, net	...	...	...	...	...	...	...	...	...	...
4 Capital transfers paid	...	...	...	...	...	...	...	...	...	...
Net lending [c]	-11203	-10094	...	-3597	5121	-10427	-12767	...	-3059	5990
Gross Accumulation [b]	3123	-7644	...	8835	5169	5574	-10187	...	10449	6055

	1980				
	Total General Government	Central Government	State or Provincial Government	Local Government	Social Security Funds
Finance of Gross Accumulation					
1 Gross saving	7866	-4509	...	6590	6681
a Consumption of fixed capital	1348	229	...	1149	9
b Net saving	6518	-4738	...	5441	6672
2 Capital transfers received [a]	-676	-6081	...	5155	-19
a From other government subsectors	...	-5880	...	5886	...
b From other resident sectors	-580	-201	...	-731	-13
c From rest of the world	-96		...		
Finance of Gross Accumulation [b]	7190	-10590	...	11745	6662
Gross Accumulation					
1 Gross capital formation	14723	2308	...	12626	51
a Increase in stocks	...	...	...	...	...
b Gross fixed capital formation	14723	2308	...	12626	51
2 Purchases of land, net	2371	357	...	2119	8
3 Purchases of intangible assets, net	...	...	...	...	...
4 Capital transfers paid	...	...	...	...	...
Net lending [c]	-9905	-13255	...	-3000	6603
Gross Accumulation [b]	7190	-10590	...	11745	6662

a) Net.
b) Columns 'Central government', 'Local government' and 'Social security funds' refer to fiscal year beginning 1 April.
c) Net lending of the Capital Accumulation Account and the Capital Finance Account have not been reconciled and are different due to different statistical sources.

3.14 General Government Capital Finance Account, Total and Subsectors

Thousand Million Japanese yen

	1970					1971				
	Total General Government	Central Government	State or Provincial Government	Local Government	Social Security Funds	Total General Government	Central Government	State or Provincial Government	Local Government	Social Security Funds
Acquisition of Financial Assets											
1 Gold and SDRs [a]	...	...	...	...	...	...	...	...	...	...
2 Currency and transferable deposits	65	83	...	96	14	131	388	...	151	22
3 Other deposits	198	8	...	121	75	214	-6	...	83	170
4 Bills and bonds, short term	43	33	...	...	1	92	58	...	...	-1
5 Bonds, long term	125	24	...	1	147	244	-31	...	...	212
6 Corporate equity securities	2	...	...	...	1	2	...	...	...	1
7 Short-term loans, n.e.c.	421	129	...	132	181	497	170	...	145	206
8 Long-term loans, n.e.c.			...					...		

Japan

3.14 General Government Capital Finance Account, Total and Subsectors
(Continued)

Thousand Million Japanese yen

	1970					1971				
	Total General Government	Central Government	State or Provincial Government	Local Government	Social Security Funds	Total General Government	Central Government	State or Provincial Government	Local Government	Social Security Funds

Acquisition of Financial Assets (continued)

9 Other receivables	...	...	...	...	...	...	...	...	...	...
10 Other assets [a]	1720	728	...	29	1227	1962	595	...	67	1387
Total Acquisition of Financial Assets [b]	2573	1005	...	378	1645	3142	1174	...	446	1998

Incurrence of Liabilities

1 Currency and transferable deposits	...	...	...	...	...	...	...	...	...	...
2 Other deposits	...	...	...	...	...	...	...	...	...	...
3 Bills and bonds, short term	245	191	...	...	...	344	343	...	...	...
4 Bonds, long term	502	358	...	169	...	1088	1142	...	397	...
5 Short-term loans, n.e.c.	462	95	...	364	84	630	244	...	588	43
6 Long-term loans, n.e.c.			...					...		
7 Other payables	...	...	...	...	...	...	...	...	...	...
8 Other liabilities	29	92	...	2	...	34	173	...	2	...
Total Incurrence of Liabilities [b]	1239	736	...	535	84	2096	1901	...	987	43
Net Lending [c]	1335	269	...	-158	1561	1046	-728	...	-541	1955
Incurrence of Liabilities and Net Worth [b]	2573	1005	...	378	1645	3142	1174	...	446	1998

	1972					1973				
	Total General Government	Central Government	State or Provincial Government	Local Government	Social Security Funds	Total General Government	Central Government	State or Provincial Government	Local Government	Social Security Funds

Acquisition of Financial Assets

1 Gold and SDRs [a]	...	...	...	...	...	...	...	...	...	...
2 Currency and transferable deposits	29	614	...	389	80	154	862	...	133	61
3 Other deposits	346	10	...	118	214	441	8	...	204	208
4 Bills and bonds, short term	89	-27	...	...	...	-44	96	...	...	...
5 Bonds, long term	121	21	...	1	171	330	30	...	2	254
6 Corporate equity securities	15	14	...	1	1	4	...	...	...	4
7 Short-term loans, n.e.c.	504	166	...	121	239	655	212	...	158	319
8 Long-term loans, n.e.c.			...					...		
9 Other receivables	...	...	...	...	...	...	...	...	...	...
10 Other assets [a]	4319	2664	...	60	1717	2336	557	...	67	1944
Total Acquisition of Financial Assets [b]	5423	3462	...	689	2421	3876	1765	...	563	2789

Incurrence of Liabilities

1 Currency and transferable deposits	...	...	...	...	...	...	...	...	...	...
2 Other deposits	...	...	...	...	...	...	...	...	...	...
3 Bills and bonds, short term	1403	1581	...	...	...	-796	-185	...	...	...
4 Bonds, long term	2766	1866	...	600	...	2222	1726	...	739	...
5 Short-term loans, n.e.c.	943	787	...	956	102	1575	21	...	1021	49
6 Long-term loans, n.e.c.			...					...		
7 Other payables	...	...	...	...	...	...	...	...	...	...
8 Other liabilities	173	280	...	4	...	41	185	...	7	...
Total Incurrence of Liabilities [b]	5284	4514	...	1559	102	3043	1748	...	1766	49
Net Lending [c]	139	-1052	...	-870	2319	883	17	...	-1203	2740
Incurrence of Liabilities and Net Worth [b]	5423	3462	...	689	2421	3876	1765	...	563	2789

	1974					1975				
	Total General Government	Central Government	State or Provincial Government	Local Government	Social Security Funds	Total General Government	Central Government	State or Provincial Government	Local Government	Social Security Funds

Acquisition of Financial Assets

1 Gold and SDRs [a]	...	...	...	...	...	...	...	...	...	...
2 Currency and transferable deposits	481	-759	...	201	142	55	-467	...	131	110
3 Other deposits	412	3	...	102	339	368	14	...	24	340
4 Bills and bonds, short term	84	60	...	...	...	111	168	...	...	...
5 Bonds, long term	192	43	...	-1	280	324	74	...	...	301
6 Corporate equity securities	3	1	...	...	2	2	1	...	...	1
7 Short-term loans, n.e.c.	954	297	...	213	490	1032	351	...	140	575
8 Long-term loans, n.e.c.			...					...		
9 Other receivables	...	...	...	...	...	...	...	...	...	...
10 Other assets [a]	3112	928	...	70	2459	3204	737	...	65	2713
Total Acquisition of Financial Assets [b]	5238	571	...	585	3712	5095	879	...	360	4040

Japan

3.14 General Government Capital Finance Account, Total and Subsectors
(Continued)

Thousand Million Japanese yen

	1974					1975				
	Total General Government	Central Government	State or Provincial Government	Local Government	Social Security Funds	Total General Government	Central Government	State or Provincial Government	Local Government	Social Security Funds

Incurrence of Liabilities

1 Currency and transferable deposits	...	...	...	...	...	...	...	...	...	...
2 Other deposits	...	...	...	...	...	...	...	...	...	...
3 Bills and bonds, short term	543	478	...	...	...	891	-45	...	...	...
4 Bonds, long term	2667	2090	...	869	...	5347	5319	...	1651	...
5 Short-term loans, n.e.c.	1060	-246	...	1182	80	2859	1500	...	1653	82
6 Long-term loans, n.e.c.										
7 Other payables	...	...	...	...	...	...	...	...	...	...
8 Other liabilities	477	659	...	12	...	107	327	...	26	...
Total Incurrence of Liabilities [b]	4747	2981	...	2064	80	9205	7101	...	3330	82
Net Lending [c]	491	-2410	...	-1479	3632	-4110	-6222	...	2970	3958
Incurrence of Liabilities and Net Worth [b]	5238	571	...	585	3712	5095	879	...	360	4040

	1976					1977				
	Total General Government	Central Government	State or Provincial Government	Local Government	Social Security Funds	Total General Government	Central Government	State or Provincial Government	Local Government	Social Security Funds

Acquisition of Financial Assets

1 Gold and SDRs [a]	...	...	...	...	...	...	...	...	...	...
2 Currency and transferable deposits	226	-60	...	366	-20	106	-101	...	274	57
3 Other deposits	917	13	...	464	448	1249	26	...	625	614
4 Bills and bonds, short term	-220	...	...	...	...	485	230	...	...	...
5 Bonds, long term	979	492	...	...	366	515	166	...	...	479
6 Corporate equity securities	2	1	...	1	1	...	2	...	1	3
7 Short-term loans, n.e.c.	1052	432	...	178	470	951	435	...	215	474
8 Long-term loans, n.e.c.										
9 Other receivables	...	...	...	...	...	...	...	...	...	...
10 Other assets [a]	4153	1669	...	110	2804	5073	2508	...	61	3580
Total Acquisition of Financial Assets [b]	7109	2547	...	1118	4069	8379	3267	...	1176	5202

Incurrence of Liabilities

1 Currency and transferable deposits	...	...	...	...	...	...	...	...	...	...
2 Other deposits	...	...	...	...	...	...	...	...	...	...
3 Bills and bonds, short term	-161	757	...	...	...	1666	1881	...	...	...
4 Bonds, long term	9907	7119	...	1996	...	10566	9835	...	1926	...
5 Short-term loans, n.e.c.	3325	1739	...	1443	134	2967	1390	...	1925	87
6 Long-term loans, n.e.c.										
7 Other payables	...	...	...	...	...	...	...	...	...	...
8 Other liabilities	289	452	...	27	...	97	354	...	18	...
Total Incurrence of Liabilities [b]	13360	10067	...	3466	134	15295	13460	...	3869	87
Net Lending [c]	-6251	-7521	...	-2348	3934	-6916	-10193	...	2695	5115
Incurrence of Liabilities and Net Worth [b]	7109	2547	...	1118	4069	8379	3267	...	1176	5202

	1978					1979				
	Total General Government	Central Government	State or Provincial Government	Local Government	Social Security Funds	Total General Government	Central Government	State or Provincial Government	Local Government	Social Security Funds

Acquisition of Financial Assets

1 Gold and SDRs [a]	...	...	...	...	...	...	...	...	...	...
2 Currency and transferable deposits	17	-744	...	523	-243	441	-2	...	1034	1171
3 Other deposits	1153	31	...	429	719	1847	50	...	884	804
4 Bills and bonds, short term	363	429	...	...	...	411	292	...	...	...
5 Bonds, long term	830	66	...	1	641	799	993	...	1	529
6 Corporate equity securities	5	1	...	...	4	1	1	...	1	...
7 Short-term loans, n.e.c.	1665	1107	...	244	418	1451	840	...	259	402
8 Long-term loans, n.e.c.										
9 Other receivables	...	...	...	...	...	...	...	...	...	...
10 Other assets [a]	7649	2623	...	72	3506	3976	834	...	142	3050
Total Acquisition of Financial Assets [b]	11682	3513	...	1269	5046	8962	3007	...	2320	5956

Incurrence of Liabilities

1 Currency and transferable deposits	...	...	...	...	...	...	...	...	...	...

Japan

3.14 General Government Capital Finance Account, Total and Subsectors
(Continued)

Thousand Million Japanese yen

	1978					1979				
	Total General Government	Central Government	State or Provincial Government	Local Government	Social Security Funds	Total General Government	Central Government	State or Provincial Government	Local Government	Social Security Funds
2 Other deposits	...	...	...	...	...	...	...	...	...	...
3 Bills and bonds, short term	5281	3092	...	...	...	-395	-1163	...	...	...
4 Bonds, long term	13548	10677	...	1944	...	13646	13652	...	2291	...
5 Short-term loans, n.e.c.	4794	1941	...	2503	66	5488	2531	...	3054	88
6 Long-term loans, n.e.c.			...					...		
7 Other payables	...	...	...	...	...	...	...	...	...	...
8 Other liabilities	66	398	...	...	...	-203	172	...	11	...
Total Incurrence of Liabilities [b]	23689	16108	...	4447	66	18536	15194	...	5355	88
Net Lending [c]	-12007	-12595	...	-3178	4980	-9610	-12187	...	3035	5869
Incurrence of Liabilities and Net Worth [b]	11682	3513	...	1269	5046	8926	3007	...	2320	5956

	1980				
	Total General Government	Central Government	State or Provincial Government	Local Government	Social Security Funds

Acquisition of Financial Assets

1 Gold and SDRs [a]	...	...	...	...	...
2 Currency and transferable deposits	-139	37	...	-744	-904
3 Other deposits	1561	-10	...	716	780
4 Bills and bonds, short term	-834	136	...	-	-
5 Bonds, long term	2337	1152	...	-	857
6 Corporate equity securities	-	-	...	-	-
7 Short-term loans, n.e.c.	1207	500	...	242	497
8 Long-term loans, n.e.c.			...		
9 Other receivables	...	...	...	...	...
10 Other assets [a]	7314	4723	...	76	5359
Total Acquisition of Financial Assets [b]	11446	6537	...	290	6589

Incurrence of Liabilities

1 Currency and transferable deposits	...	...	...	...	...
2 Other deposits	...	...	...	...	...
3 Bills and bonds, short term	1873	3460	...	-	-
4 Bonds, long term	14709	14275	...	1015	-
5 Short-term loans, n.e.c.	3974	1039	...	2764	150
6 Long-term loans, n.e.c.			...		
7 Other payables	...	...	...	...	...
8 Other liabilities	143	636	...	4	-
Total Incurrence of Liabilities [b]	20698	19410	...	3783	150
Net Lending [c]	-9253	-12872	...	-3493	6439
Incurrence of Liabilities and Net Worth [b]	11446	6537	...	290	6589

a) Item 'Gold and SDRs' is included in item 'Other assets'.
b) Columns 'Central government', 'Local government' and 'Social security funds' refer to fiscal year beginning 1 April.
c) Net lending of the Capital Accumulation Account and the Capital Finance Account have not been reconciled and are different due to different statistical sources.

3.15 General Government Balance Sheet, Total and Subsectors

Thousand Million Japanese yen

	1970					1971				
	Total General Government	Central Government	State or Provincial Government	Local Government	Social Security Funds	Total General Government	Central Government	State or Provincial Government	Local Government	Social Security Funds

Assets

Non-financial assets	32596	3054	...	7512	35	38091	3460	...	8725	41
1 Tangible assets	32596	3054	...	7512	35	38091	3460	...	8725	41
a Stocks	...	...	...	...	...	...	...	...	...	...
b Reproducible fixed assets	21996	-	...	-	-	25866	-	...	-	-
c Land and other non-reproducible tangible assets	10600	3054	...	7512	35	12226	3460	...	8725	41
2 Intangible assets [a]	...	...	...	...	...	...	...	...	...	...
Financial assets	13672	4421	...	1920	7817	16814	5396	...	2286	9756
1 Gold and SDRs [b]	...	...	...	...	...	...	...	...	...	...
2 Currency and transferable deposits	549	53	...	438	58	680	86	...	522	72

3.15 General Government Balance Sheet, Total and Subsectors
(Continued)

Japan

Thousand Million Japanese yen

	1970 Total General Government	1970 Central Government	1970 State or Provincial Government	1970 Local Government	1970 Social Security Funds	1971 Total General Government	1971 Central Government	1971 State or Provincial Government	1971 Local Government	1971 Social Security Funds
3 Other deposits	1099	42	...	690	368	1313	35	...	761	518
4 Bills and bonds, short term	78	77	...	-	1	171	169	...	-	2
5 Bonds, long term	776	91	...	7	679	1020	92	...	7	921
a Corporate	...	...	...	...	...	...	...	...	...	...
b Other government subsectors	...	...	...	...	...	...	...	...	...	...
c Rest of the world	...	...	...	...	...	...	...	...	...	...
6 Corporate equity securities	21	11	...	2	8	23	11	...	3	9
7 Short term loans, n.e.c.	2285	775	...	637	949	2782	945	...	781	1155
8 Long term loans, n.e.c.			...					...		
9 Other receivables	...	...	...	...	...	...	...	...	...	...
10 Other assets	8863	3373	...	146	5755	10825	4058	...	213	7079
Total Assets	46268	7475	...	9432	7852	54905	8856	...	11011	9797

Liabilities and Net Worth

	Total General Government	Central Government	State or Provincial Government	Local Government	Social Security Funds	Total General Government	Central Government	State or Provincial Government	Local Government	Social Security Funds
Liabilities	8848	5851	...	3195	289	10909	7251	...	3966	316
1 Currency and transferable deposits	...	...	...	...	...	...	...	...	...	...
2 Other deposits	...	...	...	...	...	...	...	...	...	...
3 Other deposits	852	852	...	-	-	1195	1195	...	-	-
4 Bonds, long term	4114	3220	...	894	-	5168	3926	...	1242	-
5 Short term loans, n.e.c.	3139	637	...	2288	289	3768	842	...	2709	316
6 Long term loans, n.e.c.			...					...		
7 Other payables	...	...	...	...	...	...	...	...	...	...
8 Other liabilities	743	1142	...	12	...	778	1288	...	15	-
Net worth	37420	1624	...	6237	7563	43996	1605	...	7045	9480
Total Liabilities and Net Worth	46268	7475	...	9432	7852	54905	8856	...	11011	9797

	1972 Total General Government	1972 Central Government	1972 State or Provincial Government	1972 Local Government	1972 Social Security Funds	1973 Total General Government	1973 Central Government	1973 State or Provincial Government	1973 Local Government	1973 Social Security Funds

Assets

Non-financial assets	48734	4402	...	11753	44	66179	5473	...	15146	70
1 Tangible assets	48734	4402	...	11753	44	66179	5473	...	15146	70
a Stocks	...	...	...	...	...	...	...	...	...	...
b Reproducible fixed assets	32536	-	...	-	-	45490	-	...	-	-
c Land and other non-reproducible tangible assets	16199	4402	...	11753	44	20689	5473	...	15146	70
2 Intangible assets [a]	...	...	...	...	...	...	...	...	...	...
Financial assets	22237	8376	...	2632	12006	26113	9094	...	3189	14796
1 Gold and SDRs [b]	...	...	...	...	...	...	...	...	...	...
2 Currency and transferable deposits	709	70	...	565	74	863	101	...	678	84
3 Other deposits	1659	45	...	881	733	2099	53	...	1099	948
4 Bills and bonds, short term	259	258	...	-	2	216	216	...	-	-
5 Bonds, long term	1142	79	...	8	1055	1472	108	...	10	1354
a Corporate	...	...	...	...	...	...	...	...	...	...
b Other government subsectors	...	...	...	...	...	...	...	...	...	...
c Rest of the world	...	...	...	...	...	...	...	...	...	...
6 Corporate equity securities	38	25	...	3	10	43	26	...	3	14
7 Short term loans, n.e.c.	3286	1110	...	902	1394	3941	1323	...	1060	1713
8 Long term loans, n.e.c.			...					...		
9 Other receivables	...	...	...	...	...	...	...	...	...	...
10 Other assets	15144	6789	...	273	8739	17480	7268	...	339	10684
Total Assets	70971	12778	...	14385	12050	92291	14567	...	18336	14866

Liabilities and Net Worth

Liabilities	16157	11355	...	5212	368	19179	12783	...	6927	436
1 Currency and transferable deposits	...	...	...	...	...	...	...	...	...	...
2 Other deposits	...	...	...	...	...	...	...	...	...	...
3 Other deposits	2598	2598	...	-	-	1802	1802	...	-	-

Japan

3.15 General Government Balance Sheet, Total and Subsectors
(Continued)

Thousand Million Japanese yen

	1972					1973				
	Total General Government	Central Government	State or Provincial Government	Local Government	Social Security Funds	Total General Government	Central Government	State or Provincial Government	Local Government	Social Security Funds
4 Bonds, long term	7898	6096	...	1802	-	10099	7676	...	2423	-
5 Short term loans, n.e.c.	4711	1072	...	3392	368	6286	1527	...	4478	436
6 Long term loans, n.e.c.			...					...		
7 Other payables	...	...	...	...	...	...	...	...	...	...
8 Other liabilities	951	1589	...	18	-	992	1778	...	25	-
Net worth	54814	1423	...	9173	11682	73112	1783	...	11409	14430
Total Liabilities and Net Worth	70971	12778	...	14385	12050	92291	14567	...	18336	14866

	1974					1975				
	Total General Government	Central Government	State or Provincial Government	Local Government	Social Security Funds	Total General Government	Central Government	State or Provincial Government	Local Government	Social Security Funds

Assets

Non-financial assets	79912	5337	...	16214	73	88820	5989	...	17662	74
1 Tangible assets	79912	5337	...	16214	73	88820	5989	...	17662	74
a Stocks	...	...	...	...	...	...	...	...	...	...
b Reproducible fixed assets	58287	-	...	-	-	65095	-	...	-	-
c Land and other non-reproducible tangible assets	21624	5337	...	16214	73	23725	5989	...	17662	74
2 Intangible assets [a]	...	...	...	...	...	...	...	...	...	...
Financial assets	31350	10434	...	3997	18116	36445	11731	...	4274	21887
1 Gold and SDRs [b]	...	...	...	...	...	...	...	...	...	...
2 Currency and transferable deposits	1344	108	...	1111	125	1399	107	...	1156	136
3 Other deposits	2512	55	...	1191	1265	2879	70	...	1219	1591
4 Bills and bonds, short term	299	299	...	-	-	411	411	...	-	-
5 Bonds, long term	1664	152	...	8	1504	1987	221	...	9	1757
a Corporate	...	...	...	...	...	...	...	...	...	...
b Other government subsectors	...	...	...	...	...	...	...	...	...	...
c Rest of the world	...	...	...	...	...	...	...	...	...	...
6 Corporate equity securities	46	26	...	3	16	47	28	...	4	16
7 Short term loans, n.e.c.	4895	1619	...	1273	2203	5927	1971	...	1413	2778
8 Long term loans, n.e.c.			...					...		
9 Other receivables	...	...	...	...	...	...	...	...	...	...
10 Other assets	20591	8175	...	409	13003	23795	8925	...	474	15609
Total Assets	111262	15771	...	20211	18190	125265	17720	...	21936	21962

Liabilities and Net Worth

Liabilities	24052	15753	...	8967	529	33232	22273	...	11802	605
1 Currency and transferable deposits	...	...	...	...	...	...	...	...	...	...
2 Other deposits	...	...	...	...	...	...	...	...	...	...
3 Other deposits	2345	2345	...	-	-	3236	3236	...	-	-
4 Bonds, long term	12891	9620	...	3272	-	18214	13560	...	4655	-
5 Short term loans, n.e.c.	7346	1360	...	5658	529	10206	2751	...	7084	605
6 Long term loans, n.e.c.			...					...		
7 Other payables	...	...	...	...	...	...	...	...	...	...
8 Other liabilities	1469	2428	...	37	-	1576	2726	...	63	-
Net worth	87210	18	...	11244	17661	92033	-4553	...	10134	21356
Total Liabilities and Net Worth	111262	15771	...	20211	18190	125265	17720	...	21936	21962

	1976					1977				
	Total General Government	Central Government	State or Provincial Government	Local Government	Social Security Funds	Total General Government	Central Government	State or Provincial Government	Local Government	Social Security Funds

Assets

Non-financial assets	101670	6128	...	19561	83	114627	6286	...	21425	93
1 Tangible assets	101670	6128	...	19561	83	114627	6286	...	21425	93
a Stocks	...	...	...	...	...	...	...	...	...	...
b Reproducible fixed assets	75898	-	...	-	-	86823	-	...	-	-
c Land and other non-reproducible tangible assets	25772	6128	...	19561	83	27804	6286	...	21425	93
2 Intangible assets [a]	...	...	...	...	...	...	...	...	...	...
Financial assets	43570	14082	...	5201	26013	51973	17060	...	6188	30900

Japan

3.15 General Government Balance Sheet, Total and Subsectors
(Continued)

Thousand Million Japanese yen

	1976					1977				
	Total General Government	Central Government	State or Provincial Government	Local Government	Social Security Funds	Total General Government	Central Government	State or Provincial Government	Local Government	Social Security Funds
1 Gold and SDRs [b]	...	...	...	...	...	...	...	...	...	...
2 Currency and transferable deposits	1639	154	...	1338	147	1743	152	...	1429	163
3 Other deposits	3797	82	...	1674	2041	5046	108	...	2294	2644
4 Bills and bonds, short term	191	191	...	-	-	676	676	...	-	-
5 Bonds, long term	2966	707	...	8	2251	3507	894	...	9	2605
a Corporate	...	...	...	...	...	...	...	...	...	...
b Other government subsectors	...	...	...	...	...	...	...	...	...	...
c Rest of the world	...	...	...	...	...	...	...	...	...	...
6 Corporate equity securities	49	28	...	4	17	49	30	...	5	15
7 Short term loans, n.e.c.	6979	2402	...	1592	3248	7930	2830	...	1807	3722
8 Long term loans, n.e.c.			...					...		
9 Other receivables	...	...	...	...	...	...	...	...	...	...
10 Other assets	27949	10518	...	585	18310	33022	12370	...	646	21752
Total Assets	145240	20210	...	24761	26096	166600	23346	...	27613	30993

Liabilities and Net Worth

	Total	Central	State/Prov	Local	Social Sec	Total	Central	State/Prov	Local	Social Sec
Liabilities	46625	32216	...	15378	758	61923	44103	...	19164	831
1 Currency and transferable deposits	...	...	...	...	...	...	...	...	...	...
2 Other deposits	...	...	...	...	...	...	...	...	...	...
3 Other deposits	3075	3075	...	-	-	4741	4741	...	-	-
4 Bonds, long term	28153	21377	...	6776	-	38736	29988	...	8748	-
5 Short term loans, n.e.c.	13531	4525	...	8511	758	16483	5772	...	10308	831
6 Long term loans, n.e.c.			...					...		
7 Other payables	...	...	...	...	...	...	...	...	...	...
8 Other liabilities	1866	3240	...	90	-	1963	3602	...	108	-
Net worth	98614	-12006	...	9384	25339	104677	-20757	...	8449	30162
Total Liabilities and Net Worth	145240	20210	...	24761	26096	166600	23346	...	27613	30993

	1978					1979				
	Total General Government	Central Government	State or Provincial Government	Local Government	Social Security Funds	Total General Government	Central Government	State or Provincial Government	Local Government	Social Security Funds

Assets

Non-financial assets	132553	6598	...	25226	108	156924	7159	...	30060	126
1 Tangible assets	132553	6598	...	25226	108	156924	7159	...	30060	126
a Stocks	...	...	...	...	...	...	...	...	...	...
b Reproducible fixed assets	100639	-	...	-	-	119578	-	...	-	-
c Land and other non-reproducible tangible assets	31914	6598	...	25226	108	37346	7159	...	30060	126
2 Intangible assets [a]	...	...	...	...	...	...	...	...	...	...
Financial assets	62806	22188	...	6864	36322	71375	23690	...	8734	41907
1 Gold and SDRs [b]	...	...	...	...	...	...	...	...	...	...
2 Currency and transferable deposits	1761	136	...	1367	257	2202	132	...	1865	205
3 Other deposits	6198	139	...	2715	3344	8045	194	...	3684	4169
4 Bills and bonds, short term	1039	1039	...	-	-	1450	1450	...	-	-
5 Bonds, long term	4337	973	...	9	3355	5136	1452	...	10	3674
a Corporate	...	...	...	...	...	...	...	...	...	...
b Other government subsectors	...	...	...	...	...	...	...	...	...	...
c Rest of the world	...	...	...	...	...	...	...	...	...	...
6 Corporate equity securities	54	31	...	5	18	55	32	...	5	18
7 Short term loans, n.e.c.	9595	3902	...	2051	4140	11046	4736	...	2309	4542
8 Long term loans, n.e.c.			...					...		
9 Other receivables	...	...	...	...	...	...	...	...	...	...
10 Other assets	39822	15968	...	718	25207	43441	15695	...	859	29301
Total Assets	195359	28787	...	32091	36430	228299	30849	...	38794	42033

Liabilities and Net Worth

Liabilities	85604	63402	...	23858	913	104109	77133	...	28925	1007
1 Currency and transferable deposits	...	...	...	...	...	...	...	...	...	...

937

Japan

3.15 General Government Balance Sheet, Total and Subsectors
(Continued)

Thousand Million Japanese yen

	1978					1979				
	Total General Government	Central Government	State or Provincial Government	Local Government	Social Security Funds	Total General Government	Central Government	State or Provincial Government	Local Government	Social Security Funds
2 Other deposits	...	...	...	...	...	...	...	...	...	...
3 Other deposits	10022	10022	...	-	-	9627	9627	...	-	-
4 Bonds, long term	52276	41612	...	10664	-	65891	53067	...	12824	-
5 Short term loans, n.e.c.	21277	7776	...	13086	913	26765	10317	...	15982	1007
6 Long term loans, n.e.c.			...					...		
7 Other payables	...	...	...	...	...	...	...	...	...	...
8 Other liabilities	2029	3992	...	108	-	1826	4121	...	119	-
Net worth	109755	-34616	...	8233	35517	124191	-46283	...	9869	41026
Total Liabilities and Net Worth	195359	28787	...	32091	36430	228300	30849	...	38794	42033

	1980				
	Total General Government	Central Government	State or Provincial Government	Local Government	Social Security Funds
Assets					
Non-financial assets	181248	7764	...	35364	137
1 Tangible assets	181248	7764	...	35364	137
a Stocks	...	...	...	...	...
b Reproducible fixed assets	137983	-	...	-	-
c Land and other non-reproducible tangible assets	43264	7764	...	35364	137
2 Intangible assets a	...	...	...	...	...
Financial assets	82901	28464	...	9641	48260
1 Gold and SDRs b	...	...	...	...	...
2 Currency and transferable deposits	2063	171	...	1695	197
3 Other deposits	9606	184	...	4444	4979
4 Bills and bonds, short term	616	616	...	-	-
5 Bonds, long term	7473	3020	...	11	4442
a Corporate	...	...	...	...	...
b Other government subsectors	...	...	...	...	...
c Rest of the world	...	...	...	...	...
6 Corporate equity securities	56	32	...	5	19
7 Short term loans, n.e.c.	12253	5245	...	2551	5039
8 Long term loans, n.e.c.			...		
9 Other receivables	...	...	...	...	...
10 Other assets	50835	19197	...	935	33584
Total Assets	264148	36228	...	45005	48397
Liabilities and Net Worth					
Liabilities	124773	94057	...	33018	1162
1 Currency and transferable deposits	...	...	...	...	...
2 Other deposits	...	...	...	...	...
3 Other deposits	11500	11500	...	-	-
4 Bonds, long term	80566	66416	...	14151	-
5 Short term loans, n.e.c.	30789	11414	...	18745	1162
6 Long term loans, n.e.c.			...		
7 Other payables	...	...	...	...	...
8 Other liabilities	1968	4728	...	122	-
Net worth	139375	-57830	...	11987	47235
Total Liabilities and Net Worth	264148	36228	...	45005	48397

a) Item 'Intangible assets' is not included in this table.
b) Item 'Gold and SDRs' is included in item 'Other assets'.

Japan

3.22 Corporate and Quasi-Corporate Enterprise Income and Outlay Account: Total and Sectors

Thousand Million Japanese yen

	1970 TOTAL	1970 Non-Financial	1970 Financial	1971 TOTAL	1971 Non-Financial	1971 Financial	1972 TOTAL	1972 Non-Financial	1972 Financial	1973 TOTAL	1973 Non-Financial	1973 Financial
Receipts												
1 Property and entrepreneurial income received	24695	16522	8173	25883	16285	9599	29887	18372	11515	35943	20851	15093
a Net operating surplus	12734	13882	-1148	11917	13291	-1374	13388	14779	-1392	14923	16853	-1929
b Withdrawals from quasi-corporate enterprises [a]	...	...	...	...	...	...	...	...	...	...	...	...
c Interest	11119	2102	9017	13015	2399	10616	15403	2923	12481	19602	3120	16482
d Dividends	721	416	304	822	465	357	957	530	426	1246	706	540
e Net land rent and royalties	122	122	-	129	129	-	140	140	-	172	172	-
2 Other current transfers received	783	251	532	871	271	600	933	294	639	1055	352	703
a Casualty insurance transactions	773	242	531	860	260	599	919	280	639	1039	337	702
Claims received	251	242	9	269	260	8	285	280	5	342	337	6
Net premiums received by insurance companies	523	-	523	591	-	591	633	-	633	697	-	697
b Current transfers received from the rest of the world [b]	...	...	...	...	...	...	...	...	...	...	...	...
c Other transfers received, except imputed [b]	...	...	...	...	...	...	...	...	...	...	...	...
d Imputed unfunded employee welfare contributions	9	9	-	12	11	1	14	14	1	17	16	1
Total Current Receipts	25478	16773	8705	26755	16556	10199	30820	18665	12155	36999	21203	15796
Disbursements												
1 Property and entrepreneurial income paid out	15168	8706	6462	17678	9957	7721	20546	11214	9332	25994	13744	12251
a Withdrawals from quasi-corporations [a]	...	...	...	...	...	...	...	...	...	...	...	...
b Interest	12581	6562	6018	14829	7657	7172	17404	8733	8670	22076	10623	11453
c Dividends	2059	1639	420	2247	1726	521	2474	1845	628	3122	2366	756
d Net land rent and royalties	529	505	24	602	574	28	669	635	33	796	755	41
2 Direct taxes and other current payments n.e.c. to general government	3147	2664	483	3446	2909	537	3595	2927	667	4878	4129	749
a Direct taxes	3104	2628	477	3400	2870	530	3545	2887	658	4814	4075	739
Income	3100	2624	476	3395	2866	529	3539	2882	657	4809	4070	739
Other	5	4	-	5	4	1	5	4	1	6	5	1
b Fines, fees, penalties and other payments n.e.c.	43	36	7	46	39	7	50	41	9	64	54	10
3 Other current transfers paid	969	384	585	1099	441	659	1204	505	699	1380	619	761
a Casualty insurance transactions	766	235	531	851	251	599	911	273	639	1035	333	703
Casualty insurance premiums paid, net	243	235	9	260	251	8	278	273	6	339	333	6
Claims paid by insurance companies	523	-	523	591	-	591	633	-	633	697	-	697
b Transfers to private non-profit institutions [b]	...	...	...	...	...	...	...	...	...	...	...	...
c Transfers to households	203	149	54	248	189	59	293	232	60	345	286	59
Unfunded employee welfare benefits	9	9	-	12	11	1	14	14	1	17	16	1
Social assistance grants and other transfers n.e.c. [b]	194	140	54	237	178	59	278	219	60	329	271	58
d Transfers to the rest of the world [b]	...	...	...	...	...	...	...	...	...	...	...	...
Net saving	6194	5020	1174	4531	3249	1282	5475	4019	1456	4746	2711	2035
Total Current Disbursements and Net Saving	25478	16773	8705	26755	16556	10199	30820	18665	12155	36999	21203	15796

	1974 TOTAL	1974 Non-Financial	1974 Financial	1975 TOTAL	1975 Non-Financial	1975 Financial	1976 TOTAL	1976 Non-Financial	1976 Financial	1977 TOTAL	1977 Non-Financial	1977 Financial
Receipts												
1 Property and entrepreneurial income received	43080	22445	20635	47439	23442	23997	52968	26935	26033	56922	28813	28109
a Net operating surplus	14401	17251	-2850	14191	17655	-3464	16473	20723	-4250	17904	22631	-4727
b Withdrawals from quasi-corporate enterprises [a]	...	...	...	...	...	...	...	...	...	...	...	...
c Interest	26942	4096	22845	31496	4683	26813	34603	5046	29557	36941	4973	31968

Japan

3.22 Corporate and Quasi-Corporate Enterprise Income and Outlay Account: Total and Sectors
(Continued)

Thousand Million Japanese yen

	1974 TOTAL	1974 Non-Financial	1974 Financial	1975 TOTAL	1975 Non-Financial	1975 Financial	1976 TOTAL	1976 Non-Financial	1976 Financial	1977 TOTAL	1977 Non-Financial	1977 Financial
d Dividends	1517	877	640	1497	849	648	1586	860	726	1742	875	868
e Net land rent and royalties	221	221	-	255	255	-	306	306	-	335	335	-
2 Other current transfers received	1364	464	900	1691	558	1133	2129	636	1492	2382	736	1646
a Casualty insurance transactions	1337	438	899	1659	527	1132	2103	612	1491	2338	695	1643
Claims received	451	438	13	552	527	25	659	612	48	763	695	69
Net premiums received by insurance companies	886	-	886	1107	-	1107	1443	-	1443	1575	-	1575
b Current transfers received from the rest of the world [b]	...	...	...	...	...	...	...	...	...	...	...	...
c Other transfers received, except imputed [b]	...	...	...	...	...	...	...	...	...	...	...	...
d Imputed unfunded employee welfare contributions	27	26	1	32	31	1	26	25	1	44	41	3
Total Current Receipts	44444	22910	21535	49130	24000	25130	55097	27571	27526	59304	29549	29755

Disbursements

	1974 TOTAL	1974 Non-Financial	1974 Financial	1975 TOTAL	1975 Non-Financial	1975 Financial	1976 TOTAL	1976 Non-Financial	1976 Financial	1977 TOTAL	1977 Non-Financial	1977 Financial
1 Property and entrepreneurial income paid out	35933	18867	17066	41180	20723	20457	44378	21622	22756	46682	21900	24783
a Withdrawals from quasi-corporations [a]	...	...	...	...	...	...	...	...	-	...	...	-
b Interest	31275	15205	16069	36530	17249	19281	39255	17937	21318	41113	18112	23001
c Dividends	3681	2736	945	3607	2499	1108	3878	2522	1357	4222	2530	1692
d Net land rent and royalties	978	926	52	1044	976	68	1246	1163	82	1348	1258	90
2 Direct taxes and other current payments n.e.c. to general government	7457	6289	1169	6757	5399	1357	6652	5273	1379	7758	6034	1724
a Direct taxes	7374	6219	1155	6669	5330	1339	6561	5201	1360	7655	5954	1701
Income	7368	6213	1155	6663	5325	1338	6546	5188	1358	7629	5932	1697
Other	6	5	1	6	5	1	14	13	2	26	22	4
b Fines, fees, penalties and other payments n.e.c.	83	70	13	87	69	18	91	73	19	103	80	23
3 Other current transfers paid	1693	721	972	2028	810	1218	2498	882	1616	2871	1021	1850
a Casualty insurance transactions	1332	433	899	1655	522	1133	2096	605	1491	2326	682	1644
Casualty insurance premiums paid, net	446	433	13	547	522	25	652	605	48	752	682	69
Claims paid by insurance companies	886	-	886	1107	-	1107	1443	-	1443	1575	-	1575
b Transfers to private non-profit institutions [b]	...	...	...	...	...	...	...	...	...	...	...	...
c Transfers to households	361	287	74	374	288	86	402	277	125	544	338	206
Unfunded employee welfare benefits	27	26	1	32	31	1	26	25	1	44	41	3
Social assistance grants and other transfers n.e.c. [b]	334	261	72	342	258	84	376	252	124	501	297	203
d Transfers to the rest of the world [b]	...	...	...	...	...	...	...	...	...	...	...	...
Net saving	-639	-2967	2328	-835	-2933	2098	1569	-206	1774	1993	595	1399
Total Current Disbursements and Net Saving	44444	22910	21535	49130	24000	25130	55097	27571	27526	59304	29549	29755

	1978 TOTAL	1978 Non-Financial	1978 Financial	1979 TOTAL	1979 Non-Financial	1979 Financial	1980 TOTAL	1980 Non-Financial	1980 Financial

Receipts

	1978 TOTAL	1978 Non-Financial	1978 Financial	1979 TOTAL	1979 Non-Financial	1979 Financial	1980 TOTAL	1980 Non-Financial	1980 Financial
1 Property and entrepreneurial income received	61765	32228	29537	68588	33296	35292	85102	38805	46297
a Net operating surplus	21890	26671	-4781	21963	27583	-5620	24864	30849	-5985
b Withdrawals from quasi-corporate enterprises [a]	...	...	...	...	...	...	...	...	...
c Interest	37808	4346	33462	44329	4380	39949	57581	6424	51157
d Dividends	1704	847	857	1898	935	963	2192	1068	1125
e Net land rent and royalties	364	364	-	398	398	-	464	464	-
2 Other current transfers received	2532	798	1734	2759	872	1887	3184	963	2221
a Casualty insurance transactions	2488	755	1733	2714	828	1886	3135	915	2220

Japan

3.22 Corporate and Quasi-Corporate Enterprise Income and Outlay Account: Total and Sectors
(Continued)

Thousand Million Japanese yen

	1978 TOTAL	1978 Non-Financial	1978 Financial	1979 TOTAL	1979 Non-Financial	1979 Financial	1980 TOTAL	1980 Non-Financial	1980 Financial
Claims received	824	755	69	890	828	62	984	915	69
Net premiums received by insurance companies	1664	-	1664	1824	-	1824	2151	-	2151
b Current transfers received from the rest of the world [b]	...	...	...	...	...	...	...	...	...
c Other transfers received, except imputed [b]	...	...	...	...	...	...	...	...	...
d Imputed unfunded employee welfare contributions	44	43	1	45	44	1	49	48	1
Total Current Receipts	64297	33026	31271	71347	34168	37179	88286	39768	48518

Disbursements

	1978 TOTAL	1978 Non-Financial	1978 Financial	1979 TOTAL	1979 Non-Financial	1979 Financial	1980 TOTAL	1980 Non-Financial	1980 Financial
1 Property and entrepreneurial income paid out	46902	20763	26139	53630	22334	31297	70965	29518	41448
a Withdrawals from quasi-corporations [a]	...	...	...	...	...	...	...	...	...
b Interest	41083	16899	24184	47023	17945	29078	63500	24541	38959
c Dividends	4438	2563	1875	5086	2950	2136	5730	3330	2399
d Net land rent and royalties	1381	1302	80	1521	1438	83	1736	1646	90
2 Direct taxes and other current payments n.e.c. to general government	8967	7012	1955	9472	7787	1685	11121	9252	1869
a Direct taxes	8855	6924	1931	9372	7704	1668	11014	9163	1851
Income	8821	6895	1926	9328	7664	1664	10968	9121	1847
Other	34	29	5	44	40	4	47	42	4
b Fines, fees, penalties and other payments n.e.c.	112	88	24	100	84	16	106	89	17
3 Other current transfers paid	3156	1176	1981	3397	1280	2117	3913	1436	2476
a Casualty insurance transactions	2474	740	1734	2704	816	1888	3118	897	2221
Casualty insurance premiums paid, net	810	740	70	880	816	64	967	897	70
Claims paid by insurance companies	1664	-	1664	1824	-	1824	2151	-	2151
b Transfers to private non-profit institutions [b]	...	...	...	...	...	...	...	...	...
c Transfers to households	682	436	247	694	464	229	795	540	255
Unfunded employee welfare benefits	44	43	1	45	44	1	49	48	1
Social assistance grants and other transfers n.e.c. [b]	639	393	246	649	420	229	746	492	254
d Transfers to the rest of the world [b]	...	...	...	...	...	...	...	...	...
Net saving	5272	4074	1198	4848	2767	2081	2287	-438	2725
Total Current Disbursements and Net Saving	64297	33026	31271	71347	34168	37179	88286	39768	48518

a) Item 'Withdrawals from quasi-corporate enterprises' is not included in this table.
b) Unrequited current transfers are recorded on a net basis, so that those net estimates are included in item 'Social assistance grants and other transfers n.e.c.'.

3.23 Corporate and Quasi-Corporate Enterprise Capital Accumulation Account: Total and Sectors

Thousand Million Japanese yen

	1970 TOTAL	1970 Non-Financial	1970 Financial	1971 TOTAL	1971 Non-Financial	1971 Financial	1972 TOTAL	1972 Non-Financial	1972 Financial	1973 TOTAL	1973 Non-Financial	1973 Financial
Finance of Gross Accumulation
1 Gross saving	13340	12000	1340	12491	11019	1472	14828	13177	1651	15868	13595	2273
a Consumption of fixed capital	7146	6980	166	7959	7769	190	9353	9158	195	11122	10884	238
b Net saving	6194	5020	1174	4531	3249	1282	5475	4019	1456	4746	2711	2035
2 Capital transfers received [a]	370	370	-	450	450	-	517	517	-	692	692	-
Finance of Gross Accumulation	13710	12370	1340	12941	11469	1472	15345	13694	1651	16560	14287	2273
Gross Accumulation
1 Gross capital formation	18531	18235	296	17269	16949	320	18303	17977	326	24004	23504	500

Japan

3.23 Corporate and Quasi-Corporate Enterprise Capital Accumulation Account: Total and Sectors
(Continued)

Thousand Million Japanese yen

	1970 TOTAL	1970 Non-Financial	1970 Financial	1971 TOTAL	1971 Non-Financial	1971 Financial	1972 TOTAL	1972 Non-Financial	1972 Financial	1973 TOTAL	1973 Non-Financial	1973 Financial
a Increase in stocks	2557	2557	-	1069	1069	-	1058	1058	-	1827	1827	-
b Gross fixed capital formation	15974	15678	296	16200	15880	320	17244	16919	326	22177	21677	500
2 Purchases of land, net	1624	1522	102	2706	2613	93	3791	3705	86	5531	5405	127
3 Purchases of intangible assets, net [b]	...	...	...	...	...	...	...	...	...	...	...	...
4 Capital transfers paid	...	...	...	...	...	...	...	...	...	...	...	...
5 Net lending [c]	-6445	-7387	942	-7033	-8092	1059	-6748	-7988	1240	-12975	-14621	1646
Gross Accumulation	13710	12370	1340	12941	11469	1472	15345	13694	1651	16560	14287	2273

	1974 TOTAL	1974 Non-Financial	1974 Financial	1975 TOTAL	1975 Non-Financial	1975 Financial	1976 TOTAL	1976 Non-Financial	1976 Financial	1977 TOTAL	1977 Non-Financial	1977 Financial
Finance of Gross Accumulation												
1 Gross saving	11978	9354	2624	11977	9515	2462	15150	12952	2198	17128	15263	1865
a Consumption of fixed capital	12617	12321	296	12812	12448	364	13582	13158	424	15135	14668	467
b Net saving	-639	-2967	2328	-835	-2933	2098	1569	-206	1774	1993	595	1399
2 Capital transfers received [a]	800	800	-	891	891	-	866	866	-	896	896	-
Finance of Gross Accumulation	12778	10154	2624	12868	10406	2462	16016	13818	2198	18024	16159	1865
Gross Accumulation												
1 Gross capital formation	28671	28091	580	24980	24395	585	25857	25300	557	28032	27458	574
a Increase in stocks	3168	3168	-	405	405	-	993	993	-	1133	1133	-
b Gross fixed capital formation	25503	24923	580	24575	23991	585	24864	24307	557	26899	26325	574
2 Purchases of land, net	2343	2243	99	1296	1142	154	749	645	104	27	-89	116
3 Purchases of intangible assets, net [b]	...	...	...	...	...	...	...	...	...	...	...	...
4 Capital transfers paid	...	...	...	...	...	...	...	...	...	...	...	...
5 Net lending [c]	-18236	-20181	1944	-13408	-15131	1723	-10590	-12127	1537	-10035	-11210	1175
Gross Accumulation	12778	10154	2624	12868	10406	2462	16016	13818	2198	18024	16159	1865

	1978 TOTAL	1978 Non-Financial	1978 Financial	1979 TOTAL	1979 Non-Financial	1979 Financial	1980 TOTAL	1980 Non-Financial	1980 Financial
Finance of Gross Accumulation									
1 Gross saving	21469	19782	1687	22352	19761	2591	21018	17738	3281
a Consumption of fixed capital	16197	15707	490	17504	16993	511	18731	18175	556
b Net saving	5272	4074	1198	4848	2767	2081	2287	-438	2725
2 Capital transfers received [a]	1335	1335	-	1492	1492	-	1279	1279	-
Finance of Gross Accumulation	22804	21117	1687	23844	21253	2591	22297	19016	3281
Gross Accumulation									
1 Gross capital formation	29984	29423	561	35079	34454	625	38985	38271	714
a Increase in stocks	790	790	...	1694	1694	-	1522	1522	-
b Gross fixed capital formation	29194	28633	561	33385	32760	625	37463	36748	714
2 Purchases of land, net	-1593	-1694	101	327	253	74	1281	1165	117
3 Purchases of intangible assets, net [b]	...	...	...	...	...	...	...	...	...
4 Capital transfers paid	...	...	...	...	...	...	...	...	...
5 Net lending [c]	-5587	-6612	1026	-11562	-13455	1892	-17970	-20419	2450
Gross Accumulation	22804	21117	1687	23844	21253	2591	22297	19016	3281

a) Net.
b) Item 'Purchases of intangible assets net' is not included in this table.
c) Net lending of the Capital Accumulation Account and the Capital Finance Account have not been reconciled and are different due to different statistical sources.

3.24 Corporate and Quasi-Corporate Enterprise Capital Finance Account: Total and Sectors

Thousand Million Japanese yen

	1970 TOTAL	1970 Non-Financial	1970 Financial	1971 TOTAL	1971 Non-Financial	1971 Financial	1972 TOTAL	1972 Non-Financial	1972 Financial	1973 TOTAL	1973 Non-Financial	1973 Financial
Acquisition of Financial Assets												
1 Gold and SDRs [a]	...	...	...	...	...	...	...	...	...	...	...	...
2 Currency and transferable deposits	1667	1586	81	4128	4132	-4	2931	2852	79	3194	1927	1267
3 Other deposits	2289	2289	-	4457	4457	-	5107	5107	-	2819	2819	-
4 Bills and bonds, short term	146	20	126	-21	128	-148	882	-185	1066	-646	114	-760

Japan

3.24 Corporate and Quasi-Corporate Enterprise Capital Finance Account: Total and Sectors
(Continued)

Thousand Million Japanese yen

	1970 TOTAL	1970 Non-Financial	1970 Financial	1971 TOTAL	1971 Non-Financial	1971 Financial	1972 TOTAL	1972 Non-Financial	1972 Financial	1973 TOTAL	1973 Non-Financial	1973 Financial
5 Bonds, long term	1724	94	1630	2800	201	2599	4907	139	4768	5273	9	5264
6 Corporate equity securities	778	326	452	1043	482	562	2424	879	1546	1841	1027	815
7 Short term loans, n.e.c.	14273	-	14273	16820	-	16820	25774	-	25774	29525	-	29525
8 Long term loans, n.e.c.												
9 Trade credits and advances	7229	7229	-	3261	3261	-	9969	9969	-	22738	22738	-
10 Other receivables	...	...	...	...	...	...	...	...	...	...	...	...
11 Other assets [a]	1441	41	1400	5873	1523	4350	3160	-115	3275	2235	1123	1112
Total Acquisition of Financial Assets	29547	11584	17963	38363	14184	24179	55154	18646	36508	66979	29755	37223

Incurrence of Liabilities

	TOTAL	Non-Fin	Fin	TOTAL	Non-Fin	Fin	TOTAL	Non-Fin	Fin	TOTAL	Non-Fin	Fin
1 Currency and transferable deposits	3391	-	3391	6672	-	6672	7463	-	7463	7842	-	7842
2 Other deposits	8158	-	8158	11804	-	11804	16819	-	16819	15739	-	15739
3 Bills and bonds, short term	-53	-53	-	-259	-259	-	-373	-373	-	93	93	-
4 Bonds, long term	2240	1030	1210	3330	1650	1680	3704	1263	2441	4695	2304	2391
5 Corporate equity securities	1097	980	117	950	842	108	1428	1207	221	1438	1183	255
6 Short-term loans, n.e.c.	11120	10326	793	12645	14382	-1737	19670	17292	2378	19650	16592	3058
7 Long-term loans, n.e.c.												
8 Net equity of households in life insurance and pension fund reserves	1464	-	1464	1675	-	1675	1994	-	1994	2269	-	2269
9 Proprietors' net additions to the accumulation of quasi-corporations	-	-	-	-	-	-	-	-	-	-	-	-
10 Trade credit and advances	5139	5139	-	2196	2196	-	8053	8048	6	19966	19966	-
11 Other accounts payable	...	...	...	...	...	...	...	...	...	...	...	...
12 Other liabilities	2623	438	2185	5382	2416	2967	5138	1272	3866	5111	1379	3731
Total Incurrence of Liabilities	35178	17861	17317	44394	21226	23168	63898	28709	35189	76802	41516	35286
Net Lending [b]	-5631	-6277	645	-6031	-7043	1011	-8744	-10063	1319	-9823	-11761	1937
Incurrence of Liabilities and Net Lending	29547	11584	17963	38363	14184	24179	55154	18646	36508	66979	29755	37223

	1974 TOTAL	1974 Non-Financial	1974 Financial	1975 TOTAL	1975 Non-Financial	1975 Financial	1976 TOTAL	1976 Non-Financial	1976 Financial	1977 TOTAL	1977 Non-Financial	1977 Financial

Acquisition of Financial Assets

1 Gold and SDRs [a]	...	...	-	...	...	-	...	...	-	...	...	-
2 Currency and transferable deposits	3107	2754	353	2575	3017	-443	3186	3376	-190	2155	2243	-87
3 Other deposits	625	625	-	3201	3201	-	3646	3646	-	3259	3259	-
4 Bills and bonds, short term	473	-84	557	1198	41	1157	212	-30	243	1501	54	1447
5 Bonds, long term	6145	164	5981	8371	383	7988	10613	457	10156	12752	176	12577
6 Corporate equity securities	903	338	565	1306	300	1006	1659	450	1210	2100	626	1474
7 Short term loans, n.e.c.	24406	-	24406	26658	-	26658	30174	-	30174	25841	1	25842
8 Long term loans, n.e.c.												
9 Trade credits and advances	8067	8067	-	8346	8346	-	14469	14469	-	2295	2295	...
10 Other receivables	...	...	...	...	...	...	...	...	...	...	...	...
11 Other assets [a]	3128	64	3063	1664	971	693	2044	605	1439	2868	791	2077
Total Acquisition of Financial Assets	46854	11929	34925	53317	16259	37059	66002	22972	43031	52772	9443	43329

Incurrence of Liabilities

1 Currency and transferable deposits	6381	-	6381	5019	-	5019	7177	-	7177	4929	-	4929
2 Other deposits	13841	-	13841	20935	-	20935	21890	-	21890	24033	-	24033
3 Bills and bonds, short term	-17	-17	-	454	454	-	226	226	-	401	401	-

Japan

3.24 Corporate and Quasi-Corporate Enterprise Capital Finance Account: Total and Sectors
(Continued)

Thousand Million Japanese yen

	1974 TOTAL	1974 Non-Financial	1974 Financial	1975 TOTAL	1975 Non-Financial	1975 Financial	1976 TOTAL	1976 Non-Financial	1976 Financial	1977 TOTAL	1977 Non-Financial	1977 Financial
4 Bonds, long term	5229	2675	2555	6729	3458	3271	6200	2821	3379	6565	2815	3751
5 Corporate equity securities	917	832	86	1331	1162	169	1099	933	166	1355	1079	276
6 Short-term loans, n.e.c.	17600	16109	1491	16958	17650	-692	18992	17783	1209	14936	13596	1340
7 Long-term loans, n.e.c.												
8 Net equity of households in life insurance and pension fund reserves	2654	-	2654	3103	-	3103	3568	-	3568	3856	-	3856
9 Proprietors' net additions to the accumulation of quasi-corporations	-	-	-	-	-	-	-	-	-	-	-	-
10 Trade credit and advances	8103	8103	-	4616	4616	-	12572	12572	-	-35	-35	-
11 Other accounts payable	...	...	...	...	...	...	...	...	...	...	...	...
12 Other liabilities	7273	823	6450	4446	502	3943	4613	-4	4617	5186	603	4583
Total Incurrence of Liabilities	61981	28525	33457	63590	27842	35749	76337	34331	42005	61227	18459	42768
Net Lending b	-15127	-16596	1469	-10273	-11583	1310	-10334	-11360	1025	-8455	-9016	561
Incurrence of Liabilities and Net Lending	46854	11929	34925	53317	16259	37059	66002	22972	43031	52772	9443	43329

	1978 TOTAL	1978 Non-Financial	1978 Financial	1979 TOTAL	1979 Non-Financial	1979 Financial	1980 TOTAL	1980 Non-Financial	1980 Financial

Acquisition of Financial Assets

	TOTAL	Non-Financial	Financial	TOTAL	Non-Financial	Financial	TOTAL	Non-Financial	Financial
1 Gold and SDRs [a]	...	...	...	...	...	...	...	...	...
2 Currency and transferable deposits	4074	3808	266	483	434	49	-429	-1485	1056
3 Other deposits	4590	4590	-	4630	4630	-	4794	4794	-
4 Bills and bonds, short term	4740	-56	4796	-275	15	-290	2393	-35	2429
5 Bonds, long term	15938	697	15241	15066	1362	13704	13018	1676	11342
6 Corporate equity securities	2520	592	1928	2380	745	1634	1549	445	1104
7 Short term loans, n.e.c.	27929	-	27930	30813	-	30813	33893	-	33894
8 Long term loans, n.e.c.									
9 Trade credits and advances	11281	11281	-	21169	21169	-	13217	13217	-
10 Other receivables	...	...	...	...	...	...	...	...	...
11 Other assets [a]	5658	1024	4634	6509	-78	6587	1737	-3273	5010
Total Acquisition of Financial Assets	76732	21936	54795	80774	28277	52497	70171	15338	54833

Incurrence of Liabilities

	TOTAL	Non-Financial	Financial	TOTAL	Non-Financial	Financial	TOTAL	Non-Financial	Financial
1 Currency and transferable deposits	9067	-	9067	3674	-	3674	-1241	-	-1241
2 Other deposits	26605	-	26605	27804	-	27804	33231	-	33231
3 Bills and bonds, short term	321	321	-	390	390	-	-303	-303	-
4 Bonds, long term	6911	3083	3827	6686	3563	3124	5537	2777	2761
5 Corporate equity securities	1291	1145	146	1450	1372	78	1532	1441	91
6 Short-term loans, n.e.c.	12604	11176	1427	14938	13359	1579	19848	18774	1074
7 Long-term loans, n.e.c.									
8 Net equity of households in life insurance and pension fund reserves	4474	-	4474	5269	-	5269	5631	-	5631
9 Proprietors' net additions to the accumulation of quasi-corporations	-	-	-	-	-	-	-	-	-
10 Trade credit and advances	10722	10722	-	19018	19019	-	10699	10700	-
11 Other accounts payable	...	...	...	...	...	...	...	...	...
12 Other liabilities	8887	1173	7713	12508	3651	8858	7050	-4095	11145
Total Incurrence of Liabilities	80882	27622	53260	91737	41353	50384	81985	29294	52691
Net Lending [b]	-4150	-5685	1535	-10963	-13076	2113	-11814	-13956	2142
Incurrence of Liabilities and Net Lending	76732	21936	54795	80774	28277	52497	70171	15338	54833

a) Item 'Gold and SDRs' is included in item 'Other assets'.
b) Net lending of the Capital Accumulation Account and the Capital Finance Account have not been reconciled and are different due to different statistical sources.

Japan

3.25 Corporate and Quasi-Corporate Enterprise Balance Sheet: Total and Sectors

Thousand Million Japanese yen

	1970 TOTAL	1970 Non-Financial	1970 Financial	1971 TOTAL	1971 Non-Financial	1971 Financial	1972 TOTAL	1972 Non-Financial	1972 Financial	1973 TOTAL	1973 Non-Financial	1973 Financial
Assets												
Non-financial assets	120616	119173	1443	140777	139114	1663	176722	174665	2057	235442	232581	2862
1 Tangible assets	120616	119173	1443	140777	139114	1663	176722	174665	2057	235442	232581	2862
a Stocks	19603	19603	-	20392	20392	-	22479	22479	-	30246	30246	-
b Reproducible fixed assets	50261	48818	1443	59806	58143	1663	73792	71735	2057	103006	100144	2862
c Land and other non-reproducible tangible assets	50753	50753	-	60579	60579	-	80452	80452	-	102191	102191	-
Financial assets	199342	86189	113153	235049	98805	136244	289386	117860	171527	355306	147931	207375
1 Gold and SDRs a	...	...	...	...	...	...	...	...	...	...	...	...
2 Currency and transferable deposits	10776	10478	298	14904	14610	295	17835	17462	374	21029	19389	1641
3 Other deposits	15147	15147	-	19605	19605	-	24711	24711	-	27530	27530	-
4 Bills and bonds, short term	2281	62	2220	2261	189	2072	3143	5	3138	2496	118	2378
a Corporate and quasi-corporate, resident	...	...	...	...	...	...	...	...	...	...	...	...
b Government	...	...	...	...	...	...	...	...	...	...	...	...
c Rest of the world	...	...	...	...	...	...	...	...	...	...	...	...
5 Bonds, long term	15525	931	14593	18268	1076	17192	23160	1199	21961	28553	1328	27225
6 Corporate equity securities	6338	2581	3758	7272	2952	4320	9352	3487	5865	10976	4296	6680
7 Short-term loans, n.e.c.	87806	41	87764	104626	41	104584	130399	41	130358	159925	41	159883
8 Long-term loans, n.e.c.												
9 Trade credits and allowances	53894	53894	-	57155	57155	-	67124	67124	-	89861	89861	-
10 Other receivables	...	...	...	...	...	...	...	...	...	...	...	...
11 Other assets b	7575	3055	4520	10959	3177	7782	13663	3831	9831	14935	5367	9568
Total Assets	319959	205363	114596	375826	237919	137907	466108	292525	173584	590748	380512	210237
Liabilities and Net Worth												
Liabilities	242154	131936	110218	284591	151719	132873	349302	181235	168067	426977	223437	203540
1 Currency and transferable deposits	24257	-	24257	30929	-	30929	38392	-	38392	46234	-	46234
2 Other deposits	52167	-	52167	63971	-	63971	80790	-	80790	96529	-	96529
3 Bills and bonds, short term	1522	1522	-	1264	1264	-	891	891	-	984	984	-
4 Bonds, long term	17413	9059	8355	20710	10675	10035	24412	11936	12476	29097	14229	14867
5 Corporate equity securities	10369	9424	945	11505	10453	1053	13320	12046	1274	13864	12335	1529
6 Short-term loans, n.e.c.	68485	63913	4572	81130	78295	2835	100800	95587	5213	120450	112179	8271
7 Long-term loans, n.e.c.												
8 Net equity of households in life insurance and pension fund reserves	8713	-	8713	10388	-	10388	12382	-	12382	14651	-	14651
9 Proprietors'net equity in quasi-corporations	...	...	...	...	...	...	...	...	...	...	...	...
1 Trade credit and advances	45000	45000	-	47221	47221	-	56164	56159	6	77833	77828	5
1 Other accounts payable	...	...	...	...	...	...	...	...	...	...	...	...
12 Other liabilities	14228	3018	11210	17474	3811	13663	22150	4615	17535	27335	5882	21453
Net worth	77805	73427	4378	91235	86200	5034	116807	111290	5517	163771	157075	6697
Total Liabilities and Net Worth	319959	205363	114596	375826	237919	137907	466108	292525	173584	590748	380512	210237

	1974 TOTAL	1974 Non-Financial	1974 Financial	1975 TOTAL	1975 Non-Financial	1975 Financial	1976 TOTAL	1976 Non-Financial	1976 Financial	1977 TOTAL	1977 Non-Financial	1977 Financial
Assets												
Non-financial assets	270227	266679	3548	290803	286948	3855	317328	307073	10255	335861	324701	11161
1 Tangible assets	270227	266679	3548	290803	286948	3855	317328	307073	10255	335861	324701	11161
a Stocks	38021	38021	-	39334	39334	-	42513	42513	-	43185	43185	-
b Reproducible fixed assets	129661	126113	3548	139473	135618	3855	155462	151125	4337	166997	162357	4640
c Land and other non-reproducible tangible assets	102545	102545	-	111997	111997	-	119353	113436	5917	125679	119158	6521
Financial assets	401927	160961	240967	454825	177223	277602	521055	200499	320555	573603	210612	362991
1 Gold and SDRs a	...	...	...	...	...	...	...	...	...	...	...	...
2 Currency and transferable deposits	24137	22142	1994	26711	25160	1552	29882	28521	1361	32039	30765	1274

Japan

3.25 Corporate and Quasi-Corporate Enterprise Balance Sheet: Total and Sectors
(Continued)

Thousand Million Japanese yen

	1974 TOTAL	1974 Non-Financial	1974 Financial	1975 TOTAL	1975 Non-Financial	1975 Financial	1976 TOTAL	1976 Non-Financial	1976 Financial	1977 TOTAL	1977 Non-Financial	1977 Financial
3 Other deposits	28155	28155	-	31356	31356	-	35002	35002	-	38261	38261	-
4 Bills and bonds, short term	2970	34	2935	4168	76	4092	4380	46	4334	5881	99	5782
a Corporate and quasi-corporate, resident	...	...	...	...	...	...	...	...	...	...	...	...
b Government	...	...	...	...	...	...	...	...	...	...	...	...
c Rest of the world	...	...	...	...	...	...	...	...	...	...	...	...
5 Bonds, long term	34598	1392	33206	42960	1766	41194	53509	2159	51350	66421	2495	63926
6 Corporate equity securities	12136	4892	7245	13510	5259	8251	15048	5588	9460	16986	6052	10934
7 Short-term loans, n.e.c.	184330	41	184289	210988	41	210946	241162	41	241120	267005	44	266962
8 Long-term loans, n.e.c.												
9 Trade credits and allowances	97928	97928	-	106274	106274	-	120743	120743	-	123038	123038	-
10 Other receivables	...	...	...	...	...	...	...	...	...	...	...	...
11 Other assets [b]	17673	6375	11298	18860	7292	11568	21329	8400	12929	23972	9858	14114
Total Assets	672155	427640	244515	745628	464171	281457	838382	507572	330810	909464	535312	374152

Liabilities and Net Worth

	1974 TOTAL	1974 Non-Financial	1974 Financial	1975 TOTAL	1975 Non-Financial	1975 Financial	1976 TOTAL	1976 Non-Financial	1976 Financial	1977 TOTAL	1977 Non-Financial	1977 Financial
Liabilities	488283	251038	237245	551141	278119	273022	632629	317587	315042	688916	331091	357825
1 Currency and transferable deposits	52615	-	52615	57634	-	57634	64811	-	64811	69741	-	69741
2 Other deposits	110370	-	110370	131306	-	131306	153196	-	153196	177228	-	177228
3 Bills and bonds, short term	967	967	-	1421	1421	-	1647	1647	-	2048	2048	-
4 Bonds, long term	34352	16930	17422	41106	20413	20693	47373	23301	24072	54106	26283	27823
5 Corporate equity securities	14217	12602	1615	16027	14244	1783	17405	15456	1949	17940	15714	2225
6 Short-term loans, n.e.c.	138049	128287	9762	155007	145937	9070	173999	163720	10279	188953	177334	11619
7 Long-term loans, n.e.c.												
8 Net equity of households in life insurance and pension fund reserves	17305	-	17305	20408	-	20408	23976	-	23976	27832	-	27832
9 Proprietors' net equity in quasi-corporations	...	...	...	...	...	...	...	...	...	...	...	...
1 Trade credit and advances	85568	85563	5	89479	89475	5	106670	106666	5	102858	102854	4
1 Other accounts payable	...	...	...	...	...	...	...	...	...	...	...	...
12 Other liabilities	34839	6688	28151	38753	6629	32123	43552	6797	36754	48212	6859	41353
Net worth	183872	176602	7270	194487	186052	8435	205753	189986	15767	220548	204221	16327
Total Liabilities and Net Worth	672155	427640	244515	745628	464171	281457	838382	507572	330810	909464	535312	374152

	1978 TOTAL	1978 Non-Financial	1978 Financial	1979 TOTAL	1979 Non-Financial	1979 Financial	1980 TOTAL	1980 Non-Financial	1980 Financial

Assets

	1978 TOTAL	1978 Non-Financial	1978 Financial	1979 TOTAL	1979 Non-Financial	1979 Financial	1980 TOTAL	1980 Non-Financial	1980 Financial
Non-financial assets	364742	352624	12117	427210	412688	14521	487209	470538	16670
1 Tangible assets	364742	352624	12117	427210	412688	14521	487209	470538	16670
a Stocks	43184	43184	-	52002	52002	-	58036	58036	-
b Reproducible fixed assets	180406	175454	4952	205574	199957	5618	230503	224389	6114
c Land and other non-reproducible tangible assets	141152	133987	7165	169633	160730	8904	198669	188113	10556
Financial assets	645645	230768	414876	721362	258752	462610	799418	279438	519980
1 Gold and SDRs [a]	...	...	...	...	...	...	...	...	...
2 Currency and transferable deposits	36113	34573	1540	36596	35007	1589	36167	33522	2644
3 Other deposits	42851	42851	-	47481	47481	-	52274	52274	
4 Bills and bonds, short term	10621	44	10577	10346	59	10287	12740	24	12716
a Corporate and quasi-corporate, resident	...	...	...	...	...	...	...	...	...
b Government	...	...	...	...	...	...	...	...	...
c Rest of the world	...	...	...	...	...	...	...	...	...
5 Bonds, long term	82133	2965	79168	96971	4100	92871	110179	5966	104213
6 Corporate equity securities	19235	6373	12862	21278	6782	14496	22591	6991	15600
7 Short-term loans, n.e.c.	294935	43	294892	325748	43	325705	359641	42	359599
8 Long-term loans, n.e.c.									
9 Trade credits and allowances	134319	134319	-	155488	155488	-	168705	168705	-

Japan

3.25 Corporate and Quasi-Corporate Enterprise Balance Sheet: Total and Sectors
(Continued)

Thousand Million Japanese yen

	1978 TOTAL	1978 Non-Financial	1978 Financial	1979 TOTAL	1979 Non-Financial	1979 Financial	1980 TOTAL	1980 Non-Financial	1980 Financial
10 Other receivables	...	...	...	...	...	...	...	...	...
11 Other assets [b]	25438	9600	15838	27455	9793	17661	37122	11915	25208
Total Assets	1010386	583393	426993	1148572	671440	477132	1286626	749976	536650

Liabilities and Net Worth

	1978 TOTAL	1978 Non-Financial	1978 Financial	1979 TOTAL	1979 Non-Financial	1979 Financial	1980 TOTAL	1980 Non-Financial	1980 Financial
Liabilities	766098	356725	409373	851265	392681	458584	942794	429720	513073
1 Currency and transferable deposits	78808	-	78808	82481	-	82481	81240	-	81240
2 Other deposits	203834	-	203834	231638	-	231638	264868	-	264868
3 Bills and bonds, short term	2369	2369	-	2759	2759	-	2457	2457	-
4 Bonds, long term	61201	29551	31650	67759	32986	34774	73416	35882	37534
5 Corporate equity securities	19124	16752	2371	20183	17734	2450	21710	19169	2541
6 Short-term loans, n.e.c.	201557	188510	13047	216495	201869	14625	236342	220643	15699
7 Long-term loans, n.e.c.									
8 Net equity of households in life insurance and pension fund reserves	32306	-	32306	37575	-	37575	43206	-	43206
9 Proprietors' net equity in quasi-corporations	...	...	...	...	...	...	...	...	...
1 Trade credit and advances	113639	113635	4	130923	130920	4	143231	143228	3
1 Other accounts payable	...	...	...	...	...	...	...	...	...
12 Other liabilities	53262	5909	47354	61452	6414	55038	76324	8342	67982
Net worth	244288	226668	17620	297307	278759	18548	343833	320256	23577
Total Liabilities and Net Worth	1010386	583393	426993	1148572	671440	477132	1286626	749976	536650

a) Item 'Gold and SDRs' is included in item 'Other assets'.
b) Item 'Intangible assets' is not included in this table.

3.26 Financial Transactions of Financial Institutions: Detail

Thousand Million Japanese yen   Fiscal year beginning 1 April

	1970 ALL FINANCIAL INSTITUTIONS	1970 Central Bank	1970 Other Monetary Institutions	1970 Insurance	1970 Other Financial Institutions	1971 ALL FINANCIAL INSTITUTIONS	1971 Central Bank	1971 Other Monetary Institutions	1971 Insurance	1971 Other Financial Institutions

Acquisition of Financial Assets

	1970 ALL	1970 CB	1970 OMI	1970 Ins	1970 OFI	1971 ALL	1971 CB	1971 OMI	1971 Ins	1971 OFI
1 Gold and SDRs [a]	...	...	...	...	...	...	...	...	...	...
2 Currency and transferable deposits	64	-	256	51	27	30	-	305	38	24
3 Other deposits	-	-	60	46	...	-	-	475	112	55
4 Bills and bonds, short term	2	-143	-	-17	162	-49	384	-	-5	-428
5 Bonds, long term	1598	-15	464	21	1128	3163	-1287	2674	176	1600
6 Corporate equity securities	409	-	231	188	-11	751	-	380	288	83
7 Short-term loans, n.e.c.	15292	439	10627	1486	3788	17611	-1778	13716	1451	5395
8 Long-term loans, n.e.c.										
9 Trade credit and advances	-	-	-	-	-	-	-	-	-	-
10 Other assets [a]	1092	589	2110	128	297	4227	4025	2255	187	303
Total Acquisition of Financial Assets [b]	18456	869	13748	1903	5396	25733	1343	19806	2246	7030

Incurrence of Liabilities

	1970 ALL	1970 CB	1970 OMI	1970 Ins	1970 OFI	1971 ALL	1971 CB	1971 OMI	1971 Ins	1971 OFI
1 Currency and transferable deposits	3662	825	3102	-	-	6855	1291	5899	-	-
2 Other deposits	8421	-	7659	-	872	12891	-	12025	-	1508
3 Bills and bonds, short term	-	-	-	-	-	-	-	-	-	-
4 Bonds, long term	1229	-	883	-	346	2017	-	1560	-	458
5 Corporate equity securities	126	-	113	2	11	118	-	89	26	4
6 Short-term loans, n.e.c.	785	-	665	-	1168	-1781	-	-1717	-	1109
7 Long-term loans, n.e.c.										
9 Net equity of households in life insurance and pension fund reserves	1514	-	-	1514	-	1728	-	-	1728	-
10 Other liabilities	2088	44	1320	387	2999	3194	52	1950	492	3952
Total Incurrence of liabilities [b]	17826	869	13748	1903	5396	25024	1343	19806	2246	7030
Net Lending [b]	631	-	-	-	-	710	-	-	-	-
Incurrence of Liabilities and Net Lending	18456	869	13748	1903	5396	25737	1343	19806	2246	7030

Japan

3.26 Financial Transactions of Financial Institutions: Detail

Thousand Million Japanese yen — Fiscal year beginning 1 April

	1972 ALL FINANCIAL INSTITUTIONS	Central Bank	Other Monetary Institutions	Insurance	Other Financial Institutions	1973 ALL FINANCIAL INSTITUTIONS	Central Bank	Other Monetary Institutions	Insurance	Other Financial Institutions
Acquisition of Financial Assets										
1 Gold and SDRs [a]	...	...	...	...	...	...	...	...	...	...
2 Currency and transferable deposits	629	-	1095	135	123	807	-	1064	99	-82
3 Other deposits	-	-	212	48	20	-	-	-10	-24	-54
4 Bills and bonds, short term	1506	-133	-	16	1623	-323	1159	-	70	-1552
5 Bonds, long term	4430	927	3278	343	-119	5645	480	1260	424	3481
6 Corporate equity securities	1547	-	728	539	280	651	-	340	243	68
7 Short-term loans, n.e.c.	28105	1875	19086	1260	7390	28389	3767	17380	1863	8098
8 Long-term loans, n.e.c.										
9 Trade credit and advances	...	...	...	...	...	...	...	...	...	...
10 Other assets [a]	2801	422	5291	256	547	2631	-1857	7231	257	849
Total Acquisition of Financial Assets [b]	39018	3091	29691	2597	9864	37800	3548	27267	2932	10809
Incurrence of Liabilities										
1 Currency and transferable deposits	9385	2988	7120	-	-	7733	3248	4758	-	-
2 Other deposits	17247	-	15570	-	1957	14147	-	12539	-	1520
3 Bills and bonds, short term	-	-	-	-	-	-	-	-	-	-
4 Bonds, long term	2480	-	1829	-	650	2432	-	1667	-	675
5 Corporate equity securities	219	-	182	11	26	235	-	170	39	26
6 Short-term loans, n.e.c.	1959	-	1859	-	1597	3476	-	3425	-	2771
7 Long-term loans, n.e.c.										
9 Net equity of households in life insurance and pension fund reserves	2083	-	-	2083	-	2331	-	-	2331	-
10 Other liabilities	3882	103	3131	503	5633	5984	300	4707	562	5817
Total Incurrence of liabilities [b]	37246	3091	29691	2597	9864	36248	3548	27267	2932	10809
Net Lending [b]	1772	-	-	-	-	1552	-	-	-	-
Incurrence of Liabilities and Net Lending	39018	3091	29691	2597	9864	37800	3548	27267	2932	10809

	1974 ALL FINANCIAL INSTITUTIONS	Central Bank	Other Monetary Institutions	Insurance	Other Financial Institutions	1975 ALL FINANCIAL INSTITUTIONS	Central Bank	Other Monetary Institutions	Insurance	Other Financial Institutions
Acquisition of Financial Assets										
1 Gold and SDRs [a]	...	...	...	...	...	...	...	...	...	...
2 Currency and transferable deposits	174	-	746	96	59	-584	-	-103	118	74
3 Other deposits	-	-	106	72	2	-	-	-82	72	7
4 Bills and bonds, short term	618	386	-	-7	240	-41	-611	-	-24	594
5 Bonds, long term	6273	1712	2511	602	1449	8865	2086	5936	911	-68
6 Corporate equity securities	620	-	224	293	103	1126	-	356	397	373
7 Short-term loans, n.e.c.	24648	-784	16153	1979	10152	27212	-1530	16811	2089	13355
8 Long-term loans, n.e.c.										
9 Trade credit and advances	...	...	...	...	...	...	...	...	...	...
10 Other assets [a]	1018	434	4814	342	364	1085	292	5714	335	475
Total Acquisition of Financial Assets [b]	33350	1747	24553	3377	12370	37664	237	28632	3898	14810
Incurrence of Liabilities										
1 Currency and transferable deposits	4583	1099	4211	-	-	6012	214	6472	-	-
2 Other deposits	15158	-	13638	-	1700	21254	-	19232	-	2020
3 Bills and bonds, short term	-	-	-	-	-	-	-	-	-	-
4 Bonds, long term	2650	-	1966	-	684	3205	-	2682	-	523
5 Corporate equity securities	98	-	71	14	12	157	-	146	-	11
6 Short-term loans, n.e.c.	1809	-	1719	-	2942	-1451	-	-1433	-	3494
7 Long-term loans, n.e.c.										
9 Net equity of households in life insurance and pension fund reserves	2762	-	-	2762	-	3217	-	-	3217	-
10 Other liabilities	4695	648	2946	600	7032	4101	24	1532	682	8762
Total Incurrence of liabilities [b]	31756	1747	24553	3377	12370	36495	237	28632	3898	14810
Net Lending [b]	1594	-	-	-	-	1168	-	-	-	-
Incurrence of Liabilities and Net Lending	33350	1747	24553	3377	12370	37664	237	28632	3898	14810

Japan

3.26 Financial Transactions of Financial Institutions: Detail

Thousand Million Japanese yen — *Fiscal year beginning 1 April*

1976 / 1977

	1976 ALL FINANCIAL INSTITUTIONS	Central Bank	Other Monetary Institutions	Insurance	Other Financial Institutions	1977 ALL FINANCIAL INSTITUTIONS	Central Bank	Other Monetary Institutions	Insurance	Other Financial Institutions
Acquisition of Financial Assets										
1 Gold and SDRs [a]	...	...	...	...	...	...	...	...	...	...
2 Currency and transferable deposits	390	-	693	128	81	4	-	486	8	28
3 Other deposits	-	-	-10	126	28	-	-	679	299	119
4 Bills and bonds, short term	1010	518	-	18	474	1839	-742	-	22	2559
5 Bonds, long term	9514	441	5934	1284	1854	13284	502	8164	1854	2764
6 Corporate equity securities	1308	-	410	487	411	1533	-	568	597	369
7 Short-term loans, n.e.c.	29310	383	17435	2064	13138	24714	-265	15123	1569	13250
8 Long-term loans, n.e.c.										
9 Trade credit and advances	...	...	...	...	...	...	...	...	...	...
10 Other assets [a]	1829	418	7184	349	924	2613	1973	8569	407	1425
Total Acquisition of Financial Assets [b]	43360	1760	31646	4456	16910	43986	1468	33588	4755	20513
Incurrence of Liabilities										
1 Currency and transferable deposits	5852	1490	4873	-	-	4527	1289	3758	-	-
2 Other deposits	22120	-	19832	-	2433	24680	-	23060	-	2718
3 Bills and bonds, short term	-									
4 Bonds, long term	3698	-	2555	-	1143	3798	-	2304	-	1494
5 Corporate equity securities	249	-	178	25	46	203	-	170	23	10
6 Short-term loans, n.e.c.	1417	-	1511	-	3615	733	-	767	-	4929
7 Long-term loans, n.e.c.										
9 Net equity of households in life insurance and pension fund reserves	3685	-	-	3685	-	4046	-	-	4046	-
10 Other liabilities	4972	269	2697	746	9674	4978	180	3529	687	11363
Total Incurrence of liabilities [b]	41993	1760	31646	4456	16910	42965	1468	33588	4755	20513
Net Lending [b]	1368	-	-	-	-	1021	-	-	-	-
Incurrence of Liabilities and Net Lending	43360	1760	31646	4456	16910	43986	1468	33588	4755	20513

1978 / 1979

	1978 ALL FINANCIAL INSTITUTIONS	Central Bank	Other Monetary Institutions	Insurance	Other Financial Institutions	1979 ALL FINANCIAL INSTITUTIONS	Central Bank	Other Monetary Institutions	Insurance	Other Financial Institutions
Acquisition of Financial Assets										
1 Gold and SDRs [a]	...	...	...	...	...	...	...	...	...	...
2 Currency and transferable deposits	60	-	117	148	41	724	-	1203	292	155
3 Other deposits	-	-	-177	220	-7	-	-	-253	-83	-44
4 Bills and bonds, short term	2462	-587	-	-22	3071	-1178	3747	3	-50	-4878
5 Bonds, long term	14637	1952	9274	2206	1205	14156	32	6134	2017	5973
6 Corporate equity securities	2038	-	772	687	578	1326	-	1086	519	-280
7 Short-term loans, n.e.c.	28014	286	16759	1280	14142	33715	1247	17213	2445	18461
8 Long-term loans, n.e.c.										
9 Trade credit and advances	...	...	...	...	...	...	...	...	...	...
10 Other assets [a]	6020	-1081	14423	727	2408	4792	-1006	11928	1140	2000
Total Acquisition of Financial Assets [b]	53230	570	41167	5247	21438	53535	4020	37315	6281	21388
Incurrence of Liabilities										
1 Currency and transferable deposits	7515	319	7440	-	-	7665	3877	4048	-	-
2 Other deposits	26539	-	23673	-	2902	25539	-	22536	-	2799
3 Bills and bonds, short term	-									
4 Bonds, long term	3669	-	2168	-	1501	2553	-	1276	-	1276
5 Corporate equity securities	121	-	86	6	29	76	-	48	9	19
6 Short-term loans, n.e.c.	2352	-	1791	-	5014	1703	-	1260	-	3436
7 Long-term loans, n.e.c.										
9 Net equity of households in life insurance and pension fund reserves	4483	-	-	4483	...	5530	-	-	5530	-
10 Other liabilities	7507	250	6010	757	11992	7834	142	8147	741	13858
Total Incurrence of liabilities [b]	52187	570	41167	5247	21438	50900	4020	37315	6281	21388
Net Lending [b]	1044	-	-	-	-	2634	-	-	-	-
Incurrence of Liabilities and Net Lending	53230	570	41167	5247	21438	53535	4020	37315	6281	21388

Japan

3.26 Financial Transactions of Financial Institutions: Detail

Thousand Million Japanese yen — *Fiscal year beginning 1 April*

	ALL FINANCIAL INSTITUTIONS	Central Bank	Other Monetary Institutions	Insurance	Other Financial Institutions
			1980		
Acquisition of Financial Assets					
1 Gold and SDRs [a]	...	...	...	...	...
2 Currency and transferable deposits	131	-	548	150	77
3 Other deposits	-	-	140	110	27
4 Bills and bonds, short term	2895	1585	-3	-25	1338
5 Bonds, long term	12574	356	4444	1871	5903
6 Corporate equity securities	1304	-	897	631	-224
7 Short-term loans, n.e.c.	32117	-2020	18850	3510	18005
8 Long-term loans, n.e.c.					
9 Trade credit and advances	-	-	-	-	-
10 Other assets [a]	6876	-81	14997	931	1662
Total Acquisition of Financial Assets [b]	55897	-160	39872	7178	26788
Incurrence of Liabilities					
1 Currency and transferable deposits	-4295	-693	-3187	-	-
2 Other deposits	35190	-	32775	-	2444
3 Bills and bonds, short term	-	-	-	-	-
4 Bonds, long term	3088	-	2068	-	1020
5 Corporate equity securities	108	-	81	12	15
6 Short-term loans, n.e.c.	-327	-	-572	1	5972
7 Long-term loans, n.e.c.					
8					
9 Net equity of households in life insurance and pension fund reserves	5665	-	-	5665	-
10 Other liabilities	13520	533	8707	1501	17337
Total Incurrence of liabilities [b]	52950	-160	39872	7178	26788
Net Lending [b]	2947	...	...	...	...
Incurrence of Liabilities and Net Lending	...	...	...	...	...

a) Item 'Gold and SDRs' is included in item 'Other assets'.
b) Japanese financial institutions are not divided into 'Monetary institutions' and 'Financial institutions'.

3.32 Household and Private Unincorporated Enterprise Income and Outlay Account

Thousand Million Japanese yen

	1970	1971	1972	1973	1974	1975	1976	1977	1978	1979	1980
Receipts											
1 Compensation of employees	31272	37147	43078	54137	68489	79745	90393	100970	108904	117741	128241
a Wages and salaries	28637	33925	39372	49591	62773	72360	81761	90629	97303	104799	113961
b Employers' contributions for social security	1645	1947	2325	2783	3679	4872	5466	6509	7363	8011	8899
c Employers' contributions for private pension & welfare plans	990	1275	1382	1763	2037	2514	3166	3832	4238	4931	5382
2 Property and entrepreneurial income received	19749	20860	24087	30074	36653	39069	42519	43930	46934	51165	57237
a Operating surplus of private unincorporated enterprises	15147	15497	17935	22498	26140	26680	29160	29819	32780	35761	35800
b Withdrawals from private quasi-corporations [a]	...	...	...	...	...	...	...	...	...	...	...
c Interest	2958	3584	4211	5194	7665	9507	10145	10680	10513	11243	16572
d Dividends	1254	1322	1402	1739	2049	2005	2161	2324	2475	2868	3283
e Net land rent and royalties	390	457	540	643	799	877	1053	1106	1166	1293	1582
3 Other current transfers received	6560	7640	9124	11169	14996	19643	23392	26977	30727	34672	38454
a Casualty insurance claims	268	318	342	348	426	546	773	798	826	919	1151
b Social security benefits	2465	2828	3474	4151	6150	8788	10834	12720	14845	16932	18908
c Social assistance grants	1136	1287	1558	1991	2498	3108	3774	4483	5147	5615	6214
d Unfunded employee welfare benefits	11	14	17	19	31	37	32	51	52	54	57
e Other current transfers received	2681	3194	3733	4660	5891	7166	7979	8925	9858	11153	12124
Total Current Receipts	57581	65647	76289	95379	120138	138457	156304	171876	186565	203578	223931
Disbursements											
1 Final consumption expenditures	37828	42711	49328	59710	72201	83935	94486	104933	115059	126147	135671

Japan

3.32 Household and Private Unincorporated Enterprise Income and Outlay Account
(Continued)

Thousand Million Japanese yen

	1970	1971	1972	1973	1974	1975	1976	1977	1978	1979	1980
2 Property income paid	1817	2115	2437	2947	3971	4962	5493	5745	5671	6136	8031
a Interest	1717	2001	2305	2792	3784	4750	5234	5484	5390	5795	7523
Consumer debt	91	108	106	127	159	174	200	230	245	287	326
Mortgage	1626	1893	2199	2665	3626	4576	5034	5254	5144	5511	7197
Other											
b Net land rent and royalties	100	114	132	155	187	212	259	261	282	339	508
3 Direct taxes, fees, fines & other payments n.e.c. to government	6117	7413	8743	11140	14345	17025	19274	22239	23837	28708	32469
a Social security contributions	3165	3718	4300	5212	6910	9503	10684	12654	13880	16049	17452
b Direct taxes	2912	3644	4381	5850	7354	7422	8472	9459	9833	12514	14862
Income taxes	2761	3468	4118	5543	6971	6967	7890	8794	9098	11671	13987
Other	151	176	263	307	382	455	582	665	734	843	875
c Fees, fines and penalties	40	50	62	77	81	100	118	127	124	145	155
4 Other current transfers paid	3386	4066	4780	5799	7167	8701	9785	10985	12199	13660	15034
a Net casualty insurance premiums	275	327	349	352	431	550	779	808	837	927	1165
b Transfers to private non-profit institutions serving households	448	564	678	792	856	983	1041	1271	1549	1618	1750
c Transfers to the rest of the world	...	...	...	...	...	...	...	...	...	...	...
d Other current transfers, except imputed	2652	3161	3737	4636	5850	7130	7933	8856	9761	11062	12062
e Imputed employee welfare contributions	11	14	17	19	31	37	32	51	52	54	57
Net saving	8434	9344	11000	15783	22453	23834	27266	27974	29799	28927	32726
Total Current Disbursements and Net Saving	57581	65647	76289	95379	120138	138457	156304	171876	186565	203578	223931

a) Item 'Withdrawals from quasi-corporate enterprises' is not included in this table.

3.33 Household and Private Unincorporated Enterprise Capital Accumulation Account

Thousand Million Japanese yen

	1970	1971	1972	1973	1974	1975	1976	1977	1978	1979	1980
					**Finance of Gross Accumulation**						
1 Gross saving a	10884	12317	14591	20152	27771	30362	34902	36649	40019	40334	45233
a Consumption of fixed capital	2375	2735	3228	3902	4837	5833	6921	7999	9129	10238	11437
b Net saving	8509	9583	11363	16250	22935	24529	27981	28650	30889	30096	33795
2 Capital transfers received b	-194	-276	-403	-446	-405	-472	-483	-525	-612	-668	-699
Total Finance of Gross Accumulation a	10690	12042	14188	19706	27366	29890	34419	36124	39407	39666	44534
					Gross Accumulation						
1 Gross Capital Formation	6809	7522	9467	12450	14416	15690	18502	19081	20915	22961	23079
a Increase in stocks	17	146	240	58	228	89	80	77	248	122	73
b Gross fixed capital formation	6793	7376	9226	12392	14189	15601	18422	19004	20668	22838	23007
2 Purchases of land, net	-2058	-3306	-4587	-6349	-3349	-2381	-1879	-1465	-211	-2302	-3653
3 Purchases of intangibles, net c	...	...	...	...	...	...	...	...	...	...	...
4 Capital transfers paid	...	...	...	...	...	...	...	...	...	...	...
5 Net lending a	5939	7826	9309	13605	16298	16581	17796	18508	18702	19008	25107
Total Gross Accumulation a	10690	12042	14188	19706	27366	29890	34419	36124	39407	39666	44534

a) Including private non-profit institutions serving households for which separate data are not available. b) Net. c) Item 'Purchases of intangible assets net' is not included in this table.

3.34 Household and Private Unincorporated Enterprise Capital Finance Account

Thousand Million Japanese yen

	1970	1971	1972	1973	1974	1975	1976	1977	1978	1979	1980
					Acquisition of Financial Assets						
1 Gold a	...	...	...	...	...	...	...	...	...	...	...
2 Currency and transferable deposits	1659	2413	4504	4494	2793	2389	3766	2668	4975	2750	-672
3 Other deposits	5602	6466	10420	12231	12627	17046	17078	18829	19486	21570	23682
4 Bills and bonds, short term	...	...	...	...	...	...	...	...	...	...	...
5 Bonds, long term	855	1191	1375	1339	1394	2598	3365	3279	2905	2634	3474
6 Corporate equity securities	483	182	-298	76	387	419	305	364	89	261	429
7 Short term loans, n.e.c.	...	...	...	...	...	...	...	...	...	...	...

Japan

3.34 Household and Private Unincorporated Enterprise Capital Finance Account
(Continued)

Thousand Million Japanese yen

	1970	1971	1972	1973	1974	1975	1976	1977	1978	1979	1980
8 Long term loans, n.e.c.	...	...	...	...	...	...	...	...	...	...	...
9 Trade credit and advances of unincorporated enterprises	...	...	...	...	...	...	...	...	...	...	...
10 Net equity of households in life insurance and pension fund reserves	1449	1650	1962	2227	2586	3020	3466	3729	4318	5074	5368
11 Proprietors' net additions to the accumulation of quasi-corporations	...	...	...	...	...	...	...	...	...	...	...
12 Other [a]	161	238	224	321	181	292	462	556	630	300	-3
Total Acquisition of Financial Assets [b]	10208	12140	18187	20688	19968	25764	28441	29425	32404	32589	32278

Incurrence of Liabilities

	1970	1971	1972	1973	1974	1975	1976	1977	1978	1979	1980
1 Short term loans, n.e.c.	3112	4042	5665	8955	6700	7872	8909	8889	12197	11838	11278
2 Long term loans, n.e.c.	...	...	...	...	...	...	...	...	...	...	...
3 Trade credit and advances of unincorporated enterprises	2087	1062	1912	2764	-50	3703	1869	2316	559	2141	2513
4 Other accounts payable	3	49	5	11	11	5	-	6	8	6	-3
5 Other liabilities											...
Total Incurrence of Liabilities [b]	5202	5153	7582	11730	6661	11581	10779	11211	12763	13985	13789
Net Lending [b]	5006	6987	10605	8958	13307	14183	17663	18214	19641	18604	18489
Incurrence of Liabilities and Net Lending [b]	10208	12140	18187	20688	19968	25764	28441	29425	32404	32589	32278

a) Item 'Gold and SDRs' is included in item 'Other assets'.
b) Including private non-profit institutions serving households for which separate data are not available.

3.35 Household and Private Unincorporated Enterprise Balance Sheet

Thousand Million Japanese yen

	1970	1971	1972	1973	1974	1975	1976	1977	1978	1979	1980
Assets											
Non-financial assets	160173	185709	247994	314002	329198	355568	389413	421777	482316	575414	662207
1 Tangible assets	160173	185709	247994	314002	329198	355568	389413	421777	482316	575414	662207
a Stocks of household enterprises	3221	3302	3886	4920	5893	6323	6876	6956	7387	8565	8988
b Dwellings	25861	30724	42279	59033							
Gross					71996	81104	96996	107561	120493	144353	158490
Less: Accumulated consumption of fixed capital	...	...	...	...							
c Other reproducible fixed assets of unincorporated enterprises	...	...	...	...							
d Land and other non-reproducible tangible assets	131091	151683	201830	250049	251309	268141	285542	307261	354436	422496	494729
2 Intangible assets [a]	...	...	...	...	...	...	...	...	...	...	...
Financial assets	67037	79142	97293	117960	138054	163793	192267	221709	254106	286663	318318
1 Gold [b]	...	...	...	...	...	...	...	...	...	...	...
2 Currency and transferable deposits	12932	15345	19848	24342	27135	29524	33290	35958	40934	43683	43011
3 Other deposits	35571	42037	52458	64688	77315	94361	111439	130268	149755	171325	195007
4 Bills and bonds, short term	...	...	...	...	...	...	...	...	...	...	...
5 Bonds, long term	4811	5967	7306	8625	10144	12718	16115	19411	22310	24913	28353
6 Corporate equitry securities	4417	4599	4302	4378	4765	5184	5489	5853	5942	6202	6413
7 Short-term loans, n.e.c.	...	...	...	...	...	...	...	...	...	...	...
8 Long-term loans, n.e.c.	...	...	...	...	...	...	...	...	...	...	...
9 Trade credit and advances of unincorporated enterprises	...	...	...	...	...	...	...	...	...	...	...
1 Net equity in life insurance and pension fund reserves	8679	10329	12291	14518	17103	20123	23589	27317	31635	36709	42077
1 Proprietors' equity in quasi-corporations	...	...	...	...	...	...	...	...	...	...	...
12 Other [b]	627	865	1089	1410	1591	1884	2346	2901	3531	3831	3457
Total Assets [c]	227210	264851	345288	431962	467252	519361	581679	643486	736422	862077	980525

Liabilities and Net Worth

	1970	1971	1972	1973	1974	1975	1976	1977	1978	1979	1980
Liabilities	27366	32494	39186	49213	56243	68528	74688	89676	102380	118099	130278

Japan

3.35 Household and Private Unincorporated Enterprise Balance Sheet
(Continued)

Thousand Million Japanese yen

	1970	1971	1972	1973	1974	1975	1976	1977	1978	1979	1980
1 Short-term loans, n.e.c.	18467	22509	28174	37130	43830	51701	60611	69499	81696	93534	104813
2 Long-term loans, n.e.c.											
3 Trade credit and advances	8879	9916	10938	11999	12317	16725	13975	20069	20569	24443	25347
4 Other accounts payable	20	69	74	85	96	101	102	108	115	121	119
5 Other liabilities											
Net worth	199844	232357	306101	382748	411009	450833	506992	553810	634042	743978	850247
Total Liabilities and Net Worth c	227210	264851	345288	431962	467252	519361	581679	643486	736422	862077	980525

a) Item 'Intangible assets' is not included in this table.
b) Item 'Gold and SDRs' is included in item 'Other assets'.
c) Including private non-profit institutions serving households for which separate data are not available.

3.41 Private Non-Profit Institutions Serving Households: Production Account

Thousand Million Japanese yen

	1970	1971	1972	1973	1974	1975	1976	1977	1978	1979	1980
Gross Output											
1 Sales	...	...	...	...	...	...	...	...	...	...	...
2 Non-marketed output	439	437	461	510	651	580	613	912	832	881	1157
a Services produced for own use	439	437	461	510	651	580	613	912	832	881	1157
Gross Output	...	...	...	...	...	...	...	...	...	...	...
Gross Input											
Intermediate consumption	443	467	562	639	784	865	999	1148	1354	1672	1699
Subtotal: Value Added	...	...	...	...	...	...	...	...	...	...	...
1 Indirect taxes, net	...	...	...	...	...	...	...	...	...	...	...
2 Consumption of fixed capital	66	73	78	90	118	127	144	151	185	220	238
3 Compensation of employees	622	730	920	1172	1616	2176	2482	2953	3297	3736	4035
Gross Input	...	...	...	...	...	...	...	...	...	...	...

3.42 Private Non-Profit Institutions Serving Households: Income and Outlay Account

Thousand Million Japanese yen

	1970	1971	1972	1973	1974	1975	1976	1977	1978	1979	1980
Receipts											
1 Property and entrepreneurial income received	70	81	98	121	134	158	152	157	173	224	272
a Withdrawals from quasi-corporations	-	-	-	-	-	-	-	-	-	-	-
b Interest	60	70	84	103	115	133	118	126	143	176	214
c Dividends	7	7	10	12	13	18	27	24	23	35	41
d Net land rent and royalties	3	4	5	6	6	7	7	6	7	12	18
2 Other current transfers received	688	875	1065	1261	1382	1642	1762	2129	2567	2696	2963
a Casualty insurance claims	3	3	3	4	5	5	6	7	7	8	9
b Other Current transfers received from resident sectors, except imputed	685	872	1061	1257	1377	1636	1755	2120	2558	2687	2952
General government	88	119	153	196	262	383	450	515	597	670	752
Corporations and quasi-corporations	149	189	340	269	259	270	264	334	412	399	450
Households and unincorporated enterprises	448	564	568	792	856	983	1041	1271	1549	1618	1750
c Current transfers received from the rest of the world	-	-	-	-	-	-	-	-	-	-	-
d Imputed unfunded employee welfare contributions	-	-	-	-	1	1	1	1	2	2	2
Total Current Receipts	758	955	1163	1382	1517	1800	1913	2285	2740	2920	3235
Disbursements											
1 Final consumption expenditures	445	450	485	520	636	633	663	857	851	919	1108
a Compensation of employees	...	...	...	...	...	...	...	...	...	...	...
b Consumption of fixed capital	65	70	71	88	105	124	139	148	177	224	...
c Purchases of goods and services, net	...	...	...	...	...	...	...	...	...	...	...

Japan

3.42 Private Non-Profit Institutions Serving Households: Income and Outlay Account
(Continued)

Thousand Million Japanese yen

	1970	1971	1972	1973	1974	1975	1976	1977	1978	1979	1980
2 Property income paid	27	30	34	41	47	55	60	87	76	74	81
3 Direct taxes and other payments to general government	...	...	...	...	...	...	...	...	...	...	...
4 Other current transfers paid	211	236	282	354	353	417	475	666	723	759	978
a Net casualty insurance premiums	3	3	3	4	5	6	6	9	10	11	12
b Current transfers to household	207	234	279	351	348	412	469	657	713	748	966
Social assistance grants	207	233	279	350	348	411	468	655	711	746	964
Unfunded employee welfare benefits	-	-	-	-	1	1	1	1	2	2	2
c Current transfers to the rest of the world	...	...	...	...	...	...	...	...	...	...	...
d Other current transfers n.e.c.	...	...	...	...	...	...	...	...	...	...	...
Net saving	75	239	363	467	481	694	715	676	1090	1169	1069
Total Current Disbursements	758	955	1163	1382	1517	1800	1913	2285	2740	2920	3235

3.43 Private Non-Profit Institutions Serving Households: Capital Accumulation Account

Thousand Million Japanese yen

	1970	1971	1972	1973	1974	1975	1976	1977	1978	1979	1980
Finance of Gross Accumulation											
1 Gross saving	140	309	439	555	586	818	854	824	1267	1630	...
a Consumption of fixed capital	65	70	76	88	105	124	139	148	177	224	...
b Net saving	75	239	363	467	481	694	715	676	1090	1406	...
2 Capital transfers received	...	...	...	...	...	...	...	...	...	...	...
Finance of Gross Accumulation	...	...	...	...	...	...	...	...	...	...	...
Gross Accumulation											
1 Gross capital formation	...	...	...	...	...	...	...	...	...	...	...
2 Purchases of land, net	...	...	...	...	...	...	...	...	...	...	...
3 Purchases of intangible assets, net	...	...	...	...	...	...	...	...	...	...	...
4 Capital transfers paid	...	...	...	...	...	...	...	...	...	...	...
5 Net lending	...	...	...	...	...	...	...	...	...	...	...
Gross Accumulation	...	...	...	...	...	...	...	...	...	...	...

3.51 External Transactions: Current Account: Detail

Thousand Million Japanese yen

	1970	1971	1972	1973	1974	1975	1976	1977	1978	1979	1980
Payments to the Rest of the World											
1 Imports of goods and services	6985	7254	7645	11261	19257	18919	21247	21267	19174	27629	35036
2 Factor income paid to the rest of the world	503	552	592	820	1436	1430	1414	1346	1306	1998	2898
a Compensation of employees	23	30	37	39	32	57	72	86	130	168	244
b Property and entrepreneurial income paid	480	523	554	781	1404	1373	1341	1259	1176	1830	2654
3 Indirect taxes paid to supranational organizations	...	...	...	...	...	...	...	...	...	...	...
4 Other current transfers to the rest of the world	75	98	106	81	94	115	129	151	183	252	342
a By general government	29	42	25	15	22	34	34	33	40	57	84
b By other resident sectors	46	55	81	66	72	81	95	118	142	195	257
5 Surplus of the nation on current transactions	744	2036	2077	11	-1285	-152	1117	2867	3504	-1896	-2481
Payments to the Rest of the World, and Surplus of the Nation on Current Transfers	8308	9940	10419	12173	19502	20313	23907	25631	24167	27984	35794
Receipts From The Rest of the World											
1 Exports of goods and services	7926	9452	9779	11291	18258	18982	22582	24308	22729	25627	32887
a Exports of merchandise f.o.b.	6873	8273	8542	9889	16190	16579	19800	21436	20144	22555	29022

Japan

3.51 External Transactions: Current Account: Detail
(Continued)

Thousand Million Japanese yen

	1970	1971	1972	1973	1974	1975	1976	1977	1978	1979	1980
b Other	1053	1179	1238	1403	2068	2403	2782	2872	2584	3072	3865
2 Factor income received from the rest of the world	347	443	598	841	1189	1273	1257	1254	1376	2276	2820
a Compensation of employees	71	80	81	95	110	154	173	189	215	227	214
b Property and entrepreneurial income received	276	363	517	746	1079	1119	1084	1065	1162	2050	2606
3 Subsidies received from supranational organizations	...	...	...	...	...	...	...	...	...	...	...
4 Other current transfers from the rest of the world	35	45	42	41	55	59	68	70	62	80	87
a To general government	2	1	2	3	8	5	10	4	11	6	10
b To other resident sectors	33	43	40	38	48	53	57	66	51	74	78
Receipts from the Rest of the World on Current Transfers	8308	9940	10419	12173	19502	20313	23907	25631	24167	27984	35794

3.52 External Transactions: Capital Accumulation Account

Thousand Million Japanese yen

	1970	1971	1972	1973	1974	1975	1976	1977	1978	1979	1980
				Finance of Gross Accumulation							
1 Surplus of the nation on current transactions	744	2036	2077	11	-1285	-152	1117	2867	3504	-1896	-2481
2 Capital transfers received from the rest of the world [a]	-35	-35	-77	-44	-44	-49	-39	-24	-20	-74	-96
a By general government	-35	-35	-77	-44	-44	-49	-39	-24	-20	-74	-96
b By other resident sectors	-	-	-	-	-	-	-	-	-	-	-
Total Finance of Gross Accumulation	709	2001	2000	-33	-1329	-200	1078	2843	3485	-1970	-2577
				Gross Accumulation							
1 Capital transfers paid to the rest of the world	...	...	...	...	...	...	...	...	...	...	...
2 Purchases of intangible assets, n.e.c., net, from the rest of the world	...	...	...	...	...	...	...	...	...	...	...
3 Net lending to the rest of the world	709	2001	2000	-33	-1329	-200	1078	2843	3485	-1970	-2577
Total Gross Accumulation	709	2001	2000	-33	-1329	-200	1078	2843	3485	-1970	-2577

a) Net.

3.53 External Transactions: Capital Finance Account

Thousand Million Japanese yen

	1970	1971	1972	1973	1974	1975	1976	1977	1978	1979	1980
				Acquisitions of Foreign Financial Assets							
1 Gold and SDR's [a]	95	102	93	40	9	-15	3	32	187	72	13
2 Currency and transferable deposits	...	...	...	...	...	...	...	...	...	...	...
3 Other deposits	...	...	...	...	...	...	...	...	...	...	...
4 Bills and bonds, short term	...	...	...	...	...	...	...	...	...	...	...
5 Bonds, long term	...	...	...	...	...	...	...	...	...	...	...
6 Corporate equity securities	...	...	...	...	...	...	...	...	...	...	...
7 Short-term loans, n.e.c.	...	...	...	...	...	...	...	...	...	...	...
8 Long-term loans	...	...	...	...	...	...	...	...	...	...	...
9 Proprietors' net additions to accumulation of quasi-corporate, non-resident enterprises		...									
10 Trade credit and advances	...	...	...	...	...	...	...	...	...	...	...
11 Other	961	4491	2375	616	1535	804	2474	2937	5081	670	3456
Total Acquisitions of Foreign Financial Assets	1056	4593	2468	656	1543	789	2477	2969	5267	742	3469
				Incurrence of Foreign Liabilities							
1 Currency and transferable deposits	...	...	...	...	...	...	...	...	...	...	...
2 Other deposits	...	...	...	...	...	...	...	...	...	...	...
3 Bills and bonds, short term	...	...	...	...	...	...	...	...	...	...	...
4 Bonds, long term	...	...	...	...	...	...	...	...	...	...	...
5 Corporate equity securities	...	...	...	...	...	...	...	...	...	...	...
6 Short-term loans, n.e.c.	...	...	...	...	...	...	...	...	...	...	...

Japan

3.53 External Transactions: Capital Finance Account
(Continued)

Thousand Million Japanese yen

	1970	1971	1972	1973	1974	1975	1976	1977	1978	1979	1980
7 Long-term loans	...	...	...	...	...	...	...	...	...	...	...
8 Non-resident proprietors' net additions to accumulation of resident quasi-corporate enterprises	...	...	...	...	...	...	...	...	...	...	...
9 Trade credit and advances	...	...	...	...	...	...	...	...	...	...	...
10 Other	303	2545	418	689	2873	990	1399	126	1783	2711	6047
Total Incurrence of Liabilities	303	2545	418	689	2873	990	1399	126	1783	2711	6047
Net Lending	753	2047	2005	-33	-1329	-200	1078	2843	3485	-1970	-2577
Total Incurrence of Liabilities and Net Lending	1056	4593	2468	656	1543	789	2477	2969	5267	742	3469

a) Excluding initial allocations of SDRs by IMF.

4.3 Derivation of Value Added by Kind of Activity, ISIC Divisions, in Current Prices

Thousand Million Japanese yen

	1970 Gross Output	1970 Intermediate Consumption	1970 Value Added	1971 Gross Output	1971 Intermediate Consumption	1971 Value Added	1972 Gross Output	1972 Intermediate Consumption	1972 Value Added	1973 Gross Output	1973 Intermediate Consumption	1973 Value Added
					All Producers							
1 Agriculture, hunting, forestry and fishing	7499	3036	4463	7383	3130	4253	8179	3147	5032	10288	3621	6667
2 Mining and quarrying	969	347	621	1006	371	635	1071	409	661	1348	527	821
3 Manufacturing	80379	54039	26340	84233	55876	28357	93010	61159	31851	118288	78831	39457
a Manufacture of food, beverages and tobacco [a]	7945	5150	2795	8887	5762	3125	9399	6259	3140	11407	7789	3619
b Textile, wearing apparel and leather industries [b]	4908	3473	1436	5116	3600	1517	5403	3873	1530	6792	4756	2036
c Manufacture of wood and wood products, including furniture	...	...	...	...	...	...	...	...	...	...	...	...
d Manufacture of paper and paper products, printing and publishing [c]	2567	1867	700	2660	1908	752	2926	2085	841	3849	2765	1084
e Manufacture of chemicals and chemical petroleum, coal, rubber and plastic products [d]	8894	5433	3461	9803	5952	3851	10733	6487	4245	12393	7628	4765
f Manufacture of non-metallic mineral products, except products of petroleum and coal	2860	1750	1110	3154	1928	1226	3548	2141	1407	4450	2622	1828
g Basic metal industries	14050	11078	2972	13318	10341	2977	14669	11100	3569	20125	15343	4782
h Manufacture of fabricated metal products, machinery and equipment	29177	18659	10518	30514	19290	11224	33723	21058	12665	42935	27257	15677
i Other manufacturing industries	9978	6630	3347	10781	7094	3687	12610	8156	4454	16338	10671	5666
4 Electricity, gas and water	2407	849	1557	2651	962	1690	2968	1178	1790	3435	1498	1937
5 Construction	15663	10001	5662	16998	10483	6514	20134	12383	7751	26834	17004	9830
6 Wholesale and retail trade, restaurants and hotels	15926	5422	10504	16995	5700	11295	19655	6605	13051	23511	7441	16070
7 Transport, storage and communication	7317	2296	5022	8161	2727	5433	8803	2979	5824	10431	3471	6960
8 Finance, insurance, real estate and business services	11422	2114	9309	13393	2458	10936	15554	2766	12788	19097	3453	15645
9 Community, social and personal services	13881	6847	7033	15766	7838	7928	18868	9036	9831	22444	11052	11392
Total, Industries	155462	84951	70511	166586	89544	77042	188239	99661	88578	235676	126896	108779
Producers of Government Services	6198	1556	4642	7272	1793	5480	8582	2114	6468	10556	2537	8020
Other Producers	1107	438	670	1233	452	781	1501	535	966	1847	626	1221
Total	162767	86945	75822	175091	91789	83302	198322	102310	96012	248079	130059	118020
Imputed bank service charge	-	2970	-2970	-	3400	-3400	-	3743	-3743	-	4961	-4961
Import duties	498	-	498	478	-	478	510	-	510	647	-	647
Value added tax	...	...	...	...	...	...	...	...	...	...	...	...
Other adjustments	-66	...	-66	251	...	251	453	...	-473	-1286	...	-1286
Total	163199	89915	73285	175821	95189	80632	198379	106053	92306	247440	135020	112420

	1974 Gross Output	1974 Intermediate Consumption	1974 Value Added	1975 Gross Output	1975 Intermediate Consumption	1975 Value Added	1976 Gross Output	1976 Intermediate Consumption	1976 Value Added	1977 Gross Output	1977 Intermediate Consumption	1977 Value Added
					All Producers							
1 Agriculture, hunting, forestry and fishing	12173	4673	7499	13123	4993	8130	14326	5504	8822	15268	5957	9310
2 Mining and quarrying	1689	744	945	1429	653	776	1540	700	840	1780	817	963
3 Manufacturing	146533	101495	45038	143936	99686	44250	164747	114016	50732	176549	121263	55286
a Manufacture of food, beverages and tobacco [a]	13753	9703	4051	17411	12540	4871	19819	14205	5614	21652	14867	6785

Japan

4.3 Derivation of Value Added by Kind of Activity, ISIC Divisions, in Current Prices
(Continued)

Thousand Million Japanese yen

	1974 Gross Output	1974 Intermediate Consumption	1974 Value Added	1975 Gross Output	1975 Intermediate Consumption	1975 Value Added	1976 Gross Output	1976 Intermediate Consumption	1976 Value Added	1977 Gross Output	1977 Intermediate Consumption	1977 Value Added
b Textile, wearing apparel and leather industries b	7167	4880	2287	7227	5154	2073	8223	5912	2311	8393	5883	2510
c Manufacture of wood and wood products, including furniture	...	...	...	...	...	...	...	...	...	...	...	...
d Manufacture of paper and paper products, printing and publishing c	5434	3799	1635	4810	3430	1380	5403	3863	1540	5686	4085	1601
e Manufacture of chemicals and chemical petroleum, coal, rubber and plastic products d	18890	14830	4061	20979	15985	4994	23831	18045	5787	25524	18918	6606
f Manufacture of non-metallic mineral products, except products of petroleum and coal	5473	3286	2187	4944	3064	1880	5399	3336	2063	5910	3686	2224
g Basic metal industries	26248	20612	5636	24053	19176	4877	28111	22410	5702	28901	23353	5548
h Manufacture of fabricated metal products, machinery and equipment	51147	32769	18378	46676	29120	17557	53670	33512	20159	59054	37148	21906
i Other manufacturing industries	18420	11617	6803	17835	11217	6619	20290	12734	7556	21429	13324	8106
4 Electricity, gas and water	4819	2668	2151	5918	2917	3002	6901	3316	3585	8181	3850	4331
5 Construction	31197	19498	11699	34014	19690	14324	37202	22186	15016	40068	24262	15806
6 Wholesale and retail trade, restaurants and hotels	29951	9551	20400	32086	10182	21904	35768	11476	24292	38585	12850	25735
7 Transport, storage and communication	12930	4830	8100	15060	5519	9541	17401	6288	11113	19689	6537	13152
8 Finance, insurance, real estate and business services	22263	4039	18224	26815	6266	20549	30287	7166	23121	34335	8019	26316
9 Community, social and personal services	27023	13264	13759	31331	15080	16251	35018	16739	18278	39731	19292	20439
Total, Industries	288577	160761	127815	303713	164986	138727	343190	187391	155799	374185	202847	171338
Producers of Government Services	13792	3181	10611	16830	3701	13128	18770	4197	14573	21034	4868	16166
Other Producers	2346	735	1611	3059	849	2210	3564	971	2593	4101	1100	3001
Total	304715	164677	140037	323602	169537	154065	365524	192559	172965	399321	208815	190506
Imputed bank service charge	-	6588	-6588	-	7253	-7253	-	7773	-7773	-	8238	-8238
Import duties	639	-	639	549	-	549	711	-	711	777	-	777
Value added tax	...	...	...	...	...	...	...	...	...	...	...	...
Other adjustments	80	...	80	670	...	670	-52	...	-52	1415	...	1415
Total	305434	171265	134169	324821	176790	148031	366183	200331	165851	401512	217053	184460

	1978 Gross Output	1978 Intermediate Consumption	1978 Value Added	1979 Gross Output	1979 Intermediate Consumption	1979 Value Added	1980 Gross Output	1980 Intermediate Consumption	1980 Value Added
				All Producers					
1 Agriculture, hunting, forestry and fishing	15375	6038	9338	16020	6512	9508	16276	7342	8935
2 Mining and quarrying	2042	912	1129	2351	1084	1267	2614	1235	1379
3 Manufacturing	183834	123062	60773	206286	140440	65847	238909	167830	71079
a Manufacture of food, beverages and tobacco a	22579	15708	6871	23388	16249	7139	26402	18618	7784
b Textile, wearing apparel and leather industries b	8152	5627	2525	8823	6066	2757	9238	6457	2781
c Manufacture of wood and wood products, including furniture	...	...	...	...	...	...	...	...	...
d Manufacture of paper and paper products, printing and publishing c	5656	3942	1714	6338	4562	1776	8127	6154	1973
e Manufacture of chemicals and chemical petroleum, coal, rubber and plastic products d	24647	16731	7917	29337	22215	7122	38247	30902	7346
f Manufacture of non-metallic mineral products, except products of petroleum and coal	6334	3889	2445	7043	4388	2655	8236	5371	2865
g Basic metal industries	29285	22742	6543	34365	26029	8336	39191	30236	8956
h Manufacture of fabricated metal products, machinery and equipment	64257	40446	23810	71427	45032	26395	82210	52788	29421
i Other manufacturing industries	22925	13977	8948	25565	15898	9667	27258	17304	9954
4 Electricity, gas and water	8602	3744	4858	9421	4625	4796	13274	6448	6825

Japan

4.3 Derivation of Value Added by Kind of Activity, ISIC Divisions, in Current Prices
(Continued)

Thousand Million Japanese yen

		1978			1979			1980	
	Gross Output	Intermediate Consumption	Value Added	Gross Output	Intermediate Consumption	Value Added	Gross Output	Intermediate Consumption	Value Added
5 Construction	44463	26394	18069	50091	29943	20148	53743	32263	21480
6 Wholesale and retail trade, restaurants and hotels	40485	13627	26858	42813	14669	28144	44665	15470	29195
7 Transport, storage and communication	21473	7288	14185	23416	8398	15018	26452	10265	16188
8 Finance, insurance, real estate and business services	38695	8967	29728	42959	9965	32995	47823	10856	36967
9 Community, social and personal services	44853	21780	23073	49747	23908	25839	54721	26608	28113
Total, Industries	399822	211811	188011	443103	239541	203562	498478	278317	220161
Producers of Government Services	23037	5509	17528	25175	6248	18927	27676	7212	20464
Other Producers	4723	1287	3436	5452	1578	3874	5932	1704	4228
Total	427581	218607	208975	473730	247367	226363	532086	287232	244854
Imputed bank service charge	-	8667	-8667	-	9705	-9705	-	11019	-11019
Import duties	759	-	759	946	-	946	924	-	924
Value added tax	...	...	...	...	...	...	...	...	...
Other adjustments	1571	...	1571	1012	...	1012	190	...	190
Total	429911	227274	202638	475688	257072	218616	533200	298251	234949

a) Excluding tobacco.
b) Textile only.
c) Excluding printing and publishing.
d) Excluding rubber and plastic products.

4.4 Derivation of Value Added by Kind of Activity, ISIC Divisions, in Constant Prices

Thousand Million Japanese yen

		1970			1971			1972			1973	
	Gross Output	Intermediate Consumption	Value Added	Gross Output	Intermediate Consumption	Value Added	Gross Output	Intermediate Consumption	Value Added	Gross Output	Intermediate Consumption	Value Added

At constant prices of: 1975

All Producers

1 Agriculture, hunting, forestry and fishing	12705	5517	7188	12350	5519	6832	13282	5490	7792	13550	5190	8360
2 Mining and quarrying	1543	723	820	1587	727	860	1663	769	894	1828	867	961
3 Manufacturing	123473	88331	35142	129674	92357	37317	141118	99829	41288	157034	110026	47008
a Manufacture of food, beverages and tobacco	12867	9444	3423	13742	10164	3578	14240	10698	3542	15652	11011	4641
b Textile, wearing apparel and leather industries a	6455	4706	1749	6836	5074	1763	7100	5349	1751	6767	4928	1839
c Manufacture of wood and wood products, including furniture	...	...	...	...	...	...	...	...	...	...	...	...
d Manufacture of paper and paper products, printing and publishing b	4565	3435	1130	4780	3546	1234	5242	3813	1430	5714	4176	1539
e Manufacture of chemicals and chemical petroleum, coal, rubber and plastic products	16932	13428	3504	18347	14319	4029	20191	15388	4803	21158	16254	4904
f Manufacture of non-metallic mineral products, except products of petroleum and coal	4877	3190	1688	5256	3423	1833	5837	3746	2092	6505	4077	2428
g Basic metal industries	20325	16733	3593	20332	16253	4079	22350	17667	4683	26484	21136	5347
h Manufacture of fabricated metal products, machinery and equipment	40606	26747	13859	42387	28005	14382	46124	30320	15804	54412	35235	19177
i Other manufacturing industries	16845	10649	6195	17994	11574	6420	20034	12850	7184	20343	13210	7133
4 Electricity, gas and water	4342	1982	2360	4764	2118	2646	5243	2540	2704	5858	3166	2692
5 Construction	27052	16095	10957	28568	16818	11749	32111	19112	12999	35922	21717	14206
6 Wholesale and retail trade, restaurants and hotels	25581	9680	15902	26829	9671	17158	30412	10616	19797	31914	10346	21568
7 Transport, storage and communication	11674	4293	7381	12476	4751	7725	12828	4941	7887	13861	5144	8718
8 Finance, insurance, real estate and business services	17183	3534	13649	19294	3946	15349	22127	4248	17878	24125	4618	19507
9 Community, social and personal services	25269	11204	14065	27022	12455	14568	30130	14000	16130	31780	15261	16518
Total, Industries	248823	141360	107463	262564	148362	114203	288914	161545	127369	315872	176335	139537
Producers of Government Services	12926	2389	10537	13596	2711	10885	14409	3161	11248	15099	3412	11686

Japan

4.4 Derivation of Value Added by Kind of Activity, ISIC Divisions, in Constant Prices
(Continued)

Thousand Million Japanese yen

	1970 Gross Output	1970 Intermediate Consumption	1970 Value Added	1971 Gross Output	1971 Intermediate Consumption	1971 Value Added	1972 Gross Output	1972 Intermediate Consumption	1972 Value Added	1973 Gross Output	1973 Intermediate Consumption	1973 Value Added
				At constant prices of:1975								
Other Producers	2263	654	1609	2297	664	1633	2520	761	1759	2695	814	1881
Total	264013	144404	119609	278457	151736	126721	305843	165467	140375	333665	180562	153104
Imputed bank service charge	-	4426	-4426	-	5106	-5106	-	6197	-6197	-	6901	-6901
Import duties	1620	-	1620	1470	-	1470	1461	-	1461	1605	-	1605
Value added tax	...	...	...	...	...	...	...	...	...	...	...	...
Other adjustments	1041	...	1041	187	...	187	-1499	...	-1499	-1862	...	-1862
Total	266674	148829	117844	280116	156842	123272	305804	171664	134140	333408	187463	145945

	1974 Gross Output	1974 Intermediate Consumption	1974 Value Added	1975 Gross Output	1975 Intermediate Consumption	1975 Value Added	1976 Gross Output	1976 Intermediate Consumption	1976 Value Added	1977 Gross Output	1977 Intermediate Consumption	1977 Value Added
				At constant prices of:1975								
				All Producers								
1 Agriculture, hunting, forestry and fishing	13222	5006	8216	13123	4993	8130	13024	5308	7716	13187	5631	7556
2 Mining and quarrying	1660	844	816	1429	653	776	1564	651	913	1731	727	1004
3 Manufacturing	151181	105096	46085	143936	99686	44250	157350	107211	50139	165414	111611	53803
a Manufacture of food, beverages and tobacco	15230	10448	4782	17411	12540	4871	18517	13590	4927	19280	13794	5487
b Textile, wearing apparel and leather industries [a]	7042	4816	2227	7227	5154	2073	7451	5279	2172	7708	5393	2315
c Manufacture of wood and wood products, including furniture	...	...	...	...	...	...	...	...	...	...	...	...
d Manufacture of paper and paper products, printing and publishing [b]	5269	3900	1370	4810	3430	1380	5397	3749	1649	5426	3857	1569
e Manufacture of chemicals and chemical petroleum, coal, rubber and plastic products	21562	16995	4567	20979	15985	4994	22279	16796	5483	23619	17496	6123
f Manufacture of non-metallic mineral products, except products of petroleum and coal	5794	3508	2286	4944	3064	1880	5183	3237	1945	5436	3440	1996
g Basic metal industries	25469	20694	4775	24053	19176	4877	26130	20518	5613	26636	21005	5631
h Manufacture of fabricated metal products, machinery and equipment	52625	33128	19496	46676	29120	17557	53042	32333	20710	57569	34671	22898
i Other manufacturing industries	18191	11607	6583	17835	11217	6619	19350	11710	7640	19740	11955	7784
4 Electricity, gas and water	5883	3172	2711	5918	2917	3002	6178	3067	3112	6416	3488	2927
5 Construction	32701	19671	13030	34014	19690	14324	34771	21025	13746	35980	22015	13964
6 Wholesale and retail trade, restaurants and hotels	31693	10369	21325	32086	10182	21904	33690	10671	23019	35084	11116	23968
7 Transport, storage and communication	14671	5364	9307	15060	5519	9541	15666	5751	9914	15577	5683	9894
8 Finance, insurance, real estate and business services	23349	4327	19027	26815	6266	20549	28055	6596	21459	30402	6962	23440
9 Community, social and personal services	30657	14472	16185	31331	15080	16251	31984	15624	16361	33953	17080	16873
Total, Industries	305023	168322	136701	303713	164986	138727	322282	175903	146378	337744	184314	153430
Producers of Government Services	15565	3389	12176	16657	3703	12955	17495	3929	13566	18349	4326	14023
Other Producers	2716	782	1934	3063	850	2213	3235	917	2319	3471	976	2494
Total	323304	172494	150810	323433	169539	153894	343012	180749	162263	359563	189616	169947
Imputed bank service charge	-	6434	-6434	-	7253	-7253	-	7426	-7426	-	8129	-8129
Import duties	703	-	703	549	-	549	714	-	714	857	-	857
Value added tax	...	...	...	...	...	...	...	...	...	...	...	...
Other adjustments	-649	...	-649	625	...	625	101	...	101	1161	...	1161
Total	323358	178928	144430	324607	176792	147815	343827	188174	155653	361581	197445	163836

	1978 Gross Output	1978 Intermediate Consumption	1978 Value Added	1979 Gross Output	1979 Intermediate Consumption	1979 Value Added	1980 Gross Output	1980 Intermediate Consumption	1980 Value Added
				At constant prices of:1975					
				All Producers					
1 Agriculture, hunting, forestry and fishing	13600	5979	7622	13728	6054	7674	13166	5798	7368
2 Mining and quarrying	1860	839	1021	1882	902	980	1849	801	1049
3 Manufacturing	174541	116789	57752	187097	123609	63488	195701	126240	69462
a Manufacture of food, beverages and tobacco	20113	15444	4669	20623	15278	5345	21451	15838	5613

Japan

4.4 Derivation of Value Added by Kind of Activity, ISIC Divisions, in Constant Prices
(Continued)

Thousand Million Japanese yen

	1978 Gross Output	1978 Intermediate Consumption	1978 Value Added	1979 Gross Output	1979 Intermediate Consumption	1979 Value Added	1980 Gross Output	1980 Intermediate Consumption	1980 Value Added
				At constant prices of: 1975					
b Textile, wearing apparel and leather industries [a]	7354	5166	2188	7619	5262	2358	7459	5063	2396
c Manufacture of wood and wood products, including furniture	...	...	...	...	...	...	...	...	...
d Manufacture of paper and paper products, printing and publishing [b]	5832	4144	1688	6267	4414	1853	6300	4601	1699
e Manufacture of chemicals and chemical petroleum, coal, rubber and plastic products	24578	17177	7402	25956	19369	6587	25200	18593	6607
f Manufacture of non-metallic mineral products, except products of petroleum and coal	5496	3620	1876	5725	3759	1966	5770	3689	2081
g Basic metal industries	26518	20665	5853	29082	21983	7099	29988	22384	7604
h Manufacture of fabricated metal products, machinery and equipment	63345	37663	25682	70108	40688	29421	78832	43927	34906
i Other manufacturing industries	21304	12910	8394	21717	12857	8860	20701	12145	8557
4 Electricity, gas and water	6793	3654	3140	7368	3929	3439	7461	3801	3659
5 Construction	38771	23510	15262	40026	24468	15557	38670	23411	15259
6 Wholesale and retail trade, restaurants and hotels	36690	11616	25075	38496	11900	26596	38564	11198	27366
7 Transport, storage and communication	16207	6389	9819	16937	6579	10358	18283	6337	11946
8 Finance, insurance, real estate and business services	32867	7640	25227	34404	8005	26399	36003	7884	28119
9 Community, social and personal services	36544	19356	17188	38934	20260	18675	39877	20034	19843
Total, Industries	357873	195770	162103	378871	205707	173165	389574	205503	184071
Producers of Government Services	19509	4892	14617	20444	5273	15171	21000	5395	15605
Other Producers	3843	1152	2691	4266	1354	2912	4348	1328	3020
Total	381225	201813	179412	403581	212334	191247	414922	212226	202695
Imputed bank service charge	-	8573	-8573	-	8902	-8902	-	9416	-9416
Import duties	1036	-	1036	1068	-	1068	792	-	792
Value added tax	...	...	...	...	...	...	...	...	...
Other adjustments	201	...	201	-2507	...	-2507	-5274	...	-5274
Total	382461	210386	172076	402142	221236	180906	410440	221642	188797

a) Textile only.
b) Excluding printing and publishing.

4.6 Cost Components of Value Added, ISIC Divisions

Thousand Million Japanese yen

	1970 Compensation of Employees	1970 Capital Consumption	1970 Net Operating Surplus	1970 Indirect Taxes	1970 Less: Subsidies Received	1970 Value Added	1971 Compensation of Employees	1971 Capital Consumption	1971 Net Operating Surplus	1971 Indirect Taxes	1971 Less: Subsidies Received	1971 Value Added
					All Producers							
1 Agriculture, hunting, forestry and fishing	578	644	3233	8	...	4463	634	707	2934	-22	...	4253
2 Mining and quarrying	266	172	210	-27	...	621	299	190	181	-36	...	635
3 Manufacturing	10439	3475	10148	2278	...	26340	12075	4047	9711	2525	...	28357
a Manufacture of food, beverages and tobacco [a]	766	209	991	830	...	2795	851	237	1101	936	...	3125

Japan

4.6 Cost Components of Value Added, ISIC Divisions
(Continued)

Thousand Million Japanese yen

	1970						1971					
	Compensation of Employees	Capital Consumption	Net Operating Surplus	Indirect Taxes	Less: Subsidies Received	Value Added	Compensation of Employees	Capital Consumption	Net Operating Surplus	Indirect Taxes	Less: Subsidies Received	Value Added
b Textile, wearing apparel and leather industries [b]	698	178	523	37	...	1436	820	201	450	45	...	1517
c Manufacture of wood and wood products, including furniture	...	...	...	...	...	...	...	...	...	...	...	...
d Manufacture of paper and paper products, printing and publishing [c]	267	147	265	22	...	700	311	158	259	24	...	752
e Manufacture of chemicals and chemical petroleum, coal, rubber and plastic products [d]	787	615	1393	667	...	3461	901	704	1501	744	...	3851
f Manufacture of non-metallic mineral products, except products of petroleum and coal	490	189	401	31	...	1110	536	214	441	35	...	1226
g Basic metal industries	795	620	1475	82	...	2972	912	701	1279	86	...	2977
h Manufacture of fabricated metal products, machinery and equipment	4811	1186	4026	495	...	10518	5537	1375	3781	531	...	11224
i Other manufacturing industries	1826	336	1075	111	...	3347	2207	457	899	124	...	3687
4 Electricity, gas and water	407	491	499	161	...	1557	492	559	457	182	...	1690
5 Construction	2768	664	2105	125	...	5662	3382	626	2365	141	...	6514
6 Wholesale and retail trade, restaurants and hotels	4586	691	4807	421	...	10504	5379	725	4727	465	...	11295
a Wholesale and retail trade	4586	691	4807	421	...	10504	5379	725	4727	465	...	11295
b Restaurants and hotels [e]	...	...	...	...	...	...	...	...	...	...	...	...
7 Transport, storage and communication	3181	1203	487	151	...	5022	3754	1296	243	140	...	5433
8 Finance, insurance, real estate and business services	1596	1478	5984	251	...	9309	1996	1705	6923	311	...	10936
9 Community, social and personal services	2494	639	3379	522	...	7033	3274	768	3274	612	...	7928
Total, Industries	26314	9456	30851	3889	...	70511	31286	10624	30814	4318	...	77042
Producers of Government Services	4311	327	-	5	...	4642	5105	369	-	6	...	5480
Other Producers	600	65	-	5	...	670	706	70	-	5	...	781
Total	31225	9848	30851	3899	...	75822	37096	11063	30814	4329	...	83302
Imputed bank service charge	-	-	-2970	-	...	-2970	-	-	-3400	-	...	-3400
Import duties	-	-	-	498	...	498	-	-	-	478	...	478
Value added tax	...	...	...	...	...	...	...	...	...	...	...	...
Other adjustments	...	...	...	...	...	-66	...	...	...	...	...	251
Total	31225	9848	27881	4397	...	73285	37096	11063	27414	4808	...	80632

	1972						1973					
	Compensation of Employees	Capital Consumption	Net Operating Surplus	Indirect Taxes	Less: Subsidies Received	Value Added	Compensation of Employees	Capital Consumption	Net Operating Surplus	Indirect Taxes	Less: Subsidies Received	Value Added
	All Producers											
1 Agriculture, hunting, forestry and fishing	696	788	3590	-42	...	5032	819	899	4921	28	...	6667
2 Mining and quarrying	280	190	214	-22	...	661	257	216	360	-11	...	821
3 Manufacturing	13868	4695	10404	2884	...	31851	17547	5450	13147	3313	...	39457
a Manufacture of food, beverages and tobacco [a]	963	289	784	1105	...	3140	1142	347	951	1177	...	3619

Japan

4.6 Cost Components of Value Added, ISIC Divisions
(Continued)

Thousand Million Japanese yen

	\multicolumn{6}{c	}{1972}	\multicolumn{6}{c}{1973}
	Compensation of Employees	Capital Consumption	Net Operating Surplus	Indirect Taxes	Less: Subsidies Received	Value Added	Compensation of Employees	Capital Consumption	Net Operating Surplus	Indirect Taxes	Less: Subsidies Received	Value Added
b Textile, wearing apparel and leather industries [b]	905	238	340	46	...	1530	1113	293	570	61	...	2036
c Manufacture of wood and wood products, including furniture	...	...	...	...	...	...	...	...	...	...	...	...
d Manufacture of paper and paper products, printing and publishing [c]	354	182	278	27	...	841	445	209	392	37	...	1084
e Manufacture of chemicals and chemical petroleum, coal, rubber and plastic products [d]	1019	822	1608	796	...	4245	1245	874	1774	870	...	4765
f Manufacture of non-metallic mineral products, except products of petroleum and coal	603	259	507	38	...	1407	783	306	686	54	...	1828
g Basic metal industries	1022	798	1648	101	...	3569	1306	999	2336	141	...	4782
h Manufacture of fabricated metal products, machinery and equipment	6421	1546	4080	619	...	12665	8219	1798	4889	772	...	15677
i Other manufacturing industries	2581	562	1160	151	...	4454	3291	624	1550	201	...	5666
4 Electricity, gas and water	568	671	348	204	...	1790	748	690	258	241	...	1937
5 Construction	4059	733	2793	166	...	7751	5158	1062	3372	238	...	9830
6 Wholesale and retail trade, restaurants and hotels	6054	883	5579	536	...	13051	7800	1038	6547	686	...	16070
a Wholesale and retail trade	6054	883	5579	536	...	13051	...	...	...	...	...	...
b Restaurants and hotels [e]	...	...	...	...	...	...	...	...	...	...	...	...
7 Transport, storage and communication	4218	1484	25	97	...	5824	5247	1700	-118	131	...	6960
8 Finance, insurance, real estate and business services	2420	2048	7962	359	...	12788	2866	2573	9668	537	...	15645
9 Community, social and personal services	3946	1015	4150	721	...	9831	4975	1309	4227	881	...	11392
Total, Industries	36107	12506	35065	4901	...	88578	45417	14936	42382	6044	...	108779
Producers of Government Services	6045	416	-	8	...	6468	7539	471	-	10	...	8020
Other Producers	883	76	-	7	...	966	1125	88	-	9	...	1221
Total	43035	12997	35065	4915	...	96012	54081	15495	42382	6063	...	118020
Imputed bank service charge	-	-	-3743	-	...	-3743	-	-	-4961	-	...	-4961
Import duties	-	-	-	510	...	510	-	-	-	647	...	647
Value added tax	...	...	...	...	...	...	...	...	...	...	...	...
Other adjustments	...	...	...	...	...	-473	...	...	...	...	...	-1286
Total	43035	12997	31323	5425	...	92306	54081	15495	37421	6709	...	112420

	\multicolumn{6}{c	}{1974}	\multicolumn{6}{c}{1975}
	Compensation of Employees	Capital Consumption	Net Operating Surplus	Indirect Taxes	Less: Subsidies Received	Value Added	Compensation of Employees	Capital Consumption	Net Operating Surplus	Indirect Taxes	Less: Subsidies Received	Value Added
	\multicolumn{12}{c}{All Producers}
1 Agriculture, hunting, forestry and fishing	1025	1119	5234	122	...	7499	1162	1104	5850	14	...	8130
2 Mining and quarrying	307	253	383	3	...	945	393	166	243	-25	...	776
3 Manufacturing	22035	6276	13772	2955	...	45038	23827	6082	10689	3651	...	44250
a Manufacture of food, beverages and tobacco [a]	1459	393	1729	470	...	4051	1750	448	1794	879	...	4871

Japan

4.6 Cost Components of Value Added, ISIC Divisions
(Continued)

Thousand Million Japanese yen

	1974						1975					
	Compensation of Employees	Capital Consumption	Net Operating Surplus	Indirect Taxes	Less: Subsidies Received	Value Added	Compensation of Employees	Capital Consumption	Net Operating Surplus	Indirect Taxes	Less: Subsidies Received	Value Added
b Textile, wearing apparel and leather industries [b]	1252	339	623	73	...	2287	1270	308	417	78	...	2073
c Manufacture of wood and wood products, including furniture	...	...	...	...	...	...	...	...	...	...	...	...
d Manufacture of paper and paper products, printing and publishing [c]	590	262	729	55	...	1635	621	248	455	56	...	1380
e Manufacture of chemicals and chemical petroleum, coal, rubber and plastic products [d]	1613	911	544	993	...	4061	1718	924	1170	1181	...	4994
f Manufacture of non-metallic mineral products, except products of petroleum and coal	1001	354	766	67	...	2187	1092	317	400	72	...	1880
g Basic metal industries	1676	1168	2615	177	...	5636	1820	1158	1701	198	...	4877
h Manufacture of fabricated metal products, machinery and equipment	10327	2102	5081	868	...	18378	10932	1970	3722	932	...	17557
i Other manufacturing industries	4119	746	1686	252	...	6803	4625	709	1030	255	...	6619
4 Electricity, gas and water	872	704	269	306	...	2151	1053	775	828	346	...	3002
5 Construction	6343	1055	4003	298	...	11699	7559	1561	4902	302	...	14324
6 Wholesale and retail trade, restaurants and hotels	9846	1262	8448	843	...	20400	11479	1284	8285	856	...	21904
a Wholesale and retail trade	9846	1262	8448	843	...	20400	11479	1284	8285	856	...	21904
b Restaurants and hotels [e]	...	...	...	...	...	...	...	...	...	...	...	...
7 Transport, storage and communication	6541	1906	-487	140	...	8100	7612	1878	-6	57	...	9541
8 Finance, insurance, real estate and business services	3691	3233	10599	702	...	18224	4592	3975	11206	777	...	20549
9 Community, social and personal services	6209	1541	4908	1101	...	13759	7451	1697	6128	976	...	16251
Total, Industries	56868	17349	47129	6470	...	127815	65128	18522	48124	6954	...	138727
Producers of Government Services	10046	553	-	12	...	10611	12446	668	-	15	...	13128
Other Producers	1497	105	-	10	...	1611	2074	124	-	12	...	2210
Total	68411	18006	47129	6492	...	140037	79648	19313	48124	6980	...	154065
Imputed bank service charge	-	-	-6588	-	...	-6588	-	-	-7253	-	...	-7253
Import duties	-	-	-	639	...	639	-	-	-	549	...	549
Value added tax	...	...	...	...	...	...	...	...	...	...	...	...
Other adjustments	...	...	...	...	...	80	...	...	...	...	...	670
Total	68411	18006	40541	7131	...	134169	79648	19313	40871	7529	...	148031

	1976						1977					
	Compensation of Employees	Capital Consumption	Net Operating Surplus	Indirect Taxes	Less: Subsidies Received	Value Added	Compensation of Employees	Capital Consumption	Net Operating Surplus	Indirect Taxes	Less: Subsidies Received	Value Added
	All Producers											
1 Agriculture, hunting, forestry and fishing	1280	1304	6108	130	...	8822	1462	1499	6305	45	...	9310
2 Mining and quarrying	464	168	231	-23	...	840	516	188	277	-18	...	963
3 Manufacturing	26327	6180	13898	4326	...	50732	28929	6672	14364	5321	...	55286
a Manufacture of food, beverages and tobacco [a]	2046	475	1843	1250	...	5614	2234	482	2404	1665	...	6785

Japan

4.6 Cost Components of Value Added, ISIC Divisions
(Continued)

Thousand Million Japanese yen

	1976						1977					
	Compensation of Employees	Capital Consumption	Net Operating Surplus	Indirect Taxes	Less: Subsidies Received	Value Added	Compensation of Employees	Capital Consumption	Net Operating Surplus	Indirect Taxes	Less: Subsidies Received	Value Added
b Textile, wearing apparel and leather industries b	1396	299	530	86	...	2311	1399	310	697	105	...	2510
c Manufacture of wood and wood products, including furniture	...	...	...	...	...	...	...	...	...	...	...	...
d Manufacture of paper and paper products, printing and publishing c	697	268	514	61	...	1540	743	265	521	73	...	1601
e Manufacture of chemicals and chemical petroleum, coal, rubber and plastic products d	1864	1008	1571	1344	...	5787	1995	1096	1916	1599	...	6606
f Manufacture of non-metallic mineral products, except products of petroleum and coal	1177	296	511	79	...	2063	1298	298	532	97	...	2224
g Basic metal industries	1895	1217	2370	220	...	5702	2079	1390	1825	254	...	5548
h Manufacture of fabricated metal products, machinery and equipment	12018	1896	5242	1004	...	20159	13440	2064	5204	1199	...	21906
i Other manufacturing industries	5234	721	1318	283	...	7556	5742	768	1265	331	...	8167
4 Electricity, gas and water	1213	928	1048	396	...	3585	1271	1131	1457	472	...	4331
5 Construction	8449	1563	4696	308	...	15016	9356	1823	4279	349	...	15806
6 Wholesale and retail trade, restaurants and hotels	13642	1416	8251	983	...	24292	15341	1568	7708	1119	...	25735
a Wholesale and retail trade	13642	1416	8251	983	...	24292	15341	1568	7708	1119	...	25735
b Restaurants and hotels e	...	...	...	...	...	...	...	...	...	...	...	...
7 Transport, storage and communication	8663	2264	283	-97	...	11113	9339	2446	1395	-28	...	13152
8 Finance, insurance, real estate and business services	5245	4706	12336	835	...	23121	6033	5465	13906	912	...	26316
9 Community, social and personal services	8800	1835	6556	1088	...	18278	10537	2194	6270	1439	...	20439
Total, Industries	74083	20364	53406	7947	...	155799	82784	22985	55961	9609	...	171338
Producers of Government Services	13770	786	-	17	...	14573	15245	900	-	21	...	16166
Other Producers	2440	139	-	15	...	2593	2839	148	-	14	...	3001
Total	90292	21288	53406	7978	...	172965	100867	24034	55961	9645	...	190505
Imputed bank service charge	-	-	-7773	-	...	-7773	-	-	-8238	-	...	-8238
Import duties	-	-	-	711	...	711	-	-	-	777	...	777
Value added tax	...	...	...	...	...	...	...	...	...	...	...	...
Other adjustments	...	...	...	...	...	-52	...	...	...	...	...	1415
Total	90292	21288	45634	8690	...	165851	100867	24034	47723	10421	...	184460

	1978						1979					
	Compensation of Employees	Capital Consumption	Net Operating Surplus	Indirect Taxes	Less: Subsidies Received	Value Added	Compensation of Employees	Capital Consumption	Net Operating Surplus	Indirect Taxes	Less: Subsidies Received	Value Added
	All Producers											
1 Agriculture, hunting, forestry and fishing	1468	1668	6248	-46	...	9338	1513	1729	6303	-37	...	9508
2 Mining and quarrying	457	192	501	-21	...	1129	434	227	646	-40	...	1267
3 Manufacturing	30496	7037	17095	6144	...	60773	32800	7479	18587	6981	...	65847
a Manufacture of food, beverages and tobacco a	2376	529	1824	2142	...	6871	2550	562	1803	2223	...	7139

Japan

4.6 Cost Components of Value Added, ISIC Divisions
(Continued)

Thousand Million Japanese yen

	1978						1979					
	Compensation of Employees	Capital Consumption	Net Operating Surplus	Indirect Taxes	Less: Subsidies Received	Value Added	Compensation of Employees	Capital Consumption	Net Operating Surplus	Indirect Taxes	Less: Subsidies Received	Value Added
b Textile, wearing apparel and leather industries [b]	1437	291	694	104	...	2525	1543	290	796	128	...	2757
c Manufacture of wood and wood products, including furniture	...	...	...	...	...	...	...	...	...	...	...	...
d Manufacture of paper and paper products, printing and publishing [c]	775	275	591	74	...	1714	817	285	586	87	...	1775
e Manufacture of chemicals and chemical petroleum, coal, rubber and plastic products [d]	2096	1141	2914	1766	...	7917	2315	1166	1566	2075	...	7122
f Manufacture of non-metallic mineral products, except products of petroleum and coal	1425	313	608	98	...	2445	1515	337	682	121	...	2655
g Basic metal industries	2126	1368	2781	268	...	6543	2233	1458	4299	346	...	8336
h Manufacture of fabricated metal products, machinery and equipment	14117	2297	6052	1345	...	23810	15223	2508	7074	1590	...	26395
i Other manufacturing industries	6144	824	1632	349	...	8948	6603	871	1781	412	...	9667
4 Electricity, gas and water	1372	1314	1685	486	...	4858	1558	1504	1192	542	...	4796
5 Construction	10509	1961	5214	385	...	18069	11536	2063	6047	502	...	20148
6 Wholesale and retail trade, restaurants and hotels	16383	1605	7686	1185	...	26858	17217	1893	7562	1471	...	28144
a Wholesale and retail trade	16383	1605	7686	1185	...	26858	...	...	...	...	...	...
b Restaurants and hotels [e]	...	...	...	...	...	...	...	...	...	...	...	...
7 Transport, storage and communication	9984	2762	1568	-129	...	14185	10635	2935	1527	-79	...	15018
8 Finance, insurance, real estate and business services	6521	6221	15927	1060	...	29728	7182	6977	17526	1309	...	32995
9 Community, social and personal services	11939	2389	7413	1331	...	23073	13465	2728	8039	1606	...	25839
Total, Industries	89129	25150	63337	10395	...	188011	96341	27534	67429	12258	...	203562
Producers of Government Services	16451	1053	-	25	...	17528	17702	1197	-	28	...	18927
Other Producers	3240	177	-	19	...	3436	3639	208	-	27	...	3874
Total	108819	26379	63337	10440	...	208975	117682	28939	67429	12312	...	226363
Imputed bank service charge	-	-	-8667	-	...	-8667	-	-	-9705	-	...	-9705
Import duties	-	-	-	759	...	759	-	-	-	946	...	946
Value added tax	...	...	...	...	...	...	...	...	...	...	...	...
Other adjustments	...	...	...	...	...	1571	...	...	...	...	...	1012
Total	108819	26379	54670	11198	...	202638	117682	28939	57724	13258	...	218616

	1980					
	Compensation of Employees	Capital Consumption	Net Operating Surplus	Indirect Taxes	Less: Subsidies Received	Value Added
		All Producers					
1 Agriculture, hunting, forestry and fishing	1670	1767	5580	-82	...	8935
2 Mining and quarrying	418	234	771	-44	...	1379
3 Manufacturing	35809	8224	19511	7534	...	71079
a Manufacture of food, beverages and tobacco [a]	2759	612	1989	2423	...	7784

Japan

4.6 Cost Components of Value Added, ISIC Divisions
(Continued)

Thousand Million Japanese yen

	Compensation of Employees	Capital Consumption	Net Operating Surplus	Indirect Taxes	Less: Subsidies Received	Value Added
			1980			
b Textile, wearing apparel and leather industries [b]	1660	279	702	141	...	2781
c Manufacture of wood and wood products, including furniture	...	...	...	...	...	...
d Manufacture of paper and paper products, printing and publishing [c]	909	339	626	99	...	1973
e Manufacture of chemicals and chemical petroleum, coal, rubber and plastic products [d]	2483	1335	1309	2218	...	7346
f Manufacture of non-metallic mineral products, except products of petroleum and coal	1703	366	660	136	...	2865
g Basic metal industries	2456	1562	4549	389	...	8956
h Manufacture of fabricated metal products, machinery and equipment	16830	2833	8085	1675	...	29421
i Other manufacturing industries	7010	899	1592	453	...	9954
4 Electricity, gas and water	1577	1924	2581	744	...	6825
5 Construction	12756	2164	5975	586	...	21480
6 Wholesale and retail trade, restaurants and hotels	19701	1891	5999	1604	...	29195
a Wholesale and retail trade	...	...	...	...	...	...
b Restaurants and hotels [e]	...	...	...	...	...	...
7 Transport, storage and communication	11350	3101	1833	-97	...	16188
8 Finance, insurance, real estate and business services	7881	7758	20039	1289	...	36967
9 Community, social and personal services	14051	2873	9394	1795	...	28113
Total, Industries	105213	29936	71683	13330	...	220161
Producers of Government Services	19086	1348	-	30	...	20464
Other Producers	3972	232	-	24	...	4228
Total	128271	31516	71683	13384	...	244854
Imputed bank service charge	-	-	-11019	-	...	-11019
Import duties	-	-	-	924	...	924
Value added tax	...	...	...	...	...	...
Other adjustments	...	...	...	...	...	190
Total	128271	31516	60664	14308	...	234949

a) Excluding tobacco.
b) Textile only.
c) Excluding printing and publishing.
d) Excluding rubber and plastic products.
e) Restaurants and hotels are included in item 'Community, social and personal services'.

4.9 Supply of Goods and Services, in Current Prices

Thousand Million Japanese yen

	Gross Domestic Output Marketed	Non-Marketed	Imports c.i.f.	Import Duties	Trade & Transport Margins	Value Added Tax	TOTAL SUPPLY
				1970			
1 Agriculture, hunting, forestry and fishing	7062	...	1637	47	1431	...	10176
2 Mining and quarrying	990	...	2146	120	382	...	3638
3 Manufacturing	80794	...	3042	331	14568	...	98735
4 Electricity, gas and water	2475	...	1	-	-	...	2476
5 Construction	16085	...	-	-	-	...	16085
6 Wholesale and retail trade, restaurants and hotels [a]	131	...	119	-	-	...	250
7 Transport and communications	5225	...	339	-	-	...	5564
8 Finance, insurance, real estate and business services	11392	...	14	-	-	...	11406
9 Community, social and personal services [a]	14931	...	271	-	-	...	15202
Total, Industries	139084	...	7568	498	16381	...	163531
Producers of Government Services	...	...	...	...	...	...	...
Other Producers	...	7306	...	...	...	...	7306
Total	139084	7306	7568	498	16381	...	170837

Japan

4.9 Supply of Goods and Services, in Current Prices
(Continued)

Thousand Million Japanese yen

	Gross Domestic Output - Marketed	Gross Domestic Output - Non-Marketed	Imports c.i.f.	Import Duties	Trade & Transport Margins	Value Added Tax	TOTAL SUPPLY
1971							
1 Agriculture, hunting, forestry and fishing	6944	...	1620	44	1442	...	10049
2 Mining and quarrying	1030	...	2417	127	401	...	3974
3 Manufacturing	84592	...	2906	308	15744	...	103551
4 Electricity, gas and water	2728	...	1	-	-	...	2728
5 Construction	17456	...	-	-	-	...	17456
6 Wholesale and retail trade, restaurants and hotels [a]	128	...	139	-	-	...	267
7 Transport and communications	5875	...	420	-	-	...	6294
8 Finance, insurance, real estate and business services	13359	...	5	-	-	...	13363
9 Community, social and personal services [a]	16883	...	346	-	-	...	17229
Total, Industries	148995	...	7852	478	17587	...	174912
Producers of Government Services	...	...	...	...	...	...	...
Other Producers	...	8505	...	...	...	...	8505
Total	148995	8505	7852	478	17587	...	183417
1972							
1 Agriculture, hunting, forestry and fishing	7717	...	1637	36	1565	...	10955
2 Mining and quarrying	1093	...	2435	134	395	...	4057
3 Manufacturing	93294	...	3168	340	18277	...	115079
4 Electricity, gas and water	3050	...	1	-	-	...	3051
5 Construction	20676	...	-	-	-	...	20676
6 Wholesale and retail trade, restaurants and hotels [a]	153	...	140	-	-	...	292
7 Transport and communications	6377	...	408	-	-	...	6785
8 Finance, insurance, real estate and business services	15514	...	3	-	-	...	15517
9 Community, social and personal services [a]	20138	...	459	-	-	...	20597
Total, Industries	168013	...	8249	510	20237	...	197009
Producers of Government Services	...	...	...	...	...	...	...
Other Producers	...	10082	...	...	...	...	10082
Total	168013	10082	8249	510	20237	...	207091
1973							
1 Agriculture, hunting, forestry and fishing	9786	...	2474	37	2008	...	14306
2 Mining and quarrying	1377	...	3217	156	480	...	5231
3 Manufacturing	118353	...	4705	453	21710	...	145220
4 Electricity, gas and water	3523	...	1	-	-	...	3524
5 Construction	27557	...	-	-	-	...	27557
6 Wholesale and retail trade, restaurants and hotels [a]	216	...	167	-	-	...	383
7 Transport and communications	7546	...	557	-	-	...	8103
8 Finance, insurance, real estate and business services	19050	...	3	-	-	...	19053
9 Community, social and personal services [a]	24008	...	633	-	63	...	24704
Total, Industries	211416	...	11757	647	24261	...	248080
Producers of Government Services	...	...	...	...	...	...	...
Other Producers	...	12403	...	...	...	...	12403
Total	211416	12403	11757	647	24261	...	260483
1974							
1 Agriculture, hunting, forestry and fishing	11603	...	3224	42	2696	...	17564
2 Mining and quarrying	1731	...	8073	146	644	...	10594
3 Manufacturing	146583	...	6949	451	27332	...	181315
4 Electricity, gas and water	4932	...	1	-	-	...	4933
5 Construction	32038	...	-	-	-	...	32038

Japan

4.9 Supply of Goods and Services, in Current Prices
(Continued)

Thousand Million Japanese yen

		Gross Domestic Output - Marketed	Gross Domestic Output - Non-Marketed	Imports c.i.f.	Import Duties	Trade & Transport Margins	Value Added Tax	TOTAL SUPPLY
6	Wholesale and retail trade, restaurants and hotels [a]	298	...	243	-	-	...	541
7	Transport and communications	9327	...	883	-	-	...	10210
8	Finance, insurance, real estate and business services	22204	...	6	-	-	...	22209
9	Community, social and personal services [a]	28886	...	778	-	304	...	29968
	Total, Industries	257602	...	20157	639	30976	...	309374
	Producers of Government Services	...	...	...	...	...	...	...
	Other Producers	...	16138	...	...	...	...	16138
	Total	257602	16138	20157	639	30976	...	325512
	1975							
1	Agriculture, hunting, forestry and fishing	13049	...	2948	50	3144	...	19191
2	Mining and quarrying	1556	...	8419	141	664	...	10780
3	Manufacturing	144232	...	5990	358	29490	...	180070
4	Electricity, gas and water	6066	...	-	-	-	...	6066
5	Construction	34075	...	-	-	-	...	34075
6	Wholesale and retail trade, restaurants and hotels [a]	357	...	281	-	-	...	638
7	Transport and communications	10729	...	1195	-	-	...	11924
8	Finance, insurance, real estate and business services	26779	...	40	-	-	...	26819
9	Community, social and personal services [a]	32869	...	870	-	704	...	34443
	Total, Industries	269712	...	19742	549	34001	...	324005
	Producers of Government Services	...	...	...	...	...	...	...
	Other Producers	...	19889	...	...	...	...	19889
	Total	269712	19889	19742	549	34001	...	343893
	1976							
1	Agriculture, hunting, forestry and fishing	14239	...	3321	54	3517	...	21131
2	Mining and quarrying	1583	...	9054	148	685	...	11469
3	Manufacturing	165328	...	7090	509	33007	...	205934
4	Electricity, gas and water	7083	...	-	-	-	...	7083
5	Construction	37274	...	-	-	-	...	37274
6	Wholesale and retail trade, restaurants and hotels [a]	388	...	307	-	-	...	695
7	Transport and communications	12482	...	1444	-	-	...	13926
8	Finance, insurance, real estate and business services	30246	...	66	-	-	...	30312
9	Community, social and personal services [a]	36563	...	605	-	796	...	37964
	Total, Industries	305185	...	21887	711	38005	...	365788
	Producers of Government Services	...	...	...	...	...	...	...
	Other Producers	...	22334	...	...	...	...	22334
	Total	305185	22334	21887	711	38005	...	388122
	1977							
1	Agriculture, hunting, forestry and fishing	15185	...	3284	52	3159	...	21680
2	Mining and quarrying	1823	...	9026	178	763	...	11789
3	Manufacturing	177119	...	7060	547	36478	...	221204
4	Electricity, gas and water	8400	...	-	-	-	...	8400
5	Construction	40144	...	-	-	-	...	40144

Japan

4.9 Supply of Goods and Services, in Current Prices
(Continued)

Thousand Million Japanese yen

		Gross Domestic Output		Imports		Trade & Transport Margins	Value Added Tax	TOTAL SUPPLY
		Marketed	Non-Marketed	Imports c.i.f.	Import Duties			
6	Wholesale and retail trade, restaurants and hotels [a]	407	...	343	·	·	...	750
7	Transport and communications	14110	...	1431	·	·	...	15542
8	Finance, insurance, real estate and business services	34290	...	65	·	·	...	34355
9	Community, social and personal services [a]	41428	...	669	·	880	...	42977
	Total, Industries	332906	...	21879	777	41280	...	396841
	Producers of Government Services	...	...	...	...	...	...	...
	Other Producers	...	25135	...	...	...	...	25135
	Total	332906	25135	21879	777	41280	...	421976
				1978				
1	Agriculture, hunting, forestry and fishing	15285	...	2711	51	3243	...	21290
2	Mining and quarrying	2084	...	7103	174	859	...	10219
3	Manufacturing	184347	...	7048	534	38799	...	230728
4	Electricity, gas and water	8830	...	·	·	·	...	8830
5	Construction	44546	...	·	·	·	...	44546
6	Wholesale and retail trade, restaurants and hotels [a]	486	...	291	·	·	...	777
7	Transport and communications	14994	...	1212	·	·	...	16207
8	Finance, insurance, real estate and business services	38645	...	77	·	·	...	38722
9	Community, social and personal services [a]	46727	...	714	·	978	...	48418
	Total, Industries	355943	...	19155	759	43879	...	419736
	Producers of Government Services	...	...	...	...	...	...	...
	Other Producers	...	27760	...	...	...	...	27760
	Total	355943	27760	19155	759	43879	...	447496
				1979				
1	Agriculture, hunting, forestry and fishing	15926	...	3852	65	3360	...	23202
2	Mining and quarrying	2397	...	10237	164	958	...	13756
3	Manufacturing	206411	...	10355	717	40992	...	258474
4	Electricity, gas and water	9673	...	·	·	·	...	9673
5	Construction	50179	...	·	·	·	...	50179
6	Wholesale and retail trade, restaurants and hotels [a]	533	...	298	·	·	...	831
7	Transport and communications	16588	...	1534	·	·	...	18122
8	Finance, insurance, real estate and business services	42898	...	85	·	·	...	42983
9	Community, social and personal services [a]	52168	...	916	·	1022	...	54106
	Total, Industries	396772	...	27276	946	46332	...	471325
	Producers of Government Services	...	...	...	...	...	...	...
	Other Producers	...	30627	...	...	...	...	30627
	Total	396772	30627	27276	946	46332	...	501952
				1980				
1	Agriculture, hunting, forestry and fishing	16179	...	4052	60	3246	...	23536
2	Mining and quarrying	2676	...	16080	148	1107	...	20010
3	Manufacturing	238852	...	12262	716	43743	...	295574
4	Electricity, gas and water	13519	...	·	·	·	...	13520
5	Construction	53845	...	·	·	·	...	53845

Japan

4.9 Supply of Goods and Services, in Current Prices
(Continued)

Thousand Million Japanese yen

	Gross Domestic Output Marketed	Gross Domestic Output Non-Marketed	Imports c.i.f.	Import Duties	Trade & Transport Margins	Value Added Tax	TOTAL SUPPLY
6 Wholesale and retail trade, restaurants and hotels [a]	493	...	396	-	-	...	889
7 Transport and communications	18587	...	1975	-	-	...	20562
8 Finance, insurance, real estate and business services	47754	...	82	-	-	...	47836
9 Community, social and personal services [a]	57434	...	1038	-	1041	...	59513
Total, Industries	449339	...	35885	924	49136	...	535284
Producers of Government Services	...	...	...	...	...	...	...
Other Producers	...	33608	...	...	...	...	33608
Total	449339	33608	35885	924	49136	...	568892

a) Restaurants and hotels are included in item 'Community, social and personal services'.

4.10 Supply of Goods and Services, in Constant Prices

Thousand Million Japanese yen

	Gross Domestic Output Marketed	Gross Domestic Output Non-Marketed	Imports c.i.f.	Import Duties	Trade & Transport Margins	Value Added Tax	TOTAL SUPPLY
At constant prices of: 1975							
1970							
1 Agriculture, hunting, forestry and fishing	12011	...	2617	66	2480	...	17174
2 Mining and quarrying	1570	...	6605	646	668	...	9490
3 Manufacturing	124129	...	5129	908	25757	...	155923
4 Electricity, gas and water	4476	...	...	...	...	...	4477
5 Construction	27791	...	...	...	...	...	27791
6 Wholesale and retail trade, restaurants and hotels [a]	152	...	247	-	-	...	399
7 Transport and communications	8111	...	517	-	-	...	8628
8 Finance, insurance, real estate and business services	17126	...	18	-	-	...	17144
9 Community, social and personal services [a]	26980	...	523	1	-	...	27504
Total, Industries	222346	...	15658	1620	28905	...	268530
Producers of Government Services	...	...	...	...	...	...	...
Other Producers	...	15189	...	...	...	...	15189
Total	222346	15189	15658	1620	28905	...	283719
1971							
1 Agriculture, hunting, forestry and fishing	11659	...	2655	66	2350	...	16731
2 Mining and quarrying	1620	...	7259	593	692	...	10164
3 Manufacturing	130218	...	4852	811	26373	...	162253
4 Electricity, gas and water	4913	...	1	...	...	...	4914
5 Construction	29330	...	...	...	...	...	29330
6 Wholesale and retail trade, restaurants and hotels [a]	140	...	287	-	-	...	428
7 Transport and communications	8629	...	655	-	-	...	9284
8 Finance, insurance, real estate and business services	19232	...	7	-	-	...	19239
9 Community, social and personal services [a]	28827	...	665	-	-	...	29492
Total, Industries	234567	...	16381	1470	29416	...	281834
Producers of Government Services	...	...	...	...	...	...	...
Other Producers	...	15893	...	...	...	...	15893
Total	234567	15893	16381	1470	29416	...	297726
1972							
1 Agriculture, hunting, forestry and fishing	12571	...	2801	56	2440	...	17867
2 Mining and quarrying	1690	...	7942	619	725	...	10976
3 Manufacturing	141560	...	5345	785	29937	...	177626
4 Electricity, gas and water	5414	...	1	...	...	...	5415
5 Construction	32969	...	...	...	...	...	32969

Japan

4.10 Supply of Goods and Services, in Constant Prices
(Continued)

Thousand Million Japanese yen

	Gross Domestic Output Marketed	Gross Domestic Output Non-Marketed	Imports c.i.f.	Import Duties	Trade & Transport Margins	Value Added Tax	TOTAL SUPPLY
At constant prices of: 1975							
6 Wholesale and retail trade, restaurants and hotels a	158	...	303	-	-	...	460
7 Transport and communications	8809	...	650	-	-	...	9460
8 Finance, insurance, real estate and business services	22058	...	4	-	-	...	22062
9 Community, social and personal services a	32142	...	921	-	-	...	33063
Total, Industries	257369	...	17966	1461	33101	...	309897
Producers of Government Services	...	...	...	...	...	...	...
Other Producers	...	16928	...	...	...	...	16928
Total	257369	16928	17966	1461	33101	...	326826
1973							
1 Agriculture, hunting, forestry and fishing	12822	...	2840	55	2873	...	18590
2 Mining and quarrying	1860	...	9562	642	810	...	12873
3 Manufacturing	157263	...	6679	908	31612	...	196462
4 Electricity, gas and water	6052	...	1	...	...	...	6053
5 Construction	36900	...	...	...	...	...	36900
6 Wholesale and retail trade, restaurants and hotels a	225	...	299	-	-	...	524
7 Transport and communications	9711	...	871	-	-	...	10582
8 Finance, insurance, real estate and business services	24051	...	4	-	-	...	24056
9 Community, social and personal services a	33920	...	1068	-	85	...	35074
Total, Industries	282804	...	21325	1605	35380	...	341113
Producers of Government Services	...	...	...	...	...	...	...
Other Producers	...	17794	...	...	...	...	17794
Total	282804	17794	21325	1605	35380	...	358907
1974							
1 Agriculture, hunting, forestry and fishing	12516	...	3008	49	2867	...	18440
2 Mining and quarrying	1698	...	9405	171	701	...	11975
3 Manufacturing	151659	...	7382	482	29371	...	188894
4 Electricity, gas and water	6004	...	1	...	...	...	6005
5 Construction	33598	...	...	...	...	...	33598
6 Wholesale and retail trade, restaurants and hotels a	305	...	262	-	-	...	567
7 Transport and communications	10416	...	951	-	-	...	11367
8 Finance, insurance, real estate and business services	23284	...	6	-	-	...	23291
9 Community, social and personal services a	32619	...	848	-	322	...	33789
Total, Industries	272101	...	21864	703	33261	...	327929
Producers of Government Services	...	...	...	...	...	...	...
Other Producers	...	18281	...	...	...	...	18281
Total	272101	18281	21864	703	33261	...	346210
1975							
1 Agriculture, hunting, forestry and fishing	13049	...	2948	50	3143	...	19191
2 Mining and quarrying	1556	...	8419	141	664	...	10780
3 Manufacturing	144232	...	5990	358	29490	...	180071
4 Electricity, gas and water	6066	...	-	...	...	...	6066
5 Construction	34075	...	...	...	...	...	34075

Japan

4.10 Supply of Goods and Services, in Constant Prices
(Continued)

Thousand Million Japanese yen

		Gross Domestic Output - Marketed	Gross Domestic Output - Non-Marketed	Imports c.i.f.	Import Duties	Trade & Transport Margins	Value Added Tax	TOTAL SUPPLY
				At constant prices of:1975				
6	Wholesale and retail trade, restaurants and hotels [a]	357	...	281	-	-	...	638
7	Transport and communications	10729	...	1195	-	-	...	11924
8	Finance, insurance, real estate and business services	26779	...	40	-	-	...	26819
9	Community, social and personal services [a]	32869	...	870	-	704	...	34443
	Total, Industries	269712	...	19742	549	34001	...	324005
	Producers of Government Services	...	...	...	...	...	...	...
	Other Producers	...	19889	...	...	...	...	19889
	Total	269712	19889	19742	549	34001	...	343893
				1976				
1	Agriculture, hunting, forestry and fishing	12943	...	3093	51	3261	...	19348
2	Mining and quarrying	1611	...	8522	141	698	...	10972
3	Manufacturing	157753	...	6892	523	32741	...	197908
4	Electricity, gas and water	6333	...	-	...	...	...	6333
5	Construction	34848	...	...	...	...	...	34848
6	Wholesale and retail trade, restaurants and hotels [a]	367	...	290	-	-	...	657
7	Transport and communications	11158	...	1349	-	-	...	12507
8	Finance, insurance, real estate and business services	28018	...	63	-	-	...	28081
9	Community, social and personal services [a]	33447	...	568	-	800	...	34815
	Total, Industries	286478	...	20775	714	37500	...	345468
	Producers of Government Services	...	...	...	...	...	...	...
	Other Producers	...	20730	...	...	...	...	20730
	Total	286478	20730	20775	714	37500	...	366198
				1977				
1	Agriculture, hunting, forestry and fishing	13116	...	3193	48	2869	...	19226
2	Mining and quarrying	1779	...	8921	174	785	...	11659
3	Manufacturing	165685	...	7173	635	36493	...	209986
4	Electricity, gas and water	6581	...	-	...	...	...	6581
5	Construction	36052	...	...	...	...	...	36052
6	Wholesale and retail trade, restaurants and hotels [a]	350	...	338	-	-	...	688
7	Transport and communications	10765	...	1427	-	-	...	12192
8	Finance, insurance, real estate and business services	30367	...	61	-	-	...	30428
9	Community, social and personal services [a]	35520	...	651	-	921	...	37092
	Total, Industries	300214	...	21764	857	41068	...	363903
	Producers of Government Services	...	...	...	...	...	...	...
	Other Producers	...	21819	...	...	...	...	21819
	Total	300214	21819	21764	857	41068	...	385722
				1978				
1	Agriculture, hunting, forestry and fishing	13526	...	3178	54	2760	...	19518
2	Mining and quarrying	1911	...	8745	212	903	...	11770
3	Manufacturing	174716	...	8396	770	39102	...	222984
4	Electricity, gas and water	6972	...	-	...	...	...	6972
5	Construction	38844	...	...	...	...	...	38844

Japan

4.10 Supply of Goods and Services, in Constant Prices
(Continued)

Thousand Million Japanese yen

	Gross Domestic Output - Marketed	Gross Domestic Output - Non-Marketed	Imports c.i.f.	Import Duties	Trade & Transport Margins	Value Added Tax	TOTAL SUPPLY
At constant prices of: 1975							
6 Wholesale and retail trade, restaurants and hotels a	371	...	347	-	-	...	717
7 Transport and communications	11170	...	1201	-	-	...	12371
8 Finance, insurance, real estate and business services	32831	...	77	-	-	...	32907
9 Community, social and personal services a	38309	...	816	-	1043	...	40168
Total, Industries	318647	...	22760	1036	43809	...	386251
Producers of Government Services	...	...	...	...	...	...	...
Other Producers	...	23352	...	...	...	...	23352
Total	318647	23352	22760	1036	43809	...	409603
1979							
1 Agriculture, hunting, forestry and fishing	13653	...	3309	53	2590	...	19606
2 Mining and quarrying	1926	...	9598	148	891	...	12563
3 Manufacturing	186903	...	10127	866	38082	...	235978
4 Electricity, gas and water	7567	...	-	-	-	...	7567
5 Construction	40097	...	-	-	-	...	40097
6 Wholesale and retail trade, restaurants and hotels a	474	...	277	-	-	...	750
7 Transport and communications	11833	...	1199	-	-	...	13032
8 Finance, insurance, real estate and business services	34362	...	77	-	-	...	34440
9 Community, social and personal services a	40982	...	850	-	1049	...	42880
Total, Industries	337797	...	25437	1068	42612	...	406914
Producers of Government Services	...	...	...	...	...	...	...
Other Producers	...	24710	...	...	...	...	24710
Total	337797	24710	25437	1068	42612	...	431623
1980							
1 Agriculture, hunting, forestry and fishing	13092	...	3196	50	2215	...	18554
2 Mining and quarrying	1900	...	9094	74	873	...	11941
3 Manufacturing	195486	...	9841	667	37587	...	243581
4 Electricity, gas and water	7569	...	...	...	...	...	7569
5 Construction	38744	...	...	...	...	...	38744
6 Wholesale and retail trade, restaurants and hotels a	494	...	257	...	...	...	751
7 Transport and communications	12233	...	1159	...	...	...	13392
8 Finance, insurance, real estate and business services	35959	...	63	...	...	...	36022
9 Community, social and personal services a	41865	...	724	...	1070	...	43658
Total, Industries	347342	...	24334	792	41745	...	414212
Producers of Government Services	...	...	...	...	...	...	...
Other Producers	...	25348	...	...	...	...	25348
Total	347342	25348	24334	792	41745	...	439560

a) Restaurants and hotels are included in item 'Community, social and personal services'.

4.11 Disposition of Goods and Services, in Current Prices

Thousand Million Japanese yen

	Intermediate Consumption - General Government	Intermediate Consumption - Public Enterprises	Intermediate Consumption - Private	Final Consumption	Gross Capital Formation - General Government	Gross Capital Formation - Public Enterprises	Gross Capital Formation - Private	Exports	TOTAL DISPOSITION
1970									
1 Agriculture, hunting, forestry and fishing	...	7460	...	2598	...	17	...	102	10176
2 Mining and quarrying	...	3545	...	5	...	81	...	8	3638
3 Manufacturing	...	59603	...	18384	...	13793	...	6954	98735
4 Electricity, gas and water	...	1757	...	714	...	-	...	5	2476
5 Construction	...	1379	...	-	...	14706	...	-	16085

Japan

4.11 Disposition of Goods and Services, in Current Prices
(Continued)

Thousand Million Japanese yen

	Intermediate Consumption: General Government	Intermediate Consumption: Public Enterprises	Intermediate Consumption: Private	Final Consumption	Gross Capital Formation: General Government	Gross Capital Formation: Public Enterprises	Gross Capital Formation: Private	Exports	TOTAL DISPOSITION
6 Wholesale and retail trade, restaurants and hotels [a]	...	125	...	77	...	19	...	30	250
7 Transport and communications	...	2491	...	2008	...	-	...	1065	5564
8 Finance, insurance, real estate and business services	...	5281	...	6110	...	-	...	14	11406
9 Community, social and personal services [a]	...	8362	...	6616	...	-	...	224	15202
Total, Industries	...	90002	...	36512	...	28616	...	8401	163531
Producers of Government Services	...	93	...	6106	...	-	...	-	6198
Other Producers	...	18	...	1090	...	-	...	-	1107
Total	...	90112	...	43707	...	28616	...	8401	170837

1971

	General Government	Public Enterprises	Private	Final Consumption	General Government	Public Enterprises	Private	Exports	TOTAL
1 Agriculture, hunting, forestry and fishing	...	7545	...	2691	...	-287	...	101	10049
2 Mining and quarrying	...	3911	...	4	...	51	...	9	3974
3 Manufacturing	...	61519	...	20540	...	13093	...	8399	103551
4 Electricity, gas and water	...	1907	...	817	...	-	...	5	2728
5 Construction	...	1482	...	-	...	15974	...	-	17456
6 Wholesale and retail trade, restaurants and hotels [a]	...	133	...	82	...	20	...	32	267
7 Transport and communications	...	2770	...	2262	...	-	...	1262	6294
8 Finance, insurance, real estate and business services	...	9107	...	7142	...	-	...	17	13363
9 Community, social and personal services [a]	...	9417	...	7556	...	-	...	256	17229
Total, Industries	...	94887	...	41094	...	28852	...	10079	174912
Producers of Government Services	...	113	...	7159	...	-	...	-	7272
Other Producers	...	18	...	1214	...	-	...	-	1233
Total	...	95020	...	¡467	...	28852	...	10079	183417

1972

	General Government	Public Enterprises	Private	Final Consumption	General Government	Public Enterprises	Private	Exports	TOTAL
1 Agriculture, hunting, forestry and fishing	...	7940	...	2941	...	7	...	67	10955
2 Mining and quarrying	...	4023	...	3	...	18	...	12	4057
3 Manufacturing	...	68999	...	23455	...	13807	...	8819	115079
4 Electricity, gas and water	...	2141	...	905	...	-	...	5	3051
5 Construction	...	1709	...	-	...	18967	...	-	20676
6 Wholesale and retail trade, restaurants and hotels [a]	...	150	...	94	...	23	...	26	292
7 Transport and communications	...	3106	...	2524	...	-	...	1155	6785
8 Finance, insurance, real estate and business services	...	7201	...	8301	...	-	...	16	15517
9 Community, social and personal services [a]	...	11257	...	9037	...	-	...	304	20597
Total, Industries	...	106525	...	47260	...	32822	...	10402	197009
Producers of Government Services	...	146	...	8436	...	-	...	-	8582
Other Producers	...	25	...	1476	...	-	...	-	1501
Total	...	106695	...	57172	...	32822	...	10402	207091

1973

	General Government	Public Enterprises	Private	Final Consumption	General Government	Public Enterprises	Private	Exports	TOTAL
1 Agriculture, hunting, forestry and fishing	...	10491	...	3585	...	153	...	78	14306
2 Mining and quarrying	...	5128	...	2	...	89	...	11	5231
3 Manufacturing	...	89290	...	28860	...	17062	...	10009	145220
4 Electricity, gas and water	...	2489	...	1031	...	-	...	4	3524
5 Construction	...	2117	...	-	...	25440	...	-	27557

Japan

4.11 Disposition of Goods and Services, in Current Prices
(Continued)

Thousand Million Japanese yen

	Intermediate Consumption			Final Consumption	Gross Capital Formation			Exports	TOTAL DISPOSITION
	General Government	Public Enterprises	Private		General Government	Public Enterprises	Private		
6 Wholesale and retail trade, restaurants and hotels [a]	...	197	...	118	...	37	...	31	383
7 Transport and communications	...	3717	...	2973	...	-	...	1413	8103
8 Finance, insurance, real estate and business services	...	9154	...	9888	...	-	...	11	19053
9 Community, social and personal services [a]	...	13670	...	10623	...	43	...	369	24704
Total, Industries	...	136252	...	57079	...	42824	...	11925	248080
Producers of Government Services	...	170	...	10387	...	-	...	-	10556
Other Producers	...	31	...	1816	...	-	...	-	1847
Total	...	136453	...	69281	...	42824	...	11925	260483

1974

1 Agriculture, hunting, forestry and fishing	...	12718	...	4475	...	280	...	91	17564
2 Mining and quarrying	...	10361	...	6	...	213	...	14	10594
3 Manufacturing	...	109940	...	35423	...	19735	...	16218	181315
4 Electricity, gas and water	...	3704	...	1225	...	-	...	5	4933
5 Construction	...	2413	...	-	...	29625	...	-	32038
6 Wholesale and retail trade, restaurants and hotels [a]	...	253	...	161	...	73	...	55	541
7 Transport and communications	...	4796	...	3528	...	-	...	1886	10210
8 Finance, insurance, real estate and business services	...	10923	...	11269	...	-	...	17	22209
9 Community, social and personal services [a]	...	16482	...	12761	...	166	...	560	29968
Total, Industries	...	171589	...	68848	...	50091	...	18846	309374
Producers of Government Services	...	192	...	13600	...	-	...	-	13792
Other Producers	...	43	...	2303	...	-	...	-	2346
Total	...	171824	...	84751	...	50091	...	18846	325512

1975

1 Agriculture, hunting, forestry and fishing	...	13766	...	4960	...	409	...	56	19191
2 Mining and quarrying	...	10682	...	6	...	79	...	14	10780
3 Manufacturing	...	107191	...	40175	...	16010	...	16695	180070
4 Electricity, gas and water	...	4485	...	1579	...	-	...	2	6066
5 Construction	...	2498	...	-	...	31577	...	-	34075
6 Wholesale and retail trade, restaurants and hotels [a]	...	274	...	202	...	106	...	56	638
7 Transport and communications	...	5300	...	4098	...	-	...	2526	11924
8 Finance, insurance, real estate and business services	...	13603	...	13163	...	-	...	53	26819
9 Community, social and personal services [a]	...	18205	...	15297	...	330	...	612	34443
Total, Industries	...	176003	...	79479	...	48511	...	20012	324005
Producers of Government Services	...	181	...	16649	...	-	...	-	16830
Other Producers	...	58	...	3001	...	-	...	-	3059
Total	...	176241	...	99129	...	48511	...	20012	343893

1976

1 Agriculture, hunting, forestry and fishing	...	14924	...	5626	...	507	...	74	21131
2 Mining and quarrying	...	11452	...	7	...	-9	...	19	11469
3 Manufacturing	...	123434	...	44978	...	17459	...	20063	205934
4 Electricity, gas and water	...	5275	...	1806	...	-	...	3	7083
5 Construction	...	2764	...	-	...	34510	...	-	37274

Japan

4.11 Disposition of Goods and Services, in Current Prices
(Continued)

Thousand Million Japanese yen

		Intermediate Consumption			Gross Capital Formation				TOTAL
		General Government	Public Enterprises	Private	Final Consumption	General Government	Public Enterprises	Private	Exports	DISPOSITION
6	Wholesale and retail trade, restaurants and hotels [a]	...	324	...	210	...	108	...	53	695
7	Transport and communications	...	6477	...	4612	...	-	...	2837	13926
8	Finance, insurance, real estate and business services	...	15076	...	15149	...	-	...	88	30312
9	Community, social and personal services [a]	...	20354	...	16829	...	374	...	407	37964
	Total, Industries	...	200079	...	89216	...	52950	...	23543	365788
	Producers of Government Services	...	321	...	18449	...	-	...	-	18770
	Other Producers	...	64	...	3500	...	-	...	-	3564
	Total	...	200464	...	111164	...	52950	...	23543	388122

1977

1	Agriculture, hunting, forestry and fishing	...	15701	...	5325	...	593	...	61	21680
2	Mining and quarrying	...	11500	...	9	...	263	...	17	11789
3	Manufacturing	...	131759	...	48853	...	18787	...	21805	221204
4	Electricity, gas and water	...	6210	...	2187	...	-	...	3	8400
5	Construction	...	2930	...	-	...	37214	...	-	40144
6	Wholesale and retail trade, restaurants and hotels [a]	...	343	...	232	...	121	...	55	750
7	Transport and communications	...	7463	...	5368	...	-	...	2710	15542
8	Finance, insurance, real estate and business services	...	16733	...	17550	...	-	...	73	34355
9	Community, social and personal services [a]	...	22673	...	19410	...	410	...	484	42977
	Total, Industries	...	215313	...	98935	...	57388	...	25206	396841
	Producers of Government Services	...	440	...	20595	...	-	...	-	21034
	Other Producers	...	70	...	4031	...	-	...	-	4101
	Total	...	215823	...	123560	...	57388	...	25206	421976

1978

1	Agriculture, hunting, forestry and fishing	...	15356	...	5492	...	376	...	65	21290
2	Mining and quarrying	...	10276	...	11	...	-85	...	17	10219
3	Manufacturing	...	137700	...	51206	...	21195	...	20627	230728
4	Electricity, gas and water	...	6443	...	2384	...	-	...	3	8830
5	Construction	...	3193	...	-	...	41353	...	-	44546
6	Wholesale and retail trade, restaurants and hotels [a]	...	358	...	244	...	126	...	48	777
7	Transport and communications	...	7858	...	6015	...	-	...	2334	16207
8	Finance, insurance, real estate and business services	...	18537	...	20098	...	-	...	87	38722
9	Community, social and personal services [a]	...	25128	...	22399	...	456	...	436	48418
	Total, Industries	...	224849	...	107849	...	63421	...	23617	419736
	Producers of Government Services	...	548	...	22489	...	-	...	-	23037
	Other Producers	...	81	...	4642	...	-	...	-	4723
	Total	...	225478	...	134979	...	63421	...	23617	447496

1979

1	Agriculture, hunting, forestry and fishing	...	16895	...	5841	...	385	...	81	23202
2	Mining and quarrying	...	13448	...	16	...	271	...	22	13756
3	Manufacturing	...	156533	...	55264	...	24151	...	22527	258474
4	Electricity, gas and water	...	7148	...	2523	...	-	...	2	9673
5	Construction	...	3554	...	-	...	46625	...	-	50179

Japan

4.11 Disposition of Goods and Services, in Current Prices
(Continued)

Thousand Million Japanese yen

		Intermediate Consumption			Final Consumption	Gross Capital Formation			Exports	TOTAL DISPO-SITION
		General Government	Public Enterprises	Private		General Government	Public Enterprises	Private		
6	Wholesale and retail trade, restaurants and hotels [a]	...	380	...	256	...	133	...	61	831
7	Transport and communications	...	8615	...	6624	...	-	...	2883	18122
8	Finance, insurance, real estate and business services	...	20702	...	22161	...	-	...	120	42983
9	Community, social and personal services [a]	...	28050	...	24975	...	500	...	581	54106
	Total, Industries	...	255324	...	117660	...	72065	...	26277	471325
	Producers of Government Services	...	596	...	24578	...	-	...	-	25175
	Other Producers	...	95	...	5357	...	-	...	-	5452
	Total	...	256016	...	147595	...	72065	...	26277	501952
					1980					
1	Agriculture, hunting, forestry and fishing	...	17741	...	5957	...	-269	...	107	23536
2	Mining and quarrying	...	20132	...	39	...	-186	...	25	20010
3	Manufacturing	...	180225	...	59229	...	26636	...	29483	295574
4	Electricity, gas and water	...	10648	...	2869	...	-	...	2	13520
5	Construction	...	3818	...	-	...	50026	...	-	53845
6	Wholesale and retail trade, restaurants and hotels [a]	...	397	...	269	...	139	...	84	889
7	Transport and communications	...	9934	...	6792	...	-	...	3836	20562
8	Finance, insurance, real estate and business services	...	23106	...	24617	...	-	...	114	47836
9	Community, social and personal services [a]	...	31346	...	26933	...	441	...	793	59514
	Total, Industries	...	297347	...	126705	...	76788	...	34444	535284
	Producers of Government Services	...	811	...	26866	...	-	...	-	27676
	Other Producers	...	113	...	5819	...	-	...	-	5932
	Total	...	298271	...	159390	...	76788	...	34444	568892

a) Restaurants and hotels are included in item 'Community, social and personal services'.

4.12 Disposition of Goods and Services, in Constant Prices

Thousand Million Japanese yen

		Intermediate Consumption			Final Consumption	Gross Capital Formation			Exports	TOTAL DISPO-SITION
		General Government	Public Enterprises	Private		General Government	Public Enterprises	Private		
					At constant prices of: 1975					
					1970					
1	Agriculture, hunting, forestry and fishing	...	12757	...	4274	...	-17	...	160	17174
2	Mining and quarrying	...	9284	...	11	...	181	...	14	9490
3	Manufacturing	...	95494	...	31211	...	19364	...	9854	155923
4	Electricity, gas and water	...	3517	...	952	...	-	...	8	4477
5	Construction	...	2374	...	-	...	25418	...	-	27791
6	Wholesale and retail trade, restaurants and hotels [a]	...	199	...	125	...	30	...	46	399
7	Transport and communications	...	3676	...	3430	...	-	...	1522	8628
8	Finance, insurance, real estate and business services	...	7792	...	9329	...	-	...	23	17144
9	Community, social and personal services [a]	...	15066	...	12120	...	-	...	318	27504
	Total, Industries	...	150159	...	61452	...	44975	...	11944	268530
	Producers of Government Services	...	498	...	12428	...	-	...	-	12926
	Other Producers	...	179	...	2085	...	-	...	-	2264
	Total	...	150835	...	75965	...	44975	...	11944	283719
					1971					
1	Agriculture, hunting, forestry and fishing	...	12781	...	4358	...	-554	...	146	16731
2	Mining and quarrying	...	10021	...	9	...	118	...	16	10164
3	Manufacturing	...	99513	...	32771	...	18235	...	11734	162253
4	Electricity, gas and water	...	3817	...	1069	...	-	...	8	4914
5	Construction	...	2483	...	-	...	26847	...	-	29330

Japan

4.12 Disposition of Goods and Services, in Constant Prices
(Continued)

Thousand Million Japanese yen

	Intermediate Consumption			Final Consumption	Gross Capital Formation			Exports	TOTAL DISPO-SITION
	General Government	Public Enterprises	Private		General Government	Public Enterprises	Private		

At constant prices of: 1975

6 Wholesale and retail trade, restaurants and hotels a	...	213	...	133	...	32	...	49	428
7 Transport and communications	...	3937	...	3651	...	-	...	1695	9284
8 Finance, insurance, real estate and business services	...	9289	...	10104	...	-	...	28	19239
9 Community, social and personal services a	...	16326	...	12810	...	-	...	357	29492
Total, Industries	...	158196	...	64924	...	44679	...	14033	281834
Producers of Government Services	...	442	...	13154	...	-	...	-	13596
Other Producers	...	153	...	2143	...	-	...	-	2297
Total	...	158794	...	80221	...	44679	...	14033	297726

1972

1 Agriculture, hunting, forestry and fishing	...	13077	...	4724	...	-16	...	82	17867
2 Mining and quarrying	...	10905	...	8	...	39	...	25	10976
3 Manufacturing	...	109895	...	36222	...	18933	...	12576	177626
4 Electricity, gas and water	...	4222	...	1186	...	-	...	7	5415
5 Construction	...	2743	...	-	...	30226	...	-	32969
6 Wholesale and retail trade, restaurants and hotels a	...	235	...	150	...	36	...	39	460
7 Transport and communications	...	4109	...	3723	...	-	...	1628	9460
8 Finance, insurance, real estate and business services	...	11105	...	10932	...	-	...	25	22062
9 Community, social and personal services a	...	18572	...	14057	...	-	...	433	33063
Total, Industries	...	174864	...	71001	...	49218	...	14815	309897
Producers of Government Services	...	493	...	13916	...	-	...	-	14408
Other Producers	...	190	...	2330	...	-	...	-	2520
Total	...	175546	...	87247	...	49218	...	14815	326826

1973

1 Agriculture, hunting, forestry and fishing	...	13373	...	4949	...	182	...	86	18590
2 Mining and quarrying	...	12606	...	5	...	244	...	19	12873
3 Manufacturing	...	121461	...	39915	...	21824	...	13263	196462
4 Electricity, gas and water	...	4731	...	1316	...	-	...	7	6053
5 Construction	...	2920	...	-	...	33979	...	-	36900
6 Wholesale and retail trade, restaurants and hotels a	...	267	...	164	...	51	...	42	524
7 Transport and communications	...	4633	...	4017	...	-	...	1932	10582
8 Finance, insurance, real estate and business services	...	12081	...	11960	...	-	...	15	24056
9 Community, social and personal services a	...	19447	...	15089	...	58	...	480	35074
Total, Industries	...	191518	...	77414	...	56338	...	15843	341113
Producers of Government Services	...	396	...	14702	...	-	...	-	15098
Other Producers	...	115	...	2580	...	-	...	-	2695
Total	...	192030	...	94692	...	56338	...	15843	358907

1974

1 Agriculture, hunting, forestry and fishing	...	13213	...	4824	...	323	...	81	18440
2 Mining and quarrying	...	11694	...	11	...	250	...	21	11975
3 Manufacturing	...	113349	...	38992	...	20364	...	16189	188894
4 Electricity, gas and water	...	4624	...	1376	...	-	...	5	6006
5 Construction	...	2519	...	-	...	31079	...	-	33598

Japan

4.12 Disposition of Goods and Services, in Constant Prices
(Continued)

Thousand Million Japanese yen

	Intermediate Consumption — General Government	Intermediate Consumption — Public Enterprises	Intermediate Consumption — Private	Final Consumption	Gross Capital Formation — General Government	Gross Capital Formation — Public Enterprises	Gross Capital Formation — Private	Exports	TOTAL DISPOSITION
At constant prices of: 1975									
6 Wholesale and retail trade, restaurants and hotels [a]	...	257	...	176	...	78	...	57	567
7 Transport and communications	...	5254	...	4153	...	-	...	1960	11367
8 Finance, insurance, real estate and business services	...	10892	...	12380	...	-	...	18	23291
9 Community, social and personal services [a]	...	18325	...	14747	...	171	...	547	33789
Total, Industries	...	180125	...	76660	...	52265	...	18879	327929
Producers of Government Services	...	280	...	15285	...	-	...	-	15565
Other Producers	...	28	...	2688	...	-	...	-	2716
Total	...	180432	...	94633	...	52265	...	18879	346210
1975									
1 Agriculture, hunting, forestry and fishing	...	13766	...	4960	...	409	...	56	19191
2 Mining and quarrying	...	10682	...	...	...	79	...	14	10780
3 Manufacturing	...	107191	...	40175	...	16010	...	16695	180070
4 Electricity, gas and water	...	4485	...	1579	...	-	...	2	6066
5 Construction	...	2498	...	-	...	31577	...	-	34075
6 Wholesale and retail trade, restaurants and hotels [a]	...	274	...	202	...	106	...	56	638
7 Transport and communications	...	5300	...	4098	...	-	...	2526	11924
8 Finance, insurance, real estate and business services	...	13603	...	13163	...	-	...	53	26819
9 Community, social and personal services [a]	...	18205	...	15297	...	330	...	612	34443
Total, Industries	...	176003	...	79479	...	48511	...	20012	324005
Producers of Government Services	...	181	...	16649	...	-	...	-	16830
Other Producers	...	58	...	3001	...	-	...	-	3060
Total	...	176241	...	99129	...	48511	...	20012	343893
1976									
1 Agriculture, hunting, forestry and fishing	...	13737	...	5074	...	475	...	62	19348
2 Mining and quarrying	...	10956	...	6	...	-9	...	19	10972
3 Manufacturing	...	118017	...	42318	...	17262	...	20311	197908
4 Electricity, gas and water	...	4711	...	1619	...	-	...	2	6333
5 Construction	...	2580	...	-	...	32268	...	-	34848
6 Wholesale and retail trade, restaurants and hotels [a]	...	310	...	195	...	102	...	50	657
7 Transport and communications	...	5739	...	4088	...	-	...	2681	12507
8 Finance, insurance, real estate and business services	...	14220	...	13778	...	-	...	84	28061
9 Community, social and personal services [a]	...	18846	...	15201	...	356	...	412	34815
Total, Industries	...	189115	...	82279	...	50454	...	23620	345468
Producers of Government Services	...	471	...	17024	...	-	...	-	17495
Other Producers	...	253	...	2983	...	-	...	-	3235
Total	...	189839	...	102286	...	50454	...	23620	366198
1977									
1 Agriculture, hunting, forestry and fishing	...	14181	...	4483	...	516	...	46	19226
2 Mining and quarrying	...	11385	...	8	...	251	...	16	11659
3 Manufacturing	...	124707	...	43957	...	18211	...	23111	209986
4 Electricity, gas and water	...	4815	...	1764	...	-	...	2	6581
5 Construction	...	2654	...	-	...	33398	...	-	36052

Japan

4.12 Disposition of Goods and Services, in Constant Prices
(Continued)

Thousand Million Japanese yen

	Intermediate Consumption: General Government	Intermediate Consumption: Public Enterprises	Intermediate Consumption: Private	Final Consumption	Gross Capital Formation: General Government	Gross Capital Formation: Public Enterprises	Gross Capital Formation: Private	Exports	TOTAL DISPOSITION
At constant prices of: 1975									
6 Wholesale and retail trade, restaurants and hotels [a]	...	324	...	205	...	108	...	50	688
7 Transport and communications	...	5600	...	3995	...	-	...	2597	12192
8 Finance, insurance, real estate and business services	...	15821	...	14536	...	-	...	71	30428
9 Community, social and personal services [a]	...	19885	...	16316	...	383	...	508	37092
Total, Industries	...	199370	...	85263	...	52868	...	26402	363903
Producers of Government Services	...	626	...	17723	...	-	...	-	18349
Other Producers	...	358	...	3113	...	-	...	-	3471
Total	...	200354	...	106099	...	52868	...	26402	385722
1978									
1 Agriculture, hunting, forestry and fishing	...	14571	...	4555	...	339	...	53	19518
2 Mining and quarrying	...	11867	...	11	...	-126	...	18	11770
3 Manufacturing	...	133964	...	44988	...	20709	...	23323	222984
4 Electricity, gas and water	...	5054	...	1916	...	-	...	2	6972
5 Construction	...	2864	...	-	...	35980	...	-	38844
6 Wholesale and retail trade, restaurants and hotels [a]	...	350	...	210	...	112	...	45	717
7 Transport and communications	...	5623	...	4260	...	-	...	2488	12371
8 Finance, insurance, real estate and business services	...	17329	...	15489	...	-	...	89	32907
9 Community, social and personal services [a]	...	21733	...	17514	...	437	...	484	40168
Total, Industries	...	213356	...	88942	...	57451	...	26502	386251
Producers of Government Services	...	922	...	18587	...	-	...	-	19509
Other Producers	...	551	...	3293	...	-	...	-	3843
Total	...	214829	...	110821	...	57451	...	26502	409603
1979									
1 Agriculture, hunting, forestry and fishing	...	14528	...	4685	...	329	...	64	19606
2 Mining and quarrying	...	12282	...	12	...	249	...	20	12563
3 Manufacturing	...	141282	...	47393	...	23743	...	23560	235978
4 Electricity, gas and water	...	5571	...	1994	...	-	...	2	7567
5 Construction	...	2957	...	-	...	37141	...	-	40097
6 Wholesale and retail trade, restaurants and hotels [a]	...	364	...	216	...	113	...	58	750
7 Transport and communications	...	5732	...	4469	...	-	...	2831	13032
8 Finance, insurance, real estate and business services	...	18083	...	16251	...	-	...	106	34440
9 Community, social and personal services [a]	...	22903	...	18937	...	447	...	594	42880
Total, Industries	...	223701	...	93956	...	62022	...	27234	406914
Producers of Government Services	...	993	...	19450	...	-	...	-	20444
Other Producers	...	627	...	3639	...	-	...	-	4266
Total	...	225322	...	117045	...	62022	...	27234	431623
1980									
1 Agriculture, hunting, forestry and fishing	...	14406	...	4282	...	-213	...	79	18554
2 Mining and quarrying	...	12009	...	19	...	-105	...	19	11941
3 Manufacturing	...	141472	...	47483	...	25911	...	28716	243581
4 Electricity, gas and water	...	5797	...	1771	...	-	...	1	7569
5 Construction	...	2832	...	-	...	35912	...	-	38744

Japan

4.12 Disposition of Goods and Services, in Constant Prices
(Continued)

Thousand Million Japanese yen

	Intermediate Consumption: General Government	Intermediate Consumption: Public Enterprises	Intermediate Consumption: Private	Final Consumption	Gross Capital Formation: General Government	Gross Capital Formation: Public Enterprises	Gross Capital Formation: Private	Exports	TOTAL DISPOSITION
At constant prices of: 1975									
6 Wholesale and retail trade, restaurants and hotels [a]	...	351	...	212	...	109	...	79	751
7 Transport and communications	...	6028	...	4270	...	-	...	3094	13392
8 Finance, insurance, real estate and business services	...	18730	...	17208	...	-	...	84	36022
9 Community, social and personal services [a]	...	23185	...	19394	...	334	...	744	43658
Total, Industries	...	224810	...	94639	...	61948	...	32815	414212
Producers of Government Services	...	1093	...	19901	...	-	...	-	21000
Other Producers	...	603	...	3745	...	-	...	-	4348
Total	...	226506	...	118291	...	61948	...	32815	439560

a) Restaurants and hotels are included in item 'Community, social and personal services'.

4.13 Gross Output of Goods and Services by Kind of Activity of Producer (Make Matrix), at Current Prices

Thousand Million Japanese yen

CHARACTERISTIC PRODUCTS OF:

	Agriculture, Hunting, Forestry, Fishing	Mining & Quarrying	Manufacturing	Electricity, Gas & Water	Construction	Wholesale & Retail Trade, Restaurants & Hotels	Transport & Communications	Finance Insurance, Real Estate & Business Services	Community Social & Personal Services	TOTAL
1970										
1 Agriculture, hunting, forestry and fishing	7056	-	442	-	-	-	-	-	-	
2 Mining and quarrying	-	963	2	3	-	-	-	-	988	
3 Manufacturing	-	6	78841	123	421	-	-	-	988	
4 Electricity, gas and water	-	-	-	2403	2	-	-	-	1	
5 Construction	-	-	-	-	15661	-	-	-	2	
6 Wholesale and retail trade, restaurants and hotels [a]	-	-	1464	-	-	14427	-	-	36	
7 Transport and communications	-	-	-	-	1	-	7312	-	5	
8 Finance, insurance, real estate and business services	-	-	-	10	1	-	-	11392	19	
9 Community, social and personal services [a]	-	-	-	-	-	-	-	-	13881	
Statistical discrepancy	...	...	...	...	...	...	...	...	...	
Total, Industries	7056	969	80748	2539	16087	14427	7312	11392	14931	
Producers of Government Services	...	...	...	...	...	...	...	...	...	
Other Producers	...	...	...	...	...	...	...	...	...	
Total	7056	969	80748	2539	16087	14427	7312	11392	14931	
1971										
1 Agriculture, hunting, forestry and fishing	6939	-	444	-	-	-	-	-	-	
2 Mining and quarrying	-	1000	2	4	-	-	-	-	1045	
3 Manufacturing	-	7	82589	135	457	-	-	-	1045	
4 Electricity, gas and water	-	-	-	2648	2	-	-	-	1	
5 Construction	-	-	-	-	16996	-	-	-	2	
6 Wholesale and retail trade, restaurants and hotels [a]	-	-	1508	-	-	15446	-	-	41	
7 Transport and communications	-	-	-	-	2	-	8154	-	5	
8 Finance, insurance, real estate and business services	-	-	-	11	2	-	-	13359	22	
9 Community, social and personal services [a]	-	-	-	-	-	-	-	-	15766	
Statistical discrepancy	...	...	...	...	...	...	...	...	...	
Total, Industries	6939	1007	84543	2797	17458	15446	8154	13359	16883	
Producers of Government Services	...	...	...	...	...	...	...	...	...	
Other Producers	...	...	...	...	...	...	...	...	...	
Total	6939	1007	84543	2797	17458	15446	8154	13359	16883	
1972										
1 Agriculture, hunting, forestry and fishing	7711	-	467	-	-	-	-	-	-	
2 Mining and quarrying	-	1064	3	4	-	-	-	-	-	
3 Manufacturing	-	7	91127	149	541	-	-	-	1185	
4 Electricity, gas and water	-	-	-	2964	3	-	-	-	2	
5 Construction	-	-	-	-	20131	-	-	-	2	

Japan

4.13 Gross Output of Goods and Services by Kind of Activity of Producer (Make Matrix), at Current Prices
(Continued)

Thousand Million Japanese yen

	Agriculture, Hunting, Forestry, Fishing	Mining & Quarrying	Manu- facturing	Electricity, Gas & Water	Construction	Wholesale & Retail Trade, Restaurants & Hotels	Transport & Communi- cations	Finance Insurance, Real Estate & Business Services	Community Social & Personal Services	TOTAL
6 Wholesale and retail trade, restaurants and hotels [a]	-	-	1638	-	-	17967	-	-	49	
7 Transport and communications	-	-	-	-	2	-	8795	-	6	
8 Finance, insurance, real estate and business services	-	-	-	12	2	-	-	15514	27	
9 Community, social and personal services [a]	-	-	-	-	-	-	-	-	18866	
Statistical discrepancy	...	...	...	...	...	...	...	...	...	
Total, Industries	7711	1071	93235	3129	20679	17967	8795	15514	20138	
Producers of Government Services	...	...	...	...	...	...	...	...	...	
Other Producers	...	...	...	...	...	...	...	...	...	
Total	7711	1071	93235	3129	20679	17967	8795	15514	20138	
1973										
1 Agriculture, hunting, forestry and fishing	9778	-	509	-	-	-	-	-	-	
2 Mining and quarrying	-	1339	4	5	-	-	-	-	-	
3 Manufacturing	-	10	115926	170	722	-	-	-	1461	
4 Electricity, gas and water	-	-	-	3429	4	-	-	-	2	
5 Construction	-	-	-	-	26831	-	-	-	3	
6 Wholesale and retail trade, restaurants and hotels [a]	-	-	1845	-	-	21607	-	-	59	
7 Transport and communications	-	-	-	-	2	-	10421	-	7	
8 Finance, insurance, real estate and business services	-	-	-	13	2	-	-	19050	32	
9 Community, social and personal services [a]	-	-	-	-	-	-	-	-	22444	
Statistical discrepancy	...	...	...	...	...	...	...	...	...	
Total, Industries	9778	1349	118284	3617	27561	21607	10421	19050	24008	
Producers of Government Services	...	...	...	...	...	...	...	...	...	
Other Producers	...	...	...	...	...	...	...	...	...	
Total	9778	1349	118284	3617	27561	21607	10421	19050	24008	
1974										
1 Agriculture, hunting, forestry and fishing	11595	-	577	-	-	-	-	-	-	
2 Mining and quarrying	-	1678	5	7	-	-	-	-	-	
3 Manufacturing	-	12	143695	245	839	-	-	-	1742	
4 Electricity, gas and water	-	-	-	4812	4	-	-	-	2	
5 Construction	-	-	-	-	31194	-	-	-	3	
6 Wholesale and retail trade, restaurants and hotels [a]	-	-	2191	-	-	27691	-	-	69	
7 Transport and communications	-	-	-	...	3	-	12918	-	9	
8 Finance, insurance, real estate and business services	-	-	-	19	3	-	-	22204	37	
9 Community, social and personal services [a]	-	-	-	-	-	-	-	-	27023	
Statistical discrepancy	...	...	...	...	...	...	...	...	...	
Total, Industries	11595	1690	146469	5083	32042	27691	12918	22204	28886	
Producers of Government Services	...	...	...	...	...	...	...	...	...	
Other Producers	...	...	...	...	...	...	...	...	...	
Total	11595	1690	146469	5083	32042	27691	12918	22204	28886	
1975										
1 Agriculture, hunting, forestry and fishing	13039	-	84	-	-	-	-	-	-	
2 Mining and quarrying	-	1417	7	5	-	-	-	-	-	
3 Manufacturing	-	99	142084	262	62	-	-	-	1428	
4 Electricity, gas and water	-	-	-	5915	1	-	-	-	2	
5 Construction	-	-	-	-	34011	-	-	-	3	

Japan

4.13 Gross Output of Goods and Services by Kind of Activity of Producer (Make Matrix), at Current Prices
(Continued)

Thousand Million Japanese yen

	Agriculture, Hunting, Forestry, Fishing	Mining & Quarrying	Manu-facturing	Electricity, Gas & Water	Construction	Wholesale & Retail Trade, Restaurants & Hotels	Transport & Communi-cations	Finance Insurance, Real Estate & Business Services	Community Social & Personal Services	TOTAL
6 Wholesale and retail trade, restaurants and hotels [a]	-	-	1964	-	-	30053	-	-	70	
7 Transport and communications	-	-	-	10	8	-	15034	-	8	
8 Finance, insurance, real estate and business services	-	-	-	-	-	-	-	26779	36	
9 Community, social and personal services [a]	-	-	-	11	-	-	-	-	31321	
Statistical discrepancy	...	...	...	...	...	...	...	...	...	
Total, Industries	13039	1516	144138	6203	34083	30053	15034	26779	32869	
Producers of Government Services	...	...	...	...	...	...	...	...	...	
Other Producers	...	...	...	...	...	...	...	...	...	
Total	13039	1516	144138	6203	34083	30053	15034	26779	32869	
1976										
1 Agriculture, hunting, forestry and fishing	14226	-	99	-	-	-	-	-	-	
2 Mining and quarrying	-	1527	6	6	-	-	-	-	-	
3 Manufacturing	-	14	162933	304	69	-	-	-	1427	
4 Electricity, gas and water	-	-	-	6898	2	-	-	-	1	
5 Construction	-	-	-	-	37202	-	-	-	-	
6 Wholesale and retail trade, restaurants and hotels [a]	-	-	2187	-	-	33503	-	-	78	
7 Transport and communications	-	-	-	11	9	-	17371	-	10	
8 Finance, insurance, real estate and business services	-	-	-	-	-	-	-	30246	41	
9 Community, social and personal services [a]	-	-	-	12	-	-	-	-	35005	
Statistical discrepancy	...	...	...	...	...	...	...	...	...	
Total, Industries	14226	1541	165226	7232	37282	33503	17371	30246	36563	
Producers of Government Services	...	...	...	...	...	...	...	...	...	
Other Producers	...	...	...	...	...	...	...	...	...	
Total	14226	1541	165226	7232	37282	33503	17371	30246	36563	
1977										
1 Agriculture, hunting, forestry and fishing	15173	-	94	-	-	-	-	-	-	
2 Mining and quarrying	-	1765	7	7	-	-	-	-	-	
3 Manufacturing	-	14	174532	360	73	-	-	-	1570	
4 Electricity, gas and water	-	-	-	8178	2	-	-	-	1	
5 Construction	-	-	-	-	40068	-	-	-	-	
6 Wholesale and retail trade, restaurants and hotels [a]	-	-	2359	-	-	36142	-	-	84	
7 Transport and communications	-	-	-	13	9	-	19655	-	11	
8 Finance, insurance, real estate and business services	-	-	-	-	-	-	-	34290	44	
9 Community, social and personal services [a]	-	-	-	15	-	-	-	-	39716	
Statistical discrepancy	...	...	...	...	...	...	...	...	...	
Total, Industries	15173	1779	176992	8573	40153	36142	19655	34290	41428	
Producers of Government Services	...	...	...	...	...	...	...	...	...	
Other Producers	...	...	...	...	...	...	...	...	...	
Total	15173	1779	176992	8573	40153	36142	19655	34290	41428	
1978										
1 Agriculture, hunting, forestry and fishing	15273	-	102	-	-	-	-	-	-	
2 Mining and quarrying	-	2025	9	8	-	-	-	-	-	
3 Manufacturing	-	20	181624	373	80	-	-	-	1738	
4 Electricity, gas and water	-	-	-	8599	2	-	-	-	2	
5 Construction	-	-	-	-	44463	-	-	-	-	

Japan

4.13 Gross Output of Goods and Services by Kind of Activity of Producer (Make Matrix), at Current Prices
(Continued)

Thousand Million Japanese yen

	Agriculture, Hunting, Forestry, Fishing	Mining & Quarrying	Manu-facturing	Electricity, Gas & Water	Construction	Wholesale & Retail Trade, Restaurants & Hotels	Transport & Communi-cations	Finance Insurance, Real Estate & Business Services	Community Social & Personal Services	TOTAL
6 Wholesale and retail trade, restaurants and hotels [a]	-	-	2475	-	-	37922	-	-	88	
7 Transport and communications	-	-	-	14	10	-	21437	-	12	
8 Finance, insurance, real estate and business services	-	-	-	-	-	-	-	38646	49	
9 Community, social and personal services [a]	-	-	-	15	-	-	-	-	44838	
Statistical discrepancy	...	...	...	...	...	...	...	...	...	
Total, Industries	15273	2044	184209	9008	44556	37922	21437	38646	46727	
Producers of Government Services	...	...	...	...	...	...	...	...	...	
Other Producers	...	...	...	...	...	...	...	...	...	
Total	15273	2044	184209	9008	44556	37922	21437	38646	46727	
					1979					
1 Agriculture, hunting, forestry and fishing	15913	-	107	-	-	-	-	-	-	
2 Mining and quarrying	-	2331	11	8	-	-	-	-	-	
3 Manufacturing	-	19	203535	409	91	-	-	-	2232	
4 Electricity, gas and water	-	-	-	9415	2	-	-	-	4	
5 Construction	-	-	-	-	50085	-	-	-	6	
6 Wholesale and retail trade, restaurants and hotels [a]	-	-	2616	-	-	40078	-	-	119	
7 Transport and communications	-	-	-	15	12	-	23375	-	14	
8 Finance, insurance, real estate and business services	-	-	-	-	-	-	-	42898	61	
9 Community, social and personal services [a]	-	-	-	17	-	-	-	-	49731	
Statistical discrepancy	...	...	...	...	...	...	...	...	...	
Total, Industries	15913	2351	206267	9864	50190	40078	23375	42898	52168	
Producers of Government Services	...	...	...	...	...	...	...	...	...	
Other Producers	...	...	...	...	...	...	...	...	...	
Total	15913	2351	206267	9864	50190	40078	23375	42898	52168	
					1980					
1 Agriculture, hunting, forestry and fishing	16166	-	110	-	-	-	-	-	1	
2 Mining and quarrying	-	2593	11	9	-	-	-	-	-	
3 Manufacturing	-	23	235775	499	103	-	-	-	2509	
4 Electricity, gas and water	-	-	-	13266	3	-	-	-	5	
5 Construction	-	-	-	-	53737	-	-	-	6	
6 Wholesale and retail trade, restaurants and hotels [a]	-	-	2729	-	-	41812	-	-	125	
7 Transport and communications	-	-	-	18	13	-	26405	-	16	
8 Finance, insurance, real estate and business services	-	-	-	-	-	-	-	47754	69	
9 Community, social and personal services [a]	-	-	-	18	-	-	-	-	54703	
Statistical discrepancy	...	...	...	...	...	...	...	...	...	
Total, Industries	16166	2616	238626	13810	53856	41812	26405	47754	57434	
Producers of Government Services	...	...	...	...	...	...	...	...	...	
Other Producers	...	...	...	...	...	...	...	...	...	
Total	16166	2616	238626	13810	53856	41812	26405	47754	57434	

a) Restaurants and hotels are included in item 'Community, social and personal services'.

Japan

4.14 Gross Output of Goods and Services by Kind of Activity of Producer (Make Matrix), at Constant Prices

Thousand Million Japanese yen

	Agriculture, Hunting, Forestry, Fishing	Mining & Quarrying	Manu-facturing	Electricity, Gas & Water	Construction	Wholesale & Retail Trade, Restaurants & Hotels	Transport & Communi-cations	Finance Insurance, Real Estate & Business Services	Community Social & Personal Services	TOTAL

At constant prices of: 1975

1970

1 Agriculture, hunting, forestry and fishing	12001	-	703	-	-	-	-	-	-	
2 Mining and quarrying	-	1534	4	6	-	-	-	-	-	
3 Manufacturing	-	9	120917	231	727	-	-	-	1589	
4 Electricity, gas and water	-	-	-	4336	4	-	-	-	2	
5 Construction	-	-	-	-	27049	-	-	-	3	
6 Wholesale and retail trade, restaurants and hotels a	-	-	2354	-	-	23159	-	-	69	
7 Transport and communications	-	-	-	-	2	-	11663	-	9	
8 Finance, insurance, real estate and business services	-	-	-	18	2	-	-	17126	37	
9 Community, social and personal services a	-	-	-	-	-	-	-	-	25269	
Statistical discrepancy	...	...	...	...	...	...	...	...	...	
Total, Industries	12001	1542	123978	4591	27785	23159	11663	17126	26979	
Producers of Government Services	...	...	...	...	...	...	...	...	...	
Other Producers	...	...	...	...	...	...	...	...	...	
Total	12001	1542	123978	4591	27785	23159	11663	17126	26979	

1971

1 Agriculture, hunting, forestry and fishing	11650	-	700	-	-	-	-	-	-	
2 Mining and quarrying	-	1576	4	7	-	-	-	-	-	
3 Manufacturing	-	11	126966	254	768	-	-	-	1675	
4 Electricity, gas and water	-	-	-	4758	4	-	-	-	2	
5 Construction	-	-	-	-	28564	-	-	-	4	
6 Wholesale and retail trade, restaurants and hotels a	-	-	2388	-	-	24369	-	-	73	
7 Transport and communications	-	-	-	-	3	-	12464	-	9	
8 Finance, insurance, real estate and business services	-	-	-	20	2	-	-	19232	40	
9 Community, social and personal services a	-	-	-	-	-	-	-	-	27022	
Statistical discrepancy	...	...	...	...	...	...	...	...	...	
Total, Industries	11650	1587	130058	5038	29342	24369	12464	19232	28826	
Producers of Government Services	...	...	...	...	...	...	...	...	...	
Other Producers	...	...	...	...	...	...	...	...	...	
Total	11650	1587	130058	5038	29342	24369	12464	19232	28826	

1972

1 Agriculture, hunting, forestry and fishing	12562	-	720	-	-	-	-	-	-	
2 Mining and quarrying	-	1651	4	8	-	-	-	-	-	
3 Manufacturing	-	11	138095	281	863	-	-	-	1869	
4 Electricity, gas and water	-	-	-	5236	5	-	-	-	2	
5 Construction	-	-	-	-	32107	-	-	-	4	
6 Wholesale and retail trade, restaurants and hotels a	-	-	2540	-	-	27792	-	-	81	
7 Transport and communications	-	-	-	-	3	-	12815	-	10	
8 Finance, insurance, real estate and business services	-	-	-	22	3	-	-	22058	44	
9 Community, social and personal services a	-	-	-	-	-	-	-	-	30130	
Statistical discrepancy	...	...	...	...	...	...	...	...	...	
Total, Industries	12562	1661	141359	5546	32981	27792	12815	22058	32141	
Producers of Government Services	...	...	...	...	...	...	...	...	...	
Other Producers	...	...	...	...	...	...	...	...	...	
Total	12562	1661	141359	5546	32981	27792	12815	22058	32141	

Japan

4.14 Gross Output of Goods and Services by Kind of Activity of Producer (Make Matrix), at Constant Prices
(Continued)

Thousand Million Japanese yen

	Agriculture, Hunting, Forestry, Fishing	Mining & Quarrying	Manufacturing	Electricity, Gas & Water	Construction	Wholesale & Retail Trade, Restaurants & Hotels	Transport & Communications	Finance Insurance, Real Estate & Business Services	Community Social & Personal Services	TOTAL
At constant prices of: 1975										
1973										
1 Agriculture, hunting, forestry and fishing	12811	-	739	-	-	-	-	-	-	
2 Mining and quarrying	-	1814	6	8	-	-	-	-	-	
3 Manufacturing	-	13	153751	312	966	-	-	-	1992	
4 Electricity, gas and water	-	-	-	5851	5	-	-	-	3	
5 Construction	-	-	-	-	35918	-	-	-	4	
6 Wholesale and retail trade, restaurants and hotels a	-	-	2565	-	-	29265	-	-	84	
7 Transport and communications	-	-	-	-	3	-	13847	-	11	
8 Finance, insurance, real estate and business services	-	-	-	25	3	-	-	24051	46	
9 Community, social and personal services a	-	-	-	-	-	-	-	-	31780	
Statistical discrepancy	...	...	...	...	...	...	...	...	...	
Total, Industries	12811	1827	157060	6196	36895	29265	13847	24051	33919	
Producers of Government Services	...	...	...	...	...	...	...	...	...	
Other Producers	...	...	...	...	...	...	...	...	...	
Total	12811	1827	157060	6196	36895	29265	13847	24051	33919	
1974										
1 Agriculture, hunting, forestry and fishing	12506	-	715	-	-	-	-	-	-	
2 Mining and quarrying	-	1647	5	8	-	-	-	-	-	
3 Manufacturing	-	11	148174	295	879	-	-	-	1821	
4 Electricity, gas and water	-	-	-	5876	5	-	-	-	2	
5 Construction	-	-	-	-	32698	-	-	-	4	
6 Wholesale and retail trade, restaurants and hotels a	-	-	2519	-	-	29094	-	-	80	
7 Transport and communications	-	-	-	-	3	-	14658	-	10	
8 Finance, insurance, real estate and business services	-	-	-	23	3	-	-	23284	43	
9 Community, social and personal services a	-	-	-	-	-	-	-	-	30657	
Statistical discrepancy	...	...	...	...	...	...	...	...	...	
Total, Industries	12506	1658	151413	6202	33587	29094	14658	23284	32619	
Producers of Government Services	...	...	...	...	...	...	...	...	...	
Other Producers	...	...	...	...	...	...	...	...	...	
Total	12506	1658	151413	6202	33587	29094	14658	23284	32619	
1975										
1 Agriculture, hunting, forestry and fishing	13039	-	84	-	-	-	-	-	-	
2 Mining and quarrying	-	1417	7	5	-	-	-	-	-	
3 Manufacturing	-	99	142084	262	62	-	-	-	1426	
4 Electricity, gas and water	-	-	-	5915	1	-	-	-	2	
5 Construction	-	-	-	-	34011	-	-	-	3	
6 Wholesale and retail trade, restaurants and hotels a	-	-	1964	-	-	30053	-	-	70	
7 Transport and communications	-	-	-	10	8	-	15034	-	8	
8 Finance, insurance, real estate and business services	-	-	-	-	-	-	-	26779	36	
9 Community, social and personal services a	-	-	-	11	-	-	-	-	31321	
Statistical discrepancy	...	...	...	...	...	...	...	...	...	
Total, Industries	13039	1516	144138	6203	34083	30053	15034	26779	32869	
Producers of Government Services	...	...	...	...	...	...	...	...	...	
Other Producers	...	...	...	...	...	...	...	...	...	
Total	13039	1516	144138	6203	34083	30053	15034	26779	32869	

Japan

4.14 Gross Output of Goods and Services by Kind of Activity of Producer (Make Matrix), at Constant Prices
(Continued)

Thousand Million Japanese yen

	Agriculture, Hunting, Forestry, Fishing	Mining & Quarrying	Manufacturing	Electricity, Gas & Water	Construction	Wholesale & Retail Trade, Restaurants & Hotels	Transport & Communications	Finance Insurance, Real Estate & Business Services	Community Social & Personal Services	TOTAL
				At constant prices of:1975						
					1976					
1 Agriculture, hunting, forestry and fishing	12934	-	90	-	-	-	-	-	-	
2 Mining and quarrying	-	1553	6	6	-	-	-	-	-	
3 Manufacturing	-	15	155636	276	64	-	-	-	1359	
4 Electricity, gas and water	-	-	-	6176	1	-	-	-	1	
5 Construction	-	-	-	-	34771	-	-	-	-	
6 Wholesale and retail trade, restaurants and hotels [a]	-	-	1963	-	-	31659	-	-	69	
7 Transport and communications	-	-	-	10	8	-	15639	-	9	
8 Finance, insurance, real estate and business services	-	-	-	-	-	-	-	28018	36	
9 Community, social and personal services [a]	-	-	-	11	-	-	-	-	31973	
Statistical discrepancy	...	...	...	...	...	...	...	...	...	
Total, Industries	12934	1567	157695	6479	34845	31659	15639	28018	33447	
Producers of Government Services	...	...	...	...	...	...	...	...	...	
Other Producers	...	...	...	...	...	...	...	...	...	
Total	12934	1567	157695	6479	34845	31659	15639	28018	33447	
					1977					
1 Agriculture, hunting, forestry and fishing	13107	-	80	-	-	-	-	-	-	
2 Mining and quarrying	-	1718	7	6	-	-	-	-	-	
3 Manufacturing	-	15	163581	285	66	-	-	-	1467	
4 Electricity, gas and water	-	-	-	6413	1	-	-	-	1	
5 Construction	-	-	-	-	35980	-	-	-	-	
6 Wholesale and retail trade, restaurants and hotels [a]	-	-	1968	-	-	33050	-	-	66	
7 Transport and communications	-	-	-	11	9	-	15549	-	9	
8 Finance, insurance, real estate and business services	-	-	-	-	-	-	-	30367	35	
9 Community, social and personal services [a]	-	-	-	12	-	-	-	-	33942	
Statistical discrepancy	...	...	...	...	...	...	...	...	...	
Total, Industries	13107	1733	165636	6726	36056	33050	15549	30367	35520	
Producers of Government Services	...	...	...	...	...	...	...	...	...	
Other Producers	...	...	...	...	...	...	...	...	...	
Total	13107	1733	165636	6726	36056	33050	15549	30367	35520	
					1978					
1 Agriculture, hunting, forestry and fishing	13516	-	84	-	-	-	-	-	-	
2 Mining and quarrying	-	1846	8	6	-	-	-	-	-	
3 Manufacturing	-	18	172484	302	71	-	-	-	1666	
4 Electricity, gas and water	-	-	-	6791	2	-	-	-	1	
5 Construction	-	-	-	-	38771	-	-	-	-	
6 Wholesale and retail trade, restaurants and hotels [a]	-	-	1992	-	-	34634	-	-	65	
7 Transport and communications	-	-	-	11	9	-	16178	-	9	
8 Finance, insurance, real estate and business services	-	-	-	-	-	-	-	32831	36	
9 Community, social and personal services [a]	-	-	-	12	-	-	-	-	36532	
Statistical discrepancy	...	...	...	...	...	...	...	...	...	
Total, Industries	13516	1864	174567	7122	38853	34634	16178	32831	38309	
Producers of Government Services	...	...	...	...	...	...	...	...	...	
Other Producers	...	...	...	...	...	...	...	...	...	
Total	13516	1864	174567	7122	38853	34634	16178	32831	38309	

Japan

4.14 Gross Output of Goods and Services by Kind of Activity of Producer (Make Matrix), at Constant Prices
(Continued)

Thousand Million Japanese yen

	Agriculture, Hunting, Forestry, Fishing	Mining & Quarrying	Manu-facturing	Electricity, Gas & Water	Construction	Wholesale & Retail Trade, Restaurants & Hotels	Transport & Communi-cations	Finance Insurance, Real Estate & Business Services	Community Social & Personal Services	TOTAL
At constant prices of: 1975										
1979										
1 Agriculture, hunting, forestry and fishing	13641	-	87	-	-	-	-	-	-	
2 Mining and quarrying	-	1866	9	7	-	-	-	-	-	
3 Manufacturing	-	15	184753	332	73	-	-	-	1924	
4 Electricity, gas and water	-	-	-	7364	2	-	-	-	2	
5 Construction	-	-	-	-	40022	-	-	-	4	
6 Wholesale and retail trade, restaurants and hotels [a]	-	-	2053	-	-	36363	-	-	79	
7 Transport and communications	-	-	-	12	9	-	16906	-	10	
8 Finance, insurance, real estate and business services	-	-	-	-	-	-	-	34362	41	
9 Community, social and personal services [a]	-	-	-	13	-	-	-	-	38921	
Statistical discrepancy	...	...	...	...	...	...	...	...	...	
Total, Industries	13641	1882	186901	7728	40106	36363	16906	34362	40982	
Producers of Government Services	...	...	...	...	...	...	...	...	...	
Other Producers	...	...	...	...	...	...	...	...	...	
Total	13641	1882	186901	7728	40106	36363	16906	34362	40982	
1980										
1 Agriculture, hunting, forestry and fishing	13081	-	85	-	-	-	-	-	-	
2 Mining and quarrying	-	1836	8	5	-	-	-	-	-	
3 Manufacturing	-	17	193480	272	74	-	-	-	1858	
4 Electricity, gas and water	-	-	-	7455	2	-	-	-	3	
5 Construction	-	-	-	-	38666	-	-	-	4	
6 Wholesale and retail trade, restaurants and hotels [a]	-	-	2040	-	-	36446	-	-	78	
7 Transport and communications	-	-	-	10	10	-	18253	-	10	
8 Finance, insurance, real estate and business services	-	-	-	-	-	-	-	35959	43	
9 Community, social and personal services [a]	-	-	-	10	-	-	-	-	39867	
Statistical discrepancy	...	...	...	...	...	...	...	...	...	
Total, Industries	13081	1853	195614	7752	38753	36446	18253	35959	41865	
Producers of Government Services	...	...	...	...	...	...	...	...	...	
Other Producers	...	...	...	...	...	...	...	...	...	
Total	13081	1853	195614	7752	38753	36446	18253	35959	41865	

a) Restaurants and hotels are included in item 'Community, social and personal services'.

4.15 Intermediate Consumption by Kind of Activity of User (Use Matrix), in Current Prices

Thousand Million Japanese yen

	Agriculture, Hunting, Forestry, Fishing	Mining & Quarrying	Manu-facturing	Electricity, Gas & Water	Construction	Wholesale & Retail Trade, Restaurants & Hotels	Transport & Communi-cations	Finance Insurance, Real Estate & Business Services	Community Social & Personal Services	TOTAL
1975										
1 Agriculture, hunting, forestry and fishing	1509	6	9027	1	61	1919	7	7	1108	13645
2 Mining and quarrying	-	7	9158	804	822	-	2	-	138	10931
3 Manufacturing	3095	435	69645	1475	15526	3049	2389	578	9044	105236
4 Electricity, gas and water	34	36	2493	113	250	266	219	92	678	4181
4 Construction	21	3	156	147	9	41	70	1800	78	2325
6 Wholesale and retail trade, restaurants and hotels [a]	-	-	-	-	-	282	-	-	-	282
7 Transport and communications	73	47	1120	38	355	909	1664	314	559	5079
8 Finance, insurance, real estate and business services	132	33	1238	78	343	1521	368	1887	556	6156
9 Community, social and personal services [a]	128	86	6811	259	2311	2179	794	1583	2882	17033
Statistical discrepancy	...	...	...	...	...	...	...	...	...	...
Total	4993	653	99647	2915	19677	10166	5513	6260	15042	164866

a) Restaurants and hotels are included in item 'Community, social and personal services'.

Jordan

General note. The preparation of national accounts statistics in the Hashemite Kingdom of Jordan is undertaken by the Department of Statistics, Amman. The annual official estimates together with methodological notes are published in a series of publications entitled 'National Accounts'. A comprehensive description of the concepts and definitions underlying the various tables is contained in 'The National Accounts 1970-1974', published in 1976 by the Department of Statistics. The estimates are generally in accordance with the classifications and definitions recommended in the United Nations System of National Accounts (SNA). Input-output tables were published for the first time in 1963 and followed up annually until 1969 in 'The National Accounts and Input-Output Analysis'. The following tables have been prepared from successive replies to the United Nations national accounts questionnaire. Tables of the period 1960-1966 cover both the West Bank and the East Bank of Jordan, while tables of the period 1967 and onward cover only the East Bank of Jordan. When the scope and coverage of the estimates differ for conceptual or statistical reasons from the definitions and classifications recommended in SNA, a footnote is indicated to the relevant tables.

Sources and methods:

(a) Gross domestic product. Gross domestic product is estimated mainly through the production approach.

(b) Expenditure on the gross domestic product. All components of GDP by expenditure type are estimated through the expenditure approach except private consumption expenditure and investment in machinery and equipment which are estimated by using the commodity-flow approach. The estimates of government final consumption expenditure are obtained from the records of the Ministry of Finance, National Planning Council and municipalities. The estimates of private final consumption expenditure are built up from studies of the origin and use of the country's economic resources and from the input-output analysis made for the years 1960-1969. Estimates of gross fixed capital formation of the private sector are based on building licence statistics, a special survey and on imports of machinery and equipment, while that of the government sector are mainly obtained from records of the Ministry of Finance. Estimates of increase in stocks are approximate and in most cases based on inquiries in the manufacturing industry. Imports and exports of goods and services are mainly estimated from the external trade statistics. GDP by expenditure at constant prices is not estimated.

(c) Cost-structure of the gross domestic product. The sources and methods applied in estimating the cost-structure components of GDP are based on income estimates. Separate estimates are made for income of agricultural workers, income of skilled labourers, and for income from property and capital assets. Gross operating surplus (i.e. including consumption of fixed capital) is arrived at as a residual.

(d) Gross domestic product by kind of economic activity. The table of GDP by kind of economic activity is prepared at factor costs. The production approach is used to estimate the value added of most industries, such as agriculture, forestry and fishing, mining and manufacturing, wholesale and retail trade, while the income approach is used for a number of service sectors. Annual agricultural sample surveys are undertaken on a country-wide basis providing production estimates for crops. The quantities obtained from these surveys are valued at farm prices which are assumed to be a certain percentage of the relevant wholesale or retail prices. Livestock estimates are obtained from the municipalities and the Ministry of Reconstruction and Development, adjusted to arrive at a total number of slaughtering for the country. The estimates of industrial production are based on the 1967 and 1974 Industrial Censuses, balance sheets and income and expenditure statements in 1970, and on analysis of large industrial companies and industrial sample surveys for the remaining years. Value added of private building construction is calculated from cost estimates obtained from special inquiries, while value of public construction is obtained from the records of the Ministry of Finance, National Planning Council and municipalities. Special sample surveys of wholesale and retail trade were conducted in the years 1967-1971 and supplemented by a systematic study of the origin and use of all goods imported and produced in the economy for the year 1975. For passenger and freight transport, the source of information is mainly the records of the authority or the corporation concerned. As for road transport, estimates are based on a survey undertaken in 1974 and on special inquiries. The estimates for banking are based on returns sent to the Department of Statistics by the various banks. Information on the operation of insurance companies has been collected by means of special surveys undertaken during 1970-1974, covering also information on the activities of foreign exchange dealers. The income arising from ownership of dwellings represents the net rental value of all dwellings based initially on the assessments of the Ministry of Finance. For other services, data are provided by the Ministry of Finance or by the institutions concerned. GDP by kind of economic activity at constant prices is not estimated.

1.1 Expenditure on the Gross Domestic Product, in Current Prices

Million Jordanian dinars

	1970	1971	1972	1973	1974	1975	1976	1977	1978	1979	1980
1 General government final consumption expenditure a	58.7	60.4	68.3	80.0	97.7	110.1	155.9	156.6	190.0	235.0	260.5
2 Private final consumption expenditure	152.8	161.7	177.4	183.1	199.8	280.9	328.5	420.2	517.4	681.7	752.4
3 Gross capital formation b	22.1	35.2	42.3	39.2	65.6	88.8	150.2	202.5	223.0	280.0	356.3
a Increase in stocks b	-3.1	4.5	6.0	-8.0	2.4	0.9	12.2	5.5	-6.1	-14.5	6.3
b Gross fixed capital formation c	25.2	30.7	36.3	47.2	63.2	87.9	138.0	197.0	229.1	294.5	350.0
Residential buildings	9.4	7.4	11.6	15.1	16.8	24.2	35.2	42.5	47.7	59.3	77.4
Non-residential buildings	0.9	0.6	1.1	1.6	1.7	2.8	3.6	5.1	6.3	9.8	12.3
Other construction and land improvement etc.	8.1	9.8	14.8	17.9	24.9	35.3	60.0	68.8	74.5	90.5	110.0
Other	6.8	12.9	8.8	12.6	19.8	25.6	39.2	80.6	100.6	134.9	150.3
4 Exports of goods and services	17.6	17.8	37.0	52.4	80.3	118.9	192.1	242.0	264.3	339.5	462.4
5 Less: Imports of goods and services	76.8	88.9	117.8	136.4	196.1	301.1	422.0	540.3	605.6	824.5	962.6
Statistical discrepancy	...	...	...	...	...	-19.0	...	...	...	...	...
Equals: Gross Domestic Product	174.4	186.2	207.2	218.3	247.3	278.6	404.7	481.0	589.1	712.0	869.0

a) Including pension payments less employees' pension contributions. Some non-capital development expenditure of the central government is included in gross domestic fixed capital formation.
b) Data not strictly comparable with those of other tables because estimates are based on a wide variety of statistical sources with varying degrees of accuracy.
c) Including some non-capital development expenditure of the central government.

1.2 Expenditure on the Gross Domestic Product, in Constant Prices

Million Jordanian dinars

	1970	1971	1972	1973	1974	1975	1976	1977	1978	1979	1980
	At constant prices of: 1972											
1 General government final consumption expenditure	...	...	...	...	...	...	...	...	...	...	...
2 Private final consumption expenditure	...	...	...	...	...	...	...	...	...	...	...
3 Gross capital formation	...	...	...	...	...	...	...	...	...	...	...
4 Exports of goods and services	...	...	...	...	...	...	...	...	...	...	...
5 Less: Imports of goods and services	...	...	...	...	...	...	...	...	...	...	...
Equals: Gross Domestic Product	194.2	196.0	207.2	193.5	193.5	191.9	219.0	...	...	...	...

Jordan

1.3 Cost Components of the Gross Domestic Product

Million Jordanian dinars

	1970	1971	1972	1973	1974	1975	1976	1977	1978	1979	1980
1 Indirect taxes, net	19.7	20.2	24.4	29.4	4.9	9.2	43.6	74.3	81.0	84.4	106.6
2 Consumption of fixed capital	7.7	7.9	8.1	8.3	8.5	9.0	10.0	11.0	13.7	20.4	28.0
3 Compensation of employees paid by resident producers to:	72.1	74.3	82.8	88.6	107.2	120.1	161.3	174.0	208.7	269.4	324.2
4 Net operating surplus	74.9	83.8	91.9	92.0	126.7	140.3	189.8	221.7	285.7	337.8	410.2
Equals: Gross Domestic Product	174.4	186.2	207.2	218.3	247.3	278.6	404.7	481.0	589.1	712.0	869.0

1.7 External Transactions on Current Account, Summary

Million Jordanian dinars

	1970	1971	1972	1973	1974	1975	1976	1977	1978	1979	1980
Payments to the Rest of the World											
1 Imports of goods and services [a]	89.9	93.0	119.9	136.4	184.6	304.4	422.0	540.3	605.6	824.5	962.6
a Imports of merchandise c.i.f.	65.5	76.2	94.9	107.8	155.7	232.9	338.7	436.2	458.9	588.3	721.0
b Other	24.4	16.8	25.0	28.6	28.9	71.5	83.3	104.1	146.7	236.2	241.6
2 Factor income paid to the rest of the world	0.7	1.0	1.1	1.6	2.1	3.1	4.7	5.9	7.2	14.7	23.5
3 Indirect taxes paid to supranational organizations	...	...	...	...	...	...	...	...	...	...	...
4 Current transfers to the rest of the world	0.1	0.1	0.1	0.1	0.1	0.1	8.1	17.9	20.7	30.3	48.3
5 Surplus of the nation on current transactions [a]	-7.8	-22.9	-0.8	-3.7	9.3	21.6	35.5	14.9	-86.0	-2.3	104.4
Payments to the Rest of the World and Surplus of the Nation on Current Transactions [a]	82.8	71.1	120.2	134.3	196.0	329.1	470.3	579.0	547.5	867.2	1138.8
Receipts From The Rest of the World											
1 Exports of goods and services [a]	32.3	20.8	51.8	50.3	85.5	129.5	192.1	242.0	264.3	339.5	462.4
a Exports of merchandise f.o.b.	12.2	11.4	17.0	19.0	49.8	48.9	68.7	83.1	90.9	120.9	169.6
b Other	20.1	9.4	34.8	31.3	35.7	80.6	123.4	158.9	173.4	218.6	293.3
2 Factor income received from rest of the world	13.3	14.2	14.9	24.4	34.1	67.0	13.9	14.2	16.6	26.7	38.6
3 Subsidies received from supranational organisations	...	...	...	...	...	...	...	...	...	...	...
4 Current transfers from rest of the world	37.2	36.2	53.6	59.6	76.5	132.6	264.3	323.3	266.6	501.0	637.8
Receipts from the Rest of the World on Current Transactions [a]	82.8	71.2	120.2	134.3	196.1	329.1	470.3	579.0	547.5	867.2	1138.8

a) For 1970-1975, estimates derived from Balance of Payment Accounts, therefore are not strictly comparable to those in other tables.

1.8 Capital Transactions of The Nation, Summary

Million Jordanian dinars

	1970	1971	1972	1973	1974	1975	1976	1977	1978	1979	1980
Finance of Gross Capital Formation											
Gross saving	16.2	13.9	43.6	43.0	68.5	110.3	177.5	204.9	151.3	302.5	433.0
1 Consumption of fixed capital	7.7	7.9	8.1	8.3	8.5	9.0	10.0	11.0	13.7	20.4	28.0
2 Net saving	8.5	6.0	35.5	34.7	60.0	101.3	167.5	193.9	137.6	282.1	405.0
Less: Surplus of the nation on current transactions [a]	-7.8	-22.9	-0.8	-3.7	9.3	21.6	35.5	14.9	-86.0	-2.3	104.4
Statistical discrepancy	-1.9	-1.6	-2.1	-7.5	6.4	-0.1	8.2	12.5	-14.3	-24.8	27.7
Finance of Gross Capital Formation	22.1	35.2	42.3	39.2	65.6	88.8	150.2	202.5	223.0	280.0	356.3
Gross Capital Formation											
Increase in stocks	-3.1	4.5	6.0	-8.0	2.4	0.9	12.2	5.5	-6.1	-14.5	6.3
Gross fixed capital formation	25.2	30.7	36.3	47.2	63.2	87.9	138.0	197.0	229.1	294.5	350.0
Gross Capital Formation	22.1	35.2	42.3	39.2	65.6	88.8	150.2	202.5	223.0	280.0	356.3

a) For 1970-1975, estimates derived from Balance of Payment Accounts, therefore are not strictly comparable to those in other tables.

1.10 Gross Domestic Product by Kind of Activity, in Current Prices

Million Jordanian dinars

	1970	1971	1972	1973	1974	1975	1976	1977	1978	1979	1980
1 Agriculture, hunting, forestry and fishing	15.6	23.9	26.6	17.6	30.3	26.0	37.3	41.7	58.6	43.9	58.5
2 Mining and quarrying	3.7	2.3	3.3	4.0	10.8	16.3	17.8	19.9	22.9	27.5	34.3
3 Manufacturing	19.0	19.6	22.8	28.5	20.8	24.8	40.3	51.1	61.4	74.5	89.4
4 Electricity, gas and water	1.9	2.2	2.5	2.8	3.0	3.1	3.6	4.1	5.2	6.5	7.3
5 Construction	7.8	7.6	9.4	15.4	17.0	16.3	23.3	27.0	35.0	43.0	75.6

Jordan

1.10 Gross Domestic Product by Kind of Activity, in Current Prices
(Continued)

Million Jordanian dinars

	1970	1971	1972	1973	1974	1975	1976	1977	1978	1979	1980
6 Wholesale and retail trade, restaurants and hotels	33.6	34.6	37.6	40.2	34.5	36.7	61.5	68.6	87.0	94.0	138.0
7 Transport, storage and communication	15.6	16.2	19.1	19.8	24.8	26.8	36.5	42.0	67.3	76.0	86.3
8 Finance, insurance, real estate and business services	19.3	19.8	21.0	22.5	25.2	29.7	33.4	43.6	53.1	60.0	103.8
9 Community, social and personal services	3.0	2.9	3.9	3.9	4.3	8.5	6.1	8.8	9.8	11.5	13.8
Total, Industries	119.5	129.1	146.0	154.5	170.7	188.2	259.8	306.8	400.3	436.9	607.0
Producers of Government Services	42.5	43.6	45.9	46.7	54.3	65.2	81.7	84.4	93.6	102.3	155.8
Other Producers	3.6	3.6	3.8	4.6	5.6	5.7	6.2	9.9	13.2	15.4	17.0
Subtotal	165.6	176.3	195.7	205.8	230.6	259.1	347.7	401.1	507.1	554.6	779.8
Less: Imputed bank service charge	1.3	1.4	1.4	1.6	2.7	2.9	3.0	3.4	12.4	13.8	20.4
Plus: Import duties	10.1	11.3	12.9	14.1	19.4	22.4	57.0	79.9	82.0	93.0	109.6
Plus: Value added tax	...	...	...	...	...	...	...	...	...	...	...
Plus: Other adjustments	...	...	...	...	...	...	3.0	3.4	12.4	78.2	...
Equals: Gross Domestic Product	174.4	186.2	207.2	218.3	247.3	278.6	404.7	481.0	589.1	712.0	869.0

1.12 Relations Among National Accounting Aggregates

Million Jordanian dinars

	1970	1971	1972	1973	1974	1975	1976	1977	1978	1979	1980
Gross Domestic Product	174.4	186.2	207.2	218.3	247.3	278.6	404.7	481.0	589.1	712.0	869.0
Plus: Net factor income received from abroad	7.1	8.2	6.4	8.5	7.9	10.6	9.2	8.3	9.4	12.0	15.1
Factor income received	...	...	...	...	...	...	13.9	14.2	16.6	26.7	38.6
Less: Factor income paid	...	...	...	...	...	...	4.7	5.9	7.2	14.7	23.5
Equals: Gross National Product	181.5	194.4	213.6	226.8	255.2	289.2	413.9	489.3	598.5	724.0	884.1
Less: Consumption of fixed capital	7.7	7.9	8.1	8.3	8.5	9.0	10.0	11.0	13.7	20.4	28.0
Less: Net indirect taxes paid to supranational organisations	...	...	...	...	...	...	...	...	...	...	...
Equals: National Income at Market Prices	173.8	186.5	205.5	218.5	246.7	280.2	403.9	478.3	584.8	703.6	856.1
Plus: Net current transfers received from abroad	46.2	41.6	75.7	79.3	110.8	193.1	256.2	305.4	245.9	470.8	589.5
Current transfers received	...	...	...	...	...	...	264.3	323.3	266.6	501.0	637.8
Less: Current transfers paid	...	...	...	...	...	...	8.1	17.9	20.7	30.3	48.3
Equals: National Disposable Income at Market Prices	220.0	228.1	281.2	297.8	357.5	473.3	660.1	783.7	830.7	1174.4	1445.6
Less: Final consumption a	211.5	222.1	245.7	263.1	297.5	391.0	484.4	576.8	707.4	916.7	1012.9
Statistical discrepancy	...	...	...	...	...	19.0	-8.2	-13.0	14.3	24.4	-27.7
Equals: Net Saving	8.5	6.0	35.5	34.7	60.0	101.3	167.5	193.9	137.6	282.1	405.0
Less: Surplus of the nation on current transactions b	-7.8	-22.9	-0.8	-3.7	9.3	21.6	35.5	14.9	-86.0	-2.3	104.4
Statistical discrepancy	-1.9	-1.6	-2.1	-7.5	6.4	-0.1	8.2	12.5	-14.3	-24.8	27.7
Equals: Net Capital Formation cd	14.4	27.3	34.2	30.9	57.1	79.8	140.2	191.5	209.3	259.6	328.3

a) Including pension payments less employees' pension contributions. Some non-capital development expenditure of the central government is included in gross domestic fixed capital formation.
b) For 1970-1975, estimates derived from Balance of Payment Accounts, therefore are not strictly comparable to those in other tables.
c) Including some non-capital development expenditure of the central government.
d) Data not strictly comparable with those of other tables because estimates are based on a wide variety of statistical sources with varying degrees of accuracy.

2.1 General Government Final Consumption Expenditure by Function, in Current Prices

Million Jordanian dinars

	1970	1971	1972	1973	1974	1975	1976	1977	1978	1979	1980
1 General public services									...	...	...
2 Defence	39.9	40.3	43.8	52.5	63.4	60.5	118.1	97.8	...	...	...
3 Public order and safety									...	...	...
4 Education	6.5	6.0	6.2	7.7	11.5	14.2	15.9	18.2	21.4	26.8	33.7
5 Health	2.2	2.3	2.3	2.4	3.3	3.6	3.6	5.3	6.0	7.5	7.9
6 Social security and welfare	1.8	1.7	1.9	2.2	2.7	3.1	3.3	4.5	5.1	6.5	14.5
7 Housing and community amenities	...	...	...	...	...	...	...	...	...	...	...
8 Recreational, cultural and religious affairs	...	...	...	...	...	...	...	...	...	...	...
9 Economic services	8.3	10.1	14.1	15.2	16.8	28.7	15.0	30.8	...	...	...
10 Other functions	...	...	...	...	...	...	...	...	...	...	...
Total General Government Final Consumption Expenditure	58.7	60.4	68.3	80.0	97.7	110.1	155.9	156.6	190.0	235.0	260.5

Jordan

2.5 Private Final Consumption Expenditure by Type, in Current Prices

Million Jordanian dinars

	1970	1971	1972	1973	1974	1975	1976	1977	1978	1979	1980
Final Consumption Expenditure of Resident Households											
1 Food, beverages and tobacco	82.0	87.1	93.1	95.3	103.8	149.9	173.0	230.8	290.2	347.6	441.1
a Food	76.4	80.8	85.7	87.5	94.9	140.2	162.5	217.6	273.9	328.9	411.2
b Non-alcoholic beverages	1.3	1.8	1.9	2.0	2.3	2.9	3.1	4.5	4.9	5.3	10.0
c Alcoholic beverages											3.4
d Tobacco	4.3	4.5	5.5	5.8	6.6	6.8	7.4	9.2	11.4	13.5	16.5
2 Clothing and footwear	13.0	13.2	14.5	15.2	16.4	22.1	25.6	32.5	36.3	42.4	65.4
3 Gross rent, fuel and power	12.8	12.5	12.9	13.4	14.3	18.3	20.1	25.0	27.7	30.1	65.2
4 Furniture, furnishings and household equipment and operation	10.1	8.6	9.7	10.9	12.5	16.4	18.3	23.9	29.7	37.0	46.6
a Household operation	...	...	...	...	...	...	...	...	...	...	44.1
b Other	...	...	...	...	...	...	...	...	...	...	2.5
5 Medical care and health expenses [a]	6.9	6.9	7.1	7.6	8.1	10.2	12.1	17.9	19.8	22.8	30.8
6 Transport and communication	13.8	14.1	15.0	16.1	17.6	20.2	23.2	26.9	29.9	35.2	45.3
7 Recreational, entertainment, education and cultural services	4.9	5.4	6.5	7.5	9.3	11.6	15.0	19.2	25.4	31.9	40.0
a Education	2.8	3.2	4.0	4.7	5.5	6.9	8.1	9.4	12.5	15.2	17.3
b Other	2.1	2.2	2.5	2.8	3.8	4.7	6.9	9.8	12.9	16.7	22.7
8 Miscellaneous goods and services	17.6	17.8	22.6	23.7	26.3	30.7	36.7	40.9	44.6	49.8	61.2
a Personal care [a]	15.7	15.6	19.6	20.4	22.2	25.8	30.9	33.4	34.8	37.7	39.1
b Expenditures in restaurants, cafes and hotels	1.9	2.2	3.0	3.3	4.1	4.9	5.8	7.5	9.8	12.1	16.5
c Other	...	...	...	...	...	...	...	...	...	...	5.6
Statistical discrepancy	...	...	...	...	...	5.6	7.9	8.6	12.8	15.8	...
Total Final Consumption Expenditure in the Domestic Market by Households, of which	161.3	166.2	181.9	190.2	209.1	285.0	331.9	425.7	516.4	612.6	795.6
Plus: Direct purchases abroad by resident households	9.4	7.7	8.5	8.9	10.7	18.1	20.1	26.5	30.1	35.2	42.2
Less: Direct purchases in the domestic market by non-resident households	18.0	12.0	13.0	16.0	20.0	22.2	26.5	35.3	37.1	38.5	85.4
Equals: Final Consumption Expenditure of Resident Households	152.7	161.9	177.4	183.1	199.8	280.9	325.5	416.8	509.5	609.3	752.4
Final Consumption Expenditure of Private Non-profit Institutions Serving Households											
Equals: Final Consumption Expenditure of Private Non-profit Organisations Serving Households	...	...	...	...	...	...	...	...	...	...	...
Statistical discrepancy	...	...	...	...	...	...	3.0	3.4	7.9	72.4	...
Private Final Consumption Expenditure	152.8	161.7	177.4	183.1	199.8	280.9	328.5	420.2	517.4	681.7	752.4

a) Personal care is included in item 'Medical care and health expenses'.

2.17 Exports and Imports of Goods and Services, Detail

Million Jordanian dinars

	1970	1971	1972	1973	1974	1975	1976	1977	1978	1979	1980
Exports of Goods and Services											
1 Exports of merchandise, f.o.b.	12.2	11.4	17.0	19.0	49.8	48.9	68.7	83.6	90.9	120.9	169.1
2 Transport and communication	4.2	3.1	8.3	10.7	17.3	35.7	68.9	95.2	...	...	138.4
3 Insurance service charges									...	...	
4 Other commodities	15.9	6.2	26.5	20.6	18.5	44.9	54.6	63.7	...	...	154.9
5 Adjustments of merchandise exports to change-of-ownership basis	...	...	...	...	...	...	...	...	...	...	...
6 Direct purchases in the domestic market by non-residential households	...	...	...	...	...	...	...	...	...	...	...
7 Direct purchases in the domestic market by extraterritorial bodies	...	...	...	...	...	...	...	...	...	...	...
Total Exports of Goods and Services [a]	32.3	20.8	51.8	50.3	85.5	129.5	192.1	242.5	264.3	339.5	462.4
Imports of Goods and Services											
1 Imports of merchandise, c.i.f.	65.5	76.2	94.9	107.8	155.7	232.9	338.7	436.2	458.9	588.3	721.0

Jordan

2.17 Exports and Imports of Goods and Services, Detail
(Continued)

Million Jordanian dinars

	1970	1971	1972	1973	1974	1975	1976	1977	1978	1979	1980
2 Adjustments of merchandise imports to change-of-ownership basis	...	...	...	...	...	...	...	...	...	...	...
3 Other transport and communication	9.4	7.7	11.3	11.3	17.4	33.8	32.1	35.2	63.9	89.7	107.6
4 Other insurance service charges	...	...	...	...	...	...	...	...	...	...	...
5 Other commodities	5.6	1.4	5.2	8.4	0.8	20.6	31.1	42.4	52.7	111.3	91.8
6 Direct purchases abroad by government	...	...	...	...	...	...	...	...	...	...	...
7 Direct purchases abroad by resident households	9.4	7.7	8.5	8.9	10.7	17.1	20.1	26.5	30.1	35.2	42.2
Total Imports of Goods and Services [a]	89.9	93.0	119.9	136.4	184.6	304.4	422.0	540.3	605.6	824.5	962.6
Balance of Goods and Services	-57.6	-72.2	-68.1	-86.1	-99.1	-174.9	-229.9	-297.8	-341.3	-485.0	-500.2
Total Imports and Balance of Goods and Services	32.3	20.8	51.8	50.3	85.5	129.5	192.1	242.5	264.3	339.5	462.4

a) For 1970-1975, estimates derived from Balance of Payment Accounts, therefore are not strictly comparable to those in other tables.

4.3 Derivation of Value Added by Kind of Activity, ISIC Divisions, in Current Prices

Million Jordanian dinars

	1970 Gross Output	1970 Intermediate Consumption	1970 Value Added	1971 Gross Output	1971 Intermediate Consumption	1971 Value Added	1972 Gross Output	1972 Intermediate Consumption	1972 Value Added	1973 Gross Output	1973 Intermediate Consumption	1973 Value Added
						All Producers						
1 Agriculture, hunting, forestry and fishing	19.3	3.7	15.6	27.8	3.9	23.9	30.4	3.8	26.6	22.3	4.7	17.6
2 Mining and quarrying	5.1	1.4	3.7	3.2	0.9	2.3	4.6	1.3	3.3	5.5	1.5	4.0
3 Manufacturing	61.1	42.1	19.0	63.1	43.5	19.6	73.3	50.5	22.8	91.0	62.7	28.3
4 Electricity, gas and water	2.1	0.2	1.9	2.5	0.3	2.2	2.8	0.3	2.5	3.2	0.4	2.8
5 Construction	23.2	15.4	7.8	22.6	15.0	7.6	28.0	18.6	9.4	45.8	30.4	15.4
6 Wholesale and retail trade, restaurants and hotels	41.6	8.0	33.6	42.8	8.2	34.6	46.4	8.8	37.6	49.6	9.4	40.2
7 Transport, storage and communication	22.8	7.2	15.6	23.7	7.5	16.2	27.9	8.8	19.1	28.5	8.7	19.8
8 Finance, insurance, real estate and business services	20.3	1.0	19.3	20.8	1.0	19.8	22.1	1.1	21.0	23.6	1.1	22.5
9 Community, social and personal services	3.5	0.5	3.0	3.4	0.5	2.9	4.2	0.5	3.7	4.4	0.5	3.9
Total, Industries	199.0	79.5	119.5	209.9	80.8	129.1	239.7	93.7	146.0	273.9	119.4	154.5
Producers of Government Services	58.7	16.2	42.5	60.4	16.8	43.6	68.3	22.4	45.9	80.0	33.3	46.7
Other Producers	3.9	0.3	3.6	3.9	0.3	3.6	4.1	0.3	3.8	4.9	0.3	4.6
Total	261.6	96.0	165.6	274.2	97.9	176.3	312.1	116.4	195.7	358.8	153.0	205.8
Imputed bank service charge	-	1.3	-1.3	-	1.4	-1.4	-	1.4	-1.4	-	1.6	-1.6
Import duties	10.1	-	10.1	11.3	-	11.3	12.9	-	12.9	14.1	-	14.1
Value added tax	...	...	...	...	...	...	...	...	...	...	...	...
Total	271.7	97.3	174.4	285.5	99.3	186.2	325.0	117.8	207.2	372.9	154.6	218.3

	1974 Gross Output	1974 Intermediate Consumption	1974 Value Added	1975 Gross Output	1975 Intermediate Consumption	1975 Value Added
			All Producers			
1 Agriculture, hunting, forestry and fishing	37.2	6.9	30.3	36.4	10.4	26.0
2 Mining and quarrying	15.0	4.2	10.8	22.6	6.3	16.3
3 Manufacturing	66.9	46.1	20.8	79.8	55.0	24.8
4 Electricity, gas and water	3.4	0.4	3.0	3.5	0.4	3.1
5 Construction	51.0	34.0	17.0	48.5	32.2	16.3
6 Wholesale and retail trade, restaurants and hotels	42.5	8.0	34.5	45.6	8.9	36.7
7 Transport, storage and communication	36.0	11.2	24.8	39.2	12.4	26.8
8 Finance, insurance, real estate and business services	26.4	1.2	25.2	31.1	1.4	29.7
9 Community, social and personal services	5.0	0.7	4.3	9.5	1.0	8.5

Jordan

4.3 Derivation of Value Added by Kind of Activity, ISIC Divisions, in Current Prices
(Continued)

Million Jordanian dinars

	1974 Gross Output	1974 Intermediate Consumption	1974 Value Added	1975 Gross Output	1975 Intermediate Consumption	1975 Value Added
Total, Industries	283.4	112.7	170.7	316.2	128.0	188.2
Producers of Government Services	97.4	43.1	54.3	110.1	44.9	65.2
Other Producers	5.8	0.2	5.6	6.0	0.3	5.7
Total	386.6	156.0	230.6	432.3	173.2	259.1
Imputed bank service charge	-	2.7	-2.7	-	2.9	-2.9
Import duties	19.4	-	19.4	22.4	-	22.4
Value added tax	...	...	...	...	...	...
Total	406.0	158.7	247.3	454.7	176.1	278.6

4.6 Cost Components of Value Added, ISIC Divisions

Million Jordanian dinars

	1970 Compensation of Employees	1970 Capital Consumption	1970 Net Operating Surplus	1970 Indirect Taxes	1970 Less: Subsidies Received	1970 Value Added	1971 Compensation of Employees	1971 Capital Consumption	1971 Net Operating Surplus	1971 Indirect Taxes	1971 Less: Subsidies Received	1971 Value Added
All Producers												
1 Agriculture, hunting, forestry and fishing	1.6	0.2	13.8	...	...	15.6	2.4	0.3	21.2	...	...	23.9
2 Mining and quarrying	0.4	0.9	2.4	...	...	3.7	0.6	0.9	0.8	...	...	2.3
3 Manufacturing	4.0	1.7	6.5	6.8	...	19.0	4.2	1.7	8.2	5.5	...	19.6
4 Electricity, gas and water	0.7	0.4	0.8	...	...	1.9	0.7	0.5	1.0	...	...	2.2
5 Construction	4.6	0.1	3.0	0.1	...	7.8	4.4	0.1	2.9	0.2	...	7.6
6 Wholesale and retail trade, restaurants and hotels	5.8	0.2	26.2	1.4	...	33.6	5.8	0.2	27.0	1.6	...	34.6
7 Transport, storage and communication	6.7	1.5	6.1	1.3	...	15.6	6.8	1.5	6.3	1.6	...	16.2
8 Finance, insurance, real estate and business services	1.6	1.9	15.8	...	...	19.3	1.7	1.9	16.2	...	...	19.8
9 Community, social and personal services	1.0	0.4	1.6	...	...	3.0	0.9	0.4	1.6	...	...	2.9
Total, Industries	26.4	7.3	76.2	9.6	...	119.5	27.5	7.5	85.2	8.9	...	129.1
Producers of Government Services	42.2	0.3	...	...	...	42.5	43.3	0.3	...	...	...	43.6
Other Producers	3.5	0.1	...	...	...	3.6	3.5	0.1	...	...	...	3.6
Total	72.1	7.7	76.2	9.6	...	165.6	74.3	7.9	85.2	8.9	...	176.3
Imputed bank service charge	...	...	-1.3	...	...	-1.3	...	...	-1.4	...	...	-1.4
Import duties	...	...	...	10.1	...	10.1	...	...	...	11.3	...	11.3
Value added tax	...	...	...	...	...	...	...	...	...	...	...	...
Other adjustments	...	...	...	...	...	...	...	...	...	...	...	...
Total	72.1	7.7	74.9	19.7	...	174.4	74.3	7.9	83.8	20.2	...	186.2

	1972 Compensation of Employees	1972 Capital Consumption	1972 Net Operating Surplus	1972 Indirect Taxes	1972 Less: Subsidies Received	1972 Value Added	1973 Compensation of Employees	1973 Capital Consumption	1973 Net Operating Surplus	1973 Indirect Taxes	1973 Less: Subsidies Received	1973 Value Added
All Producers												
1 Agriculture, hunting, forestry and fishing	2.7	0.3	23.6	...	...	26.6	1.8	0.4	15.4	...	...	17.6
2 Mining and quarrying	0.7	0.9	1.7	...	...	3.3	2.0	0.9	1.1	...	...	4.0
3 Manufacturing	5.0	1.7	8.5	7.6	...	22.8	5.5	1.7	10.0	11.1	...	28.5
4 Electricity, gas and water	0.8	0.5	1.2	...	...	2.5	0.7	0.6	1.5	...	...	2.8
5 Construction	5.5	0.2	3.5	0.2	...	9.4	9.1	0.2	5.9	0.2	...	15.4
6 Wholesale and retail trade, restaurants and hotels	7.3	0.2	28.2	1.9	...	37.6	7.1	0.2	30.8	2.1	...	40.2
7 Transport, storage and communication	8.4	1.5	7.4	1.8	...	19.1	8.4	1.5	8.0	1.9	...	19.8
8 Finance, insurance, real estate and business services	1.8	2.0	17.2	...	...	21.0	1.9	2.0	18.6	...	...	22.5
9 Community, social and personal services	1.3	0.4	2.0	...	...	3.9	1.2	0.4	2.3	...	...	3.9
Total, Industries	33.5	7.7	93.3	11.5	...	146.0	37.7	7.9	93.6	15.3	...	154.5
Producers of Government Services	45.6	0.3	...	...	...	45.9	46.4	0.3	...	...	...	46.7
Other Producers	3.7	0.1	...	...	...	3.8	4.5	0.1	...	...	...	4.6
Total	82.8	8.1	93.3	11.5	...	195.7	88.6	8.3	93.6	15.3	...	205.8
Imputed bank service charge	...	...	-1.4	...	...	-1.4	...	...	-1.6	...	...	-1.6
Import duties	...	...	...	12.9	...	12.9	...	...	...	14.1	...	14.1
Value added tax	...	...	...	...	...	...	...	...	...	...	...	...
Other adjustments	...	...	...	...	...	...	...	...	...	...	...	...
Total	82.8	8.1	91.9	24.4	...	207.2	88.6	8.3	92.0	29.4	...	218.3

Jordan

4.6 Cost Components of Value Added, ISIC Divisions

Million Jordanian dinars

1974

	Compensation of Employees	Capital Consumption	Net Operating Surplus	Indirect Taxes	Less: Subsidies Received	Value Added
			All Producers			
1 Agriculture, hunting, forestry and fishing	3.1	0.4	26.8	...	...	30.3
2 Mining and quarrying	2.4	0.9	7.5	...	...	10.8
3 Manufacturing	7.8	1.8	20.1	-8.9	...	20.8
4 Electricity, gas and water	1.2	0.5	1.3	...	...	3.0
5 Construction	10.0	0.1	6.7	0.2	...	17.0
6 Wholesale and retail trade, restaurants and hotels	7.3	0.2	34.8	-7.8	...	34.5
7 Transport, storage and communication	11.7	1.6	9.5	2.0	...	24.8
8 Finance, insurance, real estate and business services	2.2	2.2	20.8	...	...	25.2
9 Community, social and personal services	2.0	0.4	1.9	...	...	4.3
Total, Industries	47.7	8.1	129.4	-14.5	...	170.7
Producers of Government Services	53.9	0.4	...	...	...	54.3
Other Producers	5.6	-	...	...	...	5.6
Total	107.2	8.5	129.4	-14.5	...	230.6
Imputed bank service charge	...	...	-2.7	...	...	-2.7
Import duties	...	...	...	19.4	...	19.4
Value added tax	...	...	...	...	...	...
Other adjustments	...	...	...	...	...	...
Total	107.2	8.5	126.7	4.9	...	247.3

1975

	Compensation of Employees	Capital Consumption	Net Operating Surplus	Indirect Taxes	Less: Subsidies Received	Value Added
1 Agriculture, hunting, forestry and fishing	4.5	0.4	21.1	...	...	26.0
2 Mining and quarrying	2.8	1.0	12.5	...	...	16.3
3 Manufacturing	9.3	1.8	19.4	-5.7	...	24.8
4 Electricity, gas and water	1.5	0.6	1.0	...	...	3.1
5 Construction	9.6	0.2	6.3	0.2	...	16.3
6 Wholesale and retail trade, restaurants and hotels	9.8	0.3	36.2	-9.6	...	36.7
7 Transport, storage and communication	7.0	1.6	16.3	1.9	...	26.8
8 Finance, insurance, real estate and business services	2.3	2.1	25.3	...	...	29.7
9 Community, social and personal services	2.9	0.5	5.1	...	...	8.5
Total, Industries	49.7	8.7	143.2	-13.2	...	188.2
Producers of Government Services	64.8	0.4	...	...	...	65.2
Other Producers	5.6	0.1	...	...	...	5.7
Total	120.1	9.2	143.2	-13.2	...	259.1
Imputed bank service charge	...	...	-2.9	...	...	-2.9
Import duties	...	...	...	22.4	...	22.4
Value added tax	...	...	...	...	...	...
Other adjustments	...	...	...	...	...	...
Total	120.1	9.2	140.3	9.2	...	278.6

1976

	Compensation of Employees	Capital Consumption	Net Operating Surplus	Indirect Taxes	Less: Subsidies Received	Value Added
			All Producers			
1 Agriculture, hunting, forestry and fishing	4.8	0.5	32.1	...	...	37.3
2 Mining and quarrying	3.0	1.1	13.6	...	...	17.8
3 Manufacturing	14.7	1.9	38.1	-14.4	...	40.3
4 Electricity, gas and water	1.7	0.7	1.1	...	...	3.6
5 Construction	15.0	0.3	8.1	0.6	...	23.3
6 Wholesale and retail trade, restaurants and hotels	14.5	0.4	50.0	-3.4	...	61.5
7 Transport, storage and communication	14.0	1.7	16.7	4.0	...	36.5
8 Finance, insurance, real estate and business services	2.7	2.3	28.5	...	...	33.4
9 Community, social and personal services	3.6	0.5	2.0	...	...	6.1
Total, Industries	74.0	9.4	190.2	-13.8	...	259.8
Producers of Government Services	81.2	0.5	...	...	...	81.7
Other Producers	6.1	0.1	...	...	...	6.2
Total	161.3	10.0	190.2	-13.8	...	347.7
Imputed bank service charge	...	...	-3.0	...	...	-3.0
Import duties	...	...	...	57.0	...	57.0
Value added tax	...	...	...	...	...	...
Other adjustments	...	...	...	...	...	...
Total	161.3	10.0	187.2	43.2	...	401.7

1977

	Compensation of Employees	Capital Consumption	Net Operating Surplus	Indirect Taxes	Less: Subsidies Received	Value Added
1 Agriculture, hunting, forestry and fishing	5.0	...	36.3	...	...	41.7
2 Mining and quarrying	3.1	...	15.5	...	...	19.9
3 Manufacturing	15.9	...	47.0	...	...	51.1
4 Electricity, gas and water	1.9	...	1.3	...	...	4.1
5 Construction	16.0	...	10.8	...	...	27.0
6 Wholesale and retail trade, restaurants and hotels	14.3	...	51.6	...	...	68.6
7 Transport, storage and communication	15.2	...	18.7	...	...	42.0
8 Finance, insurance, real estate and business services	3.0	...	38.3	...	...	43.6
9 Community, social and personal services	4.2	...	4.0	...	...	8.8
Total, Industries	78.6	...	223.5	-5.6	...	306.8
Producers of Government Services	83.8	...	...	...	...	84.4
Other Producers	9.8	...	...	...	...	9.9
Total	172.2	11.0	223.5	-5.6	...	401.1
Imputed bank service charge	...	...	-3.4	...	...	-3.4
Import duties	...	...	...	79.9	...	79.9
Value added tax	...	...	...	...	...	...
Other adjustments	...	...	...	...	...	...
Total	172.2	11.0	220.1	74.3	...	477.6

1978

	Compensation of Employees	Capital Consumption	Net Operating Surplus	Indirect Taxes	Less: Subsidies Received	Value Added
			All Producers			
1 Agriculture, hunting, forestry and fishing	6.8	0.5	51.3	...	...	58.6
2 Mining and quarrying	3.6	1.5	17.8	...	...	22.9
3 Manufacturing	17.0	2.8	54.6	-13.0	...	61.4
4 Electricity, gas and water	2.1	1.0	2.1	...	...	5.2

1979

	Compensation of Employees	Capital Consumption	Net Operating Surplus	Indirect Taxes	Less: Subsidies Received	Value Added
1 Agriculture, hunting, forestry and fishing	6.2	0.6	37.1	...	...	43.9
2 Mining and quarrying	5.0	1.9	20.6	...	...	27.5
3 Manufacturing	20.3	3.5	64.7	-14.0	...	74.5
4 Electricity, gas and water	2.4	1.4	2.7	...	...	6.5

Jordan

4.6 Cost Components of Value Added, ISIC Divisions
(Continued)

Million Jordanian dinars

	1978						1979					
	Compensation of Employees	Capital Consumption	Net Operating Surplus	Indirect Taxes	Less: Subsidies Received	Value Added	Compensation of Employees	Capital Consumption	Net Operating Surplus	Indirect Taxes	Less: Subsidies Received	Value Added
5 Construction	16.8	0.3	17.9	...	...	35.0	18.1	0.5	24.4	...	...	43.0
6 Wholesale and retail trade, restaurants and hotels	17.9	0.6	64.5	4.0	...	87.0	19.3	0.8	69.9	4.0	...	94.0
7 Transport, storage and communication	26.3	2.4	30.6	8.0	...	67.3	27.1	3.5	36.4	9.0	...	76.0
8 Finance, insurance, real estate and business services	3.9	2.8	46.4	...	...	53.1	4.5	3.2	52.3	...	...	60.0
9 Community, social and personal services	110.3	1.8	4.5	...	...	116.6	121.5	2.5	5.2	...	...	129.2
Total, Industries	204.7	13.7	289.7	-1.0	...	507.1	224.4	17.9	313.3	-1.0	...	554.6
Producers of Government Services	...	...	...	...	...	...	...	...	...	...	...	...
Other Producers	...	...	...	...	...	...	...	...	...	...	...	...
Total	204.7	13.7	289.7	-1.0	...	507.1	224.4	17.9	313.3	-1.0	...	554.6
Imputed bank service charge	...	...	-12.4	...	...	-12.4	...	...	-13.8	...	...	-13.8
Import duties	...	...	...	82.0	...	82.0	...	...	...	93.0	...	93.0
Value added tax	...	...	...	...	...	...	...	...	...	...	...	...
Other adjustments	...	...	...	...	...	...	...	...	...	...	...	...
Total	204.7	13.7	277.3	81.0	...	576.7	224.4	17.9	299.5	92.0	...	633.8

	1980					
	Compensation of Employees	Capital Consumption	Net Operating Surplus	Indirect Taxes	Less: Subsidies Received	Value Added
	All Producers					
1 Agriculture, hunting, forestry and fishing	8.5	1.0	49.0	...	...	58.5
2 Mining and quarrying	6.3	2.5	25.5	...	...	34.3
3 Manufacturing	24.8	4.5	79.1	...	19.0	89.4
4 Electricity, gas and water	2.8	1.6	2.9	...	...	7.3
5 Construction	29.2	1.9	44.5	...	...	75.6
6 Wholesale and retail trade, restaurants and hotels	28.9	2.1	102.0	5.0	...	138.0
7 Transport, storage and communication	32.1	5.4	37.8	11.0	...	86.3
8 Finance, insurance, real estate and business services	15.1	4.9	83.8	...	...	103.8
9 Community, social and personal services	6.4	1.4	6.0	...	...	13.8
Total, Industries	154.1	25.3	430.6	16.0	19.0	607.0
Producers of Government Services	153.8	2.0	...	...	...	155.8
Other Producers	16.3	0.7	...	...	...	17.0
Total	324.2	28.0	430.6	16.0	19.0	779.8
Imputed bank service charge	...	...	-20.4	...	...	-20.4
Import duties	...	...	...	109.6	...	109.6
Value added tax	...	...	...	...	...	...
Other adjustments	...	...	...	...	...	...
Total	324.2	28.0	410.2	125.6	19.0	869.0

Kenya

General note. The preparation of national accounts statistics in Kenya is undertaken by the Central Bureau of Statistics, Nairobi. The official estimates are published annually in the 'Statistical Abstract'. The estimates are generally in accordance with the classifications and definitions recommended in the United Nations System of National Accounts (SNA). A full revision of previous estimates for the years 1972-1975 were published in 1976, implementing improved methods and sources of estimation. Input-out tables for 1967 and 1971 were published in 1972 and 1976 respectively in 'Input-Output Tables for Kenya'. The following tables have been prepared from successive replies to the United Nations national accounts questionnaire. When the scope and coverage of the estimates differ for conceptual or statistical reasons from the definitions and classifications recommended in SNA, a footnote is indicated to the relevant tables.

Sources and methods:

(a) Gross domestic product. Gross domestic product is estimated mainly through the production approach.

(b) Expenditure on the gross domestic product. The expenditure approach is used to estimate government final consumption expenditure and exports and imports of goods and services. A combination of the commodity-flow and expenditure approaches is used to estimate gross capital formation. The estimates of government final consumption expenditure are derived from the accounts of the central and local government, the East African Community, the relevant statutory boards and the National Security Fund. All accounts are prepared on a cash basis. Private consumption expenditure is obtained as a residual. Changes in stocks are recorded for agriculture, industrial activity, building and construction and wholesale and retail trade sectors. The sources of information are the large-farm censuses, the integrated rural survey, annual surveys or reports from concerned sectors and the survey of Distribution. The estimate of capital formation in building and construction is derived from 'completions' reported by municipalities and from expenditure on other construction undertaken by government and industry. Included in gross fixed capital formation is the value of development of permanent crops. Expenditure estimates on machinery and equipment are derived by using the commodity-flow method. For import items, import duties are added to the c.i.f. values. For domestic production, the annual surveys of manufacturing are the source of information. The figures derived are converted to purchasers' values by adding transport and distribution margins. Exports and imports of goods and services are based on foreign trade reports and balance of payments estimates. For the constant price estimates, government expenditure on wages and salaries are extrapolated by an index of employment, while purchases of goods and services are deflated by various price indexes. Private consumption expenditure is obtained as a residual. For the remaining expenditure items, price deflation is used.

(c) Cost-structure of the gross domestic product. Wages and salaries paid in most industries are obtained from the annual surveys of employees and self-employed persons. Other sources include the integrated rural survey for small farms, logger licences and wage rate for forestry, reports and special surveys for transport, government accounts for the government sector and annual questionnaires for the private non-profit services. Information on indirect taxes and subsidies is obtained from concerned enterprises and from government records. Operating surplus, including consumption of fixed capital, is obtained as a residual.

(d) Gross domestic product by kind of economic activity. The table of gross domestic product by kind of economic activity is prepared in factor values. The production approach is used to estimate value added of most industries. The expenditure approach is used for construction and capital formation in residential and non-residential buildings while the income approach is used for insurance and real estate. For the agricultural sector, the main sources of information are the annual large-farm censuses, annual integrated rural surveys and purchases by boards, co-operatives and large factories. The Ministry of Agriculture provides supplementary information. The censuses and surveys provide information on quantity and value of sales and quantity consumed at the farms. The prices for agricultural products sold to boards and co-operatives are those paid by the boards while prices used for other products are those obtained from integrated rural survey, reflecting prices in the local markets. Estimates for forestry and fishing are obtained from concerned departments. Information on gross output and intermediate consumption of mining and quarrying and electricity is obtained from the companies concerned. A census of manufacturing industry was held in 1972 covering all establishments. Annual surveys are undertaken for all firms employing 50 or more persons and a sample is taken for firms employing between 20 and 49 persons. For firms with less than 20 employees, estimates are derived by inflating the value of gross output and intermediate consumption obtained in the 1972 census. The bench-mark estimate for construction contractors is based on the 1972 census of industry and the rural enterprise survey. Information from large contractors are available annually while those with less than 4 employees are covered by the labour force survey. Their estimates are obtained by applying an increasing factor to the census figures. The estimates of own-account construction are obtained from the large-farm censuses. Certain percentages are added for maintenance and labour costs. The East African Power and Lighting co., Ministry of Works, Forests Department and other local authorities provide information on their own-account construction activities. In the non-monetary sector, the value of output is the number of huts built multiplied by its current cost and 15 percent added for maintenance. For trade, the Survey of Distribution 1967 provided bench-mark information on the value of output and intermediate consumption. Value added by each sub-division is then extrapolated by using various indicators. The rural enterprise survey in 1972 provided bench-mark estimates for the rural areas. The sources of information for railway, shipping and air transports are the annual reports of the concerned companies and special questionnaires. For buses, data are obtained from the Kenya Bus Services Co. only and their ratios are applied to other bus firms. For the financial sector, the Central Bank of Kenya provides the information needed. Value added of real estate is calculated as net trade receipts of companies and individuals and 50 per cent of the rentals of companies. For ownership of dwellings, a stratified multi-stage sample is taken annually. The estimates of producers of government services are obtained from the accounts of the government, East-African Community and National Security Fund. For private services, bench-mark estimates are derived from a survey conducted in 1972. Domestic services are calculated from the estimated number of servants and their wage rates. For the constant price estimates, double deflation is used for agriculture, with current year's quantities revalued at base-year prices. Double deflation is also used for mining and quarrying, manufacturing and construction. For electricity, gas and water, trade, transport and community services, value added is extrapolated by various quantity indicators and indexes. Current values of financial institutions, insurance and real estate are deflated by price indexes.

1.1 Expenditure on the Gross Domestic Product, in Current Prices

Million Kenyan pounds

		1970	1971	1972	1973	1974	1975	1976	1977	1978	1979	1980
1	General government final consumption expenditure	93.10	114.23	127.30 / 132.73	144.48	180.68	219.30	253.79	322.05	398.60	447.31	510.26
2	Private final consumption expenditure	344.69	410.59	438.91 / 467.91	518.35	683.40	816.40	895.44	1034.00	1248.86	1469.14	1705.71
3	Gross capital formation	139.66	151.92	161.67 / 167.96	226.70	273.19	217.08	294.27	441.23	610.63	516.25	694.39
a	Increase in stocks	26.96	7.72	1.30 / 4.20	47.09	70.39	-24.81	3.84	51.22	96.62	-24.20	142.55
b	Gross fixed capital formation	112.70	144.20	160.37 / 163.76	179.61	202.80	241.89	290.43	390.01	514.01	540.45	551.84
	Residential buildings	18.66	23.73	24.38 / 29.30	28.22	34.41	42.47	39.21	49.41	70.36	93.08	93.42
	Non-residential buildings	14.09	16.98	20.47 / 20.91	23.25	30.57	31.42	36.75	41.43	45.75	69.35	73.98
	Other construction and land improvement etc.	22.80	32.49	39.93 / 41.34	48.78	54.14	62.96	71.57	83.98	93.98	93.51	96.32
	Other	57.15	70.99	75.59 / 72.21	79.35	83.67	105.04	142.90	215.19	303.92	284.49	285.62
4	Exports of goods and services	170.83	181.93	200.11 / 200.11	240.58	357.20	356.90	471.70	650.20	593.10	580.40	734.80
5	Less: Imports of goods and services	175.62	223.53	216.17 / 216.16	251.78	433.80	413.00	461.60	587.60	793.00	736.50	1051.00
	Equals: Gross Domestic Product	572.66	635.14	711.82 / 752.55	878.33	1060.67	1196.68	1453.60	1859.88	2058.19	2276.60	2594.16

Kenya

1.2 Expenditure on the Gross Domestic Product, in Constant Prices

Million Kenyan pounds

		1970	1971	1972	1973	1974	1975	1976	1977	1978	1979	1980
				At constant prices of:								
			1964					1976				
1	General government final consumption expenditure	84.58	97.30	104.36 / 186.91	194.54	211.05	236.16	253.79	284.78	328.84	322.61	331.34
2	Private final consumption expenditure	320.85	362.03	367.25 / 866.73	820.80	914.63	935.81	895.44	967.37	1086.06	1198.41	1189.20
3	Gross capital formation	122.48	121.50	110.67 / 335.55	405.91	383.77	262.84	294.27	399.82	495.25	361.19	435.26
a	Increase in stocks	26.96	7.72	1.30 / 5.79	82.96	93.80	-30.40	3.84	47.86	84.06	-23.55	92.24
b	Gross fixed capital formation	95.52	113.78	109.37 / 329.76	322.95	289.97	293.24	290.43	351.96	411.19	384.74	343.02
	Residential buildings	13.40	16.50	15.74 / 52.40	45.66	44.87	49.56	39.21	44.43	57.77	66.58	55.15
	Non-residential buildings	10.11	11.81	13.21 / 41.57	41.75	40.87	37.23	36.75	39.16	39.47	51.99	45.98
	Other construction and land improvement etc.	16.64	22.77	25.77 / 77.96	78.79	73.87	72.23	71.57	79.37	80.21	69.96	60.94
	Other	55.37	62.70	54.65 / 157.82	156.75	130.36	134.22	142.90	189.00	233.74	196.21	180.95
4	Exports of goods and services	159.65	166.91	168.16 / 418.27	454.81	523.71	463.18	471.70	484.92	493.32	453.19	494.36
5	Less: Imports of goods and services	164.13	191.05	165.02 / 527.65	519.74	622.30	474.28	461.60	545.95	695.83	562.30	620.03
	Equals: Gross Domestic Product	523.43	556.69	585.42 / 1279.81	1356.32	1410.86	1423.71	1453.60	1590.94	1707.64	1773.10	1830.13

1.3 Cost Components of the Gross Domestic Product

Million Kenyan pounds

		1970	1971	1972	1973	1974	1975	1976	1977	1978	1979	1980
1	Indirect taxes, net	53.72	65.08	63.30 / 63.76	88.85	121.83	139.67	175.50	219.23	269.78	296.98	373.28
a	Indirect taxes paid	54.88	66.12	64.60 / 65.06	91.11	123.66	140.48	176.27	219.78	270.25	297.58	373.98
b	Less: Subsidies received	1.16	1.04	1.30 / 1.30	2.26	1.83	0.81	0.77	0.55	0.47	0.60	0.70
2	Consumption of fixed capital	...	...	...	...	...	...	...	...	...	...	...
3	Compensation of employees paid by resident producers to:	236.86	267.39	302.46 / 309.85	335.91	386.58	447.09	509.14	594.29	692.83	802.42	910.53
4	Net operating surplus	282.08	302.67	346.06 / 378.93	453.54	552.26	609.92	768.96	1046.36	1095.58	1177.21	1310.35
	Statistical discrepancy	...	...	0.01	0.03	-	-	-	-	-	-	...
	Equals: Gross Domestic Product	572.66	635.14	711.82 / 752.55	878.33	1060.67	1196.68	1453.60	1859.88	2058.19	2276.60	2594.16

1.10 Gross Domestic Product by Kind of Activity, in Current Prices

Million Kenyan pounds

		1970	1971	1972	1973	1974	1975	1976	1977	1978	1979	1980
1	Agriculture, hunting, forestry and fishing	172.77	178.87	209.50 / 242.42	279.98	331.99	361.38	484.44	688.29	657.23	678.85	722.84
2	Mining and quarrying	2.41	2.93	2.13 / 2.22	3.20	3.20	3.42	3.41	4.17	4.41	5.04	5.73
3	Manufacturing	62.16	71.68	84.35 / 77.93	95.62	119.42	127.00	144.18	179.94	219.32	249.84	295.14
4	Electricity, gas and water	11.96	12.68	13.61 / 13.93	14.50	15.71	19.98	23.10	31.07	35.71	41.61	47.35
5	Construction	26.39	28.86	34.85 / 46.51	51.08	56.02	63.65	67.08	79.93	97.88	119.45	135.86
6	Wholesale and retail trade, restaurants and hotels [a]	48.67	51.16	54.58 / 66.18	71.75	97.91	114.88	132.54	164.63	189.34	214.07	252.07
7	Transport, storage and communication	40.84	43.50	47.03 / 38.21	44.16	53.73	60.25	69.15	78.62	100.84	114.65	128.63
8	Finance, insurance, real estate and business services [b]	53.04	59.37	65.74 / 82.51	94.40	114.24	132.56	155.45	186.16	217.80	247.51	277.47
9	Community, social and personal services [ab]	20.08	21.68	26.27 / 16.25	19.36	20.76	23.33	27.00	30.80	35.46	39.59	47.07

Kenya

1.10 Gross Domestic Product by Kind of Activity, in Current Prices
(Continued)

Million Kenyan pounds

	1970	1971	1972	1973	1974	1975	1976	1977	1978	1979	1980
Total, Industries	438.32	470.73	538.06 586.16	674.05	812.98	906.45	1106.35	1443.61	1558.00	1710.61	1912.16
Producers of Government Services	76.48	94.49	105.34 110.56	120.59	136.71	162.07	184.70	215.40	250.66	289.26	326.13
Other Producers	4.14	4.84	5.12 5.12	6.15	7.27	8.86	10.93	13.44	17.06	21.72	28.13
Subtotal [c]	518.94	570.06	648.52 701.84	800.79	956.96	1077.38	1301.98	1672.45	1825.71	2021.59	2266.42
Less: Imputed bank service charge	...	...	... 13.05	11.31	18.12	20.37	23.88	31.80	37.31	41.97	45.54
Plus: Import duties	28.58	35.23	29.40 29.40	35.05	46.57	47.37	66.47	81.84	106.42	90.30	120.97
Plus: Value added tax	...	...	... ...	...	...	...	...	...	...	...	...
Plus: Other adjustments [d]	25.14	29.85	33.90 34.36	53.80	75.26	92.30	109.03	137.39	163.36	206.67	252.31
Equals: Gross Domestic Product	572.66	635.14	711.82 752.55	878.33	1060.67	1196.68	1453.60	1859.88	2058.19	2276.60	2594.16

a) For series 1, item 'Restaurants and hotels' is included in item 'Community, social and personal services'
b) For series 1, business services are included in item 'Community, social and personal services'.
c) Gross domestic product in factor values.
d) Relating to net indirect taxes other than import duties.

1.11 Gross Domestic Product by Kind of Activity, in Constant Prices

Million Kenyan pounds

	1970	1971	1972	1973	1974	1975	1976	1977	1978	1979	1980
		1964	At constant prices of:				1976				
1 Agriculture, hunting, forestry and fishing	173.58	175.87	189.29 441.83	453.86	459.61	475.38	484.44	532.86	553.38	549.78	543.10
2 Mining and quarrying	2.60	2.72	2.50 2.23	2.98	2.74	3.11	3.41	4.05	4.14	4.08	4.05
3 Manufacturing	52.49	59.29	63.61 120.97	137.69	144.90	145.77	144.18	167.10	188.16	201.56	210.79
4 Electricity, gas and water	9.81	10.56	11.64 18.99	19.17	20.22	21.55	23.10	25.83	27.38	29.20	30.92
5 Construction	18.98	20.22	23.05 74.41	74.98	69.83	68.40	67.08	72.05	78.58	83.70	85.00
6 Wholesale and retail trade, restaurants and hotels	43.81[a]	44.27[a]	42.64[a] 143.14	137.36	141.53	136.21	132.54	143.59	155.92	165.37	168.38
7 Transport, storage and communication	41.18	43.12	42.43 58.80	65.31	64.52	62.59	69.15	73.74	81.40	87.26	93.46
8 Finance, insurance, real estate and business services	45.00[b]	47.76[b]	49.62[b] 125.64	128.57	140.46	147.71	155.45	163.05	171.94	185.05	190.41
9 Community, social and personal services	20.33[ab]	22.64[ab]	26.58[ab] 23.60	24.37	25.38	26.29	26.99	28.69	30.46	32.86	35.06
Total, Industries	407.79	426.44	451.37 1009.61	1044.29	1069.19	1087.01	1106.35	1210.96	1291.36	1338.86	1361.17
Producers of Government Services	73.75	81.75	92.21 142.45	151.47	161.83	175.67	184.71	194.05	206.43	221.09	232.81
Other Producers	3.55	3.85	3.80 6.57	7.30	8.28	9.52	10.93	12.04	13.91	16.39	19.28
Subtotal	485.09[c]	512.04[c]	547.38[c] 1158.63	1203.06	1239.30	1272.20	1301.98	1417.05	1511.70	1576.34	1613.26
Less: Imputed bank service charge	...	...	... 21.42	16.91	23.15	24.09	23.88	26.79	28.76	31.60	31.24
Plus: Import duties	26.72	31.64	24.81 84.42	81.76	91.73	69.13	66.47	81.10	94.39	77.11	88.41
Plus: Value added tax	...	...	... ...	...	...	...	...	...	...	...	...
Plus: Other adjustments	11.62[d]	13.01[d]	13.23[d] 57.53	87.79	102.80	106.69	109.03	120.30	130.31	151.26	160.20
Equals: Gross Domestic Product	523.43	556.69	585.42 1279.16	1355.70	1410.86	1423.56	1453.60	1590.94	1707.64	1773.10	1830.13

a) Restaurants and hotels are included in item 'Community, social and personal services'.
b) Business services are included in item 'Community, social and personal services'.
c) Gross domestic product in factor values.
d) Relating to net indirect taxes other than import duties.

Kenya

1.12 Relations Among National Accounting Aggregates

Million Kenyan pounds

	1970	1971	1972	1973	1974	1975	1976	1977	1978	1979	1980
Gross Domestic Product	572.66	635.14	711.82 / 752.55	878.33	1060.67	1196.68	1453.60	1859.88	2058.19	2276.60	2594.16
Plus: Net factor income received from abroad	-20.99	-19.09	-21.68 / -21.69	-43.98	-42.30	-46.30	-68.10	-78.70	-90.60	-64.00	-68.40
Equals: Gross National Product	551.67	616.05	690.14 / 730.86	834.35	1018.37	1150.38	1385.50	1781.18	1967.59	2212.60	2525.76
Less: Consumption of fixed capital	...	...	...	...	...	...	...	...	...	...	...
Less: Net indirect taxes paid to supranational organisations	...	...	...	...	...	...	...	...	...	...	...
Equals: National Income at Market Prices [a]	551.67	616.05	690.14 / 730.86	834.35	1018.37	1150.38	1385.50	1781.18	1967.59	2212.60	2525.76
Plus: Net current transfers received from abroad	9.13	20.81	13.60 / 5.70	7.80	6.90	12.30	-2.30	15.50	26.10	26.70	29.90
Equals: National Disposable Income at Market Prices [a]	560.80	636.86	703.74 / 736.56	842.15	1025.27	1162.68	1383.20	1796.68	1993.69	2239.30	2555.66
Less: Final consumption	437.79	524.82	566.21 / 600.64	662.83	864.08	1035.70	1149.23	1356.05	1647.46	1916.45	2215.97
Statistical discrepancy	...	...	...	...	...	0.21	...	...	...	...	...
Equals: Net Saving	123.01	112.04	137.53 / 135.92	179.32	161.19	126.98	233.97	440.63	346.23	322.85	339.69
Less: Surplus of the nation on current transactions	...	...	...	...	...	...	...	...	...	...	...
Equals: Net Capital Formation	...	...	...	...	...	...	...	...	...	...	...

a) Including consumption of fixed capital.

2.1 General Government Final Consumption Expenditure by Function, in Current Prices

Million Kenyan pounds

	1970	1971	1972	1973	1974	1975	1976	1977	1978	1979	1980
1 General public services	28.54	32.86	35.86 / 38.00	40.22	47.35	53.12	59.64	70.44	82.29	94.76	...
2 Defence	8.03	8.86	10.59 / 12.43	14.07	19.28	23.37	36.56	67.98	96.41	...	...
3 Public order and safety	...	...	...	...	...	...	...	...	...	...	...
4 Education	25.81	33.07	35.90 / 41.16	46.54	60.82	77.68	90.06	100.37	114.82	134.98	...
5 Health	11.03	13.27	15.21 / 16.15	16.96	21.14	24.78	27.01	33.55	42.54	48.11	...
6 Social security and welfare										...	...
7 Housing and community amenities	19.69	26.17	29.74 / 24.99	26.69	32.09	40.35	40.52	49.71	62.54		
8 Recreational, cultural and religious affairs										...	...
9 Economic services	...	...	...	...	...	...	...	...	...	...	...
10 Other functions	...	...	...	...	...	...	...	...	...	...	...
Total General Government Final Consumption Expenditure	93.10	114.23	127.30 / 132.73	144.48	180.68	219.30	253.79	322.05	398.60	447.31	510.26

2.9 Gross Capital Formation by Kind of Activity of Owner, ISIC Major Divisions, in Current Prices

Million Kenyan pounds

	1972			1973			1974			1975		
	Total Gross Capital Formation	Increase in Stocks	Gross Fixed Capital Formation	Total Gross Capital Formation	Increase in Stocks	Gross Fixed Capital Formation	Total Gross Capital Formation	Increase in Stocks	Gross Fixed Capital Formation	Total Gross Capital Formation	Increase in Stocks	Gross Fixed Capital Formation

All Producers

1 Agriculture, hunting, fishing and forestry	...	...	13.52	...	...	12.82	...	...	20.40	...	...	22.69
2 Mining and quarrying	...	...	1.70	...	...	1.46	...	...	3.60	...	...	1.53
3 Manufacturing	...	...	28.19	...	...	31.84	...	...	29.86	...	...	31.23
4 Electricity, gas and water	...	...	8.51	...	...	12.17	...	...	10.03	...	...	17.19

Kenya

2.9 Gross Capital Formation by Kind of Activity of Owner, ISIC Major Divisions, in Current Prices
(Continued)

Million Kenyan pounds

	1972 TGCF	1972 IS	1972 GFCF	1973 TGCF	1973 IS	1973 GFCF	1974 TGCF	1974 IS	1974 GFCF	1975 TGCF	1975 IS	1975 GFCF
5 Construction	...	...	8.50	...	...	9.14	...	...	7.00	...	...	7.81
6 Wholesale and retail trade, restaurants and hotels [a]	...	...	8.19	...	...	8.86	...	...	10.19	...	...	14.47
7 Transport, storage and communication	...	...	22.47	...	...	28.03	...	...	35.46	...	...	50.39
8 Finance, insurance, real estate and business services [b]	...	...	31.99	...	...	30.94	...	...	39.00	...	...	47.97
9 Community, social and personal services [a,b]	...	...	7.60	...	...	8.92	...	...	8.52	...	...	7.16
Total Industries	...	...	130.67	...	...	144.18	...	...	164.06	...	...	200.44
Producers of Government Services	...	...	33.10	...	...	35.43	...	...	38.73	...	...	41.45
Private Non-Profit Institutions Serving Households	...	...	...	...	...	...	...	...	...	...	...	...
Total	167.96	4.20	163.76	226.70	47.09	179.61	273.19	70.39	202.80	217.08	-24.81	241.89

	1976 TGCF	1976 IS	1976 GFCF	1977 TGCF	1977 IS	1977 GFCF	1978 TGCF	1978 IS	1978 GFCF	1979 TGCF	1979 IS	1979 GFCF

All Producers

	1976 TGCF	1976 IS	1976 GFCF	1977 TGCF	1977 IS	1977 GFCF	1978 TGCF	1978 IS	1978 GFCF	1979 TGCF	1979 IS	1979 GFCF
1 Agriculture, hunting, fishing and forestry	...	...	25.28	...	...	43.61	...	...	51.86	...	...	42.74
2 Mining and quarrying	...	...	1.62	...	...	1.94	...	...	4.95	...	...	4.10
3 Manufacturing	...	...	45.96	...	...	63.27	...	...	83.71	...	...	88.52
4 Electricity, gas and water	...	...	33.15	...	...	33.72	...	...	40.20	...	...	31.99
5 Construction	...	...	9.72	...	...	15.50	...	...	32.25	...	...	25.68
6 Wholesale and retail trade, restaurants and hotels [a]	...	...	20.61	...	...	21.42	...	...	20.24	...	...	17.30
7 Transport, storage and communication	...	...	50.41	...	...	79.41	...	...	110.50	...	...	101.65
8 Finance, insurance, real estate and business services [b]	...	...	43.59	...	...	55.05	...	...	79.50	...	...	103.00
9 Community, social and personal services [a,b]	...	...	11.63	...	...	17.25	...	...	20.33	...	...	31.76
Total Industries	...	...	241.97	...	...	331.17	...	...	443.44	...	...	446.74
Producers of Government Services	...	...	48.46	...	...	58.84	...	...	70.56	...	...	93.70
Private Non-Profit Institutions Serving Households	...	...	...	...	...	...	...	...	...	...	...	...
Total	294.27	3.84	290.43	441.23	51.22	390.01	610.63	96.62	514.01	516.25	-24.20	540.45

	1980 Total Gross Capital Formation	1980 Increase in Stocks	1980 Gross Fixed Capital Formation

All Producers

	1980 TGCF	1980 IS	1980 GFCF
1 Agriculture, hunting, fishing and forestry	...	...	42.72
2 Mining and quarrying	...	...	4.08
3 Manufacturing	...	...	84.15
4 Electricity, gas and water	...	...	26.61
5 Construction	...	...	28.20
6 Wholesale and retail trade, restaurants and hotels [a]	...	...	19.06
7 Transport, storage and communication	...	...	92.64
8 Finance, insurance, real estate and business services [b]	...	...	105.35
9 Community, social and personal services [a,b]	...	...	32.12
Total Industries	...	...	434.93
Producers of Government Services	...	...	116.91
Private Non-Profit Institutions Serving Households	...	...	...
Total	694.39	142.55	551.84

a) For series 1, item 'Restaurants and hotels' is included in item 'Community, social and personal services'

b) For series 1, business services are included in item 'Community, social and personal services'.

Kenya

2.10 Gross Capital Formation by Kind of Activity of Owner, ISIC Major Divisions, in Constant Prices

Million Kenyan pounds

	1972			1973			1974			1975		
	Total Gross Capital Formation	Increase in Stocks	Gross Fixed Capital Formation	Total Gross Capital Formation	Increase in Stocks	Gross Fixed Capital Formation	Total Gross Capital Formation	Increase in Stocks	Gross Fixed Capital Formation	Total Gross Capital Formation	Increase in Stocks	Gross Fixed Capital Formation

At constant prices of: 1976

All Producers

1 Agriculture, hunting, fishing and forestry	...	...	26.70	...	...	23.29	...	...	30.17	...	...	28.78
2 Mining and quarrying	...	...	3.66	...	...	2.72	...	...	5.36	...	...	2.05
3 Manufacturing	...	...	62.09	...	...	62.22	...	...	44.38	...	...	40.75
4 Electricity, gas and water	...	...	16.64	...	...	20.18	...	...	13.84	...	...	19.90
5 Construction	...	...	18.57	...	...	18.01	...	...	10.84	...	...	10.21
6 Wholesale and retail trade, restaurants and hotels	...	...	17.62	...	...	17.36	...	...	15.76	...	...	18.93
7 Transport, storage and communication	...	...	45.07	...	...	50.65	...	...	52.56	...	...	58.74
8 Finance, insurance, real estate and business services	...	...	58.22	...	...	51.04	...	...	51.48	...	...	56.44
9 Community, social and personal services	...	...	16.11	...	...	16.94	...	...	12.34	...	...	8.71
Total Industries	...	...	264.69	...	...	262.40	...	...	236.73	...	...	244.51
Producers of Government Services	...	...	65.07	...	...	60.54	...	...	53.23	...	...	48.73
Private Non-Profit Institutions Serving Households	...	...	...	...	...	...	...	...	...	...	...	...
Total	335.55	5.79	329.76	405.91	82.96	322.95	383.77	93.80	289.97	262.84	-30.40	293.24

	1976			1977			1978			1979		
	Total Gross Capital Formation	Increase in Stocks	Gross Fixed Capital Formation	Total Gross Capital Formation	Increase in Stocks	Gross Fixed Capital Formation	Total Gross Capital Formation	Increase in Stocks	Gross Fixed Capital Formation	Total Gross Capital Formation	Increase in Stocks	Gross Fixed Capital Formation

At constant prices of: 1976

All Producers

1 Agriculture, hunting, fishing and forestry	...	...	25.28	...	...	39.75	...	...	41.64	...	...	31.61
2 Mining and quarrying	...	...	1.62	...	...	1.70	...	...	3.81	...	...	2.88
3 Manufacturing	...	...	45.96	...	...	55.82	...	...	64.87	...	...	62.49
4 Electricity, gas and water	...	...	33.15	...	...	31.46	...	...	33.72	...	...	23.45
5 Construction	...	...	9.72	...	...	13.71	...	...	24.99	...	...	18.01
6 Wholesale and retail trade, restaurants and hotels	...	...	20.61	...	...	19.05	...	...	15.80	...	...	12.21
7 Transport, storage and communication	...	...	50.41	...	...	71.08	...	...	86.38	...	...	69.26
8 Finance, insurance, real estate and business services	...	...	43.60	...	...	49.48	...	...	65.10	...	...	73.73
9 Community, social and personal services	...	...	11.63	...	...	15.67	...	...	16.48	...	...	22.71
Total Industries	...	...	241.97	...	...	297.72	...	...	352.80	...	...	316.35
Producers of Government Services	...	...	48.46	...	...	54.24	...	...	58.39	...	...	68.38
Private Non-Profit Institutions Serving Households	...	...	...	...	...	...	...	...	...	...	...	...
Total	294.27	3.84	290.43	399.82	47.86	351.96	495.25	84.06	411.19	361.19	-23.55	384.74

	1980		
	Total Gross Capital Formation	Increase in Stocks	Gross Fixed Capital Formation

At constant prices of: 1976

All Producers

1 Agriculture, hunting, fishing and forestry	...	...	26.51
2 Mining and quarrying	...	...	2.60
3 Manufacturing	...	...	53.35
4 Electricity, gas and water	...	...	16.32
5 Construction	...	...	17.89
6 Wholesale and retail trade, restaurants and hotels	...	...	12.08
7 Transport, storage and communication	...	...	58.32
8 Finance, insurance, real estate and business services	...	...	62.65
9 Community, social and personal services	...	...	20.25
Total Industries	...	...	269.97
Producers of Government Services	...	...	73.07
Private Non-Profit Institutions Serving Households	...	...	...
Total	435.26	92.24	343.02

Kenya

3.12 General Government Income and Outlay Account: Total and Subsectors

Million Kenyan pounds — Fiscal year ending 30 June

	\multicolumn{5}{c	}{1972}	\multicolumn{5}{c	}{1973}
	Total General Government	Central Government	State or Provincial Government	Local Government	Social Security Funds	Total General Government	Central Government	State or Provincial Government	Local Government	Social Security Funds

Receipts

1 Property and entrepreneurial income	...	12.16	...	...	...	...	9.78	...	...	...
a Net operating surplus	...	-1.59	...	...	...	...	-1.19	...	...	...
b Withdrawals from public quasi-corporations	...	-	...	...	...	...	-	...	...	...
c Interest	...		...	...	...	...		...	...	...
d Dividends	...	13.75	...	...	...	...	10.97	...	...	...
e Net land rent and royalties	...		...	...	...	...		...	...	...
2 Taxes, fees and contributions	...	108.55	...	...	...	...	118.14	...	...	...
a Indirect taxes	...	59.70	...	...	...	...	62.25	...	...	...
b Direct taxes	...	47.48	...	...	...	...	54.14	...	...	...
Income	...	46.86	...	...	...	...	53.45	...	...	...
Other	...	0.62	...	...	...	...	0.69	...	...	...
c Social security contributions	...	-	...	...	...	...	-	...	...	...
d Fees, fines and penalties	...	1.37	...	...	...	...	1.75	...	...	...
3 Other current transfers received	...	28.54	...	...	...	...	28.00	...	...	...
a Casualty insurance claims	...	-	...	...	...	...	-	...	...	...
b Transfers from other government subsectors	...	0.74	...	...	...	...	0.60	...	...	...
c Transfers from abroad	...	12.05	...	...	...	...	10.68	...	...	...
d Other transfers, except imputed	...	-	...	...	...	...	-	...	...	...
e Imputed unfunded employee welfare contributions	...	15.75	...	...	...	...	16.72	...	...	...
Total Current Receipts [a]	...	149.25	...	...	...	...	155.92	...	...	...

Disbursements

1 General government final consumption expenditures	...	109.04	...	...	...	...	116.37	...	...	...
a Compensation of employees	...	...	...	...	...	...	...	...	...	...
b Consumption of fixed capital	...	1.55	...	...	...	...	1.29	...	...	...
c Goods and services purchased, net	...	...	...	...	...	...	...	...	...	...
d Less: Own account production of fixed assets	...	...	...	...	...	...	...	...	...	...
e Indirect taxes paid, net	...	...	...	...	...	...	...	...	...	...
2 Property income paid	...	8.72	...	...	...	...	10.64	...	...	...
a Interest	...	...	...	...	...	...	...	...	...	...
b Net land rent and royalties	...	...	...	...	...	...	...	...	...	...
3 Subsidies	...	0.82	...	...	...	...	1.77	...	...	...
4 Other current transfers paid	...	15.06	...	...	...	...	16.60	...	...	...
a Casualty insurance premiums, net	...	-	...	...	...	...	-	...	...	...
b Transfers to other government subsectors	...	6.77	...	...	...	...	7.58	...	...	...
c Transfers to households	...	3.92	...	...	...	...	4.39	...	...	...
Social security benefits	...	-	...	...	...	...	-	...	...	...
Social assistance grants	...	0.48	...	...	...	...	0.70	...	...	...
Unfunded employee welfare benefits	...	3.44	...	...	...	...	3.69	...	...	...
d Transfers to private non-profit institutions serving households	...	3.95	...	...	...	...	4.08	...	...	...
e Transfers to the rest of the world	...	0.42	...	...	...	...	0.55	...	...	...
Net saving [a]	...	15.61	...	...	...	...	10.55	...	...	...
Total Current Disbursements and Net Saving [a]	...	149.25	...	...	...	...	155.92	...	...	...

Kenya

3.12 General Government Income and Outlay Account: Total and Subsectors

Million Kenyan pounds — Fiscal year ending 30 June

	1974 Total General Government	1974 Central Government	1974 State or Provincial Government	1974 Local Government	1974 Social Security Funds	1975 Total General Government	1975 Central Government	1975 State or Provincial Government	1975 Local Government	1975 Social Security Funds
Receipts										
1 Property and entrepreneurial income	...	6.33	...	...	...	...	4.65	...	...	...
a Net operating surplus	...	-1.52	...	...	...	...	-2.58	...	...	...
b Withdrawals from public quasi-corporations	...	-	...	...	...	...	-	...	...	...
c Interest	...	⎱	...	...	...	...	⎱	...	...	...
d Dividends	...	7.85	...	...	...	...	7.23	...	...	...
e Net land rent and royalties	...	⎰	...	...	...	...	⎰	...	...	...
2 Taxes, fees and contributions	...	161.37	...	...	...	...	199.80	...	...	...
a Indirect taxes	...	102.03	...	...	...	...	119.90	...	...	...
b Direct taxes	...	57.73	...	...	...	...	77.15	...	...	...
Income	...	57.73	...	...	...	...	77.15	...	...	...
Other	...	-	...	...	...	...	-	...	...	...
c Social security contributions	...	-	...	...	...	...	-	...	...	...
d Fees, fines and penalties	...	1.61	...	...	...	...	2.75	...	...	...
3 Other current transfers received	...	29.85	...	...	...	...	20.79	...	...	...
a Casualty insurance claims	...	-	...	...	...	...	-	...	...	...
b Transfers from other government subsectors	...	0.79	...	...	...	...	0.04	...	...	...
c Transfers from abroad	...	10.02	...	...	...	...	8.45	...	...	...
d Other transfers, except imputed	...	-	...	...	...	...	-	...	...	...
e Imputed unfunded employee welfare contributions	...	19.04	...	...	...	...	12.30	...	...	...
Total Current Receipts [a]	...	197.55	...	...	...	...	225.72	...	...	...
Disbursements										
1 General government final consumption expenditures	...	134.04	...	...	...	...	128.83	...	...	...
a Compensation of employees	...	...	...	...	...	...	...	...	...	...
b Consumption of fixed capital	...	1.53	...	...	...	...	2.51	...	...	...
c Goods and services purchased, net	...	...	...	...	...	...	...	...	...	...
d Less: Own account production of fixed assets	...	...	...	...	...	...	...	...	...	...
e Indirect taxes paid, net	...	...	...	...	...	...	...	...	...	...
2 Property income paid	...	11.98	...	...	...	...	14.53	...	...	...
a Interest	...	...	...	...	...	...	...	...	...	...
b Net land rent and royalties	...	...	...	...	...	...	...	...	...	...
3 Subsidies	...	2.77	...	...	...	...	0.89	...	...	...
4 Other current transfers paid	...	21.26	...	...	...	...	61.94	...	...	...
a Casualty insurance premiums, net	...	-	...	...	...	...	-	...	...	...
b Transfers to other government subsectors	...	8.90	...	...	...	...	54.35	...	...	...
c Transfers to households	...	6.17	...	...	...	...	4.95	...	...	...
Social security benefits	...	-	...	...	...	...	-	...	...	...
Social assistance grants	...	0.95	...	...	...	...	0.83	...	...	...
Unfunded employee welfare benefits	...	5.22	...	...	...	...	4.12	...	...	...
d Transfers to private non-profit institutions serving households	...	5.28	...	...	...	...	1.45	...	...	...
e Transfers to the rest of the world	...	0.91	...	...	...	...	1.19	...	...	...
Net saving [a]	...	27.49	...	...	...	...	19.51	...	...	...
Total Current Disbursements and Net Saving [a]	...	197.54	...	...	...	...	225.70	...	...	...

Kenya

3.12 General Government Income and Outlay Account: Total and Subsectors

Million Kenyan pounds — *Fiscal year ending 30 June*

	1976 Total General Government	1976 Central Government	1976 State or Provincial Government	1976 Local Government	1976 Social Security Funds	1977 Total General Government	1977 Central Government	1977 State or Provincial Government	1977 Local Government	1977 Social Security Funds
Receipts										
1 Property and entrepreneurial income	...	7.40	...	...	...	...	12.48	...	...	...
a Net operating surplus	...	-4.50	...	...	...	...	-2.80	...	...	...
b Withdrawals from public quasi-corporations	...	...	...	...	...	...	...	...	...	...
c Interest	...		...	...	...	...		...	...	...
d Dividends	...	11.90	...	...	...	...	15.28	...	...	...
e Net land rent and royalties										
2 Taxes, fees and contributions	...	232.02	...	...	...	...	271.06	...	...	...
a Indirect taxes	...	138.19	...	...	...	...	157.83	...	...	...
b Direct taxes	...	90.24	...	...	...	...	108.03	...	...	...
Income	...	90.24	...	...	...	...	107.47	...	...	...
Other	...	...	...	...	...	...	0.56	...	...	...
c Social security contributions	...	...	...	...	...	...	...	...	...	...
d Fees, fines and penalties	...	3.59	...	...	...	...	5.20	...	...	...
3 Other current transfers received	...	25.67	...	...	...	...	25.71	...	...	...
a Casualty insurance claims	...	...	...	...	...	...	...	...	...	...
b Transfers from other government subsectors	...	0.81	...	...	...	...	0.03	...	...	...
c Transfers from abroad	...	9.12	...	...	...	...	8.65	...	...	...
d Other transfers, except imputed	...	0.53	...	...	...	...	0.60	...	...	...
e Imputed unfunded employee welfare contributions	...	15.21	...	...	...	...	16.43	...	...	...
Total Current Receipts [a]	...	265.30	...	...	...	...	309.28	...	...	...
Disbursements										
1 General government final consumption expenditures	...	147.86	...	...	...	...	173.48	...	...	...
a Compensation of employees	...	...	...	...	...	...	...	...	...	...
b Consumption of fixed capital	...	2.61	...	...	...	...	3.95	...	...	...
c Goods and services purchased, net	...	...	...	...	...	...	...	...	...	...
d Less: Own account production of fixed assets	...	...	...	...	...	...	...	...	...	...
e Indirect taxes paid, net	...	...	...	...	...	...	...	...	...	...
2 Property income paid	...	19.53	...	...	...	...	23.95	...	...	...
a Interest	...	...	...	...	...	...	...	...	...	...
b Net land rent and royalties	...	...	...	...	...	...	...	...	...	...
3 Subsidies	...	0.81	...	...	...	...	0.74	...	...	...
4 Other current transfers paid	...	74.38	...	...	...	...	78.77	...	...	...
a Casualty insurance premiums, net	...	...	...	...	...	...	...	...	...	...
b Transfers to other government subsectors	...	65.38	...	...	...	...	67.45	...	...	...
c Transfers to households	...	6.96	...	...	...	...	8.50	...	...	...
Social security benefits	...	...	...	...	...	...	...	...	...	...
Social assistance grants	...	2.60	...	...	...	...	4.01	...	...	...
Unfunded employee welfare benefits	...	4.36	...	...	...	...	4.49	...	...	...
d Transfers to private non-profit institutions serving households	...	1.06	...	...	...	...	1.56	...	...	...
e Transfers to the rest of the world	...	0.98	...	...	...	...	1.26	...	...	...
Net saving [a]	...	22.72	...	...	...	...	32.34	...	...	...
Total Current Disbursements and Net Saving [a]	...	265.30	...	...	...	...	309.28	...	...	...

Kenya

3.12 General Government Income and Outlay Account: Total and Subsectors

Million Kenyan pounds — Fiscal year ending 30 June

	1978 Total General Government	1978 Central Government	1978 State or Provincial Government	1978 Local Government	1978 Social Security Funds	1979 Total General Government	1979 Central Government	1979 State or Provincial Government	1979 Local Government	1979 Social Security Funds
Receipts										
1 Property and entrepreneurial income	...	22.34	...	...	...	...	24.24	...	...	...
a Net operating surplus	...	-3.91	...	...	...	...	-6.05	...	...	...
b Withdrawals from public quasi-corporations	...	...	...	...	...	...	...	...	...	...
c Interest	...		...	...	...	...		...	...	...
d Dividends	...	26.25	...	...	...	...	30.29	...	...	...
e Net land rent and royalties	...		...	...	...	...		...	...	...
2 Taxes, fees and contributions	...	404.54	...	...	...	...	426.87	...	...	...
a Indirect taxes	...	256.76	...	...	...	...	267.98	...	...	...
b Direct taxes	...	143.01	...	...	...	...	151.73	...	...	...
Income	...	142.33	...	...	...	...	151.07	...	...	...
Other	...	0.68	...	...	...	...	0.68	...	...	...
c Social security contributions	...	...	...	...	...	...	...	...	...	...
d Fees, fines and penalties	...	4.77	...	...	...	...	7.16	...	...	...
3 Other current transfers received	...	36.49	...	...	...	...	41.09	...	...	...
a Casualty insurance claims	...	...	...	...	...	...	...	...	...	...
b Transfers from other government subsectors	...	0.02	...	...	...	...	0.02	...	...	...
c Transfers from abroad	...	15.06	...	...	...	...	17.60	...	...	...
d Other transfers, except imputed	...	...	...	...	...	...	...	...	...	...
e Imputed unfunded employee welfare contributions	...	21.41	...	...	...	...	23.47	...	...	...
Total Current Receipts [a]	...	463.38	...	...	...	...	493.37	...	...	...
Disbursements										
1 General government final consumption expenditures	...	263.91	...	...	...	...	309.15	...	...	...
a Compensation of employees	...	...	...	...	...	...	...	...	...	...
b Consumption of fixed capital	...	6.68	...	...	...	...	8.53	...	...	...
c Goods and services purchased, net	...	...	...	...	...	...	...	...	...	...
d Less: Own account production of fixed assets	...	...	...	...	...	...	...	...	...	...
e Indirect taxes paid, net	...	...	...	...	...	...	...	...	...	...
2 Property income paid	...	32.80	...	...	...	...	42.50	...	...	...
a Interest	...	...	...	...	...	...	...	...	...	...
b Net land rent and royalties	...	...	...	...	...	...	...	...	...	...
3 Subsidies	...	0.37	...	...	...	...	1.29	...	...	...
4 Other current transfers paid	...	96.48	...	...	...	...	115.47	...	...	...
a Casualty insurance premiums, net	...	...	...	...	...	...	...	...	...	...
b Transfers to other government subsectors	...	82.90	...	...	...	...	91.48	...	...	...
c Transfers to households	...	10.73	...	...	...	...	18.71	...	...	...
Social security benefits	...	...	...	...	...	...	...	...	...	...
Social assistance grants	...	6.81	...	...	...	...	...	...	...	...
Unfunded employee welfare benefits	...	3.92	...	...	...	...	...	...	...	...
d Transfers to private non-profit institutions serving households	...	1.33	...	...	...	...	1.78	...	...	...
e Transfers to the rest of the world	...	1.52	...	...	...	...	3.50	...	...	...
Net saving [a]	...	69.80	...	...	...	...	24.93	...	...	...
Total Current Disbursements and Net Saving [a]	...	463.36	...	...	...	...	493.37	...	...	...

Kenya

3.12 General Government Income and Outlay Account: Total and Subsectors

Million Kenyan pounds — Fiscal year ending 30 June

	Total General Government	Central Government	State or Provincial Government	Local Government	Social Security Funds
Receipts					
1 Property and entrepreneurial income	...	19.69	...	...	...
a Net operating surplus	...	-7.09	...	...	...
b Withdrawals from public quasi-corporations	...	...	...	...	...
c Interest	...	7.17	...	...	...
d Dividends	...	16.54	...	...	...
e Net land rent and royalties	...	3.07	...	...	...
2 Taxes, fees and contributions	...	526.45	...	...	...
a Indirect taxes	...	341.49	...	...	...
b Direct taxes	...	173.64	...	...	...
Income	...	171.85	...	...	...
Other	...	1.79	...	...	...
c Social security contributions	...	...	...	...	...
d Fees, fines and penalties	...	11.32	...	...	...
3 Other current transfers received	...	43.96	...	...	...
a Casualty insurance claims	...	...	...	...	...
b Transfers from other government subsectors	...	*	...	...	...
c Transfers from abroad	...	16.70	...	...	...
d Other transfers, except imputed	...	...	...	...	...
e Imputed unfunded employee welfare contributions	...	26.21	...	...	...
Total Current Receipts [a]	...	590.10	...	...	...
Disbursements					
1 General government final consumption expenditures	...	350.97	...	...	...
a Compensation of employees	...	...	...	...	...
b Consumption of fixed capital	...	...	...	...	...
c Goods and services purchased, net	...	...	...	...	...
d Less: Own account production of fixed assets	...	...	...	...	...
e Indirect taxes paid, net	...	...	...	...	...
2 Property income paid	...	48.05	...	...	...
a Interest	...	48.05	...	...	...
b Net land rent and royalties	...	...	...	...	...
3 Subsidies	...	0.98	...	...	...
4 Other current transfers paid	...	123.65	...	...	...
a Casualty insurance premiums, net	...	...	...	...	...
b Transfers to other government subsectors	...	101.28	...	...	...
c Transfers to households	...	19.53	...	...	...
Social security benefits	...	...	...	...	...
Social assistance grants	...	...	...	...	...
Unfunded employee welfare benefits	...	...	...	...	...
d Transfers to private non-profit institutions serving households	...	1.61	...	...	...
e Transfers to the rest of the world	...	1.23	...	...	...
Net saving [a]	...	66.44	...	...	...
Total Current Disbursements and Net Saving [a]	...	590.10	...	...	...

a) Data in this table refer to fiscal year ending 30 June.

Kenya

3.13 General Government Capital Accumulation Account: Total and Subsectors

Million Kenyan pounds — Fiscal year ending 30 June

	1972 Total General Government	1972 Central Government	1972 State or Provincial Government	1972 Local Government	1972 Social Security Funds	1973 Total General Government	1973 Central Government	1973 State or Provincial Government	1973 Local Government	1973 Social Security Funds
Finance of Gross Accumulation										
1 Gross saving	...	17.16	...	...	...	...	11.84	...	...	...
a Consumption of fixed capital	...	1.55	...	...	...	...	1.29	...	...	...
b Net saving	...	15.61	...	...	...	...	10.55	...	...	...
2 Capital transfers received [a]	...	1.04	...	...	...	...	0.29	...	...	...
a From other government subsectors	...	...	...	...	...	...	...	...	...	...
b From other resident sectors	...	...	...	...	...	...	...	...	...	...
c From rest of the world	...	1.04	...	...	...	...	0.29	...	...	...
Statistical discrepancy	...	...	...	...	...	...	...	...	...	...
Finance of Gross Accumulation [b]	...	18.20	...	...	...	...	12.14	...	...	...
Gross Accumulation										
1 Gross capital formation	...	33.65	...	...	...	...	39.26	...	...	...
2 Purchases of land, net	...	0.84	...	...	...	...	0.86	...	...	...
3 Purchases of intangible assets, net	...	0.87	...	...	...	...	1.12	...	...	...
4 Capital transfers paid	...	...	...	...	...	...	...	...	...	...
Net lending	...	-17.16	...	...	...	...	-29.09	...	...	...
Gross Accumulation [b]	...	18.20	...	...	...	...	12.14	...	...	...

	1974 Total General Government	1974 Central Government	1974 State or Provincial Government	1974 Local Government	1974 Social Security Funds	1975 Total General Government	1975 Central Government	1975 State or Provincial Government	1975 Local Government	1975 Social Security Funds
Finance of Gross Accumulation										
1 Gross saving	...	29.02	...	...	...	...	22.02	...	...	...
a Consumption of fixed capital	...	1.53	...	...	...	...	2.51	...	...	...
b Net saving	...	27.49	...	...	...	...	19.51	...	...	...
2 Capital transfers received [a]	...	3.23	...	...	...	...	4.58	...	...	...
a From other government subsectors	...	...	...	...	...	...	-3.65	...	...	...
b From other resident sectors	...	...	...	...	...	...	...	...	...	...
c From rest of the world	...	3.23	...	...	...	...	8.23	...	...	...
Statistical discrepancy	...	...	...	...	...	...	...	...	...	...
Finance of Gross Accumulation [b]	...	32.25	...	...	...	...	26.62	...	...	...
Gross Accumulation										
1 Gross capital formation	...	40.71	...	...	...	...	53.36	...	...	...
2 Purchases of land, net	...	0.31	...	...	...	...	1.29	...	...	...
3 Purchases of intangible assets, net	...	1.24	...	...	...	...	...	...	...	...
4 Capital transfers paid	...	...	...	...	...	...	...	...	...	...
Net lending	...	-10.01	...	...	...	...	-28.03	...	...	...
Gross Accumulation [b]	...	32.25	...	...	...	...	26.62	...	...	...

	1976 Total General Government	1976 Central Government	1976 State or Provincial Government	1976 Local Government	1976 Social Security Funds	1977 Total General Government	1977 Central Government	1977 State or Provincial Government	1977 Local Government	1977 Social Security Funds
Finance of Gross Accumulation										
1 Gross saving	...	25.33	...	...	...	...	36.29	...	...	...
a Consumption of fixed capital	...	2.61	...	...	...	...	3.95	...	...	...
b Net saving	...	22.72	...	...	...	...	32.34	...	...	...
2 Capital transfers received [a]	...	4.16	...	...	...	...	8.06	...	...	...
a From other government subsectors	...	-2.85	...	...	...	...	-0.31	...	...	...
b From other resident sectors	...	...	...	...	...	...	-2.15	...	...	...
c From rest of the world	...	7.01	...	...	...	...	10.52	...	...	...
Statistical discrepancy	...	...	...	...	...	...	...	...	...	...
Finance of Gross Accumulation [b]	...	29.50	...	...	...	...	44.38	...	...	...

Kenya

3.13 General Government Capital Accumulation Account: Total and Subsectors
(Continued)

Million Kenyan pounds — Fiscal year ending 30 June

1976 and 1977

	Total General Government 1976	Central Government 1976	State or Provincial Government 1976	Local Government 1976	Social Security Funds 1976	Total General Government 1977	Central Government 1977	State or Provincial Government 1977	Local Government 1977	Social Security Funds 1977
Gross Accumulation										
1 Gross capital formation	...	63.73	...	...	...	...	76.64	...	...	...
2 Purchases of land, net	...	2.30	...	...	...	...	1.95	...	...	...
3 Purchases of intangible assets, net	...	...	...	...	...	...	...	...	...	...
4 Capital transfers paid	...	...	...	...	...	...	...	...	...	...
Net lending	...	-36.52	...	...	...	...	-34.21	...	...	...
Gross Accumulation [b]	...	29.50	...	...	...	...	44.38	...	...	...

1978 and 1979

	Total General Government 1978	Central Government 1978	State or Provincial Government 1978	Local Government 1978	Social Security Funds 1978	Total General Government 1979	Central Government 1979	State or Provincial Government 1979	Local Government 1979	Social Security Funds 1979
Finance of Gross Accumulation										
1 Gross saving	...	76.48	...	...	...	...	33.46	...	...	...
a Consumption of fixed capital	...	6.68	...	...	...	...	8.53	...	...	...
b Net saving	...	69.80	...	...	...	...	24.93	...	...	...
2 Capital transfers received [a]	...	4.53	...	...	...	...	6.69	...	...	...
a From other government subsectors	...	-4.52	...	...	...	...	...	...	...	...
b From other resident sectors	...	...	...	...	...	...	...	...	...	...
c From rest of the world	...	9.06	...	...	...	...	...	...	...	...
Statistical discrepancy	...	...	...	...	...	...	0.12	...	...	...
Finance of Gross Accumulation [b]	...	81.04	...	...	...	...	40.27	...	...	...
Gross Accumulation										
1 Gross capital formation	...	101.93	...	...	...	...	123.87	...	...	...
2 Purchases of land, net	...	1.65	...	...	...	...	1.79	...	...	...
3 Purchases of intangible assets, net	...	...	...	...	...	...	...	...	...	...
4 Capital transfers paid	...	...	...	...	...	...	...	...	...	...
Net lending	...	-22.53	...	...	...	...	-85.39	...	...	...
Gross Accumulation [b]	...	81.04	...	...	...	...	40.27	...	...	...

1980

	Total General Government	Central Government	State or Provincial Government	Local Government	Social Security Funds
Finance of Gross Accumulation					
1 Gross saving	...	74.47	...	...	...
a Consumption of fixed capital	...	8.03	...	...	...
b Net saving	...	66.44	...	...	...
2 Capital transfers received [a]	...	14.11	...	...	...
a From other government subsectors	...	...	...	...	...
b From other resident sectors	...	...	...	...	...
c From rest of the world	...	...	...	...	...
Statistical discrepancy	...	0.10	...	...	...
Finance of Gross Accumulation [b]	...	88.69	...	...	...
Gross Accumulation					
1 Gross capital formation	...	151.05	...	...	...
2 Purchases of land, net	...	2.85	...	...	...
3 Purchases of intangible assets, net	...	...	...	...	...
4 Capital transfers paid	...	...	...	...	...
Net lending	...	-65.22	...	...	...
Gross Accumulation [b]	...	88.69	...	...	...

a) Net.
b) Data in this table refer to fiscal year ending 30 June.

Kenya

3.14 General Government Capital Finance Account, Total and Subsectors

Million Kenyan pounds — Fiscal year ending 30 June

	1972 Total General Government	1972 Central Government	1972 State or Provincial Government	1972 Local Government	1972 Social Security Funds	1973 Total General Government	1973 Central Government	1973 State or Provincial Government	1973 Local Government	1973 Social Security Funds
Acquisition of Financial Assets										
1 Gold and SDRs	...	...	...	...	...	...	...	...	...	...
2 Currency and transferable deposits	...	...	...	...	...	...	...	...	...	...
3 Other deposits	...	...	...	...	...	...	...	...	...	...
4 Bills and bonds, short term	...	...	...	...	...	...	...	...	...	...
5 Bonds, long term	...	...	...	...	...	...	...	...	...	...
6 Corporate equity securities	...	...	...	...	...	...	...	...	...	...
7 Short-term loans, n.e.c.	...	...	...	...	...	...	...	...	...	...
8 Long-term loans, n.e.c.	...	...	...	...	...	...	...	...	...	...
a Mortgages	...	...	...	...	...	...	...	...	...	...
b Other	...	...	...	...	...	...	...	...	...	...
9 Other receivables	...	...	...	...	...	...	...	...	...	...
10 Other assets	...	...	...	...	...	...	...	...	...	...
Total Acquisition of Financial Assets [a]	...	26.64	...	...	...	...	24.50	...	...	...
Incurrence of Liabilities										
1 Currency and transferable deposits	...	8.95	...	...	...	...	0.04	...	...	...
2 Other deposits	...	-0.32	...	...	...	...	-1.52	...	...	...
3 Bills and bonds, short term	...	6.09	...	...	...	...	7.07	...	...	...
4 Bonds, long term	...	15.56	...	...	...	...	21.30	...	...	...
5 Short-term loans, n.e.c.	...	-	...	...	...	...	-	...	...	...
6 Long-term loans, n.e.c.	...	11.49	...	...	...	...	24.66	...	...	...
7 Other payables	...	...	...	...	...	...	...	...	...	...
8 Other liabilities	...	2.04	...	...	...	...	2.03	...	...	...
Total Incurrence of Liabilities [a]	...	43.81	...	...	...	...	53.58	...	...	...
Net Lending [a]	...	-17.16	...	...	...	...	-29.09	...	...	...
Incurrence of Liabilities and Net Worth	...	26.65	...	...	...	...	24.49	...	...	...

	1974 Total General Government	1974 Central Government	1974 State or Provincial Government	1974 Local Government	1974 Social Security Funds	1975 Total General Government	1975 Central Government	1975 State or Provincial Government	1975 Local Government	1975 Social Security Funds
Acquisition of Financial Assets										
1 Gold and SDRs	...	...	...	...	...	...	...	...	...	...
2 Currency and transferable deposits	...	...	...	...	...	...	1.10	...	...	...
3 Other deposits	...	...	...	...	...	...	...	...	...	...
4 Bills and bonds, short term	...	...	...	...	...	...	0.68	...	...	...
5 Bonds, long term	...	...	...	...	...	...		...	...	...
6 Corporate equity securities	...	...	...	...	...	...	...	...	...	...
7 Short-term loans, n.e.c.	...	...	...	...	...	...	...	...	...	...
8 Long-term loans, n.e.c.	...	...	...	...	...	...	...	...	...	...
a Mortgages	...	...	...	...	...	...	...	...	...	...
b Other	...	...	...	...	...	...	...	...	...	...
9 Other receivables	...	...	...	...	...	...	...	...	...	...
10 Other assets	...	...	...	...	...	...	39.68	...	...	...
Total Acquisition of Financial Assets [a]	...	31.28	...	...	...	...	43.71	...	...	...
Incurrence of Liabilities										
1 Currency and transferable deposits	...	7.20	...	...	...	...	17.97	...	...	...
2 Other deposits	...	-1.63	...	...	...	...	1.80	...	...	...
3 Bills and bonds, short term	...	0.60	...	...	...	...	4.40	...	...	...
4 Bonds, long term	...	18.85	...	...	...	...	15.49	...	...	...
5 Short-term loans, n.e.c.	...	0.34	...	...	...	...	4.40	...	...	...
6 Long-term loans, n.e.c.	...	14.00	...	...	...	...	20.07	...	...	...
7 Other payables	...	...	...	...	...	...	...	...	...	...
8 Other liabilities	...	1.92	...	...	...	...	7.61	...	...	...
Total Incurrence of Liabilities [a]	...	41.28	...	...	...	...	71.74	...	...	...
Net Lending [a]	...	-10.01	...	...	...	...	-28.03	...	...	...
Incurrence of Liabilities and Net Worth	...	31.27	...	...	...	...	43.71	...	...	...

Kenya

3.14 General Government Capital Finance Account, Total and Subsectors

Million Kenyan pounds — Fiscal year ending 30 June

1976 / 1977

		1976				1977			
	Total General Government	Central Government	State or Provincial Government	Local Government	Social Security Funds	Total General Government	Central Government	State or Provincial Government	Local Government	Social Security Funds

Acquisition of Financial Assets

		1976 Central					1977 Central			
1	Gold and SDRs	...	...	...	...	...	...	...	...	...
2	Currency and transferable deposits	...	31.94	...	...	...	...	5.73	...	...	...
3	Other deposits	...	...	...	...	...	...	...	...	...	...
4	Bills and bonds, short term	...	...	...	...	...	...	...	...	...	...
5	Bonds, long term	...	...	...	...	...	...	...	...	...	...
6	Corporate equity securities	...	...	...	...	...	...	...	...	...	...
7	Short-term loans, n.e.c.	...	...	...	...	...	...	...	...	...	...
8	Long-term loans, n.e.c.	...	...	...	...	...	...	...	...	...	...
	a Mortgages	...	...	...	...	...	...	...	...	...	...
	b Other	...	...	...	...	...	...	...	...	...	...
9	Other receivables	...	...	...	...	...	...	...	...	...	...
10	Other assets	...	61.76	...	...	...	...	49.04	...	...	...
	Total Acquisition of Financial Assets [a]	...	96.88	...	...	...	...	56.82	...	...	...

Incurrence of Liabilities

1	Currency and transferable deposits	...	...	...	...	...	...	3.06	...	...	...
2	Other deposits	...	10.68	...	...	...	...	6.51	...	...	...
3	Bills and bonds, short term	...	24.08	...	...	...	...	27.60	...	...	...
4	Bonds, long term	...	52.78	...	...	...	...	25.00	...	...	...
5	Short-term loans, n.e.c.	...	...	...	...	...	...	-4.40	...	...	...
6	Long-term loans, n.e.c.	...	36.91	...	...	...	...	29.77	...	...	...
7	Other payables	...	...	...	...	...	...	...	...	...	...
8	Other liabilities	...	8.95	...	...	...	...	3.49	...	...	...
	Total Incurrence of Liabilities [a]	...	133.40	...	...	...	...	91.03	...	...	...
	Net Lending [a]	...	-36.52	...	...	...	...	-34.21	...	...	...
	Incurrence of Liabilities and Net Worth	...	96.88	...	...	...	...	56.82	...	...	...

1978 / 1979

		1978				1979			
	Total General Government	Central Government	State or Provincial Government	Local Government	Social Security Funds	Total General Government	Central Government	State or Provincial Government	Local Government	Social Security Funds

Acquisition of Financial Assets

1	Gold and SDRs	...	...	...	...	...	...	...	...	...	...
2	Currency and transferable deposits	...	...	...	...	...	...	...	...	...	...
3	Other deposits	...	...	...	...	...	...	44.73	...	...	...
4	Bills and bonds, short term	...	29.34	...	...	...	...	...	...	...	...
5	Bonds, long term	...	...	...	...	...	...	...	...	...	...
6	Corporate equity securities	...	18.04	...	...	...	...	12.59	...	...	...
7	Short-term loans, n.e.c.	...	...	...	...	...	...	...	...	...	...
8	Long-term loans, n.e.c.	...	57.10	...	...	...	...	63.38	...	...	...
	a Mortgages	...	56.98	...	...	...	...	62.81	...	...	...
	b Other	...	0.12	...	...	...	...	0.57	...	...	...
9	Other receivables	...	27.82	...	...	...	...	22.93	...	...	...
10	Other assets	...	...	...	...	...	...	...	...	...	...
	Total Acquisition of Financial Assets [a]	...	132.42	...	...	...	...	144.20	...	...	...

Incurrence of Liabilities

1	Currency and transferable deposits	...	28.35	...	...	...	...	.	...	...	...
2	Other deposits	...	13.48	...	...	...	...	6.90	...	...	...
3	Bills and bonds, short term	...	...	...	...	...	...	56.43	...	...	...
4	Bonds, long term	...	66.94	...	...	...	...	88.54	...	...	...
5	Short-term loans, n.e.c.	...	...	...	...	...	...	...	...	...	...
6	Long-term loans, n.e.c.	...	43.23	...	...	...	...	73.44	...	...	...
7	Other payables	...	...	...	...	...	...	...	...	...	...
8	Other liabilities	...	2.95	...	...	...	...	4.27	...	...	...
	Total Incurrence of Liabilities [a]	...	154.95	...	...	...	...	229.58	...	...	...
	Net Lending [a]	...	-22.53	...	...	...	...	-85.38	...	...	...
	Incurrence of Liabilities and Net Worth	...	132.42	...	...	...	...	144.20	...	...	...

Kenya

3.14 General Government Capital Finance Account, Total and Subsectors

Million Kenyan pounds — Fiscal year ending 30 June

	Total General Government	Central Government	State or Provincial Government	Local Government	Social Security Funds
1980					

Acquisition of Financial Assets

	Total General Government	Central Government	State or Provincial Government	Local Government	Social Security Funds
1 Gold and SDRs	...	...	...	...	...
2 Currency and transferable deposits	...	...	...	...	...
3 Other deposits	...	...	...	...	...
4 Bills and bonds, short term	...	33.56	...	...	...
5 Bonds, long term	...	...	...	...	...
6 Corporate equity securities	...	9.48	...	...	...
7 Short-term loans, n.e.c.	...	...	...	...	...
8 Long-term loans, n.e.c.	...	53.61	...	...	...
a Mortgages	...	...	...	...	...
b Other	...	...	...	...	...
9 Other receivables	...	30.72	...	...	...
10 Other assets	...	0.05	...	...	...
Total Acquisition of Financial Assets [a]	...	127.42	...	...	...

Incurrence of Liabilities

	Total General Government	Central Government	State or Provincial Government	Local Government	Social Security Funds
1 Currency and transferable deposits	...	52.53	...	...	...
2 Other deposits	...	4.42	...	...	...
3 Bills and bonds, short term	...	...	...	...	...
4 Bonds, long term	...	48.63	...	...	...
5 Short-term loans, n.e.c.	...	...	...	...	...
6 Long-term loans, n.e.c.	...	83.58	...	...	...
7 Other payables	...	...	...	...	...
8 Other liabilities	...	3.48	...	...	...
Total Incurrence of Liabilities [a]	...	192.64	...	...	...
Net Lending [a]	...	-65.22	...	...	...
Incurrence of Liabilities and Net Worth	...	127.42	...	...	...

a) Data in this table refer to fiscal year ending 30 June.

4.3 Derivation of Value Added by Kind of Activity, ISIC Divisions, in Current Prices

Million Kenyan pounds

	1972 Gross Output	1972 Intermediate Consumption	1972 Value Added	1973 Gross Output	1973 Intermediate Consumption	1973 Value Added	1974 Gross Output	1974 Intermediate Consumption	1974 Value Added	1975 Gross Output	1975 Intermediate Consumption	1975 Value Added
All Producers												
1 Agriculture, hunting, forestry and fishing	...	...	242.42	...	...	279.98	...	...	331.99	...	...	361.38
a Agriculture and hunting	...	...	232.63	...	...	269.00	...	...	319.37	...	...	346.30
b Forestry and logging	...	...	8.38	...	...	9.48	...	...	10.99	...	...	13.23
c Fishing	...	...	1.41	...	...	1.50	...	...	1.63	...	...	1.85
2 Mining and quarrying	...	...	2.22	...	...	3.20	...	...	3.20	...	...	3.42
a Coal mining	...	...	...	...	...	-	...	...	-	...	...	-
b Crude petroleum and natural gas production	...	...	0.03	...	...	-	...	...	-	...	...	0.01
c Metal ore mining	...	...	0.26	...	...	0.13	...	...	-	...	...	0.12
d Other mining	...	...	1.94	...	...	3.08	...	...	3.14	...	...	3.19

Kenya

4.3 Derivation of Value Added by Kind of Activity, ISIC Divisions, in Current Prices
(Continued)

Million Kenyan pounds

	1972 Gross Output	1972 Intermediate Consumption	1972 Value Added	1973 Gross Output	1973 Intermediate Consumption	1973 Value Added	1974 Gross Output	1974 Intermediate Consumption	1974 Value Added	1975 Gross Output	1975 Intermediate Consumption	1975 Value Added
3 Manufacturing	...	...	77.93	...	...	95.62	...	...	119.42	...	...	127.00
a Manufacture of food, beverages and tobacco	...	...	21.96	...	...	25.94	...	...	30.33	...	...	36.55
b Textile, wearing apparel and leather industries	...	...	9.48	...	...	11.02	...	...	12.00	...	...	13.30
c Manufacture of wood and wood products, including furniture	...	...	3.90	...	...	4.51	...	...	5.52	...	...	5.51
d Manufacture of paper and paper products, printing and publishing	...	...	5.81	...	...	7.31	...	...	11.00	...	...	10.32
e Manufacture of chemicals and chemical petroleum, coal, rubber and plastic products	...	...	12.86	...	...	17.37	...	...	22.82	...	...	24.99
f Manufacture of non-metallic mineral products, except products of petroleum and coal	...	...	4.96	...	...	6.74	...	...	7.41	...	...	8.12
g Basic metal industries	...	...	0.56	...	...	1.71	...	...	1.82	...	...	1.37
h Manufacture of fabricated metal products, machinery and equipment	...	...	16.90	...	...	18.58	...	...	26.36	...	...	25.04
i Other manufacturing industries	...	...	1.51	...	...	1.41	...	...	1.81	...	...	1.93
4 Electricity, gas and water	...	...	13.93	...	...	14.50	...	...	15.71	...	...	19.98
a Electricity, gas and steam	...	...	5.76	...	...	6.20	...	...	6.78	...	...	8.24
b Water works and supply	...	...	8.17	...	...	8.30	...	...	8.93	...	...	11.74
5 Construction	...	...	46.51	...	...	51.08	...	...	56.02	...	...	63.65
6 Wholesale and retail trade, restaurants and hotels	...	...	66.18	...	...	71.75	...	...	97.91	...	...	114.88
a Wholesale and retail trade	...	...	53.04	...	...	56.83	...	...	80.73	...	...	94.98
b Restaurants and hotels	...	...	13.14	...	...	14.92	...	...	17.18	...	...	19.90
7 Transport, storage and communication	...	...	38.21	...	...	44.16	...	...	53.73	...	...	60.25
a Transport and storage	...	...	...	...	...	44.16	...	...	53.73	...	...	60.25
b Communication	...	...	...	...	...		...	...		...	...	
8 Finance, insurance, real estate and business services	...	...	82.51	...	...	94.40	...	...	114.24	...	...	132.56
a Financial institutions	...	...	...	...	...		...	...		...	...	
b Insurance	...	...	...	...	...	94.40	...	...	114.24	...	...	132.56
c Real estate and business services	...	...	...	...	...		...	...		...	...	
Real estate, except dwellings	...	...	...	...	...		...	...		...	...	
Dwellings	...	...	...	...	...	...	...	...	...	...	...	...
9 Community, social and personal services	...	...	16.25	...	...	19.36	...	...	20.76	...	...	23.33
a Sanitary and similar services	...	...	...	...	...		...	...		...	...	
b Social and related community services	...	...	...	...	...	19.36	...	...	20.76	...	...	23.33
c Recreational and cultural services	...	...	...	...	...		...	...		...	...	
d Personal and household services	...	...	...	...	...		...	...		...	...	
Total, Industries	...	...	586.16	...	...	674.05	...	...	812.98	...	...	906.45
Producers of Government Services	...	...	110.56	...	...	120.59	...	...	136.71	...	...	162.07
Other Producers	...	...	5.12	...	...	6.15	...	...	7.27	...	...	8.86
Total	...	...	701.84	...	...	800.79	...	...	956.96	...	...	1077.38
Imputed bank service charge	...	...	-13.05	...	...	-11.31	...	...	-18.12	...	...	-20.37
Import duties	...	...	29.40	...	...	35.05	...	...	46.57	...	...	47.37
Value added tax	...	...	...	...	...	...	...	...	...	...	...	...
Other adjustments	...	...	34.36	...	...	53.80	...	...	75.26	...	...	92.30
Total	...	...	752.55	...	...	878.33	...	...	1060.67	...	...	1196.68

Kenya

4.3 Derivation of Value Added by Kind of Activity, ISIC Divisions, in Current Prices

Million Kenyan pounds

	1976 Gross Output	1976 Intermediate Consumption	1976 Value Added	1977 Gross Output	1977 Intermediate Consumption	1977 Value Added	1978 Gross Output	1978 Intermediate Consumption	1978 Value Added	1979 Gross Output	1979 Intermediate Consumption	1979 Value Added
						All Producers						
1 Agriculture, hunting, forestry and fishing	...	...	484.44	...	...	688.29	...	...	657.23	...	...	678.85
a Agriculture and hunting	...	...	466.15	...	...	668.01	...	...	631.73	...	...	648.78
b Forestry and logging	...	...	15.64	...	...	17.66	...	...	21.55	...	...	25.91
c Fishing	...	...	2.65	...	...	2.62	...	...	3.95	...	...	4.16
2 Mining and quarrying	...	...	3.41	...	...	4.17	...	...	4.41	...	...	5.04
a Coal mining	...	...	...	...	...	...	...	...	...	...	...	...
b Crude petroleum and natural gas production	...	...	...	...	...	...	...	...	...	...	...	...
c Metal ore mining	...	...	...	...	...	...	...	...	...	...	...	...
d Other mining	...	...	...	...	...	...	...	...	...	...	...	...
3 Manufacturing	...	...	144.18	...	...	179.94	...	...	219.32	...	...	249.84
a Manufacture of food, beverages and tobacco	...	...	...	...	...	...	...	...	...	...	...	...
b Textile, wearing apparel and leather industries	...	...	...	...	...	...	...	...	...	...	...	...
c Manufacture of wood and wood products, including furniture	...	...	...	...	...	...	...	...	...	...	...	...
d Manufacture of paper and paper products, printing and publishing	...	...	...	...	...	...	...	...	...	...	...	...
e Manufacture of chemicals and chemical petroleum, coal, rubber and plastic products	...	...	...	...	...	...	...	...	...	...	...	...
f Manufacture of non-metallic mineral products, except products of petroleum and coal	...	...	...	...	...	...	...	...	...	...	...	...
g Basic metal industries	...	...	...	...	...	...	...	...	...	...	...	...
h Manufacture of fabricated metal products, machinery and equipment	...	...	...	...	...	...	...	...	...	...	...	...
i Other manufacturing industries	...	...	...	...	...	...	...	...	...	...	...	...
4 Electricity, gas and water	...	...	23.10	...	...	31.07	...	...	35.71	...	...	41.61
a Electricity, gas and steam	...	...	7.85	...	...	13.40	...	...	16.16	...	...	20.04
b Water works and supply	...	...	15.25	...	...	17.67	...	...	19.55	...	...	21.57
5 Construction	...	...	67.08	...	...	79.93	...	...	97.88	...	...	119.45
6 Wholesale and retail trade, restaurants and hotels	...	...	132.54	...	...	164.63	...	...	189.34	...	...	214.07
a Wholesale and retail trade	...	...	105.21	...	...	130.12	...	...	155.90	...	...	178.99
b Restaurants and hotels	...	...	27.33	...	...	34.51	...	...	33.44	...	...	35.08
7 Transport, storage and communication	...	...	69.15	...	...	78.62	...	...	100.84	...	...	114.65
a Transport and storage	...	...	...	...	...	...	...	...	...	...	...	...
b Communication	...	...	...	...	...	...	...	...	...	...	...	...
8 Finance, insurance, real estate and business services	...	...	155.45	...	...	186.16	...	...	217.80	...	...	247.51
a Financial institutions	...	...	...	...	...	...	...	...	...	...	...	...
b Insurance	...	...	...	...	...	...	...	...	...	...	...	...
c Real estate and business services	...	...	...	...	...	...	...	...	...	...	...	...
Real estate, except dwellings	...	...	...	...	...	...	...	...	...	...	...	...
Dwellings	...	...	...	...	...	...	...	...	...	...	...	...
9 Community, social and personal services	...	...	27.00	...	...	30.80	...	...	35.46	...	...	39.59
a Sanitary and similar services	...	...	...	...	...	...	...	...	...	...	...	...
b Social and related community services	...	...	...	...	...	...	...	...	...	...	...	...
c Recreational and cultural services	...	...	...	...	...	...	...	...	...	...	...	...
d Personal and household services	...	...	...	...	...	...	...	...	...	...	...	...
Total, Industries	...	...	1106.35	...	...	1443.61	...	...	1558.00	...	...	1710.61
Producers of Government Services	...	...	184.70	...	...	215.40	...	...	250.66	...	...	289.26

Kenya

4.3 Derivation of Value Added by Kind of Activity, ISIC Divisions, in Current Prices
(Continued)

Million Kenyan pounds

	1976 Gross Output	1976 Intermediate Consumption	1976 Value Added	1977 Gross Output	1977 Intermediate Consumption	1977 Value Added	1978 Gross Output	1978 Intermediate Consumption	1978 Value Added	1979 Gross Output	1979 Intermediate Consumption	1979 Value Added
Other Producers	...	...	10.93	...	...	13.44	...	...	17.06	...	...	21.72
Total	...	...	1301.98	...	...	1672.45	...	...	1825.71	...	...	2021.59
Imputed bank service charge	...	...	-23.88	...	...	-31.80	...	...	-37.31	...	...	-41.97
Import duties	...	...	66.47	...	...	81.84	...	...	106.42	...	...	90.30
Value added tax	...	...	...	...	...	...	...	...	...	...	...	...
Other adjustments	...	...	109.03	...	...	137.39	...	...	163.36	...	...	206.67
Total	...	...	1453.60	...	...	1859.88	...	...	2058.19	...	...	2276.60

	1980 Gross Output	1980 Intermediate Consumption	1980 Value Added
			All Producers
1 Agriculture, hunting, forestry and fishing	...	...	722.84
a Agriculture and hunting	...	...	688.13
b Forestry and logging	...	...	30.33
c Fishing	...	...	4.38
2 Mining and quarrying	...	...	5.73
a Coal mining	...	...	...
b Crude petroleum and natural gas production	...	...	...
c Metal ore mining	...	...	...
d Other mining	...	...	...
3 Manufacturing	...	...	295.14
a Manufacture of food, beverages and tobacco	...	...	...
b Textile, wearing apparel and leather industries	...	...	...
c Manufacture of wood and wood products, including furniture	...	...	...
d Manufacture of paper and paper products, printing and publishing	...	...	...
e Manufacture of chemicals and chemical petroleum, coal, rubber and plastic products	...	...	...
f Manufacture of non-metallic mineral products, except products of petroleum and coal	...	...	...
g Basic metal industries	...	...	...
h Manufacture of fabricated metal products, machinery and equipment	...	...	...
i Other manufacturing industries	...	...	...
4 Electricity, gas and water	...	...	47.35
a Electricity, gas and steam	...	...	23.85
b Water works and supply	...	...	23.50
5 Construction	...	...	135.86
6 Wholesale and retail trade, restaurants and hotels	...	...	252.07
a Wholesale and retail trade	...	...	211.92
b Restaurants and hotels	...	...	40.15
7 Transport, storage and communication	...	...	128.63
a Transport and storage	...	...	...
b Communication	...	...	...
8 Finance, insurance, real estate and business services	...	...	277.47
a Financial institutions	...	...	...
b Insurance	...	...	...
c Real estate and business services	...	...	...
Real estate, except dwellings	...	...	...

Kenya

4.3 Derivation of Value Added by Kind of Activity, ISIC Divisions, in Current Prices
(Continued)

Million Kenyan pounds

	1980 Gross Output	1980 Intermediate Consumption	1980 Value Added
Dwellings	...	...	...
9 Community, social and personal services	...	...	47.07
a Sanitary and similar services	...	...	...
b Social and related community services	...	...	...
c Recreational and cultural services	...	...	...
d Personal and household services	...	...	...
Total, Industries	...	...	1912.16
Producers of Government Services	...	...	326.13
Other Producers	...	...	28.13
Total	...	...	2266.42
Imputed bank service charge	...	...	-45.54
Import duties	...	...	120.97
Value added tax	...	...	...
Other adjustments	...	...	252.31
Total	...	...	2594.16

4.4 Derivation of Value Added by Kind of Activity, ISIC Divisions, in Constant Prices

Million Kenyan pounds

At constant prices of: 1976 — All Producers

	1972 Gross Output	1972 Interm. Cons.	1972 Value Added	1973 Gross Output	1973 Interm. Cons.	1973 Value Added	1974 Gross Output	1974 Interm. Cons.	1974 Value Added	1975 Gross Output	1975 Interm. Cons.	1975 Value Added
1 Agriculture, hunting, forestry and fishing	...	...	441.83	...	...	453.86	...	...	459.61	...	...	475.38
a Agriculture and hunting	...	...	426.04	...	...	437.38	...	...	442.19	...	...	458.38
b Forestry and logging	...	...	13.25	...	...	14.14	...	...	15.28	...	...	14.87
c Fishing	...	...	2.54	...	...	2.34	...	...	2.14	...	...	2.13
2 Mining and quarrying	...	...	2.23	...	...	2.98	...	...	2.74	...	...	3.11
3 Manufacturing	...	...	120.97	...	...	137.69	...	...	144.90	...	...	145.77
4 Electricity, gas and water	...	...	18.99	...	...	19.17	...	...	20.22	...	...	21.55
a Electricity, gas and steam	...	...	5.10	...	...	5.58	...	...	6.18	...	...	6.95
b Water works and supply	...	...	13.89	...	...	13.59	...	...	14.04	...	...	14.60
5 Construction	...	...	74.41	...	...	74.98	...	...	69.83	...	...	68.40
6 Wholesale and retail trade, restaurants and hotels	...	...	143.14	...	...	137.36	...	...	141.53	...	...	136.21
a Wholesale and retail trade	...	...	121.82	...	...	114.41	...	...	117.88	...	...	110.31
b Restaurants and hotels	...	...	21.32	...	...	22.95	...	...	23.65	...	...	25.90
7 Transport, storage and communication	...	...	58.80	...	...	65.31	...	...	64.52	...	...	62.59
8 Finance, insurance, real estate and business services	...	...	125.64	...	...	128.57	...	...	140.46	...	...	147.71
9 Community, social and personal services	...	...	23.60	...	...	24.37	...	...	25.38	...	...	26.29
Total, Industries	...	...	1009.61	...	...	1044.29	...	...	1069.19	...	...	1087.01
Producers of Government Services	...	...	142.45	...	...	151.47	...	...	161.83	...	...	175.67
Other Producers	...	...	6.57	...	...	7.30	...	...	8.28	...	...	9.52
Total	...	...	1158.63	...	...	1203.06	...	...	1239.30	...	...	1272.20
Imputed bank service charge	...	...	-21.42	...	...	-16.91	...	...	-23.15	...	...	-24.09
Import duties	...	...	84.42	...	...	81.76	...	...	91.73	...	...	69.13
Value added tax	...	...	...	...	...	...	...	...	...	...	...	...
Other adjustments	...	...	57.53	...	...	87.79	...	...	102.80	...	...	106.69
Total	...	...	1279.16	...	...	1355.70	...	...	1410.86	...	...	1423.56

Kenya

4.4 Derivation of Value Added by Kind of Activity, ISIC Divisions, in Constant Prices

Million Kenyan pounds

	1976 Gross Output	1976 Intermediate Consumption	1976 Value Added	1977 Gross Output	1977 Intermediate Consumption	1977 Value Added	1978 Gross Output	1978 Intermediate Consumption	1978 Value Added	1979 Gross Output	1979 Intermediate Consumption	1979 Value Added
At constant prices of: 1976												
All Producers												
1 Agriculture, hunting, forestry and fishing	...	...	484.44	...	...	532.86	...	...	553.38	...	...	549.78
a Agriculture and hunting	...	...	466.15	...	...	513.60	...	...	533.31	...	...	529.05
b Forestry and logging	...	...	15.64	...	...	16.60	...	...	16.98	...	...	17.49
c Fishing	...	...	2.65	...	...	2.66	...	...	3.09	...	...	3.24
2 Mining and quarrying	...	...	3.41	...	...	4.05	...	...	4.14	...	...	4.08
3 Manufacturing	...	...	144.18	...	...	167.10	...	...	188.16	...	...	201.56
4 Electricity, gas and water	...	...	23.10	...	...	25.83	...	...	27.38	...	...	29.20
a Electricity, gas and steam	...	...	7.85	...	...	8.74	...	...	10.12	...	...	11.49
b Water works and supply	...	...	15.25	...	...	17.09	...	...	17.26	...	...	17.71
5 Construction	...	...	67.08	...	...	72.05	...	...	78.58	...	...	83.70
6 Wholesale and retail trade, restaurants and hotels	...	...	132.54	...	...	143.59	...	...	155.92	...	...	165.37
a Wholesale and retail trade	...	...	105.21	...	...	113.90	...	...	124.73	...	...	133.48
b Restaurants and hotels	...	...	27.33	...	...	29.69	...	...	31.19	...	...	31.89
7 Transport, storage and communication	...	...	69.15	...	...	73.74	...	...	81.40	...	...	87.26
8 Finance, insurance, real estate and business services	...	...	155.45	...	...	163.05	...	...	171.94	...	...	185.05
9 Community, social and personal services	...	...	26.99	...	...	28.69	...	...	30.46	...	...	32.86
Total, Industries	...	...	1106.35	...	...	1210.96	...	...	1291.36	...	...	1338.86
Producers of Government Services	...	...	184.71	...	...	194.05	...	...	206.43	...	...	221.09
Other Producers	...	...	10.93	...	...	12.04	...	...	13.91	...	...	16.39
Total	...	...	1301.98	...	...	1417.05	...	...	1511.70	...	...	1576.34
Imputed bank service charge	...	...	-23.88	...	...	-26.79	...	...	-28.76	...	...	-31.60
Import duties	...	...	66.47	...	...	81.10	...	...	94.39	...	...	77.11
Value added tax	...	...	...	...	...	...	...	...	...	...	...	...
Other adjustments	...	...	109.03	...	...	120.30	...	...	130.31	...	...	151.26
Total	...	...	1453.60	...	...	1590.94	...	...	1707.64	...	...	1773.10

	1980 Gross Output	1980 Intermediate Consumption	1980 Value Added
At constant prices of: 1976			
All Producers			
1 Agriculture, hunting, forestry and fishing	...	...	543.10
a Agriculture and hunting	...	...	522.03
b Forestry and logging	...	...	18.20
c Fishing	...	...	2.87
2 Mining and quarrying	...	...	4.05
3 Manufacturing	...	...	210.79
4 Electricity, gas and water	...	...	30.92
a Electricity, gas and steam	...	...	12.49
b Water works and supply	...	...	18.43
5 Construction	...	...	85.00
6 Wholesale and retail trade, restaurants and hotels	...	...	168.38
a Wholesale and retail trade	...	...	133.64
b Restaurants and hotels	...	...	34.74
7 Transport, storage and communication	...	...	93.46
8 Finance, insurance, real estate and business services	...	...	190.41
9 Community, social and personal services	...	...	35.06
Total, Industries	...	...	1361.17
Producers of Government Services	...	...	232.81

Kenya

4.4 Derivation of Value Added by Kind of Activity, ISIC Divisions, in Constant Prices
(Continued)

Million Kenyan pounds

	1980 Gross Output	Intermediate Consumption	Value Added	
				At constant prices of: 1976
Other Producers	...	...	19.28	
Total	...	...	1613.26	
Imputed bank service charge	...	...	-31.24	
Import duties	...	...	88.41	
Value added tax	...	...	...	
Other adjustments	...	...	160.20	
Total	...	...	1830.13	

4.6 Cost Components of Value Added, ISIC Divisions

Million Kenyan pounds

	1970 Compensation of Employees	Capital Consumption	Net Operating Surplus	Indirect Taxes	Less: Subsidies Received	Value Added	1971 Compensation of Employees	Capital Consumption	Net Operating Surplus	Indirect Taxes	Less: Subsidies Received	Value Added
				All Producers								
1 Agriculture, hunting, forestry and fishing	24.80	...	147.95	...	...	172.77	26.42	...	152.46	...	...	178.87
a Agriculture and hunting	22.74	...	141.52	...	...	164.26	24.02	...	145.18	...	...	169.19
b Forestry and logging	1.76	...	5.41	...	...	7.17	2.04	...	6.27	...	...	8.31
c Fishing	0.30	...	1.02	...	...	1.33	0.36	...	1.01	...	...	1.37
2 Mining and quarrying	1.20	...	1.21	...	...	2.41	1.37	...	1.56	...	...	2.93
a Coal mining	...	...	...	...	...	-	...	...	...	...	...	-
b Crude petroleum and natural gas production	...	...	...	...	...	0.44	...	...	...	...	...	0.45
c Metal ore mining	...	...	...	...	...	0.05	...	...	...	...	...	0.12
d Other mining	...	...	...	...	...	1.92	...	...	...	...	...	2.36
3 Manufacturing	31.95	...	30.21	...	...	62.16	35.88	...	35.79	...	...	71.68
a Manufacture of food, beverages and tobacco	8.08	...	8.64	...	...	16.72	8.36	...	9.05	...	...	17.41
b Textile, wearing apparel and leather industries	3.40	...	2.49	...	...	5.89	4.19	...	2.82	...	...	7.01
c Manufacture of wood and wood products, including furniture	2.01	...	0.79	...	...	2.80	2.26	...	1.63	...	...	3.89
d Manufacture of paper and paper products, printing and publishing	2.97	...	1.57	...	...	4.54	3.52	...	1.39	...	...	4.91
e Manufacture of chemicals and chemical petroleum, coal, rubber and plastic products	2.47	...	4.75	...	...	7.22	3.06	...	7.27	...	...	10.33
f Manufacture of non-metallic mineral products, except products of petroleum and coal	1.24	...	2.90	...	...	4.14	1.53	...	3.16	...	...	4.69
g Basic metal industries	11.07	...	8.04	...	...	19.11	12.16	...	9.38	...	...	21.54
h Manufacture of fabricated metal products, machinery and equipment		...		...	...			...		...	...	
i Other manufacturing industries	0.70	...	1.04	...	...	1.74	0.80	...	1.10	...	...	1.90
4 Electricity, gas and water	2.25	...	9.71	...	...	11.96	2.29	...	10.39	...	...	12.68
a Electricity, gas and steam	2.25	...	9.71	...	...	11.96	2.29	...	10.39	...	...	12.68
b Water works and supply		...		...	...			...		...	...	
5 Construction	23.49	...	2.90	...	...	26.39	25.43	...	3.43	...	...	28.86
6 Wholesale and retail trade, restaurants and hotels	22.58	...	26.09	...	...	48.67	21.57	...	29.59	...	...	51.16
a Wholesale and retail trade	22.58	...	26.09	...	...	48.67	21.57	...	29.59	...	...	51.16
b Restaurants and hotels		...		...	...	...		...		...	...	...
7 Transport, storage and communication	25.77	...	15.07	...	...	40.84	28.46	...	15.04	...	...	43.50

Kenya

4.6 Cost Components of Value Added, ISIC Divisions
(Continued)

Million Kenyan pounds

	1970						1971					
	Compensation of Employees	Capital Consumption	Net Operating Surplus	Indirect Taxes	Less: Subsidies Received	Value Added	Compensation of Employees	Capital Consumption	Net Operating Surplus	Indirect Taxes	Less: Subsidies Received	Value Added
a Transport and storage	25.77	...	15.07	...	...	40.84	28.46	...	15.04	...	...	43.50
b Communication		...		...	...			...		...	...	
8 Finance, insurance, real estate and business services	10.46	...	42.59	...	...	53.04	11.85	...	47.53	...	...	59.37
a Financial institutions		...		...	...			...		...	...	
b Insurance	10.46	...	42.59	...	...	53.04	11.85	...	47.53	...	...	59.37
c Real estate and business services		...		...	...			...		...	...	
9 Community, social and personal services	13.74	...	6.34	...	...	20.08	14.79	...	6.89	...	...	21.68
a Sanitary and similar services	...	...	...	...	...	...	...	...	...	...	...	...
b Social and related community services		...		...	...			...		...	...	
c Recreational and cultural services	13.75	...	6.34	...	...	20.09	14.79	...	6.87	...	...	21.68
d Personal and household services		...		...	...			...		...	...	
Total, Industries	156.24	...	282.08	...	...	438.32	168.06	...	302.67	...	...	470.73
Producers of Government Services	76.48	...	-	...	...	76.48	94.49	...	-	...	...	94.49
Other Producers	4.14	...	-	...	...	4.14	4.84	...	-	...	...	4.84
Total	236.86	...	282.08	...	...	518.94	267.39	...	302.67	...	...	570.06
Imputed bank service charge	...	...	...	...	...	...	...	...	...	...	...	...
Import duties	...	...	...	28.58	...	28.58	...	...	...	35.23	...	35.23
Value added tax	...	...	...	...	...	...	...	...	...	...	...	...
Other adjustments	...	...	...	25.14	...	25.14	...	...	...	29.14	...	29.85
Total	236.86	...	282.08	53.72	...	572.66	267.39	...	302.67	64.37	...	635.14

	1972						1973					
	Compensation of Employees	Capital Consumption	Net Operating Surplus	Indirect Taxes	Less: Subsidies Received	Value Added	Compensation of Employees	Capital Consumption	Net Operating Surplus	Indirect Taxes	Less: Subsidies Received	Value Added

All Producers

1 Agriculture, hunting, forestry and fishing	37.69	...	204.73	...	...	242.42	40.04	...	239.94	...	...	279.98
a Agriculture and hunting	34.52	...	198.11	...	...	232.63	36.52	...	232.48	...	...	269.00
b Forestry and logging	2.83	...	5.55	...	...	8.38	3.16	...	6.32	...	...	9.48
c Fishing	0.34	...	1.07	...	...	1.41	0.36	...	1.14	...	...	1.50
2 Mining and quarrying	1.24	...	0.99	...	...	2.22	1.41	...	1.79	...	...	3.20
a Coal mining	...	...	...	...	...	-	...	...	...	...	...	-
b Crude petroleum and natural gas production	...	...	...	...	...	0.03	...	...	...	...	...	-
c Metal ore mining	...	...	...	...	...	0.26	...	...	...	...	...	0.13
d Other mining	...	...	...	...	...	1.94	...	...	...	...	...	3.08
3 Manufacturing	38.49	...	39.44	...	...	77.93	42.82	...	52.80	...	...	95.62
a Manufacture of food, beverages and tobacco	9.50	...	12.46	...	...	21.96	10.72	...	15.22	...	...	25.94
b Textile, wearing apparel and leather industries	4.69	...	4.79	...	...	9.48	5.39	...	5.63	...	...	11.02
c Manufacture of wood and wood products, including furniture	2.59	...	1.31	...	...	3.90	2.82	...	1.69	...	...	4.51
d Manufacture of paper and paper products, printing and publishing	3.84	...	1.97	...	...	5.81	4.43	...	2.88	...	...	7.31
e Manufacture of chemicals and chemical petroleum, coal, rubber and plastic products	4.56	...	8.30	...	...	12.86	5.21	...	12.16	...	...	17.37
f Manufacture of non-metallic mineral products, except products of petroleum and coal	1.80	...	3.16	...	...	4.96	2.11	...	4.63	...	...	6.74
g Basic metal industries	10.95	...	6.50	...	...	17.46	11.62	...	9.70	...	...	21.32
h Manufacture of fabricated metal products, machinery and equipment		...		...	...			...		...	...	
i Other manufacturing industries	0.56	...	0.95	...	...	1.51	0.52	...	0.89	...	...	1.41
4 Electricity, gas and water	2.17	...	11.76	...	...	13.93	2.08	...	12.41	...	...	14.50
a Electricity, gas and steam	...	...	...	...	...	5.76	...	...	...	...	...	6.20
b Water works and supply	...	...	...	...	...	8.17	...	...	...	...	...	8.30

Kenya

4.6 Cost Components of Value Added, ISIC Divisions
(Continued)

Million Kenyan pounds

	1972						1973					
	Compensation of Employees	Capital Consumption	Net Operating Surplus	Indirect Taxes	Less: Subsidies Received	Value Added	Compensation of Employees	Capital Consumption	Net Operating Surplus	Indirect Taxes	Less: Subsidies Received	Value Added
5 Construction	29.61	...	16.90	...	...	46.51	30.15	...	20.93	...	...	51.08
6 Wholesale and retail trade, restaurants and hotels	30.01	...	36.18	...	...	66.18	32.37	...	39.38	...	...	71.75
a Wholesale and retail trade	...	...	...	...	...	53.04	...	...	...	...	...	56.83
b Restaurants and hotels	...	...	...	...	...	13.14	...	...	...	...	...	14.92
7 Transport, storage and communication	26.99	...	11.22	...	...	38.21	30.73	...	13.43	...	...	44.16
a Transport and storage	...	...	...	...	...	...	...	...	...	...	...	...
b Communication	...	...	...	...	...	...	...	...	...	...	...	...
8 Finance, insurance, real estate and business services	17.08	...	65.42	...	...	82.51	17.55	...	76.85	...	...	94.40
a Financial institutions	...	...	...	...	...	...	...	...	...	...	...	...
b Insurance	...	...	...	...	...	...	...	...	...	...	...	...
c Real estate and business services	...	...	...	...	...	...	...	...	...	...	...	...
9 Community, social and personal services	11.54	...	4.71	...	...	16.25	12.69	...	6.67	...	...	19.36
a Sanitary and similar services	...	...	...	...	...	...	...	...	...	...	...	...
b Social and related community services	...	...	...	...	...	...	...	...	...	...	...	...
c Recreational and cultural services	...	...	...	...	...	...	...	...	...	...	...	...
d Personal and household services	...	...	...	...	...	...	...	...	...	...	...	...
Total, Industries	194.82	...	391.35	...	...	586.16	209.84	...	464.20	...	...	674.05
Producers of Government Services	109.91	...	0.66	...	...	110.56	119.92	...	0.67	...	...	120.59
Other Producers	5.12	...	-	...	...	5.12	6.15	...	-	...	...	6.15
Total	309.85	...	392.01	...	...	701.84	335.91	...	464.87	...	...	800.79
Imputed bank service charge	...	...	-13.05	...	...	-13.05	...	...	-11.31	...	...	-11.31
Import duties	...	...	...	29.40	...	29.40	...	...	...	35.05	...	35.05
Value added tax	...	...	...	...	...	...	...	...	...	...	...	...
Other adjustments	...	...	...	34.36	...	34.36	...	...	...	53.80	...	53.80
Total	309.85	...	378.93	63.76	...	752.55	335.91	...	453.54	88.85	...	878.33

	1974						1975					
	Compensation of Employees	Capital Consumption	Net Operating Surplus	Indirect Taxes	Less: Subsidies Received	Value Added	Compensation of Employees	Capital Consumption	Net Operating Surplus	Indirect Taxes	Less: Subsidies Received	Value Added

All Producers

1 Agriculture, hunting, forestry and fishing	40.76	...	291.22	...	...	331.99	47.07	...	314.31	...	...	361.38
a Agriculture and hunting	36.58	...	282.79	...	...	319.37	41.76	...	304.54	...	...	346.30
b Forestry and logging	3.78	...	7.20	...	...	10.99	4.90	...	8.33	...	...	13.23
c Fishing	0.40	...	1.23	...	...	1.63	0.41	...	1.44	...	...	1.85
2 Mining and quarrying	1.64	...	1.57	...	...	3.20	1.92	...	1.50	...	...	3.42
a Coal mining	...	...	...	...	...	-	...	...	...	...	...	-
b Crude petroleum and natural gas production	...	...	...	...	...	-	...	...	...	...	...	0.01
c Metal ore mining	...	...	...	...	...	...	...	...	...	...	...	0.12
d Other mining	...	...	...	...	...	3.14	...	...	...	...	...	3.19

Kenya

4.6 Cost Components of Value Added, ISIC Divisions
(Continued)

Million Kenyan pounds

	\multicolumn{6}{c	}{1974}	\multicolumn{6}{c}{1975}
	Compensation of Employees	Capital Consumption	Net Operating Surplus	Indirect Taxes	Less: Subsidies Received	Value Added	Compensation of Employees	Capital Consumption	Net Operating Surplus	Indirect Taxes	Less: Subsidies Received	Value Added
3 Manufacturing	53.89	...	65.54	...	...	119.42	57.25	...	69.75	...	...	127.00
a Manufacture of food, beverages and tobacco	13.52	...	16.81	...	...	30.33	15.38	...	21.17	...	...	36.55
b Textile, wearing apparel and leather industries	6.54	...	5.46	...	...	12.00	7.14	...	6.16	...	...	13.30
c Manufacture of wood and wood products, including furniture	3.44	...	2.08	...	...	5.52	3.50	...	2.01	...	...	5.51
d Manufacture of paper and paper products, printing and publishing	6.53	...	4.47	...	...	11.00	5.78	...	4.54	...	...	10.32
e Manufacture of chemicals and chemical petroleum, coal, rubber and plastic products	6.85	...	15.97	...	...	22.82	7.54	...	17.45	...	...	24.99
f Manufacture of non-metallic mineral products, except products of petroleum and coal	2.99	...	4.42	...	...	7.41	2.92	...	5.20	...	...	8.12
g Basic metal industries	13.33	...	15.21	...	...	28.18	14.03	...	12.25	...	...	26.41
h Manufacture of fabricated metal products, machinery and equipment		...		...	...			...		...	...	
i Other manufacturing industries	0.69	...	1.12	...	...	1.81	0.96	...	0.97	...	...	1.93
4 Electricity, gas and water	2.62	...	13.09	...	...	15.71	4.83	...	15.15	...	...	19.98
a Electricity, gas and steam	...	...	...	...	...	6.78	...	...	...	...	...	8.24
b Water works and supply	...	...	...	...	...	8.93	...	...	...	...	...	11.74
5 Construction	32.22	...	23.80	...	...	56.02	35.68	...	27.97	...	...	63.65
6 Wholesale and retail trade, restaurants and hotels	43.67	...	54.24	...	...	97.91	51.33	...	63.55	...	...	114.88
a Wholesale and retail trade	...	...	...	...	...	80.73	...	...	...	...	...	94.98
b Restaurants and hotels	...	...	...	...	...	17.18	...	...	...	...	...	19.90
7 Transport, storage and communication	33.30	...	20.43	...	...	53.73	36.54	...	23.71	...	...	60.25
a Transport and storage	...	...	...	...	...	...	...	...	...	...	...	...
b Communication	...	...	...	...	...	...	...	...	...	...	...	...
8 Finance, insurance, real estate and business services	20.70	...	93.55	...	...	114.24	26.21	...	106.35	...	...	132.56
a Financial institutions	...	...	...	...	...	...	...	...	...	...	...	...
b Insurance	...	...	...	...	...	...	...	...	...	...	...	...
c Real estate and business services	...	...	...	...	...	...	...	...	...	...	...	...
9 Community, social and personal services	14.71	...	6.05	...	...	20.76	16.69	...	6.65	...	...	23.33
a Sanitary and similar services	...	...	...	...	...	...	...	...	...	...	...	...
b Social and related community services	...	...	...	...	...	...	...	...	...	...	...	...
c Recreational and cultural services	...	...	...	...	...	...	...	...	...	...	...	...
d Personal and household services	...	...	...	...	...	...	...	...	...	...	...	...
Total, Industries	243.51	...	569.49	...	...	812.98	277.52	...	628.94	...	...	906.45
Producers of Government Services	135.80	...	0.90	...	...	136.71	160.71	...	1.35	...	...	162.07
Other Producers	7.27	...	-	...	...	7.27	8.86	...	-	...	...	8.86
Total	386.58	...	570.39	...	...	956.96	447.09	...	630.29	...	...	1077.38
Imputed bank service charge	...	...	-18.12	...	...	-18.12	...	...	-20.37	...	...	-20.37
Import duties	...	...	...	46.57	...	46.57	...	...	...	47.37	...	47.37
Value added tax	...	...	...	...	...	...	...	...	...	...	...	...
Other adjustments	...	...	...	75.26	...	75.26	...	...	...	92.30	...	92.30
Total	386.58	...	552.26	121.83	...	1060.67	447.09	...	609.92	139.67	...	1196.68

	\multicolumn{6}{c	}{1976}	\multicolumn{6}{c}{1977}
	Compensation of Employees	Capital Consumption	Net Operating Surplus	Indirect Taxes	Less: Subsidies Received	Value Added	Compensation of Employees	Capital Consumption	Net Operating Surplus	Indirect Taxes	Less: Subsidies Received	Value Added
\multicolumn{13}{c}{All Producers}
1 Agriculture, hunting, forestry and fishing	59.46	...	424.97	...	...	484.44	60.69	...	627.61	...	...	688.29
a Agriculture and hunting	53.23	...	412.92	...	...	466.15	53.70	...	614.31	...	...	668.01
b Forestry and logging	5.58	...	10.05	...	...	15.64	6.35	...	11.32	...	...	17.66
c Fishing	0.65	...	2.00	...	...	2.65	0.64	...	1.98	...	...	2.62

Kenya

4.6 Cost Components of Value Added, ISIC Divisions
(Continued)

Million Kenyan pounds

		1976					1977					
	Compensation of Employees	Capital Consumption	Net Operating Surplus	Indirect Taxes	Less: Subsidies Received	Value Added	Compensation of Employees	Capital Consumption	Net Operating Surplus	Indirect Taxes	Less: Subsidies Received	Value Added
2 Mining and quarrying	1.86	...	1.55	...	...	3.41	2.27	...	1.90	...	...	4.17
a Coal mining	...	...	...	...	...	...	...	...	...	...	...	...
b Crude petroleum and natural gas production	...	...	...	...	...	...	...	...	...	...	...	...
c Metal ore mining	...	...	...	...	...	...	...	...	...	...	...	...
d Other mining	...	...	...	...	...	...	...	...	...	...	...	...
3 Manufacturing	59.48	...	84.69	...	...	144.18	79.76	...	100.19	...	...	179.94
a Manufacture of food, beverages and tobacco	...	...	...	...	...	...	...	...	...	...	...	...
b Textile, wearing apparel and leather industries	...	...	...	...	...	...	...	...	...	...	...	...
c Manufacture of wood and wood products, including furniture	...	...	...	...	...	...	...	...	...	...	...	...
d Manufacture of paper and paper products, printing and publishing	...	...	...	...	...	...	...	...	...	...	...	...
e Manufacture of chemicals and chemical petroleum, coal, rubber and plastic products	...	...	...	...	...	...	...	...	...	...	...	...
f Manufacture of non-metallic mineral products, except products of petroleum and coal	...	...	...	...	...	...	...	...	...	...	...	...
g Basic metal industries	...	...	...	...	...	...	...	...	...	...	...	...
h Manufacture of fabricated metal products, machinery and equipment	...	...	...	...	...	...	...	...	...	...	...	...
i Other manufacturing industries	...	...	...	...	...	...	...	...	...	...	...	...
4 Electricity, gas and water	5.23	...	17.87	...	...	23.10	6.39	...	24.69	...	...	31.07
a Electricity, gas and steam	...	...	...	...	...	7.85	...	...	...	...	...	13.40
b Water works and supply	...	...	...	...	...	15.25	...	...	...	...	...	17.67
5 Construction	38.41	...	28.67	...	...	67.08	43.54	...	36.40	...	...	79.93
6 Wholesale and retail trade, restaurants and hotels	58.69	...	73.84	...	...	132.54	70.53	...	94.10	...	...	164.63
a Wholesale and retail trade	...	...	...	...	...	105.21	...	...	...	...	...	130.12
b Restaurants and hotels	...	...	...	...	...	27.33	...	...	...	...	...	34.51
7 Transport, storage and communication	41.20	...	27.95	...	...	69.15	46.96	...	31.66	...	...	78.62
a Transport and storage	...	...	...	...	...	...	...	...	...	...	...	...
b Communication	...	...	...	...	...	...	...	...	...	...	...	...
8 Finance, insurance, real estate and business services	32.07	...	123.37	...	...	155.45	36.72	...	149.45	...	...	186.16
a Financial institutions	...	...	...	...	...	...	...	...	...	...	...	...
b Insurance	...	...	...	...	...	...	...	...	...	...	...	...
c Real estate and business services	...	...	...	...	...	...	...	...	...	...	...	...
9 Community, social and personal services	19.02	...	7.99	...	...	27.00	22.16	...	8.64	...	...	30.80
a Sanitary and similar services	...	...	...	...	...	...	...	...	...	...	...	...
b Social and related community services	...	...	...	...	...	...	...	...	...	...	...	...
c Recreational and cultural services	...	...	...	...	...	...	...	...	...	...	...	...
d Personal and household services	...	...	...	...	...	...	...	...	...	...	...	...
Total, Industries	315.42	...	790.90	...	...	1106.35	369.02	...	1074.64	...	...	1443.61
Producers of Government Services	182.79	...	1.91	...	...	184.70	211.83	...	3.58	...	...	215.40
Other Producers	10.93	...	-	...	...	10.93	13.44	...	-	...	...	13.44
Total	509.14	...	792.81	...	...	1301.98	594.29	...	1078.22	...	...	1672.45
Imputed bank service charge	...	...	-23.88	...	...	-23.88	...	...	-31.80	...	...	-31.80
Import duties	...	...	...	66.47	...	66.47	...	...	...	81.84	...	81.84
Value added tax	...	...	...	...	...	...	...	...	...	...	...	...
Other adjustments	...	...	...	109.03	...	109.03	...	...	...	137.39	...	137.39
Total	509.14	...	768.96	175.50	...	1453.60	594.29	...	1046.36	219.23	...	1859.88

Kenya

4.6 Cost Components of Value Added, ISIC Divisions

Million Kenyan pounds

	1978 Compensation of Employees	1978 Capital Consumption	1978 Net Operating Surplus	1978 Indirect Taxes	1978 Less: Subsidies Received	1978 Value Added	1979 Compensation of Employees	1979 Capital Consumption	1979 Net Operating Surplus	1979 Indirect Taxes	1979 Less: Subsidies Received	1979 Value Added
All Producers												
1 Agriculture, hunting, forestry and fishing	69.75	...	587.48	...	...	657.23	77.78	...	601.08	...	...	678.85
a Agriculture and hunting	61.32	...	570.41	...	...	631.73	67.59	...	581.19	...	...	648.78
b Forestry and logging	7.55	...	14.00	...	...	21.55	9.26	...	16.65	...	...	25.91
c Fishing	0.88	...	3.07	...	...	3.95	0.97	...	3.24	...	...	4.16
2 Mining and quarrying	2.40	...	2.01	...	...	4.41	2.74	...	2.29	...	...	5.04
a Coal mining	...	...	...	...	...	...	...	...	...	...	...	...
b Crude petroleum and natural gas production	...	...	...	...	...	...	...	...	...	...	...	...
c Metal ore mining	...	...	...	...	...	...	...	...	...	...	...	...
d Other mining	...	...	...	...	...	...	...	...	...	...	...	...
3 Manufacturing	91.94	...	127.38	...	...	219.32	103.54	...	146.30	...	...	249.84
a Manufacture of food, beverages and tobacco	...	...	...	...	...	...	...	...	...	...	...	...
b Textile, wearing apparel and leather industries	...	...	...	...	...	...	...	...	...	...	...	...
c Manufacture of wood and wood products, including furniture	...	...	...	...	...	...	...	...	...	...	...	...
d Manufacture of paper and paper products, printing and publishing	...	...	...	...	...	...	...	...	...	...	...	...
e Manufacture of chemicals and chemical petroleum, coal, rubber and plastic products	...	...	...	...	...	...	...	...	...	...	...	...
f Manufacture of non-metallic mineral products, except products of petroleum and coal	...	...	...	...	...	...	...	...	...	...	...	...
g Basic metal industries	...	...	...	...	...	...	...	...	...	...	...	...
h Manufacture of fabricated metal products, machinery and equipment	...	...	...	...	...	...	...	...	...	...	...	...
i Other manufacturing industries	...	...	...	...	...	...	...	...	...	...	...	...
4 Electricity, gas and water	6.67	...	29.04	...	...	35.71	10.45	...	31.17	...	...	41.61
a Electricity, gas and steam	...	...	...	...	...	16.16	...	...	...	...	...	20.04
b Water works and supply	...	...	...	...	...	19.55	...	...	...	...	...	21.57
5 Construction	53.95	...	43.93	...	...	97.88	65.62	...	53.83	...	...	119.45
6 Wholesale and retail trade, restaurants and hotels	81.80	...	107.53	...	...	189.34	94.17	...	119.90	...	...	214.07
a Wholesale and retail trade	...	...	...	...	...	155.90	...	...	...	...	...	178.99
b Restaurants and hotels	...	...	...	...	...	33.44	...	...	...	...	...	35.08
7 Transport, storage and communication	56.49	...	44.35	...	...	100.84	65.52	...	49.13	...	...	114.65
a Transport and storage	...	...	...	...	...	...	...	...	...	...	...	...
b Communication	...	...	...	...	...	...	...	...	...	...	...	...
8 Finance, insurance, real estate and business services	42.23	...	175.58	...	...	217.80	47.51	...	200.00	...	...	247.51
a Financial institutions	...	...	...	...	...	...	...	...	...	...	...	...
b Insurance	...	...	...	...	...	...	...	...	...	...	...	...
c Real estate and business services	...	...	...	...	...	...	...	...	...	...	...	...
9 Community, social and personal services	25.11	...	10.35	...	...	35.46	30.29	...	9.31	...	...	39.59
a Sanitary and similar services	...	...	...	...	...	...	...	...	...	...	...	...
b Social and related community services	...	...	...	...	...	...	...	...	...	...	...	...
c Recreational and cultural services	...	...	...	...	...	...	...	...	...	...	...	...
d Personal and household services	...	...	...	...	...	...	...	...	...	...	...	...
Total, Industries	430.34	...	1127.65	...	...	1558.00	497.61	...	1213.01	...	...	1710.61
Producers of Government Services	245.43	...	5.22	...	...	250.66	283.09	...	6.17	...	...	289.26

Kenya

4.6 Cost Components of Value Added, ISIC Divisions
(Continued)

Million Kenyan pounds

	1978						1979					
	Compensation of Employees	Capital Consumption	Net Operating Surplus	Indirect Taxes	Less: Subsidies Received	Value Added	Compensation of Employees	Capital Consumption	Net Operating Surplus	Indirect Taxes	Less: Subsidies Received	Value Added
Other Producers	17.06	...	-	...	...	17.06	21.72	...	-	...	...	21.72
Total	692.83	...	1132.87	...	...	1825.72	802.42	...	1219.18	...	...	2021.59
Imputed bank service charge	...	...	-37.31	...	...	-37.31	...	...	-41.97	...	...	-41.97
Import duties	...	...	...	106.42	...	106.42	...	...	...	90.30	...	90.30
Value added tax	...	...	...	...	...	...	...	...	...	...	...	...
Other adjustments	...	...	...	163.36	...	163.36	...	...	...	206.68	...	206.68
Total	692.83	...	1095.58	269.78	...	2058.19	802.42	...	1177.21	296.98	...	2276.60

	1980					
	Compensation of Employees	Capital Consumption	Net Operating Surplus	Indirect Taxes	Less: Subsidies Received	Value Added

All Producers

	Comp.	Cap.	NOS	IT	Sub	VA
1 Agriculture, hunting, forestry and fishing	89.70	...	633.14	...	...	722.84
a Agriculture and hunting	78.03	...	610.11	...	...	688.13
b Forestry and logging	10.70	...	19.63	...	...	30.33
c Fishing	0.97	...	3.40	...	...	4.38
2 Mining and quarrying	2.71	...	3.02	...	...	5.73
a Coal mining	...	...	...	...	...	...
b Crude petroleum and natural gas production	...	...	...	...	...	...
c Metal ore mining	...	...	...	...	...	...
d Other mining	...	...	...	...	...	...
3 Manufacturing	116.11	...	179.03	...	...	295.14
a Manufacture of food, beverages and tobacco	...	...	...	...	...	...
b Textile, wearing apparel and leather industries	...	...	...	...	...	...
c Manufacture of wood and wood products, including furniture	...	...	...	...	...	...
d Manufacture of paper and paper products, printing and publishing	...	...	...	...	...	...
e Manufacture of chemicals and chemical petroleum, coal, rubber and plastic products	...	...	...	...	...	...
f Manufacture of non-metallic mineral products, except products of petroleum and coal	...	...	...	...	...	...
g Basic metal industries	...	...	...	...	...	...
h Manufacture of fabricated metal products, machinery and equipment	...	...	...	...	...	...
i Other manufacturing industries	...	...	...	...	...	...
4 Electricity, gas and water	13.15	...	34.19	...	...	47.35
a Electricity, gas and steam	...	...	...	...	...	23.85
b Water works and supply	...	...	...	...	...	23.50
5 Construction	75.30	...	60.56	...	...	135.86
6 Wholesale and retail trade, restaurants and hotels	109.87	...	142.20	...	...	252.07
a Wholesale and retail trade	...	...	...	...	...	211.92
b Restaurants and hotels	...	...	...	...	...	40.15
7 Transport, storage and communication	68.61	...	60.02	...	...	128.63
a Transport and storage	...	...	...	...	...	...
b Communication	...	...	...	...	...	...
8 Finance, insurance, real estate and business services	51.55	...	225.92	...	...	277.47
a Financial institutions	...	...	...	...	...	...

Kenya

4.6 Cost Components of Value Added, ISIC Divisions
(Continued)

Million Kenyan pounds

	\multicolumn{6}{c}{1980}
	Compensation of Employees	Capital Consumption	Net Operating Surplus	Indirect Taxes	Less: Subsidies Received	Value Added
b Insurance	...	...	...	...	...	...
c Real estate and business services	...	...	...	...	...	...
9 Community, social and personal services	36.37	...	10.71	...	...	47.07
a Sanitary and similar services	...	...	...	...	...	...
b Social and related community services	...	...	...	...	...	...
c Recreational and cultural services	...	...	...	...	...	...
d Personal and household services	...	...	...	...	...	...
Total, Industries	563.37	...	1348.79	...	...	1912.16
Producers of Government Services	319.03	...	7.10	...	...	326.13
Other Producers	28.13	...	-	...	...	28.13
Total	910.53	...	1355.89	...	...	2266.42
Imputed bank service charge	...	...	-45.54	...	...	-45.54
Import duties	...	...	...	120.97	...	120.97
Value added tax	...	...	...	...	...	...
Other adjustments	...	...	...	252.31	...	252.31
Total	910.53	...	1310.35	373.28	...	2594.16

Kiribati

Source. Reply to the United Nations National Accounts Questionnaire from the Planning Office, Ministry of Finance, Tarawa.

General note. The estimates shown in the following tables have been prepared in accordance with the United Nations System of National Accounts so far as the existing data would permit. It should be noted that the estimates for 1972-1974 include data for Tuvalu (former Ellice Islands).

1.1 Expenditure on the Gross Domestic Product, in Current Prices

Thousand Australian dollars

	1970	1971	1972	1973	1974	1975	1976	1977	1978	1979	1980
1 General government final consumption expenditure	...	...	4720	5677	6238	...	...	...	7700	7900	7600
2 Private final consumption expenditure	...	...	9527	10645	13068	...	...	...	20200	21000	19400
3 Gross capital formation	...	...	1519	2419	2096	...	...	...	8200	8200	9200
a Increase in stocks	...	...	85	562	426	...	...	...	300	...	...
b Gross fixed capital formation	...	...	1434	1857	1670	...	...	...	7900	...	...
4 Exports of goods and services	...	...	6834	12177	24749	...	...	...	21600	22700	4700
5 Less: Imports of goods and services	...	...	6871	8484	9282	...	...	...	18200	21300	20000
Statistical discrepancy	...	...	83	-208	-370	...	...	...	-100	...	...
Equals: Gross Domestic Product	...	...	15812	22226	36499	42077	33641	34943	39400	38500	20900

1.3 Cost Components of the Gross Domestic Product

Thousand Australian dollars

	1970	1971	1972	1973	1974	1975	1976	1977	1978	1979	1980
1 Indirect taxes, net	...	...	692	1166	1684	...	...	...	...	...	...
a Indirect taxes paid	...	...	1266	1909	2601	...	...	...	...	...	...
b Less: Subsidies received	...	...	574	743	917	...	...	...	...	...	...
2 Consumption of fixed capital	...	...	1723	1742	1640	...	...	...	...	...	...
3 Compensation of employees paid by resident producers to:	...	...	8199	9259	10971	...	...	...	...	...	...
a Resident households	...	...	8199	9259	10971	...	...	...	...	...	...
b Rest of the world	...	...	-	-	-	...	...	...	...	...	...
4 Net operating surplus	...	...	5198	10059	22204	...	...	...	...	...	...
a Corporate and quasi-corporate enterprises	...	...	...	...	...	...	...	...	...	...	...
b Private unincorporated enterprises	...	...	2359	3168	3609	...	...	...	...	...	...
c General government	...	...	86	102	117	...	...	...	...	...	...
Equals: Gross Domestic Product	...	...	15812	22226	36499	...	...	...	...	...	...

1.4 General Government Current Receipts and Disbursements

Thousand Australian dollars

	1970	1971	1972	1973	1974	1975	1976	1977	1978	1979	1980
Receipts											
1 Property and entrepreneurial income	...	...	3234	3599	12331	...	...	...	...	...	...
2 Taxes, fees and contributions	...	...	1685	2485	3442	...	...	...	...	...	...
a Indirect taxes	...	...	1266	1909	2601	...	...	...	...	...	...
b Direct taxes	...	...	296	402	468	...	...	...	...	...	...
c Social security contributions	...	...	-	2	-	...	...	...	...	...	...
d Compulsory fees, fines and penalties	...	...	123	172	373	...	...	...	...	...	...
3 Other current receipts	...	...	1728	2027	2643	...	...	...	...	...	...
Total Current Receipts of General Government	...	...	6647	8111	18416	...	...	...	...	...	...
Disbursements											
1 General government final consumption expenditure	...	...	4720	5677	6238	...	...	...	...	...	...
a Compensation of employees	...	...	...	...	...	...	...	...	...	...	...
b Consumption of fixed capital	...	...	352	427	441	...	...	...	...	...	...
c Purchases of goods and services, net	...	...	...	...	...	...	...	...	...	...	...
d Less: Own account production of fixed assets	...	...	...	...	...	...	...	...	...	...	...
e Indirect taxes paid, net	...	...	...	...	...	...	...	...	...	...	...

Kiribati

1.4 General Government Current Receipts and Disbursements
(Continued)

Thousand Australian dollars

	1970	1971	1972	1973	1974	1975	1976	1977	1978	1979	1980
2 Property income paid	...	...	47	78	604	...	...	...	...	...	...
3 Subsidies	...	...	574	743	917	...	...	...	...	...	...
4 Other current transfers paid	...	...	384	455	404	...	...	...	...	...	...
a Social security benefits and social assistance grants	...	...	-	-	-	...	...	...	...	...	...
b Other	...	...	384	455	404	...	...	...	...	...	...
5 Net saving	...	...	922	1158	10253	...	...	...	...	...	...
Total Current Disbursements and Net Saving of General Government	...	...	6647	8111	18416	...	...	...	...	...	...

1.6 Current Income and Outlay of Households and Non-Profit Institutions

Thousand Australian dollars

	1970	1971	1972	1973	1974	1975	1976	1977	1978	1979	1980
					Receipts						
1 Compensation of employees	...	...	8229	9269	10981	...	...	...	...	...	...
a From resident producers	...	...	8199	9259	10971	...	...	...	...	...	...
b From rest of the world	...	...	30	10	10	...	...	...	...	...	...
2 Property and entrepreneurial income received	...	...	2400	3224	3807	...	...	...	...	...	...
3 Current transfers received	...	...	789	859	945	...	...	...	...	...	...
a Social security benefits and social assistance grants received	...	...	-	-	-	...	...	...	...	...	...
b Other	...	...	789	859	945	...	...	...	...	...	...
Total Current Receipts	...	...	11418	13352	15733	...	...	...	...	...	...
					Disbursements						
1 Private final consumption expenditure	...	...	9527	10645	13068	...	...	...	...	...	...
2 Property income paid	...	...	...	...	...	...	...	...	...	...	...
3 Direct taxes and other payments n.e.c. to general government	...	...	377	518	785	...	...	...	...	...	...
a Social security contributions	...	...	-	2	-	...	...	...	...	...	...
b Direct taxes	...	...	254	346	412	...	...	...	...	...	...
c Fees, fines and penalties	...	...	123	172	373	...	...	...	...	...	...
4 Other current transfers paid	...	...	1713	1706	1737	...	...	...	...	...	...
Statistical discrepancy	...	...	-147	-199	-196	...	...	...	...	...	...
5 Net saving	...	...	-53	679	337	...	...	...	...	...	...
Total Current Disbursements and Net Saving	...	...	11418	13352	15733	...	...	...	...	...	...

1.7 External Transactions on Current Account, Summary

Thousand Australian dollars

	1970	1971	1972	1973	1974	1975	1976	1977	1978	1979	1980
					Payments to the Rest of the World						
1 Imports of goods and services	...	...	6871	8484	9282	...	...	...	...	...	...
2 Factor income paid to the rest of the world	...	...	717	703	2096	...	...	...	...	...	...
a Compensation of employees	...	...	-	-	-	...	...	...	...	...	...
b Property and entrepreneurial income paid	...	...	717	703	2096	...	...	...	...	...	...
3 Indirect taxes paid to supranational organizations	...	...	...	...	...	...	...	...	...	...	...
4 Current transfers to the rest of the world	...	...	1626	1628	1677	...	...	...	...	...	...
5 Surplus of the nation on current transactions	...	...	544	4766	16023	...	...	...	...	...	...
Payments to the Rest of the World and Surplus of the Nation on Current Transactions	...	...	9758	15581	29078	...	...	...	...	...	...

Kiribati

1.7 External Transactions on Current Account, Summary
(Continued)

Thousand Australian dollars

	1970	1971	1972	1973	1974	1975	1976	1977	1978	1979	1980
Receipts From The Rest of the World
1 Exports of goods and services	...	...	6834	12177	24749	...	...	...	...	...	...
2 Factor income received from rest of the world	...	...	498	540	776	...	...	...	...	...	...
a Compensation of employees	...	...	30	10	10	...	...	...	...	...	...
b Property and entrepreneurial income received	...	...	468	530	766	...	...	...	...	...	...
3 Subsidies received from supranational organisations	...	...	...	...	...	...	...	...	...	...	...
4 Current transfers from rest of the world	...	...	2426	2864	3553	...	...	...	...	...	...
Receipts from the Rest of the World on Current Transactions	...	...	9758	15581	29078	...	...	...	...	...	...

1.8 Capital Transactions of The Nation, Summary

Thousand Australian dollars

	1970	1971	1972	1973	1974	1975	1976	1977	1978	1979	1980
Finance of Gross Capital Formation
Gross saving	...	...	2146	6977	17749	...	...	...	...	...	...
1 Consumption of fixed capital	...	...	1723	1742	1640	...	...	...	...	...	...
a General government	...	...	352	427	441	...	...	...	...	...	...
b Corporate and quasi-corporate enterprises	...	...	1346	1268	1157	...	...	...	...	...	...
c Other	...	...	25	47	42	...	...	...	...	...	...
2 Net saving	...	...	423	5235	16109	...	...	...	...	...	...
a General government	...	...	922	1158	10253	...	...	...	...	...	...
b Corporate and quasi-corporate enterprises	...	...	-673	3093	5295	...	...	...	...	...	...
c Other	...	...	174	984	561	...	...	...	...	...	...
Less: Surplus of the nation on current transactions	...	...	544	4766	16023	...	...	...	...	...	...
Statistical discrepancy	...	...	-83	208	370	...	...	...	...	...	...
Finance of Gross Capital Formation	...	...	1519	2419	2096	...	...	...	...	...	...
Gross Capital Formation
Increase in stocks	...	...	85	562	426	...	...	...	...	...	...
Gross fixed capital formation	...	...	1434	1857	1670	...	...	...	...	...	...
Gross Capital Formation	...	...	1519	2419	2096	...	...	...	...	...	...

1.10 Gross Domestic Product by Kind of Activity, in Current Prices

Thousand Australian dollars

	1970	1971	1972	1973	1974	1975	1976	1977	1978	1979	1980
1 Agriculture, hunting, forestry and fishing	...	...	2054	2853	3310	...	...	...	7300	...	...
2 Mining and quarrying	...	...	5739	8984	18797	...	...	...	16800	...	...
3 Manufacturing	...	...				...	...	...	700	...	...
4 Electricity, gas and water	...	...	229	189	301	...	...	...	600	...	...
5 Construction	...	...	590	636	437	...	...	...	3100	...	...
6 Wholesale and retail trade, restaurants and hotels	...	...	1568	2317	4618	...	...	...	2400	...	...
7 Transport, storage and communication	...	...	252	534	1213	...	...	...	1000	...	...
8 Finance, insurance, real estate and business services	...	...	281	354	272	...	...	...	600	...	...
9 Community, social and personal services [a]	...	...	2244	3109	3840	...	...	...	4700	...	...
Total, Industries	...	...	12957	18976	32788	...	...	...	37100	...	...
Producers of Government Services	...	...	...	...	...	...	...	...	...	...	...
Other Producers	...	...	...	...	...	...	...	...	...	...	...

Kiribati

1.10 Gross Domestic Product by Kind of Activity, in Current Prices
(Continued)

Thousand Australian dollars

	1970	1971	1972	1973	1974	1975	1976	1977	1978	1979	1980
Subtotal [b]	...	...	12957	18976	32788	...	...	...	... 37100	...	...
Less: Imputed bank service charge	...	...	59	17	.	...	...	...	...	...	...
Plus: Import duties	...	...	1157	1363	1389	...	...	...	...	...	...
Plus: Value added tax	...	...	...	...	...	...	...	...	...	...	...
Plus: Other adjustments [cd]	...	...	1757	1904	2322	...	...	...	... 2300	...	...
Equals: Gross Domestic Product	...	...	15812	22226	36499	...	...	...	... 39400	...	...
Memorandum Item: Mineral fuels and power	...	...	12957	18976	32788	...	...	...	...	...	...

a) Including public services n.e.c. and 'Other producers'.
b) Second series, gross domestic product in factor values.
c) First series, relating to compensation of employees received in kind.
d) Second series, relating to indirect taxes net of subsidies.

1.12 Relations Among National Accounting Aggregates

Thousand Australian dollars

	1970	1971	1972	1973	1974	1975	1976	1977	1978	1979	1980
Gross Domestic Product	...	...	15812	22226	36499	...	...	...	...	...	...
Plus: Net factor income received from abroad	...	...	-219	-163	-1320	...	...	...	...	...	...
Factor income received	...	...	498	540	776	...	...	...	...	...	...
Less: Factor income paid	...	...	717	703	2096	...	...	...	...	...	...
Equals: Gross National Product	...	...	15593	22063	35179	...	...	...	...	...	...
Less: Consumption of fixed capital	...	...	1723	1742	1640	...	...	...	...	...	...
Less: Net indirect taxes paid to supranational organisations	...	...	...	...	...	...	...	...	...	...	...
Equals: National Income at Market Prices	...	...	13870	20321	33539	...	...	...	...	...	...
Plus: Net current transfers received from abroad	...	...	800	1236	1876	...	...	...	...	...	...
Current transfers received	...	...	2426	2864	3553	...	...	...	...	...	...
Less: Current transfers paid	...	...	1626	1628	1677	...	...	...	...	...	...
Equals: National Disposable Income at Market Prices	...	...	14670	21557	35415	...	...	...	...	...	...
Less: Final consumption	...	...	14247	16322	19306	...	...	...	...	...	...
Statistical discrepancy	...	...	-83	208	370	...	...	...	...	...	...
Equals: Net Saving	...	...	423	5235	16109	...	...	...	...	...	...
Less: Surplus of the nation on current transactions	...	...	544	4766	16023	...	...	...	...	...	...
Equals: Net Capital Formation	...	...	-204	677	456	...	...	...	...	...	...

2.1 General Government Final Consumption Expenditure by Function, in Current Prices

Thousand Australian dollars

		1970	1971	1972	1973	1974	1975	1976	1977	1978	1979	1980
1	General public services	...	...	1104	1405	1312	...	...	...	...	...	...
2	Defence	...	...	...	...	...	...	...	...	...	...	...
3	Public order and safety	...	...	...	...	...	...	...	...	...	...	...
4	Education	...	...	720	749	892	...	...	...	...	...	...
5	Health	...	...	488	624	624	...	...	...	...	...	...
6	Social security and welfare	...	...	18	15	20	...	...	...	...	...	...
7	Housing and community amenities	...	...	...	...	...	...	...	...	...	...	...
8	Recreational, cultural and religious affairs [a]	...	...	40	273	271	...	...	...	...	...	...
9	Economic services	...	...	...	...	...	...	...	...	...	...	...
	a Fuel and energy	...	...				...	...	...	...	...	...
	b Agriculture, forestry, fishing and hunting	...	...				...	...	...	...	...	...
	c Mining, manufacturing and construction, except fuel and energy	...	...	768	1005	1178	...	...	...	...	...	...
	d Transportation and communication	...	...				...	...	...	...	...	...
	e Other economic affairs	...	...				...	...	...	...	...	...
10	Other functions [b]	...	...	1582	1606	1941	...	...	...	...	...	...
	Total General Government Final Consumption Expenditure	...	...	4720	5677	6238	...	...	...	...	...	...

a) Relating to disasters and other calamities
b) Relating to value of goods and services received in kind.

Kiribati

2.5 Private Final Consumption Expenditure by Type, in Current Prices

Thousand Australian dollars

	1970	1971	1972	1973	1974	1975	1976	1977	1978	1979	1980
Final Consumption Expenditure of Resident Households											
1 Food, beverages and tobacco	...	...	6127	6663	8247	...	...	...	...	...	...
2 Clothing and footwear	...	...	423	456	722	...	...	...	...	...	...
3 Gross rent, fuel and power	...	...	803	944	1125	...	...	...	...	...	...
4 Furniture, furnishings and household equipment and operation	...	...	1518	1880	2256	...	...	...	...	...	...
5 Medical care and health expenses	...	...	6	5	9	...	...	...	...	...	...
6 Transport and communication	...	...	536	600	560	...	...	...	...	...	...
7 Recreational, entertainment, education and cultural services	...	...	180	189	282	...	...	...	...	...	...
a Education	...	...	146	132	163	...	...	...	...	...	...
b Other	...	...	35	57	119	...	...	...	...	...	...
8 Miscellaneous goods and services	...	...	29	32	37	...	...	...	...	...	...
Total Final Consumption Expenditure in the Domestic Market by Households, of which	...	...	9622	10769	13238	...	...	...	...	...	...
Plus: Direct purchases abroad by resident households	...	...	...	...	...	...	...	...	...	...	...
Less: Direct purchases in the domestic market by non-resident households	...	...	95	124	170	...	...	...	...	...	...
Equals: Final Consumption Expenditure of Resident Households	...	...	9527	10645	13068	...	...	...	...	...	...
Final Consumption Expenditure of Private Non-profit Institutions Serving Households											
Equals: Final Consumption Expenditure of Private Non-profit Organisations Serving Households	...	...	...	...	...	...	...	...	...	...	...
Private Final Consumption Expenditure	...	...	9527	10645	13068	...	...	...	...	...	...

2.17 Exports and Imports of Goods and Services, Detail

Thousand Australian dollars

	1970	1971	1972	1973	1974	1975	1976	1977	1978	1979	1980
Exports of Goods and Services											
1 Exports of merchandise, f.o.b.	...	...	6600	11692	23736	...	...	...	...	...	...
2 Transport and communication	...	...	118	230	155	...	...	...	...	...	...
a In respect of merchandise imports	...	...	118	230	155	...	...	...	...	...	...
b Other	...	...	-	-	-	...	...	...	...	...	...
3 Insurance service charges	...	...	...	...	...	...	...	...	...	...	...
4 Other commodities	...	...	21	131	688	...	...	...	...	...	...
5 Adjustments of merchandise exports to change-of-ownership basis	...	...	...	...	...	...	...	...	...	...	...
6 Direct purchases in the domestic market by non-residential households	...	...	95	124	170	...	...	...	...	...	...
7 Direct purchases in the domestic market by extraterritorial bodies	...	...	...	...	...	...	...	...	...	...	...
Total Exports of Goods and Services	...	...	6834	12177	24749	...	...	...	...	...	...
Imports of Goods and Services											
1 Imports of merchandise, c.i.f.	...	...	6227	7842	8678	...	...	...	...	...	...
a Imports of merchandise, f.o.b.	...	...	5415	6819	7546	...	...	...	...	...	...
b Transport of services on merchandise imports	...	...	812	1023	1132	...	...	...	...	...	...
By residents	...	...	118	230	155	...	...	...	...	...	...

Kiribati

2.17 Exports and Imports of Goods and Services, Detail
(Continued)

Thousand Australian dollars

	1970	1971	1972	1973	1974	1975	1976	1977	1978	1979	1980
By non-residents	...	...	694	793	977	...	...	...	...	...	
c Insurance service charges on merchandise imports	...	...	...	...	...	...	...	...	...	...	
2 Adjustments of merchandise imports to change-of-ownership basis	...	...	-	-	-	...	...	...	...	...	
3 Other transport and communication	...	...	470	490	460	...	...	...	...	...	
4 Other insurance service charges	...	...	...	...	...	...	...	...	...	...	
5 Other commodities	...	...	50	70	100	...	...	...	...	...	
6 Direct purchases abroad by government	...	...	124	82	44	...	...	...	...	...	
7 Direct purchases abroad by resident households	...	...				...	...	...	...	...	
Total Imports of Goods and Services	...	...	6871	8484	9282	...	...	...	...	...	
Balance of Goods and Services	...	...	-37	3693	15467	...	...	...	...	...	
Total Imports and Balance of Goods and Services	...	...	6834	12177	24749	...	...	...	...	...	

3.12 General Government Income and Outlay Account: Total and Subsectors

Thousand Australian dollars

	1972					1973				
	Total General Government	Central Government	State or Provincial Government	Local Government	Social Security Funds	Total General Government	Central Government	State or Provincial Government	Local Government	Social Security Funds

Receipts

1 Property and entrepreneurial income	3234	3234	...	...	...	3599	3594	...	...	...
a Net operating surplus	86	86	...	...	...	102	102	...	...	...
b Withdrawals from public quasi-corporations	...	-	...	...	...	...	-	...	...	...
c Interest	...	...	...	...	...	...	...	...	...	...
d Dividends	...	...	...	...	...	...	...	...	...	...
e Net land rent and royalties	...	...	...	...	...	...	...	...	...	...
2 Taxes, fees and contributions	1685	1572	...	...	...	2485	2304	...	...	...
a Indirect taxes	1266	1227	...	...	...	1909	1851	...	...	...
b Direct taxes	296	236	...	...	...	402	301	...	...	...
Income	266	236	...	...	...	359	301	...	...	...
Other	30	-	...	...	...	43	-	...	...	...
c Social security contributions	-	-	...	...	...	2	-	...	...	...
d Fees, fines and penalties	123	108	...	...	...	172	150	...	...	...
3 Other current transfers received	1728	1721	...	...	...	2027	2024	...	...	...
a Casualty insurance claims	-	-	...	...	...	-	-	...	...	...
b Transfers from other government subsectors	...	...	...	...	...	...	...	...	...	...
c Transfers from abroad	1715	1715	...	...	...	2015	2015	...	...	...
d Other transfers, except imputed	13	6	...	...	...	12	9	...	...	...
e Imputed unfunded employee welfare contributions	...	...	...	...	...	...	...	...	...	...
Total Current Receipts	6647	6527	...	...	...	8111	7922	...	...	...

Disbursements

1 General governement final consumption expenditures	4720	4615	...	...	...	5677	5555	...	...	...
a Compensation of employees	...	...	...	...	...	...	...	...	...	...
b Consumption of fixed capital	352	352	...	...	...	427	427	...	...	...
c Goods and services purchased, net	...	...	...	...	...	...	...	...	...	...
d Less: Own account production of fixed assets	...	...	...	...	...	...	...	...	...	...
e Indirect taxes paid, net	...	...	...	...	...	...	...	...	...	...
2 Property income paid	47	44	...	...	...	78	75	...	...	...

Kiribati

3.12 General Government Income and Outlay Account: Total and Subsectors
(Continued)

Thousand Australian dollars

	1972					1973				
	Total General Government	Central Government	State or Provincial Government	Local Government	Social Security Funds	Total General Government	Central Government	State or Provincial Government	Local Government	Social Security Funds
3 Subsidies	574	574	...	...	...	743	743	...	...	...
4 Other current transfers paid	384	463	...	...	...	455	511	...	...	...
a Casualty insurance premiums, net	·	·	...	...	...	·	·	...	...	...
b Transfers to other government subsectors	...	79	...	...	...	...	56	...	...	...
c Transfers to households	283	283	...	...	...	289	289	...	...	...
Social security benefits	·	·	...	...	...	·	·	...	...	...
Social assistance grants	1	1	...	...	...	1	1	...	...	...
Unfunded employee welfare benefits	282	282	...	...	...	288	288	...	...	...
d Transfers to private non-profit institutions serving households	86	86	...	...	...	150	150	...	...	...
e Transfers to the rest of the world	15	15	...	...	...	16	16	...	...	...
Net saving	922	831	...	...	...	1158	1038	...	...	...
Total Current Disbursements and Net Saving	6647	6527	...	...	...	8111	7922	...	...	...

	1974				
	Total General Government	Central Government	State or Provincial Government	Local Government	Social Security Funds

Receipts

1 Property and entrepreneurial income	12331	12329	...	...	...
a Net operating surplus	117	117	...	...	...
b Withdrawals from public quasi-corporations	...	·	...	...	...
c Interest	...	...	...	...	...
d Dividends	...	...	...	...	...
e Net land rent and royalties	...	...	...	...	...
2 Taxes, fees and contributions	3442	3244	...	...	...
a Indirect taxes	2601	2537	...	...	...
b Direct taxes	468	353	...	...	...
Income	418	353	...	...	...
Other	50	·	...	...	...
c Social security contributions	·	·	...	...	...
d Fees, fines and penalties	373	354	...	...	...
3 Other current transfers received	2643	2643	...	...	...
a Casualty insurance claims	·	·	...	...	...
b Transfers from other government subsectors	...	...	...	...	...
c Transfers from abroad	2643	2643	...	...	...
d Other transfers, except imputed	·	·	...	...	...
e Imputed unfunded employee welfare contributions	...	...	...	...	...
Total Current Receipts	18416	18216	...	...	...

Disbursements

1 General government final consumption expenditures	6238	6095	...	...	...
a Compensation of employees	...	...	...	...	...
b Consumption of fixed capital	441	441	...	...	...
c Goods and services purchased, net	...	...	...	...	...
d Less: Own account production of fixed assets	...	...	...	...	...
e Indirect taxes paid, net	...	...	...	...	...
2 Property income paid	604	600	...	...	...

Kiribati

3.12 General Government Income and Outlay Account: Total and Subsectors
(Continued)

Thousand Australian dollars

	Total General Government	Central Government	State or Provincial Government	Local Government	Social Security Funds
			1974		
3 Subsidies	917	917	...	...	...
4 Other current transfers paid	404	448	...	...	...
a Casualty insurance premiums, net	2	-	...	...	...
b Transfers to other government subsectors	...	46	...	...	...
c Transfers to households	285	285	...	...	...
Social security benefits	-	-	...	...	...
Social assistance grants	-	-	...	...	...
Unfunded employee welfare benefits	285	285	...	...	...
d Transfers to private non-profit institutions serving households	90	90	...	...	...
e Transfers to the rest of the world	27	27	...	...	...
Net saving	10253	10156	...	...	...
Total Current Disbursements and Net Saving	18416	18216	...	...	...

3.13 General Government Capital Accumulation Account: Total and Subsectors

Thousand Australian dollars

	\multicolumn{5}{c}{1972}	\multicolumn{5}{c}{1973}
	Total General Government	Central Government	State or Provincial Government	Local Government	Social Security Funds	Total General Government	Central Government	State or Provincial Government	Local Government	Social Security Funds

Finance of Gross Accumulation

1 Gross saving	1274	1183	...	...	...	1585	1465	...	...	...
a Consumption of fixed capital	352	352	...	...	...	427	427	...	...	...
b Net saving	922	831	...	...	...	1158	1038	...	...	...
2 Capital transfers received a	1556	1460	...	...	...	1458	1394	...	...	...
a From other government subsectors	...	...	...	...	...	...	...	...	...	...
b From other resident sectors	-299	-395	...	...	...	-505	-569	...	...	...
c From rest of the world	1855	1855	...	...	...	1963	1963	...	...	...
Finance of Gross Accumulation	2830	2643	...	...	...	3043	2859	...	...	...

Gross Accumulation

1 Gross capital formation	1195	1132	...	...	...	1500	1357	...	...	...
2 Purchases of land, net	-	-	...	...	...	-	-	...	...	...
3 Purchases of intangible assets, net	...	-	...	...	...	...	...	...	...	...
4 Capital transfers paid	...	...	...	...	...	...	...	...	...	...
Net lending	1635	1511	...	...	...	1543	1502	...	...	...
Gross Accumulation	2830	2643	...	...	...	3043	2859	...	...	...

	\multicolumn{5}{c}{1974}
	Total General Government	Central Government	State or Provincial Government	Local Government	Social Security Funds

Finance of Gross Accumulation

1 Gross saving	10694	10597	...	...	...
a Consumption of fixed capital	441	441	...	...	...
b Net saving	10253	10156	...	...	...
2 Capital transfers received a	1484	1352	...	...	...
a From other government subsectors	...	...	...	...	...
b From other resident sectors	-427	-559	...	...	...
c From rest of the world	1911	1911	...	...	...
Finance of Gross Accumulation	12178	11949	...	...	...

Gross Accumulation

1 Gross capital formation	1260	1066	...	...	...
2 Purchases of land, net	-	-	...	...	...
3 Purchases of intangible assets, net	...	-	...	...	...
4 Capital transfers paid	...	...	...	...	...
Net lending	10918	10883	...	...	...
Gross Accumulation	12178	11949	...	...	...

a) Net.

Kiribati

3.51 External Transactions: Current Account: Detail

Thousand Australian dollars

	1970	1971	1972	1973	1974	1975	1976	1977	1978	1979	1980
Payments to the Rest of the World
1 Imports of goods and services	...	...	6871	8484	9282	...	...	...	...	...	...
2 Factor income paid to the rest of the world	...	...	717	703	2096	...	...	...	...	...	...
a Compensation of employees	...	...	.	.	.	...	...	...	...	...	...
b Property and entrepreneurial income paid	...	...	717	703	2096	...	...	...	...	...	...
3 Indirect taxes paid to supranational organizations	...	...	...	...	...	...	...	...	...	...	...
4 Other current transfers to the rest of the world	...	...	1626	1628	1677	...	...	...	...	...	...
a By general government	...	...	15	16	27	...	...	...	...	...	...
b By other resident sectors	...	...	1611	1612	1650	...	...	...	...	...	...
5 Surplus of the nation on current transactions	...	...	544	4766	16023	...	...	...	...	...	...
Payments to the Rest of the World, and Surplus of the Nation on Current Transfers	...	...	9758	15581	29078	...	...	...	...	...	...
Receipts From The Rest of the World
1 Exports of goods and services	...	...	6834	12177	24749	...	...	...	...	...	...
2 Factor income received from the rest of the world	...	...	...	...	...	...	...	...	...	...	...
a Compensation of employees	...	...	30	10	10	...	...	...	...	...	...
b Property and entrepreneurial income received	...	...	468	530	766	...	...	...	...	...	...
3 Subsidies received from supranational organizations	...	...	...	...	...	...	...	...	...	...	...
4 Other current transfers from the rest of the world	...	...	2426	2864	3553	...	...	...	...	...	...
a To general government	...	...	1715	2015	2643	...	...	...	...	...	...
b To other resident sectors	...	...	711	849	910	...	...	...	...	...	...
Receipts from the Rest of the World on Current Transfers	...	...	9758	15581	29078	...	...	...	...	...	...

Korea, Republic of

General note. The preparation of national accounts statistics in the Republic of Korea is undertaken by the Statistics Department of the Bank of Korea, Seoul. The official estimates and methodological notes on sources and methods are published annually by the Bank in 'National Income Statistics Yearbook'. The following presentation is based mainly on information contained in 'National Accounts in Developing Countries in Asia' issued by the Development Centre of the Organization for Economic Co-operation and Development in 1972. The estimates are generally in accordance with the classifications and definitions recommended in the United Nations System of National Accounts (SNA). Input-output tables have been compiled and published by the Bank. The following tables have been prepared from successive replies to the United Nations national accounts questionnaire. When the scope and coverage differ for conceptual or statistical reasons from the definitions and classifications recommended in SNA, a footnote is indicated to the relevant tables.

Sources and methods:

(a) Gross domestic product. Gross domestic product is estimated mainly through the production approach.

(b) Expenditure on the gross domestic product. All items of GDP by expenditure type are estimated through the expenditure approach except part of private final consumption expenditure and the purchases of producers' durable equipment which are estimated through the commodity-flow approach. The estimates of government consumption expenditure are derived from government fiscal data. Expenditure on all consumer goods, except food grain, is estimated by the commodity-flow method using industry's production data, export and import data, changes in stocks and input-output tables. Adjustment are made for net expenditure abroad by residents. For food grain, consumption per household or per head is multiplied by the total number of household or population. Changes in stocks of grain, livestock and imported raw materials are estimated by deducting total domestic demand from total domestic supply, valued at average prices. For mining and manufacturing products, estimates are based on the ratio of change in stocks to total production, this ratio is applied to the value of output by subgroups. Investment in the government sector is derived from government accounts. For the private sector, estimates of investment in construction are derived from output data adding incidental costs and excluding repair cost and construction for defence. Estimates for durable equipment are based on production data, import and exports and changes in stocks. Estimates for exports and imports of goods and services are based on balance-of-payments statements. For the constant price estimates, price deflation is used for government consumption expenditure, net expenditure abroad by resident and exports and imports of goods and services. Private expenditure on food grain is extrapolated by the index of consumption while other expenditure are based on constant value of production, imports and exports and increase in stocks. This latter source and method is also used for estimating producers' durable equipment. For increase in stocks of mineral and manufactured goods, the constant output value is multiplied by the rate of inventory change while for agricultural products and imported raw materials, the method is the same as the one used to estimate these items at current market prices.

(c) Cost-structure of the gross domestic product. The cost-structure estimates of GDP are compiled by aggregating the value added at factor cost of each industry, making adjustments for net indirect taxes which are obtained from taxation statistics.

(d) Gross domestic product by kind of economic activity. The table of GDP by kind of economic activity is prepared at market prices, i.e., producers' values. The production approach is used to estimate the value added of most industries. The income approach is used for electricity, gas and water, part of transport and communication and part of other services. The value of output of agriculture is obtained by multiplying the quantities produced by the corresponding prices, the data of which are supplied by the National Agricultural Co-operative Federation. The financial data contained in the 'Yearbook of Agriculture and Forestry Statistics' are used to obtain the value added of agricultural services. The value added of forestry is obtained by multiplying the value of production by the value- added ratio calculated from the input-output tables. For fisheries, the current value of output is obtained from fishing and marine statistics while the constant price value of intermediate inputs, extrapolated by the index of tonnage of fishing boats, is revalued at current prices by using the appropriate price indexes. Value added of the mining and manufacturing sectors is estimated by applying the value-added ratio to current value of output. Value-added ratio of subsectors are calculated from the input-output table and the Financial Statement Analysis of Enterprises. For mining, output is estimated by multiplying quantities produced by unit prices collected from wholesale price, export unit value and representative producers' prices while quantity data are obtained from the mineral production statistics. For manufacturing, output is obtained by inflating the constant-price of output by a weighted price index while quantity data are obtained from industrial production and shipment index statistics. Value added of electricity, gas and water is derived from the financial data of concerned enterprises. Value added of the construction sector is obtained by multiplying the construction value of each sector by a corresponding value-added ratio. The construction unit cost and value added ratio are specially calculated by using the base-year composition of input to total construction value. The construction value is estimated by multiplying total floor area by construction unit cost for the private sector and for the public sector, derived from fiscal data. Value added of the trade sector is estimated by multiplying total mark-up by the value-added ratio calculated from the input-output table. For restaurants and hotels, value-added in the base-year is extrapolated by volume indicators and re-valued at current prices. Value added of railway and air transportation and communication is derived directly from the respective financial data while for other transportation and storage, the gross earnings in the base-year are extrapolated by a quantity index and then revalued by appropriate price indexes. The value-added of financing and insurance and real-estate is obtained from financial data and taxation data, respectively. For business services, value added is estimated by extrapolating the base-year estimate. The government executed budget is used to estimate the contribution of public administration and defence to GDP. For the private services, estimates are calculated by multiplying the constant price estimate by appropriate price index, using such sources as Statistical Yearbook of Education and Yearbook of Public Health and Social Statistics. For the constant price estimates, double deflation is used for agriculture and fishing. Current estimates of agriculture services, government construction, financial institutions and insurance and government services are deflated by appropriate price indexes. For the remaining sectors of the economic activity, value added in the base-year is extrapolated by quantity indicators.

1.1 Expenditure on the Gross Domestic Product, in Current Prices

Thousand Million Korean won

	1970	1971	1972	1973	1974	1975	1976	1977	1978	1979	1980
1 General government final consumption expenditure	279.7	352.8	438.7	481.4	744.1	1024.7	1498.8	1988.6	2634.5	3237.2	4446.8
2 Private final consumption expenditure	1939.1	2435.9	2957.1	3523.4	5086.6	6944.8	8711.6	10754.4	14238.7	18106.5	23042.6
3 Gross capital formation	719.1	831.4	873.8	1341.0	2274.4	2881.9	3378.2	4645.0	7137.8	10293.5	10812.6
a Increase in stocks	65.0	89.0	45.3	85.4	403.8	337.9	225.8	224.1	114.7	835.3	-427.4
b Gross fixed capital formation	654.1	742.4	828.5	1255.6	1870.6	2544.0	3152.4	4420.9	7023.1	9458.2	11240.0
Residential buildings	89.7	106.3	110.1	173.6	328.1	445.0	453.6	723.3	1363.1	1615.2	1811.1
Non-residential buildings	141.0	144.7	153.1	279.7	333.4	455.6	596.7	801.3	1211.8	1732.5	2341.1
Other construction and land improvement etc.	189.8	183.0	191.0	241.4	318.4	461.4	690.2	988.0	1366.2	2162.4	2931.4
Other	233.5	308.5	374.4	560.9	890.8	1182.0	1411.8	1908.4	3082.0	3948.1	4156.5
4 Exports of goods and services	381.7	516.9	819.1	1577.7	2071.2	2748.4	4358.5	5966.8	7714.8	8806.6	12945.2
5 Less: Imports of goods and services	643.2	866.6	1015.1	1739.6	2916.4	3612.6	4595.1	5967.4	8355.6	10745.3	15385.9
Statistical discrepancy	-4.3	28.0	-29.2	91.4	138.3	-35.5	4.6	-264.7	-339.9	-343.4	-480.8
Equals: Gross Domestic Product	2672.1	3298.3	4044.4	5275.3	7398.1	9951.7	13356.5	17122.7	23030.3	29357.1	35380.5

1.2 Expenditure on the Gross Domestic Product, in Constant Prices

Thousand Million Korean won

	1970	1971	1972	1973	1974	1975	1976	1977	1978	1979	1980
	At constant prices of: 1975											
1 General government final consumption expenditure	710.2	784.6	821.8	847.8	968.7	1024.7	1134.4	1262.3	1454.7	1446.6	1474.2
2 Private final consumption expenditure	4757.4	5258.6	5574.0	6090.6	6535.4	6944.8	7534.1	8024.1	8854.0	9624.5	9491.5
3 Gross capital formation	1787.2	1955.0	1780.2	2280.3	2805.1	2881.9	3112.4	3860.0	5247.0	6164.6	4660.6
a Increase in stocks	174.3	227.5	65.0	111.1	478.2	337.9	193.9	164.6	94.3	511.2	-315.8
b Gross fixed capital formation	1612.9	1727.5	1715.2	2169.2	2326.9	2544.0	2918.5	3695.4	5152.7	5653.4	4976.4

Korea, Republic of

1.2 Expenditure on the Gross Domestic Product, in Constant Prices
(Continued)

Thousand Million Korean won

	1970	1971	1972	1973	1974	1975	1976	1977	1978	1979	1980
	\multicolumn{11}{c}{At constant prices of:1975}										
Residential buildings	215.6	232.8	211.5	285.7	406.7	445.0	403.1	549.8	844.8	720.3	617.0
Non-residential buildings	340.6	324.6	294.5	463.4	412.5	455.6	529.3	610.0	732.4	759.2	808.1
Other construction and land improvement etc.	398.0	361.5	347.1	395.5	389.0	461.4	628.0	769.9	868.5	1025.8	1096.2
Other	658.6	808.6	862.1	1024.5	1118.7	1182.0	1358.1	1765.8	2707.0	3148.1	2455.1
4 Exports of goods and services	949.7	1143.5	1565.4	2432.3	2357.0	2748.4	3931.5	4941.9	5805.2	5596.2	6148.3
5 Less: Imports of goods and services	1841.6	2229.2	2256.2	3087.9	3604.5	3612.6	4582.6	5673.8	7326.6	7957.5	7346.1
Statistical discrepancy	-48.1	38.2	-108.2	-59.0	145.0	-35.5	203.1	57.6	-149.2	-4.9	-86.7
Equals: Gross Domestic Product	6314.8	6950.5	7377.0	8504.2	9206.0	9951.7	11333.0	12472.0	13884.9	14869.5	14341.8

1.3 Cost Components of the Gross Domestic Product

Thousand Million Korean won

	1970	1971	1972	1973	1974	1975	1976	1977	1978	1979	1980
1 Indirect taxes, net	258.5	303.2	341.5	427.5	501.0	947.6	1475.7	1899.6	2620.9	3487.7	4395.4
a Indirect taxes paid	263.4	311.7	353.7	459.9	718.6	1150.2	1647.8	2132.3	2928.4	3827.8	4864.9
b Less: Subsidies received	5.0	8.5	12.2	32.4	217.6	202.6	172.1	232.7	307.5	340.1	469.5
2 Consumption of fixed capital	169.3	207.9	293.5	441.7	646.7	789.5	1049.7	1382.8	1649.9	2170.0	2941.3
3 Compensation of employees paid by resident producers to:	867.6	1071.5	1297.5	1594.6	2204.2	3056.2	4239.2	5705.8	8421.4	10630.0	13167.6
a Resident households	855.7	1063.0	1286.9	1579.5	2178.3	3017.4	4194.7	5615.7	8243.6	10452.0	12920.7
b Rest of the world	11.9	8.5	10.6	15.1	25.9	38.8	44.5	90.2	177.8	177.9	246.9
4 Net operating surplus	1376.8	1715.8	2112.0	2811.6	4046.2	5158.4	6591.9	8134.5	10338.1	13069.4	14876.2
a Corporate and quasi-corporate enterprises	422.4	514.9	643.9	884.7	1297.6	1794.7	2403.8	3112.9	4273.0	5731.0	7194.6
b Private unincorporated enterprises	920.5	1170.5	1416.2	1888.2	2696.2	3283.7	4078.7	4886.3	5883.7	7080.3	7272.3
c General government	33.9	30.4	51.9	38.7	52.4	80.0	109.4	135.3	181.4	258.1	409.3
Equals: Gross Domestic Product	2672.1	3298.3	4044.4	5275.3	7398.1	9951.7	13356.5	17122.7	23030.3	29357.1	35380.5

1.4 General Government Current Receipts and Disbursements

Thousand Million Korean won

	1970	1971	1972	1973	1974	1975	1976	1977	1978	1979	1980
	\multicolumn{11}{c}{Receipts}										
1 Property and entrepreneurial income	56.1	56.1	77.3	60.2	79.6	116.9	174.6	211.8	273.7	392.2	596.6
2 Taxes, fees and contributions	393.6	480.0	519.2	649.9	1016.3	1533.6	2289.0	2940.1	4078.3	5342.3	6538.1
a Indirect taxes	263.4	311.7	353.7	459.9	718.6	1150.2	1647.8	2132.3	2928.4	3827.8	4865.0
b Direct taxes	130.2	168.3	165.5	190.0	297.7	383.4	641.2	807.8	1149.9	1514.5	1673.1
c Social security contributions	...	...	...	...	...	...	...	...	...	...	...
d Compulsory fees, fines and penalties	...	...	...	...	...	...	...	...	...	...	...
3 Other current receipts	58.5	57.0	65.5	73.5	100.7	130.5	227.0	238.5	308.2	416.6	502.2
Total Current Receipts of General Government	508.2	593.0	662.0	783.6	1196.7	1780.9	2690.5	3390.4	4660.2	6151.1	7636.9
	\multicolumn{11}{c}{Disbursements}										
1 General government final consumption expenditure	279.7	352.8	438.7	481.4	744.1	1024.7	1498.8	1988.6	2634.5	3237.2	4446.8
a Compensation of employees	114.6	137.2	164.3	173.7	230.2	324.6	477.5	646.5	808.0	1015.3	1345.7
b Consumption of fixed capital	12.3	15.9	16.2	22.5	32.0	47.5	66.1	78.4	95.2	126.8	150.3
c Purchases of goods and services, net	51.3	72.3	96.9	99.9	224.8	328.2	448.0	598.6	856.4	956.3	1447.1
d Less: Own account production of fixed assets	...	...	...	...	...	...	...	...	...	...	...
e Indirect taxes paid, net	101.6	127.3	161.3	185.3	257.1	324.4	507.1	665.1	874.9	1138.8	1503.6
2 Property income paid	4.8	6.7	7.8	4.6	5.2	6.4	4.8	7.3	8.4	10.9	11.6
3 Subsidies	5.0	8.5	12.2	32.4	217.6	202.6	172.1	232.7	307.5	340.1	469.5
4 Other current transfers paid	29.4	40.6	56.1	54.8	68.2	169.8	189.2	260.4	305.8	565.4	707.0
a Social security benefits and social assistance grants	...	...	...	...	...	...	...	...	...	...	...
b Other	29.4	40.6	56.1	54.8	68.2	169.8	189.2	260.4	305.8	565.4	707.0
5 Net saving	189.3	184.5	147.3	210.3	161.7	377.6	825.8	901.4	1404.1	1997.5	2002.0
Total Current Disbursements and Net Saving of General Government	508.2	593.0	662.0	783.6	1196.7	1780.9	2690.5	3390.4	4660.2	6151.1	7636.9

Korea, Republic of

1.6 Current Income and Outlay of Households and Non-Profit Institutions

Thousand Million Korean won

	1970	1971	1972	1973	1974	1975	1976	1977	1978	1979	1980
Receipts											
1 Compensation of employees	890.7	1100.1	1337.4	1626.4	2236.8	3092.9	4305.6	5845.0	8589.3	10836.2	13320.7
a From resident producers	855.7	1063.0	1286.9	1579.5	2178.3	3017.4	4194.7	5615.7	8243.5	10451.9	12920.9
b From rest of the world	35.0	37.1	50.6	47.0	58.5	75.5	110.9	229.4	345.8	384.3	399.8
2 Property and entrepreneurial income received	1234.8	1522.5	1835.3	2443.0	3461.6	4308.0	5536.4	6772.3	8489.3	10622.6	12027.7
3 Current transfers received	74.8	96.7	134.4	165.5	194.3	338.5	405.3	521.3	721.8	1046.6	1518.0
a Social security benefits and social assistance grants received	...	...	...	...	...	...	...	...	...	...	...
b Other	74.8	96.7	134.4	165.5	194.3	338.5	405.3	521.3	721.8	1046.6	1518.0
Total Current Receipts	2200.3	2719.3	3307.1	4234.9	5892.7	7739.4	10247.3	13138.6	17800.4	22505.4	26866.4
Disbursements											
1 Private final consumption expenditure	1939.1	2435.9	2957.1	3523.4	5086.6	6944.8	8711.6	10754.4	14238.7	18106.5	23042.6
2 Property income paid	15.5	11.4	13.2	12.9	17.9	28.9	36.3	67.2	91.8	147.7	237.5
3 Direct taxes and other payments n.e.c. to general government	87.2	111.3	109.9	136.9	182.0	232.9	400.9	470.4	620.6	794.4	896.9
4 Other current transfers paid	38.8	42.5	57.8	84.5	95.1	127.8	208.2	292.8	339.8	455.7	558.5
5 Net saving	119.6	118.1	169.3	477.2	511.1	405.1	890.2	1553.7	2509.4	3001.1	2130.9
Total Current Disbursements and Net Saving	2200.3	2719.3	3307.1	4234.9	5892.7	7739.4	10247.3	13138.6	17800.4	22505.4	26866.4

1.7 External Transactions on Current Account, Summary

Thousand Million Korean won

	1970	1971	1972	1973	1974	1975	1976	1977	1978	1979	1980
Payments to the Rest of the World											
1 Imports of goods and services	643.2	866.6	1015.1	1739.6	2916.4	3612.6	4595.1	5967.4	8355.6	10745.3	15385.9
a Imports of merchandise c.i.f.	603.3	816.1	956.1	1650.2	2783.3	3388.4	4229.3	5270.0	7263.4	9614.7	13738.0
b Other	39.9	50.4	59.0	89.5	133.0	224.2	365.9	697.4	1092.2	1130.6	1648.0
2 Factor income paid to the rest of the world	35.2	50.5	74.3	100.2	158.1	258.1	302.7	462.1	703.7	929.2	1906.5
a Compensation of employees	11.9	8.5	10.6	15.1	25.9	38.8	44.5	90.2	177.8	177.9	246.9
b Property and entrepreneurial income paid	23.3	42.0	63.7	85.1	132.1	219.3	258.2	371.9	525.9	751.3	1659.6
3 Indirect taxes paid to supranational organizations	...	...	...	...	...	...	...	...	...	...	...
4 Current transfers to the rest of the world	7.8	8.3	13.0	25.0	22.4	32.8	55.2	79.8	49.7	58.8	86.7
5 Surplus of the nation on current transactions	-193.5	-294.7	-144.6	-123.2	-820.4	-913.3	-151.7	6.0	-525.3	-2009.2	-3224.3
Payments to the Rest of the World and Surplus of the Nation on Current Transactions	492.7	630.7	957.7	1741.6	2276.4	2990.2	4801.4	6515.2	8583.7	9724.1	14154.8
Receipts From The Rest of the World											
1 Exports of goods and services	381.7	516.9	819.1	1577.7	2071.2	2748.4	4358.5	5966.8	7714.8	8808.6	12945.2
a Exports of merchandise f.o.b.	274.4	396.5	661.3	1302.6	1824.7	2421.5	3782.3	4862.5	6151.9	7117.0	10514.4
b Other	107.3	120.4	157.8	275.1	246.5	326.9	576.2	1104.3	1562.9	1691.6	2430.8
2 Factor income received from rest of the world	47.1	47.0	58.7	63.2	92.4	99.2	218.8	360.8	591.0	644.3	847.6
a Compensation of employees	35.0	37.1	50.6	47.0	58.5	75.5	110.9	229.4	345.8	384.3	399.8
b Property and entrepreneurial income received	12.1	9.9	8.2	16.2	33.9	23.7	108.0	131.4	245.2	260.0	447.8
3 Subsidies received from supranational organisations	...	...	...	...	...	...	...	...	...	...	...
4 Current transfers from rest of the world	63.9	66.8	79.9	100.7	112.8	142.5	224.0	187.7	277.9	271.2	362.0
Receipts from the Rest of the World on Current Transactions	492.7	630.7	957.7	1741.6	2276.4	2990.2	4801.4	6515.2	8583.7	9724.1	14154.8

Korea, Republic of

1.8 Capital Transactions of The Nation, Summary

Thousand Million Korean won

	1970	1971	1972	1973	1974	1975	1976	1977	1978	1979	1980
	\multicolumn{11}{c}{Finance of Gross Capital Formation}
Gross saving	521.3	564.6	700.0	1309.2	1592.2	1933.1	3231.0	4386.2	6272.6	7940.9	7107.5
1 Consumption of fixed capital	169.3	207.9	293.5	441.7	646.7	789.5	1049.7	1382.8	1649.9	2170.0	2941.3
a General government	12.3	15.9	16.2	22.5	32.0	47.5	66.1	78.4	95.2	126.8	150.3
b Corporate and quasi-corporate enterprises	99.7	121.2	170.9	271.5	395.9	488.6	645.8	870.4	1026.6	1501.3	2136.9
c Other	57.3	70.9	106.4	147.7	218.8	253.4	337.8	434.0	528.1	541.9	654.1
2 Net saving	352.0	356.7	406.5	867.5	945.5	1143.6	2181.3	3003.4	4622.7	5770.9	4166.2
a General government	189.3	184.5	147.3	210.3	161.7	377.6	825.8	901.4	1404.1	1997.5	2001.9
b Corporate and quasi-corporate enterprises	43.1	54.2	89.9	180.1	272.7	360.9	465.4	548.3	709.2	772.3	33.4
c Other	119.6	118.1	169.3	477.2	511.2	405.2	890.2	1553.7	2509.4	3001.1	2130.9
Less: Surplus of the nation on current transactions	-193.5	-294.7	-144.6	-123.2	-820.4	-913.3	-151.7	6.0	-525.3	-2009.2	-3224.3
Statistical discrepancy	4.3	-28.0	29.2	-91.4	-138.3	35.5	-4.6	264.7	339.9	343.4	480.8
Finance of Gross Capital Formation	719.1	831.4	873.8	1341.0	2274.4	2881.9	3378.2	4645.0	7137.8	10293.5	10812.6
	\multicolumn{11}{c}{Gross Capital Formation}
Increase in stocks	65.0	89.0	45.3	85.4	403.8	337.9	225.8	224.1	114.7	835.3	-427.4
Gross fixed capital formation	654.1	742.4	828.5	1255.6	1870.6	2544.0	3152.4	4420.9	7023.1	9458.2	11240.0
1 General government	13.0	25.6	28.7	26.3	29.4	40.4	60.2	93.2	188.3	349.6	523.6
2 Corporate and quasi-corporate enterprises	...	...	...	...	...	...	...	...	...	...	...
3 Other	...	...	...	...	...	...	...	...	...	...	...
Gross Capital Formation	719.1	831.4	873.8	1341.0	2274.4	2881.9	3378.2	4645.0	7137.8	10293.5	10812.6

1.10 Gross Domestic Product by Kind of Activity, in Current Prices

Thousand Million Korean won

	1970	1971	1972	1973	1974	1975	1976	1977	1978	1979	1980
1 Agriculture, hunting, forestry and fishing	718.5	890.7	1063.1	1307.7	1816.4	2441.7	3160.6	3913.7	5016.9	5964.5	5590.0
2 Mining and quarrying	39.0	44.5	47.9	61.8	91.8	148.2	162.6	248.9	313.9	325.2	475.3
3 Manufacturing	558.7	692.6	896.2	1299.8	1910.2	2590.4	3661.8	4594.0	6193.7	7823.1	9891.0
4 Electricity, gas and water	44.0	53.2	68.3	76.9	66.6	126.2	180.6	260.6	296.5	541.4	774.3
5 Construction	146.8	162.0	184.1	258.8	344.1	497.8	673.4	1081.8	1907.2	2750.4	3221.5
6 Wholesale and retail trade, restaurants and hotels	437.7	553.0	705.9	957.2	1379.1	1717.7	2173.3	2604.9	3270.7	4308.4	5415.1
7 Transport, storage and communication	182.3	224.2	270.1	365.1	466.0	606.7	787.9	1017.2	1388.9	1705.1	2146.3
8 Finance, insurance, real estate and business services	158.4	203.1	244.7	305.4	430.8	575.7	758.0	1033.2	1456.6	1877.8	2661.9
9 Community, social and personal services	193.1	249.0	296.5	335.1	462.6	649.5	914.9	1161.4	1497.4	2006.4	2703.7
Total, Industries	2478.3	3072.2	3776.8	4967.8	6967.5	9353.8	12473.0	15915.8	21341.8	27302.3	32879.1
Producers of Government Services	134.6	163.1	195.2	209.4	282.3	389.1	575.2	785.2	996.0	1262.6	1674.2
Other Producers	8.3	10.9	13.3	15.7	21.6	27.8	32.8	35.8	46.1	59.9	61.1
Subtotal	2621.2	3246.2	3985.3	5192.9	7271.4	9770.7	13081.0	16736.8	22383.9	28624.8	34614.4
Less: Imputed bank service charge [a]	...	...	...	...	...	...	...	...	...	...	...
Plus: Import duties	50.9	52.2	59.1	82.4	126.7	181.0	275.5	385.9	646.4	732.3	766.1
Plus: Value added tax	...	...	...	...	...	...	...	...	...	...	...
Equals: Gross Domestic Product	2672.1	3298.3	4044.4	5275.3	7398.1	9951.7	13356.5	17122.7	23030.3	29357.1	35380.5

a) Item 'Less: Imputed bank service charges' is subtracted from individual industries.

1.11 Gross Domestic Product by Kind of Activity, in Constant Prices

Thousand Million Korean won

	1970	1971	1972	1973	1974	1975	1976	1977	1978	1979	1980
	\multicolumn{11}{c}{At constant prices of:1975}
1 Agriculture, hunting, forestry and fishing	1933.5	2005.4	2045.6	2173.8	2319.4	2441.7	2702.7	2759.3	2650.3	2828.6	2207.5
2 Mining and quarrying	104.7	105.8	104.6	124.4	132.0	148.2	151.7	169.6	176.9	173.4	171.6
3 Manufacturing	1135.6	1349.4	1538.2	1987.8	2301.1	2590.4	3176.6	3633.6	4386.9	4818.0	4763.8
4 Electricity, gas and water	57.4	68.3	76.6	93.5	106.0	126.2	149.4	172.5	205.1	235.2	249.3
5 Construction	343.5	335.9	332.3	425.9	437.1	497.8	559.0	699.8	876.9	891.9	884.5

Korea, Republic of

1.11 Gross Domestic Product by Kind of Activity, in Constant Prices
(Continued)

Thousand Million Korean won	1970	1971	1972	1973	1974	1975	1976	1977	1978	1979	1980
					At constant prices of: 1975						
6 Wholesale and retail trade, restaurants and hotels [a]	1121.7	1318.7	1441.3	1681.7	1781.5	1898.7	2131.8	2307.4	2561.0	2661.4	2613.5
7 Transport, storage and communication	319.0	365.2	400.8	506.8	543.5	606.7	712.2	841.3	996.2	1134.4	1172.8
8 Finance, insurance, real estate and business services	416.0	453.7	466.8	500.8	545.8	575.7	638.2	727.8	813.0	842.2	947.8
9 Community, social and personal services	498.4	546.2	572.1	606.3	629.5	649.5	684.3	723.4	769.0	824.8	860.4
Total, Industries	5929.8	6548.7	6978.2	8100.9	8795.9	9534.8	10906.0	12034.8	13435.3	14409.9	13871.2
Producers of Government Services	364.5	377.7	373.9	376.4	383.1	389.1	398.6	409.0	419.9	430.5	447.0
Other Producers	20.5	24.1	25.0	26.9	27.6	27.8	28.4	28.2	29.7	29.1	23.6
Subtotal	6314.8	6950.5	7377.1	8504.2	9206.6	9951.7	11333.0	12472.0	13884.9	14869.5	14341.8
Less: Imputed bank service charge [b]	...	...	...	...	...	...	...	...	...	...	...
Plus: Import duties [a]	...	...	...	...	...	...	...	...	...	...	...
Plus: Value added tax	...	...	...	...	...	...	...	...	...	...	...
Equals: Gross Domestic Product	6314.8	6950.5	7377.0	8504.2	9206.6	9951.7	11333.0	12472.0	13884.9	14869.5	14341.8

a) Item 'Import duties' is included in item 'Wholesale and retail trade'.
b) Item 'Less: Imputed bank service charges' is subtracted from individual industries.

1.12 Relations Among National Accounting Aggregates

Thousand Million Korean won	1970	1971	1972	1973	1974	1975	1976	1977	1978	1979	1980
Gross Domestic Product	2672.1	3298.3	4044.4	5275.3	7398.1	9951.7	13356.5	17122.7	23030.3	29357.1	35380.5
Plus: Net factor income received from abroad	11.9	-3.5	-15.5	-37.0	-65.6	-158.9	-83.9	-101.3	-112.7	-285.0	-1059.0
Factor income received	47.1	47.0	58.7	63.2	92.4	99.2	218.8	360.8	591.0	644.3	847.6
Less: Factor income paid	35.2	50.5	74.3	100.2	158.1	258.1	302.7	462.1	703.7	929.3	1906.6
Equals: Gross National Product	2684.0	3294.8	4028.9	5238.3	7332.5	9792.9	13272.6	17021.4	22917.6	29072.1	34321.6
Less: Consumption of fixed capital	169.3	207.9	293.5	441.7	646.7	789.5	1049.7	1382.8	1649.9	2170.0	2941.3
Less: Net indirect taxes paid to supranational organisations	...	...	...	...	...	...	...	...	...	...	...
Equals: National Income at Market Prices	2514.7	3086.9	3735.4	4796.6	6685.8	9003.4	12222.9	15638.6	21267.7	26902.1	31380.3
Plus: Net current transfers received from abroad	56.1	58.5	66.8	75.7	90.4	109.7	168.8	107.9	228.3	212.4	275.3
Current transfers received	63.9	66.8	79.9	100.7	112.8	142.5	224.0	187.7	277.9	271.2	362.0
Less: Current transfers paid	7.8	8.3	13.0	25.0	22.4	32.8	55.2	79.8	49.7	58.8	86.7
Equals: National Disposable Income at Market Prices	2570.8	3145.4	3802.3	4872.4	6776.2	9113.1	12391.7	15746.4	21495.9	27114.5	31655.6
Less: Final consumption	2218.8	2788.7	3395.8	4004.8	5830.7	7969.5	10210.4	12743.0	16873.2	21343.6	27489.4
Equals: Net Saving	352.0	356.7	406.5	867.5	945.5	1143.6	2181.3	3003.4	4622.7	5770.9	4166.2
Less: Surplus of the nation on current transactions	-193.5	-294.7	-144.6	-123.2	-820.4	-913.3	-151.7	6.0	-525.3	-2009.2	-3224.3
Statistical discrepancy	4.3	-28.0	29.2	-91.4	-138.3	35.5	-4.6	264.7	339.9	343.4	480.8
Equals: Net Capital Formation	549.8	623.5	580.4	899.4	1627.6	2092.4	2328.5	3262.2	5487.9	8123.5	7871.3

2.1 General Government Final Consumption Expenditure by Function, in Current Prices

Thousand Million Korean won	1970	1971	1972	1973	1974	1975	1976	1977	1978	1979	1980
1 General public services	44.6	56.4	68.3	75.3	418.8	607.2	863.3	1164.7	1565.4	1843.4	2616.4
2 Defence	100.0	131.6	166.3	173.4							
3 Public order and safety											
4 Education	5.6	7.3	9.1	9.0	13.5	18.0	28.2	33.3	44.0	57.7	75.7
5 Health	1.3	1.1	1.9	1.5	2.1	2.6	4.3	8.2	8.7	9.2	14.2
6 Social security and welfare	2.6	2.7	2.8	2.8	3.9	5.1	6.7	10.5	12.6	15.3	17.7
7 Housing and community amenities	0.5	-0.1	0.3	0.2	0.8	1.3	1.5	2.5	2.7	3.9	5.6
8 Recreational, cultural and religious affairs	1.9	2.1	4.0	4.0	4.9	6.3	8.2	8.9	13.9	15.3	15.3
9 Economic services	9.4	8.4	8.6	7.4	10.9	12.4	13.4	16.9	17.1	26.8	47.9
10 Other functions	-	-	-	-	-	-	-	-	-	-	-
Total General Government Final Consumption Expenditure [a]	165.9	209.5	261.2	273.6	455.0	652.7	925.5	1245.1	1664.4	1971.6	2792.8

a) Excluding local authorities.

Korea, Republic of

2.3 Total General Government Outlays by Function and Type

Thousand Million Korean won

	Final Consumption Expenditures Total	Compensation of Employees	Other	Subsidies	Other Current Transfers & Property Income	Total Current Disbursements	Gross Capital Formation	Other Capital Outlays	Total Outlays
1970									
1 General public services	44.6	27.6	17.0	-	3.4	48.0	7.7	1.1	56.8
2 Defence	100.0	76.1	23.9	-	0.8	100.8	...	1.7	102.6
3 Public order and safety							...		
4 Education	5.6	4.2	1.4	-	48.2	53.8	1.5	19.0	74.4
5 Health	1.3	1.0	0.3	-	1.6	2.9	1.0	0.5	4.4
6 Social security and welfare	2.6	0.7	1.9	-	8.3	10.9	0.3	0.9	12.1
7 Housing and community amenities	0.5	0.4	-	-	0.3	0.8	0.9	-	1.6
8 Recreation, culture and religion	1.9	0.6	1.3	-	1.4	3.3	19.3	4.4	26.9
9 Economic services	9.4	4.0	5.4	5.0	9.9	24.3	48.2	19.9	92.3
10 Other functions	-	-	-	-	58.7	58.7	-	1.5	60.2
Total a	165.9	114.6	51.3	5.0	132.5	303.4	78.9	49.0	431.2
1971									
1 General public services	56.4	34.2	22.2	-	3.8	60.2	8.6	0.5	69.3
2 Defence	131.6	90.2	41.4	-	2.7	134.3	...	1.7	135.9
3 Public order and safety							...		
4 Education	7.3	4.9	2.5	0.3	66.4	74.0	3.4	22.4	99.8
5 Health	1.1	1.3	-0.2	-	2.2	3.3	1.6	0.4	5.2
6 Social security and welfare	2.7	0.8	1.9	-	9.6	12.3	0.5	1.0	13.6
7 Housing and community amenities	-0.1	0.5	-0.6	-	-	-0.1	0.8	-	0.7
8 Recreation, culture and religion	2.1	0.7	1.4	-	2.1	4.2	9.4	5.3	18.8
9 Economic services	8.4	4.6	3.9	8.2	12.9	29.5	58.5	21.1	109.2
10 Other functions	-	-	-	-	68.0	68.0	-	-	68.0
Total a	209.5	137.2	72.3	8.5	167.5	385.5	82.8	52.2	520.5
1972									
1 General public services	68.3	39.9	28.4	-	13.5	81.8	9.0	0.2	91.0
2 Defence	166.3	109.7	56.7	-	4.4	170.7	...	1.5	172.2
3 Public order and safety							...		
4 Education	9.1	6.1	3.0	0.4	83.7	93.2	5.0	21.2	119.5
5 Health	1.9	1.6	0.3	-	1.8	3.7	2.0	0.4	6.1
6 Social security and welfare	2.8	1.0	1.8	-	16.8	19.6	0.7	1.1	21.3
7 Housing and community amenities	0.3	0.9	-0.6	-	1.3	1.6	2.1	-	3.7
8 Recreation, culture and religion	4.0	1.2	2.8	-	2.5	6.5	30.0	8.8	45.3
9 Economic services	8.6	4.2	4.5	11.8	15.8	36.2	75.3	25.1	136.6
10 Other functions	-	-	-	-	67.3	67.3	-	3.0	70.3
Total a	261.2	164.3	96.9	12.2	207.2	480.6	124.1	61.3	666.0
1973									
1 General public services									
2 Defence	248.7	157.5	91.2	-	9.6	258.3	8.2	1.0	267.5
3 Public order and safety									
4 Education	9.0	7.0	2.0	-	89.7	98.7	7.0	15.6	121.3
5 Health	1.5	1.7	-0.2	-	1.8	3.3	1.9	0.1	5.3
6 Social security and welfare	2.8	1.2	1.6	-	14.5	17.3	0.9	0.5	18.7
7 Housing and community amenities	0.2	0.4	-0.2	-	1.2	1.4	1.5	0.3	3.3
8 Recreation, culture and religion	4.0	1.1	2.8	-	5.5	9.5	37.9	6.6	54.0
9 Economic services	7.4	4.7	2.8	32.4	18.3	58.1	110.7	26.6	195.3
10 Other functions	-	-	-	-	73.5	73.5	-	6.4	79.8
Total a	273.6	173.7	99.9	32.4	213.9	519.9	168.1	57.1	745.2

Korea, Republic of

2.3 Total General Government Outlays by Function and Type
(Continued)

Thousand Million Korean won

		Final Consumption Expenditures			Other Current Transfers & Property Income	Total Current Disbursements	Gross Capital Formation	Other Capital Outlays	Total Outlays
		Total	Compensation of Employees	Other	Subsidies				

1974

1	General public services	418.8	206.7	212.1	-	13.5	432.3	10.0	2.8	445.1
2	Defence									
3	Public order and safety									
4	Education	13.5	9.3	4.2	-	121.5	135.0	9.7	11.1	155.8
5	Health	2.1	2.3	-0.2	-	2.2	4.3	1.7	0.1	6.0
6	Social security and welfare	3.9	1.7	2.2	-	33.9	37.8	2.3	0.3	40.4
7	Housing and community amenities	0.8	0.5	0.3	-	0.3	1.1	1.4	0.4	2.9
8	Recreation, culture and religion	4.9	1.6	3.3	-	5.9	10.8	38.1	10.3	59.3
9	Economic services	10.9	8.2	2.8	217.6	17.8	246.3	86.4	34.7	367.5
10	Other functions	-	-	-	-	81.4	81.4	-	48.6	130.0
	Total a	455.0	230.2	224.8	217.6	276.5	949.1	149.6	108.3	1207.0

1975

1	General public services	607.2	292.8	314.4	-	30.1	637.3	16.1	6.2	659.7
2	Defence									
3	Public order and safety									
4	Education	18.0	12.6	5.4	-	178.2	196.2	11.4	21.1	228.5
5	Health	2.6	3.4	-0.8	-	2.8	5.4	2.5	0.2	8.1
6	Social security and welfare	5.1	2.4	2.7	-	52.9	58.0	2.9	0.4	61.3
7	Housing and community amenities	1.3	0.7	0.6	-	0.4	1.7	1.7	1.2	4.6
8	Recreation, culture and religion	6.3	2.0	4.4	-	7.9	14.2	64.5	24.2	102.9
9	Economic services	12.4	10.8	1.6	202.6	34.3	249.3	333.1	75.1	657.5
10	Other functions	-	-	-	-	117.7	117.7	-	9.0	126.7
	Total a	652.7	324.6	328.2	202.6	424.2	1279.5	432.2	137.5	1849.2

1976

1	General public services	863.3	430.6	432.7	-	46.2	909.5	16.4	6.2	932.1
2	Defence									
3	Public order and safety									
4	Education	28.2	18.7	9.5	-	291.4	319.6	9.2	20.0	348.8
5	Health	4.3	5.5	-1.2	-	8.7	13.0	4.8	0.1	17.9
6	Social security and welfare	6.7	3.6	3.1	-	47.6	54.3	4.6	2.1	61.0
7	Housing and community amenities	1.5	1.1	0.5	0.1	0.3	1.9	1.9	1.1	4.9
8	Recreation, culture and religion	8.2	2.6	5.6	-	11.1	19.3	72.0	21.1	112.3
9	Economic services	13.4	15.5	-2.1	172.0	47.6	233.0	267.5	84.2	584.7
10	Other functions	-	-	-	-	151.5	151.5	-	10.7	162.2
	Total a	925.5	477.5	448.0	172.1	604.2	1701.8	376.3	145.6	2223.8

1977

1	General public services	1164.7	585.3	579.5	-	62.5	1227.2	23.0	8.0	1258.2
2	Defence									
3	Public order and safety									
4	Education	33.3	23.5	9.8	-	384.8	418.1	18.0	33.4	469.6
5	Health	8.2	7.9	0.4	-	10.3	18.5	8.1	1.7	28.2
6	Social security and welfare	10.5	4.6	5.9	-	69.3	79.8	2.7	5.2	87.7
7	Housing and community amenities	2.5	1.8	0.8	0.1	0.6	3.2	4.3	3.1	10.5
8	Recreation, culture and religion	8.9	3.5	5.4	-	19.2	28.1	110.9	39.5	178.4
9	Economic services	16.9	20.1	-3.2	232.6	55.2	304.7	469.8	108.9	883.3
10	Other functions	-	-	-	-	183.4	183.4	-	-	183.4
	Total a	1245.1	646.5	598.6	232.7	785.2	2263.0	636.8	199.7	3099.3

Korea, Republic of

2.3 Total General Government Outlays by Function and Type
(Continued)

Thousand Million Korean won

	Final Consumption Expenditures Total	Compensation of Employees	Other	Subsidies	Other Current Transfers & Property Income	Total Current Disbursements	Gross Capital Formation	Other Capital Outlays	Total Outlays
				1978					
1 General public services	⎡								⎤
2 Defence	1565.3	726.5	838.8	-	70.7	1636.0	31.6	11.1	1678.7
3 Public order and safety	⎣								⎦
4 Education	44.0	31.5	12.5	-	492.5	536.5	31.1	46.4	614.0
5 Health	8.7	9.3	-0.6	-	19.2	27.9	12.3	2.8	43.1
6 Social security and welfare	12.6	5.7	6.9	-	88.4	101.0	4.6	5.7	111.3
7 Housing and community amenities	2.7	1.7	1.0	0.1	0.5	3.3	2.4	6.3	12.0
8 Recreation, culture and religion	13.9	6.7	7.2	-	20.8	34.7	149.4	44.2	228.3
9 Economic services	17.1	26.6	-9.5	307.4	63.4	387.8	398.4	127.8	914.1
10 Other functions	-		-	-	248.4	248.4	-	-	248.4
Total a	1664.4	808.0	856.4	307.4	1003.9	2975.7	629.8	244.3	3849.9
				1979					
1 General public services	⎡								⎤
2 Defence	1843.4	904.8	938.6	-	98.9	1942.3	53.5	19.0	2014.8
3 Public order and safety	⎣								⎦
4 Education	57.7	42.8	14.9	-	750.3	808.0	46.5	92.0	946.5
5 Health	9.2	11.8	-2.6	-	28.2	37.4	5.4	4.2	47.0
6 Social security and welfare	15.3	7.9	7.4	-	172.1	187.4	6.4	3.4	197.2
7 Housing and community amenities	3.9	2.3	1.6	0.1	0.9	4.9	1.4	18.3	24.6
8 Recreation, culture and religion	15.3	9.6	5.7	-	60.4	75.7	162.3	44.0	282.0
9 Economic services	26.8	36.1	-9.3	340.0	106.5	473.3	570.1	227.3	1270.7
10 Other functions	-	-	-	-	337.8	337.8	-	-	337.8
Total a	1971.6	1015.3	956.3	340.1	1555.1	3866.8	845.6	408.2	5120.6
				1980					
1 General public services	⎡								⎤
2 Defence	2616.4	1197.6	1418.8	-	129.0	2745.4	76.8	27.1	2849.3
3 Public order and safety	⎣								⎦
4 Education	75.7	57.5	18.2	-	881.1	956.8	54.2	114.0	1125.0
5 Health	14.2	17.0	-2.8	-	45.9	60.1	8.9	11.2	80.2
6 Social security and welfare	17.7	9.5	8.2	-	212.9	230.6	10.0	5.2	245.8
7 Housing and community amenities	5.6	3.3	2.3	-	1.1	6.7	4.7	4.3	15.7
8 Recreation, culture and religion	15.3	12.0	3.3	-	65.8	81.1	202.4	78.4	361.9
9 Economic services	47.9	48.8	-0.9	469.5	199.2	716.6	796.0	213.0	1725.6
10 Other functions	-	-	-	-	411.6	411.6	-	-	411.6
Total a	2792.8	1345.7	1447.1	469.5	1946.6	5208.9	1153.0	453.2	6815.1

a) Excluding local authorities.

2.5 Private Final Consumption Expenditure by Type, in Current Prices

Thousand Million Korean won

	1970	1971	1972	1973	1974	1975	1976	1977	1978	1979	1980
	Final Consumption Expenditure of Resident Households										
1 Food, beverages and tobacco	1093.7	1376.7	1672.0	1974.4	2856.4	3876.8	4899.5	5931.3	7753.5	9538.5	11979.2
a Food	918.6	1156.9	1412.3	1642.8	2383.0	3202.2	4084.4	4898.7	6306.1	7598.9	3898.6
b Non-alcoholic beverages	11.9	17.2	18.2	24.3	29.6	55.9	73.5	96.8	153.2	210.9	124.8
c Alcoholic beverages	88.6	113.0	127.1	158.6	248.5	330.2	390.5	507.4	740.7	1040.1	606.6
d Tobacco	74.6	89.6	114.4	148.7	195.3	288.5	351.1	428.3	553.5	688.6	374.8
2 Clothing and footwear	192.3	235.0	267.7	374.2	468.6	676.2	819.3	1036.2	1322.5	1527.2	1820.1
3 Gross rent, fuel and power	174.8	216.4	256.8	292.8	410.7	555.1	691.6	890.4	1144.8	1526.7	2094.4
4 Furniture, furnishings and household equipment and operation	59.9	75.0	92.4	121.8	179.3	223.9	316.4	382.2	581.7	753.1	692.3
a Household operation	19.9	23.5	30.0	36.3	53.1	61.5	72.0	82.6	108.5	148.5	178.7
b Other	40.0	51.6	62.4	85.6	126.2	162.5	244.3	299.7	473.2	604.6	513.6
5 Medical care and health expenses	60.0	75.1	106.5	135.7	212.6	272.9	342.0	474.4	694.3	1034.9	1351.1
6 Transport and communication	127.3	158.2	210.3	260.5	365.2	491.8	591.0	717.3	1017.7	1371.2	1968.9
a Personal transport equipment	4.6	5.7	9.4	11.5	17.5	22.4	28.6	36.8	52.4	63.3	48.4

Korea, Republic of

2.5 Private Final Consumption Expenditure by Type, in Current Prices
(Continued)

Thousand Million Korean won

	1970	1971	1972	1973	1974	1975	1976	1977	1978	1979	1980
b Other	122.7	152.6	201.0	249.0	347.7	469.4	562.4	680.5	965.3	1307.9	1920.5
7 Recreational, entertainment, education and cultural services	98.6	119.3	133.9	168.4	253.2	370.3	508.3	651.2	816.8	1045.4	1349.1
a Education	35.9	46.1	58.3	70.2	103.7	167.0	265.2	346.5	429.5	551.4	726.6
b Other	62.7	73.3	75.6	98.2	149.4	203.3	243.1	304.7	387.3	494.0	622.5
8 Miscellaneous goods and services	136.3	186.9	241.7	289.3	394.6	538.9	665.3	832.1	1067.2	1386.8	1913.2
a Personal care	54.8	76.6	101.8	118.3	165.6	222.1	266.3	341.8	450.1	633.0	901.4
b Expenditures in restaurants, cafes and hotels	55.9	76.0	100.5	125.0	164.6	216.4	280.1	343.5	424.9	475.9	601.7
c Other	25.6	34.3	39.3	46.0	64.3	100.4	119.0	146.8	192.2	277.9	410.1
Total Final Consumption Expenditure in the Domestic Market by Households, of which	1942.9	2442.7	2981.3	3617.0	5140.5	7005.9	8833.5	10915.0	14398.5	18183.8	23168.3
a Durable goods	57.2	71.7	80.7	101.6	164.2	215.0	295.4	369.1	581.8	763.6	750.9
b Semi-durable goods	223.1	281.8	348.6	478.7	612.2	889.7	1092.2	1371.9	1727.8	2018.0	2410.6
c Non-durable goods	1274.4	1606.2	1981.0	2359.2	3437.5	4329.0	5450.4	6620.0	8634.3	10794.4	13633.1
d Services	388.2	482.9	571.0	677.5	926.5	1572.2	1995.5	2554.0	3454.6	4607.8	6373.7
Plus: Direct purchases abroad by resident households	1.4	2.3	1.9	2.7	4.4	3.8	5.0	10.0	27.4	71.8	85.5
Less: Direct purchases in the domestic market by non-resident households	5.2	9.1	26.1	96.4	58.2	64.9	126.9	170.6	187.2	149.1	211.2
Equals: Final Consumption Expenditure of Resident Households [a]	1939.1	2435.9	2957.1	3523.3	5086.6	6944.8	8711.6	10754.4	14238.7	18106.5	23042.6

Final Consumption Expenditure of Private Non-profit Institutions Serving Households

Equals: Final Consumption Expenditure of Private Non-profit Organisations Serving Households	...	...	...	...	...	...	...	...	...	...	...
Private Final Consumption Expenditure	1939.1	2435.9	2957.1	3523.4	5086.6	6944.8	8711.6	10754.4	14238.7	18106.5	23042.6

a) Including consumption expenditure of private non-profit institutions.

2.6 Private Final Consumption Expenditure by Type, in Constant Prices

Thousand Million Korean won

	1970	1971	1972	1973	1974	1975	1976	1977	1978	1979	1980
					At constant prices of: 1975						

Final Consumption Expenditure of Resident Households

	1970	1971	1972	1973	1974	1975	1976	1977	1978	1979	1980
1 Food, beverages and tobacco	2842.1	3082.2	3250.6	3494.2	3689.3	3876.8	4191.6	4375.9	4643.2	5028.6	...
a Food	2473.1	2638.0	2780.5	2969.5	3084.0	3202.2	3460.7	3573.2	3666.3	3907.1	...
b Non-alcoholic beverages	22.1	31.5	30.5	40.0	35.9	55.9	68.8	76.1	112.4	136.7	...
c Alcoholic beverages	176.9	218.8	218.3	259.6	306.4	330.2	360.0	404.5	520.2	627.6	...
d Tobacco	170.1	193.9	221.4	225.2	263.0	288.5	302.1	322.1	344.3	357.2	...
2 Clothing and footwear	422.3	503.6	521.3	620.3	646.5	676.2	737.4	765.1	839.5	787.2	...
3 Gross rent, fuel and power	432.8	456.1	467.8	500.9	526.0	555.1	586.5	628.7	674.4	730.1	...
4 Furniture, furnishings and household equipment and operation	119.5	136.0	164.7	194.4	208.8	223.9	282.8	320.8	467.2	544.6	...
a Household operation	42.0	47.3	53.8	58.5	62.5	61.5	64.1	67.7	76.4	81.9	...
b Other	77.5	88.8	110.8	136.0	146.4	162.5	218.6	253.1	390.8	462.7	...
5 Medical care and health expenses	122.2	141.5	176.4	208.3	245.8	272.9	315.9	356.3	414.6	493.2	...
6 Transport and communication	277.1	308.6	343.5	421.0	442.0	491.8	549.8	646.1	762.1	829.5	...
a Personal transport equipment	8.7	9.5	13.5	16.3	20.1	22.4	26.7	32.5	44.8	48.5	...
b Other	268.5	299.1	330.0	404.7	421.9	469.4	523.1	613.5	717.3	781.0	...
7 Recreational, entertainment, education and cultural services	251.5	283.0	289.5	331.7	360.6	370.3	397.4	436.9	486.4	523.7	...
a Education	113.1	127.3	132.8	147.1	157.1	167.0	174.1	181.2	189.4	201.0	...
b Other	138.4	155.8	156.7	184.6	203.5	203.3	223.3	255.7	297.0	322.7	...
8 Miscellaneous goods and services	299.1	362.3	405.7	453.4	485.7	538.9	578.5	620.6	673.7	720.2	...
a Personal care	108.2	135.5	162.6	173.8	192.0	222.1	237.5	255.8	284.3	302.6	...
b Expenditures in restaurants, cafes and hotels	129.9	153.6	169.0	196.4	206.8	216.4	236.3	247.6	262.1	261.5	...

Korea, Republic of

2.6 Private Final Consumption Expenditure by Type, in Constant Prices
(Continued)

Thousand Million Korean won

	1970	1971	1972	1973	1974	1975	1976	1977	1978	1979	1980
				At constant prices of:1975							
c Other	60.9	73.2	74.2	83.2	86.9	100.4	104.7	117.2	127.3	156.1	...
Total Final Consumption Expenditure in the Domestic Market by Households, of which	4766.6	5273.3	5619.5	6224.2	6604.7	7005.9	7639.7	8150.4	8961.1	9657.1	...
Plus: Direct purchases abroad by resident households	2.9	4.3	3.1	4.1	5.7	3.8	4.7	8.7	22.3	54.2	...
Less: Direct purchases in the domestic market by non-resident households	12.1	19.0	48.6	137.8	75.0	64.9	110.3	135.0	129.4	86.8	...
Equals: Final Consumption Expenditure of Resident Households [a]	4757.4	5258.7	5574.1	6090.6	6535.5	6944.8	7534.1	8024.1	8854.0	9624.5	...

Final Consumption Expenditure of Private Non-profit Institutions Serving Households

	1970	1971	1972	1973	1974	1975	1976	1977	1978	1979	1980
Equals: Final Consumption Expenditure of Private Non-profit Organisations Serving Households	...	...	...	...	...	...	...	...	...	...	...
Private Final Consumption Expenditure	4757.4	5258.6	5574.0	6090.6	6535.4	6944.8	7534.1	8024.1	8854.0	9624.5	...

a) Including consumption expenditure of private non-profit institutions.

2.9 Gross Capital Formation by Kind of Activity of Owner, ISIC Major Divisions, in Current Prices

Thousand Million Korean won

	1970			1971			1972			1973		
	Total Gross Capital Formation	Increase in Stocks	Gross Fixed Capital Formation	Total Gross Capital Formation	Increase in Stocks	Gross Fixed Capital Formation	Total Gross Capital Formation	Increase in Stocks	Gross Fixed Capital Formation	Total Gross Capital Formation	Increase in Stocks	Gross Fixed Capital Formation

All Producers

1 Agriculture, hunting, fishing and forestry	...	...	52.5	...	...	59.9	...	...	86.6	...	...	122.2
2 Mining and quarrying	...	...	3.6	...	...	5.5	...	...	5.7	...	...	9.3
3 Manufacturing	...	...	128.3	...	...	144.1	...	...	161.0	...	...	369.9
4 Electricity, gas and water	...	...	73.0	...	...	60.9	...	...	43.6	...	...	56.7
5 Construction	...	...	8.0	...	...	8.4	...	...	11.4	...	...	22.6
6 Wholesale and retail trade, restaurants and hotels	...	...	55.4	...	...	64.5	...	...	55.3	...	...	96.4
7 Transport, storage and communication	...	...	169.7	...	...	200.6	...	...	265.5	...	...	271.5
8 Finance, insurance, real estate and business services	...	...	99.4	...	...	115.3	...	...	119.3	...	...	184.6
9 Community, social and personal services	...	...	51.2	...	...	57.6	...	...	51.4	...	...	96.2
Total Industries	...	...	641.1	...	...	716.8	...	...	799.8	...	...	1229.4
Producers of Government Services	...	...	13.0	...	...	25.6	...	...	28.7	...	...	26.3
Private Non-Profit Institutions Serving Households	...	...	...	...	...	...	...	...	...	...	...	...
Total	719.1	65.0	654.1	831.4	89.0	742.4	873.8	45.3	828.5	1341.0	85.4	1255.6

	1974			1975			1976			1977		
	Total Gross Capital Formation	Increase in Stocks	Gross Fixed Capital Formation	Total Gross Capital Formation	Increase in Stocks	Gross Fixed Capital Formation	Total Gross Capital Formation	Increase in Stocks	Gross Fixed Capital Formation	Total Gross Capital Formation	Increase in Stocks	Gross Fixed Capital Formation

All Producers

1 Agriculture, hunting, fishing and forestry	...	...	220.0	...	...	228.4	...	...	297.6	...	...	401.8
2 Mining and quarrying	...	...	17.6	...	...	31.5	...	...	36.9	...	...	37.4
3 Manufacturing	...	...	419.7	...	...	536.6	...	...	716.4	...	...	922.2
4 Electricity, gas and water	...	...	125.3	...	...	172.3	...	...	330.2	...	...	420.9
5 Construction	...	...	18.3	...	...	35.1	...	...	38.7	...	...	80.4
6 Wholesale and retail trade, restaurants and hotels	...	...	142.2	...	...	178.1	...	...	245.3	...	...	418.3
7 Transport, storage and communication	...	...	433.8	...	...	703.4	...	...	729.4	...	...	971.6
8 Finance, insurance, real estate and business services	...	...	348.1	...	...	484.1	...	...	495.4	...	...	760.7
9 Community, social and personal services	...	...	116.2	...	...	134.0	...	...	202.4	...	...	314.3
Total Industries	...	...	1841.2	...	...	2503.6	...	...	3092.2	...	...	4327.7
Producers of Government Services	...	...	29.4	...	...	40.4	...	...	60.2	...	...	93.2
Private Non-Profit Institutions Serving Households	...	...	...	...	...	...	...	...	...	...	...	...
Total	2274.4	403.8	1870.6	2881.9	337.9	2544.0	3378.2	225.8	3152.4	4645.0	224.1	4420.9

Korea, Republic of

2.9 Gross Capital Formation by Kind of Activity of Owner, ISIC Major Divisions, in Current Prices

Thousand Million Korean won

	1978 Total Gross Capital Formation	1978 Increase in Stocks	1978 Gross Fixed Capital Formation	1979 Total Gross Capital Formation	1979 Increase in Stocks	1979 Gross Fixed Capital Formation	1980 Total Gross Capital Formation	1980 Increase in Stocks	1980 Gross Fixed Capital Formation
				All Producers					
1 Agriculture, hunting, fishing and forestry	...	...	569.0	...	...	669.5	...	...	762.5
2 Mining and quarrying	...	...	55.3	...	...	47.9	...	...	53.4
3 Manufacturing	...	...	1615.8	...	...	2176.8	...	...	1887.1
4 Electricity, gas and water	...	...	602.1	...	...	1030.2	...	...	1395.0
5 Construction	...	...	97.5	...	...	81.2	...	...	89.7
6 Wholesale and retail trade, restaurants and hotels	...	...	531.0	...	...	919.3	...	...	1501.9
7 Transport, storage and communication	...	...	1608.5	...	...	1966.0	...	...	2429.5
8 Finance, insurance, real estate and business services	...	...	1423.3	...	...	1677.6	...	...	1895.3
9 Community, social and personal services	...	...	332.3	...	...	540.1	...	...	702.0
Total Industries	...	...	6834.7	...	...	9108.6	...	...	10716.4
Producers of Government Services	...	...	188.3	...	...	349.6	...	...	523.6
Private Non-Profit Institutions Serving Households	...	...	...	...	...	...	...	...	...
Total	7137.8	114.7	7023.1	10293.5	835.3	9458.2	10812.6	-427.4	11240.0

2.10 Gross Capital Formation by Kind of Activity of Owner, ISIC Major Divisions, in Constant Prices

Thousand Million Korean won

	1970 Total Gross Capital Formation	1970 Increase in Stocks	1970 Gross Fixed Capital Formation	1971 Total Gross Capital Formation	1971 Increase in Stocks	1971 Gross Fixed Capital Formation	1972 Total Gross Capital Formation	1972 Increase in Stocks	1972 Gross Fixed Capital Formation	1973 Total Gross Capital Formation	1973 Increase in Stocks	1973 Gross Fixed Capital Formation
					At constant prices of:1975							
					All Producers							
1 Agriculture, hunting, fishing and forestry	...	...	120.0	...	...	134.0	...	...	176.9	...	...	204.8
2 Mining and quarrying	...	...	10.9	...	...	15.8	...	...	14.3	...	...	17.2
3 Manufacturing	...	...	364.6	...	...	389.4	...	...	383.5	...	...	665.3
4 Electricity, gas and water	...	...	168.9	...	...	134.3	...	...	83.9	...	...	95.2
5 Construction	...	...	24.3	...	...	23.4	...	...	28.5	...	...	43.1
6 Wholesale and retail trade, restaurants and hotels	...	...	129.7	...	...	143.5	...	...	108.5	...	...	160.1
7 Transport, storage and communication	...	...	406.9	...	...	460.2	...	...	538.5	...	...	473.0
8 Finance, insurance, real estate and business services	...	...	236.5	...	...	251.2	...	...	228.9	...	...	303.1
9 Community, social and personal services	...	...	122.5	...	...	128.2	...	...	103.0	...	...	166.8
Total Industries	...	...	1584.3	...	...	1680.1	...	...	1666.0	...	...	2128.5
Producers of Government Services	...	...	28.6	...	...	47.4	...	...	49.2	...	...	40.7
Private Non-Profit Institutions Serving Households	...	...	...	...	...	...	...	...	...	...	...	...
Total	1787.2	174.3	1612.9	1955.0	227.5	1727.5	1780.2	65.0	1715.2	2280.3	111.1	2169.2

	1974 Total Gross Capital Formation	1974 Increase in Stocks	1974 Gross Fixed Capital Formation	1975 Total Gross Capital Formation	1975 Increase in Stocks	1975 Gross Fixed Capital Formation	1976 Total Gross Capital Formation	1976 Increase in Stocks	1976 Gross Fixed Capital Formation	1977 Total Gross Capital Formation	1977 Increase in Stocks	1977 Gross Fixed Capital Formation
					At constant prices of:1975							
					All Producers							
1 Agriculture, hunting, fishing and forestry	...	...	274.7	...	...	228.4	...	...	273.4	...	...	311.0
2 Mining and quarrying	...	...	22.4	...	...	31.5	...	...	35.3	...	...	34.2
3 Manufacturing	...	...	531.2	...	...	536.6	...	...	684.0	...	...	781.1
4 Electricity, gas and water	...	...	153.9	...	...	172.3	...	...	281.5	...	...	393.5

Korea, Republic of

2.10 Gross Capital Formation by Kind of Activity of Owner, ISIC Major Divisions, in Constant Prices
(Continued)

Thousand Million Korean won

	1974 Total Gross Capital Formation	1974 Increase in Stocks	1974 Gross Fixed Capital Formation	1975 Total Gross Capital Formation	1975 Increase in Stocks	1975 Gross Fixed Capital Formation	1976 Total Gross Capital Formation	1976 Increase in Stocks	1976 Gross Fixed Capital Formation	1977 Total Gross Capital Formation	1977 Increase in Stocks	1977 Gross Fixed Capital Formation
					At constant prices of:1975							
5 Construction	...	...	23.2	...	...	35.1	...	...	37.0	...	...	70.5
6 Wholesale and retail trade, restaurants and hotels	...	...	104.9	...	...	178.1	...	...	226.9	...	...	323.7
7 Transport, storage and communication	...	...	535.7	...	...	703.4	...	...	701.3	...	...	873.1
8 Finance, insurance, real estate and business services	...	...	431.1	...	...	484.1	...	...	442.4	...	...	578.9
9 Community, social and personal services	...	...	145.4	...	...	134.0	...	...	181.2	...	...	253.9
Total Industries	...	...	2292.4	...	...	2503.6	...	...	2862.9	...	...	3619.8
Producers of Government Services	...	...	34.4	...	...	40.4	...	...	55.6	...	...	75.6
Private Non-Profit Institutions Serving Households	...	...	...	...	...	...	...	...	...	...	...	...
Total	2805.1	478.2	2326.9	2881.9	337.9	2544.0	3112.4	193.9	2918.5	3860.0	164.6	3695.4

	1978 Total Gross Capital Formation	1978 Increase in Stocks	1978 Gross Fixed Capital Formation	1979 Total Gross Capital Formation	1979 Increase in Stocks	1979 Gross Fixed Capital Formation
		At constant prices of:1975				
		All Producers				
1 Agriculture, hunting, fishing and forestry	...	...	399.4	...	...	378.7
2 Mining and quarrying	...	...	49.2	...	...	33.1
3 Manufacturing	...	...	1276.4	...	...	1502.9
4 Electricity, gas and water	...	...	456.1	...	...	645.1
5 Construction	...	...	81.1	...	...	56.9
6 Wholesale and retail trade, restaurants and hotels	...	...	369.0	...	...	517.6
7 Transport, storage and communication	...	...	1281.3	...	...	1283.7
8 Finance, insurance, real estate and business services	...	...	884.9	...	...	753.7
9 Community, social and personal services	...	...	237.9	...	...	324.6
Total Industries	...	...	5035.5	...	...	5496.3
Producers of Government Services	...	...	117.2	...	...	157.1
Private Non-Profit Institutions Serving Households	...	...	...	...	...	...
Total	5247.0	94.3	5152.7	6164.6	511.2	5653.4

2.17 Exports and Imports of Goods and Services, Detail

Thousand Million Korean won

	1970	1971	1972	1973	1974	1975	1976	1977	1978	1979	1980
				Exports of Goods and Services							
1 Exports of merchandise, f.o.b.	274.4	396.5	661.3	1302.6	1824.7	2421.5	3782.3	4862.5	6151.9	7117.0	10514.4
2 Transport and communication	18.7	25.5	41.8	60.6	91.0	136.0	166.4	260.1	331.4	495.5	963.9
3 Insurance service charges	0.3	0.4	0.9	1.0	1.6	2.6	4.8	9.9	12.8	19.3	28.4
4 Other commodities	83.2	85.4	89.0	117.1	95.7	123.5	278.1	663.8	1031.5	1027.7	1227.3
5 Adjustments of merchandise exports to change-of-ownership basis	...	...	...	...	...	...	...	...	...	...	...
6 Direct purchases in the domestic market by non-residential households	5.2	9.1	26.1	96.4	58.2	64.9	126.9	170.6	187.2	149.1	211.2
7 Direct purchases in the domestic market by extraterritorial bodies	...	...	...	...	...	...	...	...	...	...	...
Total Exports of Goods and Services	381.7	516.9	819.1	1577.7	2071.2	2748.4	4358.5	5966.8	7714.8	8808.6	12945.2
				Imports of Goods and Services							
1 Imports of merchandise, c.i.f.	603.3	816.1	956.1	1650.2	2783.3	3388.4	4229.3	5270.0	7263.4	9614.7	13738.0
a Imports of merchandise, f.o.b.	561.0	757.9	885.8	1528.3	2609.9	3230.4	4068.1	5093.2	7013.9	9244.5	13164.4
b Transport of services on merchandise imports	39.2	54.8	65.0	111.7	168.4	157.7	157.7	165.0	235.5	352.7	549.0
By residents	...	...	...	...	...	...	...	...	...	...	...

… Korea, Republic of

2.17 Exports and Imports of Goods and Services, Detail
(Continued)

Thousand Million Korean won

	1970	1971	1972	1973	1974	1975	1976	1977	1978	1979	1980
By non-residents	39.2	54.8	65.0	111.7	168.4	157.7	157.7	165.0	235.5	352.7	549.0
c Insurance service charges on merchandise imports	3.0	3.4	5.3	10.2	5.0	0.3	3.6	11.8	14.0	17.5	24.5
By residents	...	...	...	...	...	...	...	...	...	...	...
By non-residents	3.0	3.4	5.3	10.2	5.0	0.3	3.6	11.8	14.0	17.5	24.5
2 Adjustments of merchandise imports to change-of-ownership basis	...	...	...	...	...	...	...	...	...	...	...
3 Other transport and communication	6.9	11.4	16.0	33.5	56.9	97.7	139.4	248.8	328.4	428.0	843.5
4 Other insurance service charges	...	...	...	...	...	...	...	...	...	...	...
5 Other commodities	29.1	33.9	38.0	49.2	64.9	111.6	204.1	398.9	663.1	630.8	719.0
6 Direct purchases abroad by government	3.9	5.1	5.0	6.8	11.2	14.9	22.4	49.7	100.7	71.8	85.5
7 Direct purchases abroad by resident households											
Total Imports of Goods and Services	643.2	866.6	1015.1	1739.6	2916.4	3612.6	4595.1	5967.4	8355.6	10745.3	15385.9
Balance of Goods and Services	-261.5	-349.7	-196.0	-161.9	-845.2	-864.1	-236.6	-0.6	-640.8	-1936.7	-2440.7
Total Imports and Balance of Goods and Services	381.7	516.9	819.1	1577.7	2071.2	2748.4	4358.5	5966.8	7714.8	8808.6	12945.2

3.12 General Government Income and Outlay Account: Total and Subsectors

Thousand Million Korean won

	1970					1971				
	Total General Government	Central Government	State or Provincial Government	Local Government	Social Security Funds	Total General Government	Central Government	State or Provincial Government	Local Government	Social Security Funds

Receipts

1 Property and entrepreneurial income	56.1	49.2	...	6.9	...	56.1	48.1	...	8.0	...
2 Taxes, fees and contributions	393.6	360.2	...	33.5	...	480.0	439.8	...	40.2	...
a Indirect taxes	263.4	232.1	...	31.4	...	311.7	274.5	...	37.2	...
b Direct taxes	130.2	128.1	...	2.1	...	168.3	165.3	...	3.0	...
Income	130.2	128.1	...	2.1	...	168.3	165.3	...	3.0	...
Other	...	...	...	...	...	...	...	...	...	...
c Social security contributions	...	...	...	...	...	...	...	...	...	...
d Fees, fines and penalties [a]	...	...	...	...	...	...	...	...	...	...
3 Other current transfers received	58.5	43.8	...	123.0	...	57.0	35.3	...	158.0	...
a Casualty insurance claims	...	...	...	...	...	...	...	...	...	...
b Transfers from other government subsectors	...	...	...	...	...	...	...	...	...	...
c Transfers from abroad	27.0	27.0	...	14.7	...	22.5	22.5	...	21.7	...
d Other transfers, except imputed [a]	31.5	16.8	...	108.3	...	34.5	12.8	...	136.3	...
e Imputed unfunded employee welfare contributions	...	...	...	...	...	...	...	...	...	...
Total Current Receipts [b]	508.2	453.1	...	163.5	...	593.0	523.0	...	206.2	...

Disbursements

1 General governement final consumption expenditures	279.7	173.7	...	106.1	...	352.8	217.7	...	135.1	...
2 Property income paid	4.8	4.4	...	0.4	...	6.7	5.1	...	1.7	...

Korea, Republic of

3.12 General Government Income and Outlay Account: Total and Subsectors
(Continued)

Thousand Million Korean won

	1970					1971				
	Total General Government	Central Government	State or Provincial Government	Local Government	Social Security Funds	Total General Government	Central Government	State or Provincial Government	Local Government	Social Security Funds
3 Subsidies	5.0	5.0	...	...	...	8.5	8.5	...	...	...
4 Other current transfers paid	29.4	130.9	...	6.8	...	40.6	165.8	...	11.1	...
a Casualty insurance premiums, net	...	...	...	...	...	...	...	...	...	...
b Transfers to other government subsectors	...	108.3	...	...	...	...	136.3	...	...	...
c Transfers to households	28.9	22.1	...	6.8	...	40.2	29.1	...	11.1	...
Social security benefits	...	...	...	...	...	...	...	...	...	...
Social assistance grants	28.9	22.1	...	6.8	...	40.2	29.1	...	11.1	...
Unfunded employee welfare benefits	...	...	...	...	...	...	...	...	...	...
d Transfers to private non-profit institutions serving households	...	...	...	...	...	...	...	...	...	...
e Transfers to the rest of the world	0.5	0.5	...	-	...	0.4	0.4	...	-	...
Net saving	189.3	139.2	...	50.2	...	184.5	126.1	...	58.3	...
Total Current Disbursements and Net Saving [b]	508.2	453.1	...	163.5	...	593.0	523.0	...	206.2	...

	1972					1973				
	Total General Government	Central Government	State or Provincial Government	Local Government	Social Security Funds	Total General Government	Central Government	State or Provincial Government	Local Government	Social Security Funds

Receipts

1 Property and entrepreneurial income	77.3	69.7	...	7.8	...	60.2	59.1	...	1.1	...
2 Taxes, fees and contributions	519.2	472.1	...	47.1	...	649.9	574.8	...	75.1	...
a Indirect taxes	353.7	310.2	...	43.5	...	459.9	399.6	...	60.3	...
b Direct taxes	165.5	161.9	...	3.6	...	190.0	175.2	...	14.8	...
Income	165.5	161.9	...	3.6	...	190.0	175.2	...	14.8	...
Other	...	...	...	...	...	...	...	...	...	...
c Social security contributions	...	...	...	...	...	...	...	...	...	...
d Fees, fines and penalties [a]	...	...	...	...	...	...	...	...	...	...
3 Other current transfers received	65.5	37.1	...	194.2	...	73.5	39.2	...	201.1	...
a Casualty insurance claims	...	...	...	...	...	...	...	...	...	...
b Transfers from other government subsectors	...	...	...	...	...	...	...	...	...	...
c Transfers from abroad	20.3	20.3	...	28.4	...	14.0	14.0	...	34.3	...
d Other transfers, except imputed [a]	45.2	16.8	...	165.8	...	59.5	25.2	...	166.8	...
e Imputed unfunded employee welfare contributions	...	...	...	...	...	...	...	...	...	...
Total Current Receipts [b]	662.0	578.8	...	249.0	...	783.6	673.1	...	277.2	...

Disbursements

1 General governement final consumption expenditures	438.7	270.0	...	168.7	...	481.4	286.5	...	194.9	...
2 Property income paid	7.8	5.8	...	2.0	...	4.6	3.2	...	1.4	...
3 Subsidies	12.2	12.2	...	...	...	32.4	32.4	...	...	...
4 Other current transfers paid	56.1	207.7	...	14.2	...	54.8	208.6	...	13.0	...
a Casualty insurance premiums, net	...	...	...	...	...	...	...	...	...	...
b Transfers to other government subsectors	...	165.8	...	...	...	...	166.8	...	...	...
c Transfers to households	55.6	41.4	...	14.2	...	54.8	41.8	...	13.0	...
Social security benefits	...	...	...	...	...	...	...	...	...	...
Social assistance grants	55.6	41.4	...	14.2	...	54.8	41.8	...	13.0	...
Unfunded employee welfare benefits	...	...	...	...	...	...	...	...	...	...
d Transfers to private non-profit institutions serving households	...	...	...	...	...	...	...	...	...	...
e Transfers to the rest of the world	0.5	0.5	...	-	...	-	-	...	-	...
Net saving	147.3	83.3	...	64.1	...	210.3	142.4	...	67.9	...
Total Current Disbursements and Net Saving [b]	662.0	578.8	...	249.0	...	783.6	673.1	...	277.2	...

Korea, Republic of

3.12 General Government Income and Outlay Account: Total and Subsectors

Thousand Million Korean won

	1974 Total General Government	1974 Central Government	1974 State or Provincial Government	1974 Local Government	1974 Social Security Funds	1975 Total General Government	1975 Central Government	1975 State or Provincial Government	1975 Local Government	1975 Social Security Funds
Receipts										
1 Property and entrepreneurial income	79.6	76.2	...	3.5	...	116.9	113.0	...	3.9	...
2 Taxes, fees and contributions	1016.3	906.5	...	109.9	...	1533.6	1372.3	...	161.4	...
a Indirect taxes	718.6	626.8	...	91.9	...	1150.2	1018.8	...	131.4	...
b Direct taxes	297.7	279.7	...	18.0	...	383.4	353.5	...	30.0	...
Income	297.7	279.7	...	18.0	...	383.4	353.5	...	30.0	...
Other	...	...	...	...	...	...	...	...	...	...
c Social security contributions	...	...	...	...	...	...	...	...	...	...
d Fees, fines and penalties [a]	...	...	...	...	...	...	...	...	...	...
3 Other current transfers received	100.7	51.4	...	268.2	...	130.5	67.2	...	384.0	...
a Casualty insurance claims	...	...	...	...	...	...	...	...	...	...
b Transfers from other government subsectors	...	...	...	...	...	...	...	...	...	...
c Transfers from abroad	28.0	28.0	...	49.4	...	34.1	34.1	...	63.2	...
d Other transfers, except imputed [a]	72.7	23.4	...	218.6	...	96.4	33.1	...	320.8	...
e Imputed unfunded employee welfare contributions	...	...	...	...	...	...	...	...	...	...
Total Current Receipts [b]	1196.7	1034.0	...	381.3	...	1780.9	1552.5	...	549.2	...
Disbursements										
1 General governement final consumption expenditures	744.1	471.6	...	272.4	...	1024.7	679.4	...	345.3	...
2 Property income paid	5.2	4.8	...	0.4	...	6.4	5.5	...	0.9	...
3 Subsidies	217.6	217.6	...	...	...	202.6	202.6	...	...	...
4 Other current transfers paid	68.2	267.0	...	19.7	...	169.8	420.3	...	70.2	...
a Casualty insurance premiums, net	...	...	...	...	...	...	...	...	...	...
b Transfers to other government subsectors	...	218.6	...	...	...	...	320.8	...	...	...
c Transfers to households	68.1	48.3	...	19.7	...	168.3	98.0	...	70.2	...
Social security benefits	...	...	...	...	...	...	...	...	...	...
Social assistance grants	68.1	48.3	...	19.7	...	168.3	98.0	...	70.2	...
Unfunded employee welfare benefits	...	...	...	...	...	...	...	...	...	...
d Transfers to private non-profit institutions serving households	...	...	...	...	...	...	...	...	...	...
e Transfers to the rest of the world	0.1	0.1	...	-	...	1.5	1.5	...	-	...
Net saving	161.7	72.9	...	88.8	...	377.6	244.8	...	132.8	...
Total Current Disbursements and Net Saving [b]	1196.7	1034.0	...	381.3	...	1780.9	1552.5	...	549.2	...

	1976 Total General Government	1976 Central Government	1976 State or Provincial Government	1976 Local Government	1976 Social Security Funds	1977 Total General Government	1977 Central Government	1977 State or Provincial Government	1977 Local Government	1977 Social Security Funds
Receipts										
1 Property and entrepreneurial income	174.6	160.8	...	13.8	...	211.8	189.1	...	22.6	...
2 Taxes, fees and contributions	2289.0	2071.4	...	217.6	...	2940.1	2600.9	...	339.2	...
a Indirect taxes	1647.8	1472.4	...	175.4	...	2132.3	1864.5	...	267.8	...
b Direct taxes	641.2	599.0	...	42.2	...	807.8	736.4	...	71.4	...
Income	641.2	599.0	...	42.2	...	807.8	736.4	...	71.4	...
Other	...	...	...	...	...	...	...	...	...	...
c Social security contributions	...	...	...	...	...	...	...	...	...	...
d Fees, fines and penalties [a]	...	...	...	...	...	...	...	...	...	...
3 Other current transfers received	227.0	128.0	...	561.1	...	238.5	104.7	...	731.1	...
a Casualty insurance claims	...	...	...	...	...	...	...	...	...	...
b Transfers from other government subsectors	...	...	...	...	...	...	...	...	...	...

Korea, Republic of

3.12 General Government Income and Outlay Account: Total and Subsectors
(Continued)

Thousand Million Korean won

	1976 Total General Government	1976 Central Government	1976 State or Provincial Government	1976 Local Government	1976 Social Security Funds	1977 Total General Government	1977 Central Government	1977 State or Provincial Government	1977 Local Government	1977 Social Security Funds
c Transfers from abroad	74.0	74.0	...	99.0	...	25.4	25.4	...	133.8	...
d Other transfers, except imputed [a]	153.0	54.0	...	462.1	...	213.1	79.3	...	597.3	...
e Imputed unfunded employee welfare contributions	...	...	...	...	...	...	...	...	...	...
Total Current Receipts [b]	2690.5	2360.2	...	792.5		3390.4	2894.8	...	1092.8	...

Disbursements

1 General government final consumption expenditures	1498.8	972.4	...	526.4	...	1988.6	1299.5	...	689.1	...
2 Property income paid	4.8	3.8	...	0.9	...	7.3	6.5	...	0.9	...
3 Subsidies	172.1	172.1	...	...	...	232.7	232.7	...	...	...
4 Other current transfers paid	189.2	604.2	...	47.0	...	260.4	778.6	...	79.1	...
a Casualty insurance premiums, net	...	...	...	...	...	...	...	...	...	...
b Transfers to other government subsectors	...	462.1	...	...	...	...	597.3	...	...	...
c Transfers to households	189.2	142.1	...	47.0	...	260.3	181.2	...	79.1	...
Social security benefits	...	...	...	...	...	...	...	...	...	...
Social assistance grants	189.2	142.1	...	47.0	...	260.3	181.2	...	79.1	...
Unfunded employee welfare benefits	...	...	...	...	...	...	...	...	...	...
d Transfers to private non-profit institutions serving households	...	...	...	...	...	...	...	...	...	...
e Transfers to the rest of the world	-	-	...	-	...	0.1	0.1	...	-	...
Net saving	825.8	607.6	...	218.2	...	901.4	577.6	...	323.8	...
Total Current Disbursements and Net Saving [b]	2690.5	2360.2	...	792.5	...	3390.4	2894.8	...	1092.8	...

	1978 Total General Government	1978 Central Government	1978 State or Provincial Government	1978 Local Government	1978 Social Security Funds	1979 Total General Government	1979 Central Government	1979 State or Provincial Government	1979 Local Government	1979 Social Security Funds

Receipts

1 Property and entrepreneurial income	273.7	215.6	...	58.1	...	392.2	331.7	...	60.5	...
2 Taxes, fees and contributions	4078.3	3632.6	...	445.7	...	5342.2	4743.0	...	599.2	...
a Indirect taxes	2928.4	2574.1	...	354.3	...	3827.7	3356.7	...	471.0	...
b Direct taxes	1149.9	1058.5	...	91.4	...	1514.5	1386.3	...	128.2	...
Income	1149.9	1058.5	...	91.4	...	1514.5	1386.3	...	128.2	...
Other	...	...	...	...	...	...	...	...	...	...
c Social security contributions	...	...	...	...	...	...	...	...	...	...
d Fees, fines and penalties [a]	...	...	...	...	...	...	...	...	...	...
3 Other current transfers received	308.2	133.7	...	933.9	...	416.7	178.2	...	1316.9	...
a Casualty insurance claims	...	...	...	...	...	...	...	...	...	...
b Transfers from other government subsectors	...	...	...	...	...	...	...	...	...	...
c Transfers from abroad	18.1	18.1	...	174.5	...	19.6	19.6	...	238.5	...
d Other transfers, except imputed [a]	290.1	115.6	...	759.4	...	397.1	158.6	...	1078.4	...
e Imputed unfunded employee welfare contributions	...	...	...	...	...	...	...	...	...	...
Total Current Receipts [b]	4660.2	3981.9	...	1437.7	...	6151.1	5252.9	...	1976.6	...

Disbursements

1 General governement final consumption expenditures	2634.5	1729.6	...	904.9	...	3237.2	2048.9	...	1188.3	...
2 Property income paid	8.4	6.0	...	2.4	...	10.9	5.4	...	5.5	...

Korea, Republic of

3.12 General Government Income and Outlay Account: Total and Subsectors
(Continued)

Thousand Million Korean won

	1978					1979				
	Total General Government	Central Government	State or Provincial Government	Local Government	Social Security Funds	Total General Government	Central Government	State or Provincial Government	Local Government	Social Security Funds
3 Subsidies	307.5	307.5	...	...	...	340.1	340.1	...	...	...
4 Other current transfers paid	305.8	988.4	...	76.8	...	565.4	1527.0	...	116.8	...
a Casualty insurance premiums, net	...	...	...	...	...	...	...	...	...	...
b Transfers to other government subsectors	...	759.4	...	...	...	...	1078.4	...	...	...
c Transfers to households	305.8	229.0	...	76.8	...	565.4	448.6	...	116.8	...
Social security benefits	...	...	...	...	...	...	...	...	...	...
Social assistance grants	305.8	229.0	...	76.8	...	565.4	448.6	...	116.8	...
Unfunded employee welfare benefits	...	...	...	...	...	...	...	...	...	...
d Transfers to private non-profit institutions serving households	...	...	...	...	...	...	...	...	...	...
e Transfers to the rest of the world	-	-	...	-	...	-	-	...	-	...
Net saving	1404.1	950.4	...	453.7	...	1997.5	1331.5	...	666.0	...
Total Current Disbursements and Net Saving [b]	4660.2	3981.9	...	1437.7	...	6151.1	5252.9	...	1976.6	...

	1980				
	Total General Government	Central Government	State or Provincial Government	Local Government	Social Security Funds

Receipts

1 Property and entrepreneurial income	596.6	484.4	...	112.2	...
2 Taxes, fees and contributions	6538.0	5770.3	...	767.7	...
a Indirect taxes	4864.9	4257.6	...	607.3	...
b Direct taxes	1673.1	1512.7	...	160.4	...
Income	1673.1	1512.7	...	160.4	...
Other	...	...	...	...	...
c Social security contributions	...	...	...	...	...
d Fees, fines and penalties [a]	...	...	...	...	...
3 Other current transfers received	502.3	223.6	...	1678.5	...
a Casualty insurance claims	...	...	...	...	...
b Transfers from other government subsectors	...	...	...	...	...
c Transfers from abroad	30.4	30.4	...	278.6	...
d Other transfers, except imputed [a]	471.9	193.2	...	1399.9	...
e Imputed unfunded employee welfare contributions	...	...	...	...	...
Total Current Receipts [b]	7636.9	6478.3	...	2558.4	...

Disbursements

1 General governement final consumption expenditures	4446.8	2882.1	...	1564.7	...
2 Property income paid	11.6	6.4	...	5.2	...
3 Subsidies	469.5	469.5	...	...	...
4 Other current transfers paid	707.0	1923.7	...	183.2	...
a Casualty insurance premiums, net	...	...	...	...	...
b Transfers to other government subsectors	...	1399.9	...	...	...
c Transfers to households	707.0	523.8	...	183.2	...
Social security benefits	...	...	...	...	...
Social assistance grants	707.0	523.8	...	183.2	...
Unfunded employee welfare benefits	...	...	...	...	...
d Transfers to private non-profit institutions serving households	...	...	...	...	...
e Transfers to the rest of the world	-	-	...	-	...
Net saving	2002.0	1196.6	...	805.3	...
Total Current Disbursements and Net Saving [b]	7636.9	6478.3	...	2558.4	...

a) Item 'Fees, fines and other n.e.c.' is included in item 'Other transfers except imputed'.
b) Column 'State or Provincial government' is included in column 'Local government'.

Korea, Republic of

3.13 General Government Capital Accumulation Account: Total and Subsectors

Thousand Million Korean won

	\multicolumn{5}{c|}{1970}	\multicolumn{5}{c}{1971}
	Total General Government	Central Government	State or Provincial Government	Local Government	Social Security Funds	Total General Government	Central Government	State or Provincial Government	Local Government	Social Security Funds
\multicolumn{11}{c}{**Finance of Gross Accumulation**}
1 Gross saving	201.6	147.9	...	53.7	...	200.4	137.2	...	63.1	...
a Consumption of fixed capital	12.3	8.8	...	3.5	...	15.9	11.1	...	4.8	...
b Net saving	189.3	139.2	...	50.2	...	184.5	126.1	...	58.3	...
2 Capital transfers received	-10.2	-37.5	...	27.2	...	-12.2	-40.9	...	28.8	...
a From other government subsectors	...	-33.5	...	33.5	...	...	-37.8	...	37.8	...
b From other resident sectors	-10.2	-4.0	...	-6.3	...	-12.2	-3.2	...	-9.0	...
c From rest of the world	-	-	...	-	...	-	-	...	-	...
Finance of Gross Accumulation [a]	191.4	110.5	...	80.9	...	188.2	96.3	...	91.9	...
\multicolumn{11}{c}{**Gross Accumulation**}
1 Gross capital formation	170.3	78.9	...	91.4	...	194.0	82.8	...	111.2	...
2 Purchases of land, net	...	...	...	...	...	...	...	...	...	...
3 Purchases of intangible assets, net	...	...	...	...	...	...	...	...	...	...
4 Capital transfers paid	...	...	...	...	...	...	...	...	...	...
Net lending	21.1	31.6	...	-10.5	...	-5.8	13.5	...	-19.2	...
Gross Accumulation [a]	191.4	110.5	...	80.9	...	188.2	96.3	...	91.9	...

	\multicolumn{5}{c|}{1972}	\multicolumn{5}{c}{1973}
	Total General Government	Central Government	State or Provincial Government	Local Government	Social Security Funds	Total General Government	Central Government	State or Provincial Government	Local Government	Social Security Funds
\multicolumn{11}{c}{**Finance of Gross Accumulation**}
1 Gross saving	163.5	94.4	...	69.1	...	232.8	157.3	...	75.5	...
a Consumption of fixed capital	16.2	11.1	...	5.0	...	22.5	14.9	...	7.6	...
b Net saving	147.3	83.3	...	64.1	...	210.3	142.4	...	67.9	...
2 Capital transfers received	-24.5	-51.5	...	27.1	...	-27.3	-48.6	...	21.3	...
a From other government subsectors	...	-41.8	...	41.8	...	...	-37.2	...	37.2	...
b From other resident sectors	-24.5	-9.7	...	-14.8	...	-27.3	-11.4	...	-15.9	...
c From rest of the world	-	-	...	-	...	-	-	...	-	...
Finance of Gross Accumulation [a]	139.0	42.9	...	96.2	...	205.5	108.7	...	96.8	...
\multicolumn{11}{c}{**Gross Accumulation**}
1 Gross capital formation	219.6	124.1	...	95.5	...	269.7	168.1	...	101.6	...
2 Purchases of land, net	...	...	...	...	...	...	...	...	...	...
3 Purchases of intangible assets, net	...	...	...	...	...	...	...	...	...	...
4 Capital transfers paid	...	...	...	...	...	...	...	...	...	...
Net lending	-80.6	-81.3	...	0.7	...	-64.2	-59.5	...	-4.8	...
Gross Accumulation [a]	139.0	42.9	...	96.2	...	205.5	108.7	...	96.8	...

	\multicolumn{5}{c|}{1974}	\multicolumn{5}{c}{1975}
	Total General Government	Central Government	State or Provincial Government	Local Government	Social Security Funds	Total General Government	Central Government	State or Provincial Government	Local Government	Social Security Funds
\multicolumn{11}{c}{**Finance of Gross Accumulation**}
1 Gross saving	193.7	94.3	...	99.4	...	425.1	277.4	...	147.7	...
a Consumption of fixed capital	32.0	21.5	...	10.6	...	47.5	32.6	...	14.9	...
b Net saving	161.7	72.9	...	88.8	...	377.6	244.8	...	132.8	...
2 Capital transfers received	-83.9	-96.9	...	13.0	...	-58.5	-95.1	...	36.6	...
a From other government subsectors	...	-36.9	...	36.9	...	...	-61.3	...	61.3	...
b From other resident sectors	-83.9	-60.0	...	-23.9	...	-58.5	-33.8	...	-24.7	...
c From rest of the world	-	-	...	-	...	-	-	...	-	...
Finance of Gross Accumulation [a]	109.8	-2.6	...	112.3	...	366.6	182.3	...	184.3	...
\multicolumn{11}{c}{**Gross Accumulation**}
1 Gross capital formation	292.2	149.6	...	142.7	...	631.4	432.2	...	199.2	...
2 Purchases of land, net	...	...	...	...	...	...	...	...	...	...
3 Purchases of intangible assets, net	...	...	...	...	...	...	...	...	...	...
4 Capital transfers paid	...	...	...	...	...	...	...	...	...	...
Net lending	-182.5	-152.1	...	-30.3	...	-264.9	-249.9	...	-15.0	...
Gross Accumulation [a]	109.8	-2.6	...	112.3	...	366.6	182.3	...	184.3	...

Korea, Republic of

3.13 General Government Capital Accumulation Account: Total and Subsectors

Thousand Million Korean won

	1976					1977				
	Total General Government	Central Government	State or Provincial Government	Local Government	Social Security Funds	Total General Government	Central Government	State or Provincial Government	Local Government	Social Security Funds

Finance of Gross Accumulation

1 Gross saving	891.9	653.4	...	238.5	...	979.8	632.2	...	347.7	...
a Consumption of fixed capital	66.1	45.8	...	20.3	...	78.4	54.6	...	23.9	...
b Net saving	825.8	607.6	...	218.2	...	901.4	577.6	...	323.8	...
2 Capital transfers received	-70.9	-104.0	...	33.1	...	-111.2	-146.7	...	35.5	...
a From other government subsectors	...	-63.8	...	63.8	...	...	-86.2	...	86.2	...
b From other resident sectors	-70.9	-40.2	...	-30.7	...	-111.2	-60.5	...	-50.7	...
c From rest of the world	-	-	...	-	...	-	-	...	-	...
Finance of Gross Accumulation [a]	821.0	549.4	...	271.6	...	868.6	485.5	...	383.1	...

Gross Accumulation

1 Gross capital formation	657.2	376.3	...	280.8	...	1044.3	636.8	...	407.5	...
2 Purchases of land, net	...	...	...	...	...	...	...	...	...	...
3 Purchases of intangible assets, net	...	...	...	...	...	...	...	...	...	...
4 Capital transfers paid	...	...	...	...	...	...	...	...	...	...
Net lending	163.9	173.1	...	-9.2	...	-175.7	-151.2	...	-24.4	...
Gross Accumulation [a]	821.0	549.4	...	271.6	...	868.6	485.5	...	383.1	...

	1978					1979				
	Total General Government	Central Government	State or Provincial Government	Local Government	Social Security Funds	Total General Government	Central Government	State or Provincial Government	Local Government	Social Security Funds

Finance of Gross Accumulation

1 Gross saving	1499.3	1016.8	...	482.5	...	2124.3	1418.4	...	705.9	...
a Consumption of fixed capital	95.2	66.4	...	28.8	...	126.8	86.9	...	39.9	...
b Net saving	1404.1	950.4	...	453.7	...	1997.5	1331.5	...	666.0	...
2 Capital transfers received	-127.9	-181.8	...	53.9	...	-200.5	-327.6	...	127.1	...
a From other government subsectors	...	-110.3	...	110.3	...	...	...	...	216.1	...
b From other resident sectors	-127.9	-71.5	...	-56.4	...	-200.5	...	...	-89.0	...
c From rest of the world	-	-	...	-	...	-	-	...	-	...
Finance of Gross Accumulation [a]	1371.4	835.0	...	536.4	...	1923.8	1090.8	...	833.0	...

Gross Accumulation

1 Gross capital formation	1261.2	629.8	...	631.4	...	1823.9	845.6	...	978.3	...
2 Purchases of land, net	...	...	...	...	...	...	...	...	...	...
3 Purchases of intangible assets, net	...	...	...	...	...	...	...	...	...	...
4 Capital transfers paid	...	...	...	...	...	...	...	...	...	...
Net lending	110.2	205.3	...	-95.1	...	99.9	245.2	...	-145.3	...
Gross Accumulation [a]	1371.4	835.0	...	536.4	...	1923.8	1090.8	...	833.0	...

	1980				
	Total General Government	Central Government	State or Provincial Government	Local Government	Social Security Funds

Finance of Gross Accumulation

1 Gross saving	2152.3	1293.3	...	859.0	...
a Consumption of fixed capital	150.3	96.7	...	53.6	...
b Net saving	2002.0	1196.6	...	805.4	...
2 Capital transfers received	-220.3	-371.2	...	150.9	...
a From other government subsectors	...	-277.4	...	277.4	...
b From other resident sectors	-220.3	-93.8	...	-126.5	...
c From rest of the world	-	-	...	-	...
Finance of Gross Accumulation [a]	1932.0	922.1	...	1009.9	...

Korea, Republic of

3.13 General Government Capital Accumulation Account: Total and Subsectors
(Continued)

Thousand Million Korean won

		1980			
	Total General Government	Central Government	State or Provincial Government	Local Government	Social Security Funds
Gross Accumulation					
1 Gross capital formation	2376.4	1153.0	...	1223.4	...
2 Purchases of land, net	...	...	...	...	...
3 Purchases of intangible assets, net	...	...	...	...	...
4 Capital transfers paid	...	...	...	...	...
Net lending	-444.4	-230.9	...	-213.5	...
Gross Accumulation [a]	1932.0	922.1	...	1009.9	...

a) Column 'State or Provincial government' is included in column 'Local government'.

3.32 Household and Private Unincorporated Enterprise Income and Outlay Account

Thousand Million Korean won

	1970	1971	1972	1973	1974	1975	1976	1977	1978	1979	1980
Receipts											
1 Compensation of employees	890.7	1100.1	1337.4	1626.4	2236.8	3092.9	4305.6	5845.0	8589.3	10836.2	13320.7
2 Property and entrepreneurial income received	1234.8	1522.5	1835.3	2443.0	3461.6	4308.0	5536.4	6772.3	8489.3	10622.6	12027.7
a Operating surplus of private unincorporated enterprises	920.5	1170.5	1416.2	1888.2	2696.2	3283.7	4078.7	4886.3	5883.7	7080.3	7272.3
b Withdrawals from private quasi-corporations	...	...	...	...	...	...	...	...	...	...	...
c Interest	159.0	175.3	200.9	230.1	320.1	471.5	679.9	843.6	1262.9	1895.6	2772.5
d Dividends	38.6	34.3	41.3	102.6	155.6	163.5	298.4	372.3	405.1	405.9	408.5
e Net land rent and royalties	116.7	142.4	176.9	222.0	289.8	389.4	479.4	670.1	937.6	1240.8	1574.4
3 Other current transfers received	74.8	96.6	134.5	165.5	194.3	338.5	405.3	521.3	721.8	1046.6	1518.0
a Casualty insurance claims	...	...	...	...	...	...	...	...	...	...	...
b Social security benefits	...	...	...	...	...	...	...	...	...	...	...
c Social assistance grants	...	...	...	...	...	...	...	...	...	...	...
d Unfunded employee welfare benefits	...	...	...	...	...	...	...	...	...	...	...
e Other current transfers received	74.8	96.6	134.5	165.5	194.3	338.5	405.3	521.3	721.8	1046.6	1518.0
From general government	...	...	...	...	...	...	...	...	...	...	...
From the rest fo the world	36.9	44.4	59.5	86.8	84.8	108.4	150.0	162.2	259.9	251.6	331.6
Other	37.9	52.3	74.9	78.7	109.5	230.1	255.3	359.1	461.9	795.0	1186.4
Total Current Receipts	2200.3	2719.3	3307.1	4234.9	5892.7	7739.4	10247.3	13138.6	17800.4	22505.4	26866.4
Disbursements											
1 Final consumption expenditures	1939.1	2435.9	2957.1	3523.4	5086.6	6944.8	8711.6	10754.4	14238.7	18106.5	23042.6
2 Property income paid	15.5	11.4	13.2	12.9	17.9	28.9	36.3	67.2	91.8	147.7	237.5
a Interest	15.5	11.4	13.2	12.9	17.9	28.9	36.3	67.2	91.8	147.7	237.5
Consumer debt	15.5	11.4	13.2	12.9	17.9	28.9	36.3	67.2	91.8	147.7	237.5
Mortgage	...	...	...	...	...	...	...	...	...	...	...
Other	...	...	...	...	...	...	...	...	...	...	...
b Net land rent and royalties	...	...	...	...	...	...	...	...	...	...	...
3 Direct taxes, fees, fines & other payments n.e.c. to government	87.2	111.3	109.9	136.9	182.0	232.9	400.9	470.4	620.6	794.4	896.9
Income taxes	87.2	111.3	109.9	136.9	182.0	232.9	400.9	470.4	620.6	794.4	896.9
Other	...	...	...	...	...	...	...	...	...	...	...
4 Other current transfers paid	38.8	42.5	57.8	84.5	95.1	127.8	208.2	292.8	339.8	455.7	558.5
a Net casualty insurance premiums	...	...	...	...	...	...	...	...	...	...	...
b Transfers to private non-profit institutions serving households	...	...	...	...	...	...	...	...	...	...	...
c Transfers to the rest of the world	7.3	8.0	12.6	25.0	22.4	31.4	55.2	79.7	49.7	58.8	86.7
d Other current transfers, except imputed	31.5	34.5	45.2	59.5	72.7	96.4	153.0	213.1	290.1	396.9	471.8
e Imputed employee welfare contributions	...	...	...	...	...	...	...	...	...	...	...
Net saving	119.6	118.1	169.3	477.2	511.1	405.1	890.2	1553.7	2509.4	3001.1	2130.9
Total Current Disbursements and Net Saving	2200.3	2719.3	3307.1	4234.9	5892.7	7739.4	10247.3	13138.6	17800.4	22505.4	26866.4

Korea, Republic of

3.33 Household and Private Unincorporated Enterprise Capital Accumulation Account

Thousand Million Korean won

	1970	1971	1972	1973	1974	1975	1976	1977	1978	1979	1980
Finance of Gross Accumulation											
1 Gross saving	176.9	189.0	275.7	624.9	729.9	658.5	1228.0	1987.7	3022.7	3543.0	2785.0
a Consumption of fixed capital	57.3	70.9	106.4	147.7	218.8	253.4	337.8	434.0	513.3	541.9	654.1
b Net saving	119.6	118.1	169.3	477.2	511.1	405.1	890.2	1553.7	2509.4	3001.1	2130.9
2 Capital transfers received	-4.0	-4.7	-2.8	-2.6	-4.8	-13.6	-13.5	-14.0	-12.9	...	...
Total Finance of Gross Accumulation	172.9	184.3	272.9	622.3	725.1	644.9	1214.5	1973.7	3009.8	...	...
Gross Accumulation											
1 Gross Capital Formation	153.8	145.5	155.1	282.4	553.3	554.4	792.9	1043.6	1850.5	2467.1	...
2 Purchases of land, net	...	...	...	...	...	...	...	...	...	...	...
3 Purchases of intangibles, net	...	...	...	...	...	...	...	...	...	...	...
4 Capital transfers paid	...	...	...	...	...	...	...	...	...	...	...
5 Net lending	19.1	38.8	117.8	339.9	171.8	90.5	421.6	930.1	1159.3	...	...
Total Gross Accumulation	172.9	184.3	272.9	622.3	725.1	644.9	1214.5	1973.7	3009.8	...	...

4.3 Derivation of Value Added by Kind of Activity, ISIC Divisions, in Current Prices

Thousand Million Korean won

	1970 Gross Output	1970 Intermediate Consumption	1970 Value Added	1971 Gross Output	1971 Intermediate Consumption	1971 Value Added	1972 Gross Output	1972 Intermediate Consumption	1972 Value Added	1973 Gross Output	1973 Intermediate Consumption	1973 Value Added
All Producers												
1 Agriculture, hunting, forestry and fishing	...	...	718.5	...	...	890.7	...	...	1063.1	...	...	1307.7
a Agriculture and hunting	...	...	617.7	...	...	766.7	...	...	924.8	...	...	1097.3
b Forestry and logging	...	...	53.6	...	...	60.7	...	...	68.6	...	...	85.8
c Fishing	...	...	47.3	...	...	63.2	...	...	69.6	...	...	124.6
2 Mining and quarrying	...	...	38.9	...	...	44.5	...	...	47.9	...	...	61.8
a Coal mining	...	...	14.4	...	...	17.1	...	...	22.5	...	...	26.5
b Crude petroleum and natural gas production	...	...	-	...	...	-	...	...	-	...	...	-
c Metal ore mining	...	...	8.1	...	...	7.9	...	...	6.5	...	...	8.6
d Other mining	...	...	16.4	...	...	19.5	...	...	18.9	...	...	26.7
3 Manufacturing	...	...	558.7	...	...	692.6	...	...	896.2	...	...	1299.8
a Manufacture of food, beverages and tobacco	...	...	160.6	...	...	189.5	...	...	252.5	...	...	285.6
b Textile, wearing apparel and leather industries	...	...	119.3	...	...	149.8	...	...	220.1	...	...	341.1
c Manufacture of wood and wood products, including furniture	...	...	17.6	...	...	21.9	...	...	28.1	...	...	43.7
d Manufacture of paper and paper products, printing and publishing	...	...	26.4	...	...	34.0	...	...	43.5	...	...	54.2
e Manufacture of chemicals and chemical petroleum, coal, rubber and plastic products	...	...	110.0	...	...	147.2	...	...	168.9	...	...	232.1
f Manufacture of non-metallic mineral products, except products of petroleum and coal	...	...	27.4	...	...	33.6	...	...	41.9	...	...	56.8
g Basic metal industries	...	...	14.0	...	...	17.0	...	...	27.1	...	...	75.7
h Manufacture of fabricated metal products, machinery and equipment	...	...	70.3	...	...	86.7	...	...	98.7	...	...	181.1
i Other manufacturing industries	...	...	13.1	...	...	13.0	...	...	15.5	...	...	29.6
4 Electricity, gas and water	...	...	44.0	...	...	53.2	...	...	68.3	...	...	76.9
a Electricity, gas and steam	...	...	37.7	...	...	44.8	...	...	59.3	...	...	66.8
b Water works and supply	...	...	6.3	...	...	8.4	...	...	9.0	...	...	10.1
5 Construction	...	...	146.8	...	...	162.0	...	...	184.1	...	...	258.8
6 Wholesale and retail trade, restaurants and hotels	...	...	437.7	...	...	553.0	...	...	705.9	...	...	957.2
a Wholesale and retail trade	...	...	372.1	...	...	467.0	...	...	595.8	...	...	819.4
b Restaurants and hotels	...	...	65.6	...	...	86.0	...	...	110.1	...	...	137.8
7 Transport, storage and communication	...	...	182.3	...	...	224.2	...	...	270.1	...	...	365.1
8 Finance, insurance, real estate and business services	...	...	158.4	...	...	203.1	...	...	244.7	...	...	305.4
9 Community, social and personal services	...	...	193.1	...	...	249.0	...	...	296.5	...	...	335.1

Korea, Republic of

4.3 Derivation of Value Added by Kind of Activity, ISIC Divisions, in Current Prices
(Continued)

Thousand Million Korean won

	1970 Gross Output	1970 Intermediate Consumption	1970 Value Added	1971 Gross Output	1971 Intermediate Consumption	1971 Value Added	1972 Gross Output	1972 Intermediate Consumption	1972 Value Added	1973 Gross Output	1973 Intermediate Consumption	1973 Value Added
Total, Industries	...	...	2478.3	...	...	3072.1	...	...	3776.8	...	...	4967.8
Producers of Government Services	...	...	134.6	...	...	163.1	...	...	195.2	...	...	209.4
Other Producers	...	...	8.3	...	...	10.9	...	...	13.3	...	...	15.7
Total	...	...	2621.2	...	...	3246.1	...	...	3985.3	...	...	5192.9
Imputed bank service charge	...	...	...	...	...	...	...	...	...	...	...	...
Import duties	...	...	50.9	...	...	52.2	...	...	59.1	...	...	82.4
Value added tax	...	...	...	...	...	...	...	...	...	...	...	...
Total	...	...	2672.1	...	...	3298.3	...	...	4044.4	...	...	5275.3

	1974 Gross Output	1974 Intermediate Consumption	1974 Value Added	1975 Gross Output	1975 Intermediate Consumption	1975 Value Added	1976 Gross Output	1976 Intermediate Consumption	1976 Value Added	1977 Gross Output	1977 Intermediate Consumption	1977 Value Added
All Producers												
1 Agriculture, hunting, forestry and fishing	...	...	1816.4	...	...	2441.7	...	...	3160.6	...	...	3913.7
a Agriculture and hunting	...	...	1574.9	...	...	2118.4	...	...	2728.4	...	...	3284.9
b Forestry and logging	...	...	112.2	...	...	136.3	...	...	160.2	...	...	211.8
c Fishing	...	...	129.3	...	...	187.0	...	...	272.0	...	...	416.9
2 Mining and quarrying	...	...	91.8	...	...	148.2	...	...	162.6	...	...	248.9
a Coal mining	...	...	36.3	...	...	68.2	...	...	65.7	...	...	96.9
b Crude petroleum and natural gas production	...	...	-	...	...	-	...	...	-	...	...	-
c Metal ore mining	...	...	16.9	...	...	22.5	...	...	29.4	...	...	35.0
d Other mining	...	...	38.6	...	...	57.5	...	...	67.4	...	...	116.9
3 Manufacturing	...	...	1910.2	...	...	2590.4	...	...	3661.8	...	...	4594.0
a Manufacture of food, beverages and tobacco	...	...	377.1	...	...	584.6	...	...	803.3	...	...	1009.8
b Textile, wearing apparel and leather industries	...	...	389.0	...	...	551.2	...	...	783.4	...	...	870.9
c Manufacture of wood and wood products, including furniture	...	...	36.1	...	...	50.7	...	...	62.2	...	...	88.7
d Manufacture of paper and paper products, printing and publishing	...	...	85.9	...	...	102.8	...	...	137.4	...	...	181.8
e Manufacture of chemicals and chemical petroleum, coal, rubber and plastic products	...	...	435.3	...	...	594.7	...	...	839.4	...	...	1024.5
f Manufacture of non-metallic mineral products, except products of petroleum and coal	...	...	78.8	...	...	125.6	...	...	143.5	...	...	199.6
g Basic metal industries	...	...	165.2	...	...	108.3	...	...	194.1	...	...	277.1
h Manufacture of fabricated metal products, machinery and equipment	...	...	306.7	...	...	418.7	...	...	624.6	...	...	842.2
i Other manufacturing industries	...	...	36.2	...	...	53.7	...	...	73.9	...	...	99.5
4 Electricity, gas and water	...	...	66.6	...	...	126.2	...	...	180.6	...	...	260.6
a Electricity, gas and steam	...	...	55.2	...	...	114.4	...	...	159.3	...	...	237.3
b Water works and supply	...	...	11.4	...	...	11.9	...	...	21.3	...	...	23.3
5 Construction	...	...	344.1	...	...	497.8	...	...	673.4	...	...	1081.8
6 Wholesale and retail trade, restaurants and hotels	...	...	1379.1	...	...	1717.7	...	...	2173.3	...	...	2604.9
a Wholesale and retail trade	...	...	1196.4	...	...	1477.0	...	...	1874.2	...	...	2259.9
b Restaurants and hotels	...	...	182.7	...	...	240.7	...	...	299.1	...	...	345.0
7 Transport, storage and communication	...	...	466.0	...	...	606.7	...	...	787.9	...	...	1017.2
8 Finance, insurance, real estate and business services	...	...	430.8	...	...	575.7	...	...	758.0	...	...	1033.2
9 Community, social and personal services	...	...	462.6	...	...	649.5	...	...	914.7	...	...	1161.4
Total, Industries	...	...	6967.5	...	...	9353.8	...	...	12473.0	...	...	15915.7
Producers of Government Services	...	...	282.3	...	...	389.1	...	...	575.2	...	...	785.2
Other Producers	...	...	21.6	...	...	27.8	...	...	32.8	...	...	35.8
Total	...	...	7271.4	...	...	9770.6	...	...	13081.0	...	...	16736.7
Imputed bank service charge	...	...	...	...	...	...	...	...	...	...	...	...
Import duties	...	...	126.7	...	...	181.0	...	...	275.5	...	...	385.9
Value added tax	...	...	...	...	...	...	...	...	...	...	...	...
Total	...	...	7398.1	...	...	9951.7	...	...	13356.5	...	...	17122.7

Korea, Republic of

4.3 Derivation of Value Added by Kind of Activity, ISIC Divisions, in Current Prices

Thousand Million Korean won

	1978 Gross Output	1978 Intermediate Consumption	1978 Value Added	1979 Gross Output	1979 Intermediate Consumption	1979 Value Added	1980 Gross Output	1980 Intermediate Consumption	1980 Value Added
			All Producers						
1 Agriculture, hunting, forestry and fishing	...	...	5016.9	...	...	5964.5	...	...	5590.0
a Agriculture and hunting	...	...	4224.0	...	...	5152.3	...	...	4838.7
b Forestry and logging	...	...	264.5	...	...	269.9	...	...	343.5
c Fishing	...	...	528.4	...	...	542.4	...	...	746.5
2 Mining and quarrying	...	...	313.9	...	...	325.2	...	...	475.3
a Coal mining	...	...	134.6	...	...	151.1	...	...	216.4
b Crude petroleum and natural gas production	...	...	-	...	...	-	...	...	-
c Metal ore mining	...	...	33.7	...	...	26.0	...	...	38.2
d Other mining	...	...	145.6	...	...	148.1	...	...	220.7
3 Manufacturing	...	...	6193.7	...	...	7823.1	...	...	9891.0
a Manufacture of food, beverages and tobacco	...	...	1335.2	...	...	1658.4	...	...	2049.8
b Textile, wearing apparel and leather industries	...	...	1203.2	...	...	1424.2	...	...	1615.6
c Manufacture of wood and wood products, including furniture	...	...	123.4	...	...	136.2	...	...	104.5
d Manufacture of paper and paper products, printing and publishing	...	...	230.3	...	...	269.7	...	...	365.2
e Manufacture of chemicals and chemical petroleum, coal, rubber and plastic products	...	...	1243.0	...	...	1636.3	...	...	2425.8
f Manufacture of non-metallic mineral products, except products of petroleum and coal	...	...	247.2	...	...	343.9	...	...	467.7
g Basic metal industries	...	...	441.9	...	...	701.3	...	...	984.5
h Manufacture of fabricated metal products, machinery and equipment	...	...	1257.4	...	...	1518.5	...	...	1685.0
i Other manufacturing industries	...	...	112.1	...	...	134.6	...	...	192.9
4 Electricity, gas and water	...	...	296.5	...	...	541.4	...	...	774.3
a Electricity, gas and steam	...	...	270.3	...	...	509.2	...	...	735.9
b Water works and supply	...	...	26.2	...	...	32.2	...	...	38.4
5 Construction	...	...	1907.2	...	...	2750.4	...	...	3221.5
6 Wholesale and retail trade, restaurants and hotels	...	...	3270.7	...	...	4308.4	...	...	5415.2
a Wholesale and retail trade	...	...	2815.0	...	...	3796.9	...	...	4768.3
b Restaurants and hotels	...	...	455.7	...	...	511.5	...	...	646.9
7 Transport, storage and communication	...	...	1388.9	...	...	1705.1	...	...	2146.3
8 Finance, insurance, real estate and business services	...	...	1456.6	...	...	1877.8	...	...	2661.9
9 Community, social and personal services	...	...	1497.4	...	...	2006.4	...	...	2703.7
Total, Industries	...	...	21341.8	...	...	27302.3	...	...	32879.1
Producers of Government Services	...	...	996.0	...	...	1262.6	...	...	1674.2
Other Producers	...	...	46.1	...	...	59.9	...	...	61.1
Total	...	...	22383.9	...	...	28624.8	...	...	34614.4
Imputed bank service charge	...	...	...	...	...	...	...	...	...
Import duties	...	...	646.4	...	...	732.3	...	...	766.1
Value added tax	...	...	...	...	...	...	...	...	...
Total	...	...	23030.3	...	...	29357.1	...	...	35380.5

4.4 Derivation of Value Added by Kind of Activity, ISIC Divisions, in Constant Prices

Thousand Million Korean won

	1970 Gross Output	1970 Intermediate Consumption	1970 Value Added	1971 Gross Output	1971 Intermediate Consumption	1971 Value Added	1972 Gross Output	1972 Intermediate Consumption	1972 Value Added	1973 Gross Output	1973 Intermediate Consumption	1973 Value Added
				At constant prices of: 1975								
				All Producers								
1 Agriculture, hunting, forestry and fishing	...	...	1933.5	...	...	2005.4	...	...	2045.6	...	...	2173.8
a Agriculture and hunting	...	...	1715.9	...	...	1778.1	...	...	1789.8	...	...	1868.5
b Forestry and logging	...	...	136.5	...	...	138.9	...	...	140.8	...	...	152.6
c Fishing	...	...	81.1	...	...	88.3	...	...	115.0	...	...	152.7

Korea, Republic of

4.4 Derivation of Value Added by Kind of Activity, ISIC Divisions, in Constant Prices
(Continued)

Thousand Million Korean won

	1970 Gross Output	1970 Intermediate Consumption	1970 Value Added	1971 Gross Output	1971 Intermediate Consumption	1971 Value Added	1972 Gross Output	1972 Intermediate Consumption	1972 Value Added	1973 Gross Output	1973 Intermediate Consumption	1973 Value Added
					At constant prices of:1975							
2 Mining and quarrying	...	...	104.7	...	...	105.8	...	...	104.6	...	...	124.4
a Coal mining	...	...	48.0	...	...	49.6	...	...	48.1	...	...	52.6
b Crude petroleum and natural gas production	...	...	-	...	...	-	...	...	-	...	...	-
c Metal ore mining	...	...	19.9	...	...	19.2	...	...	19.6	...	...	21.4
d Other mining	...	...	36.8	...	...	37.1	...	...	36.9	...	...	50.4
3 Manufacturing	...	...	1135.6	...	...	1349.4	...	...	1538.2	...	...	1987.8
a Manufacture of food, beverages and tobacco	...	...	343.4	...	...	402.8	...	...	430.9	...	...	481.2
b Textile, wearing apparel and leather industries	...	...	185.7	...	...	235.0	...	...	297.7	...	...	413.1
c Manufacture of wood and wood products, including furniture	...	...	30.3	...	...	34.4	...	...	38.1	...	...	44.5
d Manufacture of paper and paper products, printing and publishing	...	...	57.0	...	...	66.1	...	...	72.9	...	...	85.8
e Manufacture of chemicals and chemical petroleum, coal, rubber and plastic products	...	...	283.3	...	...	342.2	...	...	376.9	...	...	471.5
f Manufacture of non-metallic mineral products, except products of petroleum and coal	...	...	63.7	...	...	76.2	...	...	80.2	...	...	110.4
g Basic metal industries	...	...	26.9	...	...	33.4	...	...	43.4	...	...	70.6
h Manufacture of fabricated metal products, machinery and equipment	...	...	114.2	...	...	129.5	...	...	162.9	...	...	267.5
i Other manufacturing industries	...	...	31.1	...	...	29.9	...	...	35.1	...	...	43.2
4 Electricity, gas and water	...	...	57.4	...	...	68.3	...	...	76.6	...	...	93.5
a Electricity, gas and steam	...	...	51.1	...	...	61.0	...	...	68.6	...	...	85.0
b Water works and supply	...	...	6.3	...	...	7.4	...	...	8.0	...	...	8.5
5 Construction	...	...	343.5	...	...	335.9	...	...	332.3	...	...	425.9
6 Wholesale and retail trade, restaurants and hotels	...	...	1121.7	...	...	1318.7	...	...	1441.3	...	...	1681.7
a Wholesale and retail trade [a]	...	...	956.2	...	...	1126.8	...	...	1235.3	...	...	1446.4
b Restaurants and hotels	...	...	165.5	...	...	191.9	...	...	206.0	...	...	235.3
7 Transport, storage and communication	...	...	319.0	...	...	365.2	...	...	400.8	...	...	506.8
8 Finance, insurance, real estate and business services	...	...	416.0	...	...	453.7	...	...	466.8	...	...	500.8
9 Community, social and personal services	...	...	498.4	...	...	546.2	...	...	572.1	...	...	606.3
Total, Industries	...	...	5929.8	...	...	6548.7	...	...	6978.1	...	...	8100.9
Producers of Government Services	...	...	364.5	...	...	377.7	...	...	373.9	...	...	376.4
Other Producers	...	...	20.5	...	...	24.1	...	...	25.0	...	...	26.9
Total	...	...	6314.8	...	...	6950.4	...	...	7377.0	...	...	8504.2
Imputed bank service charge	...	...	...	...	...	...	...	...	...	...	...	...
Import duties	...	...	...	...	...	...	...	...	...	...	...	...
Value added tax	...	...	...	...	...	...	...	...	...	...	...	...
Total	...	...	6314.8	...	...	6950.4	...	...	7377.0	...	...	8504.2

	1974 Gross Output	1974 Intermediate Consumption	1974 Value Added	1975 Gross Output	1975 Intermediate Consumption	1975 Value Added	1976 Gross Output	1976 Intermediate Consumption	1976 Value Added	1977 Gross Output	1977 Intermediate Consumption	1977 Value Added
					At constant prices of:1975							
					All Producers							
1 Agriculture, hunting, forestry and fishing	...	...	2319.4	...	...	2441.7	...	...	2702.7	...	...	2759.3
a Agriculture and hunting	...	...	2007.3	...	...	2118.4	...	...	2334.0	...	...	2368.5
b Forestry and logging	...	...	145.3	...	...	136.3	...	...	129.2	...	...	137.8
c Fishing	...	...	166.8	...	...	187.0	...	...	239.5	...	...	253.0
2 Mining and quarrying	...	...	132.0	...	...	148.2	...	...	151.7	...	...	169.6
a Coal mining	...	...	59.2	...	...	68.2	...	...	63.7	...	...	66.9
b Crude petroleum and natural gas production	...	...	-	...	...	-	...	...	-	...	...	-
c Metal ore mining	...	...	21.1	...	...	22.5	...	...	24.9	...	...	26.5
d Other mining	...	...	51.7	...	...	57.5	...	...	63.1	...	...	76.3

Korea, Republic of

4.4 Derivation of Value Added by Kind of Activity, ISIC Divisions, in Constant Prices
(Continued)

Thousand Million Korean won

	1974 Gross Output	1974 Intermediate Consumption	1974 Value Added	1975 Gross Output	1975 Intermediate Consumption	1975 Value Added	1976 Gross Output	1976 Intermediate Consumption	1976 Value Added	1977 Gross Output	1977 Intermediate Consumption	1977 Value Added
				At constant prices of: 1975								
3 Manufacturing	...	...	2301.1	...	...	2590.4	...	...	3176.6	...	...	3633.6
a Manufacture of food, beverages and tobacco	...	...	540.7	...	...	584.6	...	...	633.6	...	...	705.6
b Textile, wearing apparel and leather industries	...	...	458.3	...	...	551.2	...	...	674.9	...	...	703.9
c Manufacture of wood and wood products, including furniture	...	...	43.2	...	...	50.7	...	...	59.4	...	...	67.0
d Manufacture of paper and paper products, printing and publishing	...	...	99.1	...	...	102.8	...	...	126.4	...	...	146.8
e Manufacture of chemicals and chemical petroleum, coal, rubber and plastic products	...	...	512.6	...	...	594.7	...	...	724.8	...	...	841.7
f Manufacture of non-metallic mineral products, except products of petroleum and coal	...	...	120.7	...	...	125.6	...	...	146.4	...	...	177.1
g Basic metal industries	...	...	102.1	...	...	108.3	...	...	152.2	...	...	178.6
h Manufacture of fabricated metal products, machinery and equipment	...	...	373.0	...	...	418.8	...	...	585.0	...	...	722.1
i Other manufacturing industries	...	...	51.5	...	...	53.7	...	...	74.0	...	...	90.9
4 Electricity, gas and water	...	...	106.0	...	...	126.2	...	...	149.4	...	...	172.5
a Electricity, gas and steam	...	...	96.5	...	...	114.4	...	...	135.0	...	...	157.1
b Water works and supply	...	...	9.4	...	...	11.9	...	...	14.4	...	...	15.4
5 Construction	...	...	437.1	...	...	497.8	...	...	559.0	...	...	699.8
6 Wholesale and retail trade, restaurants and hotels	...	...	1781.5	...	...	1898.7	...	...	2131.8	...	...	2307.4
a Wholesale and retail trade [a]	...	...	1543.2	...	...	1658.0	...	...	1880.4	...	...	2046.9
b Restaurants and hotels	...	...	238.3	...	...	240.7	...	...	251.4	...	...	260.5
7 Transport, storage and communication	...	...	543.5	...	...	606.7	...	...	712.2	...	...	841.3
8 Finance, insurance, real estate and business services	...	...	545.8	...	...	575.7	...	...	638.2	...	...	727.8
9 Community, social and personal services	...	...	629.5	...	...	649.5	...	...	684.3	...	...	723.4
Total, Industries	...	...	8795.9	...	...	9534.8	...	...	10906.0	...	...	12034.8
Producers of Government Services	...	...	383.1	...	...	389.1	...	...	398.6	...	...	409.0
Other Producers	...	...	27.6	...	...	27.8	...	...	28.4	...	...	28.2
Total	...	...	9206.5	...	...	9951.6	...	...	11333.0	...	...	12472.0
Imputed bank service charge	...	...	...	...	...	...	...	...	...	...	...	...
Import duties	...	...	...	...	...	...	...	...	...	...	...	...
Value added tax	...	...	...	...	...	...	...	...	...	...	...	...
Total	...	...	9206.5	...	...	9951.6	...	...	11333.0	...	...	12472.0

	1978 Gross Output	1978 Intermediate Consumption	1978 Value Added	1979 Gross Output	1979 Intermediate Consumption	1979 Value Added
	At constant prices of: 1975					
	All Producers					
1 Agriculture, hunting, forestry and fishing	...	...	2650.3	...	...	2828.6
a Agriculture and hunting	...	...	2291.0	...	...	2475.7
b Forestry and logging	...	...	145.6	...	...	130.2
c Fishing	...	...	213.7	...	...	222.7
2 Mining and quarrying	...	...	176.9	...	...	173.4
a Coal mining	...	...	69.9	...	...	70.5
b Crude petroleum and natural gas production	...	...	-	...	...	-
c Metal ore mining	...	...	25.2	...	...	25.0
d Other mining	...	...	81.8	...	...	77.8

Korea, Republic of

4.4 Derivation of Value Added by Kind of Activity, ISIC Divisions, in Constant Prices
(Continued)

Thousand Million Korean won

	1978 Gross Output	1978 Intermediate Consumption	1978 Value Added	1979 Gross Output	1979 Intermediate Consumption	1979 Value Added
			At constant prices of: 1975			
3 Manufacturing	...	...	4386.9	...	...	4818.0
a Manufacture of food, beverages and tobacco	...	...	825.1	...	...	947.0
b Textile, wearing apparel and leather industries	...	...	791.1	...	...	782.0
c Manufacture of wood and wood products, including furniture	...	...	78.8	...	...	76.5
d Manufacture of paper and paper products, printing and publishing	...	...	171.2	...	...	190.9
e Manufacture of chemicals and chemical petroleum, coal, rubber and plastic products	...	...	985.7	...	...	1083.4
f Manufacture of non-metallic mineral products, except products of petroleum and coal	...	...	196.9	...	...	219.4
g Basic metal industries	...	...	224.4	...	...	290.0
h Manufacture of fabricated metal products, machinery and equipment	...	...	1014.7	...	...	1131.9
i Other manufacturing industries	...	...	99.0	...	...	97.0
4 Electricity, gas and water	...	...	205.1	...	...	235.2
a Electricity, gas and steam	...	...	187.8	...	...	215.8
b Water works and supply	...	...	17.3	...	...	19.4
5 Construction	...	...	876.9	...	...	891.9
6 Wholesale and retail trade, restaurants and hotels	...	...	2561.0	...	...	2661.4
a Wholesale and retail trade a	...	...	2284.8	...	...	2385.8
b Restaurants and hotels	...	...	276.2	...	...	275.6
7 Transport, storage and communication	...	...	996.2	...	...	1134.4
8 Finance, insurance, real estate and business services	...	...	813.0	...	...	842.2
9 Community, social and personal services	...	...	769.0	...	...	824.8
Total, Industries	...	...	13435.3	...	...	14409.9
Producers of Government Services	...	...	419.9	...	...	430.5
Other Producers	...	...	29.7	...	...	29.1
Total	...	...	13884.9	...	...	14869.5
Imputed bank service charge	...	...	...	...	...	...
Import duties	...	...	...	...	...	...
Value added tax	...	...	...	...	...	...
Total	...	...	13884.9	...	...	14865.9

a) Item 'Import duties' is included in item 'Wholesale and retail trade'.

4.6 Cost Components of Value Added, ISIC Divisions

Thousand Million Korean won

	1970 Compensation of Employees	1970 Capital Consumption	1970 Net Operating Surplus	1970 Indirect Taxes	1970 Less: Subsidies Received	1970 Value Added	1971 Compensation of Employees	1971 Capital Consumption	1971 Net Operating Surplus	1971 Indirect Taxes	1971 Less: Subsidies Received	1971 Value Added
				All Producers								
1 Agriculture, hunting, forestry and fishing	73.6	...	630.2	...	...	718.5	89.9	...	781.8	...	...	890.7
2 Mining and quarrying	26.4	...	5.4	...	...	39.0	31.1	...	5.1	...	...	44.5
3 Manufacturing	214.1	...	163.1	...	...	558.7	268.5	...	201.1	...	...	692.6
4 Electricity, gas and water	9.8	...	19.5	...	...	44.0	12.6	...	22.9	...	...	53.2
5 Construction	86.0	...	51.3	...	...	146.8	99.9	...	51.5	...	...	162.0
6 Wholesale and retail trade, restaurants and hotels	58.0	...	330.8	...	...	437.7	70.8	...	425.9	...	...	553.0
7 Transport, storage and communication	95.2	...	41.0	...	...	182.3	107.2	...	58.0	...	...	224.2
8 Finance, insurance, real estate and business services	47.5	...	75.2	...	...	158.4	62.4	...	97.9	...	...	203.1
9 Community, social and personal services	118.3	...	60.5	...	...	193.2	159.6	...	72.0	...	...	249.0
Total, Industries	728.7	...	1376.9	...	...	2478.3	902.0	...	1716.1	...	...	3072.1
Producers of Government Services	130.6	...	-0.1	...	...	134.6	158.6	...	-0.4	...	...	163.1

Korea, Republic of

4.6 Cost Components of Value Added, ISIC Divisions
(Continued)

Thousand Million Korean won

1970 / 1971

	Compensation of Employees	Capital Consumption	Net Operating Surplus	Indirect Taxes	Less: Subsidies Received	Value Added	Compensation of Employees	Capital Consumption	Net Operating Surplus	Indirect Taxes	Less: Subsidies Received	Value Added
Other Producers	8.3	...	-	...	...	8.3	10.9	...	-	...	...	10.9
Total	867.6	...	1376.8	...	...	2621.2	1071.5	...	1715.7	...	...	3246.1
Imputed bank service charge a	...	...	...	...	...	...	...	...	...	...	...	...
Import duties	...	...	...	...	...	50.9	...	...	...	...	...	52.2
Value added tax	...	...	...	...	...	...	...	...	...	...	...	...
Other adjustments	...	...	...	...	...	...	...	...	...	...	...	...
Total	867.6	...	1376.8	...	...	2672.1	1071.5	...	1715.7	...	...	3298.3

1972 / 1973

	Compensation of Employees	Capital Consumption	Net Operating Surplus	Indirect Taxes	Less: Subsidies Received	Value Added	Compensation of Employees	Capital Consumption	Net Operating Surplus	Indirect Taxes	Less: Subsidies Received	Value Added
					All Producers							
1 Agriculture, hunting, forestry and fishing	102.6	...	935.4	...	...	1063.1	119.4	...	1146.7	...	...	1307.7
2 Mining and quarrying	34.6	...	5.7	...	...	47.9	43.9	...	8.5	...	...	61.8
3 Manufacturing	341.7	...	274.9	...	...	896.2	440.7	...	484.5	...	...	1299.8
4 Electricity, gas and water	16.3	...	27.4	...	...	68.3	16.8	...	29.8	...	...	76.9
5 Construction	122.4	...	49.7	...	...	184.1	163.0	...	76.5	...	...	258.8
6 Wholesale and retail trade, restaurants and hotels	79.0	...	541.8	...	...	705.9	95.9	...	755.1	...	...	957.2
7 Transport, storage and communication	131.5	...	76.6	...	...	270.1	180.7	...	86.1	...	...	365.1
8 Finance, insurance, real estate and business services	71.0	...	120.2	...	...	244.7	87.2	...	142.4	...	...	305.4
9 Community, social and personal services	197.5	...	78.3	...	...	296.5	230.3	...	79.9	...	...	335.1
Total, Industries	1096.7	...	2109.8	...	...	3776.8	1377.8	...	2809.6	...	...	4967.8
Producers of Government Services	187.5	...	2.1	...	...	195.2	201.1	...	2.1	...	...	209.4
Other Producers	13.3	...	-	...	...	13.3	15.7	...	-	...	...	15.7
Total	1297.5	...	2112.0	...	...	3985.3	1594.6	...	2811.6	...	...	5192.9
Imputed bank service charge a	...	...	...	...	...	...	...	...	...	...	...	...
Import duties	...	...	...	...	...	59.1	...	...	...	...	...	82.4
Value added tax	...	...	...	...	...	...	...	...	...	...	...	...
Other adjustments	...	...	...	...	...	...	...	...	...	...	...	...
Total	1297.5	...	2112.0	...	...	4044.4	1594.6	...	2811.6	...	...	5275.3

1974 / 1975

	Compensation of Employees	Capital Consumption	Net Operating Surplus	Indirect Taxes	Less: Subsidies Received	Value Added	Compensation of Employees	Capital Consumption	Net Operating Surplus	Indirect Taxes	Less: Subsidies Received	Value Added
					All Producers							
1 Agriculture, hunting, forestry and fishing	138.1	...	1615.0	...	...	1816.4	189.9	...	2154.9	...	...	2441.7
2 Mining and quarrying	65.4	...	22.4	...	...	91.8	104.0	...	28.6	...	...	148.2
3 Manufacturing	668.6	...	658.4	...	...	1910.2	935.1	...	782.9	...	...	2590.4
4 Electricity, gas and water	19.3	...	33.7	...	...	66.6	30.0	...	48.5	...	...	126.2
5 Construction	221.3	...	89.9	...	...	344.1	339.1	...	121.2	...	...	497.8
6 Wholesale and retail trade, restaurants and hotels	125.0	...	1205.5	...	...	1379.1	150.2	...	1434.2	...	...	1717.7
7 Transport, storage and communication	227.6	...	118.0	...	...	466.0	264.5	...	194.8	...	...	606.7
8 Finance, insurance, real estate and business services	119.3	...	202.6	...	...	430.8	157.9	...	266.9	...	...	575.7
9 Community, social and personal services	328.1	...	98.6	...	...	462.6	483.6	...	124.7	...	...	649.6
Total, Industries	1912.5	...	4044.0	...	...	6967.5	2654.3	...	5156.8	...	...	9353.8
Producers of Government Services	270.1	...	2.1	...	...	282.3	374.2	...	1.6	...	...	389.1
Other Producers	21.6	...	-	...	...	21.6	27.8	...	-	...	...	27.8
Total	2204.2	...	4046.2	...	...	7271.4	3056.2	...	5158.4	...	...	9770.6
Imputed bank service charge a	...	...	...	...	...	...	...	...	...	...	...	...
Import duties	...	...	...	...	...	126.7	...	...	...	...	...	181.0
Value added tax	...	...	...	...	...	...	...	...	...	...	...	...
Other adjustments	...	...	...	...	...	...	...	...	...	...	...	...
Total	2204.2	...	4046.2	...	...	7398.1	3056.2	...	5158.4	...	...	9951.7

Korea, Republic of

4.6 Cost Components of Value Added, ISIC Divisions

Thousand Million Korean won

1976

	Compensation of Employees	Capital Consumption	Net Operating Surplus	Indirect Taxes	Less: Subsidies Received	Value Added
All Producers						
1 Agriculture, hunting, forestry and fishing	263.5	...	2782.7	...	...	3160.6
2 Mining and quarrying	115.6	...	30.5	...	...	162.6
3 Manufacturing	1368.6	...	1092.4	...	...	3661.8
4 Electricity, gas and water	37.1	...	70.4	...	...	180.6
5 Construction	407.8	...	191.5	...	...	673.4
6 Wholesale and retail trade, restaurants and hotels	197.3	...	1678.2	...	...	2173.3
7 Transport, storage and communication	375.2	...	212.6	...	...	787.9
8 Finance, insurance, real estate and business services	186.3	...	372.8	...	...	758.0
9 Community, social and personal services	697.3	...	159.2	...	...	914.9
Total, Industries	3648.6	...	6590.2	...	...	12473.0
Producers of Government Services	557.8	...	1.7	...	...	575.2
Other Producers	32.8	...	-	...	...	32.8
Total	4239.2	...	6591.9	...	...	13081.0
Imputed bank service charge [a]	...	...	...	...	...	...
Import duties	...	...	...	...	...	275.5
Value added tax	...	...	...	...	...	...
Other adjustments	...	...	...	...	...	...
Total	4239.2	...	6591.9	...	...	13356.5

1977

	Compensation of Employees	Capital Consumption	Net Operating Surplus	Indirect Taxes	Less: Subsidies Received	Value Added
1 Agriculture, hunting, forestry and fishing	370.8	...	3395.5	...	...	3913.7
2 Mining and quarrying	183.4	...	29.4	...	...	248.9
3 Manufacturing	1748.9	...	1217.3	...	...	4594.0
4 Electricity, gas and water	61.1	...	109.5	...	...	260.6
5 Construction	617.4	...	389.3	...	...	1081.8
6 Wholesale and retail trade, restaurants and hotels	249.0	...	2009.8	...	...	2604.9
7 Transport, storage and communication	505.4	...	284.9	...	...	1017.2
8 Finance, insurance, real estate and business services	262.6	...	511.2	...	...	1033.2
9 Community, social and personal services	907.2	...	184.8	...	...	1161.4
Total, Industries	4905.7	...	8131.8	...	...	15915.7
Producers of Government Services	764.4	...	2.6	...	...	785.2
Other Producers	35.8	...	-	...	...	35.8
Total	5705.8	...	8134.4	...	...	16736.7
Imputed bank service charge [a]	...	...	...	...	...	...
Import duties	...	...	...	...	...	385.9
Value added tax	...	...	...	...	...	...
Other adjustments	...	...	...	...	...	...
Total	5705.8	...	8134.4	...	...	17122.7

1978

	Compensation of Employees	Capital Consumption	Net Operating Surplus	Indirect Taxes	Less: Subsidies Received	Value Added
All Producers						
1 Agriculture, hunting, forestry and fishing	496.0	...	4331.7	...	...	5016.9
2 Mining and quarrying	225.7	...	38.9	...	...	313.9
3 Manufacturing	2640.5	...	1528.0	...	...	6193.7
4 Electricity, gas and water	79.1	...	136.8	...	...	296.5
5 Construction	1236.3	...	538.6	...	...	1907.2
6 Wholesale and retail trade, restaurants and hotels	384.3	...	2490.5	...	...	3270.7
7 Transport, storage and communication	769.8	...	314.1	...	...	1388.9
8 Finance, insurance, real estate and business services	403.7	...	711.4	...	...	1456.6
9 Community, social and personal services	1171.2	...	244.7	...	...	1497.4
Total, Industries	7406.6	...	10334.7	...	...	21341.8
Producers of Government Services	968.8	...	3.3	...	...	996.0
Other Producers	46.1	...	-	...	...	46.1
Total	8421.4	...	10338.0	...	...	22383.9
Imputed bank service charge [a]	...	...	...	...	...	...
Import duties	...	...	...	...	...	646.4
Value added tax	...	...	...	...	...	...
Other adjustments	...	...	...	...	...	...
Total	8421.4	...	10338.0	...	...	23030.3

1979

	Compensation of Employees	Capital Consumption	Net Operating Surplus	Indirect Taxes	Less: Subsidies Received	Value Added
1 Agriculture, hunting, forestry and fishing	520.0	...	5204.4	...	...	5964.5
2 Mining and quarrying	270.9	...	22.6	...	...	325.2
3 Manufacturing	3064.7	...	1848.9	...	...	7823.2
4 Electricity, gas and water	100.8	...	298.3	...	...	541.4
5 Construction	1849.1	...	677.3	...	...	2750.4
6 Wholesale and retail trade, restaurants and hotels	487.3	...	3415.3	...	...	4308.4
7 Transport, storage and communication	919.4	...	403.0	...	...	1705.1
8 Finance, insurance, real estate and business services	524.9	...	912.5	...	...	1877.8
9 Community, social and personal services	1602.2	...	283.9	...	...	2006.3
Total, Industries	9339.3	...	13066.2	...	...	27302.3
Producers of Government Services	1230.8	...	3.2	...	...	1262.6
Other Producers	59.9	...	-	...	...	59.9
Total	10630.0	...	13069.4	...	...	28624.8
Imputed bank service charge [a]	...	...	...	...	...	...
Import duties	...	...	...	...	...	732.3
Value added tax	...	...	...	...	...	...
Other adjustments	...	...	...	...	...	...
Total	10630.0	...	13069.4	...	...	29357.1

1980

	Compensation of Employees	Capital Consumption	Net Operating Surplus	Indirect Taxes	Less: Subsidies Received	Value Added
All Producers						
1 Agriculture, hunting, forestry and fishing	628.9	...	4671.6	...	...	5590.0
2 Mining and quarrying	408.9	...	55.8	...	...	475.3
3 Manufacturing	3760.2	...	2248.1	...	...	9891.0
4 Electricity, gas and water	142.8	...	460.7	...	...	774.3

Korea, Republic of

4.6 Cost Components of Value Added, ISIC Divisions
(Continued)

Thousand Million Korean won

	1980					
	Compensation of Employees	Capital Consumption	Net Operating Surplus	Indirect Taxes	Less: Subsidies Received	Value Added
5 Construction	2243.6	...	717.4	...	...	3221.5
6 Wholesale and retail trade, restaurants and hotels	510.8	...	4389.4	...	...	5415.1
7 Transport, storage and communication	1112.0	...	474.9	...	...	2146.3
8 Finance, insurance, real estate and business services	717.8	...	1389.6	...	...	2661.9
9 Community, social and personal services	1951.2	...	464.2	...	...	2703.8
Total, Industries	11476.2	...	14871.7	...	...	32879.1
Producers of Government Services	1630.3	...	4.5	...	...	1674.2
Other Producers	61.1	...	-	...	...	61.1
Total	13167.6	...	14876.2	...	...	34614.4
Imputed bank service charge [a]	...	...	...	...	...	...
Import duties	...	...	...	...	...	766.1
Value added tax	...	...	...	...	...	...
Other adjustments	...	...	...	...	...	...
Total	13167.6	...	14876.2	...	...	35380.5

a) Item 'Less: Imputed bank service charges' is subtracted from individual industries.

Kuwait

Source. Reply to the United Nations National Accounts Questionnaire from the Central Office of Statistics, Ministry of Planning, Kuwait City. Official estimates are published by the same Office in 'National Accounts Statistics' and 'National Accounts and Input-output Tables of Kuwait', 1976.

General note. The estimates shown in the following tables have been prepared in accordance with the United Nations System of National Accounts so far as the existing data would permit.

1.1 Expenditure on the Gross Domestic Product, in Current Prices

Million Kuwaiti dinars

	1970	1971	1972	1973	1974	1975	1976	1977	1978	1979	1980
1 General government final consumption expenditure	139	173	199	215	279	386	432	589	616	757	857
2 Private final consumption expenditure	396	420	427	439	564	759	1030	1319	1478	1742	2200
3 Gross capital formation	124	130	136	153	259	444	635	983	863	883	984
a Increase in stocks	-2	3	9	7	37	26	72	129	69	93	105
b Gross fixed capital formation	126	127	127	146	222	418	563	854	794	790	879
Residential buildings											
Non-residential buildings	63	75	86	90	141	155	264	337	421	508	513
Other construction and land improvement etc.											
Other	63	52	41	56	81	263	299	517	373	282	366
4 Exports of goods and services	614	917	1004	1154	3239	2806	2992	2918	3008	5333	6065
5 Less: Imports of goods and services	248	258	303	356	528	907	1250	1760	1700	1971	2655
Statistical discrepancy	1	...	1	-1	...	-1	1	...	...	-1	...
Equals: Gross Domestic Product	1026	1382	1464	1604	3813	3487	3840	4049	4265	6743	7451

1.2 Expenditure on the Gross Domestic Product, in Constant Prices

Million Kuwaiti dinars

	1970	1971	1972	1973	1974	1975	1976	1977	1978	1979	1980
	\multicolumn{11}{c}{At constant prices of: 1972}											
1 General government final consumption expenditure	153	177	199	213	238	270	297	358	369	379	411
2 Private final consumption expenditure	430	432	427	405	459	605	730	867	888	977	1155
3 Gross capital formation	132	133	136	136	186	290	400	606	496	468	481
a Increase in stocks	-3	3	9	6	27	18	46	78	42	53	54
b Gross fixed capital formation	135	130	127	130	159	272	354	528	454	415	427
Residential buildings											
Non-residential buildings	67	77	86	81	92	96	169	201	232	258	232
Other construction and land improvement etc.											
Other	68	53	41	49	67	176	185	327	222	157	195
4 Exports of goods and services	891	945	1004	937	825	763	831	784	842	1024	870
5 Less: Imports of goods and services	269	265	303	347	432	659	859	1152	1090	1147	1379
Statistical discrepancy	-52	-36	1	78	56	38	74	61	109	90	70
Equals: Gross Domestic Product	1285	1386	1464	1422	1332	1307	1473	1524	1614	1791	1608

1.7 External Transactions on Current Account, Summary

Million Kuwaiti dinars

	1970	1971	1972	1973	1974	1975	1976	1977	1978	1979	1980
	\multicolumn{11}{c}{Payments to the Rest of the World}											
1 Imports of goods and services	248	258	303	356	528	907	1250	1760	1700	1971	2655
2 Factor income paid to the rest of the world	213	373	432	434	513	106	36	57	81	115	173
3 Indirect taxes paid to supranational organizations	...	...	...	...	...	...	...	...	...	...	...
4 Current transfers to the rest of the world	81	81	23	219	362	310	157	358	339	356	427
5 Surplus of the nation on current transactions	175	314	322	237	2068	1813	2026	1318	1703	3926	4595
Payments to the Rest of the World and Surplus of the Nation on Current Transactions	717	1026	1080	1246	3471	3136	3469	3493	3823	6368	7850

Kuwait

1.7 External Transactions on Current Account, Summary
(Continued)

Million Kuwaiti dinars

	1970	1971	1972	1973	1974	1975	1976	1977	1978	1979	1980
Receipts From The Rest of the World											
1 Exports of goods and services	614	917	1004	1154	3239	2806	2992	2918	3008	5333	6065
2 Factor income received from rest of the world	103	109	70	92	232	330	477	575	815	1035	1785
a Compensation of employees	...	...	...	...	...	...	...	...	...	...	...
b Property and entrepreneurial income received	...	...	...	...	...	...	477	575	815	1035	1785
3 Subsidies received from supranational organisations	...	...	...	...	...	...	...	...	...	...	...
4 Current transfers from rest of the world	...	...	6	...	...	...	...	...	...	...	...
Receipts from the Rest of the World on Current Transactions	717	1026	1080	1246	3471	3136	3469	3493	3823	6368	7850

1.8 Capital Transactions of The Nation, Summary

Million Kuwaiti dinars

	1970	1971	1972	1973	1974	1975	1976	1977	1978	1979	1980
Finance of Gross Capital Formation											
Gross saving	300	443	458	390	2328	2257	2661	2301	2566	4809	5516
1 Consumption of fixed capital	58	64	70	76	81	93	107	126	155	181	208
2 Net saving	242	379	388	314	2247	2164	2554	2175	2411	4628	5308
Less: Surplus of the nation on current transactions	175	313	322	237	2069	1813	2026	1318	1703	3926	4595
Finance of Gross Capital Formation	124	130	136	153	259	444	635	983	863	883	984
Gross Capital Formation											
Increase in stocks	-2	3	9	7	37	26	72	129	69	93	105
Gross fixed capital formation	126	127	127	146	222	418	563	854	794	790	879
Gross Capital Formation	124	130	136	153	259	444	635	983	863	883	984

1.10 Gross Domestic Product by Kind of Activity, in Current Prices

Million Kuwaiti dinars

	1970	1971	1972	1973	1974	1975	1976	1977	1978	1979	1980
1 Agriculture, hunting, forestry and fishing	3	3	4	5	6	9	10	13	14	17	17
2 Mining and quarrying	619	908	914	997	3023	2459	2524	2483	2530	4420	5062
3 Manufacturing	42	54	65	78	169	195	230	240	280	574	440
4 Electricity, gas and water	7	9	11	12	13	13	19	20	24	27	25
5 Construction	28	33	38	44	63	74	123	158	176	210	220
6 Wholesale and retail trade, restaurants and hotels	85	94	111	117	147	221	303	371	390	426	468
7 Transport, storage and communication	29	32	35	42	50	60	72	77	91	106	124
8 Finance, insurance, real estate and business services	78	85	95	105	117	150	208	239	292	347	401
9 Community, social and personal services	20	23	26	28	35	43	52	55	60	66	75
Statistical discrepancy	1	1	...	-1	-2	-1	...	...	...	...	1
Total, Industries	912	1242	1299	1427	3621	3223	3541	3656	3857	6193	6833
Producers of Government Services	107	132	156	167	178	240	265	345	365	501	553
Other Producers	...	...	...	...	...	...	...	...	...	...	...
Subtotal	1019	1374	1455	1594	3799	3463	3806	4001	4222	6694	7386
Less: Imputed bank service charge	...	...	...	...	...	...	...	...	...	...	...
Plus: Import duties	7	8	9	10	14	24	33	48	42	49	65
Plus: Value added tax	...	...	...	...	...	...	...	...	...	...	...
Equals: Gross Domestic Product	1026	1382	1464	1604	3813	3487	3840	4049	4265	6743	7451

1.11 Gross Domestic Product by Kind of Activity, in Constant Prices

Million Kuwaiti dinars

	1970	1971	1972	1973	1974	1975	1976	1977	1978	1979	1980
At constant prices of: 1972											
1 Agriculture, hunting, forestry and fishing	4	4	4	4	5	5	6	6	6	7	7
2 Mining and quarrying	830	888	914	840	708	580	600	549	594	698	465
3 Manufacturing	55	61	65	78	85	100	101	98	115	138	140
4 Electricity, gas and water	8	9	11	12	13	15	18	21	25	29	29
5 Construction	31	34	38	41	51	55	87	104	106	118	115

Kuwait

1.11 Gross Domestic Product by Kind of Activity, in Constant Prices
(Continued)

Million Kuwaiti dinars

	1970	1971	1972	1973	1974	1975	1976	1977	1978	1979	1980
	\multicolumn{11}{c}{At constant prices of:1972}										
6 Wholesale and retail trade, restaurants and hotels	92	96	111	106	118	162	206	233	232	238	242
7 Transport, storage and communication	30	31	35	36	43	50	74	83	91	97	101
8 Finance, insurance, real estate and business services	87	95	95	100	105	115	133	148	160	168	187
9 Community, social and personal services	25	25	27	29	31	32	36	35	33	33	35
Statistical discrepancy	-1	3	...	...	-2	...	-1	...	...	-2	...
Total, Industries	1161	1246	1300	1246	1157	1114	1260	1277	1362	1524	1321
Producers of Government Services	116	133	155	166	163	175	191	216	225	238	253
Other Producers	...	...	...	...	...	...	...	...	...	...	...
Subtotal	1277	1378	1455	1412	1320	1289	1450	1493	1587	1762	1574
Less: Imputed bank service charge	...	...	...	...	...	...	...	...	...	...	...
Plus: Import duties	8	8	9	10	11	17	23	31	27	29	34
Plus: Value added tax	...	...	...	...	...	...	...	...	...	...	...
Equals: Gross Domestic Product	1285	1386	1464	1422	1332	1307	1473	1524	1614	1791	1608

1.12 Relations Among National Accounting Aggregates

Million Kuwaiti dinars

	1970	1971	1972	1973	1974	1975	1976	1977	1978	1979	1980
Gross Domestic Product	1026	1382	1464	1604	3813	3487	3840	4049	4265	6743	7451
Plus: Net factor income received from abroad	-110	-265	-362	-342	-281	224	441	518	734	920	1612
Equals: Gross National Product	917	1117	1102	1262	3532	3711	4281	4567	4999	7663	9063
Less: Consumption of fixed capital	58	64	70	76	81	93	107	126	155	181	208
Less: Net indirect taxes paid to supranational organisations	...	...	...	...	...	...	...	...	...	...	...
Equals: National Income at Market Prices	859	1053	1032	1186	3451	3618	4173	4441	4844	7482	8855
Plus: Net current transfers received from abroad	-81	-81	-17	-219	-362	-310	-157	-358	-339	-356	-427
Current transfers received	...	...	6	...	...	...	...	...	...	...	...
Less: Current transfers paid	81	81	23	219	362	310	157	358	339	356	427
Equals: National Disposable Income at Market Prices	778	972	1015	967	3089	3308	4016	4083	4505	7126	8428
Less: Final consumption	536	593	626	653	843	1144	1462	1908	2094	2499	3057
Statistical discrepancy	...	...	-1	...	...	...	...	...	...	1	-63
Equals: Net Saving	242	379	388	314	2247	2164	2554	2175	2411	4628	5308
Less: Surplus of the nation on current transactions	175	313	322	237	2069	1813	2026	1318	1703	3926	4595
Statistical discrepancy	-1	...	...	...	1	...	...	...	...	...	63
Equals: Net Capital Formation	66	66	66	77	178	351	528	857	708	702	776

2.1 General Government Final Consumption Expenditure by Function, in Current Prices

Million Kuwaiti dinars

	1970	1971	1972	1973	1974	1975	1976	1977	1978	1979	1980
1 General public services											
2 Defence	60	76	85	94	144	195	225	314	333	362	418
3 Public order and safety											
4 Education	33	43	51	55	63	90	97	127	130	190	197
5 Health	16	20	22	23	26	39	40	56	59	73	101
6 Social security and welfare	2	2	3	3	4	6	6	9	9	17	22
7 Housing and community amenities	7	9	11	12	13	18	20	26	27	35	38
8 Recreational, cultural and religious affairs	6	7	8	9	10	16	16	20	23	34	32
9 Economic services	15	16	19	19	19	22	28	37	35	46	49
10 Other functions	...	...	...	...	...	...	...	...	...	...	...
Total General Government Final Consumption Expenditure	139	173	199	215	279	386	432	589	616	757	857

Kuwait

2.2 General Government Final Consumption Expenditure by Function, in Constant Prices

Million Kuwaiti dinars

	1970	1971	1972	1973	1974	1975	1976	1977	1978	1979	1980
				At constant prices of:1972							
1 General public services											
2 Defence	49	73	85	90	109	122	139	169	171	164	175
3 Public order and safety											
4 Education	44	45	51	57	63	70	74	91	95	101	109
5 Health	19	20	22	23	24	29	31	35	39	39	52
6 Social security and welfare	3	3	3	3	4	5	5	6	6	9	10
7 Housing and community amenities	10	10	11	12	13	14	15	15	17	18	18
8 Recreational, cultural and religious affairs	8	8	8	9	8	11	12	14	14	19	17
9 Economic services	20	18	19	19	17	19	21	28	27	29	30
10 Other functions	...	...	...	...	...	...	...	...	...	...	...
Total General Government Final Consumption Expenditure	153	177	199	213	238	270	297	358	369	379	411

4.3 Derivation of Value Added by Kind of Activity, ISIC Divisions, in Current Prices

Million Kuwaiti dinars

	1970 Gross Output	1970 Intermediate Consumption	1970 Value Added	1971 Gross Output	1971 Intermediate Consumption	1971 Value Added	1972 Gross Output	1972 Intermediate Consumption	1972 Value Added	1973 Gross Output	1973 Intermediate Consumption	1973 Value Added
						All Producers						
1 Agriculture, hunting, forestry and fishing	...	...	3	...	...	3	...	...	4	...	...	5
a Agriculture and hunting	...	...	1	...	...	1	...	...	2	...	...	3
b Forestry and logging	...	...	...	...	...	...	...	...	...	...	...	...
c Fishing	...	...	2	...	...	2	...	...	2	...	...	2
2 Mining and quarrying	...	...	619	...	...	908	...	...	914	...	...	996
a Coal mining	...	...	...	...	...	...	...	...	...	...	...	...
b Crude petroleum and natural gas production	...	...	618	...	...	907	...	...	913	...	...	994
c Metal ore mining	...	...	...	...	...	...	...	...	...	...	...	...
d Other mining	...	...	1	...	...	1	...	...	1	...	...	2
3 Manufacturing	...	...	43	...	...	55	...	...	65	...	...	77
a Manufacture of food, beverages and tobacco	...	...	6	...	...	6	...	...	7	...	...	8
b Textile, wearing apparel and leather industries	...	...	4	...	...	4	...	...	5	...	...	8
c Manufacture of wood and wood products, including furniture	...	...	3	...	...	6	...	...	6	...	...	5
d Manufacture of paper and paper products, printing and publishing	...	...	1	...	...	1	...	...	2	...	...	2
e Manufacture of chemicals and chemical petroleum, coal, rubber and plastic products	...	...	23	...	...	29	...	...	35	...	...	39
f Manufacture of non-metallic mineral products, except products of petroleum and coal	...	...	2	...	...	4	...	...	5	...	...	6
g Basic metal industries	...	...	...	...	...	1	...	...	1	...	...	1
h Manufacture of fabricated metal products, machinery and equipment	...	...	4	...	...	4	...	...	4	...	...	8
i Other manufacturing industries	...	...	-	...	...	-	...	...	-	...	...	-
4 Electricity, gas and water	...	...	7	...	...	9	...	...	11	...	...	12
a Electricity, gas and steam	...	...	3	...	...	4	...	...	5	...	...	6
b Water works and supply	...	...	4	...	...	5	...	...	6	...	...	6
5 Construction	...	...	28	...	...	33	...	...	38	...	...	44
6 Wholesale and retail trade, restaurants and hotels	...	...	85	...	...	94	...	...	110	...	...	118
a Wholesale and retail trade	...	...	81	...	...	90	...	...	106	...	...	113
b Restaurants and hotels	...	...	4	...	...	4	...	...	4	...	...	5
7 Transport, storage and communication	...	...	29	...	...	31	...	...	35	...	...	41
a Transport and storage	...	...	27	...	...	29	...	...	32	...	...	38
b Communication	...	...	2	...	...	2	...	...	3	...	...	3
8 Finance, insurance, real estate and business services	...	...	78	...	...	85	...	...	94	...	...	104
a Financial institutions	...	...	20	...	...	22	...	...	23	...	...	24

Kuwait

4.3 Derivation of Value Added by Kind of Activity, ISIC Divisions, in Current Prices
(Continued)

Million Kuwaiti dinars

	1970			1971			1972			1973		
	Gross Output	Intermediate Consumption	Value Added	Gross Output	Intermediate Consumption	Value Added	Gross Output	Intermediate Consumption	Value Added	Gross Output	Intermediate Consumption	Value Added
b Insurance	...	...	2	...	...	1	...	...	2	...	...	3
c Real estate and business services	...	...	56	...	...	62	...	...	69	...	...	77
9 Community, social and personal services	...	...	20	...	...	24	...	...	27	...	...	30
a Sanitary and similar services	...	...	-	...	...	-	...	...	-	...	...	1
b Social and related community services	...	...	4	...	...	5	...	...	6	...	...	6
Educational services	...	...	2	...	...	3	...	...	3	...	...	3
Medical, dental, other health and veterinary services	...	...	2	...	...	2	...	...	3	...	...	3
c Recreational and cultural services	...	...	1	...	...	2	...	...	2	...	...	2
d Personal and household services	...	...	15	...	...	17	...	...	19	...	...	21
Statistical discrepancy [a]	...	...	...	...	...	...	...	...	...	...	...	...
Total, Industries	...	...	912	...	...	1242	...	...	1299	...	...	1427
Producers of Government Services	...	...	107	...	...	132	...	...	156	...	...	167
Other Producers	...	...	...	...	...	...	...	...	...	...	...	...
Total	...	...	1019	...	...	1374	...	...	1455	...	...	1594
Imputed bank service charge	...	...	...	...	...	...	...	...	...	...	...	...
Import duties	...	...	...	...	...	...	...	...	...	...	...	...
Value added tax	...	...	...	...	...	...	...	...	...	...	...	...
Total	...	...	...	...	...	...	...	...	...	...	...	...

	1974			1975			1976			1977		
	Gross Output	Intermediate Consumption	Value Added	Gross Output	Intermediate Consumption	Value Added	Gross Output	Intermediate Consumption	Value Added	Gross Output	Intermediate Consumption	Value Added
All Producers											
1 Agriculture, hunting, forestry and fishing	...	...	6	...	...	9	15	5	10	...	...	13
a Agriculture and hunting	...	...	3	...	...	6	12	5	7	...	...	10
b Forestry and logging	...	...	...	...	...	...	...	...	...	...	...	...
c Fishing	...	...	3	...	...	3	3	-	3	...	...	3
2 Mining and quarrying	...	...	3023	...	...	2459	2544	20	2524	...	...	2483
a Coal mining	...	...	...	...	...	...	...	...	...	...	...	...
b Crude petroleum and natural gas production	...	...	3020	...	...	2457	2536	16	2520	...	...	2478
c Metal ore mining	...	...	...	...	...	...	...	...	...	...	...	...
d Other mining	...	...	3	...	...	2	8	4	4	...	...	5
3 Manufacturing	...	...	170	...	...	194	771	541	228	...	...	239
a Manufacture of food, beverages and tobacco	...	...	7	...	...	13	39	24	15	...	...	18
b Textile, wearing apparel and leather industries	...	...	7	...	...	9	15	4	11	...	...	13
c Manufacture of wood and wood products, including furniture	...	...	5	...	...	9	28	12	16	...	...	15
d Manufacture of paper and paper products, printing and publishing	...	...	2	...	...	4	11	5	6	...	...	9
e Manufacture of chemicals and chemical petroleum, coal, rubber and plastic products	...	...	129	...	...	125	597	465	132	...	...	139
f Manufacture of non-metallic mineral products, except products of petroleum and coal	...	...	8	...	...	15	32	12	21	...	...	22
g Basic metal industries	...	...	2	...	...	6	13	5	7	...	...	4
h Manufacture of fabricated metal products, machinery and equipment	...	...	9	...	...	12	33	13	19	...	...	18
i Other manufacturing industries	...	...	1	...	...	1	3	1	1	...	...	1
4 Electricity, gas and water	...	...	12	...	...	13	25	6	19	...	...	20
a Electricity, gas and steam	...	...	6	...	...	6	12	4	8	...	...	8
b Water works and supply	...	...	6	...	...	7	13	2	11	...	...	12

Kuwait

4.3 Derivation of Value Added by Kind of Activity, ISIC Divisions, in Current Prices
(Continued)

Million Kuwaiti dinars

	1974 Gross Output	1974 Intermediate Consumption	1974 Value Added	1975 Gross Output	1975 Intermediate Consumption	1975 Value Added	1976 Gross Output	1976 Intermediate Consumption	1976 Value Added	1977 Gross Output	1977 Intermediate Consumption	1977 Value Added
5 Construction	...	...	63	...	...	74	283	160	123	...	...	158
6 Wholesale and retail trade, restaurants and hotels	...	...	147	...	...	221	396	93	304	...	...	370
a Wholesale and retail trade	...	...	140	...	...	211	369	80	289	...	...	352
b Restaurants and hotels	...	...	7	...	...	10	27	13	15	...	...	18
7 Transport, storage and communication	...	...	50	...	...	61	110	38	73	...	...	78
a Transport and storage	...	...	46	...	...	55	100	36	64	...	...	66
b Communication	...	...	4	...	...	6	10	2	9	...	...	12
8 Finance, insurance, real estate and business services	...	...	117	...	...	149	235	27	207	...	...	240
a Financial institutions	...	...	26	...	...	39	72	15	57	...	...	73
b Insurance	...	...	4	...	...	6	10	1	8	...	...	12
c Real estate and business services	...	...	87	...	...	104	153	11	142	...	...	155
9 Community, social and personal services	...	...	33	...	...	43	68	16	52	...	...	55
a Sanitary and similar services	...	...	1	...	...	1	3	-	3	...	...	1
b Social and related community services	...	...	6	...	...	9	13	2	11	...	...	13
Educational services	...	...	3	...	...	4	6	1	5	...	...	6
Medical, dental, other health and veterinary services	...	...	3	...	...	4	5	1	4	...	...	6
c Recreational and cultural services	...	...	2	...	...	2	1	-	1	...	...	4
d Personal and household services	...	...	24	...	...	31	51	14	37	...	...	37
Statistical discrepancy [a]	...	...	...	...	...	...	4	4	...	...	...	...
Total, Industries	...	...	3621	...	...	3223	4451	910	3541	...	...	3656
Producers of Government Services	...	...	178	...	...	240	437	172	265	...	...	345
Other Producers	...	...	...	...	...	...	...	...	...	...	...	...
Total	...	...	3799	...	...	3463	4888	1082	3806	...	...	4001
Imputed bank service charge	...	...	...	...	...	...	...	...	...	...	...	...
Import duties	...	...	...	...	...	...	...	...	...	...	...	...
Value added tax	...	...	...	...	...	...	...	...	...	...	...	...
Total	...	...	...	...	...	...	...	...	...	...	...	...

	1978 Gross Output	1978 Intermediate Consumption	1978 Value Added	1979 Gross Output	1979 Intermediate Consumption	1979 Value Added	1980 Gross Output	1980 Intermediate Consumption	1980 Value Added
				All Producers					
1 Agriculture, hunting, forestry and fishing	...	...	13	...	...	17	...	...	18
a Agriculture and hunting	...	...	9	...	...	13	...	...	14
b Forestry and logging	...	...	...	...	...	...	...	...	...
c Fishing	...	...	4	...	...	4	...	...	4
2 Mining and quarrying	...	...	2531	...	...	4420	...	...	5063
a Coal mining	...	...	...	...	...	...	...	...	...
b Crude petroleum and natural gas production	...	...	2525	...	...	4414	...	...	5056
c Metal ore mining	...	...	...	...	...	...	...	...	...
d Other mining	...	...	6	...	...	6	...	...	7

Kuwait

4.3 Derivation of Value Added by Kind of Activity, ISIC Divisions, in Current Prices
(Continued)

Million Kuwaiti dinars

	1978			1979			1980		
	Gross Output	Intermediate Consumption	Value Added	Gross Output	Intermediate Consumption	Value Added	Gross Output	Intermediate Consumption	Value Added
3 Manufacturing	...	...	280	...	...	574	...	...	441
a Manufacture of food, beverages and tobacco	...	...	20	...	...	24	...	...	28
b Textile, wearing apparel and leather industries	...	...	13	...	...	15	...	...	18
c Manufacture of wood and wood products, including furniture	...	...	22	...	...	27	...	...	30
d Manufacture of paper and paper products, printing and publishing	...	...	6	...	...	7	...	...	8
e Manufacture of chemicals and chemical petroleum, coal, rubber and plastic products	...	...	151	...	...	420	...	...	263
f Manufacture of non-metallic mineral products, except products of petroleum and coal	...	...	39	...	...	48	...	...	56
g Basic metal industries	...	...	3	...	...	3	...	...	4
h Manufacture of fabricated metal products, machinery and equipment	...	...	24	...	...	28	...	...	32
i Other manufacturing industries	...	...	2	...	...	2	...	...	2
4 Electricity, gas and water	...	...	24	...	...	27	...	...	25
a Electricity, gas and steam	...	...	9	...	...	11	...	...	10
b Water works and supply	...	...	15	...	...	16	...	...	15
5 Construction	...	...	176	...	...	210	...	...	220
6 Wholesale and retail trade, restaurants and hotels	...	...	390	...	...	426	...	...	468
a Wholesale and retail trade	...	...	371	...	...	408	...	...	449
b Restaurants and hotels	...	...	19	...	...	18	...	...	19
7 Transport, storage and communication	...	...	91	...	...	107	...	...	124
a Transport and storage	...	...	76	...	...	87	...	...	96
b Communication	...	...	15	...	...	20	...	...	28
8 Finance, insurance, real estate and business services	...	...	291	...	...	346	...	...	402
a Financial institutions	...	...	104	...	...	135	...	...	169
b Insurance	...	...	12	...	...	13	...	...	15
c Real estate and business services	...	...	175	...	...	198	...	...	218
9 Community, social and personal services	...	...	61	...	...	66	...	...	76
a Sanitary and similar services	...	...	1	...	...	1	...	...	1
b Social and related community services	...	...	17	...	...	18	...	...	22
Educational services	...	...	7	...	...	8	...	...	9
Medical, dental, other health and veterinary services	...	...	9	...	...	9	...	...	12
c Recreational and cultural services	...	...	4	...	...	4	...	...	4
d Personal and household services	...	...	39	...	...	43	...	...	49
Statistical discrepancy [a]	...	...	...	...	...	...	...	...	...
Total, Industries	...	...	3857	...	...	6193	...	...	6837
Producers of Government Services	...	...	365	...	...	501	...	...	553
Other Producers	...	...	...	...	...	...	...	...	...
Total	...	...	4222	...	...	6694	...	...	7390
Imputed bank service charge	...	...	...	...	...	...	...	...	...
Import duties	...	...	...	...	...	...	...	...	...
Value added tax	...	...	...	...	...	...	...	...	...
Total	...	...	...	...	...	...	...	...	...

a) Relating to social security and welfare services.

Kuwait

4.4 Derivation of Value Added by Kind of Activity, ISIC Divisions, in Constant Prices

Million Kuwaiti dinars

At constant prices of: 1972

All Producers

		1970 Gross Output	1970 Intermediate Consumption	1970 Value Added	1971 Gross Output	1971 Intermediate Consumption	1971 Value Added	1972 Gross Output	1972 Intermediate Consumption	1972 Value Added	1973 Gross Output	1973 Intermediate Consumption	1973 Value Added
1	Agriculture, hunting, forestry and fishing	...	...	5	...	...	5	...	...	4	...	...	4
a	Agriculture and hunting	...	...	2	...	...	2	...	...	2	...	...	2
b	Forestry and logging	...	...	...	...	...	...	...	...	...	...	...	...
c	Fishing	...	...	3	...	...	3	...	...	2	...	...	2
2	Mining and quarrying	...	...	830	...	...	888	...	...	914	...	...	840
a	Coal mining	...	...	...	...	...	...	...	...	...	...	...	...
b	Crude petroleum and natural gas production	...	...	829	...	...	887	...	...	913	...	...	838
c	Metal ore mining	...	...	...	...	...	...	...	...	...	...	...	...
d	Other mining	...	...	1	...	...	1	...	...	1	...	...	2
3	Manufacturing	...	...	55	...	...	62	...	...	65	...	...	78
a	Manufacture of food, beverages and tobacco	...	...	6	...	...	6	...	...	7	...	...	7
b	Textile, wearing apparel and leather industries	...	...	4	...	...	4	...	...	5	...	...	7
c	Manufacture of wood and wood products, including furniture	...	...	3	...	...	6	...	...	6	...	...	4
d	Manufacture of paper and paper products, printing and publishing	...	...	1	...	...	1	...	...	2	...	...	2
e	Manufacture of chemicals and chemical petroleum, coal, rubber and plastic products	...	...	35	...	...	36	...	...	35	...	...	42
f	Manufacture of non-metallic mineral products, except products of petroleum and coal	...	...	2	...	...	4	...	...	5	...	...	8
g	Basic metal industries	...	...	...	...	...	1	...	...	1	...	...	1
h	Manufacture of fabricated metal products, machinery and equipment	...	...	4	...	...	4	...	...	4	...	...	7
i	Other manufacturing industries	...	...	...	...	...	...	...	...	·	...	...	...
4	Electricity, gas and water	...	...	7	...	...	9	...	...	11	...	...	12
a	Electricity, gas and steam	...	...	3	...	...	4	...	...	5	...	...	6
b	Water works and supply	...	...	4	...	...	5	...	...	6	...	...	6
5	Construction	...	...	31	...	...	34	...	...	38	...	...	41
6	Wholesale and retail trade, restaurants and hotels	...	...	92	...	...	97	...	...	110	...	...	106
a	Wholesale and retail trade	...	...	88	...	...	93	...	...	106	...	...	101
b	Restaurants and hotels	...	...	4	...	...	4	...	...	4	...	...	5
7	Transport, storage and communication	...	...	30	...	...	31	...	...	35	...	...	36
a	Transport and storage	...	...	28	...	...	29	...	...	32	...	...	33
b	Communication	...	...	2	...	...	2	...	...	3	...	...	3
8	Finance, insurance, real estate and business services	...	...	87	...	...	96	...	...	94	...	...	100
a	Financial institutions	...	...	21	...	...	27	...	...	23	...	...	27
b	Insurance	...	...	2	...	...	2	...	...	2	...	...	2
c	Real estate and business services	...	...	64	...	...	67	...	...	69	...	...	71
9	Community, social and personal services	...	...	24	...	...	24	...	...	27	...	...	29
a	Sanitary and similar services	...	...	·	...	...	·	...	...	·	...	...	1
b	Social and related community services	...	...	6	...	...	5	...	...	6	...	...	6
	Educational services	...	...	3	...	...	3	...	...	3	...	...	3
	Medical, dental, other health and veterinary services	...	...	3	...	...	2	...	...	3	...	...	3
c	Recreational and cultural services	...	...	2	...	...	2	...	...	2	...	...	2
d	Personal and household services	...	...	16	...	...	17	...	...	19	...	...	20

Kuwait

4.4 Derivation of Value Added by Kind of Activity, ISIC Divisions, in Constant Prices
(Continued)

Million Kuwaiti dinars

	1970 Gross Output	1970 Intermediate Consumption	1970 Value Added	1971 Gross Output	1971 Intermediate Consumption	1971 Value Added	1972 Gross Output	1972 Intermediate Consumption	1972 Value Added	1973 Gross Output	1973 Intermediate Consumption	1973 Value Added
					At constant prices of: 1972							
Total, Industries	...	...	1161	...	...	1246	...	...	1300	...	...	1246
Producers of Government Services	...	...	116	...	...	133	...	...	155	...	...	166
Other Producers	...	...	...	...	...	...	...	...	...	...	...	...
Total	...	...	1277	...	...	1379	...	...	1455	...	...	1412
Imputed bank service charge	...	...	...	...	...	...	...	...	...	...	...	...
Import duties	...	...	...	...	...	...	...	...	...	...	...	...
Value added tax	...	...	...	...	...	...	...	...	...	...	...	...
Total	...	...	...	...	...	...	...	...	...	...	...	...

	1974 Gross Output	1974 Intermediate Consumption	1974 Value Added	1975 Gross Output	1975 Intermediate Consumption	1975 Value Added	1976 Gross Output	1976 Intermediate Consumption	1976 Value Added	1977 Gross Output	1977 Intermediate Consumption	1977 Value Added
					At constant prices of: 1972							
					All Producers							
1 Agriculture, hunting, forestry and fishing	...	...	4	...	...	5	...	...	6	...	...	6
a Agriculture and hunting	...	...	2	...	...	3	...	...	4	...	...	5
b Forestry and logging	...	...	...	...	...	...	...	...	...	...	...	...
c Fishing	...	...	2	...	...	2	...	...	2	...	...	1
2 Mining and quarrying	...	...	708	...	...	580	...	...	600	...	...	549
a Coal mining	...	...	...	...	...	...	...	...	...	...	...	...
b Crude petroleum and natural gas production	...	...	706	...	...	578	...	...	597	...	...	546
c Metal ore mining	...	...	...	...	...	...	...	...	...	...	...	...
d Other mining	...	...	2	...	...	2	...	...	3	...	...	3
3 Manufacturing	...	...	84	...	...	100	...	...	100	...	...	98
a Manufacture of food, beverages and tobacco	...	...	5	...	...	9	...	...	9	...	...	10
b Textile, wearing apparel and leather industries	...	...	5	...	...	6	...	...	7	...	...	7
c Manufacture of wood and wood products, including furniture	...	...	4	...	...	6	...	...	10	...	...	9
d Manufacture of paper and paper products, printing and publishing	...	...	1	...	...	3	...	...	4	...	...	6
e Manufacture of chemicals and chemical petroleum, coal, rubber and plastic products	...	...	53	...	...	55	...	...	41	...	...	41
f Manufacture of non-metallic mineral products, except products of petroleum and coal	...	...	7	...	...	8	...	...	11	...	...	10
g Basic metal industries	...	...	1	...	...	4	...	...	5	...	...	3
h Manufacture of fabricated metal products, machinery and equipment	...	...	7	...	...	8	...	...	12	...	...	11
i Other manufacturing industries	...	...	1	...	...	1	...	...	1	...	...	1
4 Electricity, gas and water	...	...	13	...	...	15	...	...	17	...	...	20
a Electricity, gas and steam	...	...	6	...	...	7	...	...	8	...	...	9
b Water works and supply	...	...	7	...	...	8	...	...	9	...	...	11
5 Construction	...	...	51	...	...	55	...	...	87	...	...	104
6 Wholesale and retail trade, restaurants and hotels	...	...	118	...	...	162	...	...	206	...	...	233
a Wholesale and retail trade	...	...	111	...	...	154	...	...	198	...	...	225
b Restaurants and hotels	...	...	7	...	...	8	...	...	8	...	...	8
7 Transport, storage and communication	...	...	43	...	...	49	...	...	74	...	...	83
a Transport and storage	...	...	39	...	...	45	...	...	69	...	...	77
b Communication	...	...	4	...	...	4	...	...	5	...	...	6
8 Finance, insurance, real estate and business services	...	...	105	...	...	116	...	...	132	...	...	148
a Financial institutions	...	...	31	...	...	35	...	...	43	...	...	54

Kuwait

4.4 Derivation of Value Added by Kind of Activity, ISIC Divisions, in Constant Prices
(Continued)

Million Kuwaiti dinars

	1974			1975			1976			1977		
	Gross Output	Intermediate Consumption	Value Added	Gross Output	Intermediate Consumption	Value Added	Gross Output	Intermediate Consumption	Value Added	Gross Output	Intermediate Consumption	Value Added
At constant prices of: 1972											
b Insurance	...	...	2	...	...	3	...	...	4	...	...	4
c Real estate and business services	...	...	72	...	...	78	...	...	85	...	...	90
9 Community, social and personal services	...	...	31	...	...	32	...	...	36	...	...	35
a Sanitary and similar services	...	...	1	...	...	1	...	...	1	...	...	1
b Social and related community services	...	...	7	...	...	6	...	...	7	...	...	7
Educational services	...	...	4	...	...	3	...	...	4	...	...	4
Medical, dental, other health and veterinary services	...	...	3	...	...	3	...	...	3	...	...	3
c Recreational and cultural services	...	...	2	...	...	1	...	...	2	...	...	3
d Personal and household services	...	...	21	...	...	24	...	...	26	...	...	24
Total, Industries	...	...	1157	...	...	1114	...	...	1260	...	...	1277
Producers of Government Services	...	...	163	...	...	175	...	...	191	...	...	216
Other Producers	...	...	...	...	...	...	...	...	...	...	...	...
Total	...	...	1320	...	...	1289	...	...	1451	...	...	1493
Imputed bank service charge	...	...	...	...	...	...	...	...	...	...	...	...
Import duties	...	...	...	...	...	...	...	...	...	...	...	...
Value added tax	...	...	...	...	...	...	...	...	...	...	...	...
Total	...	...	...	...	...	...	...	...	...	...	...	...

	1978			1979			1980		
	Gross Output	Intermediate Consumption	Value Added	Gross Output	Intermediate Consumption	Value Added	Gross Output	Intermediate Consumption	Value Added
At constant prices of: 1972								
All Producers								
1 Agriculture, hunting, forestry and fishing	...	...	5	...	...	7	...	...	7
a Agriculture and hunting	...	...	4	...	...	6	...	...	6
b Forestry and logging	...	...	...	...	...	...	...	...	...
c Fishing	...	...	1	...	...	1	...	...	1
2 Mining and quarrying	...	...	594	...	...	697	...	...	465
a Coal mining	...	...	...	...	...	...	...	...	...
b Crude petroleum and natural gas production	...	...	591	...	...	694	...	...	462
c Metal ore mining	...	...	...	...	...	...	...	...	...
d Other mining	...	...	3	...	...	3	...	...	3
3 Manufacturing	...	...	117	...	...	139	...	...	140
a Manufacture of food, beverages and tobacco	...	...	12	...	...	12	...	...	14
b Textile, wearing apparel and leather industries	...	...	8	...	...	9	...	...	9
c Manufacture of wood and wood products, including furniture	...	...	14	...	...	15	...	...	15
d Manufacture of paper and paper products, printing and publishing	...	...	4	...	...	4	...	...	4
e Manufacture of chemicals and chemical petroleum, coal, rubber and plastic products	...	...	44	...	...	51	...	...	44
f Manufacture of non-metallic mineral products, except products of petroleum and coal	...	...	17	...	...	29	...	...	35
g Basic metal industries	...	...	2	...	...	2	...	...	2
h Manufacture of fabricated metal products, machinery and equipment	...	...	15	...	...	16	...	...	16
i Other manufacturing industries	...	...	1	...	...	1	...	...	1
4 Electricity, gas and water	...	...	25	...	...	28	...	...	29
a Electricity, gas and steam	...	...	11	...	...	13	...	...	14
b Water works and supply	...	...	14	...	...	15	...	...	15

Kuwait

4.4 Derivation of Value Added by Kind of Activity, ISIC Divisions, in Constant Prices
(Continued)

Million Kuwaiti dinars

	1978 Gross Output	1978 Intermediate Consumption	1978 Value Added	1979 Gross Output	1979 Intermediate Consumption	1979 Value Added	1980 Gross Output	1980 Intermediate Consumption	1980 Value Added
				At constant prices of:1972					
5 Construction	...	...	106	...	...	118	...	...	116
6 Wholesale and retail trade, restaurants and hotels	...	...	232	...	...	238	...	...	241
a Wholesale and retail trade	...	...	224	...	...	230	...	...	234
b Restaurants and hotels	...	...	8	...	...	8	...	...	7
7 Transport, storage and communication	...	...	91	...	...	96	...	...	101
a Transport and storage	...	...	85	...	...	89	...	...	93
b Communication	...	...	6	...	...	7	...	...	8
8 Finance, insurance, real estate and business services	...	...	159	...	...	168	...	...	187
a Financial institutions	...	...	61	...	...	68	...	...	78
b Insurance	...	...	5	...	...	5	...	...	6
c Real estate and business services	...	...	93	...	...	95	...	...	103
9 Community, social and personal services	...	...	33	...	...	33	...	...	35
a Sanitary and similar services	...	...	1	...	...	1	...	...	1
b Social and related community services	...	...	8	...	...	8	...	...	9
Educational services	...	...	5	...	...	4	...	...	5
Medical, dental, other health and veterinary services	...	...	3	...	...	4	...	...	4
c Recreational and cultural services	...	...	2	...	...	2	...	...	2
d Personal and household services	...	...	22	...	...	22	...	...	23
Total, Industries	...	...	1362	...	...	1524	...	...	1321
Producers of Government Services	...	...	225	...	...	238	...	...	253
Other Producers	...	...	...	...	...	...	...	...	...
Total	...	...	1587	...	...	1762	...	...	1574
Imputed bank service charge	...	...	...	...	...	...	...	...	...
Import duties	...	...	...	...	...	...	...	...	...
Value added tax	...	...	...	...	...	...	...	...	...
Total	...	...	...	...	...	...	...	...	...

4.6 Cost Components of Value Added, ISIC Divisions

Million Kuwaiti dinars

	1976 Compensation of Employees	Capital Consumption	Net Operating Surplus	Indirect Taxes	Less: Subsidies Received	Value Added
			All Producers			
1 Agriculture, hunting, forestry and fishing	1	-	9	-	-	10
a Agriculture and hunting	1	-	6	-	-	7
b Forestry and logging	...	...	...	...	...	...
c Fishing	-	-	3	-	-	3
2 Mining and quarrying	25	8	2490	1	-	2524
a Coal mining	...	...	...	...	...	...
b Crude petroleum and natural gas production	24	7	2488	1	-	2520
c Metal ore mining	...	...	...	...	...	...
d Other mining	1	1	3	-	-	4

Kuwait

4.6 Cost Components of Value Added, ISIC Divisions
(Continued)

Million Kuwaiti dinars

	1976					
	Compensation of Employees	Capital Consumption	Net Operating Surplus	Indirect Taxes	Less: Subsidies Received	Value Added
3 Manufacturing	55	19	159	2	5	230
a Manufacture of food, beverages and tobacco	7	2	10	1	5	15
b Textile, wearing apparel and leather industries	5	-	7	-	-	11
c Manufacture of wood and wood products, including furniture	5	-	11	-	-	16
d Manufacture of paper and paper products, printing and publishing	3	-	3	-	-	6
e Manufacture of chemicals and chemical petroleum, coal, rubber and plastic products	22	11	98	1	-	132
f Manufacture of non-metallic mineral products, except products of petroleum and coal	5	1	15	-	-	21
g Basic metal industries	1	4	3	-	-	8
h Manufacture of fabricated metal products, machinery and equipment	7	1	12	-	-	19
i Other manufacturing industries	-	-	1	-	-	1
4 Electricity, gas and water	18	12	-11	-	-	19
a Electricity, gas and steam	11	8	-11	-	-	8
b Water works and supply	7	4	-	-	-	11
5 Construction	50	10	63	-	-	123
6 Wholesale and retail trade, restaurants and hotels	61	7	241	1	6	303
a Wholesale and retail trade	55	7	232	1	6	289
b Restaurants and hotels	6	-	9	-	-	15
7 Transport, storage and communication	30	18	25	-	-	72
a Transport and storage	22	11	30	-	-	64
b Communication	8	6	-5	-	-	9
8 Finance, insurance, real estate and business services	22	21	163	2	-	208
a Financial institutions	11	1	46	-	-	57
b Insurance	2	-	6	-	-	8
c Real estate and business services	9	20	111	2	-	142
9 Community, social and personal services	17	2	23	-	-	42
a Sanitary and similar services	2	-	-	-	-	3
b Social and related community services	5	-	4	-	-	9
Educational services	4	-	1	-	-	5
Medical, dental, other health and veterinary services	1	-	.3	-	-	4
c Recreational and cultural services	1	-	1	-	-	2
d Personal and household services	9	1	18	-	-	28
Total, Industries	279	96	3161	6	11	3531
Producers of Government Services	255	11	-	-	-	266
Other Producers	10	-	-	-	-	10
Total	544	107	3161	6	11	3806
Imputed bank service charge	...	...	...	...	...	...
Import duties	...	...	...	33	...	33
Value added tax	...	...	...	...	...	...
Other adjustments	...	...	...	...	...	...
Total	544	107	3161	39	11	3840

Kuwait

4.9 Supply of Goods and Services, in Current Prices

Million Kuwaiti dinars

	Gross Domestic Output — Marketed	Gross Domestic Output — Non-Marketed	Imports c.i.f.	Import Duties	Trade & Transport Margins	Value Added Tax	TOTAL SUPPLY
				1976			
1 Agriculture, hunting, forestry and fishing	15	...	61	-	43	...	119
2 Mining and quarrying	2545	...	2	-	-	...	2547
3 Manufacturing	771	...	1022	33	337	...	2163
4 Electricity, gas and water	25	...	-	-	-	...	25
5 Construction	283	...	-	-	-	...	283
6 Wholesale and retail trade, restaurants and hotels	27	...	-	-	-	...	27
7 Transport and communications	99	...	23	-	-	...	122
8 Finance, insurance, real estate and business services	235	...	36	-	-	...	271
9 Community, social and personal services	60	...	-	-	-	...	60
Total, Industries	4060	...	1144	33	380	...	5617
Producers of Government Services	449	...	106	-	-	...	555
Other Producers		...				...	
Total	4509	...	1250	33	380	...	6172

4.11 Disposition of Goods and Services, in Current Prices

Million Kuwaiti dinars

	Intermediate Consumption — General Government	Intermediate Consumption — Public Enterprises	Intermediate Consumption — Private	Final Consumption	Gross Capital Formation — General Government	Gross Capital Formation — Public Enterprises	Gross Capital Formation — Private	Exports	TOTAL DISPOSITION
				1976					
1 Agriculture, hunting, forestry and fishing	-	...	3	111	-	...	-	5	119
2 Mining and quarrying	-	...	408	-	-	...	-14	2153	2547
3 Manufacturing	107	...	302	607	14	...	380	754	2163
4 Electricity, gas and water	1	...	10	13	-	...	-	-	25
5 Construction	17	...	23	4	71	...	168	-	283
6 Wholesale and retail trade, restaurants and hotels	2	...	3	22	-	...	-	-	27
7 Transport and communications	8	...	59	16	-	...	3	37	122
8 Finance, insurance, real estate and business services	23	...	98	132	-	...	13	5	271
9 Community, social and personal services	1	...	4	55	-	...	-	-	60
Total, Industries	159	...	910	960	85	...	550	2954	5617
Producers of Government Services	13	...	-	502	-	...	-	39	555
Other Producers		...				...			
Total	172	...	910	1462	85	...	550	2992	6172

4.15 Intermediate Consumption by Kind of Activity of User (Use Matrix), in Current Prices

Million Kuwaiti dinars

	Agriculture, Hunting, Forestry, Fishing	Mining & Quarrying	Manufacturing	Electricity, Gas & Water	Construction	Wholesale & Retail Trade, Restaurants & Hotels	Transport & Communications	Finance Insurance, Real Estate & Business Services	Community Social & Personal Services	TOTAL
					1976					
1 Agriculture, hunting, forestry and fishing	-	-	1	-	-	-	-	-	-	1
2 Mining and quarrying	-	5	397	-	6	-	-	-	-	408
3 Manufacturing	3	2	67	4	102	14	10	2	102	306
4 Electricity, gas and water	-	1	5	-	-	2	-	-	2	11
4 Construction	-	6	8	-	4	1	1	1	18	39
6 Wholesale and retail trade, restaurants and hotels	2	1	43	1	34	17	6	3	17	124
7 Transport and communications	-	2	7	-	4	19	9	2	9	53
8 Finance, insurance, real estate and business services	-	2	13	-	10	37	11	18	28	120
9 Community, social and personal services	-	1	1	-	-	1	-	1	2	6
Statistical discrepancy	...	...	...	...	...	...	...	...	...	...
Total	5	20	542	5	160	92	38	27	179	1068

كيفية الحصول على منشورات الامم المتحدة

يمكن الحصول على منشورات الامم المتحدة من المكتبات ودور التوزيع في جميع انحاء العالم . استعلم عنها من المكتبة التي تتعامل معها أو اكتب الى : الامم المتحدة ،قسم البيع في نيويورك او في جنيف .

如何购取联合国出版物

联合国出版物在全世界各地的书店和经售处均有发售。请向书店询问或写信到纽约或日内瓦的联合国销售组。

HOW TO OBTAIN UNITED NATIONS PUBLICATIONS

United Nations publications may be obtained from bookstores and distributors throughout the world. Consult your bookstore or write to: United Nations, Sales Section, New York or Geneva.

COMMENT SE PROCURER LES PUBLICATIONS DES NATIONS UNIES

Les publications des Nations Unies sont en vente dans les librairies et les agences dépositaires du monde entier. Informez-vous auprès de votre libraire ou adressez-vous à : Nations Unies, Section des ventes, New York ou Genève.

КАК ПОЛУЧИТЬ ИЗДАНИЯ ОРГАНИЗАЦИИ ОБЪЕДИНЕННЫХ НАЦИЙ

Издания Организации Объединенных Наций можно купить в книжных магазинах и агентствах во всех районах мира. Наводите справки об изданиях в вашем книжном магазине или пишите по адресу: Организация Объединенных Наций, Секция по продаже изданий, Нью-Йорк или Женева.

COMO CONSEGUIR PUBLICACIONES DE LAS NACIONES UNIDAS

Las publicaciones de las Naciones Unidas están en venta en librerías y casas distribuidoras en todas partes del mundo. Consulte a su librero o diríjase a: Naciones Unidas, Sección de Ventas, Nueva York o Ginebra.

Printed in U.S.A.　　　　　　12500 (Vols. I and II)　　　　　　United Nations publication
40102—May 1983—4,350　　(only clothbound edition for sale)　　Sales No. E.83.XVII.3, Vol. I, Part 1